PROJECT ROAR PUBLISHING
LIONEL POSTWAR ENCYCLOPEDIA SERIES

AUTHORITATIVE GUIDE TO
LIONEL'S PROMOTIONAL OUFITS

1960 - 1969

John W. Schmid

Edited by:
Roger Carp & George J. Schmid

PROJECT ROAR™
PUBLISHING

Copyright © 2007 John W. Schmid

Published by Project Roar Publishing

P.O. Box 599
Winfield, IL 60190
630-653-ROAR (7627)

Visit our website or email us for additional product and ordering information.
www.projectroar.com
orders@projectroar.com

Publisher's Cataloging-In-Publication Data
(Prepared by The Donohue Group, Inc.)

Schmid, John W.
    Authoritative guide to Lionel's promotional outfits, 1960-1969 / John W. Schmid ; edited by Roger Carp & George J. Schmid.

    p. : ill. ; cm. -- (Lionel postwar encyclopedia series)

    Includes index.
    ISBN-13: 978-1-933600-03-1 (hardcover)
    ISBN-10: 1-933600-03-9 (hardcover)
    ISBN-13: 978-1-933600-02-4 (pbk.)
    ISBN-10: 1-933600-02-0 (pbk.)

1. Lionel Corporation. 2. Railroads--Models--Encyclopedias. 3. Railroads--Models--Collectors and collecting. 4. Advertising specialties--Encyclopedias. 5. Advertising specialties--Collectors and collecting. 6. Packaging--Collectors and collecting. I. Carp, Roger. II. Schmid, George J. III. Title. IV. Title: Lionel's promotional outfits, 1960-1969

TF197 .S36 2007
625.1/9

Design and Layout: Kristi Ludwig
Image Management: Mardi Callahan
Production Management: Helene Tsigistras

Printed in China
Lionel® is the registered trademark of Lionel L.L.C., Chesterfield, Michigan.

All photographs by John W. Schmid unless otherwise indicated.
Photos (pages 159, 399, 426, 484, 541, 544, 601 and 700) used with permission of Kalmbach Publishing Co.
Catalog images (pages 451 and 597) used with permission of Western Auto Supply Company.
Catalog image (page 330) used with permission of S&H Solutions.
Catalog image (page 196) used with permission of NHB Assignments LLC, as Plan Administrator of Montgomery Ward LLC.
Catalog images (pages 20 and 378) used with permission of Sears, Roebuck and Co.
The publisher has made every effort to provide appropriate credit to image sources. Any omission is unintentional and regretted.

TABLE OF CONTENTS

Acknowledgments

The task of explaining the history and components of Lionel's promotional outfits from 1960 through 1969 should have been simple. After all, I had the "cheat sheets," the Lionel Factory Orders that documented what went into every outfit. All I had to do was summarize this information in a database and hit the "print" function.

Well, the information contained in those documents took years to corroborate, analyze and digest. For every question answered, I added another three to my list. The ever-increasing list of questions could never have been answered and this volume never completed without the assistance and expertise of the individuals listed below. I am grateful to them and the entire toy train community for their support and encouragement.

First, I want to thank Joseph Algozzini, the guru of postwar collecting. His love and energy for postwar Lionel is unsurpassed. Being able to spend time with him was like attending a graduate seminar in train collecting. Thanks, Joseph, for sharing the gems in your collection and the knowledge you have gained over four decades in reviewing the content of this volume. I will never forget the day we figured out what the suffixes "-1" and "-25" meant, a groundbreaking moment that solved numerous mysteries.

Roger Carp, the senior editor of *Classic Toy Trains* magazine, provided unbelievable guidance and assistance. When asked to write an overview of Lionel's promotional outfits in the 1960's, he researched and wrote the entire history of promotional outfits and then some. Roger's contributions to this volume will enlighten all of us. His knowledge of Lionel's history and his contacts in the hobby made many things happen.

Thanks to my sister, Christy, for relentlessly researching and documenting Lionel's customers and retailers. She never gave up even with the obscure ones. Christy also deserves thanks for providing the initial pass of the outfit diagrams and design of the database used in cataloging all this information.

The photographs presented in this volume show fascinating items from some of the top Lionel collectors in the United States. Yes, people have been collecting promotional outfits for years. By allowing me to photograph and document their promotional outfits, these individuals will benefit the entire collector community for generations. Individuals sharing their collections include: George Schmid, Ed Mullin, Joseph Algozzini, Joe Astorg, Paul Ambrose, Dave Gierzsal, Barry Keener, Mike Toth, Bob Pasztor, Mark Stephens, Peter Fankhauser, Russ Dixon, Michael Garcia, L. Jay Budzon of Jays Trains Mishawaka, Terry Vittorio, Vernon Johnson and Charles Powell.

Deciphering all the data included on the Factory Orders took the assistance of many individuals with countless hours of Lionel experience. They raised the questions that have baffled the Lionel collector community for years and then pooled their knowledge to seek answers. Specifically, I would like to thank:

- Manny Piazza for all his assistance in deciphering Lionel envelopes, boxes, paper and other peripherals.
- Dan Mega, "the box man," for reviewing my box research and providing information about the notorious third line of data on the Box Manufacturing Certificate.
- Greg Hake, for sharing what the "X" suffix on motive power boxes meant and providing the photographs for the Halloween General.
- Max Knoecklein for providing the best definition of "NA" and internal document assistance.
- Bob Osterhoff for providing guidance on the Factory Orders we had and how to get them published.
- Paul Ambrose for the many hours spent sharing his postwar knowledge and lore.
- Ron Hollander for sharing his vast knowledge of Lionel's history.
- Frank Piazza for deciphering Lionel's financials and costing policies.
- Tom Pagano, Bruce Parmett and the many other former Lionel employees for the hours they spent tirelessly sharing their experiences.
- Jan Athey at the Toy Train Reference Library (administered by the Train Collectors Association in Strasburg, Pennsylvania) for always being there to help.

Information from many other sources enhanced my understanding and appreciation of the Factory Orders. Besides thanking all the collectors who have submitted insights about promotional outfits, I want to thank Alan Stewart for unselfishly sharing his years of research on promotional outfits, Raymond Fetzner for providing advertising and catalogs and Bill Williams for providing additional documentation that filled many holes in my research. Douglas Cotts for generously sharing information obtained from the estate of former Lionel employee Helen J. Graham. Andy Lamonna for access to seldom seen instruction sheets. I also want to thank Anita Lovelock and Sylvia Striebeck, two women who have carried on and generously shared the research and passion for the hobby that characterized their late husbands, Harry Lovelock and Lewis Striebeck.

I extend thanks and congratulations to the creativity of Kristi Ludwig, Mardi Callahan and Helene Tsigristras, the trio of experts, who made the presentation of photographs and the design and production of this volume proceed so smoothly. Steve Streit merits special thanks for providing his expertise in artwork and graphics.

Finally, thanks to all the individuals at the Lionel Corporation who had a dream and made it happen. Thanks to the engineers there who documented everything as well as the packrats that preserved these extraordinary documents for more than four decades until I could share them with you.

To all, I am deeply grateful!

Dedication

To my wife, Laura, and children Collin, Zachary and Alexandria: Thank you for all your love and support, especially during all the times that I was locked away working. And to answer your question once again, **"Yes, this book is finally done!"**

To my mother and father, thank you for all the support and for fostering my love of toy trains. Thanks for making this Lionel "adventure" and Project Roar Publishing a reality.

Forward

WOW!! My eyes bulged and my hands trembled as I opened the first binder in the three-foot-high stack of Lionel historical documents. Nobody in the toy train hobby knew that these records, acquired from the highly esteemed train collection of Richard Kughn, existed. The binders contained Lionel Factory Orders for all outfits (cataloged and promotional O27, O, Super O and HO Trains as well as Raceway) manufactured by Lionel from 1960 through 1966. These documents were what Lionel used when manufacturing, packing and shipping each outfit. They contained information on every component in each outfit, including quantities, substitutions and customers. The amount of information was overwhelming.

Acquiring these documents began another stage in the journey of giving back to the hobby what it has given to my father and me. Joshua Lionel Cowen's dream of using trains to bring fathers and sons closer has been repeated time and time again. My father and I are one of the many beneficiaries of Cowen's insights and hopes.

Many collectors feared that these rare documents would again be buried away or, even worse, be lost in storage. My father and I had no intention of hiding what we had learned. Instead, we decided to publish this information as a way of helping others and enabling the toy train community to learn more about Lionel and its promotional outfits. Thus, Project Roar Publishing was formed, the team created and research began.

Initially, my father and I did not comprehend the full significance of what we now owned. We eventually realized that these Factory Orders represent the "Holy Grail" of Lionel outfit documentation. The first step was to go through the Factory Orders in detail. We found discovery after discovery locked away for years waiting to be documented, including the different use of suffixes for boxed and unboxed items, the outfit number of the Halloween General, item variations not previously known and outfits produced in quantities as low as six. Every day was a new adventure.

Hobbyists enthusiastically came on board and graciously shared their collections and assisted us in the research. Thousands of outfits were observed and photographed. The top train researchers also lent their time and expertise. Thousands of additional Lionel documents were uncovered and used to enrich our research.

This volume brings fresh and authoritative information to the toy train community. Never before has such in-depth Lionel information been presented in one volume. Hopefully, you will experience the same reaction as we did upon first viewing this information.

One major part of our journey has ended with the publication of this volume. Many more books will be coming from Project Roar Publishing as we continue to give back to the hobby what it has given to us: enjoyment, cooperation, and friendship.

My father and I at the auction in 2001, when we acquired the Lionel Factory Orders.

PART I

The Background

ELECTRIC TOYS—
A Profitable Line.

(FOR THE TOY BUYER)

LIONEL ELECTRIC TOYS

PULLMAN AND DAY COACH TRAINS WITH STEAM TYPE LOCOMOTIVES
(Electrically Operated)

THESE numbers are all packed complete, and should it be found desirable, the user can substitute the freight cars numbered 11, 12, 13, 14, 15, 16 and 17, described on page 11, for the Pullman Cars or Day Coaches which come with the outfits. An endless variety of combinations may thus be formed.

Outfit No. 50.

Outfit No. 50. Consists of one No. 51 Locomotive and Tender described on page 5, and one of the Pullman Cars numbered 180, 181 and 182, described on page 11, and 4 straight sections of track, measuring 15½ feet. Operates on 8 to 10 dry batteries, or the reduced house lighting current, described on pages 12 and 13. The complete train is 5 feet in length. Code word "Jersey" Price, attractively packed....................$22.00

Outfit No. 43.

Outfit No. 43. Consists of one No. 51 Locomotive and Tender described on page 5, two No. 29 Day Coaches, described on page 10, together with 8 curved and 4 straight sections of track, measuring 15½ feet. Operates on 8 to 10 dry batteries, or on the reduced house lighting current, described on pages 12 and 13. The complete train is 4 feet 5 inches in length. Code word "Leeds." Price, attractively packed....................$17.50

Outfit No. 6, with Large Pullman Cars

The above illustration shows No. 6 Locomotive in combination with large Pullman Cars numbered 18, 19 and 190. No. 7 Locomotive may be substituted for the one shown and the outfit can be converted into a freight train by the use of the cars numbered 11, 12, 13, 14, 15, 16 and 17, described on page 11. The train shown will operate on 8 to 12 dry batteries, or on the reduced house lighting current, described on pages 12 and 13. The complete train is 6 feet in length.

How to Use This Volume

This volume is intended for individuals who are interested in the promotional outfits developed by Lionel during the 1960s. Complete information on the history and everything about these outfits appears here for the first time. This volume is also aimed at postwar collectors seeking all the rich authoritative information that can be gleaned from the thousands of internal Lionel documents used to prepare this volume.

Lionel began offering promotional outfits to its customers in the early prewar years. However, the only authoritative and complete documentation for promotional outfits that is currently known to exist is the Lionel Factory Orders from 1960 through 1966. Information on the handful of promotional outfits issued from 1967 through 1969 included in this volume is derived from other internal documents as well as observations. Accordingly, this volume provides complete listings of components, along with pricing and rarity evaluations, for Lionel promotional outfits for the last decade of the postwar era (1960-69).

Because this volume contains so much information, we have placed its contents in four sections for the convenience of readers and collectors.

Part I - The Background
- **Baseline Information** - Definitions and terminology as well as how to navigate this volume is covered.
- **Historical Overview** - Roger Carp provides the history of Lionel promotional outfits from the prewar and postwar eras.

Part II - The Reference
- **Detailed Reference** - Information regarding the components included in promotional outfits and how to identify and date variations. Boxes, inserts, suffixes, outfit numbering, trucks and couplers are all covered in detail. This section also provides pricing and rarity definitions.
- **Lionel's Customers** - Lionel created unique promotional outfits for more than 170 different customers. Lionel's customers and their background are detailed.

Part III - The Outfits
- **Outfit Listings** - All promotional outfits from 1960 through 1969 are listed sequentially by the Lionel outfit number. Outfit components are listed exactly as they appeared on the original Lionel Factory Order. Each item number is Lionel's finished good number followed by a description.
- **Price and Rarity** - Outfit prices and rarity definitions are provided as part of each outfit listing.

Part IV - The Appendices
- **Appendices** - The appendices provide different views and analyses of data contained in this volume.

Definitions and Terminology

The selection and meaning of key terms in this volume are derived from Lionel documentation. For that reason, the ways such terms are defined and used may differ slightly from customary practices in the toy train hobby. Readers should, therefore, become familiar with how those terms are used and the explanations offered here.

Set versus Outfit

Collectors have long used the terms "set" and "outfit" interchangeably. However, Lionel employees generally referred to their trains as outfits in Factory Orders and other internal documents ("set" did appear on occasion). Because this volume is based on Lionel Factory Orders and other internal documents, the listings will be described as "outfits."

Uncataloged versus Promotional

Collectors have tended to refer to train outfits that did not appear in any Lionel catalog as "uncataloged." However, Lionel did not use such a term in its Factory Orders or other internal documents. Employees used "special," "non-cataloged" and "promotional" to describe such outfits. Descriptions in this volume will rely on the term "promotional."

Advance and Consumer Catalogs

For most of the postwar years, Lionel issued what are known as an "advance catalog" and a "consumer catalog." The advance catalog came out early in the year and targeted dealers, jobbers and distributors. Functional in design, it contained an early preview of items and outfits for the current year. The consumer catalog came out later in the same year (usually in the early autumn) and was aimed at the general public. Some items listed in the advance catalog did not make it to the consumer catalog because either the demand was not as great as expected or manufacturing issues arose.

Beginning in 1959, Lionel offered outfits in its advance catalog that intentionally were not shown in the consumer catalog. Collectors refer to these items as "advance catalog" outfits; Lionel employees called them "non-cataloged." The first of these was outfit no. 1105, which was created, according to the advance catalog, "To meet the needs of the low-priced mass toy market."

Classification of Promotional Outfits

Before delving into the history of Lionel's promotional outfits, particularly for the years covered by the Factory Orders, the author wishes to explain the methods by which those outfits will be distinguished and classified in this volume. The information provided in the Factory Orders regarding customers and items contained in different outfits is so rich and varied that previous systems of classifying promotional items, both prewar and postwar, are too limited.

Any attempt at creating an all-encompassing naming convention for classifying Lionel's prewar and postwar promotional outfits must begin with the recognition that these outfits can be differentiated by three criteria.

1. **Lionel's Customer** - To whom did Lionel sell a particular outfit?

2. **Outfit Exclusivity** - Was an outfit available to one or several customers?

3. **Outfit Items** - Were the items cataloged as regular-production, promotional-only, or a combination of the two?

Lionel's Customer

Lionel produced more than 700 promotional outfits between 1960 and 1969 and sold these to over 170 different customers. Combining this information with previous prewar and postwar research shows that Lionel's customers fall into the following eight categories (the first six qualify as retailers of some sort and the final two are manufacturers):

1. Retail department stores (examples include Sears, Penney and Ward)

2. Distributors (Arkwright and Associated Merchandising Corporation)

3. Catalog houses (Aldens, Penney, Sears and Spiegel)

4. Premium houses (Richie Premium, Sperry & Hutchinson and Top Value Stamps)

5. Automotive and tire dealers (Firestone and Western Auto)

6. Hardware and hobby retailers (Madison Hardware and Polk's Hobbies)

7. Manufacturer of consumer goods (Libby's, Quaker Oats and Stokely-Van Camp)

8. Business associations (National Organization of Railroad Business Women)

Among these diverse customers, those that fall into the six categories of retailers bought Lionel product for the purpose of selling it to obtain revenue. The two groups consisting of manufacturers and business associations bought Lionel items to promote product they developed and/or marketed, to advance their reputation, or to motivate and/or reward employees or members.

Category Used in this Volume	Includes	Example
Retailers	Retail Department Stores	Sears, Penney, Ward
	Distributors	Arkwright, Associated Merchandising Corporation
	Catalog Houses	Aldens, Penney, Sears, Spiegel
	Premium Houses	Ritchie Premium, Sperry & Hutchinson (S&H), Top Value Stamps
	Automotive and Tire Dealers	Firestone, Western Auto
	Hardware and Hobby Retailers	Madison Hardware, Polk's Hobbies
Manufacturers	Manufacturer of Consumer goods	Libby's, Quaker Oats, Stokely-Van Camp
	Business Associations	National Organization of Railroad Business Women

Outfit Exclusivity

Lionel designed its promotional outfits to be different from its cataloged outfits. On the one hand, Lionel could produce a promotional outfit for a specific customer. Thus, the outfit that Lionel designated no. 12885-500 went to Sears and was assigned a Sears-specific catalog number (no. 9836). Such an item will be referred to as a "Promotional Outfit."

On the other hand, Lionel could offer the same outfit to multiple customers. For example, Lionel outfit no. 19507 was offered by Penney as its no. X 924-8279 A and by Spiegel as its no. R36 J 5260. Such an item will be referred to as a "General Release Promotional Outfit."

The Lionel Factory Orders are clear in differentiating a cataloged outfit from a promotional outfit. Specifically, any train outfit that did not appear in a Lionel consumer catalog is classified as a non-cataloged or promotional outfit. Although advance catalog outfits technically appeared in a catalog (albeit advance catalog), they were classified on the Factory Orders as "non-cataloged" outfits and sold to many different customers. As such, they are classified and referred to as a "General Release Promotional Outfit."

Besides the two types of promotional outfits, Lionel sold cataloged outfits to retailers, who assigned them one of their own retail catalog numbers. Retailers used these numbers in their own catalogs as order and stock numbers. Retail numbers were often handwritten on the outfit or stamped by the retailer beneath or next to the Lionel catalog number. Sometimes the only identification of the retail number was through the price tag placed on the outfit. Thus, the S&H no. 6-P4807 outfit was a Lionel no. 11201 with the S&H number stamped below the Lionel number.

The Factory Orders that are used as the basis of this volume do not refer to the outfits described in the previous paragraph as promotionals for the simple reason that they were nothing more than cataloged outfits. Therefore, these outfits are not included in this volume, but will be included in a future volume.

Category Used in this Volume	Definition	Example
Promotional Outfit	Promotional outfit exclusive for a particular customer.	Sears 9836 or Lionel no. 12885-500. This outfit was produced exclusively for Sears.
General Release Promotional	Promotional outfit that was offered to numerous customers.	Lionel no. 19507 was a promotional outfit offered to numerous retailers. This was cataloged by Penney as X 924-8279 A and Spiegel R36 J 5260. Lionel no. 1123 was an advance cataloged outfit sold to numerous retailers. Lionel referred to this as a "non-cataloged" or promotional outfit.
Catalog Outfit	Catalog outfit that was also sold to a customer who labeled it with their own retail number. This is NOT a promotional outfit.	Sperry and Hutchinson (S&H) sold no. 11201 as 6-P4807. This is a no. 11201 stamped with S&H's number on the box. Penney sold no. 12820 as X 924-3700 A. These are both just cataloged outfits offered by a Lionel customer.

Outfit items

Lionel produced three types of items: cataloged, promotional, and unique promotional. Promotional outfits could include any combination of such items.

Cataloged items are those that appeared in Lionel's consumer catalog and were regular-production models. Sometimes these items appeared in promotional outfits before showing up in a Lionel catalog.

Promotional items are those that were offered only as a component of one or more promotional outfits and never appeared in a Lionel catalog. They might have started out as a unique promotional item, only to be included in subsequent outfits. Examples include the nos. 6050-150 Stokely-Van Camp boxcar and 6651-25 "Big John" cannon car.

Unique promotional items are those that were offered only as part of one promotional outfit and were unique to that outfit. For example, the no. 2347 Chesapeake & Ohio GP7 road switcher that's found only in the Sears no. 9836 (no. 12885-500) outfit.

Summary

Combining the categories of Lionel's customer (retailer or manufacturer), outfit exclusivity (promotional or general release promotional) and outfit items (cataloged, promotional or unique promotional) creates eight possible categories of promotional

outfits.

For example, the Sears no. 9836 (Lionel no. 12885-500) from 1965 is a promotional outfit sold to only a single retailer and containing at least one unique item. It therefore is considered a Retailer Promotional with Unique Items (the accompanying table defines this outfit as a Type Ic).

The Quaker Oats no. X-600 from 1961 is a promotional outfit sold to only a single manufacturer and containing both catalog and promotional items. It therefore is considered a Manufacturer Promotional with Promotional Items (the accompanying table defines this outfit as a Type IIIb).

The S&H no. 6-P4807 (Lionel no. 11201) is a cataloged outfit sold to a retailer and containing only catalog items. It therefore is considered a Cataloged Outfit and is not included in this volume.

This terminology is used throughout this volume.

Type of Promotional Outfit	Items in Outfit	Lionel's Customer	
		Retailer	**Manufacturer**
Promotional Outfit Sold to Exclusive Customer	*Catalog Items Only*	Retailer Promotional with Catalog Items Type Ia	Manufacturer Promotional with Catalog Items Type IIIa
	Promotional Item(s)	Retailer Promotional with Promotional Items Type Ib	Manufacturer Promotional with Promotional Items Type IIIb
	Unique Item(s)	Retailer Promotional with Unique Items Type Ic	Manufacturer Promotional with Unique Items Type IIIc
Promotional Outfit Sold to Multiple Customers **(General Release Promotional)**	*Catalog Items Only*	Retailer General Release Promotional with Catalog Items Type IIa	None Observed
	Promotional Item(s)	Retailer General Release Promotional with Promotional Items Type IIb	

How to Navigate This Volume

Most collectors of promotional outfits seek to verify the components of an existing or desired outfit. By comparing the outfit number on the box to the outfit listing in Part III, they will obtain the list of items originally included in that outfit, along with an optional picture, description and other information.

Once collectors have found the outfit in Part III, they can use Part II for further analysis of the individual components. This section will help to ensure that the outfit is 100 percent correct for the year it was manufactured. Collectors needing more assistance to identify an outfit should turn to the section on Completing an Outfit in Part II.

Other collectors may begin with a locomotive and seek information about the outfit in which it came. For this purpose, the Appendices in Part IV are a good starting point. Still other collectors may be interested in the outfits that Lionel manufactured for a particular customer. This information is included in the section on Lionel's Distribution and Customers.

Here's an example of what we're talking about. Suppose that outfit no. X-600 from 1961 is found partially complete in its original box. A collector trying to determine the outfit's components should start by looking up the X-600 in Part III to identify which items came with it. Since this outfit listing also has a photograph, he or she should compare each individual item to the photo.

If there is no photograph or additional information is needed, a collector should turn to the appropriate section in Part II. For example, if the no. 1103-12 packed envelope is missing, he or she should go to the Outfit Peripherals section in Part II to find the correct version of a 1103-12 for outfits in 1961.

As for the customer, outfit no. X-600 was a Manufacturer Promotional (Type IIIb) created exclusively for Quaker Oats. Information regarding Quaker Oats and its relationship with Lionel can be found in the section on Lionel's Distribution and Customers, another section in Part II.

Sources of Authoritative Information

Anatomy of a Factory Order

True to Project Roar Publishing's overall mission, the foundation of this publication is internal Lionel documentation combined with expert observations. Thousands of documents, memos, reports, catalogs as well as many hours of interviews with former Lionel employees have been condensed and summarized for this volume. Thousands of train outfits were observed, photographed and documented. Numerous postwar Lionel experts reviewed, assessed and augmented the contents. All of these sources led to countless new discoveries and clarifications of many past assertions. Overall, this authoritative volume provides information that will live on for generations.

The jewel of the documents and the foundation of this volume are Lionel train outfit Factory Orders. A Factory Order documents the process of "ordering" a product (individual part, component item or complete train outfit) to be manufactured from the factory. For train outfits, this was a bill of material listing all the items meant to be packaged in an outfit, along with detailed assembly instructions. Items were identified by specific suffixes outlining the unique variations used in a particular outfit. All item substitutions were documented. Instructions also detailed how many outfits should be made, how to stamp the boxes, how many outfits to include in a master shipper and where to deliver the outfits once the order had been completed.

Historically, the Factory Orders represent the "Holy Grail" of Lionel train outfit documents. Taken as a whole, they list every outfit item manufactured from 1960 through 1966.

An outfit began when sales and factory personnel worked together to finalize its components. Then the Outfit Packing Department would engineer the boxing and inserts required. Members of the Production Planning and Scheduling team would coordinate all inventory management to determine which additional items had to be manufactured or could be substituted as needed for specific outfits.

On receiving the finished Factory Order, the Outfit Packing Department would pull the designated items from stock and assemble the outfit. Once everything was complete, they would deliver the outfit to Finished Goods. This entire process was all held together by the Factory Orders.

Factory Orders for a particular outfit evolved as requirements changed. If an outfit were successful, subsequent orders could be issued; if it flopped, orders might be canceled. Either way, the results could well affect the available stock of existing items. That, in turn, led to inventory changes and possible substitutions, all normal inventory management issues that arise in any manufacturing concern. Factory Orders were updated accordingly.

The Anatomy of a Factory Order

The original Factory Order for promotional train outfit no. 19212 from 1963. It is annotated to describe the level of information the Factory Orders provide. This authoritative information - never before published or available to general readers - is the basis of this volume.

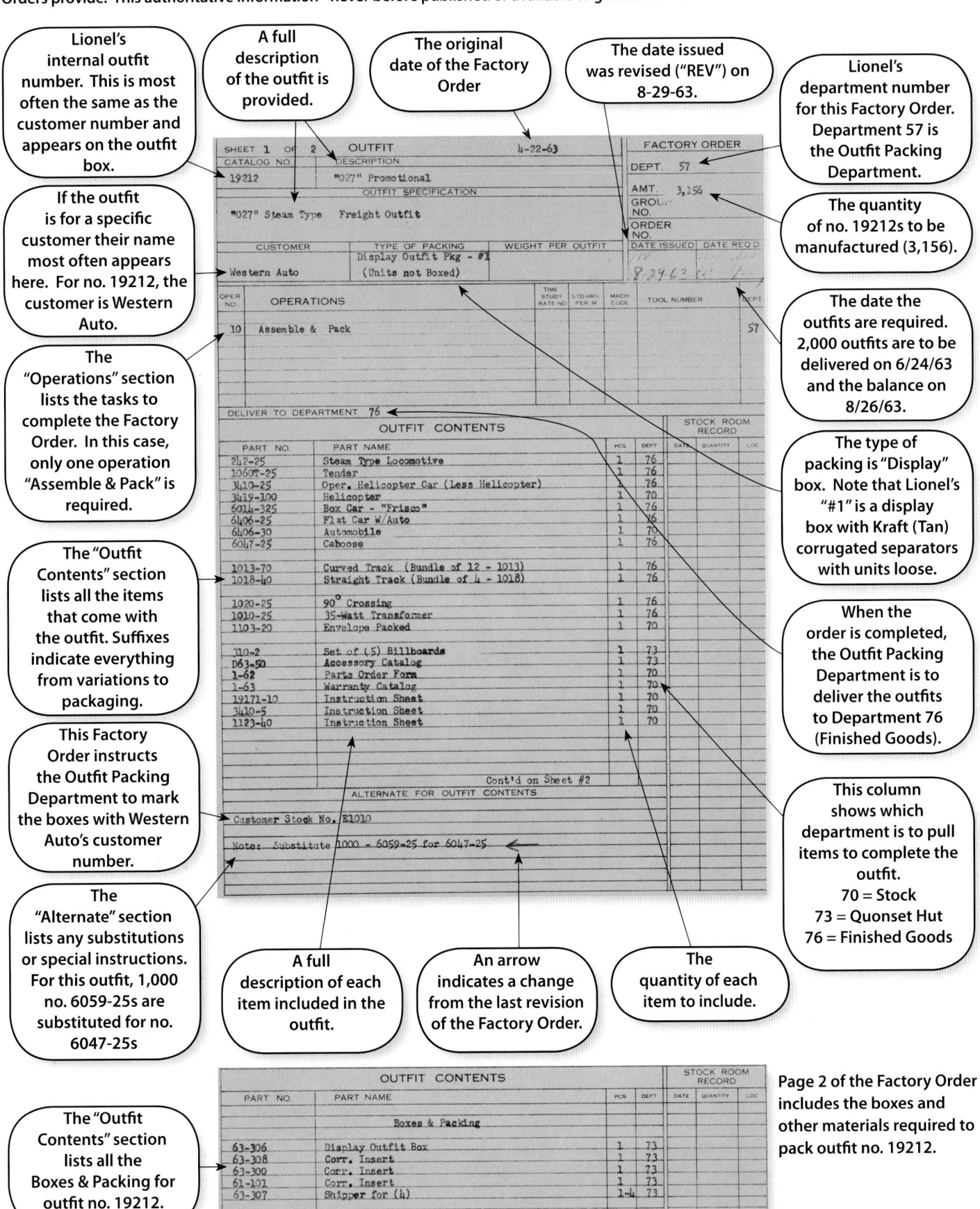

Lionel's internal outfit number. This is most often the same as the customer number and appears on the outfit box.

A full description of the outfit is provided.

The original date of the Factory Order

The date issued was revised ("REV") on 8-29-63.

Lionel's department number for this Factory Order. Department 57 is the Outfit Packing Department.

If the outfit is for a specific customer their name most often appears here. For no. 19212, the customer is Western Auto.

The quantity of no. 19212s to be manufactured (3,156).

The "Operations" section lists the tasks to complete the Factory Order. In this case, only one operation "Assemble & Pack" is required.

The date the outfits are required. 2,000 outfits are to be delivered on 6/24/63 and the balance on 8/26/63.

The type of packing is "Display" box. Note that Lionel's "#1" is a display box with Kraft (Tan) corrugated separators with units loose.

The "Outfit Contents" section lists all the items that come with the outfit. Suffixes indicate everything from variations to packaging.

When the order is completed, the Outfit Packing Department is to deliver the outfits to Department 76 (Finished Goods).

This Factory Order instructs the Outfit Packing Department to mark the boxes with Western Auto's customer number.

The "Alternate" section lists any substitutions or special instructions. For this outfit, 1,000 no. 6059-25s are substituted for no. 6047-25s

This column shows which department is to pull items to complete the outfit.
70 = Stock
73 = Quonset Hut
76 = Finished Goods

A full description of each item included in the outfit.

An arrow indicates a change from the last revision of the Factory Order.

The quantity of each item to include.

The "Outfit Contents" section lists all the Boxes & Packing for outfit no. 19212.

Page 2 of the Factory Order includes the boxes and other materials required to pack outfit no. 19212.

11

The Anatomy of a Factory Order - Continued

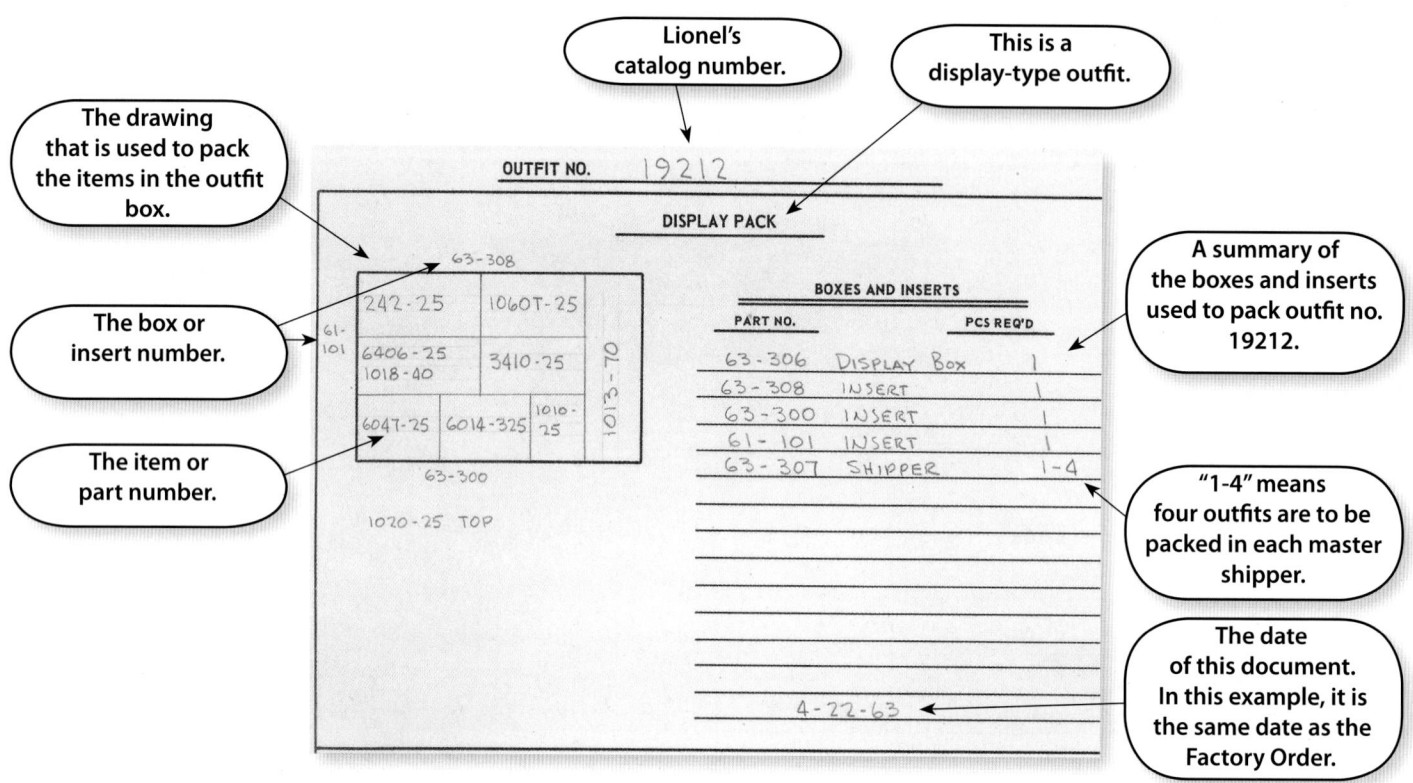

Lionel's catalog number.

This is a display-type outfit.

The drawing that is used to pack the items in the outfit box.

The box or insert number.

The item or part number.

A summary of the boxes and inserts used to pack outfit no. 19212.

"1-4" means four outfits are to be packed in each master shipper.

The date of this document. In this example, it is the same date as the Factory Order.

Attached to the Factory Order is the Outfit Packing Diagram, which shows how to pack the trains using the required boxes and inserts.

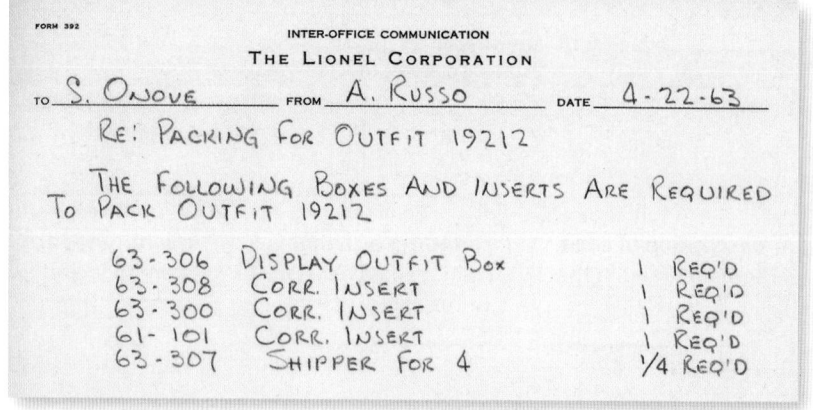

This is a memo from the Outfit Packing Department to the Production Control Department dated 4/22/63. It specifies the boxes and inserts required so they can be added (typed on) to the Factory Order.

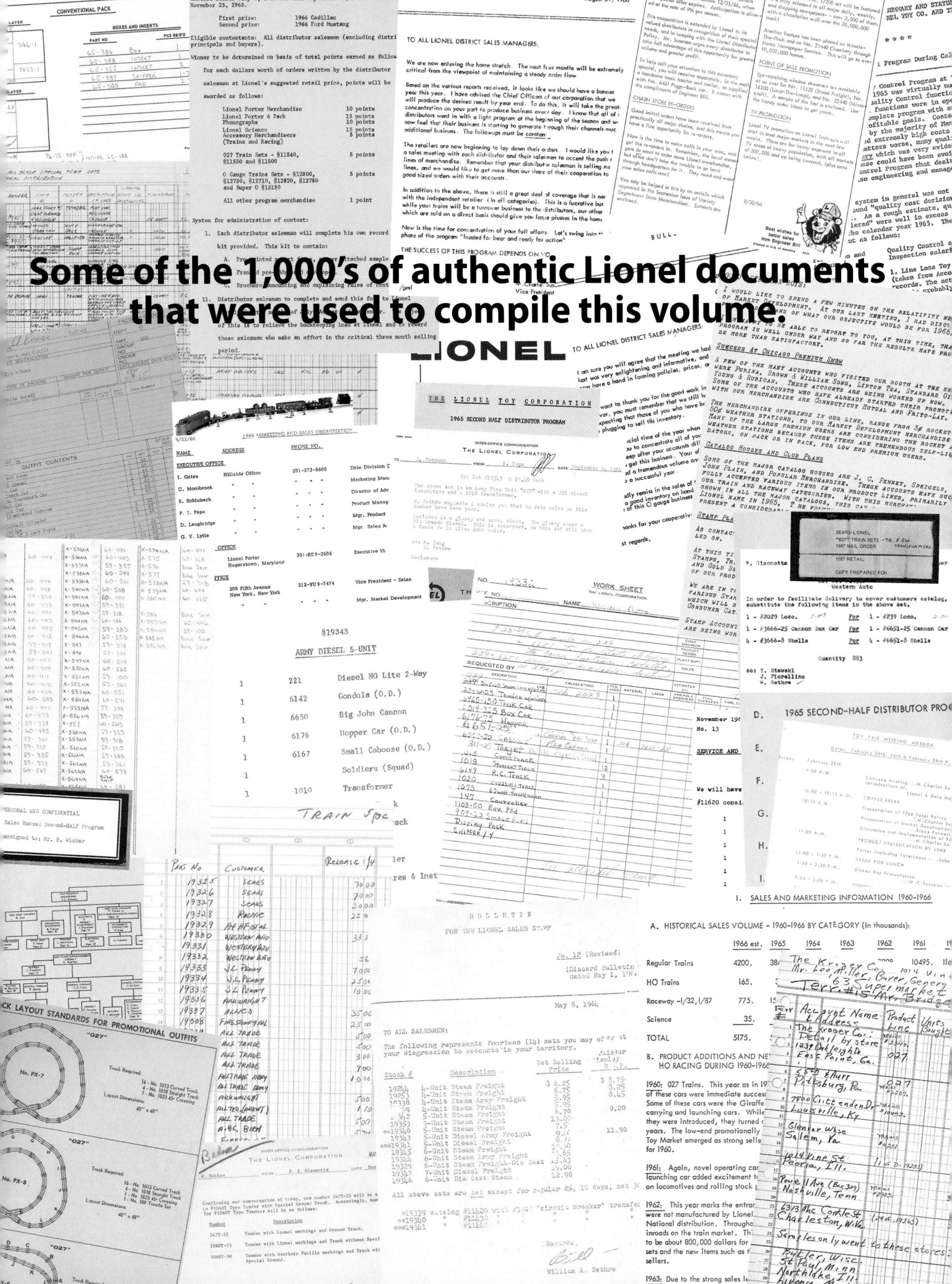

Some of the 1,000's of authentic Lionel documents that were used to compile this volume.

The History of Lionel's Promotional and Special Outfits

By Roger Carp

I. Mysteries and Clues

The more involved with Lionel electric trains collectors become, the more questions that arise in their minds. The number of their queries is all but endless: When did Lionel first issue this steam locomotive? Which passenger cars went into that outfit? Why didn't Lionel catalog that boxcar for more than two years? What kind of stamping was used on this caboose? Where did Lionel obtain the load for that flatcar? And on and on.

But beyond this enormous list of specific when's and what's, two overarching questions emerge. The first of these relates to how many of certain trains, outfits, and accessories Lionel produced. The search for the paperwork that might contain that information ("production figures") has lasted for decades, with only occasional documents surfacing that contain partial or tentative answers. The Holy Grail, in short, has yet to be discovered. As a result, collectors may never be certain that items they consider "scarce" truly are.

The second question that has perplexed experienced collectors relates to those items, particularly outfits, which Lionel created but did not describe in its annual catalogs. Certain outfits and occasionally a particular model were either not mentioned or depicted in the advance catalog (a black-and-white document issued by Lionel early each year, usually for the annual American Toy Fair in New York City, to show dealers what they might order) or the consumer catalog (the color "wish book" that Lionel distributed in the autumn and winter, in quantities generally exceeding one million in the postwar years, to show customers what they could buy).

Outfits that didn't appear in the advance or consumer catalogs remain shrouded in mystery. In fact, collectors can't even agree on what to call them. Some refer to these outfits as "uncataloged" or "noncataloged" because these items were not shown in a Lionel catalog. However, to be fair, they may have appeared in a catalog put out by a wholesale or retail firm or been advertised in some manner by Lionel.

Dave McEntarfer, who has studied these outfits in depth and written about them in the fourth volume of *Greenberg's Guide to Lionel Trains, 1901-1942* (published in 1995), chides his fellow enthusiasts by reminding them that Lionel never used the word "uncataloged." He prefers the terms "promotional outfits" and "specials," mainly because Lionel used them in the prewar documents he consulted. (The records from the 1960s that form the basis of this volume support the use of the terms "non-catalog," "promotional," "promotional outfit," and "special"; nowhere in these documents is an outfit described as "uncataloged.") According to McEntarfer, outfit boxes might be stamped or carry a label in the 1930s with the word "SPECIAL." Or they might display a number with the prefix "PO," which he believes stood for "Promotional Outfit."

Regardless of the terminology that collectors employ, they admit to being exasperated because complete information about what Lionel offered beyond its catalogs and when these mysterious outfits were made available has eluded them. Some researchers may have even wondered whether, after Lionel expanded its line in the 1960s with such items as slot-car raceways, science kits, and juvenile phonographs, it included those items in its promotional offerings.

(The documents that form the basis of this volume offer evidence that Lionel did create promotionals using road racing sets, and HO scale trains. However, unless noted otherwise, when the terms "promotionals" and "specials" are used in this introduction, they refer strictly to Standard, Super O, O, and O27 gauge toy trains.)

The questions asked by Lionel enthusiasts about promotional outfits have increased over the time. Unfortunately for them, about all that they have been able to do in their search for answers is keep chasing after train outfits that they can somehow verify have not been modified. Only by examining such "specimens" can they hope to learn more about Lionel's use of specials.

Tantalized by promotional outfits and frustrated by the lack of information, collectors have not abandoned their hunt for original paperwork that describes these special trains. Even packaging, outfit boxes in particular, has value, although a box may be missing the locomotive, cars, and other items originally put in it. The goal has always been to determine what Lionel offered (as well as when) and where various items not mentioned in the catalog appeared.

Thanks to a number of dedicated collectors, our understanding of the myriad Lionel promotional trains has grown. Among the many sleuths who have advanced research in this fascinating area, a handful deserves special mention. Besides Dave McEntarfer, Stuart Armstrong, James Havey, and Charles Weber have uncovered vast amounts of information about prewar outfits. Joe Algozzini, Paul Ambrose, and the late Harry Lovelock, along with Weber, have analyzed non-cataloged items from the postwar era, especially the years between 1956 and 1969. They have searched for facts and trains. Then they have generously shared what they have learned.

Gaps nonetheless remain. No one knows precisely what Lionel did in the area of promotional items. Conclusions about when Lionel offered specific pieces or in what quantities remain vague, to the consternation of collectors. They know that only original and complete sets of documents from Lionel can shed light on this murky field and ultimately provide the full story.

Information of this nature, covering the years between 1960 and 1966, became available a few years ago. Stout Auctions announced that it was selling a stack of loose-leaf binders filled with typed and mimeographed sheets describing more than 700 promotional and 140 cataloged Super O, O, and O27 gauge train outfits and hundreds of HO scale train and road racing outfits. The documents also contained information about the contents and packaging of outfits and the destinations of outfits created by Lionel for special clients. These notebooks belonged to Richard Kughn, the former owner of Lionel Trains Inc.

Great excitement surrounded the news that so much information about promotional items had surfaced. Bidding for this set of binders was expected to be fierce, and that certainly proved to be true. When the dust had cleared and the competition was over, George and John Schmid were the proud owners of this treasure trove of information.

To the benefit of everyone in the toy train hobby, this father-

and-son team soon made clear its intention to share the valuable information about Lionel's train outfits and (eventually) its slot-car raceways. This volume is the result of the Schmids' determination and generosity.

The notebooks that the Schmids now own are indeed overflowing with descriptions and diagrams related to more than 700 promotional outfits that Lionel created for retail and wholesale firms throughout the United States in the 1960s. The contents of each promotional outfit are carefully described and accounted for. There are instructions on how to pack the box containing the various models, and data concerning the quantity of outfits to be produced. Dates by which each promotional train was required and to which business it was promised are also included. Many outfits even have internal costing and pricing information. For collectors of postwar Lionel trains, not to mention any hobbyist interested in the marketing strategies of America's main manufacturer of toy trains in the twentieth century, this information is nothing short of extraordinary.

Since these documents represent a complete listing of items in outfits from 1960 to 1966, questions that collectors have pondered for years can now be answered with certainty: When was the no. 6651-25 "Big John" cannon car produced? Which sets contained a no. 215P Santa Fe Alco A diesel? How many of the no. R36 J 5287 (no. 19237) outfits were ordered by Spiegel? What were the correct contents of the no. 19328 outfit? Which retail outlet sold the no. 19260 outfit? What is the real number and customer for the "Halloween Set"?

These topics are just the beginning. Much remains to be learned as the Schmids share what they acquired and knowledgeable collectors analyze those documents (to be referred to as Factory Orders). Much of that research and the conclusions drawn from it appear in this volume. Other information will appear in subsequent volumes as well as articles in *Classic Toy Trains* magazine. All Lionel enthusiasts await opportunities to be enlightened and better understand what they may own or have seen elsewhere.

II. Lionel Develops its First Outfits: 1910-15

To understand the significance of the Factory Orders and the information contained in them, the place of promotional outfits and specials in Lionel's history must first be considered. Lionel was not the first American toy train manufacturer to sell what collectors recognize as a set of trains - individual cars and the locomotive to pull them. The general opinion among historians of the toy train industry is that an outfit first appeared in a Lionel catalog in 1910, four years after the firm began producing what it advertised as three-rail, sectional "Standard gauge" track and the engines, trolleys, and rolling stock to run on that track.

Long before 1910, other American toy makers were offering customers the opportunity to purchase entire trains and not just individual items. Originally, of course, these trains were pulled or pushed along floors without the benefit or need of track. Then, before the turn of the twentieth century, Carlisle & Finch, a Cincinnati-based manufacturer of what were known as "electrical novelties," added a miniature mining train to its list of products for the home and the military.

Ives Manufacturing Corporation, among the leaders in the domestic toy industry and certainly the primary manufacturer of miniature trains, also marketed sets before Lionel did. The Ives

trains generally relied on windup, or clockwork motors, although a few did use battery power. (Ives did not bring out an electrified set until 1910.)

Looking at the matter from a broader perspective suggests that Lionel and its domestic rivals were slow to see what had been apparent to German toy producers since the 1880s. These firms, the preeminent makers of toys in the world, realized the advantages of matching a locomotive powered by dry-cell batteries or household current with two or three freight or passenger cars and a complete network of track. A manufacturer could raise the price of this full-fledged railroad by promising that buyers would obtain everything they needed at once.

This marketing ploy, so obvious in retrospect, was pioneered by Marklin and Bing, two well-established toy companies based in Nuremberg. Executives there recognized that the concept of a set enabled a retail merchant to sell multiple items instead of individual ones. In other words, consumers, rather than buying a

Lionel's founder, Joshua Lionel Cowen

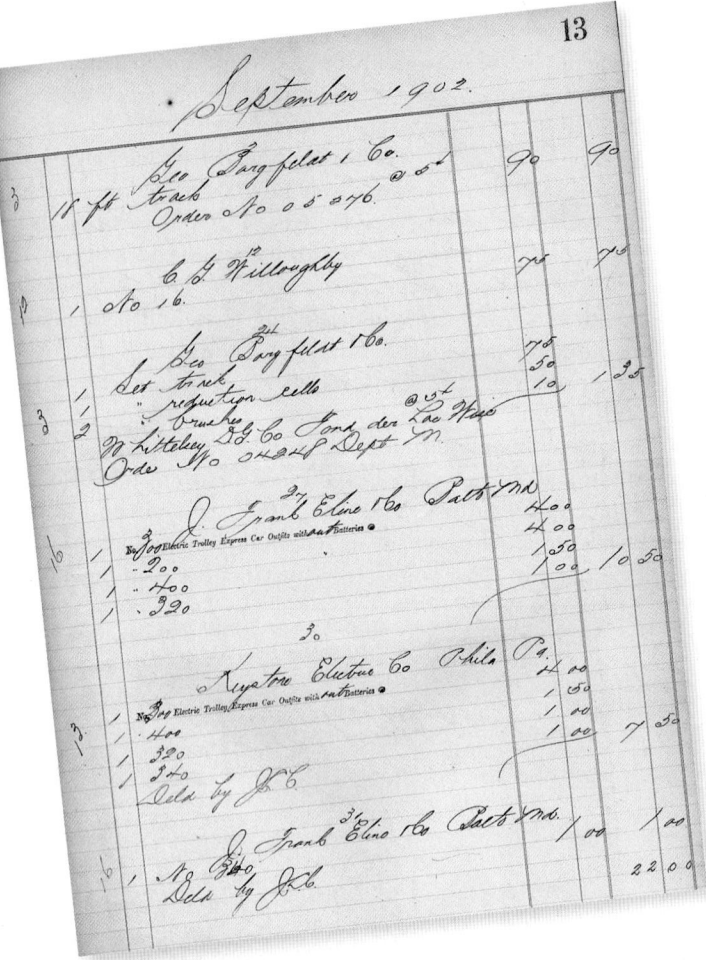

Lionel's first ledger from September 1902 featured an order from Keystone Electric Company of Philadelphia, for the nos. 300 Electronic Trolley Express Car Outfit, 320 Switch and Signal, 340 Bridge and 400 Express Trailer Car. Subsequent correspondence with Lionel indicated that this window display led to "quite a few orders". Note this order was delivered by "JLC" himself.

locomotive and rolling stock that they freely chose, had to buy a complete package as designed by the manufacturer. There was no opportunity to omit or substitute; a set was an all-or-nothing deal.

Lionel may have been slow to introduce full-fledged sets, but there was never a doubt that the marketing savvy shown by the company's founder, born Joshua Lionel Cohen, would bring great success. By the time the first real sets were shown in the 1910 catalog, Cohen had taken a number of significant steps. For one thing, he was imitating Ives - and soon surpassing this rival - in putting out a splashy catalog every year, in time for the holiday season, when sales increased. For another thing, Cohen made sure that Lionel had a presence at the American Toy Fair, which was first organized in 1903 and then scheduled annually right before the start of spring. Wholesalers and representatives from department and chain stores arrived in New York City to see what toy makers were offering and to place orders for the upcoming buying periods. In the meantime, Cohen placed advertisements in trade journals that served the toy, hardware, and electrical novelty fields. He was determined to present his wares in as many venues as possible to bolster sales.

A determination to increase revenue led Cohen, as early as

1902, to push the notion of selling an individual motorized unit and track so that consumers and merchandisers could set up electrified displays in their homes or retail establishments. In 1904 and 1905, he supplemented his firm's "Special Show Window Display" to include a gondola as well as the locomotive, track, and a crude miniature bridge. Cohen introduced a new line of trains in 1906 that he brashly called "Standard gauge." He offered in the same package a trolley, an assortment of track on which it could run, and two dry-cell batteries. This combination Cohen called an "outfit."

Not until four more years had passed did Lionel present the first of what enthusiasts would recognize as outfits. Eager, as was Ives, to mimic and then surpass the Germans, Lionel sought in 1910 to provide consumers with an alternative to the individual trolley or locomotive operated over Standard gauge track. So the company showed two items in its catalog that consisted of an electric-profile locomotive pulling two types of freight cars over a circle of track.

Lionel, by offering for sale a designated group of items at a specified price, gave consumers a gentle ultimatum: either buy the outfit the manufacturer has already prepared or pay more to obtain the individual pieces desired. Thus was accelerated the firm's marketing strategy. That strategy, along with breakthroughs in engineering design, production technology, and painting, would enable Lionel to dominate the toy train industry and become one of the most important toy makers in American history.

In the early 1910s, Joshua Cowen (he Anglicized his name in 1910) slowly increased the number of outfits shown for sale in the annual Lionel catalogs. Passenger outfits joined freight trains. Some outfits included more than one of the same car; most of the others contained all different components. As early as 1913, one freight outfit boasted five pieces of rolling stock to go with its locomotive and 12 sections of track. A power source had to be purchased separately, probably because not all the families buying Lionel sets lived in homes with household current.

Despite the advantages to Lionel and its retail dealers of selling outfits, consumers discovered a few flaws. For one thing, cataloged outfits didn't always have exactly what the buyer wanted. A boy might desire a cattle car when only a gondola was offered. Or the cars that a youngster preferred came with a locomotive that didn't appeal to him. The only solution was to make a separate purchase of the item that he yearned for.

A related problem was that buying an outfit didn't provide a consumer with something unique. Instead, the train he bought might duplicate what his friend ended up with. The latter problem affected retailers, too. For example, the department stores that had become the primary venue for Lionel's sales network by the 1920s ended up advertising the same outfits at the same specified prices. Consequently, dealers felt frustrated that they could not rise above their competitors by claiming to have something special for their customers.

III. The First Lionel Promotional Outfits: 1913-15

There were, in short, good reasons for Lionel to offer its best clients - those that placed large orders on a consistent basis - something special. Ives had already learned this lesson. Frank M. Reichenbach, writing in the second volume of *Greenberg's Guide to Ives Trains* (published in 1992), states that as early as 1908, Ives created specially lettered tenders to accompany steam locomotives that it supplied to Montgomery Ward, which was then the second leading mail-order merchandiser in the United States.

Lionel followed suit a few years later. As early as 1913, it developed a Standard gauge outfit that differed from what consumers found in the current annual catalog. McEntarfer identifies this earliest "special" as a midnight blue version of cataloged outfit no. 34. Ward announced this outfit in its catalog, complete with an illustration.

What Lionel provided Ward (and perhaps a few similar retailers, although no verification has been reported) was a regular-production outfit painted in a color otherwise unavailable. The creation of something special through decoration (painting, lettering, or later molding), whether an entire train or a single car, remained a part of Lionel's marketing strategy throughout the prewar and postwar eras. Even if this item were separated from its packaging, a knowledgeable observer would recognize that it was different from its regular-production counterpart.

A second way of developing something different became evident just two years later in 1915. Cowen, assisted by his national sales manager Mark Harris, a veteran in the toy field, took the next and logical step. Lionel took cataloged outfits consisting of regular-production items and modified one of the components. Laborers at the Lionel factory stamped the electric-profile locomotives with the name of a specific customer and then added a unique number. As was true of the midnight blue items prepared for Ward, these engines couldn't be confused with models packed in cataloged outfits or sold individually. Their markings made them unlike any other locomotive.

The committee of experts that researched and compiled Lionel Trains: Standard of the World, 1900-1943 (published by the Train Collectors Association in 1989) pinpointed five such promotional outfits as dating from 1915 or possibly 1916. Three were Standard gauge passenger outfits that went to F.A.O. Schwarz, the famed toy emporium. Inside each box were two or three regular-production cars pulled by an electric-profile locomotive that was rubber-stamped with initials ("F.A.O.S.") that identified the business plus a two-digit number seen nowhere else. With these outfits, Schwarz, a major Lionel client and a leader in toy merchandising, could announce that it sold trains unavailable to its rivals.

The Ward and Schwarz outfits each qualify as what is referred to here as a "Retailer Promotional with Unique Items" (Type Ic); McEntarfer called them "Department Store Specials." Some or all of the items that Lionel prepared for these two retailers were recognizably different from regular-production versions.

A second group of promotional outfits from 1915 can be placed in a related though separate category. Lionel negotiated with the Quaker Oats Company to decorate the electric-profile locomotives that led two regular-production O gauge passenger sets with markings that identified that business. (Lionel brought out its first models in this smaller gauge in 1915.) Like the Schwarz outfits, these two trains came with engines resembling ones pictured in the annual catalog but stamped with the name of a particular customer and unique numbers

These outfits can be classified as "Manufacturer Promotionals with Unique Items" (Type IIIc); McEntarfer called them "Factory Specials." This designation acknowledges the fact that, while the locomotives were distinctive beyond their packaging, Quaker Oats was not a retail operation. Indeed, how or even why that firm marketed these trains remains undocumented.

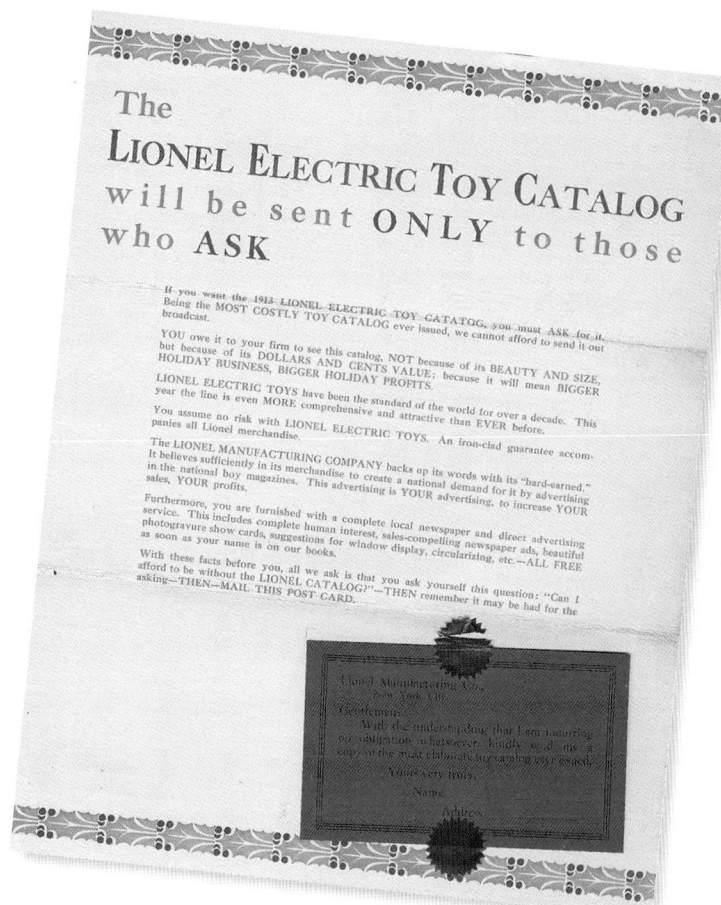

Lionel's 1913 catalog was the "Most Costly Toy Catalog ever issued". As such, Lionel mailed 2,000 flyers to potential customers who in turn had to request a catalog. Note the still attached return request card.

IV. Retailer Promotional Outfits: 1925-32

A decade passed before there appeared further signs of Lionel making promotional or special trains. Why this lapse occurred is yet another puzzle. Certainly, if sales of the F.A.O. Schwarz outfits had been disappointing, interest in having Lionel create a similar special would have vanished. Evidence to support this hypothesis lies in the fact that, starting in 1916 and continuing through 1919, F.A.O. Schwarz turned to Ives to create at least two special sets for it. One of these Retailer Promotionals with Unique Items (Type Ic) featured a No. 1 gauge electric-profile locomotive with "F.A.O.S." stamped at each end. The other, an O gauge steam train, came with a locomotive having the same initials added beneath its cab windows. Ives seemed to have reasserted its supremacy, at least in the area of specials.

Knowing that Cowen and Harris were sharp, hard-driving businessmen makes it difficult to imagine that they had given up on negotiating with retailers to purchase special Lionel trains after 1915. All the same, the first group of Retailer Promotionals documented after World War I were made by Ives. In 1924, three years after Ives introduced a line of Wide gauge trains to compete directly with Lionel's Standard gauge outfits, it created unique items in that size and in O gauge for John Wanamaker, a major retailer in Philadelphia and New York. Locomotives included in these sets boasted paint schemes different from regular-production Ives models. These engines, in addition to the passenger cars they pulled, were stamped in gold, "Wanamaker Railway Lines."

Not until 1925 or '26 did Lionel return to making promotional outfits. Buyers for eastern department stores, aware of Wanamaker's relationship with Ives and perhaps believing that the special Ives trains had sold well, might have turned to Lionel for something similar. Decision-makers at Lionel could have taken the initiative, too, and found an audience willing to listen, particularly since Lionel trains dominated the domestic market.

Cowen and Harris undoubtedly recognized the potential benefits of selling promotionals. Credit for promoting the idea should possibly also go at this time to Arthur Raphael. Hired as a junior salesman in 1921, he climbed the ladder rapidly at Lionel and soon was overseeing sales for New York City. Within a decade after joining the firm, Raphael had successfully challenged Harris for the position of national sales manager and emerged as Cowen's right-hand man. A brilliant marketer, Raphael could have been a driving force in Lionel's again promoting its trains through specials.

Regardless of where the spur came from, the trend of offering promotionals, once launched, became a critical tactic in Lionel's marketing strategy right up to the time it had to cease manufacturing electric trains because of the demands of the war effort in 1942. The number of promotional outfits rose steadily during this nearly 20-year period, especially after Lionel emerged from equity receivership in January of 1935 and regained financial stability in subsequent years.

More than 100 prewar Standard, O, and O27 gauge promotional outfits have been documented or reported thus far. To the dismay of collectors, few of them qualify as Retailer Promotionals with Unique Items (Type Ic). The vast majority of promotional outfits contained only regular-production locomotives and passenger or freight cars that were not decorated in any manner that would cause them to stand out. The only way hobbyists can link these items with a special of any kind is to discover them inside an original outfit box that, in turn, was marked with a label, stamping, or sticker to indicate that Lionel or a retailer considered the train to be a special at the time it was originally sold. Remove most trains from their special outfit box and they are easily lost amid their twins placed in cataloged outfits.

Collectors may lament the fact that so many prewar promotional outfits were special in name and packaging only, but Cowen and his lieutenants would hardly have minded. If they could create an outfit that might satisfy a key customer and increase sales without having to allocate revenue to cover additional steps in the decorating process, so much the better. What counted by the mid-1920s was using train outfits (cataloged or otherwise) to attract huge numbers of new customers - youngsters and families - into this growing niche in the toy field. Outfits enabled those consumers, through a single purchase, to obtain virtually everything necessary to enjoy a miniature train. Thereafter, they might supplement that initial purchase with additional rolling stock, an assortment of accessories (signals, tunnels, stations, street lamps, and more), and plenty of track and switches to create an entire railroad system in Standard or O gauge at home.

Given the central role of outfits in Lionel's marketing, Cowen and Harris could, quite sensibly, have sought to fill their catalogs with a selection of outfits that was broad enough to cater to every potential customer. Such an approach would have dictated at the very least offering O gauge outfits with only a locomotive (with a cheap electric or even a clockwork motor), freight car, and caboose to poor urban families or to rural households that had yet to be connected to the nation's expanding grid of electrical power.

But Lionel's leaders did not strive to design a cataloged train set for every American. They had no interest in emulating Henry Ford and developing the toy equivalent of a Model T. Executives at Lionel followed their chief in adopting a different philosophy, one that ultimately affected the outfits shown in the firm's annual catalogs as well as those made available as specials.

From the time that Cowen had launched his enterprise, he had portrayed Lionel as the producer of high-quality, innovative miniature trains that utilized the revolutionary power source of electricity. The fact that not every family could afford a Standard or O gauge train was not a disadvantage that Cowen struggled to overcome. On the contrary, he wanted his wares to be viewed as sophisticated, a bit complicated, and truly upscale. Fulfilling demands for "cheap trains" would undermine the urbane image he pursued. Let upstarts like American Flyer Manufacturing Company and Hafner Manufacturing Company (and later Louis Marx & Company) appeal to low-income groups with small, inexpensive trains. Lionel would, like the metropolitan department stores carrying the firm's trains, aim for the middle and upper classes.

Having taken that stance, the leaders of Lionel nonetheless looked for ways to avoid surrendering any segment of the market, even the low end, to competitors. Specials and promotional outfits struck them as the best answer. These items could include fewer components than similar cataloged outfits. They might contain locomotives or cars that had been superseded by newer items in the cataloged line. Either way, specials could be tagged with lower prices than cataloged outfits had and still not make dangerous inroads into Lionel's traditional market.

Another aspect of the philosophy behind the creation of promotional outfits related to where they were sold. Lionel tended to make these less desirable outfits available to a few hardware accounts and large mail-order chains, such as Sears, Roebuck and Co. and Montgomery Ward. These retailers dealt with a different, less affluent and urban clientele than did leading department stores. Lionel could, therefore, reach out to Sears without offending the buyers from Gimbel's or Macy's. Of course, the latter establishments might also want something unique to advertise, but would expect it to be more upscale and expensive. Even better would be an outfit that met the requirements of a Retailer Promotional with Unique Items (Type Ic) and was decorated to herald a particular retailer.

This two-pronged approach (appeal to middle- and upper-income consumers with cataloged items and a handful of better promotional outfits while offering low-end specials to consumers with more limited means) characterized Lionel's marketing strategy for approximately a decade after it resumed making specials around 1925. Two types of promotional outfits exemplify this marketing strategy, each of which collectors associate with a particular retailer. On the one hand, Lionel created some of its most desirable Standard and O gauge outfits, each unique in some indisputable manner, for R.H. Macy & Company department stores in New York City. On the other hand, Lionel formed a relationship with mail-order giant Sears that lasted well into the postwar period and involved the sale of a huge number of inexpensive outfits. Most of these "Sears Sets" either came with fewer items than comparable cataloged outfits or were identical with what Lionel was showing in its catalog at a higher price.

The "Macy Specials" have taken their place among the most celebrated of all prewar outfits in the eyes of collectors, who avidly pursue them. Between 1926 and 1932, Macy's, a leader in retail merchandising, offered Standard and O gauge outfits produced in limited quantities. Like the trains that Ives had made for Wanamaker, these were Retailer Promotionals with Unique Items (Type Ic) in the finest sense, returning to what Lionel had done for F.A.O. Schwarz in 1915. Virtually every Macy Special contained regular-production locomotives and passenger cars (a couple of freight sets have been reported) that were decorated in unique paint schemes and lettered with the name of this renowned store.

These promotional outfits would have required extra planning and decorating steps at the Lionel factory, thereby raising production costs. Lionel assuredly passed along these higher costs to Macy's, which responded by hiking up the retail prices. This arrangement, a bit extravagant for everyone involved, was another casualty of the Great Depression. Sales of electric trains suffered, and Macy's quit ordering specially decorated trains even before Lionel sank into equity receivership in May of 1934. Little did Cowen and his staff realize that the era of true Retailer Promotionals with Unique Items (Type Ic) had ended.

How many different Macy Specials did Lionel develop? Collectors have pondered that basic question for a generation. According to McEntarfer, nine different Standard gauge and eleven different O gauge Macy Specials have been either verified or claimed as having been sold. Some of these outfits featured combinations of locomotives and cars unlike anything cataloged by Lionel. One example of a unique group is the O gauge "Macy's Railroad Terminal" outfit from 1931. It came with a renumbered no. 253 locomotive and three no. 610-series passenger cars.

Other Macy Specials duplicated outfits advertised in the Lionel catalog, except that the components had been painted in schemes never offered there. In 1930, for example, Lionel transformed cataloged Standard gauge outfit no. 387 into a Macy Special by painting the three passenger cars brown and cream instead of peacock and orange. In almost every one of these promotional outfits, locomotives and cars that typically have "Lionel Lines" stamped or etched onto their shells were instead marked "Macy Special." Similarly, the observation cars in Macy Specials were equipped with celluloid drumheads announcing their unique designation.

Collectors remain fascinated with these Macy outfits, especially because such a mystique envelops them. Who, they wonder, was responsible for the creation of Macy Specials? Did department store executives approach Lionel and request something unique? Or did someone at Lionel, perhaps Harris or Raphael (then overseeing sales in New York City), offer to put together something special? Finally, why after 1932 did the specials carried by Macy's no longer contain unique items? From that time on, Lionel offered Macy's only the same promotional outfits (what McEntarfer terms "General Release" outfits and here are called "Retailer General Release Promotionals") with either cataloged or promotional items that it made available to other department stores and mail-order firms.

Unfortunately for hobbyists, no documents have surfaced thus far to shed light on these matters. The notion that Macy's

This undated photograph from the postwar era shows (left to right) Arthur Raphael (executive vice-president and national sales manager), Lawrence Cowen (president) and Joshua Cowen (chairman of the board of directors).

earned such distinction by being the top-selling distributor of Lionel trains has no merit. Starting in the late 1920s, General Electric placed enormous orders each year for the many appliance retailers carrying its merchandise across the United States. Even more important, according to McEntarfer, was Sears. Based on the number of Lionel outfits sold to the public, it deserves to be considered Lionel's number one client in the prewar era.

As for why Lionel stopped making Macy Specials, the obvious answer is that declining sales of toy trains during the Great Depression forced Macy's to stop carrying these fairly expensive sets. Not until 1960, with the release of outfit no. X-583NA, does it appear that Macy's returned to selling Lionel promotionals.

To repeat, Retailer Promotionals with Unique Items (Type Ic) on a par with what Lionel offered Macy's were the exception when it came to prewar promotional outfits. They combined with mid-level and high-end cataloged trains to reach Lionel's preferred clientele.

By contrast, most specials, particularly after 1925, revealed a simpler approach directed at typical households with restricted budgets. This approach represented the flip side of Lionel's marketing strategy. Executives might have wanted to camouflage this side through the creation of Retailer General Release Promotionals (Type II), but it likely accounted for a sizable portion of the company's sales during the 1930s and early '40s.

V. Retailer General Release Promotionals: 1925-42

Most prewar promotionals, especially those sold by Sears, amounted to cataloged outfits whose contents had been subtly changed. Usually, that meant removing one car or substituting another, less-desirable model. No more would Lionel go to the trouble of altering regular-production locomotives or cars in ways that made them distinctive. Modifying cataloged outfits proved to be less expensive and more efficient; as such, it met the demands of an array of customers.

The first option when creating a promotional (deleting an

item or two from a cataloged outfit) appeared early on. Sometime between 1925 and 1928, Gimbel's Department Store offered an O gauge special with two passenger cars. This train was identical to a cataloged outfit (Lionel no. 98 from 1925), except that the latter had three cars (a second Pullman) and more sections of track.

A few years later, as an example of the second method of putting together a promotional, Lionel offered a Standard gauge passenger special that contained two Pullmans and an observation. Outfit no. 360 appeared in the catalog at the same time (1931) with the same contents save one difference. It came with a baggage car rather than a second Pullman.

Still other promotional outfits from the late 1920s featured items that Lionel had dropped from its cataloged line. Presumably, then, it relied upon these promotionals to use up leftover inventory otherwise of no use. For example, Lionel did not catalog no. 100-series freight cars in its Standard gauge line after 1926. However, a promotional outfit from the next year included five of those cars and a current-production no. 10 locomotive.

Also in 1927, two different department stores (Rosenbaum and Snellenberg) offered the same special that included three no. 600-series passenger cars, which had last appeared in the Lionel catalog two years earlier. Around 1931, Lionel created a Standard gauge promotional headed by a no. 9U, an electric-profile engine with an 0-4-0 wheel arrangement, last shown in the catalog two years before. Having redesigned the no. 9E as a 2-4-2 electric making its debut in 1931, Lionel was eager to get rid of older stock.

Retailer General Release Promotionals (Type II) worked well for Lionel and the different retailers ordering them in the late 1920s and '30s. Sears joined the crowd and soon became the main buyer of specials from Lionel. Surprisingly, this mail-order leader didn't establish a formal relationship with Lionel until 1925. That was 15 years after Sears first carried Ives trains and about 10 years after it began showing Hafner trains in its catalogs. No explanation has surfaced as to why Sears and Lionel had not previously done business; Cowen and Harris were too astute and aggressive not to have recognized the dominance of Sears in the nation's retail merchandising.

Credit for finally matching the two American icons went to Raphael, at least according to an article reprinted in the February 1949 issue of *Toys and Novelties*, a publication for the toy and hobby industries. "At the time," the story went, "Sears was selling a low-priced German train. Raphael offered them a Lionel set for $22.50, which the mail order house took with some misgivings."

How did Raphael, still a junior salesman in 1925, pull off such a coup? Had he really succeeded where his bosses had failed? Or was he claiming a victory that actually belonged to the deceased and all-but-forgotten Harris two decades after the fact? The truth, it should be plain, can hardly be ascertained. Neither is it clear that Sears had quit selling its Ives and Hafner outfits and replaced them with nothing more than only "a low-priced German train." All that can be verified is that in 1925 the sole annual Sears catalog, distributed in the fall and winter, announced that Lionel outfits could be ordered.

The Lionel outfits offered by Sears ranged from five to ten in number per year. They were identical to what was depicted in the Lionel catalog, although surviving examples in boxes with a Sears sticker have been found with minor modifications. For example, a freight outfit might have a different car, but only as a result of a substitution made at the Lionel factory based on what was available at the moment. Changes of this nature were unplanned; Lionel intended that Sears outfits duplicate what was in its catalog and so treated Sears as only another outlet, albeit an important one, for its trains. As such, the vast majority of Lionel outfits sold through Sears in the 1920s and early '30s fit the definition given here of Cataloged Outfits.

To be sure, customers placing orders at that time did specify a Sears catalog number and not whatever designation Lionel had assigned to an outfit. However, as McEntarfer observes in his Greenberg reference guide to prewar Lionel outfits, the outfits sent from Sears "were shipped in the original Lionel boxes, with the Lionel outfit number printed on the label. None of the trains were ever marked with the Sears name or any other special name to identify them as Sears."

By and large, none of the outfit or component boxes of what were Cataloged Outfits contained any reference to Sears. In fact, only the presence of a sticker on the outside of the outfit box signaled that this outfit had come from Sears.

This practice changed during the Depression years, certainly by 1933, when Sears began distributing two catalogs annually (the bigger fall and winter catalog soon followed by the Christmas catalog). For the first time, as indicated by the original outfits examined by Dave McEntarfer, Charles Weber, and other

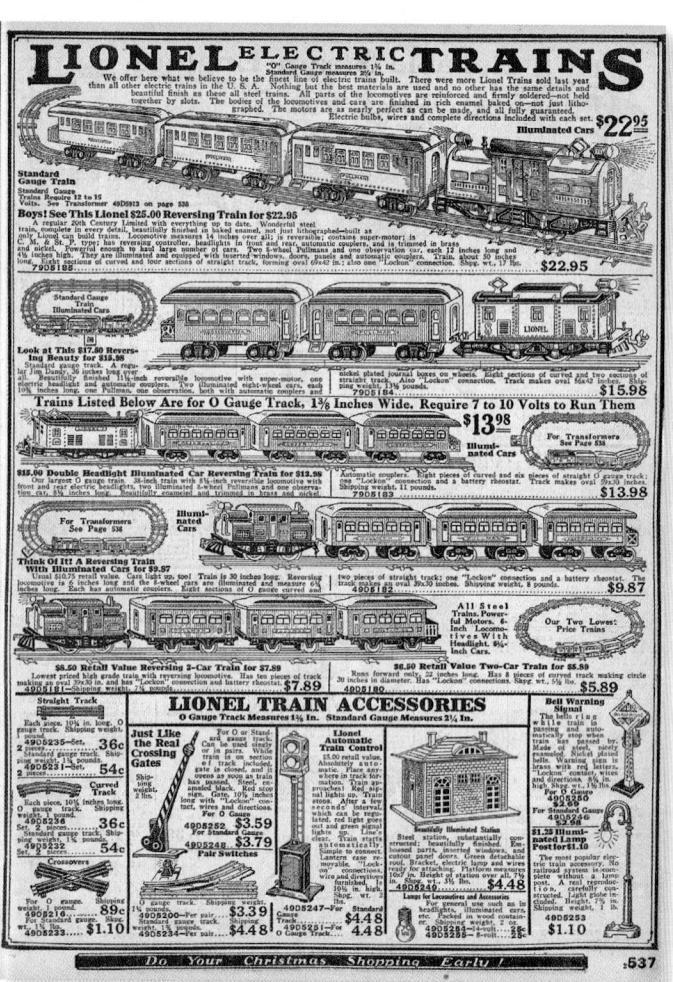

Lionel's relationship with Sears, Roebuck and Co. began in 1925 when Lionel trains first appeared in the Sears Fall and Winter Catalog. The six outfits offered were Lionel catalog outfits.

hobbyists, Lionel outfits packaged in boxes with a Sears sticker on them displayed differences with the versions of those outfits cataloged by Lionel.

This change occurred when, with the advent of a second catalog geared for the holiday season, Sears moved most of the Lionel outfits out of its fall and winter catalog. Among the handful of outfits still shown there, one tended to be a mail-order special, an exclusive O or O27 item not available from even another outside source. These "Sears Specials," McEntarfer writes, are the key to dating other Lionel promotional outfits between 1937 and 1942 because they differed each year and were assigned unique numbers by both Lionel and Sears.

The Lionel outfits advertised in the Sears Christmas catalog after 1933 usually came straight out of the Lionel catalog. Nonetheless, exceptions have surfaced. Some outfits were identical, not to what was shown in the Lionel catalog, but to the promotional outfits offered to other department stores and dealers. These Retailer General Release Promotionals (Type II) might be marked "Special" or have a unique number with a distinguishing prefix ("PO," used between 1928 and 1930 and most likely standing for "Promotional Outfit") or suffix ("X"). Because Sears purchased such enormous amounts of these specials, Lionel may have dropped the wholesale price far below what it asked other customers to pay.

As reported by collectors Stuart Armstrong, James Havey, and Weber, the promotional outfits made available to Sears, plus other Retailer General Release Promotionals (Type II), were varied and produced in huge quantities, so much so that more of these promotional outfits may have been available in a given year than were cataloged ones. Lionel's goal, again, was to increase sales by giving Sears and other major accounts something that was unique yet priced extremely low.

At the same time, these promotional outfits enabled Lionel to use up unsold merchandise, particularly locomotives that had been superseded by newer models. For example, Sears O gauge outfits nos. 5178 (1931) and 5187 (1933) were led by early versions of the no. 258, an engine that Lionel deleted from its catalog after only one appearance back in 1930.

Armstrong and Havey contend that from the late 1930s until the onset of World War II, Lionel used Sears Specials, among other promotional outfits, to dispose of surplus assembled rolling stock that lacked the features found on better models. Cars in Sears outfits (nos. 5994 from 1938 and 5992 from 1938-41 are examples) might come with manual latch couplers at a time when Lionel was avidly plugging automatic couplers in its catalogs and advertisements. Or, as with no. 5971 from 1939, a Sears outfit might come with an RCS uncoupling section yet have only one model with the electric coupler to benefit from it.

Other Sears Specials were designed to finish supplies of less sophisticated equipment. Steam outfits that came with a tender lacking a whistle stand out. Lionel enthusiastically promoted its whistle from 1935 on, yet still built tenders without that improvement to provide a low-cost alternative, especially for promotionals.

Similarly, Lionel assembled freight and passenger cars without lights or such neat touches as air tanks, steps, and journals to fill in promotional outfits. In fact, between 1937 and 1942, it put together versions of the nos. 607 and 608 passenger cars without journals and air tanks and then gave them new numbers. The stripped-down nos. 609 and 611 appeared in Sears Specials and other promotionals.

Finally, Lionel depended on these outfits to deplete inventories of non-powered dump or log cars after operating versions of those models made their debut.

Sears occasionally got something that was noticeably different from, possibly superior to, what Lionel saved for its cataloged line. In 1935, Sears outfit no. 5155 featured eight-wheel red-and-cream nos. 629 and 630 passenger cars while cataloged outfits came with only four-wheel versions. The no. 238 Torpedo streamlined steam locomotive showed up in promotional outfits for Sears and other retailers in 1939 and 1940 painted black, but was gunmetal when cataloged by Lionel from 1936 through 1938. Only Sears Specials and some other promotionals ever came with versions of the no. 1690-series passenger cars painted peacock with cream trim.

Some of the most interesting promotional outfits reveal how determined Cowen and Raphael were to lure buyers into the toy train hobby. Besides having a locomotive, cars, and track like cataloged outfits, some promotionals included one or two switches and a transformer. Better still were outfits that came with an accessory of some sort. The nos. 6300E/W from 1938 as well as nos. 6401F and 6713WCF from 1939 had a no. 1045 operating flagman. Depending on the version, outfits nos. 7003, 7004, and 7005 from 1940 and '41 could offer a no. 316 trestle bridge or a 1045 operating flagman.

Increasing sales in general, appealing to the lower end of the market, attracting first-time buyers, getting rid of unwanted merchandise, and rewarding large accounts - these factors help explain why Lionel developed many promotional outfits. Sales of these unique items may have surpassed that of cataloged outfits because retailers were free to set their own prices for the promotional outfits. They weren't bound by law or the dictates of Lionel to hold prices at a particular level lest they undercut competing retailers.

These Retailer General Release Promotionals (Type II) and even those exclusives offered to Sears were, by and large, only slightly different from what Lionel offered in its catalog. Overall, they were low-priced outfits aimed at the bottom of the market. By offering a growing array of promotional outfits, Lionel could go on pretending that it directed its trains at only the middle sector and high end of the toy-buying public (as suggested by the prices in its catalog). Promotionals met consumer demands for inexpensive Lionel trains and enabled thousands of families to enjoy an electric train at a low price.

These practices continued through 1942. In May of that year, a federal decree prohibited Lionel and its rivals from using "strategic materials" (notably metals) to produce toy trains. Lionel likely hurried to create as many outfits as possible to maintain sales levels in 1942 and assist retailers struggling to meet the demands of consumers. A number of unique and inexpensive outfits were put together because executives at Lionel had learned over the years that promotionals were an integral and lucrative part of their marketing strategy. They would not forget this lesson while World War II raged and plans for what to do next were being made.

VI. Dry Spell After World War II: 1946-54

By the spring of 1945, Americans had no doubt that the war in Europe would soon be over. How long the Allies would need to subdue Japan was unknown, although some experts estimated that fighting would continue in the Pacific Theater for another two or even three years before Tokyo surrendered. Fortunately for Lionel and other toy makers, the federal government lifted its restrictions on their use of various metals in June of 1945. Production of electric trains could resume, and Lionel rushed to solicit orders for the upcoming holiday season.

The sense of urgency felt by Lionel's brain trust heightened after the United States dropped two atomic bombs on Japan in August and the war officially ended the following month. J.L. Cowen, now chairman of the board, and his son, Lawrence, promoted to president, pressed factory superintendents to have an abbreviated line of trains ready for Christmas. The two Cowens worked hand in hand with their friend, Arthur Raphael, who held the posts of executive vice-president and national sales manager. To their delight, Lionel was able to offer retailers one cataloged O gauge train set in 1945. The next year, executives vowed, would be better.

They were right. Given an entire year to develop a line of trains and accessories, Lionel performed beautifully. The consumer catalog featured an enormous array of outfits. Having ten O gauge outfits (three of which could be purchased with a slightly more expensive whistle tender) and thirteen O27 outfits (six of which could be upgraded with a whistle tender) would seem to have been more than enough to meet the demands of every consumer. Prices for these cataloged outfits ranged from $24.95 to $85.00.

With so many outfits cataloged at a wide assortment of prices, buyers for department stores, appliance and hardware distributors, and toy shops must have been ecstatic. But what about the promotionals that had been so essential to Lionel's marketing strategy just a few years earlier? Did the Cowens and Raphael recommend that outfits with different combinations of locomotives and cars, and perhaps an accessory or switches, be created to increase sales? Was Lionel ready to pick up where it had left off with Sears and other retailers? Would any Retailer Promotionals with Unique Items appear again?

Definitive answers to these elementary yet critical questions remain elusive. The documents - sales agreements, contracts, packing orders, and correspondence - that might reveal the truth have yet to surface, if they even exist. Instead, interested collectors have, as with most prewar specials, been forced to pore through old retail catalogs and newspaper advertisements while trying to authenticate the promotional outfits that have come to their attention. The picture remains murky, at least until 1960, when the Factory Orders offer the necessary information.

Ambrose and Algozzini, writing in the fourth volume of *Greenberg's Guide to Lionel Trains, 1945-1969* (published in 1992), state that Sears, the nation's premier retailer during the postwar period, again carried Lionel trains in its annual Christmas catalog. Three such outfits, all identical to what was shown in the Lionel consumer catalog, were listed in 1946. Furthermore, note Ambrose and Algozzini, both O27 outfits as well as the O gauge train "were packaged in the same manner and were retailed at the same price as Lionel suggested in their own consumer catalog." However, these three outfits were given four-digit numbers for Sears orders rather than their Lionel designation. Missing is information as to whether the Sears numbers were printed by Lionel on the outfit boxes or merely "assigned" by Sears and then handwritten or hand-stamped by Sears retailers. Either way, these outfits cannot fairly and accurately be described as promotionals. They qualify as only Cataloged Outfits that were sold to a retailer.

This pattern of selling cataloged outfits at regular prices through Sears continued through 1954. Lionel managed every year to provide Sears with at least four outfits, one of which was an O gauge train. Nothing changed even during the Korean War, when shortages of materials might have detrimentally affected production schedules. Indeed, that conflict did drastically limit the number of American Flyer S gauge train sets, cataloged as well as promotional, that Lionel's chief rival, the A.C. Gilbert Company, manufactured. By the same token, whether Lionel also created true promotional outfits in the early 1950s and for whom it did so have yet to be determined.

We do know, thanks to American Flyer collector Robert J. Tufts, that Gilbert kept releasing a few promotional sets every year as a means of ridding itself of excessive inventory, particularly of models superseded by newer versions. Tufts observes in *The Almost Complete Guide to American Flyer S Gauge Sets* (published in 1999) that Gilbert, whose S gauge trains first challenged Lionel in the market in 1946, seems to have been plagued by significant amounts of unsold trains far beyond what Lionel experienced. Consequently, Gilbert rushed in the late 1940s to put out a handful of sets with no cataloged equivalent to make up for lost sales. These promotionals also enabled Gilbert to deplete its stock of items that had been made obsolete by the development of improved models.

The records Tufts consulted indicate that a few of the American Flyer sets he analyzed can be classified as promotionals (most were Retailer General Release Promotionals [Type II], although some were intended for particular retailers only and so were Retailer Promotional outfits [Type I]). By contrast, Ambrose and Algozzini state that every one of the Lionel outfits they examined or reported that came out before 1955 matched a cataloged one. Looking at Sears, they observe that corporate purchasing agents based in Sears' central office in Chicago ordered Lionel outfits as mail-order items for national catalogs, especially the Christmas book, and as over-the-counter ("display") items at Sears retail outlets. Regional buyers met with Lionel salesmen to order more product for stores in a specific area, in addition to mail-order purchases through regional Sears catalogs. These arrangements, conclude Ambrose and Algozzini, went on at least through 1967.

Firestone Tire & Rubber Company followed the same course. Raphael had first ironed out an agreement with this automotive distributor to carry electric trains in 1940. Firestone, according to the article reprinted in the February 1949 issue of *Toys and Novelties*, hoped to change its specialty stores into "a more general type of outlet." By 1948, Firestone dealers reported sales of Lionel trains exceeding $1.21 million, which was more than 10 percent of its total annual volume of toys. The earliest observed postwar outfits with a Firestone number (the contents duplicated what was found in the Lionel catalog) date from 1950, according to Ambrose and Algozzini.

No evidence has appeared, even after the exhaustive research conducted by Ambrose and Algozzini, to suggest that Lionel and major retailers had negotiated deals for promotionals - unique combinations of equipment - between 1946 and 1954. Only one such promotional outfit has been documented, the no. 3103W steam freight outfit from 1946. Lionel created this O gauge four-car train for New York's Madison Hardware Company, purported to have been its top-selling retail outlet. An advertisement for this outfit, which included a mix of cars unlike that found in any cataloged outfit, appeared in the October 1946 issue of *Model Builder*, a magazine put out by Lionel to promote its trains and the model railroad hobby.

Then all notice of this promotional outfit disappeared, and Madison Hardware never offered anything like it. Perhaps other retailers, feeling slighted by this special, pressured Lionel to withdraw it from the market or make it available to them as a Retailer General Release Promotional (Type II). At the same time, nothing close to a Retailer Promotional with Unique Items (Type Ic) or a Manufacturer Promotional with Unique Items (Type IIIc) was being made by Lionel either.

It's worth noting that Gilbert did create a Retailer Promotional with Unique Items (Type Ic) in 1947 and a Retailer Promotional outfit the following year. First came set no. 4605F for the G. Fox Company, a department store with outlets in Connecticut. Besides a specially decorated boxcar with the firm's name, this set came with a whistling billboard advertising FoxMart. In 1948, besides some Retailer General Release Promotionals (Type II) containing obsolete items, Gilbert put together its first S gauge promotional outfit for a specific retailer. Set no. 4850 went to Montgomery Ward, a business that, according to Ambrose and Algozzini, didn't carry Lionel outfits in the postwar era until 1955. (Marx trains were regular additions to the Ward catalog by 1955, as Robert C. Whitacre shows in the third volume of *Greenberg's Guide to Marx Trains*.)

We can only speculate as to why Lionel limited its options and offered retailers only cataloged outfits through 1954. Popular demand for its products may have been so strong that company executives saw no reason to create specials. Tales abound that during the years immediately after the war Lionel regularly shipped less than what wholesalers and other key accounts requested as a means of whetting the public's appetite for electric trains. A second possible explanation relates to the role of promotionals in undercutting competitors' attempts to capture the low end of the market. Lionel dealt with this problem by introducing the Scout line of bottom-of-the-barrel trains in 1948. Assembling basic specials might, therefore, strike executives as counterproductive and even damaging to Lionel's reputation.

Still another answer may relate to enforcement of Fair Trade Laws. According to this legislation, retailers had to respect the price levels set by a manufacturer. Thus, when Lionel specified in its catalog and price lists that a certain outfit had a price of $49.95, every store carrying that outfit was required to sell it for that amount. Discounting was prohibited. To avoid giving any of its accounts an advantage, Lionel may have deliberately refused to create specials, which could be sold for lower prices. Retailers, in turn, may have been satisfied selling American Flyer or Marx trains, which invariably cost less and were marked below comparable Lionel outfits.

This picture differs in notable respects from what Tufts suggests was going on at Gilbert's headquarters in New Haven, Connecticut. The manufacturer of American Flyer trains depended on specials to eliminate unsold inventory as well as supplies of items rendered out of date by ongoing development of better motors in locomotives, smoke units in tenders, and the mechanism used for operating cars. Promotionals played a major role in depleting inventory of S gauge freight and passenger cars equipped with old-fashioned link couplers after Gilbert started bringing out items with realistic knuckle couplers in 1952.

If, as Ambrose and Algozzini suggest, Lionel assembled

Madison Hardware Company, located in New York City, advertised the no. 3103W in 1946. This is the only Retailer Promotional outfit documented between 1946 and 1954.

virtually no promotional outfits between 1946 and '54, the reason must be that its sales staff and plant superintendents were able to avoid or compensate for the kinds of problems that hit Gilbert. Careful planning and coordination between what was ordered and how much was actually made must have prevented excessive quantities of Lionel trains from being produced and then filling storage areas after the annual buying period.

Improved production control, inventory management, and planning at Lionel were probably a result of the company installing International Business Machines (IBM) equipment in the 1950s and using it for production control. "Counting components became more precise, and that helped us plan and schedule production and track the movement of parts and subassemblies," recalls Peter Giannotta, a longtime Lionel employee, who supervised production planning there in the late 1940s and '50s (see "Keeping track of track - and trains - at Lionel," in the March 2003 issue of *Classic Toy Trains*).

Lionel could, as a result, reduce any leftover inventory through cataloged outfits the next year and not have to turn to low-priced specials. In addition, the firm's engineering and production personnel must have been more successful than their counterparts at Gilbert in planning ahead to ensure a smooth transition between the introduction of improved parts that could cause everything they replaced to be considered out of date and useless and, therefore, without value on the market.

Couplers would be a prime case. Lionel was fortunate to have introduced a knuckle coupler incompatible with earlier couplers immediately after the war. By then, thanks to a three-year production hiatus caused by wartime restrictions, inventory with the older couplers was all but gone. Moreover, consumers were so eager to buy electric trains that they willingly accepted that their prewar equipment would not work with the new trains. Similarly, refining the new smoke unit for 1947 did not compel Lionel to create specials to handle the high-end steam locomotives it had produced with an inferior unit in 1946. Luck and planning clearly worked in Lionel's favor.

Circumstances changed significantly for Lionel after 1954. To start, sales figures no longer climbed at spectacular rates; eventually a decline would be evident, one that would continue for more than a decade. Among the disappointments in the line were the Scout trains. Lionel's campaign to defeat Marx in the low end of the market had failed. Something else had to be tried if sales were to grow.

As important, legal challenges to the Fair Trade Laws by disgruntled retailers had collapsed and opened the floodgates to stores eager to slash prices on electric trains and other toys. Lionel had fought these new retailers and thrown its support behind its traditional network of stores. Unfortunately for them, times were changing. The public begged for enhanced competition, particularly from discount houses, and searched for bargains on everything from refrigerators and televisions to baseballs and electric trains. Once state and federal courts threw out fair trade legislation, the scramble was on. Lionel, like Gilbert, had no choice but to join the throngs of manufacturers revamping their pricing policies.

VII. Retailer Promotional Outfits at Sears, Ward, and Firestone: 1955-59

The year 1955 represents a watershed for Lionel's marketing policies in general and its approach to promotional outfits in particular. Signs of change at Lionel regarding the demise of Fair Trade Laws cropped up in the 1955 consumer catalog. The previous year, Lionel indicated the components of each of its O and O27 outfits and specified a retail price. Consumers knew exactly what they were getting and for how much. In 1955, however, thanks to the breakdown of the Fair Trade Laws, catalog descriptions were remarkably vague. On a typical two-page spread in the consumer catalog, Lionel showed a couple of locomotives and an assortment of rolling stock. The implication was clear: an outfit could be assembled with either of the locomotives pulling some but not all of these cars. And no outfit number or price was shown.

Consequently, dealers typically ordered what they wanted from Lionel or through a distributor, paid the wholesale price, and then attached a retail value of their choosing. One store might sell a three-car freight train for $25. Its rival down the street could, without penalty, offer the same item for $22 in an effort to lure in more business and make up the loss by selling a greater quantity of those and other discounted outfits.

This dramatic change, coupled with Lionel's sense of foreboding, augured well for retailers and consumers. Three major retailers - Sears, Ward, and Firestone - deserve special consideration for a few reasons. To start, unlike toy shops or department stores, Sears and the other two offered both traditional "on-site" sales and mail-order business based on their own catalogs. Put another way, a consumer could purchase the wares offered by any of these three giants either by stopping at one of its authorized retail outlets and paying in person or by mailing in payment and having the items ordered shipped to his or her home or local post office. Second, the sales networks of all three retailers stretched across the entire United States rather than being limited to a handful of cities or a single geographic region. Finally, the size of the orders for cataloged and promotional outfits that Sears, Ward, and Firestone placed with Lionel between 1955 and 1959 surpassed those of other mail-order retail firms.

Ward, for example, showed Lionel outfits in its holiday catalog for the first time in the postwar period in 1955. According to Ambrose and Algozzini, these outfits "were identical in content to Lionel cataloged sets and…were packed in the same manner as the Lionel outfits." Those writers assume that most of these Ward outfits "did *not* have a preprinted Ward outfit number." However, Ward did assign its own inventory numbers to the train sets it sold.

Firestone followed the same procedures. Ambrose and Algozzini contend that "all Lionel outfits sold through Firestone before 1956 were just regular production sets, with Lionel outfit numbers, that were packaged in ordinary Lionel set cartons." Consumers paging through Firestone catalogs might have found these sets identified by the numbering system developed by that firm. Firestone numbers would then have been handwritten on the set boxes or printed on a price sticker. In 1956, however, Firestone offered three low-end cataloged outfits packaged in set boxes that Lionel stamped at its factory with the special designation ("11-L") used by Firestone.

As an aside, one of Firestone's rivals in the tire and automotive field may also have been stocking Lionel cataloged outfits. Tufts reports that B.F. Goodrich, which also boasted a nationwide sales network, sold Gilbert and Lionel trains. Thus far, however, no first-hand observations have been made or documents reported to show that Goodrich offered Lionel outfits in the 1950s.

The real breakthrough in Lionel's changing marketing strategy appeared at Sears. Among the five Lionel outfits offered in 1955, all of which were O27, was one unlike what was depicted in the firm's catalog. There, Lionel showed a four-car freight outfit headed by a no. 2328 Burlington GP7 road switcher. It identified this cataloged outfit as no. 1531W/505. Ward also advertised this set in its catalog.

Sears, however, offered the Burlington freight outfit with a no. 3484-25 operating boxcar in place of the no. 6462 gondola that Lionel specified as a component of its cataloged set. Then, to indicate that the Sears outfit differed from the Lionel (and Ward) version, Lionel stamped a special number on the set box: 505X. (Sears assigned its own inventory number to this outfit, 9652.)

This Sears Special has interest for a couple of reasons. First, the item that distinguishes it from the cataloged outfit - an operating boxcar - is superior to the gondola that Lionel was offering. Second, that cataloged outfit could also be purchased through Ward in 1955. Therefore, Sears could honestly claim to have a special whereas its principal rival offered no more than what every other Lionel retailer was stocking that year.

With the demise of Fair Trade Laws and the benefits of promotional outfits apparent to retailers large and small, specials again became central elements in Lionel's marketing program. These unique, often collectible trains demonstrate that, starting in the second half of the 1950s and continuing throughout the '60s, sales executives were far more imaginative and motivated than Lionel enthusiasts have assumed. Generally speaking, contemporary observers believe that every aspect of the company suffered as the postwar period came to a close. Innovative marketing and a huge array of promotional train and later road racing outfits disprove this notion.

The purposes behind Lionel's promotional items had scarcely changed since the 1920s and '30s. The Cowens, along with Alan Ginsburg (who replaced Raphael as executive vice-president after the latter's death in 1952) and Sam Belser, the firm's national sales manager, understood the advantages of selling outfits, even low-priced specials. First-time buyers wanted a complete package that included a locomotive, cars, track, and a transformer. Newcomers liked the fact that an outfit tended to cost, on average, 20 percent less than the total value of the components as priced separately.

Lionel's leaders knew that once consumers had bought one of its introductory outfits, whether cataloged or not, they were then likely to want to expand and improve what they had. For that, people need not go far, as most outfits included a Lionel accessory catalog, which became the dream book for building their railroad empire. A sense of brand loyalty had been established with that first train. Now, to obtain more desirable rolling stock and locomotives, not to mention operating accessories and powerful transformers, buyers needed to see what their favorite toy train manufacturer offered and to order it, usually at full price.

Additional benefits accrued from the sale of Lionel promotionals, just as they had during the prewar decades. Retailer outfits, even if they were merely cataloged outfits selling for less, helped Lionel dominate the lower end of the market at the expense of Marx without sullying its heritage of excellent, upscale trains. Cheap items, sometimes produced with minimal decoration, found a home in various promotional outfits. So did unsold, overstocked merchandise, which did amass no matter how stringent Lionel's production control might be. Rolling stock that had outdated trucks or couplers could well be sold off via specials. In fact, some merchants specialized in buying obsolete inventory. Lionel was grateful to earn money in this manner and avoid having to keep extraneous items in stock and thus sacrifice storage needed for new models.

The trend launched with Sears outfit no. 9652 gathered momentum only slowly. Prior to 1960, when the Factory Orders permit more than generalizations, most of the outfits shown by Sears, Ward, and Firestone were, according to Ambrose and Algozzini, still identical to what Lionel was cataloging. Those outfits might come in boxes stamped with unique inventory numbers: Firestone used the prefix "11-L," and Ward relied on "48 T" and in 1966 went to "48 HT." The prices of promotional outfits typically were 15 to 20 percent lower than what Lionel charged, depending on shipping fees from the site of origin (in the case of Sears and Ward, that was Chicago, so discounts in the Midwest exceeded those in the Far West and Deep South).

Examples of Retailer Promotionals with Cataloged Items (Type Ia) appeared in the Sears and Ward catalogs in the late 1950s. Sears advertised the nos. 9602 and 9606 outfits in 1956, both of which differed in notable ways from what Lionel cataloged that year. Indeed, the only outfit ever to feature the no. 626 Baltimore & Ohio center-cab locomotive was the 9602. Lionel didn't even catalog this 44-ton switcher until 1957 and then only as a separate-sale item. As for the 9606, it was the only outfit, promotional or cataloged, that included a no. 6464-350 Missouri-Kansas-Texas boxcar. That Sears outfit also came with a scarce variation of the no. 3484-25 Santa Fe operating boxcar.

For Sears to offer something before Lionel did, such as the 626 Baltimore & Ohio center-cab, was quite unusual. About the best that Ward could hope for at this time was to announce something exclusive that came with an outstanding new model. It had the good fortune in 1960 to offer the no. 48 T 3073 four-car military outfit (no. X-535NA) that was led by a no. 45 U.S.M.C. mobile

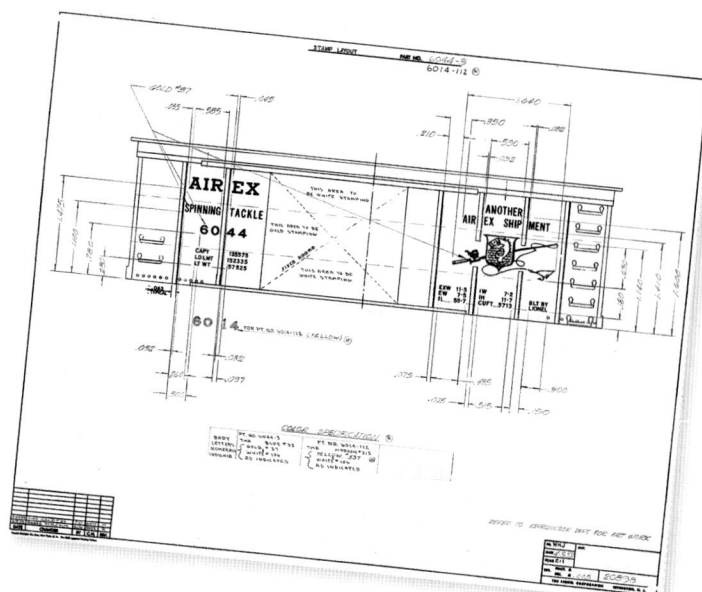

The red no. 6014-100 and blue no. 6044-25 Airex boxcars were available only in promotional outfits.

missile launcher the same year that this motorized unit made its debut in the Lionel catalog.

Both Sears and Ward revived the custom of packing switches or an accessory in a special. Ward no. 48 T 3048 diesel freight outfit from 1957, identical in motive power and rolling stock to Lionel no. 1545/701 from 1956, boasted more sections of track, including two manual switches.

After Lionel contracted with Bachmann Bros. to package Plasticville items in its boxes (a trend launched in 1958), one of those items occasionally showed up in a special. Ward no. 48 T 3001 from 1958 included a no. 957 farm building and animal set; the next year, Sears no. 9666 steam freight train had a no. 963 frontier set. Better still was Sears no. 9682 military outfit from 1959; it came with a no. 175 rocket launcher, a poor seller that Lionel was trying to get rid of.

Sometimes the promotional outfits offered contained leftover items. Take, for example, Sears no. 9665 from 1959. This diesel freight outfit featured a no. 2348 Minneapolis & St. Louis GP7 road switcher and nos. 6572 Railway Express Agency refrigerator car and 6818 flatcar with transformer, all of which had been cataloged by Lionel in the previous year but not in 1959. Or Sears no. 9694 freight outfit from 1960. It came with a no. 746 Norfolk & Western 4-8-4 Northern and tender, items that hadn't led a Lionel cataloged outfit since 1959.

Of course, Lionel could also turn around and offer Sears an item that never appeared in its catalog. Consider Sears no. 9655 from 1958. This Retailer Promotional with Promotional Items (Type Ib) was led by a no. 248 locomotive, a 2-4-2 steamer that never appeared in a Lionel catalog. Two years later, Sears listed the no. 9653 freight outfit, which came with a no. 6014-100 Airex boxcar. That unpainted red model never appeared in a Lionel catalog, but showed up in at least twelve other promotional outfits. Also missing from a Lionel catalog were the nos. 226P/226C Boston & Maine Alco A-B diesels. Those locomotives provided motive power for Sears freight outfit no. 9654 from 1960, along with two other promotional outfits and a never-cataloged variation of Lionel outfit no. 1649 from 1961 that was numbered 1649NE (the letters perhaps designating "New England" as the main market

Druggists' Service Council advertised outfit no. 149 in its 1956 Gifts Galore catalog. The 149 was awarded to the winner of an in-store drawing.

for that outfit).

The status of promotionals in the Lionel line before 1960 seems decidedly mixed when only Sears, Ward, and Firestone are studied. Even after fair trading was dissolved after 1954, the vast majority of outfits available through these three nationwide retailers amounted to cataloged outfits from the same year packed in Lionel boxes with only a label or a stamped number to differentiate them from what Lionel sold. A handful of exclusives did show up. Some of those outfits contained models that collectors prize; others consisted of a combination of items with inherent interest.

VIII. Promotional Outfits from Other Outlets: 1956-58

Information about the Lionel promotional outfits offered through Sears, Ward, and Firestone remains limited and can shed only partial light on the questions that continue to baffle Lionel researchers about the second half of the 1950s. Overshadowing all other matters is the question of how many different Lionel promotional outfits, whether identical to cataloged outfits or special in some manner, were developed. This query naturally spurs questions regarding the businesses that sponsored those promotional outfits and their reasons for doing so. Were these firms seeking to win new customers? Provide incentives for employees? Advertise their names?

So much of what happened from 1956 through 1958, particularly outside the realm of Sears, Ward, and Firestone, is still unclear. This situation is made more frustrating for Lionel collectors because Tufts, working from detailed records, lists sizable numbers of American Flyer promotional sets being released during the same three years. He counts 56 sets in 1956, 82 in 1957, and 45 in 1958. The contents of most of these American Flyer sets differed from that of the sets shown in the consumer catalogs of the same year

because Gilbert's executives used its promotional sets to unload unsold inventory. Did Lionel adopt the same strategy in those years?

Unfortunately for Lionel enthusiasts, records of its promotional outfits (their contents, quantities, and sponsors) for 1956, '57, and '58 are not known to exist. The picture improves with 1959. In a year that, according to Tufts' findings, Gilbert assembled 27 specials, a Lionel Box Ledger indicates that Lionel had 116 promotional outfits (more than four times as many as its chief rival). Of those 116, only nine went to Sears (these Retailer Promotionals included three HO scale outfits). Firestone accounted for a mere two outfits (likely cataloged items) and Ward none.

This last statistic leaves researchers wondering about the retailers and other businesses placing orders, large and small, for Lionel promotional outfits between 1956 and '59. For example, Tufts states that B.F. Goodrich carried American Flyer trains as early as 1950 and then adds in passing that it also stocked Lionel, but nothing definitive is known. He refers as well to such other major accounts for Gilbert as Allied, Goodyear, W.W. Grainger, S.S. Kresge, and May Company (which owned department stores throughout the country).

In the absence of records on Lionel's promotional outfits from 1956 through 1958, research falls back on the investigation of authenticated outfits from those years as well as examination of any documents that have surfaced. The reminiscences of former Lionel employees involved with promotional outfits also assume importance. Taken as a whole, these sources enable us to glean some understanding of what went on at the country's largest manufacturer of toy trains in the late 1950s and to gain insights into Lionel's marketing. Then, thanks to the information in the Box Ledger for 1959, the story can pick up with greater accuracy and thoroughness.

Fascinating hints of Lionel's approach to promotional outfits appeared in 1956. In that year, Alan Ginsburg (the firm's executive vice-president) and his right-hand man, Ronald Saypol, stood behind a pair of outfits that reflected a twofold strategy for this segment of Lionel's marketing. One outfit, no. 149, qualifies as a Retailer Promotional with Cataloged Items (Type Ia) because it featured a unique combination of models already part of Lionel's cataloged line in 1956. The other outfit, no. X-150, is classified as a Manufacturer Promotional with Unique Items (Type IIIc) because it came with a car that was never available through the annual consumer catalog.

The 149 went to Druggists' Service Council, Inc., a non-profit organization composed of drug manufacturers and wholesalers. Druggists' Service Council created generic catalogs containing general merchandise for its member stores. The catalogs were titled "Gifts Galore", which was likely a name created solely for these catalogs. This four-car steam freight outfit resembled but did not duplicate outfits cataloged by Lionel. Neither did it, as far as can be determined, duplicate any promotional offered by another retailer, such as Sears or Firestone.

The X-150 also did not duplicate any cataloged outfit or, as far as can be determined, any promotional outfit. To create this three-car freight train pulled by a no. 520 boxcab electric, Lionel simply removed the no. X6014 red boxcar advertising Baby Ruth candybars that was used in one of the low-end outfits cataloged in 1956 (no. 1542/750) and substituted a red boxcar advertising

Chun King canned and frozen Chinese food.

Who sponsored this promotional outfit and why haven't been ascertained. Indeed, the origins of the Chun King boxcar and the origins of the X-150 Manufacturer Promotional with Unique Items (Type IIIc) may not be identical.

A spokesman for Jeno Paulucci, the founder of Chun King Foods, surmises that the firm approached Lionel about developing a special car as a component in a small number of outfits. Chun King likely offered these trains as incentives for either sales representatives to increase distribution or wholesalers to purchase more Chun King products.

The story makes sense to Saypol, although he cannot verify it so many years later. He adds, however, that Lionel executives would have been reluctant to decorate a special freight car for only a single customer requesting so limited a quantity (probably fewer than 100 outfits). They would have authorized only a larger production run, which Saypol estimates as no fewer than 5,000 units (but contemporary records suggest was probably closer to 2,500 models). Either quantity of cars surpassed what Chun King would have requested.

Taking these matters into consideration leads to the conclusion that Lionel would have had to find other uses for the leftover cars. Instead of adding the 6014-30 Chun King boxcars to the cataloged line, Lionel evidently used them in a three-car promotional outfit (X-150) whose purpose remains uncertain. Collectors speculate that this outfit may have been a prize in a contest organized by a regional chain of supermarkets or a wholesaler handling grocery stores.

What began as a small-scale experiment in 1956 seems to have evolved into a full-fledged marketing program a year later, at least according to the Lionel annual report for the year ended December 31, 1957. That document states, "In 1957 we made available to Department Stores, on a cooperative advertising basis, exclusive promotional sets based upon regular cataloged outfits, to which additional accessories and cars were added at the buyer's individual option and selection."

Despite this announcement, the only Lionel promotional outfits linked with 1957 do not fall under the category of a Retailer Promotional (Type I) or a Retailer General Release Promotional (Type II). Instead, outfit nos. X-444 and X-589 qualify as Manufacturer Promotionals with Promotional Items (Type IIIb).

The X-589, notwithstanding its higher number, came first. This four-car steam freight outfit featured a no. 6024-50 red boxcar that Lionel lettered with the name and emblem of the RCA Whirlpool brand of home appliances. This promotional outfit was made available to employees of at least one Whirlpool plant in the Midwest.

Faced with a sizable overrun of these RCA Whirlpool boxcars, just as occurred with the Chun King boxcar the previous year, Lionel packed the additional 6024-50s into a promotional outfit. It then offered the no. X-444, a five-car train pulled by a no. 250 steam locomotive and tender, to unidentified retailers. Interestingly, the RCA Whirlpool car, like the Chun King, was never included in a Lionel cataloged outfit.

Lionel's use of promotional outfits was expected to grow in

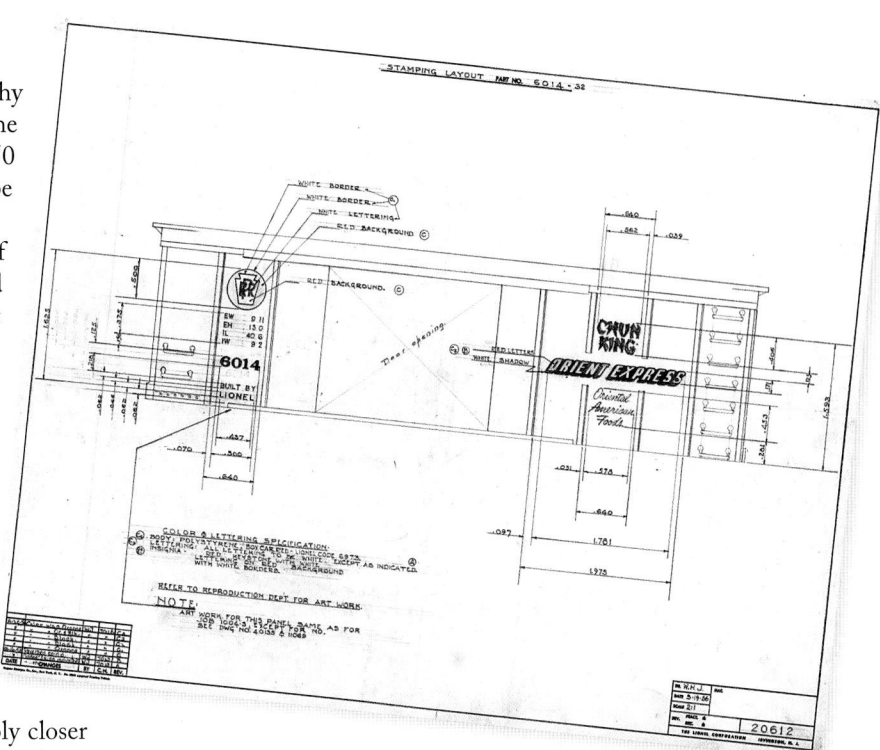

The no. 6014-30 Chun King boxcar appeared in promotional outfit no. X-150 from 1956. The 6014-30 began the trend of promotional-only plug-door boxcars.

1958, or so comments in the annual report for the year ended December 31, 1957, suggested. After mentioning the exclusive promotionals that had been made available to department stores in 1957, the report announces, "This policy of building such exclusive sets will be extended to include our wholesale trade for the first time in 1958."

Other customers were also poised to benefit from Lionel's new marketing strategy. "In 1958," the annual report continues, "Lionel will offer a non-catalogued line of train sets to a carefully selected, small group of catalog houses on an experimental basis."

Again, however, the number of promotional outfits that can actually be connected with 1958 proves to be extremely low. One Retailer Promotional with Cataloged Items (Type Ia) that has drawn much interest because of its packaging is no. X-617, which Lionel developed for Gifts Galore. This diesel four-car freight outfit, unlike any of the sets that Lionel cataloged in 1958, was packaged in a special die-cut flat pack with a speckled filler and a cardboard sleeve used as a cover.

(The Gifts Galore chapter ended two years later in 1960 with promotional outfit no. X-507NA, nicknamed the "Halloween set" and erroneously claimed to be Sears no. 9666. This Retailer Promotional with Unique Items [Type Ic] came with a no. 1882 General steam locomotive and tender plus three cars and a special version of the Plasticville frontier set [no. 963-100].)

Also in 1958 Seabrook Farms, a New Jersey-based wholesale supplier for grocery and convenience stores, worked with Lionel to bring out a Retailer Promotional with Cataloged Items (Type Ia). Outfit no. X-643 featured military items (no. 212 U.S. Marine Corps Alco A unit, four flatcars hauling Pyro loads, a flatcar with a rocket, and a caboose), plus two manual switches and a no. 253 block signal. Seabrook Farms arranged for this promotional outfit

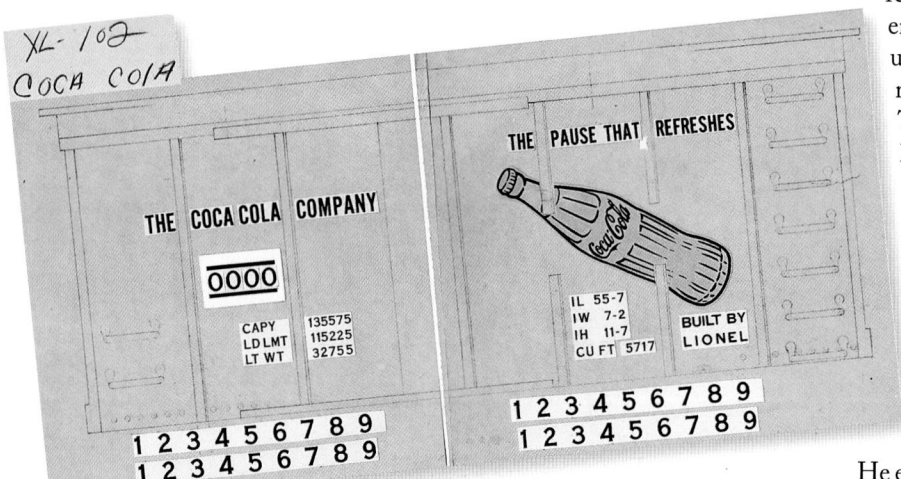

XL-102
COCA COLA

THE COCA COLA COMPANY

0000

CAPY 135575
LD LMT 115225
LT WT 32755

1 2 3 4 5 6 7 8 9
1 2 3 4 5 6 7 8 9

THE PAUSE THAT REFRESHES

IL 55-7
IW 7-2
IH 11-7
CU FT 5717

BUILT BY
LIONEL

1 2 3 4 5 6 7 8 9
1 2 3 4 5 6 7 8 9

Number XL-102 was assigned to the artwork that Lionel created for a mock-up of a plug-door boxcar for Coca Cola. Neither records of an actual mock-up nor an actual car has been observed.

to be sent to merchants who ordered a specified dollar amount of its products.

Seabrook Farms must have been pleased with its arrangement with Lionel because it placed an order for a second Retailer Promotional with Cataloged Items (Type Ia) in 1958. Outfit no. X-714 included a no. 602 Seaboard diesel switcher, five freight cars, and a no. 128 animated newsstand. Tom Costello, vice president of sales at Seabrook Farms in 1958, estimates that his firm bought no more than 40 of each outfit from Lionel. (To learn more about the Seabrook Farms promotionals, see "Recognizing the real thing," in the April 1992 issue of *Classic Toy Trains*.)

Was a third Seabrook Farms promotional outfit considered? A Lionel brochure from 1959 announced that a steam freight set would be the top prize in a contest sponsored by Seabrook Farms. Supermarkets in "80 major cities" would promote this train, which was supposed to include a special car decorated for that firm.

No evidence of what would have qualified as a Retailer Promotional with Unique Items (Type Ic) actually being marketed has been reported. However, a black-and-white photo of a Seabrook Farms boxcar said to be in Lionel's archives appears in *Lionel: A Collector's Guide & History, Vol. 5: The Archives* (published in 1981).

IX. Lionel Enters the Premium Field: 1958-59

Promotional outfits like the ones Lionel created for RCA Whirlpool and Seabrook Farms are known in marketing circles as "premiums." Whether electric train sets or other articles of merchandise, premiums are used by their sponsoring businesses to reward dealers who buy more of their product, motivate sales personnel to bring in larger orders, or boost the morale and loyalty of employees. Businesses can also offer premiums to consumers who purchase some of their goods in the form of direct benefits (additional goods priced below comparable items available to the general public) or indirect benefits (prizes in contests and bonuses for buying other products).

Lionel saw the benefits of entering the premium field on a

regular basis. As the firm's annual report for the year ended December 31, 1957, declared, "We are now set up to pursue aggressively the premium and incentive markets to which train sets lend themselves so well." The key to success in this competitive yet potentially lucrative field, believed Ginsburg (whose title had changed to "vice president - marketing and sales"), was hiring a specialist. In early 1958, he brought aboard Frank Lynch, employed as a writer on the staff of *Premium Practice*, which was then the major publication in the field.

Lynch, who is now deceased, recalled that after he settled in at Lionel he approached E.F. McDonald and Merritt, two of America's leading "incentive houses," about carrying Lionel trains.

He explained that incentive houses serve as "distributors" for makers of housewares, toys, and so forth that want to reach new "markets." They identify potential clients who may be willing to buy quantities of those housewares, toys, and other products to use as incentives or premiums.

Contacting the principal incentive firms was an obvious yet smart step for Lynch to take because it connected Lionel with large numbers of potential clients. At the same time, he worked with individual customers, hoping to convince them to capitalize on the popularity of Lionel trains and use train sets as premiums. Seabrook Farms may have been one of those customers, although Lynch confessed to having no memories of the deal Lionel made with that food distributor.

Real success came in 1959. To start, General Mills and Colgate-Palmolive-Wildroot selected Lionel layouts and outfits as the prizes in contests they conducted. These contests represent the kind of premiums that McDonald or Merritt could have engineered for Lionel.

Of greatest interest to us are promotional outfits awarded by Colgate-Palmolive-Wildroot to consumers who satisfactorily completed a jingle. A pamphlet describes a Super O outfit that featured a no. 2242 New Haven F3 A and B units pulling "5 Deluxe cars" (including nos. 3444 animated gondola and 6805 atomic waste disposal car). Twenty-five of these Manufacturer Promotionals with Cataloged Items (Type IIIa) were given away as second prizes.

The O27 four-car freight outfit put together for third prize also qualifies as a Manufacturer Promotional with Cataloged Items (Type IIIa). Colgate sent one of these sets, led by a no. 218 Santa Fe Alco A unit, to each of the 125 recipients.

Besides selling thousands of dollars worth of trains and accessories through these two contests, Lionel sought to expand its premium program in 1959 by pitching specially decorated models to an array of businesses. Lynch collaborated with Saypol and the latter's assistant, Norman Wyner, on this campaign. They hoped that such items, generally small, plug-door boxcars, might prove tempting as individual premiums or as a part of a complete train set.

The best-known of these promotional outfits from 1959 was engineered by Lynch for the Wix Corporation, a North Carolina-based manufacturer of oil filters for trucks and automobiles. That firm, according to an advertisement placed in the October 1959 issue of *Chilton's Motor Age*, offered a certificate for a promotional outfit to retailers who ordered twenty-four of its oil or air filter cartridges. That certificate entitled the bearer to purchase for only

$12.95 a no. DX 837 steam three-car freight outfit or an assortment of Lionel accessories and trading cards (probably no. X-838), either of which was said to be worth $30.00.

The DX 837 (the actual inventory number may have been X-837, with "D" added for only an example intended for display purposes) deserves to be classified as a Manufacturer Promotional with Unique Items (Type IIIc) because it included the no. 6014-150 boxcar. Lionel heat-stamped the Wix name and logo in red across the model's white plastic sides. As with the Chun King and RCA Whirlpool cars, this boxcar never appeared in a Lionel cataloged outfit.

Other proposed Lionel promotional cars did not go beyond the drawing board or the paint shop. Artwork and photographs of these experimental models languished in Lionel's archives until recently. Those documents, along with letters and memoranda, shed light on ideas sent to banks, mail-order firms, and the makers of a host of food products and consumer goods, all aimed at winning their support for premium items.

Boxcars suggested by Lynch, Saypol, and their assistants would advertise Coca-Cola, Pillsbury flour, Hot Point appliances, Electric Auto Lite spark plugs, Coast to Coast grocery stores, Willard Batteries, Lipton Tea, Mercantile National Bank of Chicago, Birdseye Frozen Foods - the list goes on and on. Typically, Lionel went only as far as developing black-and-white illustrations of the proposed rolling stock. In some cases, however, Lionel lettered cars to show the public relations departments of certain firms what was possible.

Photographs of models made for Colgate-Palmolive, Hot Point, and Pillsbury appear in the fifth volume of *Greenberg's Guide to Lionel Trains, 1945-1969* (published in 1993). Samples of two no. 6464-series boxcars, produced on request for Minnesota Mining & Manufacturing Company (makers of Scotch Cellophane Tape), are shown in the January 1994 issue of *Classic Toy Trains*.

Yet even painting and lettering O gauge models did not assure success for Lionel. All the companies named here ultimately rejected the special cars. However, as is explained elsewhere in this volume, three prominent businesses (A&P supermarkets, Popular Club Plans, and Top Value trading stamps) that did spurn Lionel's overtures eventually coordinated promotional outfits with it.

Nevertheless, what might have been added to the Lionel line in the late 1950s is interesting to contemplate. Like Retailer Promotionals (Type I) from that time, these proposed premium cars show how imaginative sales executives were in their quest to increase sales and find new outlets to promote electric trains at a time when business was slipping.

X. New Directions in Premiums under Joe Kavanagh: 1960-62

Lionel's commitment to premiums scarcely lost a beat after Lynch resigned in mid-1960 to join Lawrence Cowen, the firm's former president, at Schick Incorporated, a manufacturer of electric razors. The younger Cowen had left Lionel in December of 1959 after being removed from his post as president two months earlier following the decision of his father and sister to sell their Lionel stock to a group headed by Roy Cohn, the grand-nephew of Joshua Cowen.

Number XL-289 was assigned to the artwork that Lionel created for a mock-up of a plug-door boxcar for Lipton Tea. Neither records of an actual mock-up nor an actual car has been observed.

Ginsburg hired Joe Kavanagh to handle premiums and quickly discovered that the diminutive young man was a dynamo, filled with ideas on how to heighten Lionel's presence. Said one veteran in the field, "Joe reminded me of a leprechaun - clever yet always honest."

Kavanagh supported Lionel's efforts to place promotional outfits in discount houses and mail-order firms. The grudging acceptance that Lionel had once accorded these innovative businesses needed to give way to easy cooperation. "Lionel had to work with discounters," Kavanagh states, even if doing so bothered the hardware stores, appliance dealers, and department stores that had long constituted the main part of its retail base during the holiday shopping season.

Lionel's wish to give preference to traditional merchandisers was evident in a form letter dated February 1959 and sent to "Toy Department Merchandising Management." In that document, Lawrence Cowen referred to eight specially priced promotional outfits that Lionel would make available to just "department stores," as opposed to distributors and local retail chain stores. Furthermore, those six O27 and two HO promotional outfits would be offered to only one department store per city in 1959. (This letter and the press releases describing those promotional outfits are reproduced in the January 1993 issue of *Train Collectors Quarterly*.)

If Cowen had hoped to invigorate Lionel's traditional retail network of large, metropolitan department stores, he was probably several years too late. Instead, Kavanagh held, Lionel should eagerly strive to develop promotional outfits for any and all preferred customers, including discount retailers, who submitted enormous orders for electric trains.

Somebody at Lionel must have been listening because, according to the Factory Orders, the company produced more than 700 promotional outfits, including those shown only in advance catalogs (approximately 1,597,000 total quantity) between 1960 and 1969. Those figures surpassed the more than 140 cataloged outfits (approximately 879,000 total quantity) from the same period.

Among the first deals that Kavanagh negotiated for Lionel in 1960 was one with Channel Master. Based in Ellenville, New York, Channel Master manufactured television aerials and related

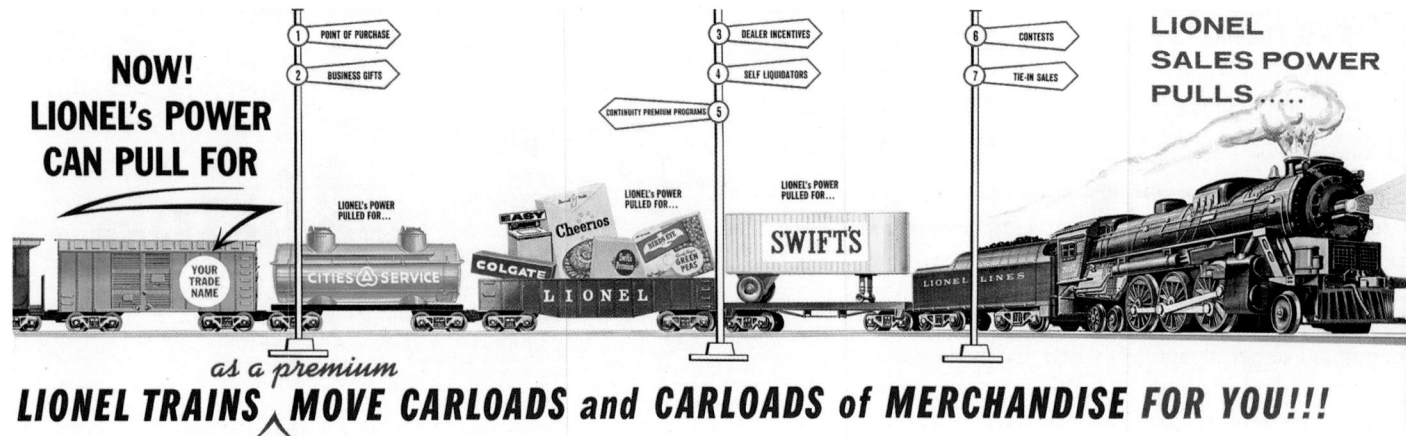

Lionel boasted its success in sales promotions in this 1961 multi-page foldout that appeared in *Premium Practice* magazine. A subsequent advertisement featured Lionel's Porter, Spear and Scalextric product lines.

electric items for appliance and home-furnishing stores. Seven versions of one such Manufacturer Promotional with Unique Items (Type IIIc) have surfaced; each contains a poor-selling accessory that Lionel wanted to sell off as well as a unique Channel Master billboard. Five of these outfits bear two numbers (X-573NA and 9745), while the other two outfits bear the sole number 9745.

Information in the Factory Orders indicates that Lionel originally received an order from Channel Master for 3,000 of the no. X-573NAs, each to have a no. 128 animated newsstand. Filling the order presented no problem because Lionel still had 3,279 of those accessories in stock.

However, when Channel Master requested an additional 1,500 promotional outfits, Lionel scrambled to find other accessories to fill the order. It came up with 279 of the 128 animated newsstand, 100 of the no. 334 operating dispatching board, 682 of the no. 464 lumber mill, and 439 of the no. 55 tie-jector motorized unit - hence five of the variations of the X-573NA. Channel Master must have then ordered another 5,000 outfits, which Lionel filled by creating the no. 9745 that came with a no. 175 rocket launcher. (Greater information on the Channel Master outfits and their use as premiums by that firm appears elsewhere in this volume.)

Kavanagh worked out a similar arrangement in 1961 with Masters, a wholesaler and independent retailer with locations in New York and New Jersey. That firm advertised a pair of Retailer Promotionals with Cataloged Items (Type Ia): nos. X-702 and X-703.

Better yet was the Retailer Promotional with Promotional Items (Type Ib) that Kavanagh offered to Masters in 1961. The no. X-714 came with a no. 45 U.S. Marines mobile missile launcher, four military-oriented cars, and two great accessories - nos. 910 Navy Yard cardboard "atomic submarine base" and 943 ammo dump. (After skipping a year, Lionel renewed its relationship with Masters with one promotional outfit in 1963 and another in 1964.)

Besides customers like Channel Master and Masters, trading stamp companies impressed Kavanagh as excellent candidates for Lionel premiums. He knew how popular these stamps were becoming, with consumers expecting to obtain them with each purchase they made at supermarkets, pharmacies, and other retail establishments. They pasted the stamps in booklets before redeeming them for appliances, cutlery, linens, sporting goods, and toys.

Lionel had entered the fast-paced world of trading stamps under Lynch's tenure, going directly to Sperry & Hutchinson, the New York-based giant of the industry. Kavanagh kept the ball rolling, and S&H showed in its catalog for 1960 outfit no. 6-P4803. This Retailer Promotional with Cataloged Items (Type Ia) was designated by Lionel as no. X-516NA.

Kavanagh offered S&H another Retailer Promotional with Promotional Items (Type Ib) in 1961. What Lionel designated as no. X-612 went by no. 6 P4805 in the S&H catalog, with the "6" prefix indicating that a consumer needed six books of stamps to acquire the train set.

Relations with Sperry & Hutchinson remained pleasant under Kavanagh's watch. In 1962 and 1963, S&H affixed its own numbers to Lionel cataloged outfits, with its no. 6-P4807 being a Lionel no. 11201 and its no. 6-P4810 being a Lionel no. 11331.

Abandoning S&H would have been foolish for Kavanagh - so would ignoring its rivals. Therefore, he reached out to two other key players in the trading stamp field - Blue Chip and Top Value. These two brands were, stated an article in the September 1960 issue of *Premium Practice*, used by a few of the major regional grocery chains. A&P and Safeway on the West Coast handed out Blue Chip stamps. Top Value, which was developed by the Kroger chain in the Midwest, was distributed at those markets as well as Winn-Dixie stores in the South. (Four of the ten leading supermarket chains used S&H stamps exclusively or partially, according to the article cited.)

"I always offered the executives at stamp companies three train sets, knowing they would select only one of them," Kavanagh relates. "The sets, which might come right out of the catalog or be something I cooked up, hit different price levels. I wanted to appeal to the egos of the guys I was talking to by offering each one an exclusive set."

Kavanagh's strategy bore fruit. Top Value, which had spurned Lionel's proposal for a special boxcar, contracted for a Retailer Promotional with Promotional Items (Type Ib). Top Value showed the no. X-604 promotional outfit in its catalogs for 1961 and '62.

Of course, Kavanagh had to be sure that Lionel would fill the orders he made. A few weeks after climbing onboard in 1960, he learned from the head of Blue Chip stamps that Lionel kept dragging its feet about how many items it would make available if that firm placed an order. "How can I submit anything when I don't know what I'll get?" the executive at Blue Chip bellowed.

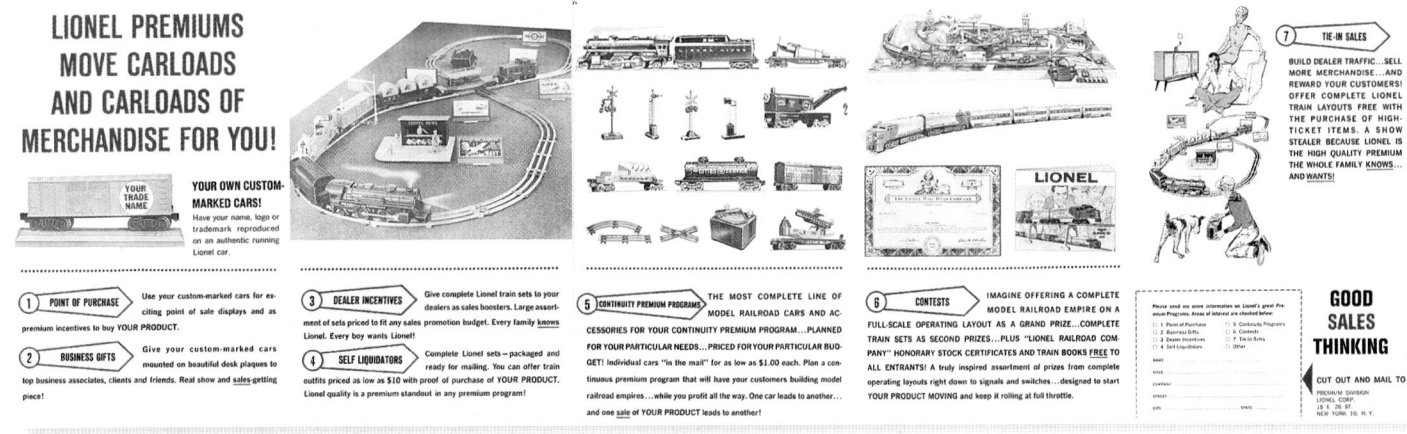

The flip-side of the multi-page foldout outlined six areas where trains could be used as premiums as well as a request card for more information. The second page from the left featured a Channel Master no. X-573NA.

Kavanagh agreed that the arrangement was unacceptable and pressured Ginsburg to fix it, which was done immediately.

Kavanagh worried that upper management at Lionel was undermining his efforts or losing sight of the advantages that premiums offered. He drove himself to secure more contracts for Lionel, and several of the ideas for specially decorated boxcars previously described date from his years there.

A multiple-page foldout printed in *Premium Practice* toward the end of Kavanagh's second year at Lionel showed how much he had already accomplished. It mentioned using Lionel promotional items in contests and "continuity premium programs" and as dealer incentives and "self liquidators." One of the Channel Master no. X-573NA outfits was illustrated.

Also shown was rolling stock lettered for Cities Service and Swift, accounts that Kavanagh acquired for Lionel. He enthusiastically backed the idea, heralded in the *Premium Practice* ad, of businesses paying Lionel for "custom-marked cars" to be used as point-of-purchase displays and incentives: "Have your name, logo or trademark reproduced on an authentic running Lionel car."

"One of my favorites," Kavanagh says with a smile, "was developed for Cities Service. We mounted a Lionel tank car and a small Cities Service billboard we did on a special wood plaque. We gave some of these desk displays to executives at Cities Service to thank them for sponsoring the [no. 6465] green tank car with their name."

Another desk ornament, sponsored by the National Broadcasting Company, featured an HO scale switcher, switching tracks, and a billboard to encourage 1,000 "time buyers and clients" to switch their affiliation to N.B.C. A photograph and description of this promotional item created by Kavanagh appeared in the September 1960 issue of *Premium Practice*.

Certainly the biggest news for Kavanagh in 1961 began with a conversation he had with managers at the Quaker Oats Company. He spoke of the advantages of using a Lionel outfit as a premium, and they worked out a deal that, Kavanagh told Ginsburg, might be worth $1 million for Lionel: "We can seal it by guaranteeing 25,000 outfits."

Ginsburg agreed to push production to meet this level, and the crews at Lionel's factory reached this goal in six weeks. Eventually, Kavanagh says, 75,000 of these specials were made, with Quaker's customers paying $11.95 per outfit to help Lionel earn a healthy profit on the transaction.

Quaker Oats then inaugurated an aggressive advertising campaign for the no. X-600 steam freight outfit. That campaign, according to the October 1961 issue of *Premium Practice*, included various point-of-purchase displays and materials; announcements in *Better Homes & Gardens*, *Good Housekeeping*, and *Woman's Day*, among other magazines; and ads in *Parade* and *This Week* Sunday newspaper supplements. Consumers were told they could "Get complete $25.00 Lionel Electronic Train Set for only $11.95 with two Quaker Oats or Mother's Oats box tops."

Outfit no. X-600, a Manufacturer Promotional with Promotional Items (Type IIIb), took off. By October of 1963, Quaker had shipped 70,775 outfits and was still actively receiving orders. Arthur F. Marquette, writing a few years later, heralded this Lionel promotional outfit as Quaker's "biggest puller, in terms of dollars" in his book, *Brands, Trademarks and Good Will: The Story of the Quaker Oats Company* (published in 1967).

Lionel had its own hopes for this inexpensive steam four-car freight outfit. The low price would, the company advised its authorized service stations, generate sales of additional track and cars to consumers buying the train set. Whether those hobby shops and other retail outlets did receive a spike in sales has yet to be determined. By the same token, the question must be asked why, with this promotional outfit being such a huge success from the standpoint of Quaker Oats, a follow-up offer never appeared.

The year after making such a splash with the outfit for Quaker Oats, Kavanagh put together a Manufacturer Promotional with Promotional Items (Type IIIb). As reported in the November 1962 issue of *Premium Practice*, "A Lionel electric train set is offered by Stokely-Van Camp Inc., Indianapolis for $11.95 and one Van Camp pork & beans label."

What Lionel designated promotional outfit no. 19142 came with a steam locomotive and tender, three freight cars, a caboose, track, transformer, and sheet of billboards and had a retail value of $25.00. Stokely-Van Camp paid Lionel to create the no. 6050-150 Van Camp's boxcar, along with a billboard that also advertised the company. The number heat-stamped on the sides of the boxcar - 638-2361 - was the telephone number for Stokely-Van Camp's corporate office in 1962.

Lionel Factory Orders called for it to assemble the outfit in three ways. First, there were 25,000 of the no. 19142 outfits (the mail-order version, which came in the same box used for the

Quaker Oats promotional and had nothing printed on the top in order to accommodate a mailing label). Second, there were 25,000 of the no. 19142-100 outfits (it came in a regular outfit box with "Lionel" printed on the top). Third, there were 450 of the no. 19142-50 outfits (the display version). However, only 2,886 of these three promotional outfits were sold between October 1962 and July 1963.

What may have been a disappointment to Stokely-Van Camp actually benefited Lionel because it was losing 48 cents on each outfit. Lionel's unit cost was, according to the Factory Orders, $11.13. However, because postage, handling, insurance, and freight amounted to $1.30, Lionel netted only $10.65 for each outfit ($11.95 minus $1.30), which came to a 48-cent loss.

No one has ascertained what happened to the enormous surplus of Stokely-Van Camp outfits. Lionel could have dumped them through a third party or cannibalized them for other outfits.

The frequency with which no. 6050-150 boxcars ended up in other promotional outfits supports the latter contention. Those models appeared in twenty-three outfits totaling 36,019 units. Those outfits more than likely were a combination of leftover inventory and new production. The presence of different body types on the Stokely-Van Camp boxcars supports the notion that Lionel made more than one production run.

By the time the Stokely-Van Camp promotional outfit was being advertised, Kavanagh had severed his ties with Lionel. He resigned in August of 1962, disappointed with the direction the toymaker was going and frustrated that his efforts were not more appreciated.

Before leaving, though, Kavanagh arranged another Manufacturer Promotional with Promotional Items (Type IIIb) with Cities Service. The steam three-car freight set was publicized in a feature article on Cities Service (a gasoline and automotive retailer) and its "effective use of consumer premiums" that appeared in the December 1962 issue of *Premium Practice*.

Like the Stokely-Van Camp promotional, this outfit came in three ways. Factory Orders indicate there were 7,390 of the no. 19106 (the mail-order version in a box with no printing on the top), 360 of the no. 19106-100 (in a box with "Lionel" printed on the top), and 250 of the no. 19106-50 (the display version).

XI. Expanding Ties with the Largest Retail and Mail-Order Firms: 1960-63

Lionel maintained and generally broadened its commercial ties with America's leading retailers, especially mail-order firms, in the early 1960s. So important and potentially lucrative were these connections to Lionel that the captains of its sales and marketing "team" (such as Ginsburg and Saypol) handled them rather than anyone below, even someone as trusted as Kavanagh.

Sears, the country's premier retailer, stood at the top of Lionel's sales chart at least to 1967 and possibly through the end of the decade. Previous research on which Lionel promotional outfits Sears and other major retailers offered has concentrated on national catalogs and surviving outfits while overlooking the fact that these retailers also used regional catalogs, flyers, and special promotions for some of these outfits. As a result, many promotional outfits have been a mystery. What is now known is that Sears offered far

It took a Lionel premium to help Stokely Van Camp knock the beans out of competition.

Lionel's Stokely-Van Camp promotion was the centerpiece of this advertisement that appeared in the April 1963 issue of *Premium Practice* magazine. By 1963, promotional outfits outnumbered catalog outfits more than seven to one.

more variety and quantity than its catalogs indicate.

Sears actually sold seven promotional outfits in both 1960 and 1961, five in 1962, and twenty-five in 1963. Many of these outfits were Retailer Promotionals (Type I) that were unique to Sears. However, it increasingly cataloged Retailer General Release Promotionals (Type II). Although Sears marketed so many different outfits in 1963, the total quantity produced was on a par with 1960.

As opposed to the 1950s, Sears offered much more than unexceptional O27 outfits in the early 1960s. In 1960, for example, it cataloged the no. 9694 outfit headed by a no. 746 Norfolk & Western streamlined 4-8-4 Northern with a "long-stripe" tender and five desirable freight cars. A year later, three of the four Super O promotional outfits were designated for Sears. One, the no. 9674, was led by a no. 616 Santa Fe NW2 diesel switcher and came with a no. 6827 flatcar with a tractor shovel and other desirable rolling stock.

Beyond these two great outfits, there is much to appreciate in the Sears specials from the early 1960s. In some cases, Lionel upgraded O27 trains by substituting Super O track for the customary tubular sections (nos. 9692 and 9693 from 1960). In others, the selection of rolling stock was superior to what Lionel packed in a comparable outfit (compare Sears no. 9657 six-car freight outfit from 1962 with Lionel's cataloged no. 11278).

Montgomery Ward was also busy selling Lionel promotional outfits in the late 1950s and early '60s. The number of outfits Ward showed in its annual catalog remained relatively steady from four in 1957 to three in both 1958 and 1959. In 1960, only two outfits were in the Ward catalog, but the Factory Orders indicate that a third was produced.

The notebooks also list three Ward outfits in 1961, four in 1962, and one in 1963 (actually, there were three, but two outfits were canceled). For unknown reasons, Ward did not show these outfits in its annual catalogs. Perhaps they were mentioned only in special promotional flyers yet to be discovered or were promoted strictly through store displays.

Lionel sales executives sought to make further inroads into the sphere of national retail and mail-order firms in the early 1960s. They won support from Spiegel, a Chicago-based retailer that was heavily involved in the mail-order business. Spiegel, write Ambrose and Algozzini in the fourth volume of *Greenberg's Guide to Lionel Trains, 1945-1969*, had carried American Flyer S gauge trains and Marx O27 sets as early as the late 1940s. The firm's relationship with Marx continued into the following decade, and Spiegel listed Gilbert trains in the 1960s. Both brands offered Spiegel inexpensive trains that were intended to appeal to the low end of the market.

Not until 1960 did Lionel obtain Spiegel as a customer with promotional outfit no. X-523NA. Spiegel was a natural fit for Lionel, which already had Sears and Ward as customers. Spiegel had been selling other brands of toy trains for years and may have used Lionel outfits to supplement its offerings or to replace less-popular selections.

Spiegel issued its catalog several times each year and likely printed different ones for different regions of the country. Lionel trains showed up in the Christmas editions, a trend that went on through 1967. In 1961, '62, and '63, three sets were cataloged, each given the prefix "R36 J." What Spiegel offered represented the low end of the Lionel line: inexpensive models in outfits that were priced 20 percent below comparable Lionel offerings.

Many of Spiegel's early outfits were just Lionel cataloged outfits and so don't qualify as promotional outfits. As such, some of these outfits are not listed in this volume. These include the nos. R36 J 5261 (Lionel cataloged outfit no. 1646) and R36 J 5263 (Lionel no. 1649), both from 1961, along with no. R36 J 5276 (Lionel no. 11288), from 1962. No observation of Spiegel providing special packaging has been made.

Most important to collectors are the Retailer Promotionals (Type I) offered by only Spiegel, some of which contained a desirable item. For example, no. R36 J 5260 (no. X-651) from 1961 came with a no. 3330-25 flatcar with submarine and a no. 3330-200 submarine kit, neither of which came in an individual component box. And outfit no. R36 J 5287 (no. 19237) from 1963 included a no. 6407 flatcar with rocket.

Spiegel wasn't the only significant account that Ginsburg and his lieutenants added. In 1960, they hammered out a deal with J. C. Penney, a New York-based retail and mail-order firm, which was larger and better known than Spiegel at that time. Penney had advertised American Flyer trains since 1958, so having it carry Lionel outfits was a triumph.

Although Penney did advertise items that came in a Lionel no. 1806 twelve-car assortment in 1960, it really launched a relationship with Lionel the next year when it first carried Retailer Promotionals (Type I). The two outfits in 1961 (nos. X-665 and X-666) were followed by another pair in 1962 (nos. 19148 and 19149).

In 1962, Penney entered into the catalog business by acquiring General Merchandise Corporation. Penney issued its first catalogs the following year, and they showed three Lionel cataloged outfits: nos. X 923-4782 A (Lionel no. 11375), X 923-4881 A (Lionel no. 11341), and X 923-4889 A (Lionel no. 11351). Prices for these outfits tended to be 23 to 25 percent less than what Lionel indicated in its catalogs for 1963.

Sales personnel at Lionel did their best to maintain strong ties with Sears, Penney, and other major mail-order firms in the early 1960s because those businesses placed orders for significant quantities of train sets. The challenge at Lionel was how to satisfy these customers without alienating smaller yet equally loyal ones, such as department and hardware stores and toy and hobby shops (what Ambrose and Algozzini refer to as "full-price wholesale customers").

Had the overall market for miniature electric trains been healthier, Lionel might have succeeded in keeping its different clients happy. Unfortunately for the company, toy trains and accessories were losing their appeal in the early 1960s. Children and families, who had once put an electric train at the top of their annual wish list, now prized other playthings and engaged in other activities. Younger boys dreamed of becoming test pilots and rocket scientists rather than locomotive engineers. Meanwhile, their older brothers cast aside their trains and asked for sports equipment and even automobiles instead.

In a national market where interest in toy trains was plainly ebbing, merchants concluded that it was imprudent to pay the "purchase order price" for cataloged outfits. They felt betrayed when Lionel demanded that they do so. The only solution likely to keep retailers stocking trains was for Lionel to develop promotional outfits that retailers could buy at prices below those assigned to cataloged outfits.

Healthy sales of these outfits might, executives at Lionel told themselves, please their customers to the point that they again made sizable orders of cataloged sets. Such a rationale helps explain why Lionel forged ahead with a promotional program that was not making much money for the company. The Factory Orders provide ample "costing data" for 1962, when Lionel released 132 promotional outfits. Information exists on one hundred of those outfits, with twenty-nine forecasted to lose money. Of the remaining seventy-one outfits, approximately 137,000 examples were produced, with a net profit of just $10,309 expected.

Lionel's attempts to satisfy each of its dealers created headaches for more than just sales and advertising personnel. Supervisors at the company's factory were stuck having to produce and package an incredible assortment of promotional outfits.

Peter Giannotta, named Division Director of Special Services in 1963, remembers that department stores and chains such as Sears and Ward demanded something unique to sell. Lionel's sales staff was willing to make promises that factory supervisors struggled to keep. "Assembling the components and then packaging everything was a nightmare," he says. "I'm not sure we made any money in the deals that Ginsburg made" (a point that the Factory Orders support). Yet there was no doubt that Lionel would continue down this same path as long as necessary.

XII. Changes in Lionel's Sales Philosophy and Organization: 1964-65

What was apparent by the early and middle 1960s was that promotional outfits had assumed a different role in Lionel's marketing strategy. To be sure, they still were used to deplete leftover inventory of poor sellers and to empty shelves filled with formerly cataloged pieces that had been superseded in some manner, as demonstrated by outfits whose components were equipped with varying combinations of trucks and couplers. In fact, some of the least impressive, blandest items that the company ever made, right down to rolling stock without any decoration, filled the plain tan or white boxes that Lionel used for promotional outfits in 1964, '65, and '66.

However, where Lionel had once relied on promotional outfits to undercut the strength of Marx in the low end of a strong market that Lionel dominated, it increasingly depended on promotional outfits to bolster a market that was slowly yet undeniably declining. Prior to the 1960s, promotionals had complemented the cataloged line because they were either intended to be options for households that otherwise could not afford a Lionel train or targeted at high-end customers that wanted unique items not found in the catalogs.

Now, though, promotional outfits were competing with whatever was shown in the catalogs, regardless of whether it was geared for the low end of the market, the high end, or somewhere in between. Executives at Lionel recognized this change and accepted the fact that just getting a family to buy a train set - any train set - had become their principal goal.

Despite Lionel's willingness to assemble a promotional outfit for virtually any customer in almost any quantity, it no longer designed unique items for those outfits. A trend highlighted by the RCA Whirlpool, Wix, and Stokely-Van Camp plug-door boxcars (not to mention all the cars proposed by Lynch and Kavanagh for diverse businesses) came to an end after the release of a premium for Libby, McNeill & Libby, a Chicago-based maker of food products, in late 1963.

The no. 19263 steam freight train was widely advertised on the West Coast (and an announcement in the February 1964 issue of *Premium Practice* suggests this promotional outfit was available only there). An ad in the October 1963 issue of *Sunset* magazine declared, "Libby's brings you a lot of train ($24.95 value) for only $10.95 ... and it's a real Lionel!" Consumers had only to mail their check with four labels from certain Libby's canned products by December 31, 1963.

This four-car Manufacturer Promotional with Promotional Items (Type IIIb) came with a few desirable items, starting with the no. 1060T-50 Southern Pacific tender and two items originally made as exclusive components of this outfit: nos. 6050-175 Libby's Tomato Juice boxcar and 6475-50 Libby's Pineapple vat car.

Sales of this premium failed to meet expectations, which is most likely why various components appeared in other promotional outfits. The no. 6050-175 boxcar was included in at least eleven other outfits, the no. 6475-50 vat car in seven, and the no. 6167-75 Union Pacific SP-Type caboose in six before being depleted in 1969.

The disappointing response to the Libby set helped curtail the sale of Manufacturer Promotional outfits (Type III). Lionel chose, instead, to emphasize Retailer Promotional outfits (Type I) from 1964 until 1969, when General Mills secured the rights to produce Lionel trains. Some of these promotional outfits were Retailer General Release Promotionals (Type II) that several retailers offered in a given year; others were exclusives that, because of information in the Factory Orders, can be linked with a specific merchant.

The many promotional outfits dating from 1964 and later reflected a significant change in Lionel's sales philosophy. Robert Wolfe, Lionel's chief executive officer and president of its newly organized toy division, saw a need for changes because sales were declining. Along with Charles Sussman, hired as vice president of sales in 1963 after Ginsburg retired due to poor health, Wolfe supervised what amounted to a retrenchment of the sales organization.

For at least 30 years to this point, Lionel had handled sales through three centers. The best known of these was the fabulous showroom open to the public at Lionel's corporate headquarters in New York City. Less familiar were two regional showrooms, open only to the trade, in Chicago and San Francisco. Prior to 1963, most of Lionel's seventeen sales representatives were based in one of these three locations (the remainder worked out of offices in areas far from one of the offices). As salaried employees, these sales representatives worked exclusively for Lionel and were expected to handle the entire line when meeting with buyers, distributors, and wholesalers. At least twice each year, they went on the road and met with clients, usually major retailers, in their territory.

The Lionel sales force experienced two noteworthy changes in 1963. First, in January, company executives designated a sales manager and ten sales representatives to handle only the company's lines of science kits, chemistry labs, and juvenile phonographs. Another sales manager and thirteen other Lionel sales representatives (including some newly hired people) concentrated on selling electric trains and road racing sets.

How these twenty-three sales representatives helped with the development of promotional outfits is unclear. Lionel's principal accounts were national in scope and so their representatives expected in the late 1950s and early '60s to deal with Lionel's corporate leadership, namely, Ginsburg, Saypol, Sussman, and Wolfe. Other promotional deals as well as assorted premiums also went through the New York City office, as Lynch and Kavanagh explained. So only the regional representatives of national accounts or sales personnel whose business was geographically limited would have worked directly with Lionel's scattered sales representatives to arrange specials.

In June of 1963, decision-makers announced a second key change. They decided to consolidate the two groups of sales representatives into one organization that would consist of only eleven individuals. Each of those salaried sales representatives would supervise a sales district (the United States was divided into eleven such areas), and all would report to the vice president of sales. Three additional sales representatives were assigned to handle toy sales to U.S. Army and Air Force post exchanges and the U.S. Navy ship stores.

In early 1964, Lionel closed all three of its showrooms and shifted its sales office in New York City to a sixth-floor room in the Toy Building (at 200 Fifth Avenue) characterized by small display layouts and cramped offices. Wolfe and Sussman justified these moves by noting that they would cut costs, stabilize marketing, and centralize sales support. From this point on, all communications from field sales and trade would be funneled through the newly created Sales Administration Department, where sharing of overall corporate knowledge was leveraged. This change alone helped streamline the sales process.

About half of the district sales managers lived in or around New York City and worked out of Lionel's office there. They stayed on the payroll to sell Lionel's toy, science, and phonograph lines. Myles Walsh, William Gaston, Ken Negri, and other veterans continued to serve accounts in the Northeast, Mid-Atlantic States, and Upper Midwest. They, like the other district sales managers in the United States and Canada, had to work much harder to win sales from longtime customers, who were increasingly skeptical about the sales potential of electric trains and accessories. District sales managers elsewhere tried to scrounge up new business accounts beyond what executives in the New York office brought in and provide local assistance for securing orders when asked.

Among the people working as district sales managers were Jack Caffrey and Mack Mostman, who had supervised Lionel's offices in Chicago and San Francisco, respectively (the salesmen connected with those offices had lost their jobs). District sales managers not previously associated with Lionel had already established careers for themselves in the toy field (Rodney Haggard in Dallas, Texas, and Joe Hammond in northern California stand out). Most district sales managers worked out of offices in metropolitan areas; others were based in their homes.

District sales managers knew the appeal of Lionel trains was waning. They therefore took steps to boost sales. Doing so required that they actively promote the entire line of Lionel O and HO trains, road racing sets, chemistry and science kits, and phonographs and records. Haggard, Mostman, and their peers promised customers specials priced below what was shown in the annual Lionel catalog. They dealt with department stores, discount houses, and chains - anyone that would listen to their spiel and place an order, even if it were as low as 100 items.

Sussman must have recognized how difficult it was becoming to sell Lionel merchandise because the firm created incentives to motivate distributors (who placed orders with district sales managers). From July through September of 1965, for example, individuals who accumulated the most points based on sales of products (note in the table below, the emphasis on science-oriented items from Porter) could earn prizes, with the winner getting a 1966 Cadillac and the runner-up a 1966 Ford Mustang.

Lionel Product	Points
Lionel-Porter Merchandise	10 Points
Lionel Porter Six-Pack	15 Points
Phonographs	10 Points
Lionel Science Items	15 Points
Accessory Merchandisers (Trains and Racing)	5 Points
O27 Outfits (nos. 11500, 11540, and 11550)	5 Points
O Gauge Outfits (nos. 12710, 12730, 12780, 12800, 12820, and Super O no. 13150)	5 Points
Other Program Merchandise	1 Point

Front: This 1966 year-end report summarizes the changes that occurred with Lionel's Marketing Organization during the early 1960s. The two major changes in 1963 may help to explain why there was such a large drop of in sales during that year. **Rear:** This March 1965 Salesmen and Representatives phone list details Lionel's territorial breakdown. It also distinguishes Lionel employed salespeople from outside representatives.

By rewarding the most points for science-oriented items, Lionel was determined to broaden the company's public image beyond toy electric trains.

At the same time, Lionel took steps to persuade consumers to revise their perceptions of the company and what it sold. It conducted television and radio promotions, set up store displays, and advertised in print media ranging from *Batman* and *Superman* comic books to *Model Railroader*, *Parents*, and *Scholastic* magazines. Lionel even signed up legendary TV star and radio personality Arthur Godfrey as its spokesmen. No one could accuse Sussman and his associates of not trying.

Yet little seemed to matter. Lionel annual reports (based on discontinued operations that most likely included electric trains and road racing sets) and other documents suggest that district sales managers sold approximately $5,865,000 of product in 1965, but still lost approximately $560,000.

This is Mr. Parmett our Market Development Manager.
Ignore Him!

Concentrate instead, on part of the great line of Lionel Toys.

The world famous, excitement packed Lionel Trains and Racing Sets. The wondrous Lionel-Porter Science Kits. The brand new U-Drive Boat. The Rocket Age Helios-21 Spaceship. And the Electronic Age Lionel-Spear Phonographs.

Great toys—every one of them!

"Sane toys for healthy kids." Toys that don't kill, scream, shoot or frighten.

Toys that are made to last. So durable they're all covered by a Warranty.

Toys that are made to sell!

And that's where Mr. Parmett comes in.

He can fill you in on all the details of Lionel's Unique Program for Profits. And specifically what it can mean to you.

Just call him at YU 9-7474. Or write: The Lionel Toy Corporation, 200 Fifth Avenue, Suite 1316, New York City, N.Y.

sane toys for healthy kids   LIONEL

Bruce Parmett's efforts and creativity boosted Lionel's promotional outfit business during the mid-1960s. His deal with Montgomery Ward provided four memorable promotional outfits. Unfortunately for Lionel, his efforts could not overcome the decline in demand for its products.

XIII. Bruce Parmett and the Market Development Division: 1964-66

While district sales managers promoted the Lionel lines with distributors and wholesalers (selling to discount houses and small retailers was left to local "jobbers"), Sussman struggled to build up a marketing staff in New York City; in particular, he looked for younger men with new ideas. One whom he knew from another toy company and thought would prove valuable to Lionel was Bruce Parmett. So Sussman offered his former colleague a position in early 1964. Parmett accepted the job and influenced Lionel's use of promotionals over the two years he stayed there.

Parmett began by calling on accounts with Myles Walsh, notably chain stores, discount houses, and Lionel service stations in Connecticut and Massachusetts. Then Sussman turned Parmett loose, telling him to meet with clients in Pennsylvania and New Jersey. Those "clients" were seldom the owners of toy or hobby shops. Instead, Parmett made appointments to see representatives of chain stores, discount drug firms, and premium accounts to tout Lionel products and receive orders.

"And those guys didn't want stacks of the Lionel outfits shown

in the annual catalog," Parmett picks up the story. "They asked for something different, an exclusive set that each could promote as unique to increase sales. Typically, they wanted something special, with low-end trains, slashed pricing, and innovative packaging (corrugated backing with clear plastic blister packs holding the trains). I did my best to fulfill their wishes."

To facilitate the development of promotional outfits for prominent retail clients, Lionel set up the Market Development Division in 1965. This sector was intended to handle direct sales to national mail-order accounts, trading stamp companies, nationwide chains of variety stores and automotive dealers, and other key accounts. Clients included Bennett Brothers, Goodyear Tire & Rubber, Maritz, Penney, Richie Premium, Sperry & Hutchinson, Spiegel, and Western Auto.

The Market Development Division was also charged with identifying customers that, in Parmett's words, "normally would not use our regular catalog line of goods." These customers fit between cataloged outfit buyers and major promotional outfit buyers. Retailer General Release Promotionals (Type II) - what Lionel termed, "Market Development Sets" - became the solution for this segment.

Parmett was given the reins of this new division and then permitted to bring over Roger Elson, a junior salesman at Lionel, to assist with sales and administration. They realized that flexibility was essential if Lionel hoped to attract new outlets. As Parmett commented before the American Toy Fair in 1966, "In certain instances, if you have an account that can use a considerable quantity of merchandise in a particular product line, specials other than the existing Market Development line can be made available through this division, providing the quantities constitute several thousand sets."

Parmett's key clients still included the drug and variety store chains he had been serving so well, including Woolworth, J.J. Newberry, McCrory's, Walgreens, and Rite Aid. For these and similar firms, he offered Retailer General Release Promotionals (Type II). The same kinds of outfits went to the trading stamp companies that joined the list of Parmett's accounts.

"Stamps were big business when I worked at Lionel," Bruce remarks, "and S&H green stamps were the biggest." In his first year at Lionel, Bruce developed what turned out to be the final Lionel premium shown in an S&H catalog. Outfit no. 6P-4811, had four different Lionel numbers and contents: nos. 19350 (1964), 19350-500 (1964 version), 19350-500 (1965 version), and 19350-501 (1965 version).

No additional Lionel trains - only Marx sets - appeared in subsequent S&H catalogs for 1965. There is a Lionel factory order for a promotional outfit (Lionel no. 19520) in 1966, but it was canceled. Sperry & Hutchinson stopped listing any electric trains that year, which was also the last time it carried Lionel's Spear brand of children's phonographs. By 1967, Lionel and S&H were no longer doing business together. (Top Value stamps quit carrying Lionel trains after 1963.)

Spiegel and Penney worked out better for Parmett. Three promotional outfits were shown in the Spiegel catalogs in 1965 and '66. These outfits qualify as Retailer General Release Promotional outfits (Type II).

Penney, from 1964 to 1966, apparently purchased both display and mail-order versions of the same promotional outfits, most likely for retail and catalog distribution. In 1964 (probably before Parmett handled the account), it offered four outfits, including Lionel nos. 19334 display and 19334-500 mail order. The number found in the Penney catalog (X 924-0680 A) is most likely attributed to 19334-500 mail order. Observations of a no. 19334 display have been made with "923-5361" on its price tag.

The Penney no. X 924-0680 A is prized by Lionel collectors. Led by a no. 221 U.S. Marine Corps Alco A unit, this Retailer Promotional with Promotional Items (Type Ib) military train featured three olive drab cars, all of which are desirable, and the no. 3309-50 olive drab turbo missile launcher, which is considered scarce. The no. 6119-125 olive drab first aid medical caboose packed in this promotional outfit is difficult to find, too.

Also in 1964, Penney offered the no. X 924-0672 A (Lionel no. 19335). The promotional diesel freight outfit contained a no. 3364-25 flatcar with logs a year before Lionel cataloged that model.

In 1965, Penney fulfilled some leftover orders from the previous year (Lionel nos. 19334-500 and 19335). Better yet, it offered five new Retailer General Release Promotionals (Type II), two of which were also offered in display and mail-order versions, along with a cataloged outfit (Lionel no. 12820 cataloged by Penney as no. X 924-3700 A).

Among these Penney promotional outfits for 1965, one stands out: no. X 924-3734 A (Lionel no. 19438-502). This steam freight outfit came with the scarce die-cast metal no. 241 steam locomotive and no. 6651-25 "'Big John' Missile/Shell Launching Car," neither of which ever appeared in a Lionel catalog as an outfit component or separate-sale item. (The production history of the desirable 6651-25 cannon car, including how it ended up in a Penney promotional outfit, is covered in detail in the September 2004 issue of *Classic Toy Trains*.)

Other Penney promotional outfits for 1965 were available elsewhere. To name one outfit, the no. X 924-3726 A (Lionel no. 19437-502) was offered by Aldens (no. 34 Y 5618E), Spiegel (no. R36 J 5262), and perhaps others. To name another, the no. X 924-3734 A (Lionel no. 19438-502) could also be obtained from Aldens (no. 34 Y 5615E).

In 1966, Penney offered six Retailer General Release Promotional outfits (Type II), three in display and three in mail-order versions. One outfit was a repeat from 1965 that Penney renumbered from X 924-3718 A (Lionel no. 19442) to X 924-8287 A (Lionel no. 19511) and increased in price from $34.44 to $37.77. Differences in Penney retail store and catalog numbers from 1966 were validated via internal Lionel documents. For example a no. 9808 (Lionel no. 19506) is the retail store display version of no. 924-8279 (Lionel no. 19507), which was a mail-order set packed for catalog customers.

Missing from Parmett's list of clients was Sears, Roebuck and Co. He learned that Wolfe had grabbed that important account and made sure the nation's largest retailer offered outstanding promotional and cataloged outfits each year. "Bob Wolfe had a special relationship with Sears," Parmett remembers, "and he would do anything to keep it as his 'pet.'"

Wolfe's favoritism explains why the number of Lionel outfits offered by Sears jumped from three in 1964 to fourteen in 1965. All of these outfits were Retailer Promotionals (Type I) unique to Sears.

Thanks to Wolfe, Sears stocked much more than unexceptional O27 outfits. In 1964, Sears carried the no. 9820, a Retailer Promotional with Promotional Items (Type Ib). This steam military freight outfit (Lionel no. 19326) featured the first issue of the scarce no. 240 steam locomotive. Moreover, the nos. 347 cannon firing range set, 958-75 olive tank (a load on the no. 6401-25 gray flatcar), and 3666 Minuteman boxcar with cannon each came as regular items in only one other promotional outfit. Even the version of the no. 6814 first aid medical caboose was different and received its own number - 6824-50 - in Factory Orders and the *Lionel Service Manual.*

Even more exciting to collectors is a Retailer Promotional with Unique Items (Type Ic) from 1965. The Sears no. 9836 (Lionel no. 12885-500) O gauge diesel six-car freight outfit came with the highly prized no. 2347 Chesapeake & Ohio GP7 road switcher, which never showed up in Lionel's cataloged line. To enhance this outfit's appeal, Lionel added an operating car (no. 3662 automatic refrigerated milk car) and three accessories (nos. 76 street lamps, 321-100 trestle bridge, and 346 operating culvert unloader).

The Sears no. 9836 outfit was so large that it required a box measuring 29½ by 16¼ by 10 inches. Based on the size and weight, and the quality of the cardboard used for the box, it's amazing that any of these outfits have survived complete.

Beyond these two classic promotional outfits, there is much to appreciate in the Sears specials offered in 1964, '65, and '66. Occasionally, Lionel upgraded O27 trains by including a pair of manual switches, as it did in Sears no. 9834 from 1965 (Lionel no. 19453). Other Sears outfits promised kids more fun by including Plasticville sets, even though Lionel had dropped these ancillary items from its line after 1962. Examples are Sears no. 9807 from 1964 (Lionel no. 19327) as well as Sears nos. 9808 and 9810 from 1966 (Lionel nos. 19557 and 19561, respectively).

In addition, Sears outfits occasionally came with an accessory. A no. 110-75 modified trestle set (eighteen pieces sealed in a plastic bag) was packed in a few outfits, notably the no. 9813 steam freight train from 1964 (Lionel no. 19325). The no. 9835 diesel freight outfit from 1965 (Lionel no. 19454-500) had a no. 145 automatic gateman plus three no. 76 street lamps. Finally, four other Sears outfits - nos. 9807 from 1964, 9834 and 9836 from 1965, and 9810 from 1966 - featured a no. 346 manual culvert unloader. (These outfits were Lionel nos. 19327, 19453, 12885-500, and 19561, respectively.)

While Lionel's relationship with Sears was growing, something odd was happening with Montgomery Ward. The second largest retailer in America did not list a single Lionel outfit in its catalogs in 1964 or '65. No mention of Lionel's making anything for Ward in those two years appears in the Factory Orders either.

Parmett, determined to show his superiors that he could win new accounts and increase sales at Lionel, decided to do what he thought was a "good deed" and get Lionel trains back in the Ward catalog. "We were desperate in 1965," he says, "scrapping for every bit of business we could find." To Parmett's credit, he won over executives at Ward and returned to Lionel's headquarters with sizable orders for four exclusive promotional outfits for 1966, with the total number requested being 50 percent greater than the amount ordered over the five previous years.

Charlie Sussman was thrilled - and Bob Wolfe was livid!

"Neither Charlie nor I had any idea," Parmett explains, "that Bob had decided that helping his friends at Sears also meant freezing out Ward." After offering Lionel trains for many years, Ward found itself on the outs after Wolfe assumed the presidency of Lionel's toy division. He refused to let any Lionel trains appear in the Ward catalogs for 1964 and '65.

"Bob was pretty mad that I had somehow offended Sears," Parmett continues. "But he calmed down - Lionel was barely doing $2 million a year on trains. We couldn't afford to stay away from Ward just because we wanted to make Sears feel better."

The deal Parmett negotiated with Ward called for it to receive four outfits. Three of the four outfits appeared in the annual Ward catalog. It also ordered a special display version of the no. 19546 promotional outfit.

Thanks to Parmett's reviving Lionel's relationship with Ward, that retailer did an estimated $180,000 in toy train sales in 1966, nearly three times the total reached for the previous five years ($58,000). Sears still surpassed its top rival, but by only $70,000 in 1966.

Besides renewing Lionel's account with Ward, Parmett sought new clients in 1965 and '66. With Elson, he approached firms that put together catalogs of housewares, appliances, toys, and other items that either consumers bought at special outlet centers or manufacturers used as incentives and rewards for their employees.

"Popular Merchandise and Bennett Brothers were good examples," Parmett says. He made a deal to provide Popular Merchandise with five exclusive train sets to show in its catalogs and arranged for eight outfits for Bennett Brothers. "Those sets were offered at a discount to employees of various companies," Parmett continues. "Richie Premium worked the same way - we called these businesses 'fulfillment houses.'"

Another customer was Grace Homes. "It offered toys and other consumer goods for individuals to sell at discounts to their friends," explains Parmett. "Grace was a lot like Tupperware, and it was one more outlet for Lionel exclusives. It would order a certain number of sets for people involved in its 'party plan' to sell."

To enhance various promotional outfits, Parmett became a master at creating "piece-count sets." He would find ancillary items to sell with a train - Plasticville structures, cardboard signs, plastic trestles, additional sections of O27 track, and leftover operating accessories.

"Then we would advertise a '40-piece' or a '55-piece' Lionel exclusive for clients," Parmett recalls. I worked with Pat Papa, one of the product managers at the Lionel, on these sets." Imaginative as these promotional outfits were, they failed to stem the tide of falling sales. There was no doubt, Parmett concludes grimly, that electric trains were losing their appeal.

AGREEMENT made April 24, 1969, between THE LIONEL TOY CORPORATION (hereafter "Lionel"), a Delaware corporation, with offices at Hoffman Place, Hillside, New Jersey, and GENERAL MILLS, INC. (hereafter "Mills"), a Delaware corporation, with offices at 9200 Wayzata Boulevard, Minneapolis, Minnesota, WITNESSETH:

WHEREAS Lionel is and has been in the business of manufacturing and selling toy trains and other toy products; and

WHEREAS Mills desires to purchase some of the assets, and to acquire an option to lease the remaining assets, used in the manufacture of said toy trains and other toy products, and Lionel desires Mills' assistance in connection with the train and toy business, all on the terms and conditions hereafter set forth.

NOW, THEREFORE in consideration of the premises and the mutual covenants and conditions herein set forth, it is hereby agreed as follows:

1. Sale.

For $65,000, receipt of which is acknowledged, Lionel hereby sells and assigns to Mills the molds, jigs, tools, dies, fixtures, designs and specifications described in Schedule A annexed hereto and which relate to the manufacture of a line of "O" gauge trains. To the extent that the items on Schedule A are common to other trains, they will not be included in this sale but Lionel will make such items available to Mills for its production.

2. Option.

For $100,000, receipt of which is acknowledged, Lionel grants to Mills the option to lease for a ten (10) year term all (except those sold pursuant to paragraph 1) Lionel's machinery, equipment, jigs, fixtures, molds, dies, designs, patterns and drawings, wheresoever situated, and used or available for use in the manufacture, assembly, handling or packaging of, and the production samples relating to, the following toy products, accessories and parts (hereafter sometimes called "the products"):

trains (Lionel)

trains (American Flyer)

On April, 24 1969, Lionel signed a contract with General Mills to acquire certain assets and obtain an option to lease others. This contract also granted General Mills the license to manufacture Lionel trains.

XIV. The Demise of Promotional Outfits: 1966-69

Bruce Parmett remembers well the feeling of desperation that touched everyone at Lionel in 1966, the year he tendered his resignation. Executives realized to their dismay that tastes in toys and entertainment were changing rapidly, with electric trains losing popularity. They tried to diversify not just their toy offerings but the company's entire product line. By the mid-1960s, the firm no longer concentrated on manufacturing toys. Indeed, the Lionel Toy Corporation was merely one division within a multi-faceted conglomerate.

Lionel's sales and marketing organization pulled out all the stops, trying valiantly to design a few creative and interesting promotional outfits. Packing also became more consumer-oriented, with display packs and boxes enabling customers to see what they were thinking of buying. Little, however, succeeded in the depressed toy market faced by Lionel and its longtime rival, the A.C. Gilbert Co. The latter reported losing $2.95 million in 1965, and trading of Gilbert's stock was temporarily halted in April 1966.

Eventually, high overhead and poor quality led to a difficult decision for Lionel's board of directors. They had been trying to figure out what to do with operations at the firm's plant in Hillside, New Jersey. The need for a solution became more acute after a labor strike hit the factory in April 1965. By the autumn the board was discussing what needed to be done to stop the dissipation of other subsidiaries by the significant losses recorded by Lionel's toy division.

To make matters worse, an internal study revealed that poor quality would cost the toy division approximately $675,000 in 1965. This included line loss, rework, and customer rejects. The irony was that the poor quality of Lionel's products could most likely be blamed on the austerity programs company decision-makers had implemented over the previous few years.

The board of directors could not, however, discontinue the business in 1965 because of "large inventories, etc." So, beginning in 1966, it rolled the toy division under Dale Electronics, one subsidiary of Lionel then recording a noticeable profit. The managers sent from Dale to supervise the toy division implemented a four-point program aimed at leveraging train experts, negotiating with the union, reducing inventory, and operating as cheaply as possible.

Wolfe concluded that moving production from Hillside would be uneconomical. Therefore, he had five alternatives: sell, close down, move part, any combination of the above, or continue operations. Unfortunately even with some great promotional outfits and strong effort by the sales and marketing organization, sales from discontinued operations (most likely the entire toy division) in 1966 were only $5.18 million while losses exceeded $3 million. These figures compared poorly with those from the previous year, when sales reached $5,865,000 and losses had been $560,000.

The deteriorating situation must have shocked sales executives because on August 31, 1966, Sussman had advised Lionel's officers that his staff would produce the desired results by year's end. In October, the sales organization was meeting to consider the product line for 1967. Before the end of the month, signs had appeared that circumstances were not auspicious. A memorandum from Sussman to the district sales managers stated, "We are sadly remiss in the sales of O gauge trains. As you heard at the meeting we have a good inventory on hand and I would like this to be moved out."

When the desired results didn't appear in November and December, executives looked frantically for answers. They chose to let virtually every member of Lionel's sales staff go, a troubling occurrence noted in the January 8, 1967, issue of *Playthings* (a publication for the toy industry). Sometime in 1967, company leaders made another significant decision. They decided that, rather than issue a new consumer catalog for that year, Lionel would reuse its catalog for 1966. This move meant that it would not directly market anything new or different for the coming year.

Robert Stein, who served as treasurer at Lionel in the middle and late 1960s, recalls that a plethora of catalogs and trains filled the company's factory at the end of 1966. "We had such a large inventory of trains that our priority was not to introduce a new line, but to sell what we had." Under such circumstances, as Stein explains in the May 1999 issue of *Classic Toy Trains*, the most sensible course was to use the same catalog for a second year.

Falling back on the existing catalog did not curtail production of promotional outfits in 1967. Lionel evidently kept busy filling orders for retailers who wanted those outfits. The company either had committed to these orders in 1966 or was stuck with existing contracts that it couldn't waive. Or maybe executives decided that if customers were willing to buy some of the inventory on hand, they would be foolish not to sell that stock.

Sears catalogs and sales flyers for 1967 mention three Lionel outfits: nos. 9723 (Lionel no. 19701), 9724 (Lionel no. 19703), and 9733 (Lionel no. 19705). A fourth Sears set, no. 9732 (Lionel no. 19706), has been observed but not yet been found in a catalog.

Other promotional outfits numbered up to 19707 have also been observed. This implies that Lionel made or planned to make at least seven promotional outfits in 1967.

The situation at Lionel grew more problematic in 1968. Executives did elect to issue a consumer catalog with an abbreviated train line (only a single outfit). However, they would not be able to produce what they needed in the plant in Hillside. More than a year before, as announced in the annual report for 1966, Lionel's board of directors had decided to close that facility. They would "discontinue the manufacturing of certain … product lines and … transfer certain other product lines to other of its facilities." The first step in that process had occurred in August of 1967 with an auction that disposed of most of the major machinery there. (The factory itself was not sold until September of 1969, when it went for a price of $2,050,000.)

In the meantime, Lionel executives had to find a way to

Lionel shall not produce or arrange for the production of finished goods relating to its 1969 line which, when added to finished goods for the 1969 line not shipped on the date of this Agreement, will exceed in the aggregate $1,200,000 at Lionel's net selling price.

Although exact sales figures for 1969 are unknown, paragraph 7 of the Lionel-General Mills contract of April, 24 1969, puts a $1.2 million cap on sales.

put out a train line for 1968. They could draw upon the leftover inventory stored at the factory in Hillside, but needed to be able to manufacture additional trains and track or contract with other firms to do so. The solution, they realized, lay with a facility in Hagerstown, Maryland, where Porter Chemical Co. had been based. Lionel had acquired that business in 1961 for its chemistry sets; seven years later, executives authorized the shipment to Hagerstown of all the special purpose equipment still left at the plant in Hillside so that new items could be produced.

How much Lionel needed to manufacture is uncertain. The cataloged line was small, and orders for promotional outfits likely declined. Keep in mind that accurate comments about promotional outfits from 1968 must depend on observations of actual outfits and examination of retail catalogs because the Factory Orders do not cover that year.

Only one such outfit (no. 11620) has been identified for 1968, though it is likely that others do exist. The 11620 included a no. 2029 steam engine that featured a motor made in Japan. All the other items in outfit 11620 appear to be left over from previous years.

Sears and Penney, two of Lionel's best customers in the past, did not mention Lionel outfits, cataloged or promotional, in 1968. This was the second year in a row that Penney did not feature any Lionel trains in its catalogs. With these key retailers showing no interest in Lionel trains and other problems emerging, it comes as no surprise that Lionel's sales fell to somewhere between $3 and $4 million for 1968.

Looking ahead to 1969, Ronald Saypol, the new president and chief executive officer of Lionel, wanted the firm to assemble as many outfits as possible, his goal being to make Lionel look attractive to any potential buyers. But the facility in Hagerstown could not be used because Lionel had sold Porter Chemical Co. to Gabriel Industries (another toy firm). So Lionel moved equipment back to New Jersey and relied on its factory in Hillside to put out a line for 1969.

Robert Stein asked three key people still working at the factory - Vincent Cardinale (tooling), Lenny Dean (service), and Charles Duggan (purchasing) - to assess the inventory of parts on hand to determine what could most efficiently be put together and sold. Based on what that trio reported, Stein and Saypol selected the locomotives, cars, track, and so forth that went into the six outfits cataloged in 1969 (produced in quantities ranging from 400 to 500, according to Stein).

Besides those cataloged outfits, Lionel managed to put out promotional outfits, although the Factory Orders do not cover this year either. To date, only two promotional outfits have been identified: nos. 10613SF and 10653 SF. Both were low-end outfits surely intended to reduce inventory on hand. No specific retailers have been identified as having ordered these outfits. Penney did return to the fold, but the two sets in its catalog for 1969 were Lionel cataloged outfits.

By this time, Lionel had let its sales force dwindle while cutting its ties with manufacturers representatives around the country. Executives in New York City may have solicited orders for promotional outfits. Or sales personnel associated with specific retailers may have placed them direct to the individuals overseeing product development at the Lionel plant. Either way, just as the glorious years of the postwar period ended so quietly and meekly, so too did the long tradition at Lionel of developing promotional items, primarily outfits, for retailers and other customers.

XV. Gems within Lionel Promotional Outfits: 1960-66

For too long, Lionel's practice of offering promotional outfits has been all but ignored by mainstream collectors of the company's prewar and postwar trains. Perhaps the mystery veiling specials of all varieties has limited their appeal. Certainly, the lack of knowledge about these promotional outfits has frustrated collectors.

Now, because of the stack of binders acquired and shared by the Schmids, all of us fascinated by Lionel's marketing programs and its promotional models will be able to learn more about the *hundreds* of specials created in the 1960s. For the Factory Orders, combined with other sources, provide information for more than 800 different promotional outfits between 1959 and 1969, nearly five times the number of cataloged outfits from those years.

Most promotional outfits were considered introductory or beginner train sets for the youngster who had no other Lionel train. To compensate for the minimal amount of cars or simple locomotives, Lionel might stick in enough sections of track and a crossover to create a figure-eight layout. Or there might be an accessory, an engineer's cap, a cardboard railroad accessory set, Lionel trading cards, or a group of billboards - something to increase the play value of that outfit.

All the same, collectors would be mistaken if they assume that Lionel in focusing its promotional outfits on the low end of the market during the postwar decades neglected the upper echelon. Gems can be uncovered among the Retailer Promotionals (Type I) as well as Retailer General Release Promotionals (Type II) that are mentioned in the Factory Orders.

Seen from one perspective, these gems are the Lionel items that appeared in promotional outfits rather than in the cataloged line. Take a look at these cursory listings of trains and cardboard accessories to get a sense of how many great items were limited to promotionals:

Locomotives:
- 215P Santa Fe Alco A: fourteen outfits between 1964 and 1967
- 220P Santa Fe Alco: thirteen outfits
- 227P Canadian National Alco A: ten outfits
- 241 steamer with die-cast metal boiler: eleven outfits from 1965-66
- 251 steamer with die-cast metal boiler: outfit no. 19583 from 1966

- 635 Union Pacific NW2 switcher: six outfits from 1965-66

Rolling stock:
- 3386 operating giraffe car: ten outfits from 1960
- 6014-100 red Airex boxcar: at least twelve outfits from 1960
- 6045-50 Cities Service tank car: nine outfits and one blister display between 1960 and 1963
- 6045-150 orange Lionel Lines tank car: fourteen outfits between 1963 and 1966
- 6410-25 flatcar with two autos: five outfits from 1963

Cardboard accessories:
- 902 cardboard trestle set: eight outfits from 1960-61
- 903 trading cards: ten outfits between 1960 and 1964
- 908 scenic station with tunnels: five outfits between 1960 and 1964
- 910 Navy yard cardboard display: nine outfits between 1960 and 1964
- X625-20 cardboard scenic set: nine outfits between 1961 and 1966

Seen from another perspective, the gems associated with Lionel's promotional outfits are a handful of the outfits themselves because their contents, even if all cataloged items, create something so large and special as to be highly valued. Consider that the Factory Orders refer to twenty-three Super O and thirteen O gauge promotional outfits, most of which matched or even surpassed the best of their cataloged peers.

In 1960, for example, Lionel developed outfit no. 9694 for Sears. This Retailer Promotional with Cataloged Items (Type Ia) included the no. 746 Norfolk & Western streamlined 4-8-4 Northern with a "long-stripe" tender and five desirable freight cars.

In 1961, outfit no. X-693, a Retailer General Release Promotional with Cataloged Items (Type IIa), featured a no. 2360 GG1 electric with seven pieces of rolling stock. The roster of models included the nos. 6119-100 work caboose, 6416 four boat transport car, 6440 twin piggyback van car, 6530 fire fighting instruction car, 6560 Bucyrus-Erie crane car, 6827 flatcar with tractor shovel, and 6828 flatcar with mobile construction crane car.

In 1962, Lionel produced two Super O promotional outfits. The no. 19178 was made for Joe, the Motorists' Friend, Inc. Headed by a 2360 GG1, it came with various pieces of high-end rolling stock. Outfit no. 19196 went to Broadway Stores and had a no. 637 die-cast metal 2-6-4 steam locomotive and tender, high-end freight cars, and a no. 470 missile launching platform.

In 1963, Lionel developed seven Super O promotional outfits (most remain unknown and unreported; the only documentation is Lionel Factory Orders). The no. 19309 had a 736 pulling nine freight cars plus the nos. 163 single target block signal, 195 floodlight tower, 299 code transmitter set, 988 Plasticville railroad structure set, and a KW transformer (separately shipped but marked to be included with this outfit).

Also noteworthy from 1963 is promotional outfit no. 19315. Like the cataloged no. 13148, it boasts nos. 2383 Santa Fe F3

A-A units leading no. 2520-series "Presidential" passenger cars. However, the 19315 differed from the 13148 in that it came with one no. 2523 *President Garfield* Pullman (not two) and had a KW transformer.

In 1964, Lionel produced Super O promotional outfits for the last time. The most notable of those seven outfits was the no. 13267 made for Jersey Model Distributors. It was identical to the cataloged no. 13150 Hudson freight set, except that it contained more rolling stock (nos. 6315 chemical tank car, 6402 flatcar, two 6464 boxcars, and 6465-150 tank car) and featured a no. 1044 transformer instead of a ZW. Having eleven cars made this promotional outfit one of the largest Lionel sets known.

Two other memorable promotional outfits from 1964 were expanded versions of the cataloged no. 12780 O gauge passenger outfit, which featured nos. 2383 Santa Fe F3 A-A diesels pulling four Presidential passenger cars. The no. 12817, sold by Polk's Hobbies of New York City, featured additional track, a trestle set, and a ZW transformer.

By 1966, Lionel's O gauge promotional outfits represented nothing more than the repackaging of cataloged outfits, with only minor changes in the rolling stock and the addition of "X" as the suffix to the number. For example, outfit no. 12710X duplicates the cataloged no. 12710 Berkshire five-car freight outfit, except that it had a no. 6431-1 piggyback car with trailer trucks and tractor in place of a no. 6476-135 hopper.

Two other Retailer General Release Promotionals (Type IIa) from 1966 deserve attention. The no. 12800X took some of the components of the cataloged no. 12800 diesel five-car freight outfit, put them in individual boxes, changed the outfit packaging to a regular slotted carton, and added a no. 6414 Evans auto loader. Outfit no. 12850X kept everything its cataloged diesel seven-car freight twin had, but substituted a no. 6822-1 night crew searchlight car for a no. 6476-135 hopper and a no. 6464-450 Great Northern boxcar for a no. 6315-60 chemical tank car.

These noteworthy outfits, although comparatively small in number, prove that well into the 1960s Lionel remained committed to the high end of its product line, even for promotional items. Customers demanded variety and uniqueness. Lionel aimed to please and took the best of what it had, combining trains with accessories and other add-ons to create some of the most sought-after outfits and individual items from the postwar era.

Nevertheless, the vast majority of promotional outfits documented in the Factory Orders do not impress on the basis on their contents. To put these sets together quickly, Lionel selected locomotives and cars that were either leftover stock or common items that required just a short production run. That way the company would not have to invest in new tooling or spend much if anything to paint and stamp the models packed into typical promotional outfits.

Similarly, the merchants placing orders for these Lionel outfits wouldn't find the cost overwhelming. The unit prices of typical promotionals weren't great; usually enough, however, for Lionel to make a small profit on nearly every outfit ordered. Retailers, in turn, sold these specials at fairly low prices, which meant that consumers didn't have to pay very much to receive a complete train set.

What does impress us from studying the Factory Orders is the overall marketing strategy that underlay Lionel's commitment to offering promotional outfits to retailers of almost any size, along with so many other types of clients. No wonder the number of promotionals developed and the quantities of these outfits made skyrocketed during the 1960s - lean years at Lionel when sales executives would go after any customer whose order might help bolster the bottom line. Consequently, during the middle and late 1960s, as was true during the late 1930s and early '40s, Lionel sold more promotional outfits than cataloged ones

Only by using the Schmids' notebooks can anyone interested in Lionel's history and the train sets available in the 1960s reach knowledgeable conclusions about its promotional outfits and their customers, contents, packaging, and more. Consulting these records enables us to appreciate what the decision-makers there hoped to achieve; analyzing them sheds powerful light on a period in Lionel's history that has remained hidden in the shadows and misunderstood for too long. These notebooks, like the outfits they describe, can be seen as treasures, finally available to the world.

The notebooks used as the basis of this volume contain thousands of documents that remained out of sight for decades. They provide complete and authoritative information straight from Lionel.

General Motors F3 Type Diesel

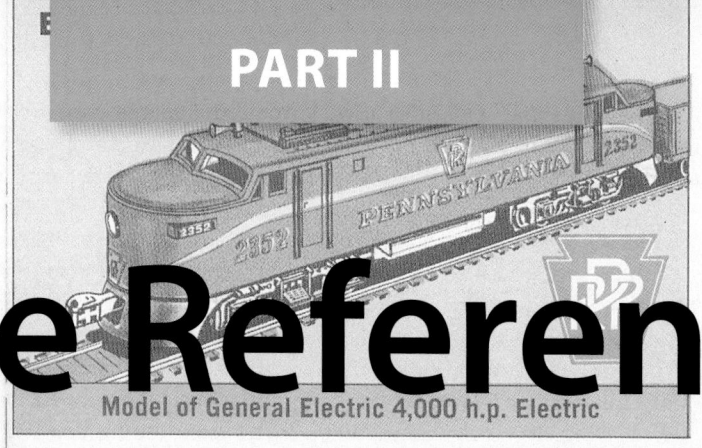

PART II

The Reference

Model of General Electric 4,000 h.p. Electric

Model of General M

'S M-K-T "SPECIAL" DIESEL

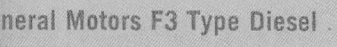

eneral Motors F3 Type Diesel

LIONEL'S "SANTA FE" DIESEL

Santa Fe

Model of General Motors F3 Type Diesel

LIONEL'S "M

Model of General

S "WESTERN PACIFIC" DIESEL

WESTERN PACIFIC

WESTERN PACIFIC

eneral Motors F3 Type Diesel

LIONEL'S "UNION PACIFIC" DIESEL SWITCHER

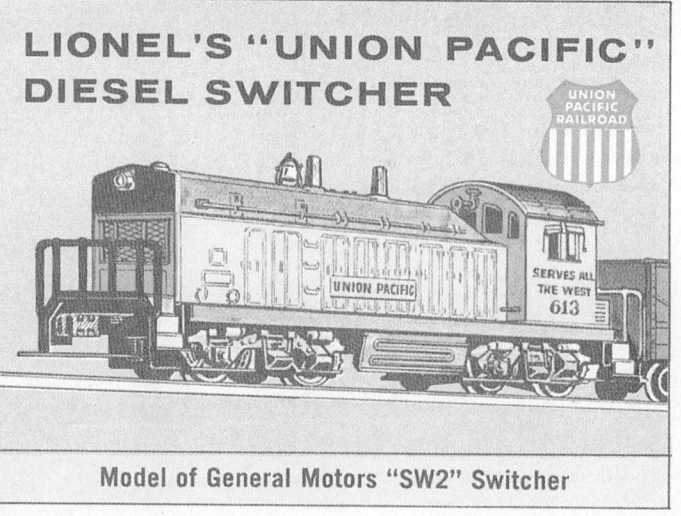

UNION PACIFIC RAILROAD

UNION PACIFIC 613

SERVES ALL THE WEST

Model of General Motors "SW2" Switcher

LIONEL'S " RECTIFIER

Model of General Ele

"NORFOLK & STERN" STEAMER

N&W RAILWAY

W's 4-8-4 Class J Locomotive

LIONEL'S "CANADIAN PACIFIC" DIESEL

Canadian Pacific

Model of General Motors F3 Type Diesel

LIONEL'S "B

Burlington Route

Model of General

Pricing, Condition, Rarity and Demand

Promotional outfits are exciting to read about, but the real fun comes with collecting them. Traditionally, there has been scant pricing information supporting the purchase or sale of a promotional outfit. This volume provides comprehensive pricing guidance for these transactions as well as for evaluating existing collections.

This volume is unique in that it is developed using actual quantities from authoritative Lionel internal records and other related sources. These production quantities will be used to determine overall outfit rarity, thereby bringing a new level of objectivity to setting a price in the marketplace.

The perceived market price for any promotional outfit can be expressed as an equation of condition, rarity, demand and other related factors. These variables are all correlated in that each one affects all the others, specifically:

Price = Condition (Grading) : Rarity (Current Supply) : Demand : Other Factors

This formula is used as a baseline in determining the price of each of the promotional outfits listed in this volume. The remainder of this section provides an overview and breakdown of this formula.

Determining Outfit Condition Grading Standards

The first variable in the formula, "condition (grading)," is determined by a rollup of the condition of each component of the outfit, including the outfit box, individual items and their boxes as well as instruction sheets and assorted peripherals. A 10-point grading scale is established, with 10 representing the highest classification. This scale is easily understandable; when an outfit moves up the scale, the better is its condition.

Our goal at Project Roar Publishing is to provide comprehensive pricing information. As such, pricing for both a complete promotional outfit and its outfit box alone is provided. This is the first reference guide to provide this level of detail, which is what collectors have told us they are seeking.

How to Read the Table

The following table summarizes the condition of each outfit component. Gray, green, yellow and orange mean that the shaded components as specified in the outfit listings (Factory Order) are required to achieve the condition rating. Pricing and rarity are provided for outfits in C8, C7 and C6 condition. For the purposes of this volume, the components required and priced for a C8, C7 and C6 outfit are shaded in green, yellow or orange, respectively.

As an example, reading across the C8 row, green indicates that the outfit requires *all* the components listed on the Factory Order, including the outfit box, items, item boxes, instruction sheets, packed envelope, major and minor peripherals and, depending on how it is boxed (display or RSC - see the section on Types of Outfit Packaging for a definition of display and RSC), all inserts, to achieve a C8 rating. A C7 outfit also requires all components (yellow). A C6 outfit does not require minor peripherals or RSC inserts. A C5 or lower condition outfit requires only the outfit box and individual items. All other components are desirable, but not required to achieve the condition rating. Note that at all times, an outfit box must be present for the group of train components to be considered an outfit.

Major peripherals are defined as items that add substantial value to a train outfit. They include accessories, cardboard punch-outs, special billboards, Plasticville sets and certain envelopes.

Minor Peripherals are easily obtainable and do not add a substantial value to an outfit. They include most track, common transformers, wire, etcetera.

The condition of peripherals and inserts is not specifically listed because they mirror the grading of outfit boxes, items, item boxes and instruction sheets. For example, to grade a no. 264-1 Operating Fork Lift Platform Set, compare its corrugated box, no. 6264 Lumber Car Complete, instruction sheet and inserts to the corresponding categories (outfit box, items and instruction sheets) already defined.

DETERMINING OUTFIT CONDITION

An outfit is the appropriate combination of an outfit box, items, item boxes, instruction sheets, packed envelopes, peripherals and inserts.

The gray, green, yellow and orange shaded outfit components are required to achieve a complete outfit in the desired condition.

GRADING SCALE	OUTFIT BOX	ITEMS *	ITEM BOXES	INSTRUCTION SHEETS	PACKED ENVELOPE	MAJOR PERIPHERALS	DISPLAY INSERTS	MINOR PERIPHERALS	RSC INSERTS
C10	Brand new square with no creases on sides. All flaps present and opened only a few times, still stiff to open. Color appears as if it just came out of master shipping carton, bright, no fading or darkening. No box rubs, tears, holes, dents or punctures. No marks or writing. No water damage.	Mint – Brand new, all original, unused and unblemished.	Brand new, square with all flaps present and never opened or opened only once or twice, flaps stiff to open, perforation (Orange Perforated) present and unpunched. No creases. Color appears as if it just came out of master shipping carton, bright, no fading or darkening. No box rubs, tears, holes, dents or punctures. No marks, price tags, or writing. No water damage. All liners, inserts, and outer sleeve included.	Brand new with square edges, bold and sharp printing. If a folded sheet, has never been opened. No marks, creases, folds or tears.	Envelope sealed, never opened. Condition of envelope mirrors instruction sheets. Contents all present and mirror condition of items.	Compare to other ratings that best represent the peripheral.	Use "Outfit Box" condition ratings.	Compare to other ratings that best represent the peripheral.	Use "Outfit Box" condition ratings.
C9	Same as C10 but may have affixed price tag indicating the "original price" of the box's contents.	Factory New - Brand new, all original and unused. May have evidence of factory rubs and the slightest evidence of handling. May have been test run at factory.	Same as C10 but may have affixed price tag indicating the "original price" of the box's contents.	Same as C10 but individual pages may have been opened. Original paper folds are crisp with no signs of damage.					
C8	Same as C9 except show signs of opening. Small box rub, but no, tears, holes, dents or punctures. One small mark or writing.	Like New – Complete, no rust, no missing original parts. May show effects of being on display and/or age. May have been run.	Same as C9, except flaps show signs of opening but still stiff. One small mark. Inserts required.	Same as C9, except shows some sign of handling, i.e. if folded, can tell item has been opened. Corners sharp and square.	May have been opened but resealed. Envelope same as instruction sheet. Contents all present same as items.				
C7	Same as C8 with nice color but not as crisp as C8 due to minimal fading. Small box rub and minimal dents, but no holes, tears or punctures. Minimal marks. No water damage.	Excellent – Minor scratches and paint nicks, no rust, no missing original parts. No distortion of component parts.	Same as C8 with nice color, but not as crisp as C8 due to minimal fading. Small box rub and minimal dents, but no holes, tears or punctures. Minimal marks. No water damage. Inserts or liners optional. Perforation shows wear but not split.	May have small crease or fold. One corner may not be perfectly square. Printing may have some slight fading.	Could be opened, but all contents present. Condition same as instruction sheet and items.				
C6	Cardboard is slightly rounded at one corner, not completely square. One small crease possible. All flaps there, but are beginning to get floppy (not stiff). Color shows signs of minimal fading or darkening. Minimal box rubs, dents, tears or punctures, but no holes. Minimal marks. No water damage.	Very Good – Minor scratches and paint nicks, minor spots of surface rust, free of dents. May have minor parts replaced.	Cardboard is slightly rounded at one corner, not completely square. One small crease possible. All flaps there, but are beginning to get floppy (not stiff). May be reinforced with tape. Color shows signs of minimal fading or darkening. Minimal box rubs, dents, but no punctures, holes or tears. Minimal marks. No water damage. Perforation beginning to separate. No inserts or liners.	Shows signs of wear and use. Corner(s) slightly off square, minor folds, or dog ears, present. May have some small pencil marks present.	Has been opened. Major contents present. Condition same as instruction sheet and items.				

DETERMINING OUTFIT CONDITION - Continued

An outfit is the appropriate combination of an outfit box, items, item boxes, instruction sheets, packed envelopes, peripherals and inserts.
The gray shaded outfit components are required to achieve a complete outfit in the desired condition.

GRADING SCALE	OUTFIT BOX	ITEMS *	ITEM BOXES	INSTRUCTION SHEETS	PACKED ENVELOPE	MAJOR PERIPHERALS	DISPLAY INSERTS	MINOR PERIPHERALS	RSC INSERTS
C5	Same as C6 but more than one side losing squareness. One or more small creases. All flaps there but can be floppy. Hinged display tops also floppy. Moderate rubs, dents and a few puncture marks but still no holes. Writing or other marks present. Slight water damage on bottom.	Good – Some sign of play wear with scratches and minor paint loss. Small dents, minor surface rust, minor parts may be missing or replaced.	Same as C6, but more than one side losing squareness. One or more small creases. Can be missing one or more interior flaps. Exterior end flaps present but may be reinforced with tape. Moderate rubs, dents, and a few puncture marks. Writing or other marks present. Perforation separated but present.	Same as C6, but may have small tear(s) that were fixed with transparent tape. Some dirt present.	Opened, missing most contents. Condition same as instruction sheet and items.				
C4	Rounded corners with creases. May be missing an interior flap or locking flap on hinged display. Remaining flaps floppy or starting to detach. Fading, darkening or skinning present. Many box rubs, dents, punctures and a small hole possible. Flaps and hinged top may have small tears. Many markings with some water damage.	Fair – Scratched, moderate paint loss, dented, missing parts, surface rust. Evidence of heavy use.	Rounded corners with creases, may be missing interior flaps or one or more exterior flaps. Remaining flaps floppy or starting to detach or are reinforced with tape. Fading very noticeable. Many box rubs and dents. Flaps may have small tears. Many markings. Perforation separated and missing.	Has been used. If folded sheet, fold is floppy and may need repair. Marks present in pen or pencil. Has tears or rips that were fixed.		Compare to other ratings that best represent the peripheral.	Use "Outfit Box" condition ratings.	Compare to other ratings that best represent the peripheral.	Use "Outfit Box" condition ratings.
C3	Same as C4 but missing more than one flap. Detached hinged display but still present.	Poor – Requires major body repair. Heavily scratched, major rust and missing parts. Restoration candidate.	Same as C4, but at least one flap remains.	Major tears, parts of pages missing, paper is disintegrating in sections.	Envelope only. Condition same as instruction sheet.				
C2	All flaps missing, not square, major rubs, marks, dents, creases, punctures, water damage or holes.	Restoration required.	All flaps missing, not square, major rubs, marks, dents, creases, punctures, water damage or holes.	Pages missing if multiple-page sheet. Rips, tears, and partial pages remain.					
C1	No flaps, just sides.	Junk, parts value only.	Just a piece of the box remains.	Just part of the instruction sheet remains.					

* Item grading descriptions as defined by the Train Collectors Association (TCA).

Outfit Rarity (Current Supply)

The second variable in determining an outfit's price is the rarity of the overall outfit and its individual components. Rarity is defined as how frequently an outfit appears in the public, or how hard it is to find. Simply put, rarity can be thought of as the current supply of an outfit.

To date, the Factory Orders and other internal Lionel documentation used as reference for this volume provide the most accurate picture of the original supply of promotional outfits and their individual components. The author has spent years analyzing these and other documents in order to obtain a comprehensive understanding of Lionel's production quantities. Typical production runs of promotional outfits ranged from 500 to 1,000; common outfits could reach 80,000 or more. Limited production runs could be as low as six outfits.

Unfortunately, all the outfits and items produced by Lionel have not survived. Even with the knowledge of original production quantities, it is difficult to identify what still remains. Still, the author has spent years in the hobby marketplace and so has a firm knowledge of how often a promotional outfit appears for sale. He also knows, regarding some of the rarer outfits, how many there are and where they currently can be found.

Taking this expertise and applying it to the original quantities leads to informed estimates of the current supply of the promotional outfits listed in this volume. This process is called "factoring."

Rarity (Current Supply) = Original Supply x Factor

How Rarity (Current Supply) is Determined

Most promotional outfits were entry level and sold through general retailers to families for children to operate. Boxes were torn open, cardboard cutouts punched and assembled and flat car loads broken or lost. As such, factoring of the original outfit supply occurs because many outfits did not stand up to this use. The original outfit supply number is lowered (factored) based on the experiences and observations of the author.

Factoring of the original supply also occurs for promotional outfit components. Components of an outfit are often fragile or contain removable parts and so did not survive complete. For example, there are many more no. 6402 Flat Cars available without their loads than there are complete examples. The same can be said for items that came with no Lionel markings. Many of the cardboard and paper items were lost or destroyed because they were so fragile. During a conversation concerning a no. 19201 (2) outfit that contains a no. 910-1 Navy Yard Cardboard Display (Atomic Sub Base), the owner said he was going to burn the Sub Base because he did not know what it was.

Many promotional outfits are extremely difficult to complete due to the inclusion of a non-train item. A 910-1, no. 908-10 Scenic Station W/Tunnels - Packed, no. X625-20 Cardboard Scenic Set, no. 975-1 Squad of Soldiers, no. 110-75 Modified Trestle Set (complete with a no. 110-78 envelope and bag) and no. 903 Set of (2) Sheets Trading Cards are just a few of the items that are often worth more than the remainder of the outfit. Accordingly, the original quantity is factored downward to determine current outfit rarity.

Outfit boxes also have faced difficult survival over the years. An outfit box was considered a place to store trains and not an item with intrinsic value. Initial openings of outfit boxes, even if done carefully, could result in ripped flaps (Lionel often applied too much glue when it sealed boxes). Other outfit boxes were improperly stored and took on water, heat, cold, fading, and insect, rodent or pet damage. Corrugated cardboard becomes brittle over years of heat exposure in an attic. Boxes were frequently marked or marred by the retailer or owner. Finally, many promotional outfit boxes were considered worthless and so were thrown out because the item contents were unknown.

Individual boxes can also skew the rarity and price of an outfit. Many boxed items placed solely in promotional outfits were produced in smaller quantities than was customary. Examples include the boxes for a no. 6027-1 Alaskan Caboose or a no. 6017-200 U.S. Navy Caboose, both of which are almost very difficult to find.

Individual item boxes also did not hold up as well as the trains they protected. Many boxes were initially discarded or severely damaged by rough treatment. These boxes, for similar reasons as outfit boxes and accessories, did not survive. As boxes were opened, they were damaged and so lost their value. Consequently, a boxed item is more difficult to find than the same item unboxed.

In this volume, rarity ratings are provided for both the individual outfit box and the entire outfit. Rarity is assigned based on the following current supply (factored original supply) quantities:

Outfit Rarity Rating	Current Supply	Example
R10	1 to 100	19248 from 1963
R9	101 to 250	19142-502 from 1963
R8	251 to 400	19192 from 1962
R7	401 to 600	19218 from 1963
R6	601 to 1,000	X-650 from 1961
R5	1,001 to 2,000	X-519NA from 1960
R4	2,001 to 3,500	19701 from 1967
R3	3,501 to 6000	9653 from 1960
R2	6,001 to 25, 000	19500 from 1966
R1	25,000 or more	11415 from 1963

Demand

Demand is the other side of rarity. It does not matter how rare a promotional outfit is or what its condition. If there is no demand for it, price will be reflected accordingly. The opposite is also true. An outfit in moderate demand, such as a no. 19142-100 Van Camp's outfit in C8 condition, continues to sell well even though the quantities produced were very high (25,000).

Other Factors

Besides condition, rarity and demand, a few intangible factors can lead to temporary price fluctuations of promotional outfits:

Short-Term Supply

Short-term supply fluctuations can influence pricing. Even if an outfit is rare with high demand, should two of them appear at the same train show or at different auctions at the same time, prices may be temporarily affected. Also, if someone pays a higher than listed price for an outfit, this circumstance may coax collectors who have owned such an outfit for years to sell in hopes of making a nice profit.

Regional Supply

Due to the Internet, this is not as much of a factor as it used to be. Still, certain outfits do sell better in different regions. Specifically, an outfit with a particular road name or an outfit sold through a particular retailer will likely sell well in its local region.

Eagerness to Sell

Some sellers may be willing to sell at a reduced price just to move an outfit. Others, in contrast, will hold on to an outfit for months, even years, until they get their desired price. Still others may have short-term financial needs that drive them to sell quickly.

Eagerness to Buy

Collectors, especially those searching for a rare piece, may be willing to pay whatever it takes to acquire that outfit. Egos may lead to bidding wars at auctions, which can drive prices to unprecedented levels.

Sales Savvy

How well an outfit is advertised or promoted also influences its price. Good auctioneers can work a room and drive up prices. Well-listed and photographed outfits from a reputable seller tend to sell better on the Internet. Finally, good old-fashioned salesmanship and relationships lead to better sales.

Access to Information

In a perfect market where all information is known, an outfit will likely sell for the same price everywhere. However, information is not evenly spread and buyers and sellers will pay a premium or discount for an outfit because they are unaware of issues, such as an outfit's completeness or the quantity produced. There are thousands of promotional outfits (complete and partially complete) and empty boxes that have not commanded any price because the buyer had no idea as to the completeness of the outfit. Volumes such as this will enhance the market for promotional outfits by making such information available.

Access to Distribution

Easy worldwide distribution of train outfits is a few clicks away. Promotional outfits that would never have found their way into the collector community are now available through online auctions and other Internet sale channels.

Assembled Outfits Versus Complete Unmarred Outfits

Over the years, most outfits have been found to be less than 100 percent complete and so collectors have assembled, upgraded or completed their outfits based on the current information. See the section on Completing an Outfit.

Even if an outfit were assembled or upgraded with the proper components for that year, it does not necessarily ensure that it was the way it was shipped from the factory. There were many individual item nuances even within a manufacturing year. Specific versions of many items appeared in outfits only and not for separate sale. Therefore, it is fairly difficult to get an outfit 100 percent correct as it left the factory. While most collectors do not make a distinction, some are willing to pay a premium for an outfit that came from its original owner and is factory complete and unmarred.

Prices in this Volume

The prices for outfits listed in this volume are determined by applying the pricing formula to each outfit and its components:

Price = Condition (Grading) : Rarity (Current Supply) : Demand : Other Factors

The resulting prices are the selling prices (in U.S. dollars) known by the author and publisher. These prices come from train shows held across America, gleaned from major auction houses, and outfits sold on eBay and other Internet sources. Asking prices for outfits listed for sale on individual websites and in toy train club publications are also used for the pricing criteria.

How Prices are Displayed

Pricing and rarity are summarized in a pricing table as part of each promotional outfit listing. The table for outfit no. X-603 from 1961 is shown below:

X-603 (1961)	C6	C7	C8	Rarity
Complete Outfit	510	950	1,300	R8
Outfit Box no. 60-409	150	300	400	R8

Pricing is included for promotional outfits as described below:

- C8 pricing includes the entire promotional outfit and all peripherals as listed on the original Lionel Factory Order. This includes the outfit box, all items with their individual boxes, instruction sheets, packed envelope(s), inserts and any other peripherals, all in C8 condition. This is color-coded green.
- C7 pricing includes the entire promotional outfit and all peripherals as listed on the original Lionel Factory Order. This includes the outfit box, all items with their individual boxes, instruction sheets, packed envelope(s), inserts and any other peripherals, all in C7 condition. This is color-coded yellow.
- C6 pricing includes the outfit box, all items with their individual boxes, instruction sheets, packed envelope(s) display inserts and any major peripherals, all in C6 condition. It excludes minor peripherals and RSC inserts. This is color-coded orange.
- Pricing is also included for the C8, C7 and C6 promotional outfit box by itself and is shown with a white background.

Note that C10 and C9 pricing is not included in this volume, as these promotional outfits are most often in limited quantities and collectors frequently pay whatever it takes to obtain them.

Selling Your Trains

Train dealers, brokers and individuals who resell trains are in the business to make a profit. For that reason, if you sell your trains to one of these individuals, you can expect to receive less than the prices listed in this volume. Depending on the profit they are seeking, and all the other variables listed in this section, you may obtain 50 to 80 percent of the prices in this volume.

If you are selling your trains directly to an individual who does not intend to resell them (they are being added to a collection), the actual prices in this volume apply. Once again, all prices in this volume are only guidelines based on observations of current market conditions. Your experiences may vary.

How to Collect Promotional Outfits

Until now, collecting promotional outfits has been a mystery and a crapshoot. A collector could never be sure of what he or she was buying because there was never an official Lionel catalog on promotional outfits. Even with this uncertainty, there has always been a market for promotional outfits. Leveraging the authoritative information in this volume should dramatically increase interest in and the marketability of promotional outfits. Outfit boxes with previously unknown contents, once considered worthless, will now have value. As a side benefit, we predict the demand for outfit peripherals will also increase as collectors seek the correct paperwork, envelopes and add-ons to complete their existing outfits.

So how does one go about collecting promotional outfits? With more than 700 promotional outfits having been created between 1960 and 1969, only a few individuals have the funds or space necessary to attempt to collect them all. Therefore, as a first step it is best to formulate a strategy to segment this market. Possible segment strategies include:

Segment	Description or Example
Outfits with a particular item	All the outfits with a no. 6407-25 or -1.
Outfits from a particular year	All the outfits from 1963.
Outfits with a particular add-on	All outfits with a no. 910-1 Submarine Base. This is an interesting segment that can now be fully exploited due to the information in this volume.
Space and Military Outfits	This is a popular segment among collectors and very well represented by promotional outfits.
Particular Retailer	Collecting outfits for a specific retailer like Sears, Ward or Penney.
Condition	Collect only outfits that meet a minimum condition level better.
Outfits with a production quantity lower than a particular amount	A new segment now possible because of production quantities provided with the Factory Orders.
Empty Boxes Only	Some collectors like to collect the empty promotional outfit boxes and leave them empty or fill them.

Once a collector knows what he or she is looking for, the next step is to find it. Promotional outfits can be found at almost any venue that sells postwar outfits. These include:

- Hobby Stores
- Trains Shows
- Auctions
- Online
- Ads in Newspapers
- Friends
- Garage Sales

The good news is that the advent of the Internet and eBay has driven a lot of these outfits out of attics into the mainstream as individuals now have easy access to numerous distribution channels.

Once an outfit is found that meets a particular target segment, the next step is to assess it and decide whether to buy. Using the information in this volume, a collector should fully examine the outfit box and items to ensure they are all there, all complete, original and in the preferred condition. For any items missing, he or she should adjust the appropriate condition price as listed. Once the decision has been made to buy the outfit, the buyer and seller should work out a fair price.

If someone is collecting empty boxes with the intent to fill, the same process can be used. The only caveat here is to ensure that he or she fully assesses the items required to fill an outfit. Some items were unique to only one or a few outfits and are extremely difficult to obtain. Refer to the section on Completing an Outfit, to help in filling the outfit box.

I have been successfully adding to my promotional outfit collection over the past couple of years. Focusing on condition and rarity alone, I have been able to find some unique deals. Now that everybody has this information, the playing field is leveled. Have FUN!!

Completing an Outfit

The information in this volume enables collectors to fill an empty outfit box, complete a partial outfit or verify an existing outfit. The outfit descriptions in Part III provide complete listings of the box, inserts, items and peripherals comprising an outfit. This volume also includes sections on properly dating items and outfit peripherals. Collectors can therefore make certain that the correct item in the correct box for the proper year is included.

Empty Box

Identification of the proper outfit box is the first step to assembling an outfit. This may sound trivial as the Lionel outfit number is most often on the box, but it becomes more complex because many outfits came with multiple box variations and outfit numbers were sometimes reused.

1. Collectors should begin by becoming familiar with the styles of outfit boxes that Lionel used from 1960 through 1969. These are described in the section on Outfit Box Printing, Graphics and Labels. Lionel used only certain boxes between 1960 and 1969, so if the style isn't shown here, the box you have is from a year beyond the scope of this volume.

2. Collectors may also want to become familiar with Lionel's outfit box part numbers (see the section on Outfit Boxes and Inserts). This information will help in identifying outfits that came in more than one type of box.

3. Next, collectors should proceed to Part III and look up the outfit number that appears on the box. The outfits are listed sequentially. If only one outfit box variation is listed and the description and photograph (if provided) match, or if there are multiple boxes listed but all contain the same components, then continue assembling.

4. If there is more than one variation of the outfit box and each variation contains different components, then it is important to identify the correct box version. Use the section on Outfit Boxes and Inserts to identify the proper box part number. Then continue assembling.

5. If a part number cannot be found, measure the box. Then consult the dimensions of the box(es) as listed in the outfit description. Compare the dimensions to the unidentified box. The dimensions that match are most likely for that box. If a positive match cannot be made, a collector can try to find another outfit that uses the same box (based on part number), review its outfit listing and see whether a positive match can be made. Then, continue assembling.

6. A few outfits were provided to customers without outfit numbers printed on the box. These boxes were usually stamped by the customer with only a retailer number. An example includes outfit no. 11520-500 from 1965, which was stamped with only Mercury Model's number 2058. Some of these retailer numbers were referenced on the Lionel Factory Order and included in the outfit listings. Also, blank outfit boxes were provided to customers who hand-stamped them with their own numbers as described in the Outfit Box Printing, Graphics and Labels section. These would not have outfit listings because they were not produced by Lionel. In either case, there may be no listing for these outfits.

Inserts

The section on Outfit Boxes and Inserts explains how to identify inserts by insert number. This section can be used to verify the inserts needed to complete an outfit.

Outfit Items

The outfit listings detail each item that came with the outfit, including a full description. Many of these items were issued over more than one year and may have subtle differences. Thus, proper dating of items is required to ensure that an outfit is 100 percent complete. Many variations are as simple as updated truck and couplers; other differences include color and decoration. The section on Trucks and Couplers assists in properly dating individual items. The pictures and descriptions that go with specific outfit listings also aid in item dating. Other sources covering individual items in detail should be check to properly date variations. Individual item boxes can be properly dated using the section on Individual Item Boxes.

Outfit Peripherals

Dating outfit peripherals is the final key to ensuring that a train outfit is 100 percent complete. The section on Outfit Peripherals explains the dating of envelopes, paper and other outfit components.

Overall, completing an outfit takes time, patience and practice. Many diverse segments of knowledge are necessary to ensure an outfit is 100 percent complete. Many collectors may know about individual items, but not track or paper. Others may be familiar with boxes, but not accessories.

Completing outfits is challenging because it stretches a person's knowledge across all these postwar segments. Collectors should take their time and enjoy their search because every outfit brings a new challenge in finding the correct item as well as the discovery of the components Lionel packaged together as an outfit.

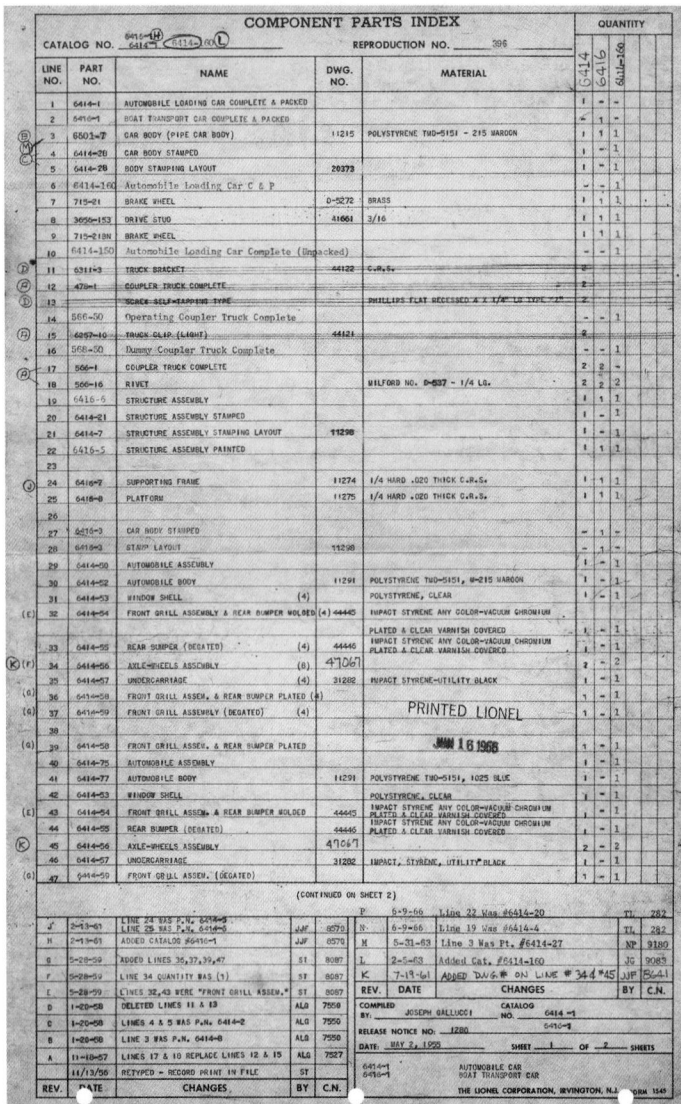

The Component Parts Index for the no. 6414-1 Automobile Loading Car Complete lists all the suffixes for every part and subassembly required for manufacturing this item.

The ways that Lionel used suffixes to identify fully assembled individual items (defined as "finished goods") continues to puzzle toy train collectors. They know that Lionel used suffixes on finished goods to distinguish differences in colors, road names, decoration, trucks and couplers, loads, wheel configurations and traction aids. Suffixes also specified the inclusion or exclusion of items in a box or an altogether different item.

Questions remain, though, concerning how Lionel assigned suffixes and what individual suffixes meant. Deciphering the meaning of various suffixes will answer many questions and uncover information related to items included in this volume.

What might be called the "suffix challenge" exists because no comprehensive external Lionel document has surfaced to explain how suffixes were used and what they meant. By far the best source of suffixes known so far is the *Lionel Service Manual*. It provides detailed component and subcomponent part suffix information and

descriptions. It also contains finished good part numbers, except that these descriptions are not always consistent. Specifically, there are many listings with identical components but with different finished good part numbers. Some items have suffixes, but others do not.

Other sources of suffix information including advance and consumer catalogs, parts lists and customer order sheets were designed for external consumer use. Consequently, they seldom have full descriptions of suffixes.

Fortunately for collectors, the Lionel Factory Orders as well as Component Parts Indexes and Production Control Files used in writing this volume resolve the "suffix challenge." These internal Lionel documents provide an authoritative and comprehensive listing of items, their suffixes and the suffix definition. They surpass the *Lionel Service Manual*, which was for external use and lists only components and sub-components released to authorized service stations for repair purposes. Information gleaned from the Factory Orders and other internal documents (primarily Component Parts Indexes and Production Control Files) can solve mysteries and aid in understanding all the items included in the promotional outfits listed in this volume.

Component Parts Index

Component Parts Indexes are paired with blueprints to provide the complete list of parts and subassemblies used to manufacture a complete item or finished good. They also provide a master index of each fully assembled item's individual blueprints.

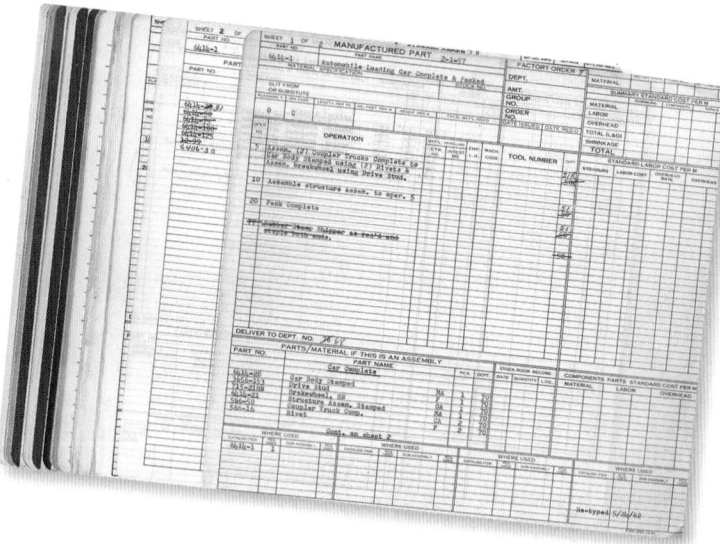

The Production Control File for the no. 6414-1 Automobile Loading Car Complete provides complete instructions on how to manufacture a 6414, including all parts and subassemblies. It also provides a history of the suffixes that were used and their replacements.

Production Control Files

Every Lionel finished good included a packet of documents that, when taken as a whole, was the bill of materials for the fully assembled (boxed or unboxed) finished good. These files list every part, subassembly and process required to make the finished good. Also included was the boxing and packing information.

Lionel's Number System

To comprehend Lionel's use of finished good suffixes, start by looking at the company's item numbering system. Every new item was assigned a base number, and any newly designed components or sub-components for this item were assigned a part number that consisted of the base number followed by a dash and another number. This dash and other number constitute the suffix.

Internally to Lionel, fully assembled and boxed finished goods were defined by the base number followed by -1. So a component boxed no. 6414 Automobile Loading Car would be known internally at Lionel as a no. 6414-1 Automobile Loading Car Complete & Packed. Consumers never saw the -1. An automobile loading car was simply a no. 6414.

It appears that Lionel assigned suffixes to the parts and subassemblies sequentially starting with "-2" and incremented as they went along. For major sub-component or finished good variations, suffixes were most often assigned in a multiple of twenty-five (e.g. -25, -50, -75) or ten (e.g. -10, -20, -110). This led to suffixes being skipped, as not every number was sequentially used.

The Advent of Unboxed Finished Goods

Before 1956, all finished goods were individually boxed and, as discussed earlier, most likely had the -1 suffix assumed as in the no. 6414 (items most often did not appear in external documentation with -1, but were known internally as ending in -1). If more than one version of an item existed, Lionel used suffixes to denote the difference between those versions. Lionel primarily used suffix increments of twenty-five to number the first major variation in a product family.

Notable examples where -1 and -25 were revealed to consumers were the nos. 2340-1 Tuscan Red and 2340-25 Green GG1's from 1955 and the nos. 2360-1 Tuscan Red and 2360-25 Green GG1's from 1956. Here, the suffixes indicated a difference in color.

Lionel's 6464 series of box cars (launched in 1953) also demonstrates the explicit use of -1 and -25 suffixes. The first boxcar in the series was no. 6464-1 Western Pacific followed by the no. 6464-25 Great Northern, no. 6464-50 Minneapolis & St. Louis, and so on. Before 1956, all items were boxed, and -1, -25 and other suffixes signified boxed items with differences in road name, color, or markings.

In 1956 cost reduction methods found their way to the outfit packing process because Lionel began packaging train outfits without individual component boxes. These expensive pre-printed individual boxes were replaced by corrugated cardboard inserts in low-end O27 outfits. Besides saving on materials, this change reduced the amount of labor needed to place items in an outfit box separated by inserts as opposed to individually boxing the items and then placing them in the outfit box. This change in packaging led to numerous downstream requirements. The most significant

Part Number	Description
6414-1	Completed finished good number for a boxed 6414 auto loader
6414-2	Car body stamped (Version for Bar End metal trucks and assembly). Later replaced by 6414-28
6414-4	Structure Assembly
6414-5	Supporting Frame
6414-6	Platform
6414-7	Structure Assembly Stamping Layout
6414-8	Car Body
6414-11	Folding Box (Replaced by 6414-29)
6414-12	Corr. Box for 24 (Replaced by 6414-30)
6414-15	Set of Cars Packed (Replaced by 6414-17)
6414-16	Set of Cars Packed (Replaced by 6414-18)
6414-17	Set of Cars Packed
6414-18	Set of Cars Packed
6414-20	Structure Assembly Painted
6414-21	Structure Assembly Stamped
6414-25	Set of Cars Packed
6414-26	Folding Box
6414-27	Car Body Unstamped (Version for AAR plastic trucks). Later replaced by 6501-7
6414-28	Car Body Stamped (Version for AAR plastic trucks)
6414-29	Folding Box
6414-30	Corr. Box for 12
6414-31	Folding Box / Imprinted
6414-50	Automobile Complete (Maroon)
6414-52	Automobile Body Maroon
6414-53	Window Shell
6414-55	Red Bumper
6414-56	Wheel & Axle Assembly
6414-57	Undercarriage
6414-59	Front Grill Assembly
6414-61	Wheel
6414-62	Axle
6414-75	Automobile Complete (Blue). Later this suffix was reused and became Automobile Transport Car Complete (Unpacked) on 2/21/64
6414-77	Automobile Body (Blue)
6414-85	Automobile Transport Car Packed (a 6414-75 in a box)
6414-86	Folding Box
6414-100	Automobile Complete (Yellow)
6414-102	Automobile Body (Yellow)
6414-125	Automobile Complete (White)
6414-127	Automobile Body (White)
6414-150	Automobile Loading Car Complete (Unpacked)
6414-160	Automobile Loading Car Complete & Packed

As an example of Lionel's number system, the no. 6414-1 Automobile Loading Car Complete & Packed used the suffixes shown in the table above.

required the Outfit Packing Department to distinguish between packing individually boxed or unboxed items. To that point, Lionel had used -1 to indicate boxed finished goods; it naturally followed that an unboxed item, being the first major variation, would be assigned a -25 suffix. As a result, Lionel adopted the rule of -1 for boxed items and -25 for unboxed items. Therefore a -1 item was a boxed version of a -25 item.

First Mystery Solved (1956 Service Station Listings)

The discovery outlined above explains many of the *Lionel Service Manual* listings that began appearing in August 1956. As Joe Algozzini observes, 1956 was the first year for the no. 6121 Pipe Car. This item was included unboxed in outfit no. 1547S and made available for separate sale. The unboxed item was assigned no. 6121-25, and the boxed separate-sale item was no. 6121-1. Both items were inadvertently listed in the *Lionel Service Manual*, even though from a service standpoint they were the same item. It appears the Service Station Department was getting acquainted with the new use of suffixes. This dual listing of many items (boxed and unboxed) has led to confusion over the years. Collectors can stop searching for many -25 variations of boxes because most do not exist.

Exceptions to -1 and -25 for Boxed and Unboxed Items

Many carryover items that were issued prior to 1956 already had -1, -25 or other suffixes allocated to indicate color or decorating schemes. This was common for hoppers, gondolas, large box cars, cabooses and other cars. When this occurred, Lionel would use suffixes to indicate boxed and unboxed items in an increment of ten or twenty-five.

A specific example is the no. 6414-1 Automobile Loading Car described earlier. This item was originally issued boxed in 1955 with an assumed -1 (not exposed to the consumer). It was known internally as no. 6414-1 Automobile Loading Car Complete & Packed. At the same time, no. 6414-25 was assigned to four autos packaged for separate sale. So in 1963, when Lionel issued an unboxed no. 6414, it could not use -25 (no longer available), so it incremented the last-used suffix (-125) by twenty-five and issued the no. 6414-150 Automobile Loader unboxed. Similar logic applied in 1964 when Lionel issued the unboxed version with cheapie autos. This time it reused the -75 suffix (the 6414-75 Blue Auto had been discontinued) and issued the no. 6414-75 Automobile Loader with Cheapie Autos unboxed and the no. 6414-85 Automobile Loader with Cheapie Autos boxed.

Many additional suffixes for boxed and unboxed items are listed in the Factory Orders, Component Parts Indexes and Production Control Files used to write this volume. Some notable examples include:

Part Number Boxed	Part Number Unboxed	Description
3330-100	3330-200	Operating Submarine Kit
6014-335	6014-325	Frisco Box Car
6119-100	6119-110	Work Caboose
6167-85	6167-75	Union Pacific Caboose
6436-110	6436-100	Lehigh Valley Hopper
6464-475	6464-485	Boston and Maine Box Car
6464-735	6464-750	New Haven Box Car
6464-900	6464-925	New York Central Box Car
6476-135	6476-125	Lehigh Valley Hopper

Suffixes for Trucks and Couplers

Another substantial change in suffixes occurred in 1963. In an attempt to further reduce costs, Lionel planned to cheapen many two operating coupler rolling stock items by changing one coupler from an operating to a non-operating coupler. This change led to new versions of many items and hence new suffixes.

For example the no. 3349 Turbo Missile Firing car was originally issued in 1962 as no. 3349-1 boxed and no. 3349-25 unboxed. Both of these items included two operating couplers, along with a no. 3349-8 instruction sheet indicating the same. In 1963, the swapping of one operating coupler with a non-operating coupler changed the unboxed suffix to no. 3349-100. This change also led to a change in the instruction sheet, and the no. 3349-105 was issued.

Other notable examples for 1963 include:

Part Number	Instruction Sheet	Description
3413-150	3413-152	Mercury Capsule Launching Car – with one operating coupler
3619-100	3619-105	Reconnaissance Copter Car – Instruction sheet changed, but apparently car was never manufactured with one operating coupler
3665-100	3665-105	Minuteman Missile Launching Car – with one operating coupler

UNCOUPLING

This car is equipped with an operating and a non-operating coupler. Make sure to join the non-operating coupler to the operating coupler of another car.

The couplers may be uncoupled by No. 1008 Cam-Trol or by electro-magnetic track sections such as No. 37 for Super"0", No. 6029 or No. 6019 for "027" and UCS for "0".

EXTRA MISSILES

Part No. 0349-10 Turbo-missiles are available at 35¢ each from Approved Service Stations or direct from The Lionel Service Department. If ordering from The Lionel Service Department include 35¢ additional on all orders totaling less than $1.00.

THE LIONEL CORPORATION
SERVICE DEPARTMENT: Hoffman Place, Hillside, N.J.

Printed in U.S. of America   3349-105 4/63

**INSTRUCTIONS
LIONEL
No.3349 TURBO - MISSILE CAR**

This Turbo-missile Car is equipped with a catapult designed to launch missiles for both long and short range flights.

The catapult is mounted so that it can be turned in a complete circle. In addition, it can be elevated from horizontal to point straight up (90° angle). These features make it possible to aim the catapult in all directions.

Turbo-missiles fired low from the side of this car will "explode" No. 6448 Target Car on contact. The car is designed to operate efficiently on "027", "0", and Super "0" track.

The no. 3349-105 instruction sheet shows that the no. 3349-100 Turbo Missile Car has one non-operating coupler.

Suffixes for Color, Decoration, Wheel Configuration and Traction Aid

Lionel continued to use suffixes to distinguish different versions of similar items. This practice allowed the company to create series of items with similar base item numbers without having to create entirely new numbers. Examples of base item numbers with different suffixes to signify differences in colors, decorations, wheel configurations, traction aids and packaging include:

Part Number	Description
211P-25	*Texas Special* Alco Diesel Power Unit – Unboxed with Magnetraction
211P-150	*Texas Special* Alco Diesel Power Unit – Unboxed with traction tires
1060T-25	Tender with Lionel markings and truck without special ground
1060T-50	Tender with Southern Pacific markings and truck without special ground
1062-25	Steam Type Loco – 0-4-0 with no traction tire
1062-50	Steam Type Loco – 0-4-0 with traction tire
1062-75	Steam Type Loco – 2-4-2 with traction tire
1062-125	Steam Type Loco – 2-4-0 with traction tire
3309-25	Turbo Missile Firing Car – (Red)
3309-50	Turbo Missile Firing Car – (Olive Drab)
3419-25	Operating Helicopter Car – Unboxed with 3419-100 Helicopter
3419-250	Operating Helicopter Car – Unboxed without Helicopter
6017-100	Boston and Maine Caboose – Boxed
6017-110	Boston and Maine Caboose – Unboxed
6017-200	U.S. Navy Caboose – Boxed
6017-210	U.S. Navy Caboose – Unboxed
6017-225	Santa Fe Caboose – Unboxed
6017-235	Santa Fe Caboose – Boxed
6050-1	Savings Bank Car – Boxed (White)
6050-25	Savings Bank Car – Unboxed (White)
6050-50	Swift Box Car – Unboxed with non-operating Archbar trucks and couplers
6050-100	Swift Box Car – Unboxed with two operating or one operating and one non-operating AAR truck and coupler
6050-110	Swift Box Car – Boxed
6050-150	Van Camp's Box Car – Unboxed
6050-175	Libby's Box Car – Unboxed

Use of "X" as a Suffix

Lionel used an "X" throughout the Factory Orders to signify a change with a finished good, such as the addition of items, deletion of items, special item markings and indication of an older version of an item. The X did not always appear on the item itself. The significant uses of X are grouped by item category and listed as follows.

Motive Power

An X added to a diesel or steam unit part number as in 2383PX-1, meant the boxed finished good did not include a lockon. This indicator help determine which type of packed envelope to include with the outfit. When an outfit was packed with motive power that included an X, the outfit's lockon was included in the packed envelope or loose in the outfit box. If the motive power did not have an X, then a separate lockon was not needed in the outfit. Therefore, if an envelope were included, it was a version that did not include a lockon.

Packed Envelopes and Track

An X as part of a packed envelope part number signified either the inclusion or exclusion of an item. For example, in late 1961 Lionel began placing power bus connectors on Super O track. Therefore, it no longer needed to include a separate envelope of no. 31-7's. This change also required that two 31-7's be added to the no. 39-25 and no. 39-35 envelopes for the uncoupling and power track sections. To signify the older envelopes without the 31-7's, X's were added to the part number. The X was also added to Super O Track part numbers to signify older track without the power bus connectors. Some examples include:

Part Number	Description
31-60X	Curved Track - Without Power Bus Connector (Bundle of 6 -31X)
31-65X	Curved Track - Without Power Bus Connector (Bundle of 6 - 31 With 2 Wires)
32-50X	Straight Track - Without Power Bus Connector (Bundle of 5 - 32)
39-25X	Operating Track Set - Without Power Bus Connector
39-35X	Operating Track Set - Without Power Bus Connector

Individual Items

An X on an individual item number signified a change in packaging or decorating. The no. 3361X was an operating lumber car that came without its bin.

Mysteries Exposed

A thorough knowledge of suffixes helps unravel many mysteries, in particular, questions relating to items in the 1963 and 1964 catalogs. For example, the use of suffixes with the nos. 6414-150 Auto Loader unboxed and 6464-750 (no. 6464-735 New Haven box car unboxed) as well as truck and coupler variations now makes sense. Many other suffixes that have appeared over the years can now be explained as either boxed or unboxed versions. The mysterious *Lionel Service Manual* listings with identical components but different finished good part numbers are also now known. The Factory Orders, Component Part Indexes and Production Control Files provide much information summarized in this volume.

Outfit Peripherals

Lionel took great care to ensure that its outfits came with all peripherals necessary to get the train up and running. Peripherals (track, transformers, lockons, paperwork, and more) were included based on the type of train outfit sold: ready-to-run, ready-to-run without a transformer or gift pack.

Lionel created more than 765 cataloged and promotional O27 outfits from 1960 through 1969. All but six of the cataloged outfits (these were gift packs) and three of the promotional outfits were ready-to-run. Ready-to-run outfits included trains, track, wires, lockon, oil, lubricant, transformer, and, if necessary, battery, smoke (pellets or liquid) and a smokestack cleaner. Also included were the relevant instruction sheets, billboards, service station lists and catalogs or flyers.

The O27 outfits were traditionally starter outfits sold to first-time train buyers. During the 1960s, many of these outfits were sold through self-service retailers who lacked the expertise needed to guide customers to a transformer or other required peripherals. As such, it was important that everything necessary to operate the outfit was included, hence the ready-to-run requirements.

Lionel also sold outfits that included everything as a ready-to-run outfit, except a transformer. Most often these were O gauge or Super O outfits targeted as a second or third outfit to customers that already owned a transformer. Only three O27 promotional outfits were sold without a transformer: one was a bulk shipment, and the other two went to retailers that added their own transformer.

The third type of outfit sold by Lionel was gift packs. The six different gift packs were targeted to customers who already had track and transformer but wanted another set of trains. These outfits included minimal peripherals, in most cases, just oil and lubricant and associated paperwork.

In determining the components of an outfit, Lionel first took inventory of the peripherals packaged with the individual outfit components to determine whether any additional peripherals were required. This process was important because the added cost of the duplicate peripherals could make an outfit unprofitable. By default, boxed motive power included many peripherals, such as lockons, oil, lubricant, smoke and smokestack cleaners. Sometimes this motive power was included in outfits.

Lionel also created different packaging of motive power specifically for outfits that did not include these peripherals. Boxed motive power without any additional peripherals was designated by an "X" on the Factory Orders. Therefore, the Outfit Packing Department would know which motive power to include in the outfit as well as which additional peripherals were required.

Lionel's engineers did a remarkable job of ensuring that each outfit did not have any duplication of peripherals. The remainder of this section details these peripherals.

Track

All outfits except gift packs included track, and many also included an uncoupling track section. Low-end O27 outfits came with a manual no. 1008-50 Cam-Trol Uncoupling Track Section, and higher-end O27 outfits included a remote control uncoupling track section (whichever was the one currently shipping that year).

All O gauge outfits (except one promotional) were packed with a UCS remote control uncoupling track with attached controller.

Super O outfits included a no. 37-25 Uncoupling Track Section in a no. 39-25 or 39-35 Remote Control Set packed envelope. Super O track required no. 31-7 Power Bus Connectors to connect sections of track. From 1957 through mid 1961, these bus bars came in separate no. 31-7 packed envelopes included in outfits. During the middle of 1961, Lionel began shipping Super O track with one bus bar attached to each track section, thus eliminating the need for the no. 31-7 packed envelope.

From 1960 through 1969, O27 track had silver/gray ties and O gauge had black ties. Super O most often came with silver conducting clips underneath the track, but the earlier version with black ties has also been observed in some outfits from the 1960s.

Transformers

Ready-to-run outfits came with a transformer of the appropriate wattage. If the transformer were component boxed, it most often came with wires; thus, additional wires for the transformer were not required with the outfit. If the transformer came unboxed, wires were included loose in the outfit box or in a packed envelope.

Lockons

For cataloged and promotional O27 outfits, lockons were included inside the boxed motive power, provided loose in the outfit box or placed in a packed envelope. Lionel used an "X" suffix on Factory Orders to indicate whether the motive power came prepackaged with the lockon. Specifically, no "X" meant that it included a lockon. If the motive power came unboxed or was boxed with an "X", (i.e. the lockon was not in the motive power box), the lockon would be included in a packed envelope or placed loose in the outfit box.

O gauge cataloged outfits always included motive power without a lockon; therefore, the lockon was placed loose in the outfit box. O gauge promotional outfits most often included motive power with an enclosed lockon.

Super O outfits used no. 43 Power Track Sections instead of the incompatible O27 lockon. Therefore, all boxed Super O motive power came without lockons.

Oil and Lubricant

Lionel included oil and lubricant in outfits through 1961 with some carryover into 1963. The no. 927-60 Tube of Oil and no. 927-65 Tube of Grease were included in the motive power box or, if the motive power were unboxed, in a packed envelope included in the outfit. In 1962, lubricant was discontinued and only oil was included with outfits. The nos. 927-60 and 927-65 tubes were replaced by no. 927-85 Oiler capsule packaged in a small cellophane wrapper numbered 927-90 Lubricating Oil Packed. By 1963, Lionel no longer included oil or lubricant in its outfits.

A no. 927-60 Tube of Oil and/or 927-65 Tube of Grease (lubricant) were included with boxed motive power or in the outfit packed envelope.

In 1962, the tube of oil was replaced by a no. 927-85 Oiler packaged as no. 927-90 Lubricating Oil Packed.

Wire

Number 81-32 Wires were included in outfits loose or in a packed envelope, or they were packaged with an accessory or transformer. Wires have been observed in numerous colors, including multiple shades of green, yellow, white, red, blue, maroon and possibly others.

Smoke

Steam locomotive outfits came equipped with smoke and, if necessary, a stack cleaner. If the locomotive were boxed, the smoke (pellets or liquid) and optional smokestack cleaner came sealed in the engine box. If the steamer were unboxed, then the appropriate smoke and stack cleaner came loose in the train outfit. In 1960 and 1961 with some carryover into 1962, a no. 909-10 Bottle of Liquid Smoke was included in outfits requiring liquid smoke. From 1962 through 1967, the bottle was replaced with a no. 909-20 Smoke Fluid, which contained three capsules filled with smoke in a cellophane front and paper-backed wrapper.

Batteries

From 1960 through 1962, Lionel included batteries in outfits as needed. Boxed items requiring a battery included one in their individual box. For unboxed items, a battery would be placed loose in the outfit box. In 1961 and 1962, a no. 2333-140 "D" Battery was included with outfits containing an unboxed no. 147-25 Horn and Whistle Controller. In 1961, a no. 601-13 "C" Battery was included with outfits containing an unboxed Alco diesel with horn. By 1963, Lionel no longer included batteries loose in any outfit.

As an interesting side note, the battery's base number indicates the diesel in which the battery first appeared. For example, the no. 2333-140 "D" Battery was first used with a no. 2333 New York Central or Santa Fe F3 Diesel in 1948. The no. 601-13 "C" Battery was first used with a no. 601 Seaboard Diesel Switcher in 1956. These were the first two diesels to use "D" and "C" batteries for horns.

Billboards

Colorful cardboard billboards were included with most train outfits from 1960 through 1966. Billboards came in perforated strips of three or five and when separated could be placed in Lionel billboard frames. Billboards were most often placed loose in outfit boxes without frames, but a few outfits included frames loose or boxed in separate-sale packaging. Three versions of these billboards were used in outfits from 1960 through 1966 (see the Paper Included in Outfits by Year summary). In 1962, Lionel introduced a strip of three billboards. There appears to be no pattern to which outfit (O27, O gauge or Super O) received a strip of three or five billboards from 1962 through 1966.

At least two special billboards were issued during this period. The first was an unnumbered billboard advertising Channel Master antennas, radios, hi-fis and tubes. This billboard came in

The Channel Master billboard came with only promotional outfit nos. 9745 and X-573NA.

311-25 8/64

Lionel issued a special no. 311-25 Target Bulls Eye billboard with Western Auto promotional outfit no. 19332.

promotional outfit nos. 9745 and X-573NA. In 1964, a plain white background version of the target range billboard was numbered 311-25 and included in Western Auto promotional outfit no. 19332. Lionel ceased providing billboards in train outfits after 1966.

Buttons and Controllers

Buttons and controllers were required to operate the trains, uncoupling tracks and accessories. From 1960 through 1969, various combinations included in outfits were the no. 80 Controller, no. 90 Uncoupling Track Controller, no. 92 Circuit Breaker Controller, no. 147 Horn and Whistle Controller, no. 364C Contactor, no. 413 Count Down Control Panel and no. 0190-25 Controller.

As with all other peripherals, great care was taken to ensure there was no duplication of items. If an accessory or track section already came with the appropriate controller, another was not added. Most often these items were included in a packed envelope, but they could also be found loose in the outfit box.

Outfit Packed Envelopes

Outfit packed envelopes were used to ease outfit packing by ensuring that smaller peripherals were not overlooked or lost. These small tan (Kraft) or white envelopes were either self-sealing or stapled closed. They were printed with the contents most often listed on the envelope front.

O27 Operating Packed Envelopes

O27 operating packed envelopes included some combination of wires, lockon, oil, lubricant, controller or other small items. From 1960 through 1969, many different outfit packed envelopes were manufactured based on combinations of these peripherals. These are detailed in the O27 Operating Packed Envelope summary.

O Gauge Operating Packed Envelopes

O Gauge outfits did not include packed envelopes. All peripherals were provided with the boxed motive power or placed loose in the outfit box.

Super O Operating Packed Envelopes

During the 1960s, two different packed envelopes were used to consolidate small outfit peripherals required for Super O outfits. From 1960 through 1966, the no. 39-25 Remote Control Set was used. From 1960 through 1963, the no. 39-35 Remote Control Set was used. Both included a power track section, uncoupling track section, no. 90 controller(s), wires and instruction sheet. The no. 39-35 added remote control blades and screws to support operating cars included in the outfit.

In the middle of 1961, Lionel eliminated separate no. 31-7 packed envelopes and placed bus bars directly on the track sections. This left outfits without the two no. 31-7s required to connect the uncoupling and power track sections. New versions of no. 39-25 and no. 39-35 were issued with two

no. 31-7s. During this transition year, Lionel used an "X" on Factory Orders to indicate outfits requiring the old envelopes without the extra no. 31-7s.

All the cataloged and most of the promotional Super O outfits included boxed motive power that came without lockons (because they were not needed). All these packed envelopes and variations are detailed in the Super O Remote Control Set Packed Envelope summary.

Super O 31-7 Power Bus Packed Envelopes

Super O track's middle rail was connected using no. 31-7 Power Bus Connectors. From 1957 through 1961, Lionel packaged these connectors in an envelope that was included in Super O outfits. The quantity of 31-7s in an envelope equaled the number of pieces of track. These envelopes and variations are detailed in the Super O 31-7 Power Bus Packed Envelope summary.

Paper

All paperwork necessary to assemble, operate and maintain a train outfit was included loose in the outfit box. As with other peripherals, if the paperwork was already included in a boxed item, Lionel ensured that additional copies weren't also duplicated in the outfit. The paperwork provided all the instructions for:

- Assembling the Lionel Outfit
- Connecting the transformer to O gauge and O27 track
- Assembling Super O track
- Placing a train on the track
- Operating the train
- Running automatic operating cars
- Working with Lionel track
- Maintaining the trains

These instructions were printed in booklet form or individual instruction sheets. Other paperwork included catalogs, warranty cards, special operating flyers, notification of substituted items, track layout diagrams and notification of inclusion of third-party products. All paperwork included in outfits from 1960 through 1969 is listed in the Paper Included in Outfits by Year summary.

Instruction Books

From 1953 through 1960, an instruction book titled, *How to Operate Lionel Trains and Accessories*, was included in high-end O27 and all O gauge and Super O outfits. This book was all-inclusive, providing the information necessary to assemble and operate every type of train outfit. With thousands of possible combinations of transformers, track, accessories, operating cars, and more, *How to Operate Lionel Trains and Accessories* became a rather large book. Maintaining and printing this book was expensive because any content change led to an update. Lionel provided yearly updates with the last being the 61-page version in 1960.

Later in 1965 and 1966, Lionel reissued this instruction book for separate sale in an 8½ x 11-inch format at $1.00. Only a handful of updates and corrections were made to this version, most notably the table of contents now correctly referenced the proper pages. Otherwise, it referred to many accessories and operating cars no longer available.

Train Outfit Instruction Sheets

From 1960 through 1969, Lionel used a single 8½ x 11-inch folded in half or 8½ x 17-inch tri-folded sheet of paper printed on both sides to create Train Outfit instruction sheets. These were used in low-end O27 outfits through 1960 and all outfits from 1961 through 1969. Low-end outfits included these sheets instead of instruction books most likely due to lower printing costs. Also, cost was probably the reason Train Outfit instruction sheets eventually were used across the entire outfit line.

In moving from the instruction books to Train Outfit instruction sheets, only essential information specific to the particular train outfit was included. No longer was every type of track, transformer, motive power, operating car, and maintenance procedure documented.

These sheets most often included a section on assembling the outfit, along with a picture of the track assembly, instructions on connecting the specific transformer to the track, features of the transformer including direction control or circuit breaker, instructions on how to operate the train and the uncoupling track section, information and features regarding the motive power, guidelines on taking care of the track, and in most cases warranty information.

As always, great care was used to eliminate any duplication of information. For example, if the motive power or individual operating car came with their own instructions, this information was not duplicated on the Train Outfit sheet. Basically, all the information in the discontinued instruction book was now divided among these individual instruction sheets.

Each year for each O27 outfit, Lionel would evaluate the need for a new instruction sheet. If an existing sheet met the outfit requirements, it was reused for the outfit; if not, a new one was created. The new instruction sheet's part number matched that of the outfit number.

This approach led to fewer printed pages, though you could argue that it was offset by a more time-consuming and complex process. Now every outfit instruction sheet needed to be engineered. A full assessment of every item, peripheral and instruction sheet was required. Since many outfits included unique track plans, different transformer features, remote or manual uncoupling, and so forth, many outfit instruction sheets were unique. More than 110 new Train Outfit instruction sheets were created from 1960 through 1969.

For Super O outfits, once the instruction book was discontinued, Lionel relied on the no. 39-7 instruction sheet that came with the no. 39-25 and 39-35 Remote Control Set packed envelope. Cataloged O Gauge outfits used only one instruction sheet, a no. 12700-10.

Numerous variations of Train Outfit instruction sheets exist. Most of the variations are slight changes in features. For example, the no. 11311-10 Train Outfit instruction sheet dated 5/63 is for a no. 1062 Steam Type Locomotive With Light & Reversing Unit, whereas no. 11311-20 dated 5/63

is the same except it is for a 1061 Steam Type Locomotive. The only difference on these sheets is the graphic showing a replacement lamp for the 1062. Others sheets, such as the no. 11331-10 and no. 11331-20, are for outfits with a no. 6139-25 and no. 6029-25 Uncoupling Track Section respectively. New instruction sheets were issued for even changes as slight as these.

Other variations went undocumented with no item number change or only date changes on the instruction sheets. In 1963, when Lionel went to a 90-day warranty, warranty information was changed for existing Train Outfit instruction sheets without updating the instruction sheet part number. Other changes include differences documenting the change in the name of the Service Department to the Service Company. Finally, when an "X" suffix was used on the Factory Orders, it indicated that the old version of the instruction sheet should be placed in the outfit rather than the one currently being used.

Train Outfit Instruction sheets assist in dating changes in Lionel's history, in particular, when batteries were no longer included in outfits and when maintenance kits changed. Pricing of certain items can also be pinpointed. The change from Lionel Corporation to Lionel Toy Corporation first appeared on Train Outfit instruction sheet no. 11341-10 dated 6/63. The change from Lionel Service Department to Lionel Service Company first appeared on a Train Outfit instruction sheet no. 12700-10 dated 8/64.

Individual Item Instruction Sheets

From 1960 through 1968, Lionel packed individual instruction sheets for motive power and operating cars with its train outfits. If the individual item were boxed, Lionel packaged the instruction sheet inside the item box; otherwise, it was included loose in the outfit box. These sheets would normally include information about the operation, maintenance and the warranty of the item.

The sheets came in many different sizes and colors. Most instruction sheets included the instruction sheet number followed by the date it was designed at the bottom right-hand corner of the back or last page. Lionel numbered instruction sheets in the same fashion as it did individual items, with the item's base number and a suffix. If possible, Lionel would use the same instruction sheet for more than one similar item. Therefore, the number on the instruction sheet did not always match the number of the item in which it came.

New versions of the same instruction sheet were often issued when a reference in the sheet changed, a mistake was made or the item was changed. As an example, the no. 6361-16 instruction sheet can come with "Lionel Corporation" or "Lionel Toy Corporation". Both versions of this sheet had the same item number. Instruction sheet no. 212-64 dated 4/64 incorrectly referenced a plate cover that was not part of the no. 212 Santa Fe Diesel. A new sheet no. 212-64 dated 4/65 corrected this problem and updated the warranty information and service department name.

Most often, a change led to the creation of a newly numbered sheet. These changes could also help document and date item production changes. For example, a no. 211-6

Lionel Alco Diesel Locomotive sheet dated 4-62 indicated the diesel came with Magnetraction, whereas no. 211-151 dated 5/63 indicated the diesel came with tire traction. This knowledge helped to identify the differences in the no. 211 *Texas Special* Diesel and determine that the no. 211-25 is the version with Magne-Traction and the no. 211-150 is the one with traction tire. Additional observations of individual instruction sheet changes are noted in outfit descriptions included in this volume.

The change from a one-year to a 90-day warranty in 1963 through 1964 led to numerous undocumented variations in item instruction sheets. In most cases, Lionel merely changed the warranty information and did not change the instruction sheet number or date. When Lionel went back to a one-year warranty again in 1965, all the sheets needed to be changed again.

Items that spanned these years might have two or three different instruction sheets. For example, there are versions of no. 6470-17 with a one-year and a 90-day warranty and both are dated 8-59. Another example was the 3410-5 instruction sheet, which had two warranty versions, both with the same 6-61 date.

LIONEL WARRANTY

All Lionel model railroad equipment is carefully made and inspected and is guaranteed against defects in materials or in our workmanship. If any such defects develop, we will repair or replace the defective part or parts, without charge, within one year of the date of purchase. If in the future this equipment should ever require servicing, you may either send it to the Factory Service Department or take it to your nearest Lionel Approved Service Station.

The LIONEL CORPORATION

New York, N. Y.

SERVICE DEPARTMENT: Hoffman Place, Hillside, N.J.

Printed in U.S. of America   3410-5   6-61

The no. 3410-5 instruction sheet from 1961-62 describes a one-year warranty and is dated 6-61.

LIONEL WARRANTY

All Lionel Model Railroad equipment is carefully made and inspected and is guaranteed against defects in materials or in our workmanship. If any such defects develop, we will repair or replace the defective part or parts, without charge within 90 DAYS OF THE DATE OF PURCHASE.

If your equipment requires servicing, under warranty, bring it to your nearest LIONEL APPROVED SERVICE STATION.

If you prefer, however, you may send it carefully packed and insured to:

THE LIONEL TOY CORPORATION
SERVICE DEPARTMENT: Hoffman Place, Hillside, N.J.

Please enclose $1.00, with your letter, to help defray the cost of postage and handling.

Printed in U.S. of America   3410-5   6-61

The no. 3410-5 instruction sheet from 1963-64 describes a 90-day warranty but it is still dated 6-61.

Special Track Layout Sheets

Train Outfit instruction sheets detailed generic track layouts, specifically circles, ovals and some figure-eights. When an outfit layout was more complex, Lionel included a separate Special Track Layout instruction sheet (see the Paper Included in Outfits by Year summary). These small (4¼ x 5½ or 5½ x 8½ inches) or large (8½ x 11 inches) sheets detailed how to assemble the track, switches, accessories, trestles and uncoupling tracks. Some sheets explained how to assemble cardboard scenery used in the layout. These were included as needed with both cataloged and promotional O27, O gauge and Super O outfits from 1960 through 1968.

Catalogs

Lionel included accessory catalogs, consumer catalogs or flyers in most outfits from 1960 through 1967. These catalogs were designed to sell add-on items to the outfit just purchased. As such, they advertised individual items, accessories, HO items, track, transformers and more. They also included sample track layouts and layout building information (see the Paper Included in Outfits by Year summary).

Warranty Cards

Warranty information was provided with the Train Outfit instruction sheet, individual item instruction sheets and list of service stations, or as a separate warranty card. For all years from 1960 through 1969 (except 1963 and 1964), Lionel's warranty was one year from the date of purchase. In 1963, Lionel changed its warranty to 90 days and started to charge a $1.00 handling fee. The warranty changed back to one year in 1965, but the fee remained.

Separate warranty sheets first appeared in 1962 with the inclusion of a no. 19106-20 warranty certificate. This same certificate was part of the no. 19142-10 Train Outfit instruction sheet. Warranty cards were included in outfits from 1963 through 1969 (see the Paper Included in Outfits by Year summary). The cards stated that the warranty was void unless they were filled out and returned within ten days of purchase. At least six variations of this card exist and are summarized below.

Part No.	Yr	Warranty	Description
1-63	'63	90 days	Orange and blue design. Changed warranty to 90 days and charged $1.00 for handling. Also had a unique serial number.
1-64	'63 – '64	90 days	Same as above but added a line about taking item to a Lionel Approved Service Station. Serial number was removed. ZIP code was added to address.
1-65	'64 – '65	90 days	Same as 1-64 but removed ZIP code.
1-165	'65 – '66	1 Year	New blue design. Address was listed as "Lionel Service Company". Serial number was added in red and began with "T".
1-166	'66 – '68	1 Year	Same as 1-165 and printed as 1-165 but part number listed as 1-166. Serial number was replaced with "T99".
1-165	'69	1 Year	Same content as above but with "P68" instead of "T99". Design was changed slightly and address was now "The Lionel Toy Corporation".

Service Station Lists

Service station lists were included with each outfit from 1960 through 1969. From 1960 through 1963, these were included as the last few pages of the accessory catalog. From 1964 through 1969, service station lists were printed separately and included in outfits (see the Paper Included in Outfits by Year summary).

Parts Order Forms

From 1963 through 1969, Lionel included parts order forms in its train outfits. In 1963, the no. 1-62 form (8½ x 11 inches) first appeared. In 1964, the smaller no. 3063 form (8½ x 5½ inches) dated 10/64 was used and stated the address as The Lionel Toy Corporation, Service Department. Another

variation of this form dated 10/65 included the change in the name of the department to The Lionel Service Company.

In 1966 and 1967, the name changed back to the "Service Department" but the date stayed 10/65. The final version, dated 10/68, mentioned the increase in the postage and handling to 65 cents (see the Paper Included in Outfits by Year summary).

Advertisements

In 1963 and 1964, Lionel included advertisements in train outfits for its track make-up kits. Form no. 2869 advertised the no. 2001 Track Make-up Kit no. 2001; form no. 2870 was double-sided and advertised track make-up kits nos. 2002 and 2003.

Important Maintenance Instructions

From 1961 through 1964, Lionel included an 8½ x 3¾-inch sheet instructing users how to lubricate and remove glaze from wheels. In 1961, the no. 1123-20 sheet dated 2-61 was used. From 1962 through 1964, the sheet was updated with a change in the maintenance kit referenced. It was numbered 1123-40 and dated 2-62 (see the Paper Included in Outfits by Year summary).

Other Flyers and Special Notices

Often Lionel would include instruction sheets that referenced specific features of an outfit or items included in the outfit. Some examples include special notices in Sears outfits about substitutions of track or items, a notice saying that the automobiles included in the outfit were not manufactured or warranted by Lionel, notices about trains uncoupling if the outfit surface was not flat and notices regarding information not covered in other instruction sheets (see the Paper Included in Outfits by Year summary).

OUTFIT PERIPHERALS
1960 - 1963 O27 OPERATING PACKED ENVELOPES

From 1960 through 1963, six different operating envelopes were used in O27 outfits. These envelopes included a combination of the lockon, wires, lubricant and controllers necessary to connect the transformer, uncoupling track, and whistle controller and maintain the motive power.

Note that lockons were included with boxed motive power unless the motive power included an "X" suffix on the Factory Order. In that case, a lockon was included in a packed envelope or loose.

1103-12 O27 OPERATING ENVELOPE 1960 - 1962

The no. 1103-12 Operating Envelope included two wires and a lockon to connect a transformer and lubricant to maintain the motive power. This envelope was included in O27 outfits with unboxed motive power (individually boxed motive power included a lockon and lubricant). Each envelope was tan and measured 5½ x 3⅛ inches. The part number for the empty envelope, no. 1103-11, was printed at the bottom right-hand corner.

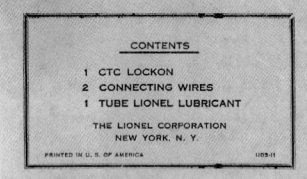 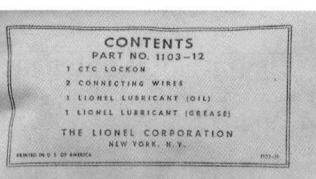 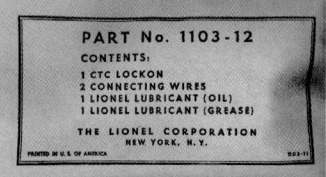 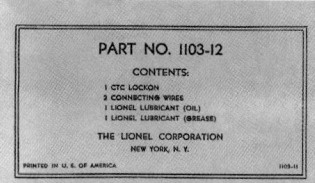

Type I: Pre-1960
"Contents" underlined
One tube of lubricant
Not included in outfits in 1960s
A variation (not shown) exists with slightly different layout and spacing

Type II: 1960 - 1961
Change of font and layout
"Part NO." now included
"Contents" no longer underlined
Oil and grease included

Type III: Mid-1960 - 1961
Bolder font and new layout
"Contents" and "Part No." switched

Type IV: Mid-1961 - 1962
Change of font and layout

6812-40 O27 OPERATING ENVELOPE 1960 - 1961

The no. 6812-40 Operating Envelope included two wires to connect a transformer and a no. 3562-62 figure. This envelope was included in O27 outfits with boxed motive power (individually boxed motive power included a lockon and lubricant) and an unboxed no. 6812-25 Track Maintenance Car. The envelope was tan and measured 4½ x 2½ inches. The part number for the empty envelope, no. 6812-41, was printed at the bottom right-hand corner.

Type I: 1960 - 1961
No. 3562-62 Figure for no. 6812-25 was included

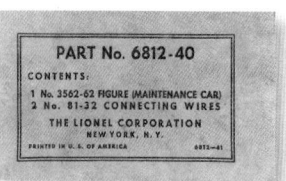

1645-12 O27 OPERATING ENVELOPE 1961 - 1963

The no. 1645-12 Operating Envelope included three wires and a lockon to connect a transformer and a no. 147 Whistle Controller. It also included oil and lubricant to maintain the motive power. This envelope was included in O27 outfits with unboxed motive power (individually boxed motive power included a lockon and lubricant). Each envelope was tan and measured 4½ x 3 inches. The part number for the empty envelope, no. 1645-13, was printed at the bottom right-hand corner.

Type I: 1961 - 1963
Oil and lubricant included

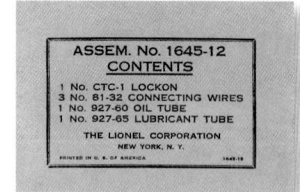

1645-15 O27 OPERATING ENVELOPE 1962 - 1963

The no. 1645-15 Operating Envelope was an update to no. 1645-12 and also included three wires and a lockon to connect a transformer and a no. 147 Whistle Controller. In 1962 no. 927-60 Oil Tube and no. 927-65 Lubricant Tube were replaced with a no. 927-85 Oil Capsule. The no. 1645-15 was included in O27 outfits with unboxed motive power (individually boxed motive power included a lockon and lubricant). Each envelope was tan and measured 4¼ x 2½ inches. The part number for the empty envelope, no. 1645-16, was printed at the bottom right-hand corner.

Type I: 1962
Included no. 927-85 Oil Capsule

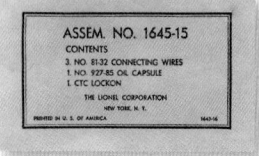

Type II: 1963
No. 927-85 Oil Capsule no longer included

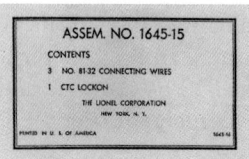

OUTFIT PERIPHERALS
1960 - 1963 O27 OPERATING PACKED ENVELOPES

1103-14 O27 OPERATING ENVELOPE 1960

The no. 1103-14 Operating Envelope included three wires and a controller to connect a transformer. This envelope was included in O27 outfits with boxed motive power (boxed motive power included a lockon and lubricant). Each envelope was tan and measured 6 x 3⅜ inches. The part number for the empty envelope, no. 1103-15, was printed at the bottom right-hand corner.

Type I: 1960
No. 2085 Instruction Sheet
was included

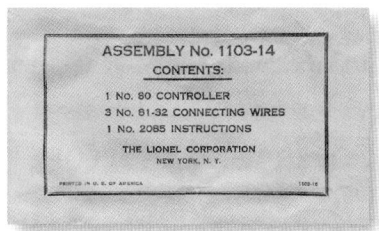

90-30 O27 OPERATING ENVELOPE 1960 - 1963

The no. 90-30 Operating Envelope included four wires and a controller to connect the transformer and remote control uncoupling track. This envelope was included in O27 outfits with boxed motive power (boxed motive power included a lockon and lubricant). Each envelope was tan and measured 5½ x 3⅛ inches. The part number for the empty envelope, no. 90-31, was printed at the bottom right-hand corner.

Type I: 1960 - 1963
"Contents" underlined

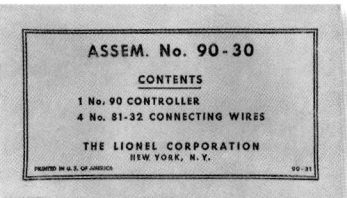

Type II: 1960 - 1963
"Assem. No." instead of "Part No."
Different line spacing

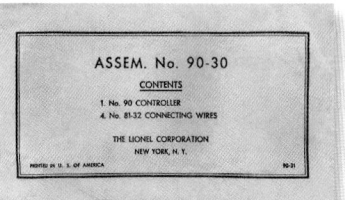

Type III: 1960 - 1963
Change of font and layout

90-40 O27 OPERATING ENVELOPE 1960 - 1963

The no. 90-40 Operating Envelope was the same as a no. 90-30 but was used when the motive power was unboxed (lockon and lubricant not included). Therefore, it also included a lockon and lubricant. Each envelope was tan and measured 6½ x 3½ inches. The part number for the empty envelope, no. 90-41, was printed at the bottom right-hand corner.

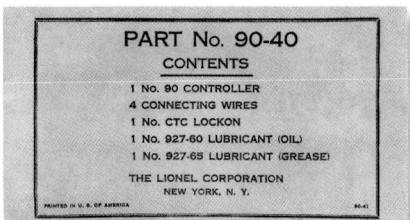

Type I: 1960 - 1963
"Contents" underlined

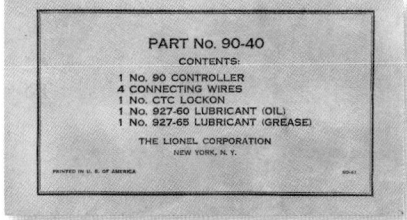

Type II: 1960 - 1963
Different font and layout
"Contents" not underlined

OUTFIT PERIPHERALS
1962 - 1969 O27 OPERATING PACKED ENVELOPES

From 1962 through 1969, earlier operating envelopes were consolidated and updated to reflect the elimination of lubricant and oil and the change in operating controllers used in outfits. Four different O27 operating envelopes were used from 1962 through 1969. These envelopes included a combination of the lockon, wires and controllers necessary to connect the transformer, uncoupling track and whistle controller. Some early envelopes included an oil capsule as well.

Note that lockons were included with boxed motive power unless the motive power included an "X" suffix on the Factory Order. In that case, a lockon was included in a packed envelope or loose.

1103-20 O27 OPERATING ENVELOPE (1962 - 1969)

The no. 1103-20 Operating Envelope was an update to the no. 1103-12 and included two wires and a lockon to connect a transformer. Type I no. 1103-20 also included a no. 927-85 Oil Capsule to maintain the motive power. This envelope was included in O27 outfits with unboxed motive power (individually boxed motive power included a lockon). Each envelope was tan or white and measured 4¼ x 2½ inches. The part number for the empty envelope, no. 1103-21, was printed at the bottom right-hand corner of the tan envelopes.

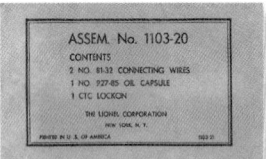

Type I: 1962 - 1963 (Carryover)
Replaces no. 1103-12
Included no. 927-85 Oil Capsule

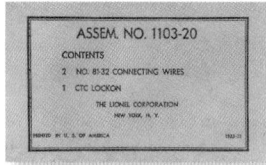

Type II: 1963 - 1966
No. 927-85 Oil Capsule no longer included

Type III: 1966 - 1969
New design and logo on white envelope
"The Lionel Toy Corporation"
No envelope number

1103-30 O27 OPERATING ENVELOPE (1963)

The no. 1103-30 Operating Envelope included four wires and a no. 0190-25 Controller to connect a transformer and a no. 147 Whistling Controller or no. 6139 Uncoupling Track Section. This envelope was included in O27 outfits with boxed motive power (individually boxed motive power included a lockon). When used with only a no. 147, it appears the controller was not needed. The envelope was tan and measured 4½ x 3 inches. The part number for the empty envelope, no. 1103-31, was printed at the bottom right-hand corner.

Type I: 1963
"The Lionel Toy Corporation"

1103-40 O27 OPERATING ENVELOPE (1963 - 1969)

The no. 1103-40 Operating Envelope was an update to the no. 90-40 and included four wires, a lockon and a no. 0190-25 Controller to connect a transformer and a remote control uncoupling track. This envelope was included in O27 outfits with unboxed motive power (individually boxed motive power included a lockon). Each envelope was tan. The part number for the empty envelope, no. 1103-41, was printed at the bottom right-hand corner.

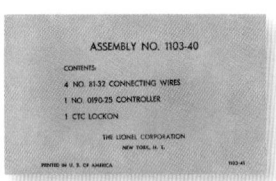

Type I: 1963 - 1965
Measures 4¼ x 2½ inches
"The Lionel Corporation"

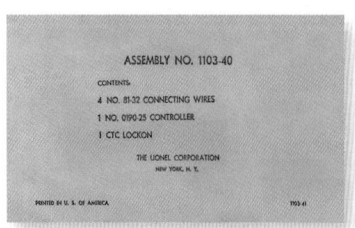

Type II: 1963 - 1964
Measures 5½ x 3⅛ inches
Layout same as Type I

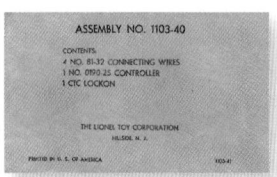

Type III: 1965 - 1969
Measures 4¼ x 2½ inches
"The Lionel Toy Corporation"
Tighter line spacing

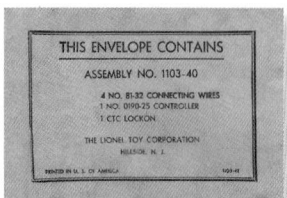

Type IV: 1965 - 1969
Measures 4½ x 3⅛ inches
"The Lionel Toy Corporation"
Different layout
Used in a few outfits

OUTFIT PERIPHERALS
1963 - 1968 O27 OPERATING PACKED ENVELOPES

1103-50 O27 OPERATING ENVELOPE (1963 - 1968)

The no. 1103-50 Operating Envelope included five wires, a lockon and a no. 0190-25 Controller to connect a transformer, a remote control uncoupling track and whistle controller. This envelope was included in O27 outfits with unboxed motive power (individually boxed motive power included a lockon). Each envelope was tan or white and measured 4¼ x 2½ inches. The part number for the empty envelope, no. 1103-51, was printed at the bottom right-hand corner of the tan envelopes.

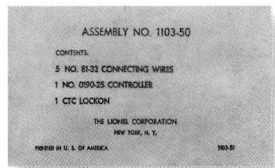

Type I: 1963 - 1966
"The Lionel Corporation"

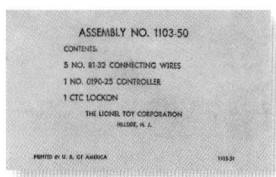

Type II: 1966
"The Lionel Toy Corporation"

Type III: 1966 - 1968
New design and logo on white
envelope
"The Lionel Toy Corporation"
No envelope number

OUTFIT PERIPHERALS
SUPER O REMOTE CONTROL SET PACKED ENVELOPES

Super O Remote Control Set packed envelopes included everything needed to connect a transformer and an uncoupling track section to Super O track. The no. 39-35 also included remote control blades and a controller necessary to run operating cars. These envelopes were included loose in Super O outfits as needed. The envelopes were tan and measured 7½ x 5 inches. The part number for the empty envelope (no. 39-26 or 39-36) was printed at the bottom right-hand corner.

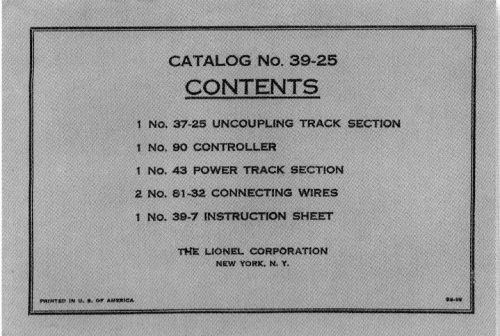

1959 - 1960
TYPE I

From 1959 through 1960, the no. 39-25 and 39-35 Remote Control Set packed envelopes included "Contents" underlined.

The no. 39-7 Instruction Sheet was dated 5-59

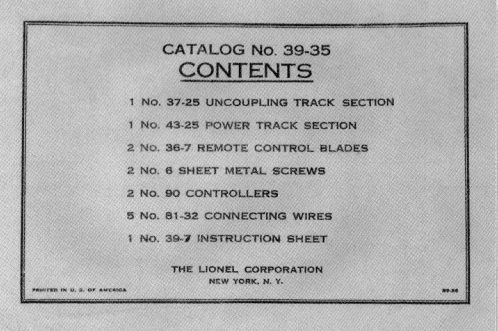

1960 - PART OF 1961
TYPE II

From 1960 through part of 1961, the no. 39-25 and 39-35 Remote Control Set packed envelopes were printed in a different font than Type I and "Contents" was no longer underlined.

The no. 39-7 Instruction Sheet was dated 5-59 or 5-61

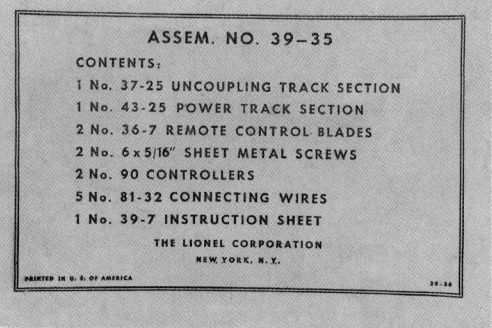

MID-1961 - 1963
TYPE III

From mid-1961 through 1963, the no. 39-25 and 39-35 Remote Control Set packed envelopes were printed with a new larger bold font and included two extra no. 31-7 Power Bus Connectors. Power bus connectors that were previously included in separate no. 31-7 envelopes were now included on the track. These two no. 31-7s were for the power track and uncoupling track sections.

The no. 39-7 Instruction Sheet was dated 5-61

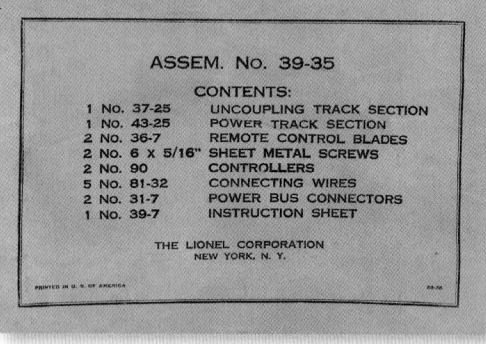

1962 - 1966
(1963 FOR 39-35)
TYPE IV

From the 1962 through 1966 (no. 39-25) and through 1963 (no. 39-35) Remote Control Set packed envelopes included the same contents as Type III and used the same font as Type II.

The no. 39-7 Instruction Sheet was dated 2-62

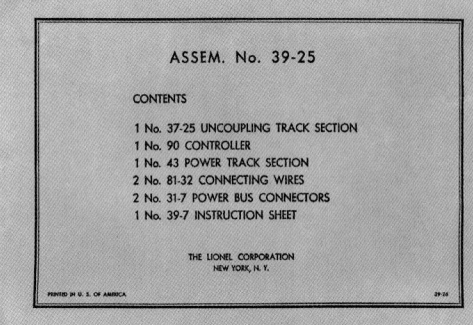

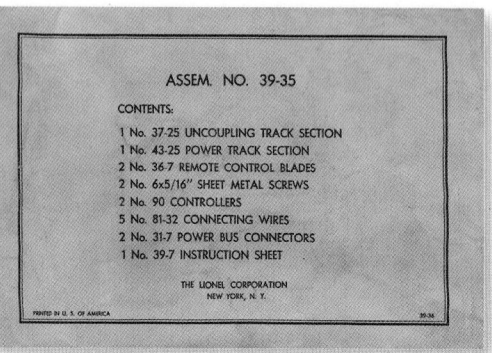

OUTFIT PERIPHERALS
SUPER O 31-7 POWER BUS PACKED ENVELOPES

Super O Outfits included a separate no. 31-7 Power Bus packed envelope from 1957 through 1961. These were used to connect the middle rail of Super O track sections. In mid-1961, power bus connectors were pre-attached to Super O track and the inclusion of envelopes ceased. The envelopes were tan and measured 4¼ x 2½ inches or 4½ x 3 inches. The part number for the empty envelope was printed at the bottom right-hand corner.

NO. 31 ENVELOPE (NO QUANTITY STATED) 1957

In 1957, a no. 31 envelope with 2 through 20 (no quantity was stated on the envelope) no. 31-7 Power Bus Connectors was included in outfits. This envelope was also included with accessories and other items. The part number for the empty envelope was no. 31-12.

NO. 31-9 ENVELOPE (QUANTITY 16) 1958 - 1961

From 1958 through 1961, a no. 31-9 envelope with 16 no. 31-7 Power Bus Connectors was included in outfits. This was the same envelope as used in 1957, but the quantity was explicitly stated. The empty envelope number was no. 31-12.

NO. 31-10 ENVELOPE (QUANTITY 18) 1958 - 1960

From 1958 through 1960, a no. 31-10 envelope with 18 no. 31-7 Power Bus Connectors was included in outfits. The empty envelope number was no. 31-18.

NO. 31-11 ENVELOPE (QUANTITY 20) 1958 - 1961

From 1958 through 1961, a no. 31-11 envelope with 20 no. 31-7 Power Bus Connectors was included in outfits. The empty envelope number was no. 31-20. A version of this exists as an overstamped no. 31-10 envelope.

NO. 31-23 ENVELOPE (QUANTITY 28) 1961

In 1961, a no. 31-23 envelope with 28 no. 31-7 Power Bus Connectors was included in outfit nos. 2549W and X-586. The empty envelope number was no. 31-27. Two versions have been observed.

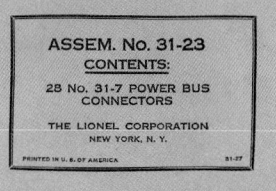
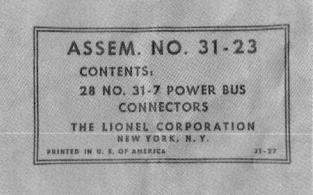

NO. 31-24 ENVELOPE (QUANTITY 36) 1961

In 1961, a no. 31-24 envelope with 36 no. 31-7 Power Bus Connectors was included in outfit no. 2553WS. The empty envelope number was no. 31-28.

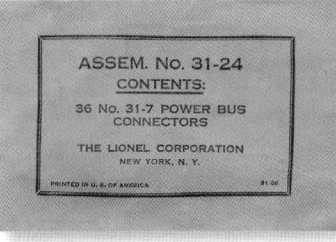

NO. 31-25 ENVELOPE (QUANTITY 40) 1961

In 1961, a no. 31-25 envelope with 40 no. 31-7 Power Bus Connectors was included in outfit nos. 2551W and X-522NA. The empty envelope number was no. 31-26.

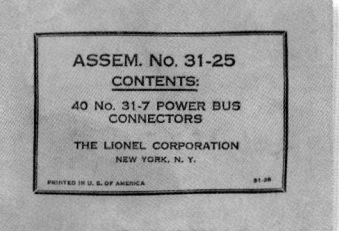

This section provides an overview of instruction sheets and other paper items included with most outfits. Individual rolling stock, motive power and accessory instruction sheets (not shown) would also come separate in the outfit if the item were unboxed.

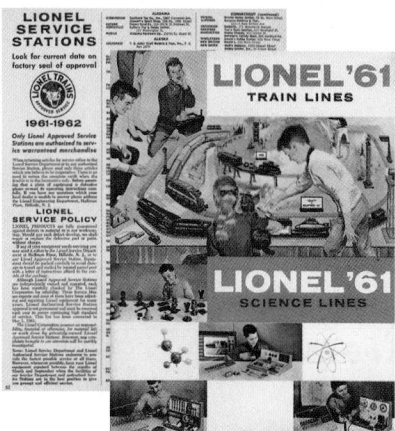

From 1960 through 1963, Lionel included an accessory catalog with each outfit. These catalogs also included a list of service stations and warranty and repair information.

In 1960, high-end O27 and all Super O outfits included a 62-page no. 926-60 *How To Operate Lionel Trains and Accessories* instruction book.

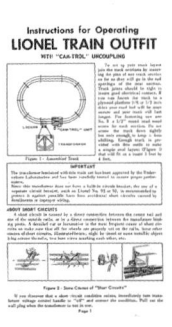

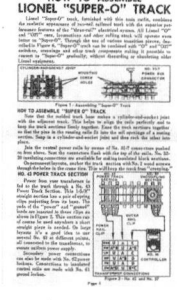

In 1960, low-end O27 outfits included a Lionel Train Outfit instruction sheet. Super O instruction sheet no. 39-7 was included as part of no. 39-25 or 39-35 envelopes.

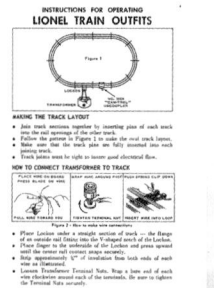

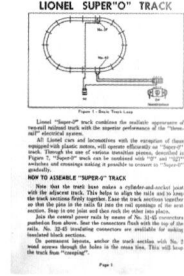

From 1961 through 1969, all outfits included a Lionel Train Outfit instruction sheet. From 1961 through 1966 Super O instruction sheet no. 39-7 was included as part of no. 39-25 or 39-35 envelopes.

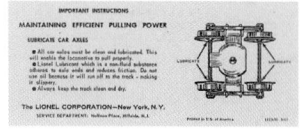

In 1960, this strip of five no. 310-2 billboards was included in most outfits.

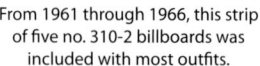

From 1961 through 1966, this strip of five no. 310-2 billboards was included with most outfits.

In 1961, a no. 1123-20 instruction sheet was included in many outfits.

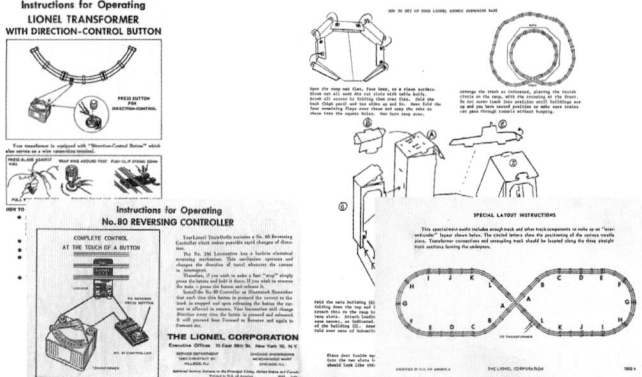

From 1960 through 1969, additional paperwork was included as needed. Examples include Special Track Layout Instructions, advertisements, supplemental transformer, controller and uncoupler instruction sheets and special notes, notices or flyers.

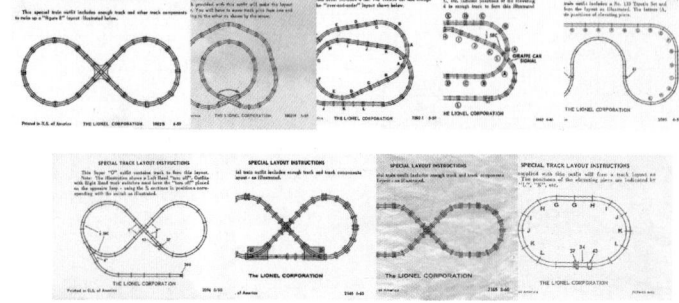

1962

1963

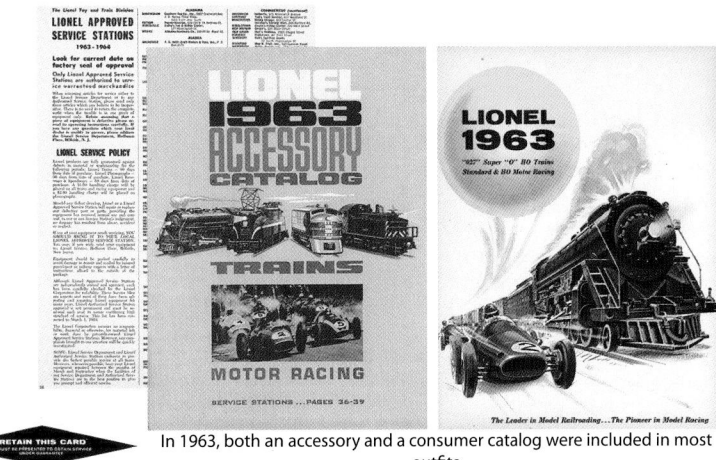

In 1963, both an accessory and a consumer catalog were included in most outfits.

In 1962, at least two promotional outfits included separate warranty sheets.

In 1963, Lionel began including a separate warranty card (no. 1-63 and then 1-64), which included some updates.

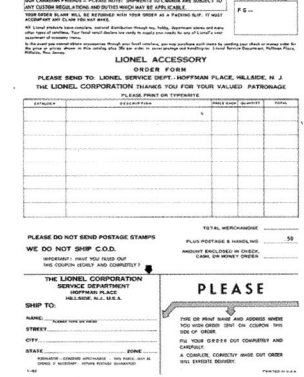

In 1963, a no. 1-62 Lionel Parts Order form was included in most outfits.

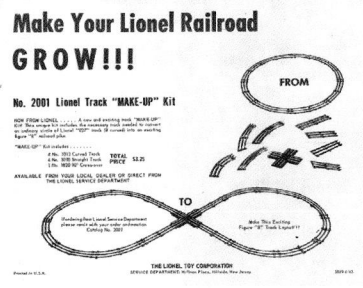

In 1963 and 1964, some outfits included a no. 2869 or 2870 form advertising Lionel's track make-up kits.

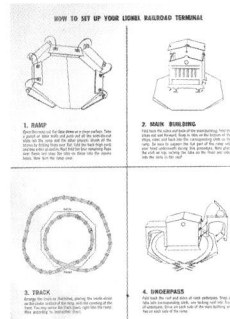

Example of additional outfit paper included as needed.

From 1962 through 1966, a strip of three no. 310-62 or strip of five no. 310-2 billboards was included with most outfits.

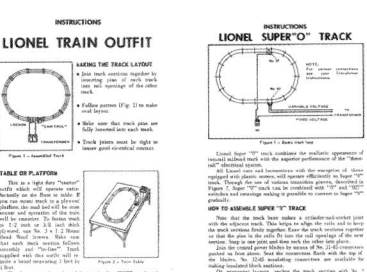

In 1962 and 1963, all outfits included a Lionel Train Outfit instruction sheet or Super O instruction sheet.

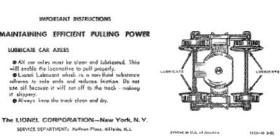

From 1962 through 1965, a no. 1123-40 instruction sheet replaced the no. 1123-20 included in many outfits. The no. 1123-40 updated the text from a no. 928 to a no. 5159 Maintenance Kit.

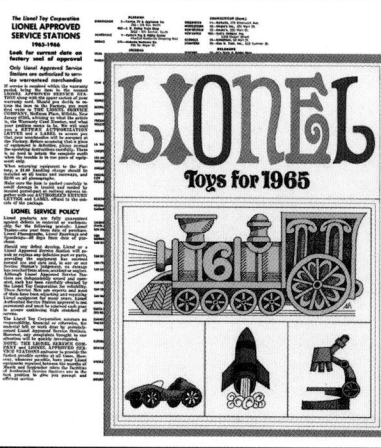

In 1964 and 1965, consumer catalogs were included in most outfits. Service station lists were printed and included separately in outfits. Some outfits in 1964 included a no. D64-50 accessory catalog.

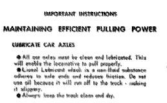

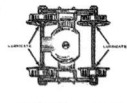

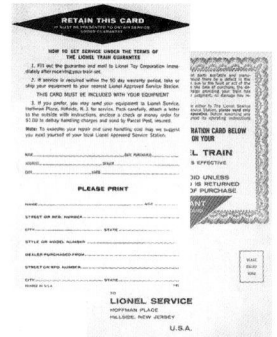

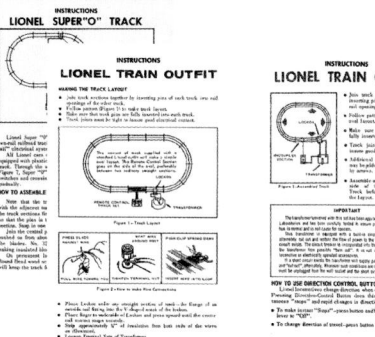

From 1962 through 1965, a no. 1123-40 instruction sheet replaced the no. 1123-20 included in many outfits. The no. 1123-40 updated the text from a no. 928 to a no. 5159 Maintenance Kit.

In 1964 and part of 1965, Lionel included a no. 1-65 warranty card. In 1964, some outfits included a no. 1-64 warranty card.

In 1964 and 1965, all O27 and O Gauge outfits included a Lionel Train Outfit instruction sheet. For Super O outfits a no. 39-7 was included as part of no. 39-25 or 39-35 envelopes.

From 1962 through 1966, a strip of three no. 310-62 or strip of five no. 310-2 billboards was included with most outfits.

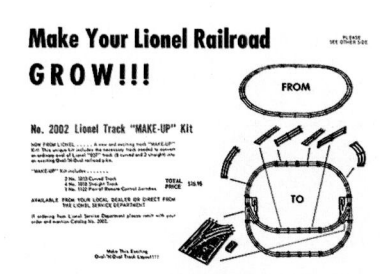

In 1963 and 1964, some outfits included a no. 2869 or 2870 form advertising Lionel's track make-up kits.

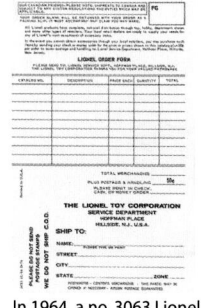

In 1964, a no. 3063 Lionel Parts Order form dated 10/64 and with "Service Department" was included.

In 1965, a no. 3063 Lionel Parts Order form dated 4/65 with "The Lionel Service Company" was included.

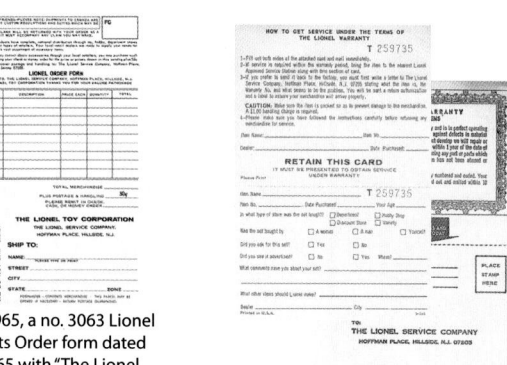

In 1965 through 1969, Lionel included a warranty card with part no. 1-165 printed on it. In 1965 and 1966, the card also included a unique serial number following a pre-printed "T".

Additional examples of paperwork included as needed.

Additional examples of paperwork included as needed.

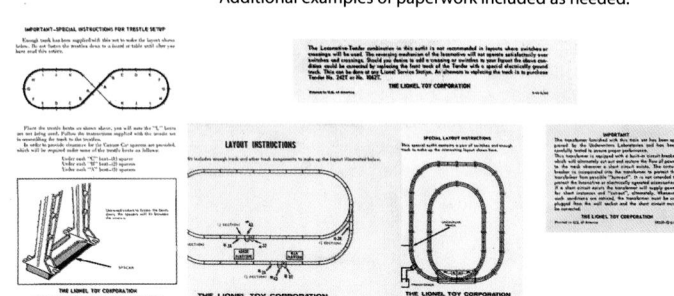

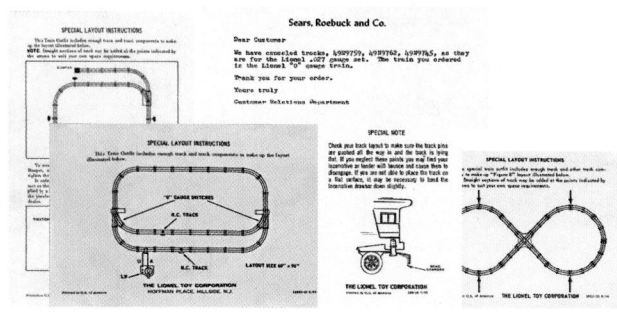

OUTFIT PERIPHERALS - PAPER INCLUDED IN OUTFITS BY YEAR

1966 1967 1968 1969

In 1966 and 1967, a flyer titled "Welcome to the Wonderful World of Lionel" was included in outfits. The 1966 - 1967 service station list was also included.

In 1968, service station lists were printed and included separately in outfits.

In 1969, service station lists were printed and included separately in outfits.

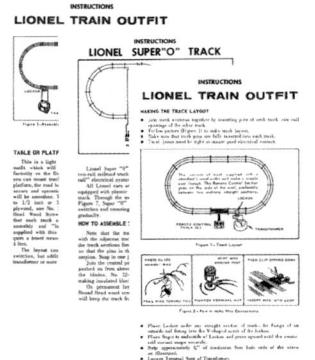

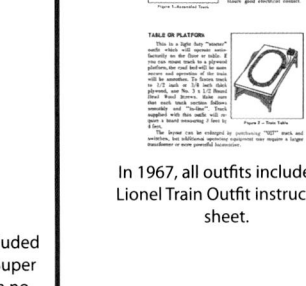

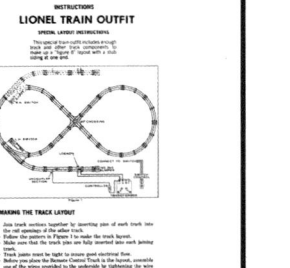

In 1966, all O27 and O Gauge outfits included a Lionel Train Outfit instruction sheet. Super O outfits included a no. 39-7 as part of a no. 39-25 envelope.

In 1967, all outfits included a Lionel Train Outfit instruction sheet.

In 1968, outfit 11600 included a Lionel Train Outfit instruction sheet.

In 1969, all cataloged outfits included a How to Assemble and Operate Your Lionel Outfit instruction sheet. Promotional outfits included a Train Outfit instruction sheet.

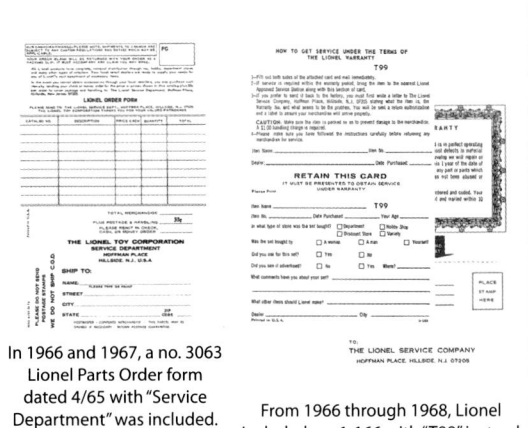

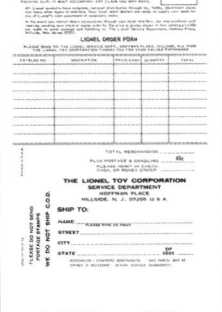

In 1968, a no. 3063 Lionel Parts Order form dated 10/68 was included. Price increased to 65¢.

In 1969, Lionel included no. 1-165 with "P68" warranty cards instead of "T99".

In 1966 and 1967, a no. 3063 Lionel Parts Order form dated 4/65 with "Service Department" was included.

From 1966 through 1968, Lionel included no. 1-166 with "T99" instead of serial number. Warranty card actually marked 1-165.

From 1962 through 1966, a strip of three no. 310-62 or strip of five no. 310-2 billboards was included with most outfits.

From 1966 through 1968, many additional sheets or notices were used.

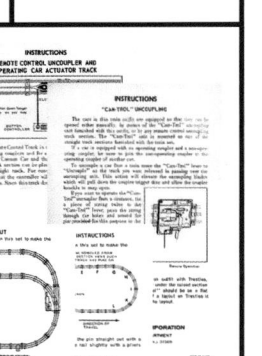

69

Lionel always tried to maximize what sales executives referred to as the "play value" of its outfits. As interest in toy trains waned in the 1960s, Lionel became even more creative in executing this strategy. Outfits began to include additional items of high play value, such as accessories, Plasticville sets, structures and scenery, bridges, trestles and tunnels, flat car and gondola loads, signals, signs and lights, toy soldiers and other train related items. Packing these additional pieces in an outfit meant the owner had more than a train running around an oval of track and so the enjoyment of the outfit increased. Although Lionel used this strategy mainly for promotional outfits, a few accessories and trestles also found their way into cataloged outfits.

Besides increasing the fun of an electric train outfit, these additional items left the impression on consumers that the outfits delivered more value than trains alone. Early on, the emphasis was to provide at least one unique item in an outfit. In later years, the concept of "piece count" was applied, linking overall outfit value to the number of pieces included.

Outfit no. 19567-500 from 1966 included 87 pieces, which increased its perceived value.

This strategy was executed at minimal additional cost. Most often the added accessories were leftover inventory. Other items were inexpensive paper, cardboard or plastic. Many of these items bore no Lionel markings. Often they were extremely fragile, which meant that they were easily damaged and discarded. Ironically, many of these low-cost items are now among the rarest postwar items and are difficult to find in a complete or usable state.

Accessories

Accessories have always been part of Lionel's strategy to provide motion and excitement with its trains. Most of the larger and more impressive accessories available after 1955 made their way into at least one promotional outfit. These additions included the no. 128-1 Animated Newsstand, no. 264-1 Operating Fork Lift Platform, no. 334-1 Dispatching Board, no. 346-1 Culvert Unloader, no. 350-1 Transfer Table, no. 375-1 Turntable, no. 461-1 Unloading Platform and the no. 464-1 Operating Lumber Mill. Several of the space and military accessories were added, such as the no. 175-1 Rocket Launcher, no. 299-1 Code Transmitter Set, no. 347-25 Rocket Launching Platform, no. 419-1 Heliport,

no. 443-1 Missile Launching Platform, no. 448-1 Missile Firing Range Set, no. 470-1 Missile Launching Platform and the no. 943-1 Exploding Ammo Dump.

Lionel included the no. 128-1 Animated Newsstand in promotional outfits to increase their play value while reducing excess inventory at its factory.

Plasticville

Lionel's relationship with Bachmann Bros. (the manufacturer of Plasticville) was the source of numerous Plasticville sets included with train outfits. Originally, Bachmann made versions of its sets exclusively for Lionel and packaged them under a Lionel part number and in orange-and-blue boxes with Lionel markings. By 1966 the sets were regular Plasticville sets, packaged and listed with just the Plasticville part number. In 1964 Lionel even used a plain white box to package the no. 958-100 Auto Set With Signs & Poles for outfit no. 19327 (Sears no. 9807).

The inclusion of a Plasticville set provided the opportunity to add buildings and scenery to a train outfit and so enhance its scenic value. An interesting Plasticville add-in is the no. 963-100 Frontier Set unique to outfit no. X-507NA (known as the "Halloween General"). Another desirable Lionel item is the no. 1640-100 Whistle Stop Audience Set Packed with outfit no. 1640W. This set includes paper signs to attach to no. 2400-series passenger cars as well as a set of Plasticville figures.

Structures and Scenery

Structures and scenery added dimension and life to train outfits. Among the notable structures packed in promotional

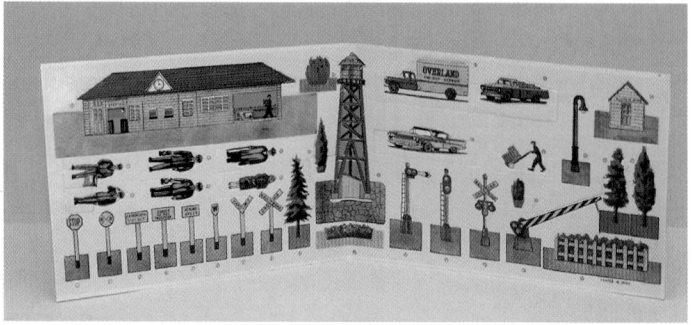

With no markings besides "Printed in Japan", the no. X625-20 Cardboard Scenic Set was frequently lost or discarded.

outfits are the no. 908-10 Scenic Station With Tunnels and no. 910-1 Navy Yard Cardboard Display, also known as the Atomic Submarine Base. Scenery included the no. X625-20 Cardboard Scenic Set and no. 19567-511 Mercury Model Cutouts.

These items do not have any sort of Lionel marking on them. For that reason, once they have been separated from their Lionel outfits, they were most often lost or destroyed. Besides cardboard scenery, two outfits even included a no. 972-1 Landscape Tree Assortment while another included a no. 920-8 Bag of Lychen.

Bridges, Trestles and Tunnels

Yet another way that Lionel increased the play value of its promotional outfits was by including an item that enabled the owner to create a more exciting track arrangement. Many of the more intricate layouts included trestles or a bridge.

Lionel used at least seven different trestle sets for its outfits. These included the no. 110-1 Trestle Set (24 or 22 pieces), no. 110-75 Modified Trestle Set (18 pieces), no. 110-125 Set of Six Trestle Piers, no. 109-25 Half Trestle Set (12 pieces), no. 111-50 Set of 20 High Bent Trestle Set, no. 111-1 Trestle Set (ten A piers) and no. 902-1 Cardboard Trestle With Girder Bridge & Tunnel.

Among the different bridges packed in promotional outfits were the no. 214 Girder Bridge, no. 321-1 Trestle Bridge, no. 321-100 Bridge and no. 332-1 Arch Under Bridge.

Number 110-75 Modified Trestle Sets came in five promotional outfits and were packaged in inexpensive plastic bags.

Flat Car and Gondola Loads

Creating new flat car or gondola loads was a quick and inexpensive way for Lionel to increase an outfit's play value. Flat car and gondola loads included automobiles, boats, trucks, vans, bridges, barrels, canisters, pipes, logs, cable reels and horses. Lionel also went to outside vendors, notably Pyro and Payton, to add the no. 958-75 Tank, no. 958-175 Cannon Assembled, no. 958-150 Jeep Assembled and other vehicles to the line.

Signals, Signs and Lights

Signals, signs and lights helped to complete a train layout by increasing the light and motion. Crossing gates, banjo signals, automatic gatemen, gantry signals, rotary beacons and lampposts were some of the items included in outfits.

Lionel went to Payton, an outside vendor, to add the no. 958-75 Tank to some of its promotional outfits with a space or military theme.

Toy Soldiers

The no. 975-1 Squad of Soldiers was a notable item included in military-themed train outfits. These were similar to the toy soldiers available in dime stores during that time.

A no. 975-1 Squad of Soldiers was the perfect addition to Lionel's space and military outfits.

Train-Related Items

Lionel also put different train-related items in several of its promotional outfits. One such item was the no. 903-1 Set of (2) Sheets Trading Cards, which provided twenty-four cards with a Lionel train on the front and a story on the back. Another add-in, the no. 19583-16 Engineer Cap, enabled a young railroader to pretend he or she was a real train engineer.

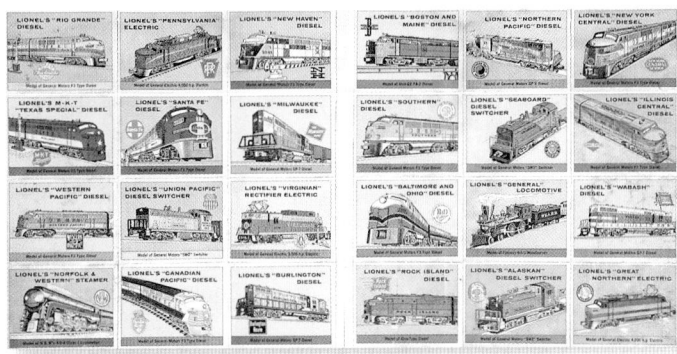

A no. 903-1 Set of (2) Sheets of Trading Cards provided interesting facts about the Lionel train and railroad on which it was modeled.

By including accessories, Plasticville items, structures and scenery as well as other low-cost items, Lionel quickly and inexpensively increased the overall play and scenic value of its train outfits.

During the early postwar years, Lionel spent its marketing dollars on majestic catalogs, in-store displays, a neatly coiffed and superbly trained sales organization and department store demonstrators to help sell its trains. Lionel's marketing department was less concerned about how its train outfits were packaged. This functional approach to packaging led to unassuming and inexpensive tan corrugated cardboard boxes. But as times changed and more trains were sold through traditional retail stores, Lionel also had to change. Beginning in the late 1950's, Lionel began using new and creative outfit packaging. This included colorful boxes, new artwork and new packaging designs.

Lionel's outfit packaging can be summarized in three categories namely, regular slotted carton or RSC, display (hinged, lift-off or tray) and blister packaging.

Regular Slotted Carton (RSC) Outfit Packaging

The formal packaging term (which Lionel used internally) for the corrugated cartons used to pack outfits is "regular slotted carton" or RSC. Lionel was also known to use "conventional pack" for RSC packaged outfits. Regular slotted cartons are corrugated boxes on which all flaps are the same length, so that, when folded shut, the flaps meet in the center. Lionel RSCs came from the box manufacturer with the fourth side glued, stapled or taped with reinforced tape. Lionel sealed the box top and bottom with glue, staple or tape. RSCs were manufactured for Lionel in different colors, including Kraft (tan), orange, yellow and white. Different graphics were also used over the years.

The tan corrugated boxes Lionel used to package its outfits were known internally by their formal packaging term, "regular slotted cartons" or RSCs.

Train items were either individually boxed and packed in an RSC or, beginning in 1956, left unboxed and separated by corrugated cardboard inserts. Some other outfits had a combination of boxed and unboxed components or items only packed in tissue. The next section on Outfit Box Printing, Graphics and Labels provides a detailed history of Lionel RSC outfit boxes from 1960 through 1969. It defines and dates box types, colors, graphics, box numbering and company (Lionel Corporation or Lionel Toy Corporation).

Display Outfit Packaging

Display outfits first appeared in 1957 with issuance of HO outfit no. 5700. The first O27 display box was for the Gifts Galore promotional outfit no. X-617 in 1958. By 1959, display boxes entered the mainstream when Lionel packaged O27 and Super O cataloged outfits in this manner. O gauge display outfits appeared in 1965.

Display outfit items were most often unboxed and separated by corrugated inserts or, in some instances, individually boxed. There are even outfits with a combination of boxed and unboxed items. Outfit inserts could be Kraft (tan) or colored (yellow, white or orange); there were also die-cut trays (yellow, green or white).

In "A String of Orange" (published in the out-of-print second volume of *Greenberg's Guide to Lionel Trains, 1945-1969*, Thomas S. Rollo (assisted by Paul V. Ambrose) offers some guidelines for categorizing display outfit packaging. This volume expands that information to include:

TYPE	DISPLAY BOX DESCRIPTION	CONTENTS	INSERTS
A	One-piece attached hinged top.	Unboxed (sometimes with one or two items boxed)	Colored or tan corrugated inserts.
B		Unboxed	Die-cut platform
C		Boxed	Colored inserts used for filler.
D	Two-piece lift-off telescoping top and bottom tray.	Unboxed (sometimes with one or two items boxed)	White or tan corrugated inserts
E	Colored tray bottom and tan corrugated sleeve.	Unboxed	Die-cut platform

Display boxes came in five versions. The first three (Type A, B and C) were made from one piece of corrugated cardboard folded in such a way to create a tray where the trains were placed and the top was hinged to the tray. The top had a perforated cutout such that, when it was opened, folded and locked back into the tray, the top would form a display back.

A hinged-top display box allowed trains to be displayed within the outfit box. Gift pack outfit no. 1810 is shown set up for display in a Type A box.

The differences in the hinged top display were determined by way the trains were packaged in the box. Trains were either primarily unboxed (with possibly one or two items boxed) with inserts separating them (Type A) or unboxed and placed in a die-cut platform (Type B). Another hinged top display had all the trains boxed with one or two inserts to fill the empty space (Type C).

Type A – 1963 outfit no. 11331 comes in a hinged display with unboxed items separated by tan corrugated inserts.

Type B – 1960 outfit no. 1805 comes in a hinged display with unboxed items placed in a die-cut platform.

Type C – 1960 outfit no. 2527 comes in a hinged display with boxed items and two colored inserts used for filler.

The next version of display outfit packing (Type D) came with a lift-off (telescoping) top. These outfit boxes came in two pieces. The bottom was a stand-alone tray on which the trains lay flat. The top was a mirror of the bottom, but slightly larger so it could telescope over the bottom.

Type D – 1965 outfit no. 11520 comes in a two-piece lift-off telescoping top and bottom tray with unboxed items separated by white corrugated inserts.

The last version of display box packing (Type E) contained only a bottom tray with a die-cut platform for the trains to be inserted. The top consisted of a sleeve that slid over the tray to protect the trains.

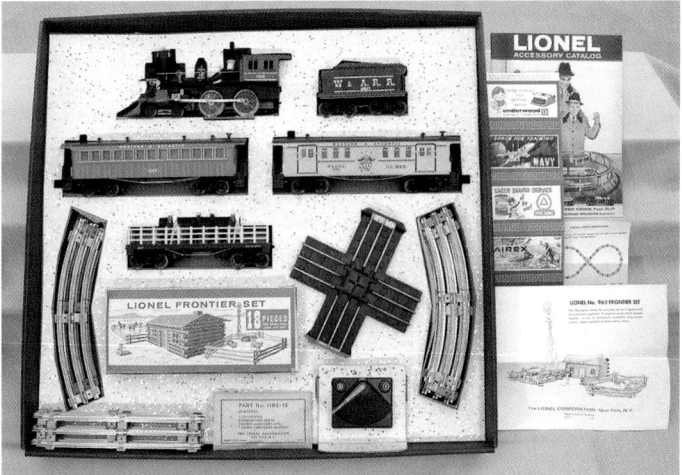

Type E – 1960 outfit no. X-507NA comes in a red colored tray that is covered by a corrugated sleeve (not shown). The items are unboxed and placed in a die-cut platform.

All five versions of display boxes were known generically as "display" within Lionel. Employees at Lionel also used the term "gift pack" for display outfits that did not include track or transformer. Gift packs followed the same characteristics of regular display outfit packaging.

Other features of display boxes:
- All made from corrugated cardboard.
- Ranged in colors, including yellow, orange, white, red and blue.
- Graphics changed over the years.

Some display outfits included a no. 61-107 Acetate Dust Cover to place over the outfit to protect items from dust, damage and theft. 1963 display outfit no. D19239 called for the entire display to be shrink-packed.

Blister display outfits were shipped in their own box with inserts to protect the blisters.

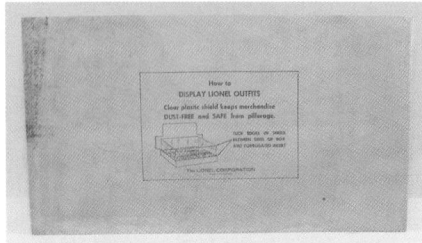

Lionel provided a no. 61-107 Plastic (acetate) Cover to keep display outfits "Dust 'Free" and "Safe from Pilferage".

The next section on Outfit Box Printing, Graphics and Labels provides a detailed history of Lionel display outfit boxes from 1960 through 1969. It defines and dates box types, colors, graphics, box numbering and company (Lionel Corporation or Lionel Toy Corporation).

Master Shipper Packaging

When shipping train outfits, Lionel would place them in a larger tan RSC master shipper carton. The RSC master shipper provided a way to consolidate one to six train outfits for shipping. Lionel would then attach an address label and ship the outfits to its customer. The markings, dating, outfit numbering and box manufacturers on master shipper cartons follow that of tan RSC boxes. Shippers were stamped with Lionel Corporation or Lionel Toy Corporation at the box manufacturer.

Display outfits were always shipped in a tan RSC master carton. RSC outfits were most often shipped in a master shipper carton.

Blister Packaging

Lionel RSC and lift-off display packaging, though functional and cost-effective, did little for the display and promotion of trains. Also, as more outfits were being sold through self-service channels and used as promotions in non-traditional channels, the need for a better way to display trains became a priority.

Enter blister packaging. Blister packaging consists of a transparent plastic overlay affixed to a cardboard backing to display and protect the trains. Blister packaging allowed retailers and dealers to hang a blister-packaged sample of a train outfit, write its price in the area provided and, when requested for purchase, provide a customer with the boxed version of the outfit. Blistered outfits began appearing in 1963 and continued until 1966. Technically, these were dealer display items; however, some are included in this volume as reference for the train outfits they helped to sell.

Blister displays were assembled with each train item placed into an individual plastic blister. In later years, the entire outfit was placed in a one-piece blister. The blister backing was stapled to the blister. The individual blister(s) were then sandwiched between two pieces of heavier cardboard that were stapled together. Two holes were punched out at the top of the blister, and pegs were provided to hang the blister on a wall. When the blister displays were shipped, four inserts were placed over them to protect them from being crushed. The displays were then placed into a shipper for delivery.

Four no. 19440 display outfits as they came packed in their master shipper.

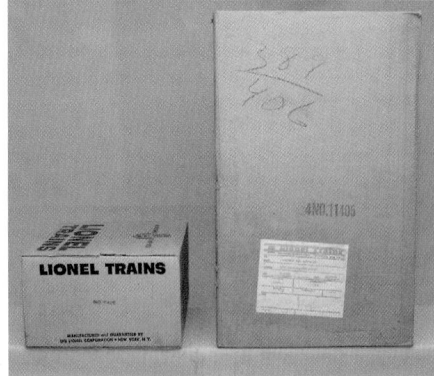

RSC outfit no. 11405 and its master shipper carton.

Blister outfit no. D19213 was hung on a wall to help sell Western Auto outfit no. 19213.

Lionel would sometimes sell RSC outfits one at a time. When this occurred, outfits were most often shipped in their own master shipper carton, although sometimes these outfits were shipped only in their outfit box. Ironically, some of Lionel's most expensive Super O outfits were shipped this way. Outfit no. 2555W (the Father and Son Set) from 1960 was one of these outfits. This fact explains why these high-end Super O boxes are so difficult to find in good condition. If the initial shipment went well a box may have survived in excellent condition; otherwise as is most often the case, it was dented, scuffed or marred.

Other Lionel RSC outfits were also designed to be shipped without shipper cartons, but not by Lionel. These were RSC Mailers or outfits designed for direct fulfillment via mail order. Lionel would ship these outfits in master shipper cartons to a retailer, distributor or liquidator, who in turn would ship the individual outfits directly to the customer.

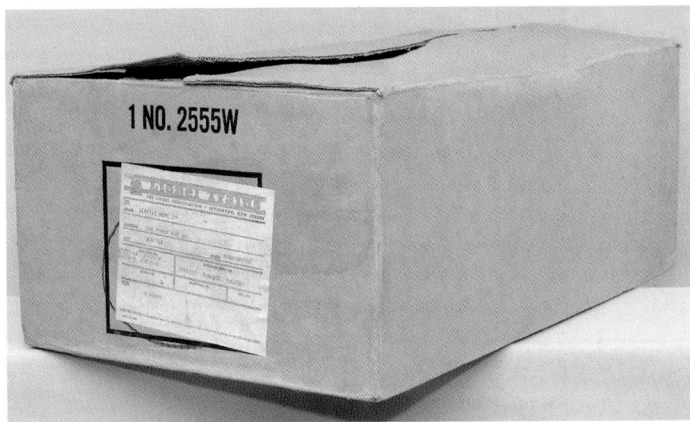

Many high-end outfits, such as no. 2555W, were shipped in their outfit box and not in a master shipper. This explains why these boxes are difficult to find in good condition.

Other Outfit and Shipper Packaging

As with any rule, there are always exceptions. When it came to getting trains out the door, sometimes every rule would be broken. Lionel often provided bulk shipments to customers and assigned them an outfit number. Factory orders for these outfits simply said "ship in bulk". Other outfits used any available packaging.

Some individually shipped outfits came in Full Overlap Slotted Container shippers for additional strength. These boxes were tan RSC's on which the end flaps fully overlapped (a good example is outfit no. 12850X). Some outfits had train items wrapped in tissue paper. Other train items did not completely fill the outfit box, so "Bogus Paper" was provided to fill out the outfit box.

Outfit no. 12850X came in its own master shipper with full overlapping flaps for extra strength and protection.

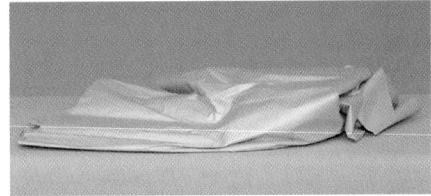

Outfit no. 19567-500 from 1966 included "Bogus Paper" to fill out the extra space in the outfit box.

Outfit Box Printing, Graphics and Labels

All of Lionel's train outfits came in some form of corrugated cardboard box. Corrugated cardboard is manufactured by sandwiching a fluted medium between two outer liner sheets. The outside liner can be left in its original color, laminated, printed or bleached either before or after being assembled into a box. Lionel's box manufacturers used all of these processes in decorating outfit boxes.

From 1959 through 1969, Lionel's outfit boxes came in Kraft (tan), orange, yellow, red, blue or white. Tan boxes used natural corrugated cardboard. Orange boxes were coated with a thin orange laminated sheet. Yellow, red and blue boxes were printed with color. White boxes contained a thin veneer of bleached white paper as part of the outer linerboard.

Lionel box graphics were printed using a letterpress process. Letterpress printing uses rubber or polymer (plastic) plates that include a raised version of the image to be printed. These plates are coated with ink via rollers and subsequently applied to the corrugated material. Lionel continuously updated its box graphics as detailed in the Dating O27, O and Super O Outfit Box summary.

Outfit numbers were also letterpress printed by the box manufacturer. This changed in 1961 for RSCs and in 1962 for display boxes, when Lionel changed to unnumbered generic outfit boxes. Lionel created custom stamps and began machine- or hand-stamping outfit numbers on these generic boxes. The quantity of many outfits numbered well into the thousands, so this was not a trivial task. An Arial-style font appears to be most commonly used.

Instances of outfits hand-stamped using a number-dial, flat-band rubber stamp have also been observed. The stamp's font is distinctly different from the more commonly used Arial font.

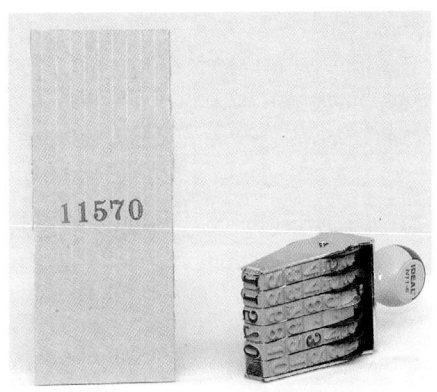

A common rubber hand-stamp was used to stamp some outfits. The font used by Lionel is the same available today.

Hand-stamped versions of outfit nos. 11570 and 12780 were likely assembled after regular production to eliminate excess inventory.

Hand-stamped variations of regular-production outfits can likely be explained as last-minute changes on the production line, an effort to eliminate inventory, repackaged returns of poor-selling items or outfits that were special promotions. Other outfits that do not correspond to any Lionel outfit number are most likely explained as custom outfits assembled and numbered by large retail stores or distributors, such as Madison Hardware Co. in New York City. Madison Hardware had many generic boxes that its employees could uniquely stamp. These undocumented outfits are discussed in the section on Undocumented Outfits.

Some of the many hand-stamped outfits observed include:

Outfit Number	Usually Came As	Hand-Stamped Version
244	Not Applicable	See Section on Undocumented Outfits
11242	No. 61-140 Type A Display (machine-stamped)	No. 61-140 Type A Display (hand-stamped)
11361	No. 61-439 Type A Display	Orange RSC
11530	Type A Display	Tan RSC
11570	No. 64-162 White RSC	Tan RSC Mailer
12780	No. 66-106 White	No. 66-102 White RSC
19233-500	No. 62-270 Tan RSC	No. 61-230 Orange RSC
19236	No. 61-170 Tan RSC	No. 63-361 Tan RSC

Two of these outfits, nos. 11570 and 12780, are 1966 outfits that may have been assembled and hand-stamped in an effort by Lionel to eliminate inventory during late 1966 or later. The RSC version of outfit no. 11530 is from 1968, when Lionel was still using up leftover inventory. Outfit no. 11242 was most likely created during regular production as a replacement for depleted machine-stamped boxes. The other outfits, nos. 11361, 19233-500 and 19236 may have been box changes on the production line. The true origin of many of these boxes still remains a mystery.

Outfit Components on the Box

Traditionally, Lionel's outfit boxes seldom provided insights regarding what was in the box. Then in 1964, promotional outfits for Sears and J. C. Penney listed all the outfit components. By 1965, Lionel issued the Type D, White Lift-Off with Full-Color 2037 Steam Freight Graphic display box. The five standard features included with every outfit were printed on the box. When one or more of these features did not apply, it would be covered by white tape.

At the same time, it became common practice for Lionel to stamp a description of the outfit, along with the outfit number, on many display and some RSC boxes. In 1966, Lionel began using labels on RSC sides and display box ends. Now, instead of looking at a blank tan or white box, consumers could see first-hand the outfit they were receiving. It appears that the labels on display outfits occurred midstream in 1966, as there are versions of outfits with and without labels. Thus after years of blank outfit boxes, Lionel began to leverage its marketing expertise to make the train outfits more attractive to consumers.

In 1965, Lionel introduced the Type D, White Lift-Off with Full-Color 2037 Steam Freight Graphic display box that included a listing of the five features of the train outfit.

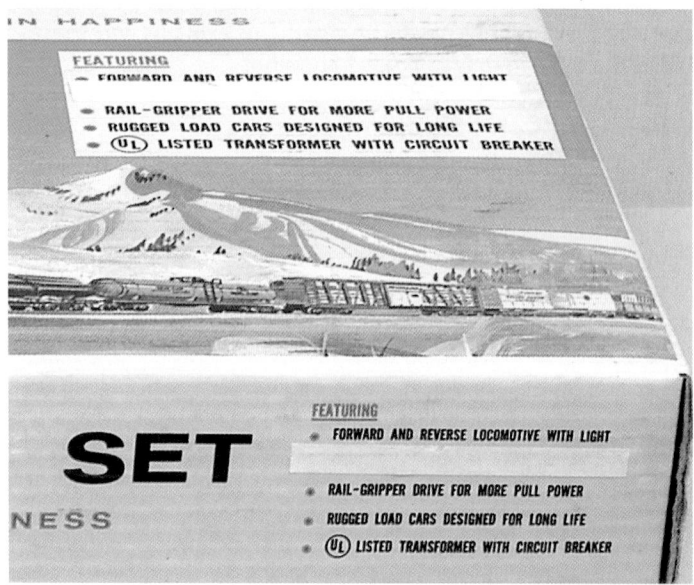

When features did not apply to the outfit, Lionel used white tape to "delete" them. In this example, the second line "Couple and Uncouple by Remote Control" is taped over.

By 1965, it was common practice to stamp both the outfit number as well as the description. Outfit no. 19516 is stamped "Steam Type Freight with Smoke and Whistle".

During 1966, Lionel began using labels showing the outfit contents on the end of display outfits. Outfit no. 11560 is shown.

During 1966, Lionel also placed descriptive labels on some RSCs. Outfit no. 19583 is shown.

"Lionel Corporation" versus "Lionel Toy Corporation"

Until 1963, "Lionel Corporation" served as the corporate name for all Lionel companies. Train outfit boxes were printed as such, "Manufactured and Guaranteed by the Lionel Corporation, New York, NY". Lionel changed its corporate structure in 1963 by combining Lionel Trains, Porter, Spear, and all other toys into the Lionel Toy Corporation subsidiary.

The first external use of "Lionel Toy Corporation" in printed material appeared in the 1963 consumer catalog. The Orange Picture box for the no. 6429 Caboose also uses "Lionel Toy Corporation" in 1963. The first appearance on an outfit box occurred in 1964 for the special graphic RSCs produced for Sears and J. C. Penney. Also, the 1964 version of cataloged Super O outfit no. 13150 has "Lionel Toy Corporation" on its RSC outfit box. "Lionel Toy Corporation" began appearing regularly in 1965 on both cataloged and promotional outfits.

Customer-Applied Markings

Once an outfit was received from Lionel, distributors or end customers often applied their own retail number or markings directly on the outfit box. These have been observed in the form of grease pen, rubber stampings, pencil/pen and price tags.

Instances when customers requested no markings on outfit boxes include 1965 outfit no. 11520-500. The Factory Order instructed that each outfit remain unstamped but the master shipper carton was to be stamped "2058". The individual outfits were subsequently augmented and stamped "2058" by the customer, Mercury Model. Other post-Lionel markings are summarized in the individual listings in this volume.

Salesman Samples

Samples of train outfits were provided to Lionel's salesmen to demonstrate the outfit and packaging to customers. Since these were early in the sales cycle, the packaging and box markings often did not match the final released outfit.

Lionel salesman Ken Negri's no. 11450 outfit sample came in a Type A display box with "#17" handwritten on the end; whereas, the final version came in Type D lift-off telescoping box.

OUTFIT BOX PRINTING, GRAPHICS AND LABELS
DATING O27 REGULAR SLOTTED CARTON (RSC) OUTFIT BOXES

	1960	**1961**	**1962**

Tan RSC with Black Graphics
(Catalog and Advance Catalog / Promotional Outfits)

From 1960 through 1969, Lionel used tan corrugated cardboard boxes. Black graphics were printed on all four sides and top. In 1960, each outfit box was unique with traditional-style outfit numbers printed as part of the box manufacturing process. Stickers were added to reuse older boxes. In 1961, generic outfit boxes were rubber-stamped by Lionel with the outfit number. Outfit numbers changed from traditional to five-digit in 1962 (except Sears four-digit through 1963). Lionel Corporation or Lionel Toy Corporation appeared as the manufacturer.

- Graphics all four sides and top
- Unique boxes
- Use of stickers to reuse boxes
- Traditional numbering
- The Lionel Corporation

- Generic boxes with rubber-stamped numbers
- Use of stickers to reuse boxes
- The Lionel Corporation

- New five-digit outfit numbering with a few carryover traditional outfit numbers
- Sears four-digit numbering
- Use of stickers to reuse boxes
- The Lionel Corporation

Tan RSC Mailer with Black Graphics
(Promotional Outfits)

From 1961 through 1966, Lionel used tan corrugated cardboard boxes for direct shipment of outfits. These were similar to tan corrugated RSC boxes, but had only black graphics on one (or no) side(s) and the bottom. This left room for the shipping label and postage. Most boxes were stronger cardboard (rated at a higher gross weight) needed to withstand the rigors of individual shipping. Generic outfit boxes were rubber-stamped by Lionel with the outfit number. Outfit numbers changed from traditional to five-digit in 1962. Lionel Corporation or Lionel Toy Corporation appeared as the manufacturer.

- Graphics one side and blank top
- Generic boxes with rubber-stamped numbers
- Traditional numbering
- The Lionel Corporation

- New five-digit outfit numbering with a few carryover traditional outfit numbers
- The Lionel Corporation

Orange RSC with Black Graphics
(Catalog and Promotional Outfits)

From 1961 through 1962 (cataloged) and 1961 through 1964 (promotional), Lionel used orange laminated corrugated cardboard boxes. Black graphics were printed on all four sides and top. Generic outfit boxes were rubber-stamped by Lionel with the outfit number. Outfit numbers changed from traditional to five-digit in 1962 (except Sears four-digit through 1962). Lionel Corporation appeared as the manufacturer.

- Graphics all four sides and top
- Generic boxes with rubber-stamped numbers
- Traditional numbering
- The Lionel Corporation

- New five-digit outfit numbering
- Sears four-digit numbering
- The Lionel Corporation

White RSC with Orange Graphics
(Promotional Outfits)

From 1964 through 1967 and in 1969, Lionel used white corrugated cardboard boxes. Orange graphics were printed on all four sides and top. Generic outfit boxes were rubber-stamped by Lionel with five-digit outfit numbers. Picture labels were added in 1966. Lionel Corporation or Lionel Toy Corporation appeared as the manufacturer.

Yellow RSC with Black Graphics
(Catalog and Promotional Outfits)

From 1960 through 1961 (promotional) and in 1960 (cataloged), Lionel used yellow corrugated cardboard boxes. Black graphics were printed on all four sides and top. All outfit boxes were leftover inventory from 1959 and stickers were added to cover the old number. Lionel Corporation appeared as the manufacturer.

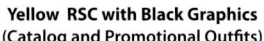

- Graphics all four sides and top
- Unique box
- Use of stickers to reuse box
- Traditional numbering
- The Lionel Corporation

White RSC Allstate By Lionel With 0-4-0 Blue Steamer (No Smoke) and Orange and Blue Graphics
White RSC Allstate By Lionel With Blue Steamer (With Smoke and Trees) and Orange and Blue Graphics
White RSC Allstate By Lionel With Blue Steamer (With Smoke and Trees) and Orange and Blue Gift of Lifetime Graphics
(Promotional Outfits)

From 1964 through 1966, Lionel used special white corrugated cardboard boxes for Sears outfits. Orange and blue graphics were printed on all four sides and top. Outfit numbers were most often unique and printed as part of the box manufacturing process or rubber-stamped by Lionel. Outfit numbers were either Sears four-digit number or both Sears and Lionel five-digit number. Outfit layout diagrams and contents were also printed on the box. Picture labels were added in 1966. Manufactured exclusively for Allstate or Sears by the Lionel Toy Corporation, or Built by the Lionel Toy Corporation, appeared as the manufacturer. Gift of Lifetime graphics were added in 1966.

White RSC Montgomery Ward Design with Black and Orange (or Black Only) Graphics
White RSC Penney Design with Blue Engine and Orange and Blue Graphics
(Promotional Outfits)

In 1964 and 1966, Lionel used special white corrugated cardboard boxes for J. C. Penney and Montgomery Ward outfits. J. C. Penney used orange and blue graphics printed on all four sides and top. The five-digit Lionel outfit number was unique and printed as part of the box manufacturing process. An outfit layout diagram and contents were printed on the box.

For Ward, black and orange or black only graphics were printed on all four sides and the top. Both Ward seven-digit and Lionel five-digit numbers were printed on the box as part of the manufacturing process. Outfit contents were listed on the box. The Lionel Toy Corporation appeared as the manufacturer on both Penney and Ward boxes.

OUTFIT BOX PRINTING, GRAPHICS AND LABELS
DATING O27 REGULAR SLOTTED CARTON (RSC) OUTFIT BOXES

1963	1964	1965	1966	1967	-	1969

- Sears four-digit numbering through 1963
- The Lionel Corporation

- The Lionel Toy Corporation

- Labels added to some promotional outfits beginning in 1966
- Both Lionel and Sears four-digit numbering

- Lionel five-digit numbering

- No graphics
- Both five-digit outfit numbering and Sears four-digit numbering

- Outfit box that has characteristics of mailer but was not used as mailer
- The Lionel Toy Corporation on one side only and blank top
- Most likely 1965 or 1966 only

- Graphics one side and blank top
- Generic box with rubber-stamped numbers
- Five-digit outfit numbering (also seven-digit Ward number)
- The Lionel Toy Corporation

- Promotional outfits only
- Five-digit outfit numbering
- The Lionel Corporation

- Graphics all four sides and top
- Generic boxes with rubber-stamped numbers
- Five-digit outfit numbering
- The Lionel Corporation

- The Lionel Toy Corporation

- Label added

White RSC with Light Blue Steamer and Red and Light Blue Graphics (Catalog Outfits)

In 1969, Lionel used white corrugated cardboard boxes. Light blue and red graphics were printed on all four sides, but not the top. A label with a photograph of the outfit, its contents and the five-digit outfit number was attached to the box. The Lionel Toy Corporation appeared as the manufacturer.

- Label with outfit photo, contents and number attached
- The Lionel Toy Corporation

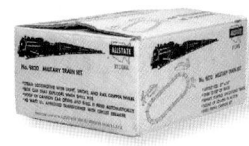

- White Allstate By Lionel With 0-4-0 Blue Steamer (No Smoke) and Orange and Blue Graphics
- Sears four-digit or Sears and Lionel five-digit numbering
- Manufactured exclusively for Allstate by the Lionel Toy Corporation

- White Allstate By Lionel With Blue Steamer (With Smoke and Trees) and Orange and Blue Graphics
- Sears four-digit numbering
- Manufactured exclusively for Sears by the Lionel Toy Corporation

- White Allstate By Lionel With Blue Steamer (With Smoke and Trees) and Orange and Blue Gift of Lifetime Graphics
- Label added
- Sears four-digit or Sears and Lionel five-digit numbering
- Built by the Lionel Toy Corporation

- White Penney Design with Blue Engine and Orange and Blue Graphics
- Lionel five-digit outfit numbering
- Layout diagram on box
- The Lionel Toy Corporation

- White Montgomery Ward Design with Black and Orange Graphics
- Ward seven-digit and Lionel five-digit numbering
- Lionel Toy Corporation

- White Montgomery Ward Design with Black Graphics
- Ward seven-digit and Lionel five-digit numbering
- The Lionel Toy Corporation

OUTFIT BOX PRINTING, GRAPHICS AND LABELS
DATING O27 DISPLAY OUTFIT BOXES

Yellow Hinged Display with Steamer, General and F3 Graphics
(Catalog and Promotional Outfits)

Yellow Hinged Display with General Graphics
(Catalog Outfits)

From 1959 through 1961, Lionel used yellow corrugated cardboard boxes. Two styles were used: Type A display boxes with an attached hinged top and unboxed items or Type B display boxes (1959 and 1960) with an attached hinged top, die-cut platform and unboxed items. Black, red and green graphics were printed on all sides of the box. Outfit boxes were unique with traditional-style outfit numbers printed as part of the box manufacturing process. Stickers were added to reuse older boxes. Lionel Corporation appeared as the manufacturer.

- Yellow Hinged Display with General Graphics
- Type B
- Graphics all sides
- Unique boxes
- Traditional numbering
- The Lionel Corporation

Orange Hinged Gift Pack with USMC Graphics
(Catalog Outfit)

In 1960, Lionel used a white corrugated cardboard box for outfit 1805. This was a Type B display box with an attached hinged top, die-cut platform and unboxed items. Orange, black and olive drab graphics were printed on all sides of the box. The outfit box was unique with a traditional-style outfit number printed as part of the box manufacturing process. Lionel Corporation appeared as the manufacturer.

Red Corrugated Tray, Sleeve Top with Black Graphics
(Promotional Outfit)

In 1960, Lionel used a red corrugated cardboard tray for outfit no. X-507NA. This was a Type E display box with a tan corrugated sleeve top, die-cut platform and unboxed items. The graphics were printed black on the tan corrugated slip cover top. The outfit box had no outfit number. No manufacturer was listed.

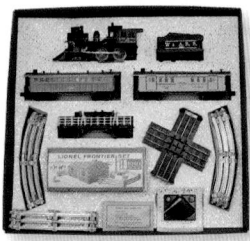

White Hinged Display with Red *Texas Special* Alco Graphics and Track Layout Plan
(Promotional Outfits)

From 1959 through 1960, Lionel used a white corrugated cardboard box made for outfit no. X-829. This was a Type A display box with an attached hinged top and unboxed items. Red and blue graphics were printed on all sides of the box. The outfit box was unique with a traditional-style outfit number printed as part of the box manufacturing process. Lionel Corporation appeared as the manufacturer.

White Hinged Display with Red *Texas Special* Alco Graphics
White Hinged Display with Green Canadian National Alco Graphics
(Advance Catalog / Promotional Outfits)

From 1959 through 1960 (*Texas Special*) and 1960 (Canadian National), Lionel used white corrugated cardboard boxes. These were Type A display boxes with an attached hinged top and unboxed items. The graphics were printed red and blue (*Texas Special*) or green and blue (Canadian National) on all sides of the box. The outfit boxes were unique with traditional-style outfit numbers printed as part of the box manufacturing process. Lionel Corporation appeared as the manufacturer.

- White Hinged Display with Red *Texas Special* Alco Graphics
- Type A
- Graphics all sides
- Unique box
- Traditional numbering
- The Lionel Corporation

White Hinged Display with 1050 Blue Steamer and Red/Orange Graphics
(Advance Catalog / Promotional Outfits)

From 1959 through 1960, Lionel used white corrugated cardboard boxes. These were Type A display boxes with an attached hinged top and unboxed items. Blue and red/orange graphics were printed on all sides of the box. In 1959 and 1960, the graphics were an 0-4-0 no. 1050 steam engine. In 1960, a 2-4-2 version (numbers only) was added. Some 0-4-0 boxes were reused and were stickered over with a red "2-4-2" sticker. The outfit boxes were unique with traditional-style outfit numbers printed as part of the box manufacturing process. Stickers were also added to cover outfit numbers of older boxes. Lionel Corporation appeared as the manufacturer.

- White Hinged Display with 1050 Blue Steamer and Red/Orange Graphics
- Type A
- Graphics all sides
- Unique box
- Traditional numbering
- The Lionel Corporation

1960

1961

- Yellow Hinged Display with Steamer, General and F3 Graphics
- Type A
- Graphics all sides
- Unique boxes
- Traditional numbering
- The Lionel Corporation

- Orange Hinged Gift Pack with USMC Graphics
- Type B
- Graphics all sides
- Unique box
- Traditional numbering
- The Lionel Corporation

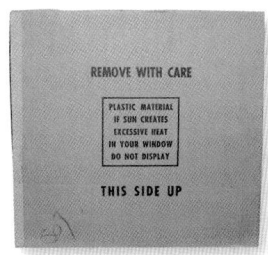

- Red Corrugated Tray, Sleeve Top with Black Graphics
- Type E
- Graphics on slip cover top
- No numbering
- No manufacturer

- White Hinged Display with Red *Texas Special* Alco Graphics and Track Layout Plan
- Type A
- Graphics all sides
- Unique box
- Traditional numbering
- The Lionel Corporation

- White Hinged Display with Green Canadian National Alco Graphics
- Type A
- Graphics all sides
- Unique box
- Traditional numbering
- The Lionel Corporation

- White Hinged Display with 1050 Blue Steamer and Red/Orange Graphics
- Type A
- Unique box
- Sticker variation to cover 0-4-0
- Traditional numbering
- Use of stickers to reuse boxes
- The Lionel Corporation

DISPLAY OUTFIT PACKAGING TYPES

TYPE	DISPLAY BOX DESCRIPTION	CONTENTS	INSERTS
A	One-piece attached hinged top.	Unboxed (sometimes with one or two items boxed)	Colored or tan corrugated inserts.
B		Unboxed	Die-cut platform
C		Boxed	Colored inserts used for filler.
D	Two-piece lift-off telescoping top and bottom tray.	Unboxed (sometimes with one or two items boxed)	White or tan corrugated inserts
E	Colored tray bottom and tan corrugated sleeve.	Unboxed	Die-cut platform

OUTFIT BOX PRINTING, GRAPHICS AND LABELS
DATING O27 DISPLAY OUTFIT BOXES

Orange, White and Gray O27 Hinged Display with 4-6-2 Steam Display Graphics
(Catalog and Promotional Outfits)

From 1960 through 1962, Lionel used white corrugated cardboard boxes known as Type A display boxes with an attached hinged top and unboxed items or Type C display boxes (1960 only) with an attached hinged top and individually boxed items. Orange, white, black and gray graphics were on all sides of the box. In 1960 and 1961, outfit boxes were unique with traditional-style outfit numbers printed as part of the box manufacturing process. In 1962, generic outfit boxes were rubber-stamped by Lionel with five-digit outfit numbers. Stickers were added to reuse older boxes. Lionel Corporation appeared as the manufacturer.

- Orange, White and Gray O27 Hinged Display with 4-6-2 Steam Display Graphics
- Type A or C (1960 only)
- Graphics all sides
- Unique boxes
- Traditional numbering
- The Lionel Corporation

- White 4-6-4 Steamer and F3 Hinged Display with Red or Red/Orange and Blue Graphics
- Type A
- Graphics all sides
- Unique boxes
- Traditional numbering
- The Lionel Corporation

White 4-6-4 Steamer and F3 Hinged Display with Red, Red/Orange or Orange and Blue Graphics
(Catalog, Advance Catalog / Promotional Outfits)

From 1961 through 1963 (advance catalog / promotional) and from 1962 through 1963 (catalog), Lionel used white corrugated cardboard boxes known as Type A display boxes with an attached hinged top and unboxed items. The graphics were printed in dark red (or reddish orange) and blue from 1961 through 1963. In 1963, the graphics also appeared in orange and blue. In all years they were printed on all sides of the box. In 1961, outfit boxes came in both unique and generic versions with traditional-style outfit numbers printed as part of the box manufacturing process or rubber-stamped by Lionel. Stickers were also used to reuse unique boxes. In 1962 and 1963, generic outfit boxes were rubber-stamped by Lionel with five-digit outfit numbers and stickers were added to reuse 1961 boxes. By 1963, it appears all older boxes had been used and stickers were no longer needed. Lionel Corporation appeared as the manufacturer.

- Use of stickers to reuse boxes

- Generic boxes with rubber-stamped numbers

White 4-6-4 Steamer and F3 Lift-Off with Orange and Blue Graphics
(Catalog and Promotional Outfits)

From 1964 through 1965, Lionel used a white corrugated cardboard box known as a Type D display box with a lift-off telescoping top and unboxed items. Orange and blue graphics were printed on all sides of the box. These generic outfit boxes were rubber-stamped by Lionel on the end with five-digit outfit numbers. Lionel Corporation appeared as the manufacturer.

White Lift-Off with Full-Color 2037 Steam Freight Graphics
(Catalog and Promotional Outfits)

From 1965 through 1966, Lionel used a white corrugated cardboard box known as a Type D display box with a lift-off telescoping top and unboxed items. Full-color graphics of a 2037 steam engine, tender and six cars were printed on all sides of the box. These generic outfit boxes were rubber-stamped on the end by Lionel with five-digit outfit numbers. White labels were applied to certain outfits to cover features that were not part of a particular outfit. In 1966, a label with a photograph of the outfit, its contents and the five-digit outfit number was attached to some of the outfit boxes. Lionel Toy Corporation appeared as the manufacturer.

White Lift-Off with Full-Color 2037 Steam Freight, Hagerstown Graphics
(Catalog Outfit)

In 1968, Lionel used a white corrugated cardboard box for its only O27 gauge display outfit no. 11600. This is known as a Type D display box with a lift-off telescoping top and unboxed items. Full-color graphics of a 2037 steam engine, tender and six cars were printed on all sides of the box. The outfit box was unique with a five-digit outfit number printed as part of the box manufacturing process. Also printed were the contents of the outfit. Lionel Toy Corporation, Hagerstown Maryland appeared as the manufacturer.

OUTFIT BOX PRINTING, GRAPHICS AND LABELS
DATING O27 DISPLAY OUTFIT BOXES

1962	1963	1964	1965	1966	1967	1968

- Orange, White and Gray O27 Hinged Display with 4-6-2 Steam Display Graphics
- Type A
- Graphics all sides
- Generic boxes with rubber-stamped numbers
- New five-digit outfit numbering
- Use of stickers to reuse boxes
- The Lionel Corporation

- New five-digit outfit numbering
- Generic boxes with rubber-stamped numbers

- New five-digit outfit numbering
- Use of stickers to reuse boxes

- Orange and Blue Graphics
- Five-digit outfit numbering
- Generic boxes with rubber-stamped numbers

- White 4-6-4 Steamer and F3 Lift-Off with Orange and Blue Graphics
- Type D
- Graphics all sides
- Generic boxes with rubber-stamped numbers
- Five-digit outfit numbering
- The Lionel Corporation

- White Lift-Off with Full-Color 2037 Steam Freight Graphics
- Type D
- Graphics all sides
- Generic boxes with rubber-stamped numbers
- Five-digit outfit numbering
- The Lionel Toy Corporation

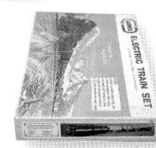

- Label added

- White Lift-Off with Full-Color 2037 Steam Freight, Hagerstown Graphics
- Type D
- Graphics all sides
- Unique box
- Five-digit outfit numbering
- The Lionel Toy Corporation, Hagerstown, Maryland

OUTFIT BOX PRINTING, GRAPHICS AND LABELS
DATING O GAUGE REGULAR SLOTTED CARTON (RSC) & DISPLAY OUTFIT BOXES

Tan RSC with Black Graphics
(Catalog and Promotional Outfits)

From 1964 through 1966, Lionel used tan corrugated cardboard boxes. If there was printing, the graphics were printed in black on one side. In 1966, one blank outfit box had the manufacturing information on the bottom printed in pink. Generic outfit boxes were rubber-stamped by Lionel with five-digit outfit numbers. Lionel Corporation, Lionel Toy Corporation or nothing appeared as the manufacturer.

Orange RSC with Black Graphics
(Catalog and Promotional Outfits)

In 1962 (promotional) and 1964 (catalog), Lionel used orange laminated corrugated cardboard boxes. Black graphics were printed on all four sides and the top. These generic outfit boxes were rubber-stamped by Lionel with four-digit customer specific (Sears 1962) and five-digit (1964) outfit numbers. Lionel Corporation appeared as the manufacturer.

- Graphics all four sides and top
- Generic boxes with rubber-stamped numbers
- Sears four-digit numbering
- The Lionel Corporation

White RSC with Orange Graphics
(Catalog and Promotional Outfits)

From 1964 through 1966, Lionel used white corrugated cardboard boxes. Orange graphics were printed on all four sides and the top. These generic outfit boxes were rubber-stamped by Lionel with five-digit outfit numbers. Lionel Corporation or Lionel Toy Corporation appeared as the manufacturer.

White RSC with Allstate By Lionel With Blue Steamer (With Smoke and Trees) and Red and Blue Graphics
(Promotional Outfit)

In 1965, Lionel used a special white corrugated cardboard box for the O gauge outfit sold to Sears. Blue and red graphics were printed on all four sides and the top. The outfit number was Sears four-digit number and was printed as part of the box manufacturing process. An outfit layout diagram and contents were printed on the box. Manufactured exclusively for Sears by the Lionel Toy Corporation.

White Lift-Off Display with Full-Color 2037 Steam Freight Graphics
(Catalog Outfit)

From 1965 through 1966, Lionel used a white corrugated cardboard box for its only O gauge display outfit. This is known as a Type D display box with a lift-off telescoping top and unboxed items. The graphics were printed in full-color with a 2037 steam engine, tender and six cars on all sides of the box. The outfit boxes were rubber-stamped by Lionel on the end with five-digit outfit numbers. A label identified this as an O gauge outfit. Another label covered the "UL Listed Transformer..." information with "Realistic Sounding Electronic Horn". Lionel Toy Corporation appeared as the manufacturer.

OUTFIT BOX PRINTING, GRAPHICS AND LABELS
DATING O GAUGE REGULAR SLOTTED CARTON (RSC) & DISPLAY OUTFIT BOXES

1964	1965	1966	1967 - 1969

- Graphics on one side and blank top
- Generic boxes with rubber-stamped number
- Five-digit outfit numbering
- The Lionel Corporation

- No graphics
- Generic boxes with rubber-stamped numbers
- Five-digit outfit numbering
- No manufacturer listed

- Graphics on one side and blank top
- Generic boxes with rubber-stamped numbers
- Five-digit outfit numbering
- The Lionel Toy Corporation

- No graphics
- Generic boxes with rubber-stamped numbers
- Five-digit outfit numbering
- No manufacturer listed

- Graphics all four sides and top
- Generic boxes with rubber-stamped numbers
- Five-digit outfit numbering
- The Lionel Corporation

- Graphics all four sides and top
- Generic boxes with rubber-stamped numbers
- Five-digit outfit numbering
- The Lionel Corporation

- Graphics all four sides and top
- Generic boxes with rubber-stamped numbers
- Five-digit outfit numbering
- The Lionel Toy Corporation

- White Allstate By Lionel With Blue Steamer (With Smoke and Trees) and Red and Blue Graphics
- Sears four-digit outfit numbering
- Manufactured exclusively for Sears by the Lionel Toy Corporation

- White Lift-Off Display with Full-Color 2037 Steam Freight Graphics
- Type D
- Five-digit outfit numbering
- Lionel Toy Corporation

OUTFIT BOX PRINTING, GRAPHICS AND LABELS
DATING SUPER O REGULAR SLOTTED CARTON (RSC) & DISPLAY OUTFIT BOXES

	1960	**1961**

Yellow RSC with Rio Grande and Norfolk and Western Graphics
(Catalog Outfits)

From 1959 through 1960, Lionel used yellow corrugated cardboard boxes. Black and red graphics were printed on all four sides and top. Outfit boxes were unique with traditional-style outfit numbers printed as part of the box manufacturing process. Lionel Corporation appeared as the manufacturer.

- Graphics all four sides and top
- Unique boxes
- Traditional numbering
- The Lionel Corporation

Orange RSC with Rio Grande and Norfolk and Western Graphics
(Catalog Outfits)

In 1960, Lionel used orange laminated corrugated cardboard boxes. Black and white graphics were printed on all four sides and top. Outfit boxes were unique with traditional-style outfit numbers printed as part of the box manufacturing process. Lionel Corporation appeared as the manufacturer.

- Graphics all four sides and top
- Unique boxes
- Traditional numbering
- The Lionel Corporation

- Graphics all four sides and top
- Unique boxes
- Use of stickers to reuse boxes
- Traditional numbering
- The Lionel Corporation

Tan RSC with Black Graphics
(Catalog and Promotional Outfits)

From 1960 through 1966, Lionel used tan corrugated cardboard boxes Black graphics were printed on all four sides and top or as noted. It appears many of these boxes were used as self-mailers, and the lack of graphics allowed room for shipping labels. In 1960, outfit boxes were unique with traditional-style outfit numbers printed as part of the box manufacturing process. Stickers were added to reuse older boxes. In 1961, generic outfit boxes were rubber-stamped by Lionel with outfit numbers. Outfit numbers changed from traditional to five-digit in 1962. Lionel Corporation or Lionel Toy Corporation appeared as the manufacturer.

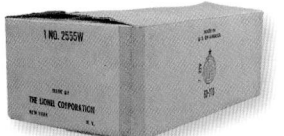

- Graphics three sides and blank top
- Unique box
- Traditional numbering
- The Lionel Corporation

- Graphics three sides and blank top
- Generic boxes with rubber-stamped numbers
- Traditional numbering
- The Lionel Corporation

Orange RSC with Black Graphics
(Catalog Outfits)

From 1961 through 1963, Lionel used orange laminated corrugated cardboard boxes. Black graphics were printed on all four sides and top. These generic outfit boxes were rubber-stamped by Lionel with the outfit number. Outfit numbers changed from traditional to five-digit in 1962. Lionel Corporation appeared as the manufacturer.

- Graphics all four sides and top
- Generic boxes with rubber-stamped numbers
- Traditional numbering
- The Lionel Corporation

Yellow Hinged Display with Steamer, General and F3 Graphics
Yellow Hinged Display with General Graphics
(Catalog Outfits)

From 1959 through 1961, Lionel used yellow boxes made from corrugated cardboard. These are known as Type C display boxes with an attached hinged top and individually boxed items (1959 and 1960) or Type B display boxes with an attached hinged top, die-cut platform and unboxed items. The graphics were printed black, red and green (General only box) on all sides of the box. The outfit boxes were unique with traditional-style outfit numbers printed as part of the box manufacturing process. Lionel Corporation appeared as the manufacturer.

- Yellow Hinged Display with Steamer, General and F3 Graphics
- Type C
- Graphics all sides
- Unique boxes
- Traditional numbering
- The Lionel Corporation

Orange, White and Gray Super O Hinged Display with 4-6-2 Steam Display Graphics
(Catalog Outfits)

In 1960, Lionel used white boxes made from corrugated cardboard. These are known as Type C display boxes with an attached hinged top and individually boxed items. The graphics were printed in orange, white, black and gray on all sides of the box. The outfit boxes were unique with traditional-style outfit numbers printed as part of the box manufacturing process. Lionel Corporation appeared as the manufacturer.

- Orange, White and Gray Super O Hinged Display with 4-6-2 Steam Display Graphics
- Type C
- Graphics all sides
- Unique boxes
- Traditional numbering
- The Lionel Corporation

OUTFIT BOX PRINTING, GRAPHICS AND LABELS
DATING SUPER O REGULAR SLOTTED CARTON (RSC) & DISPLAY OUTFIT BOXES

1962	1963	1964	1965	1966	1967 - 1969

- Graphics all four Sides and Top
- Generic Boxes
- Five-digit outfit numbering
- The Lionel Corporation

- New five-digit outfit numbering
- The Lionel Corporation

- No graphics
- Generic boxes with rubber-stamped numbers
- Five-digit outfit numbering
- No manufacturer

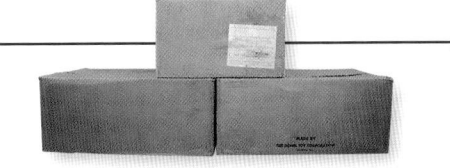

- Graphics on one side and blank top
- Generic boxes with rubber-stamped numbers
- Five-digit outfit numbering
- The Lionel Toy Corporation

- New five-digit outfit numbering
- The Lionel Corporation

- Yellow Hinged Display with General Graphics
- Type B
- Graphics all sides
- Unique boxes
- Traditional numbering
- The Lionel Corporation

While Lionel's sales executives determined which outfits the firm would offer as cataloged and promotional items, members of the Outfit Packing Department (Department 57) had to figure out the most efficient method of packing all the items designated for a particular outfit into an appropriate box. If you have ever tried to repack an outfit, you've experienced the challenge of getting all the items to fit back into the box. Multiply this task by hundreds of outfits (electric trains, raceways, Spear phonographs and Porter science kits, cataloged and promotional) each year and you can begin to understand how demanding and yet significant this job must have been.

Box and Insert Numbering Process

Lionel was a well-structured manufacturing organization with processes and numbers assigned to most everything. The Outfit Packing Department was also part of this culture, as every box, insert, blister, shipper and label had an associated part number. A familiarity with this numbering process is helpful in deciphering the Factory Orders used as a basis for this volume and ensuring that a train outfit is 100 percent correct and complete.

Each year, the Outfit Packing Department would begin a three-step process to ensure that all outfits were properly packaged and delivered to the Finished Goods Department. Members of that critical department began by creating a list, or Box Ledger, of Lionel product numbers eventually allocated to outfit boxes, inserts and other packaging.

For example, in 1960, boxes and inserts began with Lionel part no. 60-125 and numbers were reserved through no. 60-709. The "60" represented 1960, and "125" was the part number; the resulting no. 60-125 being the complete part number. Later in the outfit-packing process, these reserved numbers were sequentially assigned to specific boxes and inserts.

Gaps or unassigned part numbers existed from 1959 through 1961, as it appears the Outfit Packing Department started numbering new outfit boxes and inserts in increments of five. In 1962, when Lionel went to generic boxes for both display and RSCs, such gaps occurred less often. The outfit-box numbering system of using the year first and the part number second began in 1955.

As the second step in the packing process, the Outfit Packing Department received a memorandum (in the form of an Outfit Contents sheet in 1960 and, in subsequent years, a handwritten Factory Order or Factory Worksheet), containing a list of all outfit items and peripherals. Additional details included required packaging (display, RSC, mailer, bulk or blister), special instructions for graphics and labeling, customer number requirements, inclusion of third-party items, individual item packing instructions (boxed or unboxed) and any third-party packaging requirements.

Page 1 - No. 60-125 was the first box part number reserved (for diplay box no. 1609) in 1960

Page 2 - Assigned numbers for RSC version of outfit no. 1629

Assigned numbers for display version of outfit no. 1629

Page 3 - No. 60-709 was the last number reserved

In 1960, Lionel created a three-page Box Ledger of reserved outfit box part numbers ranging from nos. 60-125 through 60-709. Pages two and three are shown as insets.

An Outfit Contents sheet was sent to the Outfit Packing Department listing the components of an outfit.

The Outfit Packing Department would evaluate these requirements against the set of rules-of-thumb they apparently attempted to follow. Heavier items, including transformers, track and motive power, most often were placed on the bottom layer of train outfits. A cardboard insert separated train items. Boxes were packed to their capacity to minimize movement of items. Other complex requirements entailed inventory control of existing boxes and inserts, management of quantity changes during production, "make versus buy" decisions for inserts, "required by" dates and overall cost control.

As the final step, all of these constraints were taken into consideration and the Outfit Packing Department would engineer the box and inserts for the outfit. Boxes and inserts were assigned a previously reserved Lionel part number and recorded on the Box Ledger.

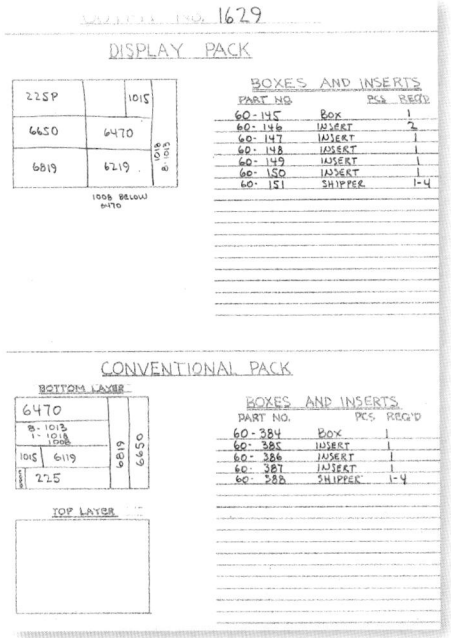

The Outfit Packing Diagram for outfit no. 1629 was hand-drawn by the Outfit Packing Department. Boxes and insert part numbers were assigned during this process.

As an example, outfit no. 1629 was offered in both display and conventional (RSC) packing. The box and inserts were assigned the following numbers and dated January 4, 1960, on the Box Ledger.

Display (Type A) Packing Assigned Box and Insert Part Numbers:

- 60-145 is the no. 1629 display outfit box
- 60-146 is an insert
- 60-147 is an insert
- 60-148 is an insert
- 60-149 is an insert
- 60-150 is an insert
- 60-151 is the shipper that held four no. 1629 outfits for shipping

Conventional (RSC) Tan Packing Assigned Box and Insert Part Numbers:

- 60-384 is the no. 1629 RSC box
- 60-385 is an insert
- 60-386 is an insert
- 60-387 is an insert
- 60-388 is the shipper that held four no. 1629 outfits for shipping

For this outfit, 12 new inserts and boxes were created, manufactured and stocked. This large number of inserts and boxes required for a single outfit stemmed from Lionel's use of unique boxes. Each box had an outfit number (in this case, no. 1629), printed by the box manufacturer. Therefore, a new box was required for every newly issued outfit. As for inserts, yellow outfit packaging was new in 1959, so not many generically sized "stock" inserts were available. Therefore, new ones were required for this outfit.

More insights about the outfit-packing process can be gleaned from additional internal documentation. In 1961, the Outfit Contents sheet became a Factory Order form while the Outfit Packing sheets became form no. 2117 5/60 (form 2117 designed in May 1960).

Also, memos between departments began to appear that listed the box and inserts required for each outfit. A good example is demonstrated with outfit no. 12885-500 from 1965 (Sears no. 9836). To begin, an early handwritten worksheet was provided to the Outfit Packing Department on 3-12-65. From this sheet, boxing and packing was engineered. Then a memo outlined the required packing and inserts, and these were incorporated on the final factory order on 8-20-65. Since this outfit consisted of individually boxed items, only two inserts and a shipper pad were required.

The progression of outfit no. 12885-500 (Sears no. 9836) began with an original handwritten worksheet that was sent to the Outfit Packing Department.

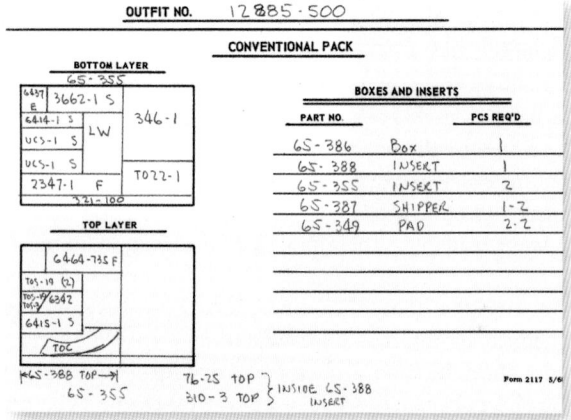

The Outfit Packing Department engineered the packaging and issued a memo of the results.

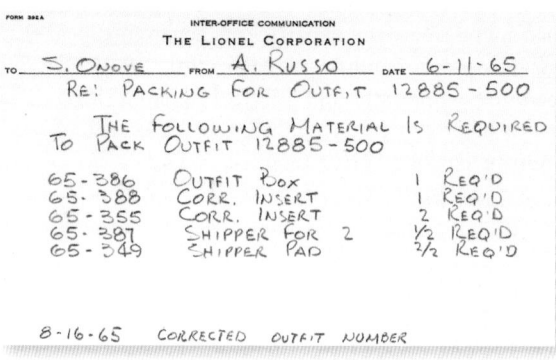

This led to the final Factory Order.

Unique Boxes

Outfit boxes were pre-printed by the box manufacturer with the Lionel outfit number. This practice was in place from 1949 through 1960 for RSCs and through 1961 for most display boxes. Other pre-printed boxes included promotional outfits for Sears, Penney's and Ward from 1964 through 1966 and cataloged outfit no. 11600 in 1968. In this volume, pre-printed boxes are defined as "Unique" boxes because they were unique to a particular outfit. If there were leftover inventory of unique boxes, they were often reused.

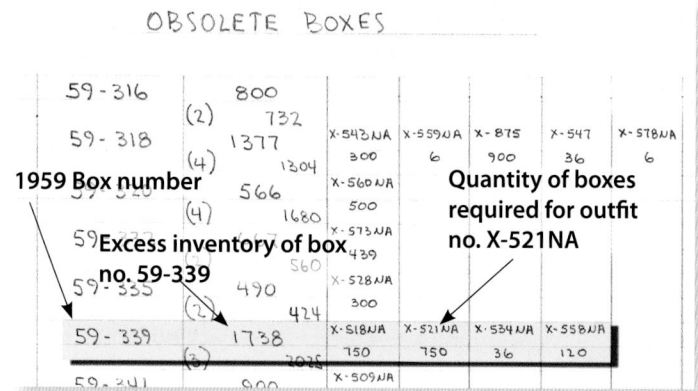

The Outfit Packing Department reused boxes if it could. In this case, in 1960, outfit no. X-521NA required 750 additional boxes. These were fulfilled by the 1,738 no. 59-339 boxes (unique box for outfit no. 9663) in inventory.

When excess inventory of no. 59-339 boxes was used, a pre-printed X-521NA sticker was glued over no. 9663.

Outfit no. 1641 from 1961 reused outfit no. 1627S's 1960 box (Lionel part no. 60-135) by applying a sticker over the "1627S". Upon close inspection, "1627S" can be seen underneath the sticker.

In some cases, a sticker was placed over a sticker. Outfit no. 1107 from 1960 reused outfit no. 1105's 1959 box (Lionel part no. 59-45). Subsequently, this outfit was sold to Firestone and another sticker was used to label it as no. 11-L-340.

Old boxes were also used when outfit order quantities changed or different sized items were substituted. That is why some outfits have as many as four different boxing variations. Outfit no.X-573NA originally started out with an order for 3,000 outfits. When the order increased by 1,500 (requiring four accessory substitutions), the Outfit Packing Department scrambled to locate enough inventory of three other boxes to meet the need. Situations like this exposed a need to move to generically sized and numbered boxes.

Generic Boxes

In 1961 for RSCs, and 1962 for display boxes, Lionel discontinued pre-numbering outfit numbers at the box manufacturer. These "Generic" boxes, as they will be called in this volume, were rubber-stamped by Lionel with the outfit number. Labels with the outfit number and contents were also used in later years.

This practice eased the burden of tracking the box inventory and presumably reduced the waste of unused boxes. It also caused a dramatic reduction in the number of new boxes and inserts. In 1960, Lionel created 338 new outfit boxes and inserts for O27, Super O and HO cataloged and promotional outfits. By moving to generic boxes, only 205 new boxes were required in 1961. A year later, only 109 were needed. By 1963, the inventory of uniquely numbered boxes had likely been depleted because the use of stickers ceased. The practice of using generic boxes also enabled Lionel to use similar boxes for numerous outfits spanning many years. These workhorse boxes, such as no. 61-170, were used in more than 70 different outfits.

Box and Insert Part Numbering

After determining the outfit packing, an order would be placed for boxes and inserts from a chosen box manufacturer. Along with the graphics, outfit number and type of packing, the order likely included the Lionel part number to be stamped on the boxes and inserts. Most Lionel boxes from 1959 through 1969 included the Lionel box part number.

For RSCs, the number is most often found on the inside bottom box flaps but it can also be found on an outside bottom box flap or on the box side. For display outfit boxes, the box number is usually found on one of the inside side flaps. The number can be checked by carefully prying open the side of the box.

The manufacturer also marked inserts with Lionel's part number, though not as consistently as boxes. Five different methods

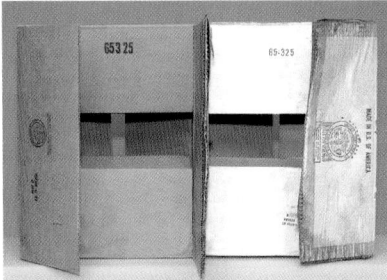

Outfit box no. 63-325 was printed on the bottom inside flap.

Outfit box no. 63-385 was printed on the bottom outside flap.

Outfit box no. 60-270 was printed on the box side.

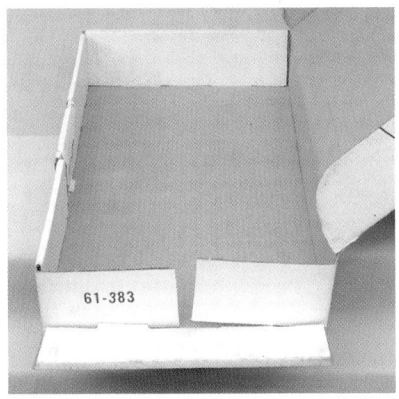

Display outfit box no. 61-383 was printed on the inside flap.

of marking the part number on inserts have been observed. They are defined as:

- Dot embossing
- Solid line embossing
- Punched pinholes
- Cut slits
- Printed writing

Each of these methods, except printed writing, was added during the insert's slotting process.

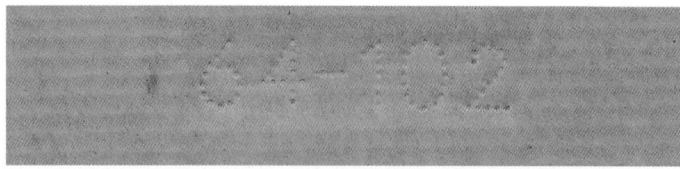

The dot embossing method (most often used) imprinted the Lionel part number by using a series of dots or dimples impressed into the corrugated cardboard. Depending upon the depth of the embossing it can be difficult to observe.

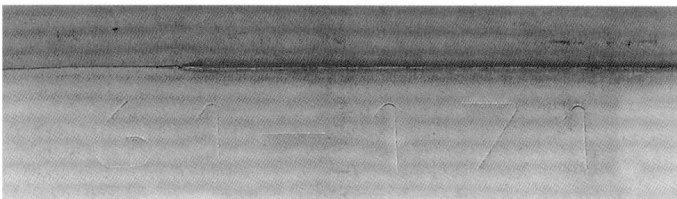

The solid line embossing method impressed the complete insert number using a solid line.

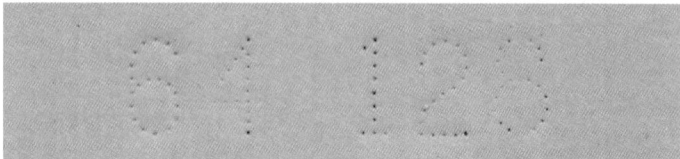

The punched pinhole method is similar to dot embossing, but it used smaller dots that most often left a pin-sized hole in the corrugated cardboard.

The cut slit method created the insert numbers by cutting small slits in the corrugated cardboard.

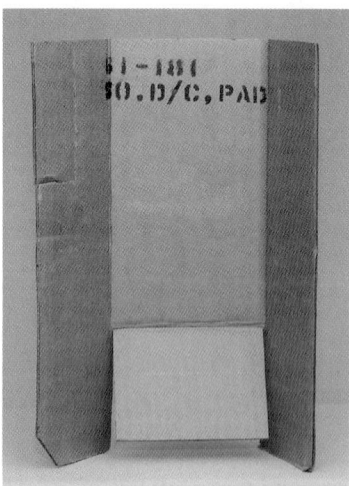

The printed writing method describes how insert manufacturers marked a bundle of inserts. The topmost insert was stamped or handwritten with the insert number. This example is also marked using the dot embossing method.

Lionel would also make its own inserts by modifying other inserts in inventory. Insert no. 64-121X was a modified version of insert no. 64-121, as described in the interoffice memo for outfit no. 19510 from 1966. Another interesting example is the insert the Lionel created for outfit no. D-19239 from 1963. At first glance, this insert appears to have been hastily put together with boxing

tape by somebody other than Lionel. After reading the Outfit Packing Memo and comparing it to insert no. 61-391, this insert can be appreciated as a creative reuse of old inventory.

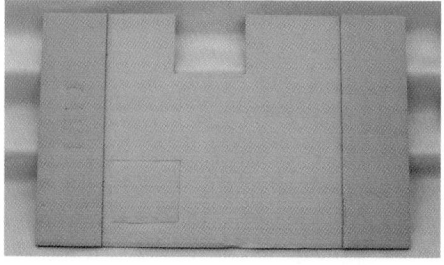

Insert no. 64-121.

Insert no. 64-121X is a modified (by the Metal Slitting Department) no. 64-121.

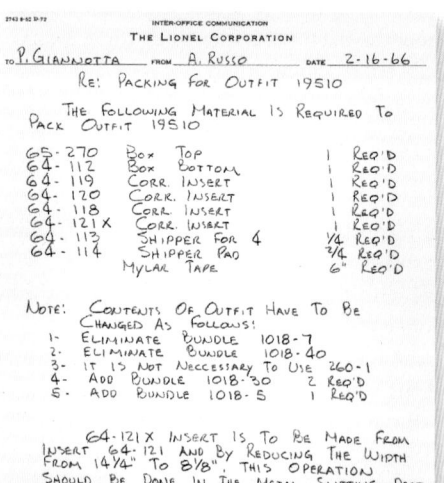

The interoffice memo with instructions on how to create a no. 64-121X insert.

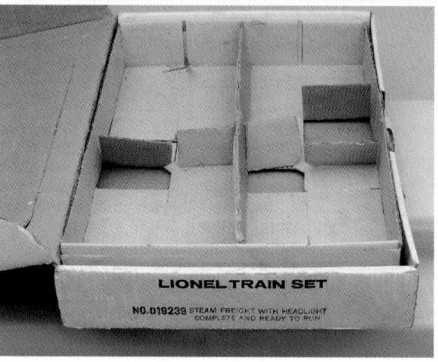

The insert in outfit no. D-19239 appears to be put together using common boxing tape by somebody other than Lionel.

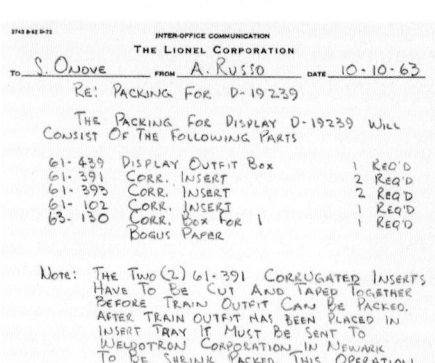

The Lionel memo instructing how to create the insert for outfit no. D-19239.

One of the no. 61-391 inserts used in creating the insert for outfit no. D-19239.

Manufacturer Markings and Dating

The same outfit box was often manufactured in multiple styles by numerous manufacturers. Their Box Manufacturer's Certificate (BMC) identifies these manufacturers. A BMC is the circular logo and all data therein stating that the box has met the Uniform Freight Classification Rule 41 as set forth by the railroads. It was required to include the manufacturer's name, city and state. Any box shipped via rail or truck (trucking firms adhered to these rail standards) required a BMC.

As for Lionel, a BMC was included on all RSCs and some display outfit boxes. Along with the BMC, manufacturers sometimes printed their own part number, the individual and crew who printed the box and other internal box classifications.

 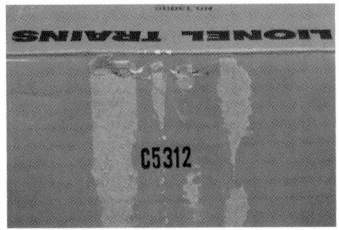

Left: Outfit box no. 61-180 used for outfit no. 19430 also included manufacturer information on the "crew" that printed the box. Right: Outfit box no. 61-250 used for outfit no. 13008 also included other manufacturer markings.

Some boxes, such as the popular no. 61-170, were manufactured by at least three manufacturers: Owens-Illinois, United Container and St. Joe Paper Company.

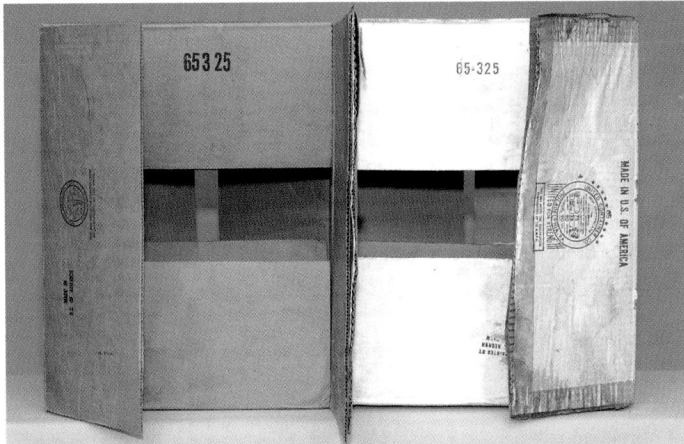

Shown are two examples of boxes used for the 1965 version of outfit no. 12780. Both have the same "65-325" box number found on the inside bottom flap; however, on the left is a Tan RSC manufactured by Gem-Bilt Container and on the right is a White RSC manufactured by United Container.

Other valuable outfit information can be obtained from changes in Box Manufacturing Certificates. It appears in 1963 that box manufacturers were required to add additional information to their BMCs describing the minimum combined weight facings ("Min Comb Wt Facings"). This changed the number of lines of data on the BMC from three to four. This fourth line of data provides a quick visual means to determine whether a box is from 1963 or later.

In 1964, some of Lionel's manufacturers stamped their boxes as compliant with the NMFC (National Motor Freight Classification as set forth by the National Motor Freight Association) requirements as well. The addition of these trucking industry requirements is another way of quickly identifying boxes manufactured in 1964 and later.

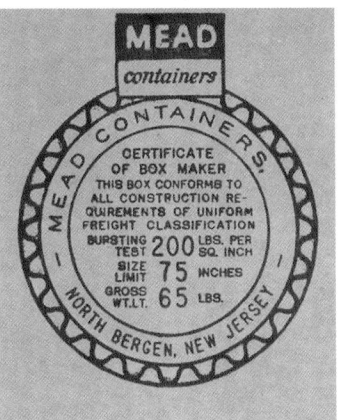 

Left: The three lines of data version of a box manufacturing certificate indicates a pre-1963 outfit box. Shown is box no. 61-385 used with outfit no. X-658. Right: The four lines of data version of a box manufacturing certificate indicates a 1963 or later outfit box. Shown is box no. 66-159 used with outfit no. 19583. Also note the "NMFC" information, which indicates that the box is from 1964 or later.

In many cases, the box manufacturers also printed information that details when a box was manufactured. Thomas S. Rollo (assisted by Paul V. Ambrose) analyzed this dating information in "A String of Orange," an essay published in the out-of-print second volume of *Greenberg's Guide to Lionel Trains, 1945-1969*. There, Rollo and Ambrose define the "Dot and Year" and the "Month-Year" dating system for dating boxes

Dot and Year Dating System

The dot and year dating system provides a way for box manufactures to keep track of when their boxes were manufactured. The system uses a series of dots, numbers or stars to indicate the month that a box was manufactured. Lionel's boxes were printed using a letterpress printing process that used rubber or polymer plates with a raised version of the image to be printed.

The plates would begin with all 12 months of the year represented by the numerals 1 through 12 or 12 dots or stars. As each month passed, the dot, star or number would likely be ground off the plate to indicate that a month had passed. Therefore, January would have 12 marks and December only one.

In some cases, the year was also shown on the outfit box. If so, it was indicated as either a two-digit number representing the decade and year or a single-digit number for the year. Four examples of dot and year dating system include: Stars, Dots, Numbers and No date shown.

MADE IN U.S. OF AMERICA

66-108

Lionel part no. 66-108 is for outfit no. 12850 from 1966. Since it has seven stars, this would most likely indicate it was manufactured in June (5 stars ground off). The year 1966 is represented by the "66" at the top of the United Container logo. The original memo from the Outfit Packing Department outlining the need for a no. 66-108 box for no. 12850 is dated 3-30-66. This means at least two months elapsed from the time Lionel engineered the box until the time it was manufactured. The "3" signifies a gross weight limit of 65 pounds.

Left: This Owens-Illinois example (Lionel part no. 60-575 for outfit no. X-573NA from 1960) demonstrates the dot system. Seven dots indicate a June manufacturing date. No year information is printed on this outfit box. The "012" is assumed to be an Owens-Illinois number. Many boxes for Owens-Illinois are marked with "012" or "9012". Right: St. Joe Paper Company utilized numbers to represent the months. This example (Lionel part no. 60-495 for outfit no. X-519NA from 1960) with "8 9 10 11 12" indicates an August manufacturing date. No year information is shown on the bottom of the box. Other St. Joe boxes have been observed with a one-digit number representing the year.

United Container did not stamp any dating information on this no. 61-170 box for outfit no. 19432 from 1965. The numeral "3" appears to be an internal United Container numbering system to signify the box weight specification. It has nothing to do with the year the box was made. A "3" or "3S" box is rated for a gross weight limit of 65 pounds whereas a "4" is 90 pounds.

Month-Year Dating System

The month-year dating system is another method used by manufactures to track when their boxes were manufactured. This system uses the number of the month followed by the two-digit representation of the year.

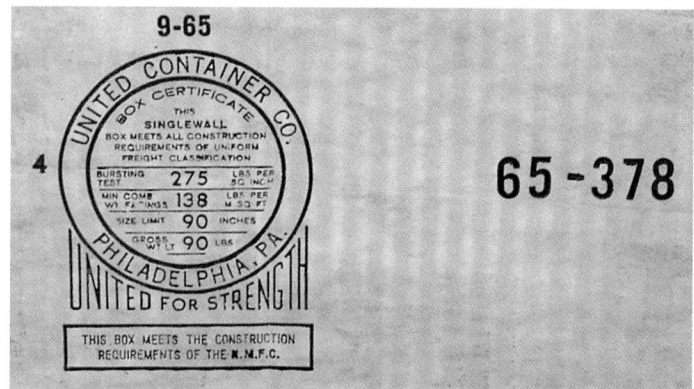

Outfit box no. 65-378 is for Sears outfit no. 9834 from 1965 (Lionel no. 19453). This United Container box is marked "9-65" or September 1965. Also note that the "4", as with other United Container boxes, represents a box rated for 90 pounds.

As a summary, from 1959 through 1969 box manufacturers primarily used the following dating methods.

Box Manufacturer	Dating Method
Bell Container	No date markings
Concora Products	No date markings
Continental Can Company, Inc.	Dots, two-digit year
Diversified Packaging Products Corp.	No date markings
Eastern Corrugated	No date markings
Express Container	No date markings
Gem-Bilt	Month year, or no date markings
Kraft Corrugated	No date markings
Mead Containers	No date markings
Owens Illinois	Dots, stars or no date markings
Robbins Container Corp.	No date markings
St. Joe Paper Company	Numbers for months, one-digit year or no date markings
St. Joe Kraft Paper Company	No date markings
Star	Month-year or no date markings
United Container, Co.	Stars, dots, month-year or no date markings

By fully understanding Lionel's box numbering system and manufacturer's markings, outfits can be accurately dated and variations identified. The individual outfit descriptions provided in this volume will highlight these variations.

Lionel's train outfits are, in the simplest terms, just a bundle of individual items (trains, track, maybe a transformer, and various peripheral items). The Production Planning and Scheduling Department (part of Production Control at the company's factory) and sales executives assigned each "bundle" an outfit number.

Outfit numbers were then used internally and externally. Internally, they were used by Lionel's supervisors and personnel, along with distributors and direct customers, to identify, order and invoice train outfits. Externally, outfit numbers made it possible for various customers to create wish lists as they perused Lionel's annual catalogs. After all, these numbers might be the only way for consumers long ago and collectors today to identify the contents of a particular outfit.

This section details the three distinct catalog outfit and promotional outfit numbering systems that Lionel used from 1959 through 1969. The earliest system is defined in this volume as "traditional" outfit numbering, and it lasted through 1961, although some carryover has been detected into 1963. From 1962 through 1969, "Five-Digit" outfit numbering was the norm. Overlapping both of these periods was "customer specific" numbering.

Outfit Numbering System	Years in Use
Traditional	1959 - 1961 with some carryover into 1963
Five-Digit	1962 - 1969
Customer Specific	Used as needed from 1959 - 1969 for specific outfits

To fully comprehend Lionel's approach to outfit numbering, it is helpful to understand both catalog and promotional outfit numbering.

Catalog Outfits

Catalog Outfit Traditional Numbering: 1959 - 1961

From 1959 through 1961, Lionel used traditional numbering for catalog outfits: four digits combined with an optional letter suffix to define an outfit. This system was intelligent in that an outfit's number provided information about its contents.

For example, if the outfit number began with "1", it was an O27 outfit. If it began with "2" it was a Super O outfit. Lionel did not catalog O gauge outfits from 1958 through 1963, but in previous years they also began with "1". In 1959 and 1960, outfits whose fourth digit was even were passenger outfits; those that ended with an odd number were freight outfits. By 1961, however, the last number had lost its significance because Lionel incremented each new outfit number sequentially.

Another key point relates to the fact that each year, Lionel numbered new outfits with a higher number than it had ended the previous year. For example, the last cataloged O27 outfit in 1960 was no. 1640W and the first outfit in 1961 was no. 1641. Super O outfits followed the same pattern.

In 1959 and 1960, Lionel used suffixes to signify motive power features, specifically:
- W - Whistle
- WS - Whistle and Smoke
- S - Smoke

By 1961, whistle and smoke designations had disappeared (except for carryover outfit no. 2528WS) and the following suffixes were used:
- C - Conventional boxing (another term for RSC – Regular Slotted Carton)
- NE – Used on only outfit no. 1649. This most likely meant "North East" or "New England" (a point made by Paul V. Ambrose in the third volume of *Greenberg's Guide to Lionel Trains, 1945-1969*. He draws this conclusion from the fact that this outfit was headed by Boston & Maine Alco diesels.) Since the 1649NE never appeared in any Lionel catalog, it is classified as a promotional outfit.

Catalog Outfit Five-Digit Numbering: 1962 - 1963

Lionel purchased Porter Chemical Company in October 1961 and Spear Electronics two months later in December. In order to eliminate any conflict among these three companies' numbering systems, Lionel introduced a new five-digit numbering system in 1962 that lasted until the end of Lionel's postwar era in 1969.

OUTFIT CODING

Due to the acquisition of the Porter Chemical Co. and Spear Electronics, Lionel has had to revise its outfit numbers in such a manner as not to conflict with its other lines:

Every train outfit will have a five digit number. The first number will be a 1 which will indicate it is in the train category. The next three numbers will refer to the outfit number and the last digit will be the packing code.

The packing code is as follows:

No. 1, 2 and 3 – Display Pack
No. 4 – Display Box with Component Packing
No. 5 and 6 – Conventional Packing
No. 7 and 8 – Conventional Box with Component Packing.

For example–No. 11001. The 1 refers to a train outfit. The 100 refers to the outfit number and the 1 means it is Display Packed.

Lionel's 1962 advance catalog described the new five-digit number system.

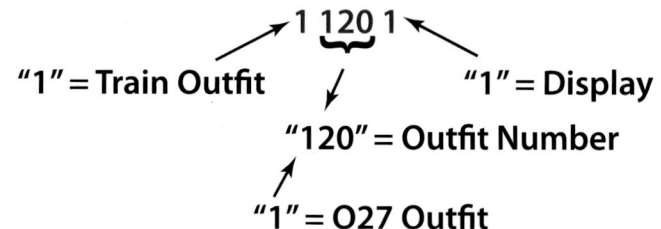

An internal memo from 1962 provides the full detail of the "Train Outfit Packing Code" (the fifth digit).

Five-Digit Numbering - Fifth Digit, 1962 – 1963	
Fifth Digit	**Description**
1	Display - Kraft (tan) Separators - Units Loose
2	Display - Colored Separators - Units Loose
3	Display - Die-Cut Platform - Units Loose
4	Display - Units Boxed
5	R.S.C. - Kraft (tan) - Units Loose
6	R.S.C. - Colored - Units Loose
7	R.S.C. - Kraft (tan) - Units Boxed
8	R.S.C. - Colored - Units Boxed
9	Display Box Inserted in R.S.C. (HO)

1 **120** 1

"1" = Train Outfit   "1" = Display

"120" = Outfit Number

"1" = O27 Outfit

As an example, outfit no. 11201 is an O27 train outfit, display packed with Kraft separators and units loose (unboxed).

- First digit "1" - Train or Raceway
- Second through fourth digit "120" - Train outfit number with the "1" signifying O27
- Fifth digit "1" - Display with Kraft (tan) separators and units loose

Whereas, outfit no. 11205, with the last digit as "5", is the same outfit in a Kraft (tan) RSC with the units loose.

The five-digit system, like its predecessor, was intelligent in that it provided information on the contents of an outfit. For the first digit, "1" signified an electric train or raceway outfit, "2" for Porter and "4" for Spear. Even though this was a five-digit numbering system, only three digits (digits two through four) actually defined the outfit number.

This terminology was confusing in that both the entire five-digit number and the three middle digits (two through four) were referred to as the "outfit number". The final digit of the five-digit outfit number specified the type of packaging to be used.

Delving deeper into digits two through four (the three-digit outfit number), the first digit of the outfit number (second digit overall) signified the type of train or raceway outfit.

Five-Digit Numbering - Second Digit of Five, 1962 – 1963	
Second Digit of Five-Digit Outfit Number	**Description**
0	HO Promotional Outfit or O27 Promotional in 1969
1	O27 Outfit
2	Gift Pack in 1962 and then O in 1964 forward
3	Super O
4	HO Catalog
5	HO Advance Catalog
6	Raceway
7	Raceway
8	Not Used
9	Promotional O27 or Super O

When Lionel assigned the Gift Pack a "2" as the second digit in 1962, it assumed there would be additional gift packs. Also, it wasn't thinking about re-issuing O gauge outfits. Therefore, when Lionel reintroduced O gauge in 1964, the meaning of "2" as the second digit changed to indicate O gauge outfits. This designation continued through the end of the postwar period.

The fifth digit identified the type of outfit packing. It was referred to as the Train Outfit Packing Code.

Lionel adhered to this system consistently in 1962 and 1963. The only exceptions occurred with Super O outfits no. 13068 and no. 13088 from 1962 and no. 13148 from 1963. Having "8" as the fifth digit should have indicated that these outfits were packed in colored RSCs. However, they actually came in Kraft (tan) RSCs. Therefore, their fifth digit should have been "7".

Each year Lionel would begin numbering new outfits with a higher number than it had used the previous year For example, the last cataloged O27 outfit in 1962 was no. 11308 (its three-digit outfit number was "130") and the first outfit in 1963 was no. 11311 (its three-digit outfit number was "131"). O and Super O outfits followed the same rule.

Catalog Outfit Five-Digit Numbering: 1964 - 1969

This creative numbering system lasted only two years. In 1964, the meaning of the first through the fourth digits remained the same. However, a new packing specification "0" was added for the fifth digit to indicate "Regular Catalog Sets and Blister Displays". In addition, the packing specification "2" was changed to "M.O." to indicate "Mail Order" pack. This revised numbering system remained in place through 1969.

PACKING SPECIFICATION

0 - Regular Catalog Sets and Blister Display Sets

1 - Display - Kraft Separators - Units Loose

2 - ~~Display - Colored Separators - Units Loose~~ *M. O. PACK*

3 - Display - Die Cut Platform - Units Loose

4 - Display - Units Boxed

5 - RSC - Kraft - Units Loose

6 - RSC - Colored - Units Loose

7 - RSC - Kraft - Units Boxed

8 - RSC - Colored - Units Boxed

9 - Display Box Inserted in RSC

EXAMPLES OF CODE

CATALOG NO.	DESCRIPTION
11420	"027" Catalog Set - Three Car Freight.
11425	"027" Special Set. Same as #11420 except units loose and packed in RSC Box.
19325	"027" Special - Five Car Diesel Freight.
19900	"027" Blister Display Set - Five Car Freight.
16064	Standard Ga. Special Road Racing Set, units packed in Display Box.
16900	Standard Ga. Road Racing Set in Blister Display.

P. J. Giannotta

Lionel's use of the fifth digit (as shown in this Packing Specification memo) to indicate the type of packaging, lasted only two years. Lionel added the description, "0 - Regular Catalog Sets and Blister Display Sets", which became the norm for the last digit of cataloged outfit numbers.

Even though all the other codes still were available for the fifth digit, they lost their significance because they were not used. Every catalog outfit ended in "0". The problem with this numbering system was that it allowed for only 100 train outfits in a gauge. For example, hypothetical outfit 11990 (its three-digit outfit number is "199") would be the last available O27 outfit number possible before a change would have to be made. Lionel eventually would have run out of numbers, which would have necessitated a modification to this system.

Promotional Outfits

Promotional Outfit Traditional Numbering "X" Series: 1959 - 1961

From 1959 through 1961, with six carryover outfits in 1962, Lionel used traditional numbering for its promotional outfits. Each outfit number began with "X", followed by a dash and a three-digit outfit number. This outfit number was optionally followed by "NA" in 1959 and 1960. Promotional outfit numbers were assigned sequentially, beginning with a multiple of 100 each year, as with X-200 in 1959.

The series of traditional outfit numbers used for promotional outfits from 1959 through 1962 includes:

Traditional Outfit "X" Series Numbering, 1959 - 1962		
Year	Outfit Number Start	Outfit Number End
1959	X-200	X-232
	X-800	X-888
1960	X-240	
	X-500NA	X-586NA
	Some X-800 Series Carryover	
1961	X-600	X-699
	X-700	X-720
1962	Some X-600 Series Carryover	
	Some X-700 Series Carryover	

The meaning of suffix NA has not been fully deciphered. Postwar collectors generally take it to stand for "No Advertising" or "No Allowance". This meant that retailers would not receive a monetary rebate for local newspaper and similar promotional expenses submitted to Lionel as they would with catalog outfits.

The origins of NA can be traced to NAA, which first appeared in 1958 with a few X-600 series outfits (X-610NAA, X-612NAA, X-644X NAA, etc). Lionel may have started out with "No Advertising Allowance" or NAA and then shortened it to NA in 1959.

The suffix NA appeared on less than one third of the 1959 X-800 series outfits. The last year that NA appeared was 1960, when only eight out of 86 X-500 series outfits did not have it. The eight outfits lacking an NA suffix were originally slated to be made in smaller quantities and so probably would have incurred lower advertising allowances, which Lionel might have been willing to provide to enable retailers to reach buyers of these outfits.

Why the NA suffix would be stamped on the box is another mystery. One theory is that Lionel could determine whether a dealer was incorrectly requesting an advertising allowance simply by looking at the outfit numbers in the advertisement. If the outfit had an NA, the request was not valid.

Another hypothesis is that for internal accounting purposes, Lionel needed to ensure that advertising dollars were not allocated to these outfits. Adding the NA suffix made it easy to do so.

Promotional Outfit Traditional Numbering Four-Digit Series: 1959 - 1961

Advance catalog outfits were defined by Lionel as non-catalog or promotional outfits. From 1959 through 1961, with outfit no. 1123 carrying over through 1963, Lionel used traditional numbering for advance catalog promotional outfits in which four digits, combined with an optional letter suffix, defined an outfit. Lionel used the same system for catalog outfits, with each number also providing information about an outfit's contents.

All advance catalog outfits were O27, and their number began with "1". As for the fourth digit, in 1959 and 1960, all outfits ended in an odd number and were freight trains. This convention disappeared in 1961, when Lionel just incremented each new outfit number sequentially.

Each year Lionel began numbering new outfits with a higher number from the previous year. For example, the final advance catalog promotional outfit in 1960 was no. 1109 and the first advance catalog outfit in 1961 was no. 1123.

From 1961 through 1963, Lionel used suffixes to specify differences in packaging or to signify whether an outfit was promotional:

- C - Conventional boxing (another term for RSC)
- P - Used to identify a promotional version (outfit no. 1124 became no. 1124P)

Promotional Outfit Five-Digit Numbering: 1962 - 1969

Promotional outfits followed the same reasoning used with catalog outfits for implementing the five-digit numbering system, namely, to eliminate the conflict of numbering systems caused by the acquisition of Porter and Spear. As with catalog outfits, the five-digit system was in place from 1962 through 1969.

For promotional outfits, Lionel used three different versions of the five-digit numbering system. One version mirrored that used with catalog outfits. Then there was one for promotional outfits only. The third was a hybrid of both that used suffixes to augment the five-digit system.

Promotional Outfit Five-Digit Numbering 10xxx, 11xxx, 12xxx and 13xxx Series: 1962 - 1969

The first version of the five-digit numbering systems followed that used for catalog outfits. It was used for advance catalog promotional outfits, customer specific RSC versions of catalog outfits (Retailer Promotional outfits) and some O and Super O outfits. The tables in the catalog outfit numbering section provide an overview of the digits used in this numbering system.

"1" = Train Outfit   **1 100 1**   **"1" = Display**

"100" = Outfit Number

"1" = O27 Outfit

As an example, advance catalog outfit no. 11001 is an O27 train outfit, display packed with Kraft separators and units loose (unboxed).

- First digit "1" - Train or Raceway
- Second through fourth digit "100" - Train outfit number with the "1" signifying O27
- Fifth digit "1" - Display with Kraft (tan) separators and units loose

Whereas, outfit no. 11005 with the last digit as "5" is the same outfit in a Kraft (tan) RSC with the units loose.

Another example, outfit no. 11315, is an O27 train outfit. It is the RSC version of catalog display outfit no. 11311 made specifically for Philco.

Other O27 promotional outfits manufactured in 1964 or later also followed the same changes to the fifth digit as used with catalog outfits (see Packing Specification memo shown earlier). These include no. 11570, no. 11580 and no. 11620, all of which end with "0", and no. 11482, which ends with "2" to signify mail-order packing.

Lionel also manufactured O and Super O promotional outfits in 1964 and assigned them outfit numbers in the same style as catalog outfits. All were made in extremely small quantities, and most were bulk-packed. The fifth digit being "5" or "7" on these outfits meant they most likely were packed in RSCs. One example is O gauge outfit no. 12807 from 1964:

- First digit "1" - Train or Raceway
- Second through fourth digit "280" - Train outfit number, with "2" signifying O gauge
- Fifth digit "7" - By definition should mean Kraft RSC with units boxed. These items were bulk-packed.

Another example is Super O outfit no. 13255 (second digit is "3"), whose three-digit number is "325".

In 1969, two O27 outfits were numbered 106xx, followed by suffix "SF". The first digit is the only one that adheres to the five-digit numbering system. The other digits defined the specific outfit number. The meaning of the suffix has yet to be determined.

Promotional Outfit Five-Digit Numbering 19xxx Series: 1962 - 1967

The second and most common version of the five-digit outfit numbering system for promotional outfits used "19" as the first two digits. The remaining three digits were incremented through the year as Lionel assigned final outfit numbers. Lionel began 1962 with promotional outfit number 19000 in July. The next outfit number jumped to no. 19100 in August and followed sequentially through no. 19206 in November. Lionel began 1963 with outfit no. 19210 and incremented the remainder of the outfits throughout the year. The "19" numbers were used for both O27 and Super O promotional outfits.

Excluding carryover, outfits ending in suffixes or outfits assigned a number but not made until the subsequent year, the range of 19xxx numbers include:

Five-Digit 19xxx Promotional Outfit Numbering		
Year	Outfit Number Start	Outfit Number End
1962	19000	19206
1963	19210	19324
1964	19325	19419
1965	19426	19455
1966	19500	19590
1966	19910	19920
1967	19701	19707

Promotional Outfit Five-Digit Numbering With Suffixes: 1962 - 1969

The final version of five-digit outfit numbering for promotional outfits supplements the first two. It clarifies how Lionel appended suffixes to five-digit catalog and promotional outfit numbers.

Production planning of hundreds of train outfits was a complex process, one made even more difficult by the frequent acceptance of any customer demand in the 1960's. This situation wreaked havoc on the outfit numbering process. Suffixes allowed the Production Planning and Scheduling Department to create new outfits without assigning an entirely new base outfit number.

Most often the suffix indicated some change or derivation of the composition of the original five-digit outfit. At other times, the new outfit with a suffix had no correlation to the original outfit.

One use of suffixes indicated differences in packaging. An outfit might originally have been packaged for mail order to satisfy a customer's direct mail business. The same customer might have also wanted the outfit to display and sell in its retail stores. Lionel assigned a five-digit number to the outfit and appended unique suffixes for each form of packaging. Stokely-Van Camp no. 19142 from 1962 illustrates this trend. The base outfit was mail-order packing; "-50" indicated display, and "-100" indicated standard RSC packaging.

Lionel might sell the same outfit to different retailers and change only the suffix of the outfit's number. The customer imagined that it was receiving something unique, and Lionel did not have to create an entirely new outfit.

Outfits sold in one year would also be used as the basis for a new outfit in subsequent years. These new outfits were exactly the same or a derivation of the original outfit. Lionel used a suffix to make it appear that this was a new outfit.

As an example of this trend, outfit no. 19240 from 1963 for Sterns Stores (dated May 7, 1963) was also sold to Kings Department Stores in October and given a "-500" suffix. Another outfit, no. 11385-500 was a promotional outfit for Maritz based on cataloged outfit no. 11385. Stokely-Van Camp 1962 outfit no. 19142 was slightly modified and sold in 1963 to two other customers. D.O. Klein purchased it as outfit no. 19142-500, and Richie Premium bought it as no. 19142-502.

The allocation of "19" series numbers could be exhausted during a year. Late in the year, the Production Planning and Scheduling Department might already have started assigning numbers for next year. In such an instance, Lionel would add suffixes to existing outfit numbers that had little or nothing in common with the original outfit.

For example, in 1963 Lionel issued outfit numbers 11341-500, 11361-500 and 11375-500. Two of them had no correlation to their cataloged equivalents. The previous year, two outfits (nos. 19203X and 19204X) had followed the same reasoning. This was a very confusing use of suffixes.

Outfits were sometimes pulled forward in the production cycle, and Lionel would cannibalize other partially fulfilled outfit orders to meet the demand. When it came time to finish filling the original outfit order, individual items might be out of stock. This situation led to the creation of similar yet not identical variations of the original outfit. In these cases, Lionel would merely assign a suffix to the outfit number to indicate the variation.

The no. 19350 series of outfits from 1964 and 1965 provide an example of suffixes assigned because of item substitutions and the inability to meet customer requirements. Outfit no. 19350 was the original outfit. When Lionel moved up the promise date, it created outfit no. 19350-500 as a substitution for no. 19350. Later in 1965, an additional order apparently resulted in a slight change to the outfit and the creation of another suffix, no. 19350-501.

		Table 1 - "19" Series Suffixes	
Yr	Suffix	Description	Example
1962	-50	Display version of base outfit.	No. 19142-50 was display version of no. 19142.
	-100	RSC non-mailer version of base outfit.	No. 19142 regularly came in a mail-order version; no. 19142-100 was regular tan RSC version.
	X	Creation of new number because all other numbers exhausted. No correlation to base outfit.	No. 19203X was assigned late in the year. It has no correlation to outfit no. 19203.
	(1) or (2)	Different items boxed versus unboxed, within the outfit.	Nos. 19201 (1) and 19201 (2). These were the same outfit, one with engines boxed, and the other with them unboxed.
1963	-500	Create new number because base numbers exhausted. No correlation to base outfit.	No. 9730-500 was a renumbered no. 19304. It has no correlation to outfit no. 9730.
		General Release version of outfit.	No. 19228-500 was a General Release version of Automotive's no. 19228.
		Outfit sold to another customer.	No. 19240-500 was sold to Kings and no. 19240 to Sterns.
	-501	Create new number because base numbers exhausted. No correlation to base outfit.	No. 19238-501 has no correlation to 19238.
		Outfit sold to another customer.	No. 19229-501, which was subsequently canceled, was the LA Sales version of no. 19229.
		General Release version of outfit.	No. 19233-501, which was subsequently canceled, was the General Release version of Goldblatt's no. 19233.
	-502	Outfit sold to another customer.	No. 19142-502 was Van Camp no. 19142 from 1962 and sold to Richie Premium.
		General Release version of outfit.	No. 19229-502 was the General Release version of Automotive's no. 19229.
	-501X	Outfit sold to another customer.	No. 19229-501X sold to Noah's Ark was based on no. 19229 for Automotive Customers.
	A	Different boxing.	No. 19317A came in a different box than no. 19317.
1964	-500	Substitution of outfit contents created substitute outfit number.	No. 19350 and no. 19350-500 both were for S&H. Different items included in the outfit created the -500 outfit substitution.
		Outfit sold to another customer.	No. 19363-500 sold to Lazarus was based on 19363 sold to Interstate White-Front.
		Mail-order version of outfit.	No. 19334-500 was mail-order version of no. 19334.
1965	-500	Substitution of outfit contents created substitute outfit number.	No. 19350 and no. 19350-500 both were for S&H. Different items included in the outfit created the -500 outfit substitution.
		Mail-order version of outfit.	No. 19334-500 was the mail-order version of no. 19334.
	-501	Substitution of outfit contents created substitute outfit number.	Nos. 19350 and 19350-501 both were for S&H. Different items included in the outfit created the -501 outfit substitution.
	-502	Mail-order version of outfit.	Many outfits in 1965 included mail-order versions. No. 19437 was display and no. 19437-502 was mail-order packaged.
1966	-500	Additional items changed outfit contents.	No. 19567-500 added cutouts to outfit no. 19567.

Table 2 - "11" and "12" Series Suffixes			
Yr	Suffix	Description	Example
1963	-500	Create new number because base numbers exhausted. No correlation to base outfit.	No. 11341-500 has no correlation to no. 11341.
1963	-500	RSC version of cataloged outfit.	Spiegel no. 11351-500 is the RSC version of cataloged outfit no. 11351.
1963	X	Cataloged outfit turned into promotional.	No. 11311X is no. 11311 sold to Army Post Exchanges (PX's).
1964	-500	Cataloged outfit turned into promotional.	No. 11385-500 for Maritz is based on cataloged outfit no. 11385.
1965	-500	Cataloged outfit turned into promotional.	No. 11520-500 is promotional version of no. 11520.
1965	-100	Addition of suffix to move excess inventory of cataloged outfits.	No. 12820-100 is based on catalog outfit no. 12820 with minor substitutions and different boxing.
1966	X	Addition of suffix to move excess inventory of cataloged outfits.	No. 12850X is catalog outfit no. 12850 with minor substitutions and issued late in the year.
1969	SF	Still to be determined.	Nos. 10613SF and 10653SF end in SF.

Outfits that made it to the Factory Order stage could still be canceled or their quantities changed. Lionel would often attempt to sell canceled outfits to other customers. If successful, it would sometimes create a new number by adding a suffix to the old number.

When quantities were decreased, Lionel often added a suffix to the number and sold these excess outfits as General Release Promotionals. When outfit no. 19314 from 1963 was canceled, Lionel managed to sell 60 outfits to Wm. H. Block that it designated as no. 19314-500. The remaining 1,040 outfits were assigned no. 11341-500.

Another example is outfit no. 19234, which had an original quantity of 2,000 on May 24, 1963. On November 14, this amount was cut to 400. A week later, on November 21, Lionel created General Release Promotional outfit no. 19234-500 to reallocate 600 of the excess.

Catalog outfits were made promotional items merely by adding a suffix to the catalog number. Outfit nos. 11520, 11540 and 11560 are all examples of Lionel adding "-500". They were then sold to a specific customer or became General Release Promotionals.

The same method of adding a suffix also served as a means of dumping excess inventory. The 1966 outfit nos. 11540X, 11560X, 12710X, 12800X and 12850X were created late in the year (November 4) to move product. They are very close to their cataloged counterparts.

The meaning of these suffixes changed from year to year, but they were used fairly consistently within a particular year. Suffixes also differed if they were appended to "19" series or "11" and "12" series of numbers. Tables 1 and 2 provide a summary of suffixes used by year.

Customer Specific Numbering: 1959 - 1965

For promotional outfits made from 1959 through 1965, Lionel sometimes provided outfits stamped with only a specific customer number. This practice would allow a customer to match its own retail numbering system.

Sears was by far the largest purchaser of promotional outfits. Its numbering system used 9000-series numbers with outfits numbered sequentially in each catalog: 9600 Series (1959 through 1962), 9700 Series (1963 and 1967) and 9800 Series (1964 through 1966).

Lionel used the same numbers internally to identify these outfits. It wasn't until 1963 that Lionel began the switch to five-digit numbers both internally and externally for Sears. Other customers for whom Lionel used only the customer number on the outfit included Firestone and Channel Master. By 1966, Lionel no longer provided outfits uniquely numbered with a customer's number.

Dual Numbered With Lionel (Traditional or Five-Digit) and Customer Number

Customers commonly requested to have their retail number provided along with the Lionel number on outfit boxes. From 1960 through 1966, numerous train outfits included both a Lionel outfit number and a customer number.

Summary of Outfit Numbering Systems by Year					
Year	Traditional Only	Traditional & Customer Number	Five-Digit Only	Five-Digit & Customer Number	Customer Number Only
1959	x				x
1960 - 1961	x	x			x
1962	Carryover		x	x	x
1963 - 1965			x	x	x
1966			x	x	
1967 - 1969			x		

Undocumented Outfits

Even with all the documentation used to compile this volume, there were still a few outfits observed that could not be substantiated. Take, for example, outfit no. 244. Several original examples of this steam freight outfit have been observed. However, no Factory Order or other Lionel documentation exists for this outfit. In fact, the only reference to it appears in a listing put out by Madison Hardware after its inventory had been purchased by Richard Kughn in 1989 and moved to Detroit. Such a listing obviously

MADISON HARDWARE C.
1915 W. Fort Street
Detroit, MI 48216-1017

LIONEL TRAIN SETS	QUANTITY	YEAR MADE
244	2	N/A

One of the first lists of outfits available for sale from the Madison Hardware Co. in Detroit included a quantity of 2 of the no. 244.

means that this outfit was in stock. The outfit box comes from 1964, and the components are from 1962 or earlier. The number "244" most likely was selected because of the motive power.

Other promotional outfits with similarly styled and stamped boxes have been observed. All of these outfits were hand-stamped using a commonly available number-dial, flat-band rubber stamp. Blank outfit boxes were available during the 1960's. Therefore, it can be assumed that these custom outfits were assembled and numbered by larger stores or distributors (including Madison Hardware) or were special outfits created by Lionel. These outfits and similar ones explain why research is a never-ending process.

Outfits such as no. 244 were likely assembled and numbered by larger stores or distributors such as Madison Hardware Company.

Trucks and Couplers

Following World War II, Lionel had the opportunity to make major changes to its entire product line. One of these changes was the transition from the prewar tinplate truck and box coupler to a realistic die-cast truck and knuckle coupler assembly. Over the next 25 years of the postwar era, Lionel made numerous improvements and versions of the truck and coupler assembly.

Fortunately for collectors, Lionel took pride in the servicing of its products. That's the reason most truck and coupler assemblies are described in Lionel's Service Station Manuals and other documentation. Combining this information with observations and previous research led to the summary in this section of the eight major types of trucks and couplers used by Lionel between 1945 and 1969. It should be noted that there are numerous minor variations in axles, wheels, rivets, pickup shoes, rollers and more within each of these categories. The majority of these variations are outside the scope of this volume.

Why should collectors care about such little details as trucks and couplers? To start, a thorough understanding of them sheds light on how Lionel designed and manufactured its trains during the postwar era, always striving to make them in more efficient and less costly ways. For example, moving from staple-end to bar-end trucks likely led to labor savings. Staple-end trucks had side truck frames that were attached in a two-step process (one for each side). The design of bar-end trucks eliminated a step in the process, as both frames could be attached simultaneously. The plastic trucks introduced in 1957 further reduced both labor and material costs while enhancing the detail of the side frame. Another example of Lionel's seeking to reduce expenses involved replacing one or both operating couplers with a less expensive non-operating coupler.

A second reason for focusing on trucks and couplers is that these critical parts help collectors identify items and determine when they were manufactured. A key change occurred in late 1951, when Lionel adopted bar-end trucks. Any item equipped with those trucks must, logically, have been made no earlier than the end of 1951.

Combining this information with other characteristics detailed in this section, such as the date that mounting clips were used and armature tabs first appeared, helps narrow down the exact date an item was produced. The changes to trucks and coupler assemblies could appear in later years as Lionel depleted inventory or the feature was just carried over, but the converse cannot be true. Thus a no. 6473 Rodeo Car with AAR trucks and couplers with open journal boxes on the operating truck and coupler was made in 1965 or later because open journal boxes on operating trucks and couplers first appeared in 1965.

More than simply dating a model, trucks and couplers may be the only way to properly identify an item. Consider the unmarked Turbo Missile Firing Car. When equipped with two non-operating trucks and couplers, it is known as a no. 3309-25. When found with one operating and one non-operating truck and coupler, it is a no. 3349-100. And when seen with two operating trucks and couplers, it can be either a no. 3349-1 (boxed) or a no. 3349-25 (unboxed).

Other models have truck and coupler variations that did not always result in a change to their number or the addition of a suffix. If an item spanned more than one year, Lionel simply manufactured it with the then-current truck and coupler combination. Since there was no change to the item's overall design, Lionel did not always assign it a new suffix.

The no. 6414 Automobile Transport Car exemplifies this trend. Lionel cataloged this freight car from 1955 through 1966. The model's truck and coupler variations include bar-end with a pivot stud, AAR with metal knuckles and AAR with Delrin® (DuPont's trade name for its plastic) knuckles with either closed or open journal boxes. All of these variations have the same 6414-1 number and suffix. It wasn't until 1963, when the Production Control File for the 6414 indicated that intended production was one operating and one non-operating truck and coupler, that Lionel changed the suffix, and the no. 6414-150 was introduced. Further changes in the suffixes added to the 6414 signified different loads and boxing, as well as trucks and couplers. This knowledge, combined with the dating of trucks and couplers, is the only practical way to complete a full, year-by-year, collection of 6414s.

Collectors, alerted to the importance of trucks and couplers, should also be aware that these parts can be repaired, modified, and replaced. Trucks and couplers took a punishment on many train layouts and are among the most common item repaired. Whoever fixed or replaced them probably didn't care about making sure the proper parts were used; what mattered was getting the car up and running again.

But collectors do need to care. If a truck or coupler does not seem correct or follow the progression explained in this section, then it may have been repaired or replaced. Such a part, especially one that is "too early" for a particular car, will confuse its dating and reduce its value.

DATING POSTWAR TRUCKS AND COUPLERS
STAPLE-END AND SCOUT TRUCKS

| 1945 | 1946 | 1947 | 1948 | 1949 | 1950 | 1951 | 1952 | - | 1955 |

STAPLE-END TRUCKS

STAPLE-END TRUCKS
METAL FRAME TRUCKS
WITH DIE-CAST "STAPLE" ATTACHED SIDES

From 1945 through 1951, metal frame trucks with die-cast sides were used for rolling stock. The die-cast sides were attached to the truck's metal frame so that when viewed from the side, it appeared that they were stapled together. Staple-end trucks first appeared with coil couplers and later with magnetic couplers.

STAPLE-END TRUCKS WITH COIL COUPLERS

Two versions of staple-end coil couplers exist. They are categorized by the way the coupler was attached to the truck.

Swedging - An operation to attach the base plate to the coupler. Used on all metal trucks.

Staking - First appeared in late 1946.

From 1945 through mid 1946, the coil coupler was attached to the metal coupler bracket.

From mid 1946 through 1948, the coil coupler was attached to a bottom frame assembly which was then attached to the trucks.

BAR-END
COIL COUPLERS

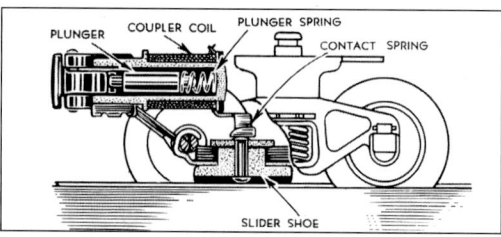

PLUNGER COUPLER COIL PLUNGER SPRING CONTACT SPRING SLIDER SHOE

From 1945 through 1948, couplers were opened by an electromagnet whose coil was integrated on the coupler, hence the name "coil coupler". Electricity passes from the track to the slider shoe. When activated, the plunger spring contracts, thereby pulling the plunger back and releasing the knuckle.

STAPLE-END TRUCKS WITH MAGNETIC COUPLERS

STAPLE-END
MAGNETIC COUPLERS

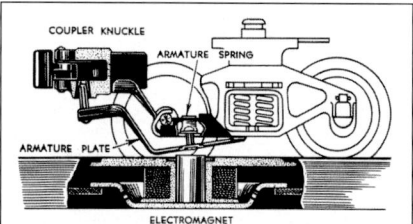

COUPLER KNUCKLE ARMATURE SPRING ARMATURE PLATE ELECTROMAGNET

From 1948 through 1951, couplers were opened by an electromagnet in the uncoupling track section. When the track section was activated, the truck's metal armature plate was pulled down, thus releasing the knuckle.

Flared end of rivet is visible. This feature appeared from 1948 into 1950.

From 1948 through 1951, staple-end trucks used magnetic couplers.

SCOUT TRUCKS

SCOUT TRUCKS
METAL FRAME TRUCKS
WITH PLASTIC SIDES

From 1948 through 1952, metal frame trucks with plastic sides were used for low-end starter outfits known as "Scout" outfits. The coupler on these trucks was not compatible with regular postwar knuckle couplers. Scout couplers can be converted to magnetic knuckle couplers by adding a no. 480-25 magnetic coupler conversion kit.

SEMI-SCOUT TRUCKS
METAL FRAME TRUCKS
WITH PLASTIC SIDES
NOT SHOWN

From 1952 through 1955, metal frame trucks with plastic sides and a "coupler frame complete" attached to the trucks were used in a few low-end starter outfits. This allowed Scout-style truck frames to be compatible with regular postwar knuckle couplers.

DATING POSTWAR TRUCKS AND COUPLERS
BAR-END TRUCKS

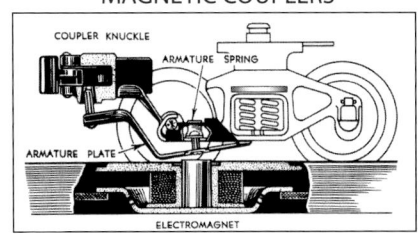

BAR-END TRUCKS
METAL FRAME TRUCKS
WITH DIE-CAST "BAR" ATTACHED SIDES

BAR-END
MAGNETIC COUPLERS

From late 1951 through 1961 and 1969, metal frame trucks with die-cast sides were used for rolling stock. The die-cast sides were attached to the metal frame via a process that resembled a bar sticking through the side of the truck. Bar-end trucks always came with magnetic couplers. Two major variations exist based on how the truck was attached to the frame: either by a pivot stud or mounting clip.

From 1957 through 1961, bar-end trucks were being replaced with plastic AAR trucks. Only a few newly issued items appeared with bar-end trucks in 1958. From 1959 through 1961, bar-end trucks were used for newly issued operating cars requiring sliding pickup shoes and some items requiring roller pickup shoes. This occurred because the AAR pickup shoe replacement was not yet available and the roller pickup version was in transition.

All bar-end couplers were opened by an electromagnet in the uncoupling track section. When the track section was activated, the truck's metal armature plate was pulled down, thus releasing the knuckle.

Pivot stud

From late 1951 through 1961, bar-end trucks were attached to the frame using a pivot stud. The pivot stud was held in place by a horseshoe shaped retaining washer.

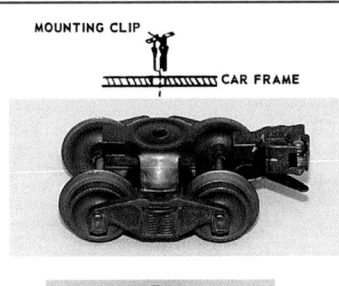

MOUNTING CLIP

CAR FRAME

From 1955 through 1958 and 1969, bar-end trucks were attached to the train's frame using a mounting clip. The mounting clip came in different sizes based on the frame thickness.

Round end of rivet is visible. This feature appeared from 1950 onward.

Truck Mounting Clips are made in three sizes to fit different car frames. For easy identification they are colored as shown

PART NO.	COLOR	"A"
6257-10	GREEN	.085
600-15	ALUMINUM	.100
1002-6	BLACK	.145

A hole in the armature plate appeared from late 1949 onward.

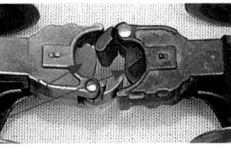

In 1957, a support hole was added to the coupler drawbar.

In 1953, couplers had a smooth knuckle top versus engraving.

In 1955, the armature assembly was changed adding a small tab to ease in manual uncoupling.

During late 1955, the knuckle pin changed from black to silver.

DATING POSTWAR TRUCKS AND COUPLERS
AAR (TIMKEN) TRUCKS

1957	1958	1959	1960	1961	1962	1963	1964	1965	1966 - 1969

AAR (TIMKEN) TRUCKS
PLASTIC FRAME TRUCKS

AAR TRUCKS

From 1957 through 1969, one-piece molded plastic trucks modeled after AAR (Association of American Railroads) trucks with Timken bearings were used. The trucks had Timken molded into the side and so are sometimes called Timken trucks.

AAR couplers were opened by an electromagnet uncoupling track section. When activated, a small metal disk shaped armature attached to the truck frame via an armature pin is pulled down, along with the spring assembly, thus releasing the knuckle. This disk has also led to the name disk operating coupler. AAR trucks included operating, non-operating and plain (truck only and no coupler mechanism) couplers.

Early AAR 1957 - 1961	**Middle AAR 1961 - 1963/64**	**Late AAR 1964/1965 -1969**
Die-Cast Knuckle and Closed Journal Boxes	Delrin (Early or Late) Knuckle and Closed Journal Boxes	Late Delrin Knuckle and Open Journal Boxes

AAR JOURNAL BOXES

In 1963, non-operating couplers had journal boxes that were closed.

From 1964 through 1969 for non-operating couplers and 1965 through 1969 for operating couplers, journal boxes were open.

From 1957 through 1964, operating couplers had journal boxes that were closed.

AAR KNUCKLES

From 1957 through 1961, a die-cast knuckle (part no. 480-8) with knuckle spring (no. 480-16) mounted by a knuckle pin or rivet (no. TC-23) was the norm.

Integrated pivot points

Notice shape of cam

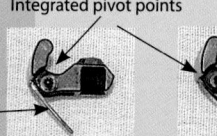

Integrated leaf spring

"Early Delrin Knuckle"
In 1961 through 1962, a one-piece Delrin plastic knuckle (part no. 566-27) with integrated leaf spring and pivot points replaced the die-cast knuckle. This was most often used with the metal leaf spring assembly with lancing. It has also been observed with the metal leaf spring with no lancing.

"Late Delrin Knuckle"
From 1962 through 1969, another version of the one-piece Delrin plastic knuckle (part no. 566-54) with integrated leaf spring was used. The shape of cam changed for the new metal leaf spring assembly with no lancing. It was most often used with this leaf spring assembly, although it has also been observed with the leaf spring with lancing.

In 1963 and 1964, some rolling stock had Delrin knuckle with an integral copper spring. This design improvement did not last more than a year.

AAR LEAF SPRING ASSEMBLY

From 1957 through 1962, the leaf spring assembly had lancing and a smaller rivet hole.

LANCING

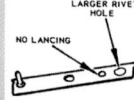
LARGER RIVET HOLE
NO LANCING

From 1962 through 1969, the leaf spring assembly had no lancing and a larger rivet hole. This redesign improved the locking and release of the coupler knuckles.

AAR WHEELS

From 1957 through 1961, the wheel hubs were flush with the wheel surface. These were used with truck frames that had pads on the sides.

WHEEL HUB PROJECTS ABOVE WHEEL SURFACE

From 1962 through 1969, the wheel hubs were raised above the wheel surface. These were used with truck frames that had smooth sides.

AAR PLASTIC SIDE FRAME

From 1957 through 1961, AAR trucks had pads on inner surfaces of truck side frames (part no. 566-5).

From 1962 through 1969, AAR trucks had smooth inner surfaces on the truck side frames. This helped improve the molding process (part no. 566-55).

AAR OTHER FEATURES

In 1960, notches appeared on top of some side frames. The inner pads also changed accordingly.

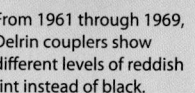

From 1961 through 1969, Delrin couplers show different levels of reddish tint instead of black.

In 1966, some trucks had a washer above or below the leaf spring rivet.

DATING POSTWAR TRUCKS AND COUPLERS
ARCHBAR COIL SPRING TRUCKS

1959	1960	1961	1962	1963

ARCHBAR COIL SPRING TRUCKS
PLASTIC FRAME TRUCKS

From 1959 through 1963, plastic trucks were styled after old-fashioned Archbar coil spring trucks. Originally designed for the General Outfits, they emulate trains of the Civil War period. They follow the same progression of changes as AAR trucks. Archbar trucks included operating, non-operating and plain (truck only and no coupler mechanism) couplers, although most cars come with non-operating couplers. Operating coupler examples include nos. 3370, 1872T and 1877. The operating couplers on nos. 1875, 1875W and 1876 were actually plain Archbar trucks with an entirely separate coupler assembly. All Archbar couplers had closed journal boxes.

Archbar operating coupler side view.

From 1959 through 1962, Archbar operating couplers were used. Bottom view with die-cast knuckle and knuckle spring both mounted by a knuckle pin. This also included a metal leaf spring assembly with lancing.

From 1959 through 1963, Archbar non-operating couplers were used.

DATING POSTWAR TRUCKS AND COUPLERS
SIX-WHEEL, 2400-SERIES AND 2500-SERIES TRUCKS

1946	1947	1948	1949	1950	1951	1952	1953	1954	1955-1966

SIX-WHEEL TRUCKS
METAL FRAME TRUCKS
WITH PLASTIC SIDES

From 1946 through 1951, six-wheel metal frame trucks with plastic sides were used for Madison Pullman "2625"-series cars, along with the no. 2460 Crane Car and nos. 2671W and 2426W Tenders. All versions include coil couplers.

2400-SERIES TRUCKS
METAL FRAME TRUCKS
WITH DIE-CAST SIDES

From 1948 through 1966, metal trucks with detailed die-cast side frames were used for 2400-series passenger cars and the no. 6517 Caboose. 2400-series trucks first appeared with coil couplers and later with magnetic couplers.

From 1948 through 1953, coil couplers were used.

From 1954 through 1966, magnetic couplers were used.

2500-SERIES TRUCKS
METAL FRAME TRUCKS
WITH DIE-CAST SIDES

From 1952 through 1966, metal trucks with die-cast side frames were used for 2500-series passenger cars. 2500-series trucks always utilized magnetic-style couplers.

From 1952 through 1966, magnetic couplers were used.

Individual Item Boxes

Lionel depended on its majestic catalogs, train department salespeople and creative advertising to sell its trains. No one expected boxes to do so, although the distinct orange and blue color scheme made Lionel's component boxes easily recognizable. Boxes were used only to protect their contents until they were sold. For this reason, early postwar boxes did not show what they contained. Instead, they identified their contents with the item number printed on the end flaps, top, bottom and sides. To see what was in a particular box, a consumer had to check a Lionel catalog or store display or remove an item from its box.

As times changed more toy trains were sold through traditional retail stores without the assistance of salespeople. This self-service approach required Lionel to place more emphasis on visual packaging. The firm responded, albeit a little late, with display packaged train outfits in 1957 (HO) and 1958 (O27). It wasn't until 1959 that individual item packaging changed. This section shows the introduction of the Orange Perforated box, which allowed dealers to remove perforated panels on the box top showing the item while it was still in the box. This process in turn left a hole the box. For some reason, Lionel reverted to fully enclosed boxes from 1961 through 1965. It wasn't until 1966, with the introduction of Cellophane Window boxes, that Lionel finally achieved a way to visually package every item without destroying the box

Cellophane Window boxes helped sell trains by allowing individuals who did not have a catalog or access to a salesperson to see what was in the box. These boxes likely were more expensive, as they required a multiple-step process to manufacture. Unfortunately for Lionel, this change occurred too late to have much impact, not with its Toy Division already deteriorating. After no new individually boxed production in 1967, Lionel again went with fully enclosed boxes in 1968 and 1969.

Boxes demonstrate Lionel's internal culture to continuously look for cost improvements. Early in the postwar years, trains were packaged using liners, inserts, paper and other protective materials. In 1955, packaging was redesigned to eliminate or simplify individual inserts and liners. In 1956, Lionel began to eliminate boxes altogether in train outfits. By the end of the postwar era, trains were loosely packed in generic sized boxes.

From a collector's perspective, boxes have achieved an increasingly level of importance. This is partially due to the way boxes were viewed in the past. Customers were purchasing trains, not the packaging; as a consequence, many boxes were destroyed or discarded. Even if saved, many were separated from the train and subsequently lost or ruined. Not surprisingly, supplies of boxes in C7 (Excellent) or better condition are now smaller than the quantities of the trains they packaged.

Today, boxes help to complete an item and thereby create another level of collecting. The addition of the correct box can dramatically increase the value of an item. Looking at such items as a no. 6401-1 Flat Car or no. 6017-200 U.S. Navy Caboose, one finds that the box is worth substantially more than the enclosed item.

That being said, it is important to know the proper year in which boxes were manufactured. This knowledge assists in matching the correct item with the correct box. It also ensures that the correct item boxes are used when assembling a train outfit.

This section details the major individual postwar box styles. The changes from box style to style are highlighted in red. The dates provided are based on when the boxes were manufactured. Sometimes boxes were used later than their manufacture date. Also, Lionel often reused older boxes by over-stamping (blocking out) the old number and stamping a new number on the box.

The rule of thumb when trying to match an item with the proper box is that an item manufactured in one year would likely be matched with the box from that year and not one from a later year. For example, a no. 6414-1 Auto Transport Car from 1960 would likely be packaged in an Orange Perforated or earlier style box and not an Orange Picture box because that style of box was not released until 1961. Although anything is possible as Lionel would sometimes package leftover inventory for sale in later years.

Matching trains and boxes gets tricky for items that were issued or repeated over many years. For example the 6414-1 was issued from 1955 through 1966. This period covered five different individual box styles. A thorough knowledge of boxes as outlined in this section, combined with trucks and couplers and other individual decorating variations, is required to ensure that the item is matched with its proper box.

DATING POSTWAR INDIVIDUAL ITEM BOXES

1945　　1946	1947	1948　　1949

ART DECO
1945 - 1946

From 1945 through 1946, Art Deco orange and blue boxes were used to package Lionel trains. The term "Art Deco" was used because the Lionel font resembled the one used on Radio City Music Hall and surrounding buildings' Art Deco motif.

The most distinguishable feature was that the bold blue lettered Lionel on both sides and end flaps touched the blue border above and below. The company was listed as The Lionel Corporation in New York, Chicago and San Francisco. Item numbers were listed on both sides, the top and bottom. The overall cardboard had a heavier textured feel.

The Lionel Corporation touches the blue borders.
Item number on both sides, top and bottom.
New York, Chicago and San Francisco.

Item number on top and bottom (above) and sides (below).

ART DECO TOY LOGO
VARIATION OF ART DECO
1947 - 1948

In 1947 and 1948, Lionel used an Art Deco Toy Logo box. This was an exact copy of the Art Deco box except it included the Toy Manufacturers Association logo on top of the box.

The Lionel Corporation touches the blue borders.
Item number on both sides, top and bottom.
New York, Chicago and San Francisco.

Toy Manufacturers Association logo on top.

Item number on bottom (above) and sides (below).

Toy Manufacturers Association logo on top.

EARLY CLASSIC
Early 1948 - 1949

In early 1948 and 1949, Lionel used the Early Classic orange and blue box. This style of box and subsequent variations were in use for over ten years, making it one of the most recognizable boxes of the postwar era. The most distinguishable feature from previous boxes is that the blue lettered Lionel on both sides and end flaps no longer touched the blue border above and below. All other features remained the same. The company was still listed as The Lionel Corporation in New York, Chicago and San Francisco. Item numbers were listed on both sides, the top and bottom of the boxes.

The Lionel Corporation does not touch the blue borders.
Item number on both sides, top and bottom.
New York, Chicago and San Francisco.

Toy Manufacturers Association logo on top.

Item number on bottom (above) and sides (below).

Changes from previous style shown in red.

DATING POSTWAR INDIVIDUAL ITEM BOXES

1949		1955	1956		1958

MIDDLE CLASSIC
Late 1949 - 1955

From late 1949 through 1955, Lionel used a Middle Classic style box. This box was the same as the Early Classic, except San Francisco was eliminated from the box sides.

In 1950, the box part number (previously not shown) began to appear on the tuck flap. In 1955, individual item boxes were redesigned to eliminate or simplify individual inserts and liners. This cheapening of the packaging process led to both smaller item boxes and different box variations.

The Lionel Corporation does not touch the blue borders.
Item number on both sides, top and bottom.
New York and Chicago (no San Francisco).

Toy Manufacturers Association logo and item number on top.

Item number on bottom (above) and sides (below).

LATE CLASSIC
Late 1955 - 1958

From late 1955 through 1958, Lionel used a Late Classic style box. This box was the same as the Middle Classic, except the item number was eliminated from the box sides, top and bottom.

There is also a Late Classic Generic (not shown) a box used from late 1955 to 1956. These boxes were purchased blank and rubber-stamped as needed. The no. 6464-275 Box Car (box part no. 12-6) is one notable example.

The Lionel Corporation does not touch the blue borders.
Item number eliminated from both sides, top and bottom.
New York and Chicago (no San Francisco)

Toy Manufacturers Association logo and no item number on top.

No Item number on bottom (above) and sides (below).

OPS CLASSIC
VARIATION OF MIDDLE CLASSIC
1952

In 1952, Lionel used an OPS Classic style box. This box was the same as the Middle Classic, except it was printed with an Office of Price Stabilization (OPS) price. These "retail ceiling" prices were required due to high inflation during the Korean War. OPS stickers first appeared in 1951 and were used internally and provided to dealers for items already in the channel.

OPS logo and price on top.
The Lionel Corporation does not touch the blue borders.
Item number on both sides, top and bottom.
New York and Chicago (no San Francisco)

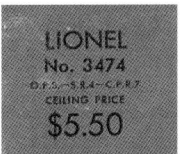

OPS logo and price on top.

BOLD CLASSIC
VARIATION OF LATE CLASSIC
1958

In 1958, Lionel used a Bold Classic style box for part of the product line. This box had the same graphics as the Late Classic, except the item number and description were printed in bold dark blue lettering on the end flaps.

Bold dark blue font on end flaps.

Lionel Corporation does not touch the blue borders.
Item number eliminated from both sides, top and bottom.
New York and Chicago (no San Francisco).

GLOSSY CLASSIC
VARIATION OF LATE CLASSIC
1959 - 1961

From 1958 through 1961, Lionel used a Glossy Classic style box. This box had the same graphics as the Late Classic, except it was printed on a glossy coated cardboard versus the textured cardboard used in the past. This box was used for only a few items. Two examples include the no. 55 Tie-Jector (1959) and no. 3366-100 Figures for Circus Car (1959).

Glossy coated cardstock.

The Lionel Corporation does not touch the blue borders.
Item number eliminated from both sides, top and bottom.
New York and Chicago (no San Francisco).

DATING POSTWAR INDIVIDUAL ITEM BOXES

1959	1960	1961	1962	1963

ORANGE PERFORATED
1959 - 1960

From 1959 through 1960, Lionel used an Orange Perforated style box. This new design coincided with the introduction of individually boxed display pack outfits. The perforated top allowed dealers to punch out the top perforated panel and display items individually or within a display packed outfit. The graphics were printed on glossy coated stock. The company was listed as The Lionel Corporation in New York and Chicago on the box top and sides. The bottom included a Lionel Lion graphic.

Perforated top.
The Lionel Corporation New York and Chicago.

Lion graphic on bottom.

The Lionel Corporation New York and Chicago on sides.
Made in USA on one side.

ORANGE PICTURE
1961 - 1965

From 1961 through 1965, Lionel used an Orange Picture style box. This box was the same as Orange Perforated, but it eliminated the punched-out section, replacing it with new top panel graphics. It was also a lighter shade of orange. The graphics were of a 4-6-4 steamer and F3 diesel and were also used for a new version of hinged display pack outfits. The company was listed as The Lionel Corporation in New York and Chicago on the top and sides. The bottom included a Lionel Lion graphic.

Solid top (no perforations).
4-6-4 steamer and F3 diesel graphic.
The Lionel Corporation New York and Chicago.

Lion graphic on bottom.

ORANGE PERFORATED PICTURE
VARIATION OF ORANGE PICTURE
1961 - 1962

From 1961 through 1962, Lionel used an Orange Perforated Picture style box for some items. It used the same graphics as the Orange Picture, except it was printed on leftover Orange Perforated cardboard. It has been observed on some rolling stock items, but most often can be found with 2500-series Presidential passenger cars.

Perforated top.
Same graphics as Orange Picture.
The Lionel Corporation New York and Chicago.

Lion graphic on bottom.

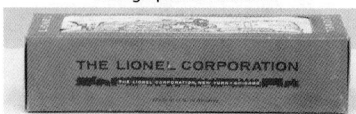

The Lionel Corporation New York and Chicago on sides.
Made in USA on one side.

ORANGE NON PERFORATED
VARIATION OF ORANGE PERFORATED
1963

In 1963, Lionel used an Orange Non Perforated style box. It was the same as the Orange Perforated, except without the perforations. It has been observed on only the no. 6827 Harnischfeger Power Shovel Car.

Orange Perforated graphics but no perforations.
The Lionel Corporation New York and Chicago.

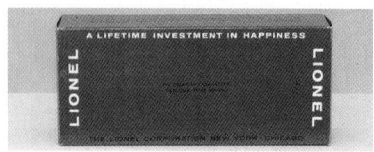

HILLSIDE ORANGE PICTURE
VARIATION OF ORANGE PICTURE
1963 - 1965

From 1963 through 1965, Lionel used a Hillside Orange Picture style box. This box was the same as the Orange Picture, except the company was now listed as The Lionel Toy Corporation on the top and sides. This reflected the change in corporate structure that took place in 1963. New York and Chicago were replaced with the location of the factory, Hillside, New Jersey, on the top of the box only, not the sides. Only one 1963 item, the no. 6429 Work Caboose, used this new box. Over time, as old boxes were depleted, new boxes were printed with this new artwork.

DATING POSTWAR INDIVIDUAL ITEM BOXES

1963	**1964**	**1965**

The Lionel Corporation New York and Chicago on sides.
Made in USA on one side.

In 1964, a variation of the Orange Picture box exists where the top panel white corners are more rounded than normal.

From 1964 through 1965, the texture of the cardboard changed for some items. The cardboard felt stiffer and more brittle than in the past. Some items also have a lighter shade of orange.

DARK ORANGE PICTURE
VARIATION ORANGE PICTURE
1963

In 1963, Lionel used a Dark Orange Picture style box. This box was the same as the Orange Picture, except it was printed using a darker shade of orange. All new and repeat item boxes printed in 1963 were this color. Most boxes were dated on the inside flap as being manufactured in 1963.

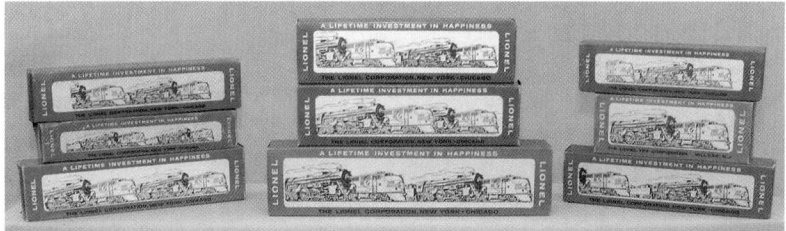

From 1961 through 1965, Lionel repeated fully or partially the 4-6-4 steamer and F3 diesel graphic for items that came in a longer Orange Picture box.

From 1964 through 1965, the new Lionel double arrow oval logo (introduced in 1963) replaced the Lionel lion on the bottom of some Hillside Orange Picture boxes.

Solid (no perforations) top.
4-6-4 steamer and F3 diesel graphic.
The Lionel Toy Corporation, Hillside, N.J.

Lion graphic on bottom.

**The Lionel Toy Corporation.
No mention of location.
Made in USA on one side.**

New Lionel double arrow oval logo on bottom.

DATING POSTWAR INDIVIDUAL ITEM BOXES

1966	1967

CELLOPHANE WINDOW
1966

In 1966, Lionel used a Cellophane Window style box. This redesigned box provided a window through which the item could be viewed without removing it from the box. The window was cut into the top of the box and covered with flimsy cellophane. Following a practice that began with outfit boxes in 1961, these boxes were generic in that the item number was not preprinted by the box manufacturer, but rubber-stamped by Lionel.

The graphics now included the phrase The Leader in Model Railroading on the top and sides. The company name remained The Lionel Toy Corporation, Hillside, N.J. and appeared on the sides. The bottom had the Lionel double arrow oval logo.

Viewing window covered with cellophane.
The Leader in Model Railroading.
Generic rubber-stamped box.

Lionel double arrow oval logo on bottom.

The Lionel Toy Corporation, **Hillside, N.J.**
Made in USA on one side.
The Leader in Model Railroading.

PLAIN WHITE
LATE 1960s

During the late 1960s, Lionel used a Plain White style box. These boxes were undecorated with rubber-stamped or occasionally preprinted item numbers. They were most likely used when stock regularly decorated boxes were depleted.

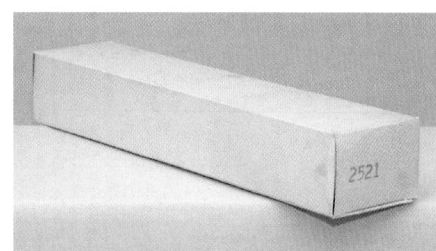

Plain white cardboard box.
Rubber-stamped number.

NO BOXED PRODUCTION
1967

During 1967, there was no cataloged train production. All promotional train outfits assembled came with unboxed items. There were no new box designs in 1967.

DATING POSTWAR INDIVIDUAL ITEM BOXES

<table>
<tr><td>

HAGERSTOWN CHECKERBOARD
1968 - 1969

In 1968 and 1969, Lionel used a Hagerstown Checkerboard style box. This was the final new postwar design that accompanied Lionel's move of production to the Lionel Porter factory in Hagerstown, Maryland.

The orange box had Lionel printed in a "checkerboard" pattern that wrapped around the top, bottom and both sides. The majority of these boxes were generic, with the item number rubber-stamped on the side. Many items shared the same size box and were padded using what Lionel called bogus paper (Kraft paper). A few items had their own preprinted boxes. The company name was listed as The Lionel Toy Corporation, Hagerstown, Maryland on the end flaps.

Checkerboard Lionel pattern.
Rubber-stamped item number.

Checkerboard Lionel pattern wraps around bottom and sides.

The Lionel Toy Corporation, Hagerstown, Maryland on both ends.

</td><td>

HILLSIDE CHECKERBOARD
1969

In 1969, Lionel used a Hillside Checkerboard style box. This box was exactly the same as Hagerstown Checkerboard, except the company location was changed from Hagerstown, Maryland to Hillside, New Jersey on the end flaps. This reflected the move back to the Hillside location. Lionel had to leave Hagerstown because Porter's chemistry line was sold in January 1969, and by March, the entire Porter company had been sold. Even though the Hillside building was for sale, it was not sold until September 1969.

Checkerboard Lionel pattern.
Rubber-stamped item number.

Checkerboard Lionel pattern wraps around bottom and sides.

The Lionel Toy Corporation, Hillside, New Jersey on both ends.

</td></tr>
</table>

Distribution Overview

The toy retail environment was diverse and growing during the 1960s. Companies introduced new products and distribution techniques almost daily.

Lionel was no exception. Its executives considered Lionel to be a toy company and created strategies to exploit this market. Besides adding new train products, Lionel diversified into science kits (through the acquisition of Porter Chemical Co. and the development of new products for the Lionel line), juvenile phonographs and records (via the acquisition of Spear) and raceways (originally with Scalextric and then Lionel's own line). Other products brought out in the 1960s included the Helios 21 remote-controlled spaceship and the U-Drive Boat. Company leaders evaluated other acquisitions and projects, but ultimately rejected them.

As for distribution, toy manufacturers used various channels in their quest to reach every potential customer in the marketplace. Dealing directly with department stores was still a common practice, yet manufacturers recognized that providing the benefits of credit and promotional advertising was too great a task for them to handle. Nevertheless, in order to be competitive in the marketplace, manufacturers relied heavily on selling to resellers (distributors, wholesalers and jobbers).

Lionel operated like other toy manufacturers in the 1960s by maximizing its relationships with resellers while still selling directly to national accounts. Executives often handled Lionel's national accounts from its New York headquarters, saving costs in this manner because intermediaries were not needed to market train outfits. These customers either purchased a large volume of cataloged outfits or ordered some quantity of promotional outfits. Many of the largest retailers, such as Sears and Montgomery Ward, were handled through New York, as were a number of the major trading stamp companies and catalog houses.

While the toy industry primarily used independent sales representatives, Lionel leveraged a direct sales force to execute its distribution strategy. This team was one of Lionel's greatest assets. Many of these salespeople had been with Lionel for years and so were familiar with the industry and knew Lionel's customers. Jointly with their distributors, they would call on dealers to ensure maximum sales. Their responsibilities also included soliciting business through retailers that ranged from grocery stores and various chain stores to discount stores, hardware retailers and automotive supply and drug stores.

Lionel's sales force also assisted with national accounts and large retailers in various ways. Salesmen were known, for example, to work with local Sears and Penney outlets to set up and troubleshoot displays of trains. Overall, the sales force had full access to the product line and could sell direct to a retailer or reseller.

During the early 1960s, Lionel's distribution strategy evolved. It wasn't until 1965 that various modifications (taken as a whole) became an issue and a major change was required. Lionel realized that it had been selling far too many promotional outfits. In 1964 alone, Lionel sold more than five times the number of different promotional outfits than catalog ones. The cost of configuring and maintaining the supporting operations must have been a huge burden.

In 1965, therefore, Lionel hoped to alleviate this problem by consolidating all its promotional activities under one manager. Thus was born the Market Development Division headed by Bruce Parmett. Distributors were now limited to only catalog outfits, and all retailers had to buy from a distributor. Only a handful of national accounts were sold direct and then only through the Market Development organization. Large retailers accustomed to buying only Retailer Promotional outfits direct from Lionel at the deepest discount were upset at having to go through distributors for their merchandise.

The creation of the Market Development Division also led to less local retailer sponsored advertising. This was because most stores did not have Retailer Promotional outfits and dramatically scaled back their advertising. Lionel produced a few Market Development outfits (General Release Promotionals) to provide some exclusivity to larger retailers, but this step failed to repair the already frail relationships. The same policies carried into 1966, though Lionel offered many more Market Development outfits (General Release Promotionals).

Consolidating all promotional activities within one division and limiting the number of promotional outfits amounted to a solution to an issue that needed to be fixed. Unfortunately for Lionel, its distribution channels were too accustomed to receiving a product (Retailer Promotional outfits) that the company's internal cost structure could not sustain. As such, even though this was the correct product and distribution solution for the long run, Lionel ran out of time.

Lionel's distribution channels included resellers, retailers and companies that used trains as a premium. A classification of each follows:

Resellers

Lionel sold its train outfits direct to firms whose role was to sell them to other dealers or retailers. These firms, known as "resellers", received some of the biggest discounts. These ranged from 40/20 (40 percent off retail less an additional 20 percent) or 48 percent of the retail price in the early 1960s to 50/10 (or 45 percent of the retail price) from 1963 forward. This was a typical way to discount items in the 1960s. For example, a $100 train outfit at 50/10 would cost a reseller $45 (50 percent off the $100 for an adjusted net price of $50, less an additional 10 percent off the $50 price, or an additional $5, for a net price of $45). Resellers marked up the price of an outfit when selling it to dealers or retailers.

Buying Offices

Buying offices, also known as buying cooperatives, were made up of buyers in national or international markets that leveraged economies of scale to select and buy merchandise for their clients. The cost of membership in the cooperative also provided market trend analysis, pricing options and supply sources. Retailers benefited by receiving merchandise at a lower cost and were not required to purchase in bulk.

Lionel sold trains to many buying offices that in turn distributed them to numerous retailers. One office in particular, Associated Merchandising Corporation (AMC), distributed many of Lionel's outfits. AMC was able to provide outfits in various industries in a smaller quantity. Many of the outfits that AMC handled for Lionel ended up in different department stores as well as discount houses. Interestingly, some of the retailers that the Lionel sales team dealt with directly were also members of the same buying offices as Lionel.

Wholesaler - Distributors (Jobbers)

Wholesaler-distributors, also known as "jobbers" or merchant-wholesalers, usually operated one or more warehouses where they stored products for their clients. Wholesale-distributors were responsible for purchasing goods in large quantities and reselling them to smaller wholesalers or retailers. Lionel sold through wholesale-distributors as a way to broaden its market. Many jobbers had their own sales force, and Lionel often worked with them to improve sales. These companies would also consolidate and manage any returns and handle issues with customers. Lionel's partnership with various wholesalers-distributors helped it reduce costs associated with selling, inventory and transportation.

Companies Involved With Premiums

Lionel also sold its trains to customers that used them for promotional purposes. Trains might be designated as premiums intended to help sell other products or as gifts or service rewards to recognize positive accomplishments.

Associations

Associations represented a distribution channel that Lionel serviced with promotional outfits. Associations were organizations with some common goal or benefit. One such group, the National Association of Railroad Business Women, helps women in the railroad industry by providing guidance and scholarships. The orders for train outfits to associations were usually small in quantity.

Gasoline Service Stations

Gasoline service stations began offering branded merchandise and tie-in promotions in the 1950s. Like many retailers, service stations were looking to increase profits, bolster customer loyalty and remain competitive. Lionel sold promotional outfits to gasoline and oil companies, which then offered them as marketing incentive tools. This tactic offered another opportunity for Lionel to gain exposure and revenue from a non-traditional toy market.

Incentive Marketing Companies

Incentive marketing companies helped create and manage motivational programs for their clients. These programs ranged from awards for sale accomplishments to recognition for achieving a specific corporate goal. An example of one such goal was a specified number of days of safe driving for truckers. Incentive marketing companies published catalogs or flyers listing the products available for achieving the specified goal. Lionel sold to many of these companies during the 1960s.

Manufacturers

Manufacturers, including Quaker Oats and Libby's, purchased Lionel promotional outfits for incentive purposes. Incentive programs guaranteed product exposure for both the manufacturer and the company supplying the incentive. Lionel forged promotional relationships with manufacturers as a means to generate profits as well as attract new customers.

End Retailers

End retailers were the locations where customers could acquire train outfits that, in turn, had been purchased through a reseller or direct from Lionel. Some end retailers were also resellers. A broad range of end retailers existed through which Lionel could sell its trains.

Automotive Stores and Hardware Stores

In the 1960s, before the development of specialty stores, it became common for automotive and hardware stores to expanded their operations to include more types of consumer goods, including train outfits. Soon, automotive and hardware stores emerged as a major part of Lionel's business. Firestone, Western Auto and others (as members of the Automotive Associates buying office) spent millions of dollars on trains. Hardware stores were also a major portion of Lionel's business. Both types of outlets proved to be key advertisers of Lionel trains, and many of their catalogs and advertisements have survived to add to our base of knowledge.

Concessionaires

Concessionaires, popular in the restaurant industry, were distribution channels for the toy industry in the 1960s. These companies outsourced a department in a store, handling the fixtures, stock and shipments. One concessionaire during the 1960s, Robin Distributors, stocked Lionel outfits in every toy department it outsourced. Although concessionaires might deal direct with a Lionel sales representative, it was not out of the ordinary for them to have an agreement with another distributor for their inventory.

Dealers

Lionel used the term "dealers" generically to refer to retailers.

Department Stores

The innovation of the department store was introduced

in the mid-1800s as a new form of retailing. These stores influenced the mass production and selling of household items and apparel. Department stores brought many changes to communities as well as the entire retail sector. They introduced the notion of fixed pricing (as opposed to bartering), which consumers preferred. Department stores, because of their size, the variety of products they carried, and their use of credit, were a major force in consumer sales in the 1960s.

Department stores provided many opportunities for manufacturers to gain exposure. These stores offered media and promotional practices as well as display options. Lionel capitalized on this concept and sold the majority of its promotional outfits through department stores in the 1960s. Those stores relied on window displays as well as large toy departments to entice customers into buying the trains they carried.

Discount Retailers

During the late 1950s, Lionel abandoned its attempt to enforce fair trade practices on its trains when dealing with discount retailers. Company executives chose to revise its catalogs by eliminating stock (outfit) numbers and prices. However, sales for the discounters were growing and department stores were opening their own discount stores to compete. The industry was flourishing, thanks to the concept of low markups and the ability to consistently turn over inventory to meet consumer demand. Lionel, realizing that it could not ignore the discounters, forged promotional relationships with major discounters, such as Goldblatt's and King Stores. Lionel became swept up in the cost game, which led to lower and lower priced outfits.

Drug Store Chains

Similar to grocery store chains, drug store chains expanded their product offerings during the 1950s by adding toys and other "hard-line" items. As they did so, Lionel was there to offer promotional outfits to help differentiate their offerings, bring in new customers and boost their already thin profit margins.

Grocery Stores

Grocery stores were one of the largest industries in the late 1950s, selling more merchandise than drug, variety and department stores combined. In order to stay competitive with other retailers, grocery chains looked to diversify and expand the goods they sold. Leading the industry in marketing non-grocery items was Grand Union. It, along with other grocery chains, purchased promotional outfits from Lionel. Lionel benefited from this new channel, which provided exposure and expanded its customer base.

Hobby and Model Stores

Hobby and model stores were independent dealers in the retail industry and served as Lionel's year-round link with toy train and model railroading enthusiasts. Most retailers offered trains only during the annual holiday season, but hobby stores carried them throughout the year. Many hobby stores were also Lionel Approved Service Stations, where customers could bring their trains for service and repair. Hobby stores generally bought their trains from a distributor, although Lionel would sometimes sell them direct.

Mail-Order Retailers

Mail-order houses were first introduced in the mid-1800s as a means for the growing number of rural residents and farmers in America to purchase goods. But the earliest catalogs offered too limited a selection and left potential consumers disappointed. Success did not come until 1872, when Aaron Montgomery Ward introduced the first mail-order catalog that presented a large and diverse assortment of goods. Before long, competitors entered the mail-order business, with Sears, Roebuck and Co. leading the way.

In the 1920s, Sears and Ward supplemented their mail-order catalog business by opening department stores under their own names. This move caused mail-order sales to decline. During the 1950s, mail-order retailers experienced further changes when discount stores sprouted up across the country. While traditional retailers felt compelled to narrow their profit margins in order to compete, mail-order retailers began to flourish. Mail-order retailers were able to sell product at a lower price because of minimal overhead and staff. The lower prices and introduction of credit in 1961 enticed consumers

During the 1960s, the four leading mail-order companies - Aldens, Sears, Spiegel and Montgomery Ward - were all customers of Lionel. Mail order was a convenient channel for consumers to purchase products as well as for retailers to provide exposure. Mail-order firms extensively advertised Lionel's products; as a result, these companies placed orders for large quantities of promotional outfits.

Toy Stores

Toy stores have been around since the 1800s, with FAO Schwarz in New York City being among the first and most famous in the United States. In fact, FAO Schwarz was a Lionel customer as early as 1902, just a year after Joshua Lionel Cowen started making toy trains. Toy stores were a natural fit for trains, and Lionel leveraged this opportunity by selling many cataloged and promotional outfits to them.

Promotional Outfit Customers Overview

During the 1960s, Lionel sold promotional outfits to more than 170 unique customers. This section provides a brief overview of each customer and the outfits it purchased. Those customers, listed alphabetically in bold type, are based on Lionel Factory Orders for promotional outfits, along with other Lionel documents, various retail catalogs, advertisements and even price tags. The names found on the Factory Orders occasionally differed from common usage. For example, Lionel referred to R. H. Macy Department Stores under that name, although the public calls them "Macy's". To avoid confusion, we have cross-referenced the two names, but added the relevant information about the company under the entry, "R. H. Macy".

When customers were specified on Factory Orders, that fact and other information were used to place them in one of two categories. They might be the "End Retailer" (the retail store that eventually sold an outfit). Or they might the "Buying Office", "Reseller" or "Parent Company" (the distributor or other merchant that bought an outfit with the intention of getting it an end retailer).

To determine the end retailer, other Lionel documents might be used or a retail catalog listing, newspaper or other advertisement or even the price tag on a surviving outfit. For example, AMC (Associated Merchandising Corporation), a buying office, is listed as the customer on outfit no. 19131. This outfit was linked with Dayton's and Rike's by observing the retail catalogs for 1962. As many such "mappings" are provided as possible, although these outfits could have ended up sold to many customers.

When no customer was specified on the Factory Orders, the outfit was likely a General Release Promotional outfit offered to many resellers or retailers. In such cases, other Lionel documents, retail catalogs, advertisements, and actual observations of outfits could shed light on the end retailer.

Finally, when compiling tables of the promotional outfits a customer offered, not all information regarding customer numbers and prices could be obtained. In such instances, the appropriate cell in the table is intentionally left empty.

Listing of Lionel's Customers

*A

Lionel used *A and A* as the customer on at least eight different outfits, all of which date from 1964. The meaning of this notation has yet to be determined, although it always appeared with at least one other customer, which indicates that these outfits were General Release Promotionals. Also, because the customer *A or A* is most often paired with was an automotive supplier, this notation might have been related in some way to Automotive Associates (see that entry).

The designations *A and A* appeared on outfit nos. 19349, 19352, 19353, 19354, 19362, 19366, 19373 and 19374.

A&P

Founded in 1859 as the Great Atlantic Pacific Tea Company by George F. Gilman and George Huntington Hartford, A&P was originally a discount tea and coffee store. Headquartered in New York, A&P's offices were located at 31 Vessey Street, which is where the World Trade Center stood years later. In 1870, as business began to expand, the firm's name was changed to the Great Atlantic and Pacific Tea Company and it became the first supermarket chain in the United States. A&P expanded by introducing its own line of products, many of which it made or processed. The company was incorporated in New Jersey in 1900 with stock worth $2.1 million.

Marketing programs were introduced at A&P stores in the early 1900s. The programs consisted of coupons and incentive premiums intended to boost customer loyalty. In the 1920s and then again in the 1960s, A&P introduced Plaid Saving Stamps. The savings stamp program was a great success, although it apparently was one of the few stamp programs that did not offer Lionel trains (see E. F. MacDonald). Currently, A&P offers coupons, rebates and sweepstakes based on its customers' buying habits.

Due to a declining market, A&P sold a majority of its stores to the Tengelmann Group in the 1979. Today, A&P is headquartered in Montvale, New Jersey, and employs more than 78,000 associates. Its operations consist of more than 640 stores in the United States and Canada and a wholesale division servicing franchise stores in Canada.

As part of Lionel's effort in the early 1960s to branch out to other retailers, it created Retailer Promotional outfit no. 19244 for A&P in 1963. During the selling process, Lionel drew up artwork for an A&P box car. This model probably helped close the deal, though it was never produced.

The outfit was sold via blister display no. D-19244. A&P typically hung these displays in stores to advertise the train, which came in a plain tan RSC box. No A&P specific numbering or markings appeared on these outfits.

As a side note, A&P took action against Lionel in 1964 for the sum of $164,420, claiming this was the amount owed to it "from a consignment sale of toys…during 1963". The Supreme Court of New York County granted a summary judgment of $110,000 based on the amount of goods returned by A&P. With outfit 19244 having a net sales price of $6.25, we estimate that approximately 17,600 of the 31,700 outfits were returned. The remaining $54,420 was still to be determined by a "triable issue". This fact sheds light on why Lionel reissued outfit 19244 in 1964 as a General Release Promotional.

Besides A&P, the sale of train outfits to grocery stores in 1963 was a disaster. In 1964, Lionel was doing whatever it could to sell off remaining inventory of this and other grocery store outfits. These 1964 outfits were the returned consignment items.

A. B. C. Birmingham

A. B. C. Birmingham purchased one General Release

Promotional outfit in 1964, no. 19348. No additional information has been found about this firm.

A. Cohen

A. Cohen appeared twice as a customer for Lionel promotional outfits, first for no. 19138 in 1962 and then two years later for no. 19362. The Factory Order for 19362 is crossed out with "Not Using", which indicates that this outfit was never produced.

No other information about A. Cohen or its relationship with Lionel has been found.

Abraham & Strauss

Abraham & Straus began life in 1865 as Wechsler & Abraham, established by Abraham and Joseph Wechsler. Located in Brooklyn, New York, the store changed names to Abraham & Straus when the Straus family bought out Wechsler's interest.

Brooklyn's major department store, Abraham & Strauss, was known for clothing, electronics and a large toy department. In 1994, Abraham & Straus merged with Macy's, a newly acquired division of Federated Department Stores. The next year, Federated converted all Abraham & Straus stores into Macy's stores.

Abraham & Straus was a Lionel customer as early as December 18, 1903, with its first purchase amounting to $79.34. Between 1960 and 1963, Abraham & Straus purchased three Lionel Retailer Promotional outfits: nos. X-574NA, X-715 and 19262. Another outfit, no. X-537NA (sold to Goldblatt's), was observed with an Abraham & Straus price tag. Finally, outfit no. 19411 listed "A&S" as a customer on a Lionel document titled, *Last Numbers Used* from 1964.

No Abraham & Straus specific numbering or markings appeared on these outfits. The only reference to Abraham & Strauss is through price tags on two of the outfits observed.

Advance Stores (see Automotive Associates)

AFA, Army, Army and Air Force Exchange, PX and Service Exchanges

During the Revolutionary War, traders sold such staples as soap and razors to soldiers. Not until after the Civil War did the U. S. Army establish authorized trading posts and canteens to solve problems of corruption and the sale of inferior goods. In 1895, it set up the Army Exchange so soldiers could purchase quality products and services at a low cost. This institution was restructured after World War II as the Army and Air Force Exchange Services. It is now located in Dallas-Fort Worth and handles all ordering and buying needs for the Army Post Exchanges (each known as a "PX") and Air Force Base Exchanges (each called a "BX").

During the 1960s, military bases might have as many as sixteen stores, with at least one carrying toys. Aware of this, Lionel executives realized that no one was better than the military at selling their trains, especially space and military items, to soldiers, pilots and other service personnel. They were correct, because between 1961 and 1966, the Army and Air Force Exchange bought $528,000 worth of merchandise ($428,000 in trains and $100,000 in raceways). This amount surpassed the combined total of J. C.

Penney and Montgomery Ward for those years.

Between 1960 and 1964, these military exchanges carried ten different promotional outfits. The AFA purchased outfit nos. X-531NA, X-657 and X-658; the Army bought outfit nos. 19343 and 19344; and the Army and Air Force Exchange went for outfit nos. 11361X and 19329. Lionel sold to the PXs outfit nos. X-613, X-614 and 11311X, and to the Service Exchanges outfit nos. X-517NA, X-518NA, 19104 and 19105.

Many of these outfits contained at least one military-related item, ranging from a no. 448 Missile Firing Range Set in X-657 to a complete military train in 19343. These outfits were then, it can be assumed, distributed to the many PXs and BXs across the country.

None of the outfits observed had any Army or Air Force specific numbering or markings.

Aldens

Aldens began in 1889 as Chicago Millinery Company, a mail-order company that sold hats. In 1905, the business changed its name to Chicago Mail Order Company and added clothing, electronics, toys and home furnishings to its catalog. The name changed to Aldens in 1946, and the firm grew to be one of the largest mail-order catalog companies.

Over the years, Aldens opened 21 department stores and 13 Shoppers World discount stores. In 1965, it merged with Gamble-Skogmo (another of Lionel's customers) and continued to operate as a subsidiary under the name Aldens. The year 1980 marked the end of Aldens, as Gamble-Skogmo merged into the Wickes Corporation and closed all stores and shut down the catalog division.

Aldens originally purchased a Retailer Promotional outfit in 1960, no. X-555NA. This outfit appeared on pages 352 and 353 of Aldens Christmas Catalog for that year. Aldens assigned number 35 Y 4856E and priced it at $39.98. Lionel trains were absent from the Aldens catalogs for 1961 and 1962, but returned in 1963 with Lionel catalog outfit no. 11311 (Aldens no. 34 Y 5678E for $14.88).

After carrying no Lionel items in 1964, Aldens moved to General Release Promotional outfits. These were observed in the Aldens catalog for 1965 as nos. 19437-502 (Aldens no. 34 Y 5618E for $19.75), 19438-502 (no. 34 Y 5615E for $29.75), 19442 (no. 34 Y 5617E for $34.75), and 19444-502 (no. 34 Y 5616E for $24.75). A year later, the Aldens Christmas Catalog for 1966 carried outfit nos. 19501 (no. 34 Y 5601 for $12.88), 19507 (no. 34 Y 5616E for $27.97) and 19515 (no. 34 Y 5618 for $19.88).

Aldens would sometimes use the same number for different outfits. Aldens 34 Y 5616E was a 19444-502 in 1965 and a 19507 in 1966. The 19507 apparently was a replacement for the six-unit 19444-502. Aldens even kept the "6 Unit Diesel" description that, in fact, was incorrect for 1966 (it should have been seven-unit diesel). By 1967, Aldens issued a joint Gamble Aldens catalog that carried only Marx trains.

No matter which catalog number Aldens used, its outfits had only Lionel numbers and no Aldens markings.

All Trade

Any outfit that listed "All Trade" as the customer was a

General Release Promotional available to any qualifying customer. This designation appears frequently in 1964, when Lionel marked the Factory Orders as such. In 1965 and 1966, the Factory Order customer field was most often left blank to signify a General Release Promotional outfit. At least 18 outfits were marked "All Trade".

Allied Stores

Founded in 1935, Allied Stores was a conglomerate based in New York that owned department stores in small and large cities. Some of the many department stores owned by Allied included Jordan Marsh, Pomeroy's, Gertz, Bon Marche, Stern's, Laubach's and William H. Block. The Campeau Corporation acquired Allied in 1986, and the latter survived as a separate unit until 1992, when it was merged into Campeau's Federated Department Stores.

Allied and the stores under its supervision were important buyers of Lionel promotional outfits, buying a quantity of 32,736 outfits between 1960 and 1964. Allied purchased eleven different outfits; Jordan Marsh, Gertz and Stern's bought an additional six outfits direct from Lionel.

Outfits sold to Allied included nos. X-500NA, X-501NA, X-648, X-650, 19150, 19151, 19154, 19241, 19241-500 and 19337. It also bought display outfit no. DO19337.

No customer specific numbering was applied to the outfit boxes, so consulting retail catalogs, advertisements and price tags was the only way to determine which Allied store was the final destination. For example, the X-650 was observed with a Pomeroy's price tag for $19.99 (it carried a Pomeroy's number 9-1 830). Outfit no. 19377-500 could also be attributed to Pomeroy's. The Stern's Christmas Catalog for 1960 showed X-500NA as Stern's no. 740 (for $39.99) and X-501NA as Stern's no. 742 (for $29.99). The December 7, 1961 *Detroit Free Press* included an advertisement showing X-648 as sold by Waite's department store in Pontiac, Michigan for $29.88. The X-648 was also sold by Gertz for $29.88.

Additional information on the outfits sold direct to Allied stores can be found under the listings for Gertz, Jordan Marsh, Pomeroy's, Stern's and William H. Block.

AMC (Associated Merchandising Corporation)

Associated Merchandising Corporation (AMC) evolved from Retail Research Association, a buying cooperative founded in 1916 by Frederic Ayres and nine other retail leaders. Fred Lazarus Jr., from Lazarus Department Stores, spearheaded the transition to AMC in 1921.

The main benefit of belonging to a buying cooperative is that its non-competitive retail store members can consolidate their buying power, which results in lower costs, better inventory management and overall lower prices to consumers. AMC evolved over the years and was purchased by Target Corporation in 1998.

AMC was a large customer of Lionel. The Factory Orders show that AMC purchased 13 outfits from 1960 through 1964. Of these, a few have been linked to specific member stores. A newspaper advertisement from 1961 showed AMC member Boston Stores offering outfit no. X-640 for $29.95. Dayton's catalog for 1961 also showed outfit X-640 (Dayton no. T18-6) at the same price.

AMC, under the name Aimcee Wholesale Corporation, created generic product catalogs that it then branded with its customer's name and address. The product numbers and prices were assigned by Aimcee, so they would be the same for multiple retailers. One example includes an identical catalog issued to both Dayton's and Rike's (now owned by Federated Department Stores). The nos. 19131, 19132 and 19133 were listed with the Aimcee number. That number was the same one used by Dayton's and Rike's. Specifically, the 1962 catalog showed outfit nos. 19131 (no. T35-3 for $19.88), 19132 (no. T35-2 for $29.88) and 19133 (no. T35-1 for $39.88).

No information has surfaced regarding which AMC stores sold the remaining nine AMC outfits: nos. X-505NA, X-506NA, X-641, X-642, X-643, 19130, 19152, 19226 and 19227.

American Furniture

Founded in 1936, American Furniture was stocking furniture, appliances, general housewares and toys by the late 1950s. It relied on dealer and custom-built displays to show off the trains it carried. One such Lionel display (no. D-265, an 8 x 8 foot Super O gauge layout from 1959) is now part of a private collection. American Furniture is still in business as a home furnishings store with eight locations in New Mexico and Arizona.

In 1960, American Furniture purchased a Retailer Promotional outfit, no. X-530NA. This outfit was one of three in the 1960s to include a no. 264 Operating Fork Lift Platform. Even though no additional Retailer Promotional outfits were documented, American Furniture was a customer of Lionel to at least 1966 and likely later.

American Wholesale Toy

American Wholesale Toy was a toy jobber located in Pawtucket, Rhode Island. In 1964, it purchased the no. 19377 promotional outfit in both RSC and display (no. D-19377).

Arkwright

Arkwright, Inc. was a large buying organization that had about 100 small department store accounts. Among its most notable customers were Bergman's (Kingston, Pennsylvania), Boston Stores (Inglewood, California), The Emporium (Madison, Wisconsin), Hershey Department Store (Hershey, Pennsylvania), Kohl's Department Store (Milwaukee, Wisconsin) and Wieboldt Stores Inc. (Chicago).

From 1960 through 1964, Arkwright bought nine promotional outfits: nos. X-550NA, X-634, 19166, 19242, 19253, 19336, 19345, 19346 and 19366. How it resold them to its end clients is unknown. Making this determination more difficult is that Lionel added only its number and no Arkwright or customer specific markings to the outfits.

Arlan's Department Stores

Arlan's, a discount department store, was founded in 1948 by Lester Palestine in New Bedford, Massachusetts. It apparently went out of business in the early 1970s, and Target purchased the Arlan's stores in Colorado and Iowa. Other facilities became part of Interstate Department Stores, which went bankrupt in 1974.

Although Arlan's did not purchase promotional outfits direct from Lionel, at least three outfits have been observed with Arlan's price tags. Arlan's acquired 1962 outfit no. 19155 from MBS (Merchants Buying Syndicate) and 1966 outfit no. 19583 (Arlan's no. 66 40 for $16.88) from Mercury Model. Outfit no. 19707 (Arlan's no. -66 for $19.99) was likely a General Release Promotional.

Arlens

Arlens, not to be confused with Arlan's, was a discount department store in the 1960s that went out of business somewhere between 1973 and 1976.

Only one outfit was sold to Arlens, no. 19376. In keeping with Arlens discounter theme, this was a low-end outfit based on no. 19253 with additional track and a gondola. There was no mention of retailer markings or numbering.

Army (see AFA)

Army and Air Force Exchange (see AFA)

Associated Dry Goods

Associated Dry Goods traced its roots to the decision of Henry Siegel (Siegel-Cooper's) and John Clafin's (Lord & Taylor, McCreey's, Hahne's and thirty-eight others) to combine their interests about 1914.

Over the years, Associated purchased numerous retailers, including J. W. Robinson's, L. S. Ayres Company, Caldor discount stores, Loehmann's stores, and Sycamore specialty stores. The company was eventually combined with May Department Stores in 1986 in a $2.44 billion stock swap merger.

In 1960, Associated Dry Goods purchased one outfit, no. X-556NA. Since it then owned Stewart Dry Goods, William Hengerer Company, J. N. Adams, Powers Dry Goods, Diamond Stewart and Company, Sibley, Lindsay & Curr and J. W. Robinson's, this outfit could have been distributed through any of these retail chains.

Automotive, Automotive Associates and Automotive Chains

During the 1960s, many automotive supply stores were more like home and auto supply stores. They carried a wide range of merchandise, including toys, appliances, electronics, bicycles and more.

Lionel typically sold direct to large automotive supply customers, notably Firestone and Western Auto. For smaller ones, it sold to distributors or buying organizations, which then supplied automotive supply stores. On the Factory Orders, these were designated "Automotive", "Automotive Associates" or "Automotive Chains". No determination has been made as to whether these were the same or different customers.

Catalogs from Automotive Associates indicated that it was likely a full-service distributor/buying company that also provided a branded catalog to automotive supply stores. It had a buying office at 175 Fifth Avenue during the 1960s. Some of Automotive Associates' customers were Advance Stores, American Auto Accessories, Babcock Brothers Auto Supply, Guarantee Auto Stores, J&R Motor Supply, Kaufman & Chernick, Noah's Ark, Oklahoma Tire & Supply Co., Dean Phipps Stores and Roth Schlenger.

Seventeen outfits were sold to automotive customers: nos. X-519NA, X-520NA, X-532NA, X-533NA, X-626, X-627, X-628, X-629, X-630, 19122, 19123, 19124, 19228, 19229, 19352, 19353 and 19354.

None of these outfits called for special retailer markings. Therefore, the only way to determine which automotive supply store sold them is through observation of the outfits in retailer catalogs, as was done when compiling this chart.

Year	Lionel Number	Retailer	Retailer Catalog and Number	Retail Price
1960	X-519NA	Noah's Ark	319 2828	$33.89
	X-519NA	Advance Stores	1960 catalog	$34.44
	X-532NA			$22.95
	X-533NA			$28.95
1961	X-626	J & R Auto Stores	3007	$15.99
	X-627		3005	$19.99
	X-629		3006	$29.99
1962	19124	Oklahoma Tire & Supply	70-761-6	$35.77
	19124	Noah's Ark	301 X814	$29.88
1963	19228	Dean Phipps Stores		$12.98

B. Altman

Founded in 1906, in New York by Benjamin Altman and Michael Friedman, B. Altman Company was known for selling top-quality and top-label merchandise ranging from clothing to hard lines. B. Altman, along with Bonwitt Teller, Sakowitz and Parisian, was bought out by Hooker Corporation of Australia in 1987. It went out of business two years later.

Lionel sold two outfits to B. Altman Company during the 1960s. Outfit no. X-717 was released in 1961, and no. 19254 was available in 1963.

Beller Brothers and Beller Electric

Beller Electric of 301 - 307 Plane Street in Newark, New Jersey, was a distributor of electric appliances, such as electric sweepers and mixers and toy trains. Among the retailers it served were L. Bamberger and other department stores and toy and hobby shops, in particular, Kraft Hardware in Irvington, New Jersey, and Treasure House in Garfield, New Jersey (both were Lionel Service Stations). William Vagell, who owned Treasure House, was known to visit Beller at the start of each year to purchase its entire remaining inventory at reduced cost.

Beller's promotional outfit purchases included only bulk shipments of trains. Lionel would assign outfit numbers to these groupings and state either "Bulk Packing" or "Ship Bulk - No Outfit Box Packing" on the Factory Orders. In both cases, no outfit boxing information was provided. Buying outfits in this manner was a way to acquire individual items at a greater discount. Beller likely sold the items individually or boxed them in its own outfit boxes.

Seven outfits were connected with Beller: nos. X-582, X-585NA, X-586 Super O promotional, 19204, 19206, 19256 and 19257 Super O promotional. Also, outfit nos. X-719 and X-720 from 1961 were likely purchased by Beller, but for some reason, it was not listed on the Factory Order.

Bennett Brothers

Bennett Brothers, Inc. was founded in 1906 through the acquisition of a diamond and watch business. Bennett Brothers has grown over the years as an implementer and fulfiller of reward programs for businesses. Since the 1920s, it has published the *Blue Book of Quality Merchandise*. This large catalog featured everything from housewares and clothing to toys that included Lionel trains.

Throughout the 1960s, Bennett Brothers primarily sold Lionel catalog outfits, typically offering outfits from the previous year. Thus the Bennett catalog for 1961 featured outfits that Lionel had shown in 1960. But this changed in 1966 and 1967, when it began to carry General Release Promotional outfits. In 1966, Bennett cataloged Lionel 1965 outfits and in 1967, Bennett carried Lionel 1966 outfits, as listed in this table:

Year	Lionel Number	Bennett Catalog Number	Bennett Catalog	Retail Price
1966	19438	6369T2600	1966 Bennett Blue Book	$40.00
	19439-502	6366T1300		$20.00
	19440-502	6367T1950		$30.00
	19441	6368T2275		$35.00
	19442	6370T3250		$50.00
1967	19501	6498T1167	1967 Bennett Blue Book	$17.95
	19503	6499T1427		$21.95
	19511	6502T3250		$50.00
	19515	6500T1950		$30.00
	19517	6501T2600		$40.00

The last four digits of the Bennett Brothers number likely represented the wholesale price.

One outfit has been observed, no. 19438, with a small white label with the Bennett no. 6369T, and another, no. 19517, with no. 6501T written in grease pen.

Benny's

Founded in 1924, Benny's is a discount retailer that provides automotive supplies, toys, hardware and gardening equipment. Currently, Benny's operates thirty stores in southern New England.

In 1962, Benny's sold two Lionel Retailer Promotional outfits, nos. 19167 and 19168. There were no special markings on these boxes, only the Lionel number.

Biederman

Little can be learned about Biederman Furniture Company other than its being sold to American International Corporation (AIC) in 1966. According to Factory Orders, Biederman purchased two Retailer Promotional outfits in 1962, nos. 19114

and 19115. These were O27 outfits that included over-and-under track arrangements. No mention of Biederman markings for either outfit can be found.

To add to the mystery, outfit 19114 appears in an advertisement in the *Atlanta Journal* of December 20, 1962, for Myers-Dickson furniture. A connection between Biederman and Myers-Dickson has yet to be established. The outfit, priced at $21.88 in that ad, was described as a "61-pc. Lionel Electric Train Set. Compare at $39.95".

Boston Stores (see Arkwright, AMC, Independent Retailers Syndicate and Mutual)

Bloomingdales

Bloomingdales, established in 1872 by Lyman and Joseph Bloomingdale, was originally a store based in New York City that specialized in notions for women. Bloomingdales expanded its flagship store in 1929, and in 1930 joined Federated Department Stores. Bloomingdales continued to grow, opening a store in Queens in 1949 and then locations in New Jersey over the next decade. Federated still runs the Bloomingdales division and has expanded the operation to more than thirty stores throughout the United States.

In 1961 and 1962, Lionel provided Bloomingdales with six promotional outfits in very limited quantities (one was for 200 units, and the other five were for 100 or fewer units). Outfit nos. X-696, X-697, 19183, 19193, 19194 and 19195 were all O27 steam freight outfits.

Branch Brook Co.

Established in Hazlet, New Jersey, in 1938, Branch Brook Company is a family-owned business that is one of New Jersey's largest retailers of swimming pools, spas and patio furniture. During the winter, it focuses on selling items for Christmas, including indoor and outdoor decorations.

Branch Brook purchased three Retailer Promotional outfits in 1964: nos. 12857, 12867 and 19410. The first two were O gauge promotionals, while the 19410 was O27. All three were bulk-packed, which suggests that Branch Brook either sold the items individually or boxed them in its own outfit boxes.

Broadway Stores

Broadway Department Stores was founded in 1896 by Arthur Letts in Los Angles. In 1950, it became the Broadway-Hale Stores after purchasing Hale Brothers stores in northern California. After many successful years in retailing, the company bought out Neiman Marcus Corporation in April 1969. In the mid-1970s, Broadway Stores changed its name to Carter Hawley Stores, which lasted until 1994, when during a corporate restructure it changed back to Broadway Stores, Inc. Federated Department Stores acquired Broadway Stores, Inc. in 1995 and has since sold, closed or converted stores to Macy's or Bloomingdales.

In 1962, Broadway Stores purchased a Super O Retailer Promotional outfit, no. 19196.

Bronco Modelcraft

Bronco Modelcraft, Inc. was a distributor located in Westbury, New York, that handled Lionel trains from at least 1959 through 1966. The relationship more than likely spanned additional years.

Bronco did only $31,000 in total combined train revenue with Lionel between 1961 and 1964. Then in 1965 it purchased $106,000 worth of merchandise. By 1966, it had become one of Lionel's top distributors, buying $250,000 in trains (the same amount credited to Sears).

In 1966, Bronco purchased four Retailer Promotionals: nos. 11520-500, 11540-500, 19578 and 19580. These are interesting outfits in that Bronco asked for these display outfits not be marked or sealed. For outfits 11520-500 and 19578 the Factory Order states, "This Set to be packed in #11500 Box but omit number and do not seal lid. Master Carton (2 per) to be sealed on one side only and stamp number 3 on Master Carton." Actually these outfits were stamped "#5". Outfits 11540-500 and 19580 have the same instructions except that the numeral "5" was supposed to be stamped on the master carton. Actually the 11540-500 was stamped "11540-500" and the 19580 was stamped "#3".

Bronco might not have wanted Lionel to number or seal these outfits because it intended to make up its own outfits, just as Mercury Model did in 1966. However, outfits have been observed with "#3" or "#5". Either way, these outfits likely were not stamped by Lionel.

Brown & Williamson and Raleigh

Founded in 1893 by George Brown and his brother-in-law Robert Williamson, Brown & Williamson began manufacturing tobacco the following year. Through the years it acquired tobacco companies, such as Sir Walter Raleigh and R.P. Richardson, and went on to become a national marketer of cigarettes. Brown & Williamson Tobacco Corporation continued independently until 2004, when R. J. Reynolds Tobacco Holdings Inc. bought it and created Reynolds American Inc., now behind only Phillip Morris among the largest cigarette maker in America.

The Raleigh brand originated as Brown & Williamson's first premium cigarette in 1928. To help sell Raleighs, Brown & Williamson started putting a premium coupon on the back of each pack in 1932. Consumers collected and redeemed these coupons for housewares, toys and other merchandise shown in a catalog, just as they might do with trading stamps. These premiums were a driving factor behind Raleigh's increased sales, and it ranked in the twenty best-selling brands of cigarettes by the 1960s.

Brown & Williamson continued with its Raleigh premium catalog until the 1980s. In 1999, the firm stopped accepting any Raleigh coupons as a result of declining participation.

Two outfits appear on the Factory Orders with Brown & Williamson or Raleigh as the customer. The first was 1961 Raleigh outfit no. X-695. The second was 1963 Brown & Williamson outfit no. 19234. It was shown on page 33 of the 1963 Raleigh premium catalog. Identified as Raleigh no. 6380, this outfit required 1,900 coupons.

Interestingly, the 1961 version of outfit no. X-705 for Gift House Stamp has been observed with a Raleigh shipping label. But it was the 1962 version of the X-705 that was shown on page 33 of the 1962 Raleigh premium catalog (requiring 1,900 coupons). These outfits were likely a substitution for X-695

because the quantities of X-695 were low (only 200 were made). Outfits X-695 and X-705 were close, except that the 1961 X-705 had an upgraded locomotive (no. 246-25 in place of no. 1060-25) and tender. The 1962 version of X-705 also included an upgraded helicopter car (no. 3410-25 in place of no. 3409-25). The observed X-705 also included the Gift House Stamp no. T-013-7-0 stamped on the box.

Brown Forman Distillers Corp.

J. T. S. Brown was founded in 1870 by George Garvin Brown and his half-brother in Louisville, Kentucky. The company changed its name to Brown Forman Distillers in 1890, when George Brown and George Forman, Brown's accountant, became partners. Brown Forman was the first distiller to sell whiskey in a sealed bottle and not a barrel. Today, the firm is a multi-national corporation operated by two of Brown's grandsons. Whiskey still plays a major role in its sales, but Brown Forman has diversified into importing wines and spirits and manufacturing Lennox China and Hartmann Luggage.

Only one outfit no. X-619 showed up for Brown Forman Distillers. The Factory Order for this 1961 Retailer Promotional called for just 160 to be manufactured, so few that the outfit was likely used for a retail promotion or an employee incentive.

Canada

Canada was new territory for retailers in the early 1950s. Sears expanded by purchasing an interest in Simpson's Ltd. to form Simpsons-Sears. W. T. Grant was not far behind when it became affiliated with Zellers Limited in 1952. Other U.S. chains, including F. W. Woolworth, A&P, Kresge and Safeway, also operated in Canada to increase sales because less competition existed in Canada than in the United States.

Lionel also took advantage of the Canadian market. One outfit in 1960 (no. X-553NA) and four in 1961 (nos. X-615, X-616, X-618 and X-621) listed Canada as the customer on the Factory Orders. Of these, only X-553NA has been observed in a retail catalog (Simpsons-Sears Christmas catalog for 1960 as no. 49 N9631L for $19.98). Overall, all of these were likely General Release Promotional outfits for the Canadian market.

Canada Hudson-Bay

The Hudson-Bay Company was founded in the 1600s as a fur trade retailer. In 1881, it established its first mail-order operation. Over the next couple of decades, it expanded its product offerings to include liquor, tobacco and confectionary items. In 1911, the company began opening department stores throughout Canada and went on to acquire such stores as Zellers and mail-order operators such as Shop-Rite. Hudson-Bay currently operates The Bay, Zellers, and Home Outfitters chain stores, which together have more than 400 locations.

Canada Hudson-Bay purchased one Retailer Promotional outfit in 1962, no. 19118. At that time Hudson-Bay operated its own department stores as well as Morgan's stores. The outfit was likely offered through either outlet.

Channel Master

Founded in 1949 by Joseph and Louis Resnick in Ellenville, New York, Channel Master manufactured outdoor television antennas, accessories and black-and-white and color TV tubes. In 1967, Channel Master was sold to Avnet and, 30 years later, to Questor Partners Fund L.P. An industry-wide slowdown caused Channel Master to file for Chapter 11 bankruptcy. Andrew Corp. bought selected assets of Channel Master in November 2003.

Channel Master ran a promotion in 1960 in which it offered a Lionel outfit free with a "'Main Line' radio package consisting of 10 popular Channel Master models, including a fabulous new addition to the Channel Master line." The copy went on to state:

"Now! For every 'Main Line' radio package you buy during this limited time promotion, we will send you a 42-piece action packed set of Lionel electronic trains. Your purchase of this 'Main Line' radio package (only ten radios in all) entitles you to a set of Lionel Electric Trains absolutely free! You get a train set for every ten radios you buy. 42 pieces in all. Actual retail value $75.00. A perfectly timed promotion. Christmas is coming, stock up now on these popular Channel Master radios and get these wonderful gifts as well. Your free Lionel Trains can be used in many ways:

- They make a splendid Christmas gift for a number of your family or a young friend.
- They can be installed in you window as part of an action packed radio display to attract passersby (place a couple of the smaller radios in the gondola car when you do this.)
- You can give them away to a lucky customer as a sales promotion prize.
- Sell them and add to your Christmas profits."

Manufacturer Promotional outfit nos. X-573NA (for Channel Master Promotion no. 9745) and 9745 were created for this promotion. Due to numerous substitutions, seven variations of these outfits exist. These outfits included a unique Channel Master billboard and are marked "X-573NA" with an additional sticker saying, "Channel Master Promotion 9745" or just "9745 Channel Master Promotion".

In 1962, Channel Master offered a train set to dealers who purchased seventy-five color television receiving tubes. Although it was not a Lionel outfit, this item provides insight into the promotions conducted by Channel Master. Two years later, Lionel tried to sell Channel Master another promotional outfit (no. 19418), but the Factory Order was marked "Not Used" and has never been observed.

Children's Bargain Town USA (see Interstate Department Stores)

Children's Supermarket (see Interstate Department Stores)

Cities Service

Cities Service Company was founded by Henry L. Doherty in 1910 to supply gas and electricity to small public utilities. In 1965, Cities Service changed its marketing brand to CITGO. PDV America, Inc. purchased the firm in the 1990s, and it is currently headquartered in Houston.

In the late 1950s and 1960s, Cities Service used promotions to drive business and reward customer loyalty. It offered customers gifts with a purchase as well as discounted promotional items. Originally, the company conducted promotions on a regional basis, but in 1961 it centralized promotional management, a step that improved the organization and scheduling of various promotions.

By that time, Lionel had launched a relationship with Cities Service. In 1960, Cities Service ordered six of the no. X-559NA outfit. So small a quantity likely meant the outfits were internal offerings for Cities Service employees or executives. This outfit included a special no. 6465-100X Cities Service Tank Car - with Special Markings. In 1961, Cities Service bought outfit no. X-655, which included the no. 6465-110 Cities Service Tank Car.

The pace picked up the next year, when Cities Service sent a mailing to its dealers that promised "sales winning service station promotions to make '62 a winning year for you." Offered were four promotional items, the last being a "Lionel complete 3-Car Steam Freighter Train Set with Headlight and Magne-Traction". The mailing stated that this outfit had a retail value of $22.95 but was available for $10.95 in the mail.

What Cities Service referred to as one freight set actually had three versions: nos. 19106 (mailer), 19106-50 (display version) and 19106-100 (regular RSC). A total of 7,900 were ordered, one for every two service stations.

No other promotional outfits were listed with Cities Service after the 19106 appeared in 1962. This fact suggests that the company's relationship with Lionel had quietly ended.

Claber's

Claber's Distributing Company consisted of a chain of discount stores throughout Pennsylvania. Claber's, which also operated the Uncle Bill's stores in Cleveland, carried housewares, tools, building supplies and trains.

Claber's purchased one Retailer Promotional in 1962, outfit no. 19162.

Coast to Coast

Coast to Coast Corp. was a wholesaler in the do-it-yourself hardware market. It merged with ServiStar in the early 1990s to form Servistar Coast to Coast (SCC). SCC merged with Cotter & Company in 1997 to form TruServ, and eight years later the firm was renamed True Value.

Two 1966 outfits can be attributed to Coast to Coast. Proof of the first came from the Factory Orders, which mentioned Retailer Promotional outfit no. 19550 (Coast to Coast no. TU0106-3 Reg. $16.99 now $14.97). Indication of the second outfit came from a Coast to Coast catalog that specified General Release Promotional outfit no. 19515 (Coast to Coast no. TU0112-5 Reg. $23.99 now $19.97).

Continental

Continental Products, Inc., started in the early 1900s as a buying office in Chicago. The majority of its sales were toys and novelties. Harrison Wholesale Company, another buying office in Chicago, bought Continental in 1964, a move that helped to expand its toy division. Continental Products continued under its name as a branch of Harrison Wholesale, though operating in a separate location. It was responsible for the distribution of catalogs to its current customers, and Harrison Wholesale supervised the buying division.

In September 1965, Harrison Wholesale expanded again by merging with the wholesale merchandise division of yet another Chicago business, A. C. McClurg and Company. The new firm, operating as Continental - Harrison and Continental - McClurg, continued as a toy buyer and a catalog company until May 1966, when it filed for Chapter 11 bankruptcy.

Continental purchased one Retailer Promotional in 1961, outfit no. X-636.

Cott Beverage Co.

Established in Toronto in 1952, Cott imported carbonated beverages from the United States and distributed them to customers in Canada. In the late 1970s, Cott expanded its operations beyond Canada and is now a major supplier of branded carbonated soft drinks in the United States, Canada and Mexico.

Cott purchased one promotional outfit in 1964, no. 19282.

Cunningham Drug

Cunningham Drug was a drug store chain established in the early 1900s, with stores in Michigan, Ohio and Indiana. During the 1940s, the firm broadened its product line with toys, hardware and electrical supplies. Cunningham Drug was eventually bought by Apex, which was purchased by Perry Drug Stores in 1985. A decade later, Rite Aid purchased Perry.

A Factory Order dated June 1963 listed Cunningham Drug as the customer for outfit no. 19235. Three months later, the original order for 1,000 was canceled.

D. O. Klein

The identity of D. O. Klein remains a mystery. It may have been a distributor, or Lionel may have been referring to S. Klein, a retailer with whom Lionel conducted business.

All the same, two promotional outfits listed D. O. Klein as the customer: nos. 19197 (1962) and 19142-500 (1963).

D. S. C. Promotional (Gifts Galore)

Druggists' Service Council, Inc. was a non-profit organization composed of drug manufacturers and wholesalers. D. S. C. merged with the National Wholesale Drug Association in 1970, and subsequently changed its name to the Healthcare Distribution Management Association after the turn of the twenty-first century.

Druggists' Service Council created generic catalogs containing general merchandise for its member stores. These catalogs were then labeled (stamped) with the drug stores' names. Therefore, smaller drug stores could share advertising dollars, a common practice at that time. The catalogs were titled "Gifts Galore", which was likely a name created solely for these catalogs.

Lionel's relationship with Druggists' Service Council began in 1956 with promotional outfit no. 149. After a year's lapse, Lionel proceeded to issue outfit nos. X-617 in 1958, X-834 in 1959 and X-507NA in 1960. Outfit X-507NA, the last promotional item that Lionel sold to D. S. C., is known as the "Halloween Outfit" because the version of the General locomotive packed with it was orange and black.

Interestingly, all four of these promotional outfits were offered free as part of an in-store drawing. Customers did not have to pay a cent for any of these outfits; they merely filled out an entry form and hoped their luck was good.

Davidson's Detroit

Davidson Brothers, Inc. began in 1932 operating retail stores and a wholesale business in Michigan. The stores carried a variety of merchandise for the family. Davidson's was acquired by Macy's in the early 1980s, and all the locations were converted to Macy's stores.

Davidson's purchased one Retailer Promotional outfit in 1963, no. 19173-500.

Dayton's (see AMC)

Dean Phipps Stores (see Automotive)

Department Store Promotional

In 1960 and 1961, eleven outfits indicated "Department Store Promotional" as their customer. These were General Release Promotionals likely sold to retailers that wanted something different from what was cataloged but could not commit to the volume necessary for their own promotional outfit. Six of the outfits dated from 1960: nos. X-510NA, X-511NA, X-512NA, X-513NA, X-514NA and X-515NA. The other five came from 1961: nos. X-605, X-606, X-607, X-608 and X-609.

Two of these outfits have been observed with retailer price tags. Outfit X-511NA shows The Emporium no. 660 14B1 for $24.98. Outfit X-608 shows Gill's Portland, Oregon, for $29.95.

Department Store Special

Department Store Special is listed by Lionel as a customer for four 1962 promotional outfits: nos. 19110, 19111, 19112 and 19113.

Factory Worksheets indicate the customer as "DS", which refers to "Department Store Special" (another name for a General Release Promotional). Outfit 19110 has been observed with a "Stewart & Co." price tag, but no definitive information has been uncovered about this customer.

Drug Fair

Founded in the late 1930s, Drug Fair was a chain of variety stores that sold automotive supplies, toys, jewelry, housewares and groceries. Its success along the East Coast enabled Drug Fair to expand to 145 stores by 1973. Soon after, Gray Drug Stores purchased the chain and renamed all the stores Gray Drug Fair. Rite Aid purchased Gray Drug (then owned by Sherman Williams) in the 1980s, and the stores were given the new owner's name.

Drug Fair, one of many pharmacies buying from Lionel in the 1960s, purchased one Retailer Promotional outfit in 1961, no. X-704.

E. F. MacDonald Co.

E. F. MacDonald traces its roots to 1922, when William Cappel, the managing partner of A. Cappel & Son in Dayton, Ohio, hired Elton F. MacDonald as a stock boy. Fifteen years later, the two men were business partners; by 1958, the company went by the name of E. F. MacDonald.

E. F. MacDonald specialized in the field of incentives whereby businesses strive to increase corporate results by rewarding a higher degree of employee performance with merchandise, vacations or other valued items. Salespeople traditionally were the recipients of these awards, although E. F. MacDonald's incentives were used by other professions, including banking, air travel, over-the-road transportation and petroleum retailing.

After years of supplying incentive merchandise to Gold Bond and King Korn trading stamps and helping to form and manage Top Value trading stamps, E. F. MacDonald entered the trading stamp business on its own in 1961. It launched Plaid Stamps, which the Great Atlantic & Pacific Tea Company quickly adopted. Soon, customers at 2,500 of the approximately 4,300 A&P stores were receiving Plaid Stamps, which they could redeem by mail or at any of the 230 redemption centers maintained by E. F. MacDonald.

By 1966, E. F. MacDonald had three major domestic divisions, including merchandise incentives, travel incentives and trading stamps. International operations were also in place. Employing more than 3,000 people, E. F. MacDonald reported an annual revenue of $128 million. Carlson Companies had bought the firm by 1981.

Lionel's relationship with E. F. MacDonald lasted from 1961 through 1966. No evidence indicates that trains or toys appeared in Plaid Stamps catalogs. Instead, four promotional outfits were likely used as corporate incentives (no advertisements for these incentives have been observed). Outfit no. X-664 served as a reward for safe driving and reduced maintenance costs to the employees of trucking companies. The other three outfits (nos. 19275, 19280 and 19437) were produced in small quantities and do not have any special markings or numbering on them.

Easy Washer

Founded in 1877 in Syracuse, New York, Easy Washing Machine Company was one of the pioneers in the washing equipment industry. During the 1950s, the Murray Corporation of America absorbed the company, designating it as the Easy Laundry Appliances division. Easy was bought by Hupp Corporation in 1963; four years later, White Consolidated Industries purchased Hupp.

In 1960, Easy offered Manufacturer Promotional outfit no. X-580NA with the purchase of one of its washer/dryer combinations during the holidays. As the advertising stated, "This was the perfect gift for the youngsters and Dad, with Mom reaping the joys of the Easy appliance."

Eaton (see T. Eaton)

Ed Schock's Toy and Hobby

In the 1960s, Ed Schock was a hobby store and authorized Lionel Service Station located in the Broad Ripple area of Indianapolis. In 1960, it bought promotional outfit no. X-240, which was a version of catalog O27 outfit no. 1629 that Lionel repackaged with additional track and trestles.

Englewood Electric

Founded in 1919 in Chicago, Englewood Electric is a distributor of automation, control and industrial goods. It currently oversees more than 30 locations throughout the United States and represents over 400 product lines.

Englewood was a steady customer between 1961 and 1966. It purchased almost $1 million worth of Lionel trains during those years ($383,000, $194,000, $80,000, $67,000, $159,000 and $55,000).

In 1964, Englewood purchased Retailer Promotional outfit no. 12838, a promotional version of Super O outfit no. 13150 with "O track of equal value". Equal value turned out to be ten curve tracks, twenty-two straight tracks and a pair of O Gauge switches. Per the Factory Order, this outfit was intended for Glen's Train Shop in Akron, Ohio.

F. C. Stearns

F. C. Sterns appeared to have been a small hardware store located in Hot Springs, Arkansas. It sold housewares, electrical appliances and possibly trains.

In 1960, F. C. Stearns purchased one promotional outfit, no. X-545NA.

Famous-Barr Co. (see May Company)

In 1892, David May (founder of May Company in 1877) and three of his partners bought the Famous Clothing Store in St. Louis. Nineteen years later, after acquiring the William Barr Dry Goods Company, May combined the two businesses to form Famous-Barr. Over the next half-century, Famous-Barr sold housewares, apparel, electronics and toys. Still part of May, it operates more than 40 stores in the Midwest and Kentucky that generate approximately $1 billion in annual sales.

During the 1960s, Famous-Barr purchased both catalog and promotional outfits from Lionel. Promotional outfits include nos. 19223 and 19230 in 1963 and nos. 19347, 19352, 19353, 19354 and 19373 (Famous-Barr no. 32 M CL 12 M 264 for $9.13) in 1964. Famous-Barr also bought a display version of 19373 (no. D-19373).

Outfit 19223 is interesting in that the Factory Order lists Mutual as the customer, but a price tag links it to Famous-Barr as no. 32 B M 264 for $10.49. Also, at least one outfit sold to May has been observed with a Famous-Barr price tag, 1961 outfit no. X-602 (Famous-Barr no. 32 B 5422 for $29.99). This evidence suggests that Lionel was selling to Famous-Barr both direct and through Mutual Buying Syndicate and May Company.

FAO Schwarz

Frederick August Otto Schwarz and his three brothers opened a toy store in Baltimore in 1862. Eight years later, he turned his attention to New York City, opening Schwarz Toy Bazaar and specializing in selling the finest toys from Europe. A mail-order catalog offering high-quality playthings and games followed in 1876. FAO Schwarz, as the business was known, gained renown in New York and the rest of the United States over the ensuing decades. Its stores were veritable toy museums and playgrounds, where youngsters felt comfortable gazing at and playing with every toy imaginable.

Famed though FAO Schwarz was, it endured tough times in the final third of the twentieth century, thanks to heightened competition from discounters and chains of toy stores. It changed hands several times and filed for Chapter 11 bankruptcy protection at the end of 2003. A business based in New York, D. E. Shaw, rescued the legendary toy retailer in 2004 by purchasing its catalog and online operations, along with the flagship store in Manhattan and a large outlet in Las Vegas, Nevada.

The relationship of Lionel with FAO Schwarz was a long and illustrious one. With a purchase of $7.09 on October 16, 1902, this toy store became one of Lionel's first customers (the order consisted of seven items in the 2⅞-inch gauge train line). FAO Schwarz also broke ground by being one of the first buyers of promotional outfits in 1915. Then, after a long stretch of purchasing only catalog outfits, FAO Schwarz went ahead with promotional outfit no. X-569NA in 1960. Although the Factory Order shows Grand Union as the customer, the FAO Schwarz Christmas Catalog for 1960 shows X-569NA on page 40 as the "Cape Canaveral Freighter (Exclusive)" with its own number (36-117) selling for $39.95.

General Release Promotional outfit no. X-688 appeared in the FAO Schwarz Christmas Catalog for 1961 as the "Lionel Space Security Special (Excl.)" 836-9 for $49.95. In 1962, outfit no. 19175 appeared on page 79 of the annual Christmas catalog as the "Lionel Astronaut Rescue Special" 836-1 for $39.95. A year later, outfit no. 19267 appeared on page 79 of the 1963 Christmas catalog as the "Lionel Fast Freight Set" 836-1 for $32.50. Curiously, it reused the same FAO catalog number from a year earlier. Finally, the 19380 appeared in the FAO Schwarz Christmas Catalog for 1964 as the "Lionel Fast Freight Set (Exclusive)" 836-2 for $34.95. Lionel trains were absent from FAO catalogs for the remainder of the decade.

FAO Schwarz purchased all but X-569NA in quantities of 100 or less. This fact indicates that trains were a small part of that retailer's overall business. The declining toy train market and Lionel's poor credit caused FAO Schwarz to part ways with it after 62 years.

Federal

Federal Wholesale Toy Company was established in 1946 by Bill Bernstein and Milt Miller in Pittsburgh as a general merchandise wholesale operation. During the 1950s, the company outgrew its facilities and moved to California to focus on being a distributor of only toys, principally in California and the Southwest. In 1968, Federal moved into a larger headquarter in La Mirada, California, that housed a warehouse, showroom and offices. Data compiled by California's secretary of state on Federal has not been updated since 1994, which suggests the firm is defunct.

In 1962, Federal purchased promotional outfit no. 19169. Since Federal was a wholesaler, it probably shipped its supply to various retailers.

Federal purchased only $2,000 of trains in 1962 and another $5,000 in 1963. Not until 1965 did business pick up, when it reported $159,000 in train sales. That amount fell to $55,000 the following year. These purchases likely consisted of General Release Promotional outfits, catalog outfits or individual items.

Firestone

Firestone Tire & Rubber Company was founded in 1900 by Harvey Firestone in Akron, Ohio, as a maker of solid rubber tires for carriage wheels. Its first major triumph occurred when Henry Ford selected Firestone tires for the first mass-produced automobiles in America. Firestone continued to expand its operations throughout the United States and entered the Canadian market in the 1920s. During the early years, Firestone continued to succeed by bringing out new products that it aggressively marketed.

When, in the 1930s and 1940s, retailers began to branch out into other industries and offer diverse products to supplement their basic lines, independent tire dealers held back. But Firestone, being an advocate of private brands, jumped on the bandwagon. Eventually, its dealers introduced other manufacturers' products, especially electric appliances. Radios, refrigerators, phonographs and toys, including trains, were included in Firestone's catalogs.

After some tough years, Firestone was acquired by Bridgestone Tires in 1988, a deal that at the time represented the largest acquisition of an American manufacturer by a Japanese corporation. Bridgestone/Firestone has its headquarters in Nashville, Tennessee, and operates 38 production facilities throughout the United States.

Starting in 1940, Lionel took advantage of Firestone's retail diversification into toys. Firestone began offering catalog outfits, and by 1948 its dealers reported sales of Lionel trains exceeding $1.21 million (more than 10 percent of Firestone's annual volume of toys). This trend continued into the 1950s, and Firestone eventually started offering promotional outfits as well as catalog ones.

Merchandise in Firestone catalogs was designated with "11-L" and then a particular item's number. Most train outfits were marked with only the Lionel number. Others were also marked in black grease pen with the Firestone "11-L" number. Still others had just their Firestone number printed by Lionel, perhaps on a sticker covering the Lionel number.

Firestone purchased one catalog outfit in 1961 (no. 1643) and three in 1963 (nos. 11311, 11321, and 11351). Between 1960 and 1964, it also bought the nine promotional outfits listed in this table:

Year	Lionel Number	Firestone Catalog Number	Retail Price
1960	1107	11-L-340 Over-stickered	
1961	1123	11-L-344	$14.88
	1124	11-L-345 printed by Lionel	$17.77
	X-654	11-L-346 printed by Lionel	$23.77
1962	19109	11-L-346 printed by Lionel	
1963	19217	11-L-346	
1964	19338	No Firestone number identified	
	19345		
	19349		

Outfit nos. 1107, 1123 and 1124 were advance catalog promotional outfits. Lionel offered them as well as nos. 19338, 19345 and 19349 to more than one customer, making them General Release Promotional outfits. Only outfit nos. X-654, 19109 and 19217 appeared to be Retailer Promotional outfits that were offered exclusively to Firestone.

As an aside, Firestone used the number 11-L-346 for three outfits available in three different years. Why it chose to reuse this number remains a mystery because the contents of these outfits differed.

It appears that Firestone was a casualty of Lionel's contraction of promotional outfits and in 1965 and 1966, Firestone went back to carrying only catalog outfits. In those two years, it offered outfit nos. 11500 (Firestone no. 11-L-383), 11530 (11-L-381), 11540 (11-L-376) and 11560 (11-L-392). Lionel's long and profitable relationship with Firestone ended after 1966.

Fish Furniture

L. Fish Furniture was founded in 1858 by David Fish and his family on Wells Street in Chicago. Destroyed during the great fire of 1871, the business reopened not long after. Fish Furniture experienced tremendous growth after World War II, expanding to eleven stores in the Midwest. It was among the first furniture retailers in that region to offer credit and trading stamps. After selling its Chicago stores to Helig-Meyers Furniture Company, L. Fish Furniture decided to maintain its outlet in Indianapolis.

Although L. Fish Furniture specialized in home furnishings, it, like other retailers in that field, commonly sold toys during the holiday season. Lionel took advantage of this arrangement and provided Fish Furniture with two promotional outfits in 1962, nos. 19116 and 19117.

Foley's

Foley Brothers Dry Goods Co. opened its first store in Houston in 1900. At that time the company had a small product line of linens and men's furnishings. It grew steadily until, by 1922, it was Houston's largest department store, carrying an array of home furnishings, toys and apparel. Federated Department Stores acquired Foley's in 1945. This arrangement lasted through 1988, when May Department Stores purchased Foley's; it has continued to operate those stores in the Southwest.

In 1964, Foley's purchased one Retailer Promotional outfit, no. 19393.

Frederick Atkins

"Atkins" was listed as a customer on Lionel Factory Orders. It was short for Frederick Atkins. Frederick Atkins was a large buying cooperative incorporated in New York in 1944. It handled the purchasing of goods for department stores, including Altman & Company and Dillard's. Atkins went out of business in 2000.

Four outfits were distributed to Frederick Atkins between 1960 and 1964: nos. X-529NA, X-685, 19243 and 19375. Outfit X-529NA has been observed with a Lazarus price tag, and X-685 has been seen with a Hahne & Company tag. These were most likely the end customers of either one of these Frederick Atkins promotionals.

Frontier Savings Stamps

Frontier Trading Stamp Company was located in southern California and provided trading stamps to a variety of retailers in the 1960s, including Alpha Beta Food Markets (which owned 49 percent of Frontier). Stamps could be redeemed for goods listed in Frontier's "Saving Stamps Merchandise Catalog". Redemption centers were located in Arizona, California, Colorado, New Mexico and Texas.

The Frontier Savings Stamps catalog for 1960, which featured items that "fit the needs of people in the West and Great Southwest", included one Lionel outfit. Retailer Promotional outfit no. X-548 was listed on page 41 as item no. T-96, which was available for six books of Frontier stamps.

G. C. Murphy

G. C. Murphy Company, founded by George Clinton Murphy, opened its first store in 1906 in McKeesport, Pennsylvania. Five years later, after Murphy had died, John S. Mack and Walter C. Shaw purchased the company. G. C. Murphy operated as a variety store and expanded throughout Pennsylvania in the 1920s. Steady growth continued, and in the 1940s the company branched outside of the East Coast and purchased stores in the Midwest. Murphy remained competitive into the 1960s, competing with discount stores by opening its own outlets known as Murphy Marts. Ames Stores bought Murphy in 1985, and it was sold to McCrory Stores four years later. McCrory, known for buying older chains of variety stores, kept the G. C. Murphy stores in operation through the 1990s despite financial problems. In 2002, the Murphy stores were shut down after the firm filed for bankruptcy.

In 1960, G. C. Murphy purchased one Retailer Promotional outfit, no. X-524NA. Over the next five years, it likely carried only catalog outfits. In 1966, Murphy offered another Retailer Promotional, no. 19586. A display example exists with a label on the cover indicating it was a "G. C. Murphy Exclusive By Lionel".

G. Fox & Company

Established in Hartford, Connecticut, by Gershan Fox, G. Fox opened its first dry goods store in 1847. The company's first department store followed in the early 1900s and, after enduring a terrible fire in 1917, grew to be the largest such business in Hartford. G. Fox continued under the leadership of Gershan Fox's daughter Beatrice and eventually became the largest privately held department store in the United States. As a result, May Company took an interest in G. Fox and acquired it in 1965. May went on operating the G. Fox division until 1995, when the latter was folded into Filenes.

In 1961, G. Fox purchased one Retailer Promotional outfit, no. X-659. This was the only promotional outfit listed in the Factory Orders for G. Fox. However, G. Fox probably purchased catalog outfits, too, because no. 12760 from 1964 has been observed with a G. Fox price tag.

Gamble-Skogmo

Founded by Bertin Gamble and Phillip Skogmo, Gamble-Skogmo was originally a car dealership that sold auto parts, tires and accessories. In 1925, the company expanded its product offerings and opened its first retail store in St Cloud, Minnesota. Gamble-Skogmo grew to be a major retailer, operating discount stores, a mail-order house (Gamble-Skogmo merged with Aldens in 1965), catalog stores, drug stores, real estate firms and department stores in the United States and Canada. Such diversity enabled the firm to survive much longer than its competitors.

Bertin Gamble retired in 1977, and the company was sold in 1980 to the Wickes Company of California. The purchase of Gamble-Skogmo was too large for Wickes to handle, and the combined companies struggled financially. In 1982, Wickes filed one of the largest non-utility bankruptcies in American history. As a result, the era of Gamble-Skogmo Department Stores ended. The company's other divisions were sold off in pieces.

Between 1961 and 1964, Gamble-Skogmo purchased four promotional outfits: nos. X-667 (1961), 19189 (1962), 19245 (1963) and 19367 (1964). Outfit X-667 was also to be stamped with customer stock no. B 23-2892; outfit 19189 was also to be marked with no. 23-4483. All four outfits were made in large quantities and likely sold through Gamble-Skogmo Department Stores. However, Gamble-Skogmo operated at least twenty-six divisions, so these outfits could have been offered through Red Owl, Snyder Drug or other holdings with toy departments.

Gertz (see Allied)

Gertz was established by the Gertz family in New York City, as a flagship department store that served much of Queens and parts of Brooklyn and Long Island. Gertz Department Store continued operating under Gertz Family Enterprises until 1941, when it was sold to Allied Store Corporation.

Allied expanded the troubled Gertz division in 1982, when it opened fifteen stores throughout New York. The division was profitable within two years. In 1986, Campeau Corporation acquired Allied and its Gertz division.

From 1960 through 1964, Lionel provided Allied Stores with eleven promotional outfits, some of which were probably sold through Gertz. Allied outfit no. X-648 was observed with a Gertz price tag for $29.88. One additional outfit, no. 19143, was sold direct to Gertz.

In 1962, a price tag indicates that Gertz offered catalog outfit no. 13048 as no. 830 11 2 for $57.00.

Gift House Stamp

Gift House Stamp, Inc. was a trading stamp company incorporated in Minneapolis in 1954. Like many of the stamp companies of that time, it distributed catalogs and opened redemption centers throughout the United States. During the 1960s, the largest provider of Gift House stamps was Star Market Inc., which operated a chain of grocery stores on the East Coast.

Between 1960 and 1962, Gift House Stamp purchased three promotional outfits: no. X-875 (in 1960) and two versions of no. X-705. The 1961 version of X-705 was also stamped with Gift House Stamp number T-013-7-0. This outfit has been observed with a Raleigh Cigarette shipping label, which suggests it was used as a substitute for no. X-695 (see Brown & Williamson). Outfit X-705, ordered again in 1962, was an update to the 1961 version. A no. 242 steam locomotive replaced a no. 246, and a no. 3410 Helicopter Launching Car replaced a no. 3409.

Gill's (see Department Store Promotional)

Gifts Galore (see D. S. C. Promotional)

Gimbels

Founded in Milwaukee in 1889, Gimbel Brothers was a department store that sold clothing, housewares, automotive supplies and toys. Gimbels, named for the eight siblings that owned and managed it, expanded its operations to Philadelphia in 1894 and New York in 1910. Incorporating in 1922, Gimbels continued to grow when it acquired two Saks and Company stores in 1923 and Kaufmann & Bauer in 1925. After gaining control of Schuster's Department Stores in 1962, the firm began calling itself Gimbels Schuster's. Gimbels was sold to BAT Industries in 1973; the last of the Gimbels stores closed 14 years later.

From 1961 through 1966, Gimbels and Gimbels Schuster's purchased $405,000 worth of merchandise ($367,000 in trains and $38,000 in raceways). That amount made the company a notable customer of Lionel.

The first two of thirteen promotional outfits ordered between 1960 and 1966 were nos. X-521NA (Gimbels no. 740 F0 at $19.99) and X-522NA. In 1961, Gimbels purchased nos. X-631 (740 F1 at $19.99), X-632 and X-633; the next year saw nos. 19142-500, 19163, 19164 and 19165. For 1963, Lionel provided outfit no. 19218 (740 F3 at $19.88). In 1964 there were nos. 19345 (P740 F4 at $19.99) and 19374 (Gimbels Schuster's no. 740 F4 at $9.88) and in 1966 there was no. 19563 (740 S8 65 at $29.99).

Glen's Train Shop

Glen's Train Shop was a hobby shop and authorized Lionel Service Station owned by Glen Uhl, a retired Navy electrician residing in Akron, Ohio. Uhl, a long-time holder of Lionel stock, never hesitated to express his concerns about Lionel's management at shareholder meetings in the 1960s. He denounced what he saw as the company's poor financial management and products' declining quality. Uhl also spoke out against what he perceived as the unfair nature of selling an outfit for less than what its components cost. Even though he took advantage of this tendency by breaking up outfits, he worried that doing so weakened Lionel's overall profitability.

Glen's Train Shop appears on one Factory Order for Retailer Promotional outfit no. 12838 in 1964. This was a promotional version of Super O outfit no. 13150 with "O track of equal value." Equal value turned out to be ten curve tracks, twenty-two straight tracks and a pair of O Gauge switches. Englewood Electric and Glen's Train Shop were listed on the Factory Order, which suggests that Englewood purchased the outfit on behalf of Glen's.

Goldblatt's

Goldblatt's, established in 1914 by Maurice and Nathan Goldblatt, was a Chicago-based department store that offered a variety of goods at discounted prices. The company was one of the few chain retailers in Chicago during the 1920s, and it flourished after the Great Depression due to its daring to offer lower prices than did its competitors. Over the years, Goldblatt's expanded its operations to include furniture and appliances (these enabled Goldblatt's to account for 15 percent of retail sales in Chicago at one time). By the 1970s, however, competition from discount retailers had caused a decline in sales. This situation, combined with poor managerial decisions, led Goldblatt's to declare bankruptcy in 1981. All but six of its stores were closed before the company was purchased by JG Industries in 1982. In August 2000, the Goldblatt family bought the right to use the Goldblatt's name from JG Industries, but had to liquidate the six remaining stores within three years.

Between 1960 and 1964, Goldblatt's purchased eight promotional outfits and one display. The first of these, Retailer Promotional outfit no. X-537NA, came about in 1960. No outfits appeared again until 1962, when it offered Retailer Promotionals nos. 19139, 19140 and 19141. A year later, Goldblatt's carried outfit nos. 19233 and 19233-500 (Goldblatt's no 242 4 3 2390 for $25.00). Finally in 1964, Retailer Promotional outfits included nos. 19351 (242 4-4 for $19.99), 19351-500 and display DO19351.

Grand Union

Established in 1872 and incorporated in 1928, Grand Union Company was one of largest and most successful food chains on the East Coast. Unlike most food chains, it did not rely solely on the grocery business to prosper. Grand Union opened mini-marts, restaurants, drug stores, a trading stamp company and discount houses to supplement its revenue. The company continued to flourish until the 1990s, when Wal-Mart and other national chains began to dominate the industry. As a result, Grand Union filed for bankruptcy protection on three separate occasions and in 2001 was acquired by GU Markets, an affiliate of C&S Wholesale Grocers Inc.

In 1960, Grand Union purchased one Retailer Promotional outfit, no. X-569NA. Lionel sold other promotional outfits to Grand Union's discount store division, which was known as Grand-Way.

Grand-Way

In 1956, Grand Union Company set up a discount store division that it named Grand-Way. Located on the East Coast, the Grand-Way stores (fewer than twenty-five) were a combination of a food outlet and a discount center. Originally, about a third of their inventory consisted of non-grocery items. This arrangement lacked sufficient diversity to generate profits in the 1960s, so Grand-Way stores began offering additional products to compete with department stores. Grand-Way operated until 2001, when GU Markets purchased Grand Union Company.

Lionel and Grand-Way did a considerable amount of promotional outfit business in the early 1960s. In 1960, Grand-Way purchased two Retailer Promotional outfits, nos. X-554NA and X-561NA. In 1962, it increased to three Retailer Promotionals: nos. 19179 (Grand-Way price tag no. 16 2-22 HG 490 for $14.97), 19180 and 19181.

Grant's (see W. T. Grant)

Grossman's

Grossman's started out in the 1890s as a one-person operation peddling building products. Family-owned by 1919, it opened its first retail store in Michigan and continued to expand. In 1968, the family sold the chain to Evans Products Co., which resulted in further growth. Although Evans declared bankruptcy in 1983, it managed to reorganize because of the profitability of the Grossman's stores. In 1997, Grossman's merged with Jeld-Wen, Inc. and now operates building supply stores and outlets in Ohio and on the East Coast.

In 1960, Grossman's purchased one Retailer Promotional, no. X-549NA. It ordered only 200 of these outfits, probably allotting a few to each store.

Hahne & Company (see Frederick Atkins)

Halle Brothers

Halle Brothers Company, founded in 1891 by Salmon and Samuel Halle, operated as a dry goods store until the early 1900s. In 1910, the brothers expanded their operations by opening a department store in downtown Cleveland. The company's success, based on superior customer service and products, paved the way for growth until it had launched nine satellite stores in Ohio. During the 1970s, when many department stores merged, Marshall Field acquired Halle Brothers. Another sale occurred in 1992, when Schottenstein Stores Corporation, one of the largest retail liquidators in America, took over Halle Brothers, only to shut down its stores in Ohio.

A Lionel outfit has been observed in a Halle Brothers catalog from the late prewar period. Positive attribution of a pair of Retailer Promotional outfits going to Halle Brothers can be made for 1960 (no. X-528NA) and 1962 (no. 19184). In addition, an outfit from 1961, no. X-632, has been observed in a *Cleveland Plain Dealer* book dated 11/26/61 for "The Halle Bros. Co." as no. 40-B selling for $28.00. However, the Lionel Factory Order lists Gimbels as the customer for X-632. Most likely, Lionel sold this outfit to both Gimbels and Halle Brothers.

Hecht & Company

Samuel and Babbett Hecht set up a general store in Baltimore in 1857 that they called Hechts Company. Two younger members of the family, Moses and Alexander Hecht, carried on this tradition by opening a department store in Washington, D.C., in 1896. That store, the flagship of Hecht & Company, sold a wide range of products, ranging from apparel to toys. During the 1950s, Hecht's opened stores along the East Coast, expansion that drew attention from May Company, which purchased the organization in 1959. May continues to operate stores under the Hecht's name on the East Coast.

In 1964, Hecht's ordered 200 of General Release Promotional outfit no. 19348. The store in Washington received 150 of them; the rest went to the store in Baltimore. Lionel also sold 19348 to A. B. C. Birmingham.

Honig's Parkway

Honig's Parkway was a department store with two locations in the Bronx, New York, one on Webster Avenue and another on White Plains Road. Honig's stores sold a variety of items, including housewares, toys and electric trains. It remains in business as Honig's Appliance LLC.

In 1963, Honig's, which featured an authorized Lionel Service Station, bought one Retailer Promotional, bulk-packed outfit no. 19268. The outfit came with a unique group of items that the store either sold individually or assembled into its own outfits. If Honig's took the latter course, it probably added a caboose to each outfit from store stock because 19268 did not include a caboose.

Hudson's Detroit (see Mercury Model)

Independent Retailers Syndicate (IRS)

Independent Retailers Syndicate (IRS) was a privately held buying cooperative located in New York that provided merchandise for hundreds of retailers, including such key accounts as Aldens, Boston Stores and Grossman's. It charged members a flat monthly or yearly fee for membership, with discounts based on the quantity of items ordered. IRS operated independently until 1989, when it was acquired by Donegar Group, another well-known buying cooperative located in New York.

During the 1960s, Lionel targeted IRS and its accounts. IRS would send out information to its members while encouraging Lionel's sales force to work directly with these stores. In 1961, IRS bought a total of 24 units of Retailer Promotional outfit no. X-682. Two years later, it ordered 37 units of Retailer Promotional outfit no. 19246. The small quantities suggested that IRS distributed them to one of its accounts or used them internally.

Interstate Department Stores - Children's Bargain Town USA and Children's Supermarket

Interstate Department Stores, Inc., was a discount and department retail chain launched in 1928. It grew by expanding its own Family Fair and Topps divisions and acquiring other retailers. Among the discount houses Interstate acquired were Children's Bargain Town USA, Children's Supermarket and White Front Stores. It later acquired Toys "R" Us, yet ended up declaring bankruptcy in 1974.

In 1966, Children's Supermarket purchased two General Release Promotional outfits: nos. 19516 (sold for $34.94) and 19517 (also $34.94). In 1961, Children's Bargain Town bought advance catalog promotional outfit no. 1123 (sold for $7.99). In 1967, it bought one General Release Promotional outfit, no. 19707 (sold for $27.97).

Interstate Department Stores - White Front Stores

White Front Stores made headlines as an operator of discount houses in Los Angeles during the 1950s. Its success as a dealer of television sets and other "hard-line" merchandise led to the purchase of the chain by Interstate Department Stores in 1959. Seeing White Front Stores prosper in southern California, Interstate opened outlets in other metropolitan areas of that state.

Although White Front Stores remained one of the largest and most successful discounters on the West Coast, they closed in 1974 when Interstate declared bankruptcy.

Between 1961 and 1966, White Front Stores purchased $327,000 ($281,000 in trains and $46,000 in raceways) worth of merchandise from Lionel. Included in this amount were two Retailer Promotional outfits: nos. X-635 in 1961 and 19363 in 1964. Lionel produced both outfits in large quantities, so Interstate likely distributed what it bought among various White Front Stores as well as other chains it owned.

J & R Auto Stores (see Automotive Associates)

J. C. Penney

J. C. Penney Co., Inc. was founded by James Cash Penney in 1902 as Golden Rule Stores. By 1912, Penney owned a chain of thirty-four Golden Rule Stores that carried a variety of merchandise for the home. Within two years, the number of stores increased to seventy-two; by 1919, the name of the firm was changed to J. C. Penney. In the 1920s, Penney experienced its largest expansion by opening more than 1,000 stores. During the 1950s and 1960s, as many Americans moved to the suburbs, Penney also moved to the shopping malls that were sprouting up.

The 1980s and 1990s were profitable for J. C. Penney, which expanded outside the United States by buying 20 percent of Sarma, S. A., a Belgian retail chain. In the meantime, Penney watched its catalog division flourish while it diversified by acquiring drug stores and banks. Recently, declining sales led to the restructuring of that catalog division and the closing of some catalog fulfillment centers. Still, Penney remains one of America's largest department store, catalog, and Internet retailers. Its 1,017 department stores employ approximately 150,000 people.

During the final decade of the postwar era, J. C. Penney proved to be a steady and loyal customer of Lionel. To be sure, the accumulated value of the items purchased did not make Penney one of Lionel's most lucrative clients. It bought $15,000 worth of merchandise in 1961, followed by $20,000 in 1962, $41,000 in 1963, $104,000 in 1964, $26,000 in 1965 and $20,000 in 1966. However, because this total of $226,000 was spread across twenty-two promotional outfits, three promotional displays and numerous catalog outfits, it made Penney a key customer. The variety and quantity of the outfits that the firm ordered guaranteed that Lionel paid close attention to it.

Lionel's relationship with J. C. Penney began in 1960, with the purchase of the no. 1806 assortment of catalog rolling stock, an indication that trains were being sold in retail outlets. Documents also suggest that, in 1961 and 1962, Penney sold through its stores four Retailer Promotional outfits: nos. X-665, X-666, 19148 and 19149.

In 1962, J. C. Penney entered the mail-order business by acquiring General Merchandise Corporation (GMC), a mail-order catalog business and discount-store operation in Milwaukee. GMC was already buying catalog outfits. Its catalogs for 1961 and 1962 listed the following Lionel outfits:

Year	Lionel Number	GMC Catalog Number	GMC Catalog
1961	1641	84-1007 W	1961 General Merchandise Catalog
	1642	84-1023 W	
	1643	84-1056 W	
	1646	84-1064 W	
	1649	84-1122 W	
1962	1646	84-0876 W	1962 General Merchandise Fall and Winter Catalog
	11222	84-0900 W	
	11232	84-0892 W	
	11252	84-0801 W	
	11288	84-0991 W	

Year	Lionel Number	J. C. Penney Catalog Number	J. C. Penney Catalog	Retail Price
1960	1806		No Catalog Listing	
1961	X-665			
	X-666			
1962	19148			
	19149			
1963	11375	X 923-4782 A	1963 Penney Toy Catalog	$29.98
	11341	X 923-4881 A		$18.88
	11351	X 923-4899 A		$22.95
1964	19333	X 924-0664 A	1964 Christmas Catalog	$9.99
	19334	X 924-0680 A		$13.88
		923-5361		$14.88
	19334-500	X 924-0680 A		$13.88
	19335	X 924-0672 A		$18.88
	D-19333		No Catalog Listing	
	DO19335			
1965	19437	923 5361		$19.88
	19437-502	X 924-3726 A	1965 Christmas Catalog	$18.99
	19438		No Catalog Listing	
	19438-502	X 924-3734 A		$29.00
	19442	X 924-3718 A	1965 Christmas Catalog	$34.44
	12820	X 924-3700 A		$69.99
1966	19506	9808	No Catalog Listing	
	19507	X 924-8279 A	*1966 Christmas Catalog	$28.88
	19510	9804	No Catalog Listing	
	19511	X 924-8287 A	1966 Christmas Catalog	$37.77
	19514	9802	No Catalog Listing	
	19515	X 924-8261 A	1966 Christmas Catalog	$19.88
	1259		No Catalog Listing	

The GMC acquisition set the stage for the release of the first J. C. Penney catalog in August of 1963. Later that year, a specialty catalog was printed containing toys and three Lionel catalog outfits. Also in 1963, Penney ordered a Retailer Promotional outfit, no. 19215, but the order was subsequently canceled, perhaps due to the acquisition of GMC.

Mail-order operations were in full swing at J. C. Penney by 1964, which is when the firm compiled its first Christmas catalog filled with, among other items, toys and electric trains. Also in 1964, outfits started to appear in different versions. Display outfits were purchased for the retail stores and RSCs for mail order.

Outfit no. 19334 is the display version likely sold through retail stores, whereas no. 19334-500 is packed in an RSC and sold via mail order. Two other Retailer Promotional outfits appearing on Factory Orders were described in the Penney catalog for 1964. Outfit no. 19333 came in a custom-decorated Penney RSC, while no. 19335 was Penney's high-end outfit for the year. Displays were also produced as nos. D-19333 and DO19335.

As indicated on 1965 Factory Orders, two outfits from 1964 - nos. 19334-500 and 19335 - were carried over. The remainder of outfits for 1965 followed Lionel's move to General Release Promotional outfits. J. C. Penney purchased five of these as well as one catalog outfit.

Display outfit nos. 19437 and 19438 were likely sold in stores whereas nos. 19437-502 and 19438-502 were sold via mail order. Outfit no. 19442 was offered only in RSC. Finally, catalog outfit no. 12820 was listed for $30.01 less than the Lionel catalog price of $100.

General Release Promotional outfits in both display and RSCs were the norm again 1966. Six outfits were available as well as the no. 1259 Merchandise Display Assortment.

Two years of inactivity followed. No Lionel trains appeared in the J. C. Penney catalogs in 1967 and 1968. Then circumstances changed. In 1969, at the end of the postwar era, two Lionel catalog outfits showed up: nos. 11710 (Penney no. X 926-1082 A for $19.99) and 11740 (no. X 926-1090 A for $34.50). These outfits concluded for this period the relationship between Lionel and a major retailer known throughout the United States.

J. J. Newberry

J. J. Newberry Co. was a chain of five-and-dime variety stores founded by John Josiah Newberry in 1911. The first of his stores was located in Stroudsburg, Pennsylvania, and soon more were added until, by 1961, Newberry boasted a network of 565 stores. McCrory Corporation acquired the company in the 1980s and continued operating the Newberry chain until 2001, when it filed for bankruptcy.

In 1964, a single outfit, no. 19253-100, specifies J. J. Newberry as a customer. However, no Factory Order exists, only a listing on a 1964 Release document. Therefore, it cannot be ascertained whether Lionel ever manufactured this outfit.

J. W. Robinson's

J. W. Robinson's was founded 1883 in Los Angeles by Joseph Winchester Robinson as Boston Dry Goods. In 1891, with the opening of the company's first department store in downtown Los Angeles, the name was changed to J. W. Robinson Company. In the late 1950s, Associated Dry Goods purchased the firm with the intention of opening more stores in California. Associated Dry Goods merged with May Department Stores in 1986 and operated J. W. Robinson's as a separate entity until January 1993, when the firm was renamed Robinsons-May.

In 1960, not long after Associated Dry Goods purchased J. W. Robinson's, the latter firm ordered Retailer Promotional outfit no.

X-558NA. The Factory Order stated that only 120 of these outfits were made. A price tag on one example indicated that it retailed for $29.95. Also in 1960, Lionel provided Associated Dry Goods with a different promotional outfit, no. X-556NA.

Jersey Model Distributors

Jersey Model Distributors is a privately held toy and hobby wholesaler located in Ramsey, New Jersey. In 1964, it purchased Retailer Promotional outfit no. 13267. That outfit was based on catalog outfit no. 13150, but it substituted several pieces of rolling stock for the no. ZW-1 transformer that Lionel originally included.

Jewel Tea Company

Established in 1899 by Frank Skiff, the Jewel Tea Company originally delivered dry goods to customers in Chicago. By the 1930s, it had diversified, adding food, discount and drug stores to its delivery business (which it had renamed Jewel Home Shopping Service). Over the next three decades, the Home Shopping Service became a division of Jewel Companies, which helped Jewel emerge as one of the largest retailers in the United States.

In 1981, Jewel Companies sold each Home Shopping Service route to the operating employee. All assets and inventory were consolidated into a cooperative that became JT's General Store. In 1984, American Stores acquired Jewel Companies, thereby becoming one of the principal food retailers in the country. In 1999, Albertsons bought American Stores for $9.5 billion and continues to operate what is known as the Jewel-Osco chain of grocery and drug stores in the Midwest. In January, 2006, Albertsons agreed to sell Jewel-Osco for $17.4 billion to an investor group led by Supervalu, CVS and Cerberus.

Jewel Tea Company purchased two Retailer Promotional outfits: nos. X-689 in 1961 and 19188 in 1962. The Factory Order for X-689 called for "Customer Stock No. X 10 R 29 to appear on outfit cartons & Shippers". This number appeared below the outfit number.

Joe, The Motorists' Friend

Joe, The Motorists' Friend, Inc. was an auto parts chain established in Harrisburg, Pennsylvania, by Joe Stine. A shipping label on outfit no. 19177 reads "Joe The Motorists' Friend, Inc., 35 Super Auto - Sports Stores; Auto Accessories, Tires, Radios, Television, Sporting Goods; Stores in Penna., Maryland, Virginia and W. VA". These retail stores were known for carrying Lionel catalog and promotional outfits.

Between 1961 and 1966, Joe, The Motorists' Friend purchased ten Retailer Promotional and two General Release Promotional outfits. The biggest purchase came in 1961, when the firm ordered 900 units of no. X-690. The next year, it bought smaller quantities of three outfits: nos. 19176, 19177 and 19178. Then in 1963 came five more outfits: nos. 19247, 19248, 19249, 19250 and 19251.

In 1964, Joe, the Motorists' Friend purchased bulk-packed General Release Promotional O gauge outfit no. 12827, which it likely broke up for separate sale. Also attributed to the firm in that year was outfit no. 19390.

No Factory Orders listed Joe, The Motorists' Friend in 1965. Still, it probably bought General Release Promotional or catalog outfits. One more promotional outfit can be linked to the company.

An example of outfit no. 11570 from 1966 has been observed with a Joe, The Motorists' Friend price tag. On it, the original $27.25 has been crossed out and $10.95 written in by hand.

A November 14, 1967, letter from Joe Stine to his stores (reprinted in the July 1988 issue of the *Train Collectors Quarterly*) provides the final clue about the outfits purchased by his company. Stating that Joe, The Motorists' Friend stores were still very active in Lionel trains, this document mentions that there were in stock "special uncataloged numbers with stock numbers beginning with 19".

Johnson Dewalt

Based in Eagleville, Pennsylvania, Johnson Dewalt operates as a manufacturer's representative to the premium and incentive industry. Like a buying cooperative, it supplies goods and services to companies interested in offering premiums to their end customers.

Johnson Dewalt purchased three Retailer Promotional outfits: nos. 19170 in 1962, 19258 in 1963 and 19386 in 1964.

Jordan Marsh (see Allied)

Founded in 1841 in Boston by Eben Jordan and Benjamin L. Marsh, Jordan Marsh Department Stores carried apparel, toys and hard-line merchandise. In the early twentieth century, Jordan Marsh became one of the leading department stores on the East Coast as well as a recognized catalog company. The firm helped found the New York-based Allied Stores Corporation in the 1930s. Allied opened Jordan Marsh stores in Florida and operated them until merging with Federated Department Stores in 1991. Not long after the merger, Burdines (part of Federated) absorbed Jordan Marsh and converted all existing Jordan Marsh stores to Burdines Department Stores.

From 1960 through 1964, Lionel provided Allied Stores with eleven promotional outfits, and some might have been sold through Jordan Marsh. In fact the Lionel Outfit Cost Worksheet for outfit no. 19154 lists "Allied - J.M." as the customer. Lionel did sell four additional outfits direct to Jordan Marsh: nos. X-560NA, X-681, 19274-500 and 19385.

Joseph Horne Co. (see Mercury Model)

Katz Drug

Isaac and Mike Katz established Katz Drug Company in 1914 as a cigar confectionary store with two locations in Kansas City, Missouri. The firm grew steadily over the years and had more than forty locations by the 1950s. Adopting new merchandising methods, Katz stocked toys and hard-line merchandise at its retail outlets and provided larger shopping locations than its competitors. Aggressive marketing, including advertisements aired over local television, also fueled the company's growth.

As a result of its huge assortment of products and services, Katz exceeded per store volume of many similar stores. Such outstanding performance caused competitors to take notice and imitate the firm's practices. The Skaggs Company bought Katz Drug in December of 1970 and nine years later took over American

Stores and assumed its name. In 1984, American Stores took over Jewel Food Stores and changed the Katz stores to Osco.

Katz, which carried a variety of toys, purchased only one promotional outfit from Lionel. In 1961, it ordered Retailer Promotional outfit no. X-710.

Kaufmann's

Kaufmann's was founded as a men's store by two brothers, Jacob and Isaac Kaufmann, in 1871. By 1892 Kaufmann's Grand Depot occupied a full block in downtown Pittsburgh. The May Department Stores Company merged with Kaufmann's in 1946 and opened branches along the East Coast. May operated the more than 50 Kaufmann's Department Stores until fall of 2005 when May was acquired by Federated. All Kaufmann's stores were converted to Macy's.

The no. 19250 from 1963 listed Joe, The Motorists' Friend as its customer on the Factory Order. Along the way, some of these were purchased by Kaufmann's either through Joe, The Motorists' Friend or directly from Lionel. A Kaufmann's sales receipt listing a 19250 was included with one such outfit. In 1964, Kaufmann's purchased one General Release Promotional outfit, no. 19374. Interestingly, this outfit has also been observed with a price tag labeled for Gimbels Schuster's, a competitor of Kaufmann's.

Kiddie City

Established in 1957 by Leonard Wasserman, Kiddie City was a self-service discount store specializing in toys, furniture, children's clothing and living accessories. One of the first toy discounters in the market, Kiddie City opened eleven stores in and around Philadelphia before selling them to Penn Fruit Company in 1961. Wasserman continued as president of Kiddie City until January of 1963, when he bought back the company from Penn Fruit.

Wasserman operated the chain of Kiddie City stores until August 1969, when the Lionel Corporation acquired the Leonard Wasserman Company in exchange for shares of stock. This was shortly after the Lionel Corporation finalized the contract to leave the train business by licensing the rights to manufacture and market its electric trains to General Mills. Wasserman remained the president of the Kiddie City division for 11 years; from 1982 to 1983, he served as president and chief executive officer of the Lionel Corporation. Kiddie City stores remained in existence until 1993, when the Lionel Corporation (unaffiliated with Lionel Trains, Inc.), operating under Chapter 11 bankruptcy, liquidated the chain due to competition and financial troubles.

In 1961, Kiddie City purchased one Retailer Promotional outfit, no. X-700. It ordered 150 of these outfits from Lionel, which broke down to approximately fifteen for each Kiddie City store.

King Korn

Peter Volid established King Korn Stamp Company in Chicago, seeking business throughout the United States and eventually testing the waters in Great Britain. By the 1960s, the company boasted five major subsidiaries and could claim to be among the largest makers of trading stamps.

In 1963, King Korn purchased one Retailer Promotional outfit, no. 19211 (King Korn no. K2893). To obtain one, consumers had

to fill 6⅔ books of stamps and then place a special order because this outfit was not stocked at King Korn redemption centers.

Kings Department Stores

Kings Department Stores, Inc. consisted of a chain of about twenty self-service discount houses on the East Coast. Stores typically carried household items, clothing and toys. Based in Pennsylvania, Kings purchased merchandise direct from manufacturers, which helped to keep costs low. Kings acquired Mammoth Mart stores in the 1970s, but it ran into financial troubles after the acquisition. As a result, Kings, which had then changed its name to KDT Industries, filed for bankruptcy in 1982 and was acquired by Ames Corporation two years later.

Kings purchased two Retailer Promotional outfits: nos. 19182 in 1962 and 19240-500 in 1963.

Kroger

Barney Kroger established what was originally known as the Great Western Tea Company in 1883. Based in Cincinnati, the firm had incorporated by 1902 and changed its name to Kroger Grocery and Baking Company. In the 1940s, it again changed names, this time to The Kroger Company.

Acquisitions made during the 1950s enabled Kroger to expand beyond its base in the Midwest. The firm adopted new marketing techniques that emphasized carrying hard-line merchandise and toys. Broadening the range of products it carried helped Kroger compete with discounters and department stores. Kroger merged with Fred Meyer, Inc. in 1999, thereby creating the largest grocery company in America.

Between 1961 and 1963, Kroger purchased two Retailer Promotional outfits, one General Release Promotional outfit and one blister display. Outfit no. X-699 appeared in a Kroger advertisement printed in the December 6, 1961, edition of the *Van Wert Times Bulletin* in Van Wert, Ohio. It was listed as "Lionel Elec. Train each $9.99 Reg. $14.99 Value. Hurry - supplies limited". Since Kroger had ordered 8,000 of these outfits, supplies were more than ample.

Kroger ordered outfit no. 19125 in 1962. The next year, it made two purchases: the General Release Promotional outfit no. 19253 and blister display no. D-19253. The 19253 was also sold through Kroger grocery stores and its SupeR$_X$ drug stores (SupeR$_X$ no. ERE 4.12 for $7.98). The 19253 was also part of Lionel's attempt to sell outfits to supermarkets in 1963. It was one of the many train outfits that did not sell, and the leftover inventory became a General Release Promotional in 1964. (See A&P for more information.)

L. A. Sales

L. A. Sales Company, Inc. was a toy wholesaler and concessionaire founded in the Bronx and moved to Deer Park, New York, in 1965. The company opened its first retail concession with National Family stores in New Jersey, which turned out to be a success. During the 1960s, L. A. Sales opened stores in New Jersey and North and South Carolina under the name J. A. Rodes Park 'n Shop, supplying merchandise for toy departments. In addition, L. A. Sales owned its own merchandising company, Iceland Toys, which handled goods for the retail concessions.

An order for outfit no. 19229-501 was canceled in 1963. The next year, L. A. Sales purchased Retailer Promotional outfit no. 19382 and a display version with an acetate sheet, no. D-19382.

Lansburgh's (see Mutual)

Lazarus

Lazarus, established in 1851 by Simon Lazarus, became the signature department store in Columbus, Ohio. It operated independently until joining Federated Department Stores in 1929. Being a part of Federated gave Lazarus the opportunity to expand while retaining its name. Currently, Federated operates more than 50 Lazarus stores throughout the United States under the names Lazarus and Lazarus-Macy.

In 1964, Lazarus purchased one Retailer Promotional outfit, no. 19363-500. The same year, Lionel sold two outfits to Macy's, another part of the Federated empire.

Leonard F. Fellman and Company

It is unclear what the Leonard F. Fellman and Company was and where it operated during the 1960s. This firm did purchase one Retailer Promotional outfit in 1960, no. X-579NA. An observation of one example of this outfit shows markings for Sidles Company, which was a Nebraska distributor of household appliances, stokers, heating equipment and air conditioning. Leonard F. Fellman and Company could, therefore, have been an independent jobber or part of a buying organization that resold this outfit to Sidles.

Lever Brothers

Founded by William Lever in 1885, Lever Brothers originally sold soap and then opened a factory to produce a brand of soap called Sunlight. In 1930, Lever combined his company with the Margarine Union to compete against Procter & Gamble. The new business, named Unilever, operated Unilever PLC in Great Britain and Unilever NV in the Netherlands. Unilever continued to expand by acquiring firms that made consumer goods, including Lipton, Chesebrough-Pond's and National Starch & Chemical. Although not as profitable as Procter & Gamble, Unilever is, with more than 1,000 brands, one of the largest producers of consumer items in the world.

In 1964, Lever Brothers purchased one promotional outfit, no. 19364. Since Lever was a manufacturer and not a retailer, it likely used this outfit as an incentive or premium.

Libby

Arthur A. Libby, his brother Charles and Archibald McNeill launched the firm of Libby McNeill and Libby in 1868. The Chicago-based firm started as a meat processor that packaged its products in cans. Over time, Libby expanded its line to include baby foods and canned fruits and vegetables.

In the 1960s, Libby went through a management restructure that led to more promotional activities. Two divisions handled promotions and promotion policies. The restructuring was beneficial in that various promotions increased profits and heightened product recognition. Nestle Alimentana S.A., bought out Libby in 1975, but still uses its name.

Libby purchased one Manufacturer Promotional outfit in 1963, no. 19263. The October 1963 issue of *Sunset* magazine contained an advertisement for this outfit. It declared, "Libby's brings you a lot of train $24.95 value for only $10.95...and it's a real Lionel!" Consumers had only to mail in four labels from certain Libby's canned products, plus the money, by December 31, 1963, to receive a train outfit.

Lit Brothers

Lit Brothers was founded in 1893 by Samuel and Jacob Lit. The original department store was located at Eight and Market Streets in Philadelphia. By the 1950s, Lit Brothers had grown and operated an impressive store at Broadway and Federal Streets. Business eventually declined, and Lit Brothers filed for bankruptcy in 1977.

The relationship between Lionel and Lit Brothers can be traced as far back as December 3, 1906. Nearly 60 years later, in 1964, Lit Brothers purchased five promotional outfits as part of its relationship with Mutual Buying Syndicate.

Besides the Factory Orders, a full-page advertisement in the *Philadelphia Inquirer* of August 30, 1964, provides valuable information about the outfits Lit Brothers had ordered. Outfit nos. 19394 (30-piece set; $25 value for $12), 19395 (31-piece set; $30 value for $15), 19396 (25-piece set; $36 value for $18) and 19398 (35-piece set; $70 value for $29) were advertised as "Closeout! Lionel Trains. ½ off. Greatest sale in more than 25 years of world's most famous electric train sets! Only at Lits in Delaware Valley."

Surprisingly, this advertisement appeared in August, three months before the traditional holiday shopping season began after Thanksgiving. In addition, the outfits were already heavily discounted. Knowing that Lit Brothers had just received the trains (the Factory Orders are dated in August), leaves the impression that this "closeout" was likely just a gimmick to lure consumers into the stores. And who knows why the fifth promotional outfit that Lit Brothers purchased (no. 19405) was not included in the advertisement.

Of note, the 19394 has also been observed with a Lit Brothers price tag with nos. XY 244 for $7.99 and 8Y 244 19394 for $12.00.

Macy's (see R. H. Macy)

Madison Hardware

Madison Hardware Company, located at 105 East 23rd Street in New York City, was a major Lionel retailer during the prewar and postwar periods. According to Roger Carp's article, "Behind the Scenes at Madison Hardware Co." in the 2003 issue of *Classic Toy Trains*, Guy M. Guest founded Madison Hardware in 1909. Not until 1922 did a change in ownership list Abram Shur and his son Louis as the new owners. The store might originally have peddled hardware, but during Madison's heyday as a toy train retailer all that remained of that aspect of its business was a machine for making keys.

Lou Shur managed Madison Hardware after World War II with assistance from his brother Carl (who anglicized the family name to Shaw). Their relationships with Joshua Lionel Cowen (Lionel's founder) and Frank Pettit (its development engineer) enabled Madison Hardware to become Lionel's customer of choice for excess inventory of finished goods, parts and work in progress. Purchasing these items by the ton or for pennies on the dollar allowed Madison Hardware to amass a huge inventory of Lionel trains. Its tiny storefront contained just a sampling of what was actually available in warehouses located in adjacent neighborhoods.

In the 1970s and 1980s, train collectors were lured to Madison Hardware by stories of mint-in-box items from years past. Richard Kughn, then the owner of Lionel Trains, Inc. and an avid train collector, bought the inventory of Madison Hardware in 1989. He moved everything that could be found to Detroit. After selecting items for his collection, Kughn opened the revamped Madison Hardware to the public. Again, hobbyists discovered bargains in trains and parts there. Kughn closed Madison Hardware in 2001, and the remaining stock has been sold at auctions.

At the end of the postwar period, Madison Hardware Company stood out among retail outlets as being the most important of all "single-store" customers of Lionel. It purchased $501,000 worth of trains and raceways between 1961 and 1966. In a year-by-year analysis, this broke down to $144,000; $176,000 (including $2,000 in raceways); $46,000 ($1,000 in raceways); $54,000 ($7,000 in raceways); $26,000 ($4,000 in raceways); and $55,000.

In the 1960s, Madison Hardware purchased catalog outfits and items, along with seven Retailer Promotional outfits. In 1960, it bought four: nos. X-564NA, X-572NA, X-576 and X-577. Then came three in 1964: nos. 19400, 19417 and 19419. However, Madison seldom treated these outfits as promotionals to be sold intact. Instead, like a few other major dealers, it used these outfits as a way to beat the system and increase profits.

The idea was simple. Outfits generally sold for less than their components would if purchased separately - that was why consumers preferred outfits, especially if they did not have a train. Lou Shur sought to exploit this by purchasing promotional outfits (preferably in bulk to cut down on Lionel's expenses and Madison's time), splitting them up and selling the components. In doing so, he could easily double his profits from the individual items.

To show what this means, consider promotional outfit no. 19417, which Madison Hardware purchased in 1964. Each of these outfits had an internal Lionel cost (materials and labor) of $11.21. When Lionel sold them to Madison Hardware, it charged $29.75 for each outfit. If Madison sold one at $49.99, it would receive a 40 percent margin. But if it broke up the outfit, the suggested retail price of the individual components would add up to nearly twice as much ($99.10). To no one's surprise, Madison preferred to follow this strategy and double its profits.

Another strategy that Madison occasionally adopted by combining various components was to create its own outfits (to which it assigned numbers). However, because such outfits were not documented in Lionel Factory Orders, they should not be considered Lionel promotional outfits (and so are not described in this volume).

Maritz

Maritz, founded in 1894 by Edward Maritz, began as the Maritz Jewelry Manufacturing Company, a maker and wholesaler of jewelry and watches. By the 1920s, its primary focus had changed to wholesaling. But economic setbacks during the Great Depression forced Maritz to look for new business opportunities, and it was transformed into a sales and marketing incentive firm that assisted companies with their award program needs.

Over the years, Maritz broadened its efforts, offering an array of products and programs as incentive awards. It also provided market and customer research for clients. Today, Maritz is a $1.35 billion provider of integrated performance improvement, travel services and market research with 240 offices in more than forty countries.

Between 1960 and 1964, Maritz purchased seven Retailer Promotional outfits. In keeping with its business model, Maritz likely used them as sales incentives or other premium rewards for employees in large corporations. It ordered three outfits in 1960 (nos. X-800, X-801 and X-802) and another in 1961 (no. X-683). In 1962 and 1963, Maritz purchased the nos. 19172 and 19266.

Incentive marking firms were known to carry the same outfit for more than one year. Maritz was no different. Maritz's no. 1486 was used with four different Lionel outfits: nos. X-802, X-683, 19172 and 19266. All of these were slightly different because they included the then current items in Lionel's product line. Maritz ended its relationship with Lionel when it purchased outfit no. 11385-500 in 1964.

Masters

Established in 1937, Masters, Inc., a privately held company, operated leased departments within discount stores throughout New York City. Headquartered in Westbury, New York, it continued to operate leased spaces in more than 100 stores nationwide until the 1980s, when it opened the first of its stand-alone retail stores. These businesses, known as Masters Fashion, began in Cleveland and expanded into Baltimore, parts of New Jersey and Philadelphia.

Masters purchased five Retailer Promotional outfits, starting with nos. X-702, X-703 and X-714 in 1961. A newspaper advertisement dated November 20, 1961, pictured the X-714 and described it as "Lionel Exclusive at Masters! 36-pc. U.S. Marine Corp. Masters price $27.88 complete. Only 400 sets, 1 per customer. No dealers!" Masters returned to Lionel in 1963, when it ordered outfit no. 19276, followed by outfit no. 19412 the next year.

Maurice Pollack

Founded in Quebec in 1905, Maurice Pollack Ltd. grew to become one of the largest retail stores in the Saint Roch district of that Canadian city. Its founder retired from the business in the 1950s and established the Maurice Pollack Foundation, which serves organizations working the fields of culture and education.

In 1962, Maurice Pollack purchased one Retailer Promotional outfit, no. 19134.

May Company, May D&F and May Group

David May opened his first department store, the Great Western Auction House and Clothier Store, in Leadville, Colorado, in 1877. Eleven years later, May and his brother-in-law Moses Shoenberg formed a partnership with Louis and Joseph Shoenberg to open a store in Denver. The four partners inaugurated the long history of May acquisitions in 1892, when they purchased the Famous Clothing store in St. Louis. Then in 1898, they bought a department store in Cleveland and named it May Company

What was known as the May Department Stores Company, based in St. Louis, incorporated in 1910. Over the next 60 years, the firm grew steadily until it operated more than 100 retail stores. Growth came mainly through the acquisition of many other companies, including William Barr Dry Goods (which was combined with Famous Clothing to form Famous-Barr), The M O'Neil Co., A. Hamburger & Sons, Bernheim-Leader, Kaufmann's, Daniels & Fisher Stores, Hecht's, G. Fox and Meier & Frank.

Throughout the 1970s and 1980s May Company continued with its acquisitions and became one of the best-known retail organizations in the United States. In 1993, the company name changed after it merged with J. W. Robinson's of Los Angeles to create the Robinsons-May stores. It was not until 1996 that the parent company reincorporated in Delaware under the name May Department Stores Company.

In August 2005, May and rival Federated Department Stores completed a merger. The first post merger priority was to eliminate any overlap in stores and convert most May Company stores to Macy's.

May Company purchased eleven Retailer Promotional outfits. First, in 1960, came nos. X-502NA, X-503NA (The M. O'Neil Co. no. D33 Y for $28.33), X-504NA and X-570NA. In 1961, it bought nos. X-601, X-602 (Famous-Barr no. 32 B 5422 for $29.99) and X-603. In 1962, there were nos. 19126, 19127, 19128 (May no. 42 D 42 19128) and 19129. Finally in 1966, outfit no. 19567-500 was sold in May - Daniels & Fisher (D&F) stores as CL 12 B Dept. 63 for $23.87.

MBS (Merchants Buying Syndicate)

Founded in 1958 in New York City, Merchants Buying Syndicate (MBS) was a buying cooperative that purchased hard-line and soft-line merchandise as well as toys. Members of the syndicate included discount stores, drug stores, supermarkets, variety stores, automotive chains, department stores and wholesalers. By 1963, there were more than 150 MBS affiliates based throughout the United States. MBS ceased operating in 1970s because it could no longer compete against the larger buying organizations, such as AMC and the Donegar Group.

MBS bought two promotional outfits in 1962: nos. 19155 and 19156. The next year, it ordered a promotional outfit (no. 19239) and a display (no. D-19239). Many direct Lionel customers were also members of MBS, including Claber's, Cunningham Drug, Federal, Goldblatt's, Katz Drug, Kroger, Hecht's, Honig's Parkway, Masters and Times Square Stores. There were hundreds of additional MBS members that could have purchased these trains. Consequently, it would be impossible to link these promotional outfits to a specific MBS member.

McMahon's

The Factory Orders attribute to McMahon's three promotional outfits: nos. X-567NA and X-568NA in 1960 and no. X-698

in 1961. The quantities (500, 400 and 900, respectively) are sufficiently large to suggest that they were provided to a good number of stores, although no information on a business with this name could be found.

Mercantile Stores

Mercantile Stores Company, Inc. was founded in 1914 and incorporated in Ohio in 1935. It operated approximately 65 department stores throughout the United States, with its best-known retailers (Caster-Knott, Joslin's and McAlpin's) being based in medium-sized cities where competition was not as intense as in metropolitan areas. By 1960, Mercantile was ranked as one of the top ten department store chains and eventually operated more than 100 retailers. Dillard's, Inc. bought out Mercantile in 1998 for $2.9 million.

Mercantile purchased five promotional outfits, starting with nos. X-539NA and X-540NA in 1960. The next year, it bought nos. X-652 and X-653. For 1962, Mercantile ordered no. 19137 and repeated the X-653. These outfits probably were distributed through any of Mercantile's retailers.

Mercury Model

Located in Cleveland, Mercury Model, Inc. was a distributor established by Leonard Blum (owner of the Hobby House, a major retail outlet selling electric trains) and operated by his son, Harry N. Blum. The latter also owned a manufacturing firm and, in the 1970s, worked for Model Products Corporation, the division of General Mills that supervised production of Lionel trains.

Between 1962 and 1966, Mercury Model purchased $461,000 worth of trains and $2,000 in raceways from Lionel. The biggest years were 1965 ($128,000) and 1966 ($300,000). Like Madison Hardware, it had close ties with personnel at Lionel's factory (probably due to Leonard Blum's connections) that it used to bypass the sales organization and obtain better prices.

Mercury, like Madison, did not hesitate to buy individual items and create its own outfits. For example, it purchased Retailer Promotional no. 11520-500 in 1965. The Factory Order included special instructions for Lionel not to mark or seal the boxes. These outfits were subsequently augmented with a no. 6050-150 Van Camp Savings Bank Car or no. 6050-175 Libby Box Car, an engineer's cap and more track and stamped "2058 5-Car Steam Freight Set Headlight, Engineer's Cap, Saving Bank Boxcar Figure 8 Track Layout" by Mercury Model.

This augmentation of outfits continued in 1966, when Mercury Model purchased six more Retailer Promotional outfits and a display. Outfit nos. 19567, 19567-500 and 19571 were designated "Mercury Model to supply Auto to go with Flat Car". Outfit 19567-500 also stated, "Mercury Model to supply cutouts". Outfit no. 19583 included an engineer's cap supplied by Mercury Model. The last two outfits, nos. 19563 and 19569, were not modified by Mercury Model. The no. D19583 display was a blister version of 19583.

Mercury Model outfits were distributed across the country, and examples have been observed with price tags from different retailers:

Year	Lionel Number	Retailer	Retail Number	Retail Price
1965	11520-500	Hudson's Detroit	664*11-6	$9.99
1966	19563	Hudson's Detroit	664*11-7	$35.00
		Gimbels Schusters	740 S8 65	$29.99
	19567-500	Titche's	830 116	$19.99 crossed out and $13.88 written in
		May - D&F	CL 12 B Dept. 63	$23.87
	19569	Shillito's	06	$29.99
		Hudson's Detroit	664*12-6	$29.99
	19571	Joseph Horne Co.	661/2 19571	$33.95 crossed out and $23.95 written in
	19583	Arlan's Department. Stores	66 40 (Store Number 66)	$16.88

Myers-Dickson (see Biederman)

Montgomery Ward

Aaron Montgomery Ward founded Montgomery Ward in Chicago in 1872. Driven by a need to supply quality items at lower costs to remotely located customers, Ward created what was the first mail-order company. He eliminated the middle man and passed on the savings to his customers. Ward's first catalog was a single sheet listing 163 different items. By 1904, Ward was mailing 3 million catalogs to customers.

In 1926, Wards opened its first retail location, carrying an assortment of merchandise that ranged from appliances, toys and apparel to auto supplies and general home goods. Due to high demand and an absence of competition, Ward expanded quickly. It was operating more than 150 stores by 1929, and its fall/winter catalog offered more than 30,000 items. In the 1930s, the company turned down a merger offer from its chief rival, Sears, Roebuck and Co. Instead, Ward launched an aggressive campaign to open more retail outlets across the country. By 1950, it was the third largest and continuously profitable department store in the United States.

Unfortunately for Ward, resistance to suburban expansion and declining catalog business hurt it financially in the 1950s. To regain momentum, it merged with Container Corporation of America to form Marcor, Inc. in 1968. Eight years later, still struggling to keep up in the retail market, Ward was acquired by Mobil Oil. By 1985, Ward had closed its 113-year-old catalog business and shifted its focus to its retail stores, restructuring them into specialty stores. Nothing seemed to work, not even an acquisition by General Electric Capital Services. At the end of 2000, Ward announced that it was shutting down all its retail locations.

Montgomery Ward was one of Lionel's first customers, buying a no. 300 Trolley, wet cells and a switch on May 21, 1902. After World War II, however, Lionel catalog outfits did not appear in a Ward catalog until 1955. During the 1960s, Ward purchased Retailer Promotional outfits in 1960 through 1963 and again in 1966. Between 1961 and 1966, Ward bought $238,000 worth of merchandise from Lionel, slightly more than did J. C. Penney. The vast majority of this amount came in 1966, when after spending only $42,000 in 1962, $11,000 in 1963 and a mere $5,000 in 1964, Ward bought $180,000 worth of trains. This jump can be attributed to the efforts of Bruce Parmett, Lionel's Market Development Manager, who convinced Ward to buy four Retailer Promotional outfits in 1966.

The first Retailer Promotional outfit that Ward purchased in 1960 - no. X-534NA - did not appear in its catalog. With only thirty-six ordered, this outfit was probably a special item or a promotional piece meant for internal purposes. Two other Retailer Promotionals appeared on page 417 of the Ward Christmas Catalog for 1960: nos. X-535NA (Montgomery Ward no. 48 T 3073 M for $29.97) and X-536NA (no. 48 T 3074 M for $39.97).

Trains did not appear in any of the catalogs released by Ward between 1961 and 1965. The Retailer Promotional outfits it ordered were likely sold through its retail stores. These included nos. X-670, X-671 and X-672 (48-F1 3202) from 1961 as well as nos. 19100 (no. 48-3210), 19101 (no. 48-3211), 19102 (no. 48-3212) and 19103 (no. 48-3213) from 1962. By 1963, business apparently was declining because Ward purchased only one of the three outfits it considered. It bought no. 19259, but nos. 19221 and 19222 were marked "Cancel" on the Factory Orders.

In 1966 Ward purchased four Retailer Promotional outfits as shown on pages 352 and 353 of its Christmas Catalog. Three were available at the company's retail stores and came in specially decorated Ward RSCs: nos. 19542 (no. 48 HT 21301 for $16.99), 19544 (no. 48 HT 21302 for $24.99) and 19546 (no. 48 HT 21303 M for $39.50).

The 19542 and 19544 were also available via mail-order, but the 19546 weighed too much, so Lionel created a no. 19547. It was the same as a 19546 and had the same Ward no. 48 HT 21303 M, but it was packed in a plain tan RSC made of thicker corrugated material (rated at 90 pounds rather than the normal 65 pounds gross weight).

Also in 1966, Ward purchased a DO19546 display for 19546 (no. 21330D). There are no records of Ward carrying Lionel trains after 1966. The following table summarizes Ward purchases from 1960 through 1966.

Year	Lionel Number	Ward Catalog Number	Ward Catalog	Retail Price
1960	X-534NA		No Catalog Listing	
	X-535NA	48 T 3073 M	1960 Christmas Catalog	$29.97
	X-536NA	48 T 3074 M		$39.97
1961	X-670		No Catalog Listing	
	X-671			
	X-672	48-F1 3202		$45.95
1962	19100	48-3210		$18.88
	19101	48-3211		
	19102	48-3212		
	19103	48-3213		
1963	19221		No Catalog Listing, Canceled	
	19222			
	19259		No Catalog Listing	
1966	19542	48 HT 2101	1966 Christmas Catalog	$16.99
	19544	48 HT 21302		$24.99
	19546	48 HT 2103 M		$39.50
	19547	48 HT 2103 M		$39.50
	DO19546	21330D	No Catalog Listing	

Morley Brothers

Anton Schmitz and his partners, George and Edward Morley, founded Schmitz & Morley in 1863 in Saginaw, Michigan. Operating as a general store, it carried everything from hardware supplies to household goods. Eventually the Morleys purchased Schmitz's share and proceeded to change the name of the business to Morley Brothers. In the 1950s and 1960s, it continued to grow as a distributor of various products. The original retail store stayed open until 1977. Today, Morley Brothers operates as Morley Companies, Inc., a market research trade show organization with offices in Saginaw as well as South Norwalk, Connecticut.

In 1960, Morley Brothers purchased one Retailer Promotional outfit, no. X-563NA.

Morris Kirschman and Company

In 1914, Morris Kirschman started a small furniture store in New Orleans that he named Kirschman's. A younger generation joined the company in the 1940s and, led by Victor Kirschman, expanded into the city's suburbs in 1958. Now under the direction of a third generation, the firm has opened three more stores, all in or near the Crescent City.

In 1964, Kirschman's purchased one Retailer Promotional outfit, no. 19389.

Mutual Buying

Mutual Buying Syndicate was a major buying cooperative in New York between 1950 and 1970. As was true of other buying cooperatives, Mutual's customers ranged from department stores to small variety stores. Its most important members included Boston Stores, Younkers, and Stern's Department Store. Mutual operated into the 1980s, when many of the buying cooperatives, faced with heightened competition, consolidated or disappeared.

Mutual was a large customer of promotional outfits. As a buying cooperative, it likely purchased these outfits for one or more of its members. A few Factory Orders and price tag observations link the end customer to Mutual outfits. Specifically, nos. 19394, 19395, 19396, 19398 and 19405 were sold to Lit Brothers and nos. 19135 and 19224 were for The Fair. Outfit 19394 was also sold to Lansburgh's.

This table lists the outfits purchased by Mutual and their end customer (if available) during the 1960s:

Year	Lionel Number	End Customer	Retail Number and Price
1960	X-526NA		
	X-527NA		
1961	X-622		
	X-623		
1962	19135	The Fair	$21.88
		John A. Brown Co.	$19.97
	19136		
1963	19223	Famous-Barr	32 B M 264 for $10.49
	19224	The Fair	57 5 for $14.98
	19225		
1964	19373		
	19381		
	19394	Lansburgh's	213 10 Y 19394 for $10.00
		Lit Brothers	XY 244 for $7.99 8Y 244 19344 for $12.00
	19395	Lit Brothers	19395 for $15.00
	19396		19396 for $18.00
	19397		
	19398	Lit Brothers	19398 for $29.00
	19399		
	19405	Lit Brothers	
	19409		
	D-19373		

In 1965, Lionel sold primarily General Release Promotional outfits; as such, its records would not mention specific customers. Mutual probably continued to purchase for its customers, even if their names did not appear on the Factory Orders.

N. Friedlander Industries

N. Friedlander Industries purchased two promotional outfits in 1963. Outfit nos. 19269 and 19270 listed "'O27' Freight Set for Canada" under their Outfit Specifications. Information on N. Friedlander Industries was unavailable. However, because the quantity of both outfits was large (a total of 5,414), it is fair to surmise that the firm was a Canadian buying office or distributor that intended to resell the outfits to clients.

National Association

The 1963 Factory Order for outfit no. 19232 listed National Assoc. as the customer with a quantity of 150. No further information about this customer is known.

National Association of Railway Business Women (NARBW)

Founded in 1921, the National Association of Railway Business Women is an organization that enables women currently or formerly employed in the railroad industry to meet one another. It conducts public education programs to help reduce railroad injuries, establishes residence for retired association members and funds scholarship programs for members and dependents. The NARBW currently reports having more than 900 members, with chapters in twenty-six cities across the United States.

In 1964, the National Association of Railway Business Women purchased one promotional outfit, no. 13255. Only twenty examples of this Super O outfit were made, which suggests it was likely used as either a promotion or an award offered to members of the NARBW.

National Tea Company

In 1899, the first National Tea store opened in Chicago. Over the years, this single retail food store grew into a chain with as many as 1,627 locations. In the early 1950s, following a few years of consolidation, National Tea Company acquired various small chains. Then in 1955, Loblaw Companies of Canada bought it and continued operations until beginning to divest unprofitable locations in the 1970s. Schnuck Markets, Inc. acquired the firm's remaining assets in 1995.

In 1963, National Tea purchased one Retailer Promotional outfit (no. 19260) as well as a blister display version (no. D19260).

Navy

The Navy Exchange Service Command (NEX) was established in 1946 in Virginia to provide United States Navy personnel and their families with goods and services at substantial savings. The NEX consists of five separate units: Navy Exchange, Navy Lodges, Navy Uniform Program, Ship Store Program and Telecommunications. The Navy Exchange is the retail arm, and it stocks items ranging from apparel to toys. The Navy Ship Store Program also maintains retail stores, although they concentrate on smaller products, such as toiletries and electronics. Currently, the Navy Exchange has more than 100 locations nationwide. The Navy Ship Program operates more than 180 stores as well as a catalog program.

In 1962, the Navy purchased one Retailer Promotional outfit, no. 19145. It likely sold these through the Navy Exchange.

Niresk Industries

Niresk Discount Sales (formerly Niresk Industries) was a mail-order retailer in Chicago in the 1950s and 1960s. It marketed household items, jewelry, toys and sporting goods at discounted prices through its catalogs.

In 1960, Niresk purchased one Retailer Promotional outfit, no. X-575.

Noah's Ark

Noah's Ark Auto Accessories, Inc. was a retail chain of twenty stores with headquarters in Rochester, New York. Having already adopted catalog mailings, it began experimenting with direct mail premiums in the late 1950s. The firm sent out a letter listing various premiums, along with a comic book, six times a year. The programs proved to be successful, making it one of the more effective campaigns in the automotive chain industry.

During the 1960s, Noah's Ark, like many other auto accessories companies, was acquired by a larger corporate entity (in this case, Eckmar Corporation). Noah's Ark continued to operate as a separate division until all its stores were closed sometime after 1969.

In 1960, Noah's Ark purchased Retailer Promotional outfit no. X-519NA, which it sold as Noah's Ark no. 319 2818 for $33.89. In 1961, it purchased advance catalog promotional no. 1123, which it sold as no. X809 for $11.88 and promotional outfit nos. X-626 (no. X810A for $18.88) and X-629 (no. X814 for $29.88). One year later, it purchased Retailer Promotional outfit no. 19124 as no. 301 X814 for $29.88. In 1963, it purchased Retailer Promotional outfit no. 19229-501X. Knowing that Noah's Ark emphasized premiums leads to the conclusion that it probably sold this outfit as part of its premium offerings for 1963. If not, then Noah's Ark likely sold the outfit through its retail stores. Finally, in 1966, General Release Promotional outfit no. 11540-500 was linked to Noah's Ark via a price tag (Noah's Ark no. 693 X3803B for $21.88).

Norge

Norge Corporation, a division of Borg-Warner Corporation from 1929 through the late 1960s, was well known in the washer and dryer industry when the industry was thriving. Borg-Warner sold Norge to Fedders Corporation, and then Magic Chef acquired Norge in 1979. Norge appliances continued to be manufactured on a small scale for foreign rather than domestic markets in the years after Maytag Corporation acquired the firm in 1986.

In 1961, Norge purchased a promotional outfit, no. X-716, to be used as an incentive for its customers. During the holiday season, Norge advertised a 26-piece Lionel electric train set (a "claimed $29.95 retail value") with the purchase of any home appliance. It is unknown if the outfit was provided free or at a cost below $29.95.

Oklahoma Tire & Supply Co.

Oklahoma Tire and Supply Company (OTASCO) was established in 1918 as an auto accessories store. From one store, it expanded to more than 600 outlets located in fourteen states in the southeastern and south central parts of the country. Besides automotive tires and general hardware, OTASCO stores sold toys and sports supplies. Purchased by McCrory Corporation in 1961, the firm operated as a subsidiary until OTASCO employees bought it back in 1984. In 1988, down to 233 stores, OTASCO filed for bankruptcy protection. A bankruptcy creditor in possession of the chain liquidated all the remaining stores in 1989.

The earliest OTASCO catalog observed showed Lionel catalog outfits as early as 1953. Certainly, in the 1960s, it was a good customer. Between 1961 and 1966, OTASCO bought $286,000 worth of merchandise. This amount broke down to $79,000 in 1961; $40,000 in 1962; $25,000 in 1963; $48,000 (including $2,000 in raceways) in 1964; $44,000 in 1965 and $50,000 in 1966.

Turning to outfits, OTASCO purchased both General Release Promotional and Retailer Promotional outfits. First, in 1960, came nos. X-532NA (OTASCO no. 70-760-8 for $22.87), X-533NA (no. 70-761-4 for $27.47), X-551NA (no. 70-762-7), X-552NA (no. 70-761-8 for $33.83), 1107 (no. 70-759-5 for $12.95) and 1109 (no. 70-760-3 for $14.99). The next year, OTASCO offered nos. X-644 (no. 70-760-4), X-645 (no. 70-760-5), X-646 (no. 70-761-5 Reg. $32.95, now $23.95) and X-647 (no. 70-762).

The OTASCO Christmas Catalog for 1962 featured both catalog outfit no. 11011 (no. 70-760-2 for $14.44) and Retailer Promotional outfit no. 19124 (sold through Automotive Associates, it had an OTASCO number, 70-761-6, and sold for $35.77). The OTASCO Holiday Gifts Catalog for 1966 featured promotional outfit nos. 19507 (no. 70-761-2 for $29.97) and 19515 (no. 70-759 for $13.99). The company probably sold other catalog and promotional outfits, but they have not been observed in catalogs or other sources.

Others

For some outfits Lionel listed a customer name followed by "& Others". This notation probably indicated that these outfits were General Release Promotionals. In 1964, the no. 12827 (Joe the Motorist & Others) was designated in this manner.

Penney's (see J. C. Penney)

Peoples Credit Jewellers

Peoples Credit Jewellers was founded in 1919 in Toronto. A family business, Peoples operated a retail chain across British Columbia as well as a catalog division that offered fine jewelry and gifts. The company, which changed its name to Peoples Jewellers, grew to become the largest jeweler in Canada by the end of the 1950s. Zale Corporation purchased Peoples Jewellers in 1999 and continues to operate it as a subsidiary across Canada.

In 1962, Peoples Credit Jewellers purchased one Retailer Promotional outfit, no. 19171.

Peter King Co.

In 1962, Peter King Company purchased one promotional outfit, no. 19000 (Peter King no. 2893). Nothing more is known about this customer or its use of this outfit, although its order of 500 units suggested that Peter King was a buying office or a retail chain.

Philco

Philco began in 1906 as Philadelphia Storage Battery Company, a manufacturer of batteries for automobiles, trucks and mine locomotives. It grew with the automotive industry, but was on the verge of bankruptcy in 1926. To stave off disaster, the firm switched to producing radios, a move that improved its prospects. The company incorporated under the name Philco in 1940, and over the next two decades diversified its line with refrigerators, air conditioners and televisions. Ford Motor Company bought Philco in 1961. Later, GTE and then Phillips purchased Philco. All that exists of it today is the brand name, which is occasionally pulled out of retirement for use on promotional video products.

During the 1960s, Philco sought to enhance the sale of its products by including premiums rather than reducing prices. Therefore, the one Manufacturer Promotional outfit that it bought in 1963, no. 11315 (Philco no. AD-4158), was likely offered to consumers to promote sales of one or more of Philco's products.

Phillips Petroleum

Phillips Petroleum Company, founded in 1917 by Frank Phillips, was an Oklahoma-based company that began marketing gasoline in 1927. During that time, Phillips, which owned the patent for propane gas, experimented with propane appliances and storage and delivery systems and gained federal approval to drill for oil in Alaska. The firm expanded steadily over the ensuing decades, eventually operating more than 12,000 service stations under the Phillips 66, Circle K, and 76 brands. In 2002, Phillips merged with Conoco to create Conoco-Phillips, the third largest energy company in the United States and the sixth largest in the world.

In the 1960s, like many other oil companies, Phillips was involved in incentive marketing campaigns, including giving a "Bargain of the Month" certificate for each dollar spent at its stations. As part of its campaign in 1961, Phillips offered its customers Lionel promotional outfit no. 1124P. An advertisement in an October 1961 newspaper states, "Do your Christmas shopping early on the Bargain of the Month Plan. Phillips 66 Bargains of the Month Certificates entitle you to big savings every month on valuable merchandise you and your family have always wanted…Lionel Electric Train set, manufacturer's suggested retail $18.95 only $10.66 with 10 Bargain of the Month Certificates."

Play-More

Play-More, Inc., founded in 1942, was a wholesaler and distributor of toys located in New York. The company operated its distribution division through 1966, when it divested that division to focus on publishing value-priced children's books. Still in operation, Play-More is currently located on Fifth Avenue in New York and distributes its books throughout the United States and Canada.

In 1962, Play-More purchased a Retailer Promotional outfit

(no. 19173) and a display (no. D19173), which it likely distributed to its retail customers.

Polk

Polk Model Craft Hobbies was founded by Irwin and Nat Polk in 1933 in New Jersey. The Polk brothers opened a retail outlet in New York City the following year, specializing in model airplanes. When they expanded their stock to include train kits and locomotives, Polk became known as a hobby store and by 1965 carried products from more than 300 domestic and foreign manufacturers. The brothers diversified further, operating as a wholesaler and then a manufacturer under the name Aristo-Craft. In the 1980s, the company moved back to New Jersey and currently manufactures the Aristo-Craft line of Large scale trains.

The Polk brothers developed a business relationship with Lionel in the 1930s by selling catalog items in their store and later serving as a distributor of Lionel trains. Their purchases of trains and raceways made them a significant customer in the 1960s, as they bought $464,000 worth of merchandise between 1961 and 1966. This amount broke down to $109,000 in 1961; $98,000 in 1962 (of which $59,000 was for trains) and $28,000 in 1963 (of which $24,000 was for trains). Polk did not make any purchases of Lionel merchandise in 1964, but followed with $104,000 in 1965 (of which only $4,000 was for raceways) and $125,000 in 1966.

In 1964, the year when Polk supposedly did not purchase any merchandise from Lionel, seven promotional outfits were listed with that firm as the customer: nos. 12807, 12817, 12847, 13277, 19406, 19407 and 19408. These outfits were bulk-packed, which suggests that Polk intended to pick out components to sell individually for greater profits (just as Madison Hardware was doing). Polk likely paid Lionel for these in 1965, which explains why Lionel did not see any revenue from Polk in 1964.

The story of Polk buying promotional outfits from Lionel ended quietly in 1966. After not making any such purchases the previous year, Polk ordered Retailer Promotional outfit no. 19590.

Pomeroy's (see Allied)

Pomeroy's was founded in the early 1900s and sold household items, apparel and toys. That department store became a division of Allied Stores Corporation and later Campeau Corporation, which purchased Allied in 1986.

Lionel sold two outfits to Allied, which it distributed through Pomeroy's. One, no. X-650, has been seen with a Pomeroy's price tag (Pomeroy's no. 9-1 830 for $19.99). The second outfit was no. 19377-500. Display outfit no. DO489 can also be attributed to Pomeroy's, which probably sold other outfits that were purchased by Allied.

Popular Club Plan

Founded in 1947 in Garfield, New Jersey, Popular Club Plan operates as a catalog company selling clothing, housewares, jewelry, toys and electronics. Consumers enroll in the plan and earn credits entitling them to buy merchandise that Popular Club carries. Originally concentrating on customers in the Northeast, the firm has broadened its reach by shrewd use of the Internet. Popular Club, once owned by Texas Pacific Group (an equity investor), has been a subsidiary of Fingerhut Companies since 1998.

Between 1960 and 1964, Popular purchased seven Retailer Promotional outfits, starting with nos. X-509NA (Popular no. B 8155 S), X-541NA (no. B 8158) and X-542NA in 1960. It bought no. X-707 in both 1961 and 1962. Then came no. 19236 in 1963 and no. 11482 (no. NY-331) in 1964.

Either to gain Popular Club Plan as a customer or to cement its relationship with the firm, Lionel created artwork dated "7-18-60" for an 8½-inch-long box car with a coin slot in the roof. Then the Engineering Department was asked to develop a sample model decorated in Popular Club graphics. This sequence of events was a common practice for Lionel's promotional program in the early 1960s. A Popular box car did not become part of Lionel's regular line, but the deal to sell promotional outfits to that firm went ahead.

Premium - (Irwin Diamond)

In 1964, Premium - (Irwin Diamond) purchased promotional outfit no. 19271. No further information is known about this customer or its use of the outfit.

Premium Service Corp.

Premium Service Company, located in Akron, Ohio, operated as a premium and incentives organization into the mid-1980s. It purchased three Retail Promotional outfits: nos. X-874 in 1960, X-660 in 1961 and X-660 again in 1962.

Prophylactic Brush Company

Founded in Florence, Massachusetts, in 1866, Florence Manufacturing Company made hair, shaving and military brushes. In 1924, following the success of a tooth-cleaning product, the firm changed its name to Pro-phy-lac-tic Brush Company. To increase sales, it relied heavily on advertisements and premiums, including children's puzzles in 1933. Pro-phy-lac-tic Brush Company was sold to Standard Oil of Ohio in 1963, and the name was changed to Pro Brush. Today, the company is owned by Oral Care, a division of NutraMax Products, and continues to operate as a toothbrush manufacturer.

Pro-phy-lac-tic purchased Manufacturer Promotional outfit nos. X-620 (Pro-phy-lac-tic no. BA 6120-6) and X-706 in 1961. Based on Pro-phy-lac-tic's history of mail-in premiums, these outfits were likely offered as a promotional tie-in with some Pro-phy-lac-tic product or purchase.

PX (see AFA)

Quaker Oats

Quaker Oats traces its history back to 1901, when several oat milling companies joined forces under the Quaker name (already used by Henry D. Seymour, one of the key players in this combination). Taking advantage of the trademarked image of the "Quaker Man", the new firm introduced a variety of breakfast products, including Aunt Jemima pancake mix, Quick Oats and other cereals. Quaker took steps to diversity its line in the final decades of the twentieth century by purchasing such companies as

Fisher-Price, Igloo, Louis Marx & Company (which made electric toy trains) and Snapple. Based on the success of Quaker's line of Gatorade products, the company was purchased by PepsiCo for $13.4 billion in August of 2001.

Quaker had long been an innovator in the field of marketing, particularly the use of premiums (ironically, it had eliminated its in-house premium offices by the time PepsiCo bought it). For example, Quaker was the first company to put premiums in cereal boxes, inserting chinaware in its oat boxes in 1891. Other premiums ranged from trading cards and puzzles in the early 1900s to housewares in the 1950s. By far, the most intriguing incentive was the Great Klondike Land Giveaway in 1955 to promote *Sgt. Preston of the Yukon*, a television series that Quaker sponsored. Quaker placed 21 million one-inch land deeds in specially marked boxes of Puffed Wheat and Puffed Rice, which quickly sold out. Unfortunately for consumers, Quaker had never registered the deeds; the 19 acres of land were eventually seized for non-payment of $37.20 in property taxes.

Quaker capitalized on the popularity of Lionel trains in its promotions as early as 1915, when it purchased Manufacturer Promotional outfits. In 1947, it gave away 300 "swell new Lionel Electric Trains Sets" to push its Puffed Wheat and Puffed Rice Sparkles cereals. Fourteen years later, in what a corporate history touts as Quaker's "biggest puller, in terms of dollars," it offered Manufacturer Promotional outfit no. X-600. This promotion, advertised heavily in family magazines, promised a Lionel train valued at $25.00 for only $11.95 plus two Quaker Oats or Mother's Oats box tops.

Interestingly, Lionel and Quaker got their hands slapped by the Federal Trade Commission for stating that this outfit was worth $25.00. The FTC asserted that such a claim violated its guidelines on deceptive pricing. Lionel cleared itself in May 1962 by vowing that the promotion had ended and would not be resumed. In reality, Quaker was still fulfilling outfit requests well into 1963. Still, Lionel made sure that any future promotional statements were carefully worded to meet the demands of the FTC. Thus, when Van Camp used outfit no. 19142 as a promotion in 1962, it was described as having a $25.00 "Premium Value".

R & S

Founded in 1919 in Newark, New Jersey, R & S Auto operated as an auto supply and service retailer, eventually opening stores throughout that state. It merged with Strauss stores in 1982 and became R & S Strauss. Four years later, the company acquired Penn Jersey, another auto supply retailer. The name changed to Strauss Discount Auto in 1995, and more than 100 such stores currently operate along the East Coast.

In 1962, R & S purchased one Retailer Promotional outfit, no. 19205. It was a bulk-packed outfit.

R. H. Macy and Macy's

Rowland Hussey Macy launched R. H. Macy & Company in 1858 as a dry goods store in New York City. He revolutionized retailing by developing a "one-price system" whereby each item was available to any customer at the same price. Macy also took delight in introducing a variety of products to his customers, items that including Idaho baking potatoes, ready-made bags of tea and colored bath towels.

R. H. Macy & Company advanced marketing and retailing in 1875 by opening the first permanent toy department. Its overwhelming success encouraged other department stores to imitate Macy's and set up their own toy departments. The company continued to prosper in the first half of the twentieth century, and its store on Herald Square in New York was celebrated as the largest department store in the world. Macy's was being publicly traded, and expansion moved along through acquisitions in other parts of the country.

In the 1980s, however, the rise of specialty stores and discounters hurt Macy's and it filed for bankruptcy in 1992. Two years later, it merged with Federated Department Stores to create the largest department store company in America. Today, Federated is in the process of branding its stores under the Macy's or Bloomingdales names, including the newly acquired May Company stores from their 2005 merger with May Company.

Lionel's relationship with R. H. Macy & Company can be tracked as far back as November 14, 1904, with the purchase of two no. 100 Electric Locomotives, two no. 300 Trolley Cars, one no. 309 Trolley Trailer and six no. 320 Switches. During the prewar years, Macy's emerged as a noteworthy buyer of promotional outfits from Lionel. Then a drought of almost 30 years ensued, with no records of Macy's purchasing promotional outfits coming to light until 1960, when it bought two Retailer Promotionals: nos. X-583NA and X-584NA.

Over the next four years, Macy's again became one of Lionel's chief customers. It bought $240,000 worth of merchandise (of which all but $3,000 was for trains), which surpassed what J. C. Penney spent. This amount broke down to $149,000 in 1961; $32,000 in 1962 (of which $29,000 was for trains); $32,000 in 1963 and $27,000 in 1964.

Macy's ordered two Retail Promotional outfits in 1961 (nos. X-708 and X-709) and another pair in 1962 (nos. 19190 and 19191, the latter designated Macy no. WD 12A selling for $29.99). Then, after failing to buy any promotional outfits in 1963, Macy's ordered two Retailer Promotional outfits in 1964: nos. 19379 and 19391 (both O27 starter outfits). There are no records of the company making any purchases after 1964.

R. S. S.

This customer, of which nothing is known, purchased one promotional outfit in 1961, no. X-701. No information has surfaced regarding how the outfit was used.

R. Simpson and Simpsons-Sears

Robert Simpson opened R. Simpson Dry Goods in 1872 in Toronto. It first published a catalog in 1893. Four years later, after Simpson had died, a small group of Canadian investors purchased the store. Subsequently, the retail arm of what was then known as Simpson's Ltd. expanded, as did its mail-order business. By 1951, the company had attracted the interest of Sears, which led to a takeover of Simpson's mail-order business, a joint venture with its suburban retail stores (called Simpsons-Sears) and the publication of the first Simpsons-Sears catalogs in 1953. Five of the original R. Simpson stores survived under that name.

The joint venture lasted until 1978, when Sears Canada absorbed the mail-order arm and began issuing catalogs bearing only the Sears name. On the retail side, Canada Hudson-Bay bought the R. Simpson stores and one-third of the Simpsons-Sears stores. It left some stores alone, converted others to its own name, and sold still others.

Lionel sold outfits to R. Simpson and Simpsons-Sears. One outfit, Retailer Promotional no. 19121, identifies R. Simpson as the customer on the Factory Order. R. Simpson likely used these outfits in its stores or catalogs.

Most of the outfits that Simpsons-Sears bought were General Release Promotional or catalog outfits, so the matching of Lionel numbers to Simpsons-Sears numbers was done through catalog observations. The Simpsons-Sears Christmas Catalog for 1960 showed an unidentified pre-1960 outfit (Simpsons no. 49 N9610L) and X-553NA (no. 49 N9631L for $19.88). The latter outfit lists Canada as the customer on the Factory Orders. The Simpsons-Sears Christmas Catalog for 1961 showed Sears outfit no. 9652 from the previous year (no. 49 N 41 855 for $29.95), along with what seemed to be promotional outfit no. X-707 (no. 49N 41 856 for $19.95), but cannot be confirmed.

In 1962, outfit no. 19130 (no. 79N 41880 L for $21.99) appeared in the catalog. This outfit likely was purchased from AMC, as that is the customer specified on the Factory Order. The Factory Order for outfit 19121 lists R. Simpson as the customer, but it does not appear in the catalog.

In 1963, only Lionel catalog outfits appeared in the Simpsons-Sears catalogs. A year later, the Simpsons-Sears catalog showed the no. 19142 Van Camp outfit from 1962 as no. 49N 14 070 for $18.98. Evidently, Lionel was liquidating its unsold Van Camp inventory in Canada.

The Simpsons-Sears catalog for 1965 listed Lionel catalog outfit no. 11520 as no. 49 N 14 133 for $22.88. The next year, it featured outfit no. 11530 (no. 49 N 14 134 for $29.99). In addition, no. 11520 returned with a higher price ($26.99). Simpsons-Sears did not carry Lionel trains after 1966.

Radoff Brothers

Incorporated in Houston in 1915, Radoff Brothers was owned by J. S. Radoff. The firm operated as a toy buyer until the late 1960s.

In 1960, Radoff Brothers purchased one Retailer Promotional outfit, no. X-557.

Raleigh (see Brown & Williamson)

Retailers Representatives

Retailers Representatives, incorporated in 1956 in New York, operated as a buying cooperative that distributed goods to small department stores, specialty stores and discount retailers. In 1963, it purchased Retail Promotional outfit no. 19255. At that time, Retailers Representatives had more than 500 clients across the United States, so this outfit could have been for any of them.

Richie Premium

Richie Premium was a premium company that managed

corporate incentive programs. Like Bennett Brothers, Richie provided catalogs to its customers, who would then have their employees choose items as a reward for some task or achievement.

Between 1961 and 1966, Richie purchased $367,000 worth of trains. This amount broke down to $61,000 in 1961; $46,000 in 1962; $62,000 in 1963; $77,000 in 1964; $49,000 in 1965 and $72,000 in 1966.

Richie purchased nine promotional outfits: nos. X-508NA in 1960, X-624 and X-625 in 1961, 19147 and 19203 in 1962, 19142-502 and 19216 in 1963, 19328 in 1964 and 19555 in 1966. General Release Promotional outfit no. 19450 from 1965 and 1966 was likely purchased by Richie because it included a no. X625-20 Cardboard Scenic Set. This delicate peripheral appeared in all Richie Premium outfits. Richie's end customers have yet to be determined, so no definitive answers can be given about how these outfits were acquired by employees.

Rike's

Rike Kumler Co. (Rike's) was founded in 1853 by David L. Rike when he became a partner in the Dayton, Ohio dry goods firm of Prugh, Joice and Rike. The original partners eventually left and he entered into a partnership with his bother-in-law Samuel Kumler.

Expansion ensued until Rike's was acquired by Federated Department Stores in 1959. In 1982, Federated merged Shillito's and Rike's to form Shillito-Rikes. Finally in 1986, Federated merged Lazarus and Shillito-Rikes under the Lazarus name.

At least four promotional outfits can be linked to Rike's via a catalog and a price tag. A 1962 Rike's catalog showed outfit nos. 19131 (no. T35-3 for $19.88), 19132 (no. T35-2 for $29.88) and 19133 (no. T35-1 for $39.88). These were purchased from AMC. In 1964, outfit no. 19346 was linked to Rike's via a price tag as no. 658P 66 for $9.99. Rike's probably sold other outfits, but they have not been observed in catalogs or other sources.

RMG

RMG purchased two promotional outfits in 1962, nos. 19199 and 19200. No further information is known about this customer or its use of these outfits.

Robin Distributors

Established in Chicago in 1960 by Rudy Schwartz, Robin Distributors had become one of the largest toy concessionaires in the Midwest by 1963. The firm provided wholesale goods to several retailers, but its principal account was Consumer Mart of America (CMA) stores. Robin stocked and ran CMA's toy, sporting goods, housewares, hardware and luggage departments. In addition, it was responsible for handling the displays, fixtures, shipping and personnel in these leased departments. The company's success was short-lived, though, because Robin filed for Chapter 11 bankruptcy in February of 1964.

In 1962, Robin Distributors purchased one Retailer Promotional outfit, no. 19198.

S. Klein

Established in 1921 in Union Square in New York City, S. Klein was one of the first discount department stores in the United States. The store advertised apparel and household items. Volume purchasing and low overhead costs explained how it was able to discount its prices. Grayson-Robinson acquired S. Klein in 1946 and expanded its operations in New York and New Jersey. S. Klein was sold again in the early 1960s to McCrory Corporation, which operated its nine stores until poor sales forced their closure in 1976.

Lionel did quite a bit of promotional outfit business with S. Klein between 1960 and 1966. S. Klein purchased six Retailer Promotional outfits: nos. X-571NA in 1960, X-694 in 1961, 19192 (sold for $12.88) in 1962, 19272 in 1963, 19273 (sold for $19.77) in 1963 and 19589 (no. 12 T for $11.88) in 1966. These outfits were supplied in large quantities, which was uncommon for a discounter operating fewer than ten retail locations. S. Klein also ordered a blister display of the 19589 in 1966 that was numbered D19589. Finally in 1964, two other outfits were proposed but "not accepted": nos. 19415 and 19416.

Sears, Roebuck and Co.

Richard Sears founded R. W. Sears Watch Company in Minneapolis in 1886. The following year, he moved to Chicago and joined forces with Alvah C. Roebuck, and they officially changed the company name to Sears, Roebuck in 1893. By 1895, their company was producing a catalog with more than 500 items. In the early 1900s, Sears expanded rapidly while fiercely competing with the leader in mail-order retailing, Montgomery Ward. By 1929, Sears had expanded to more than 400 stores; two years later, its catalog division had a higher profit than the retail division.

During the 1930s and 1940s, Sears aggressively acquired companies to broaden the services offered to its customers. In the 1950s, it established a presence in Canada by purchasing both a percentage of the R. Simpson retail stores (renaming them Simpsons-Sears) and that firm's mail-order business. Sears enhanced its recognition when it rebuilt the company's headquarters as the Sears Tower, for many years the tallest building in the world.

In the 1980s, Sears diversified by acquiring Dean Witter Reynolds Organization, Inc. and Coldwell Banker & Company as well as by launching a credit card company, Discover. It also shored up its retail stores and did not flinch at closing unprofitable ones. The same business attitude explained why, in 1993, Sears shut down a catalog division that had become unprofitable. At the same time, it was divesting by selling some subsidiaries to focus on the retail division.

By 2000, Sears retail operations consisted of its retail stores in the United States and Canada, auto stores, hardware stores, tire and battery retailers and independently owned stores. Today, after merging with K-Mart Holding Corporation, Sears Holding Corporation has become the third largest retailer in the United States.

The earliest evidence of a relationship between Sears and Lionel appeared in a Sears catalog from 1925, which contained Lionel trains. Sears remained a strong and steady customer over the decades that followed, right into the 1960s. Between 1961 and 1966, it purchased $6.7 million in trains and raceways. This table shows the breakdown (with amounts given in the thousands).

Sears Purchases	1961	1962	1963	1964	1965	1966	Total
Trains	$1,000	$700	$220	$794	$498	$250	$3,462
Raceways	$0	$30	$118	$1,766	$932	$400	$3,246
Total	$1,000	$730	$338	$2,560	$1,430	$650	$6,708

The Factory Orders revealed that Sears purchased sixty-eight different promotional outfits as well as numerous displays between 1960 and 1967. Many of these outfits never appeared in a catalog. Furthermore, all but one of these outfits qualified as a Retailer Promotional. This fact confirms what collectors have long thought: Sears was a premier account of Lionel, which is why one of its corporate executives in New York (including Robert Wolfe, president of the firm in the mid-1960s) typically handled the Sears account.

Sears showed the Lionel trains it was selling in its annual Christmas Book and/or Toy Book catalogs. Trains have also been observed in regional Sears flyers.

The numbering system Sears used on its trains consists of a two-digit department number, followed by a letter indicating the season of the catalog, a four-digit product code and an optional shipping indicator (used in calculating the shipping cost). Two examples were nos. 49 N 9820 and 79 N 9870L. Sears designated toys with either "49" (the norm) or "79" (a special shipping request). If the item to be shipped exceeded the limits noted in the tables printed in the Sears catalogs (typically, 20 pounds of weight and 72 inches of combined length and width), then special plans had to be made. Sears indicated that situation with a different number for such toys, using "79" at the beginning and a suffix at the end (in this case, "L") for manual shipping calculation.

A letter indicating which catalog contained reference to the toy came after the two-digit number. "N" specified the Christmas Book, and "U" indicated the Toy Book. Sears used "C" to refer to its flyers. Other letters likely were used, though they have not yet been observed.

The four-digit product code was next. Through 1962 and three outfits in 1963, the Sears number mirrored the number that Lionel used internally and was printed on the outfit box. In 1963, however, Lionel adopted a five-digit system for numbering its outfits, which meant that the Sears number no longer duplicated Lionel's internal number. Because of this discrepancy, outfits generally were marked with both a Lionel number and a Sears number. Through 1965, outfit nos. 12885-500 (no. 9836), 19326 (no. 9820), 19327 (no. 9807), 19446 (no. 9833), 19453 (no. 9834) and 19454-500 (no. 9835) did appear with only the Sears four-digit number printed on the outfit box. But by 1966, all outfits were stamped with only the Lionel five-digit number.

To make matters a bit more confusing, the Sears catalog number was not always consistent. Different Sears catalogs might use different prefixes or catalog indicators. Thus in 1965, outfit nos. 19430 and 19433 both had a Sears number of 9837. The price of an outfit might also vary, as shown by different regional versions of catalogs and surviving price tags. Consider outfit no. 9652 from 1960. The Sears catalog for that year priced it at $25.97. However, one surviving example has a price tag with $26.95 and another one has a tag with $26.98.

This table of Sears outfits defaults to the catalog number and price as listed in a Sears catalog. If no catalog listing was available, the catalog number comes from internal Lionel documents and the price comes from a price tag (otherwise, that entry is left blank).

Year	Lionel Number*	Sears Catalog Number	Sears Catalog	Retail Price
1960	9651	9651	No catalog listing	
	9652	49 N 9652	1960 Christmas Catalog	$25.97
			1961 Simpsons- Sears Christmas Catalog	$29.95
	9653	49 N 9653	1960 Christmas Catalog	$29.44
	9654	49 N 9654		$39.44
	9692	9692	No catalog listing	
	9693	49 N 9693	1960 Christmas Catalog	$48.95
	9694	9694	No catalog listing	$59.95
1961	9670	49 N 9670	1961 Christmas Catalog	$18.88
	9671	9671	No Catalog Listing	
	9672	49 N 9672	1961 Christmas Catalog	$29.88
	9673	49 N 9673		$39.88
	9674	9674	No catalog listing	
	9675	9675		$59.98
	9692	9692		
1962	9650	9650		$19.88
	9655	49 N 9655		$29.75
	9656	49 N 9656	1962 Christmas Catalog	$39.77
	9657	49 N 9657		$49.77
	9658	49 9658		$59.95
1963	19301	9817		
	19302	9818		$19.88
	19303	9804		
	19304	9858		
	19305	9854		$29.88
	19306	9816		
	19308	9884		$49.89
	19309	9888		
	19311	9852		
	19312	9868		
	19313	9824	No catalog listing	$19.88
	19315	9887		
	19316	9885		
	19317	9866		
	19317A	9867		
	19318	9865		
	19319	9842		
	19320	9886		$37.88
	19321	9862		
	19322	9864		
	19323	9853		
	19324	9863		
	9730	49 N 9730	1963 Christmas Catalog	$29.88
	9730-500	49 9730	No catalog listing	$29.98
	9733	9733		
1964	19325	49 N 9813		$9.97
	19326 (9820)	49 N 9820	1964 Christmas Catalog	$19.89
	19327 (9807)	79 N 9807L		$29.99

continued

Year	Lionel Number*	Sears Catalog Number	Sears Catalog	Retail Price
1965	12885-500 (9836)	79 N 9836K	1965 Christmas Catalog	$99.95
	19426		No catalog listing	
	19427	4919427		$9.99
	19428	49 SPEC		$9.99
	19429			
	19430	9837		$14.99
	19431	49 19431		$9.99
	19432			$15.99
	19433	9837		$14.99
	19434	49 19434		$14.97 or $18.99
	19435			
	19446 (9833)	9833		$19.98
	19453 (9834)	79 N 9834C	1965 Christmas Catalog	$29.99
	19454-500 (9835)	79 N 9835C		$49.95
1966	19453 (9834)	49 9834	No catalog listing	$29.99
	19557	49 N 9808	1966 Christmas Catalog	$19.99
	19561	SR 9810	No catalog listing	
1967	19701	49 N 9723	1967 Christmas Catalog	$18.44
	19703	49 N 9724		$22.50
	19705	T49 C9733	1967 Promotional Flyer	$19.99
	19706	9732	No catalog listing	$32.99

* Note, from 1964 through 1966, if the Sears number only appears on the outfit box, that number is provided in parentheses.

A few years stand out when this table is studied. Factory Orders link Sears with twenty-five promotional outfits in 1963, but only one appeared in a Sears catalog (no. 9730). This odd circumstance reveals how desperate Lionel had become to make sales. For after selling $10,375,000 worth of trains and raceways in 1962, Lionel was down to $6,052,000 the following year. Robert Wolfe, president of the Lionel Toy Corporation, needed to improve sales - and quickly! So he cut a deal with Sears, as he informed his company's board of directors on November 14, 1963: "…the Company will liquidate its completed inventory by year-end and…arrangements had been made to sell surplus toy inventory to Sears, Roebuck & Company, for $410,000." This became a "Sears Special Purchase" and led to the creation of twenty-three additional outfits in late 1963 and early 1964, with most of the revenue being credited to 1964.

After purchasing only three outfits in 1964, Sears, Roebuck and Co. made a large purchase of fourteen Retailer Promotional outfits in 1965. Only three of these outfits appeared in the 1965 Sears Christmas Catalog.

Evidence suggests that Lionel offered Sears a similar deal to the "Special Purchase" granted in 1963. First, Factory Orders for eleven of these outfits were called "Special Outfit" and had similar dates of 3-23-65 or 3-24-65. Second, each of these eleven outfits included numerous substitutions, which indicated the depletion of surplus or old inventory. Third, none of these eleven outfits appeared in a Sears catalog. Finally, after 1965, Sears returned to its traditional pattern of purchasing three or four outfits each year.

Also interesting are the four outfits attributed to Sears in 1967, which was when Lionel closed its manufacturing facility in Hillside, New Jersey. Major accounts such as Sears would make decisions on what they intended to sell during one year well into the sales cycle of the previous year. Sears might, therefore, have made commitments for what it would sell in 1967 that Lionel believed it had to honor or would honor in order to keep revenue flowing into its shrinking coffers. Whatever the reason, Sears did carry four outfits in 1967, the last ones during the postwar era. Only Marx and some HO scale trains appeared in the Sears catalog for 1968.

From a collector's standpoint, Lionel's relationship with Sears during the 1960s was significant. It produced a number of rare, highly desirable outfits, including nos. 9694, 9675, 9655, 19320 (no. 9886), 19326 (no. 9820) and 12885-500 (no. 9836).

Service Exchanges (see AFA)

Shell Oil

Marcus Sameuel started an import-export business in 1833 that later became the Shell Group. His son, recognizing the need for exporting oil for cooking and illumination, commissioned the company's first tanker in 1892. From there, Shell grew and grew. Except for difficulties during World War I and World War II, it expanded into other geographic markets and product lines, including chemicals and natural gas, and is now one of the world's giants in oil and natural gas production.

Shell, which used advertising campaigns and promotional items to strengthen its market position, purchased one Manufacturer Promotional outfit in 1963, no. 19281. It probably used this outfit for a promotion in a manner similar to what Cities Service, one of its competitors, was doing, although the exact nature of such a promotion has yet to be determined. The distribution of this outfit followed that of other Manufacturer Promotional outfits, being shipped from Lionel to the customer's fulfillment organization, which mailed it to consumers. The contract with Shell permitted dissatisfied customers to ship their outfits back to Lionel within 30 days after the date of shipment and receive a refund that Lionel would provide through Shell.

Shillito's (see Mercury Model)

Signet

Signet was a common business name in various industries during the 1960s; which firm was a customer of Lionel could not be determined with assurance. Four Retailer Promotional outfits were identified with Signet: nos. X-543NA in 1960, X-668 (Signet no. A-8901) and X-669 (no. A8900) in 1961 and 19144 in 1962.

Simpsons-Sears (see R. Simpson)

Sperry & Hutchinson Co. (S&H)

Thomas Sperry and Shelley Hutchinson created the trading stamp plan in 1896 and named their venture Sperry & Hutchinson

(S&H). The company was the first independent trading stamp company to distribute stamps and books to merchants as a means of rewarding shoppers for their timely payments and loyalty to specific merchants. The program, although enticing for retailers, did not take off until the 1930s, when states began passing fair-trade laws that punished retailers for cutting prices.

Stamps became a competitive marketing advantage for retailers because consumers would frequent stores that offered the stamps they collected. The 1.7 to 2.5 percent cost of running the program was viewed as a marketing expense, although some merchants increased prices to cover the costs. Users of S&H stamps ranged from chains of grocery stores to gasoline service stations in the United States, along with foreign subsidiaries.

S&H issued full-color catalogs filled with attractive merchandise with well-known brand names. Household appliances, hobby equipment and toys predominated. Consumers took their books of S&H Green Stamps (each filled book had a redemption value of approximately $3.00) to various S&H redemption centers and exchanged them for the merchandise wanted.

By 1964, S&H had become the largest trading stamp company, printing three times as many stamps as the United States Post Office and issuing a catalog whose print run surpassed that of any other single publication in the nation. No wonder that manufacturers pushed to get their products in the S&H catalog.

In the 1970s, the use of trading stamps began to decline. Many stamp companies went out of business, although S&H survived, mostly in the Southeast. Baldwin-United Corporation acquired S&H in 1981. When Baldwin-United fell into bankruptcy in 1986, it combined its S&H Motivation and Top Value Motivation units. In 1999, S&H was bought by a group of investors led by Walter Beinecke (Sperry's great-grandson). The firm continues today over the Internet with a digital version of the stamp program called Greenpoints.

Lionel and S&H enjoyed a prosperous relationship, with the stamp company purchasing $393,000 worth of trains and raceways between 1961 and 1966, when trading stamps were at the peak of their popularity. S&H carried both catalog and Retailer Promotional outfits. All S&H outfits were offered in the catalog for six filled books or an approximate value of $18.00. The "6" before the "P" in the S&H number stood for six books. All the outfits were stamped with both a Lionel and an S&H number.

S&H began carrying promotional outfits in 1960 with no. X-516NA (S&H no. 6-P4803). S&H ordered another promotional outfit in 1961, no. X-612 (no. 6-P4805). For the next two years, the firm shifted to catalog outfits, offering nos. 11201 (no. 6-P4807) in 1962 and 11331 (no. 6-P4810) in 1963.

The last year that Lionel trains appeared in an S&H merchandise catalog was 1964. Outfit no. 19350 (no. 6P-4811) was shown on page 122. This outfit went on to be offered by Lionel in three other configurations: nos. 19350-500 in 1964 and 1965 and 19350-501 in 1965. Two factors explained why four versions of the same outfit exist. The first related to the length of time that S&H carried products. S&H catalogs were valid until April 30 of the following year. Hence, this outfit spanned two separate production years for Lionel. If it were a popular outfit requiring a reorder, Lionel would need to fulfill with what it had. The second reason related to the far-from-optimal inventory management being done at Lionel in 1964 - outfits were cannibalized to meet deadlines for other outfits. The 19350 was one such outfit. When it came time to further fulfill the order, 19350-500 was issued.

By the end of 1965, the relationship between Lionel and S&H was waning. An outfit, no. 19520, was planned for S&H in 1966, but the order was subsequently canceled. Spear phonographs were offered by S&H from 1965 to 1967, followed by Porter science items in 1968. No products from any of Lionel's lines appeared in an S&H catalog the following year.

Spiegel

In 1865, Joseph Spiegel opened a furniture retail company, Spiegel & Company, in Chicago. By 1905, he had entered the mail-order business with a 24-page booklet offering furniture, housewares and clothing and giving consumers the opportunity to purchase with credit (a new concept in this field). Three years later, the introduction of jewelry, apparel and piece goods caused the customer base to increase. Over the years, Spiegel developed a reputation for offering quality merchandise at affordable prices. Its mail-order business grew through the acquisition of various retailers until, by 1962, Spiegel was the third largest mail-order firm in the United States.

In the years that followed, however, Spiegel watched its earnings fall because of poorly planned expansion and heightened competition. It eventually filed for Chapter 11 bankruptcy and sold its catalog to Golden Gate Capital. In February of 2005, Spiegel announced that it would reorganize under the name Eddie Bauer Holding Company and again specialize in marketing apparel and home furnishings.

Spiegel purchased a number of Lionel outfits between 1960 and 1967. Its purchase of four catalog and twenty-three promotional outfits made Spiegel a notable customer. Catalog outfits included nos. 1646 and 1649 in 1961, 11288 in 1962 and (most likely) 11540 in 1967. Spiegel bought Retailer Promotional outfits from 1960 through 1964 (although Lionel trains did not appear in the Spiegel Christmas Catalog for 1964). In 1965 and 1966, following Lionel's strategy to concentrate on General Release Promotional outfits, Spiegel purchased three of them. The relationship had ended by 1968, as only Marx and some HO trains appeared in the Spiegel catalog for that year.

Year	Lionel Number	Spiegel Catalog Number	Spiegel Catalog	Retail Price
1960	X-523NA	R36 J 5219	1960 Christmas Catalog	$19.87
1961	X-651	R36 J 5260	1961 Christmas Catalog	$19.94
	1646	R 36 J 5261		$29.33
	1649	R36 J 5263		$38.88
1962	11288	R36 J 5276	1962 Christmas Catalog	$38.88
	19185	R36 J 5278		$18.87
	19186	R36 J 5277		$29.87
1963	11351-500	R36 J 5286	1963 Christmas Catalog	$23.94
	19214-500		No catalog listing	
	19237	R36 J 5287	1963 Christmas Catalog	$17.94
	19238	R36 J 5285		$29.84
1964	19238-501		No catalog listing	
	19353			
	19368			
	19369			
	19370			
	19371	36 5284		
	19371-500	5284-S		
	19372			
	19372-500	5283-S		
1965	19437-502	R36 J 5262	1965 Christmas Catalog	$19.97
	19439-502	R36 J 5261		$14.97
	19444-502	R36 J 5263		$24.97
1966	19501	R36 J 5258	1966 Christmas Catalog	$14.77
	19507	R36 J 5260		$27.97
	19541	R36 J 5259		$19.97
1967	11540	R36 J 5266	1967 Christmas Catalog	$19.97

Stern's (see Allied)

Stern Brothers Department Stores originated in New York in 1867 as a dry goods retailer. It was bought by Allied Corporation and became one of the more successful subsidiaries by catering to the middle-class market with apparel, housewares and toys in its New York and New Jersey locations. The chain was by absorbed by Campeau Corporation in 1986, when it merged with Allied, which merged with Federated Department Stores in 1992. Stern's stores operated until 2001, when Federated converted most of them into Macy's and Bloomingdales stores.

Stern's was a long-time customer of Lionel, going back to at least 1929 and probably earlier. The March 1929 issue of *Playthings* magazine (a publication for the toy industry) refers to Stern's featuring large window displays of Lionel trains. Jumping forward, two of the eleven outfits that Lionel sold to Allied from 1960 though 1964 can be attributed to Stern's. The Stern's Christmas Catalog for 1960 shows nos. X-500NA (Stern's no. 740 for $39.99) and X-501NA (no. 742 for $29.99). Another outfit, no. 19240, was sold direct to Stern's in 1963, most likely for distribution at the company's flagship store on 42nd Street in Manhattan.

Stix, Baer & Fuller

Stix, Baer & Fuller, established in 1892 by brothers Julius and Sigmund Baer, brother-in-law Aaron Fuller and Charles Stix, opened its first department store in St. Louis. The company became a member of the New York Stock Exchange in 1952. Stix, Baer

& Fuller was purchased in 1963 by Associated Dry Goods, which expanded the chain into Kansas City, Missouri, and Springfield, Illinois. Dillard's Department Stores bought all twelve of the Stix, Baer & Fuller stores in 1983 and had closed them by 2002.

In 1960, Stix, Baer & Fuller purchased one Retailer Promotional outfit, no. X-562NA. Four years later, it bought two General Release Promotional outfits: nos. 19345 and 19392. In 1966, the Factory Order for no. 19555 indicates that it was for Richie Premium, but an example has been observed with a Stix, Baer & Fuller price tag.

Stokely-Van Camp

In the late 1800s, Anna John Stokely and her two sons purchased the Van Camp Company in Indianapolis. Known for its canned pork and beans, Stokely-Van Camp went on to manufacture a complete line of canned fruits and vegetables and acquired various companies to offer frozen foods, dry cereal and oils. In 1967, Stokely-Van Camp began to market Gatorade, a sports drink developed two years earlier at the University of Florida to prevent dehydration in football players. In 1982, Stokely-Van Camp sold its canned fruit and vegetable line to Oconomowoc Canning Company. A year later, Quaker Oats purchased the advertising and such key products as Van Camp Pork and Beans and Gatorade for $230 million. Then in 1984, Stokely returned as Stokely USA, when Oconomowoc Canning Company purchased the Stokely name and trademarks from Quaker. After enduring some financial difficulties, Stokely USA was purchased by Chiquita in 1998.

Premiums, such as gifts with the purchase of a Stokely product, were widely used in the 1950s and 1960s. A majority of the products available, such as cookbooks, children's books and recipe tins, bore Stokely's name and were offered in return for a Stokely product label and a small payment.

One such promotion partnered Stokely with Lionel. On the heels of its success with Quaker in 1961, Lionel worked with Stokely on Manufacturer Promotional outfit no. 19142 in 1962. This outfit came in three versions: nos. 19142 (mail-order packed version), 19142-50 (display version) and 19142-100 (RSC version). For sending in one Van Camp Pork and Beans label and $11.95, a consumer received a "$25.00 Premium Value Electric Train".

This Manufacturer Promotional outfit was heavily pushed. Brochures were sent to Van Camp's sales force and brokerage organizations, and another estimated 7,500 went to the grocery trade. In addition, the outfit offer was publicized on approximately 80 million Van Camp Pork and Bean labels.

Yet the promotion bombed! This was unfortunate for Stokely-Van Camp, but ironically fortunate for Lionel (it actually lost 48 cents on every outfit). Out of the 50,450 Factory Orders, only 2,886 of these outfits were sold between October 1962 and July 1963. Even worse, the contract with Van Camp pledged Lionel to pay sales tax in California. There was also a question of who owed the tax in Washington, the amount of which had not been resolved as of January 1965.

This outfit introduced the no. 6050-150 Van Camp Savings Bank Car.

Strauss Stores

In 1929, I. M. Strauss opened five auto supply stores and a

warehouse in Brooklyn, New York. The firm merged with R & S Auto in 1982 to form R & S Strauss. (In 1962, R & S Auto purchased Retailer Promotional outfit no. 19205.) Currently, the company operates as Strauss Discount Auto, with more than 100 auto supply stores and fifty service stations located throughout the East Coast.

Strauss Stores purchased three Retailer Promotional outfits: nos. X-544NA in 1960, X-637 in 1961 and 19146 in 1962.

Super Markets

Super Markets was listed on one Factory Order in 1964. This was a Retailer Promotional outfit sold to many supermarkets. Outfit no. 19244-500 was a derivation of promotional outfit nos. 19244 and 19253, which Lionel developed for A&P and Kroger respectively in 1963.

SupeR$_x$ (see Kroger)

Swift

Swift, which was established in Chicago in 1875 by Gustavus Swift, became one of the largest meat-packing companies in the world. It was the first firm to offer packaged beef to eastern markets instead of live animals. Swift went on to develop the refrigerated railway car, an aspect of how the company vertically integrated its production, supply and distribution. By the 1960s, Swift was a diversified business involved with dairy products, oils, peanut butter and ice cream. In 1973, it sought to create a different image by changing its name to Esmark, Inc. The firm was acquired in 1984 by Beatrice Foods, which operates Swift under the name Armour Swift-Eckrich.

Swift was heavily involved in advertising and premium promotions. In the 1940s, it sponsored the first regularly scheduled commercial daytime television show, *The Swift Home Service Club*. During the 1950s, the company offered a wide range of products (dishes, canisters and so forth) with the purchase of one of its products.

In 1961, Lionel and Swift teamed up on a Manufacturer Promotional outfit, no. X-686. This outfit introduced the no. 6050-50 Swift Savings Bank Car.

T. Eaton

Founded by Timothy Eaton in 1869, T. Eaton was a chain of department stores based in Toronto. In 1883, it opened a larger retail location. The following year, Eaton introduced a mail-order catalog, which offered products for consumers in rural communities. Over the years, Eaton introduced fixed pricing in Canada and became one of the dominant retailers there.

In 1999, the family-run chain found it could no longer compete with the stores maintained by American retailers in Canada and so declared bankruptcy. Sears acquired the chain not long after and kept it open until 2002, when it converted all remaining T. Eaton stores to the Sears name.

Between 1960 and 1962, T. Eaton bought two General Release and three Retailer Promotional outfits that appeared in its Christmas catalogs. Outfit nos. 1115 (Eaton no. 027-B-640 for $18.98) and 1117 (no. 027-B-648 for $23.98) were purchased in 1960. They were followed in 1961 by nos. X-673 (no. 027-G-1211 for $18.96) and then 19119 (no. 027-R4018 for $28.50) and 19120 in 1962. After not ordering any outfits in 1963, Eaton purchased a catalog outfit the next year, no. 11440 (no. 27-R 4023 for $19.99). By 1965, Eaton and Lionel were no longer customers.

Taubman's

Taubman's was a Baltimore area retailer who carried Lionel trains. Whether it was part of a larger chain has yet to be learned.

Taubman's purchased at least three Retailer Promotional outfits: nos. 19241-500 (Taubman's no. LT4-441 for $34.99) and 19252 in 1963 and 19383 in 1964.

The Emporium (see Department Store Promotional)

The Emporium was a customer of Lionel as early as 1903.

The Fair (see Mutual)

The Fair was a customer of Lionel as early as October 29, 1906.

The M. O'Neil Co. (see May Company)

Times Square Stores

Established in 1910 in Brooklyn, New York, Times Square Stores were discount retail operations that originally specialized in auto supplies and sporting goods. They continually expanded their merchandise, adding stores that carried toys in 1946. Times Square Stores, unlike many discounters, leased most of its departments to outside companies with a particular product or service. The company grew to more than ten locations throughout New York that operated under the names Times Square and Bargaintown. After many years of operating as a discounter, the company found itself unable to compete with larger retailers and in 1989 filed for bankruptcy.

Times Square Stores purchased two promotional outfits between 1960 and 1962. Outfit no. 1125 from 1960 was observed with a Times Square Stores price tag for $11.89. Outfit no. 19157 from 1962 appears on a Factory Order and referenced 31-5084 as the Times Square number.

Titche's (see Allied Stores and Mercury Model)

Founded in 1894 when Edward Titche took over his uncle's store in Dallas, Edward Titche Company grew into one of the largest retail stores in the Southwest. The stores, which shortened their name to Titche's in the 1950s, eventually sold out to Allied Stores. Allied changed the name to Joske's. A buyout in 1987 led to the stores being changed to the name of the acquiring company, Dillard's.

Two outfits have been observed with a Titche's price tag: 1966 outfit no. 19567-500 (Titche's no. 830 116 for $13.88) and General Release Promotional no. 19707 (Titche's no. 19707 for $30.00).

Top Value

Founded in 1955 by Kroger and six other firms, Top Value trading stamps were distributed at Kroger stores and gasoline chains. Top Value issued catalogs advertising a wide range of products. Its stamps could be redeemed by mail or at redemption centers throughout the United States. Top Value became one of the larger stamp companies, competing against E. F. MacDonald and Sperry & Hutchinson, among others.

In the late 1960s, when the trading stamp craze was slowing, Top Value diversified its marketing activities by adding promotional programs and travel services. Top Value dissolved when it was purchased by Baldwin-United Corporation. Renamed Plcorp and based in Philadelphia, it now serves as a trading stamp and insurance company.

Top Value purchased three Retailer Promotional outfits from Lionel: no. X-604 (Top Value no. 15-198 for 5⅘ books of stamps) in 1961 and again in 1962 and no. 19210 (no. 15-198 for 5⅘ books) in 1963. All three outfits were basically the same with minor updates, such as a different locomotive and peripherals for 1963. Based on three years of repeat Factory Orders, Top Value's Lionel promotion was a success; the quantities totaled 4,300 in 1961, 3,500 in 1962 and 3,500 in 1963. From 1964 to at least 1966, Top Value offered only Marx trains.

As part of the sales process with Top Value, Lionel developed artwork for a box car. This project helped get Top Value as a customer, but the car never became part of regular production.

Town & Country

Town & Country Distributors, acquired by Lane Bryant in 1961, was a retail chain operating six discount stores in Pennsylvania. After the acquisition, Lane Bryant restructured the company by expanding the retail locations, purchasing a warehouse and introducing soft-line goods. By 1975, the discounter had nineteen retail outlets across the United States and competed with larger discounters. The company continued until the 1980s, when the Limited Stores bought Lane Bryant and closed all the Town & Country stores.

In 1962, Town & Country purchased two Retail Promotional outfits: nos. 19160 and 19161.

Uncle Bill

Cook United, Inc. (formerly Cook Coffee Company) purchased two Uncle Bill stores in 1961. Those stores were discount department stores offering apparel, hardware, toys and housewares. It appears that Cook eventually purchased all of them. Over the years, Cook expanded through acquisitions and normal growth. When discounters like Wal-Mart and Target arrived in the 1980s, the company was unable to compete because of a decline in its customer base. In 1987, Cook United filed for bankruptcy, citing years of mismanagement and retail competition from larger discount stores.

In 1961, Uncle Bill purchased three Retailer Promotional outfits: nos. X-661, X-662 and X-663.

United Trading Stamp

Established in 1926, United Trading Stamp offered stamps for redemption until the early 1970s. United was not one of the larger stamp companies on a par with Sperry & Hutchinson or E. F. MacDonald, and information has not surfaced about which retailers distributed its stamps. The firm might also have used the name Colonial United Stamps, although that could not be confirmed.

United Trading Stamp is linked with one Retailer Promotional outfit, the 1963 version of no. 11001. This was an RSC reissue of no. 11001 from 1962, intended specifically for United Trading Stamp. Outfit no. 1123 has also been observed in a 1961 Colonial United Stamps catalog as no. 1503 offered for six books.

Van Camp (see Stokely-Van Camp)

W. T. Grant

W. T. Grant, established in 1906 by William T. Grant, was a variety store that offered products ranging from toiletries to major appliances. The company expanded rapidly in select markets and was operating 1,092 stores by the end of the 1960s. W. T. Grant established a presence in Canada by purchasing 51 percent of Zellers Limited, a chain of variety stores. When times changed and discount stores entered the retail market, Grant found it difficult to compete. In 1975, the company filed for bankruptcy and closed more than 200 stores throughout the United States.

W. T. Grant purchased two Retailer Promotional outfits in 1960 (nos. X-565NA and X-566NA) and two more promotional outfits in 1964 (nos. 19365 and 19411).

Waite's (see Allied Stores)

Ward's (see Montgomery Ward)

Western Auto

Founded in 1908 by George Pepperdine, Western Auto was a Kansas City, Missouri, company originally selling auto parts by mail order. It expanded operations by opening retail stores and incorporating in 1914. In 1935, Western Auto started the "Associate Store Plan" that enabled stores using the Western Auto name to receive wholesale merchandise and Western Auto branded and created products.

By the 1950s, Western Auto had broadened its product line to include appliances, electronics, toys, hardware and sporting goods. It was purchased by Sears in 1988, and sales began to decline steadily in the 1990s because of competition from specialty retailers. Sears started converting Western Auto stores to Parts America in 1997. A year later, 1998, Sears turned over all Parts America and Western Auto stores to Advance Auto in exchange for $175 million and 40 percent of the Advance stock.

Western Auto was the fourth largest customer of Lionel trains and raceways in the 1960s, purchasing $913,000 worth of trains and raceway. The following table shows the breakdown with amounts given in the thousands.

Western Auto Purchases	1961	1962	1963	1964	1965	1966	Total
Trains	$193	$210	$176	$164	$86	$75	$904
Raceways	$0	$0	$0	$0	$9	$0	$9
Total	$193	$210	$176	$164	$95	$75	$913

Western Auto's purchases were spread across one catalog outfit, at least sixteen promotional outfits and two displays. Prices of these outfits varied, although not significantly. Different versions of catalogs and price tags revealed slightly different pricing. When more than one catalog number or price was known, the table used the ones listed in the Western Auto Christmas Gifts Catalog.

Year	Lionel Number	Western Auto Catalog Number	Western Auto Catalog	Retail Price
1960	X-538NA	EC 5010	1960 Christmas Gifts	$18.88
	X-546NA	EC 5011		$26.88
1961	X-638	EC-1007	1961 Christmas Gifts	$18.88
	X-639	EC-1008		$28.88
1962	19107	EC 5010	1962 Christmas Gifts	$19.99
	19108	EC 5011		$29.88
1963	19212	E1010	1963 Christmas Gifts	$18.95
	19213	E1007		$11.95
	19214	E1011	No catalog listing	
	D19213	E1008		$11.97
1964	19244	E5005	1964 Christmas Gifts	$10.88
	19330	E5009		$13.99
	19331		No catalog listing	
	19332	E5011	1964 Ordering Guide	$31.88
	D-19244	E5006		
1965	19436	E1002	1965 Christmas Gifts	$15.77
1966	11520	383901	No catalog listing	
	19436		No 1966 catalog listing	
	19530	E5002	1966 Christmas Gifts and 1966-1967 Fall & Winter	$15.97
	19910	E1002		$14.77

All the promotional outfits were Retailer Promotional outfits, with the exception of no. 19244 (Western Auto no. E5005), which was leftover inventory of the A&P Retailer Promotional from 1963. Another outfit, no. 19910 (no. E1002,) was a General Release Promotional that Western Auto carried in its 1967 Christmas and 1967-1968 Fall & Winter catalogs. In 1966, Lionel sold a catalog outfit, no. 11520, to Western Auto Canada as no. 383901.

All outfits through 1964 that have been observed (except 19244 and no. 19330) were jointly marked with the Lionel and the Western Auto numbers. From 1965 on, only the Lionel number appeared. Interestingly, some Western Auto numbers were repeated on outfits whose contents differed. These include no. E1002 (nos. 19436 and 19910), no. EC 5010 (nos. X-538NA and 19107) and no. EC 5011 (nos. X-546NA and 19108). All Western Auto catalog numbers (stock numbers) began with "EC" or "E" (starting in 1963) to signify "toys". The remaining four digits filled out the stock number.

A 1964 Western Auto Ordering Guide sent to its wholesale customers indicated that the stock numbers for trains and raceways ranged from E5000 to E5100; train and raceway accessories had stock numbers E5200 to E5299. This guide also provides insights into Lionel's net sale price to Western Auto and its markups to Western Auto dealers.

White Front Stores (see Interstate Department Stores)

White Stores and White Auto

White Stores, Inc., founded in Oklahoma in 1930 and later based in Wichita Falls, Texas, was a retailer and wholesaler of a broad line of merchandise. Originally an auto parts store, White diversified its line of merchandise to include toys, hardware, furniture and appliances. By 1960, White's dealer network of more than 200 stores was spread across the Southwest. It also opened a discount operation, Broome Discount Center. White was acquired in 1982 by Canadian Tire Corp., which closed all the White Stores three years later following a disappointing campaign to apply Canadian marketing methods and product lines to the stores.

White Stores were up there with J. C. Penney in terms of revenue purchased from Lionel in the 1960s, buying $216,000 worth of trains and raceways between 1961 and 1966. This amount was spread across five Retailer Promotional outfits, one General Release Promotional outfit, two displays and likely catalog or separate-sale items. The outfits included nos. 19158 (White no. 108-95 for $15.99) and 19159 (no. 108-105 for $29.97) in 1962, 19219 (no. 108-105) and 19220 (no. 108-55) in 1963 and 19355 in 1964. Interestingly, outfit nos. 19159 and 19219 both shared the same White no. 108-105, which was also stamped on the outfit box. In 1965, White Stores sold General Release Promotional outfit no. 19441 as no. 108-120 for $24.99. The displays included nos. D19220 in 1963 and DO19516 in 1966.

Wiechmanns

Established in Saginaw, Michigan, in 1900, Wm. C. Wiechmann was a small variety store operated by William Wiechmann and his wife, Emma. In 1930, the firm opened two more retail stores. Wiechmann continued to operate in Saginaw until the mid-1980s.

In 1962, Wiechmann purchased Retailer Promotional outfit no. 19187 in an extremely limited quantity of twenty-five.

Wm. H. Block Company (see Allied)

William H. Block Company was a department store located in downtown Indianapolis prior to 1950. Over the years, Block opened more stores in Indiana and expanded into Michigan and Ohio. Allied Stores bought and operated the Block stores from 1962 until Allied was purchased by Campeau Corporation in 1982. Five years later, Federated Department Stores purchased Block and rolled its stores into its Lazarus division.

In 1963, William H. Block purchased one Retailer Promotional outfit, no. 19314-500.

WM Taylor & Son

William Taylor & Son was a variety store located in downtown Cleveland in the early 1900s. In 1939, May Company acquired a large part of the business.

In 1960, William Taylor & Son purchased thirty-six units of Retailer Promotional outfit no. X-547.

The Outfits

How to Use The Listings In Part III

Part III of this volume contains detailed outfit listings for each promotional outfit from 1960 through 1969. The outfit information came from Lionel Factory Orders and other sources as explained in the Sources of Authoritative Information section of this volume. Below is a summary of a listing for outfit no. X-646 from 1961.

Photograph and Other Artwork: A photograph and/or other artwork is supplied for many outfits in this volume. This helps identify the specific variations of the outfit box, items and peripherals included in an outfit.

Header Tab: The header tab provides the Lionel outfit number and customer number (if that was the only number that appeared on the box) and year of the Factory Order.

Side Tab: Part III of this volume is sorted by Lionel's outfit number and grouped into sections. Each page includes a side tab for easy reference.

Outfit Header Section: Each outfit listing includes a header section with summary information from the Factory Order and other sources.

Customer Number on Box (not shown): This field provides the customer number that was included on the outfit box along with the Lionel number.

Description and Specification: These two fields provide Lionel's classification for this outfit.

Customer Name, Number and Price: These three fields list the customer who purchased the outfit from Lionel or the dealer/retailer who sold the outfit, the customer number assigned to the outfit and the selling price.

Original Amount: This is the quantity of this outfit that Lionel ordered from its factory to be manufactured.

Factory Order Date, Date Issued, Date Req'd (not shown): These three dates summarize when the Factory Order was created, when the final changes were issued and when the outfits were required from the Outfit Packing Department.

Packaging: This provides a summary of the type of packaging to be used for this outfit.

Photograph and Other Artwork Caption: The caption provides insight about the outfit or artwork.

X-646
1961

Oklahoma Tire & Supply Company was a good customer of Lionel, especially in 1961 when it purchased $79,000 of trains. Its high-end space and military diesel purchase was outfit no. X-646.

OTASCO
70-761-5
Reg. 37.45
$23.95

The price tag attached to Lionel outfit no. X-646 shows its customer OTASCO, the outfit no. 70-761-5 and its discounted price. Discounting of trains was commonplace during the 1960s.

Description: "O27" Promotional Outfit
Specification: "O27" Diesel Freight Outfit
Cust./No./Price: Oklahoma Tire & Supply Co.; 70-761-5; $23.95
Original Amount: 540
Factory Order Date: 4/11/1961
Date Issued: Rev. #1 8/10-61
Packaging: R.S.C. Outfit Packing (Units not Boxed)

Contents: 224P-25 Alco Diesel Power Car - "U.S. Navy"; 224C-25 "B" Unit - "U.S. Navy"; 6062-25 Gondola Car - Black (Less Cable Reels); 40-11 Cable Reels (3); 3665-25 Minuteman Missile Launching Car; 3410-25 Oper. Helicopter Launching Car (Manually); 6017-210 Caboose - "U.S. Navy"; 1013-70 Curved Track (Bundle of 12 - 1013); 1018-30 Straight Track (Bundle of 3 - 1018); 1008-50 Uncoupling Track Section; 1025-25 45-Watt Transformer; 1020-25 90° Crossing; 1103-12 Envelope Packed; 1802B Layout Instruction Sheet; IS Instruction Sheet; 310-2 Set of (5) Billboards; D61-50 Accessory Catalog

Boxes & Packing: 61-250 Corr. Outfit Box; 61-186 Corr. Insert (2); 61-191 Corr. Insert (2); 61-193 Corr. Insert; 61-251 Corr. Shipper for (4) (1-4)

Alternate For Outfit Contents: Customer Stock No. 70 - 761-5 to appear on outfit boxes & shippers.

X-646 (1961)	C6	C7	C8	Rarity
Complete Outfit	575	1,000	1,400	R9
Outfit Box no. 61-250	200	350	450	R9

Pricing Table: This table features the U.S. dollar value and rarity of the complete outfit, outfit with substitutions and outfit box alone. See the section on Pricing, Condition, Rarity and Demand for more information.

Comments: In 1961, Oklahoma Tire & Supply Company (OTASCO) purchased four (nos. X-644 through X-647) Retailer Promotional outfits. The third was this Type Ia high-end diesel offering. The other outfits included two entry-level (one steam and one diesel) as well as a high-end steam offering.

This space and military outfit was headed by a no. 224P-25 U.S. Navy Alco Diesel Power Car with Magne-Traction and a three-position reversing unit. It was paired with a no. 224C-25 "B" Unit. When included in promotional outfits, these items most often came boxed. The X-646 was one of four exceptions to this rule.

The nos. 3665-25 Minuteman Missile Launching car and 3410-25 Oper. Helicopter Launching Car (Manually) were both new for 1961. Their space and military features made them an appropriate pairing for this outfit. The no. 6062-25 Gondola Car does not appear to fit with this outfit, and a more appropriate car would have been a no. 6470-25 Exploding Target Car.

The no. 6017-210 U.S. Navy Caboose provided a nice finish

CONVENTIONAL PACK
61-250 BOX

TOP LAYER
6062-25 INSERT	3665-25	3410-25 INSERT	1013-70

1020-25 TOP OF BOTTOM LAYER
1008-50 TOP OF 6062-25

BOTTOM LAYER
1018-30 224C-25		1025-25
	6017-210	224P-25
1 40-11	2 40-11	

Comments Section: This section provides details about the outfit, Lionel customer, individual items and their boxes, outfit boxes, variations and other interesting outfit features.

Alternate For Outfit Contents Section: This is the summary of substitutions for the outfit. Lionel also used this section to record customer outfit numbers and special requests.

Outfit Packing Diagram: This diagram shows how to pack the trains using the boxes and inserts listed in the Boxes & Packing section.

Boxes & Packing Section: These are the Lionel part numbers for the boxes, inserts, master shippers and any other items required to package and ship the outfit.

Contents Section: This section lists all the items that come with the outfit. Each item includes Lionel's part number, description and quantity. Suffixes indicate everything from variations to packaging.

How to Use The Listings in Part III - Continued

In compiling the outfit listings in Part III of this volume, we kept the integrity of the information as close to original as possible. Lionel, like any corporation that manufactured numerous products over a multiple-year span, varied naming, packaging and sub-grouping of items over time. For example, in 1961 the no. 3409-25 was called an "Oper. Satellite Launching Car (Manually)" and the no. 0333-100 Satellite was included with the car. In 1962, Lionel changed the name to an "Oper. Satellite Launching Car (Less Satellite)" and the no. 0333-100 Satellite was provided separately to the Outfit Packing Department. As such, the satellite was listed separately on the Factory Order for the latter version. In either case, it is the same car with satellite.

Names of items also changed over the years. For example, the no. 3830-1 Operating Submarine Car was also called a Flat Car - with Operating Submarine. Both are identical items.

Lionel's naming conventions may have changed over time, but it was very consistent with the use of product numbers; a 3830-1 was always a flat car that carried an operating submarine no matter what the description. There are only a few instances when a number was re-used for an entirely different item; when this occurred, the item's Production Control File made note of what had happened.

The following provides background on different sections of the outfit listings provided in Part III.

Outfit Numbering

The outfits listed in Part III are sorted by the Lionel outfit number. Some outfits did not have the Lionel number on the box. For example, Sears no. 9820 ("9820" on box) was Lionel no. 19326 ("19326" not on box). The latter number was used for sorting purposes. For these outfits, the Header Tab includes the Lionel number followed by the number that appeared on the box in parentheses. The index provides a cross reference for the few outfits that are numbered in this manner.

Outfit numbers are sequential, and any gaps in outfit numbering likely occurred because an outfit was canceled. Unfortunately, information on most of these canceled outfits has yet to be uncovered, if it even exists.

Lionel occasionally re-used outfit numbers for some "X"-series promotional outfits. If an outfit is found for a listing included in this section, but the outfit contents, outfit box and description don't match, then it is likely an earlier version and entirely different outfit.

Factory Order General

Factory Orders used pre-printed forms and not every field on the form was required or provided. Fields most often left blank were the "dates" in the Outfit Header Section. For example, if a Factory Order did not go through any revisions, the "date issued" field was left blank.

The customer that purchased the outfit from Lionel most often was listed on the Factory Order. If that customer was a wholesaler, distributor or reseller, and if the end customer is known, it is also listed. Therefore, multiple customers are listed on many outfit listings.

Original amounts are provided for nearly every outfit in this section. Some outfits lacked this number on their Factory Order, and so it is not available.

Dates are provided in "xx/xx/xx", "xx-xx-xx" or "Jan. xx, 19xx" format based on how Lionel listed them on the Factory Order. Lionel used "A/O" as an abbreviation for "At Once". Lionel used "Rev" as an abbreviation for "Revision".

Contents Section

On a few occasions, Lionel did not provide a part number for an item, but only a description. Some examples include "Layout Instruction Sheet", "Instruction Sheet", "RSC Outfit Box" and "Sticker". For naming consistency, part numbers were provided as, "LIS", "IS", the "'Outfit Number'-RSC" and "ST" respectively.

If the quantity of an item included in an outfit is greater than one, that amount is provided in parentheses after the item's description. For example, "40-11 Cable Reels (3)" indicates that there are three cable reels included. In addition, when the quantity is listed as "(1-3)", this indicates that there is one item for every three outfits.

Boxes & Packing Section

Many outfits list multiple outfit boxes. If the outfit boxes share the same inserts, then the inserts are usually listed once. If different inserts are used for each box, each outfit box is listed followed by its appropriate inserts

All box and insert information provided by Lionel is included in the outfit listing. Some outfits did not list a complete set of inserts.

Alternates For Outfit Contents Section

Some Factory Orders specified that the customer stock number should be included on the box. However, actual observations sometimes indicate otherwise. If it can be determined that the number was included, then it is included in the Outfit Header section.

Occasionally, substitutions are provided without quantities. This most often meant that all of the original items were substituted out.

Comments Section

Individual item boxes are often referred to by their folding box part number. This is the part number of the box itself that appeared on the tuck flap of the box. For example, a no. 6465-110 Cities Service 2-Dome Tank Car - Green came in a no. 6465-103 Folding Box. The "6465-103" number appears on the tuck flap, and the "6465-110" number is on the box end. This is how Lionel referred to the boxes.

Many items are referred to as a new item in the comments section. New meant that Lionel created an entirely new Production

Control File with a new product number or suffix. One example is the no. 6014-325 Frisco Box Car from 1963. This was the new version of the unboxed no. 6014-50 Frisco Box Car from 1957.

The term "carried over" is generally used to indicate cases when a particular item was offered from one year to the next. For example, a no. 3830-1 Flat Car - with Operating Submarine first appeared in 1960. In 1961, it was a carried-over model from 1960.

When comments are made about the number of outfits or years that a customer dealt with Lionel, we are referring to O, O27 and Super O outfits. The customer may have also purchased HO, Raceway or Science products in a similar year.

The types of trucks and couplers used on individual items are provided when available. Be aware that due to transition, leftover inventory and other factors, other combinations are possible. See the section on Trucks and Couplers.

Outfit Packing Diagram

The outfit packing diagrams were hand-drawn guides created by the Outfit Packing Department to instruct its factory workers on how to pack the outfit box. This department often used item numbers and conventions that differed slightly from those found on the Factory Orders. For example, a no. 6424-1 Flat Car – with 2 Autos appeared as a "6424" on the packing diagram. As another example, track was sometimes listed one way on the Factory Order, but bundled differently by the Outfit Packing Department. Small peripherals were not always listed on the outfit packing diagram.

In addition, items that came with a car, such as the nos. 3413-18 Mercury Capsule & Parachute Assem. and 3413-27 Missile, were sometimes listed separately on the outfit packing diagram but not on the Factory Order All of these inconsistencies and discrepancies reflect how Lionel conducted its business. Fortunately, they are easy to decipher when filling an outfit box.

The Outfit Packing Department used "F" when an item was packed flat, "S" when an item was placed on its side and "E" when an item was placed on its end.

The forms that Lionel's Outfit Packing Department used listed RSC boxes as "Conventional Pack". This is what appears in the outfit packing diagrams.

Lionel did not provide outfit packing diagrams for every outfit.

The RSC version of catalog outfit no. 1629 was packed inside promotional outfit no. X-240. It is shown here for reference.

Description: 1960 Outfit
Specification: "O27" Ga. Diesel Freight Outfit
Customer: Ed Schock's Toy & Hobby
Original Amount: 150
Factory Order Date: 3/21/1960
Date Issued: March 21, 1960
Packaging: Conventional Outfit Packing

Contents of X-240: 1629X-1 Outfit - (Complete & Packed in Conventional Outfit Box); 110-1 Graduated Trestle Set; 1013 Curved Track (8); 1018 Straight Track (9)

Contents of 1629X-1: 225P-25 Alco Diesel Power Car - Blue - "Chesapeake & Ohio" - Yellow Lettering with Headlight and Magne-Traction - with 2 Position Reversing Unit - Less Lockon and Lubricant; 6650-25 Missile Launching Flat Car (Less Missile Assembly); 6650-80 Missile Assembly, Red - (Or 1 - 6650-84 Missile Assembly - White); 6470-25 Exploding Target Car; 6819-25 Flat Car - Red - (Less Helicopter); 3419-125 Helicopter; 6219-25 Work Caboose - Black Frame - Blue Cab and Tray - "Chesapeake & Ohio" - Markings in Yellow; 1013 Curved Track (8); 1018 Straight Track; 1008-50 Uncoupling Unit - with (1) 1018 Straight Track; 1015-25 45-Watt Transformer; CTC-1 Lockon; 81-32 Wires (2); 927-60 Lubricant (Oil); 927-65 Lubricant (Grease); 1103-12 Envelope Packed With CTC-1, 81-32, 927-60 and 927-65; 1627-2 Instruction Sheet; 310-2 Set of (5) Billboard Signs; AC Accessory Catalog

Boxes & Packing for X-240: 60-444 Box; 60-445 Shipper (1-3)
Boxes & Packing for 1629X-1: 60-384 Box; 60-385 Insert; 60-386 Insert; 60-387 Insert

X-240 (1960)	C6	C7	C8	Rarity
Complete Outfit	900	1,500	2,075	R10
Outfit Box no. 60-444	550	800	1,000	R10

Comments: Ed Schock's Toy and Hobby was an authorized Lionel Service Station located in Indianapolis, Indiana. It purchased this Retailer Promotional Type Ia outfit in 1960.

The no. X-240 was merely an RSC version of catalog outfit no. 1629 that Lionel packaged inside another box after adding more sections of track and a trestle set. The resulting outfit had 16 pieces of curved track, 10 straights and one no. 1008-50 Uncoupling Unit.

The practice of packaging one outfit inside another was not unique to this outfit. Lionel did so with some other promotional outfits in the late 1950s as well as in 1960 with famed catalog outfit

no. 2555W (commonly known as the "Father and Son Set").

The RSC version of the 1629 is more difficult to find than the display version. The two outfits came with the same locomotive and rolling stock. Both were headed by a no. 225P-25 Chesapeake & Ohio Alco Diesel Power Car (new for 1960). It featured an open pilot and the large ledge that was added to Alcos as reinforcement in 1960.

The nos. 6470-25 Exploding Target Car and 6650-25 Missile Launching Flat Car were two pieces of commonly paired space and military rolling stock. Hours could be spent blowing up the 6470-1. The 6470-1 included "slotted" sides and a smooth roof door guide (without the nubs added later to help hold on the sides). Except for the no. 6219-25 Work Caboose (new for 1960), all the rolling stock was carried over from 1959. This caboose appeared in only one other promotional outfit in 1960 and one catalog outfit in 1961.

Pay attention to the no. 6819-25 Flat Car - Red - (Less Helicopter). The flat may be common, but finding an original, unbroken no. 3419-125 Non-Operating Helicopter Complete can be a challenge. According to the 3419's Lionel Production Control File, early non-operating helicopters included "Navy" heat-stamping, opaque-yellow tails and a single blade with tips on the end. The tail changed to translucent on 11-19-1959. Although 6819s are also found with non-operating helicopters with no markings (which were used as a load for Lionel HO scale cars), that was not Lionel's intended production for this car. A non-operating "Navy" helicopter with a yellow or translucent tail and a single-blade rotor with tips is most appropriate for this outfit.

All the cars in the X-240 and 1629 were equipped with early AAR trucks and couplers. Every model except the 6219-25 came with two operating types; that work caboose had one operating and one plain type.

An interesting tri-fold version of the no. 1627-2 Instruction Sheet came with the 1629. It offered instructions for the 225P-25, 6470-25 and 6650-25 and included the same 1627-2 number and 1-60 date as the earlier bi-fold version. The latter, different in many ways, was created for steam-powered catalog outfit no. 1627.

The X-240 used the no. 60-444 RSC outfit box. It likely was a Tan RSC with Black Graphics outfit box.

The 1629 used the no. 60-384 Tan RSC with Black Graphics outfit box. It was manufactured by St. Joe Kraft, St. Joe Paper Co. Container Division and measured 17½ x 11 x 4½ inches. This outfit box had "5 6 7 8 9 10 11 12" and the box number printed on the bottom. It was rated at 90 pounds rather than the typical 65 pounds gross weight.

The X-240 is desirable due to its unique configuration and the small quantity produced. Finding a 1629 in RSC packaging to complete an X-240 it not easy, but it is simple when compared with finding the X-240 box.

CONVENTIONAL PACK
60-444 BOX FOR X-240

1629X-1	8-1013
110-1 S	

9-1018 TOP 1013

CONVENTIONAL PACK
60-384 BOX FOR 1629X-1

6470-25		
8-1013 1-1018 1-1008-50	6819-25	6650-25
1015 -25	6219-25	
C O R D	225P-25	

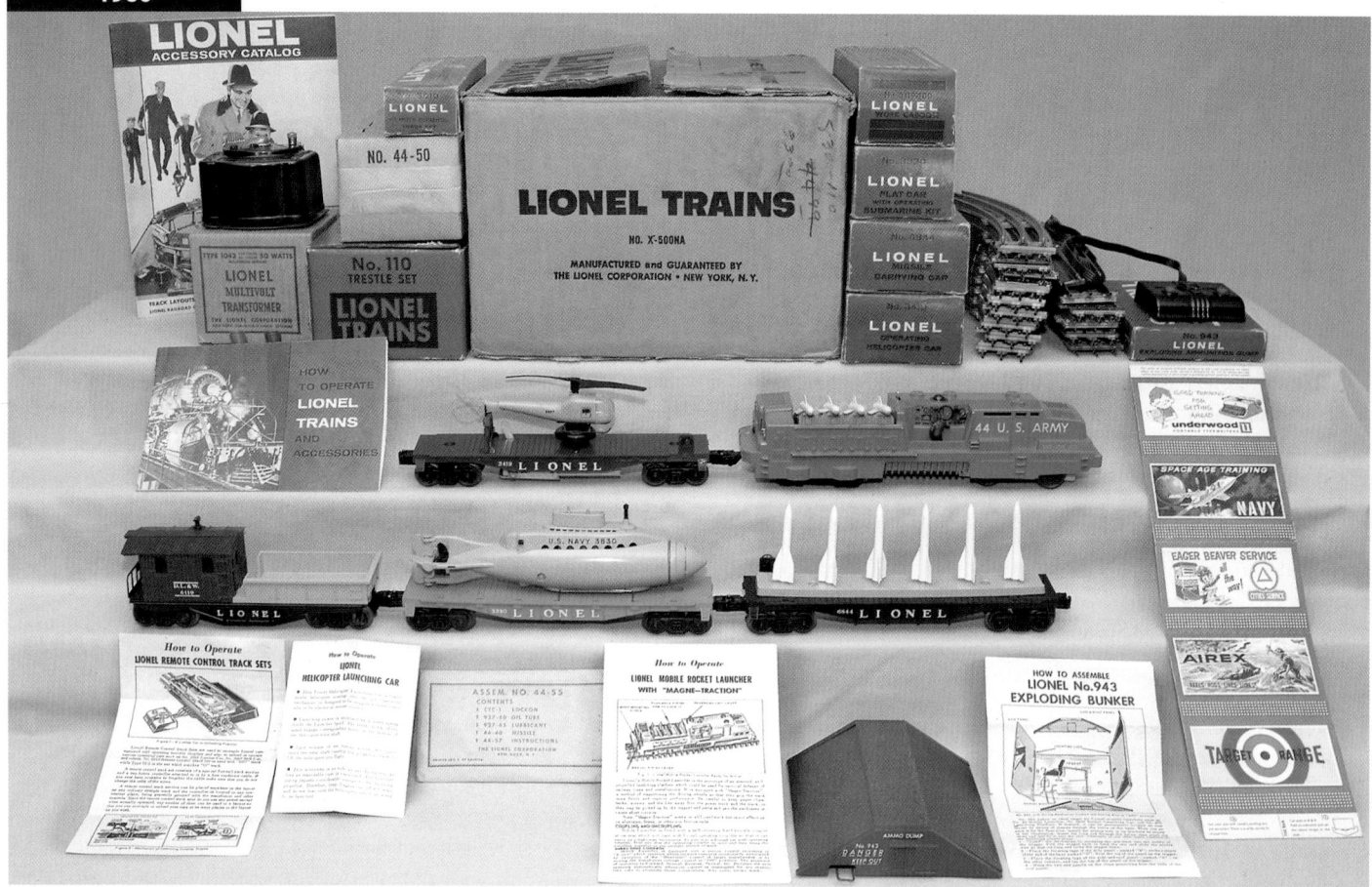

Outfit no. X-500NA listed Allied Stores on its Factory Order. It was illustrated on page 39 of the 1960 Stern's Christmas Catalog as no. 740 for $39.99. Based on the markings ("830-110" and 44.99) on the box pictured, this outfit was likely sold through other Allied company-owned retailers as well. Also note that it is shown with the no. 44-55 Envelope Packed.

Description: 1960 Outfit
Specification: "O27" Ga. Diesel Freight Outfit
Customer: Allied Stores
Customer/No./Price: Stern's; #740; $39.99
Original Amount: 1,000
Factory Order Date: 2/26/1960
Date Issued: October 12, 1960
Packaging: Conventional Outfit Packing

Contents: 44-50 Mobile Rocket Firing Car; 3419-1 Operating Helicopter Car; 6844-1 Rocket Transport Car; 3330-1 Flat Car - with Operating Submarine Kit; 6119-100 Work Caboose; 1013 Curved Track (17); 1018 Straight Track (9); 6019-1 Remote Control Track Set; 1043-50 60-Watt Transformer; 943-1 Exploding Ammo Dump; 110-1 Graduated Trestle Set; 81-32 Wires (2); 926-60 Instruction Book; 310-2 Set of (5) Billboard Signs; AC Accessory Catalog; 1802I Layout Instruction Sheet

Boxes & Packing: 60-446 Box; 60-447 Shipper (1-3)

Alternate For Outfit Contents:
Note: Substitute 765 - 1043-1 for 1043-50; 600 Sets with 44-45 Envelope in 44-50 Locomotive; Balance with 44-55 Envelope in 44-50 Locomotive.

X-500NA (1960)	C6	C7	C8	Rarity
Complete Outfit	665	1,200	1,900	R8
Outfit Box no. 60-446	150	325	450	R8

Comments: The nos. X-500NA and X-501NA outfits were Allied Stores' purchases in 1960. Allied owned many retailers and often would purchase outfits on their behalf. One of those retailers, Stern's, displayed the X-500NA and X-501NA in its 1960 Christmas Catalog. The X-500NA, a Retailer Promotional Type Ia outfit, appeared on page 39 as "Jet Express Set by Lionel". Designated item no. 740, it was priced at $39.99. It may have been available at other Allied company-owned retailers.

The X-500NA, a space and military outfit, packed a lot of action into its large (16 x 12¾ x 8¾ inch) no. 60-446 Tan RSC with Black Graphics outfit box. The box was manufactured by Star Corrugated Box Company, Inc. and had a star and "8-60" printed on the bottom.

This was the only promotional outfit appearance for the no. 44-50 Mobile Rocket Firing Car. The "-50" suffix indicated that it came packed with a no. 44-55 Envelope Packed, whereas a "-1" meant it came with a no. 44-45 Envelope Packed. The substitution of no. 44-45s in no. 44-50s would technically change the latter to no. 44-1s.

The 44-45 Envelope Packed included everything necessary to operate a Mobile Rocket Firing Car, including a no. OTC Contactor and a no. 90 Controller. However, a no. 44-55 Envelope Packed did not provide the peripherals necessary to operate the 44's missiles. A separate remote-control track was required.

Since the X-500NA came with a no. 6019-1 Remote Control Set, a 44-45 was not necessary and so either envelope would work. The only difference was that the 44-45 also included six no. 44-40 Missiles; the 44-55 included only one.

All the rolling stock in this outfit came with early operating AAR trucks and couplers and was packaged in Orange Perforated boxes. The no. 3330-1 Flat Car - with Operating Submarine Kit is a difficult item to find unassembled in C8 condition with its no. 3330-108 Submarine Kit Parts Packed still sealed in its plastic bag.

The track layout was an elevated pretzel layout (as detailed on the no. 1802I Instruction Sheet). All the rolling stock instruction sheets came packed inside their individual item boxes.

The X-500NA was an exciting space and military outfit sure to provide hours of fun for any child who was lucky enough to receive one. Unfortunately, few of these outfits have survived intact and so one is seldom seen in collectible condition.

The item substitutions have only a minimal effect on the price.

CONVENTIONAL PACK
60-446 BOX

TOP LAYER	
3419-1 S	
6119-100 S	
9-1013	8-1013
3-1018	
6-1018	

943 TOP TRACK

BOTTOM LAYER	
3330-1 S	
6844-1 S	1043 -50
44-50 S	
110-1 S	

Outfit no. X-501NA listed Allied Stores on its Factory Order. It was illustrated on page 39 of the 1960 Stern's Christmas Catalog as no. 742 for $29.99. Based on the high quantity produced, it is likely that Allied sold this outfit to many of its company-owned retailers.

Description: 1960 Outfit
Specification: "O27" Ga. Steam Type Freight Outfit with Smoke
Customer: Allied Stores
Customer/No./Price: Stern's; #742; $29.99
Original Amount: 4,000
Factory Order Date: 2/8/1960
Date Issued: April 18, 1960
Packaging: Conventional Outfit Packing

Contents: 247-1 Locomotive - with Smoke and Headlight - Blue Striping - "B & O" Markings - with 2-Position Reversing Unit - without Magne-Traction - with Lockon & Lubricant; 247T-1 Tender - Blue Striping - "B & O" Markings; 3419-1 Operating Helicopter Car; 3330-1 Flat Car - with Operating Submarine Kit; 470-1 IRBM Missile Launching Platform with Exploding Target Car; 6017-1 Caboose - Brick Brown; 1013 Curved Track (12); 1018 Straight Track (3); 1008-50 Uncoupling Unit - with (1) 1018 Straight Track; 1015-60 45-Watt Transformer; 1020-1 90° Crossover; 81-32 Wires (2); 310-2 Set of (5) Billboard Signs; 1627-2 Instruction Sheet; AC Accessory Catalog

Boxes & Packing: 60-448 Box; 60-449 Shipper (1-3)

Alternate For Outfit Contents:
Substitute 244LT for 247LT if necessary.

X-501NA (1960)	C6	C7	C8	Rarity
Complete Outfit	470	775	1,300	R5
Outfit Box no. 60-448	100	200	300	R5

Comments: The nos. X-500NA and X-501NA outfits were Allied Stores' purchases in 1960. Allied owned many retailers and often would purchase outfits on their behalf. One of those retailers, Stern's, displayed the X-500NA and X-501NA in its 1960 Christmas Catalog. The X-501NA, a Retailer Promotional Type Ia outfit, appeared on page 39 as "Clear Tracks for the B&O". Designated item no. 742, it was priced at $29.99. This outfit may have been available at other Allied company-owned retailers.

The X-501NA was Allied's steam-outfit purchase for the year and was headed by a no. 247-1 Blue-Striped B&O Locomotive. This Scout steamer pulled a space and military themed outfit that included a no. 470-1 IRBM Missile Launching Platform with Exploding Target Car. The Exploding Target Car, also known as the no. 6470-1, included "slotted" sides and a smooth roof door guide (without the nubs added later to help hold on the sides).

The no. 3330-1 Flat Car - with Operating Submarine Kit (new for 1960) provided hours of fun as youngsters assembled the submarine, a step that saved time and effort for Lionel. The 3330's Orange Perforated box is difficult to find in C8 condition because the submarine kit would easily damage the box upon removal and re-insertion. Also, a no. 3330-108 Submarine Kit Parts Packed is tough to find still sealed in its original plastic bag.

All the rolling stock in this outfit was equipped with early operating AAR trucks and couplers and came in Orange Perforated boxes.

The no. 60-448 Tan RSC with Black Graphics outfit box was manufactured by Star Corrugated Box Company and measured 16½ x 13 x 7½ inches. It had a star and "8 60 L" printed on the bottom.

With 4,000 of this outfit manufactured, Allied likely provided the X-501NA to many of its company-owned retailers. Although this outfit frequently appears, it is still difficult to find in C8 condition.

The no. 244LT substitution does not affect the price.

CONVENTIONAL PACK
60-448 BOX

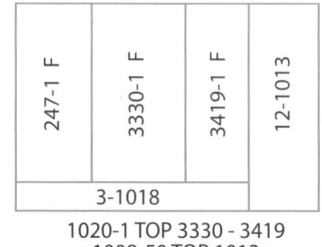

TOP LAYER

247-1 F | 3330-1 F | 3419-1 F | 12-1013
3-1018
1020-1 TOP 3330 - 3419
1008-50 TOP 1013

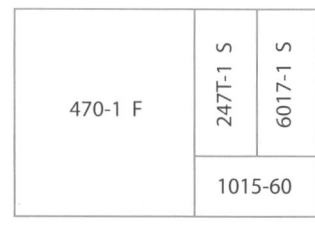

BOTTOM LAYER

470-1 F | 247T-1 S | 6017-1 S
1015-60

X-502NA
1960

Description: 1960 Outfit
Specification: "O27" Ga. Steam Type Freight Outfit
Customer: May Group
Original Amount: 3,500
Factory Order Date: 3/7/1960
Date Issued: 11-16-60
Packaging: Conventional Outfit Packing

Contents: 246-1 Locomotive - with Headlight and Magne-Traction - with Lockon and Lubricant; 1130T-1 Tender; 6826-1 Flat Car - with Trees - Red Frame; 6465-85 2-Dome Tank Car - Black; 6825-1 Flat Car - Red - with Trestle Bridge - Black; 6017-1 Caboose - Brick Brown; 1013 Curved Track (8); 1018 Straight Track (5); 1008-50 Uncoupling Unit - with (1) 1018 Straight Track; 1015-25 45-Watt Transformer; 1103-14 Envelope Packed; 310-2 Set of (5) Billboard Signs; 1609-4 Instruction Sheet; AC Accessory Catalog

Boxes & Packing: 59-324 Box; 59-325 Shipper (1-4); ST Sticker

Alternate For Outfit Contents:
Dept. 57 Note: In the event 1 - 1015-60 Transformer is included in outfit, substitute: 2 - 81-32 Wires for 1 - 1103-14 Envelope Packed; Use 1,000 - 6465-100; Substitute 1,000 - 6062-1 for 6826-1.

X-502NA (1960)	C6	C7	C8	Rarity
Complete Outfit As Listed	550	850	1,400	R9
Complete Outfit With All Substitutions	225	400	625	R6
Outfit Box no. 59-324	90	175	225	R6

Comments: The May Company purchased four promotional outfits in 1960: nos. X-502NA, X-503NA, X-504NA and X-570NA. May owned numerous retailers during the 1960s, and these outfits were likely sold through many of them.

The X-502NA, a Retailer Promotional Type Ib outfit, was May's entry-level steam-powered offering. With a quantity of 3,500, it was likely sold through several of May's retailers.

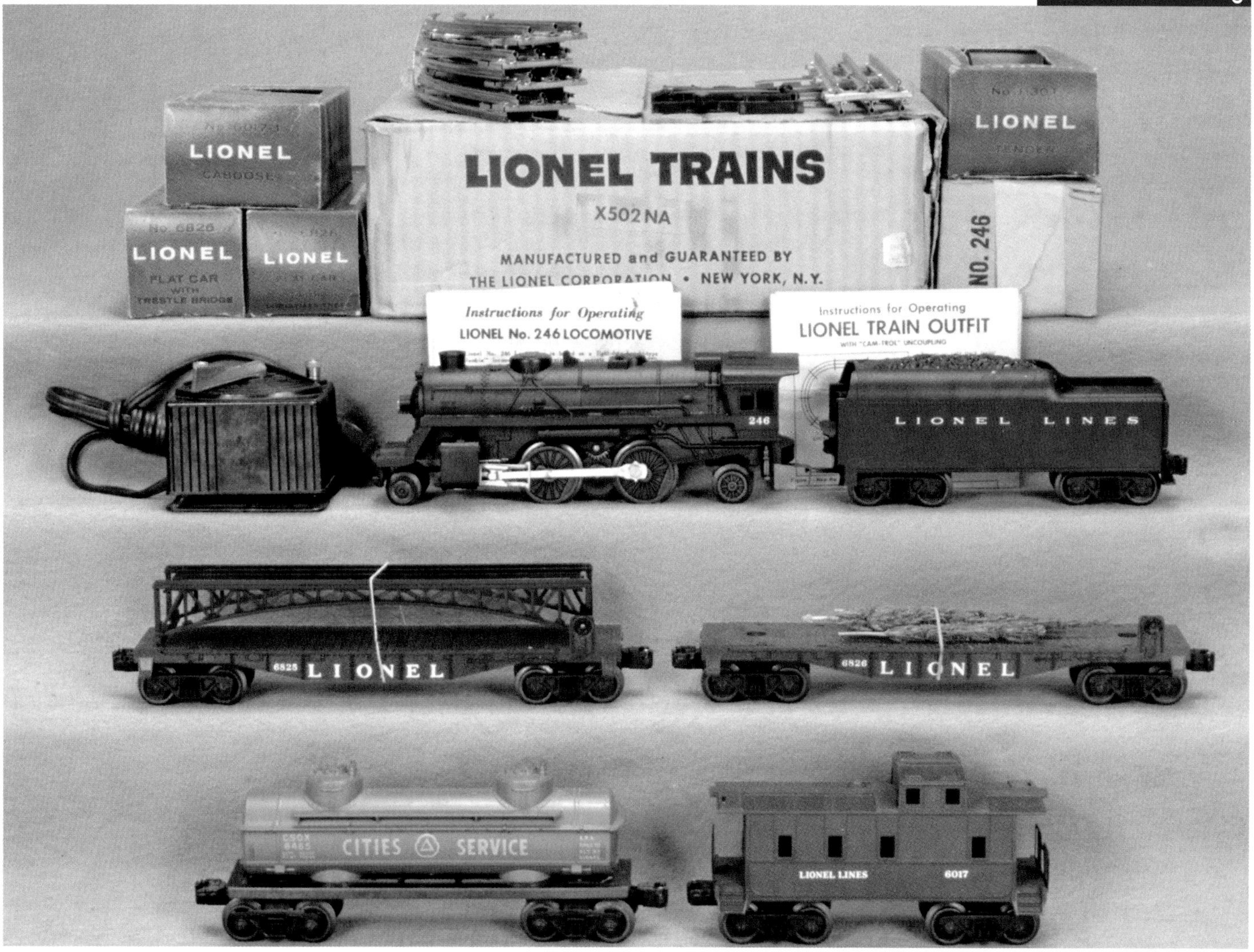

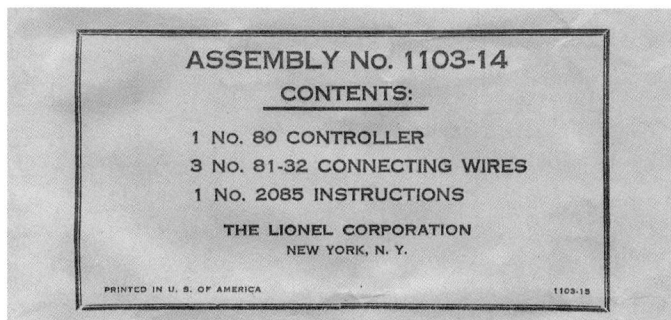

Outfit no. X-502NA came in an overstickered single-tier no. 59-324 Tan RSC with Black Graphics. It is shown with the no. 6465-100 Cities Service Two Dome Tank Car ("-100" meant unboxed) substitution. Not shown is the no. 1103-14 Envelope Packed.

ASSEMBLY No. 1103-14

CONTENTS:

1 No. 80 CONTROLLER
3 No. 81-32 CONNECTING WIRES
1 No. 2085 INSTRUCTIONS

THE LIONEL CORPORATION
NEW YORK, N. Y.

PRINTED IN U. S. OF AMERICA 1103-15

The no. 1103-14 Envelope Packed was used in three promotional outfits and designated a potential substitution in eight others. It is a rare item that is seldom seen.

Instructions for Operating
No. 80 REVERSING CONTROLLER

Your Lionel Train Outfit contains a No. 80 Reversing Controller which makes possible rapid changes of direction.

The No. 246 Locomotive has a built-in electrical reversing mechanism. This mechanism operates and changes the direction of travel whenever the current is interrupted.

Therefore, if you wish to make a fast "stop" simply press the button and hold it down. If you wish to reverse the train -- press the button and release it.

Install the No. 80 Controller as illustrated. Remember that each time this button is pressed the current to the track is stopped and upon releasing the button the current is allowed to resume. Your locomotive will change direction every time the button is pressed and released. It will proceed from Forward to Reverse and again to Forward etc.

THE LIONEL CORPORATION
Executive Offices 15 East 26th St. New York 10, N.Y.

SERVICE DEPARTMENT
1460 CHESTNUT ST.
HILLSIDE, N.J.

CHICAGO SHOWROOMS
MERCHANDISE MART
CHICAGO, ILL.

Approved Service Stations in the Principal Cities, United States and Canada
Printed in U.S. of America 2085 3-60

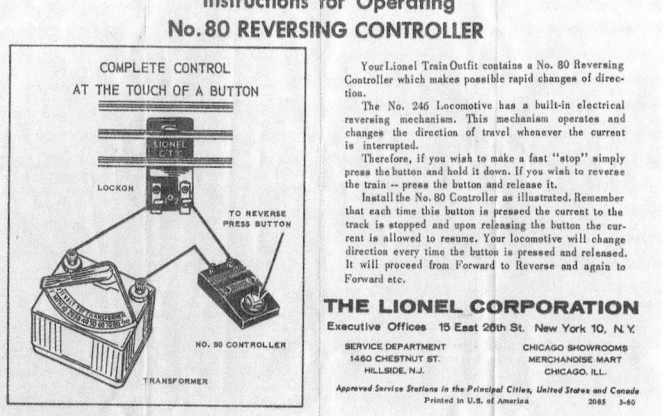

The no. 2085 Instruction Sheet that came packed in the no. 1103-14 Envelope Packed explains how to hook up the no. 80 Controller and operate the no. 246 Locomotive. Note, 80 Controllers look identical to the common no. 90 Controller, but are clearly marked "80". An 80 Controller is somewhat difficult to find.

A no. 246-1 Locomotive, a steamer equipped with Magne-Traction, headed this outfit. All the rolling stock was equipped with operating AAR trucks and couplers and came in Orange Perforated boxes.

In 1960, the no. 6826-1 Flat Car - with trees - Red Frame appeared in only this and catalog outfit no. 1635WS. Both of these outfits included substitutions for this car, indicating that this was likely the remaining inventory. Finding a C8 car with a box in matching condition and the original trees (so often lost) takes some work.

The no. 6465-85 Black 2-Dome Tank Car was being depleted in this and two other promotional outfits. Its Orange Perforated no. 6465-86 Folding Box is what is difficult to find. However, the unboxed version of that tank car (no. 6465-75) is common and was found in catalog outfit no. 1611 from 1959.

By far the toughest item in this outfit to obtain is the no. 1103-14 Envelope Packed. There's an interesting story behind this item. Lionel was depleting its inventory of no. 1015-25 45-Watt Transformers with the newly issued no. 1015-60 45-Watt Transformer. The difference between the two was that the "-25" had no circuit breaker or direction control, whereas the "-60" added direction control.

Therefore, for the X-502NA and other outfits that included a no. 246 Locomotive, direction control was needed. Lionel reinstated the previously "Obsolete" (per its Production Control File) no. 80-1 Controller and created a packed envelope for it, along with three no. 81-32 Wires and the new no. 2085 Instruction Sheet. This no. 1013-14 Envelope Packed and the included no. 2085 Instruction

CONVENTIONAL PACK
59-324 BOX
STICKER

246 S		1015	
1130T S	CORD		
6825 S		6017 S	6465 S
6826 S			
8-1013			

5-1018 TOP 6826
1008 TOP 1130T

Sheet are rare.

The no. 59-324 Tan RSC with Black Graphics outfit box was manufactured by Express Container Corp. and measured 14⅞ x 12⅝ x 4¼ inches. It originally was used for catalog outfit no. 1609 from 1959.

Substitutions for the X-502NA greatly affect its value and rarity. As such, pricing and rarity are provided for the outfit as listed *and* with all substitutions.

X-503NA
1960

Description: 1960 Outfit
Specification: "O27" Ga. Diesel Freight Outfit
Customer: May Company
Customer/No./Price: The M. O'Neil Co.; D33 Y; $28.83
Original Amount: 1,750
Factory Order Date: 2/16/1960
Date Issued: 11-17-60
Packaging: Conventional Outfit Packing, All Units Packed Except 1015, 1008

Contents: 220P-1 Alco Diesel Power Unit - "Santa Fe" - with Headlight, 2 Magnets, Non-Operating Coupler, Lockon & Lubricant; 220T-1 Motorless Unit - "S.F."; 6830-1 Flat Car - with Non-Operating Submarine - Blue Car Body; 6819-1 Flat Car - Red - with Helicopter; 6823-1 Flat Car - with missile; 6017-1 Caboose - Brick Brown; 1013 Curved Track (17); 1018 Straight Track (9); 1008-50 Uncoupling Unit - with (1) 1018 Straight Track; 1015-25 45-Watt Transformer; 110-1 Graduated Trestle Set; 81-32 Wires (2); 1569-11 Instruction Sheet; 310-2 Set of (5) Billboard Signs; AC Accessory Catalog; 1802I Layout Instruction Sheet

Boxes & Packing: 60-423 Box; 60-424 Insert; 60-425 Shipper (1-3)

X-503NA (1960)	C6	C7	C8	Rarity
Complete Outfit	550	925	1,325	R6
Outfit Box no. 60-423	100	175	230	R6

Comments: The May Company purchased four promotional outfits in 1960: nos. X-502NA, X-503NA, X-504NA and X-570NA. May owned numerous retailers during the 1960s, and these outfits were likely sold through many of them.

The X-503A, a Retailer Promotional Type Ia outfit, has been linked to one of those retailers, M. O'Neil Co., as no. D33 Y for $28.33. It was likely sold at other May Company stores as well because of the large quantities purchased.

This space and military outfit was May's only diesel-powered

purchase for 1960. The no. 220P-1 Santa Fe Alco Diesel Power Unit was an example of an item that appeared in promotional outfits (1960) before it became a regular-production item (it appeared in the 1961 consumer catalog).

The no. 6830-1 Flat Car - with Non-Operating Submarine - Blue Car Body (new for 1960) appeared in seven promotional outfits. It was a non-operating version of the no. 3830-1 Operating Submarine Car. The no. 6830-100 Submarine was stamped "6830" to match the car. The flat car and submarine are fairly common, but the Orange Perforated no. 6830-9 Folding Box is not the easiest to find in C8 condition.

Also of note was the no. 6819-1 Flat Car - Red - with Helicopter. The flat car is common, but finding an original, unbroken no. 3419-125 Non-Operating Helicopter Complete as well as its Orange Perforated folding box can be a challenge. According to the 3419-125's Lionel Production Control File, early non-operating helicopters included "Navy" heat-stamping, opaque-yellow tails and a single blade with tips on the end. The tail changed to translucent on 11-19-1959. Although 6819s also have been found with non-operating helicopters with no markings, those items were originally meant to be used on Lionel HO scale cars and not the 6819 cars.

Late in 1960, Lionel Production Control Files stated that it was Lionel's intended production to include a no. 3429-100 Operating Helicopter Complete (with U.S. Marine Corps markings) with the no. 6819-1. Although such a variation has never been reported, helicopters are easily exchanged on 6819s. So this variation could

CONVENTIONAL PACK
60-423 BOX
ALL UNITS PACKED, EXCEPT 1015, 1008

TOP LAYER

8-1013	
9-1013	6017 S
6823 S	
6830 S	
6819 S	

6-1018 TOP 9-1013
3-1018 TOP 8-1013
1008 TOP 6-1018

BOTTOM LAYER

110 F	
220P F	
220T F	1015

Outfit no. X-503NA was the May Company's space and military diesel offering in 1960. It included a no. 220P-1 Santa Fe Alco Diesel Power Unit that appeared in promotional outfits before becoming a catalog item. Note the no. 6830-1 Flat Car - Non-Operating Submarine and its matching no. 6830-100 Submarine with "6830" stamped on its top.

be created, but verification that it originally came this way would be nearly impossible. In any case, the pricing for this outfit assumes a 3419-125 Non-Operating Helicopter Complete.

All the rolling stock in the X-503NA included operating AAR trucks and couplers and came packaged in Orange Perforated boxes. The track plan was an elevated pretzel layout (as detailed on the no. 1802I Layout Instruction Sheet).

The no. 60-423 Tan RSC with Black Graphics outfit box was manufactured by Kraft Corrugated Containers, Inc. and measured

15¾ x 14 x 7½ inches. The X-503NA has also been observed in an overstickered (number below sticker unknown) Tan RSC with Black Graphics box. It was likely that this outfit box was needed due to increased orders on 5/24/60 from 600 to 1,500 and another increase on 11/17/60 to 1,750. With these changes occurring late in the year, Lionel found it easier to use leftover inventory of other boxes than to order more of the no. 60-423 Box. This is another reason why Lionel eventually adopted generic boxes that its workers could stamp themselves.

X-504NA
1960

Description: 1960 Outfit
Specification: "O27" Ga. Steam Type Freight Outfit with Smoke
Customer: May Company
Original Amount: 600
Factory Order Date: 2/16/1960
Date Issued: February 16, 1960
Packaging: Conventional Outfit Packing

Contents: 2018-1 Locomotive - with Smoke, Lockon & Lubricant - without Magne-Traction; 6026W-1 Whistle Tender; 6014-1 Box Car - Red; 6825-1 Flat Car - Red - with Trestle Bridge - Black; 6062-1 Gondola Car - Black - with (3) Cable Reels; 3419-1 Operating Helicopter Car; 6162-1 Gondola Car - Blue - with (3) White Canisters; 6017-1 Caboose - Brick Brown; 1013 Curved Track (16); 1018 Straight Track (3); 6029-25 Uncoupling Track Section; 1063-25 Transformer; 1023-1 45° Crossover; 90-1 Uncoupling Track Controller; 81-32 Wires (4); 90-30 Envelope Packed With 90-1 and 81-32; 926-60 Instruction Book; 310-2 Set of (5) Billboard Signs; AC Accessory Catalog; 1802H Layout Instruction Sheet

Boxes & Packing: 60-401 Box; 60-402 Shipper (1-4)

X-504NA (1960)	C6	C7	C8	Rarity
Complete Outfit	525	775	1,125	R8
Outfit Box no. 60-401	175	325	450	R8

Comments: The May Company purchased four promotional outfits in 1960: nos. X-502NA, X-503NA, X-504NA and X-570NA. May owned numerous retailers during the 1960s, and these outfits were likely sold through many of them. The X-504NA, a Retailer Promotional Type Ia, was May's high-end steam outfit purchase of the year.

The no. 2018-1 Steam Type Locomotive With Smoke last appeared in a catalog outfit in 1959, but was still being used in promotional outfits in the 1960s. When boxed, it included a no. CTC-1 Lockon. This, along with the no. 90-30 Envelope Packed that came with four no. 81-32 24" R.C. Wires and a no. 90-1 Controller, provided all the peripherals necessary to hook up the transformer and a no. 6029-25 R.C. Uncoupling Track.

The rolling stock in the X-504NA (all equipped with operating AAR trucks and couplers) created a basic freight outfit. The only exception to this description was the space and military no. 3419-1 Operating Helicopter Car. Introduced in 1959, this car went through many changes in 1960. The car included in this outfit would likely exhibit the 1960 features of a small winder and a single-blade Navy helicopter. With this Factory Order dated early in the year, it is unknown whether this helicopter would have been an early version without the hole in the fuselage that was added for the no. 6820's missile launching rack. Helicopters are easily swapped out, so the helicopter that came with this outfit may never be known. In either case, this is a minor variation that doesn't affect the price.

A no. 2018 necessitated additional transformer wattage, so Lionel included a no. 1063-25 75-Watt Transformer. The track layout was a pretzel layout, as detailed on the difficult-to-find no. 1802H Layout Instruction Sheet.

The no. 60-401 Box was likely a Tan RSC with Black Graphics, although one has yet to be observed. It was used for only this outfit.

With just 600 of these outfits made, it was likely sold through one or two of May's higher-end retailers.

CONVENTIONAL PACK
60-401 BOX

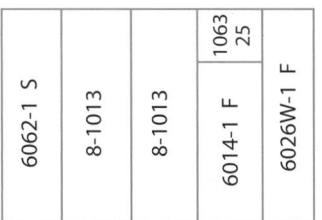

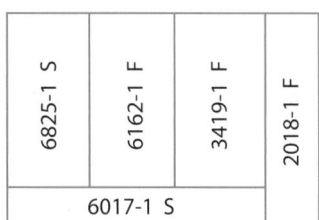

TOP LAYER						BOTTOM LAYER			
6062-1 S	8-1013	8-1013	1063-25 / 6014-1 F	6026W-1 F		6825-1 S	6162-1 F	3419-1 F	2018-1 F
							6017-1 S		

1023-1 TOP
3-1018 TOP
6029-25 TOP

AMC's outfit no. X-505NA is shown with the Bold Classic no. 1625-51 Folding Box that was overstamped with "244T". This space and military outfit was AMC's entry-level steam offering for 1960.

Description: 1960 Outfit
Specification: "O27" Ga. Steam Type Freight Outfit with Smoke
Customer/No.: AMC; 240001 2999
Original Amount: 1,250
Factory Order Date: 5/27/1960
Date Issued: June 24, 1960
Packaging: Conventional Outfit Packing, All Units Packed Except 1043 - 6029

Contents: 244-1 Locomotive - with Smoke & Headlight - with 2 Position Reversing Unit - with Lockon & Lubricant - without Magne-Traction; 244T-1 Tender; 6650-1 Missile Launching Flat Car; 6470-1 Exploding Target Car; 3419-1 Operating Helicopter Car; 6017-1 Caboose - Brick Brown; 1013 Curved Track (8); 1018 Straight Track (3); 6029-25 Uncoupling Track Section; 1043-50 60-Watt Transformer; 943 Exploding Ammo Dump; 90-1 Uncoupling Track Controller; 81-32 Wires (4); 90-30 Envelope Packed With 90-1 and 81-32; X-836-10 Instruction Sheet; AC

Accessory Catalog; 310-2 Set of (5) Billboard Signs

Boxes & Packing: 60-403 Box; 60-404 Shipper (1-4)

Alternate For Outfit Contents:
Note: Substitute 250 - 1053-50 for 1043-50.

X-505NA (1960)	C6	C7	C8	Rarity
Complete Outfit	375	615	950	R7
Outfit Box no. 60-403	115	175	250	R7

Comments: Buying cooperatives, such as AMC (Associated Merchandising Corporation), were large customers of Lionel trains. In 1960, AMC purchased two promotional outfits: nos. X-505NA and X-506NA. One X-505NA has been observed with "240001 2999" stamped on the box. It is unknown whether this was a retailer number or a retailer number with a price ($29.99). AMC sold to many stores, so linking this example to a specific

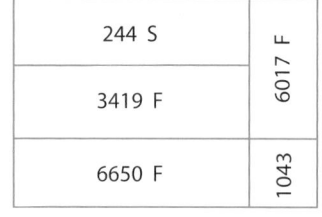

retailer will require additional information.

The X-505NA, a Retailer Promotional Type Ia outfit, was AMC's entry-level steam offering. It was headed by a no. 244-1 Locomotive (new for 1960) equipped with smoke, a headlight, a two-position reversing unit and ballast weights. This engine pulled a no. 244T-1 Tender, which came in a difficult-to-find no. 1625T overstamped Bold Classic no. 1625-51 Folding Box.

The nos. 3419-1 Operating Helicopter Car, 6470-1 Exploding Target Car and 6650-1 Missile Launching Flat Car were an exciting group of space and military rolling stock. Hours could be spent blowing up the 6470-1 Exploding Target Car as well as the no. 943 Exploding Ammo Dump.

The 3419-1 came with a no. 3419-100 Operating Helicopter Complete, whose fuselage had a hole on the bottom. The 6470-1 included "slotted" sides and a smooth roof door guide (without the nubs added later to help hold on the sides).

These two cars, like the 6650-1, were repeats from 1959. All three were equipped with early operating AAR trucks and couplers. Some of the cars also had notches on their AAR side frames. The caboose and tender were equipped with one operating AAR truck and coupler.

Other than the no. 244T-1, all the cars were packaged in Orange Perforated boxes with their appropriate instruction sheet inside.

This outfit came packed in a no. 60-403 Tan RSC with Black Graphics outfit box that was manufactured by St. Joe Kraft, St. Joe Paper Co. Container Division and measured 15 x 11¾ x 5¾ inches. It had "60-403" and "7 8 9 10 11 12" printed on the bottom and was used for only this outfit.

The X-505NA often appears on the market in collectible condition. The transformer substitution minimally affects the price because both types of transformers are readily available.

CONVENTIONAL PACK
60-403 BOX
ALL UNITS PACKED, EXCEPT 1043 - 6029

TOP LAYER		BOTTOM LAYER	
		244 S	
3-1018	244T F	3419 F	6017 F
8-1013			
6470 F		6650 F	1043

6029 TOP 1018
943 TOP 244 - TRACK

X-506NA
1960

Description: 1960 Outfit
Specification: "O27" Ga. Steam Type Freight Outfit with Smoke & Whistle
Customer: AMC
Original Amount: 1,750
Factory Order Date: 2/16/1960
Date Issued: June 24, 1960
Packaging: Conventional Outfit Packing, All Units Packed Except 1063 - 1008

Contents: 2037-1 Locomotive - with Magne-Traction, Smoke, Lockon & Lubricant; 6026W-1 Whistle Tender; 6819-1 Flat Car - Red - with Helicopter; 6062-1 Gondola Car - Black - with (3) Cable Reels; 6465-85 2-Dome Tank Car - Black; 6017-1 Caboose - Brick Brown; 1013 Curved Track (17); 1018 Straight Track (9); 1008-50 Uncoupling Unit - with (1) 1018 Straight Track; 1063-25 Transformer; 110-1 Graduated Trestle Set; 81-32 Wires (2); 926-60 Instruction Book; 310-2 Set of (5) Billboard Signs; AC Accessory Catalog; 1802I Layout Instruction Sheet

Boxes & Packing: 60-405 Box; 60-406 Shipper (1-3)

Alternate For Outfit Contents:
Note: Substitute 250 - 6465-110 for 6465-85; Substitute 250 - 243W for 6026W.

X-506NA (1960)	C6	C7	C8	Rarity
Complete Outfit As Listed	400	650	900	R7
Complete Outfit With Substitutions	350	630	845	R7
Outfit Box no. 60-405	100	150	225	R7

Comments: Buying cooperatives, such as AMC (Associated Merchandising Corporation), were large customers of Lionel trains. In 1960, AMC purchased two Retailer Promotional Type Ia outfits: nos. X-505NA and X-506NA. The X-506NA, the "high-end" outfit, has yet to be linked to a specific AMC customer.

This outfit is similar in contents to AMC's no. X-642 from 1961. Both were headed by the common no. 2037-1 Steam Type Locomotive. Originally introduced in 1953, the no. 2037 was the workhorse of one Super O and 22 O27 outfits during the 1960s.

The X-506NA, like the X-642, included three pieces of rolling stock and a caboose. Both promotional outfits came with a no. 6062-1 Gondola Car and a no. 6017-1 Caboose, but that is where the similarities ended. The two other cars in the X-506NA were a no. 6819-1 Flat Car with Helicopter (see the entry for outfit X-503NA for detailed information on this car) and a no. 6465-85 Black 2-Dome Tank Car. The 6465-85 was being depleted in this and two other promotional outfits. Its Orange Perforated no. 6465-86 Folding Box is difficult to find. However, the unboxed version of that tank car (no. 6465-75) is common and was found in catalog outfit no. 1611 from 1959.

All the cars in the X-506NA came equipped with early operating AAR trucks and couplers. The sole exception was the no. 6026W-1 Whistle Tender, which had bar-end trucks and couplers.

The elevated pretzel track layout was detailed on the no. 1802I Layout Instruction Sheet.

In 1960, the all-inclusive instruction book was being phased out in favor of separate train layout instruction sheets. In fact, only 19 of the promotional outfits included the 1960 version (no. 926-60 Instruction Book).

The X-506NA came in a no. 60-405 Tan RSC with Black Graphics outfit box. This box was manufactured by St. Joe Paper

Outfit no. X-506NA was AMC's high-end steam offering for 1960. Interestingly, the outfit shown here was never glued or stapled shut. It was only taped. This outfit included the difficult-to-find Orange Perforated box for the no. 6465-85 Black 2-Dome Tank Car.

Co. - Container Div. and measured 15½ x 14⅛ x 7 inches. It also had "7 8 9 10 11 12" printed as part of the box manufacturer's certificate.

Although the higher than average quantity produced would lead to the assumption that the X-506NA is readily available, this outfit appears infrequently on the market.

Pricing is provided with and without the substitutions.

CONVENTIONAL PACK
60-405 BOX
ALL UNITS PACKED, EXCEPT 1063 - 1008

TOP LAYER				BOTTOM LAYER		
8-1013	9-1013	6465 F			110 F	
		9-1018			2037 S	
		6819 F		1063	6062 S	
		6017 F			6026W S	

1008 TOP 1013

Description: 1960 Outfit
Specification: "D. S. C." Promotional Outfit - "The General"
Customer: D. S. C. Promotional
Original Amount: 7,300
Factory Order Date: 2/29/1960
Date Issued: June 28, 1960
Packaging: Special Display Packing - per D.S.C. Specifications, Units not Boxed

Contents: 1882-25 Locomotive - with Headlight - without Magne-Traction - with 2 Position Reversing Unit - Less Lockon and Lubricant; 1882T-25 Tender - with Non-Operating Coupler; 1866-25 Mail & Baggage Car - with Non-Operating Couplers - with Windows; 1885-25 Passenger Car - with Non-Operating Couplers - with windows; 1887-25 Flat Car - with (6) Horses - with Non-Operating Couplers; 1013 Curved Track (No. 1013-73 - Bundles of 6 each with 2 Wires) (12); 1018 Straight Track (No. 1018-10 Loose) (4); 1015-25 45-Watt Transformer; 1020-25 90° Crossing; 963-100 Frontier Set; CTC Lockon; 81-32 Wires (2); 927-60 Lubricant (Oil); 927-65 Lubricant (Grease); 1103-12 Envelope Packed With CTC, 81-32, 927-60 and 927-65; 1612-10 Instruction Sheet; 310-2 Set of (5) Billboard Signs; AC Accessory Catalog; 1802B Layout Instruction Sheet

Boxes & Packing: 60-415 Tray; 60-416 Platform; 60-416X Insert; 60-417 Trans. Cover; 60-418 Insert; 60-499 Insert; 60-419 Tube; 60-420 Track Sleeve (2); 60-421 Sleeve; 60-422 Shipper (1-4)

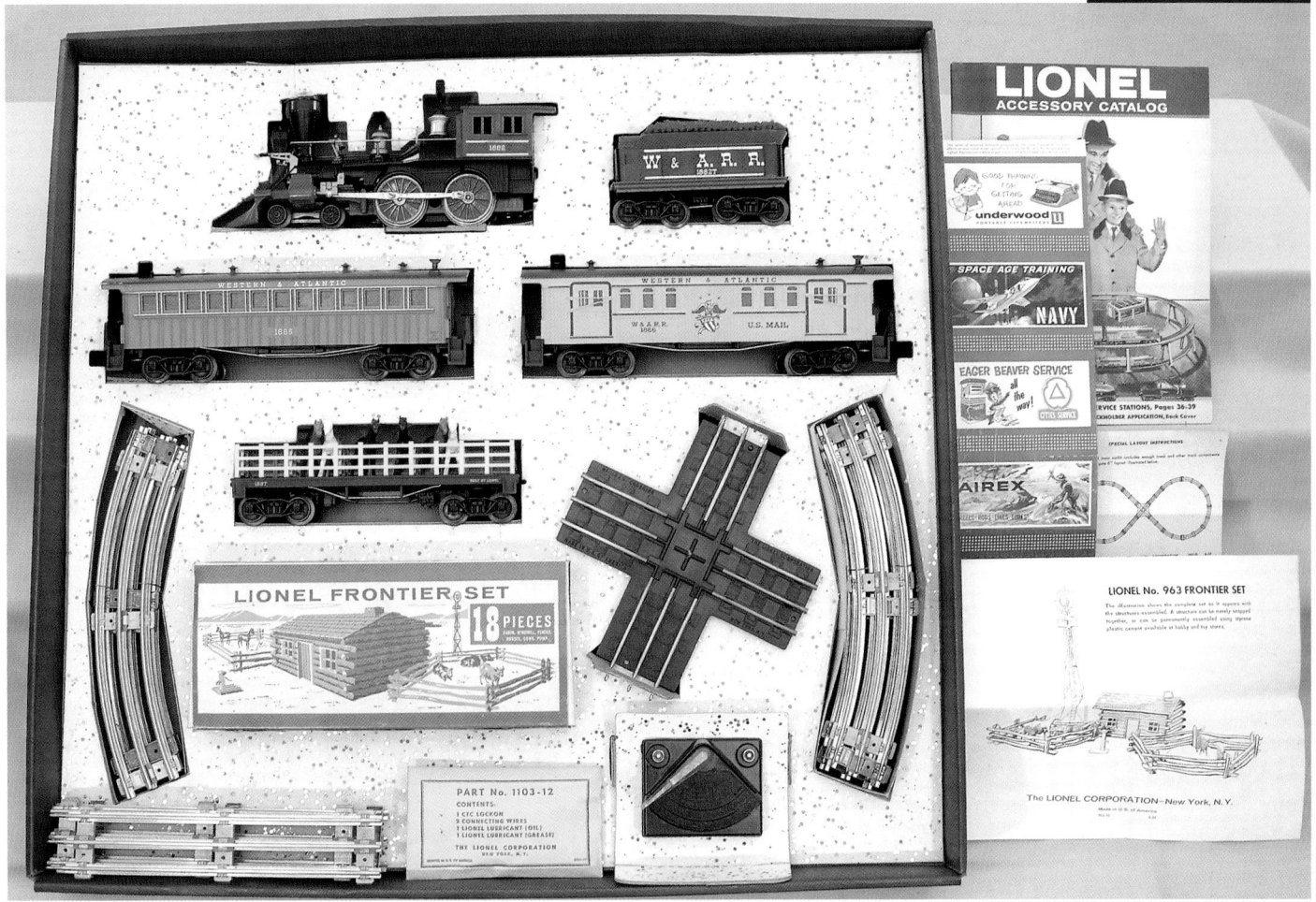

The Factory Orders identify the outfit known as the "Halloween General" as the no. X-507NA. This celebrated Retailer Promotional Type Ic came in a Type E Red Corrugated Tray with a speckled die-cut platform. It was the last of four outfits that were sold to Druggists' Service Council and advertised in that firm's Gifts Galore catalog.

Alternate For Outfit Contents:
Note: Use 1015-60 if 1015-25 not available.

X-507NA (1960)	C6	C7	C8	Rarity
Complete Outfit	3,000	5,000	7,100	R7
Outfit Tray no. 60-415 And Platform no. 60-416	2,000	3,600	5,000	R7

Comments: One of the many mysteries solved by the authoritative information used in compiling this volume is the true identity of this outfit. To date, it has been known only as the "Halloween General" (because of its orange and black color scheme) from Gifts Galore, but its true identity is actually outfit no. X-507NA from D. S. C. (Druggists' Service Council, Inc.). It took years to uncover the meaning of D. S. C. and its tie-in with Gifts Galore. (See D. S. C. Promotional in the section on Lionel's Distribution and Customers.)

The X-507NA was the fourth and last of the D. S. C. outfits (no. 149 from 1956, no. X-617 from 1958 and no. X-834 from 1959). Each of these outfits was offered free as part of a pharmacy in-store drawing. Marketing and advertising support (banners, signs and entry forms) was also created for each of these outfits. The advertising material used for the X-507NA is shown in the accompanying pictures.

Except for the 149, all of these outfits came in "Special Display Packing - per D. S. C. Specifications". To be precise, they used a tray with a die-cut platform in which the trains were held. Then a sleeve was slid over the entire box.

For the X-507NA, the no. 60-415 Type E display box, which measured 26 x 24½ x 3¼ inches, was classified as a Red Corrugated Tray. The no. 60-421 Sleeve Top with Black Graphics measured 26½ x 24 x 3⅝ inches. Neither of these items included any manufacturer markings.

Based on the listing of a no. 60-422 Shipper for four outfits, it seems likely the outfits were shipped to D. S. C., which then shipped them to the end customer drug stores. One outfit was observed in a no. 58-208 Shipper that might have been used for individual shipping of the outfit.

This Retailer Promotional Type Ic was made up of mostly promotional-only items. Only the no. 1866-25 Mail & Baggage Car appeared in catalog outfits. The no. 1882-25 Locomotive was the same as a no. 1862-25 Locomotive, but featured an orange and black color scheme. It included a two-position reversing unit and a headlight.

The 1866-25 and no. 1885-25 Passenger Car were equipped with Archbar trucks with separate non-operating and non-centering couplers. The no. 1882T-25 Tender was equipped with non-operating Archbar trucks and couplers.

The no. 1887-25 Flat Car - with (6) Horses was similar to the no. 1877-25 Flat Car - with (6) Horses, except that the numbers on the cars are different. The 1887-25 included non-operating couplers and came with yellow fence rails.

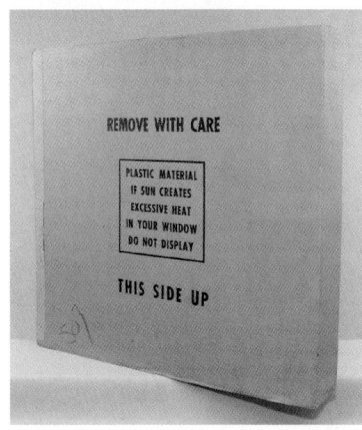

Each outfit was slid into a no. 60-421 Sleeve before being placed in its shipper. Note the "507" in the lower left-hand corner. Somewhere along the way, an individual knew the outfit number and marked it on the sleeve.

The no. 963-100 Frontier Set was unique to no. X-507NA. Its contents were identical to those of a no. 963-1 Frontier Set, except that it came in this specially decorated and numbered box.

Druggists' Service Council developed advertising and marketing support for each of its four Lionel promotional outfits. Shown is a banner advertising the no. X-507NA. The one shown here came from the original owner, who received it with the outfit he won. He safely stored the banner in the outfit box for almost 50 years.

This sign was designed to attach to outfit no. X-507NA as part of the in-store display. Similar signs and banners were created for D. S. C. outfit nos. 149 (1956), X-617 (1958) and X-834 (1959). Ad mats and other promotional materials exist as well, but are not shown.

The X-507NA also included the no. 963-100 Frontier Set, which was unique to this outfit. The contents and instruction sheet of this Plasticville item were identical to those of the no. 963-1 Frontier Set. The only difference was the unique box with "Lionel Frontier Set" and a log cabin printed on the cover and "963-100" printed on the end panel. This fragile box is rare and difficult to find in collectible condition.

In fact, all the packaging for the X-507NA deserves our attention because it was unique and consisted of many small inserts that are easily lost. The trains are readily available, but a complete outfit with all the inserts and a no. 60-421 Sleeve and an individual shipper would be the ultimate find.

Therefore, this outfit merits a high price, even though 7,300 examples were produced. In that respect, the X-507NA is similar to outfit no. 19326 from 1964 (Sears no. 9820), of which 5,500 were made. Both of these outfits have high prices because of the

unique items they feature and the consistently strong demand for them on the part of collectors.

As a result, the X-507NA boasts an R7 rarity and enhanced value. Specifically, C6 pricing minimally includes the 60-415 Tray and 60-416 Platform. C7 pricing adds the requirement of all the inserts. C8 includes all the inserts as well as the 60-421 Sleeve.

The no. X-507NA, formerly known only as the Halloween General, is a requirement for any promotional outfit collector.

DISPLAY PACK 60-415 TRAY REVISED 7-27-60			
	1882-25	1882T-25	
6	1885-25	1866-25	6
-	1887-25	1020-25	-
1			1
0		1015	0
1		25	1
3	963-100		3
	2-1018 BELOW 1013	2-1018 BELOW 1013	

Description: 1960 Outfit
Specification: "O27" Ga. Steam Type Freight Outfit
Customer: Richie Premium
Original Amount: 10,500
Factory Order Date: 7/19/1960
Date Issued: 9-21-60
Packaging: Display Outfit Packing (Use X-869 Outfit Packing in Inventory)

Contents: 1060-25 Steam Type Locomotive - with Headlight,

Front and Rear Trucks - without Magne-Traction, Reversing Unit, Lockon and Lubricant; 1060T-25 Tender; 6044-25 Box Car - Blue - "Airex" Markings - Non-Operating Trucks; 6042-25 Gondola Car - Blue - (Less 2 Red Canisters) - with Non-Operating Trucks; 6112-5 Red Canisters (2); 6045-25 Two Dome Tank Car - Gray - Non-Operating Trucks; 6047-25 Caboose - Brick Brown - Non-Operating Trucks; 1013 Curved Track (12); 1018 Straight Track (4); 1026-25 25-Watt Transformer; 1020-1 90° Crossover; 951-1 Farm Set; CTC Lockon; 81-32 Wires (2); 927-60 Lubricant (Oil); 927-65 Lubricant (Grease); 1103-12 Envelope Packed With CTC, 81-32, 927-60 and 927-65; 1119-10 Instruction Sheet; 310-2 Set of (5) Billboard Signs; AC Accessory Catalog

Outfit no. X-508NA was Richie Premium's highly successful (due to reorders) promotional outfit purchase for 1960. The gem in the outfit was the inclusion of a no. 951-1 Farm Set. Shown is the version in a no. 59-419 Box that is an overstickered no. X-869.

Boxes & Packing: 59-419 Box; 59-420 Insert; 59-421 Insert; 59-423 Insert; 59-47 Insert; 60-377 Tube; 59-424 Shipper (1-6); LBLS 5 Labels Blue on White (5); LBLS 2 Labels Red - Reversed (2); 60-530 Box; 59-420 Insert; 59-421 Insert; 59-423 Insert; 59-47 Insert; 59-44 Tube; 60-531 Shipper (1-6)

Alternate For Outfit Contents:
Note: 5,400 sets - use 980-1; 3,600 sets - use 951-1.

X-508NA (1960)	C6	C7	C8	Rarity
Complete Outfit With A no. 951-1 And no. 59-419 Box	265	410	780	R4
Outfit Box no. 59-419	75	90	130	R4
Complete Outfit With 980-1 And 60-530 Box	270	430	810	R4
Outfit Box no. 60-530	90	110	160	R4

Comments: Richie Premium was an incentive merchandiser that purchased this Retailer Promotional Type Ib outfit in 1960. The no. X-508NA was likely a huge success because the quantities increased from 7,000 to 9,000 and finally to 10,500.

This entry-level offering included low-end motive power and cars that were common to many other outfits. In fact, this outfit and the no. X-543NA were identical, except for a change in the Plasticville set and the outfit packing.

Notable items in the X-508NA included the nos. 6044-25 Blue Box Car - "Airex" Markings and 6045-25 Gray Two Dome Tank Car. The 6044-25, which was originally introduced in 1959, appeared in 13 promotional outfits in 1960. As for the tank car, gray and beige versions exist. According to Lionel Production Control Files, the material changed from "TMD 6000 Polystyrene Gray #55" to "Utility gray / high impact (special opaque)" and then back again. No specific dates were provided, but the gray version was the one included in this outfit.

These two cars, like all the rolling stock in this outfit, were equipped with non-operating Archbar trucks and couplers.

At least two outfit boxes were used. Both were Type A White Hinged Display with 1050 Blue Steamer and Red/Orange Graphics. One, the no. 59-419, was an overstickered no. X-869 from 1959 that was manufactured by Concora Container Corp. (CCA) and measured 19¾ x 14½ x 3¼ inches. The second, the no. 60-530, was unique to the X-508NA. Its manufacturer and size are still to be determined.

Lionel differentiated its promotional outfits by adding items like Plasticville sets. What drives the value of the X-508NA was the inclusion of a no. 951-1 Farm Set or its substitution of a no. 980-1 Ranch Set. Both are comparably valued, so the substitution does not affect the outfit's price. The 951-1 came with the version in a 59-419 Box, whereas the 980-1 came with the 60-530 Box.

As the quantities of the X-508NA increased, so did the boxing requirements. As stated on the Factory Order, 5,400 sets were listed as using a 980-1 and 3,600 as using a 951-1 for a total of 9,000. When the quantity increased yet again to 10,500, the Outfit Packing Department did not update the boxing information on the Factory Order, so it is unknown how these additional 1,500 outfits were fulfilled. It is likely they used 59-419s in inventory, as this is the version that most often appears.

DISPLAY PACK

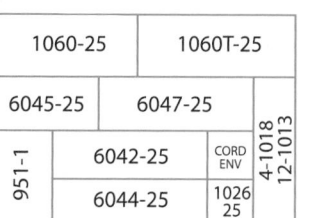

59-419 BOX

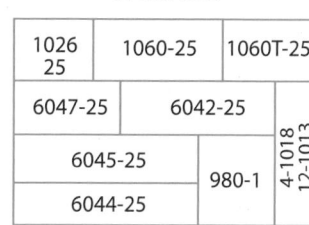

60-530 BOX

1020-1 BELOW 6042 - 6044
5 LABELS BLUE ON WHITE
2 LABELS RED - REVERSED

1020-1 BELOW 6045 - 6044

X-509NA
1960

Customer No. On Box: B 8155 S
Description: 1960 Outfit
Specification: "O27" Ga. Diesel Freight Outfit
Customer/No.: Popular Club Plan; B 8155 S
Original Amount: 250
Factory Order Date: 4/26/1960
Date Issued: June 14, 1960
Packaging: Conventional Outfit Packing

Contents: 225P-1 Alco Diesel Power Car - Blue - "Chesapeake & Ohio" - Yellow Lettering with Headlight and Magne-Traction - with 2 Position Reversing Unit - with Lockon & Lubricant; 6476-1 Hopper Car - Red; 6820-1 Flat Car - with Missile Transport Helicopter - Blue Car Body; 6062-1 Gondola Car - Black - with (3) Cable Reels; 6802-1 Flat Car - Red - with (2) Girder Bridge Sides - Black with White Lettering - U.S. Steel; 6017-1 Caboose - Brick Brown; 1013 Curved Track (8); 1018 Straight Track; 1008-50 Uncoupling Unit - with (1) 1018 Straight Track; 1015-60 45-Watt Transformer; 252 Automatic Crossing Gate; 960 Barnyard Set; 972 Landscape Tree Assortment; 81-32 Wires (2); 310-2 Set of (5) Billboard Signs; 1613-10 Instruction Sheet; AC Accessory Catalog

Boxes & Packing: 59-341 Box; 59-342 Shipper, Note: Print Stock No. on Shipper (1-3); ST Sticker

Alternate For Outfit Contents:
Note: If necessary - Substitute 1 - 1015-25; Print Customers Stock Number (B 8155 S) on Outfit Cartons & Shippers.

X-509NA (1960)	C6	C7	C8	Rarity
Complete Outfit	1,350	2,400	3,700	R10
Outfit Box no. 59-341	500	900	1,300	R10

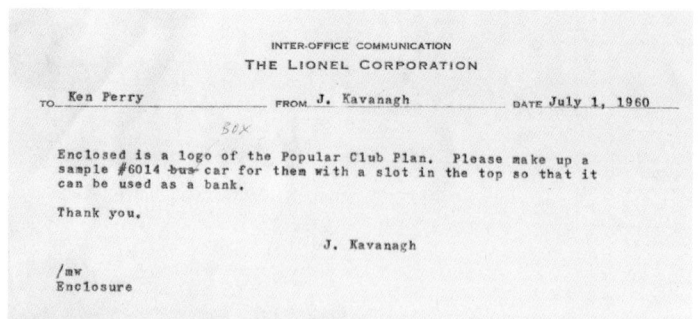

Lionel would frequently make prototype cars to help sell a prospect on doing business with it. Although a Popular Club Plan box car never became regular production, this memo documents its likely existence.

Comments: Popular Club Plan is a catalog company selling an assortment of clothing, housewares, jewelry, toys and electronics. In 1960 it purchased three Retailer Promotional outfits: nos. X-509NA, X-541NA and X-542NA.

The X-509NA, a Type Ia outfit, was Popular's high-end diesel purchase and included some highly collectible items. It was headed by a no. 225P-1 Chesapeake & Ohio Alco Diesel Power Car. New for 1960, this locomotive featured an open pilot and the large ledge that Lionel added to Alcos as reinforcement in 1960.

As with many items, it is the box for this diesel that is rare. The no. 225-20 Corrugated Box and no. 217-16 Sleeve were included only for 225s that were placed in outfits. Separate-sale items used a no. 217-15 Corrugated Box. According to a Lionel Changes Affecting Future Production document, "For the 200 items required for single sales, use corrugated box (217-15) with 2 ends imprinted in place of corr. box (225-20)." There were only 9,035 of the 225P-1s included in outfits. This helps to explain its infrequent appearance in the market.

Although the no. 6820-1 Flat Car - with Missile Transport Helicopter was offered for separate sale in 1960 and 1961, as well as being a component of nine promotional outfits, its box seldom

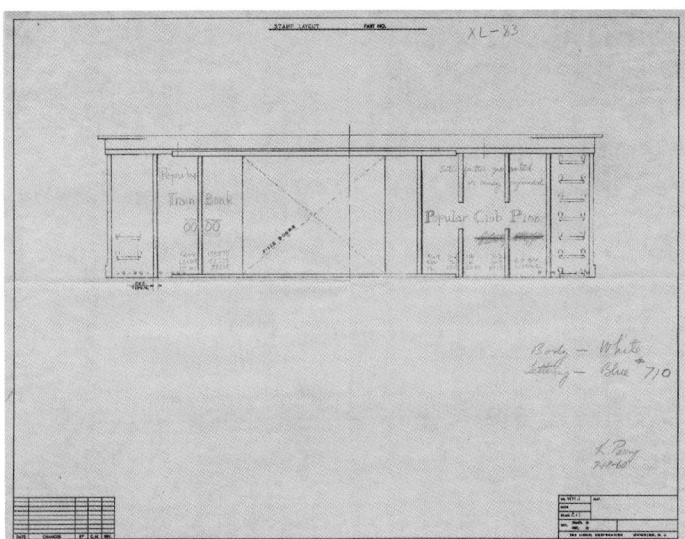

A little more than two weeks after the memo was sent, a hand-drawn stamp layout was created. The number XL-83 was assigned to this project.

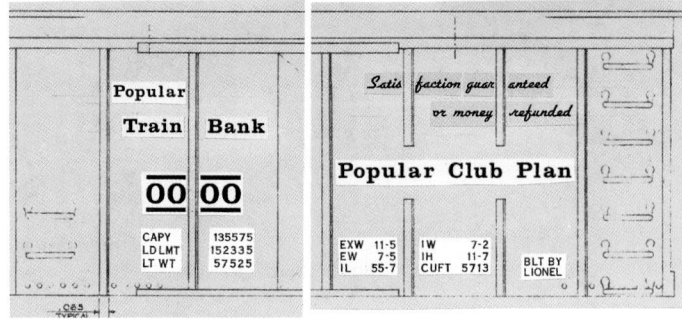

Artwork was then created as the next and likely final step before producing a prototype.

appears in collectible condition. The no. 6820-40 Non-Operating Missile Helicopter Complete is also becoming hard to find with original, unbroken parts.

The red no. 6802-1 Flat Car was being depleted through promotional outfits and as a substitution in catalog outfits. It, along with the other rolling stock in the X-509NA, was equipped with early operating AAR trucks and couplers and came packaged in Orange Perforated boxes.

All the Popular Club Plan outfits included Plasticville sets. This outfit included a no. 960 Barnyard Set as well as a Lionel no. 972 Landscape Tree Assortment. The fragile packaging for both of these items makes them difficult to obtain in collectible condition.

The X-509NA came in a no. 59-341 Tan RSC with Black Graphics outfit box. It was an overstickered no. 9665 box from 1959. It was manufactured by Star Corrugated Box Company, Inc. and included a star printed on the bottom.

Of the three Popular outfits, the X-509NA was produced in the smallest quantity and is seldom seen.

CONVENTIONAL PACK
59-341 BOX
STICKER
NOTE: PUT STOCK NO. ON SHIPPER

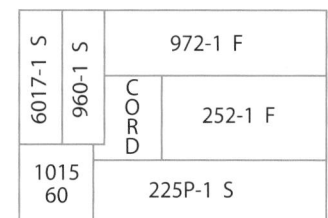

1018 TOP 6802
1008-50 TOP 6820

Description: 1960 Outfit
Specification: "O27" Ga. Steam Type Freight Outfit
Customer: Department Store Promotional
Original Amount: 1,300
Factory Order Date: 3/7/1960
Date Issued: June 24, 1960
Packaging: Conventional Outfit Packing, All Units Packed Except 1015 - 1008 - 6045-25

Contents: 246-1 Locomotive - with Headlight and Magne-Traction - with Lockon & Lubricant; 1130T-1 Tender; 6045-25 Two Dome Tank Car - Gray - with Non-Operating Trucks; 6825-1 Flat Car - Red - with Trestle Bridge - Black; 6014-100 Box Car - Red; 6017-1 Caboose - Brick Brown; 1013 Curved Track (12); 1018 Straight Track (3); 1008-50 Uncoupling Unit - with (1) 1018 Straight Track; 1015-25 45-Watt Transformer; 1020-1 90° Crossover; 960-1 Barnyard Set; 1103-14 Envelope Packed; 310-2 Set of (5) Billboard Signs; 1609-4 Instruction Sheet; AC Accessory Catalog

Boxes & Packing: 60-407 Box; 60-408 Shipper (1-3)

X-510NA
1960

Alternate For Outfit Contents:
Note: Substitute 1,300 - 6027-1 for 6017-1; Dept 57 Note: In the event 1 - 1015-60 Transformer is included in outfit, substitute: 2 - 81-32 Wires for 1 - 1103-14 Envelope Packed.

X-510NA (1960)	C6	C7	C8	Rarity
Complete Outfit With no. 6027-1	700	1,200	2,025	R9
Outfit Box no. 60-407	100	175	275	R7

Comments: This was the first of six (nos. X-510NA through X-515NA) General Release Promotional outfits from 1960 with the customer listed as "Department Store Promotional". Of these O27 gauge outfits, three were steam and three diesel. They were configured for low-, mid- and high-end customers. Lionel likely sold all of these outfits to small retailers seeking a promotional outfit yet unable to make the volume commitment to receive an exclusive one.

The no. X-510NA, a Type IIb outfit, was the entry-level offering of the 1960 Department Store Promotional outfits and included rolling stock commonly available in that year. In fact, the no. 6825 Trestle Bridge Flat Car appeared in more than 40 promotional outfits. Every item was carryover, equipped with early operating AAR trucks and couplers and packaged in an Orange

Outfit no. X-510NA is shown with the rare no. 1103-14 Envelope Packed and no. 6027-1 Alaskan Caboose with its no. 6027-3 Folding Box. The no. 960-1 Barnyard Set also helps to increase the value of this entry-level offering.

Perforated box.

The no. 246-1 Steam Type Locomotive was also a low-end item, but was equipped with Magne-Traction. First released in 1959, it was still being used in outfits as late as 1962.

The no. 960-1 Barnyard Set retailed for $1.50 in the 1960 catalog. It was a low-cost way for Lionel to enhance this outfit and, in today's market, increase the value.

The two interesting items that make this entry-level outfit a rare, high-end collectible are the no. 1103-14 Envelope Packed (see outfit no. X-502NA) and no. 6027-3 Folding Box for the no. 6027-1 Alaskan Caboose.

Lionel was depleting its inventory of the no. 1015-25 45-Watt Transformer without direction control. The 1103-14 included a no. 80-1 Controller that added direction control for the 246 steamer. This rare envelope and its included 80-1 and Form 2085 are seldom seen.

The statement, "Substitute 1,300 - 6027-1 for 6017-1", effectively replaced all the 6017s with 6027s. Therefore, all of these outfits came with the no. 6027-1 substitution.

This modification likely was recorded as a substitution rather than just a change on the Factory Order for one of two reasons. One possibility was that the outfit quantity may originally have exceeded 1,300. Therefore, when it was reduced, the change included all 6017s. Another possibility is that this change might have been a last-minute substitution that was easier to record on the Factory Order in this manner. In either case, the pricing

reflects that change.

The 6027-1 Alaskan Caboose was originally boxed in the 1959 RSC version of outfit no. 1611. The remaining inventory was depleted in 1960 promotional and 1961 catalog outfits. This Orange Perforated box is difficult to find in collectible condition.

The no. 60-407 Tan RSC with Black Graphics outfit box was manufactured by Star Corrugated Box Company, Inc. and measured 13½ x 11¾ x 6¼ inches. It had a star printed on the bottom.

When Lionel created the X-510NA, it could not have known that it was adding rare components. How ironic that entry-level outfits sometimes become some of the most difficult to obtain complete and in C8 condition.

CONVENTIONAL PACK
60-407 BOX
ALL UNITS PACKED, EXCEPT 1015 - 1008 - 6045-25

TOP LAYER			BOTTOM LAYER		
6045			6825 F		
3-1018		6027 F	6014 F		1015
12-1013 E			1130T F		
960 F			246 F		
1008 TOP			1020 TOP 1130T - 6014		

This no. X-511NA General Release Promotional outfit included a price tag from The Emporium department store with "660 14B1, $24.98". This outfit was likely sold to numerous retailers. The Classic box for the no. 6424-1 Flat Car - with 2 Autos is missing. Note that the difficult-to-find no. 2093 Layout Instruction Sheet is included.

Description: 1960 Outfit
Specification: "O27" Ga. Diesel Freight Outfit
Customer: Department Store Promotional
Customer/No./Price: The Emporium; 660 14B1; $24.98
Original Amount: 3,500
Factory Order Date: 4/8/1960
Date Issued: June 24, 1960
Packaging: Conventional Outfit Packing, All Units Packed Except 1015, 1008, 6045-25

Contents: 225P-1 Alco Diesel Power Car - Blue - "Chesapeake & Ohio" - Yellow Lettering with Headlight and Magne-Traction - with 2 Position Reversing Unit - with Lockon & Lubricant; 6424-1 Flat Car - with 2 Autos; 6045-25 Two Dome Tank Car - Gray - with Non-Operating Trucks; 3376-1 Operating Giraffe Car; 6017-1 Caboose - Brick Brown; 1013 Curved Track (16); 1018 Straight Track (11); 1013-65 1/2 Section Curved Track; 1008-50 Uncoupling Unit - with (1) 1018 Straight Track; 1015-25 45-Watt Transformer; 110-1 Graduated Trestle Set; 81-32 Wires (2); 310-2 Set of (5) Billboard Signs; 1613-10 Instruction Sheet; AC Accessory Catalog; 2093 Layout Instruction Sheet

Boxes & Packing: 60-409 Box; 60-410 Shipper (1-3)

Alternate For Outfit Contents:
Note: Substitute 6812-1 Car for 6424-1 in 2,000 sets.

X-511NA (1960)	C6	C7	C8	Rarity
Complete Outfit With no. 6424-1	400	700	1,050	R5
Complete Outfit With no. 6812-1	450	800	1,125	R5
Outfit Box no. 60-409	75	125	175	R5

Comments: This was the second of six (nos. X-510NA through X-515NA) General Release Promotional outfits from 1960 with the customer listed as "Department Store Promotional". Of these O27 gauge outfits, three were steam and three diesel. They were configured for low-, mid- and high-end customers. Lionel likely sold all of these outfits to small retailers seeking a promotional outfit yet unable to make the volume commitment to receive an exclusive one.

The no. X-511NA was a Type IIb entry-level outfit that featured a diesel locomotive. Its motive power was a no. 225P-1 Chesapeake & Ohio Alco Diesel Power Car. This Alco included an open pilot and the large ledge that Lionel added to Alcos as reinforcement in 1960. (See outfit no. X-509NA for details about this locomotive's difficult-to-obtain no. 225-20 Corrugated Box.)

Promotional outfits were often the dumping grounds of obsolete inventory. The no. 6424-1 Flat Car with 2 Autos (introduced in 1957) was such an item, being depleted in this outfit. According to its Production Control File, the various 6424 suffixes indicated the colors of autos included on the flat car. Lionel's intended production for a "-1" was originally a white and a yellow automobile in a sleeve, followed by a maroon and a blue automobile in a sleeve. Eventually, Lionel stopped including the sleeve. The X-511NA likely came with the last version of the 6424-1, which had early operating AAR trucks and couplers and came in a Classic-style box.

The no. 6045-25 Gray Two Dome Tank Car was equipped with non-operating Archbar trucks and couplers, whereas the remaining rolling stock included operating AAR trucks and couplers. Except for the 6045-25 and 6424-1, all of these cars were packed in Orange Perforated boxes.

By far the most difficult item to obtain in this outfit is its no. 2093 Layout Instruction Sheet. This item has been linked to the X-511NA and outfit no. X-672. The layout was very similar to the elevated pretzel shown on the no. 1802I, but it included an extra straight and a half-curve to accommodate the "Giraffe Car Signal". These instructions were almost always discarded or lost.

The no. 60-409 Tan RSC with Black Graphics outfit box was manufactured by Star Corrugated Box Company and measured 15½ x 13¾ x 7 inches. It also had a star and "7-22T" printed on the bottom.

CONVENTIONAL PACK
60-409 BOX
ALL UNITS PACKED EXCEPT 1015, 1008, 6045-25

TOP LAYER	
3376 F	1015
6424 F	
8-1013	
8-1013	

5-1018 TOP 6424
6-1018 TOP 6424
1008 TOP 1018
1013-65 TOP

BOTTOM LAYER	
225P F	
6017 F	6045 F
110 F	

X-512NA
1960

The no. X-512NA is shown with the nos. 6424-85 Flat Car - with 2 Autos and 6017-100 Caboose substitutions. Also shown is a no. 6014-100 Box Car - Red - "Airex Lettering", which replaced the no. 6014-1 Box Car - Red.

Description: 1960 Outfit
Specification: "O27" Ga. Steam Type Freight Outfit with Smoke
Customer: Department Store Promotional
Original Amount: 1,000
Factory Order Date: 2/16/1960
Date Issued: February 26, 1960
Packaging: Conventional Outfit Packing, All Units Packed Except 1015, 1008

Contents: 2018-1 Locomotive - with Smoke, Lockon & Lubricant - without Magne-Traction; 1130T-1 Tender; 6424-1 Flat Car - with 2 Autos; 6803-1 Flat Car - Red - with (1) 6151-22 Single Gun Tank & (1) 6151-17 Mobile Listening Post; 6844-1 Rocket Transport Car; 6802-1 Flat Car - Red - with (2) Girder Bridge Sides - Black with White Lettering - U.S. Steel; 6014-1 Box Car - Red; 6017-1 Caboose - Brick Brown; 1013 Curved Track (16); 1018 Straight Track (3); 1008-50 Uncoupling Unit -

with (1) 1018 Straight Track; 1015-25 45-Watt Transformer; 1023 45° Crossover; 81-32 Wires (2); 310-2 Set of (5) Billboard Signs; 1613-10 Instruction Sheet; AC Accessory Catalog; 1802H Layout Instruction Sheet

Boxes & Packing: 60-411 Box; 60-412 Shipper (1-3)

Alternate For Outfit Contents:
Note: Substitute 488 - 6017-85 for 6017-1; Substitute 512 - 6017-100 for 6017-1; Substitute 366 - 6424-85 for 6424-1; Substitute 100 - 6424-60 for 6424-1.

X-512NA (1960)	C6	C7	C8	Rarity
Complete Outfit With no. 6017-85	575	1,050	1,625	R7
Complete Outfit With no. 6017-100	550	1,000	1,550	R7
Outfit Box no. 60-411	125	225	300	R7

Comments: This was the third of six (nos. X-510NA through X-515NA) General Release Promotional outfits from 1960 with the customer listed as "Department Store Promotional". Of these O27 gauge outfits, three were steam and three diesel. They were configured for low-, mid- and high-end customers. Lionel likely sold all of these outfits to small retailers seeking a promotional outfit yet unable to make the volume commitment to receive an exclusive one.

The no. X-512NA outfit was Lionel's Type IIb mid-level steam offering for Department Store Promotional customers. It was headed by a no. 2018-1 Locomotive - with Smoke.

As with the X-511NA and other promotional outfits, Lionel used this outfit to deplete obsolete inventory. The nos. 6424-1, 6424-60 and 6424-85 Flat Car with 2 Autos were first introduced in 1957. According to their Production Control Files, the various 6424 suffixes indicated the colors of autos included on the flat car. Lionel's intended production for a "-1" was originally a white and a yellow automobile in a sleeve, followed by a maroon and a blue automobile in a sleeve. The "-60" included a yellow and a blue automobile, and the "-85" would have a maroon and a white automobile. Eventually, Lionel stopped including the sleeve. All of these versions came in various types of Classic-style boxes, none of which affects the price of this outfit.

The Factory Order for the X-512NA listed a no. 6014-1 Box Car - Red. Outfits that listed this car have been observed with a no. 6014-100 Box Car - Red - "Airex Lettering" in an Orange Perforated box. It appears that Lionel was depleting inventory of 6014-1s, and so the no. 6014-100 became the norm. These two cars were so similar that customers likely didn't care which one they received.

Also being depleted was the no. 6803-1 Flat Car - Red. It last appeared in this and outfit no. X-527NA.

The final items being depleted were the no. 6017-85 Caboose and the Orange Perforated boxed version of the no. 6017-100 Caboose. Neither car is easy to find with the proper box in collectible condition.

All no. 6017-1 Cabooses were substituted out. This substitution affects the price of the X-512NA enough that separate listings are provided. None of the substitutions affects the outfit's rarity, although the Bold Classic box for the 6017-85 Caboose (no. 6017-88 Folding Box) is more difficult to find than the 6017-100 Caboose (no. 6017-105 Folding Box).

All the cars in the X-512NA were equipped with early operating AAR trucks and couplers and came packed in a Classic-style or an Orange Perforated box.

The no. 60-411 Tan RSC with Black Graphics outfit box was manufactured by Star Corrugated Box Company. It measured 16¾ x 12 x 6¼ inches and had a star printed on the bottom.

CONVENTIONAL PACK
60-411 BOX
ALL UNITS PACKED EXCEPT 1015, 1008

TOP LAYER

3-1018		
8-1013	6017 F	6014 S
8-1013		
6844 F		
6802 F		

1008 TOP

BOTTOM LAYER

6803 F		1130T F
6424 F		
2018 F	1015	

1023 TOP 6803 - 6424

Description: 1960 Outfit
Specification: "O27" Ga. Diesel Switcher Freight Outfit
Customer: Department Store Promotional
Original Amount: 600
Factory Order Date: 2/16/1960
Date Issued: September 28, 1960
Packaging: Conventional Outfit Packing, All Units Packed Except 1015, 1008, 109-25

Contents: 614-1 Diesel Switcher - Blue with Yellow Brake Hatch - "Alaskan" Markings in Yellow - with (1) Magnet - with Headlight and 2-Position Reversing Unit - with Non-Operating Coupler in Front - Dummy Coupler in Rear with Lockon & Lubricant; 6817-1 Flat Car - Red - with Road Scraper; 6812-1 Track Maintenance Car; 6361-1 Log Car - Dark Green Frame; 6670-1 Crane Car; 6119-100 Work Caboose; 1013 Curved Track (16); 1018 Straight Track (3); 1008-50 Uncoupling Unit - with (1) 1018 Straight Track; 1015-25 45-Watt Transformer; 1023-1 45° Crossover; 109-25 Half Trestle Set; 109-2 Envelope Packed; 81-32 Wires (2); 310-2 Set of (5) Billboard Signs; IS Instruction Sheet; AC Accessory Catalog; 1802J Layout Instruction Sheet

Boxes & Packing: 60-413 Box; 60-414 Shipper (1-3)

X-513NA (1960)	C6	C7	C8	Rarity
Complete Outfit	1,550	2,200	3,100	R10
Outfit Box no. 60-413	300	400	525	R8

Comments: This was the fourth of six (nos. X-510NA through X-515NA) General Release Promotional outfits from 1960 with the customer listed as "Department Store Promotional". Of these O27 gauge outfits, three were steam and three diesel. They were configured for low-, mid- and high-end customers. Lionel likely sold all of these outfits to small retailers seeking a promotional outfit yet unable to make the volume commitment to receive an exclusive one.

The no. X-513NA outfit was Lionel's Type IIa mid-level diesel offering for Department Store Promotional customers. From the standpoint of value, time has been good to this outfit, with its contents becoming more difficult to find each day.

To begin, an unboxed no. 614 Alaskan Diesel Switcher is fairly common. It was part of 1959 catalog outfit no. 1611 and offered for separate sale in 1959 and 1960. But when boxed as the no. 614-1, its Orange Perforated no. 614-7 Folding Box is extremely difficult to find in collectible condition. This inexpensive method of packaging switchers did not bode well for the boxes. Finding a C8 box will test any collector's patience.

The no. 6817-1 Flat Car - Red - with Road Scraper is also an expensive item to find in collectible condition. Although Lionel made thousands of these flat car loads, the scraper and Orange Perforated box are fragile.

The X-513NA represented at least the third time that a no. 109-25 Half Trestle Set appeared in a promotional outfit. This item can be linked to promotional outfit nos. X-814NA and X-

Outfit no. X-513NA came with a few expensive and rare individual items. These included the no. 109-2 Envelope Packed, Orange Perforated no. 614-7 Folding Box and no. 6817-1 Flat Car -Red - with Road Scraper.

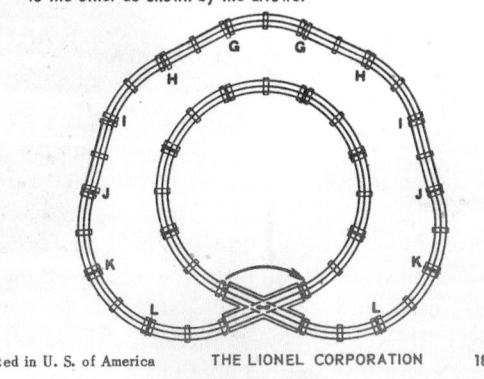

SPECIAL LAYOUT INSTRUCTIONS

This special train outfit includes a No. 109 Trestle Set and enough track to make up the layout shown below. You will have to transfer track pins from one end of the crossing to the other as shown by the arrows.

Printed in U. S. of America   THE LIONEL CORPORATION   1802J 5-59

A no. 1802J Layout Instruction Sheet was included in outfits that had a no. 109-25 Half Trestle Set.

834 from 1959. The Half Trestle Set was also used in 1961 catalog outfit no. 2574. Although the trestles are commonly available and a grouping of 12 is easily created, the no. 109-2 Envelope Packed is rare. Two versions have been observed: one with "Contents" and the other with "Assem. No. 109-2" on the top of the envelope. The contents and envelope number (109-3) were identical. The 109-25 was paired with a no. 1802J Layout Instruction Sheet, which detailed the elevated pretzel layout.

All the cars in the X-513NA were equipped with early operating AAR trucks and couplers and came packed in Orange Perforated boxes, although the no. 6119-100 Work Caboose has been observed in a Bold Classic box.

The no. 60-413 Tan RSC with Black Graphics outfit box was manufactured by Star Corrugated Box Company, Inc. It measured 13½ x 12¾ x 7½ inches and had a star printed on the bottom.

Although the rolling stock in this outfit is the same as Lionel included in Sears outfit no. 9652 from 1960, the locomotive and track layout, plus the small quantity produced, make this outfit much more desirable. It is seldom seen complete in collectible condition. The nos. 109-2 Envelope Packed and 614-7 Folding Box increase the rarity of this outfit to an R10.

CONVENTIONAL PACK
60-413 BOX
ALL UNITS PACKED EXCEPT 1015, 1008, 109-25

TOP LAYER	
109-25	
8-1013	
8-1013	3-1018
6119 F	
6670 S	

1008 TOP 1018

BOTTOM LAYER	
6361 S	
6812 S	
6817 S	1015
614 F	

1023 TOP 6812 - 6817

Description: 1960 Outfit
Specification: "O27" Ga. Steam Type Freight Outfit with Smoke
Customer: Department Store Promotional
Original Amount: 1,500
Factory Order Date: 2/17/1960
Date Issued: 6-23-60
Packaging: Conventional Outfit Packing, All Units Packed Except 1063, 1008

Contents: 243-1 Locomotive - with Smoke and Headlight - with (2) Position Reversing Unit, Lockon and Lubricant - without Magne-Traction; 243W-1 Whistle Tender; 6650-1 Missile Launching Flat Car; 6830-1 Flat Car - with Non-Operating Submarine - Blue Car Body; 3419-1 Operating Helicopter Car; 3535-1 Operating Security Car; 1013 Curved Track (12); 1018 Straight Track (3); 1008-50 Uncoupling Unit - with (1) 1018 Straight Track; 1063-25 Transformer; 1020 90° Crossover; 943 Exploding Ammo Dump; 81-32 Wires (2); 310-2 Set of (5) Billboard Signs; 926-60 Instruction Book; AC Accessory Catalog

Boxes & Packing: 60-426 Box; 60-427 Insert; 60-428 Shipper (1-3)

X-514NA (1960)	C6	C7	C8	Rarity
Complete Outfit	585	950	1,400	R6
Outfit Box no. 60-426	125	200	275	R6

Comments: This was the fifth of six (nos. X-510NA through X-515NA) General Release Promotional outfits from 1960 with the customer listed as "Department Store Promotional". Of these O27 gauge outfits three, were steam and three diesel. They were configured for low-, mid- and high-end customers. Lionel likely sold all of these outfits to small retailers seeking a promotional outfit yet unable to make the volume commitment to receive an exclusive one.

Outfit no. X-514NA was Lionel's high-end Type IIa Department Store Promotional offering. A space and military outfit, it was headed by a no. 243-1 Locomotive - with Smoke and Headlight. This engine, new for 1960, typically was followed by a no. 243W-1 Whistle Tender.

The nos. 3419-1, 6650-1 and 6830-1 provided excitement and enhanced the play value of this outfit. The 3419 and 6650 were repeats from 1959. The same three items also came in outfit no. X-531NA.

The no. 6830-1 Flat Car - with Non-Operating Submarine - Blue Car Body (new for 1960) appeared in this and six other promotional outfits. It was a non-operating version of the no. 3830-1 Operating Submarine Car. The no. 6830-100 Submarine was stamped "6830" to match the car. The flat car and submarine are fairly common, but the Orange Perforated no. 6830-9 Folding Box is not easy to find in C8 condition.

All the rolling stock in the X-514NA was equipped with early operating AAR trucks and couplers and came packaged in Orange Perforated boxes. The no. 60-426 was likely a Tan RSC with Black Graphics outfit box, and it was unique to this outfit.

Lionel was overly optimistic when it predicted the demand for this outfit. The original quantity on the Factory Order was 2,500 on February 17, 1960. The selling season didn't go well because on 6-23-60, that figure was reduced to 1,500.

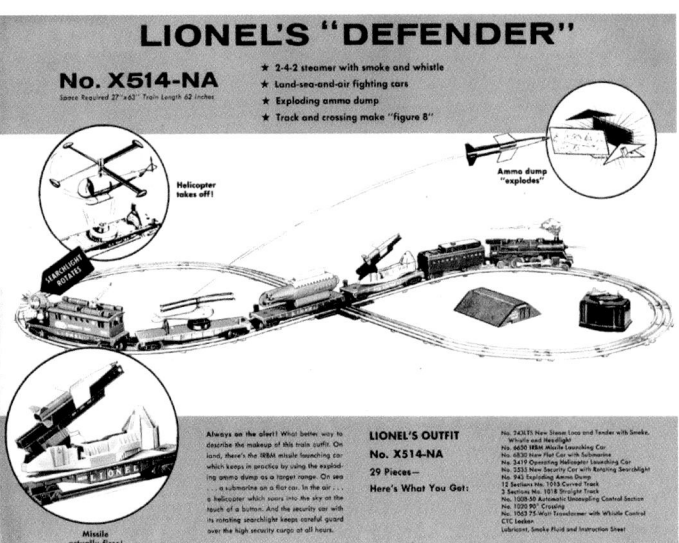

To assist in selling its outfits, Lionel provided one-page brochures to its sales department and directly to dealers. This brochure for the no. X-514NA reveals that Lionel named the outfit the "Defender".

This photograph was likely taken early in the year because the Factory Order was dated February 17, 1960. As such, the brochure illustrates a 1959 version of the no. 3419-1 Operating Helicopter Car with a large winder and dual-blade helicopter and an engineering mock-up of the no. 6830-1 Flat Car - with Non-Operating Submarine - Blue Car Body.

CONVENTIONAL PACK
60-426 BOX
ALL UNITS PACKED EXCEPT 1063, 1008

TOP LAYER

12-1013	
243W F	
3419 S	
6650 S	

3-1018 TOP 243W
1020 TOP 1018 - 1013
1008 TOP 1020

BOTTOM LAYER

243 F	943 E
3535 F	
6830 F	1063

Description: 1960 Outfit
Specification: "O27" Ga. Diesel Freight Outfit
Customer: Department Store Promotional
Original Amount: 300
Factory Order Date: 2/17/1960
Date Issued: October 12, 1960
Packaging: Conventional Outfit Packing

Contents: 45-50 Mobile Rocket Firing Car - Khaki Color - with "U.S. Marine Markings" - with Lockon and Lubricant; 3419-1 Operating Helicopter Car; 6830-1 Flat Car - with Non-Operating Submarine - Blue Car Body; 470-1 IRBM Missile Launching Platform with Exploding Target Car; 6119-100 Work Caboose; 1013 Curved Track (16); 1018 Straight Track (3); 6019-1 Remote Control Track Set; 1015-25 45-Watt Transformer; 1023 45° Crossover; 943 Exploding Ammo Dump; 910 Navy Yard Cardboard Display; 81-32 Wires (2); 310-2 Set of (5) Billboard Signs; 926-60 Instruction Book; AC Accessory Catalog; 1802H Layout Instruction Sheet

Boxes & Packing: 60-503 Box; 60-504 Shipper (1-3)

Alternate For Outfit Contents:
36 Sets with 1008-50 and 44-45 Envelope in Locomotive; Balance - As per revised specifications with 44-55 Envelope in Locomotive.

X-515NA (1960)	C6	C7	C8	Rarity
Complete Outfit	7,700	11,500	16,000	R10
Outfit Box no. 60-503	750	1,100	1,500	R10

Comments: This was the last of six (nos. X-510NA through X-515NA) General Release Promotional outfits from 1960 with the customer listed as "Department Store Promotional". Of these O27 gauge outfits, three were steam and three diesel. They were configured for low-, mid- and high-end customers. Lionel likely sold all of these outfits to small retailers seeking a promotional outfit yet unable to make the volume commitment to receive an exclusive one.

The no. X-515NA, a Type IIb outfit, was the high-end Department Store Promotional offering for 1960. It may also classify as one of the top promotional outfits. After all, the X-515NA was the first outfit to include the rare no. 910 Navy Yard Cardboard Display (also known as the Atomic Sub Base). It is unknown why Lionel would introduce such a unique item in a General Release Promotional outfit, especially since the other outfits that were designated Department Store Promotional consisted mostly of carryover items.

The rarity of the 910 can be directly linked to its lack of

CONVENTIONAL PACK
60-503 BOX

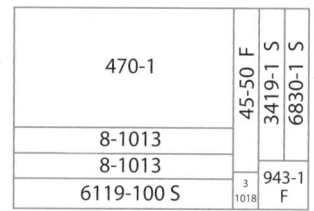

		45-50 F	3419-1 S	6830-1 S
470-1				
8-1013				
8-1013				
6119-100 S		3 1018	943-1 F	

1023 TOP 1013, 6119-100
910 BOTTOM
1015-25 TOP 943
6019-1 TOP 45

Lionel markings and fragility. Stories exist of individuals who discarded a 910 Navy Yard Cardboard Display because they did not know what it was. Even if the 910 stayed with the no. X-515NA outfit, it was extremely fragile and was likely assembled or damaged due to handling over time.

Although it is the sub base that makes this outfit so desirable, the other contents were all high-end 1960s offerings that provided the appropriate space and military theme to this outfit. It was headed by a no. 45-50 Mobile Rocket Firing Car - Khaki Color. The "-50" suffix indicated that this motorized unit came with a no. 44-55 Envelope Packed, whereas a no. 45-1 came with a no. 44-45 Envelope Packed. Since a no. 6019-1 Remote Control Track Set was included, the additional peripherals required to operate the Mobile Rocket Firing Car (included in a 44-45 Envelope Packed) were not needed. Therefore, a 45-50 came with a 44-55 Envelope. Once a no. 1008-50 was substituted for the 6019-1, a 44-45 was required to operate the 45.

Another notable item included in the X-515NA was the no. 6830-1 Flat Car - with Non-Operating Submarine. This was a natural addition to a sub-base outfit, as it could deliver a submarine to the base. The 6830-1, like all the other rolling stock in this outfit, was equipped with early operating AAR trucks and couplers and then packaged in Orange Perforated boxes.

This outfit provided plenty of fun. There were many items to shoot and be shot. The nos. 943 and 6470-1 Exploding Target Car (included in the no. 470-1) were the targets of the nos. 45-50 and 470-1 missiles.

The pretzel layout, as outlined on the no. 1802H Layout Instruction Sheet, was included with this and most other sub-base outfits. It provided additional excitement, as the train would weave in and out of the sub-base tunnels. Also common with sub-base outfits was the unnumbered "How to Assemble Your Lionel Atomic Submarine Base" instruction sheet.

The no. 60-503 Box used with this outfit was subsequently overstickered and used for sub-base outfit no. X-625 as well as outfit no. X-691.

The X-515NA was the first of nine outfits to include a no. 910 Navy Yard Cardboard Display. That fact alone, combined with its extremely low quantity and lack of market appearance, makes this one of the most difficult of the promotional outfits to find, hence its R10 rarity.

Customer No. On Box: 6-P4803
Description: 1960 Outfit
Specification: "O27" Ga. Steam Type Freight Outfit
Cust./No./Price: Sperry & Hutchinson Co.; 6-P4803; 6 Books
Original Amount: 4,000

Factory Order Date: 3/16/1960
Date Issued: April 8, 1960
Packaging: Conventional Outfit Packing

Contents: 246-1 Locomotive - with Headlight and Magne-Traction - with Lockon and Lubricant; 1130T-1 Tender; 6062-1 Gondola Car - Black - with (3) Cable Reels; 6825-1 Flat Car - Red - with Trestle Bridge - Black; 6017-1 Caboose - Brick Brown; 1013

Lionel no. X-516NA was also stamped with S&H's no. "6P4803". A common, low-end promotional outfit, it frequently appears in the contemporary toy train marketplace.

Curved Track (8); 1018 Straight Track; 1008-50 Uncoupling Unit - with (1) 1018 Straight Track; 1016-60 35-Watt Transformer; 81-32 Wires (2); 1609-4 Instruction Sheet; 310-2 Set of (5) Billboard Signs; AC Accessory Catalog

Boxes & Packing: 60-442 Box; 60-443 Shipper (1-6)

X-516NA (1960)	C6	C7	C8	Rarity
Complete Outfit	175	300	500	R4
Outfit Box no. 60-442	40	90	150	R4

Comments: Sperry & Hutchinson Co. (S&H) offered Retailer Promotional Type Ia outfit no. X-516NA in the firm's 1960 catalog on page 84 as item no. X-P4803. The X-516NA was available in exchange for six filled S&H stamp books (hence the prefix "6" in "6-P4803").

As with many promotional outfits, the pictures in the retailer's catalog do not match the actual contents of the outfit. In the case of the X-516NA, a black (and not gray) trestle bridge and an HO scale power pack were pictured.

The X-516NA was a low-end outfit featuring rolling stock with early operating AAR trucks and couplers. The no. 246-1 Steam Locomotive included a two-position reversing unit, a headlight and Magne-Traction. This outfit included the later version, which had a solid pilot and lacked generator detail on the body. All additional peripherals followed normal progression.

The outfit came in a no. 60-442 Tan RSC with Black Graphics outfit box manufactured by Kraft Corrugated Containers, Inc. and measuring 13¼ x 12¾ x 4¼ inches.

The Factory Order for the X-516NA instructed the Outfit Packing Department to stamp the boxes with S&H's "6 P 4803". Also handwritten on the Factory Order was "250 Display".

This is one of the more common promotional outfits. Its low rarity reflects its frequent occurrence in the marketplace.

CONVENTIONAL PACK
60-442 BOX

6017-1 S	8-1013	1018
	6825-1	1008-50
	6062-1 S	
1016-60	1130T-1 S	
246-1 S		

Description: 1960 Outfit
Specification: "O27" Ga. Steam Type Freight Outfit
Customer: Service Exchanges
Original Amount: 1,000
Factory Order Date: 4/20/1960
Date Issued: April 20, 1960
Packaging: Conventional Outfit Packing

Contents: 246-1 Locomotive - with Headlight and Magne-Traction - with Lockon and Lubricant; 1130T-1 Tender; 6062-1 Gondola Car - Black - with (3) Cable Reels; 3376-1 Operating Giraffe Car; 6465-110 2 Dome Tank Car - Green - ("Cities Service"); 6017-1 Caboose - Brick Brown; 1013 Curved Track (8); 1018 Straight Track; 1008-50 Uncoupling Unit - with (1) 1018 Straight Track; 1015-60 45-Watt Transformer; 81-32 Wires (2); 1609-4 Instruction Sheet; 310-2 Set of (5) Billboard Signs; AC Accessory Catalog

Boxes & Packing: 60-479 Box; 60-480 Shipper (1-4)

Alternate For Outfit Contents:
Note: If necessary - Substitute 1- 1015-25, 1- 1103-14 For 1 - 1015-60, 2 - 81-32.

X-517NA (1960)	C6	C7	C8	Rarity
Complete Outfit	340	650	900	R7
Complete Outfit With A no. 1103-14 Substitution	440	850	1,350	R9
Outfit Box no. 60-479	120	250	350	R7

Comments: In 1960, the U.S. military's Service Exchanges purchased two promotional outfits: nos. X-517NA and X-518NA. Both were Retailer Promotional outfits headed by steam engines. Outfit no. X-517NA was a Type Ib outfit when the no. 1103-14 Envelope Packed was substituted; otherwise it was a Type Ia.

Headed by a no. 246-1 Locomotive, the X-517NA was the Service Exchanges' low-end offering. Although the 246-1 was equipped with Magne-Traction, it had a plastic motor mechanism and lacked smoke.

The Orange Perforated box for the no. 6465-110 Green Cities Service Dome 2 Tank Car (new for 1960) takes some work to find in C8 condition. Also new was the no. 3376-1 Operating Giraffe Car. It was packed with a no. 3376-118 Envelope Packed as well as a no. 6809-12 Tube to protect one of its couplers.

All the rolling stock in this outfit was equipped with early operating AAR trucks and couplers and packaged in Orange Perforated boxes.

As listed on the Factory Order for the X-517NA, this was a standard freight outfit with readily available items (except for the 6465-110's box). However, when the no. 1015-60 45-Watt Transformer was swapped out for a no. 1015-25 and a no. 1103-14 Envelope Packed (see outfit no. X-502NA), this becomes a difficult outfit to complete.

Lionel was depleting the inventory of the no. 1015-25 45-Watt Transformer without direction control. The no. 1103-14 included a no. 80-1 Controller that added direction control for the 246 steamer. This rare envelope and its included 80-1 and Form 2085 are seldom seen.

The no. 60-479 Box was unique to this outfit.

Even with 1,000 made, this outfit is seldom seen. When the 1103-14 Envelope Packed is added, the rarity of the X-517NA climbs to R9.

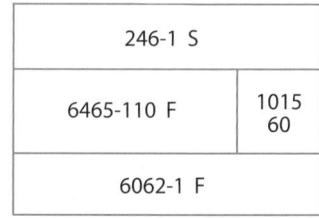

CONVENTIONAL PACK
60-479 BOX

TOP LAYER / **BOTTOM LAYER**

Boxes & Packing: 59-339 Box; 69-340 Shipper (1-3); ST Sticker

X-518NA (1960)	C6	C7	C8	Rarity
Complete Outfit	550	875	1,325	R8
Outfit Box no. 59-339	200	300	400	R8

Description: 1960 Outfit
Specification: "O27" Ga. Steam Type Freight Outfit with Smoke
Customer: Service Exchanges
Original Amount: 750
Factory Order Date: 4/20/1960
Date Issued: 6-23-60
Packaging: Conventional Outfit Packing

Contents: 244-1 Locomotive - with Smoke & Headlight with 2 Position Reversing Unit - with Lockon and Lubricant - without Magne-Traction; 244T-1 Tender; 3419-1 Operating Helicopter Car; 6544-1 Missile Firing Trail Car - Blue Car Body; 6844-1 Rocket Transport Car; 6017-1 Caboose - Brick Brown; 1013 Curved Track (8); 1018 Straight Track (3); 1008-50 Uncoupling Unit - with (1) 1018 Straight Track; 1015-25 45-Watt Transformer; 943 Exploding Ammo Dump; 81-32 Wires (2); 1627-2 Instruction Sheet; 310-2 Set of (5) Billboard Signs; AC Accessory Catalog

Comments: In 1960, the U.S. military's Service Exchanges purchased two promotional outfits: nos. X-517NA and X-518NA. Both were Retailer Promotional outfits headed by steam engines.

The X-518NA was led by a no. 244-1 Locomotive - with Smoke & Headlight. With all of its motive power and rolling stock boxed, this was the Service Exchanges' high-end Type Ia offering for 1960.

As with many military outfit purchases, the cars were space and military themed. The no. 3419-1 Operating Helicopter Car was in its second year of production that brought many changes. Specifically, the 1960 version included a small winder and a single-blade no. 3419-100 Operating Helicopter Complete. The no. 6544-1 Missile Firing Trail Car (new for 1960) contained two brake wheels attached to the plastic frame ends. Over time, the frame can easily be cracked or broken off where the wheels attach. All the cars in this outfit came with early operating AAR trucks and couplers and were packaged in Orange Perforated boxes.

The no. 943 Exploding Ammo Dump was a low-cost addition to outfits and provided a great target for the 6544-1. The 943 retailed separately for $1.95 in 1960.

The no. 59-339 Tan RSC with Black Graphics outfit box was a no. 9663 overstickered. It was manufactured by Star Corrugated Box Company, Inc. and measured 13¾ x 12 x 6 inches. It included a star on the bottom of the box.

The quantity of outfits ordered was originally 500 on April 20, 1960. This was increased to 750 on 6-23-60. Even with this increase, an X-518NA seldom appears on the market.

CONVENTIONAL PACK
59-339 BOX
STICKER

TOP LAYER					BOTTOM LAYER	
6544-1 F					244-1 F	
943-1 F	6017-1 F	3-1018	8-1013		3419-1 F	1015 25
244T-1 S					6844-1 F	
1008-50 TOP						

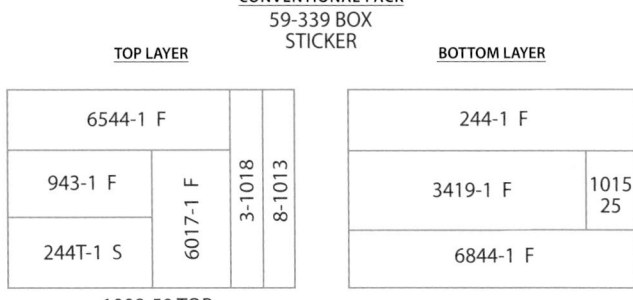

Outfit no. X-519NA was Automotive Chains' mid-level diesel offering for 1960. This space and military outfit provided plenty of play value with a no. 943 Exploding Ammo Dump and a no. 6470-1 Exploding Target Car awaiting their fate from the no. 6650-1 Missile Launching Flat Car.

Description: 1960 Outfit
Specification: "O27" Ga. Diesel Freight Outfit
Customer/Price: Advance Stores; $34.44
Customer: Automotive Chains
Cust./No./Price: Jack and Harry's Automotive; T1-512; $29.88
Customer/No./Price: Noah's Ark; 319 2818; $33.89
Original Amount: 3,000
Factory Order Date: 4/21/1960
Date Issued: 6-23-60
Packaging: Conventional Outfit Packing

Contents: 225P-1 Alco Diesel Power Car - Blue - "Chesapeake & Ohio" - Yellow Lettering with Headlight and Magne-Traction - with 2 Position Reversing Unit - with Lockon & Lubricant; 6650-1 Missile Launching Flat Car; 6470-1 Exploding Target Car; 6820-1 Flat Car - with Missile Transport Helicopter - Blue Car Body; 6830-1 Flat Car - with Non-Operating Submarine - Blue Car Body; 6017-1 Caboose - Brick Brown; 1013 Curved Track (17); 1018 Straight Track (9); 1008-50 Uncoupling Unit - with (1) 1018 Straight Track; 1015-25 45-Watt Transformer; 943 Exploding Ammo Dump; 110-1 Graduated Trestle Set; 81-32

Wires (2); 1613-10 Instruction Sheet; 310-2 Set of (5) Billboard Signs; AC Accessory Catalog; 1802I Layout Instruction Sheet

Boxes & Packing: 60-495 Box; 60-496 Shipper (1-3)

X-519NA (1960)	C6	C7	C8	Rarity
Complete Outfit	700	1,200	1,700	R5
Outfit Box no. 60-495	100	150	200	R5

Comments: In 1960, Lionel listed Automotive Chains as the customer for four outfits: nos. X-519NA, X-520NA, X-532NA and X-533NA. The X-519NA was Automotive Chains' mid-level diesel locomotive offering and included all catalog items, hence its Retailer Promotional Type Ia classification.

Linking a Lionel Automotive Chains customer to the eventual end customer is done by studying price tags, advertisements or other markings and listings. As for the X-519NA, it appeared on pages 28 and 29 of a 1960 Advance Stores catalog. It was listed as "Lionel Missile Train Outfit". The catalog went on to state that if the items in this outfit were purchased separately, the total value would be $67.30. However, Advance Stores' discount price was $34.44. This is just one example of how heavily discounted Lionel trains were during the early 1960s.

Of note, the description incorrectly states that the no. 6830 "Sub actually moves under water", while in fact it was a non-operating submarine. Somewhere along the way, either a no. 3830-1 Oper. Submarine Car was replaced or an incorrect description was printed.

Two other price tag observations link the X-519NA to Noah's Ark as no. 319 2818 for $33.89 and Jack and Harry's Automotive as no. T1-512 for $29.88. This outfit was likely sold to numerous other automotive stores, as the quantity increased from 1,000 on

April 21, 1960, to 3,000 on 6-23-60.

The X-519NA contained a no. 225P-1 Chesapeake & Ohio Alco Diesel Power Car (new for 1960). This locomotive included an open pilot and the large ledge that Lionel added to Alcos as reinforcement in 1960. (See the entry for outfit no. X-509NA for this diesel's difficult-to-obtain no. 225-20 Corrugated Box.)

Also new for 1960 were the nos. 6820-1 Flat Car - with Missile Transport Helicopter and 6830-1 Flat Car - with Non-Operating Submarine. Although the 6820-1 was offered for separate sale in 1960 and 1961, and served as a component of nine promotional outfits, its Orange Perforated no. 6820-11 Folding Box appears only infrequently in collectible condition. The no. 6820-40 Non-Operating Missile Helicopter Complete is also becoming hard to find with original, unbroken parts.

All the rolling stock in the X-519NA was equipped with early operating AAR trucks and couplers and came packaged in Orange Perforated boxes.

The no. 60-495 Tan RSC with Black Graphics outfit box was manufactured by St. Joe Paper Co. and measured 15¼ x 14¾ x 6⅞ inches. It had "60-495" and "8 9 10 11 12" printed on the bottom.

The X-519NA was a successful offering in that the quantities ordered kept increasing. Automotive Chains were a large customer of Lionel's promotional outfits.

CONVENTIONAL PACK
60-495 BOX

TOP LAYER		
6830-1 F		
9-1018	1008-50	6017-1 F
17-1013		
6470-1 S		
6820-1 S		

BOTTOM LAYER		
110-1 F		
6650-1 F	1015 25	943-1 S
225P-1 F		

Description: 1960 Outfit
Specification: "O27" Ga. Diesel Freight Outfit
Customer: Automotive Chains
Original Amount: 250
Factory Order Date: 6/24/1960
Date Issued: October 12, 1960
Packaging: Conventional Outfit Packing

Contents: 45-50 Mobile Rocket Firing Car - Khaki Color - with "U.S. Marine" Markings - with Lockon and Lubricant; 3419-1 Operating Helicopter Car; 3830-1 Flat Car - with Operating Submarine; 6650-1 Missile Launching Flat Car; 6470-1 Exploding Target Car; 6017-1 Caboose - Brick Brown; 1013 Curved Track (8); 1018 Straight Track (5); 6019-1 Remote Control Track Set; 1043-50 60-Watt Transformer; 443 IRBM Missile Launching Platform - with Exploding Ammo Dump; 81-32 Wires (2); 926-60 Instruction Book; 310-2 Set of (5) Billboard Signs; AC Accessory Catalog

Boxes & Packing: 59-361 Box; 59-362 Shipper (1-3); ST Sticker

Alternate For Outfit Contents:
Note: Substitute 150 - 1053-50 for 1043-50; 130 Sets with 6029-25 - 90-30 and 44-45 Envelope in 45-50 Locomotive; Balance - as per revised specifications with 44-55 Envelope in Locomotive.

X-520NA (1960)	C6	C7	C8	Rarity
Complete Outfit	825	1,375	2,100	R10
Outfit Box no. 59-361	300	525	800	R10

Comments: In 1960, Lionel listed Automotive Chains as the customer for four outfits: nos. X-519NA, X-520NA, X-532NA and X-533NA. The X-520NA was Automotive Chains' high-end diesel locomotive offering. It included all catalog items, hence its Retailer Promotional Type Ia classification.

Linking a Lionel Automotive Chains customer to the eventual end customer is done by studying price tags, advertisements or other markings and listings. Unfortunately, the X-520NA has yet to be linked to a specific end customer.

This space and military outfit was headed by a no. 45-50 Mobile Rocket Firing Car - Khaki Color. The "-50" suffix indicated that it came with a no. 44-55 Envelope Packed, whereas a no. 45-1 came with a no. 44-45 Envelope Packed.

Since a no. 6019-1 Remote Control Track Set was included, the additional peripherals required to operate the Mobile Missile

Outfit no. X-520NA is shown as listed on the Factory Order without any substitutions. Only 250 were manufactured, making it an R10 based on original quantity alone. When you add in the fact that it was a space and military outfit with four operating cars, the demand and value increase as well.

Firing Car included in a no. 44-45 Envelope Packed were not needed, hence the creation of a no. 45-50 with a no. 44-55 Envelope. Once a no. 6029-25 Uncoupling Track, which couldn't operate a 45-50, was substituted for the 6019-1, a 44-45 was required to operate the Mobile Rocket Firing Car.

The rolling stock in the X-520NA consisted of space and military operating cars, all of which were equipped with early operating AAR trucks and couplers.

The X-520NA provided plenty of play value, thanks to its four operating cars and a no. 443 IRBM Missile Launching Platform - with Exploding Ammo Dump. The only other time the nos. 3419-1, 3830-1, 6470-1 and 6650-1 were included together was in outfit no. X-579NA. All of these cars and the caboose were packed in Orange Perforated boxes.

The no. 3419-1 Operating Helicopter car was a carryover from 1959, but it appeared in this outfit with 1960 features (small winder and single-blade no. 3419-100 Operating Helicopter Complete). The no. 6470-1 Exploding Target Car included "slotted" sides and a smooth roof door guide (without the nubs added later to help hold on the sides).

The no. 59-361 Tan RSC with Black Graphics outfit box was an overstickered no. X-831NA from 1959. Manufactured by Continental Can Company, Inc., it measured 15½ x 14¾ x 7⅜ inches and had "59" and five dots printed on the bottom.

Although the substitution of the no. 1053-50 and the no. 6029-25 with a no. 90-30 affect the price of the X-520NA, the difference is negligible based on the overall value of the outfit.

Of the four 1960 Automotive Chains outfits, this is by far the most collectible.

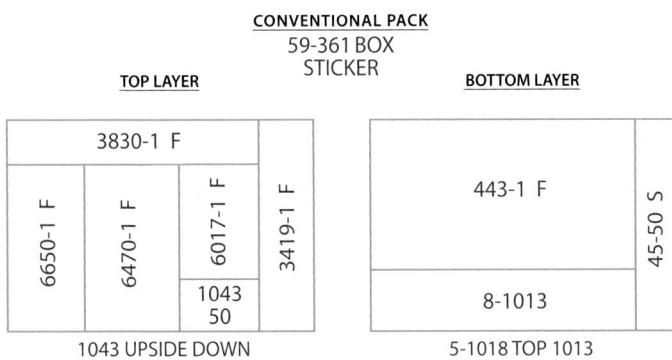

CONVENTIONAL PACK
59-361 BOX
STICKER

TOP LAYER				BOTTOM LAYER	
3830-1 F				443-1 F	
6650-1 F	6470-1 F	6017-1 F	3419-1 F		45-50 S
		1043 50		8-1013	

1043 UPSIDE DOWN   5-1018 TOP 1013
6019-1 TOP 3830

This no. X-521NA came with the rare no. 1103-14 Envelope Packed, which included Form 2085, a no. 80-1 Controller and three no. 81-32 Wires. The version with a no. 59-339 Box includes a Gimbels price tag with "740 F0, 19.99".

Description: 1960 Outfit
Specification: "O27" Ga. Steam Type Freight Outfit
Customer/No./Price: Gimbels; 740 F0; $19.99
Original Amount: 2,650
Factory Order Date: 4/21/1960
Date Issued: 12-1-60
Packaging: Conventional Outfit Packing

Contents: 246-1 Locomotive - with Headlight and Magne-Traction - with Lockon & Lubricant; 1130T-1 Tender; 6062-1 Gondola Car - Black - with (3) Cable Reels; 6825-1 Flat Car - Red - with Trestle Bridge - Black; 6821-1 Flat Car - with Cargo; 6014-100 Box Car - Red; 6017-1 Caboose - Brick Brown; 1013 Curved Track (16); 1018 Straight Track (3); 1008-50 Uncoupling Unit - with (1) 1018 Straight Track; 1015-60 45-Watt Transformer; 1023-1 45° Crossover; 81-32 Wires (2); 1609-4 Instruction Sheet; 310-2 Set of (5) Billboard Signs; AC Accessory Catalog; 1802H Layout Instruction Sheet

Boxes & Packing: 59-339 Box; 59-340 Shipper (1-3); ST Sticker; 60-595 Box; 60-596 Shipper (1-4); 60-389 Box; 60-392 Shipper (1-4); ST Sticker

Alternate For Outfit Contents:
Note: If necessary - Substitute 1- 1015-25, 1- 1103-14 For 1 - 1015-60, 2 - 81-32.

X-521NA (1960)	C6	C7	C8	Rarity
Complete Outfit With no. 59-339 Box	325	575	875	R8
Outfit Box no. 59-339	150	250	350	R8
Complete Outfit With no. 60-595 Box	275	525	800	R7
Outfit Box no. 60-595	100	200	275	R7
Complete Outfit With no. 60-389 Box And A no. 6821-1	355	625	925	R8
Complete Outfit With no. 60-389 Box And A no. 6844-1	360	665	980	R8
Outfit Box no. 60-389	200	300	400	R8
Any Outfit With A no. 1103-14 Substitution, Add The Following	100	200	450	R9

Comments: In 1960, Gimbels department stores purchased two Retailer Promotional outfits: nos. X-521NA and X-522NA. The no. X-521NA was a Type Ia (or a Type Ib with the no. 1103-14 substitution) steam locomotive outfit. Several examples of the X-521NA have been observed with a price tag printed, "Gimbels, 740 F0, 19.99".

The X-521NA was a basic starter outfit headed by the common no. 246-1 Locomotive - with Headlight and Magne-Traction. This outfit included the later version with a solid pilot and without generator detail on the body.

All the rolling stock in the X-521NA came with early operating AAR trucks and couplers and was packaged in Orange Perforated boxes. The no. 6821-1 Flat Car - with Cargo appeared in only six outfits, with more than 22,000 of them used. It appears that Lionel did not have enough to fill its entire order of X-521NA because the Outfit Packing Sheet shows a no. 6844-1 Rocket Transport Car being substituted in the last 650 of these outfits.

Also included in this outfit was a no. 6014-100 Box Car - Red. This was an Airex car that appeared in at least 12 promotional outfits in 1960.

The track layout was a pretzel layout, as detailed on the no. 1802H Layout Instruction Sheet.

By far the toughest item in this outfit is the "substitute if necessary" no. 1103-14 Envelope Packed. (See the entry for outfit no. X-502NA for complete information about this rare packed envelope.) Since this was a substitution, pricing is provided separately for it.

The X-521NA is also interesting in that the original quantity on the Factory Order was 1,000, but decreased to 750 on 6-23-60. On 9-21-60, this increased to 2,000 and finally 2,650 on 12-1-60. Gimbels likely placed follow-up orders based on customer demand.

These changes demonstrate the challenges faced by the Outfit Packing Department, which ended up using three different boxes for this outfit. Originally, the X-521NA used a no. 59-339 Tan RSC with Black Graphics outfit box manufactured by Star Corrugated Box Company, Inc. that measured 13¾ x 12 x 6 inches. It had a star printed on the box bottom.

The increase on 9-21-60 was enough to require the creation of a new box for the X-521NA. However, a no. 60-595 has yet to be observed. Finally on 12-1-60, the last of the outfits were packaged in a no. 60-389 Tan RSC with Black Graphics outfit box manufactured by Owens-Illinois Paper Products, Div. and measuring 12 x 11½ x 6½ inches. It included 12 dots as part of the box manufacturer's certificate.

These changes evidently affected the items included in the outfit. It appears that the 6821-1 was swapped out for a 6844-1 for the last outfits. This change did not appear on the Factory Order, but did appear on the Outfit Packing Sheet.

Without an 1103-14 Envelope Packed, this outfit is just one of the many starter outfits of the era. When included, its rarity jumps to R9.

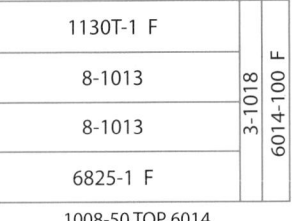

CONVENTIONAL PACK
59-339 BOX STICKER

TOP LAYER

3-1018	
6017-1 F	8-1013
8-1013	
6821-1 F	

1008-50 TOP 3-1018
1023 TOP

BOTTOM LAYER

6062-1 S	1015 60
1130T-1 F	6014-100 S
6825-1 F	
246-1 F	

60-595 BOX
1250 REVISED 9-14-60

TOP LAYER

1130T-1 F	
8-1013	3-1018 / 6014-100 F
8-1013	
6825-1 F	

1008-50 TOP 6014

BOTTOM LAYER

246-1 F	1015 60
6062-1 F	6017-1 F
6821-1 F	

1023-1 TOP 6017-6062-6821

60-389 BOX
600 REVISED 12-1-60 STICKER

TOP LAYER

	16-1013	
1015 60	1130T-1 S	1008-50
	6014-100 S	
	3-1018	
	6825-1 F	

1023-1 TOP

BOTTOM LAYER

6844-1 F	
6062-1 F	6017-1 F
246-1 F	

Description: 1960 Outfit
Specification: Super "O" Ga. Diesel Freight Outfit with Horn
Customer: Gimbels
Original Amount: 240
Factory Order Date: 4/22/1960
Date Issued: 11-17-60
Packaging: Conventional Outfit Packing

Contents: 218P-1 Alco Diesel Power Unit - "Santa Fe" - with Horn, Headlight, Magne-Traction, Non-Operating Coupler, Lockon and Lubricant; 218T-1 Alco Diesel Motorless Unit - "Santa Fe" - with Non-Operating Couplers - without Headlight; 6424-1 Flat Car - with 2 Autos; 3512-1 Operating Fireman and Ladder Car; 6470-1 Exploding Target Car; 3419-1 Operating Helicopter Car; 3330-1 Flat Car - with Operating Submarine Kit; 6017-1 Caboose - Brick Brown; 31 Curved Track (24); 32 Straight Track (13); 39-25 Remote Control Set; 31-25 Envelope of 40 - 31-7; 48 Insulated Straight Track; 1063-25 Transformer; 443 IRBM Missile Launching Platform - with Exploding Ammo Dump; 110 Graduated Trestle Set; 81-32 Wires (2); 926-60 Instruction Book; 310-2 Set of (5) Billboard Signs; AC Accessory Catalog; 2095 Layout Instruction Sheet

Boxes & Packing: 59-355 Box; 59-356 Shipper (1-2); ST Sticker

X-522NA (1960)	C6	C7	C8	Rarity
Complete Outfit	1,175	1,900	2,700	R10
Outfit Box no. 59-355	450	600	750	R10

Comments: In 1960, Gimbels department stores purchased two Retailer Promotional outfits: nos. X-521NA and X-522NA. The X-522NA was a Type Ia Super O diesel freight outfit. Of the six Super O promotional outfits in 1960, this was the only one that wasn't intended for Sears or bulk packed.

The X-522NA was a space and military outfit headed by the premier no. 218P-1 Santa Fe Alco Diesel Power Unit equipped with a three-position reversing unit, a headlight, two-axle Magne-Traction and an open pilot with a large ledge.

Notable to collectors was the no. 3330-1 Flat Car - with Operating Submarine Kit. Finding one in C8 condition with an unassembled no. 3330-200 Submarine Kit with its parts still sealed in their plastic bag and a matching C8 Orange Perforated box is becoming difficult.

The no. 6424-1 Flat Car - with 2 Autos (introduced in 1957) was being depleted in this outfit. (See outfit no. X-512NA for a detailed description of this car and its progression.)

All the cars in the X-522NA included early operating AAR

SPECIAL TRACK LAYOUT INSTRUCTIONS

This special train outfit includes a No. 110 Trestle Set and enough track to form the layout as illustrated. The letters (A, B, C, etc.) indicate positions of elevating piers.

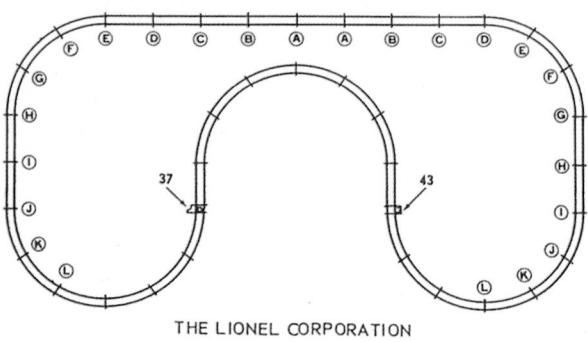

THE LIONEL CORPORATION

Printed in U.S. of America   2095   6-60

CONVENTIONAL PACK
59-355 BOX
STICKER

TOP LAYER

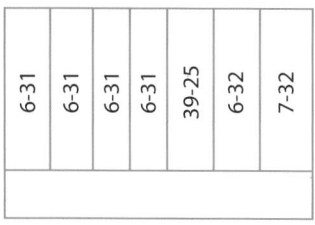

6-31	6-31	6-31	6-31	39-25	6-32	7-32

48-1 TOP 31

MIDDLE LAYER

6470-1 F		6017-1 S	
3330-1 F		1063 25	3512-1 S
6424-1 F			
110-1 S			

BOTTOM LAYER

218P-1 S		
443-1	3419-1 S	218T-1 S

Super O promotional outfit no. X-522NA and catalog outfit no. 2551W were the only outfits to include a no. 2095 Track Layout Instruction Sheet. The Production Control File for this sheet states that 1,500 were to be printed. This small quantity, combined with low survivability, makes this instruction sheet extremely difficult to find.

trucks and couplers. Except for the 6424-1, all cars came packaged in Orange Perforated boxes.

As with many Super O outfits, the peripherals in the X-522NA are the most difficult items to find. The no. 31-25 Envelope of 40 - 31-7 is rare. It was used only in this and catalog outfit no. 2551W from 1960. Also shared with the 2551W was the track plan, as outlined on the extremely difficult-to-find no. 2095 Layout Instruction Sheet.

A Type I or Type II no. 39-25 Remote Control Set provided the remainder of the peripherals necessary to assemble and operate an X-522NA. (See the section on Outfit Peripherals for information about Super O peripherals.)

Catalog Super O outfits generally did not include a transformer.

However, because promotional outfits were most often destined for retailers that probably did not have a train department, Lionel included a no. 1063-25 75-Watt Transformer with the X-522NA outfits.

The no. 443 IRBM Missile Launching Platform - with Exploding Ammo Dump topped off this outfit. It appeared only in four promotional outfits and necessitated a large outfit box.

The no. 59-355 Tan RSC with Black Graphics outfit box was manufactured by Star Corrugated Box Company, Inc. and measured 17⅜ x 14½ x 10¼ inches. It was an overstickered Sears no. 9682.

With a little more than 20 different Super O promotional outfits produced in the 1960s and the fact that only 240 of the X-522NA were made, these outfits are in extreme demand. Collectors should not pass up an opportunity to add an X-522NA – if one ever comes on the market.

X-523NA
1960

X-523NA (1960)	C6	C7	C8	Rarity
Complete Outfit	410	665	940	R9
Outfit Box no. 59-324	250	400	500	R9

Description: 1960 Outfit
Specification: "O27" Ga. Steam Type Freight Outfit
Customer/No./Price: Spiegel; R36 J 5219; $19.87
Original Amount: 500
Factory Order Date: 8/2/1960
Date Issued: August 2, 1960
Packaging: Conventional Outfit Packing

Contents: 246-1 Locomotive - with Headlight and Magne-Traction - with Lockon & Lubricant; 1130T-1 Tender; 6650-1 Missile Launching Flat Car; 6470-1 Exploding Target Car; 6017-1 Caboose - Brick Brown; 1013 Curved Track (8); 1018 Straight Track (3); 1008-50 Uncoupling Unit - with (1) 1018 Straight Track; 1015-60 45-Watt Transformer; 81-32 Wires (2); 310-2 Set of (5) Billboard Signs; 1609-4 Instruction Sheet; AC Accessory Catalog

Boxes & Packing: 59-324 Box; 59-325 Shipper (1-4); ST Sticker

Comments: Spiegel purchased this Retailer Promotional Type Ia outfit in 1960. Outfit no. X-523NA was shown on page 374 of its 1960 Christmas Catalog as Spiegel no. R36 J 5219 for $19.87. This item appears to be the first Lionel outfit offered by Spiegel, as other catalogs and records make no mention of Lionel.

Spiegel advertised the X-523NA as "Big Christmas Savings - outfit would cost you $41.75 if bought separately elsewhere." This advertising practice demonstrates how heavily discounted Lionel trains were during the early 1960s.

The X-523NA was a basic starter outfit with space and military items. It was headed by a no. 246-1 Steam Locomotive, which included a two-position reversing unit, a headlight and Magne-Traction. This engine, first released in 1959, was still being used in outfits as late as 1962.

Lionel often paired the nos. 6650-1 Missile Launching Flat Car and 6470-1 Exploding Target Car in outfits. They, like the other cars in this outfit, were equipped with early operating AAR trucks and couplers and came packaged in Orange Perforated boxes.

all aboard for Funsville

See page 376 for additional .027 ga. track and accessories

Boxcar "explodes" when hit by fired missile

FAMOUS LIONEL ACTION-PACKED ELECTRIC TRAIN
- Magne-Traction, missile firing car
- Save to $21.88 on 5-unit layout! **19.87**

Big Christmas Savings—outfit would cost you $41.75 if bought separately elsewhere. World famous Lionel quality and construction—top performance, authentic detail; real railroading action. The Iron Horse with Space Age action—a thrilling new combination for loads of fun. Steam-type electric locomotive with Magne-Traction, headlight, 2-4-2 drive; tender. IRBM missile firing car "exploding" target box car and caboose. Hi-impact plastic with 4 wheel trucks. Cars couple, uncouple automatically. 45-Watt UL appr. transformer; .027-gauge track (8 curved, 3 straight, 1 uncoupler). Lubricant, wires, CTC lock-on, instr. included. R36 J 5219. 46-in. long train. Mailable. (9 lbs.)...........19.87

The Spiegel Christmas Catalog for 1960 shows outfit no. X-523NA (Spiegel no. R36 J 5219) for $19.87. The advertising copy mentions the $41.75 price if all items were purchased separately. This was a common advertising practice for Lionel promotional outfits.

CONVENTIONAL PACK
59-324 BOX
STICKER

6650-1 F		6017-1 S	8-1013
6470-1 S			
246-1 S			
1130T-1 S	1015 60		

1008-50 TOP 6650
3-1018 TOP 1008

The no. 59-324 was a single-layer Tan RSC with Black Graphics outfit box. It was first used with catalog outfit no. 1609 in 1959 and subsequently with this and six other outfits. It was manufactured by Express Container Corp. and measured 14⅞ x 12⅝ x 4¼ inches.

The X-523NA was likely Spiegel's first Lionel offering; as such, it is a required outfit for any Spiegel collector. With only 500 made, it does not often appear on the market, hence its R9 rarity.

Description: 1960 Outfit
Specification: "O27" Ga. Steam Type Freight Outfit with Smoke
Customer: G. C. Murphy
Original Amount: 575
Factory Order Date: 8/3/1960
Date Issued: August 3, 1960
Packaging: Colored Corrugated Partitions in Display Box

Contents: 2018-1 Locomotive - with Smoke, Lockon & Lubricant - without Magne-Traction; 1130T-1 Tender; 3419-25 Operating Helicopter Car; 6544-25 Missile Firing Trail Car - Blue Car Body; 6175-25 Rocket Car; 6017-25 Caboose - Brick Brown; 1013 Curved Track (8); 1018 Straight Track (3); 1008-50 Uncoupling Unit - with (1) 1018 Straight Track; 1015-25 45-Watt Transformer; 81-32 Wires (2); IS Instruction Sheet; 310-2 Set of (5) Billboard Signs; AC Accessory Catalog

Boxes & Packing: 60-567 Box; 60-568 Insert; 60-569 Insert; 60-166 Insert (2); 60-167 Insert; 60-168 Insert; 60-170 Insert; 60-171 Insert; 60-570 Shipper (1-4)

X-524NA (1960)	C6	C7	C8	Rarity
Complete Outfit	525	800	1,200	R9
Outfit Box no. 60-567	225	350	465	R9

Comments: Retailer G. C. Murphy purchased this Retailer Promotional Type Ia outfit in 1960. Six years passed before the firm purchased its next Retailer Promotional outfit, the no. 19586 in 1966.

The no. X-524NA was a mid-level, space and military outfit headed by a no. 2018-1 Locomotive - with Smoke. This engine last appeared in a catalog outfit in 1959, but was still being used in promotional outfits in the 1960s. This was the only time in the 1960s that Lionel included the 2018 in a display-packed outfit. Interestingly, this locomotive was individually boxed, as was the no. 1130T-1 Tender.

The remainder of the rolling stock was unboxed, which was not the norm for these cars. The nos. 3419-25 Operating Helicopter Car and 6175-25 Rocket Car each appeared unboxed in only four

outfits, and the no. 6544-25 Missile Firing Trail Car was included unboxed in just five. Leaving the 6544-25 unboxed exposed its fragile brake wheels to possible damage. All of these cars are fairly common, but it may take some patience to find an original, unbroken no. 3419-100 Operating Helicopter Complete and 6544-25.

All the rolling stock was equipped with early operating AAR trucks and couplers.

The no. 60-567 Box was unique to this outfit. An example has yet to be observed, but it likely was an Orange, White and Gray O27 Hinged Display with 4-6-2 Steam Display Graphics outfit box. Based on the size of the inserts, the box was the same size as the no. 60-165 Display Outfit Box used for catalog outfit no. 1633 and promotional outfit no. X-620. That box measured 25 x 17⅛ x 3¼ inches.

In addition, this outfit box included a no. 60-171 Insert with New York Central System and Union Pacific logos. This easily lost insert came in four other outfits. Finding one to complete an outfit takes patience and will be expensive.

An X-524NA has yet to be observed in any catalog or advertisement. It is difficult to find and has an R9 rarity.

DISPLAY PACK
60-567 BOX

2018-1	1130T-1
3419-25	6175-25 3-1018
8-1013	6017-25
6544-25	1015 25

1008-50 BELOW 3419

Outfit no. X-526NA included a no. 3386-1 Operating Giraffe Car in its rare no. 3386-10 Folding Box. Lionel sold this outfit to Mutual Buying Syndicate, which offered it to the company's members.

Description: 1960 Outfit
Specification: "O27" Ga. Steam Type Freight Outfit
Customer: Mutual Buying
Original Amount: 2,600
Factory Order Date: 4/22/1960
Date Issued: 11-17-60
Packaging: Conventional Outfit Packing

Contents: 246-1 Locomotive - with Headlight and Magne-Traction - with Lockon and Lubricant; 1130T-1 Tender; 3386-1 Operating Giraffe Car; 6062-1 Gondola Car - Black - with (3) Cable Reels; 6014-1 Box Car - Red; 6017-1 Caboose - Brick Brown; 1013 Curved Track (12); 1018 Straight Track (3); 1008-50 Uncoupling Unit - with (1) 1018 Straight Track; 1015-60 45-Watt Transformer; 1020-1 90° Crossover; 81-32 Wires (2); 310-2 Set of (5) Billboard Signs; 1609-4 Instruction Sheet; 1802B Layout Instruction Sheet; AC Accessory Catalog

Boxes & Packing: 60-497 Box; 60-498 Shipper (1-4); 60-389 Box; 60-392 Shipper (1-4); ST Sticker

Alternate For Outfit Contents:
Note: If necessary - Substitute 1- 1015-25, 1- 1103-14 For 1 - 1015-60, 2 - 81-32; 6821 for 6014 (300).

X-526NA (1960)	C6	C7	C8	Rarity
Complete Outfit With no. 60-497 Box	260	450	750	R8
Outfit Box no. 60-497	100	175	250	R5
Complete Outfit With no. 60-389 Box	385	625	950	R8
Outfit Box no. 60-389	225	350	450	R8
Either Outfit With A no. 1103-14 Substitution, Add The Following	100	200	450	R9

Comments: The no. X-526NA was the first of two (along with the no. X-527NA) outfits sold to the Mutual Buying Syndicate buying cooperative. These outfits were distributed among Mutual Buying's member stores, although neither outfit can be tied to a specific customer. The Retailer Promotional Type Ib X-526NA was Mutual's steam-powered offering, and the X-527NA was its diesel-powered outfit.

The 246-1 Locomotive with - with Headlight and Magne-Traction also included a two-position reversing unit. This outfit included the later version with a solid pilot and without generator detail on the body.

Lionel included a boxed no. 3386-1 Operating Giraffe Car (with non-operating Archbar trucks and couplers) in this and two other promotional outfits. Its rare Orange Perforated 3386-10 Folding Box appeared only in promotional outfits and is the reason that this outfit is designated a Type Ib. When available for separate sale, the no. 3386-1 was boxed in an overstamped no. 3376-120 Folding Box, which, as explained in the *Authoritative Guide to*

Lionel's Postwar Operating Cars (Project Roar Publishing), is even more difficult to find than a 3386-10.

The no. 6014-1 Box Car - Red (likely a red Bosco car) listed on the Factory Order for this outfit actually came as a no. 6014-100 Airex Box Car - Red. Be aware that 1960 was a transition year for the 6014, with the 6014-1 replaced by the 6014-100. The 6014-1 appears on early Factory Orders (through April), and the 6014-100 starts to show up in March. The original date of the Factory Order for the X-526NA was April, with revisions continuing through November. Later in the year, the "-100" was the norm. To Lionel and the customer, the 6014-1 and the 6014-100 were basically the same car.

The 6014-100 and all the remaining rolling stock (except for the 3386-1) were equipped with early operating AAR trucks and couplers. Lionel packaged these cars in Orange Perforated boxes.

The no. 1802B Layout Instruction Sheet detailed the figure-eight track layout.

Orders for the X-526NA exceeded original forecasts. The quantity increased from 1,500 on 4/22/60 to 2,000 on 6/23/60 and then 2,300 on 10/24/60 and finally up to 2,600 on 11/17/60.

These changes led to two different outfit boxes. The early version (first 2,000) included the no. 60-497 Tan RSC with Black Graphics outfit box. It was manufactured by St. Joe Paper Co. - Container Div. and measured 11¾ x 11⅝ x 7 inches. Printed as part of the box manufacturer's certificate was "6 7 8 9 10 11 12". Also, on the box bottom was the "60-497" part number.

The remaining 600 outfits were packed in a no. 60-389 Tan RSC with Black Graphics outfit box. It was manufactured by Owens-Illinois Paper Products, Div. and measured 12 x 11½ x 6½ inches. The box was an overstickered no. 1631WS outfit box from 1960.

Two substitutions are possible with the X-526NA. The first was a no. 6821 for a no. 6014. This change affects the price only

minimally, not enough to justify a separate listing. However, the inclusion of a no. 1103-14 Envelope Packed does change the value and rarity, as listed in the pricing table. (See outfit no. X-502NA for more information about this packed envelope and its contents.)

Also note that the 60-497 Box achieves an R5 rarity rating, but when its contents are added, specifically the 3386-1 Operating Giraffe Car in its 3386-10 Folding Box, the rarity jumps to R8.

The X-526NA outfit does appear on the market. Nonetheless, finding a 3386-10 Folding Box or an 1103-14 Envelope Packed complete in collectible condition is extremely difficult.

CONVENTIONAL PACK
60-497 BOX

TOP LAYER		BOTTOM LAYER	
12-1013		246-1 F	
3-1018		1130T-1 S	1015
6017-1 F		6014-1 S	60
6062-1 F		3386-1 S	

1008-50 TOP 1013
1020-1 TOP 6062 - 6017

60-389
300 REV. 10-28-60
STICKER

TOP LAYER	BOTTOM LAYER
6062-1 F	246-1 F / 3386-1 F / 1130T-1 S / 6014-1 S
6017-1 F	
3-1018	
12-1013	1015-60

1020-1 TOP 6017 - 6062
1008-50 TOP 1018 - 1013

Description: 1960 Outfit
Specification: "O27" Ga. Diesel Freight Outfit
Customer: Mutual Buying
Original Amount: 850
Factory Order Date: 4/22/1960
Date Issued: April 22, 1960
Packaging: Conventional Outfit Packing

X-527NA (1960)	C6	C7	C8	Rarity
Complete Outfit With no. 6803-1	615	1,025	1,475	R7
Complete Outfit With no. 6807-1	580	915	1,275	R7
Outfit Box no. 60-488	150	275	350	R7

Contents: 224P-1 Alco Diesel Power Car - "U.S. Navy" - Navy Color and Markings - with Headlight, Magne-Traction - with Non-Operating Coupler - Lockon and Lubricant; 6650-1 Missile Launching Flat Car; 6470-1 Exploding Target Car; 6803-1 Flat Car - Red - with (1) 6151-22 Single Gun Tank & (1) 6151-17 Mobile Listening Post; 6017-1 Caboose - Brick Brown; 1013 Curved Track (16); 1018 Straight Track (3); 1008-50 Uncoupling Unit - with (1) 1018 Straight Track; 1015-25 45-Watt Transformer; 943-1 Exploding Ammo Dump; 1023-1 45° Crossover; 81-32 Wires (2); 310-2 Set of (5) Billboard Signs; 1569-11 Instruction Sheet; AC Accessory Catalog; 1802H Layout Instruction Sheet

Boxes & Packing: 60-488 Box; 60-489 Shipper (1-3)

Alternate For Outfit Contents:
Note: Substitute 130 - 6807-1 for 6803-1.

Comments: The no. X-527NA was the second of two (along with the no. X-526NA) outfits sold to the Mutual Buying Syndicate buying cooperative. These outfits were distributed among Mutual Buying's member stores, although neither outfit can be tied to a specific customer. The Retailer Promotional Type Ia X-527NA was Mutual's diesel-powered offering, and the X-526NA was its steam-powered outfit.

The X-527NA, a space and military outfit, was headed by a no. 224P-1 U.S. Navy Alco Diesel. This locomotive featured Magne-Traction and a three-position reversing unit.

The nos. 6650-1 Missile Launching Flat Car and 6470-1 Exploding Target Car were commonly paired. Both cars, as well as the no. 6017-1 Caboose, came packaged in Orange Perforated boxes.

The X-527NA was the last outfit to include a no. 6803-1 Flat Car - Red - with Single Gun Tank & Mobile Listening Post. In fact, Lionel likely depleted its inventory before filling the entire order, as a no. 6807-1 Flat Car - Red - with DKW Truck was substituted for 130 units. This substitution affects the price as listed in the pricing table. Each of these cars came in a Classic-style box.

All the rolling stock in this outfit was equipped with early operating AAR trucks and couplers.

The no. 943-1 Exploding Ammo Dump was an inexpensive way for Lionel to provide an additional target for the 6650-1. The track layout was a pretzel layout, as detailed on the no. 1802H Layout Instruction Sheet.

The no. 60-488 Tan RSC with Black Graphics outfit box was unique to this outfit and measured 16 x 12 x 6 inches.

This outfit does not appear too often on the market; in fact, the empty box is most often found. When combined with its contents, the X-527NA makes an attractive space and military offering.

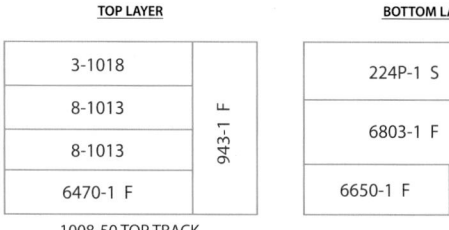

CONVENTIONAL PACK
60-488 BOX

TOP LAYER		BOTTOM LAYER	
3-1018		224P-1 S	
8-1013	943-1 F	6803-1 F	6017-1 S
8-1013			
6470-1 F		6650-1 F / 1015 25	

1008-50 TOP TRACK
1023-1 TOP

X-528NA
1960

Description: 1960 Outfit
Specification: "O27" Ga. Steam Type Freight Outfit with Smoke
Customer: Halle Brothers
Original Amount: 500
Factory Order Date: 4/25/1960
Date Issued: September 23, 1960
Packaging: Conventional Outfit Packing

Contents: 244-1 Locomotive - with Smoke and Headlight with 2 Position Reversing Unit - with Lockon & Lubricant - without Magne-Traction; 244T-1 Tender; 3419-1 Operating Helicopter Car; 6844-1 Rocket Transport Car; 6470-1 Exploding Target Car; 6544-1 Missile Firing Trail Car - Blue Car Body; 6017-1 Caboose - Brick Brown; 1013 Curved Track (12); 1018 Straight Track (3); 6029-25 Uncoupling Track Section; 1015-25 45-Watt Transformer; 1020-1 90° Crossover; 943-1 Exploding Ammo Dump; 90-1 Uncoupling Track Controller; 81-32 Wires (4); 90-30 Envelope Packed With 90-1 and 81-32; IS Instruction Sheet; 1802B Layout Instruction Sheet; 310-2 Set of (5) Billboard Signs; AC Accessory Catalog

Boxes & Packing: 59-335 Box; 59-336 Shipper (1-2); 59-100 Box; 59-101 Shipper (1-4); ST Sticker; BP Bogus Paper

Alternate For Outfit Contents:
Note: Substitute 6812-1 for 6844-1 in 200 sets.

X-528NA (1960)	C6	C7	C8	Rarity
Complete Outfit With no. 59-335 Box	600	1,100	1,675	R9
Complete Outfit With no. 59-335 Box And no. 6812-1 Substitution	685	1,185	1,760	R9
Outfit Box no. 59-335	200	425	625	R9
Complete Outfit With no. 59-100 Box	725	1,225	1,800	R10
Complete Outfit With no. 59-100 Box And no. 6812-1 Substitution	810	1,310	1,885	R10
Outfit Box no. 59-100	325	550	750	R10

Comments: Halle Brothers department stores purchased this Retailer Promotional Type Ia steam outfit in 1960. It was led by a no. 244-1 Locomotive equipped with smoke, a headlight, a two-position reversing unit and ballast weights. This new-for-1960 engine pulled a no. 244T-1 Tender that came in a difficult-to-find no. 1625T overstamped Bold Classic no. 1625-51 Folding Box.

The nos. 3419-1 Operating Helicopter Car, 6470-1 Exploding Target Car, 6844-1 Rocket Transport Car and 6544-1 Missile Firing Trail Car were an exciting combination of space and military rolling stock. Hours could be spent blowing up the no. 6470-1 Exploding Target Car as well as the no. 943-1 Exploding Ammo Dump. The no. 6470-1 included "slotted" sides and a smooth roof door guide (without the nubs added later to help hold on the sides). The no. 3419-100 Operating Helicopter Complete included the fuselage with the hole in the bottom.

The 3419-1, 6470-1 and 6844-1 made their debut in 1959, while the 6544-1 was new for 1960. All of them were equipped with early operating AAR trucks and couplers. The caboose and tender were equipped with one early operating AAR and one plain AAR truck and coupler.

Besides the 244T-1, all the rolling stock in this outfit came in Orange Perforated boxes with their appropriate instruction sheets inside. The no. 1802B Layout Instruction Sheet detailed the figure-eight track layout.

Two outfit boxes were used for the X-528NA. The no. 59-335 Tan RSC with Black Graphics outfit box was an overstickered no. 9681 that Lionel used for 300 outfits. This outfit box was manufactured by Star Corrugated Box Company, Inc. and measured 13¾ x 12½ x 7¼ inches. The no. 59-100 Yellow RSC with Black Graphics outfit box was an overstickered no. 1626W from 1959 that Lionel used for 200 outfits. This outfit box was manufactured by Star Corrugated Box Company, Inc. and measured 14⅛ x 13⅛ x 7 inches. Bogus Paper was used to fill any empty area in the box.

A no. 6812-1 Track Maintenance Car substitution affects pricing, as listed in the pricing table.

Low individual outfit quantities (200 and 300) and the infrequent appearance of an X-528NA in the market lead to the respective R10 and R9 rarities.

CONVENTIONAL PACK
(300) 59-335 BOX: STICKER
(200) 59-100 BOX: STICKER, BOGUS PAPER, REVISED 9-27-60

TOP LAYER		BOTTOM LAYER	
6470-1 S		244-1 F	
6029 / 3-1018			943-1 E
12-1013	244T-1 S	3419-1 F	
6017-1 S			
6544-1 S		6844-1 F	1015 25

1020-1 TOP 6017 - 6544

Frederick Atkins purchased outfit no. X-529NA in 1960. It was headed by a no. 220P-1 Santa Fe Alco Diesel Power Unit, which appeared in promotional outfits before becoming a catalog item.

Description: 1960 Outfit
Specification: "O27" Ga. Diesel Freight Outfit
Customer: Frederick Atkins
Original Amount: 1,200
Factory Order Date: 4/25/1960
Date Issued: August 30, 1960
Packaging: Conventional Outfit Packing

Contents: 220P-1 Alco Diesel Power Unit - "Santa Fe" - with Headlight, 2 Magnets, Non-Operating Coupler, Lockon & Lubricant; 220T-1 Motorless Unit - "Santa Fe"; 3376-1 Operating Giraffe Car; 6062-1 Gondola Car - Black - with (3) Cable Reels; 6825-1 Flat Car - Red - with Trestle Bridge - Black; 6476-1 Hopper Car - Red; 6017-1 Caboose - Brick Brown; 1013 Curved Track (12); 1018 Straight Track (13); 1008-50 Uncoupling Unit - with (1) 1018 Straight Track; 1015-25 45-Watt Transformer; 110 Graduated Trestle Set; 81-32 Wires (2); 310-2 Set of (5) Billboard Signs; 1569-11 Instruction Sheet; AC Accessory Catalog; 2099 Layout Instruction Sheet

Boxes & Packing: 60-534 Box; 60-535 Shipper (1-3)

X-529NA (1960)	C6	C7	C8	Rarity
Complete Outfit	445	800	1,200	R8
Outfit Box no. 60-534	75	175	275	R7

Comments: This Retailer Promotional Type Ia outfit was sold to Frederick Atkins (see the section on Lionel's Distribution and Customers).

The no. X-529NA was a mid-level freight outfit headed by a no. 220P-1 Santa Fe Alco Diesel Power Unit, which included two-axle Magne-Traction, a three-position reversing unit and a headlight. The only feature missing was a horn. The no. 220P-

1 is an example of an item that appeared in promotional outfits before it became a regular-production item (it appeared in the 1961 consumer catalog).

Except for the no. 3376-1 Operating Giraffe Car, all the items in this outfit were carryover from previous years. The 3376-1 was packed with a no. 3376-118 Envelope Packed as well as a no. 6809-12 Tube to protect its coupler. This car, like all the rolling stock in the X-529NA, included early operating AAR trucks and couplers and came in Orange Perforated boxes.

The track layout was detailed on the rare no. 2099 Layout Instruction Sheet. This sheet was included in only this and outfit nos. X-552NA and X-562NA. Its Production Control File list orders for 2,500. So small a quantity and the fragility of this sheet led to the R8 rarity for a complete outfit as opposed to the R7 for the box alone.

The no. 60-534 Tan RSC with Black Graphics outfit box was manufactured by Star Corrugated Box Company, Inc. and measured 16¼ x 14 x 7¼ inches. It included a star printed above the box manufacturer's certificate.

Curiously, empty boxes appear in the market, but complete outfits are seldom seen.

CONVENTIONAL PACK
60-534 BOX

TOP LAYER

6476-1 F	
6825-1 F	12-1013
13-1018	
3376-1 F	1015
6062-1 S	25

1008-50 TOP - 6476

BOTTOM LAYER

110-1 F	
220P-1 F	6017-1 S
220T-1 F	

The no. X-530NA was American Furniture's promotional outfit purchase for 1960. The no. 264-1 Operating Fork Lift Platform Set inside came with the later version of the no. 6264-25 Lumber Car Complete, which was equipped with early operating AAR trucks and couplers. A large no. 60-536 Box was necessary to fit the accessory and all the rolling stock.

Description: 1960 Outfit
Specification: "O27" Ga. Steam Type Freight Outfit
Customer: American Furniture
Original Amount: 1,400
Factory Order Date: 5/9/1960
Date Issued: May 9, 1960
Packaging: Conventional Outfit Packing

Contents: 246-1 Locomotive - with Headlight and Magne-Traction - with Lockon & Lubricant; 1130T-1 Tender; 3419-1 Operating Helicopter Car; 6062-1 Gondola Car - Black - with (3) Cable Reels; 6825-1 Flat Car - Red - with Trestle Bridge - Black; 6017-1 Caboose - Brick Brown; 1013 Curved Track (9); 1018 Straight Track (5); 1008-50 Uncoupling Unit - with (1) 1018 Straight Track; 1015-60 45-Watt Transformer; 264-1 Operating Fork Lift Platform Set; 1022-75 Manual Switch - Left Hand; 260-1 Illuminated Bumper; 81-32 Wires (2); 310-2 Set of (5) Billboard Signs; 1609-4 Instruction Sheet; AC Accessory Catalog; LIS Layout Instruction Sheet

Boxes & Packing: 60-536 Box; 60-537 Shipper (1-3)

Alternate For Outfit Contents:
Note: If necessary - Substitute 1- 1015-25, 1- 1103-14 For 1 - 1015-60, 2 - 81-32.

X-530NA (1960)	C6	C7	C8	Rarity
Complete Outfit	575	875	1,225	R6
Complete Outfit With A no. 1103-14 Substitution	675	1,075	1,675	R9
Outfit Box no. 60-536	150	200	250	R6

Comments: American Furniture is a retailer that sells home furnishings in Arizona and New Mexico. In 1960, the firm purchased this Retailer Promotional Type Ia outfit (or Type Ib with the no. 1103-14 substitution).

The no. X-530NA consisted of repeat items from previous years. It was headed by the later version of the no. 246-1 Locomotive with Headlight and Magne-Traction; it featured a closed pilot and lacked generator detail.

The sole operating car in this freight outfit was a no. 3419-1 Operating Helicopter Car. Its 3419-100 Operating Helicopter Complete had the square hole in the bottom that appeared with the introduction of the no. 6820-1 in 1960. All the rolling stock in the X-530NA was equipped with early operating AAR trucks and couplers and came packaged in Orange Perforated boxes.

Receiving a large accessory as part of an outfit always pleased consumers, even if Lionel had first issued that item several years earlier. Such was the case with the no. 264-1 Operating Fork Lift Platform Set included with the X-530NA. Promotional outfits were commonly used to deplete the inventory of accessories. This was one of three promotional outfits that Lionel used to retire the 264-1.

The Operating Fork Lift Platform Set came with a no. 6264-25 Lumber Car Complete. Included was the later version with early operating AAR trucks and couplers and "6264" to the left of "Lionel".

The track layout was an oval with a spur. This included a no. 1022-75 Left Hand Manual Switch and no. 260-1 Illuminated Bumper. A Layout Instruction Sheet has yet to be observed.

The no. 60-536 Tan RSC with Black Graphics outfit box was manufactured by Star Corrugated Box Company, Inc. and measured 19¼ x 15⅝ x 7 inches. Because of the 264-1, this box was rather large. It also included a star printed above the box manufacturer's certificate.

The substitution of an 1103-14 Envelope Packed changes the value and rarity, as listed in the pricing table. (See the entry for outfit no. X-502NA for more information about this packed envelope and its contents.)

When on the market, the X-530NA often does not include an Operating Fork Lift Platform Set. Fortunately, this item can easily be obtained to complete an outfit.

CONVENTIONAL PACK
60-536 BOX

TOP LAYER			
		1015	
		60	
9-1013		5-1018	
1130T-1 S		6062-1 S	

1008-50 TOP 1018

BOTTOM LAYER				
264-1 F	3419-1 S	246-1 S	1022-75 S	
	260			
6825-1 F	6017-1 F			

The Air Force sold outfit no. X-531NA through its AFA exchange stores in 1960. This example came from its original owner, who was a mere two years old when he received it from his father, an Air Force recruiter.

Description: 1960 Outfit
Specification: "O27" Ga. Diesel Freight Outfit
Customer: AFA
Original Amount: 1,200
Factory Order Date: 5/9/1960
Date Issued: May 9, 1960
Packaging: Conventional Outfit Packing

Contents: 220P-1 Alco Diesel Power Unit - "Santa Fe" - with Headlight, 2 Magnets, Non-Operating Coupler, Lockon & Lubricant; 220T-1 Motorless Unit - "S. F."; 6650-1 Missile Launching Flat Car; 6830-1 Flat Car - with Non-Operating Submarine - Blue Car Body; 3419-1 Operating Helicopter Car; 6017-1 Caboose - Brick Brown; 1013 Curved Track (17); 1018 Straight Track (9); 1008-50 Uncoupling Unit - with (1) 1018 Straight Track; 1015-25 45-Watt Transformer; 470-1 IRBM Missile Launching Platform with Exploding Target Car; 110-1 Graduated Trestle Set; 81-32 Wires (2); 1569-11 Instruction Sheet; AC Accessory Catalog; 1802I Layout Instruction Sheet

Boxes & Packing: 60-538 Box; 60-539 Shipper (1-3)

X-531NA (1960)	C6	C7	C8	Rarity
Complete Outfit	650	1,050	1,550	R6
Outfit Box no. 60-538	150	225	300	R6

Comments: In 1960, the Air Force (AFA) purchased this Retailer Promotional Type Ia outfit. Fittingly, the no. X-531NA had a space and military theme.

The outfit was headed by a no. 220P-1 Santa Fe Alco Diesel Power Unit, which included two-axle Magne-Traction, a three-position reversing unit and a headlight. The only feature missing was a horn. The no. 220P-1 is an example of an item that appeared in promotional outfits before it became a regular-production item (it appeared in the 1961 consumer catalog).

With the exception of the no. 6830-1 Flat Car - with Non-Operating Submarine, all the items in the X-531NA were carryover from previous years. The brand-new 6830-1 appeared in seven promotional outfits. It was a non-operating version of the no. 3830-1 Operating Submarine Car. The no. 6830-100 Submarine was stamped "6830" to match the car. The flat car and submarine are fairly common, but an Orange Perforated no. 6830-9 Folding Box is not the easiest to find in C8 condition.

The no. 470-1 IRBM Missile Launching Platform included a no. 6470-1 Exploding Target Car. The 6470-1 included "slotted" sides and a smooth roof door guide (without the nubs added later to help hold on the sides).

The nos. 3419-1 Operating Helicopter Car and 6650-1 Missile Launching Flat Car rounded out the X-531NA. They and the other pieces of rolling stock were equipped with early operating AAR trucks and couplers and came packaged in Orange Perforated boxes. Most of the cars had notches on their AAR side frames.

The track layout was an elevated pretzel layout (as detailed on the no. 1802I Layout Instruction Sheet). The no. 110-1 Graduated Trestle Set has been observed in a yellow 1959 style box as well as an orange 1960 version.

The inclusion of an IRBM Missile Launching Platform, a large accessory, necessitated a large box for the X-531NA. The no. 60-538 Tan RSC with Black Graphics outfit box was manufactured by Star Corrugated Box Company, Inc. and measured 17½ x 16⅛ x 8⅞ inches. It had "9-26V" and a star printed on its bottom.

Examples of the X-531NA frequently appear on the market, but are difficult to find in collectible condition. As with all space and military outfits, they are in high demand.

CONVENTIONAL PACK
60-538 BOX

TOP LAYER				BOTTOM LAYER	
220T-1 F		9-1018		110-1 S	3419-1 F
220P-1 S					
6650-1 S	1015 25			470-1 F	
6830-1 S					
17-1013					

1008-50 TOP 1018   6017-1 (F) TOP 3419

The no. X-532NA was a basic starter outfit sold through automotive chain stores. It was headed by a no. 244-25 Locomotive - with Smoke & Headlight (new for 1960).

Description: 1960 Outfit
Specification: "O27" Ga. Steam Type Freight Outfit with Smoke
Customer/Price: Advance Stores; $22.95
Customer: Automotive Chains
Cust./No./Price: Oklahoma Tire & Supply Co.; 70-760-8; $22.87
Original Amount: 6,000
Factory Order Date: 4/25/1960
Date Issued: August 20, 1960
Packaging: Colored Corrugated Partitions in Display Box, Units not Boxed

Contents: 244-25 Locomotive - with Smoke & Headlight with 2 Position Reversing Unit - without Magne-Traction, Lockon and Lubricant; 244T-25 Tender; 6062-25 Gondola Car - Black - with 3 Cable Reels; 3376-25 Operating Giraffe Car; 3376-118 Envelope Packed; 6465-100 2 Dome Tank Car ("Cities Service"); 6017-25 Caboose - Brick Brown; 1013 Curved Track (8); 1018 Straight Track; 1008-50 Uncoupling Unit - with (1) 1018 Straight Track; 1015-25 45-Watt Transformer; CTC Lockon; 81-32 Wires (2); 927-60 Lubricant (Oil); 927-65 Lubricant (Grease); 1103-12 Envelope Packed With CTC, 81-32, 927-60 and 927-65; 1627-2 Instruction Sheet; 310-2 Set of (5) Billboard Signs; AC Accessory Catalog; 909-10 Bottle of Liquid Smoke

Boxes & Packing: 60-540 Box; 60-541 Insert; 60-542 Insert; 60-146 Insert (2); 60-147 Insert; 60-148 Insert; 60-149 Insert; 60-543 Shipper (1-4)

X-532NA (1960)	C6	C7	C8	Rarity
Complete Outfit	225	350	450	R4
Outfit Box no. 60-540	50	75	125	R4

The no. 60-540 Yellow Hinged Display with Steamer, General and F3 Graphics Type A outfit box was unique to outfit no. X-532NA.

The no. 60-541 Insert covered and protected the no. 244T-25 Tender in outfit no. X-532NA. It was removed from the outfit picture so that the tender could be seen.

Comments: In 1960, Lionel listed Automotive Chains as the customer for four outfits: nos. X-519NA, X-520NA, X-532NA and X-533NA. The X-532NA was Automotive Chains' only steam locomotive offering and included all catalog items, hence its Retailer Promotional Type Ia classification.

Linking a Lionel Automotive Chains customer to the eventual end customer is done by studying price tags, advertisements or other markings and listings. As for the X-532NA, it appeared on page 29 of a 1960 Advance Stores catalog. It was listed simply as "Lionel Train Outfit". The catalog went on to state that if purchased separately, the total value of the items included would be $46.20, but Advance Stores' discount price was $22.95. Other manufacturers' trains were shown in the catalog, though only this one from Lionel made such a comparison. This information revealed how heavily discounted Lionel trains were in the early 1960s.

The X-532NA also appeared on page 20 of the 1960 Oklahoma Tire & Supply Co. Christmas Gifts Catalog as no. 70-760-8 for $22.87.

Almost all the items in this outfit were new for 1960, beginning with the no. 244-25 Locomotive - with Smoke & Headlight. Since this steamer was unboxed, the peripherals normally included in its box were placed loose in the outfit box. They included the contents of the no. 1103-12 Envelope Packed and a no. 909-10 Bottle of Smoke Liquid.

The same point held true for the no. 3376-25 Operating Giraffe Car. Its no. 3376-118 Envelope Packed was placed loose in the outfit box. Also new was the no. 6465-100 Cities Service 2 Dome Tank Car. These cars and their companions came with early operating AAR trucks and couplers and were not boxed. The no. 60-540 Yellow Hinged Display with Steamer, General and F3 Graphics Type A outfit box was manufactured by Kraft Corrugated Containers, Inc. and measured 25¾ x 11½ x 3⅛ inches.

With 6,000 manufactured, this outfit should appear more frequently than it does. Even so, the contents were nothing too special. Therefore, when an X-532NA does appear, it doesn't command high value.

DISPLAY PACK
60-540 BOX

244-25	244T-25	1015 25	
6062-25	6017-25		1-1018 8-1013
3376-25	6465-100		

1008-50 BELOW 6017

Automotive Chains' no. X-533NA was a space and military outfit headed by a no. 228P-25 Canadian National Alco Diesel Power Car. This diesel appeared in only five outfits and was produced in relatively low numbers.

The no. 60-555 box was unique to outfit no. X-533NA. Its number was printed by the box manufacturer. The $24.99 handwritten price is close to the $28.95 listed in the catalog from Advance Stores.

Description: 1960 Outfit
Specification: "O27" Ga. Diesel Freight Outfit
Customer/Price: Advance Stores; $28.95
Customer: Automotive Chains
Cust./No./Price: Oklahoma Tire & Supply Co.; 70-761-4; $27.47
Original Amount: 1,500
Factory Order Date: 5/11/1960
Date Issued: 5-24-60
Packaging: Colored Corrugated Partitions in Display Box, Units not Boxed (Except 943-1)

Contents: 228P-25 Alco Diesel Power Car - Blue - "Canadian National" - Yellow Lettering with Headlight and Magne-Traction - with 2 Position Reversing Unit; 3419-25 Operating Helicopter Car; 6544-25 Missile Firing Trail Car - Blue Car Body; 6844-25 Rocket Transport Car; 6017-25 Caboose - Brick Brown; 1013 Curved Track (8); 1018 Straight Track (3); 1008-50 Uncoupling Unit - with (1) 1018 Straight Track; 1015-25 45-Watt Transformer; 943-1 Exploding Ammo Dump; CTC-1 Lockon; 81-32 Wires (2); 927-60 Lubricant (Oil); 927-65 Lubricant (Grease); 1103-12 Envelope Packed With CTC, 81-32, 927-60 and 927-65; 1613-10 Instruction Sheet; 310-2 Set of (5) Billboard Signs; AC Accessory Catalog

Boxes & Packing: 60-555 Box; 60-556 Insert; 60-166 Insert (2); 60-168 Insert; 60-169 Insert; 60-170 Insert; 60-171 Insert; 60-557 Shipper (1-4)

X-533NA (1960)	C6	C7	C8	Rarity
Complete Outfit	575	850	1,200	R6
Outfit Box no. 60-555	200	300	400	R6

Comments: In 1960, Lionel listed Automotive Chains as the customer for four outfits: nos. X-519NA, X-520NA, X-532NA and X-533NA. The X-533NA was Automotive Chains' low-level diesel locomotive offering and included all catalog items, hence its Retailer Promotional Type Ia classification.

Linking a Lionel Automotive Chains customer to the eventual end customer is done by studying price tags, advertisements or other markings and listings. As for the X-533NA, it appeared on pages 28 and 29 of a 1960 Advance Stores catalog. It was listed as "Exciting Lionel Train Set" with a price of $28.95.

The X-533NA also appeared on page 20 of the 1960 Oklahoma Tire & Supply Co. Christmas Gifts Catalog as no. 70-761-4 for $27.47.

This space and military outfit was headed by a no. 228P-25 Canadian National Alco Diesel Power Car equipped with two-axle Magne-Traction, an open pilot and a two-position reversing unit. This new-for-1960 Alco was never offered for separate sale but was included in five outfits (four promotional and a substitution in catalog outfit no. 1643). The Factory Orders show a total of 5,228 produced of which 2,650 were boxed. These low numbers explain why this locomotive doesn't appear too often.

The rolling stock in the X-533NA featured a no. 6544-25 Missile Firing Trail Car and a no. 6844-25 Rocket Transport Car. They and the other items were equipped with early operating AAR trucks and couplers and came unboxed. Leaving the 6544-25 unboxed exposes its fragile brake wheels to possible damage.

The 6544-25 and 6844-25 provided plenty of missiles to shoot at the sitting duck no. 943-1 Exploding Ammo Dump. This low-cost addition to outfits retailed separately for $1.95 in 1960

The no. 60-555 Orange, White and Gray O27 Hinged Display with 4-6-2 Steam Display Graphics Type A outfit box was manufactured by UCC (United Container Co.) and measured 25¼ x 17¼ x 3¼ inches. It included a no. 60-171 Insert with New York Central System and Union Pacific logos. This insert came in the X-533NA and four other outfits. Finding this insert to complete an outfit takes patience because it is easily lost, so be prepared to pay a decent price for one.

Automotive Chains' low-end offering for 1960 compared favorably to other vendors' high-end offerings. With a space and military theme, the difficult-to-find 228P-25 Canadian National Alco and its Orange, White and Gray Type A display box, an X-533NA would be an attractive addition to any promotional outfit collection.

DISPLAY PACK
60-555 BOX

228P-25	3419-25	
1008-25 943-1	6844-25	
6544-25	6017-25	
8-1013 3-1018		1015 25

Description: 1960 Outfit
Specification: "O27" Ga. Diesel Freight Outfit
Customer: Montgomery Ward
Original Amount: 36
Factory Order Date: 8/3/1960
Date Issued: August 3, 1960
Packaging: Conventional Outfit Packing

Contents: 220P-1 Alco Diesel Power Unit - "Santa Fe" - with Headlight, 2 Magnets, Non-Operating Coupler, Lockon & Lubricant; 220T-1 Motorless Unit - "S.F."; 3419-1 Operating Helicopter Car; 6062-1 Gondola Car - Black - with (3) Cable Reels; 6014-100 Box Car - Red; 6017-1 Caboose - Brick Brown; 1013 Curved Track (8); 1018 Straight Track; 1008-50 Uncoupling Unit - with (1) 1018 Straight Track; 1015-25 45-Watt Transformer; 81-32 Wires (2); 310-2 Set of (5) Billboard Signs; 1569-11 Instruction Sheet; AC Accessory Catalog

Boxes & Packing: 59-339 Box; 59-340 Shipper (1-3); ST Sticker

X-534NA (1960)	C6	C7	C8	Rarity
Complete Outfit	1,700	2,500	3,300	R10
Outfit Box no. 59-339	1,300	2,000	2,500	R10

Comments: In 1960, Montgomery Ward purchased three Retailer Promotional outfits: nos. X-534NA, X-535NA and X-536NA. With only 36 of the X-534NA manufactured, this Type Ib outfit was likely a special item or a promotional piece used for internal purposes. As such, it did not appear in the 1960 Ward catalog, whereas nos. X-535NA and X-536NA did.

The components of the X-534NA were items commonly used in promotional outfits of 1960. The no. 220P-1 Santa Fe Alco Diesel Power Unit included all the high-end features available to

Alco power units – a headlight, Magne-Traction, a three-position reversing unit and an open pilot – but no horn. This locomotive came boxed in a no. 220-10 Corrugated Box. Originally a promotional-only item, the 220P-1 eventually appeared in the 1961 catalog.

The no. 3419-1 Operating Helicopter Car was the sole operating car in this outfit. It came with early operating AAR trucks and couplers, as did all the rolling stock.

The no. 6014-100 Red Airex Box Car appeared only in promotional outfits, with at least 12 of these outfits having been identified. This car, like the other pieces of rolling stock in the X-534NA, came packaged in Orange Perforated boxes.

The no. 59-339 Tan RSC with Black Graphics outfit box was an overstickered no. 9663. Manufactured by Star Corrugated Box Company, Inc., it measured 13¾ x 12 x 6 inches and included a star on the bottom.

What makes this outfit special is the extremely low quantity produced. It ranks eighth on the list of fewest outfits produced in the 1960s. That fact, combined with its being a Montgomery Ward outfit, easily led to its R10 ranking and price.

CONVENTIONAL PACK
59-339 BOX
STICKER

TOP LAYER

6017-1 F	
3419-1 F	1018
8-1013	
6014-100 S	

1008-50 TOP 6017

BOTTOM LAYER

220T-1 F	
220P-1 F	
6062-1 F	1015 25

Montgomery Ward cataloged the no. X-535NA as no. 48 T 3073 M for $29.97 (item 32) in its 1960 Christmas Catalog. Outfit no. X-536NA is shown as item 33. Lionel began its selling cycle with customers like Ward well in advance of the targeted catalog year. That is why the items shown in the catalog are 1959 vintage or prototypes of the 1960 versions. Also, the caboose shown is a work caboose whereas the final version was a no. 6017-1.

Description: 1960 Outfit
Specification: "O27" Ga. Diesel Freight Outfit
Customer/No./Price: Montgomery Ward; 48 T 3073 M; $29.97
Original Amount: 1,500
Factory Order Date: 5/26/1960
Date Issued: October 12, 1960
Packaging: Conventional Outfit Packing

Contents: 45-50 Mobile Rocket Firing Car - Khaki Color - with "U.S. Marine Markings" - with Lockon and Lubricant; 3419-1 Operating Helicopter Car; 6844-1 Rocket Transport Car; 6830-1 Flat Car - with Non-Operating Submarine - Blue Car Body; 6017-1 Caboose - Brick Brown; 1013 Curved Track (12); 1018 Straight Track (3); 6019-1 Remote Control Track Set; 1043-50 60-Watt Transformer; 1020 90° Crossover; 81-32 Wires (2); 1802B Layout Instruction Sheet; 926-60 Instruction Book; 310-2 Set of (5) Billboard Signs; AC Accessory Catalog

Boxes & Packing: 60-481 Box; 60-482 Shipper (1-4)

Alternate For Outfit Contents:
Note: Use - 166 - 1043-1 for 1043-50; 934 - 1043-500 for 1043-50; 400 - 1043-50; 695 Sets with 6029-25, 90-30 and 44-45 Envelope in Locomotive; Balance as per revised specifications with 44-55 Envelope in Locomotive.

X-535NA (1960)	C6	C7	C8	Rarity
Complete Outfit With A no. 1043-50 Or no. 1043-1	675	1,100	1,700	R7
Complete Outfit With no. 1043-500	710	1,175	1,800	R7
Outfit Box no. 60-481	175	250	400	R7

Comments: In 1960, Montgomery Ward purchased three Retailer Promotional outfits: nos. X-534NA, X-535NA and X-536NA. The X-535NA, a Type Ia outfit, appeared on page 417 of the 1960 Ward Christmas Catalog as no. 48 T 3073M for $29.97.

A space and military outfit, the X-535NA was headed by a no. 45-50 Mobile Rocket Firing Car - Khaki Color. The "-50" suffix indicated that it came with a no. 44-55 Envelope Packed, whereas a no. 45-1 came with a no. 44-45 Envelope Packed.

Because this outfit came with a no. 6019-1 Remote Control

Track Set, the additional peripherals required to operate the Mobile Rocket Firing Car (included in a 44-45 Envelope Packed) were not needed. Consequently, the 45-50 came with a 44-55 Envelope. However, once a no. 6029-25 Uncoupling Track, which couldn't operate the 45-50, was substituted for the 6019-1, a 44-45 was required to operate the Mobile Rocket Firing Car.

The no. 6830-1 Flat Car - with Non-Operating Submarine (new for 1960) appeared in seven promotional outfits. It was a non-operating version of the no. 3830-1 Operating Submarine Car. The no. 6830-100 Submarine was stamped "6830" to match the car. The flat car and submarine are fairly common, but an Orange Perforated no. 6830-9 Folding Box is not the easiest to find in C8 condition.

The nos. 3419-1 Operating Helicopter Car, 6844-1 Rocket Transport Car and 6017-1 Caboose rounded out the rolling stock for this outfit. These were included in many 1960 promotional outfits. They were equipped with early operating AAR trucks and couplers and, like the other items in the X-535NA, were packaged in Orange Perforated boxes.

Lionel was slowly depleting its inventory of no. 1043 60-Watt Transformers. This outfit included three versions: the "-1" was boxed with two no. 81-32 Wires, the "-50" was unboxed and the "-500" was the boxed white version first used with outfit no. 1587S, the Lady Lionel, or "Girl's Set," cataloged in 1957 and 1958. The "-500" version adds a premium, as outlined in the pricing table.

The no. 60-481 Box was unique to this outfit. Though it has yet to be observed, it was likely a Tan RSC with Black Graphics.

Lionel produced 1,500 of the X-535NA, but examples do not appear too often.

CONVENTIONAL PACK
60-481 BOX

TOP LAYER		
3419-1 F		6017-1 F
4-1013 / 3-1018		
8-1013		

1020 TOP TRACK - 3419
6019-1 TOP 8-1013

BOTTOM LAYER		
45-50 F		1043-50
6844-1 S		
6830-1 S		

The no. X-536NA appeared in the 1960 Ward catalog as no. 48 T 3074 M for $39.97. A space and military offering, all its rolling stock was individually packaged in Orange Perforated boxes. This outfit also included a dual oval layout using a pair of no. 1022-1 Manual Switches. This arrangement was outlined on the no. 1802E Layout Instruction Sheet (not shown).

Description: 1960 Outfit
Specification: "O27" Ga. Steam Type Freight Outfit with Smoke
Customer/No./Price: Montgomery Ward; 48 T 3074 M; $39.97
Original Amount: 1,500
Factory Order Date: 4/25/1960
Date Issued: 5-24-60
Packaging: Conventional Outfit Packing

Contents: 2018-1 Locomotive - with Smoke, Lockon & Lubricant - without Magne-Traction; 243W-1 Whistle Tender; 6650-1 Missile Launching Flat Car; 6470-1 Exploding Target Car; 6825-1 Flat Car - Red - with Trestle Bridge - Black; 6062-1 Gondola Car - Black - with (3) Cable Reels; 6017-1 Caboose - Brick Brown; 1013 Curved Track (10); 1018 Straight Track (5); 1008-50 Uncoupling Unit - with (1) 1018 Straight Track; 1053-50 60-Watt Transformer; 1022-1 Manual Switches (1Pr.); 81-32 Wires (2); 926-60 Instruction Book; 310-2 Set of (5) Billboard Signs; AC Accessory Catalog; 1802E Layout Instruction Sheet

Boxes & Packing: 60-483 Box; 60-484 Insert; 60-485 Shipper (1-3)

X-536NA (1960)	C6	C7	C8	Rarity
Complete Outfit	435	675	950	R6
Outfit Box no. 60-483	175	250	300	R6

Comments: In 1960, Montgomery Ward purchased three Retailer Promotional outfits: nos. X-534NA, X-535NA and X-536NA. The X-536NA, a Type Ia outfit appeared on page 417 of the 1960 Ward Christmas Catalog as no. 48 T 3074 M for $39.97. Ward listed this steam-powered outfit as a "7-Unit Military Action Train."

The no. 2018-1 Locomotive - with Smoke last appeared in a catalog outfit in 1959, but was still being used in promotional outfits in the 1960s. When boxed in its no. 2018-10 Corrugated Box, it included the nos. 675-33 Smoke Stack Cleaner, SP-1 Pellets Bottled, 927-60 Tube of Oil, 927-65 Tube of Grease, 2018-11 Instruction Sheet and CTC-1 Lockon.

The nos. 6470-1 Exploding Target Car and 6650-1 Missile Launching Flat Car were a nice matching pair, as kids could never get enough of blowing up the Exploding Target Car. These cars came together in 14 promotional outfits in 1960. The 6470-1 included "slotted" sides and a smooth roof door guide (without the nubs added later to help hold on the sides).

All the rolling stock in the X-536NA came with early operating AAR trucks and couplers and was packaged in Orange Perforated boxes.

The track layout was, according to the Ward catalog, an "interesting oval layout with inner switch track." As outlined on the no. 1802E Layout Instruction Sheet, it required a pair of no. 1022-1 Manual Switches. This is just one of the many enhanced track layouts that Lionel used in promotional outfits.

The no. 60-483 Tan RSC with Black Graphics outfit box was

manufactured by Star Corrugated Box Company, Inc. and measured 15½ x 11¼ x 7¼ inches. A star was printed on the bottom.

An example of the X-536NA has been observed with a Ward shipping label on the box. This indicates that Ward may not have repackaged the outfits for shipping, something that could have led to potential damage on initial shipment.

Ward underestimated the original demand for this outfit, as the quantity increased from 1,000 to 1,500 on 5-24-60. Even with such an increase in quantity, examples of the X-536NA do not often appear in the market.

CONVENTIONAL PACK
60-483 BOX

TOP LAYER		
5-1018		
243W-1 F		6062-1 S
6825-1 F		
6017-1 F	1053 50	

BOTTOM LAYER		
6470-1 F		
6650-1 F		10-1013
2018-1 S		

1022-1 TOP 6650 - 6470
1008-50 TOP 1013

The no. X-537NA demonstrates the variety of items that Lionel included in its promotional outfits. Besides a nice grouping of rolling stock, it included an accessory and a motorized unit as well as an interesting track layout. The few Goldblatt's customers who were lucky enough to acquire this outfit were rewarded with hours of fun and excitement.

Description: 1960 Outfit
Specification: "O27" Ga. Diesel Type Freight Outfit with Smoke & Whistle
Customer/No.: Abraham & Strauss; 0F 660
Customer: Goldblatt's
Original Amount: 275
Factory Order Date: 4/26/1960
Date Issued: 11-17-60
Packaging: Conventional Outfit Packing

Contents: 2037-1 Locomotive - with Magne-Traction, Smoke, Lockon and Lubricant; 243W-1 Whistle Tender; 3512-1 Operating Fireman and Ladder Car; 6361-1 Log Car - Dark Green Frame; 6812-1 Track Maintenance Flat Car - Red Frame - Structure in Gray and Black; 6670-1 Crane Car; 6119-100 Work Caboose; 1013 Curved Track (10); 1018 Straight Track (5); 6029-25 Uncoupling Track Section; 1063-25 Transformer; 1020-1 90° Crossover; 1022-1 Manual Switches (1Pr.); 264-1 Operating Fork Lift Platform Set; 55-1 Tie-Jector Car; 90-1 Uncoupling Track Controller; 81-32 Wires (4); 90-30 Envelope Packed With 90-1 and 81-32; 926-60 Instruction Book; 310-2 Set of (5) Billboard Signs; AC Accessory Catalog; 2146 Layout Instruction Sheet

Boxes & Packing: 59-355 Box; 59-356 Shipper (1-2); ST Sticker

X-537NA (1960)	C6	C7	C8	Rarity
Complete Outfit	1,275	2,100	2,800	R10
Outfit Box no. 59-355	400	625	800	R10

Comments: Chicago-based retailer Goldblatt's ran department stores that offered a variety of goods at discount prices. It purchased one Retailer Promotional Type Ia outfit in 1960. This outfit has been observed with an Abraham & Strauss price tag, but the linkage between the two retailers has not been established.

The no. X-537NA was a large outfit headed by a no. 2037-1 Locomotive with Magne-Traction and Smoke. Originally introduced in 1953, this steam engine was the workhorse of one Super O and 22 O27 outfits during the 1960s.

Three operating cars provided a lot of action in the X-537NA. The no. 3512-1 Operating Fireman and Ladder Car appeared in only six promotional outfits in 1960. The no. 6812-1 Track Maintenance Car was the gray-over-black version. The no. 6670-1 Crane Car was packaged in an overstamped Bold Classic no. 6660-55 Folding Box.

All the rolling stock in this outfit was equipped with early operating AAR trucks and couplers and came packaged (except for the 6670) in Orange Perforated boxes. The Orange Perforated boxes for the nos. 6361-1 Log Car and 6119-100 Work Caboose are more fragile and difficult to find than their Orange Picture versions. To be correct for this outfit, Orange Perforated boxes are required.

Receiving a large accessory as part of an outfit always pleased consumers, even if Lionel had first issued that item several years earlier. Such was the case with the no. 264-1 Operating Fork Lift Platform Set included with the X-537NA. Promotional outfits were commonly used to deplete the inventory of accessories. This was one of three promotional outfits that Lionel used to retire the 264-1.

The Operating Fork Lift Platform Set came with a no. 6264-25 Lumber Car Complete. Included was the later version with early operating AAR trucks and couplers and "6264" to the left of "Lionel".

This was also one of the last two outfits to include a no. 55-1 Tie-Jector Car. Although this motorized unit increased the play value of this outfit, it appeared out of place. It was packed in a Late Classic-style box.

The track layout was a figure-eight with two switches, as detailed on the difficult-to-find no. 2146 Layout Instruction Sheet.

The no. 59-355 Tan RSC with Black Graphics outfit box was manufactured by Star Corrugated Box Company, Inc. and measured 17⅜ x 14½ x 10¼ inches. This overstickered Sears no. 9682 box had a star printed on the bottom.

The original quantity for this outfit was 150, but it was increased to 200 on 6-23-60 and finally 275 on 11-17-60. This small quantity and large box size meant few of the boxes survived. Also, the desirable contents of the X-537NA were likely to be broken up and sold separately over the years. Thus, finding one of these outfits complete in collectible condition is a true challenge.

CONVENTIONAL PACK
59-355 BOX
STICKER

TOP LAYER

BOTTOM LAYER

6670-1 S				6361-1 S	1063 25
6812-1 S	3512-1 S	1022-1 S			
243W-1 S				264-1 F	55-1 F
6119-100 S					
2037-1 S					

10-1013 TOP 6670
5-1018 TOP 3512
6029-25 TOP TRACK
1020-1 TOP

The commonly available no. X-538NA was a basic, low-end starter outfit offered by Western Auto in 1960.

Customer No. On Box: EC 5010
Description: 1960 Outfit
Specification: "O27" Ga. Steam Type Freight Outfit
Customer/No./Price: Western Auto; EC 5010; $18.88
Original Amount: 5,000
Factory Order Date: 4/26/1960
Date Issued: April 26, 1960
Packaging: Color Corrugated Partitions in Display Box, Units Not Boxed (Except No. 1020 Crossing)

Contents: 246-25 Locomotive - with Headlight and Magne-Traction - Less Lockon and Lubricant; 1130T-25 Tender; 6476-25 Hopper Car - Red; 6825-25 Flat Car - Red - with Trestle Bridge - Black; 6017-25 Caboose - Brick Brown; 1013 Curved Track (12); 1018 Straight Track (3); 1008-50 Uncoupling Unit - with (1) 1018 Straight Track; 1016-60 35-Watt Transformer; 1020-1 90° Crossover; CTC-1 Lockon; 81-32 Wires (2); 927-60 Lubricant (Oil); 927-65 Lubricant (Grease); 1103-12 Envelope Packed With CTC-1, 81-32, 927-60 and 927-65; 1609-4 Instruction Sheet; 310-2 Set of (5) Billboard Signs; AC Accessory Catalog; 1802B Layout Instruction Sheet

Boxes & Packing: 60-544 Box; 60-545 Insert (2); 60-126 Tube; 60-128 Insert; 60-129 Insert; 60-130 Insert; 60-132 Insert; 60-546 Shipper (1-4)

Alternate For Outfit Contents:
Customer No. EC 5010 (Printed on Boxes).

X-538NA (1960)	C6	C7	C8	Rarity
Complete Outfit	200	290	410	R4
Outfit Box no. 60-544	100	125	150	R4

Comments: Western Auto Stores purchased two steam-powered promotional outfits in 1960: nos. X-538NA and X-546NA. Both were Retailer Promotional Type Ia outfits.

Western Auto outfits for 1960 came in Yellow Hinged Display with Steamer, General and F3 Graphics Type A outfit boxes. The no. 60-544 was unique to the X-538NA.

The X-538NA was Western Auto's low-end steam purchase in 1960. This basic starter outfit was headed by the later version of the no. 246-25 Steam Type Locomotive. That engine featured Magne-Traction, a two-position reversing unit and a closed pilot. There was no generator detail on its body.

DISPLAY PACK
60-544 BOX

246-25	1130T-25	
6476-25	1016-60	12-1013
6825-25 3-1018	6017-25	

1020-1 BELOW 6476 - 6825
1008-50 BELOW 6825

All the rolling stock in this mundane outfit was equipped with early operating AAR trucks and couplers. Lionel attempted to spruce it up by providing a figure-eight layout, as outlined on the no. 1802B Layout Instruction Sheet.

The no. 60-544 Yellow Hinged Display with Steamer, General and F3 Graphics Type A outfit box was manufactured by Owens Illinois and measured 24⅛ x 11¾ x 3⅛ inches.

A segment of collectors focus on specific retailer offerings, and Western Auto outfits have a following among them. Therefore, although the X-538NA was produced in high quantities and is readily available, many enthusiasts will want to add it to their collections.

Description: 1960 Outfit
Specification: "O27" Ga. Steam Type Freight Outfit
Customer: Mercantile Stores
Original Amount: 900
Factory Order Date: 5/2/1960
Date Issued: May 2, 1960
Packaging: Conventional Outfit Packing

Contents: 246-1 Locomotive - with Headlight and Magne-Traction - with Lockon and Lubricant; 1130T-1 Tender; 6544-1 Missile Firing Trail Car - Blue Car Body; 6844-1 Rocket Transport Car; 3419-1 Operating Helicopter Car; 6017-1 Caboose - Brick Brown; 1013 Curved Track (12); 1018 Straight Track (3); 1008-50 Uncoupling Unit - with (1) 1018 Straight Track; 1015-60 45-Watt Transformer; 1020-1 90° Crossover; 943-1 Exploding Ammo Dump; 81-32 Wires (2); 1609-4 Instruction Sheet; 1802B Layout Instruction Sheet; 310-2 Set of (5) Billboard Signs; AC Accessory Catalog

Boxes & Packing: 60-561 Box; 60-562 Shipper (1-3)

Alternate For Outfit Contents:
Note: If necessary - Substitute 1- 1015-25, 1- 1103-14 For 1 - 1015-60, 2 - 81-32.

X-539NA (1960)	C6	C7	C8	Rarity
Complete Outfit	650	975	1,425	R8
Complete Outfit With A no. 1103-14 Substitution	750	1,175	1,875	R9
Outfit Box no. 60-561	300	400	500	R8

Comments: Mercantile Stores Company, Inc. operated department stores in medium-sized cities during the 1960s. In 1960, it purchased two Retailer Promotional outfits: nos. X-539NA and X-540NA. One outfit featured a steam locomotive, and the other had a diesel. Either could have been sold to any of Mercantile's customers.

The Type Ia (or Type Ib with the no. 1103-14 substitution) outfit no. X-539NA was powered by a no. 246-1 Locomotive with Headlight and Magne-Traction. This steam engine was first released in 1959 and was still being used in outfits as late as 1962.

The rolling stock in this outfit was space and military themed. The no. 3419-1 Operating Helicopter Car was in its second year of production that brought many changes along with it. Specifically, the 1960 version included a small winder and a single-blade no. 3419-100 Operating Helicopter Complete.

The no. 6544-1 Missile Firing Trail Car (new for 1960) contained two brake wheels attached to the plastic frame ends. Over time, the frame is easily cracked or broken off where the wheels attach. The no. 6844-1 Rocket Transport Car rounded out the rolling stock and provided extra missiles for the 6544-1.

All the rolling stock was equipped with early operating AAR trucks and couplers and came in Orange Perforated boxes.

The no. 943 Exploding Ammo Dump was a low-cost addition to outfits and provided a great target for the 6544-1. It retailed separately for $1.95 in 1960.

The substitution of a no. 1103-14 Envelope Packed changes the value and rarity of the X-539NA, as listed in the pricing table.

(See the entry for outfit no. X-502NA for more information about this packed envelope and its contents.)

The no. 60-561 Box was unique to this outfit. It is difficult to find and has an R8 rarity.

CONVENTIONAL PACK
60-561 BOX

TOP LAYER

12-1013	
1130T-1 F	3-1018
3419-1 F	

1020-1 TOP 3419 - 1130T
1008-50 TOP

BOTTOM LAYER

246-1 F	1015 60
6544-1 F	6017-1 S	943-1 S
6844-1 F		

Description: 1960 Outfit
Specification: "O27" Ga. Diesel Freight Outfit
Customer: Mercantile Stores
Original Amount: 700
Factory Order Date: 5/9/1960
Date Issued: May 9, 1960
Packaging: Conventional Outfit Packing

Contents: 224P-1 Alco Diesel Power Car - "U.S. Navy" - Navy Color and Markings - with Headlight, Magne-Traction - with Non-Operating Coupler - Lockon and Lubricant; 6361-1 Log Car - Dark Green Frame; 6812-1 Track Maintenance Flat Car - Red Frame - Structure in Gray and Black; 6817-1 Flat Car - Red - with Road Scraper; 6414-1 Automobile Car; 6017-1 Caboose - Brick Brown; 1013 Curved Track (17); 1018 Straight Track (9); 1008-50 Uncoupling Unit - with (1) 1018 Straight Track; 1015-25 45-Watt Transformer; 110-1 Graduated Trestle Set; 81-32 Wires (2); 310-2 Set of (5) Billboard Signs; 1569-11 Instruction Sheet; AC Accessory Catalog; 1802I Layout Instruction Sheet

Boxes & Packing: 60-508 Box; 60-509 Shipper (1-3)

X-540NA (1960)	C6	C7	C8	Rarity
Complete Outfit	1,250	1,675	2,325	R8
Outfit Box no. 60-508	400	475	550	R8

Comments: Mercantile Stores Company, Inc. operated department stores in medium-sized cities during the 1960s. In 1960, it purchased two Retailer Promotional outfits: nos. X-539NA and X-540NA. One outfit featured a steam locomotive, and the other had a diesel. Either could have been sold to any of Mercantile's customers.

The X-540NA, a Type Ia diesel outfit, was headed by the collectible no. 224P-1 U.S. Navy Alco Diesel Power Car with Magne-Traction and a three-position reversing unit. When boxed, this locomotive included the nos. CTC-1 Lockon, 927-60 Tube of Oil, 927-65 Tube of Grease and no. 217-17 Instruction Sheet in its corrugated box.

Even though the engine was a space and military item, the remainder of the rolling stock consisted of regular freight offerings. The no. 6414-1 Automobile Car came in two promotional outfits in 1960 and was equipped with four premium autos with chrome bumpers. The no. 6817-1 Flat Car - Red - With Road Scraper was the most collectible item in this outfit. It included the extremely fragile no. 6817-111 Earth Scraper Complete. Finding these models in original, unbroken condition is becoming a challenge.

All the rolling stock in the X-540NA was equipped with early operating AAR trucks and couplers and came packaged in Orange Perforated boxes. The demand for collectible versions of these fragile boxes continues to grow.

The track layout was an elevated pretzel layout, as detailed on the no. 1802I Layout Instruction Sheet.

The no. 60-508 Box was unique to this outfit. As with the no. X-539NA, an example of the X-540NA is difficult to find.

CONVENTIONAL PACK
60-508 BOX

TOP LAYER

6817-1 F	
9-1018	6017-1 S
9-1013	
6361-1 S	
6812-1 F	

8-1013 TOP 6812
1008-50 TOP

BOTTOM LAYER

110-1 F	
224P-1 F	
6414-1 F	1015 25

X-541NA
1960

The no. 60-490 Box for outfit no. X-541NA included both the Lionel and Popular Club Plan numbers printed on the box.

Customer No. On Box: B 8158
Description: 1960 Outfit
Specification: "O27" Ga. Diesel Freight Outfit
Customer/No.: Popular Club Plan; B 8158
Original Amount: 1,000
Factory Order Date: 4/26/1960
Date Issued: April 26, 1960
Packaging: Units not Boxed - In Conventional Outfit Packing

Contents: 1055-25 Alco Diesel Power Car - "MKT" Markings - with Headlight and Non-Operating Coupler - without Reversing Unit, Magne-Traction, Lockon and Lubricant; 6042-25 Gondola Car - Blue - with 2 Red Canisters - with Non-Operating Trucks; 6045-25 Two Dome Tank Car - Gray - Non-Operating Trucks; 6044-25 Box Car - Blue - "Airex" Markings - Non-Operating Trucks; 6047-25 Caboose - Brick Brown - Non-Operating Trucks; 1013 Curved Track (8); 1018 Straight Track (2); 1026-25 25-Watt Transformer; 981-1 Freight Yard Set; CTC-1 Lockon; 81-32 Wires (2); 927-60 Lubricant (Oil); 927-65 Lubricant (Grease); 1103-12 Envelope Packed With CTC-1, 81-32, 927-60 and 927-65; 1105-10 Instruction Sheet; 310-2 Set of (5) Billboard Signs; AC Accessory Catalog

Boxes & Packing: 60-490 Box; 60-491 Insert; 60-492 Insert; 60-493 Insert; 60-494 Shipper (1-4)

Alternate For Outfit Contents:
Note: Print Customers Stock Number (B 8158) on Outfit Cartons & Shippers.

X-541NA (1960)	C6	C7	C8	Rarity
Complete Outfit	390	650	1,025	R7
Outfit Box no. 60-490	150	250	325	R7

Comments: Popular Club Plan is a catalog company selling an assortment of clothing, housewares, jewelry, toys and electronics. In 1960 it purchased three Retailer Promotional outfits: nos. X-509NA, X-541NA and X-542NA.

The X-541NA, a Retailer Promotional Type Ib outfit, was Popular's low-end diesel purchase. The locomotive and cars in this outfit, all of which came unboxed, are similar to those in advance catalog outfit no. 1105 and promotional outfit no. X-829.

Leading the X-541NA was a no. 1055-25 "MKT" Alco Diesel Power Car, which went only forward. The most notable of the cars that this low-end locomotive pulled were the nos. 6045-25 Gray Two Dome Tank Car and 6044-25 Blue Box Car - "Airex" Markings. Both freight cars were included in promotional outfits only. They, like the other cars in this outfit, came equipped with non-operating Archbar trucks and couplers, which was the norm with low-end outfits in the 1960s.

As with the other two Popular Club offerings, Lionel included a Plasticville item in this outfit. For the X-541NA, it was a no. 981-1 Freight Yard Set. This is by far the most expensive individual item in this outfit.

This outfit was packed in a no. 60-490 Tan RSC with Black Graphics outfit box manufactured by St. Joe Paper Co. - Container Div. and measuring 14½ x 11 x 6 inches. It had "60-490" printed on the bottom and "10 11 12" printed as part of the box manufacturer's certificate.

(See the entry for outfit no. X-509NA for discussion of a prototype Popular Club Plan box car.)

CONVENTIONAL PACK
60-490 BOX

TOP LAYER		BOTTOM LAYER	
6042-25		6044-25 F	
1026 25 / 6047-25		6045-25 F	981-1 S
CORD / 1055-25		2-1018 / 8-1013	

X-542NA
1960

Customer No. On Box: B 8164S
Description: 1960 Outfit
Specification: "O27" Ga. Steam Type Freight with Smoke
Customer/No.: Popular Club Plan; B 8164S
Original Amount: 500
Factory Order Date: 4/26/1960
Date Issued: April 26, 1960
Packaging: Conventional Outfit Packing

Contents: 244-1 Locomotive - with Smoke & Headlight - with 2 Position Reversing Unit - with Lockon and Lubricant - without Magne-Traction; 244T-1 Tender; 6062-1 Gondola Car - Black - with (3) Cable Reels; 6825-1 Flat Car - Red - with Trestle Bridge - Black; 6476-1 Hopper Car - Red; 6017-1 Caboose - Brick Brown; 1013 Curved Track (8); 1018 Straight Track; 1008-50 Uncoupling Unit - with (1) 1018 Straight Track; 1015-25 45-Watt Transformer; 953-1 Figure Set; 81-32 Wires (2); 1627-2 Instruction Sheet; 310-2 Set of (5) Billboard Signs; AC Accessory Catalog

Boxes & Packing: 59-351 Box; 59-352 Shipper (1-4); ST Sticker

Alternate For Outfit Contents:
Note: Print Customers Stock Number (B 8164S) on Outfit Cartons and Shippers.

X-542NA (1960)	C6	C7	C8	Rarity
Complete Outfit	475	800	1,250	R8
Outfit Box no. 59-351	200	375	475	R8

Comments: Popular Club Plan is a catalog company selling an assortment of clothing, housewares, jewelry, toys and electronics. In 1960 it purchased three Retailer Promotional outfits: nos. X-509NA, X-541NA and X-542NA.

The X-542NA, a Retailer Promotional Type Ia, was Popular's only steam outfit purchase. It was headed by a no. 244-1 Locomotive - with Smoke & Headlight (new for 1960). This steamer was equipped with a metal motor, but included only ballast weights as a traction aid.

The components of this basic outfit were nothing special, although most of them came in Orange Perforated boxes (the no. 244T-1 Tender came in an overstamped Bold Classic no. 1625T Folding Box). Each of the freight cars was equipped with early operating AAR trucks and couplers.

The X-542NA, like the other two Popular Club Plan outfits, included a Plasticville item that is by far the most desirable component. This outfit came with a no. 953-1 Figure Set.

The no. 59-351 Tan RSC with Black Graphics outfit box was leftover inventory from 1959. It was first used for promotional outfit no. A-608-6. Manufactured by Express Container Corp., it measured 14 x 10½ x 6¾ inches.

The Popular Club Plan outfits attract some interest because of the Plasticville items. Any of them would be a nice addition to a promotional outfit collection as an example of Lionel's use of Plasticville sets to differentiate an outfit.

(See the entry for outfit no. X-509NA for discussion of a prototype Popular Club Plan box car.)

CONVENTIONAL PACK
59-351 BOX
STICKER, PRINT STOCK NO. ON SHIPPER

TOP LAYER		
244T-1 F		
6017-1 F	8-1013	
1-1018		
6825-1 S		

1008-50 TOP 6825

BOTTOM LAYER	
6476-1 F	
6062-1 F	
244-1 F	1015 25

953 TOP 6476 - 6062

The no. 60-384 Box version of the no. X-543NA was an oversticckered single-layer no. 1629 outfit box. This was the third and last variation of this outfit. The other versions are both dual-layer RSCs. The inclusion of a no. 953-1 Figure Set makes this a desirable starter outfit.

Description: 1960 Outfit
Specification: "O27" Ga. Steam Type Freight Outfit
Customer: Signet
Original Amount: 1,350
Factory Order Date: 4/26/1960
Date Issued: 11-17-60
Packaging: Units Not Boxed (Except 1020-1 and 953-1) - In

Conventional Outfit Packing

Contents: 1060-25 Steam Type Locomotive - with Headlight, Front and Rear Trucks - without Magne-Traction, Reversing Unit, Lockon and Lubricant; 1060T-25 Tender; 6044-25 Box Car - Blue - "Airex" Markings - Non-Operating Trucks; 6042-25 Gondola Car - Blue - with 2 Red Canisters - with Non-Operating

Trucks; 6045-25 Two Dome Tank Car - Gray - Non-Operating Trucks; 6047-25 Caboose - Brick Brown - Non-Operating Trucks; 1013 Curved Track (12); 1018 Straight Track (4); 1026-25 25-Watt Transformer; 1020-1 90° Crossover; 953-1 Figure Set; CTC-1 Lockon; 81-32 Wires (2); 927-60 Lubricant (Oil); 927-65 Lubricant (Grease); 1103-12 Envelope Packed With CTC-1, 81-32, 927-60 and 927-65; 1119-10 Instruction Sheet; 1802B Layout Instruction Sheet; 310-2 Set of (5) Billboard Signs; AC Accessory Catalog

Boxes & Packing: 59-318 Box; 59-377 Insert; 60-380 Insert; 60-493 Insert; 59-319 Shipper (1-4); ST Sticker; 60-600 Box; 59-377 Insert; 60-380 Insert; 60-493 Insert; 60-601 Shipper (1-4); 60-384 Box; 60-385 Insert; 60-386 Insert; 60-388 Shipper (1-4); ST Sticker

X-543NA (1960)	C6	C7	C8	Rarity
Complete Outfit With no. 59-318 Box	550	825	1,300	R9
Outfit Box no. 59-318	350	475	600	R9
Complete Outfit With no. 60-600 Box	475	725	1,175	R8
Outfit Box no. 60-600	275	375	475	R8
Complete Outfit With no. 60-384 Box	450	700	1,150	R8
Outfit Box no. 60-384	250	350	450	R8

Comments: Signet was listed as the customer for this 1960 promotional outfit. A common 1960s company name, the identity of Signet has yet to be determined. As such, this outfit could have been a Retailer Promotional (Type Ib) or a Manufacturer Promotional (Type IIIb) outfit.

An entry-level offering, the no. X-543NA included low-end motive power and rolling stock that were common to many other outfits. In fact, this outfit and no. X-508NA were identical except for a change in the Plasticville and the outfit packing.

The no. 1060-25 Steam Type Locomotive was new for 1960. It was a low-end steamer that went forward only. Interestingly, it was included in only five promotional outfits in 1960, but appeared in more than 65 outfits over the next few years.

Among the notable items in the X-543NA was the no. 6045-25 Gray Two Dome Tank Car. Two distinct colors of this car exist: gray and beige. According to Lionel Production Control Files, the material changed from "TMD 6000 Polystyrene Gray #55" to "Utility gray / high impact (special opaque)" and then back again. No specific dates were provided, but the gray version is the one included in this outfit.

Also worthwhile was the no. 6044-25 Blue Box Car - "Airex" Markings. Originally introduced in 1959, it appeared in 13 promotional outfits in 1960.

All the rolling stock in this outfit was equipped with non-operating Archbar trucks and couplers.

What drives up the value of this outfit was the inclusion of a no. 953-1 Figure Set. Lionel differentiated its promotional outfits by adding items like Plasticville sets.

Three different Tan RSC with Black Graphics outfit boxes were used for the X-543NA. The first 300 used a no. 59-318 Box that was an overstickered Sears no. 9664. This version is identifiable by its dual-layer configuration. The increase of 550 outfits on 9-26-60 led to the no. 60-600 Box. This was unique (no sticker) to this outfit.

The final increase of 500 was packaged in the single-layer no. 60-384 Box. It was an overstickered no. 1629 that was manufactured by St. Joe Kraft, St. Joe Paper Co. Container Division and measured 17½ x 11 x 4½ inches. This box had "5 6 7 8 9 10 11 12" and the box number printed on the bottom. It was rated at 90 pounds rather than the typical 65 pounds gross weight.

The three outfit boxes used in this outfit are easily distinguishable and, as such, are priced and rated separately. Each is difficult to find, but the version in a no. 60-384 Box appears most often.

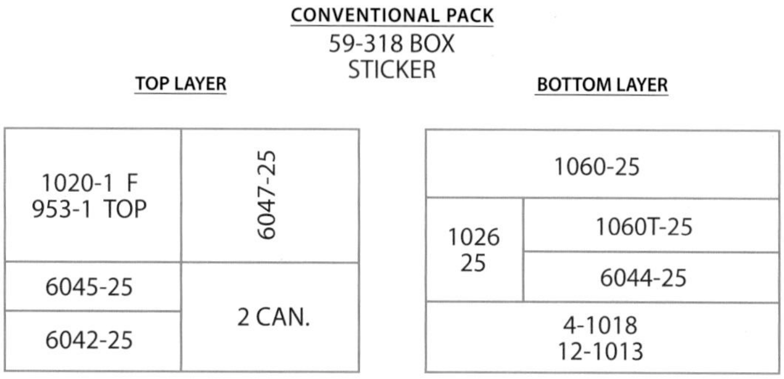

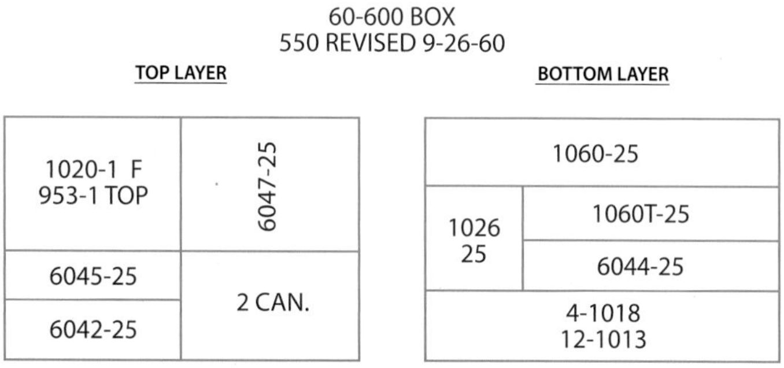

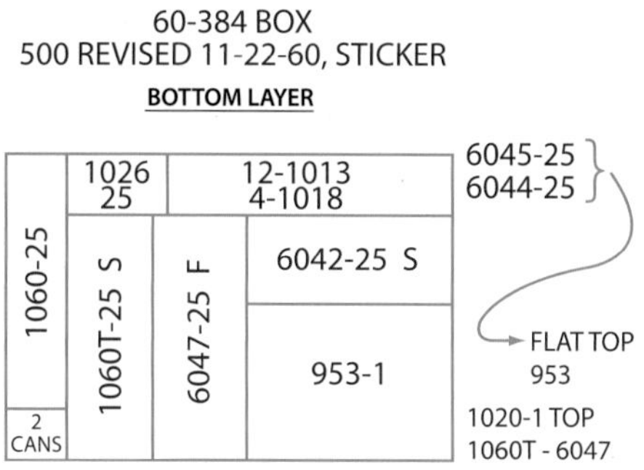

CONVENTIONAL PACK
59-318 BOX
STICKER

60-600 BOX
550 REVISED 9-26-60

60-384 BOX
500 REVISED 11-22-60, STICKER

Outfit no. X-544NA includes the nos. 902 Cardboard Trestle With Girder Bridge & Tunnel, 953-1 Figure Set and 960 Barnyard Set. These three items turn a basic outfit into a highly collectible one.

Description: 1960 Outfit
Specification: "O27" Ga. Steam Type Freight Outfit
Customer: Strauss Stores
Original Amount: 2,000
Factory Order Date: 4/26/1960
Date Issued: April 26, 1960
Packaging: Conventional Outfit Packing

Contents: 246-1 Locomotive - with Headlight and Magne-Traction - with Lockon & Lubricant; 1130T-1 Tender; 6162-1 Gondola Car - Blue - with (3) White Canisters; 6476-1 Hopper Car - Red; 6057-1 Caboose - Red; 1013 Curved Track (8); 1018 Straight Track; 1008-50 Uncoupling Unit - with (1) 1018 Straight Track; 1016-60 35-Watt Transformer; 953-1 Figure Set; 960 Barnyard Set; 902 Cardboard Trestle With Girder Bridge & Tunnel; 81-32 Wires (2); 310-2 Set of (5) Billboard Signs; 1609-4 Instruction Sheet; AC Accessory Catalog

Boxes & Packing: 60-486 Box; 60-487 Shipper (1-4)

X-544NA (1960)	C6	C7	C8	Rarity
Complete Outfit	630	1,000	1,900	R6
Outfit Box no. 60-486	175	275	350	R6

Comments: In 1960, Strauss Stores (an auto supply chain founded in Brooklyn, New York) purchased this Retailer Promotional Type Ib outfit.

Outfit no. X-544NA was headed by a no. 246-1 Locomotive with headlight and Magne-Traction. Included was the later version, which had a solid pilot but lacked generator detail. All the rolling stock in this outfit was equipped with early operating AAR trucks and couplers and came in Orange Perforated boxes. Some of the cars had notches on their AAR side frames.

Outfit no. X-544NA is a good example of Lionel taking an outfit filled with low-end rolling stock and sprucing it up with not one but two Plasticville sets. The nos. 953-1 Figure Set and 960 Barnyard Set are the items that are difficult to find in collectible condition when trying to complete this outfit. Their boxes were made of a thin cardstock that was easily torn or ripped. The instruction sheets and original, complete Plasticville pieces can also be a challenge to uncover.

Also difficult to find is the no. 902 Cardboard Trestle With Girder Bridge & Tunnel. This item is always difficult to find in C8 condition because, like other cardboard items placed in outfits, it was fragile and intended to be assembled. Once used, it retained minimal value.

The no. 60-486 Tan RSC with Black Graphics outfit box was manufactured by St. Joe Paper Co. - Container Div. and measured 13¼ x 11¾ x 6½ inches. It had "7 8 9 10 11 12" and "60-486" printed on its bottom.

This highly desirable outfit is difficult to find complete in collectible condition. One can find the empty box, but the components are almost always missing. Patience and funds are required to assemble one in C8 condition.

CONVENTIONAL PACK
60-486 BOX

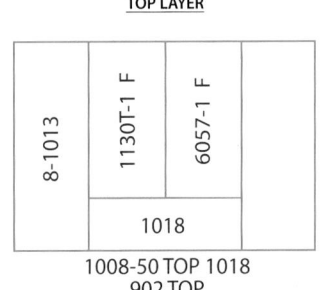

TOP LAYER

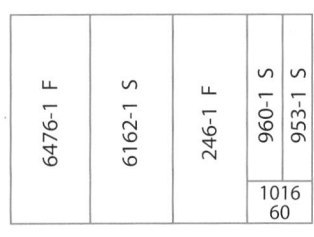

BOTTOM LAYER

Description: 1960 Outfit
Specification: "O27" Ga. Steam Type Freight Outfit
Customer: F. C. Stearns
Original Amount: 40
Factory Order Date: 4/27/1960
Date Issued: April 27, 1960
Packaging: Conventional Outfit Packing

Contents: 246-1 Locomotive - with Headlight and Magne-Traction - with Lockon and Lubricant; 1130T-1 Tender; 6162-1 Gondola Car - Blue - with (3) White Canisters; 6476-1 Hopper Car - Red; 6057-1 Caboose - Red; 1013 Curved Track (8); 1018 Straight Track (3); 1008-50 Uncoupling Unit - with (1) 1018 Straight Track; 1016-60 35-Watt Transformer; 963-1 Frontier Set; 81-32 Wires (2); 1609-4 Instruction Sheet; 310-2 Set of (5) Billboard Signs; AC Accessory Catalog

Boxes & Packing: 59-383 Box; 59-384 Shipper (1-4); ST Sticker

X-545NA (1960)	C6	C7	C8	Rarity
Complete Outfit	1,975	2,600	3,200	R10
Outfit Box no. 59-383	1,750	2,250	2,500	R10

Comments: This outfit lists F. C. Sterns as its customer. Our research indicates that this business was likely a hardware store in Hot Springs, Arkansas, that also sold Lionel trains in the 1960s. A Retailer Promotional Type Ia outfit, only 40 of the no. X-545NA were made, which ranks it tenth on the list of fewest promotional outfits. If not for its Factory Order, the existence of this outfit would surely be lost.

Outfit X-545NA included the same motive power and rolling stock as the no. X-544NA. They differed only in that the X-545NA came with one Plasticville set and lacked a no. 902 Cardboard Trestle With Girder Bridge & Tunnel.

Adding Plasticville items to an outfit was a low-cost way for Lionel to create a unique outfit. The no. 963-1 Frontier Set appeared only in this outfit during 1960. It was listed for $2.00 as a separate-sale item in the 1960 catalog. Today, this is the most difficult item to find in collectible condition when trying to complete this outfit. Its box was made of a thin cardstock that was easily torn or ripped. The instruction sheet and original, complete Plasticville pieces can also be a challenge to uncover.

All the rolling stock in the X-545NA included early operating AAR trucks and couplers and came in Orange Perforated boxes.

The no. 59-383 Tan RSC with Black Graphics outfit box was manufactured by Express Container Corp. and measured 13¼ x 12 x 6 inches. It was an overstickered no. X-860 outfit box from 1959.

With only 40 made, this is one of the rarest and most difficult promotional outfits to find. Based on the original quantity alone, it easily achieves an R10 rating.

Collectors will be scouring the area in and around Arkansas, hoping to find one of these promotional outfits, or at worst, an empty box.

CONVENTIONAL PACK
59-383 BOX
STICKER

TOP LAYER		BOTTOM LAYER

6057-1 S	
3-1018	1008-50
8-1013	
6476-1 S	
1130T-1 F	1016-60

6162-1 F
963-1 F
246-1 F

Customer No. On Box: EC 5011
Description: 1960 Outfit
Specification: "O27" Ga. Steam Type Freight Outfit with Smoke with Smoke
Customer/No./Price: Western Auto; EC 5011; $26.88
Original Amount: 2,000
Factory Order Date: 4/29/1960
Date Issued: August 20, 1960
Packaging: Color Corrugated Partitions in Display Box, Units not Boxed

Contents: 244-25 Locomotive - with Smoke & Headlight - with 2 Position Reversing Unit - without Magne-Traction, Lockon and Lubricant; 244T-25 Tender; 6062-25 Gondola Car - Black - with (3) Cable Reels; 6825-25 Flat Car Red - with Trestle Bridge - Black; 3419-25 Operating Helicopter Car; 6017-25 Caboose - Brick Brown; 1013 Curved Track (8); 1018 Straight Track; 1008-50 Uncoupling Unit - with (1) 1018 Straight Track; 1015-25 45-Watt Transformer; CTC-1 Lockon; 81-32 Wires (2); 927-60 Lubricant (Oil); 927-65 Lubricant (Grease); 1103-12 Envelope Packed With CTC-1, 81-32, 927-60 and 927-65; 1627-2 Instruction Sheet; 310-2 Set of (5) Billboard Signs; AC Accessory Catalog; 909-10 Bottle of Liquid Smoke

Boxes & Packing: 60-553 Box; 60-541 Insert; 60-542 Insert; 60-146 Insert (2); 60-147 Insert; 60-148 Insert; 60-149 Insert; 60-554 Shipper (1-4)

Alternate For Outfit Contents:
Customer No. EC 5011 (Printed on Boxes).

X-546NA (1960)	C6	C7	C8	Rarity
Complete Outfit	285	465	700	R6
Outfit Box no. 60-553	110	160	210	R6

Comments: Western Auto Stores purchased two steam-powered promotional outfits in 1960: nos. X-538NA and X-546NA. Both were Retailer Promotional Type Ia outfits, with the X-546NA being the better of the two based on its components.

This outfit was headed by a no. 244-25 Locomotive with Smoke & Headlight, a two-position reversing unit and a metal motor casing. The rolling stock in the X-546NA was also a slight upgrade from the X-538NA, thanks to the addition of a no. 3419-25 Operating Helicopter Car. Since this car came unboxed (not the norm), the no. 3419-100 Operating Helicopter Complete was

Western Auto cataloged the no. X-546NA as no. EC 5011 for $26.88 (item F) in its 1960 Christmas Catalog. In the picture, the tender is backwards and the no. 3419-25 is shown in red (never manufactured that way) with a 1959 vintage winder and helicopter.

included loose in the outfit box.

All the cars in this outfit were equipped with early operating AAR trucks and couplers.

The no. 60-553 was a Yellow Hinged Display with Steamer, General and F3 Graphics Type A outfit box. Measuring 25½ x 12½ x 3 inches, it was unique to this outfit.

The X-546NA was produced in large quantities, many of which likely went to gleeful kids at the holidays. Although examples of this outfit do appear, they're seldom in collectible condition. Western Auto outfit collectors may have to wait to find one good enough to add to their display cases.

DISPLAY PACK
60-553 BOX

244-25	244T-25	1015 25	
3419-25	6062-25		1-1018 8-1013
6825-25	6017-25		

1008-50 BELOW 6062

Description: 1960 Outfit
Specification: "O27" Ga. Steam Type Freight Outfit with Smoke
Customer: WM Taylor & Son
Original Amount: 36
Factory Order Date: 6/14/1960
Date Issued: September 7, 1960
Packaging: Conventional Outfit Packing

Contents: 244-1 Locomotive - with Smoke & Headlight - with 2 Position Reversing Unit - without Magne-Traction - with Lockon and Lubricant; 244T-1 Tender; 3376-1 Operating Giraffe Car; 6062-1 Gondola Car - Black - with (3) Cable Reels; 6825-1 Flat Car - Red - with Trestle Bridge - Black; 6017-1 Caboose - Brick Brown; 1013 Curved Track (8); 1018 Straight Track (3); 1008-50 Uncoupling Unit - with (1) 1018 Straight Track; 1015-60 45-Watt Transformer; 81-32 Wires (2); 310-2 Set of (5) Billboard Signs; 1627-2 Instruction Sheet; AC Accessory Catalog

Boxes & Packing: 59-318 Box; 59-319 Shipper (1-4); ST Sticker

Alternate For Outfit Contents:
Note: If necessary, substitute 1- 1015-25.

X-547 (1960)	C6	C7	C8	Rarity
Complete Outfit	2,050	2,675	3,100	R10
Outfit Box no. 59-318	1,850	2,350	2,600	R10

Comments: WM Taylor & Son was a variety store located in Cleveland. They purchased one Retailer Promotional Type Ia outfit during the 1960s. With only 36 ordered, the no. X-547 likely was intended as an internal promotion or a one-time sale or promotional item. This mundane freight outfit is tied for eighth

on the list of fewest manufactured.

The X-547 was headed by a no. 244-1 Locomotive with Smoke & Headlight and a two-position reversing unit. This steamer's motor was metal, but it included only ballast weights as a traction aid.

The nos. 244-1, 244T-1 Tender and 3376-1 Operating Giraffe car were all new for 1960. The remainder of the rolling stock was carryover from previous years.

All the cars were equipped with early operating AAR trucks and couplers. Except for the 244T-1 (which came in an overstamped Bold Classic no. 1625T Folding Box), everything came packaged in Orange Perforated boxes.

The no. 59-318 Tan RSC with Black Graphics outfit box was an overstickered Sears no. 9664 from 1959.

It is unknown why the number of this outfit does not include "NA". (See the section on Outfit Numbering for a discussion of "NA" and its uses.)

Collectors will be scouring hobby stores and resale shops in and around Cleveland looking for one of these outfits.

CONVENTIONAL PACK
59-318 BOX
STICKER

TOP LAYER

6825-1 S	
3-1018	
8-1013	
244T-1 F	1015 60
6017-1 S	

1008-50 TOP

BOTTOM LAYER

244-1 F
3376-1 S
6062-1 F

Description: 1960 Outfit
Specification: "O27" Ga. Steam Type Freight Outfit
Customer/No./Price: Frontier Savings Stamps; T-96; 6 Books
Original Amount: 1,600
Factory Order Date: 4/14/1960
Date Issued: 9-9-60
Packaging: Conventional Outfit Packing

Contents: 246-1 Locomotive - with Headlight and Magne-Traction - with Lockon & Lubricant; 1130T-1 Tender; 6045-25 Two Dome Tank Car - Gray - with Non-Operating Trucks; 6825-1 Flat Car - Red - with Trestle Bridge - Black; 6057-1 Caboose - Red; 1013 Curved Track (8); 1018 Straight Track; 1008-50 Uncoupling Unit - with (1) 1018 Straight Track; 1016-60 35-Watt Transformer; 81-32 Wires (2); 1609-4 Instruction Sheet; 310-2 Set of (5) Billboard Signs; AC Accessory Catalog

Boxes & Packing: 59-324 Box; 59-325 Shipper (1-4); BP Bogus Paper; ST Sticker

X-548 (1960)	C6	C7	C8	Rarity
Complete Outfit	285	425	500	R6
Outfit Box no. 59-324	150	200	250	R6

Comments: Frontier Savings Stamps was one of the many stamp companies that offered Lionel trains during the 1960s. In Frontier's 1960 catalog, it listed the no. X-548 as no. T-96 for six filled books of stamps. This Retailer Promotional Type Ib was the only outfit linked to Frontier.

Business must have been good, as the original Factory Order listed 500 on April 14, 1960, and then was increased to 1,600 on 9-9-60. With this success, it is unknown why Frontier did not purchase another Retailer Promotional outfit in subsequent years.

The X-548 was typical of starter outfits from 1960 and similar to the no. X-516NA, the competitive offering from Sperry & Hutchinson. It was headed by a no. 246-1 Locomotive with Headlight and Magne-Traction that came in a no. 246-6 Corrugated Box.

The rolling stock in this outfit was, with a single exception, packaged in Orange Perforated boxes and equipped with early operating AAR trucks and couplers. No wonder the no. 6045-25 Gray Two Dome Tank Car seemed out of place in this outfit. It was unboxed and came with non-operating Archbar trucks and couplers.

The no. 59-324 was a single-layer Tan RSC with Black Graphics outfit box. It was first used with catalog outfit no. 1609 from 1959 and subsequently with at least six other outfits. It was manufactured by Express Container Corp. and measured 14⅞ x 12⅝ x 4¼ inches.

It is unknown why the number of this outfit does not include "NA". (See the section on Outfit Numbering for a discussion of "NA" and its uses.)

CONVENTIONAL PACK
59-324 BOX
BOGUS PAPER, STICKER

246-1 S	1016	1-1018
6045-25 S		TOP 6825
1130T-1 S	6057-1 F	1008 TOP
8-1013		1018
6825-1 S		

Description: 1960 Outfit
Specification: "O27" Ga. Steam Type Freight Outfit
Customer: Grossman's
Original Amount: 200
Factory Order Date: 6/13/1960
Date Issued: August 1, 1960
Packaging: Display Outfit Packing - Corrugated Separators, Units not Boxed

Contents: 246-25 Locomotive - with Headlight and Magne-Traction - Less Lockon and Lubricant; 1060T-25 Tender; 6476-25 Hopper Car - Red; 3386-25 Operating Giraffe Car - with Non-Operating Trucks; 3376-118 Envelope Packed; 6045-25 Two Dome Tank Car - Gray - Non-Operating Trucks; 6047-25 Caboose - Brick Brown - Non-Operating Trucks; 1013 Curved Track (8); 1018 Straight Track (2); 1016-60 35-Watt Transformer; 902 Cardboard Trestle With Girder Bridge & Tunnel; 907 Set of 15 Billboard signs; 903 Set of (2) Sheets Trading Cards; CTC Lockon; 81-32 Wires (2); 927-60 Lubricant (Oil); 927-65 Lubricant (Grease); 1103-12 Envelope Packed With CTC, 81-32, 927-60 and 927-65; 1109-10 Instruction Sheet; 310-2 Set of (5) Billboard Signs; AC Accessory Catalog

Boxes & Packing: 60-514 Box; 60-515 Insert; 60-516 Insert; 59-44 Tube; 60-517 Shipper (1-6); ST 5 Stickers

X-549NA (1960)	C6	C7	C8	Rarity
Complete Outfit Without A no. 907	1,225	2,600	4,650	R10
Outfit Box no. 60-514	500	700	850	R10

Comments: Grossman's was a retailer that purchased its only promotional outfit, a Retailer Promotional Type Ib, in 1960. The no. X-549NA was a steam-powered outfit led by an unboxed no. 246-25 Locomotive with Headlight and Magne-Traction.

The rolling stock in this outfit primarily included low-end items. All were equipped with non-operating AAR trucks and couplers, with the exception of a no. 6476-25 Hopper Car - Red, which came with early operating AAR trucks and couplers. A notable item was the no. 3386-25 Operating Giraffe Car (new for 1960). This car appeared in only 10 promotional outfits. When unboxed, its no. 3376-118 Envelope Packed was placed loose in the outfit box.

By far the two items that drive up the price of this outfit are the no. 902 Cardboard Trestle With Girder Bridge & Tunnel and the no. 903 Set of (2) Sheets Trading Cards. Both of them were fragile and intended to be separated and played with. Many more examples of the 902 have survived intact than have 903s.

The 903 included 24 two-sided Lionel trading cards printed on a sheet of perforated cardstock. On the front of each card was a Lionel locomotive, and on the back was historical information about its road name as well as a trivia quiz. Two 11 x 11 inch sets of 12 cards were connected by a "folding" strip. The entire sheet of 24 was folded in half along the strip and placed loose in the outfit box. The cards were perforated and are almost always found separated as individual cards with the "folding" strip long gone. In fact, if it weren't for the complete sheets that came out of Madison Hardware over the years, it is likely that few of these items would be intact.

The no. 907 Set of 15 Billboard Signs was first issued in 1959 and appeared only in this outfit in 1960. These have yet to be seen, and the only other information available came from a Lionel "No. Book" that lists the 907 as a "Set of (3) 310-2 Billboard Signs - Purch'd". Why Lionel would issue a new part number for three common billboards is unknown. Perhaps the billboards came as a single sheet or were special in some way. Because no information on the 907 exists, the X-549NA is priced without it.

The no. 60-514 White Hinged Display with 1050 Blue Steamer and Red/Orange Graphics Type A outfit box was manufactured by Kraft Corrugated Containers and measured 19¼ x 13⅞ x 3 inches. It was an overstickered no. 1119 outfit box.

With only 200 of this outfit manufactured and distributed through a smaller retailer, it is seldom seen. Add in the inclusion of the 902 and 903 and you'll see why the X-549NA has been given its R10 rarity and high price.

DISPLAY PACK 60-514 BOX 5 STICKERS	
246-25	1060T-25
6476-25	6045-25
6047-25	3376-118 3386-25
2-1018 8-1013	1016-60
902 TOP 907 TOP	

Arkwright's offering to its customers in 1960 was the no. X-550NA. This is an exciting space and military outfit headed by the promotional-only no. 228P-1 Green Canadian National Alco Diesel. Hours of fun could be had blowing up the no. 6470-1 Exploding Target Car or the no. 943 Exploding Ammo Dump packed with it.

Description: 1960 Outfit
Specification: "O27" Ga. Diesel Freight Outfit
Customer: Arkwright
Original Amount: 1,500
Factory Order Date: 6/14/1960
Date Issued: June 14, 1960
Packaging: Conventional Outfit Packing

Contents: 228P-1 Alco Diesel Power Car - Green - "Canadian National" - Yellow Lettering with Headlight and Magne-Traction - with 2 Position Reversing Unit, Lockon & Lubricant; 6544-1 Missile Firing Trail Car - Blue Car Body; 3419-1 Operating Helicopter Car; 6470-1 Exploding Target Car; 6017-1 Caboose - Brick Brown; 1013 Curved Track (17); 1018 Straight Track (9); 1008-50 Uncoupling Unit - with (1) 1018 Straight Track; 1015-60 45-Watt Transformer; 110-1 Graduated Trestle Set; 943 Exploding Ammo Dump; 81-32 Wires (2); 310-2 Set of (5) Billboard Signs; 1613-10 Instruction Sheet; AC Accessory Catalog; 1802I Layout Instruction Sheet

Boxes & Packing: 60-565 Box; 60-566 Shipper (1-3)

Alternate For Outfit Contents:
Note: If necessary, substitute 1- 1015-25.

X-550NA (1960)	C6	C7	C8	Rarity
Complete Outfit	630	1,025	1,500	R6
Outfit Box no. 60-565	175	275	350	R6

Comments: Outfit no. X-550NA was Arkwright's (a large buying organization) promotional outfit purchase for 1960. A Retailer Promotional Type Ib outfit, it likely was resold to Arkwright's many small customers, although no connections have been made.

This space and military outfit was headed by a no. 228P-1 Green Canadian National Alco Diesel Power Car equipped with two-axle Magne-Traction, an open pilot and a two-position reversing unit. This new-for-1960 locomotive was never offered for separate sale, but it was included in five outfits (four promotional and a substitution in catalog outfit no. 1643). The Factory Orders show a total of 5,228 produced, of which 2,650 were boxed. According to Lionel Production Control Files, the 228P-1 came in an overstamped no. 210-54 or no. 208-10 Corrugated Box. These low numbers explain why it doesn't appear too often.

The nos. 3419-1 Operating Helicopter Car, 6470-1 Exploding Target Car and 6544-1 Missile Firing Trail Car were an exciting combination of space and military rolling stock. Hours could be spent blowing up the 6470-1 Exploding Target Car as well as the no. 943 Exploding Ammo Dump. The first two cars were carryover from 1959, and the 6544-1 was new for 1960. The 6470-1 included "slotted" sides and a smooth roof door guide (without the nubs added later to help hold on the sides).

The rolling stock in the X-550NA was equipped with early operating AAR trucks and couplers. The caboose, however, was equipped with one early operating AAR and one plain AAR truck

and coupler. All the cars came packaged in Orange Perforated boxes with their appropriate instruction sheets inside. The no. 1802I Layout Instruction Sheet detailed the elevate pretzel track layout.

The no. 60-565 Tan RSC with Black Graphics outfit box was manufactured by Owens Illinois Paper Products Division and measured 15½ x 13¾ x 6¾ inches. It had 12 dots printed as part of the box manufacturer's certificate.

Examples of the X-550NA do appear on the market from time to time, though generally all that is found is the empty outfit box. This circumstance is usually due to the fact that, as with many promotional outfits, the contents have been cannibalized and sold off separately because they are always in demand.

That being said, the X-550NA is an exciting space and military outfit headed by the relatively scarce 228P-1 Alco Diesel Power Car. This outfit would be a nice addition for any space and military or promotional outfit collector.

CONVENTIONAL PACK
60-565 BOX

TOP LAYER				BOTTOM LAYER		
6470-1 S				6544-1 F	1015 60	
8-1013		6017-1 F				943-1 S
9-1013				228P-1 F		
9-1018				110-1 F		
3419-1 F						
1008-50						

X-551NA
1960

Description: 1960 Outfit
Specification: "O27" Ga. Steam Type Freight Outfit with Smoke
Customer/No.: Oklahoma Tire & Supply Co.; 70-762-7
Original Amount: 225
Factory Order Date: 6/6/1960
Date Issued: June 6, 1960
Packaging: Conventional Outfit Packing

Contents: 2018-1 Locomotive - with Smoke, Lockon & Lubricant - without Magne-Traction; 243W-1 Whistle Tender; 3376-1 Operating Giraffe Car; 6062-1 Gondola Car - Black - with (3) Cable Reels; 6476-1 Hopper Car - Red; 3419-1 Operating Helicopter Car; 6017-1 Caboose - Brick Brown; 1013 Curved Track (8); 1018 Straight Track (3); 1008-50 Uncoupling Unit - with (1) 1018 Straight Track; 1063-25 75-Watt Transformer; 81-32 Wires (2); 926-60 Instruction Book; 310-2 Set of (5) Billboard Signs; AC Accessory Catalog

Boxes & Packing: 59-100 Box; 59-101 Shipper (1-4); ST Sticker; BP Bogus Paper

Alternate For Outfit Contents:
Note: Customer Stock No. 70-762-7 (Printed on Boxes).

X-551NA (1960)	C6	C7	C8	Rarity
Complete Outfit	700	1,000	1,325	R10
Outfit Box no. 59-100	450	550	650	R10

Comments: In 1960, Oklahoma Tire & Supply Company (OTASCO) purchased six promotional outfits: nos. X-532NA, X-533NA, X-551NA, X-552NA, 1107 and 1109. The X-551NA and X-552NA were Retailer Promotional Type Ia outfits unique to OTASCO. The X-551NA was headed by a steam locomotive, and the X-552NA was led by a diesel.

The X-551NA was headed by a no. 2018-1 Locomotive with Smoke. This steamer last appeared in a catalog outfit in 1959, but it was used in promotional outfits in the 1960s. When boxed in its 2018-10 Corrugated Box, it included the nos. 675-33 Smoke Stack Cleaner, SP-1 Pellets Bottled, 927-60 Tube of Oil, 927-65

CONVENTIONAL PACK
59-100 BOX
REVISED 9-22-60, STICKER, BOGUS PAPER

TOP LAYER			BOTTOM LAYER		
243W-1 S			2018-1 F		
6476-1 S		1008-50			
8-1013			6062-1 F		1063 25
6017-1 S					
3376-1 S			3419-1 F		
3-1018 TOP 6476					

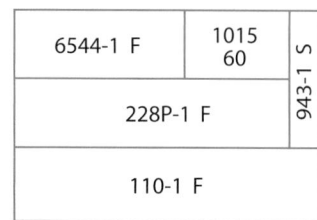

Tube of Grease, 2018-11 Instruction Sheet and CTC-1 Lockon.

The no. 243W-1 Whistle Tender and no. 3376-1 Operating Giraffe Car were both new for 1960. They, as well as the carryover items, were equipped with early operating AAR trucks and couplers. They also came packaged in Orange Perforated boxes with their appropriate instruction sheets and packed envelopes inside.

The no. 59-100 Yellow RSC with Black Graphics outfit box was manufactured by Star Corrugated Box Company, Inc. and measured 14⅛ x 13⅛ x 7 inches. It was an overstickered no. 1626W outfit box from 1959.

OTASCO was a good customer of Lionel and purchased numerous promotional and catalog outfits. This outfit, with only 225 made, is extremely difficult to find, hence its R10 rarity.

Description: 1960 Outfit
Specification: "O27" Ga. Diesel Freight Outfit
Cust./No./Price: Oklahoma Tire & Supply Co.; 70-761-8; $33.83
Original Amount: 275
Factory Order Date: 6/6/1960
Date Issued: June 14, 1960
Packaging: Conventional Outfit Packing

Contents: 220P-1 Alco Diesel Power Unit - "Santa Fe" - with Headlight, 2 Magnets, Non-Operating Coupler, Lockon & Lubricant; 220T-1 Motorless Unit - "Santa Fe"; 6812-1 Track Maintenance Car; 6062-1 Flat Car - Black - with (3) Cable Reels; 6825-1 Flat Car - Red - with Trestle Bridge - Black; 6476-1 Hopper Car - Red; 6017-1 Caboose - Brick Brown; 1013 Curved Track (12); 1018 Straight Track (13); 1008-50 Uncoupling Unit - with (1) 1018 Straight Track; 1015-60 45-Watt Transformer; 110-1 Graduated Trestle Set; 81-32 Wires (2); 310-2 Set of (5) Billboard Signs; 1569-11 Instruction Sheet; AC Accessory Catalog; 2099 Layout Instruction Sheet

Boxes & Packing: 59-361 Box; 59-362 Shipper (1-3); ST Sticker

Alternate For Outfit Contents:
Note: Customer Stock No. 70-761-8 (Printed on Boxes); Note: If necessary - substitute 1- 1015-25.

X-552NA (1960)	C6	C7	C8	Rarity
Complete Outfit	865	1,225	1,625	R10
Outfit Box no. 59-361	425	525	625	R10

Comments: In 1960, Oklahoma Tire & Supply Company (OTASCO) purchased six promotional outfits: nos. X-532NA, X-533NA, X-551NA, X-552NA, 1107 and 1109. The X-551NA and X-552NA were Retailer Promotional Type Ia outfits unique to OTASCO. The X-551NA was headed by a steam locomotive, and the X-552NA was led by a diesel.

The X-552NA appeared on page 21 of the 1960 Oklahoma Tire & Supply Co. Christmas Gifts Catalog as no. 70-761-8 for $33.83.

The X-552NA was headed by a no. 220P-1 Santa Fe Alco Diesel Power Unit, which included two-axle Magne-Traction, a three-position reversing unit and a headlight. The only feature missing was a horn. The no. 220P-1 is an example of an item that appeared in promotional outfits before it became a regular-production item (it appeared in the 1961 consumer catalog). When boxed in its no. 220-10 Corrugated Box, this locomotive included the nos. CTC-1 Lockon, 927-60 Tube of Oil, 927-65 Tube of Grease and 220-11 Instruction Sheet. The box was surrounded by a no. 217-16 Sleeve.

All the rolling stock in this outfit was carryover from previous years. The cars were equipped with early operating AAR trucks and couplers and came packaged in Orange Perforated boxes. The only notable item was a no. 6812-1 Track Maintenance Car. To be in collectible condition, this item must include original figures and an original, unbroken platform.

The track layout was detailed on a no. 2099 Layout Instruction Sheet. This sheet was included in only this and outfit nos. X-529NA and X-562NA. Its Production Control File list orders for 2,500. So small a quantity and the lack of survivability make it rare.

The no. 59-361 Tan RSC with Black Graphics outfit box was an overstickered 1959 no. X-831NA manufactured by Continental Can Company, Inc. It measured 15½ x 14¾ x 7⅜ inches and had "59" and five dots printed on the bottom.

Other than its locomotive, the X-552NA was identical to outfit no. X-562NA.

OTASCO was a good customer of Lionel and purchased numerous promotional and catalog outfits. However, as is true of the X-551NA, the small quantity of this outfit makes examples difficult to find.

CONVENTIONAL PACK
59-361 BOX
STICKER

TOP LAYER		BOTTOM LAYER	
6476-1 S		110-1 F	
6825-1 S	6017-1 F	220P-1 S	
13-1018		220T-1 S	
12-1013			
6062-1 S		6812-1 F	1015 60
1008-50 TOP			

Description: 1960 Outfit
Specification: "O27" Ga. Steam Type Freight Outfit
Customer: Canada
Customer/No./Price: Simpsons-Sears; 49 N9631L; $19.98
Original Amount: 1,000
Factory Order Date: 6/3/1960
Date Issued: June 3, 1960
Packaging: Snake Insert Outfit Packing, Units not Boxed

Contents: 1050-25 Steam Type Locomotive - with Headlight - without Pilot Trucks, Magne-Traction and Reversing Unit - Less Lockon & Lubricant; 1050T-25 Tender - with Non-Operating Truck; 6042-25 Gondola Car - Blue - with 2 Red Canisters - with Non-Operating Trucks; 6044-25 Box Car - Blue - "Airex" Markings - Non-Operating Trucks; 6045-25 Two Dome Tank Car - Gray - Non-Operating Trucks; 6047-25 Caboose - Brick Brown - Non-Operating Trucks; 1013 Curved Track (8); 1018 Straight Track (2); 1026-25 25-Watt Transformer; 81-32 Wires (2); CTC Lockon; 927-60 Lubricant (Oil); 927-65 Lubricant (Grease); 1103-12 Envelope Packed With CTC, 81-32, 927-60 and 927-65; 310-2 Set of (5) Billboard Signs; IS Instruction Sheet; AC Accessory Catalog

Boxes & Packing: 60-551 Box; 60-515 Insert; 60-516 Insert; 59-47 Insert; 59-44 Tube; 60-552 Shipper (1-6)

Alternate For Outfit Contents:
Note: Identical to X-833 (1959).

X-553NA (1960)	C6	C7	C8	Rarity
Complete Outfit	425	600	800	R7
Outfit Box no. 60-551	225	300	350	R7

Comments: Canada was listed as the customer on the Factory Order for this Retailer Promotional Type Ib outfit. The no. X-553NA has been observed in the 1960 Simpson-Sears Christmas Catalog as a "Value-Packed 0-4-0 Stem Freighter" with no. 49 N9631L for $19.98.

This and promotional outfit no. 1103 were the only two outfits in 1960 to include a no. 1050-25 Steam Type Locomotive. Originally introduced in 1959, this was Lionel's promotional-only low-end steamer. Its no. 1050-100 Motor Complete went forward only. Even though the 1050-25 was a low-end locomotive, Lionel produced it in small numbers (2,000 in 1960 and minimally 1,200 in outfit no. X-833 and 3,398 in outfit no. 1103, both from 1959). As a result, this steam locomotive is difficult to find in collectible condition. Eventually, Lionel replaced it with the no. 1060-25 Locomotive.

The rolling stock in the X-553NA was low-end, with all the cars equipped with non-operating Archbar trucks and couplers. All items except the tender and caboose appeared only in promotional outfits.

This outfit came in a no. 60-551 Type A display outfit box that was unique to this outfit.

Overall, the X-553NA was typical of many low-end and advance catalog outfits of the time. Other than its box, this outfit is identical to the no. X-833 from 1959 (that came in a no. 59-425 Box). And the contents of the X-553NA match those of the 1103 from 1960, except that the former outfit included a no. 6045-25 Gray Two Dome Tank Car.

DISPLAY PACK
60-551 BOX

1050-25	1050T-25
6044-25	6045-25
6047-25	6042-25
2-1018 8-1013	1026-25

Description: 1960 Outfit
Specification: "O27" Ga. Steam Type Freight Outfit
Customer: Grand-Way
Original Amount: 800
Factory Order Date: 6/13/1960
Date Issued: June 13, 1960
Packaging: Conventional Outfit Packing

Contents: 246-1 Locomotive - with Headlight and Magne-Traction - with Lockon and Lubricant; 1130T-1 Tender; 1877-1 Flat Car - with (6) Horses in White - Automatic Uncoupling; 3376-1 Operating Giraffe Car; 6825-1 Flat Car - Red - with Trestle Bridge - Black; 6017-1 Caboose - Brick Brown; 1013 Curved Track (8); 1018 Straight Track; 1008-50 Uncoupling Unit - with (1) 1018 Straight Track; 1015-60 45-Watt Transformer; 81-32 Wires (2); 310-2 Set of (5) Billboard Signs; AC Accessory Catalog; 1609-4 Instruction Sheet

Boxes & Packing: 60-571 Box; 60-572 Shipper (1-4)

X-554NA (1960)	C6	C7	C8	Rarity
Complete Outfit	365	650	950	R8
Outfit Box no. 60-571	150	275	375	R8

Comments: Grand-Way was Grand Union's discount store chain, and it carried Lionel trains during the 1960s. In 1960, it purchased two Retailer Promotional outfits: nos. X-554NA and X-561NA. Both featured steam locomotives.

The X-554NA was Grand-Way's low-end offering. A no. 246-1 Locomotive with Headlight and Magne-Traction led the

CONVENTIONAL PACK
60-571 BOX

TOP LAYER

8-1013
1877-1 S
6017-1 S
6825-1 F

1008-50 TOP 6825
1018 TOP

BOTTOM LAYER

246-1 F	
1130T-1 F	1015 60
3376-1 F	

Type Ia outfit. This steamer came in a no. 246-6 Corrugated Box.

The no. 1877-1 Flat Car with (6) Horses in White appeared only twice in its no. 1877-14 Folding Box during the 1960s. The X-554NA was its first appearance, and outfit no. X-719 was its last appearance in 1961. The 1877-1 was equipped with operating Archbar trucks and couplers.

The no. 3376-1 Operating Giraffe Car was the only new item in this outfit. Its no. 3376-118 Envelope Packed was placed in a no. 3376-120 Folding Box. Also included was a no. 6809-12 Tube

to protect the one coupler that, due to the giraffe mechanism, could not be turned under the car for protection. This and all the other cars were equipped with early operating AAR trucks and couplers and packaged in Orange Perforated boxes.

The X-554NA came in a no. 60-571 RSC outfit box that was unique to it.

With only 800 made, this outfit or its empty box is rarely seen.

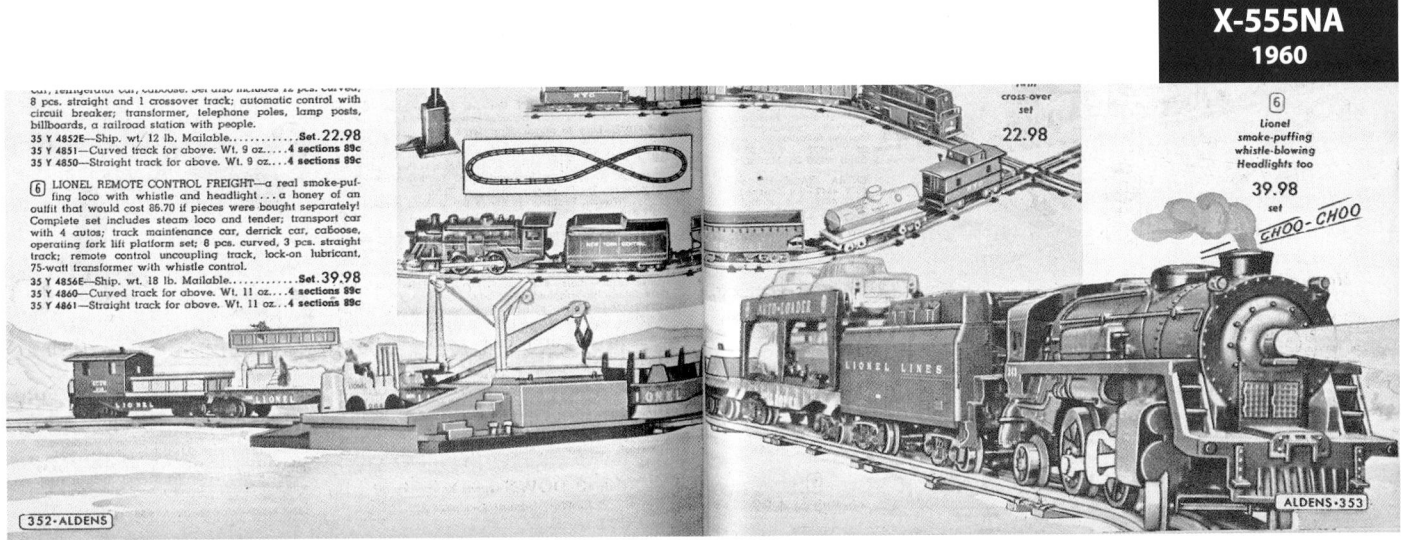

Aldens' Christmas Catalog for 1960 lists the no. X-555NA as no. 35 Y 4856E (item 6) for $39.98. It states that if purchased separately, the cost would be $86.70. This comparison-style pricing was common with promotional outfits during the 1960s. Note that the outfit appeared to be correctly illustrated, which was generally not the case with retail catalogs.

Description: 1960 Outfit
Specification: "O27" Ga. Steam Type Freight Outfit with Whistle & Smoke
Customer/No./Price: Aldens; 35 Y 4856E; $39.98
Original Amount: 150
Factory Order Date: 6/3/1960
Date Issued: June 3, 1960
Packaging: Conventional Outfit Packing

Contents: 243-1 Locomotive - with Smoke and Headlight - with (2) Position Reversing Unit, Lockon and Lubricant - without Magne-Traction; 243W-1 Whistle Tender; 6414-1 Automobile Transport Car; 6812-1 Track Maintenance Car; 6670-1 Crane Car; 6119-100 Work Caboose; 1013 Curved Track (8); 1018 Straight Track (3); 6029-25 Uncoupling Track Section; 1063-25 Transformer; 264-1 Operating Fork Lift Platform Set; 90-1 Uncoupling Track Controller; 81-32 Wires (4); 90-30 Envelope Packed With 90-1 and 81-32; 926-60 Instruction Book; 310-2 Set of (5) Billboard Signs; AC Accessory Catalog

Boxes & Packing: 59-396 Box; 59-397 Shipper (1-2); ST Sticker; BP Bogus Paper

X-555NA (1960)	C6	C7	C8	Rarity
Complete Outfit	1,350	1,925	2,400	R10
Outfit Box no. 59-396	700	925	1,025	R10

Comments: Aldens was a mail-order retailer headquartered in Chicago during the 1960s. It purchased this Retailer Promotional Type Ia outfit in 1960. The no. X-555NA was the only Lionel O27 gauge purchase to appear in its 1960 Christmas catalog. All the other Lionel items listed there were from the HO line.

A no. 243-1 Locomotive - with Smoke and Headlight headed the X-555NA. Other features on this steamer included a metal motor and a two-position reversing unit. This engine was nearly identical to the no. 244-1 Locomotive, except that the 243 included an extra weight as part of its mechanism. The locomotive and its tender were the only new items in this outfit.

Lionel frequently used promotional outfits to deplete its inventory of many items, especially accessories. This practice helped Lionel while providing consumers with unique outfits that had plenty of play value. In the case of the X-555NA, Lionel included a no. 264-1 Operating Fork Lift Platform Set. This was the last of three promotional outfits used to retire Lionel's stock of this accessory. The Operating Fork Lift Platform Set came with a no. 6264-25 Lumber Car Complete.

The cars included in this outfit were repeated from earlier years. The no. 6414-1 Automobile Car came in two promotional outfits in 1960 and had four premium autos with chrome bumpers. The nos. 6670-1 Crane Car and 6812-1 Track Maintenance Car were new in 1959.

Even though many of these items were originally issued earlier, every car likely was equipped with early operating AAR trucks and couplers and came packaged in Orange Perforated boxes. It's possible that the no. 6670-1 Crane Car came in its Bold Classic-style box because this packaging has been observed in outfits in 1960s.

A large outfit box was required to fit the Operating Fork Lift Platform Set. Lionel used a no. 59-396 Tan RSC with Black Graphics, which was an overstickered no. X-853 outfit box from 1959

With only 150 of these outfits made, it is seldom seen.

CONVENTIONAL PACK
59-396 BOX
STICKER, BOGUS PAPER

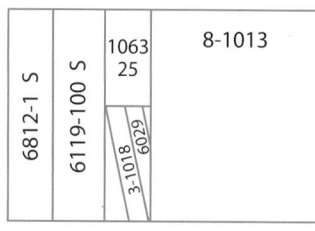

TOP LAYER

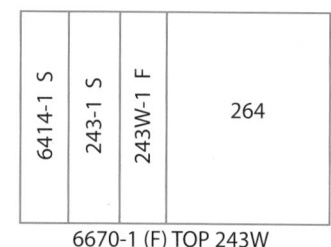

BOTTOM LAYER

6670-1 (F) TOP 243W

X-556NA
1960

Description: 1960 Outfit
Specification: "O27" Ga. Diesel Freight Outfit
Customer: Associated Dry Goods
Original Amount: 175
Factory Order Date: 6/22/1960
Date Issued: September 23, 1960
Packaging: Conventional Outfit Packing

Contents: 225P-1 Alco Diesel Power Car - Blue - "Chesapeake & Ohio" - Yellow Lettering with Headlight and Magne-Traction - with 2 Position Reversing Unit - with Lockon & Lubricant; 6812-1 Track Maintenance Car; 6650-1 Missile Launching Flat Car; 6470-1 Exploding Target Car; 3419-1 Operating Helicopter Car; 6219-1 Work Caboose - Black Frame - Blue Cab and Tray - "Chesapeake & Ohio" - Markings in Yellow; 1013 Curved Track (8); 1018 Straight Track; 6029-25 Uncoupling Track Section; 1015-60 45-Watt Transformer; 90-1 Uncoupling Track Controller; 81-32 Wires (4); 90-30 Envelope Packed With 90-1 and 81-32; IS Instruction Sheet; 310-2 Set of (5) Billboard Signs; AC Accessory Catalog

Boxes & Packing: 59-359 Box; 59-360 Shipper (1-4); ST Sticker

Alternate For Outfit Contents:
Note: Substitute 220P-1 for 225P-1 in 115 sets.

X-556NA (1960)	C6	C7	C8	Rarity
Complete Outfit With no. 225P-1	1,075	1,500	2,000	R10
Complete Outfit With no. 220P-1 Substitution	1,050	1,450	1,900	R10
Outfit Box no. 59-359	650	800	900	R10

Comments: Associated Dry Goods owned numerous retailers during the 1960s. The no. X-556NA, a Retailer Promotional Type Ia outfit, could have been sold through any of these stores. The extremely low quantity of this outfit (175 examples) suggested that it was destined for one of Associated's smaller chains.

This outfit was headed by a no. 225P-1 Chesapeake & Ohio Alco Diesel Power Car. New for 1960, it included an open pilot and the large ledge that Lionel added to Alcos as reinforcement in 1960. (See the entry for outfit no. X-509NA for detail on its difficult-to-obtain no. 225-20 Corrugated Box.)

The nos. 3419-1 Operating Helicopter Car, 6470-1 Exploding Target Car and 6650-1 Missile Launching Flat Car were an exciting combination of space and military rolling stock. Hours could be spent blowing up the 6470-1 Exploding Target Car. All three cars, as well as the no. 6812-1 Track Maintenance Car, were carryover from 1959. They were equipped with early operating AAR trucks and couplers and came packaged in Orange Perforated boxes.

The no. 6219-1 Work Caboose was equipped with one early operating AAR and one plain AAR truck and couplers. The "-1" usually meant an item was boxed. The Outfit Packing Diagram also leads us to believe that it was boxed. The only problem is that a box for this item has never been observed. In the end, the Outfit Packing Department probably inherited the task to find some kind of box to fulfill this small order.

The no. 59-359 Tan RSC with Black Graphics outfit box was manufactured by Star Corrugated Box Company, Inc. and measured 13¾ x 11⅞ x 6⅝ inches. An overstamped no. X-826 outfit box from 1959, it also had "8-4B" and a star printed on the bottom.

As the entry for the no. X-558NA reveals, the contents of that outfit are almost the same as those of the X-556NA. This is intriguing because Lionel sold the X-558NA directly to J. W. Robinson's, a department store chain that was one of Associated Dry Goods retail chains. In fact, both outfits have the same Factory Order date.

Pricing for the X-556NA is provided with and without the no. 220P-1 substitution. Pricing also assumes no box for the no. 6219-1 because one has yet to be seen and its price cannot be determined. It would likely bring a substantial premium.

CONVENTIONAL PACK
59-359 BOX
STICKER

TOP LAYER

8-1013
6219-1 S
6812-1 S
6470-1 S

1-1018 TOP
6029-25 TOP

BOTTOM LAYER

225P-1 S	
3419-1 F	1015 60
6650-1 F	

Description: 1960 Outfit
Specification: "O27" Ga. Steam Type Freight Outfit
Customer: Radoff Brothers
Original Amount: 1,000
Factory Order Date: 6/6/1960
Date Issued: 7-25-60
Packaging: Conventional Outfit Packing

Contents: 246-1 Locomotive - with Headlight and Magne-Traction - with Lockon and Lubricant; 1130T-1 Tender; 6476-1 Hopper Car - Red; 6162-1 Gondola Car - Blue - with (3) White Canisters; 6057-1 Caboose - Red; 1013 Curved Track (12); 1018 Straight Track (3); 1008-50 Uncoupling Unit - with (1) 1018 Straight Track; 1016-60 35-Watt Transformer; 1020-1 90° Crossover; 214-1 Girder Bridge; 953 Figure Set; 981 Freight Yard Set; 81-32 Wires (2); 1609-4 Instruction Sheet; 310-2 Set of (5) Billboard Signs; AC Accessory Catalog

Boxes & Packing: 60-563 Box; 60-564 Shipper (1-3)

X-557 (1960)	C6	C7	C8	Rarity
Complete Outfit	575	900	1,525	R7
Outfit Box no. 60-563	175	250	325	R7

Comments: Radoff Brothers was a toy buyer that purchased only this Retailer Promotional Type Ia outfit from Lionel during the 1960s.

The no. X-557 was a freight outfit that contained common items from the 1960 line. It was headed by a no. 246-1 Locomotive with Headlight and Magne-Traction that came packaged in a no. 246-6 Corrugated Box. The rolling stock was equipped with early operating AAR trucks and couplers and came in Orange Perforated boxes.

This item is a good example of Lionel taking an outfit filled with common rolling stock and sprucing it up with two Plasticville sets. The nos. 953 Figure Set and 981 Freight Yard Set are the two items that are difficult to find in collectible condition when trying to complete this outfit. Their boxes were made of a thin cardstock that was easily torn or ripped. The instruction sheets and original, complete Plasticville pieces can also be a challenge to obtain. This outfit was also one of two to include a no. 214-1 Girder Bridge.

The addition of these items must have worked because Radoff increased its original order from 100 to 1,000 on 7-25-60. The change was initialed "Per V.N", the initials indicating Victor Nigro, a manager in the Production Scheduling Production Planning Department in 1960.

The no. 60-563 was a Tan RSC with Black Graphics outfit box.

It is unknown why the number of this outfit does not include "NA". (See the section on Outfit Numbering for a discussion of "NA" and its uses.)

As with many promotional outfits, the X-557 does appear from time to time. Unfortunately, few of those examples are complete or in collectible condition.

CONVENTIONAL PACK
60-563 BOX

TOP LAYER		BOTTOM LAYER	
12-1013		246-1 S	
1130T-1 F	3-1018	6476-1 F	214-1 S
		6162-1 F	
6057-1 F		981-1 S	

1008-50 TOP 1018
1020-1 TOP 1130T - 1013

953-1 (F) TOP 6476 - 6162
1016-60 TOP 6476

Description: 1960 Outfit
Specification: "O27" Ga. Diesel Freight Outfit
Customer/No./Price: J. W. Robinson's; 19 558NA; $29.95
Original Amount: 120
Factory Order Date: 6/22/1960
Date Issued: 9-28-60
Packaging: Conventional Outfit Packing

Contents: 220P-1 Alco Diesel Power Unit - "Santa Fe" - with Headlight, 2 Magnets, Non-Operating Coupler, Lockon & Lubricant; 6812-1 Track Maintenance Car; 6650-1 Missile Launching Flat Car; 6470-1 Exploding Target Car; 3419-1 Operating Helicopter Car; 6017-185 Caboose - Gray - "Santa Fe"; 1013 Curved Track (8); 1018 Straight Track; 6029-25 Uncoupling Track Section; 1015-60 45-Watt Transformer; 90-1 Uncoupling Track Controller; 81-32 Wires (4); 90-30 Envelope Packed With 90-1 and 81-32; IS Instruction Sheet; 310-2 Set of (5) Billboard Signs; AC Accessory Catalog

Boxes & Packing: 59-339 Box; 59-340 Shipper (1-3); ST Sticker; 59-359 Box; ST Sticker

X-558NA (1960)	C6	C7	C8	Rarity
Complete Outfit With Either Box	1,225	1,600	2,100	R10
Outfit Box no. 59-339 Or no. 59-359	800	950	1,100	R10

Comments: J. W. Robinson's was one of the many retailers that Associated Dry Goods owned during the 1960s. The no. X-558NA was the only Retailer Promotional Type Ia outfit it purchased during that time. As noted in the entry for the no. X-556NA, this outfit is almost identical to that item, whose customer was listed as Associated Dry Goods. Only the locomotive and caboose differed. Associated Dry Goods probably was purchasing the same outfit for different retail chains and wanted this slight variation to help differentiate its offerings.

The X-558NA was headed by a no. 220P-1 Santa Fe Alco Diesel Power Unit, which included two-axle Magne-Traction, a three-position reversing unit and a headlight. The only feature missing was a horn.

The 220P-1 is an example of an item that appeared in promotional outfits before it became a regular-production item (it

Outfit no. X-558NA included a no. 220P-1 Santa Fe Alco and a matching no. 6017-185 Santa Fe Caboose. The space and military rolling stock provided plenty of fun and excitement. The version with a no. 59-359 Box is shown.

Original price tags, mailing labels and markings on outfit boxes provide additional information about promotional outfits. In this case, the J. W. Robinson Co. price tag provides outfit no. X-558NA's retail price of $29.95.

appeared in the 1961 consumer catalog). When boxed in its no. 220-10 Corrugated Box, this locomotive included the nos. CTC-1 Lockon, 927-60 Tube of Oil, 927-65 Tube of Grease and 220-11 Instruction Sheet. The box was surrounded by a no. 217-16 Sleeve.

The nos. 3419-1 Operating Helicopter Car, 6470-1 Exploding Target Car and 6650-1 Missile Launching Flat Car were an exciting combination of space and military rolling stock. Hours could be spent blowing up the 6470-1 Exploding Target Car. All three cars, as well as the no. 6812-1 Track Maintenance Car, were repeats from 1959. They were equipped with early operating AAR trucks and couplers and came packaged in Orange Perforated boxes.

The no. 6017-185 Caboose was equipped with one early operating AAR truck and coupler as well as one plain truck. The Production Control Files indicate that this item always came in a box, specifically, an Orange Perforated no. 6017-190 Folding Box.

The X-558NA came in two different boxes. It was originally packaged in a no. 59-339 Tan RSC with Black Graphics outfit box. This was an overstickered no. 9663 outfit box manufactured by Star Corrugated Box Company, Inc. and measuring 13¾ x 12 x 6 inches. It included a star on the bottom of the box.

The other outfit box was likely used when the quantity of outfits increased from 60 to 120 on 9-28-60. The no. 59-359 Tan RSC with Black Graphics outfit box was manufactured by Star Corrugated Box Company, Inc. and measured 13¾ x 11⅞ x 6⅝ inches. It was an overstamped no. X-826 outfit box from 1959 and included "8-4B" and a star printed on the bottom.

Even though two different outfit boxes were used, the differences are minimal and the total original quantity of 120 is used to determine price and rarity. Either box version of the X-558NA is a true find.

CONVENTIONAL PACK
59-339 BOX
REVISED 8-10-60, STICKER

TOP LAYER			BOTTOM LAYER	
6017-185 F	8-1013		6812-1 F	
6470-1 F			220P-1 F	
3419-1 F			6650-1 F	1015 60

1-1018 TOP 3419
6029-25 TOP 3419

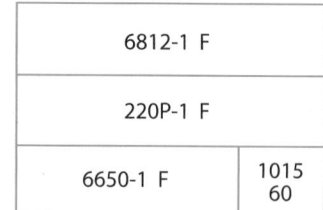

Description: 1960 Outfit
Specification: "O27" Ga. Steam Type Freight Outfit
Customer: Cities Service
Original Amount: 6
Factory Order Date: 5/25/1960
Date Issued: May 25, 1960
Packaging: Conventional Outfit Packing

Contents: 246-1 Locomotive - with Headlight and Magne-Traction - with Lockon & Lubricant; 1130T-1 Tender; 6465-100X Cities Service Tank Cars - with Special Markings (4); 6017-1 Caboose - Brick Brown; 1013 Curved Track (8); 1018 Straight Track (3); 1008-50 Uncoupling Unit - with (1) 1018 Straight Track; 1015-25 45-Watt Transformer; 1103-14 Envelope Packed; 310-2 Set of (5) Billboard Signs; 1609-4 Instruction Sheet; AC Accessory Catalog

Boxes & Packing: 59-318 Box; 59-319 Shipper (1-4); ST Sticker

X-559NA (1960)	C6	C7	C8	Rarity
Complete Outfit With no. 6465-100X	Identity Of no. 6465-100X Unknown			
Outfit Without no. 6465-100X	3,200	4,825	5,700	R10
Outfit Box no. 59-318	3,000	4,500	5,000	R10

Comments: Cities Service, which later changed its name to CITGO, purchased this Manufacturer Promotional Type IIIb outfit in 1960. This represented the beginning of a relationship with Lionel that lasted at least until the end of 1962.

Outfit nos. X-559NA and X-578NA are the two rarest promotional outfits based on original quantity produced. Only six of each of these outfits were manufactured. They rank first on the list of least produced catalog and promotional outfits.

The X-559NA was likely destined for Cities Service employees or executives. They may also have been created to commemorate

the beginning of the Lionel and Cities Service relationship.

The X-559NA included four no. 6465-100X Cities Service Tank Cars - with Special Markings. What these cars were is a mystery, as neither a car nor an outfit box has been observed.

The remaining trains included in this outfit were commonly available items from 1960. The outfit was headed by a no. 246-1 Locomotive with Headlight and Magne-Traction that came in a no. 246-6 Corrugated Box.

The nos. 1130T-1 Tender and 6017-1 Caboose included one early operating AAR and one plain AAR truck and coupler and came in Orange Perforated boxes.

Making this outfit even more interesting was the inclusion of a no. 1103-14 Envelope Packed. (See the entry for outfit no. X-502NA for more information about this rare packed envelope.)

The no. 59-318 Tan RSC with Black Graphics outfit box was an overstickered Sears no. 9664 from 1959.

Pricing is provided for the outfit box alone and the outfit without the no. 6465-100Xs. The value of a 6465-100X has yet to be determined because the true identity and features of this car are unknown.

Needless to say, this outfit is by far one of the toughest of any Lionel outfit to find.

CONVENTIONAL PACK
59-318 BOX
STICKER

TOP LAYER

6465-100X F	1015 25
1130T-1 S	
6465-100X S	
8-1013	

3-1018 TOP 6465 (F)
1008-50 TOP 1130T

BOTTOM LAYER

246-1 F	
6465-100X F	6017-1 S
6465-100X F	

Description: 1960 Outfit
Specification: "O27" Ga. Steam Type Freight Outfit
Customer: Jordan Marsh
Original Amount: 500
Factory Order Date: 6/22/1960
Date Issued: June 22, 1960
Packaging: Conventional Outfit Packing

Contents: 246-1 Locomotive - with Headlight and Magne-Traction - with Lockon & Lubricant; 1130T-1 Tender; 6825-1 Flat Car - Red - with Trestle Bridge - Black; 3376-1 Operating Giraffe Car; 6465-110 2-Dome Tank Car - Green - ("Cities Service"); 6027-1 Caboose - Blue - "Alaskan Markings"; 1013 Curved Track (8); 1018 Straight Track (5); 1008-50 Uncoupling Unit - with (1) 1018 Straight Track; 1015-60 45-Watt Transformer; 81-32 Wires (2); 310-2 Set of (5) Billboard Signs; 1609-4 Instruction Sheet; AC Accessory Catalog

Boxes & Packing: 59-320 Box; 59-321 Shipper (1-4); ST Sticker

Alternate For Outfit Contents:
Note: If necessary - Substitute 1- 1015-25, 1- 1103-14 For 1 - 1015-60, 2 - 81-32.

X-560NA (1960)	C6	C7	C8	Rarity
Complete Outfit	850	1,250	1,600	R9
Complete Outfit With A no. 1103-14 Substitution	950	1,450	2,050	R9
Outfit Box no. 59-320	325	450	550	R9

Comments: Allied Stores owned several department stores in the 1960s and was a major customer of Lionel. Among the stores owned by Allied was Jordan Marsh, which likely obtained outfits through Allied as well as direct from Lionel. The no. X-560NA was purchased from Lionel and was a Retailer Promotional Type Ia outfit (or a Type Ib with the inclusion of the no. 1103-14 substitution).

A no. 246-1 Locomotive with Headlight and Magne-Traction headed 23 different promotional outfits in 1960, including the X-560NA. It came in a no. 246-6 Corrugated Box.

The rolling stock in this outfit represented Lionel's mid-range offerings for 1960. All of these cars were equipped with early operating AAR trucks and couplers.

All of the cars came packaged in Orange Perforated boxes, two of which are difficult to find. The no. 6465-110 Green Cities Service 2-Dome Tank Car came in a no. 6465-103 Folding Box. This box takes patience to find in collectible condition. The boxed version of the no. 6027-1 Alaskan Caboose first appeared in the RSC version of catalog outfit no. 1611 from 1959. The remaining inventory of this caboose was depleted in 1960 promotional and 1961 catalog outfits. Its Orange Perforated no. 6027-3 Folding Box is difficult to find in collectible condition.

The no. 59-320 Tan RSC with Black Graphics outfit box was manufactured by Express Container Corp. and measured 11½ x 10⅝ x 7¼ inches.

The substitution of a no. 1103-14 Envelope Packed changes the value of the outfit, as listed in the pricing table. (See the entry for outfit no. X-502NA for more information about this packed envelope and its contents.)

Just finding an empty box for an X-560NA can be a challenge. The real fun begins when trying to find the Alaskan Caboose's 6027-3 Folding Box to fill this box.

CONVENTIONAL PACK
59-320 BOX
STICKER

TOP LAYER
6027-1 S
6825-1 S
5-1018
8-1013
6465-110 S
1008-50 TOP

BOTTOM LAYER	
246-1 F	
3376-1 F	
1130T-1 F	1015 60

This empty box for the no. X-561NA Retailer Promotional Type Ib outfit was manufactured by the Express Container Corp. The box was originally used for promotional outfit no. X-860 from 1959, but was overstickered with an "X-561NA" sticker. The original Grand-Way price tag is still attached with a price of $23.97.

Description: 1960 Outfit
Specification: "O27" Ga. Steam Type Freight Outfit with Smoke
Customer/Price: Grand-Way; $23.97
Original Amount: 400
Factory Order Date: 6/15/1960
Date Issued: June 15, 1960
Packaging: Conventional Outfit Packing

Contents: 244-1 Locomotive - with Smoke & Headlight - with 2 Position Reversing Unit - with Lockon and Lubricant - without Magne-Traction; 244T-1 Tender; 6809-1 Anti-Aircraft and Medical Truck Car; 6014-100 Box Car - Red; 3419-1 Operating Helicopter Car; 6062-1 Gondola Car - Black - with (3) Cable Reels; 6017-1 Caboose - Brick Brown; 1013 Curved Track (12); 1018 Straight Track (3); 1008-50 Uncoupling Unit - with (1) 1018 Straight Track; 1015-25 45-Watt Transformer; 1020-1 90° Crossover; 81-32 Wires (2); 310-2 Set of (5) Billboard Signs; 1627-2 Instruction Sheet; 1802B Layout Instruction Sheet; AC Accessory Catalog

Boxes & Packing: 59-383 Box; 59-384 Shipper (1-4); ST Sticker

X-561NA (1960)	C6	C7	C8	Rarity
Complete Outfit	750	1,075	1,500	R9
Outfit Box no. 59-383	400	475	550	R9

Comments: Grand-Way was Grand Union's discount store chain, and it carried Lionel during the 1960s. In 1960, it purchased two Retailer Promotional outfits: nos. X-554NA and X-561NA. Both featured steam locomotives, with the X-561NA being Grand-Way's high-end offering.

This Type Ib outfit included a no. 244-1 Locomotive with Smoke & Headlight and a two-position reversing unit. The no. 244-1 was equipped with a metal motor, but it included only ballast weights as a traction aid. It was new for 1960, as was its matching no. 244T-1 Tender. The tender came in a difficult-to-find no. 1625T overstamped Bold Classic no. 1625-51 Folding Box.

The no. 6809-1 Anti-Aircraft & Medical Truck Car was making its final appearance in this outfit and the no. X-564NA. Originally issued in 1958, it came packaged in a Classic-style box with two no. 6809-12 Tubes to protect its load.

Also included in the X-561NA was a no. 6014-100 Airex Box Car - Red. This car appeared in at least 12 promotional outfits in 1960. It and the remaining pieces of rolling stock were equipped with early operating AAR trucks and couplers and packaged in Orange Perforated boxes.

The track layout was a figure-eight, as outlined on the no. 1802B Layout Instruction Sheet.

The no. 59-383 Tan RSC with Black Graphics outfit box was manufactured by Express Container Corp. and measured 13¼ x 12 x 6 inches. It was an overstickered no. X-860 outfit box from 1959.

Finding an X-561NA can be quite a challenge because the number produced was small. Also, very few of these outfits have survived.

CONVENTIONAL PACK
59-383 BOX
STICKER

TOP LAYER			
6014-100 S			
244T-1 S	1015 25	3-1018	
12-1013			
244-1 F			

1020-1 TOP 244T - 1013
1008-50 TOP 244

BOTTOM LAYER	
3419-1 F	6017-1 S
6062-1 F	
6809-1 F	

Description: 1960 Outfit
Specification: "O27" Ga. Diesel Freight Outfit
Customer: Stix, Baer & Fuller
Original Amount: 75
Factory Order Date: 6/22/1960
Date Issued: August 1, 1960
Packaging: Conventional Outfit Packing

Contents: 224P-1 Alco Diesel Power Car - "U.S. Navy" - Navy Color and Markings - with Headlight, Magne-Traction - with Non-Operating Coupler - Lockon and Lubricant; 224C-1 "B" Unit - Navy Color and Markings; 6812-1 Track Maintenance Car; 6062-1 Gondola Car - Black - with (3) Cable Reels; 6825-1 Flat Car - Red - with Trestle Bridge - Black; 6476-1 Hopper Car - Red; 6017-1 Caboose - Brick Brown; 1013 Curved Track (12); 1018 Straight Track (13); 1008-50 Uncoupling Unit - with (1) 1018 Straight Track; 1015-60 45-Watt Transformer; 110-1 Graduated Trestle Set; 81-32 Wires (2); 310-2 Set of (5) Billboard Signs; 1569-11 Instruction Sheet; AC Accessory Catalog; 2099 Layout Instruction Sheet

Boxes & Packing: 59-361 Box; 59-362 Shipper (1-3); ST Sticker

X-562NA (1960)	C6	C7	C8	Rarity
Complete Outfit	1,425	2,000	2,500	R10
Outfit Box no. 59-361	900	1,200	1,400	R10

Comments: Retailer Stix, Baer and Fuller purchased this Retailer Promotional Type Ia outfit in 1960. As was the case with many promotional outfits, Lionel merely changed the motive power of another outfit (no. X-552NA) and created this outfit.

The no. X-562NA was headed by a no. 224P-1 U.S. Navy Alco Diesel Power Car with Magne-Traction and a three-position reversing unit. When boxed, this locomotive included the nos. CTC-1 Lockon, 927-60 Tube of Oil, 927-65 Tube of Grease and 217-17 Instruction Sheet in its corrugated box.

All the rolling stock in this outfit was carryover from previous years, with the cars equipped with early operating AAR trucks and couplers and packaged in Orange Perforated boxes. The only notable item among them was the no. 6812-1 Track Maintenance Car. To be in collectible condition, it must include original figures and an original, unbroken platform.

The track layout was detailed on the no. 2099 Layout Instruction Sheet. This sheet was included in only this and outfit nos. X-529NA and X-552NA. Its Production Control File list orders for 2,500. This small quantity and the item's fragility make it rare.

The no. 59-361 Tan RSC with Black Graphics outfit box was an overstickered no. X-831NA from 1959. Manufactured by Continental Can Company, Inc., it measured 15½ x 14¾ x 7⅜ inches and had "59" and five dots printed on the bottom.

The low quantity manufactured ranks the X-562NA as 18th on the list of least-produced catalog and promotional outfits.

CONVENTIONAL PACK
59-361 BOX
STICKER

TOP LAYER		BOTTOM LAYER	
6825-1 S		110-1 F	
12-1013			
6812-1 S	6017-1 F	224P-1 F	
6476-1 S			
6062-1 S		224C-1 F	1015 60
13-1018			

1008-50 TOP 6476

Description: 1960 Outfit
Specification: "O27" Ga. Steam Type Freight Outfit
Customer: Morley Brothers
Original Amount: 500
Factory Order Date: 6/22/1960
Date Issued: June 22, 1960
Packaging: Conventional Outfit Packing

Contents: 246-1 Locomotive - with Headlight and Magne-Traction - with Lockon & Lubricant; 1130T-1 Tender; 6045-25 Two Dome Tank Car - Gray - Non-Operating Trucks; 6825-1 Flat Car - Red - with Trestle Bridge - Black; 6014-100 Box Car - Red - "Airex Lettering"; 6062-1 Gondola Car - Black - with (3) Cable Reels; 6017-1 Caboose - Brick Brown; 1013 Curved Track (12); 1018 Straight Track (3); 1008-50 Uncoupling Unit - with (1) 1018 Straight Track; 1053-50 60-Watt Transformer; 1020-1 90° Crossover; 960-1 Barnyard Set; 128 Animated News Stand; 334 Operating Dispatching Board; 81-32 Wires (2); 310-2 Set of (5) Billboard Signs; IS Instruction Sheet; AC Accessory Catalog; LIS Layout Instruction Sheet & Operating Accessory Sheet

Boxes & Packing: 60-579 Box; 60-580 Shipper (1-3)

Alternate For Outfit Contents:
Note: Substitute 300 - 6027-1 for 6017-1.

X-563NA (1960)	C6	C7	C8	Rarity
Complete Outfit	925	1,350	2,100	R9
Complete Outfit With no. 6027-1 Substitution	1,175	1,750	2,600	R9
Outfit Box no. 60-579	325	450	550	R9

Comments: Morely Brothers was a distributor and retailer founded in Saginaw, Michigan. The no. X-563NA was the only Retailer Promotional outfit it purchased during the 1960s. This Type Ib outfit was an exciting one, thanks to its two accessories and one Plasticville item.

Lionel frequently used promotional outfits to deplete its inventory of many items, especially accessories. This practice helped Lionel while providing consumers with unique outfits that had plenty of play value. The X-563NA was one of the few outfits that included two accessories: nos. 128 Animated Newsstand and 334 Operating Dispatching Board. These two accessories were paired in only outfit nos. X-563NA and X-565NA.

In addition, the no. 960-1 Barnyard Set is a challenge to find in collectible condition when trying to complete this outfit. Its box was made of a thin cardstock that was easily torn or ripped. The instruction sheet as well as original, complete Plasticville pieces can be difficult to uncover.

The X-563NA was led by a no. 246-1 Locomotive with Headlight and Magne-Traction that came in a no. 246-6 Corrugated Box.

The rolling stock included a no. 6014-100 Red Airex Box Car, which appeared in at least 12 promotional outfits in 1960. It and all but one of the other cars were equipped with early operating AAR trucks and couplers and packaged in Orange Perforated boxes. The exception was the no. 6045-25 Gray Two Dome Tank Car; besides having non-operating Archbar trucks and couplers, it was unboxed.

With two accessories, the X-563NA required a large outfit box. The no. 60-579 Tan RSC with Black Graphics outfit box was manufactured by Owens Illinois Paper Products Division and measured 18 x 15¼ x 8 inches.

The substitution of a no. 6027-1 Alaskan Caboose and its difficult-to-find no. 6027-3 Folding Box substantially increases the value of this outfit. Separate pricing is provided for this substitution.

Any outfit with two accessories and a Plasticville set is in demand. When you combine the high demand with the small quantity made, you understand why an X-563NA is so difficult to acquire.

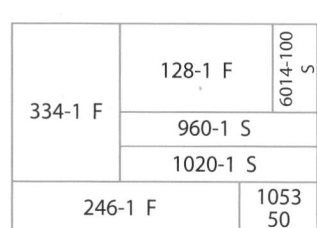

CONVENTIONAL PACK
60-579 BOX

TOP LAYER | BOTTOM LAYER

Description: 1960 Outfit
Specification: Super "O" Ga. Steam Type Frt. Outfit with Smoke & Whistle
Customer: Madison Hardware
Original Amount: 200
Factory Order Date: 7/1/1960
Date Issued: September 15, 1960
Packaging: Ship Bulk - No Outfit Packaging

Contents: 736-1 Locomotive - with Lubricant - with Smoke & Magne-Traction - with Lockon; 736W-1 Whistle Tender; 3512-1 Operating Fireman and Ladder Car; 6804-1 Flat Car - Red; 6807-1 Flat Car - Red; 6809-1 Flat Car - Red; 6812-1 Track Maintenance Car; 3419-1 Operating Helicopter Car; 961-1 School Set; 965-1 Farm Set; 350-1 Transfer Table; 350-50 Transfer Table Extension; 175 Rocket Launcher; 112 Remote Control Switches (1pr.); ZW Transformer; 32 Straight Track (36)

Alternate For Outfit Contents:
Note: Substitute - 125 - 6809, 75 - 6807 for 6804.

X-564NA (1960)	C6	C7	C8	Rarity
Items Only	2,175	3,275	4,725	N/A
Items Only With no. 6807-1 Substitution	2,130	3,165	4,525	N/A

Comments: Madison Hardware Co. of New York purchased what were known as "bulk outfits." (For an explanation of the practice of buying "bulk outfits," consult the entry on Madison Hardware Co. in the section on Lionel's Distribution and Customers.)

Madison purchased bulk-packed outfits nos. X-564NA, X-572NA, X-576 and X-577 in 1960. The first two were Retailer Promotional Type Ia outfits, and the other two were Type Ib outfits.

No individual outfit boxes have been observed for any bulk outfit listed in this volume. As a result, we cannot ascertain whether these items were ever assembled and sold as an outfit. Even if they were, we cannot prove that Madison Hardware designated the groupings as no. X-564NA, X-572NA, X-576 or X-577.

When you look at the contents of the X-564NA as well as those of the other three bulk outfits from 1960, it becomes obvious that Madison was merely splitting up its separate-sale order across multiple "outfits" to take advantage of the inherent outfit discount. As such, this outfit included a little bit of everything.

The X-564NA did not, however, contain any new items. To the contrary, it represented the last or nearly last appearance of several items. Specifically, the nos. 6804-1, 6807-1 and 6809-1 Red Flat Cars all made their final appearance in this outfit. The nos. 350-1 Transfer Table and 350-50 Transfer Table Extension also were last seen in this and the no. X-572NA. The no. 175 Rocket Launcher was being depleted in this and a few other outfits in 1960.

A listing for this outfit is provided here because a Factory Order exists for the X-564NA. Pricing is provided as reference for the items alone. However, as stated earlier in this volume, items alone do not constitute an outfit; an outfit box is required.

Overall, it appears that Lionel took the opportunity to clean out some old inventory, sending it to a willing customer. Finding a box with any sort of markings for this outfit would be quite a discovery.

The no. X-565NA was a large outfit that paired the nos. 128 Animated Newsstand and 334 Operating Dispatching Board. Also Included was a no. 3386-1 Operating Giraffe Car in its rare no. 3386-10 Folding Box.

The W. T. Grant shipping label identifies the store to which this no. X-565NA was delivered. It also indicates that these outfits were individually shipped from W. T. Grant's distribution center. Outfit boxes are rarely found in C8 condition after exposure to individual shipping.

Description: 1960 Outfit
Specification: "O27" Ga. Diesel Freight Outfit
Customer: W. T. Grant
Original Amount: 1,000
Factory Order Date: 8/3/1960
Date Issued: August 3, 1960
Packaging: Conventional Outfit Packing

Contents: 220P-1 Alco Diesel Power Unit - "Santa Fe" - with Headlight, 2 Magnets, Non-Operating Coupler, Lockon & Lubricant; 220T-1 Motorless Unit - "S.F."; 6812-1 Track Maintenance Car; 6062-1 Gondola Car - Black - with (3) Cable Reels; 3386-1 Operating Giraffe Car - with Non-Operating Trucks; 6017-1 Caboose - Brick Brown; 1013 Curved Track (8); 1018 Straight Track (5); 1008-50 Uncoupling Unit - with (1) 1018 Straight Track; 1053-50 60-Watt Transformer; 128 Animated News Stand; 334 Dispatching Board; 81-32 Wires (2); 310-2 Set of (5) Billboard Signs; 926-60 Instruction Book; AC Accessory Catalog

Boxes & Packing: 60-581 Box; 60-582 Shipper (1-3)

Alternate For Outfit Contents:
Note: Substitute 1063-25 for 1053-50 if necessary.

X-565NA (1960)	C6	C7	C8	Rarity
Complete Outfit	935	1,400	2,100	R7
Outfit Box no. 60-581	275	375	450	R7

Comments: W. T. Grant was a variety store chain that purchased two promotional outfits in 1960. The no. X-565NA was a diesel-powered Retailer Promotional Type Ib outfit, whereas the no. X-566NA was a steam-powered Retailer Promotional Type Ia outfit.

The X-565NA was headed by a no. 220P-1 Santa Fe Alco Diesel Power Unit, which included two-axle Magne-Traction, a three-position reversing unit and a headlight. The only feature missing was a horn.

The 220P-1 is an example of an item that appeared in promotional outfits before it became a regular-production item (it appeared in the 1961 consumer catalog). When boxed in its no. 220-10 Corrugated Box, this locomotive included the nos. CTC-1 Lockon, 927-60 Tube of Oil, 927-65 Tube of Grease and 220-11 Instruction Sheet. The box was surrounded by a no. 217-16 Sleeve.

Lionel included a boxed no. 3386-1 Operating Giraffe Car in this and two other promotional outfits. This car's rare Orange Perforated 3386-10 Folding Box appeared only in promotional outfits, which is the reason the X-565NA is classified as a Type Ib outfit. When available for separate sale, the 3386-1 was boxed in an overstamped no. 3376-120 Folding Box, which, as explained in the *Authoritative Guide to Lionel's Postwar Operating Cars* (Project Roar Publishing), is even more difficult to find than a 3386-10.

While the 3386-1 came equipped with non-operating Archbar trucks and couplers, all the other cars in this outfit had early operating AAR trucks and couplers. All of the cars came packaged in Orange Perforated boxes.

Lionel frequently used promotional outfits to deplete its inventory of many items, especially accessories. This practice helped Lionel while providing consumers with unique outfits that had plenty of play value. The X-565NA was one of the few outfits that included two accessories: nos. 128 Animated Newsstand and 334 Operating Dispatching Board. These two accessories were paired only in outfit nos. X-563NA and X-565NA.

The no. 60-581 Tan RSC with Black Graphics outfit box was manufactured by Owens-Illinois Paper Products, Div. and measured 17¼ x 14½ x 7⅝ inches. It had 12 dots printed as part of the box manufacturer's certificate.

This big outfit is difficult to find complete with all its accessories and rolling stock. Over the years, as with many promotional outfits, the contents of X-565NA outfits have been cannibalized and sold off separately because they are always in demand. Empty outfit boxes do appear from time to time. The transformer substitution does not affect the price.

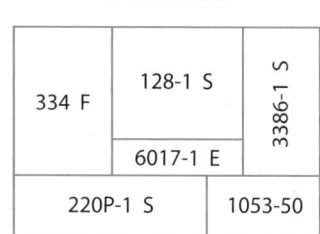

CONVENTIONAL PACK
60-581 BOX

TOP LAYER

6062-1 F	5-1018	6812-1 F		220T-1 S	1008-50
8-1013					

BOTTOM LAYER

334 F	128-1 S		3386-1 S
	6017-1 E		
220P-1 S		1053-50	

Description: 1960 Outfit
Specification: "O27" Ga. Steam Type Freight Outfit with Smoke
Customer: W. T. Grant
Original Amount: 1,000
Factory Order Date: 8/2/1960
Date Issued: September 7, 1960
Packaging: Conventional Outfit Packing

Contents: 244-50 Locomotive - with Smoke & Headlight - with 2 Position Reversing Unit - without Mage-Traction - with Lockon and Lubricant; 244T-1 Tender; 3512-1 Operating Fireman and Ladder Car; 6670-1 Crane Car; 3361X-1 Operating Lumber Car; 160-2 Unloading Bin; 6817-1 Flat Car - with Motor Scraper; 6361-1 Log Car; 6119-100 Work Caboose; 1013 Curved Track (10); 1018 Straight Track (5); 6019-1 Remote Control Track Set; 1053-50 60-Watt Transformer; 1022 Manual Switches (1Pr.); 464 Operating Lumber Mill; 81-32 Wires (2); 310-2 Set of (5) Billboard Signs; IS Instruction Sheet; 1802E Layout Instruction Sheet

Boxes & Packing: 60-583 Box; 60-584 Shipper (1-3)

Alternate For Outfit Contents:
Note: Substitute 1063-25 Transformer if necessary.

X-566NA (1960)	C6	C7	C8	Rarity
Complete Outfit	1,225	1,825	2,400	R8
Outfit Box no. 60-583	225	300	350	R7

Comments: W. T. Grant was a variety store chain that purchased two promotional outfits in 1960. The no. X-566NA was a steam-powered Retailer Promotional Type Ia outfit, whereas the no. X-565NA was a diesel-powered Retailer Promotional Type Ib outfit.

The X-566NA is interesting in that it lists a no. 244-50 Locomotive with Smoke & Headlight as its motive power. According to Lionel Engineering Specifications, a normal no. 244-25 or 244-1 was "For use with train sets including tender and (5)

light cars." The X-566NA had a tender and six cars, some of which were heavy. Somewhere along the way, W. T. Grant desired or was sold on having a Scout steam locomotive head this outfit. Instead of swapping out the engine for a no. 2018 or 2037, Lionel modified the 244 for this outfit. The "-50" suffix indicated additional ballast weight. The remaining inventory of this engine was depleted as a substitution for a no. 244-25 Steam Type Locomotive in catalog outfit no. 1642 in 1961.

Lionel appeared to be cleaning out inventory in this outfit, as all but two items (nos. 244T-1 Tender and 6361-1 Log Car) were repeated from previous years. The no. 3361X-1 Operating Lumber Car with its bar-end trucks and couplers was still being depleted into 1961. The no. 6817-1 Flat Car - with Motor Scraper included a scraper with a windshield and black lettering. The 6817-1 as well as all the remaining rolling stock were equipped with early AAR trucks and couplers.

Packaging included Late Classic (3361X-1), overstamped Classic (6670-1 and 244T-1) and Orange Perforated boxes. The 6817-1 used the no. 6817-22 Folding Box and not the no. 6817-20 Folding Box.

The track layout was an oval layout with an inner switch track. As outlined on the no. 1802E Layout Instruction Sheet, it required a pair of no. 1022-1 Manual Switches. This is just one of the many enhanced track layouts included in promotional outfits.

The no. 464 Operating Lumber Mill was being depleted in this and two other promotional outfits in the 1960s. The X-566NA included a quantity of 1,000 while the no. X-573NA used 682, and the no. X-680 included the last 287.

CONVENTIONAL PACK
60-583 BOX

TOP LAYER

6670-1 F		10-1013	5-1018	6019-1 S
3361X-1 S				
3512-1 F				

160-2 TOP 6670

BOTTOM LAYER

464-1 S			
6361-1 F	244T-1 F	6119-100 F	1022-1 S
244-50 F			
6817-1 S	1053-50		

This large accessory necessitated a large outfit box for the X-566NA. The no. 60-583 Tan RSC with Black Graphics outfit box was manufactured by Owens Illinois and measured 20 x 16½ x 6¾ inches. It was used one other time – for the no. X-680 in 1960, an outfit that also included a 464 Operating Lumber Mill.

The no. 244-50 appeared in only two outfits and is often overlooked. Even though this locomotive is rare, the variation is minor and to date it has had a low demand. This is mainly due to the lack of information about it. In either case, the "-50" version is more valuable than a normal 244-25, and it increases the rarity of this outfit to an R8. The transformer substitution does not affect the price.

Description: 1960 Outfit
Specification: "O27" Ga. Steam Type Freight Outfit
Customer: McMahon's
Original Amount: 500
Factory Order Date: 8/2/1960
Date Issued: August 2, 1960
Packaging: Display Packing - Merchandise Loose

Contents: 246-25 Locomotive - with Headlight and Magne-Traction - Less Lockon and Lubricant; 1130T-25 Tender; 6476-25 Hopper Car - Red; 3386-25 Operating Giraffe Car - with Non-Operating Trucks; 6045-25 Two Dome Tank Car - Gray - Non-Operating Trucks; 6047-25 Caboose - Brick Brown - Non-Operating Trucks; 1013 Curved Track (8); 1018 Straight Track (2); 1016-60 35-Watt Transformer; 902 Cardboard Trestle With Girder Bridge & Tunnel; 903 Set of (2) Sheets Trading Cards; 980 Ranch Set; CTC-1 Lockon; 81-32 Wires (2); 927-60 Lubricant (Oil); 927-65 Lubricant (Grease); 1103-12 Envelope Packed With CTC-1, 81-32, 927-60 and 927-65; 1109-10 Instruction Sheet; 310-2 Set of (5) Billboard Signs; AC Accessory Catalog

Boxes & Packing: 59-419 Box; 59-420 Insert; 59-423 Insert; 59-47 Insert (2); 60-377 Tube; 59-424 Shipper (1-6); ST 5 Stickers

X-567NA (1960)	C6	C7	C8	Rarity
Complete Outfit	1,200	2,550	4,700	R9
Outfit Box no. 59-419	350	450	525	R9

Comments: McMahon's was listed as the customer on the Factory Orders for the nos. X-567NA (steam-powered outfit) and X-568NA (diesel-powered outfit). Unfortunately, the identity of this customer, including what kind of business it did and where it was located, has yet to be determined. We can't even verify whether the X-567NA was a Retailer Promotional Type Ib or a Manufacturer Promotional IIIb. It was, however, similar to the no. X-574NA ordered by Abraham & Straus.

The no. 246-25 Locomotive with Headlight and Magne-Traction included in the X-567NA also featured a two-position reversing unit. Since it came unboxed (as indicated by the "-25"), a no. CTC-1 Lockon was required separately and included in the no. 1103-12 Envelope Packed.

The rolling stock in this outfit included a combination of items equipped with early operating AAR trucks and couplers (nos. 1130T-25 Tender and 6476-25 Hopper Car) and non-operating Archbar trucks and couplers (all the remaining rolling stock). A notable item was the no. 3386-25 Operating Giraffe Car (new for 1960). This car appeared in only 10 promotional outfits. When unboxed, its no. 3376-118 Envelope Packed was placed loose in the outfit box.

By far the two items that drive up the price of this outfit are the no. 902 Cardboard Trestle With Girder Bridge & Tunnel and the no. 903 Set of (2) Sheets Trading Cards. Both of them were fragile and intended to be separated and played with. Many more examples of the 902 have survived intact than have 903s.

The 903 included 24 two-sided Lionel trading cards printed on a sheet of perforated cardstock. On the front of each card was a Lionel locomotive, and on the back was historical information about its road name as well as a trivia quiz. A "folding" strip connected two 11 x 11 inch sets of 12 cards. The entire sheet of 24 was folded in half along the strip and placed loose in the outfit box. The cards were perforated and are almost always found separated as individual cards with the "folding" strip long gone. In fact if it weren't for the complete sheets that came out of Madison Hardware over the years, it is likely that few of these items would be intact.

The inclusion of a no. 980 Ranch Set also increases the value of this outfit. This Plasticville item came in a fragile box that takes patience to find in C8 condition.

The no. 59-419 White Hinged Display with 1050 Blue Steamer and Red/Orange Graphics Type A outfit box was manufactured by Concora Container Corp. (CCA) and measured 19¾ x 14½ x 3¼ inches. It was an overstickered no. X-869 from 1959.

Finding an example of the X-567NA is a challenge. Finding one with a 903 Set of (2) Sheets Trading Cards in C8 condition is a *true* challenge.

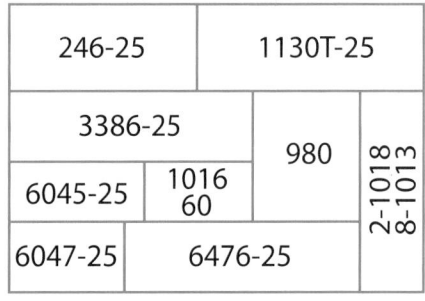

DISPLAY PACK
59-419 BOX
5 STICKERS

902, 903 TOP

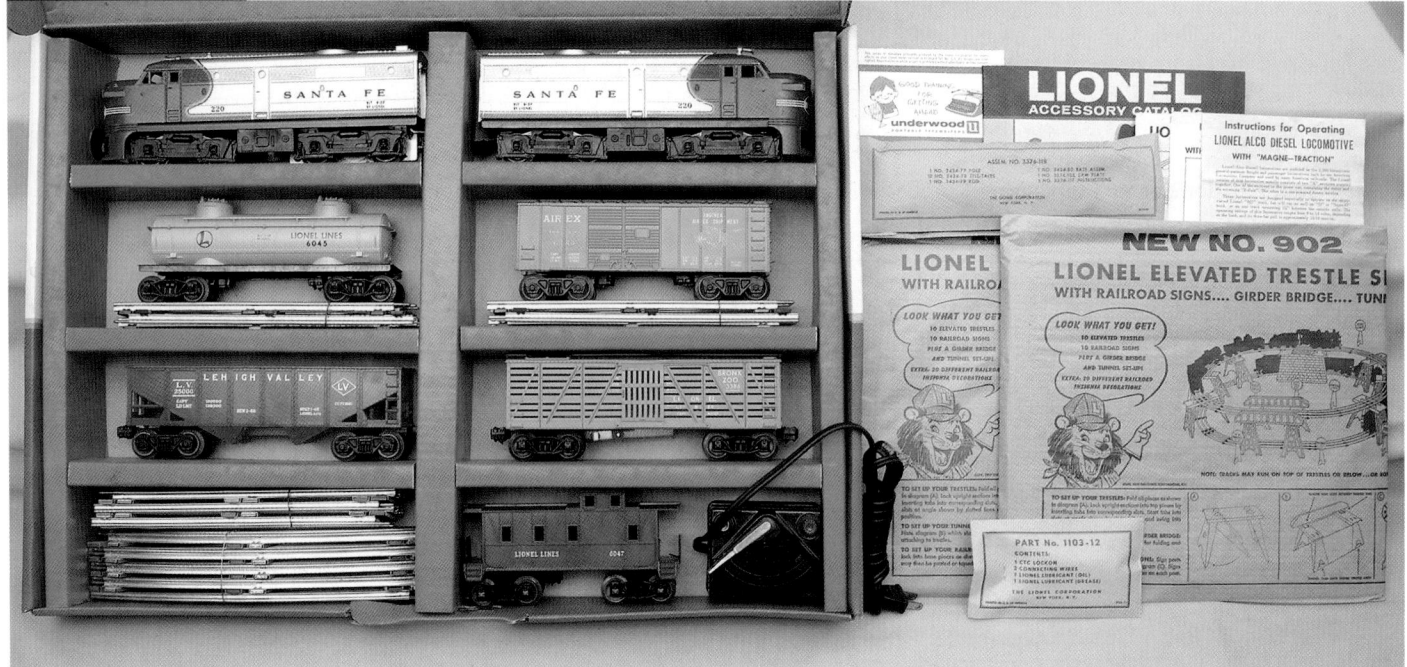

The no. X-568NA shown here was one of the 38 that were available from Madison Hardware in the early 1990s after its inventory was moved from New York City to Detroit. This outfit was the only appearance of unboxed nos. 220P-25 Santa Fe Alco Diesel Power Unit and 220T-25 Santa Fe Motorless Units in the 1960s. The X-568NA was one of only two 1960s outfits to include two of the no. 902 Cardboard Trestle With Girder Bridge & Tunnel. These cardboard trestles came packaged in tan bags and were placed loose on top of the outfit. Note the AAR version of the no. 6044-25 Blue Box Car - "Airex" Markings.

The no. 60-585 Orange, White and Gray O27 Hinged Display with 4-6-2 Steam Display Graphics Type A outfit box was unique to the no. X-568NA.

Description: 1960 Outfit
Specification: "O27" Ga. Diesel Freight Outfit
Customer: McMahon's
Original Amount: 400
Factory Order Date: 8/3/1960
Date Issued: August 20, 1960
Packaging: Display Packing Merchandise Loose

Contents: 220P-25 Alco Diesel Power Unit - "Santa Fe" - with Headlight, 2 Magnets, Non-Operating Coupler - Less Lockon and Lubricant; 220T-25 Motorless Unit - "Santa Fe"; 3386-25 Operating Giraffe Car - with Non-Operating Trucks; 6045-25 Two Dome Tank Car - Gray - Non-Operating Trucks; 6044-25 Box Car - Blue - "Airex" Markings - Non-Operating Trucks; 6476-25 Hopper Car; 6047-25 Caboose - Brick Brown - Non-Operating Trucks; 1013 Curved Track (8); 1018 Straight Track (10); 1015-25 45-Watt Transformer; 902 Cardboard Trestle With Girder Bridge & Tunnel (2); CTC-1 Lockon; 81-32 Wires (2); 927-60 Lubricant (Oil); 927-65 Lubricant (Grease); 1103-12 Envelope Packed With CTC-1, 81-32, 927-60 and 927-65; IS Instruction Sheet; 310-2 Set of (5) Billboard Signs; AC Accessory Catalog

Boxes & Packing: 60-585 Box; 60-166 Insert (2); 60-167 Insert; 60-168 Insert; 60-169 Insert; 60-170 Insert; 60-171 Insert; 60-586 Shipper (1-4)

Alternate For Outfit Contents:
Note: 400 - 220P-1 and 400 - 220T-1 to be converted to 220P-25 and 220T-25.

X-568NA (1960)	C6	C7	C8	Rarity
Complete Outfit	825	1,325	2,100	R9
Outfit Box no. 60-585	350	475	550	R9

Comments: McMahon's was listed as the customer on the Factory Orders for the nos. X-567NA (steam-powered outfit) and X-568NA (diesel-powered outfit). Unfortunately, the identity of this customer, including what kind of business it did and where it was located, has yet to be determined. We can't even verify whether the X-568NA was a Retailer Promotional Type Ib or a Manufacturer Promotional IIIb.

The X-568NA was the only time that the nos. 220P-25 Santa Fe Alco Diesel Power Unit and 220T-25 Santa Fe Motorless Unit appeared unboxed in an outfit. In fact, it was up to the Outfit Packing Department to convert 400 boxed units to unboxed versions (see Alternate For Outfit Contents for this outfit).

The no. 220P-25 was equipped with two-axle Magne-Traction, a three-position reversing unit, an open pilot with a large ledge and a headlight. The only feature missing was a horn. Since this locomotive came unboxed (as indicated by the "-25"), a no. CTC-1 Lockon was required separately and included in a Type III no. 1103-12 Envelope

The rolling stock in this outfit normally included a combination of items equipped with early operating AAR trucks and couplers (no. 6476-25 Hopper Car) and non-operating Archbar trucks and couplers (all the remaining rolling stock).

However, more than one C8 example of this outfit has been observed with a no. 6044-25 Blue Box Car - "Airex" Markings equipped with early operating AAR trucks and couplers (non-operating Archbar trucks and couplers were the norm). This outfit appeared later in 1960 than did most of the other outfits that included this car. The AAR trucks and couplers may indicate a last-minute change made to fulfill orders.

A notable item was the no. 3386-25 Operating Giraffe Car (new for 1960). This car appeared in only 10 promotional outfits. When unboxed, its no. 3376-118 Envelope Packed was placed loose in the outfit box.

The X-568NA was one of only two outfits to include two of the no. 902 Cardboard Trestle With Girder Bridge & Tunnel. This item is always difficult to find in C8 condition because, like other cardboard items placed in outfits, it was fragile and intended to be assembled. Once used, it retained minimal value.

The no. 60-585 Orange, White and Gray O27 Hinged Display with 4-6-2 Steam Display Graphics Type A outfit box was manufactured by UCC (United Container Co.) and measured 25 x 17¼ x 3¼ inches.

In 1989, Richard Kughn, then the owner of Lionel Trains, Inc.,

purchased Madison Hardware Co. and transferred its inventory from New York City to a facility he owned in Detroit. One of the first lists of outfits available for sale from the "new" Madison included a quantity of 38 of the X-568NA. That is why, although only 400 of this outfit were manufactured, they are frequently found in C8 condition. Even so, this is an attractive outfit in high demand, due mainly to its diesel locomotives, operating giraffe car and two sets of cardboard signs and details.

DISPLAY PACK
60-585 BOX

220P-25	220T-25	
6045-25 3-1018	6044-25 3-1018	
6476-25	3386-25	
8-1013 4-1018	6047-25	1015 25

2 - 902 TOP

Description: 1960 Outfit
Specification: "O27" Ga. Steam Type Freight Outfit
Customer/No./Price: FAO Schwarz; 36-117; $39.95
Customer: Grand Union
Original Amount: 2,250
Factory Order Date: 8/2/1960
Date Issued: 11-17-60
Packaging: Conventional Outfit Packing

Contents: 246-1 Locomotive - with Headlight and Magne-Traction - with Lockon & Lubricant; 1130T-1 Tender; 6465-110 2 Dome Tank Car - Green - ("Cities Service"); 6825-1 Flat Car - Red - with Trestle Bridge - Black; 6014-100 Box Car - Red; 6062-1 Gondola Car - Black - with (3) Cable Reels; 6017-1 Caboose - Brick Brown; 1013 Curved Track (12); 1018 Straight Track (3); 1008-50 Uncoupling Unit - with (1) 1018 Straight Track; 1053-50 60-Watt Transformer; 1020-1 90° Crossover; 960 Barnyard Set; 175 Rocket Launcher; 81-32 Wires (2); 310-2 Set of (5) Billboard Signs; IS Instruction Sheet; AC Accessory Catalog; 1802B Layout Instruction Sheet

Boxes & Packing: 60-573 Box; 60-574 Shipper (1-3)

Alternate For Outfit Contents:
Note: Substitute 1063-25 for 1053-50 if necessary; Substitute 100 - 980-1 for 960-1; 376 - 965-1 for 960-1; 461 - 961-1 for 960-1; 6821 for 6014.

X-569NA (1960)	C6	C7	C8	Rarity
Complete Outfit	700	1,125	1,650	R5
Outfit Box no. 60-573	125	200	250	R5

Comments: Grand Union appears as the customer on the Factory Order for this 1960 outfit. Grand Union was a food chain on the

East Coast that also purchased trains. In fact, the outfit pictured included a mailing label listing Grand Union Company, Manchester, New Hampshire, as its origination.

The no. X-569NA also appears in the 1960 FAO Schwarz Christmas Catalog as the "Cape Canaveral Freighter (Exclusive)". There it was listed as FAO no. 36-117 for $39.95. Even though this outfit had at least two customers, it only listed Grand Union on its Factory Order; therefore, we have classified it as a Retailer Promotional Type Ib outfit.

The X-569NA was quite a large outfit. To begin, it was headed by a no. 246-1 Locomotive with Headlight and Magne-Traction (the later version, which had a solid pilot but lacked generator detail). This steam engine came in a no. 246-6 Corrugated Box.

This outfit included the notable no. 6465-110 Green Cities Service Two Dome Tank Car that came in an Orange Perforated no. 6465-103 Folding Box. This box takes patience to find in collectible condition. Also included was a no. 6014-100 Red Airex Box Car (a promotional item only). It, like all the remaining rolling stock, was packaged in Orange Perforated boxes. All the cars in the X-569NA featured early operating AAR trucks and couplers.

The ancillary items make this an exciting outfit. The no. 175 Rocket Launcher is a fun accessory that provides hours of excitement. It was being depleted in this and three other outfits in 1960.

The no. 960 Barnyard Set is difficult to find in collectible condition when trying to complete this outfit. Its box was made of a thin cardstock that was easily torn or ripped. The instruction sheet and original, complete Plasticville pieces can also be challenges to obtain.

The track layout was a figure-eight, as outlined on the no. 1802B Layout Instruction Sheet.

Many substitutions are possible with the X-569NA. First, this outfit was used to deplete three other Plasticville items: nos. 961

The no. X-569NA was a large outfit that was one of four outfits used to deplete the no. 175 Rocket Launcher. The outfit is shown as listed on the Factory Order without any substitutions.

School Set, 965 Farm Set and 980 Ranch Set. Also, the no. 6821 Flat Car with Crates was substituted for the no. 6014. A quantity was not listed, and the outfit has been observed with either car. None of these substitutions affects the price.

The large no. 60-573 Tan RSC with Black Graphics outfit box was manufactured by Star Corrugated Box Company, Inc. and measured 16 x 15¼ x 10⅜ inches. It also had a star printed on the bottom

The original quantity for this outfit was 1,000, but it was increased to 2,250 on 11-17-60. This increase was likely due to the sale of this outfit to FAO Schwarz. Even though FAO Schwarz was not listed on the original Factory Order, the X-569NA does appear in its catalog.

Both empty outfit boxes and partially complete outfits frequently appear on the market. When an outfit appears, it is almost always missing its Plasticville item.

CONVENTIONAL PACK
60-573 BOX
REVISED 8-17-60

TOP LAYER				BOTTOM LAYER		
	960-1 S	12-1013	1020-1 S	175	6465-110 S	6014-100 F
1008-50						
1130T-1 S	6017-1 S			246-1 S	1053-50	

3-1018 TOP 1013

6062-1 (S) TOP 6014
6825-1 (F) TOP 246

Description: 1960 Outfit
Specification: "O27" Ga. Steam Type Freight Outfit
Customer: May Company
Original Amount: 100
Factory Order Date: 8/3/1960
Date Issued: August 3, 1960
Packaging: Conventional Outfit Packing

Contents: 245X-1 Locomotive - with Headlight & Magne-Traction - with Lockon & Lubricant - (With 2 Magnets & Weights); 1130T-1 Tender; 3376-1 Operating Giraffe Car; 6650-1 Missile Launching Flat Car; 6470-1 Exploding Target Car; 6017-1 Caboose - Brick Brown; 1013 Curved Track (12); 1018 Straight Track (13); 1008-50 Uncoupling Unit - with (1) 1018 Straight Track; 1015-60 45-Watt Transformer; 110-1 Graduated Trestle Set; 334 Dispatching Board; 81-32 Wires (2); 310-2 Set of (5) Billboard Signs; IS Instruction Sheet; AC Accessory Catalog; 1802A Layout Instruction Sheet; SNS Special Notice Sheet for Operating 334

Boxes & Packing: 60-536 Box; 60-537 Shipper (1-3); ST Sticker

X-570NA (1960)	C6	C7	C8	Rarity
Complete Outfit	1,015	1,600	2,325	R10
Outfit Box no. 60-536	600	900	1,200	R10

Comments: The May Company purchased four promotional outfits in 1960: the nos. X-502NA, X-503NA, X-504NA and X-570NA. May owned numerous retailers during the 1960s, and these outfits were likely sold through many of them.

The X-570NA, a Retailer Promotional Type Ib, was May's mid-level steam outfit purchase of the year. Its contents closely resemble those in the no. X-571NA ordered by S. Klein.

The X-570NA, a basic freight outfit, was led by a no. 245X-1 Steam Type Locomotive. This promotional-only Scout-type engine was the only Scout to include both a ballast weight and Magne-Traction, which was likely required for it to handle the incline outlined on the no. 1802A Layout Instruction Sheet.

The use of the "X" suffix with this steamer's number was inconsistent with other motive power in that it usually meant the absence of a no. CTC-1 Lockon. In this instance, the "X" might indicate that this locomotive was the later version equipped with a no. 245-200 Motor Complete.

Except for the no. 3376-1 Operating Giraffe Car, all the items in the X-570NA were carryover from previous years. All the rolling stock included early operating AAR trucks and couplers and came in Orange Perforated boxes.

The nos. 6650-1 Missile Launching Flat Car and 6470-1

Exploding Target Car were paired in 14 promotional outfits in 1960. These two cars added excitement to any outfit.

The X-570NA was one of five promotional outfits to include a no. 334 Dispatching Board. Introduced in 1957, this accessory did not appear in a catalog or an outfit after 1960. Lionel evidently managed to deplete its entire stock of Dispatching Boards.

The no. 60-536 Tan RSC with Black Graphics outfit box was originally used for outfit no. X-530NA. It was overstickered for the X-570NA. Manufactured by Star Corrugated Box Company, Inc., this large box measured 19¼ x 15⅝ x 7 inches and had a star printed above the box manufacturer's certificate.

With only 100 outfits manufactured, the X-570NA was likely destined for a specific May-owned retailer. However, no connection to a particular customer has yet been made. So small a quantity has meant that examples of this outfit are seldom scene, hence its R10 rating.

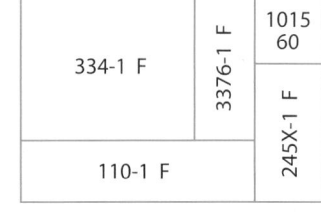

CONVENTIONAL PACK
60-536 BOX
STICKER

Description: 1960 Outfit
Specification: "O27" Ga. Steam Type Freight Outfit
Customer: S. Klein
Original Amount: 500
Factory Order Date: 8/16/1960
Date Issued: August 16, 1960
Packaging: Conventional Outfit Packing

Contents: 245X-1 Locomotive - with Headlight & Magne-Traction - with Lockon & Lubricant - (with 2 Magnets & Weights); 1130T-1 Tender; 3376-1 Operating Giraffe Car; 6544-1 Missile Firing Trail Car; 6470-1 Exploding Target Car; 6017-1 Caboose - Brick Brown; 1013 Curved Track (12); 1018 Straight Track (13); 6029-25 Uncoupling Track Section; 1015-60 45-Watt Transformer; 110-1 Graduated Trestle Set; 334 Dispatching Board; 90-1 Uncoupling Track Controller; 81-32 Wires (4); 90-30 Envelope Packed With 90-1 and 81-32; 310-2 Set of (5) Billboard Signs; IS Instruction Sheet; AC Accessory Catalog; 1802A Layout Instruction Sheet

Boxes & Packing: 60-587 Box; 60-588 Shipper (1-3)

X-571NA (1960)	C6	C7	C8	Rarity
Complete Outfit	850	1,275	1,850	R9
Outfit Box no. 60-587	350	450	525	R9

Comments: S. Klein was a discount retailer that purchased numerous promotional Lionel outfits in the 1960s. The no. X-

X-571NA
1960

571NA, a Retailer Promotional Type Ib outfit, was its only purchase for 1960.

With only one notable exception, this outfit duplicated the no. X-570NA ordered by May Company. Both were led by a no. 245X-1 Steam Type Locomotive. This promotional-only Scout-type engine was the only Scout to include both a ballast weight and Magne-Traction, which was likely required for it to handle the incline as outlined on the no. 1802A Layout Instruction Sheet.

The use of the "X" suffix with this steamer's number was inconsistent with other motive power in that it usually meant the absence of a no. CTC-1 Lockon. In this instance, the "X" might indicate that this locomotive was the later version equipped with a no. 245-200 Motor Complete.

When it came to the cars for the X-571NA, Lionel used the

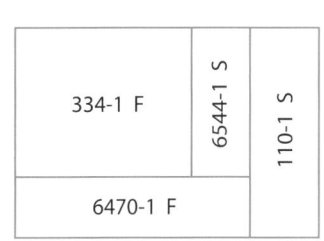

CONVENTIONAL PACK
60-587 BOX

same ones it put in the X-570NA, except that it replaced the no. 6650-1 Missile Launching Flat Car with a no. 6544-1 Missile Firing Trail Car. In addition, the no. 6029-25 Uncoupling Track Section that was substituted for the no. 1008-50 Uncoupling Unit in the X-570NA required a no. 90-30 Envelope Packed.

All the rolling stock in the X-571NA, other than the 6544-1 and the no. 3376-1 Operating Giraffe Car, were carryover items from previous years. These two cars entered the line in 1960. Be aware that cracks or breakage can occur on a 6544-1 where the

two brake wheels were attached to the plastic frame ends. That exciting car, like all the others, had early operating AAR trucks and couplers and came in an Orange Perforated box.

The X-571NA was one of five promotional outfits to include a no. 334 Dispatching Board. Introduced in 1957, this accessory did not appear in a catalog or an outfit after 1960. Lionel evidently managed to deplete its entire stock of Dispatching Boards.

The no. 60-587 Box was unique to this outfit. As with the X-570NA, an example of the X-571NA is difficult to find.

Description: 1960 Outfit
Specification: Super "O" Ga. Diesel Power Outfit with Horn
Customer: Madison Hardware
Original Amount: 100
Factory Order Date: 10/31/1960
Date Issued: October 31, 1960
Packaging: Ship in Bulk

Contents: 2383P-1 Diesel Power Unit - "Santa Fe" - with Horn, Magne-Traction, Twin Motors - with Lockon and Lubricant; 2383T-1 Motorless Unit "Santa Fe"; 3927-1 Track Cleaning Car; 68-1 Executive Inspection Car; 52-1 Fire Fighting Car; 175-1 Rocket Launcher; LW Transformer; 2432-1 Vista Dome - "Clifton"; 2436-1 Observation - "Mooseheart"; 6428-1 Non-Oper. Mail Car; 6464-900 Box Car - NYC - Green; 6544-1 Missile Firing Car; 1122 Remote Control Switches (1Pr.); 6560-25 Cane Car - Black & Red; 32 Straight Track (30); 332-1 Arch under Bridge; 350-1 Transfer Table; 350-50 Transfer Table Extension; 321-1 Trestle Bridge

X-572NA (1960)	C6	C7	C8	Rarity
Items Only	1,950	3,000	4,135	N/A

Comments: Madison Hardware Co. of New York purchased what were known as "bulk outfits." (For an explanation of the practice of buying "bulk outfits," consult the entry on Madison Hardware Co. in the section on Lionel's Distribution and Customers.)

Madison purchased bulk-packed outfits nos. X-564NA, X-

572NA, X-576 and X-577 in 1960. The first two were Retailer Promotional Type Ia outfits, and the other two were Type Ib outfits.

No individual outfit boxes have been observed for any bulk outfit listed in this volume. As a result, we cannot ascertain whether these items were ever assembled and sold as an outfit. Even if they were, we cannot prove that Madison Hardware designated the groupings as no. X-564NA, X-572NA, X-576 or X-577.

When you look at the contents of the X-572NA as well as those of the other three bulk outfits from 1960, it becomes obvious that Madison was merely splitting up its separate-sale order across multiple "outfits" to take advantage of the inherent outfit discount. As such, the X-572NA included a little bit of everything, starting with the nos. 2383 Santa Fe F3 Diesels that explain why it was labeled a "Super 'O' Ga. Diesel Power Outfit with Horn".

The rolling stock was a neat assortment of new and old. The nos. 6428-1 Mail Car, 6464-900 Green NYC Box Car and 6544-1 Missile Firing Car joined the line in 1960. By contrast, making their last or nearly last appearance were the nos. 52-1 Fire Fighting Car, 68-1 Executive Inspection Car, 175-1 Rocket Launcher, 350-1 Transfer Table, 350-50 Transfer Table Extension, 2432-1 Clifton Vista Dome, 2436-1 Mooseheart Observation and 3927-1 Track Cleaning Car.

A listing for this outfit is provided here because a Factory Order exists for the X-572NA. Pricing is provided as reference for the items alone. However, as stated earlier in this volume, items alone do not constitute an outfit; an outfit box is required.

Overall, it appears that Lionel took the opportunity to clean out some old inventory, sending it to a willing customer. Finding a box with any sort of markings for this outfit would be quite a discovery.

Customer No. On Box: 9745
Description: 1960 Outfit
Specification: "O27" Ga. Steam Type Freight Outfit with Smoke
Customer/No.: Channel Master; 9745
Original Amount: 4,500
Factory Order Date: 9/7/1960
Date Issued: September 13, 1960
Packaging: Conventional Outfit Packing

Contents: 243-1 Locomotive - with Smoke and Headlight - with (2) Position Reversing Unit, Lockon and Lubricant - without Magne-Traction; 1130T-1 Tender; 3512-1 Operating Fireman

and Ladder Car; 3376-1 Operating Giraffe Car; 6162-1 Gondola Car - Blue - with (3) White Canisters; 6812-1 Track Maintenance Car; 6017-1 Caboose - Brick Brown; 1013 Curved Track (12); 1018 Straight Track (7); 1008-50 Uncoupling Unit - with (1) 1018 Straight Track; 1015-25 45-Watt Transformer; 1020-1 90° Crossover; 128-1 Animated News Stand; 310-3 Billboard Frame; 81-32 Wires (2); 1627-2 Instruction Sheet; 2165 Layout Instruction Sheet; 310-2 Set of (5) Billboard Signs; AC Accessory Catalog

Boxes & Packing: 60-575 Box; 60-576 Shipper (1-4); 60-593 Box; 60-594 Shipper (1-3); 59-332 Box; 59-333 Shipper (1-2); ST Sticker; 60-423 Box; 60-425 Shipper (1-3); ST Sticker

Variation 1 of outfit no. X-573NA included a no. 128-1 Animated Newsstand in a no. 60-575 Box. This box was unique to this outfit. Factory orders for 3,000 of Variation 1 exist. Note the rare Channel Master billboard that was exclusive to this and outfit no. 9745.

Alternate For Outfit Contents:

Note: Substitutions for increase of 1,500 sets: Use 400 - 3512-1; Use 300 - 3435 for 3512-1; Use 800 - 3535 for 3512-1; Use 279 - 128-1; Use 100 - 334-1 for 128-1; Use 682 - 464 for 128-1; Use 439 - 55-1 for 128-1.

The side of the outfit box for Variation 1 includes a label with the Channel Master promotion no. 9745 identified.

X-573NA (1960)	C6	C7	C8	Rarity
Variation 1 - Complete Outfit With no. 128-1 And no. 60-575 Box	800	1,400	1,950	R8
Outfit Box no. 60-575	125	175	225	R5
Variation 2 - Complete Outfit With no. 464-1 And no. 60-593 Box	875	1,575	2,200	R8
Variation 3 - Complete Outfit With no. 334-1 And no. 60-593 Box	900	1,650	2,400	R8
Outfit Box no. 60-593	250	325	450	R8
Variation 4 - Complete Outfit With no. 55-1 And no. 59-332 Box	950	1,715	2,500	R9
Outfit Box no. 59-332	300	425	525	R9
Variation 5 - Complete Outfit With no. 128-1 And 60-423 Box	1,025	1,875	2,700	R10
Outfit Box no. 60-423	400	650	750	R10
Variations 2 Through 5 With A no. 3435-1 Substitution, Add The Following	15	25	50	Same
Variations 2 Through 5 With A no. 3535-1 Substitution, Subtract The Following	25	50	75	Same

Comments: The no. X-573NA was the number that Lionel assigned to Channel Master's no. 9745 promotion. Channel Master manufactured outdoor television antennas, accessories and black-and-white and color TV tubes. In 1960, it ran promotion no. 9745, in which it offered a Lionel outfit free with a "Main Line" radio package. (See the section on Lionel's Distribution and Customers for a full description of this promotion.) The X-573NA was a Manufacturer Promotional Type IIIc outfit.

Information in the Factory Orders indicates that Lionel originally received an order from Channel Master for 3,000 of the X-573NAs, each to have a no. 128-1 Animated Newsstand. Filling the order presented no problem because Lionel still had 3,279 of those accessories in stock.

However, when Channel Master requested an additional 1,500 promotional outfits, Lionel scrambled to find other accessories to fill the order. It came up with 279 more of the 128-1 Animated Newsstand and then provided 100 of the no. 334-1 Operating Dispatching Board, 682 of the no. 464-1 Lumber Mill and 439 of the no. 55-1 Tie-Jector motorized unit. These substitutions created five variations of the X-573NA.

Channel Master must have then ordered another 5,000 outfits, which Lionel filled by creating what it designated as outfit no. 9745. This outfit came with a no. 175-1 Rocket Launcher and replaced the no. 3512-1 Operating Fireman and Ladder Car with a no. 6476-25 Hopper Car - Red and the no. 6017-1 Brick Brown Caboose with a no. 6057-25 Red Caboose. Two variations of the 9745 outfit exist to make a total of seven Channel Master outfit variations. (See the entry for the 9745 for more information about that outfit.)

The X-573NA was headed by a no. 243-1 Locomotive - with Smoke and Headlight (new for 1960). Other features included a metal motor and a two-position reverse unit. This steam engine was nearly identical to the no. 244-1 Locomotive, except that the 243

Variation 4 of the no. X-573NA, which came in an overstickered no. 59-332 Box, included a no. 55-1 Tie-Jector in its Late Classic box and a Channel Master billboard. It has also been observed with a no. 3435-1 Operating Aquarium Car.

Variation 5 of the no. X-573NA also included a no. 128-1 Animated Newsstand, but now the outfit came in an overstickered no. 60-423 Box. This is the most difficult of the five variations to find, as only 279 were manufactured in this box. Note the rare Channel Master billboard that was exclusive to this and outfit no. 9745.

included an extra weight as part of its mechanism.

Notable items in this outfit included the no. 3512-1 with black ladders and the no. 6812-1 Track Maintenance Car with a gray platform and black base or vice versa. The no. 3376-1 Operating Giraffe Car was the only new piece of rolling stock. These and the other cars were equipped with early operating AAR trucks and couplers and came packaged in Orange Perforated boxes.

A no. 2165 Layout Instruction Sheet appeared only in outfits X-573NA and 9745. It outlined the extended figure-eight layout and was dated 8-60.

The X-573NA, 9745 and the no. 19332 were the only outfits from the 1960s to include a unique billboard. In this case, a Channel Master billboard was included in each outfit, along with a single no. 310-3 Billboard Frame. This billboard is frequently separated from the outfit and lost. Finding this rare billboard in collectible condition is a challenge.

Two types of substitutions exist, one for individual cars and one for accessories. Both were due to the increase of 1,500 additional outfits ordered. First, the 3512-1 was included in only 400 of the 1,500 additional outfits, even though the outfit packing sheets always listed it.

The remaining outfits (most of Variations 2 through 5 below) might have either a no. 3435-1 Operating Aquarium Car or a no. 3535-1 Operating Security Car. The Factory Orders do not break down how those substitutions were made, but observations are noted in the variations listed below. The incremental price is included in the pricing table.

The second group of substitutions involved accessories. These changes caused Lionel to use different outfit boxes so that the combination of the accessory provided and outfit box used led to five different variations.

Variation 1 included the items listed on the Factory Order. The accessory was the 128-1 Animated Newsstand. The no. 60-575 Tan RSC with Black Graphics outfit box was manufactured by Owens-Illinois Paper Products, Div. and measured 19 x 12⅞ x 6¼ inches. It had seven dots and "012" on the bottom. It was unique to this outfit. With 3,000 manufactured, this is the most common version.

Variation 2 included a 464-1 Lumber Mill. It came in a no. 60-593 Tan RSC with Black Graphics outfit box, which was unique to the X-573NA. Be aware that this variation has been observed with the no. 3535-1 Operating Security Car substitution. Factory orders for 682 of this variation were issued.

Variation 3 included a 334-1 Operating Dispatching Board. It came in the same box as Variation 2. Factory orders for 100 of this variation were issued.

Variation 4 included a 55-1 Tie-Jector Car. Although this motorized unit was a lot of fun, it seemed out of place in this outfit. The no. 59-332 Tan RSC with Black Graphics outfit box was manufactured by Star Corrugated Box Company, Inc. and measured 15½ x 13½ x 6½ inches. It was an overstickered no. X-824 outfit box from 1959 with a star printed on the bottom. Of note, this variation has been observed with the 3435-1 Operating Aquarium Car substitution. Factory orders for 439 of this variation were issued.

Variation 5 also included a 128-1 Animated Newsstand. The no. 60-423 Tan RSC with Black Graphics outfit box was manufactured by Kraft Corrugated Containers, Inc. and measured 15¾ x 14 x 7½ inches. It was an overstickered no. X-503NA outfit box from 1960. Factory orders for 279 of this variation were issued.

The outfit box variations and Channel Master billboard are the keys to determining overall price and rarity. Variation 5 is the toughest to find, followed by Variation 4. Although only 100 of Variation 3 were made, it is easily created from Variation 2 and so it achieves only an R8 rarity. Variation 1 is the easiest to find, but it jumps to R8 when the billboard is included.

Collecting each Channel Master variation is an exciting pursuit. Expect to need lots of time and patience when searching for Variation 5.

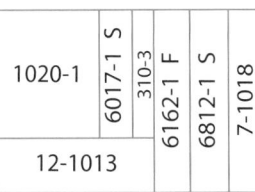

CONVENTIONAL PACK
60-575 BOX

TOP LAYER / BOTTOM LAYER

1008-50 TOP 6162

(2 OF 5) 682 WITH 464: 60-593 BOX, REVISED 9-6-60
TOP LAYER / BOTTOM LAYER

7-1018 TOP 1013
1020-1 TOP 464
1008-50 TOP 243

(3 OF 5) 100 WITH 334: 60-593 BOX, REVISED 9-6-60
TOP LAYER / BOTTOM LAYER

1020-1 TOP 6812 - 1008-50

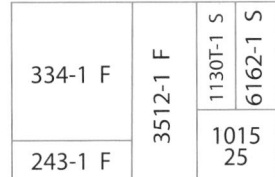

(4 OF 5) 439 WITH 55-1: 59-332 BOX, REVISED 9-6-60, STICKER
TOP LAYER / BOTTOM LAYER

1020-1 TOP 6812 - 1130T
1008-50 TOP 6017

(5 OF 5) BALANCE WITH 128-1: 60-423 BOX, REVISED 9-7-60, STICKER
TOP LAYER / BOTTOM LAYER

1008-50 TOP 1130T
1020-1 TOP

The Abraham & Straus no. X-574NA in its no. 60-591 Box. The nos. 902 Cardboard Trestle With Girder Bridge & Tunnel, 903 Set of (2) Sheets Trading Cards and 981 Freight Yard Set make this a highly desirable outfit. All of them are difficult to find in collectible condition.

An Abraham & Straus advertisement (from an unknown newspaper) for the no. X-574NA. One key message of the advertisement was a comparison to the list price of the components purchased separately. This was a common practice for promotional outfits in the 1960s.

Boxes & Packing: 60-591 Box; 60-592 Shipper (1-3); 59-100 Box; 59-101 Shipper (1-4); ST Sticker

X-574NA (1960)	C6	C7	C8	Rarity
Complete Outfit With no. 60-591 Box	1,200	2,800	5,350	R9
Outfit Box no. 60-591	200	325	450	R8
Complete Outfit With no. 59-100 Box	1,350	3,000	5,500	R9
Outfit Box no. 59-100 Box	350	500	600	R9

Comments: Longtime Lionel customer Abraham & Strauss, a department store based in Brooklyn, New York, purchased one Retailer Promotional Type Ib outfit in 1960. This outfit is similar to the no. X-567NA ordered by McMahon's.

The X-574NA was advertised by Abraham & Straus as a "79-Piece Train Set With Steam Locomotive". Only six of those "pieces" were the actual train. The advertisement went on to state that if the contents were purchased separately, the total value would be $47.60, but the A&S sale price was only $19.99. This is yet another example of how heavily discounted Lionel trains were during the early 1960s.

The outfit was headed by a no. 246-1 Locomotive with Headlight and Magne-Traction. This steamer came boxed in a no. 246-6 Corrugated Box.

The X-574NA featured some interesting pieces of rolling stock. A boxed no. 3386-1 Operating Giraffe Car appeared in only this and two other promotional outfits. This car's rare Orange Perforated 3386-10 Folding Box appeared only in promotional outfits, which is the reason the X-574NA is classified as a Type Ib outfit. When available for separate sale, the 3386-1 was boxed in an overstamped no. 3376-120 Folding Box which, as explained in the *Authoritative Guide to Lionel's Postwar Operating Cars* (Project Roar Publishing), is even more difficult to find than a 3386-10.

Two other cars deserved attention. First, the X-574NA was the first outfit to mention the no. 6045-50 Cities Service Tank Car.

Description: 1960 Outfit
Specification: "O27" Ga. Steam Type Freight Outfit
Customer/Price: Abraham & Strauss; $19.99
Original Amount: 1,100
Factory Order Date: 8/18/1960
Date Issued: August 18, 1960
Packaging: Conventional Outfit Packing

Contents: 246-1 Locomotive - with Headlight and Magne-Traction - with Lockon & Lubricant; 1130T-1 Tender; 6476-1 Hopper Car - Red; 3386-1 Operating Giraffe Car; 6045-50 Tank Car - "Cities Service"; 6047-1 Caboose - Brick Brown; 1013 Curved Track (8); 1018 Straight Track (10); 1016-60 35-Watt Transformer; 902 Cardboard Trestle With Girder Bridge & Tunnel (2); 903 Set of (2) Sheets Trading Cards; 981 Freight Yard Set; 81-32 Wires (2); 310-2 Set of (5) Billboard Signs; 1609-4 Instruction Sheet; AC Accessory Catalog

In late 1960, it superseded the no. 6045-25 Gray Two Dome Tank Car. Also, this was the only outfit in the 1960s to list a boxed no. 6047-1 Caboose. Its Orange Perforated no. 6047-3 Folding Box is difficult to find in collectible condition.

The 3386-1, 6045-50 and 6047-1 were equipped with non-operating Archbar trucks and couplers. All the remaining items in the X-574NA came with early operating AAR trucks and couplers.

By far the two items that drive up the price of this outfit are the no. 902 Cardboard Trestle With Girder Bridge & Tunnel and the no. 903 Set of (2) Sheets Trading Cards. Both of them were fragile and intended to be separated and played with. Many more examples of the 902-1 have survived intact than have 903-1s.

The 903 included 24 two-sided Lionel trading cards printed on a sheet of perforated cardstock. On the front of each card was a Lionel locomotive, and on the back was historical information about its road name as well as a trivia quiz. A "folding" strip connected two 11 x 11 inch sets of 12 cards. The entire sheet of 24 was folded in half along the strip and placed loose in the outfit box. The cards were perforated and are almost always found separated as individual cards with the "folding" strip long gone. In fact if it weren't for the complete sheets that came out of Madison Hardware over the years, it is likely that few of these items would be intact.

The inclusion of a no. 981 Freight Yard Set also increases the value of this outfit. This Plasticville set came boxed in a fragile box that takes patience to find in C8 condition.

The X-574NA was a success, as the original order of 600 was increased to 1,100 on 11-23-60. The first 600 outfits came in a no. 60-591 Tan RSC with Black Graphics outfit box manufactured by St. Joe Paper Co. - Container Div. and measuring 14½ x 12⅜ x 6⅛ inches. It also had "9 10 11 12" and "60-591" printed on the bottom.

The remaining 500 outfits were packaged in a no. 59-100 Yellow RSC with Black Graphics outfit box manufactured by Star

Corrugated Box Company, Inc. and measuring 14⅛ x 13⅛ x 7 inches. It was an overstickered no. 1626W outfit box from 1959.

Complete examples of the X-574NA do appear on the market from time to time, though generally all that is found is the empty outfit box. This circumstance is usually due to the fact that, as with many promotional outfits, the contents have been cannibalized and sold off separately because they are always in demand.

Regarding the empty boxes, examples of the 60-591 appear more often than do those of the 59-100. But finding either box takes time, patience and plenty of funds.

CONVENTIONAL PACK
60-591 BOX

TOP LAYER

6047-1 F	6476-1 F
	6045-50 F
	10-1018
	8-1013

2 - 902 TOP
903 TOP

BOTTOM LAYER

1016 60	246-1 F
1130T-1 F	981-1 F
	3386-1 S

59-100 BOX
500, REVISED 11-23-60, STICKER

TOP LAYER

1016-60	10-1018
	8-1013
	6045-50 S
	981-1 F

2 - 902 TOP
903 TOP

BOTTOM LAYER

| 6476-1 S |
6047-1 F	3386-1 F
	1130T-1 F
	246-1 F

Description: 1960 Outfit
Specification: "O27" Ga. Steam Type Freight Outfit
Customer: Niresk Industries
Original Amount: 200
Factory Order Date: 9/26/1960
Date Issued: September 26, 1960
Packaging: Display Outfit Packing - Corrugated Separators

Contents: 1060-25 Steam Type Locomotive - with Headlight, Front and Rear Trucks - without Magne-Traction, Reversing Unit, Lockon and Lubricant; 1060T-25 Tender; 6404-25 Single Auto Car - Black Frame - Red Auto - with Non-Operating Trucks; 3386-25 Operating Giraffe Car - with Non-Operating Trucks; 3376-118 Envelope Packed; 6047-25 Caboose - Brick Brown - Non-Operating Trucks; 1013 Curved Track (8); 1018 Straight Track (2); 1016-60 Transformer; 902 Cardboard Trestle With Girder Bridge & Tunnel; CTC Lockon; 81-32 Wires (2); 927-60 Lubricant (Oil); 927-65 Lubricant (Grease); 1103-12 Envelope Packed With CTC, 81-32, 927-60 and 927-65; 1109-10 Instruction Sheet; 310-2 Set of (5) Billboard Signs; AC Accessory Catalog

Boxes & Packing: 60-368 Box; 60-369 Insert; 60-370 Insert; 59-44 Tube; 60-371 Shipper (1-5); ST Sticker (5) Blue on White

Alternate For Outfit Contents:
Note: Use 1109 Outfit Box and Stock Shipper.

X-575 (1960)	C6	C7	C8	Rarity
Complete Outfit	750	1,100	1,550	R10
Outfit Box no. 60-368	500	675	800	R10

Comments: Mail-order retailer Niresk Industries purchased the no. X-575 Retailer Promotional Type Ib outfit in 1960. This was the only outfit attributed to Niresk in the 1960s.

The X-575 was identical to the no. 1109 display outfit, except that it also included a no. 902 Cardboard Trestle With Girder Bridge & Tunnel. Lionel simply took the 1109, added a 902 and placed stickers on the outfit box to create the X-575. (See the entry for outfit 1109 for more information.)

The 902 is always difficult to find in C8 condition because, like other cardboard items placed in outfits, it was fragile and intended to be assembled. Once used, it retained minimal value. Few examples have survived, and this cardboard item alone is worth more than all the rolling stock included in the outfit.

The no. 60-368 White Hinged Display with 1050 Blue Steamer and Red/Orange Graphics Type A outfit box was manufactured by Kraft Corrugated Containers, Inc. and measured 20⅝ x 11⅝ x 3⅛ inches.

It is unknown why the number of this outfit does not include "NA". (See the section on Outfit Numbering for a discussion of "NA" and its uses.)

With only 200 of the X-575 manufactured, this outfit is rarely seen for sale.

DISPLAY PACK
60-368 BOX
STICKER (5) BLUE ON WHITE

1060-25		1060T-25	
1016 60	3386-25	6047-25	
CORD 8-1013 2-1018		6404-25 3376-118	

902-1 TOP

X-576
1960

Description: 1960 Outfit
Specification: Special Promotional Outfit
Customer: Madison Hardware
Original Amount: 100
Factory Order Date: 9/26/1960
Date Issued: September 26, 1960
Packaging: Ship Bulk - No Outfit Packing

Contents: 226P-1 Alco Diesel Power Unit - "Boston & Maine" - with Horn, Headlight, Magne-Traction, Non-Operating Coupler, Lockon and Lubricant; 226C-1 "B" Unit - Blue & White - "Boston & Maine" Markings; 3672-1 Operating Bosco Car; 3361-1 Operating Lumber Car; 1875-1 Illuminated Passenger Car; 1876-1 Illuminated Mail & Passenger Car; 260-1 Illuminated Bumper; 110 Graduated Trestle Set; 52 Fire Fighting Car; 111 Elevated Trestle Set; 140-1 Banjo Signal; 353-1 Trackside Control Signal; 2432-1 Vista Dome - "Clifton"; 92 Circuit Breaker Controller; LTC Lockon; 3376-1 Operating Giraffe Car; ZW Transformer; 6464-900 Box Car - "New York Central"; 3927 Track Cleaning Car; 252-1 Crossing Gate; 50 Gang Car; 3830 Flat Car - with Operating Submarine; 6428 U. S. Mail Car; OS Straight Track (36); O22 Remote Control Switches Pr.

X-576 (1960)	C6	C7	C8	Rarity
Items Only	1,650	2,750	3,950	N/A

Comments: Madison Hardware Co. of New York purchased what were known as "bulk outfits." (For an explanation of the practice of buying "bulk outfits," consult the entry on Madison Hardware Co. in the section on Lionel's Distribution and Customers.)

Madison purchased bulk-packed outfits nos. X-564NA, X-572NA, X-576 and X-577 in 1960. The first two were Retailer Promotional Type Ia outfits, and the other two were Type Ib outfits.

No individual outfit boxes have been observed for any bulk outfit listed in this volume. As a result, we cannot ascertain whether these items were ever assembled and sold as an outfit. Even if they were, we cannot prove that Madison Hardware designated the groupings as no. X-564NA, X-572NA, X-576 or X-577.

When you look at the contents of the X-576 as well as those of the other three bulk outfits from 1960, it becomes obvious that Madison was merely splitting up its separate-sale order across multiple "outfits" to take advantage of the inherent outfit discount. As such, the X-576 included a little bit of everything.

The rolling stock was a neat assortment of new and old. The nos. 3376-1 Operating Giraffe Car, 3830 Flat Car with Operating Submarine, 6428 U.S. Mail Car and 6464-900 New York Central Box Car joined the line in 1960. By contrast, making their last or nearly last outfit appearance were the nos. 1875-1 Illuminated Passenger Car, 2432-1 *Clifton* Vista Dome, 3672-1 Operating Bosco Car and 3927 Track Cleaning Car.

The X-576 was, with four exceptions, identical to the X-577 described below. The nos. 140-1 Banjo Signal, 1876-1 Illuminated Mail & Passenger Car, 6428 U.S. Mail Car and 6464-900 New York Central Box Car in the X-576 were replaced by, respectively, the nos. 151 Semaphore, 6560-1 Crane Car, 6361 Timber Transport Car and 6475-1 Pickle Car.

A listing for this outfit is provided here because a Factory Order exists for the X-576. By the way, it is unknown why the number of this outfit does not include "NA". (See the section on Outfit Numbering for a discussion of "NA" and its uses.)

Pricing is provided as reference for the items alone. However, as stated earlier in this volume, items alone do not constitute an outfit; an outfit box is required.

Overall, it appears that Lionel took the opportunity to clean out some old inventory, sending it to a willing customer. Finding a box with any sort of markings for this outfit would be quite a discovery.

Description: 1960 Outfit
Specification: Special Promotional Outfit
Customer: Madison Hardware
Original Amount: 100
Factory Order Date: 9/23/1960
Date Issued: September 23, 1960
Packaging: Ship Bulk - No Outfit Packing

Contents: 226P-1 Alco Diesel Power Unit - "Boston & Maine" - with Horn, Headlight, Magne-Traction, Non-Operating Coupler, Lockon and Lubricant; 226C-1 "B" Unit - Blue & White - "Boston & Maine" Markings; 3672-1 Operating Bosco Car; 3361-1 Operating Lumber Car; 1875-1 Illuminated Passenger Car; 6560-1 Crane Car; 260-1 Illuminated Bumper; 110 Graduated Trestle Set; 52 Fire Fighting Car; 111 Elevated Trestle Set; 151 Semaphore; 353 Trackside Control Signal; 2432-1 Vista Dome - "Clifton"; 92 Circuit Breaker Controller; LTC Lockon; 3376-1 Operating Giraffe Car; ZW Transformer; 6475-1 Pickle Car; 3927-1 Track Cleaning Car; 252-1 Crossing Gate; 50 Gang Car; 3830-1 Flat Car - with Operating Submarine; 6361 Timber Transport Car; OS Straight Track (36); O22 Remote Control Switches Pr.

X-577 (1960)	C6	C7	C8	Rarity
Items Only	1,600	2,700	3,850	N/A

Comments: Madison Hardware Co. of New York purchased what were known as "bulk outfits." (For an explanation of the practice of buying "bulk outfits," consult the entry on Madison Hardware Co. in the section on Lionel's Distribution and Customers.)

Madison purchased bulk-packed outfits nos. X-564NA, X-572NA, X-576 and X-577 in 1960. The first two were Retailer Promotional Type Ia outfits, and the other two were Type Ib outfits.

No individual outfit boxes have been observed for any bulk outfit listed in this volume. As a result, we cannot ascertain whether these items were ever assembled and sold as an outfit. Even if they were, we cannot prove that Madison Hardware designated the groupings as no. X-564NA, X-572NA, X-576 or X-577.

When you look at the contents of the X-577 as well as those of the other three bulk outfits from 1960, it becomes obvious that Madison was merely splitting up its separate-sale order across multiple "outfits" to take advantage of the inherent outfit discount. As such, the X-577 included a little bit of everything. The nos. 3376-1 Operating Giraffe Car, 3830-1 Flat Car with Operating Submarine, 6361 Timber Transport Car and 6475-1 Pickle Car joined the line in 1960. By contrast, making their last or nearly last outfit appearance were the nos. 1875-1 Illuminated Passenger Car, 2432-1 *Clifton* Vista Dome, 3672-1 Operating Bosco Car and 3927-1 Track Cleaning Car.

The X-577 was, with four exceptions, identical to the X-576 described above. The nos. 151 Semaphore, 6560-1 Crane Car, 6361 Timber Transport Car and 6475-1 Pickle Car in the X-577 replaced, respectively, the nos. 140-1 Banjo Signal, 1876-1 Illuminated Mail & Passenger Car, 6428 U.S. Mail Car and 6464-900 New York Central Box Car.

A listing for this outfit is provided here because a Factory Order exists for the X-577. By the way, it is unknown why the number of this outfit does not include "NA". (See the section on Outfit Numbering for a discussion of "NA" and its uses.)

Pricing is provided as reference for the items alone. However, as stated earlier in this volume, items alone do not constitute an outfit; an outfit box is required.

Overall, it appears that Lionel took the opportunity to clean out some old inventory, sending it to a willing customer. Finding a box with any sort of markings for this outfit would be quite a discovery.

Description: 1960 Outfit
Specification: "O27" Ga. Freight Outfit
Original Amount: 6
Factory Order Date: 9/23/1960
Date Issued: September 23, 1960
Packaging: Conventional Outfit Packing, Wrap Cars in Tissue Paper

Contents: 58-1 Rotary Snow Plow; 6042-25 Gondola Car - Blue (less 2 Red Canisters) with Non-Operating Trucks; 6044-25 Box Car - Blue - "Airex" Markings - Non-Operating Trucks; 6045-25 Two Dome Tank Car - Gray - Non-Operating Trucks; 6047-25 Caboose - Brick Brown - Non-Operating Trucks; 1013 Curved Track (8); 1018 Straight Track (2); 1243 Transformer; 927-60 Lubricant (Oil); 927-65 Lubricant (Grease); IS Instruction Sheet; 310-2 Set of (5) Billboard Signs; AC Accessory Catalog

Boxes & Packing: 59-318 Box; 59-319 Shipper (1-4); ST Sticker; BP Bogus Paper

X-578NA (1960)	C6	C7	C8	Rarity
Complete Outfit	3,525	5,400	6,300	R10
Outfit Box no. 59-318	3,000	4,500	5,000	R10

Comments: Based on the original quantity produced, the no. X-578NA ties with the no. X-559NA as the rarest outfit. Only six of each of these outfits were manufactured. They rank first on the list of least produced catalog and promotional outfits.

Other than what is specified on the Factory Order, no information exists about the X-578NA. Unfortunately, the name of the customer was not noted. The tiny quantity ordered suggests that this outfit was likely intended for a specific retailer or manufacturer. Therefore, it was either a Retailer Promotional Type

CONVENTIONAL PACK
59-318 BOX
STICKER, BOGUS PAPER, WRAP CARS IN TISSUE PAPER

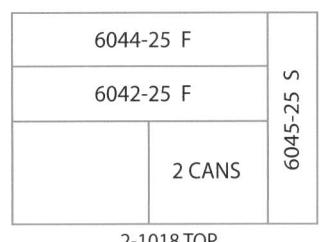

TOP LAYER

6044-25 F	
6042-25 F	6045-25 S
2 CANS	

2-1018 TOP

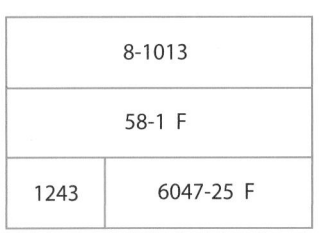

BOTTOM LAYER

8-1013	
58-1 F	
1243	6047-25 F

Ib or a Manufacturer Promotional Type IIIb outfit. Furthermore, the inclusion of a no. 1243 Transformer (the international version of the no. 1043/1053 Transformer) leads to the conclusion that this outfit probably was made for a customer outside the United States.

The X-578NA was among the handful of Lionel outfits headed by a motorized unit. It was the only one to include a no. 58-1 Rotary Snow Plow during the 1960s.

All the other pieces of rolling stock in this outfit were low-end items that were equipped with non-operating Archbar trucks and couplers.

The no. 59-318 Tan RSC with Black Graphics outfit box was an overstickered Sears no. 9664 from 1959. This is the only outfit to state that the cars were to be wrapped in tissue paper.

Needless to say, the X-578NA is by far one of the most difficult of any Lionel outfit to find.

X-579NA
1960

The no. X-579NA included five space and military operating cars and was headed by the collectible no. 224P-1 U.S. Navy Alco Diesel Power Car. With only 350 manufactured, this outfit is difficult to complete in C8 condition, yet both promotional outfit and space and military collectors desire it.

A shipping label on a no. X-579NA indicates this that outfit was shipped from Sidles, Co. The relationship between Sidles and Leonard F. Fellman (the customer listed on the Factory Order) has not been determined. The postmark (not shown) was stamped November 30, 1960.

SIDLES COMPANY

DISTRIBUTORS
Household Appliances, Stokers, Heating Equipment, Air Conditioning
7302 Pacific St.   P.O. Box 1276   OMAHA, NEBRASKA

TO   Joseph Quartoroli
6540 North 33rd Street
Omaha, Nebraska

POSTMASTER: CONTS · MDSE · RETURN   ◆   THIS PARCEL MAY BE OPENED FOR
POSTAGE GUARANTEED   POSTAL INSPECTION IF NECESSARY

Description: 1960 Outfit
Specification: "O27" Ga. Diesel Freight Outfit
Customer: Leonard F. Fellman and Company
Original Amount: 350
Factory Order Date: 10/12/1960
Date Issued: October 12, 1960
Packaging: Conventional Packing

Contents: 224P-1 Alco Diesel Power Car - "U.S. Navy" - Navy Color and Markings - with Headlight, Magne-Traction - with Non-Operating Coupler - Lockon and Lubricant; 224C-1 "B" Unit - Navy Color and Markings; 3419-1 Operating Helicopter Car; 6650-1 Missile Launching Flat Car; 3830-1 Flat Car - with Operating Submarine; 6544-1 Missile Firing Trail Car; 6017-1 Caboose - Brick Brown; 470-1 IRBM Missile Launching Platform with Exploding Target Car; 1013 Curved Track (8); 1018 Straight Track (5); 6029-25 Uncoupling Track Section; 1015-60 45-Watt Transformer; 90-1 Uncoupling Track Controller; 81-32 Wires (4); 90-30 Envelope Packed With 90-1 and 81-32; IS Instruction Sheet; 310-2 Set of (5) Billboard Signs; AC Accessory Catalog

Boxes & Packing: 60-604 Box; 60-605 Shipper (1-3)

X-579NA (1960)	C6	C7	C8	Rarity
Complete Outfit	1,075	1,600	2,250	R9
Outfit Box no. 60-604	350	500	600	R9

Comments: This was the only outfit to list Leonard F. Fellman as the customer on the Factory Order. Unfortunately, the identity and location of this customer have yet to be determined. We can't even verify whether the no. X-579NA was a Retailer Promotional Type Ia or a Manufacturer Promotional IIIa outfit.

The contents of the X-579NA show that it was an exciting and highly desirable space and military outfit headed by a no. 224P-1 U.S. Navy Alco Diesel Power Car with Magne-Traction and a three-position reversing unit. When boxed, this locomotive included the nos. CTC-1 Lockon, 927-60 Tube of Oil, 927-65

Tube of Grease and no. 217-17 Instruction Sheet in its corrugated box.

With four operating cars and a no. 470-1 IRBM Launching Platform with Exploding Target Car, this outfit provided plenty of play value. The only other time the nos. 3419-1, 3830-1, 6470-1 and 6650-1 were all combined was in outfit no. X-520NA. All of these cars, as well as the nos. 6544-1 Missile Firing Trail Car and 6017-1 Caboose, included early operating AAR trucks and couplers and were packaged in Orange Perforated boxes.

The 3419-1 Operating Helicopter car was a carryover from 1959 but appears in this outfit with 1960 features (small winder and single-blade no. 3419-100 Operating Helicopter Complete). The 6470-1 Exploding Target Car included "slotted" sides and a smooth roof door guide (without the nubs added later to help hold on the sides). The 6544-1 joined the line in 1960. Be aware that cracks or breakage can occur on this car where the two brake wheels were attached to the plastic frame ends.

The no. 60-604 Tan RSC with Black Graphics outfit box was manufactured by Owens-Illinois Paper Products, Div. and measured 17¼ x 14½ x 7 inches. It also had six dots and "012" printed on the bottom.

This is an attractive space and military outfit produced in a smaller than average quantity. It does appear on the market, but not always in collectible condition. A C8 outfit would be a nice addition to any promotional or space and military collection.

CONVENTIONAL PACK
60-604 BOX

TOP LAYER

3419-1 F	3830-1 F	6650-1 F	6017-1 S	224C-1 S
5-1018 8-1013		1015 60		

6029-25 TOP 1018

BOTTOM LAYER

470-1 F	224P-1 F
6544-1 S	

Description: 1960 Outfit
Specification: "O27" Ga. Steam Type Freight Outfit
Customer: Easy Washer
Original Amount: 2,000
Factory Order Date: 10/25/1960
Date Issued: October 25, 1960
Packaging: Display Box Packing, Merchandise not in folding boxes

Contents: 1060-25 Steam Type Locomotive - with Headlight, Front and Rear Trucks - without Magne-Traction, Reversing Unit, Lockon and Lubricant; 1060T-25 Tender; 6404-25 Single Auto Car - Black Frame - Red Auto - with Non-Operating Trucks; 6404-30 Automobile - Maroon - without Chromium Plating; 6044-25 Box Car - Blue - "Airex" Markings - Non-Operating Trucks; 6042-25 Gondola Car - Blue - (Less 2 Red Canisters) with Non-Operating Trucks; 6112-5 Red Canisters (2); 6047-25 Caboose - Brick Brown - Non-Operating Trucks; 1013 Curved Track (8); 1018 Straight Track (4); 1026-25 25-Watt Transformer; CTC Lockon; 81-32 Wires (2); 927-60 Lubricant (Oil); 927-65

Lubricant (Grease); 1103-12 Envelope Packed With CTC, 81-32, 927-60 and 927-65; 1119-10 Instruction Sheet; 310-2 Set of (5) Billboard Signs; AC Accessory Catalog

Boxes & Packing: 60-125 Box; 60-126 Tube; 60-127 Insert (2); 60-128 Insert; 60-129X Insert; 60-130 Insert; 60-132 Insert; 60-131 Shipper (1-4); ST 5 Stickers Per Outfit

X-580NA (1960)	C6	C7	C8	Rarity
Complete Outfit	285	445	515	R6
Outfit Box no. 60-125	150	225	300	R6

Comments: Easy Washer offered this Manufacturer Promotional Type IIIb outfit with the purchase of one of its washer/dryer combinations in 1960. The no. X-580NA was the only outfit purchased by Easy Washer during the 1960s.

A basic starter outfit, the X-580NA was headed by a no. 1060-25 Steam Type Locomotive - with Headlight (new for 1960). This low-end steamer went forward only. Interestingly, it was included in only five promotional outfits in 1960, but appeared in more than 65 outfits over the next few years.

The no. 6404-25 Black Frame Single Auto Car appeared in only this and three other promotional outfits. With more than 59,000 of these four outfits produced, this freight car is more common than previously thought. The red automobile with gray bumpers was a no. 6404-30 Automobile - Maroon. Lionel here used the term "maroon" to designate an item that looks red.

All the rolling stock in the X-580NA was equipped with non-operating Archbar trucks and couplers.

The no. 60-125 Yellow Hinged Display with Steamer, General and F3 Graphics Type A outfit box was manufactured by Owens Illinois and measured 24 x 11¾ x 3¼ inches. It was an overstickered no. 1609 outfit box from 1960.

Although 2,000 of this outfit were manufactured, examples do not appear too often. As with many promotional outfits, when one does, it is seldom in collectible condition.

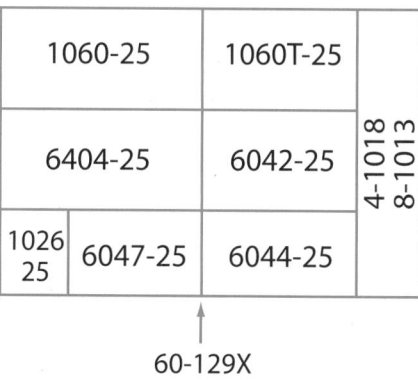

DISPLAY PACK
60-125 BOX
5 STICKERS PER OUTFIT

1060-25	1060T-25	
6404-25	6042-25	4-1018 8-1013
1026 25	6047-25	6044-25	

↑
60-129X

Description: 1960 Outfit
Specification: "O27" Ga. Diesel Freight Outfit
Customer: Beller Electric
Original Amount: 50
Factory Order Date: 10/27/1960
Date Issued: October 27, 1960
Packaging: Ship Bulk - No Outfit Box Packing

Contents: 224P-1 Alco Diesel Power Car - "U.S. Navy" - Navy Color and Markings - with Headlight, Magne-Traction - with Non-Operating Coupler - Lockon and Lubricant; 6544-1 Missile Firing Trail Car - Blue Car Body; 6470-1 Exploding Target Car; 3419-1 Operating Helicopter Car; 6670-1 Crane Car; 6017-1 Caboose - Brick Brown; 1013 Curved Track (16); 1018 Straight Track (3); 1008-50 Uncoupling Unit - with (1) 1018 Straight Track; 1015-60 45-Watt Transformer; 1023-1 45° Crossover

X-582 (1960)	C6	C7	C8	Rarity
Items Only	515	800	1,200	N/A

Comments: In the early 1960s, Beller Electric and Madison Hardware were the two big purchasers of what were known as "bulk outfits." (For an explanation of the practice of buying "bulk outfits," consult the entry on Madison Hardware Co. in the section on Lionel's Distribution and Customers.)

Beller purchased bulk-packed outfits nos. X-582, X-585NA and X-586 in 1960. All of these were Retailer Promotional Type Ia outfits.

Beller's purchases are curious because customers typically bought in bulk from Lionel as a ploy to further reduce the price paid for individual items intended for separate sale. Yet it appears that Beller was actually purchasing outfit components in bulk with the intention of assembling this outfit on its own. For the X-582, no outfit box was provided, only bulk packaging. It's assumed that Lionel packaged all the individual items in master shipping cartons.

No individual outfit boxes have been observed for any bulk outfit listed in this volume. As a result, we cannot ascertain whether these items were ever assembled and sold as an outfit. Even if they were, we cannot prove that Beller Electric designated the groupings as no. X-582, X-585NA or X-586.

The contents of the X-582 and X-585NA were identical. Only their motive power differed. The X-582 was headed by a no. 224P-1 U.S. Navy Alco Diesel Power Car, whereas the X-585NA was led by a no. 243-1 Locomotive with Smoke and Headlight.

A listing for this outfit is provided here because a Factory Order exists for the X-582. By the way, it is unknown why the number of this outfit does not include "NA". (See the section on Outfit Numbering for a discussion of "NA" and its uses.)

Pricing is provided as reference for the items alone. However, as stated earlier in this volume, items alone do not constitute an outfit; an outfit box is required.

Overall, it appears that Lionel took the opportunity to clean out some old inventory, sending it to a willing customer. Finding a box with any sort of markings for this outfit would be quite a discovery.

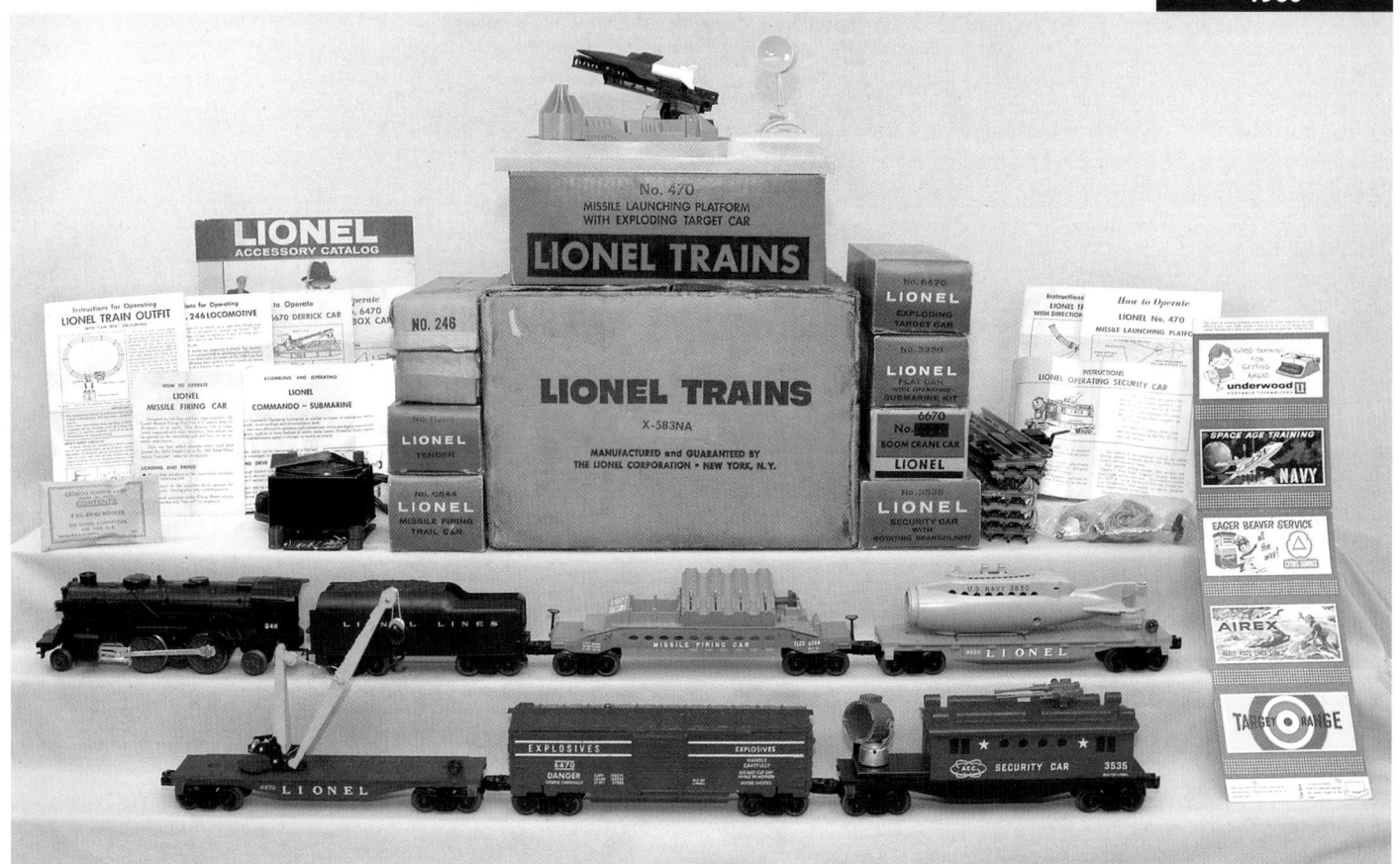

The no. X-583NA was R. H. Macy's steam-powered outfit for 1960. This outfit is highly desirable due to its low production and space and military theme. A large no. 60-446 Tan RSC with Black Graphics outfit box was required to package this outfit. Note the faint black stamp that reads "Retailed By Macy's" above "Lionel" on the outfit.

Description: 1960 Outfit
Specification: "O27" Ga. Steam Type Freight Outfit
Customer: R. H. Macy
Original Amount: 200
Factory Order Date: 11/22/1960
Date Issued: November 22, 1960
Packaging: Conventional Outfit Packing

Contents: 246-1 Locomotive - with Headlight and Magne-Traction - with Lockon and Lubricant; 1130T-1 Tender; 6544-1 Missile Firing Trail Car; 3330-1 Flat Car - with Operating Submarine Kit; 6670-1 Crane Car; 3535-1 Operating Security Car; 470-1 IRBM Missile Launching Platform with Exploding Target Car; 1013 Curved Track (8); 1018 Straight Track (3); 1008-50 Uncoupling Unit - with (1) 1018 Straight Track; 1015-60 45-Watt Transformer; 81-32 Wires (2); 310-2 Set of (5) Billboard Signs; 1609-4 Instruction Sheet; AC Accessory Catalog

Boxes & Packing: 60-446 Box; 60-447 Shipper (1-3); ST Sticker

X-583NA (1960)	C6	C7	C8	Rarity
Complete Outfit	1,200	1,650	2,300	R10
Outfit Box no. 60-446	600	750	850	R10

Comments: R. H. Macy, commonly known as Macy's, is a retailer that purchased numerous promotional outfits in the 1960s. For 1960, it ordered the nos. X-583NA (a steam-powered outfit) and X-584NA (a diesel-powered outfit).

The X-583NA was a well-equipped space and military outfit headed by a no. 246-1 Locomotive - with Headlight and Magne-Traction. This steamer headed 23 different promotional outfits in 1960. For this outfit, the later version (with a solid pilot but lacking generator detail) was included. It came packaged in a no. 246-6 Corrugated Box.

The no. 3330-1 Flat Car - with Operating Submarine Kit (new for 1960) provided hours of fun for the youngsters assembling the submarine while saving Lionel time and effort. This item's Orange Perforated box is difficult to find in C8 condition because the submarine kit would easily damage the box upon removal and reinsertion. Also, a no. 3330-108 Submarine Kit Parts Packed is tough to find still sealed in its original plastic bag.

Also new to the line was the no. 6544-1 Missile Firing Trail Car. Be aware that cracks or breakage can occur on this car where the two brake wheels were attached to the plastic frame ends.

These cars, like the other pieces of rolling stock in the X-583NA, were equipped with early operating AAR trucks and couplers. Everything except for the no. 6670-1 Crane Car was packaged in Orange Perforated boxes. The 6670-1 came in an overstamped Bold Classic no. 6660-55 Folding Box.

The no. 470-1 IRBM Missile Launching Platform included a no. 6470-1 Exploding Target Car. The no. 6470-1 included "slotted" sides and a smooth roof door guide (without the nubs added later to help hold on the sides).

The inclusion of this large accessory necessitated a large box, in this case a no. 60-446 Tan RSC with Black Graphics outfit box that measured 16 x 12¾ x 8¾ inches. The box was manufactured by Star Corrugated Box Company, Inc. and had a star and "8-60" printed on the bottom.

With only 200 manufactured, the X-583NA is a tough outfit to find in collectible condition. Demand for space and military themed outfits is high; that fact, combined with the small quantity of this outfit, justifies its R10 rating.

CONVENTIONAL PACK
60-446 BOX
STICKER

TOP LAYER						BOTTOM LAYER	
246-1 S	3330-1 S	6544-1 S	1015-60 / 1130T-1 S	8-1013	3535-1 S	470-1 F	6670-1 F

3-1018 BELOW 1013
1008-50 TOP 3535

X-584NA
1960

The no. X-584NA was R. H. Macy's diesel-powered outfit for 1960. This outfit is highly desirable due to its low production and space and military theme. As with the X-583NA, note the faint black stamp that reads "Retailed By Macy's". This was stamped over the word "Manufactured".

Description: 1960 Outfit
Specification: "O27" Ga. Diesel Freight Outfit
Customer/No.: R. H. Macy; D12 M
Original Amount: 200
Factory Order Date: 11/22/1960
Date Issued: November 22, 1960
Packaging: Conventional Outfit Packing

Contents: 224P-1 Alco Diesel Power Car - "U.S. Navy" - Navy Color and Markings - with Headlight, Magne-Traction - with Non-Operating Coupler - Lockon and Lubricant; 224C-1 "B" Unit - Navy Color and Markings; 6650-1 Missile Launching Flat Car; 3376-1 Operating Giraffe Car; 3419-1 Operating Helicopter Car; 6470-1 Exploding Target Car; 6017-1 Caboose - Brick Brown; 1013 Curved Track (8); 1018 Straight Track (3); 1008-50 Uncoupling Unit - with (1) 1018 Straight Track; 1015-60 45-Watt Transformer; 81-32 Wires (2); 310-2 Set of (5) Billboard Signs; 1569-11 Instruction Sheet; AC Accessory Catalog

Boxes & Packing: 59-100 Box; 59-101 Shipper (1-4); ST Sticker; BP Bogus Paper

X-584NA (1960)	C6	C7	C8	Rarity
Complete Outfit	1,050	1,525	2,100	R10
Outfit Box no. 59-100	550	700	800	R10

Comments: R. H. Macy, commonly known as Macy's, is a retailer that purchased numerous promotional outfits in the 1960s. For 1960, it ordered the nos. X-583NA (a steam-powered outfit) and X-584NA (a diesel-powered outfit).

The X-584NA, like its companion X-583NA, was a space and military outfit. For that reason, the inclusion of a no. 3376-1 Operating Giraffe Car was out of place.

This outfit was headed by a no. 224P-1 U.S. Navy Alco Diesel Power Car with Magne-Traction and a three-position reversing unit. When boxed, this locomotive included the nos. CTC-1 Lockon, 927-60 Tube of Oil, 927-65 Tube of Grease and no. 217-17 Instruction Sheet in its corrugated box.

The nos. 3419-1 Operating Helicopter Car, 6470-1 Exploding Target Car and 6650-1 Missile Launching Flat Car were an exciting combination of space and military rolling stock, all being carried over from 1959. Hours could be spent blowing up the Exploding Target Car. The 6470-1 included "slotted" sides and a smooth roof door guide (without the nubs added later to help hold on the sides).

All the rolling stock in the X-584NA was equipped with early operating AAR trucks and couplers and came packaged in Orange Perforated boxes.

The no. 59-100 Yellow RSC with Black Graphics outfit box was manufactured by Star Corrugated Box Company, Inc. and measured 14⅛ x 13⅛ x 7 inches. It was an overstickered no. 1626W outfit box from 1959.

With only 200 manufactured, the X-584NA is a tough outfit to find in collectible condition. Demand for space and military themed outfits is high; that fact, combined with the small quantity of this outfit, justifies its R10 rating.

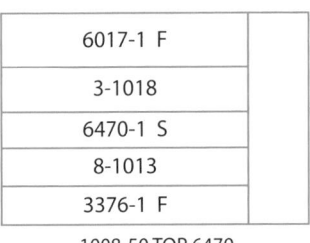

CONVENTIONAL PACK
59-100 BOX
STICKER, BOGUS PAPER

TOP LAYER

| 6017-1 F |
| 3-1018 |
| 6470-1 S |
| 8-1013 |
| 3376-1 F |

1008-50 TOP 6470

BOTTOM LAYER

6650-1 S	1015 -60
3419-1 S	
224C-1 F	
224P-1 F	

X-585NA
1960

Description: 1960 Outfit
Specification: "O27" Ga. Steam Type Freight Outfit with Smoke
Customer: Beller Electric
Original Amount: 50
Factory Order Date: 11/22/1960
Date Issued: November 22, 1960
Packaging: Ship Bulk - No Outfit Box Packing

Contents: 243-1 Locomotive - with Smoke and Headlight - with (2) Position Reversing Unit, Lockon and Lubricant - without Magne-Traction; 243W-1 Whistle Tender; 6544-1 Missile Firing Trail Car - Blue Car Body; 6470-1 Exploding Target Car; 3419-1 Operating Helicopter Car; 6670-1 Crane Car; 6017-1 Caboose - Brick Brown; 1013 Curved Track (16); 1018 Straight Track (3); 1008-50 Uncoupling Unit - with (1) 1018 Straight Track; 1015-60 45-Watt Transformer; 1023-1 45° Crossover

X-585NA (1960)	C6	C7	C8	Rarity
Items Only	435	700	1,050	N/A

Comments: In the early 1960s, Beller Electric and Madison Hardware were the two big purchasers of what were known as "bulk outfits." (For an explanation of the practice of buying "bulk outfits," consult the entry on Madison Hardware Co. in the section on Lionel's Distribution and Customers.)

Beller purchased bulk-packed outfits nos. X-582, X-585NA and X-586 in 1960. All of these were Retailer Promotional Type Ia outfits.

Beller's purchases are curious because customers typically bought in bulk from Lionel as a ploy to further reduce the price paid for individual items intended for separate sale. Yet it appears that Beller was actually purchasing outfit components in bulk with the intention of assembling this outfit on its own. For the X-585NA, no outfit box was provided, only bulk packaging. It's assumed that Lionel packaged all the individual items in master shipping cartons.

No individual outfit boxes have been observed for any bulk outfit listed in this volume. As a result, we cannot ascertain whether these items were ever assembled and sold as an outfit. Even if they were, we cannot prove that Beller Electric designated the groupings as no. X-582, X-585NA or X-586.

The contents of the X-582 and X-585NA were identical. Only their motive power differed. The X-585NA was headed by a no. 243-1 Locomotive with Smoke and Headlight, whereas the X-582 was led by a no. 224P-1 U.S. Navy Alco Diesel Power Car.

A listing for this outfit is provided here because a Factory Order exists for the X-585NA.

Pricing is provided as reference for the items alone. However, as stated earlier in this volume, items alone do not constitute an outfit; an outfit box is required.

Overall, it appears that Lionel took the opportunity to clean out some old inventory, sending it to a willing customer. Finding a box with any sort of markings for this outfit would be quite a discovery.

Description: 1960 Outfit
Specification: Super "O" Ga. Diesel Freight Outfit with Horn
Customer: Beller Brothers
Original Amount: 40
Factory Order Date: 12/8/1960
Date Issued: December 8, 1960
Packaging: Bulk Packing

Contents: 2349X GP-9 Diesel - "Northern Pacific" - Black and Gold - with Horn, Magne-Traction and Lubricant - Less Lockon; 3419-1 Operating Helicopter Car; 6470-1 Exploding Target Car; 6475-1 Pickle Car; 6650-1 Missile Launching Flat Car; 3535-1 Operating Security Car - Black Frame; 6544-1 Missile Firing Trail Car; 6844-1 Rocket Transport Car; 31 Curved Track (18); 32 Straight Track (2); 34 Half straight Track (5); 48 Insulated Straight Track; 39-25 Remote Control Set; 31-23 Envelope of 28 - 31-7; 120 90° Crossing

X-586 (1960)	C6	C7	C8	Rarity
Items Only	925	1,510	2,140	N/A

Comments: In the early 1960s, Beller Electric and Madison Hardware were the two big purchasers of what were known as "bulk outfits." (For an explanation of the practice of buying "bulk outfits," consult the entry on Madison Hardware Co. in the section on Lionel's Distribution and Customers.)

Beller purchased bulk-packed outfits nos. X-582, X-585NA and X-586 in 1960. All of these were Retailer Promotional Type Ia outfits.

Beller's purchases are curious because customers typically bought in bulk from Lionel as a ploy to further reduce the price paid for individual items intended for separate sale. Yet it appears that Beller was actually purchasing outfit components in bulk with the intention of assembling this outfit on its own. For the X-586, no outfit box was provided, only bulk packaging. It's assumed that Lionel packaged all the individual items in master shipping cartons.

No individual outfit boxes have been observed for any bulk outfit listed in this volume. As a result, we cannot ascertain whether these items were ever assembled and sold as an outfit. Even if they were, we cannot prove that Beller Electric designated the groupings as no. X-582, X-585NA or X-586.

The X-586 was Beller's Super O bulk purchase for 1960. It was the only time a no. 2349X Northern Pacific GP-9 Diesel appeared in a promotional outfit during the 1960s. The use of the "X" suffix meant the absence of a no. CTC-1 Lockon, which was unnecessary in a Super O outfit.

The space and military rolling stock was similar to those in the two other Beller outfits; however, the X-586 included two additional cars.

A listing for this outfit is provided here because a Factory Order exists for the X-586. By the way, it is unknown why the number of this outfit does not include "NA". (See the section on Outfit Numbering for a discussion of "NA" and its uses.)

Pricing is provided as reference for the items alone. However, as stated earlier in this volume, items alone do not constitute an outfit; an outfit box is required.

Overall, it appears that Lionel took the opportunity to clean out some old inventory, sending it to a willing customer. Finding a box with any sort of markings for this outfit would be quite a discovery.

Quaker Oats Manufacturer Promotional outfit no. X-600 is shown with an original 1961 Quaker Oats container with the offer printed on the cover as well as the mail coupon. The outfit is shown without any of the substitutions.

The Quaker "Lionel Electric Train Set" promotion was also available to Mother's Oats customers in 1961. Two versions of the offer coupon (front and back side) are shown.

Description: "O27" Promotional Outfit
Specification: "O27" Steam Type Freight Outfit
Customer/Price: Quaker Oats; $11.95 + 2 Box Tops
Original Amount: 75,000
Factory Order Date: 11/9/1961
Date Issued: Rev. #2 12-4-61
Packaging: R.S.C Outfit Packing (Individual Mailer), (Units not Boxed)

Contents: 246-25 Steam Type Locomotive; 1060T-25 Tender; 6406-25 Single Automobile Car (Less Auto); 6406-30 Automobile; 6042-25 Gondola Car (Less 2 Canisters); 6112-5 Canister - Red (2); 6076-75 Hopper Car - Black; 6067-25 Caboose; 1013-8 Curved Track (8 per bundle); 1018-10 Straight Track (Loose) (2); 1016-60 35-Watt Transformer; 1103-12 Envelope Packed; 1123-10 Instruction Sheet; 310-2 Set of (5) Billboards; D61-50 Accessory Catalog

Boxes & Packing: 61-399 Corr. Outfit Box; 61-171 Corr. Insert; 61-172 Corr. Insert; 61-173 Corr. Insert; 61-174 Corr. Shipper for (6) (1-6); 61-440 Insert (Added insert, to be used in production starting 10/26/61)

Alternate For Outfit Contents:
Note: When stock of 6076-75 is depleted, use 6076-25; Note: When stock of 1016-60 (Amount - 36,015) is depleted - Sub. 1010-25; Note: When stock of 1060T-25 is depleted, use 1130T-25; Note: When stock of 6067-25 is depleted, use 6017-25.

X-600 (1961)	C6	C7	C8	Rarity
Complete Outfit	135	260	410	R1
Outfit Box no. 61-399	20	40	70	R1

Comments: One of Lionel's most successful promotional outfits, Quaker Oats Manufacturer Promotional Type IIIb no. X-600 sold at least 70,508 units per a fulfillment report dated 10/4/63. For only $11.95 and two box tops from either Quaker Oats or Mother's Oats, you would receive this outfit.

The outfit was a true bargain because the stated list price of the trains in this promotion was $25.00. In reality, the list price was $35.40, as determined by memos between Lionel and the Federal Trade Commission, which investigated Lionel and Quaker's statement of claims about this outfit (see the section on Lionel's Distribution and Customers). Of note, Lionel's internal cost for this outfit was $10.52 (before shipping and insurance) and it received only $11.95.

Lionel expected this heavily advertised outfit to be a big hit. It issued a note in its December 1961 newsletter (*The Lionel Herald*) to service stations, stating that the X-600 customers "are asking where to buy more track and accessories to add to this set." The note added that any parts of damaged outfits could be returned to service stations for repair or replacement under Lionel's normal guarantee.

The X-600 introduced the no. 61-399 Tan RSC Mailer with Black Graphics for shipping outfits directly in the outfit box. Lionel printing and graphics were omitted from the box top to allow room for a shipping label. These were made of a thicker corrugated material (rated at 90 pounds rather than the normal 65 pounds gross weight) that allowed Quaker to ship the outfits in their outfit box.

This box has been observed with two different font styles, both from Mead Containers (11¼ x 10¼ x 6½ inches). The outfits were fulfilled by Advertising Distributors of America (ADA) in Brooklyn, New York. Lionel likely shipped the outfits to ADA, which in turn fulfilled the orders from the Quaker customers.

The cars, which were equipped with Archbar trucks and couplers, came unboxed and separated by corrugated inserts. A yellow automobile with gray bumpers was included, along with two red canisters. The outfit is readily observed with both red and black hoppers. The substitutions do not alter the pricing stated. All other peripherals followed the norm for 1961.

Although the X-600 is a common outfit, it still sells for a respectable price because it is in fairly high demand. A complete, high-grade example with proper peripherals and a C8 box with all inserts should be a prerequisite for any promotional outfit collector. Advanced collectors enjoy seeking original magazine advertisements, an original order form or, best yet, an original Quaker or Mother's Oats container advertising this promotion.

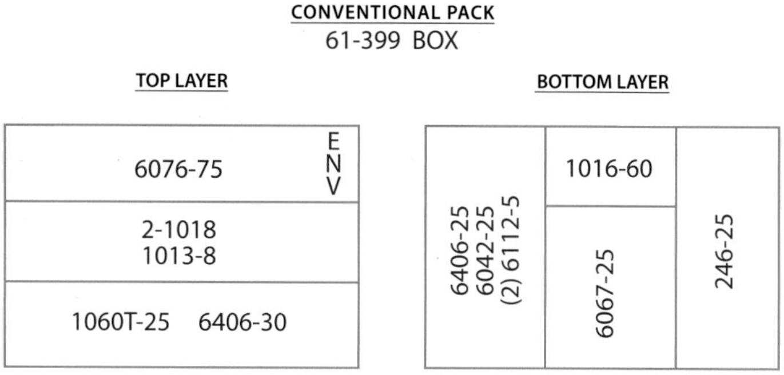

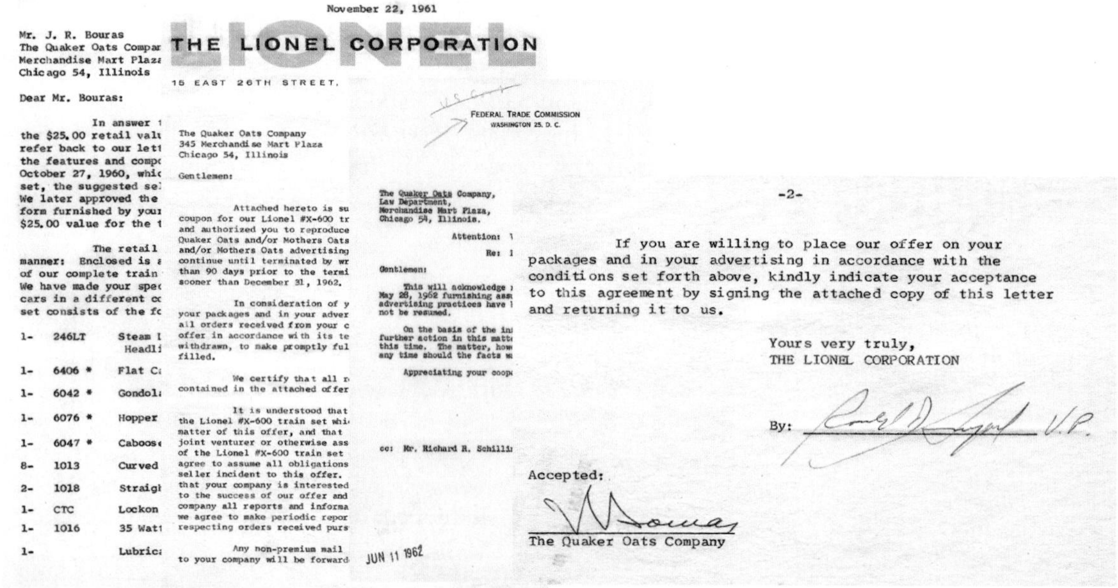

CONVENTIONAL PACK
61-399 BOX

TOP LAYER

6076-75	E N V
2-1018 1013-8	
1060T-25 6406-30	

BOTTOM LAYER

| 6406-25 6042-25 (2) 6112-5 | 1016-60 | 246-25 |
| | 6067-25 | |

Memos between Lionel and Quaker discussed the selling of outfit no. X-600 and the investigation by the Federal Trade Commission.

X-601
1961

Description: "O27" Promotional Outfit
Specification: "O27" Steam Type Freight Outfit
Customer: May Group
Original Amount: 2,000
Date Issued: Rev. #1 5-29-61
Packaging: RSC Outfit Packing (Units not Boxed)

Contents: 246-25 Steam Type Locomotive; 1130T-25 Tender; 6062-25 Gondola Car - Black (Less Cable Reels); 40-11 Cable Reels (3); 6050-25 Savings Bank Car; 6476-25 Hopper Car - Red; 6017-25 Caboose; 1013-8 Curved Track (Bundle of 8 - 1013); 1018-30 Straight Track (Bundle of 3 - 1018); 1008-50 Uncoupling Track Section; 1025-25 45-Watt Transformer; 1103-12 Envelope Packed; 1641-10 Instruction Sheet; 310-2 Set of (5) Billboards; D61-50 Accessory Catalog

Boxes & Packing: 61-180 Outfit Box; 61-181 Corr. Insert; 61-182 Corr. Insert; 61-183 Corr. Insert; 61-184 Corr. Insert; 61-185 Shipper for (4) (1-4)

X-601 (1961)	C6	C7	C8	Rarity
Complete Outfit	170	300	450	R6
Outfit Box no. 61-180	60	100	150	R6

Comments: This is the first of three 1961 Retailer Promotional Type Ia outfits purchased by the May Group (May Company). Outfit no. X-601 featured the (new for 1961) Type I no. 6050-25

Outfit no. X-601 is shown complete as listed on its Factory Order. Pictured is the Type I no. 6050-25 Savings Bank Car with two complete and two almost-complete sets of rivets to the right of its doors. Also shown is the later version of the no. 246-25 Steam Type Locomotive without the small generator detail on its top in front of the cab.

Savings Bank Car with "Blt By Lionel" and a coin slot. Early AAR trucks and couplers were the norm.

The no. 61-180 Tan RSC with Black Graphics outfit box used for this outfit was manufactured by Mead Containers and measured 12¾ x 10 x 6¾ inches. All the other peripherals followed normal progression. Although the Factory Order called for 2,000 outfits to be manufactured, the X-601 is fairly difficult to find, hence the R6 rarity rating.

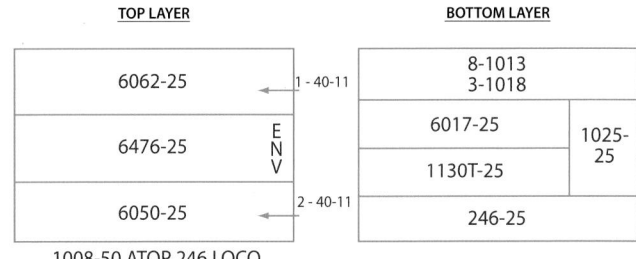

CONVENTIONAL PACK
61-180 BOX

TOP LAYER

6062-25	1 - 40-11
6476-25	E N V
6050-25	2 - 40-11

1008-50 ATOP 246 LOCO

BOTTOM LAYER

8-1013 3-1018	
6017-25	1025-25
1130T-25	
246-25	

Description: "O27" Promotional Outfit
Specification: "O27" Steam Type Freight Outfit With Smoke
Customer/No./Price: Famous-Barr Co.; 32 B 5422; $29.99
Customer: May Group
Original Amount: 2,000
Factory Order Date: 9/27/1961
Date Issued: Rev. #3 9-27-61
Packaging: R.S.C. Outfit Packing (Units Boxed)

Contents: 236-1 Steam Type Locomotive With Smoke; 1130T-1 Tender; 3830-1 Operating Submarine Car; 6470-1 Exploding Target Car; 6650-1 Missile Launching Car; 6017-1 Caboose; 1013-8 Curved Track (Bundle of 8 - 1013); 1013-90 Curved Track (Bundle of 9 - 1013); 1018-30 Straight Track (Bundle of 3 - 1018); 1018-75 Straight Track (Bundle of 6 - 1018); 1008-50 Uncoupling Track Section; 1025-25 45-Watt Transformer; 110-1 Trestle Set; 81-32 24" R.C. Wire (2); 1802I Layout Instruction Sheet; X602-10 Instruction Sheet; 310-2 Set of (5) Billboards; D61-50 Accessory Catalog

Boxes & Packing: 60-495 Outfit Box (With Sticker); 60-496 Shipper for 3 (1-3); 60-448 Outfit Box; 60-449 Shipper for 3 (1-3)

Alternate For Outfit Contents:
Note: Use 600 - 60-495 Outfit Box; Use 1,400 - 60-448 Outfit Box; Use 200 - 60-496 Shipper for 3; Use 467 - 60-449 Shipper for 3.

X-602 (1961)	C6	C7	C8	Rarity
Complete Outfit With no. 60-495 Box	490	775	1,100	R8
Outfit Box no. 60-495	225	325	425	R8
Complete Outfit With no. 60-448 Box	415	650	925	R6
Outfit Box no. 60-448	150	200	250	R6

Comments: The second of the three 1961 May Group (May Company) Retailer Promotional Type Ia outfits, its contents and track layout were a step up from the no. X-601. Headed by a steamer with space and military rolling stock, all its items were boxed and the track layout was the commonly used 1961 elevated pretzel layout (as detailed on the no. 1802I Layout Instruction Sheet). Most items still appeared in Orange Perforated boxes, which were last manufactured in 1960. The no. 6650-1 Missile Launching Car came in an Orange Picture box. The trucks and

This is the no. 60-448 Tan RSC with Black Graphics outfit box version of outfit no. X-602, which was the second Retailer Promotional Type Ia outfit purchased by the May Group in 1961. This outfit was a step up from the no. X-601, with all its items being individually boxed and an elevated pretzel track layout included.

couplers were early AAR; all other peripherals followed the normal progression.

Two versions of the Tan RSC with Black Graphics outfit boxes were used. Both were leftover inventory from the X-500 series (no. 60-495 was used for the no. X-519NA and no. 60-448 for the no. X-501NA). The 60-495 was manufactured by St. Joe Paper Co. and measured 15¼ x 14¾ x 6⅞ inches. The 60-448 was manufactured by Star Corrugated Box Company and measured 16½ x 13 x 7½ inches.

The 60-495 version of this outfit was produced in lower quantities (600); hence, it is more difficult to find and commands a higher rarity rating and price. Both outfit boxes had a no. X-602 sticker applied to cover the old X-500 series number.

Lionel's Outfit Packing Department created a packing diagram for only the 60-495 version of this outfit.

CONVENTIONAL PACK
60-495 BOX

TOP LAYER			BOTTOM LAYER	
6017-1 F	1013-8 / 1013-90 S		6470-1 S	1018-75 F
	3830-1 F			6650-1 F
1025-25	1130T-1 F			236-1 F
				110-1 S

1018-30 ATOP 1130T-1
1008-50 ATOP 3830-1

Description: "O27" Promotional Outfit
Specification: "O27" Diesel Freight Outfit With Horn
Customer: May Group
Original Amount: 750
Factory Order Date: 3/16/1961
Date Issued: Rev. #2 5-29-61
Packaging: R.S.C. Outfit Packing (Units Boxed), Except Crossing & 6519-25

Contents: 218P-1 Alco Diesel Power Unit W/Horn - "Santa Fe"; 218T-1 Motorless Unit - "Santa Fe"; 3419-1 Operating Helicopter Car; 6343-1 Barrel Ramp Car; 6361-1 Timber Transport Car; 6519-25 Allis-Chalmers Car; 6017-1 Caboose; 1013-8 Curved Track (Bundle of 8 - 1013) (2); 1018-30 Straight Track (Bundle of 3 - 1018); 1008-50 Uncoupling Track Section; 1053-50 60-

Watt Transformer; 1023-25 45° Crossing; 81-32 24" R.C. Wire (2); 1802H Layout Instruction Sheet; 1649-10 Instruction Sheet; 310-2 Set of (5) Billboards; D61-50 Accessory Catalog

Boxes & Packing: 60-409 Outfit Box (With Sticker); 60-410 Shipper for (3) (1-3); 60-390 Corr. Insert

X-603 (1961)	C6	C7	C8	Rarity
Complete Outfit	510	950	1,300	R8
Outfit Box no. 60-409	150	300	400	R8

Comments: The third and best of the three Retailer Promotional Type Ia outfits ordered by the May Group (May Company) in 1961. All rolling stock was carryover and came packaged in Orange Perforated boxes, except for the new no. 6343-1 Barrel Ramp Car. It came in an Orange Picture box. Early AAR trucks and couplers were the norm. The track layout was a pretzel layout as detailed on the no. 1802H Layout Instruction Sheet.

Outfit no. X-603 was the third Retailer Promotional outfit purchased by the May Group in 1961. This top-of-the-line offering was headed by Santa Fe Alcos and came with individually boxed items (except the no. 6519-25 Allis-Chalmers Car) and a pretzel track layout.

The Tan RSC with Black Graphics outfit box was an overstickered no. X-511NA 60-409 box from the Star Corrugated Box Company that measured 15½ x 13¾ x 7 inches. Besides the outfit box, finding an 1802H Layout Instruction Sheet is not always an easy task.

CONVENTIONAL PACK
60-409 BOX

TOP LAYER			BOTTOM LAYER	
6361-1 S			6519-25 S	6017-1 S
6343-1 S	INSERT		218T-1 F	
3419-1 F			3 1018 S / 1008-50 S	
8 1013 S / 8 1013 S	1053-50		218P-1 F	

1023-25 ATOP 218T-1

Description: "O27" Promotional Outfit
Specification: "O27" Steam Type Freight Outfit
Customer/No./Price: Top Value; 15-198; 5⅘ Books
Original Amount: 4,300
Factory Order Date: 3/15/1961
Date Issued: Revised #3 12-4-61
Packaging: R.S.C. Outfit Packing (Units not Boxed)

Contents: 246-25 Steam Type Locomotive; 1050T-25 Tender; 6045-50 Tank Car - "Cities Service"; 6406-25 Single Automobile Car (Less Auto); 6406-30 Automobile; 6067-25 Caboose; 1013-8 Curved Track (Bundle of 8 - 1013); 1018-10 Straight Track (Loose) (2); 1026-25 25-Watt Transformer; 1103-12 Envelope Packed; 1119-10 Instruction Sheet; 310-2 Set of (5) Billboards; D61-50 Accessory Catalog

Boxes & Packing: 61-170 Outfit Box; 61-171 Corr. Insert; 61-172 Corr. Insert; 61-173 Corr. Insert; 61-174 Shipper for (6) (1-6)

X-604 (1961)	C6	C7	C8	Rarity
Complete Outfit	135	225	345	R3
Outfit Box no. 61-170	25	50	75	R3

Comments: This was the first of three (nos. X-604 from 1961, X-604 from 1962 and 19210 in 1963) Top Value Retailer Promotional Type Ib outfits offered for 5⅘ filled books of Top Value trading stamps. Page 28 of the 1961 Top Value catalog incorrectly illustrates the X-604 (Top Value no. 15-198) with a black no. 6404-25 Flat Car.

The items were typical for 1961, being equipped with non-

Top Value 1961 outfit no. X-604 (Top Value no. 15-198) as listed on the Factory Order.

Number XL-290 was assigned to the artwork Lionel created for a mock-up of a no. 6050-style box car for Top Value. The artwork was likely used during the sales process to help close a deal. Neither records of an actual mock-up nor an actual car has been observed.

operating Archbar trucks. The no. 246-25 Steam Type Locomotive came in the later version without the small generator detail on its top in front of the cab. The no. 6406-30 Automobile came in red on a maroon flat.

All paperwork and peripherals were typical for 1961, including a Type IV no. 1103-12 Envelope Packed and instruction sheets dated 1960 or 1961. The outfit came in a no. 61-170 Tan RSC with Black Graphics (Owens-Illinois) that measured 11⅜ x 10¼ x 6½ inches. This box is often found with Top Value's catalog no. "15-198" marked in grease pen or with a Top Value mailing label. There appears to be no difference between the 1961 and 1962 outfit boxes; therefore, the outfit box's rarity is determined by adding the 1961 and 1962 current supply numbers.

CONVENTIONAL PACK
61-170 BOX

TOP LAYER			BOTTOM LAYER			
6406-30 6406-25					1026-25	
1050T-25	ENV.		6045-50	6067-25		246-25
2-1018 8-1013						

Description: "O27" Promotional Outfit
Specification: "O27" Steam Type Freight Outfit
Customer/No./Price: Top Value; 15-198; 5⅘ Books
Original Amount: 3,500
Factory Order Date: 8/14/1962
Date Issued: 8-16-62
Packaging: R.S.C. Outfit Packing (Units not Boxed)

Contents: 246-25 Steam Type Locomotive; 1060T-25 Tender;

6045-50 Tank Car - "Cities Service"; 6406-25 Single Automobile Car (Less Auto); 6406-30 Automobile; 6067-25 Caboose; 1013-8 Curved Track (Bundle of 8 - 1013); 1018-10 Straight Track (Loose) (2); 1026-25 25-Watt Transformer; 1103-20 Envelope Packed; 310-2 Set of (5) Billboards; D62-50 Accessory Catalog; 246-7 Instruction Sheet; 1119-10 Instruction Sheet; 1123-40 Instruction Sheet

Boxes & Packing: 61-170 Outfit Box - Use this box and the following packing when Loco is unboxed: 61-171 Insert; 61-172 Insert; 62-202 Insert; 61-175 Shipper for (4) (1-4); 61-170 Outfit Box - Use this box and the following packing when Loco is boxed:

61-172 Insert; 62-202 Insert; 61-175 Shipper for (4) (1-4)

Alternate For Outfit Contents:
Note: Use inventory of 1,230 - 246-1; Use inventory of 1,361 - 246-25; Use inventory of 114 - 245-1; Balance - Use 795 - 242-25.

X-604 (1962)	C6	C7	C8	Rarity
Complete Outfit With nos. 246-25 Or 242-25 Substitution	135	225	345	R3
Complete Outfit With no. 245-1 Substitution	155	300	440	R3
Complete Outfit With no. 246-1 Substitution	140	235	370	R3
Outfit Box no. 61-170	25	50	75	R3

Comments: This, the second of three (nos. X-604 from 1961, X-604 from 1962 and 19210 in 1963) Top Value Retailer Promotional Type Ib outfits, was an almost exact repeat of the X-604 from 1961. However, some minor changes were made, including a streamlined no. 1060T-25 Tender and substitutions for the locomotive. Also, the automobile now came in yellow on a maroon flat car.

Lionel must have found 114 of the no. 245-1 Steam Type Locomotive lying around, as this is the last outfit in which that Scout-type engine appears. First manufactured in 1959 and used only in promotional outfits, that steamer included both ballast weights and Magne-Traction.

When a boxed no. 246-1 Steam Type Locomotive was included, the Outfit Packing Department created a second packing diagram.

The X-604 was shown on page 113 of the 1962 Top Value catalog still requiring 5⅘ filled books of stamps. However, it was incorrectly shown with a no. 1050T-25 Tender.

All peripherals were updated for 1962 and included a no. 1103-20 Envelope Packed replacing the discontinued no. 1103-12. There are no noticeable differences in the no. 61-170 Tan RSC with Black Graphics outfit boxes used in 1961 and 1962, which leads to the combined current supply and R3 rarity.

The locomotive substitutions add a premium as listed in the pricing table. See the 1961 listing for X-604 for more information.

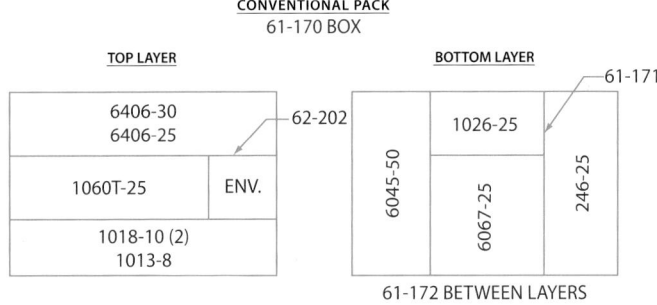

CONVENTIONAL PACK
61-170 BOX

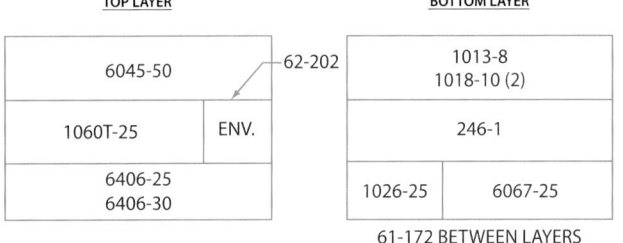

CONVENTIONAL PACK
61-170 BOX
ALTERNATE PACKING WITH 246-1 BOXED

Description: "O27" Promotional Outfit
Specification: "O27" Steam Type Freight Outfit
Customer: Department Store Promotional
Original Amount: 500
Factory Order Date: 3/15/1961
Date Issued: Revised #2 9-12-61
Packaging: R.S.C. Outfit Packing (Units not Boxed)

Contents: 246-25 Steam Type Locomotive; 244T-25 Tender; 6825-25 Trestle Bridge Flat Car (Less Trestle Bridge); 6825-3 Trestle Bridge - Black; 6343-25 Barrel Ramp Car (Less Barrels); 362-78 Barrel (6); 6062-25 Gondola Car - Black (Less Cable Reels); 40-11 Cable Reels (3); 6017-25 Caboose; 1013-8 Curved Track (Bundle of 8 - 1013); 1018-10 Straight Track (Loose); 1008-50 Uncoupling Track Section; 1025-25 45-Watt Transformer; 1103-12 Envelope Packed; 1641-10 Instruction Sheet; 310-2 Set of (5) Billboards; D61-50 Accessory Catalog

Boxes & Packing: 61-180 Outfit Box; 61-181 Corr. Insert; 61-182 Corr. Insert; 61-183 Corr. Insert; 61-184 Corr. Insert; 61-185 Shipper for (4) (1-4)

X-605 (1961)	C6	C7	C8	Rarity
Complete Outfit	325	500	700	R9
Outfit Box no. 61-180	200	275	350	R9

Comments: This was the first of five (nos. X-605 through X-609) 1961 General Release Promotional outfits that listed "Department Store Promotional" as the customer. Lionel likely sold all of these outfits to small retailers that sought a promotional outfit but were unable to make the volume commitment to receive an exclusive one.

The Type IIa X-605 was on the low end of the five 1961 outfits for Department Store Promotional and included commonly available rolling stock from that year. In fact, the no. 6825-25 Trestle Bridge Flat Car appeared in more than 40 promotional outfits. The only item new for 1961 was the no. 6343-25 Barrel Ramp Car.

CONVENTIONAL PACK
61-180 BOX

TOP LAYER		BOTTOM LAYER	
3 40-11 6062-25	ENV.	8-1013 1-1018	
6343-25		244T-25	1025-25
		6017-25	
6825-25 6825-3		246-25	

1008-25 ATOP 246 LOCO

The no. 246-25 Steam Type Locomotive was also a low-end item, though it was still equipped with Magne-Traction. First released in 1959, it was being used in outfits as late as 1962.

All rolling stock was equipped with operating AAR trucks and couplers. All peripherals followed the normal progression.

X-606
1961

Description: "O27" Promotional Outfit
Specification: "O27" Diesel Freight Outfit
Customer: Department Store Promotional
Original Amount: 478
Factory Order Date: 11/9/1961
Date Issued: Rev. #4 11-16-61
Packaging: R.S.C. Outfit Packing (Units Boxed) Except Crossing

Contents: 220P-1 Alco Diesel Power Unit - "Santa Fe"; 3330-1 Flat Car With Operating Submarine (Kit); 6476-1 Hopper Car - Red; 6050-1 Savings Bank Car; 6017-1 Caboose; 1013-70 Curved Track (Bundle of 12 - 1013); 1018-30 Straight Track (Bundle of 3 - 1018); 1008-50 Uncoupling Track Section; 1025-25 45-Watt Transformer; 1020-25 90° Crossing; 81-32 24" R.C. Wire (2); 1802B Layout Instruction Sheet; IS Instruction Sheet; 310-2 Set of (5) Billboards; D61-50 Accessory Catalog

Boxes & Packing: 61-380 Outfit Box; 61-381 Shipper for (4) (1-4)

X-606 (1961)	C6	C7	C8	Rarity
Complete Outfit	500	775	1,150	R9
Outfit Box no. 61-380	225	325	425	R9

Comments: This was the second of five (nos. X-605 through X-609) 1961 General Release Promotional outfits that listed "Department Store Promotional" as the customer. All of these outfits were likely sold to small retailers seeking a promotional outfit yet unable to make the volume commitment to receive an exclusive one.

The Type IIa no. X-606 was a major step up from the X-605 since all its items were boxed and it included a figure-eight track layout. Notable to collectors is the no. 3330-1 Flat Car With Operating Submarine (Kit). Finding one in C8 condition with an unassembled no. 3330-200 Submarine Kit with its parts still sealed in their plastic bag is becoming difficult.

CONVENTIONAL PACK
61-380 BOX

220P-1 S		
6476-1 S		6050-1 S
6017-1 S	1025-25	
3330-1 S		
12 1013 3 1018		

1008-50 ATOP 6476-1
1020-25 ATOP 6017-1

The no. 220P-1 Santa Fe Alco Diesel Power Unit is an example of an item that appeared in promotional outfits before it became a regular-production item (it appeared in the 1961 consumer catalog). Outfit X-606 likely represented the last appearance of this diesel in any outfit, as its Factory Order was dated 11/9/1961. Also the X-606 was a General Release Promotional, which meant there was no specific customer order to fulfill. Therefore, the odd outfit quantity of 478 could have been derived from the number of 220 diesels left in inventory.

All the rolling stock in this outfit featured operating AAR trucks and couplers. The no. 61-380 Tan RSC with Black Graphics outfit box used for it was manufactured by St. Joe Kraft, St. Joe Paper Company and measured 13¾ x 14 x 5⅛ inches. This was a single-level RSC in which all the trains were packed on one layer. This outfit had only 478 original factory orders and is seldom seen, which leads to its rarity rating of R9.

The no. 61-180 Tan RSC with Black Graphics outfit box used for this outfit measured 12¾ x 10 x 6¾ inches. This outfit had only 500 original factory orders and is seldom seen, which leads to its rarity rating of R9.

X-607
1961

Description: "O27" Promotional Outfit
Specification: "O27" Steam Type Freight Outfit With Smoke
Customer: Department Store Promotional
Original Amount: 500
Date Issued: Rev. #2 9-12-61
Packaging: R.S.C. Outfit Packing (Units Boxed), Except Crossing

Contents: 236-1 Steam Type Locomotive With Smoke (See below); 1130T-1 Tender; 3410-1 Operating Helicopter Launching Car (Manually); 6062-1 Gondola Car - Black - With 3 Cable Reels; 6405-1 Flat Car With Van; 6017-1 Caboose; 1013-70 Curved Track (Bundle of 12 - 1013); 1018-30 Straight Track (Bundle of 3 - 1018); 1008-50 Uncoupling Track Section; 1025-25 45-Watt Transformer; 1020-25 90° Crossing; 81-32 24" R.C. Wire (2); 1802B Layout Instruction Sheet; X602-10 Instruction Sheet; 310-2 Set of (5) Billboards; D61-50 Accessory Catalog

Boxes & Packing: 61-250 Outfit Box; 61-251 Shipper for (4) (1-4); 60-390 Insert

Alternate For Outfit Contents:
Substitute - 233-1 for 236-1.

X-607 (1961)	C6	C7	C8	Rarity
Complete Outfit With no. 233-1 Substitution	365	650	1,025	R8
Outfit Box no. 61-250	150	250	350	R8

Comments: This was the third of five (nos. X-605 through X-609) 1961 General Release Promotional outfits that listed "Department Store Promotional" as the customer. Lionel likely sold all of these outfits to small retailers that sought a promotional outfit but were

Outfit no. X-607 is shown with the no. 233-1 Steam Type Locomotive substitution and its difficult-to-find no. 233-10 Corrugated Box.

unable to make the volume commitment to receive an exclusive one.

The Type IIb no. X-607 was a slight step up from the X-605, with all items now boxed and a figure-eight track layout included. The Factory Order stated, "Substitute - 233-1 for 236-1". This usually indicated an after-the-fact change in which all items (in this case the no. 236-1) were swapped out. As such, pricing is based on the outfit having a no. 233-1 Steam Type Locomotive with its difficult-to-find no. 233-10 Corrugated Box. The nos. 233 and 236 steamers (both new for 1961) had similar features, except the 233 included a motor with two magnets whereas the 236 had only one. These two engines were commonly substituted.

Also included in X-607 was a no. 3410-1 Oper. Helicopter Launching Car (Manually). This car was never offered for separate sale; therefore, the only way to obtain a boxed version was through a promotional outfit.

All the rolling stock featured operating AAR trucks and couplers, and all peripherals followed the normal progression. The

no. 61-250 Orange RSC with Black Graphics outfit box used for this outfit was manufactured by Mead Containers and measured 13 x 12 x 7 inches.

The original Factory Order called for only 500 to be manufactured, but this outfit does show up from time to time, hence its R8 rating.

CONVENTIONAL PACK
61-250 BOX

TOP LAYER		
6062-1 F		6405-1 S
3410-1 F		
INSERT		

1018 ATOP 6062-1
1020 ATOP 3410-1

BOTTOM LAYER				
236-1 F	6017-1 F	1025-25	1130T-1 S	12-1013

Description: "O27" Promotional Outfit
Specification: "O27" Diesel Freight Outfit
Customer: Department Store Promotional
Customer/Price: Gill's; $29.95
Original Amount: 800
Factory Order Date: 9/27/1961
Date Issued: Rev. #3 11-2-61
Packaging: R.S.C. Outfit Packing (Units Boxed)

Contents: 231P-1 Alco Diesel Power Car - "Rock Island"; 3330-1 Flat Car With Operating Submarine (Kit); 6476-1 Hopper Car - Red; 3410-1 Operating Helicopter Launching Car (Manually); 6017-1 Caboose; 1013-8 Curved Track (Bundle of 8 - 1013); 1013-90 Curved Track (Bundle of 9 - 1013); 1018-30 Straight Track (Bundle of 3 - 1018); 1018-75 Straight Track (Bundle of 6 - 1018); 1008-50 Uncoupling Track Section; 1025-25 45-Watt

Transformer; 110-1 Trestle Set; 81-32 24" R.C. Wire (2); 1802I Layout Instruction Sheet; X602-10 Instruction Sheet; 310-2 Set of (5) Billboards; D61-50 Accessory Catalog

Boxes & Packing: 60-448 Outfit Box; 60-449 Shipper for (3) (1-3); 60-495 Outfit Box; 60-496 Shipper for 3 (1-3)

Alternate For Outfit Contents:
Note: Use 268 - 60-448 Outfit Box; Use 532 - 60-495 Outfit Box; Use 90 - 60-449 Shipper for 3; Use 177 - 60-496 Shipper for 3.

Outfit no. X-608 is shown with a no. 60-448 Tan RSC with Black Graphics outfit box.

X-608 (1961)	C6	C7	C8	Rarity
Complete Outfit With no. 60-448 Box	600	1,000	1,500	R9
Outfit Box no. 60-448	250	400	550	R9
Complete Outfit With no. 60-495 Box	500	900	1,400	R8
Outfit Box no. 60-495	150	300	450	R8

Comments: This was the fourth of five (nos. X-605 through X-609) 1961 General Release Promotional outfits that listed "Department Store Promotional" as the customer. All of these outfits were likely sold to small retailers seeking a promotional outfit yet unable to make the volume commitment to receive an exclusive one. A no. X-608 was observed with a "Gill's Portland, Oregon" price tag for $29.95.

The Type IIb X-608 was the top-of-the-line diesel-powered 1961 outfit for Department Store Promotional, with all its items boxed and an elevated pretzel track layout included. It came with two operating cars: the nos. 3330-1 Flat Car With Operating Submarine (Kit) and 3410-1 Operating Helicopter Launching Car. Both of these cars included difficult-to-find boxes. Finding a 3330-1 in C8 condition with an unassembled no. 3330-200 Submarine Kit with its parts still sealed in their plastic bag is becoming difficult.

All rolling stock included early AAR trucks and couplers. The cars, like all the peripherals, followed the normal progression.

Two versions of the Tan RSC with Black Graphics outfit boxes were used. Both were leftover inventory from the X-500 series (no. 60-448 was used for the no. X-501NA and no. 60-495 for the no. X-519NA). The 60-448 was manufactured by Star Corrugated Box Company, measured 16½ x 13 x 7½ inches and had "8 60L" stamped on the bottom. The 60-495 was manufactured by St. Joe Paper Co., and measured 15¼ x 14¾ x 6⅞ inches. Lionel applied "X-608" stickers over the X-501NA and X-519NA.

Outfit packing information was available for only the 60-448 version of this outfit, which was produced in lower quantities than its companion. For that reason, it is more difficult to find and commands a higher rarity rating and price.

CONVENTIONAL PACK
60-448 BOX

TOP LAYER	
6-1018 S	3410-1 F / 6476-1 F (6017-1 F) / 9-1013 S 8-1013 F

1008-50 ATOP 6476-1

BOTTOM LAYER	
110-1 F / 1025-25, 3330-1 S / 231P-1 S	3-1018 S

Description: "O27" Promotional Outfit
Specification: "O27" Steam Type Freight Outfit With Smoke & Whistle
Customer: Department Store Promotional
Original Amount: 500
Factory Order Date: 3/15/1961
Date Issued: Rev. #1 5-6-61

Packaging: R.S.C. Outfit Packing (Units Boxed) Except Crossing

Contents: 233-1 Steam Type Locomotive With Smoke; 233W-1 Whistle Tender; 3419-1 Operating Helicopter Car; 6650-1 Missile Launching Car; 6470-1 Exploding Target Car; 3330-1 Flat Car With Operating Submarine (Kit); 6017-1 Caboose; 1013-70 Curved Track (Bundle of 12 - 1013); 1018-30 Straight Track (Bundle of 3 - 1018); 1008-50 Uncoupling Track Section; 1063-100 75-Watt Transformer; 1020-25 90° Crossing; 81-32 24"

R.C. Wire (2); 1802B Layout Instruction Sheet; IS Instruction Sheet; 310-2 Set of (5) Billboards; D61-50 Accessory Catalog

Boxes & Packing: 61-250 Outfit Box; 61-251 Shipper for 4 (1-4)

X-609 (1961)	C6	C7	C8	Rarity
Complete Outfit	715	1,150	1,700	R9
Outfit Box no. 61-250	300	450	550	R9

Comments: This was the fifth and last (nos. X-605 through X-609) of the 1961 General Release Promotional outfits that listed "Department Store Promotional" as the customer. All of these outfits were likely sold to small retailers that sought a promotional outfit but were unable to make the volume commitment to receive an exclusive one.

The Type IIb X-609 was the top-of-the-line steam-powered 1961 outfit for Department Store Promotional, with all items boxed and a figure-eight track layout included. With a space and military theme, all the rolling stock consisted of operating cars, including the difficult-to-find complete and unassembled no. 3330-1 Flat Car With Operating Submarine (Kit).

The no. 1063-100 75-Watt Transformer included a green whistle control button to indicate changes made to the whistle control circuitry to prevent the Scout-type locomotives from inadvertently reversing. Its Production Control File states, "Rubber Stamp '1063-100' on Bottom of Base Plate Assembly using White Ink." This transformer is harder to find than a regular no. 1063-25 75-Watt Transformer (with a red whistle button).

The no. 233-10 Corrugated Box for the no. 233-1 Steam Type Locomotive With Smoke is difficult to find and is often the only item missing from outfits.

Overall, Lionel put together a nice consist of rolling stock for this outfit. All cars included early AAR trucks and couplers and followed the normal progression, as did all the peripherals.

The no. 61-250 Orange RSC with Black Graphics outfit box used for this outfit was manufactured by Mead Containers and measured 13 x 12 x 7 inches. This outfit had only 500 manufactured and is seldom seen, which leads to its rarity rating of R9.

CONVENTIONAL PACK
61-250 BOX

TOP LAYER

6470-1 S	3330-1 F	1063-100	1013-70 S
		6017-1 F	

1018-30 ATOP 1013
1020-25 ATOP 6017-1

BOTTOM LAYER
1008-50 SIDE OF BOX

233-1 F	3419-1 S	233W-1 S	6650-1 F

Lionel's no. X-612 was also stamped with Sperry & Hutchinson's no. 6-P-4805.

Customer No. On Box: 6-P4805
Description: "O27" Promotional Outfit
Specification: "O27" Steam Type Freight Outfit
Cust./No./Price: Sperry & Hutchinson Co.; 6-P-4805; 6 Books
Original Amount: 13,000
Factory Order Date: 10/9/1961
Date Issued: Rev. #1 10-9-61
Packaging: R.S.C. Outfit Packing (Units not Boxed)

Contents: 246-25 Steam Type Locomotive; 1050T-25 Tender; 6042-25 Gondola Car (Less 2 Canisters); 6112-5 Canister - Red (2); 6076-75 Hopper Car - Black; 6067-25 Caboose; 1013-8 Curved Track (Bundle of 8 - 1013); 1018-10 Straight Track (Loose) (2); 1010-25 35-Watt Transformer; 1103-12 Envelope Packed; IS Instruction Sheet; 310-2 Set of (5) Billboards; D61-50 Accessory Catalog

Boxes & Packing: 61-170 Corr. Outfit Box; 61-171 Corr. Insert; 61-172 Corr. Insert; 61-173 Corr. Insert; 61-174 Shipper for 6 (1-6)

Alternate For Outfit Contents:

Note: Substitute 1026-25 for immediate orders until 1010-25 is available in May; SPECIAL INSTRUCTIONS: Customer Number - 6 P 4805 - to appear on outfit box and shipper.

X-612 (1961)	C6	C7	C8	Rarity
Complete Outfit	95	160	285	R2
Outfit Box no. 61-170	20	30	75	R2

Comments: Sperry & Hutchinson (S&H) offered Retailer Promotional Type Ib outfit no. X-612 in the firm's 1961 catalog on page 116 as item no. 6-P4805. A follow-up to its 1960 no. X-516NA (S&H no. 6-P4803), the X-612 was available in exchange for six filled S&H stamp books (hence the "6" in its "6-P4805" number).

As with many promotional outfits, the pictures in the retailer catalog do not exactly match the outfit. The hopper in the catalog was red rather than black, there were no canisters and the caboose was shown as a no. 6167 and not a no. 6067-25.

This was a bare-bones outfit featuring rolling stock with non-operating Archbar trucks and couplers. The no. 246-25 Steam Locomotive included a two-position reversing unit, a headlight and Magne-Traction. This outfit included the later version with a solid pilot and lacked the small generator detail on its top in front of the cab. All additional peripherals followed the normal progression.

The outfit came in a no. 61-170 Tan RSC with Black Graphics outfit box manufactured by Owens-Illinois with 11 dots and "9012" printed on the bottom. It measured 11½ x 10¼ x 6¼ inches. The Factory Order instructed the Outfit Packing Department to also stamp the boxes with S&H's "6 P 4805".

Factory orders totaled 13,000 outfits, leading to the assumption that this outfit would be readily available in today's market. Although not extremely difficult to find, the current supply is lower than expected, especially in C8 condition. Our assumption is that many of these outfits were obtained by individuals, played with and still kept in basement or attics rather than making their way into the collector community.

The transformer substitution does not affect the price.

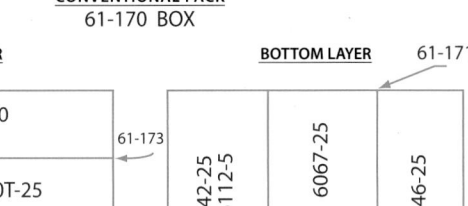

CONVENTIONAL PACK
61-170 BOX

X-613
1961

Description: "O27" Promotional Outfit
Specification: "O27" Steam Type Freight Outfit With Smoke
Customer: PX
Original Amount: 600
Date Issued: Rev. #1 5-29-61
Packaging: R.S.C. Outfit Packing (Units not Boxed), (Except Loco. & Tender)

Contents: 247-1 Steam Type Locomotive (Boxed); 247T-1 Tender (Boxed); 6062-25 Gondola Car - Black (Less Cable Reels); 40-11 Cable Reels (3); 6050-25 Savings Bank Car; 6017-25 Caboose; 1013-8 Curved Track (Bundle of 8 - 1013); 1018-30 Straight Track (Bundle of 3 - 1018); 1008-50 Uncoupling Track Section; 1010-25 35-Watt Transformer; 81-32 24" R.C. Wire (2); IS Instruction Sheet; 310-2 Set of (5) Billboards; D61-50 Accessory Catalog

Boxes & Packing: 61-170 Corr. Box; 61-171 Corr. Insert; 61-172 Corr. Insert; 61-174 Shipper for (6) (1-6)

X-613 (1961)	C6	C7	C8	Rarity
Complete Outfit	225	420	700	R8
Outfit Box no. 61-170	100	200	350	R8

Comments: This was the first of two 1961 Retailer Promotional Type Ia outfits sold to the Army's Post Exchange (PX), with the no. X-614 being the other. The no. X-613 was a basic starter outfit that consisted primarily of leftover inventory. One item, the no. 247-1 Steam Type Locomotive, though last manufactured in 1959, was still being depleted in this and three other 1961 outfits.

The only new item in the X-613 was the no. 6050-25 Savings Bank Car. It, like all the rolling stock, came equipped with operating AAR trucks and couplers.

The outfit came in a no. 61-170 Tan RSC with Black Graphics outfit box that measured 11¼ x 10¼ x 6¼ inches. Although all the components are fairly common, the outfit box, with only 600 factory orders, is seldom seen.

CONVENTIONAL PACK
61-170 BOX

TOP LAYER		BOTTOM LAYER	
3-1018 8-1013		247-1 S	
247T-1 F		6017-25	1010-25
6050-25		6062-25 3-40-11	

1008-50 ATOP 247-1

Description: "O27" Promotional Outfit
Specification: "O27" Diesel Freight Outfit
Customer: PX
Original Amount: 400
Date Issued: Rev. #2 6-22-61
Packaging: R.S.C. Outfit Packing (Units not Boxed)

Contents: 231P-25 Alco Diesel Power Car - "Rock Island"; 6825-25 Trestle Bridge Flat Car (Less Trestle Bridge); 6825-3 Trestle Bridge - Black; 3330-25 Flat Car With Operating Submarine (Less Kit); 3330-200 Submarine Kit; 6017-25 Caboose; 1013-8 Curved Track (Bundle of 8 - 1013); 1018-30 Straight Track (Bundle of 3 - 1018); 1008-50 Uncoupling Track Section; 1010-25 35-Watt Transformer; 1103-12 Envelope Packed; X602-10 Instruction Sheet; 310-2 Set of (5) Billboards; D61-50 Accessory Catalog

Boxes & Packing: 61-190 Corr. Outfit Box; 61-191 Corr. Insert; 61-192 Corr. Insert; 61-193 Corr. Insert; 61-194 Shipper for (6) (1-6)

X-614 (1961)	C6	C7	C8	Rarity
Complete Outfit	375	700	1,150	R9
Outfit Box no. 61-190	175	350	600	R9

Comments: This 1961 Retailer Promotional outfit was the companion to the no. X-613. Both outfits were sold to the Army's Post Exchange (PX).

The Type Ia no. X-614 included the newly issued no. 231P-25 Rock Island Alco Diesel whereas the X-613 included steam power. This outfit's cars were also an upgrade from the X-613. Notably, the unboxed 3330-25 Flat Car With Operating Submarine (Less Kit) was included in this and five other promotional outfits. When unboxed, the 3330-25's highly desirable no. 3330-200 Submarine Kit was placed loose in the outfit box. Finding the kit unassembled with its unopened plastic bag is required to complete a C8 outfit.

All cars included early operating AAR trucks and couplers. They followed the normal progression, as did all the peripherals.

The X-614 came in a no. 61-190 Tan RSC with Black Graphics outfit box that measured 12¼ x 9⅞ x 6¼ inches. Factory Orders were issued for only 400, and this outfit is seldom seen, which leads to its R9 rarity rating.

CONVENTIONAL PACK
61-190 BOX

TOP LAYER		BOTTOM LAYER	
3330-25 3330-200		8-1013	
ENV.	3-1018 1-1008-50	6017-25	1010-25
6825-3 6825-25		231P-25	

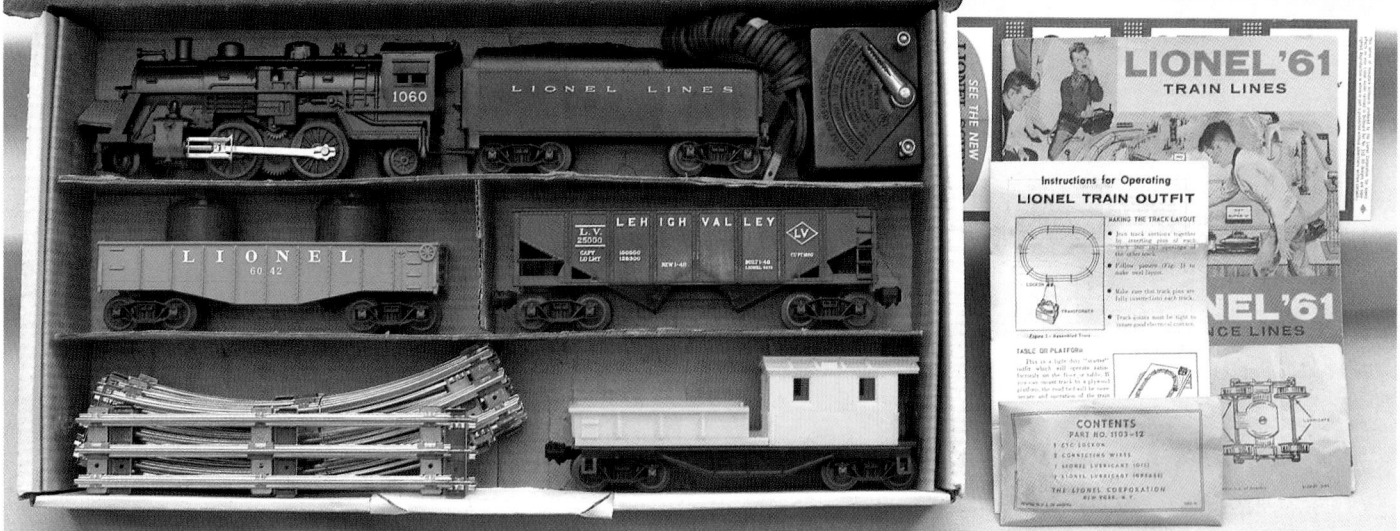

Display outfit no. X-615 included the unmarked yellow no. 6120-25 Work Caboose, which appeared only in promotional outfits.

Description: "O27" Promotional Outfit
Specification: "O27" Steam Type Freight Outfit
Customer: Canada
Original Amount: 1,000
Factory Order Date: 5/10/1961
Date Issued: Rev. #1 7-21-61
Packaging: Display Outfit Packing (Units not Boxed)

Contents: 1060-25 Steam Type Locomotive; 1060T-25 Tender; 6042-25 Gondola Car (Less 2 Canisters); 6112-5 Canister - Red (2); 6076-75 Hopper Car - Black; 6120-25 Work Caboose - "Union Pacific"; 1013-8 Curved Track (Bundle of 8 - 1013); 1018-10 Straight Track (Loose) (2); 1026-25 25-Watt Transformer; 1103-12 Envelope Packed; 1123-10 Instruction Sheet; 310-2 Set of (5) Billboards; D61-50 Accessory Catalog

The no. 61-389 hinged display outfit box had "No. X-615" printed as part of the box manufacturing process.

and X-621) 1961 General Release Promotional Type IIb outfits that listed Canada as the customer on the Factory Order.

This low-end outfit was headed by a no. 1060-25 Steam Type Locomotive. That engine, which moved just forward, was used only in promotional outfits. The only notable item in this outfit was the unmarked yellow no. 6120-25 Work Caboose, which appeared only in promotional outfits from 1961 through 1963. The rolling stock was equipped with non-operating Archbar trucks and couplers, and all the peripherals followed the normal progression.

The no. 61-389 White 4-6-4 Steamer and F3 Hinged Display with Red/Orange and Blue Graphics Type A outfit box was manufactured by Express Container, Corp. and measured 22¾ x 11½ x 3⅛ inches. Although this was a uniquely numbered box, leftover inventory was overstickered and used for promotional outfit no. 11001.

DISPLAY PACK
61-389 BOX

1060-25	1060T-25	1026 25
6042-25 E N V	6076-75	
2-1018 8-1013	6120-25	

Boxes & Packing: 61-389 Display Outfit Box; 61-101 Corr. Insert; 61-102 Corr. Insert (2); 61-103 Corr. Shipper for (6) (1-6)

X-615 (1961)	C6	C7	C8	Rarity
Complete Outfit	170	360	450	R6
Outfit Box no. 61-389	90	200	300	R6

Comments: This was the first of four (nos. X-615, X-616, X-618

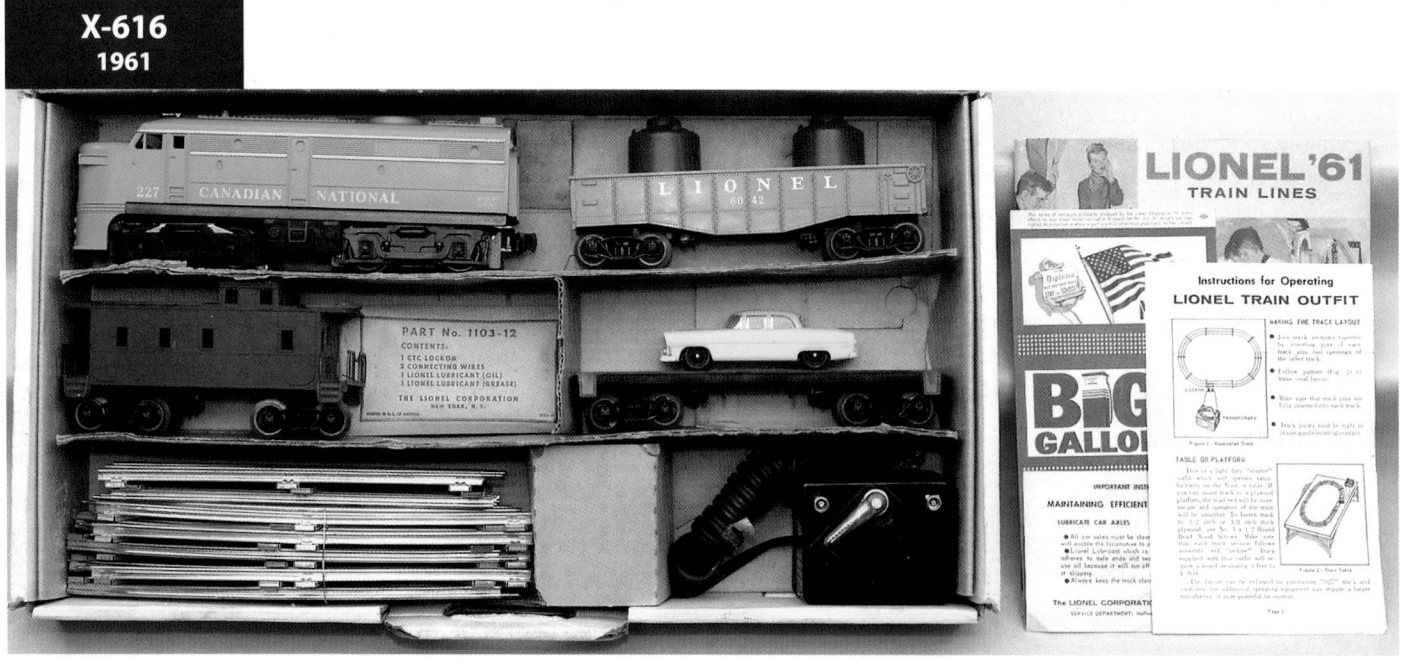

The no. 227P-25 Canadian National Alco Diesel Power Car often appeared in outfits distributed in Canada.

The no. 61-382 hinged display outfit box had "No. X-616" printed as part of the box manufacturing process.

Description: "O27" Promotional Outfit
Specification: "O27" Diesel Freight Outfit
Customer: Canada
Original Amount: 1,500
Date Issued: 3-27-61
Packaging: Display Outfit Packing (Units not Boxed)

Contents: 227P-25 Alco Diesel Power Car; 6406-25 Single Automobile Car (Less Auto); 6406-30 Automobile; 6042-25 Gondola Car (Less 2 Canisters); 6112-5 Canister - Red (2); 6067-25 Caboose; 1013-8 Curved Track (Bundle of 8 - 1013); 1018-10 Straight Track (Loose) (2); 1026-25 25-Watt Transformer; 1103-12 Envelope Packed; 1125-10 Instruction Sheet; 310-2 Set of (5) Billboards; D61-50 Accessory Catalog

Boxes & Packing: 61-382 Display Outfit Box; 61-101 Corr. Insert; 61-102 Corr. Insert (2); 61-103 Corr. Shipper for (6) (1-6)

X-616 (1961)	C6	C7	C8	Rarity
Complete Outfit	275	425	650	R6
Outfit Box no. 61-382	100	150	250	R6

Comments: This was the second of four (nos. X-615, X-616, X-618 and X-621) 1961 General Release Promotional Type IIb outfits that listed Canada as the customer on the Factory Order.

Outfit X-616 included the collectible no. 227P-25 Canadian National Alco Diesel Power Car, which moved only forward, was equipped with a closed pilot and a headlight and lacked any traction aid. This locomotive often was a component of Canadian-market outfits. All rolling stock came with non-operating Archbar trucks and couplers, and all the peripherals were appropriate for 1961.

DISPLAY PACK
61-382 BOX

227P-25		6112-5 (2) 6042-25
6067-25	E N V	6406-30 6406-25
8-1013 2-1018	INSERT	1026-25

The no. 61-382 White 4-6-4 Steamer and F3 Hinged Display with Red/Orange and Blue Graphics Type A outfit box was manufactured by Express Container, Corp. and measured 22 x 11¼ x 3¼ inches. Despite the fact that this was a uniquely numbered box, leftover inventory was overstickered and used for promotional outfit no. 11011.

Although the quantity produced is on the edge of making this a common outfit, the highly desirable 227P-25 Alco diesel drives up its overall demand.

Description: "O27" Promotional Outfit
Specification: "O27" Steam Type Freight Outfit
Customer: Canada
Original Amount: 1,000
Factory Order Date: 5/10/1961
Date Issued: Rev. #1 9-12-61
Packaging: Display Outfit Packing (Units not Boxed)

Contents: 1060-25 Steam Type Locomotive; 1050T-25 Tender; 6042-25 Gondola Car (Less 2 Canisters); 6112-5 Canister - Red (2); 6076-75 Hopper Car - Black; 6406-25 Single Automobile Car (Less Auto); 6406-30 Automobile; 6067-25 Caboose; 1013-8 Curved Track (Bundle of 8 - 1013); 1018-10 Straight Track (Loose) (2); 1026-25 25-Watt Transformer; 1103-12 Envelope Packed; 1123-10 Instruction Sheet; 310-2 Set of (5) Billboards; D61-50 Accessory Catalog

Boxes & Packing: 61-390 Display Outfit Box; 61-391 Insert; 61-392 Insert; 61-393 Insert; 61-394 Insert; 61-395 Shipper for (6) (1-6)

X-618 (1961)	C6	C7	C8	Rarity
Complete Outfit	200	385	550	R7
Outfit Box no. 61-390	100	200	275	R7

Comments: This, the third of four (nos. X-615, X-616, X-618 and X-621) 1961 General Release Promotional Type IIb outfits that

listed Canada as the customer on the Factory Order, was likely sold to general retailers in the Canadian marketplace.

The rolling stock was a combination of items from outfits no. X-615 and X-616. The cars came with non-operating Archbar trucks and couplers, and all the peripherals were 1961 vintage.

DISPLAY PACK
61-390 BOX

1060-25	1050T-25
6042-25	6406-25
6076-75	6067-25 1103-12
2-1018 8-1013	1026-25

The X-618 was headed by the low-end no. 1060-25 Steam Type Locomotive. The only exciting features of this forward-only engine were its side rods with cross heads and its headlight. In subsequent years, Lionel removed even these features when it introduced the no. 1061 steamer.

The no. 61-390 White 4-6-4 Steamer and F3 Hinged Display with Red/Orange and Blue Graphics Type A outfit box was manufactured by UCC (United Container Co.) and measured 22½ x 14½ x 3¼ inches. This outfit box was also used for outfit nos. X-715, X-716 and 19197.

The only collectible item in this outfit is its outfit box. With only 1,000 made, this outfit appears infrequently, which leads to its R7 rarity rating.

Description: "O27" Promotional Outfit
Specification: "O27" "General" Freight Outfit
Customer: Brown Forman Distillers Corp.
Original Amount: 160
Date Issued: Rev. #1 5-29-61
Packaging: R.S.C. Outfit Packing (Units not Boxed), Except 1862-1 & 1862T-1

Contents: 1862-1 "General" Locomotive; 1862T-1 Tender; 1877-25 Horse Transport Car; 1865-25 Passenger Car; 6120-25 Work Caboose - "Union Pacific"; 1013-8 Curved Track (Bundle of 8 - 1013); 1015-60 45-Watt Transformer; 1103-12 Envelope Packed;

IS Instruction Sheet; 310-2 Set of (5) Billboards; D61-50 Accessory Catalog

Boxes & Packing: 60-389 Outfit Box; 60-380 Corr. Insert; 60-391 Corr. Insert; 60-392 Shipper for (4) (1-4); ST Sticker; BP Bogus Paper if Required

X-619 (1961)	C6	C7	C8	Rarity
Complete Outfit	975	1,500	2,000	R10
Outfit Box no. 60-389	700	1,000	1,250	R10

Comments: In 1961, Brown Forman Distillers Corp. ordered 160 of this Retailer Promotional Type Ib outfit. The purpose of this outfit is still unknown, though the small quantity suggests that it was likely used as a promotional giveaway or an employee incentive.

The no. X-619 was the only outfit headed by a General old-time locomotive to include a caboose. Also, this was the only 1961 outfit to include a no. 1015-60 45-Watt Transformer with direction control. Lionel was probably depleting its remaining inventory, as it had already replaced this transformer in 1961 with the no. 1025-25 45-Watt Transformer.

The remainder of the outfit's consist appeared to have been cobbled together from readily available inventory, with all items equipped with Archbar trucks and couplers. The no. 1862-1 General Locomotive came in a no. 1862-86 Corrugated Box, and the no. 1862T-1 Tender was packaged in an Orange Perforated box.

The no. 60-389 Tan RSC with Black Graphics outfit box

was manufactured by Owens-Illinois Paper Products, Div. and measured 12 x 11½ x 6½ inches. The box was an overstickered no. 1631WS outfit box from 1960.

With only 160 factory orders, this is one of the toughest promotional outfits to find. Its collectibility and value are driven by its R10 rarity rating.

CONVENTIONAL PACK
60-389 BOX
STICKER, BOGUS PAPER IF REQUIRED

TOP LAYER		BOTTOM LAYER
6120-25 F		1013-8
1877-25 F		1862-1 F
1862T-1 F	1015-60	1865-25 F

LIONEL TRAIN SET
X-620...Complete and Ready to Run
FIVE-CAR STEAM FREIGHT

The Factory Order states to "obliterate old printing" when re-using the no. 1633 outfit box for no. X-620. As shown, the large label does the task, although it has deteriorated over time.

Description: "O27" Promotional Outfit
Specification: "O27" Steam Type Freight Outfit
Customer/No.: Prophylactic Brush Company; BA 6120-6
Original Amount: 904
Factory Order Date: 9/29/1961
Date Issued: Rev. #3 10-5-61
Packaging: Display Outfit Packing (Units not Boxed)

Contents: 1060-25 Steam Type Locomotive; 1050T-25 Tender; 6050-25 Savings Bank Car; 6042-25 Gondola Car (Less 2 Canisters); 6112-5 Canister - Red (2); 6076-75 Hopper Car - Black; 6406-25 Single Automobile Car (Less Auto); 6406-30 Automobile; 6067-25 Caboose; 1013-8 Curved Track (Bundle of 8 - 1013); 1018-10 Straight Track (Loose) (2); 1026-25 25-Watt Transformer; 1103-12 Envelope Packed; 1123-10 Instruction Sheet; 310-2 Set of (5) Billboards; D61-50 Accessory Catalog

Boxes & Packing: 60-165 Display Outfit Box; 60-166 Corr. Insert (2); 60-167 Corr. Insert; 60-168 Corr. Insert; 60-169 Corr. Insert; 60-170 Corr. Insert; 60-171 Corr. Insert; 60-172 Shipper for 4 (1-4)

Alternate For Outfit Contents:
Note: Providing labels to obliterate old printing; Customer Stock Number - BA 6120-6 - to appear on outfit box and shipper; Note: See schedule for production - important.

X-620 (1961)	C6	C7	C8	Rarity
Complete Outfit	295	450	750	R7
Outfit Box no. 60-165	135	200	350	R7

Comments: Prophylactic Brush Company purchased two Manufacturer Promotional Type IIIb outfits: nos. X-620 and X-706 in 1961. These were likely used as promotional tie-ins with one of Prophylactic Brush's products.

Other than the no. 6050-25 Savings Bank Car (new for 1961), the outfit components were common items found in most low-end promotional outfits. With five pieces of rolling stock, the X-620 offered more value than most other low-end outfits.

DISPLAY PACK
60-165 BOX

1060-25	1050T-25
6050-25	6042-25
6076-75	6067-25
8-1013 2-1018	6406-25 / 1026-25

This outfit was headed by the no. 1060-25 Steam Type Locomotive found in many promotional outfits. This engine, which moved only forward, was Lionel's low-end steam offering in 1961, its only feature of note being a headlight.

By far the best part of this outfit was its over-stickered no. 60-165 Orange, White and Gray O27 Hinged Display with 4-6-2 Steam Display Graphics Type A outfit box. This box, manufactured by UCC (United Container Co.) and measuring 25 x 17⅛ x 3¼ inches, was originally used for catalog outfit no. 1633 in 1960.

Although the Factory Order instructed to print the "BA 6120-6" customer stock number on the outfit box, this has yet to be observed. Finding an X-620 in collectable condition is not an easy task.

Description: "O27" Promotional Outfit
Specification: "O27" Steam Type Freight Outfit
Customer: Canada
Original Amount: 100
Factory Order Date: 7/31/1961
Date Issued: 8-8-61
Packaging: Display Outfit Packing (Units not Boxed)

Contents: 1060-25 Steam Type Locomotive; 1050T-25 Tender; 6630-25 Missile Launching Car (Less Missile); 6650-80 Missile Complete (or 6650-84); 6480-25 Exploding Target Car; 6120-25 Work Caboose - "Union Pacific"; 1013-8 Curved Track (Bundle of 8 - 1013); 1018-10 Straight Track (Loose) (2); 1026-25 25-Watt Transformer; 1103-12 Envelope Packed; 1123-10 Instruction Sheet; 310-2 Set of (5) Billboards; D61-50 Accessory Catalog

Boxes & Packing: 61-105 Display Outfit Box (W/Stickers); 61-101 Corr. Insert; 61-102 Corr. Insert (2); 61-103 Corr. Shipper for (6) (1-6)

X-621 (1961)	C6	C7	C8	Rarity
Complete Outfit	760	1,275	1,700	R10
Outfit Box no. 61-105	600	1,000	1,300	R10

Comments: This was the fourth and last (nos. X-615, X-616, X-618 and X-621) of the 1961 General Release Promotional Type IIb outfits for Canada.

The X-621 was the top-of-the-line 1961 General Release

Canadian outfit, which isn't saying much because it still offered a forward-only no. 1060-25 Steam Type Locomotive as its power.

This outfit, with its space and military theme, did include two new operating cars: nos. 6630-25 Missile Launching Car and 6480-25 Exploding Box Car. Neither car was actually new, since they represented low-end versions of the previously issued nos. 6650 and 6470, respectively. They, like the other pieces of rolling stock in this outfit, were equipped with non-operating Archbar trucks and couplers.

As with the X-615, this outfit also included the unmarked yellow no. 6120-25 Work Caboose. That item was used only in promotional outfits from 1961 through 1963.

The no. 61-105 White 4-6-4 Steamer and F3 Hinged Display with Red/Orange and Blue Graphics Type A outfit box used for this outfit was manufactured by Express Container Corp. and measured 21½ x 11½ x 3⅛ inches. The outfit box was a no. 1123 outfit overstickered with X-621.

As with many promotional outfits, the real value is in the outfit box. Only 100 examples of this outfit were made, which explains its R10 rating and resulting high value.

DISPLAY PACK
61-105 BOX

1060-25	1050T-25	1026-25
6480-25	E N V	6630-25
2-1018 8-1013	6120-25	

The no. X-622 is shown complete with a no. 3330-25 Flat Car with Operating Submarine (Less Kit) and an unassembled no. 3330-200 Submarine Kit. Also shown is the no. 1802B Layout Instruction Sheet. These sheets were always dated 6-59.

Description: "O27" Promotional Outfit
Specification: "O27" Steam Type Freight Outfit
Customer: Mutual Buying
Original Amount: 2,200
Factory Order Date: 11/9/1961
Date Issued: Rev. #2 11-16-61
Packaging: R.S.C. Outfit Packing (Units not Boxed)

Contents: 246-25 Steam Type Locomotive; 244T-25 Tender; 3330-25 Flat Car With Operating Submarine (Less Kit); 3330-200 Submarine Kit; 6476-25 Hopper Car - Red; 6057-25 Caboose - Red; 1013-70 Curved Track (Bundle of 12 - 1013); 1018-30 Straight Track (Bundle of 3 - 1018); 1008-50 Uncoupling Track Section; 1025-25 45-Watt Transformer; 1020-25 90° Crossing; 1103-12 Envelope Packed; 1802B Layout Instruction Sheet; 1641-10 Instruction Sheet; 310-2 Set of (5) Billboards; D61-50 Accessory Catalog

Boxes & Packing: 61-170 Corr. Outfit Box; 61-171 Corr. Insert; 61-172 Corr. Insert; 61-173 Corr. Insert; 61-174 Corr. Shipper for (6) (1-6)

X-622 (1961)	C6	C7	C8	Rarity
Complete Outfit	250	430	645	R6
Outfit Box no. 61-170	100	150	200	R6

Comments: The no. X-622 was the first of two (along with the no. X-623) outfits sold to the Mutual Buying Syndicate buying cooperative. These Retailer Promotional Type Ia outfits were distributed among Mutual Buying's member stores, although neither outfit can be tied to a specific customer.

The X-622 was Mutual's entry-level purchase. The nos. 3330-25 Flat Car With Operating Submarine (Less Kit) and no. 3330-200 Submarine Kit are the desirable items in this outfit. The 3330-200 was placed loose in the outfit box and is required to be unassembled with its plastic bag still sealed to achieve a C8 outfit rating.

With this outfit coming late in the year, most cars were equipped with middle operating AAR trucks and couplers. The no. 6057-25 Caboose was equipped with one early operating and one plain AAR truck and coupler. The no. 1802B Layout Instruction Sheet detailed the figure-eight track layout. All the other peripherals were appropriate for 1961.

The no. 61-170 Tan RSC with Black Graphics outfit box was manufactured by Owens-Illinois with six dots and "9012" printed on the bottom. It measured 11¼ x 10¼ x 6¼ inches.

Overall, this is a nice entry-level outfit that is readily available in today's market.

CONVENTIONAL PACK
61-170 BOX

TOP LAYER

3330-25 3330-200	
ENV.	244T-25
12-1013	

BOTTOM LAYER

3-1018 1-1008-50 6476-25	1025-25	246-25
	6057-25	

1020 TOP OF 6057

The no. X-623 included the new-for-1961 no. 230P-1 Chesapeake & Ohio Alco diesel. All items came individually boxed, except the darker orange version of the no. 6519-25 Allis-Chalmers Car.

Description: "O27" Promotional Outfit
Specification: "O27" Diesel Freight Outfit
Customer: Mutual Buying
Original Amount: 1,000
Factory Order Date: 3/24/1961
Date Issued: 5-25-61
Packaging: R.S.C. Outfit Packing (Units Boxed), Except 6519-25

Contents: 230P-1 Alco Diesel Power Unit - "Chesapeake & Ohio"; 3519-1 Automatic Satellite Launching Car; 6519-25 Allis-Chalmers Car; 6062-1 Gondola Car - Black - With 3 Cable Reels; 6017-1 Caboose; 1013-8 Curved Track (Bundle of 8 - 1013); 1013-90 Curved Track (Bundle of 9 - 1013); 1018-30 Straight Track (Bundle of 3 - 1018); 1018-75 Straight Track (Bundle of 6 - 1018); 6029-25 R.C. Uncoupling Track; 1025-25 45-Watt Transformer; 110-1 Trestle Set; 90-30 Envelope Packed; 1802I Layout Instruction Sheet; 9670-10 Instruction Sheet; 310-2 Set of (5) Billboards; D61-50 Accessory Catalog

Boxes & Packing: 61-220 Corr. Outfit Box; 61-193 Corr. Insert; 61-221 Corr. Shipper for (2) (1-2)

X-623 (1961)	C6	C7	C8	Rarity
Complete Outfit	350	625	900	R6
Outfit Box no. 61-220	100	175	250	R6

Comments: The no. X-623 was the second of two (along with the no. X-622) outfits sold to the Mutual Buying Syndicate buying cooperative. These Retailer Promotional Type Ia outfits were distributed among Mutual Buying's member stores, although neither outfit can be tied to a specific customer.

The X-623 was Mutual's high-end purchase. All items were boxed, except the no. 6519-25 Allis-Chalmers Car. Leaving that car unboxed and protected by only a no. 61-193 Corr. Insert was odd because its brake wheels frequently cracked or broke off their plastic mountings.

This outfit also included a no. 230P-1 Chesapeake & Ohio Alco rather than the steam locomotive packed in the companion outfit X-622. The 230P-1 (new for 1961) came equipped with a two-position reversing unit, a headlight and two-axle Magne-Traction. Also new was the no. 3519-1 Automatic Satellite Launching Car.

The track layout was the commonly used 1961 elevated pretzel layout (as detailed on the no. 1802I Layout Instruction Sheet). All cars came equipped with early operating AAR trucks and couplers. All the other peripherals were appropriate for 1961.

The no. 61-220 Orange RSC with Black Graphics outfit box was manufactured by Mead Containers and measured 16⅜ x 13⅛ x 6¼ inches.

Mutual offered its customers two nice choices in 1961, both of which are fine additions to a promotional outfit collection.

CONVENTIONAL PACK
61-220 BOX

TOP LAYER — BOTTOM LAYER

The no. X-624 included the no. X625-20 Cardboard Scenic Set. That item, so difficult to find complete and unassembled, was printed on chipboard, and the figures were perforated for easy removal. The entire sheet was folded in half so it would fit in a small outfit box. Surviving examples are extremely fragile and tend to fall apart over time.

Description: "O27" Promotional Outfit
Specification: "O27" Steam Type Freight Set
Customer: Richie Premium
Original Amount: 5,544
Factory Order Date: 11/9/1961
Date Issued: Rev. #3 12-12-61
Packaging: R.S.C. Outfit Packing (Units not Boxed)

Contents: 1060-25 Steam Type Locomotive; 1050T-25 Tender; 6042-25 Gondola Car (Less 2 Canisters); 6112-5 Canister - Red (2); 6076-75 Hopper Car - Black; 6406-25 Single Automobile Car (Less Auto); 6406-30 Automobile; 6067-25 Caboose; 1013-70 Curved Track (Bundle of 12 - 1013); 1018-40 Straight Track (Bundle of 4 - 1018); 1026-25 25-Watt Transformer; 1020-25 90° Crossing; 1103-12 Envelope Packed; X625-20 Cardboard Scenic Set; 1802B Layout Instruction Sheet; 1123-10 Instruction Sheet; 310-2 Set of (5) Billboards (2); D61-50 Accessory Catalog

Boxes & Packing: 61-170 Outfit Box; 61-171 Corr. Insert; 61-172 Corr. Insert; 61-173 Corr. Insert; 61-174 Corr. Shipper for (6) (1-6)

Alternate For Outfit Contents:

Note: When Stock of 6076-75 is depleted, use 6076-25; Increase of 36 sets - less X625-20.

X-624 (1961)	C6	C7	C8	Rarity
Complete Outfit	460	1,020	1,670	R9
Outfit Box no. 61-170	40	65	100	R5

Comments: This was the first of two (along with the no. X-625) 1961 outfits purchased by incentive merchandiser Richie Premium. A Retailer Promotional Type Ib outfit, the no. X-624 included items that, except for the rare no. X625-20 Cardboard Scenic Set, are considered commonly available.

The X625-20 Cardboard Scenic Set included figures, railroad signs, automobiles and buildings that could be punched out, assembled and placed around a layout. Its high rarity is linked to its lack of Lionel markings (it said only "Printed in Japan"), which led to it frequently being separated from the trains and discarded. Also, the Cardboard Scenic Set was extremely fragile and almost always assembled and destroyed.

As for the other components, this outfit was headed by the common forward-only no. 1060-25 Steam Type Locomotive with a headlight. All the cars came equipped with non-operating Archbar trucks and couplers. The X-624 was the only outfit to list two no. 310-2 Set of (5) Billboards.

The no. 61-170 Tan RSC with Black Graphics outfit box was manufactured by Owens-Illinois with two dots and "9012" printed on the bottom. It measured 11½ x 10¼ x 6¼ inches.

The X-624 is one of those unusual outfits whose components, specifically the X625-20, make it an R9. Just the box drops it to only R5.

CONVENTIONAL PACK
61-170 BOX

TOP LAYER			BOTTOM LAYER		

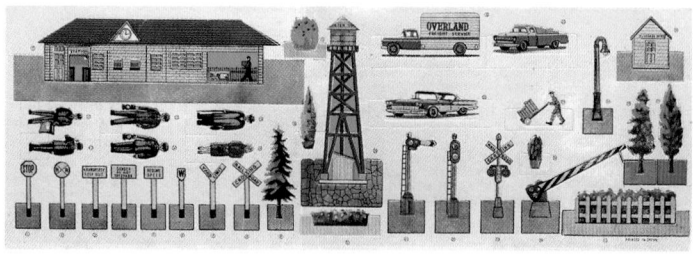

1020-25 ATOP 6067-25

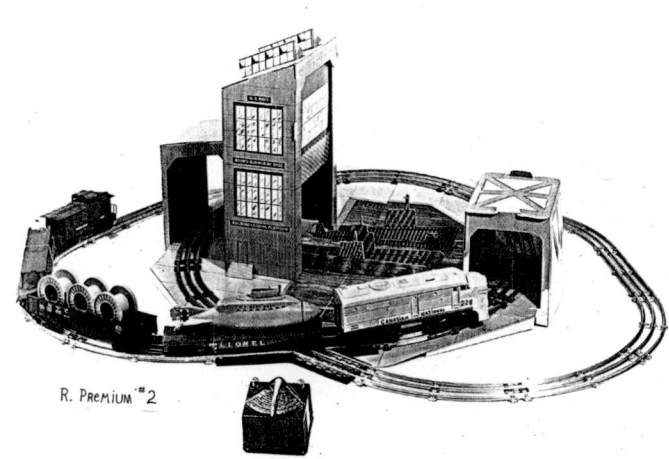

R. Premium #2

To assist in selling its outfits, Lionel provided specification sheets and glossy photographs to its sales department and to dealers. This photograph of outfit no. X-625 shows a complete and fully assembled no. 910-1 Navy Yard Cardboard Display. Upon closer inspection, the no. 3330-1 Flat Car With Operating Submarine (Kit) was shown as a no. 6830-1 Flat Car - with Non-Operating Submarine. Also, it appears that Lionel didn't have a no. 228P-1 Canadian National Alco available for this picture. As a result, one was created by sticking on handwritten labels.

Description: "O27" Promotional Outfit
Specification: "O27" Diesel Freight Outfit
Customer: Richie Premium
Original Amount: 1,000
Factory Order Date: 5/1/1961
Date Issued: 5-6-61
Packaging: R.S.C. Outfit Packing (Units Boxed)

The no. X625-20 Cardboard Scenic Set was first included in this outfit, hence the "X-625" base number. The X625-20 was printed on chipboard, and the figures were perforated for easy removal. The entire sheet was folded in half so it would fit in a small outfit box. Examples are extremely fragile and tend to fall apart over time.

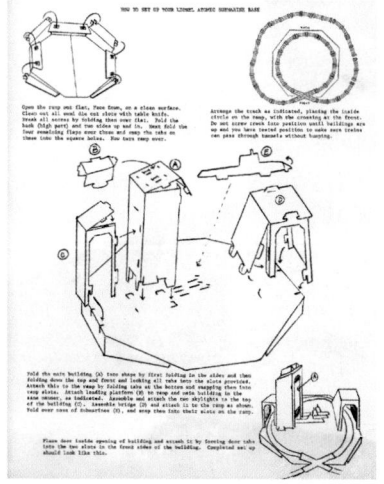

The no. X-625 included an unnumbered "How to Assemble Your Lionel Atomic Submarine Base" instruction sheet. This difficult-to-find item was printed on low-grade paper that deteriorates over time. Few examples are in full-sheet condition, as is the one shown here.

Contents: 228P-1 Alco Diesel Power Unit - "Canadian National"; 3330-1 Flat Car With Operating Submarine (Kit); 6825-1 Trestle Bridge Flat Car; 6062-1 Gondola Car - Black; 6017-1 Caboose;

1013-8 Curved Track (Bundle of 8 - 1013) (2); 1018-30 Straight Track (Bundle of 3 - 1018); 1008-50 Uncoupling Track Section; 1025-25 45-Watt Transformer; 1023-25 45° Crossing; 910-1 Navy Yard Cardboard Display; 81-32 24" R.C. Wire (2); X625-20 Cardboard Scenic Set; 1802H Layout Instruction Sheet; IS Instruction Sheet; 310-2 Set of (5) Billboards; D61-50 Accessory Catalog

Boxes & Packing: 61-385 Corr. Outfit Box; 61-386 Corr. Insert; 61-387 Corr. Shipper for (3) (1-3); 60-503 Box; 61-386 Insert; 60-504 Shipper (1-3)

Alternate For Outfit Contents:
Note: Use Inventory of 60-503 Box and 60-504 Shipper First.

X-625 (1961)	C6	C7	C8	Rarity
Complete Outfit With Either A no. 60-503 Or 61-385 Box	7,250	11,000	15,200	R10
Outfit Box no. 60-503	400	700	1,000	R9
Outfit Box no. 61-385	400	700	1,000	R9

Comments: This was the second and last (along with the no. X-624) of the 1961 outfits purchased by incentive merchandiser Richie Premium. A Retailer Promotional Type Ib outfit, the no. X-625 included two premier postwar collectible peripherals: the no. 910-1 Navy Yard Cardboard Display (also known as the Atomic Sub Base) and the no. X625-20 Cardboard Scenic Set.

The rarity of both of these items can be directly linked to their fragility and the absence of any Lionel markings on them. Stories are told of individuals discarding a 910-1 Navy Yard Cardboard Display because they did not know what it was. Even if the X625-20 and 910-1 stayed with the X-625 outfit, they were likely assembled or fell apart due to handling over time.

Other outfit items, notably the nos. 3330-1 Flat Car With Operating Submarine (Kit) and 228P-1 Canadian National Alco with two-axle Magne-Traction, are some of the nicer and more collectible items from the 1960s. However, obtaining them is far easier than getting either a 910-1 or an X625-20. All items

came with two operating AAR trucks and couplers, and the other peripherals were appropriate for 1961.

Common with sub-base outfits was the pretzel track layout detailed on the no. 1802H Layout Instruction Sheet as well as the unnumbered "How to Assemble Your Lionel Atomic Submarine Base" instruction sheet.

CONVENTIONAL PACK
60-503 OR 61-385 BOX

1025-25	228P-1 S
3330-1 S	6062-1 F
16-1013 F	6825-1 S
FILLER INSERT 61-386	

1023-25 TOP OF 1013
6017-1 TOP OF 6062-1
1018-30 TOP OF 6825-1
1008-50 TOP OF 1025-25

Two different Tan RSC with Black Graphic outfit boxes were used. First, the no. 60-503 was an overstickered no. X-515NA sub-base outfit box from 1960. The other outfit box was no. 61-385, manufactured by Mead Containers and measuring 22 x 18¼ x 5¼ inches. It was also used for the next five sub-base outfits issued in 1961 and 1962: nos. X-676, X-714, 19201 (1), 19201 (2) and 19203.

These early sub-base outfits included the 910-1 inside the outfit box. This arrangement required a large insert to fill the empty space, which led to these outfits being unevenly balanced.

The X-625 is another example of outfit items demanding a higher rarity than the box alone, although finding an X-625 outfit box in C8 condition is extremely difficult.

Note that the price of this outfit assumes the unnumbered "How to Assemble Your Lionel Atomic Submarine Base" instruction sheet as well.

The Factory Orders indicate that 1,000 of these outfits were manufactured, but few of these boxes survived. For one thing, it was a large and clumsy outfit box that did not hold up well. For another, when this box was shipped, half of it was filled with an insert. Once removed, the box provided substantially more space than necessary to store the trains. Most boxes were likely discarded, a fact that is reflected in its pricing and rarity.

Description: "O27" Promotional Outfit
Specification: "O27" Diesel Freight Outfit
Customer: Automotive
Customer/No./Price: J & R Auto Stores; 3007; $15.99
Original Amount: 3,000
Factory Order Date: 4/6/1961
Date Issued: Rev. #1 9-12-61
Packaging: Display Outfit Packing (Units not Boxed)

Contents: 1065-25 Alco Diesel Power Unit - "Union Pacific"; 3370-25 Animated Sheriff & Outlaw Car; 6050-25 Savings Bank Car; 6076-75 Hopper Car - Black; 6067-25 Caboose; 1013-8 Curved Track (Bundle of 8 - 1013); 1018-10 Straight Track (Loose) (2); 1026-25 25-Watt Transformer; 1103-12 Envelope Packed; 1125-10 Instruction Sheet; 310-2 Set of (5) Billboards; D61-50 Accessory Catalog

Boxes & Packing: 61-383 Corr. Display Outfit Box; 61-101 Corr. Insert; 61-102 Corr. Insert (2); 61-103 Corr. Shipper for (6) (1-6)

X-626 (1961)	C6	C7	C8	Rarity
Complete Outfit	200	425	575	R5
Outfit Box no. 61-383	50	100	125	R5

Comments: Lionel listed Automotive as the customer for five outfits in 1961: nos. X-626 through X-630. The X-626 was Automotive's entry-level diesel locomotive offering and included two promotional-only items, hence its classification as a Retailer Promotional Type Ib outfit.

Linking a Lionel Automotive customer to the eventual end customer is performed via price tags, advertisements or other markings or listings. Regarding the X-626, it appeared on page 12 of the 1961 J & R Auto Stores catalog as J & R no. 3007. It was listed as "Union Pacific Diesel with Savings Bank Car, Outlaw and Sheriff Car, Coal Hopper and Caboose." The catalog went on to state that if purchased separately, the total value would be $41.05,

The no. X-626 was the entry-level diesel locomotive offering for Automotive customers in 1961. It included the promotional-only no. 1065-25 Union Pacific Alco.

The no. 61-383 outfit box was pre-printed by the box manufacturer with "X-626". It was also overstickered and used for promotional outfit no. 11011 in 1962.

but J & R's discount price was $15.99. This is just one example of how heavily discounted Lionel trains were during the early 1960s.

The X-626 contained the no. 1065-25 Union Pacific Alco with headlight (new for 1961). This forward-only diesel locomotive appeared just in promotional outfits. Also new for 1961 was the no. 6050-25 Savings Bank Car with coin slot.

This outfit has been observed with a two operating Archbar truck and coupler version of the no. 3370-25 Animated Sheriff & Outlaw Car. This tough-to-find car appeared in only a few promotional and catalog outfits. The outfit pricing reflects the inclusion of this variation. Except for the locomotive, the contents of outfit no. X-645 exactly duplicate those of the X-626.

The no. 61-383 White 4-6-4 Steamer and F3 Hinged Display with Red/Orange and Blue Graphics Type A outfit box was manufactured by Express Container, Corp. and measured 21¾ x 11¼ x 3¼ inches.

These outfits are commonly available, thus indicating that they were widely distributed among many automotive retail chains.

DISPLAY PACK 61-383 BOX		
1065-25	3370-25	
2-1018 8-1013 ENV.	6076-75	
6050-25	6067-25	1026 -25

Description: "O27" Promotional Outfit
Specification: "O27" Steam Type Freight Outfit
Customer: Automotive
Customer/No./Price: J & R Auto Stores; 3005; $19.99
Original Amount: 2,500
Factory Order Date: 3/24/1961
Date Issued: 6-7-61
Packaging: Display Outfit Packing (Units not Boxed)

Contents: 246-25 Steam Type Locomotive; 244T-25 Tender; 3509-25 Operating Satellite Launching Car (Manually); 3330-25 Flat Car With Operating Submarine (Less Kit); 3330-200 Submarine Kit; 6062-25 Gondola Car - Black (Less Cable Reels); 40-11 Cable Reels (3); 6017-25 Caboose; 1013-8 Curved Track (Bundle of 8 - 1013); 1018-30 Straight Track (Bundle of 3 - 1018); 1008-50 Uncoupling Track Section; 1025-25 45-Watt Transformer; 1103-12 Envelope Packed; 1641-10 Instruction Sheet; 310-2 Set of (5) Billboards; D61-50 Accessory Catalog

Boxes & Packing: 61-396 Display Outfit Box; 61-391 Insert; 61-392 Insert; 61-393 Insert; 61-394 Insert; 61-395 Shipper for (6) (1-6)

X-627 (1961)	C6	C7	C8	Rarity
Complete Outfit	265	465	675	R5
Outfit Box no. 61-396	75	125	150	R5

Comments: This was the second of five 1961 outfits (nos. X-626 through X-630) that listed Automotive as the customer on the Factory Orders. The no. X-627 was classified as a Retailer Promotional Type Ia outfit. Of the five Automotive outfits, it was the entry-level steam locomotive outfit.

Like the X-626, the X-627 can be linked to J & R Auto Stores. It appeared on page 12 of the 1961 J & R Auto Stores catalog as J & R no. 3005. It was listed as "Steam Engine with Magne-Traction

DISPLAY PACK
61-396 BOX

246-25	244T-25
3330-25 3330-200	6062-25
3509-25	6017-25
1018-30 1013-8 1008-50	1025-25

and Satellite Car, Operating Submarine Car, Gondola Car with Cable Reels and Caboose." The catalog went on to state that if purchased separately, the total value would be $48.70, but J & R's discount price was $19.99. This is another example of how heavily discounted Lionel trains were during the early 1960s.

The X-627 was headed by a no. 246-25 Steam Type Locomotive.

That engine, first manufactured in 1959, featured Magne-Traction, a two-position reversing unit and a headlight.

For an entry-level offering, this outfit included decent rolling stock, most notably the no. 3330-25 Flat Car With Operating Submarine (Less Kit) and its no. 3330-200 Submarine Kit. Finding an original, unopened plastic bag of parts that the 3330-200 came with makes this a difficult outfit to complete. The no. 3509-25 Satellite Launching Car was new for 1961 and came equipped with the same AAR trucks and couplers as the other cars.

The no. 61-396 White 4-6-4 Steamer and F3 Hinged Display with Red/Orange and Blue Graphics Type A outfit box was manufactured by UCC (United Container Co.) and measured 22⅝ x 14¾ x 3¼ inches.

Because of its space and military theme, operating rolling stock and extremely rare Orange Perforated no. 6017-200 U.S. Navy Caboose box, outfit no. X-628 is one of the premier promotional outfits.

Description: "O27" Promotional Outfit
Specification: "O27" Diesel Freight Outfit
Customer: Automotive
Original Amount: 1,500
Factory Order Date: 4/6/1961
Date Issued: 5-19-61
Packaging: R.S.C. Outfit Packing (Units Boxed)

Contents: 224P-1 Alco Diesel Power Car - "U.S. Navy"; 224C-1 "B" Unit - "U.S. Navy"; 3830-1 Operating Submarine Car; 3665-1 Minuteman Missile Launching Car; 3410-1 Oper. Helicopter Launching Car (Manually); 6017-200 Caboose - "U.S. Navy"; 1013-70 Curved Track (Bundle of 12 - 1013); 1018-30 Straight Track (Bundle of 3 - 1018); 1008-50 Uncoupling Track Section; 1025-25 45-Watt Transformer; 1020-25 90° Crossing; 81-32 24"

R.C. Wire (2); 1802B Layout Instruction Sheet; IS Instruction Sheet; 310-2 Set of (5) Billboards; D61-50 Accessory Catalog

Boxes & Packing: 61-200 Corr. Outfit Box; 60-541 Corr. Insert; 61-201 Corr. Shipper for (4) (1-4)

Alternate For Outfit Contents:
Note: Use inventory 594 - 6017-200 (Boxed); Balance - Use 6017-210 (Not Boxed).

X-628 (1961)	C6	C7	C8	Rarity
Complete Outfit With no. 6017-200	1,025	1,670	2,500	R9
Complete Outfit With no. 6017-210	725	1,170	1,700	R6
Outfit Box no. 61-200	110	200	300	R6

Comments: The Lionel Factory Order listed Automotive as the customer for this, the third of five 1961 Automotive outfits (nos. X-626 through X-630). Of the five, outfit no. X-628 was the high-end diesel locomotive Retailer Promotional Type Ib. This outfit was likely resold to other automotive end customers, but a linkage has yet to be made.

The key item in this outfit with a space and military theme was the difficult-to-find Orange Perforated no. 6017-200 Caboose box (overstamped on a no. 6017-185 box). Thanks to the Factory Orders, the number for an unboxed U.S. Navy Caboose was revealed as no. 6017-210. But when boxed, it became a "-200" and was included in outfit X-628 and catalog outfit no. 1633(X). Total factory orders for both of these outfits were 1,594. Outfit pricing and rarity are based on the inclusion of this seldom-seen box.

Also difficult to obtain is the Orange Picture no. 3410-10 Folding Box. The no. 3410-1 Oper. Helicopter Launching Car (Manually) was never offered for separate sale; therefore, the only way to obtain a boxed version was through a promotional outfit.

Each item of rolling stock was equipped with early AAR trucks and couplers. Individual boxes included a combination of Orange Perforated (nos. 224C-1 and 6017-200) and Orange Picture (nos. 3830-1, 3665-1 and 3410-1). All the other peripherals followed the normal progression.

The no. 61-200 Orange RSC with Black Graphics outfit box was manufactured by Mead Bonded Containers and measured 14½ x 12 x 7 inches. Also included was a no. 60-541 Insert (yellow corrugated) that filled the empty space on the bottom layer. This, a difficult insert to find, was originally included with outfit no. X-532NA. Lionel was using this leftover insert for filler.

Outfit X-628's space and military theme, operating rolling stock and caboose box make it one of the premier promotional outfits. It is the individual Orange Perforated 6017-200 Caboose box that leads to the outfit having an R9 rarity, whereas the outfit box alone is R6.

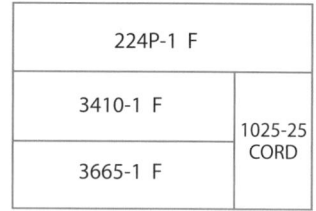

CONVENTIONAL PACK
61-200 BOX

TOP LAYER

224C-1 F	
6017-200 S	INSERT 60-541
3830-1 S	
1013-70 / 1008-50 / 1018-30	

BOTTOM LAYER

224P-1 F	
3410-1 F	1025-25 CORD
3665-1 F	

1020-25 CROSSING TOP OF INSERT

Description: "O27" Promotional Outfit
Specification: "O27" Steam Type Freight Outfit With Smoke
Customer: Automotive
Customer/No./Price: J & R Auto Stores; 3006; $29.99
Original Amount: 2,500
Factory Order Date: 4/7/1961
Date Issued: Rev. #2 8/10/61
Packaging: R.S.C. Outfit Packing (Units Boxed)

Contents: 236-1 Steam Type Locomotive With Smoke; 1130T-1 Tender; 3519-1 Automatic Satellite Launching Car; 6470-1 Exploding Target Car; 6650-1 Missile Launching Car; 6017-1 Caboose; 1013-8 Curved Track (Bundle of 8 - 1013); 1013-90 Curved Track (Bundle of 9 - 1013); 1018-30 Straight Track (Bundle of 3 - 1018); 1018-75 Straight Track (Bundle of 6 - 1018); 1008-50 Uncoupling Track Section; 1025-25 45-Watt Transformer; 110-1 Trestle Set; 81-32 24" R.C. Wire (2); 1802I Layout Instruction Sheet; X602-10 Instruction Sheet; 310-2 Set of (5) Billboards; D61-50 Accessory Catalog

Boxes & Packing: 61-220 Corr. Outfit Box; 61-221 Corr. Shipper for (2) (1-2)

X-629 (1961)	C6	C7	C8	Rarity
Complete Outfit	300	515	775	R5
Outfit Box no. 61-220	90	125	175	R5

Comments: The fourth outfit that Automotive purchased in 1961 became its mid-level steam locomotive offering. This Retailer Promotional Type Ia was one of the five outfits (nos. X-626 through X-630) purchased by Automotive in that year.

Outfit no. X-629 was linked to one of its eventual end customers via a catalog observation. It appeared on page 12 of the 1961 J & R Auto Stores catalog as J & R no. 3006. It was listed as "Steam Engine with Satellite Car, Exploding Box Car, Missile Launching Car and Caboose." The catalog went on to state that if purchased separately, the total value would be $64.40, but J & R's discount price was $29.99. This is another example of how heavily discounted Lionel trains were during the early 1960s.

This outfit featured a no. 236-1 Steam Type Locomotive and space and military rolling stock. All the items were now boxed (as compared to the entry-level Automotive X-626 steam outfit), and the track layout was the commonly used 1961 elevated pretzel layout (as detailed on the no. 1802I Layout Instruction Sheet). A J & R catalog sidebar refers to this as "Complete with Over 'N Under Trestle Set. Builds a mammoth set up…"

The no. 3519-1 Automatic Satellite Launching Car (new for 1961) was included with middle operating AAR trucks and couplers. All other cars had early operating AAR trucks and couplers. The boxes were a mixture of Orange Perforated (nos. 1130T-1, 6017-1 and 6470-1) and Orange Picture (nos. 3519-1 and 6650-1). All the other peripherals were appropriate for 1961.

The 6470-1 Exploding Target Car and 6650-1 Missile Launching Car were a nice matching pair, as kids could never get

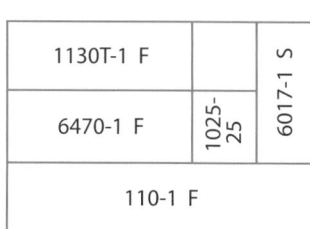

CONVENTIONAL PACK
61-220 BOX

TOP LAYER

236-1 S	
3519-1 S	1008-50 / 1018-30 / 1018-75 / 1013-8
6650-1 F	
1013-90 F	

BOTTOM LAYER

1130T-1 F		6017-1 S
6470-1 F	1025-25	
110-1 F		

The no. X-629 was the mid-level steam outfit offering purchased by Lionel's Automotive customer in 1961. The outfit had a space and military theme and featured an elevated pretzel track layout.

enough of blowing up the 6470-1. The 6470-1 included "slotted" sides and a smooth roof door guide (without the nubs added later to help hold on the sides).

The no. 61-220 Orange RSC with Black Graphics outfit box was manufactured by Mead Containers and measured 16⅜ x 13⅛

x 6¼ inches.

Except for the engine, this outfit is an exact copy of outfit nos. X-634 and X-641. With 2,500 examples manufactured, this outfit frequently appears on the market.

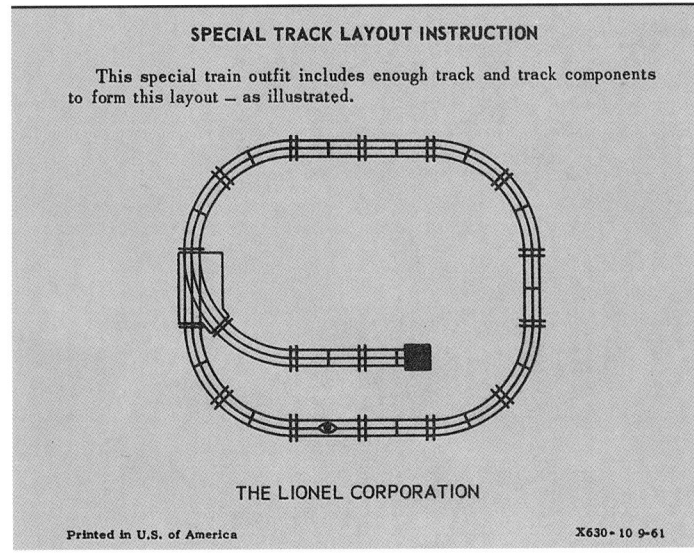

SPECIAL TRACK LAYOUT INSTRUCTION

This special train outfit includes enough track and track components to form this layout — as illustrated.

THE LIONEL CORPORATION

Printed in U.S. of America   X630-10 9-61

The no. X630-10 Layout Instruction Sheet was unique to outfit no. X-630. With only 100 outfits produced, this rare sheet is seldom seen.

Description: "O27" Promotional Outfit
Specification: "O27" Steam Type Freight Outfit With Smoke & Whistle
Customer: Automotive
Original Amount: 100
Factory Order Date: 6/2/1961
Date Issued: 6-7-61
Packaging: R.S.C. Outfit Packing (Units Boxed)

Contents: 2018-1 Steam Type Locomotive With Smoke; 243W-1 Whistle Tender; 6812-1 Track Maintenance Car; 6827-1 Flat

Car With Tractor Shovel; 6828-1 Flat Car With Construction Crane; 6519-1 Allis-Chalmers Car; 6817-1 Flat Car - With Motor Scraper - Red; 6130-1 Work Caboose - "Santa Fe"; 1013-90 Curved Track (Bundle of 9 - 1013); 1018-75 Straight Track (Bundle of 6 - 1018); 6029-25 R.C. Uncoupling Track; 1063-25 75-Watt Transformer; 1022-75 L. H. Switch; 260-1 Illuminated Bumper; 90-30 Envelope Packed; X630-10 Layout Instruction Sheet; 1650-10 Instruction Sheet; 310-2 Set of (5) Billboards; D61-50 Accessory Catalog

Boxes & Packing: 61-416 Corr. Outfit Box; 61-191 Corr. Insert; 61-417 Corr. Shipper for (3) (1-3)

X-630 (1961)	C6	C7	C8	Rarity
Complete Outfit	1,765	2,500	3,500	R10
Outfit Box no. 61-416	700	900	1,300	R10

Comments: This was the last of the five 1961 outfits (nos. X-626 through X-630) that listed Automotive as the customer on its Factory Order. Outfit X-630 was a Retailer Promotional Type Ia outfit. No connection has been established to a specific end customer.

The X-630 was the top-of-the-line steam locomotive outfit purchased by Automotive in 1961. It was made up entirely of Lionel's high-end rolling stock, though the only new item was the no. 6130-1 Santa Fe Work Caboose. Individually, all the cars in this outfit are collectible; when combined, though, they create an outfit that is the pride of any promotional outfit collection.

Interestingly, the no. 2018-1 Steam Type Locomotive With Smoke appeared only in promotional outfits in the 1960s. When boxed, it included a no. CTC-1 Lockon. This, along with the no.

90-30 Envelope Packed (containing four no. 81-32 24" R.C. Wires and a no. 90-1 Controller), provided all the peripherals necessary to hook up the transformer and no. 6029-25 R.C. Uncoupling Track.

The nos. 6827-1 Flat Car With Tractor Shovel and no. 6828-1 Flat Car With Construction Crane were boxed with Harnischfeger construction machines. If unboxed and assembled, these fragile pieces are difficult to get back in their boxes. That's why C8 versions of these cars require that all the peripherals and instruction sheets be present in C8 condition.

Probably the most collectible item in the X-630 was the no. 6817-1 Flat Car - Red - With Motor Scraper. It included the extremely fragile no. 6817-111 Earth Scraper Complete. Finding these models in original, unbroken condition is becoming a challenge.

All the cars included two operating AAR trucks and couplers, and all the peripherals were appropriate for 1961. The track layout was an oval with an inside spur. It was outlined on the rare no.

X630-10 Layout Instruction Sheet dated 9-61.

The Factory Orders called for only 100 of these outfits to be made, thus the R10 rarity. The no. 61-416 RSC outfit box, combined with the premier rolling stock, makes this a difficult outfit to obtain in any condition.

CONVENTIONAL PACK
61-416 BOX

TOP LAYER

6827-1 S		
243W-1 S	9-1018	INSERT 61-191
6817-1 F		
6812-1 F		
6029-25 6-1018		

BOTTOM LAYER

6519-1 F		6130-1 F
6828-1 F	260-1 CORD	
2018-1 F		1063 25

Outfit no. X-631 is shown with a Gimbels price tag still attached. All items were unboxed and packed in the outfit box separated by inserts.

Description: "O27" Promotional Outfit
Specification: "O27" Steam Type Freight Outfit
Customer/No./Price: Gimbels; 740 F1; $19.99
Original Amount: 1,500
Date Issued: 4-7-61
Packaging: R.S.C. Outfit Packing (Units not Boxed)

Contents: 246-25 Steam Type Locomotive; 244T-25 Tender; 6519-25 Allis-Chalmers Car; 3410-25 Oper. Helicopter Launching Car (Manually); 6062-25 Gondola Car - Black (Less Cable Reels); 40-11 Cable Reels (3); 6057-25 Caboose (Red); 1013-70 Curved Track (Bundle of 12 - 1013); 1018-30 Straight Track (Bundle of 3 - 1018); 1008-50 Uncoupling Track Section; 1025-25 45-Watt Transformer; 1020-25 90° Crossing; 1103-12 Envelope Packed;

1802B Layout Instruction Sheet; 1641-10 Instruction Sheet; 310-2 Set of (5) Billboards; D61-50 Accessory Catalog

Boxes & Packing: 61-250 Outfit Box; 61-251 Shipper for (4) (1-4); 61-181 Corr. Insert; 61-182 Corr. Insert; 61-184 Corr. Insert; 61-186 Corr. Insert

X-631 (1961)	C6	C7	C8	Rarity
Complete Outfit	285	500	750	R5
Outfit Box no. 61-250	110	150	225	R5

Comments: Gimbels department store purchased three Retailer Promotional outfits (nos. X-631, X-632 and X-633) in 1961. Outfit X-631 was its entry-level Type Ia steam locomotive outfit.

An X-631 was observed with a price tag printed, "Gimbels, Return Limit 7 Days, 740 F1, 19.99".

This freight outfit was headed by the late variation of the no. 246-25 Steam Type Freight Locomotive. That 2-4-2 Scout engine featured a solid pilot and lacked the small generator detail on its top in front of the cab. It came equipped with Magne-Traction and a two-position reversing unit.

The new-for-1961 no. 3410-25 Oper. Helicopter Launching Car (Manually) with its no. 3419-100 Operating Helicopter Complete is the most notable item in this outfit. Original, unbroken helicopters are not always easy to find. Neither are no. 6519-25 Allis-Chalmers Cars with their brake wheels not cracked or broken off at the base.

All the cars in this outfit were equipped with early AAR trucks and couplers. The other peripherals followed the normal progression.

The commonly used no. 61-250 Orange RSC with Black Graphics outfit box was manufactured by Mead Containers and measured 13 x 12 x 7 inches.

This outfit frequently appears in collectible condition.

CONVENTIONAL PACK
61-250 BOX

TOP LAYER	BOTTOM LAYER

TOP LAYER
6519-25
INSERT
6062-25 3410-25

1020-25 - TOP OF BOTTOM LAYER
(3) 40-11 ON BOTTOM OF BOX

	BOTTOM LAYER
	246-25
1025-25 ENV. TOP	244T-25
	6057-25
	1008-50 12-1013 3-1018

Gimbels outfit no. X-632 included the difficult-to-find boxed version of the no. 6820-1 Aerial Missile Transport Car. This space and military outfit was pulled by a no. 230P-1 Chesapeake & Ohio Alco Diesel.

Description: "O27" Promotional Outfit
Specification: "O27" Diesel Freight Outfit
Customer: Gimbels
Customer/No./Price: Halle Brothers; 40-B; $28.00
Original Amount: 600
Date Issued: 4-7-61
Packaging: R.S.C. Outfit Packing (Units Boxed) Except Crossing

Contents: 230P-1 Alco Diesel Power Unit - "Chesapeake & Ohio"; 6820-1 Aerial Missile Transport Car; 3665-1 Minuteman Missile Launching Car; 3519-1 Automatic Satellite Launching Car; 6470-1 Exploding Target Car; 6017-1 Caboose; 1013-70 Curved Track (Bundle of 12 - 1013); 1018-30 Straight Track (Bundle of 3 - 1018); 6029-25 R.C. Uncoupling Track; 1025-25 45-Watt Transformer; 1020-25 90° Crossing; 90-30 Envelope

Packed; 1802B Layout Instruction Sheet; 9670-10 Instruction Sheet; 310-2 Set of (5) Billboards; D61-50 Accessory Catalog

Boxes & Packing: 60-393 Outfit Box (With Sticker); 60-394 Shipper for (4) (1-4)

X-632 (1961)	C6	C7	C8	Rarity
Complete Outfit	675	1,200	1,650	R8
Outfit Box no. 60-393	175	350	450	R8

Comments: This was the second of three Retailer Promotional outfits (along with outfit nos. X-631 and X-633) that Gimbels purchased in 1961. This Type Ia outfit was the only one led by a diesel locomotive.

The no. X-632 was a space and military outfit headed by the newly issued no. 230P-1 Chesapeake & Ohio Alco Diesel equipped with a two-position reversing unit, a headlight and two-axle Magne-Traction. The most difficult item in this outfit to find in collectible condition is the Orange Perforated no. 6820-1 Aerial Missile Transport Car box. Although the 6820-1 was offered for separate sale in 1960 and 1961 and was a component of nine promotional outfits, this box seldom appears in collectible condition. (See outfit no. 9658 for more information about the no. 6820-100 Operating Missile Helicopter Complete.)

All the items came boxed in a combination of Orange Perforated and Orange Picture boxes and included early AAR trucks and couplers. The no. 1802B Layout Instruction Sheet detailed the figure-eight track layout. All the other peripherals were appropriate for 1961.

Interestingly, the X-632 has been observed in a *Cleveland Plain Dealer* book dated 11/26/61 for "The Halle Bros. Co." as no. 40-B selling for $28.00. Most likely, Lionel sold this outfit to both Gimbels and Halle Brothers, as there appears to be no relation between the two.

The over-stickered no. 60-393 Tan RSC with Black Graphics outfit box was first used with the RSC version of catalog outfit no.

1633, which was known as no. "1633(X)" per its Factory Order. It was manufactured by Kraft Corrugated Containers and measured 11½ x 11⅝ x 6 inches.

Although the X-632 is a tough box to find, collectors may be more interested in the box that lies below the sticker – the RSC version of the 1633. Either way, the overstickered X-632 is harder to find.

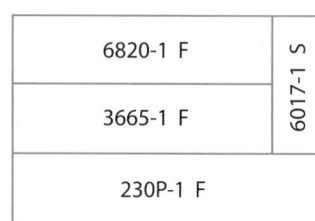

CONVENTIONAL PACK
60-393 BOX

TOP LAYER		
12-1013 / 3-1018 / 6029-25	ENV. CORD	
6470-1 F		
3519-1 F	1025 -25	

BOTTOM LAYER	
6820-1 F	6017-1 S
3665-1 F	
230P-1 F	

1020-25 ATOP BOTTOM LAYER

Description: "O27" Promotional Outfit
Specification: "O27" Steam Type Frt. Outfit With Smoke & Whistle
Customer: Gimbels
Original Amount: 1,400
Factory Order Date: 4/7/1961
Date Issued: Rev. #1 5-6-61
Packaging: R.S.C. Outfit Packing (Units Boxed)

Contents: 233-1 Steam Type Locomotive With Smoke; 233W-1 Whistle Tender; 3410-1 Oper. Helicopter Launching Car (Manually); 3330-1 Flat Car With Operating Submarine (Kit); 6530-1 Fire Prevention Training Car; 6017-1 Caboose; 1013-8 Curved Track (Bundle of 8 - 1013); 1013-90 Curved Track (Bundle of 9 - 1013); 1018-30 Straight Track (Bundle of 3 - 1018); 1018-75 Straight Track (Bundle of 6 - 1018); 1008-50 Uncoupling Track Section; 1063-100 75-Watt Transformer; 110-1 Trestle Set; 81-32 24" R.C. Wire (2); 1802I Layout Instruction Sheet; IS Instruction Sheet; 310-2 Set of (5) Billboards; D61-50 Accessory Catalog

Boxes & Packing: 60-495 Outfit Box (With Stickers); 60-496 Shipper for (3) (1-3)

X-633 (1961)	C6	C7	C8	Rarity
Complete Outfit	550	890	1,375	R6
Outfit Box no. 60-495	100	150	200	R6

Comments: This was the last of three Retailer Promotional outfits (along with nos. X-631 and X-632) that Gimbels purchased in 1961. The no. X-633, the high-end steam-powered outfit, was a Type Ib outfit.

The X-633 included a no. 3410-1 Oper. Helicopter Launching Car (Manually). This car was never offered for separate sale; therefore, the only way to obtain a boxed version was through a

promotional outfit. Also included was the never-cataloged no. 1063-100 75-Watt Transformer with a green whistle control button. This transformer included whistle control circuitry to prevent the Scout-type locomotive from inadvertently reversing.

Of note was the no. 3330-1 Flat Car With Operating Submarine (Kit). Finding one in C8 condition with an unassembled no. 3330-200 Submarine Kit and its parts still sealed in their plastic bag is becoming difficult.

This outfit was headed by a no. 233-1 Steam Type Locomotive with smoke and Magne-Traction (new for 1961). Its no. 233-10 Corrugated Box is difficult to find and is often the only missing item in outfits.

All the items came boxed in a combination of Orange Perforated and Orange Picture boxes and included early AAR trucks and couplers. All the other peripherals followed the normal progression.

The overstickered no. 60-495 Tan RSC with Black Graphics outfit box was manufactured by St. Joe Paper Co. - Container Div. and measured 15¼ x 14¾ x 6⅞ inches. It also had "8 9 10 11 12" printed as part of the box manufacturer's certificate.

Of note, the original Factory Order called for 500 of this outfit to be manufactured, but this figure was crossed out and 1,400 written in by hand. Gimbels likely sold more outfits than expected and increased its order.

CONVENTIONAL PACK
60-495 BOX

TOP LAYER		
6017-1 F	8-1013 S	
	6530-1 F	
1063-100	233W-1 F	

BOTTOM LAYER	
3330-1 F	9-1013 S
	3410-1 F
	233-1 F
	110-1 S

5-1018 ATOP 1013-8, 4-1018 ATOP 6530-1, 1008-50 ATOP 110-1

Description: "O27" Promotional Outfit
Specification: "O27" Diesel Freight Outfit
Customer: Arkwright
Original Amount: 1,500
Factory Order Date: 6/2/1961
Date Issued: 6-7-61
Packaging: R.S.C. Outfit Packing (Units Boxed)

Contents: 230P-1 Alco Diesel Power Unit - "Chesapeake & Ohio"; 6650-1 Missile Launching Car; 3519-1 Automatic Satellite Launching Car; 6470-1 Exploding Target Car; 6017-1 Caboose; 1013-8 Curved Track (Bundle of 8 - 1013); 1013-90 Curved Track (Bundle of 9 - 1013); 1018-30 Straight Track (Bundle of 3 - 1018); 1018-75 Straight Track (Bundle of 6 - 1018); 1008-50 Uncoupling Track Section; 1025-25 45-Watt Transformer; 110-1 Trestle Set; 81-32 24" R.C. Wire (2); 1802I Layout Instruction Sheet; X602-10 Instruction Sheet; 310-2 Set of (5) Billboards; D61-50 Accessory Catalog

Boxes & Packing: 61-220 Corr. Outfit Box; 61-221 Corr. Shipper for (2) (1-2)

X-634 (1961)	C6	C7	C8	Rarity
Complete Outfit	350	610	925	R6
Outfit Box no. 61-220	100	150	225	R6

Comments: Outfit no. X-634 was Arkwright's (a large buying organization) 1961 promotional outfit purchase. A Retailer Promotional Type Ia outfit, it was likely resold to Arkwright's many small customers, although no connections have been made.

Outfit X-634 was a space and military outfit that, except for its motive power, was an exact copy of outfit nos. X-629 and X-641. Leading the way was a no. 230P-1 Chesapeake & Ohio Alco. New for 1961, this diesel came equipped with a two-position reversing unit, a headlight and two-axle Magne-Traction. When boxed in its no. 230-5 Corrugated Box, the locomotive included a no. CTC-1 Lockon, 927-60 Tube of Oil, 230-6 Instruction Sheet and 927-65 Tube of Grease. This was then slid into an orange no. 217-16 Box Sleeve.

The rolling stock included the newly issued no. 3519-1 Automatic Satellite Launching Car. The no. 6650-1 Missile Launching Car was frequently paired with a no. 6470-1 Exploding Target Car to provide lots of play value. These and the other cars were equipped with two operating AAR trucks and couplers.

Also of note was the commonly used elevated-pretzel track plan outlined on the no. 1802I Layout Instruction Sheet. All the peripherals followed the 1961 progression.

The no. 61-220 Orange RSC with Black Graphics outfit box was manufactured by Mead and measured 16⅜ x 13⅛ x 6¼ inches.

CONVENTIONAL PACK
61-220 BOX

TOP LAYER

1008-50	8-1013
	9-1013
9-1018	6470-1 S
	3519-1 S

BOTTOM LAYER

110-1 S		
6017-1 S	230P-1 F	
	1025 25	6650-1 F

Description: "O27" Promotional Outfit
Specification: "O27" Steam Type Freight Outfit
Customer: Interstate Department Stores - White Front Stores
Original Amount: 3,500
Factory Order Date: 4/7/1961
Date Issued: Rev. #1 7-21-61
Packaging: Display Outfit Packing (Units not Boxed)

Contents: 1060-25 Steam Type Locomotive; 1060T-25 Tender; 6076-75 Hopper Car - Black; 6042-25 Gondola Car (Less 2 Canisters); 6112-5 Canister - Red (2); 6067-25 Caboose; 1013-8 Curved Track (Bundle of 8 - 1013); 1018-10 Straight Track (Loose) (2); 1026-25 25-Watt Transformer; 1103-12 Envelope Packed; 1123-10 Instruction Sheet; 310-2 Set of (5) Billboards; D61-50 Accessory Catalog

Boxes & Packing: 61-384 Display Outfit Box; 61-101 Corr. Insert; 61-102 Corr. Insert (2); 61-103 Corr. Shipper for (6) (1-6)

X-635 (1961)	C6	C7	C8	Rarity
Complete Outfit	90	190	300	R6
Outfit Box no. 61-384	25	50	80	R6

Comments: Discount house Interstate Department Stores - White Front Stores purchased this Retailer Promotional Type Ib outfit in 1961.

With its low-end rolling stock, the no. X-635 was typical of other outfits offered by discounters during the 1960s.

All the components of this outfit are easily obtainable. In fact, the most expensive item in a C8 outfit is the set of billboards in comparable condition.

The nos. 1060-25 Steam Type Locomotive, 6042-25 Gondola Car and 6067-25 Caboose appeared only in promotional outfits. All the items had non-operating Archbar trucks and couplers.

DISPLAY PACK
61-384 BOX

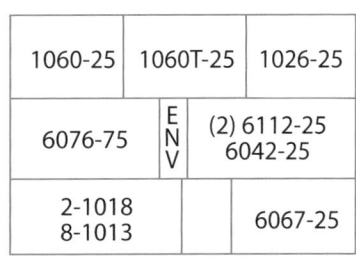

1060-25	1060T-25	1026-25
6076-75	ENV	(2) 6112-25 6042-25
2-1018 8-1013		6067-25

The X-635 came in a no. 61-384 White 4-6-4 Steamer and F3 Hinged Display with Red/Orange and Blue Graphics outfit box. Although this was a uniquely numbered box, leftover inventory was overstickered and used for promotional outfit no. 11001.

The Factory Order listed a quantity of 3,500 to be produced. With numbers this high, these outfits should be easily obtainable. In reality, they do not show up too often.

Description: "O27" Promotional Outfit
Specification: "O27" Diesel Freight Outfit With Horn
Customer: Continental
Original Amount: 264
Factory Order Date: 11/21/1961
Date Issued: Rev. #1 11-21-61
Packaging: R.S.C. Outfit Packing (Units Boxed)

Contents: 218P-1 Alco Diesel Power Unit with Horn - "Santa Fe"; 218C-1 "B" Unit - "Santa Fe"; 6343-1 Barrel Ramp Car; 6445-1 Ft. Knox Gold Bullion Transport Car; 6405-1 Single Van Flat Car; 6475-1 Pickle Car; 6017-1 Caboose; 1013-70 Curved Track (Bundle of 12 - 1013); 1018-30 Straight Track (Bundle of 3 - 1018); 1008-50 Uncoupling Track Section; 1063-25 75-Watt Transformer; 1020-25 90° Crossing; 252-1 Automatic Crossing Gate; 984-1 Railroad Set; 81-32 24" R.C. Wire (2); 1802B Layout Instruction Sheet; 1649-10 Instruction Sheet; 310-2 Set of (5) Billboards; D61-50 Accessory Catalog

Boxes & Packing: 60-409 Outfit Box (W/Sticker); 60-410 Shipper for (3) (1-3)

Alternate For Outfit Contents:
Use 6445-25 in 90 Sets and substitute 981 for 984.

X-636 (1961)	C6	C7	C8	Rarity
Complete Outfit	950	1,500	2,150	R10
Outfit Box no. 60-409	400	550	700	R10

Comments: This is the only promotional outfit purchased by Continental Products, Inc., a Chicago-based buying office. It was a Retailer Promotional Type Ia outfit that was repeated in 1962.

The motive power and rolling stock of the no. X-636 duplicated those of catalog outfit no. 1649, with the addition of a no. 252-1 Automatic Crossing Gate and a no. 984-1 Railroad Set. This is just one example of a catalog outfit being supplemented with other items (additional track and peripherals) to create a promotional outfit.

The X-636 was headed by the premier no. 218P-1 Santa Fe Alco Diesel Power Unit equipped with a three-position reversing unit, a headlight, two-axle Magne-Traction and an open pilot with a large ledge. The nos. CTC-1 Lockon and 218-11 Instruction Sheet were included inside its no. 218-10 Corrugated Box. The 218P-1 was one of the few Alcos to include a horn. Until 1963, Lionel included a no. 601-13 "C" Battery with horn-equipped boxed Alcos.

Four items (nos. 218C-1 Santa Fe "B" Unit, 6343-1 Barrel Ramp Car, 6405-1 Single Van Flat Car and 6445-1 Ft. Knox Gold Bullion Transport Car) were new for 1961. All the cars came with two operating AAR trucks and couplers. The boxes were a combination of Orange Picture (the new items in 1961) and Orange Perforated (the repeated items). A no. 1802B Layout Instruction Sheet was included and described the figure-eight track layout.

Outfit box no. 60-409 was an overstickered no. X-511NA Tan RSC with Black Graphics box. This box was also used for outfit no. X-603 and was manufactured by Star Corrugated Box Company, Inc. It measured 15½ x 13¾ x 7 inches and had a star and "7-22T" printed on the bottom.

The additional 12 outfits ordered in 1962 represented either a repeat order or the sale of the identical outfit to another customer. No customer is listed on the Factory Order for 1962, so the latter explanation is assumed.

The 1962 version of this outfit was an almost exact duplicate except for an updated accessory catalog (1962), a boxed (versus unboxed) no. 1020-1 90° Crossing and an additional no. 1123-40 Instruction Sheet.

There are not enough differences between the 1961 and 1962 versions of this outfit to tell them apart. Therefore, pricing and rarity are combined for both outfits. Even by combining the 1961 and 1962 versions of this outfit, the low quantities made and the fact that it is seldom seen lead to its R10 rarity rating.

The substitutions listed have a negligible effect on the pricing and rarity of this outfit.

CONVENTIONAL PACK
60-409 BOX
STICKER

TOP LAYER				BOTTOM LAYER	
6343-1 S				3-1018	1063
6445-1 S	12-1013	6475-1 S		984-1 F	25
6405-1 S				218C-1 F	
6017-1 S				218P-1 F	
252-1 S					

1008-50 BETWEEN 6405 - 6445
1020-25 TOP 6405 - 6343

Description: "O27" Promotional Outfit
Specification: "O27" Diesel Freight Outfit With Horn
Original Amount: 12
Factory Order Date: 11/9/1962
Packaging: R.S.C. Outfit Packing (Units Boxed)

Contents: 218P-1 Alco Diesel Power Unit with Horn - "Santa Fe"; 218C-1 "B" Unit - "Santa Fe"; 6343-1 Barrel Ramp Car; 6445-1 Ft. Knox Gold Bullion Transport Car; 6405-1 Single Van Flat Car; 6475-1 Pickle Car; 6017-1 Caboose; 1013-70 Curved Track (Bundle of 12 - 1013); 1018-30 Straight Track (Bundle of 3 - 1018); 1008-50 Uncoupling Track Section; 1063-25 75-Watt Transformer; 1020-1 90° Crossing; 252-1 Automatic Crossing Gate; 984-1 Railroad Set; 81-32 24" R.C. Wire (2); 310-2 Set of (5) Billboards; D62-50 Accessory Catalog; 1802B Layout Instruction Sheet; 1123-40 Instruction Sheet; 1649-10 Instruction Sheet

Boxes & Packing: 60-409 Outfit Box (W/Sticker); 60-410 Shipper for (3) (1-3)

Comments: This is an almost exact repeat of the no. X-636 from 1961. The only changes were an updated accessory catalog (1962), a boxed (versus unboxed) no. 1020-1 90° Crossing and an additional no. 1123-40 Instruction Sheet. From a pricing and rarity perspective, these updates have no effect. See the 1961 listing for X-636 for more information.

Outfit no. X-637 included the Plasticville nos. 953-1 Figure Set and 960-1 Barn Yard Set. These sets improved an otherwise commonplace outfit. They also provided Strauss Stores with something different from what their competitors offered, which was the main purpose of promotional outfits.

Description: "O27" Promotional Outfit
Specification: "O27" Steam Type Freight Outfit
Customer: Strauss Stores
Original Amount: 2,500
Factory Order Date: 6/2/1961
Date Issued: 6-7-61
Packaging: R.S.C. Outfit Packing (Units not Boxed)

Contents: 1060-25 Steam Type Locomotive; 1050T-25 Tender; 3409-25 Oper. Helicopter Launching Car (Manually); 6076-75 Hopper Car - Black; 6406-25 Single Automobile Car (Less Auto); 6406-30 Automobile; 6067-25 Caboose; 1013-70 Curved Track (Bundle of 12 - 1013); 1018-40 Straight Track (Bundle of 4 - 1018); 1026-25 25-Watt Transformer; 1020-25 90° Crossing; 953-1 Figure Set; 960-1 Barn Yard Set; 1103-12 Envelope Packed; 1802B Layout Instruction Sheet; 1123-10 Instruction Sheet; 310-2 Set of (5) Billboards; D61-50 Accessory Catalog

Boxes & Packing: 61-250 Corr. Outfit Box; 61-171 Corr. Insert; 61-172 Corr. Insert; 61-173 Corr. Insert; 61-192 Corr. Insert; 61-251 Corr. Shipper for (4) (1-4)

X-637 (1961)	C6	C7	C8	Rarity
Complete Outfit	475	725	1,400	R5
Outfit Box no. 61-250	75	100	175	R5

Comments: In 1961, Strauss Stores (an auto supply chain founded in Brooklyn, New York) purchased a Retailer Promotional Type Ib outfit.

Outfit no. X-637 is a good example of Lionel taking an outfit filled with lower-end rolling stock and sprucing it up with two Plasticville sets. The nos. 953-1 Figure Set and 960-1 Barn Yard Set are the two items that are most difficult to find when trying to complete this outfit. Their boxes were made of a thin cardstock that was easily torn or ripped. The instruction sheets and original, complete Plasticville pieces can also be a challenge to uncover.

The no. 3409-25 Oper. Helicopter Launching Car (Manually) appeared only in promotional outfits. But with 20 appearances and more than 51,000 factory orders, the 3409-25 is fairly common. Obtaining one with an original, unbroken no. 3419-100 Operating Helicopter Complete is more difficult. The 3409-25 and all the other cars were equipped with Archbar trucks and couplers.

The no. 1802B Layout Instruction Sheet detailed the figure-eight track layout. All the peripherals followed the normal progression.

The no. 61-250 Orange RSC with Black Graphics outfit box used for this outfit was manufactured by Mead Containers and measured 13 x 12 x 7 inches.

CONVENTIONAL PACK
61-250 BOX

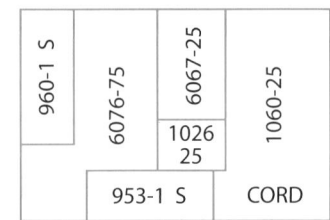

TOP LAYER

4-1018	3409-25	
	6406-25	1050T-25
	12-1013	

1020-25 TOP

BOTTOM LAYER

960-1 S	6076-75	6067-25	1060-25
		1026-25	
	953-1 S	CORD	

X-653
1962

Description: "O27" Promotional Outfit
Specification: "O27" Steam Type Freight Outfit with Smoke
Customer: Mercantile Stores
Original Amount: 150
Factory Order Date: 10/31/1962
Date Issued: 10-31-62
Packaging: R.S.C. Outfit Packing (Units Boxed), & Not Boxed

Contents: 233-1 Steam Type Locomotive With Smoke; 1130T-25 Tender; 3509-1 Oper. Satellite Launching Car; 3830-1 Oper. Submarine Car; 6820-25 Flat Car W/Oper. Missile Helicopter Car; 6017-1 Caboose; 1013-8 Curved Track (Bundle of 8 - 1013); 1013-90 Curved Track (Bundle of 9 - 1013); 1018-30 Straight Track (Bundle of 3 - 1018); 1018-75 Straight Track (Bundle of 6 - 1018); 1008-50 Uncoupling Unit; 1025-25 45-Watt Transformer; 110-1 Trestle Set; 81-32 24" R.C. Wire (2); 1123-40 Instruction Sheet; 233-11 Instruction Sheet; 122-10 Instruction Sheet; 1802I Layout Instruction Sheet

Boxes & Packing: 62-260 Outfit Box; 62-265 Shipper for (4) (1-4)

X-653 (1962)	C6	C7	C8	Rarity
Complete Outfit	925	1,600	2,200	R10
Outfit Box no. 62-260	500	800	1,050	R10

Comments: This was an almost exact repeat of Mercantile Stores' 1961 outfit no. X-653. Also a Retailer Promotional Type Ib, it was likely placed in one of Mercantile's retailer stores, as explained in the entry on outfit X-653 from 1961.

As with many carryover outfits, the original components were not always available in the subsequent year. Still a space and military outfit with some desirable upscale components, the 1962 version substituted a no. 233-1 Steam Type Locomotive for the no. 236-1. Both locomotives included smoke, a headlight and Magne-Traction. The no. 3509-1 Oper. Satellite Launching Car (Manually) remained. When boxed, it was available only in promotional outfits. The Orange Picture box for the 3509-1 is

difficult to find in collectible condition. (See outfit no. X-647 for more information on this car and its instruction flyer.)

Lionel used all but 69 units of the remaining no. 3330-1 Flat Car With Operating Submarine (Kit) in catalog outfit no. 11298 in 1962. Therefore, the no. 3830-1 Oper. Submarine Car replaced the 3330-1 in the 1962 version of this outfit. This car is common, especially compared to a 3330-1.

Two items now came unboxed: the nos. 1130T-25 Tender and 6820-25 Flat Car W/Oper. Missile Helicopter Car. Unfortunately, without its Orange Perforated no. 6820-11 Folding Box, this car is fairly common. (See outfit no. 9658 for more information about the no. 6820-100 Operating Missile Helicopter Complete.)

All the rolling stock came with operating AAR trucks and couplers. All the item instruction sheets came packaged within the item boxes. The nos. 122-10 Instruction Sheet, 1802I Layout Instruction Sheet and other peripherals were placed loose in the outfit box.

The no. 62-260 Tan RSC with Black Graphics outfit box measured 16¼ x 13 x 6⅜ inches and was used for six other outfits. This version of the X-653 came in a different box than did the 1961 version, so each outfit has its own price and rarity (in other words, they cannot be combined).

As with all space and military outfits, the 1962 version of the X-653 is highly desirable. That fact, combined with its extremely low production, leads to an R10 rating and the higher than normal price for the outfit box.

CONVENTIONAL PACK
62-260 BOX
1962 PRODUCTION

TOP LAYER

1018-75 / 1018-30 / 1008-50	1013-8
	1013-90
	3509-1 S
	6820-25
	1130T-25 F

BOTTOM LAYER

6017-1 S	1025-25	110-1 F
		3830-1 F
		233-1 F

X-654
1961

Description: "O27" Promotional Outfit
Specification: "O27" Diesel Freight Outfit
Customer/No./Price: Firestone; 11-L-346; $23.77
Original Amount: 1,000
Factory Order Date: 4/11/1961
Date Issued: Rev. #1 9-12-61
Packaging: Display Outfit Packing (Units not Boxed)

Contents: 1065-25 Alco Diesel Power Unit - "Union Pacific"; 6630-25 Missile Launching Car (Less Missile); 6650-80 Missile Complete (or 6650-84); 6480-25 Exploding Target Car; 3409-25 Operating Helicopter Launching Car (Manually); 6120-25 Work Caboose - "Union Pacific"; 1013-8 Curved Track (Bundle of 8 - 1013); 1018-10 Straight Track (Loose) (2); 1026-25 25-Watt Transformer; 1103-12 Envelope Packed; 1125-10 Instruction Sheet; 310-2 Set of (5) Billboards; D61-50 Accessory Catalog

Boxes & Packing: 61-398 Display Outfit Box; 61-391 Insert; 61-392 Insert; 61-393 Insert; 61-394 Insert; 61-395 Shipper for (6) (1-6)

Alternate For Outfit Contents:
Customer No. 11-L-346 to appear on outfit boxes & shippers.

X-654 (1961)	C6	C7	C8	Rarity
Complete Outfit	350	575	875	R7
Outfit Box no. 61-398	100	175	250	R7

Comments: Firestone Tire & Rubber Company purchased three promotional outfits in 1961, the no. X-654 and two advance catalog promotional outfits (nos. 1123 and 1124). This Retailer Promotional Type Ib was Firestone's high-end promotional offering in 1961.

A space and military outfit, the X-654 included all new-for-1961 rolling stock. Actually these new items were just low-end

Outfit no. X-637 included the Plasticville nos. 953-1 Figure Set and 960-1 Barn Yard Set. These sets improved an otherwise commonplace outfit. They also provided Strauss Stores with something different from what their competitors offered, which was the main purpose of promotional outfits.

Description: "O27" Promotional Outfit
Specification: "O27" Steam Type Freight Outfit
Customer: Strauss Stores
Original Amount: 2,500
Factory Order Date: 6/2/1961
Date Issued: 6-7-61
Packaging: R.S.C. Outfit Packing (Units not Boxed)

Contents: 1060-25 Steam Type Locomotive; 1050T-25 Tender; 3409-25 Oper. Helicopter Launching Car (Manually); 6076-75 Hopper Car - Black; 6406-25 Single Automobile Car (Less Auto); 6406-30 Automobile; 6067-25 Caboose; 1013-70 Curved Track (Bundle of 12 - 1013); 1018-40 Straight Track (Bundle of 4 - 1018); 1026-25 25-Watt Transformer; 1020-25 90° Crossing; 953-1 Figure Set; 960-1 Barn Yard Set; 1103-12 Envelope Packed; 1802B Layout Instruction Sheet; 1123-10 Instruction Sheet; 310-2 Set of (5) Billboards; D61-50 Accessory Catalog

Boxes & Packing: 61-250 Corr. Outfit Box; 61-171 Corr. Insert; 61-172 Corr. Insert; 61-173 Corr. Insert; 61-192 Corr. Insert; 61-251 Corr. Shipper for (4) (1-4)

X-637 (1961)	C6	C7	C8	Rarity
Complete Outfit	475	725	1,400	R5
Outfit Box no. 61-250	75	100	175	R5

Comments: In 1961, Strauss Stores (an auto supply chain founded in Brooklyn, New York) purchased a Retailer Promotional Type Ib outfit.

Outfit no. X-637 is a good example of Lionel taking an outfit filled with lower-end rolling stock and sprucing it up with two Plasticville sets. The nos. 953-1 Figure Set and 960-1 Barn Yard Set are the two items that are most difficult to find when trying to complete this outfit. Their boxes were made of a thin cardstock that was easily torn or ripped. The instruction sheets and original, complete Plasticville pieces can also be a challenge to uncover.

The no. 3409-25 Oper. Helicopter Launching Car (Manually) appeared only in promotional outfits. But with 20 appearances and more than 51,000 factory orders, the 3409-25 is fairly common. Obtaining one with an original, unbroken no. 3419-100 Operating Helicopter Complete is more difficult. The 3409-25 and all the other cars were equipped with Archbar trucks and couplers.

The no. 1802B Layout Instruction Sheet detailed the figure-eight track layout. All the peripherals followed the normal progression.

The no. 61-250 Orange RSC with Black Graphics outfit box used for this outfit was manufactured by Mead Containers and measured 13 x 12 x 7 inches.

CONVENTIONAL PACK
61-250 BOX

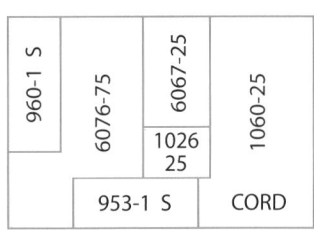

TOP LAYER

4-1018	3409-25	
	6406-25	1050T-25
	12-1013	

1020-25 TOP

BOTTOM LAYER

960-1 S	6076-75	6067-25	1060-25
		1026 25	
	953-1 S	CORD	

Outfit no. X-638 was Western Auto's entry-level outfit for 1961. Western Auto outfits most often were jointly stamped with the Lionel and Western Auto catalog numbers.

Even though the catalog listed this outfit as selling for $18.88, the tag on this example indicates that one Western Auto store priced it at $19.44.

Customer No. On Box: EC-1007
Description: "O27" Promotional Outfit
Specification: "O27" Steam Type Freight Outfit
Customer/No./Price: Western Auto; EC-1007; $18.88
Original Amount: 4,400
Factory Order Date: 11/9/1961
Date Issued: Rev. #2 11-9-61
Packaging: R.S.C. Outfit Packing (Units not Boxed)

Contents: 246-25 Steam Type Locomotive; 1050T-25 Tender; 3409-25 Oper. Helicopter Launching Car (Manually); 6076-75 Hopper Car - Black; 6406-25 Single Automobile Car (Less Auto); 6406-30 Automobile; 6067-25 Caboose; 1013-8 Curved Track (Bundle of 8 - 1013); 1018-10 Straight Track (Loose) (2); 1026-25 25-Watt Transformer; 1103-12 Envelope Packed; 1119-10 Instruction Sheet; 310-2 Set of (5) Billboards; D61-50 Accessory Catalog

Boxes & Packing: 61-170 Corr. Outfit Box; 61-171 Corr. Insert; 61-172 Corr. Insert; 61-173 Corr. Insert; 61-174 Corr. Shipper for (6) (1-6)

Alternate For Outfit Contents:
Note: Customers Stock No. EC-1007 to appear on outfit boxes and shippers.

Comments: Western Auto Stores purchased two steam-powered promotional outfits in 1961: nos. X-638 and X-639. The X-638 was a Retailer Promotional Type Ib.

This was Western Auto's low-end steam purchase in 1961. It was headed by the later version of the no. 246-25 Steam Type Locomotive. That engine featured Magne-Traction and a two-position reversing unit, came with a closed pilot and lacked the small generator detail on its top in front of the cab.

The X-638, like other entry-level outfits from the early 1960s, included cars that were equipped with Archbar trucks and couplers. The one notable item was the no. 3409-25 Oper. Helicopter Launching Car (Manually). It was available only in promotional outfits. All the peripherals followed the normal progression for 1961.

The no. 61-170 Tan RSC with Black Graphics outfit box was stamped by Lionel with "X-638" as well as Western Auto's "EC-1007" catalog number. It was manufactured by Owens-Illinois Paper Products, Div., measured 11¼ x 10¼ x 6¼ inches and was stamped with six dots and "9012" as part of the box manufacturer's certificate.

There is a segment of collectors who collect specific retailer offerings, and Western Auto outfits have a following among them. Therefore, although the X-638 was produced in high quantities and is readily available, many enthusiasts will want to add it to their collections.

X-638 (1961)	C6	C7	C8	Rarity
Complete Outfit	180	300	465	R4
Outfit Box no. 61-170	30	50	75	R4

CONVENTIONAL PACK
61-170 BOX

TOP LAYER

E N V	6406-25 6076-75	
	1050T-25	6406-30
	2-1018 8-1013	

BOTTOM LAYER

246-25		1026-25	
	6067-25		3409-25

This outfit was jointly stamped with Lionel's X-639 and Western Auto's EC-1008 catalog numbers. This was Western Auto's high-end offering for 1961.

Customer No. On Box: EC-1008
Description: "O27" Promotional Outfit
Specification: "O27" Steam Type Freight Outfit With Smoke
Customer/No./Price: Western Auto; EC-1008; $28.88
Original Amount: 3,100
Factory Order Date: 4/10/1961
Date Issued: Rev. #1 7-31-61
Packaging: R.S.C. Outfit Packing (Units not Boxed)

Contents: 236-25 Steam Type Locomotive With Smoke; 1130T-25 Tender; 6650-25 Missile Launching Car (Less Missile); 6650-80 Missile Complete (or 6650-84); 6470-25 Exploding Target Car; 6062-25 Gondola Car - Black (Less Cable Reels); 40-11 Cable Reels (3); 6017-25 Caboose; 1013-70 Curved Track (Bundle of 12 - 1013); 1018-30 Straight Track (Bundle of 3 - 1018); 1008-50 Uncoupling Track Section; 1025-25 45-Watt Transformer; 1020-25 90° Crossing; 909-10 Bottle Smoke Fluid; 1103-12 Envelope Packed; 1802B Layout Instruction Sheet; X602-10 Instruction Sheet; 310-2 Set of (5) Billboards; D61-50 Accessory Catalog

Boxes & Packing: 61-250 Corr. Outfit Box; 61-181 Corr. Insert; 61-182 Corr. Insert; 61-184 Corr. Insert; 61-186 Corr. Insert; 61-251 Corr. Shipper for (4) (1-4)

Alternate For Outfit Contents:
Note: Customers Stock No. EC-1008 to appear on outfit cartons & shippers; Note: Substitute 1,900 - 233-25 for 236-25 (Use 236-25 first).

X-639 (1961)	C6	C7	C8	Rarity
Complete Outfit	210	385	590	R5
Outfit Box no. 61-250	50	85	150	R5

Comments: This was the second of two (nos. X-638 and X-639) steam-powered promotional outfits purchased by Western Auto

Stores in 1961. With all items also illustrated in Lionel catalogs, it was classified as a Retailer Promotional Type Ia.

Outfit X-639 was Western Auto's high-end offering from Lionel in 1961. It was a space and military outfit headed by a no. 236-25 Steam Type Locomotive (new for 1961). That engine featured a two-position reversing unit and Magne-Traction.

When smoke-equipped engines were placed unboxed in an outfit, the no. 909-10 Bottle Smoke Fluid was placed loose in the outfit box. It would normally come inside the engine box. This concept also held true for any other peripherals paired with individually boxed items. When unboxed, these peripherals were placed loose in the outfit box. For this outfit, that would include the nos. 236-11, 6470-17 and 6650-92 instruction sheets.

All the rolling stock was equipped with operating AAR trucks and couplers. The no. 6650-25 Missile Launching Car (Less Missile) was frequently paired with a no. 6470-25 Exploding Target Car. This provided the operator with "Hours of Exciting Action Fun!" according to the Western Auto catalog.

All the peripherals were appropriate for 1961, and the commonly provided figure-eight track layout was described on the no. 1802B Layout Instruction Sheet.

The no. 61-250 Orange RSC with Black Graphics outfit box was stamped by Lionel with "X-639" as well as Western Auto's

CONVENTIONAL PACK
61-250 BOX

TOP LAYER	BOTTOM LAYER	
6650-25	236-25	
6062-25	1130T-25	1025-25
	6017-25	
6470-25	3-1018 12-1013	
1008-50 UNDER 6470-25	1020-25 TOP OF LAYER	

"EC-1008" catalog number. It was manufactured by Mead Containers and measured 13 x 12 x 7 inches.

The values provided are based on the outfit having either a no. 236-25 or a no. 233-25. When unboxed, these are comparably priced steam locomotives.

X-640
1961

Outfit no. X-640 was a seven-unit train outfit with some of the better rolling stock of the era. This was an exceptional outfit for an entry-level offering. AMC's customers had a good selection of quality Lionel merchandise to choose from in 1961.

Description: "O27" Promotional Outfit
Specification: "O27" Steam Type Freight Outfit
Customer: AMC
Customer/Price: Boston Stores; $29.88
Customer/No./Price: Dayton's; T18-6; $29.88
Original Amount: 4,000
Factory Order Date: 4/12/1961
Date Issued: Rev. #2 7-21-61
Packaging: R.S.C. Outfit Packing (Units Boxed)

Contents: 236-1 Steam Type Locomotive With Smoke; 1130T-1 Tender; 3370-1 Animated Sheriff & Outlaw Car; 6445-1 Ft. Knox Gold Bullion Transport Car; 6519-25 Allis-Chalmers Car; 6361-1 Timber Transport Car; 6017-1 Caboose; 1013-70 Curved Track (Bundle of 12 - 1013); 1018-30 Straight Track (Bundle of 3 - 1018); 1008-50 Uncoupling Track Section; 1025-25 45-Watt Transformer; 1020-25 90° Crossing; 81-32 24" R.C. Wire (2); 1802B Layout Instruction Sheet; X602-10 Instruction Sheet; 310-2 Set of (5) Billboards; D61-50 Accessory Catalog

Boxes & Packing: 61-250 Corr. Outfit Box; 61-251 Corr. Shipper for (4) (1-4)

Alternate For Outfit Contents:
Substitute 350 - 233-1 for 236-1 (Last 350 sets to be assembled).

X-640 (1961)	C6	C7	C8	Rarity
Complete Outfit With no. 236-1	420	650	915	R4
Complete Outfit With no. 233-1 Substitution	465	710	1,005	R4
Outfit Box no. 61-250	60	90	125	R4

Comments: Buying cooperatives, such as AMC (Associated Merchandising Corporation), were large customers of Lionel trains. In 1961, AMC purchased four promotional outfits (nos. X-640 through X-643). Each outfit fulfilled a different price point, with the X-640 being the entry-level steam-powered Retailer Promotional Type Ia offering.

Outfit X-640 has been linked to at least two end retailers. It appeared in Dayton's 1961 catalog as well as a newspaper advertisement for Boston Stores (see the section on Lionel's Distribution and Customers).

Even though the X-640 was AMC's entry-level outfit, it came with seven items, including some of the better rolling stock of the era. All items (with the exception of the no. 6519-25 Allis-Chalmers Car) came individually boxed in Orange Perforated (nos. 1130T-1 Tender, 6017-1 Caboose and 6361-1 Timber Transport Car) or Orange Picture (nos. 3370-1 Animated Sheriff & Outlaw Car and 6445-1 Ft. Knox Gold Bullion Car) boxes. It is likely that Lionel had an inventory problem with the Orange Perforated no. 6519-10 Folding Box for the Allis-Chalmers car, as it makes no sense why a car with fragile brakewheel connections would be placed unboxed in an outfit.

The no. 236-1 Steam Type Locomotive included a two-position reversing unit and Magne-Traction. When this engine was boxed, a no. CTC-1 Lockon was included.

All the rolling stock included early operating AAR trucks and couplers. All the peripherals followed the normal progression for 1961.

The no. 61-250 Orange RSC with Black Graphics outfit box was manufactured by Mead Containers and measured 13 x 12 x 7 inches.

The no. 233-1 Steam Type Locomotive With Smoke substitution adds a premium as listed in the pricing table.

CONVENTIONAL PACK
61-250 BOX

TOP LAYER		BOTTOM LAYER
1025-25	1130T-1 F	236-1 F
6017-1 S	1013-70	6519-25 F
	6445-1 S	
	3370-1 S	6361-1 F

1020-25 TOP OF 1130T-1
1008-50 TOP OF 1130T-1
1018-30 TOP OF 1130T-1

The no. X-641 outfit, which featured a space and military theme, included the new nos. 231P-1 Rock Island Alco Diesel and 3519-1 Automatic Satellite Launching Car, as well as an elevated pretzel track layout.

Description: "O27" Promotional Outfit
Specification: "O27" Diesel Freight Outfit
Customer: AMC
Original Amount: 1,800
Factory Order Date: 4/11/1961
Date Issued: 5-17-61
Packaging: R.S.C. Outfit Packing (Units Boxed)

Contents: 231P-1 Alco Diesel Power Car - "Rock Island"; 6650-1 Missile Launching Car; 6470-1 Exploding Target Car; 3519-1 Automatic Satellite Launching Car; 6017-1 Caboose; 1013-8 Curved Track (Bundle of 8 - 1013); 1013-90 Curved Track (Bundle of 9 - 1013); 1018-30 Straight Track (Bundle of 3 - 1018); 1018-75 Straight Track (Bundle of 6 - 1018); 1008-50 Uncoupling Track Section; 1025-25 45-Watt Transformer; 110-1 Trestle Set; 81-32 24" R.C. Wire (2); 1643-10 Instruction Sheet; 1802I Layout Instruction Sheet; 310-2 Set of (5) Billboards; D61-50 Accessory Catalog

Boxes & Packing: 61-220 Corr. Outfit Box; 61-221 Corr. Shipper for (2) (1-2)

X-641 (1961)	C6	C7	C8	Rarity
Complete Outfit	325	585	900	R6
Outfit Box no. 61-220	75	125	200	R6

Comments: In 1961, buying cooperative AMC (Associated Merchandising Corporation) purchased four promotional outfits (nos. X-640 through X-643), with the no. X-641 being the entry-level diesel-powered Retailer Promotional Type Ia offering. No connection to an end retailer has been made.

Except for the locomotive, this space and military outfit was an exact duplicate of Automotive's no. X-629 and Arkwright's no. X-634. There were only so many different combinations of rolling stock that Lionel could offer its customers, and the nos. 3519-1 Automatic Satellite Launching Car, 6470-1 Exploding Target Car and 6650-1 Missile Launching Car were popular items.

The X-641 was headed by a no. 231P-1 Rock Island Alco

Diesel Power Car (new for 1961). That locomotive featured a two-position reversing unit and two-axle Magne-Traction. By contrast, the X-629 was led by a no. 236-1 steamer and the X-634 by a no. 230P-1 Chesapeake & Ohio diesel.

All the items in this outfit were individually boxed and included operating AAR trucks and couplers.

The no. 1802I Layout Instruction Sheet detailed the elevated pretzel layout. All the peripherals followed the normal progression for 1961.

The no. 61-220 Orange RSC with Black Graphics outfit box was manufactured by the Mead Corporation and measured 16¼ x 13¼ x 6⅜ inches.

CONVENTIONAL PACK
61-220 BOX

TOP LAYER

6470-1 F	1018-75 / 1008-50	1018-30
1013-90		
1013-8		

BOTTOM LAYER

110-1 S		
231P-1 F		6017-1 S
3519-1 S	1025-25	
6650-1 S		

X-642
1961

Description: "O27" Promotional Outfit
Specification: "O27" Steam Type Freight Outfit With Smoke & Whistle
Customer: AMC
Original Amount: 750
Factory Order Date: 4/12/1961
Date Issued: Rev. #1 9-12-61
Packaging: R.S.C. Outfit Packing (Units Boxed)

Contents: 2037-1 Steam Type Locomotive With Smoke; 243W-1 Whistle Tender; 3419-1 Operating Helicopter Car; 6062-1 Gondola Car - Black - With 3 Cable Reels; 6405-1 Flat Car With Van; 6017-1 Caboose; 1013-70 Curved Track (Bundle of 12 - 1013); 1018-30 Straight Track (Bundle of 3 - 1018); 1008-50 Uncoupling Track Section; 1063-25 75-Watt Transformer; 1020-25 90° Crossing; 81-32 24" R.C. Wire (2); 1802B Layout Instruction Sheet; 1648-10 Instruction Sheet; 310-2 Set of (5) Billboards; D61-50 Accessory Catalog

Boxes & Packing: 61-250 Corr. Outfit Box; 61-171 Corr. Insert; 61-251 Corr. Shipper for (4) (1-4)

X-642 (1961)	C6	C7	C8	Rarity
Complete Outfit	420	700	1,025	R8
Outfit Box no. 61-250	200	300	400	R8

Comments: This was the third of four (nos. X-640 through X-643) promotional outfits purchased by AMC (Associated Merchandising Corporation) buying cooperative in 1961. It was a Retailer Promotional Type Ia offering. AMC likely sold this to many of its member retailers, but no tie to an end retailer has been made.

The no. X-642 was the high-end steam-powered outfit purchased by AMC. It included the common no. 2037-1 Steam Type Locomotive With Smoke, which was the workhorse of one Super O and 22 O27 outfits during the 1960s.

Although the engine was an upgrade, better rolling stock was included in AMC outfit nos. X-640 and X-641. The only new item in the X-642 was the no. 6405-1 Flat Car With Van. All the items were individually boxed and equipped with operating AAR trucks and couplers.

The no. 1802B Layout Instruction Sheet detailed the figure-eight layout. The no. 61-250 Orange RSC with Black Graphics outfit box measured 13 x 12 x 7 inches.

The Factory Order called for only 750 of this outfit to be made. The X-642 is seldom seen, hence its R8 rating.

CONVENTIONAL PACK
61-250 BOX

TOP LAYER

1013-70	243W-1 S
	INSERT 61-171 / 1018-30 / 1008-50
	6017-1 F

1020-25 TOP OF INSERT

BOTTOM LAYER

6062-1 S	
3419-1 S	1063-25
6405-1 S	
2037-1 S	

X-643
1961

Description: "O27" Promotional Outfit
Specification: "O27" Diesel Freight Outfit With Horn
Customer/Price: AMC; $29.88
Original Amount: 750
Factory Order Date: 5/1/1961
Date Issued: Rev. #1 9-12-61
Packaging: R.S.C. Outfit Packing (Units Boxed)

Contents: 218P-1 Alco Diesel Power Unit W/Horn - "Santa Fe"; 3665-1 Minuteman Missile Launching Car; 6470-1 Exploding Target Car; 3330-1 Flat Car With Operating Submarine (Kit); 6812-1 Track Maintenance Car; 6017-1 Caboose; 1013-8 Curved Track (Bundle of 8 - 1013); 1013-90 Curved Track (Bundle of 9 - 1013); 1018-30 Straight Track (Bundle of 3 - 1018); 1018-75 Straight Track (Bundle of 6 - 1018); 1008-50 Uncoupling Track Section; 1063-25 75-Watt Transformer; 110-1 Trestle Set; 81-32 24" R.C. Wire (2); 1802I Layout Instruction Sheet; 1649-10 Instruction Sheet; 310-2 Set of (5) Billboards; D61-50 Accessory Catalog

Boxes & Packing: 61-230 Corr. Outfit Box; 61-181 Corr. Insert; 61-231 Corr. Shipper for (2) (1-2)

AMC's high-end diesel offering for 1961 was the no. X-643, a space and military outfit that included an elevated pretzel layout. Also shown are the difficult-to-find no. 3330-1 Flat Car With Operating Submarine (Kit) and its unassembled no. 3330-200 Submarine Kit.

X-643 (1961)	C6	C7	C8	Rarity
Complete Outfit	675	1,100	1,575	R8
Outfit Box no. 61-230	200	300	400	R8

Comments: This, the last of four (nos. X-640 through X-643) promotional outfits purchased by buying cooperative AMC (Associated Merchandising Corporation), was a Retailer Promotional Type Ia outfit. The X-643 was AMC's high-end diesel freight outfit purchase for 1961. The AMC member retailers who purchased this outfit have yet to be identified.

An exciting space and military outfit, the X-643 was headed by the top-of-the-line no. 218P-1 Santa Fe Alco Diesel Power Unit equipped with a horn, two-axle Magne-Traction, three-position reversing unit and a headlight.

Of note was the no. 3330-1 Flat Car With Operating Submarine (Kit). Finding one in C8 condition with an unassembled no. 3330-200 Submarine Kit and its parts still sealed in their plastic bag is becoming difficult. The no. 3665-1 Minuteman Missile Launching car was new for 1961.

All the rolling stock was equipped with a combination of early and middle operating AAR trucks and couplers.

The commonly used in 1961 elevated pretzel layout was documented by the no. 1802I Layout Instruction Sheet. All the peripherals followed the normal progression for 1961.

The no. 61-230 Orange RSC with Black Graphics outfit box was manufactured by the Mead Corporation and measured 16 x 15½ x 7⅛ inches.

With only 750 of these outfits made, examples do not appear too often in the marketplace, hence the R8 rating. If only we could go back in time and purchase a few of this great outfit!

CONVENTIONAL PACK
61-230 BOX

TOP LAYER

1013-8 1018-30			
1013-90 1008-50	3665-1 F	INSERT 61-181	218P-1 F

BOTTOM LAYER

110-1 F	6812-1 S	3330-1 S	6017-1	1018-75
			1063-25	
		6470-1 S		

Description: "O27" Promotional Outfit
Specification: "O27" Diesel Freight Outfit
Customer/No.: Oklahoma Tire & Supply Co.; 70-760-4
Original Amount: 1,000
Factory Order Date: 4/11/1961
Date Issued: 5-17-61
Packaging: Display Outfit Packing (Units not Boxed)

Contents: 1065-25 Alco Diesel Power Unit - "Union Pacific"; 3409-25 Operating Helicopter Launching Car (Manually); 6076-75 Hopper Car - Black; 6067-25 Caboose; 1013-8 Curved Track (Bundle of 8 - 1013); 1018-10 Straight Track (Loose) (2); 1026-25 25-Watt Transformer; 1103-12 Envelope Packed; 1125-

10 Instruction Sheet; 310-2 Set of (5) Billboards; D61-50 Accessory Catalog

Boxes & Packing: 61-388 Display Outfit Box; 61-101 Corr. Insert; 61-102 Corr. Insert (2); 61-103 Shipper for (6) (1-6)

Alternate For Outfit Contents:
Customer Stock No. 70 - 760-4 to appear on outfit boxes and shippers.

X-644 (1961)	C6	C7	C8	Rarity
Complete Outfit	225	375	600	R7
Outfit Box no. 61-388	90	125	200	R7

Comments: This was the first of four (nos. X-644 through X-647) 1961 Retailer Promotional outfits for Oklahoma Tire & Supply Company (OTASCO). OTASCO was similar to other large Lionel customers in that it purchased a combination of outfits at different price points. The X-644 was its entry-level diesel offering.

Outfit X-644 included three items unique to promotional outfits: nos. 1065-25, 3409-25 and 6067-25, thus making it a Type Ib outfit. The forward-only no. 1065-25 Union Pacific Alco Diesel Power Unit was Lionel's low-end offering.

All of this outfit's components were new for 1961, with the most notable being the 3409-25 Oper. Helicopter Launching Car (Manually). Obtaining one with an original, unbroken no. 3419-100 Operating Helicopter Complete takes a little effort. The 3409-25 and all the other rolling stock were equipped with Archbar trucks and couplers. All the paperwork and peripherals were appropriate for 1961.

The no. 61-388 was a White 4-6-4 Steamer and F3 Hinged Display with Red/Orange and Blue Graphics outfit box and measured 22 x 11¼ x 3¼ inches. Although this was a uniquely numbered box, leftover inventory was overstickered and used for 1962 promotional outfit no. 11011. At that time, Lionel noted it had 131 in inventory.

DISPLAY PACK
61-388 BOX

1065-25	6067-25	E N V
6076-75	3409-25	
1013-8 1018-10 (2)	1026-25	

The Factory Order stated, "Customer Stock No. 70-760-4 to appear on outfit box…", but it appears this never occurred. All the outfits observed had only the Lionel number on them.

Description: "O27" Promotional Outfit
Specification: "O27" Steam Type Freight Outfit
Customer/No.: Oklahoma Tire & Supply Co.; 70-760-5
Original Amount: 1,500
Factory Order Date: 4/11/1961
Date Issued: 6-7-61
Packaging: Display Outfit Packing (Units not Boxed)

Contents: 246-25 Steam Type Locomotive; 1050T-25 Tender; 3370-25 Animated Sheriff & Outlaw Car; 6050-25 Savings Bank Car; 6076-75 Hopper Car - Black; 6067-25 Caboose; 1013-8 Curved Track (Bundle of 8 - 1013); 1018-10 Straight Track (Loose) (2); 1026-25 25-Watt Transformer; 1103-12 Envelope Packed; 1119-10 Instruction Sheet; 310-2 Set of (5) Billboards; D61-50 Accessory Catalog

Boxes & Packing: 61-397 Display Outfit Box; 61-391 Insert; 61-392 Insert; 61-393 Insert; 61-394 Insert; 61-395 Shipper for (6) (1-6)

Alternate For Outfit Contents:
Customer Stock No. 70-760-5 to appear on outfit boxes & shippers.

X-645 (1961)	C6	C7	C8	Rarity
Complete Outfit	255	450	625	R6
Outfit Box no. 61-397	125	175	250	R6

Comments: This was the second of four (nos. X-644 through X-647) Retailer Promotional outfits for Oklahoma Tire & Supply Company (OTASCO) in 1961. OTASCO purchased two entry-level (one steam and one diesel) and two high-end (one steam and

one diesel) outfits. The Retailer Promotional Type Ib no. X-645 was its entry-level steam-powered offering.

Besides the engine and tender, the X-645 included all new items for 1961. The no. 6050-25 Savings Bank Car included early operating AAR trucks and couplers. The remaining items were equipped with Archbar trucks and couplers.

Except for the locomotive and tender, the contents of Automotive outfit no. X-626 duplicated what came in the X-645. This fact suggests that, even though OTASCO wanted something special, Lionel didn't stray too far from what it offered its other automotive customers.

Per Lionel Production Control Files for the no. 3370-25 Animated Sheriff & Outlaw Car, normal production for this new car included Archbar trucks but was changed to AAR. On 7-18-61, this file detailed that for 1961 production (4,000 units), coupler truck complete no. 566-1 (AAR) should be used in place of coupler truck complete no. 560-50 (operating Archbar). The tough-to-find Archbar version appeared in only a

DISPLAY PACK
61-397 BOX

246-25	1050T-25
6050-25	3370-25
6076-75	6067-25
2-1018 8-1013	1026-25

few promotional and catalog outfits. Observations of this outfit exist with the two operating Archbar truck and coupler version. As such, the outfit pricing reflects the inclusion of this variation.

The no. 61-397 White 4-6-4 Steamer and F3 Hinged Display with Red/Orange and Blue Graphics outfit box measured 22½ x 14¾ x 7⅛ inches. Although this was a uniquely numbered box, leftover inventory was overstickered and 25 units were used for 1962 promotional outfit no. 19197.

Oklahoma Tire & Supply Company was a good customer of Lionel, especially in 1961 when it purchased $79,000 of trains. Its high-end space and military diesel purchase was outfit no. X-646.

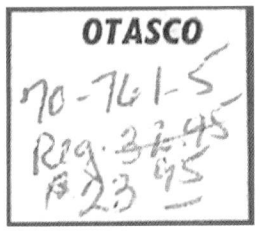

The price tag attached to Lionel outfit no. X-646 shows its customer OTASCO, the outfit no. 70-761-5 and its discounted price. Discounting of trains was commonplace during the 1960s.

X-646 (1961)	C6	C7	C8	Rarity
Complete Outfit	575	1,000	1,400	R9
Outfit Box no. 61-250	200	350	450	R9

Description: "O27" Promotional Outfit
Specification: "O27" Diesel Freight Outfit
Cust./No./Price: Oklahoma Tire & Supply Co.; 70-761-5; $23.95
Original Amount: 540
Factory Order Date: 4/11/1961
Date Issued: Rev. #1 8/10-61
Packaging: R.S.C. Outfit Packing (Units not Boxed)

Contents: 224P-25 Alco Diesel Power Car - "U.S. Navy"; 224C-25 "B" Unit - "U.S. Navy"; 6062-25 Gondola Car - Black (Less Cable Reels); 40-11 Cable Reels (3); 3665-25 Minuteman Missile Launching Car; 3410-25 Oper. Helicopter Launching Car (Manually); 6017-210 Caboose - "U.S. Navy"; 1013-70 Curved Track (Bundle of 12 - 1013); 1018-30 Straight Track (Bundle of 3 - 1018); 1008-50 Uncoupling Track Section; 1025-25 45-Watt Transformer; 1020-25 90° Crossing; 1103-12 Envelope Packed; 1802B Layout Instruction Sheet; IS Instruction Sheet; 310-2 Set of (5) Billboards; D61-50 Accessory Catalog

Boxes & Packing: 61-250 Corr. Outfit Box; 61-186 Corr. Insert (2); 61-191 Corr. Insert (2); 61-193 Corr. Insert; 61-251 Corr. Shipper for (4) (1-4)

Alternate For Outfit Contents:
Customer Stock No. 70 - 761-5 to appear on outfit boxes & shippers.

Comments: In 1961, Oklahoma Tire & Supply Company (OTASCO) purchased four (nos. X-644 through X-647) Retailer Promotional outfits. The third was this Type Ia high-end diesel offering. The other outfits included two entry-level (one steam and one diesel) as well as a high-end steam offering.

This space and military outfit was headed by a no. 224P-25 U.S. Navy Alco Diesel Power Car with Magne-Traction and a three-position reversing unit. It was paired with a no. 224C-25 "B" Unit. When included in promotional outfits, these items most often came boxed. The X-646 was one of four exceptions to this rule.

The nos. 3665-25 Minuteman Missile Launching car and 3410-25 Oper. Helicopter Launching Car (Manually) were both new for 1961. Their space and military features made them an appropriate pairing for this outfit. The no. 6062-25 Gondola Car does not appear to fit with this outfit, and a more appropriate car would have been a no. 6470-25 Exploding Target Car.

The no. 6017-210 U.S. Navy Caboose provided a nice finish

CONVENTIONAL PACK
61-250 BOX

TOP LAYER

6062-25 INSERT	3665-25	3410-25 INSERT	1013-70

BOTTOM LAYER

1018-30 224C-25	6017-210	224P-25
	1025-25	
1 40-11	2 40-11	

1020-25 TOP OF BOTTOM LAYER
1008-50 TOP OF 6062-25

when paired with the U.S. Navy Alco. Except for two outfits in 1962 and 1963, when Lionel was depleting the final inventory of these cabooses, it was always paired with the U.S. Navy Alco.

All the rolling stock was equipped with a combination of early and middle operating AAR trucks and couplers. The peripherals followed the normal progression for 1961.

The no. 61-250 Orange RSC with Black Graphics outfit box was manufactured by Mead Containers and measured. 13 x 12 x 7 inches.

The Factory Order stated, "Customer Stock No. 70-761-5 to appear on outfit box…", but it appears this never occurred. All the outfits observed had only the Lionel number on them.

Only 540 of these outfits were ordered from the factory, which is why examples are seldom seen. The R9 rarity and values reflect these facts.

X-647
1961

IMPORTANT

FLIGHT INFORMATION FOR NO. 3509
SATELLITE LAUNCHING CAR

The spring mechanism in this car is exceptionally strong. If it is fully wound the satellite may strike the ceiling. Therefore, it is recommended that the spool should be turned for only ten (10) "clicks" when it is being operated in an average size room.

Printed in U.S. of America   The LIONEL CORPORATION—New York, N. Y.   3509-7 9-61

Outfit no. X-647 included an Orange Picture boxed no. 3509-1 Operating Satellite Launching Car (Manually). This item only came boxed in promotional outfits and is not the easiest box to find. Included in the box was the difficult-to-find no. 3509-7 Instruction Flyer. That sheet warned users not to over-wind the mechanism, ostensibly to protect a ceiling but most likely to prevent people from being injured.

This Changes Affecting Future Production document details that for the remainder of the 1961 no. 3509-1 production, a no. 3509-7 Instruction Flyer was included. Also note the change of the no. 465-7X Antenna to a no. 465-7.

Description: "O27" Promotional Outfit
Specification: "O27" Steam Type Freight Outfit With Smoke
Customer/No.: Oklahoma Tire & Supply Co.; 70 - 762
Original Amount: 275
Factory Order Date: 4/11/1961
Date Issued: 6-13-61
Packaging: R.S.C. Outfit Packing (Units Boxed)

Contents: 236-1 Steam Type Locomotive With Smoke; 1130T-1 Tender; 3509-1 Operating Satellite Launching Car (Manually); 470-1 Missile Launching Platform; 3330-1 Flat Car With Operating Submarine (Kit); 6017-1 Caboose; 1013-8 Curved Track (Bundle of 8 - 1013); 1013-90 Curved Track (Bundle of 9 - 1013); 1018-30 Straight Track (Bundle of 3 - 1018); 1018-75 Straight Track (Bundle of 6 - 1018); 1008-50 Uncoupling Track Section; 1025-25 45-Watt Transformer; 110-1 Trestle Set; 81-

32 24" R.C. Wire (2); 1802I Layout Instruction Sheet; X602-10 Instruction Sheet; 310-2 Set of (5) Billboards; D61-50 Accessory Catalog

Boxes & Packing: 61-385 Corr. Outfit Box; 61-387 Corr. Shipper for (3) (1-3)

Alternate For Outfit Contents:
Customer Stock No. 70 - 762 to appear on outfit boxes & shippers; Note: Break up 1018-75 Bundle of 6 into 2 threes.

X-647 (1961)	C6	C7	C8	Rarity
Complete Outfit	675	1,200	1,775	R10
Outfit Box no. 61-385	275	500	625	R10

Comments: This was the last of four Retailer Promotional outfits purchased in 1961 by Oklahoma Tire & Supply Company (OTASCO). Of the four outfits (nos. X-644 through X-647), this Type Ib was OTASCO's high-end steam offering, with all the items being individually boxed and an elevated pretzel track layout included.

This space and military outfit came with a no. 3509-1 Operating Satellite Launching Car (Manually) that was never offered for separate sale. Therefore, the only way to obtain its Orange Picture no. 3509-6 Folding Box was in this or eight other promotional outfits. In fact, these outfits total 5,537, making this a difficult box to find in collectible condition.

Even more difficult to obtain is the no. 3509-7 Instruction Flyer included with boxed 3509s. This flyer cautioned against over-winding the spring to protect your ceiling. In reality, it was likely printed to protect the individual from being struck by a satellite launched from this manually operated car. No equivalent flyer has been observed for a no. 3519-1 Automatic Satellite Launching Car.

The X-647 also included a no. 3330-1 Flat Car With Operating Submarine (Kit). Finding one in C8 condition with an

CONVENTIONAL PACK
61-385 BOX
NOTE: BREAK UP 1018-75 BUNDLE OF 6 INTO 2 THREES

TOP LAYER

BOTTOM LAYER

unassembled no. 3330-200 Submarine Kit and its parts still sealed in their plastic bag is becoming difficult. The 3330-1 as well as the other rolling stock included operating AAR trucks and couplers.

Topping off the collectible items in this outfit was the no. 470-1 Missile Launching Platform. Lionel included it in 12 promotional outfits in the 1960s. This large and flat accessory necessitated a rather large outfit box.

The no. 61-385 Tan RSC with Black Graphic outfit box was manufactured by Mead Containers and measured 22 x 18¼ x 5¼

inches. It generally was used with sub-base outfits; the nos. X-647 and X-658 were the only two outfits lacking a sub base that used it.

The Factory Order stated, "Customer Stock No. 70-762 to appear on outfit box…", but it appears this never occurred.

The large, cumbersome box used for this outfit seldom survived in collectible condition. The small quantity of outfits manufactured and their infrequent appearance on the market lead to this outfit's R10 rating

This space and military outfit was the only way to obtain a no. 235-1 Steam Type Locomotive either boxed or unboxed. Also included in the no. X-648 was the desirable Orange Picture no. 3509-6 Folding Box manufactured by Shuttleworth.

Description: "O27" Promotional Outfit
Specification: "O27" Steam Type Freight Outfit
Customer: Allied Stores
Customer/Price: Gertz; $29.88
Customer/Price: Waite's; $29.88
Original Amount: 3,300
Factory Order Date: 6/2/1961
Date Issued: Rev. #2 12-8-61
Packaging: R.S.C. Outfit Packing (Units Boxed)

Contents: 235-1 Steam Type Locomotive; 1130T-1 Tender; 3665-1 Minuteman Missile Launching Car; 6470-1 Exploding Target Car; 3509-1 Oper. Satellite Launching Car (Manually); 6017-1 Caboose; 1013-8 Curved Track (Bundle of 8 - 1013); 1013-90 Curved Track (Bundle of 9 - 1013); 1018-30 Straight Track (Bundle of 3 - 1018); 1018-75 Straight Track (Bundle of 6 - 1018); 1008-50 Uncoupling Track Section; 1025-25 45-Watt Transformer; 110-1 Trestle Set; 81-32 24" R.C. Wire (2); 1802I Layout Instruction Sheet; X602-10 Instruction Sheet; 310-2 Set of (5) Billboards; D61-50 Accessory Catalog

Boxes & Packing: 61-220 Corr. Outfit Box; 61-221 Corr. Shipper for (2) (1-2)

Alternate For Outfit Contents:
Note: Substitute 2018 Locomotive for 235 in 100 sets.

X-648 (1961)	C6	C7	C8	Rarity
Complete Outfit With no. 235-1	580	940	1,450	R7
Complete Outfit With no. 2018 Substitution	410	815	1,075	R5
Outfit Box no. 61-220	90	125	150	R5

Comments: This was first of two outfits sold to Allied Stores in 1961. This Retailer Promotional Type Ic outfit was Allied's high-end offering, whereas no. X-650 filled the entry-level market.

The Allied Stores conglomerate owned many retailers across the country. It likely sold these outfits to any number of customers. Specifically, the December 7, 1961 edition of the *Detroit Free Press* included an advertisement for outfit no. X-648 as sold by Waite's Department Store in Pontiac, Michigan, for $29.88. Other examples of this outfit have been observed with price tags marked Gertz and Read's Store.

The X-648 is a unique space and military outfit because, although the outfit box is readily obtainable, the contents are not. To begin, the no. 235-1 Steam Type Locomotive was never offered for separate sale or in any other outfit. This outfit was the only way it and its no. 235-5 Corrugated Box could be obtained. This engine had the same features, no smoke and Magne-Traction, as the no. 246. It appeared to be the 246's replacement because the 246 was first introduced in 1959. However, this change didn't occur and the 246 went on to be offered in outfits through 1962. Allied, which purchased a total of 32,736 outfits during its relationship with Lionel, must have requested something different and had the pull to obtain it.

A Factory Order for 3,300 units, with 100 no. 235s being swapped out, meant that only 3,200 of the 235 steamers were manufactured. This is a relatively low number.

Another promotional-only item included in this outfit was the Orange Picture box for the no. 3509-1 Oper. Satellite Launching Car (Manually). (See outfit no. X-647 for more information on this car and its instruction flyer.)

Finally, the no. 6470-1 Exploding Target Car included "slotted" sides and a smooth roof door guide (without the nubs added later to help hold on the sides).

All the cars in the X-648 came with operating AAR trucks and couplers and a combination of Orange Perforated and Orange Picture boxes. The no. 1802I Layout Instruction Sheet detailed the elevated pretzel track layout. All the paperwork and peripherals were vintage 1961.

The no. 61-220 Orange RSC with Black Graphics outfit box was manufactured by the Mead Corporation and measured 16⅜ x 13⅛ x 6¼ inches.

The box achieves a rarity rating of R5 and frequently appears. When combined with its components, the complete outfit achieves an R7 rating. Finding both the 235-1 and 3509-1 in collectible condition can be a challenge.

When a no. 2018 Steam Type Locomotive With Smoke is substituted for the 235-1, the values and rarity are reduced, as indicated in the pricing table.

CONVENTIONAL PACK
61-220 BOX

TOP LAYER					BOTTOM LAYER	
					110-1 S	
6017-1 S	6-1018		1008-50 / 3-1018	1130T-1 F	235-1 S	
	8-1013				3665-1 S	
	9-1013				3509-1 F	
	1025-25	6470-1 S				

Space and military outfit no. X-650 included low-end versions of previously released rolling stock now equipped with non-operating Archbar trucks and couplers. The nos. 3409-25, 6480-25 and 6630-25 were low-end versions of the nos. 3419-25, 6470-25 and 6650-25, respectively, and are more difficult to find than their high-end counterparts.

Description: "O27" Promotional Outfit
Specification: "O27" Steam Type Freight Outfit
Customer: Allied Stores
Customer/No./Price: Pomeroy's; 9-1 830; $19.99
Original Amount: 2,500

Factory Order Date: 6/22/1961
Date Issued: Rev. #2 9-12-61
Packaging: R.S.C. Outfit Packing (Units not Boxed)

Contents: 246-25 Steam Type Locomotive; 1050T-25 Tender; 3409-25 Oper. Helicopter Launching Car (Manually); 6630-25 Missile Launching Car (Less Missile); 6650-80 Missile Complete (or 6650-84); 6480-25 Exploding Target Car; 6067-25 Caboose; 1013-70 Curved Track (Bundle of 12 - 1013); 1018-40 Straight Track (Bundle of 4 - 1018); 1026-25 25-Watt Transformer; 1020-25 90° Crossing; 1103-12 Envelope Packed; 1802B Layout Instruction Sheet; 1119-10 Instruction Sheet; 310-2 Set of (5) Billboards; D61-50 Accessory Catalog

Boxes & Packing: 61-250 Outfit Box; 61-181 Corr. Insert; 61-182 Corr. Insert; 61-186 Corr. Insert; 61-193 Corr. Insert (2); 61-251 Shipper for (4) (1-4)

X-650 (1961)	C6	C7	C8	Rarity
Complete Outfit	300	485	735	R6
Outfit Box no. 61-250	75	125	175	R6

Comments: This was second and last of the outfits purchased by Allied Stores in 1961. This Retailer Promotional Type Ib outfit was its entry-level offering, whereas no. X-648 filled the high-end market.

The no. X-650 was observed with a Pomeroy's price tag (no. "9-1 830") for $19.99. Pomeroy's was one of the many retailers that Allied Stores owned. Allied likely also sold this outfit to other retailers in its family.

A space and military outfit, the X-650 included all new-for-1961 operating cars. Actually these new items were just low-end

versions of previously released cars now equipped with non-operating Archbar trucks and couplers. The nos. 3409-25, 6480-25 and 6630-25 were low-end versions of the nos. 3419-25, 6470-25 and 6650-25, respectively. That being said, these cars appeared only in promotional outfits and are harder to find than their high-end counterparts, especially with original, unbroken helicopters and missiles.

The 6480-25 Exploding Target Car included "slotted" sides and a smooth roof door guide (without the nubs added later to help hold on the sides).

The paperwork and peripherals were all appropriate for 1961, with the no. 1119-60 Instruction Sheet dated 5-60. The outfit included a no. 1802B Layout Instruction Sheet detailing the figure-eight track layout.

The no. 61-250 Orange RSC with Black Graphics outfit box used for this outfit was manufactured by Mead Containers and measured 13 x 12 x 7 inches.

Even with a large quantity manufactured, this outfit does not appear too frequently, as reflected in its R6 rarity.

CONVENTIONAL PACK
61-250 BOX

TOP LAYER

6630-25	INSERT 61-193 HELICOPTER	INSERT 61-193 3409-25	246-25

1020-25 TOP

BOTTOM LAYER

12-1013 4-1018		61-181
6067-25	1026 25	
1050T-25		
6480-25		

61-182

61-186 BETWEEN LAYERS

The Spiegel Christmas Catalog for 1961 shows outfit no. X-651 (Spiegel no. R36 J 5260) as item number "3" at the bottom of the three outfits listed. The Lionel catalog outfits shown are "1" (no. 1649) and "2" (no. 1646).

Description: "O27" Promotional Outfit
Specification: "O27" Steam Type Freight Outfit
Customer/No./Price: Spiegel; R36 J 5260; $19.94
Original Amount: 1,200
Date Issued: Rev. #1 7-26-61
Packaging: R.S.C. Outfit Packing (Individual Mailer), (Units not Boxed)

Contents: 246-25 Steam Type Locomotive; 1050T-25 Tender; 3330-25 Flat Car With Operating Submarine (Less Kit); 3330-200 Submarine Kit; 6050-25 Savings Bank Car; 6057-25 Caboose; 1013-8 Curved Track (Bundle of 8 - 1013); 1018-30 Straight Track (Bundle of 3 - 1018); 1008-50 Uncoupling Track Section; 1010-25 35-Watt Transformer; 1103-12 Envelope Packed; 1640-10 Instruction Sheet; 310-2 Set of (5) Billboards; D61-50 Accessory Catalog

Boxes & Packing: 61-399 Outfit Box; 61-171 Corr. Insert; 61-172 Corr. Insert; 61-173 Corr. Insert; 61-174 Shipper for (6) (1-6)

X-651 (1961)	C6	C7	C8	Rarity
Complete Outfit	350	450	675	R7
Outfit Box no. 61-399	100	175	250	R7

Comments: Spiegel purchased three outfits in 1961, two catalog and one Retailer Promotional Type Ia. Outfit no. X-651 was shown on page 386 of its 1961 Christmas Catalog as Spiegel no. R36 J 5260. The outfit was Spiegel's low-end Lionel offering and

285

retailed for $19.94.

Outfit X-651 included the newly released no. 3330-25 Flat Car With Operating Submarine (Less Kit) and its difficult-to-find no. 3330-200 Submarine Kit. The "-200" Kit included a sealed no. 3330-108 Submarine Kit Parts Packed plastic bag that must be left unopened to achieve a C8 rating. Also included was the no. 6050-25 Savings Bank Car with coin slot (new for 1961). All the items came with operating AAR trucks and couplers.

Spiegel touted this outfit as "Exclusive at Spiegel...separately elsewhere $40.75." This advertising is interesting because, if the X-651 were an exclusive, why would Spiegel advertise that you could get it elsewhere? This claim also demonstrates that promotional outfits were frequently promoted on the basis of price. By contrast, the descriptions of the two catalog outfits in that Christmas catalog make no mention of comparable prices.

The X-651 reused the no. 61-399 Tan RSC Mailer with Black Graphics outfit box first used with outfit no. X-600. It was manufactured by Mead Containers and measured 11¼ x 10¼ x 6½

inches. These boxes were made of a thicker corrugated material (rated at 90 pounds rather than the normal 65 pounds gross weight) that allowed Spiegel to ship the outfits in their outfit box.

With quantities of 1,200 being made and then offered by a major retailer, these outfits should, in theory, be readily available. In fact, they don't appear too often, as is reflected in the R7 rating.

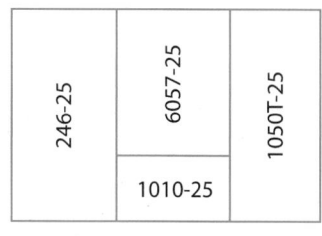

CONVENTIONAL PACK
61-399 BOX

TOP LAYER

3330-200 3330-25	
6050-25	E N V
1013-8 1018-3	

1008-50 ATOP 6050

BOTTOM LAYER

| 246-25 | 6057-25 | 1050T-25 |
| | 1010-25 | |

Description: "O27" Promotional Outfit
Specification: "O27" Diesel Freight Outfit
Customer: Mercantile Stores
Original Amount: 500
Factory Order Date: 4/11/1961
Date Issued: Rev. #1 9-12-61
Packaging: R.S.C. Outfit Packing (Units Boxed)

Contents: 231P-1 Alco Diesel Power Car - "Rock Island"; 3376-1 Operating Giraffe Car; 6062-1 Gondola Car - Black; 6825-1 Trestle Bridge Flat Car; 6017-1 Caboose; 1013-70 Curved Track (Bundle of 12 - 1013); 1018-30 Straight Track (Bundle of 3 - 1018); 1008-50 Uncoupling Track Section; 1025-25 45-Watt Transformer; 1020-25 90° Crossing; 81-32 24" R.C. Wire (2); 1802B Layout Instruction Sheet; X602-10 Instruction Sheet; 310-2 Set of (5) Billboards; D61-50 Accessory Catalog

Boxes & Packing: 61-380 Corr. Outfit Box; 61-381 Corr. Shipper for (4) (1-4)

X-652 (1961)	C6	C7	C8	Rarity
Complete Outfit	400	725	1,050	R9
Outfit Box no. 61-380	150	325	450	R9

Comments: Mercantile Stores Company, Inc. operated department stores in medium-sized cities during the 1960s. In

1961, it purchased two Retailer Promotional outfits (nos. X-652 and X-653). One outfit featured a steam locomotive, and the other had a diesel. Either could have been sold to any of Mercantile's customers.

The Type Ia outfit X-652 was powered by the new no. 231P-1 Rock Island Alco Diesel Power Car, which included a headlight and two-axle Magne-Traction. The no. 3376-1 Operating Giraffe Car never came boxed in a catalog outfit. The boxed version was available only for separate sale and in promotional outfits. All the rolling stock included operating AAR trucks and couplers and came in a combination of Orange Perforated and Orange Picture boxes.

CONVENTIONAL PACK
61-380 BOX

3376-1 F	6062-1 S
	1013-70
	1025-25 S	6017-1 S
	6825-1 F
231P-1 S	

1008-50 TOP OF 3376-1
1018-30 TOP OF 6825-1
1020-25 UNDER 1013-70

A commonly included figure-eight track layout was provided, as detailed on the 1802B Layout Instruction Sheet.

The no. 61-380 Tan RSC with Black Graphics outfit box was manufactured by St. Joe Kraft, St. Joe Paper Company and measured 13¾ x 14 x 5⅛ inches. This was a single-level RSC, in that all the trains were packed on one layer.

Only 500 examples of this outfit were made, which explains why few have been reported.

Description: "O27" Promotional Outfit
Specification: "O27" Steam Type Freight Outfit With Smoke
Customer: Mercantile Stores
Original Amount: 500
Factory Order Date: 4/11/1961

Date Issued: Rev. #1 9-12-61
Packaging: R.S.C. Outfit Packing (Units Boxed)

Contents: 236-1 Steam Type Locomotive With Smoke; 1130T-1 Tender; 3509-1 Operating Satellite Launching Car (Manually); 3330-1 Flat Car With Operating Submarine (Kit); 6820-1 Aerial Missile Transport Car; 6017-1 Caboose; 1013-8 Curved Track (Bundle of 8 - 1013); 1013-90 Curved Track (Bundle of 9 - 1013);

Space and military outfit no. X-653 contained highly desirable upscale components that are difficult to find complete with original, unbroken peripherals. The Orange Perforated no. 6820-11 Folding Box and the Orange Picture no. 3509-6 Folding Box make this a highly desirable outfit.

1018-30 Straight Track (Bundle of 3 - 1018); 1018-75 Straight Track (Bundle of 6 - 1018); 1008-50 Uncoupling Track Section; 1025-25 45-Watt Transformer; 110-1 Trestle Set; 81-32 24" R.C. Wire (2); 1802I Layout Instruction Sheet; X602-10 Instruction Sheet; 310-2 Set of (5) Billboards; D61-50 Accessory Catalog

Boxes & Packing: 61-220 Corr. Outfit Box; 61-221 Corr. Shipper for (2) (1-2)

X-653 (1961)	C6	C7	C8	Rarity
Complete Outfit	700	1,325	2,000	R8
Outfit Box no. 61-220	200	400	600	R8

Comments: This was the second of two 1961 outfits purchased by Mercantile Stores Company, Inc. (the no. X-652 was the other one). Mercantile operated department stores in medium-sized cities during the 1960s. This Retailer Promotional Type Ib steam outfit could have been sold to any of its stores.

This space and military outfit included highly desirable upscale components. The no. 236-1 Steam Type Locomotive was new for 1961 and included smoke, a headlight and Magne-Traction. The Orange Picture box for the no. 3509-1 Oper. Satellite Launching Car (Manually) was available only in promotional outfits. (See outfit no. X-647 for more information on this car and its instruction flyer.)

A difficult item in this outfit to find in collectible condition is the Orange Perforated no. 6820-1 Aerial Missile Transport Car box. Although the 6820-1 was offered for separate sale in 1960 and 1961 and was a component of nine promotional outfits, this box seldom appears in collectible condition. (See outfit no. 9658

for more information about the no. 6820-100 Operating Missile Helicopter Complete.)

The X-653 also included a no. 3330-1 Flat Car With Operating Submarine (Kit). Finding one in C8 condition with an unassembled no. 3330-200 Submarine Kit and its parts still sealed in their plastic bag is becoming difficult.

All the rolling stock was equipped with operating AAR trucks and couplers. All the item instruction sheets came packaged within the item boxes. The nos. X602-10 Instruction Sheet, 1802I Layout Instruction Sheet and other peripherals were placed loose in the outfit box.

The no. 61-220 Orange RSC with Black Graphics outfit box was manufactured by Mead Containers, Inc. and measured 16⅜ x 13⅛ x 6¼ inches.

As with all space and military outfits, the no. X-653 is highly desirable. That fact, combined with its low production, leads to an R8 rating and the higher than normal price for the outfit box.

Be aware that this outfit was repeated in 1962, but with slightly different components and a different outfit box.

CONVENTIONAL PACK
61-220 BOX

TOP LAYER

1013-8 1018-75 1008-50	1018-30 1013-90
	3509-1 F
	3330-1 S
	236-1 S

BOTTOM LAYER

6017-1 S	1025-25	110-1 F
		6820-1 F
		1130T-1 F

Description: "O27" Promotional Outfit
Specification: "O27" Steam Type Freight Outfit with Smoke
Customer: Mercantile Stores
Original Amount: 150
Factory Order Date: 10/31/1962
Date Issued: 10-31-62
Packaging: R.S.C. Outfit Packing (Units Boxed), & Not Boxed

Contents: 233-1 Steam Type Locomotive With Smoke; 1130T-25 Tender; 3509-1 Oper. Satellite Launching Car; 3830-1 Oper. Submarine Car; 6820-25 Flat Car W/Oper. Missile Helicopter Car; 6017-1 Caboose; 1013-8 Curved Track (Bundle of 8 - 1013); 1013-90 Curved Track (Bundle of 9 - 1013); 1018-30 Straight Track (Bundle of 3 - 1018); 1018-75 Straight Track (Bundle of 6 - 1018); 1008-50 Uncoupling Unit; 1025-25 45-Watt Transformer; 110-1 Trestle Set; 81-32 24" R.C. Wire (2); 1123-40 Instruction Sheet; 233-11 Instruction Sheet; 122-10 Instruction Sheet; 1802I Layout Instruction Sheet

Boxes & Packing: 62-260 Outfit Box; 62-265 Shipper for (4) (1-4)

X-653 (1962)	C6	C7	C8	Rarity
Complete Outfit	925	1,600	2,200	R10
Outfit Box no. 62-260	500	800	1,050	R10

Comments: This was an almost exact repeat of Mercantile Stores' 1961 outfit no. X-653. Also a Retailer Promotional Type Ib, it was likely placed in one of Mercantile's retailer stores, as explained in the entry on outfit X-653 from 1961.

As with many carryover outfits, the original components were not always available in the subsequent year. Still a space and military outfit with some desirable upscale components, the 1962 version substituted a no. 233-1 Steam Type Locomotive for the no. 236-1. Both locomotives included smoke, a headlight and Magne-Traction. The no. 3509-1 Oper. Satellite Launching Car (Manually) remained. When boxed, it was available only in promotional outfits. The Orange Picture box for the 3509-1 is

difficult to find in collectible condition. (See outfit no. X-647 for more information on this car and its instruction flyer.)

Lionel used all but 69 units of the remaining no. 3330-1 Flat Car With Operating Submarine (Kit) in catalog outfit no. 11298 in 1962. Therefore, the no. 3830-1 Oper. Submarine Car replaced the 3330-1 in the 1962 version of this outfit. This car is common, especially compared to a 3330-1.

Two items now came unboxed: the nos. 1130T-25 Tender and 6820-25 Flat Car W/Oper. Missile Helicopter Car. Unfortunately, without its Orange Perforated no. 6820-11 Folding Box, this car is fairly common. (See outfit no. 9658 for more information about the no. 6820-100 Operating Missile Helicopter Complete.)

All the rolling stock came with operating AAR trucks and couplers. All the item instruction sheets came packaged within the item boxes. The nos. 122-10 Instruction Sheet, 1802I Layout Instruction Sheet and other peripherals were placed loose in the outfit box.

The no. 62-260 Tan RSC with Black Graphics outfit box measured 16¼ x 13 x 6⅜ inches and was used for six other outfits. This version of the X-653 came in a different box than did the 1961 version, so each outfit has its own price and rarity (in other words, they cannot be combined).

As with all space and military outfits, the 1962 version of the X-653 is highly desirable. That fact, combined with its extremely low production, leads to an R10 rating and the higher than normal price for the outfit box.

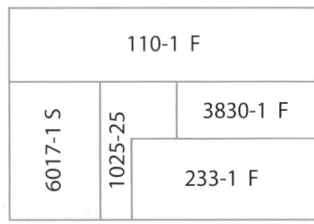

CONVENTIONAL PACK
62-260 BOX
1962 PRODUCTION

Description: "O27" Promotional Outfit
Specification: "O27" Diesel Freight Outfit
Customer/No./Price: Firestone; 11-L-346; $23.77
Original Amount: 1,000
Factory Order Date: 4/11/1961
Date Issued: Rev. #1 9-12-61
Packaging: Display Outfit Packing (Units not Boxed)

Contents: 1065-25 Alco Diesel Power Unit - "Union Pacific"; 6630-25 Missile Launching Car (Less Missile); 6650-80 Missile Complete (or 6650-84); 6480-25 Exploding Target Car; 3409-25 Operating Helicopter Launching Car (Manually); 6120-25 Work Caboose - "Union Pacific"; 1013-8 Curved Track (Bundle of 8 - 1013); 1018-10 Straight Track (Loose) (2); 1026-25 25-Watt Transformer; 1103-12 Envelope Packed; 1125-10 Instruction Sheet; 310-2 Set of (5) Billboards; D61-50 Accessory Catalog

Boxes & Packing: 61-398 Display Outfit Box; 61-391 Insert; 61-392 Insert; 61-393 Insert; 61-394 Insert; 61-395 Shipper for (6) (1-6)

Alternate For Outfit Contents:
Customer No. 11-L-346 to appear on outfit boxes & shippers.

X-654 (1961)	C6	C7	C8	Rarity
Complete Outfit	350	575	875	R7
Outfit Box no. 61-398	100	175	250	R7

Comments: Firestone Tire & Rubber Company purchased three promotional outfits in 1961, the no. X-654 and two advance catalog promotional outfits (nos. 1123 and 1124). This Retailer Promotional Type Ib was Firestone's high-end promotional offering in 1961.

A space and military outfit, the X-654 included all new-for-1961 rolling stock. Actually these new items were just low-end

Space and military outfit no. X-654 included all new-for-1961 promotional-only components. It was shown on page 34 of Firestone's 1961 catalog with a retail price of $23.77.

The no. 61-398 hinged display outfit box had "No. X-654" printed as part of the box manufacturing process.

versions of previously released cars that had been given non-operating Archbar trucks and couplers. The nos. 3409-25, 6480-25 and 6630-25 were low-end versions of the nos. 3419-25, 6470-25 and 6650-25, respectively. That being said, these cars appeared only in promotional outfits and are harder to find than their high-end counterparts, especially with original, unbroken helicopters and missiles.

The 6480-25 Exploding Target Car included "slotted" sides and a smooth roof door guide (without the nubs added later to help hold on the sides).

Also new for 1961 was the no. 1065-25 Union Pacific Alco Diesel Power Unit. This model was a follow-up to the no. 1055-25 *Texas Special* Alco. It moved forward only and lacked a traction tire and Magne-Traction. These low-end Alcos were used in promotional outfits.

The no. 61-398 White 4-6-4 Steamer and F3 Hinged Display with Red/Orange and Blue Graphics Type A outfit box measured 22½ x 14¾ x 3⅛ inches. This box was unique to outfit X-654, but it was also over-stickered and used for outfit nos. X-666 and 19197.

The Factory Order for this outfit says that the customer number "11-L-346" was to appear on the outfit boxes and shippers. Although some outfits have been observed with "11-L-346" written on them in grease pen, it does not appear that Lionel performed this task.

DISPLAY PACK
61-398 BOX

1065-25	3409-25
6480-25	6630-25
6120-25	
2-1018 8-1013	1026-25

X-655
1961

Description: "O27" Promotional Outfit
Specification: "O27" Steam Type Freight Outfit With Smoke
Customer: Cities Service
Original Amount: 200
Factory Order Date: 8/10/1961
Date Issued: 8-15-61
Packaging: R.S.C. Outfit Packing (Single Unit Packing), (Units Boxed)

Contents: 236-1 Steam Type Locomotive With Smoke; 1130T-1 Tender; 6062-1 Gondola Car - Black - With 3 Cable Reels; 6465-110 Two Dome Tank Car - "Cities Service"; 6519-1 Allis-Chalmers Car; 6017-1 Caboose; 1013-8 Curved Track (Bundle of 8 - 1013); 1013-90 Curved Track (Bundle of 9 - 1013); 1018-40 Straight Track (Bundle of 4 - 1018); 1018-5 Straight Track (Bundle of 5 - 1018); 1008-50 Uncoupling Track Section; 1025-25 45-Watt Transformer; 110-1 Trestle Set; 81-32 24" R.C. Wire (2); 1802I Layout Instruction Sheet; 1125-10 Instruction Sheet; 310-2 Set of (5) Billboards; D61-50 Accessory Catalog

Boxes & Packing: 61-220 Outfit Box; 61-221 Shipper for (2) (1-2)

Cities Service's only promotional outfit purchase in 1961, the no. X-655, contained the difficult-to-find boxed version of the no. 6465-110 Cities Service Two Dome Tank Car.

X-655 (1961)	C6	C7	C8	Rarity
Complete Outfit	670	1,050	1,425	R10
Outfit Box no. 61-220	450	650	850	R10

Comments: Cities Service, which later changed its name to CITGO, began purchasing promotional outfits in 1960. This Manufacturer Promotional Type IIIa was its only purchase for 1961.

Except for the no. 236-1 Steam Type Locomotive With Smoke (new for 1961), all the components were repeat items. As such, they came with early operating AAR trucks and couplers.

The most notable inclusion was the Orange Perforated no. 6465-103 Folding Box. It is difficult to find in collectable condition; in fact, this box is worth more than the no. 6465-110 Cities Service Two Dome Tank Car it holds.

All the peripherals were 1961 vintage, and the no. 1802I Layout Instruction Sheet (dated 5-59) detailed the elevated pretzel track layout.

The no. 61-220 Orange RSC with Black Graphics outfit box was manufactured by Mead Containers and measured 16⅜ x 13⅛ x 6¼ inches.

Despite being a smaller customer, Cities Service received major advertising exposure from Lionel. Besides two versions of its own tank car (the nos. 6045-50 and 6465-100), it received its own billboard on the 1961 and later no. 310-2 Set of (5) Billboards and the 1963 and later no. 310-62 Set of (3) Billboards.

With only 200 examples manufactured, the no. X-655 is a difficult outfit to find and has an R10 rarity.

CONVENTIONAL PACK
61-220 BOX

TOP LAYER

9-1013		5-1018	6465-110 F
8-1013			
6062-1 F			
1130T-1 F	1025-25		

4-1018 TOP 1130T

BOTTOM LAYER

110-1 F		1008-50
236-1 S	6017-1 S	
6519-1 F		

Description: "O27" Promotional Outfit
Specification: "O27" Steam Type Freight Outfit
Customer: AFA
Original Amount: 400
Factory Order Date: 9/12/1961
Date Issued: Rev. #1 9/12/61
Packaging: R.S.C. Outfit Packing (Units Boxed)

Contents: 246-1 Steam Type Locomotive; 244T-1 Tender; 6825-1 Trestle Bridge Flat Car; 6062-1 Gondola Car - Black - With 3 Cable Reels; 448-1 Missile Firing Range Set With Exploding Target Car; 6017-1 Caboose; 1013-8 Curved Track (Bundle of

8 - 1013); 1018-5 Straight Track (Bundle of 5 - 1018); 1008-50 Uncoupling Track Section; 1025-25 45-Watt Transformer; 260-1 Illuminated Bumper; 1022-75 L.H. Switch - Manual; 81-32 24" R.C. Wire (2); X657-10 Layout Instruction Sheet; X602-10 Instruction Sheet; 310-2 Set of (5) Billboards; D61-50 Accessory Catalog

Boxes & Packing: 61-250 Corr. Outfit Box; 61-251 Corr. Shipper for (4) (1-4)

X-657 (1961)	C6	C7	C8	Rarity
Complete Outfit	400	880	1,325	R9
Outfit Box no. 61-250	225	425	625	R9

The Air Force was a large customer of Lionel, offering its outfits in base exchange stores. The no. X-657 included one space and military item and the no. 244T-1 Tender in a no. 1625T overstamped Bold Classic Box.

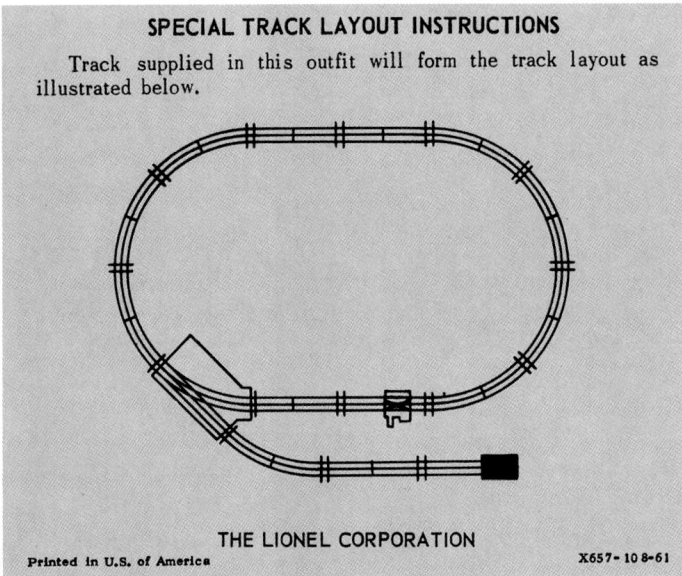

SPECIAL TRACK LAYOUT INSTRUCTIONS

Track supplied in this outfit will form the track layout as illustrated below.

THE LIONEL CORPORATION

Printed in U.S. of America   X657-10 8-61

The no. X657-10 Layout Instruction Sheet was unique to outfit no. X-657. With only 400 outfits produced, this rare sheet is seldom seen.

Comments: In 1961, the Air Force (AFA) purchased two promotional outfits (nos. X-657 and X-658). Fittingly, both outfits had a space and military theme, with the X-657 being headed by a steam locomotive and the X-658 by a diesel. Both were Retailer Promotional Type Ia outfits.

With the exception of the no. 448-1 Missile Firing Range Set With Exploding Target Car (both new for 1961), all items were carried over from previous years. The 448-1 was included in only two promotional (this was the only one in 1961) and two catalog outfits. It came boxed with a no. 6448-1 Exploding Target Range Car and the difficult-to-find in its original bag no. 448-5 Lichen Packed. A complete and collectible condition 448-1 is becoming difficult to find, as its Orange Picture box was fragile. This is the only space and military item in this outfit.

As noted, the 6448-1 Exploding Target Range Car was new

for 1961. According to the Production Control Files, as many of the variation with red sides and a white roof were made as the variation with white sides and a red roof. The version included in this outfit would be the early one with slots in the sides.

The X-657 was the last outfit – and the only one from 1961 – to include the no. 244T-1 Tender in its difficult-to-find no. 1625T overstamped Bold Classic Box. This was one of a few instances of a "Classic" box being used this far into the 1960s. Lionel probably did not expect the 244T to last this long; otherwise, it would have printed Orange Perforated or Orange Picture boxes.

The remainder of the rolling stock was commonly available, and all the items included operating AAR trucks and couplers.

The track layout was an oval with a spur. It was outlined on a no. X657-10 Layout Instruction Sheet that is extremely difficult to find.

The no. 61-250 Orange RSC with Black Graphics outfit box used for the X-657 was manufactured by Mead Containers and measured 13 x 12 x 7 inches.

Only 400 of these outfits were manufactured. So few are seen that it merits an R9 rating.

CONVENTIONAL PACK
61-250 BOX

TOP LAYER		
6825-1 F		
6062-1 F		1013-8
244T-1 S	1025-25	
6017-1 S		

1008 TOP OF 1013-8

BOTTOM LAYER	
246-1 F	
1018-5	
448-1 F	260-1

1022-75 TOP OF 448-1

The Air Force sold Lionel outfits in its base exchange stores. The no. X-658 is a big outfit that offered a lot of play value. Its space and military theme as well as its overall size create a high demand.

Description: "O27" Promotional Outfit
Specification: "O27" Diesel Freight Outfit
Customer: AFA
Original Amount: 500
Factory Order Date: 4/12/1961
Date Issued: Rev. #1 9-12-61
Packaging: R.S.C. Outfit Packing (Units Boxed)

Contents: 231P-1 Alco Diesel Power Car - "Rock Island"; 3665-1 Minuteman Missile Launching Car; 3519-1 Automatic Satellite Launching Car; 3830-1 Operating Submarine Car; 470-1 Missile Launching Platform; 6017-1 Caboose; 1013-8 Curved Track (Bundle of 8 - 1013); 1013-90 Curved Track (Bundle of 9 - 1013); 1018-30 Straight Track (Bundle of 3 - 1018); 1008-50 Uncoupling Track Section; 1025-25 45-Watt Transformer; 110-1 Trestle Set; 81-32 24" R.C. Wire (2); 1802I Layout Instruction Sheet; X602-10 Instruction Sheet; 310-2 Set of (5) Billboards; D61-50 Accessory Catalog

Boxes & Packing: 61-385 Corr. Outfit Box; 61-387 Corr. Shipper for (3) (1-3)

X-658 (1961)	C6	C7	C8	Rarity
Complete Outfit	800	1,225	1,650	R9
Outfit Box no. 61-385	350	500	600	R9

Comments: This was the second promotional outfit that the Air Force (AFA) purchased in 1961. Fittingly, both outfits had a space and military theme, with the no. X-657 headed by a steam locomotive and the no. X-658 by diesel. Both were Retailer Promotional Type Ia outfits.

This outfit was big and fun! The no. 6470-1 Exploding Target Car that was included in the no. 470-1 Missile Launching Platform didn't stand a chance. Both the no. 3665-1 Minuteman Missile Launching Car and the no. 470-1 Missile Launching Platform included missiles to fire at it.

The nos. 231P-1, 3519-1 and 3665-1 were all new for 1961. The 231P-1 Rock Island Alco was equipped with two-axle Magne-Traction, essential for this outfit's load. Also included was an elevated pretzel track layout.

The 470-1 appeared in 12 promotional and one catalog outfit in the 1960s. A 6470-1 Exploding Target Car came in the orange 470-1 corrugated box.

All rolling stock included a combination of early and middle operating AAR trucks and couplers. The boxes were a combination of Orange Perforated and Orange Picture.

Obtaining all 11 instructions sheets included with this outfit is a task unto itself. These as well as all the other peripherals were appropriate for 1961.

The no. 61-385 Tan RSC with Black Graphic outfit box was traditionally used with sub-base outfits and tightly packed this outfit. The X-658 and no. X-647 were the only two outfits without a sub base to use this box, which was manufactured by Mead Containers and measured 22 x 18¼ x 5¼ inches.

Even though only 500 of these outfits were manufactured, they still appear on the market, albeit in less than collectible condition. But the X-658 remains in high demand (hence, its stated value), thanks to its large configuration and exciting rolling stock and the generally high demand for space and military outfits.

CONVENTIONAL PACK
61-385 BOX

TOP LAYER

3519-1 F TOP OF 3365-1		
1013-8 TOP OF 3830-1		
1013-90 TOP OF 3830-1		
(3) 1018-30 TOP OF 110-1		
1008-50 TOP OF 470-1		

BOTTOM LAYER

470-1 F	3665-1 F	110-1 F	
3830-1 F	1025-25		
231P-1 S		6017-1 S	

Description: "O27" Promotional Outfit
Specification: "O27" Steam Type Freight Outfit
Customer: G. Fox & Company
Original Amount: 125
Factory Order Date: 6/2/1961
Date Issued: 6-7-61
Packaging: Display Outfit Packing (Units not Boxed)

Contents: 246-25 Steam Type Locomotive; 1050T-25 Tender; 6406-25 Single Automobile Car (Less Auto); 6406-30 Automobile; 6042-25 Gondola Car (Less 2 Canisters); 6112-5 Canister - Red (2); 6067-25 Caboose; 1013-8 Curved Track (Bundle of 8 - 1013); 1018-10 Straight Track (Loose) (2); 1026-25 25-Watt Transformer; 1103-12 Envelope Packed; 1119-10 Instruction Sheet; 310-2 Set of (5) Billboards; D61-50 Accessory Catalog

Boxes & Packing: 61-105 Display Outfit Box (with Stickers); 61-101 Corr. Insert; 61-102 Corr. Insert (2); 61-103 Corr. Shipper for (6) (1-6); ST 5 Stickers Per Box

X-659 (1961)	C6	C7	C8	Rarity
Complete Outfit	650	965	1,350	R10
Outfit Box no. 61-105	550	800	1,100	R10

Comments: This was the only promotional outfit purchased by G. Fox & Company department stores. It was a Retailer Promotional Type Ib outfit.

A typical low-end 1960s outfit, the no. X-659 did not contain any standout items. The most exciting item in today's market is the no. 6406-30 Automobile. A verified original postwar automobile with a gray bumper is always in demand.

The no. 246-25 Steam Type Locomotive was also a low-end item, though it did come with Magne-Traction.

The nos. 6042-25 Gondola Car, 6067-25 Caboose and 6406-25 Single Automobile Car were available in promotional outfits only, but the quantities produced were so large that they are readily available. All the rolling stock was equipped with non-operating Archbar trucks and couplers.

DISPLAY PACK
61-105 BOX
5 STICKERS PER BOX

246-25	1050T-25	1026-25
6042-25	6406-25	
2-1018 8-1013	6067-25	

As with most outfits, a no. 310-2 Set of (5) Billboards was included with the X-659. This item and the no. 1103-12 Envelope Packed are likely the most difficult items in this outfit to find in collectible condition.

The value of an X-659 depends largely on its over-stickered no. 61-105 White 4-6-4 Steamer and F3 Hinged Display with Red/Orange and Blue Graphics Type A outfit box. The box was manufactured by Express Container Corp. and measured 21½ x 11½ x 3⅛ inches.

Only 125 of these outfits were made, so it easily achieves an R10 rarity and a high price for its outfit box.

Description: "O27" Promotional Outfit
Specification: "O27" Steam Type Freight Outfit
Customer: Premium Service Corp.
Original Amount: 200
Factory Order Date: 4/28/1961
Date Issued: 5-19-61
Packaging: R.S.C. Outfit Packing (Units not Boxed)

Contents: 246-25 Steam Type Locomotive; 1060T-25 Tender; 6050-25 Savings Bank Car; 6406-25 Single Automobile Car (Less Auto); 6406-30 Automobile; 6162-25 Gondola Car - Blue (Less Canisters); 6112-88 Canisters (White) (3); 6067-25 Caboose; 1013-8 Curved Track (Bundle of 8 - 1013); 1018-30 Straight Track (Bundle of 3 - 1018); 1008-50 Uncoupling Track Section; 1025-25 45-Watt Transformer; 1103-12 Envelope Packed; 1641-10 Instruction Sheet; 310-2 Set of (5) Billboards; D61-50 Accessory Catalog

Boxes & Packing: 61-170 Corr. Outfit Box; 61-171 Corr. Insert; 61-172 Corr. Insert; 61-173 Corr. Insert; 61-175 Corr. Shipper for (4) (1-4)

X-660 (1961)	C6	C7	C8	Rarity
Complete Outfit	250	500	800	R8
Outfit Box no. 61-170	125	300	500	R8

Comments: Premium Service was an incentive merchandise company that purchased this Retailer Promotional Type Ib outfit in 1961 and again in 1962. Carrying over an outfit was a common practice with incentive merchandise and stamp companies, as the catalogs they provided to their customers could span several of Lionel's production years.

This outfit included three new items for 1961, including the unboxed nos. 6050-25 Savings Bank Car, 6067-25 Caboose and 6406-25 Single Automobile Car. Both the 6067-25 and 6406-25 appeared only in promotional outfits. The no. 246-25 Steam Type Locomotive was the low-end steam offering without smoke.

The no. X-660 came with a combination of non-operating Archbar (nos. 1060T-25, 6067-25 and 6406-25) as well as two operating AAR (nos. 6050-25 and 6162-25) trucks and couplers.

Both the 1961 and 1962 versions of this outfit came in a no. 61-170 Tan RSC with Black Graphics outfit box that measured 11½ x 10¼ x 6¼ inches.

Although there are some slight differences in components, the 1961 and 1962 versions of this outfit are basically the same. In fact, they both came in the same outfit box, so it would be difficult to tell them apart. Therefore, the quantities are combined for a total of 500 originally manufactured. This leads to a current supply R8 rarity. The only difference in value relates to changes involving the steam locomotive and no. 6050 box car.

CONVENTIONAL PACK
61-170 BOX

TOP LAYER

1008-50 ENV. 6050-25 1 CAN.
1060T-25 2 CAN.
8-1013 3-1018

BOTTOM LAYER

246-25	6067-25	1025-25 / 6406-30 6162-25 6406-25

293

Description: "O27" Promotional Outfit
Specification: "O27" Steam Type Freight Outfit
Customer: Premium Service Corp.
Original Amount: 300
Factory Order Date: 11/1/1962
Date Issued: 11-2-62
Packaging: RSC Outfit Packing (Units not Boxed)

Contents: 242-25 Steam Type Locomotive; 1060T-25 Tender; 6050-150 Savings Bank Car; 6406-25 Single Automobile Car; 6406-30 Automobile; 6162-25 Gondola Car (Less 3 Canisters); 6112-88 Canisters (White) (3); 6067-25 Caboose; 1013-8 Curved Track (Bundle of 8 - 1013); 1018-30 Straight Track (Bundle of 3 - 1018); 1008-50 Uncoupling Unit; 1025-25 45-Watt Transformer; 1103-20 Envelope Packed; 310-2 Set of (5) Billboards; D62-50 Accessory Catalog; 1123-40 Instruction Sheet; 1641-10 Instruction Sheet

Boxes & Packing: 61-170 Corr. Outfit Box; 61-171 Corr. Insert; 61-172 Corr. Insert; 61-173 Corr. Insert; 61-175 Corr. Shipper for (4) (1-4)

X-660 (1962)	C6	C7	C8	Rarity
Complete Outfit	265	525	830	R8
Outfit Box no. 61-170	125	300	500	R8

Comments: This is a repeat of outfit no. X-660 from 1961 with a few minor changes. Both outfits were Retailer Promotional Type Ib outfits purchased by Premium Service Corp., as explained in the entry on outfit X-660 from 1961.

This version of the X-660 included the no. 242-25 Steam Type Locomotive (new for 1962). This low-end steamer went on to become Lionel's workhorse, replacing the no. 246 as the basic steamer of choice and appearing in more than 55 catalog and promotional outfits through 1967. It had no smoke and used a rubber tire as a traction aid.

Also new in this outfit (as a replacement for the no. 6050-25 Savings Bank Car) was the no. 6050-150 Van Camp Savings Bank Car with Archbar trucks and couplers. Previously, this car has been incorrectly known as the number printed on the car "638-2361". However, the Factory Orders correctly identify this model by its proper number.

The remainder of this outfit was the same as in 1961, with the exception of the updated peripherals, instruction sheets and accessory catalog.

Both the 1961 and 1962 versions of the X-660 came in a no. 61-170 Tan RSC with Black Graphics outfit that measured 11½ x 10¼ x 6¼ inches.

Although there are some slight differences in components, the 1961 and 1962 versions of this outfit were basically the same. Indeed, both came in the same outfit box and are difficult to tell apart. Therefore, the quantities are combined for a total of 500 originally manufactured. This leads to a current supply R8 rarity. The only difference in value relates to changes involving the steam locomotive and 6050 box car.

See the entry for the X-660 from 1961 for a packing diagram.

Description: "O27" Promotional Outfit
Specification: "O27" Steam Type Freight Outfit
Customer: Uncle Bill
Original Amount: 855
Factory Order Date: 11/9/1961
Date Issued: Rev. #3 11-9-61
Packaging: Display Outfit Packing (Units not Boxed)

Contents: 1060-25 Steam Type Locomotive; 1050T-25 Tender; 3409-25 Oper. Helicopter Launching Car (Manually); 6406-25 Single Automobile Car (Less Auto); 6406-30 Automobile; 6067-25 Caboose; 1013-8 Curved Track (Bundle of 8 - 1013); 1018-10 Straight Track (Loose) (2); 1026-25 25-Watt Transformer; 1103-12 Envelope Packed; 1123-10 Instruction Sheet; 310-2 Set of (5) Billboards; D61-50 Accessory Catalog

Boxes & Packing: 61-105 Corr. Display Box; 61-101 Corr. Insert; 61-102 Corr. Insert (2); 61-103 Corr. Shipper for (6) (1-6)

X-661 (1961)	C6	C7	C8	Rarity
Complete Outfit	315	550	800	R7
Outfit Box no. 61-105	125	225	350	R7

Comments: The next three outfits (nos. X-661, X-662 and X-663) were purchased by Uncle Bill discount department stores. All three were Retail Promotional Type Ib outfits.

Outfit X-661 was Uncle Bill's steam-powered freight offering. It included low-end components common in entry-level outfits in the 1960s. The no. 1060-25 Steam Type Locomotive went only forward yet did include an operating headlight.

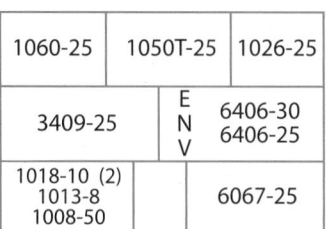

DISPLAY PACK
61-105 BOX

1060-25	1050T-25	1026-25
3409-25	ENV	6406-30 / 6406-25
1018-10 (2) / 1013-8 / 1008-50		6067-25

The no. 3409-25 Operating Helicopter Launching Car was the manual version of the no. 3419-25 and included Archbar trucks and couplers. It came only in promotional outfits. Its no. 3419-100 Operating Helicopter Complete had the square hole on the bottom that appeared with the introduction of the no. 6820-1 in 1960. All the remaining items were equipped with Archbar trucks and couplers and are readily available.

The no. 61-105 White 4-6-4 Steamer and F3 Hinged Display with Red/Orange and Blue Graphics Type A outfit box used for this outfit was manufactured by Express Container Corp. and measured 21½ x 11½ x 3⅛ inches. The outfit box was a no. 1123 outfit overstickered with X-661.

Description: "O27" Promotional Outfit
Specification: "O27" Diesel Freight Outfit
Customer: Uncle Bill
Original Amount: 550
Factory Order Date: 4/28/1961
Date Issued: Rev. #1 5-29-61
Packaging: Display Outfit Packing (Units not Boxed)

Contents: 1065-25 Alco Diesel Power Unit - "Union Pacific"; 3370-25 Animated Sheriff & Outlaw Car; 3330-25 Flat Car With Operating Submarine (Less Kit); 3330-200 Submarine Kit; 6042-25 Gondola Car (Less 2 Canisters); 6112-5 Canister - Red (2); 6067-25 Caboose; 1013-8 Curved Track (Bundle of 8 - 1013); 1018-10 Straight Track (Loose) (2); 1026-25 25-Watt Transformer; 1103-12 Envelope Packed; 1125-10 Instruction Sheet; 310-2 Set of (5) Billboards; D61-50 Accessory Catalog

Boxes & Packing: 60-145 Display Outfit Box; 60-146 Corr. Insert (2); 60-147 Corr. Insert; 60-148 Corr. Insert; 60-149 Corr. Insert; 60-150 Corr. Insert; 60-151 Corr. Shipper for (4) (1-4); ST 5 Stickers Per Box

X-662 (1961)	C6	C7	C8	Rarity
Complete Outfit	350	685	950	R8
Outfit Box no. 60-145	150	225	300	R8

Comments: This was the second of three 1961 outfits (nos. X-661 through X-663) purchased by Uncle Bill discount department stores. All three were Retail Promotional Type Ib outfits.

This outfit was Uncle Bill's diesel freight purchase headed by the no. 1065 Union Pacific Alco Diesel Power Unit (new for 1961). This model represented further cost "improvements" to the Alco line, as it had a closed pilot and went forward only.

The no. 3330-200 Submarine Kit (new for 1961) was included with the unboxed no. 3330-25 Flat Car With Operating Submarine (Less Kit). It consisted of the nos. 3330-108 Submarine Kit Parts Packed, 3830-103 Hull Half R.H Stamped, 3830-104 Hull Half L.H. Stamped, 4-7 Elastic Band and 3330-17 Instruction Sheet. The 3330-108 is the key item required in completing this outfit. Finding an all original one still sealed in its bag is becoming difficult.

The remaining nos. 3370-25 Animated Sheriff & Outlaw Car and 6067-25 Caboose were both new for 1961, but the no. 6042-25 Gondola Car was a repeat item. It is unknown whether the 3370-25 included in this outfit was the version with two operating Archbar trucks and couplers or the one with AAR trucks and couplers. The early Factory Order date would imply that it was the Archbar version and the outfit prices are based on that assumption.

DISPLAY PACK
60-145 BOX
5 STICKERS PER BOX

1065-25		1026-25	
3330-200 3330-25		3370-25	1018-10 (2) 1013-8
6067-25		2-6112-5 6042-25	

As with almost all promotional outfits, the required outfit box is the most difficult item to find. The X-662 came in a no. 60-145 Yellow Hinged Display with Steamer, General and F3 Graphic that was an over-stickered no. 1629 Type A outfit box. It measured 25½ x 12½ x 3 and was manufactured by KCC (Kraft Corrugated Containers).

These outfit boxes do appear on the market, but they are not the easiest to obtain in collectible condition.

Description: "O27" Promotional Outfit
Specification: "O27" Mobile Missile Launcher Freight Outfit
Customer: Uncle Bill
Original Amount: 200
Factory Order Date: 4/28/1961
Date Issued: Rev. #3 5-29-61
Packaging: R.S.C. Outfit Packing (Units not Boxed)

Contents: 45-25 Mobile Rocket Firing Car; 44-45 Envelope Packed; 6630-25 Missile Launching Car (Less Missile); 6650-80 Missile Complete (or 6650-84); 6480-25 Exploding Target Car; 3409-25 Operating Helicopter Launching Car (Manually); 6067-25 Caboose; 1013-8 Curved Track (Bundle of 8 - 1013); 1018-10 Straight Track (Loose) (2); 1025-25 45-Watt Transformer; 943-1 Exploding Ammo Dump; 81-32 24" R.C. Wire (2); CTC-1 Lockon; IS Instruction Sheet; 310-2 Set of (5) Billboards; D61-50 Accessory Catalog

Boxes & Packing: 61-250 Corr. Outfit Box; 61-173 Corr. Insert; 61-191 Corr. Insert; 61-193 Corr. Insert (2); 61-186 Corr. Insert; 61-251 Corr. Shipper for (4) (1-4)

X-663 (1961)	C6	C7	C8	Rarity
Complete Outfit	925	1,450	2,000	R10
Outfit Box no. 61-250	500	800	1,000	R10

Comments: This was the last of the three 1961 outfits (nos. X-661 through X-663) purchased by Uncle Bill discount department stores. All three were Retail Promotional Type Ib outfits.

This space and military outfit was headed by the unboxed no. 45-25 Mobile Rocket Firing Car. The X-663 was the only promotional outfit to include this desirable engine unboxed. When unboxed, it required a no. 44-45 Envelope Packed. This envelope did not include a no. CTC-1 Lockon, so Lionel had a dilemma. It could include a no. 1103-12 Envelope Packed, but doing so would duplicate the nos. 927-60 Oil Tube and 927-65 Lubricant already included in the 44-45. So Lionel simply added a CTC-1 Lockon loose in the outfit box. This is just one example of how an outfit was "engineered" to ensure that everything was included and nothing duplicated. It wasn't until 1962 that versions of outfit-packed envelopes were created with only wires and a lockon.

All the rolling stock in the X-663 was new for 1961. Actually, these new items were just low-end versions of previously released cars that had been given non-operating Archbar trucks and couplers. The nos. 3409-25, 6480-25 and 6630-25 were low-end versions of the nos. 3419-25, 6470-25 and 6650-25, respectively. That being said, these cars appeared only in promotional outfits and are harder to find than their high-end counterparts, especially with original, unbroken helicopters and missiles.

The 6480-25 Exploding Target Car included "slotted" sides and a smooth roof door guide (without the nubs added later to help hold on the sides).

A no. 943-1 Exploding Ammo Dump was a nice addition to any outfit and always came boxed and included a no. 943-11 Instruction Sheet dated 9-59.

The no. 61-250 Orange RSC with Black Graphics outfit box used for this outfit measured 13 x 12 x 7 inches. This generic box was used for more than 35 promotional and catalog outfits. Finding one stamped for outfit X-663 is a challenge, hence its R10 rating.

CONVENTIONAL PACK
61-250 BOX

TOP LAYER

1013-8 2 1018-10	44-45 ENV. 6630-25	943-1 6480-25	INSERT

BOTTOM LAYER

3409-25	
INSERT	
1025-25	6067-25
45-25	

X-664
1961

Outfit no. X-664 was offered to employees of trucking companies as a reward for safe driving and reduced maintenance costs.

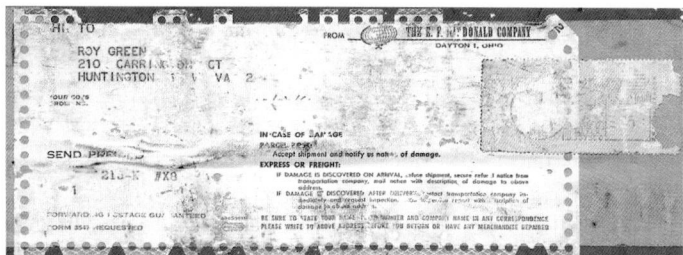

The shipping label from E. F. MacDonald on this no. X-664 outfit reveals that it was sent to Huntington, West Virginia. Note the E. F. MacDonald stock number "215-K", which also appears elsewhere on the outfit in grease pen. Unfortunately, the postmark is unreadable, so an exact date of shipment cannot be determined.

Description: "O27" Promotional Outfit
Specification: "O27" Steam Type Freight Outfit With Smoke & Whistle
Customer: E. F. MacDonald Co.
Original Amount: 1,000
Factory Order Date: 4/28/1961
Date Issued: 5-19-61

Packaging: R.S.C. Outfit Packing (Units not Boxed), Except Loco. & Tender & 6175-1 Car

Contents: 2037-1 Steam Type Locomotive With Smoke; 243W-1 Whistle Tender; 6162-25 Gondola Car - Blue (Less Canisters); 6112-88 Canisters (White) (3); 6050-25 Savings Bank Car; 6175-1 Rocket Car; 6405-25 Single Van Flat Car (Less Van); 6405-150 Van; 6057-25 Caboose (Red); 1013-8 Curved Track (Bundle of 8 - 1013); 1018-30 Straight Track (Bundle of 3 - 1018); 1008-50 Uncoupling Track Section; 1063-25 75-Watt Transformer; 81-32 24" R.C. Wire (2); 1648-10 Instruction Sheet; 310-2 Set of (5) Billboards; D61-50 Accessory Catalog

Boxes & Packing: 61-250 Corr. Outfit Box; 61-181 Corr. Insert; 61-182 Corr. Insert; 61-186 Corr. Insert; 61-191 Corr. Insert; 61-251 Corr. Shipper for (4) (1-4)

X-664 (1961)	C6	C7	C8	Rarity
Complete Outfit	280	500	710	R7
Outfit Box no. 61-250	60	100	150	R7

Comments: E. F. MacDonald Co., a leader in employee incentive rewards, purchased this outfit in 1961. The no. X-664 was offered as a reward for safe driving and reduced maintenance costs to the employees of trucking companies. It may have been used for other rewards as well. This Retailer Promotional Type Ia outfit was E. F. MacDonald's only purchase from Lionel in 1961.

The outfit retail cost was unknown. However, because the X-664 was a reward, we assume that it had a minimal – or no – retail cost.

This would have been a nice outfit to receive, as it included a no. 2037-1 Steam Type Locomotive With Smoke. This workhorse steamer spanned from 1953 through 1963 (except for 1956) and powered one Super O and 22 O27 outfits during the 1960s. When boxed as a "-1", it included the nos. 675-33 Smoke Stack Cleaner, SP-1 Smoke Pellets, 927-60 Tube of Oil, 2037-16 Instruction Sheet and CTC-1 Lockon.

The no. 243W-1 Tender came equipped with AAR trucks and ran from 1960 through 1963. Both the Type I no. 6050-25 Savings Bank Car and no. 6405-25 Single Van Flat Car (Less Van)

were new for 1961. When the 6405-25 was unboxed, as indicated by the "-25", the yellow no. 6405-150 Van was packed separately in the outfit box.

All the rolling stock featured operating AAR trucks and couplers. The no. 61-250 Orange RSC with Black Graphics outfit box used for this outfit was manufactured by Mead Containers and measured 13 x 12 x 7 inches.

CONVENTIONAL PACK
61-250 BOX

TOP LAYER			
6175-1	(3) 6112-88 6162-25	1013-8	243W-1 F

1008 TOP 243W-1

BOTTOM LAYER	
6405-25 6405-150 1018-30	
6050-25	1063-25
6057-25	
2037-1 F	

Description: "O27" Promotional Outfit
Specification: "O27" Steam Type Freight Outfit
Customer: J. C. Penney Co., Inc.
Original Amount: 750
Factory Order Date: 6/30/1961
Date Issued: 8-8-61
Packaging: Display Outfit Packing (Units not Boxed)

Contents: 1060-25 Steam Type Locomotive; 1050T-25 Tender; 6630-25 Missile Launching Car (Less Missile); 6650-80 Missile Complete (or 6650-84); 6480-25 Exploding Target Car; 3409-25 Operating Helicopter Launching Car (Manually); 6067-25 Caboose; 1013-8 Curved Track (Bundle of 8 - 1013); 1018-10 Straight Track (Loose) (2); 1026-25 25-Watt Transformer; 1103-12 Envelope Packed; 1123-10 Instruction Sheet; 310-2 Set of (5) Billboards; D61-50 Accessory Catalog

Boxes & Packing: 61-430 Display Outfit Box; 61-391 Corr. Insert; 61-392 Corr. Insert; 61-393 Corr. Insert; 61-394 Corr. Insert; 61-395 Shipper for (6) (1-6)

X-665 (1961)	C6	C7	C8	Rarity
Complete Outfit	330	575	925	R8
Outfit Box no. 61-430	125	225	400	R8

Comments: Lionel Factory Orders indicate that the next two outfits were the first to appear in J. C. Penney stores. J. C. Penney didn't enter the mail-order catalog business until 1963; therefore, this was the only known record of these outfits. Both outfits were Retailer Promotional Type Ib. Outfit no. X-665 was powered by a steamer, and no. X-666 was led by a diesel.

The Penney / Lionel relationship slowly began with this order for 750 outfits. Slowly, because Penney had 1,686 stores in 1961; so in the best case an outfit appeared in less than half of those outlets.

The X-665 was a space and military offering that had all new-for-1961 operating cars. Actually these new items were just low-end versions of previously released cars that had been given non-operating Archbar trucks and couplers. The nos. 3409-25, 6480-25 and 6630-25 were low-end versions of the nos. 3419-25, 6470-25 and 6650-25, respectively. That being said, these cars appeared only in promotional outfits and are harder to find than their high-end counterparts, especially with original, unbroken helicopters and missiles.

The remaining two items, nos. 1050T-25 Tender and 6067-25 Caboose, also were equipped with non-operating Archbar trucks and couplers.

DISPLAY PACK
61-430 BOX

1060-25	1050T-25
6630-25	6480-25
3409-25	6067-25
8-1013 2-1018	1026-25

Lastly, this low-end outfit was headed by the no. 1060-25 Steam Type Locomotive, which moved forward only. It took another two years before Lionel figured out a way to further cheapen this locomotive by releasing the no. 1061-25 without a headlight or crossheads.

The no. 61-430 White 4-6-4 Steamer and F3 Hinged Display with Red/Orange and Blue Graphics Type A outfit box measured 22½ x 14½ x 3⅛ inches. This outfit box was never reused for another outfit.

Collectors desire this outfit because it was the first of two outfits made exclusively for J. C. Penney. Even though 750 were made, it is seldom seen.

Description: "O27" Promotional Outfit
Specification: "O27" Diesel Freight Outfit
Customer: J. C. Penney Co., Inc.
Original Amount: 300
Factory Order Date: 6/30/1961
Date Issued: 8-8-61
Packaging: Display Outfit Packing (Units not Boxed)

Contents: 231P-25 Alco Diesel Power Car - "Rock Island"; 6406-25 Single Automobile Car (Less Auto); 6406-30 Automobile; 3509-25 Operating Satellite Launching Car (Manually); 3370-25 Animated Sheriff & Outlaw Car; 6050-25 Savings Bank Car; 6067-25 Caboose; 1013-8 Curved Track (Bundle of 8 - 1013); 1018-10 Straight Track (Loose) (2); 1026-25 25-Watt Transformer; 1103-12 Envelope Packed; 1125-10 Instruction Sheet; 310-2 Set of (5) Billboards; D61-50 Accessory Catalog

Boxes & Packing: 61-398 Display Outfit Box (W/Sticker); 61-391 Corr. Insert; 61-392 Corr. Insert; 61-393 Corr. Insert; 61-394 Corr. Insert; 61-395 Shipper for (6) (1-6); ST 5 Stickers Per Box

X-666 (1961)	C6	C7	C8	Rarity
Complete Outfit	475	700	1,000	R9
Outfit Box no. 61-398	225	450	625	R9

Comments: This is the second of the two outfits, along with no. X-665, to first appear in J. C. Penney stores. Since J. C. Penney didn't enter the mail-order catalog business until 1963, there is no record of these outfits beyond their Lionel Factory Orders. Both outfits were Retailer Promotional Type Ib. Outfit X-665 was powered by a steamer, and no. X-666 was headed by a diesel.

This outfit was made in lower quantities than was the X-665; therefore, it's even more difficult to find. J. C. Penney was still developing a business relationship with Lionel and so appeared reluctant to place large orders. That situation changed in later years.

The X-666 represented a step up from the X-665. Every item was new for 1961, including the no. 231P-25 Rock Island Alco Diesel Power Car. This locomotive included two-axle Magne-Traction, a headlight and a two-position reversing unit. A no. 6050-25 Savings Bank Car with two operating AAR trucks and couplers was also a nice upgrade from the non-operating Archbar trucks of the X-665.

The remainder of the rolling stock was equipped with either non-operating Archbar or operating AAR trucks and couplers. It is unknown if the no. 3370-25 Animated Sheriff & Outlaw Car was the early version with two operating Archbar or the later version with AAR trucks and couplers. The price of the outfit assumes the presence of the former variation.

The nos. 6067-25 Caboose and 6406-25 Single Automobile Car appeared only in promotional outfits, although they are both very common items.

The no. 61-398 White 4-6-4 Steamer and F3 Hinged Display with Red/Orange and Blue Graphics Type A outfit box was manufactured by UCC (United Container Co.) and measured 22½ x 14¾ x 3⅛ inches. This box was an overstickered outfit box from outfit no. X-654.

Collectors desire this outfit because it was one of the first two outfits made exclusively for J. C. Penney. With 300 made, it is seldom seen.

DISPLAY PACK 61-398 BOX 5 STICKERS PER BOX	
231P-25	3509-25
6050-25	3370-25
6406-25	6067-25
2-1018 8-1013	1026-25

Description: "O27" Promotional Outfit
Specification: "O27" Steam Type Freight Outfit With Smoke
Customer/No.: Gamble-Skogmo; B 23-2892
Original Amount: 3,000
Factory Order Date: 6/22/1961
Date Issued: Rev. #2 9/12/61
Packaging: Display Outfit Packing (Units not Boxed)

Contents: 236-25 Steam Type Locomotive With Smoke; 1060T-25 Tender; 3409-25 Operating Helicopter Launching Car (Manually); 6630-25 Missile Launching Car (Less Missile); 6650-80 Missile Complete (or 6650-84); 6480-25 Exploding Target Car; 6076-75 Hopper Car - Black; 6067-25 Caboose; 1013-70 Curved Track (Bundle of 12 - 1013); 1018-10 Straight Track (Loose) (4); 1025-25 45-Watt Transformer; 1020-25 90° Crossing; 909-10 Bottle Smoke Fluid; 1103-12 Envelope Packed; 1802B Layout Instruction Sheet; IS Instruction Sheet; 310-2 Set of (5) Billboards; D61-50 Accessory Catalog

Boxes & Packing: 61-420 Display Outfit Box; 61-392 Corr. Insert; 61-391 Corr. Insert; 61-421 Corr. Insert; 61-395 Shipper for (6) (1-6)

Alternate For Outfit Contents:
Special Instructions: Customer Stock No. B 23-2892 to appear on outfit box & shipper.

X-667 (1961)	C6	C7	C8	Rarity
Complete Outfit	300	500	750	R5
Outfit Box no. 61-420	75	100	150	R5

Comments: Discount retailer Gamble-Skogmo purchased this Retailer Promotional Type Ib outfit in 1961. Outfit no. X-667 was its only promotional outfit purchased in that year, as documented on the Factory Orders.

All the contents of this outfit, with the exception of the no. 1060T-25 Tender, were new for 1961. The no. 236-25 Steam Type Locomotive was Lionel's high-end Scout offering in 1961, and it was equipped with smoke, a headlight, a two-position reversing unit and Magne-Traction. When the 236-25 was unboxed ("-25" suffix), the nos. 909-10 Bottle of Smoke Fluid and 236-11 Instruction Sheet (dated 8-61) were placed loose in the outfit box.

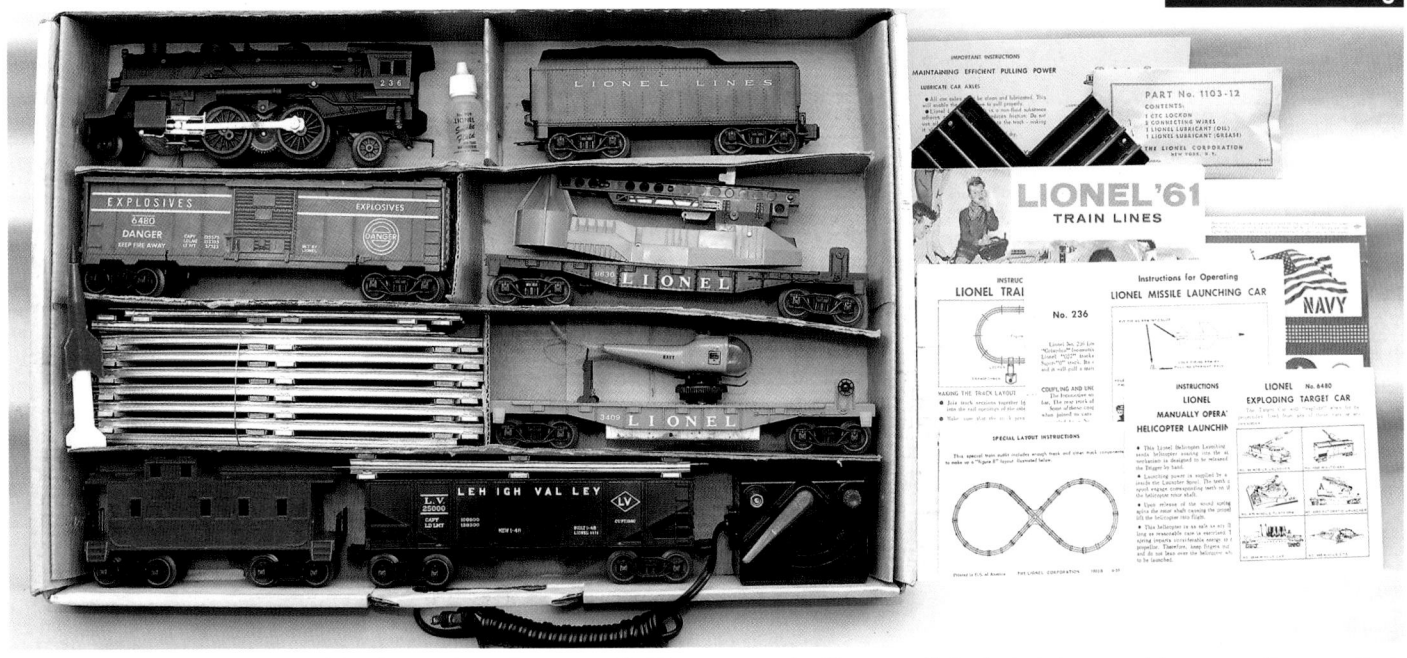

Lionel no. X-667 became Gamble-Skogmo's no. "B23-2892". This space and military outfit included three exciting operating cars that provided plenty of play value.

The no. 61-420 hinged display outfit box had "No. X-667" printed as part of the box manufacturing process.

Gamble-Skogmo's no. "B23-2892" was likely stamped by the retailer.

This space and military outfit included low-end versions of previously released cars with non-operating Archbar trucks and couplers. The nos. 3409-25, 6480-25 and 6630-25 were low-end versions of the nos. 3419-25, 6470-25 and 6650-25, respectively. That being said, these cars appeared only in promotional outfits and are harder to find than their high-end counterparts, especially with original, unbroken helicopters and missiles.

The 6480-25 Exploding Target Car included "slotted" sides and a smooth roof door guide (without the nubs added later to help hold on the sides).

DISPLAY PACK
61-420 BOX

236-25	909-10	1060T-25	E N V
6480-25		6630-25	
2-1018-10 1013-70		3409-25	
6067-25	2-1018-10 6076-75	1025-25	

1020-25 IN CUT OUT OF INSERT (61-421)

The commonly available nos. 1060T-25 and 6067-25 Caboose also included non-operating Archbar trucks and couplers.

A no. 1802B Layout Instruction Sheet detailed the figure-eight track layout. All the paperwork and peripherals followed the normal progression.

The no. 61-420 White 4-6-4 Steamer and F3 Hinged Display with Red/Orange and Blue Graphics Type A outfit box was manufactured by UCC (United Container Co.) and measured 22½ x 14¾ x 3⅛ inches. This box was unique to outfit X-667, but it was also over-stickered and used for 1962 outfit no. 19197.

The X-667 frequently appears on the market and has been observed with Gamble's "B23-2892" stamped on the front.

Description: "O27" Promotional Outfit
Specification: "O27" Steam Type Freight Outfit
Customer/No.: Signet; A-8901
Original Amount: 600
Factory Order Date: 3/24/1961
Date Issued: 5-19-61
Packaging: R.S.C. Outfit Packing (Units not Boxed)

Contents: 1060-25 Steam Type Locomotive; 1050T-25 Tender; 3409-25 Operating Helicopter Launching Car (Manually); 6076-75 Hopper Car - Black; 6406-25 Single Automobile Car (Less Auto); 6406-30 Automobile; 6067-25 Caboose; 1013-8 Curved Track (Bundle of 8 - 1013); 1018-10 Straight Track (Loose) (2); 1026-25 25-Watt Transformer; 1103-12 Envelope Packed; 1123-10 Instruction Sheet; 310-2 Set of (5) Billboards; D61-50 Accessory Catalog

Boxes & Packing: 61-170 Corr. Outfit Box; 61-171 Corr. Insert; 61-172 Corr. Insert; 61-173 Corr. Insert; 61-175 Corr. Shipper for (4) (1-4)

Alternate For Outfit Contents:
Customer Stock No. A-8901 to appear on outfit boxes & shippers.

X-668 (1961)	C6	C7	C8	Rarity
Complete Outfit	290	625	800	R8
Outfit Box no. 61-170	150	275	400	R8

Comments: Signet was listed on the Factory Orders for both this outfit and the no. X-669 in 1961. A common 1960s company name, the provenance of Signet has yet to be determined. As such, this outfit could have been a Retailer Promotional (Type Ib) or a Manufacturer Promotional (Type IIIb) outfit.

The no. X-668 was Signet's entry-level offering, headed by a promotional-only no. 1060-25 Steam Type Locomotive. This was Lionel's low-end (forward-only) steamer for 1961. With the exception of the no. 1050T-25 Tender, all the rolling stock was promotional only and new for 1961. The most notable car was the no. 3409-25 Operating Helicopter Launching Car (Manually). Obtaining one with an original, unbroken no. 3419-100 Operating Helicopter Complete takes a little effort.

All the rolling stock was equipped with non-operating Archbar trucks and couplers.

As with many low-end outfits, a no. 1026-25 25-Watt Transformer without a circuit breaker was included. Instruction sheets recommended that the customer purchase a separate no. 92 Circuit Breaker Controller.

The commonly used no. 61-170 Tan RSC with Black Graphics outfit box measured 11½ x 10¼ x 6¼ inches. With common components and outfit box and an unknown customer, the only thing this outfit has going for it is its low original quantity and high rarity.

CONVENTIONAL PACK
61-170 BOX

TOP LAYER

6406-30	3409-25
	1050T-25 6406-25
	2-1018 8-1013

BOTTOM LAYER

6076-75	1026-25	1060-25
	6067-25	

Description: "O27" Promotional Outfit
Specification: "O27" Steam Type Freight Outfit
Customer/No.: Signet; A8900
Original Amount: 400
Factory Order Date: 4/28/1961
Date Issued: Rev. #1 10-26-61
Packaging: R.S.C. Outfit Packing (Units not Boxed)

Contents: 246-25 Steam Type Locomotive; 244T-25 Tender; 3509-25 Oper. Satellite Launching Car (Manually); 3330-25 Flat Car With Operating Submarine (Less Kit); 3330-200 Submarine Kit; 6062-25 Gondola Car - Black (Less Cable Reels); 40-11 Cable Reels (3); 6017-25 Caboose; 1013-8 Curved Track (Bundle of 8 - 1013); 1018-30 Straight Track (Bundle of 3 - 1018); 1008-50 Uncoupling Track Section; 1025-25 45-Watt Transformer; 1103-12 Envelope Packed; 1641-10 Instruction Sheet; 310-2 Set of (5) Billboards; D61-50 Accessory Catalog

Boxes & Packing: 61-180 Outfit Box; 61-181 Corr. Insert; 61-182 Corr. Insert; 61-183 Corr. Insert; 61-184 Corr. Insert; 61-185 Shipper for (4) (1-4)

Alternate For Outfit Contents:
Note: Customer No. A8900 to appear on outfit boxes & shippers.

X-669 (1961)	C6	C7	C8	Rarity
Complete Outfit	390	650	1,025	R9
Outfit Box no. 61-180	200	325	500	R9

Comments: This was the second and last outfit to list Signet on its 1961 Factory Order. A common 1960s company name, the provenance of Signet has yet to be determined. As such, this outfit could have been a Retailer Promotional (Type Ia) or a Manufacturer Promotional (Type IIIa) outfit.

The no. X-669 was an upgrade from the no. X-668 and Signet's high-end offering for 1961. It was powered by a no. 246-25 Steam Type Locomotive (equipped with Magne-Traction), which Lionel introduced in 1959. In 1960, Lionel made noticeable changes to the 246 body, including closing the pilot and removing the small generator detail from the top in front of the cab. The X-669 included this later version of the steamer.

All the rolling stock, including the highly desirable no. 3330-25 Flat Car With Operating Submarine (Less Kit), was equipped with operating AAR trucks and couplers. Actually it is the no. 3330-200 Submarine Kit that makes this car desirable. To complete a C8 outfit, this kit must be all original and include a no. 3330-108 Submarine Kit Parts Packed still sealed in its plastic bag (a difficult item to find). Also notable was the no. 3509-25 Oper. Satellite Launching Car (Manually) (new for 1961).

CONVENTIONAL PACK
61-180 BOX

TOP LAYER

8-1013 3-1018
3-40-11 3330-25
3509-25

BOTTOM LAYER

246-25	
6017-25	1025-25
244T-25	
6062-25 3330-200	

1008-50 TOP OF 246-25

Although not listed on the Factory Order, all the individual item instruction sheets came loose in the outfit box. They, like all the peripherals, followed the normal progression for 1961.

A no. 61-180 Tan RSC with Black Graphics outfit box was used for this outfit and measured 12¾ x 10 x 6¾ inches.

The X-669 contained a better locomotive and rolling stock than did its companion X-668. That fact, along with its low original quantity, makes it a desirable outfit.

Description: "O27" Promotional Outfit
Specification: "O27" Diesel Freight Outfit
Customer: Montgomery Ward
Original Amount: 450
Factory Order Date: 11/9/1961
Date Issued: Rev. #2 11-9-61
Packaging: R.S.C. Outfit Packing (Units not Boxed)

Contents: 227P-25 Alco Diesel Power Car; 3370-25 Animated Sheriff & Outlaw Car; 6050-25 Savings Bank Car; 6042-25 Gondola Car (Less 2 Canisters); 6112-5 Canister - Red (2); 6120-25 Work Caboose - "Union Pacific"; 1013-8 Curved Track (Bundle of 8 - 1013); 1018-10 Straight Track (Loose) (2); 1026-25 25-Watt Transformer; 1103-12 Envelope Packed; 1125-10 Instruction Sheet; 310-2 Set of (5) Billboards; D61-50 Accessory Catalog

Boxes & Packing: 61-190 Corr. Outfit Box; 61-191 Corr. Insert; 61-192 Corr. Insert; 61-193 Corr. Insert; 61-195 Corr. Shipper for 4 (1-4)

X-670 (1961)	C6	C7	C8	Rarity
Complete Outfit	370	690	1,000	R9
Outfit Box no. 61-190	150	350	525	R9

Comments: Although Lionel trains did not appear in the Montgomery Ward catalog for 1961, they were still likely sold through its retail stores. Factory Orders list Montgomery Ward as the customer on the next three outfits (nos. X-670, X-671 and X-672).

Outfit X-670 was the entry-level diesel Retailer Promotional Type Ib Ward purchase. It featured a combination of low- and mid-level components. On the low end was the no. 227P-25 Canadian National Alco Diesel Power Car. This locomotive moved forward only and featured a closed pilot and a weight to aid in traction. Ironically, this low-end Alco is now a desirable collector piece.

The no. 6120-25 Union Pacific Work Caboose and no. 6042-25 Gondola Car were also low-end rolling stock with Archbar trucks and couplers. As with the 227P-25, the 6120-25 has become collectible. The last two cars were both mid-level Lionel offerings, including a no. 6050-25 Savings Bank Car with operating AAR couplers and a no. 3370-25 Animated Sheriff & Outlaw Car. It has yet to be determined whether the 3370-25 was the early version with Archbar trucks and couplers or the later version with AAR ones. However, the date of the Factory Order was late in the year, so the price of this outfit assumes the presence of the latter variation.

The remaining peripherals were placed loose in the outfit box, and all were appropriate for 1961.

The no. 61-190 Tan RSC with Black Graphics outfit box measured 12¼ x 9⅞ x 6¼ inches and was manufactured by Mead Containers.

After purchasing 3,036 outfits in 1960, Ward drastically scaled back its purchases in 1961. Of the 900 total outfits, half were the X-670. These do not show up too often, hence the R9 rating.

CONVENTIONAL PACK
61-190 BOX

TOP LAYER		BOTTOM LAYER	
6120-25		227P-25	
6042-25 (2) 6112-5		3370-25	1026-25
(2) 1018-10 1013-8		6050-25	

Description: "O27" Promotional Outfit
Specification: "O27" Diesel Freight Outfit
Customer: Montgomery Ward
Original Amount: 300
Factory Order Date: 5/8/1961
Date Issued: 5-23-61
Packaging: R.S.C. Outfit Packing (Units Boxed)

Contents: 231P-1 Alco Diesel Power Car - "Rock Island"; 3330-1 Flat Car With Operating Submarine (Kit); 3419-1 Operating Helicopter Car; 3545-1 Operating TV Monitor Car; 6017-1 Caboose; 1013-70 Curved Track (Bundle of 12 - 1013); 1018-30 Straight Track (Bundle of 3 - 1018); 6029-25 R.C. Uncoupling Track; 1025-25 45-Watt Transformer; 1020-25 90° Crossing; 90-30 Envelope Packed; 1802B Layout Instruction Sheet; 9670-10 Instruction Sheet; 310-2 Set of (5) Billboards; D61-50 Accessory Catalog

Boxes & Packing: 61-210 Corr. Outfit Box; 61-171 Corr. Insert; 61-184 Corr. Insert; 61-211 Corr. Shipper for (4) (1-4)

X-671 (1961)	C6	C7	C8	Rarity
Complete Outfit	670	1,150	1,750	R9
Outfit Box no. 61-210	200	400	600	R9

Comments: This was the second of three purchases made by Montgomery Ward in 1961 (nos. X-670, X-671 and X-672). These outfits were likely sold through its stores, as the Factory Orders are the only documentation available.

Outfit X-671 was Ward's high-end diesel Retailer Promotional Type Ia purchase. High-end in that all the items were boxed, and all the rolling stock was equipped with operating AAR trucks and couplers.

The new no. 231P-1 Rock Island Alco Diesel Power Car

included a headlight, two-axle Magne-Traction and an open pilot. The no. 3330-1 Flat Car With Operating Submarine (Kit) included the difficult-to-find no. 3330-200 Submarine Kit. Finding a 3330-1 in C8 condition with an unassembled 3330-200 and its parts still sealed in their plastic bag is becoming difficult.

When boxed ("-1" suffix), the no. 3419-1 Operating Helicopter Car included a no. 3419-100 Operating Helicopter Complete. Also included in the box was the no. 3419-51 Instruction Sheet.

The no. 3545-1 Operating TV Monitor Car was new for 1961 and the X-671 marked its only promotional outfit appearance during the year.

Ten outfits, all promotional items, came with a no. 6029-25 R.C. Uncoupling Track. This upgrade allowed the remote uncoupling of cars as opposed to the manual no. 1008-50 Uncoupling Track Section. A no. 90-30 Envelope Packed included the no. 90 Controller to operate the 6029-25.

The X-671 also included a figure-eight track layout. It and the other common peripherals and paperwork were packed loose in most 1961 outfits.

The no. 61-210 Orange RSC with Black Graphics outfit box was manufactured by Mead Containers and measured 13⅞ x 13¼ x 6½ inches.

As with the X-670 and X-672, this outfit was produced in low quantities. With only 300 examples manufactured, this outfit does not show up too often, hence the R9 rating.

CONVENTIONAL PACK
61-210 BOX

TOP LAYER		
3419-1 F		
INSERT 61-171		1018-30 INSERT 61-184
6017-1 S	ENV.	
3330-1 S		

BOTTOM LAYER		
6029-25 1013-70 S		1025-25
231P-1 F		
3545-1 F		

1020-25 TOP OF LAYER

Outfit no. X-672, Montgomery Ward's high-end offering for 1961, is a true collectible. Besides the fact that only 150 were made, it included the rare no. 2093 Layout Instruction Sheet and no. 233-10 Corrugated Box.

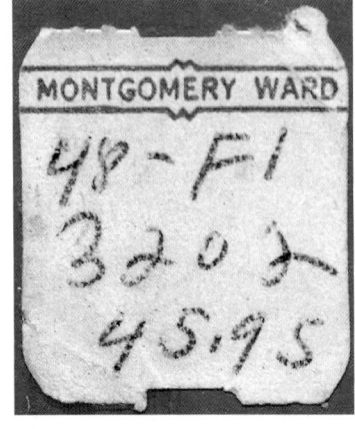

The price tag confirms that this outfit was offered through Montgomery Ward retail stores. It also provides the Ward number and retail price.

Description: "O27" Promotional Outfit
Specification: "O27" Steam Type Freight Outfit With Smoke & Whistle
Customer/No./Price: Montgomery Ward; 48-F1 3202; $45.95
Original Amount: 150
Factory Order Date: 5/8/1961
Date Issued: Rev. #1 5-29-61
Packaging: R.S.C. Outfit Packing (Units Boxed)

Contents: 233-1 Steam Type Locomotive With Smoke; 233W-1 Whistle Tender; 3519-1 Automatic Satellite Launching Car; 6343-1 Barrel Ramp Car; 3376-1 Operating Giraffe Car; 6017-1 Caboose; 1013-8 Curved Track (Bundle of 8 - 1013) (2); 1013-65

Curved Track - ½ Section; 1018-5 Straight Track (Bundle of 5 - 1018); 1018-30 Straight Track (Bundle of 3 - 1018) (2); 1008-50 Uncoupling Track Section; 1063-100 75-Watt Transformer; 110-1 Trestle Set; 81-32 24" R.C. Wire (2); 2093 Layout Instruction Sheet; IS Instruction Sheet; 310-2 Set of (5) Billboards; D61-50 Accessory Catalog

Boxes & Packing: 61-220 Corr. Outfit Box; 61-221 Corr. Shipper for (2) (1-2)

X-672 (1961)	C6	C7	C8	Rarity
Complete Outfit	830	1,325	1,900	R10
Outfit Box no. 61-220	500	750	1,000	R10

Comments: This was the last of three purchases made by Montgomery Ward in 1961 (nos. X-670, X-671 and X-672). These outfits were likely sold through its stores, as the Factory Orders are the only documentation available.

Of the three outfits, the X-672 is by far the most collectible. Besides having only 150 manufactured, this Retailer Promotional Type Ib included an attractive consist of rolling stock and a track plan used only once before.

The new no. 233-1 Steam Type Locomotive With Smoke was Lionel's high-end Scout offering in 1961. Finding its matching no. 233-10 Corrugated Box is a true challenge. The 233-1 included smoke, a two-position reversing unit and Magne-Traction. Better yet, it was paired with a no. 233W-1 Whistle Tender.

As with other outfits that included a Scout steamer and whistling tender, the "-100" version of the no. 1063-100 75-Watt Transformer was used. This transformer included a green whistle control button to indicate changes to the whistle control circuitry to prevent Scout-type locomotives from inadvertently reversing. Its Lionel Production Control File states, "Rubber Stamped '1063-

100' on Bottom of Base Plate Assembly using White Ink." This transformer is harder to find than a regular no. 1063-25 75-Watt Transformer (with a red whistle button).

The cars included the nos. 3519-1 Automatic Satellite Launching Car and 6343-1 Barrel Ramp Car (both new for 1961) in Orange Picture boxes as well as the previously issued nos. 3376-1 Operating Giraffe Car and 6017-1 Caboose. All the cars were equipped with operating AAR trucks and couplers.

The commonly used no. 61-220 Orange RSC with Black Graphics outfit box was manufactured by Mead Containers and measured 13⅞ x 13¼ x 6½ inches.

Along with the no. 61-220 Corr. Outfit Box and 233-10 Corrugated Box, the no. 2093 Layout Instruction Sheet is a difficult item to find. Its Lionel Production Control File indicates that 4,000 were ordered on 6/29/60 (for outfit no. X-511NA) and then another 200 on 8/1/61. A quantity of 4,200 may sound like a lot, but most did not survive and so are seldom seen. The layout was a slightly modified elevated-pretzel layout, with a place for the "Giraffe Car Signal".

For collectors specializing in promotional outfits, especially those sold through Montgomery Ward, the X-672 is a desirable item, although it is difficult to complete.

CONVENTIONAL PACK
61-220 BOX

TOP LAYER: 6343-1 F; 3519-1 F; (2) 1013-8 S; 1013-65; 1018-5; 1008-50; 1018-30

BOTTOM LAYER: 233-1 S; 3376-1 S; 233W-1 S; 110-1 S; 1063-100 S; 6017-1 S; 1018-30

Description: "O27" Promotional Outfit
Specification: "O27" Steam Type Freight Outfit
Customer/No./Price: T. Eaton; 027-G-1211; $18.96
Original Amount: 2,000
Factory Order Date: 6/23/1961
Date Issued: Rev. #2 10/9/61
Packaging: Display Outfit Packing (Units not Boxed)

Contents: 1060-25 Steam Type Locomotive; 1050T-25 Tender; 6406-25 Single Automobile Car (Less Auto); 6406-30 Automobile; 6042-25 Gondola Car (Less 2 Canisters); 6112-5 Canister - Red (2); 6067-25 Caboose; 1013-8 Curved Track (Bundle of 8 - 1013); 1018-10 Straight Track (Loose) (2); 1025-25 45-Watt Transformer; 1103-12 Envelope Packed; 1123-30 Instruction Sheet; D61-50 Accessory Catalog; 310-2 Set of (5) Billboards

Boxes & Packing: 61-422 Display Outfit Box; 61-101 Corr. Insert; 61-102 Corr. Insert (2); 61-103 Corr. Shipper for (6) (1-6); 61-105 Display Outfit Box With 5 Stickers

Alternate For Outfit Contents:
Note: Use 300 - 61-105 Display Outfit Box With 5 Stickers in place of 61-422 Box.

X-673 (1961)	C6	C7	C8	Rarity
Complete Outfit With no. 61-422 Box	150	300	460	R6
Outfit Box no. 61-422	50	125	200	R6
Complete Outfit With no. 61-105 Box	200	425	660	R9
Outfit Box no. 61-105	100	250	400	R9

Comments: T. Eaton was a Canadian retailer that sold Lionel outfits in its catalog. In 1961, the firm purchased one Retailer Promotional Type Ib outfit. It appeared on page 240 of the Eaton Christmas Catalog for 1961 as no. 027-G-1211 for $18.96.

The no. X-673 was a low-end display-packed outfit that included nothing special. The no. 1060-25 Steam Type Locomotive, which moved only forward, was about as cheap as you could get in 1961.

Although the nos. 6042-25 Gondola Car, 6067-25 Caboose and 6406-25 Single Automobile Car were all promotional-only items, they are commonly available today. All the items featured non-operating Archbar trucks and couplers.

Three pieces would make this outfit somewhat of a challenge

303

T. Eaton featured outfit no. X-673 in its 1961 Christmas Catalog. The most exciting items in this outfit are the nos. 6406-30 Automobile, 310-2 Set of (5) Billboards and the surprisingly uncommon 1123-30 Instruction Sheet.

The no. 61-422 hinged display outfit box had "No. X-673" printed as part of the box manufacturing process.

DISPLAY PACK 61-422 BOX		
1060-25	1050T-25	1025-25
6042-25	E N V	6406-30
		6406-25
2-1018 8-1013		6067-25

Two versions of a White 4-6-4 Steamer and F3 Hinged Display with Red/Orange and Blue Graphics Type A outfit box were used for this outfit. The first, no. 61-422, was stamped from the manufacturer with "X-673" and measured 21¾ x 11⅜ x 3⅛ inches. The second, no. 61-105 (no. 1123 overstickered), was manufactured by Express Container Corp. and measured 21½ x 11½ x 3⅛ inches.

to complete: an original yellow with gray-bumpers no. 6406-30 Automobile; a complete strip of no. 310-2 Set of (5) Billboards; and the surprisingly uncommon no. 1123-30 Instruction Sheet.

The no. 61-422 box version of this outfit appears frequently, although not often in collectible condition. By contrast, the no. 61-105 version is seldom seen.

Description: "O27" Promotional Outfit
Specification: "O27" Mobile Missile Launcher Freight Outfit
Original Amount: 200
Factory Order Date: 8/22/1961
Date Issued: Rev. #1 8/22/61
Packaging: R.S.C. Outfit Packing (Units Boxed)

Contents: 45-1 Mobile Rocket Firing Car; 6530-1 Fire & Safety Training Car; 3519-1 Automatic Satellite Launching Car; 3830-1 Operating Submarine Car; 470-1 Missile Launching Platform; 3535-1 Security Car; 1013-8 Curved Track (Bundle of 8 - 1013) (2); 1018-30 Straight Track (Bundle of 3 - 1018); 1008-50 Uncoupling Track Section; 1043-50 60-Watt Transformer; 943-1 Exploding Ammo Dump; 1023-25 45° Crossing; 910-1 Navy Yard Cardboard Display; 1802H Layout Instruction Sheet; IS Instruction Sheet; 310-2 Set of (5) Billboards; D61-50 Accessory Catalog

Boxes & Packing: 61-385 Corr. Outfit Box; 61-387 Corr. Shipper (1-3); BP Bogus Paper

Alternate For Outfit Contents:
Note: Use 64 - 1043-50; Use 136 - 1043-1; Include 2 - 81-32 when using unpacked transformer.

X-676 (1961)	C6	C7	C8	Rarity
Complete Outfit	7,750	11,250	15,550	R10
Outfit Box no. 61-385	800	1,200	1,500	R10

Comments: This was the second of three (see also the entries for the nos. X-625 and X-714) 1961 outfits to include a no. 910-1 Navy Yard Cardboard Display (also known as the Atomic Sub Base). This General Release Promotional Type IIb outfit was the same as the X-714 (Retailer Promotional for Masters) with the exception that the no. X-676 also included a no. 470-1 Missile Launching Platform.

Factory Orders for both of these outfits have the same creation

The extremely rare no. 910-1 Navy Yard Cardboard Display (sub base) included 10 cardboard pieces and an unnumbered instruction sheet, all placed in a tan-colored paper bag (not shown).

date, making it a possibility that Lionel developed this General Release Promotional outfit to provide its smaller customers with an opportunity to purchase a sub-base outfit. The X-676 was likely manufactured concurrently with the 413 units of X-714.

As with other outfits including a sub base, it is the 910-1 Navy Yard Cardboard Display that makes this outfit extremely rare today. The 910-1 was a fragile cardboard display intended to be assembled by the customer. There were no Lionel markings on this item, and it frequently became separated from the train outfit and destroyed. Stories exist of individuals who discarded a 910-1 Navy Yard Cardboard Display because they did not know what it was.

All 10 cardboard pieces that made up the sub base were placed in a plain tan-colored flat paper bag, which was laid on the bottom of the outfit box.

Even though it is the sub base that makes this outfit so desirable, the other contents were all high-end 1960s offerings that fit the space and military theme. Specifically, a complete olive drab no. 45-1 Mobile Rocket Firing Car is a collectible item when combined with its no. 45-20 Corrugated Box, no. 44-43 Corrugated Insert and no. 44-45 Envelope Packed.

Other notable items included the Orange Perforated boxed nos. 6530-1 Fire & Safety Training Car and 3535-1 Security

Car. These items always added color to outfits. The no. 3830-1 Operating Submarine Car was appropriate for this outfit.

The only new car was the Orange Picture boxed no. 3519-1 Automatic Satellite Launching Car. It was equipped, as were all the cars, with operating AAR trucks and couplers.

This outfit provided youngsters with lots to do, including plenty of items to shoot and be fired on. The nos. 943-1 Exploding Ammo Dump and 6470-1 Exploding Target Car (included in the no. 470-1) were the targets of missiles launched by the 45-1 and 470-1. The pretzel layout that was included with this and other sub-base outfits also provided excitement, as the train would weave in and out of the sub-base tunnels.

The no. 61-385 Tan RSC with Black Graphics outfit box was the same as used on the other 1961 and 1962 sub-base outfits. It was manufactured by Mead Containers and measured 22 x 18¼ x 5¼ inches. "Bogus Paper", which was actually wadded Kraft paper, was used to fill the empty space in this large outfit box.

There is a small but dedicated group of collectors that strives to obtain all the sub-base outfits. Doing so will become more difficult now that, thanks to this volume, the true number of different outfits that included the 910-1 is known. Of these outfits, the X-676 and no. 19203 from 1962 were produced in the lowest quantities and so are most difficult to obtain.

Note that the price of this outfit assumes the unnumbered "How to Assemble Your Lionel Atomic Submarine Base" instruction sheet as well. The no. 1043-50 Transformer substitution does not affect the price.

CONVENTIONAL PACK
61-385 BOX

910 BOTTOM

3535-1 F	943-1 F	1043 50	1008-50 3-1018
3519-1 S			
		45-1 S	TOP 3535
470-1	6530-1 F	3830-1 S	1023-25 TOP 3519
			8-1013 TOP 6530

Description: "O27" "General" Promotional
Specification: "O27" "General" Freight Outfit With Smoke & Whistle
Original Amount: 30
Factory Order Date: 7/24/1961
Date Issued: 8/2/61
Packaging: R.S.C. Outfit Packing (Units Boxed)

Contents: 1872X-1 "General" Locomotive - With Smoke; 1872T-1 Tender; 3370-1 Animated Sheriff & Outlaw Car; 6445-1 Ft. Knox Gold Bullion Transport Car; 1876-1 Illuminated Mail & Baggage Car; 1875W-1 Illuminated Passenger Car With Whistle; 1013-8 Curved Track (Bundle of 8 - 1013); 1018-30 Straight Track (Bundle of 3 - 1018); 1008-50 Uncoupling Track Section; 1063-25 75-Watt Transformer; CTC Lockon; 81-32 24" R.C. Wire (2); IS Instruction Sheet; 310-2 Set of (5) Billboards; D61-50 Accessory Catalog

Boxes & Packing: 60-250 Outfit Box (W/Sticker); 60-251 Shipper for (4) (1-4)

X-677 (1961)	C6	C7	C8	Rarity
Complete Outfit	1,765	2,700	3,300	R10
Outfit Box no. 60-250	1,200	1,700	2,000	R10

Comments: In what turns out to have been a preview of things to come, General Release Promotional Type IIa outfit no. X-677 included the same trains as did Super O catalog outfit no. 13036 from 1962, except that the 13036 cars were all unboxed. Of course, with only 30 factory orders, this outfit is far more difficult to obtain than the 13036, which had 675 examples ordered.

The no. 1872X-1 General Locomotive was Lionel's premier old-time locomotive, being equipped with smoke, a three-position reversing unit and Magne-Traction. This outfit was the only time it was cataloged as an O27 item.

As described in the Outfit Peripherals section, when motive power included an "X" suffix (as in 1872X), it meant that the locomotive came boxed without a no. CTC Lockon inside. The CTC Lockon was loose in the outfit box. The "X" did not appear on the no. 1872-70 Corrugated Box and was likely an indicator for the Outfit Packing Department.

The nos. 3370-1 Animated Sheriff & Outlaw Car and 6445-1 Fort Knox Gold Bullion Transport Car were both new items for 1961 and came boxed in Orange Picture boxes. Pay careful attention to 6445-1s, as the little nubs below the windows are easily broken off. A C8 item would include all of these. The 6445-1 came equipped with operating AAR trucks and couplers.

The two passenger cars were both equipped with Archbar trucks and operating couplers. When in other outfits, they were most often unboxed.

By far the biggest difference between this outfit and the 13036 is that this was an O27 entry and the latter was Super O. Therefore, all the track and peripherals were different. Also, catalog Super O outfits typically did not come with transformers.

The no. 60-250 Tan RSC with Black Graphics outfit box used for this outfit was an overstickered RSC version of the no. 2547WS.

The reason Lionel produced only 30 of this outfit has yet to be determined. It wasn't to deplete inventory – all the items were available in 1962.

With only 30 factory orders, the X-677 ranks sixth on the list of lowest original quantities and is one of the most difficult outfits to find.

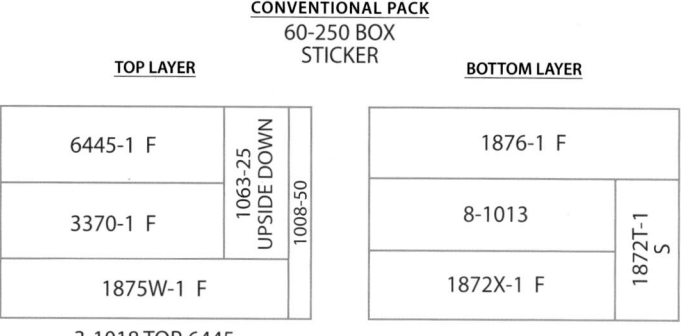

CONVENTIONAL PACK
60-250 BOX

X-678
1961

Description: "O27" Promotional Outfit
Specification: "O27" Steam Type Freight Outfit
Original Amount: 375
Factory Order Date: 5/17/1961
Date Issued: 6-7-61
Packaging: R.S.C. Outfit Packing (Units Boxed)

Contents: 246-1 Steam Type Locomotive; 1130T-1 Tender; 3370-1 Animated Sheriff & Outlaw Car; 6519-1 Allis-Chalmers Flat Car; 6428-1 U. S. Mail Car; 6817-1 Flat Car - Red - With Motor Scraper; 6017-1 Caboose; 1013-8 Curved Track (Bundle of 8 - 1013); 1018-30 Straight Track (Bundle of 3 - 1018); 1008-50 Uncoupling Track Section; 1025-25 45-Watt Transformer; 81-32 24" R.C. Wire (2); X602-10 Instruction Sheet; 310-2 Set of (5) Billboards; D61-50 Accessory Catalog

Boxes & Packing: 61-250 Corr. Outfit Box; 61-251 Corr. Shipper for (4) (1-4)

X-678 (1961)	C6	C7	C8	Rarity
Complete Outfit	950	1,350	1,800	R9
Outfit Box no. 61-250	300	450	550	R9

Comments: This General Release Promotional Type IIa has yet to be linked to a particular retailer. Without a specific customer in mind, it appears that Lionel was assembling a mid-level freight outfit for its sales staff to offer smaller retailers.

The corrugated boxed no. 246-1 Steam Type Locomotive was still heading outfits some two years after its original appearance in 1959. It went through body changes in 1960, including the addition of a solid pilot and the deletion of the small generator detail on its top in front of the cab. Equipped with a two-position reverse unit as well as Magne-Traction, it was a respectable little low-end engine.

The no. 3370-1 Animated Sheriff & Outlaw Car was new for 1961, whereas the other items were all repeats and included operating AAR trucks and couplers. The most notable piece was the inclusion of the no. 6817-1 Flat Car - Red - With Motor Scraper. It included the extremely fragile no. 6817-111 Earth Scraper Complete. Finding these in original, unbroken condition is becoming a real challenge.

The nos. 6428-1 U.S. Mail Car and 6519-1 Allis-Chalmers Flat Car are fairly common and can be obtained in collectable condition with some patience. All the rolling stock was boxed in either Orange Perforated or Orange Picture boxes.

The no. 61-250 Orange RSC with Black Graphics outfit box measured 13 x 12 x 7 inches. This outfit had only 375 original factory orders and is seldom seen, which leads to its rarity rating of R9.

CONVENTIONAL PACK
61-250 BOX

Description: "O27" Promotional Outfit
Specification: "O27" Diesel Freight Outfit
Original Amount: 460
Factory Order Date: 5/17/1961
Date Issued: 6-7-61
Packaging: R.S.C. Outfit Packing (Units Boxed)

Contents: 231P-1 Alco Diesel Power Car - "Rock Island"; 3419-1 Operating Helicopter Car; 6428-1 U.S. Mail Car; 6530-1 Fire & Safety Training Car; 6817-1 Flat Car - Red - With Motor Scraper; 6017-1 Caboose; 1013-8 Curved Track (Bundle of 8 - 1013); 1013-90 Curved Track (Bundle of 9 - 1013); 1018-30 Straight Track (Bundle of 3 - 1018); 1018-75 Straight Track (Bundle of 6 - 1018); 1008-50 Uncoupling Track Section; 1043-50 60-Watt Transformer; 110-1 Trestle Set; 81-32 24" R.C. Wire (2); 1802I Layout Instruction Sheet; IS Instruction Sheet; 310-2 Set of (5) Billboards; D61-50 Accessory Catalog

Boxes & Packing: 61-416 Corr. Outfit Box; 61-417 Corr. Shipper for (3) (1-3); BP Bogus Paper

X-679 (1961)	C6	C7	C8	Rarity
Complete Outfit	985	1,500	2,075	R9
Outfit Box no. 61-416	275	400	525	R9

Comments: Another in a series of General Release Promotional outfits for 1961, the Type IIa no. X-679 was probably aimed at smaller retailers seeking a promotional outfit.

The Factory Order was assigned a date that was early in Lionel's outfit cycle: 5-17-61. This fact demonstrates that General Release Promotional outfits were part of Lionel's overall planning and not just end-of-year afterthoughts. They were created early enough for salesmen to actively peddle to their accounts. Outfit X-679 could be considered the diesel counterpart to the no. X-678 because all the rolling stock was comparable.

The corrugated boxed no. 231P-1 Rock Island Alco included a two-position reversing unit, an open pilot and two-axle Magne-Traction. This last feature was necessary for the locomotive to pull the attached cars up the elevated pretzel layout.

All the rolling stock came equipped with two operating AAR trucks and couplers. If an item came with an instruction sheet, it was included in its individual box; otherwise, all the remaining instruction sheets and peripherals were placed loose in the outfit box.

The notable items included the no. 3419-1 Operating Helicopter Car and no. 6817-1 Flat Car - Red - With Motor Scraper. Ensuring a C8 outfit requires an original, unbroken no. 3419-100 Operating Helicopter Complete and an extremely fragile no. 6817-111 Earth Scraper Complete. Finding the latter is becoming a challenge.

The X-679 also included the no. 1802I Layout Instruction Sheet, which detailed the elevated pretzel track layout. This sheet, dated 5-59, was used as late as 1963. It, along with all the other peripherals, was appropriate for 1961.

The no. 61-416 RSC outfit box, combined with the mid-level and boxed rolling stock, makes this a difficult outfit to obtain in any condition.

CONVENTIONAL PACK
61-416 BOX
BOGUS PAPER

TOP LAYER

3-1018
6-1018
6530-1 F
6817-1 F

1008-50 TOP 6817

BOTTOM LAYER

9-1013 TOP 1013	8-1013		110-1 S	
			231P-1 S	
		1043-50	3419-1 S	
		6017-1 S	6428-1 F	

Description: "O27" Promotional Outfit
Specification: "O27" Steam Type Freight Outfit With Smoke
Original Amount: 287
Factory Order Date: 5/18/1961
Date Issued: Rev. 6-15-61
Packaging: R.S.C. Outfit Packing (Units Boxed)

Contents: 247-1 Steam Type Locomotive; 247T-1 Tender; 6817-1 Flat Car Red - With Motor Scraper; 6519-1 Allis-Chalmers Flat Car; 6428-1 U.S. Mail Car; 3361X-1 Operating Lumber Car; 160-2 Unloading Bin; 6017-1 Caboose; 1013-8 Curved Track (Bundle of 8 - 1013); 1018-5 Straight Track (Bundle of 5 - 1018); 6019-1 Remote Control Track Set; 1043-1 60-Watt Transformer; CTC-1 Lockon; 464-1 Operating Lumber Mill; 81-32 24" R.C. Wire (2); 364C-1 Contactor; 1122-234 Fibre Pin (2); X680-10 Layout Instruction Sheet; IS Instruction Sheet; 310-2 Set of (5) Billboards; D61-50 Accessory Catalog

Boxes & Packing: 60-583 Corr. Outfit Box; 60-332 Corr. Insert (2); 60-584 Corr. Shipper (3) (1-3)

X-680 (1961)	C6	C7	C8	Rarity
Complete Outfit	1,120	1,725	2,450	R9
Outfit Box no. 60-583	300	550	775	R9

Comments: This General Release Promotional Type IIa outfit was created to further deplete the inventory of the nos. 464-1 Operating Lumber Mill, 247-1 Steam Type Locomotive and 3361X-1 Operating Lumber Car. As with other General Release outfits, it was probably sold to one or many small retailers but has yet to be linked to a specific one.

Receiving a large accessory as part of an outfit always pleased consumers, even if Lionel first issued that item several years earlier. That was the case with the 464-1. Lionel introduced it in 1956 and, when burdened with leftover inventory, sought to deplete the supply by including a lumber mill in promotional outfit no. X-573NA in 1960. Whatever inventory remained ended up in outfit no. X-680 a year later. As such, the odd quantity that the Factory Order called for – 287 – probably represented the number of lumber mills gathering dust at Lionel's plant.

X-600 Series

TRACK LAYOUT - WIRING DIAGRAM

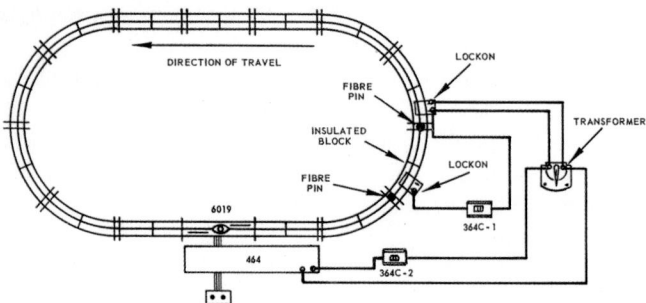

OPERATING INSTRUCTION FOR THIS OUTFIT

- The track and accessories must be placed and wired exactly as in this illustration.

- The train must be placed on the track facing in "Direction of Travel" as indicated by the arrow. Install Fibre Pins in place of the metal pins in the center rail of the same track section as illustrated.

- Place cars behind the locomotive and tender so that the Operating Lumber Car will be directly over the No. 6019 Track Section when the locomotive is stopped on the Insulated Block.

- Turn reversing unit switch "off" on locomotive; otherwise it will automatically reverse after it has stopped at Insulated Block.

- To stop the train in correct position turn No. 364C-1 Switch "off" as the locomotive is approaching the insulated block. To set HO 464 Saw Mill in operation turn No. 364C-2 "on".

- To allow train to proceed, turn No. 364C-2 Switch "off" and move No. 364C-1 Switch to "on". Increase or decrease voltage on transformer as required. No. 464 Saw Mill operates best at low voltage.

The LIONEL CORPORATION
SERVICE DEPARTMENT: Hoffman Place, Hillside, N.J.

Printed in U.S. of America   X680-10 9-61

The no. X680-10 Layout Instruction Sheet was unique to outfit no. X-680. With only 287 outfits produced, this rare sheet is seldom seen.

Generally speaking, the X-680 contained a few great models, even if the 464-1 was a bit dated. The blue stripe 247-1 Steam Locomotive in its no. 247-12 Corrugated Box was first manufactured in 1959 and included a two-position reversing unit, smoke and ballast weights.

All the rolling stock was equipped with operating AAR trucks and couplers, with the exception of the 3361X-1. This car had bar-end trucks and couplers and came in a Late Classic box. The "X" meant that the no. 160-2 Bin was not included, hence its placement loose in the outfit box.

The no. 6817-1 Flat Car - Red - With Motor Scraper was notable in that it included the extremely fragile no. 6817-111 Earth Scraper Complete. Beware as the smokestack on this scraper easily breaks.

The no. X680-10 Layout Instruction Sheet illustrated the track layout and accessory wiring requirements. It was dated 9-61 and is extremely difficult to find.

The no. 60-583 Tan RSC with Black Graphics outfit box was manufactured by Owens Illinois and measured 20 x 16½ x 6¾ inches. It was an overstickered no. X-566NA from 1960.

This outfit, as noted, was created to help Lionel dump excess inventory. Whether the X-680 met corporate expectations cannot be determined. We can say that, with an original quantity of 287 and an infrequent appearance on the market, this outfit deserves its R9 rating.

CONVENTIONAL PACK
60-583 BOX

TOP LAYER

247T-1 F	6817-1 F
6019-1 1018-5 160-2	6428-1 F
	1013-8

BOTTOM LAYER

	464-1 F	
1043 -1		6519-1 F
6017-1		3361X F
		247-1 S

Description: "O27" Promotional Outfit
Specification: "O27" Steam Type Freight Outfit
Customer: Jordan Marsh
Original Amount: 4,686
Factory Order Date: 12/4/1961
Date Issued: Rev. #8 12-13-61
Packaging: Display Outfit Packing (Units not Boxed)

Contents: 1060-25 Steam Type Locomotive; 1050T-25 Tender; 6045-50 Tank Car - "Cities Service"; 6076-75 Hopper Car - Black; 6067-25 Caboose; 1013-8 Curved Track (Bundle of 8 - 1013); 1018-10 Straight Track (Loose) (2); 1026-25 25-Watt Transformer; 1103-12 Envelope Packed; 1123-10 Instruction Sheet; 310-2 Set of (5) Billboards; D61-50 Accessory Catalog

Boxes & Packing: 61-105 Display Outfit Box; 61-101 Corr. Insert; 61-102 Corr. Insert (2); 61-103 Corr. Shipper for (6) (1-6); 61-110 Display Outfit Box With Stickers (Increase of 1,000); 61-101 Corr. Insert; 61-102 Corr. Insert (2); 61-103 Shipper for (6) (1-6); 61-432 Display Outfit Box W/Sticker (Increase of 800); 61-101 Corr. Insert; 61-102 Corr. Insert (2); 61-103 Shipper for (6) (1-6)

Alternate For Outfit Contents:
For 1,000 increase - Use 61-110 With Stickers, Inserts and shipper as above; For 800 increase - Use 61-432 Display Outfit Box W/ Sticker, Inserts and shipper as above.

X-681 (1961)	C6	C7	C8	Rarity
Complete Outfit With no. 61-105 Box	150	300	450	R5
Outfit Box no. 61-105	75	100	150	R5
Complete Outfit With no. 61-110 Box	175	400	600	R7
Outfit Box no. 61-110	100	200	300	R7
Complete Outfit With no. 61-432 Box	200	450	650	R7
Outfit Box no. 61-432	125	250	350	R7

Comments: Allied Stores owned several department stores in the 1960s and was a major customer of Lionel's. Among the stores

Jordan Marsh sold this no. X-681 starter outfit in 1961. The notable item is the no. 6045-50 Cities Service Tank Car, which was a low-end version of the no. 6465-100 Cities Service Two Dome Tank Car.

If you look closely at this no. 61-432 version of outfit no. X-681, you can see part of the "9" underneath the sticker. This indicates outfit no. X-699, which used the same box.

owned by Allied was Jordan Marsh, which may have received outfits through Allied. Jordan Marsh did obtain outfits direct from Lionel, including the no. X-681, a Retailer Promotional Type Ib, in 1961.

This was a basic, low-end starter outfit in the display packing that was typical for 1961. The no. 1060-25 Steam Locomotive was the cheapest engine at that time. It moved forward only and pulled low-end cars equipped with non-operating Archbar trucks and couplers. The only notable item in this outfit was the no. 6045-50 Cities Service Tank Car, the low-end version of the no. 6465-100 Cities Service Two Dome Tank Car. The 6045-50 appeared only in promotional outfits, showing up in nine of them.

The only other interesting characteristic of this outfit is the three versions of White 4-6-4 Steamer and F3 Hinged Display with Red/Orange and Blue Graphics Type A outfit boxes. It appears that the quantities for this outfit kept increasing. To accommodate the staggering eight revisions (as listed on the Factory Order) in a nine-day period, the Alternate for Outfit Contents section of the Factory Order listed two additional outfit boxes for "1,000 increase" and "800 increase".

This information suggests that the original order totaled 2,886 for the Express Container Corporation's no. 61-105 outfit box (originally used for outfit no. 1123). The remaining 1,800 outfits were split between 1,000 of the no. 61-110 outfit box (originally used for outfit no. 1124) and the Express Container Corp. no. 61-432 (originally used for outfit no. X-699). All of these boxes measured approximately 22 x 11½ x 3¼ inches.

The latter two boxes have a rarity two points higher than does the no. 61-105. This is because they were manufactured in slightly lower quantities. In any case, the X-681 is a common outfit with easily attainable components.

DISPLAY PACK
61-105 BOX

1060-25	1050T-25	1026-25
6045-25	6076-75	
2-1018 1013-8		6067-25

Description: "O27" Promotional Outfit
Specification: "O27" Steam Type Freight Outfit With Whistle
Customer: Independent Retailers Syndicate
Original Amount: 24
Factory Order Date: 9/27/1961
Date Issued: Rev. #1 9-29-61
Packaging: R.S.C. Outfit Packing (Units Boxed)

Contents: 247-1 Steam Type Locomotive; 247T-1 Tender; 3665-1 Minuteman Missile Launching Car; 6428-1 Non-Operating Mail Car; 6812-1 Track Maintenance Car; 6017-1 Caboose; 1013-70 Curved Track (Bundle of 12 - 1013); 1018-30 Straight Track (Bundle of 3 - 1018); 1008-50 Uncoupling Track Section;

1043-1 60-Watt Transformer; 1020-25 90° Crossing; 943-1 Exploding Ammo Dump; 1802B Layout Instruction Sheet; IS Instruction Sheet; 310-2 Set of (5) Billboards; D61-50 Accessory Catalog

Boxes & Packing: 59-351 Outfit Box (With Stickers); 59-352 Shipper for (4) (1-4)

X-682 (1961)	C6	C7	C8	Rarity
Complete Outfit	1,725	2,575	3,400	R10
Outfit Box no. 59-351	1,350	2,000	2,500	R10

309

Comments: The Factory Order for this outfit listed the customer as IRS, which was better known as Independent Retailers Syndicate, a privately held buying cooperative in New York. That firm purchased only two Retailer Promotional outfits: nos. X-682 and 19246. Both were purchased in extremely small quantities of 24 and 37, respectively. Neither outfit has been linked to a specific end retailer. Most likely, IRS just used them internally.

This Type Ia Factory Order was dated 9/27/61, which is the latest date that a no. 247-1 Steam Type Locomotive was listed in an outfit. These were likely the last, or close to the last 24 in inventory. The blue stripe 247-1 Steam Locomotive in its no. 247-12 Corrugated Box was first manufactured in 1959 and included a two-position reversing unit, smoke and ballast weights.

The only new item in this outfit was the no. 3665-1 Minuteman Missile Launching Car. This space and military item seems out of place with the previously released no. 6428-1 Non-Operating Mail Car and no. 6812-1 Track Maintenance Car. With only 24 of this outfit being made, it didn't matter how poor a mix of rolling stock was used because only a few customers would ever see this outfit.

In 1961, the 6812-1 most often included a black platform over a gray base or vice versa. It also had operating AAR trucks and couplers, as did all the other rolling stock. A combination of Orange Perforated and Orange Picture boxes was the norm in 1961.

The no. 1802B Layout Instruction Sheet details the figure-eight track layout that was commonly used in 1961. This sheet was dated 6-59.

The no. 1043-1 60-Watt Transformer came boxed in only five

promotional outfits in the 1960s, this being one of them. When boxed, it included two no. 81-32 24" Wires, which explains why the wires were not included separately in this outfit, as they were with most other 1961 outfits.

The no. 59-351 Tan RSC with Black Graphics outfit box was left over from two years before. It was first used for promotional outfit no. A-608-6 and subsequently overstickered and used for the nos. X-542NA, X-701 and X-708. It was manufactured by Express Container Corp. and measured 14 x 10½ x 6¾ inches.

Lionel made so few of this outfit – it ranks fourth in terms of low quantity – that the X-682 stands as one of the rarest promotional outfits. Collectors who desire every outfit manufactured or search for one-of-a-kind items would easily pay the listed price to own an X-682.

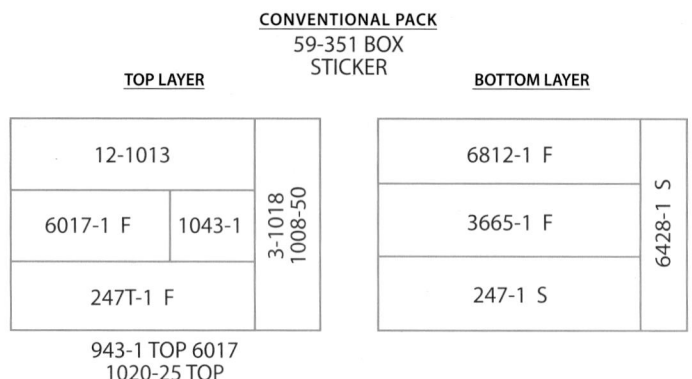

CONVENTIONAL PACK
59-351 BOX STICKER

TOP LAYER — BOTTOM LAYER

TOP LAYER:
12-1013	
6017-1 F	1043-1
247T-1 F	

3-1018 1008-50

943-1 TOP 6017
1020-25 TOP

BOTTOM LAYER:
| 6812-1 F |
| 3665-1 F |
| 247-1 S |

6428-1 S

Description: "O27" Promotional Outfit
Specification: "O27" Diesel Freight Outfit With Horn
Customer/No.: Maritz; 1486
Original Amount: 240
Factory Order Date: 5/18/1961
Date Issued: 6-7-61
Packaging: R.S.C. Outfit Packing (Units Boxed)

Contents: 218P-1 Alco Diesel Power Unit With Horn - "Santa Fe"; 6812-1 Track Maintenance Car; 6343-1 Barrel Ramp Car; 6530-1 Fire Prevention Training Car; 6817-1 Flat Car - Red - With Motor Scraper; 6357-1 Illuminated Caboose; 1013-8 Curved Track (Bundle of 8 - 1013); 1018-30 Straight Track (Bundle of 3 - 1018); 6029-25 R.C. Uncoupling Track; 1063-25 75-Watt Transformer; 90-30 Envelope Packed; 1651-10 Instruction Sheet; 310-2 Set of (5) Billboards; D61-50 Accessory Catalog

Boxes & Packing: 61-200 Corr. Outfit Box; 61-191 Corr. Insert; 61-201 Corr. Shipper for (4) (1-4)

X-683 (1961)	C6	C7	C8	Rarity
Complete Outfit	1,185	1,750	2,300	R9
Outfit Box no. 61-200	400	600	750	R9

Comments: Maritz, a well-known marketing incentive firm, purchased this Retailer Promotional Type Ia outfit in 1961. It

has been observed with a shipping label direct from Maritz in St. Louis, Missouri. The postmark was Nov. 1961.

This outfit was headed by the premier no. 218P-1 Santa Fe Alco Diesel Power Unit equipped with a three-position reversing unit, a headlight, two-axle Magne-Traction and an open pilot with a large ledge. The nos. CTC-1 Lockon and 218-11 Instruction Sheet were included inside its no. 218-10 Corrugated Box. This was also one of the few Alcos to include a horn. Until 1963, Lionel included a no. 601-13 "C" Battery with horn-equipped boxed Alcos.

The remainder of the rolling stock also included some of the better items for 1961. All of them were equipped with early AAR trucks and couplers. And, with the exception of the no. 6343-1 Barrel Ramp Car (new for 1961), all the cars were repeat items and came in Orange Perforated boxes. The 6343-1 was packed in an Orange Picture box.

In 1961, no. 6812 Track Maintenance Cars came with a black platform over a gray base or vice versa. Either variation would likely be found in this outfit, although one example has been observed with a yellow platform over a yellow base. Finding that variation in an X-683 was possible because, as noted in the *Authoritative Guide to Lionel's Postwar Operating Cars* (Project Roar Publishing), Lionel made 6812s in that scheme into 1960. With the low quantity of this outfit, a few of those older variations may have been left over and so been used for this outfit a year later.

Production Control Files indicate that early 6343-1s included a no. 4-9 Elastic Band, which was probably used to hold the barrels in place. This band was subsequently replaced by a no. 6343-7 Corrugated Insert.

Outfit no. X-683 was headed by a no. 218P-1 Santa Fe Alco Power Unit with two-axle Magne-Traction and a horn. It was followed by some of the better and colorful items still being offered in 1961. On the front left is the no. 6817-23 Corrugated Insert for the no. 6817-1 Flat Car – Red – With Motor Scraper. Lionel added that insert to help stabilize the Earth Scraper in the box.

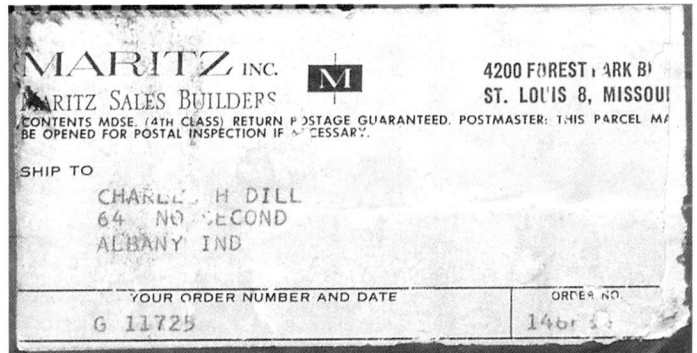

As with many incentive merchandisers, it appears that Maritz did its own fulfillment. This outfit was shipped direct in its outfit box from Maritz's location in St. Louis, Missouri.

The no. 6817-1 Flat Car - Red - With Motor Scraper is the single most expensive item in this outfit. Finding its fragile no. 6817-111 Earth Scraper Complete and Orange Perforated box in collectible condition is difficult.

The X-683 came packed in the commonly used no. 61-200 Orange RSC with Black Graphics outfit box that was manufactured by Mead Containers and measured 14½ x 12 x 7 inches.

The R9 rarity and value of this outfit are derived from its having a high-end locomotive and colorful rolling stock as well as the small quantity manufactured (a mere 240).

CONVENTIONAL PACK
61-200 BOX

TOP LAYER		
6817-1 S		INSERT 61-191
6812-1 F		
8-1013 3-1018	ENV.	

6029-25 TOP OF 6812-1

BOTTOM LAYER		
218P-1 F		
6357-1 S	1063-25	
6530-1 S		
6343-1 S		

Description: "O27" Promotional Outfit
Specification: "O27" Diesel Freight Outfit
Original Amount: 100
Factory Order Date: 7/31/1961
Date Issued: 8-8-61
Packaging: R.S.C. Outfit Packing (Units Boxed)

Contents: 231P-1 Alco Diesel Power Car - "Rock Island"; 3370-1 Animated Sheriff & Outlaw Car; 6519-1 Allis-Chalmers Car; 6050-1 Savings Bank Car; 6017-1 Caboose; 1013-70 Curved Track (Bundle of 12 - 1013); 1018-30 Straight Track (Bundle of 3 - 1018); 1008-50 Uncoupling Track Section; 1025-25 45-Watt Transformer; 1020-25 90° Crossing; 81-32 24" R.C. Wire (2); 1802B Layout Instruction Sheet; X602-10 Instruction Sheet;

310-2 Set of (5) Billboards; D61-50 Accessory Catalog

Boxes & Packing: 60-250 Outfit Box (W/Stickers); 60-251 Shipper for (4) (1-4); BP Bogus Paper

X-684 (1961)	C6	C7	C8	Rarity
Complete Outfit	900	1,450	1,950	R10
Outfit Box no. 60-250	600	1,000	1,300	R10

Comments: Another of the many General Release Promotional Type IIa outfits from 1961, the no. X-684 was likely assembled to provide Lionel's sales staff with something special to offer their smaller clients. Or, it may have been offered to Frederick

Atkins (but not listed on the Factory Order), which was listed as the customer on outfit no. X-685. These two outfits appeared in numerical sequence and were basically the same, with the no. X-684 being the diesel version with individually boxed items of the X-685.

The overall combination of cars and motive power in the X-684 included commonly available mid-level offerings from 1961. All the rolling stock in this outfit was boxed in a combination of Orange Perforated and Orange Picture boxes and came equipped with operating AAR trucks and couplers. Interestingly, the Type I no. 6050-1 Savings Bank Car (new for 1961) came boxed in only three outfits: nos. X-606, X-684 and X-698.

Also new for 1961, the no. 231P-1 Rock Island Alco Diesel Power Car was equipped with a two-position reversing unit, a headlight, an open pilot and two-axle Magne-Traction. This locomotive had plenty of power to pull this outfit around its figure-eight track layout.

What was really special about the X-684 was the rare no.

60-250 Tan RSC with Black Graphics outfit box. It was an overstickered RSC version of catalog outfit no. 2547WS (also a difficult outfit to find).

Only 100 of these outfits were made, and it is unknown where they were sold. Finding one of these outfits is a true challenge.

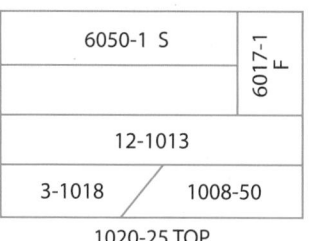

CONVENTIONAL PACK
60-250 BOX
STICKER
BOGUS PAPER

TOP LAYER		BOTTOM LAYER	
6050-1 S	6017-1 F	3370-1 F	1025-25
12-1013		6519-1 F	
3-1018 / 1008-50		231P-1 S	
1020-25 TOP			

The no. X-685 featured a steam locomotive and unboxed components, whereas its companion no. X-684 had a diesel and boxed components. Outfit X-685 is shown with a price tag (also a shipping label on top) identifying its end retailer as Hahne & Company, "39 60 L4" for $24.95.

Description: "O27" Promotional Outfit
Specification: "O27" Steam Type Freight Outfit
Customer: Frederick Atkins
Customer/No./Price: Hahne & Company; 39 60 L4; $24.95
Original Amount: 150
Factory Order Date: 7/31/1961
Date Issued: 8-8-61
Packaging: R.S.C. Outfit Packing (Units not Boxed)

Contents: 246-25 Steam Type Locomotive; 244T-25 Tender; 3370-25 Animated Sheriff & Outlaw Car; 6519-25 Allis-Chalmers Car; 6050-25 Savings Bank Car; 6017-25 Caboose; 1013-70 Curved Track (Bundle of 12 - 1013); 1018-30 Straight Track (Bundle of 3 - 1018); 1008-50 Uncoupling Track Section; 1025-25 45-Watt

Transformer; 1020-25 90° Crossing; 1103-12 Envelope Packed; 1802B Layout Instruction Sheet; 1641-10 Instruction Sheet; 310-2 Set of (5) Billboards; D61-50 Accessory Catalog

Boxes & Packing: 61-180 Outfit Box; 61-171 Corr. Insert; 61-183 Corr. Insert; 61-191 Corr. Insert; 61-185 Shipper for (4) (1-4); BP Bogus Paper

X-685 (1961)	C6	C7	C8	Rarity
Complete Outfit	800	1,100	1,525	R10
Outfit Box no. 61-180	600	800	1,100	R10

Comments: This Retailer Promotional Type Ia outfit was sold to Frederick Atkins (see the section on Lionel's Distribution and

Customers). It has been observed with a Hahne & Company, Newark, New Jersey, price tag listing it as "39 60 L4" for $24.95

Outfit no. X-684 and this outfit appear to have been created simultaneously. They have the same Factory Order date as well as date issued. Their contents are identical, except that the no. X-685 included a steamer with unboxed items, whereas the X-684 had a diesel locomotive and boxed items. Differences in the contents and packaging of these outfits, along with their quantities, explain why the X-684 is slightly more desirable than the X-685.

The no. 246-25 Steam Type Locomotive included in the X-685 featured Magne-Traction, a two-position reversing unit and the later body version with a closed pilot and lack of the small generator detail on its top in front of the cab. Since it came unboxed (as indicated by the "-25"), a no. CTC-1 Lockon was required separately and included in the no. 1103-12 Envelope Packed. This differs from the X-684: its diesel came boxed and so the CTC-1 Lockon was packed in the engine box.

The Type I no. 6050-25 Savings Bank Car (new for 1961) was equipped with operating AAR trucks and couplers, as was all the rolling stock. The no. 6519-25 Allis-Chalmers Car was left unboxed, a short-sighted decision because its fragile plastic brake wheels frequently crack or break off their mountings. That fact and the placement of these models next to the track and transformer

inside the outfit box probably contributed to any damage they suffered during shipping.

The figure-eight track plan was detailed on the 6-59 dated no. 1802B Layout Instruction Sheet. This sheet and all the other peripherals were appropriate for 1961.

The commonly used no. 61-180 Tan RSC with Black Graphics outfit box was manufactured by the Mead Corporation and measured 12¾ x 10 x 6¾ inches.

Only 150 of these outfits were made and distributed through Frederick Atkins and its member retailers or customers, making it a difficult outfit to find.

CONVENTIONAL PACK
61-180 BOX

TOP LAYER				BOTTOM LAYER		
246-25 F	BOGUS PAPER	61-191 →		6519-25 F		3-1018
6017-25 F	244T-25 F			1008-50 3370-25 F	1025-25	
12-1013		61-171 ↙		6050-25 S	CORD	
1020-25 TOP 6017				61-183 BETWEEN LAYERS		

The no. X-686, along with the no. X-713, introduced the no. 6050-50 Box Car - Red - "Swift". The Factory Orders for these outfits help to properly date the introduction of the Type IIa 8½-inch box car body. They also validate the Archbar version "-50" of the Swift box car.

Description: "O27" Promotional Outfit
Specification: "O27" Steam Type Freight Outfit
Customer: Swift
Original Amount: 3,800
Factory Order Date: 10/23/1961
Date Issued: Rev. #2 11-16-61
Packaging: R.S.C. Outfit Packing (Units not Boxed)

Contents: 1060-25 Steam Type Locomotive; 1050T-25 Tender; 6042-25 Gondola Car (Less 2 Canisters); 6112-5 Canister - Red (2); 3409-25 Oper. Helicopter Launching Car (Manually); 6050-50 Box Car - Red - "Swift"; 6067-25 Caboose; 1013-8 Curved Track (Bundle of 8 - 1013); 1018-10 Straight Track (Loose) (2); 1026-25 25-Watt Transformer; 1103-12 Envelope Packed; 1123-10 Instruction Sheet; 310-2 Set of (5) Billboards; D61-50 Accessory Catalog

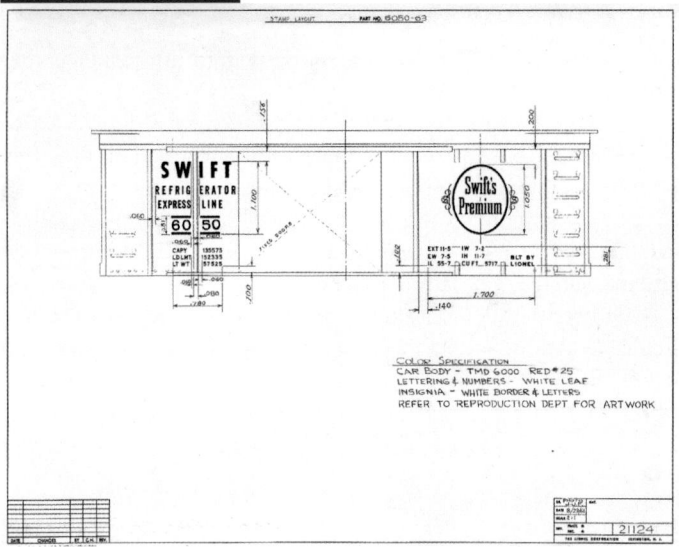

The Stamping Layout for the Swift box car body (stamped no. 6050-63) was dated 8/23/61. This clearly shows a Type IIa body (rivets removed so there was room for the Swift logo). This information, combined with the Factory Order for outfit no. X-686, confirms that Lionel first issued this body type in 1961.

Boxes & Packing: 61-170 Outfit Box; 61-171 Corr. Insert; 61-172 Corr. Insert; 61-173 Corr. Insert; 61-174 Shipper for (6) (1-6)

X-686 (1961)	C6	C7	C8	Rarity
Complete Outfit	200	350	525	R4
Outfit Box no. 61-170	75	100	140	R4

Comments: The Factory Order lists Swift as the customer for this outfit, thus making the no. X-686 a Manufacturer Promotional Type IIIb. This is the only outfit to list Swift as a customer. Although Swift was known for offering promotional items with the purchase of some of its products, no documentation has been uncovered linking this outfit to any sort of Swift-sponsored promotion or direct sale.

The relationship between Swift and Lionel flourished in 1961. Besides receiving its own no. 6050-50 Box Car, Swift was featured on a billboard included with the no. 310-2 Set of (5) Billboards. These billboards were included in almost every outfit.

The X-686 was one of two 1961 outfits (General Release Promotional no. X-713 being the other) to list the no. 6050-50

Box Car – Red – "Swift" on its Factory Order. That car, though just an entry-level item equipped with non-operating Archbar trucks and couplers, has historical importance.

To be specific, the 6050-50 was the first car to use a Type IIa 8½-inch box car body. A Type IIa has two complete rows of rivets to the left of its door and two complete and two incomplete (one rivet at the top and two at the bottom) on the right. Extra rivets were removed from the Type I 8½-inch box car to facilitate the application of the Swift logo.

Previously, this change was thought to have been effected in 1962, because that is when the 6050-50 first appeared in a catalog. But, as with numerous other items, that item was introduced in a promotional outfit before becoming a catalog item.

The 6050-50 was also significant in that its "-50" suffix indicated an Archbar variation of the Swift box car previously undocumented in the collector community. This car went on to be used only in promotional outfits until 1963. Both of these previously unknown facts were revealed by the authoritative information used in compiling this volume.

Regarding other rolling stock in the X-686, the no. 3409-25 Oper. Helicopter Launching Car (Manually) is easy to find, but its no. 3419-100 Operating Helicopter Complete requires care to find with original, unbroken parts. Other items weren't very exciting, with the gondola and caboose being quite common, and the no. 1060-25 Steam Type Locomotive and its tender being low-end motive power.

This outfit's no. 61-170 Tan RSC with Black Graphics outfit box is readily available. It was manufactured by Owens-Illinois, measured 11½ x 10¼ x 6¼ inches and had "9012" printed below the box manufacturer's certificate.

With 3,800 ordered from the factory, this box frequently appears on the market.

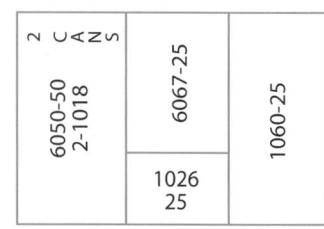

CONVENTIONAL PACK
61-170 BOX

TOP LAYER

8-1013
1050T-25

6042-25 3409-25	HELICOPTER

BOTTOM LAYER

6050-50 2-1018	2 UANS	6067-25	1060-25
		1026 25	

Description: "O27" Promotional Outfit
Specification: "O27" Steam Type Freight Outfit
Original Amount: 3,000
Factory Order Date: 6/30/1961
Date Issued: Rev. #1 9-27-61
Packaging: Display Outfit Packing (Units not Boxed)

Contents: 1060-25 Steam Type Locomotive; 1050T-25 Tender; 6042-25 Gondola Car (Less 2 Canisters); 6112-5 Canister - Red (2); 6076-75 Hopper Car - Black; 6406-25 Single Automobile Car (Less Auto); 6406-30 Automobile; 6067-25 Caboose; 1013-

8 Curved Track (Bundle of 8 - 1013); 1018-10 Straight Track (Loose) (2); 1026-25 25-Watt Transformer; 1103-12 Envelope Packed; 1123-10 Instruction Sheet; 310-2 Set of (5) Billboards

Boxes & Packing: 61-429 Display Outfit Box; 61-391 Corr. Insert; 61-392 Corr. Insert; 61-393 Corr. Insert; 61-394 Corr. Insert; 61-395 Shipper for (6) (1-6)

X-687 (1961)	C6	C7	C8	Rarity
Complete Outfit	190	300	415	R5
Outfit Box no. 61-429	90	125	150	R5

Outfit nos. X-687 and X-715 both used the no. 61-429 Display Outfit Box. An overstickered no. X-715 outfit is shown with part of the "X-715" sticker removed. Underneath is the "No. X-687" as it was stamped by the box manufacturer.

Comments: Another of the General Release Promotional Type IIb outfits issued in 1961, this entry-level outfit has yet to be linked to a particular retailer.

As with other low-end outfits, keeping the cost down was the goal when developing the no. X-687. As a result, all the rolling stock was equipped with non-operating Archbar trucks and couplers. The no. 1060-25 Steam Locomotive was available only in promotional outfits. That 2-4-2 steamer moved forward only and didn't include much except for a headlight. The freight cars were also inexpensive items found only in promotional outfits.

The most exciting item in today's market is the no. 6406-30 Automobile. A verified original postwar automobile with a gray bumper is always in demand.

The no. 61-429 White 4-6-4 Steamer and F3 Hinged Display with Red/Orange and Blue Graphics Type A outfit box was manufactured by United Container Co. and measured 22½ x 14½ x 3¼ inches. It was uniquely numbered by the box manufacturer with X-687 and over-stickered when used for outfit no. X-715.

Although many examples of the X-687 were made, this outfit does not appear on the market too often.

DISPLAY PACK 61-429 BOX	
1060-25	1050T-25
6042-25	6076-75
6406-25 6406-30	6067-25
8-1013 2-1018	1026-25

LIONEL "HO" and "O" Gauge Trains

G LIONEL SPACE SECURITY SPECIAL (Excl.) 5 car Space Security Special is always on the alert! As it speeds to trouble spot, helicopter is launched to fly scouting mission; then satellite orbits off to monitor enemy activities. Finally missile blasts off with pinpoint accuracy to explode (by spring action) enemy "high explosives" car. All action by remote control, including reversing of twin unit diesel locomotive with headlight, and automatic coupling and uncoupling.
836-9 "O" GAUGE SPACE SECURITY SPECIAL Ship. wt. 16 lbs.....................49.95 Complete, with 16 curved and 8 straight track sections, uncoupler, 90° crossing, trestle set, instruction sheet and 75 watt transformer. Track layout 63" x 41", train length 70".
836-13 "HO" GAUGE SPACE SECURITY SPECIAL Ship. wt. 9 lbs.............49.95 Complete, with 27 curved and 10 straight track sections, uncoupler, 30° crossing, trestle set, instruction sheet, and power pack. Layout 75" x 47", train length 46".

As shown on page 67 of the FAO Schwarz Christmas Catalog for 1961, outfit no. X-688 (FAO Schwarz no. 836-9), when paired with its HO no. 5834 counterpart (FAO Schwarz no. 836-13), could be considered the Father and Son Outfit of 1961. Note the always-elevated track layout that appeared with this outfit only.

Description: "O27" Promotional Outfit
Specification: "O27" Diesel Freight Outfit
Customer/No./Price: FAO Schwarz; 836-9; $49.95
Original Amount: 50
Factory Order Date: 6/30/1961
Date Issued: 8/2/61
Packaging: R.S.C. Outfit Packing (Units Boxed)

Contents: 220P-1 Alco Diesel Power Unit - "Santa Fe"; 218C-1 "B" Unit - "Santa Fe"; 3509-1 Operating Satellite Launching Car (Manually); 3410-1 Operating Helicopter Launching Car (Manually); 6650-1 Missile Launching Car; 6470-1 Exploding Target Car; 6017-1 Caboose; 1013-8 Curved Track (Bundle of 8 - 1013) (2); 1018-40 Straight Track (Bundle of 4 - 1018) (2); 1008-50 Uncoupling Track Section; 1073-25 60-Watt Transformer; 1020-25 90° Crossing; 111-1 Trestle Set; 110-1 Graduated Trestle Set; 81-32 24" R.C. Wire (2); X688-10 Layout Instruction Sheet; 1649-10 Instruction Sheet; 310-2 Set of (5) Billboards; D61-50 Accessory Catalog

Boxes & Packing: 60-536 Outfit Box (W/Sticker); 60-537 Shipper for (3) (1-3); BP Bogus Paper

X-688 (1961)	C6	C7	C8	Rarity
Complete Outfit	1,775	2,500	3,300	R10
Outfit Box no. 60-536	1,200	1,500	1,700	R10

Comments: As with any General Release Promotional outfit, the challenge is to discover the end retailer. This Type IIb was found on page 67 of the FAO Schwarz Christmas Catalog for 1961. It was listed as FAO number 836-9 and "Lionel Space Security Special (Excl.)" for $49.95. Also shown was an HO Space Security

SPECIAL TRACK LAYOUT

This track layout shows the track and components of HO outfit No. 5834 and "027" track of outfit No. X688.

These layouts can be set up together (as illustrated) or individually. The alphabetical letters such as A,B,C, etc. indicate the positions of the elevating piers.

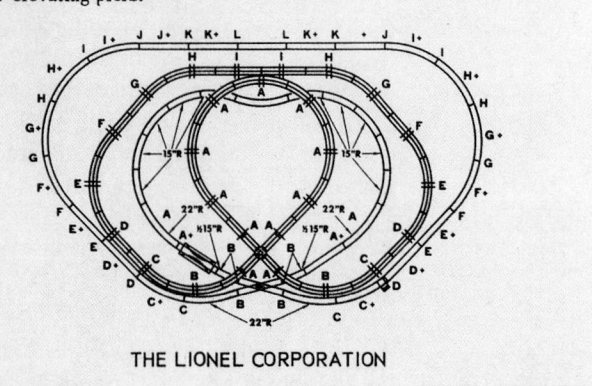

THE LIONEL CORPORATION

Printed in U.S. of America   X688-10 9-61

The no. X688-10 Layout Instruction Sheet was included in O27 outfit no. X-688 and HO outfit no. 5834. With only 100 combined outfits produced, this rare sheet is seldom seen.

Special for $49.95.

As shown with the HO outfit in the catalog, this unique offering could be considered the Father and Son Outfit of 1961. Its matching HO no. 5834 (FAO Schwarz no. 836-13) outfit had similar items and track plan. Finding both of these outfits would be a collector's dream come true.

FAO Schwarz typically offered higher-end Lionel outfits. The no. X-688 was no exception. The outfit's no. 220P-1 Santa Fe Alco Diesel Power Unit included two-axle Magne-Traction, a three-position reversing unit, an open pilot with a large ledge and a headlight. The only thing missing was a horn.

Both the nos. 3509-1 Operating Satellite Launching Car

(Manually) and 3410-1 Operating Helicopter Launching Car (Manually) were new for 1961 and came in Orange Picture boxes. In fact, the only way to obtain the Orange Picture no. 3509-6 Folding Box was in this or eight other promotional outfits. (See outfit no. X-647 for more information on this car and its paperwork.)

The nos. 6650-1 Missile Launching Car and 6470-1 Exploding Target Car were both repeat items. They, like all the items in the X-688, included operating AAR trucks and couplers.

The most interesting feature of this outfit was its always-elevated pretzel track layout. Both a no. 110-1 Graduated Trestle and a no. 111-1 Trestle Set were included. The no. X688-10 Layout Instruction Sheet detailed both the HO and O27 layouts. This rare sheet was dated 9-61.

The no. 60-536 Tan RSC with Black Graphics outfit box was originally used for outfit no. X-530NA. It was overstickered for this and outfit nos. X-570NA and X-693. The box measured 19¼ x 15⅝ x 7 inches and was manufactured by Star Corrugated Box Company. It also had a star printed above the box manufacturer's certificate.

Factory orders called for only 50 of these to be manufactured. So small a quantity, along with the outfit's higher-end rolling stock, unique track plan and potential to pair up with its matching 5834 HO outfit, makes finding it truly exciting.

	CONVENTIONAL PACK 60-536 BOX STICKER BOGUS PAPER		
TOP LAYER		**BOTTOM LAYER**	

218C-1 F			110-1 F	1073-25
4-1018				
6470-1 S	1020-25			
3509-1 S	1008-50		220P-1 F	
4-1018				
8-1013	6017-1 F	111-1 F	3410-1 S	
8-1013			6650-1 S	

Customer No. On Box: X 10 R 29
Description: "O27" Promotional Outfit
Specification: "O27" Steam Type Freight Outfit
Customer/No.: Jewel Tea Company; X 10 R 29
Original Amount: 500
Factory Order Date: 6/30/1961
Date Issued: 8/2/61
Packaging: R.S.C. Outfit Packing (Units not Boxed)

Contents: 246-25 Steam Type Locomotive; 244T-25 Tender; 3376-25 Operating Giraffe Car (Less 3376-118 Env.); 3376-118 Envelope Packed; 6162-25 Gondola Car - Blue (Less Canisters); 6112-88 Canisters (White) (3); 6057-25 Caboose (Red); 1013-70 Curved Track (Bundle of 12 - 1013); 1018-30 Straight Track (Bundle of 3 - 1018); 1008-50 Uncoupling Track Section; 1026-25 25-Watt Transformer; 1020-25 90° Crossing; 1103-12 Envelope Packed; 1802B Layout Instruction Sheet; IS Instruction Sheet; 310-2 Set of (5) Billboards; D61-50 Accessory Catalog

Boxes & Packing: 61-170 Outfit Box; 61-171 Corr. Insert; 61-172 Corr. Insert; 61-173 Corr. Insert; 61-174 Shipper for (6) (1-6)

Alternate For Outfit Contents:
Note: Customer Stock No. X 10 R 29 to appear on outfit cartons & shippers.

X-689 (1961)	C6	C7	C8	Rarity
Complete Outfit	270	520	835	R8
Outfit Box no. 61-170	135	300	500	R8

Comments: Jewel Tea Company purchased this Retailer Promotional Type Ia outfit in 1961. The outfit box was stamped with both Lionel and Jewel Tea Company's "X 10 R 29" numbers.

A typical mid-level promotional outfit, the no. X-689 was headed by the no. 246-25 Steam Type Locomotive with a two-position reversing unit, a headlight and Magne-Traction. The body type was the later version with a solid pilot and lack of the small generator detail on its top in front of the cab.

The no. 3376-118 Envelope Packed was placed loose in the outfit box. This occurred when a no. 3376-25 Operating Giraffe Car was unboxed. The remaining rolling stock didn't include any items that stood out, although they were equipped with operating AAR trucks and couplers.

The Factory Order for outfit no. X-689 stated, "Customer Stock No. X 10 R 29 to appear on outfit cartons & shippers". The Jewel Tea Company number was printed below Lionel's number.

The figure-eight track layout was detailed on the no. 1802B Layout Instruction Sheet. This sheet was dated 6-59.

A no. 61-170 Tan RSC with Black Graphics outfit box was manufactured by Owens-Illinois and measured 11½ x 10¼ x 6¼ inches.

Forty-three promotional outfits had a quantity of at least 500. The X-689 was among them; still, only one example has been reported over the past two or three years. As a consequence, this outfit falls at the high end of the R8 rating.

CONVENTIONAL PACK
61-170 BOX

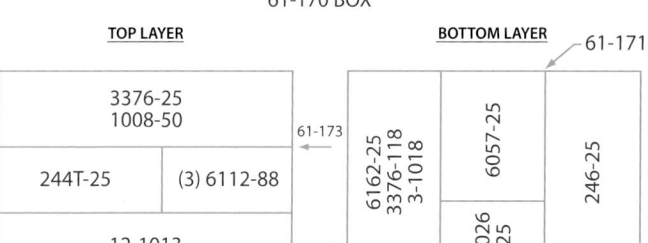

TOP LAYER

3376-25 1008-50	
244T-25	(3) 6112-88
12-1013	

61-173

BOTTOM LAYER — 61-171

6162-25 / 3376-118 / 3-1018 · 6057-25 · 246-25 · 1026 25

1020-25 TOP 6057
61-172 BETWEEN LAYERS

Description: "O27" Promotional Outfit
Specification: "O27" Steam Type Freight Outfit
Customer: Joe, The Motorists' Friend
Original Amount: 900
Factory Order Date: 6/30/1961
Date Issued: Rev #2 8/10/61
Packaging: R.S.C. Outfit Packing (Units not Boxed)

Contents: 1060-25 Steam Type Locomotive; 1050T-25 Tender; 3409-25 Operating Helicopter Launching Car (Manually); 6076-75 Hopper Car - Black; 6406-25 Single Automobile Car (Less Auto); 6406-30 Automobile; 6067-25 Caboose; 1013-8 Curved Track (Bundle of 8 - 1013); 1018-10 Straight Track (Loose) (2); 1026-25 25-Watt Transformer; 1103-12 Envelope Packed; 1123-10 Instruction Sheet; 310-2 Set of (5) Billboards; D61-50 Accessory Catalog

Boxes & Packing: 61-170 Outfit Box; 61-171 Corr. Insert; 61-172 Corr. Insert; 61-173 Corr. Insert; 61-174 Shipper for (6) (1-6)

X-690 (1961)	C6	C7	C8	Rarity
Complete Outfit	230	375	575	R7
Outfit Box no. 61-170	90	125	175	R7

Comments: This was the first of many train outfits purchased by Joe, The Motorists' Friend during the 1960s. This Retailer Promotional Type Ib outfit was a low- to mid-level starter outfit that included rolling stock with non-operating Archbar trucks and couplers. Except for the tender, all the items were found only in promotional outfits.

The no. 1060-25 Steam Type Locomotive was Lionel's low-end offering. That engine, which moved forward only, pulled a new-for-1961 no. 3409-25 Operating Helicopter Launching Car (Manually) that carried a no. 3419-100 Operating Helicopter

CONVENTIONAL PACK
61-170 BOX

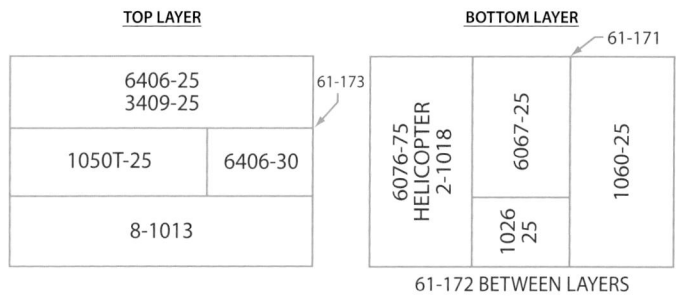

TOP LAYER

6406-25 3409-25	
1050T-25	6406-30
8-1013	

61-173

BOTTOM LAYER — 61-171

6076-75 HELICOPTER 2-1018 · 6067-25 · 1060-25 · 1026 25

61-172 BETWEEN LAYERS

X-600 Series

Complete. The hopper car, automobile flat car and caboose were also new for 1961. All of these items are very common in today's market.

The no. 61-170 Tan RSC with Black Graphics outfit box was used for at least 81 outfits, almost all of which were promotional. It measured 11½ x 10¼ x 6¼ inches.

With 900 of this outfit made, examples should appear for sale on a regular basis. However, the converse has proved to be true.

X-691
1961

Description: "O27" Promotional Outfit
Specification: "O27" Steam Type Freight Outfit With Smoke
Original Amount: 150
Factory Order Date: 6/30/1961
Date Issued: 8/2/61
Packaging: R.S.C. Outfit Packing (Units Boxed)

Contents: 236-1 Steam Type Locomotive With Smoke; 1130T-1 Tender; 3519-1 Automatic Satellite Launching Car; 3830-1 Operating Submarine Car; 6017-1 Caboose; 1013-8 Curved Track (Bundle of 8 - 1013); 1013-90 Curved Track (Bundle of 9 - 1013); 1018-30 Straight Track (Bundle of 3 - 1018) (3); 1008-50 Uncoupling Track Section; 1025-25 45-Watt Transformer; 110-1 Trestle Set; 470-1 Missile Launching Platform; 81-32 24" R.C. Wire (2); 1802I Layout Instruction Sheet; X602-10 Instruction Sheet; 310-2 Set of (5) Billboards; D61-50 Accessory Catalog

Boxes & Packing: 60-503 Outfit Box (W/Sticker); 60-504 Shipper for (3) (1-3)

X-691 (1961)	C6	C7	C8	Rarity
Complete Outfit	825	1,500	2,000	R10
Outfit Box no. 60-503	500	1,000	1,200	R10

Comments: Another of the many 1961 General Release Promotional outfits, this Type IIa outfit included items that were also available for separate sale or in catalog outfits.

The no. X-691 should be considered a mid-level offering because all items came boxed and equipped with operating AAR trucks and couplers. The addition of a no. 470-1 Missile Launching Platform and an elevated pretzel track layout made it even more exciting for potential customers.

The no. 236-1 Steam Type Locomotive was one of three new Scout offerings in 1961. It included a two-position reversing unit, a headlight, smoke and Magne-Traction. When boxed in its no. 236-10 Corrugated Box, it included the nos. CTC-1 Lockon, 236-11 Instruction Sheet, 909-10 Smoke Fluid, 927-60 Tube of Oil and 927-65 Tube of Grease. The only other peripherals required to operate this outfit were the two no. 81-32 24" R.C. Wires, which were placed loose in the outfit box.

The no. 3519-1 Automatic Satellite Launching Car was also new for 1961 and came in an Orange Picture box. All the other items came in either an Orange Perforated or an Orange Picture box, with the appropriate instruction sheets included.

With the 470-1 in this space and military outfit, Lionel added a no. 6470-1 Exploding Target Car. The inclusion of this large accessory necessitated a large box. The no. 60-503 was an overstickered no. X-515NA sub-base outfit box from 1960. It was also used for outfit no. X-625.

The no. X-691 was packaged in a large, clumsy and easily destroyed outfit box. This fact, combined with the low quantity manufactured, makes this an extremely hard outfit to find.

CONVENTIONAL PACK
60-503 BOX
STICKER

236-1 S		3830-1 S	
110-1 F	6017-1 S	1025-25	3519-1 F
	1130T-1 S	8-1013	470-1

9-1013 TOP 3519
3-1018 TOP 8-1013, 236, AND 1130T
1008-50 TOP 470

X-692
1961

Description: "O27" Promotional Outfit
Specification: "O27" Steam Type Freight Outfit With Smoke & Whistle
Original Amount: 75
Factory Order Date: 7/17/1961
Date Issued: 8/2/61
Packaging: R.S.C. Outfit Packing (Units Boxed)

Contents: 2018-1 Steam Type Locomotive With Smoke; 243W-1 Whistle Tender; 3370-1 Animated Sheriff & Outlaw Car; 6445-1 Ft. Knox Gold Bullion Transport Car; 3376-1 Operating Giraffe Car; 6812-1 Track Maintenance Car; 6519-1 Allis Chalmers Car; 6357-1 Illuminated Caboose; 1013-8 Curved Track (Bundle of 8 - 1013); 1018-5 Straight Track (Bundle of 5 - 1018); 6029-25 R.C. Uncoupling Track; 1063-25 75-Watt Transformer; 90-30 Envelope Packed; 1650-10 Instruction Sheet; 310-2 Set of (5) Billboards; D61-50 Accessory Catalog

Boxes & Packing: 61-210 Outfit Box; 61-211 Shipper for (4) (1-4)

X-692 (1961)	C6	C7	C8	Rarity
Complete Outfit	1,425	1,850	2,600	R10
Outfit Box no. 61-210	850	1,000	1,400	R10

Comments: This was an exciting General Release Promotional Type IIa outfit that has yet to be linked to a particular retailer.

To be sure, no single piece in the no. X-692 stands out. Nonetheless, the combination of eight items makes for an attractive, colorful and larger-than-average outfit.

Interestingly, the no. 2018-1 Steam Type Locomotive With Smoke appeared only in promotional outfits in the 1960s. When boxed, it included a no. CTC-1 Lockon. This, along with the no. 90-30 Envelope Packed, with four no. 81-32 24" R.C. Wires and a no. 90-1 Controller, provided all the peripherals necessary to hook up the transformer and no. 6029-25 R.C. Uncoupling Track.

All items were Lionel's mid- to high-level 1961 offerings that came in a combination of Orange Perforated and Orange Picture boxes. They were all equipped with operating AAR trucks and couplers.

The nos. 3370-1 Animated Sheriff & Outlaw Car and 6445-1 Fort Knox Gold Bullion Transport Car were new for 1961, while the remaining rolling stock was repeated. The no. 6357-1 Illuminated Caboose was a nice addition and appeared in only two other promotional outfits.

The no. 61-210 Orange RSC with Black Graphics outfit box was manufactured by Mead Containers and measured 13⅞ x 13¼ x 6½ inches.

This outfit achieves its R10 rarity based on its extremely low original production quantity and lack of availability in the market.

CONVENTIONAL PACK
61-210 BOX

TOP LAYER				BOTTOM LAYER		
6445-1 F				3376-1 F		1063 -25
3370-1 F	5-1018	8-1013		243W-1 S		
6357-1 F				2018-1 S		
6812-1 S				6519-1 F		

6029-25 TOP 6519

Description: Super "O" Promotional Outfit
Specification: Super "O" GG-1 Freight Outfit
Original Amount: 97
Factory Order Date: 7/16/1961
Date Issued: Rev. #1 11-28-61
Packaging: R.S.C. Outfit Packing (Units Boxed)

Contents: 2360X-1 Penn GG-1 Electric Locomotive With Horn; 6530-1 Fire Prevention Training Car; 6440-1 Twin Piggyback Van Transport Car; 6827-1 Flat Car With Tractor Shovel; 6828-1 Flat Car With Construction Crane; 6560-25 Crane Car; 6416-1 Boat Transport Car; 6119-100 Work Caboose; 31-60 Curved Track - With Power Bus Connector (Bundle of 6 - 31) (2); 32-60 Straight Track - With Power Bus Connector (Bundle of 3 - 32) (2); 39-35 Operating Track Set - Without Power Bus Connector; 1044-1 90-Watt Transformer; IS Instruction Sheet; 310-2 Set of (5) Billboards; D61-50 Accessory Catalog

Boxes & Packing: 60-536 Outfit Box (W/Sticker); 60-537 Shipper for (3) (1-3)

X-693 (1961)	C6	C7	C8	Rarity
Complete Outfit	2,900	4,300	5,800	R10
Outfit Box no. 60-536	1,200	1,800	2,000	R10

Comments: Lionel made only four Super O promotional outfits in 1961. Three were for Sears, and the no. X-693 was a General Release Promotional Type IIa outfit.

For this outfit, as with all its Super O outfits, Lionel combined a high-end locomotive with comparable rolling stock. The X-693 was headed by the newly, per Production Control Files, "Re-instated 3-1-61" no. 2360X-1 Penn GG-1 Electric Locomotive With Horn. As described in the section on Outfit Peripherals, an "X" signified that a no. CTC-1 Lockon was not included in the no. 2360-10 Corrugated Box. Including a Lockon in a Super O outfit would be a waste.

All rolling stock was equipped with operating AAR trucks and couplers and came in a combination of Orange Perforated and Orange Picture boxes. The nos. 6440-1 Twin Piggyback Van Transport Car and 6416-1 Boat Transport Car were new for 1961, and both came in Orange Picture boxes. The Vans were attached to the 6440-1 with two no. 4-6 Elastic Bands. The Boat Transport Car came in 10 promotional outfits.

The nos. 6827-1 Flat Car With Tractor Shovel and 6828-1 Flat Car With Construction Crane were each boxed with a model of a Harnischfeger construction machine. When unboxed and assembled, these fragile pieces are difficult to get back in their boxes. C8 versions of these cars require that all peripherals and instruction sheets be present in C8 condition.

The no. 6560-25 Crane Car was the boxed version of the crane with a red cab and a black base. The 6560 Crane Car was first manufactured in 1955, one year before Lionel began using the "-25" suffix to indicate unboxed items (see the section on Item Numbering and Suffixes). As such, the "-1" was assigned to the boxed gray cab / black base 6560 and the "-25" to the boxed red cab / black base.

As with most Super O outfits, the track layout of the X-693 was a basic oval. In mid-1961, Super O track started to come with the Power Bus Connectors attached to the track. Therefore, a Type III no. 39-35 Envelope Packed was included with this outfit.

The no. 60-536 Tan RSC with Black Graphics outfit box was originally used for outfit no. X-530NA. It was overstickered for the X-693 as well as outfit nos. X-570NA and X-688. The box measured 19¼ x 15⅝ x 7 inches and was manufactured by Star Corrugated Box Company. It also had a star printed above the box manufacturer's certificate.

The locomotive and four of the seven pieces of rolling stock mirrored the contents of catalog outfit no. 2575 from 1961. That outfit is very desirable and commands a high price even though 1,200 were made. Only 8 percent as many units of the X-693 were manufactured (a quantity of 97), which accounts for its rarity and market price.

And why such an odd quantity? The X-693 was a General Release Promotional with no items being depleted from inventory, so Lionel typically would have manufactured a multiple of an even number. The "Date Issued" on the Factory Order stated, "Rev. #1 11-28-61". This revision was for the quantity and was likely based on a customer's specific order. Unfortunately, this customer has yet to be determined.

CONVENTIONAL PACK
60-536 BOX
STICKER

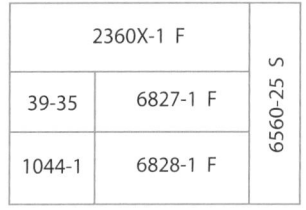

TOP LAYER					BOTTOM LAYER			
3-32 3-32			6416-1 F			2360X-1 F		6560-25 S
	6-31	6-31	6530-1 S	6119-100 S	6440-1 F	39-35	6827-1 F	
						1044-1	6828-1 F	

Description: "O27" Promotional Outfit
Specification: "O27" Steam Type Freight Outfit
Customer: S. Klein
Original Amount: 2,030
Factory Order Date: 11/16/1961
Date Issued: Rev. #5 11-28-61
Packaging: R.S.C. Outfit Packing (Units not Boxed)

Contents: 246-25 Steam Type Locomotive; 244T-25 Tender; 3665-25 Minuteman Missile Launching Car; 3509-25 Oper. Satellite Launching Car (Manually); 6470-25 Exploding Target Car; 6057-25 Caboose (Red); 1013-70 Curved Track (Bundle of 12 - 1013); 1018-30 Straight Track (Bundle of 3 - 1018); 1008-50 Uncoupling Track Section; 1025-25 45-Watt Transformer; 1020-25 90° Crossing; 1103-12 Envelope Packed; 1802B Layout Instruction Sheet; 1641-10 Instruction Sheet; 310-2 Set of (5) Billboards; D61-50 Accessory Catalog

Boxes & Packing: 59-320 Corr. Outfit Box (With Stickers); 61-171 Corr. Insert; 61-172 Corr. Insert; 61-173 Corr. Insert; 59-321 Shipper for (4) (1-4); 61-250 Outfit Box (Increase of 300); 61-181 Corr. Insert; 61-182 Corr. Insert; 61-184 Corr. Insert; 61-186 Corr. Insert; 61-251 Shipper for 4 (1-4); 61-250 Outfit Box (Increase of 1,400); 61-181 Corr. Insert; 61-182 Corr. Insert; 61-184 Corr. Insert; 61-183 Corr. Insert; 61-251 Shipper for 4 (1-4)

Alternate For Outfit Contents:
Note: For increase of 300 - use 61-250 box, inserts and shipper as listed above; Note: For increase of 1,400 - use 61-250 box, inserts and shipper as listed above.

X-694 (1961)	C6	C7	C8	Rarity
Complete Outfit With no. 59-320 Box	385	700	1,075	R9
Outfit Box no. 59-320	175	350	575	R9
Complete Outfit With no. 61-250 Box	310	500	725	R6
Outfit Box no. 61-250	100	150	225	R6

Comments: S. Klein was a discount retailer that purchased numerous promotional Lionel outfits in the 1960s. This Retailer Promotional Type Ia outfit was its only purchase for 1961.

A space and military outfit, the no. X-694 was headed by a no. 246-25 Steam Type Locomotive (new in 1959). This engine featured Magne-Traction, a two-position reverse unit and the later body version with a closed pilot and lack of the small generator detail on its top in front of the cab.

Since it came unboxed (as indicated by the "-25"), a no. CTC-1 Lockon was required separately and included in the no. 1103-12 Envelope Packed.

The rolling stock included some of the nicer items from 1961. The nos. 3665-25 Minuteman Missile Launching Car and 3509-25 Oper. Satellite Launching Car (Manually) were both new items. They were paired with the no. 6470-25 Exploding Target Car and no. 6057-25 Caboose (Red). All the items were unboxed and equipped with operating AAR trucks and couplers.

When items were unboxed, their individual instruction sheets were placed loose in the outfit box. These, along with the outfit instruction sheets and the other peripherals, were all appropriate for 1961.

The no. 1802B Layout Instruction Sheet detailed the figure-eight track layout.

As with many other outfits, revisions to the X-694 were made along the way. This outfit included at least five such changes, at least one of which increased the number of factory orders. When this revision occurred, the inventory of outfit boxes may have been depleted, which would have necessitated a switch.

The X-694 used a no. 59-320 Tan RSC with Black Graphics outfit box. That box was manufactured by Express Container Corp. and measured 11½ x 10⅝ x 7¼ inches. The increase in orders led to the adoption of a no. 61-250 Orange RSC with Black Graphics outfit box. It measured 13 x 12 x 7 inches.

The Tan RSC version of this outfit was manufactured in lower quantities and has a higher rarity rating.

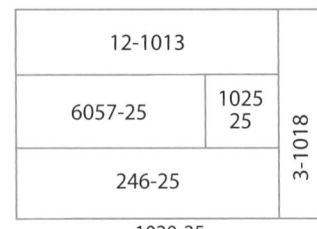

CONVENTIONAL PACK
59-320 BOX
STICKER

TOP LAYER

| 244T-25 |
| 6470-25 |
| 3509-25 |
| 3665-25 |

BOTTOM LAYER

12-1013	
6057-25	1025-25
246-25	

3-1018

1020-25
1008-50

CONVENTIONAL PACK
61-250 BOX
300 INCREASE

TOP LAYER

| 3509-25 |
| 6470-25 |
| 3665-25 |

1020-25 TOP

BOTTOM LAYER

3-1018 12-1013	1008-50
6057-25	1025-25
244T-25	
246-25	

Description: "O27" Promotional Outfit
Specification: "O27" Steam Type Freight Outfit
Customer/Price: Raleigh; 1900 Coupons
Original Amount: 200
Factory Order Date: 7/24/1961
Date Issued: Rev. #1 11-28-61
Packaging: R.S.C. Outfit Packing (Units not Boxed)

Contents: 1060-25 Steam Type Locomotive; 1050T-25 Tender; 3409-25 Operating Helicopter Launching Car (Manually); 6076-75 Hopper Car - Black; 6406-25 Single Automobile Car (Less Auto); 6406-30 Automobile; 6067-25 Caboose; 1013-8 Curved Track (Bundle of 8 - 1013); 1018-10 Straight Track (Loose) (2); 1026-25 25-Watt Transformer; 1103-12 Envelope Packed; 1123-10 Instruction Sheet; 310-2 Set of (5) Billboards; D61-50 Accessory Catalog

Boxes & Packing: 61-170 Outfit Box; 61-171 Corr. Insert; 61-172 Corr. Insert; 61-173 Corr. Insert; 61-174 Shipper for (6) (1-6)

X-695 (1961)	C6	C7	C8	Rarity
Complete Outfit	590	900	1,200	R10
Outfit Box no. 61-170	450	650	800	R10

Comments: Brown & Williamson and its Raleigh brand of cigarettes operated a successful promotional coupon program that was in full gear during the 1960s.

A Factory Order exists for the no. X-695 and indicates that the customer for this Retailer Promotional Type IIIb outfit was Raleigh. However, the X-695 did not appear in the Raleigh premium catalog for 1961. In fact, no outfit was shown there.

To add to this mystery, a no. X-705 Gift House Stamp Retailer Promotional Type Ib outfit for 1961 has been observed with a Raleigh shipping label. This label suggests that the X-705 was a substitution made by Raleigh in 1961.

One possible explanation for this substitution is that the Raleigh promotion was so successful that it sold out of the X-695. Raleigh then went to Gift House Stamp instead of Lionel to obtain additional outfits to fulfill its orders since it was a common practice at the time for stamp companies to fulfill products for other firms. Gift House Stamp in turn supplied Raleigh with outfit X-705 (the 1961 version of that outfit was almost an exact substitute for the X-695).

It appears that the promotion continued its success into 1962. Raleigh likely kept its relationship with Gift House Stamp, as the 1962 version of the X-705 appeared in the Raleigh premium catalog for 1962. This version of the X-705 was a slight upgrade. (For more information, see the entry for outfit X-705.)

The X-695 was an entry-level offering with the no. 1060-25 Steam Type Locomotive, which moved forward only. Except for the promotional-only no. 3409-25 Operating Helicopter Launching Car (Manually), the cars were low-end items with non-operating Archbar trucks and couplers and were offered in several promotional outfits. The 3409's matching no. 3419-100 Operating Helicopter Complete requires care to find with original, unbroken parts.

The no. 61-170 Tan RSC with Black Graphics outfit box measured 11½ x 10¼ x 6¼ inches.

If it weren't for the extremely low quantity of the X-695, it would be just one of the many low-end offerings of the 1960s. With only 200 manufactured, this outfit becomes a true collectible.

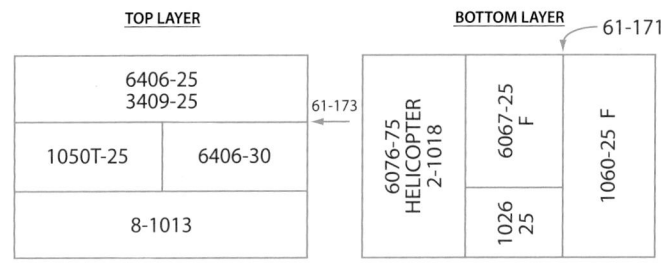

CONVENTIONAL PACK
61-170 BOX

Description: "O27" Promotional Outfit
Specification: "O27" Steam Type Freight Outfit
Customer: Bloomingdales
Original Amount: 200
Factory Order Date: 7/24/1961
Date Issued: Rev. #1 12-4-61
Packaging: R.S.C. Outfit Packing (Units not Boxed)

Contents: 1060-25 Steam Type Locomotive; 1050T-25 Tender; 6406-25 Single Automobile Car (Less Auto); 6406-30 Automobile; 6042-25 Gondola Car (Less 2 Canisters); 6112-5 Canister - Red (2); 3376-25 Oper. Giraffe Car (Less 3376-118 Envelope); 3376-118 Envelope Packed; 6067-25 Caboose; 1013-8 Curved Track (Bundle of 8 - 1013); 1018-10 Straight Track (Loose) (2); 1026-25 25-Watt Transformer; 1103-12 Envelope Packed; 1123-10 Instruction Sheet; 310-2 Set of (5) Billboards; D61-50 Accessory Catalog

Boxes & Packing: 61-170 Outfit Box; 61-171 Corr. Insert; 61-172 Corr. Insert; 61-173 Corr. Insert; 61-174 Shipper for (6) (1-6)

X-696 (1961)	C6	C7	C8	Rarity
Complete Outfit	565	785	1,125	R10
Outfit Box no. 61-170	425	625	775	R10

Comments: Bloomingdales purchased two Retailer Promotional Type Ib outfits in 1961. Although both were steam freight outfits, the locomotive and cars included in the no. X-696 made it a lower-end offering than its companion no. X-697.

A no. 1060-25 Steam Type Locomotive, a promotional-only model that ran just forward, headed the X-696. It pulled cars that, with the exception of the no. 3376-25 Oper. Giraffe Car, could be considered as low-end, common items.

The 3376-25 was the only component of this outfit that came with two operating AAR trucks and couplers; everything else had non-operating Archbar trucks and couplers. When included in outfits, it was most often individually boxed. When unboxed, though, its no. 3376-118 Envelope Packed was placed loose in the outfit box.

This outfit's common no. 61-170 Tan RSC with Black Graphics outfit box measured 11½ x 10¼ x 6¼ inches.

Only the small quantity of the X-696 that Lionel assembled accounts for the value of this outfit. Otherwise, its common items and outfit box make it just one of the many low-end outfits of the 1960s.

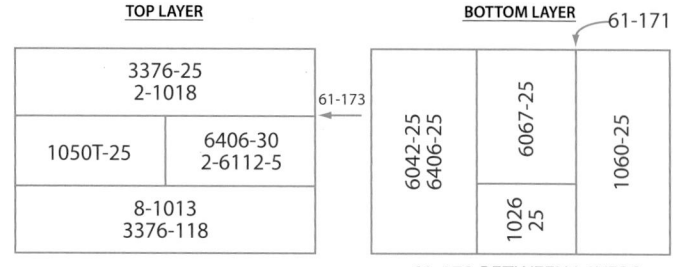

CONVENTIONAL PACK
61-170 BOX

X-697
1961

Description: "O27" Promotional Outfit
Specification: "O27" Steam Type Freight Outfit With Smoke
Customer: Bloomingdales
Original Amount: 75
Factory Order Date: 7/24/1961
Date Issued: 8/2/61
Packaging: R.S.C. Outfit Packing (Units Boxed)

Contents: 247-1 Steam Type Locomotive; 247T-1 Tender; 3509-1 Oper. Satellite Launching Car (Manually); 6530-1 Fire & Safety Training Car; 6017-1 Caboose; 1013-8 Curved Track (Bundle of 8 - 1013); 1018-30 Straight Track (Bundle of 3 - 1018); 1008-50 Uncoupling Track Section; 1025-25 45-Watt Transformer; 81-32 24" R.C. Wire (2); 1642-10 Instruction Sheet; 310-2 Set of (5) Billboards; D61-50 Accessory Catalog

Boxes & Packing: 61-170 Outfit Box; 61-174 Shipper for (6) (1-6)

X-697 (1961)	C6	C7	C8	Rarity
Complete Outfit	1,025	1,700	2,100	R10
Outfit Box no. 61-170	750	1,150	1,300	R10

Comments: This Retailer Promotional Type Ib was Bloomingdales' second and more desirable outfit (along with the no. X-696) in 1961.

Like its companion, the no. X-697 was powered by a steamer. In fact, it was one of the last outfits to include a no. 247-1 Steam Type Locomotive. Lionel was depleting its inventory in promotional outfits such as this one. This steamer first appeared in 1959 and included a two-position reversing unit, smoke and ballast weights.

Packed inside its no. 247-12 Corrugated Box were the nos. CTC-1 Lockon, 927-60 Tube of Oil, 247-11 Instruction Sheet, 909-10 Smoke Fluid and 927-65 Tube of Grease. Consequently, all that was required to operate this outfit were the two no. 81-32 24" Wires included loose in the outfit box. The 247-12 Corrugated Box was placed inside an orange no. 247-14 Box Sleeve.

The no. 3509-1 Oper. Satellite Launching Car (Manually) was available only in boxed form in promotional outfits. As such, this was the only way to obtain its Orange Picture box. (See the entry for outfit no. X-647 for information about its instruction sheets.)

All the rolling stock in the X-697 came equipped with operating AAR trucks and couplers and a combination of Orange Perforated and Orange Picture boxes.

The generic no. 61-170 Tan RSC with Black Graphics outfit box, measuring 11½ x 10¼ x 6¼ inches, was extremely common. However, when stamped with no. X-697, it became rare.

This outfit has yet to be observed in any sort of Bloomingdales literature. With quantities this low, it was likely just offered in stores and never cataloged. The quantity of the X-697 is the reason for its R10 rarity and price.

CONVENTIONAL PACK
61-170 BOX

TOP LAYER

| 8-1013 3-1018 |
| 247T-1 F |
| 6530-1 S |

1008-50 TOP 247T

BOTTOM LAYER

1025-25	6017-1 S
247-1 F	
3509-1 F	

X-698
1961

Description: "O27" Promotional Outfit
Specification: "O27" Diesel Freight Outfit
Customer: McMahon's
Original Amount: 900
Factory Order Date: 7/24/1961
Date Issued: Rev. #2 10-31-61
Packaging: R.S.C. Outfit Packing (Units Boxed)

Contents: 220P-1 Alco Diesel Power Unit - "Santa Fe"; 3330-1 Flat Car With Operating Submarine (Kit); 6476-1 Hopper Car - Red; 6050-1 Savings Bank Car; 6825-1 Trestle Bridge Flat Car; 6017-1 Caboose; 1013-70 Curved Track (Bundle of 12 - 1013); 1018-5 Straight Track (Bundle of 5 - 1018); 1018-75 Straight Track (Bundle of 6 - 1018); 1008-50 Uncoupling Track Section; 1025-25 45-Watt Transformer; 1020-25 90° Crossing; 81-32 24" R.C. Wire (2); LIS Layout Instruction Sheet; IS Instruction Sheet; 310-2 Set of (5) Billboards; D61-50 Accessory Catalog

Boxes & Packing: 61-210 Outfit Box; 61-191 Corr. Insert; 61-211 Shipper for (4) (1-4)

Alternate For Outfit Contents:
Note: Sub. 231P-1 for 220P-1 in 150 sets.

X-698 (1961)	C6	C7	C8	Rarity
Complete Outfit	460	750	1,175	R7
Outfit Box no. 61-210	150	250	350	R7

Comments: McMahon's was listed as the customer on this Factory Order. Unfortunately, this was a common name in the 1960s and no additional information about it is available. This Promotional Type Ib or IIIb was this customer's only promotional outfit purchase in 1961.

Outfit nos. X-606, X-688 and X-698 were the last three to include a no. 220P Santa Fe Alco Diesel Power Unit. Lionel was depleting the final items in stock. In fact, with the substitution of 150 of the 220P-1 Santa Fe for the no. 231P-1 Rock Island, it appears the remaining quantity was falling short of completing its assigned outfits.

The "-1" boxed version of the 220P-1 included in this outfit came equipped with two-axle Magne-Traction, a three-position reversing unit, a headlight and an open pilot with a large ledge. The only feature missing was a horn.

All rolling stock was boxed in a combination of Orange Perforated and Orange Picture boxes. The cars were all equipped with operating AAR trucks and couplers.

The no. 3330-1 Flat Car With Operating Submarine (Kit) is difficult to find in C8 condition with an unassembled no. 3330-200 Submarine Kit and its parts still sealed in their plastic bag. The Type I no. 6050-1 Savings Bank Car was new for 1961. The remaining cars were repeat items.

Of note is the track plan for this outfit. The exact Layout Instruction Sheet has yet to be identified, although it probably was the no. 2165, dated 8-60. That sheet can be linked to outfit no. X-573NA, which has a similar track plan but four fewer sections of straight track.

The no. 61-210 Orange RSC with Black Graphics outfit box was manufactured by Mead Containers and measured 13⅞ x 13¼ x 6½ inches.

The substitution of a 231P-1 for a 220P-1 has little effect on the price or rarity of this outfit.

CONVENTIONAL PACK
61-210 BOX

TOP LAYER	
12-1013 1008-50	
5-1018 6-1018	
1025-25	6017-1 F
INSERT 61-191	

1020-25 TOP

	BOTTOM LAYER	
6050-1 S	3330-1 F	
	6825-1 S	
	6476-1 S	
	220P-1 F	

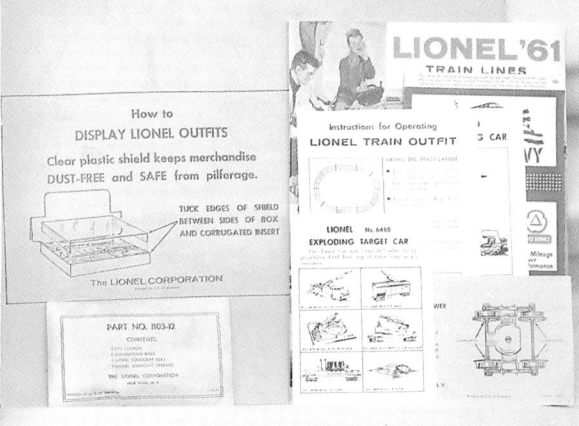

Kroger space and military outfit no. X-699, though small, was one of the nicer entry-level offerings in 1961. The two cars provided plenty of play value. Also shown is the no. 61-104 Envelope Packed with the no. 61-107 Acetate Dust Cover enclosed.

The no. 61-432 hinged display outfit box had "No. X-699" printed as part of the box manufacturing process.

Description: "O27" Promotional Outfit
Specification: "O27" Steam Type Freight Outfit
Customer/Price: Kroger; $9.99
Original Amount: 8,000
Factory Order Date: 8/15/1961
Date Issued: Rev. #2 10-11-61
Packaging: Display Outfit Packing (Units not Boxed)

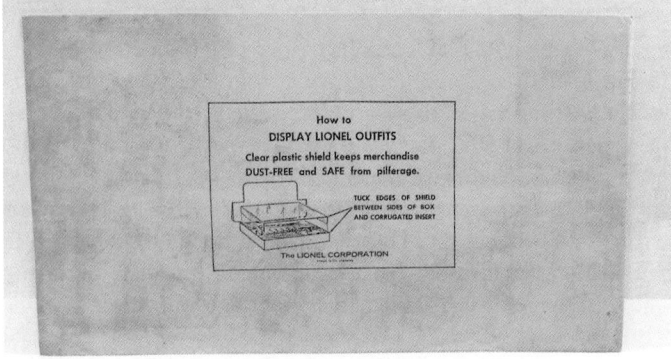

Lionel provided a no. 61-104 Envelope Packed to retailers with every six outfits. This allowed them to display the trains and keep them "dust free" and protected from "pilferage." This rare item is shown with the no. 61-108 Envelope and the no. 61-107 Acetate Dust Cover.

Contents: 1060-25 Steam Type Locomotive; 1050T-25 Tender; 6630-25 Missile Launching Car (Less Missile); 6650-80 Missile Complete (or 6650-84); 6480-25 Exploding Target Car; 6067-25 Caboose; 1013-8 Curved Track (Bundle of 8 - 1013); 1018-10 Straight Track (Loose) (2); 1026-25 25-Watt Transformer; 1103-12 Envelope Packed; 1123-10 Instruction Sheet; 310-2 Set of (5) Billboards; D61-50 Accessory Catalog

Boxes & Packing: 61-432 Display Outfit Box; 61-101 Corr. Insert; 61-102 Corr. Insert (2); 61-103 Shipper for (6) (1-6); 61-104 Env. Packed 1 per shipper (1-6)

X-699 (1961)	C6	C7	C8	Rarity
Complete Outfit	200	325	525	R3
Outfit Box no. 61-432	40	75	150	R3
Complete Outfit With no. 61-104	800	1,125	1,525	R10

Comments: Kroger grocery stores purchased 8,000 of these Retailer Promotional Type Ib outfits in 1961. Quaker's no. X-600, S&H's no. X-612 and Sears' no. 9670 were the only Retailer and Manufacturer Promotional outfits from 1961 that were produced in larger quantities than the no. X-699.

Outfit X-699 appeared in a Kroger advertisement printed in the December 6, 1961, edition of the *Van Wert Times Bulletin* in Van Wert, Ohio. It was listed as "Lionel Elec. Train each $9.99 Reg. $14.99 Value. Hurry – supplies limited". Since Kroger had ordered 8,000 of these outfits, supplies were more than ample.

A space and military outfit, the X-699 was headed by a no. 1060-25 Steam Type Locomotive (found only in promotional outfits). This low-end engine, which moved only forward, had a headlight and a 2-4-2 wheel configuration.

Even though the X-699 had only two cars and a caboose, it was a nice starter outfit. The nos. 6480-25 Exploding Target Car and 6630-25 Missile Launching Car were both new for 1961 and provided plenty of play value. They were low-end versions of the nos. 6470 and 6650, respectively.

All the rolling stock came with non-operating Archbar trucks and couplers. The billboards, instruction sheets and packed envelope were all appropriate for 1961.

The no. 61-432 White 4-6-4 Steamer and F3 Hinged Display with Red/Orange and Blue Graphics Type A outfit box was manufactured by Express Container, Corp. and measured 22¾ x 11⅜ x 3⅛ inches. Although this was a uniquely numbered box, leftover inventory was overstickered and used for promotional outfit nos. X-681 and 11001.

With every shipper of six outfits Lionel packaged a no. 61-104 Envelope Packed. This envelope included a no. 61-107 Acetate Dust Cover in a no. 61-108 Envelope. The printing on the envelope states that the "clear plastic shield keeps merchandise dust free and safe from pilferage." These were likely used to display the outfits in Kroger stores. Pricing and rarity are provided separately for this seldom seen item. In 1963, Lionel developed the blister display to serve the same purpose.

With 8,000 of these outfits manufactured, the X-699 is readily available. But as with any outfit, finding a C8 example, complete with all its peripherals, takes some work.

DISPLAY PACK
61-432 BOX

1060-25	1050T-25	1026-25
6480-25	6630-25	
2-1018 8-1013	6067-25	

Description: "O27" Promotional Outfit
Specification: "O27" Steam Type Freight Outfit
Customer: Kiddie City
Original Amount: 150
Factory Order Date: 8/10/1961
Date Issued: 8-15-61
Packaging: R.S.C. Outfit Packing (Units not Boxed)

Contents: 1060-25 Steam Type Locomotive; 1050T-25 Tender; 3409-25 Oper. Helicopter Launching Car (Manually); 6076-75 Hopper Car - Black; 6042-25 Gondola Car (Less 2 Canisters); 6112-5 Canister - Red (2); 6406-25 Single Automobile Car (Less Auto); 6406-30 Automobile; 6067-25 Caboose; 1013-8 Curved Track (Bundle of 8 - 1013); 1018-10 Straight Track (Loose) (2); 1026-25 25-Watt Transformer; 1103-12 Envelope Packed; 1123-10 Instruction Sheet; 310-2 Set of (5) Billboards; D61-50 Accessory Catalog

Boxes & Packing: 61-170 Outfit Box; 61-171 Corr. Insert; 61-172 Corr. Insert; 61-173 Corr. Insert; 61-174 Shipper for (6) (1-6)

X-700 (1961)	C6	C7	C8	Rarity
Complete Outfit	650	1,000	1,350	R10
Outfit Box no. 61-170	500	750	950	R10

Comments: Kiddie City discount stores purchased this Retailer Promotional Type Ib outfit in 1961. It was that chain's only promotional outfit purchase. As explained in the section on Lionel's Distribution and Customers, Kiddie City subsequently was purchased by Lionel in 1969.

A basic starter outfit, the no. X-700 included the same engine and rolling stock as did outfit no. X-706. Both outfits were headed by the no. 1060-25 Steam Type Locomotive. That engine, which moved forward only, was used exclusively in promotional outfits.

The most notable item in this outfit was the promotional-only no. 3409-25 Oper. Helicopter Launching Car (Manually). Its flat car is fairly common, but finding its no. 3419-100 Operating Helicopter Complete in original, unbroken condition is more of a challenge. That car would have come with a no. 3409-10 Instruction Sheet (dated "5-61 Rev.") packed loose with the other peripherals in the outfit box. The 3409-25 and all the other rolling stock were equipped with non-operating Archbar trucks and couplers.

The X-700 came in a no. 61-170 Tan RSC with Black Graphics outfit box that measured 11¼ x 10¼ x 6¼ inches. Although all the components are fairly common, the outfit box, with only 150 factory orders, is rare and seldom seen.

CONVENTIONAL PACK
61-170 BOX

TOP LAYER

6076-75 3409-25	1 CAN
6406-30 1 CAN	1050T-25
8-1013	

2-1018 TOP 6076

BOTTOM LAYER

6042-25 HELICOPTER 6406-25	6067-25	1060-25
	1026 25	

Description: "O27" Promotional Outfit
Specification: "O27" Diesel Freight Outfit
Customer: R. S. S.
Original Amount: 200
Factory Order Date: 8/9/1961
Date Issued: Rev. #2 10-5-61
Packaging: R.S.C. Outfit Packing (Units Boxed)

Contents: 231P-1 Alco Diesel Power Car - "Rock Island"; 3665-1 Minuteman Missile Launching Car; 6470-1 Exploding Target Car; 6825-1 Trestle Bridge Flat Car; 3410-1 Operating Helicopter Launching Car (Manually); 6017-1 Caboose; 1013-70 Curved Track (Bundle of 12 - 1013); 1018-30 Straight Track (Bundle of 3 - 1018); 1008-50 Uncoupling Track Section; 1025-25 45-Watt Transformer; 1020-25 90° Crossing; 81-32 24" R.C. Wire (2); 1802B Layout Instruction Sheet; X602-10 Instruction Sheet; 310-2 Set of (5) Billboards; D61-50 Accessory Catalog

Boxes & Packing: 59-351 Outfit Box (W/Stickers); 59-352 Shipper for (4) (1-4)

X-701 (1961)	C6	C7	C8	Rarity
Complete Outfit	850	1,275	1,725	R10
Outfit Box no. 59-351	475	650	825	R10

Comments: This is the only promotional outfit purchased by R. S. S. Without any additional information, the true identity of R. S. S. cannot be determined. As such, this is either a Retailer Promotional Type Ib or a Manufacturer Promotional Type IIIb outfit.

This space and military outfit was headed by the new no. 231P-1 Rock Island Alco Diesel Power Car. That locomotive included a two-position reversing unit, two-axle Magne-Traction and a headlight. Except for the out-of-place inclusion of a no. 6825-1 Trestle Bridge Flat Car, the rolling stock was typical for space and military outfits. This was the only time a no. 3410 Operating Helicopter Launching Car (Manually), a no. 3665 Minuteman Missile Launching Car and a no. 6470 Exploding Target Car appeared together in the same outfit.

The Orange Picture no. 3410-10 Folding Box is difficult to

CONVENTIONAL PACK
59-351 BOX
STICKER

TOP LAYER

3410-1 F	
12-1013	6017-1 S
6470-1	

3-1018 TOP 3410
1008-50 TOP 1013
1020-25 TOP

BOTTOM LAYER

231P-1 F	
3665-1 F	1025-25
6825-1 S	

obtain. The 3410-1 was never offered for separate sale; therefore, the only way to obtain a boxed version was through a promotional outfit. It appeared boxed in only eight outfits.

All the rolling stock came in a combination of Orange Perforated and Orange Picture boxes. The cars were equipped with operating AAR trucks and couplers.

Also included in the X-701 was a figure-eight track layout, as detailed on the no. 1802B Layout Instruction Sheet.

X-702
1961

Description: "O27" Promotional Outfit
Specification: "O27" Steam Type Freight Outfit W/Smoke
Customer: Masters
Original Amount: 600
Factory Order Date: 8/10/1961
Date Issued: Rev. #1 11-16-61
Packaging: R.S.C. Outfit Packing (Units not Boxed)

Contents: 236-25 Steam Type Locomotive With Smoke; 1130T-25 Tender; 3370-25 Animated Sheriff & Outlaw Car; 6062-25 Gondola Car - Black (Less Cable Reels); 40-11 Cable Reels (3); 6050-25 Savings Bank Car; 6057-25 Caboose (Red); 1013-8 Curved Track (Bundle of 8 - 1013); 1018-10 Straight Track (Loose); 1008-50 Uncoupling Track Section; 1025-25 45-Watt Transformer; 1103-12 Envelope Packed; 909-10 Bottle Smoke Fluid; X602-10 Instruction Sheet; 310-2 Set of (5) Billboards; D61-50 Accessory Catalog

Boxes & Packing: 61-180 Corr. Outfit Box; 61-181 Corr. Insert; 61-182 Corr. Insert; 61-183 Corr. Insert; 61-184 Corr. Insert; 61-185 Shipper for (4) (1-4)

X-702 (1961)	C6	C7	C8	Rarity
Complete Outfit	325	550	800	R8
Outfit Box no. 61-180	175	300	425	R8

Comments: Masters purchased three Retailer Promotional outfits in 1961. All of them – nos. X-702, X-703 and X-714 – were likely offered through Masters' leased departments within discount stores.

X-703
1961

Description: "O27" Promotional Outfit
Specification: "O27" Diesel Freight Outfit
Customer: Masters
Original Amount: 1,398
Factory Order Date: 12/4/1961
Date Issued: Rev. #3 12-11-61
Packaging: R.S.C. Outfit Packing (Units not Boxed)

Contents: 1065-25 Alco Diesel Power Unit - "Union Pacific"; 6406-25 Single Automobile Car (Less Auto); 6406-30 Automobile; 6042-25 Gondola Car (Less 2 Canisters); 6112-5 Canister -

The no. 59-351 Tan RSC with Black Graphics outfit box was left over from two years prior. It was first used for promotional outfit no. A-608-6 and subsequently overstickered and used for the nos. X-542NA, X-682 and X-708. It was manufactured by Express Container Corp. and measured 14 x 10½ x 6¾ inches.

The R10 rarity is attributed to the low original quantity of this outfit and the fact that examples are seldom seen.

As with many retailers, Masters purchased outfits to fulfill different customer segments. Type Ia outfit X-702 was a mid-level steam-powered outfit, whereas X-703 was diesel-powered. The X-714 was headed by a no. 45-1 Mobile Rocket Firing Car.

The unboxed no. 236-25 Steam Type Locomotive with Smoke (new for 1961) headed the X-702. That engine included Magne-Traction, a headlight and a two-position reversing unit. The peripherals normally included with a boxed no. 236-1 were placed loose in the outfit box or included in the no. 1103-12 Envelope Packed. These included the nos. 909-10 Bottle Smoke Fluid, CTC-1 Lockon, 927-60 Tube of Oil, 927-65 Tube of Grease and 236-11 Instruction Sheet.

The nos. 3370-25 Animated Sheriff & Outlaw Car and 6050-25 Savings Bank Car were also new for 1961. They and the other cars were equipped with operating AAR trucks and couplers.

The no. 61-180 Tan RSC with Black Graphics outfit box used for this outfit measured 12¾ x 10 x 6¾ inches. Although the original quantity of these outfit was 600, it is seldom seen, which leads to its R8 rarity.

CONVENTIONAL PACK
61-180 BOX

TOP LAYER			BOTTOM LAYER		
6062-25 1018	40-11		8-1013		
6050-25	40-11		6057-25		1025 25
			1130T-25		
3370-25	40-11		236-25		

1008-50 TOP

Red (2); 6067-25 Caboose; 1013-8 Curved Track (Bundle of 8 - 1013); 1018-10 Straight Track (Loose) (2); 1026-25 25-Watt Transformer; 1103-12 Envelope Packed; 902-1 Cardboard Trestle W/Girder Bridge & Tunnel; 1125-10 Instruction Sheet; 310-2 Set of (5) Billboards; D61-50 Accessory Catalog

Boxes & Packing: 59-324 Outfit Box (W/Stickers); 61-171 Corr. Insert; 61-173 Corr. Insert; 59-325 Shipper for (4) (1-4)

Alternate For Outfit Contents:
Increase of 970 outfits - less 902; Substitute 227P-25 for 1065-25 in 895 outfits.

X-703 (1961)	C6	C7	C8	Rarity
Complete Outfit With no. 902-1	335	600	1,000	R7
Complete Outfit Without no. 902-1	235	400	525	R7
Either Outfit With A no. 227P-25 Substitution, Add The Following	55	80	100	R7
Outfit Box no. 59-324	115	200	235	R7

Comments: This was the second of three (nos. X-702, X-703 and X-714) outfits purchased by Masters in 1961. Masters leased departments within discount stores, and that is where this Retailer Promotional Type Ib outfit was likely sold.

As with many retailers, Masters purchased outfits to fulfill different customer segments. Outfit X-703 was its diesel-powered outfit, whereas X-702 was steam-powered. The X-714 was headed by a no. 45-1 Mobile Rocket Firing Car.

A low-end outfit, the X-703 was headed by the no. 1065-25 Union Pacific Alco Diesel Power Unit. This forward-only locomotive was as stripped down as Lionel could make an Alco in 1961. The rolling stock wasn't much better, as all the cars were equipped with non-operating Archbar trucks and couplers. The most exciting item from a collectibility standpoint is the no. 902-1 Cardboard Trestle W/Girder Bridge & Tunnel.

The original quantity of this outfit before revisions was 428. This odd quantity was likely linked to the number of 902-1s remaining in inventory, as the X-703 was the last outfit to include that cardboard item. When the quantity of this outfit increased to 1,398, Lionel appeared unable to meet the demand for the extra 902s; therefore, the remaining outfits did not include them.

It also appears that, being so late in the year, the 1961 inventory of 1065s was depleted in this outfit. It was substituted out for the no. 227P-25 Canadian National Alco, another low-end diesel that moved only forward.

Like other cardboard items placed in outfits, the 902-1 was fragile and intended to be assembled. Once used, it retained minimal value. This item was clearly marked Lionel; therefore, it did not become as easily separated from its train outfit as did the no. 910-1 Navy Yard Cardboard Display and the no. X625-20 Cardboard Scenic Set. Even so, an unassembled 902-1 in C8 condition is an expensive item.

The outfit pricing table includes pricing with and without the 902-1. If the 227P-25 is substituted, add the amounts as indicated in the table.

The no. 59-324 was a single-layer Tan RSC with Black Graphics outfit box. It was first used with outfit no. 1609 and subsequently with six other outfits including this one. It was manufactured by Express Container Corp. and measured 14⅞ x 12⅝ x 4¼ inches. Even with 1,398 examples produced, the X-703 is seldom seen.

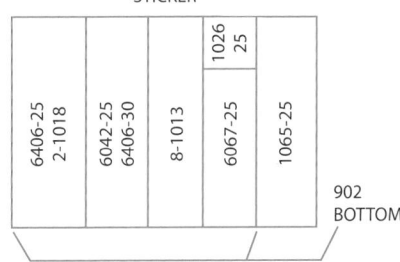

CONVENTIONAL PACK
59-324 BOX
STICKER

X-700 Series

Description: "O27" Promotional Outfit
Specification: "O27" Steam Type Freight Outfit
Customer/Price: Drug Fair; $14.85
Original Amount: 500
Factory Order Date: 8/10/1961
Date Issued: 8-15-61
Packaging: Display Outfit Packing (Units not Boxed)

Contents: 246-25 Steam Type Locomotive; 1060T-25 Tender; 6045-50 Tank Car - "Cities Service"; 6812-25 Track Maintenance Car; 3409-25 Oper. Helicopter Launching Car (Manually); 6067-25 Caboose; 1013-8 Curved Track (Bundle of 8 - 1013); 1018-10 Straight Track (Loose) (2); 1026-25 25-Watt Transformer; 1103-12 Envelope Packed; 6812-40 Envelope - (2 - 81-32 Wires and 1 - 3562-62 Figure); 902-1 Cardboard Trestle W/Girder Bridge & Tunnel; 903-1 Set of (2) Sheets Trading Cards; 1123-10 Instruction Sheet; 310-2 Set of (5) Billboards; D61-50 Accessory Catalog

Boxes & Packing: 61-431 Outfit Box; 61-391 Corr. Insert; 61-392 Corr. Insert; 61-393 Corr. Insert; 61-394 Corr. Insert; 61-395 Shipper for (6) (1-6)

X-704 (1961)	C6	C7	C8	Rarity
Complete Outfit	1,125	2,475	4,550	R9
Outfit Box no. 61-431	250	350	475	R8

Comments: This is the only Retailer Promotional Type Ib outfit purchased by variety chain store Drug Fair. It was common for drug stores to carry Lionel trains in the early 1960s.

This freight outfit included both low-end and mid-level components. It was headed by Lionel's workhorse Scout engine, the no. 246-25 Steam Type Locomotive. This engine was introduced in 1959 and appeared in outfits through 1962. The version included in the no. X-704 was the later one with a solid pilot and a lack of generator detail on top.

The items equipped with non-operating Archbar trucks and couplers included the nos. 1060T-25 Tender, 6045-50 Cities Service Tank Car, 3409-25 Oper. Helicopter Launching Car (Manually) and 6067-25 Caboose. The 3409-25 was available only in promotional outfits. Obtaining it with an original, unbroken no. 3419-100 Operating Helicopter Complete is more of a challenge.

The unboxed no. 6812-25 Track Maintenance Car with its two operating AAR trucks and couplers was an odd item to include with this outfit. Every other item was low-end, and the 6812-25 could be considered one of Lionel's mid-level items for 1961. Also, it appeared unboxed in only four outfits. When it did, the difficult-to-find no. 6812-40 Envelope - (2 - 81-32 Wires and 1 - 3562-62 Figure) was included. According to the 6812-25's Production Control File, Lionel originally intended to provide the no. 3562-62 Figure loose with the car, but this was changed and the 6812-40 Envelope Packed was created. Even though the inclusion of wires was redundant, it prevented the 3562-62 Figure for the top platform from being lost.

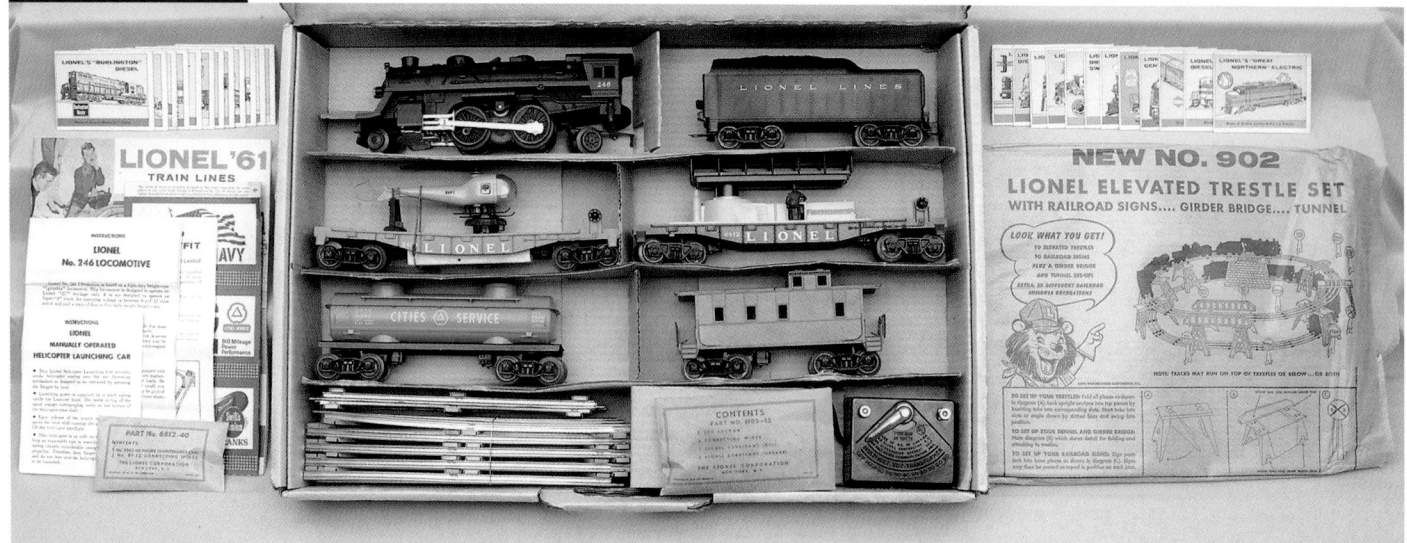

Outfit no. X-704 included the no. 903-1 Set of (2) Sheets Trading Cards as well as the no. 902-1 Cardboard Trestle W/Girder Bridge & Tunnel. These cardboard items are worth more than the outfit they came with because they are fragile and frequently assembled or lost.

The no. 61-431 Outfit Box was uniquely numbered for outfit no. X-704. Note the Drug Fair price tag with a price of $16 and unreadable change. That price was crossed out with a grease pen, and $14.85 was written on the box top.

By far the two items that drive the price of this outfit are the no. 902-1 Cardboard Trestle W/Girder & Tunnel and the no. 903-1 Set of (2) Sheets Trading Cards. Both of these items were fragile and intended to be separated and played with. Many more 902-1s survived intact than 903-1s.

The 903 included 24 two-sided Lionel trading cards printed on a sheet of perforated cardstock. On the front of each card was a Lionel locomotive, and on the back was historical information about its road name as well as a trivia quiz. Two 11 x 11 inch sets

of 12 cards were connected by a "folding" strip. The entire sheet of 24 was folded in half along the strip and placed loose in the outfit box. The cards were perforated and are almost always found separated as individual cards with the "folding" strip long gone. In fact, if it weren't for the complete sheets that came out of Madison Hardware over the years, it is likely that few of these items would be intact.

The no. 61-431 White 4-6-4 Steamer and F3 Hinged Display with Red/Orange and Blue Graphics Type A outfit box was manufactured by United Container Co. and measured 22½ x 15 x 3⅛ inches. Also printed as part of the box manufacturing certificate were an "E" and five dots. Although this was a uniquely numbered box, leftover inventory was overstickered and used for promotional outfit no. 19167 for 1962.

This outfit does show up from time to time, but it is almost always missing the 903-1 Set of (2) Sheets Trading Cards. It achieves an

DISPLAY PACK
61-431 BOX

246-25	1060T-25
3409-25	6812-25
6045-50	6067-25
2-1018 8-1013	1026-25

1-902 } TOP
1-903

R9 rarity rating due to these cards. To find an outfit with a set of 903s in C8 condition is a true challenge.

Customer No. On Box: T-013-7-0
Description: "O27" Promotional Outfit
Specification: "O27" Steam Type Freight Outfit
Customer/No.: Gift House Stamp; T-013-7-0
Original Amount: 700

Factory Order Date: 8/15/1961
Date Issued: Rev. #1 9-27-61
Packaging: R.S.C. Outfit Packing (Units not Boxed)

Contents: 246-25 Steam Type Locomotive; 1060T-25 Tender; 3409-25 Operating Helicopter Launching Car (Manually); 6076-75 Hopper Car - Black; 6406-25 Single Automobile Car (Less

Two empty boxes for the 1961 version of outfit no. X-705. Both are stamped with the Lionel number as well as Gift House Stamp's customer number.

The mailing label on a no. X-705 outfit from 1961 links the customer to Raleigh. It is likely this outfit was a substitution for Brown & Williamson's outfit no. X-695. Note that the shipment date was November, 1961 from Louisville, Ky., where Brown & Williamson had its headquarters.

turn, the stamps could be redeemed for merchandise chosen out of a catalog or at one of its redemption centers. Gift House Stamp purchased a total of three promotional outfits (nos. X-875, X-705 in 1961 and again in 1962). All were Retailer Promotional Type Ib outfits.

The X-705 included rolling stock that was commonly combined together. At least seven outfits for 1961 included the nos. 3409-25 Operating Helicopter Launching Car (Manually), 6076-75 Hopper Car - Black and 6406-25 Single Automobile Car. Beside the steamer and tender, all the rolling stock was new for 1961 and available only in promotional outfits. All the items had non-operating Archbar trucks and couplers.

In the 1960s, it was common for trading stamp companies to offer fulfillment services for other organizations. It appears that Gift House Stamp provided this service to Brown & Williamson for its Raleigh brand of cigarettes because this outfit has been observed with a Raleigh mailing label.

In 1961, Raleigh offered outfit no. X-695 to its customers. Outfit X-705 was almost an exact substitute for the X-695. One likely assumption is that the Raleigh promotion was so successful that it sold out of its supply of X-695. Instead of going to Lionel for additional outfits, Raleigh went to Gift House Stamp to obtain and fulfill its orders. Gift House Stamp supplied Raleigh with a quantity of the X-705.

To further confuse matters, the 1962 version of X-705 was a slight upgrade and it was shown in the 1962 Raleigh Premium catalog. Brown & Williamson likely continued to have Gift House Stamp fulfill its outfits.

The no. 61-170 Tan RSC with Black Graphics outfit box measured 11½ x 10¼ x 6¼ inches.

This outfit has yet to be observed in any Gift House Stamp literature. If it weren't for the Factory Orders, the true identity of the customer of this outfit would still be unknown.

As specified in the Factory Order, the Gift House Stamp "T-013-7-0" customer number appears, along with Lionel's number on this 1961 version. This information makes it easy to differentiate between the 1961 and 1962 versions.

Auto); 6406-30 Automobile; 6067-25 Caboose; 1013-8 Curved Track (Bundle of 8 - 1013); 1018-10 Straight Track (Loose) (2); 1026-25 25-Watt Transformer; 1103-12 Envelope Packed; 1119-10 Instruction Sheet; 310-2 Set of (5) Billboards; D61-50 Accessory Catalog

Boxes & Packing: 61-170 Outfit Box; 61-171 Corr. Insert; 61-172 Corr. Insert; 61-173 Corr. Insert; 61-174 Shipper for (6) (1-6)

Alternate For Outfit Contents:
Customer Stock No. T-013-7-0 to appear on outfit boxes and shippers.

X-705 (1961)	C6	C7	C8	Rarity
Complete Outfit	300	525	800	R8
Outfit Box no. 61-170	150	275	400	R8

Comments: Gift House Stamp, Inc. was one of the many companies that offered trading stamps for goods purchased. In

CONVENTIONAL PACK
61-170 BOX

TOP LAYER
1060T-25
3409-25
8-1013 2-1018

BOTTOM LAYER		
6076-75 6406-25	6067-25	246-25
	1026-25	

Description: "O27" Promotional Outfit
Specification: "O27" Steam Type Freight Outfit
Customer: Gift House Stamp
Customer/Price: Raleigh; 1900 Coupons
Original Amount: 1,000
Factory Order Date: 8/30/1962
Packaging: R S C Outfit Packing (Units not Boxed)

Contents: 242-25 Steam Type Locomotive; 1060T-25 Tender; 3410-25 Oper. Heli. Car - Manually Oper. - Less Heli.; 3419-100 Helicopter; 6076-25 Hopper Car; 6406-25 Single Automobile Car (Less Auto); 6406-30 Auto; 6067-25 Caboose; 1013-8 Curved Track (Bundle of 8 - 1013); 1018-10 Straight Track (Loose) (2); 1026-25 25-Watt Transformer; 1103-20 Envelope Packed; 310-2 Set of (5) Billboards; D62-50 Accessory Catalog;

In 1962, outfit no. X-705 was a repeat of the 1961 version but with some upgraded components. The upgrades were due to previous items no longer being available from Lionel.

O. Lionel Electric Train—Steam locomotive and tender, helicopter car, hopper car, flat car with auto, and caboose. Oval track has 8 curved sections and 2 straight sections. Transformer and wires......1900 Coupons

The Raleigh premium catalog for 1962 illustrates a train outfit on page 33 for 1,900 coupons. The picture matches Gift House Stamp outfit no. X-705 rather than Raleigh no. X-695. It is likely that Gift House Stamp provided fulfillment services for Raleigh in 1961 and 1962. Note that a no. 6405-25 Single Auto Car is incorrectly shown.

1123-40 Instruction Sheet; 3410-5 Instruction Sheet; 19106-10 Instruction Sheet

Boxes & Packing: 61-170 Outfit Box; 61-171 Insert; 61-172 Insert; 61-173 Insert; 61-174 Shipper for (6) (1-6)

X-705 (1962)	C6	C7	C8	Rarity
Complete Outfit	250	475	725	R7
Outfit Box no. 61-170	100	200	300	R7

Comments: This was the 1962 version of Gift House Stamp outfit no. X-705 (see the entry for the X-705 for 1961). Trading stamp companies would often repeat outfits because their redemption catalogs sometimes spanned calendar years.

It also appears that the relationship with Brown & Williamson was still in place because this outfit was shown in the Raleigh premium catalog for 1962. For a mere 1,900 coupons, you could

obtain this outfit from Raleigh. It was likely easier for Brown & Williamson to outsource its fulfillment than to do so in house.

This Retailer Promotional Type Ib outfit attempted to mirror the version for 1961, but Lionel had discontinued some of the components. Specifically, the X-705 was now headed by a no. 242-25 Steam Type Locomotive, which was new for 1962. This low-end locomotive replaced the no. 246-25 and included a traction tire, a two-position reversing unit and a headlight.

The no. 3409-25 Operating Helicopter Launching Car (Manually) was no longer available, so a no. 3410-25 Oper. Heli. Car - Manually Oper. - Less Heli. was used instead. It was equipped with two operating AAR trucks and couplers. Interestingly, in 1962 Lionel gave the task of adding the no. 3419-100 Operating Helicopter Complete to the Outfit Packing Department (as noted on the 3410-25 Production Control File).

In 1962, the Production Control File for the 3419-100 Operating Helicopter Complete changed from a gray Navy stamped two-piece helicopter body to an unmarked helicopter with a one-piece yellow helicopter body. Although this was Lionel's intended production, many 3419-100 Navy helicopters still appeared on 3410s in 1962.

All the remaining rolling stock was equipped with non-operating Archbar trucks and couplers.

CONVENTIONAL PACK
61-170 BOX

TOP LAYER

1060T-25
3419-100 3410-25
8-1013 2-1018

61-173

BOTTOM LAYER

61-171

6076-25 6406-30 6406-25	6067-25	242-25
	1026-25	

61-172 BETWEEN LAYERS

The X-705 for 1962, like the one for the previous year, came in a no. 61-170 Tan RSC with Black Graphics outfit box. It was manufactured by St. Joe Kraft and measured 11½ x 10¼ x 6¼ inches.

Be aware that the updated X-705 does not have the Gift House Stamp "T-013-7-0" customer number, an omission that helps to differentiate it from the 1961 version. With quantities slightly higher than the previous year, this outfit is a little easier to find and hence has a lower rarity rating.

Description: "O27" Promotional Outfit
Specification: "O27" Steam Type Freight Outfit
Customer: Prophylactic Brush Company
Original Amount: 300
Factory Order Date: 10/9/1961
Date Issued: 10-9-61
Packaging: R.S.C. Outfit Packing (Units not Boxed)

Contents: 1060-25 Steam Type Locomotive; 1050T-25 Tender; 3409-25 Operating Helicopter Launching Car (Manually); 6076-75 Hopper Car - Black; 6042-25 Gondola Car (Less 2 Canisters); 6112-5 Canister - Red (2); 6406-25 Single Automobile Car (Less Auto); 6406-30 Automobile; 6067-25 Caboose; 1013-70 Curved Track (Bundle of 12 - 1013); 1018-40 Straight Track (Bundle of 4 - 1018); 1026-25 25-Watt Transformer; 1020-25 90° Crossing; 1103-12 Envelope Packed; 1802B Layout Instruction Sheet; 1123-10 Instruction Sheet; 310-2 Set of (5) Billboards; D61-50 Accessory Catalog

Boxes & Packing: 61-180 Corr. Outfit Box; 61-171 Corr. Insert; 61-183 Corr. Insert; 61-184 Corr. Insert; 61-185 Shipper for (4) (1-4)

X-706 (1961)	C6	C7	C8	Rarity
Complete Outfit	385	625	1,025	R9
Outfit Box no. 61-180	225	350	575	R9

Comments: This was the second of two (see no. X-620) Prophylactic Brush Company Manufacturer Promotional Type IIIb outfits purchased in 1961.

The no. X-706 is very similar to outfit X-620, except that the no. 6050-25 Savings Bank Car was replaced by a no. 3409-25 Operating Helicopter Launching Car (Manually).

The track layout was more elaborate, now being a figure-eight pretzel layout. Otherwise it was the same outfit. This may have been an add-on order to the X-620 or an RSC version to fulfill different customer needs.

In either case, the X-706 was a low-end steam outfit powered by the no. 1060-25 Steam Type Locomotive found in many promotional outfits. This was Lionel's low-end, forward-only steam offering in 1961 whose only feature of note was a headlight. The rolling stock was also low-end and came equipped with non-operating Archbar trucks and couplers. The most exciting item was the promotional-only 3409-25 with its no. 3419-100 Operating Helicopter Complete.

The no. 61-180 Tan RSC with Black Graphics outfit box measured 12¾ x 10 x 6¾ inches.

It is unknown why Prophylactic Brush would purchase two so similar outfits during the same year. This outfit, because fewer examples were manufactured, is more difficult to find than the X-620 and is seldom seen, hence its R9 rarity.

CONVENTIONAL PACK
61-180 BOX

TOP LAYER

| 12-1013 4-1018 |
| 3409-25 |
| HELICOPTER |
| 6406-25 6042-25 |

BOTTOM LAYER

| 6112-5 (2) | 6067-25 | 1060-25 |
| 6076-75 6406-30 1050T-25 | 1026-25 | |

Description: "O27" Promotional Outfit
Specification: "O27" Steam Type Freight Outfit
Customer: Popular Club Plan
Original Amount: 481
Factory Order Date: 8/15/1961
Date Issued: Rev. #2 12-6-61
Packaging: R.S.C. Outfit Packing (Individual Mailers), (Units not Boxed)

Contents: 1060-25 Steam Type Locomotive; 1050T-25 Tender; 6042-25 Gondola Car (Less 2 Canisters); 6112-5 Canister - Red (2); 6076-75 Hopper Car - Black; 6406-25 Single Automobile Car (Less Auto); 6406-30 Automobile; 6067-25 Caboose; 1013-8 Curved Track (Bundle of 8 - 1013); 1018-10 Straight Track (Loose) (2); 1026-25 25-Watt Transformer; 1103-12 Envelope Packed; 1123-10 Instruction Sheet; 310-2 Set of (5) Billboards; D61-50 Accessory Catalog

Boxes & Packing: 61-399 Outfit Box; 61-171 Corr. Insert; 61-172 Corr. Insert; 61-173 Corr. Insert; 61-174 Shipper for (6) (1-6)

X-707 (1961)	C6	C7	C8	Rarity
Complete Outfit	225	400	600	R7
Outfit Box no. 61-399	125	225	340	R7

Comments: Popular Club Plan is a catalog company selling an assortment of clothing, housewares, jewelry, toys and electronics. In 1961 and 1962, it offered a Retailer Promotional Type Ib outfit to its customers.

Outfit no. X-707 was repeated for both years with almost the same contents. Both outfits were headed by a no. 1060-25 Steam Type Locomotive with a headlight. That engine, which moved just forward, was used only in promotional outfits.

All the rolling stock represented Lionel's low-end offerings, with many items found only in promotional outfits. The sole difference in rolling stock was that the 1961 version had a slope-back no. 1050T-25 Tender whereas the 1962 included a streamlined no. 1060T-25 Tender. These and all other cars were equipped with non-operating Archbar trucks and couplers.

As with many of these low-end outfits, the no. 6406-30 Automobile is the most difficult item to obtain. Finding an original postwar yellow with gray bumper is becoming a challenge. There are many reproductions or modern-era reissues on the market.

All the paperwork and peripherals were appropriate for either 1961 or 1962. The biggest difference was the inclusion of the new no. 1103-20 Envelope Packed in the version for 1962. This envelope was a replacement for the no. 1103-12 Envelope Packed.

The X-707 reused the no. 61-399 Tan RSC Mailer with Black Graphics first used with outfit no. X-600. It was manufactured by Mead Containers and measured 11¼ x 10¼ x 6½ inches. These were made of a thicker corrugated material (rated at 90 pounds rather than the normal 65 pounds gross weight) that allowed Popular to ship the outfit in its outfit box.

The 1962 version used a no. 62-246 Tan RSC Mailer with Black

Graphics outfit box that was manufactured by Mead Containers and measured 11¼ x 10¼ x 6¼ inches. Unfortunately, this box was nearly identical to the no. 61-399. Since the contents of the 1961 and 1962 versions of the X-707 were also nearly identical, we could not justify having them stand alone from a rarity and value perspective. As such, the original quantities are combined, which leads to a rarity of R7.

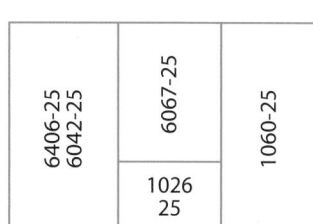

CONVENTIONAL PACK
61-399 BOX

TOP LAYER		BOTTOM LAYER		
6076-75 6406-30		6406-25 6042-25	6067-25	1060-25
1050T-25	2-6112-5			
8-1013 2-1018			1026 25	

X-707
1962

Description: "O27" Promotional Outfit
Specification: "O27" Steam Type Freight Outfit
Customer: Popular Club Plan
Original Amount: 400
Factory Order Date: 9/28/1962
Date Issued: Rev. 10-1-62
Packaging: R.S.C. Outfit Packing (Individual Mailers), (Units not Boxed)

Contents: 1060-25 Steam Type Locomotive; 1060T-25 Tender; 6042-25 Gondola Car (Less 2 Canisters); 6112-5 Canister - Red (2); 6076-75 Hopper Car - Black; 6406-25 Single Automobile Car (Less Auto); 6406-30 Automobile; 6067-25 Caboose; 1013-8 Curved Track (Bundle of 8 - 1013); 1018-10 Straight Track (Loose) (2); 1026-25 25-Watt Transformer; 1103-20 Envelope Packed; 310-2 Set of (5) Billboards; D62-50 Accessory Catalog; 1123-10 Instruction Sheet; 1123-40 Instruction Sheet

Boxes & Packing: 62-246 Outfit Box; 61-171 Corr. Insert; 61-172 Corr. Insert; 61-173 Corr. Insert; 62-247 Shipper for (4) (1-4)

X-707 (1962)	C6	C7	C8	Rarity
Complete Outfit	225	400	600	R7
Outfit Box no. 62-246	125	225	340	R7

Comments: This outfit was a near identical repeat of the 1961 version that is described in the previous entry. Even though the no. X-707 for 1962 was made in smaller quantities than its predecessor, there is not enough difference between them to justify rarity based on its numbers alone. Therefore the total quantity of both outfits – 881 – is used in calculating rarity.

Of note, if a collector wanted to collect both the 1961 and 1962 versions of this outfit, the only way to accurately determine the differences in the outfit boxes would be to open the bottom box flaps and expose the box number. (See the section on Outfit Boxes and Inserts for more information in identifying boxes.)

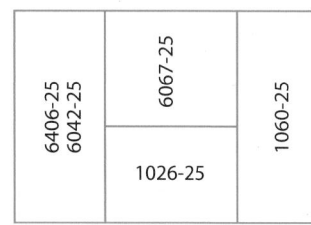

CONVENTIONAL PACK
62-246 BOX
REVISED 9-28-62

TOP LAYER		BOTTOM LAYER		
6076-75	(2) 6112-5	6406-25 6042-25	6067-25	1060-25
1060T-25	6406-30			
(2) 1018-10 1013-8			1026-25	

X-708
1961

Description: "O27" Promotional Outfit
Specification: "O27" Diesel Freight Outfit
Customer: R. H. Macy
Original Amount: 286
Factory Order Date: 8/15/1961

Date Issued: Rev. #2 12/4/61
Packaging: R.S.C. Outfit Packing (Units Boxed)

Contents: 231P-1 Alco Diesel Power Car - "Rock Island"; 3370-1 Animated Sheriff & Outlaw Car; 6445-1 Ft. Knox Gold Bullion Transport Car; 3376-1 Operating Giraffe Car; 6812-1 Track Maintenance Car; 6017-1 Caboose; 1013-8 Curved Track (Bundle of 8 - 1013); 1018-5 Straight Track (Bundle of 5 - 1018); 1008-50

Outfit no. X-708 was packed in an overstickered no. A-608-6 Outfit Box first used in 1959. There actually are two stickers covering this number. The contents are typical of Lionel's mid-level offerings in the 1960s.

Uncoupling Track Section; 1025-25 45-Watt Transformer; 81-32 24" R.C. Wire (2); X602-10 Instruction Sheet; 310-2 Set of (5) Billboards; D61-50 Accessory Catalog

Boxes & Packing: 59-351 Outfit Box (With Stickers); 59-352 Shipper for (4) (1-4)

X-708 (1961)	C6	C7	C8	Rarity
Complete Outfit	850	1,250	1,700	R9
Outfit Box no. 59-351	350	500	650	R9

Comments: R. H. Macy, commonly known as Macy's, is a retailer that purchased numerous promotional outfits in the 1960s. The following two were purchased in 1961. The no. X-708 was a Retailer Promotional Type Ia diesel-powered outfit, and the no. X-709 was a Retailer Promotional Type Ib steam-powered outfit.

The X-708 was headed by the no. 231P-1 Rock Island Alco Diesel Power Car equipped with a two-position reversing unit and two-axle Magne-Traction. It was new for 1961 and pulled some of Lionel's nicer 1960s rolling stock, all equipped with operating AAR trucks and couplers.

The nos. 3370-1 Animated Sheriff & Outlaw Car and 6445-1 Ft. Knox Gold Bullion Transport Car were both new items for 1961 and came in Orange Picture boxes. Pay attention to the 6445-1s because the little nubs below the windows are easily broken off. A C8 example would include all of these nubs.

The remaining rolling stock was individually boxed in a combination of Orange Perforated and Orange Picture boxes. When individually boxed, the instruction sheets and associated peripherals came within the item box. As such, the 231P-1 included the no. CTC Lockon for the outfit, and all that was required to hook up the outfit were the two no. 81-32 24" R.C. Wires.

The no. 59-351 Tan RSC with Black Graphics outfit box was left over from two years before. It was first used for promotional outfit no. A-608-6 and subsequently overstickered and used for the nos. X-542NA, X-682 and X-701. It was manufactured by Express Container Corp. and measured 14 x 10½ x 6¾ inches.

The quantities manufactured for both this and the X-709 were not even numbers. Based on the revisions, it appears that R. H. Macy was likely adjusting its orders to exactly meet the demand and thus retain no additional inventory past the holiday season. The low quantity leads to the R9 rarity rating.

CONVENTIONAL PACK
59-351 BOX
STICKERS

TOP LAYER			BOTTOM LAYER	
3376-1 F			231P-1 F	
1008-50 5-1018	3370-1 S		6445-1 F	1025-25
6017-1 S				
8-1013			6812-1 S	

Description: "O27" Promotional Outfit
Specification: "O27" Steam Type Freight Outfit With Smoke
Customer: R. H. Macy
Original Amount: 387
Factory Order Date: 8/15/1961
Date Issued: Rev. #2 12-18-61
Packaging: R.S.C. Outfit Packing (Units Boxed)

Contents: 236-1 Steam Type Locomotive With Smoke; 1130T-1 Tender; 3665-1 Minuteman Missile Launching Car; 3830-1 Operating Submarine Car; 3509-1 Oper. Satellite Launching Car (Manually); 6470-1 Exploding Target Car; 6017-1 Caboose; 1013-8 Curved Track (Bundle of 8 - 1013); 1018-30 Straight Track (Bundle of 3 - 1018); 1008-50 Uncoupling Track Section; 1025-25 45-Watt Transformer; 81-32 24" R.C. Wire (2);

X602-10 Instruction Sheet; 310-2 Set of (5) Billboards; D61-50 Accessory Catalog

Boxes & Packing: 61-250 Outfit Box; 61-251 Shipper for (4) (1-4)

X-709 (1961)	C6	C7	C8	Rarity
Complete Outfit	675	1,150	1,580	R9
Outfit Box no. 61-250	300	425	560	R9

Comments: The no. X-709 was the second R. H. Macy promotional outfit purchase in 1961 (see no. X-708). This Retailer Promotional Type Ib outfit was Macy's steam-powered offering, whereas the X-708 was its diesel offering.

The X-709 was a space and military outfit headed by the no. 236-1 Steam Type Locomotive with Smoke (new for 1961). It pulled two cars that also were new in 1961: nos. 3665-1 Minuteman Missile Launching Car and 3509-1 Oper. Satellite Launching Car (Manually). When boxed, the 3509-1 was available only in promotional outfits. The Orange Picture box for the 3509-1 is difficult to find in collectible condition. (See the entry for the no. X-647 for more information on this car and its instruction flyer.)

The other items in the X-709 were repeated from previous years. All of them were equipped with operating AAR trucks and couplers and came in Orange Picture Boxes, except the 6017-1, which came in an Orange Perforated box.

The no. 61-250 Orange RSC with Black Graphics outfit box used for this outfit measured 13 x 12 x 7 inches.

The X-709 was an attractive space and military outfit. That fact, combined with the small quantity originally made, makes this outfit desirable and leads to its R9 rarity.

CONVENTIONAL PACK
61-250 BOX

TOP LAYER

3509-1 S	
1130T-1 S	
3665-1 S	
8-1013	
6017-1	1025-25

BOTTOM LAYER

236-1 F	
3830-1 F	3-1018 / 1008-50
6470-1 F	

Description: "O27" Promotional Outfit
Specification: "O27" Steam Type Freight Outfit
Customer: Katz Drug
Original Amount: 1,000
Factory Order Date: 8/22/1961
Date Issued: Rev. #1 9/21/61
Packaging: Display Outfit Packing (Units not Boxed)

Contents: 246-25 Steam Type Locomotive; 1050T-25 Tender; 3370-25 Animated Sheriff & Outlaw Car; 6445-25 Ft. Knox Gold Bullion Transport Car; 6076-75 Hopper Car - Black; 6067-25 Caboose; 1013-8 Curved Track (Bundle of 8 - 1013); 1018-10 Straight Track (Loose) (2); 1025-25 45-Watt Transformer; 1103-12 Envelope Packed; 1119-10 Instruction Sheet; 310-2 Set of (5) Billboards; D61-50 Accessory Catalog

Boxes & Packing: 61-436 Display Outfit Box; 61-391 Corr. Insert; 61-392 Corr. Insert; 61-393 Corr. Insert; 61-394 Corr. Insert; 61-395 Shipper for (6) (1-6)

X-710 (1961)	C6	C7	C8	Rarity
Complete Outfit	325	510	725	R7
Outfit Box no. 61-436	125	200	275	R7

Comments: Katz Drug was one of the many drug-store chains to carry Lionel's promotional outfits. This Retailer Promotional Type Ib was its only purchase in the 1960s.

Steam freight outfits were common, especially when headed by the no. 246-25 Steam Type Locomotive. This engine headed at least 58 outfits in the 1960s before being replaced by the no. 242 in 1962.

Besides the tender, all the rolling stock in the no. X-710 was new for 1961. The nos. 3370-25 Animated Sheriff & Outlaw Car and 6445-25 Ft. Knox Gold Bullion Transport Car were paired together at least eight times. Both were equipped with two operating AAR trucks and couplers. Be aware that this appearance of the 3370-25 came after its Production Control File stated that the trucks and couplers should be changed from Archbar to AAR. Therefore, the X-710 probably included the version with AAR trucks and couplers. All the other items included non-operating Archbar trucks and couplers.

The no. 61-436 White 4-6-4 Steamer and F3 Hinged Display with Red/Orange and Blue Graphics Type A outfit box measured 22½ x 14½ x 3⅛ inches. This outfit box was overstickered and also used for outfit no. 19167.

This outfit contained two upscale items, which was unusual for a drug-store purchase. Although 1,000 were made, the X-710 seldom appears on the market.

DISPLAY PACK
61-436 BOX

246-25	1050T-25
6445-25	6076-75
3370-25	6067-25
8-1013 / 2-1018	1025-25

The no. X-713, along with the no. X-686, was the only outfit in 1961 to include the no. 6050-50 Swift Box Car. This was the first car to use the Type IIa 8½-inch box car shell. This demonstrates how some features first appeared as part of promotional outfits before they became regular-production items.

Customer No. On Box: S33-208
Description: "O27" Promotional Outfit
Specification: "O27" Diesel Freight Outfit
Original Amount: 1,000
Factory Order Date: 8/22/1961
Date Issued: 9/8/61
Packaging: R.S.C. Outfit Packing (Units not Boxed)

Contents: 1065-25 Alco Diesel Power Unit - "Union Pacific"; 6050-50 Box Car - Red - "Swift"; 6042-25 Gondola Car (Less 2 Canisters); 6112-5 Canister - Red (2); 6067-25 Caboose; 1013-8 Curved Track (Bundle of 8 - 1013); 1018-10 Straight Track (Loose) (2); 1026-25 25-Watt Transformer; 1103-12 Envelope Packed; 1125-10 Instruction Sheet; 310-2 Set of (5) Billboards; D61-50 Accessory Catalog

Boxes & Packing: 61-170 Outfit Box; 61-171 Corr. Insert; 61-172 Corr. Insert; 61-173 Corr. Insert; 61-174 Shipper for (6) (1-6)

Alternate For Outfit Contents:
Sub. 24 - 6050-25 for 6050-50 for initial shipment; Customer Stock No. S33-208 to appear on outfit box and shipper.

X-713 (1961)	C6	C7	C8	Rarity
Complete Outfit	225	380	535	R6
Outfit Box no. 61-170	100	200	275	R6

Comments: This is an interesting outfit because there was no customer provided on the Factory Order, though it instructs the Outfit Packing Department to stamp the customer stock number "S33-208" on the outfit box and shipper. Therefore, this could be a Type Ib, IIb or IIIb outfit, depending on the actual customer. No other marking or documentation exists to link the no. X-713 to a specific retailer.

This low-end outfit, headed by a no. 1065-25 Union Pacific Alco Diesel Power Unit that went only forward, initially seemed to be just another promotional outfit. In reality, however, the X-713, like the X-686, provided important information regarding the development of Lionel's 8½-inch plug-door box cars.

The X-713 was one of two 1961 outfits (the X-686 being the other) to list the no. 6050-50 Box Car – Red – "Swift" on its Factory Order. That car, though just an entry-level item equipped with non-operating Archbar trucks and couplers, has historic importance.

To be specific, the 6050-50 was the first car to use a Type IIa 8½-inch box car body. A Type IIa has two complete rows of rivets to the left of its door and two complete and two incomplete (one rivet at the top and two at the bottom) on the right. Extra rivets were removed from the Type I 8½-inch box car to facilitate the application of the Swift logo.

Previously, this change was thought to have been effected in 1962, because that is when the 6050-50 first appeared in a catalog. But, as with numerous other items, that item was introduced in a promotional outfit before becoming a catalog item.

The 6050-50 was also significant in that its "-50" suffix indicated an Archbar variation of the Swift box car previously undocumented in the collector community. This car went on to be used only in promotional outfits until 1963. Both of these previously unknown facts were revealed by the authoritative information used in compiling this volume. The remainder of the outfit also included non-operating Archbar trucks and couplers.

The outfit came in a no. 61-170 Tan RSC with Black Graphics outfit box manufactured by Owens-Illinois with "9012" printed on the bottom. It measured 11½ x 10¼ x 6¼ inches.

Although the X-713 is mysterious in its Lionel customer, it still appears on the market with the "S33-208" clearly stamped below the Lionel number.

CONVENTIONAL PACK
61-170 BOX

TOP LAYER

8-1013	
2-1018	
1065-25	ENV

BOTTOM LAYER

6042-25	6067-25	6050-50
	1026-25	

LIONEL Exclusive at MASTERS!

36-PC. U.S. MARINE CORP.
MISSILE LAUNCHING TRAIN SET WITH 4 ACTION CARS, SUB BASE, EXPLODING AMMO DUMP, 50 WATT TRANSFORMER and MAGNE TRACTION

Mfr.'s Open Stock Sugg. List* 73.10

masters price
27 88 COMPLETE

Special!
MISSILE LAUNCHING PLATFORM WITH EXPLODING TARGET CAR
Mfr's Orig. Sugg. List Price* 10.95
masters price **4.97**
Press firing lever & missile "blasts off" ... Target car "explodes" when hit. Easily reassembled.

SORRY, NO MAIL OR PHONE ORDERS ON THESE 3-DAY SPECIALS

FOUR ACTION CARS INCLUDED
OPERATING SUBMARINE CAR CRUISES & DIVES
SECURITY CAR WITH ROTATING SEARCH LIGHT
MOBILE MISSILE LAUNCHER with FIRING LIGHT & MAGNE TRACTION
OPERATING SATELLITE LAUNCHING CAR

Sensational 36-Piece U.S. Marine Corp. Missile Launching Train Set with 4 play-packed action cars to delight any youngster. Purchase it now and save, at masters' fantastically low, low price. Only 400 sets, 1 per customer. No dealers!

masters for everything you need

LAKE SUCCESS, Long Island
SHOPPING CENTER, 1510 UNION TPKE.
10 to 9:30 Daily • 9 to 6 P.M. Saturday

HEMPSTEAD, Long Island
250 FULTON AVENUE
10 to 9:30 P.M. Daily • 10 to 6 P.M. Saturday

Delivery is an additional charge. *The list prices shown are the manufacturer's original suggested list prices. These are not necessarily the normal selling prices in the local trading area.

This 1961 advertisement from an unknown newspaper listed Masters' outfit no. X-714 for $27.88 complete. The advertisement went on to say that only 400 sets were made, with only one offered to each customer. Also note that the no. 470-1 Missile Launching Platform, which was included with outfit no. X-676, could be purchased separately for $4.97.

Description: "O27" Promotional Outfit
Specification: "O27" Mobile Missile Launcher Freight Outfit
Customer/Price: Masters; $27.88
Original Amount: 413
Factory Order Date: 8/22/1961
Date Issued: 9/8/61
Packaging: R.S.C. Outfit Packing (Units Boxed)

Contents: 45-1 Mobile Rocket Firing Car; 6530-1 Fire & Safety Training Car; 3519-1 Automatic Satellite Launching Car; 3830-1 Operating Submarine Car; 3535-1 Security Car; 1013-8 Curved Track (Bundle of 8 - 1013) (2); 1018-30 Straight Track (Bundle of 3 - 1018); 1008-50 Uncoupling Track Section; 1043-50 60-Watt Transformer; 943-1 Exploding Ammo Dump; 1023-25 45° Crossing; 910-1 Navy Yard Cardboard Display; 1802H Layout Instruction Sheet; 310-2 Set of (5) Billboards; D61-50 Accessory Catalog

Boxes & Packing: 61-385 Outfit Box; 61-435 Corr. Insert; 61-387 Shipper for (3) (1-3)

Alternate For Outfit Contents:
Note: Use 59 - 1043-50; Use 354 - 1043-500; Include 2 - 81-32 when using unpacked transformer.

X-714 (1961)	C6	C7	C8	Rarity
Complete Outfit	7,500	11,250	15,000	R10
Outfit Box no. 61-385	900	1,200	1,500	R10

Comments: This was the third and last of the three outfits, including the nos. X-702 and X-703, purchased by Masters in 1961. Masters leased departments within discount stores, and that is where this Retailer Promotional Type Ib outfit was likely sold. As with many retailers, Masters purchased outfits to fulfill different customer segments. Outfit no. X-714 was its high-end offering.

This outfit was the third (see the entries for nos. X-625 and X-676) and last outfit in 1961 to include a no. 910-1 Navy Yard Cardboard Display (also known as the Atomic Sub Base).

The X-714 was identical to General Release Promotional no. X-676, except that the latter outfit also included a no. 470-1 Missile Launching Platform. Factory Orders for these two outfits have the same creation date, which suggests that Lionel developed the X-676 to provide its smaller customers with an opportunity to purchase a sub-base outfit. These outfits probably were manufactured concurrently.

As with other outfits including a sub base, it is that item which makes the X-714 extremely rare today. The no. 910-1 Navy Yard Cardboard Display was a fragile model intended to be assembled by the customer. There were no Lionel markings on this item, and it frequently became separated from the train outfit and destroyed. Stories exist of individuals who discarded a 910-1 because they did not know what it was.

All 10 cardboard pieces that made up the sub base were placed in a plain tan-colored flat paper bag, which was laid on the bottom of the outfit.

Even though it is the sub base that makes this outfit so desirable, all the other contents were high-end offerings that fit the space and military theme. Specifically, a complete olive drab no. 45-1 Mobile Rocket Firing Car is a collectible item when combined with its nos. 45-20 Corrugated Box, 44-43 Corrugated Insert and 44-45 Envelope Packed.

Other notable items included the Orange Perforated boxed nos. 6530-1 Fire & Safety Training Car and 3535-1 Security Car. These items always added color to outfits. The no. 3830-1 Operating Submarine Car was appropriate for this outfit.

The only new car was the Orange Picture boxed no. 3519-1 Automatic Satellite Launching Car. It was equipped, as were all the cars, with operating AAR trucks and couplers.

Lionel was busy depleting the inventory of no. 1043 60-Watt Transformers in 1961. When filling the order for the X-714, workers evidently found some white no. 1043-500 60-Watt

Transformers still packed in their box. They used these in 354 of the 413 outfits ordered. The outfit pricing assumes this transformer since its inclusion is more likely.

The pretzel layout that was included with this and other sub-base outfits also provided excitement, as the train would weave in and out of the sub-base tunnels.

The no. 61-385 Tan RSC with Black Graphics outfit box was the same as used on the other sub-base outfits for 1961 and '62. It was manufactured by Mead Containers and measured 22 x 18¼ x 5¼ inches. A no. 61-435 Corr. Insert took the place of the 470-1 included in outfit no. X-676. As with other outfits that use the 61-385 box, it was oversized and seldom saved.

These early sub-base outfits included the 910-1 inside the outfit box. This arrangement required a large insert to fill the empty space, which caused these outfits to be unevenly balanced. This likely led to some of them being accidentally dropped.

Among the nine sub-base outfits, the X-714 ranks fourth in smallest quantity produced. The high demand and low supply easily lead to its R10 rarity.

Note that the price of this outfit assumes the unnumbered "How to Assemble Your Lionel Atomic Submarine Base" instruction sheet for the sub base.

CONVENTIONAL PACK
61-385 BOX

45-1 S		1043 50

910-1 BOTTOM
943-1 (F) TOP
1013

3830-1 S
6530-1 F
8-1013
8-1013
3535-1 S

3519-1 S

INSERT 61-435

1018
1008-50

TOP 6530

1023 TOP

Description: "O27" Promotional Outfit
Specification: "O27" Steam Type Freight Outfit
Customer/No./Price: Abraham & Strauss; 1F15660; $14.55
Original Amount: 4,624
Factory Order Date: 12/4/1961
Date Issued: Rev. #4 12-4-61
Packaging: Display Outfit Packing (Units not Boxed)

Contents: 1060-25 Steam Type Locomotive; 1050T-25 Tender; 6076-75 Hopper Car - Black; 3376-25 Oper. Giraffe Car (Less 3376-118 Envelope); 3376-118 Envelope Packed; 6042-25 Gondola Car (Less 2 Canisters); 6112-5 Canister - Red (2); 6067-25 Caboose; 1013-8 Curved Track (Bundle of 8 - 1013); 1018-10 Straight Track (Loose) (2); 1026-25 25-Watt Transformer; 1103-12 Envelope Packed; 1123-10 Instruction Sheet; 310-2 Set of (5) Billboards; D61-50 Accessory Catalog

Boxes & Packing: 61-437 Display Outfit Box; 61-391 Corr. Insert; 61-392 Corr. Insert; 61-393 Corr. Insert; 61-394 Corr. Insert; 61-395 Shipper for (6) (1-6); 61-390 Display Outfit Box with 5 Stickers; 61-429 Display Outfit Box with 5 Stickers

Alternate For Outfit Contents:
Note: Use 500 - 61-390 Display Outfit Box with 5 Stickers in place of 61-437 Box; Use 2,624 - 61-429 Display Outfit Box with 5 Stickers in place of 61-437 Box.

X-715 (1961)	C6	C7	C8	Rarity
Complete Outfit With no. 61-437 Box	215	385	570	R6
Outfit Box no. 61-437	100	175	250	R6
Complete Outfit With no. 61-390 Box	265	510	820	R8
Outfit Box no. 61-390	150	300	500	R8
Complete Outfit With no. 61-429 Box	200	335	490	R5
Outfit Box no. 61-429	85	125	170	R5

Comments: Longtime Lionel customer Abraham & Strauss, a department store based in Brooklyn, New York, purchased one Retailer Promotional Type Ib outfit in 1961.

With all low-end items, outfit no. X-715 included nothing

The no. X-715 was a low-end starter outfit carried by Abraham & Strauss. It likely was a very successful offering, as the original order of 1,500 swelled to 4,624 outfits.

Outfit no. X-715 was packaged in three different outfit boxes. Although they appear the same, the box underneath the sticker is different. Shown is the no. 61-437 (with X-715 printed by the box manufacturer) on the top and no. 61-429 (X-687 overstickered) on the bottom.

special. Its no. 1060-25 Steam Type Locomotive (forward only) was common in low-end outfits.

With the exception of the no. 3376-25 Oper. Giraffe Car (Less 3376-118 Env.), all the rolling stock was equipped with non-

operating Archbar trucks and couplers. The no. 3376-25 seemed out of place because it was equipped with two operating AAR trucks and couplers. Lionel may have been planning originally to include an Archbar-equipped no. 3386-25 Operating Giraffe Car - with Non-Operating Trucks instead. An early version of the Outfit Packing Sheet had the 3386-25 on it, but these cars were no longer available in 1961. Either way, when the giraffe car was unboxed, the no. 3376-118 Envelope Packed was placed loose in the outfit box.

The X-715 came in one of three versions of a White 4-6-4 Steamer and F3 Hinged Display with Red/Orange and Blue Graphics Type A outfit box. All three were manufactured by

DISPLAY PACK 61-437 BOX	
1060-25	1050T-25
6042-25	6076-75
3376-25	6067-25
8-1013 2-1018	1026-25

United Container Co. (no. 61-390 identified United Container as "UCC") and measured 22½ x 14½ x 3¼ inches. The no. 61-437 was printed specifically for this outfit. The nos. 61-390 and 61-429 were overstickered nos. X-618 and X-687, respectively.

Although this is a fairly common outfit, collecting the box variations makes it more interesting. The 61-390 Display Outfit Box is the most difficult of the trio to find, whereas the other two frequently appear. Rarity and values for each box variation have been provided.

Description: "O27" Promotional Outfit
Specification: "O27" Steam Type Freight Outfit
Customer: Norge
Original Amount: 6,300
Factory Order Date: 11/20/1961

Date Issued: Rev. #5 12-4-61
Packaging: Display Outfit Packing (Units not Boxed)

Contents: 1060-25 Steam Type Locomotive; 1050T-25 Tender; 6042-25 Gondola Car (Less 2 Canisters); 6112-5 Canister - Red (2); 6076-75 Hopper Car - Black; 6050-25 Savings Bank Car; 6067-25 Caboose; 1013-8 Curved Track (Bundle of 8 - 1013); 1018-40 Straight Track (Bundle of 4 - 1018); 1026-25 25-Watt

Outfit no. X-716 was available to customers of Norge appliances. It featured the Type I no. 6050-25 Savings Bank Car with coin slot. This example is shown with the no. 6076-25 Hopper Car - Red substitution.

Outfit no. X-716 was packaged in three different outfit boxes. Although they appear the same, the box underneath the sticker is different. Shown is the no. 61-438 with "No. X-716" printed as part of the box manufacturing process.

Transformer; 1103-12 Envelope Packed; 1123-10 Instruction Sheet; 310-2 Set of (5) Billboards; D61-50 Accessory Catalog

Boxes & Packing: 61-438 Corr. Outfit Box (Amount 3,000); 61-391 Corr. Insert; 61-392 Corr. Insert; 61-393 Corr. Insert; 61-394 Corr. Insert; 61-395 Shipper for (6) (1-6); 61-390 Display Outfit Box (Amount 97); 61-391 Corr. Insert; 61-392 Corr. Insert; 61-393 Corr. Insert; 61-394 Corr. Insert; 61-395 Shipper for (6) (1-6); 61-439 Corr. Outfit Box (Stamp No.) (Use for Balance); 61-391 Corr. Insert; 61-392 Corr. Insert; 61-393 Corr. Insert; 61-394 Corr. Insert; 61-395 Shipper for (6) (1-6)

Alternate For Outfit Contents:
For 3,000 Outfits use 61-438 Corr. Outfit Box, Inserts and Shipper as listed above; For 97 Outfits use 61-390 Box, Inserts and Shipper as listed above; Balance Use: 61-439 (Stamp No.) Box, Inserts and Shipper as listed above; Note: Use 6076-25 when stock of 6076-75 is depleted.

X-716 (1961)	C6	C7	C8	Rarity
Complete Outfit With no. 61-438 Box	160	300	450	R5
Outfit Box no. 61-438	70	100	125	R5
Complete Outfit With no. 61-390 Box	215	450	725	R10
Outfit Box no. 61-390	125	250	400	R10
Complete Outfit With no. 61-439 Box	160	300	450	R5
Outfit Box no. 61-439	70	100	125	R5

Comments: Norge, a manufacturer of appliances during the 1960s, purchased this Manufacturer Promotional Type IIIb outfit in 1961. During the holiday season, Norge advertised a 26-piece Lionel electric train set (a "claimed $29.95 retail value") with the purchase of any home appliance. The promotion must have been a success because 6,300 of these outfits were sold.

Another of the many low-end promotional outfits from the 1960s, the no. X-716 included the no. 1060-25 Steam Type Locomotive, which went forward only. The one stand-out item was the Type I no. 6050-25 Savings Bank Car with coin slot (new for 1961). It came equipped with two operating AAR trucks and couplers.

All the other items had non-operating Archbar

DISPLAY PACK
61-438 BOX

1060-25	1050T-25
6042-25	6050-25
6076-75	6067-25
4-1018 8-1013	1026-25

1103-12

X-700 Series

trucks and couplers. All the outfit's paperwork was appropriate for 1961.

As with the no. X-715, this outfit came in three different outfit boxes. This was due to an increase in the order and Lionel's use of unique boxes preprinted with the outfit number by the box manufacturer. (See the section on Outfit Boxes and Inserts.)

All three boxes were a White 4-6-4 Steamer and F3 Hinged Display with Red/Orange and Blue Graphics Type A outfit box. They were manufactured by United Container Co. (no. 61-390 identified United Container as "UCC") and measured 22½ x 14½ x 3¼ inches. The no. 61-438 was printed specifically for this outfit.

The no. 61-390 was an overstickered no. X-618, and the no. 61-439 was the first generic display box. It was stamped by Lionel with the outfit number.

The X-716 is a very common outfit that is readily available on the market. Its price is not affected by substitution that Lionel made of a no. 6076-25 Hopper Car - Red.

The only difficult to obtain version is the one that came in the no. 61-390 Corr. Outfit Box. Although this version achieves an R10 rarity rating because of its low original quantity, demand for it remains confined to a niche of the most dedicated collectors.

X-717
1961

Description: "O27" Promotional Outfit
Specification: "O27" Steam Type Freight Outfit With Smoke
Customer: B. Altman
Original Amount: 100
Factory Order Date: 10/24/1961
Date Issued: 10-24-61
Packaging: R.S.C. Outfit Packing (Units Boxed)

Contents: 236-1 Steam Type Locomotive With Smoke; 1130T-1 Tender; 3665-1 Minuteman Missile Launching Car; 3509-1 Oper. Satellite Launching Car (Manually); 3330-1 Flat Car With Operating Submarine (Kit); 6812-1 Track Maintenance Car; 6017-1 Caboose; 1013-70 Curved Track (Bundle of 12 - 1013); 1018-30 Straight Track (Bundle of 3 - 1018); 1008-50 Uncoupling Track Section; 1025-25 45-Watt Transformer; 1020-25 90° Crossing; 81-32 24" R.C. Wire (2); 1802B Layout Instruction Sheet; X602-10 Instruction Sheet; 310-2 Set of (5) Billboards; D61-50 Accessory Catalog

Boxes & Packing: 61-250 Outfit Box; 61-251 Shipper for (4) (1-4)

X-717 (1961)	C6	C7	C8	Rarity
Complete Outfit	1,090	1,825	2,450	R10
Outfit Box no. 61-250	600	950	1,150	R10

Comments: B. Altman was a retailer known for selling top-quality merchandise. This Retailer Promotional Type Ib outfit was an appropriate offering, and it contained some of Lionel's higher-end items.

The no. X-717 featured a no. 236-1 Steam Type Locomotive With Smoke and Magne-Traction (new for 1961) pulling an impressive combination of space and military rolling stock. To start, there was a no. 3509-1 Operating Satellite Car (Manually), a car that was never offered for separate sale. The only way to obtain its Orange Picture no. 3509-6 Folding Box was in this or the eight other promotional outfits that had it. The fact that only 5,537 of those nine different outfits were made means this a difficult box to find in collectible condition.

Even more difficult to obtain is the no. 3509-7 Instruction Flyer included with boxed 3509s. This flyer cautioned against over-winding the spring to protect your ceiling. In reality, it was likely printed to protect the individual from being struck by a satellite launched from this manually operated car. No equivalent flyer has been observed for a no. 3519-1 Automatic Satellite Launching Car.

The X-717 also included the no. 3330-1 Flat Car With Operating Submarine (Kit). A no. 3330-108 Submarine Kit Parts Packed still sealed in its plasstic bag is difficult to find in collectible condition. The 3330-1 as well as all the other rolling stock had operating AAR trucks and couplers.

A no. 3665-1 Minuteman Missile Launching Car added to the excitement of this outfit. Interestingly, no other outfit, catalog or promotional, ever came with the nos. 3330, 3509 and 3665 together.

The figure-eight track layout was described on the no. 1802B Layout Instruction Sheet dated 6-59. All the other peripherals were appropriate for 1961.

The no. 61-250 Corrugated Box was an Orange RSC with Black Graphics and measured 13 x 12 x 7 inches.

B. Altman purchased this outfit late in the year, as indicated by the Factory Order date of October 24, 1961. With only 100 examples ordered, the X-717 is seldom seen and achieves a well-deserved R10 rarity.

CONVENTIONAL PACK
61-250 BOX

TOP LAYER

3665-1 F	
6017-1 S	1025-25
3-1018	1008-50
12-1013	

1020-25 TOP

BOTTOM LAYER

236-1 F	
3509-1 F	1130T-1 S
3330-1 S	
6812-1 S	

Description: "O27" Promotional Outfit
Specification: "O27" Steam Type Freight Outfit W/Smoke
Original Amount: 700
Factory Order Date: 11/10/1961
Date Issued: 11-10-61
Packaging: R.S.C. Outfit Packing (Units Boxed)

Contents: 2018-1 Steam Type Locomotive With Smoke; 1130T-1 Tender; 3509-1 Oper. Satellite Launching Car (Manually); 3665-1 Minuteman Missile Launching Car; 3820-25 Flat Car W/Oper. Submarine; 3830-12 Envelope; 3410-1 Operating Helicopter Launching Car (Manually); 6017-1 Caboose; 1013-8 Curved Track (Bundle of 8 - 1013); 1018-30 Straight Track (Bundle of 3 - 1018); 1008-50 Uncoupling Track Section; 1025-25 45-Watt Transformer; 81-32 24" R.C. Wire (2); IS Instruction Sheet; 310-2 Set of (5) Billboards; D61-50 Accessory Catalog

Boxes & Packing: 59-100 Outfit Box W/Sticker; 59-101 Shipper for (4) (1-4); 61-250 Box; 61-251 Shipper (1-4)

X-718 (1961)	C6	C7	C8	Rarity
Complete Outfit With Either Box	775	1,275	1,775	R8
Outfit Box no. 59-100 Or no. 61-250	300	400	500	R8

Comments: General Release Promotional outfits sometimes included interesting groupings of items. The no. X-718, a Type IIb outfit, was one of them.

Lionel likely created this space and military outfit to reduce its inventory of the no. 2018-1 Steam Type Locomotive With Smoke and deplete the inventory of the olive drab no. 3820-25 Flat Car W/Oper. Submarine. Its November 10, 1961, Factory Order was the latest that a 2018-1 and a 3820-25 appeared.

The X-718 was the only promotional outfit to contain the no. 3820-25, which first appeared in the no. 1805 Land Sea and Air Gift Pack, an item cataloged in 1960. The following year, the same Flat Car W/Oper. Submarine was offered in a different catalog outfit, the no. 1810 Space Age Gift Pack. The Factory Order for the 1810 was last revised on October 5, 1961, and the quantity was changed. Most likely, the total was revised downward, thus leading

to extra 3820s that needed to be depleted, hence the creation of the X-718. Although the Factory Order states, "Units Boxed", the 3820-25 was unboxed.

Whether found in one of those two catalog outfits or in the promotional X-718, this Flat Car W/Oper. Submarine is a collectible item. Admittedly, with a total quantity of 7,300 units produced, it is not as difficult to obtain as previously thought, but it's still a challenge to find in C8 condition with no chips in its painted frame.

Two other items in this outfit are also very collectible: the nos. 3410-1 Operating Helicopter Launching Car (Manually) and 3509-1 Oper. Satellite Car (Manually). Neither was ever offered for separate sale. In fact, both cars were available in their difficult-to-find Orange Picture boxes only in promotional outfits. They, like the other cars, were equipped with two operating AAR trucks and couplers.

The X-718 listed a no. 59-100 Yellow RSC with Black Graphics outfit box (manufactured by Star Corrugated Box Company, Inc. and measuring 14⅛ x 13⅛ x 7 inches) on its Factory Order and a no. 61-250 Orange RSC with Black Graphics outfit box (measuring 13 x 12 x 7 inches) on its Outfit Packing Sheet. The 59-100 was an overstickered version of the box used for catalog O27 outfit no. 1626W in 1959. This was the final use of that box and the only time it was used in 1961. Packing information was available for only the 61-250 version.

The exact quantity of each box used is unknown, so individual rarity by box type cannot be determined. Either way, the X-718 is a difficult outfit to find in any condition in either box.

CONVENTIONAL PACK
61-250 BOX

TOP LAYER		BOTTOM LAYER	
6017-1 F	1025-25	2018-1 S	
1130T-1 S			
3509-1 F		3820-25 F	
3665-1 S		3410-1 F	

1008-50 TOP 6017
3-1018 TOP 1130T
8-1013 TOP 3509

Description: "O27" Promotional Outfit
Specification: "O27" Steam Type Freight Outfit W/Smoke
Original Amount: 139
Factory Order Date: 11/9/1961
Date Issued: 11-9-61
Packaging: Bulk Packing

Contents: 2018-1 Steam Type Locomotive With Smoke; 1130T-1 Tender; 3361-1 Operating Lumber Car; 1877-1 Horse Car; 3370-1 Animated Sheriff & Outlaw Car; 3376-1 Operating Giraffe Car; 6437-1 Illuminated Caboose; 1013-10 Curved Track (Bundle of 10 - 1013); 1018-5 Straight Track (Bundle of 5 - 1018); 6019-1 Remote Control Track Set; 1022-1 Manual Switches (pr); 1073-25 Transformer; 81-32 24" R.C. Wire (2)

Alternate For Outfit Contents:
Note: Use inventory 85 - 3361-1; Use 54 - 3361X-1 with one (1) 160-2 Bin; Ship 1013 in cartons of 200; Ship 1018 in cartons of 200.

X-719 (1961)	C6	C7	C8	Rarity
Items Only - With no. 3361-1	340	600	900	N/A
Items Only - With no. 3361X-1	330	540	800	N/A

Comments: The Factory Order for this outfit did not include a customer name, but it probably was destined for Beller Electric. In the early 1960s, Beller and Madison Hardware were the two big purchasers of what were known as "bulk outfits." (For an explanation of the practice of buying "bulk outfits," consult the entry on Madison Hardware Co. in the section on Lionel's Distribution and Customers.)

Beller purchased bulk-packed outfits nos. X-582, X-585NA

and X-586 in 1960 and nos. 19204 and 19206 in 1962. These were all similar to the nos. X-719 and X-720 from 1961. Somehow, Beller's name may have been missed and not added to this Factory Order. If Beller were the customer, the X-719 would be classified as a Retailer Promotional Type Ia outfit.

Beller's purchases are curious because customers typically bought in bulk from Lionel as a ploy to further reduce the price paid for individual items intended for separate sale. Yet it appears that Beller was actually purchasing outfit components in bulk with the intention of assembling this outfit on its own. For the X-719, no outfit box was provided, only bulk packaging. It's assumed that Lionel packaged all the individual items in master shipping cartons.

No individual outfit boxes have been observed for any bulk outfit listed in this volume. As a result, we cannot ascertain whether these items were ever assembled and sold as an outfit. Even if they were, we cannot prove that Beller assigned the no. X-719 or the no. X-720 to the groupings.

The X-719 represented the final appearance of three items: the no. 2018-1 Steam Type Locomotive With Smoke (also in the no. X-718), the Late Classic boxed nos. 3361-1 and 3361X-1 Operating Lumber Car (one of the last times that a Late Classic boxed item appeared in the 1960s) and the no. 1877-1 Horse Car in its no. 1877-14 Folding Box (also in the no. X-554NA).

A listing for this outfit is provided here because a Factory Order exists for the X-719. Pricing is provided as reference for the items alone. However, as stated earlier in this volume, items alone do not constitute an outfit; an outfit box is required.

Overall, it appears that Lionel took the opportunity to clean out old inventory to a willing customer. Finding a box with any sort of markings for this outfit would be a true discovery.

X-720
1961

Description: "O27" Freight Outfit
Specification: "O27" Alco Diesel Freight Outfit
Original Amount: 200
Factory Order Date: 11/9/1961
Date Issued: 11-9-61
Packaging: Bulk Packing

Contents: 224P-1 Alco Diesel Power Car - "U.S. Navy"; 6820-1 Aerial Missile Transport Car; 6530-1 Fire Prevention Training Car; 3419-1 Operating Helicopter Car; 6650-1 Missile Launching Car; 6437-1 Illuminated Caboose; 1013-10 Curved Track (Bundle of 10 - 1013); 1018-5 Straight Track (Bundle of 5 - 1018); 6029-1 R.C. Uncoupling track; 1122-1 Remote Control Switches (pr); 1025-25 45-Watt Transformer; 81-32 24" R.C. Wire (2)

Alternate For Outfit Contents:
Ship 1013 in boxes of 200; Ship 1018 in boxes of 200.

X-720 (1961)	C6	C7	C8	Rarity
Items Only	675	1,250	1,750	N/A

Comments: The Factory Order for this outfit did not include a customer name, but it probably was destined for Beller Electric. In the early 1960s, Beller and Madison Hardware were the two big purchasers of what were known as "bulk outfits." (For an explanation of the practice of buying "bulk outfits," consult the entry on Madison Hardware Co. in the section on Lionel's Distribution and Customers.)

Beller purchased bulk-packed outfits nos. X-582, X-585NA and X-586 in 1960 and nos. 19204 and 19206 in 1962. These were all similar to the nos. X-719 and X-720 from 1961. Somehow, Beller's name may have been missed and not added to this Factory Order. If Beller were the customer, the X-720 would be classified as a Retailer Promotional Type Ia outfit. (See the entry for the X-719 for more information on Beller.)

As with the no. X-719, some of the contents in this outfit were near the end of their product cycle. The boxed versions of the nos. 224P-1 U.S. Navy Alco Diesel Power Unit, 6820-1 Aerial Missile Transport Car and 6530-1 Fire Prevention Training Car all appeared in their last few outfits in late 1961 and 1962. The 6820-1's Orange Perforated box makes this item highly collectible.

Also included was the boxed no. 6029-1 R.C. Uncoupling Track. Finding its rare individual box in C8 condition is difficult and very expensive.

A listing for this outfit is provided here because a Factory Order exists for the X-720. Pricing is provided as reference for the items alone. However, as stated earlier in this volume, items alone do not constitute an outfit; an outfit box is required.

Overall, it appears that Lionel took the opportunity to clean out old inventory to a willing customer. Finding a box with any sort of markings for this outfit would be a true discovery.

Description: 1960 Outfit
Specification: "O27" Ga. Steam Type Freight Outfit with Smoke
Customer: Maritz
Original Amount: 400
Factory Order Date: 5/2/1960
Date Issued: June 14, 1960
Packaging: Conventional Outfit Packing

Contents: 2018-1 Locomotive - with Smoke, Lockon & Lubricant - without Magne-Traction; 1130T-1 Tender; 6014-100 Box Car - Red - "Airex Lettering"; 6162-1 Gondola Car - Blue - with (3) White Canisters; 6825-1 Flat Car - Red - with Trestle Bridge - Black; 6476-1 Hopper Car - Red; 6844-1 Rocket Transport Car; 6017-1 Caboose - Brick Brown; 1013 Curved Track (8); 1018 Straight Track (3); 1008-50 Uncoupling Unit - with (1) 1018 Straight Track; 1015-60 45-Watt Transformer; 81-32 Wires (2); 310-2 Set of (5) Billboard Signs; IS Instruction Sheet; AC Accessory Catalog

Boxes & Packing: 59-413 Box; 59-414 Shipper (1-3)

Alternate For Outfit Contents:
Note: If necessary substitute 1- 1015-25.

X-800 (1960)	C6	C7	C8	Rarity
1960 Complete Outfit With no. 59-413 Box	500	800	1,150	R9
1960 Outfit Box no. 59-413	275	425	575	R9
1959 Complete Outfit With no. 58-205 Box		1959 Version - Contents Unknown		
1959 Outfit Box no. 58-205				

Comments: Incentive marketer Maritz purchased three Retailer Promotional outfits in 1960. These included the nos. X-800 steam-freight, X-801 diesel-passenger and X-802 diesel-freight outfits. All three included some of Lionel's higher-end products. The outfits were likely used as sales incentives or other premium rewards for employees in large corporations.

The Type Ib X-800 was led by a no. 2018-1 Locomotive - with Smoke. The 2018 last appeared in a catalog outfit in 1959, but was still being used in promotional outfits in the 1960s. When boxed in its no. 2018-10 Corrugated Box, it included the nos. 675-33 Smoke Stack Cleaner, SP-1 Pellets Bottled, 927-60 Tube of Oil, 927-65 Tube of Grease, 2018-11 Instruction Sheet and CTC-1 Lockon.

All the items in this outfit came from previous years. In fact the entire outfit was likely a carryover, as an internal Lionel Promotional Outfit List from 1959 records the X-800 in a no. 58-205 outfit box with a quantity of 144. This is the only information available about the 1959 version.

The no. 6014-100 Red Airex Box Car appeared only in promotional outfits. The remaining cars in the X-800 were commonly included in outfits during 1960. One item, the no. 6844-1 Rocket Transport Car, was out of place because of its space and military quality.

All the rolling stock in the X-800 was equipped with early operating AAR trucks and couplers and came packaged in Orange Perforated boxes.

The no. 59-413 RSC outfit box was an overstamped no. X-850 from 1959.

The transformer substitution does not affect the price.

CONVENTIONAL PACK
59-413 BOX

TOP LAYER

3-1018	8-1013	
	6017-1 S	1015 60
	1130T-1 F	
	6825-1 S	

1008-50 TOP 1013

BOTTOM LAYER

6014-100 S	6162-1 S
	6844-1 F
	6476-1 S
	2018-1 F

Description: 1960 Outfit
Specification: "O27" Ga. Diesel Freight Outfit
Customer: Maritz
Original Amount: 50
Factory Order Date: 6/3/1960
Date Issued: June 15, 1960
Packaging: Conventional Outfit Packing

Contents: 220P-1 Alco Diesel Power Unit - "Santa Fe" - with Headlight, 2 Magnets, Non-Operating Coupler, Lockon & Lubricant; 6428-1 U.S. Mail Car; 2432 Illuminated Vista-Dome Car; 2436 Illuminated Observation Car; 1013 Curved Track (8); 1018 Straight Track (3); 6029-25 Uncoupling Track Section; 1015-60 45-Watt Transformer; 90 Uncoupling Track Controller; 81-32 Wires (4); 90-30 Envelope Packed With 90 and 81-32; 310-2 Set of (5) Billboard Signs; IS Instruction Sheet; AC Accessory Catalog

Boxes & Packing: 59-324 Box; 59-325 Shipper (1-4); ST Sticker

Alternate For Outfit Contents:
Note: If necessary - substitute 1- 1015-25.

X-801 (1960)	C6	C7	C8	Rarity
Complete Outfit	1,275	1,950	2,450	R10
Outfit Box no. 59-324	1,000	1,500	1,800	R10

Comments: Incentive marketer Maritz purchased three Retailer Promotional outfits in 1960. These included the nos. X-800 steam-freight, X-801 diesel-passenger and X-802 diesel-freight outfits. All three included some of Lionel's higher-end products. The outfits were likely used as sales incentives or other premium rewards for employees in large corporations.

The Type Ia X-801 was led by a no. 220P-1 Santa Fe Alco Diesel Power Unit. This locomotive featured two-axle Magne-Traction, a three-position reversing unit and a headlight. The only feature it did not include was a horn.

The 220P-1 is an example of an item that appeared in promotional outfits before it became a regular-production item (it appeared in the 1961 consumer catalog). When boxed in its no.

220-10 Corrugated Box, it came with the nos. CTC-1 Lockon, 927-60 Tube of Oil, 927-65 Tube of Grease and 220-11 Instruction Sheet. The box was surrounded by a no. 217-16 Sleeve.

This outfit, along with a few other 1960 outfits, was used to deplete the remaining inventory of the nos. 2432 Illuminated Vista-Dome Car and 2436 Illuminated Observation Car. With the addition of a no. 6428-1 U. S. Mail Car (new for 1960), this was an attractive little passenger outfit. It also was very similar to catalog outfit no. 1640W. In fact, both of those illuminated passenger cars can be found in the 1640W as substitutions.

The 6428-1 was equipped with two early operating AAR trucks and couplers and came in an Orange Perforated box.

The no. 59-324 was a single-layer Tan RSC with Black Graphics outfit box. It was first used with catalog outfit no. 1609 from 1959

DISPLAY PACK
59-324 BOX
STICKER

220P-1 F		
6428-1 F	1015 60	3-1018
2432-1 S		
2436-1 S		

3-1013 TOP 220P
6029-25 TOP 220P
5-1013 TOP 6428

and subsequently with this and five other promotional outfits. It was manufactured by Express Container Corp. and measured 14⅞ x 12⅝ x 4¼ inches.

The transformer substitution does not affect the price of the X-801.

With only 50 of these outfits made, the X-801 ranks among the 20 catalog and promotional outfits of which Lionel made the fewest examples. This fact is reflected in the R10 rarity and price of this outfit.

X-802
1960

Description: 1960 Outfit
Specification: "O27" Ga. Diesel Freight Outfit with Horn
Customer: Maritz; 1486
Original Amount: 400
Factory Order Date: 5/2/1960
Date Issued: May 2, 1960
Packaging: Conventional Outfit Packing

Contents: 218P-1 Alco Diesel Power Unit - "Santa Fe" - with Horn, Headlight, Magne-Traction, Non-Operating Coupler, Lockon and Lubricant; 6175-1 Rocket Car; 6519-1 Allis-Chalmers Flat Car; 6820-1 Flat Car - with Missile Transport Helicopter - Blue Car Body; 6464-475 Box Car - Blue - "Boston & Maine"; 6517-1 Bay Window Caboose - Illuminated; 1013 Curved Track (8); 1018 Straight Track (3); 6029-25 Uncoupling Track Section; 1053-50 60-Watt Transformer; 90-1 Uncoupling Track Controller; 81-32 Wires (4); 90-30 Envelope Packed With 90-1 and 81-32; 926-60 Instruction Book; 310-2 Set of (5) Billboard Signs; AC Accessory Catalog

Boxes & Packing: 59-359 Box; 59-360 Shipper (1-4); ST Sticker

X-802 (1960)	C6	C7	C8	Rarity
1960 Complete Outfit With no. 59-359 Box	825	1,300	1,800	R9
1960 Outfit Box no. 59-359	275	425	575	R9
1959 Complete Outfit With no. 58-51 Box	1959 Version - Contents Unknown			
1959 Outfit Box no. 58-51				

Comments: Incentive marketer Maritz purchased three Retailer Promotional outfits in 1960. These included the nos. X-800 steam-freight, X-801 diesel-passenger and X-802 diesel-freight outfits. All three included some of Lionel's higher-end products. The outfits were likely used as sales incentives or other premium rewards for employees in large corporations.

The Type Ia X-802 was led by a no. 218P-1 Santa Fe Alco Diesel Power Unit. This locomotive featured a three-position reversing unit, a headlight, two-axle Magne-Traction, a horn and

an open pilot with a large ledge. This was Lionel's premier Alco offering for 1960. Being one of the few Alcos to include a horn, the 218P-1 came with a no. 601-13 "C" Battery. This practice lasted until 1963. The nos. CTC-1 Lockon and 218-11 Instruction Sheet were included inside the diesel's no. 218-10 Corrugated Box.

Although the no. 6820-1 Flat Car - with Missile Transport Helicopter was offered for separate sale in 1960 and 1961, as well as being a component of nine promotional outfits, its Orange Perforated no. 6820-11 Folding Box appears infrequently in collectible condition. The no. 6820-40 Non-Operating Missile Helicopter Complete is also becoming hard to find with original, unbroken parts.

Also included in this outfit were a Type III no. 6464-475 Boston & Maine Box Car and a no. 6517-1 Bay Window Caboose (the later version without an underlined built date). The caboose was equipped with 2400-series die-cast metal trucks and couplers and came packaged in a Late Classic style box. Lionel depleted the remaining quantity of 547 6517-1s in this and catalog outfit no. 2551W from 1960.

With the exception of the caboose, all the rolling stock in the X-802 was equipped with two early operating AAR trucks and couplers. All items were packaged in Orange Perforated boxes.

The no. 59-359 Tan RSC with Black Graphics outfit box was manufactured by Star Corrugated Box Company, Inc. and measured 13¾ x 11⅞ x 6⅝ inches. It was a 1959 overstamped no. X-826 outfit box and included "8-4B" and a star printed on the bottom.

The X-802 has been observed with Maritz no. 1486. This same number was also on the Maritz outfits from 1961, 1962 and 1963.

In addition, a 1959 version of the X-802 was planned. An internal Lionel Promotional Outfit List from 1959 includes the

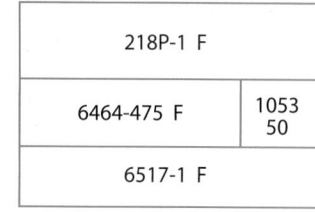

CONVENTIONAL PACK
59-359 BOX
STICKER

TOP LAYER

6519-1 F
6175-1 S
8-1013
6820-1 S

3-1018 TOP 6175
6029-25 TOP 6519

BOTTOM LAYER

218P-1 F	
6464-475 F	1053 50
6517-1 F	

X-802 in a no. 58-51 box with a quantity of 212. If it is the same outfit, there had to have been some changes made, if only because the 6820-1 didn't appear until 1960. This is the only information available about the 1959 version.

With a high-end Alco, a 6464-475 Box Car and a 6517-1 Bay Window Caboose, the X-802 is an interesting outfit. Combined with its lower-than-average quantity of 400, this is an outfit that shouldn't be passed up.

General Release Promotional outfit no. X-829 was first issued in 1959. A new Factory Order was issued for 350 in 1960. Its motive power and rolling stock mirrored that of advance catalog outfit no. 1105 from 1959. All the rolling stock in this outfit was equipped with non-operating Archbar trucks and couplers. Somewhere along the way, the outfit used for this photograph had its 6047-25 Caboose incorrectly swapped for a no. 6047-25 produced later with AAR trucks and couplers.

The no. 59-402 White Hinged Display with Red *Texas Special* Alco Graphics and Track Layout Plan Type A outfit box was unique to outfit no. X-829.

Description: 1960 Outfit
Specification: "O27" Ga. Diesel Freight Outfit
Original Amount: 1,113
Factory Order Date: 6/3/1960
Date Issued: June 13, 1960
Packaging: Conventional Outfit Packing, Units not Boxed except as noted

Contents: 1055-25 Alco Diesel Power Car - "MKT" Markings - with Headlight and Non-Operating Coupler - without Reversing Unit, Magne-Traction, Lockon and Lubricant; 6044-25 Box Car - Blue - "Airex" Markings - Non-Operating Trucks; 6045-25 Two Dome Tank Car - Gray - Non-Operating Trucks; 6042-25 Gondola Car - Blue - with 2 Red Canisters - with Non-Operating Trucks; 6047-25 Caboose - Brick Brown - Non-Operating Trucks; 1013 Curved Track (16); 1018 Straight Track (4); 1026-25 25-Watt

Transformer; 1023-1 45° Crossover; 920-8 Lychen; 903 Set of two (2) Sheets Trading Cards; 951 Farm Set; 81-32 Wires (2); CTC Lockon; 927-60 Lubricant (Oil); 927-65 Lubricant (Grease); 1103-12 Envelope Packed With CTC, 81-32, 927-60 and 927-65; 310-2 Set of (5) Billboard Signs; AC Accessory Catalog; 1105-10 Instruction Sheet; 1802H Layout Instruction Sheet

Boxes & Packing: 59-402 Box; 59-46 Insert; 59-47 Insert; 59-49 Insert; 59-403 Shipper (1-6)

Alternate For Outfit Contents:
Note: Production 350 Sets; Balance - Inventory.

X-829 (1960)	C6	C7	C8	Rarity
Complete Outfit	950	2,200	4,250	R9
Outfit Box no. 59-402	200	325	450	R8

Comments: This General Release Promotional Type IIb outfit included identical motive power and rolling stock as the no. 1105 advance catalog outfit from 1959.

Originally issued in 1959 with a quantity of 1,250, the no. X-829 was carried over into 1960. The 1960 version called for another 350 to be manufactured, or a total of 1,600 over the two years. The 1959 and 1960 outfits were likely the same.

A starter outfit, the X-829 was headed by a no. 1055-25 Alco Diesel Power Car - "MKT" Markings. This was Lionel's low-end

345

diesel offering that went forward only. It was a carryover item from 1959 that appeared in three promotional outfits in 1960.

The rolling stock in the X-829 was low-end, with all the cars equipped with non-operating Archbar trucks and couplers. The most notable item was the no. 6044-25 Blue Box Car - "Airex" Markings. Originally introduced in 1959, it appeared in 13 promotional outfits in 1960. All the items, except for the caboose, appeared only in promotional outfits.

What makes the X-829 much more collectible and valuable than the 1105 was the inclusion of the nos. 920-8 Lychen, 903 Set of two (2) Sheets Trading Cards and 951 Farm Set. This outfit represents the only one to include the 920-8 Lychen in the 1960s. That item typically showed up only as part of the no. 920 Scenic Display Set.

The 903 included 24 two-sided Lionel trading cards printed on a sheet of perforated cardstock. On the front of each card was a Lionel locomotive, and on the back was historical information about its road name as well as a trivia quiz. Two 11 x 11 inch sets of 12 cards were connected by a "folding" strip. The entire sheet of 24 was folded in half along the strip and placed loose in the outfit box. The cards were perforated and are almost always found separated as individual cards with the "folding" strip long gone. In fact, if it weren't for the complete sheets that came out of Madison Hardware over the years, it is likely that few of these items would be intact.

The inclusion of a Plasticville 951 Farm Set also increases the value of this outfit. It came boxed in a fragile box that takes patience to find in C8 condition.

The pretzel layout was detailed on the no. 1802H Layout Instruction Sheet.

The no. 59-402 White Hinged Display with Red *Texas Special* Alco Graphics and Track Layout Plan Type A outfit box was manufactured by Concora Products CCA Specialty Division Container Corp. and measured 20 x 15¼ x 3 inches.

Even though Lionel produced 1,600 of these outfits over a two-year span, an X-829 is seldom seen. Its unique box and highly collectible contents make this an extremely desirable and difficult outfit to find. The inclusion of the trading cards increases the outfit rarity to an R9.

DISPLAY PACK
59-402 BOX

1026-25	1055-25	2-1018 8-1013
6042-25	6044-25	
6047-25	6045-25	
951	8-1013/2-1018	
	920-8	

1023-1 BELOW CARS AND TRACK

X-835
1960

Description: 1960 Outfit
Specification: "O27" Ga. Steam Type Freight Outfit with Smoke & Whistle
Original Amount: 1,000
Factory Order Date: 6/3/1960
Date Issued: June 3, 1960
Packaging: Conventional Outfit Packing

Contents: 2037-1 Locomotive - with Magne-Traction, Smoke, Lockon & Lubricant; 243W-1 Whistle Tender; 6844-1 Rocket Transport Car; 6014-100 Box Car - Red; 6175-1 Rocket Car; 6162-1 Gondola Car - Blue - with (3) White Canisters; 6017-1 Caboose - Brick Brown; 1013 Curved Track (8); 1018 Straight Track (3); 6029-25 Uncoupling Track Section; 1053-50 60-Watt Transformer; 90-1 Uncoupling Track Controller; 81-32 Wires (4); 90-30 Envelope Packed With 90-1 and 81-32; 310-2 Set of (5) Billboard Signs; IS Instruction Sheet; AC Accessory Catalog

Boxes & Packing: 60-532 Box; 60-533 Shipper (1-3)

Alternate For Outfit Contents:
Note: Inventory - 150 Sets; Production - 850 Sets.

X-835 (1960)	C6	C7	C8	Rarity
1960 Complete Outfit With no. 60-532 Box	425	725	1,050	R7
1960 Outfit Box no. 60-532	175	275	375	R7
1959 Complete Outfit With no. 58-54 Box	1959 Version - Contents Unknown			
1959 Outfit Box no. 58-54				

Comments: This General Release Promotional Type IIb outfit was issued in both 1959 and 1960. An internal Lionel Promotional Outfit List from 1959 records the X-835 in a no. 58-54 Tan and White Basket Weave RSC with Blue Graphics overstickered outfit box with a quantity of 200. If the contents are the same outfit as the 1960 version, there would be some changes because the no. 243W-1 Whistle Tender didn't appear until 1960. This is the only information available about the 1959 version.

The 1960 version was headed by a no. 2037-1 Locomotive - with Magne-Traction and Smoke. This workhorse steamer spanned the years 1953 through 1963 (except for 1956) and powered one Super O and 22 O27 outfits during the 1960s. When boxed as a "-1", it included the nos. 675-33 Smoke Stack Cleaner, SP-1 Smoke Pellets, 927-60 Tube of Oil, 2037-16 Instruction Sheet and CTC-1 Lockon.

Except for the 243W-1 Whistle Tender, all the cars were carryover items. The no. 6014-100 Red Airex Box Car appeared only in promotional outfits. The nos. 6844-1 Rocket Transport Car and 6175-1 Rocket Car provided space and military loads.

All the rolling stock was equipped with early operating AAR trucks and couplers and came packaged in Orange Perforated boxes.

The no. 60-532 Tan RSC with Black Graphics outfit box was manufactured by Star Corrugated Box Company, Inc. and measured 13 x 12 x 6¼ inches. It had a star printed on the bottom.

The 1960 version of this outfit has been observed with a mailing label from incentive merchandiser E. F. MacDonald. (See the section on Lionel's Distribution and Customers.)

Pricing and rarity are provided only for the 1960 version of the X-835 because the contents of the 1959 version have yet to be determined.

CONVENTIONAL PACK
60-532 BOX

TOP LAYER

8-1013
243W-1 F
3-1018
6029-25

1053-50	6017-1 F

CORD BELOW 6017

BOTTOM LAYER

2037-1 S	
6162-1 S	6014-100 S
6175-1 S	
6844-1 F	

Description: 1960 Outfit
Specification: "O27" Ga. Steam Type Freight Outfit
Original Amount: 150
Factory Order Date: 6/6/1960
Date Issued: June 6, 1960
Packaging: Conventional Outfit Packing

Contents: 246-1 Locomotive - with Headlight and Magne-Traction - with Lockon and Lubricant; 1130T-1 Tender; 6162-1 Gondola Car - Blue - with (3) White Canisters; 6014-100 Box Car - Red; 6057-1 Caboose - Red; 1013 Curved Track (12); 1018 Straight Track (3); 1008-50 Uncoupling Unit - with (1) 1018 Straight Track; 1015-60 45-Watt Transformer; 1020 90° Crossover; 81-32 Wires (2); AC Accessory Catalog; 310-2 Set of (5) Billboard Signs; 1609-4 Instruction Sheet; 1802B Layout Instruction Sheet

Boxes & Packing: 59-324 Box; 59-325 Shipper (1-4); ST Sticker

Alternate For Outfit Contents:
Note: If necessary - Substitute 1- 1015-25, 1- 1103-14 For 1 - 1015-60, 2 - 81-32.

X-837 (1960)	C6	C7	C8	Rarity
1960 Complete Outfit With no. 59-324 Box	350	625	950	R10
1960 Complete Outfit With A no. 1103-14 Substitution And no. 59-324 Box	450	825	1,400	R10
1960 Outfit Box no. 59-324	200	400	600	R10
1959 Complete Outfit With no. 6014-150 And no. 59-344 Box	350	550	825	R5
1959 Outfit Box no. 59-344	75	125	150	R4

Comments: The no. X-837 was issued in both 1959 and 1960. The 1959 Manufacturer Promotional Type IIIb version is commonly known as one of the "WIX" outfits because it was available for $12.95 plus a C.O.D. charge with the purchase of 24 WIX Oil or Air Filter Cartridges. An internal Lionel Promotional Outfit List from 1959 records the X-837 in a no. 59-344 Tan RSC with Black Graphics outfit box with a quantity of 6,000. This box was manufactured by Star Corrugated Box Company, Inc. and measured 15 x 12¾ x 4½ inches. The number "X-837" was printed as part of the box manufacturing process.

The 1959 version of the X-837 was the same as the 1960

version, except that it included the no. 6014-150 WIX Box Car. The 1960 version included a promotional-only no. 6014-100 Red Airex Box Car.

The 1960 version listed here was a General Release Promotional Type IIb outfit. It was headed by a no. 246-1 Locomotive - with Headlight and Magne-Traction. This steam engine headed 23 different promotional outfits in 1960. It came boxed in a no. 246-6 Corrugated Box.

All the cars in this outfit were originally issued in earlier years. They came equipped with early operating AAR trucks and couplers and were packaged in Orange Perforated boxes.

The no. 59-324 Tan RSC with Black Graphics outfit box was an overstickered no. 1609 from 1959. It was manufactured by Express Container Corp. and measured 14⅞ x 12⅝ x 4¼ inches.

Two major features help to identify the rare 1960 version of this outfit box. First, it was overstickered; second, it was manufactured by Express Container instead of Star Corrugated Box Company, Inc.

The 1959 version is a popular outfit among collectors because it likely was the only outfit to include a 6014-150 WIX Box Car and its Orange Perforated no. 6014-154 Folding Box.

The low quantity of the 1960 version is what determines its rarity and price. Also influencing the rarity and price is the substitution of a no. 1103-14 Envelope Packed, a point indicated in the pricing table. (See the entry for outfit no. X-502NA for more information about this packed envelope and its contents.)

CONVENTIONAL PACK
59-324 BOX
STICKER

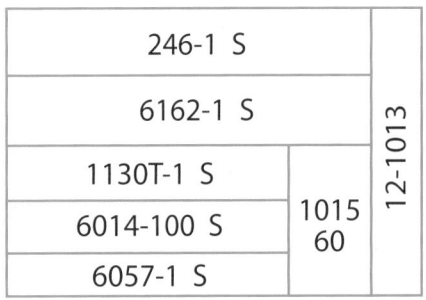

246-1 S	
6162-1 S	
1130T-1 S	
6014-100 S	1015 60
6057-1 S	

With 12-1013 on right side.

3-1018 TOP 1013
1008-50 TOP
1020 TOP 6162 - 6014

Description: 1960 Outfit
Specification: "O27" Ga. Steam Type Freight Outfit
Customer: Premium Service Corp.
Original Amount: 72
Factory Order Date: 4/29/1960
Date Issued: April 29, 1960
Packaging: Conventional Outfit Packing

Contents: 249-1 Locomotive - without Magne-Traction - Headlight or Smoke - Striped - with 2 Position "E" Unit - with Lockon & Lubricant; 250T-1 Tender - Striped - "Pennsylvania"; 6476-1 Hopper Car - Red; 6162-1 Gondola Car - Blue - with (3) White Canisters; 6807-1 Flat Car - Red - with (1) 6151-21 DKW Truck; 6017-1 Caboose - Brick Brown; 1013 Curved Track (8); 1018 Straight Track; 1008-50 Uncoupling Unit - (With (1) 1018 Straight Track); 1015-25 45-Watt Transformer; 81-32 Wires (2); 310-2 Set of (5) Billboard Signs; AC Accessory Catalog; IS Instruction Sheet

Boxes & Packing: 59-383 Box; 59-384 Shipper (1-4); BP Bogus Paper

Alternate For Outfit Contents:
Substitute 24 - 247LT for 24 - 249LT.

X-874 (1960)	C6	C7	C8	Rarity
1960 Complete Outfit With no. 59-383 Box	1,125	1,535	1,925	R10
1960 Outfit Box no. 59-383	900	1,200	1,400	R10
1959 Complete Outfit With no. 58-33 Box		1959 Version - Contents Unknown		
1959 Outfit Box no. 58-33				

Comments: Premium Service was an incentive merchandise company that purchased this Retailer Promotional Type Ia outfit in 1960.

Two versions of the no. X-874 exist, one for 1959 and another for 1960. An internal Lionel Promotional Outfit List from 1959 records the X-874 in a no. 58-33 Box with a quantity of 100. The 1959 and 1960 versions might be identical, as the contents were readily available in 1959. Also, Premium Service was known to carry the same outfit for more than one year (see the entry for outfit no. X-660 in 1961 and 1962). In either case, a 1959 version has yet to be observed and verified.

The 1960 version was headed by a no. 249-1 Locomotive - without Magne-Traction - Headlight or Smoke. This red-striped Scout steamer was first issued in 1958. It, along with the no. 250T-1 Red-Striped Pennsylvania Tender, made a last appearance in this outfit. In fact, it appears that Lionel did not have the inventory to cover the quantity of 72 required, as the no. 247LT Baltimore & Ohio Locomotive and Tender was used as a substitution. This substitution only minimally affects the outfit price.

The no. 6807-1 Flat Car - Red - with DKW Truck was also making a final appearance in outfits during 1960. It was first released two years prior.

All the rolling stock in the X-874 was equipped with early operating AAR trucks and couplers. The items were boxed in a combination of Orange Perforated (nos. 6017-1, 6162-1 and 6476-1) and Classic style boxes.

The no. 59-383 Tan RSC with Black Graphics outfit box was manufactured by Express Container Corp. and measured 13¼ x 12 x 6 inches. It was a 1959 overstickered no. X-860 outfit box.

With only 72 manufactured, the X-874 ranks right up there as one of the rarest outfits.

CONVENTIONAL PACK
59-383 BOX
BOGUS PAPER

TOP LAYER		BOTTOM LAYER	
1018	1008-50	8-1013	
250T-1 S	1015 25	6476-1 F	
6162-1 S		6807-1 F	
6017-1 F		249-1 F	

Description: 1960 Outfit
Specification: "O27" Ga. Steam Type Freight Outfit
Customer: Gift House Stamp
Customer: All Trade
Original Amount: 5,000
Factory Order Date: 8/18/1960
Date Issued: September 7, 1960
Packaging: Conventional Outfit Packing

Contents: 246-1 Locomotive - with Headlight and Magne-Traction - with Lockon & Lubricant; 1130T-1 Tender; 6014-100 Box Car - Red - "Airex" Lettering"; 6476-1 Hopper Car - Red; 6465-110 2 Dome Tank Car - Green - ("Cities Service"); 6017-1 Caboose - Brick Brown; 1013 Curved Track (8); 1018 Straight Track (3); 1008-50 Uncoupling Unit - (with (1) 1018 Straight Track); 1015-60 45-Watt Transformer; 81-32 Wires (2); 310-2 Set of (5) Billboard Signs; AC Accessory Catalog; 1609-4 Instruction Sheet

Boxes & Packing: 59-318 Box; 59-319 Shipper (1-4); ST Sticker; 60-577 Box; 60-578 Shipper (1-4)

Alternate For Outfit Contents:
Note: If necessary - Substitute 1- 1015-25, 1- 1103-14 For 1 - 1015-60, 2 - 81-32; Note: 813 Outfits assembled with one (1) 1018; Balance with 3 sections of 1018 as per revised outfit contents sheet (above); Substitute - 6821-1 for 6014-100 in 2,500 sets.

X-875 (1960)	C6	C7	C8	Rarity
Complete Outfit With no. 59-318 Box	325	550	775	R7
Outfit Box no. 59-318	150	225	300	R7
Complete Outfit With no. 60-577 Box	270	450	650	R4
Outfit Box no. 60-577	95	135	175	R4
Either Outfit With A no. 1103-14 Substitution, Add The Following	100	200	450	R9

The no. X-875 is shown with its no. 60-577 Box and the no. 6821-1 Flat Car - with Cargo substitution.

Comments: Gift House Stamp, Inc. was one of the many companies that offered trading stamps for goods purchased. In turn, consumers could redeem the stamps for merchandise selected from a catalog or at one of the Gift House Stamp redemption centers. The Factory Order for the no. X-875 listed "Gift House, etc." as the customer, making this a General Release Promotional Type IIb outfit.

There is also a 1959 version of this outfit. An internal Lionel Promotional Outfit List from 1959 (the only source of information for this earlier version) records the X-875 in a no. 59-318 box with a quantity of 60. If it is the same outfit, changes would be required because the no. 6465-110 Green Cities Service Two Dome Tank Car didn't appear until 1960.

The 1960 version of the X-875 was headed by a no. 246-1 Locomotive - with Headlight and Magne-Traction. Included in the outfit was the later version of this steamer with a solid pilot and lack of generator detail. This engine, which headed 23 different promotional outfits in 1960, came boxed in a no. 246-6 Corrugated Box.

Rolling stock in the X-875 included the notable 6465-110 Green Cities Service Two Dome Tank Car that came in an Orange Perforated no. 6465-103 Folding Box. This box takes patience to find in collectible condition. Also included was the promotional-only no. 6014-100 Red Airex Box Car. All the cars in this outfit were equipped with early operating AAR trucks and couplers and came packaged in Orange Perforated boxes.

This outfit came boxed in two different Tan RSC with Black Graphics outfit boxes. One, the no. 59-318, was an overstickered Sears no. 9664 from 1959 that also was used for the 1959 version of the X-875.

The other outfit box, the no. 60-577, was manufactured by Owens-Illinois Paper Products, Div. and measured 12⅛ x 10¾ x 6 inches. It had 12 dots printed as part of the box manufacturer's certificate. The 60-577 boxed version appears more often than does the overstickered 59-318 box.

Pricing and rarity are provided for the 1960 versions of this outfit, as the 1959 version has yet to be seen. Also, since the 1959 version came in the same box as one of the 1960 versions, they are likely indistinguishable.

Regarding substitutions, as shown in the pricing table, the substitution of a no. 1103-14 Envelope Packed changes the value of the X-875. (See the entry for outfit no. X-502NA for more information about this packed envelope and its contents.) However, the substitution of a no. 6821-1 Flat Car - with Cargo affects the price only minimally.

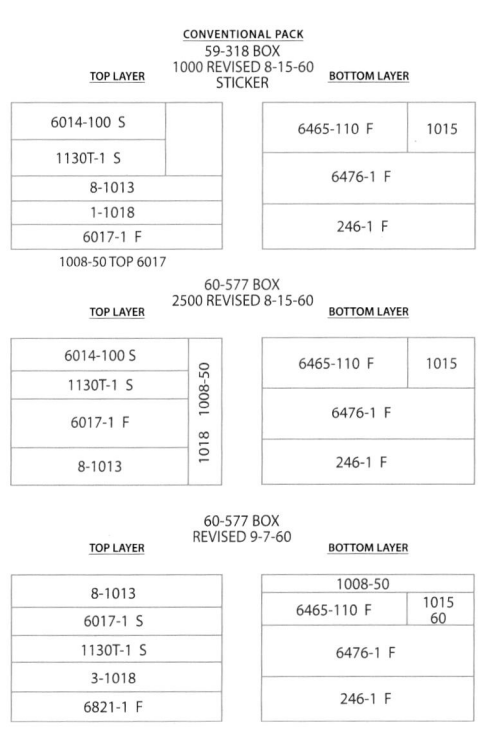

General Release Promotional outfit no. 1103 was a repeat outfit from 1959. A new Factory Order was issued for 1,000 in 1960. All the rolling stock in this outfit was equipped with non-operating Archbar trucks and couplers. Somewhere along the way, the outfit used for this photograph had its no. 6047-25 Caboose incorrectly swapped for a later production 6047-25 with AAR trucks and couplers.

Display outfit box no. 59-40 was pre-printed by the manufacturer with "No. 1103".

Description: 1960 Outfit
Specification: "O27" Ga. Steam Type Freight Outfit
Original Amount: 1,000
Factory Order Date: 6/6/1960
Date Issued: June 6, 1960
Packaging: Snake Insert Outfit, Units not boxed

Contents: 1050-25 Steam Type Locomotive - with Headlight - without Pilot Trucks, Magne-Traction and Reversing Unit - Less Lockon & Lubricant; 1050T-25 Tender - with Non-Operating Truck; 6042-25 Gondola Car - Blue with 2 Red Canisters with Non-Operating Trucks; 6044-25 Box Car - Blue - "Airex" Markings - Non-Operating Trucks; 6047-25 Caboose - Brick Brown - Non-Operating Trucks; 1013 Curved Track (8); 1018 Straight Track (2); 1026-25 25-Watt Transformer; 81-32 Wires (2); CTC Lockon; 927-60 Lubricant (Oil); 927-65 Lubricant (Grease); 1103-12 Envelope Packed With CTC, 81-32, 927-60 and 927-65; 1103-10 Instruction Sheet; 310-2 Set of (5) Billboard Signs; AC Accessory Catalog

Boxes & Packing: 59-40 Box; 59-41 Insert; 59-42 Insert; 59-44 Tube; 59-43 Shipper (1-6)

1103 (1960)	C6	C7	C8	Rarity
Complete Outfit	250	400	550	R6
Outfit Box no. 59-40	75	125	150	R6

Comments: This Type IIb outfit was the first of eight 1100-series General Release Promotional outfits that Lionel issued in 1960.

The no. 1103 first appeared in 1959 with a quantity of 3,398 produced. It was likely the sister steam outfit to the no. 1105 advance catalog diesel outfit for 1959. Why the 1103 did not appear in the 1959 advance catalog is a mystery. In any case, it was reissued in 1960 and a new Factory Order was created.

This outfit and the no. X-553NA were the only two outfits in 1960 to include a no. 1050-25 Steam Type Locomotive (new in 1959). In fact, except for the fact that the X-553NA also included a no. 6045-25 Gray Two Dome Tank Car, the two outfits are identical.

The 1050-25 steam locomotive was Lionel's promotional-only low-end steamer. Its no. 1050-100 Motor Complete went forward only. Even though the 1050-25 was a low-end engine, Lionel produced it in low numbers (2,000 in 1960 and minimally 1,200 in outfit no. X-833 and 3,398 in outfit 1103, both from 1959). As a result, this steam locomotive is difficult to find in collectible condition. Eventually, Lionel replaced it with the no. 1060-25 Locomotive.

DISPLAY PACK
59-40 BOX

1050-25	1050T-25	
1026-25	6042-25	2-1018 8-1013
6047-25	6044-25	

The rolling stock in the 1103 was low-end, and all the cars were equipped with non-operating Archbar trucks and couplers. All the items, except for the tender and caboose, appeared only in promotional outfits.

The no. 59-40 White Hinged Display with 1050 Blue Steamer and Red/Orange Graphics Type A outfit box was manufactured by Concora Products CCA Specialty Division Container Corp. and measured 19⅞ x 11⅜ x 2⅞ inches.

Despite Lionel's having produced a total of 4,398 examples of this low-end outfit between 1959 and 1960, it is surprisingly difficult to find in collectible condition. Even when found, most outfits have been stripped of their 1050-25 steam locomotive due to its individual value.

General Release Promotional outfit no. 1107 appeared in the Lionel 1960 advance catalog. It was Lionel's diesel-powered offering, whereas outfit no. 1109 featured a steam locomotive.

Display outfit box no. 60-375 was pre-printed by the manufacturer with "No. 1107".

The no. 59-45 White Hinged Display with Red *Texas Special* Alco Graphics Type A outfit box version of the no. 1107 was an overstickered no. 1105 outfit from 1959.

Description: 1960 Outfit (Non-Catalog)
Specification: "O27" Ga. Diesel Freight Outfit
Customer/No.: Firestone; 11-L-340
Customer/No.: Lionel Advance Catalog; 1107
Cust./No./Price: Oklahoma Tire & Supply Co.; 70-759-5; $12.95
Original Amount: 65,000
Factory Order Date: 3/28/1960
Date Issued: 6-23-60
Packaging: Display Outfit Packing - Corrugated Separators, Units not Boxed; Also in Conventional Outfit Packing (Units not Boxed)

Contents: 1055-25 Alco Diesel Power Car - "MKT" Markings - with Headlight and Non-Operating Coupler - without Reversing Unit, Magne-Traction, Lockon and Lubricant; 6042-25 Gondola Car - Blue (Less 2 Red Canisters) with Non-Operating Trucks; 6112-5 Red Canisters (2); 6044-25 Box Car - Blue - "Airex" Markings - Non-Operating Trucks; 6047-25 Caboose - Brick Brown - Non-Operating Trucks; 1013 Curved Track (8); 1018 Straight Track (2); 1026-25 25-Watt Transformer; CTC Lockon; 81-32 Wires (2); 927-60 Lubricant (Oil); 927-65 Lubricant (Grease); 1103-12 Envelope Packed With CTC, 81-32, 927-60 and 927-65; 1105-10 Instruction Sheet; 310-2 Set of (5) Billboard Signs; AC Accessory Catalog

Boxes & Packing: 60-375 Box; 59-46 Insert; 59-49 Insert; 60-376 Shipper (1-6); 59-45 Box; 59-46 Insert; 59-49 Insert; 59-48 Shipper (1-6); ST 5 Stickers Blue On White; 59-374 Box; 59-375 Insert; 59-376 Insert; 59-378 Insert; 59-379 Shipper (1-6); ST Sticker

Alternate For Outfit Contents:
Note: Substitute 12,875 - 6042-50 for 6042-25.

1107 (1960)	C6	C7	C8	Rarity
Complete Outfit With no. 60-375 Display Box	125	210	340	R1
Display Outfit Box no. 60-375	40	60	100	R1
Complete Outfit With no. 59-45 Display Box	125	210	340	R1
Display Outfit Box no. 59-45	40	60	100	R1
Complete Outfit With no. 59-374 RSC Box	160	275	380	R6
RSC Outfit Box no. 59-374	75	125	150	R6

Comments: This Type IIb outfit was the second of eight 1100-series General Release Promotional outfits that Lionel issued in 1960. An illustration of the no. 1107 appeared on the inside cover of the Lionel 1960 advance catalog. The description stated that the nos. 1107 and 1109 "are designed for the toy market and will not be included in the Lionel consumer catalog." These advance catalog outfits were part of Lionel's promotional outfit strategy to offer retailers something different even if they couldn't commit to the quantity necessary for a unique promotional outfit.

The 1107 was the follow-up outfit to the no. 1105 from 1959. The outfits were identical except that the 1105 also included a no. 6045-25 Gray Two Dome Tank Car.

A basic starter outfit, the 1107 was headed by a no. 1055-25 Alco Diesel Power Car - "MKT" Markings. This was Lionel's low-end diesel offering that went forward only. It was a carryover item from 1959 that appeared in three promotional outfits in 1960.

The rolling stock was low-end, with all the cars equipped with non-operating Archbar trucks and couplers. The most notable item was the no. 6044-25 Blue Box Car - "Airex" Markings. Originally introduced in 1959, it appeared in 13 promotional outfits in 1960. All the items, except for the caboose, appeared only in promotional outfits.

Three versions of this outfit exist, as based on differences in outfit packing. The first was the no. 60-375 White Hinged Display with Red *Texas Special* Alco Graphics Type A outfit box. It was manufactured by Kraft Corrugated and measured 19⅞ x 11⅜ x 2⅞ inches.

The second version was an overstickered no. 59-45 White Hinged Display with Red *Texas Special* Alco Graphics Type A outfit box. It was manufactured by Concora Products CCA Specialty Division Container Corp. and measured 20 x 11¼ x 3 inches. This box was originally used for promotional outfit 1105 from 1959.

The last version of the 1107 was a no. 59-374 Tan RSC with Black Graphics outfit box. It was manufactured by Express Container Corp. and measured 16 x 9½ x 4 inches. This box was also originally used for promotional outfit 1105 from 1959.

The substitution of a no. 6042-50 Black Gondola Car does not affect the outfit's price or rarity.

With the very large quantities of the 1107 that Lionel produced, this outfit frequently appears in display packaging. As for the RSC version, it is seldom seen and so is much more collectible.

It appears that most of these outfits achieved their goal of reaching the "toy market," as examples are often found in well-used condition. As such, finding a complete C8 outfit takes some patience.

DISPLAY PACK 60-375 OR 59-45 BOX WITH 5 STICKERS BLUE ON WHITE			
1026	1055		8-1013 2-1018
6042	6044		
6047	CATALOG		

CONVENTIONAL PACK 59-374 BOX STICKER			
1055			
6044		1026	6047
CATALOG			6042
8-1013 2-1018			

Description: 1960 Outfit (Non-Catalog)
Specification: "O27" Ga. Steam Type Freight Outfit
Cust./Price: Augusta Hardware & Plumbing Company; $13.88
Customer/No./Price: Duckwall's; J109 J/0; $12.88
Customer/No.: Lionel Advance Catalog; 1109
Cust./No./Price: Oklahoma Tire & Supply Co.; 70-760-3; $14.99
Original Amount: 50,000
Factory Order Date: 3/28/1960
Date Issued: 5-24-60
Packaging: Display Outfit Packing - Corrugated Separators, Units not Boxed; Also in conventional Outfit Packing (Units not Boxed)

Contents: 1060-25 Steam Type Locomotive - with Headlight, Front and Rear Trucks - without Magne-Traction, Reversing Unit, Lockon and Lubricant; 1060T-25 Tender; 6404-25 Single Auto Car - Black Frame - (Less Auto) - with Non-Operating Trucks; 6404-30 Automobile - Maroon; 3386-25 Operating Giraffe Car - with Non-Operating Trucks; 3376-118 Envelope Packed; 6047-25 Caboose - Brick Brown - Non-Operating Trucks; 1013 Curved Track (8); 1018 Straight Track (2); 1016-25 35-Watt Transformer; CTC Lockon; 81-32 Wires (2); 927-60 Lubricant (Oil); 927-65 Lubricant (Grease); 1103-12 Envelope Packed With CTC, 81-32, 927-60 and 927-65; 1109-10 Instruction Sheet; 310-2 Set of (5) Billboard Signs; AC Accessory Catalog

Boxes & Packing: 60-368 Box; 60-369 Insert; 60-370 Insert; 59-44 Tube; 60-371 Shipper (1-6); 60-372 Box; 60-373 Insert; 60-380 Insert; 59-377 Insert; 60-374 Shipper (1-6)

Alternate For Outfit Contents:
Note: When entire inventory of 22,800 - 1016-25 is depleted, balance substitute 1016-60 Transformers.

General Release Promotional outfit no. 1109 appeared in the Lionel 1960 advance catalog. A basic starter outfit, it was one of four promotional outfits to include the no. 6404-25 Black Frame Single Auto Car. This car included the no. 6404-30 Automobile – Maroon, which was a red automobile with gray bumpers.

The display version of the no. 1109 came in the no. 60-368 White Hinged Display with 1050 Blue Steamer and Red/Orange Graphics Type A outfit box.

DISPLAY PACK 60-368 BOX		
1060		1060T
1016	3386	6047
CORD 8-1013 2-1018	6404 3376-118	

CONVENTIONAL PACK 60-372 BOX				
1060	CORD			
6047	1016		3386	6404
1060T				
8-1013 2-1018				

1109 (1960)	C6	C7	C8	Rarity
Complete Outfit With no. 60-368 Display Box	200	300	450	R1
Display Outfit Box no. 60-368	25	50	75	R1
Complete Outfit With no. 60-372 RSC Box	235	350	500	R3
RSC Outfit Box no. 60-372	60	100	125	R3

A basic starter outfit, the 1109 was headed by a no. 1060-25 Steam Type Locomotive - with Headlight. The low-end no. 1060-25 was new in 1960 and went forward only. Interestingly, it was included with only five promotional outfits in 1960, but appeared in more than 65 outfits over the next few years.

The no. 6404-25 Black Frame Single Auto Car appeared only in this and three other promotional outfits. With more than 59,000 of these four outfits produced, this freight car is more common than previously thought. The red automobile with gray bumpers was a no. 6404-30 Automobile - Maroon. Lionel here used the term "maroon" to designate an item that looks red.

Also included in the 1109 was the no. 3386-25 Operating Giraffe Car (new for 1960), which appeared in only 10 promotional outfits. When the 3386-25 was unboxed, its no. 3376-118 Envelope Packed was placed loose in the outfit box.

All the rolling stock in the 1109 was equipped with non-operating Archbar trucks and couplers.

This outfit came boxed both in display and RSC versions. The display was a no. 60-368 White Hinged Display with 1050 Blue Steamer and Red/Orange Graphics Type A outfit box. It was

Comments: This Type IIb outfit was the third of eight 1100-series General Release Promotional outfits that Lionel issued in 1960. An illustration of the no. 1109 appeared on the inside cover of the Lionel 1960 advance catalog. The description stated that the nos. 1107 and 1109 "are designed for the toy market and will not be included in the Lionel consumer catalog." These advance catalog outfits were part of Lionel's promotional outfit strategy to offer retailers something different even if they couldn't commit to the quantity necessary for a unique promotional outfit.

1000 Series

The RSC version of the no. 1109 included the same components as the display version, but it was produced in smaller quantities (5,000 for RSC compared with 45,000 for display). Packaging outfits in both RSC and display was a common practice in 1960.

manufactured by Kraft Corrugated Containers, Inc. and measured 20⅝ x 11⅝ x 3⅛ inches.

The no. 60-372 Tan RSC with Black Graphics outfit box was the RSC version. It was manufactured by Owens Illinois Paper Products Division and measured 17 x 10¼ x 4⅛ inches. It also had "9" printed below the box manufacturer's certificate.

Of the 50,000 examples of this outfit that Lionel produced, 45,000 were display and 5,000 RSC. The display is easily found; the RSC takes more effort.

It appears that most of these outfits achieved their goal of reaching the "toy market," as they're often found in well-used condition. As such, finding a complete C8 outfit takes some patience.

1111
1960

Description: 1960 Outfit (Non-Catalog)
Specification: "O27" Ga. Steam Type Freight Outfit
Original Amount: 7,500
Factory Order Date: 2/17/1960
Date Issued: 9-9-60
Packaging: Display Outfit Packing - Corrugated Separators, Units not boxed; Also in Conventional Outfit Packing (Units not Boxed)

Contents: 246-25 Locomotive - with Headlight and Magne-Traction - Less Lockon and Lubricant; 1060T-25 Tender; 6476-25 Hopper Car; 3386-25 Operating Giraffe Car - with Non-Operating Trucks; 3376-118 Envelope Packed; 6045-25 Two Dome Tank Car - Gray - Non-Operating Trucks; 6047-25 Caboose - Brick Brown - Non-Operating Trucks; 1013 Curved Track (8); 1018 Straight Track (2); 1016-60 35-Watt Transformer; CTC Lockon; 81-32 Wires (2); 927-60 Lubricant (Oil); 927-65 Lubricant (Grease); 1103-12 Envelope Packed With CTC, 81-32, 927-60 and 927-65; 1109-10 Instruction Sheet; 310-2 Set of (5) Billboard Signs; AC Accessory Catalog

Boxes & Packing: 60-360 Box; 60-361 Insert; 60-362 Insert; 60-363 Insert; 59-44 Tube; 60-364 Shipper (1-6); 60-365 Box; 60-366 Insert; 60-379 Insert; 60-380 Insert; 60-377 Insert; 59-44 Tube; 60-367 Shipper (1-6)

1111 (1960)	C6	C7	C8	Rarity
Complete Outfit With no. 60-360 Display Box	215	325	475	R4
Display Outfit Box no. 60-360	75	100	150	R4
Complete Outfit With no. 60-365 RSC Box	290	575	775	R9
RSC Outfit Box no. 60-365	150	350	450	R9

Comments: This Type IIb outfit was the fourth of eight 1100-series General Release Promotional outfits that Lionel issued in 1960. The no. 1111 was a step up from the nos. 1103, 1107 and 1109 because the motive power and rolling stock were slightly better. As an aside, Lionel used the same number for a cataloged O27 outfit in 1948.

This version of the 1111, like the other 1100-series promotional outfits, was a starter outfit. It was headed by a no. 246-25 Locomotive - with Headlight and Magne-Traction. Since

General Release Promotional outfit no. 1111 was the fourth outfit issued in the 1100-series from 1960. It included similar rolling stock to other outfits in the series.

that steamer came unboxed (as indicated by the "-25"), a no. CTC-1 Lockon was required separately and included in the no. 1103-12 Envelope Packed.

The rolling stock in this outfit was very similar to that included in the other 1100-series outfits. A notable item was the no. 3386-25 Operating Giraffe Car. This item, new for 1960, appeared in only 10 promotional outfits. When the 3386-25 was unboxed, its no. 3376-118 Envelope Packed was placed loose in the outfit box.

The no. 6476-25 Hopper Car was equipped with two operating AAR trucks and couplers. All the remaining rolling stock was equipped with non-operating Archbar trucks and couplers.

The 1111 came boxed in display and RSC versions. The display was a no. 60-360 White Hinged Display with 1050 Blue Steamer and Red/Orange Graphics Type A outfit box. It was manufactured by Kraft Corrugated Containers, Inc. and measured 23⅞ x 11¾ x 3 inches.

The no. 60-365 was likely a Tan RSC with Black Graphics, although an example has yet to be observed.

Of the 7,500 examples of this outfit that Lionel produced, 7,000 were display and 500 RSC. The display is easily found, although most often without inserts.

DISPLAY PACK 60-360 BOX			
246	1060T		2-1018 8-1013
6476	6045		
3376-118 3386	6047	1016	

CONVENTIONAL PACK 60-365 BOX						
6476			3376-118	3386	6045	246
1060T	1016					
6047						
8-1013 2-1018						

1000 Series

Description: 1960 Outfit
Specification: "O27" Ga. Diesel Freight Outfit
Original Amount: 7,500
Factory Order Date: 4/20/1960
Date Issued: 8-1-60
Packaging: Display Outfit Packing - Corrugated Separators; Illustrate Canadian National Locomotive on Outfit Box, Units not Boxed

Contents: 227P-25 Alco Diesel Power Car - "Canadian National" Markings - with Headlight and Non-Operating Coupler - without Reversing Unit, Magne-Traction, Lockon and Lubricant; 6042-25 Gondola Car - Blue - with 2 Red Canisters - with Non-Operating

Trucks; 6044-25 Box Car - Blue - "Airex" Markings - Non-Operating Trucks; 6047-25 Caboose - Brick Brown - Non-Operating Trucks; 1013 Curved Track (8); 1018 Straight Track (2); 1026-25 25-Watt Transformer; CTC-1 Lockon; 81-32 Wires (2); 927-60 Lubricant (Oil); 927-65 Lubricant (Grease); 1103-12 Envelope Packed With CTC-1, 81-32, 927-60 and 927-65; 1105-10 Instruction Sheet; 310-2 Set of (5) Billboards; AC Accessory Catalog

Boxes & Packing: 60-475 Box; 59-46 Insert; 59-49 Insert; 60-476 Shipper (1-6)

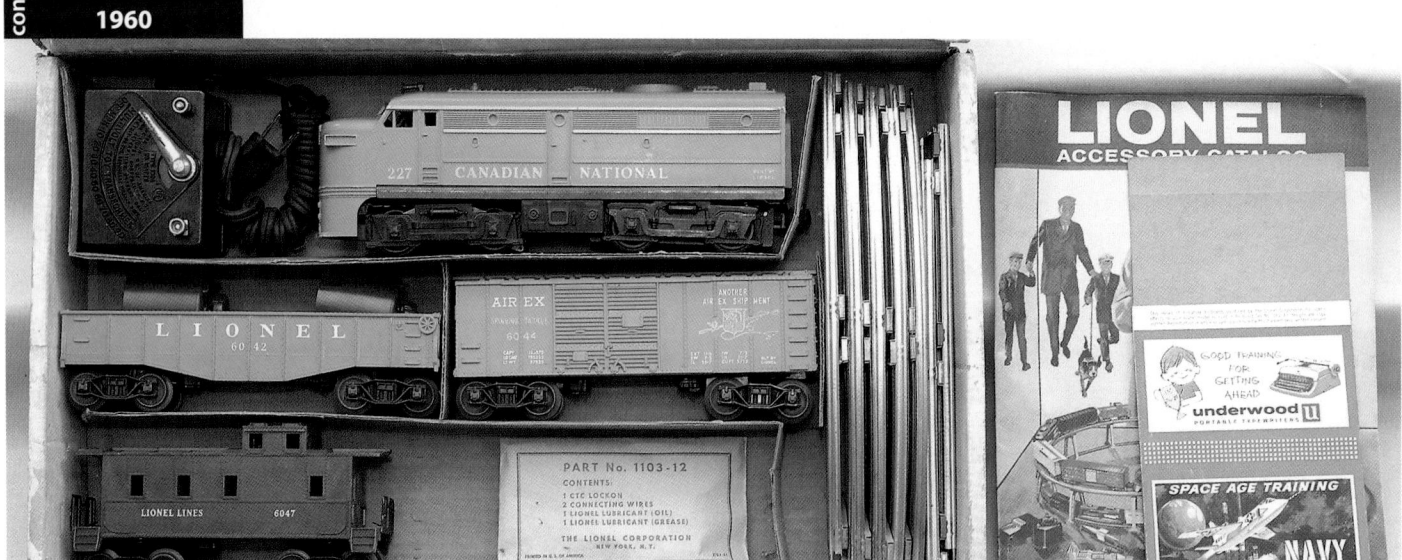

General Release Promotional outfit no. 1113 is a highly desirable starter outfit. Although the quantities produced were fairly high, it seldom appears on the market in collectible condition. Also, its Canadian National outfit box graphics and no. 227P-25 Alco add to the desirability of the 1113.

Outfit no. 1113 came packaged in a no. 60-475 White Hinged Display with Green Canadian National Alco Graphics Type A outfit box. These graphics were used for only this and outfit no. 1115.

The rolling stock in this outfit was low-end and similar to that included in other 1100-series outfits. The cars were equipped with non-operating Archbar trucks and couplers. All of them, except for the caboose, appeared only in promotional outfits.

The no. 60-475 White Hinged Display with Green Canadian National Alco Graphics Type A outfit box was manufactured by KCC, Kraft Corrugated Containers and measured 19⅞ x 11½ x 3⅛ inches.

The 1113 was a success based on the increase of outfits on the Factory Order. The original quantity was 3,500 in April of 1960, but over the next four months it incrementally increased to 7,500.

Even so, this is a difficult outfit to find in collectible condition. Its unique Canadian National graphics (used for only the nos. 1113 and 1115) and 227P-25 Alco make it a highly desirable outfit. With high demand and low collectible supply, this is an expensive starter outfit.

1113 (1960)	C6	C7	C8	Rarity
Complete Outfit	425	700	950	R5
Outfit Box no. 60-475	275	450	600	R5

Comments: This Type IIb outfit was the fifth of eight 1100-series General Release Promotional outfits that Lionel issued in 1960. The no. 1113 outfit was similar to the no. 1115, except the 1115 included an additional car. As an aside, Lionel used the same number for a cataloged O27 outfit in 1950.

This version of the 1113, like the other 1100-series promotional outfits, was a starter outfit. It was headed by a no. 227P-25 Canadian National Alco Diesel Power Car. This locomotive moved forward only and featured a closed pilot and a weight to aid in traction. Ironically, this low-end Alco, which often was a component of Canadian-market outfits, is now a desirable collector piece.

DISPLAY PACK
60-475 BOX

1026 25	227P-25	
6042-25	6044-25	2-1018 8-1013
6047-25	CATALOG	

Outfit no. 1115 was offered to Canadian customers via T. Eaton's 1960 Christmas Catalog for $18.98 delivered. This outfit included the gray (versus beige) variation of the no. 6045-25 Gray Two Dome Tank Car. The outfit is highly desirable and does not appear too often.

Outfit no. 1115 came packaged in a no. 60-477 White Hinged Display with Green Canadian National Alco Graphics Type A outfit box. These graphics were used for only this and outfit no. 1113.

Wires (2); 927-60 Lubricant (Oil); 927-65 Lubricant (Grease); 1103-12 Envelope Packed With CTC, 81-32, 927-60 and 927-65; 1105-10 Instruction Sheet; 310-2 Set of (5) Billboards; AC Accessory Catalog

Boxes & Packing: 60-477 Box; 59-46 Insert; 59-47 Insert; 59-49 Insert; 60-478 Shipper (1-6)

1115 (1960)	C6	C7	C8	Rarity
Complete Outfit	620	925	1,200	R6
Outfit Box no. 60-477	450	650	800	R6

Description: 1960 Outfit
Specification: "O27" Ga. Diesel Freight Outfit
Customer/No./Price: T. Eaton; 027-B-640; $18.98
Original Amount: 2,500
Factory Order Date: 4/20/1960
Date Issued: 6-14-60
Packaging: Display Outfit Packing - Corrugated Separators, Units not Boxed; Illustrate Canadian National Locomotive on Outfit Box

Contents: 227P-25 Alco Diesel Power Car - "Canadian National" Markings - with Headlight and Non-Operating Coupler - without Reversing Unit, Magne-Traction, Lockon and Lubricant; 6045-25 Two Dome Tank Car - Gray - with Non-Operating Trucks; 6044-25 Box Car - Blue - "Airex" Markings - Non-Operating Trucks; 6042-25 Gondola Car - Blue - with 2 Red Canisters - with Non-Operating Trucks; 6047-25 Caboose - Brick Brown - Non-Operating Trucks; 1013 Curved Track (8); 1018 Straight Track (2); 1026-25 25-Watt Transformer; CTC Lockon; 81-32

Comments: This was the sixth of eight 1100-series General Release Promotional outfits issued in 1960. The no. 1115 appeared on page 244 of the T. Eaton (a Canadian retailer) 1960 Christmas Catalog for $18.98 delivered. The listing stated that "a special company-wide purchase enables us to offer this outstanding Electric Train Set at a savings of $9.00!" Since no customer was listed on the Factory Order for the 1115, it might have appeared at other retail locations. Therefore, we classify it as a Type IIb outfit.

This outfit was identical to the no. 1113, except that the 1115 also included a no. 6045-25 Gray Two Dome Tank Car. As an aside,

DISPLAY PACK
60-477 BOX

1026 25	227P-25	
6042-25	6044-25	2-1018 8-1013
6045-25	6047-25	

Lionel used the same number for a cataloged O27 outfit in 1949.

This version of the 1115, like the other 1100-series promotional outfits, was a starter outfit. It was headed by a no. 227P-25 Canadian National Alco Diesel Power Car. This locomotive moved forward only and featured

357

a closed pilot and a weight to aid in traction. Ironically, this low-end Alco is now a desirable collector piece.

Of note, the photo in the T. Eaton catalog incorrectly showed a no. 1055 Alco Diesel Power Car with Canadian National markings. This model may have been the prototype of the 227P-25.

The rolling stock in the 1115 was low-end and similar to what was packed in the other 1100-series outfits. The cars were equipped with non-operating Archbar trucks and couplers. All of them, except for the caboose, appeared only in promotional outfits.

The 6045-25 Gray Two Dome Tank Car included in this outfit was the gray (rather than the beige) plastic variation.

The no. 60-477 White Hinged Display with Green Canadian National Alco Graphics Type A outfit box was manufactured by KCC, Kraft Corrugated Containers and measured 19½ x 11⅜ x 2⅞ inches.

The original quantity of this outfit was 1,500, but it was increased to 2,500 on 6-14-60.

The 1115 was produced in smaller quantities than the 1113, and it is more difficult to find in collectible condition. Its unique Canadian National graphics (only used for the 1113 and 1115) and 227P-25 Alco make it a highly desirable outfit. With high demand and low collectible supply, this is an expensive starter outfit.

Outfit no. 1117 was shown on page 245 of the T. Eaton (a Canadian retailer) 1960 Christmas Catalog as no. 027-B-648 for $23.98 delivered. The listing stated, "Set would ordinarily sell for 33.98 - you save $10.00".

Description: 1960 Outfit
Specification: "O27" Ga. Steam Type Freight Outfit
Customer/No./Price: T. Eaton; 027-B-648; $23.98
Original Amount: 2,000
Factory Order Date: 5/2/1960
Date Issued: May 2, 1960
Packaging: Display Outfit Packing - Corrugated Separators, Units not Boxed

Contents: 246-25 Locomotive - with Headlight and Magne-Traction Less Lockon and Lubricant; 1060T-25 Tender; 6476-25 Hopper Car - Red; 3386-25 Operating Giraffe Car - with Non-Operating Trucks; 6045-25 Two Dome Tank Car - Gray - Non-Operating Trucks; 6044-25 Box Car - Blue - "Airex" Markings - Non-Operating Trucks; 6047-25 Caboose - Brick Brown - Non-Operating Trucks; 1013 Curved Track (8); 1018 Straight Track (2); 1016-60 35-Watt Transformer; CTC-1 Lockon; 81-32 Wires (2); 927-60 Lubricant (Oil); 927-65 Lubricant (Grease); 1103-12 Envelope Packed With CTC-1, 81-32, 927-60 and 927-65; 1109-10 Instruction Sheet; 310-2 Set of (5) Billboard Signs; AC Accessory Catalog

Boxes & Packing: 60-518 Box; 60-519 Insert; 60-515 Insert; 60-363 Insert; 60-370 Insert; 59-47 Insert; 59-44 Tube; 60-520 Shipper (1-6)

Comments: This was the seventh of eight 1100-series General Release Promotional outfits that Lionel issued in 1960. The no. 1117 appeared on page 245 of the T. Eaton (a Canadian retailer) 1960 Christmas Catalog for $23.98 delivered. The listing stated, "Set would ordinarily sell for 33.98 - you save $10.00". Since no customer was listed on the Factory Order for the 1117, it might have appeared at other retail locations. Therefore, we classify it as a Type IIb outfit.

This outfit was identical to the no. 1111, except that the 1117 also included a 6044-25 Blue Box Car - "Airex" Markings. As an aside, Lionel used the same number for a cataloged O27 outfit in 1949.

This version of the 1117, like the other 1100-series promotional outfits, was a starter outfit. It was headed by a no. 246-25 Locomotive - with Headlight and Magne-Traction. Since that steamer came unboxed (as indicated by the "-25"), a no. CTC-1 Lockon was required separately and included in the no. 1103-12 Envelope Packed.

DISPLAY PACK 60-518 BOX REVISED 6/15/60		
246-25	1060T-25	
6047-25	3386-25	2-1018 8-1013
6044-25	6045-25	
6476-25	1016-60	

The rolling stock in this outfit was similar to that found in the other 1100-series outfits. A notable item included in the 1117 was the no. 3386-25 Operating Giraffe Car. This car, new for 1960, appeared in only 10 promotional outfits. When the 3386-25 was

1117 (1960)	C6	C7	C8	Rarity
Complete Outfit	225	400	575	R6
Outfit Box no. 60-518	100	200	275	R6

unboxed, its no. 3376-118 Envelope Packed was placed loose in the outfit box.

The no. 6476-25 Hopper Car was equipped with two operating

AAR trucks and couplers, but all the remaining rolling stock was equipped with non-operating Archbar trucks and couplers.

The 1117 and its no. 60-518 Box are seldom seen.

General Release Promotional outfit no. 1119 was the last of the eight 1100-series outfits issued in 1960. A basic starter outfit, it was one of four promotional outfits to include the no. 6404-25 Black Frame Single Auto Car. This car included the no. 6404-30 Automobile – Maroon, which was a red automobile with gray bumpers.

Outfit no. 1119 came in a no. 60-514 White Hinged Display with 1050 Blue Steamer and Red/Orange Graphics Type A outfit box.

Description: 1960 Outfit
Specification: "O27" Ga. Steam Type Freight Outfit
Original Amount: 7,000
Factory Order Date: 3/21/1960
Date Issued: 9-28-60
Packaging: Display Outfit Packing - Corrugated Separators, Units not Boxed

Contents: 246-25 Locomotive - with Headlight and Magne-Traction - Less Lockon & Lubricant; 1060T-25 Tender; 6045-25 Two Dome Tank Car - Gray - Non-Operating Trucks; 6404-25 Single Auto Car - Black Frame - Red Auto - with Non-Operating Trucks; 6042-25 Gondola Car - Blue - with 2 Red Canisters - with Non-Operating Trucks; 6047-25 Caboose - Brick Brown - Non-Operating Trucks; 1013 Curved Track (8); 1018 Straight Track (2); 1016-60 35-Watt Transformer; CTC Lockon; 81-32 Wires (2); 927-60 Lubricant (Oil); 927-65 Lubricant (Grease); 1103-12 Envelope Packed With CTC, 81-32, 927-60 and 927-65; 1119-10 Instruction Sheet; 310-2 Set of (5) Billboard Signs; AC Accessory Catalog

Boxes & Packing: 60-514 Box; 60-515 Insert; 60-516 Insert; 59-47 Insert; 59-44 Tube; 60-517 Shipper (1-6)

1119 (1960)	C6	C7	C8	Rarity
Complete Outfit	220	325	450	R4
Outfit Box no. 60-514	90	125	150	R4

Comments: This Type IIb outfit was the last of the eight 1100-series General Release Promotional outfits that Lionel issued in 1960. As an aside, Lionel used the same number for a cataloged O27 outfit in 1951.

This version of the no. 1119, like all the other 1100-series promotional outfits, was a starter outfit. It was headed by a no. 246-25 Locomotive - with Headlight and Magne-Traction. Since it came unboxed (as indicated by the "-25"), a no. CTC-1 Lockon was required separately and included in the no. 1103-12 Envelope Packed.

The no. 6404-25 Black Frame Single Auto Car appeared only in this and three other promotional outfits. With more than 59,000 of these four outfits produced, this car is more common than previously thought. The red automobile with gray bumpers was a no. 6404-30 Automobile - Maroon. Lionel here used the term "maroon" to designate an item that looks red.

All the rolling stock was equipped with non-operating Archbar trucks and couplers.

The no. 60-514 White Hinged Display with 1050 Blue Steamer and Red/Orange Graphics Type A outfit box was manufactured by Kraft Corrugated Containers and measured 19¼ x 13⅞ x 3 inches.

The original Factory Order listed 5,000 outfits, but on 9-28-60, this was increased to 7,000. The inclusion of the 6404-25 makes the 1119 somewhat of a desirable outfit.

246-25	1060T-25
6045-25	6042-25
6404-25	6047-25
2-1018 8-1013	1016-60

1123
1961

General Release Promotional outfit no. 1123 was one of three Lionel advance catalog offerings for 1961. A basic starter outfit, it included the no. 6406-30 Automobile, which was a yellow automobile with gray bumpers.

Outfit no. 1123 came in a no. 61-105 White 4-6-4 Steamer and F3 Hinged Display with Red/Orange and Blue Graphics Type A outfit box.

Customer/No./Price: Firestone; 11-L-344; $14.88
Customer/No.: Lionel Advance Catalog; 1123
Original Amount: 69,000
Factory Order Date: 9/29/1961
Date Issued: Rev. #3 10-5-61
Packaging: Display Outfit Packing (Units not Boxed)

Contents: 1060-25 Steam Type Locomotive; 1050T-25 Tender; 6406-25 Single Automobile Car (Less Auto); 6406-30 Automobile; 6042-25 Gondola Car (Less 2 Canisters); 6112-5 Canister - Red (2); 6067-25 Caboose; 1013-8 Curved Track (Bundle of 8 - 1013); 1018-10 Straight Track (Loose) (2); 1026-25 25-Watt Transformer; 1103-12 Envelope Packed; 1123-10 Instruction Sheet; 310-2 Set of (5) Billboards; D61-50 Accessory Catalog

Description: 1961 Non-Catalog Outfit
Specification: "O27" Steam Type Freight Outfit
Customer/Price: Children's Bargain Town USA; $7.99

Boxes & Packing: 61-105 Display Outfit Box; 61-101 Corr. Insert; 61-102 Corr. Insert (2); 61-103 Shipper for 6 (1-6); 61-104 Envelope Packed (1-6); 61-100 Box Unprinted; 61-101 Insert; 61-102 Insert (2); 61-103 Shipper Unprinted (1-6)

Alternate For Outfit Contents:
Use inventory 13,457 - 6047-25 for 6067-25.

1123 (1961)	C6	C7	C8	Rarity
Complete Outfit With no. 61-105 Box	150	250	375	R1
Outfit Box no. 61-105	50	75	100	R1
Complete Outfit With no. 61-104	750	1,050	1,375	R10

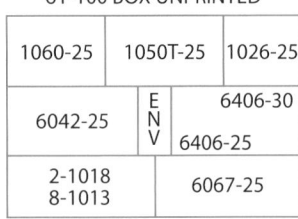

DISPLAY PACK
61-105 BOX PRINTED OR
61-100 BOX UNPRINTED

1060-25	1050T-25	1026-25
6042-25	E N V	6406-30
		6406-25
2-1018 8-1013		6067-25

Comments: This Type IIb outfit was the first of three 1100-series General Release Promotional outfits issued in 1961. The no. 1123 appeared on page 15 of the Lionel 1961 advance catalog. The description stated that the nos. 1123, 1124, and 1125 "were designed to meet the needs of the low priced toy train market. These 'O27' outfits will not be included in the Lionel full-color consumer catalog." These advance catalog outfits were part of Lionel's promotional outfit strategy to offer retailers something different even if they couldn't commit to the quantity necessary for a unique promotional outfit.

A basic starter outfit, the 1123 was Lionel's low-end steam-powered advance catalog outfit for 1961. It was led by the no. 1060-25 Steam Type Locomotive found in many promotional outfits. This was Lionel's low-end, forward-only steam offering in 1961 whose only feature of note was a headlight.

All the rolling stock in the 1123 represented Lionel's low-end

offerings, with many items found only in promotional outfits. The cars were equipped with non-operating Archbar trucks and couplers.

As with many of these low-end outfits, the no. 6406-30 Automobile is the most difficult item to obtain. Finding an original postwar yellow with gray bumper version is becoming a challenge. There are many reproductions or modern-era reissues on the market.

The no. 61-105 White 4-6-4 Steamer and F3 Hinged Display with Red/Orange and Blue Graphics Type A outfit box was manufactured by Express Container Corp. and measured 21½ x 11½ x 3⅛ inches. A no. 61-100 Box Unprinted is also mentioned but has yet to be observed.

With every six outfits shipped, Lionel packaged a no. 61-104 Envelope Packed. This envelope included a no. 61-107 Acetate Dust Cover in a no. 61-108 Envelope. The printing on the envelope states that the "clear plastic shield keeps merchandise dust free and safe from pilferage." This rare item adds a substantial premium to the outfit price.

The substitution of the caboose does not affect the price.

With 69,000 made, the 1123 ranks third as the most produced catalog or promotional outfit during the 1960s. Only the X-600 and 11415 were produced in larger quantities. The 1123 was sold to numerous retailers, a few of which have been identified by price tags or catalog listings. This outfit is readily available; however, finding a C8 or better example is not always easy.

Description: 1962 Non-Catalog Outfit
Specification: "O27" Steam Type Freight Outfit
Customer/No.: Lionel Advance Catalog; 1123
Original Amount: 406
Factory Order Date: 5/9/1962
Date Issued: 5-9-62
Packaging: Display Outfit Packing (Units not Boxed)

Contents: 1060-25 Steam Type Locomotive; 244T-25 Tender; 6406-25 Single Automobile Car (Less Auto); 6406-30 Automobile; 6042-25 Gondola Car (Less 2 Canisters); 6112-5 Canister - Red (2); 6067-25 Caboose; 1013-8 Curved Track (Bundle of 8 - 1013); 1018-10 Straight Track (Loose) (2); 1026-25 25-Watt Transformer; 1103-12 Envelope Packed; 1123-10 Instruction Sheet; 310-2 Set of (5) Billboards; D61-50 Accessory Catalog

Boxes & Packing: 61-105 Display Outfit Box; 61-101 Corr. Insert; 61-102 Corr. Insert (2); 61-103 Shipper for 6 (1-6); 61-104 Envelope Packed (1-6)

1123 (1962)	C6	C7	C8	Rarity
Complete Outfit With no. 61-105 Box	150	250	375	R1
Outfit Box no. 61-105	50	75	100	R1
Complete Outfit With no. 61-104	750	1,050	1,375	R10

Comments: This General Release Promotional Type IIb outfit was a repeat of the 1961 advance catalog outfit no. 1123. However, the 1123 did not appear in the 1962 advance catalog.

The only difference between these two outfits was a change in tenders. The 1962 version included a no. 244T-25, whereas the 1961 outfit came with a no. 1050T-25. The 244T-25 tender was equipped with one operating and one plain AAR truck and coupler.

Even with 69,000 of the 1123 produced in 1961, an additional 406 were required in 1962, hence the Factory Order and this listing. (See the entry for the 1123 from 1961 for more information.)

1000 Series

Description: 1961 Non-Catalog Outfit
Specification: "O27" Steam Type Freight Outfit
Customer/No.: Lionel Advance Catalog; 1123C
Original Amount: 11,000
Factory Order Date: 11/20/1961
Date Issued: Rev. #2 11-20-61
Packaging: Conv. Outfit Packing (Units not Boxed)

Contents: 1060-25 Steam Type Locomotive; 1050T-25 Tender; 6406-25 Single Automobile Car (Less Auto); 6406-30 Automobile; 6042-25 Gondola Car (Less 2 Canisters); 6112-5 Canister - Red (2); 6067-25 Caboose; 1013-8 Curved Track (Bundle of 8 - 1013); 1018-10 Straight Track (Loose) (2); 1026-25 25-Watt Transformer; 1103-12 Envelope Packed; 1123-10 Instruction Sheet; 310-2 Set of (5) Billboards; D61-50 Accessory Catalog

Boxes & Packing: 61-170 Outfit Box; 61-171 Corr. Insert; 61-172 Corr. Insert; 61-173 Corr. Insert; 61-174 Shipper for 6 (1-6)

1123C (1961)	C6	C7	C8	Rarity
Complete Outfit	160	260	400	R4
Outfit Box no. 61-170	60	85	125	R4

Comments: This General Release Promotional Type IIb outfit was

the RSC version of display-packed no. 1123 from 1961. The only differences related to the packaging and the quantity produced. The "C" stood for "Conventional", another term that Lionel used for RSC packaging.

The no. 61-170 Tan RSC with Black Graphics outfit box measured 11½ x 10¼ x 6¼ inches. This box was manufactured by numerous box manufacturers, including United Container Co.; Owens-Illinois Paper Products, Div.; and St. Joe Kraft, St. Joe Paper Co. Container Division.

As with the 1123, a large number of these outfits were produced. But finding an example in C8 condition is not easy. (See the entry for the 1123 from 1961 for more information.)

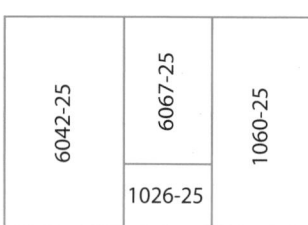

CONVENTIONAL PACK
61-170 BOX

TOP LAYER

2-1018 8-1013	
6406-25 6406-30	ENV
1050T-25	

BOTTOM LAYER

| 6042-25 | 6067-25 | 1060-25 |
| | 1026-25 | |

Description: 1962 Non-Catalog Outfit
Specification: "O27" Steam Type Freight Outfit
Customer/No.: Lionel Advance Catalog; 1123C
Original Amount: 500
Factory Order Date: 6/14/1962
Date Issued: 6-15-62
Packaging: Conv. Outfit Packing (Units not Boxed)

Contents: 1060-25 Steam Type Locomotive; 1050T-25 Tender; 6406-25 Single Automobile Car (Less Auto); 6406-30 Automobile; 6042-25 Gondola Car (Less 2 Canisters); 6112-5 Canister - Red (2); 6067-25 Caboose; 1013-8 Curved Track (Bundle of 8 - 1013); 1018-10 Straight Track (Loose) (2); 1026-25 25-Watt Transformer; 1103-20 Envelope Packed; 1123-10 Instruction Sheet; 310-2 Set of (5) Billboards; D62-50 Accessory Catalog

Boxes & Packing: 61-170 Outfit Box; 61-171 Corr. Insert; 61-172 Corr. Insert; 61-173 Corr. Insert; 61-174 Shipper for 6 (1-6)

1123C (1962)	C6	C7	C8	Rarity
Complete Outfit	160	260	400	R4
Outfit Box no. 61-170	60	85	125	R4

Comments: This General Release Promotional Type IIb outfit was a repeat of the 1961 advance catalog outfit no. 1123C. However, the 1123C did not appear in the 1962 advance catalog.

The only differences between these two outfits were changes to the then-current packed envelope (no. 1103-20 versus no. 1103-12) and accessory catalog (no. D62-50 versus no. D61-50).

Orders for the 1123C must still have been coming in during 1962 because an additional 500 outfits were required.

There are no noticeable differences between the 1961 and 1962 versions. As such, both of them are considered the same, and the pricing and rarity of the 1962 outfit mirror those of the 1961 version.

As with the no. 1123, a large number of these outfits were produced. But finding an example in C8 condition is not easy. (See the entries for the 1123 and 1123C from 1961 for more information.)

Description: "O27" Promotional Outfit
Specification: "O27" Steam Type Freight Outfit
Customer/No.: Lionel Advance Catalog; 1123C
Original Amount: 500
Factory Order Date: 5/29/1963
Date Issued: 6-11-63
Date Req'd: Aug.
Packaging: RSC Outfit Packing (Units not Boxed)

Contents: 1060-25 Steam Type Locomotive; 1061T-25 Tender; 6406-25 Flat Car W/Auto; 6406-30 Automobile; 6042-25 Gondola Car - Blue; 6112-5 Canister (2); 6067-25 Caboose; 1013-8 Curved Track (Bundle of 8 - 1013); 1018-10 Straight Track (Loose) (2); 1026-25 25-Watt Transformer; 1103-20 Envelope Packed; 1123-40 Instruction Sheet; 1123-10 Instruction Sheet; Form 2870 Printed Sheet

Boxes & Packing: 61-170 Outfit Box; 61-171 Corr. Insert; 61-172 Corr. Insert; 61-173 Corr. Insert; 61-174 Shipper for (6) (1-6)

1123C (1963)	C6	C7	C8	Rarity
Complete Outfit	165	270	415	R4
Outfit Box no. 61-170	60	85	125	R4

Comments: This General Release Promotional Type IIb outfit was a repeat of the 1961 and 1962 advance catalog outfit no. 1123C. However, the 1123C did not appear in the 1963 advance catalog.

The only differences between this and the 1961 version were changes to the then-current packed envelope (no. 1103-20 versus no. 1103-12), new tender (no. 1061T-25 versus. no. 1050T-25) and some additional paperwork common to 1963 outfits. The 1061T-25 was a plain unpainted black slope-back tender.

Orders for the 1123C must still have been coming in during 1963 because an additional 500 outfits were required.

The differences between the 1963 version of the 1123C and the 1961 and 1962 versions are minimal and easily replicated. The slight changes in paperwork explain the variation in price from the 1961 and 1962 versions.

As with the no. 1123, a large number of these outfits were produced. But finding an example in C8 condition is not easy. (See the entries for the 1123 and 1123C from 1961 for more information.)

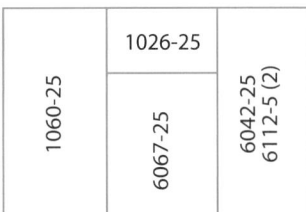

CONVENTIONAL PACK
61-170 BOX
5-20-63

Description: 1961 Non-Catalog Outfit
Specification: "O27" Steam Type Freight Outfit
Customer/No./Price: Firestone; 11-L-345; $17.77
Customer/No.: Lionel Advance Catalog; 1124
Original Amount: 25,000
Date Issued: Rev. #2 7-26-61
Packaging: Display Outfit Packing (Units not Boxed)

Contents: 1060-25 Steam Type Locomotive; 1060T-25 Tender; 3409-25 Oper. Helicopter Launching Car (Manually); 6076-75 Hopper Car - Black; 6067-25 Caboose; 1013-8 Curved Track (Bundle of 8 - 1013); 1018-10 Straight Track (Loose) (2); 1026-25 25-Watt Transformer; 1103-12 Envelope Packed; 1123-10 Instruction Sheet; 310-2 Set of (5) Billboards; D61-50 Accessory Catalog

Boxes & Packing: 61-110 Display Outfit Box; 61-101 Corr. Insert; 61-102 Corr. Insert (2); 61-103 Shipper for 6 (1-6); 61-104 Envelope Packed (1-6); 61-100 Box Unprinted; 61-101 Insert; 61-102 Insert (2); 61-103 Shipper Unprinted (1-6)

1124 (1961)	C6	C7	C8	Rarity
Complete Outfit	175	300	425	R2
Outfit Box no. 61-110	50	75	100	R2
Complete Outfit With no. 61-104	775	1,100	1,425	R10

Comments: This Type IIb outfit was the second of three 1100-series General Release Promotional outfits issued in 1961. The no. 1124 appeared on page 15 of the Lionel 1961 advance catalog. The description stated that the nos. 1123, 1124, and 1125 "were designed to meet the needs of the low priced toy train market. These 'O27' outfits will not be included in the Lionel full-color consumer catalog." These advance catalog outfits were part of Lionel's promotional outfit strategy to offer retailers something different even if they couldn't commit to the quantity necessary for a unique promotional outfit.

A basic starter outfit, the 1124 was Lionel's high-end steam-powered advance catalog offering for 1961. It was headed by the no. 1060-25 Steam Type Locomotive found in many promotional outfits. This was Lionel's low-end, forward-only steam offering in 1961 whose only feature of note was a headlight.

The rolling stock was low-end and came equipped with non-operating Archbar trucks and couplers. The most exciting item was the promotional-only no. 3409-25 Oper. Helicopter Launching Car (Manually) with its no. 3419-100 Operating Helicopter Complete.

The no. 61-110 White 4-6-4 Steamer and F3 Hinged Display with Red/Orange and Blue Graphics Type A outfit box measured 21½ x 11½ x 3¼ inches. A no. 61-100 Box Unprinted is also mentioned, but one has yet to be observed.

With every six outfits shipped, Lionel packaged a no. 61-104 Envelope Packed. This envelope included a no. 61-107 Acetate Dust Cover in a no. 61-108 Envelope. The printing on the envelope

363

General Release Promotional outfit no. 1124 was one of three Lionel advance catalog offerings for 1961. A basic starter outfit, it included a no. 3409-25 Oper. Helicopter Launching Car (Manually) with a no. 3419-100 Operating Helicopter Complete.

Outfit no. 1124 came in a no. 61-110 White 4-6-4 Steamer and F3 Hinged Display with Red/Orange and Blue Graphics Type A outfit box.

DISPLAY PACK
61-110 BOX PRINTED OR
61-100 BOX UNPRINTED

1060-25	1060T-25	1026-25
6076-75		3409-25
2-1018 8-1013	6067-25	E N V

states that the "clear plastic shield keeps merchandise dust free and safe from pilferage." This rare item adds a substantial premium to the outfit price.

An extremely large number (25,000) of 1124s were produced. It was sold to numerous retailers, a few of which have been identified by price tags or catalog listings. This outfit is readily available, but even with so many produced, finding a C8 or better example is not easy.

Description: 1961 Non-Catalog Outfit
Specification: "O27" Steam Type Freight Outfit
Customer/No.: Lionel Advance Catalog; 1124C
Original Amount: 2,500
Date Issued: Rev. #1 7-26-61
Packaging: Conv. Outfit Packing (Units not Boxed)

Contents: 1060-25 Steam Type Locomotive; 1060T-25 Tender; 3409-25 Oper. Helicopter Launching Car (Manually); 6076-75 Hopper Car - Black; 6067-25 Caboose; 1013-8 Curved Track (Bundle of 8 - 1013); 1018-10 Straight Track (Loose) (2); 1026-25 25-Watt Transformer; 1103-12 Envelope Packed; 1123-10 Instruction Sheet; 310-2 Set (5) Billboards; D61-50 Accessory Catalog

Boxes & Packing: 61-170 Outfit Box; 61-171 Corr. Insert; 61-172 Corr. Insert; 61-173 Corr. Insert; 61-174 Shipper for 6 (1-6)

1124C (1961)	C6	C7	C8	Rarity
Complete Outfit	200	450	500	R5
Outfit Box no. 61-170	75	125	175	R5

Comments: This General Release Promotional Type IIb outfit was the RSC version of display-packed no. 1124 from 1961. The only differences related to the packaging and the quantity produced. The "C" stood for "Conventional", another term that Lionel used for RSC packaging.

The no. 61-170 Tan RSC with Black Graphics outfit box was manufactured by Owens-Illinois Paper Products, Div. and measured 11½ x 10¼ x 6¼ inches. Also printed as part of the box manufacturer's certificate were 11 dots and "9012".

Only 10 percent as many 1124Cs were made as 1124s. That fact explains why the RSC version is harder to find than the display version.

CONVENTIONAL PACK
61-170 BOX

TOP LAYER		BOTTOM LAYER		
2-1018 8-1013		1060T-25	6067-25	1060-25
3409-25				
6076-75	E N V		1026-25	

When General Release Promotional outfit no. 1124 was packaged in a Tan RSC with Black Graphics outfit box, it became the no. 1124C. The "C" stood for "Conventional" packing, a term that Lionel used interchangeably with RSC.

A few examples of the 1124C have been observed with a label from Advertising Distributors of America (ADA) in Brooklyn, New York. Lionel likely shipped some outfits to ADA, which in turn fulfilled direct orders for other customers. (See the entry for the 1124 from 1961 for more information.)

Description: 1961 Non-Catalog Outfit
Specification: "O27" Steam Type Freight Outfit
Customer/Price: Phillips Petroleum; $10.66 With 10 Bargain of the Month Certificates
Original Amount: 750
Factory Order Date: 9/21/1961
Date Issued: 9/21/61
Packaging: Display Outfit Packing (Units not Boxed)

Contents: 1060-25 Steam Type Locomotive; 1060T-25 Tender; 3409-25 Oper. Helicopter Launching Car (Manually); 6076-75 Hopper Car - Black; 6067-25 Caboose; 1013-8 Curved Track (Bundle of 8 - 1013); 1018-10 Straight Track (Loose) (2); 1026-25 25-Watt Transformer; 1103-12 Envelope Packed; 1123-10 Instruction Sheet; 310-2 Set of (5) Billboards; D61-50 Accessory Catalog

Boxes & Packing: 61-110 Display Outfit Box; 61-101 Corr. Insert; 61-102 Corr. Insert (2); 61-103 Shipper for 6 (1-6); 61-107 Dust Cover; 61-100 Box Unprinted; 61-101 Insert; 61-102 Insert (2); 61-103 Shipper Unprinted (1-6)

1124P (1961)	C6	C7	C8	Rarity
Complete Outfit	325	525	725	R2
Outfit Box no. 61-110	200	300	400	R2
Complete Outfit With no. 61-107	475	725	975	R10

Comments: Lionel sold trains to numerous oil and gas companies during the 1960s. This Manufacturer Promotional Type IIIb outfit was sold to Phillips Petroleum, which offered the no. 1124P to its customers as "...Lionel Electric Train set, manufacturer's suggested retail $18.95 only $10.66 with 10 Bargain of the Month Certificates."

The contents of this outfit were an exact duplicate of the no. 1124 (see the entry for 1124 from 1961). It appears that Lionel sold Phillips the 1124 and designated it with "P" for Phillips Petroleum.

The only other difference between the two Factory Orders occurred in the packaging. The 1124P Factory Order indicates that each outfit came with a no. 61-107 Acetate Dust Cover, whereas the 1124 included one no. 61-104 Envelope Packed (a no. 61-107 inside a no. 61-108 Envelope) for every six outfits. According to Lionel, the 61-107 was a "clear plastic shield [that] keeps merchandise dust free and safe from pilferage."

For unknown reasons, Phillips never purchased another Retailer Promotional outfit from Lionel.

DISPLAY PACK
61-110 BOX PRINTED

1060-25	1060T-25	1026-25
6076-75	3409-25	
2-1018 8-1013	6067-25	E N V

1125 **1961**

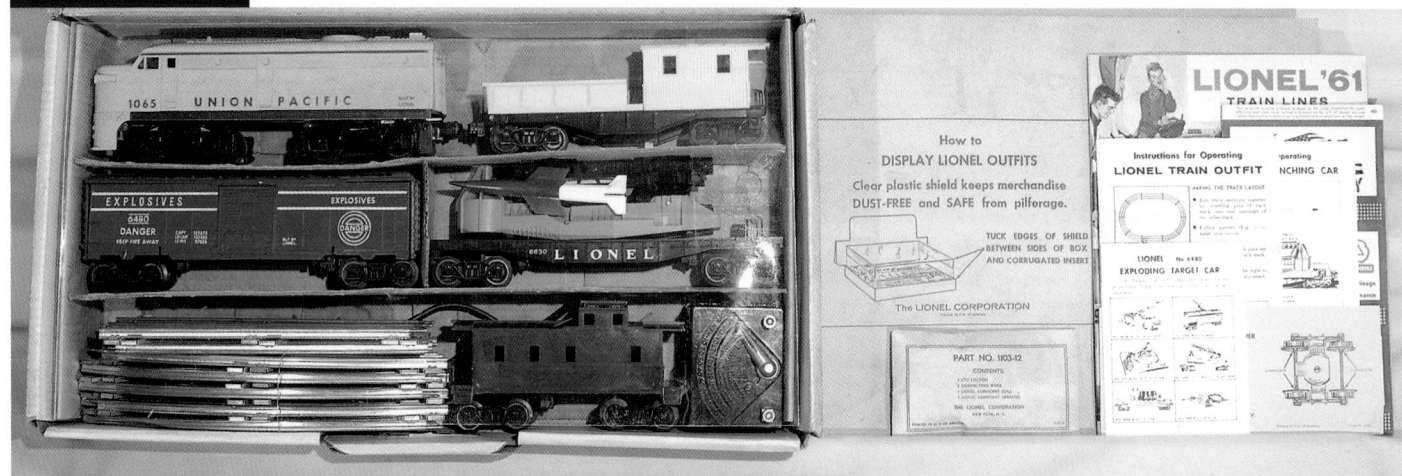

General Release Promotional outfit no. 1125 was the last of three Lionel advance catalog offerings for 1961. It was Lionel's high-end advance catalog outfit, featuring a space and military theme. All the items included were new for 1961. The 1125 is shown with its no. 61-107 Acetate Dust Cover placed over the trains to keep them dust free and safe from pilferage.

Outfit no. 1125 came in a no. 61-115 White 4-6-4 Steamer and F3 Hinged Display with Red/Orange and Blue Graphics Type A outfit box.

Description: 1961 Non-Catalog Outfit
Specification: "O27" Diesel Freight Outfit
Customer/No.: Lionel Advance Catalog; 1125
Customer/Price: Times Square Stores; $11.89
Original Amount: 27,000
Date Issued: Rev. #1 3-30-61
Packaging: Display Outfit Packing (Units not Boxed)

Contents: 1065-25 Alco Diesel Power Unit - "Union Pacific"; 6630-25 Missile Launching Car (Less Missile); 6650-80 Missile Complete (or 6650-84); 6480-25 Exploding Target Car; 6120-25

Work Caboose - "Union Pacific"; 1013-8 Curved Track (Bundle of 8 - 1013); 1018-10 Straight Track (Loose) (2); 1026-25 25-Watt Transformer; 1103-12 Envelope Packed; 1125-10 Instruction Sheet; 310-2 Set of (5) Billboards; D61-50 Accessory Catalog

Boxes & Packing: 61-115 Display Outfit Box; 61-101 Corr. Insert; 61-102 Corr. Insert (2); 61-103 Shipper for 6 (1-6); 61-104 Envelope Packed (1-6); 61-100 Box Unprinted; 61-101 Insert; 61-102 Insert (2); 61-103 Shipper Unprinted (1-6)

Alternate For Outfit Contents:
Use inventory of 1,990 - 1055-25 for 1065-25; Use inventory of 334 - 227P-25 for 1065-25.

1125 (1961)	C6	C7	C8	Rarity
Complete Outfit With nos. 1055-25 Or 1065-25	225	385	550	R2
Complete Outfit With no. 227P-25	275	465	650	R2
Outfit Box no. 61-115	60	90	115	R2
Either Outfit With no. 61-104, Add The Following	600	800	1,000	R10

Comments: This Type IIb outfit was the last of the three 1100-series General Release Promotional outfits issued in 1961. The no. 1125 appeared on page 15 of the Lionel 1961 advance catalog. The description stated that the nos. 1123, 1124, and 1125 "were designed to meet the needs of the low priced toy train market. These 'O27' outfits will not be included in the Lionel full-color consumer catalog." These advance catalog outfits were part of Lionel's promotional outfit strategy to offer retailers something different even if they couldn't commit to the quantity necessary for a unique promotional outfit.

A basic starter outfit, the 1125 was Lionel's high-end advance catalog offering for 1961. All the items were new for 1961, including the no. 1065-25 Union Pacific Alco Diesel Power Unit. This model was a follow-up to the no. 1055-25 *Texas Special* Alco. It moved forward only and lacked a traction tire and Magne-Traction. These low-end Alcos were used in promotional outfits.

The 1125, with its space and military theme, included two new operating cars: nos. 6630-25 Missile Launching Car and 6480-25 Exploding Box Car. Neither car was actually new, since they represented low-end versions of the previously issued nos. 6650-25 and 6470-25, respectively. They, like the other pieces of rolling stock in this outfit, were equipped with non-operating Archbar trucks and couplers.

This outfit also included the unmarked yellow no. 6120-25 Work Caboose. That item was used only in promotional outfits from 1961 through 1963.

Lionel used the 1125 to deplete the inventory of the 1055-25

Texas Special Alco. Also listed as a substitution was the no. 227P-25 Canadian National Alco Diesel Power Car. This low-end Alco is now a desirable collector piece. (The pricing table for the 1125 accounts for the substitution of these Alcos.)

The no. 61-115 White 4-6-4 Steamer and F3 Hinged Display with Red/Orange and Blue Graphics Type A outfit box was manufactured by Express Container Corp. and measured 22 x 11½ x 3¼ inches. A no. 61-100 Box Unprinted is also mentioned but has yet to be observed.

With every six outfits shipped, Lionel packaged a no. 61-104 Envelope Packed. This envelope included a no. 61-107 Acetate Dust Cover in a no. 61-108 Envelope. The printing on the envelope states that the "clear plastic shield keeps merchandise dust free and safe from pilferage." This rare item adds a substantial premium to the outfit price.

An extremely large number (27,000) of 1125s were produced. It was sold to numerous retailers, a few of which have been identified by price tags or catalog listings. This outfit is readily available, but even with so many produced, finding a C8 or better example is not easy. Overall, the 1125 is the most desirable of the three advance catalog outfits from 1961.

DISPLAY PACK
61-115 BOX PRINTED OR
61-100 BOX UNPRINTED

1065-25	6120-25	
6480-25	6630-25	
2-1018 8-1013	6650-80	1026-25

Description: 1961 Non-Catalog Outfit
Specification: "O27" Diesel Freight Outfit
Customer/No.: Lionel Advance Catalog; 1125C
Original Amount: 1,000
Date Issued: Rev. #1 10-9-61
Packaging: Conv. Outfit Packing (Units not Boxed)

Contents: 1065-25 Alco Diesel Power Unit - "Union Pacific"; 6630-25 Missile Launching Car (Less Missile); 6650-80 Missile Complete (or 6650-84); 6480-25 Exploding Target Car; 6120-25 Work Caboose - "Union Pacific"; 1013-8 Curved Track (Bundle of 8 - 1013); 1018-10 Straight Track (Loose) (2); 1026-25 25-Watt Transformer; 1103-12 Envelope Packed; IS Instruction Sheet; 310-2 Set of (5) Billboards; D61-50 Accessory Catalog

Boxes & Packing: 61-190 Outfit Box; 61-191 Corr. Insert; 61-192 Corr. Insert; 61-193 Corr. Insert; 61-194 Shipper for 6 (1-6)

1125C (1961)	C6	C7	C8	Rarity
Complete Outfit	375	600	850	R7
Outfit Box no. 61-190	175	300	400	R7

Comments: This General Release Promotional Type IIb outfit was the RSC version of display-packed no. 1125 from 1961. The

1125C
1961

only differences related to the packaging and the quantity produced. The "C" stood for "Conventional", another term that Lionel used for RSC packaging.

The no. 61-190 Tan RSC with Black Graphics outfit box was manufactured by Mead Containers and measured 12¼ x 9⅞ x 6¼ inches.

Only 1,000 of the 1125Cs were made, far fewer than the 27,000 of the 1125. That discrepancy explains why the RSC version is so much more difficult to find than the display version.

(See the entry for the 1125 from 1961 for more information.)

CONVENTIONAL PACK
61-190 BOX

TOP LAYER		BOTTOM LAYER	
6630-25		8-1013	
2-1018 6650-80	ENV	6120-25	1026-25
6480-25		1065-25	

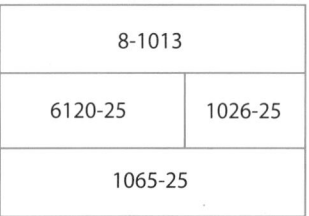

The no. 1649NE was an almost exact duplicate of catalog outfit no. 1649. The only difference was the no. 226P-1 Boston & Maine Alco and its matching no. 226C-1 "B" Unit that came with this and three other promotional outfits. The "NE" likely meant "New England" or "North East" to fit with the outfit's Boston & Maine motive power.

Description: 1961 Catalog Outfit
Specification: "O27" Boston & Maine Diesel Freight Outfit With Horn
Customer/Price: Miller's; $32.88
Original Amount: 425
Date Issued: Revised 3-17-61
Packaging: R.S.C. Outfit Packing (Units Boxed)

Contents: 226P-1 Alco Diesel Power Unit W/Horn - "Boston & Maine"; 226C-1 "B" Unit - "Boston & Maine"; 6343-1 Barrel Ramp Car; 6475-1 Pickle Car; 6445-1 Ft. Knox Gold Bullion Transport Car; 6405-1 Flat Car With Van; 6017-1 Caboose; 1013-8 Curved Track (Bundle of 8 - 1013); 1018-30 Straight Track (Bundle of 3 - 1018); 1008-50 Uncoupling Track Section; 1063-25 75-Watt Transformer; 81-32 24" R.C. Wire (2); 1649-10 Instruction Sheet; 310-2 Set of (5) Billboards; D61-50 Accessory Catalog

Boxes & Packing: 61-200 Outfit Box; 61-201 Shipper for 4 (1-4)

1649NE (1961)	C6	C7	C8	Rarity
Complete Outfit	660	1,175	1,700	R9
Outfit Box no. 61-200	300	500	700	R9

Comments: Except for its Boston & Maine Alcos, this General Release Promotional Type IIb outfit was an exact duplicate of catalog outfit no. 1649 from 1961.

The "NE" most likely meant "North East" or "New England" (a conclusion drawn by Paul V. Ambrose in the third volume of *Greenberg's Guide to Lionel Trains, 1945-1969*, based on the fact that this outfit was headed by Boston & Maine Alco diesels).

Catalog outfit no. 1649 was headed by a no. 218P-1 Santa Fe Alco Diesel Power Unit and its matching no. 218C-1 Santa Fe "B" Unit, whereas the 1649NE was headed by a no. 226P-1 Boston & Maine Alco Diesel Power Unit and its matching no. 226C-1 Boston & Maine "B" Unit. This was Lionel's high-end Alco that included all the features available at the time, notably a three-position reversing unit, open pilot, horn, headlight and two-axle Magne-Traction. It appeared only in four promotional outfits, of which a total of 6,625 were produced.

When this Alco was boxed in its no. 226-7 Corrugated Box, it included the nos. 601-13 "C" Battery, CTC-1 Lockon, 927-60 Tube of Oil, 218-11 Instruction Sheet and a 927-65 Tube of Grease.

Two of the outfits that included the 226P-1 (nos. X-576 and X-577) were bulk packed for Madison Hardware Co. in New York City. This bulk packaging was the likely source of the 226Ps in C10 condition that Madison Hardware was selling well into the 1980s. Hence, even though this Alco was a promotional-only item and produced in smaller than normal quantities, many survived in C10 condition.

The nos. 6343-1 Barrel Ramp Car, 6445-1 Ft. Knox Gold Bullion Transport Car and 6405-1 Single Van Flat Car were all new for 1961. All the cars in the 1649NE came equipped with two

The no. 1649 is one of the more desirable catalog O27 freight outfits from the 1960s. Its Factory Order, dated 3-17-61, listed a quantity of 7,575 units. The original quantity likely was 8,000 units, with 425 of them being redirected for outfit no. 1649NE.

operating AAR trucks and couplers and were packaged in Orange Picture boxes.

The no. 61-200 Orange RSC with Black Graphics outfit box was manufactured by Mead Bonded Containers and measured 14½ x 12 x 7 inches.

This outfit was likely sold to numerous retailers, a few of which have been identified by price tags.

The Factory Order for this outfit lists it as a "1961 Catalog Outfit". Even so, since it never appeared in any Lionel catalog, it is included in this volume

Many collectors view this outfit as a variation of catalog outfit 1649. Therefore, even if they don't collect promotional outfits, they still want this one. Since the 1649NE was made in lower than average quantities, the net result is a high price and a high rarity.

CONVENTIONAL PACK
61-200 BOX

TOP LAYER			
8-1013			
6475-1 S			
6405-1 F	3-1018		
6017-1 S			

1008-50 TOP 6405

BOTTOM LAYER		
226P-1 S		
6343-1 S	1063-25	
6445-1 S		
226C-1 F		

1000 Series

369

9650
1962

Description: "O27" Promotional Outfit
Specification: "O27" Steam Type Freight Outfit
Customer/No./Price: Sears, Roebuck and Co.; 9650; $19.88
Original Amount: 5,000
Factory Order Date: 6/29/1962
Date Issued: Rev. #1 7-27-62
Packaging: R.S.C. Outfit Packing (Units not Boxed)

Contents: 242-25 Steam Type Locomotive; 1060T-25 Tender; 6476-25 Hopper Car - Red; 6162-25 Gondola Car (Less 3 Canisters); 6112-88 Canisters (White) (3); 6825-25 Trestle Bridge Flat Car (Less Trestle Bridge); 6825-3 Trestle Bridge; 6473-25 Rodeo Car; 6057-25 Caboose; 1013-8 Curved Track (Bundle of 8 - 1013); 1018-10 Straight Track (Loose); 6029-25 Uncoupling Track Section; 1010-25 35-Watt Transformer; 90-40 Envelope Packed; 310-2 Set of (5) Billboards; 1123-40 Instruction Sheet; 9650-10 Instruction Sheet

Boxes & Packing: 61-180 Outfit Box; 61-181 Corr. Insert; 61-182 Corr. Insert; 61-183 Corr. Insert; 62-248 Corr. Insert; 62-249 Corr. Insert; 61-185 Shipper for (4) (1-4)

9650 (1962)	C6	C7	C8	Rarity
Complete Outfit	225	345	475	R4
Outfit Box no. 61-180	90	125	150	R4

Comments: The no. 9650 was the first of five Sears outfits from 1962. This Retailer Promotional Type Ia outfit never appeared in a Sears catalog.

The 9650 was Sears' entry-level O27 steam-powered offering for 1962. It was led by a no. 242-25 Steam Type Locomotive (new for 1962). This low-end steamer appeared in more than 55 catalog and promotional outfits through 1967. It had no smoke and used a rubber tire as a traction aid. The version with wide running boards was included in this outfit.

The no. 6473-25 Rodeo Car (new in 1962) had a Type I body style with a partially filled slot caused by a flaw in the original tool. This model featured red heat-stamped lettering.

The remaining pieces of rolling stock in this outfit were carryover items from earlier years. These included the no. 6825-25 Trestle Bridge Flat Car, which was making its sixth appearance in an outfit since 1960. This car, like all the other ones in the 9650, was equipped with operating AAR trucks and couplers.

The Sears O27 outfits from 1962 came with a no. 6029-25 Uncoupling Track Section. For this outfit, that meant a no. 90-40 Envelope Packed was required. It also meant that a new instruction sheet was required for the combination of the 242-25 and 6029-25 plus a no. 1010-25 Transformer. The resulting no. 9650-10 Instruction Sheet was unique to this outfit. Both it and the 90-40 account for a good portion of the value of a C8 outfit.

The commonly used no. 61-180 Tan RSC with Black Graphics outfit box was manufactured by United Container Co. and measured 12¾ x 10 x 6¾ inches.

The 9650, like all Sears outfits, even entry-level ones, is always in demand.

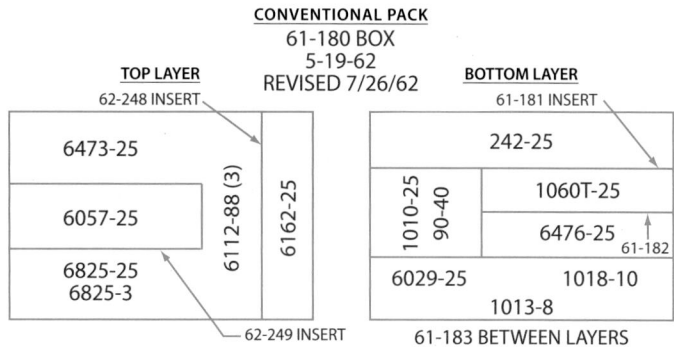

9651
1960

Description: 1960 Outfit
Specification: "O27" Ga. Steam Type Freight Outfit
Customer/No.: Sears, Roebuck and Co.; 9651
Original Amount: 9,100
Factory Order Date: 3/16/1960
Date Issued: 9-7-60
Packaging: Conventional Outfit Packing, All units packed except 1016, 1008

Contents: 246-1 Locomotive - with Headlight and Magne-Traction - with Lockon & Lubricant; 1130T-1 Tender; 6825-1 Flat Car - Red - with Trestle Bridge - Black; 6062-1 Gondola Car - Black - with (3) Cable Reels; 6465 2 Dome Tank Car; 6476-1 Hopper Car - Red; 6057-1 Caboose - Red; 1013 Curved Track (8); 1018 Straight Track; 1008-50 Uncoupling Unit - with (1) 1018 Straight Track; 1016-60 35-Watt Transformer; 81-32 Wires (2); 1609-4 Instruction Sheet; 310-2 Set of (5) Billboard Signs; AC Accessory Catalog

Boxes & Packing: 60-429 Box; 60-430 Shipper (1-4)

Alternate For Outfit Contents:
Note: Re: 6465 Tank Cars - Use - inventory 570 - 6465-1; Use - inventory 557- 6465-60; Use - inventory 608 - 6465-85; Use - inventory 6,265 - 6465-110.

9651 (1960)	C6	C7	C8	Rarity
Complete Outfit With no. 6465-1	190	365	530	R4
Complete Outfit With no. 6465-60	175	325	465	R4
Complete Outfit With no. 6465-85	240	445	650	R5
Complete Outfit With no. 6465-110	200	420	575	R4
Outfit Box no. 60-429	35	55	75	R4

Comments: The no. 9651 was the first of seven Sears outfits from 1960. This Retailer Promotional Type Ia outfit never appeared in a Sears catalog.

The 9651 was a success based on the increase of outfits on the Factory Order. The original quantity was 8,000 on March 16, 1960, but it was increased to 9,100 on 9-7-60.

The 9651 was Sears' entry-level O27 steam-powered offering for 1960. It was led by the later version of the no. 246-1 Locomotive

The no. 9651 was Sears' entry-level O27 steam-powered offering for 1960. It came with one of four different tank cars. Shown is the no. 6465-110 Green Cities Service Two Dome Tank Car version with its Orange Perforated Box.

- with Headlight and Magne-Traction. This version came with a solid pilot but lacked any generator detail. This steamer, which headed 23 different promotional outfits in 1960, came packaged in a no. 246-6 Corrugated Box.

The Factory Order generically listed a "6465 2 Dome Tank Car" and then provided all the possible inclusions in the Alternates Section. These included the black no. 6465-1 Two Dome Tank Car - Gulf, gray no. 6465-60 Two Dome Tank Car - Gulf, no. 6465-85 Black 2-Dome Tank Car with Lionel Lines markings and no. 6465-110 Green Cities Service Two Dome Tank Car.

The remaining inventory of the 6465-1, 6465-60 and 6465-85 was depleted in this outfit. The "-1" and "-60" came in Classic style boxes, and the "-85" came in the difficult-to-find Orange Perforated no. 6465-86 Folding Box.

The norm for a 6465-110 was an Orange Perforated no. 6465-103 Folding Box. A rare Bold Classic version of a 6465-60 box has been observed with the "60" overstamped with "110". Due to all the tank car substitutions, this box was likely used in this outfit, although its inclusion has not been verified. As such, pricing is provided for the Orange Perforated version. All the remaining rolling stock in the 9651 was packaged in Orange Perforated boxes.

When the outfit quantity was increased on 9-7-60 from 8,000 to 9,100, the 6465-110 was likely used as the tank car in this version.

All the rolling stock in the 9651 was equipped with early operating AAR trucks and couplers.

The no. 60-429 Tan RSC with Black Graphics outfit box was manufactured by United Container Co. and measured 15¼ x 11 x 5⅜ inches. One observed example also included six dots and an "E" as part of the box manufacturer's certificate.

This outfit does not appear as often as one would think considering the large amount produced. When it does, it is almost always found with a 6465-110.

CONVENTIONAL PACK
60-429 BOX
ALL UNITS PACKED
EXCEPT 1016, 1008

TOP LAYER				BOTTOM LAYER	
8-1013		6465 F		246 F	1130T F
1018					
6057 F	1016			6476 F	
6825 S				6062 F	

1008 TOP 6465

Description: 1960 Outfit
Specification: "O27" Ga. Diesel Freight Outfit
Customer/No./Price: Sears, Roebuck and Co.; 9652; $25.97
Customer/No./Price: Simpsons-Sears; 49 N 41 855; $29.95
Original Amount: 2,400
Factory Order Date: 3/17/1960
Date Issued: 9-7-60
Packaging: Conventional Outfit Packing, All units packed except 1015, 6029

Contents: 225P-1 Alco Diesel Power Car - Blue - "Chesapeake & Ohio" - Yellow Lettering with Headlight and Magne-Traction - with 2 Position Reversing Unit - with Lockon & Lubricant; 6361-1 Log Car - Dark Green Frame; 6812-1 Track Maintenance Car; 6817-1 Flat Car - Red - with Road Scraper; 6670-1 Crane Car; 6119-100 Work Caboose; 1013 Curved Track (8); 1018 Straight Track (3); 6029-25 Uncoupling Track Section; 1015-25 45-Watt Transformer; 90 Uncoupling Track Controller; 81-32 Wires (4); 90-30 Envelope Packed With 90 and 81-32; 9663-10 Instruction Sheet; 310-2 Set of (5) Billboard Signs; AC Accessory Catalog

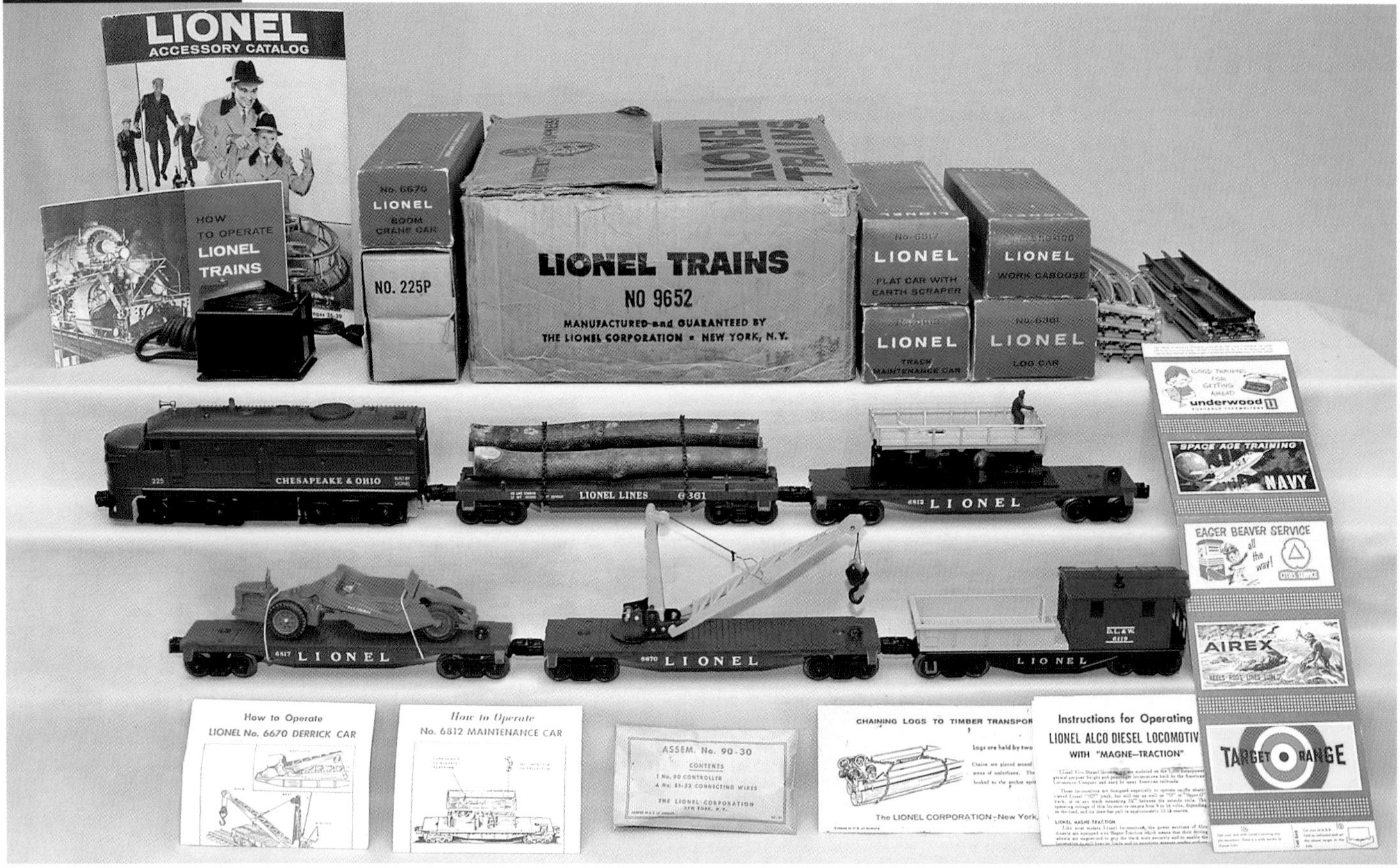

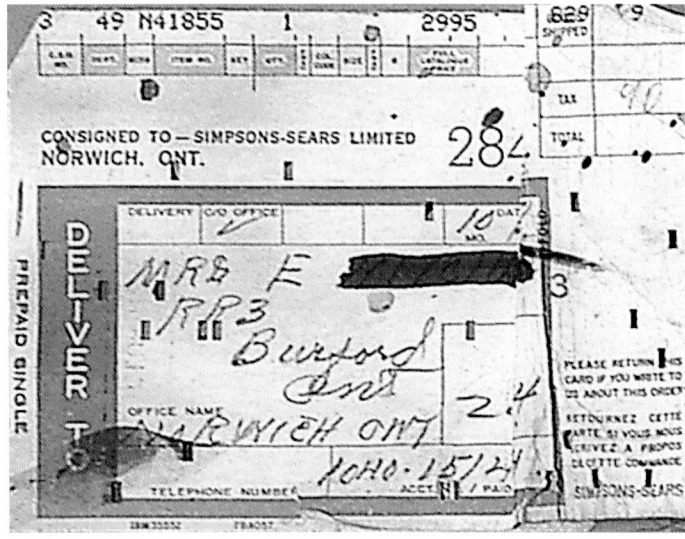

The no. 9652 was Sears' entry-level O27 diesel-powered offering for 1960. This outfit contained the collectible no. 6817-1 Flat Car - Red - with Road Scraper and no. 225P-1 Chesapeake & Ohio Alco in its tough no. 225-20 Corrugated Box. Examples of the 9652 have been observed with its no. 6119-100 Work Caboose in a Bold Classic box.

3 49 N41855 1 2995
CONSIGNED TO—SIMPSONS-SEARS LIMITED
NORWICH, ONT.
284
TAX
TOTAL
DELIVER TO
PREPAID SINGLE
DELIVERY C/O OFFICE
MRS E [redacted]
RR 3
Burford Ont
OFFICE NAME
NORWICH ONT
PLEASE RETURN THIS CARD IF YOU WRITE TO US ABOUT THIS ORDER
RETOURNEZ CETTE CARTE SI VOUS ECRIVEZ A PROPOS DE CETTE COMMANDE
SIMPSONS-SEARS
TELEPHONE NUMBER

The no. 9652 also appeared in the 1961 Simpsons-Sears Christmas Catalog as no. 49 N 41 855 for $29.95. The Simpsons-Sears shipping label from a 9652 is shown. The upper left identifies the Simpsons-Sears number and price.

Boxes & Packing: 60-431 Box; 60-432 Shipper (1-3)

9652 (1960)	C6	C7	C8	Rarity
Complete Outfit	965	1,500	2,000	R5
Outfit Box no. 60-431	125	200	250	R5

Comments: The no. 9652 was the second of seven Sears outfits from 1960. This Retailer Promotional Type Ia outfit appeared in the 1960 Sears Christmas Catalog as well as the 1961 Simpsons-Sears Christmas Catalog. This was not the first time that a Simpsons-Sears catalog included an outfit from the previous year. The same thing occurred in its 1960 Christmas Catalog.

Was Sears dumping its excess inventory through its Canadian arm? That is one likely scenario, as the 9652 did not meet Sears' expectations. The original quantity on the Factory Order was 3,000, but that was reduced to 2,400 on 9-7-60.

The 9652 was Sears' entry-level O27 diesel-powered offering for 1960. It was headed by a no. 225P-1 Chesapeake & Ohio Alco Diesel Power Car. New for 1960, this locomotive featured an open pilot and the large ledge that was added to Alcos as reinforcement in 1960. It also included a two-position reversing unit, a headlight and two-axle Magne-Traction. (See the entry for outfit no. X-509NA for detail on this diesel's difficult-to-obtain no. 225-20 Corrugated Box.)

The no. 6817-1 Flat Car - Red - with Road Scraper is the most expensive item in the 9652. Finding its Orange Perforated box and fragile no. 6817-111 Earth Scraper Complete in collectible condition is difficult. This outfit has been observed with the early version of the scraper with a no. 6817-105 Wire Windshield Frame and white "Allis Chalmers" on the scraper drawbar. With this being a 1960 outfit, the 9652 might also have come with the later version of the scraper, which lacked a windshield and any stamping.

All the pieces of rolling stock in this outfit came equipped with early operating AAR trucks and couplers. And all but one of the cars were packaged in Orange Perforated boxes. The exception was the no. 6119-100 Work Caboose, which also has been observed in a Bold Classic box.

The no. 60-431 Tan RSC with Black Graphics outfit box was manufactured by United Container Co. and measured 13⅞ x 12½ x 6 inches. Many, yet not all, examples have been observed with additional markings: seven dots and an "E" as part of the box manufacturer's certificate.

Ironically, the entry-level 9652 is more collectible then the no. 9654, its higher-end counterpart. That's because its items are more collectible and it was produced in lower quantities.

CONVENTIONAL PACK
60-431 BOX
ALL UNITS PACKED
EXCEPT 1015, 6029

TOP LAYER		
6361 F		
6812 F	6029	
3-1018		
6817 F		

BOTTOM LAYER	
225P F	
6119 S	1015
8-1013 E	
6670 F	

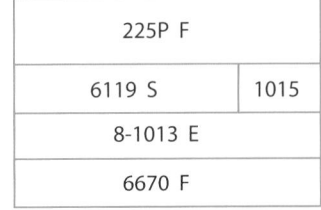

The no. 9653 was Sears' high-end O27 steam-powered offering for 1960. The nos. 243-1 Locomotive - with Smoke and Headlight and 243W-1 Whistle Tender provided two key features (smoke and whistle) to this otherwise plain outfit.

Description: 1960 Outfit
Specification: "O27" Ga. Steam Type Freight Outfit with Whistle & Smoke
Customer/No./Price: Sears, Roebuck and Co.; 9653; $29.44
Original Amount: 8,300
Factory Order Date: 3/17/1960
Date Issued: 9-7-60
Packaging: Conventional Outfit Packing, All units packed except 1063, 6029

Contents: 243-1 Locomotive - with Smoke and Headlight - with (2) Position Reversing Unit, Lockon and Lubricant - without Magne-Traction; 243W-1 Whistle Tender; 6062-1 Gondola Car - Black - with (3) Cable Reels; 6014-1 Box Car - Red; 6825-1 Flat Car - Red - with Trestle Bridge - Black; 6017-1 Caboose - Brick Brown; 1013 Curved Track (8); 1018 Straight Track (3); 6029-25 Uncoupling Track Section; 1063-25 75-Watt Transformer; 90 Uncoupling Track Controller; 81-32 Wires (4); 90-30 Envelope Packed With 90 and 81-32; 926-60 Instruction Book; 310-2 Set of (5) Billboard Signs; AC Accessory Catalog

Boxes & Packing: 60-433 Box; 60-434 Shipper (1-4)

9000 Series

9653 (1960)	C6	C7	C8	Rarity
Complete Outfit	240	375	525	R3
Outfit Box no. 60-433	60	85	100	R3

Comments: The no. 9653 was the third of seven Sears outfits from 1960. This Retailer Promotional Type Ib outfit appeared in the 1960 Sears Christmas Catalog on page 444 for $29.44.

The 9653 was Sears' high-end O27 steam-powered offering for 1960. A no. 243-1 Locomotive - with Smoke and Headlight led this outfit. This engine featured a metal motor and a two-position reversing unit and was followed by a no. 243W-1 Whistle Tender. The locomotive and tender were the only new items in this outfit.

The no. 6014-1 Box Car - Red (likely a Bosco car) listed on the Factory Order for this outfit was actually a no. 6014-100 Red Airex Box Car. That's because 1960 turned out to be a transition year for the 6014, with the 6014-1 being replaced by the 6014-100 in Lionel's product line. Having a 6014-100, which appeared only as a promotional item, is what makes this outfit a Type Ib.

The 6014-100 and the other pieces of rolling stock in the 9653 were equipped with early operating AAR trucks and couplers and came packaged in Orange Perforated boxes.

The no. 60-433 Tan RSC with Black Graphics single-layer

outfit box was manufactured by United Container Co. and measured 15 x 12½ x 4¼ inches.

This outfit exceeded Sears' expectations, as the quantity was increased from 8,000 to 8,300 on 9-7-60. With a large number produced and no standout rolling stock, this is a common outfit. The 9653's only highlight is that there are many dedicated Sears outfit collectors that hunt for all of its offerings.

CONVENTIONAL PACK
60-433 BOX
ALL UNITS BOXED
EXCEPT 1063, 6029

6014 S	6017 S	243W S
		6062 S
		6825 S
1063		243 S
		8-1013

6029 TOP 243W
3-1018 TOP 6825

Description: 1960 Outfit
Specification: "O27" Ga. Diesel Freight Outfit with Horn
Customer/No./Price: Sears, Roebuck and Co.; 9654; $39.44
Original Amount: 6,000
Factory Order Date: 3/17/1960
Date Issued: 9-7-60
Packaging: Conventional Outfit Packing, All units packed except 1063, 6029

Contents: 226P-1 Alco Diesel Power Unit - "Boston & Maine" - with Horn, Headlight, Magne-Traction, Non-Operating Coupler, Lockon and Lubricant; 226C-1 "B" Unit - Blue & White - "Boston & Maine" Markings; 3419-1 Operating Helicopter Car; 6830-1 Flat Car - with Non-Operating Submarine - Blue Car Body; 6650-1 Missile Launching Flat Car; 6470-1 Exploding Target Car; 6017-1 Caboose - Brick Brown; 1013 Curved Track (8); 1018 Straight Track (5); 6029-25 Uncoupling Track Section; 1063-25 75-Watt Transformer; 90-1 Uncoupling Track Controller; 81-32 Wires (4); 90-30 Envelope Packed With 90-1 and 81-32; 926-60 Instruction Book; 310-2 Set of (5) Billboard Signs; AC Accessory Catalog

Boxes & Packing: 60-435 Box; 60-436 Shipper (1-3)

Alternate For Outfit Contents:
Note: Use inventory of 826 - 217C-1 for 226C-1.

9654 (1960)	C6	C7	C8	Rarity
Complete Outfit	540	925	1,350	R4
Outfit Box no. 60-435	100	150	200	R4

Comments: The no. 9654 was the fourth of seven Sears outfits from 1960. This Retailer Promotional Type Ib outfit appeared in the 1960 Sears Christmas Catalog on page 445 for $39.44.

The 9654 was Sears' high-end O27 diesel-powered offering for 1960. It exceeded Sears' expectations, as the quantity was increased from 5,500 to 6,000 on 9-7-60.

This exciting space and military outfit was led by a no. 226P-1 Boston & Maine Alco Diesel Power Unit. A high-end Alco (new for 1960), the 226P-1 came with all the features that were available at that time, including a three-position reversing unit, an open pilot, a horn, a headlight and two-axle Magne-Traction. Combined with its no. 226C-1 "B" Unit, it appeared in only four promotional outfits, with a total of 6,625 units being produced.

When packaged in its no. 226-7 Corrugated Box, the Boston & Maine diesel came with the nos. 601-13 "C" Battery, CTC-1 Lockon, 927-60 Tube of Oil, 218-11 Instruction Sheet and 927-65 Tube of Grease.

Two of the outfits that included a 226P-1 (nos. X-576 and X-577) were bulk-packed for Madison Hardware Co. in New York City. This is the likely source of the 226Ps in C10 condition that Madison Hardware was selling well into the 1980s. Hence, even though this Alco was a promotional-only item and was produced in smaller-than-normal quantities, a number of them have survived in C10 condition.

The nos. 3419-1 Operating Helicopter Car, 6470-1 Exploding Target Car, 6650-1 Missile Launching Flat Car and 6830-1 Flat Car - with Non-Operating Submarine were an exciting combination of space and military rolling stock. Hours could be spent blowing up the Exploding Target Car. The 6470-1 included "slotted" sides and a smooth roof door guide (without the nubs added later to help hold on the sides).

Except for the brand-new 6830-1, all the cars in this outfit were carried over from 1959. Each of them was equipped with early operating AAR trucks and couplers. In addition, all of them

The no. 9654 was Sears' high-end O27 diesel-powered offering for 1960. It included the promotional-only no. 226P-1 Boston & Maine Alco Diesel Power Unit. The rolling stock was an exciting assortment of space and military items.

came packaged in Orange Perforated boxes.

The no. 60-435 Tan RSC with Black Graphics outfit box was manufactured by United Container Co. and measured 14⅝ x 11½ x 7 inches. It has been observed with six dots and an "E" as part of the box manufacturer's certificate.

The substitution of a no. 217C-1 Boston & Maine "B" Unit minimally affects the price.

This outfit accounts for almost all the 226Ps and 226Cs that Lionel produced. That fact alone makes the 9654 collectible. Combined with its Sears origins, this outfit becomes highly desirable. The good news is that with large quantities produced, it does appear on the market.

CONVENTIONAL PACK
60-435 BOX
ALL UNITS PACKED
EXCEPT 1063, 6029

TOP LAYER

8-1013	
6470 F	6017
6830 S	
6650 S	

5-1018 TOP 6470
6029 TOP 1018

BOTTOM LAYER

226P S	
226C F	
3419 F	1063

Description: "O27" Promotional
Specification: "O27" GP-7 Freight Outfit
Customer/No./Price: Sears, Roebuck and Co.; 9655; $29.75
Original Amount: 6,000
Factory Order Date: 7/26/1962
Date Issued: Rev. 9-19-62
Packaging: R.S.C. Outfit Packing (Units Boxed)

Contents: 2365-1 GP-7 Diesel Power Unit - "Chesapeake & Ohio"; 3349-1 Turbo Missile Firing Car; 6463-1 Rocket Fuel Car; 6448-1 Exploding Target Range Car; 6413-1 Mercury Capsule Transport Car; 6057-1 Caboose; 1013-8 Curved Track (Bundle of 8 - 1013); 1018-10 Straight Track (Loose); 6029-25 Uncoupling Track Section; 1025-25 45-Watt Transformer; 90-30 Envelope

Packed; 310-2 Set of (5) Billboards; 1123-40 Instruction Sheet; 126-10 Instruction Sheet

Boxes & Packing: 62-274 Outfit Box; 62-256 Corr. Insert; 62-266 Corr. Insert; 62-275 Shipper for (4) (1-4)

9655 (1962)	C6	C7	C8	Rarity
Complete Outfit	740	1,175	1,650	R4
Outfit Box no. 62-274	150	300	450	R4

Comments: The no. 9655 was the second of five Sears outfits from 1962. This Retailer Promotional Type Ia outfit appeared in the 1962 Sears Christmas Catalog on page 437 for only $29.75.

The no. 9655 was Sears' entry-level O27 diesel-powered offering for 1962. This space and military outfit was one of three outfits to include a no. 2365-1 Chesapeake & Ohio GP-7 Diesel Power Unit. It now ranks among the most desirable of all the entry-level Sears offerings.

The 9655 was Sears' entry-level O27 diesel-powered offering for 1962. It was led by a no. 2365-1 Chesapeake & Ohio GP-7 Diesel Power Unit. This new-for-1962 locomotive also led catalog outfit no. 11268 from 1962 and Sears no. 19305 from 1963. It featured Magne-Traction, a three-position reversing unit and a light at both ends. When packaged in its no. 2365-12 Corr. Box, the Chesapeake & Ohio GP-7 included a no. 2365-11 Instruction Sheet, 927-60 Tube of Oil, 927-65 Tube of Grease and a CTC-1 Lockon.

The space and military rolling stock led to an exciting outfit that was well worth the price. All but one of the cars as well as the caboose was brand new to the Lionel line. The no. 6448-1 Exploding Target Range Car was a carryover from 1961. According to the Production Control Files, as many of the variation with red sides and a white roof were made as the variation with white sides and a red roof. The version included in this outfit included "non-slotted" sides and nubs on the roof door guide to help hold on the sides.

All the pieces of rolling stock in the 9655 were equipped with middle operating AAR trucks and couplers. Everything came packaged in Orange Picture boxes.

The Sears O27 outfits from 1962 came with a no. 6029-25 Uncoupling Track Section. For this outfit, that meant a no. 90-30 Envelope Packed was required.

The no. 62-274 Orange RSC with Black Graphics outfit box was manufactured by the Mead Corporation and measured 16⅜ x 11¼ x 6¼ inches. It was used for two other outfits, catalog items nos. 11268 and 13028.

The 9655 is probably the most desirable of any of the entry-level Sears outfits. It does appear on the market, but takes some patience to find in C8 condition.

CONVENTIONAL PACK
62-274 BOX
5-22-62

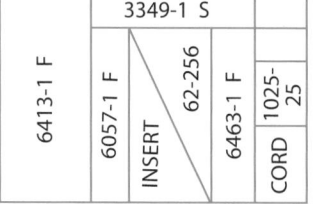

TOP LAYER

		3349-1 S			
6413-1 F	6057-1 F	INSERT 62-256	6463-1 F	1025-25	CORD

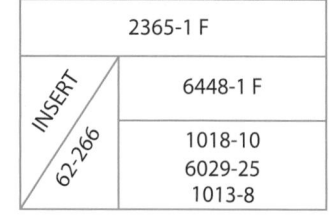

BOTTOM LAYER

	2365-1 F
INSERT 62-266	6448-1 F
	1018-10 6029-25 1013-8

The no. 9656 was Sears' high-end O27 diesel-powered offering for 1962. It introduced the no. 223P-1 Santa Fe Alco Diesel Power Unit with Horn. This promotional-only Alco pulled a no. 218C-1 Santa Fe "B" Unit and space and military rolling stock.

Description: "O27" Promotional
Specification: "O27" Diesel Freight Outfit with Horn
Customer/No./Price: Sears, Roebuck and Co.; 9656; $39.77
Original Amount: 4,500
Factory Order Date: 8/9/1962
Date Issued: Rev. 8-21-62
Packaging: R.S.C. Outfit Packing (Units Boxed)

Contents: 223P-1 "Santa Fe" Alco Diesel Power Unit with Horn; 218C-1 "B" Unit - "Santa Fe"; 3419-1 Operating Helicopter Car; 3665-1 Minuteman Missile Launching Car; 6448-1 Exploding Target Range Car; 3349-1 Turbo Missile Firing Car; 6017-235 Caboose - "Santa Fe" Markings; 1013-8 Curved Track (Bundle of 8 - 1013); 1018-30 Straight Track (Bundle of 3 - 1018); 6029-25 Uncoupling Track Section; 1073-25 60-Watt Transformer; 147-25 Horn & Whistle Controller; 2333-140 Flashlight Cell; 81-32 24" R.C. Wire (3); 90-30 Envelope Packed; 310-2 Set of (5) Billboards; 1123-40 Instruction Sheet; 9656-10 Instruction Sheet

Boxes & Packing: 61-210 Outfit Box; 61-193 Insert; 61-211 Shipper for (4) (1-4)

9656 (1962)	C6	C7	C8	Rarity
Complete Outfit	675	1,175	1,725	R5
Outfit Box no. 61-210	175	350	500	R5

Comments: The no. 9656 was the third of five Sears outfits from 1962. This Retailer Promotional Type Ib outfit appeared in the 1962 Sears Christmas Catalog on page 436 for $39.77.

The 9656 was Sears' high-end O27 diesel-powered offering for 1962. It was led by a no. 223P-1 Santa Fe Alco Diesel Power Unit with Horn. This locomotive featured a two-position reversing unit, a headlight, one-axle Magne-Traction and an open pilot with a large ledge. The 223P-1 appeared only in promotional outfits in 1962 and 1963. When packaged in its no. 223-8 Corr. Box, the 223P-1 included a no. 229-7 Instruction Sheet, 927-90 Lubricating Oil Packed, 601-13 "C" Battery and a CTC-1 Lockon.

The space and military cars make this a highly desirable Sears outfit. The only new items were the nos. 3349-1 Turbo Missile Firing Car and boxed no. 6017-235 Santa Fe Caboose. The 6017-235 totaled 7,600 units between this outfit and catalog outfit no. 13018. The relatively low number is why its box takes some patience to find.

In 1962, the no. 3419-100 Operating Helicopter Complete changed from a gray Navy stamped two-piece helicopter body to an unmarked helicopter with a one-piece yellow helicopter body. Although this was Lionel's intended production, many more 3419-100 Navy helicopters still appeared on 3419s in 1962. Both of these helicopters were frequently lost or broken.

All the pieces of rolling stock in the 9656 were equipped with operating AAR trucks and couplers. Everything came packaged in Orange Picture boxes.

The Sears O27 outfits from 1962 came with a no. 6029-25 Uncoupling Track Section. For this outfit, that meant a no. 90-30 Envelope Packed was required.

When a no. 147-25 Horn & Whistle Controller was included, Lionel provided a no. 2333-140 Flashlight Cell loose in the outfit box. This practice lasted until 1963. The no. 9656-10 Instruction Sheet was introduced with this outfit and also used for outfit no. 19165.

The no. 61-210 Orange RSC with Black Graphics outfit box was manufactured by the Mead Corporation and measured 13⅞ x 13¼ x 6½ inches.

As with all space and military and Sears outfits, the 9656 is in high demand.

TOP LAYER		
3665-1 F	1018-30 ON TOP	1013-8
3419-1 F	6029-25 ON TOP	
3349-1 F		
61-193 INSERT		

BOTTOM LAYER		
218C-1 F		1073-25
223P-1 F		
147-25 2333-140 81-32	6017-235 S	
6448-1 S		

9657
1962

Lionel Matching Outfits

"027"
Outside rails 1¼ in. apart
Engine about 4 in. high

HO-gauge
Rails 2⅛ in. apart
Engine about 2 in. high

"027"-gauge 8-unit Train $49⁷⁷ cash NO MONEY DOWN

HO-gauge 8-unit Train $44⁷⁷ cash NO MONEY DOWN

"027"-gauge 7-unit Train $39⁷⁷ cash NO MONEY DOWN

8 units with whistle .. smoke .. 3 action cars

Freight whistles by remote control, speeds ahead puffing smoke .. head-lamp beams. Pulls tender, "gold" bullion car, "log" car, "battling sheriff-and-outlaw" car, giraffe car, car with bobbing horses, caboose. Plastic, steel. UL listed transformer or powerpack for 110-120-v, 60-cycle AC. Un-coupling track. Both uncouple by remote control; HO has N.M.R.A. couplers.
75-in. "027"-gauge Train. Die-cast Mag-ne-Traction engine. 12 tracks make 27x45-in. oval. 75-w. circuit-breaker transformer.
49 N 9657—Shipping weight 13 lbs. .. $49.77

47-inch HO-gauge Train, 8 tracks .. 36x45-in. oval. 1¼-amp. DC-AC powerpack.
79 N 9906C–Wt. 11 lbs. $44.77

7-unit Twin Diesel with horn

Twin diesel locomotive has bright headlamp, w let you launch a helicopter, fire a "Minuteman fire "Turbo" missile. Caboose. Run train fast, uncouple cars, sound horn—all by remote contr transformer or powerpack for 110-120-volt, 60-72-in. "027"-ga.Train. Power unit diesel. Magne-Traction drive, more pull power. 12 tracks .. 27x45-in. oval. 60-w circuit break transformer.
49 N 9656—Shipping weight 13 lbs. $39.77

Left: The no. 9657 was Sears' high-end O27 steam-powered offering for 1962. This exciting, western-oriented outfit included three operating cars. Middle: The catalog listing also illustrates Sears' strategy for 1962 of selling matching HO scale outfits. The no. 9906C was the HO counterpart to the 9657.

Description: "O27" Promotional
Specification: "O27" Steam Type Freight Outfit W/Smoke & Whistle
Customer/No./Price: Sears, Roebuck and Co.; 9657; $49.77
Original Amount: 3,200
Factory Order Date: 7/25/1962
Date Issued: 7-26-62
Packaging: RSC Outfit Packing (Units Boxed)

Contents: 2037-1 Steam Type Locomotive With Smoke; 234W-1 Whistle Tender; 3370-1 Animated Sheriff & Outlaw Car; 6445-1 Ft. Knox Gold Bullion Transport Car; 3376-160 Operating Giraffe Car; 6473-1 Rodeo Car; 6361-1 Timber Transport Car; 6017-1 Caboose; 1013-8 Curved Track (Bundle of 8 - 1013); 1018-30 Straight Track (Bundle of 3 - 1018); 6029-25 Uncoupling Track Section; 1063-25 75-Watt Transformer; 90-30 Envelope Packed;

310-2 Set of (5) Billboards; 1123-40 Instruction Sheet; 1650-10 Instruction Sheet

Boxes & Packing: 61-210 Outfit Box; 61-211 Shipper for (4) (1-4)

9657 (1962)	C6	C7	C8	Rarity
Complete Outfit	600	925	1,350	R5
Outfit Box no. 61-210	125	225	350	R5

Comments: The no. 9657 was the fourth of five Sears outfits from 1962. This Retailer Promotional Type Ia outfit appeared in the 1962 Sears Christmas Catalog on page 436 for $49.77.

The 9657 was Sears' high-end O27 steam-powered offering for 1962. It was led by a no. 2037-1 Steam Type Locomotive with Smoke and Magne-Traction. This workhorse steamer spanned from 1953 through 1963 (except for 1956) and powered one Super O and 22 O27 outfits during the 1960s. When boxed as a "-1", it included the nos. 675-33 Smoke Stack Cleaner, SP-1 Smoke Pellets, 927-90 Lubricating Oil Packed, 2037-16 Instruction Sheet and a CTC-1 Lockon inside its 2037-13 Corr. Box.

The no. 234W-1 Whistle Tender was new for 1962. For that year it was equipped with one non-operating and one plain Archbar truck and coupler.

The rolling stock in this outfit created an exciting, western-oriented theme. Sears provided three operating cars, including the green no. 3376-160 Operating Giraffe Car (new for 1962). This was the only 1962 outfit to include a boxed version of that car. Other than the 3376-160 and no. 6473-1 Rodeo Car, the rolling stock in the 9657 was repeated from earlier years.

All the cars in this outfit were equipped with operating AAR trucks and couplers and came packaged in Orange Picture boxes. The 6361-1 Timber Transport Car has also been observed in an

TOP LAYER		
1013-8	90-30	6017-1 F
234W-1 F		
6473-1 F		
3370-1 F		

BOTTOM LAYER		
2037-1 S		1018-30 6029-25
6361-1 F		
6445-1 S		
3376-160 S	1063-25	

Orange Perforated box.

The Sears O27 outfits from 1962 came with a no. 6029-25 Uncoupling Track Section. For this outfit, that meant a no. 90-30 Envelope Packed was required.

The no. 61-210 Orange RSC with Black Graphics outfit box was manufactured by the Mead Corporation and measured 13⅞ x 13¼ x 6½ inches.

This high-end Sears O27 offering included colorful, action-packed rolling stock, which makes it highly desirable among Sears outfit collectors. Demand is high for the 9657. Unfortunately, examples of this outfit do not appear too often in collectible condition.

The no. 9658 was Sears' high-end offering for 1962. This was the first O gauge outfit issued by Lionel in at least two years. Even though all items were carried over from previous years, the 9658 was still an exciting offering and so remains highly desirable.

Description: "O" Ga. Promotional
Specification: "O" Ga. Steam Type Freight W/Smoke & Whistle
Customer/No./Price: Sears, Roebuck and Co.; 9658; $59.95
Original Amount: 600
Factory Order Date: 7/25/1962
Date Issued: 7-26-62
Packaging: R.S.C. Outfit Packing (Units Boxed)

Contents: 736X-1 Steam Type Locomotive With Smoke; 736W-1 Whistle Tender; 3362-1 Helium Tank Unloading Car; 6519-1 Allis-Chalmers Car; 6820-1 Flat Car W/Oper. Missile Helicopter Car; 6475-1 Pickle Car; 6437-1 Illuminated Cupola Caboose; TOC-8 Curved Track (8 per Bundle); TOS-3 Straight Track (3 per Bundle); UCS-1 Remote Control Track Section; 1063-25 75-Watt Transformer; 81-32 24" R.C. Wire (2); CTC-1 Lockon; 310-2 Set of (5) Billboards; 1123-40 Instruction Sheet; 1650-10 Instruction Sheet

Boxes & Packing: 61-220 Outfit Box; 61-184 Insert; 61-221 Shipper for (2) (1-2)

9658 (1962)	C6	C7	C8	Rarity
Complete Outfit	1,075	1,625	2,225	R8
Outfit Box no. 61-220	300	500	700	R8

Comments: The no. 9658 was the last of five Sears outfits from 1962. This Retailer Promotional Type Ia outfit was likely sold over the counter in retail stores, as it has yet to be observed in a catalog. This was Sears' high-end O gauge offering for 1962, and it carried the highest price. One outfit was observed with a Sears price tag of $59.95. Lionel Factory Pricing Worksheets confirm this price.

The 9658 marked the return of O gauge outfits to the Lionel line. The last catalog O gauge outfit appeared in 1957. A few promotional O gauge outfits were likely produced in 1958 and 1959, but then no O gauge outfits of any kind were attributed to 1960 or 1961. After the 9658, O gauge outfits did not return to the Lionel line until 1964.

This outfit was led by a no. 736X-1 Steam Type Locomotive With Smoke and Magne-Traction. Originally introduced in 1950, the 736 appeared in at least 17 outfits during the 1960s. When packaged in its no. 736-36 Corr. Box, it included the nos. 675-33 Smoke Stack Cleaner, SP-1 Smoke Pellets Bottled, 682-16 Instruction Sheet and appropriate lubrication. As described in the section on Outfit Peripherals, an "X" signified that a no. CTC-1 Lockon was not included in the locomotive box; therefore, it was included separately in the outfit box.

Even though the 9658 was Sears' high-end O gauge outfit, all the items included were carried over from previous years. Furthermore, Lionel appeared to be using this outfit to empty its shelves. Most of the cars were at the end of their product life, with 1962 being their last or next-to-last year in an outfit.

The most notable item in the 9658 was the no. 6820-1 Flat Car W/Oper. Missile Helicopter Car. Late in 1960, Lionel Production Control Files indicated that the intended production of the helicopter with the 6820-1 changed from a no. 6820-40 Non-Operating Missile Helicopter Complete to a no. 6820-100 Operating Missile Helicopter Complete.

An intriguing point is that the body used for the 6820-100 is a USMC no. 3429-33 Body Stamped (the same body that Lionel used on a USMC 3429-100 Operating Helicopter Car Complete). A 6820-1 with a USMC 6820-100 Operating Missile Helicopter Complete has never been reported. This may be due to the fact that helicopters are easily exchanged on 6820s. Thus, it may never be verified that the 6820-1 came with a USMC helicopter. For that reason, the pricing for this outfit assumes a 6820-40 Non-

Operating Missile Helicopter, which is becoming hard to find with original unbroken parts.

All the rolling stock in this outfit was equipped with operating AAR trucks and couplers. Everything came packaged in Orange Picture or Orange Perforated boxes.

The no. 61-220 Orange RSC with Black Graphics outfit box was manufactured by Mead Bonded Containers and measured 16⅜ x 13⅛ x 6¼ inches.

This was Lionel's first O gauge offering in at least two years and the last until 1964. That fact, combined with the 9658's Sears origins and its low production, makes this outfit highly collectible.

CONVENTIONAL PACK
61-220 BOX

TOP LAYER		**BOTTOM LAYER**	

UCS-1 S / TOS-3	TOC - 8			3362-1 S	1063-25	6519-1 F
	81-32 CTC-1				6820-1 S
	6437-1 F				736W-1 S
	6475-1 F				736X-1 F

61-184 INSERT

The no. 9670 was Sears' entry-level O27 steam-powered offering for 1961. Its one stand-out item was the Type I no. 6050-25 Savings Bank Car. Other than the outfit box, the no. 90-40 Envelope Packed is the most difficult item to find in completing a 9670.

Description: "O27" Promotional Outfit
Specification: "O27" Steam Type Freight Outfit
Customer/No./Price: Sears, Roebuck and Co.; 9670; $18.88
Original Amount: 9,000
Date Issued: Rev. #1 9-12-61
Packaging: R.S.C. Outfit Packing (Units not Boxed)

Contents: 246-25 Steam Type Locomotive; 244T-25 Tender; 6476-25 Hopper Car - Red; 6050-25 Savings Bank Car; 6162-25 Gondola Car - Blue (Less Canisters); 6112-88 Canisters (White)

(3); 6825-25 Trestle Bridge Flat Car (Less Trestle Bridge); 6825-3 Trestle Bridge - Black; 6057-25 Caboose - Red; 1013-8 Curved Track (Bundle of 8 - 1013); 1018-10 Straight Track (Loose); 6029-25 R.C. Uncoupling Track; 1010-25 35-Watt Transformer; 90-40 Envelope; 9670-10 Instruction Sheet; 310-2 Set of (5) Billboards

Boxes & Packing: 61-180 Outfit Box; 61-181 Corr. Insert; 61-182 Corr. Insert; 61-183 Corr. Insert; 61-184 Corr. Insert; 61-185 Shipper for (4) (1-4)

9670 (1961)	C6	C7	C8	Rarity
Complete Outfit	200	325	450	R4
Outfit Box no. 61-180	75	115	150	R4

Comments: The no. 9670 was the first of seven Sears outfits from 1961. This Retailer Promotional Type Ia outfit appeared in the 1961 Sears Christmas Catalog on page 402 for $18.88. It was the follow-up to no. 9651 from 1960, an outfit with similar contents.

The 9670 was Sears' entry-level O27 steam-powered offering for 1961. It was led by a no. 246-25 Steam Type Locomotive, which was equipped with a two-position reversing unit, a headlight and Magne-Traction. This outfit included the later version that had a solid pilot and lacked generator detail on the body.

The one standout item in the 9670 was the Type I no. 6050-25 Savings Bank Car with coin slot (new for 1961). All the other pieces of rolling stock were carried over from previous years. Everything in this outfit was equipped with early operating AAR trucks and couplers.

The Sears O27 outfits from 1961 came with a no. 6029-25 R.C. Uncoupling Track. For this outfit, that meant a no. 90-40 Envelope Packed was required. A complete C8 envelope is the most difficult item to find in completing a 9670.

This outfit introduced the no. 9670-10 Instruction Sheet, which subsequently was used in many outfits.

The commonly used no. 61-180 Tan RSC with Black Graphics outfit box was manufactured by the Mead Corporation and measured 12¾ x 10 x 6¾ inches.

Based on its contents, the 9670 should not receive much attention from collectors. However, because it was a Sears outfit – and Sears outfits always are in demand – it does attract a lot of interest. In fact, finding a 9670 in C8 condition can be a challenge.

CONVENTIONAL PACK
61-180 BOX

TOP LAYER
6825-25 6162-25
1013-8 1018-10 1-6029-25
244T-25

BOTTOM LAYER
6112-88 (3) HERE

6476-25 6825-3 TOP	
6050-25	1010-25
6057-25	
246-25	

The no. 9671 was Sears' entry-level O27 diesel-powered offering for 1961. Its contents offered a less-than-appealing combination of colors. Among the cars, the no. 6640-25 Missile Launching Car - Khaki Color was making its last appearance in this outfit.

Description: "O27" Promotional Outfit
Specification: "O27" Diesel Freight Outfit
Customer/No.: Sears, Roebuck and Co.; 9671
Original Amount: 1,200
Factory Order Date: 4/20/1961
Date Issued: Rev. #2 9/12/61
Packaging: R.S.C. Outfit Packing (Units not Boxed)

Contents: 224P-25 Alco Diesel Power Car - "U.S. Navy"; 224C-25 "B" Unit - "U.S. Navy"; 6650-25 Missile Launching Flat Car; 6650-80 Missile Complete (or 6650-84); 6470-25 Exploding Target Car; 6465-100 Two Dome Tank Car - "Cities Service"; 6017-210 Caboose - "U. S. Navy"; 1013-8 Curved Track (Bundle of 8 - 1013); 1018-10 Straight Track (Loose); 6029-25 R.C. Uncoupling Track; 1025-25 45-Watt Transformer; 90-40 Envelope; 9670-10 Instruction Sheet; 310-2 Set of (5) Billboards

Boxes & Packing: 61-250 Corr. Outfit Box; 61-181 Corr. Insert; 61-182 Corr. Insert; 61-186 Corr. Insert; 61-191 Corr. Insert; 61-193 Corr. Insert; 61-251 Corr. Shipper for (4) (1-4)

Alternate For Outfit Contents:
Note: Use inventory of 6640-25 for 6650-25.

9671 (1961)	C6	C7	C8	Rarity
Complete Outfit With no. 6640-25	626	1,200	1,600	R7
Outfit Box no. 61-250	275	500	600	R7

Comments: The no. 9671 was the fifth of seven Sears outfits from 1961. This Retailer Promotional Type Ia never appeared in a Sears catalog.

It appears that this outfit did not meet Sears' original expectations, as the Factory Order was reduced to its final quantity of 1,200 on 9/12/61.

The 9671 was Sears' entry-level O27 diesel-powered offering for 1961. This space and military outfit was led by a no. 224P-25 U.S. Navy Alco Diesel with Magne-Traction and a three-position reversing unit. It was paired with a no. 224C-25 "B" Unit. The 224P most often was individually boxed when included with an outfit. However, the 9671 was one of five outfits to contain an unboxed 224P.

All the rolling stock (equipped with operating AAR trucks and couplers) was carried over from earlier years. This outfit was used to deplete the inventory of the no. 6640-25 Missile Launching Car - Khaki Color. That car's first and only other appearance was in catalog outfit no. 1805 Land Sea and Air Gift Pack from 1960. The 6640-25 replaced all the no. 6650-25 Missile Launching Flat Cars.

The no. 6470-25 Exploding Target Car in the 9671 was the early version that included "slotted" sides and a smooth roof door guide (without the nubs added later to help hold on the sides).

The no. 6017-210 U.S. Navy Caboose was the appropriate caboose for the U.S. Navy Alco. Except for two outfits in 1962 and 1963, when Lionel was depleting its final inventory of these cabooses, the 6017-210 was always paired with the U.S. Navy Alco.

What was interesting about the rolling stock in this outfit was the bizarre combination of colors. Think about it: khaki, red, green and light blue. They hardly go together, which made the 9671 one of the ugliest outfits that Lionel issued.

The Sears O27 outfits from 1961 came with a no. 6029-25 R.C. Uncoupling Track. For this outfit, that meant a no. 90-40 Envelope Packed was required.

The no. 61-250 Orange RSC with Black Graphics outfit box was manufactured by the Mead Containers and measured 13 x 12 x 7 inches.

This outfit is difficult to obtain in collectible condition. As with all Sears outfits, it is in high demand.

CONVENTIONAL PACK
61-250 BOX

TOP LAYER
224C-25
6470-25
CATALOG 6650-25

BOTTOM LAYER		
224P-25		
6465-100		1025-25
6017-210		
FILLER INSERT		
1013-8		

6029-25 AND 1018-10 TOP OF INSERT

9672 (1961)	C6	C7	C8	Rarity
Complete Outfit	235	385	550	R3
Outfit Box no. 61-180	65	100	125	R3

Description: "O27" Promotional Outfit
Specification: "O27" Steam Type Freight Outfit With Smoke & Whistle
Customer/No./Price: Sears, Roebuck and Co.; 9672; $29.88
Original Amount: 7,500
Factory Order Date: 5/5/1961
Date Issued: 5-6-61
Packaging: R.S.C. Outfit Packing (Units not Boxed)

Contents: 233-25 Steam Type Locomotive With Smoke; 233W-25 Whistle Tender; 6825-25 Trestle Bridge Flat Car (Less Trestle Bridge); 6825-3 Trestle Bridge - Black; 6162-25 Gondola Car - Blue (Less Canisters); 6112-88 Canisters (White) (3); 6465-100 Two Dome Tank Car - "Cities Service"; 6017-25 Caboose; 1013-8 Curved Track (Bundle of 8 - 1013); 1018-30 Straight Track (Bundle of 3 - 1018); 6029-25 R.C. Uncoupling Track; 1063-100 75-Watt Transformer; 90-40 Envelope; 909-10 Bottle Smoke Fluid; IS Instruction Sheet; 310-2 Set of (5) Billboards

Boxes & Packing: 61-180 Outfit Box; 61-181 Corr. Insert; 61-182 Corr. Insert; 61-183 Corr. Insert; 61-184 Corr. Insert; 61-185 Corr. Shipper for (4) (1-4)

Comments: The no. 9672 was the third of seven Sears outfits from 1961. This Retailer Promotional Type Ib outfit appeared in the 1961 Sears Christmas Catalog on page 402 for $29.88. It was the follow-up outfit to no. 9653 from 1960.

The 9672 was Sears' high-end O27 steam-powered offering for 1961. This outfit was led by a no. 233-25 Steam Type Locomotive With Smoke and Magne-Traction. The 9672 represented one of the few times that Lionel paired this steamer with a no. 233W-25 Whistle Tender in an outfit. The engine and tender were both new for 1961.

All the rolling stock in this outfit was carried over from earlier years and included in many 1961 outfits. Everything was equipped with operating AAR trucks and couplers.

As with other outfits that included a Scout steamer and whistle tender, the "-100" version of the no. 1063-100 75-Watt Transformer was used. This transformer included a green whistle control button to indicate changes to the whistle control circuitry and thereby prevent Scout-type locomotives from inadvertently reversing. Its Lionel Production Control File states, "Rubber Stamped '1063-100' on Bottom of Base Plate Assembly using White Ink." This transformer is harder to find than a regular no. 1063-25 75-Watt Transformer, which had a red whistle button.

The no. 9672 was Sears' high-end O27 steam-powered offering for 1961. It was headed by Lionel's high-end Scout, the no. 233-25 Steam Type Locomotive With Smoke and Magne-Traction, which also boasted a headlight. This outfit represented one of the few times that this steamer came with a no. 233W-25 Whistle Tender.

The Sears O27 outfits from 1961 came with a no. 6029-25 R.C. Uncoupling Track. For this outfit, that meant a no. 90-40 Envelope Packed was required.

The commonly used no. 61-180 Tan RSC with Black Graphics outfit box was manufactured by the Mead Corporation and measured 12¾ x 10 x 6¾ inches.

Based on its contents, the 9672 should not receive much attention from collectors. However, because it was a Sears outfit – and Sears outfits always are in demand – it does attract a lot of interest. In fact, finding a 9672 in C8 condition can be a challenge.

CONVENTIONAL PACK
61-180 BOX

TOP LAYER	BOTTOM LAYER	
8-1013 3-1018	3-6112-88 6162-25	
6825-25 6825-3 6029-25	6465-100	1063-100
	6017-25	
233W-25	233-25	

Description: "O27" Promotional Outfit
Specification: "O27" Diesel Freight Outfit With Horn
Customer/No./Price: Sears, Roebuck and Co.; 9673; $39.88
Original Amount: 6,000
Factory Order Date: 4/21/1961
Date Issued: Rev. #1 8-16-61
Packaging: R.S.C. Outfit Packing (Units Boxed)

Contents: 218P-1 Alco Diesel Power Unit With Horn - "Santa Fe"; 218C-1 "B" Unit - "Santa Fe"; 3419-1 Operating Helicopter Car; 6476-1 Hopper Car - Red; 3665-1 Minuteman Missile Launching Car; 6162-1 Gondola Car - Blue; 6017-1 Caboose; 1013-8 Curved Track (Bundle of 8 - 1013); 1018-5 Straight Track (Bundle of 5 - 1018); 6029-25 R.C. Uncoupling Track; 1063-25 75-Watt Transformer; 90-30 Envelope Packed; 9670-10 Instruction Sheet; 310-2 Set of (5) Billboards

Boxes & Packing: 61-200 Corr. Outfit Box; 61-201 Corr. Shipper for (4) (1-4)

9673 (1961)	C6	C7	C8	Rarity
Complete Outfit	500	825	1,100	R4
Outfit Box no. 61-200	150	225	300	R4

Comments: The no. 9673 was the fourth of seven Sears outfits from 1961. This Retailer Promotional Type Ia outfit appeared in the 1961 Sears Christmas Catalog on page 402 for $39.88.

The 9673 was Sears' high-end O27 diesel-powered offering for 1961. This outfit was led by a no. 218P-1 Santa Fe Alco Diesel Power Unit equipped with a three-position reversing unit, a headlight, two-axle Magne-Traction and an open pilot. The nos. CTC-1 Lockon and 218-11 Instruction Sheet were included inside its no. 218-10 Corrugated Box. This was also one of the few Alcos to include a horn. Until 1963, Lionel included a no. 601-13 "C" Battery with boxed Alcos that were equipped with a horn.

The no. 9673 was Sears' high-end O27 diesel-powered offering for 1961. This space and military outfit was led by Lionel's high-end Alco offering, the no. 218P-1 Santa Fe Alco Diesel Power Unit. This example still has its Sears price tag attached.

In 1960, Sears cataloged the 218P-1 in Super O outfit no. 9693. Now just a year later, Sears' customers could receive the same engine in the 9673 for about $10 less.

The rolling stock in this outfit was a combination of space and military and freight items. The only new item in this outfit was the no. 3665-1 Minuteman Missile Launching Car. The others were carried over from earlier years.

All the rolling stock was equipped with operating AAR trucks and couplers. Cars came packaged in either an Orange Perforated or an Orange Picture box.

The Sears O27 outfits from 1961 came with a no. 6029-25 R.C. Uncoupling Track. For this outfit, that meant a no. 90-30 Envelope Packed was required.

The no. 61-200 Orange RSC with Black Graphics outfit box was manufactured by Mead Bonded Containers and measured 14½ x 12 x 7 inches.

The 9673 is on the wish list of every collector of Sears outfits. Demand is high, and so it takes time to find an example of this outfit in C8 condition.

CONVENTIONAL PACK
61-200 BOX

TOP LAYER

3419-1 F	
3665-1 F	8-1013 / 1-6029-25
6162-1 F	

BOTTOM LAYER

6017-1 F	1063-25
218C-1 S	
6476-1 S	
218P-1 S	

1018-5 TOP OF 6017-1

Description: Super "O" Promotional Outfit
Specification: Super "O" Diesel Switcher Freight Outfit With Horn
Customer/No.: Sears, Roebuck and Co.; 9674
Original Amount: 1,000
Factory Order Date: 4/25/1961
Date Issued: Rev. #1 9-12-61
Packaging: R.S.C. Outfit Packing (Units Boxed)

Contents: 616X-1 Diesel Switcher - "Santa Fe" - With Horn; 6822-1 Searchlight Car; 6812-1 Track Maintenance Car; 6827-1 Flat Car With Tractor Shovel; 6519-25 Allis Chalmers Car; 6416-1 Boat Transport Car; 6130-1 Work Caboose - "Santa Fe"; 31-60 Curved Track - With Power Bus Connector (Bundle of 6 - 31) (2); 32-5 Straight Track - With Power Bus Connector (Loose) (2); 39-25 Operating Track Set; 1063-25 75-Watt Transformer; IS Instruction Sheet; 310-2 Set of (5) Billboards

Boxes & Packing: 61-230 Corr. Outfit Box; 61-171 Corr. Insert; 61-191 Corr. Insert; 61-231 Corr. Shipper for (2) (1-2)

LIONEL ENGINEERING SPECIFICATION

CATALOG NO.: 616-1 ITEM: DIESEL SWITCHER

1ST YEAR OF PRODUCTION: 1961

DESCRIPTION:

SAME AS (614-1) WITH 3 POSITION "E" UNIT, MAGNETRACTION (2 MAGNETS),
HEADLIGHT, OPERATING HORN, NON-OPERATING COUPLERS, FRONT & REAR -
NO AIR TANKS - NO CHANGE IN TRUCK DESIGN

FUNCTION:

TO BE USED IN 1961 OUTFIT WHICH CONSISTS OF THE FOLLOWING:

6828, 6812, 6822, 6560, 6130 (CARS)
31 TRACK (12 USED)
32 TRACK (2 USED)
39-25 OPERATING TRACK SET

MECHANICAL &
ELECTRICAL REQUIREMENTS:

USE INSPECTION DEPT. STANDARD

PACKAGING INFORMATION

ACCESSORIES REQUIRED: LUBRICANT, OIL, WIRES AND INSTRUCTION SHEET

OVERALL DIMENSIONS: SIMILAR TO (614-1)

WEIGHT: 1230 GRAMS (LESS BATTERY)

SPECIAL COMMENTS:

DESIGNER JJF
DATE 2-3-61   46536
DATE CHANGES BY C.N. REV. THE LIONEL CORPORATION, IRVINGTON, N. J.

The no. 9674 was Sears' Super O diesel-powered offering for 1961. It was headed by a no. 616X-1 Santa Fe Diesel Switcher. The no. 616-1 Lionel Engineering Specification shows, based on the contents listed, that this locomotive originally was created for catalog outfit no. 2570.

9674 (1961)	C6	C7	C8	Rarity
Complete Outfit	1,135	1,725	2,450	R7
Outfit Box no. 61-230	300	450	600	R7

Comments: The no. 9674 was the fifth of seven Sears outfits from 1961. This Retailer Promotional Type Ia did not appear in a Sears catalog.

The 9674 was Sears' Super O diesel-powered offering for 1961. Its brand-new no. 616X-1 Santa Fe Diesel Switcher was created for catalog outfit no. 2570 in that same year (see Lionel Engineering Specification) and subsequently used in this outfit. According to the Lionel Component Parts Index of the 616 as well as observations of examples of the 9674, the locomotive included in this outfit was the early version without an ornamental no. 600-19 Bell or a no. 600-25 Horn. Lionel added these features in late 1961, but for some reason removed them early the next year.

As described in the section on Outfit Peripherals, an "X" signified that a no. CTC-1 Lockon was left out because it wasn't necessary in a Super O outfit. The fragile Orange Picture no. 616-7 Folding Box is difficult to find in C8 condition because it did not withstand the weight of the engine.

The rolling stock in the 9674 was typical of that included in a Super O freight outfit. Notable items included the desirable nos. 6416-1 Boat Transport Car and 6827-1 Flat Car With Tractor Shovel. These and the other cars were equipped with operating AAR trucks and couplers. All the rolling stock came packaged in Orange Picture boxes.

In mid-1961, Lionel began placing the no. 31-7 Power Bus Connectors on the track. As a consequence, this outfit included a Type III version of the no. 39-25 Operating Track Set.

The no. 61-230 Orange RSC with Black Graphics outfit box was manufactured by the Mead Corporation and measured 16 x 15½ x 7⅛ inches.

Sears outfits and Super O outfits are always in demand. Therefore, it stands to reason that a Sears Super O promotional outfit will draw even more attention, which is the case with the 9674. Unfortunately for Lionel enthusiasts, this outfit is difficult to find complete in collectible condition.

CONVENTIONAL PACK
61-230 BOX

TOP LAYER

6827-1 F	6812-1 F	
	31-60 / 39-25	6416-1 F
	31-60 UNDER INSERT 61-191	

BOTTOM LAYER

| | 1063-25 | INSERT 61-171 | | |
| 616X-1 F | 6519-25 F | 6130-1 F | 6822-1 S | (2) 32-5 |

Description: Super "O" Promotional Outfit
Specification: Super "O" Steam Type Freight Outfit With Smoke & Whistle
Customer/No./Price: Sears, Roebuck and Co.; 9675; $59.98
Original Amount: 700
Factory Order Date: 4/25/1961
Date Issued: 6-13-61
Packaging: R.S.C. Outfit Packing (Units Boxed)

Contents: 736X-1 Steam Type Locomotive With Smoke; 736W-1 Whistle Tender; 6428-1 U. S. Mail Car; 3361X Operating Lumber Car (Less Bin); 160-2 Unloading Bin; 6530-1 Fire Prevention Training Car; 6736-1 Hopper Car - "Mackinac Mac"; 6357-1 Illuminated Caboose; 31-60 Curved Track - With Power Bus Connector (Bundle of 6 - 31) (2); 32-75 Straight Track - With Power Bus Connectors (Bundle of 4 - 32); 39-35 Remote Control Set (With Clips); 1063-25 75-Watt Transformer; 1123-20 Instruction Sheet; 310-2 Set of (5) Billboards

Boxes & Packing: 61-220 Corr. Outfit Box; 61-221 Corr. Shipper for (2) (1-2)

9675 (1961)	C6	C7	C8	Rarity
Complete Outfit	1,100	1,600	2,100	R8
Outfit Box no. 61-220	450	650	800	R8

Comments: The no. 9675 was the sixth of seven Sears outfits from 1961. This Retailer Promotional Type Ia did not appear in a Sears catalog. One outfit was observed with a Sears price tag of $59.98.

The no. 9675 was one of Sears' two Super O steam-powered offerings for 1961. This outfit consisted of carryover items. In fact, the no. 3361X-1 Operating Lumber Car (Less Bin) was first issued in 1955. This example of the 9675 included a Sears price tag (not shown) with a price of $59.98.

The 9675 as well as the carryover no. 9692 were the only two Super O steam-powered offerings for 1961. The 9675 was led by a no. 736X-1 Steam Type Locomotive With Smoke and Magne-Traction. Originally introduced in 1950, the 736 appeared in at least 17 outfits during the 1960s. When packaged in its no. 736-36 Corr. Box, this steamer included the nos. 675-33 Smoke Stack Cleaner, SP-1 Smoke Pellets Bottled, 682-16 Instruction Sheet and appropriate lubrication. The use of the "X" suffix indicated the absence of a no. CTC-1 Lockon, which was unnecessary in a Super O outfit.

All the rolling stock in this outfit was carried over from previous years. In fact, the no. 3361X-1 Operating Lumber Car (Less Bin) entered the line in 1955 and was making its final appearance in this and two other promotional outfits in 1961. The "X" indicated that the no. 160-2 Bin was not included in the component box but was, instead, placed loose in the outfit box.

The 3361X-1 was the only model in this outfit that was not equipped with early operating AAR trucks and couplers. It came, instead, with bar-end types. While this car was packaged in a Late Classic box, everything else came in Orange Perforated boxes.

The no. 6357-1 Illuminated Caboose was a nice addition to the 9675. It appeared in only seven outfits during the 1960s.

In mid-1961, Lionel began placing the no. 31-7 Power Bus

Connectors on the track. As a result, this outfit included a Type III version of the no. 39-35 Remote Control Set.

The no. 61-220 Orange RSC with Black Graphics outfit box was manufactured by Mead Bonded Containers and measured 16⅜ x 13⅛ x 6¼ inches.

Sears outfits and Super O outfits are always in demand. Therefore, it stands to reason that a Sears Super O promotional outfit will draw even more attention, which is the case with the 9675. Unfortunately for Lionel enthusiasts, this outfit is difficult to find complete in collectible condition.

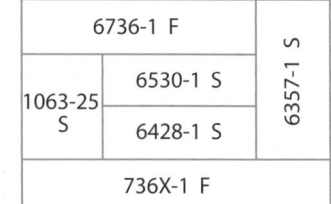

CONVENTIONAL PACK
61-220 BOX

TOP LAYER		
3361X S		32-75
31-60	39-35	
31-60		
736W-1 F		

160-2 BIN TOP OF 3361X

BOTTOM LAYER		
6736-1 F		6357-1 S
1063-25 S	6530-1 S	
	6428-1 S	
736X-1 F		

Description: 1960 Outfit

Specification: Super "O" Ga. Steam Type Freight Outfit with Smoke & Whistle

Customer/No.: Sears, Roebuck and Co.; 9692

Original Amount: 1,300

Factory Order Date: 3/17/1960

Date Issued: 9-7-60

Packaging: Conventional Outfit Packing, All units packed except 1063

Contents: 2037-1 Locomotive - with Magne-Traction, Smoke, Lockon & Lubricant; 243W-1 Whistle Tender; 6361-1 Log Car - Dark Green Frame; 6825-1 Flat Car - Red - with Trestle Bridge - Black; 6062-1 Gondola Car - Black - with (3) Cable Reels; 6821-1 Flat Car - with Cargo; 6017-1 Caboose - Brick Brown; 31 Curved Track (12); 32 Straight Track; 48 Insulated Straight Track; 39-25 Remote Control Set; 31-9 Power Blade Connectors (Env. of 16 - 31-7); 1063-25 75-Watt Transformer; 81-32 Wires (2); 926-60 Instruction Book; 310-2 Set of (5) Billboard Signs; AC Accessory Catalog

The no. 9692 was Sears' entry-level Super O steam-powered offering for 1960. It was configured as a Super O outfit, which makes it highly desirable among Sears outfit collectors. Handwritten in pencil on the box is "Replaces 9681". The no. 9681 was Sears' diesel-powered Super O offering from 1959.

Boxes & Packing: 60-437 Box; 60-438 Insert; 60-439 Shipper (1-3)

9692 (1960)	C6	C7	C8	Rarity
Complete Outfit	375	675	1,000	R6
Outfit Box no. 60-437	100	200	275	R6

Comments: The no. 9692 was the fifth of seven Sears outfits from 1960. This Retailer Promotional Type Ia outfit never appeared in a Sears catalog.

The 9692 was Sears' entry-level Super O steam-powered offering for 1960. It did not meet Sears' expectations, as the quantity was decreased from 2,500 to 1,700 on 5-24-60 and finally to 1,300 on 9-7-60.

Except for the fact that it was a Super O outfit, there was nothing extraordinary about the 9692. It was led by a no. 2037-1 Steam Type Locomotive With Smoke and Magne-Traction. This workhorse steamer spanned from 1953 through 1963 (except for 1956) and powered this particular Super O as well as 22 O27 outfits during the 1960s. When boxed as a "-1", it included the nos. 675-33 Smoke Stack Cleaner, SP-1 Smoke Pellets, 927-60 Tube of Oil, 2037-16 Instruction Sheet and a CTC-1 Lockon inside its 2037-13 Corr. Box.

The rolling stock in this outfit consisted of common freight items found in numerous 1960 outfits. All the cars were equipped with early operating AAR trucks and couplers and came packaged in Orange Perforated boxes.

The only brand-new items in the 9692 were the nos. 243W-1 Whistle Tender and 6361-1 Log Car. The latter's Orange

Perforated no. 6361-14 Folding Box is correct for this outfit and more difficult to find in collectible condition than its later Orange Picture box. Another car, the no. 6821-1 Flat Car - with Cargo, was making its final appearance in outfits during 1960.

A Type I or Type II no. 39-25 Remote Control Set was included in this outfit because the no. 31-7 Power Bus Connectors were provided in a separate no. 31-9 Envelope.

The no. 60-437 Tan RSC with Black Graphics outfit box was manufactured by United Container Co. and measured 14¾ x 12¼ x 6¾ inches. It has been observed with eight dots and an "E" as part of the box manufacturer's certificate.

Sears outfits are highly desirable among collectors. This one is a sleeper in that it includes O27 items but was packaged as a Super O outfit. Because the 9692 never appeared in a Sears catalog, its contents could not be confirmed until the documents used for this volume were examined.

CONVENTIONAL PACK
60-437 BOX
ALL UNITS PACKED
EXCEPT 1063

TOP LAYER		BOTTOM LAYER	
6825 F		2037 S	
6-31	6062	6361 F	6017 S
6-31		243W S	
6821 F		6062 S	1063

1-32
1-48 } TOP 6-31
39-25 INSIDE INSERT

Description: Super "O" Promotional Outfit
Specification: Super "O" Steam Type Freight Outfit W/Smoke & Whistle
Customer/No.: Sears, Roebuck and Co.; 9692
Original Amount: 34
Factory Order Date: 10/17/1961
Date Issued: 10-18-61
Packaging: R.S.C. Outfit Packing (Units Boxed)

Contents: 2037-1 Steam Type Locomotive With Smoke; 243W-1 Whistle Tender; 6361-1 Timber Transport Car; 6825-1 Flat Car - Red - With Trestle Bridge; 6062-1 Gondola Car - Black - With 3 Cable Reels; 6440-1 Flat Car W/2 Piggy Back Vans; 6017-1 Caboose; 31-60 Curved Track - With Power Bus Connector (Bundle of 6 - 31) (2); 32-5 Straight Track - With Power Bus Connector (Loose); 48-1 Insulated Straight Track; 39-25 Operating Track Set (With Power Bus Connector); 1063-25 75-Watt Transformer; 81-32 24" R.C. Wire (2); IS Instruction Sheet; 310-2 Set of (5) Billboards; D61-50 Accessory Catalog

Boxes & Packing: 61-200 Corr. Outfit Box; 61-201 Corr. Shipper for (4) (1-4)

9692 (1961)	C6	C7	C8	Rarity
Complete Outfit	2,100	2,800	3,300	R10
Outfit Box no. 61-200	1,800	2,250	2,500	R10

Comments: The no. 9692 was the last of the seven Sears outfits from 1961. A Retailer Promotional Type Ia, it was a repeat of outfit no. 9692 from 1960. (See the entry for the 9692 from 1960 for more information on that outfit.)

As with the 1960 version, the 9692 from 1961 did not appear in any catalog. The Factory Order for this outfit was dated late in the year, so it is unlikely that these were required to fulfill 1960 orders. Somehow in late 1961 Sears required an additional 34 of the 9692.

For the most part, the 9692 from 1961 duplicated the 9692

from 1960. All the rolling stock had operating AAR trucks and couplers and came in a combination of Orange Perforated and Orange Picture boxes.

However, the 1961 version of this outfit included a few changes that, from a collector's perspective, were significant. First, not all the items in the 1960 version were available for the later outfit. Specifically the no. 6821-1 Flat Car - with Cargo was updated to a no. 6440-1 Flat Car W/2 Piggy Back Vans. The latter, new for 1961, had its vans secured with two no. 4-6 Elastic Bands.

A second difference related to the track. In mid-1961, Lionel began to place the no. 31-7 Power Bus Connectors on the track. Therefore, it included a Type III version of no. 39-25 Operating Track Set (With Power Bus Connector) with the 9692 from 1961.

Third and most important, the 1961 version came in a no. 61-200 Orange RSC with Black Graphics outfit box. This box, which was manufactured by Mead Bonded Containers and measured 14½ x 12 x 7 inches, differed noticeably from the no. 60-437 Tan RSC with Black Graphics outfit box that Lionel used for the 9692 from 1960.

The small quantity produced and the Orange RSC with Black Graphics outfit box used make this a highly collectible variation. In fact, the 9692 from 1961 may be one of the toughest Sears outfits to find. It ranks seventh on the list of fewest outfits produced in the 1960s.

CONVENTIONAL PACK
61-200 BOX

TOP LAYER			BOTTOM LAYER	

TOP LAYER:
6062-1 S	39-25
243W-1 S	
6-31 1-32 / 1-48	6017-1 F
6-31	
6825-1 S	

BOTTOM LAYER:
6440-1 F	1063-25
6361-1 F	
2037-1 F	

Description: 1960 Outfit
Specification: Super "O" Ga. Diesel Freight Outfit with Horn
Customer/No./Price: Sears, Roebuck and Co.; 9693; $48.95
Original Amount: 1,600
Factory Order Date: 3/17/1960
Date Issued: 9-7-60
Packaging: Conventional Outfit Packing, All units packed except 1063

Contents: 218P-1 Alco Diesel Power Unit - "Santa Fe" - with Horn, Headlight, Magne-Traction, Non-Operating Coupler, Lockon and Lubricant; 218T-1 Alco Diesel Motorless Unit - "Santa Fe" with Non-Operating Couplers - without Headlight; 3444-1 Animated Gondola Car; 3512-1 Operating Fireman and Ladder Car; 3419-1 Operating Helicopter Car; 6816-1 Flat Car - with Tractor Dozer; 6017-1 Caboose - Brick Brown; 31 Curved Track (12); 32 Straight Track; 48 Insulated Straight Track; 39-25

Remote Control Set; 31-9 Power Blade Connectors (Env. of 16 - 31-7); 1063-25 75-Watt Transformer; 81-32 Wires (2); 926-60 Instruction Book; 310-2 Set of (5) Billboard Signs; AC Accessory Catalog

Boxes & Packing: 60-440 Box; 60-441 Shipper (1-3)

9693 (1960)	C6	C7	C8	Rarity
Complete Outfit	935	1,575	2,125	R6
Outfit Box no. 60-440	135	185	225	R6

Comments: The no. 9693 was the sixth of seven Sears outfits from 1960. This Retailer Promotional Type Ia outfit appeared in the 1960 Sears Christmas Catalog on page 445 for $48.95.

The 9693 was Sears' only Super O diesel-powered offering for 1960. It slightly exceeded Sears' expectations, as the quantity was increased from 1,500 to 2,000 on 5-24-60 and then reduced to 1,600 on 9-7-60.

All the items in this outfit actually were parts of Lionel's O27 line, which the firm combined with Super O track and peripherals

The no. 9693 was Sears' only Super O diesel-powered offering for 1960. It featured the last appearance of the no. 3444-1 Animated Gondola Car as well as the only promotional outfit appearance of the no. 6816-1 Flat Car - with Tractor Dozer in the 1960s.

to create what was an exciting offering for both Sears and Lionel. To begin, this outfit was led by a no. 218P-1 Santa Fe Alco Diesel Power Unit equipped with a three-position reversing unit, a headlight, two-axle Magne-Traction and an open pilot with a large ledge. The nos. CTC-1 Lockon and 218-11 Instruction Sheet were included inside its no. 218-10 Corrugated Box. This was also one of the few Alcos to include a horn. Until 1963, Lionel included a no. 601-13 "C" Battery with boxed Alcos that were equipped with a horn.

The 9693 represented the final appearance of the no. 3444-1 Animated Gondola Car, which was first cataloged in 1957. It was equipped with bar-end trucks and couplers with two pickup rollers, as was first noted in the *Authoritative Guide to Lionel's Postwar Operating Cars* (Project Roar Publishing). This outfit was also the only promotional outfit in the 1960s to include the fragile no. 6816-1 Flat Car - with Tractor Dozer.

Other than the 3444-1, all the rolling stock in the 9693 had early operating AAR trucks and couplers. Everything except that model was packaged in Orange Perforated boxes. The Animated Gondola Car came in a Late Classic box.

Being a Super O outfit, the 9693 included a no. 39-25 Remote Control Set. A Type I or Type II variation is possible.

The no. 60-440 Tan RSC with Black Graphics outfit box was manufactured by United Container Co. and measured 14½ x 12⅜ x 7 inches.

Sears outfits and Super O outfits are always in demand. Therefore, it stands to reason that a Sears Super O promotional outfit will draw even more attention, which is the case with the 9693. Unfortunately for Lionel enthusiasts, this outfit is difficult to find complete in collectible condition.

CONVENTIONAL PACK
60-440 BOX
ALL UNITS PACKED EXCEPT 1063

TOP LAYER			BOTTOM LAYER
6816 S	1063		218P F
6-31			218P F
6-31	6017 S		218T F
3444 S			3512 F
3419 S			3512 F

1-32 TOP 6-31
1-48 TOP 3444
39-25 TOP TRACK

Description: 1960 Outfit
Specification: Super "O" Ga. Steam Type Freight Outfit with Smoke & Whistle
Customer/No./Price: Sears, Roebuck and Co.; 9694; $59.95
Original Amount: 900
Factory Order Date: 3/17/1960
Date Issued: 9-7-60
Packaging: Conventional Outfit Packing

Contents: 746-1 Locomotive - with Smoke, Magne-Traction - with Lockon & Lubricant; 746W-1 Whistle Tender - "Norfolk and Western" - Striped; 3419-1 Operating Helicopter Car; 3330-1 Flat Car - with Operating Submarine Kit; 6544-1 Missile Firing Trail Car - Blue Car Body; 3540-1 Operating Radar Searchlight Car; 3535-1 Operating Security Car - Black Frame; 31 Curved Track (12); 32 Straight Track; 48 Insulated Straight Track; 39-25 Remote Control Set; 31-9 Power Blade Connectors (Env. of 16 - 31-7); 1063-25 75-Watt Transformer; 81-32 Wires (2); 926-60 Instruction Book; 310-2 Set of (5) Billboard Signs; AC Accessory Catalog

Boxes & Packing: 60-450 Box; 60-451 Shipper (1-3)

Alternate For Outfit Contents:
Note: Use inventory of 642 - 746LTS; Balance substitute 736LTS.

The no. 9694 was Sears' high-end Super O steam-powered offering for 1960. It never appeared in a Sears catalog and was likely sold over the counter in Sears stores. It marked the last appearance by the no. 746-1 Norfolk & Western Locomotive - with Smoke and Magne-Traction and included space and military rolling stock.

9694 (1960)	C6	C7	C8	Rarity
Complete Outfit With no. 746LTS	1,525	2,425	3,700	R8
Complete Outfit With no. 736LTS	1,050	2,050	2,875	R8
Outfit Box no. 60-450	300	550	700	R8

Comments: The no. 9694 was the last of the seven Sears outfits from 1960. This Retailer Promotional Type Ia outfit never appeared in a Sears catalog. An example has been observed with a Sears price tag with "OR 9494 $59.95" printed on it. This outfit was likely sold over the counter at Sears stores and not through a mail-order catalog. In any case, the 9694 did not meet expectations because the original Factory Order was reduced from 1,260 to 900 on 9-7-60.

The 9694 was Sears' high-end Super O steam-powered offering for 1960. It was used to deplete the remaining inventory of the no. 746-1 Norfolk & Western Locomotive - with Smoke and Magne-Traction. According to the Factory Order, a quantity of 642 of the no. 746LTS (first cataloged in 1957) was in inventory. Once this was depleted, Lionel planned to fill the rest of the order with no. 736LTS Locomotive and Tender Sets. The 746-1 was paired with a long-striped no. 746W-1 Tender that was equipped with bar-end trucks and couplers and packaged in a Late Classic box.

The space and military rolling stock was made up entirely of operating cars. Notable items included the no. 3330-1 Flat Car - with Operating Submarine Kit. It provided hours of fun as youngsters assembled the submarine, a step that saved time and effort for Lionel. The 3330's Orange Perforated box is difficult to find in C8 condition because the submarine kit would easily damage the box upon removal and re-insertion. Also, a no. 3330-

108 Submarine Kit Parts Packed is tough to find still sealed in its original plastic bag.

The no. 6544-1 Missile Firing Trail Car (new for 1960) featured two brake wheels attached to the plastic frame ends. Over time, the frame is easily cracked or broken off where the wheels attach.

All the rolling stock in this outfit was equipped with early operating AAR trucks and couplers. All cars, except the tender, came packaged in Orange Perforated boxes.

Being a Super O outfit, the 9694 included a no. 39-25 Remote Control Set. A Type I or Type II variation is possible.

The no. 60-450 Tan RSC with Black Graphics outfit box was manufactured by Star Corrugated Box Company, Inc. and measured 16¼ x 12¼ x 7½ inches. The box also had a star and "8-3V" printed on the bottom.

There have been reports of this outfit including a boxed no. 1063-1 75-Watt Transformer, but the Factory Order specifies a

CONVENTIONAL PACK
60-450 BOX

TOP LAYER			
746W-1 S			
6-31		6-31 S	6544-1 S
3330-1 S			
1-32	1-48		

BOTTOM LAYER		
746-1 F		
3535-1 F		1063-25
3540-1 S		

3419-1 F ON TOP 3540, 32 AND 48

1063-25 75-Watt Transformer. The "-25" suffix meant that it came unboxed.

Pricing is provided for outfits with the either the 746LTS (746-1 and 746W-1) or the 736LTS (nos. 736-1 Steam Type Locomotive With Smoke and 736W-1 Whistle Tender).

Sears outfits and Super O outfits are always in demand.

Therefore, it stands to reason that a Sears Super O promotional outfit will draw even more attention, which is the case with the 9694. To add to its appeal, this outfit represented the last appearance of the 746. Unfortunately for Lionel enthusiasts, the 9694 is difficult to find complete in collectible condition.

The no. 9730 was the only Lionel outfit to appear in the 1963 Sears Christmas Catalog. Shown on page 187, it retailed for $29.88. This colorful outfit was one of only four to include two no. 6464-series box cars during the 1960s. All the components of this outfit came unboxed.

Description: "O27" Promotional Outfit
Specification: "O27" "Santa Fe" "AA" Diesel Freight Outfit W/ Horn
Customer/No./Price: Sears, Roebuck and Co.; 9730; $29.88
Original Amount: 5,000
Factory Order Date: 6/18/1963
Date Issued: Rev 11-12-63
Date Req'd: W/O 7-22-63 Bal 9-23-63
Packaging: RSC Outfit Packing (Units not Boxed)

Contents: 218P-25 Alco Diesel Power Unit With Horn - "Santa Fe"; 218T-25 Motorless Unit; 6469-50 Miscellaneous Car; 6469-52 Cardboard Container Stamped; 6465-150 Tank Car; 6464-925 "New York Central" Box Car; 6464-750 "New Haven" Box Car; 6476-25 Hopper Car - Red; 6473-25 Rodeo Car; 6017-25 Caboose; 1013-8 Curved Track (Bundle of 8 - 1013); 1018-5 Straight Track (Bundle of 5 - 1018); 1073-25 60-Watt Transformer; 147-25 Horn

& Whistle Controller; 6139-25 Uncoupling Track Section; 1103-50 Envelope Packed; 310-2 Set of (5) Billboards; 1-62 Parts Order Form; 1-63 Warranty Card; 1123-40 Instruction Sheet; 218-11 Instruction Sheet; 11385-10 Instruction Sheet

Boxes & Packing: 63-354 Outfit Box; 61-181 Corr. Insert; 61-182 Corr. Insert (2); 62-248 Corr. Insert (3); 63-311 Corr. Insert; 63-315 Corr. Insert; 63-316 Corr. Insert (2); 61-201 Shipper for (4) (1-4); 63-354 Outfit Box (Use when 6315-60 car is used); 61-181 Corr. Insert; 61-182 Corr. Insert (2); 62-248 Corr. Insert (2); 63-315 Corr. Insert; 63-316 Corr. Insert (2); 61-201 Shipper for (4) (1-4)

Alternate For Outfit Contents:
Note: For 800 outfits use the following: 6315-60 in place of 6465-150, 6059-50 in place of 6017-25, 1063-100 in place of 1073-25, 9730-10 (Inst. Sheet) also (when using 1063-100), and do not use 147-25.

9000 Series

Sears purchased the no. D1250 "O27" Track Accessories & Train Set Display (Sears no. 9755D) to sell additional track and accessories for outfit nos. 9730 and 9733. Remarkably, at least one of the 208 produced has survived. The right-hand panel shows the 9730. Unfortunately, the left-hand panel showing the 9733 is missing (a second 9730 panel is shown in its place). A no. 1250 (Sears no. 9755) Special Assortment included the salable items for this display.

9730 (1963)	C6	C7	C8	Rarity
Complete Outfit	410	650	980	R4
Complete Outfit With All Substitutions	465	725	1,075	R4
Outfit Box no. 63-354	50	100	150	R4

Comments: After including three outfits in the Sears Christmas Catalog for 1962, Sears included only one Lionel outfit in its 1963 catalog. The no. 9730, a Retailer Promotional Type Ib outfit, appeared in the Sears Christmas Catalog for that year on page 183 for only $29.88

In addition to the 9730, Sears ordered outfit no. 9733, which was sold over the counter in Sears stores. These were intended to be the only two Sears outfits for 1963, and both were dated 6-18-63. This decision meant that Sears ordered at least 12,000 fewer outfits from Lionel in 1963 than it did in 1962. However, Sears conducted a "Special Purchase" late in 1963 that more than made up for this drop in quantity. (See the entry for Sears, Roebuck and Co. in the section on Lionel's Distribution and Customers.)

The 9730 was led by the nos. 218P-25 Santa Fe Alco Diesel Power Unit With Horn and 218T-25 Motorless Unit. The 218P-25 featured a three-position reversing unit, a headlight, two-axle Magne-Traction and an open pilot with a large ledge.

This outfit was one of only five from the 1960s to include more than one no. 6464-series box car. The orange New Haven box car that was heat-stamped "6464725" was designated no. 6464-735 when it came in a box and no. 6464-750 when unboxed. The "-750" version made its first appearance in this and two other promotional outfits from Sears.

Next came the unboxed version of the no. 6464-900 New York Central Box Car. This model, the no. 6464-925, first came unboxed in 1963. Like the New Haven box car, it featured a Type IV body.

The no. 6473-25 Rodeo Car featured a Type IIb body type (cadmium yellow plastic with red lettering). The Type IIb body included a partially filled slot caused by broken tooling, a point noted in the *Authoritative Guide to Lionel's Postwar Operating Cars* (Project Roar Publishing).

The two box cars, along with the nos. 6315-60 Chemical Tank Car and 6476-25 Hopper Car – Red, were equipped with operating AAR trucks and couplers. The remaining cars came with one operating and one non-operating AAR type. And the caboose (either a no. 6017-25 or a no. 6059-25) had one operating and one plain AAR truck and coupler.

When the nos. 147-25 Horn & Whistle Controller and 6139-25 Uncoupling Track Section were included in an outfit, five wires were required to connect these peripherals to the transformer. Lionel created the no. 1103-50 Envelope Packed for this purpose. It came with five wires, a no. CTC-1 Lockon and a no. 0190-25 Controller. A Type I no. 1103-50 version was included.

The substitutions affect the outfit price, as listed in the pricing table. Of note, the 9730 was one of the final six outfits to include a no. 1063-100 75-Watt Transformer, which was last used in 1961. (See outfit no. 9672 from 1961 for more information about this transformer.)

All the paperwork reflected the 90-day warranty policy that Lionel instituted in 1963. The no. 218-11 Instruction Sheet was dated 7-60, but it listed a 90-day warranty. The no. 9730-10 Instruction Sheet that replaced the no. 11385-10 in 800 outfits is very difficult to find. It was dated 11/63.

The no. 63-354 Tan RSC with Black Graphics outfit box was manufactured by St. Joe Kraft, St. Joe Paper Co. Container Division and measured 14¼ x 12 x 7⅛ inches. It included four lines of data as part of the box manufacturer's certificate.

With a quantity of 5,000 manufactured, the 9730 is fairly easy to obtain. As with all Sears outfits, it is in demand.

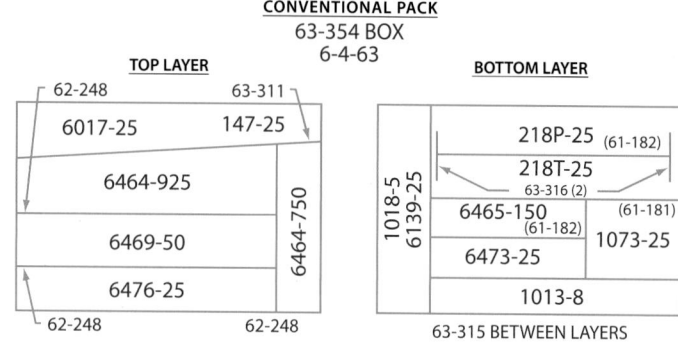

CONVENTIONAL PACK
63-354 BOX
6-4-63

Outfit no. 9730-500 was one of the 23 Sears "Special Purchase" outfits from late 1963. Although the 9730-500 shares the same base number as Sears outfit no. 9730, they have almost nothing in common. The 9730-500 was the only outfit to list a no. 6820-100 Operating Missile Helicopter Complete. Shown is a no. 6820-40 Non-Operating Missile Helicopter Complete, as the 6820-100 has yet to be verified. (See outfit no. 9658 regarding the 6820-100.)

Description: "O27" Promotional Outfit
Specification: "O27" Diesel Freight Outfit
Customer/No./Price: Sears, Roebuck and Co.; 49 9730; $29.98
Original Amount: 1,300
Factory Order Date: 11/27/1963
Date Issued: 11-27-63
Date Req'd: 11-27-63
Packaging: RSC (Units Loose)

Contents: 229P-1 "Minn. St. Louis" Alco Diesel Power Car with Horn; 229C-1 "B" Unit; 6820-25 Flat Car W/Oper. Missile Helicopter Car; 6820-100 Operating Missile Helicopter Complete; 6630-25 Missile Launching Car; 6408-25 Flat Car W/5 Pipes; 6511-15 Pipes (5); 6014-325 Frisco Box Car; 6142-25 Gondola Car (Less 2 Canisters); 6112-88 Canister (2); 6076-100 Hopper Car - Gray; 6059-50 Caboose; 262-1 Highway Crossing Gate; 903 Set of (2) Sheets Trading Cards; 40-1 Cable Reel W/Wire (Any Color); 1013-8 Curved Track (Bundle of 8 - 1013); 1018-30 Straight Track (Bundle of 3 - 1018); 1008-50 Uncoupling Unit; 1063-100 75-Watt Transformer; 1103-20 Envelope Packed; 310-62 Set of (3) Billboards; D63-50 Accessory Catalog; 1-62 Parts Order Form; 1-63 Warranty Card; 1648-10 Instruction Sheet; 6630-6 Instruction Sheet; 229-7 Instruction Sheet

Boxes & Packing: 62-316 Outfit Box; 63-311 Corr. Insert; 62-264 Corr. Insert; 62-278 Corr. Insert (2); COR-25 Corr. Insert; 62-319 Shipper for (3) (1-3)

Alternate For Outfit Contents:
Note: Substitute 251 - 6480-25 for 6820-25; Substitute 167 -

6440-50 for 6820-25; Note: #40 Cable Reel to be taken from set of 8 in finished goods Stockroom.

9730-500 (1963)	C6	C7	C8	Rarity
Complete Outfit	1,250	2,700	4,650	R9
Complete Outfit With no. 6480-25 Substitution	1,150	2,500	4,350	R9
Complete Outfit With no. 6440-50 Substitution	1,170	2,540	4,405	R9
Outfit Box no. 62-316	150	250	300	R7

Comments: In late 1963, Robert Wolfe, president of the Lionel Toy Corporation, worked out a deal - "Special Purchase" - with Sears, Roebuck and Co. to quickly bring additional revenue to Lionel by liquidating surplus toy inventory. This deal accounted for 23 of the 25 Super O and O27 Retailer Promotional outfits purchased by Sears in late 1963. None of these "Special Purchase" outfits has been observed in a Sears catalog. Internal Lionel and Sears documents revealed the link to Sears, along with the proper Sears number. (See the entry for Sears, Roebuck and Co. in the section on Lionel's Distribution and Customers.)

The no. 9730-500, a Type Ib outfit, was one of the many diesel-powered outfits purchased by Sears in 1963. Even though an example has been observed with a Sears price tag listing "49 9730" for $29.98", the 9730-500 has almost nothing in common with the no. 9730.

Instead, the 9730-500 began as an early version of outfit no. 19304. An early 19304 Factory Order had "Replaced by 9730-500" handwritten beneath the 19304 number. The final Factory Order for the 9730-500 was based on this outfit. The final 19304 was an entirely different outfit.

The 9730-500 was the last outfit to be led by a no. 229P-1 Minn. St. Louis Alco Diesel Power Car with Horn. The 229P-1 featured a two-position reversing unit, a headlight and one-axle Magne-Traction and came packaged in a no. 229-8 Corr. Box. It was trailed by a no. 229C-1 "B" Unit that was packaged in an Orange Picture box. The 229C-1 was also making its last outfit appearance.

In spite of Lionel's determination to liquidate its surplus inventory, not everything in this outfit was a carryover item. In fact most of the cars were brand-new except for the carryover nos. 6480-25 Exploding Target Car, 6630-25 Missile Launching Car and 6820-25 Flat Car W/Oper. Missile Helicopter Car. This fact supports the contention that Lionel had overestimated production for 1963.

The 6820-25 made its last appearance in this outfit. When it was replaced by a no. 6440-50 Flat Car W/2 Piggy Back Vans or a 6480-25, the outfit price was affected, as listed in the pricing table. The 9730-500 was the only outfit to list a no. 6820-100 Operating Missile Helicopter Complete as a separate item. (See outfit no. 9658 for more information about the 6820-100.)

The transition from Archbar to AAR trucks and couplers that began in 1962 continued into 1963. As part of this, Lionel sought to cut costs by introducing a non-operating AAR type. Therefore, starting in 1963, most cars equipped with AAR trucks and couplers had at least one non-operating type.

The 9730-500 presented a slightly different story. True, most of the cars in this outfit were equipped with AAR trucks and couplers. However, not every model had even one non-operating AAR type. Specifically, the 6480-25 and 6630-25 were equipped with non-operating Archbar trucks and couplers, and the 6820-25 had two operating AAR types. The no. 6076-100 Hopper Car - Gray usually had two non-operating AAR types although Archbar was also possible. The norm for the nos. 6014-325 Frisco Box Car, 6408-25 Flat Car with W/5 Pipes and 6142-25 Gondola Car was one operating and one non-operating AAR type. The no. 6059-50 Caboose was equipped with one operating and one plain AAR truck and coupler.

For the Sears "Special Purchase" outfits, Lionel took the opportunity to reduce its inventory of accessories and other peripherals. Thus, the 9730-500 included a no. 262-1 Highway Crossing Gate (new for 1962). This outfit also was one of the last six to include a no. 1063-100 75-Watt Transformer, which was last used in 1961. (See outfit no. 9672 from 1961 for more information about this transformer.)

The inclusion of the no. 903 Set of (2) Sheets Trading Cards makes the 9730-500 a very desirable outfit. The 903 included 24 two-sided Lionel trading cards printed on a sheet of perforated cardstock. On the front of each card was a Lionel locomotive, and on the back was historical information about its road name as well as a trivia quiz. Two 11 x 11 inch sets of 12 cards were connected by a "folding" strip. The entire sheet of 24 was folded in half along the strip and placed loose in the outfit box. The cards were perforated and are almost always found separated as individual cards, with the "folding" strip long gone. In fact, if it weren't for the complete sheets that came out of Madison Hardware over the years, it is likely that few of these items would be intact.

The no. 62-316 Tan RSC with Black Graphics outfit box was manufactured by the Mead Corporation and measured 17⅜ x 13¼ x 6⅞ inches. It included four lines of data as part of the box manufacturer's certificate.

An empty 9730-500 outfit box can be found, but complete outfits are extremely difficult to uncover. As with all Sears outfits, the 9730-500 is in high demand.

CONVENTIONAL PACK
62-316 BOX
11-26-63

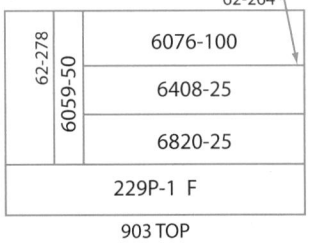
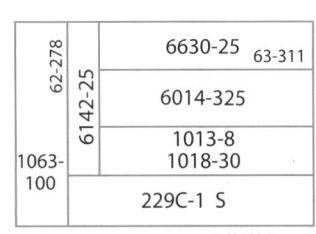

9733 1963

Description: "O27" Promotional Outfit
Specification: "O27" Steam Type Freight Outfit W/Smoke & Whistle
Customer/No.: Sears, Roebuck and Co.; 9733
Original Amount: 2,000
Factory Order Date: 6/18/1963
Date Issued: Rev 11-21-63
Date Req'd: W/O 7/29/63
Packaging: RSC Outfit Packing (Units not Boxed), Except Loco. & Tender

Contents: 2037-1 Steam Type Locomotive With Smoke; 234W-1 Whistle Tender; 6413-25 Mercury Capsule Transport Car; 6413-4 Capsules (2); 6413-10 Envelope Packed; 6407-25 Flat Car W/Sterling Missile; 6407-11 Sterling Missile; 6448-25 Exploding Target Car; 6463-25 Rocket Fuel Car; 6650-25 Missile Launching Flat Car; 6650-80 Missile; 6162-25 Gondola Car (Less 3 Canisters); 6112-88 Canister (3); 6017-25 Caboose; 1013-8 Curved Track (Bundle of 8 - 1013); 1018-5 Straight Track (Bundle of 5 - 1018); 6139-25 Uncoupling Track Section; 1063-25 75-Watt Transformer; 1103-30 Envelope Packed; 310-2 Set of (5) Billboards; 1-63 Warranty Card; 1-62 Parts Order Form; 1123-40 Instruction Sheet; 6448-14 Instruction Sheet; 6650-92 Instruction Sheet; 11351-10 Instruction Sheet

Boxes & Packing: 63-309 Outfit Box; 61-182 Corr. Insert; 62-223 Corr. Insert; 62-248 Corr. Insert; 63-311 Corr. Insert; 63-310 Shipper for (4) (1-4)

9733 (1963)	C6	C7	C8	Rarity
Complete Outfit	730	1,185	1,800	R6
Outfit Box no. 63-309	150	225	300	R6

The no. 9733 was sold to Sears for over-the-counter retail sales only. As such, it did not appear in the Sears Christmas Catalog. This space and military outfit was reminiscent of ones from 1962. Notable items included the no. 6407-25 Flat Car W/Sterling Missile with its no. 6407-11 Sterling Missile and the difficult-to-find no. 1103-30 Envelope Packed.

Comments: The nos. 9733 and 9730, both Retailer Promotional outfits, were intended to be the only two Sears outfits for 1963. Both were dated 6-18-63. This decision meant that Sears ordered at least 12,000 fewer outfits from Lionel in 1963 than it did in 1962. However, Sears conducted a "Special Purchase" late in 1963 that more than made up for this drop in quantity. (See the entry for Sears, Roebuck and Co. in the section on Lionel's Distribution and Customers.)

The 9733, a Type Ia outfit that Sears sold over the counter, was led by a no. 2037-1 Steam Type Locomotive With Smoke and Magne-Traction. This workhorse steamer spanned the years 1953 through 1963 (except for 1956) and powered one Super O and 22 O27 outfits during the 1960s. When boxed as a "-1", it included the nos. 675-33 Smoke Stack Cleaner, SP-1 Smoke Pellets, 927-90 Lubricating Oil Packed, 2037-16 Instruction Sheet and a CTC-1 Lockon inside its 2037-13 Corr. Box. The 2037-1 pulled a no. 234W-1 Whistle Tender that came in an Orange Picture box.

The space and military cars included in this outfit were the same as listed for outfit no. 19241-500 from 1963. The only difference was that the 9733 also included a no. 6162-25 Gondola Car (Less 3 Canisters).

Of note was the unboxed no. 6407-25 Flat Car W/Sterling Missile (new for 1963). It was included in 11 different outfits, with a total of 13,124 cars produced. This highly collectible item was also available for separate sale as a no. 6407-1. The flat car was a common red no. 6511-series model with "Lionel" stamped on each side. It featured a brake wheel plus one operating and one non-operating AAR truck and coupler. The same flat car was used with the no. 6408-25 Flat Car W/5 Pipes.

The flat car might be common, but the no. 6407-11 Sterling Missile was not. This load, manufactured by Sterling Plastics, was frequently separated from its flat car because it lacked Lionel markings. An authentic original would have "Sterling Plastics" molded into the capsule bottom and rocket base.

The remaining cars in this outfit were carryover items being

depleted in promotional outfits, a common occurrence in 1963. The no. 6448-25 Exploding Target Car had "non-slotted" sides and nubs on the roof door guide to help hold on the sides. The unboxed no. 6650-25 Missile Launching Flat Car was making its final outfit appearances in 1963.

All the paperwork reflected the 90-day warranty policy that Lionel instituted in 1963. Many of these instruction sheet versions are the most difficult ones to find, especially the 90-day version of the no. 6448-14 Instruction Sheet, which was still dated 3-61.

Lionel used a no. 1103-30 Envelope Packed in this outfit and two others. It included four wires and a no. 0190-25 Controller. This difficult-to-find envelope was one of the first to list "The Lionel Toy Corporation" instead of "The Lionel Corporation" as the company name.

The transition from Archbar to AAR trucks and couplers that began in 1962 continued into 1963. As part of this, Lionel sought to cut costs by introducing a non-operating AAR type. Therefore, starting in 1963, most cars equipped with AAR trucks and couplers had at least one non-operating type.

The 9733 presented a slightly different story. True, most of the cars in this outfit were equipped with AAR trucks and couplers. However, not every model had even one non-operating AAR type. Specifically, the 234W-1 was equipped with one non-operating

CONVENTIONAL PACK
63-309 BOX
6-6-63

TOP LAYER		
6448-25		62-248
6407-25		
6407-11		6413-25 6413-10
6162-25		
1018-5 1013-8 6139-25		

63-311

BOTTOM LAYER		
6650-25	6413-4 (2) 6112-88	
2037-1 S		
6463-25		1063-25
6017-25	6112-88 (2)	
234W-1 S		

62-223 BETWEEN LAYERS   61-182

395

and one plain Archbar truck and coupler. Also, the nos. 6413-25 Mercury Capsule Transport Car, 6448-25 and 6650-25 had two operating AAR types. The norm for the nos. 6162-25, 6407-25 and 6463-25 Rocket Fuel Car was one operating and one non-operating AAR type. Finally, the no. 6017-25 Caboose came with one operating and one plain AAR truck and coupler.

The no. 63-309 Tan RSC with Black Graphics outfit box was manufactured by the Mead Corporation and measured 13¼ x 12½ x 6¾ inches. It included four lines of data as part of the box manufacturer's certificate.

Even with 2,000 manufactured, the 9733 seldom appears. As with all Sears outfits, this one is in demand.

9745
1960

Variation 1 of the no. 9745 included mostly unboxed trains (not shown are the boxes for the nos. 243-1 Locomotive - with Smoke and Headlight and 3376-1 Operating Giraffe Car). The 9745 and promotional outfit no. X-572NA were the last two outfits to come with a no. 175-1 Rocket Launcher. Note the rare Channel Master billboard that was exclusive to this and outfit no. X-573NA. Variation 1 came in a no. 60-597 Box.

Description: 1960 Outfit
Specification: "O27" Ga. Steam Type Freight Outfit with Smoke
Customer: Channel Master
Original Amount: 5,000
Factory Order Date: 9/20/1960
Date Issued: September 20, 1960
Packaging: Conventional Outfit Packing

9745 (1960)	C6	C7	C8	Rarity
Variation 1 - Complete Outfit With no. 60-597 Box	700	1,350	1,800	R8
Outfit Box no. 60-597	125	175	200	R4
Variation 2 - Complete Outfit With no. 860L Box	800	1,550	2,100	R8
Outfit Box no. 860L	250	350	475	R8

Contents: 243-1 Locomotive - with Smoke and Headlight - with (2) Position Reversing Unit, Lockon and Lubricant - without Magne-Traction; 1130T-25 Tender; 3376-1 Operating Giraffe Car; 6162-25 Gondola Car - Blue - with (3) White Canisters; 6476-25 Hopper Car - Red; 6812-25 Track Maintenance Flat Car - Red Frame - Structure in Gray and Black; 6057-25 Caboose - Red; 1013 Curved Track (12); 1018 Straight Track (7); 1008-50 Uncoupling Unit - with (1) 1018 Straight Track; 1015-60 45-Watt Transformer; 1020-1 90° Crossover; 175-1 Rocket Launcher; 310-3 Billboard Frame; 81-32 Wires (2); 6812-40 Envelope - (2 - 81-32 Wires and 1 - 3562-62 Figure); 1627-2 Instruction Sheet; 2165 Layout Instruction Sheet; 310-2 Set of (5) Billboard Signs; AC Accessory Catalog

Boxes & Packing: 60-597 Box; 60-598 Insert; 60-492 Insert; 60-380 Insert; 59-377 Insert; 60-599 Shipper (1-2); 860L Box

Comments: The Channel Master no. 9475 was likely a follow-up order to that firm's no. X-573NA. Channel Master manufactured outdoor television antennas, accessories and black-and-white and color TV tubes. In 1960 it ran promotion no. 9745 in which it offered a Lionel outfit free with a "Main Line" radio package. (See the section on Lionel's Distribution and Customers for an overview of this promotion.)

Information in the Factory Orders indicates that Lionel received orders from Channel Master for 4,500 of the X-573NA. However, this promotion was so successful that Lionel needed additional outfits.

Channel Master must have ordered another 5,000 outfits, which Lionel filled by creating the 9745, a Manufacturer Promotional Type IIIc. This outfit came with the nos. 175-1 Rocket Launcher, 6057-25 Caboose and 6476-25 Hopper Car - Red instead of the nos. 128-1 Animated Newsstand, 6017-1 Brick Brown Caboose and 3512-1 Operating Fireman and Ladder Car listed on the Factory Order for the X-573NA. Combined with the five variations of the X-573NA, a total of seven Channel Master outfits can be documented.

Variation 2 of the no. 9745 had the same components as Variation 1 except that they were individually boxed. This outfit also included the rare Channel Master billboard, which appeared only in this and outfit no. X-573NA. Variation 2 came in a no. 860L Box.

Shown is the master shipper no. 60-599 (right) for Variation 1 of no. 9745. This shipper was sent to "Hargis Austin Inc. in Austin Texas". The 9745 was shipped two at a time.

The 9745 was headed by a no. 243-1 Locomotive - with Smoke and Headlight (new for 1960). Other features of this steam engine included a metal motor and a two-position reverse unit. The 243-1 was nearly identical to the no. 244-1 Locomotive, except that the former included an extra weight as part of its mechanism.

Notable among the cars was the no. 6812-25 Track Maintenance Car. It could have a gray platform and a black base or a black platform and a gray base. The no. 3376-1 Operating Giraffe Car was the only new piece of rolling stock.

These cars, like all the rolling stock in this outfit, were equipped with early operating AAR trucks and couplers. All boxed rolling stock came packaged in Orange Perforated boxes.

A no. 2165 Layout Instruction Sheet appeared in only the X-573NA and 9745. It outlined the extended figure-eight layout and was dated 8-60.

The 9745, X-573NA and the no. 19332 were the only outfits from the 1960s to include a unique billboard. In this case, a Channel Master billboard was packed in each outfit, along with a single no. 310-3 Billboard Frame. This rare billboard is frequently separated from the outfit and lost. Finding one in collectible condition is a challenge.

The 9745 and promotional outfit no. X-572NA marked the final appearance of the 175-1 Rocket Launcher. A space and military accessory seemed out of place in this freight outfit.

Two packing variations of this outfit have been observed.

Variation 1 included the items as listed on the Factory Order. The no. 60-597 Tan RSC with Black Graphics outfit box was manufactured by St. Joe Paper Co. - Container Div. and measured 19¼ x 12 x 10½ inches. It had "9 10 11 12" printed as part of the box manufacturer's certificate.

Variation 2 also included the items on the Factory Order except they all were individually boxed. The Tan RSC with Black Graphics outfit box was manufactured by Star Corrugated Box Company, Inc. and measured 16 x 15 x 10⅜ inches. It had "860L" printed on the bottom.

Of the two outfits, Variation 2 is more difficult to find. It likely represented the end of production of Channel Master outfits. Variation 1 frequently appears on the market, but seldom does it have a Channel Master billboard.

CONVENTIONAL PACK
60-597 BOX

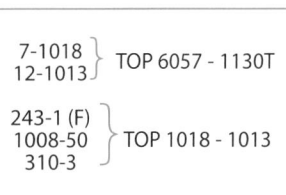

TOP LAYER

7-1018
12-1013 } TOP 6057 - 1130T

243-1 (F)
1008-50
310-3 } TOP 1018 - 1013

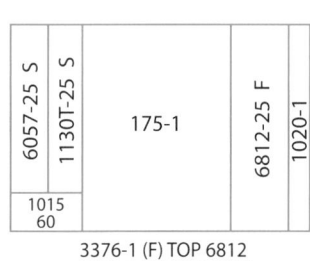

BOTTOM LAYER

6057-25 S	1130T-25 S		175-1		6812-25 F	1020-1
1015 60						

3376-1 (F) TOP 6812
6476-25 (F) TOP 3376
6162-25 (F) TOP 6476

9000 Series

397

The no. 10613SF represented what Lionel had become by 1969. It was a bland outfit assembled from leftover inventory. From a collector's viewpoint, the 10613SF is somewhat desirable because it featured the unstamped no. 1061-75 Steam Type Locomotive and was the last steam-powered promotional outfit produced by Lionel in the postwar era.

Description: "O27" Promotional Outfit
Specification: "O27" Steam Type Freight Outfit
Packaging: R.S.C. Outfit Packing

Contents: 1061-75 Steam Type Locomotive; 1062T-25 Tender; 6402-50 Flat Car W/2 Cable Reels; 40-11 Cable Reels (2); 6176-25 Hopper Car; 6167-100 Caboose; 1013 Curved Track (8); 1018 Straight Track (2); 1025-25 45-Watt Transformer; 1103-20 Envelope Packed; Form 3063 Parts Order Form; 1-165 Warranty Card; 1968-1969 Service Station List; 11570-10 Instruction Sheet

Boxes & Packing: 65-410 Outfit Box; 62-254 Insert

10613SF (1969)	C6	C7	C8	Rarity
Complete Outfit	250	425	600	R8
Outfit Box no. 65-410	100	175	250	R8

Comments: In 1969, Lionel issued two General Release Promotional Type IIb outfits: nos. 10613SF and 10653SF. The 10613SF was steam-powered, and the 10653SF was diesel-powered. Neither outfit has thus far been linked to an end retailer. The meaning of the suffix "SF" is unknown.

These outfits were created as part of Lionel's effort to generate additional train revenue before licensing the train division to General Mills. As such, these outfits were hastily configured primarily with what was available in inventory.

The 10613SF was led by a no. 1061-75 Steam Type Locomotive. This low-end Scout steamer featured a 2-4-2 wheel arrangement and a rubber tire as a traction aid. It went forward only and lacked a headlight and lens. Other than its wheel arrangement, the 1061-75 was identical to the no. 1061-50 Steam Type Loco W/Tire. The version included in this outfit featured an unstamped body. Lionel apparently was assembling whatever it had lying around and didn't take the time or have the capability to heat-stamp "1061" on these locomotives. This version does command a premium, especially among Scout collectors.

The rolling stock in this outfit was all low-end. The unmarked gray hopper car was designated the no. 6176-25 Hopper Car because it came with an operating truck and coupler. Some outfits included two red no. 6112-5 Canisters.

The rolling stock in the 10613SF followed the normal truck and coupler progression for 1969, with all the cars having late AAR types. All but one were equipped with one operating and one non-operating truck and coupler. The no. 1062T-25 Tender had one non-operating and one plain type.

The no. 65-410 Tan RSC with Black Graphics outfit box was manufactured by Eastern Corrugated Container Corp. and measured 11½ x 10 x 6¼ inches. These boxes were made of a thicker corrugated material (rated at 90 pounds rather than the normal 65 pounds gross weight) that allowed each outfit to be shipped in its outfit box. It featured four lines of data as part of the box manufacturer's certificate.

Finding either of the two promotional outfits from 1969 complete with their original components is somewhat difficult because they do not appear too often.

CONVENTIONAL PACK
65-410 BOX

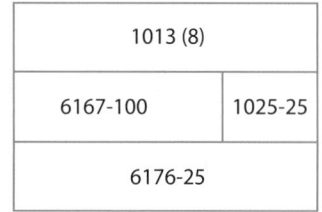

TOP LAYER — 40-11 (2), 6402-50; 1061-75; 1062T-25; 1018 (2)

BOTTOM LAYER — 1013 (8); 6167-100; 1025-25; 6176-25

The no. 10653SF was a slight step up from the no. 10613SF that Lionel also released in 1969. Two items of note were the no. 1065-25 Union Pacific Alco Diesel Power Unit, which last appeared in 1963, and the unboxed orange no. 6014-75 Frisco Box Car, which was reissued in 1969. The 10653SF attracts interest because it was the last diesel-powered promotional outfit produced by Lionel in the postwar era.

Description: "O27" Promotional Outfit
Specification: "O27" Diesel Freight Outfit
Packaging: R.S.C. Outfit Packing

Contents: 1065-25 Alco Diesel Power Unit - "Union Pacific"; 6142-50 Gondola Car; 6112-88 Canister (2); 6402-50 Flat Car W/2 Cable Reels; 40-11 Cable Reels (2); 6014-75 Frisco Box Car; 6167-100 Caboose; 1013 Curved Track (8); 1018 Straight Track (2); 1025-25 45-Watt Transformer; 1103-20 Envelope Packed; 19152-10 Instruction Sheet

Boxes & Packing: 65-410 Outfit Box; 10653SF-White RSC Outfit Box

10653SF (1969)	C6	C7	C8	Rarity
Complete Outfit With Either Outfit Box	215	365	515	R8
Outfit Box no. 65-410	100	175	250	R8
Outfit Box no. 10653SF-White RSC	100	175	250	R8

Comments: In 1969, Lionel issued two General Release Promotional Type IIb outfits: nos. 10613SF and 10653SF. The 10613SF was steam-powered, and the 10653SF was diesel-powered. Neither outfit has thus far been linked to an end retailer. The meaning of the suffix "SF" is unknown.

These outfits were created as part of Lionel's effort to generate additional train revenue before licensing the train division to General Mills. As such, these outfits were hastily configured primarily with what was available in inventory.

The 10653SF was led by a no. 1065-25 Union Pacific Alco Diesel Power Unit, a low-end locomotive that moved forward only and whose sole feature of note was a headlight. This Alco had not

appeared since 1963, but Lionel must have found enough in its inventory to complete the 10653SF.

The rolling stock in this outfit was all low-end. The most notable item was an orange no. 6014-75 Frisco Box Car with blue heat-stamped lettering. The "-75" meant that it came unboxed. It was last cataloged in 1957 and, according to its Production Control File, was reinstated on 1-9-69.

The norm for the gondola included in the 10653SF was an unmarked green no. 6142-50 Gondola Car, though other models were possible. Green no. 40-11 Cable Reels have been observed.

The rolling stock in the 10653SF followed the normal truck and coupler progression for 1969, with all the cars having late AAR types. Each was equipped with one operating and one non-operating truck and coupler.

The no. 19152-10 Instruction Sheet was dated 5/66.

Two different outfit boxes were used for the 10653SF. The first, a no. 65-410 Tan RSC with Black Graphics outfit box, was manufactured by Eastern Corrugated Container Corp. and measured 11½ x 10 x 6¼ inches. These boxes were made of a thicker corrugated material (rated at 90 pounds rather than the normal 65 pounds gross weight) that allowed each outfit to be shipped in its outfit box.

Lionel used the 65-410 for many RSC outfits from 1967 through 1969. It apparently exhausted the inventory with the 10653SF and so substituted a White RSC with Orange Graphics outfit box. Both outfit boxes appear as often, and there is no price premium for either of them.

Finding either of the two promotional outfits from 1969 complete with their original components is somewhat difficult because they do not appear too often.

General Release Promotional advance catalog outfit no. 11001 was Lionel's steam-powered advance catalog offering for 1962. It was a follow-up to the advance catalog no. 1123 from 1961. The 11001 introduced the no. 6402-25 Flat Car, which was Tuscan Red and equipped with non-operating Archbar trucks and couplers.

Display outfit box no. 62-200 was a generic box that Lionel stamped with "No. 11001".

11001 (1962)	C6	C7	C8	Rarity
Complete Outfit With no. 62-200 Box	100	200	300	R1
Outfit Box no. 62-200	50	75	100	R1
Complete Outfit With Any Overstickered Box	175	325	475	R7
Overstickered Outfit Box nos. 61-110, 61-384, 61-389 Or 61-432	125	200	275	R7
Any Outfit With no. 61-104, Add The Following	600	800	1,000	R10

Description: Non-Catalog Steam Type Freight Outfit - "O27"
Specification: "O27" Steam Type Freight Outfit
Customer/No.: Lionel Advance Catalog; 11001; $9.98 or $10.98
Original Amount: 55,000
Factory Order Date: 2/13/1962
Date Issued: Revised #1 3-7-62
Packaging: Display Outfit Packing (Units not Boxed)

Contents: 1060-25 Steam Type Locomotive; 1060T-25 Tender; 6402-25 Flat Car (Less 2 Cable Reels); 40-11 Cable Reels (2); 6042-25 Gondola Car (Less 2 Canisters); 6112-5 Canister - Red (2); 6067-25 Caboose; 1013-8 Curved Track (Bundle of 8 - 1013); 1018-10 Straight Track (Loose) (2); 1026-25 25-Watt Transformer; 1103-20 Envelope Packed; 310-2 Set of (5) Billboards; D62-50 Accessory Catalog; 1123-10 Instruction Sheet; 1123-40 Instruction Sheet

Boxes & Packing: 61-110 Outfit Box (Inv. 631) W/Stickers; 61-384 Outfit Box (Inv. 250) W/Stickers; 61-389 Outfit Box (Inv. 397) W/Stickers; 61-432 Outfit Box; 62-200 Display Outfit Box - Unprinted; 61-101 Corr. Insert; 61-102 Corr. Insert (2); 61-103 Corr. Shipper for 6 (1/6); 61-104 Env. Packed (1/6)

Alternate For Outfit Contents:
Note: Use inventory of 1103-12 Envelope first.

Comments: In 1962, Lionel issued two no. 11000-series General Release Promotional Type IIb advance catalog outfits: nos. 11001 and 11011.

An illustration of the 11001 appeared on the inside cover of the Lionel advance catalog for 1962. The accompanying description stated that the 11001 and 11011 were "Styled and Priced to Meet the Demands of the Mass Toy Market". These advance catalog outfits were part of Lionel's promotional outfit strategy of offering retailers something different even if they couldn't commit to the quantity necessary for a unique promotional outfit.

Lionel sold the 11001 to jobbers and national retail chains for $7.50 each and other retail chains and department stores for $7.98 each. The suggested selling price was $9.98 for national retail chains and $10.98 for dealers.

The 11001 was a basic starter outfit and a follow-up to the advance catalog no. 1123 from 1961. Both were led by a no. 1060-25 Steam Type Locomotive, which was used in many promotional outfits. This was Lionel's low-end, forward-only steam offering in 1962, and its only feature of note was a headlight.

All the rolling stock in the 11001 represented Lionel's low-end offerings, with many items found only in promotional outfits. The cars were equipped with non-operating Archbar trucks and couplers. However, the nos. 1060T-25 Tender and 6067-25 Caboose have been observed with one non-operating Archbar and one plain AAR truck and coupler.

The 11001 and its RSC counterpart, the no. 11005, introduced the no. 6402-25 Flat Car (Less 2 Cable Reels). This model is most often found in 1962 as a Tuscan Red flat car equipped with two non-operating Archbar trucks and couplers. Some examples of the 6402-25 were molded in gray plastic. The no. 40-11 Cable Reels were listed separately.

Lionel used the 11001 and many other early 1962 outfits to deplete its inventory of pre-printed White 4-6-4 Steamer and F3 Hinged Display with Red/Orange and Blue Graphics Type A outfit boxes. This outfit used four overstickered versions as well as the no. 62-200 Display Outfit Box - Unprinted. The 62-200, the most common of these outfit boxes, was manufactured by United Container Co. and measured 21⅝ x 11½ x 3¼ inches.

The remaining four outfit box variations were overstickered with an "11001" label. They were produced in small quantities and so bring a premium on today's market:

- The no. 61-110 was an overstickered no. 1124 and measured 21½ x 11½ x 3¼ inches.
- The no. 61-384 was an overstickered no. X-635.
- The no. 61-389 was an overstickered no. X-615 that was manufactured by Express Container, Corp. and measured 22¾ x 11½ x 3⅛ inches.
- The no. 61-432 was an overstickered no. X-699 that was manufactured by Express Container, Corp. and measured 22¾ x 11⅜ x 3⅛ inches.

With every shipment of six outfits Lionel packaged a no. 61-104 Envelope Packed. This envelope included a no. 61-107 Acetate Dust Cover in a no. 61-108 Envelope. The printing on the envelope stated that the "clear plastic shield keeps merchandise dust free and safe from pilferage." These covers likely were used to display the outfits in stores.

DISPLAY PACK
62-200 BOX UNPRINTED
61-110, 61-389, 61-384 OR
61-432 BOX
5 STICKERS PER BOX
2-29-62

61-102 INSERT →

1060-25	1060T-25	1026-25
6112-5 (2) 6042-25	1103-20 ENV.	40-11 (2) 6402-25
1018-10 (2) 1013-8	INSERT 61-102	6067-25

61-101 INSERT

This outfit was also used to deplete the no. 1103-12 Envelope Packed. It was being replaced by the no. 1103-20 Envelope Packed in 1962. This substitution does not affect the price.

With a quantity of 55,000 outfits produced, the 11001 is very common. What is not common are the overstickered box versions. Striving to collect all four makes this a more interesting outfit.

In 1963, United Trading Stamp purchased this Retailer Promotional Type Ib outfit. The RSC packed no. 11001 almost duplicated RSC packed no. 11005 from 1962. The only difference was that the paperwork in this outfit had been updated for 1963.

1013-8 Curved Track (Bundle of 8 - 1013); 1018-10 Straight Track (Loose) (2); 1026-25 25-Watt Transformer; 1103-20 Envelope Packed; 310-2 Set of (5) Billboards; D63-50 Accessory Catalog; 1-62 Parts Order Form; 1-63 Warranty Card; 1123-10 Instruction Sheet; 1123-40 Instruction Sheet; Form 2870 Printed Sheet

Description: "O27" Promotional Outfit
Specification: "O27" Steam Type Freight Outfit
Customer: United Trading Stamp
Original Amount: 1,000
Factory Order Date: 5/15/1963
Date Issued: 5-24-63
Packaging: RSC Outfit Packing #5 (Units not Boxed)

Contents: 1060-25 Steam Type Locomotive; 1060T-25 Tender; 6402-25 Flat Car W/2 Cable Reels; 40-11 Cable Reels (2); 6042-25 Gondola Car - Blue; 6112-5 Canister (2); 6067-25 Caboose;

Boxes & Packing: 61-170 Outfit Box; 61-171 Corr. Insert; 61-172 Corr. Insert; 62-202 Corr. Insert (Inv. 525 pcs.) Bal use 61-173; 61-174 Shipper for (6) (1-6)

11001 (1963)	C6	C7	C8	Rarity
Complete Outfit	175	325	485	R7
Outfit Box no. 61-170	90	175	250	R7

Comments: United Trading Stamp was a small stamp redemption company that purchased the Retailer Promotional Type Ib outfit no. 11001 in 1963.

Except for the paperwork, this outfit was identical to the no. 11005 from 1962. (See the entry for the 11005 from 1962 for information about the outfit contents.)

The paperwork for the 11001 from 1963 was updated to 1963 standards. Included were a no. D63-50 Accessory Catalog for 1963 as well as a 1-62 Parts Order Form, 1-63 Warranty Card and Form 2870. (See the section on Outfit Peripherals for more information on the paperwork included in 1963.)

The no. 61-170 Tan RSC with Black Graphics outfit box was manufactured by St. Joe Kraft, St. Joe Paper Co. Container Division and measured 11½ x 10¼ x 6¼ inches.

The 11005 was the RSC version of 11001 from 1962, whereas the 11001 from 1963 was a separate "'O27' Promotional Outfit" for United Trading Stamp. Even so, the 11001 from 1963 is often mistakenly identified as the RSC outfit box version of display-packed 11001 from 1962.

With only 1,000 examples made, the 11001 from 1963 is more difficult to find than either the 11005 or the display-packed 11001 from 1962.

CONVENTIONAL PACK
61-170 BOX
4-29-63

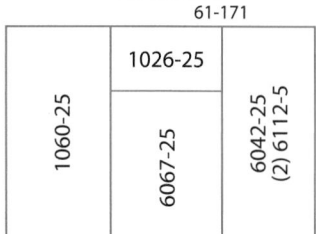

TOP LAYER

1018-10 (2) 1013-8	
1060T-25	1103-20
6402-25 40-11 (2)	↑ 62-202

BOTTOM LAYER
61-171

| 1060-25 | 1026-25 | 6042-25 (2) 6112-5 |
| | 6067-25 | |

61-172 BETWEEN LAYERS

General Release Promotional outfit no. 11005 was the RSC version of advance catalog outfit no. 11001 from 1962. It was produced in much lower quantities than the display version and so does not appear as often.

Description: Non-Catalog Steam Type Outfit - "O27"
Specification: "O27" Steam Type Freight Outfit
Customer/No.: Lionel Advance Catalog; 11005
Original Amount: 5,000
Factory Order Date: 1/29/1962
Date Issued: 3-12-62
Packaging: R.S.C. Outfit Packing (Units not Boxed)

Contents: 1060-25 Steam Type Locomotive; 1060T-25 Tender; 6402-25 Flat Car (Less 2 Cable Reels); 40-11 Cable Reels (2); 6042-25 Gondola Car (Less 2 Canisters); 6112-5 Canister - Red (2); 6067-25 Caboose; 1013-8 Curved Track (Bundle of 8 - 1013); 1018-10 Straight Track (Loose) (2); 1026-25 25-Watt Transformer; 1103-20 Envelope Packed; 310-2 Set of (5) Billboards; D62-50 Accessory Catalog; 1123-10 Instruction Sheet; 1123-40 Instruction Sheet

Boxes & Packing: 61-170 Corr. Outfit Box; 61-171 Corr. Insert; 61-172 Corr. Insert; 62-202 Corr. Insert; 61-174 Shipper for (6) (1-6)

Alternate For Outfit Contents:
Note: Use inventory of 1103-12 Envelope first.

11005 (1962)	C6	C7	C8	Rarity
Complete Outfit	115	200	325	R4
Outfit Box no. 61-170	50	75	125	R4

Comments: This General Release Promotional Type IIb outfit was the RSC version of display-packed no. 11001 from 1962. The only differences related to the packaging, the quantity produced and the color of the no. 6402-25 Flat Car (Less 2 Cable Reels).

The use of "5" as the last digit of the outfit number indicated "R.S.C - Kraft (tan) - Units Loose". (See the section on Outfit Numbering for more information on Lionel's five-digit numbering system.)

The 11005 was led by a no. 1060-25 Steam Type Locomotive, which was found in many promotional outfits. This was Lionel's low-end, forward-only steam offering in 1962, and its only feature of note was a headlight.

All the rolling stock in the 11005 represented Lionel's low-end offerings, with many items found only in promotional outfits. The cars were equipped with non-operating Archbar trucks and couplers. However, the nos. 1060T-25 Tender and 6067-25 Caboose have been observed with one non-operating Archbar and one plain AAR truck and coupler.

The 11005 and its display-packed counterpart, the no. 11001, introduced the 6402-25 Flat Car (Less 2 Cable Reels). It is most often found in the 11005 as a gray flat car with two non-operating Archbar trucks and couplers. These cars were also molded in Tuscan Red plastic. The no. 40-11 Cable Reels were listed separately.

The no. 61-170 Tan RSC with Black Graphics outfit box was manufactured by St. Joe Kraft, St. Joe Paper Co. Container Division and measured 11½ x 10¼ x 6¼ inches.

A quantity of 5,000 of the 11005 was made as compared to

55,000 of the 11001. That fact explains why the RSC version is harder to find than the display version.

CONVENTIONAL PACK
61-170 BOX
3-7-62

TOP LAYER		
1013-8 (2) 1018-10		
1103-20 ENV.	1060T-25	62-202 ← INSERT
(2) 6112-5 6042-25		

BOTTOM LAYER		
	— 61-171 INSERT	
1060-25	1026-25	(2) 40-11 6402-25
	6067-25	

61-172 INSERT BETWEEN LAYERS

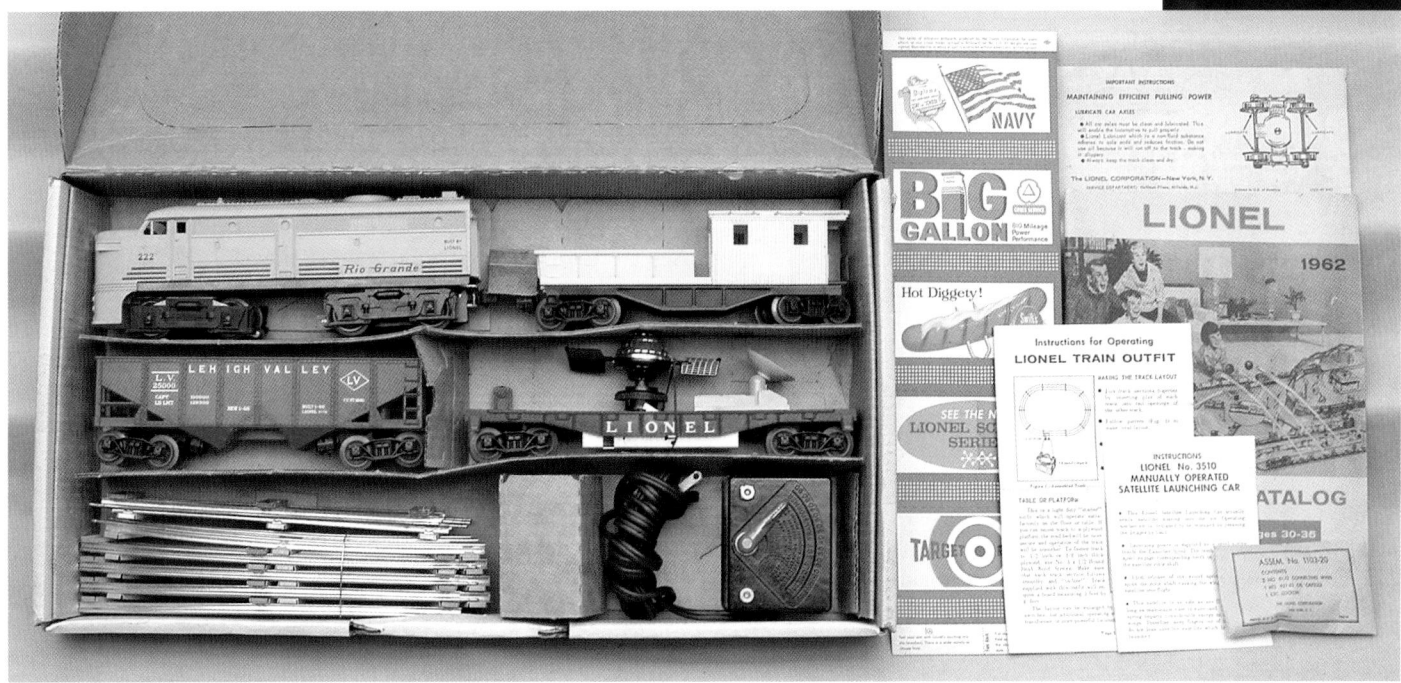

General Release Promotional advance catalog outfit no. 11011 was Lionel's diesel-powered advance catalog offering for 1962. It was a follow-up to the advance catalog no. 1125 from 1961. The 11011 introduced the no. 3510-25 Satellite Launching Car (Less Satellite), which was a red version of a no. 3509-25 Satellite Launching Car.

Outfit no. 11011 used four different overstamped boxes. Shown is the no. 61-115, which was an overstamped no. 1125 from 1961.

Cust./No./Price: Oklahoma Tire & Supply Co.; 70-760-2; $14.44
Original Amount: 20,000
Factory Order Date: 3/9/1962
Date Issued: Revised #1 3-8-62
Packaging: Display Outfit Packing (Units not Boxed)

Contents: 222P-25 "Denver & Rio Grande" Alco Diesel Power Unit; 3510-25 Satellite Launching Car (Less Satellite); 0333-100 Satellite; 6076-25 Hopper Car - Red; 6120-25 Work Caboose; 1013-8 Curved Track (Bundle of 8 - 1013); 1018-10 Straight Track (Loose) (2); 1026-25 25-Watt Transformer; 1103-20 Envelope Packed; 310-2 Set of (5) Billboards; D62-50 Accessory Catalog; 1123-40 Instruction Sheet; 1125-10 Instruction Sheet; 3510-5 Instruction Sheet

Description: Non-Catalog Outfit - Diesel Freight - "O27"
Specification: "O27" Diesel Freight Outfit
Cust./No.: Lionel Advance Catalog; 11011; $11.98 or $12.98

Boxes & Packing: 61-115 Display Box (Inv. 4,739) W/Stickers; 61-382 Display Box (Inv. 557) W/Stickers; 61-383 Display Box (Inv. 1,514) W/Stickers; 61-388 Display Box (Inv. 131) W/Stickers; 62-200 Display Box; 61-101 Corr. Insert; 61-102 Corr. Insert (2); 61-103 Shipper for (6) - Unprinted (1-6); 61-104 Envelope Packed (1-6)

Alternate For Outfit Contents:

Note: Use Inventory of 1103-12 Envelope first.

11011 (1962)	C6	C7	C8	Rarity
Complete Outfit With no. 62-200 Box	255	390	575	R2
Outfit Box no. 62-200	30	50	75	R2
Complete Outfit With Overstickered nos. 61-115, 61-382 Or 61-383 Box	325	365	650	R6
Overstickered Outfit Box nos. 61-115, 61-382 Or 61-383	100	125	150	R6
Complete Outfit With Overstickered no. 61-388 Box	425	740	1,100	R10
Overstickered Outfit Box no. 61-388	200	400	600	R10
Any Outfit With no. 61-104, Add The Following	600	800	1,000	R10

Comments: In 1962, Lionel issued two no. 11000-series General Release Promotional Type IIb advance catalog outfits: nos. 11001 and 11011.

An illustration of the 11011 appeared on the inside cover of the Lionel advance catalog for 1962. The accompanying description stated that the 11001 and 11011 were "Styled and Priced to Meet the Demands of the Mass Toy Market". These advance catalog outfits were part of Lionel's promotional outfit strategy of offering retailers something different even if they couldn't commit to the quantity necessary for a unique promotional outfit. Lionel sold the 11011 to jobbers and national retail chains for $8.95 each and other retail chains and department stores for $9.50 each. The suggested selling price was $11.98 for national retail chains and $12.98 for dealers.

Many retailers likely carried the 11011. One that can be documented as having done so was Oklahoma Tire & Supply Co. The 11011 was listed on page 16 of that retailer's 1962 Christmas Toys and Gift Catalog as no. 70-760-2 for $14.44.

The 11011 was a basic starter outfit and a follow-up to the advance catalog no. 1125 from 1961. Both were led by low-end Alcos found in many promotional outfits. The 11011 was led by a no. 222P-25 Denver & Rio Grande Alco Diesel Power Unit (new

for 1962). This locomotive moved forward only and featured a traction tire, a headlight and a closed pilot.

This 11011 and its RSC counterpart, the 11015, introduced the no. 3510-25 Satellite Launching Car (Less Satellite). This car featured a red frame, had "Lionel" stamped on each side and used the same mechanism as the no. 3509-25 Satellite Launching Car. It is the most difficult of the satellite launching cars to find.

This outfit also included the unmarked yellow no. 6120-25 Work Caboose. That model was used only in promotional outfits from 1961 through 1963. It, like the other pieces of rolling stock in the 11011, was equipped with non-operating Archbar trucks and couplers.

Lionel used the 11011 and many other early 1962 outfits to deplete its inventory of pre-printed White 4-6-4 Steamer and F3 Hinged Display with Red/Orange and Blue Graphics Type A outfit boxes. This outfit used four overstickered versions as well as the no. 62-200 Display Outfit Box - Unprinted. The 62-200 was manufactured by United Container Co. and measured 21⅝ x 11½ x 3¼ inches.

All the overstickered boxes measured 22 x 11½ x 3¼ inches. They were, with the exception of the no. 61-388, manufactured by Express Container Corp. The company that made the 61-388 has yet to be identified.

With every shipment of six outfits Lionel packaged a no. 61-104 Envelope Packed. This envelope included a no. 61-107 Acetate Dust Cover in a no. 61-108 Envelope. The printing on the envelope states that the "clear plastic shield keeps merchandise dust free and safe from pilferage." These covers likely were used to display the outfits in stores.

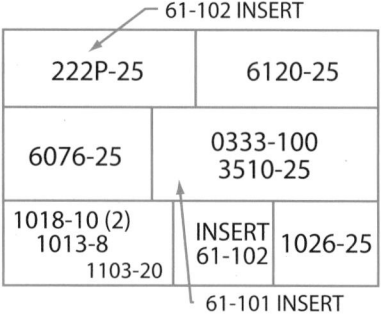

DISPLAY PACK
62-200 BOX UNPRINTED
61-115, 61-382, 61-383
OR 61-388 BOX
5 STICKERS PER BOX
1-27-62

This outfit was also used to deplete the no. 1103-12 Envelope Packed. It was being replaced by the no. 1103-20 Envelope Packed in 1962. This substitution does not affect the price.

The original quantity of this outfit was 22,000 units, but it was decreased to 20,000. This large quantity of outfits explains why examples of the 11011 frequently appear.

11015 (11011)
1962

Customer No. On Box: 11011
Description: Non-Catalog Outfit - Diesel Freight - "O27"
Specification: "O27" Diesel Freight Outfit
Customer/No.: Lionel Advance Catalog; 11015
Original Amount: 3,000
Factory Order Date: 1/29/1962
Date Issued: 3-12-62

Packaging: R.S.C. Outfit Packing (Units not Boxed)

Contents: 222P-25 "Denver & Rio Grande" Alco Diesel Power Unit; 3510-25 Satellite Launching Car (Less Satellite); 0333-100 Satellite; 6076-25 Hopper Car - Red; 6120-25 Work Caboose; 1013-8 Curved Track (Bundle of 8 - 1013); 1018-10 Straight Track (Loose) (2); 1026-25 25-Watt Transformer; 1103-20 Envelope Packed; 310-2 Set of (5) Billboards; D62-50 Accessory Catalog; 1123-40 Instruction Sheet; 1125-10 Instruction Sheet; 3510-5 Instruction Sheet

Left: The RSC version of no. 11011 was listed on its Factory Order as 11015; however, it actually was stamped "11011". **Right:** the display-packed version came with the same contents.

Boxes & Packing: 61-170 Corr. Outfit Box; 61-171 Corr. Insert; 61-172 Corr. Insert; 61-173 Corr. Insert; 61-174 Shipper for (6) (1-6)

Alternate For Outfit Contents:
Note: Use Inventory of 1103-12 Envelope first.

11015 (11011) (1962)	C6	C7	C8	Rarity
Complete Outfit	275	415	635	R5
Outfit Box no. 61-170	50	75	125	R5

Comments: This General Release Promotional Type IIb outfit was the RSC version of display-packed no. 11011 from 1962. The only differences between them related to the packaging and the quantity produced.

The "5" that served as the last digit of the outfit number indicated "R.S.C - Kraft (tan) - Units Loose". (See the section on Outfit Numbering for more information on Lionel's five-digit numbering system.)

Interestingly, the RSC version of the no. 11015 was actually stamped "11011" on a no. 61-170 Tan RSC with Black Graphics outfit box. The box was manufactured by St. Joe Kraft, St. Joe Paper Co. Container Division and measured 11½ x 10¼ x 6¼ inches. (See the entry for the display-packed 11011 from for information about the outfit contents.)

Only 3,000 of this outfit were made, far fewer than the 20,000 of the 11011. That discrepancy explains why the RSC version is harder to find than the display version.

CONVENTIONAL PACK
61-170 BOX
3-7-62

TOP LAYER

| 6076-25 | 0333-100 1103-20 ENV. | 6120-25 |
| | 1026-25 | |

└ 61-171 INSERT

BOTTOM LAYER

| 1013-8 (2) 1018-10 |
| 222P-25 ← 61-173 INSERT |
| 3510-25 |

61-172 INSERT BETWEEN LAYERS

Description: "O27" Special Outfit
Specification: "O27" Steam Type Freight Outfit
Customer: PX
Original Amount: 2,200
Factory Order Date: 3/27/1963
Date Issued: Rev 10-30-63
Packaging: #1-Display Outfit Packing (Units not Boxed)

Contents: 1061-25 Steam Type Locomotive; 1061T-25 Tender; 6409-25 Flat Car W/3 Pipes; 6511-15 Pipes (3); 6076-100 Hopper Car - Gray; 6167-25 Caboose; 1013-8 Curved Track (Bundle of 8 - 1013); 1026-25 25-Watt Transformer; 1103-20 Envelope Packed; 310-2 Set of (5) Billboards; D63-50 Accessory Catalog; 1-63 Warranty Card; 1-62 Parts Order Form; 1123-40

Instruction Sheet; 11311-20 Instruction Sheet; Form 2869 Printed Sheet

Boxes & Packing: 62-200 Display Outfit Box; 61-101 Corr. Insert; 61-102 Corr. Insert (2); 61-103 Shipper for (6) (1-6)

11311X (1963)	C6	C7	C8	Rarity
Complete Outfit	175	300	435	R6
Outfit Box no. 62-200	75	135	175	R6

Comments: The no. 11311X was the Retailer Promotional Type Ib version of catalog outfit no. 11311 from 1963. The 11311X was sold to the Army's Post Exchange (PX).

The main difference between the low-end promotional outfit

10000 Series

405

The Army's Post Exchange (PX) purchased outfit no. 11311X in 1963. This promotional outfit was nearly identical to catalog outfit no. 11311, except that it was led by a no. 1061-25 Steam Type Locomotive. The 11311X also included a no. 11311-20 Instruction Sheet.

Few examples of the no. 11311X's no. 62-200 White 4-6-4 Steamer and F3 Hinged Display with Red/Orange and Blue Graphics Type A outfit box have survived in collectible condition. The one shown has seen better days. Even so, this complete example verifies the Factory Order.

11311X and catalog outfit 11311 was that the former was led by a no. 1061-25 Steam Type Locomotive and the latter by a no. 1062-25 Steam Type Loco. W/Light & Reversing Unit. The stripped-down 1061-25 Scout steamer (new for 1963) featured an 0-4-0 wheel arrangement and went forward only. It lacked a headlight, a lens and any sort of traction aid.

All the rolling stock in the 11311X was new for 1963. The no. 6409-25 Flat Car W/3 Pipes was a red no. 6511-series flat car that had "Lionel" stamped on each side and lacked a car number and a brake wheel.

The nos. 1061T-25 Tender, 6076-100 Hopper Car - Gray and 6167-25 Caboose were all low-end models made out of unpainted plastic with no stamped decoration. The lack of features and markings epitomized the ways that Lionel was cheapening its product line in 1963.

The transition from Archbar to AAR trucks and couplers that began in 1962 continued into 1963. As part of this, Lionel sought to cut costs by introducing a non-operating AAR type. For the 11311X, the 6076-100 was equipped with non-operating Archbar trucks and couplers. All other cars included AAR types. The 6409-25 included non-operating trucks and couplers. The 1061T-25 and 6167-25 included one non-operating and one plain truck and coupler.

The Form 2869 advertising the no. 2001 Track Make-Up Kit was dated 6/63. It is one of the more difficult and expensive items to find in completing a C8 outfit.

The no. 62-200 White 4-6-4 Steamer and F3 Hinged Display with Red/Orange and Blue Graphics Type A outfit box was manufactured by United Container Co. and measured 21⅝ x 11½ x 3¼ inches.

The 11311X was a success for the PX because its quantity was increased from 1,500 to 2,200. Even so, few examples have survived in collectible condition, thereby making it more difficult to find than catalog outfit 11311.

DISPLAY PACK
62-200 BOX
3-12-63

1061-25	1061T-25	1026-25 ⟵61-102
6076-100	6409-25	
	61-101	
1013-8	61-102	6167-25

Customer No. On Box: AD-4158
Description: "O27" Promotional Outfit
Specification: "O27" Steam Type Freight Outfit
Customer/No.: Philco; AD-4158
Original Amount: 1,000
Factory Order Date: 6/24/1963
Date Issued: 6-24-63

Packaging: RSC Outfit Packing (Units not Boxed), Individual Mailers

Contents: 1062-25 Steam Type Loco. W/Light & Reversing Unit; 1061T-25 Tender; 6409-25 Flat Car W/3 Pipes; 6511-15 Pipes (3); 6076-100 Hopper Car - Gray; 6167-25 Caboose; 1013-8 Curved Track (Bundle of 8 - 1013); 1026-25 25-Watt Transformer; 1103-20 Envelope Packed; 310-2 Set of (5) Billboards; D63-50 Accessory Catalog; 1-62 Parts Order Form; 1-63 Warranty Card; Form 2869 Printed Sheet; 1123-40 Instruction Sheet; 11311-10 Instruction Sheet

Boxes & Packing: 62-246 Outfit Box; 61-171 Corr. Insert; 61-172 Corr. Insert; 61-173 Corr. Insert; 62-255 Corr. Insert (2)

Alternate For Outfit Contents:
Do not provide master shipper. Customer Stock No. AD-4158 to appear on carton.

11315 (1963)	C6	C7	C8	Rarity
Complete Outfit	200	370	565	R8
Outfit Box no. 62-246	100	200	300	R8

Comments: The no. 11315 was the Manufacturer Promotional Type IIIa version of catalog outfit no. 11311 from 1963. Lionel sold the 11315 to Philco, which likely used this outfit to promote the sales of one or more of its products.

The only difference between promotional outfit 11315 and catalog outfit 11311 involved their packaging. Specifically, the 11315 came RSC boxed in a no. 62-246 Tan RSC Mailer with Black Graphics outfit box while the 11311 was display packed.

The low-end 11315 was led by a no. 1061-25 Steam Type Locomotive (new for 1963). This stripped-down Scout steamer featured an 0-4-0 wheel arrangement and went forward only. It lacked a headlight, a lens and any sort of traction aid.

All the rolling stock in the 11315 was new for 1963. The no. 6409-25 Flat Car W/3 Pipes was a red no. 6511-series flat car that had "Lionel" stamped on each side and lacked a car number and a brake wheel.

The nos. 1061T-25 Tender, 6076-100 Hopper Car - Gray and 6167-25 Caboose were all low-end models made out of unpainted plastic with no stamped decoration. The lack of features and markings epitomized the ways that Lionel was cheapening its product line in 1963.

The transition from Archbar to AAR trucks and couplers that began in 1962 continued into 1963. As part of this, Lionel sought to cut costs by introducing a non-operating AAR type. Therefore, starting in 1963, most of the cars that came with AAR trucks and couplers had at least one non-operating type. For the 11315, it was possible for any of the cars to come with AAR, Archbar or a combination of trucks and couplers. The 6076-100 and 6409-25 were equipped with non-operating trucks and couplers. The 1061T-25 and 6167-25 included one non-operating and one plain truck and coupler.

The Form 2869 advertising the no. 2001 Track Make-Up Kit was dated 6/63. It is one of the more difficult and expensive items to find in completing a C8 outfit.

The 62-246 Outfit Box was manufactured by Mead Containers and measured 11½ x 10¼ x 6¼ inches. These boxes were made of a thicker corrugated material (rated at 90 pounds rather than the normal 65 pounds gross weight) that allowed each outfit to be shipped in its outfit box. The manufacturer omitted any Lionel printing on the box top to leave room for a mailing label.

With only 1,000 examples of the 11315 manufactured, one is seldom seen. This promotional outfit is much more difficult to find than its catalog counterpart, the 11311.

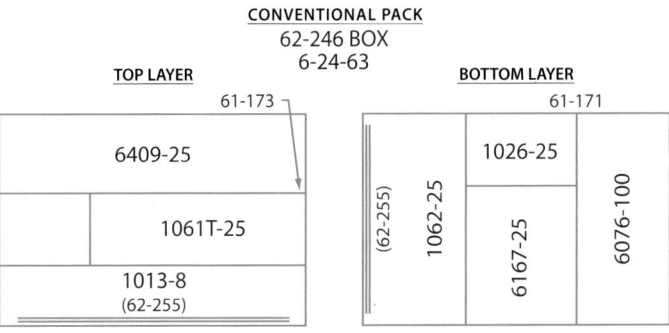

CONVENTIONAL PACK
62-246 BOX
6-24-63

Description: "O27" Promotional Outfit
Specification: "O27" Diesel Freight Outfit
Original Amount: 1,040
Factory Order Date: 11/20/1963
Date Issued: 11-20-63
Date Req'd: At Once
Packaging: RSC

Contents: 221P-25 Diesel Locomotive; 6062-1 Gondola Car With Cable Reels; 6445-1 Ft. Knox Gold Bullion Transport Car; 6463-25 Rocket Fuel Car; 3519-1 Operating Satellite Launching Car; 6059-50 Caboose; 1013-8 Curved Track (Bundle of 8 - 1013); 1018-10 Straight Track (Loose); 1008-50 Uncoupling Unit; 1010-25 35-Watt Transformer; 1103-20 Envelope Packed; 310-62 Set of (3) Billboards; D63-50 Accessory Catalog; 1-62 Parts Order Form; 1-63 Warranty Card; 122-10 Instruction Sheet

Boxes & Packing: 62-243 Outfit Box; 62-254 Corr. Insert; 62-244 Shipper for (4) (1-4)

Alternate For Outfit Contents:
Note: Substitute 140 - 222P-25 for 221P-25; Substitute 96 - 6413-25 for 6445-1 using 2 - 6413-4 and 6413-10; Substitute 50 - 6416-1 for 6445-1; Substitute 460 - 6402-25 for 6463-25.

11341-500 (1963)	C6	C7	C8	Rarity
Complete Outfit	395	700	950	R7
Complete Outfit With no. 6416-1 Substitution, Add The Following	45	70	100	R7
Outfit Box no. 62-243	125	250	300	R7

Comments: This General Release Promotional Type IIa or IIb (depending on the substitutions) was one of the many outfits that Lionel issued late in 1963 in an attempt to deplete excess inventory. Outfit no. 11341-500, which had no correlation to catalog outfit no. 11341, began as outfit no. 19314. The latter might have been one of the outfits that Lionel offered to Sears as part of its year-end "Special Purchase", but it was rejected.

The Factory Order for the 19314 was handwritten and listed 11341-500 beneath its number. The final Factory Order for the 11341-500 was typewritten.

The 11341-500 was led by a 221P-25 Rio Grande Diesel Locomotive (new for 1963). This low-end, unpainted yellow Alco featured a two-position reversing unit, a traction tire and a closed pilot and lacked a headlight.

As with other outfits created late in 1963, the 11341-500

was intended to help Lionel clean its shelves of old inventory. Among those carryover items, the nos. 3519-1 Operating Satellite Launching Car, 6062-1 Gondola Car With Cable Reels and 6445-1 Ft. Knox Gold Bullion Transport Car were still equipped with early operating AAR trucks and couplers, which were last used in 1961. All three cars came in Orange Picture boxes.

The 6062-1 may have been a carryover item, but it included three gray no. 40-11 Cable Reels, which first appeared in late 1963. In fact, the production sample for the gray reels was dated 10-22-63. The gray versions are more desirable and provide a slight premium.

The norm for the no. 6463-25 Rocket Fuel Car was one operating and one non-operating AAR truck and coupler, although two operating types are possible. The no. 6059-50 Caboose came with one operating and one plain AAR truck and coupler.

The only substitution that materially affects the outfit price was the no. 6416-1 Boat Transport Car, which replaced the 6445-1. The price difference is noted in the pricing table.

Be aware that the no. 6402-25 Flat Car Without Load substitution was the gray plastic version equipped with non-operating Archbar trucks and couplers.

The nos. 122-10 Instruction Sheet made reference to the new 90-day warranty policy that Lionel instituted in 1963.

The no. 62-243 Tan RSC with Black Graphics outfit box measured 12⅛ x 11½ x 6⅜ inches.

With a higher-than-average quantity of 1,040 units, the 11341-500 should appear on the market. Experience shows that one seldom shows up.

CONVENTIONAL PACK
62-243 BOX
11-19-63

TOP LAYER	BOTTOM LAYER
3519-1 F	221P-25 ← 62-254
1013-8	6059-50 · 1010-25
6062-1 F · 1018-10 · 1008-50	6445-1 F
6463-25	2 CATALOGS BETWEEN LAYERS

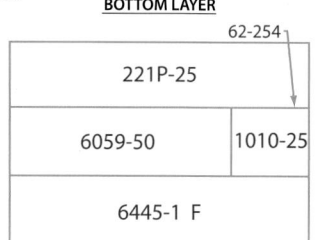

11351-500
1963

The no. 11351-500 listed Spiegel on its Factory Order. It was stamped with Spiegel's no. "5286S". The 11351-500 was likely the mail-order version of the no. R36 J 5286 (Lionel catalog outfit no. 11351), which was featured in the 1963 Spiegel Christmas Catalog.

Contents: 237-25 Steam Type Locomotive with Smoke; 1060T-25 Tender; 6050-150 Van Camp Savings Bank Car; 6162-25 Gondola Car (Less 3 Canisters); 6112-88 Canister (3); 6076-100 Hopper Car - Gray; 6045-150 Tank Car; 6119-100 Work Caboose; 1013-8 Curved Track (Bundle of 8 - 1013); 1018-10 Straight Track (Loose); 6139-25 Uncoupling Track Section; 1103-40 Envelope Packed; 1025-25 45-Watt Transformer; 909-20 Smoke Fluid; 310-62 Set of (3) Billboards; D63-50 Accessory Catalog; D63-52 Accessory Catalog; 1-62 Parts Order Form; 1-63 Warranty Card; 11351-10 Instruction Sheet; 1123-40 Instruction Sheet; 237-11 Instruction Sheet

Boxes & Packing: 61-180 Outfit Box; 63-311 Corr. Insert; 62-264 Corr. Insert; 62-254 Corr. Insert; 61-185 Shipper for (4) (1-4)

Customer No. On Box: 5286S
Description: "O27" Non-Catalog Outfit
Specification: "O27" Steam Type Freight Outfit W/Smoke
Customer/No./Price: Spiegel; R36 J 5286; $23.94
Customer/No./Price: Spiegel; 5286S; $23.94
Original Amount: 275
Factory Order Date: 12/6/1963
Date Issued: Rev 12-12-63
Date Req'd: At Once
Packaging: RSC

11351-500 (1963)	C6	C7	C8	Rarity
Complete Outfit	500	800	1,150	R9
Outfit Box no. 61-180	300	500	700	R9

Comments: In 1963, five promotional outfits listed Spiegel as the customer on the Factory Order: nos. 11351-500, 19214-500, 19237, 19238 and 19238-501. The 11351-500 was a Retailer Promotional Type Ib outfit.

For background on this outfit, keep in mind that catalog outfit no. 11351 was shown on page 380 of the 1963 Christmas Catalog as Spiegel no. R36 J 5286 for $23.94. The description said that the outfit was "Mailable". However, the 11351 was a display-packed outfit and so likely was not what was mailed by Spiegel.

The Factory Order for outfit 11351-500 listed Spiegel as the customer, and the box was stamped with "5286S". Even though the contents of this outfit differed slightly from those of the 11351, it stands to reason that the 11351-500 was the outfit mailed by Spiegel to its customers.

The 11351-500 was led by a no. 237-25 Steam Type Locomotive with Smoke (new for 1963). This Scout steamer featured a two-position reversing unit and a headlight and used a rubber tire as a traction aid. The harder-to-find early version with wide running boards came in this outfit. Except for its 237 number, it was the same engine as a no. 238.

The nos. 6045-150 Tank Car and 6076-100 Hopper Car - Gray with no markings were both new for 1963. All the other rolling stock in this outfit was carried over from earlier years.

As with most cars in 1963, the truck and coupler combinations varied from those of earlier years. The no. 6050-150 Van Camp Savings Bank Car was equipped with non-operating Archbar trucks and couplers. The no. 1060T-25 Tender included one non-operating and one plain AAR truck and coupler. The no. 6119-

100 Work Caboose came with one operating and one plain AAR type. The nos. 6045-150 and 6076-100 had non-operating AAR trucks and couplers. Finally, the no. 6162-25 Gondola Car (Less 3 Canisters) included one operating and one non-operating AAR truck and coupler.

By the way, Lionel must have had extra Orange Picture boxed 6119-100s lying around because one found its way into this outfit.

The paperwork was appropriate for the new 90-day warranty policy that Lionel instituted in 1963. Many of these instruction sheet versions are the most difficult to find. Pay particular attention to the no. 11351-10 Instruction Sheet, as it must be dated 5/63.

The commonly used no. 61-180 Tan RSC with Black Graphics outfit box was manufactured by St. Joe Kraft, St. Joe Paper Co. Container Division and measured 12¾ x 10 x 6¾ inches.

With only 275 examples of the 11351-500 produced, this is a very difficult outfit to find.

CONVENTIONAL PACK
61-180 BOX
12-6-63

TOP LAYER				BOTTOM LAYER
62-264		63-311		62-254
6045-150				237-25
6119-100				
6162-25	1060T-25		6050-150	1025-25
6076-100			1013-8 1018-10	

CATALOGS

Description: "O27" Promotional Outfit
Specification: "O27" Diesel Freight Outfit
Original Amount: 246
Factory Order Date: 12/2/1963
Date Issued: Rev 12-11-63
Date Req'd: 12-3-63
Packaging: RSC (Units Loose)

Contents: 211P-150 *"Texas Special"* Diesel; 211T-25 *"Texas Special"* Motorless Unit; 6408-25 Flat Car W/5 Pipes; 6511-15 Pipes (5); 3349-1 Turbo Missile Firing Car; 6480-25 Exploding Target Car; 6463-25 Rocket Fuel Car; 6142-25 Gondola Car (Less 2 Canisters); 6112-5 Canister (2); 6059-50 Caboose; 1013-8 Curved Track (Bundle of 8 - 1013); 1018-30 Straight Track (Bundle of 3 - 1018); 1008-50 Uncoupling Unit; 1025-25 45-Watt Transformer; 1103-20 Envelope Packed; 310-62 Set of (3) Billboards; D63-50 Accessory Catalog; 1-62 Parts Order Form; 1-63 Warranty Card; 122-10 Instruction Sheet; 6480-5 Instruction Sheet; 211-151 Instruction Sheet

Boxes & Packing: 63-309 Outfit Box; 62-224 Corr. Insert; 62-245 Corr. Insert (2); 62-248 Corr. Insert; 62-254 Corr. Insert; 63-310 Shipper for (4) (1-4)

Alternate For Outfit Contents:
Note: Substitute 90 - 211T-1 for 211T-25; Substitute 50 - 218P-25 for 211P-150; Substitute 50 - 218T-25 for 211T-25.

11361-500 (1963)	C6	C7	C8	Rarity
Complete Outfit As Listed	550	985	1,350	R9
Complete Outfit With no. 211T-1 Substitution	560	1,015	1,390	R9
Outfit Box no. 63-309	300	550	750	R9

Comments: This General Release Promotional Type IIb was one of the many outfits that Lionel issued late in 1963 in an attempt to deplete excess inventory. Outfit no. 11361-500, which had no correlation to catalog outfit no. 11361, began as outfit no. 19310 with a quantity of 296 units. The latter outfit might have been one of those that Lionel offered to Sears as part of its year-end "Special Purchase", but it was rejected.

The Factory Order for the 19310 was handwritten and listed 11361-500 beneath its number. The final Factory Order for outfit 11361-500 was typewritten with a quantity of 246. The extra 50 outfits went on to become outfit no. 19238-502 (see the entry for the 19238-502 from 1963).

The space and military 11361-500 was led by a 211P-150 *Texas Special* Diesel (new for 1963). The 211P-150 was a cost-reduced version of the no. 211P-25 *Texas Special* Alco Diesel Power Unit. The "-150" featured a two-position reversing unit, two traction tires, a headlight, a weight and an open pilot with a large ledge. This variation has not stirred much interest in the collector community.

This outfit used substitutions to deplete the remaining

General Release Promotional outfit no. 11361-500 was created at the end of 1963 as a way for Lionel to deplete as much inventory as possible. It marked one of the final appearances of the no. 6480-25 Exploding Target Car and the boxed no. 3349-1 Turbo Missile Firing Car.

inventory of unboxed no. 218s. The nos. 218P-25 Santa Fe Alco Diesel Power Car and 218T-25 Motorless Unit made their last outfit appearance in the 11361-500.

Some of the unboxed 211T-25s were swapped out for a boxed no. 211T-1 *Texas Special* Motorless Unit. The 211T-1 made its second-to-last appearance in this outfit. Its Orange Picture box slightly increases the outfit value, as listed in the pricing table.

The only new rolling stock in the 11361-500 were the nos. 6142-25 Gondola Car (Less 2 Canisters), 6408-25 Flat Car W/5 Pipes and 6059-50 Caboose. Actually these were just color, decorating or coupler variations of other cars.

The 6408-25 first appeared in catalog outfit no. 11351 earlier in the year. It was a red no. 6511-series flat car with "Lionel" stamped on each side. It was almost the same car as a no. 6409-25 Flat Car W/3 Pipes, but the 6408 also included a brake wheel and one operating and one non-operating AAR truck and coupler. The 6142-25 was a short gondola molded in black with one non-operating and one operating AAR truck and coupler. The no. 6059-50 Caboose was the unpainted version of the no. 6059-25 Caboose with an operating and plain AAR truck and coupler.

The Orange Picture boxed no. 3349-1 Turbo Missile Firing Car made its second-to-last appearance in this outfit. It came equipped with operating AAR trucks and couplers. The no. 6480-25 Exploding Target Car was making its final appearance in this outfit and the 19238-502. It included non-operating Archbar

trucks and couplers.

Lastly, the no. 6463-25 Rocket Fuel Car came with one operating and one non-operating AAR truck and coupler.

The nos. 122-10 and 211-151 Instruction Sheets made reference to the new 90-day warranty policy that Lionel instituted in 1963.

The no. 63-309 Tan RSC with Black Graphics outfit box was manufactured by the Mead Corporation and measured 13¼ x 12½ x 6¾ inches. It included four lines of data as part of the box manufacturer's certificate.

Both the 11361-500 and 19238-502 were created in small quantities and are very difficult to find.

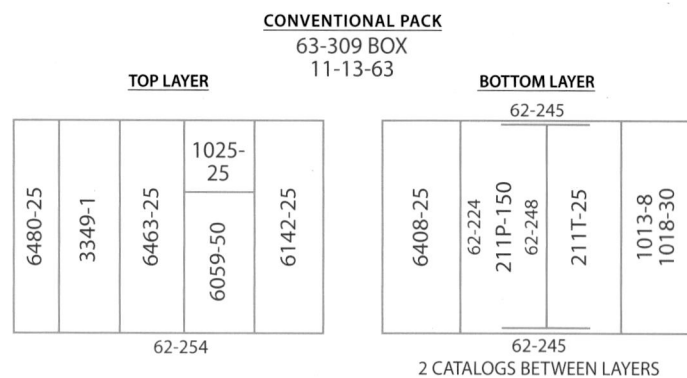

CONVENTIONAL PACK
63-309 BOX
11-13-63

TOP LAYER

6480-25	3349-1	6463-25	1025-25	6142-25
			6059-50	

62-254

BOTTOM LAYER

62-245

6408-25	62-224	211P-150	62-248	211T-25	1013-8 1018-30

62-245
2 CATALOGS BETWEEN LAYERS

Description: "O27" Promotional Outfit
Specification: "O27" *Texas Special* Diesel Freight Outfit
Customer: Army and Air Force Exchange
Original Amount: 200
Factory Order Date: 6/18/1963
Date Issued: Rev 6-24-63
Date Req'd: Aug
Packaging: #1 Display Outfit Packing (Units not Boxed)

Contents: 211P-150 *"Texas Special"* Diesel; 3413-150 Mercury Capsule Launching Car; 3665-100 Minuteman Missile Launching Car; 6413-25 Mercury Capsule Transport Car; 6413-4 Capsules (2); 6413-10 Env. Packed; 6470-25 Exploding Target Car; 6257-100 Caboose; 1013-8 Curved Track (Bundle of 8 - 1013); 1018-30 Straight Track (Bundle of 3 - 1018); 6139-25 Uncoupling Track Section; 1025-25 45-Watt Transformer; 1103-40 Envelope Packed; 310-2 Set of (5) Billboards; D63-50 Accessory Catalog; 1-62 Parts Order Form; 1-63 Warranty Card; 1123-40 Instruction Sheet; 211-151 Instruction Sheet; 11351-10 Instruction Sheet; 3665-30 Instruction Sheet; 6470-17 Instruction Sheet

Boxes & Packing: 63-306 Display Outfit Box; 61-101 Corr. Insert; 62-257 Corr. Insert; 63-300 Corr. Insert; 63-307 Shipper for (4) (1-4)

Alternate For Outfit Contents:
Note: Same as 11361 less 1 - 211T-25 Motorless Unit.

11361X (1963)	C6	C7	C8	Rarity
Complete Outfit	990	1,475	1,960	R10
Outfit Box no. 63-306	550	750	900	R10

Comments: The Army and Air Force Exchange was listed on the Factory Order for outfit no. 11361X from 1963. The 11361X, a Retailer Promotional Type Ia outfit, fittingly had a space and military theme.

According to its Factory Order, the contents of the 11361X duplicated those in catalog outfit no. 11361 with two differences. For one thing, this promotional outfit did not have a no. 211T-25 *Texas Special* Motorless Unit. For another thing, different display packing was used. Be aware that promotional outfit no. 19232 included the same items.

The 11361X was led by a no. 211P-150 *Texas Special* Diesel (new for 1963). The 211P-150 was a cost-reduced version of the no. 211P-25 *Texas Special* Alco Diesel Power Unit. The "-150" featured a two-position reversing unit, two traction tires, a headlight, a weight and an open pilot with a large ledge. This variation has not stirred much interest in the collector community.

The transition from Archbar to AAR trucks and couplers that began in 1962 continued into 1963. As part of this, Lionel sought to cut costs by introducing a non-operating AAR type. Therefore, starting in 1963, most cars equipped with AAR trucks and couplers

had at least one non-operating type. For the 11361X, all but one of the pieces of rolling stock were 1963 versions equipped with one operating and one non-operating AAR truck and coupler. The no. 6257-100 Caboose had one operating and one plain AAR type.

This transition in trucks and couplers led to new suffixes for the nos. 3413 Mercury Capsule Launching Car and 3665 Minuteman Missile Launching Car. Specifically, when equipped with one operating and one non-operating type, they became the nos. 3413-150 and 3665-100, respectively. The nos. 6413-25 Mercury Capsule Transport Car and 6470-25 Exploding Target Car did not receive new suffixes even though their truck and coupler combinations were changed.

On 3-5-63, the Lionel 3665 Blueprints indicated that the material used to mold the roof sections changed from Lionel Blue #6964 to Blue #6978 (a lighter shade of blue plastic). This light shade of blue plastic was intended as the norm for 3665-100s and is likely proper for this outfit. The version with a light blue roof demands a premium.

Cars equipped with one non-operating truck and coupler, which are correct for this outfit, are harder to find than the two operating type versions. However, they do not demand any sort of premium.

What do bring premiums are the 1963 versions of the instruction sheets in the 11361X. All of these sheets made reference to the 90-day warranty policy that Lionel put in place in 1963. The nos. 3665-30 and 3413-152 Instruction Sheets were new for 1963. Both mentioned the truck-and-coupler configuration change for 1963.

The no. 63-306 White 4-6-4 Steamer and F3 Hinged Display with Red/Orange and Blue Graphics Type A outfit box listed the manufacturer as "SJPC" (likely St. Joe Paper Company). It measured 24½ x 11½ x 3⅛ inches.

Finding this outfit complete with the proper 1963 components is extremely difficult. Even if a collector manages to find an empty box, obtaining a proper 1963 version of every item listed on the Factory Order demands great patience.

DISPLAY PACK
63-306 BOX
6-10-63

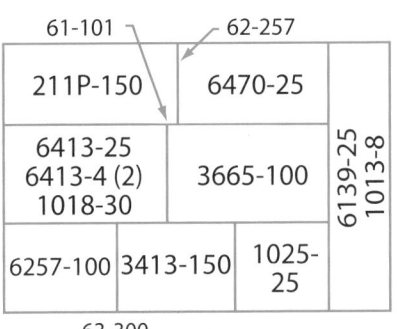

General Release Promotional outfit no. 11375-500 was produced in small quantities and so is difficult to find. It was made late in 1963 in an attempt to deplete excess inventory. Notable items included the version of the no. 237-25 Steam Type Locomotive with Smoke that had wide running boards as well as a no. 6464-900 New York Central Box Car.

Description: "O27" Non-Catalog Outfit
Specification: "O27" Steam Type Freight Outfit W/Smoke & Whistle
Original Amount: 330
Factory Order Date: 11/25/1963
Date Issued: 11-25-63
Date Req'd: 11-25-63
Packaging: RSC

Contents: 237-25 Steam Type Locomotive with Smoke; 234W-1 Whistle Tender; 6162-25 Gondola Car (Less 3 Canisters); 6112-88 Canister (3); 6822-50 Searchlight Car; 6076-100 Hopper Car - Gray; 6464-900 "New York Central" Box Car; 6343-25 Barrel Ramp Car; 362-78 Wood Barrels (6); 6059-50 Caboose; 1013-8 Curved Track (Bundle of 8 - 1013); 1018-30 Straight Track (Bundle of 3 - 1018); 6139-25 Uncoupling Track Section; 1103-50 Envelope Packed; 1063-25 75-Watt Transformer; 909-20 Smoke Fluid; 310-62 Set of (3) Billboards; D63-50 Accessory Catalog; 1-62 Parts Order Form; 1-63 Warranty Card; 237-11 Instruction Sheet; 9730-10 Instruction Sheet

Boxes & Packing: 61-380 Outfit Box; 62-255 Corr. Insert (4); 61-381 Shipper for (4) (1-4)

11375-500 (1963)	C6	C7	C8	Rarity
Complete Outfit	635	950	1,285	R9
Outfit Box no. 61-380	325	475	575	R9

Comments: This General Release Promotional Type IIa outfit was one of the many outfits that Lionel issued late in 1963 in an attempt to deplete excess inventory. Outfit no. 11375-500 had no correlation to catalog outfit no. 11375.

The 11375-500 was led by a no. 237-25 Steam Type Locomotive with Smoke (new for 1963). This Scout steamer featured a two-position reversing unit and a headlight and used a rubber tire as a traction aid. The harder-to-find early version with wide running boards came in this outfit. Except for its 237 number, it was the same engine as a no. 238. The 237-25 pulled a no. 234W-1 Whistle Tender that came in an Orange Picture box.

Three of the cars in this outfit were new versions for 1963. The no. 6822-50 Searchlight Car was an unboxed 6822 equipped with one operating and one non-operating AAR truck and coupler. The no. 6076-100 Hopper Car - Gray was an undecorated model, and the no. 6059-50 Caboose was the unpainted red-plastic version of the no. 6059-25 Caboose. Of note was the inclusion of a Type IV no. 6464-900 New York Central Box Car in this outfit. It came in an Orange Picture box.

All but one piece of rolling stock in the 11375-500 came with AAR trucks and couplers. The 234W-1 had one non-operating and one plain Archbar type. Among the cars with AAR types, the no. 6162-25 Gondola Car had one operating and one non-operating truck and coupler. The nos. 6343-25 Barrel Ramp Car and 6464-900 had two operating types, and the 6076-100 had non-operating types. Finally, the 6059-50 was equipped with one operating and one plain truck and coupler

The appropriate instruction sheets for this outfit refer to the

90-day warranty policy that Lionel instituted in 1963. The no. 9730-10 Instruction Sheet, which was dated 11/63, is very difficult to find.

The no. 61-380 Tan RSC with Black Graphics outfit box was manufactured by St. Joe Kraft, St. Joe Paper Company and measured 13¾ x 14 x 5⅛ inches. It had "61-380" printed on the box bottom.

With only 300 examples produced, the 11375-500 is difficult to find.

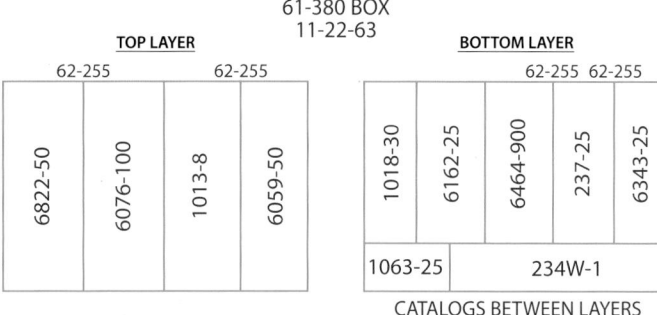

CONVENTIONAL PACK
61-380 BOX
11-22-63

TOP LAYER

6822-50	6076-100	1013-8	6059-50

62-255   62-255

BOTTOM LAYER

62-255 62-255

1018-30	6162-25	6464-900	237-25	6343-25

| 1063-25 | 234W-1 |

CATALOGS BETWEEN LAYERS

Description: "O27" Train Set
Customer: Maritz
Original Amount: 300
Date Issued: 7/24/64
Packaging: RSC Pack (Units Loose)

Contents: 212P-25 "Santa Fe" "A" Diesel W/Horn; 212T-25 "Santa Fe" "A" Unit; 6544-25 Missile Firing Car; 6176-50 Hopper Car - Black; 3349-100 Turbo Missile Firing Car; 0349-100 Turbo Missile (2); 3470-100 Aerial Target Launching Car; 3470-20 Env. Packed; 3470-4 Basket; 3830-75 Oper. Submarine Car; 6407-25 Flat Car W/Sterling Missile; 6407-11 Sterling Missile; 6257-100 Caboose; 1013-8 Curved Track (Bundle of 8 - 1013); 1018-30 Straight Track (Bundle of 3 - 1018); 1073-25 60-Watt Transformer; 147-25 Horn & Whistle Controller; 6139-25 Uncoupling Track Section; 1103-50 Envelope Packed; 310-2 Set of (5) Billboards; 1-62 Parts Order Form; 11385-10 Instruction Sheet; 212-64 Instruction Sheet; 3349-105 Instruction Sheet; 3330-107 Instruction Sheet

Boxes & Packing: 61-210 Outfit Box; 62-224 Insert; 62-245 Insert (2)

11385-500 (1964)	C6	C7	C8	Rarity
Complete Outfit	1,165	1,850	2,700	R9
Outfit Box no. 61-210	400	600	800	R9

Comments: This was the last of seven outfits from the 1960s that listed Maritz, a well-known marketing incentive firm, on its Factory Order. This Retailer Promotional Type Ia outfit was based on catalog outfit no. 11385 from 1963. In fact the Factory Order stated that the no. 11385-500 was "same as 1963 Set #11385 except eliminate 223P-25, 218C-25 and 3619-100 and add 212P-25, 212T-25, 6544-25 and 6176-50 from stock." As an aside, promotional outfit no. 19271 from 1964 was also based on the 11385.

As with the 11385, the 11385-500 is a very desirable and collectible space and military outfit. The latter was led by a no. 212P-25 Santa Fe "A" Diesel W/Horn. This new-for-1964 Alco featured a two-position reversing unit, a headlight and two rubber tires as traction aids. Except for the shell's decoration, it was the same as the no. 223P-50 Santa Fe Alco Diesel Power Car W/Horn, which it replaced. By the way, the nos. 212P-25 and 212T-25 Santa Fe "A" Unit have been observed with "BLT 8-57" stamped on them.

The rolling stock in the 11385-500 duplicated what was packed in the 11385 with one key exception. The no. 3619-100 Reconnaissance Copter Car in the catalog outfit was replaced by the nos. 6176-50 Hopper Car - Black and 6544-25 Missile Firing Car. The 6176-50 was equipped with one operating and one non-operating AAR truck and coupler, and the 6544-25 had operating AAR trucks and couplers. The unboxed 6544-25 was making its final appearance in an outfit. It contained two brake wheels attached to the plastic frame ends. Over time, the frame can easily be cracked or broken off where the wheels were attached.

The no. 3470-100 Aerial Target Launching Car in this outfit was the difficult-to-find version with a light blue frame. The "-100" indicated a change from two operating AAR trucks and couplers to one operating and one non-operating type. Its no. 3470-103 Instruction Sheet is very difficult to find.

The no. 3349-100 Turbo Missile Firing Car was the same as a no. 3349-25 Turbo Missile Firing Car, except that it was equipped with one operating and one non-operating AAR truck and coupler. Its no. 3349-105 Instruction Sheet is also hard to find.

The no. 3830-75 Oper. Submarine Car was, with one difference, identical to the no. 3830-25 Oper. Submarine Car. According to the 3830-75's Production Control File, it was equipped with one operating and one non-operating AAR truck and coupler. This outfit marked the last time a 3830-75 appeared on a Factory Order.

The no. 6407-25 Flat Car W/Sterling Missile is highly collectible. It was part of 11 different outfits, with a total of 13,124 cars produced. It was also available for separate sale. The car was a red no. 6511-series flat car with a brake wheel and "Lionel" stamped on each side. The same flat car was used with the no. 6408-25 Flat Car W/5 Pipes.

The flat car is common, but the no. 6407-11 Sterling Missile is not. It was frequently separated from its flat car because it lacked Lionel markings. Manufactured by Sterling Plastics, it would have "Sterling Plastics" molded into the capsule bottom and rocket base.

Finally, the no. 6257-100 Caboose with a smokestack was reissued in 1963 with one operating and one plain AAR truck and coupler.

As with the 11385 and 19271, the appropriate paperwork for this outfit is very difficult to obtain. The instruction sheets made reference to the 90-day warranty policy that Lionel instituted in 1963. The no. 11385-10 Instruction Sheet was dated 6/63; the no. 212-64 Instruction Sheet was dated 6/64.

The no. 61-210 Orange RSC with Black Graphics outfit box was manufactured by Mead Containers and measured 13⅞ x 13¼

The no. 11385-500 was Maritz's last outfit purchase in the 1960s. This space and military outfit was based on catalog outfit no. 11385 from 1963. It included the highly desirable light blue version of the no. 3470-100 Aerial Target Launching Car and a no. 6407-25 Flat Car W/ Sterling Missile. The instruction sheets included in this outfit are some of the most difficult versions to find.

x 6½ inches. It included three lines of data as part of the box manufacturer's certificate.

This is a difficult outfit box to find and even more so to complete. Some of the variations included in this outfit are subtle, and others are not. Even if the items are found, lots of patience is

required to find the correct versions of the instruction sheets. The 11385-500 was produced in smaller quantities than the 11385 and is likely to generate as much collector interest now that its contents have been verified.

11415
1963

11415 (1963)	C6	C7	C8	Rarity
Complete Outfit	115	175	275	R1
Outfit Box no. 63-320	10	25	35	R1

Description: "O27" Non Catalog Outfit
Specification: "O27" Steam Type Freight Outfit
Customer/No.: Lionel Advance Catalog; 11415
Original Amount: 85,000
Factory Order Date: 4/1/1963
Date Issued: Rev 9-30-63
Packaging: #5 RSC Outfit Packing (Units not Boxed)

Contents: 1061-25 Steam Type Locomotive; 1061T-25 Tender; 6502-50 Girder Transport Car; 6502-3 Girder Bridge; 6167-25 Caboose; 1013-8 Curved Track (Bundle of 8 - 1013); 1026-25 25-Watt Transformer; 1103-20 Envelope Packed; 310-62 Set of (3) Billboards; D63-50 Accessory Catalog; 1-62 Parts Order Form; 1-63 Warranty Card; 1123-40 Instruction Sheet; 11311-20 Instruction Sheet; Form 2869 Printed Sheet

Boxes & Packing: 63-320 Outfit Box; 63-322 Corr. Insert; 63-323 Corr. Insert; 62-251 Corr. Insert; 63-321 Shipper for (6) (1-6)

Alternate For Outfit Contents:
Note: Substitute inventory of 6502-25 for 6502-50 (Amount - 4,065).

Comments: The no. 11415 was Lionel's sole new advance catalog offering for 1963. It was a General Release Promotional Type IIb outfit.

An illustration of the 11415 appeared in the Lionel advance catalog for 1963 with the caption, "A new, complete Lionel net priced outfit at an all-time low, low price". These advance catalog outfits were part of Lionel's promotional outfit strategy of offering retailers something different even if they couldn't commit to the quantity necessary for a unique promotional outfit.

The 11415 was nearly identical to outfit no. 19253. In fact, the latter likely was derived from the 11415 because the 19253's Factory Order appeared later in the year.

Lionel was able to offer the 11415 at a "low, low price" because it was a "low, low-end" outfit. Its rolling stock consisted of one freight car and a caboose.

The 11415 was led by a no. 1061-25 Steam Type Locomotive (new for 1963). This stripped-down steamer featured an 0-4-0 wheel arrangement, went forward only and lacked a headlight, a lens and any sort of traction aid.

The other items in this outfit were also new for 1963 and equipped with non-operating AAR trucks and couplers. The no. 6502-50 Girder Transport Car was an unmarked blue plastic version of the black no. 6502-25 Girder Transport Car. Both light

Outfit no. 11415 was Lionel's sole new advance catalog outfit for 1963. It was as low end as Lionel could make an outfit. The no. 310-62 Set of (3) Billboards and Form 2869 advertising the no. 2001 Track Make-Up Kit are the two most difficult items to obtain.

Two variations exist of the no. 63-320 Tan RSC with Black Graphics outfit box, one with "Lionel Trains" (left) and one without "Lionel Trains" (right).

This version of outfit no. 11415 mounted on a display board belonged to former Lionel salesman Ken Negri, and he might have used it to help sell the 11415. Note that the "1061" on the locomotive was a decal, a no. 1050T-style tender was used ("Lionel Lines" was blackened out) and the caboose was painted.

The two items that are most difficult to find in completing this outfit are the no. 310-62 Set of (3) Billboards and Form 2869 advertising the no. 2001 Track Make-Up Kit. Both are worth more than the other items in this outfit.

The no. 63-320 Tan RSC with Black Graphics outfit box was manufactured by St. Joe Kraft, St. Joe Paper Co. Container Division and measured 11 x 7⅞ x 5½ inches. It included four lines of data as part of the box manufacturer's certificate.

With 85,000 units made, the 11415 ranks first among all outfits from the 1960s, catalog or promotional, in terms of the quantity produced. The 11415 was sold to numerous retailers, a few of which have been identified by price tags or catalog listings. This outfit is easily obtained, but its paperwork and billboards are frequently absent.

Blister Display no. D463 was created to help sell outfit no. 11415. It was designed to be hung on the wall of a store.

and dark blue plastic versions have been observed. Some outfits included the 6502-25 as a substitution, but this does not affect the outfit price. The no. 6502-3 Girder Bridge was orange.

The two pieces of rolling stock were made out of unpainted plastic with no stamped decoration. The lack of features and markings epitomized the ways that Lionel was cheapening its product line in 1963.

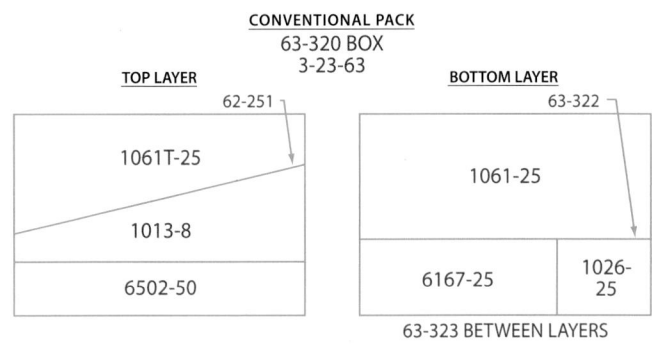

CONVENTIONAL PACK
63-320 BOX
3-23-63

TOP LAYER		BOTTOM LAYER	
62-251		63-322	
1061T-25		1061-25	
1013-8			
6502-50		6167-25	1026-25

63-323 BETWEEN LAYERS

Outfit no. 11482 was Popular Club Plan's last promotional outfit purchase from Lionel. Stamped below Lionel's no. 11482 was "NY-331". This likely was Popular Club Plan's catalog number, although it has yet to be observed in any documentation. This colorful outfit was identical to catalog outfit no. 11480 from 1964, except that it came in an RSC outfit box.

Customer No. On Box: NY-331
Specification: 7 Unit "O27" Diesel Freight
Customer/No.: Popular Club Plan; NY-331
Original Amount: 300
Factory Order Date: 7/23/1964
Date Issued: 7-21-64
Packaging: MO Pack

Contents: 213P-25 "Minn. & St. Louis" Diesel Power Car; 213T-25 Motorless Unit; 6473-25 Rodeo Car; 6176-50 Hopper Car - Black; 6142-150 Gondola Car; 40-11 Cable Reels (2); 6014-325 Frisco Box Car; 6257-100 Caboose; 1013-70 Curved Track (Bundle of 12 - 1013); 1018-30 Straight Track (Bundle of 3 - 1018); 6149-25 Remote Control Track; 1020-25 90° Crossing; 1025-25 45-Watt Transformer; 1103-40 Envelope Packed; 310-62 Set of (3) Billboards; D64-50 Accessory Catalog; 1-62 Parts Order Form; 1-65 Warranty Card; 927-64 Service Station List; 1123-40 Instruction Sheet; 211-151 Instruction Sheet; 19214-10 Instruction Sheet

Boxes & Packing: 62-243 Outfit Box; 62-224 Corrugated Insert; 62-245 Corrugated Insert (2)

11482 (1964)	C6	C7	C8	Rarity
Complete Outfit	525	850	1,200	R9
Outfit Box no. 62-243	300	450	600	R9

Comments: Popular Club Plan is a catalog company that sells an assortment of clothing, housewares, jewelry, toys and electronics. In 1964, it offered a Retailer Promotional Type Ia outfit to its customers. The no. 11482 was an RSC outfit box version of catalog outfit no. 11480 from 1964. This was the last Factory Order to list Popular as a customer.

Each outfit had "NY-331" stamped below the Lionel number. This was likely Popular's catalog number for the 11482, although it has yet to be found in any Popular catalog or documentation.

The 11482 was led by a no. 213P-25 Minn. & St. Louis Diesel Power Car. This new-for-1964 Alco featured a two-position reversing unit, two traction tires, a headlight, a weight and an open pilot with a large ledge. This was one of four promotional outfits from 1964 to include a 213P-25, which was paired with a no. 213T-25 Motorless Unit (also new for 1964).

The cars in this outfit were, with three exceptions, new for 1964. Of those three, the no. 6014-325 Frisco Box Car had a Type III body and the no. 6257-100 Caboose (reissued in 1963) came with a smokestack. The third carryover – no. 6473-25 Rodeo Car – used a Type IIb body (cadmium yellow plastic with red lettering). The Type II body included a partially filled slot caused by broken tooling.

All the rolling stock in the 11482 followed the normal truck and coupler progression for 1964, with each of the cars having AAR types. All but one were equipped with one operating and one non-operating truck and coupler. The 6257-100 had one operating and one plain type.

The proper instruction sheets made reference to the 90-day warranty that Lionel instituted in 1963.

The no. 62-243 Tan RSC with Black Graphics outfit box was manufactured by St. Joe Kraft, St. Joe Paper Co. Container Division and measured 12⅛ x 11½ x 6⅜ inches. It included four lines of data as part of the box manufacturer's certificate. Printed on the bottom of the outfit box was a reference to the N.M.F.C.

The 11482 was produced in smaller than average quantities and does not appear too often.

When it left Lionel's factory, the no. 11520-500 had the contents of catalog outfit no. 11520 from 1965 but came in a larger display box. Mercury Model added a box car, an engineer's cap and additional track and then stamped the outfit no. 2058. This example has a Type IIb no. 6050-150 Van Camp Savings Bank Car with early operating AAR trucks and couplers (this car typically came with Archbar types). The 11520-500 represented the final outfit appearance of a 6050-150.

Customer No. On Box: 2058
Description: "O27" Promotional Outfit
Specification: "O27" Steam Type Freight Outfit
Customer/No./Price: Hudson's Detroit; 664*11-6; $9.99
Customer/No.: Mercury Model; 2058
Original Amount: 2,300
Factory Order Date: 10/25/1965
Date Issued: 10-25-65
Date Req'd: 10/25/65
Packaging: Display

Contents: 242-25 Steam Type Locomotive; 1062T-25 Tender; 3364-25 Log Dump Car; 3364-8 Logs (3); 6176-75 Hopper Car; 6142-100 Gondola Car; 6112-88 Canister (2); 6050-150 Van Camp Savings Bank Car; 6059-50 Caboose; 1013-70 Curved Track (Bundle of 12 - 1013); 1018-10 Straight Track (Loose) (3); 6149-25X Remote Control Track; 1020-25 90° Crossing; 1010-25 35-Watt Transformer; 1103-40 Envelope Packed; D65-50 Accessory Catalog; Form 3063 Parts Order Form; 1-165 Warranty Card; 926-65 Service Station List; 11450-10 Instruction Sheet; 3364-10 Instruction Sheet; CAP Engineer Cap

Boxes & Packing: 65-270 Box Top; 64-115 Box Bottom; 64-119 Corr. Insert; 64-120 Corr. Insert; 64-118 Corr. Insert; 64-116 Shipper for 4 (1-4); 64-117 Shipper Pad (2-4)

Alternate For Outfit Contents:
Note: The Master Carton to be marked 2058 instead of our normal 11520-500.

11520-500 (2058) (1965)	C6	C7	C8	Rarity
Complete Outfit	260	390	565	R6
Outfit Box no. 65-270	100	125	150	R6

Comments: In 1965, Lionel sold outfit no. 11520-500, a Retailer Promotional Type Ib, to Mercury Model, an important Lionel distributor, for $9.00 each. Surprisingly, at least at first glance, the Factory Order included special instructions for Lionel *not* to mark or seal the outfit boxes. This made sense, however, because Mercury Model did not hesitate to buy individual items with which to augment the outfits it purchased and thereby create something that was unique to it. (Be aware that the 11520-500 was issued from Lionel in a similar unstamped fashion for Bronco Modelcraft in 1966. See the entry for 11520-500 from 1966.)

In the case of the 11520-500 from 1965, Mercury subsequently augmented each outfit with a no. 6050-150 Van Camp Savings Bank Car or no. 6050-175 Libby Box Car, an engineer's cap and additional track. The outfit box was then stamped "2058 5-Car Steam Freight Set Headlight, Engineer's Cap, Saving Bank Boxcar Figure 8 Track Layout". The 11520-500 likely was offered to numerous Mercury customers. One example has been linked via a price tag to Hudson's Detroit as no. 664*11-6 for $9.99.

Before Mercury added the extra components, the 11520-

500 from 1965 was nothing more than catalog outfit no. 11520 in a larger display box. It was led by a no. 242-25 Steam Type Locomotive. This low-end Scout steamer featured a two-position reversing unit and a headlight, lacked smoke and used a rubber tire as a traction aid. The later version with narrow running boards was included in this outfit.

The rolling stock consisted of carryover items that were commonly used in outfits from 1965. The most notable item was the no. 3364-25 Log Dump Car, which was identical to the no. 3362-25 Helium Tank Unloading Car except that it carried logs instead of helium tanks. The yellow no. 6176-75 Hopper Car was stamped "BUILT 1-48" and "LIONEL 6176".

Mercury Model added a no. 6050-150 Van Camp Savings Bank Car or no. 6050-175 Libby Box Car. Interestingly, the 6050-150 has been observed with a Type IIb or Type III body and with AAR trucks and couplers. These cars were either assembled by Mercury or purchased this way from Lionel. In either case, this may be the source of the AAR-equipped 6050-150s that appear on the market. As for the 6050-175, it has been observed with a Type III body and late AAR trucks and couplers, both of which were the norm for 1965.

The rolling stock in the 11520-500 followed the normal truck and coupler progression for 1965, with each of the cars having AAR types. Most were equipped with one late operating and one late non-operating truck and coupler. However, the no. 1062T-25 Tender had one late non-operating and one plain type, and the no. 6059-50 Caboose had one late operating and one plain type. Also of note, some 6050-150s have been observed with early operating AAR types.

The engineer's cap was also added by Mercury Model and appeared only in two promotional outfits during the 1960s, both from Mercury Model. It was likely the version that featured "Engineer" in yellow paint, although the version with "Lionel Engineer" was possible.

The 11520-500 as shipped from Lionel included only eight pieces of curved track, one straight and a no. 6149-25X Remote Control Track. Mercury added four additional pieces of curved track, two straights and a no. 1020-25 90° Crossing to create a figure-eight layout

The no. 65-270 White Lift-Off with Full-Color 2037 Steam Freight Graphics Type D display outfit box was manufactured by Mead Containers and measured 24½ x 15½ x 3⅛ inches. It provided the extra room necessary to fit the items added by Mercury Model. Since the boxes came blank and unsealed, Mercury simply stamped its no. 2058 on each box.

The "2058" has baffled collectors and researchers for years. Even after discovering the Factory Order for the 11520-500, we were stumped on its history and true contents. It wasn't until conducting further research on Mercury Model and interviewing former Lionel employees that light was shed on Mercury's practices of augmenting outfits. Once revealed, the true identity of the contents of the 11520-500 were confirmed and documented.

Mercury's 2058 was produced in fairly large quantities. It is a collector's favorite due to the inclusion of the engineer's cap. There is no difference in pricing or rarity for a 6050-150 or 6050-175.

This outfit is fairly common, but finding a C8 outfit with an original cap takes some patience to find.

Customer No. On Box: #5
Description: "O27" Promotional Outfit
Specification: "O27" Steam Type Freight Outfit
Customer/No.: Bronco Modelcraft; #5
Original Amount: 3,500
Factory Order Date: 6/16/1966
Date Issued: Rev 6-20-66
Date Req'd: 6-16-66
Packaging: Display (Units not Boxed)

Contents: 242-25 Steam Type Locomotive; 1062T-25 Tender; 3364-25 Log Dump Car; 3364-8 Logs (3); 6176-75 Hopper Car; 6142-100 Gondola Car; 6112-88 Canister (2); 6059-50 Caboose; 1013-8 Curved Track (Bundle of 8 - 1013); 1018-10 Straight Track (Loose); 6149-25 Remote Control Track; 1025-25 45 Watt Transformer; 1103-40 Envelope Packed; Form 3063 Parts Order Form; 1-166 Warranty Card; 926-66 Service Station List; 11450-10 Instruction Sheet; 3364-10 Instruction Sheet

Boxes & Packing: 65-270 Box Top; 64-112 Box Bottom; 64-118 Corr. Insert; 64-119 Corr. Insert; 64-120 Corr. Insert; 64-121 Corr. Insert; 65-274 Shipper for 2 (1-2)

Alternate For Outfit Contents:
Note: Set to be packed in #11500 Box but omit number and do not seal lid. Master carton to be sealed on one side and stamp number 3 on master carton.

11520-500 (#5) (1966)	C6	C7	C8	Rarity
Complete Outfit	200	335	500	R6
Outfit Box no. 65-270	100	175	250	R6

Comments: In 1966, Bronco Modelcraft, a notable Lionel distributor, purchased four Retailer Promotional outfits: nos. 11520-500, 11540-500, 19578 and 19580.

The 11520-500, a Type Ia, was identical to catalog outfit no. 11520 from 1966, but it came packaged in a larger display box. This outfit was also a follow-up to Mercury Model's no. 11520-500 from 1965.

Bronco likely sold the 11520-500 to numerous customers. However, an end customer has yet to be identified.

The Factory Order instructed Lionel not to stamp or seal the outfit boxes, only to stamp "No. 3" on the master carton. Even so, individual outfit boxes have been observed stamped "#5". Bronco also purchased outfit no. 19578, which was identical to this outfit except that it included additional bulk-packed items. It is believed that the outfit box for the 19578 was stamped "#5" as well. (See the entry for 19578 from 1966.)

The 11520-500 was led by a no. 242-25 Steam Type Locomotive. This low-end Scout steamer featured a two-position

The no. 11520-500 (Bronco Modelcraft #5) was Bronco Modelcraft's low-end purchase for 1966. Bronco was likely responsible for stamping it with the "#5". It was identical to catalog outfit no. 11520 from 1966 except it came in a larger display box. Of note was the version of the no. 6176-75 Hopper Car that was missing "6176" from its heat-stamping.

and one late non-operating truck and coupler. The no. 1062T-25 Tender had one late non-operating and one plain type, and the no. 6059-50 Caboose had one late operating and one plain type.

The no. 65-270 White Lift-Off with Full-Color 2037 Steam Freight Graphics Type D display outfit box was manufactured by Mead Containers and measured 24½ x 15½ x 3⅛ inches.

Since the outfit boxes were not sealed, it is highly possible that Bronco augmented the outfits with additional

reversing unit and a headlight, lacked smoke and used a rubber tire as a traction aid. The later version with narrow running boards was included in this outfit.

The rolling stock consisted of carryover items that were commonly used in outfits from 1965. The most notable item was the no. 3364-25 Log Dump Car, which was identical to the no. 3362-25 Helium Tank Unloading Car except that it carried logs instead of helium tanks. The yellow no. 6176-75 Hopper Car was stamped "BUILT 1-48" and "LIONEL". This interesting variation did not include the "6176" number as part of its heat-stamping.

The rolling stock in the 11520-500 followed the normal truck and coupler progression for 1966, with each of the cars having AAR types. All but two were equipped with one late operating

track and rolling stock. To date, most #5s are found as listed on the Factory Order and some are found with enough additional track to make a figure-eight layout.

Interestingly, even though the Factory Order specified that the master carton for the 11520-500 was to be stamped with a "No. 3", the outfit boxes are observed stamped "#5". The opposite is true for Bronco's 19580: The Factory Order instructs that the master carton be stamped "No. 5", but the 19580's outfit box is observed stamped "#3".

It is our belief that the #5 was stamped on both Bronco's 11520-500 and 19578. As such, quantities are combined to determine rarity and pricing.

Description: "O27" Promotional Outfit
Specification: "O27" Steam Type Freight Outfit W/Smoke
Original Amount: 1,150
Factory Order Date: 8/25/1965
Date Issued: Rev. 8-24-65
Packaging: (Units not Boxed)

Contents: 239-25 Steam Locomotive With Smoke; 242T-25 Tender; 6473-25 Rodeo Car; 6465-150 Tank Car; 6176-50 Hopper Car; 6119-110 Work Caboose; 1013-8 Curved Track (Bundle of 8 - 1013); 1018-10 Straight Track (Loose); 6149-25 Remote Control Track; 1025-25 45-Watt Transformer; 1103-40 Envelope Packed; 909-20 Smoke Fluid; D65-50 Accessory Catalog; Form

3063 Parts Order Form; 1-165 Warranty Card; 926-65 Service Station List; 11450-10 Instruction Sheet; 237-11 Instruction Sheet; 239-18 Flyer

Boxes & Packing: 65-270 Box Top; 64-115 Box Bottom; 64-118 Corr. Insert; 64-119 Corr. Insert; 64-120 Corr. Insert; 64-116 Shipper for 4 (1-4); 64-117 Shipper Pad (2-4)

Alternate For Outfit Contents:

Note: No outfit number or description is to be printed on box or shipper.

Comments: In 1965, Lionel offered Retailer Promotional outfits to only Mercury Model, Sears and Western Auto. Other retailers, many of whom were accustomed to obtaining exclusive promotional outfits, were now limited to General Release Promotional outfits. They had to compete head-to-head with other retailers with similar offerings.

Outfit no. 11540-500, a Type IIa, has yet to be linked to a particular retailer. Lionel's cost to retailers was $13.50 for each 11540-500. Except for one insert, the outfit was identical to catalog outfit no. 11540 from 1965.

The 11540-500 is an interesting outfit that's difficult to decipher. It was issued in 1965 and 1966 with three subtle differences between the two years. These included a different outfit box bottom and updated paperwork, along with updated versions of the rolling stock.

Specifically, the no. 64-115 Box Bottom for the 1965 version measured only 3 inches high versus 3⅞ inches for the no. 64-112 Box Bottom used for the 1966 version. This deeper bottom meant the no. 65-270 Box Top did not fully telescope the bottom.

The paperwork included year appropriate service station lists, warranty cards and accessory catalogs.

As far as the rolling stock was concerned, most no. 6176-50 Hopper Cars still included a built date and item number heat-stamped on the car in 1965. A year later, some of the cars in this outfit featured a washer riveted above or below the leaf spring on their trucks and couplers.

The Factory Order for both the 1965 and 1966 versions indicated that an outfit number was not to be stamped on the outfit box. Although 11540-500s have been observed stamped as "No. 11540-500", they all exhibit the features for 1966 mentioned above and were likely stamped by Bronco Modelcraft, the customer for 11540-500 from 1966. (See the entry for 11540-500 from 1966.)

It is unknown where the 1965 versions of this outfit went and if and how they were eventually stamped. Unfortunately, an 11540-500 with 1965 features has yet to be observed. Since we do not know how the outfit box was stamped, pricing and rarity are unavailable.

11540-500
1966

Description: "O27" Promotional Outfit
Specification: "O27" Steam Type Freight Outfit W/Smoke
Customer: Bronco Modelcraft
Customer/No./Price: Noah's Ark; 693 X3803B; $21.88
Original Amount: 1,550
Factory Order Date: 6/16/1966
Date Issued: Rev 9-1-66
Date Req'd: 9-1-66
Packaging: Display (Units not Boxed)

Contents: 239-25 Steam Locomotive With Smoke; 242T-25 Tender; 6473-25 Rodeo Car; 6465-150 Tank Car; 6176-50 Hopper Car; 6119-110 Work Caboose; 1013-8 Curved Track (Bundle of 8 - 1013); 1018-10 Straight Track (Loose); 6149-25 Remote Control Track; 1025-25 45-Watt Transformer; 1103-40 Envelope Packed; 909-20 Smoke Fluid; Form 3063 Parts Order Form; 1-166 Warranty Card; 926-66 Service Station List; 11450-10 Instruction Sheet; 237-11 Instruction Sheet

Boxes & Packing: 65-270 Box Top; 64-112 Box Bottom; 64-118 Corr. Insert; 64-119 Corr. Insert; 64-120 Corr. Insert; 64-121 Corr. Insert; 65-274 Shipper for 2 (1-2)

Alternate For Outfit Contents:
Note: This set to be packed in #11500 Box but omit number and do not seal lid. Master carton to be sealed but on one side only and stamp number 5 on master carton.

11540-500 (1966)	C6	C7	C8	Rarity
Complete Outfit	250	375	550	R6
Outfit Box no. 65-270	100	175	250	R6

Comments: In 1966, Bronco Modelcraft, a notable Lionel distributor, purchased four Retailer Promotional outfits: nos. 11520-500, 11540-500, 19578 and 19580.

The 11540-500, a Type Ia, was a follow-up to General Release Promotional outfit no. 11540-500 from 1965. The contents of the 1966 version were nearly identical to those of catalog outfit no. 11540 from 1966. The only differences related to the box bottom, two inserts and an instruction sheet. In fact, this outfit was likely created from excess inventory of the 11540. The quantity of 11540s was cut by 1,500 on 6/8/66, and the Factory Order for the 11540-500 was issued on 6/16/66 with a quantity of 1,500. An additional 50 units of the 11540-500 were added on 9/1/66.

The 11540-500 likely was offered to numerous Bronco customers. One example has been linked to Noah's Ark Auto Accessories, Inc. as no. 695 X3803B for $21.88.

The Factory Order instructed Lionel not to stamp or seal the outfit boxes, only to stamp "No. 5" on the master carton. Even so, individual outfit boxes have been observed stamped "No. 11540-500". Since the outfit boxes were not sealed, it is highly likely that Bronco augmented the outfits with additional track and rolling stock. To date, most 11540-500s are found as listed on the Factory Order, but more than one has been observed with an additional no. 6162-100 Gondola Car with two no. 6112-88 Canisters.

The 11540-500 was led by a no. 239-25 Steam Locomotive With Smoke. This die-cast Scout steamer featured a two-position reversing unit, a headlight and a rubber tire as a traction aid. Except for its 239 number and lack of stripe, it was the same engine as a no. 241.

The rolling stock consisted of carryover items that were commonly used in outfits from 1966. The no. 6473-25 Rodeo Car used a Type IIIc body (cadmium yellow plastic with maroon lettering). That body no longer exhibited the filled slot caused by broken tooling. During the course of 1966, Lionel finished removing the new date, a built date and number data from the heat-stamping of the black no. 6176-50 Hopper Car. This minimal decoration became the norm for the 6176-50. The "-110" suffix for the no. 6119-110 Work Caboose meant that it came unboxed.

The rolling stock in the 11540-500 followed the normal truck and coupler progression for 1966, with each of the cars having AAR types. All but two were equipped with one late operating and one late non-operating truck and coupler. The no. 242T-25

The no. 11540-500 was one of the four Retailer Promotional outfits purchased by Bronco Modelcraft in 1966. The Factory Order instructed Lionel not to stamp or seal the outfit boxes. As such, these were likely hand-stamped by Bronco with just the outfit number and no description. The outfit shown was one of those that came out of Madison Hardware after it was moved to Detroit.

Mead Containers and measured 24½ x 15½ x 3⅛ inches.

Interestingly, even though the Factory Order specified that the master carton for the 11540-500 was to be stamped with a "No. 5", the outfit boxes are observed stamped "11540-500". Bronco also purchased outfit no. 19580, which was identical to this outfit except that it included one additional instruction sheet and additional bulk-packed items. Its outfit box was stamped "#3".

In 1989, Richard Kughn, then the owner of Lionel Trains Inc., purchased Madison Hardware Co. of New York City and reopened it in Detroit shortly thereafter. One of the first lists of outfits available for sale included five of the 11540-500. With 1,550 originally manufactured and the fact that new outfits were still available from Madison into the late 1980s, the 11540-500 can be obtained with some patience.

Tender had one late non-operating and one plain type, and the 6119-110 had one late operating and one plain type. Be aware that some 6176-50s featured a washer riveted above or below the leaf spring on its trucks and couplers.

The no. 65-270 White Lift-Off with Full-Color 2037 Steam Freight Graphics Type D display outfit box was manufactured by

---

Description: "O27" Promotional Outfit
Original Amount: 500
Factory Order Date: 11/4/1966
Date Issued: 11-4-66
Date Req'd: 11-5-66

Contents: 239-25 Steam Locomotive With Smoke; 242T-25 Tender; 6473-25 Rodeo Car; 6465-150 Tank Car; 6014-325 Frisco Box Car; 6062-25 Gondola Car; 6112-88 Canister (2); 6119-110 Work Caboose; 1013-8 Curved Track (Bundle of 8 - 1013); 1018-10 Straight Track (Loose); 6149-25 Remote Control Track; 1025-25 45-Watt Transformer; 1103-40 Envelope Packed; 909-20 Smoke Fluid; Form 3063 Parts Order Form; 1-166 Warranty Card; 926-66 Service Station List; 11450-10 Instruction Sheet; 237-11 Instruction Sheet; 239-18 Flyer

Boxes & Packing: 65-270 Box Top; 64-115 Box Bottom; 64-119 Corr. Insert; 64-120 Corr. Insert; 64-118 Corr. Insert; 64-116 Shipper for 4 (1-4); 64-117 Shipper Pad (2-4); MT Mylar Tape (6")

11540X (1966)	C6	C7	C8	Rarity
Complete Outfit	365	650	950	R9
Outfit Box no. 65-270	150	300	400	R9

Comments: On November 4, 1966, Lionel issued Factory Orders for five General Release Promotional Type IIa outfits: nos. 11540X, 11560X, 12710X, 12800X and 12850X. All five were based on catalog outfits, with an "X" suffix added to the catalog number. Lionel created these outfits to reduce its excess inventory of unsold stock from 1966.

The 11540X was based on catalog outfit no. 11540 from 1966. The 11540X replaced the no. 6176-50 Hopper Car in the 11540 with a no. 6014-325 Frisco Box Car and a no. 6062-25 Gondola Car with two red no. 6112-88 Canisters. Also, one insert was changed. The 11540X has yet to be linked to a specific end retailer.

The 11540X was led by a no. 239-25 Steam Locomotive With Smoke. This die-cast Scout steamer featured a two-position reversing unit, a headlight and a rubber tire as a traction aid. Except for its 239 number and lack of stripe, it was the same engine as a no. 241.

The rolling stock was all carryover. Except for the no. 6062-25 Gondola Car, all the items were commonly used in outfits from 1966. The no. 6473-25 Rodeo Car used a Type IIIa body (cadmium yellow plastic with red lettering). That body no longer exhibited the filled slot caused by broken tooling.

Outfit no. 11540X was one of five promotional outfits from late 1966 that were based on a catalog outfit. It is very similar to catalog outfit no. 11540 issued earlier in the year. Of note was the inclusion of the no. 6119-110 Work Caboose that came with "BUILT BY LIONEL" on its own builder's plate. Also note "LIONEL" in "sans-serif" lettering on the frame.

and coupler progression for 1966, with each of the cars having AAR types. All but two were equipped with one late operating and one late non-operating truck and coupler. The no. 242T-25 Tender had one late non-operating and one plain type, and the 6119-110 had one late operating and one plain type. Be aware that the no. 6465-150 Tank Car featured a washer riveted above or below the leaf spring on its trucks and couplers.

In 1966, the 6112-88 Canisters could be found molded in red plastic. Also the no. 909-20 Smoke Fluid began to appear with a white paper backing.

The no. 65-270 White Lift-Off with Full-Color 2037 Steam Freight Graphics Type D display outfit box was manufactured by Mead Containers and measured 24½ x 15½ x 3⅛ inches.

The 11540X is a highly desirable promotional outfit for a couple of reasons. First, only 500 units were manufactured and so one appears only infrequently. Second, it included the difficult-to-find version of the 6119-110 with a separate builder's plate.

The no. 6119-110 Work Caboose was the difficult-to-find version that featured wood slats below the number plate and "BUILT BY LIONEL" on its own builder's plate. It also had "LIONEL" stamped on the frame in "sans-serif" lettering. The "-110" suffix meant that it came unboxed. This variation adds a premium to the outfit price.

The rolling stock in the 11540X followed the normal truck

11560-500
1965

Description: "O27" Promotional Outfit
Specification: "O27" Diesel Freight Outfit
Original Amount: 596
Factory Order Date: 9/1/1965
Date Issued: Rev. 9-1-65
Date Req'd: 9-3-65
Packaging: Display Packing (Units not Boxed)

Contents: 211P-150 *"Texas Special"* Diesel; 211T-25 *"Texas Special"* Motorless Unit; 6473-25 Rodeo Car; 6176-50 Hopper Car; 6142-100 Gondola Car; 6112-88 Canister (2); 6465-150 Tank Car; 6059-50 Caboose; 1013-70 Curved Track (Bundle of 12 - 1013); 1018-30 Straight Track (Bundle of 3 - 1018); 1020-25 90° Crossing; 6149-25 Remote Control Track; 1025-25 45-Watt Transformer; 1103-40 Envelope Packed; D65-50 Accessory Catalog; Form 3063 Parts Order Form; 1-165 Warranty Card;

926-65 Service Station List; 211-151 Instruction Sheet; 19214-10 Instruction Sheet

Boxes & Packing: 65-270 Box Top; 64-115 Box Bottom; 64-118 Corr. Insert; 64-122 Corr. Insert; 64-116 Shipper for 4 (1-4); 64-117 Shipper Pad (2-4); MT Mylar Tape (5")

Alternate For Outfit Contents:
Note: This set is identical to set #11560 except do not stamp outfit identification number on display box.

Comments: In 1965, Lionel offered Retailer Promotional outfits to only Mercury Model, Sears and Western Auto. Other retailers, many of whom were accustomed to obtaining exclusive promotional outfits, were now limited to General Release Promotional outfits. They had to compete head-to-head with other retailers with similar offerings.

The 11560-500, a Type IIa, was identical to catalog outfit no. 11560 from 1965. In fact they were both created at the same time. When the quantity of the 11560 was increased from 6,000 to 12,404 outfits, Lionel issued a Factory Order for the 11560-500 and its quantity of 596. This was likely done to make the production run a round number of 13,000 outfits. Lionel's cost to retailers was $16.87 for each 11560-500.

The Factory Order stated that no number was to be stamped on the box. Consequently, where examples of this outfit went cannot be determined. Neither can whether they eventually were stamped and, if so, in what manner.

Omissions like these mean that an authentic example of the 11560-500 may never be found. Even if an unstamped 11560 showed up, it would be impossible to prove that it actually was an 11560-500 without definite provenance from the time it left Lionel.

To make matters still more confusing and frustrating for collectors, unstamped no. 65-270 Box Tops were provided to Lionel's Service Department. As a result, this outfit could easily have been created with a blank top and a 11560 bottom.

Since the 11560-500 was produced at the same time as the 11560, the contents of the two outfits likely were identical. For that reason, a description of the catalog outfit follows.

The 11560 was led by a no. 211P-150 *Texas Special* Diesel. The 211P-150 was a cost-reduced version of the no. 211P-25 *Texas Special* Alco Diesel Power Unit. The "-150" featured a two-position reversing unit, two traction tires, a headlight, a weight and an open pilot with a large ledge.

The rolling stock consisted of carryover items that were commonly used in outfits from 1965. The no. 6473-25 Rodeo Car typically came with a Type IIIa body (cadmium yellow plastic with red lettering). However, a Type IIIc body (cadmium yellow plastic with maroon lettering) has been observed, and a Type IIIb body (lighter lemon yellow plastic with maroon lettering) is also possible. The Type IIIb variation would command a slight premium. The Type III body no longer exhibited the filled slot caused by broken tooling.

The black no. 6176-50 Hopper Car was actually stamped "BUILT 1-48" and "LIONEL 6076". However, this car still was considered a 6176 because it included an operating truck and coupler.

A green no. 6142-100 Gondola Car was listed on the Factory Order, but this outfit has also been observed with a blue no. 6142-125 Gondola Car.

The rolling stock in the 11560 (and presumably the 11560-500) followed the normal truck and coupler progression for 1965, with each of the cars having AAR types. All but one were equipped with one late operating and one late non-operating truck and coupler. The no. 6059-50 Caboose had one late operating and one plain type.

The no. 65-270 White Lift-Off with Full-Color 2037 Steam Freight Graphics Type D display outfit box measured 24½ x 15½ x 3⅛ inches.

Even though the contents of the 11560-500 were identical to those of the 11560, we do not know how the outfit box was stamped. As such, pricing and rarity are unavailable.

Description: "O27" Promotional Outfit
Original Amount: 500
Factory Order Date: 11/4/1966
Date Issued: 11-4-66
Date Req'd: 11-5-66

Contents: 211P-150 *"Texas Special"* Diesel; 211T-25 *"Texas Special"* Motorless Unit; 6473-25 Rodeo Car; 6176-50 Hopper Car; 6014-325 Frisco Box Car; 6401-25 Flat Car; 3364-8 Logs (3); 6059-50 Caboose; 1013-70 Curved Track (Bundle of 12 - 1013); 1018-30 Straight Track (Bundle of 3 - 1018); 1020-25 90° Crossing; 6149-25 Remote Control Track; 1025-25 45-Watt Transformer; 1103-40 Envelope Packed; Form 3063 Parts Order Form; 1-166 Warranty Card; 926-66 Service Station List; 211-151 Instruction Sheet; 19214-10 Instruction Sheet

Boxes & Packing: 65-270 Box Top; 64-115 Box Bottom; 64-118 Corr. Insert; 64-122 Corr. Insert; 64-116 Shipper for 4 (1-4); 64-117 Shipper Pad (2-4); MT Mylar Tape (6")

11560X (1966)	C6	C7	C8	Rarity
Complete Outfit	310	600	850	R9
Outfit Box no. 65-270	150	300	400	R9

Comments: On November 4, 1966, Lionel issued Factory Orders for five General Release Promotional Type IIa outfits: nos. 11540X, 11560X, 12710X, 12800X and 12850X. All five were based on catalog outfits, with an "X" suffix added to the catalog number. Lionel created these outfits to reduce its excess inventory of unsold stock from 1966.

The 11560X, which has yet to be linked to a specific end retailer, was based on catalog outfit no. 11560 from 1966. The 11560X replaced the nos. 6142-100 Gondola Car, two 6112-88 Canisters and 6465-150 Tank Car found in the 11560 with the nos. 6014-325 Frisco Box Car, 6401-25 Flat Car and three 3364-8 Logs.

The 11560X was led by a no. 211P-150 *Texas Special* Diesel. The 211P-150 was a cost-reduced version of the no. 211P-25 *Texas Special* Alco Diesel Power Unit. The "-150" featured a two-position reversing unit, two traction tires, a headlight, a weight and an open pilot with a large ledge.

The rolling stock in this outfit consisted of carryover items that were commonly used in outfits from 1966. The no. 6473-25 Rodeo Car used a Type IIIc body (cadmium yellow plastic with maroon lettering), which no longer exhibited the filled slot caused by broken tooling. During the course of 1966, Lionel finished removing the new date, a built date and number data from the heat-stamping of the black no. 6176-50 Hopper Car. This minimal decoration became the norm for the 6176-50. Also in 1966, Lionel began to pair the no. 6401-25 Flat Car with three no. 3364-8 Logs.

The rolling stock in the 11560X followed the normal truck and coupler progression for 1966, with each of the cars having AAR types. All were equipped with one late operating and one late non-operating truck and coupler. However the no. 6059-50 Caboose could come with one late operating and one plain type.

A no. 19214-10 Instruction Sheet detailed the figure-eight track layout and was dated 6/66.

The no. 65-270 White Lift-Off with Full-Color 2037 Steam Freight Graphics Type D display outfit box measured 24½ x 15½ x 3⅛ inches. Per the Factory Order, the outfit box was simply stamped "11560X" with no additional information about the train outfit.

The contents of the 11560X are no more exciting than those

in its 11560 counterpart. What is exciting from a collectibility perspective is the small quantity produced and the infrequent appearance of an example on the market. For these reasons, the 11560X is more desirable than its catalog counterpart.

11570
1966

Outfit no. 11570 was available to any Lionel customer that desired an outfit other than what was listed in the consumer catalog. In earlier years, Lionel would have classified it as an advance catalog outfit. Be aware that the no. 1061-75 Steam Type Locomotive featured a 2-4-2 wheel arrangement and the no. 6167-25 Caboose now came with two non-operating late AAR trucks and couplers.

Two variations of the no. 64-162 White RSC with Orange Graphics outfit box. Left: This still-sealed sales sample was the early version manufactured by St. Joe Paper Co. Container Div. It still referred to "The Lionel Corporation". Right: A later version, manufactured by United Container, made reference to "The Lionel Toy Corporation".

Description: "O27" Promotional Outfit
Specification: "O27" Steam Type Freight Outfit
Customer/Price: E.J. Korvette; $7.77
Customer/No./Price: Joe, The Motorists' Friend; 11570; $10.95
Original Amount: 50,000
Factory Order Date: 2/18/1966
Date Issued: Rev 6-16-66
Date Req'd: 5-19-66
Packaging: WRSC

Contents: 1061-75 Steam Type Locomotive; 1062T-25 Tender;

The sales flyer for the nos. 11570 and D11570 Blister Display states, "Priced to walk off the shelf!" These flyers, along with black-and-white glossy photographs, were provided to the sales force to use as needed.

6042-250 Gondola Car; 6112-88 Canister (2); 6402-25 Flat Car W/2 Cable Reels; 40-11 Cable Reels (2); 6167-25 Caboose; 1013-8 Curved Track (Bundle of 8 - 1013); 1018-10 Straight Track (Loose) (2); 1025-25 45-Watt Transformer; 1103-20 Envelope Packed; 11570-10 Instruction Sheet; 1-166 Warranty Card; 926-66 Service Station List; Form 3063 Parts Order Form

Boxes & Packing: 64-162 Outfit Box; 62-254 Corr. Insert; 61-173 Corr. Insert; 64-319 Corr. Insert; 63-384 Shipper for 4 (1-4); 64-106 Shipper Pad (2-4)

Alternate For Outfit Contents:

Note: Sub. 8,800 - 1010-25 for 1025-25.

11570 (1966)	C6	C7	C8	Rarity
Complete Outfit	80	140	210	R2
Outfit Box no. 64-162	15	25	35	R2

Comments: In 1966, Lionel issued two low-cost General Release Promotional Type IIb outfits: nos. 11570 and 11580. This pair probably would have been classified as advance catalog outfits had Lionel still been issuing special advance catalogs to retailers. Instead, the two outfits were part of Lionel's promotional outfit strategy of offering retailers something different even if they couldn't commit to the quantity necessary for a unique promotional outfit.

The 11570 was sold to numerous retailers, a few of which have been identified by price tags or catalog listings. Retailers paid Lionel $7.50 for each outfit.

The 11570 was the less desirable of the two outfits. It was led by a no. 1061-75 Steam Type Locomotive (new for 1966). This low-end Scout steamer featured a 2-4-2 wheel arrangement and a rubber tire as a traction aid. It went forward only and lacked a headlight and lens. Other than its wheel arrangement, the 1061-75 was identical to the no. 1061-50 Steam Type Loco W/Tire.

The other contents of this outfit consisted of carryover items. The no. 1062T-25 Tender was stamped with "Lionel Lines", but all the other cars were unmarked. The no. 6042-250 Gondola Car has been observed in light and dark shades of blue plastic.

The rolling stock in the 11570 followed the normal truck and coupler progression for 1966, with all the cars having late AAR types. Every model except for the 1062T-25 was equipped with two non-operating trucks and couplers; it came with one non-operating and one plain type. The no. 6167-25 Caboose had two non-operating trucks and couplers, reflecting the trend at Lionel to replace the plain one with a non-operating type on most cabooses in 1966.

This outfit introduced the no. 11570-10 Instruction Sheet that was dated 2/66.

The transformer substitution does not affect the outfit price.

Originally, 25,000 units of the 11570 were supposed to be manufactured. This amount was subsequently increased to 50,000. This quantity means the 11570 ranks seventh as the most produced catalog or promotional outfit during the 1960s.

With so many outfits produced, there are variations in its outfit box. The 11570 is most often found in a no. 64-162 White RSC with Orange Graphics outfit box manufactured by United Container Co. and measuring 11⅜ x 9¾ x 6⅛ inches. This outfit box included four lines of data and has been observed with an "8-66" or "66" and seven, eight or nine stars as part of the box manufacturer's certificate. Other combinations likely exist. Printed on the bottom of the outfit box were "64-162" and a reference to the N.M.F.C.

An early, hand-stamped sales sample of the 11570 also came in a 64-162 White RSC with Orange Graphics outfit box with the same dimensions. However, it was manufactured by St. Joe Paper Co. Container Div.

A Tan RSC Mailer that was hand-stamped has also been observed. This likely came from the latter part of 1966 or even later, and it probably was an attempt to reduce excess inventory. (See the section on Outfit Box Printing, Graphics and Labels.)

The 11570 was produced in such large quantities that many examples have survived. For that reason, adding one to a collection is easy.

CONVENTIONAL PACK
64-162 BOX

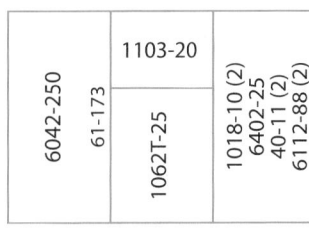

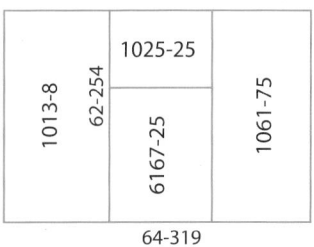

Description: "O27" Promotional Outfit
Specification: "O27" Steam Type Freight Outfit
Original Amount: 18,000
Factory Order Date: 2/18/1966
Date Issued: Rev 10-28-66
Date Req'd: 10-28-66
Packaging: WRSC

Contents: 1062-75 Steam Type Loco. W/Light & Reversing Unit; 1062T-25 Tender; 6401-25 Flat Car; 3364-8 Logs (3); 6176-50 Hopper Car; 6167-100 Caboose; 4-5 Elastic Band; 1013-8 Curved Track (Bundle of 8 - 1013); 1018-10 Straight Track (Loose); 1008-50 Uncoupling Unit; 1025-25 45-Watt Transformer; 1103-20 Envelope Packed; 11580-15 Instruction Sheet; 1-166 Warranty Card; 926-66 Service Station List; Form 3063 Parts Order Form

Boxes & Packing: 64-162 Outfit Box; 62-254 Corr. Insert; 61-173 Corr. Insert; 64-319 Corr. Insert; 63-384 Shipper for 4 (1-4); 64-106 Shipper Pad (2-4)

Alternate For Outfit Contents:

Note: 11580-20 Printed Label to be applied to box.

11580 (1966)	C6	C7	C8	Rarity
Complete Outfit	95	165	260	R3
Outfit Box no. 64-162	25	45	75	R3
Complete Outfit With no. 11580-20 Printed Label	105	180	280	R3
Outfit Box no. 64-162 With no. 11580-20 Printed Label	35	60	95	R3

Comments: In 1966, Lionel issued two low-cost General Release Promotional Type IIb outfits: nos. 11570 and 11580. This pair probably would have been classified as advance catalog outfits had Lionel still been issuing special advance catalogs to retailers. Instead, the two outfits were part of Lionel's promotional outfit strategy of offering retailers something different even if they couldn't commit to the quantity necessary for a unique promotional outfit.

The 11580 was sold to numerous retailers, a few of which

Outfit no. 11580 was available to any customer that desired an outfit other than what was listed in the consumer catalog. In earlier years, Lionel would have classified this as an advance catalog outfit. Be aware that the black no. 6176-50 Hopper Car omitted the new date, a built date and number data from its heat-stamping and the no. 6167-100 Caboose came with one operating and one non-operating late AAR truck and coupler.

The sales flyer for the nos. 11580 and D11580 Blister Display states, "New Value-Packed Promotional Set from Lionel". These flyers, along with black-and-white glossy photographs, were provided to the sales force to use as needed.

Some examples of the no. 11580 came with a no. 11580-20 Printed Label applied on the box end. Adding labels to outfit boxes to help promote the contents was becoming a common practice by 1966. An 11580 with a label is more difficult to find than one without it.

have been identified by price tags or catalog listings. Retailers paid Lionel $9.00 for each outfit.

The 11580 was the more desirable of the two outfits. It was led by a no. 1062-75 Steam Type Loco. W/Light & Reversing Unit (new for 1966). This low-end Scout steamer featured a 2-4-2 wheel arrangement and a rubber tire as a traction aid. Except for its wheel arrangement, the 1062-75 was identical to the no. 1062-50 Steam Type Loco. W/Light & Reversing Unit.

The rolling stock in this outfit consisted of carryover items that were commonly used in outfits from 1966. During the course of that year, Lionel finished removing the new date, a built date and number data from the heat-stamping of the black no. 6176-50 Hopper Car. This minimal decoration became the norm for the 6176-50. Also in 1966, Lionel began to pair the no. 6401-25 Flat Car with three no. 3364-8 Logs.

The no. 6167-100 Caboose most often featured an unpainted red plastic shell, but it has also been observed painted red on a gray shell. The latter version commands a premium.

The rolling stock in the 11580 followed the normal truck and

coupler progression for 1966, with all the cars having late AAR types. Every model except for the 1062T-25 Tender was equipped with one operating and one non-operating truck and coupler; it came with one non-operating and one plain type. The no. 6167-100 Caboose had one operating and one non-operating truck and coupler, reflecting the trend at Lionel to replace the plain one with a non-operating type on most cabooses in 1966.

Early Factory Orders created for sales samples of the 11580 listed a no. 11580-10 Instruction Sheet dated 1/66. It appears this difficult-to-find sheet was never used, probably because it omitted information about the locomotive. It was replaced by a no. 11580-15 Instruction Sheet dated 5/66. Both sheets were newly created for the 11580.

A white Type III no. 1103-20 Envelope Packed has been observed in this outfit.

The no. 64-162 White RSC with Orange Graphics outfit box was manufactured by United Container Co. and measured 11⅜ x 9¾ x 6⅛ inches. It included four lines of data and has been observed with an "8-66" or "66" and eight stars as part of the box manufacturer's certificate. Other combinations likely exist. Printed on the bottom were "64-162" and a reference to the N.M.F.C.

Even though a no. 11580-20 Printed Label was to be applied to the outfit box, most outfits are found without this label. A no. 11580 is more difficult to find with the label, a point that is noted in the pricing table.

An original quantity of 50,000 units of the 11580 was to have been manufactured. This amount was subsequently reduced to 18,000. As a result, this outfit is more difficult to find than its companion 11570, but it is still a common promotional outfit.

CONVENTIONAL PACK
64-162 BOX

TOP LAYER

| 6176-50 | 61-173 | 1103-20 | | 1018-10 1008-50 6401-25 3364-8 (3) |
| | | 1062T-25 | | |

BOTTOM LAYER

| 1013-8 | 62-254 | 1025-25 | 1062-75 |
| | | 6167-100 | |

64-319

During 1968, when Lionel issued a single catalog outfit (no. 11600), it was still committed to producing promotional outfits. Outfit no. 11620 was the only General Release Promotional outfit issued by Lionel in that year. Its no. 2029-25 Steam Type Locomotive With Smoke relied on a motor assembly manufactured in Japan. The no. 234T-25 Tender (Without Whistle) was stamped "234W" even though it did not include a whistle. Note that the 2029-25's body appears dull with faded heat-stamping – that is how many new outfits are found. This example was one of the 44 that were available from Madison Hardware Co. in Detroit.

Description: "O27" Promotional Outfit
Specification: "O27" Steam Type Freight Outfit With Smoke
Factory Order Date: 11/1/1968
Date Issued: 12/4/68
Packaging: R.S.C. Outfit Packing

Contents: 2029-25 Steam Type Locomotive With Smoke; 234T-25 Tender (Without Whistle); 6402-50 Flat Car W/2 Cable Reels; 40-11 Cable Reels (2); 6476-125 Hopper Car; 6062-25 Gondola Car; 6130-25 Work Caboose - "Santa Fe"; 1025-25 45-Watt Transformer; 1013 Curved Track (8); 1018 Straight Track (3); 6149-25 Remote Control Track; 1103-50 Envelope Packed; 1-165 Warranty Card; Form 3063 Parts Order Form; 2029-5 Instruction Sheet; 6149-17 Instruction Sheet; SP-1 Smoke Pellets; 675-33 Smoke Stack Cleaner

Boxes & Packing: 65-410 Outfit Box; 62-248 Insert (4)

11620 (1968)	C6	C7	C8	Rarity
Complete Outfit	210	330	465	R6
Outfit Box no. 65-410	50	75	100	R6

Comments: In 1968, Lionel issued two outfits: catalog outfit no. 11600 and General Release Promotional Type IIa outfit no.

11620. The latter was announced in *Lionel Service News* no. 13 from November 1968. The suggested retail was $45.00, and the dealer cost was $22.50 each. This outfit has yet to be linked to an end retailer.

The 11620 was led by a new version of the no. 2029-25 Steam Type Locomotive With Smoke that featured a motor assembly made in Japan. The nameplate listed Hagerstown as Lionel's address, and the trailing truck had "JAPAN" embossed on it. The motor assembly was paired with a no. 2029-2 Boiler & Cab Assembly, which likely came from inventory. This may explain why many new examples appear dull and have off-white "2029" heat-stamping that was poorly applied.

This steamer featured a two-position reversing unit, a headlight and a rubber tire as a traction aid. Since the 2029-25 came unboxed (as indicated by the "-25"), the nos. SP-1 Smoke Pellets, 675-33 Smoke Stack Cleaner and 2029-5 Instruction Sheet were provided separately in the outfit box. The no. CTC-1 Lockon came in the 1103-50 Envelope Packed.

Lionel also introduced the no. 234T-25 Tender (Without Whistle) in 1968. This model had "234W" heat-stamped on each side, but a whistle was not installed. The 234T-25 was assembled to deplete excess tender bodies and frames. It came with one operating and one plain AAR truck and coupler.

The remaining rolling stock in this outfit appeared to be

assembled from leftover inventory. The yellow no. 6476-125 Hopper Car omitted the new date, a built date and number data from its heat-stamping. The "-125" suffix meant that it came unboxed. It was considered a 6476 because it had operating AAR trucks and couplers.

The unpainted black no. 6062-25 Gondola Car omitted the "New 2-49" from its heat-stamping. It was equipped with one operating AAR truck and coupler and one non-operating AAR or Archbar truck and coupler. Some outfits included two red no. 6112-5 Canisters as a load for this car.

Different variations of the no. 6130-25 Santa Fe Work Caboose have been observed with the 11620. The one most often found featured an unpainted and unstamped black frame, had a builder's plate, lacked slats below the Santa Fe herald and came with two operating AAR trucks and couplers. Other, earlier versions of the 6130-25 have been observed as well as a no. 6119-110 Work Caboose substitution.

The no. 6402-50 Flat Car was equipped with one operating and one non-operating AAR truck and coupler.

Except for the Archbar truck and coupler on some 6062-25s, the rolling stock in the 11620 followed the normal truck and coupler progression for 1968. All the cars came with late AAR types.

The no. 6149-17 Instruction Sheet dated 3/65 and the 1968 version of Form 3063 dated 10/68 are both difficult to find.

The no. 65-410 Tan RSC with Black Graphics outfit box was manufactured by Eastern Corrugated Container Corp. and measured 11½ x 10 x 6¼ inches. These boxes were made of a thicker corrugated material (rated at 90 pounds rather than the normal 65 pounds gross weight) that allowed each outfit to be shipped in its outfit box. Two versions have been observed. Both featured four lines of data as part of the box manufacturer's certificate, but a second version also included a reference to the N.M.F.C. Some outfits were overstickered with a strip of packing tape on the box end and the "11620" stamped on the tape.

Lionel had more than 6,225 units of 65-410 boxes in inventory during the middle of 1967. Exactly how many remained by 1968 and were used for the 11620 cannot be determined. What is known is that many 11620s did survive.

In 1989, Richard Kughn, then the owner of Lionel Trains Inc., purchased Madison Hardware Co. of New York City and reopened it in Detroit soon thereafter. One of the first lists of outfits available for sale included 44 of the 11620.

CONVENTIONAL PACK
65-410 BOX

TOP LAYER			BOTTOM LAYER	
6476-125			1013 (8)	
6062-25	40-11 (2)	6402-50	1025-25	234T-25
6130-25			2029-25	
6149-25 1018 (3)				

Description: "O" Gauge Promotional Outfit
Original Amount: 200
Factory Order Date: 11/4/1966
Date Issued: 11-4-66
Date Req'd: 11-5-66

Contents: 736-1 Steam Type Locomotive With Smoke; 736W-1 Whistle Tender; 6464-735 "New Haven" Box Car; 6162-110 Gondola W/Canisters; 6414-1 Auto Transport Car; 6431-1 Trailer Flat Car W/2 Trailers; 6437-1 Illuminated Caboose; TOC-8 Curved Track (8 per Bundle); TOS-19 Straight Track (5 per Bundle); UCS-1 Remote Control Track Section; LW-1 125-Watt Transformer; CTC-1 Lockon; Form 3063 Parts Order Form; 1-166 Warranty Card; 926-66 Service Station List; 12700-10 Instruction Sheet

Boxes & Packing: 66-102 Outfit Box; 66-103 Shipper (1-1); 65-367 Corr. Insert (2)

12710X (1966)	C6	C7	C8	Rarity
Complete Outfit	1,325	1,950	2,650	R10
Outfit Box no. 66-102	500	700	900	R10

Comments: On November 4, 1966, Lionel issued Factory Orders for five General Release Promotional Type IIa outfits: nos. 11540X, 11560X, 12710X, 12800X and 12850X. All five were based on catalog outfits, with an "X" suffix added to the catalog number.

Lionel created these outfits to reduce its excess inventory of unsold stock from 1966.

The 12710X, which has yet to be linked to a specific end retailer, was based on O gauge catalog outfit no. 12710 from 1966. Their contents were identical, except that the 12710X replaced the no. 6476-135 Hopper Car found in the 12710 with a no. 6431-1 Trailer Flat Car W/2 Trailers.

The 12710X was led by a no. 736-1 Steam Type Locomotive With Smoke and Magne-Traction. Originally introduced in 1950, this engine was included in at least 17 outfits during the 1960s. In this outfit, the 736-1 came packaged in a no. 736-36 Corr. Box. It appears that later versions of this steamer were packaged without a no. CTC-1 Lockon; therefore, it was included separately in the outfit box.

The desirable 6431-1 was the only new-for-1966 item in this outfit. As with many cars from the middle and late 1960s, "new" meant that it was derived from other cars. To be specific, the car was stamped "6430" and Lionel added a die-cast red no. 6431-150 Toy Tractor purchased from Midgetoy and two white no. 6430-150 Trailer Assemblies. Then it packaged everything in a Cellophane Window box that was stamped "6431" on the end flap and "12-247" on its tuck flap. The 6431-1 made its final appearance in this outfit.

All the other pieces of rolling stock in this outfit were carryover items from earlier years and, with the exception of the no. 6414-1 Auto Transport Car, would remain in the product line through 1968. The 6414-1 was making its last appearance in this outfit and the no. 12800X. The orange New Haven box car that was heat-stamped "6464725" was designated no. 6464-735 when it came in a box and no. 6464-750 when unboxed. The "-735" version was included in this outfit.

Outfit no. 12710X was one of five promotional outfits from late 1966 that were based on a catalog outfit. It was identical to the 1966 version of catalog outfit no. 12710, except that it substituted a no. 6431-1 Trailer Flat Car W/2 Trailers for the 6476-135 Hopper Car found in the 12710. Notice that the "X" stamped on the outfit box is crooked and appears to have been stamped separately from the "12710". Lionel had 700 extra units of the no. 66-102 Outfit Box because the factory orders for the 12710 were reduced. Lionel likely took the already stamped boxes and added an "X".

As was the tendency in 1966, all but one of the cars could come packaged in either Orange Picture or Cellophane Window boxes. The 6431-1, as noted, came only in a Cellophane Window box.

The rolling stock in the 12710X followed the normal truck and coupler progression for 1966, with each of the cars having AAR types. All but two were equipped with operating trucks and couplers. The nos. 736W-1 Whistle Tender and 6437-1 Illuminated Caboose came with one operating and one plain type.

The no. 66-102 White RSC with Orange Graphics outfit box was manufactured by Bell Container Corp. and measured 19 x 12½ x 7¼ inches. It was unique to the 12710 and 12710X. The box included four lines of data as part of the box manufacturer's certificate. Printed on the bottom was a reference to the N.M.F.C.

The 12710X is a very desirable promotional outfit, thanks to the small number that was produced and the addition of a 6431-1. This outfit is seldom seen, which leads to its R10 rarity rating.

Description: "O" Gauge Promotional Outfit
Specification: "O" Ga. Diesel Freight Outfit
Original Amount: 300
Factory Order Date: 11/4/1966
Date Issued: 11-7-66
Date Req'd: 11-8-66

Contents: 2346-1 GP-9 Diesel - "Boston & Maine"; 6414-1 Auto Transport Car; 6428-25 Mail Car; 6436-100 Hopper Car; 6464-485 Box Car - "Boston & Maine"; 6415-25 Tank Car; 6017-110 Caboose - "Boston & Maine"; TOC-45 Curved Track (Loose) (2); TOC-10 Curved Track (6 per Bundle); TOS-19 Straight Track (5 per Bundle); UCS-25 Remote Control Track Section; CTC-1 Lockon; 926-66 Service Station List; Form 3063 Parts Order Form; 1-166 Warranty Card; 12700-10 Instruction Sheet

Boxes & Packing: 66-119 Outfit Box; 62-248 Corr. Insert (2); 62-273 Corr. Insert; 64-168 Corr. Insert; 62-225 Corr. Insert (4); 66-120 Shipper (1-4); 64-114 Shipper Pad (2-4)

12800X (1966)	C6	C7	C8	Rarity
Complete Outfit	775	1,250	1,750	R9
Outfit Box no. 66-119	300	450	600	R9

Comments: On November 4, 1966, Lionel issued Factory Orders for five General Release Promotional Type IIa outfits: nos. 11540X, 11560X, 12710X, 12800X and 12850X. All five were based on catalog outfits, with an "X" suffix added to the catalog number. Lionel created these outfits to reduce its excess inventory of unsold stock from 1966.

The 12800X, which has yet to be linked to a specific end retailer, was based on O gauge catalog outfit no. 12800 from 1966. Their contents were identical, except that the 12800X added a no. 6414-1 Auto Transport Car and a box for the no. 2346-1 Boston & Maine GP-9 Diesel and came in a Tan RSC Mailer with Black Graphics outfit box.

The 12800X was led by the 2346-1 Boston & Maine GP-9 Diesel. This locomotive featured Magne-Traction, a three-position reversing unit, a horn, operating couplers and a light at both ends. It came packed with nos. 1-165 Warranty Card and 2346-5 Instruction Sheet in a no. 2346-6 Corrugated Box.

The rolling stock in this outfit consisted of carryover items. The nos. 6017-110 Boston & Maine Caboose, 6414-1 and 6428-25 Mail Car were making their last or next-to-last appearance in this outfit. In 1966, the 6414-1 could come in either an Orange Picture or a Cellophane Window box.

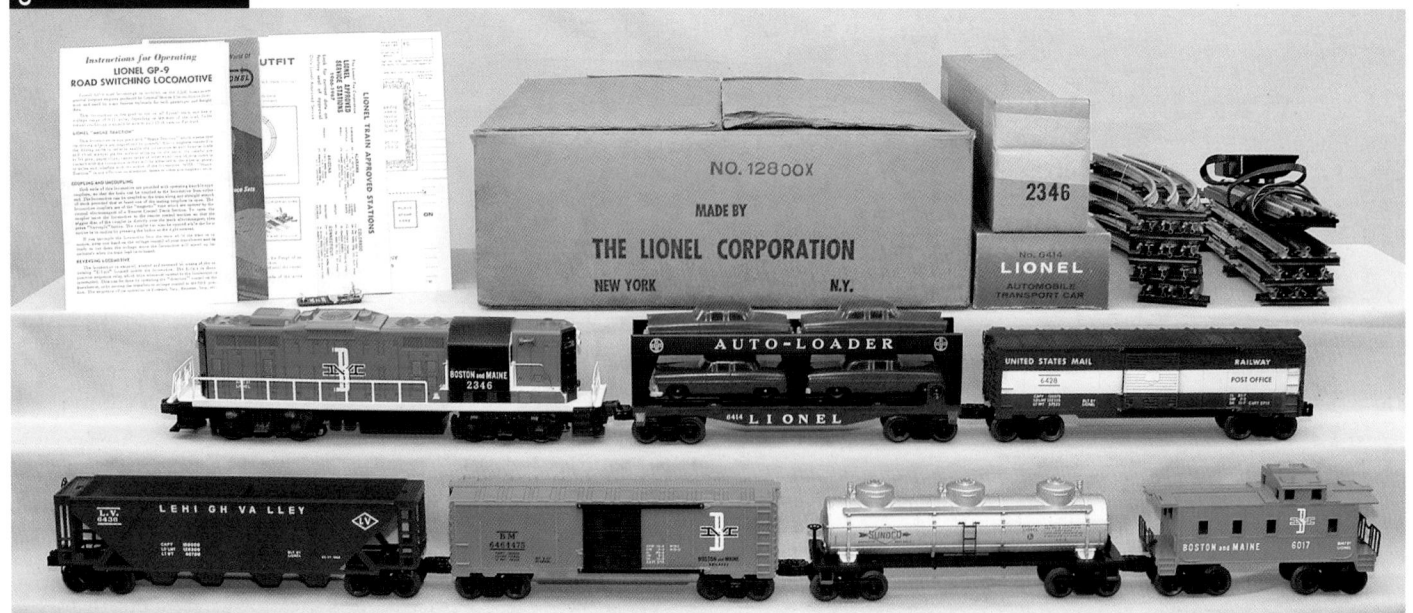

Outfit no. 12800X was one of five promotional outfits from late 1966 that were based on a catalog outfit. The 12800X was the RSC version of catalog outfit no. 12800. The "X" version added a no. 6414-1 Auto Transport Car and a boxed version of the no. 2346-1 Boston & Maine GP-9 Diesel. Like its catalog counterpart, this O gauge outfit did not include a transformer.

When Lionel issued catalog outfit no. 12800 in 1965, it assigned new suffixes to items that previously were available only in boxed form. These items were the same as those used in the 12800X. Specifically, the nos. 6415-25 Tank Car, 6428-25 Mail Car, 6436-100 Hopper Car, 6464-485 Boston & Maine Box Car were the unboxed versions of the nos. 6415-1, 6428-1, 6436-110 and 6464-475, respectively. The 6017-110 was the unboxed version of the no. 6017-100 Caboose. The 6017-110 first appeared as a substitution in catalog outfit nos. 11331 and 11341 from 1963.

The rolling stock in the 12800X followed the normal truck and coupler progression for 1966, with each of the cars having AAR types. All but one were equipped with late operating trucks and couplers. The 6017-110 came with one late operating and one plain type.

The no. 66-119 Tan RSC Mailer with Black Graphics outfit box was manufactured by United Container Co. and measured 15¾ x 15¾ x 5½ inches. This box was made of a thicker corrugated material (rated at 90 pounds rather than the normal 65 pounds gross weight) that allowed each outfit to be shipped in its outfit box. It included four lines of data as part of the box manufacturer's certificate. Printed on the bottom was a reference to the N.M.F.C.

Lionel produced fewer of the 12800X than it did the 12800. That fact, along with the 12800X having a boxed diesel and a 6414-1, explains why it is considered the more desirable of the two outfits. Unfortunately for hobbyists, complete and collector-grade 12800Xs do not appear too often, hence the R9 rarity rating.

Description: "O" Gauge Special
Specification: "O" Gauge Special
Customer: Polk
Original Amount: 30
Factory Order Date: 8/30/1964
Date Issued: 8-27-64
Packaging: Individually Boxed for Bulk Packing

Contents: 736LTS Steam Type Locomotive & Tender With Smoke & Whistle; 3662-1 Operating Milk Car; 6415-1 Tank Car; TOC Curve Track (16); TOS Straight Track (30); UCS-1 Remote Control Track Section; 375-1 Motorized Turntable; 110-1 Trestle Set; 494-1 Rotary Beacon; KW-1 Transformer; 260-1 Illuminated Bumper; TO20-1 90° Crossing; TO22-1 Remote Control Switches

12807 (1964)	C6	C7	C8	Rarity
Items Only	1,000	1,475	1,985	N/A

Comments: In 1964, longtime Lionel customer Polk Model Craft Hobbies purchased what were known as "bulk outfits." (For an explanation of the practice of buying "bulk outfits," consult the entry on Madison Hardware Co. in the section on Lionel's Distribution and Customers.)

Polk purchased bulk-packed O27 outfits nos. 19406, 19407 and 19408; O gauge outfits nos. 12807, 12817 and 12847; and Super O outfit no. 13277. All were Retailer Promotional Type Ia outfits.

When you look at the contents of all these outfits and weigh the fact that all the Factory Orders recorded the same date, it becomes obvious that Polk was merely splitting up its separate-sale order across multiple "outfits" to take advantage of the inherent outfit discount. As such, each of these outfits offered a little bit of everything.

In 1964, Lionel reinstated many cars that had previously been marked obsolete on their Production Control Files. The 12807, for which Polk paid $67.00 each, included two of these reissues (the nos. 3662-1 Operating Milk Car and 6415-1 Tank Car) as well as accessories and track.

A listing for this outfit is provided here because a Factory

Order exists for the 12807. Pricing is provided as reference for the items alone. However, as stated earlier in this volume, items alone do not constitute an outfit; an outfit box is required.

It is unknown what Polk did with these items. For that reason, finding a box with 12807 markings would be a true discovery.

Description: "O" Gauge Special
Specification: "O" Gauge Special
Customer: Polk
Original Amount: 30
Factory Order Date: 8/30/1964
Date Issued: 8-27-64
Packaging: Individually Boxed For Bulk Packing

Contents: 2383-1 "Santa Fe" "AA" Diesel Unit With Horn; 2521-1 Illuminated Observation Car; 2522-1 Illuminated Vista Dome; 2523-1 Illuminated Pullman Car (2); TOC Curve Track (16); TOS Straight Track (30); UCS-1 Remote Control Track Section (2); TO22-1 Remote Control Switches (2); ½ TOC ½ Curve Track (4); ½ TOS ½ Straight Track (4); TO20-1 90° Crossing; TO11-43 Fibre Pins (12 Doz.); TOC-51 Steel Pins (24 Doz.); ZW-1 Transformer; 110-1 Trestle Set; 111-1 Trestle Set

12817 (1964)	C6	C7	C8	Rarity
Items Only	1,100	1,800	2,800	N/A

Comments: In 1964, longtime Lionel customer Polk Model Craft Hobbies purchased what were known as "bulk outfits." (For an explanation of the practice of buying "bulk outfits," consult the entry on Madison Hardware Co. in the section on Lionel's Distribution and Customers.)

Polk purchased bulk-packed O27 outfits nos. 19406, 19407 and 19408; O gauge outfits nos. 12807, 12817 and 12847; and Super O outfit no. 13277. All were Retailer Promotional Type Ia outfits.

When you look at the contents of all these outfits and weigh the fact that all the Factory Orders recorded the same date, it becomes obvious that Polk was merely splitting up its separate-sale order across multiple "outfits" to take advantage of the inherent outfit discount. As such, each of these outfits offered a little bit of everything.

Out of all the Polk purchases for 1964, the 12817 came closest to actually being considered a stand-alone outfit. This item, for which Polk paid $100.00 each, was similar to catalog outfit no. 12780 from 1964.

The 12817 featured a no. 2383-1 Santa Fe "AA" Diesel Unit With Horn. The 2383-1 included a no. 2383PX-1 Santa Fe Power Diesel Unit With Horn and a no. 2383T-1 Santa Fe Motorless Unit inside a no. 12-94 Outfit Box (master carton).

A listing for this outfit is provided here because a Factory Order exists for the 12817. Pricing is provided as reference for the items alone. However, as stated earlier in this volume, items alone do not constitute an outfit; an outfit box is required.

It is unknown what Polk did with these items. For that reason, finding a box with 12817 markings would be a true discovery.

Description: "O" Gauge Promotional Outfit
Specification: "O" Ga. Diesel Freight Outfit
Packaging: RSC (Units Boxed)

Contents: 2322-1 "Virginian" Diesel Locomotive; 6822-1 Searchlight Car; 6361-1 Timber Transport Car; 6464-735 "New Haven" Box Car; 6436-110 Hopper Car; 6315-60 Chemical Tank Car; 6437-1 Illuminated Caboose; D65-50 Accessory Catalog; 1-165 Warranty Card

Boxes & Packing: SE-60 Outfit Box

12820-100 (1965)	C6	C7	C8	Rarity
Complete Outfit	1,200	1,750	2,425	R10
Outfit Box no. SE-60	500	650	800	R10

Comments: In 1965, Lionel offered Retailer Promotional outfits to only Mercury Model, Sears and Western Auto. Other retailers, many of whom were accustomed to obtaining exclusive promotional outfits, were now limited to General Release Promotional outfits. They had to compete head-to-head with other retailers with similar offerings.

The no. 12820-100, a Type IIa, was similar to catalog outfit no. 12820 from 1965. It has yet to be linked to a specific retailer.

The 12820-100 was led by no. 2322-1 Virginian Diesel Locomotive (new for 1965). This Fairbanks-Morse Train Master typically came with an unpainted blue body and featured Magne-

Traction, a three-position reversing unit and a headlight at both ends. The 2322-1 was wrapped in no. TP-2 Tissue Paper and included a no. 1-165 Instruction Sheet when it was packaged in its no. 2322-15 Corrugated Box.

The cars in this outfit were, with the omission of a no. 3662-1 Operating Milk Car, identical to those in the 12820. All of them were carryover items; some were Lionel's higher-end models for 1965.

The orange New Haven box car that was heat-stamped "6464725" was designated no. 6464-735 when packaged in a box and no. 6464-750 when unboxed. The "-735" version came in this outfit. All the cars came in Orange Picture or Hillside Orange Picture boxes.

The rolling stock in the 12820-100 followed the normal truck and coupler progression for 1965, with each of the cars having AAR types. All but one were equipped with either late operating or one late operating and one late non-operating truck and coupler. The no. 6437-1 Illuminated Caboose had one late operating and one plain type.

The no. SE-60 Tan RSC with Black Graphics outfit box was manufactured by Gem-Bilt Container Corp. and measured 23¼ x 12½ x 6¼ inches. The box included four lines of data as part of the box manufacturer's certificate. Printed on the bottom was a reference to the N.M.F.C. The SE-60 was similar in style to the 19326 from 1965. Both were marked "Made By the Lionel Toy Corporation" on the box side.

The no. 12820-100 from 1965 was a stripped-down version of catalog outfit no. 12820. This promotional outfit did not come with the no. 3662-1 Operating Milk Car, track and transformer included in the 12820. The "-100" was likely assembled to deplete excess inventory. Even so, the no. 2322-1 Virginian Diesel Locomotive and higher-end rolling stock make it a desirable O gauge promotional outfit.

The 12820-100 was likely assembled by Lionel to deplete excess inventory. In any case, this outfit is much more difficult to find than its catalog counterpart and always commands a premium price.

12827
1964

Description: Special "O" Gauge Set
Specification: Special "O" Gauge Set
Customer: Joe, The Motorists' Friend
Customer: Others
Original Amount: 60
Factory Order Date: 7/28/1964
Date Issued: 7/28/64
Packaging: All Units Individually Packed & Then Bulk Packed

Contents: 773LTS Steam Type Locomotive & Tender With Smoke & Whistle; 6414-85 Auto Transport Car; 3356-1 Operating Horse Car And Corral; 3434-1 Operating Poultry Car; 6560-1 Crane Car; 6415-1 Tank Car; 3662-1 Operating Milk Car; 6822-1 Searchlight Car; TOC Curve Track (16); TOS Straight Track (90); UCS-1 Remote Control Track Section (4); 375-1 Motorized Turntable; 110-1 Trestle Set (2); 260-1 Illuminated Bumper (2); TO20-1 90° Crossing; TO22-1 Remote Control Switches (2); ZW Transformer

12827 (1964)	C6	C7	C8	Rarity
Items Only	2,250	3,250	4,650	N/A

Comments: In 1964, Joe, The Motorists' Friend purchased two Lionel outfits: nos. 12827 and 19390. The 12827, a General Release Promotional Type IIa outfit, listed Joe, The Motorists' Friend and "Others" on its Factory Order. However, this outfit, which cost $125.00 each from Lionel, has yet to be linked to any other retailer.

The 12827 was the second of two "bulk outfits" purchased by Joe, The Motorists' Friend. The other was promotional outfit no. 19251 from 1963. For the 12827, no outfit box was provided, only bulk packaging. It's assumed that Lionel packaged all the individual items in master shipping cartons.

The 12827 was part of a bulk-packed O gauge series of promotional outfits from 1964. All six outfits in this series were numbered "128x7" with the "x" being the only difference in outfit numbers.

When you look at the contents of the 128x7 series of outfits, it becomes obvious that the customers were merely placing their separate-sale orders in the form of an outfit. This practice allowed them to take advantage of the inherent outfit discount. (For an explanation of the practice of buying "bulk outfits," consult the entry on Madison Hardware Co. in the section on Lionel's Distribution and Customers.)

The 12827 included a no. 773-1 Steam Type Locomotive With Smoke and a no. 736W-1 Whistle Tender packed in a no. 12-149 Corr. Box (master carton). This master carton pairing was called a no. 773LTS Steam Type Locomotive & Tender With Smoke & Whistle. The 773-1 was a New York Central 4-6-4 Hudson steamer that was first cataloged in 1950 and returned to the line in 1964. Inside its individual no. 773-131 Corr. Box were the nos. CTC-1 Lockon, SP-1 Smoke Pellets, 675-33 Smoke Stack Cleaner and 773-132 Instruction Sheet.

In 1964, Lionel reinstated many cars that had previously been marked obsolete on their Production Control Files. It also updated some cars with new loads or decoration. With the exception of the carried-over Orange Picture boxed no. 6822-1 Searchlight Car, all the cars in the 12827 were new-for-1964 versions. This was further proof that the 12827 was actually a grouping of separate-sale items.

The nos. 3356-1 Operating Horse Car And Corral, 3434-1 Operating Poultry Car, 3662-1 Operating Milk Car and 6415-1 Tank Car in this outfit were four of the previously obsolete cars. All came in Orange Picture boxes.

The no. 6414-85 Auto Transport Car was a boxed 6414 with four "cheapie" automobiles, which consisted of just the plastic car frame with simulated wheels molded as part of the body. To be complete, a 6414-85 must include its difficult-to-find Orange Picture box stamped "6414-85". (See outfit no. 19380 for more information about this car.)

The addition of a no. 6560-1 Crane Car in this outfit was curious because it was last listed on a Factory Order from 1960.

The 6560-1 was the version with a gray cab and a black base that last appeared in a Late Classic style box. Whether it came that way in this grouping is unknown.

All the cars in the 12827 followed the normal truck and coupler progression for 1964.

A listing for this outfit is provided here because a Factory Order exists for the 12827. Pricing is provided as reference for the items alone. However, as stated earlier in this volume, items alone do not constitute an outfit; an outfit box is required.

It is unknown what Joe, The Motorists' Friend or other retailers did with these items. For that reason, finding a box with 12827 markings would be a true discovery.

Description: "O" Gauge Special Train Set
Specification: "O" Gauge Special Train Set
Customer: Englewood Electric
Customer: Glen's Train Shop
Original Amount: 25
Factory Order Date: 8/4/1964
Date Issued: 8-4-64
Packaging: RSC Pack (Units Individually Boxed)

Contents: 773-1 Steam Type Locomotive With Smoke; 736W-1 Whistle Tender; 3434-1 Operating Poultry Car; 6361-1 Timber Transport Car; 3662-1 Operating Milk Car; 6415-1 Tank Car; 3356-1 Operating Horse Car And Corral; 6436-110 Hopper Car; 6437-1 Illuminated Caboose; TO22-1 Remote Control Switches; TOC Curve Track (10); TOS Straight Track (22); UCS-1 Remote Control Track Section; ZW-1 Transformer; 310-2 Set of (5) Billboards; 1-65 Warranty Card; Form 3063 Parts Order Form; D64-50 Accessory Catalog; 927-64 Service Station List

Boxes & Packing: 12838-RSC Outfit Box

12838 (1964)	C6	C7	C8	Rarity
Complete Outfit	3,100	4,150	5,600	R10
Outfit Box no. 12838-RSC	1,750	2,250	2,750	R10

Comments: In 1964, Englewood Electric purchased Retailer Promotional Type Ia outfit no. 12838, a promotional version of Super O outfit no. 13150 with "O track of equal value". Equal value turned out to be 10 curve tracks, 22 straight tracks and a pair

of O gauge switches. According to the Factory Order, this outfit was intended for Glen's Train Shop in Akron, Ohio.

The 12838, for which Englewood paid $96.00 each, was led by a no. 773-1 Steam Type Locomotive With Smoke. The 773-1 was a New York Central 4-6-4 Hudson steamer that was first cataloged in 1950 and returned to the line in 1964. Inside its individual no. 773-131 Corr. Box were the nos. CTC-1 Lockon, SP-1 Smoke Pellets, 675-33 Smoke Stack Cleaner and 773-132 Instruction Sheet. For this year, the 773-1 was paired with a no. 736W-1 Whistle Tender.

In 1964, Lionel reinstated many cars that had previously been marked obsolete on their Production Control Files. The nos. 3356-1 Operating Horse Car And Corral, 3434-1 Operating Poultry Car, 3662-1 Operating Milk Car and 6415-1 Tank Car in this outfit were four of the previously obsolete cars.

The nos. 6436-110 Hopper Car and 6437-1 Illuminated Caboose were carryover items. They, like the other cars in this outfit, came packed in Orange Picture boxes.

All the rolling stock in the 12838 followed the normal truck and coupler progression for 1964. The 736W-1 and 6437-1 were equipped with one operating and one plain AAR type. All other cars were equipped with operating AAR trucks and couplers.

The box for the 12838 was likely the same as that used for the 13150, which was a Tan RSC with Black Graphics outfit box.

Lionel made so few examples of this outfit – it ties for fifth in terms of low quantity – that the 12838 stands as one of the rarest promotional outfits. Finding a 12838 in any condition is a great find.

Description: "O" Gauge Special
Specification: "O" Gauge Special
Customer: Polk
Original Amount: 60
Factory Order Date: 8/30/1964
Date Issued: 8-27-64
Packaging: Individually Boxed for Bulk Packing

Contents: 773LTS Steam Type Locomotive & Tender With Smoke & Whistle; 3356-1 Operating Horse Car And Corral; 6415-1 Tank Car; 3662-1 Operating Milk Car; TOC Curve Track (8); TOS Straight Track (60); UCS-1 Remote Control Track Section (2); 375-1 Motorized Turntable; 110-1 Trestle Set (2); 260-1 Illuminated Bumper (2); TO20-1 90° Crossing; TO22-1 Remote Control Switches (2); ZW-1 Transformer

12847 (1964)	C6	C7	C8	Rarity
Items Only	1,425	2,115	3,125	N/A

Comments: In 1964, longtime Lionel customer Polk Model Craft Hobbies purchased what were known as "bulk outfits." (For an explanation of the practice of buying "bulk outfits," consult the entry on Madison Hardware Co. in the section on Lionel's Distribution and Customers.)

Polk purchased bulk-packed O27 outfits nos. 19406, 19407 and 19408; O gauge outfits nos. 12807, 12817 and 12847; and Super O outfit no. 13277. All were Retailer Promotional Type Ia outfits.

When you look at the contents of all these outfits and weigh the fact that all the Factory Orders recorded the same date, it becomes obvious that Polk was merely splitting up its separate-sale order across multiple "outfits" to take advantage of the inherent outfit discount. As such, each of these outfits offered a little bit of everything.

The 12847, for which Polk paid $105.00 each, included a no. 773-1 Steam Type Locomotive With Smoke and a no. 736W-1 Whistle Tender packed in a no. 12-149 Corr. Box (master carton). This master carton pairing was called a no. 773LTS Steam Type Locomotive & Tender With Smoke & Whistle. The 773-1 was a New York Central 4-6-4 Hudson steamer that was first cataloged in 1950 and returned to the line in 1964. Inside its individual no. 773-

131 Corr. Box were the nos. CTC-1 Lockon, SP-1 Smoke Pellets, 675-33 Smoke Stack Cleaner and 773-132 Instruction Sheet.

In 1964, Lionel reinstated many cars that had previously been marked obsolete on their Production Control Files. The 12847, like the 12807, included two of these reissues: the nos. 3662-1 Operating Milk Car and 6415-1 Tank Car.

A listing for this outfit is provided here because a Factory Order exists for the 12847. Pricing is provided as reference for the items alone. However, as stated earlier in this volume, items alone do not constitute an outfit; an outfit box is required.

It is unknown what Polk did with these items. For that reason, finding a box with 12847 markings would be a true discovery.

12850X
1966

Description: "O" Gauge Promotional Outfit
Original Amount: 150
Factory Order Date: 11/4/1966
Date Issued: 11-4-66
Date Req'd: 11-5-66

Contents: 2322-1 "Virginian" Diesel Locomotive; 3662-1 Operating Milk Car; 6476-135 Hopper Car; 6361-1 Timber Transport Car; 6464-735 "New Haven" Box Car; 6436-110 Hopper Car; 6464-450 Box Car - Great Northern; 6437-1 Illuminated Caboose; TOC-5 Curved Track (5 per Bundle) (2); TOS-19 Straight Track (5 per Bundle); TOS-51 Straight Track (9 per Bundle); UCS-1 Remote Control Track Section; TO22-1 Remote Control Switches; LW-1 125-Watt Transformer; CTC-1 Lockon; Form 3063 Parts Order Form; 1-166 Warranty Card; 926-66 Service Station List; 12850-10 Layout Sheet; 12700-10 Instruction Sheet

Boxes & Packing: 66-108 Outfit Box; 41110-23 Corr. Insert (2); 66-109 Shipper for 1 (1-1)

Alternate For Outfit Contents:
Note: If any TO22-1 Switches are used from inventory, (2) O22-153 must be included in outfit.

12850X (1966)	C6	C7	C8	Rarity
Complete Outfit	1,675	2,550	4,150	R10
Outfit Box no. 66-108	500	1,000	1,500	R10

Comments: On November 4, 1966, Lionel issued Factory Orders for five General Release Promotional Type IIa outfits: nos. 11540X, 11560X, 12710X, 12800X and 12850X. All five were based on catalog outfits, with an "X" suffix added to the catalog number. Lionel created these outfits to reduce its excess inventory of unsold stock from 1966.

The 12850X, which has yet to be linked with a specific end retailer, was based on O gauge catalog outfit no. 12850 from 1966. Their contents were identical, except that the 12850X replaced the nos. 6315-60 Chemical Tank Car and 6822-1 Searchlight Car in the 12850 with the nos. 6464-450 Great Northern Box Car and 6476-135 Hopper Car.

The 12850X was led by a no. 2322-1 Virginian Diesel Locomotive. This Fairbanks-Morse Train Master featured Magne-Traction, a three-position reversing unit, operating couplers and a headlight at both ends. The 2322-1 was wrapped in no. TP-2 Tissue Paper and included a no. 1-165 Instruction Sheet when it was packaged in its no. 2322-15 Corrugated Box. The difficult-to-find version of the 2322 with a black plastic shell painted both yellow and blue was included. It was making its last outfit appearance here.

This outfit was one of only five from the 1960s to include more than one no. 6464-series box car. The orange New Haven box car that was heat-stamped "6464725" was designated no. 6464-735 when it came in a box. Next came the no. 6464-450. This was last seen cataloged in 1957 and reissued in 1966. Like the New Haven box car, it featured a Type IV body. The 6464-450 last appeared in this outfit.

The yellow no. 6476-135 Hopper Car was heat-stamped "BUILT 1-48" and "LIONEL 6176". It was classified as a 6476 because it was equipped with two operating trucks and couplers.

The no. 3662-1 Operating Milk Car was making its second-to-last appearance in this outfit. All the other cars in this outfit appeared until 1968 or 1969.

The 6464-series cars came in Cellophane Window boxes, and all the other cars were packaged in Orange Picture boxes. Be aware, however, that other combinations were possible in 1966.

The rolling stock in the 12850X followed the normal truck and coupler progression for 1966, with each of the cars having AAR types. All but one were equipped with late operating trucks and couplers. The no. 6437-1 Illuminated Caboose was equipped with one late operating and one plain type. The 6464 cars featured washers riveted as part of one or both of their leaf spring assemblies.

The no. 12850-10 Layout Sheet is very difficult to find and was dated 3/66. It was also included in catalog outfit no. 12850.

The no. 66-108 White RSC with Orange Graphics outfit box was manufactured by United Container Co. and measured 26 x 14¼ x 8⅜ inches. It included four lines of data, a "66" and seven stars as part of the box manufacturer's certificate. Printed on the bottom were "66-108" and a reference to the N.M.F.C.

As with the 12710X, the "X" stamped on the outfit box was crooked and appeared to have been stamped separately from the "12850". Lionel had 1,020 extra units of the no. 66-108 Outfit Box because the factory orders for the 12850 were reduced. Lionel likely took the already stamped boxes and added an "X".

Outfit no. 12850X was one of five promotional outfits from late 1966 that were based on a catalog outfit. The 12850X was identical to catalog outfit no. 12850, except that it replaced the nos. 6315-60 Chemical Tank Car and 6822-1 Searchlight Car in the 12850 with the nos. 6464-450 Great Northern Box Car and 6476-135 Hopper Car. Completed warranty cards included with this outfit indicate that this example was purchased on 6/6/67 from a dealer named Ted Dartt. Interestingly, the customer stated on the card that he did not ask for a 12850X. He wanted a 12850.

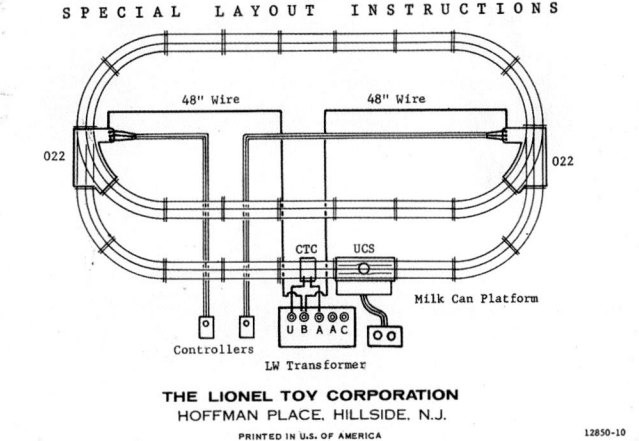

The no. 12850-10 Layout Sheet detailed the track layout that was unique to the 12850 and 12850X. It is a very difficult sheet to find.

The 12850X was produced in such small quantities that it is extremely difficult to find complete and in collectible condition. Coming up with even an empty box is quite a challenge.

CONVENTIONAL PACK
66-108 BOX
3-30-66

TOP LAYER

TOC-5 (2)	6437-1 S	6464-450 S	6464-735 S	6476-135 S	6361-1 S
TOS-19					
USC-1 F					
TOS-51					
6436-110 S					

41110-23

BOTTOM LAYER
41110-23

2322-1 F		3662-1 F
LW-1	TO22-1	

12857
1964

Description: "O" Gauge Special
Specification: "O" Gauge Special
Customer: Branch Brook Co.
Original Amount: 24
Factory Order Date: 9/17/1964
Date Issued: 9-17-64
Packaging: Indv. Boxed for Bulk Packing

Contents: 2383-1 "Santa Fe" "AA" Diesel Unit With Horn; 2521-1 Illuminated Observation Car; 2522-1 Illuminated Vista Dome (3); 2523-1 Illuminated Pullman Car (3); TOC Curve Track (16); TOS Straight Track (30); ½ TOC ½ Curve Track (4); ½ TOS ½

Straight Track (4); TO20-1 90° Crossing; TO11-43 Fibre Pins (2 Doz.); TOC-51 Steel Pins (2 Doz.); LW-1 125-Watt Transformer; 76-1 Set of (3) Lamp Posts (3); 110-1 Trestle Set; 111-1 Trestle Set

12857 (1964)	C6	C7	C8	Rarity
Items Only	1,435	2,300	3,200	N/A

Comments: In 1964, Branch Brook Company purchased three of what were known as "bulk outfits": nos. 12857, 12867 and 19410. All three were Retailer Promotional Type Ia outfits. (For an explanation of the practice of buying "bulk outfits," consult the entry on Madison Hardware Co. in the section on Lionel's Distribution and Customers.)

Even though the items in the 12857 may have been grouped together, no individual outfit box has been observed for any bulk outfit listed in this volume. As a result, we cannot ascertain whether these items were ever assembled and sold as an outfit. Even if they were, we cannot prove that Branch Brook designated the grouping as 12857.

The 12857, for which Branch Brook paid $85.64 each, featured a no. 2383-1 Santa Fe "AA" Diesel Unit With Horn. The 2383-1

included a no. 2383PX-1 Santa Fe Power Diesel Unit With Horn and a no. 2383T-1 Santa Fe Motorless Unit inside a no. 12-94 Outfit Box (master carton). With seven cars, the 12857 would have been the longest passenger outfit offered by Lionel.

A listing for this outfit is provided here because a Factory Order exists for the 12857. Pricing is provided as reference for the items alone. However, as stated earlier in this volume, items alone do not constitute an outfit; an outfit box is required.

It is unknown what Branch Brook did with these items. For that reason, finding a box with 12857 markings would be a true discovery.

12867
1964

Description: "O" Gauge Special
Specification: "O" Gauge Special
Customer: Branch Brook Co.
Original Amount: 24
Factory Order Date: 9/17/1964
Date Issued: 9-17-64
Packaging: Indv. Boxed for Bulk Packing

Contents: 773LTS Steam Type Locomotive & Tender With Smoke & Whistle; 6415-1 Tank Car; TOC Curve Track (16); TOS Straight Track (9); UCS-1 Remote Control Track Section (4); 375-1 Motorized Turntable; 110-1 Trestle Set (2); 260-1 Illuminated Bumper (2); TO20-1 90° Crossing; TO22-1 Remote Control Switches (2); LW-1 125-Watt Transformer

12867 (1964)	C6	C7	C8	Rarity
Items Only	1,125	1,650	2,350	N/A

Comments: In 1964, Branch Brook Company purchased three of what were known as "bulk outfits": nos. 12857, 12867 and 19410. All three were Retailer Promotional Type Ia outfits. (For an explanation of the practice of buying "bulk outfits," consult the entry on Madison Hardware Co. in the section on Lionel's Distribution and Customers.)

Because the 12867 included only a locomotive and one item

of rolling stock, it would appear initially that Branch Brook was purchasing a bulk outfit for separate sale. Upon closer inspection, the track and other peripherals appeared to comprise an outfit. As such, Branch Brook might have intended to add more rolling stock to create an outfit.

Even so, no individual outfit box has been observed for any bulk outfit listed in this volume. As a result, we cannot ascertain whether these items were ever assembled and sold as an outfit. Even if they were, we cannot prove that Branch Brook designated the grouping as 12867.

The 12867, for which Branch Brook paid $95.60 each, included a no. 773-1 Steam Type Locomotive With Smoke and a no. 736W-1 Whistle Tender packed in a no. 12-149 Corr. Box (master carton). This master carton pairing was called a no. 773LTS Steam Type Locomotive & Tender With Smoke & Whistle. The 773-1 was a New York Central 4-6-4 Hudson steamer that was first cataloged in 1950 and returned to the line in 1964. Inside its individual no. 773-131 Corr. Box were the nos. CTC-1 Lockon, SP-1 Smoke Pellets, 675-33 Smoke Stack Cleaner and 773-132 Instruction Sheet.

A listing for this outfit is provided here because a Factory Order exists for the 12867. Pricing is provided as reference for the items alone. However, as stated earlier in this volume, items alone do not constitute an outfit; an outfit box is required.

It is unknown what Branch Brook did with these items. For that reason, finding a box with 12867 markings would be a true discovery.

12885-500
(9836)
1965

Customer No. On Box: 9836
Description: "O" Ga. Promotional Outfit
Specification: "O" Ga. Diesel Freight Outfit W/Horn
Customer/No./Price: Sears, Roebuck and Co.; 9836; $99.95
Original Amount: 315
Factory Order Date: 8/20/1965
Date Issued: Rev 9-9-65
Packaging: (Units Boxed)

Contents: 2347-1 GP-7 Diesel Power Unit - "Chesapeake & Ohio"; 6464-735 "New Haven" Box Car; 6342-25 Culvert Car; 6414-1 Auto Transport Car; 6415-1 Tank Car; 3662-1 Operating

Milk Car; 6437-1 Illuminated Caboose; 346-1 Culvert Unloader; 321-100 Bridge; 76-25 Lamp Post (3); TOC-8 Curved Track (8 per Bundle); TOC-45 Curved Track (Loose) (2); TOS-19 Straight Track (5 per Bundle) (3); TOS-3 Straight Track (3 per Bundle); UCS-1 Remote Control Track Section (2); TO22-1 Remote Control Switches; LW-1 125-Watt Transformer; CTC-1 Lockon; 1-165 Warranty Card; 310-2 Set of (5) Billboards; 310-3 Billboard Frame (5); 12700-10 Instruction Sheet; 12885-10 Layout Sheet; 346-21 Instruction Sheet; 76-10 Instruction Sheet

Boxes & Packing: 65-386 Outfit Box; 65-388 Corr. Insert; 65-355 Corr. Insert (2); 65-387 Shipper for 2 (1-2); 65-349 Shipper Pad (2-2)

Outfit no. 12885-500 (Sears no. 9836) is one of the most desirable of all the Lionel promotional outfits offered by Sears during the postwar era. The rare nos. 2347-1 Chesapeake & Ohio GP-7 Diesel Power Unit and 12885-10 Layout Sheet could be obtained only in this outfit. Also of note were the nos. 321-100 Bridge and 346-1 Culvert Unloader. Interestingly, the outfit shown came with a memorandum from Sears, Roebuck and Co. informing the customer that his order for additional O27 track had been canceled. This occurred because, according to the memo, "The train you ordered is the Lionel 'O' gauge train."

The large outfit box for the no. 12885-500 (Sears no. 9836) was made from the same single-wall 65-pound gross weight corrugated cardboard used for most outfits. As such, few outfits survived the initial shipment from Sears without damage. Even when one did survive, the large storage space requirements for this box have led to many being damaged over the years. The one shown is one of the best we've seen.

Comments: After purchasing only three outfits in 1964, Sears, Roebuck and Co. made a large purchase of 14 Retailer Promotional outfits in 1965. Only three of these outfits appeared in the 1965 Sears Christmas Catalog.

Outfit no. 12885-500, a Type Ic, was stamped with Sears no. 9836. It appeared on page 463 of the 1965 Sears Christmas Catalog for $99.95. Sears paid Lionel $62.72 for each 12885-500.

Of all the Lionel promotional outfits offered by Sears during the postwar era, the 12885-500 is the one most desired by many collectors. Being one of only two O gauge promotional outfits for 1965 and having a scarce locomotive and several high-end components explain the interest shown in the 12885-500.

To begin, the no. 2347-1 Chesapeake & Ohio GP-7 Diesel Power Unit was unique to this outfit and never intended for separate sale. It is one of the most sought-after postwar Lionel diesels. With only a small quantity made, it achieves an R10 rarity rating. The 2347-1 featured Magne-Traction a three-position reversing unit, a horn, operating couplers and a light at both ends. It came in a no. 2359-13 Corrugated Box, which was taped shut and rubber-stamped "2347" on the tape. Included in the box were the nos. 2346-5 Instruction Sheet and 1-165 Warranty Card. Every lone 2347-1 indicates that there is one less complete 12885-500 on the market!

12885-500 (9836) (1965)	C6	C7	C8	Rarity
Complete Outfit	6,000	9,000	13,000	R10
Outfit Box no. 65-386	1,500	2,000	3,000	R10

Since this was an O gauge outfit, all the rolling stock, with the exception of the no. 6342-25 Culvert Car, was individually packaged in Orange Picture boxes. These cars were among Lionel's higher-end offerings for 1965.

Notable cars were the nos. 3662-1 Operating Milk Car and 6414-1 Auto Transport Car with four red automobiles. Also of note was the 6342-25 Culvert Car. Last seen in the 1959 consumer catalog, it was re-introduced in outfit no. 19327 from 1964. The new version was equipped with one operating and one non-operating AAR truck and coupler riveted directly to the body.

The orange New Haven box car that was heat-stamped "6464725" was designated no. 6464-735 when it came packaged in a box and no. 6464-750 when unboxed. The "-735" version was used in this outfit.

The rolling stock in the 12885-500 followed the normal truck and coupler progression for 1965, with each of the cars having AAR types. All but two were equipped with operating trucks and couplers. The 6342-25 had one operating and one non-operating type and the no. 6437-1 Illuminated Caboose had one operating and one plain type.

As with many promotional outfits, the peripherals included in the 12885-500 add to this outfit's appeal. Specifically, the no. 346-1 Culvert Unloader appeared only in five promotional outfits. The 346-1 was the manual version of the culvert unloader and was packed with seven culvert pipes in a no. 346-13 Corr. Box. The 6342-25 and no. 346-21 Instruction Sheet were included separately in the outfit.

The no. 321-100 Bridge, new in 1965, was included only in this outfit and promotional outfit no. 19454-500 (Sears no. 9835). It was the same as a no. 321-1 Trestle Bridge, except that it omitted the metal base. It also included a no. 321-101 Instruction Sheet and no. 3330-102 Plastic Cement Filled Capsule in its corrugated box. Lionel produced only 1,815 of this difficult-to-find bridge.

The 12885-500 included a unique track layout, as outlined on the rare no. 12885-10 Layout Sheet. This sheet was printed on blue paper and commands a substantial premium.

Even though the no. 12700-10 Instruction Sheet was still dated 8/64, it, like all the other sheets in this outfit, made reference to the one-year warranty reinstated in 1965. The correct 346-21 and 2346-5 were dated 8/65 and 6/65, respectively.

The no. 65-386 White RSC Allstate By Lionel With Blue Steamer (With Smoke and Trees) and Orange and Blue Graphics outfit box was manufactured by Diversified Packaging Products Corp. and measured 29½ x 16¼ x 10 inches. Surprisingly, for the largest and heaviest Sears outfit from 1965, Lionel used a single-wall corrugated cardboard box rated at 65 pounds gross weight. This lighter weight cardboard is one of the reasons why this outfit box is so difficult to find in collectible condition.

Lionel originally intended to make a quantity of 400 of the 12885-500. Unfortunately, the orders didn't match these projections and the number was reduced to 315.

The small quantity of outfits produced, combined with direct outfit shipping in a poorly chosen box and the large space required to store the box, has led to an extremely low quantity of boxes surviving in collectible condition. In fact, we have observed only two boxes that are in C7 condition or better. Even when a box is found, finding collectible versions of its components takes time and plenty of money. This is truly a "wow" outfit!

CONVENTIONAL PACK
65-386 BOX

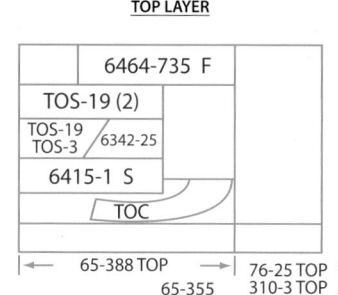

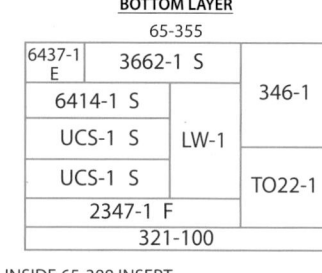

13255
1964

Description: Super "O" Promotional Outfit
Specification: Super "O" Steam Type Freight Outfit W/Smoke & Whistle
Customer: National Association of Railroad Business Women
Original Amount: 20
Factory Order Date: 5/6/1964
Date Issued: 5-8-64
Date Req'd: 5-8-64
Packaging: RSC Individual Shipper Units Boxed

Contents: 637X-1 Steam Type Locomotive with Smoke; 736W-1 Whistle Tender; 6464-735 "New Haven" Box Car; 6361-1 Timber Transport Car; 6440-1 Flat Car W/2 Piggy Back Vans; 6436-110 Hopper Car; 6437-1 Illuminated Caboose; 494-1 Rotating Beacon; 145-1 Automatic Gateman; 50-1 Gang Car; 262-1 Highway Crossing Gate; 321-1 Trestle Bridge; 260-1 Illuminated Bumper (2); 112-1 Pr. Remote Control Switches; SW-1 130-Watt Transformer; 39-25 Envelope Packed; 31-60 Bundle of 6 - 31 Curved Track (3); 31-30 Curved Track (Loose) (4); 32-50 Bundle of 5 - 32 Straight Track; 32-70 Straight Track (7 per Bundle); 34-10 Straight Track - ½ Section; 43-25 Power Track Section

Boxes & Packing: 13255-RSC Outfit Box

Alternate For Outfit Contents:
Note: Layout Diagram to be included with each set; Note: Use any available packing; Note: Each outfit to be individually shipped.

13255 (1964)	C6	C7	C8	Rarity
Complete Outfit	3,200	4,250	5,450	R10
Outfit Box no. 13255-RSC	2,250	2,750	3,250	R10

Comments: In 1964, the National Association of Railway Business Women (NARBW) purchased one Manufacturer Promotional Type IIIb outfit, the no. 13255. Only 20 examples of this Super O outfit were made, which suggests it probably was used as a promotion or an award offered to members of the NARBW.

FORM 392

INTER-OFFICE COMMUNICATION

THE LIONEL CORPORATION

TO __P. Giannotta__ FROM __S. Katzman__ DATE __5/4/64__

Please release twenty (20) pieces of #13255 Train Set for production. This is a special promotion for a women's club, and I would like to get this out as soon as possible. The outfit weight is being checked out by Ted Stawski, and you should have this shortly.

Outfit no. 13255 was the only outfit ever purchased by the National Association of Railroad Business Women. It probably was used as an award to some of its members. This internal memo authorizes the production of 20 outfits.

The 13255, for which the NARBW paid $60.00 each, was one of three promotional Super O outfits from 1964. It marked the last promotional outfit appearance in the 1960s of a no. 637X-1 Steam Type Locomotive with Smoke. This engine was equipped with Magne-Traction, a three-position reversing unit and a headlight. As described in the section on Outfit Peripherals, an "X" signified that a no. CTC-1 Lockon was left out of the no. 637-13 Corrugated Box. Including a Lockon in a Super O outfit was unnecessary.

All the cars in the 13255 were carryover items. The orange New Haven box car that was heat-stamped "6464725" was designated no. 6464-735 when it came in a box and no. 6464-750 when unboxed. The "-735" version came in this outfit. The no. 6440-1 Flat Car W/2 Piggy Back Vans was first introduced in 1961; it appeared in only one outfit after this one.

The rolling stock in this outfit followed the normal truck and coupler progression for 1964, with all the cars having AAR types. Most were equipped with operating trucks and couplers. However,

the nos. 736W-1 Whistle Tender and 6437-1 Illuminated Caboose had one operating and one plain type. The norm for all the cars were to come packed in Orange Picture boxes.

Besides the trains, the 13255 provided plenty of excitement with its accessories and a no. 50-1 Gang Car. The 50-1 was making its last outfit appearance. Adequate peripherals were provided to allow this motorized unit to operate on its own section of track.

This is one of only four outfits to include a no. SW-1 130-Watt Transformer. It provided enough power to operate all the trains and accessories.

The Factory Order indicates that a Layout Diagram was to be included with each set. Also, it stated that each outfit was to be individually shipped in any available packing. As such, Lionel may have shipped each of these outfits direct to the NARBW recipients.

With a quantity of only 20 manufactured, the 13255 ranks third on the list of fewest outfits produced. It is one of the most desirable and collectible of any outfit ever produced by Lionel.

FORM 392 /3267

INTER-OFFICE COMMUNICATION
THE LIONEL CORPORATION

TO __P. Papa__ FROM __F. Weiss__ DATE __July 1, 1964__
cc: W. Sethre

SUBJECT: Jersey Model Dist., Ramsey New Jersey

The above customer had requested 12 number 13150 train sets without ZW transformers and has agreed to take the following items with each set in lieu of the ZW (the dollar value is the same.)

1	1044
1	6315
2	6464
1	6402
1	6465-150

The customer has spread delivery of these 12 outfits among four shipments ranging from September 1 to December 1.

Please advise correct number to use for this special 13150 combination, so that the orders which I am holding may be processed.

This memorandum regarding outfit no. 13267 outlines the changes required to outfit no. 13150. It also details the delivery requirements for Jersey Model Distributors.

Description: Special "Super O" Set
Specification: Special "Super O" Set
Customer: Jersey Model Distributors
Original Amount: 12
Factory Order Date: 7/28/1964
Date Issued: 7-23-64
Date Req'd: Four shipments ranging from Sept. 1 to Dec. 1
Packaging: All Units Boxed and Then Bulk Packed

Contents: 773X-1 Steam Type Locomotive; 736W-1 Whistle Tender; 3434-1 Operating Poultry Car; 6361-1 Timber Transport Car; 3662-1 Operating Milk Car; 6415-1 Tank Car; 3356-1 Operating Horse Car And Corral; 6436-110 Hopper Car; 6402-50 Flat Car W/2 Cable Reels; 6465-150 Tank Car; 6464 Box Car (2); 6315-60 Chemical Tank Car; 6437-1 Illuminated Caboose; 112-1 Pr. Remote Control Switches; 31-30 Curved Track (Loose) (4); 31-60 Bundle of 6 - 31 Curved Track (2); 32-70 Straight Track (7 per Bundle) (2); 32-50 Straight Track (5 per bundle); 34-10 Straight Track (Loose) (4); 36-1 Oper. Car Control Set; 39-25 Remote Control Set (2); 1044-1 90-Watt Transformer

13267 (1964)	C6	C7	C8	Rarity
Items Only	1,450	2,075	3,150	N/A

Comments: In 1964, Jersey Model Distributors purchased bulk-packed outfit no. 13267 (originally assigned no. 13160 but subsequently changed to 13267). (For an explanation of the practice of buying "bulk outfits," consult the entry on Madison Hardware Co. in the section on Lionel's Distribution and Customers.)

The 13267 was a Retailer Promotional Type Ia outfit for which Jersey Model Distributors paid $96.00 each. It was based on catalog outfit no. 13150, but added five cars and swapped transformers. Specifically, the 13267 included the six freight cars and one caboose in the 13150, plus nos. 6315-60 Chemical Tank Car, 6402-50 Flat Car W/2 Cable Reels, two 6464 Box Cars and 6465-150 Tank Car. Also, Lionel substituted a no. 1044-1 90-Watt Transformer for the ZW-1 Transformer in the catalog outfit.

No individual outfit boxes have been observed for any bulk outfit listed in this volume. As a result, we cannot ascertain whether these items were ever assembled and sold as an outfit. Even if they were, we cannot prove that Jersey Model Distributors designated the grouping as a 13267.

The 13267, like the 13150, was led by a no. 773X-1 Steam Type Locomotive With Smoke. This steamer was a New York Central 4-6-4 Hudson that was first cataloged in 1950 and returned to the line in 1964. It was paired with a no. 736W-1 Tender. As described in the section on Outfit Peripherals, an "X" signified that a no. CTC-1 Lockon was not included in the no. 773-131 Corr. Box. Including a Lockon in a Super O outfit was unnecessary.

Also in that year Lionel reinstated many cars that had previously been marked obsolete on their Production Control Files. The nos. 3356-1 Operating Horse Car And Corral, 3434-1 Operating Poultry Car, 3662-1 Operating Milk Car and 6415-1 Tank Car in this outfit were four of the previously obsolete cars. The nos. 6436-110 Hopper Car and 6437-1 Illuminated Caboose were carryover items.

Of the five additional cars provided with the 13267, the inclusion of two 6464 Box Cars was noteworthy. The 13267 was one of only five outfits from the 1960s to include more than one car from that series. The specific cars were not indicated, but they likely were the nos. 6464-525 Minn & St. Louis Box Car and 6464-735 New Haven Box Car because those two cars were included in outfits in 1964. Boxed versions of these cars were packed in Orange Picture boxes.

The rolling stock in this outfit followed the normal truck and coupler progression for 1964, with all the cars having AAR types. Most were equipped with either two operating or one operating and one late non-operating truck and coupler. However, the 736W-1 and 6437-1 came with one operating and one plain type.

A listing for this outfit is provided here because a Factory Order exists for the 13267. Pricing is provided as reference for the items alone. However, as stated earlier in this volume, items alone do not constitute an outfit; an outfit box is required.

It is unknown what Jersey Model Distributors did with these items. For that reason, finding a box with 13267 markings would be a true discovery.

13277
1964

Description: Super "O" Special
Specification: Super "O" Special
Customer: Polk
Original Amount: 60
Factory Order Date: 8/30/1964
Date Issued: 8-27-64
Packaging: Individually Boxed for Bulk Packing

Contents: 773LTS Steam Type Locomotive & Tender With Smoke & Whistle; 3470-1 Aerial Target Launching Car; 3419-1 Operating Helicopter Car; 140-1 Banjo Signal; 154-1 Flashing Highway Signal; 151-1 Automatic Semaphore; 262-1 Highway Crossing Gate; SW-1 130-Watt Transformer; 112-1 Pr. Remote Control Switches; 31 Curved Track (6); 32 Straight Track (30)

13277 (1964)	C6	C7	C8	Rarity
Items Only	1,275	1,650	2,500	N/A

Comments: In 1964, longtime Lionel customer Polk Model Craft Hobbies purchased what were known as "bulk outfits." (For an explanation of the practice of buying "bulk outfits," consult the entry on Madison Hardware Co. in the section on Lionel's Distribution and Customers.)

Polk purchased bulk-packed O27 outfits nos. 19406, 19407 and 19408; O gauge outfits nos. 12807, 12817 and 12847; and Super O outfit no. 13277. All were Retailer Promotional Type Ia outfits.

When you look at the contents of all these outfits and weigh the fact that all the Factory Orders recorded the same date, it becomes obvious that Polk was merely splitting up its separate-sale order across multiple "outfits" to take advantage of the inherent outfit discount. As such, each of these outfits offered a little bit of everything.

The 13277, for which Polk paid $70.00 each, was one of three Super O promotional outfits issued in 1964. It was used to deplete the final inventory of the nos. 3419-1 Operating Helicopter Car and 3470-1 Aerial Target Launching Car. As with the 12847, the 13277 included a no. 773-1 Steam Type Locomotive With Smoke and a no. 736W-1 Whistle Tender packed in a no. 12-149 Corr. Box (master carton). This master carton pairing was called a no. 773LTS Steam Type Locomotive & Tender With Smoke & Whistle. The 773-1 was a New York Central 4-6-4 Hudson steamer that was first cataloged in 1950 and returned to the line in 1964. Inside its individual no. 773-131 Corr. Box were the nos. CTC-1 Lockon, SP-1 Smoke Pellets, 675-33 Smoke Stack Cleaner and 773-132 Instruction Sheet.

A listing for this outfit is provided here because a Factory Order exists for the 13277. Pricing is provided as reference for the items alone. However, as stated earlier in this volume, items alone do not constitute an outfit; an outfit box is required.

It is unknown what Polk did with these items. For that reason, finding a box with 13277 markings would be a true discovery.

Peter King Co. purchased outfit no. 19000 in 1962. It was marked with both Lionel's "19000" and Peter King's "2893" customer number. Most of its rolling stock represented new offerings in 1962.

Customer No. On Box: 2893
Description: "O27" Promotional Outfit
Specification: "O27" Steam Type Freight Outfit
Customer/No.: Peter King Co.; 2893
Original Amount: 500
Factory Order Date: 7/30/1962
Date Issued: 7-31-62
Packaging: R.S.C. Outfit Packing (Units not Boxed)

Contents: 1060-25 Steam Type Locomotive; 1060T-25 Tender; 6502-25 Girder Transport Car (Less Girder); 6502-3 Girder Bridge; 6050-150 Stokely Van Camp Savings Bank Car; 6042-75 Gondola Car (Less 2 Cable Reels); 40-11 Cable Reels (2); 6067-25 Caboose; 1013-8 Curved Track (Bundle of 8 - 1013); 1018-10 Straight Track (Loose) (2); 1010-25 35-Watt Transformer; 1103-20 Envelope Packed; 310-2 Set of (5) Billboards; D62-50 Accessory Catalog; 1123-30 Instruction Sheet; 1123-40 Instruction Sheet

Boxes & Packing: 61-170 Outfit Box; 61-171 Insert; 61-172 Insert; 61-173 Insert; 61-175 Shipper for (4) (1-4)

Alternate For Outfit Contents:
Customer Stock No. 2893 to appear on outfit carton & shipper.

19000 (1962)	C6	C7	C8	Rarity
Complete Outfit	350	575	775	R8
Outfit Box no. 61-170	250	400	500	R8

Comments: Peter King Co. was listed as the customer on this Factory Order. Unfortunately, the nature of its business has yet to be determined. The no. 19000, either a Retailer Promotional Type Ib or a Manufacturer Promotional IIIb outfit, was this customer's only promotional outfit purchase.

The 19000 was a low-end starter outfit. It was led by a no. 1060-25 Steam Type Locomotive, which went forward only.

Included in this outfit were nos. 6502-25 Girder Transport Car (Less Girder), 6050-150 Stokely Van Camp Savings Bank Car and 6042-75 Gondola Car (Less 2 Cable Reels), all of which were new for 1962. The 6502-25 was part of only one catalog outfit no. 11201 and its RSC version no. 11205 and three promotional outfits in 1962. It is frequently found without its orange no. 6502-3 Girder Bridge. The 6050-150 was making its rounds in 1962 promotional outfits after first being introduced in the no. 19142.

All the cars in this outfit were equipped with non-operating Archbar trucks and couplers. The no. 1103-20 Envelope Packed was a Type I, as typically found in 1962 outfits.

The common no. 61-170 Tan RSC with Black Graphics outfit

box was used for the 19000. It measured 11½ x 10¼ x 6¼ inches.

The Factory Order instructed the Outfit Packing Department to stamp Peter King's customer number "2893" on the outfit box. All examples have been observed marked in this manner.

Of note, this is the only 19000-series outfit. Lionel skipped over the next 99 numbers until it reached outfit no. 19100.

The small quantity produced of the 19000 makes it a somewhat desirable collectible. Otherwise, this outfit's low-end contents were common offerings of the era.

CONVENTIONAL PACK
61-170 BOX

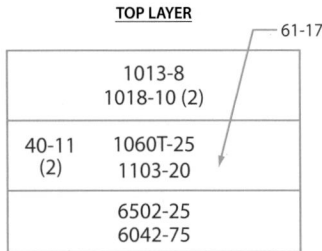

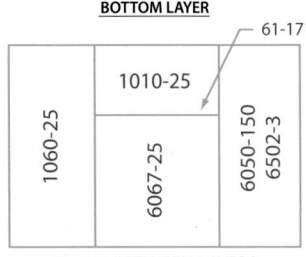

61-172 BETWEEN LAYERS

19100
1962

Customer No. On Box: 48-3210
Description: "O27" Promotional Outfit
Specification: "O27" Steam Type Freight Outfit
Customer/No.: Montgomery Ward; 48-3210
Original Amount: 150
Factory Order Date: 8/14/1962
Date Issued: 8-16-62
Packaging: R.S.C. Outfit Packing (Units not Boxed)

Contents: 1060-25 Steam Type Locomotive; 1060T-25 Tender; 3309-25 Turbo Missile Firing Car (Less Missiles); 0349-10 Turbo Missile (2); 6406-25 Single Automobile Car (Less Auto); 6406-30 Automobile; 6067-25 Caboose; 1013-8 Curved Track (Bundle of 8 - 1013); 1018-10 Straight Track (Loose) (2); 1026-25 25-Watt Transformer; 1103-20 Envelope Packed; 310-2 Set of (5) Billboards; D62-50 Accessory Catalog; 1123-40 Instruction Sheet; 3309-5 Instruction Sheet; 1123-10 Instruction Sheet

Boxes & Packing: 61-170 Outfit Box; 61-171 Corr. Insert; 61-172 Corr. Insert; 61-173 Corr. Insert; 62-248 Corr. Insert; 61-175 Shipper for (4) (1-4)

Alternate For Outfit Contents:
Customer Stock No. 48-3210.

19100 (1962)	C6	C7	C8	Rarity
Complete Outfit	615	925	1,275	R10
Outfit Box no. 61-170	500	750	1,000	R10

Comments: Lionel trains did not appear in the Montgomery Ward catalog for 1962. However, they probably were sold through

its retail stores. Factory Orders list Montgomery Ward as the customer on four outfits: nos. 19100, 19101, 19102 and 19103.

The 19100 was Ward's entry-level steam-powered Retailer Promotional Type Ib purchase for 1962. This outfit was led by a no. 1060-25 Steam Type Locomotive. This engine was Lionel's low-end, forward-only steam offering in 1962; its only feature of note was a headlight.

The cars in this outfit were low-end models equipped with non-operating Archbar trucks and couplers. The no. 3309-25 Turbo Missile Firing Car was the only new item; all the others were repeated from earlier years. The car is common but its no. 0349-10 Turbo Missiles are frequently missing or found broken.

As with many of these low-end outfits, the no. 6406-30 Automobile is the most difficult item to obtain. Finding an original, postwar model with gray bumpers is becoming a challenge. There are many reproductions and modern-era reissues on the market. But the price of a correct model is trivial when compared with the total value of this outfit.

The no. 61-170 Tan RSC with Black Graphics outfit box measured 11½ x 10¼ x 6¼ inches.

The 19100 is all about the outfit box. With only 150 made, it is extremely rare and difficult to find.

CONVENTIONAL PACK
61-170 BOX

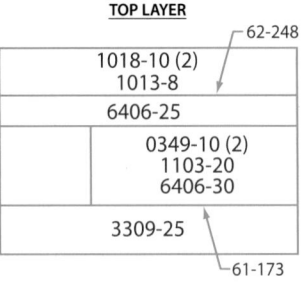

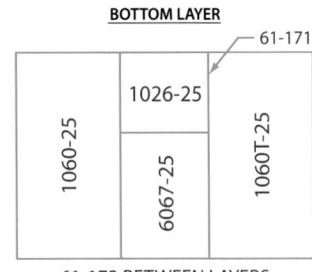

61-172 BETWEEN LAYERS

Cities Service's no. 19106-100 came in a no. 61-170 Tan RSC with Black Graphics outfit box. The outfit is shown with an orange no. 6057-50 Caboose substitution.

19106-100 (1962)	C6	C7	C8	Rarity
Complete Outfit	295	575	825	R9
Outfit Box no. 61-170	200	400	575	R9

Comments: This outfit was the regular RSC version of Cities Service's no. 19106 (see the entry for 19106 from 1962). The contents of these outfits were identical; only the packaging differed.

Some examples of the 19106-100 have been seen with an orange no. 6057-50 Caboose. This fact suggests that Lionel was depleting inventory of this model (equipped with AAR trucks and couplers) in promotional outfits.

The 19106-100 came in a common no. 61-170 Tan RSC with Black Graphics outfit box. The box was manufactured by St. Joe Kraft, St. Joe Paper Co. Container Division and measured 11½ x 10¼ x 6¼ inches.

Only 360 examples were made, and they're seldom seen. The 19106-100 is much more desirable than the 19106 version.

CONVENTIONAL PACK
61-170 BOX

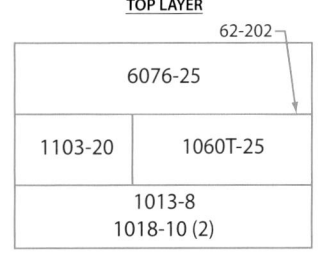

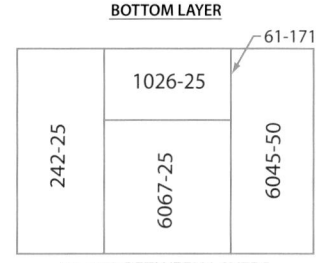

61-172 BETWEEN LAYERS

Customer No. On Box: EC 5010
Description: "O27" Promotional Outfit
Specification: "O27" Steam Type Freight Outfit
Customer/No./Price: Western Auto; EC 5010; $19.99
Original Amount: 4,000
Factory Order Date: 5/16/1962
Date Issued: Revised #1 6-18-62
Packaging: R.S.C. Outfit Packing (Units not Boxed), Except 1020 Crossing

Contents: 242-25 Steam Type Locomotive; 1060T-25 Tender; 6630-25 Missile Launching Car (Less Missile); 6650-80 Missile Complete (or 6650-84); 6480-25 Exploding Target Car; 6042-75 Gondola Car (Less 2 Cable Reels); 40-11 Cable Reels (2); 6067-25 Caboose; 1013-70 Curved Track (Bundle of 12 - 1013); 1018-40 Straight Track (Bundle of 4 - 1018); 1020-1 90° Crossing; 1026-25 25-Watt Transformer; 1103-20 Envelope Packed; 310-2 Set of (5) Billboards; D62-50 Accessory Catalog; 19107-10 Instruction Sheet; 1123-40 Instruction Sheet; 6630-6 Instruction Sheet; 6480-5 Instruction Sheet

Boxes & Packing: 60-389 Outfit Box (Inv. 1380); 60-392 Shipper for (4) (Inv.) (1-4); 62-243 Outfit Box; 62-223 Insert; 62-224 Insert; 62-225 Insert (2); 62-227 Insert; 62-244 Shipper for (4) (1-4)

Alternate For Outfit Contents:
Special Instructions: Customer Stock No. EC 5010 to appear on Outfit Box and Shipper; Use Inventory of 60-389 Box First; Use Inventory of 60-392 Shipper First.

19107 (1962)	C6	C7	C8	Rarity
Complete Outfit With no. 60-389 Box	325	500	700	R6
Outfit Box no. 60-389	150	225	275	R6
Complete Outfit With no. 62-243 Box	275	410	590	R5
Outfit Box no. 62-243	100	135	165	R5

Comments: Western Auto Stores purchased two steam-powered promotional outfits in 1962: nos. 19107 and 19108. The 19107 was a Retailer Promotional Type Ib outfit; it appeared on page 18 of the 1962 Western Auto Christmas Gifts Catalog as no. EC 5010 for $19.99.

Interestingly, the 19107 Lionel Outfit Cost Worksheet indicates that Lionel lost $0.31 on every outfit sold to Western

Western Auto purchased two steam outfits in 1962. The no. 19107, its low-end offering, is shown in the no. 60-389 Outfit Box. This outfit appeared in the 1962 Western Auto Christmas Gifts Catalog as no. EC 5010 for $19.99.

Auto. Unfortunately for Lionel, this was a common practice in 1962, with the company losing money on approximately 30 percent of all the promotional outfits it sold.

This space and military outfit was Western Auto's low-end purchase for 1962. It was led by a no. 242-25 Steam Type Locomotive (new for 1962). This low-end steamer went on to become Lionel's workhorse, replacing the no. 246 as the basic steamer of choice and appearing in more than 55 catalog and promotional outfits through 1967. It had a two-position reversing unit and a headlight, lacked smoke and used a rubber tire as a traction aid. The version with wide running boards was included in this outfit.

The nos. 6480-25 Exploding Target Car and 6630-25 Missile Launching Flat Car were low-end versions of the nos. 6470-25 and 6650-25, respectively. That being said, these cars appeared only in promotional outfits and are harder to find than their high-end counterparts. Except for the no. 6042-75 Gondola Car (Less 2 Cable Reels), all the cars in this outfit were carryover from previous years.

A transition from Archbar to AAR trucks and couplers began in 1962. For the 19107, the cars came equipped with non-operating Archbar types. However, the no. 1060T-25 Tender could come with either two Archbar types or one non-operating Archbar and one plain AAR truck and coupler.

Two Tan RSC with Black Graphics outfit boxes were used for the 19107. The no. 60-389 Outfit Box was manufactured by Owens-Illinois Paper Products, Div. and measured 12 x 11½ x 6½ inches. It was an overstickered no. 1631WS outfit box from 1960. It has been observed with 12 dots printed as part of the box manufacturer's certificate. The no. 62-243 Outfit Box measured 12⅛ x 11½ x 6⅜ inches.

Of the two Western Auto outfits for 1962, the 19107 is the easier one to find in collectible condition.

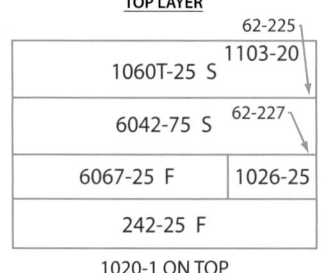

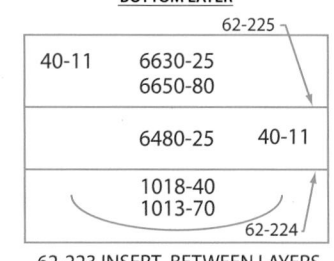

CONVENTIONAL PACK
USE INVENTORY OF 60-380 BOX FIRST
62-243 BOX

TOP LAYER

62-225
1103-20
1060T-25 S

6042-75 S   62-227

6067-25 F | 1026-25

242-25 F

1020-1 ON TOP

BOTTOM LAYER

62-225

40-11 | 6630-25
6650-80

6480-25 | 40-11

1018-40
1013-70
62-224

62-223 INSERT BETWEEN LAYERS

E **Giant Lionel 8-Car Train Set with Figure-8 Track.**
Give the high ball! Fun's on it's way with deluxe smoking locomotive with headlight and Magne-Traction! Train includes tender,
action Sheriff-and-Outlaw car, gondola with canisters, hopper
car, flat car with bridge girder, box car and caboose. Big figure
eight track layout includes crossing and uncoupling track. Set is
complete with UL Approved transformer, oil, instructions. EC5011

F **Lionel Missile Launcher Action Railroad with Figure-8
Track.** Send a missile on its way as the train whizzes along!
Aim for the exploding target car! Steam type locomotive with
headlight and Magne-Traction, tender, missile launching car,
target car, gondola car and caboose for space age thrills!
Complete set includes transformer, lockon, oil, etc. EC5010

E **29⁸⁸** Easy Terms

F **19⁹⁹** Only 1.25 Weekly

Western Auto purchased
two steam outfits in 1962.
The no. 19108 (item "E") was
its high-end offering, listed
in the 1962 Western Auto
Christmas Gifts Catalog as
no. EC 5011 for $29.88. Also
shown is outfit no. 19107
(item "F") as Western Auto
no. EC 5010 for $19.99.

SPECIAL LAYOUT INSTRUCTIONS

Track furnished with this outfit will form a layout as illustrated. Join
track section fully and firmly.

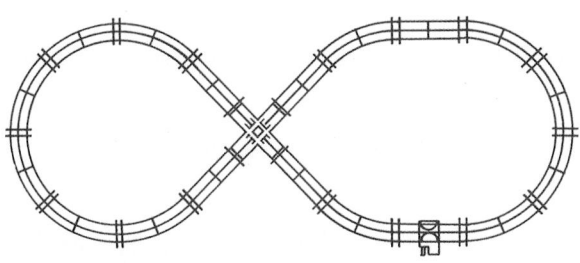

THE LIONEL CORPORATION
SERVICE DEPARTMENT: Hoffman Place, Hillside, N.J.

Printed in U.S. of America

19108-10 5-62

**The no. 19108-10 Layout Instruction Sheet was unique to this
outfit.**

Customer No. On Box: EC 5011
Description: "O27" Promotional Outfit
Specification: "O27" Steam Type Freight Outfit With Smoke
Customer/No./Price: Western Auto; EC 5011; $29.88
Original Amount: 2,000
Factory Order Date: 6/5/1962
Date Issued: 6-2-62
Packaging: R.S.C. Outfit Packing (Units not Boxed), Except 1020
Crossing

Contents: 236-25 Steam Type Loco. With Smoke; 1060T-
25 Tender; 3370-25 Animated Sheriff & Outlaw Car; 6162-25
Gondola Car (Less 3 Canisters); 6112-88 Canisters (White) (3);

6476-25 Hopper Car; 6050-25 Savings Bank Car; 6825-25 Trestle
Bridge Flat Car (Less Trestle Bridge); 6825-3 Trestle Bridge;
6057-25 Caboose; 1013-70 Curved Track (Bundle of 12 - 1013);
1018-5 Straight Track (Bundle of 5 - 1018); 1008-50 Uncoupling
Unit; 1020-1 90° Crossing; 1025-25 45-Watt Transformer; 909-
20 Smoke Fluid; 1103-20 Envelope Packed; 310-2 Set of (5)
Billboards; D62-50 Accessory Catalog; 3370-17 Instruction
Sheet; 236-11 Instruction Sheet; 1123-40 Instruction Sheet; 122-
10 Instruction Sheet; 19108-10 Layout Instruction Sheet

Boxes & Packing: 62-243 Outfit Box; 61-171 Insert; 62-223
Insert; 62-225 Insert; 62-248 Insert (2); 62-251 Insert (2); 62-258
Insert; 62-244 Shipper for (4) (1-4)

Alternate For Outfit Contents:
Special Instructions - Customer Stock No. EC 5011 to appear on
outfit box & shipper.

19108 (1962)	C6	C7	C8	Rarity
Complete Outfit	315	485	690	R5
Outfit Box no. 62-243	100	150	200	R5

Comments: Western Auto Stores purchased two steam-powered
promotional outfits in 1962: nos. 19107 and 19108. The 19108
was a Retailer Promotional Type Ia outfit; it appeared on page 18
of the 1962 Western Auto Christmas Gifts Catalog as no. EC
5011 for $29.88.

The 19108 was Western Auto's high-end purchase in 1962.
It was led by a no. 236-25 Steam Locomotive with Smoke. This
engine also came with Magne-Traction, a headlight and a two-
position reversing unit. The peripherals that normally went with
a boxed no. 236-1 were placed loose in the outfit box or put in a
no. 1103-20 Envelope Packed. These items included the nos. 909-

20 Smoke Fluid, CTC-1 Lockon, 927-90 Lubricating Oil Packed and 236-11 Instruction Sheet.

All the rolling stock in this outfit was carryover from earlier years. The no. 6050-25 Savings Bank Car was nearing the end of its run, as it appeared in only this and one other outfit in 1962. It made one final appearance in 1964. The other rolling stock in the 19108 consisted of commonly available items.

A transition from Archbar to AAR trucks and couplers began in 1962. For the 19108, the cars came equipped with operating AAR types. However, the no. 1060T-25 Tender could come with either two Archbar types or one non-operating Archbar and one plain AAR truck and coupler.

The difficult-to-find no. 19108-10 Layout Instruction Sheet was created just for this outfit. It was printed on yellow paper and dated 5-62.

The no. 62-243 Tan RSC with Black Graphics outfit box measured 12⅛ x 11½ x 6⅜ inches.

Although both this outfit and the 19107 have similar pricing and rarity, the 19108 is the more desirable of the two Western Auto outfits issued for 1962. It featured an upgraded locomotive and better cars, and a smaller quantity was produced.

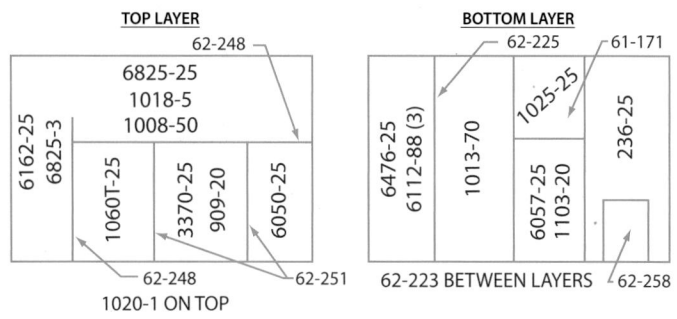

Customer No. On Box: 11-L-346
Description: "O27" Promotional Outfit
Specification: "O27" Diesel Freight Outfit
Customer/No.: Firestone; 11-L-346
Original Amount: 1,200
Factory Order Date: 8/13/1962
Date Issued: 8-16-62
Packaging: Display Outfit Packing (Units not Boxed), Except 1020-1 Crossover

Contents: 222P-25 "Denver & Rio Grande" Alco Diesel Power Unit; 3309-25 Turbo Missile Firing Car (Less Missiles); 0349-10 Turbo Missile (2); 6480-25 Exploding Target Car; 6413-25 Mercury Capsule Transport Car (Less Capsules); 6413-4 Capsules (2); 6413-10 Envelope Packed; 6067-25 Caboose; 1013-70 Curved Track (Bundle of 12 - 1013); 1018-40 Straight Track (Bundle of 4 - 1018); 1026-25 25-Watt Transformer; 1103-20 Envelope Packed; 1020-1 90° Crossing; 310-2 Set of (5) Billboards; D62-50 Accessory Catalog; 1125-10 Instruction Sheet; 1123-40 Instruction Sheet; 3309-5 Instruction Sheet; 6480-5 Instruction Sheet; 6413-8 Instruction Sheet; 1802B Layout Instruction Sheet

Boxes & Packing: 62-200 Display Outfit Box; 61-101 Insert; 61-102 Insert; 62-257 Insert (3); 61-103 Shipper for (Pack 5 per shipper) (1-5)

Alternate For Outfit Contents:
Note: Customer Stock No. 11-L-346 to appear on outfit box & shipper.

19109 (1962)	C6	C7	C8	Rarity
Complete Outfit	385	640	925	R7
Outfit Box no. 62-200	125	225	300	R7

Comments: This was Firestone Tire & Rubber Company's only promotional outfit purchase in 1962. The cars in the no. 19109

duplicated those in Grand-Way's no. 19179 from 1962; however, their motive power differed.

The 19109, a Retailer Promotional Type Ib, was led by a no. 222P-25 Denver & Rio Grande Alco Diesel Power Unit (new in 1962). It moved forward only and featured a traction tire, a headlight and a closed pilot.

The space and military rolling stock in this outfit included three operating cars that provided plenty of excitement and action. The no. 3309-25 Turbo Missile Firing Car (Less Missiles) was frequently paired with a no. 6480-25 Exploding Target Car. Both were low-end versions of the nos. 3349-25 and 6470-25, respectively. Except for the 6480-25 and no. 6067-25 Caboose, every item in the 19109 was new for 1962.

A transition from Archbar to AAR trucks and couplers began in 1962. For the 19109, all but one of the cars came equipped with non-operating Archbar types. The exception – the no. 6413-25 Mercury Capsule Transport Car – had operating AAR trucks and couplers.

The figure-eight track layout was described on the no. 1802B Layout Instruction Sheet dated 6-59. All the other peripherals in this outfit were appropriate for 1962.

The no. 62-200 White 4-6-4 Steamer and F3 Hinged Display with Red/Orange and Blue Graphics Type A outfit box was manufactured by United Container Co. and measured 21⅝ x 11½ x 3¼ inches.

The original Factory Order listed a quantity of 600, but this was eventually doubled to 1,200. Even with such an increase, examples of the 19109 do not appear too often. As with all Firestone outfits, this one is in demand.

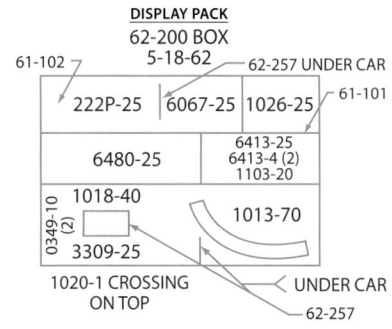

The no. 19110 was the first of four General Release Promotional outfits from 1962 with Department Store Special listed as the customer. It was the follow-up to the no. X-605 from 1961 and included comparable items. This outfit had a Stewart & Co. price tag (not shown) listing the price as $18.88.

Description: "O27" Promotional Outfit
Specification: "O27" Steam Type Freight Outfit
Customer/Price: Department Store Special; $19.95
Customer/No./Price: Stewart & Co.; 39 05; $18.88
Original Amount: 500
Factory Order Date: 6/6/1962
Date Issued: 6-8-62
Packaging: R.S.C. Outfit Packing (Units not Boxed)

Contents: 242-25 Steam Type Locomotive; 1060T-25 Tender; 3357-25 Animated Hobo & Railroad Policeman Car; 3357-27 Box Packed; 6062-25 Gondola Car (Less 3 Cable Reels); 40-11 Cable Reels (3); 6825-25 Trestle Bridge Flat Car (Less Trestle Bridge); 6825-3 Trestle Bridge; 6057-25 Caboose; 1013-8 Curved Track (Bundle of 8 - 1013); 1018-10 Straight Track (Loose); 1008-50 Uncoupling Unit; 1010-25 35-Watt Transformer; 1103-20 Envelope Packed; 310-2 Set of (5) Billboards; D62-50 Accessory Catalog; 1123-40 Instruction Sheet; 1641-10 Instruction Sheet

Boxes & Packing: 61-180 Outfit Box; 61-181 Corr. Insert; 61-182 Corr. Insert; 61-183 Corr. Insert; 61-184 Corr. Insert; 61-185 Shipper for (4) (1-4)

19110 (1962)	C6	C7	C8	Rarity
Complete Outfit	375	615	850	R8
Outfit Box no. 61-180	250	375	475	R8

Comments: This was the first of four (nos. 19110 through 19113) General Release Promotional outfits from 1962 with the customer listed as "Department Store Special". Lionel likely sold all of these

outfits to small retailers seeking a promotional outfit yet unable to make the volume commitment to receive an exclusive one.

The 19110, a Type IIa outfit, was the low end of these four outfits. It was the follow-up to General Release Promotional outfit no. X-605 from 1961. The 19110 Lionel Outfit Cost Worksheet lists the suggested retail price of $19.95. Lionel sold the outfit for $13.00, and it cost $12.08 to make. Thus a $0.92 profit, or 7.1 percent net margin, was realized. However, an example of the 19110 that specifies Stewart & Company as the customer indicates, via a price tag, a price of $18.88.

The 19110 was headed by a no. 242-25 Steam Type Locomotive. This low-end Scout steamer featured a two-position reversing unit and a headlight, lacked smoke and used a rubber tire as a traction aid. The version with wide running boards was included in this outfit.

The cars in this outfit were commonly available in 1962. In fact, the no. 6825-25 Trestle Bridge Flat Car appeared in more than 40 promotional outfits. The only item that was new for 1962 was the no. 3357-25 Animated Hobo & Railroad Policeman Car. The 3357-25 provided plenty of excitement as the cop tried to catch the hobo. Since this car came unboxed (hence the "-25" suffix), the Factory Order also listed a no. 3357-27 Box Packed.

A transition from Archbar to AAR trucks and couplers began in 1962. For the 19110, the cars came equipped with operating AAR types. However, the no. 1060T-25 Tender could come with either one non-operating and one plain Archbar types or one non-operating Archbar and one plain AAR truck and coupler.

The no. 61-180 Tan RSC with Black Graphics outfit box was manufactured by United Container Co. and measured 12¾ x 10 x 6¾ inches.

In 1989, Richard Kughn, then the owner of Lionel Trains, Inc., purchased Madison Hardware Co. and transferred its inventory from New York City to a facility he owned in Detroit. One of the first lists of outfits available for sale from the "new" Madison included a quantity of seven of the 19110.

This outfit does appear on the market, but not too often. For that reason, it achieves an R8 rarity.

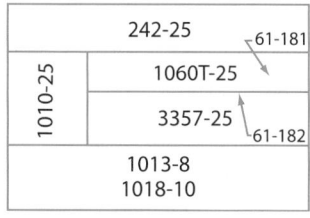

CONVENTIONAL PACK
61-180 BOX

TOP LAYER

3357-27	6057-25
40-11 (1)	6825-25 / 6825-3
1103-20	1008-50
6062-25	40-11 (2)

61-184

BOTTOM LAYER

1010-25	242-25
	1060T-25
	3357-25
	1013-8 / 1018-10

61-181
61-182

61-183 BETWEEN LAYERS

19111
1962

Description: "O27" Promotional Outfit
Specification: "O27" Steam Type Freight Outfit with Smoke
Customer/Price: Department Store Special; $24.88
Original Amount: 250
Factory Order Date: 6/7/1962
Date Issued: 6-8-62
Packaging: R.S.C. Outfit Packing (Units not Boxed), Except 1020 Crossing

Contents: 236-25 Steam Type Locomotive with Smoke; 1060T-25 Tender; 3349-25 Turbo Missile Firing Car (Less Missiles); 0349-10 Turbo Missile (2); 6413-25 Mercury Capsule Transport Car; 6413-4 Capsules (2); 6413-10 Envelope Packed; 6448-25 Exploding Target Range Car; 6057-25 Caboose; 1013-70 Curved Track (Bundle of 12 - 1013); 1018-30 Straight Track (Bundle of 3 - 1018); 1008-50 Uncoupling Unit; 1025-25 45-Watt Transformer; 1020-1 90° Crossing; 1103-20 Envelope Packed; 909-20 Smoke Fluid; 310-2 Set of (5) Billboards; D62-50 Accessory Catalog; 1123-40 Instruction Sheet; 236-11 Instruction Sheet; 3349-8 Instruction Sheet; 6448-17 Instruction Sheet; 122-10 Instruction Sheet; 1802B Layout Instruction Sheet

Boxes & Packing: 61-180 Outfit Box; 61-181 Corr. Insert; 61-191 Corr. Insert; 62-248 Corr. Insert; 62-264 Corr. Insert; 61-185 Shipper for (4) (1-4)

19111 (1962)	C6	C7	C8	Rarity
Complete Outfit	700	1,000	1,300	R10
Outfit Box no. 61-180	450	600	700	R10

Comments: This was the second of four (nos. 19110 through 19113) General Release Promotional outfits from 1962 with the customer listed as "Department Store Special". Lionel likely sold all of these outfits to small retailers seeking a promotional outfit yet unable to make the volume commitment to receive an exclusive one.

The no. 19111, a Type IIa outfit, was the follow-up to General Release Promotional outfit no. X-607 from 1961. It was a step up from the 19110, with an upgraded locomotive and better rolling stock.

The 19111 Lionel Outfit Cost Worksheet lists the suggested retail price of $24.88. Lionel sold the outfit for $16.50, and it cost $14.86 to make. Thus a $1.64 profit, or 9.9 percent net margin, was realized.

The 19111 was led by a no. 236-25 Steam Locomotive with Smoke, which also featured Magne-Traction, a headlight and a two-position reversing unit. The peripherals that normally went with a boxed no. 236-1 were placed loose in the outfit box or put in a no. 1103-20 Envelope Packed. These included the nos. 909-20 Smoke Fluid, CTC-1 Lockon, 927-90 Lubricating Oil Packed and 236-11 Instruction Sheet.

In addition, the 19111 came with a no. 3349-25 Turbo Missile Firing Car (Less Missiles). The 3349-25 was paired with a no. 6448-25 Exploding Target Range Car in at least seven outfits. The 3349-25 as well as the no. 6413-25 Mercury Capsule Transport Car in this outfit were new for 1962.

All the rolling stock in the 19111 was equipped with operating AAR trucks and couplers. However, because a transition from Archbar to AAR types began in 1962, the no. 1060T-25 Tender could come with two Archbar types or one non-operating Archbar and one plain AAR truck and coupler.

The appropriate quantity of track was included to make the figure-eight layout. That track plan was outlined on the no. 1802B Layout Instruction Sheet dated 6-59.

The no. 61-180 Tan RSC with Black Graphics outfit box measured 12¾ x 10 x 6¾ inches.

The Factory Order originally listed a quantity of 200, but that was increased to 250. Both of these numbers are small and explain why this outfit is so difficult to find in collectible condition.

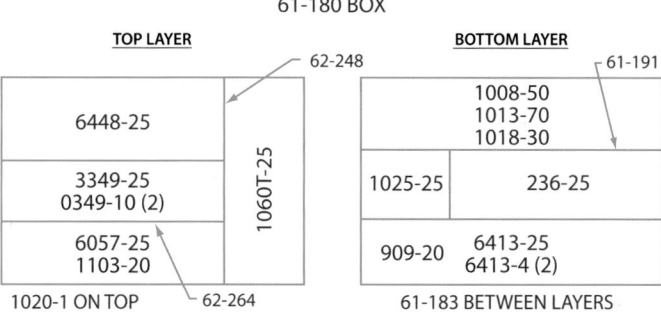

CONVENTIONAL PACK
61-180 BOX

TOP LAYER

62-248

6448-25	
3349-25 / 0349-10 (2)	1060T-25
6057-25 / 1103-20	

1020-1 ON TOP
62-264

BOTTOM LAYER

61-191

1008-50 / 1013-70 / 1018-30	
1025-25	236-25
909-20	6413-25 / 6413-4 (2)

61-183 BETWEEN LAYERS

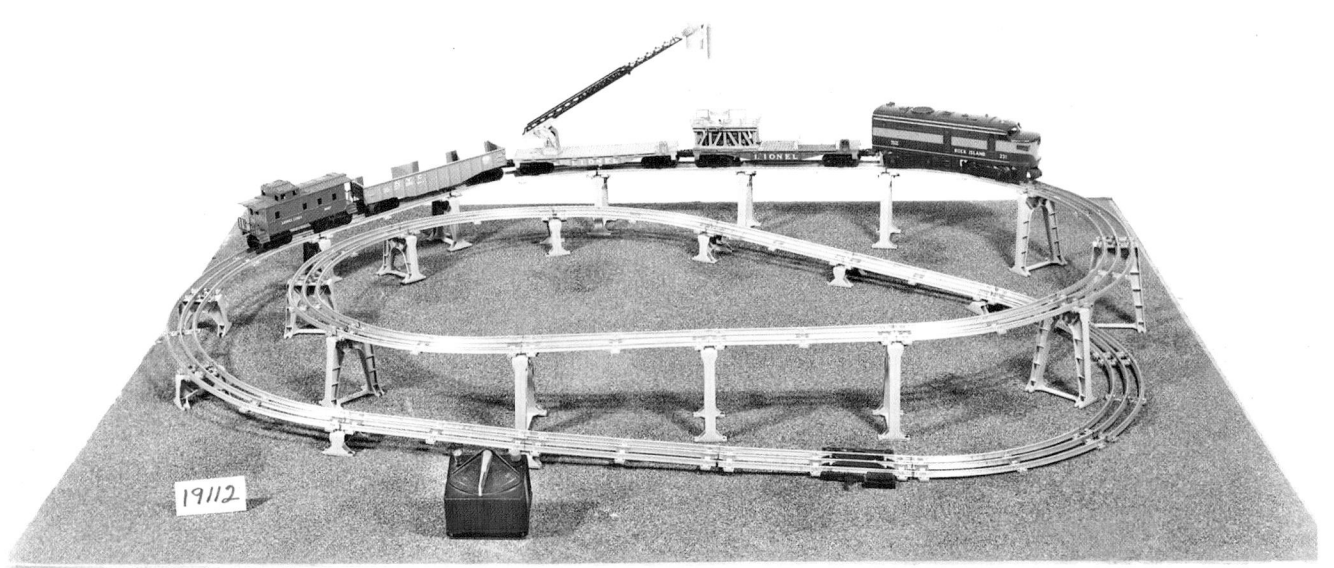

To assist in selling its outfits, Lionel provided specification sheets and glossy photographs to its sales department and to dealers. This photo of the no. 19112 came from a dealer packet sent to Schaffner's in Canton, Ohio. It was a Lionel Service Station in 1962.

Description: "O27" Promotional Outfit
Specification: "O27" Diesel Freight Outfit
Customer: Department Store Special
Original Amount: 550
Factory Order Date: 6/7/1962
Date Issued: 6-8-62
Packaging: R.S.C. Outfit Packing (Units not Boxed), Except 110-1 Trestle Set

Contents: 231P-25 Alco Diesel Power Car - "Rock Island"; 3413-25 Mercury Capsule Launching Car; 3413-18 Mercury Capsule & Parachute Assem.; 3413-27 Missile; 6512-25 Cherry Picker Car; 6162-25 Gondola Car (Less 3 Canisters); 6112-88 Canisters (White) (3); 6057-25 Caboose; 1013-8 Curved Track (Bundle of 8 - 1013); 1013-90 Curved Track (Bundle of 9 - 1013); 1018-30 Straight Track (Bundle of 3 - 1018) (3); 1008-50 Uncoupling Unit; 1010-25 35-Watt Transformer; 110-1 Trestle Set; 1103-20 Envelope Packed; 310-2 Set of (5) Billboards; D62-50 Accessory Catalog; 1123-40 Instruction Sheet; 3413-8 Instruction Sheet; 225-6 Instruction Sheet; X602-10 Instruction Sheet; 1802I Layout Instruction Sheet

Boxes & Packing: 60-483 Corr. Outfit Box; 61-172 Insert (2); 61-181 Insert; 61-182 Insert; 62-225 Insert; 62-248 Insert; 62-264 Insert; 60-485 Corr. Shipper for (3) (1-3); 62-260 Outfit Box; 61-182 Insert; 62-245 Insert; 62-248 Insert; 62-263 Insert; 62-264 Insert; 62-265 Shipper for (4) (1-4)

19112 (1962)	C6	C7	C8	Rarity
Complete Outfit With no. 60-483 Box	815	1,215	1,550	R10
Outfit Box no. 60-483	500	700	800	R10
Complete Outfit With no. 62-260 Box	615	965	1,325	R9
Outfit Box no. 62-260	300	450	575	R9

Comments: This was the third of four (nos. 19110 through 19113) General Release Promotional outfits from 1962 with the customer listed as "Department Store Special". Lionel likely sold all of these

outfits to small retailers seeking a promotional outfit yet unable to make the volume commitment to receive an exclusive one.

The no. 19112, a Type IIa outfit, was the follow-up to General Release Promotional outfit no. X-608 from 1961. The 19112 Lionel Outfit Cost Worksheet lists Lionel's selling price as $19.35 and the cost as $17.92. Thus a $1.43 profit, or 7.4 percent net margin, was realized.

This outfit was the only diesel-powered offering for Department Store Special. It was led by a no. 231P-25 Rock Island Alco Diesel Power Car that featured two-axle Magne-Traction, a headlight and a two-position reversing unit.

Two newly issued operating cars were included in the 19112. The nos. 3413-25 Mercury Capsule Launching Car and 6512-25 Cherry Picker Car were paired in at least 18 different outfits. They were designed to work together, with the 6512-25 pretending to

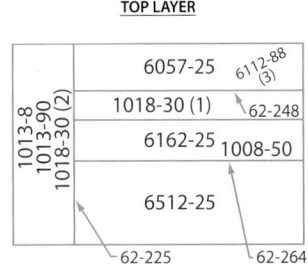

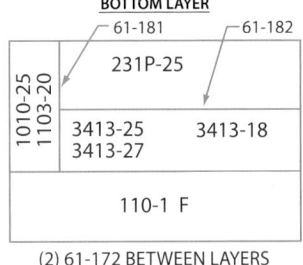

load an astronaut into the waiting Mercury capsule. The other cars were carryover from previous years.

All the rolling stock in this outfit came with operating AAR trucks and couplers. The no. 1802I Layout Instruction Sheet (dated 5-59) detailed the elevated pretzel track layout.

Two different Tan RSC with Black Graphics outfit boxes were used. The no. 60-483 Tan RSC with Black Graphics outfit box was manufactured by Star Corrugated Box Company, Inc. and measured 15½ x 11¼ x 7¼ inches. It was an overstickered no. X-536NA that had a star printed on the box bottom. The no. 62-260 Outfit Box measured 16¼ x 13 x 6⅜ inches and was used for six other outfits.

The original Factory Order called for 200 of the 19112 to be made. When the quantity was increased to 550, the new 62-260 Outfit Box was likely used. Rarity and pricing are provided for both box versions. The 60-483 Outfit Box is tougher to find than the 62-260.

19113 1962

Description: "O27" Promotional Outfit
Specification: "O27" Steam Type Freight Outfit W/Smoke & Whistle
Customer: Department Store Special
Packaging: R.S.C. Outfit Packing (Units not Boxed), Except 1020

Contents: 233-25 Steam Type Locomotive With Smoke; 234W-25 Whistle Tender; 3619-25 Reconnaissance Copter Car; 0319-100 Helicopter; 6501-25 Jet Boat Car; 6501-2 Boat Assem.; 6501-17 Fuel Pellets; 3362-25 Helium Tank Unloading Car; 6463-25 Rocket Fuel Car; 6057-25 Caboose; 1013-70 Curved Track (Bundle of 12 - 1013); 1018-30 Straight Track (Bundle of 3 - 1018); 1008-50 Uncoupling Unit; 1073-25 60-Watt Transformer; 147-25 Horn & Whistle Controller; 2333-140 Flashlight Cell; 1020-1 90° Crossing; 1645-12 Envelope Packed; 909-20 Smoke Fluid; 310-2 Set of (5) Billboards; D62-50 Accessory Catalog; 1646-10 Instruction Sheet; 1802B Layout Instruction Sheet

Boxes & Packing: 62-243 Outfit Box; 61-171 Insert; 62-223 Insert; 62-225 Insert (2); 62-449 Insert; 62-244 Shipper for (4) (1-4)

19113 (1962)	C6	C7	C8	Rarity
Complete Outfit	825	1,150	1,500	R10
Outfit Box no. 62-243	450	600	700	R10

Comments: This was the last of four (nos. 19110 through 19113) General Release Promotional outfits from 1962 with the customer listed as "Department Store Special". Lionel likely sold all of these outfits to small retailers seeking a promotional outfit yet unable to make the volume commitment to receive an exclusive one.

The 19113, a Type IIa outfit, was the follow-up to General Release Promotional outfit no. X-609 from 1961. The 19113 Lionel Outfit Cost Worksheet lists Lionel's selling price as $25.00 and cost as $22.74. Thus a $2.26 profit, or 9.0 percent net margin, was realized.

The 19113 was the high-end steam-powered offering for Department Store Special. It was led by a no. 233-25 Steam Locomotive with Smoke. This was Lionel's high-end Scout engine, and it also had a headlight and Magne-Traction.

The peripherals that normally went with a boxed no. 233-1 were placed loose in the outfit box or put in a no. 1645-12 Envelope Packed. These included the nos. 909-20 Smoke Fluid, CTC-1 Lockon, 927-60 Tube of Oil, 927-65 Tube of Grease and 233-11 Instruction Sheet.

The 233-25 was paired with a no. 234W-25 Whistle Tender instead of a no. 233W Whistle Tender because the latter was being phased out.

All the rolling stock in this outfit came from Lionel's higher-end offerings. Standing out were the nos. 3619-25 Reconnaissance Copter Car, 6463-25 Rocket Fuel Car and 6501-25 Jet Motor Boat Car (all new for 1962).

All cars were equipped with operating AAR trucks and couplers except for the 234W-25. In 1962, the 234Ws came with one non-operating and one plain Archbar truck and coupler.

When a no. 147-25 Horn & Whistle Controller was included, Lionel provided a no. 2333-140 Flashlight Cell loose in the outfit box. This practice lasted until 1963.

The 1645-12 included three wires that were required to hook up the 147-25 as well as the outfit. This is a difficult-to-find packed envelope.

The no. 62-243 Tan RSC with Black Graphics outfit box measured 12⅛ x 11½ x 6⅜ inches.

This higher-end outfit provided general retailers with a product competitive with any Retailer Promotional outfit. Original quantity numbers are not available, and rarity is based solely on actual observations.

CONVENTIONAL PACK
62-243 BOX

TOP LAYER: 62-225, 61-171, CORD, 1073-25, 233-25, 3619-25, 0319-100, 1013-70, 1018-50 ON TOP, 1645-12, 6057-25, 909-20, 1020-1 ON TOP

BOTTOM LAYER: 62-225, 62-249, 6501-25, 234W-25, 6463-25, 1018-30, 3362-25, 147-25, 2333-140, 6501-2, 6501-17, 62-223 BETWEEN LAYERS

19114 1962

Description: "O27" Promotional Outfit
Specification: "O27" Steam Type Freight Outfit
Customer: Biederman

Original Amount: 500
Factory Order Date: 10/1/1962
Date Issued: 10-2-62
Packaging: R.S.C. Outfit Packing (Units not Boxed), Except 110-1

Contents: 242-25 Steam Type Locomotive; 1060T-25 Tender; 3413-25 Mercury Capsule Launching Car; 6512-25 Cherry Picker Car; 6413-25 Mercury Capsule Transport Car; 6413-4 Capsules (2); 6413-10 Envelope Packed; 6057-25 Caboose; 1013-8 Curved Track (Bundle of 8 - 1013); 1013-90 Curved Track (Bundle of 9 - 1013); 1018-30 Straight Track (Bundle of 3 - 1018) (3); 1008-50 Uncoupling Unit; 1010-25 35-Watt Transformer; 110-1 Trestle Set; 1103-20 Envelope Packed; 310-2 Set of (5) Billboards; D62-50 Accessory Catalog; 1123-40 Instruction Sheet; 3413-8 Instruction Sheet; 6512-19 Instruction Sheet; 1802I Layout Instruction Sheet; 1641-10 Instruction Sheet

Boxes & Packing: 62-270 Outfit Box; 61-171 Insert (2); 62-223 Insert; 62-225 Insert; 62-248 Insert; 62-272 Corr. Insert; 62-271 Shipper for (3) (1-3)

19114 (1962)	C6	C7	C8	Rarity
Complete Outfit	550	935	1,335	R8
Outfit Box no. 62-270	225	375	500	R8

Comments: The no. 19114 was Biederman Furniture Company's Retailer Promotional Type Ia steam-powered offering for 1962. Biederman also purchased the diesel-powered no. 19115.

A no. 242-25 Steam Type Locomotive (new for 1962) led the 19114. This low-end Scout steamer featured a two-position reversing unit and a headlight, lacked smoke and used a rubber tire as a traction aid. The version with wide running boards was included in this outfit.

The 19114 came with the three new space and military cars that Lionel was highlighting in 1962. The nos. 3413-25 Mercury Capsule Launching Car and 6512-25 Cherry Picker Car were designed to work together, with the 6512-25 pretending to load

an astronaut into the waiting Mercury capsule. The no. 6413-25 Mercury Capsule Transport Car carried extra capsules for subsequent launches, although it turned out that the capsules were too big to fit the 3413-25's rocket. These three cars appeared together in at least five different outfits, all from 1962.

All the cars in this outfit were unboxed and equipped with operating AAR trucks and couplers. However, a transition from Archbar to AAR trucks and couplers began in 1962. As a result, the no. 1060T-25 Tender could come with either two Archbar types or one non-operating Archbar and one plain AAR truck and coupler.

The elevated pretzel track layout was detailed on the no. 1802I Layout Instruction Sheet.

The no. 62-270 Tan RSC with Black Graphics outfit box was manufactured by United Container Co. and measured 15½ x 14⅛ x 6¼ inches.

From both the contents and the quantity produced, this outfit is representative of the offerings from 1962. Because of the 19114's space and military theme and the combination of cars included, it is desired by space and military and promotional outfit collectors alike.

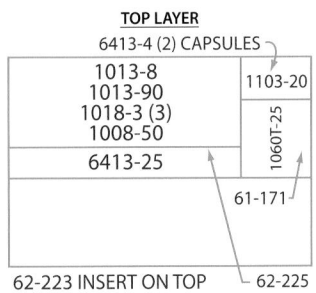
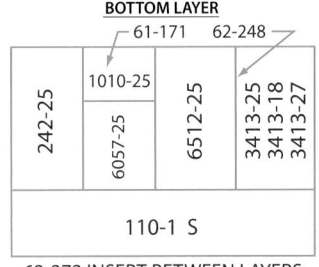

CONVENTIONAL PACK
62-270 BOX

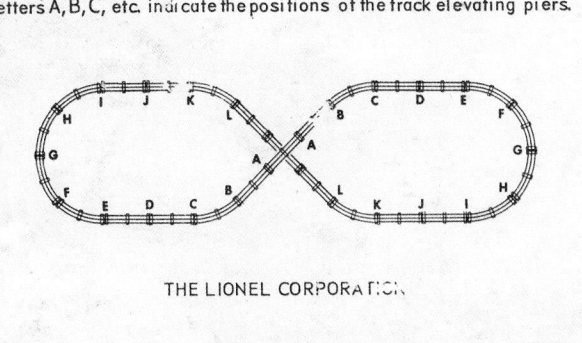

The no. 19115-10 Track Layout Instruction Sheet details the elevated and elongated figure-eight layout used with this outfit. It was subsequently used in four promotional outfits in 1963.

Description: "O27" Promotional Outfit
Specification: "O27" Diesel Freight Outfit
Customer: Biederman
Customer/Price: Meyers-Dickson; $22.88
Original Amount: 175
Factory Order Date: 8/27/1962
Date Issued: Rev 9-13-62

Packaging: R.S.C. Outfit Packing (Units not Boxed), Except 110-1

Contents: 211P-25 *"Texas Special"* Alco Diesel Power Unit; 211T-25 Motorless Unit; 3349-25 Turbo Missile Firing Car (Less Missiles); 0349-10 Turbo Missile (2); 6501-25 Jet Motor Boat Car; 6501-17 Fuel Pellets Packed; 6501-2 Boat Assem.; 3470-25 Aerial Target Launching Car; 3470-20 Envelope; 3470-4 Basket; 3410-25 Oper. Helicopter Car (Less Helicopter); 3419-100 Operating Helicopter Complete; 6017-225 Caboose - "Santa Fe"; 1013-70 Curved Track - (Bundle of 12 - 1013); 1018-7 Straight Track - (Bundle of 7 - 1018); 1018-75 Straight Track - (Bundle of 6 - 1018); 1008-50 Uncoupling Unit; 1025-25 45-Watt Transformer; 110-1 Trestle Set; 1103-20 Envelope Packed; 310-2 Set of (5) Billboards; D62-50 Accessory Catalog; 1123-40 Instruction Sheet; 211-6 Instruction Sheet; 122-10 Instruction Sheet; 3349-8 Instruction Sheet; 6501-14 Instruction Sheet; 3410-5 Instruction Sheet; 19115-10 Track Layout

Boxes & Packing: 61-230 Outfit Box; 61-173 Insert; 62-224 Insert; 62-225 Insert; 62-245 Insert (2); 62-248 Insert; 62-264 Corr. Insert; 62-272 Corr. Insert (4); 61-231 Shipper for (2) (1-2); 62-270 Box; 61-171 Insert; 62-224 Insert; 62-245 Insert (2); 62-248 Insert; 62-264 Insert; 62-272 Insert; 62-271 Shipper for (3) (1-3)

19115 (1962)	C6	C7	C8	Rarity
Complete Outfit With nos. 61-230 Or 62-270 Box	925	1,500	2,000	R10
Outfit Box nos. 61-230 Or 62-270	500	750	900	R10

Comments: The no. 19115, along with the no. 19114, was Biederman Furniture Company's promotional outfit purchase for 1962. The 19115 was a Retailer Promotional Type Ia diesel-powered offering, whereas the 19114 was steam-powered.

The 19115 Lionel Outfit Cost Worksheet lists Lionel's selling price as $24.50 and cost as $21.44. Thus a $3.06 profit, or 12.5 percent net margin, was realized. Based on the latter figure, the 19115 was Lionel's fifth most profitable promotional outfit in 1962.

A no. 211P-25 *Texas Special* Alco Diesel Power Unit led the 19115. This locomotive featured a two-position reversing unit, an open pilot, a headlight and two-axle Magne-Traction.

The space and military rolling stock consisted of almost all items that were new for 1962. The only carryover item was the no. 3410-25 Oper. Helicopter Car (Less Helicopter). In 1962, the Production Control File for the 3419-100 Operating Helicopter Complete changed from a gray Navy stamped two-piece helicopter body to an unmarked helicopter with a one-piece yellow helicopter body. Although this was Lionel's intended production, many 3419-100 Navy helicopters still appeared on 3410s in 1962.

The no. 3349-25 Turbo Missile Firing Car (Less Missiles) was paired with its primary target, a no. 3470-25 Aerial Target

Launching Car, in at least five different outfits. These and the other cars in this outfit were equipped with operating AAR trucks and couplers.

The 19115 mimicked the elevated and elongated figure-eight track layout first described on the no. 1802A Layout Instruction Sheet. The no. 19115-10 Track Layout Instruction Sheet was created for this outfit. Why Lionel issued a new sheet remains unknown. The 19115-10 was also included in four promotional outfits in 1963.

Two different outfit boxes were used for the 19115. The no. 61-230 Orange RSC with Black Graphics outfit box was manufactured by the Mead Corporation and measured 16 x 15½ x 7⅛ inches. The no. 62-270 Tan RSC with Black Graphics outfit box was manufactured by United Container Co. and measured 15½ x 14⅛ x 6¼ inches. Both box versions are equally rare.

The 19115 is an exciting outfit that is difficult to find due to its low production numbers.

CONVENTIONAL PACK
62-270 BOX
REVISED 9-7-62

TOP LAYER

6501-25 6501-2 6501-17	3349-25 0349-10 (2)	62-264 61-171 1018-7 1018-75	
		6017-225 1103-20	1025-25
		3470-25 3470-20	3470-4
1008-50			

BOTTOM LAYER

62-245 (2)	3410-25 3419-100	1013-70
	211P-25 62-248 INSERT	
	211T-25	
	110-1 S	62-224

62-272 BETWEEN LAYERS

19116
1962

Description: "O27" Promotional Outfit
Specification: "O27" Steam Type Promotional Outfit
Customer: Fish Furniture
Original Amount: 100
Factory Order Date: 9/14/1962
Date Issued: 9-17-62
Packaging: R.S.C. Outfit Packing (Units not Boxed), Except 110

Contents: 242-25 Steam Type Locomotive; 1060T-25 Tender; 3665-25 Minuteman Missile Launching Car; 6501-25 Jet Motor Boat Car; 6501-2 Boat Assem.; 6501-17 Fuel Pellets Packed; 6463-25 Rocket Fuel Car; 6057-25 Caboose; 1013-8 Curved Track (Bundle of 8 - 1013); 1013-90 Curved Track (Bundle of 9 - 1013); 1018-30 Straight Track (Bundle of 3 - 1018); 1008-50 Uncoupling Unit; 1010-25 35-Watt Transformer; 110-1 Trestle Set; 1103-20 Envelope Packed; 310-2 Set of (5) Billboards; D62-50 Accessory Catalog; 1123-40 Instruction Sheet; 3665-23 Instruction Sheet; 6501-14 Instruction Sheet; 1802I Layout Instruction Sheet; 1641-10 Instruction Sheet

Boxes & Packing: 62-270 Outfit Box; 61-171 Insert; 61-173 Insert; 62-272 Insert; 62-264 Insert (2); 62-271 Shipper for (3) (1-3)

19116 (1962)	C6	C7	C8	Rarity
Complete Outfit	950	1,450	1,850	R10
Outfit Box no. 62-270	700	1,000	1,250	R10

Comments: In 1962, Fish Furniture purchased two Retailer Promotional Type Ia outfits: nos. 19116 and 19117. Both outfits were space and military themed and consisted mainly of new items from 1962.

The 19116, Fish Furniture's steam-powered offering, was led by a no. 242-25 Steam Type Locomotive. This low-end Scout steamer featured a two-position reversing unit and a headlight, lacked smoke and used a rubber tire as a traction aid. The version with wide running boards was included in this outfit.

The rolling stock in the 19116 included two operating cars: nos. 3665-25 Minuteman Missile Launching Car and 6501-25 Jet

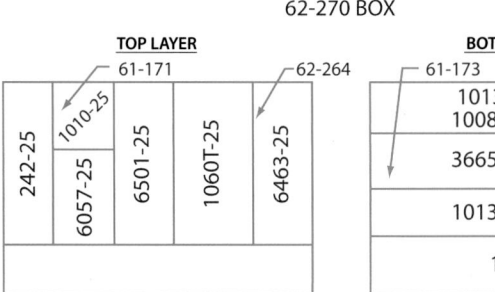

CONVENTIONAL PACK
62-270 BOX

TOP LAYER

242-25	1010-25 6057-25	6501-25	1060T-25	61-171 62-264 6463-25

BOTTOM LAYER

61-173 62-264		
1013-8 1008-50		1018-30 (3) 6501-2
3665-25		1103-20
1013-90		
110-1 S		

62-272 BETWEEN LAYERS

Motor Boat Car. A transition from Archbar to AAR trucks and couplers began in 1962. For the 19116, the cars came equipped with operating AAR types. However, the no. 1060T-25 Tender could come with either two Archbar types or one non-operating Archbar and one plain AAR truck and coupler.

The no. 1802I Layout Instruction Sheet detailed the elevated pretzel track layout.

The no. 62-270 Tan RSC with Black Graphics outfit box was manufactured by United Container Co. and measured 15½ x 14⅛ x 6¼ inches.

The 19116 and 19117 were the only time that Fish Furniture appeared as a customer on a Factory Order. The small quantity of only 450 total made between the two outfits was indicative of how Lionel was lowering the quantity requirements for unique promotional outfits. Today, that is why these two outfits are difficult to find in collectible condition.

Description: "O27" Promotional Outfit
Specification: "O27" Diesel Freight Outfit
Customer: Fish Furniture
Original Amount: 350
Factory Order Date: 10/1/1962
Date Issued: Rev 10-1-62
Packaging: R.S.C. Outfit Packing (Units not Boxed), Except 110

Contents: 211P-25 *"Texas Special"* Alco Diesel Power Unit; 211T-25 *"Texas Special"* Motorless Unit; 3413-25 Mercury Capsule Launching Car; 6512-25 Cherry Picker Car; 3410-25 Oper. Helicopter Car (Less Helicopter); 3419-100 Operating Helicopter Complete; 6413-25 Mercury Capsule Transport Car (Less Capsules); 6413-4 Capsules (2); 6017-210 Caboose "U.S. Navy"; 1013-70 Curved Track (Bundle of 12 - 1013); 1018-75 Straight Track (Bundle of 6 - 1018); 1018-7 Straight Track - (Bundle of 7 - 1018); 6029-25 Uncoupling Track Unit; 1025-25 45-Watt Transformer; 110-1 Trestle Set; 90-40 Envelope Packed; 310-2 Set of (5) Billboards; D62-50 Accessory Catalog; 1123-40 Instruction Sheet; 211-6 Instruction Sheet; 3413-8 Instruction Sheet; 3410-5 Instruction Sheet; 126-10 Instruction Sheet; 1802A Layout Instruction Sheet

Boxes & Packing: 62-270 Outfit Box; 61-171 Insert; 62-224 Insert; 62-245 Insert (2); 62-248 Insert (3); 62-272 Insert; 62-271 Shipper for (3) (1-3)

19117 (1962)	C6	C7	C8	Rarity
Complete Outfit	870	1,400	1,900	R9
Outfit Box no. 62-270	350	500	600	R9

Comments: In 1962, Fish Furniture purchased two Retailer Promotional Type Ia outfits: nos. 19116 and 19117. Both outfits were space and military themed and consisted mainly of new items from 1962.

The no. 19117 Lionel Outfit Cost Worksheet lists Lionel's selling price as $25.00 and cost as $22.01. Thus a $2.99 profit, or 12.0 percent net margin, was realized. Based on the latter figure, the 19117 was Lionel's sixth most profitable promotional outfit in 1962.

As an aside, Fish Furniture's 19116 was also very profitable for Lionel (9.1 percent net margin). Unfortunately for Lionel, these two outfits were produced in such small quantities that they could not offset all the unprofitable outfits that the company produced in 1962.

The 19117, Fish Furniture's diesel-powered offering, was led by a no. 211P-25 *Texas Special* Alco Diesel Power Unit. This

locomotive featured a two-position reversing unit, an open pilot, a headlight and two-axle Magne-Traction.

This outfit came with the three new space and military cars that Lionel was highlighting in 1962. The nos. 3413-25 Mercury Capsule Launching Car and 6512-25 Cherry Picker Car were designed to work together, with the 6512-25 pretending to load an astronaut into the waiting Mercury capsule. The no. 6413-25 Mercury Capsule Transport Car carried extra capsules for subsequent launches, although it turned out that the capsules were too big to fit the 3413-25's rocket. These three cars appeared together in at least five different outfits, all from 1962.

The two carryover items in this outfit were the nos. 3410-25 Oper. Helicopter Car (Less Helicopter) and 6017-210 U.S. Navy Caboose. They, like the other pieces of rolling stock, were equipped with operating AAR trucks and couplers.

In 1962, the Production Control File for the no. 3419-100 Operating Helicopter Complete changed from a gray Navy stamped two-piece helicopter body to an unmarked helicopter with a one-piece yellow helicopter body. Although this was Lionel's intended production, many 3419-100 Navy helicopters still appeared on 3410s in 1962.

The 19117 included the elevated and elongated figure-eight track layout that was described on the no. 1802A Layout Instruction Sheet.

With the inclusion of a no. 6029-25 R.C. Uncoupling Track, a no. 90-40 Envelope Packed was required to supply the extra wires and no. 90 Controller.

The no. 62-270 Tan RSC with Black Graphics outfit box was manufactured by United Container Co. and measured 15½ x 14 x 6¼ inches.

The original quantity of this outfit was 250, but it was increased to 350. Even so, the small number produced makes the 19117 extremely difficult to find in collectible condition.

CONVENTIONAL PACK
62-270 BOX

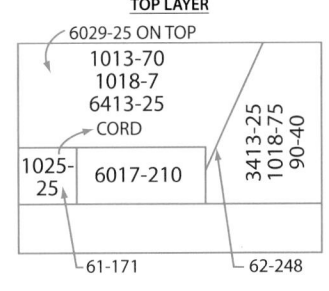

TOP LAYER

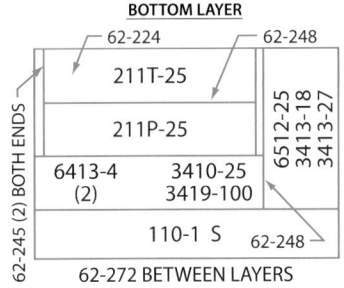

BOTTOM LAYER

Description: "O27" Promotional Outfit
Specification: "O27" Steam Type Freight Outfit
Customer: Canada Hudson-Bay
Original Amount: 750
Factory Order Date: 5/16/1962
Date Issued: Rev #1 7/31/62
Packaging: R.S.C. Outfit Packing (Units not Boxed)

Contents: 1060-25 Steam Type Locomotive; 1060T-25 Tender; 6042-25 Gondola Car (Less 2 Canisters); 6112-5 Canisters (Red) (2); 6076-25 Hopper Car; 6406-25 Single Auto Flat Car (Less Auto); 6406-30 Auto; 6050-50 Swift Savings Bank Car; 6067-25 Caboose; 1013-8 Curved Track (Bundle of 8 - 1013); 1018-10 Straight Track (Loose) (2); 1026-25 25-Watt Transformer; 1103-20 Envelope Packed; 310-2 Set of (5) Billboards; D62-50 Accessory Catalog; 1123-10 Instruction Sheet; 1123-40 Instruction Sheet

Boxes & Packing: 61-190 Outfit Box; 61-191 Insert; 61-192 Insert; 62-248 Insert; 62-249 Insert; 61-194 Shipper for (6) (1-6)

19118 (1962)	C6	C7	C8	Rarity
Complete Outfit	300	525	725	R8
Outfit Box no. 61-190	175	300	400	R8

Comments: This was the only time that Canada Hudson-Bay appeared on a Factory Order. The no. 19118 was a Retailer Promotional Type Ib outfit.

The 19118 was made up of Lionel's low-end offerings, and all the items repeated from earlier years. Powering this outfit was a no. 1060-25 Steam Type Locomotive. This engine moved forward only and had a headlight as its only key feature.

The most interesting item in this outfit was the no. 6050-50

Swift Savings Bank Car. The "-50" version was equipped with non-operating Archbar trucks and couplers, as were the other cars. It is more difficult to find than the no. 6050-100 version with AAR trucks and couplers.

As with many of these low-end outfits, the no. 6406-30 Automobile is the most difficult item to obtain. Finding an original, postwar model with gray bumpers is becoming a challenge. There are many reproductions and modern-era reissues on the market.

A transition from Archbar to AAR trucks and couplers began in 1962. As a result, the nos. 1060T-25 Tender and 6067-25 Caboose could come with either two Archbar types or one non-operating Archbar and one plain AAR truck and coupler.

The no. 61-190 Tan RSC with Black Graphics outfit box measured 12¼ x 9⅞ x 6¼ inches and was manufactured by Mead Containers.

Frankly, the 19118 is not too exciting. After all, the contents were low-end, and the outfit box was a standard Tan RSC. The only notable feature is that this was the only Retailer Promotional outfit purchased by Canadian Hudson Bay.

By the way, the 19118 was one of 29 unprofitable outfits in 1962. Lionel lost $0.84 per outfit sold.

CONVENTIONAL PACK
61-190 BOX
REVISED 7-31-62

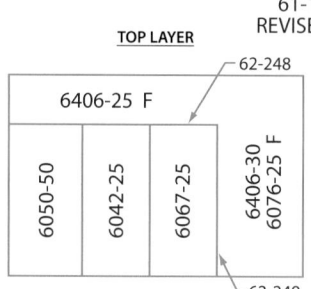

TOP LAYER

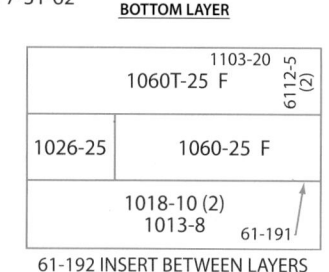

BOTTOM LAYER

61-192 INSERT BETWEEN LAYERS

Description: "O27" Promotional Outfit
Specification: "O27" Steam Type Freight Outfit
Customer/No./Price: T. Eaton; 027-R4018; $28.50
Original Amount: 700
Factory Order Date: 9/27/1962
Date Issued: 10-2-62
Packaging: Display Outfit Packing (Units not Boxed)

Contents: 1060-25 Steam Type Locomotive; 1060T-25 Tender; 3357-25 Animated Hobo & Railroad Policeman Car; 3357-27 Box Packed; 6473-25 Rodeo Car; 6067-25 Caboose; 1013-8 Curved Track (Bundle of 8 - 1013); 1018-10 Straight Track (Loose) (2); 1026-25 25-Watt Transformer; 1103-20 Envelope Packed; 310-2 Set of (5) Billboards; D62-50 Accessory Catalog; 1123-10 Instruction Sheet; 1123-40 Instruction Sheet

Boxes & Packing: 62-200 Outfit Box; 61-101 Corr. Insert; 61-102 Corr. Insert; 61-103 Corr. Shipper for (6) (1-6)

19119 (1962)	C6	C7	C8	Rarity
Complete Outfit	275	485	700	R8
Outfit Box no. 62-200	175	300	400	R8

Comments: T. Eaton was a Canadian retailer that sold Lionel outfits in its catalog. In 1962, the firm purchased two Retailer Promotional outfits: nos. 19119 and 19120. The 19119, a Type Ib outfit, appeared on page 222 of the Eaton Christmas Catalog for 1962 as no. 027-R4018 for $28.50. It also appeared in an Eaton advertisement in the *Toronto Daily Star* on December 1, 1962, as "Lionel Steam Freight Set! Eaton Opportunity Day Special, Set. $19.99."

The 19119 was a small yet enjoyable outfit that likely delighted many a child during its day. It was led by a no. 1060-25 Steam Type Locomotive, which moved forward only. The locomotive included in this outfit was the later version with a small rain shield covering the headlight.

A pair of brand-new operating cars distinguished the 19119. Since the Type IIb no. 3357-25 Animated Hobo & Railroad Policeman Car came unboxed (hence the "-25" suffix), its peripherals were listed separately as a no. 3357-27 Box Packed. The Type I no. 6473-25 Rodeo Car was the early version with a partially filled slot caused by a flaw in the original tool. It featured red heat-stamped lettering.

Both of these cars were equipped with middle operating AAR trucks and couplers. Be aware that a transition from Archbar to AAR trucks and couplers began in 1962. As a result, the no. 1060T-25 Tender came with one non-operating Archbar and one

T. Eaton featured outfit no. 19119 in its 1962 Christmas Catalog. The combination of two new operating cars made this an exciting entry-level outfit. Unfortunately for Lionel, it lost $0.44 on every 19119 sold to T. Eaton.

The no. 19119 came in the common no. 62-200 White 4-6-4 Steamer and F3 Hinged Display with Red/Orange and Blue Graphics Type A outfit box. This generic box was stamped on top by Lionel with "No. 19119".

DISPLAY PACK
62-200 BOX
5-18-62 — 61-102

		61-101
1060-25	1060T-25	1026-25
1018-10 (2) 1013-8	6473-25	
3357-25	3357-27	1103-20 6067-25

plain AAR truck and coupler and the no. 6067-25 Caboose with non-operating Archbar trucks and couplers.

The no. 62-200 White 4-6-4 Steamer and F3 Hinged Display with Red/Orange and Blue Graphics Type A outfit box was manufactured by United Container Co. and measured 21⅝ x 11½

x 3¼ inches.

The 19119 does appear from time to time. Since it was different from many starter outfits, it is a nice addition to a promotional outfit collection.

19120
1962

Description: "O27" Promotional Outfit
Specification: "O27" Steam Type Freight Outfit
Customer: T. Eaton
Packaging: R.S.C. Outfit Packing (Units not Boxed)

Contents: 242-25 Steam Type Locomotive; 1060T-25 Tender; 3413-25 Mercury Capsule Launching Car; 3413-18 Mercury Capsule & Parachute Assem.; 3413-27 Missile; 3619-25 Reconnaissance Copter Car; 0319-100 Helicopter; 6057-25 Caboose - Red; 1013-8 Curved Track (Bundle of 8 - 1013); 1018-10 Straight Track (Loose); 1008-50 Uncoupling Unit; 1010-25 35-Watt Transformer; 1103-20 Envelope Packed; 310-2 Set of (5) Billboards; D62-50 Accessory Catalog; 1641-10 Instruction Sheet

Boxes & Packing: 61-170 Outfit Box; 61-171 Insert; 61-172 Insert; 62-202 Insert; 61-175 Shipper for (4) (1-4)

19120 (1962)	C6	C7	C8	Rarity
Complete Outfit	400	715	1,050	R8
Outfit Box no. 61-170	175	350	525	R8

Comments: T. Eaton was a Canadian retailer that sold Lionel outfits in its catalog. In 1962, the firm purchased two Retailer Promotional outfits: nos. 19119 and 19120. However, the 19120, a Retailer Promotional Type Ib outfit, never appeared in the Eaton Christmas Catalog. Neither has it been observed in any other literature. As such, the Factory Order is the one document of its existence.

The 19120 Lionel Outfit Cost Worksheet lists Lionel's selling price as $14.80 and cost as $14.03. Thus a $0.77 profit, or 5.2 percent net margin, was realized.

The 19120 was Eaton's better offering for the year. It was led by a no. 242-25 Steam Type Locomotive. This low-end Scout steamer featured a two-position reversing unit and a headlight, lacked smoke and used a rubber tire as a traction aid. The version with wide running boards was included in this outfit.

As with the 19119, this outfit included two brand-new operating cars. The no. 3619-25 Reconnaissance Copter Car included a fragile and easily lost no. 0319-100 Helicopter. As part of the manufacturing process, the roof of the 3619-25 was taped shut with a ½-inch piece of Scotch tape. Examples in C8 condition still have a mark where the tape was applied. The no. 3413-25 Mercury Capsule Launching Car appeared in 24 outfits in 1962.

A transition from Archbar to AAR trucks and couplers began in 1962. For the 19120, the cars were equipped with operating AAR types. However, the no. 1060T-25 Tender could come with either two Archbar types or one non-operating Archbar and one plain AAR truck and coupler.

The no. 61-170 Tan RSC with Black Graphics outfit box measured 11½ x 10¼ x 6¼ inches.

This outfit is seldom seen; hence, it has a higher-than-average rarity and price.

CONVENTIONAL PACK
61-170 BOX

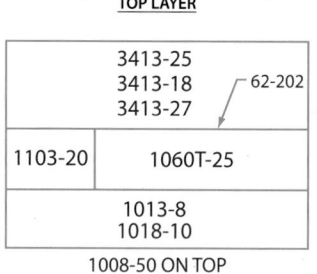

TOP LAYER

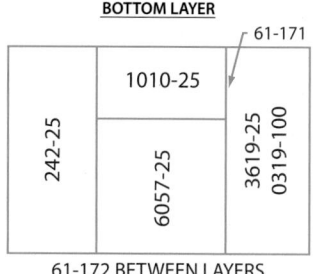

BOTTOM LAYER

19121
1962

Description: "O27" Promotional Outfit
Specification: "O27" Steam Type Freight Outfit
Customer: R. Simpson
Original Amount: 400
Factory Order Date: 9/27/1962
Date Issued: 10-2-62
Packaging: R.S.C. Outfit Packing (Units not Boxed), Except 953-1

Contents: 242-25 Steam Type Locomotive; 1060T-25 Tender; 6476-25 Hopper Car - Red; 6162-25 Gondola Car (Less 3 Canisters); 6112-88 Canisters (White) (3); 6825-25 Trestle Bridge Flat Car (Less Trestle Bridge); 6825-3 Trestle Bridge; 3357-25 Animated Hobo & Railroad Policeman Car; 3357-27 Box Packed; 6057-25 Caboose; 1013-8 Curved Track (Bundle of 8 - 1013); 1018-10 Straight Track (Loose); 1008-50 Uncoupling Unit; 1010-25 35-Watt Transformer; 1103-20 Envelope Packed; 953-1 Figure Set; 310-2 Set of (5) Billboards; D62-50 Accessory Catalog; 1641-10 Instruction Sheet; 1123-40 Instruction Sheet

Boxes & Packing: 62-243 Outfit Box; 61-171 Insert; 61-172 Insert; 62-225 Insert (2); 62-251 Insert (2); 62-244 Shipper for (4) (1-4)

19121 (1962)	C6	C7	C8	Rarity
Complete Outfit	500	850	1,325	R9
Outfit Box no. 62-243	250	425	550	R9

Comments: R. Simpson was listed as the customer on the Factory Order for this Retailer Promotional Type Ia outfit. Even so, the no. 19121 did not appear in the 1962 Simpsons-Sears Christmas Catalog. It is likely R. Simpson sold this outfit over the counter at its retail stores.

The 19121 Lionel Outfit Cost Worksheet lists Lionel's selling price as $12.83 and cost as $13.19. Thus a $0.36 (2.8 percent) loss was realized on every outfit.

The 19121 was led by a no. 242-25 Steam Type Locomotive. This low-end Scout steamer featured a two-position reversing unit and a headlight, lacked smoke and used a rubber tire as a traction aid. The version with wide running boards was included in this outfit.

The rolling stock included items that were commonly available in 1962. All of them were carryover, except for the Type IIb no. 3357-25 Animated Hobo & Railroad Policeman Car. This new operating car provided plenty of excitement as the cop tried to catch the hobo. Since the car came unboxed (hence the "-25" suffix), the Factory Order also listed a no. 3357-27 Box Packed.

A transition from Archbar to AAR trucks and couplers began in 1962. For the 19121, the cars came equipped with operating AAR types. However, the no. 1060T-25 Tender could come with either two Archbar types or one non-operating Archbar and one plain AAR truck and coupler.

The no. 953-1 Figure Set is the item that is most difficult to acquire when trying to complete this outfit. Its box was made of a thin cardstock that was easily torn or ripped. The instruction sheet and original, complete Plasticville pieces can also be a challenge to obtain. The 953-1 made its last outfit appearance in the 19121.

The no. 62-243 Tan RSC with Black Graphics outfit box measured 12⅛ x 11½ x 6⅜ inches.

The R9 rarity is due to the small quantity of outfits originally produced and the infrequent appearance of an example in the market.

CONVENTIONAL PACK
62-243 BOX

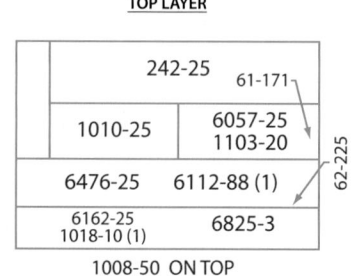

TOP LAYER

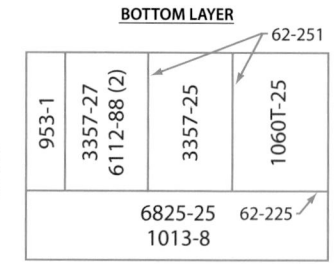

BOTTOM LAYER

Description: "O27" Promotional Outfit
Specification: "O27" Diesel Freight Outfit
Customer: Automotive Associates
Original Amount: 2,000
Factory Order Date: 6/7/1962
Date Issued: 6-8-62
Packaging: Display Outfit Packing (Units not Boxed)

Contents: 1065-25 Alco Diesel Power Unit - "Union Pacific"; 6630-25 Missile Launching Car (Less Missile); 6650-80 Missile Complete (or 6650-84); 6480-25 Exploding Target Car; 3510-25 Satellite Launching Car (Less Satellite); 0333-100 Satellite; 6067-25 Caboose; 1013-8 Curved Track (Bundle of 8 - 1013); 1018-10 Straight Track (Loose) (2); 1026-25 25-Watt Transformer; 1103-20 Envelope Packed; 310-2 Set of (5) Billboards; D62-50 Accessory Catalog; 1123-40 Instruction Sheet; 1125-10 Instruction Sheet; 6630-6 Instruction Sheet; 6480-5 Instruction Sheet; 3510-5 Instruction Sheet

Boxes & Packing: 62-200 Outfit Box; 61-101 Corr. Insert; 62-257 Corr. Insert (3); 61-103 Shipper for (6) (1-6)

19122 (1962)	C6	C7	C8	Rarity
Complete Outfit	425	650	900	R5
Outfit Box no. 62-200	125	200	250	R5

Comments: Lionel listed Automotive Associates as the customer for three outfits in 1962: nos. 19122, 19123 and 19124. The 19122 was Automotive Associates' entry-level diesel locomotive offering and included all promotional-only items – hence its classification as a Retailer Promotional Type Ib outfit. This space and military outfit was the follow-up to the no. X-626 from 1961.

The 19122 contained a no. 1065-25 Union Pacific Alco Diesel Power Unit. This forward-only locomotive was as stripped down as Lionel could make an Alco in 1962, though it did have a headlight. This diesel appeared only in promotional outfits.

Except for the no. 3510-25 Satellite Launching Car (Less Satellite), all items in this outfit were carried over from 1961. The 3510-25 included a red frame and "Lionel" stamped on the side; otherwise, its mechanism was an exact duplicate of the no. 3509-25 Satellite Launching Car. It is the most difficult of the satellite launching cars to find.

The nos. 6480-25 Exploding Target Car and 6630-25 Missile Launching Flat Car were low-end versions of the nos. 6470-25 and 6650-25, respectively. That being said, these cars appeared only in promotional outfits and are harder to find than their high-end counterparts.

A transition from Archbar to AAR trucks and couplers began in 1962. For the 19122, the cars came equipped with non-operating Archbar types. However, the no. 6067-25 Caboose could come with one non-operating Archbar and one plain AAR truck and coupler.

The no. 62-200 White 4-6-4 Steamer and F3 Hinged Display with Red/Orange and Blue Graphics Type A outfit box was manufactured by United Container Co. and measured 21⅝ x 11½ x 3¼ inches.

Many 19122s have survived over the years, although not always in collectible condition or with the correct contents. The inclusion of a 3510-25, which appeared only in 10 promotional outfits, makes this a desirable outfit.

Description: "O27" Promotional Outfit
Specification: "O27" Steam Type Freight Outfit
Customer: Automotive Associates
Original Amount: 1,500
Factory Order Date: 7/20/1962
Date Issued: Rev #1 7-23-62
Packaging: R.S.C. Outfit Packing (Units not Boxed)

Contents: 242-25 Steam Type Locomotive; 1060T-25 Tender; 3357-25 Animated Hobo & Railroad Policeman Car; 3357-27 Box Packed; 6162-25 Gondola Car (Less 3 Canisters); 6112-88 Canisters (White) (3); 6476-25 Hopper Car - Red; 6057-25 Caboose; 1013-8 Curved Track (Bundle of 8 - 1013); 1018-10 Straight Track (Loose); 1008-50 Uncoupling Unit; 1010-25 35-Watt Transformer; 1103-20 Envelope Packed; 310-2 Set of (5) Billboard Signs; D62-50 Accessory Catalog; 1123-40 Instruction Sheet; 1641-10 Instruction Sheet

Boxes & Packing: 61-170 Outfit Box; 61-171 Corr. Insert; 61-172 Corr. Insert; 62-248 Corr. Insert; 62-249 Corr. Insert; 61-175 Corr. Shipper for (4) (1-4)

19123 (1962)	C6	C7	C8	Rarity
Complete Outfit	215	415	575	R6
Outfit Box no 61-170	100	200	250	R6

Comments: Lionel listed Automotive Associates as the customer for three outfits in 1962: nos. 19122, 19123 and 19124. The 19123 was classified as a Retailer Promotional Type Ia outfit. This entry-level steam locomotive outfit was the follow-up to the no. X-627 from 1961.

The 19123 was headed by a no. 242-25 Steam Type Locomotive. This low-end Scout steamer featured a two-position reversing unit and a headlight, lacked smoke and used a rubber tire as a traction aid. The version with wide running boards was included in this outfit.

Except for the no. 3357-25 Animated Hobo & Railroad Policeman Car, all the items in this outfit were carryover from previous years. The 3357-25 provided plenty of excitement as the

CONVENTIONAL PACK
61-170 BOX

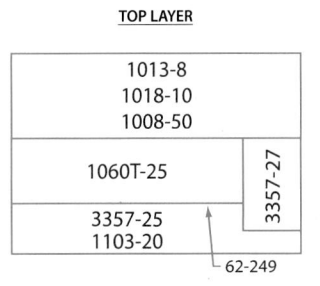

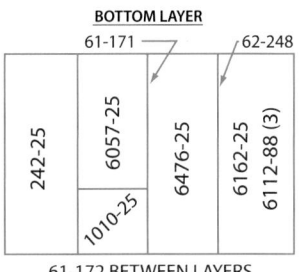

Automotive Associates purchased the no. 19123 as its entry-level steam locomotive outfit in 1962. This outfit was likely sold by one of the many Automotive Associates customers.

cop tried to catch the hobo. Since the car came unboxed (hence the "-25" suffix), the Factory Order also listed a no. 3357-27 Box Packed.

The cars came equipped with operating AAR types. However, the no. 1060T-25 Tender came with non-operating Archbar types.

The no. 61-170 Tan RSC with Black Graphics outfit box

was manufactured by St. Joe Kraft, St. Joe Paper Co. Container Division and measured 11½ x 10¼ x 6¼ inches.

The 19123 was produced in the lowest quantity of the three Automotive Associates outfits from 1962. Even so, these outfits were distributed through many automotive retail chains and so examples do appear from time to time.

19124
1962

Description: "O27" Promotional Outfit
Specification: "O27" Steam Type Freight Outfit With Smoke
Customer: Automotive Associates
Customer/No./Price: Noah's Ark; 301 X814; $29.88
Cust./No./Price: Oklahoma Tire & Supply Co.; 70-761-6; $35.77
Original Amount: 2,600
Factory Order Date: 10/2/1962
Date Issued: Rev 10-2-62
Packaging: R.S.C. Outfit Packing (Units not Boxed), Except 110

Contents: 236-25 Steam Type Locomotive with Smoke; 1060T-25 Tender; 3413-25 Mercury Capsule Launching Car; 6512-25 Cherry Picker Car; 6050-100 Swift Savings Bank Car; 3349-25 Turbo Missile Firing Car (Less Missiles); 0349-10 Turbo Missile (2); 6057-25 Caboose; 1013-8 Curved Track (Bundle of 8 - 1013); 1013-90 Curved Track (Bundle of 9 - 1013); 1018-30 Straight Track (Bundle of 3 - 1018) (3); 1008-50 Uncoupling Unit; 1025-25 45-Watt Transformer; 110-1 Trestle Set; 1103-20 Envelope Packed; 909-20 Smoke Fluid; 310-2 Set of (5) Billboards; D62-50 Accessory Catalog; 1123-40 Instruction Sheet; 236-11 Instruction

Sheet; 3413-8 Instruction Sheet; 3349-8 Instruction Sheet; 122-10 Instruction Sheet; 1802I Layout Instruction Sheet

Boxes & Packing: 62-270 Outfit Box; 61-171 Insert; 62-225 Insert; 62-264 Insert (2); 62-272 Insert; 62-271 Shipper for (3) (1-3)

Alternate For Outfit Contents:
Note: Substitute 900 - 6050-25 for 6050-100.

19124 (1962)	C6	C7	C8	Rarity
Complete Outfit	400	650	935	R5
Outfit Box no. 62-270	100	150	200	R5

Comments: Lionel listed Automotive Associates as the customer for three outfits in 1962: nos. 19122, 19123 and 19124. The 19124, a Retailer Promotional Type Ia outfit, was the follow-up to the no. X-629 from 1961.

The 19124 was linked to two of its eventual end customers through a catalog observation and a price tag. It appeared on page 17 of the 1962 Oklahoma Tire & Supply Co. Christmas Toys and Gift Catalog as no. 70-761-6 for $35.77. It was listed as "Lionel' Space Launcher". The illustration was shown with the no. 6050-

Automotive Associates purchased outfit no. 19124 in 1962. This space and military outfit has been linked to at least two automotive customers. The 19124 introduced the no. 6050-100 Swift Savings Bank Car. It was the operating AAR truck and coupler replacement to the Archbar equipped no. 6050-50 Swift Savings Bank Car. The no. 62-270 Outfit Box for the 19124 was used in more than 30 outfits from 1962 and 1963.

A price tag still attached to outfit no. 19124 links this example to Noah's Ark as no. 301 X814. The price of $29.88 is less than the $35.77 that Oklahoma Tire & Supply Co. listed in its 1962 Christmas Toys and Gift Catalog.

25 Savings Bank Car substitution. In addition, an example of the 19124 has been observed with a Noah's Ark price tag.

This outfit featured a no. 236-25 Steam Type Locomotive with Smoke. The 236-25 also featured Magne-Traction, a headlight and a two-position reversing unit. The peripherals that normally went with a boxed no. 236-1 were placed loose in the outfit box or put in a no. 1103-20 Envelope Packed. These included the nos. 909-20 Smoke Fluid, CTC-1 Lockon, 927-90 Lubricating Oil Packed and 236-11 Instruction Sheet.

The 19124 came with three new space and military cars that Lionel was featuring in 1962. The nos. 3413-25 Mercury Capsule Launching Car and 6512-25 Cherry Picker Car were paired in at least 18 different outfits. They were designed to work together, with the 6512-25 pretending to load an astronaut into the waiting Mercury capsule. A no. 3349-25 Turbo Missile Firing Car (Less Missiles) was also included, but a target was not provided. Maybe Lionel intended for it to protect the launch from unforeseen enemies. These three cars appeared together in at least six different outfits, all from 1962.

A transition from Archbar to AAR trucks and couplers began

in 1962. For the 19124, the no. 6050-100 Swift Savings Bank Car was introduced in this outfit. It was the operating AAR truck and coupler replacement to the Archbar equipped no. 6050-50 Swift Savings Bank Car. The 6050-100 and all cars were equipped with middle operating AAR types with a combination of early and late side frames. However, the no. 1060T-25 Tender could come with either two Archbar types or one non-operating Archbar and one plain AAR truck and coupler.

The no. 1802I Layout Instruction Sheet detailed the elevated pretzel track layout.

This outfit was used to thin out the inventory of the no. 6050-25 Savings Bank Car. This substitution hardly affects the overall outfit price.

The no. 62-270 Tan RSC with Black Graphics outfit box was manufactured by United Container Co. and measured 15½ x 14 x 6¼ inches.

This outfit does appear from time to time, but it is difficult to find complete and in collectible condition.

CONVENTIONAL PACK
62-270 BOX

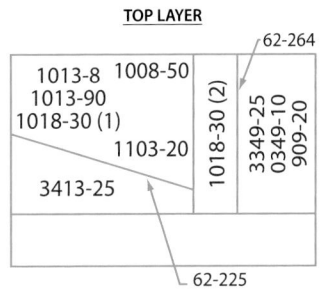

TOP LAYER

1013-8 1008-50	62-264			
1013-90				
1018-30 (1)	1018-30 (2)	3349-25	0349-10	909-20
	1103-20			
3413-25				
	62-225			

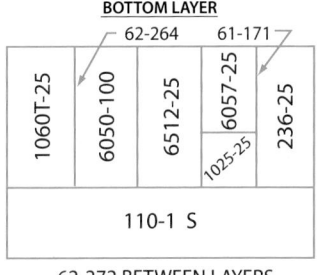

BOTTOM LAYER

	62-264		61-171	
1060T-25	6050-100	6512-25	6057-25	236-25
			1025-25	
	110-1 S			

62-272 BETWEEN LAYERS

Description: "O27" Promotional Outfit
Specification: "O27" Steam Type Freight Outfit
Customer: Kroger
Packaging: Display Outfit Packing (Units not Boxed)

Contents: 1060-25 Steam Type Locomotive; 1060T-25 Tender; 3309-25 Turbo Missile Firing Car (Less Missiles); 0349-10 Turbo Missile; 6501-25 Jet Motor Boat Car; 6067-25 Caboose; 1013-8 Curved Track (Bundle of 8 - 1013); 1018-10 Straight Track (Loose) (2); 1010-25 35-Watt Transformer; 1103-12 Envelope Packed; 310-2 Set of (5) Billboards; D62-50 Accessory Catalog; 1123-30 Instruction Sheet

Boxes & Packing: 62-200 Display Box; 61-101 Corr. Insert; 61-102 Corr. Insert (2); 61-103 Corr. Shipper for (6) (1-6); 61-104 Envelope Packed (1-6)

19125 (1962)	C6	C7	C8	Rarity
Complete Outfit	260	425	575	R6
Outfit Box no. 62-200	100	175	225	R6
Complete Outfit With no. 61-104	860	1,225	1,575	R10

Comments: Kroger grocery stores purchased this Retailer Promotional Type Ib outfit in 1962. The no. 19125 was the follow-up to Kroger's no. X-699 from 1961. This was one of the 29 unprofitable outfits from 1962. Lionel lost $0.67 per outfit sold.

The 19125 was headed by a no. 1060-25 Steam Type Locomotive. This low-end engine, which moved only forward, was a carryover from 1960.

Even though this outfit had only two cars and a caboose, the

cars were new operating models for 1962. The no. 3309-25 Turbo Missile Firing Car (Less Missiles) is common, but its no. 0349-10 Turbo Missiles are frequently missing or found broken. The car was the low-end version of the no. 3349-25 and was equipped with non-operating Archbar trucks and couplers. The no. 6501-25 Jet Motor Boat Car was equipped with operating AAR trucks and couplers. Its boat is also frequently missing from the car.

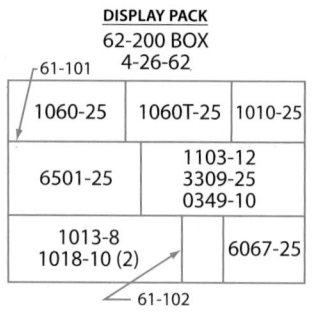

The nos. 1060T-25 Tender and 6067-25 Caboose in this outfit could come with either two Archbar trucks and couplers or one non-operating Archbar and one plain AAR truck and coupler.

With every six outfits shipped, Lionel packaged a no. 61-104 Envelope Packed. This envelope included a no. 61-107 Acetate Dust Cover in a no. 61-108 Envelope. The printing on the envelope states that the "clear plastic shield keeps merchandise dust free and safe from pilferage." This rare item adds a substantial premium to the outfit price.

The no. 62-200 White 4-6-4 Steamer and F3 Hinged Display with Red/Orange and Blue Graphics Type A outfit box was manufactured by United Container Co. and measured 21⅝ x 11½ x 3¼ inches.

Of the three outfits purchased by Kroger, the 19125 is the most difficult to find.

Original quantity numbers are not available, and rarity is based solely on actual observations.

Description: "O27" Promotional Outfit
Specification: "O27" Steam Type Freight Outfit
Customer: May Company
Original Amount: 3,600
Factory Order Date: 6/13/1962
Date Issued: 6-18-62
Packaging: Display Outfit Packing (Units not Boxed)

Contents: 1060-25 Steam Type Locomotive; 1060T-25 Tender; 6406-25 Single Automobile Car (Less Auto); 6406-30 Automobile; 6042-75 Gondola Car (Less 2 Cable Reels); 40-11 Cable Reels (2); 6067-25 Caboose; 1013-8 Curved Track (Bundle of 8 - 1013); 1018-10 Straight Track (Loose) (2); 1026-25 25-Watt Transformer; 1103-20 Envelope Packed; 310-2 Set of (5) Billboards; D62-50 Accessory Catalog; 1123-40 Instruction Sheet; 1123-10 Instruction Sheet

Boxes & Packing: 62-200 Display Outfit Box; 61-101 Corr. Insert; 61-102 Corr. Insert (2); 61-103 Corr. Shipper for (6) (1-6).

19126 (1962)	C6	C7	C8	Rarity
Complete Outfit	195	275	390	R5
Outfit Box no. 62-200	100	125	150	R5

Comments: In 1962, May Company purchased four Retailer Promotional outfits: nos. 19126, 19127, 19128 and 19129. The 19126, a Type Ib, was May's low-end starter outfit. It was led by a no. 1060-25 Steam Type Locomotive. A carryover item from 1960, this engine moved forward only.

All the rolling stock included in this outfit (equipped with non-operating Archbar trucks and couplers) is commonly available today. In fact, as with many low-end outfits, the no. 6406-30 Automobile is the most difficult item to obtain. Finding an original, postwar model with a gray bumper is becoming a challenge. There are many reproductions and modern-era reissues on the market.

The no. 62-200 White 4-6-4 Steamer and F3 Hinged Display with Red/Orange and Blue Graphics Type A outfit box was manufactured by United Container Co. and measured 21⅝ x 11½ x 3¼ inches.

Of the four May Company outfits from 1962, this one was produced in the largest quantities and is the easiest to find.

Description: "O27" Promotional Outfit
Specification: "O27" Steam Type Freight Outfit
Customer: May Company
Original Amount: 1,500
Factory Order Date: 6/14/1962
Date Issued: 6-18-62
Packaging: R.S.C. Outfit Packing (Units not Boxed), Except 1020 Crossing

Contents: 242-25 Steam Type Locomotive; 1060T-25 Tender; 6076-25 Hopper Car - Red; 6042-75 Gondola Car (Less 2 Cable Reels); 40-11 Cable Reels (2); 3357-25 Animated Hobo & Railroad Policeman Car; 3357-27 Box Packed; 6067-25 Caboose; 1013-70 Curved Track (Bundle of 12 - 1013); 1018-40 Straight Track (Bundle of 4 - 1018); 1010-25 35-Watt Transformer; 1020-1 90° Crossing; 1103-20 Envelope Packed; 310-2 Set of (5) Billboards; D62-50 Accessory Catalog; 1123-40 Instruction Sheet; 120-10 Instruction Sheet; 1802B Layout Instruction Sheet

Boxes & Packing: 62-243 Outfit Box; 61-191 Corr. Insert; 62-223 Corr. Insert; 62-225 Corr. Insert; 62-248 Corr. Insert; 62-251 Corr. Insert; 62-244 Shipper for (4) (1-4)

19127 (1962)	C6	C7	C8	Rarity
Complete Outfit	265	415	885	R6
Outfit Box no. 62-243	150	200	250	R6

Comments: In 1962, May Company purchased four Retailer Promotional outfits: nos. 19126, 19127, 19128 and 19129. The 19127, a Type Ib, was the follow-up to May's no. X-601 from 1961.

The 19127 was May's mid-level steam-powered offering. It was led by a no. 242-25 Steam Type Locomotive. This low-end

Scout steamer had a two-position reversing unit and a headlight, lacked smoke and used a rubber tire as a traction aid. The version with wide running boards was included in this outfit.

Except for the nos. 6042-75 Gondola Car (Less 2 Cable Reels) and 3357-25 Animated Hobo & Railroad Policeman Car, all the items in the 19127 were carryover from previous years. The 3357-25 provided plenty of excitement as the cop tried to catch the hobo. Since the car came unboxed (hence the "-25" suffix), the Factory Order also listed a no. 3357-27 Box Packed.

The rolling stock in this outfit came in a combination of operating AAR (3357-25) and non-operating Archbar (nos. 6042-75 and 6076-25) trucks and couplers.

Due to the transition from Archbar to AAR trucks and couplers that began in 1962, the nos. 1060T-25 Tender and 6067-25 Caboose could come with either two Archbar types or one non-operating Archbar and one plain AAR truck and coupler.

The figure-eight track layout was described on the no. 1802B Layout Instruction Sheet dated 6-59. The no. 62-243 Tan RSC with Black Graphics outfit box measured 12⅛ x 11½ x 6⅜ inches.

This outfit exceeded May's expectations, as the original quantity of 1,000 was increased to 1,500 on the Factory Order. Even so, it is fairly difficult to find in collectible condition.

CONVENTIONAL PACK
62-243 BOX

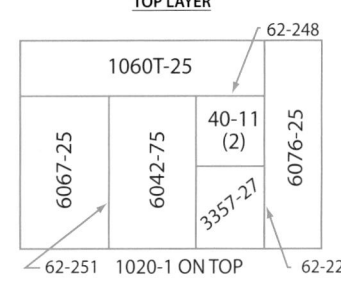

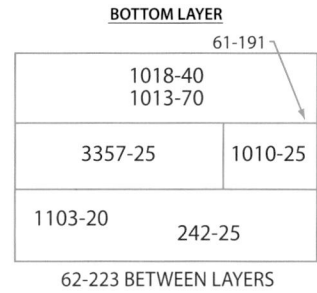

Description: "O27" Promotional Outfit
Specification: "O27" Steam Type Freight Outfit with Smoke
Customer/No.: May Company; 42 D 42 19128
Original Amount: 750
Factory Order Date: 6/13/1962
Date Issued: 6-18-62
Packaging: R.S.C. Outfit Packing (Units not Boxed), Except 110 Trestle Set

Contents: 236-25 Steam Type Locomotive with Smoke; 1060T-25 Tender; 3410-25 Oper. Helicopter Car (Less Helicopter); 3419-100 Operating Helicopter Complete; 3349-25 Turbo Missile Firing Car (Less Missiles); 0349-10 Turbo Missile (2); 6448-25 Exploding Target Range Car; 6057-25 Caboose; 1013-8 Curved Track (Bundle of 8 - 1013); 1013-90 Curved Track (Bundle of 9 - 1013); 1018-30 Straight Track (Bundle of 3 - 1018) (3); 1008-50 Uncoupling Unit; 1025-25 45-Watt Transformer; 110-1 Trestle Set; 1103-20 Envelope Packed; 909-20 Smoke Fluid; 310-2 Set of (5) Billboards; D62-50 Accessory Catalog; 1123-40 Instruction Sheet; 1802I Layout Instruction Sheet; 236-11 Instruction Sheet; 3410-5 Instruction Sheet; 3349-8 Instruction Sheet; 6448-17 Instruction Sheet; X602-10 Instruction Sheet

Boxes & Packing: 62-260 Outfit Box; 61-171 Corr. Insert; 62-248 Corr. Insert; 62-262 Corr. Insert; 62-263 Corr. Insert; 62-264 Corr. Insert; 62-265 Corr. Shipper for (4) (1-4)

19128 (1962)	C6	C7	C8	Rarity
Complete Outfit	415	700	975	R8
Outfit Box no. 62-260	200	325	400	R8

Comments: In 1962, May Company purchased four Retailer Promotional outfits: nos. 19126, 19127, 19128 and 19129. The 19128, a Type Ia, was the follow-up to May's no. X-602 from 1961, except that none of the items in the 19128 were individually boxed.

This outfit was May's high-end steam-powered offering for 1962. Headed by a no. 236-25 Steam Type Locomotive with Smoke, this space and military themed outfit included three operating cars.

Both the new-for-1962 no. 3349-25 Turbo Missile Firing Car (Less Missiles) and carryover no. 3410-25 Operating Helicopter Car carried delicate loads (nos. 0349-10 Turbo Missiles and 3419-100 Operating Helicopter Complete, respectively) that were frequently lost or broken.

The no. 19128 was May Company's high-end steam-powered offering for 1962. This outfit featured space and military rolling stock, including a no. 3349-25 Turbo Missile Firing Car (new for 1962).

In 1962, the Production Control File for the 3419-100 Operating Helicopter Complete changed from a gray Navy stamped two-piece helicopter body to an unmarked helicopter with a one-piece yellow helicopter body. Although this was Lionel's intended production, many 3419-100 Navy helicopters still appeared on 3410s in 1962.

A transition from Archbar to AAR trucks and couplers occurred in 1962. For the 19128, all the cars were equipped with operating AAR trucks and couplers. However, the no. 1060T-25 Tender could come with either two Archbar types or one non-operating Archbar and one plain AAR truck and coupler.

The no. 1802I Layout Instruction Sheet detailed the elevated pretzel track layout.

The no. 62-260 Tan RSC with Black Graphics outfit box was manufactured by St. Joe Kraft, St. Joe Paper Co. Container Division and measured 16¼ x 13 x 6⅜ inches.

As with the 19127, this outfit exceeded May's expectations, as the original quantity of 500 was increased to 750 on the Factory Order. Even with quantities below that of the 19127, the 19128 seems to appear more frequently.

CONVENTIONAL PACK
62-260 BOX

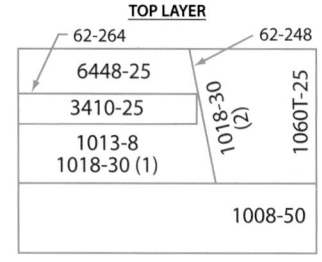

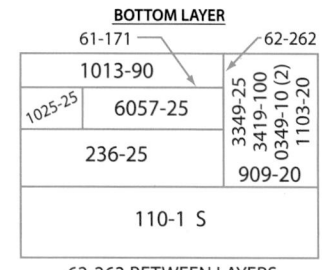

62-263 BETWEEN LAYERS

Description: "O27" Promotional Outfit
Specification: "O27" Diesel Freight Outfit With Horn
Customer: May Company
Original Amount: 500
Factory Order Date: 6/14/1962
Date Issued: 6-18-62
Packaging: R.S.C. Outfit Packing (Units Boxed)

Contents: 229P-1 "Minn. St. Louis" Alco Diesel Power Car W/ Horn; 229C-1 "B" Unit; 3519-1 Operating Satellite Launching Car; 3413-1 Mercury Capsule Launching Car; 6512-1 Cherry Picker Car; 3349-1 Turbo Missile Firing Car; 6017-1 Caboose; 1013-70 Curved Track (Bundle of 12 - 1013); 1018-30 Straight Track (Bundle of 3 - 1018); 1008-50 Uncoupling Unit; 1073-25 60-Watt Transformer; 147-25 Horn & Whistle Controller; 2333-140 Flashlight Cell; 81-32 24" R.C. Wire (3); 1020-1 90° Crossing; 310-2 Set of (5) Billboards; D62-50 Accessory Catalog; 1123-40 Instruction Sheet; 1646-10 Instruction Sheet; 1802B Layout Instruction Sheet

Boxes & Packing: 61-200 Outfit Box; 61-201 Shipper for (4) (1-4)

19129 (1962)	C6	C7	C8	Rarity
Complete Outfit	725	1,225	1,725	R9
Outfit Box no. 61-200	200	375	525	R9

Comments: In 1962, May Company purchased four Retailer Promotional outfits: nos. 19126, 19127, 19128 and 19129. The 19129, a Type Ia, was the follow-up to May's no. X-603 from 1961.

The 19129 was May's diesel-powered offering for 1962. It was one of only two promotional outfits powered by a no. 229P-1 Minn. St. Louis Alco Diesel Power Car W/Horn. The 229P-1 featured a two-position reversing unit, a headlight and one-axle Magne-Traction.

When boxed in its no. 229-8 Corr. Box, this diesel included the nos. CTC-1 Lockon, 229-7 Instruction Sheet and 927-90 Lubricating Oil Packed. Be aware that, as noted, the 229-1 was one of the few Alcos to include a horn. Until 1963, Lionel included a no. 601-13 "C" Battery with horn-equipped boxed Alcos.

The 19129 came with three new space and military cars that Lionel was featuring in 1962. The boxed nos. 3413-1 Mercury Capsule Launching Car and 6512-1 Cherry Picker Car were paired in at least six different outfits. They were designed to work together, with the 6512-1 pretending to load an astronaut into the waiting Mercury capsule. A no. 3349-1 Turbo Missile Firing Car was also included, but a target was not provided. Maybe Lionel intended for it to protect the launch from unforeseen enemies.

All the cars in this outfit were equipped with operating AAR trucks and couplers. They came packaged in Orange Picture Boxes.

The figure-eight track layout was described on the no. 1802B Layout Instruction Sheet dated 6-59. When a no. 147-25 Horn & Whistle Controller was included, Lionel provided a no. 2333-140 Flashlight Cell loose in the outfit box. This practice lasted until 1963.

The 19129 came in the common no. 61-200 Orange RSC with Black Graphics outfit box. It was manufactured by Mead Containers and measured 14½ x 12 x 7 inches.

As with both the 19127 and 19128, this outfit exceeded May's expectations, as the original quantity of 250 was increased to 500 on the Factory Order. Even though this was the smallest amount of any of the May offerings from 1962, examples of this outfit still appear from time to time.

CONVENTIONAL PACK
61-200 BOX

TOP LAYER

229C-1 F	
3413-1 F	1073-25
3349-1 F / 1008-50	81-32
147-25 2333-140 1018-30	

1020-1 ON TOP

BOTTOM LAYER

1013-70	6017-1 F
3519-1 S	
6512-1 S	
229P-1 F	

Description: "O27" Promotional Outfit
Specification: "O27" Steam Type Freight Outfit
Customer/Price: AMC; $10.98
Customer/No./Price: Simpsons-Sears; 79N 41880 L; $21.99
Original Amount: 1,500
Factory Order Date: 7/27/1962
Date Issued: 7-31-62
Packaging: R.S.C. Outfit Packing (Units not Boxed)

Contents: 1060-25 Steam Type Locomotive; 1060T-25 Tender; 6042-75 Gondola Car (Less 2 Cable Reels); 40-11 Cable Reels (2); 6076-25 Hopper Car; 6067-25 Caboose; 1013-8 Curved Track (Bundle of 8 - 1013); 1018-10 Straight Track (Loose) (2); 1026-25 25-Watt Transformer; 1103-20 Envelope Packed; 310-2 Set of (5) Billboards; D62-50 Accessory Catalog; 1123-40 Instruction Sheet; 1123-10 Instruction Sheet

Boxes & Packing: 61-170 Outfit Box; 61-171 Corr. Insert; 61-172 Corr. Insert; 61-173 Corr. Insert; 61-175 Shipper for (4) (1-4)

19130 (1962)	C6	C7	C8	Rarity
Complete Outfit	195	325	450	R6
Outfit Box no. 61-170	125	200	250	R6

Comments: Buying cooperatives, such as AMC (Associated Merchandising Corporation), were large customers of Lionel trains. In 1962, AMC purchased five promotional outfits (nos. 19130 through 19133 and 19152). Each outfit fulfilled a different

price point, with the 19130 being the entry-level steam-powered Retailer Promotional Type Ib offering.

Outfit 19130 has been linked to at least one end retailer. It appeared in the 1962 Simpsons-Sears Christmas Catalog as no. 79N 41880 L for $21.99 delivered. The 19130 Lionel Outfit Cost Worksheet lists Lionel's selling price as $8.00 and cost as $8.68. Thus a $0.68 (8.5 percent) loss was realized.

The 19130 was about as low-end as an outfit could get in 1962. The no. 1060-25 Steam Type Locomotive went forward only. The three pieces of rolling stock were entry-level cars equipped with non-operating Archbar trucks and couplers. Except for the no. 6042-75 Gondola Car (Less 2 Cable Reels), they were carryover from previous years.

Even the box used for this outfit was low-end and common. The no. 61-170 Tan RSC with Black Graphics outfit box was

CONVENTIONAL PACK
61-170 BOX

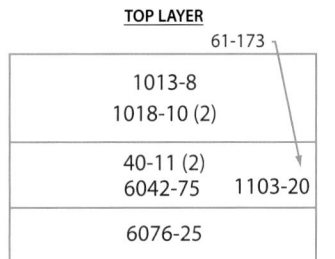

TOP LAYER — 61-173

1013-8 1018-10 (2) / 40-11 (2) 6042-75 / 1103-20 / 6076-25

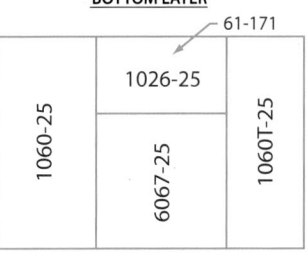

BOTTOM LAYER — 61-171

1026-25 / 1060-25 / 6067-25 / 1060T-25

61-172 BETWEEN LAYERS

The no. 19130 was AMC's entry-level steam offering for 1962 (one of five AMC outfits for the year). It appeared in the 1962 Simpsons-Sears Christmas Catalog as no. 79N 41880 L for $21.99 delivered.

manufactured by St. Joe Kraft, St. Joe Paper Co. Container Division and measured 11½ x 10¼ x 6¼ inches.

If a collector is patient, he or she can find an example of this outfit. Even an empty box is enough – the items are common, and so the outfit would be simple to complete.

The no. 19131 was AMC's mid-level steam offering for 1962. This outfit appeared in the 1962 Dayton's and Rike's catalogs as no. T35-3 for $19.88. The no. 3309-25 Turbo Missile Firing Car was new for 1962.

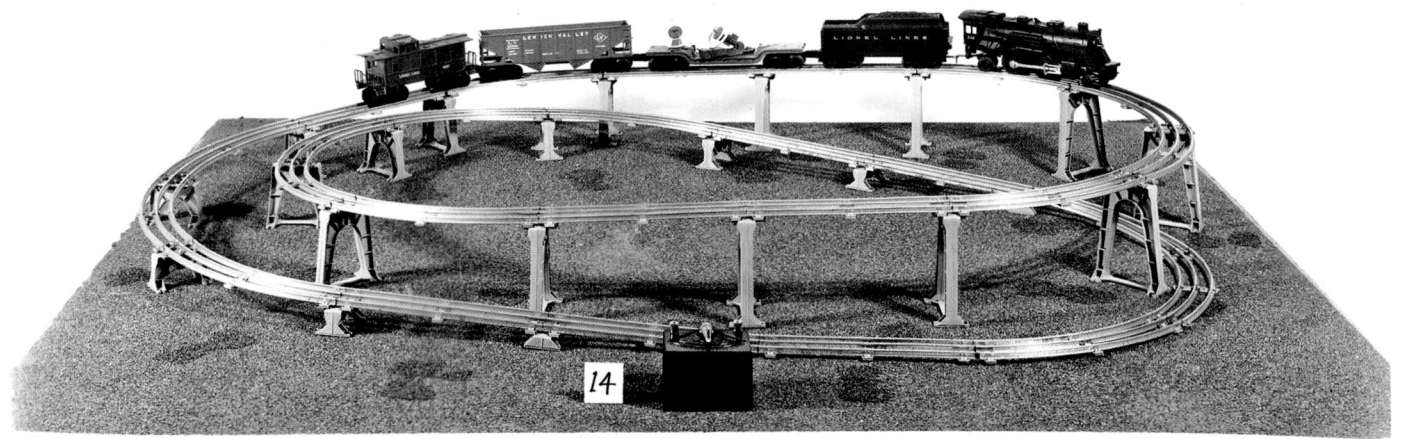

The no. 19131's glossy sales photograph was taken early in the selling process. It illustrates a few interesting facts about how Lionel configured and sold outfits during 1962. First, during the sales proposal process, outfits were numbered sequentially; outfit no. 19131 was originally no. 14. Second, the 19131 was intended to have higher-end components equipped with AAR trucks and couplers. For example the photo shows a no. 3349-25 Turbo Missile Firing Car rather than a no. 3309-25 Turbo Missile Firing Car. Third, some items may not have been available yet (a no. 246-25 Steam Type Locomotive is shown and not the no. 242-25 Steam Type Locomotive that was included). Finally, the 3349-25 was likely an early mock-up, as it does not match the final production model.

Description: "O27" Promotional Outfit
Specification: "O27" Steam Type Freight Outfit
Customer: AMC
Customer/No./Price: Dayton's; T35-3; $19.88
Customer/No./Price: Rike's; T35-3; $19.88
Original Amount: 4,000
Factory Order Date: 5/16/1962
Date Issued: 5-16-62
Packaging: R.S.C. Outfit Packing (Units not Boxed), Except 110 Trestle Set

Contents: 242-25 Steam Type Locomotive; 1060T-25 Tender; 3309-25 Turbo Missile Firing Car (Less Missiles); 0349-10 Turbo Missile (2); 6076-25 Hopper Car; 6067-25 Caboose; 1013-8 Curved Track (Bundle of 8 - 1013); 1013-90 Curved Track (Bundle of 9 - 1013); 1018-5 Straight Track (Bundle of 5 - 1018) (2); 110-1 Trestle Set; 1010-25 35-Watt Transformer; 1103-20 Envelope Packed; 310-2 Set of (5) Billboards; D62-50 Accessory Catalog; 3309-5 Instruction Sheet; 1123-40 Instruction Sheet; 120-10 Instruction Sheet; 1802I Layout Instruction Sheet

Boxes & Packing: 62-260 Outfit Box; 61-171 Corr. Insert; 62-261 Corr. Insert; 62-262 Corr. Insert; 62-263 Corr. Insert; 62-264 Corr. Insert; 62-265 Shipper for (4) (1-4)

19131 (1962)	C6	C7	C8	Rarity
Complete Outfit	185	300	425	R4
Outfit Box no. 62-260	75	100	125	R4

Comments: Buying cooperatives, such as AMC (Associated Merchandising Corporation), were large customers of Lionel trains. In 1962, AMC purchased five promotional outfits (nos. 19130 through 19133 and 19152). Each outfit fulfilled a different price point, with the no. 19131 being the mid-level steam-powered Retailer Promotional Type Ib offering.

Outfit 19131 has been linked to at least two end retailers. It appeared in both a Dayton's and a Rike's 1962 catalog as no. T35-3.

The listings went on to state, "Lots of fun and action, with plenty of 'Big Time' thrills! Special Price…$19.88".

The 19131 was a slight improvement over the 19130. It upgraded the motive power to a no. 242-25 Steam Type Locomotive. This low-end Scout steamer featured a two-position reversing unit and a headlight, lacked smoke and used a rubber tire as a traction aid. The version with wide running boards was included in this outfit.

As with the 19130, the 19131 included three pieces of rolling stock. However, one of them, the no. 3309-25 Turbo Missile Firing Car (Less Missiles), was an operating car that was new for 1962. It, like the other cars, came with non-operating Archbar trucks and couplers.

The big difference between the 19131 and the 19130 was that the former included the elevated pretzel track layout. The no. 1802I Layout Instruction Sheet detailed this layout.

The no. 62-260 Tan RSC with Black Graphics outfit box was manufactured by St. Joe Kraft, St. Joe Paper Co. Container Division and measured 16¼ x 13 x 6⅜ inches.

This outfit was made in large quantities, and many appear to have survived. Nonetheless, as with the majority of promotional outfits, finding one in C8 condition may take time.

CONVENTIONAL PACK
62-260 BOX

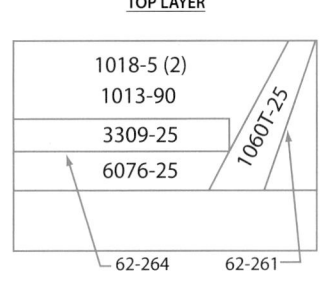

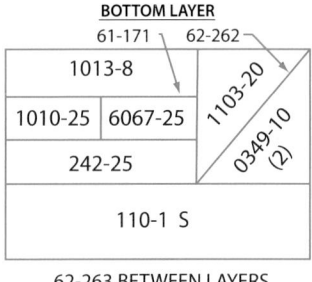

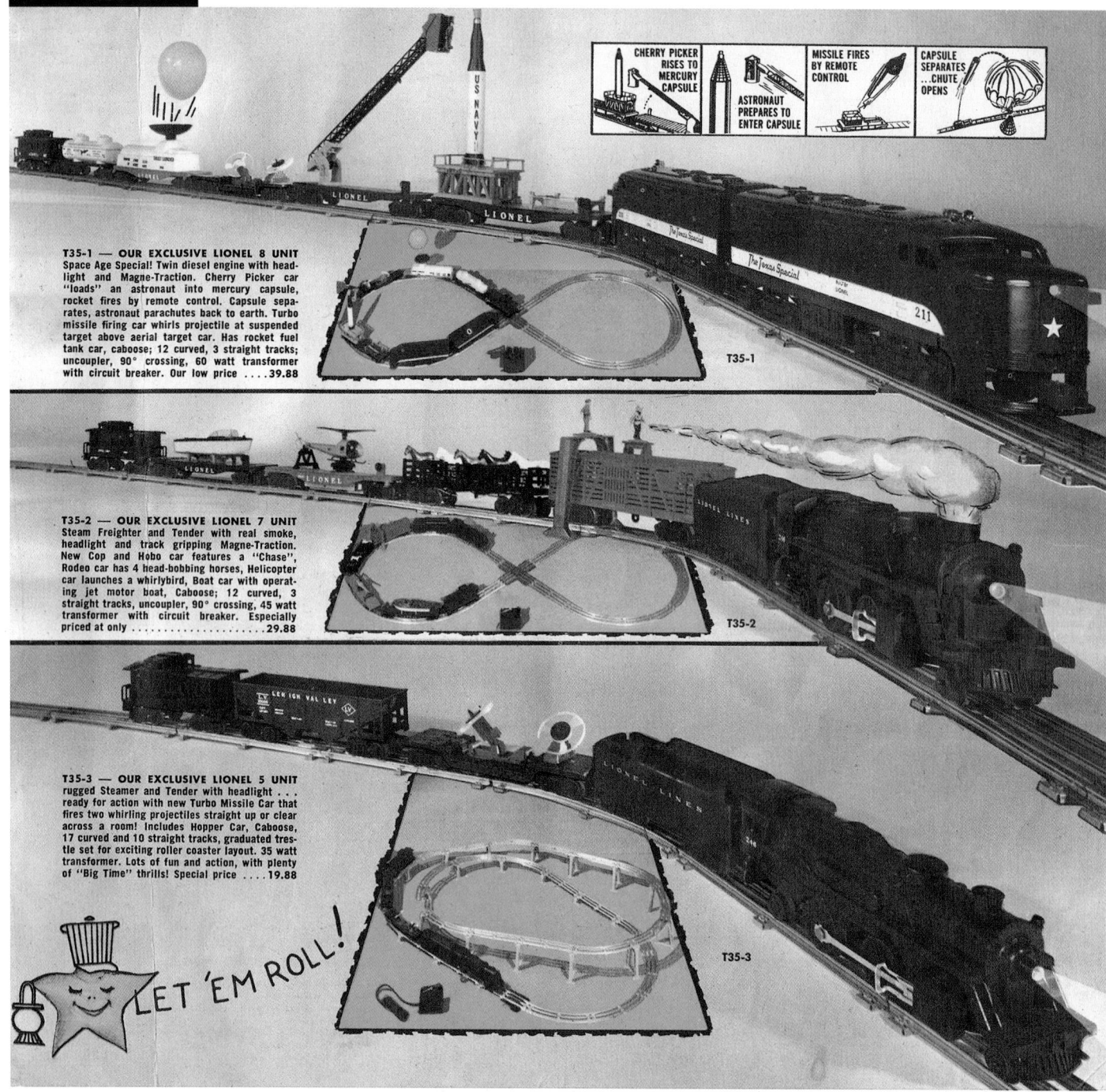

CHERRY PICKER RISES TO MERCURY CAPSULE • ASTRONAUT PREPARES TO ENTER CAPSULE • MISSILE FIRES BY REMOTE CONTROL • CAPSULE SEPARATES ...CHUTE OPENS

T35-1 — OUR EXCLUSIVE LIONEL 8 UNIT Space Age Special! Twin diesel engine with headlight and Magne-Traction. Cherry Picker car "loads" an astronaut into mercury capsule, rocket fires by remote control. Capsule separates, astronaut parachutes back to earth. Turbo missile firing car whirls projectile at suspended target car. Has rocket fuel tank car, caboose; 12 curved, 3 straight tracks; uncoupler, 90° crossing, 60 watt transformer with circuit breaker. Our low price 39.88

T35-2 — OUR EXCLUSIVE LIONEL 7 UNIT Steam Freighter and Tender with real smoke, headlight and track gripping Magne-Traction. New Cop and Hobo car features a "Chase", Rodeo car has 4 head-bobbing horses, Helicopter car launches a whirlybird, Boat car with operating jet motor boat, Caboose; 12 curved, 3 straight tracks, uncoupler, 90° crossing, 45 watt transformer with circuit breaker. Especially priced at only 29.88

T35-3 — OUR EXCLUSIVE LIONEL 5 UNIT rugged Steamer and Tender with headlight ... ready for action with new Turbo Missile Car that fires two whirling projectiles straight up or clear across a room! Includes Hopper Car, Caboose, 17 curved and 10 straight tracks, graduated trestle set for exciting roller coaster layout. 35 watt transformer. Lots of fun and action, with plenty of "Big Time" thrills! Special price 19.88

LET 'EM ROLL!

Lionel's nos. 19131, 19132 and 19133 (bottom to top) appeared in Aimcee Wholesale Corporation's (AMC) catalog from 1962. This catalog was private labeled for specific retailers that purchased from AMC. The photographs were likely taken early in the year. As such, engineering mock-ups of the nos. 3309-25 Turbo Missile Firing Car and 3357-25 Animated Hobo & Railroad Policeman Car were included. Note that a no. 246-25 Steam Locomotive was shown in place of the no. 242-25 Steam Type Locomotive eventually included in the 19131.

Description: "O27" Promotional Outfit
Specification: "O27" Steam Type Freight Outfit With Smoke
Customer/Price: AMC; $29.98
Customer/No./Price: Dayton's; T35-2; $29.88
Customer/No./Price: Rike's; T35-2; $29.88
Original Amount: 1,700
Factory Order Date: 6/13/1962
Date Issued: 6-18-62
Packaging: R.S.C. Outfit Packing (Units not Boxed), Except 1020 Crossing

Contents: 236-25 Steam Type Locomotive with Smoke; 1060T-25 Tender; 3357-25 Animated Hobo & Railroad Policeman Car; 3357-27 Box Packed; 1877-25 Horse Transport Car; 3410-25 Oper. Helicopter Car (Less Helicopter); 3419-100 Operating Helicopter Complete; 6501-25 Jet Motor Boat Car; 6501-2 Boat Assem.; 6057-25 Caboose; 1013-70 Curved Track (Bundle of 12 - 1013); 1018-30 Straight Track (Bundle of 3 - 1018); 1008-50 Uncoupling Unit; 1020-1 90° Crossing; 1025-25 45-Watt Transformer; 1103-20 Envelope Packed; 909-20 Smoke Fluid; 6501-17 Fuel Pellets Packed; 310-2 Set of (5) Billboards; D62-50 Accessory Catalog; 236-11 Instruction Sheet; 3410-5 Instruction

Sheet; 122-10 Instruction Sheet; 1123-40 Instruction Sheet; 1802B Layout Instruction Sheet

Boxes & Packing: 62-243 Outfit Box; 61-171 Corr. Insert; 62-223 Corr. Insert; 62-225 Corr. Insert; 62-248 Corr. Insert; 62-251 Corr. Insert; 62-257 Corr. Insert; 62-244 Shipper for (4) (1-4)

19132 (1962)	C6	C7	C8	Rarity
Complete Outfit	425	700	1,000	R6
Outfit Box no. 62-243	125	175	225	R6

Comments: Buying cooperatives, such as AMC (Associated Merchandising Corporation), were large customers of Lionel trains. In 1962, AMC purchased five promotional outfits (nos. 19130 through 19133 and 19152). Each outfit fulfilled a different price point, with the no. 19132 being the high-end steam-powered Retailer Promotional Type Ia offering.

Outfit 19132 has been linked to at least two end retailers. It appeared in both a Dayton's and a Rike's 1962 catalog as no. T35-2. The listings went on to state, "Especially priced at only … $29.88".

The no. 236-25 Steam Type Locomotive with Smoke that headed this outfit was one of Lionel's high-end Scout steamers. It also included a two-position reversing unit, a headlight and Magne-Traction.

Three operating cars were included in this outfit. The nos. 3357-25 Animated Hobo & Railroad Policeman Car and 6501-25 Jet Motor Boat Car were both new for 1962. However, the no. 3410-25 Oper. Helicopter Car (Less Helicopter) and all the other cars were carryover from previous year. Each of the cars in this outfit carried loads that were easily lost or separated from the train outfit.

In 1962, the Production Control File for the no. 3419-100

Operating Helicopter Complete changed from a gray Navy stamped two-piece helicopter body to an unmarked helicopter with a one-piece yellow helicopter body. Although this was Lionel's intended production, many 3419-100 Navy helicopters still appeared on 3410s in 1962.

The 19132 represented the final appearance of the no. 1877-25 Horse Transport Car. It was equipped with operating Archbar trucks and couplers. All the other cars in this outfit came with operating AAR trucks and couplers except for the no. 1060T-25 Tender. Because a transition from Archbar to AAR trucks and couplers began in 1962, it could come with either two Archbar types or one non-operating Archbar and one plain AAR truck and coupler.

The 19132, like AMC's 19133 and 19152, came with a figure-eight track layout. It was described on the no. 1802B Layout Instruction Sheet dated 6-59.

The no. 62-243 Tan RSC with Black Graphics outfit box measured 12⅛ x 11½ x 6⅜ inches.

Even though this outfit was manufactured in comparable numbers to AMC's 19130, it does not appear as often.

CONVENTIONAL PACK
62-243 BOX

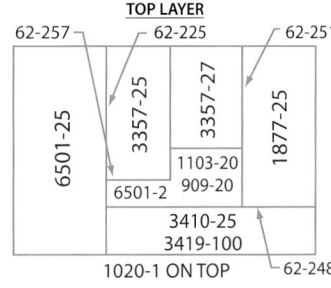
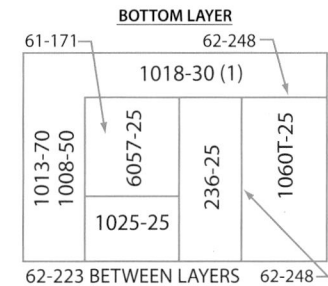

Description: "O27" Promotional Outfit
Specification: "O27" Diesel Freight Outfit
Customer: AMC
Customer/No./Price: Dayton's; T35-1; $39.88
Customer/No./Price: Rike's; T35-1; $39.88
Original Amount: 900
Factory Order Date: 5/31/1962
Date Issued: Rev 10-10-62
Packaging: R.S.C. Outfit Packing (Units not Boxed), Except 1020 Crossing

Contents: 211P-25 *"Texas Spec."* Alco Diesel Power Unit; 211T-25 *"Texas Spec."* Motorless Unit; 3349-25 Turbo Missile Firing Car (Less Missiles); 0349-10 Turbo Missile (2); 3470-25 Aerial Target Launching Car; 3470-20 Envelope Packed; 3470-4 Basket; 3413-25 Mercury Capsule Launching Car; 3413-18 Mercury Capsule & Parachute Assem.; 3413-27 Missile; 6512-25 Cherry Picker Car; 6463-25 Rocket Fuel Car; 6017-225 Caboose - "Santa Fe"; 1013-70 Curved Track (Bundle of 12 - 1013); 1018-30 Straight Track (Bundle of 3 - 1018); 1008-50 Uncoupling Unit; 1020-1 90° Crossing; 1073-25 60-Watt Transformer; 1103-20 Envelope Packed; 310-2 Set of (5) Billboards; D62-50 Accessory Catalog; 3349-8 Instruction Sheet; 3413-8 Instruction Sheet; 122-10 Instruction Sheet; 1123-40 Instruction Sheet; 211-6 Instruction Sheet; 1802B Layout Instruction Sheet

Boxes & Packing: 61-200 Outfit Box; 61-182 Insert; 61-192 Insert (2); 62-202 Insert; 62-224 Insert; 62-225 Insert; 62-245 Insert (2); 62-248 Insert; 61-201 Shipper for (4) (1-4); 61-210 Outfit Box; 61-192 Insert; 62-202 Insert; 62-224 Insert; 62-225 Insert; 62-245 Insert (2); 62-248 Insert; 61-211 Shipper for (4) (1-4)

19133 (1962)	C6	C7	C8	Rarity
Complete Outfit With Either Box	675	1,025	1,450	R7
Outfit Box nos. 61-200 Or 61-210	250	300	350	R7

Comments: Buying cooperatives, such as AMC (Associated Merchandising Corporation), were large customers of Lionel trains. In 1962, AMC purchased five promotional outfits (nos. 19130 through 19133 and 19152). Each outfit fulfilled a different price point, with the no. 19133 being the high-end diesel-powered Retailer Promotional Type Ia offering.

Outfit 19133 has been linked to at least two end retailers. It appeared in both a Dayton's and a Rike's 1962 catalog as no. T35-1. The listings went on to state, "Our low price …$39.88".

The 19133 Lionel Outfit Cost Worksheet lists Lionel's selling price as $26.40 and cost as $21.34. Thus a $5.06 profit, or 19.2 percent net margin, was realized. These figures made the 19133 Lionel's most profitable promotional outfit in 1962. Unfortunately for Lionel, it manufactured only 900 of them.

The no. 211P-25 *Texas Special* Alco Diesel Power Unit that led this outfit powered 12 different outfits in 1962. This locomotive included a two-position reversing unit, an open pilot, a headlight and two-axle Magne-Traction.

The 19133 offered plenty of action. It combined four new space and military cars that Lionel was featuring in 1962. The nos. 3413-25 Mercury Capsule Launching Car and 6512-25 Cherry Picker Car were paired in at least 18 different outfits. They were designed to work together, with the 6512-25 pretending to load an astronaut into the waiting Mercury capsule. Both came with operating AAR trucks and couplers.

The no. 3349-25 Turbo Missile Firing Car (Less Missiles) could be aimed at a no. 3470-25 Aerial Target Launching Car. They, like the other cars in this outfit, were equipped with operating AAR trucks and couplers.

The 19133, like AMC's 19132 and 19152, came with a figure-eight track layout. It was described on the no. 1802B Layout Instruction Sheet dated 6-59.

Lionel packed the 19133 in one of two different Orange RSC with Black Graphics outfit boxes. The no. 61-200 was manufactured by Mead Containers and measured 14½ x 12 x 7 inches. The no. 61-210 was manufactured by Mead Containers and measured 13⅞ x 13¼ x 6½ inches. Because the boxes are not substantially different, separate pricing and rarity ratings are not necessary.

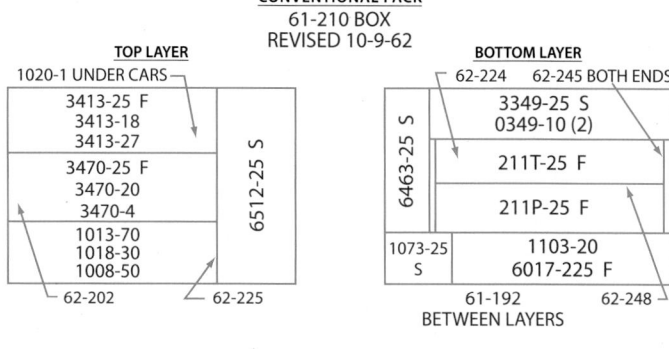

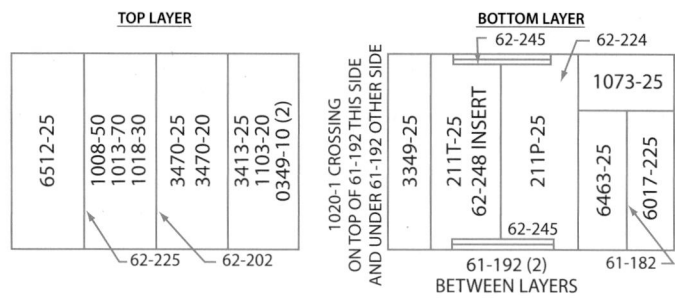

With only 900 examples of this outfit made, examples do not often appear on the market.

Description: "O27" Promotional Outfit
Specification: "O27" Steam Type Freight Outfit
Customer: Maurice Pollack
Original Amount: 200
Factory Order Date: 6/13/1962
Date Issued: 6-18-62
Packaging: R.S.C. Outfit Packing (Units not Boxed)

Contents: 242-25 Steam Type Locomotive; 1060T-25 Tender; 6050-50 Swift Savings Bank Car; 6406-25 Single Automobile Car (Less Auto); 6406-30 Automobile; 6076-25 Hopper Car - Red; 6067-25 Caboose; 1013-8 Curved Track (Bundle of 8 - 1013); 1018-10 Straight Track (Loose) (2); 1026-25 25-Watt Transformer; 1103-20 Envelope Packed; 310-2 Set of (5) Billboards; D62-50 Accessory Catalog; 1123-40 Instruction Sheet; 19106-10 Instruction Sheet

Boxes & Packing: 61-170 Outfit Box; 61-171 Corr. Insert; 61-172 Corr. Insert; 61-173 Corr. Insert; 62-248 Corr. Insert; 61-175 Shipper for (4) (1-4)

19134 (1962)	C6	C7	C8	Rarity
Complete Outfit	575	850	1,085	R10
Outfit Box no. 61-170	450	650	800	R10

Comments: This was the only Factory Order to list Canadian retailer Maurice Pollack. A Retailer Promotional Type Ib offering,

the no. 19134 was a low-end starter outfit.

The 19134 was led by a no. 242-25 Steam Type Locomotive. This low-end Scout engine appeared in more than 55 catalog and promotional outfits through 1967. A 2-4-2 steamer, it featured a two-position reversing unit and a headlight, lacked smoke and used a rubber tire as a traction aid. The version with wide running boards was included in this outfit.

The only interesting item in this outfit was the no. 6050-50 Swift Savings Bank Car. The "-50" version was equipped with non-operating Archbar trucks and couplers, as were the other cars. It is more difficult to find than the no. 6050-100 version with AAR trucks and couplers.

As with many of these low-end outfits, the no. 6406-30 Automobile is the most difficult item to obtain. Finding an original, postwar model with gray bumpers is becoming a challenge. There are many reproductions and modern-era reissues on the market.

The no. 61-170 Tan RSC with Black Graphics outfit box was manufactured by St. Joe Kraft, St. Joe Paper Co. Container

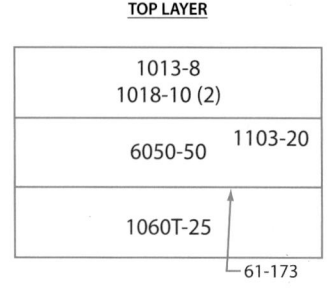

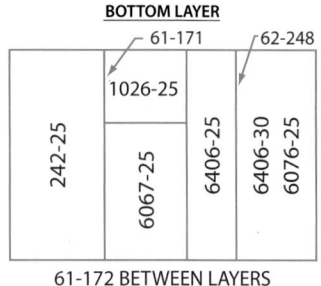

Canadian retailer Maurice Pollack purchased outfit no. 19134 in 1962. A low-end starter outfit, it included the version of the no. 6050-50 Swift Savings Bank Car equipped with Archbar trucks and couplers.

Division and measured 11½ x 10¼ x 6¼ inches.

For each 19134, it cost Maurice Pollack $9.60 and Lionel lost $0.73. Luckily, only 200 of these were made, so Lionel didn't lose much money. But with only 200 produced, the 19134 is a very difficult outfit to find. It's too bad that Lionel didn't save some of these outfits, because they are worth much more today.

Description: "O27" Promotional Outfit
Specification: "O27" Steam Type Freight Outfit
Customer/Price: John A. Brown Co.; $19.97
Customer: Mutual Buying
Customer/Price: The Fair; $21.88
Original Amount: 1,500
Factory Order Date: 5/31/1962
Date Issued: 6-8-62
Packaging: R.S.C. Outfit Packing (Units not Boxed), Except 1020 Crossing

Contents: 242-25 Steam Type Locomotive; 1060T-25 Tender; 3309-25 Turbo Missile Firing Car (Less Missiles); 0349-10 Turbo Missile (2); 6480-25 Exploding Target Car; 6463-25 Rocket Fuel Car; 6067-25 Caboose; 1013-70 Curved Track (Bundle of 12 - 1013); 1018-40 Straight Track (Bundle of 4 - 1018); 1025-25 45-Watt Transformer; 1020-1 90° Crossing; 1103-20 Envelope Packed; 310-2 Set of (5) Billboards; D62-50 Accessory Catalog; 1123-40 Instruction Sheet; 3309-10 Instruction Sheet; 6480-5 Instruction Sheet; 120-10 Instruction Sheet; 1802B Layout Instruction Sheet

Boxes & Packing: 61-180 Outfit Box; 61-171 Corr. Insert; 61-183 Corr. Insert; 62-248 Corr. Insert; 62-264 Corr. Insert; 61-185 Corr. Shipper for (4) (1-4)

19135
1962

19135 (1962)	C6	C7	C8	Rarity
Complete Outfit	250	415	625	R6
Outfit Box no. 61-180	100	175	225	R6

Comments: In 1962, Lionel sold two outfits to the Mutual Buying Syndicate cooperative: nos. 19135 and 19136. The 19135, a Retailer Promotional Type Ib outfit, was the follow-up to Mutual's no. X-622 from 1961. It was distributed among Mutual Buying's member stores.

Outfit 19135 was featured in an advertisement for The Fair that appeared in the December 13, 1962, edition of the *Chicago Daily News*. It was listed as "ours alone! Lionel Train set would be $42.34 if purchased separately. Now $21.88". Further research has revealed that "ours alone!" was a bit of an exaggeration because the 19135 has also been observed with a John A. Brown Co. price tag for $19.97.

This space and military themed outfit was headed by a no. 242-25 Steam Type Locomotive, which was a common addition to many 1962 outfits. In fact, this workhorse engine appeared in more than 55 catalog and promotional outfits through 1967. A low-end Scout steamer, it featured a two-position reversing unit and a headlight, lacked smoke and used a rubber tire as a traction aid. The version with wide running boards was included in this outfit.

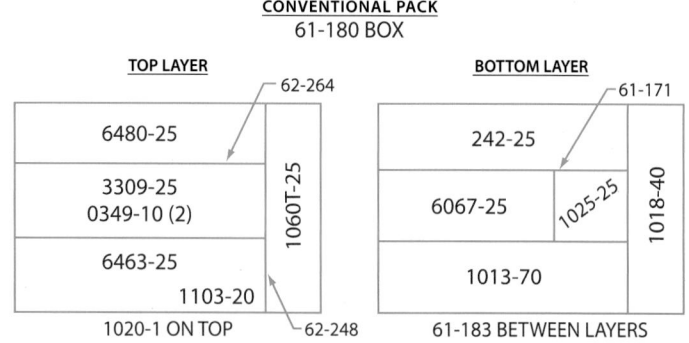

Outfit no. 19135 was Mutual Buying Syndicate's steam-powered purchase for 1962. It was sold to Mutual's member stores, including The Fair and John A. Brown Co.

The rolling stock in the 19135 included a no. 3309-25 Turbo Missile Firing Car (Less Missiles), which could be used to blow up the no. 6480-25 Exploding Target Car. The 6480-25 included "slotted" sides and a smooth roof door guide (without the nubs added later to help hold on the sides).

Except for the no. 6463-25 Rocket Fuel Car that came with operating AAR trucks and couplers, all the cars in the 19135 had non-operating Archbar types.

The appropriate quantity of track was included to make the figure-eight layout. That track plan was outlined on the no. 1802B Layout Instruction Sheet.

The commonly used no. 61-180 Tan RSC with Black Graphics outfit box was manufactured by United Container Co. and measured 12¾ x 10 x 6¾ inches.

CONVENTIONAL PACK
61-180 BOX

TOP LAYER		
6480-25		62-264
3309-25 0349-10 (2)	1060T-25	
6463-25 1103-20		
1020-1 ON TOP		62-248

BOTTOM LAYER		
242-25		61-171
6067-25	1025-25	1018-40
1013-70		
61-183 BETWEEN LAYERS		

Even with only 1,500 produced, this outfit is one of the more readily available promotional outfits on the market.

19136
1962

Description: "O27" Promotional Outfit
Specification: "O27" Diesel Freight Outfit
Customer: Mutual Buying
Original Amount: 750
Factory Order Date: 8/16/1962
Date Issued: Rev 10-18-62
Packaging: R.S.C. Outfit Packing (Units not Boxed), Except 110

Contents: 211P-25 *"Texas Special"* Alco Diesel Power Unit;

211T-25 Motorless Unit; 3413-25 Mercury Capsule Launching Car; 3413-18 Mercury Capsule & Parachute Assem.; 3413-27 Missile; 6512-25 Cherry Picker Car; 6476-25 Hopper Car; 6057-25 Caboose; 1013-8 Curved Track (Bundle of 8 - 1013); 1013-90 Curved Track (Bundle of 9 - 1013); 1018-30 Straight Track (Bundle of 3 - 1018) (3); 1008-50 Uncoupling Unit; 1025-25 45-Watt Transformer; 1103-20 Envelope Packed; 110-1 Trestle Set; 310-2 Set of (5) Billboards; D62-50 Accessory Catalog; 1123-40 Instruction Sheet; 211-6 Instruction Sheet; 3413-8 Instruction Sheet; 1802I Layout Instruction Sheet; 122-10 Instruction Sheet; 6512-19 Instruction Sheet

The no. 19136 was Mutual Buying Syndicate's diesel-powered purchase for 1962. This outfit has yet to be linked to a specific end retailer. With only 750 examples produced, it is more difficult to find than Mutual's other 1962 outfit, the no. 19135.

Boxes & Packing: 62-270 Outfit Box; 62-224 Insert; 62-225 Insert; 62-245 Insert (2); 62-248 Insert (3); 62-272 Insert; 62-271 Shipper for (3) (1-3)

19136 (1962)	C6	C7	C8	Rarity
Complete Outfit	525	875	1,250	R8
Outfit Box no. 62-270	200	300	400	R8

Comments: The no. 19136 was the last of two (along with the no. 19135) outfits sold to the Mutual Buying Syndicate cooperative in 1962. This Retailer Promotional Type Ia outfit was distributed among Mutual Buying's member stores, although it has yet to be tied to a specific end customer.

The 19136, the follow-up to Mutual's no. X-623 from 1961, was led by a no. 211P-25 *Texas Special* Alco Diesel Power Unit. This locomotive featured a two-position reversing unit, an open pilot, a headlight and two-axle Magne-Traction.

The 19136 featured the two new space and military cars that Lionel showcased on page 33 of its consumer catalog for 1962. The nos. 3413-25 Mercury Capsule Launching Car and 6512-25 Cherry Picker Car were paired in at least 18 different outfits. They were designed to work together, with the 6512-25 pretending to

load an astronaut into the waiting Mercury capsule. Like the other cars in this outfit, they came equipped with operating AAR trucks and couplers.

The 19136 included the elevated pretzel track layout. This track plan was described on the no. 1802I Layout Instruction Sheet.

The no. 62-270 Tan RSC with Black Graphics outfit box was manufactured by United Container Co. and measured 15½ x 14 x 6¼ inches.

Of the two Mutual outfits, this one is more difficult to find. Only 750 examples were made, half the number of the 19135.

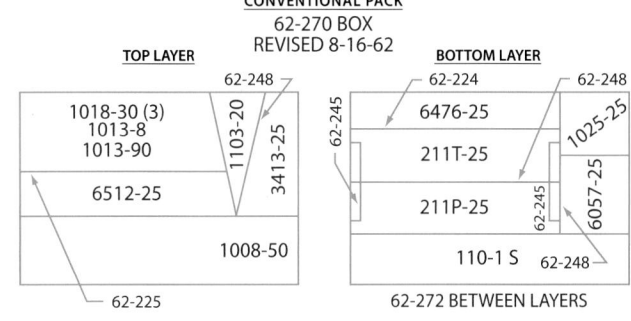

19137
1962

Description: "O27" Promotional Outfit
Specification: "O27" Steam Type Freight Outfit with Smoke
Customer: Mercantile Stores
Original Amount: 1,000
Factory Order Date: 6/29/1962
Date Issued: 9-21-62
Packaging: R.S.C. Outfit Packing (Units not Boxed), Except 110

Contents: 236-25 Steam Type Locomotive with Smoke; 1060T-25 Tender; 3410-25 Oper. Helicopter Car (Less Helicopter); 3419-100 Operating Helicopter Complete; 6501-25 Jet Motor Boat Car; 6501-2 Boat Assembly; 3349-25 Turbo Missile Firing Car

(Less Missiles); 0349-10 Turbo Missile (2); 6448-25 Exploding Target Range Car; 6057-25 Caboose; 1013-8 Curved Track (Bundle of 8 - 1013); 1013-90 Curved Track (Bundle of 9 - 1013); 1018-30 Straight Track (Bundle of 3 - 1018) (3); 1008-50 Uncoupling Unit; 1025-25 45-Watt Transformer; 110-1 Trestle Set; 1103-20 Envelope Packed; 909-20 Smoke Fluid; 6501-17 Fuel Pellets Packed; 310-2 Set of (5) Billboards; D62-50 Accessory Catalog; 122-10 Instruction Sheet; 1123-40 Instruction Sheet; 236-11 Instruction Sheet; 3410-5 Instruction Sheet; 6501-14 Instruction Sheet; 3349-8 Instruction Sheet; 6448-17 Instruction Sheet; 1802I Layout Instruction Sheet

Boxes & Packing: 62-270 Outfit Box; 61-171 Corr. Insert; 62-264 Corr. Insert (3); 62-272 Corr. Insert; 62-271 Shipper for (3) (1-3)

19137 (1962)	C6	C7	C8	Rarity
Complete Outfit	500	765	1,065	R7
Outfit Box no. 62-270	175	250	315	R7

Comments: Mercantile Stores Company, Inc. operated department stores in medium-sized cities during the 1960s. In 1962, it purchased two Retailer Promotional outfits: nos. 19137 and X-653.

The 19137, a Type Ia outfit, had a space and military theme. The no. 236-25 Steam Type Locomotive with Smoke that headed this outfit was one of Lionel's high-end Scout steamers. It also featured a two-position reversing unit, a headlight and Magne-Traction.

Among the rolling stock in this outfit was a no. 3349-25 Turbo Missile Firing Car (Less Missiles) (new for 1962). This car could be used to blow up a no. 6448-25 Exploding Target Range Car. Like all the other cars, it was equipped with operating AAR trucks and couplers.

The no. 3410-25 Oper. Helicopter Car (Less Helicopter) was a carryover from 1961. Interestingly, in 1962 Lionel gave the task of adding the no. 3419-100 Operating Helicopter Complete to the Outfit Packing Department (as noted on the no. 3410-25 Production Control File). These helicopters were frequently lost or broken.

In 1962, the Production Control File for the 3419-100 changed from a gray Navy stamped two-piece helicopter body to an unmarked helicopter with a one-piece yellow helicopter body. Although this was Lionel's intended production, many 3419-100 Navy helicopters still appeared on 3410s in 1962.

The 19137 included the elevated pretzel track layout that was described on the no. 1802I Layout Instruction Sheet.

The no. 62-270 Tan RSC with Black Graphics outfit box was manufactured by United Container Co. and measured 15½ x 14 x 6¼ inches.

The quantities produced of this outfit were higher than average, but examples appear only infrequently. As such, the 19137 achieves an R7 rarity.

CONVENTIONAL PACK
62-270 BOX

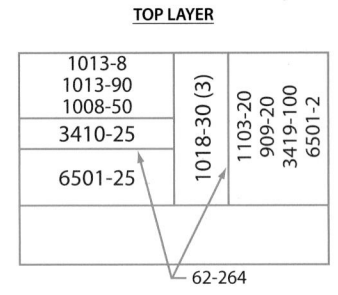

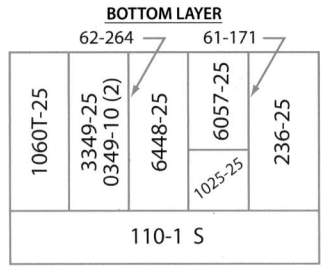

Description: "O27" Promotional Outfit
Specification: "O27" Diesel Freight Outfit
Customer: A. Cohen
Packaging: R.S.C. Outfit Packing (Units not Boxed), Except 1020

Contents: 231P-25 Alco Diesel Power Car - "Rock Island"; 3413-25 Mercury Capsule Launching Car; 3413-18 Capsule; 3413-27 Rocket; 6512-25 Cherry Picker Car; 6405-25 Single Van Flat Car (Less Van); 6405-150 Van; 3619-25 Reconnaissance Copter Car; 0319-100 Helicopter; 6057-25 Caboose; 1013-70 Curved Track (Bundle of 12 - 1013); 1018-30 Straight Track (Bundle of 3 - 1018); 1008-50 Uncoupling Unit; 1025-25 45-Watt Transformer; 1020-1 90° Crossing; 1103-20 Envelope Packed; 310-2 Set of (5) Billboards; D62-50 Accessory Catalog; 122-10 Instruction Sheet; 1802B Layout Instruction Sheet

Boxes & Packing: 62-243 Outfit Box; 61-173 Insert; 62-223 Insert; 62-224 Insert; 62-245 Insert (2); 62-248 Insert; 62-244 Shipper for (4) (1-4)

19138 (1962)	C6	C7	C8	Rarity
Complete Outfit	575	875	1,210	R7
Outfit Box no. 62-243	200	275	350	R7

Comments: This was one of two outfits with a Factory Order listing A. Cohen, a customer whose identity, including location and type of business, remains unknown. As a result, we cannot determine whether the no. 19138 is a Retailer Promotional Type Ia or a Manufacturer Promotional Type IIIa outfit.

The 19138 was headed by a no. 231P-25 Rock Island Alco Diesel Power Car. This locomotive featured two-axle Magne-Traction, a headlight and a two-position reversing unit.

This was one of many promotional outfits to feature the two new space and military cars that Lionel highlighted on page 33 of its consumer catalog for 1962. The nos. 3413-25 Mercury Capsule Launching Car and 6512-25 Cherry Picker Car were paired in at least 18 different outfits. They were designed to work together, with the 6512-25 pretending to load an astronaut into the waiting Mercury capsule.

CONVENTIONAL PACK
62-243 BOX

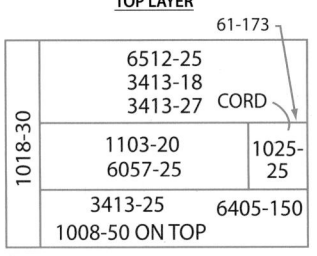

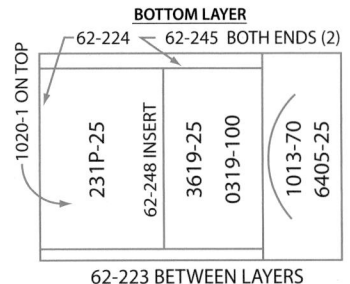

Also of note in this outfit was the new no. 3619-25 Reconnaissance Copter Car, which included a fragile and easily lost no. 0319-100 Helicopter. As part of the manufacturing process, the roof of the 3619-25 was taped shut with a ½-inch piece of Scotch tape. Even examples in C8 condition still have a mark where the tape was applied. This car, like the others in the 19138, was equipped with operating AAR trucks and couplers.

The 19138 included the figure-eight track layout that was detailed on the no. 1802B Layout Instruction Sheet.

This entire outfit came packed in a no. 62-243 Tan RSC with Black Graphics outfit box that measured 12⅛ x 11½ x 6⅜ inches.

The R7 rarity is due to the infrequent appearance of a 19138 in the marketplace.

Description: "O27" Promotional Outfit
Specification: "O27" Steam Type Freight Outfit
Customer/Price: Goldblatt's; $22.00
Original Amount: 700
Factory Order Date: 6/14/1962
Date Issued: 6-18-62
Packaging: R.S.C. Outfit Packing (Units not Boxed), Except 1020 Crossing

Contents: 1060-25 Steam Type Locomotive; 1060T-25 Tender; 3309-25 Turbo Missile Firing Car (Less Missiles); 0349-10 Turbo Missile (2); 3470-25 Aerial Target Launching Car; 3470-20 Envelope Packed; 3470-4 Basket; 3357-25 Animated Hobo & Railroad Policeman Car; 3357-27 Box Packed; 6067-25 Caboose; 1013-8 Curved Track (Bundle of 8 - 1013); 1013-5 Curved Track (Loose) (4); 1018-40 Straight Track (Bundle of 4 - 1018); 1026-25 25-Watt Transformer; 1020-1 90° Crossing; 1103-20 Envelope Packed; 310-2 Set of (5) Billboards; D62-50 Accessory Catalog; 1123-40 Instruction Sheet; 3309-10 Instruction Sheet; 1123-10 Instruction Sheet; 1802B Layout Instruction Sheet

Boxes & Packing: 62-243 Outfit Box; 61-171 Insert; 62-223 Insert; 62-225 Insert (3); 62-248 Insert; 62-251 Insert; 62-244 Shipper for (4) (1-4)

19139 (1962)	C6	C7	C8	Rarity
Complete Outfit	450	665	900	R8
Outfit Box no. 62-243	275	350	415	R8

Comments: Chicago-based retailer Goldblatt's ran department stores that offered a variety of goods at discount prices. In 1962, it purchased three Retailer Promotional outfits: nos. 19139, 19140 and 19141. The 19139 is a Type Ib. It has been observed in a Goldblatt's advertisement printed in the November 4, 1962, edition of the *Chicago Tribune*. The advertisement stated, "Get Goldblatt's Low Price! Lionel Electric 6-Unit Steam Freight Train, $22 complete. Price Would be $49.50 if Purchase Separately".

This space and military outfit was Goldblatt's entry-level steam offering. It was led by a no. 1060-25 Steam Type Locomotive, a low-end engine that went only forward, and a no. 1060T-25 Tender.

19139
1962

The rolling stock in the 19139 was not bad for an entry-level offering and included three new operating cars. To begin, the no. 3309-25 Turbo Missile Firing Car (Less Missiles) was a low-end version of a no. 3349-25. The only difference was that the 3309-25 was equipped with non-operating Archbar trucks and couplers and the 3349 had AAR trucks and couplers. Both cars were designed to bring down the balloon on a no. 3470-25 Aerial Target Launching Car.

The no. 3357-25 Animated Hobo & Railroad Policeman Car was also a nice addition. It provided plenty of excitement as the cop tried to catch the hobo. Since the car came unboxed (hence the "-25" suffix), the Factory Order also listed a no. 3357-27 Box Packed.

For the 19139, all but two of its cars came equipped with operating AAR trucks and couplers. The 1060T-25 and 3309-25 had non-operating Archbar trucks and couplers.

As with many 1962 promotional outfits, the appropriate quantity of track was included to make the figure-eight layout. That track plan was outlined on the no. 1802B Layout Instruction Sheet.

This entire outfit came packed in a no. 62-243 Tan RSC with Black Graphics outfit box that measured 12⅛ x 11½ x 6⅜ inches.

Of the three 1962 Goldblatt's offerings, this outfit was produced in the largest quantity. Even so, it is very difficult to find, hence its R8 rarity.

CONVENTIONAL PACK
62-243 BOX

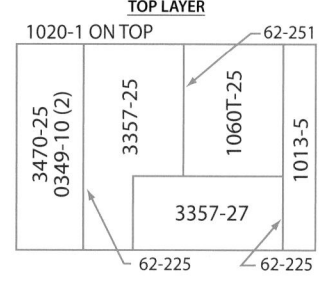

TOP LAYER
1020-1 ON TOP — 62-251
3470-25 0349-10 (2)
3357-25
1060T-25
1013-5
3357-27
62-225 — 62-225

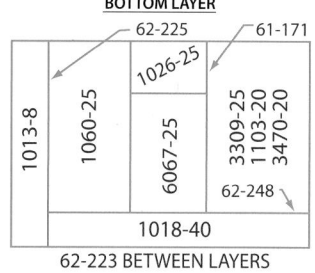

BOTTOM LAYER
62-225 — 61-171
1026-25
1013-8
1060-25
6067-25
3309-25 1103-20 3470-20
62-248
1018-40
62-223 BETWEEN LAYERS

Description: "O27" Promotional Outfit
Specification: "O27" Steam Type Freight Outfit
Customer: Goldblatt's
Original Amount: 400
Factory Order Date: 6/14/1962
Date Issued: Rev. 9-17-62
Packaging: R.S.C. Outfit Packing (Units not Boxed), Except 1020 Crossing

Contents: 246-25 Steam Type Locomotive; 1060T-25 Tender; 3357-25 Animated Hobo & Railroad Policeman Car; 3357-27 Box Packed; 6473-25 Rodeo Car; 3362-25 Helium Tank Unloading Car; 6501-25 Jet Motor Boat Car; 6501-2 Boat Assem.; 6057-25 Caboose; 1013-70 Curved Track (Bundle of 12 - 1013); 1018-30 Straight Track (Bundle of 3 - 1018); 6029-25 Uncoupling Track Section; 1073-25 60-Watt Transformer; 1020-1 90° Crossing; 90-40 Envelope Packed; 6501-17 Fuel Pellets Packed; 310-2 Set of (5) Billboards; D62-50 Accessory Catalog; 1123-40 Instruction Sheet; 3362-15 Instruction Sheet; 246-7 Instruction Sheet; 9670-10 Instruction Sheet; 1802B Layout Instruction Sheet

Boxes & Packing: 62-243 Outfit Box; 61-171 Insert; 62-223 Insert; 62-225 Insert (2); 62-251 Insert; 62-264 Insert; 62-244 Shipper for (4) (1-4)

Alternate For Outfit Contents:
Note: Substitute 242-25 if 246-25 not available.

19140 (1962)	C6	C7	C8	Rarity
Complete Outfit	575	875	1,175	R9
Outfit Box no. 62-243	325	450	550	R9

Comments: Chicago-based retailer Goldblatt's ran department stores that offered a variety of goods at discount prices. In 1962, it purchased three Retailer Promotional outfits: nos. 19139, 19140 and 19141. The 19140 is a Type Ia that was this firm's high-end steam-powered purchase in 1962.

This outfit and the no. X-604 (also from 1962) were the last ones to include a no. 246-25 Steam Type Locomotive. The no. 242-

25 Steam Type Locomotive replaced the 246-25 in the product line. In fact, the substitution for this outfit states to use the 242 if the 246 is not available. Since the locomotives were similar, the presence of one over the other does not affect the outfit's price.

The 19140 featured four new operating cars for 1962. The nos. 3357-25 Animated Hobo & Railroad Policeman Car and 6473-25 Rodeo Car were paired in at least 11 outfits. The 3357-25 provided plenty of excitement as the cop tried to catch the hobo. Since the car came unboxed (hence the "-25" suffix), the Factory Order also listed a no. 3357-27 Box Packed.

The inclusion of a no. 3362-25 Helium Tank Car required a no. 6029-25 Uncoupling Track Section. This further necessitated a no. 90-40 Envelope Packed to supply a no. 90 Controller and wires for the uncoupling track section.

A transition from Archbar to AAR trucks and couplers began in 1962. For the 19140, all the cars were equipped with operating AAR trucks and couplers. However, the no. 1060T-25 Tender could come with either two Archbar types or one non-operating Archbar and one plain AAR truck and coupler.

As with many 1962 promotional outfits, the appropriate quantity of track was included to make the figure-eight layout. That track plan was outlined on the no. 1802B Layout Instruction Sheet.

This entire outfit came packed in a no. 62-243 Tan RSC with Black Graphics outfit box that measured 12⅛ x 11½ x 6⅜ inches.

Of the three Goldblatt's outfits from 1962, the 19140's production numbers put it in the middle of the pack. As with the 19139 and 19141, it is very difficult to find.

CONVENTIONAL PACK
62-243 BOX

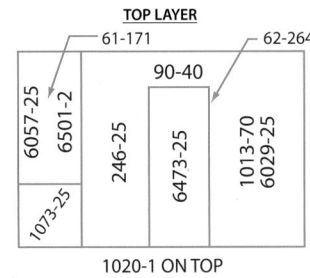
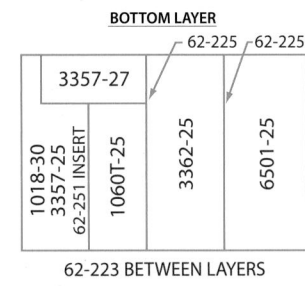

Description: "O27" Promotional Outfit
Specification: "O27" Diesel Freight Outfit
Customer: Goldblatt's
Original Amount: 300
Factory Order Date: 6/13/1962
Date Issued: 6-18-62
Packaging: R.S.C. Outfit Packing (Units not Boxed), Except 1020 Crossing

Contents: 211P-25 *"Texas Special"* Alco Diesel Power Unit; 211T-25 Motorless Unit; 3619-25 Reconnaissance Copter Car; 3413-25 Mercury Capsule Launching Car; 3413-18 Mercury Capsule & Parachute Assem.; 3413-27 Missile; 6512-25 Cherry Picker Car; 6650-25 Missile Launching Flat Car; 6650-80 Missile Complete (Or 6650-84); 3470-25 Aerial Target Launching Car; 3470-20 Envelope Packed; 3470-4 Basket; 6057-25 Caboose; 1013-70 Curved Track (Bundle of 12 - 1013); 1018-7 Straight Track - (Bundle of 7 - 1018); 1008-50 Uncoupling Unit; 1073-25 60-Watt Transformer; 1020-1 90° Crossing; 1103-20 Envelope Packed; 310-2 Set of (5) Billboards; D62-50 Accessory Catalog; 211-6 Instruction Sheet; 1123-40 Instruction Sheet; 3619-8 Instruction Sheet; 3413-8 Instruction Sheet; 6650-92 Instruction Sheet; X602-10 Instruction Sheet; 19141-10 Layout Instruction Sheet

Boxes & Packing: 62-270 Outfit Box; 61-173 Insert; 61-184 Insert; 62-224 Insert; 62-245 Insert (2); 62-248 Insert; 62-264 Insert (2); 62-272 Insert; 62-271 Shipper for (3) (1-3)

19141 (1962)	C6	C7	C8	Rarity
Complete Outfit	850	1,325	1,800	R9
Outfit Box no. 62-270	350	500	600	R9

Comments: Chicago-based retailer Goldblatt's ran department stores that offered a variety of goods at discount prices. In 1962, it purchased three Retailer Promotional outfits: nos. 19139, 19140 and 19141. The 19141, a Type Ia, was the only one of these that included a diesel locomotive.

The 19141 Lionel Outfit Cost Worksheet lists Lionel's selling price as $28.20 and cost as $23.52. Thus, a $4.68 profit, or 16.6 percent net margin, was realized, making this Lionel's third most profitable promotional outfit in 1962. Unfortunately for Lionel, Goldblatt's ordered only 300 of these outfits.

This exciting space and military outfit consisted entirely of operating cars. The nos. 3413-25 Mercury Capsule Launching Car and 6512-25 Cherry Picker Car (both new for 1962) were paired in at least 18 different outfits. They were designed to work together, with the 6512-25 pretending to load an astronaut into the waiting Mercury capsule. Two other cars worked in tandem. The no. 6650-25 Missile Launching Flat Car was intended to bring down the balloon on a no. 3470-25 Aerial Target Launching Car. Last came a no. 3619-25 Reconnaissance Copter Car, which included a fragile and easily lost no. 0319-100 Helicopter.

All the cars were equipped with operating AAR trucks and couplers. And, except for the 6650-25 and no. 6057-25 Caboose, they were new for 1962.

The no. 19141-10 Layout Instruction Sheet was unique to

this outfit. It was an elongated figure-eight layout similar to the no. 2165 Layout Instruction Sheet found in outfit no. X-573NA from 1960.

The 19141 came in a no. 62-270 Tan RSC with Black Graphics outfit box. It was manufactured by United Container Co. and measured 15½ x 14 x 6¼ inches.

This outfit exceeded the customer's projections. The Factory Order stated an original quantity of 200, which later was increased to 300.

This quantity was the lowest of the three outfits Lionel made for Goldblatt's in 1962. All three are difficult to find, but this is the toughest, hence its R9 rarity.

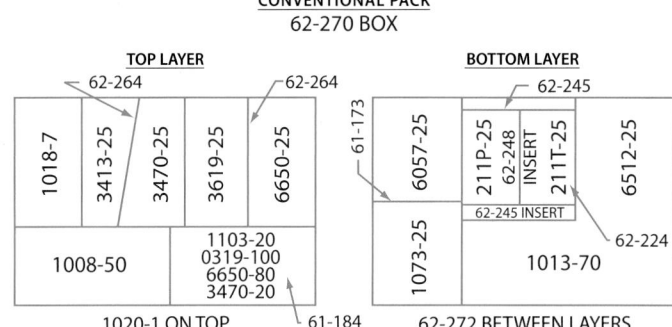

CONVENTIONAL PACK
62-270 BOX

Description: "O27" Promotional Outfit
Specification: "O27" Steam Type Freight Outfit
Customer/No./Price: Simpsons-Sears; 49 N 14 070; $18.98
Customer/Price: Stokely-Van Camp; $11.95 + 1 Label
Original Amount: 25,000
Factory Order Date: 5/16/1962
Date Issued: Revised 9-13-62
Packaging: R.S.C. Outfit Packing Mailer (Units not Boxed)

Contents: 242-25 Steam Type Locomotive; 1060T-25 Tender; 3309-25 Turbo Missile Firing Car (Less Missiles); 0349-10 Turbo Missile (2); 6406-25 Single Automobile Car (Less Auto); 6406-30 Automobile; 6050-150 Stokely Van Camp Savings Bank Car; 6067-25 Caboose; 1013-8 Curved Track (Bundle of 8 - 1013); 1018-10 Straight Track (Loose) (2); 1010-25 35-Watt Transformer; 1103-20 Envelope Packed; 310-62 Set of (3) Billboard Signs; D62-50 Accessory Catalog; 1123-40 Instruction Sheet; 3309-5 Instruction Sheet; 19142-10 Instruction Sheet

Boxes & Packing: 62-246 Outfit Box; 61-172 Insert; 62-254 Insert; 62-255 Insert; 62-256 Insert; 62-257 Insert; 62-258 Insert; 62-247 Shipper for (4) (1-4)

versions: nos. 19142 (Tan RSC Mailer version), 19142-50 (display version) and 19142-100 (regular Tan RSC version). For sending in one Van Camp's Pork and Beans label and $11.95, a consumer received a "$25.00 Premium Value Electric Train".

(See the entry for Stokely-Van Camp in the section on Lionel's Distribution and Customers. Also see the section on The History of Lionel's Promotional Outfits for more information about this outfit.)

The 19142, a Type IIIb, introduced the no. 6050-150 Stokely Van Camp Savings Bank Car as well as the no. 310-62 Set of (3) Billboards. Both of these items advertised Van Camp's Pork and Beans. They went on to become regular production offerings added to many outfits over the next few years.

The remaining cars in the 19142 were common components of outfits available in 1962. They were equipped with non-operating Archbar trucks and couplers. Keep in mind, however, that a transition from Archbar to AAR trucks and couplers began in 1962. As a result, the nos. 1060T-25 Tender and 6067-25 Caboose could come with either two Archbar types or one non-operating Archbar and one plain AAR truck and coupler.

Of note was the no. 6406-25 Single Automobile Car (Less Auto) and its no. 6406-30 Automobile. According to Lionel Production Control Files, the norm for the flat car was Tuscan Red with a yellow automobile with gray bumpers in 1962. In 1963, green automobiles with gray bumpers and brown autos with gray bumpers appeared, as did brown versions of the no. 6067-25 Caboose. All of these variations have been observed with this outfit. A value and rarity premium is added for brown or green automobiles with gray bumpers.

The no. 19142-10 Instruction Sheet was unique to this outfit and included a warranty certificate that was to be filled out and sent to Lionel. This was the precursor to the no. 1-63 Warranty

19142 (1962)	C6	C7	C8	Rarity
Complete Outfit With Yellow Automobile	200	325	500	R2
Complete Outfit With Brown Or Green Automobile	350	525	750	R3
Outfit Box no. 62-246	50	100	150	R2

Comments: On the heels of its success with Quaker in 1961, Lionel worked with Stokely-Van Camp on Manufacturer Promotional outfit no. 19142 in 1962. This outfit came in three

Stokely-Van Camp Manufacturer Promotional Type IIIb outfit no. 19142 is shown with an original Van Camp's Pork and Beans label showing the Lionel train offer. Note the Tuscan Red no. 6406-25 Single Automobile Car and the yellow no. 6406-30 Automobile with gray bumpers. The no. 62-246 Tan RSC Mailer does not have any Lionel markings on its top. This allowed room for a mailing label.

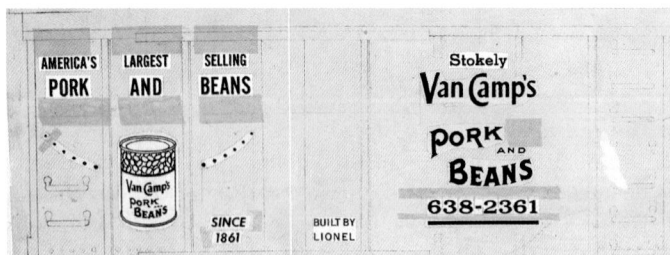

Lionel used "19142" with and without suffixes on four different RSC packed outfits. Left to right: nos. 19142 (1962 Van Camp Tan RSC Mailer), 19142-100 (1962 Van Camp regular Tan RSC), 19142-500 (1963 D. O. Klein Tan RSC Mailer) and 19142-502 (1963 Richie Premium Tan RSC).

The original mock-up artwork for the no. 6050-150 Stokely-Van Camp Savings Bank Car was likely used to help sell this outfit and the car. Over the next few years, Lionel included this car in at least 25 promotional outfits.

The 19142 also introduced the no. 62-246 Tan RSC Mailer with Black Graphics outfit box. It was manufactured by Mead Containers and measured 11½ x 10¼ x 6¼ inches. These boxes were made of a thicker corrugated material (rated at 90 pounds rather than the normal 65 pounds gross weight) that allowed each outfit to be shipped in its outfit box. The manufacturer omitted any Lionel printing on the box top to leave room for a mailing label.

The outfits were fulfilled by Custom Service Corporation in Spring Park, Minnesota. Lionel shipped the outfits to Custom Service, which fulfilled the orders from the Van Camp customers.

Unfortunately for Lionel, there weren't many orders to be fulfilled. Internal records show that only 2,886 of the 50,450 outfits called for on the Factory Orders were sold as of July 1963. Also, an outfit matching the contents of the 19142 was clearly shown on page 68 of the 1964 Simpsons-Sears Christmas Catalog as no. 49 N 14 070 for $18.98.

Card that appeared in 1963. Most examples of the Instruction Sheet observed were printed in green ink on white paper.

Van Camp's
SINCE 1861
PACKERS OF AMERICA'S LARGEST SELLING PORK & BEANS
A DIVISION OF STOKELY-VAN CAMP, INC.
INDIANAPOLIS 6, INDIANA

September 26, 1962

Mr. D. S. Cameron
The Lionel Corporation
1423 Merchandise Mart
Chicago, Illinois

Dear Doug:

Enclosed are copies of the little brochure we are sending to our
sales force and brokerage organizations for presentation to their
customers of the Lionel Train dealer incentive.

Approximately 7500 of these will be distributed into the grocery
trade, so that I am sure that everyone of our major customers
will be covered regarding the tie-in we are enjoying with the
Lionel Corporation.

I have been advised by our West Coast office that the State of
Washington is getting more stringent in their regulations per-
taining to consumer premium offers, much the same as California.
Although the agreement between our two companies states that you
will take care of the California tax requirements, I would appreciate
a letter indicating the same for the State of Washington.

Would appreciate you clearing this with your Legal Department and
advising me, so that I in turn can advise our West Coast office.

Sincerely,

STOKELY-VAN CAMP, INC.

Bob

R. E. Donnelly

RED:mp

JAN 29 1963

VAN CAMP'S Take-it-easy FOODS

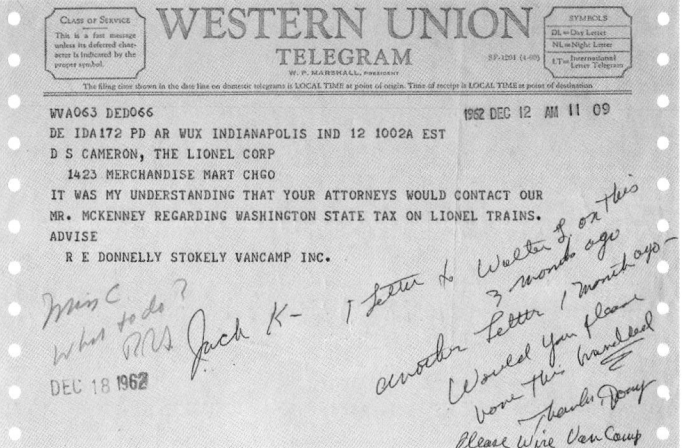

WESTERN UNION
TELEGRAM

WVA063 DED066   1962 DEC 12 AM 11 09
DE IDA172 PD AR WUX INDIANAPOLIS IND 12 1002A EST
D S CAMERON, THE LIONEL CORP
1423 MERCHANDISE MART CHGO
IT WAS MY UNDERSTANDING THAT YOUR ATTORNEYS WOULD CONTACT OUR
MR. MCKENNEY REGARDING WASHINGTON STATE TAX ON LIONEL TRAINS.
ADVISE
R E DONNELLY STOKELY VANCAMP INC.

DEC 18 1962

THE LIONEL CORPORATION

TOY AND TRAIN DIVISION
CHICAGO OFFICE • MERCHANDISE MART • CHICAGO 54, ILLINOIS
MAIN OFFICE AND SHOWROOM, 15 EAST 26TH STREET, NEW YORK 10, N. Y.

October 2, 1962

Mr. Walter Lewis
The Lionel Corporation
Hoffman Place
Hillside, New Jersey

Dear Walter:

Paragraph three and four of the attached letter from Stokely-
Van Camp is self-explanatory. Would you please correspond
directly with Mr. R. E. Donnelly concerning this tax requirement and send a copy of the letter to me.

Thanks for your cooperation, Walter, I hope this is the last we
see of these state tax envolvements.

Best personal regards,

Doug

Dougald S. Cameron

DSC:md

FORM 392   INTER-OFFICE COMMUNICATION
THE LIONEL CORPORATION

TO R. Schilling   FROM W. G. Thornhill   DATE 12-3-64

A few years back we had a Promotion with Stokely-Van Camp wherein one of
our items was shipped from Custom Service, Spring Park, Minnesota to
buyers in all states of the Country. The purchase was made by clipping
off a coupon and mailing the coupon with a check to Custom Service.
Custom Service in turn shipped our merchandise to the customer and refunded
the monies to us after deducting their Service charge.

Enclosed is a copy of a letter from Stokely-Van Camp referring to our tax
liability under this Promotion, in the state of California. We have never
paid any sales taxes to any states on this merchandise. Would you be
kind enough to tell me whether or not we have any liability for the sales
tax in California or liability in any other areas of the Country.

I am enclosing a copy of a page in our contract with Stokely-Van Camp.
You will note that this contract delegates responsibility in the sales
tax area to The Lionel Toy Corporation. However, since no sales tax was
paid since the inception of the contract, I am wondering if perhaps somewhere
along the way, we found that we do not have responsibility in this area.

I would appreciate your prompt reply since the matter is quite old and in
addition, Stokely-Van Camp is pressing for a reply.

W. G. Thornhill

As of January 1965, Lionel had not paid California taxes on
its sales of outfit no. 19142. Stokely-Van Camp and Lionel
disagreed about which of them was bound to pay those taxes as
well as any owed the state of Washington. Memos between the
two companies discuss these issues.

CONVENTIONAL PACK
62-246 BOX

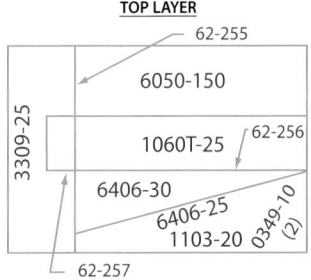

TOP LAYER

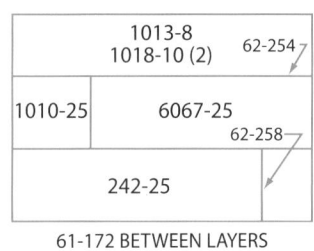

BOTTOM LAYER

61-172 BETWEEN LAYERS

This information strongly suggests that some of these outfits
were made in 1963 or later and may have been the source of the
brown and green automobile variations as well as the brown caboose.
In any case, with so many examples produced and so few sold, this
promotion could be judged a failure. Poor sales probably explained
why Stokely-Van Camp did not purchase a follow-up outfit.

In 1989, Richard Kughn, then the owner of Lionel Trains, Inc.,
purchased Madison Hardware Co. and transferred its inventory
from New York City to a facility he owned in Detroit. One of
the first lists of outfits available for sale from the "new" Madison
included a quantity of 16 of the 19142.

Although the 19142 is a common outfit, it still sells for a
respectable price because it is in fairly high demand. A complete,
high-grade example with proper peripherals and a C8 box with all

inserts should be a prerequisite for any promotional outfit collector.
Advanced collectors hunt for original magazine advertisements or,
best of all, an original Van Camp's Pork and Beans label featuring
the Lionel promotion.

The no. 19142-50 was the display version of Stokely-Van Camp no. 19142. It is rare and seldom seen. The one shown here was shipped directly from the company's headquarters in Indianapolis.

Description: "O27" Promotional Outfit
Specification: "O27" Steam Type Freight Outfit
Customer/Price: Stokely-Van Camp; $11.95 + 1 Label
Original Amount: 450
Factory Order Date: 9/12/1962
Date Issued: 9-12-62
Packaging: Display Outfit Packing (Units not Boxed)

Contents: 242-25 Steam Type Locomotive; 1060T-25 Tender; 3309-25 Turbo Missile Firing Car (Less Missiles); 0349-10 Turbo Missile (2); 6406-25 Single Automobile Flat Car (Less Auto); 6406-30 Automobile; 6050-150 Stokely Van Camp Savings Bank Car; 6067-25 Caboose; 1013-8 Curved Track (Bundle of 8 - 1013); 1018-40 Straight Track (Bundle of 4 - 1018); 1010-25 35-Watt Transformer; 1103-20 Envelope Packed; 310-62 Set of (3) Billboard Signs; 310-3 Billboard Frame; D62-50 Accessory Catalog; 1123-40 Instruction Sheet; 3309-5 Instruction Sheet; 19142-10 Instruction Sheet

Boxes & Packing: 61-439 Display Outfit Box; 61-391 Corr. Insert; 61-392 Corr. Insert; 61-421 Corr. Insert; 61-394 Corr. Insert; 61-395 Shipper for (6) (1-6)

Comments: The 19142-50 was the display version of Stokely-Van Camp's no. 19142 (see the entry for outfit 19142 from 1962). This Manufacturer Promotional Type IIIb outfit was packed in a no. 61-439 White 4-6-4 Steamer and F3 Hinged Display with Red/Orange and Blue Graphics Type A outfit box. It was manufactured by United Container Co. and measured 22½ x 14½ x 3¼ inches. Interestingly, outfit no. 19106 for Cities Service also came in three similar packaging variations.

Other than the packaging, the only difference between the 19142 and the 19142-50 was the inclusion of two additional pieces of straight track and a no. 310-3 Billboard Frame in the latter. This outfit was likely provided to stores or internally to Stokely-Van Camp offices to display the promotion.

The 19142-50 is rare and seldom seen. Many toy train enthusiasts do not even know of its existence. Still, demand is high for this and the other Van Camp outfits and will only grow as more collectors learn about the different versions.

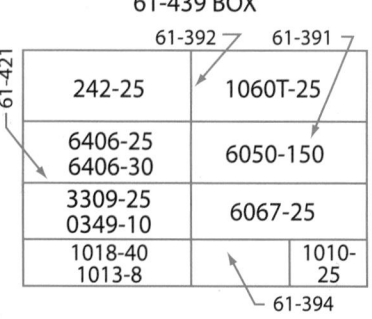

DISPLAY PACK
61-439 BOX

	61-392	61-391	
61-421	242-25	1060T-25	
	6406-25 6406-30	6050-150	
	3309-25 0349-10	6067-25	
	1018-40 1013-8		1010-25
	61-394		

19142-50 (1962)	C6	C7	C8	Rarity
Complete Outfit	600	1,025	1,250	R9
Outfit Box no. 61-439	450	800	900	R9

Stokely-Van Camp Manufacturer Promotional Type IIIb outfit no. 19142-100 is shown with a Tuscan Red no. 6406-25 Single Automobile Car and a yellow no. 6406-30 Automobile with gray bumpers. Note that the no. 61-170 Tan RSC has Lionel markings printed on its top.

Description: "O27" Promotional Outfit
Specification: "O27" Steam Type Freight Outfit
Customer/Price: Stokely-Van Camp; $11.95 + 1 Label
Original Amount: 25,000
Factory Order Date: 9/14/1962
Date Issued: 9-17-62
Packaging: R.S.C. Outfit Packing (Units not Boxed)

Contents: 242-25 Steam Type Locomotive; 1060T-25 Tender; 3309-25 Turbo Missile Firing Car (Less Missiles); 0349-10 Turbo Missile (2); 6406-25 Single Automobile Flat Car (Less Automobile); 6406-30 Automobile; 6050-150 Stokely Van Camp Savings Bank Car; 6067-25 Caboose; 1013-8 Curved Track (Bundle of 8 - 1013); 1018-30 Straight Track (Bundle of 3 - 1018); 1018-10 Straight Track (Loose); 1010-25 35-Watt Transformer; 1103-20 Envelope Packed; 310-62 Set of (3) Billboard Signs; D62-50 Accessory Catalog; 1123-40 Instruction Sheet; 3309-5 Instruction Sheet; 19142-10 Instruction Sheet

Boxes & Packing: 61-170 Outfit Box; 61-172 Insert; 62-254 Insert; 62-255 Insert; 62-256 Insert; 62-257 Insert; 62-258 Insert; 61-175 Shipper for (4) (1-4)

Comments: This outfit was the regular RSC version of Stokely-Van Camp no. 19142 (see the entry for 19142). Except for two additional pieces of straight track, the contents were exactly the same.

The real differences related to the packaging. The 19142-100 came in a common no. 61-170 Tan RSC with Black Graphics outfit box. It was manufactured by St. Joe Kraft, St. Joe Paper Co. Container Division and measured 11½ x 10¼ x 6¼ inches

The Factory Orders for the 19142 and 19142-100 both called for 25,000 of each outfit to be made. As such, they are equally as common. As with the 19142, a complete, high-grade example of the 19142-100 with proper peripherals and a C8 box with all inserts should be a prerequisite for any promotional outfit collector.

CONVENTIONAL PACK
61-170 BOX

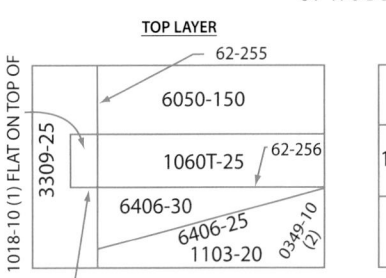

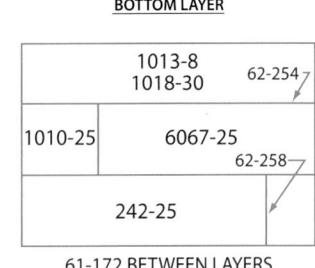

19142-100 (1962)	C6	C7	C8	Rarity
Complete Outfit With Yellow Automobile	200	325	500	R2
Complete Outfit With Brown Or Green Automobile	350	525	750	R3
Outfit Box no. 61-170	50	100	150	R2

D. O. Klein purchased the no. 19142-500 in 1963. This outfit is similar to Stokely-Van Camp no. 19142 from a year earlier, except it came with the nos. 3830-1 Operating Submarine Car, 6014-325 Frisco Box Car and 1061T-25 Tender.

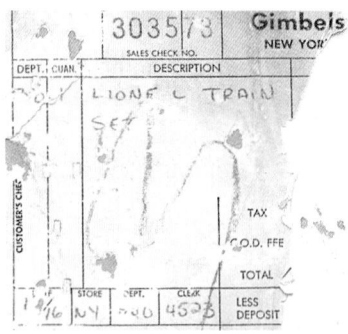

A no. 19142-500 has been observed with a Gimbels shipping label still attached to the outfit box. Also included with this outfit was a completed warranty card listing Gimbels as the dealer. The relationship between D. O. Klein and Gimbels has yet to be determined.

Description: "O27" Promotional Outfit
Specification: "O27" Steam Type Freight Outfit
Customer: D. O. Klein
Customer: Gimbels
Original Amount: 2,072
Factory Order Date: 10/23/1963
Date Issued: Rev 12-3-63
Date Req'd: 11-10-63
Packaging: RSC

Contents: 242-25 Steam Type Locomotive; 1061T-25 Tender; 3830-1 Operating Submarine Car; 6406-25 Flat Car W/Auto; 6406-30 Automobile; 6014-325 Frisco Box Car; 6067-25 Caboose; 1013-8 Curved Track (Bundle of 8 - 1013); 1018-10 Straight Track (Loose); 1008-50 Uncoupling Unit; 1010-25 35-Watt Transformer; 1103-20 Envelope Packed; 310-62 Set of (3) Billboards; D63-50 Accessory Catalog; 1-62 Parts Order Form; 1-63 Warranty Card; 1641-10 Instruction Sheet

Boxes & Packing: 62-246 Outfit Box; 62-254 Corr. Insert; 62-247 Shipper for (4) (1-4)

Alternate For Outfit Contents:
Note: Substitute 6120-25 and 6167-25 for 6067-25 as needed.

19142-500 (1963)	C6	C7	C8	Rarity
Complete Outfit With nos. 6067-25 Or 6167-25	325	500	685	R6
Complete Outfit With no. 6120-25	340	520	720	R6
Outfit Box no. 62-246	125	195	250	R6

Comments: This was the second of two Factory Orders to list D. O. Klein (see the entry for no. 19197 from 1962) as the customer. D. O. Klein's identity is unknown; therefore, we cannot determine whether this outfit should be classified as a Retailer Promotional Type Ib or a Manufacturer Promotional Type IIIb.

The nos. 19142-500 and 19142-502 are interesting outfits in that they are similar to the nos. 19142 and 19142-100, respectively. Since both the 19142 and 19142-100 were failures, Lionel may have been cannibalizing the unsold outfits or assembling new outfits from unpackaged items.

Also, the quantity of the 19142-500 was decreased from 2,500 to 2,072 on 12-3-63. The decrease of 428 went towards the creation of outfit 19142-502, which lists a quantity of 428.

The 19142-500 and 19142-502 included the same engine and rolling stock. Both were led by a no. 242-25 Steam Type Locomotive. This low-end Scout steamer featured a two-position reversing unit and a headlight, lacked smoke and used a rubber tire as a traction aid. The version with wide running boards was included in this outfit.

The 19142-500 could be considered an upgrade over the 19142. For example, it included a no. 3830-1 Operating Submarine Car, whereas the 19142 had a no. 3349-25 Turbo Missile Firing Car (Less Missiles). Lionel was starting to deplete its inventory of the 3830-1. Also, the Type III no. 6014-325 Frisco Box Car was the newly issued white Frisco car and replaced the no. 6050-150 Van Camp Box Car in the 19142.

The Factory Order for the 19142-500 indicated that the no. 6067-25 Caboose should be swapped out as needed. Early outfits likely included a 6067-25 Caboose in unpainted brown plastic, as this outfit has been observed this way. Later outfits likely included a no. 6120-25 Work Caboose or a no. 6167-25 Caboose. The inclusion of a 6120-25 receives a slight premium.

The norm for the 6167-25 Caboose was AAR trucks and couplers, but Archbar types were not unusual. Except for the 6067-25 and 6120-25 equipped with non-operating Archbar trucks and couplers, all the cars in this outfit came with AAR types. The 3830-1 came packaged in an Orange Picture box. The substitutions are listed in the pricing table.

This outfit used the no. 62-246 Tan RSC Mailer with Black Graphics outfit box. It was manufactured by Mead Containers and measured 11½ x 10¼ x 6¼ inches. These boxes were made of a thicker corrugated material (rated at 90 pounds rather than the normal 65 pounds gross weight) that allowed each outfit to be shipped in its outfit box. The manufacturer omitted any Lionel printing on the box top to leave room for a mailing label. The 62-246 Outfit Box was a 1963 version with four lines of data as part of the box manufacturer's certificate.

A 19142-500 has been observed with a Gimbels mailing label and completed warranty card. The relationship between Gimbels and D. O. Klein is unknown.

This outfit is more difficult to find than the 19142, but not as hard as the 19142-502.

Collectors have tried for years to determine whether the 19142-500 was a Stokely-Van Camp outfit. Now, thanks to the Factory Orders, we can conclude that it was intended for D. O. Klein – whoever that was.

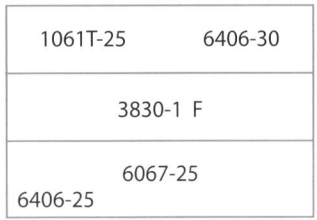

CONVENTIONAL PACK
62-246 BOX
10-22-63

TOP LAYER		BOTTOM LAYER	
1061T-25 6406-30		1008-50 1018-10 62-254 1013-8	
3830-1 F		1010-25	6014-325
6067-25 6406-25		242-25	

2 CATALOGS BETWEEN LAYERS

Description: "O27" Promotional Outfit
Specification: "O27" Steam Type Freight Outfit
Customer: Richie Premium
Original Amount: 428
Factory Order Date: 12/3/1963
Date Issued: 12-3-63
Date Req'd: At Once
Packaging: RSC

Contents: 242-25 Steam Type Locomotive; 1061T-25 Tender; 3830-1 Operating Submarine Car; 6406-25 Flat Car W/Auto; 6406-30 Automobile; 6014-325 Frisco Box Car; 6120-25 Work Caboose; 1013-70 Curved Track (Bundle of 12 - 1013); 1018-30 Straight Track (Bundle of 3 - 1018); 1008-50 Uncoupling Unit; 1020-25 90° Crossing; 1010-25 35-Watt Transformer; 1103-20 Envelope Packed; 903 Set of (2) Sheets Trading Cards; X625-20 Cardboard Scenic Set; 310-62 Set of (3) Billboards; D63-50 Accessory Catalog; 1-62 Parts Order Form; 1-63 Warranty Card; 1123-40 Instruction Sheet; 1641-10 Instruction Sheet; 1802B Layout Instruction Sheet

Boxes & Packing: 61-170 Outfit Box; 61-171 Corr. Insert; 61-174 Shipper for (6) (1-6)

Alternate For Outfit Contents:
Note: X625-20 Customer Supplied.

19142-502 (1963)	C6	C7	C8	Rarity
Complete Outfit	1,400	3,225	5,000	R9
Outfit Box no. 61-170	375	475	550	R9

Comments: This was the first of two (along with the no. 19216) outfits purchased by incentive merchandiser Richie Premium in 1963. A Retailer Promotional Type Ib, the no. 19142-502 contained items that were the same as those in the no. 19142-

500 from 1963 and similar to those in the no. 19142-100 from 1962. (See the entries for outfits 19142-100 from 1962 and 19142-500 from 1963.)

Besides the components (described in the entry for the 19142-500), the 19142-502 included some rare paper items. In this respect, it was like most of the outfits associated with Richie Premium. For example, that firm's 19142-502, 19216 and no. 19328 represent the only instances in which the nos. 903 Set of (2) Sheets Trading Cards and X625-20 Cardboard Scenic Set were paired.

The X625-20 Cardboard Scenic Set included figures, railroad signs, automobiles and buildings that could be punched out, assembled and placed around a layout. Its high rarity is linked to its lack of Lionel markings (it said only "Printed in Japan"), which led to it frequently being separated from the trains and discarded. Also, the Cardboard Scenic Set was extremely fragile and almost always assembled and destroyed.

The 903 included 24 two-sided Lionel trading cards printed on a sheet of perforated cardstock. On the front of each card was a Lionel locomotive, and on the back was historical information about its road name as well as a trivia quiz. Two 11 x 11 inch sets of 12 cards were connected by a "folding" strip. The entire sheet of 24 was folded in half along the strip and placed loose in the outfit box. The cards were perforated and are almost always found separated as individual cards, with the "folding" strip long gone. In fact, if it weren't for the complete sheets that came out of Madison Hardware over the years, it is likely that few of these items would be intact.

The only other differences between this outfit and the 19142-500 were that the no. 6120-25 Work Caboose was the norm in the 19142-502 and the figure-eight track plan outlined on the no. 1802B Layout Instruction Sheet was included with it. This was one of the last two outfits to include a 6120-25.

The no. 61-170 Box was the same as the one the 19142-100 came in, though it was manufactured by United Container

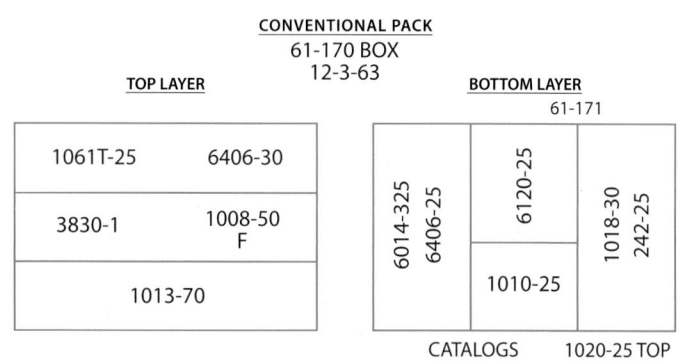

Richie Premium purchased the no. 19142-502 in 1963. This outfit represented the first of three instances when the nos. 903 Set of (2) Sheets Trading Cards and X625-20 Cardboard Scenic Set were paired. The other two also occurred in outfits associated with Richie Premium.

Co. Container Division and measured 11½ x 10¼ x 6¼ inches. This outfit box included "63" and five stars as part of the box manufacturer's certificate (BMC). It also had four lines of data in the BMC.

As with all Richie Premium outfits, the peripherals make the 19142-502 extremely difficult to complete. Empty boxes appear from time to time, but completed outfits are quite rare.

Collectors have tried for years to determine whether the 19142-502 was a Stokely-Van Camp outfit. Now, thanks to the Factory Orders, we can conclude that it was intended for Richie Premium.

CONVENTIONAL PACK
61-170 BOX
12-3-63

TOP LAYER		BOTTOM LAYER
		61-171

TOP LAYER	
1061T-25	6406-30
3830-1	1008-50 F
1013-70	

BOTTOM LAYER			
6014-325 6406-25	6120-25	1018-30 242-25
	1010-25	

CATALOGS   1020-25 TOP

19143
1962

Description: "O27" Promotional Outfit
Specification: "O27" Steam Type Freight Outfit with Smoke
Customer: Gertz
Original Amount: 50
Factory Order Date: 10/31/1962
Date Issued: 11-1-62
Packaging: R.S.C. Outfit Packing (Units not Boxed), Except 110

Contents: 236-25 Steam Type Locomotive with Smoke; 1060T-25 Tender; 3413-25 Mercury Capsule Launching Car; 6512-25 Cherry Picker Car; 3349-25 Turbo Missile Firing Car (Less Missiles); 0349-10 Turbo Missile; 6057-25 Caboose; 1013-8 Curved Track (Bundle of 8 - 1013); 1013-90 Curved Track (Bundle of 9 - 1013); 1018-30 Straight Track (Bundle of 3 - 1018) (3); 1008-50 Uncoupling Unit; 1025-25 45-Watt Transformer; 110-1 Trestle Set; 909-20 Smoke Fluid; 1103-20 Envelope Packed; 310-2 Set of (5) Billboards; D62-50 Accessory Catalog; 1123-40 Instruction Sheet; 1802I Layout Instruction Sheet; 236-11 Instruction Sheet; 122-10 Instruction Sheet; 3413-8 Instruction Sheet; 6512-19 Instruction Sheet; 3349-8 Instruction Sheet

Boxes & Packing: 62-270 Outfit Box; 61-171 Insert (2); 61-173 Insert; 62-251 Insert; 62-261 Insert; 62-272 Insert; 62-271 Shipper for 3 (1-3)

19143 (1962)	C6	C7	C8	Rarity
Complete Outfit	1,800	2,250	2,800	R10
Outfit Box no. 62-270	1,500	1,750	2,000	R10

Comments: This was the only time that Gertz, an Allied Stores' owned retailer, appeared on a Factory Order. Only 50 examples of the no. 19143, a Retailer Promotional Type Ia outfit, were manufactured. That quantity ties it for 13th on the list of the fewest outfits produced.

A space and military outfit, the 19143 was led by a no. 236-25 Steam Type Locomotive with Smoke. One of Lionel's high-end Scout steamers, it also included a two-position reversing unit, a headlight and Magne-Traction.

This outfit included the commonly paired nos. 3413-25 Mercury Capsule Launching Car and 6512-25 Cherry Picker Car. They were designed to work together, with the 6512-25 pretending to load an astronaut into the waiting Mercury capsule. A no. 3349-25 Turbo Missile Car (Less Missiles) was also part of the 19143, but a target was not provided. Maybe Lionel intended for it to protect the launch from unforeseen enemies.

These and the other cars were equipped with operating AAR trucks and couplers. Be aware, however, that a transition from Archbar to AAR trucks and couplers began in 1962. As a result, the no. 1060T-25 Tender could come with either two Archbar types or one non-operating Archbar and one plain AAR truck and coupler.

The no. 110-1 Trestle Set in this outfit was used for the elevated pretzel track layout. The no. 1802I Layout Instruction Sheet detailed this track plan.

The no. 62-270 Tan RSC with Black Graphics outfit box measured 15½ x 14 x 6¼ inches.

As with many promotional outfits, the outfit box is difficult to find, but its components are not. With only 50 manufactured, this outfit is rare. Finding a 19143 outfit box is a true challenge.

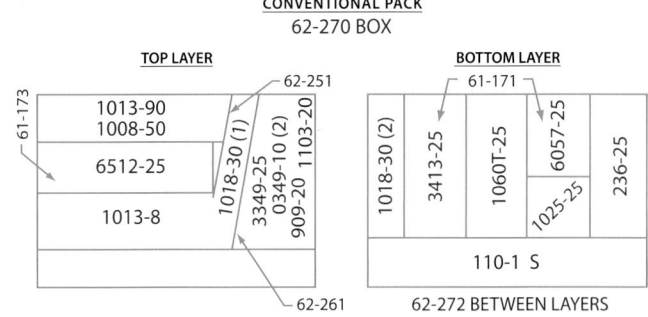

CONVENTIONAL PACK
62-270 BOX

Description: "O27" Promotional Outfit
Specification: "O27" Diesel Freight Outfit
Customer: Signet
Original Amount: 500
Factory Order Date: 6/7/1962
Date Issued: 6-8-62
Packaging: R.S.C. Outfit Packing (Units not Boxed), Except 1020 Crossing

Contents: 1065-25 Alco Diesel Power Unit - "Union Pacific"; 3309-25 Turbo Missile Firing Car (Less Missiles); 0349-10 Turbo Missile (2); 6480-25 Exploding Target Car; 6413-25 Mercury Capsule Transport Car; 6413-4 Capsules (2); 6413-10 Envelope Packed; 6067-25 Caboose; 1013-70 Curved Track (Bundle of 12 - 1013); 1018-40 Straight Track (Bundle of 4 - 1018); 1026-25 25-Watt Transformer; 1020-1 90° Crossing; 1103-20 Envelope Packed; 310-2 Set of (5) Billboards; D62-50 Accessory Catalog; 3309-10 Instruction Sheet; 6480-5 Instruction Sheet; 1123-40 Instruction Sheet; 1125-10 Instruction Sheet; 1802B Layout Instruction Sheet

Boxes & Packing: 61-170 Outfit Box; 61-171 Corr. Insert; 61-172 Corr. Insert; 62-264 Corr. Insert; 61-175 Shipper for (4) (1-4)

19144 (1962)	C6	C7	C8	Rarity
Complete Outfit	525	800	1,115	R8
Outfit Box no. 61-170	275	400	500	R8

Comments: Signet was listed on the Factory Order for this outfit in 1962. A common 1960s company name, the identity of Signet has yet to be determined. As such, this outfit could have been a Retailer Promotional Type Ib or a Manufacturer Promotional Type IIIb.

We do know that the 19144 was a space and military outfit headed by a no. 1065-25 Union Pacific Alco Diesel Power Unit. This forward-only locomotive was as stripped down as Lionel could

make an Alco in 1962, though it did have a headlight. This diesel appeared only in promotional outfits.

Although the nos. 3309-25 Turbo Missile Firing Car (Less Missiles) and 6480-25 Exploding Target Car were operating cars, they were low-end versions of the nos. 3349-25 and 6470-25, respectively. Both of the models in this outfit were equipped with non-operating Archbar trucks and couplers.

The new-for-1962 no. 6413-25 Mercury Capsule Transport Car included operating AAR trucks and couplers. Since this car came unboxed, its associated peripherals (nos. 6413-4 Capsules and 6413-10 Envelope Packed) were placed loose in the outfit box.

Finally, there was a no. 6067-25 Caboose. A transition from Archbar to AAR trucks and couplers began in 1962, so it could come with either two Archbar types or one non-operating Archbar and one plain AAR truck and coupler

The appropriate quantity of track was included to make the figure-eight layout. That track plan was outlined on the no. 1802B Layout Instruction Sheet.

The common no. 61-170 Tan RSC with Black Graphics outfit box was used for this outfit. It measured 11½ x 10¼ x 6¼ inches.

With only 500 made, examples of the 19144 don't appear too often. Then again, this outfit doesn't stand out from other promotional outfits from 1962, so collectors don't pursue it with great passion.

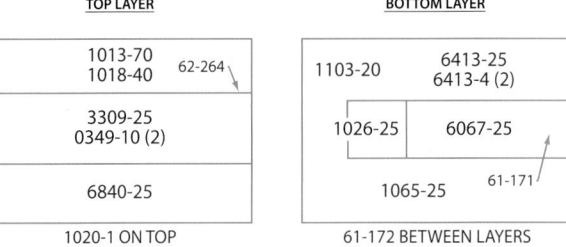

CONVENTIONAL PACK
61-170 BOX

Description: "O27" Promotional Outfit
Specification: "O27" Diesel Freight Outfit
Customer: Navy
Original Amount: 300
Factory Order Date: 6/25/1962
Date Issued: 6-17-62
Packaging: R.S.C. Outfit Packing (Units not Boxed)

Contents: 224P-25 Alco Diesel Power Car - "U.S. Navy"; 224C-25 "B" Unit - "U.S. Navy"; 6630-25 Missile Launching Car (Less Missile); 6650-80 Missile Complete (or 6650-84); 6480-25 Exploding Target Car; 6042-25 Gondola Car (Less 2 Canisters); 6112-5 Canister - Red (2); 6067-25 Caboose; 1013-8 Curved Track (Bundle of 8 - 1013); 1018-10 Straight Track (Loose) (2); 1025-25 45-Watt Transformer; 1103-20 Envelope Packed; 310-2 Set of (5) Billboards; D62-50 Accessory Catalog; 1123-40 Instruction Sheet; 6630-6 Instruction Sheet; 6480-5 Instruction Sheet; 19145-10 Instruction Sheet; 217-17 Instruction Sheet

Boxes & Packing: 62-243 Outfit Box; 61-191 Insert; 62-223 Insert; 62-224 Insert; 62-225 Insert; 62-245 Insert (2); 62-248 Insert; 62-244 Shipper for (4) (1-4)

19145 (1962)	C6	C7	C8	Rarity
Complete Outfit	725	1,050	1,375	R9
Outfit Box no. 62-243	400	550	650	R9

Comments: This was the only Factory Order to list the Navy in the 1960s. As with the Army, the Navy ran retail stores. Navy Exchange stores carried the no. 19145, a Retailer Promotional Type Ib outfit, in 1962.

Fittingly the U.S. Navy purchased a space and military outfit led by a no. 224P-25 U.S. Navy Alco Diesel Power Car. This locomotive was making its last appearance in 1962 in this and

outfit nos. 19201 (1) and 19201 (2). Luckily, there were enough examples left to fulfill the Navy's order.

Unfortunately, Lionel did not provide a matching no. 6017-200 U.S. Navy Caboose. Instead, a common, unmarked no. 6067-25 Caboose was included. This was most likely equipped with non-operating Archbar trucks and couplers.

The nos. 6480-25 Exploding Target Car and 6630-25 Missile Launching Flat Car were low-end versions of the nos. 6470-25 and 6650-25, respectively. These cars appeared only in promotional outfits and are harder to find than their high-end counterparts. Like the no. 6042-25 Gondola Car, they were equipped with non-operating Archbar trucks and couplers.

The 19145 introduced the no. 19145-10 Instruction Sheet, which was a generic Lionel Train Outfit Sheet. It made no mention of the motive power or uncoupling track. Therefore, every outfit would also need a separate motive power instruction sheet.

The 19145 came in a no. 62-243 Tan RSC with Black Graphics outfit box that measured 12⅛ x 11½ x 6⅜ inches.

As with all space and military outfits, this one is in high demand. Also, the fact that it was actually sold by the Navy in such low quantities makes it a must for promotional outfit collectors.

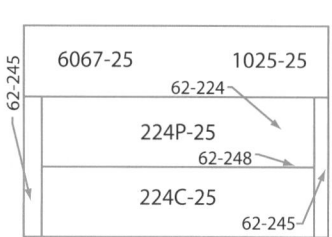

CONVENTIONAL PACK
62-243 BOX

TOP LAYER

6112-5 (1)	1018-10 (2) UNDER	62-225
6042-25	6650-80	
6112-5 (1)	6480-25	
1103-20	6630-25	
1013-8		

61-191

BOTTOM LAYER

6067-25	1025-25
	62-224
224P-25	
	62-248
224C-25	
	62-245

62-245 (left side)

62-223 BETWEEN LAYERS

Customer No. On Box: 85021
Description: "O27" Promotional Outfit
Specification: "O27" Steam Type Freight Outfit
Customer/No.: Strauss Stores; 85021
Original Amount: 2,000
Factory Order Date: 8/13/1962
Date Issued: 8-16-62
Packaging: R.S.C. Outfit Packing (Units not Boxed), Except 1020, 953 & 984

Contents: 1060-25 Steam Type Locomotive; 1060T-25 Tender; 3309-25 Turbo Missile Firing Car (Less Missiles); 0349-10 Turbo Missile (2); 6042-25 Gondola Car (Less 2 Canisters); 6112-5 Canister (Red) (2); 6076-25 Hopper Car - Red; 6067-25 Caboose; 1013-70 Curved Track (Bundle of 12 - 1013); 1018-40 Straight Track (Bundle of 4 - 1018); 1020-1 90° Crossing; 1026-25 25-Watt Transformer; 1103-20 Envelope Packed; 953-1 Figure Set; 984-1 Railroad Set; 310-2 Set of (5) Billboards; D62-50 Accessory Catalog; 1802B Layout Instruction Sheet; 1123-40 Instruction Sheet; 3309-5 Instruction Sheet; 1123-10 Instruction Sheet

Boxes & Packing: 61-200 Outfit Box; 61-171 Insert; 62-248 Insert; 62-258 Insert; 62-264 Insert; 62-326 Insert; 61-201 Shipper for (4) (1-4)

Alternate For Outfit Contents:
Customer Stock No. 85021 to appear on outfit box and shipper.

19146 (1962)	C6	C7	C8	Rarity
Complete Outfit	465	750	2,300	R5
Outfit Box no. 61-200	100	150	200	R5

Comments: Strauss Stores (an auto supply chain founded in Brooklyn, New York) purchased the no. 19146, a Retailer Promotional Type Ib outfit, in 1962. After three years of purchasing outfits, this represented the firm's last order with Lionel.

As with Strauss Stores' previous two outfits (nos. X-544NA and X-637), the 19146 was a good example of Lionel taking an outfit filled with low-end rolling stock and sprucing it up with two Plasticville sets. The nos. 953-1 Figure Set and 984-1 Railroad Set are the two items that are most difficult to find when trying to complete this outfit. Their boxes were made of a thin cardstock that was easily torn or ripped. The instruction sheets and original, complete Plasticville pieces can also be a challenge to uncover.

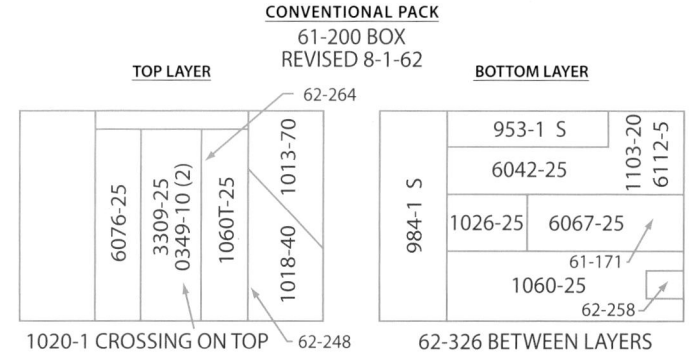

Outfit no. 19146 included the nos. 953-1 Figure Set and 984-1 Railroad Set. These Plasticville sets improved an otherwise commonplace outfit. They also provided Strauss Stores with something different from what their competitors offered, which was the main purpose of promotional outfits.

The rolling stock in the 19146 was all lower-end, and the only car of note was the no. 3309-25 Turbo Missile Firing Car (Less Missiles). All the cars were equipped with non-operating Archbar trucks and couplers.

As with the X-637, the 19146 included the figure-eight track layout that was detailed on the no. 1802B Layout Instruction Sheet

The no. 61-200 Orange RSC with Black Graphics outfit box was manufactured by Mead Containers and measured 14½ x 12 x 7 inches.

Empty outfit boxes for the 19146 do appear on the market, as do incomplete outfits. Typically missing are the Plasticville items.

CONVENTIONAL PACK
61-200 BOX
REVISED 8-1-62

TOP LAYER

6076-25	3309-25 0349-10 (2)	1060T-25	1013-70	1018-40

62-264

1020-1 CROSSING ON TOP — 62-248

BOTTOM LAYER

984-1 S	953-1 S		1103-20	6112-5
	6042-25			
	1026-25	6067-25		
		61-171		
	1060-25			
		62-258		

62-326 BETWEEN LAYERS

Description: "O27" Promotional Outfit
Specification: "O27" Steam Type Freight Outfit
Customer: Richie Premium
Original Amount: 5,000
Factory Order Date: 6/13/1962
Date Issued: 6-18-62
Packaging: R.S.C. Outfit Packing (Units not Boxed), Except 1020 Crossing

Contents: 1060-25 Steam Type Locomotive; 1060T-25 Tender; 3309-25 Turbo Missile Firing Car (Less Missiles); 0349-10 Turbo Missile (2); 6480-25 Exploding Target Car; 6042-75 Gondola Car (Less 2 Cable Reels); 40-11 Cable Reels (2); 6067-25 Caboose; 1013-70 Curved Track (Bundle of 12 - 1013); 1018-40 Straight Track (Bundle of 4 - 1018); 1026-25 25-Watt Transformer; 1020-1 90° Crossing; 1103-20 Envelope Packed; X625-20 Cardboard

Scenic Set; 310-2 Set of (5) Billboards; D62-50 Accessory Catalog; 1123-40 Instruction Sheet; 3309-10 Instruction Sheet; 6480-5 Instruction Sheet; 1123-10 Instruction Sheet; 1802B Layout Instruction Sheet

Boxes & Packing: 62-243 Outfit Box; 61-191 Insert; 61-193 Insert; 62-223 Insert; 62-248 Insert; 62-249 Insert; 62-244 Shipper for (4) (1-4)

19147 (1962)	C6	C7	C8	Rarity
Complete Outfit	525	1,150	1,500	R9
Outfit Box no. 62-243	90	125	150	R4

The no. 19147 was the follow-up to Richie Premium's no. X-624 from 1961. Both promotional outfits included the no. X625-20 Cardboard Scenic Set. That item, so difficult to find complete and unassembled, was printed on chipboard, and the figures were perforated for easy removal. The entire sheet was folded in half so it would fit in a small outfit box. Surviving examples are extremely fragile and tend to fall apart over time.

Comments: In 1962, incentive merchandiser Richie Premium purchased two outfits: nos. 19147 and 19203. The 19147, a Retailer Promotional Type Ib, was the follow-up to that firm's outfit no. X-624 from 1961. It contained items that, except for the rare no. X625-20 Cardboard Scenic Set, were common and low-end.

The 19147 (like the X-624) was led by a no. 1060-25 Steam Type Locomotive. This inexpensive engine went forward only and had a headlight. Although, this outfit featured two operating cars – nos. 3309-25 Turbo Missile Firing Car (Less Missiles) and 6480-25 Exploding Target Car – both were low-end versions of better models (nos. 3349-25 and 6470-25, respectively). The 6480-25 included "non-slotted" sides and a smooth roof door guide (without the nubs added later to help hold on the sides). It, like the other cars in the 19147, was equipped with non-operating Archbar trucks and couplers.

The X625-20 Cardboard Scenic Set included figures, railroad signs, automobiles and buildings that could be punched out, assembled and placed around a layout. The high rarity of this item is linked to its lack of Lionel markings (it said only "Printed in Japan"), which led to it frequently being separated from the trains and discarded. Also, the Cardboard Scenic Set was extremely fragile and almost always assembled and destroyed.

The appropriate quantity of track was included to make the figure-eight layout. That track plan was outlined on the no. 1802B Layout Instruction Sheet.

The no. 62-243 Tan RSC with Black Graphics outfit box was manufactured by St. Joe Kraft, St. Joe Paper Co. Container Division and measured 12⅛ x 11½ x 6⅜ inches.

The 19147, like its predecessor X-624, is one of those unusual outfits whose components, specifically the X625-20, make it an R9. The box by itself rates an R4.

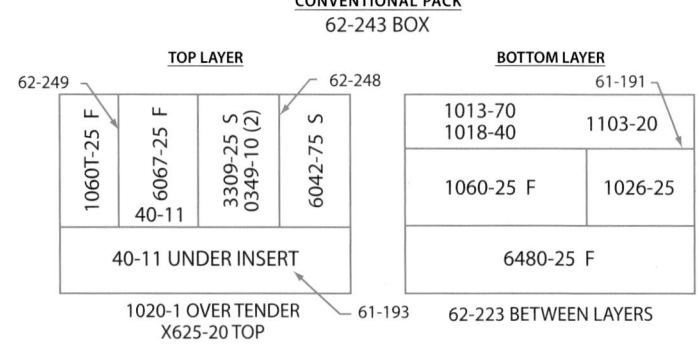

CONVENTIONAL PACK
62-243 BOX

TOP LAYER — BOTTOM LAYER

62-249 — 62-248 — 61-191

TOP LAYER				BOTTOM LAYER	
1060T-25 F	6067-25 F	3309-25 S / 0349-10 (2) S	6042-75 S	1013-70 / 1018-40	1103-20
	40-11			1060-25 F	1026-25
40-11 UNDER INSERT				6480-25 F	

1020-1 OVER TENDER / X625-20 TOP — 61-193 — 62-223 BETWEEN LAYERS

Description: "O27" Promotional Outfit
Specification: "O27" Steam Type Freight Outfit
Customer: J. C. Penney Co., Inc.
Original Amount: 1,100
Factory Order Date: 5/31/1962
Date Issued: Rev. #1 8-7-62
Packaging: R.S.C. Outfit Packing (Units not Boxed), Except 1020 Crossing

Contents: 242-25 Steam Type Locomotive; 1060T-25 Tender; 3309-25 Turbo Missile Firing Car (Less Missiles); 0349-10 Turbo Missile (2); 6463-25 Rocket Fuel Car; 6480-25 Exploding Target Car; 3510-25 Satellite Launching Car (Less Satellite); 0333-100 Satellite; 6067-25 Caboose; 1013-8 Curved Track (Bundle of 8 - 1013); 1013-5 Curved Track (Loose) (4); 1018-40 Straight Track (Bundle of 4 - 1018); 1020-1 90° Crossing; 1010-25 35-Watt Transformer; 1103-20 Envelope Packed; 310-2 Set of (5) Billboards; D62-50 Accessory Catalog; 1123-40 Instruction Sheet; 3309-10 Instruction Sheet; 6480-5 Instruction Sheet; 3510-5 Instruction Sheet; 120-10 Instruction Sheet; 1802B Layout Instruction Sheet

Promotional outfit no. 19148 was J. C. Penney's steam-powered purchase for 1962. It was a success, as the original quantity of 750 was increased to 1,100 on 8-7-62. This was one of the last two outfits from J. C. Penney before it entered the mail-order catalog business.

Boxes & Packing: 62-243 Outfit Box; 61-171 Corr. Insert; 62-223 Corr. Insert; 62-225 Corr. Insert; 62-248 Corr. Insert (3); 62-264 Corr. Insert; 62-244 Shipper for (4) (1-4)

19148 (1962)	C6	C7	C8	Rarity
Complete Outfit	400	625	900	R7
Outfit Box no. 62-243	150	225	275	R7

Comments: Lionel Factory Orders for 1962 indicated that the next two outfits were for J. C. Penney. J. C. Penney didn't enter the mail-order catalog business until 1963; therefore, the Factory Orders are the only known record of these outfits. Outfit no. 19148 was powered by a steam locomotive; the no. 19149 was led by a diesel.

The 19148, a Retailer Promotional Type Ib outfit, was the follow-up to J. C. Penney's no. X-665 from 1961. It was a space and military offering led by a no. 242-25 Steam Type Locomotive. This low-end Scout steamer featured a two-position reversing unit and a headlight, lacked smoke and used a rubber tire as a traction aid. The version with wide running boards was included in this outfit.

The nos. 3309-25 Turbo Missile Firing Car (Less Missiles), 3510-25 Satellite Launching Car (Less Satellite) and 6480-25 Exploding Target Car included in this outfit were low-end versions of the nos. 3349-25, 3519-25 and 6470-25, respectively. Lionel included the 3510-25 and 6480-25 in promotional outfits only;

they are more difficult to find than their high-end counterparts.

All the cars in the 19148 were, with one exception, equipped with non-operating Archbar trucks and couplers. The no. 6463-25 Rocket Fuel Car had operating AAR types.

The appropriate quantity of track was included to make the figure-eight layout. That track plan was outlined on the no. 1802B Layout Instruction Sheet.

The no. 62-243 Tan RSC with Black Graphics outfit box was manufactured by St. Joe Kraft, St. Joe Paper Co. Container Division and measured 12⅛ x 11½ x 6⅜ inches.

There is a segment of promotional outfit collectors that concentrates on specific retailers, including J. C. Penney. Now that the Factory Orders have documented these early J. C. Penney outfits, demand for them will increase.

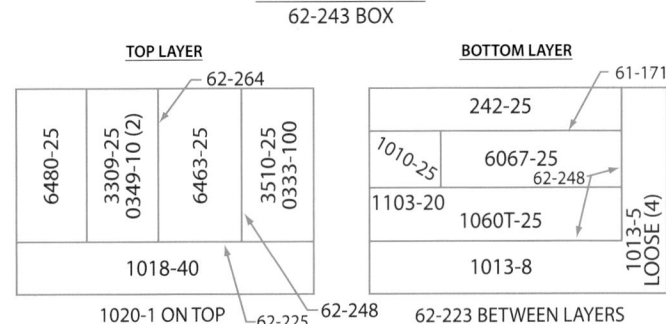

CONVENTIONAL PACK
62-243 BOX

TOP LAYER
BOTTOM LAYER

Description: "O27" Promotional Outfit
Specification: "O27" Diesel Switcher Freight Outfit
Customer: J. C. Penney Co., Inc.
Original Amount: 200
Factory Order Date: 6/14/1962
Date Issued: 6-18-62

Packaging: R.S.C. Outfit Packing (Units not Boxed), Except 110

Contents: 633-50 "Santa Fe" Diesel Switcher; 6512-25 Cherry Picker Car; 3413-25 Mercury Capsule Launching Car; 3413-18 Mercury Capsule & Parachute Assem.; 3413-27 Missile; 3410-

25 Oper. Helicopter Car (Less Helicopter); 3419-100 Operating Helicopter Complete; 6463-25 Rocket Fuel Car; 6057-25 Caboose; 1013-8 Curved Track (Bundle of 8 - 1013); 1013-90 Curved Track (Bundle of 9 - 1013); 1018-30 Straight Track (Bundle of 3 - 1018) (3); 1008-50 Uncoupling Unit; 110-1 Trestle Set; 1025-25 45-Watt Transformer; 1103-20 Envelope Packed; 310-2 Set of (5) Billboards; D62-50 Accessory Catalog; 1123-40 Instruction Sheet; 121-10 Instruction Sheet; 3413-8 Instruction Sheet; 3410-5 Instruction Sheet; 1802I Layout Instruction Sheet

Boxes & Packing: 62-270 Outfit Box; 600-26 Insert (2); 61-183 Insert; 61-191 Insert; 62-248 Insert; 62-264 Insert; 62-273 Insert; 62-271 Shipper for (3) (1-3)

19149 (1962)	C6	C7	C8	Rarity
Complete Outfit	1,000	1,525	2,025	R10
Outfit Box no. 62-270	550	800	900	R10

Comments: This is the second of two promotional outfits from 1962 to list J. C. Penney as its customer on the Factory Order (see the entry for no. 19148). Since J. C. Penney didn't enter the mail-order catalog business until 1963, there is no record of these outfits beyond their Lionel Factory Orders. Outfit no. 19149 was powered by a diesel locomotive; the 19148 was led by a steamer.

The 19149, a Retailer Promotional Type Ib outfit, was the follow-up to J. C. Penney's no. X-666 from 1961. This space and military outfit was led by a no. 633-50 Santa Fe Diesel Switcher, which was the promotional-only upgrade to the no. 633-25 that Lionel issued earlier in 1962. This low-end switcher came with a traction tire but lacked a horn. However, it was "4 wheel drive equipped", unlike the 633-25, which was driven by only two wheels. The "-50" version is more difficult (3,660 produced) to find than the "-25" (11,900 produced). According to the Lionel Engineering Specification for the 633-50, it was "primarily designed to pull 5 moderate weight cars up a trestle".

The commonly paired nos. 3413-25 Mercury Capsule Launching Car and 6512-25 Cherry Picker Car were included in the 19149. They were designed to work together, with the 6512-25 pretending to load an astronaut into the waiting Mercury capsule. Like the other cars in this outfit, they were equipped with operating AAR trucks and couplers.

The no. 3410-25 Oper. Helicopter Car (Less Helicopter) was a carryover from 1961. Interestingly, in 1962 Lionel gave the task of adding the no. 3419-100 Operating Helicopter Complete to the Outfit Packing Department (as noted on the 3410-25 Production Control File). These helicopters were frequently lost or broken.

In 1962, the Production Control File for the 3419-100 changed from a gray Navy stamped two-piece helicopter body to an unmarked helicopter with a one-piece yellow helicopter body. Although this was Lionel's intended production, many 3419-100 Navy helicopters still appeared on 3410s in 1962.

The no. 110-1 Trestle Set in this outfit was used for the elevated pretzel track layout. The no. 1802I Layout Instruction Sheet detailed this track plan.

The no. 62-270 Tan RSC with Black Graphics outfit box measured 15½ x 14 x 6¼ inches.

Based on small quantity of this outfit that Lionel produced, the 19149 achieves an R10 rating and already has a high demand. Now that it is also known to be a J. C. Penney outfit, demand will certainly increase further.

CONVENTIONAL PACK
62-270 BOX

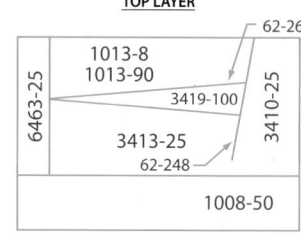

TOP LAYER

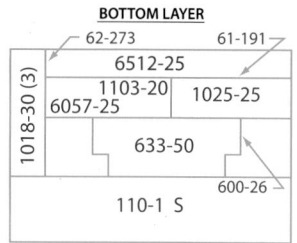

BOTTOM LAYER

61-183 BETWEEN LAYERS

Description: "O27" Promotional Outfit
Specification: "O27" Steam type Freight Outfit
Customer: Allied Stores
Original Amount: 2,000
Factory Order Date: 8/9/1962
Date Issued: 8-16-62
Packaging: R.S.C. Outfit Packing (Units not Boxed), Except 1020 Crossing

Contents: 242-25 Steam Type Locomotive; 1060T-25 Tender; 3357-25 Animated Hobo & Railroad Policeman Car; 3357-27 Box Packed; 6473-25 Rodeo Car; 6076-25 Hopper Car; 6067-25 Caboose; 1013-70 Curved Track (Bundle of 12 - 1013); 1018-40 Straight Track (Bundle of 4 - 1018); 1020-1 90° Crossing; 1026-25 25-Watt Transformer; 1103-20 Envelope Packed; 310-2 Set of (5) Billboards; D62-50 Accessory Catalog; 1123-40 Instruction Sheet; 19107-10 Instruction Sheet

Boxes & Packing: 61-180 Outfit Box; 61-171 Corr. Insert; 61-183 Corr. Insert; 62-248 Corr. Insert (2); 62-249 Corr. Insert; 61-185 Corr. Shipper for (4) (1-4)

19150 (1962)	C6	C7	C8	Rarity
Complete Outfit	240	400	550	R5
Outfit Box no. 61-180	125	190	225	R5

Comments: In 1962, Allied Stores conglomerate purchased three promotional outfits: nos. 19150, 19151 and 19154. Allied owned many retailers across the country, so it likely sold these outfits to any number of customers. However, the 19150 has not yet been linked to a specific store.

This Retailer Promotional Type Ib was Allied's high-end steam-powered purchase. It was led by a common no. 242-25 Steam Type Locomotive. This low-end Scout steamer featured a two-position reversing unit and a headlight, lacked smoke and used a rubber tire as a traction aid. The version with wide running boards was included in this outfit.

The 19150 included two operating cars that were new for 1962. The nos. 3357-25 Animated Hobo & Railroad Policeman

494

Allied Stores purchased the no. 19150 in 1962. The outfit was its high-end steam-powered offering for the year. It included two new operating cars: nos. 3357-25 Animated Hobo & Railroad Policeman Car and 6473-25 Rodeo Car.

Car and 6473-25 Rodeo Car were paired in at least 11 outfits. The 3357-25 provided plenty of excitement as the cop tried to catch the hobo. Since the car was unboxed (hence the "-25" suffix), its peripherals were listed separately on the Factory Order as a no. 3357-27 Box Packed.

All the cars in the 19150 were, with two exceptions, equipped with non-operating Archbar trucks and couplers. The nos. 3357-25 and 6473-25 had operating AAR types.

The no. 61-180 Tan RSC with Black Graphics outfit box was manufactured by United Container Co. and measured 12¾ x 10 x 6¾ inches.

Except for that fact that this outfit included two operating cars, there was nothing special about it. With 2,000 examples manufactured, it can be found with some patience.

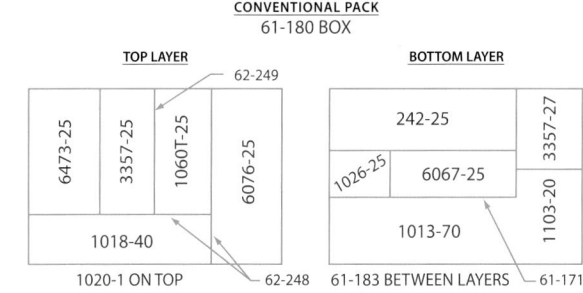

19151
1962

Description: "O27" Promotional Outfit
Specification: "O27" Diesel Switcher Freight Outfit
Customer: Allied Stores
Original Amount: 2,500
Factory Order Date: 8/14/1962
Date Issued: 8-16-62
Packaging: R.S.C. Outfit Packing (Units not Boxed), Except 110

Contents: 633-50 "Santa Fe" - Diesel Switcher; 3413-25 Mercury Capsule Launching Car; 3413-18 Mercury Capsule & Parachute Assem.; 3413-27 Missile; 3619-25 Reconnaissance Copter Car; 3349-25 Turbo Missile Firing Car (Less Missiles); 0349-10 Turbo Missile (2); 6057-25 Caboose; 1013-8 Curved Track (Bundle of 8 - 1013); 1013-90 Curved Track (Bundle of 9 - 1013); 1018-30 Straight Track (Bundle of 3 - 1018) (3); 1008-50 Uncoupling Unit; 110-1 Trestle Set; 1025-25 45-Watt Transformer; 1103-20 Envelope Packed; 310-2 Set of (5) Billboards; D62-50 Accessory Catalog; 1123-40 Instruction Sheet; 3413-8 Instruction Sheet;

3349-8 Instruction Sheet; 3619-8 Instruction Sheet; 1802I Layout Instruction Sheet; 121-10 Instruction Sheet

Boxes & Packing: 62-270 Outfit Box; 600-26 Insert (2); 61-183 Insert; 61-191 Insert; 62-264 Insert (2); 62-273 Insert; 62-271 Shipper for (3) (1-3); 60-405 Box; 600-26 Insert; 61-191 Insert; 61-183 Insert; 62-264 Insert; 62-273 Insert; 62-248 Insert; 60-406 Shipper for (3) (1-3)

19151 (1962)	C6	C7	C8	Rarity
Complete Outfit With no. 62-270 Box	535	900	1,250	R5
Outfit Box no. 62-270	135	200	250	R5
Complete Outfit With no. 60-405 Box	750	1,175	1,575	R9
Outfit Box no. 60-405	350	475	575	R9

The no. 62-270 Outfit Box version of the no. 19151 was Allied Stores' only diesel-powered offering for 1962. This space and military outfit provided plenty of color and fun. Of note was the inclusion of the no. 633-50 Santa Fe Diesel Switcher, which appeared in promotional outfits only.

Comments: In 1962, Allied Stores conglomerate purchased three promotional outfits: nos. 19150, 19151 and 19154. Allied owned many retailers across the country, so it likely sold these outfits to any number of customers. However, the 19151 has not yet been linked to a specific store.

This Retailer Promotional Type Ib was Allied's only diesel-powered purchase in 1962. This space and military outfit was led by a no. 633-50 Santa Fe Diesel Switcher, which was the promotional-only upgrade to the no. 633-25 that Lionel issued earlier in 1962. This low-end switcher came with a traction tire but lacked a horn. However, it was "4 wheel drive equipped", unlike the 633-25, which was driven by only two wheels. The "-50" version is more difficult (3,660 produced) to find than the "-25" (11,900 produced). According to the Lionel Engineering Specification for the 633-50, it was "primarily designed to pull 5 moderate weight cars up a trestle".

The 19151 featured three new-for-1962 operating cars. Of note was the no. 3619-25 Reconnaissance Copter Car, which included a fragile and easily lost no. 0319-100 Helicopter. As part of the manufacturing process, the roof of the 3619-25 was taped shut with a ½-inch piece of Scotch tape. Even examples in C8 condition still have a mark where the tape was applied. This car, like the others in this outfit, was equipped with operating AAR trucks and couplers.

The no. 110-1 Trestle Set in this outfit was used for the elevated pretzel track layout. The no. 1802I Layout Instruction

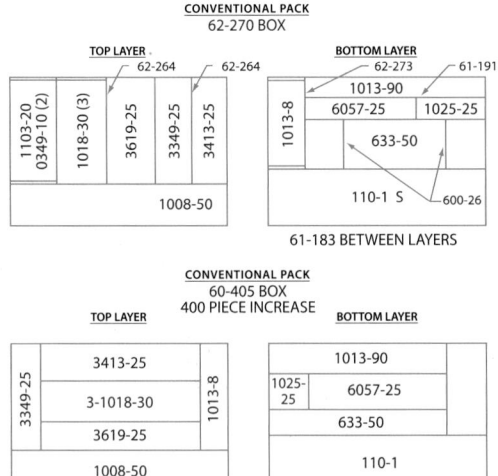

Sheet detailed this track plan.

This outfit was likely a success for Allied, as there was an increase of 400 "pieces" noted. This increase led to there being two Tan RSC with Black Graphics outfit box variations. The first was a no. 62-270 that was manufactured by United Container Co. and measured 15½ x 14 x 6¼ inches. The second was a no. 60-405 that was manufactured by St. Joe Paper Co. - Container Div. and measured 15½ x 14⅛ x 7 inches. It was an overstamped no. X-506NA from 1960.

Empty 62-270 Outfit Boxes do appear from time to time, whereas 60-405s are rare. Finding a complete outfit with the proper 633-50 Santa Fe Diesel Switcher is a challenge.

Description: "O27" Promotional Outfit
Specification: "O27" Diesel Switcher Freight Outfit
Customer/Price: AMC; $19.98
Original Amount: 500
Factory Order Date: 6/25/1962
Date Issued: 6-17-62
Packaging: R.S.C. Outfit Pkg (Units not Boxed), Except 1020 Crossing

Contents: 633-50 "Santa Fe" Diesel Switcher; 6402-25 Flat Car (Less 2 Cable Reels); 40-11 Cable Reels (2); 6630-25 Missile Launching Car (Less Missile); 6650-80 Missile Complete (or 6650-84); 6480-25 Exploding Target Car; 6067-25 Caboose; 1013-8 Curved Track (Bundle of 8 - 1013); 1013-5 Curved Track (Loose) (4); 1018-40 Straight Track (Bundle of 4 - 1018); 1020-1 90° Crossing; 1010-25 35-Watt Transformer; 1103-20 Envelope Packed; 310-2 Set of (5) Billboards; D62-50 Accessory Catalog; 1123-40 Instruction Sheet; 6630-6 Instruction Sheet; 6480-5 Instruction Sheet; 1802B Layout Instruction Sheet; 19152-10 Instruction Sheet

Boxes & Packing: 62-243 Outfit Box; 62-249 Insert; 62-251 Insert; 62-258 Insert; 62-273 Insert; 62-276 Insert; 62-277 Insert; OS-33 Insert; 62-244 Shipper for (4)

19152 (1962)	C6	C7	C8	Rarity
Complete Outfit	600	950	1,275	R9
Outfit Box no. 62-243	350	450	525	R9

Comments: Buying cooperatives, such as AMC (Associated Merchandising Corporation), were large customers of Lionel trains. In 1962, AMC purchased five promotional outfits (nos. 19130 through 19133 and 19152). Each outfit fulfilled a different price point, with the 19152 being the entry-level diesel-powered Retailer Promotional Type Ib offering. It has yet to be linked to an end retailer.

This space and military outfit was led by a no. 633-50 Santa Fe Diesel Switcher, which was the promotional-only upgrade to the no. 633-25 that Lionel issued earlier in 1962. This low-end switcher came with a traction tire but lacked a horn. However, it was "4 wheel drive equipped", unlike the 633-25, which was driven by only two wheels. The "-50" version is more difficult (3,660 produced) to find than the "-25" (11,900 produced). According to the Lionel Engineering Specification for the 633-50, it was "primarily designed to pull 5 moderate weight cars up a trestle".

The nos. 6480-25 Exploding Target Car and 6630-25 Missile Launching Flat Car in this outfit were low-end versions of the nos. 6470-25 and 6650-25, respectively. These cars appeared only in promotional outfits and are harder to find than their high-end counterparts. They, like the other cars in the 19152, were equipped with non-operating Archbar trucks and couplers.

The 19152, like AMC's nos. 19132 and 19133, came with a figure-eight track layout. It was described on the no. 1802B Layout Instruction Sheet dated 6-59.

The no. 62-243 Tan RSC with Black Graphics outfit box measured 12⅛ x 11½ x 6⅜ inches. This was one of three outfits to use the no. 62-276 Insert to hold the 633 Diesel Switcher. This triangle-shaped insert slipped over the ends of the switcher and locked it into place in the outfit box. Even with the outfit packing diagram, it takes some effort to figure out how it works.

The 19152 exceeded AMC's original projections, as the quantity on the Factory Order was increased from 250 to 500. Even so, this is the most difficult of any of the AMC offerings from 1962 to find.

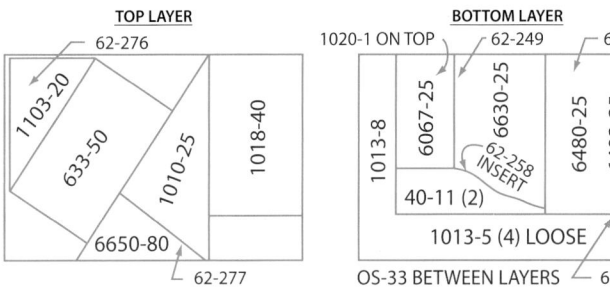

CONVENTIONAL PACK
62-243 BOX

Description: "O27" Promotional Outfit
Specification: "O27" Steam Type Freight Outfit
Original Amount: 450
Factory Order Date: 8/14/1962
Date Issued: 8-16-62
Packaging: R.S.C. Outfit Packing (Units not Boxed), Except 110

Contents: 242-25 Steam Type Locomotive; 1060T-25 Tender; 3309-25 Turbo Missile Firing Car (Less Missiles); 0349-10 Turbo Missile (2); 3470-25 Aerial Target Launching Car; 3470-20 Envelope Packed; 3470-4 Basket; 6076-25 Hopper Car; 6067-25 Caboose; 1013-8 Curved Track (Bundle of 8 - 1013); 1013-90 Curved Track (Bundle of 9 - 1013); 1018-5 Straight Track (Bundle of 5 - 1018) (2); 110-1 Trestle Set; 1010-25 35-Watt Transformer; 1103-20 Envelope Packed; 310-2 Set of (5) Billboards; D62-50 Accessory Catalog; 1123-40 Instruction Sheet; 3309-5 Instruction Sheet; 3470-8 Instruction Sheet; 1802I Layout Instruction Sheet; 120-10 Instruction Sheet

Boxes & Packing: 62-270 Outfit Box; 61-171 Insert; 62-225 Insert; 62-261 Insert; 62-264 Insert; 62-272 Insert; 62-271 Shipper for (3) (1-3)

19153 (1962)	C6	C7	C8	Rarity
Complete Outfit	450	700	965	R9
Outfit Box no. 62-270	275	400	525	R9

Comments: The Lionel Outfit Cost Worksheet originally listed Gamble-Skogmo as the customer for this outfit; it was subsequently crossed out and Claber's (see the entry for no. 19162) was written in. Listing more than one customer name on a Worksheet was common because Lionel was trying to sell certain promotional outfits to many customers.

Nonetheless, Lionel appeared to have been unsuccessful in selling this outfit to a specific customer because the final Factory Order did not list a customer. Also, an example of the no. 19153 with any sort of customer marking has yet to be observed. Therefore, we classify this outfit as a General Release Promotional Type IIb.

This space and military outfit included a no. 242-25 Steam Type Locomotive. A low-end Scout steamer introduced in 1962, it featured a two-position reversing unit and a headlight, lacked smoke and used a rubber tire as a traction aid.

The rolling stock in the 19153 included two new operating cars. The no. 3309-25 Turbo Missile Firing Car (Less Missiles) was a low-end version of a no. 3349-25. The only difference was the 3309-25 was equipped with non-operating Archbar truck and couplers in contrast to the AAR types on the 3349. Both cars were designed to bring down the balloon on a no. 3470-25 Aerial Target Launching Car. Since the 3470 came unboxed, its peripherals were placed loose in the outfit box. This car was equipped with operating AAR trucks and couplers.

The cars in this outfit came equipped with different types of trucks and couplers. The 3309-25 and no. 6076-25 Hopper Car had non-operating Archbar trucks and couplers, and the 3470-25 had operating AAR types. However, the nos. 1060T-25 Tender and 6067-25 Caboose could come with either two Archbar types or one non-operating Archbar and one plain AAR truck and coupler.

The no. 1802I Layout Instruction Sheet was included with instructions on how to assemble the elevated pretzel layout.

The no. 62-270 Tan RSC with Black Graphics outfit box measured 15½ x 14 x 6¼ inches.

The 19153 certainly doesn't stand out amid other promotional outfits from 1962. Its contents were common, and no specific customer was listed for it. All it has going for it is a lower-than-average original quantity produced. That factor leads to its R9 rarity.

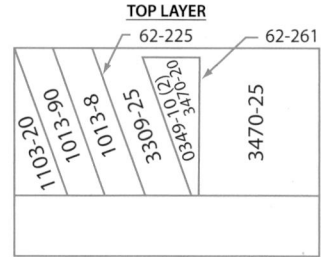

CONVENTIONAL PACK
62-270 BOX

TOP LAYER
62-225 — 62-261

1103-20 | 1013-90 | 1013-8 | 3309-25 | 0349-10 (2) 3470-20 | 3470-25

BOTTOM LAYER
62-264 — 61-171

1018-5 (2) | 6076-25 | 1060T-25 | 1010-25 | 6067-25 | 242-25

110-1 S

62-272 BETWEEN LAYERS

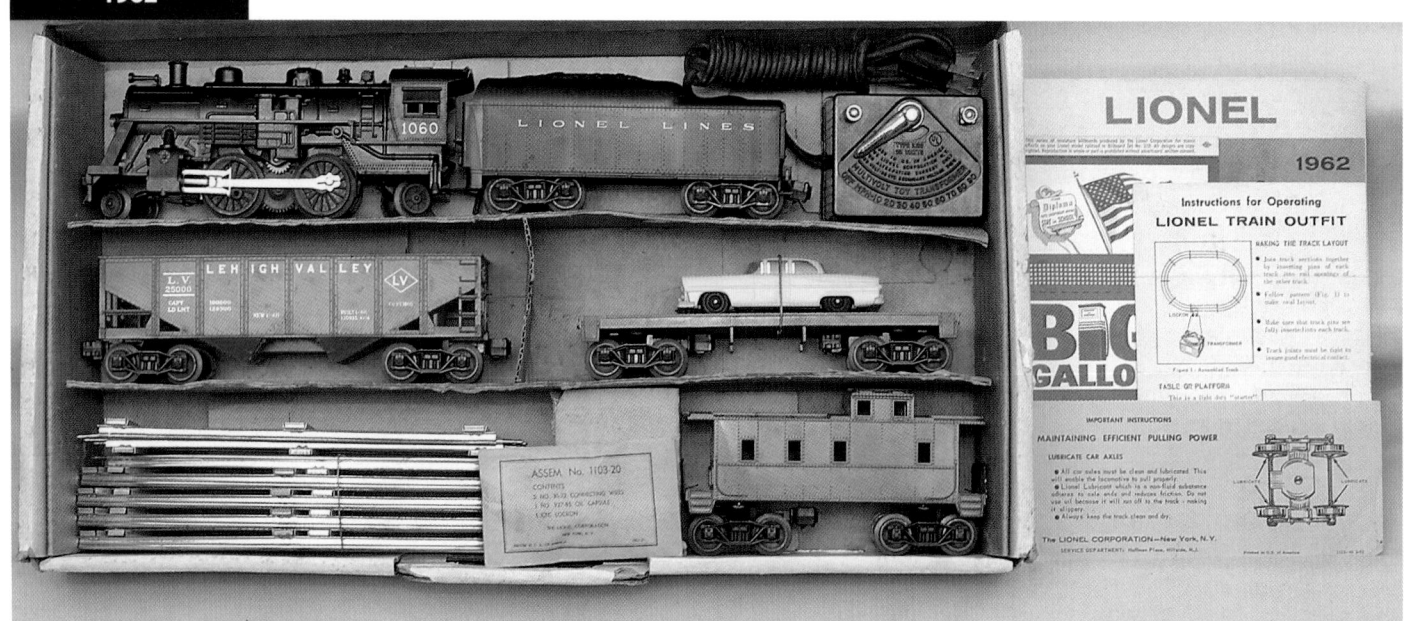

The no. 19154 was Allied's 1962 purchase for its Jordan Marsh department stores. This basic starter outfit included low-end rolling stock. The most notable item was the no. 6406-25 Single Automobile Car and its yellow no. 6406-30 Automobile with gray bumpers.

The no. 62-200 White 4-6-4 Steamer and F3 Hinged Display with Red/Orange and Blue Graphics Type A outfit box was manufactured by United Container. This generic box was used for more than 20 different outfits, each stamped by Lionel with the appropriate outfit number.

Description: "O27" Promotional Outfit
Specification: "O27" Steam Type Freight Outfit
Customer: Allied Stores
Customer: Jordan Marsh
Original Amount: 1,000
Factory Order Date: 6/22/1962
Date Issued: 6-17-62
Packaging: Display Outfit Packing (Units not Boxed)

Contents: 1060-25 Steam Type Locomotive; 1060T-25 Tender; 6406-25 Single Automobile Car (Less Auto); 6406-30 Automobile; 6076-25 Hopper Car - Red; 6067-25 Caboose; 1013-8 Curved

Track (Bundle of 8 - 1013); 1018-10 Straight Track (Loose) (2); 1026-25 25-Watt Transformer; 1103-20 Envelope Packed; 310-2 Set of (5) Billboards; D62-50 Accessory Catalog; 1123-40 Instruction Sheet; 1123-10 Instruction Sheet

Boxes & Packing: 62-200 Outfit Box; 61-101 Corr. Insert; 61-102 Corr. Insert (2); 61-103 Corr. Shipper for (6) (1-6)

19154 (1962)	C6	C7	C8	Rarity
Complete Outfit	225	375	535	R7
Outfit Box no. 62-200	125	225	300	R7

Comments: In 1962, the Allied Stores conglomerate, which owned many retailers across the country, purchased three promotional outfits: nos. 19150, 19151 and 19154. Several pieces of evidence suggested that the 19154 was destined for Allied's Jordan Marsh department stores. The Lionel Outfit Cost Worksheet for this outfit listed "Allied - J.M.". Also, one outfit observed came from its original owner and included add-on track and peripherals with Jordan Marsh price tags.

In addition, Jordan Marsh was listed as the customer on Factory Orders in 1960, 1961, 1963 and 1964. For some reason, Jordan Marsh had its parent company, Allied, purchase on its behalf in 1962. The 19154, a Retailer Promotional Type Ib outfit, would

DISPLAY PACK
62-200 BOX
5-17-62

1060-25	1060T-25	1026-25
6076-25		6406-30 / 6406-25
1018-10 (2) / 1013-8		1103-20 / 6067-25

61-101

61-102

therefore appear to be the follow-up to Jordan Marsh's no. X-681 from 1961.

The 19154 was about as low-end as Lionel could make an outfit in 1962. All its items were carryover, including the no. 1060-25 Steam Type Locomotive that went forward only.

Perhaps the most notable car in this outfit was the no. 6406-25 Single Automobile Car (equipped with non-operating Archbar trucks and couplers like its companions). That's because finding an original, postwar version of its no. 6406-30 Automobile with gray bumpers is becoming a challenge. There are many reproductions and modern-era reissues on the market.

The no. 62-200 White 4-6-4 Steamer and F3 Hinged Display with Red/Orange and Blue Graphics Type A outfit box was manufactured by United Container Co. and measured 21⅝ x 11½ x 3¼ inches.

The bad news is that Lionel lost $0.94 on each of these outfits. The good news for Lionel was that it made only 1,000 of them, so it didn't lose too much.

The no. 19155 in its no. 62-200 Type A Display Box was Merchants Buying Syndicate's (MBS) low-end steam-powered purchase for 1962. This outfit included two new cars for 1962: nos. 3309-25 Turbo Missile Firing Car and 6042-75 Gondola Car (Less 2 Cable Reels).

The no. 19155 came in the common no. 62-200 White 4-6-4 Steamer and F3 Hinged Display with Red/Orange and Blue Graphics Type A outfit box. This generic box was stamped by Lionel with "No. 19155".

Description: "O27" Promotional Outfit
Specification: "O27" Steam Type Freight Outfit
Customer: Arlan's Department Stores
Customer: MBS
Original Amount: 4,500
Factory Order Date: 6/29/1962
Date Issued: Rev 8-16-62
Packaging: Display Outfit Packing (Units not Boxed), Also RSC Pack

Contents: 1060-25 Steam Type Locomotive; 1060T-25 Tender; 3309-25 Turbo Missile Firing Car (Less Missiles); 0349-10 Turbo Missile (2); 6042-75 Gondola Car (Less 2 Cable Reels); 40-11

The no. 19155 with its no. 61-170 Tan RSC with Black Graphics outfit box was created to fulfill some of the many additional orders for this outfit. The contents were the same as the display version; however, this example came with the no. 6057-25 Caboose substitution. It had a price tag for Arlan's Dept. Stores (a customer of MBS in 1962).

Cable Reels (2); 6067-25 Caboose; 1013-8 Curved Track (Bundle of 8 - 1013); 1018-40 Straight Track (Bundle of 4 - 1018); 1026-25 25-Watt Transformer; 1103-20 Envelope Packed; 310-2 Set of (5) Billboards; D62-50 Accessory Catalog; 1123-40 Instruction Sheet; 1123-10 Instruction Sheet; 3309-10 Instruction Sheet

Boxes & Packing: 62-200 Outfit Box; 61-101 Corr. Insert; 61-102 Corr. Insert (2); 61-103 Corr. Shipper for (6) (1-6); 61-170 Box; 61-171 Insert; 61-172 Insert; 62-202 Insert; 61-174 Shipper (1-6)

Alternate For Outfit Contents:
Use 6057-25 for 6067-25 if needed.

19155 (1962)	C6	C7	C8	Rarity
Complete Outfit With no. 62-200 Display Box	180	300	440	R5
Display Outfit Box no. 62-200	90	150	200	R5
Complete Outfit With no. 61-170 RSC Box	190	325	465	R6
RSC Outfit Box no. 61-170	100	175	225	R6

DISPLAY PACK
62-200 BOX
REVISED 8/16/62

1060-25	1060T-25	1026-25	61-101
0349-10 (2) 3309-25		40-11 (2) 6042-75	
1018-40 1013-8		1103-20 6067-25	
		61-102	

CONVENTIONAL PACK
61-170 BOX
BALANCE 1962 PRODUCTION

TOP LAYER

1013-8 1018-40		
(2) 0349-10 1103-20	1060T-25	
3309-25		

BOTTOM LAYER

CORD	1026-25	
1060-25	6067-25	6042-25 (2) 40-11

Comments: In 1962, a buying cooperative known as Merchants Buying Syndicate (MBS) purchased two outfits: nos. 19155 and 19156. This Retailer Promotional Type Ib was its low-end steam-powered outfit; the 19156 was its high-end steam-powered outfit.

The 19155 was a huge success for MBS as original factory orders swelled from 1,300 to 2,600 and finally 4,500 between 6-29-62 and 8-16-62. This increase led to there being both a display

and an RSC outfit version as well as caboose substitutions.

This basic starter outfit included all low-end items, starting with the motive power. The no. 1060-25 Steam Type Locomotive was one of Lionel's low-end steamers from 1960 through 1965.

A transition from Archbar to AAR trucks and couplers began in 1962. For the 19155, all the cars were equipped with non-operating Archbar trucks and couplers. However, the no. 1060T-25 Tender came with one non-operating Archbar and one plain AAR truck and coupler.

When the no. 6067-25 Caboose was replaced by a no. 6057-25 Caboose, the latter was equipped with AAR trucks and couplers. This substitution likely occurred due to the increase in the number of outfits produced. Regardless, examples of the 19155 have been observed with either caboose, and the difference in price between the two versions is minimal.

Perhaps the most interesting characteristic of this outfit was its two types of packaging. Originally this outfit was to be produced

in display packaging only. It appears the increase in orders led to an RSC version also being produced.

The no. 62-200 White 4-6-4 Steamer and F3 Hinged Display with Red/Orange and Blue Graphics Type A outfit box was manufactured by United Container Co. and measured 21⅝ x 11½ x 3¼ inches. The no. 61-170 Tan RSC with Black Graphics outfit box was manufactured by St. Joe Kraft, St. Joe Paper Co. Container Division and measured 11½ x 10¼ x 6¼ inches.

Of the two, the display version is more prevalent. Overall, both are readily available on the market.

Description: "O27" Promotional Outfit
Specification: "O27" Steam Type Freight Outfit
Customer: MBS
Original Amount: 700
Factory Order Date: 6/7/1962
Date Issued: 6-8-62
Packaging: R.S.C. Outfit Packing (Units not Boxed), Except 1020

Contents: 242-25 Steam Type Locomotive; 1060T-25 Tender; 6630-25 Missile Launching Car (Less Missile); 6650-80 Missile Complete (or 6650-84); 6480-25 Exploding Target Car; 6413-25 Mercury Capsule Transport Car; 6413-4 Capsules (2); 6413-10 Envelope Packed; 3410-25 Oper. Helicopter Car (Less Helicopter); 3419-100 Operating Helicopter Complete; 6067-25 Caboose; 1013-82 Curved Track (Bundle of 6 - 1013) (2); 1018-40 Straight Track (Bundle of 4 - 1018); 1018-10 Straight Track (Loose) (4); 1020-1 90° Crossing; 1010-25 35-Watt Transformer; 1103-20 Envelope Packed; 310-2 Set of (5) Billboards; D62-50 Accessory Catalog; 3410-5 Instruction Sheet; 1123-40 Instruction Sheet; 120-10 Instruction Sheet; 6630-6 Instruction Sheet; 6480-5 Instruction Sheet; 1802B Layout Instruction Sheet

Boxes & Packing: 62-243 Outfit Box; 61-171 Corr. Insert; 62-223 Corr. Insert; 62-225 Corr. Insert; 62-248 Corr. Insert (5); 62-244 Shipper for (4) (1-4)

19156 (1962)	C6	C7	C8	Rarity
Complete Outfit	500	835	1,200	R8
Outfit Box no. 62-243	150	300	375	R8

Comments: In 1962, a buying cooperative known as Merchants Buying Syndicate (MBS) purchased two outfits: nos. 19155 and 19156. This Retailer Promotional Type Ib was its high-end steam-powered outfit; the 19155 was its low-end steam-powered outfit.

The 19156 was a success for MBS as original factory orders increased from 500 to 700. It has yet to be linked to any MBS end customer.

This exciting space and military outfit included four operating cars. The commonly paired nos. 6480-25 Exploding Target Car and 6630-25 Missile Launching Car (Less Missile) were low-end versions of the nos. 6470-25 and 6650-25, respectively. These cars

appeared only in promotional outfits and are harder to find than their high-end counterparts.

The no. 6413-25 Mercury Capsule Transport Car was new for 1962. Since this car came unboxed, its associated peripherals (nos. 6413-4 Capsules and 6413-10 Envelope Packed) were placed loose in the outfit box.

A transition from Archbar to AAR trucks and couplers began in 1962. For the 19156, the 6480-25 and 6630-25 were equipped with non-operating Archbar trucks and couplers. The nos. 3410-25 Oper. Helicopter Car (Less Helicopter) and 6413-25 had two operating AAR types. However, the no. 1060T-25 Tender and 6067-25 Caboose could come with either two Archbar types or one non-operating Archbar and one plain AAR truck and coupler.

In 1962, the Production Control File for the no. 3419-100 Operating Helicopter Complete changed from a gray Navy stamped two-piece helicopter body to an unmarked helicopter with a one-piece yellow helicopter body. Although this was Lionel's intended production, many 3419-100 Navy helicopters still appeared on 3410s in 1962.

The appropriate quantity of track was included to make the figure-eight layout. That track plan was outlined on the no. 1802B Layout Instruction Sheet.

The no. 62-243 Tan RSC with Black Graphics outfit box measured 12⅛ x 11½ x 6⅜ inches.

This outfit was produced in smaller quantities than the 19155. That is reflected in its infrequent appearance on the market and its R8 rarity rating.

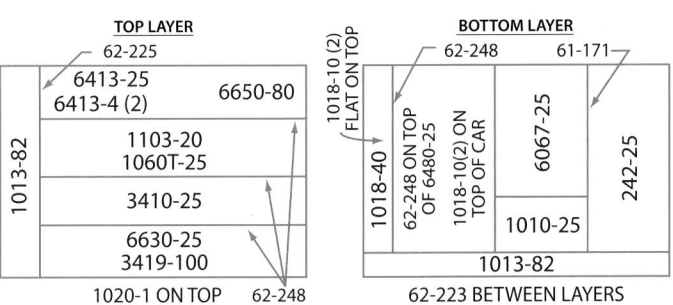

CONVENTIONAL PACK
62-243 BOX

Customer No. On Box: 31-5084
Description: "O27" Promotional Outfit
Specification: "O27" Steam Type Freight Outfit
Customer/No.: Times Square Stores; 31-5084
Original Amount: 1,500
Factory Order Date: 6/29/1962
Date Issued: Rev 8-29-62
Packaging: Display Outfit Packing (Units not Boxed)

Contents: 1060-25 Steam Type Locomotive; 1060T-25 Tender; 3510-25 Satellite Launching Car (Less Satellite); 0333-100 Satellite; 6076-25 Hopper Car; 6120-25 Work Caboose; 1013-8 Curved Track (Bundle of 8 - 1013); 1018-10 Straight Track (Loose) (2); 1026-25 25-Watt Transformer; 1103-20 Envelope Packed; 310-2 Set of (5) Billboards; D62-50 Accessory Catalog; 1123-40 Instruction Sheet; 1123-10 Instruction Sheet; 3510-5 Instruction Sheet

Boxes & Packing: 62-200 Outfit Box; 61-101 Corr. Insert; 61-102 Corr. Insert; 62-249 Corr. Insert; 61-103 Corr. Shipper for (6) (1-6)

Alternate For Outfit Contents:
Customer Stock No. 31-5084 to appear on every carton.

19157 (1962)	C6	C7	C8	Rarity
Complete Outfit	300	525	700	R6
Outfit Box no. 62-200	125	225	275	R6

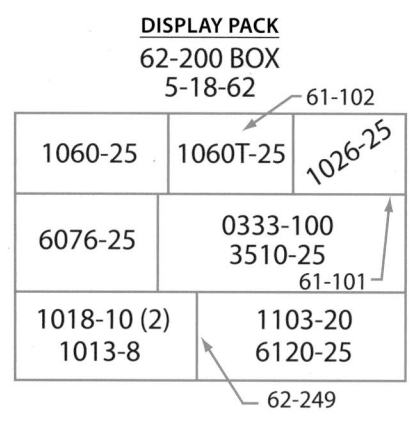

DISPLAY PACK
62-200 BOX
5-18-62

Comments: Discount retailer Times Square Stores was listed as the customer for this 1962 Retailer Promotional Type Ib outfit. This was the last outfit that can be attributed to Time Square Stores.

After purchasing advance catalog outfit no. 1125 in 1961, Times Square Stores followed up with the no. 19157. This outfit was the same as advance catalog no. 11011 from 1962, except that the no. 222P-25 Denver & Rio Grande Alco Diesel Power Unit was swapped for a no. 1060-25 Steam Type Locomotive. This low-end steamer went forward only.

(See the entry for the 11011 from 1962 for a description of the cars included in the 19157.)

The generic no. 62-200 White 4-6-4 Steamer and F3 Hinged Display with Red/Orange and Blue Graphics Type A outfit box was manufactured by United Container Co. and measured 21⅝ x 11½ x 3¼ inches.

Compared to the quantity of 20,000 of the 11011s manufactured, this outfit is a lot more difficult to find.

Description: "O27" Promotional Outfit
Specification: "O27" Steam Type Frt. Outfit
Customer/No./Price: White Auto; 108-95; $15.99
Original Amount: 3,000
Factory Order Date: 6/5/1962
Date Issued: 6-8-62
Packaging: R.S.C Outfit Packing (Units not Boxed), Except 1020 Crossing

Contents: 1060-25 Steam Type Locomotive; 1060T-25 Tender; 6050-50 Swift Savings Bank Car; 6076-25 Hopper Car - Red; 6042-25 Gondola Car (Less 2 Canisters); 6112-5 Canister - Red (2); 6406-25 Single Automobile Car (Less Auto); 6406-30 Automobile; 6067-25 Caboose; 1013-70 Curved Track (Bundle of 12 - 1013); 1018-40 Straight Track (Bundle of 4 - 1018); 1026-25 25-Watt Transformer; 1020-1 90° Crossing; 1103-20 Envelope Packed; 310-2 Set of (5) Billboards; D62-50 Accessory Catalog; 1123-10 Instruction Sheet; 1123-40 Instruction Sheet; 1802B Layout Instruction Sheet

Boxes & Packing: 62-243 Outfit Box; 61-191 Corr. Insert; 62-223 Corr. Insert; 62-225 Corr. Insert; 62-249 Corr. Insert; 62-251 Corr. Insert; 62-258 Corr. Insert; 62-244 Shipper for (4) (1-4)

Alternate For Outfit Contents:
Note: Use 800 - 6050-50 Box Cars; Balance use 6050-150.

19158 (1962)	C6	C7	C8	Rarity
Complete Outfit	250	350	490	R5
Outfit Box no. 62-243	100	125	150	R5

Comments: White Auto purchased two Retailer Promotional Type Ib outfits in 1962. The no. 19158 was its steam-powered outfit purchase, whereas the no. 19159 was its diesel-powered outfit.

An observed price tag listed White Auto's no. 108-95 and a price of $15.99. White made $6.09 on every outfit, but Lionel lost $0.89.

The 19158 was a starter outfit produced in large quantities. It was led by a no. 1060-25 Steam Type Locomotive, which moved only forward. The locomotive included in this outfit was the later version with a small rain shield covering the headlight.

The only items of note in this outfit were the no. 6050-50 Swift Savings Bank Car and its substitution no. 6050-150 Van Camp Savings Bank Car. The "-50" Swift was the harder-to-find version equipped with Archbar trucks and couplers. Both the "-50" Swift and "-150" Van Camp cars are comparably valued, so the substitution does not affect the outfit price. The no. 6406-30 Automobile is missing from many outfits. Finding an original, postwar model with gray bumpers is becoming a challenge. There are many reproductions and modern-era reissues on the market.

All the cars in this outfit were equipped with non-operating Archbar trucks and couplers. The figure-eight track layout was included, and it was outlined on the no. 1802B Layout Instruction Sheet.

The no. 62-243 Tan RSC with Black Graphics outfit box

The no. 19158 was White Auto's steam-powered purchase for 1962. It is shown with the no. 6050-150 Van Camp Savings Bank Car substitution.

White Auto price tags for outfit no. 19158 (White Auto no. 108-95 left) and outfit no. 19159 (White Auto no. 108-105 right) show the retail prices ($15.99 and $29.97, respectively) for these two outfits.

CONVENTIONAL PACK
62-243 BOX

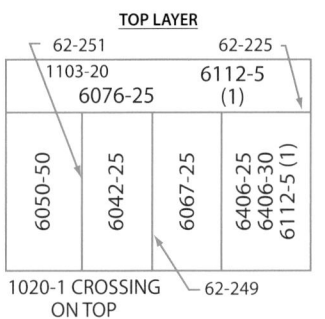

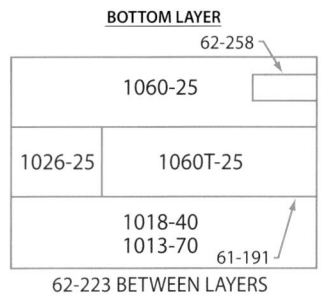

was manufactured by St. Joe Kraft, St. Joe Paper Co. Container Division and measured 12⅛ x 11½ x 6⅜ inches.

Since 3,000 outfits were produced, many examples have survived. As such, this outfit does appear for sale from time to time.

Of note, a Factory Order exists for a no. DX-19158 64 x 30 Inch Display Board. It is unknown if there were any Lionel markings on this board, and one has yet to be identified.

Customer No. On Box: 108-105
Description: "O27" Promotional Outfit
Specification: "O27" Diesel Freight Outfit
Customer/No./Price: White Auto; 108-105; $29.97
Original Amount: 1,200
Factory Order Date: 6/29/1962
Date Issued: Rev. #1 7-27-62
Packaging: R.S.C. Outfit Packing (Units not Boxed), Except 110

Contents: 211P-25 *"Texas Special"* Alco Diesel Power Unit; 211T-25 Motorless Unit; 3309-25 Turbo Missile Firing Car (Less Missiles); 0349-10 Turbo Missile (2); 6076-25 Hopper Car; 6042-75 Gondola Car (Less 2 Cable Reels); 40-11 Cable Reels (2); 6502-25 Girder Transport Car (Less Girder); 6502-3 Girder Bridge; 6050-50 Swift Savings Bank Car; 6067-25 Caboose;

1013-8 Curved Track (Bundle of 8 - 1013); 1013-90 Curved Track (Bundle of 9 - 1013); 1018-5 Straight Track (Bundle of 5 - 1018) (2); 1025-25 45-Watt Transformer; 1103-20 Envelope Packed; 110-1 Trestle Set; 310-2 Set of (5) Billboards; D62-50 Accessory Catalog; 1123-40 Instruction Sheet; 3309-10 Instruction Sheet; 1802I Layout Instruction Sheet; 19145-10 Instruction Sheet; 211-6 Instruction Sheet

Boxes & Packing: 62-270 Outfit Box; 61-171 Insert; 62-224 Insert; 62-245 Insert (2); 62-248 Insert (2); 62-264 Insert; 62-272 Insert; 62-271 Shipper for (3) (1-3)

The no. 19159 was White Auto's diesel-powered purchase for 1962. It is shown with the no. 6050-150 Van Camp Savings Bank Car substitution. The $29.97 sale price netted a profit of $11.87 for White Auto.

Alternate For Outfit Contents:

Note: Customer Stock No. 108-105 to appear on outfit box & shipper; Use 6050-150 for 6050-50 if needed.

19159 (1962)	C6	C7	C8	Rarity
Complete Outfit	375	650	925	R7
Outfit Box no. 62-270	150	225	275	R7

Comments: White Auto purchased two Retailer Promotional Type Ib outfits in 1962. The no. 19159 was its diesel-powered outfit purchase, whereas the no. 19158 was its steam-powered outfit.

The 19159 was a decent-sized outfit with six pieces of rolling stock. It could be called the "red" outfit because six of the eight items came in that color.

A no. 211P-25 *Texas Special* Alco Diesel Power Unit led this outfit. It included a two-position reversing unit, an open pilot, a headlight and two-axle Magne-Traction.

As with the 19158, the no. 6050-50 Swift Savings Bank Car was listed on the Factory Order but was freely substituted out for a no. 6050-150 Van Camp Savings Bank Car. The "-50" Swift was the harder-to-find version equipped with Archbar trucks and couplers. Both the "-50" Swift and "-150" Van Camp cars are comparably valued, so the substitution does not affect the outfit price. This was the first of three 1962 promotional outfits to come with a no. 6502-25 Girder Transport Car (Less Girder). This black flat car included an orange no. 6502-3 Girder Bridge.

The no. 3309-25 Turbo Missile Firing Car (Less Missiles) seemed out of place in this otherwise common freight outfit. It, like the other cars, was equipped with non-operating Archbar trucks and couplers.

The no. 1802I Layout Instruction Sheet was included with instructions on how to assemble the elevated pretzel layout.

The no. 62-270 Tan RSC with Black Graphics outfit box was manufactured by United Container Co. and measured 15½ x 14 x 6¼ inches.

Lionel produced fewer of the 19159 than it did the 19158, yet the former appears on the market almost as often. Interestingly, the number that White Auto gave this outfit (no. 108-105) was used in 1963 for promotional outfit no. 19219, which, except for having updated contents and lacking a no. 3309-25, was identical to the 19159.

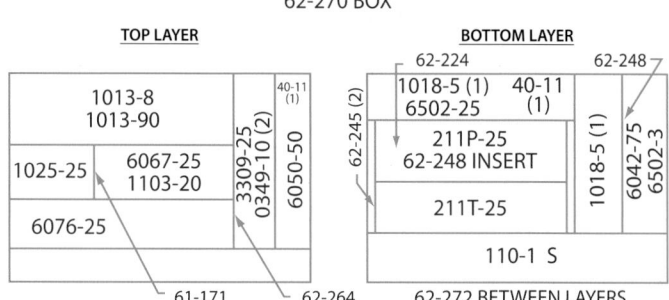

CONVENTIONAL PACK
62-270 BOX

Town & Country Distributors' no. 19160 was its lower-end steam-powered purchase for 1962. It was an exciting and fun space and military outfit. With only 150 manufactured, it is difficult to find. This example is the only one observed to date.

Description: "O27" Promotional Outfit
Specification: "O27" Steam Type Freight Outfit
Customer: Town & Country
Original Amount: 150
Factory Order Date: 8/14/1962
Date Issued: 8-16-62
Packaging: R.S.C. Outfit Packing (Units not Boxed), Except 110

Contents: 242-25 Steam Type Locomotive; 1060T-25 Tender; 3309-25 Turbo Missile Firing Car (Less Missiles); 0349-10 Turbo Missile (2); 3470-25 Aerial Target Launching Car; 3470-20 Envelope Packed; 3470-4 Basket; 3619-25 Reconnaissance Copter Car; 6067-25 Caboose; 1013-8 Curved Track (Bundle of 8 - 1013); 1013-90 Curved Track (Bundle of 9 - 1013); 1018-5 Straight Track (Bundle of 5 - 1018) (2); 1010-25 35-Watt Transformer; 110-1 Trestle Set; 1103-20 Envelope Packed; 310-2 Set of (5) Billboards; D62-50 Accessory Catalog; 120-10 Instruction Sheet; 1123-40 Instruction Sheet; 3309-5 Instruction Sheet; 3470-8 Instruction Sheet; 1802I Layout Instruction Sheet

Boxes & Packing: 62-270 Outfit Box; 61-171 Insert; 61-173 Insert; 62-248 Insert (2); 62-264 Insert; 62-272 Insert; 62-271 Shipper for (3) (1-3)

19160 (1962)	C6	C7	C8	Rarity
Complete Outfit	1,100	1,500	1,850	R10
Outfit Box no. 62-270	850	1,100	1,250	R10

Comments: Town & Country Distributors was a retailer that owned stores in Pennsylvania. It was listed on two Factory Orders in 1962: nos. 19160 and 19161. Both outfits were led by Scout steam locomotives, with the 19160 being the lower-end purchase.

The 19160 was a Retailer Promotional Type Ib outfit. This space and military outfit included a no. 242-25 Steam Type Locomotive. This low-end steamer, introduced in 1962, featured a two-position reversing unit and a headlight, lacked smoke and used a rubber tire as a traction aid.

The rolling stock in this outfit included three new operating cars. The no. 3309-25 Turbo Missile Firing Car (Less Missiles) was a low-end version of a no. 3349-25. It was designed to bring down the balloon on a no. 3470-25 Aerial Target Launching Car. Since the 3470-25 came unboxed, its peripherals were placed loose in the outfit box.

The no. 3619-25 Reconnaissance Copter Car included a fragile and easily lost no. 0319-100 Helicopter. As part of the manufacturing process, the roof of the 3619-25 was taped shut with a ½-inch piece of Scotch tape. Even examples in C8 condition still have a mark where the tape was applied.

All but two of the cars in this outfit came equipped with late non-operating Archbar trucks and couplers. The 3470-25 and 3619-25 had middle operating AAR types.

As with many 1962 outfits, a no. 110-1 Trestle Set was included with the 19160. The trestles and the appropriate quantities of track were used to build the elevated pretzel track layout. That track plan was outlined on the no. 1802I Layout Instruction Sheet.

The no. 62-270 Tan RSC with Black Graphics outfit box was manufactured by United Container Co. and measured 15½ x 14 x 6¼ inches.

This outfit is desirable for three reasons. First, it was a space and military outfit with colorful, fun higher-end cars. Next, it is one of only two outfits produced for Town & Country Distributors. Most importantly, only 150 were manufactured. These factors all lead to it easily achieving an R10 rarity.

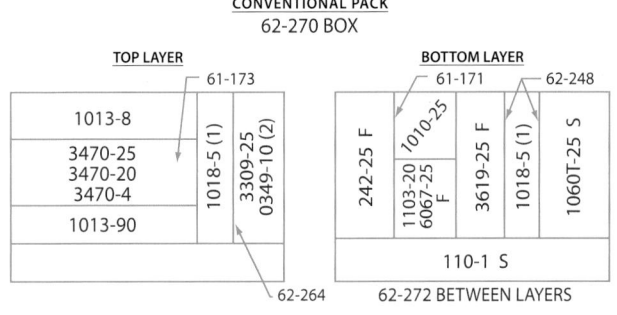

CONVENTIONAL PACK
62-270 BOX

Description: "O27" Promotional Outfit
Specification: "O27" Steam Type Freight Outfit With Smoke & Whistle
Customer: Town & Country
Original Amount: 150
Factory Order Date: 9/28/1962
Date Issued: 10-2-62
Packaging: R.S.C. Outfit Packing (Units not Boxed), Except 1020-1

Contents: 233-25 Steam Type Locomotive With Smoke; 234W-25 Whistle Tender; 3413-25 Mercury Capsule Launching Car; 6512-25 Cherry Picker Car; 6413-25 Mercury Capsule Transport Car; 6413-4 Capsules (2); 6413-10 Envelope Packed; 6463-25 Rocket Fuel Car; 6057-25 Caboose; 1013-70 Curved Track (Bundle of 12 - 1013); 1018-30 Straight Track (Bundle of 3 - 1018); 1008-50 Uncoupling Unit; 1073-25 60-Watt Transformer; 147-25 Horn & Whistle Controller; 2333-140 Flashlight Cell; 1020-1 90° Crossing; 909-20 Smoke Fluid; 1645-15 Envelope Packed; 310-2 Set of (5) Billboards; D62-50 Accessory Catalog; 1123-40 Instruction Sheet; 233-11 Instruction Sheet; 3413-8 Instruction Sheet; 1802B Layout Instruction Sheet; 1646-10 Instruction Sheet; 6512-19 Instruction Sheet

Boxes & Packing: 61-250 Outfit Box; 61-181 Insert; 61-182 Insert; 62-223 Insert; 62-225 Insert; 62-249 Insert; 61-251 Shipper for (4) (1-4)

19161 (1962)	C6	C7	C8	Rarity
Complete Outfit	1,300	1,785	2,275	R10
Outfit Box no. 61-250	875	1,125	1,275	R10

Comments: Town & Country Distributors was a retailer that owned stores in Pennsylvania. It was listed on two Factory Orders in 1962: nos. 19160 and 19161. Both outfits were led by Scout steam locomotives, with the 19161 being the high-end purchase.

The 19161 was a Retailer Promotional Type Ia outfit. This space and military outfit was led by a no. 233-25 Steam Type Locomotive with Smoke as well as a no. 234W-25 Whistle Tender. The 233-25 was paired with a 234W-25 instead of a no. 233W Whistle Tender because the latter was being phased out.

The peripherals that normally went with a boxed no. 233-1 were placed loose in the outfit box or put in a no. 1645-15 Envelope Packed. These included the nos. 909-20 Smoke Fluid, CTC-1 Lockon, 927-85 Oiler and 233-11 Instruction Sheet.

All the rolling stock in the 19161 represented higher-end offerings. These included the nos. 3413-25 Mercury Capsule Launching Car, 6413-25 Mercury Capsule Transport Car, 6463-25 Rocket Fuel Car and 6512-25 Cherry Picker Car (all new for 1962). These and the other items in this outfit (except for the 234W-25) were equipped with operating AAR trucks and couplers. In 1962, the 234Ws included one non-operating and one plain Archbar truck and coupler.

When a no. 147-25 Horn & Whistle Controller was included in this outfit, Lionel provided a no. 2333-140 Flashlight Cell loose in the outfit box. This practice lasted until 1963.

The Type I 1645-15 Envelope Packed included the three wires that were required to hook up the 147-25 as well as the outfit. This is a difficult-to-find packed envelope.

The no. 61-250 Corrugated Box was an Orange RSC with Black Graphics and measured 13 x 12 x 7 inches.

The 19161 is desirable for three reasons. First, it was a space and military outfit with colorful, fun higher-end cars. Next, it is one of only two outfits produced for Town & Country Distributors. Most importantly, only 150 were manufactured. These factors all lead to it easily achieving an R10 rarity.

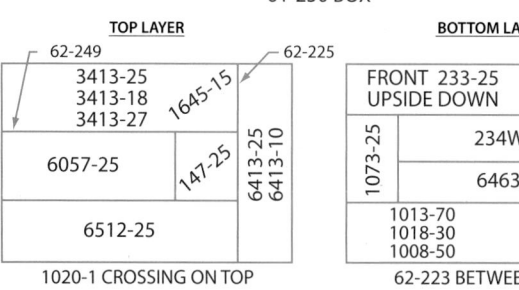

CONVENTIONAL PACK
61-250 BOX

Description: "O27" Promotional Outfit
Specification: "O27" Steam Type Freight Outfit
Customer: Claber's
Original Amount: 250
Factory Order Date: 9/12/1962
Date Issued: 9-13-62
Packaging: R.S.C. Outfit Packing (Units not Boxed)

Contents: 1060-25 Steam Type Locomotive; 1060T-25 Tender; 3510-25 Satellite Launching Car (Less Satellite); 0333-100 Satellite; 6076-25 Hopper Car; 6067-25 Caboose; 1013-8 Curved Track (Bundle of 8 - 1013); 1018-10 Straight Track (Loose) (2); 1026-25 25-Watt Transformer; 1103-20 Envelope Packed; 310-2 Set of (5) Billboards; D62-50 Accessory Catalog; 1123-40 Instruction Sheet; 3510-5 Instruction Sheet; 1123-10 Instruction Sheet

Boxes & Packing: 61-170 Outfit Box; 61-171 Insert; 61-172 Insert; 61-173 Insert; 62-257 Insert; 61-175 Shipper for (4) (1-4)

19162 (1962)	C6	C7	C8	Rarity
Complete Outfit	600	950	1,375	R9
Outfit Box no. 61-170	300	500	700	R9

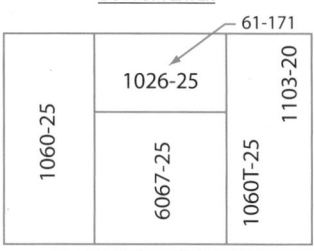

CONVENTIONAL PACK
61-170 BOX

Comments: This Retailer Promotional Type Ib outfit was purchased by Claber's Distributing Company in 1962. Lionel lost $0.71 on every outfit that it sold to Claber's

The no. 19162 was a low-end starter outfit led by a no. 1060-25 Steam Type Locomotive. The cars in this outfit were, with one exception, commonly available items from previous years. The only item of note was the no. 3510-25 Satellite Launching Car (Less Satellite). The 3510-25 included a red frame and "Lionel" stamped on the side; otherwise, its mechanism was an exact duplicate of

the no. 3509-25 Satellite Launching Car. This new-for-1962 car appeared only in 10 promotional outfits. It was equipped with non-operating Archbar trucks and couplers, as were the other cars in this outfit.

The common no. 61-170 Tan RSC with Black Graphics outfit box was used for the 19162. It measured 11½ x 10¼ x 6¼ inches.

Other than the 3510-25, there are no standout qualities to this outfit. What gives it interest is the small quantity that Lionel produced.

Description: "O27" Promotional Outfit
Specification: "O27" Steam Type Freight Outfit
Customer: Gimbels
Original Amount: 600
Factory Order Date: 9/20/1962
Date Issued: 9-21-62
Packaging: R.S.C. Outfit Packing (Units not Boxed)

Contents: 242-25 Steam Type Locomotive; 1060T-25 Tender; 3619-25 Reconnaissance Copter Car; 6062-25 Gondola Car - Black (Less 3 Cable Reels); 40-11 Cable Reels (3); 6476-25 Hopper Car - Red; 6057-25 Caboose; 1013-8 Curved Track (Bundle of 8 - 1013); 1018-10 Straight Track (Loose); 1008-50 Uncoupling Unit; 1010-25 35-Watt Transformer; 1103-20 Envelope Packed; 310-2 Set of (5) Billboards; D62-50 Accessory Catalog; 1123-40 Instruction Sheet; 3619-8 Instruction Sheet; 1641-10 Instruction Sheet

Boxes & Packing: 61-180 Outfit Box; 61-181 Insert; 61-182 Insert; 61-183 Insert; 61-184 Insert; 61-185 Shipper for (4) (1-4)

19163 (1962)	C6	C7	C8	Rarity
Complete Outfit	375	725	865	R8
Outfit Box no. 61-180	200	350	450	R8

Comments: In 1962, Gimbels department stores purchased three Retailer Promotional outfits: nos. 19163, 19164 and 19165. Outfit 19163 was its Type Ia steam locomotive outfit. This entry-level freight outfit was the follow-up to the no. X-631 from 1961.

The 19163 was led by a no. 242-25 Steam Type Freight Locomotive. This low-end Scout steamer featured a two-position reversing unit and a headlight, lacked smoke and used a rubber tire as a traction aid. The version with wide running boards was

included in this outfit.

The new-for-1962 no. 3619-25 Reconnaissance Copter Car with its no. 0319-100 Helicopter was the most notable item in this outfit. Original, unbroken helicopters are not easy to find. As part of the manufacturing process, the roof of the 3619-25 was taped shut with a ½-inch piece of Scotch tape. Even examples in C8 condition still have a mark where the tape was applied.

All the cars, except for the no. 1060T-25 Tender, were equipped with operating AAR trucks and couplers. The 1060T-25 generally was equipped with non-operating Archbar trucks and couplers, but for this outfit it probably came with one non-operating Archbar and one plain AAR truck and coupler.

The no. 61-180 Tan RSC with Black Graphics outfit box measured 12¾ x 10 x 6¾ inches.

Gimbels greatly reduced its total Lionel outfit orders from 2,600 in 1961 to 1,050 in 1962. More than one half of the 1,050 from 1962 was accounted for by the 19163, whose original quantity of 350 was increased to 600. As a result, the 19163 and the other outfits from 1962 are more difficult to find than those from the previous year.

CONVENTIONAL PACK
61-180 BOX

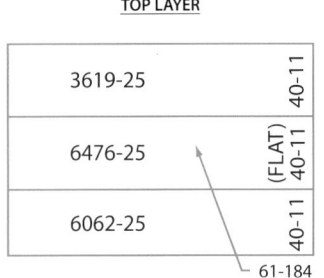
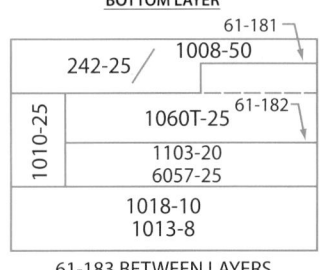

TOP LAYER

BOTTOM LAYER

61-183 BETWEEN LAYERS

Description: "O27" Promotional Outfit
Specification: "O27" Diesel Freight Outfit
Customer: Gimbels
Original Amount: 350
Factory Order Date: 9/21/1962
Date Issued: Rev 9-21-62
Packaging: R.S.C. Outfit Packing (Units not Boxed), Except 110

Contents: 231P-25 Alco Diesel Power Car - "Rock Island"; 3349-25 Turbo Missile Firing Car (Less Missiles); 0349-10 Turbo Missile (2); 3470-25 Aerial Target Launching Car; 3470-20 Envelope Packed; 3470-4 Basket; 6463-25 Rocket Fuel Car; 6413-25 Mercury Capsule Transport Car (Less Capsules); 6413-4

Capsules (2); 6413-10 Envelope Packed; 6057-25 Caboose; 1013-8 Curved Track (Bundle of 8 - 1013); 1013-90 Curved Track (Bundle of 9 - 1013); 1018-30 Straight Track (Bundle of 3 - 1018) (3); 1008-50 Uncoupling Unit; 1025-25 45-Watt Transformer; 110-1 Trestle Set; 1103-20 Envelope Packed; 310-2 Set of (5) Billboards; D62-50 Accessory Catalog; 1802I Layout Instruction Sheet; 1123-40 Instruction Sheet; 3349-8 Instruction Sheet; 3470-8 Instruction Sheet; 211-6 Instruction Sheet; 122-10 Instruction Sheet

Boxes & Packing: 62-270 Outfit Box; 62-224 Insert; 62-245 Insert (2); 62-248 Insert (2); 62-261 Insert; 62-264 Insert; 62-272 Insert; 62-271 Shipper for (3) (1-3)

19164 (1962)	C6	C7	C8	Rarity
Complete Outfit	675	1,050	1,425	R9
Outfit Box no. 62-270	325	475	575	R9

Comments: In 1962, Gimbels department stores purchased three Retailer Promotional outfits: nos. 19163, 19164 and 19165. Outfit 19164 was a Type Ia diesel locomotive outfit. This space and military outfit was the follow-up to the no. X-632 from 1961.

The 19164 was led by a no. 231P-25 Rock Island Alco Diesel Power Car equipped with a two-position reversing unit, a headlight and two-axle Magne-Traction.

The rolling stock, all new for 1962, represented some of Lionel's better offerings. The no. 3349-25 Turbo Missile Firing Car (Less Missiles) was frequently paired with a no. 3470-25 Aerial Target Launching Car. According to the Lionel catalog, it was designed to "bring down the balloon" on that car. Since both the 3470-25 and 6413-25 Mercury Capsule Transport Car (Less Capsules) were unboxed, their peripherals were placed loose in the outfit box. These and the other cars were equipped with operating AAR trucks and couplers.

The elevated pretzel track layout was part of at least 50 different outfits including the 19164. It was described on the no. 1802I Layout Instruction Sheet.

The no. 62-270 Tan RSC with Black Graphics outfit box measured 15½ x 14 x 6¼ inches.

Gimbels greatly reduced its total Lionel outfit orders from 2,600 in 1961 to 1,050 in 1962. One third of the 1,050 from 1962 was accounted for by the 19164, whose original quantity of 175 was doubled to 350. As a result, the 19164 and the other outfits from 1962 are more difficult to find than those from the previous year.

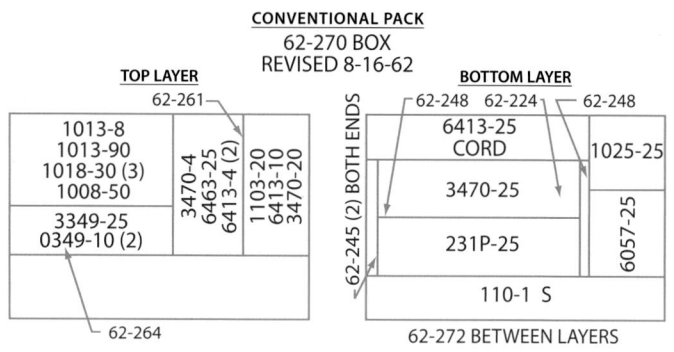

19165

1962

Description: "O27" Promotional Outfit
Specification: "O27" Steam Type Freight Outfit With Smoke & Whistle
Customer: Gimbels
Original Amount: 100
Factory Order Date: 9/21/1962
Date Issued: 9-21-62
Packaging: R.S.C. Outfit Packing (Units not Boxed), Except 1020

Contents: 233-25 Steam Type Locomotive with Smoke; 234W-25 Whistle Tender; 3357-25 Animated Hobo & Railroad Policeman Car; 3357-27 Box Packed; 6473-25 Rodeo Car; 3362-25 Helium Tank Unloading Car; 6501-25 Jet Motor Boat Car; 6501-2 Boat Assem.; 6501-17 Fuel Pellets Packed; 6057-25 Caboose; 1013-70 Curved Track (Bundle of 12 - 1013); 1018-30 Straight Track (Bundle of 3 - 1018); 6029-25 Uncoupling Track Unit; 1073-25 60-Watt Transformer; 147-25 Horn & Whistle Controller; 2333-140 Flashlight Cell; 909-20 Smoke Fluid; 1020-1 90° Crossing; 90-40 Envelope; 310-2 Set of (5) Billboards; D62-50 Accessory Catalog; 233-11 Instruction Sheet; 1123-40 Instruction Sheet; 3357-8 Instruction Sheet; 3362-15 Instruction Sheet; 6501-14 Instruction Sheet; 9656-10 Instruction Sheet

Boxes & Packing: 61-250 Outfit Box; 61-181 Insert; 61-182 Insert; 62-223 Insert; 62-251 Insert; 62-264 Insert; 61-251 Shipper for (4) (1-4)

19165 (1962)	C6	C7	C8	Rarity
Complete Outfit	1,125	1,615	2,000	R10
Outfit Box no. 61-250	800	1,100	1,250	R10

Comments: In 1962, Gimbels department stores purchased three Retailer Promotional outfits: nos. 19163, 19164 and 19165. Outfit 19165 was its high-end Type Ia steam locomotive outfit. This freight outfit was the follow-up to the no. X-633 from 1961.

The 19165 was in the minority of 1962 outfits in that it didn't include any space and military items. It was led by a no. 233-25 Steam Type Locomotive with Smoke that pulled a no. 234W-25 Whistle Tender. The 233-25 was paired with a 234W-25 instead of a no. 233W Whistle Tender because the latter was being phased out.

The peripherals that normally went with a boxed no. 233-1 were placed loose in the outfit box or put in a no. 90-40 Envelope Packed. These included the nos. 909-20 Smoke Fluid, CTC-1 Lockon, 927-60 Tube of Oil, 927-65 Tube of Grease and 233-11 Instruction Sheet.

The nos. 3357-25 Animated Hobo & Railroad Policeman Car and 6473-25 Rodeo Car were paired in at least 11 outfits. The 3357-25 provided plenty of excitement as the cop tried to catch the hobo. Since the car was unboxed, the no. 3357-27 Box Packed was listed separately on the Factory Order and placed loose in the outfit box. Interestingly, the outfit packing diagram listed a no. 3357-23. This is consistent with actual outfit observations in 1962, which included a 3357-27 with "3357-23" printed on its box. The "3357-23" was actually the number of the box and appears to have been mistakenly printed as the final assembly number on some early examples of the 3357-27 Box Packed.

Except for the nos. 3362-25 Helium Tank Unloading Car and 6057-25 Caboose, the cars in the 19165 were new for 1962. They were equipped with operating AAR trucks and couplers. However, in 1962 the 234Ws came with one non-operating and one plain Archbar truck and coupler.

When a no. 147-25 Horn & Whistle Controller was included in an outfit, Lionel provided a no. 2333-140 Flashlight Cell loose in the outfit box. This practice lasted until 1963.

The no. 61-250 Corrugated Box was an Orange RSC with Black Graphics outfit box. It was manufactured by Kraft Corrugated Containers and measured 13 x 12 x 7 inches.

Gimbels greatly reduced its total Lionel outfit orders from 2,600 in 1961 to 1,050 in 1962. Less than one tenth of the 1,050 from 1962 was accounted for by the 100 units ordered of the 19165. As a result, the 19165 has an R10 rarity rating.

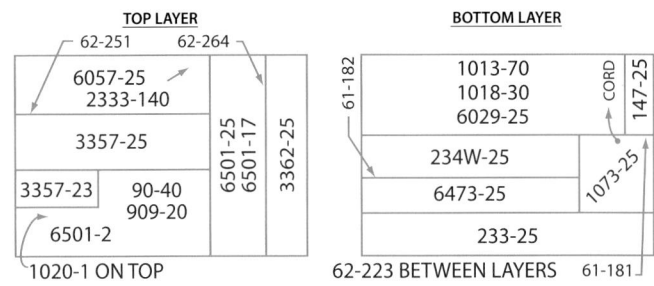

CONVENTIONAL PACK
61-250 BOX

TOP LAYER

| 62-251 | 62-264 |
| 6057-25 |
| 2333-140 |
| 3357-25 |
| 3357-23 | 90-40 |
| | 909-20 |
| 6501-2 |

6501-25
6501-17
3362-25

1020-1 ON TOP

BOTTOM LAYER

61-182
1013-70
1018-30
6029-25
234W-25
6473-25
233-25

CORD
147-25
1073-25

62-223 BETWEEN LAYERS   61-181

The no. 19166 was Arkwright's only outfit purchase in 1962. It included the frequently paired nos. 3413-25 Mercury Capsule Launching Car and 6512-25 Cherry Picker Car. The 19166 was one of more than 50 outfits to include the no. 110-1 Trestle Set needed to build the elevated pretzel track layout.

Description: "O27" Promotional Outfit
Specification: "O27" Steam Type Freight Outfit With Smoke
Customer: Arkwright
Original Amount: 700
Factory Order Date: 10/1/1962
Date Issued: 10-2-62
Packaging: R.S.C. Outfit Packing (Units not Boxed), Except 110

Contents: 236-25 Steam Type Locomotive with Smoke; 1060T-25 Tender; 6463-25 Rocket Fuel Car; 3413-25 Mercury Capsule Launching Car; 6512-25 Cherry Picker Car; 6057-25 Caboose; 1013-8 Curved Track (Bundle of 8 - 1013); 1013-90 Curved Track (Bundle of 9 - 1013); 1008-50 Uncoupling Unit; 1018-30 Straight Track (Bundle of 3 - 1018) (3); 1010-25 35-Watt Transformer; 110-1 Trestle Set; 909-20 Smoke Fluid; 1103-20 Envelope Packed; 310-2 Set of (5) Billboards; D62-50 Accessory Catalog; 1123-40 Instruction Sheet; 236-11 Instruction Sheet; 3413-8 Instruction Sheet; 1802I Layout Instruction Sheet; 122-10 Instruction Sheet; 6512-19 Instruction Sheet

Boxes & Packing: 62-270 Outfit Box; 61-171 Insert; 61-173 Insert; 62-248 Insert (2); 62-272 Insert; 62-271 Shipper for (3) (1-3)

19166 (1962)	C6	C7	C8	Rarity
Complete Outfit	625	800	1,100	R8
Outfit Box no. 62-270	250	325	400	R8

Comments: Outfit no. 19166 was Arkwright's (a large buying organization) promotional outfit purchase for 1962. This Retailer Promotional Type Ia outfit was likely resold to Arkwright's many small customers, although no connections have been made.

The 19166 was a space and military outfit led by a no. 236-25 Steam Type Locomotive with Smoke. This was one of Lionel's high-end Scout steamers and included a two-position reversing unit, a headlight and Magne-Traction.

The new-for-1962 rolling stock included the frequently paired nos. 3413-25 Mercury Capsule Launching Car and 6512-25 Cherry Picker Car. They were designed to work together, with the

6512-25 pretending to load an astronaut into the waiting Mercury capsule. Also new was the no. 6463-25 Rocket Fuel Car.

All the cars in this outfit, except for the no. 1060T-25 Tender, were equipped with middle operating AAR trucks and couplers. The 1060T-25 came with non-operating Archbar trucks and couplers.

As with many 1962 outfits, a no. 110-1 Trestle Set was included with the 19166. The trestles and the appropriate quantities of track were used to build the elevated pretzel track layout that was outlined on the no. 1802I Layout Instruction Sheet.

The no. 62-270 Tan RSC with Black Graphics outfit box was manufactured by United Container Co. and measured 15½ x 14 x 6¼ inches.

This outfit was more successful than predicted because the Factory Order indicated an increase from 500 to 700 units. Even

with this increase, the final quantity did not represent a large number of outfits produced. As such, the 19166 does not appear too often.

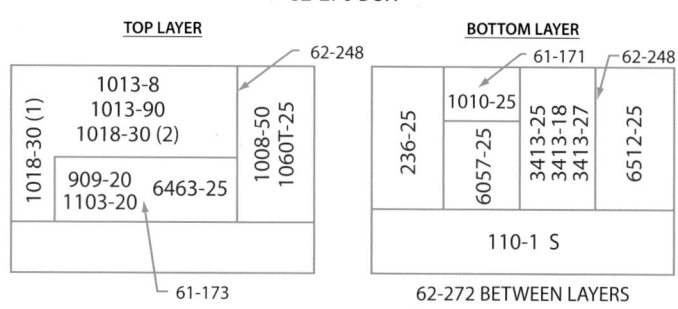

CONVENTIONAL PACK
62-270 BOX

TOP LAYER	BOTTOM LAYER

Top Layer: 1018-30 (1); 1013-8, 1013-90, 1018-30 (2); 62-248; 1008-50, 1060T-25; 909-20, 1103-20, 6463-25; 61-173

Bottom Layer: 236-25; 1010-25, 6057-25; 61-171; 3413-25, 3413-18, 3413-27; 62-248, 6512-25; 110-1 S; 62-272 BETWEEN LAYERS

Benny's purchased outfit no. 19167 as its entry-level steam offering for 1962. This starter outfit was packaged in four different versions of the White 4-6-4 Steamer and F3 Hinged Display with Red/Orange and Blue Graphics outfit box. This is the no. 61-396 version.

The no. 61-396 version of outfit no. 19167 was an overstickered no. X-627 from 1961. Lionel was depleting its inventory of leftover outfit boxes from 1961. The 19167 marked the final appearance of each of the four outfit boxes listed.

Description: "O27" Promotional Outfit
Specification: "O27" Steam Type Freight Outfit
Customer: Benny's
Original Amount: 600

Factory Order Date: 9/28/1962
Date Issued: 10-2-62
Packaging: Display Outfit Packing (Units not Boxed)

Contents: 1060-25 Steam Type Locomotive; 1060T-25 Tender; 3357-25 Animated Hobo & Railroad Policeman Car; 3357-27 Box Packed; 6042-75 Gondola Car (Less 2 Cable Reels); 40-11 Cable Reels (2); 6076-25 Hopper Car - Red; 6067-25 Caboose; 1013-8 Curved Track (Bundle of 8 - 1013); 1018-10 Straight Track (Loose) (2); 1026-25 25-Watt Transformer; 1103-20 Envelope Packed; 310-2 Set of (5) Billboards; D62-50 Accessory Catalog; 1123-40 Instruction Sheet; 1123-10 Instruction Sheet

Boxes & Packing: 61-396 Display Outfit Box W/Stickers - Amount 200; 61-436 Display Outfit Box W/Stickers - Amount 200; 61-429 Display Outfit Box W/Stickers - Amount 175; 61-431 Outfit Box W/Stickers - Amount 50; 61-391 Insert; 61-392 Insert; 61-393 Insert; 61-394 Insert; 61-395 Shipper for (6) (1-6)

19167 (1962)	C6	C7	C8	Rarity
Complete Outfit With no. 61-396 Box	500	800	1,100	R9
Outfit Box no. 61-396	400	600	800	R9
Complete Outfit With no. 61-436 Box	500	800	1,100	R9
Outfit Box no. 61-436	400	600	800	R9
Complete Outfit With no. 61-429 Box	600	900	1,200	R10
Outfit Box no. 61-429	500	700	900	R10
Complete Outfit With no. 61-431 Box	750	1,200	1,500	R10
Outfit Box no. 61-431	650	1,000	1,200	R10

Comments: Discount retailer Benny's was listed as the customer for two outfits in 1962: the nos. 19167 and 19168. Both outfits were led by steam locomotives. The 19167, a Retailer Promotional Type Ib, was the less impressive of the two.

This starter outfit was led by the very common no. 1060-25 Steam Type Locomotive. This was Lionel's low-end, forward-only steam offering in 1962; its sole feature of note was a headlight.

The only piece of rolling stock in this outfit worthy of attention was the Type IIb no. 3357-25 Animated Hobo & Railroad Policeman Car (new for 1962). The 3357-25 provided plenty of excitement as the cop tried to catch the hobo. Since this car came unboxed (hence the "-25" suffix), its peripherals were listed separately on the Factory Order as a no. 3357-27 Box Packed. It was equipped with middle operating AAR trucks and couplers.

All the other cars in the 19167 came with non-operating Archbar types.

Four different versions of the White 4-6-4 Steamer and F3 Hinged Display with Red/Orange and Blue Graphics Type A outfit box were used for this outfit:

- The no. 61-396, which was manufactured by UCC (United Container Co.) and measured 22⅝ x 14¾ x 3¼ inches. It was an overstickered no. X-627 from 1961.
- The no. 61-436, which measured 22½ x 14½ x 3⅛ inches. It was an overstickered no. X-710 from 1961.
- The no. 61-429, which was manufactured by United Container Co. and measured 22½ x 14½ x 3¼ inches. It was an overstickered no. X-687 from 1961.
- The no. 61-431, which was manufactured by United Container Co. and measured 22½ x 15 x 3⅛ inches. It was an overstickered no. X-704 from 1961.

These four boxes lead to four variations of this outfit, each of which has a separate rarity and price. The easiest way to identify the different outfit boxes is by gently prying up the side flaps to reveal the box number. (See the section on Outfit Boxes and Inserts for more information in identifying boxes.)

DISPLAY PACK
61-396, 61-436, 61-429 OR 61-431 BOX
5 STICKERS PER BOX
REVISED 8-28-62

1060-25		1060T-25	
40-11 (2) 6076-25	1103-20	6042-75	
3357-25	3357-27	6067-25	
1013-8 1018-10 (2)			1026-25

Of the four variations, the 61-431 Display Outfit Box (overstickered X-704) is the most difficult to find. Collecting all four versions is a real challenge.

Description: "O27" Promotional Outfit
Specification: "O27" Steam Type Freight Outfit
Customer: Benny's
Original Amount: 650
Factory Order Date: 10/1/1962
Date Issued: 10-2-62
Packaging: R.S.C. Outfit Packing (Units not Boxed), Except 1020

Contents: 242-25 Steam Type Locomotive; 1060T-25 Tender; 3619-25 Reconnaissance Copter Car; 3413-25 Mercury Capsule Launching Car; 3349-25 Turbo Missile Firing Car (Less Missiles); 0349-10 Turbo Missile (2); 6057-25 Caboose; 1013-70 Curved Track (Bundle of 12 - 1013); 1018-30 Straight Track (Bundle of 3 - 1018); 1008-50 Uncoupling Unit; 1010-25 35-Watt Transformer; 1020-1 90° Crossing; 1103-20 Envelope Packed; 310-2 Set of (5) Billboards; D62-50 Accessory Catalog; 1123-40 Instruction Sheet; 3619-8 Instruction Sheet; 3413-8 Instruction Sheet; 3349-8 Instruction Sheet; 1802B Layout Instruction Sheet; 1641-10 Instruction Sheet

Boxes & Packing: 62-243 Outfit Box; 61-171 Insert; 61-173 Insert; 62-223 Insert; 62-225 Insert; 62-244 Shipper for (4) (1-4)

19168 (1962)	C6	C7	C8	Rarity
Complete Outfit	500	750	1,075	R8
Outfit Box no. 62-243	200	300	400	R8

Comments: Discount retailer Benny's was listed as the customer for two outfits in 1962: the nos. 19167 and 19168. Both outfits were led by steam locomotives. The 19168, a space and military outfit, was the more impressive of the two.

This outfit is interesting for two reasons. First, the original quantity on the Factory Order was 75 units. Compared to its original forecast, this outfit was a huge success, as the numbers were increased to 650. Second, more that one of these outfits has been observed with Simpsons-Sears markings and labels. Perhaps Lionel sold this outfit to both Benny's and Simpsons-Sears, although an example has yet to be observed in any Simpsons-Sears catalog. Still, this could explain the big jump in the quantity produced. In either case, since only one name is on the Factory Order, this outfit is classified as a Retailer Promotional Type Ia outfit.

The 19168 included three new operating cars for 1962. Of note was the no. 3619-25 Reconnaissance Copter Car, which included a fragile and easily lost no. 0319-100 Helicopter. As part

The no. 19168 was the last of two outfits purchased by discount retailer Benny's in 1962. It was Benny's high-end offering and came with three new space and military operating cars and the figure-eight track layout. Interestingly, this example also had Simpsons-Sears labels (not shown) on the outfit box. Other 19168s have been observed with Simpsons-Sears markings.

of the manufacturing process, the roof of the 3619-25 was taped shut with a ½-inch piece of Scotch tape. Even examples in C8 condition still have a mark where the tape was applied.

All the cars in this outfit, except for the no. 1060T-25 Tender, were equipped with operating AAR trucks and couplers. The 1060T-25 was normally equipped with non-operating Archbar trucks and couplers, but for this outfit it probably came with one non-operating Archbar and one plain AAR truck and coupler.

The appropriate quantity of track was included to make the figure-eight layout. That track plan was outlined on the no. 1802B Layout Instruction Sheet.

The no. 62-243 Tan RSC with Black Graphics outfit box was manufactured by St. Joe Kraft, St. Joe Paper Co. Container Division and measured 12⅛ x 11½ x 6⅜ inches.

Even with only 650 made, this outfit often appears.

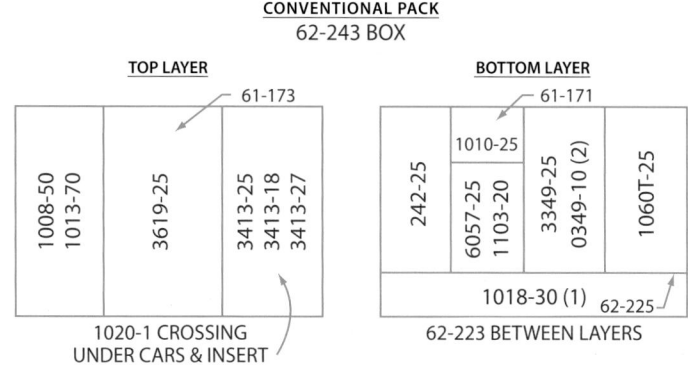

CONVENTIONAL PACK
62-243 BOX

TOP LAYER

61-173

1008-50 / 1013-70 | 3619-25 | 3413-25 / 3413-18 / 3413-27

1020-1 CROSSING UNDER CARS & INSERT

BOTTOM LAYER

61-171

242-25 | 6057-25 / 1103-20 | 1010-25 / 3349-25 / 0349-10 (2) | 1060T-25

1018-30 (1)

62-225

62-223 BETWEEN LAYERS

Description: "O27" Promotional Outfit
Specification: "O27" Steam Type Freight Outfit
Customer: Federal
Original Amount: 1,000
Factory Order Date: 8/14/1962
Date Issued: 8-16-62
Packaging: R.S.C. Outfit Packing (Units not Boxed), Except 110

Contents: 242-25 Steam Type Locomotive; 1060T-25 Tender; 6042-25 Gondola Car (Less 2 Canisters); 6112-5 Canister - Red (2); 6076-25 Hopper Car; 6502-25 Girder Transport Car (Less Girder); 6502-3 Girder Bridge; 6067-25 Caboose; 1013-8 Curved Track (Bundle of 8 - 1013); 1013-90 Curved Track (Bundle of 9 - 1013); 1018-5 Straight Track (Bundle of 5 - 1018) (2); 1010-

25 35-Watt Transformer; 110-1 Trestle Set; 1103-20 Envelope Packed; 310-2 Set of (5) Billboards; D62-50 Accessory Catalog; 1123-40 Instruction Sheet; 120-10 Instruction Sheet; 1802I Layout Instruction Sheet

Boxes & Packing: 62-270 Outfit Box; 61-171 Insert; 62-225 Insert; 62-262 Insert; 62-264 Insert; 62-272 Insert; 62-271 Shipper for (3) (1-3)

19169 (1962)	C6	C7	C8	Rarity
Complete Outfit	275	425	610	R7
Outfit Box no. 62-270	175	250	315	R7

Comments: Federal Wholesale Toy Company purchased this Retailer Promotional Type Ib outfit in 1962. A distributor of toys, Federal likely sold this outfit to many of its customers. However, a link to a specific end customer has yet to be made.

A basic starter outfit, the no. 19169 was led by a no. 242-25 Steam Type Freight Locomotive. This low-end Scout steamer featured a two-position reversing unit and a headlight, lacked smoke and used a rubber tire as a traction aid. The version with wide running boards was included in this outfit.

The rolling stock was all low-end. The 19169 was the last of three 1962 promotional outfits to feature a no. 6502-25 Girder Transport Car (Less Girder). This black flat car included an orange no. 6502-3 Girder Bridge. All the rolling stock was equipped with non-operating Archbar trucks and couplers.

The no. 1802I Layout Instruction Sheet detailed the elevated pretzel track plan. It was uncommon for this track layout to be included in an outfit with such low-end components.

The no. 62-270 Tan RSC with Black Graphics outfit box measured 15½ x 14 x 6¼ inches.

This outfit was likely a huge success for Federal because the number ordered was increased twice. The originally quantity of 500 units grew to 600 and finally 1,000. Even with these increases, the outfit seldom is seen.

Of note, a Factory Order exists for a no. D-19169 54 x 48 Inch Display Board. It is unknown if there were any Lionel markings on this board. Unfortunately, one has yet to be identified.

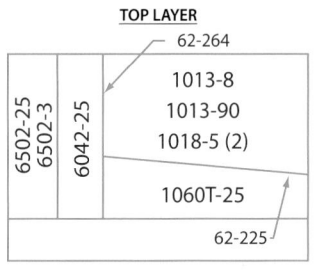
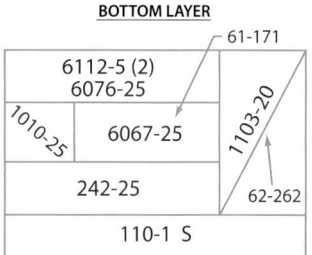

CONVENTIONAL PACK
62-270 BOX

Description: "O27" Promotional Outfit
Specification: "O27" Steam Type Freight Outfit
Customer: Johnson Dewalt
Original Amount: 1,500
Factory Order Date: 9/12/1962
Date Issued: 9-12-62
Packaging: Display Outfit Packing, Colored Inserts (Units not Boxed)

Contents: 1060-25 Steam Type Locomotive; 1060T-25 Tender; 3510-25 Satellite Launching Car (Less Satellite); 0333-100 Satellite; 6042-25 Gondola Car (Less 2 Canisters); 6112-5 Canister - Red (2); 6076-25 Hopper Car; 6067-25 Caboose; 1013-8 Curved Track (Bundle of 8 - 1013); 1018-10 Straight Track (Loose) (2); 1026-25 25-Watt Transformer; 1103-20 Envelope Packed; 310-2 Set of (5) Billboards; D62-50 Accessory Catalog; 1123-40 Instruction Sheet; 1123-10 Instruction Sheet; 3510-5 Instruction Sheet

Boxes & Packing: 61-140 Display Outfit Box; 61-141 Insert; 61-142 Insert; 61-143 Insert; 61-144 Insert; 61-145 Shipper for (4) (1-4)

19170 (1962)	C6	C7	C8	Rarity
Complete Outfit	325	500	700	R6
Outfit Box no. 61-140	150	225	275	R6

19170
1962

Comments: This was the first outfit to list Johnson Dewalt as a customer on a Factory Order. Johnson Dewalt operated as a manufacturer's representative to the premium and incentive industry. This Retailer Promotional Type Ib outfit was its only outfit purchase for 1962.

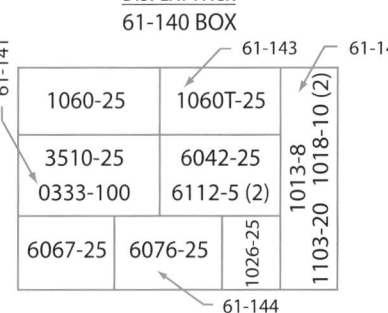

DISPLAY PACK
61-140 BOX

The no. 19170 was identical to the no. 19162, except that it added a no. 6042-25 Gondola Car (Less 2 Canisters) and was packed in a display outfit box.

(See the entry for outfit 19162 from 1962 for a description of the cars included in the 19170.)

The no. 61-140 Orange, White and Gray O27 Hinged Display with 4-6-2 Steam Display Graphics Type A outfit box was manufactured by United Container Co. and measured 26¼ x 12¼ x 3¾ inches.

With 1,500 units originally produced, the 19170 achieves an R6 rarity.

Description: "O27" Promotional Outfit
Specification: "O27" Steam Type Freight Outfit
Customer: Peoples Credit Jewellers
Original Amount: 1,000
Factory Order Date: 8/13/1962
Date Issued: 8-16-62
Packaging: R.S.C. Outfit Packing (Units not Boxed), Except 1020, 953, 984

Contents: 242-25 Steam Type Locomotive; 1060T-25 Tender; 3309-25 Turbo Missile Firing Car (Less Missiles); 0349-10 Turbo Missile (2); 6050-150 Stokely Van Camp Savings Bank Car;

19171
1962

6042-75 Gondola Car (Less 2 Cable Reels); 40-11 Cable Reels (2); 6067-25 Caboose; 1013-70 Curved Track (Bundle of 12 - 1013); 1018-40 Straight Track (Bundle of 4 - 1018); 1010-25 35-Watt Transformer; 1020-1 90° Crossing; 953-1 Figure Set; 984-1 Railroad Set; 1103-20 Envelope Packed; 310-2 Set of (5) Billboards; D62-50 Accessory Catalog; 1123-40 Instruction Sheet; 19171-10 Instruction Sheet; 3309-5 Instruction Sheet

Boxes & Packing: 61-250 Outfit Box; 61-172 Insert; 62-223 Insert; 62-225 Insert; 62-248 Insert; 62-249 Insert; 62-254 Insert; 61-251 Shipper for (4) (1-4)

19171 (1962)	C6	C7	C8	Rarity
Complete Outfit	575	885	1,450	R8
Outfit Box no. 61-250	200	275	350	R8

Comments: Canadian jeweler and retailer Peoples Credit Jewellers purchased this Retailer Promotional Type Ib outfit in 1962. The no. 19171 was the only outfit to list Peoples as a customer.

The 19171 was very similar to outfit no. 19146 in that it included two Plasticville items and almost the same rolling stock. Lionel would often use inexpensive Plasticville items to embellish otherwise bland starter outfits. The nos. 953-1 Figure Set and 984-1 Railroad Set are the two items that are most difficult to find when trying to complete this outfit. Their boxes were made of a thin cardstock that was easily torn or ripped. The instruction sheets and original, complete Plasticville pieces can be difficult to uncover.

All the rolling stock in this outfit was low-end, with the exception of the no. 3309-25 Turbo Missile Firing Car (Less Missiles). It, like the other cars, was equipped with non-operating Archbar trucks and couplers.

This outfit introduced the no. 19171-10 Instruction Sheet. Because this sheet included a figure-eight track diagram, a no. 1802B Layout Instruction Sheet was not needed.

The no. 61-250 Orange RSC with Black Graphics outfit box measured 13 x 12 x 7 inches.

The inclusion of two Plasticville items makes the 19171 a somewhat desirable outfit. Its infrequent appearance in the market leads to an R8 rarity level.

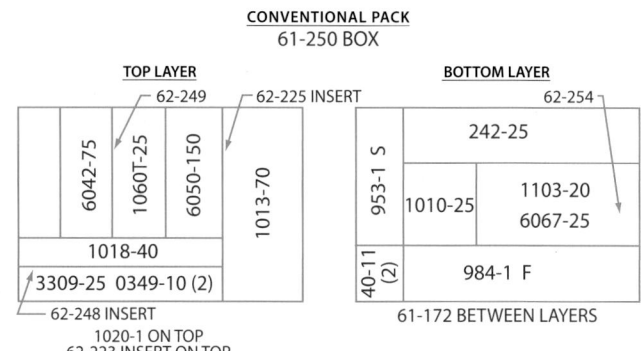

CONVENTIONAL PACK
61-250 BOX

19172
1962

This was the third year for Maritz's no. 1486 (Lionel no. 19172). It was first issued in 1960 as the no. X-802 and then in 1961 as the no. X-683. Due to updates in Lionel's product offerings, the 19172 evolved from the X-802 and X-683. The 19172 shown includes the no. 6416-1 Boat Transport Car substitution.

Customer No. On Box: 1486
Description: "O27" Promotional Outfit
Specification: "O27" Diesel Freight Outfit With Horn
Customer/No.: Maritz; 1486
Original Amount: 450
Factory Order Date: 8/7/1962
Date Issued: 8-7-62
Packaging: R.S.C. Outfit Packing (Units Boxed)

Contents: 218P-1 Alco Diesel Power Unit W/Horn - "Santa Fe"; 6812-1 Track Maintenance Car; 6343-1 Barrel Ramp Car; 6736-1 Hopper Car - "Mackinac Mac"; 6817-1 Flat Car - Red - with Motor Scraper; 6437-1 Illuminated Cupola Caboose; 1013-8 Curved Track (Bundle of 8 - 1013); 1018-30 Straight Track (Bundle of 3 - 1018); 6029-25 Remote Control Uncoupling Track; 1063-25 75-Watt Transformer; 90-30 Envelope Packed; 310-2 Set of (5) Billboards; D62-50 Accessory Catalog; 1123-40 Instruction Sheet; 1650-10 Instruction Sheet

Boxes & Packing: 60-490 Outfit Box; 60-494 Shipper for (4) (1-4)

Alternate For Outfit Contents: Important Note: Sub. 223P-1 for 218P-1 in 150 sets; Use inventory of 100 - 6817-1 then sub. 6416-1; Customer Stock No. 1486.

19172 (1962)	C6	C7	C8	Rarity
Complete Outfit As Listed	1,000	1,475	2,000	R9
Complete Outfit With no. 223P-1 Substitution	1,045	1,555	2,160	R9
Complete Outfit With no. 6416-1 Substitution	745	1,160	1,600	R9
Complete Outfit With nos. 223P-1 And 6416-1 Substitutions	790	1,240	1,760	R9
Outfit Box no. 60-490	275	400	525	R9

Comments: Maritz, a well-known marketing incentive firm, purchased this Retailer Promotional Type Ia outfit in 1962. Incentive marketing firms were known to carry the same outfit for more than one year. Maritz began a four-year run with the nos. X-802 from 1960, X-683 from 1961 and 19172 from 1962; it finished with the no. 19266 from 1963. All four outfits carried Maritz's no. 1486.

Lionel's product life-cycles didn't always span the same years as a customer's outfits. As such, there are differences in all four of the outfits linked with Maritz based on currently available items. (See the entries for outfits X-802, X-683 and 19266 for a full description of the components included.) The X-802 shares only a locomotive with the other outfits, though their other components are very similar.

In comparing the X-683 to the 19172, the no. 6357-1 Illuminated Caboose used in the former outfit was no longer available in 1962 and the no. 6530-1 Fire Prevention Car was depleted in catalog outfit no. 13068 in early 1962. Therefore the

19172 included the nos. 6437-1 Illuminated Cupola Caboose and 6736-1 Mackinac Mac Hopper Car instead.

Lionel was also digging out the last of its inventory of nos. 6817-1 Flat Car with Motor Scraper and 6812-1 Track Maintenance Car; both made their final appearance in this outfit. The nos. 6343-1 Barrel Ramp Car and 6736-1 Hopper Car were also near their last appearance here.

Lionel did its best to make the remainder of this outfit as close as possible to the X-683, but at least two more substitutions were required. They affect the price of this outfit, as listed in the pricing table.

All the cars in the 19172 were equipped with early AAR trucks and couplers, except for the 6437-1 Caboose. It had one middle operating AAR and one plain AAR truck and coupler.

The 6736-1 and 6817-1 were packaged in Orange Perforated boxes. All the other cars came in Orange Picture boxes.

The 19172 came packed in a no. 60-490 Tan RSC with Black Graphics outfit box manufactured by St. Joe Paper Co. - Container Div. It measured 14½ x 11 x 6 inches with "60-490" printed on the bottom and "10 11 12" printed as part of the box manufacturer's certificate. It was a no. X-541NA outfit box from 1960 that had that number crossed out on one side and "No. 19172" and "1486" stamped on the other side.

As with the three other versions of Maritz's 1486, these outfits were produced in low quantities and are very difficult to find.

CONVENTIONAL PACK
60-490 BOX

TOP LAYER		BOTTOM LAYER	
6817-1 OR 6416-1 } F	6437-1 F	218P-1 F	
6343-1 F		6736-1 S	
1018-30 BELOW 1013-8 TOP		1063-25	6029-25
			6812-1 F

Description: "O27" Promotional Outfit
Specification: "O27" Steam Type Freight Outfit
Customer: Play-More
Original Amount: 5,772
Factory Order Date: 8/7/1962
Date Issued: 8-7-62
Packaging: Display Outfit Packing (Units not Boxed)

Contents: 1060-25 Steam Type Locomotive; 1060T-25 Tender; 6405-25 Single Van Flat Car (Less Van); 6405-150 Van; 6042-25X Gondola Car - (Without Canisters); 6067-25 Caboose; 1013-8 Curved Track (Bundle of 8 - 1013); 1018-10 Straight Track (Loose) (2); 1026-25 25-Watt Transformer; 1103-20 Envelope Packed; 310-2 Set of (5) Billboards; D62-50 Accessory Catalog; 1123-10 Instruction Sheet; 1123-40 Instruction Sheet

Boxes & Packing: 62-200 Display Outfit Box; 61-101 Insert; 61-102 Insert; 62-201 Insert; 61-103 Shipper for (6) (1-6)

Alternate For Outfit Contents:
Note: 6042-25X - Gondola Car without Canisters; Hold 250 - 6405-25 for Outfit 19186; Sub. 6406-25 for 6405-25 - Amt. - 250.

19173 (1962)	C6	C7	C8	Rarity
Complete Outfit	150	240	350	R4
Outfit Box no. 62-200	75	100	125	R4

Comments: Play-More, Inc. was a wholesaler and distributor that purchased this Retailer Promotional Type Ib outfit in 1962. This was the only time that Play-More appeared on a Factory Order.

The no. 19173 was the least profitable outfit for Lionel in 1962. The 19173 Lionel Outfit Cost Worksheet lists Lionel's selling price as $7.50 and cost as $9.19. Thus a $1.69 (22.5 percent) loss was realized on each outfit. Unfortunately for Lionel, it produced 5,772 of these outfits, leading to a large loss for the company.

The 19173 was a low-end starter outfit that was led by a no. 1060-25 Steam Type Locomotive. This was Lionel's low-end, forward-only steam offering in 1962; its sole feature of note was a headlight. The locomotive included in this outfit was the later version with a small rain shield covering the headlight.

The Factory Order instructed employees to save 250 of the no. 6405-25 Single Van Flat Car for outfit no. 19186 from 1962 by

In 1962, Play-More, Inc. purchased the no. 19173, a Retailer Promotional Type Ib outfit. This basic starter outfit included a no. 6405-25 Single Van Flat Car (Less Van) and its no. 6405-150 Van.

The no. 19173 came in the common no. 62-200 White 4-6-4 Steamer and F3 Hinged Display with Red/Orange and Blue Graphics Type A outfit box. This generic box was stamped by Lionel with "No. 19173".

swapping them out for a no. 6406-25 Single Automobile Car (Less Auto). This substitution likely was not necessary because Lionel still had 750 of the 6405s available in 1963 for outfit no. 19228. The pricing for the 19173 was scarcely affected by this change.

The 19173 was the only outfit to list a no. 6042-25X Gondola Car (Without Canisters). There was nothing special about this car other than the suffix assigned. In 1963, Lionel officially numbered

it a no. 6042-250 Gondola Car (Without Load).

The no. 6405-25 Single Van Flat Car (Less Van) was equipped with middle operating AAR trucks and couplers. All the other cars in this outfit had non-operating Archbar trucks and couplers.

The generic no. 62-200 White 4-6-4 Steamer and F3 Hinged Display with Red/Orange and Blue Graphics Type A outfit box was manufactured by United Container Co. and measured 21⅝ x 11½ x 3¼ inches.

DISPLAY PACK
62-200 BOX

INSERT 62-201		
1060-25	1060T-25	1026-25
6042-25X / 1103-20	6405-150 / 6405-25	
1018-10 (2) / 1013-8	INSERT 61-102	6067-25
INSERT 61-101		

The 19173 is a commonly available promotional outfit. Be aware, however, that a Factory Order exists for a no. D19173 Special Display for this outfit. The order stated to "Make Base 1" x 4" x 4"" and "Paint Base & Mount Merchandise & Pack". A tiny quantity of 50 of the D19173s was ordered, which probably explains why an example has yet to be identified.

Description: "O27" Promotional Outfit
Specification: "O27" Steam Type Freight Outfit
Customer: Davidson's Detroit
Original Amount: 200
Factory Order Date: 10/3/1963
Date Issued: 10-3-63
Date Req'd: 9-27-63
Packaging: RSC (Units Loose)

Contents: 1060-25 Steam Type Locomotive; 1061T-25 Tender; 6042-250 Gondola Car - Blue; 3309-25 Turbo Missile Firing Car (Less Missiles); 0349-10 Turbo Missile (2); 6167-25 Caboose; 1013-8 Curved Track (Bundle of 8 - 1013); 1018-10 Straight Track (Loose) (2); 1026-25 25-Watt Transformer; 1103-20 Envelope Packed; 310-62 Set of (3) Billboards; D63-50 Accessory Catalog; 1-62 Parts Order Form; 1-63 Warranty Card; 1123-40 Instruction

Sheet; 19272-10 Instruction Sheet; 3309-5 Instruction Sheet

Boxes & Packing: 61-170 Outfit Box; 61-171 Corr. Insert; 61-173 Corr. Insert; 62-255 Corr. Insert (2); 61-174 Shipper for (6) (1-6); 63-383 Box; 61-173 Insert; 62-254 Insert; 63-384 Shipper (1-4)

19173-500 (1963)	C6	C7	C8	Rarity
Complete Outfit With Either Outfit Box	450	710	1,000	R10
Outfit Box nos. 61-170 Or 63-383	350	550	750	R10

Comments: This was the only Retailer Promotional Type Ia outfit purchased by Michigan retailer Davidson's Detroit. The no. 19173-500 shared a similar base number as the no. 19173 from 1962 because it was derived from that outfit. The Lionel Outfit Cost Worksheet for the 19173 includes notes from 9/23/63 showing the genesis of the "-500".

Both the 19173 and 19173-500 were starter outfits that included Lionel's lower-end offerings. The no. 1060-25 Steam Type

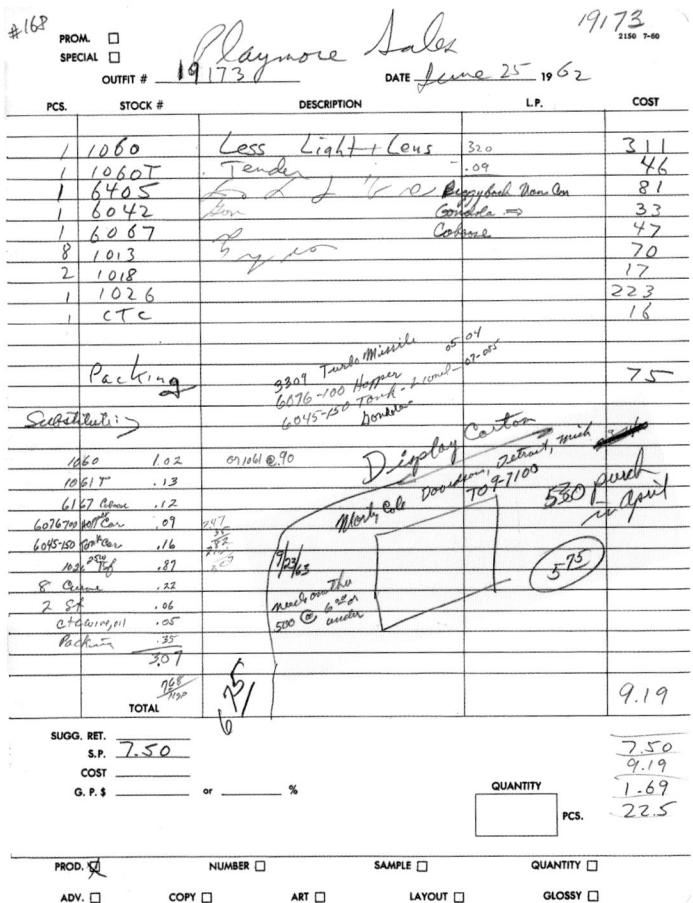

CONVENTIONAL PACK
63-383 BOX
9-30-63

TOP LAYER

1018-10 (2) 1013-8	
61-173	
0349-10 (2)	1061T-25
6042-250	

BOTTOM LAYER

1060-25	
62-254	
6167-25	1026-25
3309-25	

2 CATALOGS BETWEEN LAYERS

CONVENTIONAL PACK
61-170 BOX
REVISED 10-1-63

TOP LAYER

1018-10 (2) 1013-8	
61-173	
0349-10 (2)	1061T-25
6042-250	
62-255	

BOTTOM LAYER

61-171

62-255	1060-25	1026-25	3309-25
		6167-25	

2 CATALOGS BETWEEN LAYERS

The Lionel Outfit Cost Worksheet for the no. 19173 has notes from 9/23/63 that shed light on the genesis of the 19173-500 (see the highlighted portion of this Worksheet). The notes indicate that Davidson's Detroit ordered 530 units in April. Somehow this amount was reduced, as the final Factory Order for the 19173-500 was for 200 on October 3, 1963.

All remaining cars in the 19173-500 were new for 1963 and demonstrated the further cheapening of the product line. For example, the no. 1061T-25 Tender had no decoration on its sides. Also, the blue plastic no. 6042-250 Gondola Car no longer came with any sort of load or markings.

Regarding trucks and couplers, the 3309-25 was equipped with non-operating Archbar types while the 6042-250 had non-operating AAR types. The norm for the 1061T-25 Tender and no. 6167-25 Caboose was AAR trucks and couplers, but Archbar types were not unusual.

The common no. 61-170 Tan RSC with Black Graphics outfit box was used for this outfit. It measured 11½ x 10¼ x 6¼ inches. Also used was a no. 63-383 Tan RSC with Black Graphics outfit box. It measured 11½ x 9¾ x 6 inches.

The low quantity produced of the 19173-500 is the only reason that this starter outfit is in any demand. With only 200 produced, it easily achieves an R10 rarity.

Locomotive led most of Lionel's low-end starter outfits until 1965.

The rolling stock in the 19173-500 was similar to that in the 19173, with the no. 6405-25 Single Van Flat Car (Less Van) being replaced by a no. 3309-25 Turbo Missile Firing Car. The 3309-25 was a carryover from 1962. It provided minimal excitement because no target for the no. 0349-10 Turbo Missiles was provided.

19174
1962

Description: "O27" Promotional Outfit
Specification: "O27" Steam Type Freight Outfit
Original Amount: 150
Factory Order Date: 9/12/1962
Date Issued: 9-13-62
Packaging: R.S.C. Outfit Packing (Units not Boxed), Except 1020

Contents: 242-25 Steam Type Locomotive; 1060T-25 Tender; 3349-25 Turbo Missile Firing Car (Less Missiles); 0349-10 Turbo Missile (2); 6480-25 Exploding Target Car; 6413-25 Mercury Capsule Transport Car; 6413-4 Capsules (2); 6413-10 Envelope Packed; 6067-25 Caboose; 1013-70 Curved Track (Bundle of 12 - 1013); 1018-40 Straight Track (Bundle of 4 - 1018); 1010-25 35-Watt Transformer; 1020-1 90° Crossing; 1103-20 Envelope Packed; 310-2 Set of (5) Billboards; D62-50 Accessory Catalog;

1123-40 Instruction Sheet; 3349-8 Instruction Sheet; 6480-5 Instruction Sheet; 19171-10 Instruction Sheet

Boxes & Packing: 61-180 Outfit Box; 61-183 Insert; 62-248 Insert (2); 62-254 Insert; 62-258 Insert; 62-264 Insert; 61-185 Shipper for (4) (1-4)

19174 (1962)	C6	C7	C8	Rarity
Complete Outfit	775	1,100	1,500	R10
Outfit Box no. 61-180	500	750	950	R10

Comments: No customer was listed on the Factory Order for the no. 19174. For this reason, we classify it as a General Release Type IIb outfit. The Lionel Outfit Cost Worksheet indicates that this outfit was originally targeted for "Mutual" (Mutual Buying

Syndicate), but that notation was erased.

The 19174 was a small yet somewhat exciting space and military offering. It included the nos. 3349-25 Turbo Missile Firing Car (Less Missiles) and 6413-25 Mercury Capsule Transport Car (both new for 1962). Since these cars were unboxed, their peripherals were provided separately and loose in the outfit box. Both were equipped with operating AAR trucks and couplers.

The 3349-25 was paired with a no. 6480-25 Exploding Target Car that was equipped with non-operating Archbar trucks and couplers. This combination was puzzling in that it would be more appropriate for a 3349-25 to be paired with a no. 6470-25 Exploding Target Car because both were equipped with operating AAR trucks and couplers. For some reason 6470s were not included separately in outfits in 1962. The only way to obtain a 6470 in 1962 was through a substitution or as part of a no. 470-1 Missile Launching Platform.

The odd combination of trucks and couplers found on components of the 19174 continued with the nos. 1060T-25 Tender and 6067-25 Caboose. Because a transition from Archbar to AAR trucks and couplers began in 1962, they could come with either two Archbar types or one non-operating Archbar and one

plain AAR truck and coupler.

The no. 19171-10 Instruction Sheet included a figure-eight track layout diagram. Therefore, a no. 1802B Layout Instruction Sheet was not needed in this outfit.

The no. 61-180 Tan RSC with Black Graphics outfit box measured 12¾ x 10 x 6¾ inches.

With only 150 of the 19174 manufactured, the end customer of this outfit may never be discovered. It is an extremely difficult outfit to find.

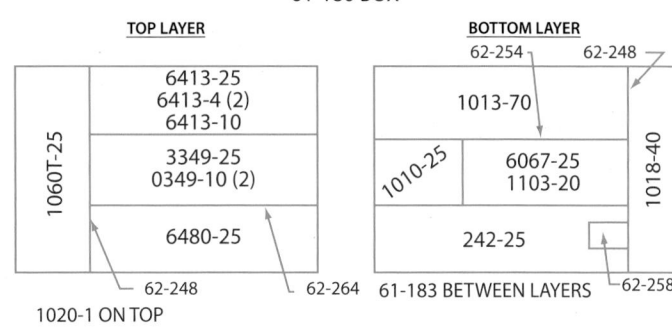

CONVENTIONAL PACK
61-180 BOX

TOP LAYER

	6413-25 6413-4 (2) 6413-10	
1060T-25	3349-25 0349-10 (2)	
	6480-25	

62-248 · 62-264

1020-1 ON TOP

BOTTOM LAYER

62-254 · 62-248

	1013-70	
1010-25	6067-25 1103-20	1018-40
	242-25	

61-183 BETWEEN LAYERS · 62-258

A 836-1 LIONEL ASTRONAUT RESCUE SPECIAL 39.95
(Exclusive) ("O" Gauge) 5 car Astronaut Rescue Special is always on the alert! Flying helicopter is launched from Heliport to scout astronaut landing position, then train speeds out on rescue mission, steam-type loco's blazing headlight illuminating the path ahead. When astronaut is spotted, arm of "Cherry Picker" Car swings out to gently pick him up, ready to place him in missile on Launching Car for another "space flight." Missile fires by remote control to launch capsule, which floats by parachute to "earth." Cable Reel Car, Rocket Fuel Car and Caboose complete train. Set includes 12 curved and 4 straight track sections, 90° crossing, 45 watt transformer, 22 piece set of signs, figures, and buildings, with automatic coupling and uncoupling. Track layout 63" x 26". Ship. wt. 18 lbs.

As shown on page 79 of the FAO Schwarz Christmas Catalog for 1962, outfit no. 19175 matches the Factory Order. The description of this outfit makes any child "got to have it". If you look closely, you can see that the nos. 3413-25 Mercury Capsule Launching Car and 6512-25 Cherry Picker Car still have "mock-up" labels attached. Also note the no. 419-1 is missing the "Lionel Heliport" markings.

Description: "O27" Promotional Outfit
Specification: "O27" Steam Type Freight Outfit
Customer/No./Price: FAO Schwarz; 836-1; $39.95
Original Amount: 60
Factory Order Date: 9/21/1962
Date Issued: Rev 10-12-62
Packaging: R.S.C. Outfit Packing (Units not Boxed), (Except 1020 - 984 & 419)

Contents: 242-25 Steam Type Locomotive; 1060T-25 Tender; 3413-25 Mercury Capsule Launching Car; 3413-18 Mercury Capsule & Parachute Assem.; 3413-27 Missile; 6512-25 Cherry Picker Car; 6062-25 Gondola Car - Black (Less 3 Cable Reels); 40-11 Cable Reels (3); 6463-25 Rocket Fuel Car; 6057-25 Caboose; 1013-70 Curved Track (Bundle of 12 - 1013); 1018-30 Straight Track (Bundle of 3 - 1018); 1008-50 Uncoupling Unit; 1020-1 90° Crossing; 1025-25 45-Watt Transformer; 1103-20 Envelope Packed; 984-1 Railroad Set; 419-1 Operating Heliport; 310-2 Set

of (5) Billboards; D62-50 Accessory Catalog; 1123-40 Instruction Sheet; 3413-8 Instruction Sheet; 1802B Layout Instruction Sheet; 1641-10 Instruction Sheet

Boxes & Packing: 61-230 Outfit Box; 62-225 Insert; 62-251 Insert (2); 62-264 Insert; 62-272 Insert; 61-231 Shipper for (2) (1-2)

19175 (1962)	C6	C7	C8	Rarity
Complete Outfit	1,850	2,700	3,750	R10
Outfit Box no. 61-230	1,250	1,500	1,750	R10

Comments: After two years of sharing outfits with other customers (nos. X-569NA from 1960 and X-688 from 1961), FAO Schwarz finally had its own Retail Promotional Type Ia outfit. The famed toy retailer was the only customer listed on this Factory Order.

The no. 19175 appeared in the 1962 FAO Schwarz Christmas Catalog as the "Lionel Astronaut Rescue Special (Exclusive)". It was listed as FAO Schwarz no. 836-1 for $39.95. For the first time, when this firm said "Exclusive" it was telling the truth.

The motive power and rolling stock in the 19175 were typical items from 1962. The no. 242-25 Steam Type Locomotive was new in 1962. This low-end Scout steamer featured a two-position reversing unit and a headlight, lacked smoke and used a rubber tire as a traction aid.

The new-for-1962 space and military items featured the frequently paired nos. 3413-25 Mercury Capsule Launching Car and 6512-25 Cherry Picker Car. They were designed to work together, with the 6512-25 pretending to load an astronaut into the waiting Mercury capsule (or, as described by FAO Schwarz, "swing out and gently pick him up"). Also new-for-1962 was the no. 6463-25 Rocket Fuel Car.

Keep in mind that a transition from Archbar to AAR trucks began in 1962. For the 19175, all the cars were equipped with operating AAR trucks and couplers. However, the no. 1060T-25 Tender could come with either two Archbar types or one non-operating Archbar and one plain AAR truck and coupler.

The inclusion of a Plasticville no. 984-1 Railroad Set and a no. 419-1 Operating Heliport is what makes the 19175 so collectible. Plasticville items were an inexpensive way for Lionel and its customer to differentiate various offerings.

The Operating Heliport was new in 1962. It was included in only one other outfit (in 1965) as a substitution. This accessory introduced the single-body yellow version of the no. 3419-100 Operating Helicopter Complete that went on to become the norm

for helicopter cars.

The appropriate quantity of track was included to make the figure-eight layout. That track plan was outlined on the no. 1802B Layout Instruction Sheet.

The no. 61-230 Orange RSC with Black Graphics outfit box was manufactured by the Mead Corporation and measured 16 x 15½ x 7⅛ inches. This large box was necessary to hold the Operating Heliport.

The 19175 Lionel Outfit Cost Worksheet lists Lionel's selling price as $23.35 and cost as $20.26. Thus a $3.09 profit (13.2 percent net margin) was realized. This was Lionel's third most profitable promotional outfit in 1962. Unfortunately for Lionel, it was asked to manufacture only 60 of these outfits.

As with FAO Schwarz's X-688 from 1961, the quantities produced are so low that both of these outfits are rarely seen.

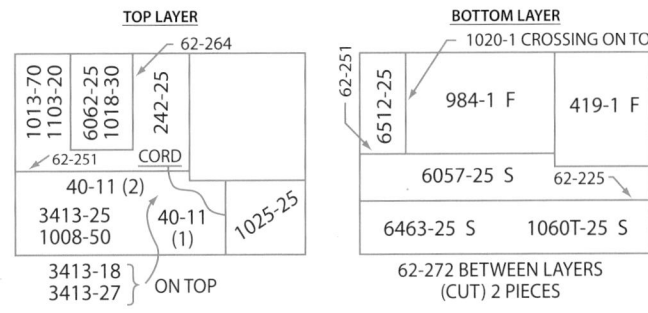

CONVENTIONAL PACK
61-230 BOX

Description: "O27" Promotional Outfit
Specification: "O27" Steam Type Freight Outfit with Smoke
Customer: Joe, The Motorists' Friend
Original Amount: 150
Factory Order Date: 9/21/1962
Date Issued: 9-21-62
Packaging: R.S.C. Outfit Packing (Units not Boxed), Except 110

Contents: 236-25 Steam Type Locomotive With Smoke; 1060T-25 Tender; 3413-25 Mercury Capsule Launching Car; 3413-18 Mercury Capsule & Parachute Assem.; 3413-27 Missile; 3619-25 Reconnaissance Copter Car; 6463-25 Rocket Fuel Car; 6501-25 Jet Motor Boat Car; 6501-2 Boat Assem.; 6501-17 Fuel Pellets Packed; 6057-25 Caboose; 1013-8 Curved Track (Bundle of 8 - 1013); 1013-90 Curved Track (Bundle of 9 - 1013); 1018-30 Straight Track (Bundle of 3 - 1018) (3); 1008-50 Uncoupling Unit; 1025-25 45-Watt Transformer; 110-1 Trestle Set; 1103-20 Envelope Packed; 909-20 Smoke Fluid; 310-2 Set of (5) Billboards; D62-50 Accessory Catalog; 1123-40 Instruction Sheet; 3413-8 Instruction Sheet; 3619-8 Instruction Sheet; 6501-14 Instruction Sheet; 1802I Layout Instruction Sheet; 122-10 Instruction Sheet; 236-11 Instruction Sheet

Boxes & Packing: 62-270 Outfit Box; 61-171 Insert; 62-225 Insert; 62-248 Insert; 62-264 Insert (2); 62-272 Insert; 62-271 Shipper for (3) (1-3)

19176 (1962)	C6	C7	C8	Rarity
Complete Outfit	1,150	1,550	1,925	R10
Outfit Box no. 62-270	750	900	1,000	R10

19176
1962

Comments: In 1962, Joe, The Motorists' Friend purchased three Lionel outfits: nos. 19176, 19177 and 19178. All three were high-end offerings that contained some of Lionel's better motive power and rolling stock from the early 1960s.

The 19176 was Joe, The Motorists' Friend's first of two steam offerings. It was a Retailer Promotional Type Ia outfit led by a no. 236-25 Steam Type Locomotive with Smoke. This engine was one of Lionel's high-end Scout steamers, and it featured a two-position reversing unit, a headlight and Magne-Traction.

Except for the tender and caboose, all the cars in this space and military outfit were new for 1962. Two cars of note were the nos. 3413-25 Mercury Capsule Launching Car and 3619-25 Reconnaissance Copter Car. They were two of Lionel's highest-priced separate-sale cars in 1962.

The 3619-25 included a fragile and easily lost no. 0319-100 Helicopter. As part of the manufacturing process, the roof of the 3619-25 was taped shut with a ½-inch piece of Scotch tape. Even examples in C8 condition still have a mark where the tape was applied.

A transition from Archbar to AAR trucks and couplers began in 1962. For the 19176, all the cars were equipped with operating AAR trucks and couplers. However, the no. 1060T-25 Tender could come with either two Archbar types or one non-operating Archbar and one plain AAR truck and coupler.

The no. 110-1 Trestle Set in this outfit was used for the elevated pretzel track layout. The no. 1802I Layout Instruction Sheet detailed this track plan.

The no. 62-270 Tan RSC with Black Graphics outfit box measured 15½ x 14 x 6¼ inches.

The 19176, like the other two outfits purchased in 1962 by Joe, The Motorists' Friend, was manufactured in extremely low quantities. It also included some of Lionel's higher-end offerings from that year. These two factors explain why each of these three outfits is extremely desirable.

CONVENTIONAL PACK
62-270 BOX
TOP LAYER
62-225
62-264
1013-90
1013-8
1018-30 (1)
3413-25
3413-18
909-20
3413-27
1018-30 (2)
6501-17
6501-25
1008-50
BOTTOM LAYER
61-171
62-264
62-248
236-25 S
1025-25
1103-20
6057-25
3619-25 S
1060T-25 S
6463-25 S
6501-2
110-1 S
62-272 BETWEEN LAYERS

19177
1962

LIONEL
1962
ACCESSORY CATALOG
NO. 2037
LIONEL TRAINS
NO.19177
MANUFACTURED and GUARANTEED BY
THE LIONEL CORPORATION • NEW YORK, N.Y.
LIONEL
LIONEL LINES
BOAT-LOADER
LIONEL
PENNSYLVANIA
NAVY
BIG GALLON
Hot Diggety!
SEE THE NEW
LIONEL SCIENCE
SERIES
TARGET RANGE

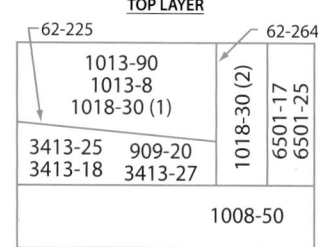

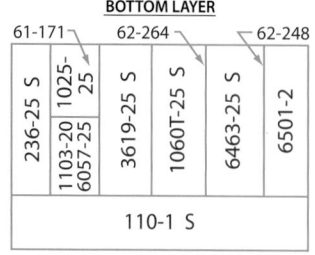

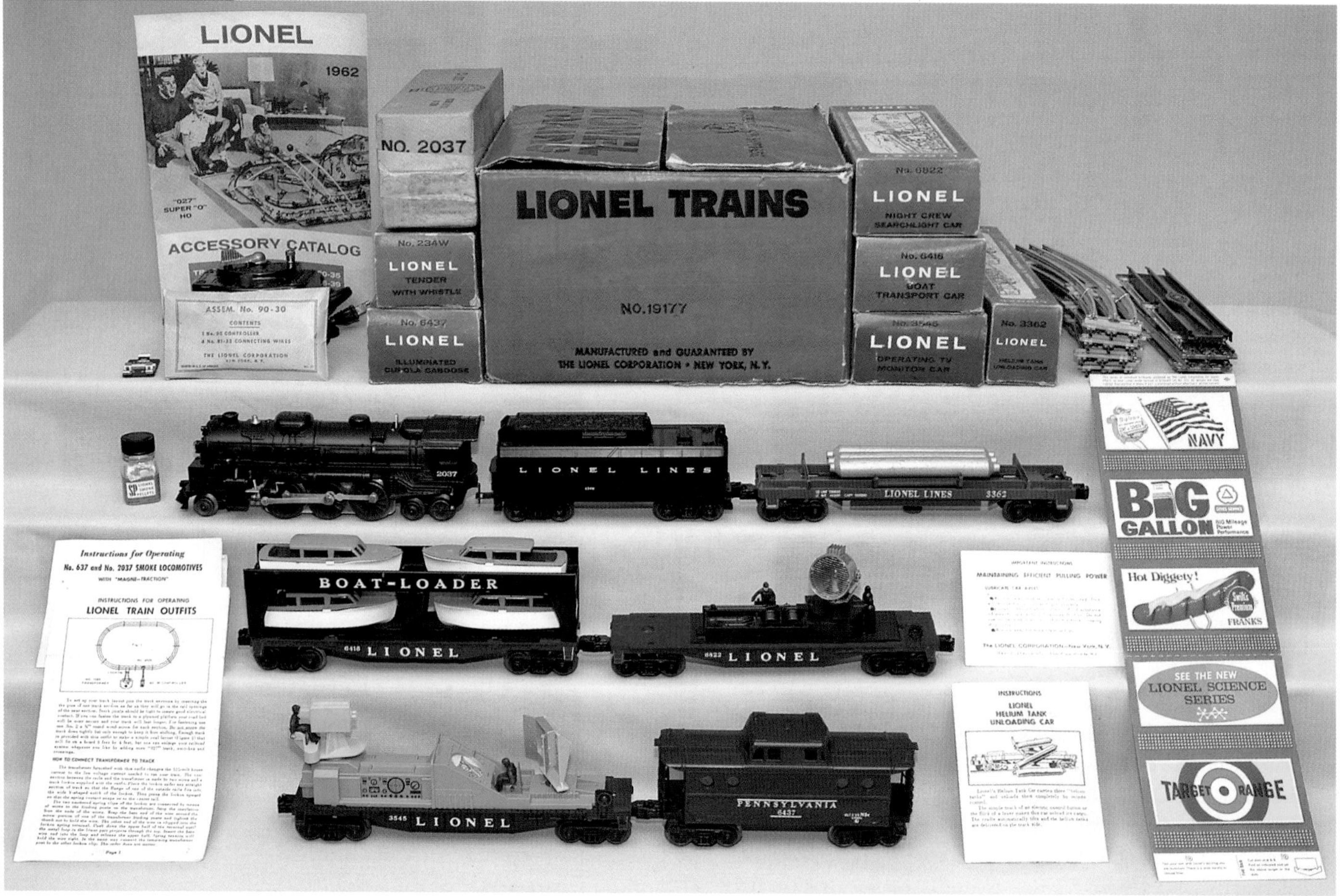

Joe, The Motorists' Friend purchased Lionel no. 19177 as its high-end steam offering for 1962. This outfit included some of Lionel's better rolling stock. Each car was packaged in an Orange Picture box. Individually boxed items were the exception in promotional outfits from 1962.

Description: "O27" Promotional Outfit
Specification: "O27" Steam Type Freight Outfit with Smoke & Whistle
Customer: Joe, The Motorists' Friend
Original Amount: 100
Factory Order Date: 9/12/1962
Date Issued: 9-12-62
Packaging: R.S.C. Outfit Packing (Units Boxed)

Contents: 2037-1 Steam Type Locomotive With Smoke; 234W-1 Whistle Tender; 3362-1 Helium Tank Unloading Car; 6416-1 Boat Transport Car; 6822-1 Illuminated Searchlight Car; 3545-1 Operating TV Monitor Car; 6437-1 Illuminated Cupola Caboose; 1013-8 Curved Track (Bundle of 8 - 1013); 1018-5 Straight Track (Bundle of 5 - 1018); 6029-25 Uncoupling Track Set; 90-30 Envelope Packed; 1063-25 75-Watt Transformer; 310-2 Set of (5) Billboards; D62-50 Accessory Catalog; 1123-40 Instruction Sheet; 1650-10 Instruction Sheet

Boxes & Packing: 61-250 Outfit Box; 61-251 Shipper for (4) (1-4)

19177 (1962)	C6	C7	C8	Rarity
Complete Outfit	1,400	1,925	2,500	R10
Outfit Box no. 61-250	850	1,100	1,300	R10

Comments: In 1962, Joe, The Motorists' Friend purchased three Lionel outfits: nos. 19176, 19177 and 19178. All three were high-end offerings that contained some of Lionel's better motive power and rolling stock from the early 1960s.

The 19177, a Retailer Promotional Type Ia outfit, was led by a no. 2037-1 Locomotive with Smoke and Magne-Traction. This workhorse steamer spanned the years 1953 through 1963 (except for 1956) and powered one Super O and 22 O27 outfits during the 1960s. When boxed as a "-1", it included the nos. 675-33 Smoke Stack Cleaner, SP-1 Smoke Pellets, 927-85 Oiler, 2037-16 Instruction Sheet and CTC-1 Lockon inside its 2037-13 Corr. Box.

The 234W-1 Whistle Tender was equipped with non-operating Archbar trucks and couplers. It required a transformer with whistle control, hence the no. 1063-25 75-Watt Transformer.

The rolling stock in this outfit included some of Lionel's higher-end items. Placing items unboxed in outfits was the norm in promotional outfits from 1962, so Joe, The Motorists' Friend likely made a special request to get the items individually boxed. As such, all rolling stock was individually packaged in Orange Picture boxes. Rounding out the higher-end items was a no. 6437-1 Illuminated Cupola Caboose.

All the cars in the 19177 were equipped with early (nos. 3662-1 Helium Tank Unloading Car, 6822-1 Illuminated Searchlight Car and 3545-1 Operating TV Monitor Car) or middle (no. 6416-1 Boat Transport Car and 6437-1) operating AAR trucks and couplers.

One would think that since this outfit was a higher-end item, Lionel would have made more money on each unit sold. Not so. The 19177 Lionel Outfit Cost Worksheet lists Lionel's selling price as $29.50 and cost as $29.32. Thus a mere $0.18 profit (0.6 percent net margin) was realized.

The no. 61-250 Corrugated Box was an Orange RSC with Black Graphics outfit box. It was manufactured by Kraft Corrugated Containers and measured 13 x 12 x 7 inches.

The 19177, like the other two outfits purchased in 1962 by Joe, The Motorists' Friend, was manufactured in extremely low quantities. It also included some of Lionel's higher-end offerings from that year. These two factors explain why each of these three outfits is extremely desirable.

CONVENTIONAL PACK
61-250 BOX

TOP LAYER		BOTTOM LAYER

Description: Super "O" Promotional Outfit
Specification: Super "O" GG-1 Freight Outfit with Horn
Customer: Joe, The Motorists' Friend
Original Amount: 100
Factory Order Date: 9/12/1962
Date Issued: 9-12-62
Packaging: R.S.C. Outfit Packing (Units Boxed)

Contents: 2360X-1 Penn. GG-1 Electric Locomotive With Horn; 6473-1 Rodeo Car; 6560-25 Crane Car; 6440-1 Flat Car With 2 Piggy Back Vans; 6820-1 Flat Car W/Oper. Missile Helicopter Car; 6736-1 Hopper Car; 6475-1 Pickle Car; 6437-1 Illuminated Cupola Caboose; 31-60 Curved Track (Bundle of 6 - 31) (2); 32-50 Straight Track (5 per bundle); 34-10 Straight Track - 1/2 Section; LW-1 Transformer; 39-35 Remote Control Set; 310-2 Set of (5) Billboards; D62-50 Accessory Catalog; 1123-40 Instruction Sheet

Boxes & Packing: 61-230 Outfit Box; 61-231 Shipper for (2) (1-2)

Alternate For Outfit Contents:
Note: Use 6820-25 and 6820-100 for 6820-1 as needed.

19178 (1962)	C6	C7	C8	Rarity
Complete Outfit With no. 6820-1	2,400	3,675	5,100	R10
Complete Outfit With no. 6820-25	2,300	3,555	4,950	R10
Outfit Box no. 61-230	900	1,300	1,500	R10

Comments: In 1962, Joe, The Motorists' Friend purchased three Lionel outfits: nos. 19176, 19177 and 19178. All three were high-end offerings that contained some of Lionel's better motive power and rolling stock from the early 1960s.

The 19178 was Joe, The Motorists' Friend Super O diesel-powered offering and was one of only two promotional Super O outfits from 1962 (the no. 19196, sold to the Broadway Stores, was the other). This Retailer Promotional Type Ia outfit was the second of four promotional outfits led by the newly "Re-instated 3-1-61" (per Production Control Files) no. 2360X-1 Penn GG-1 Electric Locomotive With Horn. As described in the section on Outfit Peripherals, an "X" signified that a no. CTC-1 Lockon was not included in the no. 2360-10 Corrugated Box. Including a Lockon in a Super O outfit was unnecessary.

The rolling stock in the 19178 included some of Lionel's higher-end items. All of them were carryover, except for the no. 6473-1 Rodeo Car, and each was equipped with operating AAR trucks and couplers.

The 19178 marked the final appearance of boxed examples of the nos. 6736-1 Hopper Car and 6820-1 Flat Car W/Oper. Missile Helicopter Car in an outfit. They came packaged in Orange Perforated boxes.

Interestingly, finding an Orange Perforated no. 6820-11 Folding Box in collectible condition is difficult. This is surprising because the 6820-1 was offered for separate sale in 1960 and 1961 and was a component of nine promotional outfits. (See outfit no. 9658 for more information about the no. 6820-100 Operating Missile Helicopter Complete.)

Some examples of the 19178 came with their 6820-1 unboxed as the no. 6820-25. This variation is reflected in the pricing table and outfit packing diagram.

The no. 6560-25 Crane Car was the boxed version of the crane with a red cab and a black base. The 6560 Crane Car was first manufactured in 1955, one year before Lionel began using the "-25" suffix to indicate unboxed items (see the section on Item Numbering and Suffixes). As such, "-1" was assigned to a boxed 6560 with a gray cab and a black base; "-25" was assigned to a boxed 6560 with a red cab and a black base.

An Orange Perforated or Orange Picture version of the 6560 box could have been used for this outfit. The specific one has yet to be identified. However, we do know that the remaining cars came in Orange Picture boxes.

As with most Super O outfits, the track layout of the 19178 was a basic oval. A Type III or Type IV no. 39-35 Envelope Packed is possible with this outfit.

Catalog Super O outfits generally did not include a transformer. However, because promotional outfits were most often destined for retailers that probably did not have a train department, Lionel included a transformer.

The no. 61-230 Orange RSC with Black Graphics outfit box was manufactured by the Mead Corporation and measured 16 x 15½ x 7⅛ inches.

The 19178, like the other two outfits purchased in 1962 by Joe, The Motorists' Friend, was manufactured in extremely low

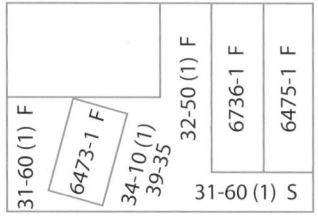

CONVENTIONAL PACK
61-230 BOX

TOP LAYER

BOTTOM LAYER

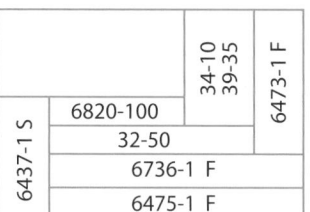

CONVENTIONAL PACK
61-230 BOX
WITH 6820-25

TOP LAYER

BOTTOM LAYER

quantities. It also included some of Lionel's higher-end offerings from that year. Add in the fact that it was a Super O outfit, and you can understand why it is the most desirable and difficult to find of this trio of outstanding promotional outfits.

Grand-Way's low-end steam-powered outfit purchase for 1962 was the no. 19179. This space and military outfit provided two operating cars for fun and excitement. Note that this example still has its yellow price tag attached (on the top of the box). The price was $14.97.

Description: "O27" Promotional Outfit
Specification: "O27" Steam Type Freight Outfit
Customer/No./Price: Grand-Way; 15 2-22 HG 490; $14.97
Original Amount: 300
Factory Order Date: 8/13/1962
Date Issued: 8-16-62
Packaging: R.S.C. Outfit Packing (Units not Boxed)

Contents: 1060-25 Steam Type Locomotive; 1060T-25 Tender; 3309-25 Turbo Missile Firing Car (Less Missiles); 0349-10 Turbo Missile (2); 6480-25 Exploding Target Car; 6413-25 Mercury Capsule Transport Car (Less Capsules); 6413-4 Capsules (2); 6413-10 Envelope Packed; 6067-25 Caboose; 1013-8 Curved Track (Bundle of 8 - 1013); 1018-10 Straight Track (Loose) (2); 1026-25 25-Watt Transformer; 1103-20 Envelope Packed; 310-2 Set of (5) Billboards; D62-50 Accessory Catalog; 1123-10 Instruction Sheet; 3309-5 Instruction Sheet; 6480-5 Instruction Sheet; 1123-40 Instruction Sheet

Boxes & Packing: 61-180 Outfit Box; 61-181 Insert; 61-182 Insert; 61-183 Insert; 61-184 Insert; 61-185 Shipper for (4) (1-4)

19179 (1962)	C6	C7	C8	Rarity
Complete Outfit	550	850	1,125	R9
Outfit Box no. 61-180	350	500	600	R9

Comments: Grand-Way was Grand Union's discount store chain that carried Lionel trains during the 1960s. In 1962, it purchased three Retailer Promotional outfits: nos. 19179, 19180 and 19181. Two were steam-powered and one diesel-powered. Except for the locomotive, the 19179 included the same rolling stock as Firestone's no. 19109 from 1962.

This Retailer Promotional Type Ib was Grand-Way's low-end steam-powered purchase. It was led by a no. 1060-25 Steam Type Locomotive. This low-end steamer went forward only. The locomotive included in this outfit was the later version with a small rain shield covering the headlight.

The space and military rolling stock included three operating cars for plenty of excitement and action. The no. 3309-25 Turbo Missile Firing Car (Less Turbo Missile) was frequently paired with a no. 6480-25 Exploding Target Car. They were low-end versions of the nos. 3349-25 and 6470-25, respectively. The no. 6480-25 included "non-slotted" sides and a smooth roof door guide (without the nubs added later to help hold on the sides). Except for the 6480-25 and the no. 6067-25 Caboose, every item in this outfit was new for 1962.

All but one of the cars in the 19179 came equipped with non-operating Archbar trucks and couplers. The no. 6413-25 Mercury Capsule Transport Car had two operating AAR types.

The commonly used no. 61-180 Tan RSC with Black Graphics outfit box was manufactured by United Container Co. and measured 12¾ x 10 x 6¾ inches.

Grand-Way's three outfits were purchased in quantities that were lower than average. As such, they are all somewhat difficult to find.

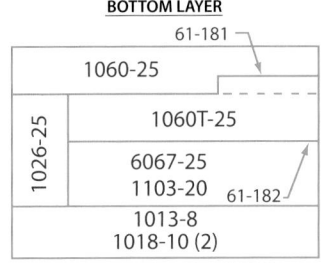

CONVENTIONAL PACK
61-180 BOX

TOP LAYER — 61-184 — 6480-25 — 3309-25, 0349-10 (2), 6413-4 (2), 6413-10 — 6413-25

BOTTOM LAYER — 61-181 — 1060-25 — 1026-25, 1060T-25, 6067-25, 1103-20, 61-182 — 1013-8, 1018-10 (2)

61-183 BETWEEN LAYERS

Description: "O27" Promotional Outfit
Specification: "O27" Steam Type Freight Outfit
Customer: Grand-Way
Original Amount: 300
Factory Order Date: 9/27/1962
Date Issued: 10-2-62
Packaging: R.S.C. Outfit Packing (Units not Boxed)

Contents: 242-25 Steam Type Locomotive; 1060T-25 Tender; 3357-25 Animated Hobo & Railroad Policeman Car; 3357-27 Box Packed; 6475-25 Pickle Car; 6162-25 Gondola Car (Less 3 Canisters); 6112-88 Canisters (White) (3); 6057-25 Caboose; 1013-8 Curved Track (Bundle of 8 - 1013); 1018-10 Straight Track (Loose); 1008-50 Uncoupling Unit; 1010-25 35-Watt Transformer; 1103-20 Envelope Packed; 310-2 Set of (5) Billboards; D62-50 Accessory Catalog; 1123-40 Instruction Sheet; 1641-10 Instruction Sheet

Boxes & Packing: 61-180 Outfit Box; 61-181 Insert; 61-182 Insert; 61-183 Insert; 61-184 Insert; 61-185 Shipper for (4) (1-4)

19180 (1962)	C6	C7	C8	Rarity
Complete Outfit	425	675	915	R9
Outfit Box no. 61-180	300	450	550	R9

Comments: Grand-Way was Grand Union's discount store chain that carried Lionel trains during the 1960s. In 1962, it purchased three Retailer Promotional outfits: nos. 19179, 19180 and 19181. Two were steam-powered and one diesel-powered.

The 19180, a Retailer Promotional Type Ia, was Grand-Way's high-end steam-powered purchase. High-end in that it was led by a no. 242-25 Steam Type Locomotive as opposed to the no. 1060-25 Steam Type Locomotive in the 19179. The 242-25 featured a two-position reversing unit and a headlight, lacked smoke and used a rubber tire as a traction aid.

The 19180 was the only outfit to have its no. 6475-25 Pickle Car unboxed. The no. 3357-25 Animated Hobo & Railroad Policeman Car (new for 1962) provided plenty of excitement as the cop tried to catch the hobo. Since this car also was unboxed, the no. 3357-27 Box Packed was listed separately on the Factory Order and placed loose in the outfit box.

523

A transition from Archbar to AAR trucks and couplers began in 1962. For the 19180, all the cars were equipped with operating AAR trucks and couplers. However, the no. 1060T-25 Tender could come with either two Archbar types or one non-operating Archbar and one plain AAR truck and coupler.

The commonly used no. 61-180 Tan RSC with Black Graphics outfit box measured 12¾ x 10 x 6¾ inches.

Grand-Way's three outfits were purchased in quantities that were lower than average. As such, they are all somewhat difficult to find.

CONVENTIONAL PACK
61-180 BOX

TOP LAYER		
6475-25	6112-88 (1)	61-184
6162-25	6112-88 (2)	
1008-50 6057-25	3357-27	

BOTTOM LAYER	
242-25	61-181
1010-25	1060T-25
	3357-25
	1103-20 61-182
1013-8 1018-10	

61-183 BETWEEN LAYERS

19181
1962

Description: "O27" Promotional Outfit
Specification: "O27" Diesel Freight Outfit
Customer: Grand-Way
Original Amount: 200
Factory Order Date: 9/27/1962
Date Issued: 10-2-62
Packaging: R.S.C. Outfit Packing (Units not Boxed), Except 1020

Contents: 211P-25 *"Texas Special"* Alco Diesel Power Unit; 3413-25 Mercury Capsule Launching Car; 6512-25 Cherry Picker Car; 6463-25 Rocket Fuel Car; 3510-25 Satellite Launching Car (Less Satellite); 0333-100 Satellite; 6057-25 Caboose; 1013-70 Curved Track (Bundle of 12 - 1013); 1018-30 Straight Track (Bundle of 3 - 1018); 1008-50 Uncoupling Unit; 1020-1 90° Crossing; 1025-25 45-Watt Transformer; 1103-20 Envelope Packed; 310-2 Set of (5) Billboards; D62-50 Accessory Catalog; 211-6 Instruction Sheet; 1123-40 Instruction Sheet; 3413-8 Instruction Sheet; 6512-19 Instruction Sheet; 3510-5 Instruction Sheet; 1802B Layout Instruction Sheet; 122-10 Instruction Sheet

Boxes & Packing: 62-243 Outfit Box; 62-224 Insert; 62-225 Insert; 62-245 Insert (2); 62-248 Insert (2); 62-264 Insert; 62-244 Shipper for (4) (1-4)

19181 (1962)	C6	C7	C8	Rarity
Complete Outfit	900	1,300	1,800	R10
Outfit Box no. 62-243	500	650	800	R10

Comments: Grand-Way was Grand Union's discount store chain that carried Lionel trains during the 1960s. In 1962, it purchased three Retailer Promotional outfits: nos. 19179, 19180 and 19181. Two were steam-powered and one diesel-powered.

This Retailer Promotional Type Ib was Grand-Way's diesel-powered purchase. A no. 211P-25 *Texas Special* Alco Diesel Power Unit led the 19181. This locomotive featured a two-position reversing unit, an open pilot, a headlight and two-axle Magne-Traction.

The new-for-1962 rolling stock included the nos. 3413-25 Mercury Capsule Launching Car and 6512-25 Cherry Picker Car. They were designed to work together, with the 6512-25 pretending to load an astronaut into the waiting Mercury capsule. Also new was the no. 6463-25 Rocket Fuel Car. These three cars came together in at least eight outfits.

This outfit also included the collectible no. 3510-25 Satellite Launching Car (Less Satellite). This new-for-1962 car appeared only in 10 promotional outfits. The 3510-25 included a red frame and "Lionel" stamped on the side; otherwise, its mechanism was an exact duplicate of the no. 3509-25 Satellite Launching Car. It was equipped with non-operating Archbar trucks and couplers. All the other cars in the 19181 were equipped with operating AAR trucks and couplers.

The figure-eight track layout was described on the no. 1802B Layout Instruction Sheet dated 6-59.

The no. 62-243 Tan RSC with Black Graphics outfit box measured 12⅛ x 11½ x 6⅜ inches.

Grand-Way's three outfits were purchased in quantities that were lower than average, with the 19181 having the smallest order. As a result, it is the most difficult of the trio to find.

CONVENTIONAL PACK
62-243 BOX

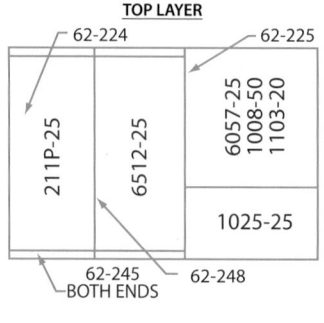

TOP LAYER

62-224 — 62-225

| 211P-25 | 6512-25 | 6057-25 1008-50 1103-20 |
| | | 1025-25 |

62-245 — 62-248
BOTH ENDS

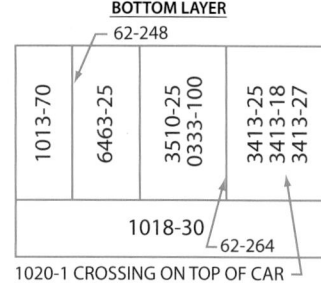

BOTTOM LAYER

62-248

| 1013-70 | 6463-25 | 3510-25 0333-100 | 3413-25 3413-18 3413-27 |
| | 1018-30 | 62-264 |

1020-1 CROSSING ON TOP OF CAR

19182
1962

Description: "O27" Promotional Outfit
Specification: "O27" Steam Type Freight Outfit
Customer: Kings Department Stores
Original Amount: 1,000

Factory Order Date: 10/3/1962
Date Issued: 10-3-62
Packaging: Display Outfit Packing (Units not Boxed)

Contents: 1060-25 Steam Type Locomotive; 1060T-25 Tender; 6402-25 Flat Car; 40-11 Cable Reels (2); 6076-25 Hopper Car - Red; 6067-25 Caboose; 1013-8 Curved Track (Bundle of 8 - 1013); 1018-10 Straight Track (Loose) (2); 1026-25 25-Watt Transformer; 1103-20 Envelope Packed; 310-2 Set of (5) Billboards; D62-50 Accessory Catalog; 1123-40 Instruction Sheet; 1123-10 Instruction Sheet

Boxes & Packing: 62-200 Display Outfit Box; 61-101 Corr. Insert; 61-102 Corr. Insert (2); 61-103 Shipper for (6) (1-6)

19182 (1962)	C6	C7	C8	Rarity
Complete Outfit	200	325	475	R7
Outfit Box no. 62-200	125	200	275	R7

Comments: This was the first outfit in the 1960s that listed Kings Department Stores as its customer. The no. 19182 was a Retailer Promotional Type Ib outfit that included low-end motive power and rolling stock.

This outfit was basically the same as advance catalog outfit no. 11001 from 1962, except that it included a no. 6076-25 Hopper Car - Red instead of a no. 6042-25 Gondola Car.

(See the entry for outfit 11001 for a description of the motive power and rolling stock.)

The no. 62-200 White 4-6-4 Steamer and F3 Hinged Display with Red/Orange and Blue Graphics Type A outfit box was manufactured by United Container Co. and measured 21⅝ x 11½ x 3¼ inches.

The 19182 and 11001 are almost the same outfit. If a collector could acquire only one of them, he or she should choose the 19182 because of its lower production quantities. That being said, the 19182 does not appear too often.

DISPLAY PACK
62-200 BOX

1060-25	1060T-25	1026-25
6402-25	6076-25	
2-1018 8-1013	6067-25	

Description: "O27" Promotional Outfit
Specification: "O27" Steam Type Freight Outfit
Customer: Bloomingdales
Original Amount: 50
Factory Order Date: 9/14/1962
Date Issued: 9-17-62
Packaging: R.S.C. Outfit Packing (Units not Boxed), Except 110

Contents: 242-25 Steam Type Locomotive; 1060T-25 Tender; 3309-25 Turbo Missile Firing Car (Less Missiles); 0349-10 Turbo Missile (2); 6076-25 Hopper Car - Red; 3413-25 Mercury Capsule Launching Car; 3413-18 Mercury Capsule & Parachute Assem.; 3413-27 Missile; 6512-25 Cherry Picker Car; 6067-25 Caboose; 1013-8 Curved Track (Bundle of 8 - 1013); 1013-90 Curved Track (Bundle of 9 - 1013); 1018-30 Straight Track (Bundle of 3 - 1018); 1008-50 Uncoupling Unit; 1010-25 35-Watt Transformer; 1103-20 Envelope Packed; 110-1 Trestle Set; 310-2 Set of (5) Billboards; D62-50 Accessory Catalog; 1123-40 Instruction Sheet; 1802I Layout Instruction Sheet; 3309-5 Instruction Sheet; 3413-8 Instruction Sheet; 1641-10 Instruction Sheet

Boxes & Packing: 62-270 Outfit Box; 61-171 Insert; 62-202 Insert; 62-248 Insert; 62-264 Insert; 62-272 Insert; 62-271 Shipper for (3) (1-3)

19183 (1962)	C6	C7	C8	Rarity
Complete Outfit	1,450	1,950	2,350	R10
Outfit Box no. 62-270	1,200	1,500	1,700	R10

Comments: In 1962, Bloomingdales purchased four Retailer Promotional Type Ib outfits: nos. 19183, 19193, 19194 and 19195. All four were space and military steam freight outfits that Lionel produced in very small quantities.

The 19183 was considered Bloomingdales' high-end offering because it came with a no. 242-25 Steam Type Locomotive whereas the other three outfits were led by the low-end no. 1060-25 Steam Type Locomotive. In addition, the 19183 included more cars than the others and cost the most. Its Lionel Outfit Cost Worksheet listed the cost to Bloomindales as $17.50.

The nos. 3413-25 Mercury Capsule Launching Car and 6512-25 Cherry Picker Car (both new for 1962) were paired in at least 18 different outfits. They were designed to work together, with the 6512-25 pretending to load an astronaut into the waiting Mercury capsule. The two cars had operating AAR trucks and couplers.

Also new was the no. 3309-25 Turbo Missile Firing Car (Less Missiles). It was the low-end version of the no. 3349-25 Turbo Missile Firing Car. The difference between the two cars was that the 3309-25 was equipped with non-operating Archbar rather than operating AAR trucks and couplers.

It seems odd that Lionel didn't include a 3349-25 in this high-end outfit. But then Bloomindales might have been trying to pack as much as it could in this outfit while holding down costs. Besides, with three components of the 19183 having Archbar trucks and couplers (nos. 1060T-25 Tender, 6067-25 Caboose and 6076-25 Hopper Car - Red), it hardly mattered whether these parts matched those on other cars.

The no. 110-1 Trestle Set in this outfit was used for the elevated pretzel track layout. The no. 1802I Layout Instruction Sheet detailed this track plan.

The no. 62-270 Tan RSC with Black Graphics outfit box measured 15½ x 14 x 6¼ inches.

Lionel produced such small quantities of all four Bloomingdales outfits that they were likely sold over the counter at Bloomingdales stores. No catalog listings or other information beyond the Factory Orders has been observed. The outfits are seldom seen, hence the R10 rarity for all four of them.

CONVENTIONAL PACK
62-270 BOX

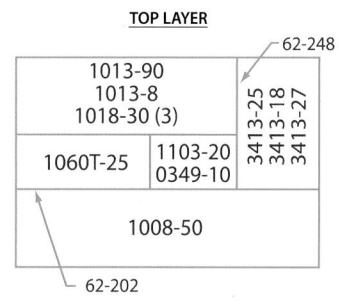

TOP LAYER

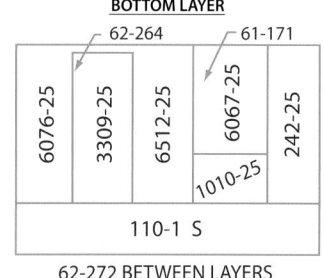

BOTTOM LAYER

Description: "O27" Promotional Outfit
Specification: "O27" Diesel Switcher Freight Outfit
Customer: Halle Brothers
Original Amount: 150
Factory Order Date: 9/27/1962
Date Issued: 10-2-62
Packaging: R.S.C. Outfit Packing (Units not Boxed), Except 1020

Contents: 633-50 "Santa Fe" Diesel Switcher; 3357-25 Animated Hobo & Railroad Policeman Car; 3357-27 Box Packed; 6473-25 Rodeo Car; 6501-25 Jet Motor Boat Car; 6501-2 Boat Assem.; 6501-17 Fuel Pellets Packed; 6162-25 Gondola Car (Less 3 Canisters); 6112-88 Canisters (White) (3); 6057-25 Caboose; 1013-70 Curved Track (Bundle of 12 - 1013); 1018-30 Straight Track (Bundle of 3 - 1018); 1008-50 Uncoupling Unit; 1025-25 45-Watt Transformer; 1103-20 Envelope Packed; 1020-1 90° Crossing; 310-2 Set of (5) Billboards; D62-50 Accessory Catalog; 1123-40 Instruction Sheet; 6501-14 Instruction Sheet; 1802B Layout Instruction Sheet; 121-10 Instruction Sheet

Boxes & Packing: 61-250 Outfit Box; 61-181 Insert; 61-182 Insert; 61-184 Insert; 62-223 Insert; 62-225 Insert; 600-26 Insert (2); 61-251 Shipper for (4) (1-4)

19184 (1962)	C6	C7	C8	Rarity
Complete Outfit	1,000	1,475	1,950	R10
Outfit Box no. 61-250	650	900	1,100	R10

Comments: Halle Brothers department stores purchased this Retailer Promotional Type Ib diesel outfit in 1962.

The no. 19184 was led by a no. 633-50 Santa Fe Diesel Switcher, which was the promotional-only upgrade to the no. 633-25 that Lionel issued earlier in 1962. This low-end switcher came with a traction tire but lacked a horn. However, it was "4 wheel drive equipped", unlike the 633-25, which was driven by only two wheels. The "-50" version is more difficult (3,660 produced) to find than the "-25" (11,900 produced). According to the Lionel

Engineering Specification for the 633-50, it was "primarily designed to pull 5 moderate weight cars up a trestle".

The 19184 featured three new-for-1962 operating cars. The nos. 3357-25 Animated Hobo & Railroad Policeman Car and 6473-25 Rodeo Car were paired in at least 11 outfits. The 3357-25 provided plenty of excitement as the cop tried to catch the hobo. Since the car came unboxed (hence the "-25" suffix), the Factory Order also listed a no. 3357-27 Box Packed. Interestingly, the outfit packing diagram listed a no. 3357-23. This is consistent with actual outfit observations in 1962, which included a 3357-27 with "3357-23" printed on its box. The "3357-23" was actually the number of the box and appears to have been mistakenly printed as the final assembly number on some early examples of the 3357-27 Box Packed.

The no. 6501-25 Jet Motor Boat Car had its no. 6501-17 Fuel Pellets Packed listed separately on the Factory Order.

All the cars in this outfit were equipped with operating AAR trucks and couplers.

A no. 1020-1 90° Crossing plus appropriate track were included to create the figure-eight layout outlined on the no. 1802B Layout Instruction Sheet.

The no. 61-250 Orange RSC with Black Graphics outfit box measured 13 x 12 x 7 inches.

The low quantity of 150 produced makes the 19184 a difficult outfit to find.

CONVENTIONAL PACK
61-250 BOX

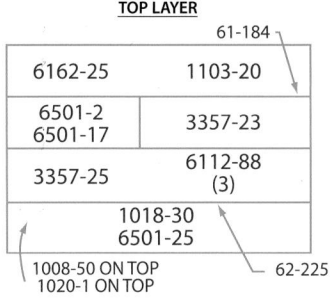

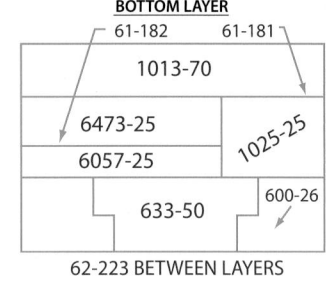

Customer No. On Box: 36 J 5278
Description: "O27" Promotional Outfit
Specification: "O27" Steam Type Freight
Customer/No./Price: Spiegel; 36 J 5278; $18.87
Original Amount: 400
Factory Order Date: 9/12/1962
Date Issued: 9-12-62
Packaging: R.S.C. Outfit Packing (Units not Boxed)

Contents: 242-25 Steam Type Locomotive; 1060T-25 Tender; 3349-25 Turbo Missile Firing Car (Less Missiles); 0349-10 Turbo Missile (2); 6448-25 Exploding Target Range Car; 6057-25 Caboose; 1013-8 Curved Track (Bundle of 8 - 1013); 1018-10 Straight Track (Loose); 1008-50 Uncoupling Unit; 1010-25 35-Watt Transformer; 1103-20 Envelope Packed; 310-2 Set of (5) Billboards; D62-50 Accessory Catalog; 1123-40 Instruction

Sheet; 3349-8 Instruction Sheet; 6448-17 Instruction Sheet; 1641-10 Instruction Sheet

Boxes & Packing: 61-170 Outfit Box; 61-171 Insert; 61-172 Insert; 61-173 Insert; 62-257 Insert; 61-175 Shipper for (4) (1-4)

Alternate For Outfit Contents:
Note: Shipment must be made by September 4th; Customer Stock No. 36 J 5278.

19185 (1962)	C6	C7	C8	Rarity
Complete Outfit	345	525	825	R9
Outfit Box no. 61-170	225	325	525	R9

Comments: In 1962, Spiegel purchased three outfits: nos. 11288 (catalog) and 19185 and 19186 (both Retail Promotional Type Ia). The 19185 was Spiegel's low-end space and military offering and retailed for $18.87. The follow-up to Spiegel's no. X-651 from 1961, it was shown on page 384 of Spiegel's 1962 Christmas

Spiegel's low-end purchase for 1962 was the no. 19185. This outfit was also stamped by Lionel with Spiegel catalog number "36-J-5278". This example was shipped solely in its Lionel RSC box (the shipping label is still attached on top). If all outfits were shipped from Spiegel this way, it would explain why so few outfit boxes have survived in any kind of condition.

Catalog as the no. R36 J 5278.

Spiegel advertised this outfit as "NEW...turbo missile train". As such, it included the new-for-1962 no. 3349-25 Turbo Missile Firing Car (Less Missiles) and its target, a no. 6448-25 Exploding Target Car. The 6448-25 included in this outfit had "non-slotted" sides and nubs on the roof door guide to help hold on the sides. According to the Production Control Files, as many of the variation with red sides and a white roof were made as the variation with white sides and a red roof. The 6448-25 was shown in the Spiegel catalog with white sides and a red roof.

The 19185 was led by a no. 242-25 Steam Type Locomotive. This low-end Scout steamer featured a two-position reversing unit and a headlight, lacked smoke and used a rubber tire as a traction aid. The version with wide running boards was included in this outfit.

The 242-25 pulled a no. 1060T-25 Tender equipped with non-operating Archbar trucks and couplers. All other cars came with operating AAR trucks and couplers.

The common no. 61-170 Tan RSC with Black Graphics outfit box was used for this outfit. It measured 11½ x 10¼ x 6¼ inches.

Spiegel purchased 1,200 of the X-651 outfit in 1961. A year later, it reduced its order of 19185 outfits to only 400 units. Both of these outfits are difficult to find in any condition.

CONVENTIONAL PACK
61-170 BOX

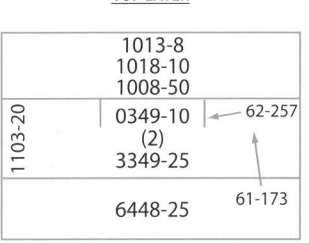

TOP LAYER

1103-20	1013-8 1018-10 1008-50	
	0349-10 (2) 3349-25	← 62-257
	6448-25	61-173

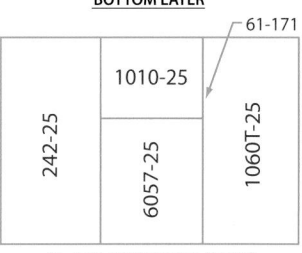

BOTTOM LAYER

		61-171
242-25	1010-25	
	6057-25	1060T-25

61-172 BETWEEN LAYERS

527

19186	
1962	

New Lionel space age train . . . ready for Cape Canaveral loaded with exciting action

the rocket and retrieving the nose cone parachute! Rocket fires by remote control. With new capsule launching car, new cherry picker car used to hoist astronaut, new mercury capsule carrying car, and new rocket fuel tank car. Mighty Minneapolis and St. Louis 2-unit twin diesel with headlight, electric horn, magne-traction, and automatic uncouplers; plus caboose car. 120 inches of running track on 27x44-in. oval layout; .027 gauge track. Complete space-age train includes uncoupling track set, lock on, horn controller, 60 watt circuit-breaker transformer, oil, wires, and instruction sheet.
R36 J 5276. Mailable. Shipping weight 14 lbs. . . . . low monthly terms . . . 38.88

6 unit train **29.87**

Continuous fun as cop 'n hobo leap from trestle to boxcar of 4-ft. train on 120-in oval

LIONEL 6-UNIT SMOKING STEAM FREIGHT with new cop 'n hobo car. Makes one of the most welcome gifts we know of. Cop 'n hobo chase is continuous fun . . . from on top the trestle cop spots hobo on approaching train . . . as cop leaps on train car hobo jumps on trestle! Situation reverses itself when train again passes under trestle. 53-inch long train is authentically detailed of hi-impact plastic and steel. Steam locomotive with headlight and magne-traction whistles and smokes as it pulls 8-wheel tender car. Followed by cop 'n hobo car, flat car with piggy-back van, gondola car with cable reels, and caboose. Cars have automatic couplers. Incl. 60 watt transformer with circuit breaker, trestle, uncoupling track set, whistle control unit, oil, wires, and instruction sheet. 27x44-in. oval layout; .027 gauge track.
R36 J 5277. Mailable. Shipping weight 11 lbs. . . . . low monthly terms . . . 29.87

NEW . . . cop and hobo train

Lionel's no. 19186 was illustrated on page 384 of the Spiegel's 1962 Christmas Catalog as Spiegel no. R36 J 5277 for $29.87. This was Spiegel's mid-level offering for the year. Note the mock-up version of the trestle shown with the no. 3357-25 Animated Hobo & Railroad Policeman Car.

Description: "O27" Promotional Outfit
Specification: "O27" Steam Type Freight Outfit With Smoke & Whistle
Customer/No./Price: Spiegel; R36 J 5277; $29.87
Original Amount: 250
Factory Order Date: 9/21/1962
Date Issued: 9-21-62
Packaging: R.S.C. Outfit Packing (Units not Boxed), Except Loco. & Tender

Contents: 233-1 Steam Type Locomotive With Smoke; 234W-1 Whistle Tender; 6062-25 Gondola Car (Less 3 Cable Reels); 40-11 Cable Reels (3); 3357-25 Animated Hobo & Railroad Policeman Car; 3357-27 Box Packed; 6405-25 Single Van Flat Car (Less Van); 6405-150 Van; 6057-25 Caboose; 1013-8 Curved Track (Bundle of 8 - 1013); 1018-30 Straight Track (Bundle of 3 - 1018); 1008-50 Uncoupling Unit; 1073-25 60-Watt Transformer; 147-25 Horn & Whistle Controller; 2333-140 Flashlight Cell; 81-32 24" R.C. Wire (3); 310-2 Set of (5) Billboards; D62-50 Accessory Catalog; 1123-40 Instruction Sheet; 3357-8 Instruction Sheet; 1646-10 Instruction Sheet

Boxes & Packing: 61-180 Outfit Box; 61-192 Insert; 62-248 Insert; 62-251 Insert (3); 61-185 Shipper for (4) (1-4)

19186 (1962)	C6	C7	C8	Rarity
Complete Outfit	575	950	1,300	R10
Outfit Box no. 61-180	350	550	700	R10

Comments: In 1962, Spiegel purchased three outfits: nos. 11288 (catalog) and 19185 and 19186 (both Retail Promotional Type Ia). The 19186 was Spiegel's mid-end Lionel offering and retailed for $29.87. The follow-up to Spiegel's purchase of Lionel catalog outfit no. 1646 from 1961, it was shown on page 384 of Spiegel's 1962 Christmas Catalog as the no. R36 J 5277.

This outfit was led by a no. 233-1 Steam Type Locomotive with Smoke in 1962. One of Lionel's high-end Scout steamers, it featured a two-position reversing unit, a headlight and Magne-Traction. The 233-1 was paired with a no. 234W-1 Whistle Tender

instead of a no. 233W Whistle Tender because the latter was being phased out.

The 19186 represented one of the last times that the 233 came boxed. Consequently, this outfit did not include a packed envelope and the no. 81-32 24" R.C. Wires were placed loose in the outfit box.

When a no. 147-25 Horn & Whistle Controller was included, Lionel provided a no. 2333-140 Flashlight Cell loose in the outfit box. This practice lasted until 1963.

Advertised as "NEW…cop and hobo train", this outfit included the new-for-1962 no. 3357-25 Animated Hobo & Railroad Policeman Car. Since the car was unboxed, the no. 3357-27 Box Packed was listed separately on the Factory Order and placed loose in the outfit box. Interestingly, the outfit packing diagram listed a no. 3357-23. This is consistent with actual outfit observations in 1962, which included a 3357-27 with "3357-23" printed on its box. The "3357-23" was actually the number of the box and appears to have been mistakenly printed as the final assembly number on some early examples of the 3357-27 Box Packed.

The 3357-25, like all but one of the components of the 19186, was equipped with operating AAR trucks and couplers. The sole exception was the 234W-1; in 1962, 234Ws had one non-operating and one plain Archbar truck and coupler.

The commonly used no. 61-180 Tan RSC with Black Graphics outfit box measured 12¾ x 10 x 6¾ inches.

Spiegel purchased only 250 of this mid-level offering in 1962. For that reason, examples do not appear often.

CONVENTIONAL PACK
61-180 BOX

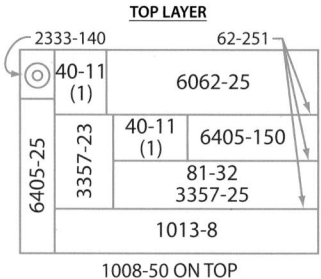

TOP LAYER

1008-50 ON TOP

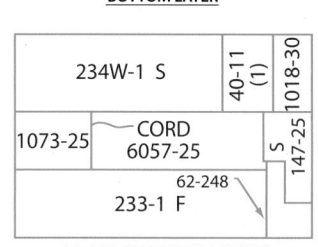

BOTTOM LAYER

61-192 BETWEEN LAYERS

Description: "O27" Promotional Outfit
Specification: "O27" Diesel Freight Outfit
Customer: Wiechmanns
Original Amount: 25
Factory Order Date: 9/12/1962
Date Issued: 9-12-62
Packaging: R.S.C. Outfit Packing (Units not Boxed), Except 110

Contents: 211P-25 *"Texas Special"* Alco Diesel Power Unit; 211T-25 Motorless Unit; 3349-25 Turbo Missile Firing Car (Less Missiles); 0349-10 Turbo Missile (2); 3470-25 Aerial Target Launching Car; 3470-20 Envelope Packed; 3470-4 Basket; 6162-25 Gondola Car (Less 3 Canisters); 6112-88 Canisters (White) (3); 6057-25 Caboose; 1013-8 Curved Track (Bundle of 8 - 1013); 1013-90 Curved Track (Bundle of 9 - 1013); 1018-30 Straight Track (Bundle of 3 - 1018) (3); 1008-50 Uncoupling Unit; 1025-25 45-Watt Transformer; 110-1 Trestle Set; 1103-20 Envelope Packed; 310-2 Set of (5) Billboards; D62-50 Accessory Catalog; 1802I Layout Instruction Sheet; 122-10 Instruction Sheet; 1123-40 Instruction Sheet; 211-6 Instruction Sheet; 3349-8 Instruction Sheet; 3470-8 Instruction Sheet

Boxes & Packing: 62-270 Outfit Box; 62-224 Insert; 62-245 Insert (2); 62-248 Insert (3); 62-264 Insert; 62-272 Insert; 62-271 Shipper for (3) (1-3)

19187 (1962)	C6	C7	C8	Rarity
Complete Outfit	1,600	2,450	3,150	R10
Outfit Box no. 62-270	1,350	1,950	2,450	R10

Comments: Wiechmanns was a small variety store headquartered in Saginaw, Michigan. This is the only Factory Order to list it as a customer. The no. 19187, a Retailer Promotional Type Ia outfit, was purchased in a quantity of 25 units, which ranks it fifth among the outfits with the fewest produced.

A space and military outfit, the 19187 was led by a no. 211P-25 *Texas Special* Alco Diesel Power Unit. This locomotive featured a two-position reversing unit, an open pilot, a headlight and two-axle Magne-Traction.

Highlighting the rolling stock were two operating cars that Lionel introduced in 1962. The no. 3349-25 Turbo Missile Firing Car (Less Missiles) was paired with its primary target, a no. 3470-25 Aerial Target Launching Car, in at least five different outfits. A description of the 3349 in the Lionel catalog explained that "by manually setting the direction…missile can be used as a projectile to bring down the balloon on the Aerial Target Car…" That car, like the others in this outfit, came with operating AAR trucks and couplers.

The track layout for this outfit was the elevated pretzel that was detailed on the no. 1802I Layout Instruction Sheet.

The no. 62-270 Tan RSC with Black Graphics outfit box measured 15½ x 14⅛ x 6¼ inches.

Lionel made so few of this outfit that the 19187 stands as one of the rarest promotional outfits.

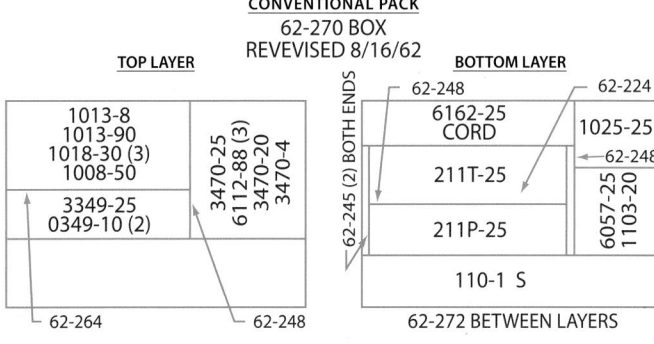

CONVENTIONAL PACK
62-270 BOX
REVEVISED 8/16/62

Description: "O27" Promotional Outfit
Specification: "O27" Steam Type Freight Outfit
Customer: Jewel Tea Company
Original Amount: 500
Factory Order Date: 9/28/1962
Date Issued: Rev 10-5-62
Packaging: R.S.C. Outfit Packing (Units not Boxed), Except 110

Contents: 242-25 Steam Type Locomotive; 1060T-25 Tender; 3357-25 Animated Hobo & Railroad Policeman Car; 3357-27 Box Packed; 6162-25 Gondola Car (Less 3 Canisters); 6112-88 Canisters (White) (3); 6057-25 Caboose; 1013-70 Curved Track (Bundle of 12 - 1013); 1018-30 Straight Track (Bundle of 3 - 1018); 1008-50 Uncoupling Unit; 1010-25 35-Watt Transformer; 1020-1 90° Crossing; 1103-20 Envelope Packed; 310-2 Set of (5) Billboards; D62-50 Accessory Catalog; 1123-40 Instruction Sheet; 1802B Layout Instruction Sheet; 1641-10 Instruction Sheet

Boxes & Packing: 61-170 Outfit Box; 61-172 Insert; 62-251 Insert (2); 62-254 Insert; 61-175 Shipper for (4) (1-4)

19188 (1962)	C6	C7	C8	Rarity
Complete Outfit	465	615	860	R9
Outfit Box no. 61-170	350	400	525	R9

Comments: Jewel Tea Company purchased this Retailer Promotional Type Ia outfit in 1962. Issued as the follow-up to its no. X-689 from 1961, the no. 19188 was updated to include items available in 1962. (See the entry for outfit X-689 from 1961 for more information.)

The 19188 was led by a no. 242-25 Steam Type Locomotive, which took the place of the discontinued no. 246-25 that Lionel used in the X-689. This replacement featured a two-position reversing unit and a rubber tire for traction aid as opposed to the Magne-Traction on the 246-25.

The no. 3357-25 Animated Hobo & Railroad Policeman Car was new for 1962 and replaced the no. 3376-25 Operating Giraffe Car included in the X-689. Since the car was unboxed, the no. 3357-27 Box Packed was listed separately on the Factory Order and placed loose in the outfit box. Interestingly, the outfit packing diagram listed a no. 3357-23. This is consistent with actual outfit observations in 1962, which included a 3357-27 with "3357-23" printed on its box. The "3357-23" was actually the number of the box and appears to have been mistakenly printed as the final assembly number on some early examples of the 3357-27 Box Packed.

Keep in mind that a transition from Archbar to AAR trucks and couplers began in 1962. As a result, while all the cars were equipped with operating AAR trucks and couplers, the no. 1060T-25 Tender could come with either two Archbar types or one non-operating Archbar and one plain AAR truck and coupler.

The no. 61-170 Tan RSC with Black Graphics outfit box measured 11½ x 10¼ x 6¼ inches.

The 19188 was produced in the same quantity as the X-689, but it is more difficult to find. Therefore, it achieves an R9 rating, different from the R8 assigned to outfit X-689.

CONVENTIONAL PACK
61-170 BOX

TOP LAYER	
1103-20	6112-88 (2)

6057-25 | 3357-23 | 3357-25 | 1018-30

6162-25

1008-50
1020-1 } ON TOP

62-251

BOTTOM LAYER

62-254

1013-70

1010-25 | 1060T-25

6112-88 (1) | 242-25

61-172 BETWEEN LAYERS

19189
1962

Following the Factory Order, Lionel stamped both the no. 19189 as well as Gamble-Skogmo's no. 23-4483 on this outfit box. The one item of note in this outfit was the Type IIb no. 3357-25 Animated Hobo & Railroad Policeman Car (new for 1962). Note that the no. 3357-27 Box Packed came in the version stamped "3357-23".

Customer No. On Box: 23-4483
Description: "O27" Promotional Outfit
Specification: "O27" Steam Type Freight Outfit
Customer/No./Price: Gamble-Skogmo; 23-4483; $17.88
Original Amount: 3,000
Factory Order Date: 9/28/1962
Date Issued: 10-2-62
Packaging: R.S.C. Outfit Packing (Units not Boxed), Except 1020 Crossing, (4 per Shipper)

Contents: 1060-25 Steam Type Locomotive; 1060T-25 Tender; 3357-25 Animated Hobo & Railroad Policeman Car; 3357-27 Box Packed; 6042-25 Gondola Car (Less 2 Canisters); 6112-5 Canister (Red) (2); 6076-25 Hopper Car - Red; 6067-25 Caboose; 1013-70 Curved Track (Bundle of 12 - 1013); 1018-40 Straight Track (Bundle of 4 - 1018); 1010-25 35-Watt Transformer; 1020-1 90° Crossing; 1103-20 Envelope Packed; 310-2 Set of (5) Billboards; D62-50 Accessory Catalog; 1123-40 Instruction Sheet; 1802B Layout Instruction Sheet; 1123-30 Instruction Sheet

Boxes & Packing: 62-243 Outfit Box; 61-191 Insert; 62-223 Insert; 62-225 Insert (2); 62-251 Insert; 62-258 Insert; 62-244 Shipper for (4) (1-4)

Alternate For Outfit Contents:
Customer Stock No. 23-4483; Pack Outfit as soon 3357-25 is available.

19189 (1962)	C6	C7	C8	Rarity
Complete Outfit	200	335	460	R5
Outfit Box no. 62-243	90	125	150	R5

Comments: Discount retailer Gamble-Skogmo purchased this Retailer Promotional Type Ib outfit in 1962. The no. 19189 was its only promotional outfit purchase in that year, as documented on the Factory Orders. It was the follow-up to Gamble's no. X-667 from 1961, although the two outfits had only three cars in common.

The 19189 was one of the least profitable outfits for Lionel in 1962. The 19189 Lionel Outfit Cost Worksheet lists Lionel's selling price as $10.50 and cost as $11.50. Thus a $1.00 loss was realized, the second highest of any outfit sold in that year.

The 19189 was led by a no. 1060-25 Steam Type Locomotive. This low-end steamer went forward only. The locomotive included in this outfit was the later version with a small rain shield covering the headlight.

The only new item in this outfit was the Type IIb no. 3357-25 Animated Hobo & Railroad Policeman Car. Since the car was unboxed, the no. 3357-27 Box Packed was listed separately on the Factory Order and placed loose in the outfit box. This outfit has been observed with the 3357-27 stamped "3357-23" on its box. The "3357-23" was actually the number of the box and appears to have been mistakenly printed as the final assembly number on some early examples of the 3357-27 Box Packed.

All but one of the cars came equipped with non-operating Archbar trucks and couplers. The exception was the 3357-25, which had middle operating AAR types.

A no. 1020-1 90° Crossing plus appropriate track were included in this outfit to create the figure-eight layout outlined on the no. 1802B Layout Instruction Sheet.

The no. 62-243 Tan RSC with Black Graphics outfit box was manufactured by St. Joe Kraft, St. Joe Paper Co. Container Division and measured 12⅛ x 11½ x 6⅜ inches.

This outfit exceeded Gamble-Skogmo's expectations, as the original quantity of 2,600 was increased to 3,000. Both the 19189 and X-667 were produced in the same quantity and so achieve the same R5 ranking. They appear equally as often on the market.

CONVENTIONAL PACK
62-243 BOX

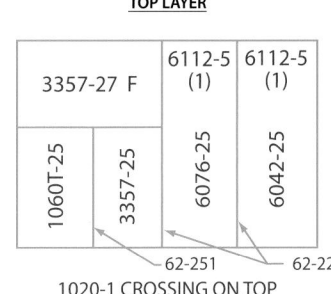
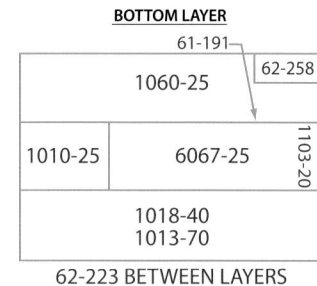

Description: "O27" Promotional Outfit
Specification: "O27" Diesel Freight Outfit
Customer: R. H. Macy
Original Amount: 150
Factory Order Date: 9/28/1962
Date Issued: 10-2-62
Packaging: R.S.C. Outfit Packing (Units not Boxed)

Contents: 231P-25 Alco Diesel Power Car - "Rock Island"; 3619-25 Reconnaissance Copter Car; 3413-25 Mercury Capsule Launching Car; 6512-25 Cherry Picker Car; 3349-25 Turbo Missile Firing Car (Less Missiles); 0349-10 Turbo Missile (2); 6057-25 Caboose; 1013-8 Curved Track (Bundle of 8 - 1013); 1018-30 Straight Track (Bundle of 3 - 1018); 1008-50 Uncoupling Unit; 1025-25 45-Watt Transformer; 1103-20 Envelope Packed; 1123-40 Instruction Sheet; 3413-8 Instruction Sheet; 211-6 Instruction Sheet; 122-10 Instruction Sheet; 6512-19 Instruction Sheet

Boxes & Packing: 62-243 Outfit Box; 62-223 Insert; 62-224 Insert; 62-225 Insert; 62-245 Insert (2); 62-248 Insert; 62-254 Insert; 62-244 Shipper for (4) (1-4)

19190 (1962)	C6	C7	C8	Rarity
Complete Outfit	900	1,400	1,850	R10
Outfit Box no. 62-243	500	800	1,000	R10

Comments: R. H. Macy, commonly known as Macy's, is a retailer that purchased numerous promotional outfits in the 1960s. In 1962, it purchased a pair of Retailer Promotional Type Ia outfits: nos. 19190 and 19191.

The 19190 was the follow-up to the no. X-708 from 1961. Both outfits included four higher-end cars and a caboose. Each was powered by a no. 231P Rock Island Diesel Power Car, which

was equipped with a two-position reversing unit, a headlight and two-axle Magne-Traction.

The space and military operating cars in the 19190 were all new for 1962. The nos. 3413-25 Mercury Capsule Launching Car and 6512-25 Cherry Picker Car were paired in at least 18 different outfits. They were designed to work together, with the 6512-25 pretending to load an astronaut into the waiting Mercury capsule.

The no. 3619-25 included a fragile and easily lost no. 0319-100 Helicopter. As part of the manufacturing process, the roof of the 3619-25 was taped shut with a ½-inch piece of Scotch tape. Even examples in C8 condition still have a mark where the tape was applied. This car, like the others in the 19190, was equipped with operating AAR trucks and couplers.

The no. 62-243 Tan RSC with Black Graphics outfit box was manufactured by St. Joe Kraft, St. Joe Paper Co. Container Division and measured 12⅛ x 11½ x 6⅜ inches.

The 19190 and 19191 were manufactured in lower quantities than their counterparts from 1961 (X-708 and no. X-709). As a consequence, they are more difficult to find.

CONVENTIONAL PACK
62-243 BOX

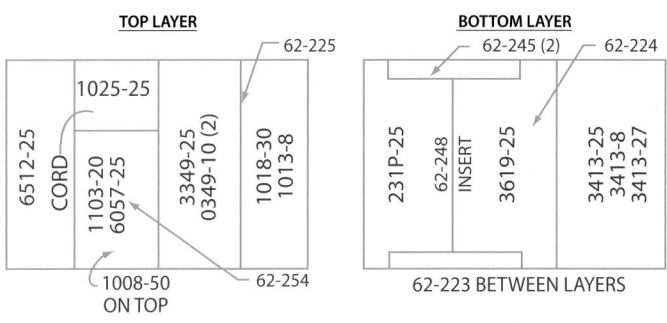

Macy's steam-powered outfit purchase for 1962 was the no. 19191. It was produced in relatively low quantities and is difficult to find. This outfit still has its original Macy's price tag attached, which listed "Macy's WD 12A 29.99". The "29.99" was crossed out and $20.99 handwritten on the price tag.

Description: "O27" Promotional Outfit
Specification: "O27" Steam Type Freight Outfit with Smoke
Customer/No./Price: R. H. Macy; WD 12A; $29.99
Original Amount: 300
Factory Order Date: 9/28/1962
Date Issued: 10-2-62
Packaging: R.S.C. Outfit Packing (Units not Boxed)

Contents: 236-25 Steam Type Locomotive with Smoke; 1060T-25 Tender; 3357-25 Animated Hobo & Railroad Policeman Car; 3357-27 Box Packed; 6473-25 Rodeo Car; 3370-25 Sheriff & Outlaw Car; 6445-25 Ft. Knox Gold Bullion Transport Car; 6057-25 Caboose; 1013-8 Curved Track (Bundle of 8 - 1013); 1018-30 Straight Track (Bundle of 3 - 1018); 1008-50 Uncoupling Unit; 1025-25 45-Watt Transformer; 1103-20 Envelope Packed; 909-20 Smoke Fluid; 310-2 Set of (5) Billboards; D62-50 Accessory Catalog; 1123-40 Instruction Sheet; 3370-17 Instruction Sheet; 236-11 Instruction Sheet; 122-10 Instruction Sheet

Boxes & Packing: 62-243 Outfit Box; 61-191 Insert; 62-223 Insert; 62-225 Insert; 62-251 Insert (3); 62-258 Insert; 62-244 Shipper for (4) (1-4)

19191 (1962)	C6	C7	C8	Rarity
Complete Outfit	600	925	1,225	R9
Outfit Box no. 62-243	350	500	600	R9

Comments: R. H. Macy, commonly known as Macy's, is a retailer that purchased numerous promotional outfits in the 1960s. In 1962, it purchased a pair of Retailer Promotional Type Ia outfits: nos. 19190 and 19191.

The 19191 was the follow-up to the no. X-709 from 1961. Both outfits included four higher-end cars and a caboose. Each was powered by a no. 236 Steam Type Locomotive with Smoke. The 19191 included an unboxed 236-25. This engine was one of Lionel's high-end Scout steamers, and it featured a two-position reversing unit, a headlight and Magne-Traction. It was paired with a no. 1060T-25 Tender. The 1060T-25 was usually equipped with non-operating Archbar trucks and couplers, but it could come with one non-operating Archbar and one plain AAR truck and coupler.

The 19191 featured two operating cars that were new in 1962. The nos. 3357-25 Animated Hobo & Railroad Policeman Car and 6473-25 Rodeo Car were paired in at least 11 outfits. The 3357-25 provided plenty of excitement as the cop tried to catch the hobo. Since the car came unboxed (hence the "-25" suffix), the Factory Order also listed a no. 3357-27 Box Packed. Interestingly, the outfit packing diagram listed a no. 3357-23. This is consistent with actual outfit observations in 1962, which indicated that a 3357-27 with "3357-23" was printed on its box. The "3357-23" was actually the number of the box and appears to have been mistakenly printed as the final assembly number on some early examples of the 3357-27 Box Packed.

The nos. 3370-25 Sheriff & Outlaw Car and 6445-25 Ft. Knox Gold Bullion Transport Car were carryover items from 1961. They and the other cars in this outfit were equipped with operating

AAR trucks and couplers.

The no. 62-243 Tan RSC with Black Graphics outfit box was manufactured by St. Joe Kraft, St. Joe Paper Co. Container Division and measured 12⅛ x 11½ x 6⅜ inches.

The 19190 and 19191 were manufactured in lower quantities than their counterparts from 1961 (no. X-708 and X-709). As a consequence, they are more difficult to find.

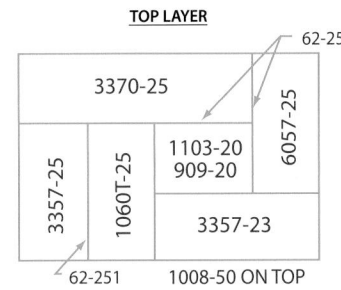
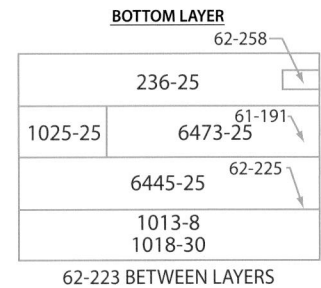

CONVENTIONAL PACK
62-243 BOX

TOP LAYER

3370-25	62-251
1103-20 / 909-20	6057-25
3357-25	1060T-25
3357-23	

62-251 — 1008-50 ON TOP

BOTTOM LAYER

| 236-25 | 62-258 |
| 1025-25 | 6473-25 61-191 |
| 6445-25 62-225 |
| 1013-8 1018-30 |

62-223 BETWEEN LAYERS

19192
1962

S. Klein purchased the no. 19192 in 1962. This outfit was interesting because it included all low-end items except for the no. 3413-25 Mercury Capsule Launching Car. The firing mechanism on the 3413-25s would not stay locked, thus causing the bowed-out insert in this example. Note Lionel's use of mixed trucks and couplers on the nos. 1060T-25 Tender and 6067-25 Caboose.

The no. 19192 came in the common no. 62-200 White 4-6-4 Steamer and F3 Hinged Display with Red/Orange and Blue Graphics Type A outfit box. This generic box was stamped by Lionel with "No. 19192". The example shown still has its S. Klein price tag attached.

Contents: 1060-25 Steam Type Locomotive; 1060T-25 Tender; 3413-25 Mercury Capsule Launching Car; 6042-75 Gondola Car (Less 2 Cable Reels); 40-11 Cable Reels (2); 6067-25 Caboose; 1013-8 Curved Track (Bundle of 8 - 1013); 1018-10 Straight Track (Loose); 1008-50 Uncoupling Unit; 1026-25 25-Watt Transformer; 1103-20 Envelope Packed; 310-2 Set of (5) Billboards; D62-50 Accessory Catalog; 19192-10 Instruction Sheet; 1123-40 Instruction Sheet; 3413-8 Instruction Sheet

Boxes & Packing: 62-200 Outfit Box; 61-101 Insert; 61-102 Insert (2); 61-103 Shipper for (6) (1-6)

19192 (1962)	C6	C7	C8	Rarity
Complete Outfit	335	575	800	R8
Outfit Box no. 62-200	175	300	400	R8

Description: "O27" Promotional Outfit
Specification: "O27" Steam Type Freight Outfit
Customer/Price: S. Klein; $12.88
Original Amount: 750
Factory Order Date: 10/2/1962
Date Issued: 10-2-62
Packaging: Display Outfit Packing (Units not Boxed)

Comments: S. Klein was a discount retailer that purchased numerous promotional Lionel outfits in the 1960s. This Retailer Promotional Type Ib outfit was its only purchase for 1962.

The no. 19192 was led by a no. 1060-25 Steam Type Locomotive, a low-end item that moved only forward. The locomotive included in this outfit was the later version with a small rain shield covering the headlight.

All the cars in the 19192 were low-end items, with the exception of a no. 3413-25 Mercury Capsule Launching Car. This car appeared unboxed in 24 outfits in 1962.

Keep in mind that a transition from Archbar to AAR trucks and couplers began in 1962. For example, the 3413-25 was equipped with middle AAR types. However, the nos. 1060T-25 Tender and 6067-25 Caboose came with one non-operating Archbar and one plain AAR truck and coupler. And the new-for-1962 no. 6042-75 Gondola Car (Less 2 Cable Reels) had two non-operating Archbar types.

The no. 19192-10 Instruction Sheet was unique to this outfit and is very difficult to find.

DISPLAY PACK
62-200 BOX

```
                            61-102
  ┌──────────┬──────────┬──────────┐
  │ 1060-25  │ 1060T-25 │ 1026-25  │
  ├──────────┼──────────┴──────────┤
  │ 40-11 (2)│     3413-25          │
  │ 6042-75  │     3413-18          │ ── 61-101
  │          │     3413-27          │
  ├──────────┼─────────────────────┤
  │ 1013-8   │                      │
  │ 1018-10  │     6067-25          │
  │ 1008-50  │     1103-20          │
  └──────────┴─────────────────────┘
                    61-102
```

The no. 62-200 White 4-6-4 Steamer and F3 Hinged Display with Red/Orange and Blue Graphics Type A outfit box was manufactured by United Container Co. and measured 21⅝ x 11½ x 3¼ inches.

Despite being given an R8 rarity rating, this outfit can be obtained. Patience is definitely required to find a C8 version.

19193
1962

Description: "O27" Promotional Outfit
Specification: "O27" Steam Type Freight Outfit
Customer: Bloomingdales
Original Amount: 100
Factory Order Date: 9/14/1962
Date Issued: 9-17-62
Packaging: R.S.C. Outfit Packing (Units not Boxed)

Contents: 1060-25 Steam Type Locomotive; 1060T-25 Tender; 3309-25 Turbo Missile Firing Car (Less Missiles); 0349-10 Turbo Missile (2); 6480-25 Exploding Target Car; 6067-25 Caboose; 1013-8 Curved Track (Bundle of 8 - 1013); 1018-10 Straight Track (Loose) (2); 1010-25 35-Watt Transformer; 1103-20 Envelope Packed; 310-2 Set of (5) Billboards; D62-50 Accessory Catalog; 1123-40 Instruction Sheet; 6480-5 Instruction Sheet; 3309-5 Instruction Sheet; 1123-30 Instruction Sheet

Boxes & Packing: 61-170 Outfit Box; 61-171 Insert; 61-172 Insert; 62-202 Insert; 61-175 Shipper for (4) (1-4)

19193 (1962)	C6	C7	C8	Rarity
Complete Outfit	815	1,200	1,500	R10
Outfit Box no. 61-170	700	1,000	1,200	R10

Comments: In 1962, Bloomingdales purchased four Retailer Promotional Type Ib outfits: nos. 19183, 19193, 19194 and 19195. All four were space and military steam freight outfits that Lionel produced in very small quantities.

The 19193 was an entry-level steam-powered outfit. It was led by a no. 1060-25 Steam Type Locomotive, which went forward only.

The rolling stock in this outfit featured a pair of operating cars. In fact, with only one difference, the contents were identical to those in the 19194. Whereas the 19193 included a no. 6480-25 Exploding Target Car, the 19194 had a no. 3470-25 Aerial Target Launching Car. Why Bloomingdales ended up with two outfits in the same year that were virtually the same remains a mystery. Did the customer request that Lionel configure them in this manner? Or did the reason stem from workings at Lionel? Either way, it would be interesting to learn which outfit sold better.

The 6480-25 in the 19193 (like the more expensive 3470-25 in the 19194) was paired with a no. 3309-25 Turbo Missing Firing Car. Either car provided a neat target for the 3309-25 to shoot.

The 3309-25 and 6480-25 were both equipped with non-operating Archbar trucks and couplers. A transition from Archbar to AAR trucks and couplers began in 1962. As a result, the nos. 1060T-25 Tender and 6067-25 Caboose could come with either two Archbar types or one non-operating Archbar and one plain AAR truck and coupler.

The common no. 61-170 Tan RSC with Black Graphics outfit box was used for the 19193. It measured 11½ x 10¼ x 6¼ inches.

Lionel produced such small quantities of all four Bloomingdales outfits that they were likely sold over the counter at Bloomingdales stores. No catalog listings or other information beyond the Factory Orders has been observed. The outfits are seldom seen, hence the R10 rarity for all four of them.

CONVENTIONAL PACK
61-170 BOX

TOP LAYER

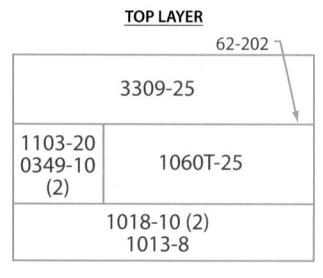

BOTTOM LAYER

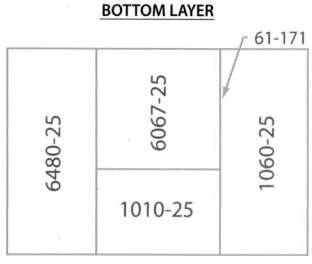

61-172 BETWEEN LAYERS

19194
1962

Description: "O27" Promotional Outfit
Specification: "O27" Steam Type Freight Outfit
Customer: Bloomingdales

Original Amount: 100
Factory Order Date: 9/14/1962
Date Issued: 9-17-62
Packaging: R.S.C. Outfit Packing (Units not Boxed)

Contents: 1060-25 Steam Type Locomotive; 1060T-25 Tender; 3309-25 Turbo Missile Firing Car (Less Missiles); 0349-10 Turbo Missile (2); 3470-25 Aerial Target Launching Car; 3470-4 Basket; 3470-20 Envelope Packed; 6067-25 Caboose; 1013-8 Curved Track (Bundle of 8 - 1013); 1018-10 Straight Track (Loose) (2); 1010-25 35-Watt Transformer; 1103-20 Envelope Packed; 310-2 Set of (5) Billboards; D62-50 Accessory Catalog; 1123-40 Instruction Sheet; 3309-5 Instruction Sheet; 1123-30 Instruction Sheet

Boxes & Packing: 61-170 Outfit Box; 61-171 Insert; 61-172 Insert; 61-173 Insert; 61-175 Shipper for (4) (1-4)

19194 (1962)	C6	C7	C8	Rarity
Complete Outfit	840	1,225	1,550	R10
Outfit Box no. 61-170	700	1,000	1,200	R10

Comments: In 1962, Bloomingdales purchased four Retailer Promotional Type Ib outfits: nos. 19183, 19193, 19194 and 19195. All four were space and military steam freight outfits that Lionel produced in very small quantities.

The 19194 was an entry-level steam-powered outfit. It was led by a no. 1060-25 Steam Type Locomotive, which went forward only.

The rolling stock in this outfit featured a pair of operating cars. In fact, with only one difference, the contents were identical to those in the 19193. Whereas the 19194 included a no. 3470-25 Aerial Target Launching Car, the 19193 had a no. 6480-25 Exploding Target Car. Why Bloomingdales ended up with two outfits in the same year that were virtually the same remains a mystery. Did the customer request that Lionel configure them in this manner? Or did the reason stem from workings at Lionel? Either way, it would be interesting to learn which outfit sold better.

The 3470-25 in the 19194 (like the less expensive 6480-25 in the 19193) was paired with a no. 3309-25 Turbo Missing Firing Car. Either car provided a neat target for the 3309-25 to shoot.

The 3309-25 was equipped with non-operating Archbar trucks and couplers, whereas the 3470-25 was equipped with operating AAR types. A transition from Archbar to AAR trucks and couplers began in 1962. As a result, the nos. 1060T-25 Tender and 6067-25 Caboose could come with either two Archbar types or one non-operating Archbar and one plain AAR truck and coupler.

The common no. 61-170 Tan RSC with Black Graphics outfit box was used for the 19194. It measured 11½ x 10¼ x 6¼ inches.

Lionel produced such small quantities of all four Bloomingdales outfits that they were likely sold over the counter at Bloomingdales stores. No catalog listings or other information beyond the Factory Orders has been observed. The outfits are seldom seen, hence the R10 rarity for all four of them.

CONVENTIONAL PACK
61-170 BOX

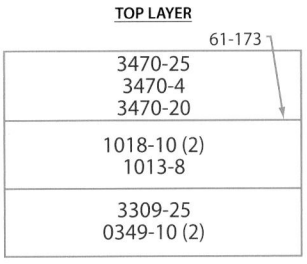
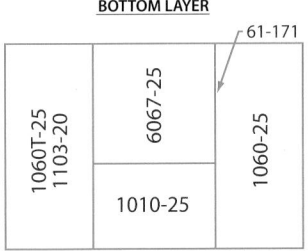

61-172 BETWEEN LAYERS

Description: "O27" Promotional Outfit
Specification: "O27" Steam Type Freight Outfit
Customer: Bloomingdales
Original Amount: 50
Factory Order Date: 9/17/1962
Date Issued: 9-17-62
Packaging: R.S.C. Outfit Packing (Units not Boxed)

Contents: 1060-25 Steam Type Locomotive; 1060T-25 Tender; 3665-25 Minuteman Missile Launching Car; 6480-25 Exploding Target Car; 3357-25 Animated Hobo & Railroad Policeman Car; 3357-27 Box Packed; 6067-25 Caboose; 1013-8 Curved Track (Bundle of 8 - 1013); 1018-10 Straight Track (Loose) (2); 1010-25 35-Watt Transformer; 1103-20 Envelope Packed; 310-2 Set of (5) Billboards; D62-50 Accessory Catalog; 1123-30 Instruction Sheet; 1123-40 Instruction Sheet; 3665-23 Instruction Sheet; 6480-5 Instruction Sheet; 3357-8 Instruction Sheet

Boxes & Packing: 62-243 Outfit Box; 61-191 Insert; 62-202 Insert; 62-223 Insert; 62-225 Insert; 62-251 Insert; 62-244 Shipper for (4) (1-4)

19195 (1962)	C6	C7	C8	Rarity
Complete Outfit	1,325	1,775	2,150	R10
Outfit Box no. 62-243	1,150	1,450	1,650	R10

Comments: In 1962, Bloomingdales purchased four Retailer Promotional Type Ib outfits: nos. 19183, 19193, 19194 and 19195. All four were space and military steam freight outfits that Lionel produced in very small quantities.

The 19195 fit right in the middle of the other Bloomingdales offerings. Led by a no. 1060-25 Steam Type Locomotive that went only forward, it did include one more piece of rolling stock than the 19193 and 19194.

The contents of the 19195 included three unboxed operating cars. This was the only time that Lionel paired a no. 3665-25 Minuteman Missile Launching Car with a no. 6480-25 Exploding Target Car. The 3665-25 was usually paired with a no. 6470 Exploding Target Car. Because Lionel was not offering the 6470 separately in outfits in 1962, it resorted to using a 6480-25.

The no. 3357-25 Animated Hobo & Railroad Policeman Car was the only new car in this outfit, although it was out of place in a space and military outfit. Since the car was unboxed, the no. 3357-27 Box Packed was listed separately on the Factory Order and placed loose in the outfit box. Interestingly, the outfit packing diagram listed a no. 3357-23. This is consistent with actual outfit observations in 1962, which included a 3357-27 with "3357-23" printed on its box. The "3357-23" was actually the number of the box and appears to have been mistakenly printed as the final assembly number on some early examples of the 3357-27 Box Packed.

The 3357-25 and 3665-25 were equipped with operating AAR trucks and couplers, whereas the 6480-25 had non-operating Archbar trucks and couplers. A transition from Archbar to AAR trucks and couplers began in 1962. As a result, the nos. 1060T-25 Tender and 6067-25 Caboose could come with either two Archbar types or one non-operating Archbar and one plain AAR truck and coupler.

The no. 62-243 Tan RSC with Black Graphics outfit box measured 12⅛ x 11½ x 6⅜ inches.

Lionel produced such small quantities of all four Bloomingdales outfits that they were likely sold over the counter at Bloomingdales stores. No catalog listings or other information beyond the Factory Orders has been observed. The outfits are seldom seen, hence the R10 rarity for all four of them.

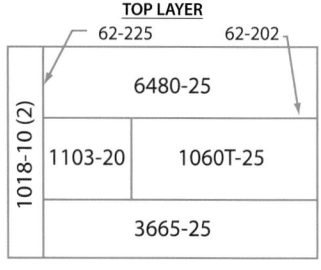

CONVENTIONAL PACK
62-243 BOX

TOP LAYER

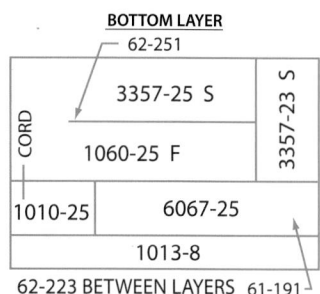

BOTTOM LAYER

62-223 BETWEEN LAYERS 61-191

Description: Super "O" Promotional Outfit
Specification: Super "O" Steam Type Freight With Smoke & Whistle
Customer: Broadway Stores
Original Amount: 60
Factory Order Date: 9/21/1962
Date Issued: 9-21-62
Packaging: R.S.C. Outfit Packing (Units Boxed)

Contents: 637X-1 Steam Type Locomotive with Smoke; 736W-1 Whistle Tender; 3619-1 Reconnaissance Copter Car; 6175-1 Rocket Car; 3830-1 Operating Submarine Car; 3545-1 Operating TV Monitor Car; 6437-1 Illuminated Cupola Caboose; 31-60 Bundle of 6 - 31 Curved Track (2); 32-60 Bundle of 3 - 32 Straight Track; 34-10 Straight Track - 1/2 Section; 39-25 Remote Control Set; 1044-1 90-Watt Transformer; 470-1 Missile Launching Platform; 310-1 Set of (5) Billboards; D62-50 Accessory Catalog; 1123-40 Instruction Sheet

Boxes & Packing: 62-279 Outfit Box; 62-280 Shipper for (2) (1-2)

19196 (1962)	C6	C7	C8	Rarity
Complete Outfit	2,300	3,000	3,650	R10
Outfit Box no. 62-279	1,500	1,800	2,000	R10

Comments: This outfit is the only one to list Broadway Stores as the customer on a Factory Order. A Retailer Promotional Type Ia outfit, it was one of only two promotional Super O outfits from 1962 (the no. 19178, sold to Joe, The Motorists' Friend, was the other).

The no. 19196 marked the first promotional outfit appearance in the 1960s of a no. 637X-1 Steam Type Locomotive with Smoke. This engine was equipped with Magne-Traction, a three-position reversing unit and a headlight. As described in the section on Outfit Peripherals, an "X" signified that a no. CTC-1 Lockon was not included in the no. 637-13 Corrugated Box. Including a Lockon in a Super O outfit was unnecessary.

The space and military rolling stock in the 19196 included some of Lionel's high-end items from 1962. All the cars were equipped with operating AAR trucks and couplers. Except for the no. 6175-1 Rocket Car that came in an Orange Perforated box, all

cars came individually packaged in Orange Picture boxes. This fact made the 19196 a high-end outfit for 1962; the norm in that year was for all cars to come unboxed.

Four operating cars were selected to make this an outfit that provided hours of fun. Cars of note included the no. 3619-1 Reconnaissance Copter Car, which came with a fragile and easily lost no. 0319-100 Helicopter. As part of the manufacturing process, the roof of the 3619-1 was taped shut with a ½-inch piece of Scotch tape. Even examples in C8 condition still have a mark where the tape was applied.

The no. 3545-1 Operating TV Monitor Car appeared only in two promotional outfits in 1962. The 6175-1 was making its last appearance in any outfit. The no. 6470-1 Exploding Target Car was included inside the no. 470-1 Missile Launching Platform.

A no. 39-25 Remote Control Set included all the Super O peripherals. It could be either a Type III or Type IV.

The 19196 was one of the few outfits to come with a no. 310-1 Set of (5) Billboards. This was the boxed version that included billboards and holders.

Catalog Super O outfits generally did not include a transformer. However, because promotional outfits were most often destined for retailers that probably did not have a train department, Lionel included a transformer. In this case, a no. 1044-1 90-Watt Transformer was included; it appeared in only 10 outfits during the 1960s.

The no. 62-279 Orange RSC with Black Graphics outfit box was manufactured by Mead Containers and measured 17½ x 15¾ x 7 inches. The same box was used for catalog outfit no. 13058 from 1962.

The 19196 was made in quantities so small that it ties for 15th on the list of fewest outfits produced. That fact, combined with this highly desirable outfit being one of only two promotional Super O outfits from 1962, easily gives this outfit an R10 rarity.

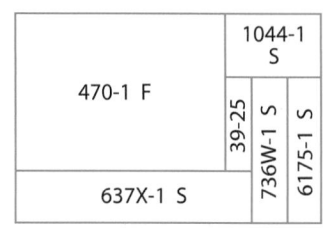

CONVENTIONAL PACK
62-279 BOX

TOP LAYER

BOTTOM LAYER

D. O. Klein was listed as the customer on the Factory Order for the no. 19197. This outfit was one of nine 1962 outfits to feature the promotional-only no. 6050-150 Van Camp Savings Bank Car. Five different box variations exist. The no. 61-420 Display Outfit Box version is shown here.

There are four overstickered and one generic stamped version of outfit no. 19197. This is the no. 61-420 Display Outfit Box version, which was an overstickered no. X-667. The easiest way to identify these variations is by prying up the side flaps to reveal the box part number.

Boxes & Packing: 61-398 Display Outfit Box W/Stickers (Amount - 465); 61-390 Display Outfit Box W/Stickers (Amount - 168); 61-420 Display Outfit Box W/Stickers (Amount - 733); 61-397 Display Outfit Box W/Stickers (Amount - 25); 61-439 Display Outfit Box; 61-391 Insert; 61-392 Insert; 61-421 Insert (Inv. 270); 61-393 Insert (Replacing 61-421); 61-394 Insert; 62-252 Insert (2); 62-253 Insert; 61-395 Shipper for (6) (1-6)

Alternate For Outfit Contents:
Substitute 6057-50 as needed for 6067-25.

Description: "O27" Promotional Outfit
Specification: "O27" Steam Type Freight Outfit
Customer: D. O. Klein
Original Amount: 3,000
Factory Order Date: 9/21/1962
Date Issued: Rev 10/12/62
Packaging: R.S.C. Outfit Packing (Units not Boxed), Except 1020 Crossing

Contents: 1060-25 Steam Type Locomotive; 1060T-25 Tender; 6042-25 Gondola Car (Less 2 Canisters); 6112-5 Canister - Red (2); 6076-25 Hopper Car - Red; 6050-150 "Van Camp" Savings Bank Car; 6067-25 Caboose; 1013-70 Curved Track (Bundle of 12 - 1013); 1018-10 Straight Track (Loose) (4); 1026-25 25-Watt Transformer; 1020-1 90° Crossing; 1103-20 Envelope Packed; 1123-40 Instruction Sheet; 1802B Layout Instruction Sheet; 1123-10 Instruction Sheet; 310-2 Set of (5) Billboards; D62-50 Accessory Catalog

19197 (1962)	C6	C7	C8	Rarity
Complete Outfit With no. 61-398 Box	350	600	800	R9
Outfit Box no. 61-398	250	400	500	R9
Complete Outfit With no. 61-390 Box	450	650	900	R10
Outfit Box no. 61-390	350	450	600	R10
Complete Outfit With no. 61-420 Box	275	475	650	R8
Outfit Box no. 61-420	175	275	350	R8
Complete Outfit With no. 61-397 Box	650	850	1,050	R10
Outfit Box no. 61-397	550	650	750	R10
Complete Outfit With no. 61-439 Box	215	400	575	R6
Outfit Box no. 61-439	115	200	275	R6

Comments: This was the first of two Factory Orders to list as the customer D. O. Klein (see the entry for the no. 19142-500 from 1963). Because our research has yet to uncover any information about the identity or location of D. O. Klein, we cannot determine whether the no. 19197 was a Retailer Promotional Type Ib outfit or a Manufacturer Promotional Type IIIb outfit.

What is clear is that the 19197 was a low-end starter outfit led by a no. 1060-25 Steam Type Locomotive, which went forward only. The locomotive included in this outfit was the later version with a small rain shield covering the headlight.

The only car of note in the 19197 was the no. 6050-150 Van Camp Savings Bank Car. This car, which appeared only in promotional outfits, was included in a mere nine outfits during its first year.

Keep in mind that a transition from Archbar to AAR trucks and couplers began in 1962. For the 19197, all the cars were equipped with non-operating Archbar types. However, the no. 1060T-25 Tender has been observed with either two Archbar types or one non-operating Archbar and one plain AAR truck and coupler.

In addition, some examples of the 19197 have been seen with an orange no. 6057-50 Caboose. This fact suggests that Lionel was depleting inventory of this model (equipped with AAR trucks and couplers) in promotional outfits.

The 19197 stood out thanks to its five outfit box variations. As with many early 1962 outfits, Lionel was depleting its inventory of pre-printed outfit boxes. The 19197 used four overstickered versions as well as the unprinted no. 61-439 Display Outfit Box. All were White 4-6-4 Steamer and F3 Hinged Display with Red/Orange and Blue Graphics Type A outfit boxes.

The 61-439 was manufactured by United Container Co. and measured 22½ x 14½ x 3¼ inches. It was stamped with "No. 19197" by Lionel.

The four overstickered versions included:

- The no. 61-398, which was manufactured by UCC (United Container Co.) and measured 22½ x 14¾ x 3⅛ inches. It was an overstickered no. X-654 from 1961.
- The no. 61-390, which was manufactured by UCC (United Container Co.) and measured 22½ x 14½ x 3¼ inches. It was an overstickered no. X-618 from 1961.
- The no. 61-420, which was manufactured by UCC (United Container Co.) and measured 22½ x 14¾ x 3⅛ inches. It was an overstickered no. X-667 from 1961.
- The no. 61-397, which measured 22½ x 14¾ x 3⅛ inches. It was an overstickered no. X-645 from 1961.

These five boxes lead to five variations of this outfit, each of which has a separate rarity and price. The easiest way to identify the different outfit boxes is by prying up the side flaps to reveal the box number. (See the section on Outfit Boxes and Inserts for more information in identifying boxes.)

Of the five variations, the 61-397 overstickered X-645 outfit box is the most difficult to find. Collecting all five versions is a real challenge.

DISPLAY PACK
61-398, 61-390, 61-420 OR 61-397 BOX
5 STICKERS PER BOX
61-439 BOX

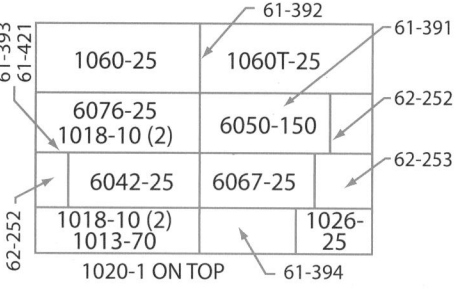

Description: "O27" Promotional Outfit
Specification: "O27" Diesel Switcher Freight Outfit
Customer: Robin Distributors
Original Amount: 144
Factory Order Date: 10/10/1962
Date Issued: 10-10-62
Packaging: R.S.C. Outfit Packing (Units not Boxed), Except 1020 Crossing

Contents: 633-50 "Santa Fe" Diesel Switcher; 3619-25 Reconnaissance Copter Car; 3413-25 Mercury Capsule Launching Car; 6512-25 Cherry Picker Car; 3349-25 Turbo Missile Firing Car (Less Missiles); 0349-10 Turbo Missile (2); 6057-25 Caboose; 1013-70 Curved Track (Bundle of 12 - 1013); 1018-30 Straight Track (Bundle of 3 - 1018); 1008-50 Uncoupling Unit; 1025-25 45-Watt Transformer; 1103-20 Envelope Packed; 1020-1 90° Crossing; 310-2 Set of (5) Billboards; D62-50 Accessory Catalog; 1123-40 Instruction Sheet; 3413-8 Instruction Sheet; 3349-8 Instruction Sheet; 1802B Layout Instruction Sheet; 121-10 Instruction Sheet; 6512-19 Instruction Sheet

Boxes & Packing: 61-250 Outfit Box; 600-26 Insert; 61-182 Insert; 61-184 Insert; 62-223 Insert; 62-225 Insert; 62-264 Insert; 61-251 Shipper for (4) (1-4)

19198 (1962)	C6	C7	C8	Rarity
Complete Outfit	1,115	1,650	2,225	R10
Outfit Box no. 61-250	650	900	1,100	R10

Comments: Robin Distributors was a large toy concessionaire during the early 1960s. The no. 19198 was the only outfit that listed it as the customer on a Factory Order.

This Retailer Promotional Type Ib was a space and military outfit that, except for the caboose, was entirely new for 1962. It was led by a no. 633-50 Santa Fe Diesel Switcher, which was the promotional-only upgrade to the no. 633-25 that Lionel issued earlier in 1962. This low-end switcher came with a traction tire but lacked a horn. However, it was "4 wheel drive equipped", unlike the 633-25, which was driven by only two wheels. The "-50" version is more difficult (3,660 produced) to find than the "-25" (11,900 produced). According to the Lionel Engineering Specification for the 633-50, it was "primarily designed to pull 5 moderate weight cars up a trestle".

Four operating cars were included in the 19198. The nos. 3413-25 Mercury Capsule Launching Car and 6512-25 Cherry

Picker Car (both new for 1962) were paired in at least 18 different outfits. They were designed to work together, with the 6512-25 pretending to load an astronaut into the waiting Mercury capsule.

The no. 3619-25 Reconnaissance Copter Car included a fragile and easily lost no. 0319-100 Helicopter. As part of the manufacturing process, the roof of the 3619-25 was taped shut with a ½-inch piece of Scotch tape. Even examples in C8 condition still have a mark where the tape was applied. This car, like the others in the 19198, was equipped with operating AAR trucks and couplers.

A no. 1020-1 90° Crossing plus appropriate track were included with this outfit to create the figure-eight layout outlined on the no. 1802B Layout Instruction Sheet.

The no. 61-250 Orange RSC with Black Graphics outfit box measured 13 x 12 x 7 inches.

The quantity of a promotional outfit that a customer ordered varied, although many were multiples of 100 or even 10. So why

were 144 of the 19198 made? That unusual number represents a "gross": an aggregate consisting of 12 dozen of an item. Not surprisingly with so low a total made, examples of this outfit are seldom seen, a fact that earns the 19198 an R10 rarity.

CONVENTIONAL PACK
61-250 BOX

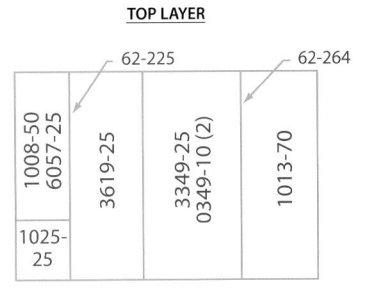

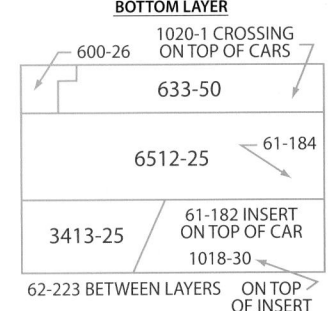

Description: "O27" Promotional Outfit
Specification: "O27" Steam Type Freight Outfit
Customer: RMG
Original Amount: 100
Factory Order Date: 10/8/1962
Date Issued: 10-8-62
Packaging: R.S.C. Outfit Packing (Units not Boxed), Except 110-1

Contents: 242-25 Steam Type Locomotive; 1060T-25 Tender; 3309-25 Turbo Missile Firing Car (Less Missiles); 0349-10 Turbo Missile (2); 6463-25 Rocket Fuel Car; 6413-25 Mercury Capsule Transport Car (Less Capsules); 6413-4 Capsules (2); 6413-10 Envelope Packed; 6067-25 Caboose; 1013-8 Curved Track (Bundle of 8 - 1013); 1013-90 Curved Track (Bundle of 9 - 1013); 1018-5 Straight Track (Bundle of 5 - 1018) (2); 1010-25 35-Watt Transformer; 110-1 Trestle Set; 1103-20 Envelope Packed; 310-2 Set of (5) Billboards; D62-50 Accessory Catalog; 1123-40 Instruction Sheet; 120-10 Instruction Sheet; 3309-10 Instruction Sheet; 1802I Layout Instruction Sheet

Boxes & Packing: 62-270 Outfit Box; 61-171 Insert; 62-264 Insert; 62-272 Insert; 62-278 Insert; 62-271 Shipper for (3) (1-3); BP Bogus Paper

19199 (1962)	C6	C7	C8	Rarity
Complete Outfit	965	1,360	1,775	R10
Outfit Box no. 62-270	750	1,000	1,200	R10

Comments: In 1962, RMG was listed as the customer on two outfits: nos. 19199 and 19200. Because our research has yet to uncover any information about the identity or location of RMG, we cannot determine whether the no. 19199 was a Retailer Promotional Type Ib outfit or a Manufacturer Promotional Type IIIb outfit.

Evidently, the 19199 was the better of RMG's two steamer purchases for 1962 – in spite of being led by a no. 242-25 Steam Type Locomotive. That low-end Scout steamer had a two-position reversing unit and a headlight, lacked smoke and used a rubber tire as a traction aid.

The rolling stock distinguished this outfit, particularly the trio of new-for-1962 space and military items. The no. 3309-25 Turbo Missile Firing Car (Less Missiles) was the low-end version of the no. 3349-25 Turbo Missile Firing Car. The difference between the two cars was that the 3309-25 was equipped with non-operating Archbar trucks and couplers rather than operating AAR types. It was unusual that Lionel didn't include a 3349-25 in this outfit, as both the nos. 6463-25 Rocket Fuel Car and 6413-25 Mercury Capsule Transport Car in it were equipped with operating AAR trucks and couplers.

Due to the transition from Archbar to AAR types that began in 1962, the nos. 1060T-25 Tender and 6067-25 Caboose in this outfit could come with either two Archbar types or one non-operating Archbar and one plain AAR truck and coupler.

The no. 110-1 Trestle Set in this outfit was used for the elevated pretzel track layout. The no. 1802I Layout Instruction Sheet detailed this track plan.

The no. 62-270 Tan RSC with Black Graphics outfit box measured 15½ x 14 x 6¼ inches.

Both of the outfits ordered by RMG were produced in extremely low quantities and so are rarely seen.

CONVENTIONAL PACK
62-270 BOX

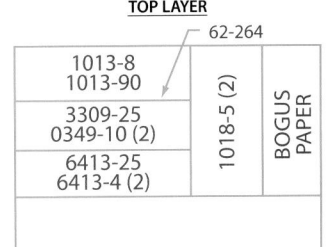

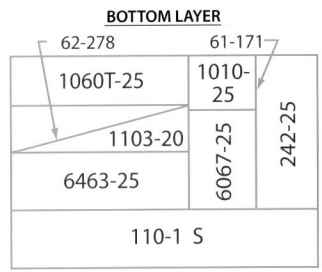

Description: "O27" Promotional Outfit
Specification: "O27" Steam Type Freight Outfit
Customer: RMG
Original Amount: 150
Factory Order Date: 10/5/1962
Date Issued: 10-5-62
Packaging: R.S.C. Outfit Packing (Units not Boxed)

Contents: 1060-25 Steam Type Locomotive; 1060T-25 Tender; 6042-75 Gondola Car (Less 2 Cable Reels); 40-11 Cable Reels (2); 6050-150 Stokely Van Camp Savings Bank Car; 6076-25 Hopper Car - Red; 6067-25 Caboose; 1013-8 Curved Track (Bundle of 8 - 1013); 1018-10 Straight Track (Loose) (2); 1026-25 25-Watt Transformer; 1103-20 Envelope Packed; 310-2 Set of (5) Billboards; D62-50 Accessory Catalog; 1123-40 Instruction Sheet; 1123-10 Instruction Sheet

Boxes & Packing: 61-170 Outfit Box; 61-171 Insert; 62-248 Insert; 62-264 Insert; 61-175 Shipper for (4) (1-4)

19200 (1962)	C6	C7	C8	Rarity
Complete Outfit	600	815	1,255	R10
Outfit Box no. 61-170	500	750	1,000	R10

Comments: In 1962, RMG was listed as the customer on two outfits: nos. 19199 and 19200. Because our research has yet to uncover any information about the identity or location of RMG, we cannot determine whether the no. 19200 was a Retailer Promotional Type Ib outfit or a Manufacturer Promotional Type IIIb outfit.

The 19200 was, however, RMG's low-end steamer purchase for 1962. It was led by a no. 1060-25 Steam Type Locomotive, which went forward only. The rolling stock was commonplace, except for the no. 6050-150 Van Camp Savings Bank Car. This car, which appeared only in promotional outfits, was included in at least nine outfits during its first year.

A transition from Archbar to AAR trucks and couplers began in 1962. For the 19200, all the cars were equipped with non-operating Archbar trucks and couplers. However, the nos. 1060T-25 Tender and 6067-25 Caboose could come with either two Archbar types or one non-operating Archbar and one plain AAR truck and coupler.

The no. 61-170 Tan RSC with Black Graphics outfit box was used for this and numerous other outfits. It measured 11½ x 10¼ x 6¼ inches.

Both of the outfits ordered by RMG were produced in extremely low quantities and so are rarely seen.

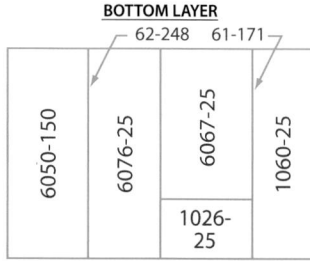

CONVENTIONAL PACK
61-170 BOX

TOP LAYER

1013-8 1018-10 (2)	62-264
1103-20 6042-75	
40-11 (2)	1060T-25

BOTTOM LAYER

62-248   61-171

6050-150	6076-25	6067-25	1060-25
		1026-25	

61-172 BETWEEN LAYERS

Description: "O27" Promotional Outfit
Specification: "O27" Diesel Freight Outfit
Original Amount: 600
Factory Order Date: 11/27/1962
Date Issued: 11-28-62
Packaging: R.S.C. Outfit Packing (Units Boxed and not Boxed)

Contents: 224P-1 Alco Diesel Power Car - "U.S. Navy"; 224C-1 "B" Unit - "U.S. Navy"; 3830-1 Operating Submarine Car; 3362-25 Helium Tank Unloading Car; 6343-25 Barrel Ramp Car (Less Barrels); 362-78 Wood Barrels (6); 6017-210 Caboose U.S. Navy; 1013-8 Curved Track (Bundle of 8 - 1013); 1018-5 Straight Track (Bundle of 5 - 1018); 1008-50 Uncoupling Unit; 1025-25 45-Watt Transformer; 910-1 Navy Yard Cardboard Display; 81-32 24" R.C. Wire (2); 310-2 Set of (5) Billboards; D62-50 Accessory Catalog; 1123-40 Instruction Sheet; 3362-15 Instruction Sheet; 122-10 Instruction Sheet

Boxes & Packing: 61-385 Outfit Box; 61-386 Insert; 61-387 Shipper for (3) (1-3)

19201 (1) (1962)	C6	C7	C8	Rarity
Complete Outfit	7,500	11,250	15,250	R10
Outfit Box no. 61-385	800	950	1,100	R9

Comments: Two General Release Promotional Type IIb outfits were listed as no. 19201. They were identical except that the "(1)" version included a boxed Alco and "B" Unit whereas the "(2)" included an unboxed Alco and "B" Unit. Neither outfit has yet to be linked to a specific end customer.

The 19201s were the sixth and seventh outfits to include a no. 910-1 Navy Yard Cardboard Display (also known as the Atomic Sub Base). As was true with the other outfits containing a sub base, that item is what makes the 19201s extremely rare today. The 910-1 Navy Yard Cardboard Display was a fragile model intended to be assembled by the customer. There were no Lionel markings on this item, and it often became separated from the train outfit and was destroyed. Stories exist of individuals who discarded a 910-1 because they did not know what it was.

All 10 cardboard pieces that made up the sub base were placed in a plain, tan-colored flat paper bag, which was laid on the bottom of the outfit.

Of all the sub-base outfits, the 19201s came with the most appropriate motive power and rolling stock. Lionel finally placed a no. 224P U.S. Navy Alco Diesel Power Car and a no. 224C U.S. Navy "B" Unit at the head of a sub-base outfit. This was the last appearance of both of these items.

The 224P featured Magne-Traction and a three-position reversing unit. It came boxed as a 224P-1 in the 19201 (1) and unboxed as a 224P-25 in the 19201 (2). When boxed, the 224P-1 included the nos. CTC-1 Lockon, 927-90 Lubricating Oil Packed and a no. 217-17 Instruction Sheet in its corrugated box. For the

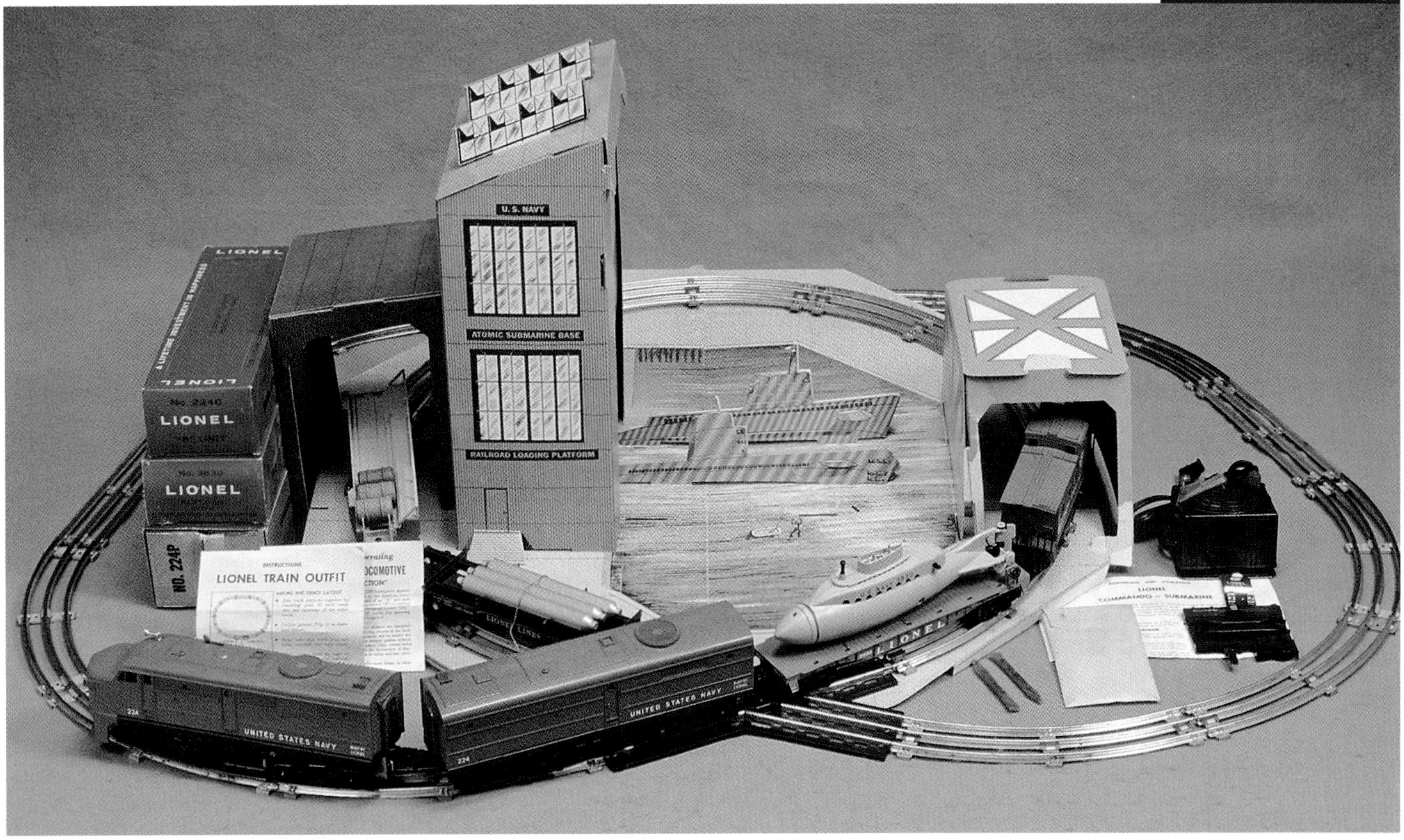

The no. 19201 (1) included a boxed no. 224P-1 U.S. Navy Alco Diesel Power Car and a no. 224C-1 U.S. Navy "B" Unit. This example is shown with an assembled no. 910-1 Navy Yard Cardboard Display (also known as the Atomic Sub Base). The track layout included with the 19201 (1) was actually an oval and not the pretzel layout shown. Obtaining a complete, unassembled 910-1 is extremely difficult. So much so that this one is missing a sub from the picture.

The Factory Order listed the outfits as nos. 19201 (1) and 19201 (2). They came stamped by Lionel as "NO. 19201-1" and "NO. 19201-2". Shown is the no. 61-385 Outfit Box for outfit 19201 (1).

19201 (2), which had an unboxed 224P-25, these items had to be included separately. The no. 19201 (2) Factory Order listed these peripherals, along with a no. 1103-20 Envelope Packed.

Also appropriate for these outfits were the nos. 3830-1 Operating Submarine Car and 6017-210 U.S. Navy Caboose. The 3830-1 came in an Orange Picture box.

For the 19201s, all but one of the cars came equipped with middle AAR types. The no. 6017-210 Caboose had one early operating AAR and one plain AAR truck and coupler. In addition, its AAR side frames had notches on top.

Interestingly, these two sub-base outfits were the only two not to include a pretzel track layout. They came with a simple oval. No other layout instruction sheet, besides the unnumbered "How to Assemble Your Lionel Atomic Submarine Base", was included.

The no. 61-385 Tan RSC with Black Graphics outfit box was the same as Lionel used on the other sub-base outfits for 1961 and 1962. It was manufactured by Mead Containers and measured 22 x 18¼ x 5¼ inches. The 19201 (2) included the extra inserts needed to protect the unboxed 224P-25 and 224C-25.

These early sub-base outfits included the 910-1 inside the outfit box. This arrangement required a large no. 61-386 Insert to fill the empty space, which caused these outfits to be unevenly balanced and might have contributed to some being dropped accidentally.

Even though the Factory Order listed the outfits as 19201 (1) and 19201 (2), the boxes were actually stamped "NO. 19201-1" and "NO. 19201-2".

Both the "(1)" version and "(2)" version do appear from time to time, but almost always without the sub base. They are equally rare. Acquiring a complete, unassembled sub base to complete an outfit is the real challenge.

CONVENTIONAL PACK
61-385 BOX
WITH 224P-1 AND 224C-1 PACKED

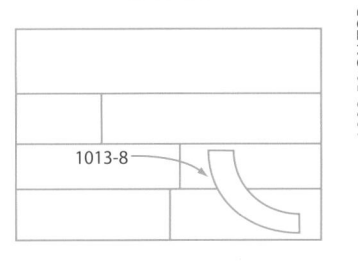

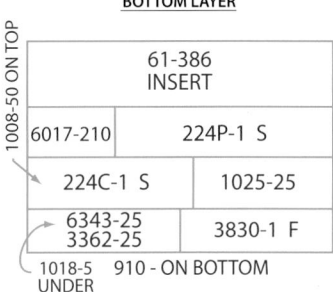

The no. 19201 (2) was the seventh of nine outfits to include a no. 910-1 Navy Yard Cardboard Display (also known as the Atomic Sub Base). It, along with the no. 19201 (1), were the only two sub-base outfits to be led by a no. 224P U.S. Navy Alco Diesel Power Car. The combination of U.S. Navy Alcos and a sub base was long overdue; unfortunately, this outfit represented the last appearance by the nos. 224P and 224C.

Early sub-base outfits included the no. 910-1 Navy Yard Cardboard Display on the box bottom. This left a large space that was filled by a no. 61-386 Insert.

Description: "O27" Promotional Outfit
Specification: "O27" Diesel Freight Outfit
Original Amount: 600
Factory Order Date: 11/27/1962
Date Issued: 11-28-62
Packaging: R.S.C. Outfit Pkg (Units Boxed and not Boxed)

Contents: 224P-25 Alco Diesel Power Car - "U.S. Navy"; 224C-25 "B" Unit - "U.S. Navy"; 3830-1 Operating Submarine Car; 3362-25 Helium Tank Unloading Car; 6343-25 Barrel Ramp Car (Less Barrels); 362-78 Wood Barrels (6); 6017-210 Caboose - "U.S. Navy"; 1013-8 Curved Track (Bundle of 8 - 1013); 1018-5 Straight Track (Bundle of 5 - 1018); 1008-50 Uncoupling Unit; 1025-25 45-Watt Transformer; 910-1 Navy Yard Cardboard Display; 1103-20 Envelope Packed; 310-2 Set of (5) Billboards; D62-50 Accessory Catalog; 1123-40 Instruction Sheet; 3362-15 Instruction Sheet; 122-10 Instruction Sheet; 217-17 Instruction Sheet

Boxes & Packing: 61-385 Outfit Box; 61-192 Insert; 61-386 Insert; 62-224 Insert; 62-245 Insert (2); 62-248 Insert; 61-387 Shipper for (3) (1-3)

19201 (2) (1962)	C6	C7	C8	Rarity
Complete Outfit	7,425	11,125	15,100	R10
Outfit Box no. 61-385	800	950	1,100	R9

Comments: See the entry for outfit no. 19201 (1) from 1962.

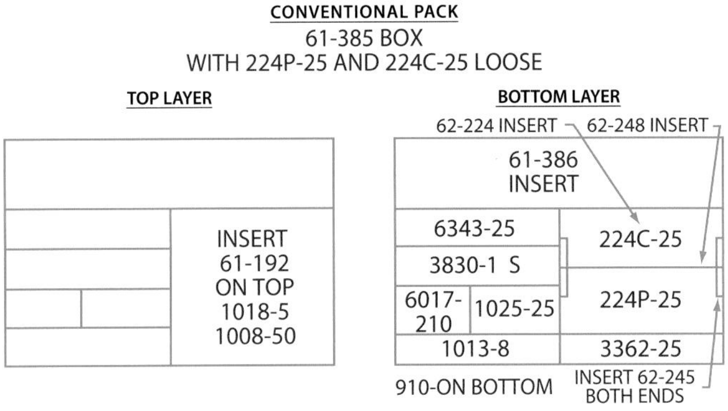

CONVENTIONAL PACK
61-385 BOX
WITH 224P-25 AND 224C-25 LOOSE

Description: "O27" Promotional Outfit
Specification: "O27" Diesel Freight Outfit
Original Amount: 5,500
Packaging: R.S.C. Outfit Packing (Units not Boxed), (Except 3830-1)

Contents: 231P-25 Alco Diesel Power Car - "Rock Island"; 3830-1 Operating Submarine Car; 6343-25 Barrel Ramp Car (Less Barrels); 362-78 Wood Barrels (6); 6062-25 Gondola Car (Less Cable Reels); 40-11 Cable Reels (3); 6630-25 Missile Launching Car (Less Missile); 6650-80 Missile Complete (or 6650-84); 6057-50 Caboose; 1013-8 Curved Track (Bundle of 8 - 1013); 1018-5 Straight Track (Bundle of 5 - 1018); 1008-50 Uncoupling Unit; 1025-25 45-Watt Transformer; 1103-20 Envelope Packed; 310-2 Set of (5) Billboards; D62-50 Accessory Catalog; 122-10 Instruction Sheet

Boxes & Packing: 62-243 Outfit Box; 62-223 Insert; 62-245 Insert (2); 62-264 Insert; 62-225 Insert; 62-244 Shipper for (4) (1-4)

19202 (1962)	C6	C7	C8	Rarity
Complete Outfit	415	625	850	R4
Outfit Box no. 62-243	90	125	150	R4

Comments: The no. 19202 was a General Release Promotional Type IIb outfit issued in 1962.

This space and military outfit was led by a no. 231P-25 Rock Island Alco Diesel Power Car. The 231P-25 was equipped with a two-position reversing unit, a headlight and two-axle Magne-Traction.

19202
1962

The rolling stock in this outfit was a peculiar mix of items that likely reflected what Lionel had in inventory rather than what went together well. The cars were, with the exception of the no. 6057-50 Caboose, all carryover items. That orange Lionel Lines caboose was first issued with catalog outfit no. 11232, which appeared earlier in the year.

For the 19202, all but one of the cars came equipped with operating AAR trucks and couplers. The no. 6630-25 Missile Launching Car (Less Missile) had non-operating Archbar types.

As for packaging, the no. 3830-1 Operating Submarine Car came in an Orange Picture box. Everything else was unboxed.

The no. 62-243 Tan RSC with Black Graphics outfit box measured 12⅛ x 11½ x 6⅜ inches.

Even though 5,500 of the 19202 were made, examples do not often show up.

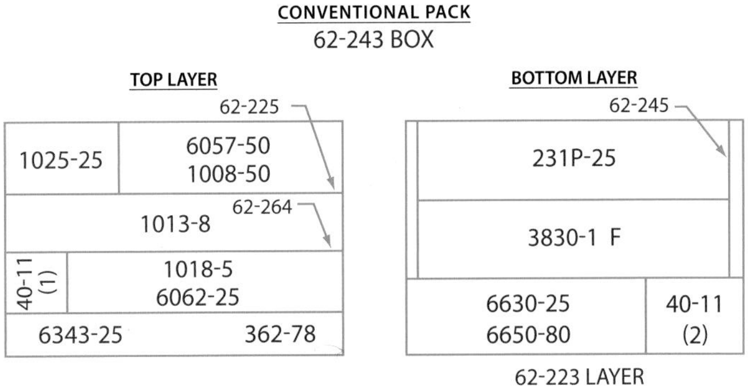

CONVENTIONAL PACK
62-243 BOX

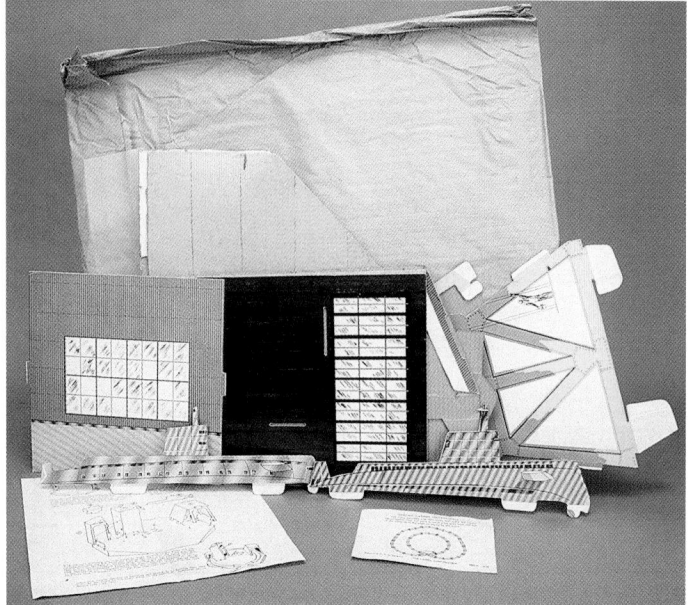

All 10 cardboard pieces that made up the no. 910-1 Navy Yard Cardboard Display (also known as the Atomic Sub Base) were placed in a plain tan-colored flat paper bag, which was laid on the bottom of the outfit. It is shown with its "How to Assemble Your Lionel Atomic Submarine Base" instruction sheet and a no. 1802H Layout Instruction Sheet.

Description: "O27" Promotional Outfit
Specification: "O27" Diesel Freight Outfit
Customer: Richie Premium
Original Amount: 50
Factory Order Date: 11/9/1962
Packaging: RSC Outfit Packing (Units Boxed)

Contents: 228P-1 Alco Diesel Power Unit - "Canadian National"; 3830-1 Flat Car with Operating Submarine; 6825-1 Trestle Bridge Flat Car; 6062-1 Gondola Car - Black; 6017-1 Caboose; 1013-8 Curved Track (Bundle of 8 - 1013) (2); 1018-30 Straight Track (Bundle of 3 - 1018); 1008-50 Uncoupling Unit; 1025-25 45-Watt Transformer; 1023-1 45° Crossing; 910-1 Navy Yard Cardboard Display; 81-32 24" R.C. Wire (2); 310-2 Set of (5) Billboards; D62-50 Accessory Catalog; 1802H Layout Instruction Sheet; 1123-40 Instruction Sheet; 122-10 Instruction Sheet

Boxes & Packing: 61-385 Corr. Outfit Box; 61-386 Corr. Insert; 61-387 Corr. Shipper for (3) (1-3)

19203 (1962)	C6	C7	C8	Rarity
Complete Outfit	8,450	12,250	16,300	R10
Outfit Box no. 61-385	1,900	2,250	2,500	R10

Comments: In 1962, incentive merchandiser Richie Premium purchased two outfits: nos. 19147 and 19203. The 19203, a Retailer Promotional Type Ib, repeated that firm's outfit no. X-625 from 1961. Richie likely needed some additional outfits to fulfill customer orders or demand.

The major differences between the 19203 and the X-625 were twofold. First, the 19203 still had a no. 910-1 Navy Yard Cardboard Display (also known as the Atomic Sub Base) but not a no. X625-20 Cardboard Scenic Set. Second, the 19203 included a no. 3830-1 Flat Car with Operating Submarine instead of a no. 3330-1 Flat Car With Operating Submarine (Kit). The paperwork in this outfit was updated for 1962.

The no. 61-385 Tan RSC with Black Graphics outfit box was manufactured by Mead Containers and measured 22 x 18¼ x 5¼ inches. It was also used for sub-base outfits issued in 1961 and 1962, including the nos. X-625, X-676, X-714, 19201 (1) and 19201 (2).

These early sub-base outfits placed the 910-1 inside the outfit box. This arrangement required a large insert to fill the empty space, which led to these outfits being unevenly balanced.

Note that the price of this outfit assumes the unnumbered "How to Assemble Your Lionel Atomic Submarine Base" instruction sheet as well.

With only 50 examples, not to mention the inclusion of the rare 910-1, the 19203 is one of the most difficult outfits to find and complete. (See the entry for outfit X-625 from 1961 for additional information on the contents and rarity of these purchases by Ritchie Premium.)

CONVENTIONAL PACK
61-385 BOX

1025-25	228P-1 S
3830-1 S	6062-1 F
16-1013 F	6825-1 S
FILLER INSERT 61-386	

1023-1 TOP OF 1013
6017-1 TOP OF 6062-1
1018-30 TOP OF 6825-1
1008-50 TOP OF 1025-25

Description: "O27" Promotional Outfit
Specification: "O27" Steam Type Freight Outfit With Smoke
Original Amount: 2,400
Factory Order Date: 11/28/1962
Date Issued: 11-28-62
Packaging: R.S.C. Outfit Packing (Units not Boxed), Except 943-1

Contents: 243-25 Steam Type Locomotive with Smoke; 1130T-25 Tender; 6630-25 Missile Launching Flat Car (Less Missile); 6650-80 Missile Complete (or 6650-84); 6343-25 Barrel Ramp Car (Less Barrels); 362-78 Wood Barrels (6); 6062-25 Gondola Car; 40-11 Cable Reels (3); 3362-25 Helium Tank Unloading Car; 6057-50 Caboose; 943-1 Exploding Ammo Dump; 1013-8 Curved Track (Bundle of 8 - 1013); 1018-5 Straight Track (Bundle of 5 - 1018); 1008-50 Uncoupling Unit; 1103-20 Envelope Packed; 909-20 Smoke Fluid; 1025-25 45-Watt Transformer; 310-2 Set of (5) Billboards; D62-50 Accessory Catalog; 1123-40 Instruction Sheet; 243-6 Instruction Sheet; 6630-6 Instruction Sheet; 3362-15 Instruction Sheet; 122-10 Instruction Sheet

Boxes & Packing: 60-490 Outfit Box (For 1,600 sets - use the following packing); 61-171 Insert; 62-248 Insert; 62-225 Insert; 62-249 Insert; 61-172 Insert; 60-494 Shipper for 4 (Inv) (1-4); 62-243 Outfit Box (For 800 sets - use the following packing); 61-171 Insert; 62-223 Insert; 62-225 Insert; 62-248 Insert; 62-244 Shipper for 4 (1-4)

Lionel probably created General Release Promotional Type IIb no. 19203X to thin out existing inventory at the end of the year. This outfit, along with the no. 19204X, marked the last appearance of the no. 243-25 Steam Type Locomotive with Smoke. The 19203X confirms that brown no. 40-11 Cable Reels began to appear in late 1962. The outfit is shown with a no. 62-243 Outfit Box.

Alternate For Outfit Contents: For 1600 sets - use 60-490 Box, Inserts and Shipper as listed above; For 800 sets - use 60-243 Box, Inserts and Shipper as listed above.

19203X (1962)	C6	C7	C8	Rarity
Complete Outfit With no. 60-490 Box	425	600	875	R6
Outfit Box no. 60-490	125	175	225	R6
Complete Outfit With no. 62-243 Box	525	700	975	R8
Outfit Box no. 62-243	225	275	325	R8

Comments: The no. 19203X was a General Release Promotional Type IIb outfit issued in 1962. It shared the same Factory Order date of 11-28-62 with outfit no. 19204X. The two outfits are similar and appear to have been created to reduce Lionel's inventory of some older items. Neither has anything in common with the nos. 19203 and 19204 outfits, respectively.

The 19203X and 19204X marked the last appearance of the no. 243-25 Steam Type Locomotive with Smoke. That engine also featured a metal motor and a two-position reverse unit. It was first introduced in 1960 and eventually was replaced in the product line by the nos. 233 and 236 Steam Locomotive with Smoke.

The components of the 19203X were, with two exceptions, identical to what came in the 19204X. The former outfit included a no. 6630-25 Missile Launching Flat Car (Less Missile), whose target was a no. 943-1 Ammo Dump. The 19204X came, instead, with a no. 470-1 Missile Launching Platform, whose target was a no. 6470-1 Exploding Target Car.

Other than its caboose, the cars in the 19203X were carryover from previous years. The 6630-25 was first introduced in 1961. Its target, the 943-1, was being reduced in this outfit, having last been offered for separate sale in 1961 for $1.95.

Also carried over was the no. 6062-25 Gondola Car, which came with no. 40-11 Cable Reels. Late in 1962, Lionel began to mold those reels in brown plastic. In fact, the production sample for the hard-to-find brown reels was dated 11-7-62.

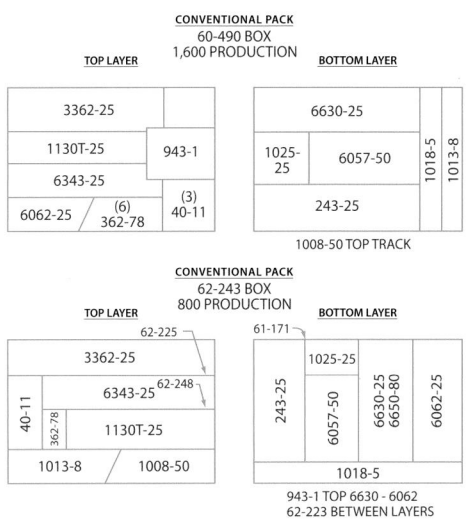

The sole new-for-1962 model found in the 19203X was the no. 6057-50 Caboose. Nevertheless, the absence of a separate-sale box for this item indicated that Lionel was dumping the remaining inventory in promotional outfits.

For the 19203X, all but two of the cars came equipped with middle operating AAR trucks and couplers. The 6630-25 had non-operating Archbar trucks and couplers, and the no. 1130T-25 Tender had early AAR types.

The 19203X came in two box variations. The first 1,600 outfits came in a no. 60-490 Tan RSC with Black Graphics outfit box. It was manufactured by St. Joe Paper Co. - Container Div. and measured 14½ x 11 x 6 inches. It was an overstickered no. X-541NA from 1960.

The last 800 examples came in a no. 62-243 Tan RSC with Black Graphics outfit box manufactured by St. Joe Kraft, St. Joe Paper Co. Container Division. It measured 12⅛ x 11½ x 6⅜ inches.

Of the two variations, the no. 62-243 Outfit Box version is more difficult to find, hence its R8 rarity rating.

Description: "O27" Promotional Outfit
Specification: "O27" Steam Type Freight Outfit with Smoke & Whistle
Customer: Beller Electric
Original Amount: 200
Factory Order Date: 11/12/1962
Packaging: Bulk Packing

Contents: 2037-1 Steam Type Locomotive With Smoke; 234W-1 Whistle Tender; 3619-1 Reconnaissance Copter Car; 3665-1 Minuteman Missile Launching Car; 3470-1 Aerial Target Launching Car; 6463-1 Rocket Fuel Car; 6512-1 Cherry Picker Car; 6437-1 Illuminated Cupola Caboose; 1013-5 Curved Track (Furnish 200 per box - Amt. 2,000 sets) (10); 1018-1 Straight Track (Furnish 200 per box - Amt. 1,200 sets) (6); 1063-1 75-Watt Transformer; 1122-1 Pr. Remote Control Switches; 6019-1 Remote Control Track Set

19204 (1962)	C6	C7	C8	Rarity
Items Only	500	850	1,250	N/A

Comments: In the early 1960s, Beller Electric and Madison Hardware Co. of New York purchased what were known as "bulk outfits." (For an explanation of the practice of buying "bulk outfits," consult the entry on Madison Hardware Co. in the section on Lionel's Distribution and Customers.)

Beller purchased bulk-packed outfits nos. 19204 and 19206 in 1962. Both of these were Retailer Promotional Type Ia outfits. The 19204 was steam-powered, and the 19206 was diesel-powered.

Beller's purchases are curious because customers typically bought in bulk from Lionel as a ploy to further reduce the price paid for individual items intended for separate sale. Yet it appears that Beller was actually purchasing outfit components in bulk with the intention of assembling this outfit on its own.

For the 19204, bulk packaging and not an outfit box was provided. Lionel likely packaged all the individual items in master shipping cartons. However, no individual outfit boxes have been observed for any of the bulk outfits listed in this volume. As a result, we cannot ascertain whether these items were ever assembled and sold as an outfit. Even if they were, we cannot prove that Beller Electric designated the groupings as 19204 or 19206.

The 19204 was led by a no. 2037-1 Steam Type Locomotive with Smoke and Magne-Traction. The space and military rolling stock included a few high-end items. The nos. 3665-1 Minuteman Missile Launching Car and 6437-1 Illuminated Cupola Caboose were carryovers from 1961. All the other cars were new for 1962.

Because of the no. 1122-1 Pr. Remote Control Switches, the track plan for this outfit was likely an oval layout with an inner reverse loop cutoff.

A listing for this outfit is provided here because a Factory Order exists for the 19204. Pricing is provided as reference for the items alone. However, as stated earlier in this volume, items alone do not constitute an outfit; an outfit box is required.

This bulk outfit appeared late in the year, and Lionel may have been thinning out inventory in a quick and inexpensive way (no outfit packaging). Finding a box with any sort of markings for this outfit would be a true discovery.

Description: "O27" Promotional Outfit
Specification: "O27" Steam Type Freight Outfit with Smoke
Original Amount: 1,200
Factory Order Date: 11/28/1962
Date Issued: 11-28-62
Packaging: RSC Outfit Packing (Units not Boxed), Except 470-1

Contents: 243-25 Steam Type Locomotive with Smoke; 1130T-25 Tender; 3362-25 Helium Tank Unloading Car; 6343-25 Barrel Ramp Car (Less Barrels); 362-78 Wood Barrels (6); 6062-25 Gondola Car; 40-11 Cable Reels (3); 6057-50 Caboose; 1013-8 Curved Track (Bundle of 8 - 1013); 1018-5 Straight Track (Bundle of 5 - 1018); 1008-50 Uncoupling Unit; 1025-25 45-Watt Transformer; 1103-20 Envelope Packed; 909-20 Smoke Fluid; 470-1 Missile Launching Platform; 310-2 Set of (5) Billboards; D62-50 Accessory Catalog; 1123-40 Instruction Sheet; 243-6 Instruction Sheet; 3362-15 Instruction Sheet; 122-10 Instruction Sheet

Boxes & Packing: 62-316 Outfit Box; 62-317 Insert; 62-318 Insert; 62-264 Insert (2); 62-248 Insert; 62-257 Insert; 61-182 Insert; 62-319 Shipper for (3) (1-3)

19204X (1962)	C6	C7	C8	Rarity
Complete Outfit	430	625	925	R7
Outfit Box no. 62-316	150	225	275	R7

Comments: The no. 19204X was a General Release Promotional Type IIa outfit issued in 1962. It shares the same Factory Order date of 11-28-62 with outfit no. 19203X. The two are similar and appear to have been created to reduce Lionel's inventory of some older items. Neither has anything in common with the nos. 19203 and 19204 outfits, respectively.

The 19203X and 19204X marked the last appearance of the no. 243-25 Steam Type Locomotive with Smoke. That engine also featured a metal motor and a two-position reverse unit. It was first introduced in 1960 and eventually was replaced in the product line by the nos. 233 and 236 Steam Locomotive with Smoke.

The components of the 19204X were, with two exceptions, identical to what came in the 19203X. The former outfit included a no. 470-1 Missile Launching Platform, whose target was a no. 6470-1 Exploding Target Car (the no. 19196 was the only other outfit to include this car in 1962). The 19203X came instead with a no. 6630-25 Missile Launching Flat Car (Less Missile), whose target was a no. 943-1 Ammo Dump.

Other than its caboose, the cars in the 19204X were carryover from previous years. The no. 6062-25 Gondola Car came with no. 40-11 Cable Reels. Late in 1962, Lionel began to mold those reels in brown plastic. In fact, the production sample for the hard-to-find brown reels was dated 11-7-62.

The sole new-for-1962 model found in the 19204X was the

General Release Promotional Type IIa no. 19204X was similar to the no. 19203X. Lionel probably created both outfits to thin out some inventory at the end of the year. These outfits marked the last appearance of the no. 243-25 Steam Type Locomotive with Smoke.

no. 6057-50 Caboose. Nevertheless, the absence of a separate-sale box for this item indicated that Lionel was dumping the remaining inventory in promotional outfits.

For the 19204X, all but one of the cars came equipped with middle operating AAR trucks and couplers. The no. 1130T-25 Tender had early AAR types.

The new no. 62-316 Tan RSC with Black Graphics outfit box was used only for this outfit in 1962. It was manufactured by St. Joe Kraft, St. Joe Paper Co. Container Division and measured 17⅜ x 13¼ x 6⅞ inches. It had "62-316" printed on the bottom.

With only half as many of the 19204X produced as the 19203X, it does not appear as often. It is more difficult to find, especially with a 470-1 Missile Launching Platform.

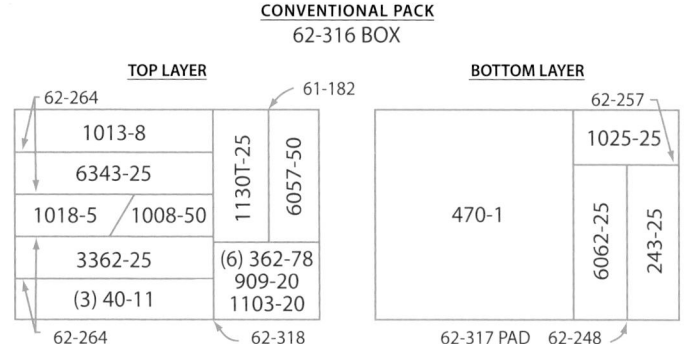

CONVENTIONAL PACK
62-316 BOX

TOP LAYER — 62-264, 61-182, 1013-8, 6343-25, 1018-5 / 1008-50, 1130T-25, 6057-50, 3362-25, (6) 362-78, 909-20, 1103-20, (3) 40-11, 62-264, 62-318

BOTTOM LAYER — 62-257, 1025-25, 470-1, 6062-25, 243-25, 62-317 PAD, 62-248

Description: "O27" Promotional Outfit
Specification: "O27" Steam Type Freight Outfit With Smoke & Whistle
Customer: R & S
Original Amount: 404
Factory Order Date: 11/15/1962
Date Issued: 11-15-62
Packaging: Bulk

Contents: 2037-1 Steam Type Locomotive With Smoke; 234W-1 Whistle Tender; 3370-1 Sheriff & Outlaw Car; 3619-1 Reconnaissance Copter Car; 3413-1 Mercury Capsule Launching Car; 3470-1 Aerial Target Launching Car; 6017-1 Caboose; 1013-5 Curved Track (Furnish 3232 sections) (8); 1018-1 Straight

Track (Furnish 808 sections) (2); 1063-1 75-Watt Transformer

19205 (1962)	C6	C7	C8	Rarity
Items Only	475	725	1,050	N/A

Comments: The no. 19205 listed R & S Auto as the customer on its Factory Order in 1962. A bulk-packed outfit, this Retailer Promotional Type Ia appeared to have been configured with the intention of being sold as an outfit. (For an explanation of the practice of buying "bulk outfits," consult the entry on Madison Hardware Co. in the section on Lionel's Distribution and Customers.)

For the 19205, bulk packaging and not an outfit box was

provided. Lionel likely packaged all the individual items in master shipping cartons. However, no individual outfit boxes have been observed for any of the bulk outfits listed in this volume. As a result, we cannot ascertain whether these items were ever assembled and sold as an outfit. Even if they were, we cannot prove that R & S designated the groupings as 19205.

This space and military outfit was led by a no. 2037-1 Steam Type Locomotive with Smoke and Magne-Traction. Higher-end rolling stock was included. All the cars were new for 1962, except for the nos. 3370-1 Sheriff & Outlaw Car and 6017-1 Caboose.

A listing for this outfit is provided here because a Factory Order exists for the 19205. Pricing is provided as reference for the items alone. However, as stated earlier in this volume, items alone do not constitute an outfit; an outfit box is required.

This bulk outfit appeared late in the year, and Lionel may have been thinning out inventory in a quick and inexpensive way (no outfit packaging). Finding a box with any sort of markings for this outfit would be a true discovery.

19206
1962

Description: Promotional (Bulk Pkg)
Specification: Promotional
Customer: Beller Electric
Original Amount: 300
Factory Order Date: 11/28/1962
Date Issued: 11-28-62
Packaging: Bulk Packing

Contents: 211PX-1 *"Texas Special"* - Alco Diesel Power Unit; 211T-1 *"Texas Special"* Motorless Unit; 6162-1 Gondola Car with 3 Canisters; 6416-1 Boat Transport Car; 6050-110 Swift Savings Bank Car; 3357-1 Animated Hobo & Railroad Policeman Car; 6437-1 Illuminated Cupola Caboose; 1013-8 Curved Track (Ship Bulk - 2400 Sections); 1018-40 Straight Track (Ship Bulk - 1200 Sections); 110-1 Trestle Set; 1044-1 90-Watt Transformer

19206 (1962)	C6	C7	C8	Rarity
Items Only	400	750	1,100	N/A

Comments: In the early 1960s, Beller Electric and Madison Hardware Co. of New York purchased what were known as "bulk outfits." (For an explanation of the practice of buying "bulk outfits," consult the entry on Madison Hardware Co. in the section on Lionel's Distribution and Customers.)

Beller purchased bulk-packed outfits nos. 19204 and 19206 in 1962. Both of these were Retailer Promotional Type Ia outfits. The 19206 was diesel-powered, and the 19204 was steam-powered.

Beller's purchases are curious because customers typically bought in bulk from Lionel as a ploy to further reduce the price paid for individual items intended for separate sale. Yet it appears that Beller was actually purchasing outfit components in bulk with the intention of assembling this outfit on its own.

For the 19206, bulk packaging and not an outfit box was provided. Lionel likely packaged all the individual items in master shipping cartons. However, no individual outfit boxes have been observed for any of the bulk outfits listed in this volume. As a result, we cannot ascertain whether these items were ever assembled and sold as an outfit. Even if they were, we cannot prove that Beller Electric designated the groupings as 19204 or 19206.

The 19206 was led by a no. 211PX-1 *Texas Special* Alco Diesel Power Unit. This locomotive was new for 1962 and featured a two-position reversing unit, an open pilot, a headlight and two-axle Magne-Traction.

The freight cars were all commonly available items in 1962, except for the no. 6050-110 Swift Savings Bank Car. The version of this car equipped with AAR trucks and couplers came boxed in only this and catalog outfit no. 11278. It also was available for separate sale in 1962.

A listing for this outfit is provided here because a Factory Order exists for the 19206. Pricing is provided as reference for the items alone. However, as stated earlier in this volume, items alone do not constitute an outfit; an outfit box is required.

This bulk outfit appeared late in the year, and Lionel may have been thinning out inventory in a quick and inexpensive way (no outfit packaging). Finding a box with any sort of markings for this outfit would be a true discovery.

19210
1963

Description: "O27" Promotional Outfit
Specification: "O27" Steam Type Freight Outfit
Customer/No./Price: Top Value; 15-198; 5⅖ Books
Original Amount: 3,500
Factory Order Date: 5/15/1963
Date Issued: Rev 10-8-63
Packaging: RSC Outfit Packing #5 (Units not Boxed)

Contents: 242-25 Steam Type Locomotive; 1060T-25 Tender; 6045-50 Two Dome Tank Car; 6406-25 Flat Car W/Auto; 6406-30 Automobile; 6067-25 Caboose; 1013-8 Curved Track (Bundle of 8 - 1013); 1018-10 Straight Track (Loose) (2); 1026-25 25-Watt Transformer; 1103-20 Envelope Packed; 310-2 Set of (5) Billboards; D63-50 Accessory Catalog; 1-63 Warranty Card; 1-62 Parts Order Form; 1123-40 Instruction Sheet; 1123-10 Instruction Sheet; Form 2870 Printed Sheet

Boxes & Packing: 61-404 Outfit Box; 61-171 Insert; 62-249 Insert; 63-353 Insert; 61-405 Shipper (1-4); 63-383 Outfit Box; 62-254 Corr. Insert; 62-264 Corr. Insert; 63-384 Shipper (4) (1-4)

Alternate For Outfit Contents:
Note: Substitute 2,250 - 1130T-25 for 1060T-25; Use inventory of 943 - 6045-50; Use inventory of 306 - 6045-60; Balance - amount 2,251 - use 6045-150; Note: All packing replaced should be used until all on hand or in shipment would be used up.

As a follow-up to the no. X-604 offered in 1961 and 1962, Top Value purchased the no. 19210 in 1963. In that year, Lionel changed the color of many items. For that reason, a brown automobile and caboose were common with the 19210. This example included a no. 1130T-25 Tender substitution. The outfit is shown with a no. 61-404 Outfit Box.

19210 (1963)	C6	C7	C8	Rarity
Complete Outfit With no. 61-404 Box And Brown Automobile	325	525	725	R5
Outfit Box no. 61-404	50	125	175	R5
Complete Outfit With no. 63-383 Box And Brown Automobile	350	575	800	R7
Outfit Box no. 63-383	75	175	250	R7
Either Outfit With Red Or Yellow Automobile, Subtract The Following	150	200	250	Same

Comments: This, the last of three (nos. X-604 from 1961, X-604 from 1962 and 19210 in 1963) Top Value Retailer Promotional Type Ib outfits, virtually duplicated the contents of the X-604 from 1962 (see the entry for outfit X-604 from 1961 and 1962). However, some minor changes were made, including an updated locomotive and outfit packaging and new colors for certain items.

The 19210, which was pictured on page 138 of the 1963 Top Value catalog, required 5⅖ filled books of stamps. This outfit was shown with a gray no. 6406-25 Flat Car W/Auto, a brown no. 6406-30 Automobile and a brown no. 6067-25 Caboose. Keep in mind that examples of this outfit have been observed with a Tuscan Red plastic version of the 6406-25.

The 19210 was led by a no. 242-25 Steam Type Locomotive, which took the place of the discontinued no. 246-25 that Lionel used in the X-604 from 1962. This replacement featured a two-position reversing unit and a rubber tire as a traction aid as opposed to the Magne-Traction on the 246-25. The version of the 242 with wide running boards was included in this outfit.

In 1963, many items that were previously molded in red plastic appeared in brown as well. The 19210 has been observed with a brown 6406-30 Automobile with gray bumpers and a brown 6067-25. The pricing table includes pricing for a brown automobile with gray bumpers. The differences in price between a brown, a red or a yellow automobile also apply when a legitimate 19210 is found that way.

The transition from Archbar to AAR trucks and couplers that

began in 1962 continued into 1963. As part of this, Lionel sought to cut costs by introducing a non-operating AAR type. Therefore, starting in 1963, most cars equipped with AAR trucks and couplers had at least one non-operating type. For the 19210, trucks and couplers were most often the non-operating Archbar types. With substitutions and variations, some items were equipped with AAR (6067-25) or combinations of AAR and Archbar (nos. 1060T-25 Tender and 6067-25) trucks and couplers.

A no. 6045-60 Two Dome Tank Car was listed as a substitution for the no. 6045-50 Two Dome Tank Car. The 6045-60 was the boxed version of the 6045-50. The Production Control File for the no. 6045-60 states to "use folding box (6465-103), block out and imprint with no. 6045-60...." This was the only outfit to list a 6045-60. A box has yet to be observed, and no pricing is available.

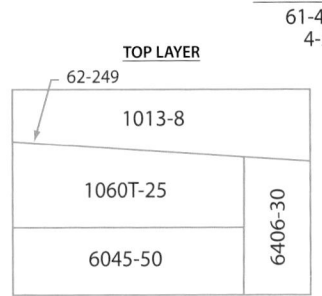

CONVENTIONAL PACK
61-404 BOX
4-29-63

| TOP LAYER | | BOTTOM LAYER |

62-249 / 1013-8 / 1060T-25 / 6406-30 / 6045-50
61-171 / 1018-10 (2) / 6406-25 / 6067-25 / 1026-25 / 242-25

CONVENTIONAL PACK
63-383 BOX
REVISED PACKING 9-17-63

| TOP LAYER | BOTTOM LAYER |

1013-8 / 1018-10 (2) / 62-264 / 6406-25 / 6406-30 / 6045-50
242-25 / 62-254 / 6067-25 / 1026-25 / 1060T-25

Two versions of a Tan RSC with Black Graphics outfit box were used for the 19210. The first and more common was a no. 61-404 Outfit Box. It was manufactured by St. Joe Kraft, St. Joe Paper Co. Container Division and measured 10¾ x 9¼ x 5½ inches. The second was a no. 63-383 Outfit Box. It was manufactured by United Container Co. and measured 11½ x 9¾ x 6 inches. Both boxes included four lines of data as part of the box manufacturer's certificate.

Of the three Top Value outfits, the 19210 is the most desirable. It contained the collectible brown version of the 6406-30 Automobile. The 19210's outfit box variations were produced in lower quantities than those of the X-604. Finding a complete 19210 is possible, but most often it is found without the automobile.

19211
1963

Description: "O27" Promotional Outfit
Specification: "O27" Steam Type Freight Outfit
Customer/No./Price: King Korn; K2893; 6⅘ Books
Original Amount: 1,500
Factory Order Date: 5/15/1963
Date Issued: 5-24-63
Packaging: RSC Outfit Packing #5 (Units not Boxed)

Contents: 1060-25 Steam Type Locomotive; 1060T-25 Tender; 6502-50 Girder Transport Car; 6502-3 Girder Bridge; 6050-150 Van Camp Savings Bank Car; 6042-75 Gondola Car (Less 2 Cable Reels); 40-11 Cable Reels (2); 6067-25 Caboose; 1013-8 Curved Track (Bundle of 8 - 1013); 1018-10 Straight Track (Loose) (2); 1010-25 35-Watt Transformer; 1103-20 Envelope Packed; 310-2 Set of (5) Billboards; D63-50 Accessory Catalog; 1-62 Parts Order Form; 1-63 Warranty Card; 1123-40 Instruction Sheet; 1123-30 Instruction Sheet; Form 2870 Printed Sheet

Boxes & Packing: 61-170 Outfit Box; 61-171 Corr. Insert; 61-172 Corr. Insert; 61-173 Corr. Insert; 61-174 Shipper for (6) (1-6)

Alternate For Outfit Contents:
Note: Substitute 1130T-25 for 1060T-25.

19211 (1963)	C6	C7	C8	Rarity
Complete Outfit	220	400	565	R6
Outfit Box no. 61-170	100	200	250	R6

Comments: Not to be left behind by other trading stamp companies, King Korn jumped on board with Lionel in 1963 with this Retailer Promotional Type Ib outfit. The no. 19211 was shown on page 62 of the 1963 King Korn Stamps Gift Book as no. K2893

for 6⅘ books.

A low-end outfit, the 19211 was led by a no. 1060-25 Steam Type Locomotive, which went forward only. The unmarked no. 6502-50 Girder Transport Car was the only new item for 1963. This plastic model was the same as the "-25" version, except that it came in blue and not black and had two non-operating AAR or Archbar trucks and couplers.

All the other rolling stock in this outfit was carryover from previous years. The transition from Archbar to AAR trucks and couplers that began in 1962 continued into 1963. As part of this, Lionel sought to cut costs by introducing a non-operating AAR type. Therefore, starting in 1963, most cars equipped with AAR trucks and couplers had at least one non-operating type. For the 19211, the cars included non-operating Archbar or a combination of non-operating Archbar and AAR types.

The no. 61-170 Tan RSC with Black Graphics outfit box measured 11½ x 10¼ x 6¼ inches.

The 1,500 outfits ordered represented a respectable first purchase for King Korn. Unfortunately, it appeared to have been King Korn's last purchase. This was the only time the name of that customer appeared on a Factory Order. Even with 1,500 made, a 19211 does not appear that often.

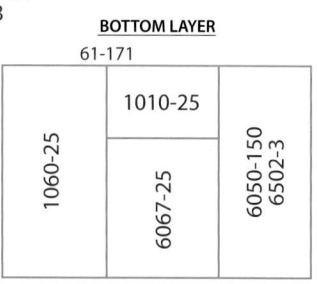

CONVENTIONAL PACK
61-170 BOX
5-1-63

| TOP LAYER | | BOTTOM LAYER |

61-172 BETWEEN LAYERS

19212
1963

Customer No. On Box: E1010
Description: "O27" Promotional Outfit
Specification: "O27" Steam Type Freight Outfit
Customer/No./Price: Western Auto; E1010; $18.95
Original Amount: 3,156
Factory Order Date: 4/22/1963
Date Issued: Rev 8-29-63
Date Req'd: 2,000 - 6/24/63, Bal 8/26/63
Packaging: Display Outfit Pkg - #1 (Units not Boxed)

Contents: 242-25 Steam Type Locomotive; 1060T-25 Tender; 3410-25 Oper. Helicopter Car (Less Helicopter); 3419-100 Operating Helicopter Complete; 6014-325 Frisco Box Car; 6406-25 Flat Car W/Auto; 6406-30 Automobile; 6047-25 Caboose; 1013-70 Curved Track (Bundle of 12 - 1013); 1018-40 Straight Track (Bundle of 4 - 1018); 1020-25 90° Crossing; 1010-25 35-Watt Transformer; 1103-20 Envelope Packed; 310-2 Set of (5) Billboards; D63-50 Accessory Catalog; 1-62 Parts Order Form; 1-63 Warranty Card; 19171-10 Instruction Sheet; 3410-5 Instruction Sheet; 1123-40 Instruction Sheet

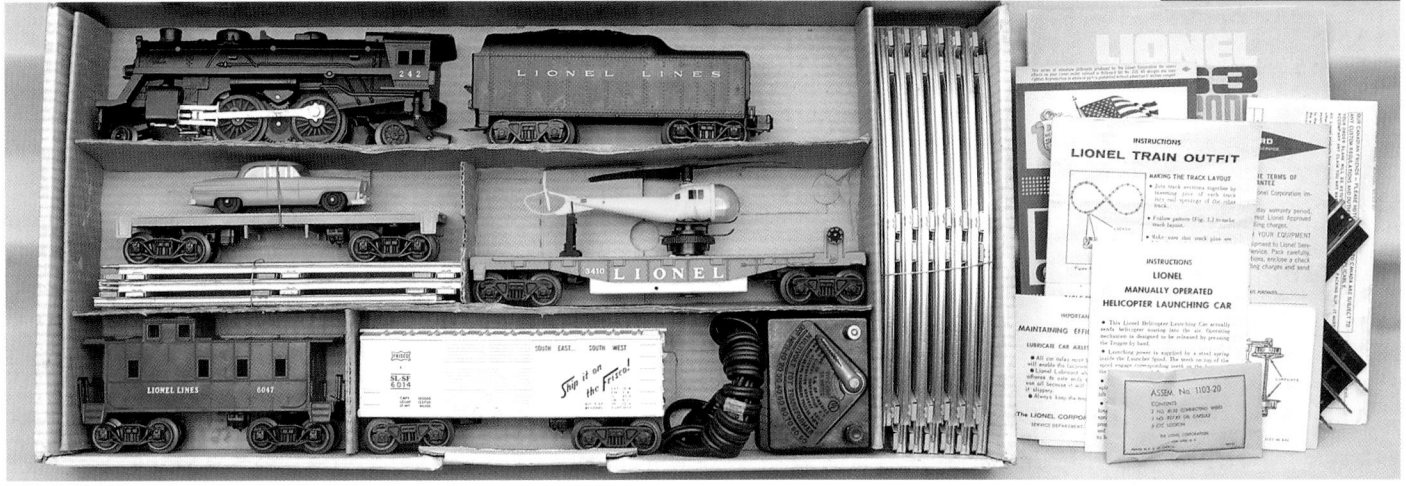

Western Auto purchased three steam outfits in 1963. The no. 19212, its mid-level offering, appeared in the 1963 Western Auto Christmas Gifts Catalog as no. E1010 for $18.95. This outfit included a green no. 6406-30 Automobile with gray bumpers and a yellow no. 3419-100 Operating Helicopter Complete.

The no. 19212 was one of the first outfits to use the no. 63-306 White 4-6-4 Steamer and F3 Hinged Display with Red/Orange and Blue Graphics Type A outfit box. This generic box was stamped with both the Lionel and Western Auto numbers (only on the box top).

Boxes & Packing: 63-306 Display Outfit Box; 63-308 Corr. Insert; 63-300 Corr. Insert; 61-101 Corr. Insert; 63-307 Shipper for (4) (1-4)

Alternate For Outfit Contents:
Customer Stock No. E1010; Note: Substitute 1000 - 6059-25 for 6047-25.

19212 (1963)	C6	C7	C8	Rarity
Complete Outfit	425	625	850	R5
Outfit Box no. 63-306	100	150	175	R5

Comments: Western Auto Stores purchased three steam-powered Retailer Promotional outfits in 1963: nos. 19212, 19213 and 19214. The 19212 appeared on page 17 of the 1963 Western Auto Christmas Gifts Catalog as no. E1010 for $18.95. It was shown with a green no. 6406-30 Automobile and a yellow no. 3419-100 Operating Helicopter Complete.

The 19212, a Type Ib outfit, was Western Auto's mid-level purchase in 1963. It was a follow-up to the no. 19107 from 1962. Both were led by a no. 242-25 Steam Type Locomotive. This low-end Scout steamer featured a two-position reversing unit and a headlight, lacked smoke and used a rubber tire as a traction aid. The version with wide running boards was included in this outfit.

The no. 3410-25 Oper. Helicopter Car (Less Helicopter) was a carryover from two years prior. It was equipped with operating AAR trucks and couplers.

In 1962, the Production Control File for the no. 3419-100

Operating Helicopter Complete changed from a gray Navy stamped two-piece helicopter body to an unmarked helicopter with a one-piece yellow helicopter body. Also in 1962, Lionel gave the task of adding the 3419-100 to the Outfit Packing Department (as noted on the 3410-25 Production Control File). These helicopters were frequently lost or broken.

The no. 6014-325 Frisco Box Car was the only new item in this outfit. It came with one operating and one non-operating AAR truck and coupler.

The gray no. 6406-25 Flat Car W/Auto was equipped with non-operating Archbar trucks and couplers. Its load was a green no. 6406-30 Automobile with gray bumpers. The green automobile provides a premium to the outfit price, as reflected in the pricing table.

The remaining rolling stock had either non-operating Archbar (no. 6047-25 Caboose) or mixed AAR and Archbar (no. 1060T-25 Tender) types.

Although the red-painted no. 6059-25 Minn. & St. Louis Caboose is more valuable than the 6047-25 Lionel Lines model, its substitution is negligible when compared to the price for the entire outfit.

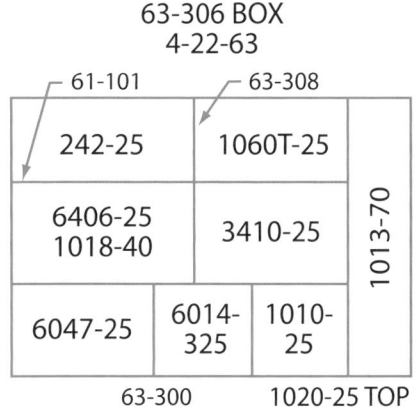

DISPLAY PACK
63-306 BOX
4-22-63

A no. 19171-10 Instruction Sheet detailed the figure-eight track layout.

The no. 63-306 White 4-6-4 Steamer and F3 Hinged Display with Red/Orange and Blue Graphics Type A outfit box listed the manufacturer as "SJPC" (likely St. Joe Paper Company). It measured 24½ x 11½ x 3⅛ inches.

This outfit is desirable because it came from Western Auto and included both a green automobile and a yellow one-piece helicopter. Finding an outfit is easy; finding it with these two items is very difficult.

Western Auto purchased a no. D19213 (Western Auto no. E1008) blister display to assist in selling the no. 19213. Containing all the items from the 19213 in a "Blister Pack", it was designed to be hung on a wall of a store with the price written on the upper right-hand corner.

Customer No. On Box: E1007
Description: "O27" Promotional Outfit
Specification: "O27" Steam Type Freight Outfit
Customer/No./Price: Western Auto; E1007; $11.95
Original Amount: 4,600
Factory Order Date: 4/22/1963
Date Issued: Rev 7-22-63
Date Req'd: 3,600 - 6/24/63, Bal - 8/26/63
Packaging: Display Outfit Packing #1 (Units not Boxed)

Contents: 1061-25 Steam Type Locomotive; 1061T-25 Tender; 6045-150 Tank Car; 6076-75 Hopper Car - Black; 6167-25 Caboose; 1013-8 Curved Track (Bundle of 8 - 1013); 1026-25 25-Watt Transformer; 1103-20 Envelope Packed; 310-2 Set of (5) Billboards; D63-50 Accessory Catalog; 1-63 Warranty Card; 1-62 Parts Order Form; 1123-40 Instruction Sheet; 11311-20 Instruction Sheet; Form 2869 Printed Sheet

Boxes & Packing: 62-200 Display Outfit Box; 61-101 Corr. Insert; 61-102 Corr. Insert (2); 61-103 Shipper for (6) (1-6)

Alternate For Outfit Contents:
Note: Customer Stock No. E-1007 to appear on all cartons.

19213 (1963)	C6	C7	C8	Rarity
Complete Outfit	190	300	420	R4
Outfit Box no. 62-200	90	125	150	R4

Comments: Western Auto Stores purchased three steam-powered Retailer Promotional outfits in 1963: nos. 19212, 19213 and 19214. The 19213 appeared on page 17 of the 1963 Western Auto Christmas Gifts Catalog as no. E1007 for $11.95.

The 19213, a Type Ib outfit, was Western Auto's low-end purchase in 1963. It was led by a no. 1061-25 Steam Type Locomotive. This new-for-1963 Scout steamer was a follow-up to the no. 1050-25 Steam Type Locomotive that was first issued in 1959. This stripped-down locomotive featured an 0-4-0 wheel arrangement and went forward only. It lacked a headlight, a lens and any sort of traction aid.

Except for the no. 6076-75 Hopper Car - Black, the rolling stock in this outfit was new for 1963. These new cars demonstrated the further cheapening of the product line. Lionel even went so far as to create the no. 1061T-25 Tender without any markings.

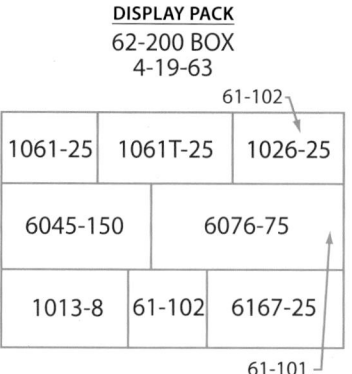

The transition from Archbar to AAR trucks and couplers that began in 1962 continued into 1963. As part of this, Lionel sought to cut costs by introducing a non-operating AAR type. Therefore, starting in 1963, most cars equipped with AAR trucks and couplers had at least one non-operating type. For the 19213, only the no. 6045-150 Tank Car included an operating coupler. All the other cars were equipped with non-operating AAR trucks and couplers.

The no. 62-200 White 4-6-4 Steamer and F3 Hinged Display with Red/Orange and Blue Graphics Type A outfit box was manufactured by United Container Co. and measured 21⅝ x 11½ x 3¼ inches.

Of the three Western Auto outfits from 1963, the 19213 is the least desirable. It was produced in large quantities and had low-end rolling stock.

Customer No. On Box: E1011
Description: "O27" Promotional Outfit
Specification: "O27" Steam Type Freight Outfit With Smoke
Customer/No.: Western Auto; E1011
Original Amount: 926
Factory Order Date: 5/7/1963
Date Issued: Rev 11-27-63
Packaging: RSC Outfit Packing #5, Units not Boxed

Contents: 238-25 Steam Type Locomotive with Smoke; 1060T-25 Tender; 6414-150 Auto Transport (Less Autos); 6406-30 Automobile (4); 6162-25 Gondola Car (Less 3 Canisters); 6112-88 Canister (3); 6465-150 Tank Car; 6476-75 Hopper Car - Black; 6822-50 Searchlight Car; 6257-100 Caboose; 1013-70 Curved Track (Bundle of 12 - 1013); 1018-5 Straight Track (Bundle of 5 - 1018); 6139-25 Uncoupling Track Section; 1103-50 Envelope Packed; 1020-25 90° Crossing; 1025-25 45-Watt Transformer; 909-20 Smoke Fluid; 310-2 Set of (5) Billboards; D63-50 Accessory Catalog; 1-62 Parts Order Form; 1-63 Warranty Card; 1123-40 Instruction Sheet; 19214-10 Instruction Sheet; 237-11 Instruction Sheet

Western Auto's no. E1011 was a Lionel no. 19214 from 1963. It was Western Auto's high-end steam offering and featured a no. 6414-150 Auto Transport with four green no. 6406-30 Automobiles with gray bumpers.

Boxes & Packing: 63-348 Outfit Box; 62-264 Corr. Insert; 62-251 Corr. Insert; 62-248 Corr. Insert; 62-225 Corr. Insert; 61-171 Corr. Insert; 63-311 Corr. Insert; 63-315 Corr. Insert; 63-349 Shipper for (4) (1-4)

Alternate For Outfit Contents:

Note: Customer Stock No. E-1011 to appear on cartons.

19214 (1963)	C6	C7	C8	Rarity
Complete Outfit With Green Automobiles	1,225	1,725	2,275	R7
Outfit Box no. 63-348	250	400	500	R7

Comments: Western Auto Stores purchased three steam-powered Retailer Promotional outfits in 1963: nos. 19212, 19213 and 19214. Of the three outfits, the 19214 was the only one that did not appear in the 1963 Western Auto Christmas Gifts Catalog.

The 19214, a Type Ia outfit, was Western Auto's high-end purchase in 1963. It was led by a no. 238-25 Steam Locomotive with Smoke. This new-for-1963 Scout steamer included a two-position reversing unit, a headlight and a rubber tire as a traction aid. The early version with wide running boards was included in this outfit. Except for its 238 number, it was the same engine as a no. 237.

Three cars in this outfit were carryover items that were given new suffixes in 1963. The no. 6414-150 Auto Transport (Less Autos) was an unboxed 6414 without automobiles. The no. 6822-50 Searchlight Car was an unboxed 6822 with one operating and one non-operating AAR truck and coupler. The no. 6257-100 Caboose was an AAR-equipped 6257.

The transition from Archbar to AAR trucks and couplers that began in 1962 continued into 1963. As part of this, Lionel sought to cut costs by introducing a non-operating AAR type. Therefore, starting in 1963, most cars equipped with AAR trucks and couplers had at least one non-operating type.

For the 19214, the no. 1060T-25 Tender was equipped with non-operating Archbar trucks and couplers. The nos. 6414-150, 6465-150 Tank Car and 6476-75 Hopper Car - Black included two operating AAR types. The nos. 6162-25 Gondola Car, 6822-50 and 6257-100 came with one operating and one non-operating AAR type.

This outfit introduced the no. 19214-10 Instruction Sheet. It was dated 6/63. Because the 19214-10 depicted the figure-eight track diagram, a no. 1802B Layout Instruction Sheet was not needed. This sheet, as well as the other sheets in this outfit, specified a 90-day warranty.

The no. 63-348 Tan RSC with Black Graphics outfit box was manufactured by St. Joe Kraft, St. Joe Paper Co. Container Division and measured 14⅜ x 12⅜ x 6 inches. It included four lines of data as part of the box manufacturer's certificate.

Of the three Western Auto outfits from 1963, the 19214 is the most desirable. It included a collectors' favorite: a 6414 with four green no. 6406-30 Automobiles with gray bumpers.

The original quantity of the 19214 was 1,000, but that number was reduced by 74 to 926 on 11-27-63. These 74 outfits became the no. 19214-500.

CONVENTIONAL PACK
63-348 BOX
4-25-63

TOP LAYER

6476-75	(1) 6112-88	
6162-25 (2) 6406-30		6822-50 6139-25
6465-150		
1060T-25	(2) 6112-88	

BOTTOM LAYER

238-25	1025-25		
	6257-100	6414-150 (2) 6406-30	1013-70
	1018-5		

1020-25 TOP 6257

Description: "O27" Promotional Outfit
Specification: "O27" Steam Type Freight Outfit W/Smoke
Customer: Spiegel
Original Amount: 74
Factory Order Date: 11/27/1963
Date Issued: Rev 12-3-63
Date Req'd: At Once
Packaging: RSC Outfit Packing. #5, Units Loose

Contents: 238-25 Steam Type Locomotive with Smoke; 1060T-25 Tender; 6414-150 Auto Transport (Less Autos); 6406-30 Automobile (4); 6162-25 Gondola Car (Less 3 Canisters); 6112-88 Canister (3); 6465-150 Tank Car; 6822-50 Searchlight Car; 6257-100 Caboose; 1013-8 Curved Track (Bundle of 8 - 1013); 1018-10 Straight Track (Loose); 6139-25 Uncoupling Track Section; 1103-50 Envelope Packed; 1025-25 45-Watt Transformer; 909-20 Smoke Fluid; 310-2 Set of (5) Billboards; D63-50 Accessory Catalog; 1-62 Parts Order Form; 1-63 Warranty Card; 1123-40 Instruction Sheet; 19214-10 Instruction Sheet; 237-11 Instruction Sheet

Boxes & Packing: 63-348 Outfit Box; 62-264 Corr. Insert; 62-251 Corr. Insert; 62-248 Corr. Insert; 62-225 Corr. Insert; 61-171 Corr. Insert; 63-311 Corr. Insert; 63-315 Corr. Insert; 63-349 Shipper for (4) (1-4)

19214-500 (1963)	C6	C7	C8	Rarity
Complete Outfit With Green Or Brown Automobiles	1,775	2,500	3,150	R10
Complete Outfit With Yellow Automobiles	1,175	1,700	2,150	R10
Outfit Box no. 63-348	800	1,200	1,400	R10

Comments: This was the second of five (nos. 11351-500, 19214-500, 19237, 19238 and 19238-501) Retailer Promotional outfits from 1963 that listed Spiegel as the customer on the Factory Order. The 19214-500, a Type Ia outfit, did not appear in the 1963 Spiegel Christmas Catalog.

Except for two differences, the 19214-500 duplicated Western Auto no. 19214. For one thing, the 19214-500 lacked a no. 6476-25 Hopper Car – Black. For another, it included an oval track plan and not a figure-eight.

The 19214-500 was led by a no. 238-25 Steam Locomotive with Smoke. This new-for-1963 Scout steamer included a two-position reversing unit, a headlight and a rubber tire as a traction aid. The early version with wide running boards was included in this outfit. Except for its 238 number, it was the same engine as a no. 237. This was the last appearance of the 238-25 in an outfit until 1965.

Three cars in this outfit were carryover items that were given new suffixes in 1963. The no. 6414-150 Auto Transport (Less Autos) was an unboxed 6414 without automobiles. It likely included four green or brown no. 6406-30 Automobiles with gray bumpers, but yellow automobiles with gray bumpers were also possible. Pricing is provided for all of these variations.

The no. 6822-50 Searchlight Car was an unboxed 6822 with one operating and one non-operating AAR truck and coupler. The no. 6257-100 Caboose was an AAR-equipped 6257.

The transition from Archbar to AAR trucks and couplers that began in 1962 continued into 1963. As part of this, Lionel sought to cut costs by introducing a non-operating AAR type. Therefore, starting in 1963, most cars equipped with AAR trucks and couplers had at least one non-operating type.

For the 19214-500, the no. 1060T-25 Tender was equipped with non-operating Archbar trucks and couplers. The norm for the nos. 6414-150 and 6465-150 Tank Car was one operating and one non-operating AAR type, although two operating types were possible. The nos. 6162-25 Gondola Car, 6822-50 and 6257-100 came with one operating and one non-operating AAR type.

The no. 63-348 Tan RSC with Black Graphics outfit box was manufactured by St. Joe Kraft, St. Joe Paper Co. Container Division and measured 14⅜ x 12⅜ x 6 inches. It included four lines of data as part of the box manufacturer's certificate.

Of the five Spiegel outfits, the 19214-500 was produced in the lowest quantity and is the rarest of them all. It is also more difficult to find than a 19214.

Description: "O27" Promotional Outfit
Specification: "O27" Steam Type Freight Outfit
Customer: J. C. Penney Co., Inc.
Original Amount: ~~3,000~~ Cancel
Factory Order Date: 5/15/1963
Date Issued: 5-24-63
Packaging: RSC Outfit Packing #5 (Units not Boxed)

Contents: 1060-25 Steam Type Locomotive; 1061T-25 Tender; 6409-25 Flat Car W/3 Pipes; 6511-15 Pipes (3); 6076-100 Hopper Car - Gray; 6014-325 Frisco Box Car; 6167-25 Caboose; 1013-8 Curved Track (Bundle of 8 - 1013); 1018-10 Straight Track (Loose) (2); 1026-25 25-Watt Transformer; 1103-20 Envelope Packed; D63-50 Accessory Catalog; 310-2 Set of (5) Billboards; 1-62 Parts Order Form; 1-63 Warranty Card; 1123-40 Instruction Sheet; 1123-10 Instruction Sheet; Form 2870 Printed Sheet

Boxes & Packing: 61-170 Outfit Box; 61-171 Corr. Insert; 61-172 Corr. Insert; 61-173 Corr. Insert; 61-174 Shipper for (6) (1-6)

Comments: The Factory Order for this J. C. Penney outfit was marked "Cancel". This listing is included for historical reference. It is likely that this outfit was canceled due to J. C. Penney's acquisition of General Merchandise Corporation to run its mail-order business. (See the entry for J. C. Penney in the section on Lionel's Distribution and Customers for information about this outfit.)

Richie Premium outfits included rare and collectible paper items, such as the nos. X625-20 Cardboard Scenic Set and 903 Set of (2) Sheets Trading Cards. But what makes the no. 19216 fascinating was the inclusion of both a steam and a diesel locomotive. The outfit is shown with its no. 1060-25 Steam Type Locomotive and 1130T-25 Tender substitutions.

Description: "O27" Promotional Outfit
Specification: "O27" Steam Type Freight Outfit
Customer: Richie Premium
Original Amount: 6,500
Factory Order Date: 5/15/1963
Date Issued: Rev 9-30-63
Date Req'd: Aug
Packaging: RSC Outfit Packing #5 (Units not Boxed)

Contents: 1061-25 Steam Type Locomotive; 1060T-25 Tender; 6045-150 Tank Car; 6050-150 Van Camp Savings Bank Car; 6062-25 Gondola Car - Black - W/3 Cable Reels; 40-11 Cable Reels (3); 6067-25 Caboose; 1013-70 Curved Track (Bundle of 12 - 1013); 1018-40 Straight Track (Bundle of 4 - 1018); 1020-25 90° Crossing; 1026-25 25-Watt Transformer; 1103-20 Envelope Packed; 903 Set of (2) Sheets Trading Cards; X625-20 Cardboard Scenic Set; 1065-25 Alco Diesel Power Unit - "Union Pacific"; 310-2 Set of (5) Billboards; D63-50 Accessory Catalog; 1-62 Parts Order Form; 1-63 Warranty Card; 1123-40 Instruction Sheet; 1802B Layout Instruction Sheet; 11311-20 Instruction Sheet

Boxes & Packing: 62-243 Outfit Box; 61-171 Corr. Insert; 62-225 Corr. Insert (2); 62-248 Corr. Insert; 62-244 Shipper for (4) (1-4)

Alternate For Outfit Contents:
Note: Substitute 1130T-25 for 1060T-25; Substitute 1060-25 for 1061-25.

19216 (1963)	C6	C7	C8	Rarity
Complete Outfit	1,020	2,675	4,550	R9
Outfit Box no. 62-243	50	75	100	R4

Comments: This was the second of two (along with the no. 19142-502) outfits purchased by incentive merchandiser Richie Premium in 1963. A Retailer Promotional Type Ib outfit, the no. 19216 was a follow-up to Richie's no. 19147 from 1962.

Richie Premium outfits are highly collectible because each of them included some rare paper items. In fact, Richie's nos. 19142-502, 19216 and 19328 represented the only instances in which the nos. 903 Set of (2) Sheets Trading Cards and X625-20 Cardboard Scenic Set were paired. (See the entry for the 19142-502 from 1963 for a discussion of these rare paper items.)

What makes Richie's 19216 and 19328 interesting is that they included *both* a steam and a diesel locomotive! Many original owners of these outfits still have complete outfits with both engines. But once an outfit leaves its original owner, one of the locomotives tends to be separated. Stories abound of collectors who purchased outfits intact and sold one engine. If it weren't for the Factory Orders, the fact that these outfits included two engines might never have been revealed.

The steam engine listed on the Factory Order was a no. 1061-25 Steam Type Locomotive, but all the outfits observed included a no. 1060-25 Steam Type Locomotive substitution. Both were low-end Scout steamers that lacked a traction aid. The diesel locomotive was a no. 1065-25 Union Pacific Alco Diesel Power Unit. This low-end Alco appeared only in promotional outfits.

Except for the orange no. 6045-150 Tank Car, all the rolling stock in the 19216 was carryover from earlier years. The no. 6062-25 Gondola Car has been observed with brown or orange no. 40-11 Cable Reels. The brown versions are more difficult to find. A brown no. 6067-25 Caboose was also common with this outfit. The no. 1130T-25 Tender substitution was the norm. It still came with early operating AAR trucks and couplers.

The transition from Archbar to AAR trucks and couplers that began in 1962 continued into 1963. As part of this, Lionel sought to cut costs by introducing a non-operating AAR type. Therefore, starting in 1963, most cars equipped with AAR trucks and couplers had at least one non-operating type. For the 19216 the nos. 6050-150 Van Camp Savings Bank Car and 6067-25 were equipped with non-operating Archbar types. The 6062-25 included operating AAR types. The 6045-150 came with non-operating AAR types. Other combinations on the 6067-25 were possible.

The no. 62-243 Tan RSC with Black Graphics outfit box was

manufactured by the Mead Corporation and measured 12⅛ x 11½ x 6⅜ inches. It included four lines of data on the box manufacturer's certificate.

In 1989, Richard Kughn, then the owner of Lionel Trains Inc., purchased Madison Hardware Co. of New York City and reopened it in Detroit soon thereafter. One of the first lists of outfits available for sale included three of the 19216.

The peripherals included in Richie Premium outfits make them extremely difficult to complete. Empty boxes are common, but completed outfits are quite rare.

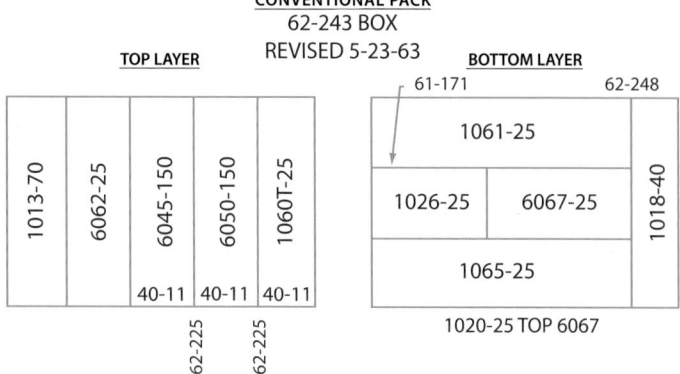

CONVENTIONAL PACK
62-243 BOX
REVISED 5-23-63

Description: "O27" Promotional Outfit
Specification: "O27" Steam Type Freight Outfit
Customer/No.: Firestone; 11 L 346
Original Amount: 1,000
Factory Order Date: 5/13/1963
Date Issued: Rev 9-3-63
Date Req'd: W/O 6-10-63
Packaging: RSC Outfit Packing #5 (Units not Boxed)

Contents: 1062-25 Steam Type Loco. W/Light & Reversing Unit; 1060T-25 Tender; 6630-25 Missile Launching Car; 6650-80 Missile; 6500-25 Beechcraft Bonanza Transport Car; 6042-25 Gondola Car - Blue; 6112-5 Canister (2); 6050-150 Van Camp Savings Bank Car; 6067-25 Caboose; 1013-70 Curved Track (Bundle of 12 - 1013); 1018-40 Straight Track (Bundle of 4 - 1018); 1020-25 90° Crossing; 1026-25 25-Watt Transformer; 943-1 Exploding Ammo Dump; 1103-20 Envelope Packed; 310-2 Set of (5) Billboards; D63-50 Accessory Catalog; 1-62 Parts Order Form; 1-63 Warranty Card; 1802B Layout Instruction Sheet; 1123-40 Instruction Sheet; 6630-6 Instruction Sheet; 6500-3 Instruction Sheet; 11311-10 Instruction Sheet

Boxes & Packing: 62-243 Outfit Box; 61-171 Corr. Insert; 61-172 Corr. Insert; 62-248 Corr. Insert; 62-249 Corr. Insert; 62-244 Shipper for (4) (1-4)

Alternate For Outfit Contents:
Note: Sub. 1130T-25 Tender for 1060T-25.

19217 (1963)	C6	C7	C8	Rarity
Complete Outfit	820	1,135	1,600	R7
Outfit Box no. 62-243	150	225	300	R7

Comments: The Firestone Tire & Rubber Company purchased only one promotional outfit in 1963. The no. 19217 was a Retailer Promotional Type Ib led by a no. 1062-25 Steam Type Loco. W/ Light & Reversing Unit. This low-end Scout steamer was new for 1963; it featured an 0-4-0 wheel arrangement and lacked a traction aid. According to its Lionel Engineering Specification, it was the "Same as #1061 but with the addition of Reversing Unit & Lamp".

In 1963, Lionel was depleting its remaining inventory of

the unboxed no. 6500-25 Beechcraft Bonanza Transport Car in promotional outfits. This item made its first of five promotional outfit appearances in the 19217. For this outfit, the 6500-25 was equipped with operating AAR trucks and couplers.

All the remaining rolling stock was carryover from previous years. The three-year run of the no. 6630-25 Missile Launching Car was coming to an end in 1963. It was making its last appearance in six promotional outfits.

The transition from Archbar to AAR trucks and couplers that began in 1962 continued into 1963. For the 19217, the norm for the nos. 6050-150 Van Camp Savings Bank Car and 6630-25 was non-operating Archbar trucks and couplers. The no. 6042-25 Gondola Car - Blue could come with either non-operating AAR or Archbar trucks and couplers, as could the no. 6067-25 Caboose and no. 1060T-25 Tender.

The no. 1130T-25 Tender substitution for the 1060T-25 Tender minimally affects the outfit price.

The no. 943-1 Exploding Ammo Dump was an inexpensive way to provide an additional target for the 6630-25.

The appropriate quantity of track was included to make the figure-eight layout. That track plan was outlined on a no. 1802B Layout Instruction Sheet.

The no. 62-243 Tan RSC with Black Graphics outfit box measured 12⅛ x 11½ x 6⅜ inches.

This outfit was produced in roughly the same quantity as the previous two Firestone promotional outfits. As with all Firestone outfits, the 19217 remains in demand.

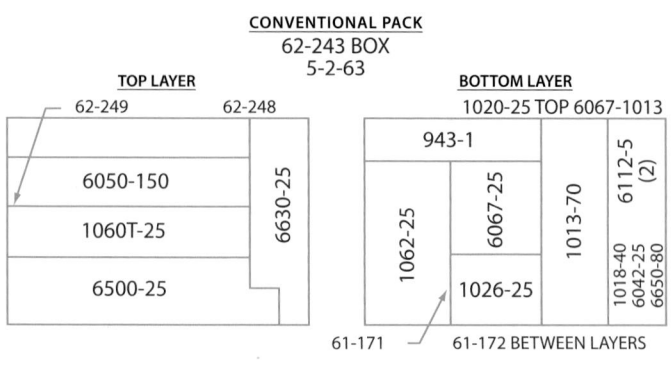

CONVENTIONAL PACK
62-243 BOX
5-2-63

Gimbels' only promotional outfit purchase in 1963 was the no. 19218. This was an example of Lionel using a promotional outfit to deplete older inventory, as all the rolling stock in it represented carryover items. The 19218 came with the early version of the no. 237-25 Steam Type Locomotive with Smoke that had wide running boards. The no. 1130T-25 Tender substitution is shown.

Description: "O27" Promotional Outfit
Specification: "O27" Steam Type Freight Outfit W/Smoke
Customer/No./Price: Gimbels; 740 F3; $19.88
Original Amount: 1,050
Factory Order Date: 5/13/1963
Date Issued: Rev 10-30-63
Packaging: RSC Outfit Packing - #5 (Units not Boxed)

Contents: 237-25 Steam Type Locomotive with Smoke; 1060T-25 Tender; 6050-150 Van Camp Savings Bank Car; 3519-25 Operating Satellite Launching Car; 0333-100 Satellite; 6500-25 Beechcraft Bonanza Transport Car; 6343-25 Barrel Ramp Car; 362-78 Wood Barrels (6); 6067-25 Caboose; 1013-70 Curved Track (Bundle of 12 - 1013); 1018-30 Straight Track (Bundle of 3 - 1018); 1008-50 Uncoupling Unit; 1020-25 90° Crossing; 1010-25 35-Watt Transformer; 1103-20 Envelope Packed; 909-20 Smoke Fluid; 310-2 Set of (5) Billboards; D63-50 Accessory Catalog; 1-62 Parts Order Form; 1-63 Warranty Card; 1802B Layout Instruction Sheet; 1123-40 Instruction Sheet; 237-11 Instruction Sheet; 3519-7 Instruction Sheet; 6500-3 Instruction Sheet; 122-10 Instruction Sheet

Boxes & Packing: 62-243 Outfit Box; 61-171 Corr. Insert; 62-223 Corr. Insert; 62-225 Corr. Insert; 62-248 Corr. Insert; 62-249 Corr. Insert; 62-251 Corr. Insert; 62-244 Shipper for (4) (1-4)

Alternate For Outfit Contents:
Note: Sub. 1,000 1130T-25 for 1060T-25.

19218 (1963)	C6	C7	C8	Rarity
Complete Outfit	730	1,125	1,600	R7
Outfit Box no. 62-243	100	225	325	R7

Comments: This was the only Retailer Promotional Type Ib outfit purchased by Gimbels in 1963. The no. 19218 was the follow-up outfit to the no. 19165 from 1962.

As noted, Gimbels purchased just one outfit in 1963. However, the quantity listed for the 19218 was 50 percent greater than that of the two outfits Gimbels ordered in 1962 (1,050 units as opposed to 700).

The 19218 was led by a no. 237-25 Steam Type Locomotive with Smoke. This new-for-1963 Scout steamer featured a two-position reversing unit and a headlight and used a rubber tire as a traction aid. The harder-to-find early version with wide running boards was included in this outfit. Except for its 237 number, it was the same engine as a no. 238.

All the rolling stock in this outfit was carryover from early years. Lionel began to deplete its remaining inventory of the no. 3519-25 Satellite Launching Car in 1963. The 19218 was one of only four outfits in which this model came unboxed. Also in 1963, Lionel was depleting the remaining inventory of the unboxed no. 6500-25 Beechcraft Bonanza Transport Car in this and other promotional outfits. The no. 6067-25 Caboose has been observed in either brown or red.

The transition from Archbar to AAR trucks and couplers that began in 1962 continued into 1963. For the 19218, the no. 6050-150 Van Camp Savings Bank Car was equipped with non-operating Archbar trucks and couplers. All the other cars were equipped with two operating (nos. 3519-25, 6500-25 and 6343-25) or one operating and one plain (nos. 6067-25 and 1130T-25) AAR trucks and couplers.

The appropriate quantity of track was included to make the figure-eight layout. That track plan was outlined on a no. 1802B Layout Instruction Sheet.

All the paperwork reflected the new 90-day warranty policy that Lionel instituted in 1963. Many of these instruction sheet versions are the most difficult ones to find.

The no. 62-243 Tan RSC with Black Graphics outfit box was manufactured by the Mead Corporation and measured 12⅛ x 11½ x 6⅜ inches. It included four lines of data as part of the box manufacturer's certificate.

The 19218 slightly exceeded Gimbels' forecast. An early Factory Order dated 7-26-63 indicated a quantity of 1,000, but this was increased to 1,050 on 10-30-63. With so many examples made, this outfit does appear on the market.

CONVENTIONAL PACK
62-243 BOX
5-2-63

TOP LAYER

62-249			62-225
6050-150	1060T-25	6343-25	3519-25
AIRPLANE 362-78 (6) 0333-100			

62-251 1008-50 TOP 1060T

BOTTOM LAYER

61-171		62-248
237-25		1018-30
1010-25	6067-25	
6500-25 1013-70		

62-223 BETWEEN LAYERS
1020-25 TOP 6067

19219
1963

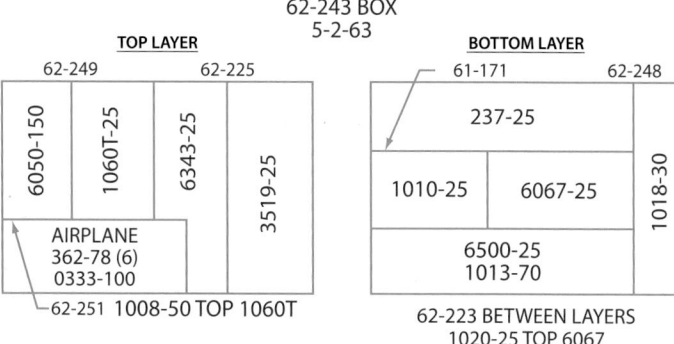

The no. 19219 was White Auto's diesel-powered purchase for 1963. It was an almost exact repeat of White's no. 19159 from 1962. Both outfits shared the White no. 108-105. The blue no. 6502-50 Girder Transport Car substitution is shown.

Customer No. On Box: 108-105
Description: "O27" Promotional Outfit
Specification: "O27" Diesel Freight Outfit
Customer/No.: White Stores; 108-105
Original Amount: 1,039
Factory Order Date: 5/13/1963
Date Issued: Rev 9-27-63
Packaging: RSC Outfit Packing #5 (Units not Boxed), Except 110

Contents: 211P-150 *"Texas Special"* Diesel; 211T-25 *"Texas Special"* Motorless Unit; 6076-25 Hopper Car - Red; 6042-75 Gondola Car (Less 2 Cable Reels); 40-11 Cable Reels (2); 6502-25 Girder Transport Car; 6502-3 Girder Bridge; 6050-150 Van Camp Savings Bank Car; 6067-25 Caboose; 1013-8 Curved Track

(Bundle of 8 - 1013); 1013-90 Curved Track (Bundle of 9 - 1013); 1018-5 Straight Track (Bundle of 5 - 1018) (2); 1010-25 35-Watt Transformer; 110-1 Trestle Set; 1103-20 Envelope Packed; 310-2 Set of (5) Billboards; D63-50 Accessory Catalog; 1-62 Parts Order Form; 1-63 Warranty Card; 1123-40 Instruction Sheet; 211-151 Instruction Sheet; 1802I Layout Instruction Sheet; 19145-10 Instruction Sheet

Boxes & Packing: 62-270 Outfit Box; 61-171 Corr. Insert; 62-224 Corr. Insert; 62-245 Corr. Insert (2); 62-248 Corr. Insert (2); 62-264 Corr. Insert; 62-272 Corr. Insert; 62-271 Shipper for (3) (1-3)

Alternate For Outfit Contents:
Note: Use 800 - 211P-25 - Balance 211P-150; Customer Stock No. 108-105 on carton & shipper; Substitute 6502-50 for 6502-25.

19219 (1963)	C6	C7	C8	Rarity
Complete Outfit	315	600	875	R7
Outfit Box no. 62-270	125	225	300	R7

Comments: In 1963, White Auto purchased two Retailer Promotional Type Ib outfits: nos. 19219 and 19220. The 19219 was its diesel-powered purchase, whereas the 19220 was its steam-powered outfit.

The 19219 almost exactly duplicated White's no. 19159 from 1962. In fact, both outfits had White's no. 108-105 stamped on the box. The only differences were that the 19219 had a smaller transformer than did the 19159 and lacked its no. 3309-25 Turbo Missile Firing Car. (See the entry for the 19159 from 1962 for complete information.)

The 19219 used 800 of the remaining no. 211P-25 *Texas Special* Alco Diesel Power Units. A no. 211P-150 *Texas Special* Alco Diesel Power Unit led the last 239 outfits. It was a cost-reduced version of the 211P-25 *Texas Special* Alco Diesel Power Unit. The 211P-150 was new for 1963 and featured a two-position reversing unit, two traction tires, a headlight, a weight and an open pilot with a large ledge. The "-150" variation has not stirred much interest in the collector community, which is why the substitution does not affect the outfit's price.

The rolling stock in the 19219 included updated versions of the items found in the 19159. For example, the no. 6042-75 Gondola Car now came with non-operating AAR trucks and couplers. Also, a blue no. 6502-50 Girder Transport Car replaced the black no. 6502-25 Girder Transport Car. Finally, a no. 6050-

150 Van Camp Savings Bank Car was now the norm. All the cars (except for the 6042-75) were equipped with non-operating Archbar trucks and couplers.

All the paperwork reflected the new 90-day warranty policy that Lionel instituted in 1963. Many of these instruction sheet versions are the most difficult ones to find.

The no. 62-270 Tan RSC with Black Graphics outfit box was manufactured by United Container Co. and measured 15½ x 14 x 6¼ inches. It included four lines of data as part of the box manufacturer's certificate (BMC). It has been observed with a "62" and three stars as part of the BMC.

Even though the 19219 was produced in smaller quantities than its earlier 19159 counterpart, it is slightly less desirable. The reason for this discrepancy is that the 19219 did not include a 3309-25 Turbo Missile Firing Car.

CONVENTIONAL PACK
62-270 BOX

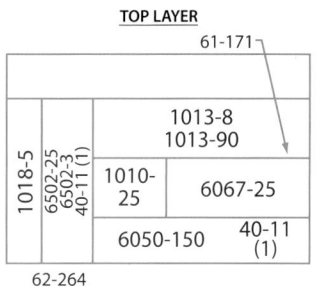

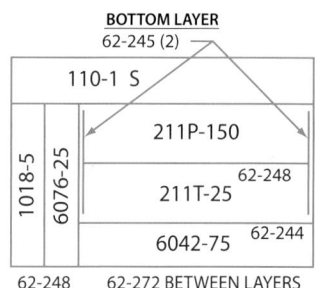

Customer No. On Box: 108-55
Description: "O27" Promotional Outfit
Customer/No.: White Stores; 108-55
Original Amount: 9,100
Factory Order Date: 5/13/1963
Date Issued: Rev 10-3-63
Date Req'd: W/O 7/22/63 Bal 9-23-63
Packaging: RSC Outfit Packing - #5 (Units not Boxed)

Contents: 1061-25 Steam Type Locomotive; 1061T-25 Tender; 6502-25 Girder Transport Car; 6502-3 Girder Bridge; 6050-150 Van Camp Savings Bank Car; 6167-25 Caboose; 1013-8 Curved Track (Bundle of 8 - 1013); 1026-25 25-Watt Transformer; 1103-20 Envelope Packed; D63-50 Accessory Catalog; 1-62 Parts Order Form; 1-63 Warranty Card; 310-62 Set of (3) Billboards; 1123-40 Instruction Sheet; 11311-20 Instruction Sheet; Form 2869 Printed Sheet

Boxes & Packing: 61-404 Outfit Box; 61-171 Insert; 62-249 Insert; 63-353 Insert; 61-405 Shipper (1-4); 63-383 Outfit Box; 62-254 Corr. Insert; 61-173 Corr. Insert; 63-384 Shipper (4) (1-4)

Alternate For Outfit Contents:
Customer Stock No. 108-55 on Carton & Shipper; Note: Substitute 6502-50 for 6502-25; Note: All packing replaced should be used until all on hand or in shipment would be used up.

19220 (1963)	C6	C7	C8	Rarity
Complete Outfit With no. 61-404 Box	180	190	425	R4
Outfit Box no. 61-404	60	95	125	R4
Complete Outfit With no. 63-383 Box	190	225	475	R5
Outfit Box no. 63-383	70	130	175	R5

Comments: In 1963, White Auto purchased two Retailer Promotional Type Ib outfits: nos. 19219 and 19220. The 19219 was its diesel-powered purchase, whereas the 19220 was its steam-powered outfit. The 19220 was assigned White Auto's no. 108-55. This number is most often found stamped on the outfit box.

The 19220 was a starter outfit produced in very large quantities. It was led by a no. 1061-25 Steam Type Locomotive. This stripped-down Scout steamer (new for 1963) featured an 0-4-0 wheel arrangement and went forward only. It lacked a headlight, a lens and any sort of traction aid. It was trailed by an unmarked no. 1061T-25 Tender.

The no. 6050-150 Van Camp Savings Bank Car was making one of its 13 appearances in 1963. It was equipped with non-operating Archbar trucks and couplers. The unmarked blue plastic no. 6502-50 Girder Transport Car replaced the black version (no. 6502-25) in 1963. It came with a no. 6502-3 Girder Bridge molded in orange plastic.

The no. 19220 was White Auto's steam-powered purchase for 1963. It was a low-end starter outfit produced in very large quantities. It is shown with the blue no. 6502-50 Girder Transport Car substitution and a no. 61-404 Outfit Box.

The transition from Archbar to AAR trucks and couplers that began in 1962 continued into 1963. As part of this, Lionel sought to cut costs by introducing a non-operating AAR type. Therefore, starting in 1963, most cars equipped with AAR trucks and couplers had at least one non-operating type. For the 19220, the 6502-50 and all the other cars were most often equipped with non-operating AAR trucks and couplers.

The Form 2869 advertising the no. 2001 Track Make-Up Kit was dated 6/63. It is one of the more difficult items to find in completing a C8 outfit.

Two versions of a Tan RSC with Black Graphics outfit box were used for the 19220. The first and more common of the two was a no. 61-404 Outfit Box. It was manufactured by St. Joe Kraft, St. Joe Paper Co. Container Division and measured 10¾ x 9¼ x 5½ inches. It included four lines of data as part of the box manufacturer's certificate. The second was a no. 63-383 Outfit Box. It was manufactured by United Container Co. and measured 11½ x 9¾ x 6 inches.

More than one outfit has been observed lacking the White no. 108-55 printed on the box.

Since 9,100 outfits were produced, the 19220 appears frequently, but in various forms of completion. The 63-383 Outfit Box version is more difficult to find, hence its rarity and pricing premium over a 61-404 Outfit Box version.

Be aware that a no. D19220 Blister Display was also produced for the 19220. However, an example of this unique item has yet to be observed.

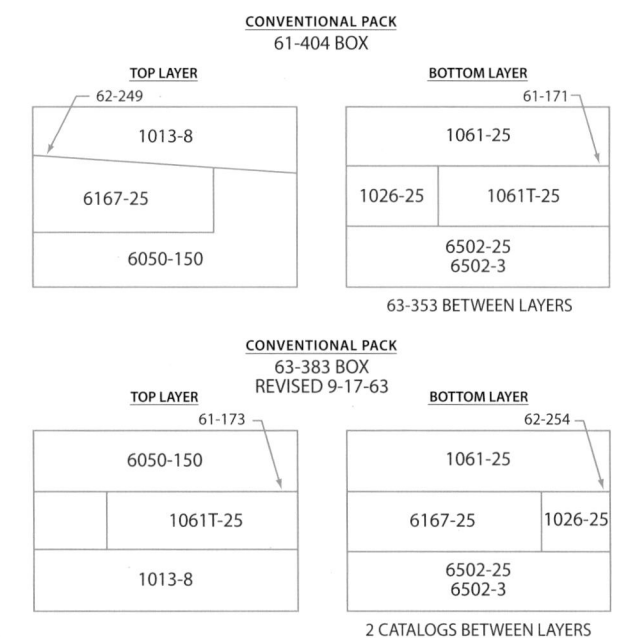

CONVENTIONAL PACK
61-404 BOX

TOP LAYER		BOTTOM LAYER	
62-249			61-171
1013-8		1061-25	
6167-25		1026-25	1061T-25
6050-150		6502-25 6502-3	

63-353 BETWEEN LAYERS

CONVENTIONAL PACK
63-383 BOX
REVISED 9-17-63

TOP LAYER		BOTTOM LAYER	
61-173			62-254
6050-150		1061-25	
1061T-25		6167-25	1026-25
1013-8		6502-25 6502-3	

2 CATALOGS BETWEEN LAYERS

Description: "O27" Promotional Outfit
Specification: "O27" Steam Type Freight Outfit
Customer: Montgomery Ward
Original Amount: ~~3,500~~ Cancel
Date Req'd: Aug

Packaging: RSC Outfit Packing #4 (Units not Boxed), 4 per shipper

Contents: 1061-25 Steam Type Locomotive; 1061T-25 Tender; 6042-25 Gondola Car - Blue; 6112-5 Canister (2); 6167-25 Caboose; 1013-8 Curved Track (Bundle of 8 - 1013); 1026-25 25-Watt Transformer; 1103-20 Envelope Packed; D63-50 Accessory Catalog; 1-62 Parts Order Form; 1-63 Warranty Card; 11311-20 Instruction Sheet

Outfit no. 19224 was Mutual Buying Syndicate's high-end steam-powered purchase for 1963. It re-introduced the no. 908-10 Scenic Station W/Tunnels - Packed. This large cardboard accessory was last seen in the nos. X-810NA and X-855 from 1959. It was the task of the retailer to provide one of the separately shipped 908-10s to each customer that bought a 19224.

The no. 908-10 Scenic Station W/Tunnels - Packed came in a Kraft paper bag stamped "908 For 19224". This is the correct version of the 908-10 included in the 19224.

Form; 1-63 Warranty Card; 1123-40 Instruction Sheet; 237-11 Instruction Sheet; 19145-10 Instruction Sheet; 1802H Layout Instruction Sheet

Boxes & Packing: 62-243 Outfit Box; 62-223 Corr. Insert; 62-225 Corr. Insert; 62-249 Corr. Insert; 62-254 Corr. Insert; 62-244 Shipper for (4) (1-4); 63-252 Box To Ship 908-1 (1-8)

Alternate For Outfit Contents:
Note: Ship on two (2); 1 - Outfit, 1 - 908-10; Outfit Box and 908 Env. to be stamped to include each other. To ship 908-1 Scenic Station Use: 63-252 Corr. Box 1/8 Req'd.

19224 (1963)	C6	C7	C8	Rarity
Complete Outfit	1,565	2,050	2,485	R9
Outfit Box no. 62-243	225	300	350	R7

Comments: In 1963, Lionel sold three outfits to the Mutual Buying Syndicate cooperative: nos. 19223, 19224 and 19225. The 19224, a Retailer Promotional Type Ib outfit, was distributed among Mutual Buying's member stores. It has been linked to at least one retailer, The Fair, through a price tag imprinted with no. 57 5 for $14.98.

The 19224 was Mutual's high-end steam-powered offering and a follow-up to its no. 19135 from 1962. This outfit is very collectible because of the inclusion of a no. 908-10 Scenic Station W/Tunnels - Packed. This large and fragile cardboard station first appeared in outfit nos. X-810NA and X-855 from 1959. After a four-year absence, it returned with the 19224 and went on to appear in four other promotional outfits through 1964. There were no Lionel markings on this item, which was intended to be assembled by the customer. The 908-10 frequently became separated from the train outfit and was destroyed.

Lionel shipped the 908-10s separately to the retailer. They came packaged eight at a time in their own no. 63-252 Corr. Box. Each 908-10 came in a large Kraft paper bag stamped "908 For 19224". There are at least three other versions of this bag. Two were stamped with outfit nos. 19394 and 19395. The third included no printing. The 908-10 also included an instruction sheet titled "How To Set Up Your Railroad Terminal". The pricing and rarity for this outfit assume the difficult-to-find "908 For 19244" Kraft bag.

The outfit box was stamped "Include 908 With This Set". Since the 908-10s came packaged separately, it was the task of the retailer to provide a 908-10 with each outfit purchased.

As for the components of the 19224, it was led by a no. 237-25 Steam Type Locomotive with Smoke. This new-for-1963 Scout steamer featured a two-position reversing unit and a headlight and used a rubber tire as a traction aid. The harder-to-find early version with wide running boards came in this outfit. Except for its 237 number, it was the same engine as a no. 238.

The orange no. 6045-150 Tank Car was the only new car in this outfit. It was equipped with non-operating AAR trucks and couplers. All the other rolling stock was carryover from earlier years and came equipped with non-operating Archbar trucks and couplers.

A no. 1802H Layout Instruction Sheet detailed the pretzel layout.

The paperwork was updated to reflect the new 90-day warranty policy that Lionel instituted in 1963. The no. 19145-10 Instruction Sheet made reference to the 90-day warranty, though it still was dated 7-62. The no. 237-11 Instruction Sheet was dated 3/63. Many of these instruction sheets are the most difficult versions to find.

The no. 62-243 Tan RSC with Black Graphics outfit box was manufactured by the Mead Corporation and measured 12⅛

x 11½ x 6⅜ inches. It included four lines of data as part of the box manufacturer's certificate.

The 19224 did not meet Mutual's original forecast because the outfit quantity was decreased from 1,500 to 1,000 on 10-29-63.

Examples of the 19224 do not often appear on the market, and when one does it tends to be missing the 908-10 Scenic Station W/Tunnels - Packed. Matching the Kraft paper bag stamped "908 For 19224" with this outfit is certainly the most difficult task in completing a C8 outfit.

CONVENTIONAL PACK
62-243 BOX

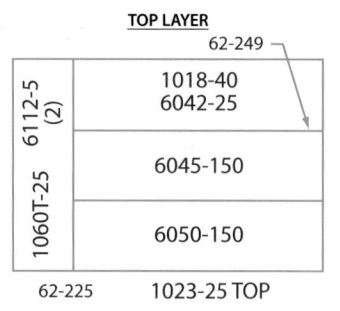

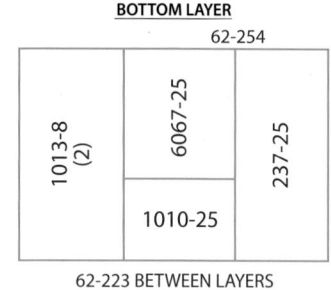

19225
1963

Description: "O27" Promotional Outfit
Specification: "O27" Diesel Freight Outfit
Customer: Mutual Buying
Original Amount: 1,000
Factory Order Date: 5/29/1963
Date Issued: Rev 10-30-63
Date Req'd: Aug
Packaging: RSC Outfit Packing #5 (Units not Boxed), Except 110

Contents: 211P-150 *"Texas Special"* Diesel; 211T-25 *"Texas Special"* Motorless Unit; 6500-25 Beechcraft Bonanza Transport Car; 6650-25 Missile Launching Flat Car; 6650-80 Missile; 6448-25 Exploding Target Range Car; 6501-25 Jet Motor Boat Car; 6501-2 Boat Assem.; 6501-17 Fuel Pellets - Packed; 6067-25 Caboose; 1013-8 Curved Track (Bundle of 8 - 1013); 1013-90 Curved Track (Bundle of 9 - 1013); 1018-40 Straight Track (Bundle of 4 - 1018); 1018-5 Straight Track (Bundle of 5 - 1018); 1008-50 Uncoupling Unit; 1025-25 45-Watt Transformer; 110-1 Trestle Set; 1103-20 Envelope Packed; 310-2 Set of (5) Billboards; D63-50 Accessory Catalog; 1-62 Parts Order Form; 1-63 Warranty Card; 122-10 Instruction Sheet; 1123-40 Instruction Sheet; 211-151 Instruction Sheet; 6500-3 Instruction Sheet; 6650-92 Instruction Sheet; 6448-17 Instruction Sheet; 6501-14 Instruction Sheet; 1802I Layout Instruction Sheet

Boxes & Packing: 62-270 Outfit Box; 62-245 Corr. Insert (2); 62-248 Corr. Insert (3); 62-272 Corr. Insert; 62-224 Corr. Insert; 62-271 Corr. Shipper for (3) (1-3)

19225 (1963)	C6	C7	C8	Rarity
Complete Outfit	910	1,335	1,875	R7
Outfit Box no. 62-270	150	225	300	R7

Comments: In 1963, Lionel sold three outfits to the Mutual Buying Syndicate cooperative: nos. 19223, 19224 and 19225. The 19225, a Retailer Promotional Type Ib outfit, was distributed among Mutual Buying's member stores. It has yet to be tied to a specific end customer.

The 19225 was a follow-up to Mutual's no. 19136 from 1962. Both outfits had a space and military theme and were headed by a no. 211P *Texas Special* Diesel. The no. 211P included in the 19225 was designated as the no. 211P-150 *Texas Special* Diesel (new for 1963). The new suffix, "-150", meant it was a cost-reduced version of the no. 211P-25 *Texas Special* Alco Diesel Power Unit included with the 19136. The 211P-150 featured a two-position reversing unit, two traction tires, a headlight, a weight and an open pilot with a large ledge. The "-150" variation has not stirred much interest in the collector community.

In 1963, Lionel was depleting its remaining inventory of the unboxed no. 6500-25 Beechcraft Bonanza Transport Car in promotional outfits. This model made one of its five promotional outfit appearances in the 19225. The nos. 6448-25 Exploding Target Car, 6501-25 Jet Motor Boat Car and 6650-25 Missile Launching Flat Car were also being depleted in promotional outfits. All of these cars were equipped with operating AAR trucks and couplers.

The 6448-25 has been observed in an all-white variation in this outfit. There is no premium for this variation because it is easily re-created. The version in this outfit came with "non-slotted" sides and nubs on the roof door guide to help hold on the sides.

The brown no. 6067-25 Caboose was equipped with one operating and one plain Archbar truck and coupler.

The no. 110-1 Trestle Set was used for the elevated pretzel track layout. A no. 1802I Layout Instruction Sheet detailed this track plan.

Outfit no. 19225 was Mutual Buying Syndicate's only diesel-powered purchase for 1963. It was a follow-up to Mutual's no. 19136 from 1962. The no. 6500-25 Beechcraft Bonanza Transport Car makes the 19225 a desirable and valuable outfit. Be aware that outfits have been observed with an all-white no. 6448-25 Exploding Target Car.

The paperwork was updated to reflect the new 90-day warranty policy that Lionel instituted in 1963. Many of these instruction sheets are the most difficult versions to find. Especially difficult to find is the no. 6448-17 Instruction Sheet. It was still dated 3-61, but included 90-day warranty information.

The no. 62-270 Tan RSC with Black Graphics outfit box was manufactured by United Container Co. and measured 15½ x 14 x 6¼ inches. It included four lines of data as part of the box manufacturer's certificate (BMC). It has been observed with a "63" and four stars as part of the BMC.

This outfit exceeded Mutual's original forecast because the quantity was increased from 900 to 1,000 on 10-30-63. Even with the extra 100 units manufactured, the 19225 is still a difficult outfit to find.

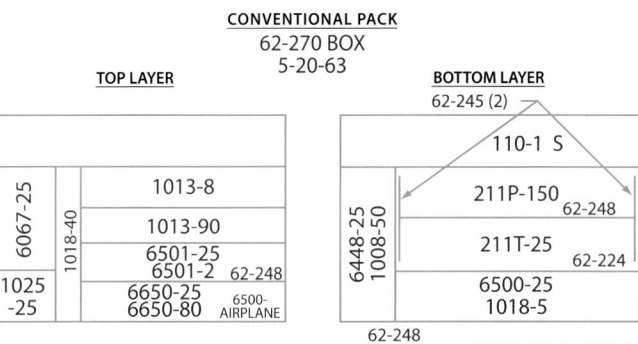

CONVENTIONAL PACK
62-270 BOX
5-20-63

TOP LAYER

6067-25	1018-40	1013-8	
		1013-90	
		6501-25	
		6501-2	62-248
1025 -25		6650-25	6500-
		6650-80	AIRPLANE

BOTTOM LAYER
62-245 (2)

110-1 S

6448-25 1008-50	211P-150	
		62-248
	211T-25	
		62-224
	6500-25	
	1018-5	

62-248
62-272 BETWEEN LAYERS

Description: "O27" Promotional Outfit
Specification: "O27" Steam Type Freight Outfit W/Smoke
Customer: AMC
Original Amount: 1,000
Factory Order Date: 5/31/1963
Date Issued: Rev 10-22-63
Date Req'd: Aug
Packaging: RSC Outfit Packing #5 (Units not Boxed), Except 110-1

Contents: 237-25 Steam Type Locomotive with Smoke; 1060T-25 Tender; 6476-25 Hopper Car - Red; 6465-150 Tank Car; 6067-25 Caboose; 1013-8 Curved Track (Bundle of 8 - 1013); 1013-90 Curved Track (Bundle of 9 - 1013); 1018-30 Straight Track (Bundle of 3 - 1018) (3); 1008-50 Uncoupling Unit;

19226
1963

110-1 Trestle Set; 1010-25 35-Watt Transformer; 1103-20 Envelope Packed; 909-20 Smoke Fluid; 310-2 Set of (5) Billboards; D63-50 Accessory Catalog; 1-62 Parts Order Form; 1-63 Warranty Card; 1123-40 Instruction Sheet; 237-11 Instruction Sheet; 122-10 Instruction Sheet; 1802I Layout Instruction Sheet

Boxes & Packing: 62-270 Outfit Box; 61-171 Corr. Insert; 61-172 Corr. Insert; 62-248 Corr. Insert; 62-273 Corr. Insert (2); 62-271 Shipper for (3) (1-3)

19226 (1963)	C6	C7	C8	Rarity
Complete Outfit	315	500	660	R7
Outfit Box no. 62-270	200	275	325	R7

Comments: Buying cooperatives, such as AMC (Associated Merchandising Corporation), were large customers of Lionel trains. In 1963, AMC purchased two promotional outfits: nos. 19226 and 19227.

The 19226, a Retailer Promotional Type Ib, was AMC's steam-powered follow-up to outfit no. 19131 from 1962. It was led by a no. 237-25 Steam Type Locomotive with Smoke. This new-for-1963 Scout steamer featured a two-position reversing unit and a headlight and used a rubber tire as a traction aid. The harder-to-find early version with wide running boards was included in this outfit. Except for its 237 number, it was the same engine as a no. 238.

The only new piece of rolling stock in the 19226 was the orange no. 6465-150 Tank Car. It came equipped with one operating and one non-operating AAR truck and coupler.

The transition from Archbar to AAR trucks and couplers that began in 1962 continued into 1963. As part of this, Lionel sought to cut costs by introducing a non-operating AAR type. Therefore, starting in 1963, most cars equipped with AAR trucks and couplers had at least one non-operating type. In 1963, it was possible for the no. 6476-25 Hopper Car - Red to come equipped with either operating AAR trucks and couplers or one operating and one non-operating AAR types. The nos. 1060T-25 Tender and 6067-25 Caboose could have Archbar or AAR trucks and couplers.

The no. 110-1 Trestle Set was used for the elevated pretzel track layout. A no. 1802I Layout Instruction Sheet detailed this track plan.

The paperwork in the 19226 was updated to reflect the new 90-day warranty policy that Lionel instituted in 1963. Many of these instruction sheets are the most difficult versions to find.

The no. 62-270 Tan RSC with Black Graphics outfit box was manufactured by United Container Co. and measured 15½ x 14 x 6¼ inches. It included four lines of data as part of the box manufacturer's certificate (BMC). It has also been observed with a "63" and four stars as part of the BMC.

The pattern of purchases that AMC made with Lionel in the early 1960s mirrored that of many other retailers. After ordering 8,600 outfits in 1962, AMC bought only 1,500 a year later. Consequently, the 19226 and 19227 are more difficult to find than the AMC outfits from 1962.

In 1989, Richard Kughn, then the owner of Lionel Trains Inc., purchased Madison Hardware Co. of New York City and reopened it in Detroit soon thereafter. One of the first lists of outfits available for sale included one 19226.

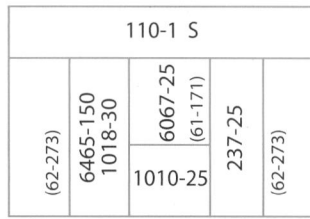

CONVENTIONAL PACK
62-270 BOX
5-21-63

TOP LAYER — BOTTOM LAYER

61-172 BETWEEN LAYERS

Description: "O27" Promotional Outfit
Specification: "O27" Diesel Freight Outfit
Customer: AMC
Original Amount: 500
Factory Order Date: 6/3/1963
Date Issued: 10-9-63
Date Req'd: Aug
Packaging: RSC Outfit Packing - #5 (Units not Boxed)

Contents: 231P-25 Alco Diesel Power Car - "Rock Island"; 3410-25 Oper. Helicopter Car (Less Helicopter); 3419-100 Operating Helicopter Complete; 6469-50 Miscellaneous Car; 6822-25 Searchlight Car; 6501-25 Jet Motor Boat Car; 6501-2 Boat Assem.; 6501-17 Fuel Pellets - Packed; 6142-25 Gondola Car (Less 2 Canisters); 6112-5 Canister (2); 6473-25 Rodeo Car; 6017-25 Caboose; 6469-52 Cardboard Container Stamped; 1013-70 Curved Track (Bundle of 12 - 1013); 1018-30 Straight Track (Bundle of 3 - 1018); 1008-50 Uncoupling Unit; 1020-25 90° Crossing; 1025-25 45-Watt Transformer; 1103-20 Envelope Packed; 310-2 Set of (5) Billboards; D63-50 Accessory Catalog; 1-62 Parts Order Form; 1-63 Warranty Card; 225-6 Instruction Sheet; 1123-40 Instruction Sheet; 3410-5 Instruction Sheet; 3419-151 Instruction Sheet; 6501-14 Instruction Sheet; 1802B Layout Instruction Sheet; 122-10 Instruction Sheet

Boxes & Packing: 63-348 Outfit Box; 61-171 Corr. Insert; 62-248 Corr. Insert (2); 62-264 Corr. Insert; 63-315 Corr. Insert; 63-349 Shipper for (4) (1-4)

Alternate For Outfit Contents:
Note: Substitute 6822-50 for 6822-25.

19227 (1963)	C6	C7	C8	Rarity
Complete Outfit	665	1,075	1,485	R9
Outfit Box no. 63-348	250	400	525	R9

Comments: Buying cooperatives, such as AMC (Associated Merchandising Corporation), were large customers of Lionel trains. In 1963, AMC purchased two promotional outfits: nos. 19226 and 19227.

The 19227, a Retailer Promotional Type Ia, was AMC's diesel-powered follow-up to outfit no. 19133 from 1962. It was led by a no. 231P-25 Rock Island Alco Diesel Power Car that featured two-axle Magne-Traction, a headlight and a two-position reversing unit.

Seven pieces of rolling stock were packed with the 19227, which included mention of a no. 6822-25 Searchlight Car. This was the only time that the 6822-25 was ever listed in Lionel documentation. This number signified an unboxed no. 6822-1 equipped with two operating AAR trucks and couplers.

In 1963, Lionel changed many items from two operating AAR trucks and couplers to one operating and one non-operating AAR types. As such, an unboxed 6822-1 became a no. 6822-50 equipped with one operating and one non-operating AAR truck

Outfit no. 19227 was AMC's diesel-powered purchase for 1963. Its empty no. 63-348 Tan RSC with Black Graphics outfit box is shown. Many promotional outfit boxes like this one have been orphaned because collectors have not known the contents.

and coupler. Lionel never offered an unboxed 6822 with two operating AAR types.

Since the "-25" existed on paper only, it was actually replaced in this outfit with the 6822-50. See the *Authoritative Guide to Lionel's Postwar Operating Cars* (Project Roar Publishing) for more information on this car.

The nos. 3410-25 Oper. Helicopter Car (Less Helicopter) and 6501-25 Jet Motor Boat Car were making their final outfit appearances in 1963. The norm for a no. 3419-100 Operating Helicopter Complete was a one-piece yellow body in 1963. This fragile helicopter was frequently lost or broken.

All the freight cars in the 19227 were equipped with one operating and one non-operating AAR truck and coupler. The caboose included one operating and one plain AAR truck and coupler.

The appropriate quantity of track was included to make the figure-eight layout. That track plan was outlined on a no. 1802B Layout Instruction Sheet.

Some of the most difficult items to find in completing this outfit are the relevant instruction sheets that made reference to the 90-day warranty policy that Lionel instituted in 1963. Even though the warranty policy changed, Lionel often did not change the date that was stamped on these sheets.

The no. 63-348 Tan RSC with Black Graphics outfit box was manufactured by St. Joe Kraft, St. Joe Paper Co. Container Division and measured 14⅜ x 12⅜ x 6 inches. It included four lines of data as part of the box manufacturer's certificate.

With only 500 made, the 19227 is a difficult outfit to find, hence its R9 rarity rating.

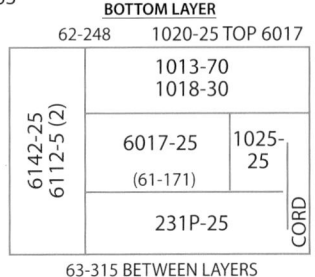

CONVENTIONAL PACK
63-348 BOX
5-22-63

TOP LAYER

6473-25 / 1008-50	6469-50 (62-248)
	6501-25
	3410-25 / 3419-100
	6822-25 / 6501-2

62-225   62-264

BOTTOM LAYER
62-248   1020-25 TOP 6017

6142-25 / 6112-5 (2)	1013-70 / 1018-30	
	6017-25 (61-171)	1025-25
	231P-25	CORD

63-315 BETWEEN LAYERS

Description: "O27" Promotional Outfit
Specification: "O27" Steam Type Freight Outfit
Customer: Automotive
Customer/Price: Dean Phipps Stores; $12.98
Original Amount: 3,862
Factory Order Date: 5/13/1963
Date Issued: Rev 10-30-63
Packaging: RSC Outfit Packing #5 (Units not Boxed)

Contents: 1062-25 Steam Type Loco. W/Light & Reversing Unit; 1061T-25 Tender; 3410-25 Oper. Helicopter Car (Less Helicopter); 3419-100 Operating Helicopter Complete; 6042-75 Gondola Car (Less 2 Cable Reels); 40-11 Cable Reels (2); 6406-25 Flat Car W/Auto; 6406-30 Automobile; 6067-25 Caboose; 1013-8 Curved Track (Bundle of 8 - 1013); 1018-10 Straight Track (Loose) (2); 1010-25 35-Watt Transformer; 1103-20 Envelope Packed; 310-62 Set of (3) Billboards; D63-50 Accessory Catalog; 1-62 Parts Order Form; 1-63 Warranty Card; 1123-40 Instruction Sheet; 3410-5 Instruction Sheet; 19288-10 Instruction Sheet; Form 2870 Printed Sheet

Boxes & Packing: 61-170 Outfit Box; 61-171 Corr. Insert; 61-172 Corr. Insert; 61-173 Corr. Insert; 61-174 Shipper for (6) (1-6)

Alternate For Outfit Contents:
Note: Sub. 700 - 6405-25 for 6406-25 and 6405-150 for 6406-30.

19228
1963

19228 (1963)	C6	C7	C8	Rarity
Complete Outfit With Green no. 6406-30 Automobile	425	660	950	R5
Complete Outfit With no. 6405-150 Substitution	260	450	700	R5
Outfit Box no. 61-170	100	175	250	R5

Comments: Lionel listed Automotive as the customer for two outfits in 1963: nos. 19228 and 19229. The 19228, a Retailer Promotional Type Ib, was the follow-up to the no. 19123 from 1962.

The 19228 was led by a no. 1062-25 Steam Type Locomotive W/Light & Reversing Unit. This low-end Scout steamer was new for 1963 and featured an 0-4-0 wheel arrangement and lacked a traction aid. According to its Lionel Engineering Specification, it was the "Same as #1061 but with the addition of Reversing Unit & Lamp". It was trailed by an unmarked no. 1061T-25 Tender with AAR trucks and couplers.

All the cars in this outfit were carryover items from previous years. The no. 3410-25 Oper. Helicopter Car (Less Helicopter) was making its final outfit appearances in 1963 and 1964. It came equipped with one operating and one non-operating AAR truck and coupler. The norm for a no. 3419-100 Operating Helicopter Complete was a one-piece yellow body in 1963. This fragile helicopter was frequently lost or broken.

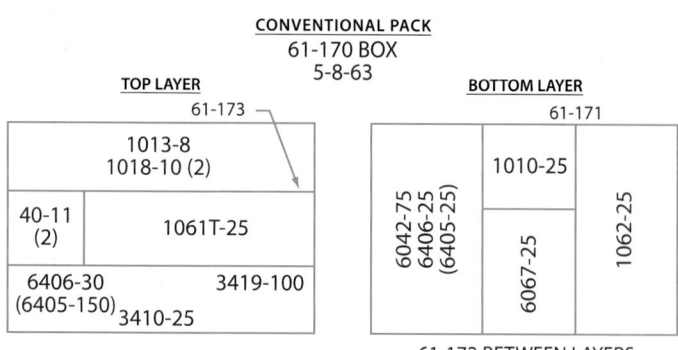

The no. 19228 listed Automotive as the customer on its 1963 Factory Order. This outfit is highly desirable because it included a green no. 6406-30 Automobile with gray bumpers. The outfit shown here was one of the three available from Madison Hardware in Detroit. Still sealed at the time of purchase, it was opened by the original owner. Even the rubber bands in this picture are original postwar Lionel.

In 1963, the no. 6406-25 Flat Car W/Auto frequently came in gray molded plastic. The 6406-25 and no. 6042-75 Gondola were equipped with non-operating Archbar trucks and couplers.

What makes this outfit desirable was the inclusion of a green no. 6406-30 Automobile with gray bumpers. This automobile provides a premium to the outfit price, as is reflected in the pricing table.

The no. 6067-25 Caboose came with one non-operating and one plain AAR truck and coupler.

The nos. 6405-25 Single Van Flat Car (Less Van) and 6405-150 Van substitutions are listed separately in the pricing table. The inclusion of these items marked the last appearance of the 6405-25. Subsequent flat cars for the 6405-150 Van were unmarked 6402-series cars.

Only the no. 3410-5 Instruction Sheet listed the 90-day warranty policy that Lionel instituted in 1963. This version is much more difficult to find than a one-year warranty version. The Form 2870 advertising the nos. 2002 and 2003 Track Make-Up Kits was dated 6/63. This outfit also introduced the undated no. 19228-10 Instruction Sheet.

The no. 61-170 Tan RSC with Black Graphics outfit box was manufactured by United Container Co. and measured 11½ x 10¼ x 6¼ inches. It included four lines of data as part of the box

manufacturer's certificate (BMC). It has also been observed with a "63" and four stars as part of the BMC.

In 1989, Richard Kughn, then the owner of Lionel Trains Inc., purchased Madison Hardware Co. of New York City and reopened it in Detroit soon thereafter. One of the first lists of outfits available for sale included three of the 19228.

The 19228 exceeded expectations, as the Factory Order indicated an increase in quantity from 3,500 to 3,862 on 10-30-63. The outfit can be found, but the yellow helicopter and green automobile are most often missing.

CONVENTIONAL PACK
61-170 BOX
5-8-63

TOP LAYER		
61-173 →		
	1013-8 1018-10 (2)	
40-11 (2)	1061T-25	
6406-30 (6405-150)		3419-100
	3410-25	

BOTTOM LAYER		
		61-171
6042-75 6406-25 (6405-25)	1010-25	1062-25
	6067-25	

61-172 BETWEEN LAYERS

Description: "O27" Promotional Outfit
Specification: "O27" Steam Type Freight Outfit
Original Amount: 252
Factory Order Date: 10/23/1963
Date Issued: Rev 11-14-63
Date Req'd: At Once
Packaging: RSC (Units Loose)

Contents: 1062-25 Steam Type Loco. W/Light & Reversing Unit; 1061T-25 Tender; 3410-25 Oper. Helicopter Car (Less Helicopter); 6042-25 Gondola Car - Blue; 40-11 Cable Reels (2); 6406-25 Flat Car W/Auto; 6406-30 Automobile; 6067-25 Caboose; 1013-8 Curved Track (Bundle of 8 - 1013); 1018-10 Straight Track (Loose) (2); 1010-25 35-Watt Transformer; 1103-20 Envelope Packed; 310-62 Set of (3) Billboards; D63-50 Accessory Catalog; 1-62 Parts Order Form; 1-63 Warranty Card; 3410-5 Instruction Sheet; 19288-10 Instruction Sheet

Boxes & Packing: 61-170 Outfit Box; 61-171 Corr. Insert; 61-174 Shipper for (6) (1-6)

Alternate For Outfit Contents:
Note: Substitute 3619-1 for 3410-25; Substitute 6167-25 for 6067-25.

19228-500 (1963)	C6	C7	C8	Rarity
Complete Outfit With no. 3619-1 Substitution And Green Or Brown Automobile	625	1,015	1,450	R9
Outfit Box no. 61-170	300	525	700	R9

Comments: The no. 19228-500 was the General Release Type IIb version of the no. 19228 issued earlier in the year. The original quantity of the 19228-500 was listed as 500 on 10-23-63. That amount was decreased to 252 on 11-14-63. This change coincided with the increase in the size of the order of 19228s recorded on 10-30-63. It is likely that Lionel allocated a portion of the 19228-500s to the 19228 when the demand for the latter was increased.

In 1963, it appears that Lionel was taking promotional outfits configured for a specific customer and adding a "-500" suffix to create a general release derivative. This overall strategy may have been a way to offer general customers a promotional outfit at a lower-than-normal quantity threshold. Or, more than likely, it was just another method for Lionel to quickly create outfits to deplete excess inventory late in the year.

The 19228-500 was, with two differences, identical to the 19228. For one thing, the no. 3619-1 Reconnaissance Copter Car replaced the no. 3410-25 Oper. Helicopter Car (Less Helicopter). For another thing, a no. 6167-25 Caboose took the place of a no. 6067-25 Caboose.

The 3619-1 came with a fragile and easily lost no. 0319-100 Helicopter. As part of the manufacturing process, the roof of the 3619-1 was taped shut with a ½-inch piece of Scotch tape. Even examples in C8 condition still have a mark where the tape was applied. This car was equipped with operating AAR trucks and couplers.

Another difference between the 19228 and 19228-500 was that the no. 6042-75 Gondola Car in the former was replaced by a no. 6042-25 Gondola Car - Blue. Both of these cars were blue gondolas stamped "6042". Normal production had the "-25" coming with canisters and the "-75" coming with cable reels. For some reason, the "-25" was listed in the 19288, along with cable reels.

In 1963, the no. 6406-30 Automobile was most often molded in brown or green plastic with gray bumpers. The specific color cannot be confirmed for this outfit, but the pricing table assumes either a green or brown version.

The only other change between the two outfits was the paperwork. The 19228-500 did not list the no. 1123-40 Instruction Sheet and the Form 2870.

(See the entry for the 19228 from 1963 for complete information about the remainder of this outfit.)

Only 252 of the 19228-500 were manufactured, leading to an R9 rarity rating. This is an extremely difficult outfit to find.

CONVENTIONAL PACK
61-170 BOX
10-21-63

TOP LAYER

| 1013-8 1018-10 (2) |
| 3619-1 F |
| 40-11 (2) 6406-30 | 1061T-25 |

BOTTOM LAYER
61-171

| 6042-25 6406-25 | 1010-25 | 1062-25 |
| | 6167-25 | |

2 CATALOGS BETWEEN LAYERS

Description: "O27" Promotional Outfit
Specification: "O27" Steam Type Freight Outfit W/Smoke
Customer: Automotive
Original Amount: 2,800
Factory Order Date: 6/3/1963
Date Issued: Rev 10-29-63
Date Req'd: Aug
Packaging: RSC Outfit Packing #5 (Units not Boxed)

Contents: 233-25 Steam Type Locomotive W/Smoke; 1060T-25 Tender; 6050-100 Swift Savings Bank Car; 6465-150 Tank Car; 6409-25 Flat Car W/3 Pipes; 6511-15 Pipes (3); 6142-25 Gondola Car (Less 2 Canisters); 6112-5 Canister (2); 3357-25 Animated Hobo & Railroad Policeman Car; 3357-27 Box Packed; 6473-25 Rodeo Car; 6067-25 Caboose; 1013-70 Curved Track (Bundle of 12 - 1013); 1018-30 Straight Track (Bundle of 3 - 1018); 1008-50 Uncoupling Unit; 1020-25 90° Crossing; 1025-25 45-Watt Transformer; 909-20 Smoke Fluid; 1103-20 Envelope Packed; 310-2 Set of (5) Billboards; D63-50 Accessory Catalog; 1-62 Parts Order Form; 1-63 Warranty Card; 122-10 Instruction Sheet; 1123-40 Instruction Sheet; 233-11 Instruction Sheet; 3357-8 Instruction Sheet; 1802B Layout Instruction Sheet

Boxes & Packing: 63-348 Outfit Box; 61-171 Corr. Insert; 62-225 Corr. Insert (2); 62-248 Corr. Insert; 62-249 Corr. Insert; 62-251 Corr. Insert; 63-315 Corr. Insert; 63-349 Shipper for (4) (1-4)

The no. 19229 listed Automotive as the customer on its 1963 Factory Order. It was likely destined for one of the many automotive supply stores that carried Lionel trains. This colorful combination of cars included two carryover operating cars from 1962. It is shown with the no. 1130T-25 Tender substitution.

Alternate For Outfit Contents:

Note: Substitute 2,000 - 1130T-25 for 1060T-25; Substitute 800 - 237-25 for 233-25; Note: Use 237-11 Inst. Sheet instead of 233-11 when substituting 237-25.

19229 (1963)	C6	C7	C8	Rarity
Complete Outfit	265	475	575	R5
Outfit Box no. 63-348	90	135	165	R5

Comments: Lionel listed Automotive as the customer for two outfits in 1963: nos. 19228 and 19229. The 19229, a Retailer Promotional Type Ib, was the follow-up to the no. 19124 from 1962.

The 19229 was led by a no. 233-25 Steam Locomotive W/ Smoke. When this engine was first introduced in 1961, it was Lionel's high-end Scout steamer and featured a headlight and Magne-Traction. It was being depleted in a few outfits in 1963. In fact, when the orders for the 19229 were increased from 2,000 to 2,800 on 10-29-63, Lionel apparently ran out of the 233. A no. 237-25 Steam Type Locomotive with Smoke was substituted.

Most 19229s included an early AAR-equipped no. 1130T-25 Tender substitution. Neither the 237-25 nor the 1130T-25 substitution affects the outfit price.

Three new-for-1963 items were included in this outfit. The nos. 6142-25 Gondola Car and orange 6465-150 Tank Car were lower-end items created by changing the color and decoration of other cars in the product line. Both were equipped with one operating and one middle non-operating AAR truck and coupler. The no. 6409-25 Flat Car W/3 Pipes was a red no. 6511-series flat car with "Lionel" stamped on each side. It lacked a car number and a brake wheel, but did come with non-operating AAR trucks and couplers.

The remaining cars in the 19229 were all carryover items from earlier years. The Type IIb no. 6050-100 Swift Savings Bank Car included one middle operating AAR and one non-operating Archbar truck and coupler. The Type IIb 3357-25 Animated Hobo & Railroad Policeman Car was equipped with middle operating AAR

trucks and couplers. The 3357-25 provided plenty of excitement as the cop tried to catch the hobo. Since the car was unboxed (hence the "-25" suffix), its peripherals were listed separately on the Factory Order as a no. 3357-27 Box Packed. The no. 6473-25 Rodeo Car was a Type IIb and included one operating and one non-operating AAR truck and coupler. Finally the no. 6067-25 Caboose was brown with non-operating Archbar trucks and couplers.

Some of the most difficult items to find in completing this outfit are the appropriate instruction sheets that made reference to the 90-day warranty policy that Lionel instituted in 1963. Even though the warranty policy changed, Lionel often did not change the date that was stamped on these sheets.

The no. 63-348 Tan RSC with Black Graphics outfit box was manufactured by St. Joe Kraft, St. Joe Paper Co. Container Division and measured 14⅜ x 12⅜ x 6 inches. It included four lines of data as part of the box manufacturer's certificate.

As stated earlier, the quantity of the 19229 was increased from 2,000 to 2,800 on 10-29-63. This change indicates that this outfit was successful and means that the odds of an example surviving are greater than is true with many other promotional outfits.

CONVENTIONAL PACK
63-348 BOX
5-22-63

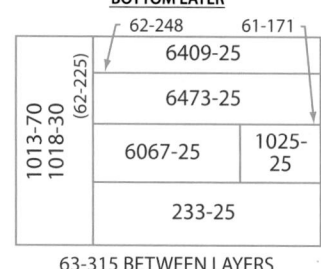

Description: "O27" Promotional Outfit
Specification: "O27" Steam Type Freight Outfit
Original Amount: ~~700~~ Cancel
Factory Order Date: 10/25/1963
Date Issued: Rev 10-29-63
Date Req'd: At Once
Packaging: RSC (Units Loose)

Contents: 233-25 Steam Type Locomotive W/Smoke; 1060T-25 Tender; 6050-150 Van Camp Savings Bank Car; 6465-150 Tank Car; 6409-25 Flat Car W/3 Pipes; 6511-15 Pipes (3); 6142-25 Gondola Car (Less 2 Canisters); 6112-88 Canister (2); 3357-25 Animated Hobo & Railroad Policeman Car; 6473-25 Rodeo Car; 6067-25 Caboose; 1013-70 Curved Track (Bundle of 12 - 1013); 1018-30 Straight Track (Bundle of 3 - 1018); 1008-50 Uncoupling Unit; 1020-25 90° Crossing; 1025-25 45-Watt Transformer; 1103-20 Envelope Packed; 310-62 Set of (3) Billboards; D63-50 Accessory Catalog; 1-62 Parts Order Form; 1-63 Warranty Card; 122-10 Instruction Sheet; 3357-8 Instruction Sheet; 1802B Layout Instruction Sheet

Boxes & Packing: 63-348 Outfit Box; 61-171 Corr. Insert; 62-249 Corr. Insert; 62-264 Corr. Insert; 63-349 Shipper for (4) (1-4)

Alternate For Outfit Contents:
Note: Substitute 242-25 for 233-25; Substitute 6162-25 for 6142-25; Substitute 3376-160 for 3357-25 and 3357-8; Substitute 50 - 6448-25 and 6448-17 for 6473-25; Substitute 650 - 6470-25 and 6470-17 for 6473-25; Substitute 6047-25 for 6067-25.

Comments: The Factory Order for outfit no. 19229-500 was marked "Cancel". It appears that Lionel was attempting to sell outfit no. 19229 to multiple customers and may have created this outfit for that purpose. When the 19229-500 was canceled, the outfit quantity was likely rolled into additional 19229s. This conclusion is derived from knowing that the dates of the 19229-500's cancellation and the increase in quantity of the 19229 are identical. This listing is provided for historical reference.

Description: "O27" Promotional Outfit
Specification: "O27" Steam Type Freight Outfit with Smoke
Customer: L. A. Sales
Original Amount: ~~150~~ Cancel
Factory Order Date: 10/25/1963
Date Issued: Rev 10-29-63
Date Req'd: At Once
Packaging: RSC (Units Loose)

Contents: 233-25 Steam Type Locomotive W/Smoke; 1060T-25 Tender; 6050-100 Swift Savings Bank Car; 6465-150 Tank Car; 6409-25 Flat Car W/3 Pipes; 6511-15 Pipes (3); 6142-25 Gondola Car (Less 2 Canisters); 6112-88 Canister (2); 3357-25 Animated Hobo & Railroad Policeman Car; 6473-25 Rodeo Car; 6067-25 Caboose; 1013-70 Curved Track (Bundle of 12 - 1013); 1018-30 Straight Track (Bundle of 3 - 1018); 1008-50 Uncoupling Unit; 1020-25 90° Crossing; 1025-25 45-Watt Transformer; 1103-20 Envelope Packed; 909-20 Smoke Fluid; 310-62 Set of (3) Billboards; D63-50 Accessory Catalog; 1-62 Parts Order Form; 1-63 Warranty Card; 3357-8 Instruction Sheet; 237-11 Instruction Sheet; 122-10 Instruction Sheet; 1802B Layout Instruction Sheet

Boxes & Packing: 63-309 Outfit Box; 62-225 Corr. Insert; 62-249 Corr. Insert; 63-312 Corr. Insert; 63-310 Shipper for (4) (1-4)

Alternate For Outfit Contents:
Note: Substitute 237X-1 for 233-25; Substitute 6162-25 for 6142-25; Substitute 3370-1 for 3357-25 and 3357-8; Substitute 6470-25 and 6470-17 for 6473-25; Substitute 6167-25 for 6067-25; Substitute 6464-925 for 6050-100.

Comments: The Factory Order for the no. 19229-501 was marked "Cancel". It appears that Lionel was attempting to sell outfit no. 19229 to other customers and convinced L. A. Sales to buy 150 of them. When the 19229-501 was canceled, the outfit quantity was likely rolled into additional 19229s. This conclusion is derived from knowing that the dates of the 19229-501's cancellation and the increase in quantity of 19229 are identical. This listing is provided for historical reference.

Description: "O27" Promotional Outfit
Specification: "O27" Steam Type Freight Outfit W/Smoke
Customer: Noah's Ark
Original Amount: 350
Factory Order Date: 10/25/1963
Date Issued: 10-25-63
Date Req'd: At Once
Packaging: RSC (Units Loose)

Contents: 233-25 Steam Type Locomotive W/Smoke; 1060T-25 Tender; 6050-100 Swift Savings Bank Car; 6465-150 Tank Car; 6409-25 Flat Car W/3 Pipes; 6511-15 Pipes (3); 6142-25 Gondola Car (Less 2 Canisters); 6112-88 Canister (2); 3357-25 Animated Hobo & Railroad Policeman Car; 6473-25 Rodeo Car; 6067-25 Caboose; 1013-70 Curved Track (Bundle of 12 - 1013); 1018-30 Straight Track (Bundle of 3 - 1018); 1008-50 Uncoupling Unit; 1020-25 90° Crossing; 1025-25 45-Watt Transformer; 1103-20 Envelope Packed; 909-20 Smoke Fluid; 310-62 Set of (3) Billboards; D63-50 Accessory Catalog; 1-62 Parts Order Form; 1-63 Warranty Card; 3357-8 Instruction Sheet; 237-11 Instruction Sheet; 122-10 Instruction Sheet; 1802B Layout Instruction Sheet

Boxes & Packing: 63-309 Outfit Box; 62-225 Corr. Insert; 62-249 Corr. Insert; 63-312 Corr. Insert; 63-310 Shipper for (4) (1-4)

Alternate For Outfit Contents:

Note: Substitute 237X-1 for 233-25; Substitute 6162-25 for 6142-25; Substitute 3370-1 for 3357-25 and 3357-8; Substitute 3519-25 for 6473-25; Substitute 6167-25 for 6067-25; Substitute 6464-925 for 6050-100.

19229-501X (1963)	C6	C7	C8	Rarity
Complete Outfit With All Substitutions	700	1,000	1,350	R9
Outfit Box no. 63-309	350	475	575	R9

Comments: After two cancellations (see outfit nos. 19229-500 and 19229-501), it appears that Lionel was finally able to sell a version of the no. 19229 to Noah's Ark Auto Accessories, Inc. The result was the no. 19229-501X, a Retailer Promotional Ia outfit.

Lionel was always looking to provide its customers with something unique. The 19229-501X provided Noah's Ark with an outfit that differed slightly from the 19229.

For some reason, instead of creating an entirely new Factory Order, Lionel used the 19229 Factory Order as the starting point and replaced every car except for the nos. 1060T-25 Tender and 6409-25 Flat Car W/3 Pipes.

The 19229-501X with all its substitutions was led by a boxed no. 237X-1 Steam Type Locomotive with Smoke. The boxed version appeared only in four promotional outfits. This new-for-1963 Scout steamer featured a two-position reversing unit and a headlight and used a rubber tire as a traction aid. The harder-to-find early version with wide running boards was included in this outfit. Except for its 237 number, it was the same engine as a no. 238.

The 237X-1 came in a no. 237-10 Corrugated Box, which is very difficult to find. The "X" meant that it lacked the nos. 909-20 and CTC-1 in its box. These two items were provided separately as part of the 19229-501X.

Lionel used substitutions in the 19229-501X to deplete its inventory of the no. 3370-1 Sheriff & Outlaw Car and reduce its inventory of the no. 3519-25 Automatic Satellite Launching Car. Also included in this outfit was a no. 6162-25 Gondola Car (Less

3 Canisters), which was first issued in 1959.

The unboxed version of the no. 6464-900 New York Central Box Car was designated no. 6464-925. It first came unboxed in 1963. The no. 6409-25 Flat Car W/3 Pipes was a red no. 6511-series flat car with "Lionel" stamped on each side. It lacked a car number and a brake wheel.

The transition from Archbar to AAR trucks and couplers that began in 1962 continued into 1963. As part of this, Lionel sought to cut costs by introducing a non-operating AAR type. Therefore, starting in 1963, most cars equipped with AAR trucks and couplers had at least one non-operating type. For the 19229-501X, all the cars were equipped with one of the possible combinations of AAR trucks and couplers.

The appropriate instruction sheets for this outfit made reference to the 90-day warranty policy that Lionel instituted in 1963.

The no. 63-309 Tan RSC with Black Graphics outfit box measured 13¼ x 12½ x 6¾ inches. It included four lines of data as part of the box manufacturer's certificate.

This outfit represented the only time that Noah's Ark purchased direct from Lionel. The small quantity produced and the lack of appearances in the market contributed to the 19229-501X having an R9 rarity rating.

CONVENTIONAL PACK
63-309 BOX
10-25-63

TOP LAYER				BOTTOM LAYER	
		62-249 → 62-225		6112-88 (2)	6409-25 6162-25
1018-30	6167-25	6465-150			
		1060T-25		237X-1 F	
	3519-25			1025-25	1013-70
	6464-925				3370-1 F

6511-15 TOP 1018-30 ← 63-312   2 CATALOGS
1008-50 TOP 6167
1020-25 TOP 6465, 1060T

Description: "O27" Promotional Outfit
Specification: "O27" Steam Type Freight Outfit W/Smoke
Original Amount: 700
Factory Order Date: 11/7/1963
Date Issued: 10-30-63
Date Req'd: 10-30-63
Packaging: RSC (Units not Boxed)

Contents: 237-25 Steam Type Locomotive with Smoke; 1060T-25 Tender; 6050-100 Swift Savings Bank Car; 6465-150 Tank Car; 6409-25 Flat Car W/3 Pipes; 6511-15 Pipes (3); 6142-25 Gondola Car (Less 2 Canisters); 6112-5 Canister (2); 3370-25 Sheriff & Outlaw Car; 6473-25 Rodeo Car; 6067-25 Caboose; 1013-70 Curved Track (Bundle of 12 - 1013); 1018-30 Straight Track (Bundle of 3 - 1018); 1008-50 Uncoupling Unit; 1020-25 90° Crossing; 1025-25 45-Watt Transformer; 909-20 Smoke Fluid;

1103-20 Envelope Packed; 310-2 Set of (5) Billboards; D63-50 Accessory Catalog; 1-62 Parts Order Form; 1-64 Warranty Card; 122-10 Instruction Sheet; 1123-40 Instruction Sheet; 237-11 Instruction Sheet; 3370-17 Instruction Sheet; 1802B Layout Instruction Sheet

Boxes & Packing: 63-348 Outfit Box; 61-171 Corr. Insert; 62-225 Corr. Insert (2); 62-248 Corr. Insert; 62-249 Corr. Insert; 62-251 Corr. Insert; 63-315 Corr. Insert; 63-349 Shipper for (4) (1-4)

19229-502 (1963)	C6	C7	C8	Rarity
Complete Outfit	430	645	880	R8
Outfit Box no. 63-348	225	325	400	R8

Comments: The no. 19229-502 was the General Release Type IIb version of the no. 19229 issued earlier in the year. (See the entry for the 19229 from 1963.)

In 1963, it appeared that Lionel was taking promotional outfits configured for a specific customer and adding a "-500" style suffix to

The no. 19229-502 was a General Release Promotional Type IIb version of the no. 19229. Both outfits came with a colorful combination of rolling stock, but only the "-502" included a no. 237-25 Steam Type Locomotive with Smoke and a no. 3370-25 Sheriff & Outlaw Car.

create a general release derivative. This overall strategy might have been intended to offer general customers a promotional outfit at a lower-than-normal quantity threshold. Or, more likely, it was just another way for Lionel to quickly create outfits late in the year that would deplete excess inventory.

The only differences between the 19229-502 and the 19229 were the presence in the former outfit of nos. 237-25 Steam Type Locomotive with Smoke and 3370-25 Sheriff & Outlaw Car, plus a no. 1-64 Warranty Card.

The 237-25 was a new-for-1963 steamer that featured a two-position reversing unit and a headlight and used a rubber tire as a traction aid. The harder-to-find early version with wide running boards was included in this outfit. Except for its 237 number, it was the same engine as a no. 238.

Lionel used the 19229-502 to deplete its inventory of the unboxed 3370-25. That car came equipped with operating AAR trucks and couplers.

The appropriate instruction sheets for this outfit made reference to the 90-day warranty policy that Lionel instituted in 1963. The no. 1-64 Warranty Card is surprisingly difficult to find. (See the section on Outfit Peripherals for more information.) The Factory Order for

the 19229-502 was the only outfit to list it separately, but it likely appeared in a few other outfits.

The no. 63-348 Tan RSC with Black Graphics outfit box was manufactured by St. Joe Kraft, St. Joe Paper Co. Container Division and measured 14⅜ x 12⅜ x 6 inches. It included four lines of data as part of the box manufacturer's certificate.

The 19229-502 was produced in smaller quantities than the 19229. It is harder to find and therefore is the more desirable of the two outfits.

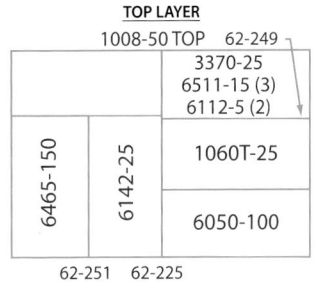

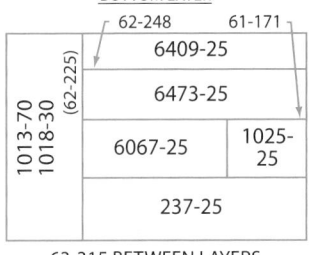

CONVENTIONAL PACK
63-348 BOX

TOP LAYER

1008-50 TOP   62-249

6465-150	6142-25	3370-25
		6511-15 (3)
		6112-5 (2)
		1060T-25
		6050-100

62-251   62-225

BOTTOM LAYER

62-248   61-171

1013-70 1018-30	(62-225)	6409-25	
		6473-25	
		6067-25	1025-25
		237-25	

63-315 BETWEEN LAYERS
1020-25 TOP 6067

The no. 19230 was a General Release Promotional Type IIa outfit from 1963. It has been observed with a Famous-Barr Co. price tag for $33.99. This high-end offering was likely sold to other retailers as well. The 19230 came with boxed nos. 2037-1 Steam Type Locomotive With Smoke and 234W-1 Whistle Tender. Placing individually boxed items in outfits was an exception in 1963.

Description: "O27" Promotional Outfit

Specification: "O27" Steam Type Freight Outfit With Smoke & Whistle

Customer/Price: Famous-Barr Co.; $33.99

Original Amount: 728

Factory Order Date: 5/21/1963

Date Issued: Rev 10-30-63

Packaging: RSC Outfit Packing (Units not Boxed), Except Loco & Tender

Contents: 2037-1 Steam Type Locomotive With Smoke; 234W-1 Whistle Tender; 6469-50 Miscellaneous Car; 6440-50 Flat Car W/2 Piggy Back Vans; 6440-150 Trailer Vans (2); 6050-100 Swift Savings Bank Car; 6476-25 Hopper Car - Red; 6017-25 Caboose; 6469-52 Cardboard Container Stamped; 1013-8 Curved Track (Bundle of 8 - 1013); 1018-30 Straight Track (Bundle of 3 - 1018); 1008-50 Uncoupling Unit; 1063-25 75-Watt Transformer; 81-32 24" R.C. Wire (2); 1123-40 Instruction Sheet; 19230-10 Instruction Sheet; Form 2870 Printed Sheet; 310-2 Set of (5) Billboards; D63-50 Accessory Catalog; 1-62 Parts Order Form; 1-63 Warranty Card

Boxes & Packing: 62-243 Outfit Box; 61-182 Corr. Insert; 62-223 Corr. Insert; 62-244 Shipper for (4) (1-4)

19230 (1963)	C6	C7	C8	Rarity
Complete Outfit	515	775	1,100	R8
Outfit Box no. 62-243	250	350	425	R8

Comments: The no. 19230 was a General Release Promotional Type IIa outfit. It has been observed with a Famous-Barr Co. price tag for $33.99.

The 19230 was a high-end outfit for 1963 in that it included

a boxed no. 2037-1 Steam Type Locomotive With Smoke and Magne-Traction. This workhorse steamer spanned the years 1953 through 1963 (except for 1956) and powered one Super O and 22 O27 outfits during the 1960s. When boxed as a "-1", it included the nos. 675-33 Smoke Stack Cleaner, SP-1 Smoke Pellets, 927-85 Oiler, 2037-16 Instruction Sheet and CTC-1 Lockon inside its 2037-13 Corr. Box. Consequently, this outfit did not include a packed envelope and the no. 81-32 24" R.C. Wires were placed loose in the outfit box.

The 2037 pulled an Archbar-equipped no. 234W-1 Whistle Tender. It came in an Orange Picture box.

All but two of the pieces of rolling stock in the 19230 were carried over from earlier years. The first newcomer was the no. 6440-50 Flat Car W/2 Piggy Back Vans. It carried a load that was easily separated and lost.

Also new was the no. 6469-50 Miscellaneous Car. When it carried a no. 6469-52 Cardboard Container Stamped, it was commonly referred to as a Liquefied Gas Tank Car. This easily lost load – a simulated tank carrying liquefied gas – was made from a cardboard tube wrapped in white paper.

The transition from Archbar to AAR trucks and couplers that began in 1962 continued into 1963. As part of this, Lionel sought to cut costs by introducing a non-operating AAR type. Therefore, starting in 1963, most cars equipped with AAR trucks and couplers had at least one non-operating type. The 19230 followed this progression, although the 6440-50 has been observed with operating AAR trucks and couplers.

The appropriate instruction sheets for this outfit made reference to the 90-day warranty policy that Lionel instituted in 1963. This outfit introduced the difficult-to-find no. 19230-10 Instruction Sheet dated 6/63. It appeared in only a handful of other outfits.

The no. 62-243 Tan RSC with Black Graphics outfit box

was manufactured by St. Joe Kraft, St. Joe Paper Co. Container Division and measured 12⅛ x 11½ x 6⅜ inches.

The 19230 was a success for Lionel in that the quantity was increased from 600 to 728 on 10-30-63. With slightly higher-than-average quantities of this outfit produced, its empty box does appear. However, patience is required to find a complete outfit in C8 condition.

CONVENTIONAL PACK
62-243 BOX
5-15-63

TOP LAYER

6440-150 (2)	
6476-25	1008-50
234W-1 F	
6469-50	

(6440-50 vertical)

BOTTOM LAYER

1018-30 1013-8	
2037-1 F	
1063-25	6017-25
	CORD
	6050-100

62-223 BETWEEN LAYERS
61-182 INSERT INTO BASE
OF TRANSFORMER

19200 Series

Description: "O27" Promotional Outfit
Specification: "O27" Steam Type Freight Outfit With Smoke & Whistle
Original Amount: 300
Factory Order Date: 10/25/1963
Date Issued: 10-25-63
Date Req'd: At Once
Packaging: RSC (Units Loose)

Contents: 2037-1 Steam Type Locomotive With Smoke; 234W-25 Whistle Tender; 6469-50 Miscellaneous Car; 6440-1 Flat Car W/2 Piggy Back Vans; 6050-150 Van Camp Savings Bank Car; 6476-25 Hopper Car - Red; 6017-25 Caboose; 1013-8 Curved Track (Bundle of 8 - 1013); 1018-30 Straight Track (Bundle of 3 - 1018); 1008-50 Uncoupling Unit; 1063-25 75-Watt Transformer; 1103-20 Envelope Packed; 909-20 Smoke Fluid; D63-50 Accessory Catalog; 1-62 Parts Order Form; 1-63 Warranty Card; 310-62 Set of (3) Billboards; 1648-10 Instruction Sheet

Boxes & Packing: 63-309 Outfit Box; 61-181 Corr. Insert; 61-182 Corr. Insert; 61-186 Corr. Insert; 62-225 Corr. Insert (2); 63-310 Shipper for (4) (1-4)

Alternate For Outfit Contents:
Note: Substitute 637X-1 for 2037-1; Substitute 6076-100 for 6476-25; Substitute 6257-100 for 6017-25.

19230-500 (1963)	C6	C7	C8	Rarity
Complete Outfit With All Substitutions	675	1,075	1,500	R9
Outfit Box no. 63-309	350	500	600	R9

Comments: The no. 19230-500 was a slightly modified version of General Release Promotional Type IIa outfit no. 19230. (See the entry for outfit 19230 from 1963.) The "-500" version of the 19230 was likely created as a quick way to configure an outfit to deplete excess inventory in late 1963. This General Release Promotional Type IIb has yet to be linked to a specific retailer.

Three substitutions differentiated the 19230-500 from the 19230. First, a no. 637X-1 Steam Type Locomotive with Smoke replaced the no. 2037-1 Steam Type Locomotive. The former locomotive was equipped with Magne-Traction, a three-position reversing unit and a headlight. As described in the section on Outfit Peripherals, an "X" signified that a no. CTC-1 Lockon was not included in the no. 637-13 Corrugated Box. Therefore, a separate no. 1103-20 Envelope Packed was required.

Second, Lionel substituted an unmarked no. 6076-100 Hopper Car – Gray for the no. 6476-25 Hopper Car - Red. Finally, a no. 6257-100 Caboose replaced the no. 6017-25 Caboose in the 19230.

In addition, the tender in the 19230-500 came unboxed rather than boxed as was case with the 19230. And the no. 6440 Flat Car With 2 Piggy Back Vans was now packed in an Orange Picture box as a no. 6440-1.

As for the trucks and couplers, the 6076-100 came equipped with non-operating AAR types. Otherwise, the trucks and couplers were the same as in the 19230.

The version of the no. 1648-10 Instruction Sheet made reference to the 90-day warranty policy that Lionel instituted in 1963. It was still dated 5-61.

The outfit box was also updated for this outfit. The no. 63-309 Tan RSC with Black Graphics outfit box measured 13¼ x 12½ x 6¾ inches. It included four lines of data as part of the box manufacturer's certificate.

Less than half as many 19230-500s were made as the 19230. As such, it is a much more difficult outfit to find.

CONVENTIONAL PACK
63-309 BOX
10-24-63

TOP LAYER

BOTTOM LAYER

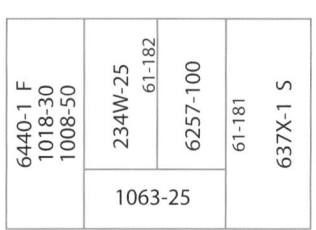

61-186 BETWEEN LAYERS

Description: "O27" Promotional Outfit
Specification: "O27" Diesel Freight Outfit with Horn
Original Amount: 1,050
Factory Order Date: 7/31/1963
Date Issued: Rev 11-14-63
Packaging: RSC Outfit Packing (Units not Boxed), Except 218P & 218T

Contents: 218P-1 Alco Diesel Power Unit With Horn - "Santa Fe"; 218T-1 Motorless Unit; 6469-50 Miscellaneous Car; 6469-52 Cardboard Container Stamped; 6440-50 Flat Car W/2 Piggy Back Vans; 6440-150 Trailer Vans (2); 6050-100 Swift Savings Bank Car; 6476-25 Hopper Car - Red; 6017-25 Caboose; 1013-8 Curved Track (Bundle of 8 - 1013); 1018-30 Straight Track (Bundle of 3 - 1018); 1008-50 Uncoupling Unit; 1063-25 75-Watt Transformer; 81-32 24" R.C. Wire (2); 1123-40 Instruction Sheet; 19230-10 Instruction Sheet; Form 2870 Printed Sheet; 310-2 Set of (5) Billboards; D63-50 Accessory Catalog; 1-62 Parts Order Form; 1-63 Warranty Card

Boxes & Packing: 63-313 Outfit Box; 61-172 Corr. Insert; 61-182 Corr. Insert; 62-225 Corr. Insert (3); 63-315 Corr. Insert; 63-314 Shipper for 4 (1-4)

Alternate For Outfit Contents:
Note: Substitute 198 - 218P-25 for 218P-1; Substitute 232 - 218T-25 for 218T-1.

19231 (1963)	C6	C7	C8	Rarity
Complete Outfit With nos. 218P-1 And 218T-1	435	750	1,035	R8
Complete Outfit With nos. 218P-25 And 218T-25 Substitutions	415	700	960	R8
Outfit Box no. 63-313	125	200	275	R8

Comments: Lionel frequently issued identical outfits that differed only in their motive power. The no. 19231 was one of those outfits. This General Release Promotional Type IIa was the diesel-powered version of no. 19230 from 1963. Whereas the latter was led by a no. 2037-1 Steam Type Locomotive With Smoke, the 19231 came with a no. 218P-1 Santa Fe Alco Diesel Power Unit With Horn and a no. 218T-1 Motorless Unit.

The 218P-1 and 218T-1 were first introduced in 1959. The 218P-1 featured a three-position reversing unit, a headlight, two-axle Magne-Traction and an open pilot with a large ledge. In 1963, Lionel made changes to the peripherals included inside its no. 218-10 Corrugated Box. No longer did Lionel provide lubricant or a no. 601-13 "C" Battery for its horn. Only the nos. CTC-1 Lockon and 218-11 Instruction Sheet (90-day warranty version dated 7-60) were included.

When the quantity of this outfit was increased from 800 to 1,050 on 11-14-63, Lionel ran out of boxed 218P-1s and 218T-1s. It issued the unboxed nos. 218P-25 Santa Fe Alco Diesel Power Car and 218T-25 Motorless Unit as substitutions. These changes do affect the price, as listed in the pricing table.

All other cars and peripherals in the 19231 were identical to 19230.

The no. 63-313 Tan RSC with Black Graphics outfit box measured 14½ x 11¾ x 7 inches.

Even though this outfit was manufactured in larger quantities than the 19230, it does not appear as often. Therefore, it achieves the same R8 rarity as the 19230.

CONVENTIONAL PACK
63-313 BOX
5-16-63

TOP LAYER

1013-8 | 6469-50 | 6440-50 6440-150 (2) | 6017-25

62-225 | 62-225 | 62-225

BOTTOM LAYER

61-182

218T-1 S

1063-25 | 6476-25

6050-100
1008-50

218P-1 F | 1018-30 (TOP)

63-315 BETWEEN LAYERS
61-172 BELOW AND INTO 1063 BASE

Description: "O27" Promotional Outfit
Specification: "O27" Diesel Freight Outfit with Horn
Original Amount: 200
Factory Order Date: 10/24/1963
Date Issued: Rev 11-18-63
Date Req'd: At Once
Packaging: RSC (Units Loose)

Contents: 218P-25 Alco Diesel Power Unit With Horn - "Santa Fe"; 218T-25 Motorless Unit; 6469-50 Miscellaneous Car; 6440-50 Flat Car W/2 Piggy Back Vans; 6440-150 Trailer Vans (2); 6050-100 Swift Savings Bank Car; 6476-25 Hopper Car - Red; 6017-25 Caboose; 1013-8 Curved Track (Bundle of 8 - 1013); 1018-30 Straight Track (Bundle of 3 - 1018); 1008-50 Uncoupling Unit; 1063-25 75-Watt Transformer; 1103-50 Envelope Packed; 310-62 Set of (3) Billboards; D63-50 Accessory Catalog; 1-62 Parts Order Form; 1-63 Warranty Card; 1648-10 Instruction Sheet; 218-11 Instruction Sheet

Boxes & Packing: 63-313 Outfit Box; 62-224 Corr. Insert; 62-245 Corr. Insert (2); 62-248 Corr. Insert; 62-264 Corr. Insert; 62-278 Corr. Insert; 63-315 Corr. Insert; 63-314 Shipper for 4 (1-4)

Alternate For Outfit Contents:
Note: Substitute 63 - 6469-1 for 6469-50; Substitute 122 - 6076-100 for 6476-25; Substitute 6257-100 for 6017-25; Substitute 78 - 6076-75 for 6476-25; Substitute 6464-925 for 6050-100.

19231-500 (1963)	C6	C7	C8	Rarity
Complete Outfit With All Substitutions	850	1,275	1,750	R10
Outfit Box no. 63-313	425	625	800	R10

Comments: The no. 19231-500 was a General Release Promotional Type IIb that Lionel created by making a few changes to the contents of outfit no. 19231 (see the entry on that outfit). It most likely did so as a quick way to configure an outfit to deplete excess inventory in late 1963 and increase sales, although the 19231-500 has not been connected to a specific retailer.

The 19231-500, like some later examples of the 19231, was led by the nos. 218P-25 Santa Fe Alco Diesel Power Unit With Horn and 218T-25 Motorless Unit. The 218P-25 featured a three-position reversing unit, a headlight, two-axle Magne-Traction and an open pilot with a large ledge. As described in the entry for the 19231, Lionel used these unboxed versions of the Santa Fe Alcos when it ran out of boxed 218P-1s and 218T-1s.

A newcomer to the line was the no. 6469 Miscellaneous Car, which appeared in 13 outfits in 1963 and 1964 and was available for separate sale in 1963. When the 6469 carried a no. 6469-52 Cardboard Container Stamped, it was commonly referred to as a Liquefied Gas Tank Car. This easily lost load – a simulated tank carrying liquefied gas – was made from a cardboard tube wrapped in white paper. In the 19231-500, the 6469 could come unboxed as a "-50" or in an Orange Picture box as a "-1".

For the 19231-500, Lionel replaced the no. 6476-25 Hopper Car – Red in the 19231 with a no. 6076-75 Hopper Car – Black or an unmarked no. 6076-100 Hopper Car – Gray. It substituted a no. 6464-925 New York Central Box Car – the unboxed version of the 6464-900 that was introduced in 1963 – for the no. 6050-100 Swift Savings Bank Car in the 19231. And a no. 6257-100 Caboose took the place of the no. 6017-25 Caboose.

The transition from Archbar to AAR trucks and couplers that began in 1962 continued into 1963. As part of this, Lionel sought to cut costs by introducing a non-operating AAR type. Therefore, starting in 1963, most cars equipped with AAR trucks and couplers had at least one non-operating type.

Most of the cars in the 19231-500 came with one operating and one non-operating AAR truck and coupler. However, the 6440-50 Flat Car W/2 Piggy Back Vans (new in 1963) has been observed with operating AAR types and the 6076-75 and 6076-100 Hopper Cars typically came with non-operating AAR types.

The version of the nos. 218-11 and 1648-10 Instruction Sheets made reference to the 90-day warranty policy that Lionel instituted in 1963. Both were still dated 7-60 and 5-61, respectively.

The no. 63-313 Tan RSC with Black Graphics outfit box measured 14½ x 11¾ x 7 inches.

Only a small quantity of the 19231-500 was made. This leads to its R10 rarity rating.

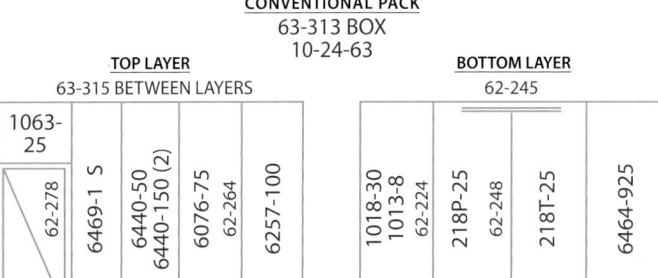

CONVENTIONAL PACK
63-313 BOX
10-24-63

Description: "O27" Promotional Outfit
Specification: "O27" *Texas Special* Diesel Freight Outfit
Customer: National Association
Original Amount: 150
Factory Order Date: 6/4/1963
Date Issued: 6-11-63
Date Req'd: Aug
Packaging: RSC Outfit Packing #5 (Units not Boxed), Except 110-1

Contents: 211P-150 *Texas Special* Diesel; 211T-25 *Texas Special* Motorless Unit; 3413-150 Mercury Capsule Launching Car; 3665-100 Minuteman Missile Launching Car; 6413-25 Mercury Capsule Transport Car; 6413-4 Capsules (2); 6413-10 Env. Packed; 6470-25 Exploding Target Car; 6257-100 Caboose; 1013-8 Curved Track (Bundle of 8 - 1013); 1013-90 Curved Track (Bundle of 9 - 1013); 1018-30 Straight Track (Bundle of 3 - 1018) (3); 6139-25 Uncoupling Track Section; 1025-25 45-Watt Transformer; 1103-40 Envelope Packed; 110-1 Trestle Set; 310-2 Set of (5) Billboards; D63-50 Accessory Catalog; 1-62 Parts Order Form; 1-63 Warranty Card; 1123-40 Instruction Sheet; 211-151 Instruction Sheet; 1802I Layout Instruction Sheet; 3413-152 Instruction Sheet; 3665-30 Instruction Sheet; 6470-17 Instruction Sheet; 11351-10 Instruction Sheet

Boxes & Packing: 62-270 Outfit Box; 61-173 Corr. Insert; 62-224 Corr. Insert; 62-245 Corr. Insert (2); 62-248 Corr. Insert (3); 62-272 Corr. Insert; 62-271 Shipper for (3) (1-3)

19232
1963

19232 (1963)	C6	C7	C8	Rarity
Complete Outfit	1,000	1,650	2,250	R10
Outfit Box no. 62-270	500	800	1,000	R10

Comments: National Association was listed on the Factory Order for this outfit in 1963. A common 1960s company name, the identity of National Association has yet to be determined. As such, the no. 19232 could have been a Retailer Promotional Type Ia or a Manufacturer Promotional Type IIIa.

A space and military outfit, the 19232 was a promotional version of catalog outfit no. 11361 from 1963. They came with the same motive power and rolling stock. Only the track layout and packaging varied.

The 19232 was led by a no. 211P-150 *Texas Special* Diesel. The 211P-150 was a cost-reduced version of the no. 211P-25 *Texas Special* Alco Diesel Power Unit. The "-150" was new for 1963 and featured a two-position reversing unit, two traction tires, a headlight, a weight and an open pilot with a large ledge. This variation has not stirred much interest in the collector community.

The transition from Archbar to AAR trucks and couplers that began in 1962 continued into 1963. As part of this, Lionel sought to cut costs by introducing a non-operating AAR type. Therefore, starting in 1963, most cars equipped with AAR trucks and couplers had at least one non-operating type. For the 19232, all the cars were 1963 versions that came with one operating and one non-operating AAR truck and coupler.

This transition led to new suffixes in 1963 for the nos. 3413 Mercury Capsule Launching Car and 3665 Minuteman Missile Launching Car. Specifically, when equipped with one operating and one non-operating types, they became the no. 3413-150 and no. 3665-100, respectively. The nos. 6413-25 Mercury Capsule Carrying Car and 6470-25 Exploding Target Car did not receive new suffixes in spite of the fact that their combination of trucks and couplers changed.

On 3-5-63, the Lionel 3665 Blueprints indicated that the material used to mold the roof sections changed from Lionel Blue #6964 to Blue #6978 (a lighter shade of blue plastic). This light shade of blue plastic was intended as the norm for 3665-100s and is likely proper for this outfit. The version with a light blue roof commands a premium.

Cars equipped with one operating and one non-operating truck and coupler are correct for this outfit. They are more difficult to find than the versions with two operating types, yet they do not command a premium.

What does command a premium are the 1963 versions of the instruction sheets in the 19232. All of them made reference to the 90-day warranty policy put in place by Lionel in 1963. The nos. 3413-152 and 3665-30 Instruction Sheets were new for 1963. Both referred to the changes in truck and coupler configurations for 1963.

The no. 110-1 Trestle Set was used for the elevated pretzel track layout. A no. 1802I Layout Instruction Sheet detailed this track plan.

The no. 62-270 Tan RSC with Black Graphics outfit box was manufactured by United Container Co. and measured 15½ x 14 x 6¼ inches.

Finding this outfit complete with the proper 1963 components is extremely difficult. Even if a collector is lucky enough to find an empty box, obtaining every item listed on the Factory Order in its correct 1963 version demands great patience.

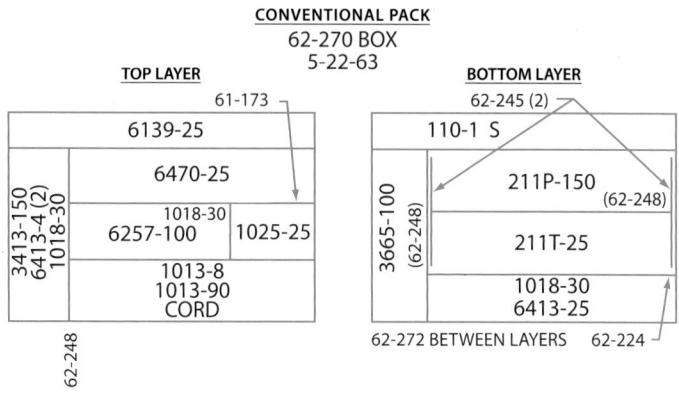

19233
1963

Description: "O27" Promotional Outfit
Specification: "O27" Steam Type Freight Outfit W/Smoke
Customer: Goldblatt's
Original Amount: 1,621
Factory Order Date: 6/4/1963
Date Issued: Rev 10-29-63
Date Req'd: Aug
Packaging: RSC Outfit Packing (Units not Boxed), Except 110-1

Contents: 233-25 Steam Type Locomotive W/Smoke; 1060T-25 Tender; 6501-25 Jet Motor Boat Car; 6501-2 Boat Assem.; 6501-17 Fuel Pellets - Packed; 6473-25 Rodeo Car; 6465-150 Tank Car; 6476-25 Hopper Car - Red; 6067-25 Caboose; 1013-70 Curved Track (Bundle of 12 - 1013); 1018-5 Straight Track (Bundle of 5 - 1018) (2); 1018-30 Straight Track (Bundle of 3 - 1018); 1008-50 Uncoupling Unit; 110-1 Trestle Set; 1073-25 60-Watt Transformer; 1103-20 Envelope Packed; 909-20 Smoke Fluid; 310-2 Set of (5) Billboards; D63-50 Accessory Catalog; 1-62 Parts Order Form; 1-63 Warranty Card; 1123-40 Instruction Sheet; 233-11 Instruction Sheet; 6501-14 Instruction Sheet; 122-10 Instruction Sheet; 19115-10 Instruction Sheet

Boxes & Packing: 62-270 Outfit Box; 61-181 Corr. Insert; 61-182 Corr. Insert (2); 62-257 Corr. Insert (4); 62-272 Corr. Insert; 62-271 Shipper for (3) (1-3)

Alternate For Outfit Contents:
Note: Substitute 1,000 - 1130T-25 for 1060T-25; Substitute 513 - 237-25 for 233-25; Substitute 108 - 238-25 for 233-25; Note:

Use 237-11 Inst. Sheet instead of 233-11 when substituting 237-25 or 238-25.

19233 (1963)	C6	C7	C8	Rarity
Complete Outfit	375	600	810	R7
Complete Outfit With no. 238-25 Substitution	440	670	920	R7
Outfit Box no. 62-270	125	200	250	R7

Comments: Chicago-based retailer Goldblatt's ran department stores that offered a variety of goods at discount prices. It purchased a Retailer Promotional Type Ib outfit (no. 19233) and a General Release Promotional Type IIa outfit (no. 19233-500) in 1963. The two outfits were almost exactly the same.

The 19233 must have exceeded the customer's expectations because the quantity ordered was increased from 1,000 units to 1,621 on 10-29-63. This increase depleted the remaining inventory of the no. 233-25 Steam Type Locomotive W/Smoke and Magne-Traction. It was replaced by a no. 237-25 or a no. 238-25 Steam Type Locomotive with Smoke. Both the 237-25 and 238-25 were new for 1963 and featured a two-position reversing unit and a headlight and used a rubber tire as a traction aid. The harder-to-find early versions with wide running boards were included in this outfit. Except for the numbers stamped on their cabs, the 237-25 and 238-25 were the same engine. The 238-25 is slightly more difficult to obtain; therefore, its substitution affects the price, as listed in the pricing table.

The no. 6501-25 Jet Motor Boat Car was making its final outfit appearances in 1963. It came with operating AAR trucks and couplers.

The first 1,000 units of this outfit included a no. 1130T-25 Tender that Lionel was still depleting in 1963. It was equipped with one operating and one plain AAR truck and coupler. The remaining quantity of outfits came with a no. 1060T-25 Tender, which was equipped with one non-operating and one plain AAR truck and coupler. The norm for all the other pieces of rolling stock in the 19233 was to include one operating and one non-operating AAR truck and coupler. Earlier 6476s with two operating AAR types are possible.

The appropriate instruction sheets for this outfit made reference to the 90-day warranty policy that Lionel instituted in 1963. The 19232 mimicked the elevated and elongated figure-eight track layout first described on the no. 1802A Layout Instruction Sheet. The no. 19115-10 Track Layout Instruction Sheet describing the track layout was used for this outfit. (See the entry for outfit no. 19115 for more information and a picture of this sheet.)

The no. 62-270 Tan RSC with Black Graphics outfit box was manufactured by United Container Co. and measured 15½ x 14 x 6¼ inches.

The 19233 was produced in fairly large quantities, but for some reason examples do not appear too often.

CONVENTIONAL PACK
62-270 BOX
5-23-63

TOP LAYER — BOTTOM LAYER

6476-25	6501-25	6465-150	6501-17 / 6501-2 / 1018-5 (2) / 1008-50

62-257 62-257 62-257 62-257

BOTTOM LAYER
61-181
110-1 S
233-25
1073-25 | 1060T-25 / 6067-25 (61-182)
1013-70
(61-182) / 6473-25 / 1018-30

62-272 BETWEEN LAYERS

Description: "O27" Promotional Outfit
Specification: "O27" Steam Type Freight Outfit W/Smoke
Customer/No./Price: Goldblatt's; 242 4 3 2390; $25.00
Original Amount: 440
Factory Order Date: 10/23/1963
Date Issued: Rev 10-29-63
Date Req'd: At Once
Packaging: RSC (Units Loose)

Contents: 237X-1 Steam Type Locomotive with Smoke; 1060T-25 Tender; 6501-1 Jet Motor Boat Car; 6465-150 Tank Car; 3370-1 Sheriff & Outlaw Car; 6476-25 Hopper Car - Red; 6167-25 Caboose; 1013-70 Curved Track (Bundle of 12 - 1013); 1018-5 Straight Track (Bundle of 5 - 1018) (2); 1018-30 Straight Track (Bundle of 3 - 1018); 1008-50 Uncoupling Unit; 110-1 Trestle Set; 1073-25 60-Watt Transformer; 1103-20 Envelope Packed; 909-20 Smoke Fluid; D63-50 Accessory Catalog; 1-62 Parts Order Form; 1-63 Warranty Card; 310-62 Set of (3) Billboards; 237-11 Instruction Sheet; 1802A Layout Instruction Sheet; 19145-10 Instruction Sheet

Boxes & Packing: 62-270 Outfit Box; 62-249 Corr. Insert; 62-273 Corr. Insert; 62-271 Shipper for (3) (1-3); 61-230 Outfit Box

Alternate For Outfit Contents:
Note: Substitute 6119-100 for 6167-25 as needed; Substitute 6045-150 for 6465-150 as needed.

19233-500 (1963)	C6	C7	C8	Rarity
Complete Outfit As Listed And no. 62-270 Box	660	1,000	1,350	R9
Complete Outfit With Substitutions And no. 62-270 Box	700	1,050	1,425	R9
Outfit Box no. 62-270	250	400	525	R9
Complete Outfit As Listed And no. 61-230 Box	810	1,300	1,725	R10
Complete Outfit With Substitutions And no. 61-230 Box	850	1,350	1,800	R10
Outfit Box no. 61-230	400	700	900	R10

Comments: Chicago-based retailer Goldblatt's ran department stores that offered a variety of goods at discount prices. It purchased a Retailer Promotional Type Ib outfit (no. 19233) and a General Release Promotional Type IIa outfit (no. 19233-500) in 1963. The two outfits are almost exactly the same.

In 1963, it appeared that Lionel was taking promotional outfits configured for a specific customer and adding a "-500" style suffix to create a general release derivative. This overall strategy might have been intended to offer general customers a promotional outfit at a lower-than-normal quantity threshold. Or, more likely, it was just another way for Lionel to quickly create outfits late in the year that would deplete excess inventory.

Specifically, the 19233-500 was a General Release version of the 19233. What is interesting is that the 19233-500 has been observed with a Goldblatt's price tag. The 19233 was likely so successful that Goldblatt's also purchased its General Release companion outfit to fulfill its orders. (See the entry for the 19233 from 1963.)

The 19233-500 was created late in the year, and the no. 233-25 Steam Type Locomotive W/Smoke included in the 19233 probably was no longer available. So Lionel used a no. 237X-1 Steam Type Locomotive With Smoke in the 19233-500. The boxed 237X-1 appeared only in four promotional outfits. This new-for-1963 Scout steamer featured a two-position reversing unit and a headlight and used a rubber tire as a traction aid. The harder-to-find early version with wide running boards was included in this outfit. Except for its 237 number, it was the same engine as a no. 238.

The 237X-1 came boxed in a difficult-to-find no. 237-10 Corrugated Box. An "X" signified that a no. CTC-1 Lockon was not included in the 237-10. Therefore, a separate no. 1103-20 Envelope Packed was required.

Lionel used this outfit to thin out its inventory of a few boxed items. These included the nos. 3370-1 Sheriff & Outlaw Car, 6119-100 Work Caboose and 6501-1 Jet Motor Boat Car. All three models came packaged in Orange Picture boxes. The no. 6476-25 Hopper Car - Red as well as all the aforementioned cars were equipped with operating AAR trucks and couplers. The 3370-1, which was still being depleted from a few years earlier, had early operating AAR trucks and couplers.

The no. 19233-500 was a General Release Promotional Type IIa outfit from 1963. This example included a Goldblatt's price tag with "242 4 3 2390" for $25.00. The outfit is shown with its no. 62-270 Outfit Box and the no. 6119-100 Work Caboose and orange no. 6045-150 Tank Car substitutions. The individual no. 237-10 Corrugated Box is very difficult to find.

The no. 61-230 Outfit Box variation of the no. 19233-500 was hand-stamped. This version was likely due to a box change at the time of production.

The no. 1060T-25 Tender came with one non-operating and one plain AAR truck and coupler. The orange no. 6465-150 Tank Car included one operating and one non-operating AAR truck and coupler.

Substitutions included the 6119-100 and orange 6045-150 Tank Car. These items affect the price of this outfit, as listed in the pricing table.

The no. 110-1 Trestle Set was used for the elevated pretzel track layout. A no. 1802A Layout Instruction Sheet detailed this track plan.

The no. 62-270 Tan RSC with Black Graphics outfit box was manufactured by United Container Co. and measured 15½ x 14 x 6¼ inches. It included four lines of data as part of the box manufacturer's certificate (BMC). It has also been observed with a "63" and four stars as part of the BMC. An outfit packing diagram is provided for this outfit box.

The 19233-500 has been observed in a hand-stamped no. 61-230 Orange RSC with Black Graphics outfit box. It was manufactured by the Mead Corporation and measured 16 x 15½ x 7⅛ inches. It included four lines of data in its BMC. This version was likely caused by a box change at the time of production. (See the section on Outfit Box Printing, Graphics and Labels for more information.)

The 19233-500 was produced in lower-than-average quantities. Even so, the no. 62-270 Outfit Box version does appear from time to time. The no. 61-230 Orange RSC version of this outfit is very difficult to find, hence its R10 rarity rating.

CONVENTIONAL PACK
62-270 BOX
10-23-63

TOP LAYER						BOTTOM LAYER		
1008-50						110-1 S		
6465-150	6476-25	6501-1 F	6119-100	3370-1 F		1018-5 / 1018-30 / 62-273	1018-5	1013-70
								237X-1 F
						1060T-25 / 62-249		1073-25

2 CATALOGS BETWEEN LAYERS

Description: "O27" Promotional Outfit
Specification: "O27" Steam Type Freight Outfit
Original Amount: ~~500~~ Cancel
Factory Order Date: 10/24/1963
Date Issued: Rev 10-29-63
Date Req'd: At Once

Packaging: RSC (Units Loose)

Contents: 242-25 Steam Type Locomotive; 1060T-25 Tender; 6501-1 Jet Motor Boat Car; 6465-150 Tank Car; 3370-1 Sheriff & Outlaw Car; 6476-25 Hopper Car - Red; 6167-25 Caboose; 1013-70 Curved Track (Bundle of 12 - 1013); 1018-5 Straight Track (Bundle of 5 - 1018) (2); 1018-30 Straight Track (Bundle of 3 - 1018); 1008-50 Uncoupling Unit; 110-1 Trestle Set; 1073-25 60-Watt Transformer; CTC-1 Lockon; 81-32 24" R.C. Wire

(2); 310-62 Set of (3) Billboards; D63-50 Accessory Catalog; 1-62 Parts Order Form; 1-63 Warranty Card; 1640-10 Instruction Sheet; 1802A Layout Instruction Sheet

Boxes & Packing: 62-270 Outfit Box; 61-182 Corr. Insert; 62-225 Corr. Insert (2); 62-272 Corr. Insert; 62-271 Shipper for (3) (1-3)

P. Lionel Electric Train #6380—Engine, tender, 4 cars. Oval track: 8 curved, 2 straight sections. Transformer.........1900 Coupons

The Raleigh and Belair Premium Catalog for 1963 mentioned outfit no. 19234 on page 33 as being available for 1,900 coupons. As with previous Raleigh catalogs, the illustration did not match what was listed on the Factory Order. In fact, the outfit matches the no. X-705 from 1962 instead of the 19234 from 1963.

Description: "O27" Promotional Outfit
Specification: "O27" Steam Type Freight Outfit
Cust./No./Price: Brown & Williamson; #6380; 1900 Coupons
Original Amount: 400
Factory Order Date: 5/13/1963
Date Issued: Rev 11-14-63
Packaging: RSC Outfit Packing #5 (Units not Boxed)

Contents: 242-25 Steam Type Locomotive; 1060T-25 Tender; 3410-25 Oper. Helicopter Car (Less Helicopter); 3419-100 Operating Helicopter Complete; 6076-100 Hopper Car - Gray; 6406-25 Flat Car W/Auto; 6406-30 Automobile; 6067-25 Caboose; 1013-8 Curved Track (Bundle of 8 - 1013); 1018-10 Straight Track (Loose) (2); 1026-25 25-Watt Transformer; 1103-20 Envelope Packed; 310-2 Set of (5) Billboards; D63-50 Accessory Catalog; 1-62 Parts Order Form; 1-63 Warranty Card; 1123-40 Instruction Sheet; 3410-5 Instruction Sheet; 19210-10 Instruction Sheet; Form 2870 Printed Sheet

Boxes & Packing: 61-170 Outfit Box; 61-171 Corr. Insert; 61-172 Corr. Insert; 62-202 Corr. Insert; 61-174 Shipper for (6) (1-6)

Alternate For Outfit Contents:
Note: Sub. 1130T-25 for 1060T-25.

19234 (1963)	C6	C7	C8	Rarity
Complete Outfit With Green Or Brown Automobile	525	885	1,300	R9
Complete Outfit With Yellow Automobile	375	685	1,050	R9
Outfit Box no. 61-170	200	400	600	R9

Alternate For Outfit Contents:
Note: Substitute 200 - 6536-25 for 6476-25; Substitute 6119-100 for 6167-25.

Comments: The Factory Order for the no. 19233-501 was marked "Cancel". This outfit was similar to the no. 19233-500, but for some reason it was canceled. This listing is provided for historical reference.

19234
1963

Comments: Brown & Williamson and its Raleigh brand of cigarettes operated a successful promotional coupon program that was in full gear during the 1960s. The Factory Order for outfit no. 19234 was the last one to list Brown & Williamson or Raleigh as a customer.

This Manufacturer Promotional Type IIIb outfit appeared on page 33 of the Raleigh and Belair Premium Catalog for 1963 as "#6380" for 1,900 coupons. This was the last Brown & Williamson catalog to include a Lionel train.

It was common for promotional coupon companies to purchase the same or similar outfits across different calendar years. As such, the 19234 followed up almost exactly Brown & Williamson's 1962 offering, the no. X-705. (See the entries for outfit no. X-695 from 1961 and X-705 from 1962 for more information.)

The 19234, like the X-705, was led by a no. 242-25 Steam Type Locomotive. This low-end Scout steamer featured a two-position reversing unit and a headlight, lacked smoke and used a rubber tire as a traction aid. The version with wide running boards was included in these outfits.

In the 19234, a no. 1130T-25 Tender took the place of the no. 1060T-25 Tender that was used in the X-705. This substitution does not affect the value of a 19234.

The transition from Archbar to AAR trucks and couplers that began in 1962 continued into 1963. As part of this, Lionel sought to cut costs by introducing a non-operating AAR type. Therefore, starting in 1963, most cars equipped with AAR trucks and couplers had at least one non-operating type. For the 19234, all three of these combinations were possible. The 1130T-25 was equipped with one plain and one operating AAR type, whereas the 1060T-25 could come with either AAR or Archbar types.

With only one exception, the rolling stock in the 19234 duplicated the cars in the X-705. The key difference was the unmarked no. 6076-100 Hopper Car - Gray. The norm in 1963 for the 6076-100 was to be equipped with non-operating AAR trucks and couplers although Archbar types were possible.

All the other cars in the 19234 were the same as those in the X-705, although they had been updated for 1963. Specifically, the no. 3410-25 Oper. Helicopter Car (Less Helicopter) was making its final outfit appearances in 1963 and 1964. It came equipped with one operating and one non-operating AAR truck and coupler. The norm for a no. 3419-100 Operating Helicopter Complete was a one-piece yellow body in 1963. This fragile helicopter was frequently lost or broken.

Other updates for 1963 included the no. 6406-25 Flat Car W/Auto. Gray molded plastic started to become the norm, but Tuscan Red was also possible. The no. 6406-30 Automobile was most often molded in brown or green plastic with gray bumpers, but a yellow automobile with gray bumpers could have been used.

Pricing is provided for these variations.

All the paperwork for this outfit was updated to reflect the new 90-day warranty policy that Lionel instituted in 1963.

The no. 61-170 Tan RSC with Black Graphics outfit box measured 11½ x 10¼ x 6¼ inches.

The Factory Order for this outfit was updated on 11-14-63. This update lowered the quantity from 2,000 to 400. This smaller-than-average amount leads to an R9 rarity rating. The 19234 is more difficult to find than its predecessor, the X-705 from 1962.

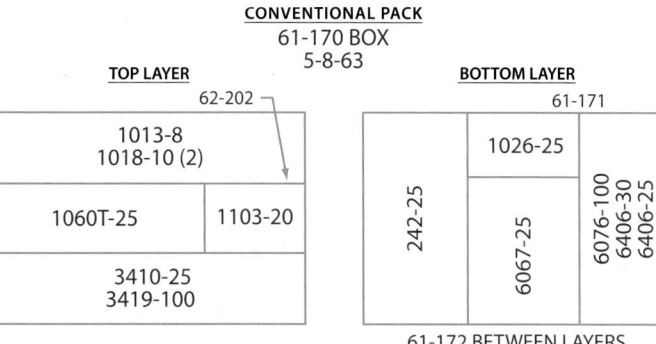

CONVENTIONAL PACK
61-170 BOX
5-8-63

TOP LAYER		BOTTOM LAYER	

61-172 BETWEEN LAYERS

19234-500
1963

Description: "O27" Promotional Outfit
Specification: "O27" Steam Type Freight Outfit
Original Amount: 600
Factory Order Date: 11/21/1963
Date Issued: 11-21-63
Date Req'd: 11-21-63
Packaging: RSC (Units Loose)

Contents: 242-25 Steam Type Locomotive; 1130T-25 Tender; 6045-150 Tank Car; 6162-25 Gondola Car (Less 3 Canisters); 6112-88 Canister (3); 6076-100 Hopper Car - Gray; 6406-25 Flat Car W/Auto; 6406-30 Automobile; 6067-25 Caboose; 1013-8 Curved Track (Bundle of 8 - 1013); 1018-10 Straight Track (Loose) (6); 1026-25 25-Watt Transformer; 1103-20 Envelope Packed; 310-62 Set of (3) Billboards; D63-50 Accessory Catalog; 1-62 Parts Order Form; 1-63 Warranty Card; 19106-10 Instruction Sheet

Boxes & Packing: 62-246 Outfit Box; 61-171 Corr. Insert; 62-247 Shipper for (4) (1-4)

19234-500 (1963)	C6	C7	C8	Rarity
Complete Outfit	450	515	980	R8
Outfit Box no. 62-246	150	300	400	R8

Comments: The no. 19234-500 was created only one week after the no. 19234 indicated a decrease in quantity from 2,000 to 400. Lionel likely took some of the leftover rolling stock and created the 19234-500. As such, this General Release Promotional Type IIb outfit is similar to outfit no. 19234 from 1963. It has yet to be tied to a specific end customer.

The 19234-500 was a basic starter outfit led by a no. 242-25 Steam Type Locomotive. This low-end Scout steamer featured a two-position reversing unit and a headlight, lacked smoke and used a rubber tire as a traction aid. The version with wide running boards was included in this outfit. It pulled a no. 1130T-25 Tender equipped with one operating and one plain AAR truck and coupler.

With two exceptions, the rolling stock in this outfit was carried over from earlier years. The new-for-1963 cars were the orange nos. 6045-150 Tank Car and the unmarked 6076-100 Hopper Car - Gray. The former was equipped with one operating and one non-operating AAR truck and coupler. The norm for the latter was non-operating AAR types.

In 1963 the no. 6406-25 Flat Car W/Auto began to appear in gray molded plastic and most often had non-operating Archbar trucks and couplers. The no. 6406-30 Automobile was generally molded in brown or green plastic with gray bumpers. The specific color cannot be confirmed for this outfit. Pricing assumes either a green or brown version.

The no. 19106-10 Instruction Sheet was similar to the no. 19210-10 Instruction Sheet included with the 19234. The only difference worth noting is that the former showed an oval layout track plan and the latter illustrated a circular plan.

The 19234-500 used the no. 62-246 Tan RSC Mailer with Black Graphics outfit box. It was manufactured by Mead Containers and measured 11½ x 10¼ x 6¼ inches. These boxes were made of a thicker corrugated material (rated at 90 pounds rather than the normal 65 pounds gross weight) that allowed each outfit to be shipped in its own box. The manufacturer omitted any Lionel printing on the box top to leave room for a mailing label.

If it were not for the inclusion of a brown or green automobile with gray bumpers, this outfit would be just one of the numerous promotional outfits from 1963. The 19234-500's R8 rarity is based on its average original production quantity and infrequent appearance on the market.

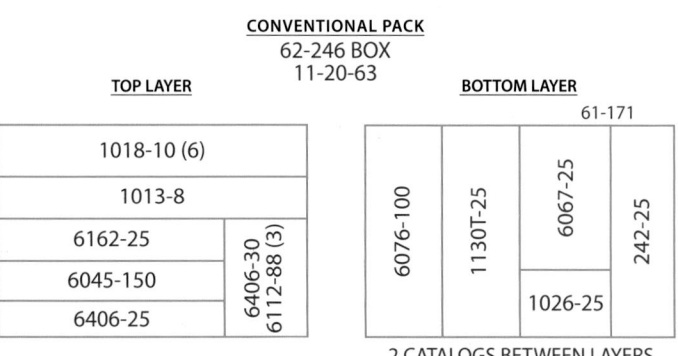

CONVENTIONAL PACK
62-246 BOX
11-20-63

TOP LAYER	BOTTOM LAYER

2 CATALOGS BETWEEN LAYERS

Description: "O27" Promotional Outfit
Specification: "O27" Diesel Freight Outfit
Customer: Cunningham Drug
Original Amount: ~~1,000~~ Cancel
Factory Order Date: 6/4/1963
Date Issued: Rev 9-23-63
Date Req'd: Aug
Packaging: Display Outfit Packing - #1 (Units not Boxed)

Contents: 221P-25 Diesel Locomotive; 3309-25 Turbo Missile Firing Car (Less Missiles); 0349-10 Turbo Missile (2); 6076-75 Hopper Car - Black; 6042-25 Gondola Car - Blue; 6112-5 Canister (2); 6473-25 Rodeo Car; 6167-25 Caboose; 1013-8 Curved Track (Bundle of 8 - 1013); 1018-10 Straight Track (Loose) (2); 1026-25 25-Watt Transformer; 1103-20 Envelope Packed; 1123-40 Instruction Sheet; 11321-10 Instruction Sheet; 3309-5 Instruction Sheet; Form 2870 Printed Sheet

Boxes & Packing: 63-306 Outfit Box; 61-101 Corr. Insert; 61-102 Corr. Insert; 63-300 Corr. Insert; 63-307 Shipper for (4) (1-4)

Comments: This was the only Factory Order to list Cunningham Drug as the customer. However, the original quantity was crossed out and the Factory Order marked "Cancel". This listing is provided for historical reference.

The no. 19236 listed Popular as the customer on its Factory Order. This low-end starter outfit included a Type IIb no. 6050-150 Van Camp Savings Bank Car and a no. 3309-25 Turbo Missile Firing Car. Two outfit box versions are available. Shown is the one that had a hand-stamped no. 63-361 Outfit Box.

Description: "O27" Promotional Outfit
Specification: "O27" Steam Type Freight Outfit
Customer: Popular Club Plan
Original Amount: 2,500
Factory Order Date: 5/15/1963
Date Issued: 5-24-63
Packaging: RSC Outfit Packing #5 (Units not Boxed)

Contents: 1062-25 Steam Type Loco. W/Light & Reversing Unit; 1061T-25 Tender; 3309-25 Turbo Missile Firing Car (Less Missiles); 0349-10 Turbo Missile (2); 6050-150 Van Camp Savings Bank Car; 6162-25 Gondola Car (Less 3 Canisters); 6112-88 Canister (3); 6067-25 Caboose; 1013-8 Curved Track (Bundle of 8 - 1013); 1018-10 Straight Track (Loose) (2); 1026-25 25-Watt Transformer; 1103-20 Envelope Packed; 310-2 Set of (5) Billboards; D63-50 Accessory Catalog; 1-62 Parts Order Form; 1-63 Warranty Card; 1123-40 Instruction Sheet; 3309-5 Instruction Sheet; 11311-10 Instruction Sheet; Form 2870 Printed Sheet

Boxes & Packing: 61-170 Outfit Box; 61-171 Corr. Insert; 61-172 Corr. Insert; 61-173 Corr. Insert; 61-174 Shipper for (6) (1-6); 63-361 Outfit Box

19236 (1963)	C6	C7	C8	Rarity
Complete Outfit With no. 61-170 Box	225	360	495	R5
Outfit Box no. 61-170	100	150	175	R5
Complete Outfit With no. 63-361 Box	325	610	820	R8
Outfit Box no. 63-361	200	400	500	R8

Comments: Popular Club Plan is a catalog company selling an assortment of clothing, housewares, jewelry, toys and electronics. In 1963, it offered a Retailer Promotional Type Ib outfit to its customers. The no. 19236 was a follow-up to the no. X-707 that Popular purchased in 1962.

The no. 19236 was a basic starter outfit led by a no. 1062-25 Steam Type Loco. W/Light & Reversing Unit. This low-end Scout steamer was new for 1963 and featured an 0-4-0 wheel arrangement and lacked a traction aid. According to its Lionel Engineering Specification, it was the "Same as #1061 but with the addition of Reversing Unit & Lamp". It was trailed by an unmarked no. 1061T-25 Tender that equipped with one non-operating and one plain AAR truck and coupler.

All the rolling stock in this outfit was carried over from earlier years. The Type IIb no. 6050-150 Van Camp Savings Bank Car was making one of its 13 appearances in 1963. The no. 3309-25 Turbo Missile Firing Car (Less Missiles) was the low-end version of the no. 3349-25 Turbo Missile Firing Car. Both the 6050-150 and 3309-25 were equipped with non-operating Archbar trucks and couplers. The no. 6067-25 Caboose came with one non-operating and one plain Archbar type.

The no. 6162-25 Gondola Car was first issued in 1959. As with many cars in 1963, it changed from two operating to one operating and one non-operating AAR truck and coupler.

The Form 2870 advertising the nos. 2002 and 2003 Track Make-Up Kits was dated 6/63.

Two outfit boxes were used for the 19236. The first was a no. 61-170 Tan RSC with Black Graphics outfit box that measured 11½ x 10¼ x 6¼ inches. This outfit has also been observed in a hand-stamped no. 63-361 Tan RSC with Black Graphics outfit box manufactured by St. Joe Paper Co. - Container Div. and measuring 12⅛ x 9⅞ x 5½ inches. Its box manufacturer's certificate included four lines of data. This version was likely due to a box change at the time of production. (See the section on Outfit Box Printing, Graphics and Labels for more information.)

Of the two boxes, the 63-361 Outfit Box is more difficult to find. Therefore, the version of the 19236 that came in that box has a higher rarity rating (R8) than does the one that came in the 61-170 (R5).

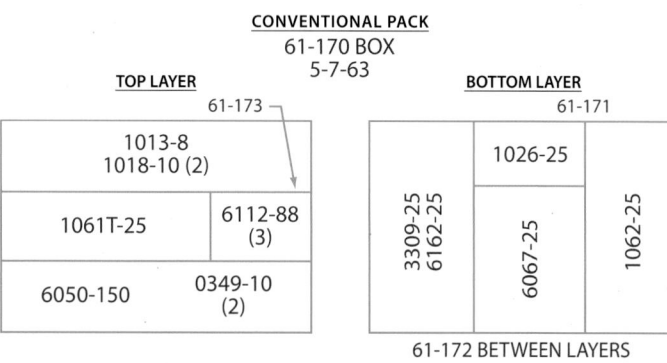

19237
1963

Description: "O27" Promotional Outfit
Specification: "O27" Diesel Freight Outfit
Customer/No./Price: Spiegel; R36 J 5287; $17.94
Original Amount: 1,500
Factory Order Date: 6/5/1963
Date Issued: Rev 9-20-63
Date Req'd: Aug
Packaging: RSC Outfit Packing - #5 (Units not Boxed)

Contents: 221P-25 Diesel Locomotive; 6407-25 Flat Car W/ Sterling Missile; 6407-11 Sterling Missile; 6014-325 Frisco Box Car; 3410-25 Oper. Helicopter Car (Less Helicopter); 3419-100 Operating Helicopter Complete; 6463-25 Rocket Fuel Car; 6059-50 Caboose; 1013-8 Curved Track (Bundle of 8 - 1013); 1018-10 Straight Track (Loose); 6139-25 Uncoupling Track Section; 1010-25 35-Watt Transformer; 1103-40X Envelope Packed; 310-2 Set of (5) Billboards; D63-50 Accessory Catalog; 1-62 Parts Order Form; 1-63 Warranty Card; 1123-40 Instruction Sheet; 3410-5 Instruction Sheet; 11351-10 Instruction Sheet; Form 2870 Printed Sheet

Boxes & Packing: 61-180 Outfit Box; 61-181 Corr. Insert; 61-182 Corr. Insert; 61-183 Corr. Insert; 62-248 Corr. Insert; 62-264 Corr. Insert; 61-185 Shipper for (4) (1-4)

Alternate For Outfit Contents:
Note: 1103-40X Env. Packed for this set must include oil & lubricant.

19237 (1963)	C6	C7	C8	Rarity
Complete Outfit	550	950	1,450	R6
Outfit Box no. 61-180	100	175	250	R6

Comments: This was the third of five (nos. 11351-500, 19214-500, 19237, 19238 and 19238-501) promotional outfits from 1963 that listed Spiegel as the customer on the Factory Order. The 19237 was a Retailer Promotional Type Ia outfit. It was shown on page 380 of the 1963 Christmas Catalog as Spiegel no. R36 J 5287 for $17.94.

The 19237 was led by a 221P-25 Rio Grande Diesel Locomotive. This low-end, unpainted yellow Alco was new for 1963. It featured a two-position reversing unit, a traction tire and a closed pilot and lacked a headlight.

Even though this space and military outfit was Spiegel's low-end diesel-powered offering, it included some collectible rolling stock. The unboxed no. 6407-25 Flat Car W/Sterling Missile (new for 1963) was included in 11 different outfits, with a total of 13,124 cars produced. This highly collectible item was also available for separate sale as a no. 6407-1. The flat car was a common red no. 6511-series model with "Lionel" stamped on each side and a brake wheel installed. The same flat car was used with the no. 6408-25 Flat Car W/5 Pipes.

Spiegel's low-end diesel-powered offering for 1963 contained the highly collectible no. 6407-25 Flat Car W/Sterling Missile. Also included was the aquamarine variation of the no. 3410-25 Oper. Helicopter Car (Less Helicopter). The outfit was shown on page 380 of the 1963 Spiegel Christmas Catalog as no. R36 J 5287 for $17.94.

The flat car might be common, but the no. 6407-11 Sterling Missile was not. This load, manufactured by Sterling Plastics, was frequently separated from its flat car because it lacked Lionel markings. An authentic original would have "Sterling Plastics" molded into the capsule bottom and rocket base.

The 6407-25, like the other cars in the 19237, was equipped with one operating and one non-operating AAR truck and coupler.

Also new were the Type IIb no. 6014-325 Frisco Box Car and the unpainted version of the no. 6059-50 Caboose.

In 1962, the no. 3419-100 Operating Helicopter Complete changed from a gray Navy stamped two-piece helicopter body to an unmarked helicopter with a one-piece yellow helicopter body. Even so, gray Navy helicopters were still appearing on cars. Both of these helicopters were frequently lost or broken.

The 19237 was one of only two promotional outfits to specify a no. 1103-40X Envelope Packed (the 19238 is the other). The "X" meant that the packed envelope also included oil and lubricant.

All the paperwork in this outfit reflected the new 90-day warranty policy that Lionel instituted in 1963. Many of these instruction sheet versions are the most difficult ones to find. Pay particular attention to the no. 11351-10 Instruction Sheet, as it must be dated 5/63. Also, even though the no. 3410-5 Instruction Sheet was still dated 6-61, it should make reference to a 90-day warranty.

The commonly used no. 61-180 Tan RSC with Black Graphics outfit box measured 12¾ x 10 x 6¾ inches.

The 19237 was produced in greater numbers than any of the other outfits connected with Spiegel in 1963. For that reason, it has the lowest rarity rating of these five outfits and examples appear most often on the market.

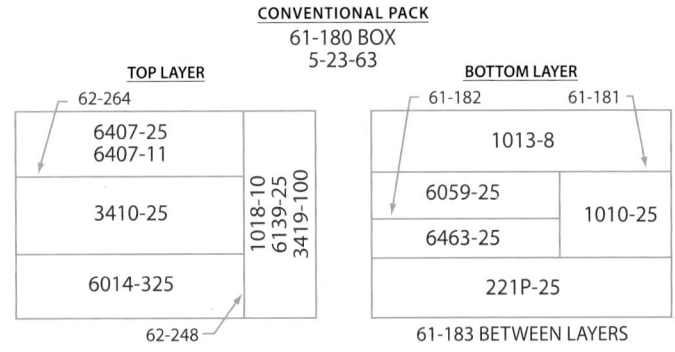

CONVENTIONAL PACK
61-180 BOX
5-23-63

TOP LAYER
62-264
6407-25
6407-11
1018-10
6139-25
3419-100
3410-25
6014-325
62-248

BOTTOM LAYER
61-182   61-181
1013-8
6059-25
6463-25
1010-25
221P-25

61-183 BETWEEN LAYERS

LIONEL TRANSPORT HIGHBALLS FREIGHT
8 unit train 29.84

DELUXE 8-UNIT DIESEL TRANSPORT by Lionel. All the fun and adventure of a big cross country freight. Operating searchlight car scans track with powerful beam. Piggy back flat car carries 2 vans, auto transport car hauls 4 automobiles. Liquefied gas tank car, 2 dome tank car and caboose. Powered by mighty Texas Special two unit, twin diesel engine. Almost 7-ft. of authentically detailed, Lionel quality train. Built of hi-impact plastic and steel. Automatic couplers on all cars. 120-in. of running .027 gauge track on 27x44-in. oval layout; 60 watt transformer with circuit breaker. Uncoupling track set, oil, wires. Instructions included. R36 J 5285. Mailable. Shipping weight 14 lbs............Low monthly terms 29.84

Searchlight car scans the track

Spiegel's high-end diesel-powered offering for 1963 was the no. 19238 (Spiegel no. R36 J 5285). Shown here in the 1963 Spiegel Christmas Catalog, it demonstrates how entries in retailer catalogs did not always match the final offering. This discrepancy occurred because Lionel began its selling cycle with customers like Spiegel well in advance of the targeted catalog year. Photographs were often taken before an outfit's components had been finalized. As such, the 19238 is incorrectly shown with a no. 6465-100 Cities Service Tank Car and a no. 6257-100 Caboose. The final version came with a no. 6465-150 Tank Car and a no. 6017-25 Caboose.

Description: "O27" Promotional Outfit
Specification: "O27" Diesel Freight Outfit
Customer/No./Price: Spiegel; R36 J 5285; $29.84
Original Amount: 500
Factory Order Date: 6/5/1963
Date Issued: Rev 9-20-63
Date Req'd: Aug
Packaging: RSC Outfit Packing - #5 (Units not Boxed)

Contents: 211P-150 *"Texas Special"* Diesel; 211T-25 *"Texas Special"* Motorless Unit; 6440-50 Flat Car W/2 Piggy Back Vans; 6440-150 Trailer Vans (2); 6414-150 Auto Transport (Less Autos); 6406-30 Automobile (4); 6465-150 Tank Car; 6822-50 Searchlight Car; 6469-50 Miscellaneous Car; 6469-52 Cardboard Container Stamped; 6017-25 Caboose; 1013-8 Curved Track (Bundle of 8 - 1013); 1018-30 Straight Track (Bundle of 3 - 1018); 6139-25 Uncoupling Track Section; 1073-25 60-Watt Transformer; 1103-40X Envelope Packed; 310-2 Set of (5) Billboards; D63-50 Accessory Catalog; 1-62 Parts Order Form; 1-63 Warranty Card; 1123-40 Instruction Sheet; 211-151 Instruction Sheet; 11351-10 Instruction Sheet

Boxes & Packing: 63-354 Outfit Box; 61-181 Corr. Insert; 61-182 Corr. Insert (2); 62-225 Corr. Insert (2); 62-264 Corr. Insert; 63-315 Corr. Insert; 63-316 Corr. Insert (2); 61-201 Corr. Shipper for (4) (1-4)

Alternate For Outfit Contents:
Note: 1103-40X Envelope Packed for this set must include oil & lubricant.

19238 (1963)	C6	C7	C8	Rarity
Complete Outfit With Green Or Brown Automobiles	1,280	1,900	2,535	R9
Complete Outfit With Yellow Automobiles	680	1,100	1,535	R9
Outfit Box no. 63-354	250	400	500	R9

Comments: This was the fourth of five (nos. 11351-500, 19214-500, 19237, 19238 and 19238-501) promotional outfits from 1963 that listed Spiegel as the customer on the Factory Order. The 19238 was a Retailer Promotional Type Ia outfit. It was shown as Spiegel's high-end diesel offering on page 380 of the 1963 Christmas Catalog as no. R36 J 5285 for $29.84.

The 19238 was led by a no. 211P-150 *Texas Special* Diesel. The 211P-150 was a cost-reduced version of the no. 211P-25 *Texas*

Special Alco Diesel Power Unit. The "-150" was new for 1963 and featured a two-position reversing unit, two traction tires, a headlight, a weight and an open pilot with a large ledge. This variation has not stirred much interest in the collector community.

Two new pieces of rolling stock were the orange no. 6465-150 Tank Car and the no. 6469-50 Miscellaneous Car. The nos. 6414-150 Auto Transport (Less Autos), 6440-50 Flat Car W/2 Piggy Back Vans and 6822-50 Searchlight Car were carryover items that were assigned new suffixes in 1963. The suffixes indicated that these items came unboxed with one operating and one non-operating AAR truck and coupler. All the other cars in this outfit were similarly equipped except the caboose. It had one operating and one plain AAR truck as well.

The 6414-150 Auto Transport Car (Less Autos) likely included four green or brown no. 6406-30 Automobiles with gray bumpers, but yellow automobiles with gray bumpers were possible. Pricing is provided for these variations.

The 19238 was one of only two promotional outfits to specify a no. 1103-40X Envelope Packed (the 19237 is the other). The "X" meant that the packed envelope also included oil and lubricant.

All the paperwork in this outfit reflected the new 90-day warranty policy that Lionel instituted in 1963. Many of these instruction sheet versions are the most difficult ones to find. Pay particular attention to the nos. 11351-10 and 211-151 Instruction Sheets. Both should be dated 5/63.

The no. 63-354 Tan RSC with Black Graphics outfit box was manufactured by St. Joe Kraft, St. Joe Paper Co. Container Division and measured 14¼ x 12 x 7⅛ inches.

The 19238 is desirable because it came from Spiegel and featured some nice rolling stock for 1963. It remains difficult to find in collectible condition.

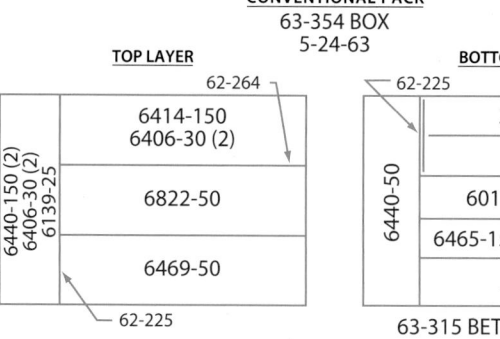

CONVENTIONAL PACK
63-354 BOX
5-24-63

TOP LAYER
62-264
6440-150 (2)
6406-30 (2)
6139-25
6414-150
6406-30 (2)
6822-50
6469-50
62-225

BOTTOM LAYER
62-225
63-316 (2)
6440-50
211P-150 (61-182)
211T-25 (61-181)
6017-25
6465-150 (61-182)
1073-25
1013-8
1018-30
63-315 BETWEEN LAYERS

Description: "O27" Promotional Outfit
Specification: "O27" Diesel Freight Outfit
Customer: Spiegel
Original Amount: 100
Factory Order Date: 12/6/1963
Date Issued: 12-6-63
Date Req'd: At Once

Contents: 231P-25 Alco Diesel Power Car - "Rock Island"; 6827-1 Flat Car With Tractor Shovel; 6822-1 Searchlight Car; 6475-50 Crushed Pineapple Car; 6045-150 Tank Car; 6050-175 Libby Box Car; 6361-1 Timber Transport Car; 6162-25 Gondola Car (Less 3 Canisters); 6112-88 Canister (3); 6167-75 Caboose; 1013-8 Curved Track (Bundle of 8 - 1013); 1018-5 Straight Track (Bundle of 5 - 1018); 6139-25 Uncoupling Track Section; 1103-40 Envelope Packed; 1073-25 60-Watt Transformer; 310-62 Set of (3) Billboards; D63-50 Accessory Catalog; D63-52 Accessory Catalog; 1-62 Parts Order Form; 1-63 Warranty Card; 11351-10 Instruction Sheet; 1123-40 Instruction Sheet; 230-6 Instruction Sheet

Boxes & Packing: 63-313 Outfit Box; 62-225 Corr. Insert; 62-251 Corr. Insert; 63-314 Shipper for (4) (1-4)

19238-501 (1963)	C6	C7	C8	Rarity
Complete Outfit	1,175	1,700	2,200	R10
Outfit Box no. 63-313	700	950	1,150	R10

Comments: This was the last of the five (nos. 11351-500, 19214-500, 19237, 19238 and 19238-501) promotional outfits from 1963 that listed Spiegel as the customer on the Factory Order. The 19238-501 was a Retailer Promotional Type Ib outfit. It did not appear in the 1963 Spiegel Christmas Catalog.

The Factory Order for the 19238-501, like that for outfit no. 19214-500, was dated late in the year. These outfits may have been quickly assembled and shopped to retailers like Spiegel to help dump inventory at the end of the year. Lionel closed a similar deal with Sears. (For an explanation of Lionel's 1963 year-end deal with Sears, consult the entry on Sears, Roebuck and Co. in the section on Lionel's Distribution and Customers.) Even though the 19238 and 19238-501 share the same base number, their contents are entirely different.

The 19238-501 was a high-end, diesel-powered outfit led by a no. 231P-25 Rock Island Alco Diesel Power Car. The 231P-25 featured two-axle Magne-Traction, a headlight and a two-position reversing unit.

The eight pieces of rolling stock in this outfit provided plenty of fun and excitement. They started with a trio of collectible items from outfit no. 19263 (known as the "Libby" outfit). They included the nos. 6050-175 Libby Box Car, 6167-75 Union Pacific Caboose and 6475-50 Crushed Pineapple Car. All three cars were equipped with non-operating AAR trucks and couplers.

Two other cars of note in the 19238-501 were the boxed nos. 6361-1 Log Car and 6822-1 Searchlight Car. Orange Picture boxes were the norm, although the 6361-1 has been observed in an Orange Perforated box through 1963. Even so, it was not the norm for Lionel to include boxed items in 1963 outfits.

The no. 6827-1 Flat Car With Tractor Shovel was making its last appearance in 1963. It, like the 6361-1 and 6822-1, came with operating AAR trucks and couplers. Be aware that a new Orange Non Perforated no. 6827-5 Folding Box was issued for the Flat Car With Tractor Shovel in 1963.

The remaining two cars in this outfit were the nos. 6045-150 Tank Car and 6162-25 Gondola Car. Both were equipped with one operating and one non-operating AAR truck and coupler.

All the paperwork reflected the new 90-day warranty policy that Lionel instituted in 1963. Many of these instruction sheet versions are the most difficult ones to find. The correct version of the no. 11351-10 for this outfit was dated 5/63.

The no. 63-313 Tan RSC with Black Graphics outfit box measured 14½ x 11¾ x 7 inches.

The 19238-501 and 19214-500 were produced in the lowest quantities of any of the Spiegel outfits. That is why they are the two most difficult of these outfits to find.

CONVENTIONAL PACK
63-313 BOX
12-6-63

TOP LAYER		BOTTOM LAYER

TOP LAYER:
- 6361-1 F
- 6162-25
- 6822-1 F / 6139-25
- 6050-175 / 1018-5
- 1013-8

BOTTOM LAYER:
- 1073-25
- 231P-25
- 6167-75
- 6045-150
- 6827-1 F
- 6475-50

Description: "O27" Promotional Outfit
Specification: "O27" Diesel Freight Outfit
Original Amount: 50
Factory Order Date: 12/12/1963
Date Issued: 12-12-63
Packaging: RSC

Contents: 211P-150 *"Texas Special"* Diesel; 211T-25 *"Texas Special"* Motorless Unit; 6408-25 Flat Car W/5 Pipes; 6511-15 Pipes (5); 6480-25 Exploding Target Car; 6463-25 Rocket Fuel Car; 6822-1 Searchlight Car; 6142-25 Gondola Car (Less 2 Canisters); 6112-5 Canister (2); 6059-50 Caboose; 1013-8 Curved Track (Bundle of 8 - 1013); 1018-30 Straight Track (Bundle of 3 - 1018); 1008-50 Uncoupling Unit; 1073-25 60-Watt Transformer; 1103-20 Envelope Packed; 310-62 Set of (3) Billboards; D63-50 Accessory Catalog; D63-52 Accessory Catalog; 1-62 Parts Order Form; 1-63 Warranty Card; 1123-40 Instruction Sheet; 19241-10 Instruction Sheet; 211-151 Instruction Sheet; 6480-5 Instruction Sheet

Boxes & Packing: 63-309 Outfit Box; 61-172 Corr. Insert; 62-224 Corr. Insert; 62-245 Corr. Insert (2); 62-248 Corr. Insert; 63-310 Shipper for (4) (1-4)

19238-502 (1963)	C6	C7	C8	Rarity
Complete Outfit	1,270	1,700	2,350	R10
Outfit Box no. 63-309	1,000	1,250	1,600	R10

Comments: This General Release Promotional Type IIb was one of many outfits issued late in 1963 in an attempt to deplete inventory. The no. 19238-502 nearly duplicated outfit no. 11361-500 from 1963 and likely was derived from it. Even though the 19238 and 19238-502 share the same base number, their contents are entirely different.

The 11361-500 began as outfit no. 19310 with a quantity of 296. On 12-11-63, that number was revised downward to 246. The next day, Lionel created the 19238-502 with a quantity of 50. These 50 were most likely leftover 11361-500s. (See the entry for the 11361-500 from 1963 for information about the motive power and rolling stock included in the 19238-502.)

The only major difference between the 11361-500 and 19238-502 was that the latter included a no. 6822-1 Searchlight Car instead of a no. 3349-1 Turbo Missile Firing Car. The 3349-1 was no longer available, but Lionel still had more than 5,200 of the 6822-1s in stock. The 6822-1 was equipped with operating AAR trucks and couplers and came packaged in an Orange Picture box.

The 19238-502 also differed in having a better power source, a no. 1073-25 60-Watt Transformer. This upgrade necessitated a change in the outfit instruction sheet, and Lionel included a no. 19241-10 Instruction Sheet. This and most of the other paperwork

in this outfit likely made reference to the 90-day warranty policy that Lionel announced in 1963.

Both the 11361-500 and 19238-502 used a no. 63-309 Tan RSC with Black Graphics outfit box. Manufactured by the Mead Corporation, it measured 13¼ x 12½ x 6¾ inches and included four lines of data as part of the box manufacturer's certificate.

The two outfits were created in limited amounts, but the quantity of the 19238-502 was extremely small. With only 50 produced, it ties for 13th on the list of the fewest outfits made. This outfit easily achieves its R10 rarity ranking.

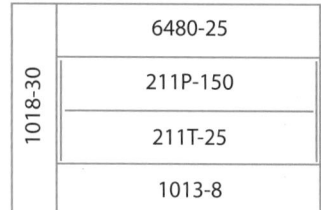

CONVENTIONAL PACK
63-309 BOX
12-12-63

TOP LAYER				BOTTOM LAYER	
6408-25				6480-25	
6822-1 F	6463-25	6142-25	6059-50	1018-30	211P-150
					211T-25
			1073-25		1013-8

Description: "O27" Promotional Outfit
Specification: "O27" Steam Type Freight Outfit
Customer: MBS
Original Amount: 2,500
Factory Order Date: 6/5/1963
Date Issued: Rev 10-30-63
Packaging: RSC Outfit Packing - #5 (Units not Boxed)

Contents: 1062-25 Steam Type Loco. W/Light & Reversing Unit; 1061T-25 Tender; 6473-25 Rodeo Car; 6050-150 Van Camp Savings Bank Car; 6042-25 Gondola Car - Blue; 6112-5 Canister (2); 6076-75 Hopper Car - Black; 6120-25 Work Caboose; 1013-8 Curved Track (Bundle of 8 - 1013); 1018-40 Straight Track (Bundle of 4 - 1018); 1026-25 25-Watt Transformer; 1103-20 Envelope Packed; 310-2 Set of (5) Billboards; D63-50 Accessory Catalog; 1-62 Parts Order Form; 1-63 Warranty Card; 1123-40 Instruction Sheet; 11311-10 Instruction Sheet

Boxes & Packing: 62-243 Outfit Box; 62-223 Corr. Insert; 62-225 Corr. Insert (2); 62-248 Corr. Insert; 62-249 Corr. Insert; 62-254 Corr. Insert; 62-244 Shipper for (4) (1-4)

Alternate For Outfit Contents:
Note: Substitute 2,000 - 6042-75 for 6042-25; Substitute 4,000 - 40-11 for 6112-5; Substitute 500 - 6119-100 for 6120-25.

19239 (1963)	C6	C7	C8	Rarity
Complete Outfit	250	425	600	R6
Outfit Box no. 62-243	125	200	250	R6

Comments: In 1963, a buying cooperative known as Merchants Buying Syndicate (MBS) purchased the no. 19239. This Retailer Promotional Type Ib was a success for MBS, as the factory orders were increased from 2,000 on 6-5-63 to 2,500 on 11-6-63.

The 19239 was led by a no. 1062-25 Steam Type Loco. W/ Light & Reversing Unit. This low-end Scout steamer was new for 1963 and featured an 0-4-0 wheel arrangement and lacked a traction aid. According to its Lionel Engineering Specification, it was the "Same as #1061 but with the addition of Reversing Unit & Lamp". It was trailed by an unmarked no. 1061T-25 Tender, which was equipped with one non-operating and one plain AAR truck and coupler.

All the rolling stock in this outfit was carried over from earlier years. The no. 6473-25 Rodeo Car had a Type IIb body type (cadmium yellow plastic with red lettering) and came with one operating and one non-operating AAR truck and coupler. All the other cars were equipped with non-operating trucks and couplers.

The no. 6050-150 Van Camp Savings Bank Car was a Type II with Archbar trucks and couplers. The nos. 6042-25 Gondola Car - Blue and 6076-75 Hopper Car - Black came with AAR types.

This outfit also included the unmarked yellow no. 6120-25 Work Caboose. That model, which had Archbar trucks and couplers, appeared only in promotional outfits from 1961 through 1963.

The no. 62-243 Tan RSC with Black Graphics outfit box measured 12⅛ x 11½ x 6⅜ inches.

MBS also purchased a dealer display version of the 19239 that was listed as the no. D-19239. This display was packaged in a no. 61-439 White 4-6-4 Steamer and F3 Hinged Display with Red/ Orange and Blue Graphics Type A outfit box. It was manufactured by United Container Co. and measured 22½ x 14½ x 3¼ inches.

Even though the 19239 was produced in fairly large quantities, it is difficult to find in C8 condition.

Merchants Buying Syndicate (MBS) purchased a no. D-19239 as a display version of no. 19239. This display was likely used to assist MBS' member retailers in the sales of the 19239. This rare display (only 100 were produced) was packaged in a Type A display box. Its Factory Order stated: "After the train outfit has been placed in insert tray, it must be sent to Weldotron Corp. to be shrink packed." The outfit shown has had its shrink pack removed.

The no. D-19239 was packaged in a no. 61-439 White 4-6-4 Steamer and F3 Hinged Display with Red/Orange and Blue Graphics Type A outfit box.

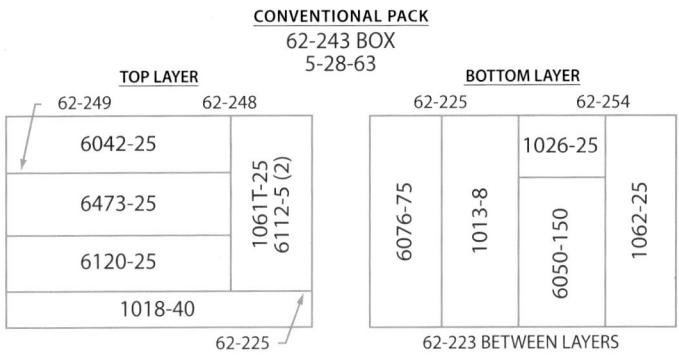

CONVENTIONAL PACK
62-243 BOX
5-28-63

TOP LAYER

62-249	62-248	
6042-25		1061T-25 6112-5 (2)
6473-25		
6120-25		
1018-40		

62-225

BOTTOM LAYER

62-225		62-254
		1026-25
6076-75	1013-8	6050-150 1062-25

62-223 BETWEEN LAYERS

19240
1963

Description: "O27" Promotional Outfit
Specification: "O27" Steam Type Freight Outfit
Customer: Stern's
Original Amount: 1,400
Factory Order Date: 5/7/1963
Date Issued: Rev 10-11-63
Packaging: RSC Outfit Packing #5 (Units not Boxed)

Boxes & Packing: 61-170 Outfit Box; 61-171 Corr. Insert; 61-172 Corr. Insert; 61-173 Corr. Insert; 61-174 Shipper for (6) (1-6)

19240 (1963)	C6	C7	C8	Rarity
Complete Outfit	300	450	615	R7
Outfit Box no. 61-170	150	225	275	R7

Contents: 1061-25 Steam Type Locomotive; 1061T-25 Tender; 6502-50 Girder Transport Car; 6502-3 Girder Bridge; 3370-25 Sheriff & Outlaw Car; 6042-75 Gondola Car (Less 2 Cable Reels); 40-11 Cable Reels (2); 6067-25 Caboose; 1013-70 Curved Track (Bundle of 12 - 1013); 1018-40 Straight Track (Bundle of 4 - 1018); 1020-25 90° Crossing; 1010-25 35-Watt Transformer; 1103-20 Envelope Packed; 310-2 Set of (5) Billboards; D63-50 Accessory Catalog; 1-62 Parts Order Form; 1-63 Warranty Card; 1123-40 Instruction Sheet; 3370-17 Instruction Sheet; 1802B Layout Instruction Sheet; 19223-10 Instruction Sheet

Comments: Stern Brothers Department Stores purchased this Retailer Promotional Type Ib outfit in 1963. Stern's typically obtained its outfits through its parent company, Allied. The no. 19240 represented the only outfit that Stern's purchased direct from Lionel.

This basic starter outfit had only one notable item, a no. 3370-25 Sheriff & Outlaw Car. This car first appeared in 1961 and was making its final unboxed appearance in promotional outfits in 1963. It was equipped with operating AAR trucks and couplers.

The 19240 was led by a no. 1061-25 Steam Type Locomotive.

This stripped-down Scout steamer (new for 1963) featured an 0-4-0 wheel arrangement and went forward only. It lacked a headlight, a lens and any sort of traction aid. It was trailed by an unmarked no. 1061T-25 Tender.

The 6502-50 Girder Transport Car was new for 1963. It was an unmarked blue plastic version of the black no. 6502-25 Girder Transport Car that Lionel first issued in 1962. The 6502-50 came equipped with non-operating AAR or non-operating Archbar trucks and couplers.

The transition from Archbar to AAR trucks and couplers that began in 1962 continued into 1963. As part of this, Lionel sought to cut costs by introducing a non-operating AAR type. Therefore, starting in 1963, most cars equipped with AAR trucks and couplers had at least one non-operating type. For the 19240, it was possible for all the remaining cars to come with AAR or Archbar trucks or couplers.

A no. 1802B Layout Instruction Sheet detailed the figure-eight track layout.

The no. 61-170 Tan RSC with Black Graphics outfit box measured 11½ x 10¼ x 6¼ inches.

This outfit was produced in fairly large quantities and sold to a well-known retailer. Even so, it does not often appear, a circumstance that is reflected in its R7 rarity rating.

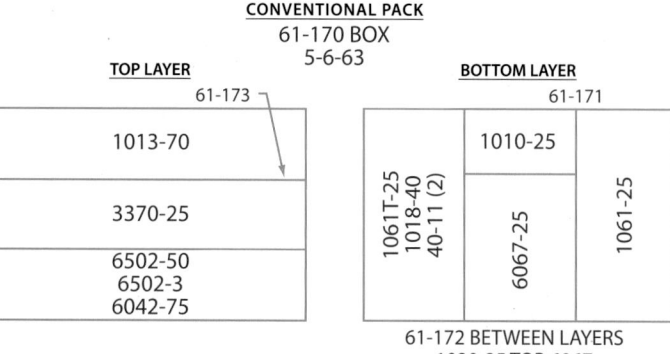

CONVENTIONAL PACK
61-170 BOX
5-6-63

19240-500
1963

Description: "O27" Promotional Outfit
Specification: "O27" Steam Type Freight Outfit
Customer: Kings Department Stores
Original Amount: 900
Factory Order Date: 10/23/1963
Date Issued: Rev 10-25-63
Date Req'd: At Once
Packaging: RSC (Units Loose)

Contents: 1061-25 Steam Type Locomotive; 1061T-25 Tender; 6502-50 Girder Transport Car; 6502-3 Girder Bridge; 3370-25 Sheriff & Outlaw Car; 6042-75 Gondola Car (Less 2 Cable Reels); 40-11 Cable Reels (2); 6067-25 Caboose; 1013-70 Curved Track (Bundle of 12 - 1013); 1018-40 Straight Track (Bundle of 4 - 1018); 1020-25 90° Crossing; 1010-25 35-Watt Transformer; 1103-20 Envelope Packed; 310-62 Set of (3) Billboards; D63-50 Accessory Catalog; 1-62 Parts Order Form; 1-63 Warranty Card; 19240-10 Instruction Sheet; 3370-17 Instruction Sheet

Boxes & Packing: 61-170 Outfit Box; 61-171 Corr. Insert; 62-248 Corr. Insert; 61-174 Shipper for (6) (1-6)

Alternate For Outfit Contents:
Note: Substitute 3376-160 for 3370-25; Substitute 6042-25 for 6042-75; Substitute 6257-100 for 6067-25.

19240-500 (1963)	C6	C7	C8	Rarity
Complete Outfit	315	470	670	R8
Complete Outfit With All Substitutions	370	540	770	R8
Outfit Box no. 61-170	175	250	325	R8

Comments: This was the second and last outfit in the 1960s to list Kings Department Stores as its customer. The no. 19240-500 was a Retailer Promotional Type Ib outfit that was almost an exact duplicate of the no. 19240 from 1963. (See the entry for outfit no.

19240 from 1963 for a detailed description of motive power and rolling stock.)

The 19240-500 was created 5½ months after the 19240. The major differences between the two outfits involved three substitutions in the 19240-500.

First, a no. 3376-160 Operating Giraffe Car replaced the no. 3370-25 Sheriff & Outlaw Car. The 3376-160 was the green version of the giraffe car in an Orange Picture box. It was equipped with operating AAR trucks and couplers.

Second, a no. 6042-25 Gondola Car - Blue replaced the no. 6042-75 Gondola Car (Less 2 Cable Reels). These cars were identical; their suffixes related to their respective loads. Both cars came with non-operating AAR trucks and couplers.

Third, a no. 6257-100 Caboose with a smokestack replaced the no. 6067-25 Caboose. The former model, the 1963 version of the 6257 Caboose, came with one operating and one plain AAR truck and coupler.

The layout instruction sheet changed from a no. 19223-10 Instruction Sheet in outfit 19240 to a no. 19240-10 Instruction Sheet in outfit 19240-500.

Both outfits were packaged in a no. 61-170 Tan RSC with Black Graphics outfit box that measured 11½ x 10¼ x 6¼ inches.

The 19240-500 was produced in smaller quantities than the 19240 and so is much more difficult to find.

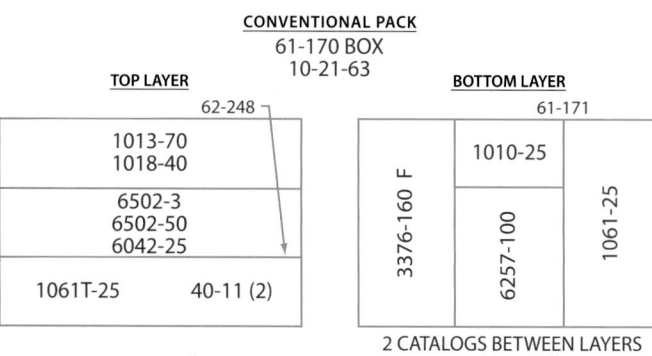

CONVENTIONAL PACK
61-170 BOX
10-21-63

The no. 19241 was likely sold through one of Allied's corporate-owned stores. This space and military outfit could well have been considered a high-end offering because it contained three operating cars. Two items of note were the harder-to-find light blue version of the no. 3419-250 Operating Helicopter Car and the version of the no. 238-25 Steam Type Locomotive with Smoke that came with wide running boards.

Description: "O27" Promotional Outfit
Specification: "O27" Steam Type Freight Outfit W/Smoke & Whistle
Customer: Allied Stores
Original Amount: 3,500
Factory Order Date: 6/27/1963
Date Issued: Rev 11-21-63
Date Req'd: July 17-19
Packaging: RSC Outfit Packing #5 (Units not Boxed), Except 110

Contents: 238-25 Steam Type Locomotive with Smoke; 234W-25 Whistle Tender; 6463-25 Rocket Fuel Car; 6413-25 Mercury Capsule Transport Car; 6413-4 Capsules (2); 6413-10 Envelope Packed; 6650-25 Missile Launching Flat Car; 6650-80 Missile; 6448-25 Exploding Target Range Car; 3419-250 Operating Helicopter Car; 3419-100 Operating Helicopter Complete; 6067-25 Caboose; 1013-70 Curved Track (Bundle of 12 - 1013); 1018-75 Straight Track (Bundle of 6 - 1018); 1018-7 Straight Track (Bundle of 7 - 1018); 1008-50 Uncoupling Unit; 110-1 Trestle Set; 1073-25 60-Watt Transformer; 147-25 Horn & Whistle Controller; 909-20 Smoke Fluid; 1645-15 Envelope Packed; D63-50 Accessory Catalog; 1-62 Parts Order Form; 1-63 Warranty Card; 310-62 Set of (3) Billboards; Form No. 1927 Instruction Sheet; 237-11 Instruction Sheet; 6650-92 Instruction Sheet; 3419-51 Instruction Sheet; 1646-10 Instruction Sheet; 19115-10 Instruction Sheet; 6448-14 Instruction Sheet

Boxes & Packing: 63-366 Outfit Box; 61-181 Corr. Insert; 61-182 Corr. Insert (2); 62-248 Corr. Insert; 62-264 Corr. Insert; 62-272 Corr. Insert; 63-367 Shipper for (3) (1-3)

Alternate For Outfit Contents:
Note: For 155 outfits following changes made: 1063-25 used instead of 1073-25; No 147-25 used; No 1646-10 used; (1) 19241-10 used (Instruction Sheet).

19241 (1963)	C6	C7	C8	Rarity
Complete Outfit	560	875	1,375	R5
Outfit Box no. 63-366	75	125	150	R5

Comments: In 1963, the Allied Stores conglomerate, which owned many retailers across the country, purchased two promotional outfits: nos. 19241 and 19241-500. The 19241 was likely sold through one or several of Allied's corporate-owned retailers. However, this outfit has yet to be linked to a specific store.

The 19241, a Retailer Promotional Type Ib outfit, was a higher-end offering for both Allied and Lionel in 1963. It was led by a no. 238-25 Steam Locomotive with Smoke. This new-for-1963 Scout steamer featured a two-position reversing unit, a headlight and a rubber tire as a traction aid. The early version with wide running boards was included in this outfit. Except for its 238 number, it was the same engine as a no. 237.

The space and military rolling stock included 1963 versions of carryover items. The no. 6650 Missile Launching Flat Car was introduced in 1959. The unboxed no. 6650-25 was making its final few outfit appearances in 1963.

The transition from Archbar to AAR trucks and couplers that began in 1962 continued into 1963. As part of this, Lionel sought to cut costs by introducing a non-operating AAR type. Therefore, starting in 1963, most cars equipped with AAR trucks and couplers had at least one non-operating type. For the 19241, the 6650-25 was equipped with early operating AAR trucks and couplers. The no. 234W-25 Whistle Tender had non-operating Archbar trucks and couplers, as did the no. 6067-25 Caboose. This caboose has been observed in brown or red plastic. All the other cars in this outfit came with one operating and one non-operating AAR truck and coupler.

Lionel created a new suffix for the no. 3419 Oper. Helicopter Car to indicate that it was configured with one non-operating AAR coupler. The no. 3419-250 Operating Helicopter Car was the result. It appeared only in one catalog and four promotional outfits, with a total of 9,966 cars produced.

Having only one non-operating coupler did not make the 3419-250 an exciting variation. However, the version included in this outfit was molded in a lighter shade of blue plastic. This version is much more difficult to find, a fact that is reflected in the outfit pricing. The norm for a no. 3419-100 Operating Helicopter Complete was a one-piece yellow body in 1963. This fragile helicopter was frequently lost or broken.

The no. 6448-25 Exploding Target Range Car has been observed in an all-red variation in this outfit. There is no premium for this variation because it is easily re-created. The version in this outfit had "non-slotted" sides and nubs on the roof door guide to help hold on the sides.

Obtaining all the paperwork included with the 19241 is quite a challenge because there were three operating car instruction sheets and an upgraded track layout. The no. 19115-10 Track Layout Instruction Sheet describing an elongated figure-eight track layout was used for this outfit. (See the entry for outfit no. 19115 for more information and a picture of this sheet.) All the other paperwork reflected the new 90-day warranty policy that Lionel instituted in 1963. Many of these instruction sheet versions are the most difficult ones to find.

The 19241 represented the sole listing in 1963 for the no. 1645-15 Envelope Packed. This envelope included the three wires required to connect the no. 147-25 Horn & Whistle Controller.

The no. 63-366 Tan RSC with Black Graphics outfit box was manufactured by the Mead Corporation and measured 15¾ x 14¾ x 6⅞ inches. It included four lines of data as part of the box manufacturer's certificate.

The transformer substitution of a no. 1063-25 75-Watt Transformer for a no. 1073-25 60-Watt Transformer does not affect the pricing.

An empty 19241 outfit box is fairly easy to obtain. Filling it with the correct items and paperwork requires time and effort.

CONVENTIONAL PACK
63-366 BOX
6-26-63

TOP LAYER				BOTTOM LAYER		
62-264						61-181
1008-50	6413-10			110-1 S		
6650-25 6650-80		234W-25			1013-70	
3419-250 3419-100		1018-75	6448-25 (61-182)	6463-25 (61-182)		1073-25
6413-25 1018-7	147-25			6413-4 (2)	6067-25	
				238-25		
62-248				62-272 BETWEEN LAYERS		

19241-500 (1963)	C6	C7	C8	Rarity
Complete Outfit	825	1,430	2,425	R9
Outfit Box no. 62-316	200	400	600	R9

Description: "O27" Promotional Outfit
Specification: "O27" Steam Type Freight Outfit W/Smoke & Whistle
Customer: Allied Stores
Customer/No./Price: Taubman's; LT4-441; $34.99
Original Amount: 400
Factory Order Date: 11/21/1963
Date Issued: Rev 12-2-63
Date Req'd: 11-22-63
Packaging: RSC

Contents: 237X-1 Steam Type Locomotive with Smoke; 234W-1 Whistle Tender; 6463-25 Rocket Fuel Car; 6413-25 Mercury Capsule Transport Car; 6413-4 Capsules (2); 6413-10 Envelope Packed; 6650-25 Missile Launching Flat Car; 6650-80 Missile; 6448-25 Exploding Target Range Car; 6407-25 Flat Car W/ Sterling Missile; 6407-11 Sterling Missile; 6017-25 Caboose; 1013-70 Curved Track (Bundle of 12 - 1013); 1018-5 Straight Track (Bundle of 5 - 1018) (2); 1018-30 Straight Track (Bundle of 3 - 1018); 1008-50 Uncoupling Unit; 110-1 Trestle Set; 1063-25 75-Watt Transformer; 1103-20 Envelope Packed; 310-62 Set of (3) Billboards; D63-50 Accessory Catalog; 1-62 Parts Order Form; 1-63 Warranty Card; 6650-92 Instruction Sheet; 6448-14 Instruction Sheet; 19241-10 Instruction Sheet; 19115-10 Instruction Sheet

Boxes & Packing: 62-316 Outfit Box; 61-182 Corr. Insert; 62-223 Corr. Insert; 63-311 Corr. Insert; 62-319 Shipper for (3) (1-3)

Comments: In 1963, the Allied Stores conglomerate, which owned many retailers across the country, purchased two promotional outfits: nos. 19241 and 19241-500. The 19241-500 appeared to be a late-in-the-year reorder of the 19241 with a few of the components having been updated. (See the entry for the 19241 from 1963.)

The 19241-500 was likely sold through one or several of Allied's corporate-owned retailers. Nonetheless, this outfit has yet to be linked to a specific Allied store. The closest we have come is a connection to Taubman's via a price tag stamped no. LT4-441 for $34.99. It is unknown whether Taubman's purchased the 19241-500 through Allied or direct from Lionel.

In either case, Allied was the only customer listed on the Factory Order, which is the reason this outfit is classified as a Retailer Promotional Type Ia. As with the 19241, this could be considered a higher-end offering for both Allied and Lionel in 1963.

The 19241-500 was created late in the year, and the no. 238-25 Steam Type Locomotive with Smoke used in the 19241 probably was no longer available. So Lionel used a no. 237X-1 Steam Type Locomotive With Smoke in the 19241-500. The boxed 237X-1 appeared only in four promotional outfits. This new-for-1963 Scout steamer featured a two-position reversing unit and a headlight and relied on a rubber tire as a traction aid. The harder-to-find early version with wide running boards was included in this outfit. Except for its 237 number, it was the same engine as a 238.

The 237X-1 came packaged in a difficult-to-find no. 237-10 Corrugated Box. An "X" signified that a no. CTC-1 Lockon was not included in the 237-10. Therefore, a separate no. 1103-20

The no. 19241-500 was likely a reorder of outfit no. 19241 made late in the year. Noteworthy components of the 19241-500 included the no. 6407-25 Flat Car W/Sterling Missile with its no. 6407-11 Sterling Missile and the boxed version of the no. 237X-1 Steam Type Locomotive with Smoke.

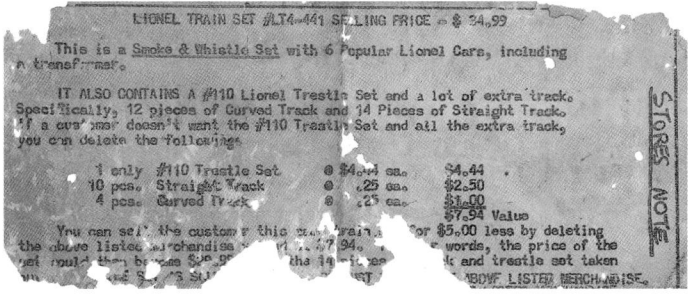

A "Stores Note" sheet from Taubman's lists the no. 19241-500 as no. LT4-441 for $34.99. The text states, "If your customer doesn't want the #110 Trestle Set, and all the extra track, you can delete the following…" Once those items were removed, the price was reduced to $29.99. Just how many outfits were cannibalized in this manner is unknown. This information explains why finding this outfit complete is difficult.

Envelope Packed was required.

As with the 19241, a no. 234W Whistle Tender was included. However, it now came packaged as a "-1" in an Orange Picture box.

The nos. 6413-25 Mercury Capsule Transport Car, 6448-25 Exploding Target Range Car, 6463-25 Rocket Fuel Car and 6650-25 Missile Launching Flat Car were the same cars and variations that Lionel added to the 19241. The only difference was that all of them now came with operating AAR trucks and couplers.

The unboxed no. 6407-25 Flat Car W/Sterling Missile (new for 1963) was included in 11 different outfits, with a total of 13,124 cars produced. This highly collectible item was also available for separate sale as a no. 6407-1. The flat car was a common red no. 6511-series model with "Lionel" stamped on each side. It featured a brake wheel plus one operating and one non-operating AAR truck and coupler. The same flat car was used with the no. 6408-25 Flat Car W/5 Pipes.

The flat car might be common, but the no. 6407-11 Sterling

Missile was not. This load, manufactured by Sterling Plastics, was frequently separated from its flat car because it lacked Lionel markings. An authentic original would have "Sterling Plastics" molded into the capsule bottom and rocket base.

The no. 6017-25 Caboose came equipped with one operating and one plain AAR truck and coupler.

A no. 19115-10 Instruction Sheet was included in both the 19241 and 19241-500. The remaining paperwork was updated to reflect the changes in the rolling stock and transformer. The warranty policy was stated as covering 90 days on the appropriate instruction sheets.

A no. 62-316 Tan RSC with Black Graphics outfit box was used with the 19241-500. It was manufactured by the Mead Corporation and measured 17⅜ x 13¼ x 6⅞ inches. It included four lines of data as part of the box manufacturer's certificate.

The 19241-500 was produced in smaller quantities than the 19241. As such, it is more desirable and harder to find than its companion.

CONVENTIONAL PACK
62-316 BOX
REVISED 12-2-63

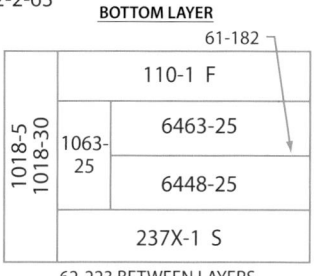

TOP LAYER		
	63-311 →	
6017-25	1018-5	
	234W-1 F	
6407-25 / 6407-11	6650-25	
	6413-25	
	1013-70	

BOTTOM LAYER		
	61-182 →	
	110-1 F	
1018-5 / 1018-30	1063-25	6463-25
		6448-25
	237X-1 S	

62-223 BETWEEN LAYERS

Description: "O27" Promotional Outfit
Specification: "O27" Steam Type Freight Outfit W/Smoke
Customer: Arkwright
Original Amount: 775
Factory Order Date: 5/15/1963
Date Issued: Rev 12-5-63
Packaging: RSC Outfit Packing #5 (Units not Boxed), Except 110 & 452

Contents: 237-25 Steam Type Locomotive with Smoke; 1060T-25 Tender; 6050-150 Van Camp Savings Bank Car; 6045-150 Tank Car; 6502-50 Girder Transport Car; 6502-3 Girder Bridge; 6042-250 Gondola Car (Without Load); 6076-75 Hopper Car - Black; 6067-25 Caboose; 1013-8 Curved Track (Bundle of 8 - 1013); 1013-90 Curved Track (Bundle of 9 - 1013); 1018-5 Straight Track (Bundle of 5 - 1018) (2); 110-1 Trestle Set; 452-1 Overhead Gantry Signal; 1025-25 45-Watt Transformer; 1103-20 Envelope Packed; 909-20 Smoke Fluid; 310-62 Set of (3) Billboards; D63-50 Accessory Catalog; 1-62 Parts Order Form; 1-63 Warranty Card; 19145-10 Instruction Sheet; 1123-40 Instruction Sheet; 237-11 Instruction Sheet; 1802I Layout Instruction Sheet

Boxes & Packing: 62-316 Outfit Box; 61-171 Corr. Insert; 61-182 Corr. Insert (2); 62-264 Corr. Insert; 63-353 Corr. Insert; 62-319 Shipper for (3) (1-3)

19242 (1963)	C6	C7	C8	Rarity
Complete Outfit	415	675	1,000	R8
Outfit Box no. 62-316	150	250	350	R8

Comments: The no. 19242 was Arkwright's (a large buying organization) promotional outfit purchase for 1963. A Retailer Promotional Type Ib, it was likely resold to Arkwright's many small customers, although no connections have been made.

The 19242 was led by a no. 237-25 Steam Type Locomotive with Smoke. This new-for-1963 Scout steamer featured a two-position reversing unit and a headlight and used a rubber tire as a traction aid. The harder-to-find early version with wide running boards was included in this outfit. Except for its 237 number, it was the same engine as a no. 238.

The 19242 featured three new cars, starting with the first outfit appearance of the unmarked blue plastic no. 6042-250 Gondola Car (Without Load). Also included were the orange no. 6045-150 Tank Car and the unmarked blue plastic no. 6502-50 Girder Transport Car with an orange girder. Even though these cars were considered new because they had new suffixes in 1963, they were just slight variations of items already in the product line. All three cars were equipped with non-operating AAR trucks and couplers.

The no. 6067-25 Caboose has been observed in the brown plastic version. It, like the no. 1060T-25 Tender, came with one non-operating and one plain Archbar truck and coupler. The remaining cars in this outfit had non-operating Archbar types.

The 19242 was one of two outfits to include a no. 452-1 Overhead Gantry Signal. Lionel was either providing something special to Arkwright or thinning existing inventory.

The no. 110-1 Trestle Set was used for the elevated pretzel track layout, which was detailed on a no. 1802I Layout Instruction Sheet. All the remaining paperwork made reference to the new 90-day warranty policy that Lionel instituted in 1963.

The no. 62-316 Tan RSC with Black Graphics outfit box measured 17⅜ x 13¼ x 6⅞ inches.

This outfit did not meet Arkwright's original expectations, as the Factory Order indicated a reduction in quantity from 1,000 to 775 on 12-5-63. While not the easiest outfit to find, the 19242 does appear from time to time.

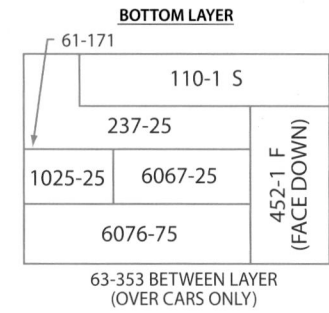

CONVENTIONAL PACK
62-316 BOX

TOP LAYER				
1013-8	6502-3 TOP 110		6042-250	1060T-25
	6050-150 (62-264)			
	6045-150			
	6502-50 1018-5 (2)			
	1013-90			
61-182	61-182			

BOTTOM LAYER	61-171		
	110-1 S		452-1 F (FACE DOWN)
	237-25		
1025-25	6067-25		
	6076-75		

63-353 BETWEEN LAYER (OVER CARS ONLY)

Description: "O27" Promotional Outfit
Specification: "O27" Steam Type Freight Outfit
Customer: Frederick Atkins
Original Amount: 700
Factory Order Date: 6/13/1963
Date Issued: Rev 9-27-63
Packaging: RSC Outfit Packing #5 (Units not Boxed)

Contents: 1062-25 Steam Type Loco. W/Light & Reversing Unit; 1061T-25 Tender; 6406-25 Flat Car W/Auto; 6406-30 Automobile; 6042-75 Gondola Car (Less 2 Cable Reels); 40-11 Cable Reels (2); 6067-25 Caboose; 1013-8 Curved Track (Bundle of 8 - 1013); 1018-10 Straight Track (Loose) (2); 1026-25 25-Watt Transformer; 1103-20 Envelope Packed; 310-2 Set of (5) Billboards; D63-50 Accessory Catalog; 1-62 Parts Order Form; 1-63 Warranty Card; 1123-40 Instruction Sheet; 11311-10 Instruction Sheet

Boxes & Packing: 61-170 Outfit Box; 61-171 Corr. Insert; 61-172 Corr. Insert; 61-173 Corr. Insert; 61-174 Shipper for (6) (1-6)

19243 (1963)	C6	C7	C8	Rarity
Complete Outfit	200	610	850	R8
Outfit Box no. 61-170	100	250	350	R8

Comments: This Retailer Promotional Type Ib outfit was sold to Frederick Atkins (see the section on Lionel's Distribution and Customers).

The no. 19243 was a low-end starter outfit led by a no. 1062-25 Steam Type Loco. W/Light & Reversing Unit. This low-end Scout steamer was new for 1963 and featured an 0-4-0 wheel arrangement and lacked a traction aid. According to its Lionel

Engineering Specification, it was the "Same as #1061 but with the addition of Reversing Unit & Lamp". It was trailed by an unmarked no. 1061T-25 Tender.

All the cars in this outfit were carryover items. The only item of note was the no. 6406-25 Flat Car W/Auto. In 1963, it began to appear in gray molded plastic. The no. 6406-30 Automobile was generally molded in brown or green plastic with gray bumpers. The specific color cannot be confirmed for this outfit. Pricing assumes either a green or brown version.

The transition from Archbar to AAR trucks and couplers that began in 1962 continued into 1963. As such, cars in this outfit could come equipped with AAR or Archbar trucks and couplers. The 1061T-25 and no. 6067-25 Caboose were equipped with one non-operating and one plain truck and coupler. All other cars were equipped with non-operating types.

The no. 61-170 Tan RSC with Black Graphics outfit box measured 11½ x 10¼ x 6¼ inches.

If it were not for the inclusion of a brown or green automobile with gray bumpers, this outfit would be just one of the numerous low-end promotional outfits from 1963. The R8 rarity of the 19243 is based on its infrequent appearance on the market.

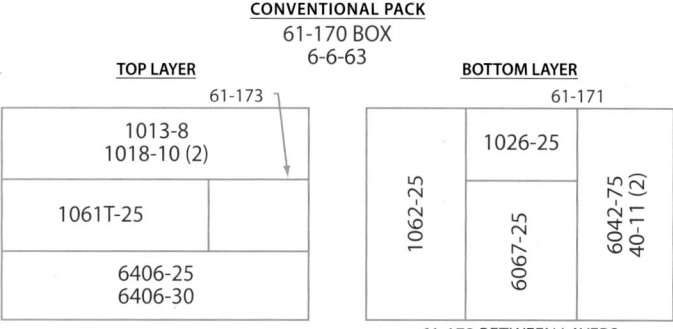

CONVENTIONAL PACK
61-170 BOX
6-6-63

TOP LAYER — 61-173: 1013-8, 1018-10 (2); 1061T-25; 6406-25, 6406-30

BOTTOM LAYER — 61-171: 1062-25; 1026-25; 6067-25; 6042-75, 40-11 (2)

61-172 BETWEEN LAYERS

Description: "O27" Promotional Outfit
Specification: "O27" Steam Type Freight Outfit
Customer/Price: A&P; $9.99
Original Amount: 31,700
Factory Order Date: 8/8/1963
Date Issued: Rev 12-2-63
Date Req'd: 9/3/63
Packaging: RSC (Units Loose)

Contents: 1061-25 Steam Type Locomotive; 1061T-25 Tender; 6042-25 Gondola Car - Blue; 6112-5 Canister (2); 6406-25 Flat Car W/Auto; 6406-30 Automobile; 6067-25 Caboose; 1013-8 Curved Track (Bundle of 8 - 1013); 1026-25 25-Watt Transformer; 40-11 Cable Reels (2); 362-78 Wood Barrels (6); 1103-20 Envelope Packed; D63-50 Accessory Catalog; 1-62 Parts Order Form; 1-63 Warranty Card; 310-62 Set of (3) Billboards (3); 1123-40 Instruction Sheet; 11311-20 Instruction Sheet; Form 2869 Printed Sheet

Boxes & Packing: 61-170 Outfit Box; 61-171 Corr. Insert; 61-172 Corr. Insert; 61-173 Corr. Insert; 61-174 Shipper for (6) (1-6); 62-246 Corr. Outfit Box; 62-247 Corr. Shipper for (4) (1-5)

Alternate For Outfit Contents:
Note: For final packing of 1,000 outfits use 62-246 Corr. Outfit Box in place of Corr. Outfit Box 61-170 and also 62-247 Corr. Shipper for (4) in place of 61-174 Corr. Shipper for (6).

19244 (1963)	C6	C7	C8	Rarity
Complete Outfit With no. 61-170 Box	190	310	500	R2
Outfit Box no. 61-170	30	60	100	R2
Complete Outfit With no. 62-246 Box	235	400	650	R8
Outfit Box no. 62-246	75	150	250	R8

Comments: The no. 19244 was A&P's only promotional outfit purchase. This Retailer Promotional Type Ib outfit was part of Lionel's strategy in 1963 to sell train outfits through large supermarket organizations. On paper, this outfit was a huge

success; after all, the Factory Orders showed an increase from 30,000 on 9-27-63 to 31,700 on 12-2-63. This was the tenth highest quantity produced of any catalog or promotional outfit in the 1960s.

Unfortunately, Lionel greatly overestimated the number of outfits that the supermarket program could sell. (See the entries for A&P and Kroger in the section on Lionel's Distribution and Customers.) Lionel *Sales Bulletin* no. 20 from June 1964 stated, "During the summer and fall of 1963, Lionel sold thousands of train and racing sets to many of the large supermarket organizations. There was a relatively heavy return on this merchandise after the first of the year...." It is estimated that 17,600 of all the 19244s were returned and became General Release Promotional outfit no. 19244 for 1964.

The 19244 was a low-end starter outfit that cost A&P $6.25 and had a suggested retail of $9.99. It was very similar to the highly successful Quaker Oats no. X-600 from 1961. Lionel was likely still touting the huge success of the X-600 when selling to new customers such as A&P. Other sales tactics included creating artwork for a mocked-up HO scale A&P box car.

A no. 1061-25 Steam Type Locomotive led this outfit. This stripped-down Scout steamer (new for 1963) featured an 0-4-0 wheel arrangement and went forward only. It lacked a headlight, a lens and any sort of traction aid. It was trailed by an unmarked no. 1061T-25 Tender.

With so many examples of the 19244 manufactured, slight variations in the rolling stock have been observed. Specifically, either gray or orange no. 40-11 Cable Reels are possible. Late in 1963, Lionel began to mold those reels in gray plastic. In fact, the production sample for the gray reels was dated 10-22-63. The gray versions are more desirable and provide a slight premium.

Another variation occurred with the no. 6067-25 Caboose. It has been observed in brown or red.

Even though the no. 6406-25 Flat Car W/Auto began to appear in gray plastic in 1963, the one packed in this outfit was Tuscan Red. The no. 6406-30 Automobile came in yellow with gray bumpers.

The transition from Archbar to AAR trucks and couplers that began in 1962 continued into 1963. As part of this, Lionel

Outfit no. 19244 was A&P's only promotional outfit purchase. It was a low-end, steam-powered outfit that contained commonly available items. Of interest was the inclusion of the nos. 40-11 Cable Reels, 362-78 Wood Barrels and 6112-5 Canisters. With so many loads, there was no room in the no. 6042-25 Gondola Car - Blue to carry them all. Although more than 14,000 of these outfits were likely sold through A&P supermarkets, Lionel produced 31,700. A&P returned the extras, which went on to become the 19244 from 1964.

Blister Display no. D-19244 was created to help sell the no. 19244 in A&P supermarkets. It was designed to be hung on a wall in the store. Note the difficult-to-find green no. 40-11 Cable Reels and absence of the no. 362-78 Wood Barrels. When this D-19244 was new and unopened, it included the barrels inside the no. 6042-25 Gondola Car - Blue.

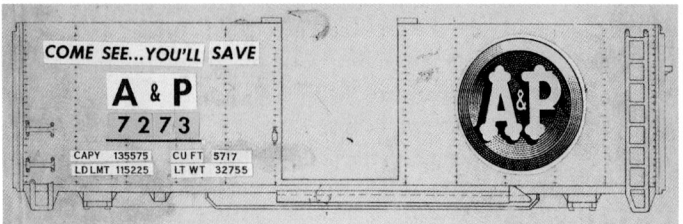

As part of the selling process, Lionel created artwork for an HO scale A&P box car. Although the car was never produced, this mock-up likely assisted in closing the deal for outfit no. 19244.

sought to cut costs by introducing a non-operating AAR type. Therefore, starting in 1963, most cars equipped with AAR trucks and couplers had at least one non-operating type. However, most of the components in the low-end 19244 came with non-operating Archbar trucks and couplers (non-operating AAR types are possible).

The Form 2869 advertising the no. 2001 Track Make-Up Kit was dated 6/63. It is one of the more difficult items to find in completing a C8 outfit.

Six no. 362-78 Wood Barrels were included with each outfit. The barrels and cable reels provided additional loads for the 6042-25 and increased the overall piece count. Unfortunately, they added little to the play value of this outfit.

Two versions of a Tan RSC with Black Graphics outfit box were used for the 19244. The first was a common no. 61-170 Outfit Box manufactured by United Container and measuring 11½ x 10¼ x 6¼ inches. It included four lines of data as part of the box manufacturer's certificate (BMC). One version was observed with a "63" and four stars and another without any additional markings as part of its BMC.

The second box was a no. 62-246 Outfit Box. It was manufactured by Mead Containers and measured 11½ x 10¼ x 6¼ inches. These were made of a thicker corrugated material (rated at 90 pounds rather than the normal 65 pounds gross weight) that allowed each outfit to be shipped in its outfit box. Also, any Lionel printing on the box top was omitted to leave room for a mailing label.

With more than 30,000 of the 19244 manufactured, it is readily available. However, finding one in a 62-246 Outfit Box is a challenge. Even tougher to find is a no. D-19244 Blister Display.

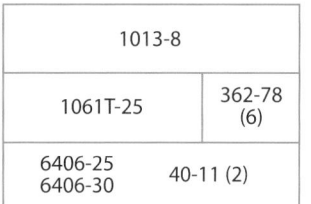
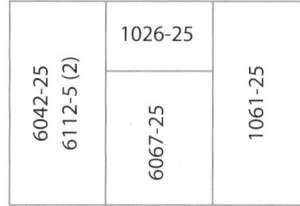

Lionel produced 1,964 of them to help supermarkets promote the 19244, and few have survived.

There are no noticeable differences between the 1963 and 1964 versions of the 19244. Lionel *Sales Bulletin* no. 20 from June of 1964 noted that "the composition of the merchandise has not been changed from 1963." Therefore, the pricing in the table applies to both the 1963 and 1964 versions.

CONVENTIONAL PACK
61-170 BOX
6-4-63

TOP LAYER | BOTTOM LAYER

1013-8			1026-25	
1061T-25	362-78 (6)	6042-25 / 6112-5 (2)	6067-25	1061-25
6406-25 6406-30	40-11 (2)			

Description: "O27" Train Set
Specification: #19244 Lionel "O27" Train Set
Customer: All Trade
Customer/No./Price: Western Auto; E5005; $10.88
Original Amount: 12,871
Packaging: RSC

Contents: 1061-25 Steam Type Locomotive; 1061T-25 Tender; 6042-25 Gondola Car - Blue; 6112-5 Canister (2); 6406-25 Flat Car W/Auto; 6406-30 Automobile; 6067-25 Caboose; 1013-8 Curved Track (Bundle of 8 - 1013); 1026-25 25-Watt Transformer; 40-11 Cable Reels (2); 362-78 Wood Barrels (6); 1103-20 Envelope Packed; 1-62 Parts Order Form; 1-63 Warranty Card; 310-62 Set of (3) Billboards (3); 1123-40 Instruction Sheet; 11311-20 Instruction Sheet; Form 2869 Printed Sheet

Boxes & Packing: 61-170 Outfit Box; 61-171 Corr. Insert; 61-172 Corr. Insert; 61-173 Corr. Insert; 61-174 Shipper for (6) (1-6); 62-246 Corr. Outfit Box; 62-247 Corr. Shipper for (4) (1-5)

Comments: The no. 19244 from 1964 was identical to the 1963 version. Keep in mind that they were nothing more than the 19244 outfits that A&P returned to Lionel. (See the entry for the 19244 from 1963.)

With so many outfits returned, Lionel was doing whatever it could to sell these trains. It turned the 19244 and no. D-19244 into General Release Promotional Type IIb outfits. They were listed on Lionel *Sales Bulletin* no. 12 from May 8, 1964, which stated, "The following represents fourteen (14) sets you may offer at your discretion to accounts in your territory". The no. 19244's cost to retailers was still $6.25.

One taker was Western Auto, which purchased the 19244 and listed it in the firm's 1964 Christmas Gifts Catalog as no. E5005 for $10.88.

The quantity of 12,871 listed for the 19244 from 1964 represented the number of outfits released to customers on August 4, 1964. These were likely part of the estimated 17,600 outfits returned from A&P rather than new production.

There are no noticeable differences between the 1963 or 1964 versions. As such, the pricing is the same as the 1963 version.

(2) Wow! Look What This Low W.A. Price Buys . . . Exciting Lionel 5-Unit Steam Train! Budget price but ruggedly designed and made by world-famous Lionel! Steam-type locomotive, tender, flat car with "piggy back" auto; gondola car with 2 cable reels and six barrels, and caboose. 8 sections of curved & straight track. CTC lock-on. 25-watt power transformer. Young "Casey-Jones" will love to send this Christmas thriller zipping 'round the track! $1 holds in layaway now at W.A.! E5005

Outfit no. 19244 was illustrated in the Western Auto Christmas Gifts Catalog for 1964 as no. E5005 for $10.88. It is shown with gray no. 40-11 Cable Reels, which first appeared in late 1963 and were carried over into 1964. The six no. 362-78 Wood Barrels are not shown, but are listed in the description.

Description: "O27" Freight
Specification: 5 Unit Steam Freighter
Customer: Super Markets
Original Amount: 10,000
Factory Order Date: 10/8/1964
Date Issued: 10-8-64
Date Req'd: 10-20-64
Packaging: RSC 6 to shipper

Contents: 1061-50 Steam Loco With Tire; 1061T-50 Tender; 6042-25 Gondola Car - Blue; 6112-5 Canister (2); 6502-50 Girder Transport Car; 6067-25 Caboose; 1026-25 25-Watt Transformer; 1013 Curved Track (8); 1103-20 Envelope Packed; 1-65 Warranty

Card; Form 3063 Parts Order Form; 11311-20 Instruction Sheet; D64-50 Accessory Catalog; 927-64 Service Station List

Boxes & Packing: 62-246 Outfit Box; 62-246 Corr. Shipper for 4 (1-4)

Alternate For Outfit Contents:
Note: Sub cars where necessary as long as appearance is the same; Do not sub. load; 6067-25 Sub. 6167-75; 6067-25 Sub. 6167-50.

19244-500 (1964)	C6	C7	C8	Rarity
Complete Outfit As Listed	100	185	275	R5
Complete Outfit With Either Caboose Substitution	105	195	290	R5
Outfit Box no. 62-246	50	100	150	R5

LIONEL 5-UNIT STEAM FREIGHTER
Complete and Ready to Run

VALUE PACKED...FOR HIGH VOLUME SALES

No. 19244-500

GREAT FUN FOR THE WHOLE FAMILY!

No. 19244 - 500
LIONEL STEAM FREIGHTER OUTFIT INCLUDES:

* No. 1061 Steam Loco w/Rail-Gripper Wheels
* No. 1061T Slope-Back Steam Tender
* No. 6042 Gondola with 2 Canisters
* No. 6502-50 Flat Car with Girder
* No. 6067-25 Caboose
* No. 1013 Curved Track (8 sections)
* CTC - Lockon
* No. 1026 U.L. Approved Transformer
* Wires and Instruction Sheet

Now model railroaders of all ages can share the excitement of owning their very own Lionel train...now at a new low price! This mighty steam freighter outfit comes complete and is chock-full of Lionel "exclusives": knuckle couplers, sturdy rolling stock, authentic detailing and Rail-Gripper wheels on the locomotive for greater traction. To insure "full-power" this Lionel outfit includes a mighty U.L. approved transformer guaranteeing many happy hours of model railroading fun and action.

Promote and profit with Lionel!

Lionel's sales brochure for the no. 19244-500 touted it as "Great Fun For The Whole Family!"

Comments: The no. 19244-500, a Retailer Promotional Type Ib outfit, was created for Lionel's supermarket customers. It is unknown why Lionel would create another supermarket outfit after the large number of returns for supermarket outfit nos. 19244 and 19253 from 1963.

At first glance, one could assume that the 19244-500 was made up of leftover inventory of the 19244 and 19253. However, observations of actual outfits and close examination of suffixes indicated otherwise. All the items included in the 19244-500

were 1964 vintage, being equipped with at least one late non-operating AAR truck and coupler. Thus, the components were new production for 1964.

Maybe after the unfortunate 1963 supermarket program, Lionel learned from its mistakes and there was sufficient new supermarket business to justify producing this outfit.

The 19244-500 was led by a no. 1061-50 Steam Type Loco W/Tire (new for 1964). This version came with a rubber tire as a traction aid, a feature that made it a slight upgrade of the no. 1061-25 Steam Type Locomotive. Even with this improvement, the 1061-50 (lacking a headlight and a lens) remained Lionel's low-end Scout steamer configured with an 0-4-0 wheel arrangement.

Lionel upgraded the no. 1061T-25 Tender in 1964 by adding Lionel Lines to each side. The result was the no. 1061T-50 Tender equipped with one late non-operating and one plain AAR truck and coupler.

All the rolling stock in this outfit was 1964 production of carryover items. The unmarked no. 6502-50 Girder Transport Car was a blue plastic version of the black no. 6502-25 Girder Transport Car that was first issued in 1962. The no. 6502-3 Girder Bridge was black. The no. 6042-25 Gondola Car - Blue had "6042" stamped on each side. All the cars as listed came with late non-operating AAR trucks and couplers.

According to the Alternates section of the Factory Order, Lionel freely substituted cars as needed. Outfits have been observed with a blue no. 6142-125 Gondola Car with "6142" stamped on each side. It was equipped with one late non-operating and one middle operating AAR truck and coupler. Also, an unboxed no. 6167-75 Union Pacific Caboose has been observed with one middle non-operating and one plain AAR truck and coupler. This model and the unmarked yellow no. 6167-50 Caboose listed as a substitution add a premium, as listed in the pricing table.

The 19244-500 used the no. 62-246 Tan RSC Mailer with Black Graphics outfit box. It was manufactured by Mead Containers and measured 11½ x 10¼ x 6¼ inches. These boxes were made of a thicker corrugated material (rated at 90 pounds rather than the normal 65 pounds gross weight) that allowed each outfit to be shipped in its own box. The manufacturer omitted any Lionel printing on the box top to leave room for a mailing label.

With 10,000 manufactured, the 19244-500 should appear more often that it does. Its R5 rarity is based on its infrequent appearance on the market. The most desirable versions of this outfit have one of the caboose substitutions.

Description: "O27" Promotional Outfit
Specification: "O27" Steam Type Freight Outfit
Customer: Gamble-Skogmo
Original Amount: 2,000
Factory Order Date: 8/28/1963
Date Issued: Rev 9-27-63
Date Req'd: 9-3-63
Packaging: RSC (Units Loose)

Contents: 1062-25 Steam Type Loco. W/Light & Reversing Unit; 1061T-25 Tender; 6042-75 Gondola Car (Less 2 Cable Reels);

40-11 Cable Reels (2); 6502-50 Girder Transport Car; 6502-3 Girder Bridge; 6076-100 Hopper Car - Gray; 3410-25 Oper. Helicopter Car (Less Helicopter); 3419-100 Operating Helicopter Complete; 6067-25 Caboose; 1013-70 Curved Track (Bundle of 12 - 1013); 1018-40 Straight Track (Bundle of 4 - 1018); 1020-25 90° Crossing; 1010-25 35-Watt Transformer; 1103-20 Envelope Packed; D63-50 Accessory Catalog; 1-62 Parts Order Form; 1-63 Warranty Card; 310-2 Set of (5) Billboards; 19223-10 Instruction Sheet; 3410-5 Instruction Sheet

Boxes & Packing: 62-243 Outfit Box; 61-173 Corr. Insert; 62-223 Corr. Insert; 62-254 Corr. Insert; 62-264 Corr. Insert; 62-244 Shipper for (4) (1-4)

19245 (1963)	C6	C7	C8	Rarity
Complete Outfit	260	420	625	R6
Outfit Box no. 62-243	100	150	200	R6

Comments: Discount retailer Gamble-Skogmo purchased the no. 19245, a Retailer Promotional Type Ib outfit, in 1963. Two years later, Lionel reissued this outfit after making some slight changes. (See the entry for the 19245 from 1965.)

When released in 1963, the 19245 was led by a no. 1062-25 Steam Type Loco. W/Light & Reversing Unit. This low-end Scout steamer was new for 1963 and featured an 0-4-0 wheel arrangement and lacked a traction aid. According to its Lionel Engineering Specification, it was the "Same as #1061 but with the addition of Reversing Unit & Lamp". The 1062-25 was trailed by an unmarked no. 1061T-25 Tender.

The unmarked no. 6076-100 Hopper Car - Gray and unmarked no. 6502-50 Girder Transport Car were new for 1963. The latter model was a blue plastic version of the black no. 6502-25 Girder Transport Car that Lionel first issued in 1962.

The no. 3410-25 Oper. Helicopter Car (Less Helicopter) was making its final outfit appearances in 1963 and 1964. The norm for a no. 3419-100 Operating Helicopter Complete was a one-piece yellow body in 1963. This fragile helicopter was frequently lost or broken.

The transition from Archbar to AAR trucks and couplers that began in 1962 continued into 1963. As part of this, Lionel sought to cut costs by introducing a non-operating AAR type. Therefore, starting in 1963, most cars equipped with AAR trucks and couplers

had at least one non-operating type. For the 19245, the norm for the no. 3410-25 was one operating and one non-operating AAR truck and coupler. The remaining cars in this outfit generally came with non-operating Archbar trucks and couplers although AAR types were possible.

A figure-eight track layout was outlined on the no. 19223-10 Instruction Sheet.

The no. 62-243 Tan RSC with Black Graphics outfit box measured 12⅛ x 11½ x 6⅜ inches.

The 1963 and 1965 versions of the 19245 used the same outfit box. Therefore, the combined quantity of 2,075 is used to determine the rarity and pricing of both outfit boxes. With 2,075 examples manufactured, the 19245 is possible to obtain, but it takes patience to find a complete outfit in C8 condition.

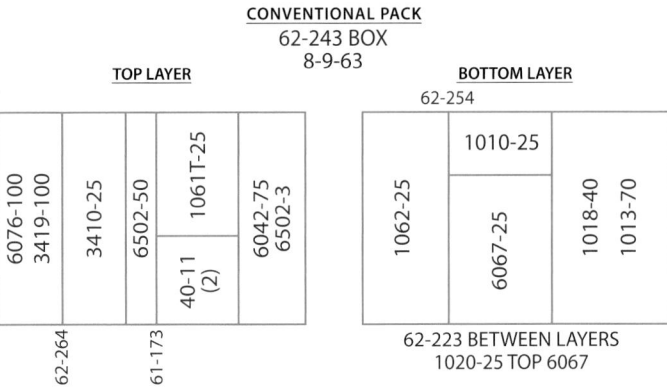

Description: "O27" Promotional Outfit
Specification: "O27" Steam Type Freight Outfit
Original Amount: 75
Factory Order Date: 9/27/1965
Date Issued: Rev 11-1-65
Packaging: (Units not Boxed)

Contents: 1062-25 Steam Type Loco. W/Light & Reversing Unit; 1061T-25 Tender; 6042-75 Gondola Car (Less 2 Cable Reels); 40-11 Cable Reels (2); 6502-50 Girder Transport Car; 6502-3 Girder Bridge; 6076-100 Hopper Car - Gray; 3510-25 Satellite Launching Car; 6067-25 Caboose; 1013-70 Curved Track (Bundle of 12 - 1013) (12); 1018-40 Straight Track (Bundle of 4 - 1018); 1020-25 90° Crossing; 1010-25 35-Watt Transformer; 1103-20 Envelope Packed; D65-50 Accessory Catalog; Form 3063 Parts Order Form; 1-165 Warranty Card; 926-65 Service Station List; 3510-5 Instruction Sheet; 19171-10 Instruction Sheet

Boxes & Packing: 62-243 Outfit Box; 61-173 Corr. Insert; 62-223 Corr. Insert; 62-254 Corr. Insert; 62-264 Corr. Insert; 62-244 Shipper for 4 (1-4)

Alternate For Outfit Contents:
Note: Sub. 6142-75 for 6042-75; Sub. 6476-75 for 6076-100; Sub. 6059-50 for 6067-25.

19245 (1965)	C6	C7	C8	Rarity
Complete Outfit	290	465	660	R6
Outfit Box no. 62-243	100	150	200	R6

Comments: A Factory Order for 75 of the no. 19245 was issued in 1965 with no customer listed. This General Release Promotional Type IIb outfit was a repeat of the 19245 from 1963. (See the entry for the 19245 from 1963.) The reason a new Factory Order was created two years after the 19245 last appeared is unknown. All that can be determined is that Lionel still had 10 outfits in inventory on October 30, 1965.

The two versions of the 19245 were nearly identical. The outfit from 1965 included slight upgrades to some pieces of rolling stock as well as the appropriate paperwork for 1965. Both outfits were led by a no. 1062-25 Steam Type Loco. W/Light & Reversing Unit as well as a no. 1061T-25 Tender.

All but one of the pieces of rolling stock included in the outfit from 1963 were replaced by similar items two years later. The exception was the no. 6502-50 Girder Transport Car.

Because the nos. 6076-100 Hopper Car - Gray and 3410-25 Oper. Helicopter Car (Less Helicopter) were no longer available in 1965, Lionel replaced them with the nos. 6476-75 Hopper Car - Black and 3510-25 Satellite Launching Car, respectively. Employees probably searched high and low at the factory to find 75 of the latter two cars because the 6476-75 had last appeared in an outfit in 1962 and the 3510-25 in 1964. The 19245 represented the final outfit appearance for both of them.

The 3510-25 appeared only in 10 promotional outfits. It featured a red frame and had "Lionel" stamped on each side; its mechanism was an exact duplicate of that on the no. 3509-25 Satellite Launching Car. The 3510-25 was equipped with non-operating Archbar trucks and couplers.

The 1965 version of the 19245 had a couple of other changes. A no. 6142-75 Gondola Car replaced the no. 6042-75 Gondola Car, and a no. 6059-50 Caboose took the place of the 6067-25 Caboose. These two substitutions, like all the rolling stock in this outfit but the Satellite Launching Car, typically came with late AAR trucks and couplers.

A figure-eight track layout was outlined on the no. 19171-10 Instruction Sheet.

19246
1963

Description: "O27" Promotional Outfit
Specification: "O27" Steam Type Freight Outfit with Smoke
Customer: Independent Retailers Syndicate
Original Amount: 37
Factory Order Date: 8/19/1963
Date Issued: Rev 9-27-63
Date Req'd: 8/19/63
Packaging: RSC (Units Loose)

Contents: 237-25 Steam Type Locomotive with Smoke; 1060T-25 Tender; 6500-25 Beechcraft Bonanza Transport Car; 6473-25 Rodeo Car; 6014-325 Frisco Box Car; 6476-25 Hopper Car - Red; 6067-25 Caboose; 1013-70 Curved Track (Bundle of 12 - 1013); 1018-5 Straight Track (Bundle of 5 - 1018) (2); 1018-30 Straight Track (Bundle of 3 - 1018); 1008-50 Uncoupling Unit; 110-1 Trestle Set; 1073-25 60-Watt Transformer; 1103-20 Envelope Packed; 909-20 Smoke Fluid; 310-2 Set of (5) Billboards; D63-50 Accessory Catalog; 1-62 Parts Order Form; 1-63 Warranty Card; 237-11 Instruction Sheet; 1123-40 Instruction Sheet; 6500-3 Instruction Sheet; 19115-10 Instruction Sheet; 122-10 Instruction Sheet

Boxes & Packing: 62-270 Outfit Box; 61-181 Corr. Insert; 61-182 Corr. Insert (2); 62-264 Corr. Insert (2); 62-272 Corr. Insert; 62-271 Shipper for (3) (1-3)

19246 (1963)	C6	C7	C8	Rarity
Complete Outfit	2,400	3,100	3,700	R10
Outfit Box no. 62-270	1,800	2,250	2,500	R10

Comments: The Factory Order for this outfit listed the customer as IRS, which was better known as Independent Retailers Syndicate, a privately held buying cooperative in New York. That firm purchased only two Retailer Promotional outfits: nos. X-682 and 19246. Both were purchased in extremely small quantities: 24 and 37, respectively. Neither outfit has been linked to a specific end retailer. Most likely, IRS just used them internally.

The 19246, a Type Ib, was led by a no. 237-25 Steam Type Locomotive with Smoke. This new-for-1963 Scout steamer featured a two-position reversing unit and a headlight and used a rubber tire as a traction aid. The harder-to-find early version with wide running boards was included in this outfit. Except for its 237 number, it was the same engine as a no. 238.

The no. 6014-325 Frisco Box Car was the only new piece of rolling stock in this outfit. It came with one operating and one non-operating AAR truck and coupler.

The no. 62-243 Tan RSC with Black Graphics outfit box measured 12⅛ x 11½ x 6⅜ inches.

Even though only 75 of the 1965 version of the 19245 were manufactured, the 1963 and 1965 versions used the same outfit box. Therefore, the combined quantity of 2,075 is used to determine the rarity and pricing of both outfit boxes. With 2,075 manufactured, the box is possible to obtain, but it takes patience to find a complete outfit in C8 condition.

In 1963, Lionel was depleting its remaining inventory of the unboxed no. 6500-25 Beechcraft Bonanza Transport Car in promotional outfits. This model, equipped with operating AAR trucks and couplers, made one of its five promotional outfit appearances in the 19246.

In 1963, the norm for a no. 6473-25 Rodeo Car was a Type IIb body type (cadmium yellow plastic with red lettering) as well as one operating and one non-operating AAR truck and coupler. This description probably fit the model packed in each 19246.

The transition from Archbar to AAR trucks and couplers that began in 1962 continued into 1963. As part of this, Lionel sought to cut costs by introducing a non-operating AAR type. Therefore, starting in 1963, most cars equipped with AAR trucks and couplers had at least one non-operating type. In 1963, it was possible for the no. 6476-25 Hopper Car - Red to come with either operating AAR trucks and couplers or one operating and one non-operating AAR types. The nos. 1060T-25 Tender and 6067-25 Caboose could be equipped with either one non-operating and one plain Archbar truck and coupler or AAR types.

The no. 19115-10 Track Layout Instruction Sheet describing an elongated figure-eight track layout was used for this outfit. (See the entry for outfit no. 19115 for more information and a picture of this sheet.) The nos. 237-11 Instruction Sheet and 122-10 Instruction Sheet made reference to the new 90-day warranty policy that Lionel instituted in 1963.

The no. 62-270 Tan RSC with Black Graphics outfit box measured 15½ x 14 x 6¼ inches.

Lionel made so few of this outfit – it ranks ninth in terms of smallest quantity – that the 19246 stands as one of the rarest promotional outfits. Collectors who desire every outfit manufactured or search for one-of-a-kind items would easily pay the listed price to own a 19246.

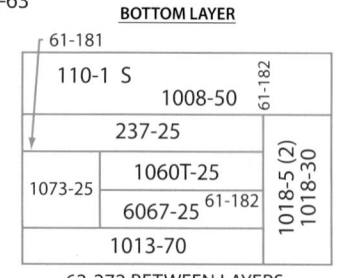

CONVENTIONAL PACK
62-270 BOX
8-12-63

TOP LAYER — BOTTOM LAYER

Outfit no. 19247 was Joe, The Motorists' Friend's low-end steam-powered purchase for 1963. It came with the desirable no. 6410-25 Flat Car W/2 Autos. The model included with the outfit shown here was stamped "Lionel" on its sides (technically making it a no. 6409-25) and came with two brown no. 6406-30 Automobiles with gray bumpers.

Description: "O27" Promotional Outfit
Specification: "O27" Steam Type Freight Outfit
Customer: Joe, The Motorists' Friend
Original Amount: 750
Factory Order Date: 6/18/1963
Date Issued: Rev 9-27-63
Date Req'd: W/O 7/15/63
Packaging: RSC Outfit Packing #5 (Units not Boxed)

Contents: 1061-25 Steam Type Locomotive; 1061T-25 Tender; 6410-25 Flat Car W/2 Autos; 6406-30 Automobile (2); 6042-25 Gondola Car - Blue; 6112-5 Canister (2); 6067-25 Caboose; 1013-8 Curved Track (Bundle of 8 - 1013); 1018-10 Straight Track (Loose) (2); 1026-25 25-Watt Transformer; 1103-20 Envelope Packed; 310-2 Set of (5) Billboards; D63-50 Accessory Catalog; 1-62 Parts Order Form; 1-63 Warranty Card; 1123-40 Instruction Sheet; 11311-20 Instruction Sheet

Boxes & Packing: 61-170 Outfit Box; 61-171 Corr. Insert; 61-172 Corr. Insert; 61-173 Corr. Insert; 61-174 Shipper for (6) (1-6)

Alternate For Outfit Contents:
Substitute 6409-25 for 6410-25 as needed.

19247 (1963)	C6	C7	C8	Rarity
Complete Outfit	715	925	1,175	R8
Outfit Box no. 61-170	175	275	350	R8

Comments: In 1963, Joe, The Motorists' Friend purchased five Lionel outfits: nos. 19247 through 19251. The 19247 and no. 19249 were low-end offerings; the other outfits were higher-end offerings containing some of Lionel's upgraded motive power and rolling stock.

The 19247 was Joe, The Motorists' Friend's low-end steam-powered offering for 1963. It was a Retailer Promotional Type Ib outfit led by a no. 1061-25 Steam Type Locomotive (new for 1963). This stripped-down Scout steamer featured an 0-4-0 wheel arrangement and went forward only. It lacked a headlight, a lens and any sort of traction aid. It was trailed by an unmarked no. 1061T-25 Tender that was equipped with one non-operating and one plain AAR truck and coupler.

This was the second of five desirable promotional outfits to include a no. 6410-25 Flat Car W/2 Autos. This model was nothing more than a red no. 6511-series flat car with no markings or a brake wheel.

Outfit Factory Orders indicated that Lionel produced a total of 6,680 of the 6410-25. Until this point, however, the Lionel part number and the quantity produced had not been documented, which meant collectors did not know that this model was a 6410-25. Now that it has been documented, hobbyists will search for this unique car to complete their collections.

Lionel freely substituted a no. 6409-25 Flat Car Complete for the 6410-25. The two cars were largely identical (both typically came with non-operating AAR trucks and couplers, although examples of the 6410-25 with non-operating Archbar types are known). Keep in mind, however, that the 6409-25 had "Lionel" stamped on each of its sides.

The two no. 6406-30 Automobiles in this outfit were brown with gray bumpers. The brown automobiles are highly desirable and are reflected in the outfit pricing.

The no. 6042-25 Gondola Car - Blue was equipped with non-operating AAR trucks and couplers. The no. 6067-25 Caboose was molded in brown plastic and included one non-operating and one plain Archbar truck and coupler.

The no. 61-170 Tan RSC with Black Graphics outfit box was manufactured by United Container and measured 11½ x 10¼ x 6¼ inches. It included four lines of data as part of the box

manufacturer's certificate (BMC). One version was observed with a "63" and four stars as part of its BMC.

Of the five Joe, The Motorists' Friend outfits from 1963, the 19246 was produced in the largest quantities. Examples do appear on the market, although they usually show up without their brown automobiles.

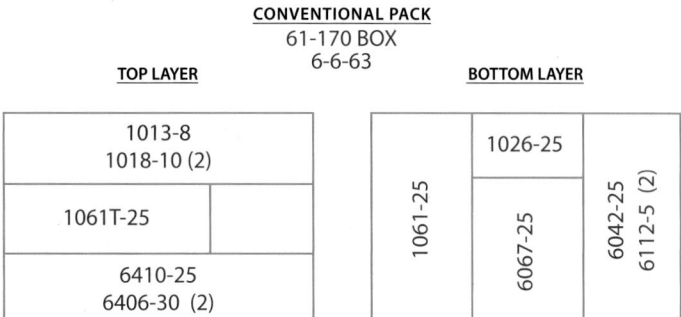

CONVENTIONAL PACK
61-170 BOX
6-6-63

TOP LAYER		BOTTOM LAYER			
1013-8 1018-10 (2)			1026-25		
1061T-25		1061-25	6067-25	6042-25	6112-5 (2)
6410-25 6406-30 (2)					

19248
1963

Description: "O27" Promotional Outfit
Specification: "O27" Switcher Freight Outfit
Customer: Joe, The Motorists' Friend
Original Amount: 100
Factory Order Date: 6/13/1963
Date Issued: 6-17-63
Date Req'd: 8/26/63
Packaging: RSC Outfit Packing (Units Boxed)

Contents: 634-1 "Santa Fe" Diesel Switcher; 6476-85 Hopper Car; 6014-335 Frisco Box Car; 3410-1 Oper. Helicopter Launching Car (Manually); 6463-1 Rocket Fuel Car; 6059-1 Caboose; 1013-8 Curved Track (Bundle of 8 - 1013); 1018-10 Straight Track (Loose); 6029-1 Uncoupling Track Connector; 1010-1 35-Watt Transformer; 310-2 Set of (5) Billboards; D63-50 Accessory Catalog; 1-62 Parts Order Form; 1-63 Warranty Card; 1123-40 Instruction Sheet; 11341-20 Instruction Sheet

Boxes & Packing: 61-380 Outfit Box; 61-381 Shipper for (4) (1-4)

19248 (1963)	C6	C7	C8	Rarity
Complete Outfit	1,500	2,500	3,500	R10
Outfit Box no. 61-380	700	1,000	1,300	R10

Comments: In 1963, Joe, The Motorists' Friend purchased five Lionel outfits: nos. 19247 through 19251. The nos. 19248, 19250 and 19251 were higher-end offerings containing some of Lionel's upgraded motive power and rolling stock. The other two were low-end outfits.

The 19248 was Joe, The Motorists' Friend's mid-level diesel-powered offering for 1963. It was a Retailer Promotional Type Ib outfit led by a no. 634-1 Santa Fe Diesel Switcher (new for 1963). According to its Lionel Engineering Specification, the 634 was the same as a 633 but a dummy front coupler had been added. It included a two-position reversing unit, a headlight and a rubber tire as a traction aid. The 1963 version had yellow-painted safety

stripes and lacked additional weights.

The boxed no. 6014-335 Frisco Box Car was the only new piece of rolling stock in this outfit. It came with one operating and one non-operating AAR truck and coupler.

The boxed no. 3410-1 Oper. Helicopter Launching Car (Manually) was making its final outfit appearance in 1963. The norm for 1963 was for it to come equipped with one operating and one non-operating AAR truck and coupler. Also the norm for a no. 3419-100 Operating Helicopter Complete was a one-piece yellow body in 1963. However, the boxed 3410 in this outfit might have been sitting in stock for a couple of years; therefore, a gray 3419-100 was possible. This fragile helicopter was frequently lost or broken.

All the remaining cars were equipped with AAR trucks and couplers that followed the typical progression.

The 19248 stands out as a collector's treasure because it was one of the few promotional outfits from 1963 that boasted all boxed items. Joe, The Motorists' Friend purchased only 100 of these outfits and likely requested individually boxed items.

The boxed 634-1 and 6014-335 first appeared on this Factory Order. With only 100 orders, it is highly unlikely that Lionel printed unique boxes. Specific boxes for these two items do exist, although they did not appear until 1964 and 1965, respectively. To add to the confusion, the 634-1 box from 1965 was overstickered with a white label, although this has been proved to be 1965 production. Lionel probably used overstamped boxes for the 634-1 and 6014-335 to fulfill the 19248's factory order; however, this conclusion has not yet been verified.

Also of interest was the listing of a boxed no. 6476-85 Hopper Car. The box used for the 6476-85 is unknown. Both a Bold Classic box and a Late Classic box exist for this car, but which was used in the 19248 – or whether Lionel opted for an overstamped box – has yet to be ascertained.

The Orange Picture no. 3410-10 Folding Box is difficult to obtain. The no. 3410-1 was never offered for separate sale. Therefore, the only way to obtain a boxed version was through a promotional outfit, and it appeared boxed in only eight outfits.

An orange box with "Lionel Electric Trains" and a lion printed on the top and bottom was used for the no. 6029-1 Uncoupling Track Section. This box is rare and adds substantial value to this

Lionel's no. 19248 was Joe, The Motorists' Friend's mid-level diesel purchase for 1963. With only 100 manufactured, it is a very difficult outfit to find. The 19248 marked the first time that the nos. 634-1 Santa Fe Diesel Switcher and 6014-335 Frisco Box Car were listed with individual boxes. Also of note was the boxed no. 6476-85 Hopper Car. Unfortunately, the outfit shown here came without these rare individual boxes.

outfit.

Finally, the 19248 was the only outfit to list a boxed no. 1010-1 Transformer. It came in a no. 12-142 Corr. Box. All the other items were packaged in Orange Picture boxes.

The no. 61-380 Tan RSC with Black Graphics outfit box was manufactured by St. Joe Kraft, St. Joe Paper Company and measured 13¾ x 14 x 5⅛ inches. It had "61-380" printed on the bottom.

Even though this was the mid-level diesel offering for Joe, The Motorists' Friend, the 19248 ranks as one of the top promotional outfits due to its interesting individual-item boxes. The outfit box is very difficult to find, but finding the correct individual-item boxes could take years.

CONVENTIONAL PACK
61-380 BOX
6-6-63

TOP LAYER					BOTTOM LAYER			
1018-10	6014-335 F	6463-1 F	6059-1 F		634-1 S	3410-1 F	1013-8	6476-85 F
	6029-1 S					1010-1		

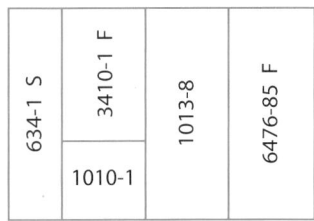

19249
1963

Description: "O27" Promotional Outfit
Specification: "O27" Diesel Freight Outfit
Customer: Joe, The Motorists' Friend
Original Amount: 193
Factory Order Date: 6/14/1963
Date Issued: Rev 10-30-63
Date Req'd: 8/26/63
Packaging: RSC Outfit Packing - #5 (Units not Boxed)

Contents: 211P-150 *"Texas Special"* Diesel; 211T-25 *"Texas Special"* Motorless Unit; 6076-25 Hopper Car; 6042-75 Gondola Car (Less 2 Cable Reels); 40-11 Cable Reels (2); 6502-25 Girder Transport Car; 6502-3 Girder Bridge; 6050-50 Swift Savings Bank Car; 6067-25 Caboose; 1013-8 Curved Track (Bundle of 8 - 1013); 1018-40 Straight Track (Bundle of 4 - 1018); 1010-25 35-Watt Transformer; 1103-20 Envelope Packed; 310-2 Set of (5) Billboards; D63-50 Accessory Catalog; 1-62 Parts Order Form; 1-63 Warranty Card; 1123-40 Instruction Sheet; 211-151 Instruction Sheet; 19145-10 Instruction Sheet

Boxes & Packing: 62-243 Outfit Box; 62-223 Corr. Insert; 62-224 Corr. Insert; 62-225 Corr. Insert (2); 62-245 Corr. Insert (2); 62-248 Corr. Insert; 62-249 Corr. Insert; 62-244 Shipper for (4) (1-4)

Alternate For Outfit Contents:
Note: Substitute 6050-100 for 6050-50; Substitute 6502-50 for 6502-25; Substitute 24 - 6076-100 for 6076-25.

19249 (1963)	C6	C7	C8	Rarity
Complete Outfit With nos. 6502-50 And 6050-100 Substitutions	625	975	1,300	R10
Outfit Box no. 62-243	450	650	800	R10

Comments: In 1963, Joe, The Motorists' Friend purchased five Lionel outfits: nos. 19247 through 19251. The 19247 and no. 19249 were low-end offerings; the others outfits were higher-end offerings containing some of Lionel's upgraded motive power and rolling stock.

Lionel's no. 19249 was Joe, The Motorists' Friend's entry-level diesel purchase for 1963. With only 193 manufactured, its outfit box is difficult to find in collectible condition. Don't overlook the brown no. 40-11 Cable Reels.

The 19249 was Joe, The Motorists' Friend's entry-level diesel-powered offering for 1963. It was a Retailer Promotional Type Ib outfit led by a no. 211P-150 *Texas Special* Diesel. The 211P-150 was a cost-reduced version of the no. 211P-25 *Texas Special* Alco Diesel Power Unit. The "-150" was new for 1963 and featured a two-position reversing unit, two traction tires, a headlight, a weight and an open pilot with a large ledge. The "-150" variation has not stirred much interest in the collector community.

All the rolling stock in this outfit was carryover from earlier years. In the case of two cars – nos. 6050-50 Swift Savings Bank Car and 6502-25 Girder Transport Car – newer versions took their place. These substitutions were, respectively, the nos. 6050-100 Swift Savings Bank Car and 6502-50 Girder Transport Car.

The 6050-100 was equipped with one operating and one non-operating AAR truck and coupler, as opposed to the non-operating Archbar trucks and couplers on the 6050-50. The unmarked 6502-50 was a blue plastic version of the black no. 6502-25 Girder Transport Car that Lionel first issued in 1962 (both came with non-operating Archbar trucks and couplers). The model's no. 6502-3 Girder Bridge was orange. The outfit price table includes the 6050-100 and 6502-50 substitutions.

The no. 6042-75 Gondola Car (Less 2 Cable Reels) was equipped with non-operating AAR trucks and couplers. Late in 1962, Lionel began to mold the no. 40-11 Cable Reels in brown plastic. In fact, the production sample for brown reels was dated 11-7-62. This outfit has been observed with these harder-to-find reels.

A brown version of the no. 6067-25 Caboose was included with the 19249. Both it and the no. 6076-25 Hopper Car were equipped with non-operating Archbar trucks and couplers. The substitution of an unmarked no. 6076-100 Hopper Car - Gray minimally affects the price. It came with non-operating AAR trucks and couplers.

The paperwork reflected the new 90-day warranty policy that Lionel instituted in 1963. The no. 19145-10 Instruction Sheet made reference to the 90-day warranty, but it was still dated 7-62.

The no. 62-243 Tan RSC with Black Graphics outfit box was manufactured by the Mead Corporation and measured 12⅛ x 11½ x 6⅜ inches. It included four lines of data as part of the box manufacturer's certificate.

The Factory Order for the 19249 originally listed a quantity of 169 outfits. This was increased to 193 on 10-30-63. With so few units produced, this outfit remains a difficult one to find.

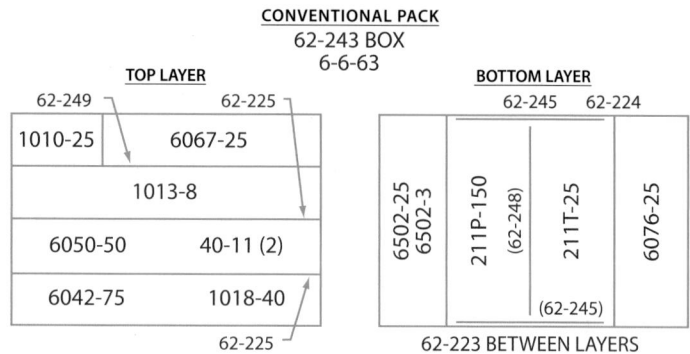

CONVENTIONAL PACK
62-243 BOX
6-6-63

TOP LAYER	
62-249	62-225
1010-25	6067-25
1013-8	
6050-50	40-11 (2)
6042-75	1018-40
62-225	

BOTTOM LAYER				
	62-245		62-224	
6502-25 6502-3	211P-150 (62-248)	211T-25	6076-25
		(62-245)	

62-223 BETWEEN LAYERS

Lionel's no. 19250 was Joe, The Motorists' Friend's high-end steam purchase for 1963. Only 200 of these outfits were made, leading to its R10 rarity. The 19250 included a no. 6410-25 Flat Car W/2 Autos, shown with two dark yellow no. 6406-30 Automobiles.

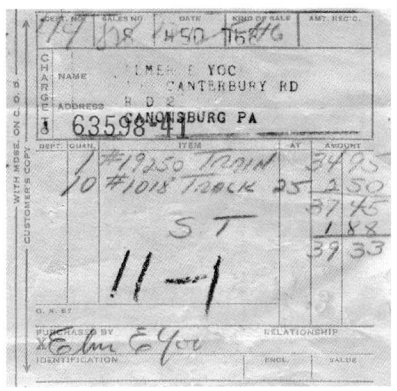

A sales receipt from Kaufmann's in Pittsburgh (identified on the back of the receipt) shows the no. 19250 selling for $34.95. Joe, The Motorists' Friend might have sold this outfit to Kaufmann's, or the latter could have purchased a quantity direct from Lionel.

Description: "O27" Promotional Outfit
Specification: "O27" Steam Type Freight Outfit W/Smoke & Whistle
Customer: Joe, The Motorists' Friend
Customer/Price: Kaufmann's; $34.95
Original Amount: 200
Factory Order Date: 6/14/1963
Date Issued: Rev 9-27-63
Date Req'd: 8/26/63
Packaging: RSC Outfit Packing #5 (Units not Boxed), (Except Loco & Tender)

Contents: 2037-1 Steam Type Locomotive With Smoke; 234W-1 Whistle Tender; 6465-150 Tank Car; 6410-25 Flat Car W/2 Autos; 6406-30 Automobile (2); 6050-50 Swift Savings Bank Car; 6476-25 Hopper Car - Red; 6017-25 Caboose; 1013-8 Curved Track (Bundle of 8 - 1013); 1018-30 Straight Track (Bundle of 3 - 1018); 1008-50 Uncoupling Unit; 1073-25 60-Watt Transformer; 147-25 Horn & Whistle Controller; 1103-30 Envelope Packed; 310-2 Set of (5) Billboards; D63-50 Accessory Catalog; 1-62 Parts Order Form; 1-63 Warranty Card; 1123-40 Instruction Sheet; 1646-10 Instruction Sheet

Boxes & Packing: 61-250 Outfit Box; 61-182 Corr. Insert; 61-186 Corr. Insert; 62-264 Corr. Insert; 62-278 Corr. Insert; 61-251 Shipper for (4) (1-4)

Alternate For Outfit Contents:
Note: Substitute 6050-100 for 6050-50; Substitute 6409-25 for 6410-25 as needed.

19250 (1963)	C6	C7	C8	Rarity
Complete Outfit With Brown Automobiles	965	1,345	1,760	R10
Complete Outfit With Yellow Automobiles	665	945	1,260	R10
Outfit Box no. 61-250	400	550	700	R10

Comments: In 1963, Joe, The Motorists' Friend purchased five Lionel outfits: nos. 19247 through 19251. The nos. 19248, 19250 and 19251 were higher-end offerings containing some of Lionel's upgraded motive power and rolling stock. The other two were low-end outfits.

The 19250 was Joe, The Motorists' Friend's high-end steam-powered offering for 1963. It was a Retailer Promotional Type Ib outfit led by a no. 2037-1 Steam Type Locomotive With Smoke and Magne-Traction. This workhorse steamer spanned the years 1953 through 1963 (except for 1956) and powered one Super O and 22 O27 outfits during the 1960s. When boxed as a "-1", it included the nos. 675-33 Smoke Stack Cleaner, SP-1 Smoke Pellets, 927-90 Lubricating Oil Packed, 2037-16 Instruction Sheet and CTC-1 Lockon inside its 2037-13 Corr. Box.

The 2037 pulled an Archbar-equipped no. 234W-1 Whistle Tender. The latter model came in an Orange Picture box.

The 19250 was the third of five desirable promotional outfits to include a no. 6410-25 Flat Car W/2 Autos. This model was nothing more than a red no. 6511-series flat car with no markings or a brake wheel.

Outfit Factory Orders indicated that Lionel produced a total of 6,680 of the 6410-25. Until this point, however, the Lionel part number and the quantity produced had not been documented, which meant collectors did not know that this model was a 6410-25. Now that it has been documented, hobbyists will search for this unique car to complete their collections.

Lionel freely substituted a no. 6409-25 Flat Car Complete for the 6410-25. The two cars were largely identical (both typically came with non-operating AAR trucks and couplers, although the 6410-25 in this outfit had non-operating Archbar types). Keep in mind, however, that the 6409-25 had "Lionel" stamped on each side.

The two no. 6406-30 Automobiles in this outfit were dark yellow or brown with gray bumpers. The brown automobiles command a premium, as outlined in the pricing table.

A no. 6050-100 Swift Savings Bank Car took the place of the no. 6050-50 Swift Savings Bank Car. The 6050-100 was equipped with either one operating and one non-operating AAR truck and coupler or a pair of operating AAR types, as opposed to the non-operating Archbar trucks and couplers on the 6050-50. The no. 6465-150 Tank Car came with one operating and one non-operating AAR truck and coupler. All the remaining cars in this outfit were equipped with operating AAR trucks and couplers.

When a no. 147-25 Horn & Whistle Controller and a transformer were included in an outfit, three wires were required. The 19250 and no. 19252 were the first two outfits to list a no. 1103-30 Envelope Packed, which came with four wires and a no.

0190-25 Controller. It is unknown why that controller and an extra wire were included. This difficult-to-find envelope was one of the first to list "The Lionel Toy Corporation" instead of "The Lionel Corporation" as the company name.

The no. 61-250 Orange RSC with Black Graphics outfit box was manufactured by Mead Containers and measured 13 x 12 x 7 inches.

A quantity of 200 of the 19250 was listed on the Factory Order. Such a small number makes this outfit difficult to find. As a side note, one example was observed with a sales receipt from Kaufmann's Department Store in Pittsburgh that showed the 19250 number and a price of $34.95. Perhaps Kaufmann's obtained this and other outfits from Joe, The Motorists' Friend.

CONVENTIONAL PACK
61-250 BOX
6-6-63

TOP LAYER				BOTTOM LAYER

19251
1963

Description: Super "O" Promotional Outfit
Specification: GG-1 Freight Outfit W/Horn
Customer: Joe, The Motorists' Friend
Original Amount: 72
Factory Order Date: 6/24/1963
Date Issued: 6-24-63
Date Req'd: 8/26/63
Packaging: Units Boxed Ship Bulk

Contents: 2360-1 Penn GG-1 Electric Locomotive With Horn; 6464-900 "New York Central" Box Car; 6436-110 Hopper Car; 6315-60 Chemical Tank Car; 6560-25 Crane Car; 6469-1 Miscellaneous Car; 6446-1 Cement Car "N & W"; 6119-100 Work Caboose; LW-1 Transformer; 31-1 Curved Track (12); 32-1 Straight Track (5); 34-1 ½ Straight Track; 39-35 Remote Control Set

19251 (1963)	C6	C7	C8	Rarity
Items Only	1,650	2,600	4,000	N/A

Comments: In 1963, Joe, The Motorists' Friend purchased five Lionel outfits: nos. 19247 through 19251. The nos. 19248, 19250 and 19251 were higher-end offerings containing some of Lionel's upgraded motive power and rolling stock. The other two were low-end outfits.

The 19251 was the first of two "bulk outfits" purchased by Joe, The Motorists' Friend. The other was promotional outfit no. 12827 from 1964. (For an explanation of the practice of buying "bulk

outfits," consult the entry on Madison Hardware Co. in the section on Lionel's Distribution and Customers.)

Customers typically bought in bulk from Lionel as a ploy to further reduce the price paid for individual items intended for separate sale. Yet it appears that Joe, The Motorists' Friend was actually purchasing outfit components in bulk with the intention of assembling this outfit on its own. For the 19251, no outfit box was provided, only bulk packaging. It's assumed that Lionel packaged all the individual items in master shipping cartons.

The 19251 was a Retailer Promotional Type Ia outfit that was the follow-up to Joe, The Motorists' Friend's no. 19178 from 1962. It was led by the "Re-instated 3-1-61" (per Production Control Files) no. 2360-1 Penn GG-1 Electric Locomotive With Horn. When boxed, this locomotive included the nos. CTC-1 Lockon, TP-2 Tissue Paper, 2360-12 Instruction Sheet, 2332-276 Corrugated Insert, 2332-278 Corrugated Insert, and 927-90 Lubricating Oil Packed in its no. 2360-10 Corrugated Box.

The rolling stock in this outfit included some of Lionel's higher-end items. The no. 6560-25 Crane Car was the boxed version of the crane with a red cab and a black base. The 6560 Crane Car was first cataloged in 1955, one year before Lionel began using the "-25" suffix to indicate unboxed items (see the section on Item Numbering and Suffixes). As such, the "-1" was assigned to a boxed 6560 with a gray cab and a black base while the "-25" designated a boxed model with a red cab and a black base. The Orange Picture version of the 6560-25's box most likely was used for this outfit.

The 19251 featured two difficult-to-find hopper cars: nos. 6436-110 Hopper Car and 6446-1 N&W Cement Car. Of the two, the 6446-1 in its Orange Picture box is the harder to find. It was a reissue of a model that Lionel introduced in 1954. The reissued 6446-1 came in one catalog and four promotional outfits, with a total of 1,527 cars produced. The "-1" meant the car was gray. Even though its number was 6446-1, the car was stamped "644625".

The no. 6315-60 Chemical Car in this outfit is interesting because early versions came in an Orange Picture box with "6315-50" stamped on the box. This quickly changed to the correct "6315-60" version. The early box is more difficult to find.

The remaining cars in the 19251 came in Orange Picture boxes. All of them were equipped with operating AAR trucks and couplers.

As with most Super O outfits, the track layout of the 19251 was a basic oval. A Type III or Type IV no. 39-35 Envelope Packed is possible with this outfit.

Even though Lionel's catalog Super O outfits generally did not include transformers, promotional ones did. These outfits had to provide a consumer with everything necessary to get a train up and running because they were not sold through regular hobby channels where a transformer could be purchased separately.

A listing for this outfit is provided here because a Factory Order exists for the 19251. Pricing is provided as reference for the items alone. However, as stated earlier in this volume, items alone do not constitute an outfit; an outfit box is required.

It is unknown what Joe, The Motorists' Friend ever did with these items. For that reason, finding any box with 19251 markings would be a true discovery.

Description: "O27" Promotional Outfit
Specification: "O27" Steam Type Freight Outfit W/Smoke & Whistle
Customer: Taubman's
Original Amount: 100
Factory Order Date: 6/14/1963
Date Issued: Rev 7-26-63
Date Req'd: W/O July 15th
Packaging: RSC Outfit Packing #5 (Units not Boxed), Except Loco. & Tender

Contents: 2037-1 Steam Type Locomotive With Smoke; 234W-1 Whistle Tender; 6502-25 Girder Transport Car; 6502-3 Girder Bridge; 6142-25 Gondola Car (Less 2 Canisters); 6112-5 Canister (2); 6050-50 Swift Savings Bank Car; 6476-25 Hopper Car - Red; 6017-25 Caboose; 1013-8 Curved Track (Bundle of 8 - 1013); 1018-30 Straight Track (Bundle of 3 - 1018); 1008-50 Uncoupling Unit; 1073-25 60-Watt Transformer; 147-25 Horn & Whistle Controller; 1103-30 Envelope Packed; 310-2 Set of (5) Billboards; D63-50 Accessory Catalog; 1-62 Parts Order Form; 1-63 Warranty Card; 1123-40 Instruction Sheet; 1646-10 Instruction Sheet

Boxes & Packing: 61-250 Outfit Box; 61-182 Corr. Insert; 61-186 Corr. Insert; 62-264 Corr. Insert; 62-278 Corr. Insert; 61-251 Shipper for (4) (1-4)

Alternate For Outfit Contents:
Note: Substitute 6050-100 for 6050-50.

19252 (1963)	C6	C7	C8	Rarity
Complete Outfit	950	1,315	1,685	R10
Outfit Box no. 61-250	750	1,000	1,200	R10

Comments: The Factory Order for Retailer Promotional Type Ia outfit no. 19252 listed Taubman's as the customer.

The 19252 was led by a no. 2037-1 Steam Type Locomotive With Smoke and Magne-Traction. This workhorse steamer spanned the years 1953 through 1963 (except for 1956) and powered one Super O and 22 O27 outfits during the 1960s. When boxed as a "-1", it included the nos. 675-33 Smoke Stack Cleaner, SP-1 Smoke Pellets, 927-90 Lubricating Oil Packed, 2037-16 Instruction Sheet and CTC-1 Lockon inside its 2037-13 Corr. Box.

The no. 2037 pulled a no. 234W-1 Whistle Tender, which could come equipped with Archbar or AAR trucks and couplers in 1963. Lionel packaged it in an Orange Picture box.

As noted on the Factory Order, a no. 6050-100 Swift Savings Bank Car took the place of the 6050-50 Swift Savings Bank Car variation. The 6050-100 was equipped with either one operating and one non-operating AAR truck and coupler or a pair of operating AAR types, as opposed to the non-operating Archbar trucks and couplers on the 6050-50.

The no. 6502-25 Girder Transport Car was making its last appearance in this and a few other promotional outfits. It could come with non-operating Archbar or AAR trucks and couplers.

The no. 6142-25 Gondola Car (Less 2 Canisters) in the 19252 was a short gondola molded in black with one non-operating and one operating AAR truck and coupler. All the remaining cars in this outfit were equipped with operating AAR trucks and couplers.

When a no. 147-25 Horn & Whistle Controller and a transformer were included in an outfit, three wires were required. The 19252 and no. 19250 were the first two outfits to list a no. 1103-30 Envelope Packed, which came with four wires and a no. 0190-25 Controller. It is unknown why that controller and an extra wire were included. This difficult-to-find envelope was one of the first to list "The Lionel Toy Corporation" instead of "The Lionel Corporation" as the company name.

The no. 61-250 Orange RSC with Black Graphics outfit box measured 13 x 12 x 7 inches.

Since Taubman's likely had only a few stores, the quantity of 100 was more than enough to meet its demand. This outfit is yet another example of Lionel lowering the minimum quantity requirements for a unique promotional outfit. This small quantity makes the 19252 highly desirable and extremely difficult to find.

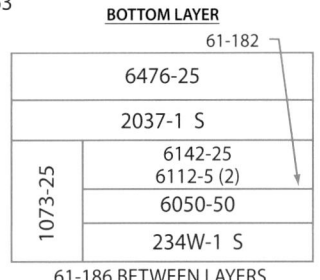

CONVENTIONAL PACK
61-250 BOX
6-6-63

607

Outfit no. 19253 listed Kroger on its Factory Order, but it was also sold to the general supermarket trade. Lionel's supermarket program was a disaster in that approximately 12,954 of the 28,500 outfits produced were returned. Lionel reissued these as a General Release Promotional outfit available to any customer in 1964.

The no. D-19253 Blister Display was created to help sell the no. 19253 in supermarkets. It was designed to be hung on a wall in the store. This promotional glossy photograph was provided to Lionel's sales staff as well as authorized dealers.

Description: "O27" Promotional Outfit
Specification: "O27" Steam Type Freight Outfit
Customer: Kroger
Customer/No./Price: SupeRX; ERE 4.12; $7.98
Original Amount: 28,500
Factory Order Date: 6/26/1963
Date Issued: Rev 12-2-63
Date Req'd: 9/1/63
Packaging: RSC Outfit Packing #5 (Units not Boxed)

Contents: 1062-25 Steam Type Loco. W/Light & Reversing Unit; 1061T-25 Tender; 6502-50 Girder Transport Car; 6502-3 Girder Bridge; 6167-25 Caboose; 1013-8 Curved Track (Bundle of 8 - 1013); 1026-25 25-Watt Transformer; 1103-20 Envelope Packed; 310-2 Set of (5) Billboards; D63-50 Accessory Catalog; 1-62 Parts Order Form; 1-63 Warranty Card; Form 2869 Printed Sheet; 1123-40 Instruction Sheet; 11311-10 Instruction Sheet

Boxes & Packing: 63-320 Outfit Box; 63-322 Corr. Insert; 63-323 Corr. Insert; 62-251 Corr. Insert; 63-321 Shipper for (6) (1-6)

19253 (1963)	C6	C7	C8	Rarity
Complete Outfit	120	200	305	R2
Outfit Box no. 63-320	30	55	75	R2

Comments: Even though the Factory Order for outfit no. 19253 listed Kroger grocery stores as the customer, this outfit was sold to numerous other supermarkets. As a result, it was classified as a General Release Promotional Type IIb outfit.

The 19253 was part of Lionel's strategy in 1963 to sell train outfits through large supermarket organizations. On paper, this outfit was a huge success; after all, the Factory Orders showed an increase from 25,000 on 9-27-63 to 28,500 on 12-2-63. This was the twelfth highest number produced of any individual catalog or promotional outfit in the 1960s.

Unfortunately, Lionel greatly overestimated the number of outfits that the supermarket program could sell. (See the entries for A&P and Kroger in the section on Lionel's Distribution and Customers.) Lionel *Sales Bulletin* no. 20 from June of 1964 stated, "During the summer and fall of 1963, Lionel sold thousands of train and racing sets to many of the large supermarket organizations. There was a relatively heavy return on this merchandise after the first of the year...." Sales forecast documents indicated that approximately 12,954 of the 19253s were returned and became General Release Promotional outfit 19253 for 1964.

The 19253 was a low-end starter outfit that cost Kroger $6.25. It was very similar to advance catalog outfit no. 11415 from 1963.

The 19253 was led by a no. 1062-25 Steam Type Loco. W/

Light & Reversing Unit. This low-end Scout steamer was new for 1963 and featured an 0-4-0 wheel arrangement and lacked a traction aid. According to its Lionel Engineering Specification, it was the "Same as #1061 but with the addition of Reversing Unit & Lamp". It was trailed by an unmarked no. 1061T-25 Tender.

All the items in this outfit were new for 1963 and came with non-operating AAR trucks and couplers. The unmarked no. 6502-50 Girder Transport Car was molded in blue plastic and carried an orange plastic no. 6502-3 Girder Bridge.

The Form 2869 advertising the no. 2001 Track Make-Up Kit was dated 6/63. It is one of the more difficult items to find in completing a C8 outfit.

The no. 63-320 Tan RSC with Black Graphics outfit box was manufactured by St. Joe Kraft, St. Joe Paper Co. Container Division and measured 11 x 7⅞ x 5½ inches. It included four lines of data as part of the box manufacturer's certificate.

Lionel *Sales Bulletin* no. 20 from June of 1964 noted that "the composition of the merchandise has not been changed from 1963."

Other than the fact that some outfits have been observed with a yellow accessory catalog from 1964, no noticeable differences exist between the 1963 and 1964 versions of the 19253. Therefore, the pricing in the table applies to both the 1963 and 1964 versions.

With more than 28,500 of these outfits manufactured, it is readily available.

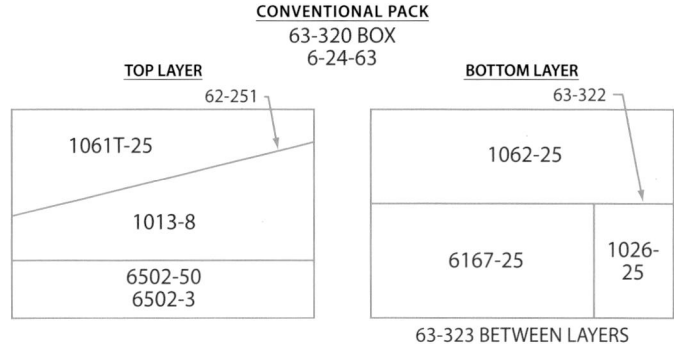

CONVENTIONAL PACK
63-320 BOX
6-24-63

TOP LAYER
62-251
1061T-25
1013-8
6502-50
6502-3

BOTTOM LAYER
63-322
1062-25
6167-25
1026-25

63-323 BETWEEN LAYERS

Description: "O27" Train Set
Specification: #19253 Lionel "O27" Train Set
Customer: All Trade
Customer: Arkwright
Original Amount: 13,000
Packaging: RSC

Contents: 1062-25 Steam Type Loco. W/Light & Reversing Unit; 1061T-25 Tender; 6502-50 Girder Transport Car; 6502-3 Girder Bridge; 6167-25 Caboose; 1013-8 Curved Track (Bundle of 8 - 1013); 1026-25 25-Watt Transformer; 1103-20 Envelope Packed; 310-2 Set of (5) Billboards; 1-62 Parts Order Form; 1-63 Warranty Card; Form 2869 Printed Sheet; 1123-40 Instruction Sheet; 11311-10 Instruction Sheet

Boxes & Packing: 63-320 Outfit Box; 63-322 Corr. Insert; 63-323 Corr. Insert; 62-251 Corr. Insert; 63-321 Shipper for (6) (1-6)

Comments: The no. 19253 from 1964 was the same as the 1963 version. These outfits were nothing more than the ones that Kroger and other supermarkets had returned to Lionel. (See the entry for

19253
1964

outfit 19253 from 1963.)

With so many outfits returned, Lionel was doing whatever it could to sell these trains. It turned the 19253 and no. D-19253 Blister Display into General Release Promotional Type IIb outfits that were available to any customer. They were listed on Lionel *Sales Bulletin* no. 12 from May 8, 1964: "The following represents fourteen (14) sets you may offer at your discretion to accounts in your territory". One additional customer, Arkwright (a large buying organization), has been linked to the 19253. The 19253's cost to retailers was reduced to $5.75.

The quantity of 13,000 listed for the 1964 version of the 19253 was the number of outfits released to customers on August 4, 1964. These were likely all of the estimated 12,954 outfits returned from 1963 and not new production. Some 19253s have been observed with a yellow accessory catalog from 1964. These were likely 1963 outfits with added paperwork.

There are no noticeable differences between the 1963 and 1964 versions. Therefore, the pricing from the 19253 from 1963 applies to both of them.

Customer: J. J. Newberry

Comments: A listing for outfit no. 19253-100 with customer J. J. Newberry appears on an internal Lionel Releases document from 1964. No quantity or date was provided. This is all the information

19253-100
1964

available, and it cannot be determined whether the outfit was produced. This listing is provided for completeness and to solicit observations.

Description: "O27" Promotional Outfit
Specification: "O27" Steam Type Freight Outfit W/Smoke & Whistle
Customer: B. Altman
Original Amount: 100
Factory Order Date: 6/26/1963
Date Issued: 6-26-63
Date Req'd: 8/15/63
Packaging: RSC Outfit Packing - #5 (Units not Boxed)

19254
1963

Contents: 238-25 Steam Type Locomotive with Smoke; 234W-25 Whistle Tender; 6414-150 Auto Transport (Less Autos); 6406-30 Automobile (4); 6465-150 Tank Car; 6476-75 Hopper Car - Black; 6162-25 Gondola Car (Less 3 Canisters); 6112-88 Canister (3); 6257-100 Caboose; 1013-82 Curved Track (Bundle of 6 - 1013) (2); 1018-30 Straight Track (Bundle of 3 - 1018); 1020-25 90° Crossing; 6139-25 Uncoupling Track Section; 1103-50 Envelope Packed; 1073-25 60-Watt

Transformer; 147-25 Horn & Whistle Controller; 909-20 Smoke Fluid; 310-2 Set of (5) Billboards; D63-50 Accessory Catalog; 1-62 Parts Order Form; 1-63 Warranty Card; 1123-40 Instruction Sheet; 237-11 Instruction Sheet; 11385-10 Instruction Sheet; 1802B Layout Instruction Sheet

Boxes & Packing: 63-309 Outfit Box; 61-181 Corr. Insert; 61-182 Corr. Insert; 61-186 Corr. Insert; 62-225 Corr. Insert; 62-248 Corr. Insert; 63-312 Corr. Insert; 63-310 Shipper for (4) (1-4)

19254 (1963)	C6	C7	C8	Rarity
Complete Outfit With Green Or Brown Automobiles	1,800	2,400	3,050	R10
Complete Outfit With Yellow Automobiles	1,200	1,600	2,050	R10
Outfit Box no. 63-309	800	1,050	1,250	R10

Comments: This Retailer Promotional Type Ia outfit was the last to list B. Altman as its customer. That firm was known for selling top-quality merchandise, so it was no surprise that the no. 19254 contained some higher-end items from Lionel's 1963 product line.

The 19254 was led by a no. 238-25 Steam Locomotive with Smoke. This new-for-1963 Scout steamer featured a two-position reversing unit, a headlight and a rubber tire as a traction aid. The early version with wide running boards was included in this outfit. Except for its 238 number, it was the same engine as a no. 237. The 238-25 pulled a no. 234W-25 Whistle Tender, which could come equipped with Archbar or AAR trucks and couplers in 1963.

The no. 6414-150 Auto Transport (Less Autos), which was new for 1963, likely included four green or brown no. 6406-30 Automobiles with gray bumpers. However, yellow automobiles with gray bumpers were possible; therefore, pricing is provided for these variations.

The suffix indicated that the 6414-150 came unboxed with one operating and one non-operating AAR truck and coupler. The

6465-150 Tank Car also had one of each type of AAR truck and coupler. So did the no. 6162-25 Gondola Car, which went from two operating AAR types to one operating and one non-operating in 1963. The no. 6476-25 had two operating AAR types and the no. 6257-100 Caboose came with one operating and one plain AAR truck and coupler.

The no. 6139-25 Uncoupling Track Section appeared in outfits only in 1963 and 1964. It was a follow-up to the no. 6029 Uncoupling Track Section.

When a no. 147-25 Horn & Whistle Controller and a 6139-25 were included in an outfit, five wires were required to connect these peripherals to the transformer. Lionel created the no. 1103-50 Envelope Packed for this purpose. It came with five wires, a no. CTC-1 Lockon and a no. 0190-25 Controller.

All the paperwork reflected the new 90-day warranty policy that Lionel instituted in 1963. Many of these instruction sheet versions are the most difficult ones to find. The correct version of the no. 11385-10 is dated 6/63. A no. 1802B Layout Instruction Sheet detailed the figure-eight track layout.

The no. 63-309 Tan RSC with Black Graphics outfit box measured 13¼ x 12½ x 6¾ inches.

With only 100 examples ordered, the 19254 is seldom seen and achieves a well-deserved R10 rarity.

CONVENTIONAL PACK
63-309 BOX
6-25-63

TOP LAYER

| 62-225 → |
| 6406-30 (4) |

| 1013-82 | 1013-82 | 1018-30 6139-25 | 6465-150 | 6162-25 |

1020-25 TOP 6465, 6162   62-248

BOTTOM LAYER

61-181 ⌐ 61-182 ⌐

238-25		
1073-25	234W-25	
	6257-100	
6414-150		
6112-88 (3)	6476-75	147-25

61-186 BETWEEN LAYERS   63-312

Description: "O27" Promotional Outfit
Specification: "O27" Steam Type Freight Outfit
Customer: Retailers Representatives
Original Amount: 500
Factory Order Date: 6/26/1963
Date Issued: 6-26-63
Date Req'd: 8/15/63
Packaging: RSC Outfit Packing - #5 (Units not Boxed), Except 1047-1

Contents: 242-25 Steam Type Locomotive; 1060T-25 Tender; 6473-25 Rodeo Car; 6476-25 Hopper Car - Red; 6142-25 Gondola Car (Less 2 Canisters); 6112-5 Canister (2); 6050-100 Swift Savings Bank Car; 6059-50 Caboose; 1013-70 Curved Track (Bundle of 12 - 1013); 1018-30 Straight Track (Bundle of 3 - 1018); 1008-50 Uncoupling Unit; 1020-25 90° Crossing; 1010-25 35-Watt Transformer; 1103-20 Envelope Packed; 1047-1 Switchman With Flag; 310-2 Set of (5) Billboards; D63-50

Accessory Catalog; 1-62 Parts Order Form; 1-63 Warranty Card; 1123-40 Instruction Sheet; 1641-10 Instruction Sheet; 1802B Layout Instruction Sheet

Boxes & Packing: 63-348 Outfit Box; 62-248 Corr. Insert (2); 62-249 Corr. Insert; 63-311 Corr. Insert; 63-365 Corr. Insert; 63-349 Shipper for (4) (1-4)

19255 (1963)	C6	C7	C8	Rarity
Complete Outfit	625	1,050	1,525	R9
Outfit Box no. 63-348	250	400	550	R9

Comments: This Retailer Promotional Type Ia outfit was the only one to list buying cooperative Retailers Representatives on its Factory Order. The no. 19255 has yet to be linked to any of Retailers Representatives' member retailers.

The 19255 was led by a no. 242-25 Steam Type Locomotive. This low-end Scout steamer featured a two-position reversing unit and a headlight, lacked smoke and used a rubber tire as a traction aid. The version with wide running boards was included in this outfit. The norm for a no. 1060T-25 Tender was to be equipped with one non-operating and one plain AAR truck and coupler, but Archbar types were possible.

The most notable item in this outfit was a no. 1047-1 Switchman With Flag, which was last seen in the Lionel catalog from 1961. Lionel began to deplete its remaining inventory of 4,740 units in this and five other promotional outfits. The accessory is enjoyable if not terribly exciting; however, its no. 1047-12 Folding Box was made of flimsy chipboard and did not survive well. It is extremely difficult to find in collectible condition with the top flap still attached, so that a boxed example adds a substantial premium to the value of this outfit.

The normal progression for the nos. 6473-25 Rodeo Car and 6050-100 Swift Savings Bank Car was one operating and one non-operating AAR truck and coupler in 1963.

The only new car in this outfit was the no. 6142-25 Gondola Car. Lionel created a "new" car by taking a commonly available short gondola and updating the decoration. The 6142-25 was equipped with one operating and one non-operating AAR truck and coupler.

The, "-50" version of the no. 6059 Caboose made its first appearance in 1963. It was the unpainted red plastic version of the nos. 6059-1 and 6059-25 Cabooses, which were first issued in 1961. The 6059-50 Caboose was equipped with one operating and

one plain AAR truck and coupler.

The appropriate quantity of track was included in the 19255 to make a figure-eight layout. That track plan was outlined on a no. 1802B Layout Instruction Sheet dated 6-59.

The no. 63-348 Tan RSC with Black Graphics outfit box measured 14⅜ x 12⅜ x 6 inches.

The inclusion of the 1047-1 Switchman With Flag makes the 19255 a desirable promotional outfit. Obtaining a 1047-1 in collectible condition with a suitable box takes patience. With a quantity of only 500 made, this outfit does not appear too often and so is rather difficult to find.

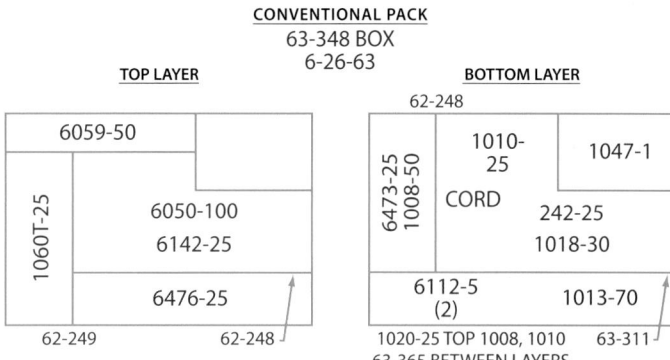

CONVENTIONAL PACK
63-348 BOX
6-26-63

Description: "O27" Promotional Outfit
Specification: "O27" Diesel Freight Outfit W/Horn
Customer: Beller Electric
Original Amount: 200
Factory Order Date: 6/25/1963
Date Issued: 6-25-63
Date Req'd: Late July
Packaging: Bulk Packing (Units Boxed)

Contents: 617X-1 Diesel Switcher W/Horn - "Santa Fe"; 3370-1 Sheriff & Outlaw Car; 3419-1 Operating Helicopter Car; 6446-1 Cement Car "N & W"; 6501-1 Jet Motor Boat Car; SW-1 130-Watt Transformer; 1122-1 Pr. Remote Control Switches; 1020-1 90° Crossing; 1018-200 Straight Track (Cartons of 200 Sections) (4,000 Sections) (20 (Boxes))

19256 (1963)	C6	C7	C8	Rarity
Items Only	870	1,345	2,015	N/A

Comments: In the early 1960s, Beller Electric and Madison Hardware were the two big purchasers of what were known as "bulk outfits." (For an explanation of the practice of buying "bulk outfits," consult the entry on Madison Hardware Co. in the section on Lionel's Distribution and Customers.)

Beller purchased bulk-packed outfits nos. 19256 and 19257 in 1963. Both of these were Retailer Promotional Type Ia outfits.

Beller's purchases are curious because customers typically bought in bulk from Lionel as a ploy to further reduce the price paid for individual items intended for separate sale. Yet it appears that Beller was actually purchasing outfit components in bulk with the intention of assembling this outfit on its own.

For the 19256, bulk packaging and not an outfit box was provided. Lionel likely packaged all the individual items in master

shipping cartons. However, no individual outfit boxes have been observed for any of the bulk outfits listed in this volume. As a result, we cannot ascertain whether these items were ever assembled and sold as an outfit. Even if they were, we cannot prove that Beller Electric designated the groupings as 19256 or 19257.

The 19256 included a high-end grouping of individually boxed Lionel items. The no. 617X-1 Santa Fe Diesel Switcher W/Horn was new for 1963. It featured a three-position reversing unit and two-axle Magne-Traction. Its Orange Picture no. 617-11 Folding Box is difficult to find in collectible condition. The use of the "X" suffix indicated the absence of a no. CTC-1 Lockon.

All the cars in this bulk-packed outfit were equipped with operating AAR trucks and couplers and came in an Orange Picture box. Standing out among them was the no. 6446-1 N&W Cement Car. A reissue of a model that Lionel introduced in 1954, it came in one catalog and four promotional outfits, with a total of 1,527 cars produced. The "-1" meant the car was gray. Even though its number was 6446-1, the car was stamped "644625". Its Orange Picture box is tough to find.

Curiously, the contents of the 19256 included only straight track and lacked a caboose. Beller likely added the necessary pieces of curved track and selected a caboose from its inventory to complete this outfit.

A listing for this outfit is provided here because a Factory Order exists for the 19256. Pricing is provided as reference for the items alone. However, as stated earlier in this volume, items alone do not constitute an outfit; an outfit box is required.

Finding a box with any sort of markings for this outfit would be quite a discovery.

Description: Super "O" Promotional Outfit
Specification: Super "O" Steam Type Freight With Smoke & Whistle
Customer: Beller Electric
Original Amount: 200
Factory Order Date: 6/25/1963
Date Issued: 6/25/63
Date Req'd: Late July
Packaging: Bulk Packing (Units Boxed)

Contents: 736X-1 Steam Type Locomotive With Smoke; 736W-1 Whistle Tender; 6827-1 Flat Car With Tractor Shovel; 6414-1 Auto Transport Car; 6560-25 Crane Car; 6429-1 Wrecking Car; ZW-1 Transformer; 112-1 Pr. Remote Control Switches; 32-100 100 Sections per box (4,000 Sections) (40 (Boxed))

19257 (1963)	C6	C7	C8	Rarity
Items Only	1,380	2,120	2,820	N/A

Comments: In the early 1960s, Beller Electric and Madison Hardware were the two big purchasers of what were known as "bulk outfits." (For an explanation of the practice of buying "bulk outfits," consult the entry on Madison Hardware Co. in the section on Lionel's Distribution and Customers.)

Beller purchased bulk-packed outfits nos. 19256 and 19257 in 1963. Both of these were Retailer Promotional Type Ia outfits.

Beller's purchases are curious because customers typically bought in bulk from Lionel as a ploy to further reduce the price paid for individual items intended for separate sale. Yet it appears that Beller was actually purchasing outfit components in bulk with the intention of assembling this outfit on its own.

For the 19257, bulk packaging and not an outfit box was provided. Lionel likely packaged all the individual items in master shipping cartons. However, no individual outfit boxes have been observed for any of the bulk outfits listed in this volume. As a result, we cannot ascertain whether these items were ever assembled and sold as an outfit. Even if they were, we cannot prove that Beller Electric designated the groupings as 19256 or 19257.

The 19257 was a Super O outfit that included all individually boxed Lionel items. It was led by a no. 736X-1 Steam Type Locomotive With Smoke and Magne-Traction. Originally introduced in 1950, the no. 736 appeared in at least 17 outfits during the 1960s. It came packaged in a no. 736-36 Corr. Box. The use of the "X" suffix indicated the absence of a no. CTC-1 Lockon.

The locomotive in this outfit was paired with a no. 736W-1 Whistle Tender, which was equipped with one operating and one plain AAR truck and coupler.

The rolling stock in the 19257 (all of which had operating AAR trucks and couplers) included items that have become very collectible. The no. 6429-1 Wrecking Car is rare because it was put in only one catalog and three promotional outfits, which called for a total of 1,433 cars. Its no. 6429-10 Folding Box was the first Hillside Orange Picture box issued by Lionel. The box listed Lionel's corporate name as "The Lionel Toy Corporation".

The no. 6560-25 Crane Car was the boxed version of the crane with a red cab and a black base. The 6560 Crane Car was first cataloged in 1955, one year before Lionel began using the "-25" suffix to indicate unboxed items (see the section on Item Numbering and Suffixes). As such, the "-1" was assigned to a boxed 6560 with a gray cab and a black base while the "-25" designated a boxed model with a red cab and a black base. The Orange Picture version of the 6560-25's box most likely was used for this outfit.

The no. 6827-1 Flat Car With Tractor Shovel was making its last appearance in 1963. A new Orange Non Perforated no. 6827-5 Folding Box was issued for this car in 1963. This box, like the ones for the Wrecking Car and the Crane Car, is difficult to find in collectible condition. Meanwhile, the nos. 6414-1 Auto Transport Car and 736W-1 Whistle Tender came in Orange Picture boxes.

The 19257 came with only straight track. Beller likely added the necessary pieces of curved track from its inventory to complete this outfit.

A listing for this outfit is provided here because a Factory Order exists for the 19257. Pricing is provided as reference for the items alone. However, as stated earlier in this volume, items alone do not constitute an outfit; an outfit box is required.

Finding a box with any sort of markings for this outfit would be quite a discovery.

Description: "O27" Promotional Outfit
Specification: "O27" Steam Type Freight Outfit
Customer: Johnson Dewalt
Original Amount: 400
Factory Order Date: 8/9/1963
Date Issued: 8-9-63
Date Req'd: Aug 26
Packaging: Display Outfit Packing #1 (Units not Boxed)

Contents: 1061-25 Steam Type Locomotive; 1061T-25 Tender; 6473-25 Rodeo Car; 3410-25 Oper. Helicopter Car (Less Helicopter); 3419-100 Operating Helicopter Complete; 6142-25 Gondola Car (Less Canisters); 6112-5 Canister (2); 6067-25 Caboose; 1013-8 Curved Track (Bundle of 8 - 1013); 1018-40 Straight Track (Bundle of 4 - 1018); 1010-25 35-Watt Transformer; 310-2 Set of (5) Billboards; D63-50 Accessory Catalog; 1-62 Parts Order Form; 1-63 Warranty Card; 1103-20 Envelope Packed; 3410-5 Instruction Sheet; 1123-40 Instruction Sheet; 19228-10 Instruction Sheet

Boxes & Packing: 63-306 Display Box; 61-101 Corr. Insert; 61-102 Corr. Insert; 63-307 Shipper for (4) (1-4)

19258 (1963)	C6	C7	C8	Rarity
Complete Outfit	425	675	925	R9
Outfit Box no. 63-306	275	425	525	R9

Comments: Johnson Dewalt operated as a manufacturer's representative to the premium and incentive industry. The no. 19258, a Retailer Promotional Type Ib, was this customer's only outfit purchase for 1963.

The 19258 was the follow-up to Johnson Dewalt's no. 19170 from 1962. The 19258 came with two operating cars and was led by a no. 1061-25 Steam Type Locomotive. This stripped-down Scout steamer was new for 1963. It featured an 0-4-0 wheel arrangement and went forward only. It lacked a headlight, a lens and any sort of traction aid.

The 1061-25 was followed by an unmarked no. 1061T-25 Tender and trailed by a no. 6067-25 Caboose. The norm for both of these cars in 1963 was one non-operating and one plain AAR truck and coupler, although a similar Archbar combination is possible.

The no. 3410-25 Oper. Helicopter Car (Less Helicopter) was making its final outfit appearances in 1963 and 1964. The norm for a no. 3419-100 Operating Helicopter Complete was a one-piece yellow body in 1963. This fragile helicopter was frequently lost or broken.

In 1963, a no. 6473-25 Rodeo Car typically had a Type IIb body type (cadmium yellow plastic with red lettering). That is most likely what was included in this outfit.

Both the 3410-25 and 6473-25 followed the normal truck and coupler progression and most often came equipped with one operating and one non-operating AAR truck and coupler in 1963. The no. 6142-25 Gondola Car was similarly equipped.

All the paperwork reflected the new 90-day warranty policy that Lionel instituted in 1963. Many of these instruction sheet versions are the most difficult ones to find.

The no. 63-306 White 4-6-4 Steamer and F3 Hinged Display with Red/Orange and Blue Graphics Type A outfit box listed the manufacturer as "SJPC" (likely St. Joe Paper Company). It measured 24½ x 11½ x 3⅛ inches.

Only 400 examples of the 19258 were made, and its outfit box is seldom seen. If an empty 19258 box were found, this outfit would not be too difficult to complete. The only items that are difficult to obtain in collectible condition are the 3419-100 and no. 19228-10 Instruction Sheet.

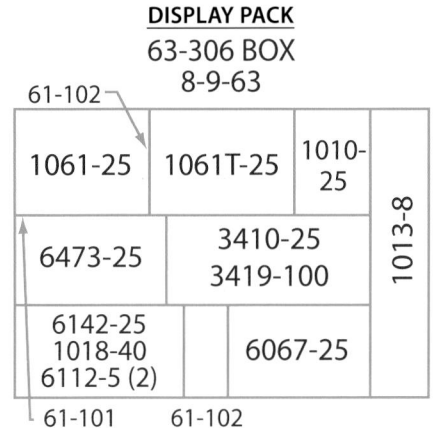

DISPLAY PACK
63-306 BOX
8-9-63

Description: "O27" Promotional Outfit
Specification: "O27" Steam Type Freight Outfit
Customer: Montgomery Ward
Original Amount: 1,000
Factory Order Date: 8/13/1963
Date Issued: 8-13-63
Date Req'd: Aug 25
Packaging: RSC (Units Loose)

Contents: 1062-25 Steam Type Loco. W/Light & Reversing Unit; 1061T-25 Tender; 6076-100 Hopper Car - Gray; 6409-25 Flat Car W/3 Pipes; 6511-15 Pipes (3); 6042-75 Gondola Car (Less 2 Cable Reels); 40-11 Cable Reels (2); 6050-150 Van Camp Savings Bank Car; 6067-25 Caboose; 1013-70 Curved Track (Bundle of 12 - 1013); 1018-40 Straight Track (Bundle of 4 - 1018); 1020-25 90° Crossing; 1010-25 35-Watt Transformer; 1103-20 Envelope Packed; D63-50 Accessory Catalog; 310-2 Set of (5) Billboards; 1-62 Parts Order Form; 1-63 Warranty Card; 19223-10 Instruction Sheet

Boxes & Packing: 62-243 Outfit Box; 61-171 Corr. Insert; 61-173 Corr. Insert; 62-223 Corr. Insert; 62-225 Corr. Insert; 63-380 Shipper for (6) (1-6)

19259 (1963)	C6	C7	C8	Rarity
Complete Outfit	315	475	535	R7
Outfit Box no. 62-243	200	275	325	R7

Comments: This was the only Montgomery Ward outfit from 1963 that was not canceled (see outfit nos. 19221 and 19222). The no. 19259 was likely sold through Montgomery Ward stores, as it has yet to be observed in any Ward catalog or literature.

The 19259, a Retailer Promotional Type Ib, was led by a no.

1062-25 Steam Type Locomotive W/ Light & Reversing Unit. This low-end Scout steamer was new for 1963 and featured an 0-4-0 wheel arrangement and lacked a traction aid. According to its Lionel Engineering Specification, it was the "Same as #1061 but with the addition of Reversing Unit & Lamp".

This outfit contained three brand-new items that were equipped with middle non-operating AAR trucks and couplers. Two these newcomers were as low-end as possible. The nos. 1061T-25 Tender and 6076-100 Hopper Car - Gray were plastic models that came unpainted and undecorated. Slightly more impressive was the no. 6409-25 Flat Car W/3 Pipes. The 6409-25 was a red no. 6511-series flat car that had "Lionel" stamped on each side and lacked a car number and a brake wheel.

The remaining cars in the 19259 were carryover items that had non-operating Archbar trucks and couplers. The no. 6067-25 Caboose came in unpainted brown plastic.

The figure-eight track layout was outlined on a no. 19223-10 Instruction Sheet.

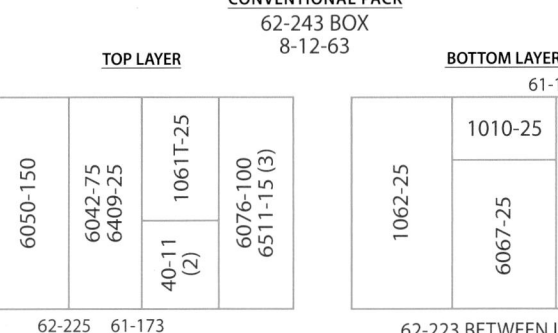

CONVENTIONAL PACK
62-243 BOX
8-12-63

The no. 19259 was the only outfit purchased by Montgomery Ward in 1963. It included three new-for-1963 cars: nos. 6076-100 Hopper Car - Gray, 1061T-25 Tender and 6409-25 Flat Car W/3 Pipes. Most new Lionel rolling stock during and after 1963 was merely a variation in decoration or load of a previously released item.

The no. 62-243 Tan RSC with Black Graphics outfit box was manufactured by the Mead Corporation and measured 12⅛ x 11½ x 6⅜ inches. It included four lines of data as part of the box manufacturer's certificate.

This was the only outfit purchased by Ward in 1963. It also marked the final Ward outfit appearance for at least another three years. As with all Ward outfits, the 19259 is highly desirable; even more so now because of the knowledge that it was the only Lionel outfit associated with that venerable firm between 1963 and 1965.

19260
1963

Description: "O27" Promotional Outfit
Specification: "O27" Steam Type Freight Outfit
Customer: National Tea Company
Original Amount: 2,000
Factory Order Date: 8/13/1963
Date Issued: 8-13-63
Date Req'd: 1,000 - 8/25/63 Bal - 9/3/63
Packaging: RSC (Units Loose)

Contents: 1061-25 Steam Type Locomotive; 1061T-25 Tender; 6411-25 Flat Car W/6 Pipes; 6511-15 Pipes (6); 6042-275 Gondola Car W/6 Horses; 1877-12 Horses (Brown) (6); 6067-25 Caboose; 1013-8 Curved Track (Bundle of 8 - 1013); 1026-25 25-Watt Transformer; 1103-20 Envelope Packed; D63-50 Accessory Catalog; 310-2 Set of (5) Billboards; 1-62 Parts Order Form; 1-63 Warranty Card; 11311-20 Instruction Sheet

Boxes & Packing: 61-170 Outfit Box; 61-172 Corr. Insert; 61-173 Corr. Insert; 62-254 Corr. Insert; 62-255 Corr. Insert; 61-174 Shipper for (6) (1-6)

Alternate For Outfit Contents:
Note: Substitute Inventory of 1877-10 & 1877-11 in place of 1877-12 until used up.

19260 (1963)	C6	C7	C8	Rarity
Complete Outfit	135	275	500	R5
Outfit Box no. 61-170	50	125	250	R5

Comments: This was the only Factory Order to list National Tea Company as the customer. The no. 19260 was likely part of Lionel's plans in 1963 to target supermarket chains. (See the entries for A&P's no. 19244 and Kroger's no. 19253 from 1963.)

As compared to the 19244 and 19253, the 19260 was produced in drastically smaller quantities. There is no record of any of these being returned to Lionel, although a few did appear at Madison Hardware. In 1989, Richard Kughn purchased Madison Hardware of New York and reopened it in Detroit soon thereafter. One of the first lists of outfits available for sale included a quantity of three of the 19260.

The 19260 was a low-end starter outfit typical of the outfits sold to supermarket chains. It was led by a no. 1061-25 Steam Type Locomotive. This stripped-down Scout steamer was new for 1963. It featured an 0-4-0 wheel arrangement, went forward only, did not include a headlight or lens, and did not include any sort of traction aid. It was followed by an unmarked no. 1061T-25 Tender

The no. 19260 was the only outfit purchased by National Tea Company. For this outfit, two new pieces of rolling stock the nos. 6042-275 Gondola Car W/6 Horses and 6411-25 Flat Car W/6 Pipes were created. In reality, both new items were simply a re-numbering of already existing items. The outfit shown here was one of the three available from Madison Hardware in Detroit. The 6411-25 is shown with only three of its six no. 6511-15 Pipes.

equipped with a one non-operating and one plain AAR truck and coupler.

For this outfit, two new pieces of rolling stock were created. In reality, both new items were simply a re-numbering of already existing items. The no. 6411-25 Flat Car W/6 Pipes was the same as a no. 6409-25 Flat Car W/3 Pipes. The only difference was the note on the 6411-25's Production Control File instructing the Outfit Packing Department to include six no. 6511-15 Pipes. The 6411-25 appeared in only one other outfit, the no. 19438 from 1965.

The 6411-25 was a red 6511-series flat car with "Lionel" stamped on the side. No car number or brake wheel was provided.

Of note, the no. 6411 was previously used from 1948 through 1950 for the no. 6411-1 Flat Car Complete and Packed.

The unmarked blue no. 6042-275 Gondola Car W/6 Horses was identical to a no. 6042-250 Gondola Car. The only difference was the note on the 6042-275's Production Control File instructing the Outfit Packing Department to include six no. 1877-12 Horses

(Brown). It appears Lionel still had horses in inventory a year after the no. 1877 Horse Transport Car last appeared. Where better to deplete the inventory then in a promotional outfit.

Since both the 6042-275 and 6411-25 are indistinguishable from the commonly available 6042-250 and 6409-25, they do not demand any sort of premium.

Lionel originally thought of placing the six horses in their own no. 63-206 Poly Bag and calling the grouping a no. 6042-276 Bag of 6 Horse Figures. It likely changed its mind because the 19260 Factory Order lists the horses separately. The substitutions of the nos. 1877-10 Horse Figure (White) or 1877-11 Horse Figure (Black) do not affect the outfit price.

All cars except the no. 6067-25 Caboose were equipped with non-operating AAR trucks and couplers. The 6067-25 has been observed in brown plastic with one non-operating and one plain Archbar truck and coupler. It has also been observed in red with one non-operating and one plain AAR truck and coupler.

The no. 61-170 Tan RSC with Black Graphics outfit box was manufactured by United Container and measured 11½ x

10¼ x 6¼ inches. It included four lines of data as part of the box manufacturer's certificate (BMC). One version was observed with a "63" and five stars as part of its BMC.

To help National Tea Company promote the 19260, Lionel created a no. D19260 Blister Display. Lionel manufactured a small quantity of these and few have survived.

Since a quantity of 2,000 of the 19260 was manufactured and at least three were still available at Madison Hardware in Detroit, this outfit can be obtained with some patience. When found, it is most often missing its horses and pipes.

CONVENTIONAL PACK
61-170 BOX
8-8-63

TOP LAYER				BOTTOM LAYER		
61-173 ⌐					62-254 ⌐	
6042-275				1013-8		
1877-12 (6)	1061T-25			1026-25	6067-25	
6411-25 6511-15 (6)				1061-25		
62-255				61-172 BETWEEN LAYERS		

19262
1963

The no. 19262 was the last example of a Factory Order listing Abraham & Strauss as a customer. This outfit included a highly desirable no. 6406-30 Automobile in green plastic with gray bumpers. It also has been observed with a brown automobile with gray bumpers. The outfit shown here was one of four available from Madison Hardware Co. in Detroit.

Description: "O27" Promotional Outfit
Specification: "O27" Steam Type Freight Outfit With Smoke
Customer: Abraham & Strauss
Original Amount: 170
Factory Order Date: 8/16/1963
Date Issued: Rev 11-22-63
Date Req'd: 9/3/63
Packaging: RSC (Units Loose)

Contents: 237-25 Steam Type Locomotive with Smoke; 1061T-25 Tender; 6076-100 Hopper Car - Gray; 6406-25 Flat Car W/Auto; 6406-30 Automobile; 3357-25 Animated Hobo & Railroad Policeman Car; 3357-27 Box Packed; 6067-25 Caboose; 1013-70 Curved Track (Bundle of 12 - 1013); 1018-40 Straight Track (Bundle of 4 - 1018); 1020-25 90° Crossing; 1010-25 35-Watt Transformer; 1103-20 Envelope Packed; 909-20 Smoke Fluid; D63-50 Accessory Catalog; 1-62 Parts Order Form; 1-63

Warranty Card; 310-2 Set of (5) Billboards; 237-11 Instruction Sheet; 1123-40 Instruction Sheet; 3357-8 Instruction Sheet; 19171-10 Instruction Sheet

Boxes & Packing: 61-170 Outfit Box; 61-171 Corr. Insert; 61-172 Corr. Insert; 62-248 Corr. Insert; 62-251 Corr. Insert; 61-174 Corr. Shipper for (6) (1-6)

19262 (1963)	C6	C7	C8	Rarity
Complete Outfit	535	875	1,275	R10
Outfit Box no. 61-170	225	400	600	R10

Comments: Longtime Lionel customer Abraham & Strauss, a department store based in Brooklyn, New York, purchased one Retailer Promotional Type Ib outfit in 1963. This was the last Factory Order to list it as a customer.

The no. 19262 was led by a no. 237-25 Steam Type Locomotive

with Smoke. This new-for-1963 Scout steamer featured a two-position reversing unit and a headlight and used a rubber tire as a traction aid. The harder-to-find early version with wide running boards was included in this outfit. Except for its 237 number, it was the same engine as a no. 238.

The nos. 1061T-25 Tender and 6076-100 Hopper Car - Gray were new for 1963. These low-end models were unpainted plastic with no stampings. The 1061T-25 came with one non-operating and one plain AAR truck and coupler and the 6076-100 came with non-operating Archbar types. Their lack of features and decoration epitomized the way Lionel was cheapening its product line at the time.

In 1963, the no. 6406-25 Flat Car W/Auto began to appear in gray molded plastic and most often was equipped with non-operating Archbar trucks and couplers. That was the version found in this outfit. The no. 6406-30 Automobile has been observed in brown or green plastic with gray bumpers. Either one of these automobiles provides a premium to the outfit price, as reflected in the pricing table.

The no. 6067-25 Caboose came in its desirable brown plastic version and was equipped with one non-operating and one plain Archbar truck and coupler.

The Type IIb no. 3357-25 Animated Hobo & Railroad Policeman Car was equipped with middle operating AAR trucks and couplers. The 3357-25 provided plenty of excitement as the cop tried to catch the hobo. Since the car was unboxed (hence the "-25" suffix), its peripherals were listed separately on the Factory Order as a no. 3357-27 Box Packed.

All the paperwork reflected the new 90-day warranty policy that Lionel instituted in 1963. The no. 19171-10 Instruction Sheet did not make reference to a warranty, but it was changed to specify the firm's name as "Lionel Toy Corporation". Its date remained 8-

62. The 1963 versions of the paperwork that were included in this outfit are the most difficult versions to find.

A figure-eight track layout was outlined on the 19171-10 Instruction Sheet.

The no. 61-170 Tan RSC with Black Graphics outfit box was manufactured by United Container and measured 11½ x 10¼ x 6¼ inches. It included four lines of data as part of the box manufacturer's certificate (BMC). One version was observed with a "63" and five stars as part of its BMC.

In 1989, Richard Kughn, then the owner of Lionel Trains Inc., purchased Madison Hardware Co. of New York City and reopened it in Detroit soon thereafter. One of the first lists of outfits available for sale included four of the 19262.

An early Factory Order lists a quantity of 2,000 for the 19262, but on 11-22-63 that was reduced significantly to only 170. It is unknown why there was such a drastic reduction.

Two of the four outfits from Madison Hardware have been observed. Other than those examples, a 19262 has seldom appeared on the market.

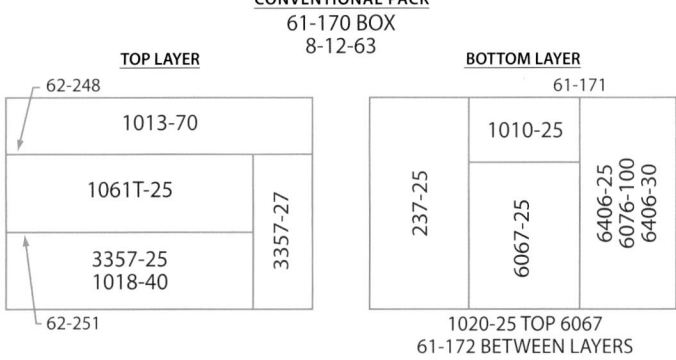

CONVENTIONAL PACK
61-170 BOX
8-12-63

Description: "O27" Promotional Outfit
Specification: "O27" Steam Type Freight Outfit
Customer/Price: Libby; $10.95 Plus Four Labels
Original Amount: 12,000
Factory Order Date: 9/9/1963
Date Issued: Rev 12-2-63
Date Req'd: 10-4-63
Packaging: RSC (Units Loose)

Contents: 1062-25 Steam Type Loco. W/Light & Reversing Unit; 1060T-50 Tender; 6050-175 Libby Box Car; 6475-50 Crushed Pineapple Car; 6076-125 Hopper Car; 6167-75 Caboose; 1013-8 Curved Track (Bundle of 8 - 1013); 1018-10 Straight Track (Loose) (2); 1010-25 35-Watt Transformer; 1103-20 Envelope Packed; D63-50 Accessory Catalog; 1-62 Parts Order Form; 1-63 Warranty Card; 19228-10 Instruction Sheet

Boxes & Packing: 61-170 Corr. Outfit Box; 61-171 Corr. Insert; 61-182 Corr. Insert; 62-202 Corr. Insert; 61-174 Shipper for (6) (1-6)

19263 (1963)	C6	C7	C8	Rarity
Complete Outfit	250	400	625	R4
Outfit Box no. 61-170	115	175	300	R4

Comments: Libby's no. 19263 was the last of the three Manufacturer Promotional Type IIIb outfits that food manufacturers purchased from Lionel during the 1960s. It was preceded by Quaker's no. X-600 from 1960 and Stokely-Van Camp's no. 19142 from 1962. (See the entry for Libby in the section on Lionel's Distribution and Customers. Also see the section on The History of Lionel's Promotional Outfits for more information about the 19263.)

The 19263 was available to Libby customers who mailed in $10.95 and four labels from certain Libby canned products. In return, they received a Lionel train with a "$24.95 value". This offer expired December 31, 1963. However, by December 2, both Libby and Lionel realized the promotion was not going as well as expected because the factory orders were reduced from 17,500 to 12,000 outfits.

Regardless of what consumers might have thought of this outfit in 1963, collectors prize the 19263 because it introduced five brand-new additions to the Lionel product line, each of which was equipped with non-operating AAR trucks and couplers.

Four of these new models appeared only in promotional outfits, starting with the no. 1060T-50 Tender. Except for being stamped "Southern Pacific," it was identical to the no. 1060T-25 Tender. Hobbyists consider the 1060T-50 one of the more desirable of the small streamlined tenders.

The no. 19263 was available by mailing in $10.95 and four labels from certain Libby canned products. It is a highly desirable outfit because it introduced the nos. 1060T-50 Tender with Southern Pacific markings, 6050-175 Libby Box Car, 6475-50 Crushed Pineapple Car, 6076-125 Hopper with ATSF markings and 6167-75 Caboose with Union Pacific markings.

Libby's brings you a lot of train ($24⁹⁵) for only $10⁹⁵

...and it's a real LIONEL!

The Lionel electric train shown here represents a $24.95 value. It comes complete with reversible engine (including headlight), tender, 4 cars, 10-piece track and 35-watt transformer with circuit-breaker. But with four Libby's labels, it's only $10.95. Get it now—have it ready for a birthday or Christmas present!

TO: LIONEL TRAIN OFFER
P.O. BOX 7767, CHICAGO 77, ILLINOIS

Send this coupon with four labels from any of the Libby's canned products shown at left, plus check or money order for $10.95. We'll send you the Lionel electric train as illustrated and described above. Offer expires on December 31, 1963.

Name_____

Address_____

City_____State_____

... the most experienced food processor in the world

Libby advertised the no. 19263 promotion during the fall of 1963 in newspapers and magazines. Shown is the November 1963 issue of *Sunset* Magazine.

Next came a pair of cars that Lionel developed to promote Libby products. The Type III no. 6050-175 Libby Box Car was a new addition to the 6050-series of 8½-inch box cars. It advertised Libby's tomato juice and went on to be included in at least nine other promotional outfits. The no. 6475-50 Crushed Pineapple Car, like many other new items, merely featured new decoration on an existing model. In this case, a no. 6475-1 Pickle Car was molded in blue with Libby artwork added to the vats. The 6475-50 came in two shades of light blue, with aquamarine being the more desirable variation.

The fourth "promotional-only" item was the gray no. 6076-125 Hopper Car that came with "ATSF" markings. It showed up in this and three other promotional outfits. Although often overlooked, this model is one of the tougher low-end hoppers to find.

The fifth new piece of rolling stock was the yellow no. 6167-75 Caboose, which included "Union Pacific" markings. Lionel was still depleting its inventory of these models in 1969 when it offered the 6167-75 as both a component of catalog outfit no. 11730 and a separate-sale item. When individually boxed for separate sale, it became a no. 6167-85 Caboose.

The no. 1062-25 Steam Type Loco. W/Light & Reversing Unit that headed this outfit was also new for 1963. This low-end Scout steamer featured an 0-4-0 wheel arrangement and lacked any sort of traction aid. According to its Lionel Engineering Specification, the 1062-25 was the "Same as #1061 but with the addition of Reversing Unit & Lamp".

The no. 61-170 Tan RSC with Black Graphics outfit box was manufactured by United Container and measured 11½ x 10¼ x 6¼ inches. It included four lines of data as part of the box manufacturer's certificate (BMC). It also included a "63" and four stars as part of its BMC.

Surprisingly, Lionel did not pack the 19263 in the corrugated boxes that it used for other self-mailing outfits. The boxes used with the X-600 and 19142 were rated at 90 pounds and had no stamping on top.

Many 19263s have been observed with a return address from a Chicago post office box. Outfits that have been through this initial mailing are seldom found in C8 condition. Others were likely never shipped, as they have been observed without any type of shipment markings.

Of the three Manufacturer Promotional outfits purchased by food manufacturers, the 19263 is not as common as the X-600 or 19142. It is in fairly high demand due to its contents and association with Libby. A complete, high-grade example with proper peripherals and a C8 box with all inserts should be a prerequisite for any promotional outfit collector.

CONVENTIONAL PACK
61-170 BOX
9-6-63

TOP LAYER

62-202

| 1013-8 1018-10 (2) |
| 1060T-50 F |
| 6475-50 F |

BOTTOM LAYER

61-171 | 61-182

| 1062-25 S | 6167-75 F | 1010-25 | 6050-175 S | 6076-125 S |

2 CATALOGS BETWEEN LAYERS

Customer No. On Box: 1486
Description: "O27" Promotional Outfit
Specification: "O27" Diesel Freight Outfit with Horn
Customer/No.: Maritz; 1486
Original Amount: 250
Factory Order Date: 8/19/1963
Date Issued: Rev 8-22-63
Date Req'd: At Once
Packaging: RSC Outfit Packing (Units Boxed)

Contents: 218P-1 "Santa Fe" Alco Diesel Power Unit - with Horn; 6469-1 Miscellaneous Car; 6343-1 Barrel Ramp Car; 6476-1 Hopper Car; 6416-1 Boat Transport Car; 6017-1 Caboose; 1013-8 Curved Track (Bundle of 8 - 1013); 1018-30 Straight Track (Bundle of 3 - 1018); 6029-25 Remote Control Uncoupling Track; 1063-25 75-Watt Transformer; 90-30 Envelope Packed; 310-62 Set of (3) Billboards; D62-50 Accessory Catalog; 1123-40 Instruction Sheet; 1650-10 Instruction Sheet

Boxes & Packing: 61-380 Outfit Box; 61-381 Shipper for (4) (1-4)

Alternate For Outfit Contents:
Note: Customer Stock No. 1486.

19266 (1963)	C6	C7	C8	Rarity
Complete Outfit	825	1,300	1,800	R10
Outfit Box no. 61-380	375	575	725	R10

Comments: Maritz, a well-known marketing incentive firm, purchased this Retailer Promotional Type Ia outfit in 1963.

Incentive marketing firms were known to carry the same outfit for more than one year. Maritz began a four-year run with the nos. X-802 from 1960, X-683 from 1961 and 19172 from 1962 and finished with the no. 19266 from 1963. All four outfits carried Maritz's no. 1486.

Lionel's product life-cycles didn't always span the same years as its customer's outfits. As such, there are differences in all four of the outfits linked with Maritz based on currently available items. (See the entries for outfit nos. X-802, X-683 and 19172 for a full description of the components included.) The X-802 shares only a locomotive with the other outfits, although their other components are very similar.

The 19266 was based on the last available version of the 19172, with the exception that the nos. 6736-1 Mackinac Mac Hopper Car and 6812-1 Track Maintenance Car were no longer available. They were replaced by the nos. 6476-1 Hopper Car and 6469-1 Miscellaneous Car, respectively. Also, a no. 6017-1 Caboose took the place of the no. 6437-1 Illuminated Cupola Caboose.

The nos. 218P-1 Santa Fe Alco Diesel Power Unit, 6343-1 Barrel Ramp Car and 6476-1 were making their last appearance as boxed items in this outfit. Lionel was well on its way to placing all items in outfits unboxed. Since this was a carryover outfit, Maritz may have requested boxed items to keep it as similar as possible to the earlier versions of the 1486.

All the cars in the 19266 came packaged in Orange Picture boxes. They were equipped with a variety of AAR trucks and couplers. The 6017-1 had one operating and one plain type. Everything else came with either two operating or one operating and one non-operating type.

The no. 61-380 Tan RSC with Black Graphics outfit box measured 13¾ x 14 x 5⅛ inches.

As with the three other versions of Maritz's 1486, these outfits were produced in small quantities and are very difficult to find.

CONVENTIONAL PACK
61-380 BOX
8-15-63

TOP LAYER

| 1018-30 |
| 6476-1 F |
| 6029-25 1013-8 |

BOTTOM LAYER

6017-1 S	6469-1 S
	6416-1 F
1063-25	6343-1 F
	218P-1 S

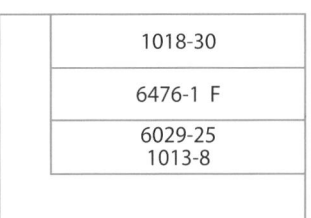

Description: "O27" Promotional Outfit
Specification: "O27" Steam Type Freight W/Smoke
Customer/No./Price: FAO Schwarz; 836-1; $32.50
Original Amount: 100
Factory Order Date: 8/19/1963
Date Issued: 8-20-63
Date Req'd: 9-20-63
Packaging: RSC Units Loose

Contents: 237-25 Steam Type Locomotive with Smoke; 1060T-25 Tender; 6500-25 Beechcraft Bonanza Transport Car; 6343-25 Barrel Ramp Car; 362-78 Wood Barrels (6); 6465-150 Tank Car; 6414-150 Auto Transport (Less Autos); 6406-30 Automobile (4); 6067-25 Caboose; 1047-1 Switchman With Flag; 310-1 Billboard Signs; 972-1 Landscape Tree Assortment; 1013-70 Curved Track (Bundle of 12 - 1013); 1018-30 Straight Track (Bundle of 3 - 1018); 1008-50 Uncoupling Unit; 1020-25 90° Crossing; 1025-25 45-Watt Transformer; 1103-20 Envelope Packed; 909-20 Smoke Fluid; 310-62 Set of (3) Billboards; D63-50 Accessory Catalog; 1-62 Parts Order Form; 1-63 Warranty Card; 122-10 Instruction Sheet; 1123-40 Instruction Sheet; 237-11 Instruction Sheet; 1802B Layout Instruction Sheet; 6500-3 Instruction Sheet

Boxes & Packing: 62-316 Outfit Box; 61-182 Corr. Insert (2); 62-248 Corr. Insert; 63-312 Corr. Insert; 62-319 Shipper for (3) (1-3)

19267 (1963)	C6	C7	C8	Rarity
Complete Outfit With Green Or Brown Automobiles	2,400	3,550	3,850	R10
Complete Outfit With Yellow Automobiles	1,800	2,750	2,850	R10
Outfit Box no. 62-316	750	1,000	1,250	R10

Comments: This Retailer Promotional Type Ib outfit listed FAO Schwarz on its Factory Order. The follow-up to that firm's no. 19175 from 1962, the no. 19267 appeared in the 1963 FAO Schwarz Christmas Catalog as the "Lionel Fast Freight Set". It was listed as FAO Schwarz no. 836-1 for $32.50. Curiously, it reused the same FAO catalog number from a year earlier.

The no. 19267 was led by a no. 237-25 Steam Type Locomotive with Smoke. This new-for-1963 Scout steamer featured a two-position reversing unit and a headlight and used a rubber tire as a traction aid. The harder-to-find early version with wide running boards was included in this outfit. Except for its 237 number, it was the same engine as a no. 238.

In 1963, Lionel was depleting its remaining inventory of the unboxed no. 6500-25 Beechcraft Bonanza Transport Car in promotional outfits. This model made one of its last five promotional outfit appearances in the 19267. The no. 6465-150 Tank Car was

an orange Lionel Lines model that was new for 1963.

The no. 6414-150 Auto Transport (Less Autos) was new for 1963. The suffix indicated that the 6414-150 came unboxed with one operating and one non-operating AAR truck and coupler. It likely included four green or brown no. 6406-30 Automobiles with gray bumpers. However, yellow automobiles with gray bumpers were possible; therefore, pricing is provided for these variations.

The norm for the nos. 1060T-25 Tender and 6067-25 Caboose in 1963 was one non-operating and one plain AAR truck and coupler, although a similar Archbar combination was possible. All the other cars in this outfit were equipped with two operating AAR trucks and couplers (nos. 6343-25 Barrel Ramp Car and 6500-25) or one operating and one non-operating type (6465-150).

The two most notable items in this outfit were the nos. 1047-1 Switchman With Flag and 972-1 Landscape Tree Assortment. The 1047-1 was last seen in the Lionel catalog from 1961, and Lionel began to deplete its remaining inventory of 4,740 units in this and five other promotional outfits. The accessory is enjoyable if not terribly exciting; however, its no. 1047-12 Folding Box was made of flimsy chipboard and did not survive well. It is extremely difficult to find in collectible condition with the top flap still attached, so that a boxed example adds a substantial premium to the value of this outfit.

The 972-1 appeared in three promotional outfits. It also included fragile packaging that did not hold up well over time and so adds a substantial premium to the value of this outfit.

The 19267 was one of the few outfits to come with a no. 310-1 Billboard Signs. This was the boxed version that included billboards and holders. A no. 310-62 Set of (3) Billboards was also put in this outfit.

All the paperwork reflected the new 90-day warranty policy that Lionel instituted in 1963. Many of these instruction sheet versions are the most difficult ones to find. A no. 1802B Layout Instruction Sheet detailed the figure-eight track layout.

The no. 62-316 Tan RSC with Black Graphics outfit box measured 17⅜ x 13¼ x 6⅞ inches.

With only 100 of the 19267s produced, it is rarely seen and easily achieves its R10 rarity rating.

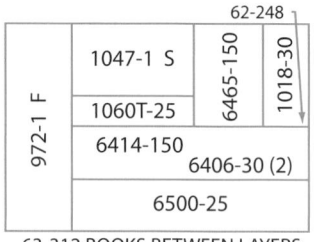

CONVENTIONAL PACK
62-316 BOX
8-16-63

TOP LAYER

6067-25 6406-30 (2)	1020-25	1025-25 362-78 (6)
	1013-70	1008-50
310-1 F	237-25 61-182	
	6343-25 6500 - AIRPLANE	

BOTTOM LAYER

62-248

972-1 F	1047-1 S	6465-150	1018-30
	1060T-25		
	6414-150		
	6406-30 (2)		
	6500-25		

63-312 BOOKS BETWEEN LAYERS

Description: Honig's Parkway Special
Customer: Honig's Parkway
Original Amount: 200
Factory Order Date: 9/6/1963

Date Issued: Rev 9-27-63
Date Req'd: 10-1-63
Packaging: All Units Individually Boxed - Ship Bulk

Contents: 2037LTS Steam Type Locomotive & Tender With Smoke & Whistle; 6414-1 Auto Transport Car; 3665-1 Minuteman Missile Launching Car; 6448-1 Exploding Target

Range Car; 3370-1 Sheriff & Outlaw Car; 494-1 Rotary Beacon; 110-1 Trestle Set; 1013 Curved Track Sections (Pack 100 per Box) (16); 1018 Straight Track Section (Pack 100 per Box) (23); 1020-1 90° Crossing; 1044-1 90-Watt Transformer; 6019-1 Remote Control Track Set; CTC-1 Lockon; 1122-1 Pr. Remote Control Switches; 145-1 Automatic Gateman; 262-1 Highway Crossing Gate

Alternate For Outfit Contents:
Note: Bulk Pack in any usable shippers - more than one permissible.

19268 (1963)	C6	C7	C8	Rarity
Items Only	835	1,425	1,900	N/A

Comments: This was the only Retailer Promotional Type Ia outfit purchased by Honig's Parkway department store, which was an authorized Lionel Service Station. The no. 19268 was a "bulk outfit". (For an explanation of the practice of buying "bulk outfits," consult the entry on Madison Hardware Co. in the section on Lionel's Distribution and Customers.)

This purchase by Honig's Parkway is curious because customers typically bought in bulk from Lionel as a ploy to further reduce the price paid for individual items intended for separate sale. Yet it appears that Honig's was actually buying outfit components in bulk with the intention of assembling this outfit on its own. Only a caboose was needed to make this into a complete outfit, and Honig's likely added one from its existing inventory.

For the 19268, no outfit box was provided, only bulk packaging. Lionel stated on the Factory Order, "Bulk Pack in any usable shippers…". However, no individual outfit boxes have been observed for any of the bulk outfits listed in this volume. As a result, we cannot ascertain whether these items were ever assembled and

sold as an outfit. Even if they were, we cannot prove that Honig's Parkway designated the grouping as 19268.

The 19268 was headed by a no. 2037LTS Steam Type Locomotive & Tender With Smoke & Whistle. What is interesting about this listing is that, even though the 2037LTS was not offered for separate sale in 1963, a 2037LTS Factory Order exists. That Factory Order included the same dates and quantity as the 19268, thus leading us to believe that the 2037LTS was available in 1963 only in this outfit.

Even more interesting is that the 2037LTS Factory Order listed a no. 637X-1 Steam Type Locomotive with Smoke with a no. 736W-1 Whistle Tender in a no. 12-77 Outfit Box. This information revealed, first, that Lionel included a 637X-1 in a 2037LTS master carton. Second, it showed that Lionel packaged a 2037LTS in 1963, even though that combination was not offered for separate sale. Consequently, the 19268 remains one of the sources of the difficult-to-find 2037LTS master cartons.

The rolling stock in this outfit was all carryover from earlier years. Lionel was likely thinning out old inventory. The norm for these items was operating AAR trucks and couplers and Orange Picture boxes.

The exact track layout is unknown, but it likely was elaborate. After all, Lionel packed with this outfit 16 sections of curved tracks, 23 straight tracks, a no. 110-1 Trestle Set and a no. 1122-1 Pr. Remote Control Switches.

A listing for the 19268 is provided here because a Factory Order exists for it. Pricing is provided as reference for the items alone. However, as stated earlier in this volume, items alone do not constitute an outfit; an outfit box is required.

Overall, it appears that with the 19268 Lionel took the opportunity to get rid of old inventory by sending it to a willing customer. Finding a box with any sort of markings for this outfit would be quite a discovery.

Description: "O27" Promotional Outfit
Specification: "O27" Freight Set for Canada
Customer: N. Friedlander Industries
Original Amount: 5,000
Factory Order Date: 9/6/1963
Date Issued: Rev 9-30-63
Date Req'd: 9-9-63
Packaging: RSC (Units Loose)

Contents: 1062-25 Steam Type Loco. W/Light & Reversing Unit; 1061T-25 Tender; 6409-25 Flat Car W/3 Pipes; 6511-15 Pipes (3); 6076-100 Hopper Car - Gray; 6402-25 Flat Car Without Load; 6405-150 Van; 6167-50 Caboose; 1013-8 Curved Track (Bundle of 8 - 1013); 1018-40 Straight Track (Bundle of 4 - 1018); 1026-25 25-Watt Transformer; 1103-20 Envelope Packed; 11311-10 Instruction Sheet; 310-62 Set of (3) Billboards; D63-50 Accessory Catalog; 1-62 Parts Order Form; 1-63 Warranty Card

Boxes & Packing: 61-170 Corr. Outfit Box; 61-171 Corr. Insert; 61-172 Corr. Insert; 61-173 Corr. Insert; 61-175 Shipper for (4) (1-4)

19269 (1963)	C6	C7	C8	Rarity
Complete Outfit	160	300	450	R4
Outfit Box no. 61-170	50	100	150	R4

Comments: N. Friedlander Industries appeared as the customer on the Factory Order for outfit nos. 19269 and 19270. Unfortunately, the identity and location of this firm have yet to be determined. As such, these outfits are either Retailer Promotional Type Ib or Manufacturer Promotional Type IIIb outfits. (See the entry for N. Friedlander in the section on Lionel's Distribution and Customers.)

The outfits were identical, except for the outfit packaging and instruction sheet. The 19269 came in a no. 61-170 Tan RSC with Black Graphics outfit box that measured 11½ x 10¼ x 6¼ inches. The 19270 came in a no. 63-306 White 4-6-4 Steamer and F3 Hinged Display with Red/Orange and Blue Graphics Type A outfit box. It listed the manufacturer as "SJPC" (likely St. Joe Paper Company) and measured 24½ x 11½ x 3⅛ inches.

The 19269 and 19270 were basic starter outfits. With the exception of the no. 6402-25 Flat Car Without Load from 1962, all the items included were new for 1963. The no. 1062-25 Steam Type Locomotive W/Light & Reversing Unit that headed the 19269 featured an 0-4-0 wheel arrangement and lacked any sort of traction aid. According to its Lionel Engineering Specification, it was the "Same as #1061 but with the addition of Reversing Unit & Lamp".

The cars in this pair of outfits offered further proof of how

Lionel was cheapening its product line in 1963: only the no. 6409-25 Flat Car W/3 Pipes had any markings. The no. 6167-50 Caboose was making its first promotional appearance in these two outfits. It was an unmarked and unpainted yellow plastic model. The no. 6405-150 Van was placed on a 6402-25 Flat Car Without Load because its normal car, the no. 6405-25 Single Van Flat Car (Less Van), had been depleted in outfit no. 19228.

Many combinations of trucks and couplers were apparent in 1963, and the cars in the 19269 showed how diverse they could be. For example, the nos. 1061T-25 Tender and 6167-50 had one plain and one non-operating truck and coupler. But AAR types were used on the Tender, and Archbar types were installed on the Caboose.

And that was just the beginning of the variety. The no. 6076-100 Hopper Car – Gray was equipped with non-operating AAR trucks and couplers. But all the remaining pieces of rolling stock had non-operating Archbar types. Anything seemed possible in 1963.

One subtle difference between the two outfits was that only the 19269 listed a no. 11311-10 Instruction Sheet.

Finally, Lionel produced more of the 19269. Even so, finding one can be as difficult as finding its companion.

CONVENTIONAL PACK
61-170 BOX
8-30-63

TOP LAYER		BOTTOM LAYER	
61-173		61-171	

TOP LAYER:
1013-8 1018-40	
	1061T-25
6409-25 6405-150 VAN	

BOTTOM LAYER:
| 1062-25 | 1026-25 | |
| | 6167-50 | 6076-100 / 6511-15 / 6402-25 |

61-172 BETWEEN LAYERS

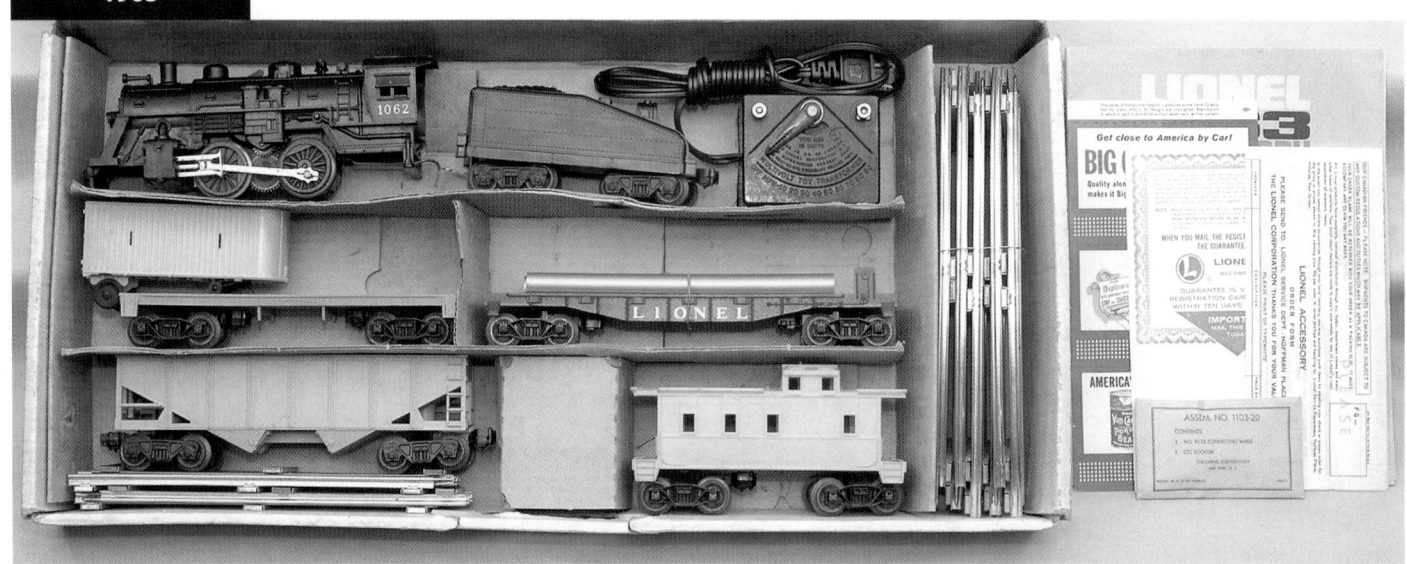

The no. 19270 was the display packaged version of outfit no. 19269. Both are representative of the further cheapening of the Lionel product line that occurred in 1963. Specifically, the no. 6167-50 Caboose was new in 1963 and had no markings. The no. 6402-25 Flat Car Without Load was used to carry a no. 6405-150 Van. All the cars were low-end models equipped with non-operating trucks and couplers.

The no. 63-306 White 4-6-4 Steamer and F3 Hinged Display with Red/Orange and Blue Graphics Type A outfit box was stamped by Lionel with "NO. 19270".

Description: "O27" Promotional Outfit
Specification: "O27" Freight Set for Canada
Customer: N. Friedlander Industries
Original Amount: 415
Factory Order Date: 9/6/1963
Date Issued: 9-6-63
Date Req'd: 9-9-63
Packaging: Display Outfit Packing (Units not Boxed)

Contents: 1062-25 Steam Type Loco. W/Light & Reversing Unit; 1061T-25 Tender; 6409-25 Flat Car W/3 Pipes; 6511-15 Pipes (3); 6076-100 Hopper Car - Gray; 6402-25 Flat Car Without Load; 6405-150 Van; 6167-50 Caboose; 1013-8 Curved Track (Bundle of 8 - 1013); 1018-40 Straight Track (Bundle of 4 - 1018); 1026-25 25-Watt Transformer; 1103-20 Envelope Packed;

310-62 Set of (3) Billboards; D63-50 Accessory Catalog; 1-62 Parts Order Form; 1-63 Warranty Card

Boxes & Packing: 63-306 Display Outfit Box; 61-101 Corr. Insert; 61-102 Corr. Insert (2); 63-307 Shipper for (4) (1-4)

19270 (1963)	C6	C7	C8	Rarity
Complete Outfit	305	585	900	R9
Outfit Box no. 63-306	200	400	600	R9

Comments: This was the display-packaged version of outfit no. 19269 from 1963. (See the listing for 19269 from 1963.)

DISPLAY PACK
63-306 BOX
9-3-63

1062-25	1061T-25	1026-25	
6402-25	6511-15 6409-25		1013-8
6076-100 1018-40	6167-50		

Description: "O27" Special Train Set
Specification: 8 Unit "O27" Special Train Set
Customer: Premium - (Irwin Diamond)
Original Amount: 750
Factory Order Date: 5/5/1964
Date Issued: 6/3/64
Date Req'd: March 1964
Packaging: White RSC Pack (Units Loose)

Contents: 223P-50 "Santa Fe" Alco Diesel Power Unit with Horn; 218C-25 "B" Unit - "Santa Fe"; 3619-100 Reconnaissance Copter Car; 3349-100 Turbo Missile Firing Car; 0349-10 Turbo Missile (2); 3470-100 Aerial Target Launching Car; 3470-20 Env. Packed; 3470-4 Basket; 3830-75 Oper. Submarine Car; 6407-25 Flat Car W/Sterling Missile; 6407-11 Sterling Missile; 6257-100 Caboose; 140-1 Banjo Signal; 1018 Straight Track (13); 1013 Curved Track (8); 1073-25 60-Watt Transformer; 147-25 Horn & Whistle Controller; 6139-25 Uncoupling Track Section; 1103-50 Envelope Packed; 310-2 Set (5) Billboards; D64-50 Accessory Catalog; Form 3063 Parts Order Form; 927-64 Service Station List; 1-65 Warranty Card; 11385-10 Instruction Sheet; 212-64 Instruction Sheet; 1123-40 Instruction Sheet; 3619-102 Instruction Sheet; 3349-105 Instruction Sheet; 3330-107 Instruction Sheet

Boxes & Packing: 19271-RSC Outfit Box; 62-224 Corr. Insert

19271 (1964)	C6	C7	C8	Rarity
Complete Outfit	1,500	2,000	3,000	R8
Outfit Box no. 19271-RSC	400	600	800	R8

Comments: Outfit no. 19271 listed Premium - (Irwin Diamond) as the customer on its Factory Order. Unfortunately, the identity and location of this company have yet to be determined. As such, this outfit is either a Retailer Promotional Type Ia or a Manufacturer Promotional Type IIIa outfit.

According to the 19271's Factory Order, it was the same as catalog outfit no. 11385 with the addition of a no. 140-1 Banjo Signal and 10 extra sections of no. 1018 Straight Track.

Lionel Worksheets indicate that this outfit originated on 8/28/63, thus the 19271 designation, which was part of the 1963 numbering sequence. For some reason, Irwin Diamond wanted delivery in 1964, and this became a 1964 outfit. Irwin Diamond paid Lionel $28.87 for each outfit.

As with the 11385, this is a very desirable space and military outfit. It was led by a no. 223P-50 Santa Fe Alco Diesel Power Unit with Horn. The 223P-50 (new in 1963) was an unboxed version

of the no. 223P-1 that had traction tires instead of Magne-Traction. This "-50" variation appeared in only this and outfit no. 11385 from the previous year. Like the 223P-1, it also featured a two-position reversing unit and a headlight. The no. 218C-25 Santa Fe "B" Unit in this outfit was an unnumbered model.

The rolling stock in the 19271 included the same difficult-to-find variations of cars and instruction sheets that first appeared in 11385 from 1963.

The no. 3619-100 Reconnaissance Copter Car included in the 19271 was likely the dark yellow variation that included a fragile and easily lost no. 0319-100 Helicopter. As part of the manufacturing process, the roof of the 3619-100 was taped shut with a ½-inch piece of Scotch tape. Even examples in C8 condition still have a mark where the tape was applied. Lionel originally intended the 3619-100 to include one operating and one non-operating AAR truck and coupler. In fact the uncommon no. 3619-102 Instruction Sheet noted, "If the car has a non-operating coupler..." A 3619-100 configured with one operating and one non-operating type has yet to be observed.

The no. 3470-100 Aerial Target Launching Car in this outfit was likely the difficult-to-find version with a light blue frame. As with the other cars, the "-100" indicated a change from two operating AAR trucks and couplers to one operating and one non-operating type. Its no. 3470-103 Instruction Sheet is very difficult to find.

The no. 3349-100 Turbo Missile Firing Car was the same as a no. 3349-25 Turbo Missile Firing Car, except that it was equipped with one operating and one non-operating AAR truck and coupler. Its no. 3349-105 Instruction Sheet is very difficult to find.

The no. 3830-75 Oper. Submarine Car was, with one difference, identical to the no. 3830-25 Oper. Submarine Car. According to the 3830-75's Production Control File, it was equipped with one operating and one non-operating AAR truck and coupler.

The unboxed no. 6407-25 Flat Car W/Sterling Missile (new for 1963) was included in 11 different outfits, with a total of 13,124 cars produced. This highly collectible item was also available for separate sale as a no. 6407-1. The flat car was a common red no. 6511-series model with "Lionel" stamped on each side. It featured a brake wheel plus one operating and one non-operating AAR truck and coupler. The same flat car was used with the no. 6408-25 Flat Car W/5 Pipes.

The flat car might be common, but the no. 6407-11 Sterling Missile was not. This load, manufactured by Sterling Plastics, was frequently separated from its flat car because it lacked Lionel markings. An authentic original would have "Sterling Plastics" molded into the capsule bottom and rocket base.

Finally, the no. 6257-100 Caboose with a smokestack was reissued in 1963 with one operating and one plain AAR truck and coupler.

The appropriate instruction sheets for the 19271 made reference to the 90-day warranty policy that Lionel instituted in 1963. The no. 11385-10 Instruction Sheet was dated 6/63.

The box for the 19271 was likely a White RSC with Orange Graphics outfit box, although a Tan RSC with Black Graphics

outfit box is possible.

This is a difficult outfit box to find and even more so to complete. Some of the variations included in the 19271 are subtle, and others are not. Even if all the cars are found, patience is required to track down the correct versions of the instruction sheets. The 19271 was produced in smaller quantities than the 11385 and is likely to generate as much collector interest now that its contents have been verified.

19272
1963

The no. 19272 was S. Klein's 1963 follow-up to its no. 19192 from 1962. The outfits were similar, with the 19272 being the better of the two. It included two often paired operating cars, the nos. 6470-25 Exploding Target Car and 6544-25 Missile Firing Car. The outfit is shown as listed on the Factory Order without the no. 6448-25 Exploding Target Car substitution. The 19272 came with the no. 310-62 Set of (3) Billboards and not the no. 310-2 Set of (5) Billboard Signs that's shown.

Description: "O27" Promotional Outfit
Specification: "O27" Steam Type Freight Outfit
Customer: S. Klein
Original Amount: 2,050
Factory Order Date: 10/3/1963
Date Issued: 10-3-63
Date Req'd: 10-1-63
Packaging: RSC (Units Loose)

Contents: 1061-25 Steam Type Locomotive; 1061T-25 Tender; 6544-25 Missile Firing Car; 6470-25 Exploding Target Car; 6042-75 Gondola Car (Less 2 Cable Reels); 40-11 Cable Reels (2); 6067-25 Caboose; 1013-8 Curved Track (Bundle of 8 - 1013); 1018-10 Straight Track (Loose) (2); 1026-25 25-Watt Transformer; 1103-20 Envelope Packed; 310-62 Set of (3) Billboards; D63-50 Accessory Catalog; 1-62 Parts Order Form; 1-63 Warranty Card;

6470-17 Instruction Sheet; 19272-10 Instruction Sheet; 1123-40 Instruction Sheet; 6544-12 Instruction Sheet

Boxes & Packing: 61-170 Outfit Box; 61-171 Corr. Insert; 61-173 Corr. Insert; 61-174 Shipper for (6) (1-6)

Alternate For Outfit Contents:
Note: Substitute 1,950 - 6448-25 for 6470-25.

19272 (1963)	C6	C7	C8	Rarity
Complete Outfit As Listed	290	475	700	R6
Complete Outfit With no. 6448-25	280	460	675	R6
Outfit Box no. 61-170	100	175	225	R6

Comments: S. Klein was a discount retailer that purchased numerous promotional Lionel outfits in the 1960s. In 1963, it ordered outfit nos. 19272 and 19273 as its respective low- and high-end purchases.

The 19272, a Retailer Promotional Type Ib, was S. Klein's follow-up to its no. 19192 from 1962. A small but exciting space and military outfit, the 19272 was led by a no. 1061-25 Steam Type Locomotive. This stripped-down Scout steamer (new for 1963) featured an 0-4-0 wheel arrangement and went forward only. It lacked a headlight, a lens and any sort of traction aid.

The 19272 included two operating cars, the nos. 6470-25 Exploding Target Car and 6544-25 Missile Firing Car. Both were old cars in the product line, having been introduced in 1959 and 1960, respectively. That they were not new would hardly have mattered to youngsters, who could spend hours blowing up the 6470-25. The unboxed 6544-25 was equipped with operating AAR trucks and couplers. By leaving the 6544-25 unboxed, Lionel exposed the car's fragile brake wheels to possible damage.

The nos. 1060T-25 Tender and 6067-25 Caboose included in this outfit were equipped with one non-operating and one plain truck and coupler. The no. 6042-75 Gondola Car (Less 2 Cable Reels) had non-operating AAR trucks and couplers. The usual configuration for the 6470-25 was one operating and one non-operating AAR truck and coupler in 1963, although two operating types were possible.

The no. 6448-25 Exploding Target Range Car substitution

affects the outfit price, as listed in the pricing table.

The appropriate instruction sheets for this outfit made reference to the 90-day warranty policy that Lionel instituted in 1963. This outfit introduced the difficult-to-find no. 19272-10 Instruction Sheet dated 9/63.

The no. 61-170 Tan RSC with Black Graphics outfit box was manufactured by United Container and measured 11½ x 10¼ x 6¼ inches. It had four lines of data as part of the box manufacturer's certificate (BMC). It also included a "63" and four stars as part of its BMC.

With 2,050 examples of the 19272 manufactured, obtaining one is possible. However, it does not appear as often as other outfits that were produced in similar quantities.

CONVENTIONAL PACK
61-170 BOX
9-30-63

Description: "O27" Promotional Outfit
Specification: "O27" Steam Type Freight W/Smoke
Customer/Price: S. Klein; $19.77
Original Amount: 800
Factory Order Date: 10/3/1963
Date Issued: Rev 10-8-63
Date Req'd: 10-1-63
Packaging: RSC (Units Loose)

19273 (1963)	C6	C7	C8	Rarity
Complete Outfit As Listed	565	875	1,250	R8
Complete Outfit With All Substitutions	575	885	1,305	R8
Outfit Box no. 63-309	200	275	350	R8

Contents: 237-25 Steam Type Locomotive with Smoke; 1060T-25 Tender; 3410-25 Oper. Helicopter Car (Less Helicopter); 3419-100 Operating Helicopter Complete; 3349-25 Turbo Missile Firing Car (Less Missiles); 0349-10 Turbo Missile (2); 6470-25 Exploding Target Car; 6650-25 Missile Launching Flat Car; 6650-80 Missile; 6413-25 Mercury Capsule Transport Car; 6413-10 Envelope Packed; 6413-4 Capsules (2); 6057-25 Caboose; 1013-70 Curved Track (Bundle of 12 - 1013); 1018-30 Straight Track (Bundle of 3 - 1018); 1008-50 Uncoupling Unit; 1020-25 90° Crossing; 1010-25 35-Watt Transformer; 1103-20 Envelope Packed; 909-20 Smoke Fluid; 310-62 Set of (3) Billboards; D63-50 Accessory Catalog; 1-62 Parts Order Form; 1-63 Warranty Card; 6470-17 Instruction Sheet; 3349-105 Instruction Sheet; 1123-40 Instruction Sheet; 19171-10 Instruction Sheet; 237-11 Instruction Sheet; 3410-5 Instruction Sheet; 6650-92 Instruction Sheet

Boxes & Packing: 63-309 Outfit Box; 61-171 Corr. Insert; 61-186 Corr. Insert; 62-264 Corr. Insert; 63-311 Corr. Insert; 63-310 Shipper for (4) (1-4)

Alternate For Outfit Contents:
Note: Substitute 3419-250 for 3410-25; Substitute 6448-25 for 6470-25; Substitute 6067-25 for 6057-25.

Comments: S. Klein was a discount retailer that purchased numerous promotional Lionel outfits in the 1960s. In 1963, it ordered outfit nos. 19272 and 19273 as its respective low- and high-end purchases.

The 19273, a Retailer Promotional Type Ia, was a space and military offering led by a no. 237-25 Steam Type Locomotive with Smoke. This new-for-1963 Scout steamer featured a two-position reversing unit and a headlight and used a rubber tire as a traction aid. The harder-to-find early version with wide running boards was included in this outfit. Except for its 237 number, it was the same engine as a no. 238.

When Lionel listed substitutions without quantities, the original items were swapped out entirely. This is what occurred with the 19273 because all the items replaced would reach the end of their product life in the coming months. Any inventory of the nos. 3410-25 Oper. Helicopter Car (Less Helicopter) and 6057-25 Caboose likely had already been assigned to other outfits and thus was not available.

Pricing is provided for the 19273 as listed on the Factory Order and with all substitutions. The outfit packing diagram showed the original items. Any substitutions would be placed in the same location.

Except for the no. 3419-250 Operating Helicopter Car, all the items in this outfit were carried over from earlier years. The 3419-250 appeared only in one catalog and four promotional outfits, with a total of 9,966 produced. Per its Factory Order, the "-250" suffix indicated that it was equipped with one operating and one non-operating AAR truck and coupler, although the one included in this outfit has been observed with two operating AAR types. The 3419-250's frame was molded in a lighter shade of blue plastic. The light blue version is much more difficult to find and is reflected in the outfit pricing. The no. 3419-100 Operating Helicopter Complete was the one-piece yellow body version. This fragile helicopter was frequently lost or broken.

The nos. 6448-25 Exploding Target Car and 6650-25 Missile Launching Car were paired in at least six catalog and promotional outfits. Both were at or near the end of their product life. The 6448-25 has been observed in an all-red variation in this outfit. There is no premium for this variation because it is easily re-created. The version in this outfit came with "non-slotted" sides and nubs on the roof door guide to help hold on the sides.

The difficult-to-find aquamarine version of the no. 6413-25 Mercury Capsule Carrying Car was included in the 19273. This car adds a premium to the outfit price.

The no. 1060T-25 Tender included one non-operating and one plain Archbar truck and coupler. The 6067-25 Caboose included one non-operating and one plain AAR truck and coupler. The nos. 3349-25 Turbo Missile Firing Car (Less Missiles), 6448-25 and 6650-25 were equipped with two operating AAR trucks and

couplers. The 6413-25 came with one operating and one non-operating AAR truck and coupler.

All the paperwork reflected the new 90-day warranty policy that Lionel instituted in 1963. Many of these instruction sheet versions are the most difficult ones to find. A no. 19171-10 Instruction Sheet detailed the figure-eight track layout.

The no. 63-309 Tan RSC with Black Graphics outfit box was manufactured by the Mead Corporation and measured 13¼ x 12½ x 6¾ inches.

Of the two S. Klein outfits from 1963, the 19273 is by far the more difficult to find and complete. Acquiring the correct versions of the instruction sheets requires lots of time and patience.

CONVENTIONAL PACK
63-309 BOX
9-30-63

TOP LAYER					BOTTOM LAYER	
					61-171	

TOP LAYER: 1018-30 · 6650-25 · 3410-25 / 3419-100 · 2 CAPS / 1060T-25 · 1013-70 / 1008-50 · 62-264

BOTTOM LAYER: 61-171 · 1010-25 · 237-25 · 6057-25 · 6470-25 · 6413-25 · 63-311 · 3349-25 · 0349-10 (2) · 1020-25 TOP 6057 · 61-186 BETWEEN LAYERS

19273-500
1963

Description: "O27" Promotional Outfit
Specification: "O27" Steam Type Freight Outfit
Original Amount: 1,000
Factory Order Date: 11/22/1963
Date Issued: 11-22-63
Date Req'd: 11-22-63
Packaging: RSC (Units Loose)

Contents: 242-25 Steam Type Locomotive; 1060T-25 Tender; 3376-160 Operating Giraffe Car; 3309-25 Turbo Missile Firing Car (Less Missiles); 0349-10 Turbo Missile (2); 3619-1 Reconnaissance Copter Car; 6406-25 Flat Car W/Auto; 6406-30 Automobile; 6076-100 Hopper Car - Gray; 6014-325 Frisco Box Car; 6067-25 Caboose; 161-1 Mail Pickup Set; 1013-70 Curved Track (Bundle of 12 - 1013); 1018-7 Straight Track (Bundle of 7 - 1018); 1008-50 Uncoupling Unit; 1020-25 90° Crossing; 1010-25 35-Watt Transformer; 1103-20 Envelope Packed; 310-62 Set of (3) Billboards; D63-50 Accessory Catalog; 1-62 Parts Order Form; 1-63 Warranty Card; 3309-5 Instruction Sheet; 19273-10 Instruction Sheet

Boxes & Packing: 63-313 Outfit Box; 61-171 Corr. Insert; 63-314 Shipper for (4) (1-4)

Alternate For Outfit Contents:
Note: Substitute 500 - 3349-1 for 3309-25; Substitute 236 - 1130T-25 for 1060T-25; Substitute 141 - 1020-1 for 1020-25.

19273-500 (1963)	C6	C7	C8	Rarity
Complete Outfit As Listed	525	800	1,165	R7
Complete Outfit With no. 3349-1	545	830	1,210	R7
Complete Outfit With Brown Or Green Automobile, Add The Following	150	200	250	R7
Outfit Box no. 63-313	100	200	300	R7

Comments: This General Release Promotional Type IIb outfit was one of the many outfits that Lionel issued late in 1963 in an attempt to deplete inventory. As such, the no. 19273-500 included a bit of everything.

As with many other outfits that included a "-500" series suffix, the 19273-500 had nothing in common with the no. 19273. The "-500" suffix was added as though it were an entirely new outfit.

The 19273-500 was led by a no. 242-25 Steam Type Locomotive. This low-end Scout steamer featured a two-position reversing unit and a headlight, lacked smoke and used a rubber tire as a traction aid. The version with wide running boards was included in this outfit. The 242-25 pulled a no. 1060T-25 Tender or a substituted no. 1130T-25 Tender. The quantity of 236 of the 1130T-25s was the last time this tender appeared in an outfit. It was equipped with one operating and one plain AAR truck and coupler.

Since this outfit was used to deplete inventory, almost anything was possible. Some items were boxed, and others weren't. Cars could be generic freight or space and military items. Whatever was on the shelves seemed to be fair game. The only brand-new items were the no. 6076-100 Hopper Car – Gray and the Type II no. 6014-325 Frisco Box Car.

Three other items worth noting were the boxed nos. 3376-160

Boxes & Packing: 63-309 Outfit Box; 61-181 Corr. Insert; 61-182 Corr. Insert; 61-186 Corr. Insert; 62-264 Corr. Insert; 63-311 Corr. Insert; 63-312 Corr. Insert; 63-310 Shipper for (4) (1-4)

19275 (1963)	C6	C7	C8	Rarity
Complete Outfit With Green Or Brown Automobiles	2,775	3,625	4,400	R10
Complete Outfit With Yellow Automobiles	2,175	2,825	3,400	R10
Outfit Box no. 63-309	1,750	2,250	2,500	R10

Comments: E. F. MacDonald Co. was a leader in employee incentive rewards. It purchased two outfits in 1963: nos. 19275 and 19280.

Only 40 of the 19275 were manufactured, making it extremely difficult to find. So small a quantity suggested that this Retailer Promotional Type Ia outfit was used as a reward for employees of one of E. F. MacDonald's customers. It also appears that E. F. MacDonald provided direct fulfillment because the Factory Order called for mail-order cartons.

The 19275 was typical of many higher-end outfits from 1963. It was led by a no. 238-25 Steam Locomotive with Smoke (new for 1963). This Scout steamer featured a two-position reversing unit, a headlight and a rubber tire as a traction aid. The early version with wide running boards was included in this outfit. Except for its 238 number, it was the same engine as a no. 237. The 238-25 pulled a no. 234W-25 Whistle Tender, which could come equipped with Archbar or AAR trucks and couplers in 1963.

The transition from Archbar to AAR trucks and couplers that began in 1962 continued into 1963. As part of this, Lionel sought to cut costs by introducing a non-operating AAR type. Therefore, starting in 1963, most cars equipped with AAR trucks and couplers had at least one non-operating type. The new suffixes assigned to many of the cars in the 19275 reflected this change.

The no. 6414-150 Auto Transport (Less Autos) was new for 1963. The "-150" indicated that it came unboxed with one operating and one non-operating AAR truck and coupler. The 6414-150 likely included four green or brown no. 6406-30 Automobiles with gray bumpers, but yellow automobiles with gray bumpers were possible. Pricing is provided for these variations.

The no. 6822-50 Searchlight Car was an unboxed 6822 with one operating and one non-operating AAR truck and coupler. The "-50" suffix version was new in 1963.

The one operating and one non-operating AAR configuration also appeared on the nos. 6162-25 Gondola Car (Less 2 Canisters) and 6465-150 Tank Car. It was probably the norm as well for the no. 6476-75 Hopper Car - Black. Finally, the no. 6257-100 Caboose with a smokestack was reissued in 1963 with one operating and one plain AAR truck and coupler.

The appropriate instruction sheets for this outfit made reference to the 90-day warranty policy that Lionel instituted in 1963. The no. 11385-10 Instruction Sheet was dated 6/63.

The no. 63-309 Tan RSC with Black Graphics outfit box measured 13¼ x 12½ x 6¾ inches.

With only 40 examples manufactured, the 19275 easily achieves an R10 rarity rating.

CONVENTIONAL PACK
63-309 BOX
9-6-63

Description: "O27" Promotional Outfit
Specification: "O27" Steam Type Freight Outfit
Customer: Masters
Original Amount: 548
Factory Order Date: 10/3/1963
Date Issued: 11-14-63
Date Req'd: 10-1-63
Packaging: RSC (Units Loose)

Contents: 1062-25 Steam Type Loco. W/Light & Reversing Unit; 1061T-25 Tender; 3410-25 Oper. Helicopter Car (Less Helicopter); 3419-100 Operating Helicopter Complete; 6042-75 Gondola Car (Less 2 Cable Reels); 40-11 Cable Reels (2); 6406-25 Flat Car W/Auto; 6406-30 Automobile; 6067-25 Caboose; 1013-8 Curved Track (Bundle of 8 - 1013); 1018-10 Straight Track (Loose) (2); 1010-25 35-Watt Transformer; 1103-20 Envelope Packed; 111-1 Trestle Set; 310-62 Set of (3) Billboards; D63-50 Accessory Catalog; 1-62 Parts Order Form; 1-63 Warranty Card; 3410-5 Instruction Sheet; 19228-10 Instruction Sheet; 1123-40 Instruction Sheet

Boxes & Packing: 62-243 Outfit Box; 61-171 Corr. Insert; 62-264 Corr. Insert; 62-244 Shipper for (4) (1-4)

19276 (1963)	C6	C7	C8	Rarity
Complete Outfit With Green Or Brown Automobile	635	900	1,200	R8
Complete Outfit With Yellow Automobile	485	700	950	R8
Outfit Box no. 62-243	300	400	475	R8

Comments: After purchasing three promotional outfits in 1961, Masters followed them up with the no. 19276 two years later. Masters leased departments within discount stores, and that is where this Retailer Promotional Type Ib outfit was likely sold.

The 19276 was a follow-up to two of the Masters outfits from 1961. It contained items of a similar value to those in outfit no. X-702. The 19276 also came with an elevated oval track layout, as had outfit no. X-703. The no. 902-1 Cardboard Trestle With Girder Bridge & Tunnel used in X-703 was no longer available, so the 19276 used a no. 111-1 Trestle Set.

A no. 1062-25 Steam Type Locomotive W/Light & Reversing Unit led the 19276. This low-end Scout steamer (new for 1963) featured an 0-4-0 wheel arrangement and lacked a traction aid.

According to its Lionel Engineering Specification, it was the "Same as #1061 but with the addition of Reversing Unit & Lamp".

The no. 3410-25 Oper. Helicopter Car (Less Helicopter) was making its final outfit appearances in 1963 and 1964. The 3410-25 followed the general truck and coupler progression and most often came equipped with one operating and one non-operating AAR type in 1963. The norm for a no. 3419-100 Operating Helicopter Complete was a one-piece yellow body in 1963. This fragile helicopter was frequently lost or broken.

In 1963, the no. 6406-25 Flat Car W/Auto began to appear in gray molded plastic and most often featured non-operating Archbar trucks and couplers. The no. 6406-30 Automobile was most often molded in brown or green plastic with gray bumpers, but a yellow automobile with gray bumpers was also possible. The specific color cannot be confirmed for this outfit. Pricing is provided for these variations.

The no. 6042-75 Gondola Car usually was equipped with non-operating AAR trucks and couplers. The norm for both the nos. 1061T-25 Tender and 6067-25 Caboose in 1963 was one non-operating and one plain AAR truck and coupler, although a similar Archbar configuration was possible.

The appropriate instruction sheets for this outfit made reference to the 90-day warranty policy that Lionel instituted in 1963.

The no. 62-243 Tan RSC with Black Graphics outfit box measured 12⅛ x 11½ x 6⅜ inches.

The 19276 exceeded Masters' forecasts because the order was increased from 300 to 548 units on 11-4-63. Even with the increase in quantity, this outfit is difficult to find in any condition.

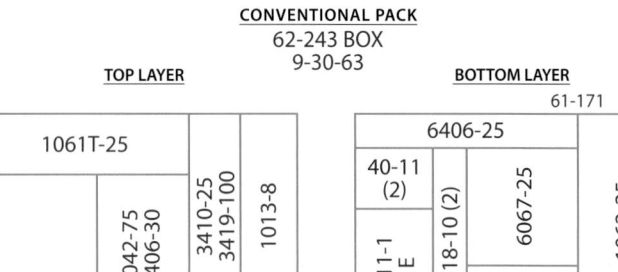

CONVENTIONAL PACK
62-243 BOX
9-30-63

TOP LAYER — BOTTOM LAYER

62-264 — 2 CATALOGS BETWEEN LAYERS

Description: "O27" Promotional Outfit
Specification: "O27" Steam Type Freight W/Smoke
Customer: E. F. MacDonald Co.
Original Amount: 500
Factory Order Date: 10/3/1963
Date Issued: 10-3-63
Date Req'd: 216 At Once; Bal 10-5-63
Packaging: RSC (Units Loose)

CONVENTIONAL PACK
61-170 BOX
9-30-63

TOP LAYER — BOTTOM LAYER

2 CATALOGS BETWEEN LAYERS

Contents: 237-25 Steam Type Locomotive with Smoke; 1060T-25 Tender; 3370-25 Sheriff & Outlaw Car; 6343-25 Barrel Ramp Car; 362-78 Wood Barrels (6); 6119-100 Work Caboose; 1013-8 Curved Track (Bundle of 8 - 1013); 1018-10 Straight Track (Loose); 1008-50 Uncoupling Unit; 1025-25 45-Watt Transformer; 1103-20 Envelope Packed; 909-20 Smoke Fluid; 310-62 Set of (3) Billboards; D63-50 Accessory Catalog; 1-62 Parts Order Form; 1-63 Warranty Card; 237-11 Instruction Sheet; 122-10 Instruction Sheet; 3370-17 Instruction Sheet

Boxes & Packing: 61-170 Outfit Box; 62-254 Corr. Insert; 62-264 Corr. Insert; 61-174 Shipper for (6) (1-6)

19280 (1963)	C6	C7	C8	Rarity
Complete Outfit	500	725	990	R9
Outfit Box no. 61-170	300	425	550	R9

Comments: E. F. MacDonald Co. was a leader in employee incentive rewards. It purchased two outfits in 1963: nos. 19275 and 19280.

The 19280, a Retailer Promotional Type Ia, was likely offered to employees of one of E. F. MacDonald's customers as a reward. This starter outfit featured a locomotive with smoke and one operating car, which made it a higher-end item.

A no. 237-25 Steam Type Locomotive with Smoke led the 19280. This new-for-1963 Scout steamer featured a two-position reversing unit and a headlight and used a rubber tire as a traction aid. The harder-to-find early version with wide running boards was included in this outfit. Except for its 237 number, this was the same engine as a no. 238.

The nos. 3370-25 Sheriff & Outlaw Car and 6343-25 Barrel Ramp Car first appeared in 1961. The 3370-25 was making its final unboxed appearance in promotional outfits in 1963. The norm for both cars was operating AAR trucks and couplers.

The no. 1060T-25 Tender in this set typically came with one non-operating and one plain AAR truck and coupler in 1963. The no. 6119-100 Work Caboose had one operating and one plain AAR type.

The appropriate instruction sheets for this outfit made reference to the 90-day warranty policy that Lionel instituted in 1963. The no. 122-10 Instruction Sheet was dated 5-62.

The no. 61-170 Tan RSC with Black Graphics outfit box measured 11½ x 10¼ x 6¼ inches.

Lionel manufactured 500 examples of the 19280. This outfit seldom appears on the market.

Outfit no. 19281 was Shell Oil's only Manufacturer Promotional Type IIIb purchase. It consisted of surplus items and was produced in large quantities. The outfit as shown includes the nos. 3349-1 Turbo Missile Firing Car, 6076-100 Hopper Car - Gray and 6167-25 Caboose substitutions.

Description: "O27" Special Outfit
Specification: "O27" Diesel Freight Outfit
Customer: Shell Oil
Original Amount: 5,000
Factory Order Date: 10/15/1963
Date Issued: 10-15-63
Date Req'd: 1,000 - 11-1; 2,000 - 11-10; 2,000 - 11-20
Packaging: RSC (Units Loose)

Contents: 231P-25 Alco Diesel Power Car - "Rock Island"; 3309-25 Turbo Missile Firing Car (Less Missiles); 0349-10 Turbo Missile (2); 6402-25 Flat Car W/2 Cable Reels; 40-11 Cable Reels (2); 6076-75 Hopper Car - Black; 6473-25 Rodeo Car; 6017-25 Caboose; 1013-70 Curved Track (Bundle of 12 - 1013); 1018-7 Straight Track (Bundle of 7 - 1018) (2); 1025-25 45-Watt Transformer; CTC-1 Lockon; 81-32 24" R.C. Wire (2); 110-1 Trestle Set; D63-50 Accessory Catalog; 1-62 Parts Order Form; 1-63 Warranty Card; 19145-10 Instruction Sheet; 225-6 Instruction Sheet; 1123-40 Instruction Sheet; 1802A Layout Instruction Sheet; 3309-5 Instruction Sheet

Boxes & Packing: 63-385 Outfit Box (Required when using 3349-1 Car); 61-171 Corr. Insert; 61-183 Corr. Insert; 62-245 Corr. Insert (2); 62-248 Corr. Insert; 62-273 Corr. Insert; 62-271 Shipper for (3) (1-3); 63-385 Outfit Box (Required when using 3309-25 Car); 61-171 Corr. Insert; 61-183 Corr. Insert; 62-245 Corr. Insert (2); 62-248 Corr. Insert; 62-264 Corr. Insert; 62-273 Corr. Insert; 62-271 Shipper for (3) (1-3)

Alternate For Outfit Contents:
Note: Lionel name must not appear on the Ind. Carton; Note: Substitute 3,109 - 3349-1 for 3309-25; Substitute 2,427 - 6076-100 for 6076-75; Substitute 400 - 6059-50 for 6017-25; Substitute 888 - 6059-25 for 6017-25; Substitute 85 - 6167-50 for 6017-25; Substitute 203 - 6167-25 for 6017-25.

19281 (1963)	C6	C7	C8	Rarity
Complete Outfit	300	525	750	R4
Complete Outfit With no. 3349-1 Substitution	320	555	795	R4
Outfit Box no. 63-385	100	200	300	R4

Comments: Shell Oil followed the lead of Cities Service, one of its competitors, when it decided to purchase this Lionel outfit. The no. 19281, a Manufacturer Promotional Type IIIb outfit, was likely used for a promotion. However, the nature of such a promotion

This no. 19281 was shipped in its no. 63-385 Outfit Box direct from Shell in New York City. Notice the Shell shipping label and metered postage dated November, 1963. Finding a direct-shipped outfit in C8 condition is difficult because of normal shipment wear. The box shown here is slightly bowed and creased. Unfortunately for Lionel and Shell, all the outfits did not sell, with several being available through Madison Hardware Co. Fortunately for collectors, those outfits were never individually shipped and are often found in C7 or C8 condition.

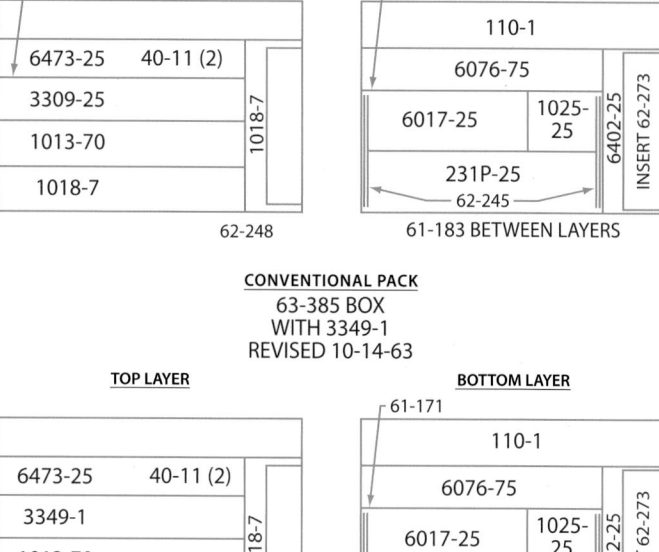

has yet to be determined. (See the entry for Shell Oil in the section on Lionel's Distribution and Customers.)

An internal memorandum sent from the Sales Department at Lionel to its Manufacturing Department shed light on the contents of the 19281. Titled "#19281 Shell Oil Train Set", this memo of 10/8/63 stated, "You will note that this outfit uses all surplus merchandise with the exception, of course, of track and transformers."

The use of surplus merchandise to create promotional outfits was typical of many of the outfits from late in 1963. In fact, the 19281 marked the last appearance of the no. 6059-25 Caboose and depleted the remaining 1963 inventory of the nos. 3309-25 Turbo Missile Firing Car and 6167-50 Caboose.

The no. 231P-25 Rock Island Alco Diesel Power Car that led this outfit was first issued in 1961. It featured two-axle Magne-Traction, a headlight and a two-position reversing unit. This locomotive was nearing the end of its product life.

The 3309-25 was the low-end version of the no. 3349-1 Turbo Missile Firing Car. The difference between the two cars was that the 3309-25 was equipped with non-operating Archbar rather than operating AAR trucks and couplers. Lionel had a quantity of 1,891 of the 3309-25s in stock and fulfilled the difference by substituting a 3349-1. This substitution affects the price, as listed in the pricing table.

The no. 6473-25 Rodeo Car has been observed with both a Type IIa body (bright yellow) and a Type IIb body (cadmium yellow); both variations had red stamping. The Type II body included a partially filled slot due to broken tooling, as was noted in the *Authoritative Guide to Lionel's Postwar Operating Cars* (Project Roar Publishing).

The 6473-25 was equipped with operating AAR trucks and couplers. The gray no. 6402-25 Flat Car in this outfit came with two non-operating Archbar types.

The no. 6076-75 Hopper Car - Black was still going strong in the Lionel product line. Lionel likely had plenty in inventory but split the quantity of 5,000 hoppers required for the 19281 between a 6076-75 and an unmarked no. 6076-100 Hopper Car - Gray.

The norm for both of these cars in 1963 was non-operating AAR trucks and couplers, although in the 19281 the 6076-100 is most often observed with non-operating Archbar types.

The no. 6017-25 Caboose was nearing its end, and Lionel made up for the shortfall by reducing the inventory of other cabooses. The 6017-25 was equipped with one operating and one plain AAR truck and coupler.

The appropriate instruction sheets for this outfit made reference to the 90-day warranty policy that Lionel instituted in 1963. The no. 19145-10 Instruction Sheet did, too, despite still being dated 7-62. A no. 1802A Layout Instruction Sheet described the elevated and elongated figure-eight track layout used for this outfit.

The no. 63-385 Tan RSC Mailer with Black Graphics outfit box was manufactured by United Container Co. and measured 15¼ x 14½ x 6¼ inches. It included four lines of data as part of the box manufacturer's certificate (BMC). It also included a "63" and three stars as part of its BMC. The box number "63-385" was printed on the bottom of the box.

The 63-385 Outfit Box was made of a thicker corrugated material (rated at 90 pounds rather than the normal 65 pounds gross weight) that allowed the outfit to be shipped in its outfit box. A Shell mailing label has been observed on at least one outfit. This indicates that Lionel first shipped the outfits to Shell's fulfillment organization, which in turn mailed them to customers.

The extent to which this promotional outfit was a success cannot be ascertained. Only a few examples have been observed with Shell mailing labels. However, after Richard Kughn, then the owner of Lionel Trains Inc., purchased Madison Hardware Co. of New York City in 1989 and reopened it in Detroit soon thereafter, one of the first lists of outfits available for sale included 16 examples of the 19281.

Like Quaker's no. X-600, Van Camp's no. 19142 and Libby's no. 19263, this outfit remains desirable because of its association with a well-known customer. The 19281 may have been produced in large quantities, but it will always be in demand.

R. Marfuggi   W. A. Sethre   10/8/63

SUBJECT: #19281 Shell Oil Train Set

Please package immediately for mail order shipment a sample of
the train set per attached outfit sheet. You will note that this
outfit uses all surplus merchandise with the exception, of course,
of track and transformers. The quantity production release will
be given within the next few days. *Release 5000 Sets*

Delivery on this set will be required commencing approximately
November 1.

NOTE: The mailer packing should not have any Lionel identification.
Also, because of the size of this outfit, special care should be
exercised in making certain the unit is packed properly for
parcel post mail order shipment. I have already discussed the
contents and packing of this set with Nunzio Palumbo.

Please advise if there are any problems.

WAS:BN
Att.

cc: P. Giannotta
    N. Palumbo ✓

**This memorandum (above) and the attached early version of
a Factory Order (right) from Lionel's Sales Department to its
Manufacturing Department provide insight into the creation
of promotional outfit no. 19281. Note the use of surplus
merchandise and the selling price to Shell of $14.25 per outfit.**

SHEET OF	OUTFIT		FACTORY ORDER	
CATALOG NO.	DESCRIPTION		DEPT.	
19281	027 Outfit — Special —		AMT. 5000	
	OUTFIT SPECIFICATION		GROUP NO.	
	Note: Lionel Name Must Not appear on the Ind. Carton.		ORDER NO.	
CUSTOMER	TYPE OF PACKING	WEIGHT PER OUTFIT	DATE ISSUED	DATE REQ'D
Shell Oil	Loose Crossaxed RSC		10/8/63	11/1/63 #1

OPERATIONS:
*1 Note: Need 1000 units by 11/1/63 — HSPrice
Need 2000 Units by 4/10/63 — 1425
Need 2000 Units by 4/20/63

DELIVER TO DEPARTMENT

OUTFIT CONTENTS				STOCK ROOM RECORD		
PART NO.	PART NAME	PCS	DEPT	DATE	QUANTITY	LOC
221 P-25	Rock Island Diesel Loco	1				
6017-25	Caboose (Have 3624 in Surplus)					
	Substitute: 6057-50 (Have 400 in Surplus)					
	: 6057-25 (Have 288 in Surplus)					
	6167-50 (Have 85 in Surplus)					
	6167-25 (use 2 from Surplus)					
3309-25	Turbo Missile Car (Have 1891 in Surplus)	1				
	Sub: 3349-1 (Use 3109 from Surplus)					
6402-25	Flat Car with 2 Cable Reels (No Sub)	1				
6076-75	Hopper Car (use 2573 from Surplus)	1				
	Sub: 6076-100 (use 2427 from Surplus)					
6473-25	Rodeo Car (Have 2769 in Surplus)	1				
	Sub: 6473-1 (Have 1697 in Surplus)					
	6473 (take 524 from Separate Sales Plan)					
110-1	Trestle Set (Have 1716 in Surplus)	1				
	Sub: 110 (384 from Separate Sales Plan)					
1025-25	Transformer	1				
1018	Straight Track	14				
1013	Curve Track	12				
OTC	Lockon					
	Wire + Instructions					
	Do Not include Billboards					
	R.S.C Packing —					

ALTERNATE FOR OUTFIT CONTENTS

Description: "O27" Special Train Set
Specification: 6 Unit "O27" Special Train Set
Customer: Cott Beverage Co.
Original Amount: 100
Factory Order Date: 9/27/1963
Date Issued: 5/2/64
Packaging: RSC Pack (MO), (Units Loose)

Contents: 1062-50 Steam Type Loco. W/Light & Reversing Unit;
1060T-25 Tender; 6014-325 Frisco Box Car (W/Slot for Bank);
6465-150 Tank Car; 6076-75 Hopper Car - Black; 6167-100
Caboose; 1013 Curved Track (8); 1018 Straight Track (2); CTC-
1 Lockon; 1010-25 35-Watt Transformer; 19228-10 Instruction
Sheet; 1-65 Warranty Card; Form 3063 Parts Order Form; 927-64
Service Station List; D64-50 Accessory Catalog

Boxes & Packing: 62-246 Outfit Box; 62-247 Shipper for 4 (1-4)

19282 (1964)	C6	C7	C8	Rarity
Complete Outfit	395	750	1,050	R10
Outfit Box no. 62-246	300	600	800	R10

Comments: The no. 19282 was the only Factory Order to list Cott
Beverage Co. as a customer. This Manufacturer Promotional Type
IIIa originally appeared on a Lionel Work Sheet dated 9/27/63,
hence the no. 19282, which was part of the 1963 numbering
sequence. The 19282 was finally approved and released on 5/2/64
at a cost from Lionel of $9.25.

The 19282 was led by a no. 1062-50 Steam Type Loco. W/
Light & Reversing Unit. This low-end
Scout steamer was new for 1964 and
featured an 0-4-0 wheel arrangement
and a rubber tire as a traction aid. Except for the rubber tire, it
was identical to the no. 1062-25 Steam Type Loco. W/Light &
Reversing Unit. The 1062-50 pulled a no. 1060T-25 Tender that
typically had one non-operating and one plain AAR truck and
coupler in 1964.

The most notable item in this outfit was a no. 6014-325 Frisco
Box Car (W/Slot for Bank). This was the only time that a Factory
Order specified using this difficult-to-find variation with a coin
slot. This car adds a premium to the price of this outfit. Like the
no. 6465-150 Tank Car in this outfit, it came with one operating
and one non-operating AAR truck and coupler.

The no. 6167-100 Caboose variation was new for 1964. It had
Lionel Lines stamped on its body. The 6167-100 was equipped
with one operating and one plain AAR truck and coupler.

The no. 6076-75 Hopper Car - Black appeared in almost 50
different outfits. In 1964, it normally was equipped with non-
operating AAR trucks and couplers.

The 19282 used the no. 62-246 Tan RSC Mailer with Black
Graphics outfit box. It was manufactured by Mead Containers
and measured 11½ x 10¼ x 6¼ inches. These boxes were made
of a thicker corrugated material (rated at 90 pounds rather than
the normal 65 pounds gross weight) that allowed each outfit to
be shipped in its own box. The manufacturer omitted any Lionel
printing on the box top to leave room for a mailing label. Packaging
of this nature likely indicated that the 19282 was to be individually
mailed to customers.

With only 100 examples manufactured, the 19282 is seldom
seen. As a result, this outfit has an R10 rarity rating.

Outfit no. 19301 (Sears no. 9817) was one of the 23 Sears "Special Purchase" outfits from late 1963. All the components were new for 1963. Except for the no. 6502-50 Girder Transport Car, the cars first appeared in Libby's outfit no. 19263 from earlier in the year.

Customer No. On Box: 9817
Specification: 5 Unit Diesel Freight
Customer/No.: Sears, Roebuck and Co.; 9817
Original Amount: 2,300
Factory Order Date: 12/31/1963
Packaging: RSC (Units Loose)

Contents: 221P-25 Diesel Locomotive; 6050-175 Libby Box Car; 6076-125 Hopper Car; 6502-50 Girder Transport Car; 6502-3 Girder Bridge; 6167-75 Caboose; 1013-8 Curved Track (Bundle of 8 - 1013); 1018 Straight Track (2); 1026-25 25-Watt Transformer; 1103-20 Envelope Packed; 310-62 Set of (3) Billboards; D63-50 Accessory Catalog; 1-62 Parts Order Form; 1-63 Warranty Card; 19301-15 Instruction Sheet; 1123-40 Instruction Sheet

Boxes & Packing: 62-246 Outfit Box; 61-172 Corr. Insert; 62-254 Corr. Insert; 62-264 Corr. Insert; 62-247 Shipper for 4 (1-4)

Alternate For Outfit Contents:
Sub. For 221P-25: Use 221P-1 Amount 100, Use 227P-25 Amount Balance needed.

19301 (1963)	C6	C7	C8	Rarity
Complete Outfit	240	360	525	R6
Complete Outfit With no. 227P-25 Substitution	295	445	640	R6
Outfit Box no. 62-246	75	100	150	R6

Comments: In late 1963, Robert Wolfe, president of the Lionel Toy Corporation, worked out a deal - "Special Purchase" - with Sears, Roebuck and Co. to quickly bring additional revenue to Lionel by liquidating surplus toy inventory. This deal accounted for 23 of the 25 Super O and O27 Retailer Promotional outfits purchased by Sears in late 1963. None of these "Special Purchase" outfits has been observed in a Sears catalog. Internal Lionel and Sears documents revealed the link to Sears, along with the proper Sears number. (See the entry for Sears, Roebuck and Co. in the section on Lionel's Distribution and Customers.)

The no. 19301, a Type Ib outfit, was one of the many diesel-powered outfits purchased by Sears in 1963. The Sears no. 9817 appeared on the box below the Lionel number.

This outfit was led by a no. 221P-25 Rio Grande Diesel Locomotive, a low-end engine that was new for 1963. This unpainted yellow Alco featured a two-position reversing unit, a traction tire and a closed pilot and lacked a headlight.

Lionel's determination to liquidate its surplus inventory didn't mean that everything in this outfit was a carryover item. To the contrary, *nothing* in the 19301 was a carryover item! This fact supports the contention that Lionel had overestimated production for 1963.

Three of the four pieces of rolling stock in this outfit duplicated those in Libby's no. 19263. This suggested that Lionel was shifting items after the Factory Order for the 19263 was decreased on December 2, 1963. (See the entry for outfit 19263).

The sole exception was the no. 6502-50 Girder Transport Car. It was molded in blue plastic and carried an orange plastic no. 6502-3 Girder Bridge. The 6502-50 came equipped with non-operating Archbar trucks and couplers.

The Type III no. 6050-175 Libby Box Car was a new addition to the no. 6050-series of 8½-inch box cars. It advertised Libby's tomato juice and went on to be a part of at least nine other promotional outfits. This model has been observed with operating AAR trucks and couplers, although other combinations are possible.

The gray no. 6076-125 Hopper Car included "ATSF" markings and appeared only in this and three other promotional outfits. Although often overlooked, this model is one of the tougher low-end hoppers to find. It was equipped with non-operating AAR trucks and couplers.

While the 6050-175, 6076-125, and 6502-50 appeared only in promotional outfits, the no. 6167-75 Caboose did show up in the catalog line. The yellow 6167-75 boasted "Union Pacific" markings. Interestingly, Lionel was still depleting its inventory of models in 1969 when it offered the 6167-75 as both a component of catalog outfit no. 11730 and a separate-sale item. When individually boxed for separate sale, it became a no. 6167-85 Caboose. It came with one non-operating and one plain AAR truck and coupler.

The substitution of a no. 227P-25 Canadian National Alco Diesel Power Unit affects the price, as listed in the pricing table. It appeared in the 19301 and two other promotional outfits in 1963. The Factory Order also lists a quantity of 100 of the no. 221P-1 Rio Grande Diesel Locomotive. The "-1" suffix indicated that it came in an individual box; however, a boxed 221P-1 has yet to be observed.

The no. 19301-15 Instruction Sheet, which was dated 12/63, was unique to this outfit. It is one of the more difficult items to find in completing this outfit.

The 19301 used the no. 62-246 Tan RSC Mailer with Black Graphics outfit box. It was manufactured by Mead Containers and measured 11½ x 10¼ x 6¼ inches. These boxes were made of a thicker corrugated material (rated at 90 pounds rather than the normal 65 pounds gross weight) that allowed each outfit to be shipped in its outfit box. The manufacturer omitted any Lionel printing on the box top to leave room for a mailing label. The 62-246 Outfit Box used for the 19301 was a 1963 version with four lines of data as part of the box manufacturer's certificate.

Even with 2,300 of the 19301 manufactured, it is surprisingly difficult to obtain. Therefore, this outfit achieves an R6 rarity rating.

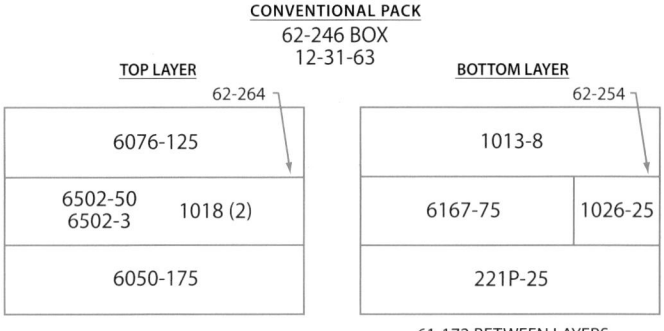

CONVENTIONAL PACK
62-246 BOX
12-31-63

TOP LAYER		BOTTOM LAYER	
62-264		62-254	
6076-125		1013-8	
6502-50 6502-3	1018 (2)	6167-75	1026-25
6050-175		221P-25	

61-172 BETWEEN LAYERS

Description: "O27" Promotional Outfit
Specification: "O27" Diesel Freight Outfit
Original Amount: 2,300
Factory Order Date: 11/11/1963
Date Issued: 11-11-63
Date Req'd: 11-18-63
Packaging: RSC (Units Loose)

Contents: 227P-25 Alco Diesel Power Unit - "Canadian National"; 6343-25 Barrel Ramp Car; 362-78 Wood Barrels (6); 6142-25 Gondola Car (Less Canisters); 6014-325 Frisco Box Car; 6059-50 Caboose; 1013-8 Curved Track (Bundle of 8 - 1013); 1018-10 Straight Track (Loose); 1008-50 Uncoupling Unit; 1026-25 25-Watt Transformer; 1645-12 Envelope Packed; 92-1 Circuit Breaker; 310-62 Set of (3) Billboards; D63-50 Accessory Catalog; 1-62 Parts Order Form; 1-63 Warranty Card; 19301-10 Instruction Sheet

Boxes & Packing: 62-246 Outfit Box; 62-254 Corr. Insert; 62-264 Corr. Insert; 62-247 Shipper for (4) (1-4)

19301(A) (1963)	C6	C7	C8	Rarity
Complete Outfit	315	525	875	R7
Outfit Box no. 62-246	100	200	400	R7

Comments: This General Release Promotional Type IIb outfit was one of the many outfits issued by Lionel late in 1963 in an attempt to deplete inventory. Although the no. 19301(A) shared the same base number as no. 19301 from 1963, it included different items.

The 19301(A) was led by a no. 227P-25 Canadian National Alco Diesel Power Unit. The 227P-25 moved forward only and featured a closed pilot, a headlight and a weight to aid in traction. It appeared in the 19301(A) and two other promotional outfits in 1963. Ironically, this low-end Alco is now a desirable collector piece.

Except for the no. 6343-25 Barrel Ramp Car, all the cars in this outfit were new or new variations for 1963. The no. 6142-25 Gondola Car (Less Canisters) was created by taking a common short gondola and updating its decoration. The same was true for the no. 6059-50 Caboose. It was the unpainted red plastic version of the nos. 6059-1 and 6059-25 Caboose that were first issued in 1961.

The norm for all the cars was AAR trucks and couplers in 1963. The no. 6014-325 Frisco Box Car and 6142-25 each boasted one operating and one non-operating type, while the 6343-25 was equipped with two operating types. The 6059-50 came with one operating and one plain truck and coupler.

The 19301(A) marked the last appearance of the no. 1645-12 Envelope Packed. That difficult-to-find item included three wires, which were required to hook up the no. 92-1 Circuit Breaker to the transformer and track.

The no. 19301-10 Instruction Sheet was dated 10/63 and made reference to the 90-day warranty policy that Lionel instituted in 1963. It is similar to the no. 19301-15 Instruction Sheet, but the "-10" includes information about the no. 1008-50 Uncoupling Unit.

The 19301(A) used the no. 62-246 Tan RSC Mailer with Black Graphics outfit box. It was manufactured by Mead Containers and measured 11½ x 10¼ x 6¼ inches. These boxes were made of a thicker corrugated material (rated at 90 pounds rather than the normal 65 pounds gross weight) that allowed each outfit to be shipped in its outfit box. The manufacturer omitted any Lionel printing on the box top to leave room for a mailing label.

Even with 2,300 manufactured, the 19301(A) is an extremely difficult outfit to find.

CONVENTIONAL PACK
62-246 BOX
11-11-63

TOP LAYER				BOTTOM LAYER	
62-264 →					62-254 →
6343-25				1013-8 1018-10	
6142-25				1026-25	6059-50
1008-50 6014-325				227P-25	

2 CATALOGS BETWEEN LAYERS

19302
1963

Outfit no. 19302 (Sears no. 9818) was one of the 23 Sears "Special Purchase" outfits from late 1963. Although this outfit has never been observed in a Sears catalog, this example had a Sears price tag (not shown) with "4R 49 9818 $19.88". The 19302 came with the no. 310-62 Set of (3) Billboards and not the no. 310-2 Set of (5) Billboard Signs that's shown.

Description: "O27" Promotional Outfit
Specification: "O27" Diesel Freight Outfit
Customer/No./Price: Sears, Roebuck and Co.; 9818; $19.88
Original Amount: 3,600
Factory Order Date: 11/12/1963
Date Issued: 12-5-63
Date Req'd: 11-18-63
Packaging: RSC (Units Loose)

Contents: 232P-25 Alco Diesel Power Car - "New Haven"; 6630-25 Missile Launching Car; 6822-50 Searchlight Car; 6014-325 Frisco Box Car; 6142-25 Gondola Car (Less 2 Canisters); 6112-5 Canister (2); 6408-25 Flat Car W/5 Pipes; 6511-15 Pipes (5); 6059-50 Caboose; 1013-8 Curved Track (Bundle of 8 - 1013); 1018-10 Straight Track (Loose); 1008-50 Uncoupling Unit; 1025-25 45-Watt Transformer; 1103-20 Envelope Packed; 310-62 Set of (3) Billboards; D63-50 Accessory Catalog; 1-62 Parts Order Form; 1-63 Warranty Card; 122-10 Instruction Sheet; 6630-6 Instruction Sheet

Boxes & Packing: 61-180 Outfit Box; 61-181 Corr. Insert; 61-182 Corr. Insert; 63-311 Corr. Insert; 61-185 Shipper for (4) (1-4); 61-183 Corr. Insert

19302 (1963)	C6	C7	C8	Rarity
Complete Outfit	325	500	710	R5
Outfit Box no. 61-180	65	95	125	R5

Comments: In late 1963, Robert Wolfe, president of the Lionel Toy Corporation, worked out a deal - "Special Purchase" - with Sears, Roebuck and Co. to quickly bring additional revenue to Lionel by liquidating surplus toy inventory. This deal accounted for 23 of the 25 Super O and O27 Retailer Promotional outfits purchased by Sears in late 1963. None of these "Special Purchase" outfits has been observed in a Sears catalog. Internal Lionel and Sears documents revealed the link to Sears, along with the proper Sears number. (See the entry for Sears, Roebuck and Co. in the section on Lionel's Distribution and Customers.)

The no. 19302, a Type Ib outfit, was one of the many diesel-powered outfits purchased by Sears in 1963. The Sears no. 9818 was not stamped on the outfit box, but it has been observed on a price tag as no. 4R 49 9818 for $19.88.

The 19302 was led by a 232P-25 New Haven Alco Diesel Power Car. The orange plastic locomotive featured a two-position reversing unit, a headlight and two-axle Magne-Traction. The 232P-25 was originally issued in 1962 in catalog outfit no. 11232 and its RSC version no. 11235.

Lionel's determination to liquidate its surplus inventory didn't mean that everything in this outfit was a carryover item. Indeed, only the no. 6630-25 Missile Launching Car had already appeared in the line. Its three-year run was coming to an end in 1963, when it appeared in this and six other promotional outfits. Otherwise, all the rolling stock in the 19302 was either a new model or a new variation for 1963. This fact supports the contention that Lionel had overestimated production for this year.

The no. 6014-325 Frisco Box Car was a Type III variation that was new in 1963. The nos. 6059-50 Caboose, 6142-25 Gondola Car (Less 2 Canisters), 6408-25 Flat Car W/5 Pipes and 6822-50 Searchlight Car were color, decorating or coupler variations of other cars. The 6059-50 was the unpainted version of the no. 6059-25 Caboose. The 6142-25 was a short gondola molded in black. The 6408-25 was a red no. 6511-series model with "Lionel" stamped on each side and a brake wheel installed. The 6822-50 was a coupler variation of the no. 6822-1 Searchlight Car.

The transition from Archbar to AAR trucks and couplers that began in 1962 continued into 1963. As part of this, Lionel sought to cut costs by introducing a non-operating AAR type. Therefore, starting in 1963, most cars equipped with AAR trucks and couplers had at least one non-operating type.

For the 19302, many combinations were possible. The 6630-25 was equipped with non-operating Archbar types. The 6059-50 was equipped with one operating and one plain AAR type. The norm for the remaining cars was one operating and one non-operating AAR truck and coupler, although the 6014-325 and 6408-25 have been observed with one non-operating Archbar and one operating AAR type.

The no. 122-10 Instruction Sheet made reference to the 90-day warranty policy that Lionel instituted in 1963. It was dated 5-62.

The commonly used no. 61-180 Tan RSC with Black Graphics outfit box was manufactured by St. Joe Kraft, St. Joe Paper Co. Container Division and measured 12¾ x 10 x 6¾ inches. It included four lines of data as part of the box manufacturer's certificate.

Of the 25 Sears outfits from 1963, the 19302 is among the easiest to find.

CONVENTIONAL PACK
61-180 BOX
11-11-63

TOP LAYER	
6511-15 (5) 6112-5 (2)	1013-8 / 1018-10
	6408-25
	6142-25
	6822-50

63-311

BOTTOM LAYER	
61-181 / 61-182	232P-25
1025-25	6059-50
	6014-325
	6630-25

2 CATALOGS BETWEEN LAYERS

Description: "O27" Promotional Outfit
Specification: "O27" Diesel Freight Outfit
Customer/No.: Sears, Roebuck and Co.; 9804
Original Amount: 3,200
Factory Order Date: 11/13/1963
Date Issued: 11-13-63
Date Req'd: 11-18-63
Packaging: RSC (Units Loose)

Contents: 1065-25 Alco Diesel Power Unit - "Union Pacific"; 6343-25 Barrel Ramp Car; 362-78 Wood Barrels (6); 6408-25 Flat Car W/5 Pipes; 6511-15 Pipes (5); 6014-325 Frisco Box Car; 6465-150 Tank Car; 6059-50 Caboose; 1013-8 Curved Track (Bundle of 8 - 1013); 1018-10 Straight Track (Loose); 1008-50 Uncoupling Unit; 1026-25 25-Watt Transformer; 1103-20 Envelope Packed; 310-62 Set of (3) Billboards; D63-50 Accessory Catalog; 1-62 Parts Order Form; 1-63 Warranty Card; 19301-10 Instruction Sheet

Boxes & Packing: 61-180 Outfit Box; 61-181 Corr. Insert; 61-182 Corr. Insert; 62-264 Corr. Insert; 61-185 Shipper for (4) (1-4)

Alternate For Outfit Contents:
Note: Substitute 990 - 6519-25 for 6465-150; Substitute 1,414 - 6413-25 for 6465-150.

19303 (1963)	C6	C7	C8	Rarity
Complete Outfit	250	375	550	R5
Complete Outfit With no. 6519-25 Substitution	295	440	625	R5
Complete Outfit With no. 6413-25 Substitution	335	505	735	R5
Outfit Box no. 61-180	95	125	165	R5

Comments: In late 1963, Robert Wolfe, president of the Lionel Toy Corporation, worked out a deal - "Special Purchase" - with Sears, Roebuck and Co. to quickly bring additional revenue to Lionel by liquidating surplus toy inventory. This deal accounted

Outfit no. 19303 (Sears no. 9804) was one of the 23 Sears "Special Purchase" outfits from late 1963. The 19303 was identical to outfit no. 19306, with the exception of one car and the outfit box. Both outfits marked the last appearance of the no. 1065-25 Union Pacific Alco Diesel Power Unit, until 1969.

for 23 of the 25 Super O and O27 Retailer Promotional outfits purchased by Sears in late 1963. None of these "Special Purchase" outfits has been observed in a Sears catalog. Internal Lionel and Sears documents revealed the link to Sears, along with the proper Sears number. (See the entry for Sears, Roebuck and Co. in the section on Lionel's Distribution and Customers.)

The no. 19303, a Type Ib outfit, was one of the many diesel-powered outfits purchased by Sears in 1963. The Sears no. 9804 was not stamped on the outfit box although at least one example has been observed with "9804" written on the box with a grease pen.

The features of this outfit were, with only slight exceptions, identical to those of Sears outfit no. 19306 (Sears no. 9816). They differed in their rolling stock and outfit packaging.

Both the 19303 and 19306 were led by a 1065-25 Union Pacific Alco Diesel Power Unit. This forward-only locomotive was as stripped down as Lionel could make an Alco in 1963, though it did have a headlight. This diesel appeared only in promotional outfits.

Lionel's determination to liquidate its surplus inventory didn't mean that everything in this outfit was a carryover item. Indeed, only the no. 6343-25 Barrel Ramp Car had appeared in the line previously. Introduced in 1961, it was being depleted in outfits through 1964. Otherwise, all the rolling stock in the 19303 was either a new model or a new variation for 1963. This fact supports the contention that Lionel had overestimated production for this year.

The no. 6014-325 Frisco Box Car was a Type III variation that was new in 1963. The nos. 6059-50 Caboose, 6408-25 Flat Car W/5 Pipes and 6465-150 Tank Car were color, decorating or coupler variations of other cars. The 6059-50 was the unpainted

version of the no. 6059-25 Caboose. The 6408-25 was a red no. 6511-series model with "Lionel" stamped on each side and a brake wheel installed. The 6465-150 was an orange tank car with Lionel Lines decoration. This car was replaced in the 19306 with a no. 6142-25 Gondola Car (Less Canisters).

Two substitutions affect the price as listed in the pricing table. The no. 6519-25 Allis-Chalmers Car was making its final appearance in this outfit, and the no. 6413-25 Mercury Capsule Transport Car was being thinned out.

The transition from Archbar to AAR trucks and couplers that began in 1962 continued into 1963. As part of this, Lionel sought to cut costs by introducing a non-operating AAR type. Therefore, starting in 1963, most cars equipped with AAR trucks and couplers had at least one non-operating type.

The 19303 generally followed this pattern. All the cars in this outfit were equipped with AAR trucks and couplers. However, not every model had even one non-operating AAR type. Specifically, the 6343-25, 6465-150 and 6519-25 had two operating types. The

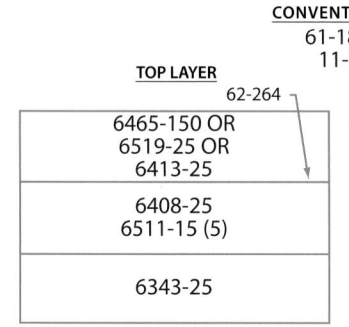

CONVENTIONAL PACK
61-180 BOX
11-11-63

TOP LAYER		
6465-150 OR 6519-25 OR 6413-25 ← 62-264		
6408-25 6511-15 (5)		
6343-25		

BOTTOM LAYER		
1013-8 ← 61-181	1018-10 1008-50 ← 61-182	
1026-25	6059-50	
	6014-325	
1065-25		

2 CATALOGS BETWEEN LAYERS

norm for the 6014-325, 6408-25 and 6413-25 was one operating and one non-operating type. Finally, the 6059-50 came with one operating and one plain truck and coupler.

The no. 19301-10 Instruction Sheet was dated 10/63 and made reference to the 90-day warranty policy that Lionel instituted in 1963. It was similar to the no. 19301-15 Instruction Sheet, but the "-10" included information about the no. 1008-50 Uncoupling Unit.

As noted, the 19303 also differed from the 19306 in its packaging. The 19303 came in the common no. 61-180 Tan RSC with Black Graphics outfit box, which was manufactured by St. Joe Kraft, St. Joe Paper Co. Container Division and measured 12¾ x 10 x 6¾ inches. It included four lines of data as part of the box manufacturer's certificate.

Lionel manufactured 3,200 of the 19303. Many have survived, but finding one in C8 condition is not easy.

Description: 7 Unit Diesel Freight
Customer/No.: Sears, Roebuck and Co.; 9858
Original Amount: 1,300
Factory Order Date: 12/31/1963
Date Issued: 1-2-64
Packaging: RSC (Units Loose)

Contents: 231P-1 Alco Diesel Power Car - "Rock Island"; 6402-25 Flat Car W/2 Cable Reels; 40-11 Cable Reels (2); 6076-75 Hopper Car - Black; 6473-25 Rodeo Car; 6475-50 Crushed Pineapple Car; 6050-175 Libby Box Car; 6017-25 Caboose; 1022-1 Pr. Manual Switches (1 Pr.); 1025-25 45-Watt Transformer; 161-1 Mail Pickup Set; 262-1 Highway Crossing Gate; 310-1 Billboard Set; 321-1 Trestle Bridge; 1013 Curved Track (14); 1018 Straight Track (20); 1103-20 Envelope Packed; 1648-10 Instruction Sheet

Boxes & Packing: 63-392 Box (Used when using 231P-1); 62-249 Insert; 62-264 Insert; 63-392 Box (Used when using 231P-25); 62-225 Insert; 62-245 Insert (2); 62-249 Insert; BP Bogus Paper

Alternate For Outfit Contents:
Note: Substitute 231P-25 as needed for 231P-1.

19304 (1963)	C6	C7	C8	Rarity
Complete Outfit	750	1,100	1,485	R8
Complete Outfit With no. 231P-25 Substitution	740	1,080	1,445	R8
Outfit Box no. 63-392	300	400	500	R8

Comments: In late 1963, Robert Wolfe, president of the Lionel Toy Corporation, worked out a deal - "Special Purchase" - with Sears, Roebuck and Co. to quickly bring additional revenue to Lionel by liquidating surplus toy inventory. This deal accounted for 23 of the 25 Super O and O27 Retailer Promotional outfits purchased by Sears in late 1963. None of these "Special Purchase" outfits has been observed in a Sears catalog. Internal Lionel and Sears documents revealed the link to Sears, along with the proper Sears number. (See the entry for Sears, Roebuck and Co. in the section on Lionel's Distribution and Customers.)

The no. 19304, a Type Ib outfit, was one of the many diesel-powered outfits purchased by Sears in 1963. It was assigned Sears no. 9858. Of note, an early version of a 19304 Factory Order was marked "Cancel" and "Replaced by 9730-500". (See the entry for outfit no. 9730-500.)

The 19304 was led by the no. 231P Rock Island Alco Diesel Power Car. This locomotive, first issued in 1961, featured two-axle Magne-Traction, a headlight and a two-position reversing unit. The 231P was nearing the end of its product life. It came either

boxed as the 231P-1 or unboxed as the 231P-25. Two different outfit packing diagrams detailed the differences for boxed or unboxed 231Ps.

Two of the pieces of rolling stock in this outfit duplicated those in Libby's no. 19263: nos. 6050-175 Libby Box Car and 6475-50 Crushed Pineapple Car. This fact suggested that Lionel was shifting items after the Factory Order for the 19263 was decreased on December 2, 1963. (See the entry for outfit 19263.)

The remainder of this outfit was used by Lionel to reduce its inventory of cars that were in the middle of their product lives.

The transition from Archbar to AAR trucks and couplers that began in 1962 continued into 1963. As part of this, Lionel sought to cut costs by introducing a non-operating AAR type. Therefore, starting in 1963, most cars equipped with AAR trucks and couplers had at least one non-operating type.

Generally speaking, the cars in the 19304 came with AAR trucks and couplers. However, because this outfit consisted of many items that represented surplus inventory, many combinations of these types were possible. Most cars had non-operating types, although they could be Archbar trucks and couplers on the nos. 6076-75 Hopper Car – Black and 6402-25 Flat Car W/2 Cable Reels. The norm for the no. 6473-25 Rodeo Car was one operating and one non-operating AAR type, while the norm for the 6017-25 Caboose was one operating and one plain AAR type.

The Sears "Special Purchase" outfits gave Lionel an opportunity

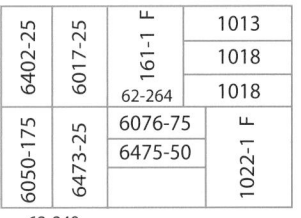

CONVENTIONAL PACK
63-392 BOX
12-31-63

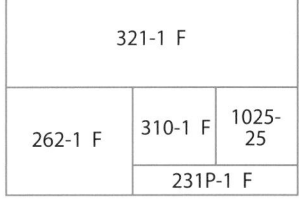

CONVENTIONAL PACK
63-392 BOX
REVISED 1-2-64

to reduce its inventory of accessories and other peripherals. Thus, the 19304 included nos. 161-1 Mail Pickup Set, 262-1 Highway Crossing Gate and 321-1 Bridge, all carried over from previous years. Adding these items as well as the no. 1022-1 Pr. Manual Switches provided a unique and intriguing promotional outfit.

The track layout was likely an outer loop with two switches arranged back to back to create an inner loop. (See outfit no. 19327 for a similar track layout.)

A large no. 63-392 Tan RSC with Black Graphics outfit box was used for the 19304. It was manufactured by Robbins Container Corp. and measured 26 x 17½ x 4½ inches.

Even with 1,300 of the 19304 manufactured, it is seldom seen and easily achieves its R8 rarity rating.

Customer No. On Box: 9854
Description: "O27" Promotional Outfit
Specification: "O27" Diesel Freight Outfit
Customer/No./Price: Sears, Roebuck and Co.; 9854; $29.88
Original Amount: 2,400
Factory Order Date: 11/12/1963
Date Issued: Rev 12-12-63
Date Req'd: 11-18-63
Packaging: RSC

Contents: 2365-1 GP-7 Diesel Power Unit - "Chesapeake & Ohio"; 6544-1 Missile Firing Trail Car; 3619-1 Reconnaissance Copter Car; 3470-1 Aerial Target Launching Car; 6476-25 Hopper Car - Red; 6014-325 Frisco Box Car; 6059-50 Caboose; 214-1 Girder Bridge; 1013-8 Curved Track (Bundle of 8 - 1013); 1018-30 Straight Track (Bundle of 3 - 1018); 1008-50 Uncoupling Unit; 1025-25 45-Watt Transformer; 1103-20 Envelope Packed; 310-62 Set of (3) Billboards; D63-50 Accessory Catalog; 1-62 Parts Order Form; 1-63 Warranty Card; 6544-12 Instruction Sheet; 3619-102 Instruction Sheet; 2365-11 Instruction Sheet; 1648-10 Instruction Sheet

Boxes & Packing: 62-260 Outfit Box; 62-273 Corr. Insert; 61-221 Shipper for (2) (1-2)

Alternate For Outfit Contents:
Note: Substitute 500 - 3413-1 for 3619-1; Substitute 252 - 3410-25 and 3419-100 for 3619-1.

19305 (1963)	C6	C7	C8	Rarity
Complete Outfit	800	1,200	1,725	R5
Complete Outfit With no. 3413-1 Substitution	810	1,225	1,750	R5
Complete Outfit With no. 3410-25 Substitution	750	1,135	1,665	R5
Outfit Box no. 62-260	75	125	200	R5

Comments: In late 1963, Robert Wolfe, president of the Lionel Toy Corporation, worked out a deal - "Special Purchase" - with Sears, Roebuck and Co. to quickly bring additional revenue to Lionel by liquidating surplus toy inventory. This deal accounted for 23 of the 25 Super O and O27 Retailer Promotional outfits purchased by Sears in late 1963. None of these "Special Purchase" outfits has been observed in a Sears catalog. Internal Lionel and Sears documents revealed the link to Sears, along with the proper Sears number. (See the entry for Sears, Roebuck and Co. in the section on Lionel's Distribution and Customers.)

The no. 19305, a Type Ia outfit, was one of the many diesel-powered outfits purchased by Sears in 1963. The Sears no. 9854 was stamped on the outfit box below the Lionel number. Outfits have been observed with a price tag with no. 49 9854 for $29.88 and no. 49 SPEC for $29.88.

The 19305 was Sears' space and military follow-up to no. 9655 from 1962. Both outfits were led by a 2365-1 Chesapeake & Ohio GP-7 Diesel Power Unit. This new-for-1962 engine also led catalog outfit no. 11268 from 1962. It featured Magne-Traction, a three-position reversing unit and a light at both ends. When packaged in its no. 2365-12 Corr. Box, the Chesapeake & Ohio GP-7 included a no. 2365-11 Instruction Sheet, 927-90 Lubricating Oil Packed and a CTC-1 Lockon.

In spite of Lionel's determination to liquidate its surplus inventory, not everything in this outfit was a carryover item. The nos. 6014-325 Frisco Box Car and the unpainted 6059-50 Caboose were new items for 1963. This fact supports the contention that Lionel had overestimated production for this year.

Still, the nos. 3470-1 Aerial Target Launching Car, 3619-1 Reconnaissance Copter Car and 6544-1 Missile Firing Car were carryover items that Lionel was thinning out in this outfit. Variations observed with the 19305 included the 3470-1 with a dark blue frame, 3619-1 with a bright yellow body and at least one example observed with a 6544-1 having a black heat-stamped control panel graphic. All of these cars came packaged in Orange Picture boxes.

The 3619-1 came with a fragile and easily lost no. 0319-100 Helicopter. As part of the manufacturing process, the roof of the 3619-1 was taped shut with a ½-inch piece of Scotch tape. Even examples in C8 condition still have a mark where the tape was applied.

The nos. 3410-25 Oper. Helicopter Car (Less Helicopter) and 3413-1 Mercury Capsule Launching Car substitutions affect the outfit price, as listed in the pricing table. The final inventory of 252 of the 3410-25 was depleted in this outfit. The 3410-25 has been observed with an aquamarine frame.

The transition from Archbar to AAR trucks and couplers that began in 1962 continued into 1963. As part of this, Lionel sought to cut costs by introducing a non-operating AAR type. Therefore, starting in 1963, most cars equipped with AAR trucks and couplers had at least one non-operating type.

The 19305 generally followed this pattern. All the cars in this outfit were equipped with AAR trucks and couplers. However, not every model had even one non-operating AAR type. Specifically, all the boxed items came with two operating types. The no. 6476-25 Hopper Car – Red could have either two operating trucks and couplers or one operating and one non-operating type in 1963. The 6014-325 did have one of each, while the 6059-50 came with one operating and one plain truck and coupler.

Outfit no. 19305 (Sears no. 9854) was one of the 23 Sears "Special Purchase" outfits from late 1963. It was a follow-up to Sears' no. 9655 from 1962. These two outfits marked the only promotional appearance of the no. 2365-1 Chesapeake & Ohio GP-7 Diesel Power Unit. This space and military offering provided plenty of excitement with its three operating cars.

The Factory Order for the 19305 listed additional instruction sheets for boxed items. Since the boxed items were all carryover, they may have included one-year warranty sheets from 1962. The extra sheets may have been used to replace the one-year sheets with the 90-day warranty versions, which are much more difficult to obtain. Be aware that the no. 1648-10 Instruction Sheet mentioned a no. 1063 75-Watt Transformer though a no. 1025-25 45-Watt Transformer was included.

The no. 62-260 Tan RSC with Black Graphics outfit box was manufactured by the Mead Corporation and measured 16¼ x 13 x 6⅜ inches. It included four lines of data as part of the box manufacturer's certificate.

Even though the 19305 featured leftover inventory, it demonstrated that Lionel could put together an exciting and respectable outfit in late 1963. With 2,400 manufactured, it does appear on the market, but is difficult to find complete in C8 condition.

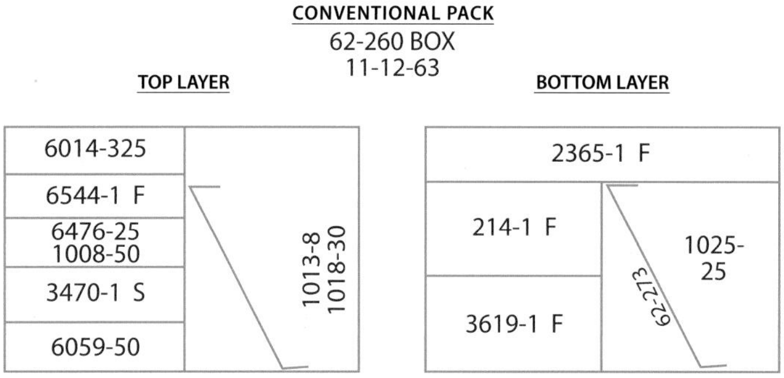

CONVENTIONAL PACK
62-260 BOX
11-12-63

TOP LAYER

| 6014-325 |
| 6544-1 F |
| 6476-25 1008-50 |
| 3470-1 S |
| 6059-50 |

1013-8 1018-30

BOTTOM LAYER

2365-1 F	
214-1 F	1025-25
3619-1 F	

62-273

Description: "O27" Promotional Outfit
Specification: "O27" Diesel Freight Outfit
Customer/No.: Sears, Roebuck and Co.; 9816
Original Amount: 900
Factory Order Date: 11/7/1963
Date Issued: 11-4-63
Date Req'd: 11-18
Packaging: RSC (Units Loose)

Contents: 1065-25 Alco Diesel Power Unit - "Union Pacific"; 6343-25 Barrel Ramp Car; 362-78 Wood Barrels (6); 6408-25 Flat Car W/5 Pipes; 6511-15 Pipes (5); 6014-325 Frisco Box Car; 6142-25 Gondola Car (Less Canisters); 6059-50 Caboose;

1013-8 Curved Track (Bundle of 8 - 1013); 1018-10 Straight Track (Loose); 1008-50 Uncoupling Unit; 1026-25 25-Watt Transformer; 1103-20 Envelope Packed; 310-62 Set of (3) Billboards; D63-50 Accessory Catalog; 1-62 Parts Order Form; 1-63 Warranty Card; 19301-10 Instruction Sheet

Boxes & Packing: 62-246 Outfit Box; 62-225 Corr. Insert; 62-254 Corr. Insert; 62-247 Shipper for (4) (1-4)

19306 (1963)	C6	C7	C8	Rarity
Complete Outfit	300	500	615	R8
Outfit Box no. 62-246	150	250	325	R8

Comments: In late 1963, Robert Wolfe, president of the Lionel Toy Corporation, worked out a deal - "Special Purchase" - with Sears, Roebuck and Co. to quickly bring additional revenue to Lionel by liquidating surplus toy inventory. This deal accounted for 23 of the 25 Super O and O27 Retailer Promotional outfits purchased by Sears in late 1963. None of these "Special Purchase" outfits has been observed in a Sears catalog. Internal Lionel and Sears documents revealed the link to Sears, along with the proper Sears number. (See the entry for Sears, Roebuck and Co. in the section on Lionel's Distribution and Customers.)

The no. 19306, a Type Ib outfit, was one of the many diesel-powered outfits purchased by Sears in 1963. It was assigned Sears no. 9816.

The features of this outfit were, with only slight exceptions, identical to those of Sears outfit no. 19303 (Sears no. 9804). They differed in one item rolling stock and outfit packaging.

Both the 19306 and 19303 were led by a 1065-25 Union Pacific Alco Diesel Power Unit. This forward-only locomotive was as stripped down as Lionel could make an Alco in 1963, though it did have a headlight. This diesel appeared only in promotional outfits.

Lionel's determination to liquidate its surplus inventory didn't mean that everything in this outfit was a carryover item. Indeed, only the no. 6343-25 Barrel Ramp Car had appeared in the line previously. Introduced in 1961, it was being depleted in outfits through 1964. Otherwise, all the rolling stock in the 19306 was either a new model or a new variation for 1963. This fact supports the contention that Lionel had overestimated production for this year.

The no. 6014-325 Frisco Box Car was a Type III variation that was new in 1963. The nos. 6059-50 Caboose, 6408-25 Flat Car W/5 Pipes and 6142-25 Gondola Car (Less Canisters) were color, decorating or coupler variations of other cars. The 6059-50 was the unpainted version of the no. 6059-25 Caboose. The 6408-25 was a red no. 6511-series model with "Lionel" stamped on each side and a brake wheel installed. The 6142-25 was molded in black. This car replaced the no. 6465-150 Tank Car in the 19303.

The transition from Archbar to AAR trucks and couplers that began in 1962 continued into 1963. As part of this, Lionel sought

to cut costs by introducing a non-operating AAR type. Therefore, starting in 1963, most cars equipped with AAR trucks and couplers had at least one non-operating type.

The 19306 generally followed this pattern. All the cars in this outfit were equipped with AAR trucks and couplers. However, not every model had even one non-operating AAR type. Specifically, the 6343-25 had two operating types. The norm for the 6014-325, 6142-25 and 6408-25 was one operating and one non-operating type. Finally, the 6059-50 came with one operating and one plain truck and coupler.

The no. 19301-10 Instruction Sheet was dated 10/63 and made reference to the 90-day warranty policy that Lionel instituted in 1963. It was similar to the no. 19301-15 Instruction Sheet, but the "-10" included information about the no. 1008-50 Uncoupling Unit.

The 19306 also differed from the 19303 in its packaging. It appeared that the 19306 might have been the mail-order version of the 19303. The former used the no. 62-246 Tan RSC Mailer with Black Graphics outfit box, which was manufactured by Mead Containers and measured 11½ x 10¼ x 6¼ inches. These boxes were made of a thicker corrugated material (rated at 90 pounds rather than the normal 65 pounds gross weight) that allowed each outfit to be shipped in its outfit box. The manufacturer omitted any Lionel printing on the box top to leave room for a mailing label.

With only 900 manufactured, the 19306 is much more difficult to find than the 19303.

CONVENTIONAL PACK
62-246 BOX
11-4-63

TOP LAYER		BOTTOM LAYER	
6343-25 / 6511-15 (5) ← 62-225		1065-25 ← 62-254	
362-78 (6)	6014-325	1026-25	6059-50
	6142-25		
	6408-25	1018-10 / 1013-8	

2 CATALOGS BETWEEN LAYERS

Customer No. On Box: 9884
Description: Super "O" Promotional Outfit
Specification: Super "O" Steam Type Freight Outfit W/Smoke & Whistle
Customer/No./Price: Sears, Roebuck and Co.; 9884; $49.89
Original Amount: 1,470
Factory Order Date: 12/12/1963
Date Issued: 12-12-63
Packaging: RSC

Contents: 637X-1 Steam Type Locomotive with Smoke; 736W-1 Whistle Tender; 6500-1 Beechcraft Bonanza Transport Car; 6464-735 "New Haven" Box Car; 6142-25 Gondola Car (Less 2 Canisters); 6112-5 Canister (2); 6512-1 Cherry Picker Car; 6463-25 Rocket Fuel Car; 6059-50 Caboose; 40-1 Cable Reel W/Wire (Any Color); 452-1 Overhead Gantry Signal; 31-60 Bundle of 6 - 31 Curved Track (2); 32-5 Straight Track - Loose (3); 34-10

Straight Track - ½ Section; 39-25 Envelope Packed; SW-1 130-Watt Transformer; 310-62 Set of (3) Billboards; 1-62 Parts Order Form; 1-63 Warranty Card; 1123-40 Instruction Sheet

Boxes & Packing: 62-316 Outfit Box; 62-319 Shipper for (3) (1-3)

Alternate For Outfit Contents:
Note: Substitute 666 - 6464-750 for 6464-735; Substitute 467 - 6464-900 for 6464-735; Note: #40 Cable Reel to be taken from set of 8 in finished goods Stock Room.

19308 (1963)	C6	C7	C8	Rarity
Complete Outfit	1,265	1,910	2,650	R7
Outfit Box no. 62-316	200	300	450	R7

Outfit no. 19308 (Sears no. 9884) was one of the 23 Sears "Special Purchase" outfits from late 1963. It was also one of the five Sears Super O purchases from the same year. The no. 637X-1 Steam Type Locomotive with Smoke appeared in only four promotional outfits during the 1960s. Still attached to the box is the Sears, Roebuck and Co. price tag stamped, "4RDIV49 $49.89". This example has the no. 6464-900 New York Central Box Car substitution.

Comments: In late 1963, Robert Wolfe, president of the Lionel Toy Corporation, worked out a deal - "Special Purchase" - with Sears, Roebuck and Co. to quickly bring additional revenue to Lionel by liquidating surplus toy inventory. This deal accounted for 23 of the 25 Super O and O27 Retailer Promotional outfits purchased by Sears in late 1963. None of these "Special Purchase" outfits has been observed in a Sears catalog. Internal Lionel and Sears documents revealed the link to Sears, along with the proper Sears number. (See the entry for Sears, Roebuck and Co. in the section on Lionel's Distribution and Customers.)

The no. 19308, a Type Ia outfit, was one of five Super O outfits purchased by Sears in 1963. The Sears no. 9884 was stamped on the outfit box below the Lionel number. At least one outfit has been observed with a price tag with no. 4RDIV49 for $49.89.

The 19308 was led by a no. 637X-1 Steam Type Locomotive with Smoke. This engine was equipped with Magne-Traction, a three-position reversing unit and a headlight. It came packaged in a no. 637-13 Corrugated Box. As described in the section on Outfit Peripherals, an "X" signified that a no. CTC-1 Lockon was left out because it wasn't necessary in a Super O outfit.

Because this was a Super O outfit, the inclusion of the low-end unboxed nos. 6059-50 Caboose, 6142-25 Gondola Car (Less 2 Canisters) and 6463-25 Rocket Fuel Car was curious. Lionel likely offered Sears such an attractive deal that it overlooked these low-end additions to a Super O outfit.

The other items included in the 19308 were typical of Super O outfits from 1963. The orange New Haven box car that was heat-stamped "6464725" was designated no. 6464-735 when it came in a box and no. 6464-750 when unboxed. The "-735" version came in this outfit. However, the "-750" was substituted in 666 of the outfits and a boxed no. 6464-900 New York Central Box Car was used in place of the 6464-735 in 467 of the outfits. These substitutions minimally affect the outfit price.

The no. 6500-1 Beechcraft Bonanza Transport Car made its first promotional outfit appearance in the Sears "Special Purchase" outfits. It is one of the few items that could come in an Orange

Perforated Picture or Orange Picture box. All the other cars in the 19308 came in Orange Picture boxes.

The transition from Archbar to AAR trucks and couplers that began in 1962 continued into 1963. As part of this, Lionel sought to cut costs by introducing a non-operating AAR type. Therefore, starting in 1963, most cars equipped with AAR trucks and couplers had at least one non-operating type.

The 19308 generally followed this pattern. All the cars in this outfit were equipped with AAR trucks and couplers. However, not every model had even one non-operating AAR type. Specifically, all the boxed items came with two operating types. The norm for the 6142-25 and 6463-25 was one operating and one non-operating type. The no. 736W-1 Tender and 6059-50 were equipped with one operating and one plain truck and coupler.

The Sears "Special Purchase" outfits gave Lionel an opportunity to reduce its inventory of accessories and other peripherals. Thus, the 19308 included the nos. 40-1 Cable Reel W/Wire (Any Color) and 452-1 Overhead Gantry Signal.

Catalog Super O outfits generally did not include a transformer. However, because promotional outfits were most often destined for retailers that probably did not have a train department, Lionel included a transformer. For the 19308, the no. SW-1 130-Watt Transformer provided plenty of power to operate this outfit. It appeared in only four outfits during the 1960s.

CONVENTIONAL PACK
62-316 BOX
12-6-63

TOP LAYER				BOTTOM LAYER			
31-60	31-60	736W-1	32-5	637X-1 S	6464-735 S	6512-1 S	SW-1
			32-5				
			32-5				
			6142-25		40-1		452-1 F
			6463-25		39-25		
6059-50		6500-1 S					
34-10 TOP							

A Type III or Type IV no. 39-25 Envelope Packed provided the remainder of the peripherals necessary to assemble and operate a 19308.

The no. 62-316 Tan RSC with Black Graphics outfit box was manufactured by the Mead Corporation and measured 17⅜ x 13¼ x 6⅞ inches. It included four lines of data as part of the box

manufacturer's certificate.

Sears outfits and Super O outfits are always in demand. Therefore, it stands to reason that a Sears Super O promotional outfit will draw even more attention, which is the case with the 19308. Unfortunately for Lionel enthusiasts, this outfit is difficult to find complete in collectible condition.

19309
1963

Description: Super "O" Promotional Outfit
Specification: Super "O" Steam Type Freight With Smoke & Whistle
Customer/No.: Sears, Roebuck and Co.; 9888
Original Amount: 200
Factory Order Date: 12/12/1963
Date Issued: 12-12-63
Packaging: RSC

Contents: 736X-1 Steam Type Locomotive With Smoke; 736W-1 Whistle Tender; 6446-1 Cement Car "N & W"; 3349-1 Turbo Missile Firing Car; 6519-1 Allis-Chalmers Car; 6825-1 Flat Car With Trestle Bridge; 6500-1 Beechcraft Bonanza Transport Car; 6476-25 Hopper Car - Red; 3470-1 Aerial Target Launching Car; 6416-1 Boat Transport Car; 6059-50 Caboose; 31-60 Bundle of 6 - 31 Curved Track (2); 32-5 Straight Track - Loose (3); 34-10 Straight Track - ½ Section; 39-25 Envelope Packed; 40-1 Cable Reel W/Wire (Any Color); 195-1 Floodlight Tower; 163-1 Single Target Control Signal; 988-1 R.R. Structure Set; 299-1 Code Transmitter Set; KW-1 190-Watt Transformer; 1103-20 Envelope Packed; 310-62 Set of (3) Billboards; 1-62 Parts Order Form; 1-63 Warranty Card; 1123-40 Instruction Sheet

Boxes & Packing: 63-387 Outfit Box

Alternate For Outfit Contents:
Note: Substitute 41 - 6407-1 for 6416-1; Substitute 37 - 6476-85 for 6476-25; Substitute 38 - 987-1 for 988-1; Note: #40 Cable Reel to be taken from set of 8 in finished goods Stockroom; Note: Outfit Box will contain all the contents of the set except the KW Transformer which will be shipped separately. Outfit Box and Transformer must be marked to show shipping on 2.

19309 (1963)	C6	C7	C8	Rarity
Complete Outfit With no. KW-1 (With no. 19309 Markings)	2,910	4,260	5,650	R10
Complete Outfit Without A no. KW-1	2,535	3,735	5,000	R10
Complete Outfit With no. 6407-1 Substitution, Add The Following	305	465	875	R10
Complete Outfit With no. 6476-85 Substitution, Add The Following	90	135	180	R10
Complete Outfit With no. 987-1 Substitution, Add The Following	300	425	500	R10
Outfit Box no. 63-387	700	850	1,000	R10

Comments: In late 1963, Robert Wolfe, president of the Lionel Toy Corporation, worked out a deal - "Special Purchase" - with Sears, Roebuck and Co. to quickly bring additional revenue to Lionel by liquidating surplus toy inventory. This deal accounted for 23 of the 25 Super O and O27 Retailer Promotional outfits purchased by Sears in late 1963. None of these "Special Purchase" outfits has been observed in a Sears catalog. Internal Lionel and Sears documents revealed the link to Sears, along with the proper Sears number. (See the entry for Sears, Roebuck and Co. in the section on Lionel's Distribution and Customers.)

The no. 19309, a Type Ia outfit, was one of five Super O outfits purchased by Sears in 1963. With a steamer, tender and nine pieces of rolling stock, it is one of the largest outfits offered by Lionel. It was assigned Sears no. 9888.

The 19309 was led by a no. 736X-1 Steam Type Locomotive With Smoke and Magne-Traction. Originally introduced in 1950, the no. 736 appeared in at least 17 outfits during the 1960s. This steamer came packaged in a no. 736-36 Corr. Box. As described in the section on Outfit Peripherals, an "X" signified that a no. CTC-1 Lockon was left out because it wasn't necessary in a Super O outfit.

The rolling stock in the 19309 included some of Lionel's most collectible items. Of note was the no. 6446-1 N&W Cement Car. Its Orange Picture box is extremely tough to find. It was a reissue of the 6446-1, which first appeared in 1954. The reissued 6446-1 came in one catalog and four promotional outfits, with a total of 1,527 cars being made. The "-1" meant the car was gray. Even though its number was 6446-1, the car was stamped "644625".

The no. 6500-1 Beechcraft Bonanza Transport Car made its first promotional outfit appearance in the Sears "Special Purchase" outfits. It is one of the few items that could come in an Orange Perforated Picture or Orange Picture box.

At least five items made their last individually boxed appearance in the 19309. These included the nos. 6407-1 Flat Car W/Sterling Missile, 6416-1 Boat Transport Car, 6476-85 Hopper Car, 6519-1 Allis-Chalmers Car and 6825-1 Flat Car With Trestle Bridge. When substitutions were made, the outfit price was affected, as shown in the pricing table.

The box used for the 6476-85 is unknown. Both a Bold Classic box and a Late Classic box exist for this car, but which was used in the 13909 – or whether Lionel opted for an overstamped box – has yet to be ascertained.

For the boxed items in this outfit, Lionel used Orange Picture boxes with one exception. The 6825-1 came in an Orange Perforated box.

Unfortunately, when Lionel got to the caboose it selected a low-end model, the no. 6059-50 Caboose. This item seemed out of place among the higher-end rolling stock.

All the cars included in the 13909 were equipped with AAR trucks and couplers, with most of them having two operating types. However, the no. 6476-25 Hopper Car - Red and 6476-

85 could come with one operating and one non-operating type in 1963. The 6407-1 also came that way, but the no. 736W-1 Whistle Tender and 6059-50 were equipped with one operating and one plain truck and coupler.

The Sears "Special Purchase" outfits gave Lionel an opportunity to reduce its inventory of accessories and other peripherals. Thus, the 19309 was the only outfit that included the nos. 163-1 Single Target Control Signal, 195-1 Floodlight Tower, 987-1 Town Set, and 988-1 R.R. Structure Set. It also was one of four outfits to come with a no. 299-1 Code Transmitter Set.

A Type III or Type IV no. 39-25 Envelope Packed provided the remainder of the peripherals necessary to assemble and operate a 19309.

The no. 63-387 Outfit Box was manufactured by Robbins Container Corp. and was unique to the 19309. Finding this rare outfit box is extremely difficult. Even more difficult is finding a properly marked no. KW-1 190-Watt Transformer box indicating that it went with the 19309. This box demands a premium, as outlined in the pricing table.

As the description should make clear, the 19309 is by far one of the most intriguing and desirable of all the Sears Super O outfits. It easily earns an R10 rarity rating.

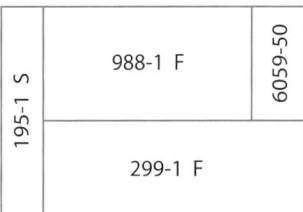

CONVENTIONAL PACK
63-387 BOX

TOP LAYER

163-1 F	6500-1 S	6476-25
	736W-1 S	
	6825-1 S	
	31-60	
	31-60 / 32-5 (3)	34-10 / 40-1
	3349-1 S	

MIDDLE LAYER

736X-1 F	6446-1 F	39-25
	6519-1 F	
	3470-1 F	
	6416-1 S	

BOTTOM LAYER

| 195-1 S | 988-1 F | 6059-50 |
| | 299-1 F | |

19300 Series

Description: "O27" Promotional Outfit
Specification: "O27" Diesel Freight Outfit
Original Amount: 296
Date Issued: 11-13-63
Packaging: RSC (Units Loose)

Contents: 211P-150 *"Texas Special"* Diesel; 211T-25 *"Texas Special"* Motorless Unit; 6408-25 Flat Car W/5 Pipes; 6511-15 Pipes (5); 3349-1 Turbo Missile Firing Car; 6480-25 Exploding Target Car; 6463-25 Rocket Fuel Car; 6142-25 Gondola Car (Less 2 Canisters); 6112-5 Canister (2); 6059-50 Caboose; 1013-8 Curved Track (Bundle of 8 - 1013); 1018-30 Straight Track (Bundle of 3 - 1018); 1008-50 Uncoupling Unit; 1025-25 45-Watt Transformer; 1103-20 Envelope Packed; 310-62 Set of (3) Billboards; D63-50 Accessory Catalog; 1-62 Parts Order Form; 1-63 Warranty Card

Boxes & Packing: 63-309 Box; 62-224 Insert; 62-245 Insert (2); 62-248 Insert; 62-254 Insert; 63-310 Shipper (1-4)

Alternate For Outfit Contents:
Note: Substitute 90 - 211T-1 for 211T-25; Substitute 50 - 218P-25 for 211P-150; Substitute 50 - 218T-25 for 211T-25.

Comments: The Factory Order for this outfit included a handwritten "11361-500" on it. This might have been one of the outfits offered to Sears as part of its year-end "Special Purchase", but which, for some reason, was rejected. The 19310 was likely never made and became the General Release Promotional Type IIb no. 11361-500. This listing is provided for historical reference. (See the entry for the 11361-500.)

Outfit no. 19311 (Sears no. 9852) was one of the 23 Sears "Special Purchase" outfits from late 1963. A space and military offering, it was one of three outfits to include a no. 59-1 Minuteman Diesel Switcher. More importantly, this 19311 had the rare no. 910-1 Navy Yard Cardboard Display (also known as the Atomic Sub Base) as well as the no. 19311-10 Instruction Sheet. A no. 63-309 Outfit Box is shown.

Customer No. On Box: 9852
Description: "O27" Promotional Outfit
Specification: "O27" Diesel Freight Outfit
Customer/No.: Sears, Roebuck and Co.; 9852
Original Amount: 875
Factory Order Date: 11/14/1963
Date Issued: 11-14-63
Packaging: RSC (Units Loose)

Contents: 59-1 Minuteman Diesel Switcher; 3519-25 Operating Satellite Launching Car; 448-1 Missile Firing Range Set With Exploding Target Car; 6014-325 Frisco Box Car; 6142-25 Gondola Car (Less 2 Canisters); 6112-5 Canister (2); 6059-50 Caboose; 910-1 Navy Yard Cardboard Display; 1013-8 Curved Track (Bundle of 8 - 1013) (2); 1018-30 Straight Track (Bundle of 3 - 1018); 1023-1 45° Crossing; 90-30 Envelope Packed; 1010-25 35-Watt Transformer; 1103-20 Envelope Packed; 6029-25 Uncoupling Track Section; 310-62 Set of (3) Billboards; D63-50 Accessory Catalog; 1-62 Parts Order Form; 1-63 Warranty Card; 3519-7 Instruction Sheet; 59-7 Instruction Sheet; 19145-10 Instruction Sheet; 19311-10 Instruction Sheet

Boxes & Packing: 63-309 Outfit Box (Used when using 448-1); 63-310 Shipper for (4) (1-4); 63-366 Outfit Box (Used when using (470-1); 62-249 Corr. Insert; 62-278 Corr. Insert (2); 63-367 Shipper for (3) (1-3)

Alternate For Outfit Contents:
Note: Substitute 345 - 470-1 for 448-1; Substitute 908-10 for 910-1 as needed; Note: The 910 used in this set will not be packed with the rest of the set. They will be shipped in carton 63-216 five (5) units per carton. Each set and each 908 or 910 must be marked to go together.

19311 (1963)	C6	C7	C8	Rarity
Complete Outfit With nos. 910-1, 448-1 And 63-309 Box	7,000	10,700	14,500	R10
Complete Outfit With nos. 908-10, 448-1 And 63-309 Box	1,900	2,900	4,000	R9
Outfit Box no. 63-309 (For no. 448-1)	250	400	500	R9
Complete Outfit With nos. 910-1, 470-1 And 63-366 Box	7,100	10,800	14,600	R10
Complete Outfit With nos. 908-10, 470-1 And 63-366 Box	2,000	3,000	4,100	R9
Outfit Box no. 63-366 (For no. 470-1)	350	500	600	R9

Another version of the no. 19311 included a no. 908-10 Scenic Station W/Tunnels - Packed. This substitution occurred in some 19311s. A no. 63-309 Outfit Box is shown.

Comments: In late 1963, Robert Wolfe, president of the Lionel Toy Corporation, worked out a deal - "Special Purchase" - with Sears, Roebuck and Co. to quickly bring additional revenue to Lionel by liquidating surplus toy inventory. This deal accounted for 23 of the 25 Super O and O27 Retailer Promotional outfits purchased by Sears in late 1963. None of these "Special Purchase" outfits has been observed in a Sears catalog. Internal Lionel and Sears documents revealed the link to Sears, along with the proper Sears number. (See the entry for Sears, Roebuck and Co. in the section on Lionel's Distribution and Customers.)

The no. 19311, a Type Ib outfit, was one of the many space and military outfits purchased by Sears in 1963. The Sears no. 9852 was stamped on the outfit box below the Lionel number.

This outfit was led by a no. 59-1 Minuteman Diesel Switcher equipped with a three-position reversing unit. Using a motorized unit to lead an outfit was not a new idea, but it was very uncommon. The 59-1 was being depleted in three outfits in 1963, all for Sears.

The 19311 was the eighth promotional outfit to include a no. 910-1 Navy Yard Cardboard Display (also known as the Atomic Sub Base). As was true with the other outfits containing a sub base, that item is what makes the 19311 extremely rare today. The 910-1 Navy Yard Cardboard Display was a fragile model intended to be assembled by the customer. There were no Lionel markings on this item, and it often became separated from the train outfit and was destroyed. Stories exist of individuals who discarded a 910-1 because they did not know what it was.

All 10 cardboard pieces that made up the sub base were placed in a plain, tan-colored flat paper bag. This was the first sub base outfit that did not pack the sub base in the outfit box. According to the Factory Order, the 910-1 was shipped separately and marked to go with the 19311.

However, not all of the 19311 outfits included a sub base. In some, Lionel substituted a no. 908-10 Scenic Station W/Tunnels - Packed. This large and fragile cardboard station was similar to the

910-1 and was packaged in the same manner, a large Kraft paper bag. The 908-10 first appeared in outfit nos. X-810NA and X-855 from 1959. After a four-year absence, it returned with outfit no. 19224 and went on to appear in four other promotional outfits through 1964. Although it is a rare item, it is nowhere near as difficult to find as a 910-1.

The Factory Order indicated that the outfit box was to be stamped to acknowledge either the 908 or 910. Since these cardboard accessories came separately boxed, it was the task of the retailer to provide a 908-10 or 910-1 with each outfit.

Compared to the 910-1 and 908-10, the other items in this

CONVENTIONAL PACK 63-309 BOX WITH 448-1 11-13-63			
TOP LAYER		**BOTTOM LAYER**	
1013-8		448-1 F	6059-50
1013-8			
6142-25		59-1 F	
3519-25 F			1010-25
6014-325		1018-30	
1023-1 TOP			

CONVENTIONAL PACK 63-366 BOX WITH 470-1 REVISED 11-13-63				
TOP LAYER			**BOTTOM LAYER**	
62-249				
1013-8		1018-30	470-1	59-1 F
6014-325	62-278	62-278		
6059-50				
6142-25			1013-8	1010-25
3519-25 F			1023-1	

outfit are easily obtained. The nos. 448-1 Missile Firing Range Set With Exploding Target Car, 470-1 Missile Launching Platform substitution and unboxed 3519-25 Operating Satellite Launching Car were making their last outfit appearances. A no. 6448-1 Exploding Target Range Car or 6470-1 Exploding Target Car were included in the 448-1 and 470-1, respectively.

The rolling stock packed with the 19311 typically came equipped with AAR trucks and couplers. To be specific, the 3519-25, 6448-1 and 6470-1 had two operating types; the nos. 6014-325 Frisco Box Car and 6142-25 Gondola Car (Less 2 Canisters) had one operating and one non-operating type; and the no. 6059-50 Caboose had one operating and one plain type.

The outfit's paperwork included the no. 19311-10 Instruction Sheet dated 12/63; this rare document showed up in no other outfit. The no. 19145-10 Instruction Sheet made reference to Lionel's new 90-day warranty policy, although it still was dated 7-62.

The substitution of a 470-1 for a 448-1 required that Lionel use two different Tan RSC with Black Graphic outfit boxes. The no. 63-309 Outfit Box measured 13¼ x 12½ x 6¾ inches, while the no. 63-366 Outfit Box measured 15¾ x 14¾ x 6⅞ inches. Both were manufactured by the Mead Corporation and included four lines of data as part of the box manufacturer's certificate.

Finding either outfit box for the 19311 takes patience, especially if a 63-366 is sought. Then come the challenges of completing this outfit with the appropriate cardboard display and paperwork.

Keep in mind that the pricing and rarity for this outfit assume the presence of either the 910-1's "How to Assemble Your Lionel Atomic Submarine Base" Instruction Sheet or the 908-10's "How To Set Up Your Railroad Terminal" Instruction Sheet. Additionally, the cardboard accessory should have its difficult-to-find paper bag.

Customer No. On Box: 9868
Description: "O27" Promotional Outfit
Specification: "O27" Diesel Freight Outfit
Customer/No.: Sears, Roebuck and Co.; 9868
Original Amount: 660
Factory Order Date: 12/16/1963
Date Issued: 12-16-63
Date Req'd: 12-20-63
Packaging: RSC

Contents: 231P-25 Alco Diesel Power Car - "Rock Island"; 230P-25 Alco Diesel Power Unit - "Chesapeake & Ohio"; 6045-150 Tank Car; 6484-25 "New Haven" Box Car; 6536-25 Hopper Car - Red - "Minn. - St. Louis"; 6825-25 Flat Car W/Trestle Bridge; 6825-3 Trestle Bridge; 3545-1 Operating TV Monitor Car; 6059-50 Caboose; 40-1 Cable Reel W/Wire (Any Color); 50-1 Gang Car; 59-1 Minuteman Diesel Switcher; 260-1 Illuminated Bumper; 375-1 Motorized Turntable; 262-1 Highway Crossing Gate; 1013-8 Curved Track (Bundle of 8 - 1013); 1018-7 Straight Track (Bundle of 7 - 1018) (4); 1018-30 Straight Track (Bundle of 3 - 1018); 6029-25 Uncoupling Track Section; 364C-50 Contactor; 1122-1 Pr. Remote Control Switches; KW-1 190-Watt Transformer; 1103-20 Envelope Packed; 310-62 Set of (3) Billboards; 1-62 Parts Order Form; 1-63 Warranty Card; 6650-92 Instruction Sheet; 230-6 Instruction Sheet; 1123-40 Instruction Sheet

Boxes & Packing: 63-390 Outfit Box; 62-224 Corr. Insert; 62-245 Corr. Insert (2); 62-248 Corr. Insert

Alternate For Outfit Contents:
Note: Substitute 27 - 211P-25 for 230P-25; Substitute 201 - 222P-25 for 230P-25; Substitute 80 - 227P-25 for 230P-25; Substitute 98 - 6650-25 for 3545-1 (With 6650-80); Note: #40 Cable Reel to be taken from set of 8 in Finished Goods Stock Room.

19312 (1963)	C6	C7	C8	Rarity
Complete Outfit	1,700	2,650	3,775	R9
Complete Outfit With no. 6650-25 Substitution	1,560	2,475	3,505	R9
Outfit Box no. 63-390	300	400	500	R9

Comments: In late 1963, Robert Wolfe, president of the Lionel Toy Corporation, worked out a deal - "Special Purchase" - with Sears, Roebuck and Co. to quickly bring additional revenue to Lionel by liquidating surplus toy inventory. This deal accounted for 23 of the 25 Super O and O27 Retailer Promotional outfits purchased by Sears in late 1963. None of these "Special Purchase" outfits has been observed in a Sears catalog. Internal Lionel and Sears documents revealed the link to Sears, along with the proper Sears number. (See the entry for Sears, Roebuck and Co. in the section on Lionel's Distribution and Customers.)

The no. 19312, a Type Ib outfit, was among the most interesting Sears or Lionel offerings because it was the only outfit to come with two diesel locomotives and two motorized units. This outfit had the Sears no. 9868 stamped on the outfit box below the Lionel number.

The 19312 included the nos. 231P-25 Rock Island Alco Diesel Power Car and 230P-25 Chesapeake & Ohio Alco Diesel Power Unit. Both locomotives featured two-axle Magne-Traction, a headlight and a two-position reversing unit.

The unboxed 230P-25 was making its last outfit appearance. In some of the 19312 outfits, it was replaced by a no. 211P-25 *Texas Special* Alco Diesel Power Unit (making its final outfit appearance), no. 222P-25 Denver & Rio Grande Alco Diesel Power Unit (also making its final outfit appearance) or no. 227P-25 Canadian National Alco Diesel Power Unit. The 211P-25 had features on a par with those of the 230P-25. By contrast, the 222P-25 and 227P-25 were downgrades that lacked even Magne-Traction. The price differential of these substitutions is minimal when compared to the overall outfit price.

Turning to the rolling stock, the 19312 was the only promotional outfit to include an unboxed no. 6484-25 New Haven Box Car, which first appeared in catalog outfit no. 11395

Outfit no. 19312 (Sears no. 9868) was one of the 23 Sears "Special Purchase" outfits from late 1963. It included a little bit of everything, as Lionel was cleaning out its inventory. The 19312 is the only outfit to include two diesel locomotives *and* two motorized units. The no. 375-1 Motorized Turntable could be used to switch this motive power on and off the layout.

from 1963. The short-lived 6484-25 was the number that Lionel assigned to an orange New Haven 6464-series box car equipped with one operating and one non-operating AAR truck and coupler. Except for the truck and coupler configuration, it was identical to the orange unboxed no. 6464-750 New Haven Box Car that was heat-stamped "6464725".

The no. 6536-25 Minneapolis and St. Louis Hopper Car - Red was a component of only three outfits. It was the unboxed reissue of the no. 6536-1 model, which last appeared in 1959. The 6536-25 and no. 6825-25 Flat Car with Trestle Bridge were making their last outfit appearances.

The Orange Picture boxed no. 3545-1 Operating TV Monitor Car was replaced by a no. 6650-25 Missile Launching Flat Car in 98 of the outfits. This represented the final quantity of unboxed 6650-25s to appear in an outfit. The outfit price was affected, as noted in the pricing table.

The rolling stock included in the 19312 typically came equipped with AAR trucks and couplers. To be specific, the 3545-1, 6650-25 and 6825-25 had two operating types; the nos. 6484-25 and 6536-25 had one operating and one non-operating type; the no. 6045-150 Tank Car had non-operating types; and the no. 6059-50 Caboose had one operating and one plain type.

The no. 375-1 Motorized Turntable was included in six promotional outfits. The track layout diagram has yet to be confirmed, but probably was similar to one found on a form provided to Lionel Service Stations (Form 2759 dated 10/62). The nos. 50-1 Gang Car, 59-1 Minuteman Diesel Switcher, 230P-25 and 231P-25 provided motive power that could be switched on and off the track using the turntable.

The no. 63-390 Tan RSC with Black Graphics outfit box was

manufactured by Robbins Container Corp. and measured 22¼ x 18⅜ x 8¼ inches. It included four lines of data as part of the box manufacturer's certificate. The box also had "2L8" printed on the bottom.

The 19312 is very difficult to find in any condition, hence its R9 rarity rating and associated price.

CONVENTIONAL PACK
63-390 BOX

TOP LAYER			
6536-25	260	6059-50	
3545-1 F	50-1 S		
	6045-150		
6484-25	59-1 S		
1013-8			
1122-1 F			

1018-30, 6825-3, TOP 1013-8
6825-25, 1018-7, TOP 1122

	BOTTOM LAYER		
1018-7 (3)	262-1 F TOP 375	375-1 F	
	231P-25 62-248	KW-1	
	230P-25		

Outfit no. 19313 (Sears no. 9824) was one of the 23 Sears "Special Purchase" outfits from late 1963. Of note were the Orange Picture-boxed no. 6445-1 Ft. Knox Gold Bullion Transport Car and 6512-1 Cherry Picker Car. Overall, the 19313 showed the signs of an outfit hastily put together to reduce inventory.

Description: "O27" Promotional Outfit
Specification: "O27" Diesel Freight Outfit
Customer/No./Price: Sears, Roebuck and Co.; 9824; $19.88
Original Amount: 1,000
Factory Order Date: 11/11/1963
Date Issued: 11-11-63
Packaging: RSC

Contents: 231P-25 Alco Diesel Power Car - "Rock Island"; 6445-1 Ft. Knox Gold Bullion Transport Car; 6630-25 Missile Launching Car; 6650-80 Missile; 6512-1 Cherry Picker Car; 6014-325 Frisco Box Car; 6142-25 Gondola Car (Less Canisters); 6059-50 Caboose; 1013-8 Curved Track (Bundle of 8 - 1013); 1018-10 Straight Track (Loose); 1008-50 Uncoupling Unit; 1025-25 45-Watt Transformer; 1103-20 Envelope Packed; 310-62 Set of (3) Billboards; D63-50 Accessory Catalog; 1-62 Parts Order Form; 1-63 Warranty Card; 122-10 Instruction Sheet; 6630-6 Instruction Sheet; 6512-19 Instruction Sheet

Boxes & Packing: 61-180 Outfit Box; 61-181 Corr. Insert; 61-182 Corr. Insert; 61-185 Shipper for (4) (1-4)

19313 (1963)	C6	C7	C8	Rarity
Complete Outfit	500	800	1,175	R7
Outfit Box no. 61-180	100	175	275	R7

Comments: In late 1963, Robert Wolfe, president of the Lionel Toy Corporation, worked out a deal - "Special Purchase" - with Sears, Roebuck and Co. to quickly bring additional revenue to Lionel by liquidating surplus toy inventory. This deal accounted for 23 of the 25 Super O and O27 Retailer Promotional outfits purchased by Sears in late 1963. None of these "Special Purchase" outfits has been observed in a Sears catalog. Internal Lionel and Sears documents revealed the link to Sears, along with the proper Sears number. (See the entry for Sears, Roebuck and Co. in the section on Lionel's Distribution and Customers.)

The no. 19313, a Type Ib outfit, was one of the many diesel-powered outfits purchased by Sears in 1963. It was assigned Sears no. 9824.

The no. 231P-25 Rock Island Alco Diesel Power Car that led this outfit was first issued in 1961. It featured two-axle Magne-Traction, a headlight and a two-position reversing unit. This locomotive was nearing the end of its product life.

The diverse assortment of rolling stock in this outfit was indicative of the inventory that Lionel was depleting. The nos. 6630-25 Missile Launching Car and 6512-1 Cherry Picker Car were carryover space and military items hastily combined with a no. 6445-1 Ft. Knox Gold Bullion Transport Car. The 6445-1 and 6512-1 came in Orange Picture boxes. The three-year run of the 6630-25 was coming to an end in 1963, and the model made its last appearance in six promotional outfits.

Lionel's determination to liquidate its surplus inventory didn't mean that everything in this outfit was a carryover item. For the 19313, the nos. 6014-325 Frisco Box Car, 6059-50 Caboose and 6142-25 Gondola Car (Less Canisters) were all new items for 1963. This fact supports the contention that Lionel had overestimated production for this year.

Except for the 6630-25, which came with non-operating Archbar trucks and couplers, the cars in this outfit were equipped with AAR types. To be specific, the 6445-1 and 6512-1 had two operating types, the 6014-325 and 6142-25 had one operating and one non-operating type and the 6059-50 had one operating and one plain type.

The no. 122-10 Instruction Sheet made reference to the 90-day warranty policy that Lionel instituted in 1963. It was dated 5-62.

The commonly used no. 61-180 Tan RSC with Black Graphics outfit box measured 12¾ x 10 x 6¾ inches.

Even though the 19313 was produced in larger quantities than many of the other Sears "Special Purchase" outfits, it is still difficult to find complete in collectible condition.

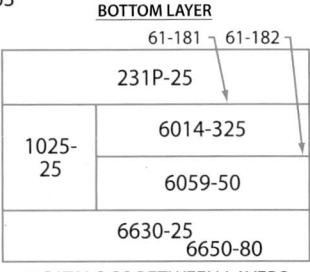

CONVENTIONAL PACK
61-180 BOX
11-11-63

TOP LAYER

6142-25	6445-1 F 1008-50
	1013-8
	6512-1 F 1018-10

BOTTOM LAYER
61-181 ┐ 61-182 ┐

	231P-25
1025-25	6014-325
	6059-50
	6630-25
	6650-80

2 CATALOGS BETWEEN LAYERS

Description: "O27" Promotional Outfit
Specification: "O27" Diesel Freight Outfit
Original Amount: 1,040
Factory Order Date: 11/20/1963
Date Req'd: At Once
Packaging: RSC

Contents: 221P-25 Diesel Locomotive; 6062-1 Gondola Car - Black - with (3) Cable Reels; 6445-1 Ft. Knox Gold Bullion Transport Car; 6463-25 Rocket Fuel Car; 3519-1 Operating Satellite Launching Car; 6059-50 Caboose; 1013-8 Curved Track (Bundle of 8 - 1013); 1018-10 Straight Track (Loose); 1008-50 Uncoupling Unit; 1010-25 35-Watt Transformer; 1103-20 Envelope Packed; 310-62 Set of (3) Billboards; D63-50 Accessory Catalog; 1-62 Parts Order Form; 1-63 Warranty Card; 122-10 Instruction Sheet

Boxes & Packing: 62-243 Outfit Box; 62-254 Corr. Insert; 62-244 Shipper for (4) (1-4)

Alternate For Outfit Contents:
Note: Substitute 140 - 222P-25 for 221P-25; Substitute 96 - 6413-25 for 6445-1 using 2 - 6413-4 and 6413-10; Substitute 50 - 6416-1 for 6445-1; Substitute 460 - 6402-25 for 6463-25.

Comments: The Factory Order for this outfit included a handwritten "11341-500" on it. This might have been one of the outfits offered to Sears as part of its year-end "Special Purchase", but which, for some reason, was rejected. The 19314 was likely never made and became the General Release Promotional no. 11341-500. This listing is provided for historical reference. (See the entry for the 11341-500.)

Description: "O27" Promotional Outfit
Specification: "O27" Diesel Freight Outfit
Customer: Wm. H. Block Company
Original Amount: 60
Factory Order Date: 11/13/1963
Date Issued: 11-13-63
Packaging: RSC

Contents: 222P-25 "Denver & Rio Grande" Alco Diesel Power Unit; 6062-1 Gondola Car - Black - with (3) Cable Reels; 6413-25 Mercury Capsule Transport Car; 6413-4 Capsules (2); 6413-10 Envelope Packed; 6463-25 Rocket Fuel Car; 3519-1 Operating Satellite Launching Car; 6059-50 Caboose; 1013-70 Curved Track (Bundle of 12 - 1013); 1018-5 Straight Track (Bundle of 5 - 1018); 1020-1 90° Crossing; 1008-50 Uncoupling Unit; 1010-25 35-Watt Transformer; 1103-20 Envelope Packed; 310-62 Set of (3) Billboards; D63-50 Accessory Catalog; 1-62 Parts Order Form; 1-63 Warranty Card; 3519-7 Instruction Sheet; 122-10 Instruction Sheet; 1802B Layout Instruction Sheet

Boxes & Packing: 61-180 Outfit Box; 61-181 Corr. Insert; 61-182 Corr. Insert; 61-185 Shipper for (4) (1-4)

19314-500 (1963)	C6	C7	C8	Rarity
Complete Outfit	1,300	1,735	2,225	R10
Outfit Box no. 61-180	1,000	1,250	1,500	R10

Comments: Before outfit no. 19314 was reassigned to outfit no. 11341-500, a quantity of 60 apparently was slightly modified to become outfit no. 19314-500. This Retailer Promotional Type Ib outfit listed Wm. H. Block Company as its customer.

The 19314-500 was led by a no. 222P-25 Denver & Rio Grande Alco Diesel Power Unit. This locomotive moved forward only and featured a traction tire, a headlight and a closed pilot.

As with other late-in-the-year outfits from 1963, Lionel was cleaning its shelves of old inventory. Except for the no. 6059-50 Caboose, all the items in this outfit were carryover from earlier years. The nos. 3519-1 Operating Satellite Launching Car and 6062-1 Gondola Car - Black - with (3) Cable Reels came in Orange Picture boxes and likely were equipped with early operating AAR trucks and couplers.

The transition from Archbar to AAR trucks and couplers that began in 1962 continued into 1963. As part of this, Lionel sought to cut costs by introducing a non-operating AAR type. Therefore, starting in 1963, most cars equipped with AAR trucks and couplers had at least one non-operating type. For the 19314-500, the no. 6413-25 Mercury Capsule Transport Car and 6463-25 Rocket Fuel Car could come with two operating or one operating and one non-operating AAR type. The 6059-50 included one operating and one plain AAR truck and coupler.

The nos. 122-10 Instruction Sheet made reference to the 90-day warranty policy that Lionel instituted in 1963. It was dated 5-62. A no. 1802B Layout Instruction Sheet detailed the figure-eight track layout.

The commonly used no. 61-180 Tan RSC with Black Graphics outfit box measured 12¾ x 10 x 6¾ inches.

The 19314-500 was made in quantities so small that it ties for 15th on the list of fewest outfits produced. Add in that this was the only outfit to list Wm. H. Block Company as its customer and the 19314-500 becomes a very desirable outfit.

CONVENTIONAL PACK
61-180 BOX
11-12-63

TOP LAYER | BOTTOM LAYER

61-181 61-182

1018-5 1008-50	6413-25
	1013-70
	3519-1 F
1020-1 TOP

1010-25	6062-1 S
	6059-50
	6463-25
	222P-25
2 CATALOGS BETWEEN LAYERS

19315
1963

Description: Super "O" Promotional Outfit
Specification: Super "O" Twin Diesel Passenger Outfit With Horn
Customer/No.: Sears, Roebuck and Co.; 9887
Original Amount: 75
Factory Order Date: 12/12/1963
Date Issued: Rev 1-21-64
Packaging: RSC

Contents: 2383PX-1 "Santa Fe" Power Diesel Unit With Horn; 2383T-1 "Santa Fe" Motorless Unit; 2521-1 Illuminated Observation Car; 2522-1 Illuminated Vista Dome; 2523-1 Illuminated Pullman Car; 31-60 Bundle of 6 - 31 Curved Track (2); 32-5 Straight Track - Loose (5); 34-10 Straight Track - ½ Section; 39-25 Envelope Packed; KW-1 190-Watt Transformer; 310-62 Set of (3) Billboards; 1-62 Parts Order Form; 1-63 Warranty Card; 1123-40 Instruction Sheet

Boxes & Packing: 63-388 Outfit Box

Alternate For Outfit Contents:
Note: Can be taken from 1964 line reserve.

19315 (1963)	C6	C7	C8	Rarity
Complete Outfit	2,800	4,350	5,550	R10
Outfit Box no. 63-388	1,750	2,500	3,000	R10

Comments: In late 1963, Robert Wolfe, president of the Lionel Toy Corporation, worked out a deal - "Special Purchase" - with Sears, Roebuck and Co. to quickly bring additional revenue to Lionel by liquidating surplus toy inventory. This deal accounted for 23 of the 25 Super O and O27 Retailer Promotional outfits purchased by Sears in late 1963. None of these "Special Purchase" outfits has been observed in a Sears catalog. Internal Lionel and Sears documents revealed the link to Sears, along with the proper Sears number. (See the entry for Sears, Roebuck and Co. in the section on Lionel's Distribution and Customers.)

The no. 19315, a Type Ia outfit, was one of five Super O outfits purchased by Sears in 1963. Assigned Sears no. 9887, it was almost an exact duplicate of catalog outfit no. 13148 from 1963. The only differences were that, first, the 19315 included one no. 2523-1 Illuminated Pullman Car instead of the two in the catalog outfit and, second, it also came with a no. KW-1 190-Watt Transformer.

The 19315 was led by the nos. 2383PX-1 Santa Fe Power

Diesel Unit With Horn and 2383T-1 Santa Fe Motorless Unit. The engine featured Magne-Traction, a three-position reversing unit and a headlight. The 2383PX-1 came packaged in a no. 2383-11 Corr. Box. As described in the section on Outfit Peripherals, an "X" signified that a no. CTC-1 Lockon was left out because it wasn't necessary in a Super O outfit.

Lionel introduced the no. 2520-series of "Presidential" streamlined passenger cars in 1962. Catalog outfit 13148's Factory Order was dated 4-3-63, so it would have consisted of any leftover 2520-series inventory from 1962 as well as 1963 production. Since the 19315 was part of the late-in-the-year Sears "Special Purchase", the passenger cars used in that outfit were likely surplus inventory from 1963.

The passenger cars are fairly common, but their boxes are difficult to obtain in collectible condition. The proper versions of the 2520-series Dark Orange Picture box for 1963 included a "4-63" date on one of the inside flaps and were a darker shade of orange. These boxes demand a premium that is reflected in the outfit price. Leftover Orange Perforated Picture boxes from 1962 are also possible, but not likely.

As with most Super O outfits, the track layout of the 19315 was a basic oval. A Type III or Type IV no. 39-25 Envelope Packed is possible with this outfit.

Catalog Super O outfits generally did not include a transformer. However, because promotional outfits were most often destined for retailers that probably did not have a train department, Lionel included a transformer. For the 19315, the KW-1 provided plenty of power to operate this outfit. It appeared in only six outfits during the 1960s.

The no. 63-388 Outfit Box was manufactured by Robbins Container Corp. and was unique to the 19315. Finding this rare outfit box is extremely difficult.

The 19315 was made in quantities so small that it ties for 18th on the list of fewest outfits produced. That fact, combined with this highly desirable outfit being one of only five promotional Super O outfits available from Sears in 1963, easily gives it an R10 rarity.

CONVENTIONAL PACK
63-388 BOX
12-11-63

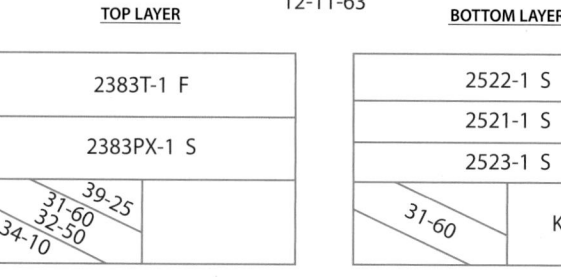

TOP LAYER | BOTTOM LAYER

| 2383T-1 F |
| 2383PX-1 S |
| 31-60 39-25 34-10 32-50 |

| 2522-1 S |
| 2521-1 S |
| 2523-1 S |
| 31-60 | KW-1 S |

Description: Super "O" Promotional Outfit
Specification: Super "O" Twin Diesel Freight Outfit With Horn
Customer/No.: Sears, Roebuck and Co.; 9885
Original Amount: 200
Factory Order Date: 12/12/1963
Date Issued: 12-12-63
Packaging: RSC

Contents: 2383PX-1 "Santa Fe" Power Diesel Unit With Horn; 2383T-1 "Santa Fe" Motorless Unit; 6315-60 Chemical Tank Car; 6142-25 Gondola Car (Less 2 Canisters); 6112-5 Canister (2); 6650-1 Missile Launching Flat Car; 3413-1 Mercury Capsule Launching Car; 6476-25 Hopper Car - Red; 6469-50 Miscellaneous Car; 6059-50 Caboose; 31-60 Bundle of 6 - 31 Curved Track (2); 32-5 Straight Track - Loose (5); 34-10 Straight Track - ½ Section; 39-25 Envelope Packed; KW-1 190-Watt Transformer; 310-62 Set of (3) Billboards; 1-62 Parts Order Form; 1-63 Warranty Card; 1123-40 Instruction Sheet

Boxes & Packing: 1S Corr. Carton

19316 (1963)	C6	C7	C8	Rarity
Complete Outfit	1,390	2,130	3,025	R10
Outfit Box no. 1S	650	900	1,200	R10

Comments: In late 1963, Robert Wolfe, president of the Lionel Toy Corporation, worked out a deal - "Special Purchase" - with Sears, Roebuck and Co. to quickly bring additional revenue to Lionel by liquidating surplus toy inventory. This deal accounted for 23 of the 25 Super O and O27 Retailer Promotional outfits purchased by Sears in late 1963. None of these "Special Purchase" outfits has been observed in a Sears catalog. Internal Lionel and Sears documents revealed the link to Sears, along with the proper Sears number. (See the entry for Sears, Roebuck and Co. in the section on Lionel's Distribution and Customers.)

The no. 19316, a Type Ia outfit, was one of five Super O outfits purchased by Sears in 1963. It was assigned Sears no. 9885.

The 19316 was led by the nos. 2383PX-1 Santa Fe Power Diesel Unit With Horn and 2383T-1 Santa Fe Motorless Unit. The engine featured Magne-Traction, a three-position reversing unit and a headlight. The 2383PX-1 came packaged in a no. 2383-11 Corr. Box. As described in the section on Outfit Peripherals, an "X" signified that a no. CTC-1 Lockon was left out because it wasn't necessary in a Super O outfit.

Since the 19316 was a Super O outfit, the inclusion of the low-end unboxed nos. 6059-50 Caboose, 6142-25 Gondola Car (Less 2 Canisters) and 6476-25 Hopper Car - Red was curious. Lionel likely offered Sears such an attractive deal that it overlooked these low-end additions to a Super O outfit.

The other items in this outfit were typical of those added to Super O outfits from 1963. The nos. 3413-1 Mercury Capsule

Launching Car and 6650-1 Missile Launching Flat Car were space and military items being depleted in this outfit. The no. 6315-60 Chemical Car is interesting because early versions came in an Orange Picture box with "6315-50" stamped on the box. This quickly changed to the correct "6315-60" version, which probably was included in this outfit. All the boxed rolling stock in the 19316 came in Orange Picture boxes.

The transition from Archbar to AAR trucks and couplers that began in 1962 continued into 1963. As part of this, Lionel sought to cut costs by introducing a non-operating AAR type. Therefore, starting in 1963, most cars equipped with AAR trucks and couplers had at least one non-operating type.

The 19316 generally followed this pattern. All the cars in this outfit were equipped with AAR trucks and couplers. However, not every model had even one non-operating AAR type. Specifically, all the boxed items came with two operating types. The no. 6476-25 Hopper Car – Red could have either two operating trucks and couplers or one operating and one non-operating type in 1963. The norm for the 6142-25 and no. 6469-50 Miscellaneous Car was one of each, while the no. 736W-1 Whistle Tender and 6059-50 came with one operating and one plain truck and coupler.

As with most Super O outfits, the track layout of the 19316 was a basic oval. A Type III or Type IV no. 39-25 Envelope Packed was possible with this outfit.

Catalog Super O outfits generally did not include a transformer. However, because promotional outfits were most often destined for retailers that probably did not have a train department, Lionel included a transformer. For the 19316, the no. KW-1 190-Watt Transformer provided plenty of power to operate this outfit. It appeared in only six outfits during the 1960s.

The no. 1S Corr. Carton was unique to the 19316. Finding this rare outfit box is extremely difficult.

Sears outfits and Super O outfits are always in demand. Therefore, it stands to reason that a Sears Super O promotional outfit will draw even more attention, which is the case with the 19316. Unfortunately for Lionel enthusiasts, so few examples of this outfit were produced that finding one in any condition proves to be quite a challenge.

CONVENTIONAL PACK
1S BOX
11-18-63

TOP LAYER

6315-60	6476-25	32-5

| 6142-25 | | |
| 6469-50 | 39-25 | |

BOTTOM LAYER

| KW-1 | 2383PX-1 F | 2383T-1 F | | | 6059-50 |
| 09-1E / 09-1E | | | 3413-1 F | 6650-1 F | |

Description: "O27" Promotional Outfit
Specification: "O27" Diesel Freight Outfit
Customer/No.: Sears, Roebuck and Co.; 9866
Original Amount: 200
Factory Order Date: 12/12/1963
Date Issued: 12-12-63
Packaging: RSC

Contents: 223P-1 "Santa Fe" Alco Diesel Power Unit with Horn; 6501-1 Jet Motor Boat Car; 6630-25 Missile Launching Car; 6650-80 Missile; 6406-25 Flat Car W/Auto; 6406-30 Automobile; 6076-100 Hopper Car - Gray; 3470-1 Aerial Target Launching Car; 6014-325 Frisco Box Car; 6167-25 Caboose; 299-1 Code Transmitter Set; 1013-8 Curved Track (Bundle of 8 - 1013); 1018-40 Straight Track (Bundle of 4 - 1018); 1063-100 75-Watt Transformer; 1103-20 Envelope Packed; 310-62 Set of (3) Billboards; 1-62 Parts Order Form; 1-63 Warranty Card; 6630-6 Instruction Sheet; 1123-40 Instruction Sheet; 19317-10 Instruction Sheet

Boxes & Packing: 63-389 Outfit Box

Alternate For Outfit Contents:
Note: Substitute 66 - 3376-160 for 3470-1.

19317 (1963)	C6	C7	C8	Rarity
Complete Outfit With Green Or Brown Automobile	1,250	1,775	2,400	R10
Complete Outfit With Yellow Automobile	1,100	1,575	2,150	R10
Outfit Box no. 63-389	450	600	750	R10

Comments: In late 1963, Robert Wolfe, president of the Lionel Toy Corporation, worked out a deal - "Special Purchase" - with Sears, Roebuck and Co. to quickly bring additional revenue to Lionel by liquidating surplus toy inventory. This deal accounted for 23 of the 25 Super O and O27 Retailer Promotional outfits purchased by Sears in late 1963. None of these "Special Purchase" outfits has been observed in a Sears catalog. Internal Lionel and Sears documents revealed the link to Sears, along with the proper Sears number. (See the entry for Sears, Roebuck and Co. in the section on Lionel's Distribution and Customers.)

The no. 19317, a Type Ib outfit, was one of the many diesel-powered outfits purchased by Sears in 1963. It was assigned Sears no. 9866.

The 19317 was led by a no. 223P-1 Santa Fe Alco Diesel Power Unit with Horn. This locomotive also featured a two-position reversing unit, a headlight, one-axle Magne-Traction and an open pilot with a large ledge. A promotional-only diesel, it came packaged in a no. 223-8 Corr. Box. The 223P-1 was available only as a component in outfits from Sears and a substitution in outfit no. 19172 from Maritz.

The diverse assortment of rolling stock in the 19317 was indicative of the inventory that Lionel was depleting. The nos. 3470-1 Aerial Target Launching Car and 6630-25 Missile Launching Car were carryover space and military items that were combined with other commonly available rolling stock.

In 1963 the no. 6406-25 Flat Car W/Auto began to appear in gray molded plastic. The no. 6406-30 Automobile was most often molded in brown or green plastic with gray bumpers, but a yellow automobile with gray bumpers was also possible. The specific color cannot be confirmed for this outfit. Pricing is provided for these variations.

In spite of Lionel's determination to liquidate its surplus inventory, not everything in this outfit was a carryover item. The nos. 6014-325 Frisco Box Car and 6167-25 Caboose were new items for 1963. This fact supports the contention that Lionel had overestimated production for this year.

The nos. 3376-160 Operating Giraffe Car, 3470-1 and 6501-1 Jet Motor Boat Car all came in Orange Picture boxes. The substitution of a 3376-160 marginally affects the outfit price.

The transition from Archbar to AAR trucks and couplers that began in 1962 continued into 1963. Most of the cars in this outfit were equipped with AAR trucks and couplers. Boxed items had two operating AAR types. The 6014-325 was equipped with one operating and one non-operating AAR type, and the 6076-100 and 6406-25 usually came with two of those non-operating types, although Archbar is also possible. The 6630-25 had non-operating Archbar trucks and couplers. The 6167-25 had one non-operating and one plain AAR or Archbar truck and coupler.

The Sears "Special Purchase" outfits gave Lionel an opportunity to reduce its inventory of accessories and other peripherals. Thus, the 19317 included a no. 299-1 Code Transmitter Set. This outfit also was one of the last six to include a no. 1063-100 75-Watt Transformer, which was last used in 1961. (See outfit no. 9672 from 1961 for more information about this transformer.)

The paperwork packed with this outfit included the no. 19317-10 Instruction Sheet dated 12/63. This rare document showed up in no other outfit.

The no. 63-389 Outfit Box was manufactured by Robbins Container Corp. and was unique to the 19317.

The 19317 is a collectible outfit because it came from Sears and was produced in small quantities. That being said, it is difficult to find an empty box or a complete outfit, hence the R10 rarity rating.

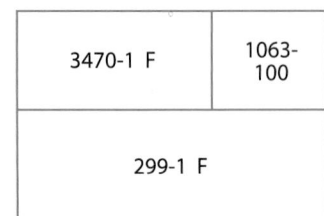

CONVENTIONAL PACK
63-389 BOX
12-11-63

Description: "O27" Promotional Outfit
Specification: "O27" Diesel Freight Outfit W/Horn
Customer/No.: Sears, Roebuck and Co.; 9867
Original Amount: 100
Factory Order Date: 12/16/1963
Date Issued: 12-16-63
Date Req'd: 12-20-63
Packaging: RSC

Contents: 223P-1 "Santa Fe" Alco Diesel Power Unit with Horn; 6630-25 Missile Launching Car; 6650-80 Missile; 6361-1 Timber Transport Car; 6162-25 Gondola Car (Less 3 Canisters); 6112-88 Canister (3); 3376-150 Operating Giraffe Car; 3413-1 Mercury Capsule Launching Car; 6436-110 Hopper Car; 6059-50 Caboose; 1013-8 Curved Track (Bundle of 8 - 1013); 1018-30 Straight Track (Bundle of 3 - 1018); 1008-50 Uncoupling Unit; 299-1 Code Transmitter Set; 1063-100 75-Watt Transformer; 1103-20 Envelope Packed; 3376-118 Envelope Packed; 310-62 Set of (3) Billboards; 1-62 Parts Order Form; 1-63 Warranty Card; 19241-10 Instruction Sheet; 1123-40 Instruction Sheet; 6630-6 Instruction Sheet

Boxes & Packing: 62-316 Outfit Box; 62-319 Shipper for (3) (1-3)

19317A (1963)	C6	C7	C8	Rarity
Complete Outfit	1,380	2,035	2,675	R10
Outfit Box no. 62-316	700	1,000	1,200	R10

Comments: In late 1963, Robert Wolfe, president of the Lionel Toy Corporation, worked out a deal - "Special Purchase" - with Sears, Roebuck and Co. to quickly bring additional revenue to Lionel by liquidating surplus toy inventory. This deal accounted for 23 of the 25 Super O and O27 Retailer Promotional outfits purchased by Sears in late 1963. None of these "Special Purchase" outfits has been observed in a Sears catalog. Internal Lionel and Sears documents revealed the link to Sears, along with the proper Sears number. (See the entry for Sears, Roebuck and Co. in the section on Lionel's Distribution and Customers.)

The no. 19317A, a Type Ib outfit, was one of the many diesel-powered outfits purchased by Sears in 1963. It was assigned Sears no. 9867. Even though the 19317A had the same base number as outfit no. 19317, they had only four items in common.

The 19317A was led by a no. 223P-1 Santa Fe Alco Diesel Power Unit with Horn. This locomotive also featured a two-position reversing unit, a headlight, one-axle Magne-Traction and an open pilot with a large ledge. A promotional-only diesel, it came packaged in a no. 223-8 Corr. Box. The 223P-1 was available only as a component in outfits from Sears and a substitution in outfit no. 19172 from Maritz.

The diverse assortment of rolling stock in the 19317 was indicative of the inventory that Lionel was depleting. The nos. 3413-1 Mercury Capsule Launching Car and 6630-25 Missile Launching Car were carryover space and military items hastily combined with other commonly available rolling stock. The three-year run of 6630-25 was coming to an end in 1963, and it made its last appearance in six promotional outfits.

The green no. 3376-150 Operating Giraffe Car made its second promotional outfit appearance in the 19317A. The "-150"

indicated that it was an unboxed no. 3376-160 Operating Giraffe Car. Since this item was unboxed, the 3376-150's no. 3376-118 Envelope Packed was placed loose in the outfit box.

In spite of Lionel's determination to liquidate its surplus inventory, not everything in this outfit was a carryover item. The nos. 6059-50 Caboose and 6436-110 Hopper Car were new items for 1963. This fact supports the contention that Lionel had overestimated production for this year.

All the boxed items came in Orange Picture types except for the no. 6361-1 Timber Transport Car. It could come packaged in an Orange Perforated box in 1963.

The transition from Archbar to AAR trucks and couplers that began in 1962 continued into 1963. Most of the cars in this outfit were equipped with AAR trucks and couplers. Boxed items had two operating AAR types, as did the 3376-150. The 6162-25 was equipped with one operating and one non-operating AAR type, and the 6059-50 had one operating and one plain AAR truck and coupler. The 6630-25 had non-operating Archbar trucks and couplers.

For the Sears "Special Purchase" outfits, Lionel also took the opportunity to reduce its inventory of accessories and other peripherals. The 19317A was one of four outfits to include a no. 299-1 Code Transmitter Set.

The no. 19241-10 Instruction Sheet appeared in only four outfits. Dated 11/63, it made reference to the 90-day warranty policy that Lionel instituted in 1963.

The no. 62-316 Tan RSC with Black Graphics outfit box measured 17⅜ x 13¼ x 6⅞ inches.

The 19317A is a collectible outfit because it came from Sears and was produced in very small quantities. That being said, it is difficult to find the empty box or complete outfit, hence the R10 rarity rating.

CONVENTIONAL PACK
62-316 BOX
12-12-63

TOP LAYER / BOTTOM LAYER

655

Description: "O27" Promotional Outfit
Specification: "O27" Diesel Freight Outfit W/Horn
Customer/No.: Sears, Roebuck and Co.; 9865
Original Amount: 100
Factory Order Date: 12/13/1963
Packaging: RSC

Contents: 617X-1 Diesel Switcher W/Horn - "Santa Fe"; 6512-1 Cherry Picker Car; 6062-1 Gondola Car - Black - with (3) Cable Reels; 6560-50 Crane Car Unpacked; 6059-50 Caboose; 908-10 Scenic Station W/Tunnels - Packed; 1013-8 Curved Track (Bundle of 8 - 1013) (2); 1018-30 Straight Track (Bundle of 3 - 1018); 1023-1 45° Crossing; 1063-100 75-Watt Transformer; 1103-20 Envelope Packed; 6139-25 Uncoupling Track Section; 310-62 Set of (3) Billboards; D63-50 Accessory Catalog; 1-62 Parts Order Form; 1-63 Warranty Card

Boxes & Packing: 61-210 Outfit Box; 61-211 Shipper for (4) (1-4); 63-252 Box To Ship 908-1 (1-8)

Alternate For Outfit Contents:
Note: 908-10 used in this set will be shipped eight (8) to a carton. The carton for this will be 63-252. Outfit box and 908-10 each have to be stamped with outfit number and showing outfit is shipped on two (2).

19318 (1963)	C6	C7	C8	Rarity
Complete Outfit	2,215	2,990	3,875	R10
Outfit Box no. 61-210	800	1,050	1,250	R10

Comments: In late 1963, Robert Wolfe, president of the Lionel Toy Corporation, worked out a deal - "Special Purchase" - with Sears, Roebuck and Co. to quickly bring additional revenue to Lionel by liquidating surplus toy inventory. This deal accounted for 23 of the 25 Super O and O27 Retailer Promotional outfits purchased by Sears in late 1963. None of these "Special Purchase" outfits has been observed in a Sears catalog. Internal Lionel and Sears documents revealed the link to Sears, along with the proper Sears number. (See the entry for Sears, Roebuck and Co. in the section on Lionel's Distribution and Customers.)

The no. 19318, a Type Ib outfit, was one of the many diesel-powered outfits purchased by Sears in 1963. It was assigned Sears no. 9865.

The 19318 was a led by a no. 617X-1 Santa Fe Diesel Switcher W/Horn. New for 1963, the 617X-1 featured a three-position reversing unit and two-axle Magne-Traction. Its Orange Picture no. 617-11 Folding Box is difficult to find in collectible condition. As described in the section on Outfit Peripherals, an "X" signified that a no. CTC-1 Lockon was not included.

The quantity of 100 locomotives used for these outfits likely represented stock left over from catalog outfit no. 13108, which Lionel issued earlier in 1963.

The no. 6062-1 Gondola Car made its last appearance in promotional outfits 19318 and no. 19321.

In spite of Lionel's determination to liquidate its surplus inventory, not everything in this outfit was a carryover item. The nos. 6059-50 Caboose and 6560-50 Crane Car were new items for 1963. This fact supports the contention that Lionel had overestimated production for this year.

The unboxed 6560-50 came with a red cab and a black base. It was the same as the 1962 version of the 6560-25 Crane Car, except that the "-50" was equipped with one operating and one non-operating AAR truck and coupler. The 19318 marked the only promotional outfit appearance of the 6560-50. The quantity of 100 included in this outfit was likely leftover from catalog outfit no. 11395, which Lionel issued earlier in the year.

The 6062-1 and no. 6512-1 Cherry Picker Car were equipped with operating AAR trucks and couplers. The 6059-50 had one operating and one plain AAR truck and coupler. All the boxed items in the 19318 came in Orange Picture boxes.

The item that makes this outfit a unique collectible was the no. 908-10 Scenic Station W/Tunnels - Packed. This large and fragile cardboard station first appeared in outfit nos. X-810NA and X-855 from 1959. After a four-year absence, it returned with the 19224 and went on to appear in four other promotional outfits through 1964. There were no Lionel markings on this item, which was intended to be assembled by the customer. The 908-10 frequently became separated from the train outfit and was destroyed.

Lionel shipped the 908-10s separately to the retailer. They came packaged eight at a time in their own no. 63-252 Corr. Box. Each 908-10 came in a large Kraft paper bag that, per the Factory Order, was "stamped with outfit number". A 908-10 with 19318 stampings has yet to be observed. There are at least four versions of this bag. Three were stamped with outfit nos. 19224, 19394 and 19395. The fourth included no printing. The 908-10 also included an instruction sheet titled, "How To Set Up Your Railroad Terminal". The pricing and rarity for this outfit assume the difficult-to-find Kraft bag.

The Factory Order indicated that the outfit box was to be stamped to acknowledge the 908-10. Since the 908-10s came packaged separately, it was the task of the retailer to provide a 908-10 with each outfit purchased.

The Sears "Special Purchase" outfits gave Lionel an opportunity to reduce its inventory of accessories and other peripherals. Thus, the 19318 was one of the last six outfits to include a no. 1063-100 75-Watt Transformer, which was last used in 1961. (See outfit no. 9672 from 1961 for more information about this transformer.)

The no. 61-210 Orange RSC with Black Graphics outfit box measured 13⅞ x 13¼ x 6½ inches.

The 19318 included two collectible items, the 617X-1 and 908-10. Those items, combined with the 19318 being a Sears outfit produced in very low quantities, make this outfit a desirable one that is difficult to obtain.

CONVENTIONAL PACK
61-210 BOX

TOP LAYER		BOTTOM LAYER	
6560-50		6512-1 F	
1018-30		617X-1 S	
1013-8		1013-8	
6059-50		1063-100	6062-1 F
1023-1 TOP			

Description: "O27" Promotional Outfit
Specification: "O27" Diesel Freight Outfit
Customer/No.: Sears, Roebuck and Co.; 9842
Original Amount: 800
Factory Order Date: 12/13/1963
Packaging: RSC (Units Loose)

Contents: 230P-25 Alco Diesel Power Unit - "Chesapeake & Ohio"; 3519-1 Operating Satellite Launching Car; 6500-1 Beechcraft Bonanza Transport Car; 6476-25 Hopper Car - Red; 6142-25 Gondola Car (Less 2 Canisters); 6112-5 Canister (2); 6059-50 Caboose; 1013-8 Curved Track (Bundle of 8 - 1013); 1018-30 Straight Track (Bundle of 3 - 1018); 1008-50 Uncoupling Unit; 1010-25 35-Watt Transformer; 1103-20 Envelope Packed; 310-62 Set of (3) Billboards; D63-50 Accessory Catalog; 1-62 Parts Order Form; 1-63 Warranty Card

Boxes & Packing: 62-246 Outfit Box; 62-247 Shipper for (4) (1-4)

Alternate For Outfit Contents:
Note: Substitute 171 - 3545-1 for 3519-1.

19319 (1963)	C6	C7	C8	Rarity
Complete Outfit	850	1,310	1,665	R8
Complete Outfit With no. 3545-1 Substitution	990	1,455	1,860	R8
Outfit Box no. 62-246	175	250	325	R8

Comments: In late 1963, Robert Wolfe, president of the Lionel Toy Corporation, worked out a deal - "Special Purchase" - with Sears, Roebuck and Co. to quickly bring additional revenue to Lionel by liquidating surplus toy inventory. This deal accounted for 23 of the 25 Super O and O27 Retailer Promotional outfits purchased by Sears in late 1963. None of these "Special Purchase" outfits has been observed in a Sears catalog. Internal Lionel and Sears documents revealed the link to Sears, along with the proper Sears number. (See the entry for Sears, Roebuck and Co. in the section on Lionel's Distribution and Customers.)

The no. 19319, a Type Ia outfit, was one of the many diesel-powered outfits purchased by Sears in 1963. It was assigned Sears no. 9842.

The 19319 was a led by a no. 230P-25 Chesapeake & Ohio Alco Diesel Power Unit. This locomotive featured two-axle Magne-Traction, a headlight and a two-position reversing unit.

In spite of Lionel's determination to liquidate its surplus inventory, not everything in this outfit was a carryover item. The nos. 6059-50 Caboose and 6142-25 Gondola Car (Less 2 Canisters) were new items for 1963. This fact supports the contention that Lionel had overestimated production for this year.

Still, all the other items were carryover. The no. 6500-1 Beechcraft Bonanza Transport Car made its first promotional outfit appearance in the Sears "Special Purchase" outfits. It is one of the few items that could come in an Orange Perforated Picture or Orange Picture box.

The no. 3545-1 Operating TV Monitor Car substitution affects the outfit price, as listed in the pricing table. Both it and the no. 3519-1 Operating Satellite Launching Car came in an Orange Picture box.

The norm for all the cars in the 19319 was AAR trucks and couplers. To be specific, all the boxed items were equipped with operating types. The no. 6476-25 Hopper Car usually was as well, although it could come with one operating and one non-operating type. The 6142-25 also came with one operating and one non-operating type. The 6059-50 Caboose had one operating and one plain truck and coupler.

This outfit used the no. 62-246 Tan RSC Mailer with Black Graphics outfit box. Manufactured by Mead Containers, these boxes measured 11½ x 10¼ x 6¼ inches. They were made of a thicker corrugated material (rated at 90 pounds rather than the normal 65 pounds gross weight) that allowed each outfit to be shipped in its outfit box. The manufacturer omitted any Lionel printing on the box top to leave room for a mailing label.

Only 800 units of the 19319 were manufactured, which explains why it is a difficult outfit to find.

CONVENTIONAL PACK
62-246 BOX
12-13-63

TOP LAYER			BOTTOM LAYER	
1013-8			3519-1 S	
6142-25		1010-25	6059-50	
6476-25			6500-1 S	
1018-30 1008-50			230P-25	

Customer No. On Box: 9886
Description: Super "O" Promotional Outfit
Specification: Super "O" GG-1 Freight Outfit W/Horn
Customer/No./Price: Sears, Roebuck and Co.; 9886; $37.88
Original Amount: 200
Factory Order Date: 12/12/1963
Packaging: RSC

Contents: 2360X-1 Penn GG-1 Electric Locomotive With Horn; 3362-1 Helium Tank Unloading Car; 6361-1 Timber Transport Car; 6343-25 Barrel Ramp Car; 362-78 Wood Barrels (6); 6440-1 Flat Car W/2 Piggy Back Vans; 6464-750 "New Haven" Box Car; 6827-1 Flat Car With Tractor Shovel; 6407-1 Flat Car W/Sterling Missile; 6407-11 Sterling Missile; 3830-1 Operating Submarine Car; 6429-1 Wrecking Car; 31-60 Bundle of 6 - 31 Curved Track (2); 32-5 Straight Track - Loose (5); 34-10 Straight Track - ½ Section; 39-25 Operating Track Set; KW-1 190-Watt Transformer; 310-62 Set of (3) Billboards; D63-50 Accessory Catalog; 1-62 Parts Order Form; 1-63 Warranty Card; Form 3063 Parts Order Form; 1123-40 Instruction Sheet

Boxes & Packing: 63-391 Box

Outfit no. 19320 (Sears no. 9886) was one of the 23 Sears "Special Purchase" outfits from late 1963. This desirable outfit is one of the longest ones offered by Lionel. Two items of note were the boxed nos. 6407-1 Flat Car W/Sterling Missile and 6429-1 Wrecking Car. Their boxes are very difficult to find in collectible condition. This 19320 was obtained from its original owner, who also purchased additional track (not shown) that came with the two no. 31-45 Envelope of 12 - 31-7 Power Bus Connectors.

NAME B.Mart   DATE PURCHASED 12/10/64
ADDRESS 518 Lancaster ████████ Sears Roebuck & Co
CITY Pasadena   STATE Texas

SEARS, ROEBUCK AND CO.
TAKE-WITH   1988 49   038.64 M-S
CUSTOMER'S VOUCHER   AMT. OF PURCHASE

Top: A portion of the original warranty card for a no. 19320 shows that it took a year before the outfit was likely sold. **Bottom:** The receipt demonstrates how heavily discounted promotional outfits were in the early 1960s. The 19320 could be purchased from Sears for $38.64 ($37.88 plus tax) whereas a similar catalog outfit (no. 13138) from 1963 retailed for $100.

19320 (1963)	C6	C7	C8	Rarity
Complete Outfit	3,065	4,565	6,575	R10
Outfit Box no. 63-391	700	900	1,000	R10

Comments: In late 1963, Robert Wolfe, president of the Lionel Toy Corporation, worked out a deal - "Special Purchase" - with Sears, Roebuck and Co. to quickly bring additional revenue to Lionel by liquidating surplus toy inventory. This deal accounted for 23 of the 25 Super O and O27 Retailer Promotional outfits purchased by Sears in late 1963. None of these "Special Purchase" outfits has been observed in a Sears catalog. Internal Lionel and Sears documents revealed the link to Sears, along with the proper Sears number. (See the entry for Sears, Roebuck and Co. in the section on Lionel's Distribution and Customers.)

The no. 19320, a Type Ia outfit, was one of five Super O outfits purchased by Sears in 1963. It had the Sears no. 9886 stamped on

the outfit box below the Lionel number.

The 19320 was the last of four promotional outfits led by the newly "Re-instated 3-1-61" (per Production Control Files) no. 2360X-1 Penn GG-1 Electric Locomotive With Horn. This engine came packaged in a no. 2360-10 Corrugated Box. As described in the section on Outfit Peripherals, an "X" signified that a no. CTC-1 Lockon was left out because it wasn't necessary in a Super O outfit.

Like the no. 19309, the 19320 included nine items of rolling stock, making it one of the largest outfits offered by Lionel. All of them, except the unboxed no. 6343-25 Barrel Ramp Car, were typical of what Lionel was packing in Super O outfits. Today, some of these items are among Lionel's most collectible pieces, notably the boxed nos. 6407-1 Flat Car W/Sterling Missile, 6429-1 Wrecking Car and 6827-1 Flat Car With Tractor Shovel.

The 6407-1 is a difficult car to obtain with an original no. 6407-11 Sterling Missile, but finding the 6407-1's Dark Orange Picture box is even more of a challenge. Lionel used it only for separate-sale cars and those used as a substitute in outfit 19309 and a component of 19320.

The 6429-1 is rare because it was included only in one catalog and three promotional outfits. A total quantity of 1,433 was included in these outfits. Its no. 6429-10 Folding Box was the first Hillside Orange Picture box issued by Lionel. The box listed Lionel's corporate name as "The Lionel Toy Corporation".

The 6827-1 made its final outfit appearance in the 19320. A new Orange Non Perforated no. 6827-5 Folding Box was issued for this car in 1963. The no. 6827-100 Harnischfeger Power Shovel included with the 6827-1 was the dark yellow variation.

The orange New Haven box car that was heat-stamped "6464725" was designated no. 6464-735 when it came in a box and no. 6464-750 when unboxed. The "-750" version first came in this outfit and two other promotional outfits from Sears.

The no. 6361-1 Timber Transport Car was packaged in an Orange Perforated box and all remaining boxed items came in Orange Picture boxes.

All but one of the pieces of rolling stock in the 19320 came equipped with two operating AAR trucks and couplers. The exception was the 6407-1, which had one operating and one non-operating type. Be aware that these cars had middle AAR trucks and couplers, but the no. 3362-1 Helium Tank Unloading Car had early types.

As with most Super O outfits, the track layout of the 19320 was a basic oval. A Type IV no. 39-25 Envelope Packed was included with this outfit.

Catalog Super O outfits generally did not include a transformer. However, because promotional outfits were most often destined for retailers that probably did not have a train department, Lionel included a transformer. For the 19320, the KW-1 190-Watt Transformer provided plenty of power to operate this outfit. It appeared in only six outfits during the 1960s.

The no. 63-391 Tan RSC with Black Graphics outfit box was manufactured by Robbins Container Corp. and measured 20 x

16½ x 8⅜ inches. It included four lines of data as part of the box manufacturer's certificate. It also had "20-8" printed on the box bottom.

Promotional outfits and Super O outfits are always in demand. But when a combined Sears Super O promotional outfit exists, demand is extremely high. Finding this rare outfit box is extremely difficult. Filling it with the correct, 1963-vintage items is an expensive challenge. In either case, the outfit easily deserves its R10 rarity rating.

CONVENTIONAL PACK
63-391 BOX
12-12-63

TOP LAYER		
	6343-25	
	6429-1 S	
	3830-1 S	
31-60	31-60	
3362-1 F		39-25
6361-1 S		

BOTTOM LAYER		
		6827-1 S
KW-1	6440-1 S	
	6464-750	
	2360X-1 F	
	6407-1 S	32-50

Customer No. On Box: 9862
Description: "O27" Promotional Outfit
Specification: "O27" Diesel Freight Outfit
Customer/No.: Sears, Roebuck and Co.; 9862
Original Amount: 200
Factory Order Date: 12/13/1963
Packaging: RSC

Contents: 633-50 "Santa Fe" Diesel Switcher; 6436-110 Hopper Car; 3376-150 Operating Giraffe Car; 6062-1 Gondola Car - Black - with (3) Cable Reels; 6059-50 Caboose; 161-1 Mail Pickup Set; 1013-8 Curved Track (Bundle of 8 - 1013); 1018-30 Straight Track (Bundle of 3 - 1018); 1008-50 Uncoupling Unit; 1010-25 35-Watt Transformer; 1103-20 Envelope Packed; 3376-118 Envelope Packed; 310-62 Set of (3) Billboards; 122-10 Instruction Sheet; D63-50 Accessory Catalog; 1-62 Parts Order Form; 1-63 Warranty Card

Boxes & Packing: 61-250 Outfit Box; 62-223 Insert; 62-255 Insert (2); 61-251 Shipper for (4) (1-4)

Alternate For Outfit Contents:
Note: Substitute 34 - 634-25 for 633-50.

19321 (1963)	C6	C7	C8	Rarity
Complete Outfit	700	1,165	1,640	R10
Complete Outfit With no. 634-25 Substitution	675	1,105	1,540	R10
Outfit Box no. 61-250	300	550	700	R10

Comments: In late 1963, Robert Wolfe, president of the Lionel Toy Corporation, worked out a deal - "Special Purchase" - with Sears, Roebuck and Co. to quickly bring additional revenue to Lionel by liquidating surplus toy inventory. This deal accounted for 23 of the 25 Super O and O27 Retailer Promotional outfits

purchased by Sears in late 1963. None of these "Special Purchase" outfits has been observed in a Sears catalog. Internal Lionel and Sears documents revealed the link to Sears, along with the proper Sears number. (See the entry for Sears, Roebuck and Co. in the section on Lionel's Distribution and Customers.)

The no. 19321, a Type Ib outfit, was one of the many diesel-powered outfits purchased by Sears in 1963. The Sears no. 9862 appeared on the box below the Lionel number.

The 19321 was led by a no. 633-50 Santa Fe Diesel Switcher, which was the promotional-only upgrade to the no. 633-25 that Lionel issued in 1962. This low-end switcher came with a traction tire but lacked a horn. However, it was "4 wheel drive equipped", unlike the 633-25, which was driven by only two wheels. The "-50" version is more difficult (3,660 produced) to find than the "-25" (11,900 produced). According to the Lionel Engineering Specification for the 633-50, it was "primarily designed to pull 5 moderate weight cars up a trestle".

In spite of Lionel's determination to liquidate its surplus inventory, not everything in this outfit was a carryover item. The nos. 6059-50 Caboose and 6436-110 Hopper Car were new items for 1963. This fact supports the contention that Lionel had overestimated production for this year.

The green no. 3376-150 Operating Giraffe Car made its first promotional outfit appearance in the 19321. The "-150" indicated that it was an unboxed no. 3376-160 Operating Giraffe Car. Since it was unboxed, the 3376-150's no. 3376-118 Envelope Packed was placed loose in the outfit box.

The no. 6062-1 Gondola Car made its last appearance in this and outfit no. 19318. That car, like the 6436-110, came in an Orange Picture box.

All the items in this outfit were equipped with two operating AAR trucks and couplers except for the 6059-50. It came with one operating and one plain AAR type.

The Sears "Special Purchase" outfits gave Lionel an opportunity

Outfit no. 19321 (Sears no. 9862) was one of the 23 Sears "Special Purchase" outfits from late 1963. It marked the last outfit appearance of the no. 161-1 Mail Pickup Set. The no. 633-50 Santa Fe Diesel Switcher in the 19321 appeared in promotional outfits only.

to reduce its inventory of accessories and other peripherals. The no. 161-1 Mail Pickup Set was making its last outfit appearance in the 19321.

The substitution of a no. 634-25 Santa Fe Diesel Switcher for the 633-50 affected the outfit price, as listed in the pricing table.

The nos. 122-10 Instruction Sheet made reference to the new 90-day warranty policy that Lionel instituted in 1963. It was dated 5-62.

The no. 61-250 Orange RSC with Black Graphics outfit box was manufactured by the Mead Containers and measured 13 x 12 x 7 inches. It included four lines of data as part of the box manufacturer's certificate.

The small quantity of 200 outfits manufactured combined with the Sears connection of the 19321 makes it a highly desirable outfit. As such, it is difficult to find complete in collectible condition.

CONVENTIONAL PACK
61-250 BOX
12-13-63

TOP LAYER	BOTTOM LAYER
161-1 F (BOTTOM) 1013-8 1018-30	1010-25 / 6059-50
3376-150	6062-1 F
3376-118	
6436-110	633-50

62-255 (left and right sides of bottom layer)

62-223 BETWEEN LAYERS

Description: "O27" Promotional Outfit
Specification: "O27" Diesel Freight Outfit
Customer/No.: Sears, Roebuck and Co.; 9864
Original Amount: 200
Factory Order Date: 12/16/1963
Packaging: RSC

Contents: 223P-1 "Santa Fe" Alco Diesel Power Unit with Horn; 6501-1 Jet Motor Boat Car; 6502-50 Girder Transport Car; 6502-3 Girder Bridge; 6448-25 Exploding Target Range Car; 6014-325 Frisco Box Car; 6059-50 Caboose; 299-1 Code Transmitter Set; 903-1 Set of (2) Sheets Trading Cards; 1013-70 Curved Track (Bundle of 12 - 1013); 1018-30 Straight Track (Bundle of 3 - 1018); 1008-50 Uncoupling Unit; 1020-1 90° Crossing; 1063-100 75-Watt Transformer; 1103-20 Envelope Packed; 310-62 Set of (3) Billboards; 19322-10 Instruction Sheet; D63-50 Accessory Catalog; 1-62 Parts Order Form; 1-63 Warranty Card

Boxes & Packing: 62-270 Outfit Box; 62-255 Insert (2); 62-271 Shipper for (3) (1-3)

19322 (1963)	C6	C7	C8	Rarity
Complete Outfit	1,485	2,940	4,900	R10
Outfit Box no. 62-270	500	700	850	R10

Comments: In late 1963, Robert Wolfe, president of the Lionel Toy Corporation, cut a deal - "Special Purchase" - with Sears, Roebuck and Co. to quickly drive additional revenue for Lionel by liquidating surplus toy inventory. This accounted for 23 of the 25 Super O and O27 Retailer Promotional outfits purchased by Sears in late 1963. None of these "Special Purchase" outfits have been observed in a Sears catalog. Internal Lionel and Sears documents provided the linkage to Sears along with the proper Sears number. (See the entry for Sears, Roebuck and Co. in the section on Lionel's Distribution and Customers.)

The no. 19322, a Type Ib outfit, was one of the many diesel-powered outfits purchased by Sears in 1963. It was assigned Sears no. 9864.

The 19322 was led by a no. 223P-1 Santa Fe Alco Diesel Power Unit with Horn. This locomotive also featured a two-position reversing unit, a headlight, one-axle Magne-Traction and an open pilot with a large ledge. A promotional-only diesel, it came packaged in a no. 223-8 Corr. Box. The 223P-1 was available only as a component in outfits from Sears and a substitution in outfit no. 19172 from Maritz.

In spite of Lionel's determination to liquidate its surplus inventory, not everything in this outfit was a carryover item. The nos. 6014-325 Frisco Box Car, 6059-50 Caboose and 6502-50 Girder Transport Car were all new items for 1963. This fact supports the contention that Lionel had overestimated production for this year.

Still, the other cars were carryover inventory being thinned out in this outfit. These included the no. 6448-25 Exploding Target Range Car and 6501-1 Jet Motor Boat Car, which came in an Orange Picture box.

The transition from Archbar to AAR trucks and couplers that began in 1962 continued into 1963. The 6502-50 could have non-operating Archbar or AAR trucks and couplers. All the other models were equipped with AAR types. However, the 6448-25 and 6501-1 had two operating types. The 6014-325 was equipped with one operating and one non-operating type, and the 6059-50 had one operating and one plain truck and coupler.

The Sears "Special Purchase" outfits gave Lionel an opportunity to reduce its inventory of accessories and other peripherals. Thus, the 19322 included a no. 299-1 Code Transmitter Set. This outfit also was one of the final six to include a no. 1063-100 75-Watt Transformer, which was last used in 1961. (See outfit no. 9672 from 1961 for more information about this transformer.)

The inclusion of the no. 903-1 Set of (2) Sheets Trading Cards made the 19322 a very desirable outfit. The 903-1 included 24 two-sided Lionel trading cards printed on a sheet of perforated cardstock. On the front of each card was a Lionel locomotive, and on the back was historical information about its road name as well as a trivia quiz. Two 11 x 11 inch sets of 12 cards were connected by a "folding" strip. The entire sheet of 24 was folded in half along the strip and placed loose in the outfit box. The cards were perforated and are almost always found separated as individual cards, with the "folding" strip long gone. In fact, if it weren't for the complete sheets that came out of Madison Hardware over the years, it is likely that few of these items would be intact.

The 19322 included the difficult-to-find no. 19322-10 Instruction Sheet dated 12/63.

The no. 62-270 Tan RSC with Black Graphics outfit box measured 15½ x 14 x 6¼ inches.

The small quantity of this outfit that Lionel produced (200), along with it being linked with Sears and containing a 903-1, explains its desirability. With so few available, the 19322 merits an R10 rarity rating.

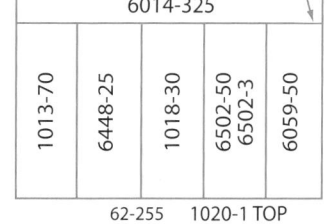

CONVENTIONAL PACK
62-270 BOX
12-16-63

TOP LAYER — 62-255 — 6014-325 — 1013-70 — 6448-25 — 1018-30 — 6502-50 / 6502-3 — 6059-50 — 62-255 — 1020-1 TOP

BOTTOM LAYER — 223P-1 F — 1063-100 F — 6501-1 F — 299-1 F

Description: "O27" Promotional Outfit
Specification: "O27" Diesel Freight Outfit
Customer/No.: Sears, Roebuck and Co.; 9853
Original Amount: 400
Factory Order Date: 12/20/1963
Date Issued: Rev 1-21-64
Packaging: RSC (Units Loose)

Contents: 231P-25 Alco Diesel Power Car - "Rock Island"; 3470-1 Aerial Target Launching Car; 443-1 IRBM Missile Launching Platform - with Exploding Ammo Dump; 6500-1 Beechcraft Bonanza Transport Car; 6630-25 Missile Launching Car; 6650-80 Missile; 6059-50 Caboose; 262-1 Highway Crossing Gate; 1013-8 Curved Track (Bundle of 8 - 1013); 1018-30 Straight Track (Bundle of 3 - 1018); 1008-50 Uncoupling Unit; 1010-25 35-Watt Transformer; 1103-20 Envelope Packed; 310-62 Set of (3) Billboards; 1-62 Parts Order Form; 1-63 Warranty Card; 6630-6 Instruction Sheet; 1123-40 Instruction Sheet; X602-10 Instruction Sheet; 230-6 Instruction Sheet

Boxes & Packing: 61-230 Outfit Box; 61-231 Shipper for (2) (1-2)

19323 (1963)	C6	C7	C8	Rarity
Complete Outfit	1,155	1,795	2,325	R9
Outfit Box no. 61-230	275	450	550	R9

Comments: In late 1963, Robert Wolfe, president of the Lionel Toy Corporation, worked out a deal - "Special Purchase" - with Sears, Roebuck and Co. to quickly bring additional revenue to Lionel by liquidating surplus toy inventory. This deal accounted for 23 of the 25 Super O and O27 Retailer Promotional outfits purchased by Sears in late 1963. None of these "Special Purchase" outfits has been observed in a Sears catalog. Internal Lionel and Sears documents revealed the link to Sears, along with the proper Sears number. (See the entry for Sears, Roebuck and Co. in the section on Lionel's Distribution and Customers.)

The no. 19323, a Type Ib outfit, was one of the many space and military outfits purchased by Sears in 1963. It was assigned

Sears no. 9853.

The 19323 was led by a no. 231P-25 Rock Island Alco Diesel Power Car, which was first issued in 1961. This locomotive, which was nearing the end of its product life, featured two-axle Magne-Traction, a headlight and a two-position reversing unit.

All but one of the pieces of rolling stock in this outfit was a carryover item. The sole exception was the no. 6059-50 Caboose (new for 1963). The no. 6500-1 Beechcraft Bonanza Transport Car made its first promotional outfit appearance in the Sears "Special Purchase" outfits. It is one of the few items that could come in an Orange Perforated Picture or Orange Picture box.

After a three-year run, the no. 6630-25 Missile Launching Car was making its last appearance in the 19323. Another space and military item, the no. 3470-1 Aerial Target Launching Car, came in an Orange Picture box.

For the 19323, the 6630-25 was equipped with non-operating Archbar trucks and couplers. All but one of the other items in this outfit were equipped with two operating AAR types. The 6059-50 had one operating and one plain AAR truck and coupler.

The Sears "Special Purchase" outfits gave Lionel an opportunity to reduce its inventory of accessories and other peripherals. Thus, the 19323 included a no. 262-1 Highway Crossing Gate. This outfit also came with a no. 443-1 IRBM Missile Launching Platform -

with Exploding Ammo Dump. This accessory appeared only in four promotional outfits and necessitated a large outfit box.

The no. 61-230 Orange RSC with Black Graphics outfit box measured 16 x 15½ x 7⅛ inches.

Interestingly, the early versions of this outfit were intended to have a no. 44X-1 Mobile Rocket Firing Car - Less Lockon. However, Lionel abandoned this idea before any outfits were so produced.

Only 400 units of the 19323 were made, which helps explain why examples are seldom seen on the market. But that small quantity and the outfit's connection with Sears merely drive up demand.

CONVENTIONAL PACK
61-230 BOX
REVISED 1-20-64

TOP LAYER			BOTTOM LAYER	
262-1 F		1018-30 / 1013-8	443-1 F	231P-25
6630-25	6059-50		6500-1 F	1010-25

3470-1 F TOP 231P

Description: "O27" Promotional Outfit
Specification: "O27" Diesel Freight Outfit
Customer/No.: Sears, Roebuck and Co.; 9863
Original Amount: 200
Factory Order Date: 12/16/1963
Packaging: RSC

Contents: 59-1 Minuteman Diesel Switcher; 6343-25 Barrel Ramp Car; 362-78 Wood Barrels (6); 6361-1 Timber Transport Car; 6162-25 Gondola Car; 6112-88 Canister (3); 6014-325 Frisco Box Car; 6059-50 Caboose; 1013-8 Curved Track (Bundle of 8 - 1013); 1018-30 Straight Track (Bundle of 3 - 1018); 1008-50 Uncoupling Unit; 1010-25 35-Watt Transformer; 1103-20 Envelope Packed; 310-62 Set of (3) Billboards; D63-50 Accessory Catalog; 1-62 Parts Order Form; 1-63 Warranty Card

Boxes & Packing: 61-180 Outfit Box; 62-264 Insert; 61-185 Shipper for (4) (1-4)

19324 (1963)	C6	C7	C8	Rarity
Complete Outfit	1,250	1,830	2,500	R10
Outfit Box no. 61-180	600	750	850	R10

Comments: In late 1963, Robert Wolfe, president of the Lionel Toy Corporation, cut a deal - "Special Purchase" - with Sears, Roebuck and Co. to quickly drive additional revenue for Lionel by liquidating surplus toy inventory. This accounted for 23 of the 25 Super O and O27 Retailer Promotional outfits purchased by Sears in late 1963. None of these "Special Purchase" outfits have been observed in a Sears catalog. Internal Lionel and Sears documents

provided the linkage to Sears along with the proper Sears number. (See the entry for Sears, Roebuck and Co. in the section on Lionel's Distribution and Customers.)

The no. 19324, a Type Ia outfit, was one of the many diesel-powered outfits purchased by Sears in 1963. It was assigned Sears no. 9863.

This outfit was led by a no. 59-1 Minuteman Diesel Switcher equipped with a three-position reversing unit. Using a motorized unit to lead an outfit was not a new idea, but it was very uncommon. The 59-1 was being depleted in three outfits in 1963, all for Sears.

In spite of Lionel's determination to liquidate its surplus inventory, not everything in this outfit was a carryover item. The nos. 6014-325 Frisco Box Car and 6059-50 Caboose were new items for 1963. This fact supports the contention that Lionel had overestimated production for this year.

Still, all the other cars in this outfit were carryover items. One of them, the no. 6361-1 Timber Transport Car, could come packaged in an Orange Perforated box in 1963.

The transition from Archbar to AAR trucks and couplers that began in 1962 continued into 1963. As part of this, Lionel sought to cut costs by introducing a non-operating AAR type. Therefore, starting in 1963, most cars equipped with AAR trucks and couplers had at least one non-operating type.

The 19324 generally followed this pattern. All the cars in this outfit were equipped with AAR trucks and couplers. However, not every model had even one non-operating AAR type. Specifically, the 6343-25 Barrel Ramp Car and 6361-1 had two operating types. The norm for the 6014-325 and 6162-25 Gondola Car was one operating and one non-operating type, although the latter could have two operating types. Finally, the 6059-50 came with one operating and one plain truck and coupler.

The commonly used no. 61-180 Tan RSC with Black Graphics outfit box measured 12¾ x 10 x 6¾ inches.

The small quantity of this outfit that Lionel produced (200), along with it being linked with Sears and containing a 59-1, explains its desirability. With so few available, the 19324 merits an R10 rarity rating.

CONVENTIONAL PACK
61-180 BOX
12-16-63

TOP LAYER

6059-50	1013-8
	6014-325
	6162-25
	6343-25

62-264

BOTTOM LAYER

1010-25	59-1 F
	1018-30
	6361-1 F

Outfit no. 19325 (Sears no. 9813) was Sears' low-end steam offering for 1964. It included the difficult-to-find no. 110-75 Modified Trestle Set, which came packed in a no. 1-41 Poly Bag. This outfit came in one of the first outfit boxes to list "The Lionel Toy Corporation" as the manufacturer. This example is shown with the no. 6142-125 Gondola Car substitution.

Customer No. On Box: 9813
Description: "O27" Special Train Set
Specification: 5 Unit "O27" Special Train Set
Customer/No./Price: Sears, Roebuck and Co.; 9813; $9.97
Original Amount: 7,000
Factory Order Date: 4/28/1964
Date Issued: 5/5/64
Packaging: RSC Pack (MO) Units Loose

Contents: 1061-50 Steam Loco With Tire; 1061T-50 Tender; 3309-25 Turbo Missile Firing Car (Less Missiles); 0349-10 Turbo Missile (2); 6042-125 Gondola Car; 6167-150 Caboose; 1013 Curved Track (12); 1018 Straight Track (6); 110-75 Modified Trestle Set; 1026-25 25-Watt Transformer; 1103-20 Envelope Packed; 310-62 Set of (3) Billboards; D64-50 Accessory Catalog; 1-62 Parts Order Form; 1-63 Warranty Card; 1123-40 Instruction Sheet; 19325-10 Instruction Sheet

Boxes & Packing: 64-170 Outfit Box

Alternate For Outfit Contents:
Substitute a 6142-125 for 6042-125 as needed.

19325 (1964)	C6	C7	C8	Rarity
Complete Outfit	200	330	600	R6
Outfit Box no. 64-170	40	65	125	R4

Comments: Even after the large year-end "Special Purchase" in 1963, Sears went on to order three more Retailer Promotional outfits in 1964. The no. 19325, the first of these three outfits, was assigned Sears' no. 9813. Both the Lionel and Sears number appeared on the outfit box.

This Type Ib outfit appeared in the 1964 Sears Christmas Catalog on page 216 for $9.97. Lionel sold this low-end starter outfit to Sears for $6.70 each.

The 19325 was led by a no. 1061-50 Steam Type Loco W/Tire (new for 1964). This version came with a rubber tire as a traction aid, a feature that made it a slight upgrade of the no. 1061-25 Steam Type Locomotive. Even with this improvement, the 1061-50 (lacking a headlight and a lens) remained Lionel's low-end

Scout steamer configured with an 0-4-0 wheel arrangement.

The rolling stock in this outfit also qualified as low-end, and everything was equipped with non-operating AAR trucks and couplers. The no. 3309-25 Turbo Missile Firing Car was the only carryover item. All the other cars represented slight updates to existing cars, enough for Lionel to assign each of them a new suffix. The no. 1061T-50 Tender was a no. 1061T-25 Tender with the addition of "Lionel Lines" stamped on its sides. The no. 6042-125 Gondola Blue was a no. 6042-25 Gondola but without a load. The no. 6167-150 Caboose was a no. 6167-25 Caboose with the addition of "Lionel Lines" and "6167" stamped on its sides.

Examples of the 19325 have been observed with a no. 6142-125 Gondola Car in place of the 6042-125. This does not affect the outfit price.

Although the rolling stock is very common, the no. 110-75 Modified Trestle Set included in this outfit is not. The 110-75 included nine pairs of graduated trestle piers, or "bents," which were designed to elevate the figure-eight track layout to a height of approximately 5 inches. A no. 110-78 Envelope Packed included the Tie Channels and Screws to assemble the trestles. All of these peripherals were sealed in a no. 1-41 Poly Bag. As with many promotional-only items, the packaging and packed envelope are very difficult to obtain, yet are necessary to complete the outfit (a point assumed in the outfit pricing).

The figure-eight layout was outlined on the difficult-to-find no. 19325-10 Instruction Sheet. Dated 6/64, this sheet made reference to the 90-day warranty policy that Lionel instituted in 1963.

The no. 64-170 White RSC Allstate By Lionel With 0-4-0 Blue Steamer (No Smoke) and Orange and Blue Graphics outfit box was manufactured by United Container Co. and measured 12¼ x 11⅜ x 6½ inches. This box was made of a thicker corrugated material (rated at 90 pounds rather than the normal 65 pounds gross weight) that allowed each outfit to be shipped in its outfit box.

This outfit box had four lines of data, a "64" and two or six stars as part of the box manufacturer's certificate (BMC). The "4" below the BMC indicated that the box was rated at 90 pounds. This box marked one of the first external appearances of "The Lionel Toy Corporation" on a Lionel product.

The unique outfit box and the Sears origin make the 19325 an outfit that is always in demand. With 7,000 manufactured, the outfit box is fairly common, but the 110-75 is extremely difficult to find complete with its original poly bag and packed envelope. That item alone makes a complete outfit an R6.

Customer No. On Box: 9820
Description: "O27" Special Train Set
Specification: 6 Unit "O27" Special Train Set
Customer/No./Price: Sears, Roebuck and Co.; 9820; $19.89
Original Amount: 5,500
Factory Order Date: 4/28/1964
Date Issued: 5/2/64
Packaging: RSC Pack (MO) Units Loose

Contents: 240-25 Steam Locomotive With Light & Smoke; 242T-25 Tender; 6470-25 Exploding Target Car; 6401-25 Flat Car; 958-75 Tank; 3666-25 Cannon Box Car; 3666-8 Shells (4); 6824-50 Work Caboose; 975-1 Squad of Soldiers; 347-25 Rocket Launching Platform; 347-5 Shell (4); 1013-8 Curved Track (Bundle of 8 - 1013); 1018-5 Straight Track (Bundle of 5 - 1018); 6149-25 Remote Control Track; 1025-25 45-Watt Transformer; 1103-40 Envelope Packed; 909-20 Smoke Fluid; 11450-10 Instruction Sheet; 1-65 Warranty Card; 347-10 Instruction Sheet; Form 3063 Parts Order Form; 6470-17 Instruction Sheet; 3666-20 Instruction Sheet; 237-11 Instruction Sheet; 927-64 Service Station List

Boxes & Packing: 64-171 Outfit Box; 64-173 Insert; 64-177 Insert

19326 (9820) (1964)	C6	C7	C8	Rarity
Complete Outfit	1,300	2,450	3,700	R7
Outfit Box no. 64-171	150	350	500	R5

Comments: Even after the large year-end "Special Purchase" in 1963, Sears went on to order three more Retailer Promotional outfits in 1964. The no. 19326, the second of these three outfits, was assigned Sears' no. 9820. Only the Sears number appeared on the outfit box.

This Type Ib outfit appeared in the 1964 Sears Christmas Catalog on page 216 for $19.89. Lionel sold this space and military outfit to Sears for $13.00 each.

The 19326 was led by a no. 240-25 Steam Locomotive With Light & Smoke (new for 1964). This promotional-only Scout steamer featured a two-position reversing unit and used a rubber tire as a traction aid. The 240-25 appeared only in this outfit and the nos. 19350-500 from 1964 and 1965. Except for its 240 number and lack of stripe, it was the same engine as a no. 237.

All the rolling stock in this outfit was new, with the exception of the no. 6470-25 Exploding Target Car. Two of the newcomers appeared only in promotional outfits and made their debut in this one. The no. 3666-25 Cannon Box Car was a component of only four promotional outfits, and the no. 6824-50 Work Caboose appeared in five. The 3666-25 is a very desirable car that included a light blue roof and an olive drab cannon firing mechanism. The car was modeled after a no. 3665-25 Minuteman Missile Launching Car, but it fired shells like a no. 6651-25 Cannon Car.

The 6824-50 is interesting because it shared the same cab and body as a no. 6814-1 First Aid Caboose, first issued in 1959. In fact both cars were numbered 6814. The most noticeable difference is that the 6824-50 came with a black frame whereas the 6814-1 came with a gray one.

The rolling stock in the 19326 followed the normal truck and coupler progression for 1964, with all the cars having AAR types. Most were equipped with one operating and one late non-operating truck and coupler. However, the no. 242T-25 Tender had one late non-operating and one plain type, and the 6824-50 had one operating and one plain type.

As with many promotional outfits, the peripherals included

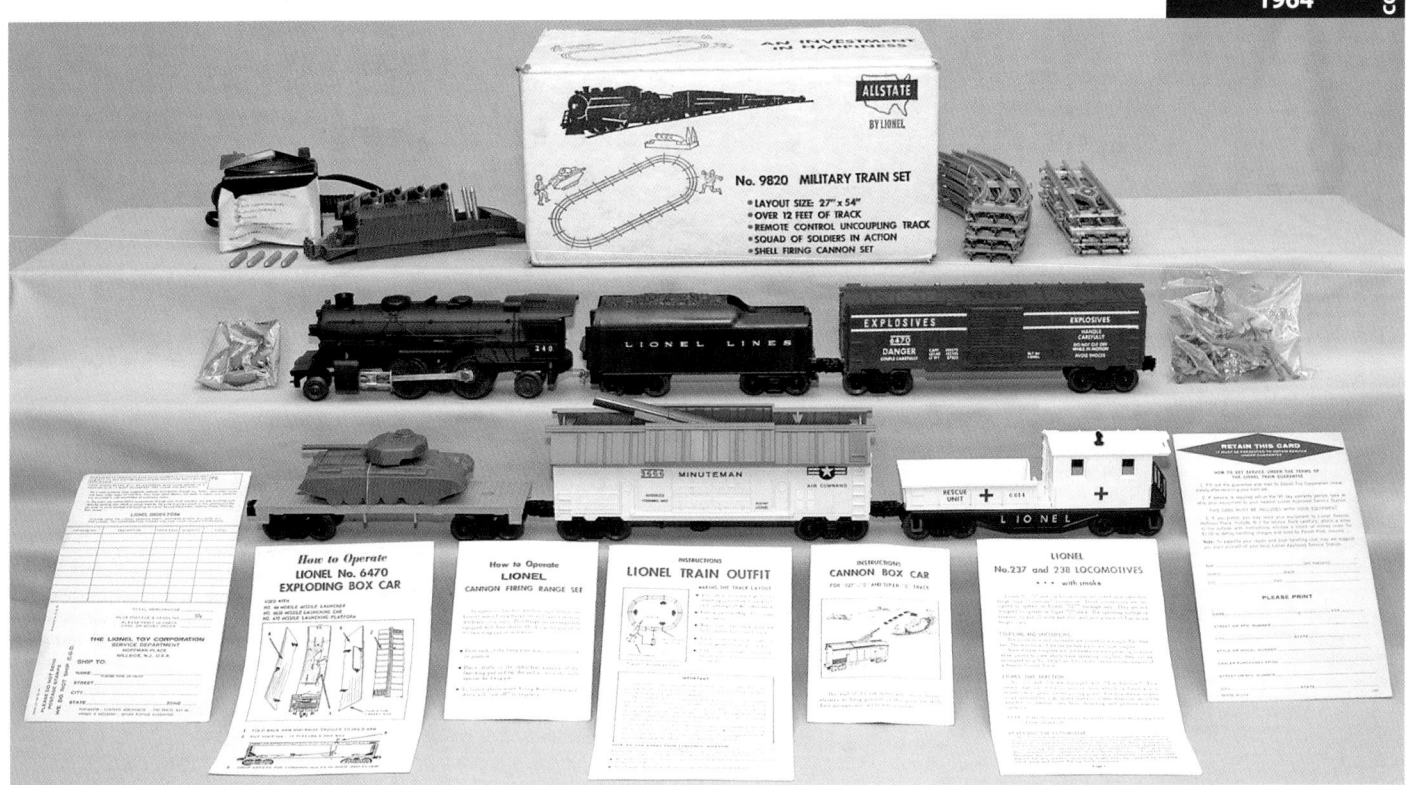

Outfit no. 19326 (Sears no. 9820) was Sears' space and military offering for 1964. It included several items that appeared only in promotional outfits: nos. 347-25 Rocket Launching Platform, 958-75 Tank, 975-1 Squad of Soldiers, 3666-25 Cannon Box Car and 6824-50 Work Caboose. When you combine this outfit's Sears origin, space and military theme, promotional-only items and unique outfit box, there is no doubt why the 19326 is one of the most desirable and collectible of any Lionel outfit. This example is shown as it came from Lionel with an original Lionel version of the Payton tank and MPC soldiers.

in the 19326 make it a highly collectible outfit. Specifically, the no. 347-25 Rocket Launching Platform appeared only in three promotional outfits. This difficult-to-find item commands a premium price. The no. 958-75 Tank was purchased from Payton Products and appeared in this outfit, outfit no. 19344 and Sears outfit no. 19434. The no. 975-1 Squad of Soldiers consisted of a polyethylene bag filled with 10 soldiers purchased from Multiple Products Corporation (MPC) of New York.

The tank and soldiers were also part of the regular Payton and MPC product lines and sold through retail stores. These items were manufactured over several years and exhibited many variations in plastic colors (including shades of green) and mold features.

Lionel made one bulk purchase from Payton (no. 958-80 Military Assortment) on 8/4/64 and three bulk purchases from MPC (no. 975-2 Soldier Figure - Assorted) on 6/8/64, 7/2/64 and 9/14/64. Lionel took these bulk-purchased items and sorted, assembled and packaged them accordingly.

Because all of these item were purchased at the same time, they exhibit the same color and mold features (admittedly, variations could exist). For the tanks, the color tends to be more green than olive drab. Verified Lionel-purchased tanks also have a raised impression on the turret bottom. As for the soldiers, the face detail on the Lionel soldiers is crisp without excess plastic or flash.

Collectors should be aware that the only way to be certain that an item came from Lionel (rather than being a separate sale Payton or MPC item) is to know the provenance of the particular outfit being examined or considered for purchase. Otherwise, they can borrow a known original Lionel item and use it to study and compare. Naturally, the pricing listed here for a 19326 assumes a Lionel version of the Payton tank and MPC soldiers.

Rounding out this outfit are the difficult-to-find 90-day warranty versions of the instruction sheets from 1964. The correct no. 11450-10 Instruction Sheet was dated 6/64. Be aware that the nos. 347-10 Instruction Sheet and 3666-20 Instruction Sheet have been reproduced. Original versions are difficult to find.

The no. 64-171 White RSC Allstate By Lionel With 0-4-0 Blue Steamer (No Smoke) and Orange and Blue Graphics outfit box was manufactured by United Container Co. and measured 13⅜ x 11⅝ x 6½ inches. This box was made of a thicker corrugated material (rated at 90 pounds rather than the normal 65 pounds gross weight) that allowed each outfit to be shipped in its outfit box.

This outfit box had four lines of data, a "64" and five stars as part of the box manufacturer's certificate (BMC). The "4" below the BMC indicated that the box was rated at 90 pounds. This box marked one of the first external appearances of "The Lionel Toy Corporation" on a Lionel product.

Of interest, early 19326 Factory Worksheets indicated that originally every car in this outfit was going to be a military item colored olive drab. The cars were listed as nos. 6448-50 Exploding Box Car, 6401-50 Flat Car, 6651-25 Cannon Car and 6119-125 Work Caboose. However, Lionel never produced olive drab versions of the 6448 and 6401.

The 19326 is one of the most popular and desirable of all promotional and catalog outfits. It included rolling stock and peripherals that can be found only in a few outfits. As such, a complete 19326 is on the wish list of many outfit collectors.

The outfit box is fairly common and achieves only an R5 rarity rating. Trying to complete an outfit can take years because the correct rolling stock, paperwork and peripherals included in the

cont. **19326 (9820)**
1964

19326 are very difficult to find. Therefore, the complete outfit has an R7 rarity rating.

Even with 5,500 of these outfits manufactured, the 19326 and its individual components are in such high demand that the price for a complete C8 outfit is high.

CONVENTIONAL PACK
64-171 BOX

TOP LAYER

958-75 / 6401-25	6824-50	3666-25	6470-25

BOTTOM LAYER

64-173

909-20	1103-40 3666-8 347-5	975-1 347-25	1013-8
240-25	242T-25	1025-25	6149-25 1018-5

19326
1965

The 1965 version of outfit no. 19326 came in a Tan RSC Mailer with Black Graphics outfit box. Except for the outfit box, no. 238-25 Steam Locomotive with Smoke and no. 6401-25 Flat Car load, it was identical to the 19326 (Sears no. 9820) from 1964. The 1965 version was likely created from excess inventory and so is much more difficult to find than the 1964 version.

Description: "O27" Special Train Set
Specification: 6 Unit "O27" Special Train Set
Packaging: RSC Pack (MO) Units Loose

Contents: 238-25 Steam Type Locomotive with Smoke; 242T-25 Tender; 6470-25 Exploding Target Car; 6401-25 Flat Car; 958-150 Jeep Assembled; 958-175 Cannon Assembled; 3666-25 Cannon Box Car; 3666-8 Shells (4); 6824-50 Work Caboose; 975-1 Squad of Soldiers; 347-25 Rocket Launching Platform; 347-5 Shell (4); 1013-8 Curved Track (Bundle of 8 - 1013); 1018-5 Straight Track (Bundle of 5 - 1018); 6149-25 Remote Control Track; 1025-25 45-Watt Transformer; 1103-40 Envelope Packed; 909-20 Smoke Fluid; 11450-10 Instruction Sheet; 1-63 Warranty Card; 347-10 Instruction Sheet; 1-62 Parts Order Form; 6470-17 Instruction Sheet; 3666-20 Instruction Sheet; 237-11 Instruction Sheet; 927-64 Service Station List

Boxes & Packing: 64-114 Outfit Box; 64-173 Insert; 64-177 Insert

19326 (1965)	C6	C7	C8	Rarity
Complete Outfit	1,850	3,000	4,750	R10
Outfit Box no. 64-114	750	1,000	1,500	R10

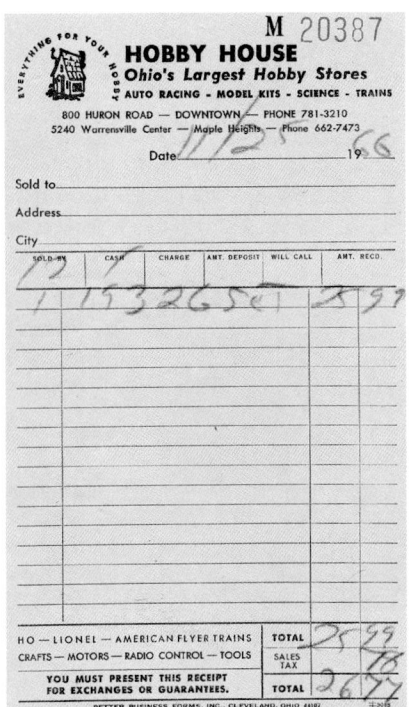

This original sales receipt dated 11/25/66 was included with the 1965 version of the 19326. It identifies the seller as Hobby House in Cleveland, Ohio. Of note, the price of $25.99 is more than the $19.89 that Sears charged for the 1964 version.

appeared after this reduction in quantity.

The main differences between the 1964 and 1965 versions were threefold. To start, the latter was led by a no. 238-25 Steam Locomotive with Smoke. This Scout steamer featured a two-position reversing unit, a headlight and a rubber tire as a traction aid. The later version with narrow running boards was included in this outfit. Except for its 238 number and stripe, it was the same engine as a no. 240-25 Steam Locomotive With Light & Smoke included in the 19326 from 1964. The 238-25 was making its last appearance in this outfit.

Second, the no. 6401-25 Flat Car in the 1965 version came with a different load. The no. 958-75 Tank included in the 19326 from 1964 was replaced by the nos. 958-150 Jeep Assembled and 958-175 Cannon Assembled. Both items were purchased from Payton Products. (See the 19326 from 1964 for more information about Payton.) All the other significant items and paperwork were identical to the 19326 from 1964.

Third, the 1965 version included different outfit packaging. Its no. 64-114 Tan RSC Mailer with Black Graphics outfit box was manufactured by Gem-Bilt Container Corp. and measured 13¼ x 11¼ x 6½ inches. This box was made of a thicker corrugated material (rated at 90 pounds rather than the normal 65 pounds gross weight) that allowed each outfit to be shipped in its outfit box. It included four lines of data as part of the box manufacturer's certificate.

The 1965 version of the 19326 is extremely difficult to find. The exact quantity produced is unknown, but examples appear so infrequently that this outfit easily achieves an R10 rarity rating.

Comments: The no. 19326 from 1965 was likely assembled from excess production of outfit no. 19326 (Sears no. 9820) from 1964. (See the 19326 from 1964.)

The original Factory Order quantity of the Sears 19326 from 1964 was 7,000. That quantity was subsequently cut to 5,500. The 19326 from 1965 was a General Release Type IIb outfit that

---

Customer No. On Box: 9807
Description: "O27" Special Train Set
Specification: 6 Unit "O27" Special Train Set
Customer/No./Price: Sears, Roebuck and Co.; 9807; $29.99
Original Amount: 7,000
Factory Order Date: 4/28/1964
Date Issued: 5/24/64
Packaging: RSC Pack (MO) Units Loose

19327 (9807) (1964)	C6	C7	C8	Rarity
Complete Outfit	875	1,375	2,050	R8
Complete Outfit With no. 6076-125 Substitution	890	1,395	2,075	R8
Outfit Box no. 64-184	100	200	450	R4

Contents: 237-25 Steam Type Locomotive with Smoke; 242T-25 Tender; 6176-75 Hopper Car; 6822-50 Searchlight Car; 6342-25 Culvert Car; 6059-50 Caboose; 346-1 Culvert Unloader; 321-1 Trestle Bridge; 958-100 Auto Set With Signs & Poles; 909-20 Smoke Fluid; 1022-1 Pr. Manual Switches; 1013 Curved Track (14); 1018 Straight Track (11); 6149-25 Remote Control Track; 1103-40 Envelope Packed; 1025-25 45-Watt Transformer; 310-62 Set of (3) Billboards; D64-50 Accessory Catalog; 1-62 Parts Order Form; 1-63 Warranty Card; 1123-40 Instruction Sheet; 346-21 Instruction Sheet; 237-11 Instruction Sheet; 11450-10 Instruction Sheet; 19327-10 Layout Sheet

Boxes & Packing: 64-184 Outfit Box

Alternate For Outfit Contents:
Note: Use 6076-125 instead of 6176-25 as necessary.

Comments: Even after the large year-end "Special Purchase" in 1963, Sears went on to order three more Retailer Promotional outfits in 1964. The no. 19327, the last of these three outfits, was assigned Sears' no. 9807. Only the Sears number appeared on the outfit box.

This Type Ic outfit appeared in the 1964 Sears Christmas Catalog on page 217 for $29.99. Lionel sold this space and military outfit to Sears for $19.50 each.

The 19327 was led by a no. 237-25 Steam Type Locomotive with Smoke. This Scout steamer featured a two-position reversing unit and a headlight and used a rubber tire as a traction aid. The later version with narrow running boards came in this outfit. Except for its 237 number, it was the same engine as a no. 238.

The only notable piece of rolling stock was the no. 6342-25 Culvert Car. Last seen in the 1959 consumer catalog, it was reintroduced in 1964. The new version was equipped with one operating and one non-operating AAR truck and coupler riveted directly to the body.

The no. 6176-75 Hopper Car has been observed in either gray or yellow. Both cars are identical in price and rarity. Lionel

Outfit no. 19327 (Sears no. 9807) was listed as a "Giant Steam Freighter Set" in the 1964 Sears Christmas Catalog. This *giant* outfit required a large outfit box that was decorated exclusively for Allstate (Sears). The 19327 is the only outfit to include the rare white-boxed no. 958-100 Auto Set With Signs & Poles.

replaced the 6176-75 Hopper Car with a no. 6076-125 Hopper Car in some outfits. The 6076-125 included "ATSF" markings and appeared only in this and three other promotional outfits. Often overlooked it is one of the tougher low-end hoppers to find.

The rolling stock in the 19327 followed the normal truck and coupler progression for 1964, with all the cars having AAR types. Most were equipped with one operating and one non-operating truck and coupler. However, the no. 242T-25 Tender had one late non-operating and one plain type, and the no. 6059-50 Caboose had one operating and one plain type.

As with many promotional outfits, the peripherals included in the 19327 make it a highly collectible outfit. Specifically, the no. 346-1 Culvert Unloader was new for 1964 and appeared only in five promotional outfits. The 346-1 was the manual version of the culvert unloader and was packed with seven culvert pipes in a no. 346-13 Corr. Box. The 6342-25 and no. 346-21 Instruction Sheet were included separately in the outfit box.

The no. 958-100 Auto Set With Signs & Poles was packed in a plain white box. This rare packing variation was included only in this outfit. Few white-boxed 958-100s have survived, thus justifying the R8 rarity rating given a complete 19327.

The track layout was an oval layout with an inner switch track. As outlined on the no. 19327-10 Instruction Sheet, it required a pair of no. 1022-1 Pr. Manual Switches.

Rounding out this outfit were the difficult-to-find 90-day warranty versions of the instruction sheets from 1964. The correct

nos. 11450-10 Instruction Sheet and 346-21 Instruction Sheet were dated 6/64 and 8/64, respectively.

The no. 64-184 White RSC Allstate By Lionel With 0-4-0 Blue Steamer (No Smoke) and Orange and Blue Graphics outfit box was manufactured by United Container Co. and measured 24¾ x 12 x 9⅞ inches. This box was made of a thicker corrugated material (rated at 90 pounds rather than the normal 65 pounds gross weight) that allowed each outfit to be shipped in its outfit box.

This outfit box had four lines of data, a "64" and two, four or five stars as part of the box manufacturer's certificate (BMC). The "4" below the BMC indicated that the box was rated at 90 pounds. This box marked one of the first external appearances of "The Lionel Toy Corporation" on a Lionel product.

The 19327 was produced in such large quantities that the outfit box is somewhat common. However, because of direct outfit shipping and the large space needed to store the box, most outfit boxes have not fared well. High-grade versions are difficult to find.

Completing a 19327 is also difficult. The correct white box for the 958-100 is seldom seen, and a boxed 346-1 is fairly expensive.

The no. 19328 was a repeat of Richie Premium's no. 19216 from 1963. It was updated to include currently available items. Richie Premium outfits always came with rare and collectible paper items, such as the nos. X625-20 Cardboard Scenic Set and 903 Set of (2) Sheets Trading Cards. But what makes the 19328 fascinating was the inclusion of both a steam and a diesel locomotive. The outfit is shown with only two of the three cable reels listed on the Factory Order.

Description: "O27" Special Train Set
Specification: 7 Unit "O27" Special Train Set.
Customer: Richie Premium
Original Amount: 7,300
Factory Order Date: 4/24/1964
Date Issued: 5/13/64
Packaging: RSC Pack (Units Loose)

Contents: 1061-25 Steam Type Locomotive; 1060T-25 Tender; 6465-150 Tank Car; 6014-325 Frisco Box Car; 6142-125 Gondola Car; 40-11 Cable Reels (3); 6167-100 Caboose; 1013-70 Curved Track (Bundle of 12 - 1013); 1018-40 Straight Track (Bundle of 4 - 1018); 1020-25 90° Crossing; 1026-25 25-Watt Transformer; 1103-20 Envelope Packed; 1066-25 Alco Diesel; X625-20 Cardboard Scenic Set; 903-25 Set of (2) Sheets Trading Cards; 310-2 Set (5) Billboards; 11311-20 Instruction Sheet; 1066-10 Instruction Sheet; 1802-10 Instruction Sheet; D64-50 Accessory Catalog; 927-64 Service Station List; 1-62 Parts Order Form; 1-65 Warranty Card

Boxes & Packing: 64-164 Outfit Box; 62-246 Shipper/4 (1-4)

Alternate For Outfit Contents:
Use no. 1060T-50 and 6167-125 as needed.

19328 (1964)	C6	C7	C8	Rarity
Complete Outfit With no. 1060T-25	1,000	2,625	4,500	R9
Complete Outfit With no. 1060T-50 Substitution	1,035	2,665	4,545	R9
Outfit Box no. 64-164	75	100	125	R3

Comments: This Retailer Promotional Type Ib outfit was the only outfit purchased by incentive merchandiser Richie Premium in 1964. Although its Factory Order stated that it was the "same as #19216 (1963)", the items were updated based on 1964 availability. (See the entry for no. 19216 from 1963.)

Richie Premium outfits are highly collectible because all of them included rare paper items. In fact Richie's nos. 19142-502, 19216 and 19328 represented the only three instances of Lionel pairing the nos. 903 Set of (2) Sheets Trading Cards and X625-20 Cardboard Scenic Set. (See the entry for 19142-502 from 1963 for a discussion of these highly collectible paper items.)

The 19328 was similar to the 19216 in that it included *both* a steam and a diesel locomotive! Many original owners of these outfits still have complete outfits with both engines. But once an outfit leaves its original owner, one of the locomotives tends to be separated. Stories abound of collectors who purchased outfits intact and sold one engine. If it weren't for the Factory Orders, the fact that these outfits included two engines might never have been revealed.

The steam engine was a low-end no. 1061-25 Steam Type Locomotive. This stripped-down Scout steamer featured an 0-4-0 wheel arrangement and went forward only. It lacked a headlight, a lens and any sort of traction aid. The diesel was a no. 1066-25 Union Pacific Alco Diesel (new for 1964). This low-end Alco, which appeared only in two promotional outfits, moved forward only, had a closed pilot and used a rubber tire as a traction aid.

The no. 1060T-25 Tender was freely replaced by a no. 1060T-50 Southern Pacific Tender. Both were equipped with one non-operating and one plain AAR truck and coupler.

The no. 6167 Caboose could come as a "-125" with no stamping or a "-100" with "Lionel Lines". Both variations were equipped with one operating and one plain AAR truck and coupler. All the other cars in this outfit came with one operating and one non-operating AAR truck and coupler.

The no. 6014-325 Frisco Box Car was a Type III variation. The no. 6142-125 Gondola Car was new for 1964; the "-125" suffix meant it had a blue body without a load.

Late in 1963, Lionel began to mold the no. 40-11 Cable Reels in gray plastic. In fact, the production sample for gray reels was dated 10-22-63. The norm for this outfit was these harder-to-find reels, although orange ones have also been observed.

The no. 1066-10 Instruction Sheet titled "Diesel Care" is difficult to find. It was dated 8/64.

The no. 64-164 White RSC with Orange Graphics outfit box was manufactured by United Container Co. and measured 12⅛ x 11⅝ x 6½ inches. It included four lines of data, a "64" and four or six stars as part of the box manufacturer's certificate (BMC).

The peripherals included in Richie Premium outfits make them extremely difficult to complete. Empty boxes are common, but completed outfits are rare.

Lionel provided this photograph of outfit no. 19329 as an attachment to *Sales Bulletin* no. 12 from May 8, 1964. Sales representatives were encouraged to use it to sell the outfit. These early photographs provide interesting observations. The no. 2029-25 Steam Type Locomotive With Smoke was likely not yet available because a no. 637-25 Steam Type Locomotive with Smoke was used with its number partially scratched off. The no. 6142-125 Gondola Car stamping is faintly visible and appears to be painted over.

Description: "O27" Special Train Set
Specification: 6 Unit "O27" Special Train Set
Customer: Army and Air Force Exchange
Customer: All Trade
Original Amount: 200
Factory Order Date: 4/23/1964
Date Issued: 5/24/64
Packaging: RSC Pack (Units Loose)

Contents: 2029-25 Steam Type Locomotive With Smoke; 242T-25 Tender; 6402-50 Flat Car W/2 Cable Reels; 6465-150 Tank Car; 6142-125 Gondola Car; 6059-50 Caboose; 1013 Curved Track (8); 1018 Straight Track (3); 6149-25 Remote Control Track; 40-11 Cable Reels (2); 1025-25 45-Watt Transformer; 1103-40 Envelope Packed; SP-1 Smoke Pellets; 675-33 Smoke Stack Cleaner; 2029-5 Instruction Sheet; Form 3063 Parts Order Form; 1-65 Warranty Card; 927-64 Service Station List; D64-50 Accessory Catalog

Boxes & Packing: 19329-RSC Outfit Box; 64-319 Corr. Insert

19329 (1964)	C6	C7	C8	Rarity
Complete Outfit	390	680	1,100	R10
Outfit Box no. 19329-RSC	300	550	900	R10

Comments: The Factory Order for the no. 19329 listed the Army and Air Force Exchange and All Trade as its customers. Therefore, this outfit is classified as a General Release Promotional Type IIa.

Lionel listed the 19329 on *Sales Bulletin* no. 12 from May 8, 1964, which stated, "The following represents fourteen (14) sets you may offer at your discretion to accounts in your territory". Lionel charged its retailers $15.63 for each 19329.

The 19329 was led by a no. 2029-25 Steam Type Locomotive With Smoke (new for 1964). This steamer featured a two-position reversing unit, a headlight and a rubber tire as a traction aid. Since the 2029-25 came unboxed (as indicated by the "-25"), the nos. SP-1 Smoke Pellets, 675-33 Smoke Stack Cleaner and 2029-5 Instruction Sheet were provided separately in the outfit box. The no. CTC-1 Lockon came in the 1103-40 Envelope Packed.

The rolling stock in this outfit was all low-end and typical of starter outfits of the era. Three new-for-1964 cars were included. The no. 242T-25 Tender was identical to a no. 1060T-25 Tender, except that it had a copper ground spring on its plain truck. The no. 6142-125 Gondola Car used a "-125" suffix to indicate its blue body and lack of a load. The no. 6402-50 Flat Car W/2 Cable Reels used a "-50" suffix to identify its gray color, load and configuration of one operating and one non-operating AAR truck and coupler.

The rolling stock in this outfit followed the normal truck and coupler progression for 1964, with all the cars having AAR types. Most were equipped with one operating and one non-operating truck and coupler. However, the no. 242T-25 had one non-operating and one plain type, and the no. 6059-50 Caboose had one operating and one plain type.

The box for the 19329 likely was either a Tan RSC with Black Graphics or a White RSC with Orange Graphics outfit box.

The no. 19330 was one of Western Auto's four outfit purchases in 1964. It was illustrated on page 11 of the 1964 Western Auto Christmas Gifts Catalog as no. E5009 for $13.99. The most notable item was a no. 3364-25 Log Dump Car. Its no. 160-2 Unloading Bin is not pictured.

Description: "O27" Special Train Set
Specification: 6 Unit "O27" Special Train Set
Customer/No./Price: Western Auto; E5009; $13.99
Original Amount: 5,300
Factory Order Date: 4/23/1964
Date Issued: 5/2/64
Packaging: Display Pack (Units Loose)

Contents: 1061-50 Steam Loco With Tire; 1061T-50 Tender; 3364-25 Log Dump Car; 3364-8 Logs (3); 160-2 Unloading Bin; 6176-50 Hopper Car; 6142-125 Gondola Car; 6167-100 Caboose; 1010-25 35-Watt Transformer; 1013-8 Curved Track (Bundle of 8 - 1013); 1018 Straight Track; 6149-25 Remote Control Track; 1103-40 Envelope Packed; 3364-10 Instruction Sheet; 19330-10 Instruction Sheet; 1-65 Warranty Card; 1-62 Parts Order Form; 927-64 Service Station List; D64-50 Accessory Catalog

Boxes & Packing: 64-111 Box Top; 64-115 Box Bottom; 64-120 Corr. Insert; 64-119 Corr. Insert; 64-118 Corr. Insert

19330 (1964)	C6	C7	C8	Rarity
Complete Outfit	135	225	390	R4
Outfit Box no. 64-111	30	50	90	R4

Comments: Western Auto Stores purchased four steam-powered promotional outfits in 1964: nos. 19244, 19330, 19331 and 19332. The 19330 appeared on page 11 of the 1964 Western Auto Christmas Gifts Catalog as no. E5009 for $13.99. Lionel sold the outfit to Western Auto for $7.40 each.

The 19330, a Retailer Promotional Type Ia outfit, was one of Western Auto's low-end purchases for 1964. It was led by a no. 1061-50 Steam Type Loco W/Tire (new for 1964). This version came with a rubber tire as a traction aid, a feature that made it a slight upgrade of the no. 1061-25 Steam Type Locomotive. Even with this improvement, the 1061-50 (lacking a headlight and a lens) remained Lionel's low-end Scout steamer configured with an 0-4-0 wheel arrangement.

All the rolling stock in this outfit was new or new versions for 1964. The most notable item was the no. 3364-25 Log Dump Car, which was identical to the no. 3362-25 Helium Tank Unloading Car except that it carried logs instead of helium tanks. A no. 160-2 Unloading Bin was provided for the logs and placed loose in the outfit box.

The no. 1061T-50 Tender was the same as a no. 1061T-25 Tender with the addition of "Lionel Lines" stamped on its sides. The no. 6142-125 Gondola Car used a "-125" suffix to indicate its blue body and lack of a load.

The rolling stock in the 19330 followed the normal truck and coupler progression for 1964, with all the cars having AAR types. Most were equipped with one operating and one late non-operating truck and coupler. However, the 1061T-50 had one late non-operating and one plain type, and the no. 6167-100 Caboose had one operating and one plain type.

The no. 19330-10 Instruction Sheet was introduced in this outfit. It was dated 7/64. The no. 3364-10 Instruction Sheet was dated 6/64.

The no. 64-111 White 4-6-4 Steamer and F3 Lift-Off with Orange and Blue Graphics Type D display outfit box was manufactured by United Container Co. and measured 24⅞ x 15¼ x 3 inches.

The 19330 was one of the first Western Auto purchases not to have its Western Auto number printed with the Lionel number. Only the latter appeared. Examples of this outfit have been observed with Western Auto price tags or pen markings identifying the 19330 as E5009.

With 5,300 manufactured, the 19330 frequently appears. It is fairly easy to obtain in collectible condition.

Description: "O27" Train Set
Specification: 7 Unit "O27" Train Set
Customer: Western Auto
Factory Order Date: 4/23/1964
Date Issued: 5/5/64
Packaging: Display Packed Units Loose

Contents: 237-25 Steam Type Locomotive with Smoke; 242T-25 Tender; 6142-75 Gondola Car; 6112-88 Canister (2); 6473-25 Rodeo Car; 6401-25 Flat Car; 958-50 Truck; 3419-25 Operating Helicopter Car; 6119-110 Work Caboose; 909-20 Smoke Fluid; 1013 Curved Track (12); 1018 Straight Track (3); 6149-25 Remote Control Track; 1020-25 90° Crossing; 1010-25 35-Watt Transformer; 1103-40 Envelope Packed; Form 3063 Parts Order Form; 1-65 Warranty Card; 927-64 Service Station List; D64-50 Accessory Catalog

Comments: Western Auto Stores purchased four steam-powered promotional outfits in 1964: nos. 19244, 19330, 19331 and 19332. A Factory Worksheet exists for the 19331, but the outfit appears never to have progressed to the Factory Order stage, which strongly suggests that it was canceled. No other documentation about this outfit from Lionel or Western Auto has been uncovered, and this listing is provided here for historical reference

Western Auto typically purchased two or three promotional O27 outfits from Lionel each year. The 19331 would have been the fourth outfit for 1964 and likely one too many. Lionel's cost to Western Auto was listed at $11.70 for each 19331.

The 19331, a Retailer Promotional Type Ib outfit, was targeted to be Western Auto's mid-level steam purchase for 1964. Its contents were better than those in the 19330 but not as high-end as those in the 19332.

Be aware that the 19331 was supposed to come with a no. 958-50 Truck. This olive drab plastic toy was purchased from Payton Products.

Customer No. On Box: E5011
Description: "O27" Train Outfit
Specification: 7 Unit "O27" Train Outfit
Customer/No./Price: Western Auto; E5011; $31.88
Original Amount: 1,050
Factory Order Date: 4/23/1964
Date Issued: 9-23-64
Packaging: Display Packed Units Loose

Contents: 2029-25 Steam Type Locomotive With Smoke; 233W-25 Whistle Tender; 6465-150 Tank Car; 6014-325 Frisco Box Car; 6176-75 Hopper Car; 3666-25 Cannon Box Car; 3666-8 Shells (4); 6059-50 Caboose; 311-25 Target Bulls Eye Billboard; 1013 Curved Track (12); 1018 Straight Track (3); 6149-25 Remote Control Track; 1020-25 90° Crossing; 1073-25 60-Watt Transformer; 147-25 Horn & Whistle Controller; 1103-50 Envelope Packed; SP-1 Smoke Pellets; 675-33 Smoke Stack Cleaner; 11460-10 Instruction Sheet; 1-65 Warranty Card; Form 3063 Parts Order Form; 2029-5 Instruction Sheet; 3666-20 Instruction Sheet; D64-50 Accessory Catalog; 927-64 Service Station List; 1802-10 Instruction Sheet

The no. 19332, which was Western Auto's high-end steam purchase for 1964, had the highly desirable nos. 3666-25 Cannon Box Car and 311-25 Target Bulls Eye Billboard. The 311-25, which is unique to this outfit, lacked any Lionel references; that's why it often was separated from the 19332 and lost.

WORK SHEET
THE LIONEL CORPORATION

NO. ___19332___

PRF. NO. _____ NAME___Western Auto___

DESCRIPTION

9-23-64 Sub. made on 239
& 6651 to facilitate delivery
to cover customer catalog.
239 & 6651 mold not available - delayed

REQUESTED BY _IN ITALY._

The no. 19332 was earmarked to be one of the first outfits to include the nos. 239-25 Steam Locomotive With Smoke and 6651-25 Cannon Car. Unfortunately, as noted on the Factory Worksheet the molds were delayed in Italy.

Boxes & Packing: 64-111 Box Top; 64-112 Box Bottom; 64-118 Corr. Insert; 64-126 Corr. Insert; 64-127 Corr. Insert; 64-121 Corr. Insert; 64-113 Shipper for 4 (1-4)

Alternate For Outfit Contents:
Substitute the following items in the above set: #2029 Loco for #239 Loco; #3666-25 Cannon Box Car for #6651-25 Cannon Car; #3666-8 Shells for #6651-8 Shells.

19332 (1964)	C6	C7	C8	Rarity
Complete Outfit	850	1,435	2,225	R9
Outfit Box no. 64-111	150	275	400	R8

Comments: Western Auto Stores purchased four steam-powered promotional outfits in 1964: nos. 19244, 19330, 19331 and 19332. The 19332 appeared on page 5 of a 1964 Western Auto Ordering Guide sent to its wholesale customers. The wholesale price was $21.75, and the suggested retail was $31.88. Lionel sold the outfit to Western Auto for $17.00 each.

The 19332, a Retailer Promotional Type Ic outfit, was Western Auto's high-end purchase for 1964. The outfit originally was to have included the nos. 239-25 Steam Locomotive With Smoke and 6651-25 Cannon Car but they were replaced by the nos. 2029-25 Steam Type Locomotive With Smoke and 3666-25 Cannon Box Car, respectively. This substitution occurred because, as stated on a Factory Worksheet, there were "mold delays in Italy".

The 19332 was led by a 2029-25 (new for 1964). This steamer featured a two-position reversing unit, a headlight and a rubber tire as a traction aid. Since the 2029-25 came unboxed (as indicated by the "-25"), the nos. SP-1 Smoke Pellets, 675-33 Smoke Stack Cleaner and 2029-5 Instruction Sheet were provided separately in the outfit box. The no. CTC-1 Lockon came in the 1103-50 Envelope Packed.

Two promotional-only items made this a highly collectible and desirable outfit. The 3666-25 appeared only in four promotional outfits. New for 1964, it featured a light blue roof and an olive drab cannon firing mechanism. The car was modeled after a no. 3665-25 Minuteman Missile Launching Car, but it fired shells like a 6651-25.

The no. 311-25 Target Bulls Eye Billboard was unique to the 19332. As with many paper items found in promotional outfits, it lacked any reference to Lionel and often was separated from the train outfit. Generally overlooked, this billboard is very difficult to find and so adds a substantial premium to this outfit.

Of minor note, the no. 6014-325 Frisco Box Car used a Type III body. The no. 233W-25 Whistle Tender, which last appeared in 1963, was making its last appearance in this outfit and outfit no. 19354. The yellow version of the no. 6176-75 Hopper Car has been observed in the 19332.

The rolling stock in the 19332 followed the normal truck and coupler progression for 1964, with all the cars having AAR types. Most were equipped with one operating and one late non-operating truck and coupler. However, the 233W-25 and no. 6059-50 Caboose had one operating and one plain type.

The proper instruction sheets made reference to the 90-day warranty that Lionel instituted in 1963. The correct no. 11460-10 Instruction Sheet was dated 6/64. A no. 1802-10 Layout Instruction Sheet detailed the figure-eight track layout. Be aware that the no. 3666-20 Instruction Sheet, which is difficult to find, has been reproduced.

The no. 64-111 White 4-6-4 Steamer and F3 Lift-Off with Orange and Blue Graphics Type D display outfit box was manufactured by United Container Co. and measured 24⅞ x 15¼ x 3 inches.

As with many promotional outfits, the outfit box can be found, but finding the proper contents is difficult. Specifically, a 19332's outfit box has an R8 rarity rating; however, the addition of the 311-25 gives the entire outfit an R9 rarity rating.

Description: "O27" Train Set
Specification: 5 Unit "O27" Train Set
Cust./No./Price: J. C. Penney Co., Inc.; X 924-0664 A; $9.99
Original Amount: 7,000
Factory Order Date: 4/23/1964
Date Issued: 5/3/64
Packaging: RSC Pack (Units Loose)

Contents: 1062-50 Steam Type Loco. W/Light & Reversing Unit; 242T-25 Tender; 6502-75 Girder Transport Car; 6502-3 Girder Bridge; 6176-75 Hopper Car; 6059-50 Caboose; 1010-25 35-Watt Transformer; 1013 Curved Track (12); 1018 Straight Track (3); 1008-50 Uncoupling Unit; 1020-25 90° Crossing; 1103-20 Envelope Packed; 19333-10 Instruction Sheet; 1-62 Parts Order Form; 927-64 Service Station List; 1-65 Warranty Card; D64-50 Accessory Catalog

Boxes & Packing: 64-223 Outfit Box; 61-173 Insert; 61-171 Insert; 61-172 Insert; 61-170 Outfit Box

Alternate For Outfit Contents:
Substitute no. 6076-125 or 6176-50 for 6176-75 as needed; Substitute no. 1062T-25 for 242T-25 as needed.

Lionel likely ran out of uniquely decorated boxes for J. C. Penney's no. 19333 and resorted to generic tan outfit boxes. The no. 61-170 Tan RSC with Black Graphics version of the 19333 is a difficult-to-find variation. The example shown has the nos. 1062T-25 Tender and 6176-50 Hopper Car substitutions.

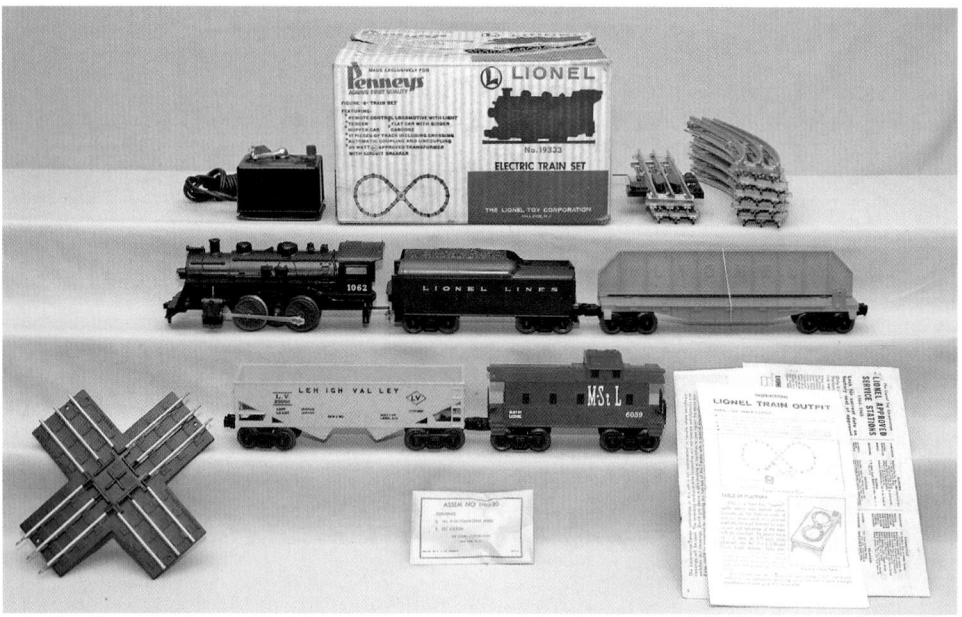

The no. 19333 was J. C. Penney's low-end steam-powered offering for 1964 and retailed for a mere $9.99. The uniquely decorated outfit box is a collector's favorite.

19333 (1964)	C6	C7	C8	Rarity
Complete Outfit With no. 64-223 Box	185	275	500	R3
Outfit Box no. 64-223	85	125	250	R3
Complete Outfit With no. 61-170 Box	200	350	600	R9
Outfit Box no. 61-170	100	200	350	R9
Either Outfit With A no. 6076-125 Substitution, Add The Following	15	20	25	Same

Comments: J. C. Penney purchased four Retailer Promotional Type Ib outfits in 1964: nos. 19333, 19334, 19334-500 and 19335. Penney's inaugural Christmas Catalog featured the 19333 on page 241 as Penney no. X 924-0664 A for $9.99. Lionel sold the outfit to Penney for $7.25 each.

The 19333 was Penney's low-end offering for 1964. This basic starter outfit was led by a no. 1062-50 Steam Type Loco. W/Light

& Reversing Unit (new for 1964). This low-end Scout steamer had an 0-4-0 wheel arrangement and featured a rubber tire as a traction aid. Except for the rubber tire, it was identical to the no. 1062-25 Steam Type Loco. W/ Light & Reversing Unit.

The rolling stock in this outfit was, with the exception of the no. 6059-50 Caboose (carried over from 1963), was either a new car or a new version of an older car. Lionel introduced the no. 6176 series of hopper cars in 1964. The "-75" version was yellow with black heat-stamping. The no. 6502-75 Girder Transport Car obtained its "-75" suffix by coming with one operating and one non-operating AAR truck and coupler. It was paired with a no. 6502-3 Girder Bridge that has been observed in orange or black plastic.

The rolling stock in the 19333 followed the normal truck and coupler progression for 1964, with all the cars having AAR types. Most were equipped with one operating and one late non-operating truck and coupler. However, the no. 242T-25 Tender had one late non-operating and one plain type, and the 6059-50 had one operating and one plain type.

Keep in mind that a no. 1062T-25 Tender is commonly found as a substitute for the 242T-25. Also, the no. 6176-75 Hopper Car was replaced by a no. 6076-125 Hopper with "ATSF" markings or a black no. 6176-50 Hopper Car. The 6076-125 commands a slight premium, as detailed in the pricing table.

Regarding the paperwork in the 19333, the no. 19333-10 Instruction Sheet was introduced in this outfit. It detailed the figure-eight track layout.

By far the most exciting feature of the 19333 was its uniquely decorated no. 64-223 Outfit Box, a concept that Lionel likely borrowed from the Sears offerings from 1964. The 64-223 White RSC Penney Design with Blue Engine and Orange and Blue Graphics outfit box was manufactured by St. Joe Kraft, St. Joe

Paper Co. and measured 11½ x 10¼ x 6¼ inches. It included four lines of data as part of the box manufacturer's certificate (BMC). It also had "64-223" printed on the bottom. This box marked one of the first external appearances of "The Lionel Toy Corporation" on a Lionel product.

A difficult-to-find variation of the 19333 was packaged in a no. 61-170 Tan RSC with Black Graphics outfit box. The box was manufactured by United Container and measured 11½ x 10¼ x 6¼ inches. It included four lines of data, a "63" and five stars as part

of its BMC. Lionel may have run out of custom-decorated boxes and so had to resort to a plain tan RSC. In either case, both boxes are the same size.

With 7,000 units of the 19333 manufactured and a low selling price, there is an abundant supply of this outfit. Curiously, finding a C8 version takes some patience. Advanced collectors desire the Tan RSC version.

Be aware that a listing for a no. D19333 Display also exists.

The no. 19334 was J. C. Penney's space and military offering for 1964. All the new-for-1964 olive drab components make this one of the most desirable Lionel outfits. Although these items are all difficult to obtain, the outfit box is truly rare.

Boxes & Packing: 64-101 Box Top; 64-102 Box Bottom; 64-107 Corr. Insert

Alternate For Outfit Contents:
Use 221P-75 in place of 221P-50 as needed.

Description: "O27" Military Train Set
Specification: 5 Unit "O27" Military Train Set
Customer/No./Price: J. C. Penney Co., Inc.; 923-5361; $14.88
Cust./No./Price: J. C. Penney Co., Inc.; X 924-0680 A; $13.88
Original Amount: 400
Factory Order Date: 4/23/1964
Date Issued: 5/2/64
Packaging: Display Pack (Units Loose)

Contents: 221P-50 Diesel Locomotive; 3309-50 Turbo Missile Firing Car; 0349-10 Turbo Missile (2); 6176-100 Hopper Car; 6142-175 Gondola Car; 6119-125 Work Caboose; 1013 Curved Track (8); 1018 Straight Track (3); 6149-25 Remote Control Track; 1010-25 35-Watt Transformer; 1103-40 Envelope Packed; 975-1 Squad of Soldiers; 19339-10 Flyer; 3349-105 Instruction Sheet; 11440-10 Instruction Sheet; Form 3063 Parts Order Form; 1-65 Warranty Card; 927-64 Service Station List; D64-50 Accessory Catalog

19334 (1964)	C6	C7	C8	Rarity
Complete Outfit	1,750	2,650	3,750	R10
Outfit Box no. 64-101	1,000	1,250	1,500	R10

Comments: J. C. Penney purchased four Retailer Promotional Type Ib outfits in 1964: nos. 19333, 19334, 19334-500 and 19335. Penney's inaugural Christmas Catalog featured the display-packed 19334 and its mail-order twin (the 19334-500) on page 241 as Penney no. X 924-0680 A for $13.88. The 19334 also was sold in J. C. Penney retail stores because a price tag with the no. 923-5361 and price of $14.88 has been observed. Lionel sold the 19334 to Penney for $9.50 each.

The 19334 is one of Lionel's most desirable space and military outfits. It was J. C. Penney's mid-level offering for 1964 and introduced many new olive drab plastic items. Be aware, however, that this outfit was incorrectly illustrated in the J. C. Penney catalog and in a Lionel promotional photograph. Both of them showed

675

many incorrect components, including a mock-up Alco diesel.

This outfit was led by a no. 221P-50 Diesel Locomotive (new for 1964). This olive drab "USMC" diesel featured a two-position reversing unit, a traction tire and a closed pilot, and it lacked a headlight.

Lionel evidently substituted a no. 221P-75 Santa Fe Diesel Locomotive for the no. 221P-50 because outfits have been observed with the former engine (also new for 1964), which had the same features as a 221P-50. Although the Santa Fe Alco is more difficult to find than the USMC, the price differential is minimal as compared to the overall outfit price.

All the rolling stock in this outfit represented olive drab versions of existing cars in the product line. These new-for-1964 items were identified by new suffixes. For example, the no. 3309-50 Turbo Missile Firing Car was the olive drab version of a no. 3349-100 Turbo Missile Firing Car. The no. 6119-125 Work Caboose represented an update of the no. 6119-style work caboose, now with an olive drab body and a black frame but without a number or a load. Finally, the no. 6142-175 Gondola Car was an unmarked olive drab no. 6142-series gondola while the no. 6176-100 Hopper Car was an unmarked olive drab no. 6176-series hopper.

The rolling stock in the 19334 followed the normal truck and coupler progression for 1964, with all the cars having AAR types.

All but one were equipped with one operating and one late non-operating truck and coupler. The 6119-125 had one operating and one plain type.

The no. 11440-10 Instruction Sheet was dated 6/64 and made reference to the 90-day warranty policy that Lionel instituted in 1963. A difficult-to-find no. 19339-10 Flyer was included in this outfit as well.

Topping off the 19334 and adding to its collectibility was a no. 975-1 Squad of Soldiers. This was one of 11 outfits to include a 975-1, which consisted of a polyethylene bag filled with 10 soldiers purchased from Multiple Products Corporation (MPC) of New York. (See outfit no. 19326 from 1964 for details about the 975-1.)

The no. 64-101 White 4-6-4 Steamer and F3 Lift-Off with Orange and Blue Graphics Type D display outfit box was manufactured by St. Joe Kraft and measured 23⅜ x 11⅝ x 3¼ inches.

The space and military items in the 19334 are difficult to obtain, but can be found with patience. More time and funds are necessary to acquire the outfit box because the original quantity of this outfit was reduced from 2,500 to only 400. So small an order makes the 19334 extremely difficult to find in collectible condition, hence its R10 rarity rating.

Description: "O27" Military Train Set
Specification: 5 Unit "O27" Military Train Set
Cust./No./Price: J. C. Penney Co., Inc.; X 924-0680 A; $13.88
Factory Order Date: 4/23/1964
Date Issued: 5/2/64
Packaging: RSC Pack (MO) Units Loose

Contents: 221P-50 Diesel Locomotive; 3309-50 Turbo Missile Firing Car; 0349-10 Turbo Missile (2); 6176-100 Hopper Car; 6142-175 Gondola Car; 6119-125 Work Caboose; 1013 Curved Track (8); 1018 Straight Track (3); 6149-25 Remote Control Track; 1010-25 35-Watt Transformer; 1103-40 Envelope Packed; 975-1 Squad of Soldiers; 19339-10 Flyer; 3349-105 Instruction Sheet; 11440-10 Instruction Sheet; Form 3063 Parts Order Form; 1-65 Warranty Card; 927-64 Service Station List; D64-50 Accessory Catalog

Boxes & Packing: 62-246 Outfit Box; 62-254 Corr. Insert; 61-172 Corr. Insert; 61-173 Corr. Insert

19334-500 (1964)	C6	C7	C8	Rarity
Complete Outfit	2,000	2,900	4,000	R10
Outfit Box no. 62-246	1,250	1,500	1,750	R10

Comments: J. C. Penney purchased four Retailer Promotional Type Ib outfits in 1964: nos. 19333, 19334, 19334-500 and 19335. Penney's inaugural Christmas Catalog featured the display-packed 19334 and its mail-order twin (the 19334-500) on page 241 as Penney no. X 924-0680 A for $13.88.

The 19334-500's Factory Order stated, "Contents same as 19334, but mail order packed." It was common for retailers to purchase a display-packed outfit to sell through their retail stores and a mail-order version to fulfill catalog orders. It is likely that the 19334-500 was what Penney shipped for catalog orders, although the firm might have shipped 19334s as well. (See the entry for 19334 from 1964 for a complete description of the contents of this outfit.)

A tiny quantity of six 19334-500s was reordered in 1965.

The 19334-500 used a no. 62-246 Tan RSC Mailer with Black Graphics outfit box. It was manufactured by Mead Containers and measured 11½ x 10¼ x 6¼ inches. These boxes were made of a thicker corrugated material (rated at 90 pounds rather than the normal 65 pounds gross weight) that allowed each outfit to be shipped in its outfit box. The manufacturer omitted any Lionel printing on the box top to leave room for a mailing label.

Original quantity numbers are not available, and rarity is based solely on actual observations.

The 19334-500 is even more difficult to find than the R10-rated 19334.

Description: "O27" Promotional Outfit
Specification: "O27" Diesel Freight Outfit
Cust./No./Price: J. C. Penney Co., Inc.; X 924-0680 A; $13.88
Original Amount: 6
Factory Order Date: 3/19/1965
Date Issued: 3-19-65
Date Req'd: 3-19-65
Packaging: MO Pack (Units not Boxed)

Contents: 221P-50 Diesel Locomotive; 3309-50 Turbo Missile Firing Car; 0349-10 Turbo Missile (2); 6176-100 Hopper Car; 6142-175 Gondola Car; 6119-125 Work Caboose; 975-1 Squad of Soldiers; 1013-8 Curved Track (Bundle of 8 - 1013); 1018-30 Straight Track (Bundle of 3 - 1018); 6149-25 Remote Control Track; 1010-25 35-Watt Transformer; 1103-40 Envelope Packed; 310-62 Set of (3) Billboards; D65-50 Accessory Catalog; Form 3063 Parts Order Form; 1-165 Warranty Card; 926-65 Service Station List; 3349-105 Instruction Sheet; 11440-10 Instruction Sheet; 19339-10 Flyer

Boxes & Packing: 62-246 Outfit Box; 62-254 Corr. Insert; 61-172 Corr. Insert; 61-173 Corr. Insert; 62-247 Shipper for 4 (1-4)

Comments: The Factory Order for outfit no. 19334-500 from 1965 was a repeat of the no. 19334-500 from 1964. J. C. Penney likely had some additional catalog orders it needed to fulfill in 1965. Since there are no noticeable differences from the 1964 version, the outfit pricing for the 1965 is unchanged from that of the previous version. (See the entry for the 19334-500 from 1964.)

CONVENTIONAL PACK
62-246 BOX

TOP LAYER	**BOTTOM LAYER** 62-254
6119-125	221P-50
3309-50 / 1018-30 / 6149-25	975-1 / 6142-175 / 1010-25
6176-100	1013-8

61-172

Description: "O27" Train Set
Specification: 6 Unit "O27" Train Set
Customer/No./Price: J. C. Penney Co., Inc.; X 924-0672 A; $18.88
Original Amount: 1,000
Factory Order Date: 4/23/1964
Date Issued: 5/2/64
Packaging: Display Pack (Units Loose)

Contents: 215P-25 "Santa Fe" Diesel Power Car; 212T-25 "Santa Fe" "A" Unit; 6142-25 Gondola Car; 40-11 Cable Reels (2); 6473-25 Rodeo Car; 3364-25 Log Dump Car; 3364-8 Logs (3); 6059-50 Caboose; 1013 Curved Track (12); 1018 Straight Track (3); 1020-25 90° Crossing; 6149-25 Remote Control Track; 1010-25 35-Watt Transformer; 1103-40 Envelope Packed; D64-50 Accessory Catalog; Form 3063 Parts Order Form; 1-65 Warranty Card; 927-64 Service Station List; 3364-10 Instruction Sheet; 211-151 Instruction Sheet; 19214-10 Instruction Sheet

Boxes & Packing: 64-111 Box Top; 64-115 Box Bottom; 64-118 Corr. Insert; 64-122 Corr. Insert

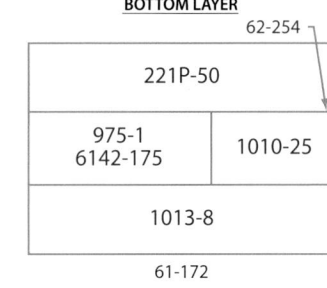

The no. 19335 was J. C. Penney's high-end offering for 1964. It was led by the promotional-only no. 215P-25 Santa Fe Diesel Power Car. This new-for-1964 Alco appeared in five outfits during its first year. It was paired with a no. 212T-25 Santa Fe "A" Unit. Also included in this outfit was the gray version of the no. 40-11 Cable Reels.

19300 Series

19335 (1964)	C6	C7	C8	Rarity
Complete Outfit	325	550	845	R7
Outfit Box no. 64-111	100	225	300	R7

Comments: J. C. Penney purchased four Retailer Promotional Type Ib outfits in 1964: nos. 19333, 19334, 19334-500 and 19335. Penney's inaugural Christmas Catalog featured the display-packed 19335 on page 241 as Penney no. X 924-0672 A for $18.88. Lionel sold the 19335, which was Penney's high-end offering for 1964, to the firm for $12.75 each.

The 19335 was incorrectly illustrated being led by a no. 223P Santa Fe Alco Diesel Power Unit in the J. C. Penney catalog and in a promotional Lionel photograph. It actually was led by a no. 215P-25 Santa Fe Diesel Power Car (new for 1964). This promotional-only Alco featured a two-position reversing unit, two traction tires, a headlight, a weight and an open pilot with a large ledge. The 215P-25 came in five promotional outfits from 1964; here, it was paired with a no. 212T-25 Santa Fe "A" Unit (also new for 1964).

The 19335 came with two operating cars. The most notable item was the no. 3364-25 Log Dump Car, which was identical to the no. 3362-25 Helium Tank Unloading Car except that it carried logs instead of helium tanks. The no. 6473-25 Rodeo Car used a Type IIb body (cadmium yellow plastic with red lettering);

the Type II body included a partially filled slot caused by broken tooling

Late in 1963, Lionel began to mold the no. 40-11 Cable Reels in gray plastic. In fact, the production sample for gray reels was dated 10-22-63. The norm for this outfit was these harder-to-find reels.

The rolling stock in this outfit followed the normal truck and coupler progression for 1964, with all the cars having AAR types. All but one were equipped with one operating and one late non-operating truck and coupler. The no. 6059-50 Caboose had one operating and one plain type. As an aside, the operating coupler on the 3364-25 included an integral copper spring.

The paperwork included the difficult-to-find 90-day warranty versions of the instruction sheets. The correct no. 19214-10 Instruction Sheet was dated 6/64.

The no. 64-111 White 4-6-4 Steamer and F3 Lift-Off with Orange and Blue Graphics Type D display outfit box was manufactured by United Container Co. and measured 24⅞ x 15¼ x 3 inches.

The 19335 was produced in larger-than-average quantities, and many have survived. Unfortunately for collectors, the outfit boxes have not fared well so finding a C8 version is difficult.

Be aware that a listing for a no. DO19335 Display also exists.

Description: "O27" Promotional Outfit
Specification: "O27" Diesel Freight Outfit
Customer/No.: J. C. Penney Co., Inc.; X 924-0672 A
Original Amount: 100
Factory Order Date: 4/23/1965
Date Issued: 3-23-65
Date Req'd: 03/25/65
Packaging: RSC Units not boxed

Contents: 215P-25 "Santa Fe" Diesel Power Car; 212T-25 "Santa Fe" "A" Unit; 6142-150 Gondola Car; 40-11 Cable Reels (2); 6473-25 Rodeo Car; 3364-25 Log Dump Car; 3364-8 Logs (3); 6059-50 Caboose; 1013-70 Curved Track (Bundle of 12 - 1013); 1018-30 Straight Track (Bundle of 3 - 1018); 1020-25 90° Crossing; 6149-25X Remote Control Track; 1010-25 35-Watt Transformer; 1103-40 Envelope Packed; 310-62 Set of (3) Billboards; D65-50 Accessory Catalog; Form 3063 Parts Order Form; 1-165 Warranty Card; 926-65 Service Station List; 3364-10 Instruction Sheet; 211-151 Instruction Sheet; 19214-10 Instruction Sheet

Boxes & Packing: 64-166 Outfit Box; 64-169 Corr. Insert (2); 62-248 Corr. Insert (2); 62-224 Corr. Insert; 62-245 Corr. Insert (2); 64-168 Corr. Insert; 64-143 Corr. Insert (2); 64-147 Shipper for 4 (1-4)

Alternate For Outfit Contents:
Sub. 6142-25 for 6142-150; Sub. 6361-1 for 6473-25; Sub. 6047-25 for 6059-50.

19335 (1965)	C6	C7	C8	Rarity
Complete Outfit With All Substitutions	800	1,205	1,850	R10
Outfit Box no. 64-166	550	800	1,200	R10

Comments: The Factory Order for outfit no. 19335 from 1965 was similar to the no. 19335 from 1964 (both were Retailer Promotional Type Ib outfits). J. C. Penney likely had additional catalog orders it needed to fulfill in 1965 and so placed a second order for 100 more outfits. (See the entry for 19335 from 1964.)

There are enough differences between the 1964 and 1965 outfits to justify additional discussion. The biggest difference was that the 1965 version was packed in a no. 64-166 White RSC with Orange Graphics outfit box that was manufactured by United Container Co. and measured 15⅜ x 10½ x 7⅛ inches.

Other differences related to the rolling stock, with Lionel replacing three items in the version from 1964. Gone were the nos. 6059-50 Caboose, 6142-150 Gondola Car and 6473-25 Rodeo Car, replaced by the nos. 6047-25 Caboose, 6142-125 Gondola

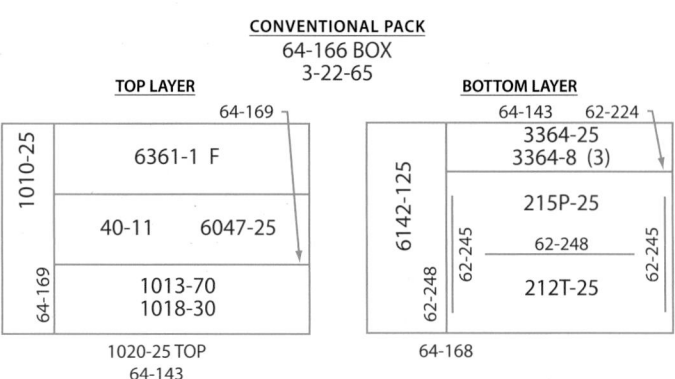

CONVENTIONAL PACK
64-166 BOX
3-22-65

Car and 6361-1 Timber Transport Car, respectively. By the way, the 6047-25 made its last appearance in this outfit and the 6361-1 came in an Orange Picture box.

The cars in this outfit followed the normal truck and coupler progression for 1965, with all but two being equipped with one operating and one non-operating AAR type. The norm for a no. 6047-25 was one non-operating and one plain Archbar type, although AAR types are also possible. The 6361-1 came with operating AAR trucks and couplers.

Although the contents of the both 19335s are similar in value, the outfit boxes are not. Only 100 of the 19335 from 1965 were made. These outfits are seldom seen and easily support an R10 rarity rating.

Be aware that additional orders for the no. DO19335 Display were placed in 1965.

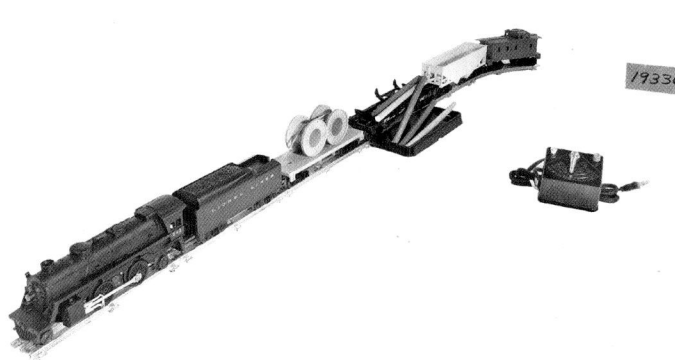

Lionel provided this photograph of outfit no. 19336 as an attachment to *Sales Bulletin* no. 13 from May 8, 1964. Sales representatives were encouraged to use it to sell the outfit. As with many early-in-the-year photographs, the items shown do not match those in the final Factory Order. Specifically, the hopper car and caboose are slightly different.

Description: "O27" Train Set
Specification: 6 Unit "O27" Train Set
Customer: Arkwright
Factory Order Date: 4/23/1964
Date Issued: 5/2/64
Packaging: RSC Pack (Units Loose)

Contents: 242-25 Steam Type Locomotive; 1060T-25 Tender; 6402-50 Flat Car W/2 Cable Reels; 40-11 Cable Reels (2); 3364-25 Log Dump Car; 3364-8 Logs (3); 160-2 Unloading Bin; 6176-50 Hopper Car; 6059-50 Caboose; 1013 Curved Track (8); 1018 Straight Track (3); 6149-25 Remote Control Track; 1010-25 35-Watt Transformer; 1103-40 Envelope Packed; Form 3063 Parts Order Form; 1-65 Warranty Card; 927-64 Service Station List; D64-50 Accessory Catalog

Boxes & Packing: 19336-RSC Outfit Box

19336 (1964)	C6	C7	C8	Rarity
Complete Outfit	395	600	850	R10
Outfit Box no. 19336-RSC	300	450	600	R10

Description: "O27" Train Set
Specification: 7 Unit "O27" Train Set
Customer/Price: Allied Stores; $29.71
Original Amount: 5,000
Factory Order Date: 4/23/1964
Date Issued: 5/4/64
Packaging: RSC Pack (Units Loose)

Comments: Arkwright (a large buying organization) purchased five promotional outfits in 1964: nos. 19253, 19336, 19345, 19346 and 19366.

Lionel initially tried to sell the 19336 to Allied, but the latter did not accept the outfit. Arkwright eventually purchased the 19336 at a cost of $9.45 each. Even so, Lionel still hoped to sell this outfit to other customers. Therefore, it listed the 19336 on *Sales Bulletin* no. 13 from May 8, 1964, which stated, "The following is a recap of O27 Train Specials restricted to accounts in individual markets on a first choice basis. If they are not selected in any one market by the account then at your discretion it is open to others." Consequently, the 19336 is classified as a General Release Promotional Type IIa outfit.

The 19336 was one of Arkwright's lower-end purchases for 1964. It was led by a no. 242-25 Steam Type Locomotive. This low-end Scout steamer featured a two-position reversing unit and a headlight, lacked smoke and used a rubber tire as a traction aid. The later version with narrow running boards was included in this outfit.

The only car of note was the no. 3364-25 Log Dump Car. This new-for-1964 car was the same as a no. 3362-25 Helium Tank Unloading Car except that the 3364-25 carried logs instead of helium tanks. A no. 160-2 Unloading Bin was provided for the logs and placed loose in the outfit box.

The rolling stock in the 19336 followed the normal truck and coupler progression for 1964, with all the cars having AAR types. Most were equipped with one operating and one non-operating truck and coupler. However, the no. 1060T-25 Tender had one non-operating and one plain type, and the no. 6059-50 Caboose had one operating and one plain type.

The box for the 19336 likely was either a Tan RSC with Black Graphics or a White RSC with Orange Graphics outfit box.

Be aware that a listing for a no. D19336 Display also exists. The cost to retailers was $11.95 each.

Contents: 239-25 Steam Locomotive With Smoke; 234W-25 Whistle Tender; 6465-150 Tank Car; 6651-25 Cannon Car; 6651-8 Shells (4); 6470-25 Exploding Target Car; 3419-250 Operating Helicopter Car; 3419-100 Operating Helicopter Complete; 6059-50 Caboose; 1013 Curved Track (12); 1018 Straight Track (13); 6149-25 Remote Control Track; 110-1 Trestle Set; 1073-25 60-Watt Transformer; 147-25 Horn

The space and military no. 19337 was Allied Stores' sole outfit purchase in 1964. It was an exciting, higher-end offering that featured a no. 6651-25 Cannon Car. This olive drab car was modeled after a no. 6650-25 / 6640-25 Missile Launching Flat Car and fired small wooden shells instead of a missile.

& Whistle Controller; 909-20 Smoke Fluid; 1103-40 Envelope Packed; 19337-10 Instruction Sheet; 6470-17 Instruction Sheet; 3419-51 Instruction Sheet; Form 3063 Parts Order Form; 6651-10 Instruction Sheet; 1-65 Warranty Card; 11460-10 Instruction Sheet; 237-11 Instruction Sheet

Boxes & Packing: 64-181 Outfit Box; 61-181 Insert; 61-182 Insert; 62-273 Insert

19337 (1964)	C6	C7	C8	Rarity
Complete Outfit	625	1,050	1,575	R5
Outfit Box no. 64-181	200	325	500	R5

Comments: In 1964, the Allied Stores conglomerate, which owned many retailers across the country, purchased Retailer Promotional Type Ib outfit no. 19337. Allied paid Lionel $19.20 for each outfit, and at least one was observed selling for $29.71.

The 19337 was a follow-up to Allied's nos. 19241 and 19241-500 from 1963. All three outfits had a space and military theme and so contained similar items.

The 19337 was led by a no. 239-25 Steam Locomotive With Smoke (new for 1964). This die-cast Scout steamer featured a two-position reversing unit, a headlight and a rubber tire as a traction aid. Except for its 239 number and lack of stripe, it was the same engine as a no. 241.

The no. 6651-25 Cannon Car was the only new-for-1964 car included in this outfit. It was derived from the no. 6650-25 / 6640-25 Missile Launching Flat Car and featured a new firing mechanism that fired shells instead of a missile. The base of the car was painted olive drab, whereas the top was molded in olive drab plastic. The 6651-25 was equipped with two operating AAR trucks and couplers. Both couplers included an integral copper spring.

The 3419-250 appeared in only one catalog and four

promotional outfits, with a quantity of 9,966 produced. Its "-250" suffix indicated that it was equipped with one operating and one late non-operating AAR truck and coupler. The norm for a no. 3419-100 Operating Helicopter Complete was a one-piece yellow body in 1963 and after. Even so, gray 3419-100s with Navy markings still appeared.

The no. 6470-25 Exploding Target Car included "non-slotted" sides and nubs on the roof door guide to help hold on the sides. The correct version for this outfit was equipped with one operating and one late non-operating AAR truck and coupler.

The remaining cars in the 19337 followed the normal truck and coupler progression for 1964, with most being equipped with one operating and one late non-operating AAR type. However, the no. 234W-25 Whistle Tender had one late non-operating and one plain AAR type and the no. 6059-50 Caboose had one operating and one plain AAR type.

The proper instruction sheets in this outfit made reference to the 90-day warranty that Lionel instituted in 1963. In fact, these are some of the most difficult versions to find. Specifically, the no. 6651-10 Instruction Sheet was dated 8/64, the no. 3419-51 was dated 3-61 but made reference to the 90-day policy and the no. 6470-17 Instruction Sheet was dated 8-59 but made reference to the 90-day warranty policy. The no. 19337-10 Instruction Sheet was unique to this outfit and detailed the track plan and use of spacers so that the 6651-25 would fit under the track.

The no. 64-181 White RSC with Orange Graphics outfit box was manufactured by United Container Co. and measured 15¼ x 14¾ x 7 inches. It included four lines of data as part of the box manufacturer's certificate.

Having a space and military theme as well as including a 6651-25 made the 19337 an exciting, collectible and a desirable outfit. Fortunately for collectors, Lionel produced a large quantity so that finding one is possible.

Be aware that a listing for a no. DO19337 Display also exists.

Lionel provided this photograph of outfit no. 19338 as an attachment to *Sales Bulletin* no. 12 from May 8, 1964. Sales representatives were encouraged to use it to sell the outfit. As with many early-in-the-year photographs, the items shown do not match those in the final Factory Order. Specifically, the gondola and caboose appear to be decaled prototypes. Curiously, the soldiers are Payton soldiers and not MPC. This suggests that Lionel originally may have thought of purchasing the soldiers from Payton.

Description: "O27" Military Train Set
Specification: 4 Unit "O27" Military Train Set
Customer: All Trade
Customer: Firestone
Original Amount: 1,160
Factory Order Date: 4/24/1964
Date Issued: 5/2/64
Packaging: RSC Pack (Units Loose)

Contents: 1061-25 Steam Type Locomotive; 1061T-50 Tender; 6042-100 Gondola Car; 6167-175 Caboose; 975-1 Squad of Soldiers; 1026-25 25-Watt Transformer; 1013 Curved Track (8); 1018 Straight Track (2); 1103-20 Envelope Packed; 19272-10 Instruction Sheet; Form 3063 Parts Order Form; 1-65 Warranty Card; 927-64 Service Station List; D64-50 Accessory Catalog

Boxes & Packing: 64-157 Outfit Box; 63-322 Insert; 63-323 Insert; 62-251 Insert

19338 (1964)	C6	C7	C8	Rarity
Complete Outfit	490	875	1,285	R7
Outfit Box no. 64-157	150	250	350	R7

Comments: Firestone Tire & Rubber Company purchased at least three promotional outfits in 1964: nos. 19338, 19345 and 19349.

Even after Firestone was assigned to the 19338 (at a cost of $5.95 each), Lionel still tried to sell this outfit to other customers. Therefore, it listed the 19338 on *Sales Bulletin* no. 12 from May 8, 1964, which stated, "The following represents fourteen (14) sets you may offer at your discretion to accounts in your territory." Consequently, it is classified as a General Release Promotional Type IIb outfit.

For a small military starter outfit, the 19338 included some highly collectible items. To begin, it was led by a no. 1061-25 Steam Type Locomotive. This stripped-down Scout steamer featured an 0-4-0 wheel arrangement and went forward only. It lacked a headlight, a lens and any sort of traction aid.

The nos. 6042-100 Gondola Car and 6167-175 Caboose (both new for 1964) were molded in olive drab plastic. These highly collectible and desirable cars included no markings or stampings. The 6042-100 appeared in only two promotional outfits, with a quantity of 2,260 made. The 6042-100 is almost identical to the more common olive drab no. 6142-175 Gondola Car except that the former came with non-operating AAR trucks and couplers and the latter had one operating and one non-operating AAR truck and coupler. Even though the 6042-100 is more difficult to find, the slight difference in trucks and couplers does not command a premium price.

All the cars in this outfit followed the normal truck and coupler progression for 1964. The nos. 1061T-50 Tender and 6167-175 were equipped with one non-operating and one plain AAR type. As noted, the 6042-100 had non-operating AAR trucks and couplers.

Topping off the 19338 and adding to its collectibility was a no. 975-1 Squad of Soldiers. This was one of 11 outfits to include a 975-1, which consisted of a polyethylene bag filled with 10 soldiers purchased from Multiple Products Corporation (MPC) of New York. (See outfit no. 19326 from 1964 for details about the 975-1.)

The no. 64-157 White RSC with Orange Graphics outfit box measured 11 x 7⅞ x 5½ inches.

This was a neat little military outfit that is in high demand by collectors. Unfortunately for them, examples are seldom seen.

Be aware that a listing and a glossy photograph for a no. D19338 Blister Display also exist. The cost to retailers was $8.45 each.

Description: "O27" Train Set
Specification: 4 Unit "O27" Train Set
Customer: All Trade
Original Amount: 500
Factory Order Date: 4/30/1964
Date Issued: 5/3/64
Packaging: RSC Pack (Units Loose)

Contents: 1061-50 Steam Loco With Tire; 1061T-50 Tender; 6042-250 Gondola Car (Without Load); 6167-25 Caboose; 1013-8 Curved Track (Bundle of 8 - 1013); 1010-25 35-Watt Transformer; 1103-20 Envelope Packed; 310-62 Set of (3) Billboards; D64-50 Accessory Catalog; 1-62 Parts Order Form; 1-65 Warranty Card; 927-64 Service Station List; 1123-40 Instruction Sheet; 11311-20 Instruction Sheet; 19339-10 Flyer; D64-50 Accessory Catalog

Boxes & Packing: 64-157 Outfit Box; 63-322 Corr. Insert; 63-323 Corr. Insert; 62-251 Corr. Insert; 63-321 Shipper for (6) (1-6)

19339 (1964)	C6	C7	C8	Rarity
Complete Outfit	200	325	500	R8
Outfit Box no. 64-157	100	175	250	R8

Comments: This was first of three General Release Promotional Type IIa outfits (nos. 19339, 19340 and 19341) based on a catalog outfit from 1964. Specifically, the Factory Order indicated that the 19339 was the same "as #11420 w/1010". The former, which cost $5.95 each from Lionel, has yet to be linked to a specific retailer.

The 19339 was a low-end starter outfit led by a no. 1061-50 Steam Type Loco W/Tire (new for 1964). This version came

IMPORTANT

The transformer furnished with this train set has been approved by the Underwriters Laboratories and has been carefully tested to assure proper performance.

This transformer is equipped with a built-in circuit breaker which will alternately cut out and restore the flow of power to the track whenever a short circuit exists. The circuit breaker is incorporated into the transformer to protect the transformer from possible "burn-out". It is not intended to protect the locomotive or electrically operated accessories. If a short circuit exists the transformer will supply power for short instances and "cut-out", alternately. Whenever such conditions are noticed, the transformer must be unplugged from the wall socket and the short circuit must be corrected.

THE LIONEL TOY CORPORATION

Printed in U.S. of America   19339-10 6/64

Outfit no. 19339 introduced the no. 19339-10 Flyer. This sheet was created to supplement Lionel Train Outfit Instruction Sheets that did not make reference to the circuit breaker included with the transformer.

with a rubber tire as a traction aid, a feature that made it a slight upgrade of the no. 1061-25 Steam Type Locomotive. Even with this improvement, the 1061-50 (lacking a headlight and a lens) remained Lionel's low-end Scout steamer configured with an 0-4-0 wheel arrangement.

The no. 1061T-50 Tender was a slope-back version with "Lionel Lines" stamped on each side. The nos. 6042-250 Gondola Car (Without Load) and 6167-25 Caboose were undecorated.

All the cars in this outfit followed the normal truck and coupler progression for 1964. The 1061T-50 and 6167-25 were equipped with one non-operating and one plain AAR type. The 6042-250 came with non-operating AAR trucks and couplers.

The 19339 differed from the 11420 in three ways. First, its power source was upgraded from a no. 1026-25 25-Watt Transformer to a no. 1010-25 35-Watt Transformer. Second, as a consequence of that change, Lionel had to introduce the no. 19339-10 Flyer for this promotional outfit. That difficult-to-find sheet (dated 6/64) explained that the transformer was equipped with a circuit breaker.

The third distinction related to the outfit packing. Specifically, the 11420 used a Tan RSC with Black Graphics outfit box, whereas the 19339 used a no. 64-157 White RSC with Orange Graphics outfit box that measured 11 x 7⅞ x 5½ inches.

The 19339-10 Flyer and the 64-157 Outfit Box are, along with the no. 310-62 Set of (3) Billboards, the key items of value in the 19339. Because this outfit was produced in much lower quantities than the 11420, it is far more difficult to find and desirable to own.

Be aware that a listing for a no. D19339 Display also exists.

19340
1964

Description: "O27" Train Set
Specification: 5 Unit "O27" Train Set
Customer: All Trade
Original Amount: 500
Factory Order Date: 4/30/1964
Date Issued: 5/3/64
Packaging: Display Pack (Units Loose)

Contents: 1062-50 Steam Type Loco. W/Light & Reversing Unit; 1061T-50 Tender; 6176-25 Hopper Car; 6142-50 Gondola Car; 6167-125 Caboose; 1013-8 Curved Track (Bundle of 8 - 1013); 1018-10 Straight Track (Loose); 6149-25 Remote Control Track; 1010-25 35-Watt Transformer; 1103-40 Envelope Packed; 310-62 Set of (3) Billboards; D64-50 Accessory Catalog; 1-62 Parts Order Form; 1-65 Warranty Card; 927-64 Service Station List; 1123-40 Instruction Sheet; 11450-10 Instruction Sheet; 1-66 Flyer

Boxes & Packing: 64-101 Box Top; 64-102 Box Bottom; 64-107 Corr. Insert; 64-103 Shipper for (6) (1-6); 64-104 Corr. Pad (2-6)

19340 (1964)	C6	C7	C8	Rarity
Complete Outfit	275	415	625	R8
Outfit Box no. 64-101	150	225	330	R8

Comments: This was second of three General Release Promotional Type IIa outfits (nos. 19339, 19340 and 19341) based on a catalog outfit from 1964. Specifically, the Factory Order indicated that the 19340 was the same "as #11430 w/1010". The former, which cost $7.55 each from Lionel, has yet to be linked to a specific retailer.

The 19340 was a starter outfit that represented a slight upgrade from the no. 19339. It was led by a no. 1062-50 Steam Type Loco. W/Light & Reversing Unit (new for 1964). This low-end Scout steamer featured an 0-4-0 wheel arrangement and a rubber tire as a traction aid. Except for the rubber tire, it was identical to the no. 1062-25 Steam Type Loco. W/Light & Reversing Unit.

The no. 1061T-50 Tender was a slope-back version with "Lionel Lines" stamped on each side. The "-50" version of the 1061T as well as the remaining cars were new for 1964. The green no. 6142-50 Gondola Car, red no. 6167-125 Caboose and yellow no. 6176-25 Hopper Car were undecorated.

The rolling stock in this outfit followed the normal truck and coupler progression for 1964, with all the cars having AAR types. Most were equipped with one operating and one non-operating truck and coupler. However, the 1061T-50 had one non-operating and one plain type, and the 6167-125 had one operating and one plain type.

The 19340 differed from the 11430 in two ways. First, its power source was upgraded from a no. 1026-25 25-Watt Transformer to a no. 1010-25 35-Watt Transformer. Second, as a consequence of that change, Lionel had to pack a no. 11450-10 Instruction Sheet with this promotional outfit. That sheet, dated 6/64, listed the 90-day warranty.

The no. 64-101 White 4-6-4 Steamer and F3 Lift-Off with Orange and Blue Graphics Type D display outfit box was manufactured by St. Joe Kraft and measured 23⅜ x 11⅝ x 3¼ inches.

The 64-101 Outfit Box and no. 310-62 Set of (3) Billboards are the key items of value in the 19340. Because this outfit was produced in much lower quantities than the 11430, it is far more difficult to find and desirable to own.

Be aware that a listing for a no. D19340 Display also exists.

General Release Promotional Type IIa outfit no. 19340 was a repeat of the no. 19340 from 1964. The motive power and rolling stock were identical. Only the paperwork and packaging were updated. Both the 1964 and 1965 versions were based on catalog outfit no. 11430 from 1964.

Comments: The no. 19340 from 1965 was a General Release Promotional Type IIa repeat of outfit no. 19340 from 1964. (See the entry for 19340 from 1964.)

The two outfits contained the same motive power and rolling stock. In fact, all the cars exhibited 1964 truck and coupler features, thus indicating that they might have been leftover production from 1964.

The 19340 from 1965 updated the paperwork and outfit packaging. The no. 11450-10 Instruction Sheet was now dated 6/65 and made reference to the one-year warranty that Lionel reinstated in 1965. The 1965 version did not include a no. 310-62 Set of (3) Billboards.

The no. 65-260 White Lift-Off with Full-Color 2037 Steam Freight Graphics Type D display outfit box was manufactured by Mead Containers and measured 23½ x 11½ x 3 inches.

Of the two versions of the 19340, the 1965 version was produced in much larger quantities. As such, it is easier to obtain and less desirable than the 1964 version.

Description: "O27" Promotional Outfit
Specification: "O27" Steam Type Freight Outfit
Original Amount: 3,000
Factory Order Date: 7/19/1965
Date Issued: Rev 7-22-65
Date Req'd: 9/7/65
Packaging: Display Pack (Units not Boxed)

Contents: 1062-50 Steam Type Loco. W/Light & Reversing Unit; 1061T-50 Tender; 6176-25 Hopper Car; 6142-50 Gondola Car; 6167-125 Caboose; 1013-8 Curved Track (Bundle of 8 - 1013); 1018-10 Straight Track (Loose); 6149-25 Remote Control Track; 1010-25 35-Watt Transformer; 1103-40 Envelope Packed; D65-50 Accessory Catalog; Form 3063 Parts Order Form; 1-165 Warranty Card; 926-65 Service Station List; 11450-10 Instruction Sheet; 1-66 Flyer

Boxes & Packing: 65-260 Box Top; 64-102 Box Bottom; 64-107 Corr. Insert; 64-105 Shipper for 4 (1-4); 64-106 Shipper Pad (2-4)

19340 (1965)	C6	C7	C8	Rarity
Complete Outfit	165	270	390	R5
Outfit Box no. 65-260	75	125	175	R5

Description: "O27" Train Set
Specification: 5 Unit "O27" Train Set
Customer: All Trade
Original Amount: 1,000
Factory Order Date: 4/30/1964
Date Issued: 5/3/64
Packaging: Display Pack (Units Loose)

Contents: 221P-25 Diesel Locomotive; 3349-100 Turbo Missile Firing Car; 0349-10 Turbo Missile (2); 6142-125 Gondola Car; 6176-50 Hopper Car; 6167-100 Caboose; 1013-8 Curved Track (Bundle of 8 - 1013); 1018-10 Straight Track (Loose); 6149-25 Remote Control Track; 1010-25 35-Watt Transformer; 1103-40 Envelope Packed; 310-62 Set of (3) Billboards; D64-50 Accessory Catalog; 1-62 Parts Order Form; 1-65 Warranty Card; 927-64 Service Station List; 1123-40 Instruction Sheet; 3349-105 Instruction Sheet; 11440-10 Instruction Sheet; Form 2870 Printed Sheet; 19339-10 Flyer

Boxes & Packing: 64-101 Box Top; 64-102 Box Bottom; 64-107 Corr. Insert

19300 Series

In 1964, Lionel issued three General Release Promotional Type IIa outfits based on a catalog counterpart. The no. 19341, which was based on catalog outfit no. 11440, contained a no. 3349-100 Turbo Missile Firing Car and its difficult-to-find no. 3349-105 Instruction Sheet.

19341 (1964)	C6	C7	C8	Rarity
Complete Outfit	285	510	715	R7
Outfit Box no. 64-101	100	225	300	R7

Comments: This was last of three General Release Promotional Type IIa outfits (nos. 19339, 19340 and 19341) based on a catalog outfit from 1964. Specifically, the Factory Order indicated that the 19341 was the same "as #11440 w/1010". The former, which cost $8.99 each from Lionel, has yet to be linked to a specific retailer.

The 19341 was led by a no. 221P-25 Rio Grande Diesel Locomotive. This low-end, unpainted yellow Alco engine featured a two-position reversing unit, a traction tire and a closed pilot and lacked a headlight.

The no. 3349-100 Turbo Missile Firing Car was the same as a no. 3349-25 Turbo Missile Firing Car except that it was equipped with one operating and one non-operating AAR truck and coupler. Its no. 3349-105 Instruction Sheet is very difficult to find.

The nos. 6142-125 Gondola Car, 6167-100 Caboose and 6176-50 Hopper Car were new-for-1964 color, decorating or coupler variations of cars already in the product line. The new suffixes indicated the changes.

The rolling stock in this outfit followed the normal truck and coupler progression for 1964, with all the cars having AAR types. All but one were equipped with one operating and one late non-operating truck and coupler. The 6167-100 had one operating and one plain type.

The 19341 differed from the 11440 in two ways. First, its power source was upgraded from a no. 1026-25 25-Watt Transformer to a no. 1010-25 35-Watt Transformer. Second, as a consequence of that change, Lionel had to include a no. 19339-10 Flyer with this promotional outfit. That difficult-to-find sheet (dated 6/64) explained that the transformer was equipped with a circuit breaker.

The no. 64-101 White 4-6-4 Steamer and F3 Lift-Off with Orange and Blue Graphics Type D display outfit box was manufactured by St. Joe Kraft and measured 23⅜ x 11⅝ x 3¼ inches.

Of the three General Release Promotional outfits based on a catalog outfit from 1964, the 19341 is the most desirable. Because this outfit was produced in much lower quantities than the 11440, it is far more difficult to find.

Be aware that a listing for a no. D19341 Display also exists.

Description: "O27" Special Train Set
Specification: 5 Unit "O27" Special Train Set
Customer: All Trade
Original Amount: 1,068
Factory Order Date: 4/24/1964
Date Issued: 5/10/64
Packaging: RSC Pack (Units Loose)

Contents: 1061-25 Steam Type Locomotive; 1061T-50 Tender; 6176-25 Hopper Car; 6042-250 Gondola Car; 6167-25 Caboose; 1010-25 35-Watt Transformer; 1013 Curved Track (8); 1018 Straight Track (4); 1103-20 Envelope Packed; Form 3063 Parts Order Form; 1-65 Warranty Card; 927-64 Service Station List; D64-50 Accessory Catalog

Boxes & Packing: 19342-RSC Outfit Box; 64-319 Corr. Insert

19342 (1964)	C6	C7	C8	Rarity
Complete Outfit	175	275	400	R7
Outfit Box no. 19342-RSC	100	175	250	R7

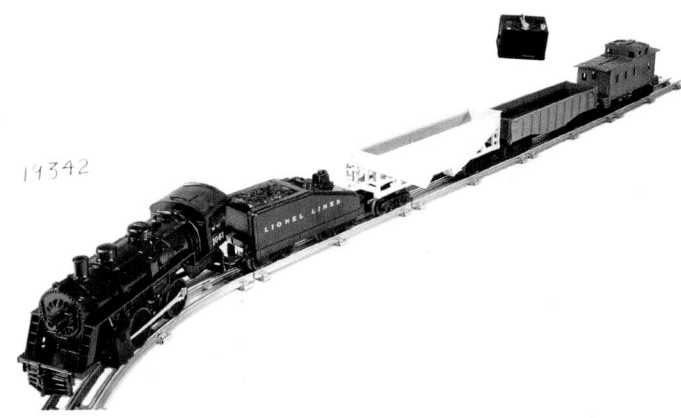

14342

Lionel provided this photograph of outfit no. 19342 as an attachment to *Sales Bulletin* no. 12 from May 8, 1964. Sales representatives were encouraged to use it to sell the outfit.

Comments: The no. 19342 was one of the many All Trade Specials that Lionel produced in 1964. This outfit, classified as a General Release Promotional Type IIb, has yet to be linked to a specific end retailer.

Lionel listed the 19342 on *Sales Bulletin* no. 12 from May 8, 1964, which stated, "The following represents fourteen (14) sets you may offer at your discretion to accounts in your territory." The

retailer's cost from Lionel was $6.70 each. Also listed was a no. D19342 Blister Display for $9.20 each.

Handwritten notes on a Sales Flyer indicated that the 19342 was similar in its contents to outfit no. 19363 from 1964. Those notes pointed out that all the items in the 19342, one of many low-end starter outfits offered by Lionel in this year, were taken from surplus inventory.

The 19342 was led by a no. 1061-25 Steam Type Locomotive. This stripped-down Scout steamer featured an 0-4-0 wheel arrangement and went forward only. It lacked a headlight, a lens and any sort of traction aid. Behind the engine was a no. 1061T-50 Tender, which was the slope-back version with "Lionel Lines" stamped on each side (new for 1964).

Among the cars in this outfit, the blue no. 6042-250 Gondola Car, red no. 6167-25 Caboose and yellow no. 6176-25 Hopper Car came undecorated. They, like the other cars, followed the normal truck and coupler progression for 1964. The 1061T-50 and 6167-25 were equipped with one non-operating and one plain AAR type. The 6176-25 came with one operating and one non-operating AAR type. The 6042-250 had non-operating AAR trucks and couplers.

The box for the 19342 likely was either a Tan RSC with Black Graphics or a White RSC with Orange Graphics outfit box.

Description: "O27" Military Train set
Specification: 5 Unit "O27" Military Train Set
Customer: All Trade
Customer: Army
Original Amount: 200
Factory Order Date: 4/24/1964
Date Issued: 6/2/64
Packaging: White RSC Pack Units Loose

Contents: 221P-75 Diesel Locomotive; 6142-175 Gondola Car; 6651-25 Cannon Car; 6651-8 Shells (4); 6176-100 Hopper Car; 6167-175 Caboose; 975-1 Squad of Soldiers; 1010-25 35-Watt Transformer; 1013 Curved Track (8); 1018 Straight Track (3); 6149-25 Remote Control Track; 1103-40 Envelope Packed; 6651-10 Instruction Sheet; 1-65 Warranty Card; 927-64 Service Station List; D64-50 Accessory Catalog; Form 3063 Parts Order Form

Boxes & Packing: 64-183 Outfit Box

19343 (1964)	C6	C7	C8	Rarity
Complete Outfit	1,550	2,500	3,350	R10
Outfit Box no. 64-183	750	1,000	1,250	R10

Comments: In 1964, the Army purchased two promotional outfits: nos. 19343 (diesel-powered) and 19344 (steam-powered). However, it seems likely that the Army did not commit to ordering sufficient outfits to justify an exclusive purchase. Therefore, Lionel listed the 19343 and 19344 on *Sales Bulletin* no. 12 from May 8, 1964, which stated, "The following represents fourteen (14) sets you may offer at your discretion to accounts in your territory." As such, the 19343 and 19344 are classified as General Release Promotional Type IIb outfits.

The 19343, which cost $9.40 each from Lionel, was similar to J. C. Penney's no. 19334 in that it consisted entirely of olive

drab items, starting with the no. 221P-75 Santa Fe Diesel Locomotive. This difficult-to-find Alco locomotive can be linked only to four promotional outfits. It featured a two-position reversing unit, a traction tire and a closed pilot and lacked a headlight.

All the cars in this outfit were new for 1964. The no. 6651-25 Cannon Car was derived from the no. 6650-25 / 6640-25 Missile Launching Flat Car and included a new firing mechanism that fired shells instead of a missile. The base of the car was painted olive drab, whereas the top was molded in olive drab plastic.

The remaining pieces of rolling stock represented olive drab versions of existing cars in the product line. These new-for-1964 items were identified by new suffixes. Thus, the no. 6142-175 Gondola Car was an unmarked olive drab no. 6142-series gondola while the no. 6176-100 Hopper Car was an unmarked olive drab no. 6176-series hopper. Finally, the no. 6167-175 Caboose was an olive drab no. 6167-series caboose.

The rolling stock in this outfit followed the normal truck and coupler progression for 1964, with all the cars having AAR types. Most were equipped with one operating and one late non-operating truck and coupler. However, the 6651-25 had two operating types, and the 6167-175 had one non-operating and one plain type. Both couplers on the 6651-25 included an integral copper spring.

The difficult-to-find 90-day warranty version of the no. 6651-10 Instruction Sheet was included in this outfit. It was dated 8/64.

Topping off the 19343 and adding to its collectibility was a no. 975-1 Squad of Soldiers. This was one of 11 outfits to include a 975-1, which consisted of a polyethylene bag filled with 10 soldiers purchased from Multiple Products Corporation (MPC) of New York. (See outfit no. 19326 from 1964 for details about the 975-1.)

The no. 64-183 White RSC with Orange Graphics outfit box was manufactured by United Container Co. and measured 12¾ x

The Army purchased the no. 19343 as its diesel-powered offering for 1964. This highly desirable outfit was one of only four to be led by the olive drab no. 221P-75 Santa Fe Diesel Locomotive. The no. 6651-25 Cannon Car appeared in only eight promotional outfits.

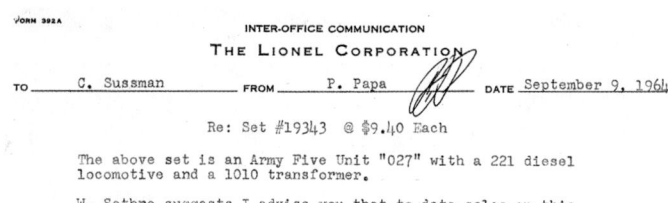

VORM 392A

INTER-OFFICE COMMUNICATION

THE LIONEL CORPORATION

TO ___C. Sussman___ FROM ___P. Papa___ DATE ___September 9, 1964___

Re: Set #19343 @ $9.40 Each

The above set is an Army Five Unit "027" with a 221 diesel locomotive and a 1010 transformer.

W. Sethre suggests I advise you that to date sales on this number have been poor.

Enclosed is a glossy and spec. sheet. The glossy shows a Rio Grande diesel. This is incorrect, as this set will have a Sante Fe in olive drab color.

cc: M. Lang
    W. Sethre

Enclosure

This memorandum, dated September 9, 1964, provides insight into the poor sales of outfit no. 19343. It also confirms that the olive drab Santa Fe Diesel Locomotive led the outfit.

10 x 6⅝ inches. It had four lines of data and "8-64" as part of the box manufacturer's certificate.

An original quantity of 1,000 units of the 19343 was to be manufactured. This was subsequently reduced to 200. This low quantity, combined with the difficult-to-obtain olive drab versions in this outfit, easily earns this outfit an R10 rarity rating.

Be aware that a listing for a no. D19343 Blister Display also exists. The cost to retailers was $11.90 each.

19344
1964

Description: "O27" Military Set
Specification: 6 Unit "O27" Military Set
Customer: All Trade
Customer: Army
Factory Order Date: 4/24/1964
Date Issued: 5/13/64
Packaging: RSC Pack (Units Loose)

Contents: 237-25 Steam Type Locomotive with Smoke; 242T-25 Tender; 6651-25 Cannon Car; 6651-8 Shells (4); 6176-100 Hopper Car; 6401-25 Flat Car; 958-75 Tank; 6119-125 Work Caboose; 975-1 Squad of Soldiers; 1013 Curved Track (12); 1018 Straight Track (3); 1020-25 90° Crossing; 6149-25 Remote Control

Track; 1010-25 35-Watt Transformer; 1103-40 Envelope Packed; 6651-10 Instruction Sheet; Form 3063 Parts Order Form; 1-65 Warranty Card; 927-64 Service Station List; D64-50 Accessory Catalog

Boxes & Packing: 19344-RSC Outfit Box

19344 (1964)	C6	C7	C8	Rarity
Complete Outfit	940	1,500	2,115	R10
Outfit Box no. 19344-RSC	500	750	1,000	R10

Comments: In 1964, the Army purchased two promotional outfits: nos. 19343 (diesel-powered) and 19344 (steam-powered). However, it seems likely that the Army did not commit to ordering sufficient outfits to justify an exclusive purchase. Therefore, Lionel listed the 19343 and 19344 on *Sales Bulletin* no. 12 from May 8,

Lionel provided this photograph of outfit no. 19344 as an attachment to *Sales Bulletin* no. 12 from May 8, 1964. Sales representatives were encouraged to use it to sell the outfit. As with many early-in-the-year photographs, the items shown do not match those in the final Factory Order. The final outfit had a no. 6651-25 Cannon Car stamped "6651" not "6640" as shown, a no. 958-75 Tank on the flat car, an unmarked no. 6176-100 Hopper Car and a no. 6119-125 Work Caboose.

1964, which stated, "The following represents fourteen (14) sets you may offer at your discretion to accounts in your territory." As such, the 19343 and 19344 are classified as General Release Promotional Type IIb outfits.

The 19344, which cost $13.65 each from Lionel, was led by a no. 237-25 Steam Type Locomotive with Smoke. This Scout steamer featured a two-position reversing unit and a headlight and used a rubber tire as a traction aid. The later version with narrow running boards came in this outfit. Except for its 237 number, it was the same engine as a no. 238.

All the cars in this outfit were new for 1964. The no. 6651-25 Cannon Car was derived from the no. 6650-25 / 6640-25 Missile Launching Flat Car and included a new firing mechanism that fired shells instead of a missile. The base of the car was painted olive drab, whereas the top was molded in olive drab plastic.

Other components included the no. 6176-100 Hopper Car, which was an unmarked olive drab no. 6176-series hopper. The no. 6119-125 Work Caboose represented an update of the no. 6119-style work caboose, now with an olive drab body and a black frame but without a number or a load.

The rolling stock in the 19344 followed the normal truck and coupler progression for 1964, with all the cars having AAR types. The 6176-100 and 6401-25 were equipped with one operating and one non-operating truck and coupler. The no. 242T-25 Tender

had one non-operating and one plain type, and the 6119-125 had one operating and one plain type. Also, the 6651-25 came with operating trucks and couplers.

Of interest, early 19344 Factory Worksheets indicated that originally every car in this outfit was going to be a military item colored olive drab. One of the cars specified was a no. 6401-50 Flat Car. However, Lionel never produced an olive drab version of the 6401.

The difficult-to-find 90-day warranty version of the no. 6651-10 Instruction Sheet was included in this outfit. It was dated 8/64.

Topping off the 19344 and adding to its collectibility were nos. 958-75 Tank and 975-1 Squad of Soldiers. The 958-75 was purchased from Payton Products and appeared in this and Sears outfit nos. 19326 and 19434. The 19344 was one of 11 outfits to include a 975-1, which consisted of a polyethylene bag filled with 10 soldiers purchased from Multiple Products Corporation (MPC) of New York. (See outfit no. 19326 from 1964 for details about the 958-75 and 975-1.)

The box for the 19344 likely was either a Tan RSC with Black Graphics or a White RSC with Orange Graphics outfit box.

The 19344's military theme and the inclusion of a 6651-25 and a 958-75 make it a collectible and desirable outfit.

Description: "O27" Special Train Set
Specification: 6 Unit "O27" Special Train Set
Customer: All Trade
Customer: Arkwright
Customer: Firestone
Customer/No./Price: Gimbels; P740 F4; $19.99
Customer/Price: Stix, Baer & Fuller; $19.99
Original Amount: 1,500
Factory Order Date: 4/24/1964
Date Issued: 5/10/64
Packaging: Display Packed

Contents: 239-25 Steam Locomotive With Smoke; 242T-25 Tender; 6014-325 Frisco Box Car; 6142-100 Gondola Car; 6112-88 Canister (2); 6465-150 Tank Car; 6167-100 Caboose;

1020-25 90° Crossing; 1010-25 35-Watt Transformer; 1013 Curved Track (12); 1018 Straight Track (3); 6149-25 Remote Control Track; 1103-40 Envelope Packed; 909-20 Smoke Fluid; 11450-10 Instruction Sheet; 1802B Instruction Sheet; 1-65 Warranty Card; Form 3063 Parts Order Form; D64-50 Accessory Catalog; 237-11 Instruction Sheet; 927-64 Service Station List

Boxes & Packing: 64-111 Box Top; 64-115 Box Bottom; 64-119 Corr. Insert; 64-120 Corr. Insert; 64-118 Corr. Insert

Alternate For Outfit Contents:
Substitute 6167-125 for 6167-100 as needed.

Lionel sold the no. 19345 to at least four different retailers in 1964. Pictured is one that included a Gimbels price tag (not shown) with Gimbels no. P740 F4 and a price of $19.99. The no. 239-25 Steam Locomotive With Smoke was the first no. 200-series Scout locomotive to have a die-cast body. The no. 6167-125 Caboose substitution is shown.

the same engine as a no. 241.

The no. 242T-25 Tender, green no. 6142-100 Gondola Car and red no. 6167-100 Caboose were new for 1964. All the other cars in this outfit were carried over from 1963. The no. 6014-325 Frisco Box Car used a Type III body. The substitution of a no. 6167-125 Caboose for the 6167-100 does not affect the outfit price.

The rolling stock in the 19345 followed the normal truck and coupler progression for 1964, with all the cars having AAR types. Most were equipped with one operating and one late non-operating truck and coupler. However, the 242T-25 had one late non-operating and one plain type, and the 6167-100 had one operating and one plain type.

The proper instruction sheets made reference to the 90-day warranty that Lionel instituted in 1963.

The no. 64-111 White 4-6-4 Steamer and F3 Lift-Off with Orange and Blue Graphics Type D display outfit box was manufactured by United Container Co. and measured 24⅞ x 15¼ x 3 inches.

This was a popular General Release Promotional outfit because it was purchased by at least four different customers. The widespread circulation of the 19345 may be the reason that examples appear frequently today. Even so, ones with a high-grade outfit box are difficult to find.

Of interest, 500 units of this outfit were cannibalized to create outfit no. 19371-500 from 1964. (See the entry for 19371-500.)

19345 (1964)	C6	C7	C8	Rarity
Complete Outfit	200	335	475	R6
Outfit Box no. 64-111	90	175	250	R6

Comments: The no. 19345 was a General Release Promotional Type IIa outfit that has been linked to at least four different retailers. Lionel documentation and real observations have identified Arkwright, Firestone Tire & Rubber Company, Gimbels and Stix Baer & Fuller as recipients of this outfit. Halle Brothers may also have purchased the 19345. Price tags indicate that Gimbels and Stix Baer & Fuller sold the outfit for $19.99. The retailer's cost from Lionel was $13.50.

The 19345 was led by a no. 239-25 Steam Locomotive With Smoke. This die-cast Scout steamer was new for 1964 and featured a two-position reversing unit, a headlight and a rubber tire as a traction aid. Except for its 239 number and lack of stripe, it was

Description: "O27" Train Set
Specification: 6 Unit "O27" Train Set
Customer: All Trade
Customer: Arkwright
Customer/No./Price: Rike's; 658P 66; $9.99
Original Amount: 150
Factory Order Date: 4/24/1964
Date Issued: 5/13/64
Packaging: RSC Pack (Units Loose)

Contents: 239-25 Steam Locomotive With Smoke; 242T-25 Tender; 6050-100 Swift Savings Bank Car; 6142-125 Gondola Car; 6112-88 Canister (2); 6465-150 Tank Car; 6119-110 Work Caboose; 1025-25 45-Watt Transformer; 1013 Curved Track (8); 1018 Straight Track (3); 6149-25 Remote Control Track; 1103-40 Envelope Packed; 909-20 Smoke Fluid; 11450-10 Instruction Sheet; 1-65 Warranty Card; Form 3063 Parts Order Form; 237-11 Instruction Sheet; D64-50 Accessory Catalog; 927-64 Service Station List

Boxes & Packing: 61-170 Outfit Box; 61-171 Corr. Insert; 61-172 Corr. Insert; 62-249 Corr. Insert

Lionel sold the no. 19346 to at least two different retailers in 1964. Pictured is a 19346 that included a Rike's price tag (not shown) with Rike's no. 658P 66 and a price of $9.99. The no. 239-25 Steam Locomotive With Smoke was the first no. 200-series Scout engine to include a die-cast body.

Research of promotional outfits is made easy when items like this are found. This is the bottom portion of the no. 1-65 Warranty Card that came with a no. 19346. It identifies the date on which it was purchased (Jan. 2, 1965) as well as the retailer (Rike's Warehouse).

19346 (1964)	C6	C7	C8	Rarity
Complete Outfit	550	815	1,115	R10
Outfit Box no. 61-170	400	600	800	R10

Comments: The no. 19346 was a General Release Promotional Type IIa outfit that has been linked to at least two different retailers. Lionel documentation and real observations identified Arkwright and Rike's Warehouse as recipients of this outfit. A Rike's price tag listed a retail price of $19.88 and a discounted price of $9.99. Since Rike's paid Lionel $12.90 for each outfit, it lost money on every one it sold.

The 19346 was led by a no. 239-25 Steam Locomotive With Smoke (new for 1964). This die-cast Scout steamer featured a two-position reversing unit, a headlight and a rubber tire as a traction aid. Except for its 239 number and lack of stripe, it was the same engine as a no. 241.

The no. 242T-25 Tender and blue no. 6142-125 Gondola Car were new items for 1964. All the other cars in this outfit were carried over from earlier years. The no. 6050-100 Swift Savings Bank Car used a Type III body. The "-110" suffix identified the no. 6119-110 Work Caboose as being unboxed.

The rolling stock in the 19346 followed the normal truck and coupler progression for 1964, with all the cars having AAR types. Most were equipped with one operating and one late non-operating truck and coupler. However, the 242T-25 had one late non-operating and one plain type, and the 6119-110 had one operating and one plain type.

The proper instruction sheets made reference to the 90-day warranty that Lionel instituted in 1963. The 90-day variations are difficult to obtain.

The no. 61-170 Tan RSC with Black Graphics outfit box was manufactured by United Container and measured 11½ x 10¼ x 6¼ inches. It included four lines of data, a "63" and five stars as part of the box manufacturer's certificate.

As with many promotional outfits, the outfit box is all that matters with the 19346. The components are common, but with only 150 units produced the outfit box is very difficult to find.

General Release Promotional outfit no. 19347 was a colorful and fun outfit that included three operating cars. It sold well despite a net selling price of $19.00 that made it one of the higher priced outfits from Lionel in 1964. Factory Orders were increased from 500 to 1,200 units.

Description: "O27" Train Set
Specification: 6 Unit "O27" Train Set
Customer: All Trade
Customer: Famous-Barr Co.
Original Amount: 1,200
Factory Order Date: 4/24/1964
Date Issued: 5/13/64
Packaging: RSC Pack (Units Loose)

Contents: 212P-25 "Santa Fe" "A" Diesel W/Horn; 212T-25 "Santa Fe" "A" Unit; 6473-25 Rodeo Car; 3364-25 Log Dump Car; 3364-8 Logs (3); 6822-50 Searchlight Car; 6119-110 Work Caboose; 1073-25 60-Watt Transformer; 147-25 Horn & Whistle Controller; 6149-25 Remote Control Track; 1013 Curved Track (16); 1018 Straight Track (3); 1103-50 Envelope Packed; 1023-25 45° Crossing; 212-64 Instruction Sheet; 3364-10 Instruction Sheet; 1-65 Warranty Card; Form 3063 Parts Order Form; 927-64 Service Station List; D64-50 Accessory Catalog

Boxes & Packing: 64-178 Outfit Box

19347 (1964)	C6	C7	C8	Rarity
Complete Outfit	375	625	925	R7
Outfit Box no. 64-178	125	200	275	R7

Comments: The no. 19347, a General Release Promotional Type IIa outfit, has been linked to Famous-Barr Co. and possibly Halle Brothers. Lionel listed it on *Sales Bulletin* no. 12 from May 8, 1964, which stated, "The following represents fourteen (14) sets you may offer at your discretion to accounts in your territory". The retailer's cost from Lionel was $19.00 for each outfit.

The 19347 was led a no. 212P-25 Santa Fe "A" Diesel W/Horn

(new for 1964). This Alco featured a two-position reversing unit, a headlight and two rubber tires as traction aids.

The outfit included three operating cars for plenty of excitement. The 3364-25 Log Dump Car (new for 1964) was the same as a no. 3362-25 Helium Tank Unloading Car except that it carried logs instead of helium tanks. The no. 6473-25 Rodeo Car used a Type IIb body (cadmium yellow plastic with red lettering). The Type II body included a partially filled slot caused by broken tooling. The no. 6822-50 Searchlight Car was an unboxed 6822 equipped with one operating and one late non-operating AAR truck and coupler. The "-50" suffix version was introduced in 1963. The "-110" suffix identified the no. 6119-110 Work Caboose as being unboxed.

The rolling stock in the 19347 followed the normal truck and coupler progression for 1964, with all the cars having AAR types. All but one were equipped with one operating and one late non-operating truck and coupler. The 6119-110 had one operating and one plain type.

When the nos. 147-25 Horn & Whistle Controller and 6149-25 Remote Control Track were included in an outfit, five wires were required to connect these peripherals to the transformer. Lionel created the no. 1103-50 Envelope Packed for this purpose. It came with five wires, a no. CTC-1 Lockon and a no. 0190-25 Controller.

The proper instruction sheets in this outfit made reference to the 90-day warranty that Lionel instituted in 1963. The nos. 212-64 Instruction Sheet and 3364-10 Instruction Sheet were both dated 6/64.

The no. 64-178 White RSC with Orange Graphics outfit box was manufactured by United Container Co. and measured 12⅞ x 10½ x 6¾ inches. It included four lines of data, a "64" and two stars as part of the box manufacturer's certificate.

This outfit was a success for Lionel because the original order of 500 units was raised to 1,200. As a General Release Promotional outfit, this increase was likely attributable to additional customers choosing to purchase it. With 1,200 made, this outfit does appear from time to time.

Description: "O27" Train Set
Specification: 6 Unit "O27" Train Set
Customer: A. B. C. Birmingham
Customer: Hecht & Company
Original Amount: 574
Factory Order Date: 4/24/1964
Date Issued: 6/2/64
Packaging: RSC Pack (Units Loose)

Contents: 237-25 Steam Type Locomotive with Smoke; 1061T-25 Tender; 6162-25 Gondola Car; 6407-25 Flat Car W/Sterling Missile; 6407-11 Sterling Missile; 6050-100 Swift Savings Bank Car; 6059-50 Caboose; 1025-25 45-Watt Transformer; 1103-40 Envelope Packed; 110-1 Trestle Set; 1013 Curved Track (12); 1018 Straight Track (13); 6149-25 Remote Control Track; 909-20 Smoke Fluid; 11450-10 Instruction Sheet; 237-11 Instruction Sheet; Form 3063 Parts Order Form; 1-65 Warranty Card; 927-64 Service Station List; D64-50 Accessory Catalog

Boxes & Packing: 19348-RSC Outfit Box

19348 (1964)	C6	C7	C8	Rarity
Complete Outfit	515	890	1,300	R7
Outfit Box no. 19348-RSC	150	250	325	R7

Comments: Outfit no. 19348 listed A. B. C. Birmingham and Hecht & Company on its Factory Order. As such, it is classified as a General Release Promotional Type IIa outfit. This outfit was likely sold to other retailers as well. The retailer's cost from Lionel was $12.00

The 19348 was led by a no. 237-25 Steam Type Locomotive with Smoke. This Scout steamer included a two-position reversing unit and a headlight and used a rubber tire as a traction aid. The later version with narrow running boards came in this outfit. Except for its 237 number, it was the same engine as a no. 238.

The no. 6407-25 Flat Car W/Sterling Missile is highly collectible. It was part of 11 different outfits, with a total of 13,124 cars produced. It was also available for separate sale. The car was a red no. 6511-series flat car that had "Lionel" stamped on each side and included a brake wheel. This was the same flat car used with the no. 6408-25 Flat Car W/5 Pipes.

The flat car is common, but the no. 6407-11 Sterling Missile is not. It was frequently orphaned from its flat car because it lacked Lionel markings. It was manufactured by Sterling Plastics, and an original would have "Sterling Plastics" molded into the capsule bottom and rocket base.

The rolling stock in the 19348 followed the normal truck and coupler progression for 1964, with all the cars having AAR types. Most were equipped with one operating and one non-operating truck and coupler. However, the no. 1061T-25 Tender had one non-operating and one plain type, and the no. 6059-50 Caboose had one operating and one plain type.

The proper instruction sheets in this outfit made reference to the 90-day warranty that Lionel instituted in 1963.

The box for the 19348 likely was either a Tan RSC with Black Graphics or a White RSC with Orange Graphics outfit box.

With only 574 of the 19348 manufactured and the inclusion of a 6407-25, this outfit is somewhat desirable. Unfortunately, it does not appear too often, hence its R7 rarity rating.

Description: "O27" Special Train Set
Specification: 6 Unit "O27" Special Train Set
Customer: *A
Customer: Firestone
Original Amount: 602
Factory Order Date: 4/24/1964
Date Issued: 5/10/64
Packaging: Display

Contents: 231P-25 Alco Diesel Power Car - "Rock Island"; 6408-25 Flat Car W/5 Pipes; 6511-15 Pipes (5); 6343-25 Barrel Ramp Car; 362-78 Wood Barrels (6); 6050-100 Swift Savings Bank Car; 6162-25 Gondola Car (Less 3 Canisters); 6112-88 Canister (3); 40-11 Cable Reel; 6047-25 Caboose; 1018 Straight Track (3); 1013 Curved Track (8); 6149-25 Remote Control Track; 1025-25 45-Watt Transformer; 1103-40 Envelope Packed; 11351-10 Instruction Sheet; 230-6 Instruction Sheet; 1-65 Warranty Card; 1-62 Parts Order Form; D64-50 Accessory Catalog; 310-62 Set of (3) Billboards; 927-64 Service Station List

Boxes & Packing: 64-101 Box Top; 64-102 Box Bottom; 64-107 Insert

19349 (1964)	C6	C7	C8	Rarity
Complete Outfit	400	665	900	R8
Outfit Box no. 64-101	200	300	400	R8

Comments: The no. 19349 was a General Release Promotional Type IIa outfit that has been linked to at least two different customers. Lionel documentation and real observations identified *A (an unknown customer) and Firestone Tire & Rubber Company as recipients of this outfit. The retailer's cost from Lionel was $9.20 each.

The 19349 was a basic diesel outfit used to thin out inventory of many items. Although the outfit has yet to be observed in any Firestone catalog or documentation, the Factory Order and a price tag confirm this connection.

The 19349 was led by a no. 231P-25 Rock Island Alco Diesel Power Car, which was first issued in 1961. It featured two-axle Magne-Traction, a headlight and a two-position reversing unit. This locomotive made one of its last two appearances in this outfit.

Firestone Tire & Rubber Company purchased the no. 19349 in 1964. Lionel used this outfit to thin out the inventory of many items that had been part of the product line for years. One example was the no. 231P-1 Rock Island Alco Diesel Power Car. First issued in 1961, it made its final appearance in this and one other outfit in 1964.

All the rolling stock in this outfit was carried over from earlier years. The no. 6343-25 Barrel Ramp Car was making its last appearance in 1964. The no. 6408-25 Flat Car W/5 Pipes was making its final promotional outfit appearances in 1964. The no. 6047-25 Caboose appeared in only two outfits in 1964 and one in 1965.

Interestingly, the no. 6162-25 Gondola Car (Less 3 Canisters) carried both the no. 6112-88 Canisters and a no. 40-11 Cable Reel. The reel has been observed in orange or gray plastic.

The rolling stock in the 19349 followed the normal truck and coupler progression for 1964, with all the cars having AAR types. The 6047-25 had one non-operating and one plain type. The nos. 6050-100 Swift Savings Bank Car and 6343-25 had operating types. All other cars were equipped with one operating and one non-operating truck and coupler.

The proper instruction sheets made reference to the 90-day warranty that Lionel instituted in 1963. In fact, these are some of the most difficult versions to find. Specifically, the no. 11351-10 Instruction Sheet was dated 6/64 and mentioned a no. 6149-25 Remote Control Track. The no. 230-6 Instruction Sheet was dated 8-61 but made reference to the 90-day warranty.

The no. 64-101 White 4-6-4 Steamer and F3 Lift-Off with Orange and Blue Graphics Type D display outfit box measured 23⅜ x 11⅝ x 3¼ inches.

The 19349 appears more often than its Factory Order quantity of 602 units would suggest.

Customer No. On Box: 6P-4811
Description: "O27" Special Train Set
Specification: 6 Unit "O27" Special Train Set
Cust./No./Price: Sperry & Hutchinson Co.; 6P-4811; 6 Books
Original Amount: 4,800
Factory Order Date: 4/24/1964
Date Issued: 5/13/64
Packaging: Display Pack (Units Loose)

Contents: 242-25 Steam Type Locomotive; 1060T-50 Tender; 6408-25 Flat Car W/3 Pipes; 6511-15 Pipes (3); 3410-25 Oper. Helicopter Car (Less Helicopter); 3419-100 Operating Helicopter Complete; 6476-25 Hopper Car - Red; 6059-50 Caboose; 1013 Curved Track (8); 1018 Straight Track; 6149-25 Remote Control Track; 1010-25 35-Watt Transformer; 1103-40 Envelope Packed; 11450-10 Instruction Sheet; 1-66 Flyer; 3410-5 Instruction Sheet; 1123-40 Instruction Sheet; Form 2870 Printed Sheet; 1-62 Parts

Order Form; 1-65 Warranty Card; 927-64 Service Station List; D64-50 Accessory Catalog

Boxes & Packing: 64-111 Box Top; 64-115 Box Bottom; 64-119 Insert; 64-120 Insert; 64-128 Insert

Alternate For Outfit Contents:
Use: 1060T-25 for 1060T-50 as needed.

19350 (1964)	C6	C7	C8	Rarity
Complete Outfit	275	425	590	R4
Complete Outfit With no. 1060T-25 Substitution	265	415	580	R4
Outfit Box no. 64-111	65	95	125	R4

Comments: After two years of featuring Lionel catalog outfits (nos. 11201 from 1962 and 11331 from 1963) in its catalog, Sperry & Hutchinson (S&H) offered Retailer Promotional Type Ib (or Ia with substitution) outfit no. 19350 in the firm's 1964 catalog on page 122 as item no. 6P-4811. The 19350 was available in

19300 Series

The no. 19350 series of outfits began when Sperry & Hutchinson purchased outfit no. 19350 in 1964. The 19350 is the most common of the series, which lasted through early 1965. It marked the final appearance of the no. 3410-25 Oper. Helicopter Car (Less Helicopter).

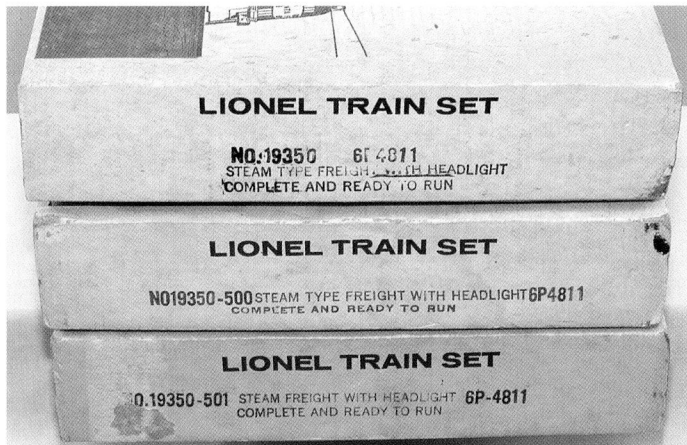

Three box examples for the no. 19350 series (top to bottom): Nos. 19350 from 1964, 19350-500 from 1964 and 1965 and 19350-501 from 1965. Versions with different styles of stamping or lacking the no. 6P-4811 number have been observed.

exchange for six filled S&H stamp books (hence the "6" in its "6P-4811" number). Lionel charged S&H $9.50 for each outfit.

This outfit went on to be offered by Lionel in three other configurations: nos. 19350-500 in 1964 and 1965 and 19350-501 in 1965. Two factors explained why four versions of the same outfit exist. The first related to the length of time that S&H carried products. Its catalogs were valid until April 30 of the following year. Hence, this outfit spanned two separate production years for Lionel. If it were a popular outfit requiring a reorder, Lionel would need to fulfill with what it had.

The second reason related to the far-from-optimal inventory management being done at Lionel in 1964. Put simply, outfits were cannibalized to meet deadlines for other outfits. The 19350 was one such outfit. When it came time to further fulfill the order, the 19350-500 was issued.

All four outfits were created to fulfill S&H's catalog listing for the 6P-4811. As such, they were to be stamped with both the 19350-series number and 6P-4811 by Lionel, although some 19350 outfits have been observed without the 6P-4811.

The 19350 was the most common of the four outfits, with 4,800 units produced. This is the version that matches the S&H catalog illustration. The outfit was led by a no. 242-25 Steam Type Locomotive. This low-end Scout steamer featured a two-position reversing unit and a headlight, lacked smoke and used a rubber tire as a traction aid. The later version with narrow running boards was included in this outfit.

Some interesting cars were included with the 19350. All were carried over from earlier years, and a few items were nearing the end of their product life. This is the main reason why, when S&H reordered, Lionel could not fulfill with the same items. The company had depleted its stock and so had to make changes with the two 19350-500s and the 19350-501.

The first item of note in the 19350 was the no. 1060T-50 Tender. It was the same as the no. 1060T-25 Tender except it was stamped "Southern Pacific". Lionel introduced this model in the no. 19263 "Libby" outfit from 1963, and it is one of the more desirable small streamlined tenders. When the 1060T-50 was replaced by a 1060T-25, the outfit price decreased, as listed in the pricing table.

After a four-year run, the no. 3410-25 Oper. Helicopter Car (Less Helicopter) was making its final appearance in this outfit. The norm for a no. 3419-100 Operating Helicopter Complete was a one-piece yellow body in 1964. This fragile helicopter was frequently lost or broken.

The no. 6408-25 Flat Car W/3 Pipes is interesting because the description of the 6408-25 changed with this outfit. It was previously called a Flat Car W/5 Pipes. It wasn't until 1966 that Lionel introduced the no. 6408-50 Flat Car W/3 Pipes. In any case, the 6408-25 in this outfit came with three no. 6511-15 Pipes.

The rolling stock in the 19350 followed the normal truck and coupler progression for 1964, with all the cars having AAR types. Most were equipped with one operating and one late non-operating truck and coupler. However, the 1060T-50 had one non-operating and one plain type, and the no. 6059-50 Caboose had one operating and one plain type. Be aware that the one operating and one non-operating AAR truck and coupler on the 3410-25 were not the late type.

The proper instruction sheets in this outfit made reference to the 90-day warranty that Lionel instituted in 1963. In fact, these are some of the most difficult versions to find. Specifically, the no. 11450-10 Instruction Sheet was dated 6/64 and mentioned a no. 6149-25 Remote Control Track. The no. 3410-5 Instruction Sheet, though dated 6-61, made reference to the 90-day warranty.

Of note, one outfit was observed with a no. 11331-10 Instruction Sheet dated 4/63. This outfit also included the no. 6139-25 Uncoupling Track Section that was described on the no. 11331-10 Instruction Sheet. This outfit lacked no. 6P-4811 markings. It likely was an early outfit that somehow omitted the S&H outfit number but kept the instruction sheets and track configuration from S&H's 1963 purchase, catalog outfit 11331.

The no. 64-111 White 4-6-4 Steamer and F3 Lift-Off with Orange and Blue Graphics Type D display outfit box was manufactured by United Container Co. and measured 24⅞ x 15¼ x 3 inches.

With so many units produced, the 19350 appears frequently. When it does, it most often is missing the yellow 3419-100 and pipes. Finding original and unbroken versions of these two items can take time.

The 19350 series of outfits are collector's favorites. Collecting all four versions requires patience, but can be accomplished.

Customer No. On Box: 6P-4811
Description: "O27" Freight
Specification: 6 Unit "O27" Freight
Cust./No./Price: Sperry & Hutchinson Co.; 6P-4811; 6 Books
Original Amount: 1,000
Factory Order Date: 12/11/1964
Date Issued: 12-11-64
Date Req'd: A/O
Packaging: Display Pack

Contents: 240-25 Steam Locomotive With Light & Smoke; 242T-25 Tender; 6402-50 Flat Car W/2 Cable Reels; 40-11 Cable Reels (2); 3619-25 Reconnaissance Copter Car; 6176-75 Hopper Car; 6059-50 Caboose; 1013 Curved Track (8); 1018 Straight Track; 6149-25 Remote Control Track; 1010-25 35-Watt Transformer; 1103-40 Envelope Packed; 909-20 Smoke Fluid; 3619-102 Instruction Sheet; 11450-10 Instruction Sheet; 237-11 Instruction Sheet; 1-62 Parts Order Form; 1-65 Warranty Card; D64-50 Accessory Catalog; 927-64 Service Station List

Boxes & Packing: 64-111 Box Top; 64-115 Box Bottom; 64-119 Insert; 64-120 Insert; 64-128 Insert

Alternate For Outfit Contents:
Outfit is substitute for 19350; Use: 1062T-25 for 242T-25 as needed.

19350-500 (1964)	C6	C7	C8	Rarity
Complete Outfit	460	700	1,040	R6
Outfit Box no. 64-111	125	175	225	R6

Comments: When Sperry & Hutchinson (S&H) placed a reorder for the no. 19350 from 1964, Lionel was unable to fulfill this request with the same items. It therefore issued the Retailer Promotional Type Ib no. 19350-500, for which S&H was charged $9.50 each. In fact, the Factory Order indicated that the 19350-500 was a substitution for the 19350. This outfit was stamped with both the 19350-500 number and 6P-4811. (See the 19350 from 1964 for more information.)

The 19350 and 19350-500 from 1964 differed in every respect except one. Both outfits came with a no. 6059-50 Caboose.

The 19350-500 from 1964 was led by a no. 240-25 Steam Locomotive With Light & Smoke (new for 1964). This promotional-only Scout steamer featured a two-position reversing unit and used a rubber tire as a traction aid. The 240-25 appeared only in this outfit, the nos. 19326 (Sears no. 9820) from 1964 and 19350-500 from 1965. Except for its 240 number and lack of stripe, it was the same engine as a no. 237.

The no. 3619-25 Reconnaissance Copter Car was making its final three appearances in the S&H no. 19350-500 series of outfits. Included was the harder-to-find darker yellow variation. The car came with a fragile and easily lost no. 0319-100 Helicopter. As part of the manufacturing process, the roof of the 3619-25 was taped shut with a ½-inch piece of Scotch tape. Even examples in C8 condition still have a mark where the tape was applied.

The 3619-25 and 6059-50 were the only carryover items in this outfit; all the remaining cars were new for 1964. The gray version of the no. 6176-75 Hopper Car was found in the 19350-500 series of outfits.

Lionel replaced the no. 242T-25 Tender with a no. 1062T-25 Tender in some outfits. This substitution has no affect on the outfit pricing.

The rolling stock in the 19350-500 followed the normal truck and coupler progression for 1964, with all the cars having AAR types. The 242T-25 had one late non-operating and one plain type, and the 6059-50 had one operating and one plain type. The 3619-25 was equipped with two operating AAR trucks and couplers; both of its couplers included an integral copper spring. All other cars were equipped with one operating and one non-operating truck and coupler.

The proper instruction sheets made reference to the 90-day warranty that Lionel instituted in 1963. In fact, these are some of the most difficult versions to find. Specifically, the no. 11450-

10 Instruction Sheet was dated 6/64 and mentioned a no. 6149-25 Remote Control Track. The no. 3619-102 Instruction Sheet is also difficult to find.

The no. 64-111 White 4-6-4 Steamer and F3 Lift-Off with Orange and Blue Graphics Type D display outfit box was manufactured by United Container Co. and measured 24⅞ x 15¼ x 3 inches. This is the same box used for both the 1964 and 1965 versions of the 19350-500. As such, even though the two outfits and one insert are slightly different, their outfit boxes are interchangeable. The R6 rarity rating is based on a combined quantity of the 1964 and 1965 versions.

The 19350 series of outfits are collector's favorites. The 19350-500 versions from 1964 and 1965 are the most desirable because they included a 240-25 as well as the darker yellow version of the 3619-25. Of the two, the 19350-500 from 1965 is more desirable because it also came with two "cheapie" automobiles.

Collecting all four versions of the 19350 requires patience, but can be accomplished.

The no. 19350-500 from 1964 was the second outfit in the no. 19350 series from Sperry & Hutchinson. It featured the promotional-only no. 240-25 Steam Locomotive With Light & Smoke as well as the darker yellow version of the no. 3619-25 Reconnaissance Copter Car. The outfit box is identical to the one used for the 19350-500 from 1965.

Customer No. On Box: 6P-4811
Description: "O27" Promotional Outfit
Specification: "O27" Steam Type Freight Outfit W/Smoke
Cust./No./Price: Sperry & Hutchinson Co.; 6P-4811; 6 Books
Original Amount: 900
Factory Order Date: 1/12/1965
Date Issued: 1-12-65
Date Req'd: 1/13/65
Packaging: Display Pack

Contents: 240-25 Steam Locomotive With Light & Smoke; 242T-25 Tender; 3619-25 Reconnaissance Copter Car; 6401-25 Flat Car; 0068-3 Automobile Body (Maroon); 0068-105 Automobile Body (Yellow); 6176-75 Hopper Car; 6059-50 Caboose; 1013-8 Curved Track (Bundle of 8 - 1013); 1018-10 Straight Track (Loose); 1010-25 35-Watt Transformer; 1103-40 Envelope Packed; 6149-25X Remote Control Track; 909-20 Smoke Fluid; 310-62 Set of (3) Billboards; D64-50 Accessory Catalog; Form 3063 Parts Order Form; 1-65 Warranty Card; 927-64 Service Station List; 1-70 Packing Brochure; 237-11 Instruction Sheet; 11450-10 Instruction Sheet; 3619-102 Instruction Sheet

19350-500
1965

Boxes & Packing: 64-111 Box Top; 64-115 Box Bottom; 64-118 Corr. Insert; 64-119 Corr. Insert; 64-120 Corr. Insert; 64-116 Shipper for 4 (1-4); 64-117 Shipper Pad (2-4)

Alternate For Outfit Contents:
Note: Sub. 7 - 242-25 for 240-25; Sub. 588 - 3619-1 for 3619-25.

19350-500 (1965)	C6	C7	C8	Rarity
Complete Outfit	575	975	1,275	R6
Complete Outfit With no. 242-25, Subtract The Following	110	180	320	R6
Complete Outfit with no. 3619-1, Add The Following	35	40	50	R6
Outfit Box no. 64-111	125	175	225	R6

Comments: Orders were flowing for the no. 19350 series of outfits. Only one month after planning the no. 19350-500 from 1964, Sperry & Hutchinson (S&H) placed an order for an additional 900 units. That increase led to the development of the no. 19350-500 from 1965. This Retailer Promotional Type Ib outfit was stamped with both the 19350-500 number and 6P-4811. (See the 19350

The no. 19350-500 from 1965 was the third outfit in the no. 19350 series from Sperry & Hutchinson. It included the promotional-only no. 240-25 Steam Locomotive With Light & Smoke, the darker yellow version of the no. 3619 Reconnaissance Copter Car and the nos. 0068-3 Automobile Body (Maroon) and 0068-105 Automobile Body (Yellow) which are commonly referred to as "cheapie" automobiles. Its outfit box is identical to the 19350-500 from 1964. This example has the Orange Picture boxed no. 3619-1 Reconnaissance Copter Car substitution.

The "cheapie" automobiles were just the plastic car frame with simulated wheels molded as part of the body. In 1964, Lionel began using these highly desirable and hard-to-find items on flat cars and the Auto Transport Car (unboxed no. 6414-75 and boxed no. 6414-85).

This outfit marked the last appearance of the no. 240-25 Steam Locomotive With Light & Smoke. It previously appeared in the nos. 19326 (Sears no. 9820) and 19350-500 both from 1964. Lionel must have had only a quantity of 893 in stock because seven outfits specified a no. 242-25 Steam Type Locomotive substitution. The no. 3619-1 Reconnaissance Copter Car substitution came in an Orange Picture box.

Since this was a January 1965 outfit, the rolling stock in the 19350-500 followed the normal truck and coupler progression for 1964, with all the cars having AAR types. The no. 242T-25 Tender had one late non-operating and one plain type, and the no. 6059-50 Caboose had one operating and one plain type. The 3619-1 and 3619-25 were equipped with two operating AAR trucks and couplers; both couplers included an integral copper spring. All other cars were equipped with one operating and one non-operating truck and coupler.

Even though this was a 1965 outfit, the paperwork was the same as the 19350-500 from 1964. The only difference was the inclusion of a no. 1-70 Packing Brochure. Also a no. 310-62 Set of (3) Billboards came with this outfit.

The no. 64-111 White 4-6-4 Steamer and F3 Lift-Off with Orange and Blue Graphics Type D display outfit box was manufactured by United Container Co. and measured 24⅞ x 15¼ x 3 inches. Both the 1964 and 1965 versions of the 19350-500 used this box. As such, even though the outfit contents and one insert are slightly different, their outfit boxes are interchangeable. The R6 rarity rating is based on a combined quantity of the 1964 and 1965 versions.

The 19350 series of outfits are collector's favorites. The 19350-500 versions from 1964 and 1965 are the most desirable because they included a 240-25 as well as the darker yellow version of the 3619. Of the two, the 19350-500 from 1965 is more desirable because it also came with two "cheapie" automobiles.

Collecting all four versions of the 19350 requires patience, but can be accomplished.

and 19350-500 from 1964 for more information.)

The 19350-500 from 1964 and 19350-500 from 1965 were nearly identical. For the 1965 version, Lionel updated the flat car load, made two substitutions and supplemented the paperwork, changes that affect the pricing. (See the 19350-500 from 1964 for more information.)

The no. 6402-50 Flat Car W/2 Cable Reels in the 1964 version was replaced by a no. 6401-25 Flat Car in the later version. The new flat car load consisted of the nos. 0068-3 Automobile Body (Maroon) and 0068-105 Automobile Body (Yellow). Commonly referred to as "cheapie" automobiles, these two models were derived from the nos. 0068-50 Motorized Stock Car - Red and 0068-100 Motorized Stock Car - Yellow. The Motorized Stock Cars were first issued as part of HO catalog outfit no. 6100 from 1961.

Customer No. On Box: 6P-4811
Description: "O27" Promotional Outfit
Specification: "O27" Steam Type Freight Outfit
Cust./No./Price: Sperry & Hutchinson Co.; 6P-4811; 6 Books
Original Amount: 1,200
Factory Order Date: 1/20/1965
Date Issued: 1-21-65
Date Req'd: 1-22-65
Packaging: Units Not Boxed

Contents: 1062-50X Steam Type Loco. W/Light & Reversing Unit; 242T-25 Tender; 3619-25 Reconnaissance Copter Car; 6401-25 Flat Car; 6511-15 Pipes (3); 6176-75 Hopper Car; 6059-50 Caboose; 1013-8 Curved Track (Bundle of 8 - 1013); 1018-10 Straight Track (Loose); 1010-25 35-Watt Transformer; 1103-40 Envelope Packed; 6149-25X Remote Control Track; 310-62 Set of (3) Billboards; D64-50 Accessory Catalog; Form 3063 Printed Sheet; 1-65 Warranty Card; 927-64 Service Station List; 1-70 Packing Brochure; 11450-10 Instruction Sheet; 3619-102 Instruction Sheet

Boxes & Packing: 64-111 Box Top; 64-115 Box Bottom; 64-118 Corr. Insert; 64-119 Corr. Insert; 64-120 Corr. Insert; 64-116 Shipper for 4 (1-4); 64-117 Shipper Pad (2-4)

Alternate For Outfit Contents:
Note: Sub. 450 - 3419-250 With (1) 3419-100 & (1) 3419-51 for 3619-25; Sub. 561 - 3665-1 for 3619-25 Less 3619-102.

19350-501 (1965)	C6	C7	C8	Rarity
Complete Outfit	375	585	835	R7
Outfit Box no. 64-111	150	225	300	R7

Comments: The final outfit in the no. 19350 series from Sperry & Hutchinson (S&H) was the no. 19350-501 from 1965. This Factory Order was dated eight days after the 19350-500 from 1965. The 19350-501 was a Retailer Promotional Type Ib version of that outfit, and it was stamped with both the 19350-501 number and 6P-4811. (See the 19350 and 19350-500 from 1964 for more information.)

The 19350-501 from 1965 was nearly identical to the 19350-500 from that year. For the former, Lionel changed the motive power, updated the flat car load, made two substitutions and supplemented the paperwork.

The 19350-501 was led by a no. 1062-50X Steam Type Loco. W/Light & Reversing Unit (new for 1964). The 1062-50 was a low-end Scout steamer featured an 0-4-0 wheel arrangement and a rubber tire as a traction aid. Except for the rubber tire, it was identical to the no. 1062-25 Steam Type Loco. W/Light & Reversing Unit. The meaning of the "X" is unknown, but more than one 1062-50X in the 19350-501 has been observed with a 2-4-2 wheel arrangement. This didn't become normal production until the no. 1062-75 Steam Type Loco. W/Light & Reversing Unit was introduced in 1966.

The no. 3619-25 Reconnaissance Copter Car made its last appearance in this outfit. Included was the harder-to-find darker yellow variation. The car came with a fragile and easily lost no. 0319-100 Helicopter. As part of the manufacturing process, the roof of the 3619-25 was taped shut with a ½-inch piece of Scotch tape. Even examples in C8 condition still have a mark where the tape was applied.

The 3619-25 and no. 6059-50 Caboose were the only carryover items in this outfit; everything else was new for 1964. The gray version of the no. 6176-75 Hopper Car was found in the 19350 series of outfits.

When Lionel ran out of the remaining quantity of 189 of the 3619-25, it replaced the car with either a light blue no. 3419-250 Operating Helicopter Car or no. 3665-1 Minuteman Missile Launching Car. This outfit marked the last appearance of the 3419-250, which appeared in only one catalog and four promotional outfits (a total of 9,966 were produced). Its "-250" suffix indicated that it was equipped with one operating

The no. 19350-501 from 1965 was the last outfit in the no. 19350 series from Sperry & Hutchinson. This outfit marked the final appearance of the no. 3619-25 Reconnaissance Copter Car, with the darker yellow version being included.

and one late non-operating AAR truck and coupler. The norm for a no. 3419-100 Operating Helicopter Complete was a one-piece yellow body in 1964. This fragile helicopter was frequently lost or broken. The 3419-250 and 3419-100 substitution does not affect the outfit price.

The 3665-1 has been observed in the harder-to-find light blue roof version and an overstamped Orange Picture 3619 box. The 3665-1 substitution does not affect the outfit price.

Since this was a January 1965 outfit, the rolling stock in the 19350-501 followed the normal truck and coupler progression for 1964, with all the cars having AAR types. The no. 242T-25 Tender had one late non-operating and one plain type, and the 6059-50 had one operating and one plain type. The 3619-25 and 3665-1 were equipped with two operating trucks and couplers, although the light blue roof version of the latter car often had one operating and one non-operating type. Both couplers on the 3619-25 included an integral copper spring. All other cars were equipped with one operating and one non-operating truck and coupler.

Even though this was a 1965 outfit, the paperwork still consisted of the 1964 versions. The proper instruction sheets made reference to the 90-day warranty that Lionel instituted in 1963. In fact, these are some of the most difficult versions to find.

The no. 64-111 White 4-6-4 Steamer and F3 Lift-Off with Orange and Blue Graphics Type D display outfit box was manufactured by United Container Co. and measured 24⅞ x 15¼ x 3 inches.

The 19350 series of outfits are collector's favorites. The 19350-501 is the most difficult outfit box in the series to find. Only 1,200 were produced as opposed to a combined 1,900 for the 19350-500s and 4,800 for the 19350. As such, the 19350-501 demands the highest empty box price and rarity for the series. Ironically, its contents are not as collectible as the no. 19350-500 versions from 1964 and 1965.

Collecting all four versions of the 19350 requires patience, but can be accomplished.

The no. 19351 was one of two outfits purchased by Chicago-based retailer Goldblatt's in 1964. It included a no. 6470-25 Exploding Target Car, but lacked any sort of firing car to blow it up. Such an odd mix probably resulted from Lionel configuring outfits based on what it had in stock rather than which items went well together. Even so, the outfit was a success and led to a reorder that became the no. 19351-500.

Description: "O27" Special Train
Specification: 7 Unit "O27" Special Train Set
Customer/No./Price: Goldblatt's; 242 4-4; $19.99
Original Amount: 1,281
Factory Order Date: 4/28/1964
Date Issued: 5/10/64
Packaging: RSC Pack (Units Loose)

Contents: 237-25 Steam Type Locomotive with Smoke; 242T-25 Tender; 6142-125 Gondola Car; 6470-25 Exploding Target Car; 6343-25 Barrel Ramp Car; 362-78 Wood Barrels (6); 6176-75 Hopper Car; 6059-50 Caboose; 1013 Curved Track (12); 1018 Straight Track (13); 6149-25 Remote Control Track; 1103-40 Envelope Packed; 1025-25 45-Watt Transformer; 110-1 Trestle Set; 909-20 Smoke Fluid; 310-62 Set of (3) Billboards; 1-65

Warranty Card; Form 3063 Parts Order Form; 237-11 Instruction Sheet; 6470-17 Instruction Sheet; D64-50 Accessory Catalog; 927-64 Service Station List

Boxes & Packing: 64-180 Outfit Box

19351 (1964)	C6	C7	C8	Rarity
Complete Outfit	310	505	735	R6
Outfit Box no. 64-180	125	200	275	R6

Comments: In 1964, Goldblatt's, a Chicago-based retailer with discount department stores, purchased two Retailer Promotional outfits: nos. 19351 and 19351-500.

The 19351, a Type Ia outfit, was purchased from Lionel at a cost of $13.00 each. It was advertised in an unknown newspaper as "Lionel 38 piece $19.99 - 3 days only 11/19 to 11/21". A Goldblatt's price tag listed the retail number as "242 4-4" for $19.99.

This outfit was led by a no. 237-25 Steam Type Locomotive with Smoke. This Scout steamer featured a two-position reversing unit and a headlight and used a rubber tire as a traction aid. The later version with narrow running boards came in this outfit. Except for its 237 number, it was the same engine as a no. 238.

The interesting mix of rolling stock was an indication of old and new. Old were the nos. 6059-50 Caboose, 6343-25 Barrel Ramp Car and 6470-25 Exploding Target Car. The 6343-25 was

making its last appearance in 1964. Including a 6470-25 with no means of triggering the explosion was a sign that Lionel was just randomly depleting surplus inventory. The remaining items were new for 1964.

The rolling stock in the 19351 followed the normal truck and coupler progression for 1964, with all the cars having AAR types. Most were equipped with one operating and one non-operating truck and coupler. However, the no. 242T-25 Tender had one late non-operating and one plain type, and the 6059-50 had one operating and one plain type. Be aware that the norm for a 6343-25 was two operating AAR trucks and couplers.

The no. 110-1 Trestle Set helped to create the elevated and elongated figure-eight track layout used for this outfit.

The proper instruction sheets made reference to the 90-day warranty that Lionel instituted in 1963. In fact, these are some of the most difficult versions to find.

The no. 64-180 White RSC with Orange Graphics outfit box was manufactured by United Container Co. and measured 15½ x 14½ x 6¼ inches. It included four lines of data as part of the box manufacturer's certificate.

This outfit was likely a success because late in the year, Goldblatt's ordered an additional 1,000 units. This went on to become the 19351-500. Of the two outfits, the "-500" version is much harder to find.

Be aware that a listing for a no. DO19351 Display also exists.

Description: "O27" Special
Specification: 7 Unit "O27" Special Substitution for 19351
Customer: Goldblatt's
Original Amount: 1,000
Factory Order Date: 11/20/1964
Date Issued: 11-20-64
Date Req'd: A/O
Packaging: Any RSC

19351-500 (1964)	C6	C7	C8	Rarity
Complete Outfit	450	700	1,035	R8
Complete Outfit With no. 6119-100 Substitution	390	600	845	R8
Complete Outfit With nos. 6017-25 or 6167-100 Substitution	365	560	785	R8
Complete Outfit With no. 6401-25 Substitution, Subtract The Following	20	30	50	R8
Outfit Box no. 19351-500-RSC	150	225	300	R8

Contents: 239-25 Steam Locomotive With Smoke; 242T-25 Tender; 6162-100 Gondola Car; 6176-100 Hopper Car; 6470-25 Exploding Target Car; 6343-25 Barrel Ramp Car; 362-78 Wood Barrels (6); 6119-125 Work Caboose; 1073-25 60-Watt Transformer; 110-1 Trestle Set; 1013 Curved Track (12); 1018 Straight Track (13); 909-20 Smoke Fluid; 1103-40 Envelope Packed; 6149-25 Remote Control Track; 6470-17 Instruction Sheet; 237-11 Instruction Sheet; 11450-10 Instruction Sheet; Form 3063 Parts Order Form; 1-65 Warranty Card; 927-64 Service Station List; D64-50 Accessory Catalog

Boxes & Packing: 19351-500-RSC Outfit Box

Alternate For Outfit Contents:
Outfit is substitution for 19351; Sub 432 - 6401-25 and 864 - 40-11 for 6343-25; Sub 131 - 6119-100 for 6119-125; Sub 137 - 6017-25 for 6119-125; Sub 108 - 6167-100 for 6119-125.

Comments: In 1964, Goldblatt's, a Chicago-based retailer with discount department stores, purchased two Retailer Promotional outfits: nos. 19351 and 19351-500.

The Type Ib 19351-500 was a reorder of the Type Ia 19351 with slightly different items. Lionel's far-from-optimal inventory management in 1964 meant that even simple outfit reorders could not be matched with identical components. This is likely why the 19351-500 differs from the 19351. This new version cost Goldblatt's $14.00 each, one dollar more than the 19351. These changes also led to the 19351-500 being much more desirable than the 19351.

The 19351-500 was led by a no. 239-25 Steam Locomotive With Smoke (new for 1964). This die-cast Scout steamer featured a two-position reversing unit, a headlight and a rubber tire as a traction aid. Except for its 239 number and lack of stripe, it was the same engine as a no. 241.

The interesting mix of rolling stock was an indication of old and new. Old were the nos. 6343-25 Barrel Ramp Car and

NO.19351-500

Outfit no. 19351-500 was the result of the reorder by Goldblatt's of outfit no. 19351. In fact, the 19351-500's Factory Order stated that it was a "substitution for 19351". The two outfits, which might seem quite different, actually were very similar. This example of the 19351-500 has the nos. 6401-25 Flat Car and 40-11 Cable Reel substitutions, but is missing the no. 110-1 Trestle Set, track and transformer.

6470-25 Exploding Target Car. The 6343-25 was making its last appearance in 1964. Including a 6470-25 with no means of triggering the explosion was a sign that Lionel was just randomly depleting surplus inventory. The 6470-25 had "non-slotted" sides and nubs on the roof door guide to help hold on the sides.

The remaining cars in the 19351-500 were new for 1964. The no. 6176-100 Hopper Car was an unmarked olive drab no. 6176-series hopper. The no. 6119-125 Work Caboose represented an update of the no. 6119-style work caboose, now with an olive drab body and a black frame but without a number or a load. Each of these desirable cars appeared in at least 10 outfits.

The substitutions for the 6119-125 affect the outfit price, as listed in the pricing table. Be aware that the 19351-500 represented the last promotional outfit appearance of the Orange Picture boxed no. 6119-100 Work Caboose and the final appearance of the no. 6017-25 Caboose.

The rolling stock in this outfit followed the normal truck and

coupler progression for 1964, with all the cars having AAR types. Most were equipped with one operating and one non-operating truck and coupler. However, the no. 242T-25 Tender had one late non-operating and one plain type, and the cabooses had one operating and one plain type. The norm for the nos. 6343-25 and 6162-100 Gondola Car was operating trucks and couplers.

The no. 110-1 Trestle Set helped to create the elevated and elongated figure-eight track layout used for this outfit.

The proper instruction sheets made reference to the 90-day warranty that Lionel instituted in 1963. In fact, these are some of the most difficult versions to find.

The box for the 19351-500 was a Tan RSC Mailer with Black Graphics outfit box.

The 19351-500 is more difficult to obtain than the 19351. It was produced in smaller quantities and has more desirable space and military items. The version as listed without any substitutions is the one that collectors desire.

The no. 19352 was one of three General Release Promotional Type IIa outfits originally offered to Automotive Associates in 1964. The 19352 was the low-end offering with basic yet colorful rolling stock.

Description: "O27" Special Train Set
Specification: 6 Unit "O27" Special Train Set
Customer: *A
Customer: Automotive Associates
Customer: Famous-Barr Co.
Original Amount: 3,000
Factory Order Date: 4/24/1964
Date Issued: 5/13/64
Packaging: RSC Pack (Units Loose)

Contents: 1062-50 Steam Type Loco. W/Light & Reversing Unit; 1061T-50 Tender; 6142-125 Gondola Car; 6176-75 Hopper Car; 6465-150 Tank Car; 6167-100 Caboose; 1013 Curved Track (8); 1018 Straight Track (5); 6149-25 Remote Control Track; 1026-25 25-Watt Transformer; 1103-40 Envelope Packed; 1-65 Warranty Card; Form 3063 Parts Order Form; D64-50 Accessory Catalog; 927-64 Service Station List

Boxes & Packing: 64-159 Outfit Box; 64-161 Corrugated Insert

19352 (1964)	C6	C7	C8	Rarity
Complete Outfit	130	230	365	R5
Outfit Box no. 64-159	50	90	150	R5

Comments: Lionel initially listed Automotive Associates as the customer for three outfits in 1964: nos. 19352, 19353 and 19354. However, as was true with many outfits in 1964, it offered these three to other customers as well. As *Sales Bulletin* no. 13 from May 8, 1964, stated, "The following is a recap of O27 Train Specials restricted to accounts in individual markets on a first choice basis. If they are not selected in any one market by the account then at your discretion it is open to others." Consequently, all three are classified as General Release Promotional Type IIa outfits.

Lionel documentation further identified *A (an unknown customer) and Famous-Barr as additional recipients of this outfit. The retailer's cost from Lionel was $8.10 each, which made the 19352 the low-end offering of the three outfits.

The 19352 was led by a no. 1062-50 Steam Type Loco. W/ Light & Reversing Unit (new for 1964). This low-end Scout steamer featured an 0-4-0 wheel arrangement and a rubber tire as a traction aid. Except for the rubber tire, it was identical to the no. 1062-25 Steam Type Loco. W/Light & Reversing Unit. The 1062-50 was paired with a no. 1061T-50 Tender, which was the slope-back version with "Lionel Lines" stamped on each side (also new for 1964).

With only one exception, all the cars in this outfit were new for 1964. The sole carryover was the no. 6465-150 Tank Car. Among the newcomers, the no. 6176-75 Hopper Car was molded in gray or yellow (these variations are identical in price and rarity).

The rolling stock in the 19352 followed the normal truck and coupler progression for 1964, with all the cars having AAR types. Most were equipped with one operating and one non-operating truck and coupler. However, the 1061T-50 had one late non-operating and one plain type, and the no. 6167-100 Caboose had one operating and one plain type.

The no. 64-159 White RSC with Orange Graphics outfit box was manufactured by United Container Co. and measured 11½ x 11¼ x 5½ inches. It included four lines of data and "8-64" as part of the box manufacturer's certificate.

The original quantity of 2,500 of the 19352 was raised to 3,000. This increase likely represented outfits being purchased by Famous-Barr. With a large quantity manufactured, the 19352 can be found and completed with minimal effort.

19353
1964

The no. 19353 was second of three General Release Promotional Type IIa outfits originally offered to Automotive Associates in 1964. It was the mid-level offering that included two operating cars and a steam locomotive.

Description: "O27" Special Train Set
Specification: 9 Unit "O27" Special Train Set
Customer: *A
Customer: Automotive Associates
Customer: Famous-Barr Co.
Customer: Spiegel
Customer: All Trade
Original Amount: 5,000
Factory Order Date: 4/24/1964
Date Issued: 5-29-64
Packaging: RSC Pack (Units Loose)

Contents: 237-25 Steam Type Locomotive with Smoke; 242T-25

Tender; 6402-50 Flat Car W/2 Cable Reels; 40-11 Cable Reels (2); 6176-75 Hopper Car; 6465-150 Tank Car; 6473-25 Rodeo Car; 3364-25 Log Dump Car; 3364-8 Logs (3); 6014-325 Frisco Box Car; 6167-100 Caboose; 1013 Curved Track (12); 1018 Straight Track (7); 1020-25 90° Crossing; 6149-25 Remote Control Track; 1025-25 45-Watt Transformer; 1103-40 Envelope Packed; 909-20 Smoke Fluid; 1802-10 Instruction Sheet; 3364-10 Instruction Sheet; 237-11 Instruction Sheet; 1-65 Warranty Card; Form 3063 Parts Order Form; D64-50 Accessory Catalog; 927-64 Service Station List

Boxes & Packing: 64-166 Outfit Box; 64-169 Corrugated Insert (2); 64-167 Corr. Shipper for 4 (1-4)

19353 (1964)	C6	C7	C8	Rarity
Complete Outfit	220	365	560	R4
Outfit Box no. 64-166	55	100	150	R4

Comments: Lionel initially listed Automotive Associates as the customer for three outfits in 1964: nos. 19352, 19353 and 19354. However, as was true with many outfits in 1964, it offered these three to other customers as well. As *Sales Bulletin* no. 13 from May 8, 1964, stated, "The following is a recap of O27 Train Specials restricted to accounts in individual markets on a first choice basis. If they are not selected in any one market by the account then at your discretion it is open to others." Consequently, all three are classified as General Release Promotional Type IIa outfits.

Lionel documentation further identified *A (an unknown customer), and Famous-Barr and Spiegel as additional recipients of this outfit. The retailer's cost from Lionel was $13.00 each, which made the 19353 the mid-level offering of the three outfits.

This outfit was led by a no. 237-25 Steam Type Locomotive with Smoke. This Scout steamer featured a two-position reversing unit and a headlight and used a rubber tire as a traction aid. The later version with narrow running boards came in this outfit. Except for its 237 number, it was the same engine as a no. 238.

The 19353 included two operating cars for plenty of excitement. The 3364-25 Log Dump Car (new for 1964) was the same as a no. 3362-25 Helium Tank Unloading Car except that it carried logs instead of helium tanks. The no. 6473-25 Rodeo Car used a Type IIb body (cadmium yellow plastic with red lettering). The Type II body included a partially filled slot caused by broken tooling.

The no. 6176-75 Hopper Car was molded in gray or yellow (these variations are identical in price and rarity). The no. 6014-325 Frisco Box Car used a Type III body.

All the rolling stock in this outfit followed the normal truck and coupler progressions for 1964, with all the cars having AAR types. Most of them were equipped with one operating and one non-operating truck and coupler. However, the no. 242T-25 Tender had one late non-operating and one plain type, and the no. 6167-100 Caboose had one operating and one plain type. Be aware that the operating coupler on the 6014-325 came with an integral copper spring.

The proper instruction sheets made reference to the 90-day warranty that Lionel instituted in 1963. A no. 1802-10 Instruction Sheet detailed the figure-eight track layout.

The no. 64-166 White RSC with Orange Graphics outfit box was manufactured by United Container Co. and measured 15⅜ x 10½ x 7⅛ inches. It included four lines of data, a "64" and two stars as part of the box manufacturer's certificate. Printed on the bottom was a reference to the N.M.F.C.

The original quantity of 2,000 of the 19353 swelled to 5,000. This increase likely represented outfits being purchased by Famous-Barr, Spiegel and others. In fact, the Factory Order states, "Sold 500 to Spiegels at $13.00 as sub for 19371." The 19353 and the no. 19371-500 were likely used to fulfill the increased orders for the no. 19371. (See the entries for the 19371 and 19371-500.)

With a large quantity manufactured, the 19353 can be found and completed with minimal effort.

Description: "O27" Train Set
Specification: 8 Unit "O27" Train Set
Customer: *A
Customer: Automotive Associates
Customer: Famous-Barr Co.
Original Amount: 1,200
Factory Order Date: 4/24/1964
Date Issued: 5/13/64
Packaging: RSC Pack (Units Loose)

Contents: 2029-25 Steam Type Locomotive With Smoke; 233W-25 Whistle Tender; 6142-125 Gondola Car; 6014-325 Frisco Box Car; 6408-25 Flat Car W/5 Pipes; 6511-15 Pipes (5); 6176-75 Hopper Car; 6465-150 Tank Car; 6167-125 Caboose; 1073-25 60-Watt Transformer; 147-25 Horn & Whistle Controller; 6149-25 Remote Control Track; 1013 Curved Track (8); 1018 Straight Track (5); 1103-50 Envelope Packed; SP-1 Smoke Pellets; 675-33 Smoke Stack Cleaner; 2029-5 Instruction Sheet; 1-65 Warranty Card; Form 3063 Parts Order Form; D64-50 Accessory Catalog; 927-64 Service Station List; 11460-10 Instruction Sheet

Boxes & Packing: 64-164 Outfit Box; 64-323 Corrugated Insert

19354 (1964)	C6	C7	C8	Rarity
Complete Outfit	190	460	675	R7
Outfit Box no. 64-164	125	200	275	R7

Comments: Lionel initially listed Automotive Associates as the customer for three outfits in 1964: nos. 19352, 19353 and 19354.

However, as was true with many outfits in 1964, it offered these three to other customers as well. As *Sales Bulletin* no. 13 from May 8, 1964, stated, "The following is a recap of O27 Train Specials restricted to accounts in individual markets on a first choice basis. If they are not selected in any one market by the account then at your discretion it is open to others." Consequently, all three are classified as General Release Promotional Type IIa outfits.

Lionel documentation further identified *A (an unknown customer), and Famous-Barr as additional recipients of this outfit. The retailer's cost from Lionel was $18.50 each, which made the 19354 the high-end offering of the three outfits.

This outfit was led by a no. 2029-25 Steam Type Locomotive With Smoke (new for 1964). This steamer featured a two-position reversing unit, a headlight and a rubber tire as a traction aid. Since the 2029-25 came unboxed (as indicated by the "-25"), the nos. SP-1 Smoke Pellets, 675-33 Smoke Stack Cleaner and 2029-5 Instruction Sheet were provided separately in the outfit box. The no. CTC-1 Lockon came in the 1103-50 Envelope Packed.

With the no. 233W-25 Whistle Tender, there were a total of seven pieces of rolling stock in the 19354. Unfortunately for consumers, the absence of any operating cars limited the play value of this outfit. Notable components included the no. 6408-25 Flat Car W/5 Pipes, which was making its last promotional outfit appearances in 1964. The 233W-25, which last appeared in 1963, was making its last appearance in this outfit and outfit no. 19332. The yellow version of the no. 6176-75 Hopper Car has been observed in this outfit.

19300 Series

NO. 19354 *Famous Barr*

8 UNIT LIONEL STEAM FREIGHTER FEATURING DIE CAST STEAM LOCOMOTIVE
AND WHISTLE TENDER

"POWER HOUSE ON WHEELS"

Big rugged and majestic is Lionel's mighty 2029 steamer equipped
with the ultimate of model railroading features...Die Cast construction, blazing, track scanning headlight, real billowing smoke and
authentic sounding whistle. The rolling stock featured on this
freighter is authentic throughout and includes a rugged Gondola, a
utilitarian Box Car, a flat car with 5 pipes, a detailed Hopper
Car, long distance Tank Car, and a colorful "crews quarters" Caboose.
This exciting steam freighter comes complete in every detail and
includes a mighty 60 watt Transformer with built-in circuit breaker.
Every boy from 6 to 60 will be proud to own this exciting Lionel
model railroad empire.

CONTENTS

	o.2029 LTS	Die cast steam type locomotive, with whistle tender, forward, reverse, headlight, smoke
	No.6142-125	Gondola car
	No.6014	Box car
	No.6408	Flat car with 5 pipes
	No. 6176-75	Hopper car
	No. 6465	Tank car
	No. 6167-100	Caboose
	No. 1073	60 Watt UL approved transformer
	No. 147	Whistle controller
	No. 6149	Remote control track section
8	No. 1013	Curved track
5	No. 1018	Straight track

Wires and instruction sheet

The above sets packed each in an individual corrugated carton, 4 to a
master shipper. Cost each: $18.50

AUTOMOTIVE ASSOCIATIONS 027 TRAIN SPECIAL

The rolling stock in the 19354 followed the normal truck and coupler progression for 1964, with all the cars having AAR types. All but two were equipped with one operating and one non-operating truck and coupler. The 233W-25 and no. 6167-125 Caboose had one operating and one plain type.

When the nos. 147-25 Horn & Whistle Controller and 6149-25 Remote Control Track were included in an outfit, five wires were required to connect these peripherals to the transformer. Lionel created the no. 1103-50 Envelope Packed for this purpose. It included five wires, a no. CTC-1 Lockon and a no. 0190-25 Controller.

The proper instruction sheets made reference to the 90-day warranty that Lionel instituted in 1963.

The no. 64-164 White RSC with Orange Graphics outfit box was manufactured by United Container Co. and measured 12⅛ x 11⅝ x 6½ inches. It included four lines of data as part of the box manufacturer's certificate.

Lionel produced a larger-than-average quantity of 1,200 of the 19354. Even so, the outfit does not often appear.

A Sales Sheet for outfit no. 19354 demonstrates Lionel's marketing creativity in selling outfits. The text titled "Power House On Wheels" is highly persuasive, making it sound as though this outfit is a must for "every boy from 6 to 60". Such a description probably went into the catalogs issued by partners of Automotive Associates. Don't overlook the handwritten notation linking this outfit to "Famous-Barr"; it was also listed as a customer on two other documents for the 19354.

SPECIAL LAYOUT INSTRUCTIONS

This special train outfit includes enough track to make up the layout shown below. You will have to transfer track pins from one end of the crossing to the other as shown by the arrow.

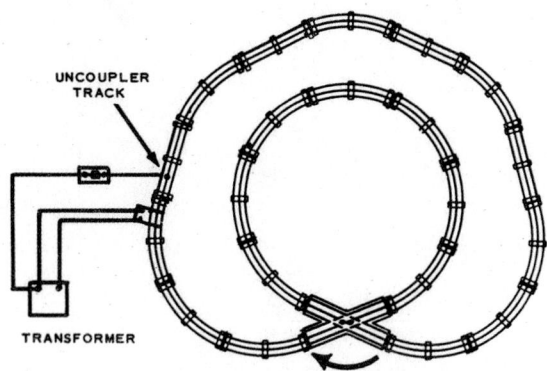

UNCOUPLER TRACK

TRANSFORMER

THE LIONEL TOY CORPORATION

Printed in U.S. of America   19355-10 6/64

Outfit no. 19355 came with the rare no. 19355-10 Instruction Sheet dated 6/64. It diagrammed the track layout and placement of the nos. 6149-25 Remote Control Track and CTC-1 Lockon.

Description: "O27" Special Train Set
Specification: 6 Unit "O27" Special Train Set
Customer: White Stores
Original Amount: 1,200

Factory Order Date: 5/12/1964
Date Issued: 5-27-64
Packaging: RSC Pack (Units Loose)

Contents: 215P-25 "Santa Fe" Diesel Power Car; 212T-25 "Santa Fe" "A" Unit; 3364-25 Log Dump Car; 3364-8 Logs (3); 6465-150 Tank Car; 6176-75 Hopper Car; 6059-50 Caboose; 1013 Curved Track (16); 1018 Straight Track (3); 6149-25 Remote Control Track; 1023-25 45° Crossing; 1025-25 45-Watt Transformer; 1103-40 Envelope Packed; D64-50 Accessory Catalog; Form 3063 Parts Order Form; 1-65 Warranty Card; 927-64 Service Station List; 3364-10 Instruction Sheet; 211-151 Instruction Sheet; 19355-10 Instruction Sheet

Boxes & Packing: 64-164 Outfit Box; 62-224 Corrugated Insert; 62-245 Corrugated Insert (2)

19355 (1964)	C6	C7	C8	Rarity
Complete Outfit	345	565	875	R8
Outfit Box no. 64-164	125	200	275	R7

Comments: The no. 19355 was White Stores' sole Retailer Promotional Type Ib outfit purchase in 1964. The cost from Lionel was $12.80 each.

The 19355 was led by a no. 215P-25 Santa Fe Diesel Power Car (new for 1964). This promotional-only Alco featured a two-position reversing unit, two traction tires, a headlight, a weight and an open pilot with a large ledge. This was one of five promotional outfits from 1964 to include a 215P-25, which was paired with a no. 212T-25 Santa Fe "A" Unit (also new for 1964).

The rolling stock consisted of commonly available items from 1964. The most notable item was the no. 3364-25 Log Dump Car, which was identical to the no. 3362-25 Helium Tank Unloading Car except that it carried logs instead of helium tanks. The no. 6176-75 Hopper Car was molded in gray or yellow (these variations are identical in price and rarity).

The rolling stock in the 19355 followed the normal truck and coupler progression for 1964, with all the cars having AAR types. All but one were equipped with one operating and one non-operating truck and coupler. The no. 6059-50 Caboose had one operating and one plain type.

The proper instruction sheets made reference to the 90-day warranty that Lionel instituted in 1963. Standing out was the rare no. 19355-10 Instruction Sheet, which detailed a pretzel layout. This is by far the most difficult item to obtain in completing this outfit. It boosts a complete 19355 to an R8 rarity level.

The no. 64-164 White RSC with Orange Graphics outfit box was manufactured by United Container Co. and measured 12⅛ x 11⅝ x 6½ inches. It included four lines of data as part of its box manufacturer's certificate.

Lionel produced a larger-than-average quantity of 1,200 of the 19355. Even so, the outfit does not often appear.

Description: "O27" Special Train Set
Specification: 5 Unit "O27" Special Train Set
Customer: All Trade
Original Amount: 1,984
Factory Order Date: 4/24/1964
Date Issued: 5/12/64
Packaging: RSC Pack White (Units Loose)

Contents: 1060-25 Steam Type Locomotive; 1061T-25 Tender; 6042-250 Gondola Car; 6050-175 Libby Box Car; 6167-50 Caboose; 1026-25 25-Watt Transformer; 1013 Curved Track (8); 1018 Straight Track (2); 1103-20 Envelope Packed; 1-65 Warranty Card; Form 3063 Parts Order Form; D64-50 Accessory Catalog; 927-64 Service Station List

Boxes & Packing: 64-162 Outfit Box; 64-319 Corr. Insert

19357 (1964)	C6	C7	C8	Rarity
Complete Outfit	165	305	450	R7
Outfit Box no. 64-162	75	150	225	R7

Comments: The no. 19357, a low-end starter outfit, was one of the many All Trade items produced in 1964. It was classified as a General Release Promotional Type IIb outfit. The 19357, which

Lionel sold for $6.00 each, has yet to be linked to a specific retailer.

This outfit was led by a no. 1060-25 Steam Type Locomotive. This steamer, which went forward only, was nearing the end of its product life; in fact, the 19357 was its only outfit appearance in 1964.

All the items were carried over from earlier years and marked "surplus sets" on the Factory Order. The outfit quantity of 1,984 units was likely determined from the remaining inventory of one of these items.

The only car of note was the no. 6050-175 Libby Box Car. First introduced in the no. 19263 "Libby" outfit from 1963, it was being depleted in outfits through 1965.

The rolling stock in the 19357 followed the normal truck and coupler progression for 1964, with all the cars having AAR types. Most were equipped non-operating trucks and couplers. However, the no. 1061T-25 Tender and unmarked yellow no. 6167-50 Caboose had one non-operating and one plain type.

The no. 64-162 White RSC with Orange Graphics outfit box was manufactured by St. Joe Paper Co. - Container Div. and measured 11⅜ x 9¾ x 6⅛ inches. It included four lines of data as part of its box manufacturer's certificate.

Even with 1,984 units produced, the 19357 is still a very difficult outfit to find.

Customer: All Trade
Original Amount: Killed
Factory Order Date: 4/24/1964
Date Issued: 5/11/64
Packaging: RSC Pack

Contents: 1062-25 Steam Type Loco. W/Light & Reversing Unit; 1061T-25 Tender; 6402-25 Flat Car W/2 Reels; 40-11 Cable Reels (2); 6042-250 Gondola Car; 6067-25 Caboose; 1013 Curved Track (8); 1018 Straight Track (2); 1026-25 25-Watt

Transformer; 1103-20 Envelope Packed; 1-65 Warranty Card; Form 3063 Parts Order Form; D64-50 Accessory Catalog; 927-64 Service Station List

Comments: The Factory Order for no. 19358 was marked "Set Not Used, Killed 5/11/64". It was intended to be a General Release Promotional Type IIb outfit. This listing is provided here for historical reference.

Description: "O27" Special Train Set
Specification: 6 Unit "O27" Special Train Set
Customer: *A
Customer: A. Cohen
Original Amount: ~~5,000~~ Not Using
Factory Order Date: 4/24/1964
Date Issued: 5/10/64
Packaging: RSC Pack (Units Loose)

Contents: 1062-50 Steam Type Loco. W/Light & Reversing Unit; 1061T-25 Tender; 6050-175 Libby Box Car; 6042-250

Gondola Car; 3309-25 Turbo Missile Firing Car (Less Missiles); 0349-10 Turbo Missile (2); 6067-25 Caboose; 1010-25 35-Watt Transformer; 1013 Curved Track (8); 1018 Straight Track (4); 1103-20 Envelope Packed; 3309-5 Instruction Sheet; 1-65 Warranty Card; Form 3063 Parts Order Form; D64-50 Accessory Catalog; 927-64 Service Station List

Comments: The Factory Order for no. 19362 was marked "Not Using". It was intended to be a General Release Promotional Type IIb outfit. This listing is provided here for historical reference.

Outfit no. 19363 was a low-end starter outfit originally sold to Interstate Department Stores - White Front Stores. Along the way, Lionel offered it to other retailers, although any particular one has yet to be identified.

Description: "O27" Special Train Set
Specification: 5 Unit "O27" Special Train Set
Customer: Interstate Department Stores - White Front Stores
Original Amount: 4,000
Factory Order Date: 4/24/1964
Date Issued: 5/10/64
Packaging: RSC Pack (Units Loose)

Contents: 1061-50 Steam Loco With Tire; 1061T-50 Tender; 6042-125 Gondola Car; 6076-75 Hopper Car - Black; 6167-25 Caboose; 1013 Curved Track (8); 1018 Straight Track (2); 1026-25 25-Watt Transformer; 1103-20 Envelope Packed; 11311-20 Instruction Sheet; 1-65 Warranty Card; Form 3063 Parts Order Form; D64-50 Accessory Catalog; 927-64 Service Station List

Boxes & Packing: 62-246 Outfit Box; 62-247 Shipper for 4 (1-4)

19363 (1964)	C6	C7	C8	Rarity
Complete Outfit	155	255	375	R5
Outfit Box no. 62-246	75	125	175	R5

Comments: Lionel listed Interstate Department Stores - White Front Stores as the customer on outfit no. 19363. As with many outfits in 1964, Lionel offered the 19363 to other customers as well, with *Sales Bulletin* no. 13 from May 8, 1964, stating, "The following is a recap of O27 Train Specials restricted to accounts in individual markets on a first choice basis. If they are not selected in any one market by the account then at your discretion it is open to others." Consequently, the 19363, which cost a retailer $5.85 each, is classified as a General Release Promotional Type IIa outfit.

The 19363 was a low-end starter outfit comprised of surplus items. It was led by a no. 1061-50 Steam Type Loco W/Tire (new for 1964). This version came with a rubber tire as a traction aid, a feature that made it a slight upgrade of the no. 1061-25 Steam Type Locomotive. Even with this improvement, the 1061-50 (lacking a headlight and a lens) remained Lionel's low-end Scout steamer configured with an 0-4-0 wheel arrangement.

There was nothing too exciting about the rolling stock in this outfit. In fact, the most intriguing features were the trucks and couplers. The no. 6076-75 Hopper Car - Black was equipped with non-operating Archbar types, thus indicating that it was carried over inventory. The no. 6142-125 Gondola Car was stamped "6142" and normally came with one operating and one non-operating AAR truck and coupler. The one in this outfit had non-operating types. The nos. 1061T-50 Tender and 6167-25 Caboose were equipped with one non-operating and one plain AAR type.

The proper instruction sheets made reference to the 90-day warranty that Lionel instituted in 1963.

The 19363 used a no. 62-246 Tan RSC Mailer with Black Graphics outfit box. It was manufactured by Mead Containers and measured 11½ x 10¼ x 6¼ inches. These boxes were made of a thicker corrugated material (rated at 90 pounds rather than the normal 65 pounds gross weight) that allowed each outfit to be shipped in its outfit box. The manufacturer omitted any Lionel printing on the box top to leave room for a mailing label. The

a headlight.

The no. 3349-100 Turbo Missile Firing Car was the same as a no. 3349-25 Turbo Missile Firing Car except that it was equipped with one operating and one non-operating AAR truck and coupler. Its no. 3349-105 Instruction Sheet is very difficult to find.

The nos. 6142-125 Gondola Car, 6167-100 Caboose and 6176-50 Hopper Car (all new for 1964) were color, decorating or coupler variations of other cars. The new suffixes indicated the changes.

The rolling stock in this outfit followed the normal truck and coupler progression for 1964, with all the cars having AAR types. All but one were equipped with one operating and one non-operating truck and coupler. The 6167-100 had one operating and one plain type.

The no. 11440-10 Instruction Sheet made reference to the 90-day warranty that Lionel instituted in 1963.

The 19370 used a no. 62-246 Tan RSC Mailer with Black Graphics outfit box. It was manufactured by Mead Containers and measured 11½ x 10¼ x 6¼ inches. These boxes were made of a thicker corrugated material (rated at 90 pounds rather than the normal 65 pounds gross weight) that allowed each outfit to be shipped in its outfit box. The manufacturer omitted any Lionel printing on the box top to leave room for a mailing label. The box bottom had four lines of data as part of its box manufacturer's certificate.

Only 400 of the 19370 were made, thus leading to its R9 rarity rating. It is one of the more difficult of the Spiegel offerings from 1964 to find.

Spiegel purchased eight promotional outfits in 1964. The no. 19371, its high-end steam-powered offering, featured a no. 237-25 Steam Type Locomotive with Smoke. This example was mailed direct from Spiegel to the customer - the shipping label is still attached to the box top.

Left: The no. 19371 was stamped by Lionel. Right: The Spiegel no. 36 5284 was hand-stamped by Spiegel.

Description: "O27" Special Train Set
Specification: 8 Unit "O27" Special Train Set
Customer/No.: Spiegel; 36 5284
Original Amount: 801
Factory Order Date: 4/30/1964
Date Issued: 7/23/64

Packaging: RSC Pack (MO), (Units Loose)

Contents: 237-25 Steam Type Locomotive with Smoke; 242T-25 Tender; 6473-25 Rodeo Car; 6014-325 Frisco Box Car; 6465-150 Tank Car; 6142-100 Gondola Car; 6112-88 Canister (2); 6176-50 Hopper Car; 6119-110 Work Caboose; 1013 Curved Track (8); 1018 Straight Track (3); 6149-25 Remote Control Track; 1025-25 45-Watt Transformer; 1103-40 Envelope Packed; 909-20 Smoke Fluid; 11450-10 Instruction Sheet; 237-11 Instruction Sheet; D64-50 Accessory Catalog; Form 3063 Parts Order Form; 1-65 Warranty Card; 927-64 Service Station List

Boxes & Packing: 64-164 Outfit Box

19371 (1964)	C6	C7	C8	Rarity
Complete Outfit	290	450	535	R7
Outfit Box no. 64-164	150	250	350	R7

Comments: In 1964, Spiegel purchased eight promotional outfits: nos. 19353, 19368, 19369, 19370, 19371, 19371-500, 19372 and 19372-500. Lionel trains did not appear in a 1964 Spiegel catalog. As such, if it weren't for the Factory Orders and outfit box markings, these Retailer Promotional outfits might never have been linked to Spiegel.

The 19371 (Spiegel no. 36 5284), a Type Ia outfit, was Spiegel's high-end steam offering. Lionel charged it $12.00 for each outfit. Its contents were very similar to those of catalog outfit no. 11470, but the 19371 included a no. 6473-25 Rodeo Car and a hopper car of a different color.

The 19371 came in at least two other configurations, the nos. 19353 and 19371-500. Because of the far-from-optimal inventory management being done at Lionel in 1964, Lionel was unable to fulfill all reorders of the 19371 with the same items. As such, the 19353 and 19371-500 were issued as substitutions.

This outfit was led by a no. 237-25 Steam Type Locomotive with Smoke. This Scout steamer included a two-position reversing unit and a headlight and used a rubber tire as a traction aid. The later version with narrow running boards came in this outfit. Except for its 237 number, it was the same engine as a no. 238.

The streamlined no. 242T-25 Tender, green no. 6142-100 and

black no. 6176-50 Hopper Car were new items for 1964. All the other cars in this outfit were carried over from earlier years.

The no. 6473-25 Rodeo Car used a Type IIb body (cadmium yellow plastic with red lettering) with a partially filled slot caused by broken tooling. The no. 6014-325 Frisco Box Car had a Type III body. The "-110" suffix identified the no. 6119-110 Work Caboose as being unboxed.

The rolling stock in the 19371 followed the normal truck and coupler progression for 1964, with all the cars having AAR types. Most were equipped with one operating and one late non-operating truck and coupler. However, the 242T-25 had one late non-operating and one plain type, and the 6119-110 had one operating and one plain type.

The instruction sheets made reference to the 90-day warranty that Lionel instituted in 1963. A Type II no. 1103-40 Envelope Packed was included.

The no. 64-164 White RSC with Orange Graphics outfit box was manufactured by United Container Co. and measured 12⅛ x 11⅝ x 6½ inches. It included four lines of data, a "64" and four stars as part of the box manufacturer's certificate.

The 19371 was a successful Spiegel offering because the original Factory Order quantity of 400 outfits was increased to 801. Further demand led to the 19353 and 19371-500 being issued as substitutions. Of the three, the 19371 was produced in the largest quantity and so is the easiest to find. As with all Spiegel outfits, the 19371 is desired by promotional outfit collectors.

19371-500
1964

Specification: 7 Unit "O27"
Customer/No.: Spiegel; 5284-S
Original Amount: 500
Factory Order Date: 11/27/1964
Date Issued: 11-27-64
Date Req'd: A/O
Packaging: Any M.O. Packing

Contents: 239-25 Steam Locomotive With Smoke; 242T-25 Tender; 6014-325 Frisco Box Car; 6142-100 Gondola Car; 6112-88 Canister (2); 6465-150 Tank Car; 6469-50 Miscellaneous Car; 6167-100 Caboose; 1010-25 35-Watt Transformer; 1013 Curved Track (8); 1018 Straight Track (3); 6149-25 Remote Control Track; 1103-40 Envelope Packed; 909-20 Smoke Fluid; 1-65 Warranty Card; Form 3063 Parts Order Form; 11450-10 Instruction Sheet; 237-11 Instruction Sheet; D64-50 Accessory Catalog; 927-64 Service Station List

Boxes & Packing: 64-183 Outfit Box

19371-500 (1964)	C6	C7	C8	Rarity
Complete Outfit	415	700	925	R8
Outfit Box no. 64-183	250	400	500	R8

Comments: In 1964, Spiegel purchased eight promotional outfits: nos. 19353, 19368, 19369, 19370, 19371, 19371-500, 19372 and 19372-500. Lionel trains did not appear in a 1964 Spiegel catalog. As such, if it weren't for the Factory Orders and outfit box markings,

these Retailer Promotional outfits might never have been linked to Spiegel.

When Spiegel placed a reorder for the no. 19371, Lionel was unable to fulfill this request with the same items. It therefore issued the Type Ia no. 19371-500 (Spiegel no. 5284-S). The Factory Order stated, "500 Pieces of 19345 being discontinued and components are to be used for 19371-500". Nearly identical to the 19345, the 19371-500 added a no. 6469-50 Miscellaneous Car and deleted some track.

The Factory Order also indicated that the 19371-500 was a substitution for the 19371. Even so, the outfits had only four cars in common. Each 19371-500 cost Spiegel $13.00, which was one dollar more than what Lionel charged for the 19371.

The 19371-500 was led by a no. 239-25 Steam Locomotive With Smoke (new for 1964). This die-cast Scout steamer featured a two-position reversing unit, a headlight and a rubber tire as a traction aid. Except for its 239 number and lack of stripe, it was the same engine as a no. 241.

The no. 242T-25 Tender, green no. 6142-100 Gondola Car and red no. 6167-100 Caboose were new for 1964. All other cars were carried over from 1963. The no. 6014-325 Frisco Box Car used a Type III body.

The rolling stock in this outfit followed the normal truck and coupler progression for 1964, with all the cars having AAR types. Most were equipped with one operating and one late non-operating truck and coupler. However, the 242T-25 had one late non-operating and one plain type, and the no. 6167-100 Caboose had one operating and one plain type.

The proper instruction sheets made reference to the 90-day warranty that Lionel instituted in 1963.

The no. 64-183 White RSC with Orange Graphics outfit box

The no. 19371-500 was created to fulfill the re-orders of outfit no. 19371. A quantity of 500 of the no. 19345 was cannibalized to obtain the items included in this outfit. With the addition of a no. 6469-50 Miscellaneous Car and RSC packaging, the 19371-500 was developed. Other than the Spiegel shipping label dated December 6, 1964, and found on the bottom of this box, it has no Spiegel identifying marks.

was manufactured by United Container Co. and measured 12¾ x 10 x 6⅝ inches. It included four lines of data and "8-64" as part of the box manufacturer's certificate.

The 19371-500 was created in response to the success of the 19371 and Lionel's poor inventory management in 1964. With only 500 made, it is more difficult to find than the 19371. As with all Spiegel outfits, the 19371-500 is desired by promotional outfit collectors.

19372
1964

Description: "O27" Special Train Set
Specification: 8 Unit "O27" Special Train Set
Customer: Spiegel
Original Amount: 400
Factory Order Date: 4/30/1964
Date Issued: 5/10/64
Packaging: RSC Pack Units Loose

19372 (1964)	C6	C7	C8	Rarity
Complete Outfit	490	850	1,200	R9
Outfit Box no. 64-164	275	450	575	R9

Contents: 213P-25 "Minn. & St. Louis" Diesel Power Car; 213T-25 Motorless Unit; 6014-325 Frisco Box Car; 3364-25 Log Dump Car; 3364-8 Logs (3); 6176-75 Hopper Car; 6176-50 Hopper Car; 6142-150 Gondola Car; 40-11 Cable Reels (2); 6059-50 Caboose; 1013 Curved Track (12); 1018 Straight Track (3); 1020-25 90° Crossing; 6149-25 Remote Control Track; 1025-25 45-Watt Transformer; 1103-40 Envelope Packed; 3364-10 Instruction Sheet; 1-65 Warranty Card; Form 3063 Parts Order Form; 19214-10 Instruction Sheet; 211-151 Instruction Sheet; D64-50 Accessory Catalog; 927-64 Service Station List

Boxes & Packing: 64-164 Outfit Box; 62-224 Corr. Insert; 62-245 Corr. Insert (2)

Comments: In 1964, Spiegel purchased eight promotional outfits: nos. 19353, 19368, 19369, 19370, 19371, 19371-500, 19372 and 19372-500. Lionel trains did not appear in a 1964 Spiegel catalog. As such, if it weren't for the Factory Orders and outfit box markings, these Retailer Promotional outfits might never have been linked to Spiegel.

The 19372, a Type Ia outfit, was Spiegel's high-end diesel offering. Lionel charged it $17.00 for each outfit, which the Factory Order stated was a "no. 11480 plus log dump car, hopper and omit rodeo car". The 19372 also included a no. 6059-50 Caboose instead of the no. 6257-100 Caboose found in the 11480.

When Spiegel placed a reorder for the no. 19372, Lionel was unable to fulfill this request with the same items. It therefore created the no. 19372-500 (Spiegel no. 5283-S).

The 19372 was one of four promotional outfits from 1964 to be led by a no. 213P-25 Minn. & St. Louis Diesel Power Car (new for 1964). This Alco featured a two-position reversing unit, two traction tires, a headlight, a weight and an open pilot with a large ledge. The 213P-25 was paired with a no. 213T-25 Motorless Unit (also new for 1964).

The cars in this outfit were, with two exceptions, new for 1964. Carried over from 1963 were the nos. 6014-325 Frisco Box Car and 6059-50. The most notable item was the no. 3364-25 Log Dump Car, which was identical to the no. 3362-25 Helium Tank Unloading Car except that it carried logs instead of helium tanks. Surprisingly, Lionel packed two different hopper cars – nos. 6176-50 Hopper Car and 6176-75 Hopper Car – in this outfit (one of the few outfits to have two of them).

The rolling stock in the 19372 followed the normal truck and coupler progression for 1964, with all the cars having AAR types. All but one were equipped with one operating and one non-operating truck and coupler. The 6059-50 had one operating and one plain type.

The instruction sheets made reference to the 90-day warranty that Lionel instituted in 1963.

The no. 64-164 White RSC with Orange Graphics outfit box was manufactured by United Container Co. and measured 12⅛ x 11⅝ x 6½ inches. It included four lines of data as part of the box manufacturer's certificate.

The 19372 was a successful offering for Spiegel because the original quantity of 400 outfits was followed by an order for an additional 650. This new order was fulfilled with the 19372-500. As with all Spiegel outfits, the 19372 is desired by promotional outfit collectors.

19372-500
1964

Description: "O27" Special
Specification: 7 Unit "O27" Special
Customer/No.: Spiegel; 5283-S
Original Amount: 650
Date Issued: 11-27-64
Date Req'd: A/O
Packaging: Any Mail Order Packing

Contents: 215P-25 "Santa Fe" Diesel Power Car; 212T-25 "Santa Fe" "A" Unit; 6014-325 Frisco Box Car; 6361-1 Timber Transport Car; 6176-100 Hopper Car; 6142-125 Gondola Car; 40-11 Cable Reels (2); 6059-50 Caboose; 1013 Curved Track (8); 1018 Straight Track (7); 1047-1 Switchman With Flag; 6149-25 Remote Control Track; 1025-25 45-Watt Transformer; 1103-40 Envelope Packed; 1-65 Warranty Card; Form 3063 Parts Order Form; 211-151 Instruction Sheet; D64-50 Accessory Catalog; 927-64 Service Station List

Boxes & Packing: 19372-500-RSC Outfit Box; 64-177 Corrugated Insert

Alternate For Outfit Contents:
Use 6176-100 for 440 sets; Substitute 6436-110 for Balance of 210 Sets.

19372-500 (1964)	C6	C7	C8	Rarity
Complete Outfit	850	1,340	1,845	R9
Outfit Box no. 19372-500-RSC	350	500	600	R9

Comments: In 1964, Spiegel purchased eight promotional outfits: nos. 19353, 19368, 19369, 19370, 19371, 19371-500, 19372 and 19372-500. Lionel trains did not appear in a 1964 Spiegel catalog. As such, if it weren't for the Factory Orders and outfit box markings, these Retailer Promotional outfits might never have been linked to Spiegel.

When Spiegel placed a reorder for the no. 19372, Lionel was unable to fulfill this request with the same items. It therefore issued the no. 19372-500 (Spiegel no. 5283-S), a Type Ib outfit for which Spiegel paid $17.00 each.

The Factory Order indicated that the 19372-500 was a substitution for the 19372. Even so, the outfits had only two cars in common.

The 19372-500 was led by a no. 215P-25 Santa Fe Diesel Power Car (new for 1964). This promotional-only Alco featured a two-position reversing unit, two traction tires, a headlight, a weight and an open pilot with a large ledge. This was one of five promotional outfits from 1964 to include a 215P-25, which here was paired with a no. 212T-25 Santa Fe "A" Unit (also new for 1964).

The cars in this outfit were, with two exceptions, carryovers. New to the line in 1964 were the blue no. 6142-125 Gondola Car and the unmarked olive drab no. 6176-100 Hopper Car.

The inclusion of a boxed no. 6361-1 Timber Transport Car was curious. The norm was for it to come in an Orange Picture box in 1964. The Orange Picture boxed no. 6436-110 Hopper Car substitution does not affect the outfit price.

The rolling stock in the 19372-500 followed the normal truck and coupler progression for 1964, with all the cars having AAR types. Most were equipped with one operating and one non-operating truck and coupler. However, the norm for the 6361-1 and 6436-110 was operating types, and the no. 6059-50 Caboose had one operating and one plain type.

The proper instruction sheets made reference to the 90-day warranty that Lionel instituted in 1963.

The no. 1047-1 Switchman With Flag last appeared in a Lionel catalog in 1961. Lionel used six promotional outfits to deplete its remaining inventory. This accessory wasn't exciting, but its no. 1047-12 Folding Box was made of flimsy chipboard and did not survive well. It is extremely difficult to find in collectible condition with the top flap still attached.

The box for the 19372-500 likely was either a Tan RSC with Black Graphics or a White RSC with Orange Graphics outfit box.

This was the last of eight promotional outfits purchased by Spiegel in 1964. As with all the other Spiegel outfits, it is highly desirable.

Mutual Buying Syndicate's no. 19373 was, with the exception of the no. 6167-25 Caboose, comprised of surplus inventory. Lionel also sold this basic starter outfit to *A (an unknown customer) and Famous-Barr. The only noteworthy item in the 19373 was the no. 6475-50 Crushed Pineapple Car, which first appeared in the no. 19263 "Libby" outfit from 1963.

Description: "O27" Special Train Set
Specification: 5 Unit "O27" Special Train Set
Customer: *A
Cust./No./Price: Famous-Barr Co.; 32 M CL 12 M 264; $9.13
Customer: Mutual Buying
Original Amount: 4,000
Factory Order Date: 5/5/1964
Date Issued: 5/10/64
Packaging: RSC Pack (Units Loose)

Contents: 1061-25 Steam Type Locomotive; 1061T-25 Tender; 6475-50 Crushed Pineapple Car; 6042-250 Gondola Car; 6167-25 Caboose; 1010-25 35-Watt Transformer; 1013 Curved Track (8); 1018 Straight Track (2); 1103-20 Envelope Packed; 1-65 Warranty Card; Form 3063 Parts Order Form; D64-50 Accessory Catalog; 927-64 Service Station List

Boxes & Packing: 63-383 Outfit Box; 64-319 Corr. Insert

19373 (1964)	C6	C7	C8	Rarity
Complete Outfit	150	250	380	R5
Outfit Box no. 63-383	55	100	150	R5

Comments: In 1964, the Mutual Buying Syndicate cooperative was listed as the customer on 10 Factory Orders. (See Mutual Buying in the section on Lionel's Distribution and Customers.)

Lionel initially listed Mutual as the customer for outfit no. 19373. However, as was the case with many outfits in 1964, Lionel offered this one to other customers as well. As stated in *Sales Bulletin* no. 13 from May 8, 1964, "The following is a recap of O27 Train Specials restricted to accounts in individual markets on a first choice basis. If they are not selected in any one market by the

account then at your discretion it is open to others."

Lionel's sales staff was successful because documentation further identified *A (an unknown customer) and Famous-Barr (no. 32 M CL 12 M 264 for $9.13) as additional recipients of this outfit, which cost $6.47 each. Consequently, the 19373 is classified as a General Release Promotional Type IIb outfit.

The 19373 was a low-end purchase for these retailers. It was led by a no. 1061-25 Steam Type Locomotive. This stripped-down Scout steamer featured an 0-4-0 wheel arrangement and went forward only. It lacked a headlight, a lens and any sort of traction aid.

All the cars in this outfit were carried over from 1963. According to the Factory Order, all were taken from surplus inventory except the no. 6167-25 Caboose. The no. 6475-50 Crushed Pineapple Car was still being depleted from the no. 19263 "Libby" outfit from 1963. The nos. 1061T-25 Tender, 6042-250 Gondola Car and 6167-25 Caboose came unmarked.

The rolling stock in the 19373 followed the normal truck and coupler progression for 1964, with all the cars having AAR types. Most were equipped with non-operating trucks and couplers. However, the nos. 1061T-25 and 6167-25 had one non-operating and one plain type.

The no. 63-383 Tan RSC with Black Graphics outfit box was manufactured by United Container Co. and measured 11½ x 9¾ x 6 inches. It included four lines of data as part of the box manufacturer's certificate.

The 19373 was a success because the quantity was increased from 1,000 to 4,000. Even so, this outfit appears less frequently than its large production quantities would normally indicate.

Be aware that a listing for a no. D-19373 Display also exists. Its cost to retailers was $8.97.

General Release Promotional outfit no. 19374 was a low-end starter outfit linked to at least three end retailers. The example shown includes a Gimbel Schuster's price tag with no. 740 F4 for $9.88. Note the unmarked and unpainted yellow no. 6167-50 Caboose and gray no. 40-11 Cable Reels.

Description: "O27" Special Train Set
Specification: 5 Unit "O27" Special Train Set
Customer: *A
Customer/No./Price: Gimbels; 740 F4; $9.88
Customer: Kaufmann's
Original Amount: 1,201
Factory Order Date: 5/5/1964
Date Issued: 5/10/64
Packaging: RSC Pack (Units Loose)

Contents: 1062-25 Steam Type Loco. W/Light & Reversing Unit; 1061T-25 Tender; 6042-250 Gondola Car; 6402-25 Flat Car W/2 Cable Reels; 40-11 Cable Reels (2); 6167-50 Caboose; 1013 Curved Track (8); 1018 Straight Track (2); 1026-25 25-Watt Transformer; 1103-20 Envelope Packed; 11311-10 Instruction Sheet; 1-65 Warranty Card; Form 3063 Parts Order Form; D64-50 Accessory Catalog; 927-64 Service Station List

Boxes & Packing: 64-162 Outfit Box; 62-254 Insert; 61-173 Insert; 64-319 Insert

19374 (1964)	C6	C7	C8	Rarity
Complete Outfit	175	325	500	R6
Outfit Box no. 64-162	100	200	300	R6

Comments: The no. 19374 was a General Release Promotional Type IIb outfit that has been linked to at least three different customers. Lionel documentation and observations of actual outfits have identified them as *A (an unknown customer) and retailers Gimbels Schuster's (Gimbels) and Kaufmann's.

The 19374, which cost a retailer $6.25 each, was led by a no. 1062-25 Steam Type Locomotive W/Light & Reversing Unit. This low-end Scout steamer featured an 0-4-0 wheel arrangement and lacked a traction aid. According to its Lionel Engineering Specification, it was the "Same as #1061 but with the addition of Reversing Unit & Lamp".

The unmarked and unpainted low-end rolling stock in this outfit was carried over from earlier years. As noted on the Factory Order, all the items were taken from surplus inventory. The yellow no. 6167-50 Caboose is the most desirable of the cars.

The rolling stock in the 19374 followed the normal truck and coupler progression for 1964, with all the cars having AAR types (although the 6402-25 still could have non-operating Archbar types). Most were equipped with non-operating trucks and couplers. However, the no. 1061T-25 Tender and 6167-50 had one non-operating and one plain type.

Late in 1963, Lionel began to mold the no. 40-11 Cable Reels in gray plastic. This practice carried over into 1964, and the norm for this outfit was these harder-to-find reels.

The no. 64-162 White RSC with Orange Graphics outfit

box was manufactured by St. Joe Paper Co. - Container Div. and measured 11⅜ x 9¾ x 6⅛ inches. It included four lines of data as part of its box manufacturer's certificate.

The 19374 did not meet expectations because the original quantity of 2,271 was reduced to 1,201, which still is larger than typical. The number of outfits produced and the low-end components in them explain why this outfit does not command much collector interest. Even so, it does take some effort to find a complete outfit in C8 condition.

Frederick Atkins purchased the no. 19375 in 1964 as a follow-up to its no. 19243 from 1963. The 19375 was an RSC version of catalog outfit no. 11430 with the addition of a no. 6402-50 Flat Car W/2 Cable Reels, two no. 40-11 Cable Reels and two additional pieces of no. 1018 Straight Track.

Description: "O27" Special Set
Specification: 6 Unit "O27" Special Set
Customer: Frederick Atkins
Original Amount: 500
Factory Order Date: 5/5/1964
Date Issued: 6/3/64
Packaging: RSC Pack (Units Loose)

Contents: 1062-50 Steam Type Loco. W/Light & Reversing Unit; 1061T-50 Tender; 6176-25 Hopper Car; 6142-50 Gondola Car; 6402-50 Flat Car W/2 Cable Reels; 40-11 Cable Reels (2); 6167-125 Caboose; 1013 Curved Track (8); 1018 Straight Track (3); 6149-25 Remote Control Track; 1026-25 25-Watt Transformer; 1103-40 Envelope Packed; D64-50 Accessory Catalog; Form 3063 Parts Order Form; 1-65 Warranty Card; 927-64 Service Station List; 11430-10 Instruction Sheet; 1-66 Flyer

Boxes & Packing: 63-383 Outfit Box; 64-319 Corr. Insert

19375 (1964)	C6	C7	C8	Rarity
Complete Outfit	305	525	750	R8
Outfit Box no. 63-383	200	350	500	R8

Comments: The no. 19375 is a Retailer Promotional Type Ia outfit that Lionel sold for $7.50 each to Frederick Atkins (see the section on Lionel's Distribution and Customers). This outfit has yet to be linked to an end customer.

The Factory Order for the 19375 stated that it was a version of catalog outfit no. 11430 that now came in an RSC outfit box and whose contents had been modified. Added to the outfit were a no. 6402-50 Flat Car W/2 Cable Reels, two no. 40-11 Cable Reels and two additional pieces of no. 1018 Straight Track.

The 19375 was a low-end starter outfit led by a no. 1062-50 Steam Type Loco. W/Light & Reversing Unit (new for 1964).

This low-end Scout steamer featured an 0-4-0 wheel arrangement and a rubber tire as a traction aid. Except for the rubber tire, it was identical to the no. 1062-25 Steam Type Loco. W/Light & Reversing Unit.

The no. 1061T-50 Tender was a slope-back version with "Lionel Lines" stamped on each side. The "-50" version of the 1061T as well as the remaining cars in this outfit were new for 1964. The gray 6042-50, green no. 6142-50 Gondola Car, red no. 6167-125 Caboose and yellow no. 6176-25 Hopper Car were undecorated.

The rolling stock in the 19375 followed the normal truck and coupler progression for 1964, with all the cars having AAR types. Most were equipped with one operating and one late non-operating truck and coupler. However, the 1061T-50 had one non-operating

and one plain type, and the 6167-125 had one operating and one plain type.

Late in 1963, Lionel began to mold the no. 40-11 Cable Reels in gray plastic. This practice carried over into 1964, and the norm for this outfit was these harder-to-find reels.

The proper instruction sheets made reference to the 90-day warranty that Lionel instituted in 1963.

The no. 63-383 Tan RSC with Black Graphics outfit box was manufactured by United Container Co. and measured 11½ x 9¾ x 6 inches. It included four lines of data as part of the box manufacturer's certificate.

Only 500 of the 19375 were manufactured, but it does appear from time to time.

Description: "O27" Train Special
Specification: 5 Unit "O27" Special Train Set
Customer: Arlens
Factory Order Date: 5/11/1964
Date Issued: 6/2/64
Packaging: RSC Pack (Units Loose)

Contents: 1062-25 Steam Type Loco. W/Light & Reversing Unit; 1061T-25 Tender; 6502-50 Girder Transport Car; 6502-3 Girder Bridge; 6042-250 Gondola Car; 6112-88 Canister (2); 6167-25 Caboose; 1013 Curved Track (8); 1018 Straight Track (4); 1026-25 25-Watt Transformer; 1103-20 Envelope Packed; 11311-10 Instruction Sheet; D64-50 Accessory Catalog; Form 3063 Parts Order Form; 1-65 Warranty Card; 927-64 Service Station List

Boxes & Packing: 61-170 Outfit Box

19376 (1964)	C6	C7	C8	Rarity
Complete Outfit	275	505	750	R9
Outfit Box no. 61-170	200	375	550	R9

Comments: This Retailer Promotional Type Ib outfit was sold to Arlens in 1964. That discount retailer paid Lionel $6.83 for each outfit.

The Factory Order for outfit no. 19376 stated that it was the same as outfit no. 19253 from 1963 with the addition of a no. 6042-250 Gondola Car and four pieces of no. 1018 Straight Track.

The 19376 was led by a no. 1062-25 Steam Type Loco. W/Light & Reversing Unit. This low-end Scout steamer featured an 0-4-0 wheel arrangement and lacked a traction aid. According to its Lionel Engineering Specification, it was the "Same as #1061 but with the addition of Reversing Unit & Lamp".

The unmarked and unpainted low-end rolling stock in this outfit was carried over from 1963. The only car of note was the no. 6502-50 Girder Transport Car. It was molded in blue plastic and carried an orange plastic no. 6502-3 Girder Bridge.

The rolling stock in the 19376 followed the normal truck and coupler progression for 1964, with all the cars having AAR types. Most were equipped with late non-operating trucks and couplers. However, the nos. 1061T-25 Tender and 6167-25 Caboose had one late non-operating and one plain type.

The no. 61-170 Tan RSC with Black Graphics outfit box was manufactured by United Container and measured 11½ x 10¼ x 6¼ inches. It included four lines of data, a "63" and two stars as part of the box manufacturer's certificate.

The 19376 had the same locomotive and rolling stock as the nos. 19377 and 19377-500. They differed only in their track components and transformers. Of the three outfits, the 19376 and 19377-500 are the most difficult to find.

Description: "O27" Special Train
Specification: 5 Unit "O27" Special Train Set
Customer: American Wholesale Toy
Original Amount: 2,188
Factory Order Date: 5/11/1964
Date Issued: 6/2/64
Packaging: RSC Pack (Units Loose)

Contents: 1062-25 Steam Type Loco. W/Light & Reversing Unit; 1061T-25 Tender; 6502-50 Girder Transport Car; 6502-3 Girder Bridge; 6042-250 Gondola Car; 6112-88 Canister (2); 6167-25

Caboose; 1013 Curved Track (8); 1026-25 25-Watt Transformer; 1103-20 Envelope Packed; 11311-10 Instruction Sheet; D64-50 Accessory Catalog; Form 3063 Parts Order Form; 1-65 Warranty Card; 927-64 Service Station List

Boxes & Packing: 61-170 Outfit Box

19377 (1964)	C6	C7	C8	Rarity
Complete Outfit	125	225	400	R6
Outfit Box no. 61-170	50	100	200	R6

Comments: This Retailer Promotional Type Ib outfit was sold to American Wholesale Toy in 1964. That toy jobber paid Lionel $6.50 for each outfit.

American Wholesale Toy purchased one promotional outfit from Lionel, the no. 19377. It was the same as promotional outfit no. 19253 with the addition of a no. 6042-250 Gondola Car. The unmarked and unpainted rolling stock was typical of many low-end starter outfits of the era.

The Factory Order for the no. 19377 stated that it was the same as outfit no. 19253 from 1963, with the addition of a no. 6042-250 Gondola Car.

The 19377 was led by a no. 1062-25 Steam Type Loco. W/ Light & Reversing Unit. This low-end Scout steamer featured an 0-4-0 wheel arrangement and lacked a traction aid. According to its Lionel Engineering Specification, it was the "Same as #1061 but with the addition of Reversing Unit & Lamp".

The unmarked and unpainted low-end rolling stock in this outfit was carried over from 1963. The only car of note was the no. 6502-50 Girder Transport Car. It was molded in blue plastic and carried an orange plastic no. 6502-3 Girder Bridge.

The rolling stock in the 19377 followed the normal truck and

coupler progression for 1964, with all the cars having AAR types. Most were equipped with late non-operating trucks and couplers. However, the nos. 1061T-25 Tender and 6167-25 Caboose had one late non-operating and one plain type.

The no. 61-170 Tan RSC with Black Graphics outfit box was manufactured by United Container and measured 11½ x 10¼ x 6¼ inches. It included four lines of data, a "63" and two stars as part of the box manufacturer's certificate.

The 19377 had the same locomotive and rolling stock as the nos. 19376 and 19377-500. They differed only in their track components and transformers. Of the three outfits, just the 19377 appears frequently; the other two are difficult to find.

Be aware that a listing for a no. D-19377 Display also exists.

Description: "O27" Special Train Set
Specification: 5 Unit "O27" Special Train Set
Customer: Allied Stores
Customer: Pomeroy's
Original Amount: 200
Factory Order Date: 5/14/1964
Date Issued: 6/2/64
Packaging: RSC Pack (Units Loose)

Contents: 1062-25 Steam Type Loco. W/Light & Reversing

Unit; 1061T-25 Tender; 6502-50 Girder Transport Car; 6502-3 Girder Bridge; 6042-250 Gondola Car; 6112-88 Canister (2); 6167-25 Caboose; 1013 Curved Track (8); 1010-25 35-Watt Transformer; 1103-20 Envelope Packed; 19228-10 Instruction Sheet; D64-50 Accessory Catalog; Form 3063 Parts Order Form; 1-65 Warranty Card; 927-64 Service Station List

Boxes & Packing: 61-170 Outfit Box; 64-319 Corrugated Insert

19377-500 (1964)	C6	C7	C8	Rarity
Complete Outfit	485	735	1,000	R10
Outfit Box no. 61-170	400	600	800	R10

Comments: This Retailer Promotional Type Ib outfit was destined for Allied's Pomeroy's stores. Allied, which paid Lionel $6.85 for each no. 19377-500, might have sold this outfit to other retailers in its organization.

The Factory Order for the 19377-500 stated that it was the same as outfit no. 19377, but with a no. 1010-25 35-Watt Transformer instead of the no. 1026-25 25-Watt Transformer included in the latter.

The 19377-500 was led by a no. 1062-25 Steam Type Loco. W/Light & Reversing Unit. This low-end Scout steamer featured an 0-4-0 wheel arrangement and lacked a traction aid. According to its Lionel Engineering Specification, it was the "Same as #1061 but with the addition of Reversing Unit & Lamp".

The unmarked and unpainted low-end rolling stock in this

outfit was carried over from 1963. The only car of note was the no. 6502-50 Girder Transport Car. It was molded in blue plastic and carried an orange plastic no. 6502-3 Girder Bridge.

The rolling stock in this outfit followed the normal truck and coupler progression for 1964, with all the cars having AAR types. Most were equipped with late non-operating trucks and couplers. However, the nos. 1061T-25 Tender and 6167-25 Caboose had one late non-operating and one plain type.

The no. 61-170 Tan RSC with Black Graphics outfit box was manufactured by United Container and measured 11½ x 10¼ x 6¼ inches. It included four lines of data, a "63" and two stars as part of the box manufacturer's certificate.

The 19377-500 had the same locomotive and rolling stock as the no. 19376 and 19377. They differed only in their track components and transformers. Of the three outfits, the 19376 and 19377-500 are the most difficult to find.

Be aware that a listing for a no. D-19377-500 Display also exists.

19378
1964

Description: "O27" Special Train
Specification: 6 Units "O27" Special Train Set
Customer: All Trade
Original Amount: Not Quoted or Assigned
Factory Order Date: 5/18/1964
Date Issued: 5-18-64
Packaging: RSC Pack (Units Loose)

Contents: 239-25 Steam Locomotive With Smoke; 1060T-25 Tender; 6014-325 Frisco Box Car; 6142-100 Gondola Car; 6112-

88 Canister (2); 6465-150 Tank Car; 6167-100 Caboose; 1023-25 45° Crossing; 1010-25 35-Watt Transformer; 1013 Curved Track (16); 1018 Straight Track (3); 6149-25 Remote Control Track; 1103-40 Envelope Packed; 909-20 Smoke Fluid; 11450-10 Instruction Sheet; 1-65 Warranty Card; Form 3063 Parts Order Form; D64-50 Accessory Catalog; 237-11 Instruction Sheet; 927-64 Service Station List

Comments: The Factory Order for no. 19378 was marked "Not Quoted or Assigned". It also stated, "same as set no. 19345 w/ addition of 4 - 1013 Curve Track & 45° Crossing in place of a 90° Crossing." The outfit was to be a General Release Promotional Type IIa outfit. This listing is provided here for historical reference.

19379
1964

Description: "O27" Special Train Set
Specification: 5 Unit "O27" Special Train Set
Customer: Macy's
Original Amount: 1,000
Factory Order Date: 5/19/1964
Date Issued: 7/23/64
Packaging: RSC Pack

Contents: 1062-25 Steam Type Loco. W/Light & Reversing Unit; 1061T-50 Tender; 6502-50 Girder Transport Car; 214-3 Bridge Side; 6473-25 Rodeo Car; 6167-25 Caboose; 1013 Curved Track (8); 1018 Straight Track (2); 1026-25 25-Watt Transformer; 1103-20 Envelope Packed; 11311-10 Instruction Sheet; 1-66 Flyer; 1-65 Warranty Card; Form 3063 Parts Order Form; D64-50 Accessory Catalog; 927-64 Service Station List

Boxes & Packing: 64-162 Outfit Box; 64-319 Corr. Insert

Alternate For Outfit Contents:
Note: Substitute 6409-25 for 6502-50 as needed.

19379 (1964)	C6	C7	C8	Rarity
Complete Outfit	250	400	555	R7
Outfit Box no. 64-162	150	250	325	R7

Comments: After failing to buy any promotional outfits in 1963, Macy's ordered two Retailer Promotional outfits in 1964: nos. 19379 and 19391. The no. 19379 was a Type Ib - or a Type Ia, depending on substitutions. This outfit, for which Macy's paid $7.30 each, was its low-end steam-powered purchase.

The Factory Order for the 19379 stated that it was the same as outfit no. 19253 from 1963, with the addition of a no. 6473-25 Rodeo Car and two sections of no. 1018 Straight Track.

The 19379 was led by a no. 1062-25 Steam Type Loco. W/ Light & Reversing Unit. This low-end Scout steamer featured an 0-4-0 wheel arrangement and lacked a traction aid. According to its Lionel Engineering Specification, it was the "Same as #1061 but with the addition of Reversing Unit & Lamp".

The no. 6473-25 Rodeo Car used a Type IIb body (cadmium yellow plastic with red lettering). The Type II body had a partially filled slot caused by broken tooling.

Two updates in the rolling stock differentiated the 19379 from the 19253. First, the tender in the 19379 was a no. 1061T-50 Tender, which had "Lionel Lines" stamped on each side. Second, a red no. 6409-25 Flat Car stamped "Lionel" replaced the unstamped

After a one-year absence, Macy's returned to Lionel to purchase two promotional outfits: nos. 19379 and 19391 in 1964. The 19379 was the same as promotional outfit no. 19253 with the addition of a no. 6473-25 Rodeo Car. The no. 6409-25 Flat Car substitution is shown with a black no. 214-3 Bridge Side.

blue no. 6502-25 Girder Transport Car in the 19253. Both flat cars carried a black no. 214-3 Bridge Side. This substitution does not affect the outfit price.

The rolling stock in the 19379 followed the normal truck and coupler progression for 1964, with all the cars having AAR types. The 1061T-50 and no. 6167-25 Caboose had one late non-operating and one plain type, and the 6473-25 had one operating and one late non-operating type. All other cars were equipped with late non-operating trucks and couplers.

The no. 64-162 White RSC with Orange Graphics outfit box was manufactured by St. Joe Paper Co. - Container Div. and measured 11⅜ x 9¾ x 6⅛ inches. It included four lines of data as part of its box manufacturer's certificate.

The 19379 was issued in 1964 with an additional Factory Order listing a quantity of 49 in 1965. Since the only major difference in these two outfits related to their paperwork and transformers, they are considered the same outfit from a pricing and rarity standpoint.

19379
1965

Description: "O27" Promotional Outfit
Specification: "O27" Steam Type Freight Outfit
Original Amount: 49
Factory Order Date: 8/4/1965
Date Issued: 8-5-65
Date Req'd: 8-9-65
Packaging: (Units not Boxed)

Contents: 1062-50 Steam Type Loco. W/Light & Reversing Unit; 1061T-50 Tender; 6502-50 Girder Transport Car; 214-3 Bridge Side; 6473-25 Rodeo Car; 6167-25 Caboose; 1013-8 Curved Track (Bundle of 8 - 1013); 1018-10 Straight Track (Loose) (2); 1026-25 25-Watt Transformer; 1103-20 Envelope Packed; D65-50 Accessory Catalog; Form 3063 Parts Order Form; 1-165 Warranty Card; 926-65 Service Station List; 11311-10 Instruction Sheet; 1-66 Flyer

Boxes & Packing: 64-162 Outfit Box; 61-171 Corr. Insert; 61-173 Corr. Insert; 64-319 Corr. Insert; 63-384 Shipper for 4 (1-4)

Alternate For Outfit Contents:
Note: Sub. 1010-25 for 1026-25 also using 19339-10 Flyer.

Comments: The no. 19379 from 1965 was a General Release Promotional Type IIa repeat of outfit no. 19379 from 1964. The 19379 from 1965 included updated paperwork, a no. 1062-50 Steam Type Loco. W/Light & Reversing Unit, 1965 versions of the rolling stock and a no. 1010-25 35-Watt Transformer substitution. Everything else was identical to the 1964 version. Since there are no differences in the outfit packing, the 1964 and 1965 versions are combined from a pricing and rarity standpoint. (See the 19379 from 1964.)

F 836-2 LIONEL FAST FREIGHT SET 34.95 (Exclusive) ("O" Gauge) Smoke-puffing 6 car fast freight thunders down the rails, headlight illuminating the path ahead. With operating Rodeo Car, operating Cop and Hobo Car, Tank Car, Auto Transporter with 4 automobiles, N. H. Box Car, and Caboose. Complete with billboard set, trees, 12 curved and 4 straight track sections, 90° crossing, and 45 watt plug-in transformer. Automatic coupling and remote control uncoupling. Track layout 63" x 26". Ship. wt. 16 lbs.

Lionel's no. 19380 was listed as the no. 836-2 Lionel Fast Freight Set (Exclusive) for $34.95 in the FAO Schwarz Christmas Catalog for 1964. It provided plenty of action with a steam locomotive, two operating cars and a figure-eight layout. This was one of only three outfits to include the no. 972-1 Landscape Tree Assortment.

Description: "O27" Freight Special
Specification: 8 Unit "O27" Freight - Special Figure 8
Customer/No./Price: FAO Schwarz; 836-2; $34.95
Original Amount: 60
Factory Order Date: 5/21/1964
Date Issued: 6/3/64
Packaging: RSC Pack (Units Loose)

Contents: 237-25 Steam Type Locomotive with Smoke; 242T-25 Tender; 6473-25 Rodeo Car; 3357-25 Animated Hobo & Railroad Policeman Car; 3357-27 Box Packed; 6465-150 Tank Car; 6414-75 Auto Transport Car; 0068-3 Automobile Body (Maroon) (2); 0068-105 Automobile Body (Yellow) (2); 6464-735 "New Haven" Box Car; 6067-25 Caboose; 972-1 Landscape Tree Assortment; 310-2 Set of (5) Billboard Signs; 1013 Curved Track (12); 1018 Straight Track (3); 6149-25 Remote Control Track; 1020-25 90° Crossing; 1025-25 45-Watt Transformer; 1103-40 Envelope Packed; 237-11 Instruction Sheet; 909-20 Smoke Fluid; 1-65 Warranty Card; Form 3063 Parts Order Form; D64-50 Accessory Catalog; 927-64 Service Station List

Boxes & Packing: 19380-RSC Outfit Box

19380 (1964)	C6	C7	C8	Rarity
Complete Outfit	1,225	1,975	2,860	R10
Outfit Box no. 19380-RSC	650	1,000	1,350	R10

Comments: This Retailer Promotional Type Ib outfit listed FAO Schwarz on its Factory Order. The follow-up to that firm's no. 19267 from 1963, the no. 19380 appeared in the 1964 FAO Schwarz Christmas Catalog as the "Lionel Fast Freight Set (Exclusive)". It was listed as FAO Schwarz no. 836-2 for $34.95 (Schwarz paid Lionel $18.95 for each outfit).

The 19380 resembled the 19267, with both being led by a no. 237-25 Steam Type Locomotive with Smoke. This Scout steamer featured a two-position reversing unit and a headlight and used a rubber tire as a traction aid. The later version with narrow running boards came in this outfit. Except for its 237 number, it was the same engine as a no. 238.

As with all the Lionel train outfits offered by FAO Schwarz,

the 19380 included some of Lionel's higher-end rolling stock. The no. 6414-75 Auto Transport was new for 1964. The "-75" indicated that it came unboxed with operating AAR trucks and couplers and a new load. The new load was two no. 0068-3 Automobile Body (Maroon) and two no. 0068-105 Automobile Body (Yellow). Commonly referred to as "cheapie" automobiles, these items were derived from the nos. 0068-50 Motorized Stock Car - Red and 0068-100 Motorized Stock Car - Yellow. The Motorized Stock Cars were first issued as part of HO catalog outfit no. 6100 from 1961. The "cheapie" automobiles consisted of just the plastic car frame with simulated wheels molded as part of the body. In 1964, Lionel began using these highly desirable and hard-to-find items on flat cars and the Auto Transport Car (unboxed no. 6414-75 and boxed no. 6414-85).

Interestingly, the 6414-75 is one example where Lionel re-assigned a suffix after it was made obsolete. The 6414-75 was originally used for the 6414-75 Automobile Complete (Blue). The Automobile Complete (Blue) was made obsolete and its number re-assigned to the Auto Transport Car on 2-21-64.

The orange New Haven box car that was heat-stamped "6464725" was designated no. 6464-735 when it came in a box and no. 6464-750 when unboxed. The "-735" version came in this outfit.

The rolling stock in the 19380 followed the normal truck and coupler progression for 1964, with all the cars having AAR types. The nos. 242T-25 Tender and 6067-25 Caboose had one non-operating and one plain type. The norm for the nos. 3357-25 Animated Hobo & Railroad Policeman Car, 6414-75 and 6464-735 was operating trucks and couplers. All other cars were equipped with one operating and one non-operating truck and coupler.

The 972-1 Landscape Tree Assortment last appeared in FAO Schwarz no. 19267 from 1963. The 972-1 included fragile packaging that did not hold up well over time and so adds a substantial premium to the value of this outfit.

The box for the 19380 likely was either a Tan RSC with Black Graphics or a White RSC with Orange Graphics outfit box.

With only 60 examples produced, the 19380 is an extremely difficult outfit to find.

Description: "O27" Special
Specification: 7 Unit "O27" Special
Customer: Mutual Buying
Original Amount: 200
Factory Order Date: 5/25/1964
Date Issued: 6/1/64
Packaging: Any Carton OK, Units Loose

Contents: 1062-25 Steam Type Loco. W/Light & Reversing Unit; 1062T-25 Tender; 6502-50 Girder Transport Car; 6502-3 Girder Bridge; 6045-150 Tank Car; 6042-75 Gondola Car; 6076-75 Hopper Car - Black; 6167-25 Caboose; 1013 Curved Track (8); 1018 Straight Track (6); 1010-25 35-Watt Transformer; 1103-20 Envelope Packed; 19228-10 Instruction Sheet; 1-65 Warranty Card; Form 3063 Parts Order Form; D64-50 Accessory Catalog; 927-64 Service Station List

Boxes & Packing: 61-180 Outfit Box

19381 (1964)	C6	C7	C8	Rarity
Complete Outfit	450	720	960	R10
Outfit Box no. 61-180	350	550	700	R10

Comments: In 1964, the Mutual Buying Syndicate cooperative was listed as the customer on 10 Factory Orders (see Mutual Buying in the section on Lionel's Distribution and Customers).

Outfit no. 19381, sold to Mutual for $8.00 each, was one of its Retailer Promotional Type Ib steam-powered purchases. This outfit has yet to be linked to an end retailer.

The 19381 was led by a no. 1062-25 Steam Type Locomotive W/Light & Reversing Unit. This low-end Scout steamer featured an 0-4-0 wheel arrangement and lacked a traction aid. According to its Lionel Engineering Specification, it was the "Same as #1061 but with the addition of Reversing Unit & Lamp".

All the cars in this outfit were low-end offerings in 1964. The only new-for-1964 car was the no. 1062T-25 Tender. It included a copper ground spring riveted as part of the plain truck assembly. This spring helped keep the steamer from inadvertently reversing when passing over switches and crossings.

The 19381 marked the only appearance in 1964 of the no. 6045-150 Tank Car. That model was nearing the end of its product life.

The rolling stock in the 19381 followed the normal truck and coupler progression for 1964, with all the cars having AAR types. Most were equipped with non-operating trucks and couplers. However, the 1062T-25 and no. 6167-25 Caboose had one non-operating and one plain type.

The common no. 61-180 Tan RSC with Black Graphics outfit box measured 12¾ x 10 x 6¾ inches.

If it weren't for the low quantity of the 19381, it would be just one of the many low-end offerings of the 1960s. With only 200 manufactured, this outfit becomes a true collectible.

Description: "O27" Diesel Display Pack
Specification: 7 Unit "O27" Diesel Display Pack
Customer: L. A. Sales
Original Amount: 200
Factory Order Date: 8/3/1964
Date Issued: 8/4/64
Packaging: Display Pack (Units Loose)

Contents: 221P-25 Diesel Locomotive; 3349-100 Turbo Missile Firing Car; 0349-10 Turbo Missile (2); 6142-25 Gondola Car; 6076-75 Hopper Car - Black; 6475-50 Crushed Pineapple Car; 6502-50 Girder Transport Car; 6502-3 Girder Bridge; 6167-25 Caboose; 1013 Curved Track (8); 1018 Straight Track; 6139-25 Uncoupling Track Section; 1010-25 35-Watt Transformer; 1103-40 Envelope Packed; 3349-105 Instruction Sheet; 1-65 Warranty Card; Form 3063 Parts Order Form; D64-50 Accessory Catalog; 927-64 Service Station List

Boxes & Packing: 64-111 Box Top; 64-112 Box Bottom; 64-118 Corr. Insert; 64-119 Corr. Insert; 64-120 Corr. Insert; 64-121 Corr. Insert

19382 (1964)	C6	C7	C8	Rarity
Complete Outfit	490	885	1,150	R10
Outfit Box no. 64-111	300	600	750	R10
Complete Outfit With no. 61-107	640	1,085	1,400	R10

Comments: Toy wholesaler L. A. Sales purchased the no. 19382, a Retailer Promotional Type Ib, from Lionel for $9.54 each.

This outfit was led by a no. 221P-25 Rio Grande Diesel Locomotive. A low-end, unpainted yellow Alco, it featured a two-position reversing unit, a traction tire and a closed pilot and lacked a headlight.

All cars in this outfit were carryover models. The no. 6475-50 Crushed Pineapple Car was still being depleted from the no. 19263 "Libby" outfit from 1963. The no. 3349-100 Turbo Missile Firing Car was the same as a no. 3349-25 Turbo Missile Firing Car except that it was equipped with one operating and one non-operating AAR truck and coupler. Its no. 3349-105 Instruction Sheet is very difficult to find. The no. 6142-25 Gondola Car was nearing the end of its product life.

The rolling stock in the 19382 followed the normal truck and coupler progression for 1964, with all the cars having AAR types. Most were equipped with non-operating trucks and couplers. However, the 6167-25 Caboose had one non-operating and one plain type, and the 3349-100 and 6142-25 had one operating and one non-operating truck and coupler.

The no. 64-111 White 4-6-4 Steamer and F3 Lift-Off with Orange and Blue Graphics Type D display outfit box was manufactured by United Container Co. and measured 24⅞ x 15¼ x 3 inches.

Of interest, early Factory Worksheets stated that Lionel may have to provide 17 pieces with an acetate cover. This was likely a no. 61-107 Acetate Dust Cover last used in 1962. According to Lionel, the 61-107 was a "clear plastic shield [that] keeps merchandise dust free and safe from pilferage." This rare item adds a substantial premium to the outfit price.

The 19382 was the only outfit purchased by L. A. Sales. With only 200 manufactured, it is a difficult outfit to obtain.

Be aware that a listing for a no. D-19382 Display Pack also exists.

Description: "O27" Special Train Set
Specification: 5 Unit "O27" Special Train Set
Customer: Taubman's
Original Amount: 120
Factory Order Date: 7/29/1964
Date Issued: 7/30/64
Packaging: Display Pack (Units Loose)

Contents: 221P-75 Diesel Locomotive; 3349-100 Turbo Missile Firing Car; 0349-10 Turbo Missile (2); 6142-125 Gondola Car; 6176-50 Hopper Car; 6167-100 Caboose; 1013 Curved Track (8); 1018 Straight Track; 6149-25 Remote Control Track; 1026-25 25-Watt Transformer; 1103-40 Envelope Packed; D64-50 Accessory Catalog; Form 3063 Parts Order Form; 1-65 Warranty Card; 927-64 Service Station List; 3349-105 Instruction Sheet; 11440-10 Instruction Sheet

Boxes & Packing: 64-101 Box Top; 64-102 Box Bottom; 64-107 Corr. Insert; 64-103 Shipper for (6) (1-6); 64-104 Corr. Pad (2-6)

19383 (1964)	C6	C7	C8	Rarity
Complete Outfit	825	1,350	1,800	R10
Outfit Box no. 64-101	550	800	1,000	R10

Comments: Taubman's, a retailer based in Baltimore, purchased the no. 19383, a Retailer Promotional Type Ib, for $8.94 each. The Factory Order indicated that, except for the locomotive, this outfit was identical to catalog outfit no. 11440.

The 19383 was led by an olive drab no. 221P-75 Santa Fe Diesel Locomotive. This difficult-to-find Alco can be linked to only four promotional outfits. It featured a two-position reversing unit, a traction tire and a closed pilot and lacked a headlight.

The no. 3349-100 Turbo Missile Firing Car was the same as a no. 3349-25 Turbo Missile Firing Car except that it was equipped with one operating and one non-operating AAR truck and coupler. Its no. 3349-105 Instruction Sheet is very difficult to find.

The nos. 6142-125 Gondola Car, 6167-100 Caboose and 6176-50 Hopper Car were new color, decorating or coupler variations of other cars. Their new suffixes indicated the changes.

The rolling stock in the 19383 followed the normal truck and coupler progression for 1964, with all the cars having AAR types. All but one were equipped with one operating and one non-operating truck and coupler. The 6167-100 had one operating and one plain type.

The no. 64-101 White 4-6-4 Steamer and F3 Lift-Off with Orange and Blue Graphics Type D display outfit box measured 23⅜ x 11⅝ x 3¼ inches.

The 19383 is highly desirable for two reasons. First, it include the difficult-to-find 221P-75. Second, only 120 of these outfits were produced, which means one is very seldom seen. These two facts contributed to the 19383 having a rarity rating of R10.

Description: "O27" Special Train Set
Specification: 6 Unit "O27" Special Train Set
Customer: Jordan Marsh
Original Amount: 2,000
Factory Order Date: 7/22/1964
Date Issued: 7/23/64
Packaging: RSC Pack

Contents: 1062-50 Steam Type Loco. W/Light & Reversing Unit; 1061T-50 Tender; 6176-25 Hopper Car; 6409-25 Flat Car W/2 Pipes; 6511-15 Pipes (2); 6142-125 Gondola Car; 6167-100 Caboose; 1013 Curved Track (8); 1018 Straight Track; 6149-25 Remote Control Track; 1010-25 35-Watt Transformer; 1103-40 Envelope Packed; 310-62 Set of (3) Billboards; D64-50 Accessory Catalog; Form 3063 Parts Order Form; 1-65 Warranty Card; 927-64 Service Station List; 11430-10 Instruction Sheet; 19339-10 Flyer; 1-66 Flyer

Boxes & Packing: 61-170 Outfit Box

Alternate For Outfit Contents:
Substitute no. 19385-10 for nos. 11430-10 and 19339-10 as needed.

19385 (1964)	C6	C7	C8	Rarity
Complete Outfit	215	350	540	R6
Outfit Box no. 61-170	75	125	200	R6

Comments: Allied Stores owned several department stores in the 1960s and was a major customer of Lionel's. Among the stores owned by Allied was Jordan Marsh, which may have received outfits through Allied. Jordan Marsh did obtain outfits direct from Lionel, including the no. 19385, a Retailer Promotional Type Ia, for which it paid $7.80 each.

The Factory Order for the 19385 stated that it was identical to catalog outfit 11430, with the addition of a no. 6409-25 Flat Car W/2 Pipes and the substitution of a no. 1010-25 35-Watt Transformer for the no. 1026-25 25-Watt Transformer in the 11430.

The 19385 was led by a no. 1062-50 Steam Type Loco. W/Light & Reversing Unit (new for 1964). This low-end Scout steamer featured an 0-4-0 wheel arrangement and a rubber tire as a traction aid. Except for the rubber tire, it was identical to the no. 1062-25 Steam Type Loco. W/Light & Reversing Unit.

All the cars in this outfit, with one exception, were new for 1964. The 6409-25 was the only carryover, and an internal Lionel memorandum indicated that it came from surplus inventory. The latter point makes sense because the 6409-25 still had non-operating Archbar trucks and couplers. Although this car normally came with three no. 6511-15 Pipes, the one with this outfit had only two.

The no. 1061T-50 Tender was a slope-back version with "Lionel Lines" stamped on each side. The "-50" version of the 1061T was new for 1964.

Even though the Factory Order said the 19385 was identical to a 11430, three minor differences characterized the rolling stock in these outfits. First, the unmarked green no. 6142-50 Gondola Car, unmarked red no. 6167-125 Caboose and unmarked yellow no. 6176-25 Hopper Car in the 11430 were replaced by a blue

The Factory Order for outfit no. 19385 was last time that Boston-based retailer Jordan Marsh was listed as a customer. The 19385 was a low-end starter outfit that was based on catalog outfit no. 11430. It included updated versions of some of the cars as well as an additional no. 6409-25 Flat Car W/2 Pipes. The no. 19385-10 Instruction Sheet substitution is shown.

no. 6142-125 Gondola Car stamped "6142", a red no. 6167-100 Caboose with "Lionel Lines" and an unmarked gray no. 6176-25 Hopper Car, respectively. Be aware that Lionel evidently used the same part number for the unmarked gray and unmarked yellow 6176-25 Hopper Car.

The rolling stock in this outfit followed the normal truck and coupler progression for 1964. All but one of the cars had AAR types; the 6409-25 came with non-operating Archbar types. Of the other cars, most were equipped with one operating and one late non-operating AAR truck and coupler. However, the 1061T-50 had one late non-operating and one plain type, and the 6167-100 had one operating and one plain type. As a final note, the operating

coupler on the 6176-25 had an integral copper spring.

The proper instruction sheets for the 19385 made reference to the 90-day warranty that Lionel instituted in 1963. Early outfits included a no. 11430-10 Instruction Sheet and no. 19339-10 Flyer, both dated 6/64. Later outfits likely included the difficult-to-find no. 19385-10 Instruction Sheet dated 11/64.

The no. 61-170 Tan RSC with Black Graphics outfit box was manufactured by United Container and measured 11½ x 10¼ x 6¼ inches. It included four lines of data, a "63" and four stars as part of the box manufacturer's certificate.

Although the 19385 was produced in large quantities, it is still fairly difficult to find complete and in collectible condition.

Description: "O27" Freight
Specification: 4 Unit "O27" Freight
Customer: Johnson Dewalt
Original Amount: 500
Packaging: Display Pack

Contents: 1061-25 Steam Type Locomotive; 1061T-25 Tender; 6042-50 Gondola Car (Less 2 Canisters); 6112-5 Canister (2); 6167-25 Caboose; 1013 Curved Track (8); 1018 Straight Track (4); 1010-25 35-Watt Transformer; 310-62 Set of (3) Billboards; 1103-20 Envelope Packed; 11311-20 Instruction Sheet; D64-50 Accessory Catalog; Form 3063 Parts Order Form; 1-65 Warranty Card; 927-64 Service Station List

Boxes & Packing: 64-101 Box Top; 64-102 Box Bottom; 64-107 Corr. Insert

19386
1964

19386 (1964)	C6	C7	C8	Rarity
Complete Outfit	230	460	695	R9
Outfit Box no. 64-101	150	325	475	R9

Comments: Johnson Dewalt operated as a manufacturer's representative to the premium and incentive industry. The no. 19386, a Retailer Promotional Type Ib, was the last time that firm appeared on a Factory Order. Johnson Dewalt's cost from Lionel for each 19386 was $6.95.

The 19386 was led by a no. 1061-25 Steam Type Locomotive. This stripped-down Scout steamer featured an 0-4-0 wheel arrangement and went forward only. It lacked a headlight, a lens and any sort of traction aid.

The 19386 included only three items of rolling stock, which were all about as low-end as Lionel could make. The nos. 1061T-25 Tender and 6167-25 Caboose were unmarked and unpainted. The black no. 6042-50 Gondola Car (Less 2 Canisters) last appeared in outfit no. 1107 from 1960. It was making one of its final outfit appearances in this outfit.

When it came to trucks and couplers, the 6042-50 probably was still equipped with non-operating Archbar types. The 1061T-25 and 6167-25 had one non-operating and one plain AAR type.

The no. 64-101 White 4-6-4 Steamer and F3 Lift-Off with Orange and Blue Graphics Type D display outfit box measured 23⅜ x 11⅝ x 3¼ inches.

As with many low-end promotional outfits, the only feature of note relating to the 19386 was the small number produced. The outfit is seldom seen, hence its R9 rarity rating.

19389
1964

The no. 19389 was the only promotional outfit purchased by Morris Kirschman, a furniture retailer based in New Orleans. It was one of a few outfits to include both a steam and a diesel locomotive. The outfit shown here came from its original owner with all the trains still intact. This 19389 as well as the others we've observed came from Louisiana.

Description: "O27" Special Train Set
Specification: "O27" Special Train Set
Customer: Morris Kirschman and Co.
Original Amount: 400
Factory Order Date: 7/28/1964
Date Issued: 7/30/64
Packaging: WRSC Pack (Units Loose)

Contents: 1062-25 Steam Type Loco. W/Light & Reversing Unit; 1062T-25 Tender; 6465-150 Tank Car; 6502-50 Girder Transport Car; 6502-3 Girder Bridge; 6475-50 Crushed Pineapple Car; 6042-50 Gondola Car (Less 2 Canisters); 40-11 Cable Reels (2); 6167-100 Caboose; 1013 Curved Track (8); 1018 Straight Track (3); 1008-50 Uncoupling Unit; 1010-25 35-Watt Transformer; 1066-25 Alco Diesel; 1641-10 Instruction Sheet; 1103-20 Envelope Packed; 1066-10 Instruction Sheet; D64-50 Accessory Catalog; Form 3063 Parts Order Form; 1-64 Warranty Card; 927-64 Service Station List

Boxes & Packing: 64-164 Outfit Box

19389 (1964)	C6	C7	C8	Rarity
Complete Outfit	370	615	900	R9
Outfit Box no. 64-164	200	350	500	R9

Comments: The Retailer Promotional Type Ib no. 19389 was the only promotional outfit purchased by Morris Kirschman furniture stores of New Orleans. Kirschman's cost from Lionel was $12.00 each.

The 19389 was similar to the Richie Premium's nos. 19216 from 1963 and 19328 from 1964 in that it also included *both* a steam and diesel engine! Many original owners of these outfits still have complete outfits with both engines. But once an outfit leaves its original owner, one of the locomotives tends to be separated. Stories exist of collectors who purchased outfits intact and sold one engine. If it weren't for the Factory Orders, the fact that these outfits came with two locomotives might never have been revealed.

The steam engine in the 19389 was a no. 1062-25 Steam Type Locomotive W/Light & Reversing Unit. This low-end Scout steamer featured an 0-4-0 wheel arrangement and lacked a traction aid. According to its Lionel Engineering Specification, it was the "Same as #1061 but with the addition of Reversing Unit & Lamp".

The diesel locomotive was a no. 1066-25 Union Pacific Alco Diesel (new for 1964). This low-end engine went only forward, had a closed pilot and used a rubber tire as a traction aid. It appeared in just two promotional outfits.

The only new-for-1964 cars were the nos. 1062T-25 Tender and 6167-100 Caboose. The tender included a copper ground spring riveted as part of the plain truck assembly. This addition helped keep the steamer from inadvertently reversing when passing over switches and crossings.

The other cars in this outfit were carryover from earlier years. The no. 6502-50 Girder Transport Car was molded in blue plastic and carried an orange plastic no. 6502-3 Girder Bridge. The no. 6475-50 Crushed Pineapple Car was still being depleted from the no. 19263 "Libby" outfit from 1963. The black no. 6042-50 Gondola Car (Less 2 Canisters) last appeared in outfit no. 1107 from 1960. It was making one of its final outfit appearances in this outfit and came equipped with non-operating Archbar trucks and couplers.

The remaining cars followed the normal truck and coupler progression for 1964. All of them had AAR types, but the particular mix proved to be quite varied. For example, the 1062T-25 was equipped with one late non-operating and one plain type, while the 6167-100 had one operating and one plain type. The 6475-50 and 6502-50 were equipped with non-operating trucks and couplers, and the no. 6465-150 Tank Car came with one operating and one non-operating type.

Late in 1963, Lionel began to mold the no. 40-11 Cable Reels in gray plastic. This practice carried over into 1964, and the norm for this outfit was these harder-to-find reels.

The no. 1066-10 Instruction Sheet is very difficult to find. It was dated 8/64.

The no. 64-164 White RSC with Orange Graphics outfit box was manufactured by United Container Co. and measured 12⅛ x 11⅝ x 6½ inches. It has been observed with four lines, a "64" and six stars as part of its box manufacturer's certificate.

The 19389 did not meet Lionel's expectations because the original quantity of 700 was decreased to 400. This lower-than-average quantity and infrequent appearances of this outfit lead to its R9 rarity.

Description: "O27" Train Set
Specification: Special "O27" Train Set
Customer: Joe, The Motorists' Friend
Original Amount: 200
Factory Order Date: 7/28/1964
Date Issued: 7/28/64
Packaging: RSC Pack (Units Loose)

Contents: 237-25 Steam Type Locomotive with Smoke; 234W-25 Whistle Tender; 6162-25 Gondola Car; 6407-25 Flat Car W/Sterling Missile; 6407-11 Sterling Missile; 6050-100 Swift Savings Bank Car; 6059-50 Caboose; 1025-25 45-Watt Transformer; 1103-50 Envelope Packed; 1013 Curved Track (8); 1018 Straight Track (3); 6149-25 Remote Control Track; 909-20 Smoke Fluid; 147-25 Horn & Whistle Controller; 11450-10 Instruction Sheet; 237-11 Instruction Sheet; Form 3063 Parts Order Form; 1-65 Warranty Card; 927-64 Service Station List; D64-50 Accessory Catalog

Boxes & Packing: 19390-RSC Outfit Box

19390 (1964)	C6	C7	C8	Rarity
Complete Outfit	825	1,300	1,885	R10
Outfit Box no. 19390-RSC	425	625	825	R10

Comments: In 1964, Joe, The Motorists' Friend purchased two Lionel outfits: nos. 12827 and 19390. The 19390, a Retailer Promotional Type Ia outfit, cost Joe, The Motorists' Friend $12.70 each from Lionel. According to its Factory Order, the 19390 had the same motive power and rolling stock as the no. 19348, except that the no. 1061T-25 Tender in the latter was replaced by a no. 234W-25 Whistle Tender.

The 19390 was led by a no. 237-25 Steam Type Locomotive with Smoke. This Scout steamer featured a two-position reversing unit and a headlight and used a rubber tire as a traction aid. The

later version with narrow running boards came in this outfit. Except for its 237 number, it was the same engine as a no. 238.

The no. 6407-25 Flat Car W/Sterling Missile is highly collectible. It was part of 11 different outfits, with a total of 13,124 cars produced. It was also available for separate sale. The car was a red no. 6511-series flat car with a brake wheel and "Lionel" stamped on each side. The same flat car was used with the no. 6408-25 Flat Car W/5 Pipes.

The flat car is common, but the no. 6407-11 Sterling Missile is not. It was frequently separated from its flat car because it lacked Lionel markings. Manufactured by Sterling Plastics, it would have "Sterling Plastics" molded into the capsule bottom and rocket base.

The rolling stock in the 19390 followed the normal truck and coupler progression for 1964, with all the cars having AAR types. Most were equipped with one operating and one non-operating truck and coupler. However, the norm for the 234W-25 was one non-operating and one plain type, and the no. 6059-50 Caboose had one operating and one plain type.

When an outfit contained the nos. 147-25 Horn & Whistle Controller and 6149-25 Remote Control Track, five wires were required to connect these peripherals to the transformer. Lionel created the no. 1103-50 Envelope Packed for this purpose. It came with five wires, a no. CTC-1 Lockon and a no. 0190-25 Controller.

The proper instruction sheets made reference to the 90-day warranty that Lionel instituted in 1963.

The box for the 19390 likely was either a Tan RSC with Black Graphics or a White RSC with Orange Graphics outfit box.

With only 200 of the 19390 manufactured, it is a difficult outfit to obtain. As such, it easily deserves its R10 rarity rating.

Description: "O27" Special
Specification: 6 Unit "O27" Special
Customer: Macy's
Original Amount: 500
Factory Order Date: 7/27/1964
Date Issued: 7/28/64
Packaging: Display Pack (Units Loose)

Contents: 239-25 Steam Locomotive With Smoke; 242T-25 Tender; 6014-325 Frisco Box Car; 6142-100 Gondola Car; 6112-88 Canister (2); 6465-150 Tank Car; 6119-125 Work Caboose; 1020-25 90° Crossing; 1010-25 35-Watt Transformer; 1013 Curved Track (12); 1018 Straight Track (3); 6149-25 Remote Control Track; 1103-40 Envelope Packed; 909-20 Smoke Fluid; 11450-10 Instruction Sheet; 1802B Instruction Sheet; 1-65 Warranty Card; Form 3063 Parts Order Form; D64-50 Accessory Catalog; 237-11 Instruction Sheet; 927-64 Service Station List

Boxes & Packing: 64-111 Box Top; 64-115 Box Bottom; 64-119 Corr. Insert; 64-120 Corr. Insert; 64-118 Corr. Insert

19391 (1964)	C6	C7	C8	Rarity
Complete Outfit	525	750	1,050	R9
Outfit Box no. 64-111	300	400	500	R9

Comments: After failing to buy any promotional outfits in 1963, Macy's ordered two Retailer Promotional outfits in 1964: nos. 19379 and 19391. The no. 19391 turned out to be Macy's high-end steam-powered purchase. This Type Ia outfit cost the chain of department stores $13.65 each.

The Factory Order for the 19391 stated that its contents were identical to those in outfit no. 19345 except that it came with a work caboose.

The 19391 was led by a no. 239-25 Steam Locomotive With Smoke (new for 1964). This die-cast Scout steamer featured a two-position reversing unit, a headlight and a rubber tire as a traction aid. Except for its 239 number and lack of stripe, it was the same engine as a no. 241.

The no. 242T-25 Tender, green no. 6142-100 Gondola Car and no. 6119-125 Work Caboose were new for 1964. The 6119-125 represented an update of the no. 6119-style work caboose, now with an olive drab body and a black frame but without a number or a load. All the other cars in this outfit were carried over from 1963. The no. 6014-325 Frisco Box Car used a Type III body.

The rolling stock in the 19391 followed the normal truck and coupler progression for 1964, with all the cars having AAR types. Most were equipped with one operating and one late non-operating truck and coupler. However, the 242T-25 had one late non-operating and one plain type, and the 6119-125 had one operating and one plain type.

The proper instruction sheets made reference to the 90-day warranty that Lionel instituted in 1963.

The no. 64-111 White 4-6-4 Steamer and F3 Lift-Off with Orange and Blue Graphics Type D display outfit box was manufactured by United Container Co. and measured 24⅞ x 15¼ x 3 inches.

Compared to the 19345, the 19391 is much more collectible because only one third as many were produced. Also, the desirable 6119-125 was a component of the 19391, although many surviving examples of this outfit are missing this collectible car.

Outfit no. 19391 was Macy's high-end steam-powered purchase for 1964. Lionel created this outfit by taking General Release Promotional outfit no. 19345 and replacing its no. 6167-100 Caboose with a no. 6119-125 Work Caboose. The olive drab 6119-125 makes this a desirable promotional outfit.

Specification: 7-Unit Diesel Freight Set
Customer: Stix, Baer & Fuller

Contents: 213P-25 "Minn. & St. Louis" Diesel Power Car; 213T-25 Motorless Unit; 6473-25 Rodeo Car; 6176-50 Hopper Car - Black; 6142-150 Gondola Car; 40-11 Cable Reels (2); 6014-325 Frisco Box Car; 6257-100 Caboose; 140-1 Banjo Signal; 1013 Curved Track (12); 1018 Straight Track (3); 6149-25 Remote Control Track; 1020-25 90° Crossing; 1025-25 45-Watt Transformer; 1103-40 Envelope Packed; D64-50 Accessory Catalog; Form 3063 Parts Order Form; 1-65 Warranty Card; 927-64 Service Station List; 211-151 Instruction Sheet; 19214-10 Instruction Sheet

Boxes & Packing: 19392-RSC Outfit Box

19392 (1964)	C6	C7	C8	Rarity
Complete Outfit	450	775	1,125	R9
Outfit Box no. 19392-RSC	200	350	500	R9

Comments: The no. 19392 was a General Release Promotional Type IIa outfit that has been linked to Stix Baer & Fuller.

Description: "O27" Special Train Set
Specification: 9 Unit Special "O27" Train Set
Customer: Foley's
Original Amount: 144
Factory Order Date: 7/30/1964
Date Issued: 8/15/64
Packaging: WRSC (Units Loose)

Contents: 2029-25 Steam Type Locomotive With Smoke; 234W-25 Whistle Tender; 6465-150 Tank Car; 6402-50 Flat Car W/2 Cable Reels; 40-11 Cable Reels (2); 6176-75 Hopper Car; 6473-25 Rodeo Car; 6014-325 Frisco Box Car; 6142-75 Gondola Car; 6112-88 Canister (2); 6257-100 Caboose; 1013 Curved Track (8); 1018 Straight Track (11); 6149-25 Remote Control Track; 1073-25 60-Watt Transformer; 147-25 Horn & Whistle Controller; 1103-50 Envelope Packed; SP-1 Smoke Pellets; 675-33 Smoke Stack Cleaner; D64-50 Accessory Catalog; 310-62 Set of (3) Billboards; Form 3063 Parts Order Form; 1-65 Warranty Card; 927-64 Service Station List; 2029-5 Instruction Sheet; 11460-10 Instruction Sheet

Boxes & Packing: 64-166 Outfit Box; 64-169 Corr. Insert; 64-167 Shipper for 4 (1-4)

19393 (1964)	C6	C7	C8	Rarity
Complete Outfit	700	1,050	1,425	R10
Outfit Box no. 64-166	500	750	950	R10

Comments: Foley Brothers Dry Goods Co. purchased one Retailer Promotional Type Ia outfit from Lionel. The no. 19393 cost it $25.50 each.

The Factory Order indicated that this outfit came with the same motive power and rolling stock as catalog outfit no. 11500, but added the nos. 6142-75 Gondola Car with two no. 6112-88 Canisters and a no. 6473-25 Rodeo Car. It also had eight additional pieces of straight track.

Lionel created this promotional outfit by adding a no. 140-1 Banjo Signal to the contents of catalog outfit no. 11480. Both were led by a no. 213P-25 Minn. & St. Louis Diesel Power Car (new for 1964). This Alco featured a two-position reversing unit, two traction tires, a headlight, a weight and an open pilot with a large ledge. The 19392 was one of four promotional outfits from 1964 to include a 213P-25, which was paired with a no. 213T-25 Motorless Unit (also new for 1964).

Everything else in this outfit was new for 1964, with the exception of the nos. 6014-325 Frisco Box Car, 6257-100 Caboose and 6473-25 Rodeo Car. The 6473-25 used a Type IIb body (cadmium yellow plastic with red lettering). That body included a partially filled slot caused by broken tooling. The 6257-100, which came with a smokestack, had been reissued in 1963.

The rolling stock in the 19392 followed the normal truck and coupler progression for 1964, with all the cars having AAR types. Each was equipped with one operating and one non-operating truck and coupler except for the 6257-100; it had one operating and one plain type.

The box for the 19392 likely was either a Tan RSC with Black Graphics or a White RSC with Orange Graphics outfit box.

This outfit is seldom seen, hence its R9 rarity rating.

The 19393 was led by a no. 2029-25 Steam Type Locomotive With Smoke (new for 1964). This steamer featured a two-position reversing unit, a headlight and a rubber tire as a traction aid. Since the 2029-25 came unboxed (as indicated by the "-25"), the nos. SP-1 Smoke Pellets, 675-33 Smoke Stack Cleaner and 2029-5 Instruction Sheet were provided separately in the outfit box. The no. CTC-1 Lockon came in a no. 1103-50 Envelope Packed.

Two cars of note in this outfit were the no. 6257-100 Caboose and 6473-25. In 1964, the latter used a Type IIb body (cadmium yellow plastic with red lettering). The Type II body included a partially filled slot caused by broken tooling. The 6257-100 was reissued in 1963 and included a smokestack. All the remaining cars in the 19393 were common components of 1964 outfits.

The rolling stock in the 19393 followed the normal truck and coupler progression for 1964, with all the cars having AAR types. Most were equipped with one operating and one non-operating truck and coupler. However, the norm for the no. 234W-25 Whistle Tender was one non-operating and one plain type, and the 6257-100 came with one operating and one plain type.

When Lionel included the nos. 147-25 Horn & Whistle Controller and 6149-25 Remote Control Track in an outfit, five wires were required to connect these peripherals to the transformer. Lionel created the 1103-50 Envelope Packed for this purpose. It came with five wires, a no. CTC-1 Lockon and a no. 0190-25 Controller.

The proper instruction sheets made reference to the 90-day warranty that Lionel instituted in 1963.

The no. 64-166 White RSC with Orange Graphics outfit box was manufactured by United Container Co. and measured 15⅜ x 10½ x 7⅛ inches.

This was the only time that Foley's appeared on a Factory Order. With only 144 manufactured, the 19393 is yet another example of Lionel lowering the minimum quantity requirements for a unique promotional outfit. This small quantity makes the 19393 highly desirable and extremely difficult to find.

Outfit no. 19394 was one of 10 outfits to list Mutual Buying Syndicate on the Factory Order in 1964. The outfit shown was linked to Lit Brothers by a price tag (not shown) with no. 8Y 244 19394 for $12.00. The last appearance of the collectible no. 227P-25 Canadian National Alco Diesel Power is overshadowed by the last appearance of the no. 910-1 Navy Yard Cardboard Display (also known as the Atomic Sub Base).

Description: "O27" Special Train Set
Specification: Special "O27" Train Set
Customer/No./Price: Lansburgh's; 213 10 Y 19394; $10.00
Customer/No./Price: Lit Brothers; 8Y 244 19394; $12.00
Customer: Mutual Buying
Original Amount: 2,300
Factory Order Date: 8/7/1964
Date Issued: 8/8/64
Packaging: RSC Pack (Units Loose)

19394 (1964)	C6	C7	C8	Rarity
Complete Outfit With no. 910-1	6,450	9,650	13,000	R10
Outfit Box no. 61-170 For 910-1	250	350	500	R9
Complete Outfit With no. 908-10	1,215	1,725	2,235	R9
Outfit Box no. 61-170 For 908-10	115	225	300	R8

Contents: 227P-25 Alco Diesel Power Unit - "Canadian National"; 6050-150 Van Camp Savings Bank Car; 6076-100 Hopper Car - Gray; 6502-50 Girder Transport Car; 6502-3 Girder Bridge; 6067-25 Caboose; 1026-25 25-Watt Transformer; 1013 Curved Track (16); 1018 Straight Track (4); 1023-25 45° Crossing; 910-1 Navy Yard Cardboard Display; 1103-20 Envelope Packed; 19394-10 Instruction Sheet; 1-65 Warranty Card; Form 3063 Parts Order Form; 1105-10 Instruction Sheet; D64-50 Accessory Catalog; 927-64 Service Station List

Boxes & Packing: 61-170 Outfit Box

Alternate For Outfit Contents:
Note: Substitute 908-10 Scenic Station W/Tunnels when out of 910-1.

Comments: In 1964, the Mutual Buying Syndicate cooperative was listed as the customer on 10 Factory Orders (see Mutual Buying in the section on Lionel's Distribution and Customers). Outfit no. 19394 was one of Mutual's Retailer Promotional Type Ib diesel-powered purchases. It paid Lionel $7.50 for each outfit.

The 19394 has been linked to Lansburgh's (no. 213 10Y 19394 for $10.00) and Lit Brothers. A Lit Brothers advertisement appeared in the *Philadelphia Inquirer* of August 30, 1964, listing the 19394 for $12.00. It was Lit's entry-level diesel offering for 1964. This outfit has also been observed with a price tag of $7.99. (See Lit Brothers in the section on Lionel's Distribution and Customers.)

The 19394 marked the last appearance of the no. 227P-25 Canadian National Alco Diesel Power Unit. That locomotive moved forward only and featured a closed pilot, a headlight and a weight to aid in traction. Ironically, this low-end Alco is now a desirable collector piece.

Outfit no. 19394 is shown with the no. 908-10 Scenic Station W/Tunnels - Packed substitution. Note that the outfit box indicates to "Include 908 With This Set" and the 908's Kraft bag indicates "To Be Included With Outfit no. 19394."

SPECIAL LAYOUT INSTRUCTIONS

This special train outfit includes enough track to make up the layout shown below. You will have to transfer track pins from one end of the crossing to the other as shown by the arrow.

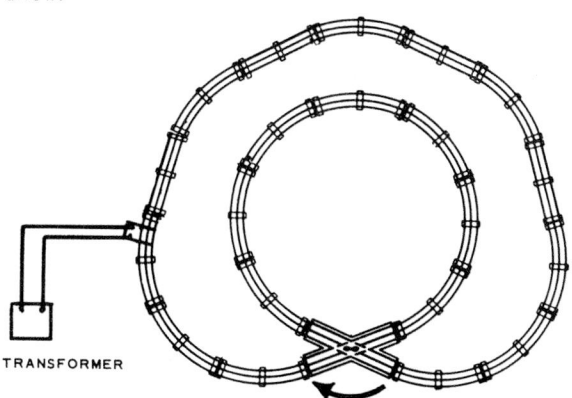

TRANSFORMER

THE LIONEL TOY CORPORATION

Printed in U.S. of America   19394-10 8/64

The rare no. 19394-10 Instruction Sheet came with outfit no. 19394.

Lionel was likely using the 19394 to dump surplus inventory. As such, all the rolling stock was carried over from earlier years. In fact, Lionel was finally depleting the last of the no. 6050-150 Van Camp Savings Bank Cars first issued in 1962. The 19394 marked one of the 6050-150's final two appearances. This car was equipped with non-operating Archbar trucks and couplers.

Also nearing the end of its product life was the no. 6067-25 Caboose. This unmarked red caboose with railings could still appear with one non-operating and one plain Archbar truck and coupler, although AAR was the norm in 1964.

The remaining cars in this outfit followed the normal truck and coupler progression for 1964. Specifically, they were equipped with non-operating AAR trucks and couplers.

The 19394 included the difficult-to-find no. 1105-10 Instruction Sheet that made reference to the 90-day warranty instituted in 1963. Lionel updated the warranty, but left the sheet date as 1-60. Also included was the rare no. 19394-10 Instruction Sheet that detailed the pretzel layout. It was dated 8/64.

What makes the 19394 one of the top promotional outfits is that it was the ninth and last outfit to include a no. 910-1 Navy Yard Cardboard Display (also known as the Atomic Sub Base). As was true with the other outfits containing a sub base, that item is what makes the 19394 extremely rare today. The 910-1 Navy Yard Cardboard Display was a fragile model intended to be assembled by the customer. There were no Lionel markings on this item, and it often became separated from the train outfit and was destroyed. Stories exist of individuals who discarded a 910-1 because they did not know what it was.

All 10 cardboard pieces that made up the sub base were placed in a plain, tan-colored flat paper bag. This was the second sub-base outfit that did not pack the sub base in the box. The 910-1 was shipped separately.

For the 19394, Lionel substituted a no. 908-10 Scenic Station W/Tunnels - Packed for the 910-1 in some outfits. The 908-10 first appeared in outfit nos. X-810NA and X-855 from 1959. After a four-year absence, it returned with outfit no. 19224 from 1963 and went on to appear in four other promotional outfits through 1964.

This large and fragile cardboard station was very similar to the 910-1 and was packaged in a large Kraft paper bag stamped, "To Be Included With Outfit no. 19394". There are at least three other versions of this bag. Two were stamped with outfit nos. 19244 and 19395. The third included no printing. Although the 908-10 is a rare item, it is nowhere near as difficult to find as a 910-1.

The pricing and rarity for this outfit assumes the inclusion of the 910-1's "How to Assemble Your Lionel Atomic Submarine Base" Instruction Sheet or the 908-10's "How To Set Up Your Railroad Terminal" Instruction Sheet as well as the difficult-to-find paper bags.

The outfit box was stamped to include a 908 or 910. Since these cardboard accessories came separately boxed, it was the task of the retailer to provide a 908-10 or 910-1 with each outfit.

The no. 61-170 Tan RSC with Black Graphics outfit box was manufactured by United Container and measured 11½ x 10¼ x 6¼ inches. It included four lines of data, a "63" and two or five stars as part of the box manufacturer's certificate.

Of the 2,300 outfits produced, almost 80 percent (1,800) were destined for Lit Brothers. Since Lit's advertisement illustrated and described a sub base – and every outfit box that we have observed with a Lit Brothers price tag was stamped, "Include 910 With This Outfit" – it's likely that at least 1,800 of the 19394s included a sub base.

Having said that, the 19394 with a 910-1 remains the much more desirable variation and easily achieves an R9 rarity rating for the empty box and an R10 for the complete outfit. Completing this outfit with the appropriate paperwork and cardboard display is a real challenge.

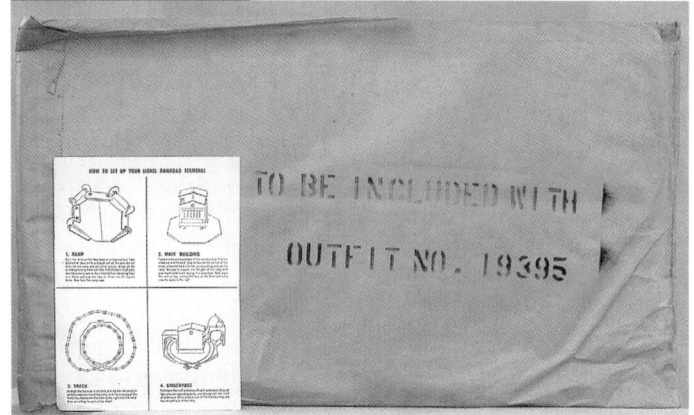

With each no. 19395 purchased, the retailer was to provide a no. 908-10 Scenic Station W/Tunnels - Packed. These fragile cardboard displays came in a Kraft bag stamped, "To Be Included With Outfit no. 19395".

Description: "O27" Special Train Set
Specification: Special "O27" Train Set
Customer/No./Price: Lit Brothers; 19395; $15.00
Customer: Mutual Buying
Original Amount: 675
Factory Order Date: 8/7/1964
Date Issued: 8/8/64
Packaging: RSC Pack (Units Loose)

Contents: 232P-25 Alco Diesel Power Car - "New Haven"; 6500-1 Beechcraft Bonanza Transport Car; 6445-1 Ft. Knox Gold Bullion Transport Car; 6409-25 Flat Car W/3 Pipes; 6511-15 Pipes (3); 6076-100 Hopper Car - Gray; 6067-25 Caboose; 1008-50 Uncoupling Unit; 908-10 Scenic Station W/Tunnels - Packed; 1013 Curved Track (16); 1018 Straight Track (3); 1023-25 45° Crossing; 1010-25 35-Watt Transformer; 1103-20 Envelope Packed; 1-65 Warranty Card; Form 3063 Parts Order Form; 122-10 Instruction Sheet; 230-6 Instruction Sheet; D64-50 Accessory Catalog; 927-64 Service Station List

Boxes & Packing: 19395-RSC Outfit Box

Alternate For Outfit Contents:
Sub. 231P-25 or 231P-1 Rock Island for 232P-25 as needed.

19395 (1964)	C6	C7	C8	Rarity
Complete Outfit	1,790	2,655	3,400	R8
Outfit Box no. 19395-RSC	150	300	400	R8

Comments: In 1964, the Mutual Buying Syndicate cooperative was listed as the customer on 10 Factory Orders (see Mutual Buying in the section on Lionel's Distribution and Customers). Outfit no. 19395 was one of Mutual's Retailer Promotional Type Ib diesel-powered purchases. It paid Lionel $9.50 for each outfit.

The 19395 has been linked to Lit Brothers through a newspaper advertisement in the *Philadelphia Inquirer* from August 30, 1964, that illustrated the outfit for $15.00. This outfit was Lit's mid-level diesel offering for 1964. Of the 675 units produced, 500 were destined for this customer. (See Lit Brothers in the section on Lionel's Distribution and Customers.)

The 19395 marked the last appearance of many items, starting with the no. 232P-25 New Haven Alco Diesel Power Car. The orange plastic 232P-25 featured a two-position reversing unit, a headlight and two-axle Magne-Traction. This locomotive was originally issued in 1962 catalog outfit no. 11232 and its RSC version no. 11235.

The unboxed no. 231P-25 and boxed no. 231P-1 Rock Island Alco Diesel Power Car substitutions do not significantly affect the overall outfit price.

Lionel used the 19395 to dump surplus inventory. As such, all the rolling stock was carried over from earlier years. The nos. 6445-1 Ft. Knox Gold Bullion Transport Car and 6500-1 Beechcraft Bonanza Transport Car were making their last appearances in this outfit. The norm for both was an Orange Picture box, although the 6500-1 could come in an Orange Perforated Picture box. Lionel must have struggled to find enough completed 6500-1s because a note on the Factory Order stated the need to "draw extra planes from the Service Department". Also nearing the end of its product life was the red unmarked no. 6067-25 Caboose.

The rolling stock in this outfit followed the normal truck and coupler progression for 1964, with all the cars having AAR types. The norm for the 6067-25 was one non-operating and one plain type. The 6445-1 and 6500-1 came with operating AAR trucks and couplers. All other cars were equipped with non-operating trucks and couplers.

The 19395 is very collectible because of the inclusion of a no. 908-10 Scenic Station W/Tunnels - Packed. This large and fragile cardboard station first appeared in outfit nos. X-810NA and X-855 from 1959. After a four-year absence, it returned with the no. 19224 from 1963 and went on to appear in four other promotional outfits through 1964. The 19395 was its last appearance. There were no Lionel markings on this item, which was intended to be assembled by the customer. The 908-10 often became separated from the train outfit and was destroyed.

Lionel shipped the 908-10s separately to the retailer. They came packaged eight at a time in their own box. Each 908-10 came in a large Kraft paper bag stamped, "To Be Included With Outfit no. 19395". There are at least three other versions of this bag. Two were stamped with outfit nos. 19224 and 19394. The third included no printing. The 908-10 also included an instruction sheet titled,

"How To Set Up Your Railroad Terminal". The pricing and rarity for this outfit assume the difficult-to-find "To Be Included With Outfit no. 19395" Kraft bag. Since the 908-10s came packaged separately, it was the task of the retailer to provide a 908-10 with each outfit purchased.

The box for the 19395 likely was either a Tan RSC with Black Graphics or a White RSC with Orange Graphics outfit box.

Finding a 19395 is a challenge. As with all five of the outfits that included the 908-10, it is highly desirable and collectible.

Outfit no. 19396 was Lit Brothers' high-end diesel offering for 1964. It marked the last appearance of the nos. 211PX-1 *Texas Special* Alco Diesel Power Unit and 211T-1 *Texas Special* Motorless Unit. With only 205 manufactured, this outfit is very difficult to obtain. The example shown has the unboxed nos. 211P-150 *Texas Special* Diesel and 211T-25 *Texas Special* Motorless Unit substitutions.

Description: "O27" Special Train Set
Specification: Special "O27" Train Set
Customer/No./Price: Lit Brothers; 19396; $18.00
Customer: Mutual Buying
Original Amount: 205
Factory Order Date: 8/7/1964
Date Issued: 8/8/64
Packaging: RSC Pack (Units Loose)

Contents: 211PX-1 *"Texas Special"* - Alco Diesel Power Unit; 211T-1 *"Texas Special"* - Motorless Unit; 6501-1 Jet Motor Boat Car; 6142-125 Gondola Car; 6050-175 Libby Box Car; 6176-50 Hopper Car; 6059-50 Caboose; 1008-50 Uncoupling Unit; 1013 Curved Track (8); 1018 Straight Track (5); 1103-20 Envelope Packed; 1010-25 35-Watt Transformer; 1-65 Warranty Card; Form 3063 Parts Order Form; 122-10 Instruction Sheet; 211-151 Instruction Sheet; D64-50 Accessory Catalog; 927-64 Service Station List

Boxes & Packing: 64-164 Outfit Box; 62-224 Corr. Insert; 62-245 Corr. Insert (2)

Alternate For Outfit Contents:
Sub. 211P-150 for 211PX-1; Sub. 211T-25 for 211T-1; Sub. 25 - no. 215P-25 for no. 211PX-1; Sub. 25 - no. 212T-25 for no. 211T-1.

19396 (1964)	C6	C7	C8	Rarity
Complete Outfit	740	1,235	1,660	R10
Complete Outfit With nos. 211P-150 And 211T-25 Substitutions	695	1,155	1,560	R10
Complete Outfit With nos. 215P-25 And 212T-25 Substitutions	725	1,160	1,570	R10
Outfit Box no. 64-164	400	650	850	R10

Comments: In 1964, the Mutual Buying Syndicate cooperative was listed as the customer on 10 Factory Orders (see Mutual Buying in the section on Lionel's Distribution and Customers). Outfit no. 19396 was one of Mutual's Retailer Promotional Type Ib diesel-powered purchases. It paid Lionel $10.80 for each outfit.

The 19396 has been linked to Lit Brothers through a newspaper advertisement in the *Philadelphia Inquirer* from August 30, 1964, that illustrated the outfit for $18.00. This outfit was Lit's high-end diesel offering for 1964. All of the 205 units produced were destined for this customer. (See Lit Brothers in the section on Lionel's Distribution and Customers.)

The 19396 marked the last outfit appearance of the boxed nos. 211PX-1 *Texas Special* Alco Diesel Power Unit and 211T-1 *Texas Special* Motorless Unit. The 211PX-1 featured a two-position reversing unit, an open pilot, a headlight and two-axle Magne-Traction.

Twenty-five of the 211PX-1s and 211T-1s were replaced by the nos. 215P-25 Santa Fe Diesel Power Car and 212T-25 Santa Fe "A" Unit. The remaining 211PX-1s were replaced by the unboxed nos. 211P-150 *Texas Special* Diesel and 211T-25 *Texas*

Special Motorless Unit. The 211P-150 was a cost-reduced version of the 211PX-1.

Both the 215P-25 and 211P-150 featured a two-position reversing unit, two traction tires, a headlight, a weight and an open pilot with a large ledge. These Alco substitutions affect the 19396's value, as listed in the pricing table.

Lionel was reducing surplus inventory with the outfits it supplied to Mutual. The no. 6501-1 Jet Motor Boat car was making one of its last two outfit appearances. It came packaged in an Orange Picture box. The no. 6050-175 Libby Box Car was first introduced in the no. 19263 "Libby" outfit from 1963. This car was still being depleted in outfits through 1965. All the other cars in the 19396 were common components of 1964 outfits.

The rolling stock in this outfit followed the normal truck and coupler progression for 1964, with all of them equipped with AAR types. Most came with one operating and one non-operating type. However, the 6501-1 had operating types, and the no. 6059-50 Caboose had one operating and one plain type. Also, the norm for the 6050-175 was non-operating AAR trucks and couplers although Archbar was possible.

The no. 64-164 White RSC with Orange Graphics outfit box was manufactured by United Container Co. and measured 12⅛ x 11⅝ x 6½ inches. It included four lines of data, a "64" and six stars as part of the box manufacturer's certificate.

With only 205 of the 19396 purchased, it is an extremely difficult outfit or outfit box to find. It easily earns an R10 rarity rating.

19397
1964

Customer: Mutual Buying
Original Amount: 350

Contents: 239-25 Steam Locomotive With Smoke; 234W-25 Whistle Tender; 6470-25 Exploding Target Car; 6651-25 Cannon Car; 6651-8 Shells (4); 6014-325 Frisco Box Car; 6401-25 Flat Car; 958-50 Truck; 6059-50 Caboose; 943-1 Exploding Ammo. Dump; 1013 Curved Track (8); 1018 Straight Track (5); 1008-50 Uncoupling Unit; 1073-25 60-Watt Transformer; 147-25 Horn & Whistle Controller; 1103-20 Envelope Packed; 81-32 24" R.C. Wire; 19398-10 Instruction Sheet; 6470-17 Instruction Sheet; 6651-10 Instruction Sheet; 1-65 Warranty Card; Form 3063 Parts Order Form; 237-11 Instruction Sheet; D64-50 Accessory Catalog; 927-64 Service Station List

Boxes & Packing: 19397-RSC Outfit Box

19397 (1964)	C6	C7	C8	Rarity
Complete Outfit	565	1,000	1,445	R10
Outfit Box no. 19397-RSC	200	400	600	R10

Comments: In 1964, the Mutual Buying Syndicate cooperative was listed as the customer on 10 Factory Orders (see Mutual Buying in the section on Lionel's Distribution and Customers). Outfit no. 19397, which Lionel sold for $15.50 each, was one of Mutual's Retailer Promotional Type Ib steam-powered purchases. It has yet to be linked to an end retailer.

The 19397 was led by a no. 239-25 Steam Locomotive With Smoke (new for 1964). This die-cast Scout steamer featured a two-position reversing unit, a headlight and a rubber tire as a traction aid. Except for its 239 number and lack of stripe, it was the same engine as a no. 241.

The 19397's space and military components make it a highly desirable and collectible outfit. The nos. 6470-25 Exploding Target Car and 6651-25 Cannon Car were paired together in this and outfit no. 19337. The 6651-25 was derived from the no. 6650-25 / 6640-25 Missile Launching Flat Car and included a new firing mechanism that fired shells instead of a missile. The base of the car was painted olive drab, whereas the top was molded in olive drab plastic.

The no. 943-1 Exploding Ammo Dump was making its final outfit appearance in the 19397. Lionel did not have enough of these in inventory to complete the factory order. As such, the Factory Order noted to "draw additional requirements from service".

The rolling stock in the 19397 followed the normal truck and coupler progression for 1964, with all the cars having AAR types. Most were equipped with one operating and one non-operating truck and coupler. However, the 6651-25 had operating types, and the no. 6059-50 Caboose came with one operating and one plain type.

The difficult-to-find 90-day warranty version of the no. 6651-10 Instruction Sheet came with this outfit. It was dated 8/64. Also included was the scarce no. 19398-10 Instruction Sheet dated 8/64.

The box for the 19397 likely was either a Tan RSC with Black Graphics or a White RSC with Orange Graphics outfit box.

This was one of eight outfits to include a 6651-25. That fact alone makes this a collectible outfit. Add in the small number of 19397s produced, and it achieves an R10 rarity rating.

19398
1964

Description: "O27" Special Train Set
Specification: Special "O27" Train Set
Customer/No./Price: Lit Brothers; 19398; $29.00
Customer: Mutual Buying
Original Amount: 400
Factory Order Date: 8/7/1964

Date Issued: 8/8/64
Packaging: RSC Pack (Units Loose)

Contents: 2029-25 Steam Type Locomotive With Smoke; 234W-25 Whistle Tender; 6473-25 Rodeo Car; 6463-1 Rocket Fuel Car; 6014-325 Frisco Box Car; 6402-50 Flat Car W/2 Cable Reels; 6059-50 Caboose; 1013 Curved Track (12); 1018 Straight Track (7); 1008-50 Uncoupling Unit; 1020-25 90° Crossing; 1073-25 60-Watt Transformer; 147-25 Horn & Whistle Controller; 252-1

Automatic Crossing Gate; 1047-1 Switchman With Flag; 1103-20 Envelope Packed; 81-32 24" R.C. Wire; SP-1 Smoke Pellets; 675-33 Smoke Stack Cleaner; 19398-10 Instruction Sheet; 2029-5 Instruction Sheet; 1802-10 Instruction Sheet; 1-65 Warranty Card; Form 3063 Parts Order Form; D64-50 Accessory Catalog; 927-64 Service Station List

Boxes & Packing: 19398-RSC Outfit Box

19398 (1964)	C6	C7	C8	Rarity
Complete Outfit	725	1,245	1,825	R9
Outfit Box no. 19398-RSC	250	425	600	R9

Comments: In 1964, the Mutual Buying Syndicate cooperative was listed as the customer on 10 Factory Orders (see Mutual Buying in the section on Lionel's Distribution and Customers). Outfit no. 19398 was one of Mutual's Retailer Promotional Type Ia steam-powered purchases. It paid Lionel $22.90 for each outfit.

The 19398 has been linked to Lit Brothers through a newspaper advertisement in the *Philadelphia Inquirer* from August 30, 1964, that illustrated the outfit for $29.00. This outfit was Lit's high-end steam offering for 1964. Of the 400 units produced, 300 were destined for this customer. (See Lit Brothers in the section on Lionel's Distribution and Customers.)

The 19398 was led by a no. 2029-25 Steam Type Locomotive With Smoke (new for 1964). This steamer featured a two-position reversing unit, a headlight and a rubber tire as a traction aid. Since the 2029-25 came unboxed (as indicated by the "-25"), the nos. SP-1 Smoke Pellets, 675-33 Smoke Stack Cleaner and 2029-5 Instruction Sheet were provided separately in the outfit box. The no. CTC-1 Lockon came in a no. 1103-20 Envelope Packed.

All but one of the cars in this outfit were carried over. The newcomer was the no. 6402-50 Flat Car W/2 Cable Reels. The 6463-1 Rocket Fuel Car was making its only outfit appearance in 1964; it came packaged in an Orange Picture box.

The rolling stock in the 19398 followed the normal truck and coupler progression for 1964, with all the cars having AAR types. Most were equipped with one operating and one non-operating truck and coupler. However, the norm for the 234W-25 Whistle Tender was one non-operating and one plain type, and the no. 6059-50 Caboose had one operating and one plain type. Be aware that the 6463-1 could come with two operating trucks and couplers.

The proper instruction sheets made reference to the 90-day warranty that Lionel instituted in 1963. The difficult-to-find no. 19398-10 Instruction Sheet was introduced with this outfit. It was dated 8/64. A no. 1802-10 Instruction Sheet detailed the figure-eight track layout.

The no. 1047-1 Switchman With Flag last appeared in a Lionel catalog in 1961. Lionel used six promotional outfits to deplete its remaining inventory. This accessory wasn't exciting, but its no. 1047-12 Folding Box was made of flimsy chipboard and did not survive well. It is extremely difficult to find in collectible condition with the top flap still attached.

The 252-1 Automatic Crossing Gate made its last outfit appearance in the 19398.

The Factory Order for this outfit stated, "pack in any RSC (cheapest)". The box likely was either a Tan RSC with Black Graphics or a White RSC with Orange Graphics outfit box.

With only 400 units produced, the 19398 is a difficult outfit to find.

Description: "O27" Special Train Set
Specification: Special "O27" Train Set
Customer: Mutual Buying
Customer: Stanley Marcus
Original Amount: 50
Factory Order Date: 8/10/1964
Date Issued: 8/10/64
Packaging: RSC Pack (Units Loose)

Contents: 215P-25 "Santa Fe" Diesel Power Car; 212T-25 "Santa Fe" "A" Unit; 6501-1 Jet Motor Boat Car; 6142-125 Gondola Car; 6050-175 Libby Box Car; 6176-50 Hopper Car; 6465-150 Tank Car; 6059-50 Caboose; 1008-50 Uncoupling Unit; 1013 Curved Track (8); 1018 Straight Track (5); 1103-20 Envelope Packed; 1010-25 35-Watt Transformer; 211-151 Instruction Sheet; 122-10 Instruction Sheet; 1-65 Warranty Card; Form 3063 Parts Order Form; D64-50 Accessory Catalog; 927-64 Service Station List

Boxes & Packing: 64-164 Outfit Box

19399 (1964)	C6	C7	C8	Rarity
Complete Outfit	1,030	1,600	2,225	R10
Outfit Box no. 64-164	700	1,100	1,500	R10

Comments: In 1964, the Mutual Buying Syndicate cooperative was listed as the customer on 10 Factory Orders (see Mutual Buying

in the section on Lionel's Distribution and Customers). Outfit no. 19399 was one of Mutual's Retailer Promotional Type Ib diesel-powered purchases. It paid Lionel $11.00 for each outfit.

The Factory Order for this outfit stated, "Mutual for Stan Marcus". In 1964, Stanley Marcus was chief executive officer of high-end retailer Neiman Marcus; it therefore was possible that these outfits were destined for that retailer.

The contents of the 19399 were, with one exception, identical to those of the no. 19396. However, the former outfit also came with a no. 6465-150 Tank Car. The original quantity of the 19396 was 255, but it was reduced to 205. The extra 50 outfits were likely used for the 19399

The 19399 was led by a no. 215P-25 Santa Fe Diesel Power Car (new for 1964). This promotional-only Alco featured a two-position reversing unit, two traction tires, a headlight, a weight and an open pilot with a large ledge. This was one of five promotional outfits from 1964 to include a 215P-25, which was paired with a no. 212T-25 Santa Fe "A" Unit (also new for 1964).

(See the entry for 19396 for information about the rolling stock and outfit packing).

As with many promotional outfits, the outfit box is difficult to find, but the components are not. With only 50 manufactured, finding a 19399 or its outfit box is a true challenge.

Description: "O27" Special
Specification: 6 Unit "O27" Special
Customer: Madison Hardware
Original Amount: 100
Date Issued: 8-11-64
Packaging: Individually Boxed for Bulk Packing

Contents: 2029-1 Steam Type Locomotive With Smoke; 234W-1 Whistle Tender; 2404-1 Vista Dome; 2405-1 Pullman Car (2); 2406-1 Observation Car; 1044-1 90-Watt Transformer; 1013 Curved Track (8); 1018 Straight Track (5); 6019-1 Remote Control Track Set; 1103-40 Envelope Packed; 32 Straight Track (24)

Alternate For Outfit Contents:
Note: Add 24 #32 Super "O" Straight track per each set to be packed in Bulk. Total 2,400.

19400 (1964)	C6	C7	C8	Rarity
Items Only	390	710	1,025	N/A

Comments: Madison Hardware Co. of New York purchased what were known as "bulk outfits." (For an explanation of the practice of buying "bulk outfits," consult the entry on Madison Hardware Co. in the section on Lionel's Distribution and Customers.)

Madison purchased bulk-packed outfits nos. 19400 and 19417 in 1964. Both were Retailer Promotional Type Ia outfits. Madison paid Lionel $29.00 for each 19400.

When you look at the contents of the 19400 and 19417, it is obvious that Madison was splitting up part of its separate-sale order across multiple "outfits" to take advantage of the inherent outfit discount. In reality, an outfit could have been created from the locomotive and cars, but the Super O straight track was added to achieve a greater discount on the track.

No individual outfit boxes have been observed for any bulk outfit listed in this volume. As a result, we cannot ascertain whether these items were ever assembled and sold as an outfit. Even if they were, we cannot prove that Madison Hardware designated the groupings as 19400 or 19417.

This bulk-packed 19400 included a no. 2029-1 Steam Type Locomotive With Smoke (new for 1964). This steamer featured a two-position reversing unit, a headlight and a rubber tire as a traction aid. Inside its individual no. 2029-6 Corr. Box were the nos. CTC-1 Lockon, SP-1 Smoke Pellets, 675-33 Smoke Stack Cleaner and 2029-5 Instruction Sheet. The 2029-1 was paired with a no. 234W-1 Whistle Tender that came in an Orange Picture box.

The three no. 2400-series Santa Fe passenger cars were new for 1964. They came individually packed in Orange Picture boxes.

A listing for this outfit is provided here because a Factory Order exists for the 19400. Pricing is provided as reference for the items alone. However, as stated earlier in this volume, items alone do not constitute an outfit; an outfit box is required.

It is unknown what Madison Hardware did with these items. For that reason, finding any box with 19400 markings would be a true discovery.

Description: "O27" Special
Specification: 5 Unit "O27" Special
Customer: Mutual Buying
Customer: Lit Brothers
Original Amount: 900
Factory Order Date: 8/21/1964
Date Issued: 8-20-64
Packaging: Any RSC

Contents: 1061-25 Steam Type Locomotive; 1061T-25 Tender; 6409-25 Flat Car W/3 Pipes; 6511-15 Pipes (3); 6042-25 Gondola Car - Blue; 6047-25 Caboose; 1013 Curved Track (8); 1018 Straight Track (2); 1103-20 Envelope Packed; 1026-25 25-Watt Transformer; 975-1 Squad of Soldiers; 958-175 Cannon Assembled; 958-150 Jeep Assembled; 958-50 Truck; 11311-20 Instruction Sheet; 1-65 Warranty Card; Form 3063 Parts Order Form; D64-50 Accessory Catalog; 927-64 Service Station List

Boxes & Packing: 19405-RSC Outfit Box

19405 (1964)	C6	C7	C8	Rarity
Complete Outfit	350	595	925	R7
Outfit Box no. 19405-RSC	150	250	350	R7

Comments: In 1964, the Mutual Buying Syndicate cooperative was listed as the customer on 10 Factory Orders (see Mutual Buying in the section on Lionel's Distribution and Customers).

Outfit no. 19405 was one of Mutual's Retailer Promotional Type Ib steam-powered purchases. It paid Lionel $5.97 for each outfit.

The 19405 has been linked to Lit Brothers through the Factory Order that stated, "Mutual for Lit Bros." This outfit was Lit's low-end steam offering for 1964. Of the 900 units produced, 400 were destined for it. (See Lit Brothers in the section on Lionel's Distribution and Customers.)

The 19405 was led by a no. 1061-25 Steam Type Locomotive. This stripped-down Scout steamer featured an 0-4-0 wheel arrangement and went forward only. It lacked a headlight, a lens and any sort of traction aid.

All the cars in this outfit were low-end items carried over from earlier years. In fact, the entire outfit was likely assembled to reduce surplus inventory. The only car of note was the no. 6409-25 Flat Car W/3 Pipes. It was a red no. 6511-series flat car with "Lionel" stamped on each side. It lacked a car number and a brake wheel.

The rolling stock in the 19405 followed the normal truck and coupler progression for 1964, with all the cars having AAR types. All but two were equipped with non-operating trucks and couplers. The nos. 1061T-25 Tender and 6047-25 Caboose had one non-operating and one plain type, although the 6047-25 could be equipped with Archbar types as well.

Lionel apparently used this outfit to reduce the inventory of plastic military figures and vehicles because it included the highly collectible nos. 958-150 Jeep Assembled, 958-175 Cannon Assembled and 975-1 Squad of Soldiers. The 958-150 and 958-175 as well as the no. 958-50 Truck were purchased from Payton Products. The 975-1 consisted of a polyethylene bag filled with 10 soldiers purchased from Multiple Products Corporation (MPC) of New York. (See outfit no. 19326 from 1964 for details about the

958s and 975-1.)

The Factory Order for the 19405 stated to use "any RSC (cheapest)". The box likely was either a Tan RSC with Black Graphics or a White RSC with Orange Graphics outfit box.

If it weren't for the highly collectible plastic figures and

vehicles from Payton and MPC that Lionel placed in this outfit, it would attract only minimal interest. But finding a complete 19405 with Lionel versions of these peripherals is a challenge. The outfit pricing assumes original Lionel versions.

Description: "O27" Special
Specification: "O27" Special
Customer: Polk
Original Amount: 42
Factory Order Date: 8/30/1964
Date Issued: 8-27-64
Packaging: Indv. Boxed for Bulk Packing

Contents: 213LT "Minn. & St. Louis" Diesel Unit; 2404-1 Vista Dome; 2405-1 Pullman Car; 2406-1 Observation Car; 2521-1 Illuminated Observation Car; 2522-1 Illuminated Vista Dome; 2523-1 Illuminated Pullman Car; 375-1 Motorized Turntable; 480-32 Conversion Coupler (18); 1122-1 Pr. Remote Control Switches (6); 1018 Straight Track (72); 1013 Curved Track (12); 313-121 Fibre Pins (18 Doz); 1013-12 Steel Pins (36 Doz)

19406 (1964)	C6	C7	C8	Rarity
Items Only	1,725	3,000	4,000	N/A

Comments: In 1964, longtime Lionel customer Polk Model Craft Hobbies purchased what were known as "bulk outfits." (For an explanation of the practice of buying "bulk outfits," consult the entry on Madison Hardware Co. in the section on Lionel's Distribution and Customers.)

Polk purchased bulk-packed O27 outfits nos. 19406, 19407 and 19408; O gauge outfits nos. 12807, 12817 and 12847; and

Super O outfit no. 13277. All were Retailer Promotional Type Ia outfits.

When you look at the contents of all these outfits and weigh the fact that all the Factory Orders recorded the same date, it becomes obvious that Polk was merely splitting up its separate-sale order across multiple "outfits" to take advantage of the inherent outfit discount. As such, each of these outfits offered a little bit of everything.

Polk's 1964 purchases included a few items that have become highly desirable among collectors. Polk paid $90.00 for each 19406, which included a no. 213LT Minn. & St. Louis Diesel Unit that consisted of a no. 213P-1 Minn. & St. Louis Diesel Power Car and a no. 213T-1 Tender inside a no. 12-67 Corr. Box (master carton). The individual boxes combined with their master carton are very difficult to find.

The 19406 also came with nos. 2404-1 Vista Dome, 2405-1 Pullman Car and 2406-1 Observation Car. Their Orange Picture boxes are difficult to find in collectible condition.

A listing for this outfit is provided here because a Factory Order exists for the 19406. Pricing is provided as reference for the items alone. However, as stated earlier in this volume, items alone do not constitute an outfit; an outfit box is required.

It is unknown what Polk did with these items. For that reason, finding any box with 19406 markings would be a true discovery.

Description: "O27" Special
Specification: "O27" Special
Customer: Polk
Original Amount: 54
Factory Order Date: 8/30/1964
Date Issued: 8-27-64
Packaging: Indv. Boxed for Bulk Packing

Contents: 238LTS Steam Type Locomotive & Tender with Smoke & Whistle; 6464-735 "New Haven" Box Car; 6361-1 Timber Transport Car; 3434-1 Operating Poultry Car; 6560-1 Crane Car; 6822-1 Searchlight Car; ZW-1 Transformer; 332-1 Arch Under Bridge; 110-1 Trestle Set; 1044-1 90-Watt Transformer; 1018 Straight Track (72); 1013 Curved Track (12); ½ 1018 Half Straight Track (24); ½ 1013 Half Curve Track (12)

19407 (1964)	C6	C7	C8	Rarity
Items Only	1,100	1,675	2,550	N/A

Comments: In 1964, longtime Lionel customer Polk Model Craft Hobbies purchased what were known as "bulk outfits." (For an explanation of the practice of buying "bulk outfits," consult the entry on Madison Hardware Co. in the section on Lionel's Distribution and Customers.)

Polk purchased bulk-packed O27 outfits nos. 19406, 19407 and 19408; O gauge outfits nos. 12807, 12817 and 12847; and Super O outfit no. 13277. All were Retailer Promotional Type Ia outfits.

When you look at the contents of all these outfits and weigh the fact that all the Factory Orders recorded the same date, it becomes obvious that Polk was merely splitting up its separate-sale order across multiple "outfits" to take advantage of the inherent outfit discount. As such, each of these outfits offered a little bit of everything.

Polk's 1964 purchases included a few items that have become highly desirable among collectors. Polk paid $55.00 for each 19407, which included a no. 238LTS Steam Type Locomotive & Tender with Smoke & Whistle. According to its Factory Order, the 238LTS consisted of a no. 237-1 Steam Type Locomotive with Smoke and a no. 234W-1 Whistle Tender inside a no. 12-77 Corr. Box (master carton). The inclusion of a different engine (237-1) instead of the one listed (238LTS) is an interesting occurrence but not a unique one. The individual boxes combined with their master carton are very difficult to find.

The addition of a no. 6560-1 Crane Car to the 19407 was curious. This model was last listed on a Factory Order from 1960. The 6560-1 was the version with a gray cab and a black base that last appeared in a Late Classic style box. Whether it came that way in this grouping is unknown.

A listing for this outfit is provided here because a Factory Order exists for the 19407. Pricing is provided as reference for the

items alone. However, as stated earlier in this volume, items alone do not constitute an outfit; an outfit box is required.

It is unknown what Polk did with these items. For that reason, finding any box with 19407 markings would be a true discovery.

19408
1964

Description: "O27" Special
Specification: "O27" Special
Customer: Polk
Original Amount: 54
Factory Order Date: 8/30/1964
Date Issued: 8-27-64
Packaging: Indv. Boxed For Bulk Packing

Contents: 2029LTS Steam Type Locomotive & Tender With Smoke & Whistle; 3665-1 Minuteman Missile Launching Car; 3519-1 Operating Satellite Launching Car; 3619-1 Reconnaissance Copter Car; 65-1 Motorized Hand Car; LW-1 125-Watt Transformer; 1022-1 Pr. Manual Switches (6); 1018 Straight Track (72); 1013 Curved Track (12)

19408 (1964)	C6	C7	C8	Rarity
Items Only	660	1,050	1,525	N/A

Comments: In 1964, longtime Lionel customer Polk Model Craft Hobbies purchased what were known as "bulk outfits." (For an explanation of the practice of buying "bulk outfits," consult

the entry on Madison Hardware Co. in the section on Lionel's Distribution and Customers.)

Polk purchased bulk-packed O27 outfits nos. 19406, 19407 and 19408; O gauge outfits nos. 12807, 12817 and 12847; and Super O outfit no. 13277. All were Retailer Promotional Type Ia outfits.

When you look at the contents of all these outfits and weigh the fact that all the Factory Orders recorded the same date, it becomes obvious that Polk was merely splitting up its separate-sale order across multiple "outfits" to take advantage of the inherent outfit discount. As such, each of these outfits offered a little bit of everything.

Other purchases made by Polk in 1964 may have included a few collectible items, but the 19408 consisted primarily of old stock that Lionel was slowly depleting. This outfit, for which Polk paid $57.00 each, marked the second-to-last appearance of the nos. 3519-1 Operating Satellite Launching Car and 3619-1 Reconnaissance Copter Car.

A listing for this outfit is provided here because a Factory Order exists for the 19408. Pricing is provided as reference for the items alone. However, as stated earlier in this volume, items alone do not constitute an outfit; an outfit box is required.

It is unknown what Polk did with these items. For that reason, finding any box with 19408 markings would be a true discovery.

19409
1964

Description: "O27" Special
Specification: "O27" Special W/No Transformer
Customer: Mutual Buying
Original Amount: 40
Factory Order Date: 9/16/1964
Date Issued: 9-14-64
Packaging: Any RSC Packing

Contents: 1061-25 Steam Type Locomotive; 1061T-25 Tender; 6409-25 Flat Car W/3 Pipes; 6511-15 Pipes (3); 6042-25 Gondola Car - Blue; 6067-25 Caboose; 1013 Curved Track (8); 1103-20 Envelope Packed; 11311-20 Instruction Sheet; 1-65 Warranty Card; Form 3063 Parts Order Form; D64-50 Accessory Catalog; 927-64 Service Station List

Boxes & Packing: 63-320 Outfit Box

19409 (1964)	C6	C7	C8	Rarity
Complete Outfit	610	1,025	1,450	R10
Outfit Box no. 63-320	550	900	1,250	R10

Comments: In 1964, the Mutual Buying Syndicate cooperative was listed as the customer on 10 Factory Orders (see Mutual Buying in the section on Lionel's Distribution and Customers).

Outfit no. 19409 was one of Mutual's Retailer Promotional Type Ib steam-powered purchases. It has yet to be linked to an end retailer. Mutual's cost from Lionel was $4.25 for each outfit.

The 19409 was a low-end starter outfit led by a no. 1061-25 Steam Type Locomotive. This stripped-down Scout steamer featured an 0-4-0 wheel arrangement and went forward only. It lacked a headlight, a lens and any sort of traction aid.

All the cars in this outfit were low-end items carried over from earlier years. In fact, the entire outfit was likely assembled with surplus inventory. The only car of note was the no. 6409-25 Flat Car W/3 Pipes, which was a red no. 6511-series flat car with "Lionel" stamped on each side. It lacked a car number and a brake wheel.

The rolling stock in the 19409 followed the normal truck and coupler progression for 1964, with all the cars having AAR types. All but two were equipped with non-operating trucks and couplers. The nos. 1061T-25 Tender and 6067-25 Caboose had one non-operating and one plain type.

The no. 63-320 Tan RSC with Black Graphics outfit box was manufactured by St. Joe Kraft, St. Joe Paper Co. Container Division and measured 11 x 7⅞ x 5½ inches. It included four lines of data as part of the box manufacturer's certificate.

If it weren't for the extremely small quantity of the 19409 that Lionel produced, it would be just one of the many low-end offerings of the 1960s. With only 40 manufactured, it ties for tenth on the list of fewest outfits produced, thus making the 19409 a true collectible.

Description: "O27" Bulk Special
Specification: "O27" Bulk Special
Customer: Branch Brook Co.
Original Amount: 100
Factory Order Date: 9/11/1964
Date Issued: 9-3-64
Packaging: Indv. Boxed For Bulk Packing

Contents: 212P-1 "Santa Fe" "A" Diesel W/Horn; 212T-1 "Santa Fe" "A" Unit; 6464-735 "New Haven" Box Car; 6415-1 Tank Car; 3662-1 Operating Milk Car; 3356-1 Operating Horse Car And Corral; 6437-1 Illuminated Caboose; 1018 Straight Track (27); 1013 Curved Track (16); 1122-1 Pr. Remote Control Switches; 110-1 Trestle Set; ZW-1 Transformer; CTC-1 Lockon; 145-1 Automatic Gateman; 262-1 Highway Crossing Gate

19410 (1964)	C6	C7	C8	Rarity
Items Only	850	1,375	2,100	N/A

Comments: In 1964, Branch Brook Company purchased three of what were known as "bulk outfits": nos. 12857, 12867 and 19410. All three were Retailer Promotional Type Ia outfits. (For an explanation of the practice of buying "bulk outfits," consult the entry on Madison Hardware Co. in the section on Lionel's Distribution and Customers.)

Although the items in the 19410 probably were intended to be grouped together, no individual outfit box has been observed for any bulk outfit listed in this volume. As a result, we cannot ascertain whether these items were ever assembled and sold as an outfit. Even if they were, we cannot prove that Branch Brook designated the grouping as 19410. Branch Brook paid $58.37 for this outfit.

The Factory Order for the 19410 was the first Lionel document to mention the boxed nos. 212P-1 Santa Fe "A" Diesel W/Horn and 212T-1 Santa Fe "A" Unit. These Alco diesels did not appear in individual boxes again until 1966.

A listing for this outfit is provided here because a Factory Order exists for the 19410. Pricing is provided as reference for the items alone. However, as stated earlier in this volume, items alone do not constitute an outfit; an outfit box is required.

It is unknown what Branch Brook did with these items. For that reason, finding any box with 19410 markings would be a true discovery.

Description: Die Cast Loco Freight
Specification: 8 Unit Die Cast Loco Freight With Smoke & Whistle
Customer: Abraham & Strauss
Customer: W. T. Grant
Original Amount: 1,000
Factory Order Date: 10/12/1964
Date Issued: 10-9-64
Packaging: RSC

Contents: 2029-25 Steam Type Locomotive With Smoke; 234W-25 Whistle Tender; 6142-125 Gondola Car; 6014-325 Frisco Box Car; 6408-25 Flat Car W/5 Pipes; 6511-15 Pipes (5); 6176-75 Hopper Car; 6465-150 Tank Car; 6167-100 Caboose; 1073-25 60-Watt Transformer; 147-25 Horn & Whistle Controller; 6149-25 Remote Control Track; 1013 Curved Track (12); 1018 Straight Track (7); 1020-25 90° Crossing; 1103-50 Envelope Packed; SP-1 Smoke Pellets; 675-33 Smoke Stack Cleaner; 2029-5 Instruction Sheet; 1-65 Warranty Card; Form 3063 Parts Order Form; D64-50 Accessory Catalog; 927-64 Service Station List; 1802-10 Instruction Sheet; 11460-10 Instruction Sheet

Boxes & Packing: 64-166 Outfit Box; 64-167 Corr. Shipper for 4 (1-4)

19411 (1964)	C6	C7	C8	Rarity
Complete Outfit	320	525	760	R7
Outfit Box no. 64-166	135	225	300	R7

Comments: For the first time since 1960, the variety store chain W. T. Grant purchased new promotional outfits in 1964: nos. 19365 and 19411. The former was Retailer Promotional Type Ia outfit, and the latter was a General Release Promotional Type IIa outfit.

The Factory Order listed W. T. Grant as the sole customer. However, a Lionel document from 1964 titled, "Last Numbers Used", listed "W. T. Grant" and "A&S" (Abraham & Strauss) as the customer of the 19411. For that reason, it is classified as a General Release Promotional outfit. The retailer's cost from Lionel was $20.50 for each outfit.

The 19411's Factory Order stated, "same as set #19354 plus 4-1013, 2-1018 and 1-1020". The 19354 was a General Release Promotional Type IIa outfit that Lionel's sales staff sold to at least three customers. One likely scenario for the genesis of the 19411 was that when W. T. Grant and Abraham & Strauss were presented with the 19354, they wanted a slightly different track plan. Therefore, Lionel updated the track plan to a figure-eight layout and created the 19411. The 19411 also included the nos. 234W-25 Whistle Tender and 6167-100 Caboose in place of the nos. 233W-25 Whistle Tender and 6167-125 Caboose found in the 19354. Other than these changes, the contents of these two outfits were the same. (See the entry for outfit 19354 for complete information about this outfit.)

The 19411 used a different outfit box – a slightly larger one – than did the 19354. The no. 64-166 White RSC with Orange Graphics outfit box was manufactured by United Container Co. and measured 15⅜ x 10½ x 7⅛ inches.

The 19411 was produced in slightly lower quantities than the 19354. Neither of these outfits appears very often.

Outfit no. 19412 marked the last time that Masters appeared on a Factory Order. This outfit featured a Type IIb no. 6473-25 Rodeo Car and gray no. 40-11 Cable Reels. The 19412 represented one of the few cases where an outfit component (the no. 111-1 Trestle Set) was provided separately.

Description: "O27" Special
Specification: 6 Unit "O27" Special
Customer: Masters
Original Amount: 600
Factory Order Date: 9/11/1964
Date Issued: 9-3-64
Packaging: R.S.C.

Contents: 1062-50 Steam Type Loco. W/Light & Reversing Unit; 1061T-25 Tender; 6142-150 Gondola Car; 40-11 Cable Reel (2); 6473-25 Rodeo Car; 6465-150 Tank Car; 6167-125 Caboose; 1013 Curved Track (8); 1018 Straight Track (5); 6149-25 Remote Control Track; 1026-25 25-Watt Transformer; 1103-40 Envelope Packed; 111-1 Trestle Set; 11430-10 Instruction Sheet; 1-66 Flyer; 927-64 Service Station List; Form 3063 Parts Order Form; D64-50 Accessory Catalog; 1-65 Warranty Card

Boxes & Packing: 61-170 Outfit Box; 62-254 Corr. Insert; 62-248 Corr. Insert; 61-172 Corr. Insert

Alternate For Outfit Contents:
Ship #111 Trestle separately.

19412 (1964)	C6	C7	C8	Rarity
Complete Outfit	265	500	750	R8
Outfit Box no. 61-170	150	300	450	R8

Comments: Masters leased departments within discount stores, and that is where the no. 19412 outfit was likely sold. This Retailer Promotional Type Ia was a follow-up to Masters' no. 19276 from 1963. Both outfits contained items of a similar value as well as a no. 111-1 Trestle Set. Masters paid $9.86 for each 19412.

The 19412 was led by a no. 1062-50 Steam Type Loco. W/ Light & Reversing Unit (new for 1964). This low-end Scout steamer featured an 0-4-0 wheel arrangement and a rubber tire as a traction aid. Except for the rubber tire, it was identical to the no. 1062-25 Steam Type Loco. W/Light & Reversing Unit.

The no. 6142-150 Gondola Car and unmarked no. 6167-125 Caboose were the only new items in this outfit; all the other cars were carryover. The no. 6473-25 Rodeo Car used a Type IIb body (cadmium yellow plastic with red lettering). The Type II body had a partially filled slot caused by broken tooling.

The rolling stock in the 19412 followed the normal truck and coupler progression for 1964, with all the cars having AAR types. All but two were equipped with one operating and one late non-operating truck and coupler. The no. 1061T-25 Tender had one late non-operating and one plain type, and the 6167-125 had one operating and one plain type.

Late in 1963, Lionel began to mold the no. 40-11 Cable Reels in gray plastic. This practice carried over into 1964, and the norm for this outfit was these harder-to-find reels.

The proper instruction sheets made reference to the 90-day warranty that Lionel instituted in 1963.

The no. 61-170 Tan RSC with Black Graphics outfit box was manufactured by United Container and measured 11½ x 10¼ x 6¼ inches. It included four lines of data, a "63" and two stars as part of the box manufacturer's certificate.

The Factory Order specified that the 111-1 Trestle Set was to be packed separately. As such, "Include 111-1 With This Set" was stamped on every outfit box.

With 600 units manufactured, empty boxes for this outfit do appear from time to time. However, complete examples of the 19412 with a 111-1 are an infrequent occurrence.

Description: "O27" Special
Specification: 6 Unit "O27" Special
Customer: S. Klein
Original Amount: ~~1,500~~ Did Not Accept
Factory Order Date: 10/15/1964
Date Issued: 10-16-64
Date Req'd: 11-1-64
Packaging: Loose RSC

Contents: 1061-50 Steam Loco With Tire; 1061T-25 Tender;

6651-25 Cannon Car; 6651-8 Shells (4); 6448-25 Exploding Target Car; 6042-25 Gondola Car - Blue; 40-11 Cable Reels (3); 6167-100 Caboose; 1013 Curved Track (8); 1018 Straight Track (2); 1103-20 Envelope Packed; 1026-25 25-Watt Transformer

Comments: The Factory Orders for S. Klein outfit nos. 19415 and 19416 were marked, "Did Not Accept". Both were to be Retailer Promotional Type Ib outfits. S. Klein was to pay Lionel $9.25 for each 19415. This listing is provided here for historical reference.

Description: "O27" Special
Specification: 8 Unit "O27" Special
Customer: S. Klein
Original Amount: ~~1,500~~ Did Not Accept
Factory Order Date: 10/15/1964
Date Issued: 10-16-64
Date Req'd: 11-1-64
Packaging: Loose RSC

Contents: 237-25 Steam Type Locomotive with Smoke; 1061T-50 Tender; 3357-25 Animated Hobo & Railroad Policeman Car; 3357-27 Box Packed; 3309-50 Turbo Missile Firing Car; 0349-10 Turbo Missile (2); 6176-100 Hopper Car; 6142-175 Gondola Car; 6413-25 Mercury Capsule Car; 6413-4 Capsules (2); 6413-10 Envelope Packed; 6119-125 Work Caboose; 1013 Curved Track

(12); 1018 Straight Track (11); 1008-50 Uncoupling Unit; 1020-25 90° Crossing; 1010-25 35-Watt Transformer; 975-1 Squad of Soldiers; 1103-20 Envelope Packed; 909-20 Smoke Fluid

Alternate For Outfit Contents:
Substitute: 1,000 #6402-50 (W/2 Cable Reels) in Place of 6413-25.

Comments: The Factory Orders for S. Klein outfit nos. 19415 and 19416 were marked, "Did Not Accept". Both were to be Retailer Promotional Type Ib outfits. S. Klein was to pay Lionel $16.50 for each 19416. This listing is provided here for historical reference.

Description: "O27" Special
Specification: "O27" Special W/Super "O" Track
Customer: Madison Hardware
Original Amount: 100
Date Issued: 10-16-64
Date Req'd: At Once
Packaging: Bulk to be Packed in Lot

Contents: 2029LTS Steam Type Locomotive & Tender With Smoke & Whistle; 6315-60 Chemical Tank Car; 6415-1 Tank Car; 6465-160 Tank Car; 6436-110 Hopper Car; 6464-525 "Minn & St. Louis" Box Car; 6414-85 Auto Transport Car; 1073 60-Watt Transformer; 6019-1 Remote Control Track Set; 147-25 Horn & Whistle Controller; 31 Curved Track (12); 32 Straight Track (10)

19417 (1964)	C6	C7	C8	Rarity
Items Only	1,100	1,550	2,115	N/A

Comments: Madison Hardware Co. of New York purchased what were known as "bulk outfits." (For an explanation of the practice of buying "bulk outfits," consult the entry on Madison Hardware Co. in the section on Lionel's Distribution and Customers.)

Madison purchased bulk-packed outfits nos. 19400 and 19417 in 1964. Both were Retailer Promotional Type Ia outfits. Madison paid Lionel $29.75 for each 19417.

When you look at the contents of the 19400 and 19417, it is obvious that Madison was splitting up part of its separate-sale order across multiple "outfits" to take advantage of the inherent outfit discount.

No individual outfit boxes have been observed for any bulk

outfit listed in this volume. As a result, we cannot ascertain whether these items were ever assembled and sold as an outfit. Even if they were, we cannot prove that Madison Hardware designated the groupings as 19400 or 19417.

This bulk-packed 19417 included a no. 2029-1 Steam Type Locomotive With Smoke (new for 1964). This steamer featured a two-position reversing unit, a headlight and a rubber tire as a traction aid. Inside its individual no. 2029-6 Corr. Box were the nos. CTC-1 Lockon, SP-1 Smoke Pellets, 675-33 Smoke Stack Cleaner and 2029-5 Instruction Sheet.

The 2029-1 was paired with a no. 234W-1 Whistle Tender in a no. 12-77 Corr. Box (master carton). This master carton pairing was called a no. 2029LTS Steam Type Locomotive & Tender With Smoke & Whistle.

The no. 6414-85 Auto Transport Car was a boxed 6414 with four "cheapie" automobiles, which consisted of just the plastic car frame with simulated wheels molded as part of the body. To be complete, a 6414-85 must include its difficult-to-find Orange Picture box stamped "6414-85". (See outfit no. 19380 for more information about this car.)

Another component of the 19417 that came in a hard-to-obtain box was the no. 6465-160 Tank Car. Its Orange Picture no. 6465-161 Folding Box was offered only on the separate-sale model in 1964 and in this bulk shipment. A total of 850 boxes was listed on its Production Control File. All remaining cars were packaged in Orange Picture boxes.

The rolling stock in this outfit followed the normal truck and coupler progression for 1964, with all the cars having AAR types. All but two were equipped with operating trucks and couplers. The norm for the no. 234W-1 was one non-operating and one plain type. Also, the 6465-160 came with one operating and one non-operating truck and coupler.

The inclusion of Super O track in an O27 outfit was yet another indication that Madison was bundling items for the inherent outfit discount.

A listing for this outfit is provided here because a Factory

Order exists for the 19417. Pricing is provided as reference for the items alone. However, as stated earlier in this volume, items alone do not constitute an outfit; an outfit box is required.

It is unknown what Madison Hardware did with these items. For that reason, finding any box with 19417 markings would be a true discovery.

19418
1964

Description: "O27" Special Freight
Specification: "O27" Special Freight 7 Unit
Customer: Channel Master
Original Amount: 2,000 Not Used
Factory Order Date: 11/10/1964
Date Issued: 11-10-64
Packaging: Any RSC

Contents: 1062-50 Steam Type Loco. W/Light & Reversing Unit; 1061T-50 Tender; 6176-100 Hopper Car; 6142-125

Gondola Car; 6473-25 Rodeo Car; 6465-150 Tank Car; 6167-175 Caboose; 1010-25 35-Watt Transformer; 6149-25 Remote Control Track; 1013 Curved Track (8); 1018 Straight Track (5); 1103-40 Envelope Packed

Alternate For Outfit Contents:
Sub Caboose if Necessary.

Comments: The Factory Order for Channel Master outfit no. 19418 was marked "Not Used". It was to be a Manufacturer Promotional Type IIIb outfit. Channel Master was to pay Lionel $9.70 for each 19418. This listing is provided here for historical reference.

19419
1964

Description: "O27" Freight
Specification: 6 Unit "O27" Freight
Customer: Madison Hardware
Original Amount: 100
Factory Order Date: 11/11/1964
Date Issued: 11-11-64
Date Req'd: A/O
Packaging: Any Packing

Contents: 239-25 Steam Locomotive With Smoke; 1060T-25 Tender; 6050-150 Van Camp Savings Bank Car; 6050-175 Libby Box Car; 6475-50 Crushed Pineapple Car; 6651-25 Cannon Car; 6651-8 Shells (4); 1010-25 35-Watt Transformer; 1013 Curved Track (8); 1018 Straight Track (3); 6149-25 Remote Control Track; 6651-10 Instruction Sheet; 1-70 Packing Brochure; 237-11 Instruction Sheet; 1103-40 Envelope Packed; 1-65 Warranty Card; Form 3063 Parts Order Form; D64-50 Accessory Catalog; 927-64 Service Station List; 909-20 Smoke Fluid

Boxes & Packing: 64-164 Outfit Box

Alternate For Outfit Contents:
Note: Customer to supply his own caboose.

19419 (1964)	C6	C7	C8	Rarity
Complete Outfit	930	1,450	1,925	R10
Outfit Box no. 64-164	600	900	1,200	R10

Comments: In 1964, Madison Hardware Co. of New York purchased three outfits: nos. 19400, 19417 and 19419. The 19419 was a Retailer Promotional Type Ib outfit that cost Madison $10.65 each.

The 19419 was led by a no. 239-25 Steam Locomotive With Smoke (new for 1964). This die-cast Scout steamer featured a two-position reversing unit, a headlight and a rubber tire as a traction aid. Except for its 239 number and lack of stripe, it was the same engine as a no. 241.

The only new piece of rolling stock in this outfit was the no. 6651-25 Cannon Car. It was derived from the no. 6650-25 / 6640-25 Missile Launching Flat Car and included a new firing mechanism that fired shells instead of a missile. The base of the car was painted olive drab, whereas the top was molded in olive drab plastic.

All the remaining cars in the 19419 were carryover items. Lionel was depleting the last of the no. 6050-150 Van Camp Savings Bank Cars first issued in 1962. This outfit represented one of the final two appearances of this car.

The nos. 6050-175 Libby Box Car and 6475-50 Crushed Pineapple Car were first introduced in the no. 19263 "Libby" outfit from 1963. Both cars were still being depleted in outfits through 1965.

The Factory Order did not list a caboose. It specified, instead, that Madison Hardware would supply its own caboose and, therefore, space should be left in the outfit box for that item.

The rolling stock in the 19419 followed the normal truck and coupler progression for 1964, with all the cars having either AAR or Archbar types. All but three were equipped with non-operating AAR trucks and couplers. The 6050-150 came with non-operating Archbar types. The norm for the no. 1060T-25 Tender was one non-operating and one plain AAR type. Also, the 6651-25 came with operating AAR trucks and couplers.

The difficult-to-find 90-day warranty version of the no. 6651-10 Instruction Sheet was included in this outfit. It was dated 8/64.

The no. 64-164 White RSC with Orange Graphics outfit box was manufactured by United Container Co. and measured 12⅛ x 11⅝ x 6½ inches.

With only 100 units of the 19419 manufactured, it is seldom seen and easily achieves an R10 rarity rating.

Description: "O27" Special Outfit
Customer: Sears, Roebuck and Co.
Original Amount: 1,100
Factory Order Date: 3/23/1965
Date Issued: Rev 4-31-65
Date Req'd: 5-26-65
Packaging: Units Loose, Kraft RSC 6/Shipper

Contents: 1061-25 Steam Type Locomotive; 1061T-25 Tender; 6042-100 Gondola Car; 6502-50 Girder Transport Car; 214-3 Bridge Side; 6167-50 Caboose; 1013-8 Curved Track (Bundle of 8 - 1013); 1018-10 Straight Track (Loose) (2); 1103-20 Envelope Packed; 1026-25 25-Watt Transformer; 11311-20X Instruction Sheet; Form 3063 Parts Order Form; 1-65 Warranty Card

Boxes & Packing: 63-383 Outfit Box; 62-254 Corr. Insert; 61-173 Corr. Insert; 64-319 Corr. Insert (2); 65-330 Shipper for 6 (1-6); 64-104 Shipper Pad (2-6)

Alternate For Outfit Contents:
Note: Sub. 83 - 1061-50 for 1061-25.

19426 (1965)	C6	C7	C8	Rarity
Complete Outfit	250	415	650	R7
Outfit Box no. 63-383	100	200	300	R7

Comments: After purchasing only three outfits in 1964, Sears, Roebuck and Co. made a large purchase of 14 Retailer Promotional outfits in 1965. Only three of these outfits appeared in the 1965 Sears Christmas Catalog.

Evidence suggests that Lionel offered Sears a similar deal to the "Special Purchase" granted in 1963. First, Factory Orders for 11 of these outfits were called "Special Outfit" and had similar dates of 3-23-65 or 3-24-65. Second, each of these 11 outfits included numerous substitutions, which indicated the depletion of surplus or old inventory. Third, none of these 11 outfits appeared in a Sears catalog. Finally, after 1965, Sears returned to its traditional pattern of purchasing three or four outfits each year.

The no. 19426, a Type Ib outfit, was one of the many steam-powered outfits purchased by Sears in 1965. This outfit, for which Sears paid $4.67 each, was nearly identical to Sears outfit no. 19427.

Both were likely sold over the counter at Sears stores because they did not appear in the 1965 Sears Christmas Catalog.

The 19426 was led by a no. 1061-25 Steam Type Locomotive. This stripped-down Scout steamer featured an 0-4-0 wheel arrangement and went forward only. It lacked a headlight, a lens and any sort of traction aid. When Lionel replaced the 1061-25 with a no. 1061-50 Steam Loco With Tire, the outfit price was not affected.

As with all the Sears "Special Outfit" purchases from 1965, the 19426 reduced or depleted the inventory of many items. The olive drab no. 6042-100 Gondola Car was making its last appearance in this outfit. The 6042-100 is almost identical to the more common olive drab no. 6142-175 Gondola Car, except that the former was equipped with non-operating AAR trucks and couplers and the latter was equipped with one operating and one non-operating AAR truck and coupler. Even though the 6042-100 is more difficult to find, the slight difference in trucks and couplers does not command a premium price.

The unmarked yellow no. 6167-50 Caboose was making its final appearance in this outfit and the 19427. The unmarked no. 1061T-25 Tender was making its last outfit appearances in 1965 and the blue no. 6502-50 Girder Transport Car was making one of its last four appearances in this outfit. It carried a black no. 214-3 Bridge Side.

The rolling stock in the 19426 followed the normal truck and coupler progression for 1965, with each of the cars having AAR types. All but two were equipped with non-operating trucks and couplers. The 1061T-25 and 6167-50 had one non-operating and one plain type.

The "X" at the end of the no. 11311-20X Instruction Sheet indicated that the version from the previous year was being used. Actually, the suffix was unnecessary because Lionel did not make any changes to this sheet in 1965.

The no. 63-383 Tan RSC with Black Graphics outfit box was manufactured by United Container Co. and measured 11½ x 9¾ x 6 inches. It included four lines of data as part of the box manufacturer's certificate. Printed on the bottom was a reference to the N.M.F.C.

This low-end outfit was produced in larger-than-average quantities. When it does appear, it is often missing its 6042-100.

Description: "O27" Special Outfit
Customer/No./Price: Sears, Roebuck and Co.; 4919427; $9.99
Original Amount: 10,000
Factory Order Date: 3/23/1965
Date Issued: Rev 4-21-65
Date Req'd: 4-19-65
Packaging: Units Loose, Kraft RSC 6/Shipper

Contents: 1061-50 Steam Loco With Tire; 1061T-25 Tender; 6042-75 Gondola Car (Less 2 Cable Reels); 6502-50 Girder Transport Car; 214-3 Bridge Side; 6167-50 Caboose; 1013-8 Curved Track (Bundle of 8 - 1013); 1018-10 Straight Track (Loose) (2); 1103-20 Envelope Packed; 1026-25 25-Watt Transformer; 11311-20X Instruction Sheet; Form 3063 Parts Order Form; 1-65 Warranty Card

Boxes & Packing: 63-383 Outfit Box; 62-254 Corr. Insert; 61-173 Corr. Insert; 64-319 Corr. Insert (2); 65-330 Shipper for 6 (1-6); 64-104 Shipper Pad (2-6)

Alternate For Outfit Contents:
Note: Sub. 7,491 - 1061T-50 for 1061T-25; Sub. 2,260 - 6167-25 for 6167-50; Sub. 3,740 - 6167-175 for 6167-50; Sub. 1,488 - 6042-125 for 6042-75; Sub. 306 - 6142-175 for 6042-75.

Outfit no. 19427 was one of the 14 outfits purchased by Sears in 1965. Eleven of these outfits, including the 19427, were labeled "Special Outfit" and used to deplete surplus inventory. This example included the nos. 1061T-50 Tender, 6042-125 Gondola and 6167-25 Caboose substitutions.

19427 (1965)	C6	C7	C8	Rarity
Complete Outfit	110	185	300	R3
Complete Outfit With no. 6167-175 Substitution, Add The Following	170	340	490	R3
Complete Outfit With no. 6142-175 Substitution, Add The Following	70	90	165	R3
Outfit Box no. 63-383	35	60	100	R3

Comments: After purchasing only three outfits in 1964, Sears, Roebuck and Co. made a large purchase of 14 Retailer Promotional outfits in 1965. Only three of these outfits appeared in the 1965 Sears Christmas Catalog.

Evidence suggests that Lionel offered Sears a similar deal to the "Special Purchase" granted in 1963. First, Factory Orders for 11 of these outfits were called "Special Outfit" and had similar dates of 3-23-65 or 3-24-65. Second, each of these 11 outfits included numerous substitutions, which indicated the depletion of surplus or old inventory. Third, none of these 11 outfits appeared in a Sears catalog. Finally, after 1965, Sears returned to its traditional pattern of purchasing three or four outfits each year.

The no. 19427, a Type Ib outfit, was one of the many steam-powered outfits purchased by Sears in 1965. This outfit, for which Sears paid $4.67 each, was nearly identical to Sears outfit no. 19426. Both were likely sold over the counter at Sears stores because they did not appear in the 1965 Sears Christmas Catalog.

The 19427 was led by a no. 1061-50 Steam Type Loco W/ Tire. This version came with a rubber tire as a traction aid, a feature that made it a slight upgrade of the no. 1061-25 Steam Type Locomotive. Even with this improvement, the 1061-50 (lacking a headlight and a lens) remained Lionel's low-end Scout steamer configured with an 0-4-0 wheel arrangement.

As with all the Sears "Special Outfit" purchases from 1965, the 19427 reduced or depleted the inventory of many items. The olive drab no. 6167-175 Caboose was making its last appearance in this outfit. The 1061-50 and olive drab no. 6142-175 Gondola Car were being depleted in the Sears outfits from 1965.

The unmarked yellow no. 6167-50 Caboose was making its final appearance in this outfit and the 19426. The unmarked no. 1061T-25 Tender was making its last outfit appearances in 1965. The blue no. 6502-50 Girder Transport Car was making one of its last four appearances in this outfit. It carried a black no. 214-3 Bridge Side.

When a 6142-175 or 6167-175 was included, the outfit price is increased, as indicated in the pricing table.

The rolling stock in the 19427 followed the normal truck and coupler progression for 1965, with each of the cars having AAR types. Most were equipped with non-operating trucks and couplers. However, the tenders and cabooses had one non-operating and one plain type, and the 6142-175 had one operating and one non-operating type.

The "X" at the end of the no. 11311-20X Instruction Sheet indicated that the version from the previous year was being used. Actually, the suffix was unnecessary because Lionel did not make any changes to this sheet in 1965.

The no. 63-383 Tan RSC with Black Graphics outfit box was manufactured by United Container Co. and measured 11½ x 9¾ x 6 inches. It included four lines of data, a "65" and 10 stars as part of the box manufacturer's certificate. Printed on the bottom was a reference to the N.M.F.C.

The 19427 is not difficult to find. However, with 10,000 units made, it should appear even more often than it does. The most desirable variation of the 19427 comes with an olive drab 6142-175 and 6167-175.

Outfit no. 19428 was one of the 14 outfits purchased by Sears in 1965. Eleven of these outfits, including the 19428, were labeled "Special Outfit" and used to deplete surplus inventory. This example appears as listed on the Factory Order without any substitutions.

Description: "O27" Special Outfit
Customer/No./Price: Sears, Roebuck and Co.; 49 SPEC; $9.99
Original Amount: 8,800
Factory Order Date: 3/23/1965
Date Issued: Rev 6-14-65
Date Req'd: 5-24-65
Packaging: Units Loose, Kraft RSC 6/Shipper

Contents: 1061-50 Steam Loco With Tire; 1061T-50 Tender; 6406-25 Flat Car W/Auto; 958-50 Truck; 6042-250 Gondola Car; 6067-25 Caboose; 6406-30 Automobile; 1020-25 90° Crossing; 1013-70 Curved Track (Bundle of 12 - 1013); 1018-40 Straight Track (Bundle of 4 - 1018); 1103-20 Envelope Packed; 1026-25 25-Watt Transformer; 11311-20X Instruction Sheet; 1802-10X Instruction Sheet; Form 3063 Parts Order Form; 1-65 Warranty Card

Boxes & Packing: 63-383 Outfit Box; 62-254 Corr. Insert; 61-173 Corr. Insert; 64-319 Corr. Insert (2); 65-330 Shipper for 6 (1-6); 64-104 Shipper Pad (2-6)

Alternate For Outfit Contents:
Note: Sub. 65 - 1062-50 for 1061-50 W/19107-10X & 1-66X less 11311-20X; Sub. 4 - 1060T-25 for 1061T-50; Sub. 687 - 1060T-50 for 1061T-50; Sub. 5,894 - 1061T-25 for 1061T-50; Sub. 19 - 1060T-1 for 1061T-50; Sub. 1,223 - 6409-25 for 6406-25; Sub. 80 - 6410-25 for 6406-25; Sub. 1,707 6402-25 for 6406-25; Sub. 526 - 6411-25 for 6406-25; Sub. 867 - 6401-25 for 6406-25; Sub. 874 - 6142-175 for 6042-250; Sub. 3,828 - 6167-75 for 6067-25; Sub. 1,431 - 6167-150 for 6067-25; Sub. 1,525 - 1010-25 for 1026-25 W/19339-10X.

19428 (1965)	C6	C7	C8	Rarity
Complete Outfit	140	230	355	R3
Complete Outfit With no. 1062-50 Substitution, Add The Following	4	10	22	R3
Complete Outfit With no. 1060T-1 Substitution, Add The Following	200	300	450	R8
Complete Outfit With Either nos. 6409-25, 6410-25 Or 6411-25 Substitutions, Add The Following	7	12	20	R3
Complete Outfit With no. 6142-175 Substitution, Add The Following	70	90	165	R3
Complete Outfit With nos. 1010-25 And 19339-10X Substitution, Add The Following	10	20	25	R3
Outfit Box no. 63-383	35	60	100	R3

Comments: After purchasing only three outfits in 1964, Sears, Roebuck and Co. made a large purchase of 14 Retailer Promotional outfits in 1965. Only three of these outfits appeared in the 1965 Sears Christmas Catalog.

Evidence suggests that Lionel offered Sears a similar deal to the "Special Purchase" granted in 1963. First, Factory Orders for 11 of these outfits were called "Special Outfit" and had similar dates of 3-23-65 or 3-24-65. Second, each of these 11 outfits included numerous substitutions, which indicated the depletion of surplus or old inventory. Third, none of these 11 outfits appeared in a Sears catalog. Finally, after 1965, Sears returned to its traditional pattern of purchasing three or four outfits each year.

The no. 19428, a Type Ib outfit, was one of the many steam-powered outfits purchased by Sears in 1965. This outfit, for which Sears paid $5.33 each, was likely sold over the counter at Sears stores because it did not appear in the 1965 Sears Christmas Catalog.

The 19428 was led by a no. 1061-50 Steam Type Loco W/ Tire. This version came with a rubber tire as a traction aid, a feature that made it a slight upgrade of the no. 1061-25 Steam Type Locomotive. Even with this improvement, the 1061-50 (lacking a headlight and a lens) remained Lionel's low-end Scout steamer configured with an 0-4-0 wheel arrangement.

As with all the Sears "Special Outfit" purchases from 1965, the 19428 reduced or depleted the inventory of many items. The nos. 958-50 Truck, 1060T-1 Tender, 6167-150 Caboose, 6406-25 Flat Car W/Auto, 6410-25 Flat Car W/2 Autos and 6411-25 Flat Car W/6 Pipes were all making their last appearance in this outfit.

The 1061-50 and olive drab no. 6142-175 Gondola Car were being depleted in the Sears outfits from 1965. The unmarked red no. 6067-25 Caboose was making its last appearance in this outfit and the 1965 version of outfit no. 19245. The unmarked no. 1061T-25 Tender was making its last outfit appearances in 1965. The substitutions that affect the outfit price are detailed in the pricing table.

Of interest, the 958-50 was the load for the gondola car because the flat car already came with the red no. 6406-30 Automobile.

The rolling stock in the 19428 followed the normal truck and coupler progression for 1965, with each of the cars having AAR types. Most were equipped with non-operating trucks and couplers. However, the tenders and cabooses had one non-operating and one plain type. Also, the 6142-175 and 6401-25 had one operating and one non-operating type.

The "X" at the end of the instruction sheet numbers indicated that the versions from the previous year were being used. Actually, the suffixes were unnecessary because Lionel did not make any changes to these sheets in 1965.

The no. 63-383 Tan RSC with Black Graphics outfit box was manufactured by United Container Co. and measured 11½ x 9¾ x 6 inches. It included four lines of data, a "65" and 10 stars as part of the box manufacturer's certificate. Printed on the bottom was a reference to the N.M.F.C.

The 19428 was produced in large quantities and readily appears. Collectors desire the version with the 6142-175 and 1060T-1, especially because that tender comes in an Orange Perforated no. 1060-26 Folding Box. That rare box demands a substantial premium and increases the outfit rarity to R8.

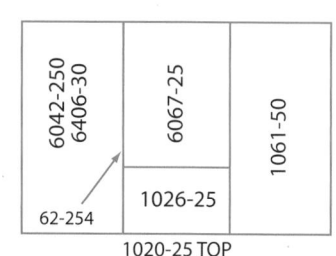

CONVENTIONAL PACK
63-383 BOX

TOP LAYER — 1018-40, 6406-25, 1061T-50, 1013-70, 958-50, 64-319 BETWEEN LAYERS, 61-173

BOTTOM LAYER — 6042-250, 6406-30, 6067-25, 1061-50, 62-254, 1026-25, 1020-25 TOP

Description: "O27" Special Outfit
Customer: Sears, Roebuck and Co.
Original Amount: 1,800
Factory Order Date: 3/23/1965
Date Issued: Rev 4-21-65
Date Req'd: 5-24-65
Packaging: Units Loose, Kraft RSC 6/Shipper

Contents: 1060-25 Steam Type Locomotive; 1061T-25 Tender; 6050-175 Libby Box Car; 6076-75 Hopper Car - Black; 6167-25 Caboose; 1013-8 Curved Track (Bundle of 8 - 1013); 1018-10 Straight Track (Loose) (2); 1026-25 25-Watt Transformer; 1103-20 Envelope Packed; 11311-20X Instruction Sheet; Form 3063 Parts Order Form; 1-65 Warranty Card

Boxes & Packing: 63-383 Outfit Box; 62-254 Corr. Insert; 61-173 Corr. Insert; 64-319 Corr. Insert (2); 65-330 Shipper for 6 (1-6); 64-104 Shipper Pad (2-6)

Alternate For Outfit Contents:
Note: Sub. 40 - 1061-50 for 1060-25.

19429 (1965)	C6	C7	C8	Rarity
Complete Outfit	155	295	335	R6
Outfit Box no. 63-383	75	150	225	R6

Comments: After purchasing only three outfits in 1964, Sears, Roebuck and Co. made a large purchase of 14 Retailer Promotional outfits in 1965. Only three of these outfits appeared in the 1965 Sears Christmas Catalog.

Evidence suggests that Lionel offered Sears a similar deal to the "Special Purchase" granted in 1963. First, Factory Orders for 11 of these outfits were called "Special Outfit" and had similar dates of 3-23-65 or 3-24-65. Second, each of these 11 outfits included numerous substitutions, which indicated the depletion of surplus or old inventory. Third, none of these 11 outfits appeared in a Sears catalog. Finally, after 1965, Sears returned to its traditional pattern of purchasing three or four outfits each year.

The no. 19429, a Type Ib outfit, was one of the many steam-powered outfits purchased by Sears in 1965. This outfit, for which Sears paid $4.67 each, was likely sold over the counter at Sears stores because it did not appear in the 1965 Sears Christmas Catalog.

The 19429 was led by a no. 1060-25 Steam Type Locomotive, which went forward only. This locomotive was making its last appearance in this outfit. As such, the outfit quantity of 1,800 probably was linked to the number of 1060-25s in inventory.

Lionel may have run out of the 1060-25 because a quantity of

40 was replaced by the no. 1061-50 Steam Loco With Tire. The 1061-50 was making its final appearance in the Sears outfits from 1965. This substitution does not affect the outfit price.

As with all the Sears "Special Outfit" purchases from 1965, the 19429 reduced or depleted the inventory of many items. The no. 6050-175 Libby Box Car was first introduced in the no. 19263 "Libby" outfit from 1963. It was making its last appearances in 1965. The unmarked no. 1061T-25 Tender was making its last outfit appearances in 1965.

The rolling stock in the 19429 followed the normal truck and coupler progression for 1965, with each of the cars having AAR types. All but two were equipped with non-operating trucks and couplers. The 1061T-25 and no. 6167-25 Caboose had one non-operating and one plain type.

The "X" at the end of the no. 11311-20X Instruction Sheet indicated that the version from the previous year was being used. Actually, the suffix was unnecessary because Lionel did not make any changes to this sheet in 1965.

The no. 63-383 Tan RSC with Black Graphics outfit box was manufactured by United Container Co. and measured 11½ x 9¾ x 6 inches. It included four lines of data as part of the box manufacturer's certificate.

With a large quantity of 1,800 examples of the 19429 manufactured, the outfit should appear on the market more frequently than it does. Yet when one does appear, collectors don't show it much interest.

Description: "O27" Special Outfit
Customer/No./Price: Sears, Roebuck and Co.; 9837; $14.99
Original Amount: 1,700
Factory Order Date: 3/24/1965
Date Issued: Rev 6-7-65
Packaging: Units Loose, Kraft RSC 6/Shipper

Contents: 1062-25 Steam Type Loco. W/Light & Reversing Unit; 1061T-25 Tender; 3357-25 Animated Hobo & Railroad Policeman Car; 3357-27 Box Packed; 6176-75 Hopper Car; 6502-75 Girder Transport Car; 214-3 Bridge Side; 6824-50 Work Caboose; 1008-50 Uncoupling Track; 1013-8 Curved Track (Bundle of 8 - 1013); 1018-30 Straight Track (Bundle of 3 - 1018); 1010-25 35-Watt Transformer; 1103-20 Envelope Packed; 1-66X Flyer; 1641-10X Instruction Sheet; Form 3063 Parts Order Form; 1-65 Warranty Card

Boxes & Packing: 61-180 Outfit Box; 61-181 Corr. Insert; 61-182 Corr. Insert; 61-183 Corr. Insert; 62-225 Corr. Insert; 62-248 Corr. Insert; 65-331 Shipper for 6 (1-6); 64-104 Shipper Pad (2-6)

Alternate For Outfit Contents:
Note: Sub. 1,700 - 1061T-50 for 1061T-25; Sub. 131 - 3357-1 for 3357-25 & 3357-27; Sub. 510 - 1026-25 for 1010-25; Sub. 510 - 19301-10 for 1641-10X.

19430 (1965)	C6	C7	C8	Rarity
Complete Outfit	235	450	665	R6
Complete Outfit With no. 3357-1 Substitution	250	475	745	R6
Outfit Box no. 61-180	75	150	225	R6

Comments: After purchasing only three outfits in 1964, Sears, Roebuck and Co. made a large purchase of 14 Retailer Promotional outfits in 1965. Only three of these outfits appeared in the 1965 Sears Christmas Catalog.

Evidence suggests that Lionel offered Sears a similar deal to the "Special Purchase" granted in 1963. First, Factory Orders for 11 of these outfits were called "Special Outfit" and had similar dates of 3-23-65 or 3-24-65. Second, each of these 11 outfits included numerous substitutions, which indicated the depletion of surplus or old inventory. Third, none of these 11 outfits appeared in a Sears catalog. Finally, after 1965, Sears returned to its traditional pattern of purchasing three or four outfits each year.

The no. 19430, a Type Ib outfit, was one of the many steam-powered outfits purchased by Sears in 1965. This outfit, for which Sears paid $7.33 each, was likely sold over the counter at Sears stores because it did not appear in the 1965 Sears Christmas Catalog.

The 19430 was led by a no. 1062-25 Steam Type Locomotive W/Light & Reversing Unit. This low-end Scout steamer featured an 0-4-0 wheel arrangement and lacked a traction aid. According to its Lionel Engineering Specification, it was the "Same as #1061 but with the addition of Reversing Unit & Lamp". The engine was making its last appearance in this outfit and outfit nos. 19245 (1965 version) and 19431.

As with all the Sears "Special Outfit" purchases from 1965, the 19430 reduced or depleted the inventory of many items. The no. 3357-25 Animated Hobo & Railroad Policeman Car, first introduced in 1962, was making it last appearance in this outfit. The Orange Picture boxed no. 3357-1 and unboxed no. 6824-50 Work Caboose were being depleted in the Sears outfits from 1965. The boxed version of the 3357-1 adds a slight premium to the outfit price.

The no. 6502-75 Girder Transport Car was making its final appearance in this outfit as well. The "-75" suffix indicated that this model was equipped with one operating and one non-operating AAR truck and coupler. It came with a black no. 214-3 Bridge Side. The yellow no. 6176-75 Hopper Car was stamped "BUILT 1-48" and "LIONEL 6176".

The 6824-50 is interesting because it shared the same cab and body as a no. 6814-1 First Aid Caboose (first issued in 1959). In fact, both cars were numbered 6814. The most noticeable difference is that the 6824-50 came with a black frame whereas the 6814-1 came with a gray one.

Lionel apparently ran out of no. 1061T-25 Tenders, as they were all replaced by the no. 1061T-50 Tender.

The rolling stock in the 19430 followed the normal truck and coupler progression for 1965, with each of the cars having AAR types. The 6176-75 and 6502-75 were equipped with one operating and one non-operating truck and coupler. The 1061T-50 had one non-operating and one plain type, and the 6824-50 had one operating and one plain type. Also, the 3357-25 and 3357-1 came with operating types.

The "X" at the end of the instruction sheet numbers indicated that the versions from the previous year were being used. Actually, the suffixes were unnecessary because Lionel did not make any changes to these sheets in 1965.

Outfit no. 19430 was one of the 14 outfits purchased by Sears in 1965. Eleven of these outfits, including the 19430, were labeled "Special Outfit" and used to deplete surplus inventory. The inclusion of the nos. 3357 Animated Hobo & Railroad Policeman Car and 1010-25 35-Watt Transformer led to a mid-tier offering for Sears and a $14.99 price. The outfit shown includes the no. 1061T-50 Tender substitution.

The commonly used no. 61-180 Tan RSC with Black Graphics outfit box was manufactured by United Container Co. and measured 12¾ x 10 x 6¾ inches. It included four lines of data, a "65" and seven stars as part of the box manufacturer's certificate.

Printed on the bottom was a reference to the N.M.F.C.

The 19430 frequently appears, although it is almost always missing its no. 3357-27 Box Packed.

19431
1965

Description: "O27" Special Outfit
Customer/No./Price: Sears, Roebuck and Co.; 49 19431; $9.99
Original Amount: 820
Factory Order Date: 3/24/1965
Date Issued: Rev 4-19-65
Date Req'd: 6-2-65
Packaging: Units Loose, Kraft RSC 6/Shipper

Contents: 1062-25 Steam Type Loco. W/Light & Reversing Unit; 1061T-25 Tender; 3357-1 Animated Hobo & Railroad Policeman Car; 6142-175 Gondola Car; 6463-1 Rocket Fuel Car; 6824-50 Work Caboose; 1008-50 Uncoupling Track; 1013-8 Curved Track (Bundle of 8 - 1013); 1018-30 Straight Track (Bundle of 3 - 1018); 1010-25 35-Watt Transformer; 1103-20 Envelope Packed; 1641-10X Instruction Sheet; 1-66X Flyer; Form 3063 Parts Order Form; 1-65 Warranty Card

Boxes & Packing: 65-332 Outfit Box; 62-254 Corr. Insert; 62-248 Corr. Insert; 64-133 Corr. Insert; 65-333 Shipper for 6 (1-6); 41110-23 Shipper Pad (2-6); 65-332 Outfit Box (Use this box and the following when using 6440-50, 6413-25 or 6463-25 Cars.);

62-254 Corr. Insert; 62-248 Corr. Insert (2); 64-133 Corr. Insert; 62-225 Corr. Insert; 65-333 Shipper for 6 (1-6); 41110-23 Shipper Pad (2-6)

Alternate For Outfit Contents:
Note: Sub. 820 - 1061T-50 for 1061T-25; Sub. 82 - 6440-50 for 6463-1; Sub. 379 - 6413-1 for 6463-1; Sub. 17 - 6413-25 W/6413-8X for 6463-1; Sub. 12 - 6463-25 for 6463-1.

19431 (1965)	C6	C7	C8	Rarity
Complete Outfit	450	735	1,100	R8
Complete Outfit With no. 6413-25 Substitution	515	815	1,200	R8
Complete Outfit With no. 6413-1 Substitution	560	860	1,350	R8
Outfit Box no. 65-332	200	275	350	R8

Comments: After purchasing only three outfits in 1964, Sears, Roebuck and Co. made a large purchase of 14 Retailer Promotional outfits in 1965. Only three of these outfits appeared in the 1965 Sears Christmas Catalog.

Evidence suggests that Lionel offered Sears a similar deal to the "Special Purchase" granted in 1963. First, Factory Orders for

Outfit no. 19431 was one of the 14 outfits purchased by Sears in 1965. Eleven of these outfits, including the 19431, were labeled "Special Outfit" and used to deplete surplus inventory. According to the Factory Order, all the tenders were replaced. For that reason, the outfit shown here includes a no. 1061T-50 Tender substitution.

11 of these outfits were called "Special Outfit" and had similar dates of 3-23-65 or 3-24-65. Second, each of these 11 outfits included numerous substitutions, which indicated the depletion of surplus or old inventory. Third, none of these 11 outfits appeared in a Sears catalog. Finally, after 1965, Sears returned to its traditional pattern of purchasing three or four outfits each year.

The no. 19431, a Type Ib outfit, was one of the many steam-powered outfits purchased by Sears in 1965. It was likely sold over the counter at Sears stores because it did not appear in the 1965 Sears Christmas Catalog. Sears paid Lionel $8.00 for each 19431. A price tag has been observed with a $9.99 price. This was likely a sales price because similar Sears outfits sold for more.

The 19431 was led by a no. 1062-25 Steam Type Locomotive W/Light & Reversing Unit. This low-end Scout steamer featured an 0-4-0 wheel arrangement and lacked a traction aid. According to its Lionel Engineering Specification, it was the "Same as #1061 but with the addition of Reversing Unit & Lamp". The engine was making its last appearance in this outfit and outfit nos. 19245 (1965 version) and 19430.

As with all the Sears "Special Outfit" purchases from 1965, the 19431 reduced or depleted the inventory of many items. In fact, the locomotive and every piece of rolling stock except for the no. 1061T-25 Tender were making its final appearance in this or other outfits in 1965.

The nos. 3357-1 Animated Hobo & Railroad Policeman Car, 6413-1 Mercury Capsule Transport Car and 6463-1 Rocket Fuel Car came in Orange Picture boxes.

The 6824-50 Work Caboose is interesting because it shared the same cab and body as a no. 6814-1 First Aid Caboose (first issued in 1959). In fact, both cars were numbered 6814. The most noticeable difference is that the 6824-50 came with a black frame whereas the 6814-1 came with a gray one.

The no. 6142-175 Gondola Car was an unmarked olive drab no. 6142-series gondola car. It is one of the most desirable in the series.

Lionel apparently ran out of 1061T-25s, as they were all replaced by the no. 1061T-50 Tender.

The nos. 6440-50 Flat Car W/2 Piggy Back Vans and 6463-25 Rocket Fuel Car substitutions minimally affect the outfit price. The 6413 substitution commands a premium, as listed in the pricing table.

The rolling stock in the 19431 followed the normal truck and coupler progression for 1965, with each of the cars having AAR types. Many were equipped with one operating and one non-operating truck and coupler. However, the 1061T-50 had one non-operating and one plain type, and the 6824-50 had one operating and one plain type. Also, the 3357-1, 6413s and 6463s could come with two operating types.

The "X" at the end of the instruction sheet numbers indicated that the versions from the previous year were being used. Actually, the suffixes were unnecessary because Lionel did not make any changes to these sheets in 1965.

The no. 65-332 Tan RSC with Black Graphics outfit box was manufactured by United Container Co. and measured 14 x 9¾ x 6¾ inches. It included four lines of data, a "65" and seven stars as part of the box manufacturer's certificate. Printed on the bottom was a reference to the N.M.F.C.

Of the 11 Sears "Special Outfit" purchases for 1965, the 19431 was produced in the lowest quantity and is one of the most difficult to find.

Outfit no. 19432 was one of the 14 outfits purchased by Sears in 1965. Eleven of these outfits, including the 19432, were labeled "Special Outfit" and used to deplete surplus inventory. Lionel apparently had extra no. 6413-4 Mercury Capsules, as they were included as a load for the no. 6142-175 Gondola Car. The no. 61-170 Outfit Box is shown with the no. 1061T-50 Tender substitution.

Description: "O27" Special Outfit
Customer/Price: Sears, Roebuck and Co.; $15.99
Original Amount: 2,500
Factory Order Date: 3/24/1965
Date Issued: Rev 6-7-65
Packaging: Units Loose, Kraft RSC 6/Shipper

Contents: 1062-50 Steam Type Loco. W/Light & Reversing Unit; 1061T-25 Tender; 3309-50 Turbo Missile Firing Car; 0349-10 Turbo Missile (2); 6142-175 Gondola Car; 6413-4 Mercury Capsules (2); 6402-25 Flat Car W/2 Cable Reels; 40-11 Cable Reels (2); 6119-125 Work Caboose; 1013-8 Curved Track (Bundle of 8 - 1013); 1018-5 Straight Track (Bundle of 5 - 1018); 1008-50 Uncoupling Unit; 1010-25 35-Watt Transformer; 1103-20 Envelope Packed; 1641-10X Instruction Sheet; 1-66X Flyer; Form 3063 Parts Order Form; 1-65 Warranty Card

Boxes & Packing: 61-170 Outfit Box; 61-171 Corr. Insert; 61-172 Corr. Insert; 62-264 Corr. Insert; 61-174 Shipper for 6 (1-6); 64-213 Corr. Pad (2-6); 62-243 Outfit Box (Use this box and the following when using 3545-1 or 3830-1); 62-254 Corr. Insert; 62-223 Corr. Insert; 63-380 Shipper for 6 (1-6); 64-213 Corr. Pad (2-6)

Alternate For Outfit Contents:
Note: Sub. 2,500 - 1061T-50 for 1061T-25; Sub. 6 - 3309-25 for 3309-50; Sub. 65 - 3545-1 for 3309-50; Sub. 43 - 3830-1 for 3309-50; Sub. 700 - 6176-100 for 6402-25 and 40-11; Sub. 1,500 - 6824-50 for 6119-125; Sub. 433 - 6429-1 for 6119-125; Sub. 143 - 6119-110 for 6119-125.

19432 (1965)	C6	C7	C8	Rarity
Complete Outfit With no. 61-170 Box	495	800	1,225	R6
Outfit Box no. 61-170	60	130	200	R6
Complete Outfit With no. 62-243 Box And no. 3545-1 Substitution	810	1,195	1,725	R10
Complete Outfit With no. 62-243 Box And no. 3830-1 Substitution	725	1,105	1,600	R10
Outfit Box no. 62-243	400	600	800	R10
Either Outfit Box With no. 3309-25 Substitution, Subtract The Following	180	270	355	Same
Either Outfit Box With no. 6176-100 Substitution, Add The Following	40	60	90	Same
Either Outfit Box With no. 6119-110 Substitution, Subtract The Following	80	130	235	Same
Either Outfit Box With no. 6429-1 Substitution, Add The Following	360	550	640	Same
Either Outfit Box With no. 6824-50 Substitution, Subtract The Following	30	40	115	Same

Comments: After purchasing only three outfits in 1964, Sears, Roebuck and Co. made a large purchase of 14 Retailer Promotional outfits in 1965. Only three of these outfits appeared in the 1965 Sears Christmas Catalog.

Evidence suggests that Lionel offered Sears a similar deal to the "Special Purchase" granted in 1963. First, Factory Orders for 11 of these outfits were called "Special Outfit" and had similar dates of 3-23-65 or 3-24-65. Second, each of these 11 outfits included numerous substitutions, which indicated the depletion of surplus or old inventory. Third, none of these 11 outfits appeared in a Sears catalog. Finally, after 1965, Sears returned to its traditional pattern of purchasing three or four outfits each year.

The no. 19432, a Type Ib outfit, was one of the many steam-powered outfits purchased by Sears in 1965. This outfit, for which Sears paid $8.00 each, was likely sold over the counter at Sears stores because it did not appear in the 1965 Sears Christmas Catalog.

The 19432 was led by a no. 1062-50 Steam Type Loco. W/ Light & Reversing Unit. This low-end Scout steamer featured an 0-4-0 wheel arrangement and a rubber tire as a traction aid. Except for the rubber tire, it was identical to the no. 1062-25 Steam Type Loco. W/Light & Reversing Unit. This locomotive pulled a no. 1061T-50 Tender because Lionel apparently ran out of the no. 1061T-25 Tender. The latter were all replaced by the 1061T-50.

In fact, like all the Sears "Special Outfit" purchases from 1965, the 19432 reduced or depleted the inventory of many items. The nos. 3309-25 Turbo Missile Firing Car, olive drab 3309-50 Turbo Missile Firing Car, 3545-1 Operating TV Monitor Car and 6429-1 Wrecking Car last appeared in this outfit. In addition to the locomotive, tender and no. 6402-25 Flat Car W/2 Cable Reels, all the remaining cars in this outfit were making their last outfit appearances in 1965.

The 3545-1 and 3830-1 substitutions came in Orange Picture boxes. They, along with many of the other substitutions, affect the outfit price, as outlined in the pricing table.

Perhaps the key substitutions involved the car at the end of the train. The no. 6119-125 Work Caboose amounted to a no. 6814-style work caboose that came with an olive drab body and a black frame and lacked a load and a number. This model was replaced by a no. 6824-50 Work Caboose in 1,500 of the outfits. The 6824-50 is interesting because it shared the cab and body used on the no. 6814-1 First Aid Caboose (first issued in 1959). In fact both cars were numbered 6814. The most noticeable difference is that the

6824-50 came with a black frame while the 6814-1 came with a gray one.

Also used as a substitution in this outfit was the no. 6429-1, a rare item that came in only one catalog and three promotional outfits. A total of 1,433 were included in these outfits. Its no. 6429-10 Folding Box was the first Hillside Orange Picture box issued by Lionel. The box listed Lionel's corporate name as "The Lionel Toy Corporation".

The rolling stock in the 19432 followed the normal truck and coupler progression for 1965, with each of the cars having AAR types. Some were equipped with non-operating trucks and couplers. However, the 1061T-50 had one non-operating and one plain type, and the nos. 6119-110 Work Caboose, 6119-125 and 6824-50 had one operating and one plain type. Also, the nos. 3309-50, 6142-175 Gondola Car and 6176-100 Hopper Car came with one non-operating and one operating type. Finally, the 3545-1, 3830-1 and 6429-1 were equipped with two operating types.

The "X" at the end of the instruction sheet numbers indicated that the versions from the previous year were being used. Actually, the suffixes were unnecessary because Lionel did not make any changes to these sheets in 1965.

The 19432 came in two different Tan RSC with Black Graphics outfit boxes. The no. 61-170 Outfit Box was manufactured by United Container Co. and measured 11½ x 10¼ x 6¼ inches. It included four lines of data as part of the box manufacturer's certificate. The no. 62-243 Outfit Box measured 12⅛ x 11½ x 6⅜ inches.

Of the two outfit boxes, the 62-243 version is extremely difficult to find and receives an R10 rarity rating. The 61-170 version is much more common.

Because of all the substitutions, the 19432 should actually be seen as many outfits in one. One of the most desirable versions featured the olive drab 6176-100 and boxed 6429-1 substitutions.

Description: "O27" Special Outfit
Customer/No./Price: Sears, Roebuck and Co.; 9837; $14.99
Original Amount: 1,190
Factory Order Date: 3/24/1965
Date Issued: Rev 6-7-65
Packaging: Units Loose, Kraft RSC 6/Shipper

Contents: 221P-25 Diesel Locomotive; 3376-160 Operating Giraffe Car; 6050-175 Libby Box Car; 6062-25 Gondola Car; 6167-25 Caboose; 1008-50 Uncoupling Unit; 1013-8 Curved Track (Bundle of 8 - 1013); 1018-5 Straight Track (Bundle of 5 - 1018); 1026-25 25-Watt Transformer; 1103-20 Envelope Packed; 1047-1 Switchman With Flag; 19301-10X Instruction Sheet; Form 3063 Parts Order Form; 1-65 Warranty Card

Boxes & Packing: 65-334 Outfit Box; 62-254 Corr. Insert; 61-172 Corr. Insert; 62-225 Corr. Insert; 64-143 Corr. Insert (2); 64-209 Corr. Insert; 65-335 Shipper for 6 (1-6); 64-104 Shipper Pad (2-6)

Alternate For Outfit Contents:
Note: Sub. 23 - 3376-1 for 3376-160; Sub. 17 - 3376-150 and 3376-118 for 3376-160; Sub. 106 - 3370-1 for 3376-160; Sub. 250

- 3357-1 for 3376-160; Sub. 290 - 3830-1 for 3376-160; Sub. 164 - 6050-100 for 6050-175; Sub. 710 - 6142-75 for 6062-25.

19433 (1965)	C6	C7	C8	Rarity
Complete Outfit	530	955	1,350	R6
Outfit Box no. 65-334	100	200	275	R6

Comments: After purchasing only three outfits in 1964, Sears, Roebuck and Co. made a large purchase of 14 Retailer Promotional outfits in 1965. Only three of these outfits appeared in the 1965 Sears Christmas Catalog.

Evidence suggests that Lionel offered Sears a similar deal to the "Special Purchase" granted in 1963. First, Factory Orders for 11 of these outfits were called "Special Outfit" and had similar dates of 3-23-65 or 3-24-65. Second, each of these 11 outfits included numerous substitutions, which indicated the depletion of surplus or old inventory. Third, none of these 11 outfits appeared in a Sears catalog. Finally, after 1965, Sears returned to its traditional pattern of purchasing three or four outfits each year.

The no. 19433, a Type Ib outfit, was one of the five diesel-powered outfits purchased by Sears in 1965. This outfit, for which

Outfit no. 19433 was one of the 14 outfits purchased by Sears in 1965. Eleven of these outfits, including the 19433, were labeled "Special Outfit" and used to deplete surplus inventory. The inclusion of a no. 1047-1 Switchman With Flag in its fragile no. 1047-12 Folding Box makes this a desirable promotional outfit.

Sears paid $9.00 each, was likely sold over the counter at Sears stores because it did not appear in the 1965 Sears Christmas Catalog.

The 19433 was led by a no. 221P-25 Rio Grande Diesel Locomotive. This low-end, unpainted yellow Alco featured a two-position reversing unit, a traction tire and a closed pilot and lacked a headlight.

As with all the Sears "Special Outfit" purchases from 1965, the 19433 reduced or depleted the inventory of many items. The no. 1047-1 Switchman With Flag and Orange Picture boxed no. 3370-1 Sheriff & Outlaw Car last appeared in this outfit. The no. 6050-175 Libby Box Car, which was introduced in the no. 19263 "Libby" outfit from 1963, was making its last appearances in 1965. The Orange Picture boxed nos. 3357-1 Animated Hobo & Railroad Policeman Car and 3830-1 Operating Submarine Car were being depleted in the Sears outfits. The 3376 Giraffe Car was making its last appearance in 1965 before it was reissued in 1969; boxed versions came in Orange Picture boxes.

The 1047-1 was the most notable component of this outfit. The accessory is nothing too exciting, but its no. 1047-12 Folding Box was made of flimsy chipboard and did not survive well. It is extremely difficult to find in collectible condition with the top flap still attached.

The rolling stock in the 19433 followed the normal truck and coupler progression for 1965, with each of the cars having AAR types. Some were equipped with one operating and one non-operating truck and coupler. However, the no. 6167-25 Caboose had one non-operating and one plain AAR type. The norm for the 6050-175 was non-operating types, although it has been observed with one operating and one non-operating type. Also, the norm for the 3357-1, 3370-1, 3376s and 3830-1 was operating types.

The "X" at the end of the no. 19301-10X Instruction Sheet indicated that the version from the previous year was being used. Actually, the suffix was unnecessary because Lionel did not make any changes to this sheet in 1965.

The no. 65-334 Tan RSC with Black Graphics outfit box was manufactured by United Container Co. and measured 15½ x 11½ x 6¼ inches. It included four lines of data, a "65" and eight stars as part of the box manufacturer's certificate. Printed on the bottom was a reference to the N.M.F.C.

Compared to the overall outfit price, the substitutions have a minimal impact on the price.

The 19433 is a desirable outfit because of the inclusion of a 1047-1. Unfortunately, most outfits are found without this fragile item. Finding a boxed 1047-1 is more difficult than finding the remaining items in the 19433.

Description: "O27" Special Outfit
Customer/No./Price: Sears, Roebuck and Co.; 49 19434; $14.97
Original Amount: 3,798
Factory Order Date: 3/24/1965
Date Issued: Rev. 6-17-65
Packaging: Units Loose, Kraft RSC 6/Shipper

Contents: 221P-50 Diesel Locomotive; 3665-1 Minuteman Missile Launching Car; 6470-25 Exploding Target Car; 6142-75 Gondola Car; 6059-50 Caboose; 975-1 Squad of Soldiers; 958-150 Jeep Assembled; 958-175 Cannon Assembled; 347-25 Rocket Launching Platform; 958-75 Tank; 6029-25 Uncoupling Track Section; 1013-8 Curved Track (Bundle of 8 - 1013); 1018-5 Straight Track (Bundle of 5 - 1018); 347-5 Shell (4); 1010-25 35-Watt Transformer; 1103-40 Envelope Packed; 347-10X Instruction Sheet; 6470-17X Instruction Sheet; 11440-10X Instruction Sheet;

19339-10X Flyer; 6029-8X Flyer; Form 3063 Parts Order Form; 1-65 Warranty Card

Boxes & Packing: 62-243 Outfit Box; 62-254 Corr. Insert; 62-223 Corr. Insert; 63-380 Shipper for 6 (1-6); 64-213 Corr. Pad (2-6); 62-243 Outfit Box (When using 3666-25 use this box and the following:); 62-254 Corr. Insert; 62-223 Corr. Insert; 62-225 Corr. Insert (2); 63-380 Shipper for 6 (1-6); 64-213 Corr. Pad (2-6); 65-336 Outfit Box (When using 443-1 or 419-1 use this box and the following:); 62-254 Corr. Insert; 61-183 Corr. Insert; 46599-12 Corr. Insert; 62-225 Corr. Insert (2); 65-337 Shipper for 6 (1-6); 41110-23 Corr. Pad (2-6)

Alternate For Outfit Contents:
Note: Sub. 1,126 - 221P-25 for 221P-50; Sub. 320 - 231P-1 for 221P-50; Sub. 7 - 213P-25 for 221P-50; Sub 221P-75 for 221P-50 as needed; Sub. 136 - 6448-1 for 6470-25 and 6470-17X; Sub. 150 - 6448-25 and 6448-14 for 6470-25 and 6470-17X; Sub. 266 - 419-1 - for 347-25 and 347-10X; Sub. 225 - 443-1 - for 347-25 and 347-10X; Sub. 12 - 462-1 for 347-25 and 347-10X; Sub. 2,351 - 3666-25, 3666-20X and (4) 3666-8 for 3665-1; Note: Use 61-183 when 419-1 is used and 46599-12 when 443-1 is used.

19434 (1965)	C6	C7	C8	Rarity
Complete Outfit With no. 62-243 Box	1,150	2,215	3,350	R7
Complete Outfit With no. 62-243 Box And no. 462-1 Substitution	960	1,695	2,550	R6
Outfit Box no. 62-243	150	300	450	R6
Complete Outfit With no. 65-336 Box And no. 419-1 Substitution	1,085	2,045	3,220	R9
Complete Outfit With no. 65-336 Box And no. 443-1 Substitution	910	1,535	2,400	R9
Outfit Box no. 65-336	250	400	650	R9
Either Outfit Box With no. 221P-25 Substitution, Subtract The Following	205	410	615	Same
Either Outfit Box With nos. 231P-1or 213P-25 Substitutions, Subtract The Following	175	335	500	Same
Either Outfit Box With no. 3666-25 Substitution, Add The Following	270	425	735	Same

Comments: After purchasing only three outfits in 1964, Sears, Roebuck and Co. made a large purchase of 14 Retailer Promotional outfits in 1965. Only three of these outfits appeared in the 1965 Sears Christmas Catalog.

Evidence suggests that Lionel offered Sears a similar deal to the "Special Purchase" granted in 1963. First, Factory Orders for 11 of these outfits were called "Special Outfit" and had similar dates of 3-23-65 or 3-24-65. Second, each of these 11 outfits included numerous substitutions, which indicated the depletion of surplus or old inventory. Third, none of these 11 outfits appeared in a Sears catalog. Finally, after 1965, Sears returned to its traditional pattern of purchasing three or four outfits each year.

The no. 19434, a Type Ib outfit, was one of the five diesel-powered outfits purchased by Sears in 1965. It was likely sold over the counter at Sears stores because it did not appear in the 1965 Sears Christmas Catalog. This space and military outfit, for which Sears paid Lionel $10.00 each, has been observed with Sears price tags for $14.97 and $18.99.

The 19434 was a follow-up to outfit no. 19326 (Sears no. 9820) from 1964. It included numerous substitutions that led to more than 150 possible outfit configurations. As with all the Sears "Special Outfit" purchases from 1965, the 19434 reduced or depleted the inventory of many items. In fact, except for the nos. 221P-25 Diesel Locomotive, 6059-50 Caboose and 6142-75 Gondola Car, all the Alcos, rolling stock and accessories in this outfit were making their last appearance. All the substitutions are listed in the Alternate For Outfit Contents Section, and if they change the outfit price, in the pricing table as well.

To begin, the 19434 most often was led by a no. 221P-50 Diesel Locomotive. This olive drab "USMC" diesel featured a two-position reversing unit, a traction tire and a closed pilot and lacked a headlight.

It appears that Lionel was also freely substituting an olive drab no. 221P-75 Santa Fe Diesel Locomotive for the no. 221P-50 because outfits have been observed with this Alco. The 221P-75 had the same features as the 221P-50. Although the Santa Fe is more difficult to find than the USMC, the price differential is minimal as compared to the outfit price.

The rolling stock in this outfit included a few notable items. The no. 6470-25 Exploding Target Car was the more difficult-to-find version with one operating and one non-operating AAR truck and coupler. All the boxed rolling stock came in Orange Picture boxes.

In addition, the no. 3665-1 Minuteman Missile Launching Car was the harder-to-find version with a light blue roof. (See outfit no. 19232 from 1963 for an explanation of this variation.) However, a no. 3666-25 Cannon Box Car replaced the 3665-1 in most outfits. The 3666-25 appeared only in four promotional outfits. It also included a light blue roof but came with an olive drab cannon firing mechanism. The car was modeled after the 3665-1 but fired shells like a no. 6651-25 Cannon Car.

The cars in the 19434 followed the normal truck and coupler progression for 1965, with each of them having AAR types. Some were equipped with operating trucks and couplers. However, the 6059-50 had one operating and one plain type. Also, the 3666-25, 6142-75 and 6470-25 came with one operating and one non-operating type.

As with many promotional outfits, the peripherals included in the 19434 make it a highly collectible outfit. Specifically, the no. 347-25 Rocket Launching Platform appeared only in three promotional outfits. This difficult-to-find item commands a premium price.

The 19434 also included three items purchased from Payton Products: nos. 958-75 Tank, 958-150 Jeep Assembled and 958-175 Cannon Assembled. It was one of 11 outfits to include a no. 975-1 Squad of Soldiers, which consisted of 10 soldiers purchased from Multiple Products Corporation (MPC) of New York and placed in a polyethylene bag. (See outfit no. 19326 from 1964 for details about the 958s and 975-1.)

The substitutions of the nos. 419-1 Operating Heliport and 462-1 Derrick Platform were interesting. Both are less valuable than the 347-25 they replaced; however, the 419-1 appeared only in one other outfit and the 462-1 only in this outfit.

The "X" at the end of the instruction sheet numbers indicated that the versions from the previous year were being used. The proper instruction sheets made reference to the 90-day warranty that Lionel

753

Outfit no. 19434 was one of the 14 outfits purchased by Sears in 1965. Eleven of these outfits, including the 19434, were labeled "Special Outfit" and used to deplete surplus inventory. With all its substitutions, more than 150 possible configurations are possible. One of the most desirable space and military outfits, this no. 62-243 Outfit Box example had the olive drab no. 221P-75 Santa Fe Diesel Locomotive substitution.

instituted in 1963. These are some of the most difficult versions to find. The correct no. 11440-10 Instruction Sheet was dated 6/64. The no. 6470-17 Instruction Sheet was dated 8-59 but made reference to the 90-day warranty policy. The no. 6029-8 Flyer is very difficult to find. Be aware that the nos. 347-10 Instruction Sheet and 3666-20 Instruction Sheet have been reproduced. Original versions are difficult and expensive to find.

Two outfit boxes were used for the 19434. The no. 62-243 Tan RSC with Black Graphics outfit box was used for 3,307 of them. Manufactured by St. Joe Kraft, St. Joe Paper Co. Container Division, it measured 12⅛ x 11½ x 6⅜ inches and had four lines of data as part of the box manufacturer's certificate. Printed on the

bottom was a reference to the N.M.F.C.

The no. 65-336 Tan RSC with Black Graphics outfit box was unique to this outfit. It was used for the 491 outfits that came with a 419-1 or 443-1.

The 62-243 Outfit Box is fairly common and achieves only an R6 rarity rating. By contrast, the 65-336 Outfit Box is very difficult to find and achieves an R9 rarity rating. Even if a box is found, trying to complete an outfit can take years because the rolling stock, paperwork and peripherals are difficult to find.

Even with 3,798 of these outfits produced, the 19434 and its individual components are in such high demand that the price for a complete C8 outfit remains high.

Description: "O27" Special Outfit
Customer: Sears, Roebuck and Co.
Original Amount: 1,200
Factory Order Date: 3/24/1965
Date Issued: Rev 6-7-65
Date Req'd: 5-27-65
Packaging: Units Loose, Kraft RSC Pack

Contents: 215P-25 "Santa Fe" Diesel Power Car; 6475-50 Crushed Pineapple Car; 6414-75 Auto Transport Car; 0068-3 Automobile Body (Maroon) (2); 0068-105 Automobile Body (Yellow) (2); 6142-125 Gondola Car; 3364-25 Log Dump Car; 3364-8 Logs (3); 3413-1 Mercury Capsule Launching Car; 6059-50 Caboose; 54-1 Track Ballast Car; 6029-1 Uncoupling Track Section; 1013-70 Curved Track (Bundle of 12 - 1013); 1018-7 Straight Track (Bundle of 7 - 1018); 1018-40 Straight Track (Bundle of 4 - 1018); 1020-25 90° Crossing; 1025-25 45-Watt Transformer; 1103-20 Envelope Packed; 1802-10X Instruction

Sheet; 19214-10X Instruction Sheet; 6029-8X Flyer; 211-151X Instruction Sheet; 3364-10X Instruction Sheet; Form 3063 Parts Order Form; 1-65 Warranty Card

Boxes & Packing: 63-313 Outfit Box; 63-315 Corr. Insert; 62-225 Corr. Insert (4); 65-338 Shipper for 6 (1-6); 41110-23 Shipper Pad (2-6)

Alternate For Outfit Contents:
Note: Sub. 36 - 6414-85 for 6414-75; Sub. 520 - 6440-1 for 6414-75; Sub. 55 - 6446-1 for 6414-75; Sub. 155 - 6446-60 for 6414-75; Sub. 82 - 3470-100 With 3470-20 & 3470-4 for 3413-1; Sub. 69 - 3330-1 for 3413-1; Sub. 255 - 3519-1 for 3413-1; Sub. 98 - 6650-1 for 3413-1; Sub. 12 - 3362-1 for 3413-1; Sub. 50 - 6512-1 for 3413-1; Sub. 169 - 6512-25 With 6512-19X for 3413-1; Sub. 76 - 6544-1 for 3413-1.

Outfit no. 19435 was one of the 14 outfits purchased by Sears in 1965. Eleven of these outfits, including the 19435, were labeled "Special Outfit" and used to deplete surplus inventory. This 19435 is shown as listed on the Factory Order without any substitutions. It included the no. 6414-75 Auto Transport Car with two no. 0068-3 Automobile Body (Maroon) and two no. 0068-105 Automobile Body (Yellow). The no. 6029-1 Uncoupling Track Section box is not shown.

19400 Series

19435 (1965)	C6	C7	C8	Rarity
Complete Outfit	845	1,500	2,135	R7
Complete Outfit With no. 6414-85 Substitution	1,220	1,960	2,660	R7
Complete Outfit With no. 6440-1 Substitution	690	1,280	1,830	R7
Complete Outfit With no. 6446-1 Substitution	850	1,560	2,260	R7
Complete Outfit With no. 6446-60 Substitution	920	1,660	2,460	R7
Complete Outfit With nos. 3470-100 or 6544-1 Substitution	850	1,525	2,200	R7
Complete Outfit With nos. 3362-1, 3519-1, 6512-1, 6512-25 or 6650-1 Substitution	800	1,400	2,025	R7
Outfit Box no. 63-313	100	200	275	R7

Comments: After purchasing only three outfits in 1964, Sears, Roebuck and Co. made a large purchase of 14 Retailer Promotional outfits in 1965. Only three of these outfits appeared in the 1965 Sears Christmas Catalog.

Evidence suggests that Lionel offered Sears a similar deal to the "Special Purchase" granted in 1963. First, Factory Orders for 11 of these outfits were called "Special Outfit" and had similar dates of 3-23-65 or 3-24-65. Second, each of these 11 outfits included numerous substitutions, which indicated the depletion of surplus or old inventory. Third, none of these 11 outfits appeared in a Sears catalog. Finally, after 1965, Sears returned to its traditional pattern of purchasing three or four outfits each year.

The no. 19435, a Type Ib outfit, was one of the five diesel-powered outfits purchased by Sears in 1965. This outfit, for which Sears paid $15.00 each, was likely sold over the counter at Sears stores because it did not appear in the 1965 Sears Christmas Catalog.

As with all the Sears "Special Outfit" purchases from 1965, the 19435 reduced or depleted the inventory of many items. In fact, except for the no. 215P-25 Santa Fe Diesel Power Car, 3364-25 Log Dump Car, 6059-50 Caboose and 6142-125 Gondola Car, all the rolling stock in this outfit was making its last appearance. All the substitutions are listed in the Alternate For Outfit Contents Section and, if they change the outfit price, in the pricing table as well.

The 19435 was led by a no. 215P-25 Santa Fe Diesel Power Car. This promotional-only Alco featured a two-position reversing unit, two traction tires, a headlight, a weight and an open pilot with a large ledge.

The rolling stock and substitutions included many notable and rare items. Start with the no. 54-1 Track Ballast Car; this was the only outfit in which this motorized unit appeared during the 1960s.

The no. 6414-75 Auto Transport was carried over from 1964. The "-75" indicated that it came unboxed with operating AAR trucks and couplers and a new load. The new load was two no. 0068-3 Automobile Body (Maroon) and two no. 0068-105 Automobile Body (Yellow). (See outfit no. 19380 for a full description of this car.)

The no. 6446-1 N&W Cement Car in its Orange Picture box is extremely tough to find. It was a reissue of the 6446-1 that first appeared in 1954. The reissued 6446-1 came in one catalog and four promotional outfits, with a total of 1,527 cars produced. The "-1" meant the car was gray. Even though its number was 6446-1, the car was stamped "644625".

The Orange Picture boxed no. 6446-60 Cement Car is also extremely difficult to find. The car was actually numbered "6436" and included a cover with hatches. It was first issued in 1963 in Super O outfit no. 13118. The 19435 was its only other outfit appearance. The quantity of 155 included in this outfit was the remaining inventory.

The no. 3470-100 Aerial Target Launching Car in this outfit was the difficult-to-find version with a light blue frame. The no. 3330-1 Flat Car With Operating Submarine (Kit) was last seen in catalog outfit no. 11298 from 1962.

The no. 6544-1 Missile Firing Trail Car had two brake wheels attached to the plastic frame ends. Over time, the frame is easily cracked or broken off where the wheels were attached. The 6544-1, like all the boxed rolling stock, came in Orange Picture boxes.

The rolling stock in the 19435 followed the normal truck and coupler progression for 1965, with each of the cars having AAR types. Some were equipped with operating trucks and couplers. However, the 6059-50 had one operating and one plain type. Also, the 3364-25, 3470-100 and 6142-125 came with one operating and one non-operating type.

The "X" at the end of the instruction sheet numbers indicated that the versions from the previous year were being used. The

proper instruction sheets made reference to the 90-day warranty that Lionel instituted in 1963. These are some of the most difficult versions to find.

Also included in the 19435 was the boxed no. 6029-1 Uncoupling Track Section. This was one of three outfits to include a boxed version. Finding its rare individual box in C8 condition is difficult and very expensive.

The no. 63-313 Tan RSC with Black Graphics outfit box was manufactured by United Container Co. and measured 14½ x 11¾ x 7 inches. It included four lines of data, a "65" and seven stars as part of the box manufacturer's certificate. Printed on the bottom was a reference to the N.M.F.C.

Lionel exhausted the inventory of some highly collectible rolling stock in this outfit. As such, this outfit is often split up and sold separately. Empty outfit boxes do appear, but filling them takes time and money.

The no. 19436 was Western Auto's only promotional outfit purchase for 1965. A low-end outfit, it did include one operating car, the no. 3364-25 Log Dump Car. This outfit was marked with "E1002 15.77" on the box top (in blue ink right below the "S" in "Set"). Western Auto purchased a slightly updated version of this outfit in 1966.

Description: "O27" Promotional Outfit
Specification: "O27" Steam Type Freight Outfit
Customer/No./Price: Western Auto; E1002; $15.77
Original Amount: 5,850
Factory Order Date: 6/16/1965
Date Issued: Rev 8-16-65

Packaging: Display Pack 4/Shipper (Units not Boxed)

Contents: 1062-50 Steam Type Loco. W/Light & Reversing Unit; 1062T-25 Tender; 3364-25 Log Dump Car; 3364-8 Logs (3); 6142-100 Gondola Car; 6112-88 Canister (2); 6059-50 Caboose; 1013-70 Curved Track (Bundle of 12 - 1013); 1018-30

Straight Track (Bundle of 3 - 1018); 1020-25 90° Crossing; 6149-25 Remote Control Track; 1010-25 35-Watt Transformer; 1103-40 Envelope Packed; D65-50 Accessory Catalog; Form 3063 Parts Order Form; 1-165 Warranty Card; 926-65 Service Station List; 3364-10 Instruction Sheet; 11450-10 Instruction Sheet; 1802-10 Instruction Sheet

Boxes & Packing: 65-260 Box Top; 64-102 Box Bottom; 65-264 Corr. Insert; 64-105 Shipper for 4 (1-4); 64-106 Shipper Pad (2-4)

19436 (1965)	C6	C7	C8	Rarity
Complete Outfit	115	190	295	R3
Outfit Box no. 65-260	15	25	40	R3

Comments: The no. 19436 was the only promotional outfit purchased by Western Auto Stores for 1965. This Retailer Promotional Type Ia, for which Lionel was paid $8.91 each, appeared on page 12 of the 1965 Western Auto Christmas Gifts Catalog as no. E1002 for $15.77. A Factory Order for a 1966 version of this outfit also lists Western Auto as the customer, but that version has yet to be observed in any Western Auto literature.

The 19436 from 1965 was led by a no. 1062-50 Steam Type Loco. W/Light & Reversing Unit. This low-end Scout steamer featured an 0-4-0 wheel arrangement and a rubber tire as a traction aid. Except for the rubber tire, it was identical to the no. 1062-25 Steam Type Loco. W/Light & Reversing Unit.

The rolling stock consisted of carryover items that were commonly used in outfits from 1965. The most notable item was the no. 3364-25 Log Dump Car, which was identical to the no. 3362-25 Helium Tank Unloading Car except that it carried logs instead of helium tanks. The green no. 6142-100 Gondola Car transported two white no. 6112-88 Canisters.

The rolling stock in the 19436 followed the normal truck and coupler progression for 1965, with each of the cars having AAR types. The no. 6059-50 Caboose had one late operating and one plain type, and the no. 1062T-25 Tender had one late non-operating and one plain type. Also, the 3364-25 came with late operating types, and the 6142-100 had one late operating and one late non-operating truck and coupler.

A no. 1802-10 Instruction Sheet detailed the figure-eight track layout.

The no. 65-260 White Lift-Off with Full-Color 2037 Steam Freight Graphics Type D display outfit box was manufactured by Mead Containers and measured 23½ x 11½ x 3 inches.

There are subtle differences between the 1965 and 1966 versions of this outfit (see the entry for the 19436 from 1966), but they do not affect the overall outfit price. Also, since the packaging is the same for both years, a combined quantity of 6,550 is used to determine the rarity and pricing.

There is a segment of collectors that collects specific retailer offerings, and Western Auto outfits have a following among them. Therefore, although the 19436 was produced in large quantities and is readily available, many enthusiasts will want to add it to their collections.

Description: "O27" Promotional Outfit
Specification: "O27" Steam Type Freight Outfit
Customer: Western Auto
Original Amount: 700
Factory Order Date: 4/29/1966
Date Issued: Rev 5-20-66
Date Req'd: 5-20-66
Packaging: Display Pack 4/ Shipper (Units not Boxed)

Contents: 1062-75 Steam Type Loco. W/Light & Reversing Unit; 1062T-25 Tender; 3364-25 Log Dump Car; 3364-8 Logs (3); 6142-100 Gondola Car; 6112-88 Canister (2); 6059-50 Caboose; 1013-70 Curved Track (Bundle of 12 - 1013); 1018-30 Straight Track (Bundle of 3 - 1018); 1020-25 90° Crossing; 6149-25 Remote Control Track; 1010-25 35-Watt Transformer; 1103-40 Envelope Packed; D65-50 Accessory Catalog; Form 3063 Parts Order Form; 1-166 Warranty Card; 926-66 Service Station List; 3364-10 Instruction Sheet; 11450-10 Instruction Sheet; 1802-10 Instruction Sheet

Boxes & Packing: 65-260 Box Top; 64-102 Box Bottom; 65-264 Corr. Insert; 64-105 Shipper for 4 (1-4); 64-106 Shipper Pad (2-4)

Alternate For Outfit Contents:
Note: Substitute 1025-25 Transformer for 1010-25 Transformer.

Comments: Western Auto Stores purchased four outfits in 1966: nos. 11520, 19436, 19530 and 19910. The Retailer Promotional Type Ib outfit 19436 from 1966 was a repeat order of the 19436 from the previous year. The 1966 version has yet to be observed in any Western Auto literature.

The 1966 version included an updated locomotive, paperwork, transformer and trucks and couplers – otherwise, it was identical to the 1965 outfit. Frankly, these changes were so small that the pricing and rarity are the same as the 1965 version.

The 19436 from 1966 was led by a no. 1062-75 Steam Type Loco. W/Light & Reversing Unit (new for 1966). This low-end Scout steamer featured a 2-4-2 wheel arrangement and a rubber tire as a traction aid. Except for its wheel arrangement, the 1062-75 was identical to the no. 1062-50 Steam Type Loco. W/Light & Reversing Unit.

The paperwork was updated to include a 1966 warranty card and service station list.

The most noticeable change involving trucks and couplers occurred with the no. 6059-50 Caboose. In 1966, it normally was equipped with one operating and one non-operating AAR truck and coupler.

The outfit box and inserts were identical, and the pricing and rarity for this outfit are the same as the 1965 version. (See the 19436 from 1965.)

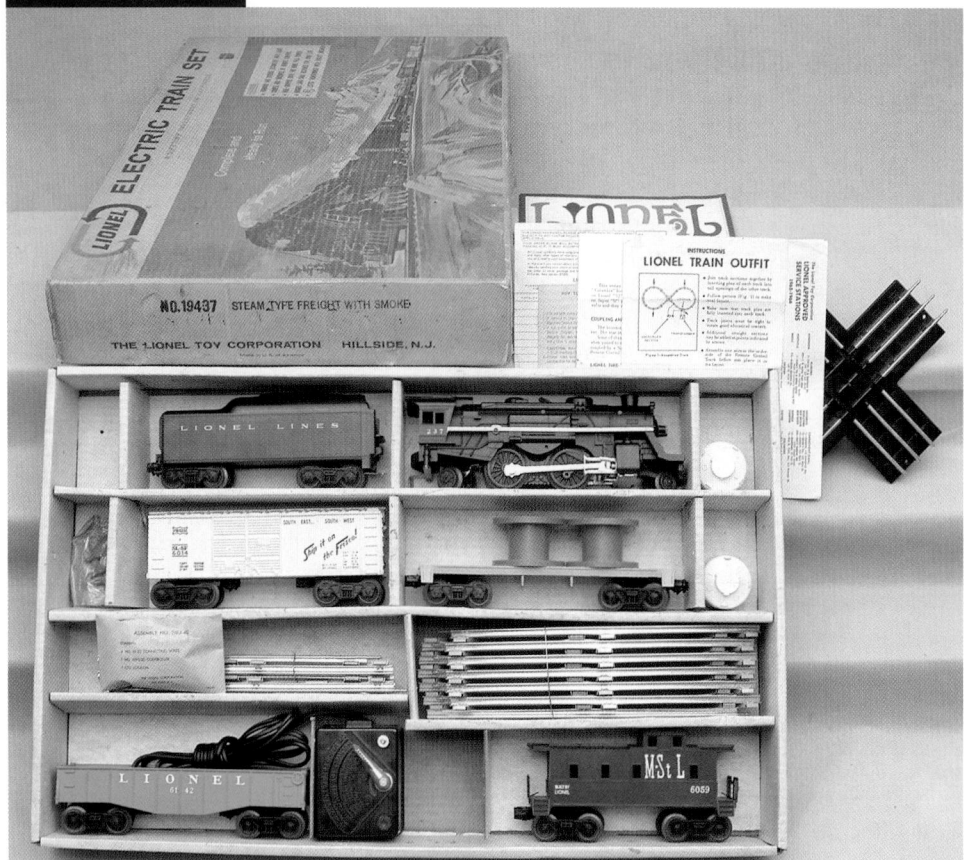

The no. 19437 was a mid-level steam-powered General Release Promotional outfit for 1965 that, like many other promotional outfits from that year, was made up of carryover items. It featured a no. 237-25 Steam Type Locomotive with Smoke and a figure-eight track layout.

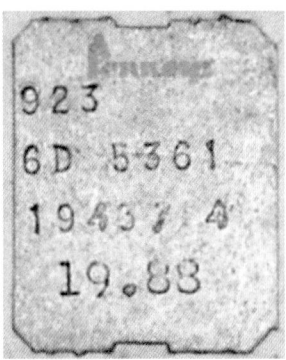

A price tag from a display-packed no. 19437 links this outfit to J. C. Penney as no. 923 5361 for $19.88. The display-packed outfit was sold over the counter, whereas the mail-order version was listed in the 1965 J. C. Penney Christmas Catalog as no. X 924-3726 A (Lionel no. 19437-502) for $18.99.

Boxes & Packing: 65-270 Box Top; 64-115 Box Bottom; 64-118 Corr. Insert; 64-119 Corr. Insert; 64-120 Corr. Insert; 64-116 Shipper for 4 (1-4); 64-117 Shipper Pad (2-4)

19437 (1965)	C6	C7	C8	Rarity
Complete Outfit	125	200	300	R4
Outfit Box no. 65-270	15	25	40	R4

Comments: In 1965, Lionel offered Retailer Promotional outfits to only Mercury Model, Sears and Western Auto. Other retailers, many of whom were accustomed to obtaining exclusive promotional outfits, were now limited to General Release Promotional outfits. They had to compete head-to-head with other retailers with similar offerings. Many of these outfits were offered in both display and mail-order RSC packed versions.

Outfit no. 19437, a General Release Promotional Type IIa outfit, was display-packed and sold over the counter at retailers, whereas its mail-order RSC counterpart, outfit no. 19437-502, was sold through retail catalogs. The 19437 has been linked to J. C. Penney as no. 923 5361 for $19.88. It likely was also sold over the counter by other retailers. Retailers paid Lionel $12.60 for each 19437.

The 19437 was a mid-level steam-powered outfit. It was led by a no. 237-25 Steam Type Locomotive with Smoke. This Scout steamer featured a two-position reversing unit and a headlight and used a rubber tire as a traction aid. The later version with narrow running boards came in this outfit.

All the cars in this outfit were carryover items that were commonly used in outfits from 1965. The most notable item was the Type III no. 6014-325 Frisco Box Car. The green no. 6142-100 Gondola Car carried two white no. 6112-88 Canisters.

The rolling stock in the 19437 followed the normal truck and

Description: "O27" Promotional Outfit
Specification: "O27" Steam Type Freight Outfit W/Smoke
Customer/No./Price: J. C. Penney Co., Inc.; 923 5361; $19.88
Original Amount: 3,660
Factory Order Date: 6/16/1965
Date Issued: Rev 8-16-65
Date Req'd: 8-16-65
Packaging: Display Pack 4/Shipper (Units not Boxed)

Contents: 237-25 Steam Type Locomotive with Smoke; 242T-25 Tender; 6142-100 Gondola Car; 6112-88 Canister (2); 6402-50 Flat Car W/2 Cable Reels; 40-11 Cable Reels (2); 6014-325 Frisco Box Car; 6059-50 Caboose; 1013-70 Curved Track (Bundle of 12 - 1013); 1018-30 Straight Track (Bundle of 3 - 1018); 1020-25 90° Crossing; 6149-25 Remote Control Track; 1010-25 35-Watt Transformer; 1103-40 Envelope Packed; 909-20 Smoke Fluid; D65-50 Accessory Catalog; Form 3063 Parts Order Form; 1-165 Warranty Card; 926-65 Service Station List; 19214-10 Instruction Sheet; 237-11 Instruction Sheet

coupler progression for 1965, with each of the cars having AAR types. All but two were equipped with one late operating and one late non-operating truck and coupler. The no. 242T-25 Tender had one late non-operating and one plain type, and the no. 6059-50 Caboose had one late operating and one plain type.

The no. 19214-10 Instruction Sheet detailed the figure-eight track layout and was dated 6/65. The no. 237-11 Instruction Sheet was dated 1/65 on the back and 4/65 on the inside.

The no. 65-270 White Lift-Off with Full-Color 2037 Steam Freight Graphics Type D display outfit box measured 24½ x 15½

x 3⅛ inches.

The 19437 was offered again in 1966 as both a General Release Promotional and a Retailer Promotional outfit for E. F. MacDonald. Comparing the 1965 and 1966 versions, we find no differences in the outfit packing and minimal differences in the contents (see the listing for 19437 from 1966). As such, the pricing and rarity are the same for all versions of the 19437.

This outfit was produced in large quantities and frequently appears on the market.

Description: "O27" Promotional Outfit
Specification: "O27" Steam Type Freight Outfit W/Smoke
Customer: E. F. MacDonald Co.
Original Amount: 648
Factory Order Date: 11/29/1966
Date Issued: 11-29-66
Date Req'd: 11-30-66
Packaging: Display Pack 4/Shipper (Units not Boxed)

Contents: 237-25 Steam Type Locomotive with Smoke; 242T-25 Tender; 6142-100 Gondola Car; 6112-88 Canister (2); 6402-50 Flat Car W/2 Cable Reels; 40-11 Cable Reels (2); 6014-325 Frisco Box Car; 6059-50 Caboose; 1013-70 Curved Track (Bundle of 12 - 1013); 1018-30 Straight Track (Bundle of 3 - 1018); 1020-25 90° Crossing; 6149-25 Remote Control Track; 1025-25 45-Watt Transformer; 1103-40 Envelope Packed; 909-20 Smoke Fluid; D65-50 Accessory Catalog; Form 3063 Parts Order Form; 1-165 Warranty Card; 926-65 Service Station List; 19214-10 Instruction Sheet; 237-11 Instruction Sheet

Boxes & Packing: 65-270 Box Top; 64-115 Box Bottom; 64-118

Corr. Insert; 64-119 Corr. Insert; 64-120 Corr. Insert; 64-116 Shipper for 4 (1-4); 64-117 Shipper Pad (2-4)

Alternate For Outfit Contents:
Note: Sub. (75) 239-25 for 237-25.

Comments: The no. 19437 from 1966 was a repeat of outfit 19437 from 1965. The contents of the two outfits were nearly identical, the only differences being that the later version came with an updated transformer and a locomotive substitution. Also, the rolling stock in the 19437 from 1966 was equipped with the trucks and couplers that were the norm for that year.

None of these changes materially affects the outfit price. In fact, the 1965 and 1966 versions are considered identical from a pricing and rarity perspective.

Of interest, two Factory Orders exist for the 19437 from 1966. The first was for a quantity of 448 for a General Release Promotional Type IIa outfit. The second was for a quantity of 200 Retailer Promotional Type Ia outfits for E. F. MacDonald. (See the entry for the 19437 from 1965.)

Description: "O27" Promotional Outfit
Specification: "O27" Steam Type Freight Outfit W/Smoke
Customer/No./Price: Aldens; 34 Y 5618E; $19.75
Cust./No./Price: J. C. Penney Co., Inc.; X 924-3726 A; $18.99
Customer/No./Price: Spiegel; R36 J 5262; $19.97
Original Amount: 1,200
Factory Order Date: 7/22/1965
Date Issued: 8-16-65
Packaging: MO Pack (Units not Boxed)

Contents: 237-25 Steam Type Locomotive with Smoke; 242T-25 Tender; 6142-100 Gondola Car; 6112-88 Canister (2); 6402-50 Flat Car W/2 Cable Reels; 40-11 Cable Reels (2); 6014-325 Frisco Box Car; 6059-50 Caboose; 1013-70 Curved Track (Bundle of 12 - 1013); 1018-30 Straight Track (Bundle of 3 - 1018); 1020-25 90° Crossing; 6149-25 Remote Control Track; 1010-25 35-Watt Transformer; 1103-40 Envelope Packed; 909-20 Smoke Fluid; D65-50 Accessory Catalog; Form 3063 Parts Order Form; 1-165 Warranty Card; 926-65 Service Station List; 19214-10 Instruction Sheet; 237-11 Instruction Sheet

Boxes & Packing: 62-246 Outfit Box; 61-172 Corr. Insert; 62-249 Corr. Insert; 62-254 Corr. Insert; 62-247 Shipper for 4 (1-4)

19437-502 (1965)	C6	C7	C8	Rarity
Complete Outfit	165	285	515	R7
Outfit Box no. 62-246	50	100	250	R7

Comments: In 1965, Lionel offered Retailer Promotional outfits to only Mercury Model, Sears and Western Auto. Other retailers, many of whom were accustomed to obtaining exclusive promotional outfits, were now limited to General Release Promotional outfits. They had to compete head-to-head with other retailers with similar offerings. Many of these outfits were offered in both display and mail-order RSC packed versions.

The no. 19437-502 was the mail-order RSC version of no. 19437 from 1965. Except for its RSC packaging, the 19437-502 was identical to the 19437. (See the 19437 from 1965.)

This General Release Promotional Type IIa outfit was sold through numerous retailers, including Aldens (1965 Christmas Catalog page 149 as no. 34 Y 5618E for $19.75), J. C. Penney (1965 Christmas Catalog page 392 as no. X 924-3726 A for $18.99) and Spiegel (1965 Christmas Catalog page 375 as no. R36 J 5262 for $19.97). Retailers paid Lionel $12.65 for each 19437-502.

The 19437-502 used a no. 62-246 Tan RSC Mailer with Black

Graphics outfit box. It was manufactured by Mead Containers and measured 11½ x 10¼ x 6¼ inches. These boxes were made of a thicker corrugated material (rated at 90 pounds rather than the normal 65 pounds gross weight) that allowed each outfit to be shipped in its outfit box. The manufacturer omitted any Lionel printing on the box top to leave room for a mailing label. The box included four lines of data as part of its box manufacturer's certificate.

The 19437-502 was produced in smaller quantities than the 19437. As such, it is more difficult to find and so achieves an R7 rarity rating.

19438
1965

The no. 19438 was a mid-level steam-powered General Release Promotional outfit for 1965. The 19438 and its mail-order RSC counterpart (the no. 19438-502) represented the last appearance of the no. 6651-25 Cannon Car in an outfit. This was also the only appearance of the 6651-25 in a display- packed outfit. Note the unique inserts required to pack this outfit. The completed warranty card lists Bennett Bros. as the dealer and a purchase date of 11-15-65.

Description: "O27" Promotional Outfit
Specification: "O27" Steam Type Freight Outfit W/Smoke & Whistle
Customer/No./Price: Bennett Brothers; 6369T2600; $40.00
Original Amount: 350
Factory Order Date: 6/16/1965
Date Issued: Rev 9-10-65
Packaging: Display Outfit Packing (Units not Boxed)

Contents: 241-25 Steam Type Locomotive with Smoke; 234W-25 Whistle Tender; 6014-325 Frisco Box Car; 6465-150 Tank Car; 6651-25 Cannon Car; 6651-8 Shells (4); 6176-50 Hopper Car; 6059-50 Caboose; 1013-8 Curved Track (Bundle of 8 - 1013); 1018-5 Straight Track (Bundle of 5 - 1018); 6149-25 Remote Control Track; 1073-25 60-Watt Transformer; 147-25 Horn & Whistle Controller; 1103-50 Envelope Packed; 909-20 Smoke Fluid; D65-50 Accessory Catalog; Form 3063 Parts Order Form; 1-165 Warranty Card; 926-65 Service Station List; 6651-10 Instruction Sheet; 11460-10 Instruction Sheet; 237-11 Instruction Sheet

Boxes & Packing: 65-270 Box Top; 64-112 Box Bottom; 64-220 Corr. Insert; 64-221 Corr. Insert; 64-222 Corr. Insert; 64-121 Corr. Insert; 64-113 Shipper for 4 (1-4); 64-114 Shipper Pad (2-4)

19438 (1965)	C6	C7	C8	Rarity
Complete Outfit	645	1,025	1,325	R9
Outfit Box no. 65-270	300	450	550	R9

Comments: In 1965, Lionel offered Retailer Promotional outfits to only Mercury Model, Sears and Western Auto. Other retailers, many of whom were accustomed to obtaining exclusive promotional outfits, were now limited to General Release Promotional outfits. They had to compete head-to-head with other retailers with similar offerings. Many of these outfits were offered in both display and mail-order RSC packed versions.

Outfit no. 19438, a General Release Promotional Type IIb outfit, was display packed and likely sold over the counter at retailers, whereas its mail-order RSC counterpart, outfit no. 19438-502, was sold through retail catalogs.

The 19438, for which retailers paid Lionel $18.70 each, has been linked to Bennett Brothers as no. 6369T2600 for $40.00. It was likely also sold over the counter at J. C. Penney and other retailers.

The 19438 was a mid-level steam-powered outfit for 1965. It was led by a no. 241-25 Steam Type Locomotive with Smoke (new for 1965). This die-cast Scout steamer, which appeared only in promotional outfits, featured a two-position reversing unit, a headlight and a rubber tire as a traction aid. The early version with a thin rubber-stamped stripe was included in this outfit. Except for its 241 number and stripe, it was the same engine as a no. 239.

The 19438 and 19438-502 marked the last appearance of the no. 6651-25 Cannon Car. It was derived from the no. 6650-25 / 6640-25 Missile Launching Flat Car and included a new firing mechanism that fired shells instead of a missile. The base of the car was painted olive drab, whereas the top was molded in olive drab plastic.

All the remaining cars in this outfit were carryover items commonly used in outfits from 1965. The no. 6014-325 Frisco

Box Car used a Type III body. The black no. 6176-50 Hopper Car was actually stamped "BUILT 1-48" and "LIONEL 6076", but it was still considered a 6176 because it included an operating truck and coupler.

The rolling stock in the 19438 followed the normal truck and coupler progression for 1965, with each of the cars having AAR types. Many were equipped with one late non-operating and one late operating truck and coupler. However, the no. 234W-25 Whistle Tender had one late non-operating and one plain type, and the no. 6059-50 Caboose had one late operating and one plain type. Also, the 6651-25 was equipped with operating types with integral copper springs.

This outfit included the 1965 version of the no. 6651-10 Instruction Sheet dated 8/65. This version is easier to find than the one dated 8/64.

The no. 65-270 White Lift-Off with Full-Color 2037 Steam Freight Graphics Type D display outfit box was manufactured by Mead Containers and measured 24½ x 15½ x 3⅛ inches.

The 19438 represents the only instance of a 6651-25 being included in a display-packed outfit. In reality, this car was intended to be included in display-packed outfit no. 19332 from 1964. According to that listing, though, the 6651-25 was replaced by a no. 3666-25 Cannon Box Car. That is why these unique inserts (nos. 64-220, 64-221 and 64-222) include 1964 part numbers. In any case, they are required for C6 or better outfits.

The inclusion of a 6651-25, thin-striped 241-25 and unique inserts make this one of the more desirable General Release Promotional outfits from 1965. The 19438 was produced in low numbers and is difficult to find.

Description: "O27" Promotional Outfit
Specification: "O27" Steam Type Freight Outfit W/Smoke & Whistle
Customer/No./Price: Aldens; 34 Y 5615E; $29.75
Cust./No./Price: J. C. Penney Co., Inc.; X 924-3734 A; $29.00
Original Amount: 1,647
Factory Order Date: 8/25/1965
Date Issued: 8-24-65
Date Req'd: 9-7-65
Packaging: (Units not Boxed)

Contents: 241-25 Steam Type Locomotive with Smoke; 234W-25 Whistle Tender; 6014-325 Frisco Box Car; 6465-150 Tank Car; 6651-25 Cannon Car; 6651-8 Shells (4); 6176-50 Hopper Car; 6059-50 Caboose; 1013-8 Curved Track (Bundle of 8 - 1013); 1018-5 Straight Track (Bundle of 5 - 1018); 6149-25 Remote Control Track; 1073-25 60-Watt Transformer; 147-25 Horn & Whistle Controller; 1103-50 Envelope Packed; 909-20 Smoke Fluid; D65-50 Accessory Catalog; Form 3063 Parts Order Form; 1-165 Warranty Card; 926-65 Service Station List; 6651-10 Instruction Sheet; 11460-10 Instruction Sheet; 237-11 Instruction Sheet

Boxes & Packing: 65-435 Outfit Box; 61-181 Corr. Insert; 61-182 Corr. Insert; 62-225 Corr. Insert; 62-249 Corr. Insert; 64-106 Corr. Insert; 64-169 Corr. Insert; 65-436 Shipper for 4 (1-4); 64-106 Shipper Pad (2-4)

Alternate For Outfit Contents:
Note: Sub. 6176-75 for 6176-50 as needed.

19438-502 (1965)	C6	C7	C8	Rarity
Complete Outfit	445	755	985	R7
Outfit Box no. 65-435	100	175	225	R7

Comments: In 1965, Lionel offered Retailer Promotional outfits to only Mercury Model, Sears and Western Auto. Other retailers, many of whom were accustomed to obtaining exclusive promotional outfits, were now limited to General Release Promotional outfits. They had to compete head-to-head with other retailers with similar offerings. Many of these outfits were offered in both display and mail-order RSC packed versions.

The no. 19438-502 was the mail-order RSC version of no. 19438 from 1965. Except for its RSC packaging and a gray no. 6176-75 Hopper Car, the 19438-502 was identical to the 19438. (See the 19438 from 1965.)

This General Release Promotional Type IIb outfit was sold through numerous retailers, including Aldens (1965 Christmas Catalog page 149 as no. 34 Y 5615E for $29.75) and J. C. Penney (1965 Christmas Catalog page 392 as no. X 924-3734 A for $29.00). Retailers paid Lionel $18.70 for each 19438-502.

The 19438-502 used a no. 65-435 Tan RSC with Black Graphics outfit box. It was manufactured by the Mead Corporation and measured 12¾ x 12 x 6⅞ inches. These boxes were made of a thicker corrugated material (rated at 90 pounds rather than the

The no. 19439 was a low-end steam-powered General Release Promotional outfit for 1965. Lionel tried to make it more attractive by adding a figure-eight layout and a no. 6149-25 Remote Control Track. Unfortunately, with 12,438 units manufactured between 1965 and 1966 and commonly available components, this outfit elicits little interest from collectors.

A no. 1802-10 Instruction Sheet detailed the figure-eight track layout.

The no. 65-260 White Lift-Off with Full-Color 2037 Steam Freight Graphics Type D display outfit box was manufactured by Mead Containers and measured 23½ x 11½ x 3 inches.

There are subtle differences between the 1965 and 1966 versions of this outfit (see the entry for the 19439 from 1966), but they do not affect the overall outfit price. Also, since the packaging is the same for both years, a combined quantity of 12,438 was used to determine the rarity and pricing.

This is a very common low-end outfit that attracts minimal collector interest.

Description: "O27" Promotional Outfit
Specification: "O27" Steam Type Freight Outfit
Original Amount: 100
Factory Order Date: 5/24/1966
Date Issued: 5-24-66
Date Req'd: 6-1-66
Packaging: Display Pack (Units not Boxed)

Contents: 1062-50 Steam Type Loco. W/Light & Reversing Unit; 1062T-25 Tender; 6402-50 Flat Car W/2 Cable Reels; 40-11 Cable Reels (2); 6142-100 Gondola Car; 6112-88 Canister (2); 6059-50 Caboose; 1013-70 Curved Track (Bundle of 12 - 1013); 1018-30 Straight Track (Bundle of 3 - 1018); 1020-25 90° Crossing; 6149-25 Remote Control Track; 1010-25 35-Watt Transformer; 1103-40 Envelope Packed; Form 3063 Parts Order Form; 1-166 Warranty Card; 926-66 Service Station List; 11450-10 Instruction Sheet; 1802-10 Instruction Sheet

Boxes & Packing: 65-260 Box Top; 64-102 Box Bottom; 65-264 Corr. Insert; 64-105 Shipper for 4 (1-4); 64-106 Shipper Pad (2-4)

Alternate For Outfit Contents:
Note: Sub. 1062-75 for 1062-50; Sub. 1025-25 for 1010-25.

Comments: The no. 19439 from 1966 was a repeat of outfit 19439 from 1965. The contents of the two outfits were nearly identical, the only differences being that the later version came with an updated transformer and paperwork and a locomotive substitution. Also, the rolling stock in the 19439 from 1966 was equipped with the trucks and couplers that were the norm for that year.

The biggest difference between these two outfits related to the locomotive. The 19439 from 1966 was led by a no. 1062-75 Steam Type Loco. W/Light & Reversing Unit (new for 1966). This low-end Scout steamer featured a 2-4-2 wheel arrangement and a rubber tire as a traction aid. Except for its wheel arrangement, the 1062-75 was identical to the no. 1062-50 Steam Type Loco. W/Light & Reversing Unit. This engine made the 19439 from 1966 a Type IIb outfit.

None of these changes materially affects the outfit price. In fact, the 1965 and 1966 versions are considered identical from a pricing and rarity perspective. (See the entry for the 19439 from 1965.)

19439-502
1965

Description: "O27" Promotional Outfit
Specification: "O27" Steam Type Freight Outfit
Customer/No./Price: Bennett Brothers; 6366T1300; $20.00
Customer/No./Price: Spiegel; R36 J 5261; $14.97
Original Amount: 3,844
Factory Order Date: 7/22/1965
Date Issued: Rev 9-3-65
Packaging: MO Pack (Units not Boxed)

Contents: 1062-50 Steam Type Loco. W/Light & Reversing Unit; 1062T-25 Tender; 6402-50 Flat Car W/2 Cable Reels; 40-11 Cable Reels (2); 6142-100 Gondola Car; 6112-88 Canister (2); 6059-50 Caboose; 1013-70 Curved Track (Bundle of 12 - 1013); 1018-30 Straight Track (Bundle of 3 - 1018); 1020-25 90° Crossing; 6149-25 Remote Control Track; 1010-25 35-Watt Transformer; 1103-40 Envelope Packed; D65-50 Accessory Catalog; Form 3063 Parts Order Form; 1-165 Warranty Card; 926-65 Service Station List; 11450-10 Instruction Sheet; 1802-10 Instruction Sheet

Boxes & Packing: 65-410 Outfit Box; 61-173 Corr. Insert; 62-254 Corr. Insert; 64-319 Corr. Insert; 63-384 Shipper for 4 (1-4); 65-330 Shipper for 6 (1-6); 64-104 Corr. Pad (2)

Alternate For Outfit Contents:
Note: For 1st 1,000 outfits substitute 65-330 Shipper for 6 together with two (2) 64-104 Corr. Pads in place of 63-384 Shipper for 4.

19439-502 (1965)	C6	C7	C8	Rarity
Complete Outfit	125	225	350	R5
Outfit Box no. 65-410	35	75	125	R5

Comments: In 1965, Lionel offered Retailer Promotional outfits to only Mercury Model, Sears and Western Auto. Other retailers, many of whom were accustomed to obtaining exclusive promotional outfits, were now limited to General Release Promotional outfits. They had to compete head-to-head with other retailers with similar offerings. Many of these outfits were offered in both display and mail-order RSC packed versions.

The no. 19439-502 was the mail-order RSC version of no. 19439 from 1965. Except for its RSC packaging, the 19439-502 was identical to the 19439. (See the 19439 from 1965.)

This General Release Promotional Type IIa outfit was sold through numerous retailers, including Bennett Brothers (1966 Bennett Blue Book page 766 as no. 6366T1300 for $20.00) and Spiegel (1965 Christmas Catalog page 375 as no. R36 J 5261 for $14.97). Retailers paid Lionel $8.50 for each 19439-502.

The 19439-502 used a no. 65-410 Tan RSC with Black Graphics outfit box. It was manufactured by Mann Kraft Container Corporation and measured 11½ x 10 x 6¼ inches. These boxes were made of a thicker corrugated material (rated at 90 pounds rather than the normal 65 pounds gross weight) that allowed each outfit to be shipped in its outfit box. It included four lines of data as part of its box manufacturer's certificate as well as a reference to the N.M.F.C.

Since the 19439-502's contents are common low-end items, a complete 19439-502 is not on the top of many collectors' wish lists. But because the 19439-502 outfit box is surprisingly difficult to find, one should not pass on an opportunity to acquire this outfit as it may be a while before it appears again.

19440
1965

Description: "O27" Promotional Outfit
Specification: "O27" Diesel Freight Outfit
Original Amount: 1,310
Factory Order Date: 6/17/1965
Date Issued: Rev 8-16-65
Packaging: Display Pack (Units not Boxed)

Contents: 635-25 "Union Pacific" Diesel Switcher; 6473-25 Rodeo Car; 6465-150 Tank Car; 3364-25 Log Dump Car; 3364-8 Logs (3); 6176-50 Hopper Car; 6059-50 Caboose; 1013-8 Curved Track (Bundle of 8 - 1013); 1018-30 Straight Track (Bundle of 3 - 1018); 6149-25 Remote Control Track; 1025-25 45-Watt Transformer; 1103-40 Envelope Packed; D65-50 Accessory Catalog; Form 3063 Parts Order Form; 1-165 Warranty Card; 926-65 Service Station List; 3364-10 Instruction Sheet; 11530-10 Instruction Sheet

Boxes & Packing: 65-270 Box Top; 64-115 Box Bottom; 64-118 Corr. Insert; 65-273 Corr. Insert; 64-116 Shipper for 4 (1-4); 64-117 Shipper Pad (2-4)

19440 (1965)	C6	C7	C8	Rarity
Complete Outfit	190	315	550	R6
Outfit Box no. 65-270	15	50	100	R6

Comments: In 1965, Lionel offered Retailer Promotional outfits to only Mercury Model, Sears and Western Auto. Other retailers, many of whom were accustomed to obtaining exclusive promotional outfits, were now limited to General Release Promotional outfits. They had to compete head-to-head with other retailers with similar offerings. Many of these outfits were offered in both display and mail-order RSC packed versions.

The no. 19440, a General Release Promotional Type IIb outfit, was display packed and likely sold over the counter at retailers, whereas its mail-order RSC counterpart, outfit no. 19440-502, was sold via retail catalogs. This higher-end diesel-powered outfit, for which retailers paid Lionel $13.25 each, has yet to be linked to a particular retailer.

The 19440 was led by a no. 635-25 Union Pacific Diesel Switcher (new for 1965). Included in promotional outfits only, this locomotive featured a two-position reversing unit, a headlight, a weight and a rubber tire as a traction aid.

The rolling stock was all carryover and included two operating cars. The no. 6473-25 Rodeo Car in this outfit commonly came with a Type IIIa body (cadmium yellow plastic with red lettering) or a Type IIIc body (cadmium yellow plastic with maroon lettering). A Type IIIb body (lighter lemon yellow plastic with maroon lettering) is also possible in 1965 and would command a slight premium. The Type III body no longer exhibited the filled slot caused by broken tooling.

The second operating car in this outfit was a no. 3364-25 Log Dump Car. It was identical to the no. 3362-25 Helium Tank

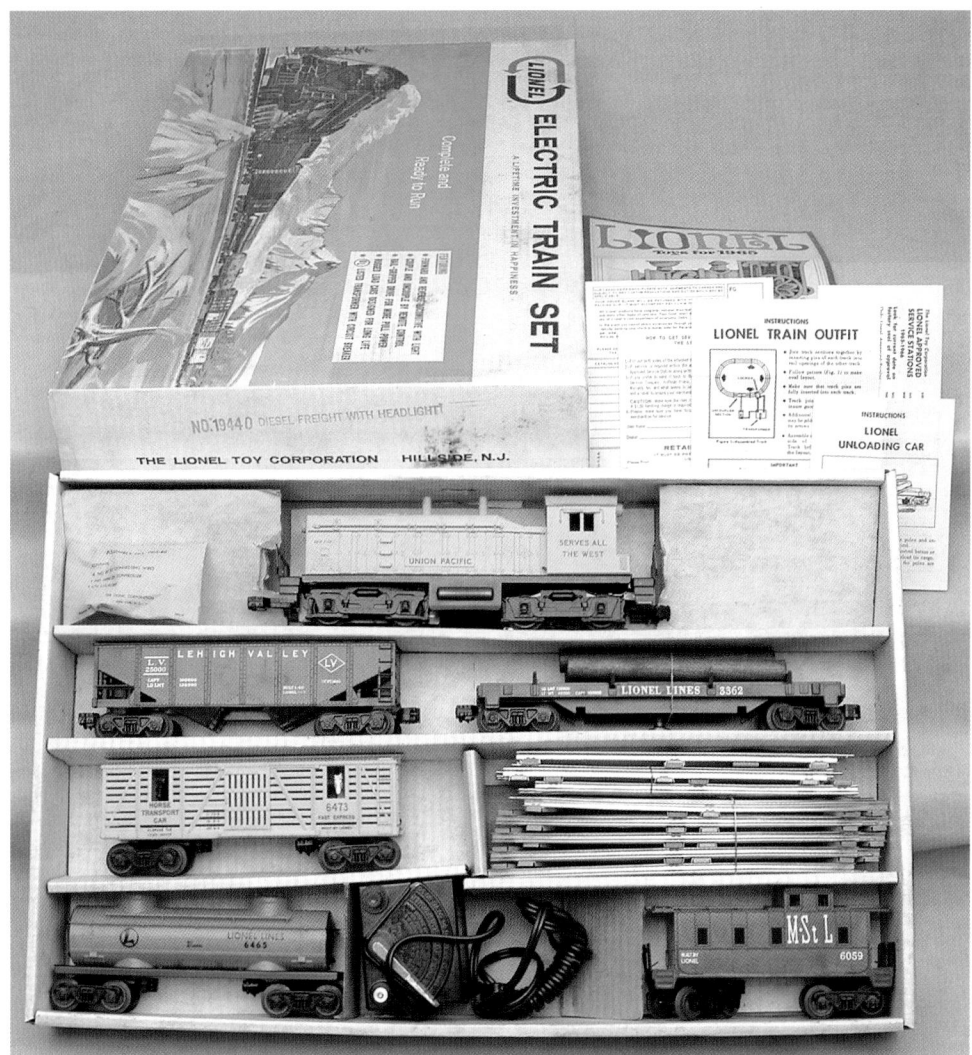

The no. 19440 was a higher-end diesel-powered General Release Promotional outfit for 1965. It introduced the promotional-only no. 635-25 Union Pacific Diesel Switcher. By including two operating cars, Lionel increased the play value and excitement for its customers. Unfortunately, this outfit did not sell too well and many outfits, including this one, ended up at Madison Hardware.

The rolling stock in the 19440 followed the normal truck and coupler progression for 1965, with each of the cars having AAR types. All but one were equipped with one late operating and one late non-operating truck and coupler. The no. 6059-50 Caboose had one late operating and one plain type.

The no. 65-270 White Lift-Off with Full-Color 2037 Steam Freight Graphics Type D display outfit box measured 24½ x 15½ x 3⅛ inches. No manufacturer was printed on the box top.

In 1989, Richard Kughn, then the owner of Lionel Trains Inc., purchased Madison Hardware Co. of New York City and reopened it in Detroit soon thereafter. One of the first lists of outfits available for sale included 22 of the 19440.

Unloading Car, except that it carried logs instead of helium tanks.

Of note was the black no. 6176-50 Hopper Car. Although stamped "BUILT 1-48" and "LIONEL 6076", this model still was considered a 6176 because it included an operating truck and coupler.

The 19440 likely did not meet expectations, and the excess inventory was depleted through Madison Hardware. This explains why the 19440 is readily available in high-grade collectible condition. For collectors, a 19440 serves as a good source for acquiring a 635-25 Union Pacific Diesel Switcher.

Description: "O27" Promotional Outfit
Specification: "O27" Diesel Freight Outfit
Customer/No./Price: Bennett Brothers; 6367T1950; $30.00
Original Amount: 900
Factory Order Date: 7/28/1965
Date Issued: 7-28-65
Date Req'd: 8-15-65
Packaging: MO Pack (Units not Boxed)

Boxes & Packing: 65-411 Outfit Box; 65-413 Corr. Insert; 65-414 Corr. Insert; 64-177 Corr. Insert (3); 600-26 Corr. Insert (2); 65-412 Shipper for 4 (1-4); 64-106 Shipper Pad (2-4)

19440-502 (1965)	C6	C7	C8	Rarity
Complete Outfit	275	440	700	R7
Outfit Box no. 65-411	100	175	250	R7

Contents: 635-25 "Union Pacific" Diesel Switcher; 6473-25 Rodeo Car; 6465-150 Tank Car; 3364-25 Log Dump Car; 3364-8 Logs (3); 6176-50 Hopper Car; 6059-50 Caboose; 1013-8 Curved Track (Bundle of 8 - 1013); 1018-30 Straight Track (Bundle of 3 - 1018); 6149-25 Remote Control Track; 1025-25 45-Watt Transformer; 1103-40 Envelope Packed; D65-50 Accessory Catalog; Form 3063 Parts Order Form; 1-165 Warranty Card; 926-65 Service Station List; 3364-10 Instruction Sheet; 11530-10 Instruction Sheet

Comments: In 1965, Lionel offered Retailer Promotional outfits to only Mercury Model, Sears and Western Auto. Other retailers, many of whom were accustomed to obtaining exclusive promotional outfits, were now limited to General Release Promotional outfits. They had to compete head-to-head with other retailers with similar offerings. Many of these outfits were offered in both display and mail-order RSC packed versions.

The no. 19440-502 was the mail-order RSC version of no. 19440 from 1965. Except for its RSC packaging, the 19440-502 was identical to the 19440. (See the 19440 from 1965.)

LIONEL TRAINS

NO.19440-502

MANUFACTURED and GUARANTEED BY
THE LIONEL CORPORATION • NEW YORK, N. Y.

The no. 19440-502 was the mail-order RSC version of outfit no. 19440. The 19440-502's contents, including the no. 635-25 Union Pacific Diesel Switcher, were identical to those of the 19440. The 19440-502 was shipped in its outfit box. In fact, the outfit shown includes remnants of a shipping label and the no. "4-71-286" stamped on its box top.

This General Release Promotional Type IIb outfit was sold through numerous retailers, including Bennett Brothers (1966 Bennett Blue Book page 766 as no. 6367T1950 for $30.00). Retailers paid Lionel $13.25 for each 19440-502.

The 19440-502 used a no. 65-411 Tan RSC with Black Graphics outfit box. It was manufactured by Mann Kraft Container Corporation and measured 13¼ x 11¼ x 6¼ inches. These boxes were made of a thicker corrugated material (rated at 90 pounds

rather than the normal 65 pounds gross weight) that allowed each outfit to be shipped in its outfit box. It included four lines of data as part of its box manufacturer's certificate as well as a reference to the N.M.F.C.

In choosing between the 19440 and 19440-502, collectors should be aware that the latter is more difficult to find and, as such, is more desirable.

19441
1965

Description: "O27" Promotional Outfit
Specification: "O27" Steam Type Freight Outfit W/Smoke & Whistle
Customer/No./Price: Bennett Brothers; 6368T2275; $35.00
Customer/No./Price: White Stores; 108-120; $24.99
Original Amount: 632
Factory Order Date: 4/16/1965
Date Issued: Rev 8-16-65
Packaging: Display Pack (Units not Boxed)

Contents: 237-25 Steam Type Locomotive with Smoke; 234W-25 Whistle Tender; 6014-325 Frisco Box Car; 6465-150 Tank Car; 6176-50 Hopper Car; 6059-50 Caboose; 1013-8 Curved Track (Bundle of 8 - 1013); 1018-30 Straight Track (Bundle of 3 - 1018); 6149-25 Remote Control Track; 1025-25 45-Watt Transformer; 147-25 Horn & Whistle Controller; 1103-50 Envelope Packed; 909-20 Smoke Fluid; D65-50 Accessory Catalog; Form 3063

Parts Order Form; 1-165 Warranty Card; 926-65 Service Station List; 237-11 Instruction Sheet; 19441-10 Instruction Sheet

Boxes & Packing: 65-270 Box Top; 64-115 Box Bottom; 64-118 Corr. Insert; 64-119 Corr. Insert; 64-120 Corr. Insert; 64-116 Shipper for 4 (1-4); 64-117 Shipper Pad (2-4)

19441 (1965)	C6	C7	C8	Rarity
Complete Outfit	350	525	775	R8
Outfit Box no. 65-270	200	300	400	R8

Comments: In 1965, Lionel offered Retailer Promotional outfits to only Mercury Model, Sears and Western Auto. Other retailers, many of whom were accustomed to obtaining exclusive promotional outfits, were now limited to General Release Promotional outfits. They had to compete head-to-head with other retailers with similar offerings.

Outfit no. 19441, a General Release Promotional Type IIa outfit, was sold through numerous retailers, including Bennett Brothers (1966 Bennett Blue Book page 766 as no. 6368T2275 for $35.00)

The no. 19441 was a mid-level steam-powered General Release Promotional outfit for 1965 that came with common rolling stock for that year. Standing out was the desirable no. 234W-25 Whistle Tender, which came in only four outfits in 1965.

The rolling stock was all carryover and commonly used in outfits from 1965. The most notable item was the Type III no. 6014-325 Frisco Box Car. Also of note was the black no. 6176-50 Hopper Car. Although stamped "BUILT 1-48" and "LIONEL 6076", this model still was considered a 6176 because it included an operating truck and coupler.

The rolling stock in the 19441 followed the normal truck and coupler progression for 1965, with each of the cars having AAR types. All but two were equipped with one late operating and one late non-operating truck and coupler. The 234W-25 had one late non-operating and one plain type, and the no. 6059-50 Caboose had one late operating and one plain type.

The no. 19441-10 Instruction Sheet was unique to this outfit and remains very difficult to find. Dated 6/65, it described how to connect the nos. 147-25 Horn & Whistle Controller and 6149-25 Remote Control Track.

The no. 65-270 White Lift-Off with Full-Color 2037 Steam Freight Graphics Type D display outfit box was manufactured by Mead Containers and measured 24½ x 15½ x 3⅛ inches.

Since only 632 of the 19441 were produced, it is one of the more difficult General Release Promotional outfits from 1965 to find.

and White Stores (1965 Christmas Savings Sale page 11 as no. 108-120 for $24.99). Retailers paid Lionel $16.00 for each 19441.

This mid-level steam-powered outfit was led by a no. 237-25 Steam Type Locomotive with Smoke. This Scout steamer featured a two-position reversing unit and a headlight and used a rubber tire as a traction aid. The later version with narrow running boards came in this outfit. It was paired with a no. 234W-25 Whistle Tender.

Description: "O27" Promotional Outfit
Specification: "O27" Steam Type Freight Outfit W/Smoke & Whistle
Customer/No./Price: Aldens; 34 Y 5617E; $34.75
Customer/No./Price: Bennett Brothers; 6370T3250; $50.00
Cust./No./Price: J. C. Penney Co., Inc.; X 924-3718 A; $34.44
Original Amount: 1,060
Factory Order Date: 6/17/1965
Date Issued: Rev 8-16-65
Packaging: White RSC (Units not boxed)

Contents: 241-25 Steam Type Locomotive with Smoke; 234W-25 Whistle Tender; 6473-25 Rodeo Car; 3364-25 Log Dump Car; 3364-8 Logs (3); 6176-50 Hopper Car; 6142-100 Gondola Car; 6112-88 Canister (2); 6130-25 Work Caboose - "Santa Fe"; 260-1 Illuminated Bumper; 1022-75 L.H. Manual Switch; 1013-8 Curved Track (Bundle of 8 - 1013); 1013-85 Curved Track (Loose); 1018-7 Straight Track (Bundle of 7 - 1018); 1018-40 Straight Track (Bundle of 4 - 1018); 6149-25 Remote Control Track; 1073-25 60-Watt Transformer; 147-25 Horn & Whistle Controller; 1103-50 Envelope Packed; 909-20 Smoke Fluid; D65-50 Accessory Catalog; Form 3063 Parts Order Form; 1-165 Warranty Card; 926-65 Service Station List; 11460-10 Instruction Sheet; 3364-10 Instruction Sheet; 19442-10 Instruction Sheet; 237-11 Instruction Sheet

Boxes & Packing: 64-166 Outfit Box; 61-181 Corr. Insert; 61-182 Corr. Insert; 62-248 Corr. Insert (2); 64-143 Corr. Insert (3); 62-225 Corr. Insert (2); 64-167 Shipper 4 (1-4)

19442 (1965)	C6	C7	C8	Rarity
Complete Outfit	375	650	950	R7
Outfit Box no. 64-166	100	200	300	R7

19400 Series

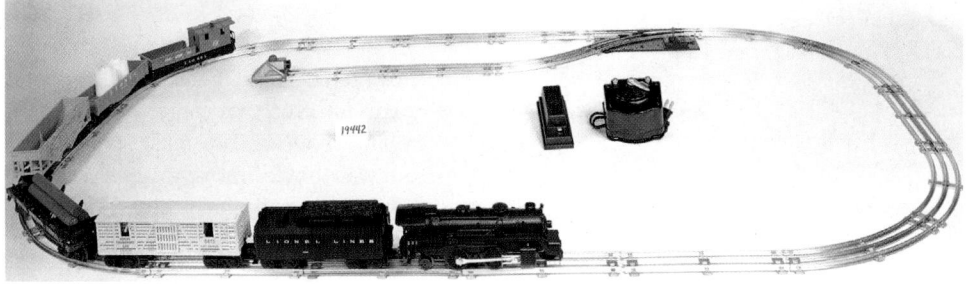

The no. 19442 was a higher-end steam-powered General Release Promotional outfit for 1965. The sales glossy that Lionel's sales staff used to sell this outfit is shown. Be aware that the engine shown is a no. 239-25 Steam Locomotive With Smoke rather than the no. 241-25 Steam Type Locomotive with Smoke actually included in this outfit.

Comments: In 1965, Lionel offered Retailer Promotional outfits to only Mercury Model, Sears and Western Auto. Other retailers, many of whom were accustomed to obtaining exclusive promotional outfits, were now limited to General Release Promotional outfits. They had to compete head-to-head with other retailers with similar offerings.

Outfit no. 19442, a General Release Promotional Type IIb outfit, was sold through numerous retailers, including Aldens (1965 Christmas Catalog page 149 as no. 34 Y 5617E for $34.75), Bennett Brothers (1966 Bennett Blue Book page 766 as no. 6370T3250 for $50.00) and J. C. Penney (1965 Christmas Catalog page 393 as no. X 924-3718 A for $34.44). Retailers paid Lionel $22.50 for each 19442.

The 19442 was a higher-end steam-powered outfit led by a no. 241-25 Steam Type Locomotive with Smoke (new for 1965). This die-cast Scout steamer, which appeared only in promotional outfits, featured a two-position reversing unit, a headlight and a rubber tire as a traction aid. The early version with a thin rubber-stamped stripe was likely included in this outfit. Except for its 241 number and stripe, it was the same engine as a no. 239. It was paired with a no. 234W-25 Whistle Tender.

The rolling stock was primarily carryover and included two operating cars. The no. 6473-25 Rodeo Car in this outfit commonly came with a Type IIIa body (cadmium yellow plastic with red lettering) or a Type IIIc body (cadmium yellow plastic with maroon lettering). A Type IIIb body (lighter lemon yellow plastic with maroon lettering) is also possible and would command a slight premium. The Type III body no longer exhibited the filled slot caused by broken tooling.

The second operating car in this outfit was a no. 3364-25 Log Dump Car. It was identical to the no. 3362-25 Helium Tank Unloading Car, except that it carried logs instead of helium tanks.

The unboxed no. 6130-25 Santa Fe Work Caboose was introduced in 1965. Previously, it always came boxed as a no. 6130-1 Santa Fe Work Caboose. The boxed version last appeared as a substitution in catalog outfit no. 13008 from 1962.

The rolling stock in the 19442 followed the normal truck and coupler progression for 1965, with each of the cars having AAR types. All but two were equipped with one late operating and one late non-operating truck and coupler. The 234W-25 had one late non-operating and one plain type, and the 6130-25 had one late operating and one plain type.

The no. 19442-10 Instruction Sheet is very difficult to find. It was dated 4/65 and detailed an oval layout with an inside spur.

The no. 64-166 White RSC with Orange Graphics outfit box was manufactured by United Container Co. and measured 15⅜ x 10½ x 7⅛ inches.

The 19442 exceeded early forecasts because its factory orders were increased from 500 to 1,060. An additional quantity of 12 outfits was required in 1966, and that change led to a new Factory Order being created. The 1965 and 1966 versions of this outfit were identical and share pricing and rarity. Even with 1,072 manufactured over a two-year period, this outfit seldom appears.

(A display-packed version of this outfit was offered in 1966 as the no. 19510. See that listing for more information.)

Description: "O27" Promotional Outfit
Specification: "O27" Steam Type Freight Outfit W/Smoke & Whistle
Original Amount: 12
Factory Order Date: 1/20/1966
Date Issued: 1-20-66
Packaging: White RSC (Units not Boxed)

Contents: 241-25 Steam Type Locomotive with Smoke; 234W-25 Whistle Tender; 6473-25 Rodeo Car; 3364-25 Log Dump Car; 3364-8 Logs (3); 6176-50 Hopper Car; 6142-100 Gondola Car; 6112-88 Canister (2); 6130-25 Work Caboose - "Santa Fe"; 260-1 Illuminated Bumper; 1022-75 L.H. Manual Switch; 1013-8 Curved Track (Bundle of 8 - 1013); 1013-85 Curved Track (Loose); 1018-7 Straight Track (Bundle of 7 - 1018); 1018-40 Straight Track (Bundle of 4 - 1018); 6149-25 Remote Control Track; 1073-25 60-Watt Transformer; 147-25 Horn & Whistle Controller; 1103-50 Envelope Packed; 909-20 Smoke Fluid; D65-50 Accessory Catalog; Form 3063 Parts Order Form; 1-165 Warranty Card; 926-65 Service Station List; 11460-10 Instruction Sheet; 3364-10 Instruction Sheet; 19442-10 Instruction Sheet; 237-11 Instruction Sheet

Boxes & Packing: 64-166 Outfit Box; 61-181 Corr. Insert; 61-182 Corr. Insert; 62-248 Corr. Insert (2); 64-143 Corr. Insert (3); 62-225 Corr. Insert (2); 64-167 Shipper 4 (1-4)

Comments: The no. 19442 from 1966 was a repeat of outfit 19442 from 1965. It appears that Lionel needed an additional 12 outfits to fulfill customer requests. As such, the outfits were identical. (See the entry for the 19442 from 1965 for a description of this outfit's contents, pricing and rarity.)

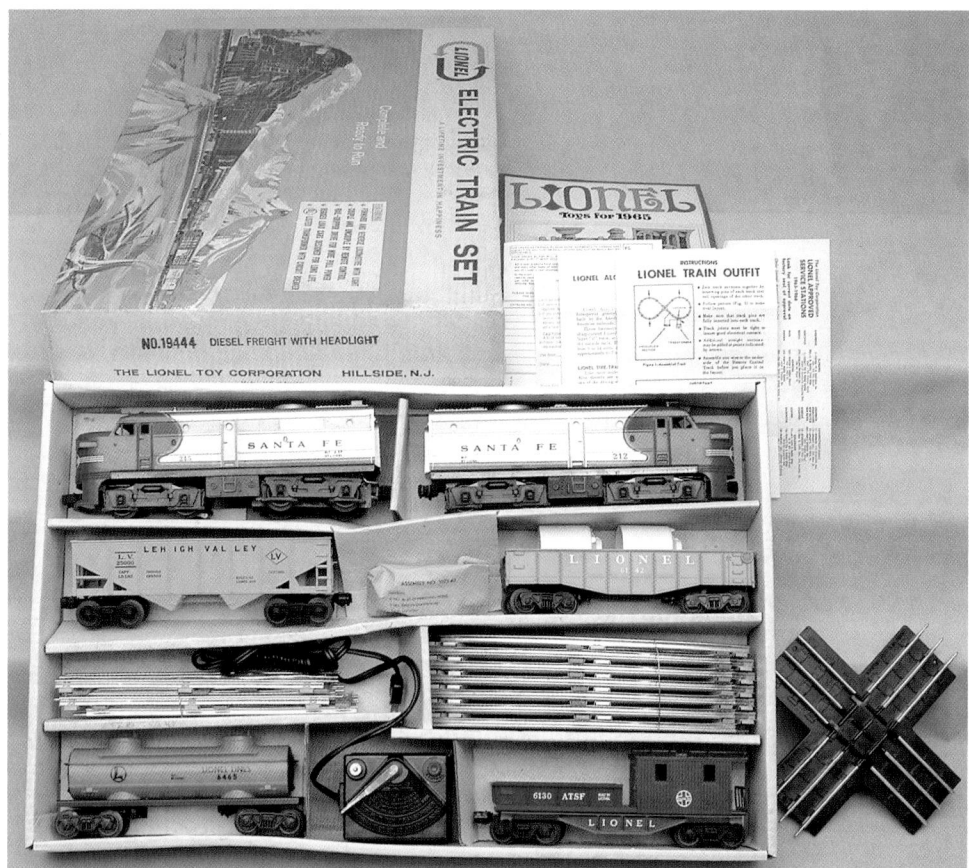

The no. 19444 was a mid-level diesel-powered General Release Promotional outfit for 1965. It paired the promotional-only no. 215P-25 Santa Fe Diesel Power Car with a no. 212T-25 Santa Fe "A" Unit. Lionel provided a matching no. 6130-25 Santa Fe Work Caboose, which was a nice addition to the otherwise bland rolling stock.

outfit, was display packed and likely sold over the counter at retailers, whereas its mail-order RSC counterpart, outfit no. 19444-502, was sold via retail catalogs.

The 19444, a mid-level diesel-powered outfit, has yet to be linked to a particular retailer. Retailers paid Lionel $15.25 for each 19444.

This outfit was led by 215P-25 Santa Fe Diesel Power Car. This promotional-only Alco featured a two-position reversing unit, two traction tires, a headlight, a weight and an open pilot with a large ledge.

The rolling stock was primarily carryover and included commonly used cars from 1965. The no. 6176-75 Hopper Car was molded in either gray or yellow. The gray and yellow versions are identical in price and rarity. The unboxed no. 6130-25 Santa Fe Work Caboose was introduced in 1965. Previously, the 6130 always came boxed as a no. 6130-1 Santa Fe Work Caboose. The boxed version last appeared as a substitution in catalog outfit no. 13008 from 1962. The common version of the 6130-25 was included; it featured a painted frame, cab and tray and had "Lionel" stamped on the frame.

The rolling stock in the 19444 followed the normal truck and coupler progression for 1965, with each of the cars having AAR types. All but one were equipped with one late operating and one late non-operating truck and coupler. The 6130-25 had one late operating and one plain type.

The no. 19214-10 Instruction Sheet was dated 6/65 and detailed the figure-eight track layout. The no. 211-151 Instruction Sheet was dated 3/65.

The no. 65-270 White Lift-Off with Full-Color 2037 Steam Freight Graphics Type D display outfit box measured 24½ x 15½ x 3⅛ inches.

The 19444 did not meet forecasts because its factory orders were decreased slightly from 1,500 to 1,450 units. An additional quantity of 50 outfits was required in 1966, a change that led to a new Factory Order being created. These may have been leftover 1965 outfits. The 1965 and 1966 versions of this outfit are nearly identical and so share pricing and rarity.

In 1989, Richard Kughn, then the owner of Lionel Trains Inc., purchased Madison Hardware Co. of New York City and reopened it in Detroit soon thereafter. One of the first lists of outfits available for sale included eight of the 19444.

Even with 1,500 manufactured over a two-year period and the quantity of eight outfits available at Madison Hardware, this outfit seldom appears.

Description: "O27" Promotional Outfit
Specification: "O27" Diesel Freight Outfit
Original Amount: 1,450
Factory Order Date: 6/29/1965
Date Issued: Rev 8-16-65
Packaging: Display Pack (Units not Boxed)

Contents: 215P-25 "Santa Fe" Diesel Power Car; 212T-25 "Santa Fe" "A" Unit; 6176-75 Hopper Car; 6142-100 Gondola Car; 6112-88 Canister (2); 6465-150 Tank Car; 6130-25 Work Caboose - "Santa Fe"; 1013-70 Curved Track (Bundle of 12 - 1013); 1018-30 Straight Track (Bundle of 3 - 1018); 1020-25 90° Crossing; 6149-25 Remote Control Track; 1025-25 45-Watt Transformer; 1103-40 Envelope Packed; D65-50 Accessory Catalog; Form 3063 Parts Order Form; 1-165 Warranty Card; 926-65 Service Station List; 211-151 Instruction Sheet; 19214-10 Instruction Sheet

Boxes & Packing: 65-270 Box Top; 64-115 Box Bottom; 64-118 Corr. Insert; 64-122 Corr. Insert; 64-116 Shipper for 4 (1-4); 64-117 Shipper Pad (2-4); MT Mylar Tape (5")

19444 (1965)	C6	C7	C8	Rarity
Complete Outfit	260	450	685	R6
Outfit Box no. 65-270	75	150	225	R6

Comments: In 1965, Lionel offered Retailer Promotional outfits to only Mercury Model, Sears and Western Auto. Other retailers, many of whom were accustomed to obtaining exclusive promotional outfits, were now limited to General Release Promotional outfits. They had to compete head-to-head with other retailers with similar offerings.

Outfit no. 19444, a General Release Promotional Type IIb

Description: "O27" Promotional Outfit
Specification: "O27" Diesel Freight Outfit
Original Amount: 50
Factory Order Date: 5/24/1966
Date Issued: 5-24-66
Date Req'd: 6-1-66
Packaging: Display Pack (Units not Boxed)

Contents: 215P-25 "Santa Fe" Diesel Power Car; 212T-25 "Santa Fe" "A" Unit; 6176-75 Hopper Car; 6142-100 Gondola Car; 6112-88 Canister (2); 6465-150 Tank Car; 6130-25 Work Caboose - "Santa Fe"; 1013-70 Curved Track (Bundle of 12 - 1013); 1018-30 Straight Track (Bundle of 3 - 1018); 1020-25 90° Crossing; 6149-25 Remote Control Track; 1025-25 45-Watt Transformer;

1103-40 Envelope Packed; Form 3063 Parts Order Form; 1-166 Warranty Card; 926-66 Service Station List; 211-151 Instruction Sheet; 19214-10 Instruction Sheet

Boxes & Packing: 65-270 Box Top; 64-115 Box Bottom; 64-118 Corr. Insert; 64-122 Corr. Insert; 64-116 Shipper for 4 (1-4); 64-117 Shipper Pad (2-4); MT Mylar Tape (5")

Comments: The no. 19444 from 1966 was a repeat of outfit 19444 from 1965. It appears that Lionel needed an additional 50 outfits to fulfill customer requests. Except for some updated paperwork, the outfits were identical. (See the entry for the 19444 from 1965 for a description of this outfit's contents, pricing and rarity.)

The no. 19444-502 was the mail-order RSC version of outfit no. 19444. The 19444-502's contents, including the promotional-only no. 215P-25 Santa Fe Diesel Power Car, were identical to those of the 19444. Both outfits also came with the common version of the no. 6130-25 Santa Fe Work Caboose that featured a painted frame, cab and tray and had "Lionel" stamped on the frame.

Description: "O27" Promotional Outfit
Specification: "O27" Diesel Freight Outfit
Customer/No./Price: Aldens; 34 Y 5616E; $24.75
Customer/No./Price: Spiegel; R36 J 5263; $24.97
Original Amount: 450
Factory Order Date: 8/2/1965
Date Issued: Rev 8-16-65
Packaging: MO Pack (Units not Boxed)

Contents: 215P-25 "Santa Fe" Diesel Power Car; 212T-25 "Santa Fe" "A" Unit; 6176-75 Hopper Car; 6142-100 Gondola Car; 6112-

88 Canister (2); 6465-150 Tank Car; 6130-25 Work Caboose - "Santa Fe"; 1013-70 Curved Track (Bundle of 12 - 1013); 1018-30 Straight Track (Bundle of 3 - 1018); 1020-25 90° Crossing; 6149-25 Remote Control Track; 1025-25 45-Watt Transformer; 1103-40 Envelope Packed; D65-50 Accessory Catalog; Form 3063 Parts Order Form; 1-165 Warranty Card; 926-65 Service Station List; 211-151 Instruction Sheet; 19214-10 Instruction Sheet

Boxes & Packing: 65-415 Outfit Box; 62-223 Corr. Insert; 62-224 Corr. Insert; 62-245 Corr. Insert (2); 62-248 Corr. Insert; 62-254 Corr. Insert; 64-177 Corr. Insert; 62-244 Shipper for 4 (1-4)

19444-502 (1965)	C6	C7	C8	Rarity
Complete Outfit	335	500	900	R9
Outfit Box no. 65-415	150	300	450	R9

Comments: In 1965, Lionel offered Retailer Promotional outfits to only Mercury Model, Sears and Western Auto. Other retailers, many of whom were accustomed to obtaining exclusive promotional outfits, were now limited to General Release Promotional outfits. They had to compete head-to-head with other retailers with similar offerings. Many of these outfits were offered in both display and mail-order RSC packed versions.

The no. 19444-502 was the mail-order RSC version of no. 19444 from 1965. Except for its RSC packaging, the 19444-502 was identical to the 19444. (See the 19444 from 1965.)

This General Release Promotional Type IIb outfit was sold through numerous retailers, including Aldens (1965 Christmas Catalog page 149 as no. 34 Y 5616E for $24.75) and Spiegel (1965 Christmas Catalog page 375 as no. R36 J 5263 for $24.97). Retailers paid Lionel $15.25 for each 19444-502.

The no. 65-415 Tan RSC with Black Graphics outfit box was manufactured by St. Joe Paper Co. - Container Div. and measured 12 x 11½ x 6⅜ inches. It included four lines of data as part of its box manufacturer's certificate as well as a reference to the N.M.F.C.

In choosing between the 19444 and 19444-502, collectors should be aware that the latter is more difficult to find and, as such, is more desirable.

Outfit no. 19446 (Sears no. 9833) was one of the 14 outfits purchased by Sears in 1965. The outfit shown came with its original sales receipt dated November 8, 1965 (not shown), with a total cost with tax of $20.58. The no. 19446-10 Layout Sheet is the most difficult item to find in completing this outfit. The outfit box details the contents and provides an illustration of the track layout on top.

Customer No. On Box: 9833
Description: "O27" Promotional Outfit
Specification: "O27" Steam Type Freight Outfit
Customer/No./Price: Sears, Roebuck and Co.; 9833; $19.98
Original Amount: 1,500
Factory Order Date: 8/4/1965
Date Issued: Rev 8-25-65
Date Req'd: 8-16-65
Packaging: (Units not Boxed)

Contents: 1062-50 Steam Type Loco. W/Light & Reversing Unit; 1062T-25 Tender; 3364-25 Log Dump Car; 3364-8 Logs (3); 6176-75 Hopper Car; 6402-50 Flat Car W/2 Cable Reels; 40-11 Cable Reels (2); 6059-50 Caboose; 260-25 Illuminated Bumper; 1013-90 Curved Track (Bundle of 9 - 1013); 1018-7 Straight Track (Bundle of 7 - 1018); 1018-40 Straight Track (Bundle of 4 - 1018); 1022-75 L.H. Manual Switch; 6149-25 Remote Control Track; 1010-25 35-Watt Transformer; 1103-40 Envelope Packed; 1-165 Warranty Card; 3364-10 Instruction Sheet; 19446-10

Layout Sheet; 11450-10 Instruction Sheet

Boxes & Packing: 65-373 Outfit Box; 65-375 Corr. Insert; 65-376 Corr. Insert (3); 65-377 Corr. Insert (3); 61-171 Corr. Insert; 65-374 Shipper for 4 (1-4); 64-106 Shipper Pad (2-4)

19446 (9833) (1965)	C6	C7	C8	Rarity
Complete Outfit	230	385	590	R7
Outfit Box no. 65-373	100	175	250	R7

Comments: After purchasing only three outfits in 1964, Sears, Roebuck and Co. made a large purchase of 14 Retailer Promotional outfits in 1965. Only three of these outfits appeared in the 1965 Sears Christmas Catalog.

The no. 19446, a Type Ia, was stamped with Sears no. 9833. This outfit, for which Sears paid $13.00 each, was curious because it was neither called a "Special Outfit" on its Factory Order nor did it appear in the 1965 Sears Christmas Catalog. Outfits have been observed with a Sears price tag and sales receipt, which suggests that the 19446 was sold over the counter at Sears stores.

The 19446 was led by a no. 1062-50 Steam Type Loco. W/ Light & Reversing Unit. This low-end Scout steamer featured an 0-4-0 wheel arrangement and a rubber tire as a traction aid. Except for the rubber tire, it was identical to the no. 1062-25 Steam Type Loco. W/Light & Reversing Unit.

The rolling stock consisted of carryover items. The most notable item was the no. 3364-25 Log Dump Car, which was identical to the no. 3362-25 Helium Tank Unloading Car except that it carried logs instead of helium tanks. The no. 6176-75 Hopper Car was molded in either gray or yellow. The gray version was included in this outfit. This model was stamped "BUILT 1-48" and "LIONEL 6076", but was still considered a 6176 because it included an operating truck and coupler.

The rolling stock in the 19446 followed the normal truck and coupler progression for 1965, with each of the cars having AAR types. All but two were equipped with one late operating and one late non-operating truck and coupler. The no. 1062T-25 Tender had one late non-operating and one plain type, and the no. 6059-

50 Caboose had one late operating and one plain type.

The instruction sheets in this outfit were updated to make reference to the one-year warranty reinstated in 1965. The no. 19446-10 Layout Sheet was unique to this outfit and is very difficult to find.

The no. 65-373 White RSC Allstate By Lionel With Blue Steamer (With Smoke and Trees) and Orange and Blue Graphics outfit box was manufactured by United Container Co. and measured 13¼ x 11 x 6¾ inches. This box was made of a thicker corrugated material (rated at 90 pounds rather than the normal 65 pounds gross weight). It included four lines of data as part of the box manufacturer's certificate. Printed on the bottom were "65-373" and a reference to the N.M.F.C.

The 19446 did not meet Lionel's expectations because the original quantity of 2,000 was reduced to 1,500. This outfit does appear, but its unique outfit box frequently has yellowed with age. The most difficult item to find in completing this outfit is the proper 19446-10 Layout Sheet.

19450
1965

The no. 19450 was a low-end steam-powered General Release Promotional outfit for 1965. It included the promotional-only no. X625-20 Cardboard Scenic Set. That item, so difficult to find complete and unassembled, was printed on chipboard, and the figures were perforated for easy removal. The entire sheet was folded in half so it would fit in a small outfit box. Surviving examples are extremely fragile and tend to fall apart over time. This outfit is shown with the gray no. 6176-75 Hopper Car substitution.

Description: "O27" Promotional Outfit
Specification: "O27" Steam Type Freight Outfit
Original Amount: 5,000
Factory Order Date: 6/17/1965
Date Issued: Rev 8-16-65
Packaging: (Units not Boxed)

Contents: 1062-50 Steam Type Loco. W/Light & Reversing Unit; 1062T-25 Tender; 6014-325 Frisco Box Car; 3364-25 Log Dump Car; 3364-8 Logs (3); 6176-50 Hopper Car; 6059-50 Caboose; 1013-70 Curved Track (Bundle of 12 - 1013); 1018-30 Straight Track (Bundle of 3 - 1018); 1020-25 90° Crossing; 6149-

25 Remote Control Track; 1010-25 35-Watt Transformer; 1103-40 Envelope Packed; X625-20 Cardboard Scenic Set; D65-50 Accessory Catalog; Form 3063 Parts Order Form; 1-165 Warranty Card; 926-65 Service Station List; 19223-10 Instruction Sheet; 3364-10 Instruction Sheet; 1802-10 Instruction Sheet

Boxes & Packing: 61-170 Outfit Box; 61-171 Corr. Insert; 61-172 Corr. Insert; 64-177 Corr. Insert (2); 61-174 Shipper for 6 (1-6)

Alternate For Outfit Contents:
Note: Sub. 6176-75 for 6176-50 as needed.

19450 (1965)	C6	C7	C8	Rarity
Complete Outfit	435	1,050	1,375	R9
Outfit Box no. 61-170	25	50	75	R4

Comments: In 1965, Lionel offered Retailer Promotional outfits to only Mercury Model, Sears and Western Auto. Other retailers, many of whom were accustomed to obtaining exclusive promotional outfits, were now limited to General Release Promotional outfits. They had to compete head-to-head with other retailers with similar offerings.

Outfit no. 19450 was a General Release Promotional Type IIb outfit for which retailers paid $10.95 each. Although it has yet to be linked to a particular retailer, evidence suggests that some if not all of the 19450s went to incentive merchandiser Richie Premium. After all, this outfit came with a no. X625-20 Cardboard Scenic Set, a highly desirable peripheral item that was included only in promotional outfits that Lionel sold to Richie Premium.

This low-end steam-powered outfit was led by a no. 1062-50 Steam Type Loco. W/Light & Reversing Unit. This low-end Scout steamer featured an 0-4-0 wheel arrangement and a rubber tire as a traction aid. Except for the rubber tire, it was identical to the no. 1062-25 Steam Type Loco. W/Light & Reversing Unit.

The rolling stock consisted of carryover items that were commonly used in outfits from 1965. The most notable item was the no. 3364-25 Log Dump Car, which was identical to the no. 3362-25 Helium Tank Unloading Car except that it carried logs instead of helium tanks. The no. 6014-325 Frisco Box Car used a Type III body.

Besides the black no. 6176-50 Hopper Car, a gray no. 6176-75 Hopper Car has been observed with this outfit. Although stamped "BUILT 1-48" and "LIONEL 6076", this model still was considered a 6176 because it included an operating truck and coupler. This substitution does not affect the outfit price.

The rolling stock in the 19450 followed the normal truck and coupler progression for 1965, with each of the cars having AAR

types. All but two were equipped with one operating and one non-operating truck and coupler. The no. 1062T-25 Tender had one non-operating and one plain type, and the no. 6059-50 Caboose had one operating and one plain type.

What makes this otherwise common and dull outfit highly collectible was the inclusion of an X625-20. This fragile item featured figures, railroad signs, automobiles and buildings that could be punched out, assembled and placed around a layout. The rarity of the X625-20 is linked to a lack of Lionel markings (it was identified with only "Printed in Japan"), which led to it frequently being separated from the trains and being discarded before or after assembly.

The nos. 19223-10 and 1802-10 Instruction Sheets in the 19450 detailed the figure-eight track layout. They were dated 7/65 and 8/64, respectively.

The no. 61-170 Tan RSC with Black Graphics outfit box was manufactured by United Container Co. and measured 11½ x 10¼ x 6¼ inches. It included four lines of data, a "64" and two stars as part of the box manufacturer's certificate. Printed on the bottom was a reference to the N.M.F.C.

The 19450 exceeded early forecasts because its factory orders were increased from 2,500 to 5,000. An additional quantity of 50 outfits was required in 1966, a change that led to a new Factory Order being created. The 1965 and 1966 versions are nearly identical and so share pricing and rarity.

In 1989, Richard Kughn, then the owner of Lionel Trains Inc., purchased Madison Hardware Co. of New York City and reopened it in Detroit soon thereafter. One of the first lists of outfits available for sale included six of the 19450.

Even with 5,050 of the 19450 manufactured over two years, completing this outfit with the Cardboard Scenic Set has proved to be very difficult. As such, the 19450 is one of those unusual outfits whose components, specifically the X625-20, make it an R9. The box by itself rates an R4.

Description: "O27" Promotional Outfit
Specification: "O27" Steam Type Freight Outfit
Original Amount: 50
Factory Order Date: 5/24/1966
Date Issued: 5-24-66
Date Req'd: 6-1-66
Packaging: (Units not Boxed)

Contents: 1062-50 Steam Type Loco. W/Light & Reversing Unit; 1062T-25 Tender; 6014-325 Frisco Box Car; 3364-25 Log Dump Car; 3364-8 Logs (3); 6176-50 Hopper Car; 6059-50 Caboose; 1013-70 Curved Track (Bundle of 12 - 1013); 1018-30 Straight Track (Bundle of 3 - 1018); 1020-25 90° Crossing; 6149-25 Remote Control Track; 1010-25 35-Watt Transformer; 1103-40 Envelope Packed; X625-20 Cardboard Scenic Set; Form 3063 Parts Order Form; 1-166 Warranty Card; 926-66 Service Station List; 19223-10 Instruction Sheet; 3364-10 Instruction Sheet; 1802-10 Instruction Sheet

Boxes & Packing: 61-170 Outfit Box; 61-171 Corr. Insert; 61-172 Corr. Insert; 64-177 Corr. Insert (2); 61-174 Shipper for 6 (1-6)

Alternate For Outfit Contents:
Note: Sub. 1062-75 for 1062-50; Sub. 1025-25 for 1010-25.

Comments: The no. 19450 from 1966 was a repeat of outfit 19450 from 1965. It appears that Lionel needed an additional 50 outfits to fulfill customer requests.

Lionel may have run out of the no. 1062-50 Steam Type Loco. W/Light & Reversing Unit used in the 1965 version and replaced it with the no. 1062-75 Steam Type Loco. W/Light & Reversing Unit (new for 1966). This low-end Scout steamer featured a 2-4-2 wheel arrangement and a rubber tire as a traction aid. Except for its wheel arrangement, the 1062-75 was identical to the no. 1062-50 Steam Type Loco. W/Light & Reversing Unit.

The transformer and some paperwork were also updated for 1966. Even so, the outfits are considered identical from a pricing and rarity perspective. (See the entry for the 19450 from 1965 for a description of this outfit's contents, pricing and rarity.)

19400 Series

Outfit no. 19453 (Sears no. 9834) was one of the 14 outfits purchased by Sears in 1965. It was a follow-up to outfit no. 19327 (Sears no. 9807) that omitted the nos. 321-1 Trestle Bridge and 958-100 Auto Set With Signs & Poles. Two items of note were the nos. 346-1 Culvert Unloader and 6342-25 Culvert Car (equipped with AAR trucks and couplers).

Customer No. On Box: 9834
Description: "O27" Promotional Outfit
Specification: "O27" Steam Type Freight Outfit W/Smoke
Customer/No./Price: Sears, Roebuck and Co.; 9834; $29.99
Original Amount: 10,000
Factory Order Date: 8/4/1965
Date Issued: Rev 8-25-65
Date Req'd: 8-25-65
Packaging: (Units not Boxed)

Contents: 237-25 Steam Type Locomotive with Smoke; 242T-25 Tender; 6176-75 Hopper Car; 6822-50 Searchlight Car; 6342-25 Culvert Car; 6059-50 Caboose; 346-1 Culvert Unloader; 1013-70 Curved Track (Bundle of 12 - 1013); 1013-85 Curved Track (Loose) (2); 1018-7 Straight Track (Bundle of 7 - 1018); 1018-40 Straight Track (Bundle of 4 - 1018); 1022-1 Pr. Manual Switches; 6149-25 Remote Control Track; 1025-25 45-Watt Transformer; 1103-40 Envelope Packed; 909-20 Smoke Fluid; 1-165 Warranty Card; 11450-10 Instruction Sheet; 237-11 Instruction Sheet; 346-21 Instruction Sheet; 19327-10 Layout Sheet

Boxes & Packing: 65-378 Outfit Box; 65-380 Corr. Insert; 65-381 Corr. Insert; 61-171 Corr. Insert; 61-172 Corr. Insert; 61-183 Corr. Insert; 62-248 Corr. Insert; 62-264 Corr. Insert; 62-273 Corr. Insert; 64-169 Corr. Insert; 41110-23 Corr. Insert (2); 65-379 Shipper for 3 (1-3); 41110-23 Shipper Pad (2-3)

19453 (9834) (1965)	C6	C7	C8	Rarity
Complete Outfit	445	700	1,065	R4
Outfit Box no. 65-378	75	150	300	R4

Comments: After purchasing only three outfits in 1964, Sears, Roebuck and Co. made a large purchase of 14 Retailer Promotional outfits in 1965. Only three of these outfits appeared in the 1965 Sears Christmas Catalog.

Outfit no. 19453, a Type Ib, was stamped with Sears no. 9834. This outfit, for which Sears paid $19.02 each, appeared on page 462 of the 1965 Sears Christmas Catalog for $29.99.

The 19453 was a repeat of outfit no. 19327 (Sears no. 9807) from 1964. The motive power, rolling stock and accessory were nearly identical. The 19453 did not include the nos. 321-1 Trestle Bridge and 958-100 Auto Set With Signs & Poles that were found in the 19327.

The 19453 was led by a no. 237-25 Steam Type Locomotive with Smoke. This Scout steamer featured a two-position reversing unit and a headlight and used a rubber tire as a traction aid. The later version with narrow running boards came in this outfit. Except for its 237 number, it was the same engine as a no. 238.

The most notable item of rolling stock was the no. 6342-25 Culvert Car. Last seen in the 1959 consumer catalog, it was re-introduced in the 19327 from 1964. The new version was equipped with one operating and one non-operating AAR truck and coupler riveted directly to the body.

The yellow no. 6176-75 Hopper Car came without the "NEW 1-48" data stamped on the car.

The rolling stock in the 19453 followed the normal truck and coupler progression for 1965, with each of the cars having AAR types. All but two were equipped with one operating and one non-operating truck and coupler. The no. 242T-25 Tender had one non-operating and one plain type, and the no. 6059-50 Caboose had one operating and one plain type.

As with many promotional outfits, the peripherals included in the 19453 make it a highly collectible outfit. Specifically, the no. 346-1 Culvert Unloader appeared only in five promotional outfits. The 346-1 was the manual version of the culvert unloader and was packed with seven culvert pipes in a no. 346-13 Corr. Box. The 6342-25 and no. 346-21 Instruction Sheet were included separately in the outfit.

The track layout was an oval layout with an inner switch track. As outlined on the no. 19327-10 Instruction Sheet, it required a no. 1022-1 Pr. Manual Switches.

The instruction sheets were updated from the 19327 and made reference to the one-year warranty reinstated in 1965. The

correct nos. 11450-10 Instruction Sheet and 346-21 Instruction Sheet were dated 6/65 and 8/65, respectively.

The no. 65-378 White RSC Allstate By Lionel With Blue Steamer (With Smoke and Trees) and Orange and Blue Graphics outfit box was manufactured by United Container Co. and measured 20¼ x 13¼ x 9¾ inches. This box was made of a thicker corrugated material (rated at 90 pounds rather than the normal 65 pounds gross weight) that allowed each outfit to be shipped in its outfit box. It included four lines of data, a "65" or "9-65" and four stars as part of the box manufacturer's certificate. Printed on the bottom were "65-378" and a reference to the N.M.F.C.

The 19453 was produced in large quantities, making the outfit box fairly common. Unfortunately, due to direct outfit shipping and the large space needed to store the box, most outfit boxes have not fared well. High-grade versions are difficult to find. Of the two similar Sears outfits, the 19327 from 1964 is more desirable.

Customer No. On Box: 9834
Description: "O27" Promotional Outfit
Specification: "O27" Steam Type Freight Outfit W/Smoke
Customer/No./Price: Sears, Roebuck and Co.; 9834; $29.99
Factory Order Date: 2/1/1966
Date Issued: 2-24-66
Date Req'd: 2-24-66
Packaging: (Units not Boxed)

Contents: 237-25 Steam Type Locomotive with Smoke; 242T-25 Tender; 6176-75 Hopper Car; 6822-50 Searchlight Car; 6342-25 Culvert Car; 6059-50 Caboose; 346-1 Culvert Unloader; 1013-70 Curved Track (Bundle of 12 - 1013); 1013-85 Curved Track (Loose) (2); 1018-7 Straight Track (Bundle of 7 - 1018); 1018-40 Straight Track (Bundle of 4 - 1018); 1022-1 Pr. Manual Switches; 6149-25 Remote Control Track; 1025-25 45-Watt Transformer; 1103-40 Envelope Packed; 909-20 Smoke Fluid; 1-165 Warranty

Card; 11450-10 Instruction Sheet; 237-11 Instruction Sheet; 346-21 Instruction Sheet; 19327-10 Layout Sheet

Boxes & Packing: 65-378 Outfit Box; 65-380 Corr. Insert; 65-381 Corr. Insert; 61-171 Corr. Insert; 61-172 Corr. Insert; 61-183 Corr. Insert; 62-248 Corr. Insert; 62-264 Corr. Insert; 62-273 Corr. Insert; 64-169 Corr. Insert; 41110-23 Corr. Insert (2); 65-379 Shipper for 3 (1-3); 41110-23 Shipper Pad (2-3)

Comments: A Factory Order for a 1966 version of outfit no. 19453 (Sears no. 9834) exists. It appears that this order was a continuation of the 1965 Factory Order for the 19453 and not a new outfit. As such, no additional outfits were manufactured and the quantity of 10,000 from 1965 is used to determine rarity. (See the entry for outfit 19453 from 1965.)

Customer No. On Box: 9835
Description: "O27" Promotional Outfit
Specification: "O27" Diesel Freight Outfit W/Horn
Customer/No./Price: Sears, Roebuck and Co.; 9835; $49.95
Original Amount: 1,500
Factory Order Date: 8/23/1965
Date Issued: Rev 9-2-65
Packaging: (Units not Boxed)

Contents: 216P-25 "Minn. & St. Louis" Diesel Power Car With Horn; 213T-25 Motorless Unit; 6176-50 Hopper Car; 6014-325 Frisco Box Car; 6142-100 Gondola Car; 6112-88 Canister (2); 6402-50 Flat Car W/2 Cable Reels; 40-11 Cable Reels (2); 6465-150 Tank Car; 6059-50 Caboose; 76-25 Lamp Post (3); 145-100 Automatic Gateman; 321-100 Bridge; 260-25 Illuminated Bumper; 110-125 Set of 6 Trestle Piers; 1013-73 Curved Track (6 per Bundle); 1013-90 Curved Track (Bundle of 9 - 1013); 1018-7 Straight Track (Bundle of 7 - 1018) (3); 1018-10 Straight Track (Loose); 1018-60 Half Section Straight Track; 1022-1 Pr. Manual Switches; 1022-75 L.H. Manual Switch; 6149-25 Remote Control Track; 310-2 Set of (5) Billboards; 310-3 Billboard Frame (5); 1073-25 60-Watt

Transformer; 147-25 Horn & Whistle Controller; 1103-50 Envelope Packed; 1-165 Warranty Card; 76-10 Instruction Sheet; 11460-10 Instruction Sheet; 212-64 Instruction Sheet; 19454-10 Layout Sheet

Boxes & Packing: 65-382 Outfit Box; 65-384 Corr. Insert; 65-385 Corr. Insert; 61-181 Corr. Insert; 61-182 Corr. Insert; 61-183 Corr. Insert; 64-177 Corr. Insert; 64-169 Corr. Insert; 63-316 Corr. Insert (2); 63-312 Corr. Insert (2); 65-302 Corr. Insert (2); 65-383 Shipper for 2 (1-2); 64-143 Shipper Pad (2-2)

Alternate For Outfit Contents:
Note: Sub. 6176-75 for 6176-50 as needed.

19454-500 (9835) (1965)	C6	C7	C8	Rarity
Complete Outfit	825	1,325	1,915	R7
Outfit Box no. 65-382	150	250	350	R7

Outfit no. 19454-500 (Sears no. 9835) was one of the 14 outfits purchased by Sears in 1965. It was Sears' high-end O27 offering for 1965 and came with a unique track plan and many promotional-only items. The no. 216P-25 Minn. & St. Louis Diesel Power Car With Horn appeared in only this and another promotional outfit. The large outfit box was unique to this outfit and long enough to fit the no. 321-100 Bridge.

Comments: After purchasing only three outfits in 1964, Sears, Roebuck and Co. made a large purchase of 14 Retailer Promotional outfits in 1965. Only three of these outfits appeared in the 1965 Sears Christmas Catalog.

Outfit no. 19454-500, a Type Ic, was stamped with Sears no. 9835. This outfit appeared on page 463 of the 1965 Sears Christmas Catalog for $49.95. Sears paid Lionel $32.34 for each 19454-500.

The 19454-500 was Sears' high-end O27 offering for 1965. It was led by a no. 216P-25 Minn. & St. Louis Diesel Power Car With Horn (new for 1965). This Alco featured a two-position reversing unit, a headlight and two rubber tires as traction aids. It appeared only in this and promotional outfit no. 19571. In both it was paired with a no. 213T-25 Motorless Unit. Lionel produced only 2,000 of these difficult-to-find Alcos.

The rolling stock was all carryover items. The no. 6014-325 Frisco Box Car used a Type III body. Some outfits have been observed with a yellow no. 6176-75 Hopper Car substitution, which does not affect the overall outfit price.

The rolling stock in the 19454-500 followed the normal truck and coupler progression for 1965, with each of the cars having AAR types. All but one were equipped with one operating and one non-operating truck and coupler. The no. 6059-50 Caboose had one operating and one plain type.

As with many promotional outfits, the peripherals included in the 19454-500 make it a highly collectible outfit. Specifically, the no. 145-100 Automatic Gateman was a common accessory, but its no. 145-59 Folding Box was made of flimsy chipboard and did not survive well. It is difficult to find in collectible condition. The 145-100 was introduced on 8/7/64 and made its sole outfit appearance in this outfit. The "-100" indicated that it included a no. 145-64

Printed Card with its $8.00 retail price prominently shown.

The no. 321-100 Bridge, new in 1965, was included only in this outfit and promotional outfit no. 12885-500 (Sears no. 9836). It was the same as a no. 321-1 Trestle Bridge, except that it omitted the metal base. It also included a no. 321-101 Instruction Sheet and no. 3330-102 Plastic Cement Filled Capsule in its corrugated box. Lionel produced only 1,815 of this difficult-to-find bridge.

The no. 110-125 Set of 6 Trestle Piers was unique to this outfit. Along with the piers, a no. 110-126 Instruction Sheet (dated 8/65), Tie Channels and Screws came in a polyethylene bag. This is an extremely difficult item to find with its original bag. A C8 outfit assumes an original instruction sheet and bag.

The track layout was unique to this outfit and was outlined on the difficult-to-find no. 19454-10 Layout Sheet.

The instruction sheets made reference to the one-year warranty reinstated in 1965. The correct nos. 11460-10 Instruction Sheet and 212-64 Instruction Sheet were both dated 4/65.

The no. 65-382 White RSC Allstate By Lionel With Blue Steamer (With Smoke and Trees) and Orange and Blue Graphics outfit box was manufactured by the Mead Corporation and measured 24¾ x 11¾ x 8¼ inches. This box was made of a thicker corrugated material (rated at 90 pounds rather than the normal 65 pounds gross weight) that allowed each outfit to be shipped in its outfit box. It included four lines of data as part of the box manufacturer's certificate as well as a reference to the N.M.F.C.

A quantity of 1,500 of the 19454-500s was manufactured. Even with this larger-than-average number, direct outfit shipping and the large space needed to store the box contributed to a small number of high-grade boxes surviving. Even when a box is found, finding collectible versions of its components takes time.

The no. 19455 was a mid-level steam-powered General Release Promotional outfit for 1965. It included the bright yellow no. 6176-75 Hopper Car variation, one of the more desirable models in the 6176 series. Also shown is a no. 6473-25 Rodeo Car with a Type IIIa body (cadmium yellow plastic with red lettering).

Comments: In 1965, Lionel offered Retailer Promotional outfits to only Mercury Model, Sears and Western Auto. Other retailers, many of whom were accustomed to obtaining exclusive promotional outfits, were now limited to General Release Promotional outfits. They had to compete head-to-head with other retailers with similar offerings.

Outfit no. 19455, a General Release Promotional Type IIa for which retailers paid $13.00 each, has yet to be linked to a particular retailer.

This mid-level steam-powered outfit was led by a no. 237-25 Steam Type Locomotive with Smoke. This Scout steamer featured a two-position reversing unit, a headlight and a rubber tire as a traction aid. The later version with narrow running boards came in this outfit.

The rolling stock was all carryover and commonly used in outfits from 1965. The most notable item was the no. 6473-25 Rodeo Car. It used a Type IIIa body (cadmium yellow plastic with red lettering). That body no longer exhibited the filled slot caused by broken tooling. The no. 6176-75 Hopper Car was bright yellow and stamped "BUILT 1-48" and "LIONEL 6176".

The rolling stock in the 19455 followed the normal truck and coupler progression for 1965, with each of the cars having AAR types. All but two were equipped with one late operating and one late non-operating truck and coupler. The no. 242T-25 Tender had one late non-operating and one plain type, and the no. 6059-50 Caboose had one late operating and one plain type.

The no. 65-270 White Lift-Off with Full-Color 2037 Steam Freight Graphics Type D display outfit box was printed by Continental Printing Corp. and measured 24½ x 15½ x 3⅛ inches.

With 1,500 units manufactured and the contents being commonplace, the 19455 does not attract much interest from collectors. Even so, finding one in C8 condition does take effort.

Description: "O27" Promotional Outfit
Specification: "O27" Steam Type Freight Outfit W/Smoke
Original Amount: 1,500
Factory Order Date: 6/29/1965
Date Issued: 6-30-65
Date Req'd: 7-5-65
Packaging: Display Pack (Units not Boxed)

Contents: 237-25 Steam Type Locomotive with Smoke; 242T-25 Tender; 6402-50 Flat Car W/2 Cable Reels; 40-11 Cable Reels (2); 6473-25 Rodeo Car; 6176-75 Hopper Car; 6465-150 Tank Car; 6059-50 Caboose; 1013-8 Curved Track (Bundle of 8 - 1013); 1018-30 Straight Track (Bundle of 3 - 1018); 6149-25 Remote Control Track; 1025-25 45-Watt Transformer; 1103-40 Envelope Packed; 909-20 Smoke Fluid; D65-50 Accessory Catalog; Form 3063 Parts Order Form; 1-165 Warranty Card; 926-65 Service Station List; 237-11 Instruction Sheet; 11450-10 Instruction Sheet

Boxes & Packing: 65-270 Box Top; 64-115 Box Bottom; 64-118 Corr. Insert; 64-119 Corr. Insert; 64-120 Corr. Insert; 64-116 Shipper for 4 (1-4); 64-117 Shipper Pad (2-4); MT Mylar Tape (5")

19455 (1965)	C6	C7	C8	Rarity
Complete Outfit	200	350	550	R6
Outfit Box no. 65-270	75	150	250	R6

Outfit no. 19500 was Lionel's entry-level market development outfit for 1966. It is fairly easy to obtain in collectible condition, but it attracts little interest because of its common and low-end rolling stock.

Description: "O27" Promotional Outfit
Specification: "O27" Steam Type Freight Outfit
Original Amount: 25,000
Factory Order Date: 2/22/1966
Date Issued: Rev 10-28-66
Date Req'd: 10/28/66
Packaging: Display

Contents: 1062-75 Steam Type Loco. W/Light & Reversing Unit; 1062T-25 Tender; 6042-125 Gondola Car; 6076-75 Hopper Car - Black; 6167-100 Caboose; 1013-8 Curved Track (Bundle of 8 - 1013); 1018-10 Straight Track (Loose) (2); 1025-25 45-Watt Transformer; 1103-20 Envelope Packed; 19500-10 Instruction Sheet; 1-166 Warranty Card; 926-66 Service Station List; Form 3063 Parts Order Form

Boxes & Packing: 65-260 Box Top; 64-102 Box Bottom; 64-107 Corr. Insert; 64-103 Shipper for 6 (1-6); 64-104 Shipper Pad (2-6); MT Mylar Tape (6")

Alternate For Outfit Contents:
Note: Substitute 6042-75 (without load) for 6042-125 for 15,000 sets; Note: Sub 1010-25 for 1025-25 for 16,000 sets.

Outfit Number	Packaging Type	Engine Number	Lionel Selling Price	Suggested Retail
19500	Display	1062-75	$7.50	$15.00
19501	RSC			
19512	Display	221P-25	$8.75	$19.00
19513	RSC			
19502	Display	242-25	$10.25	$21.95
19503	RSC			
19504	Display	635-25	$12.25	$26.95
19514	Display	237-25	$13.00	$28.88
19515	RSC			
19506	Display	215P-25	$17.50	$35.00
19507	RSC			
19516	Display	241-25	$19.00	$40.00
19517	RSC			
19510	Display	241-25	$22.50	$50.00
19511	RSC			

This table summarizes the 15 market development outfits offered by Lionel in 1966. The entries are arranged according to price rather than outfit number because Lionel did not originally plan to release a display and an RSC version of each outfit. When it changed the no. 19501 to an RSC version of the no. 19500, the original 19501 became the no. 19512. The other outfit numbers were also changed accordingly. Needless to say, this non-sequential numbering of progressively better-equipped outfits is confusing. Be aware that not every number in the sequence 19500-19517 was used.

19500 (1966)	C6	C7	C8	Rarity
Complete Outfit	70	120	200	R2
Outfit Box no. 65-260	15	20	30	R2

Comments: In 1966, Lionel issued 15 General Release Promotional outfits as part of its market development line. In reality, there were eight different outfits, seven of which were packaged in both display and RSC versions. Each outfit was created to fulfill a different price point.

The market development outfits were sold to numerous retailers, including Aldens, Bennett Brothers, J. C. Penney and Spiegel. These retailers were identified by price tags, catalog listings, newspaper advertisements and other documents. Many of these retailers were accustomed to obtaining exclusive promotional outfits. They were now limited to General Release Promotional outfits and had to compete head to head against other retailers with similar offerings. (See the section on Lionel's Distribution and Customers for more information about Lionel's Market Development Division.)

The nos. 19500 and 19501, both Type IIb outfits, included identical motive power and rolling stock. Each was led by a no. 1062-75 Steam Type Loco. W/Light & Reversing Unit (new for 1966). This low-end Scout steamer featured a 2-4-2 wheel arrangement and a rubber tire as a traction aid. Except for its wheel arrangement, the 1062-75 was identical to the no. 1062-50 Steam Type Loco. W/Light & Reversing Unit.

The rolling stock in this outfit consisted of carryover items that were commonly used in outfits from 1966. During the course of that year, Lionel finished removing the new date, a built date and number data from the heat-stamping of the no. 6076-75 Hopper Car - Black. This minimal decoration became the norm for the 6076-75. The nos. 1010-25 35-Watt Transformer and 6042-75 Gondola Car (Less 2 Cable Reels) substitutions do not affect the outfit price.

The rolling stock in the 19500 and 19501 followed the normal truck and coupler progression for 1966, with each of the cars having AAR types. All but two were equipped with non-operating trucks and couplers. The no. 6167-100 Caboose had one operating and one non-operating type, and the no. 1062T-25 Tender had one non-operating and one plain type. The 6167-100 also featured a washer riveted as part of its leaf spring assembly.

The no. 1103-20 Envelope Packed has been observed in a Type II or Type III envelope.

The no. 19500-10 Instruction Sheet was introduced in this outfit and dated 5/66.

The no. 65-260 White Lift-Off with Full-Color 2037 Steam Freight Graphics Type D display outfit box was manufactured by Mead Containers and measured 23½ x 11½ x 3 inches.

An original quantity of 15,000 units of the 19500 was to have been manufactured. This was subsequently increased to 25,000. As such, this is one of the most common and easiest to obtain of all Lionel outfits.

Outfit no. 19501 was Lionel's entry-level market development outfit for 1966. Even with 3,000 made, it is somewhat difficult to find. Its contents were identical to those of outfit no. 19500.

19500 Series

Description: "O27" Promotional Outfit
Specification: "O27" Steam Type Freight Outfit
Customer/No./Price: Aldens; 34 Y 5601; $12.88
Customer/No./Price: Bennett Brothers; 6498T1167; $17.95
Customer/No./Price: Spiegel; R36 J 5258; $14.77
Original Amount: 3,000
Factory Order Date: 5/5/1966
Date Issued: Rev 10-24-66
Date Req'd: 10/24/66
Packaging: Mail Order Pack

Contents: 1062-75 Steam Type Loco. W/Light & Reversing Unit; 1062T-25 Tender; 6042-125 Gondola Car; 6076-75 Hopper Car - Black; 6167-100 Caboose; 1013-8 Curved Track (Bundle of 8 - 1013); 1018-10 Straight Track (Loose) (2); 1025-25 45-Watt Transformer; 1103-20 Envelope Packed; 19500-10 Instruction Sheet; 1-166 Warranty Card; 926-66 Service Station List; Form 3063 Parts Order Form

Boxes & Packing: 65-410 Outfit Box; 62-254 Corrugated Insert; 64-319 Corrugated Insert; 61-173 Corrugated Insert; 65-330 Shipper for 6 (1-6); 64-104 Shipper Pad (2-6); 19501-15 Printed Label

A no. 19501-15 Printed Label was to have been applied to 19501 outfit boxes. Even though an example with a label has yet to be observed, the original artwork for the 19501-15 survived.

Alternate For Outfit Contents:
Sub. 1010-25 for 1025-25 for 3,000 sets.

19501 (1966)	C6	C7	C8	Rarity
Complete Outfit	115	175	260	R6
Outfit Box no. 65-410	45	60	90	R6

Comments: In 1966, Lionel issued 15 General Release Promotional outfits as part of its market development line. In reality, there were eight different outfits, seven of which were packaged in both display and RSC versions. Each outfit was created to fulfill a different price point. (See outfit no. 19500 for a summary of the market development outfits for 1966.)

The no. 19501, a Type IIb outfit, has been linked to Aldens (1966 Christmas Catalog page 152 as no. 34 Y 5601 for $12.88),

Bennett Brothers (1967 Bennett Blue Book page 774 as no. 6498T1167 for $17.95) and Spiegel (1966 Christmas Catalog page 398 as no. R36 J 5258 for $14.77). It likely was sold through other retailers as well.

The 19501 came with the same motive power and rolling stock as the no. 19500. (See the 19500 for information about the contents of this outfit.) The only difference was that the 19501 came in an RSC box. In this case, the no. 65-410 Tan RSC with Black Graphics outfit box, which was manufactured by Mann Kraft Container Corporation and measured 11½ x 10 x 6¼ inches. It included four lines of data as part of the box manufacturer's certificate as well as a reference to the N.M.F.C.

Even though a no. 19501-15 Printed Label was to have been applied to the outfit box, an outfit box has yet to be observed with this label. An example found with a label would command a premium.

An original quantity of 10,000 units of the 19501 was to have been manufactured. This was subsequently reduced to 3,000. The 19501 is much more difficult to find than its display-packed counterpart, the 19500.

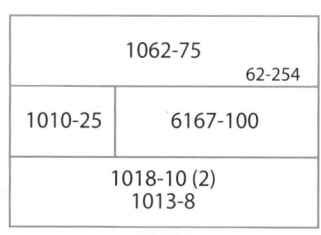

CONVENTIONAL PACK
65-410 BOX

TOP LAYER		BOTTOM LAYER	
6076-75 / 61-173		1062-75 / 62-254	
	1062T-25	1010-25	6167-100
6042-125		1018-10 (2) 1013-8	
		64-319	

Description: "O27" Promotional Outfit
Specification: "O27" Steam Type Freight Outfit
Original Amount: 1,000
Factory Order Date: 2/22/1966
Date Issued: Rev 6-2-66
Date Req'd: 5-9-66
Packaging: Display Pack

Contents: 242-25 Steam Type Locomotive; 242T-25 Tender; 6014-325 Frisco Box Car; 6402-50 Flat Car; 40-11 Cable Reels (2); 6050-100 Swift Savings Bank Car; 6059-50 Caboose; 1013-8 Curved Track (Bundle of 8 - 1013); 1018-30 Straight Track (Bundle of 3 - 1018); 6149-25 Remote Control Track; 1025-25 45-Watt Transformer; 1103-40 Envelope Packed; 11450-10 Instruction Sheet; Form 3063 Parts Order Form; 1-166 Warranty Card; 926-66 Service Station List

Boxes & Packing: 65-270 Box Top; 64-115 Box Bottom; 64-119 Corr. Insert; 64-120 Corr. Insert; 64-128 Corr. Insert; 64-116 Shipper for 4 (1-4); 64-117 Shipper Pad (2-4); MT Mylar Tape (6")

19502 (1966)	C6	C7	C8	Rarity
Complete Outfit	200	350	515	R7
Outfit Box no. 65-270	100	200	300	R7

Comments: In 1966, Lionel issued 15 General Release Promotional outfits as part of its market development line. In reality, there were eight different outfits, seven of which were packaged in both display and RSC versions. Each outfit was created to fulfill a different price point. (See outfit no. 19500 for a summary of the market development outfits for 1966.)

The nos. 19502 and 19503, both Type IIa outfits, included identical motive power and rolling stock. Each was led by a no. 242-25 Steam Type Locomotive. This low-end Scout steamer featured a two-position reversing unit and a headlight, lacked smoke and used a rubber tire as a traction aid. The later version with narrow running boards was included in this outfit.

The rolling stock in this outfit consisted of carryover items that were commonly used in outfits from 1966. The nos. 6014-325 Frisco Box Car and 6050-100 Swift Savings Bank Car, both of which used a Type III body, were paired together in only the 19502 and 19503.

The rolling stock in the 19502 and 19503 followed the normal truck and coupler progression for 1966, with each of the cars having AAR types. All but one of them, including the no. 6059-50 Caboose, were equipped with one late operating and one late

Outfit no. 19502 was Lionel's second steam-powered market development outfit for 1966. The addition of two box cars (nos. 6014-325 Frisco Box Car and 6050-100 Swift Savings Bank Car) made this a somewhat unique outfit. They were paired together in only the 19502 and no. 19503. Note the truck and coupler configuration on the no. 6059-50 Caboose – Lionel replaced the plain truck with a non-operating one in 1966.

non-operating truck and coupler. The no. 242T-25 Tender had one late non-operating and one plain type.

The no. 11450-10 Instruction Sheet was dated 6/65.

The no. 65-270 White Lift-Off with Full-Color 2037 Steam Freight Graphics Type D display outfit box was manufactured by Mead Containers and measured 24½ x 15½ x 3⅛ inches.

An original quantity of 3,500 units of the 19502 was to have been manufactured. This was subsequently slashed to 1,000. This reduction makes the 19502 a difficult outfit to find complete and in collectible condition.

Description: "O27" Promotional Outfit
Specification: "O27" Steam Type Freight Outfit
Customer/No./Price: Bennett Brothers; 6499T1427; $21.95
Original Amount: 500
Factory Order Date: 5/5/1966
Date Issued: Rev 10-28-66
Date Req'd: 10-28-66
Packaging: Mail Order Pack

Contents: 242-25 Steam Type Locomotive; 242T-25 Tender; 6014-325 Frisco Box Car; 6402-50 Flat Car; 40-11 Cable Reels (2); 6050-100 Swift Savings Bank Car; 6059-50 Caboose; 1013-8 Curved Track (Bundle of 8 - 1013); 1018-30 Straight Track (Bundle of 3 - 1018); 6149-25 Remote Control Track; 1025-25 45-Watt Transformer; 1103-40 Envelope Packed; 11450-10 Instruction Sheet; Form 3063 Parts Order Form; 1-166 Warranty Card; 926-66 Service Station List

Boxes & Packing: 61-170 Outfit Box; 62-251 Corr. Insert; 61-171 Corrugated Insert; 61-172 Corrugated Insert; 62-202 Corrugated Insert; 61-175 Shipper for 4 (1-4); 65-413 Shipper Pad (2-4)

19503 (1966)	C6	C7	C8	Rarity
Complete Outfit	250	450	715	R9
Outfit Box no. 61-170	150	300	500	R9

Comments: In 1966, Lionel issued 15 General Release Promotional outfits as part of its market development line. In reality, there were eight different outfits, seven of which were packaged in both display and RSC versions. Each outfit was created to fulfill a different price point. (See outfit no. 19500 for a summary of the market development outfits for 1966.)

The no. 19503, a Type IIa outfit, has been linked to Bennett Brothers (1967 Bennett Blue Book page 774 as no. 6499T1427 for $21.95). It was likely sold through other retailers as well.

19500 Series

The 19503 came with the same motive power and rolling stock as the no. 19502. (See the 19502 for information about the contents of this outfit.) The only difference was that the 19503 came in an RSC box. In this case, the no. 61-170 Tan RSC with Black Graphics outfit box, which likely was manufactured by United Container and measured 11½ x 10¼ x 6¼ inches.

An original quantity of 1,000 units of the 19503 was to have been manufactured. This was subsequently reduced to 500. This low quantity makes the 19503 very difficult to find, much more so than its display-packed counterpart, the 19502.

CONVENTIONAL PACK
61-170 BOX

TOP LAYER

1013-8 1018-30 6149-25	
242T-25 62-202	40-11 (2)
6050-100	

BOTTOM LAYER

242-25	61-171	1025 25		6014-325	62-251	6402-50
		6059-50				

61-172

19504
1966

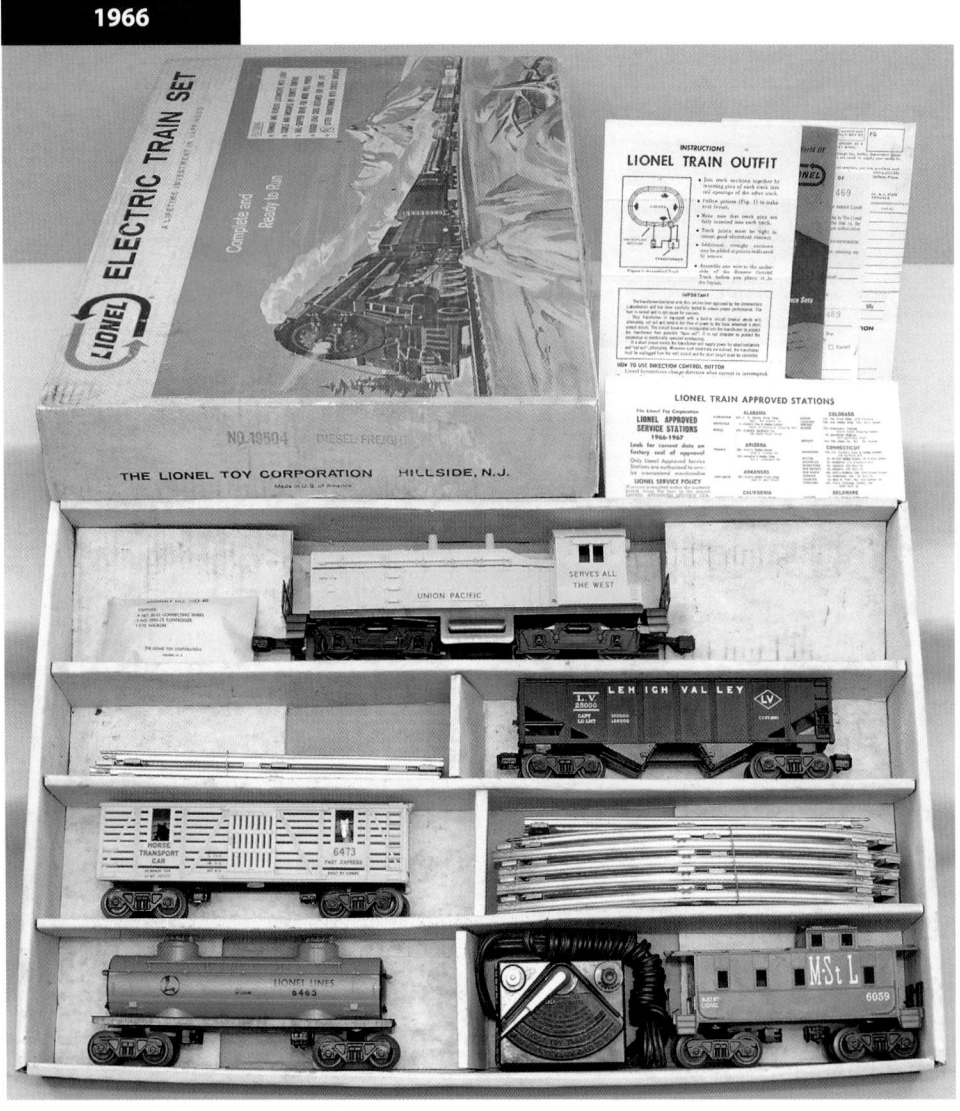

Outfit no. 19504 was Lionel's mid-level diesel-powered market development outfit for 1966. It featured the no. 635-25 Union Pacific Diesel Switcher, which appeared in only six promotional outfits. Note the truck and coupler configuration on the no. 6059-50 Caboose – Lionel replaced the plain truck with a non-operating one in 1966.

Description: "O27" Promotional Outfit
Specification: "O27" Diesel Freight Outfit
Original Amount: 600
Factory Order Date: 2/22/1966
Date Issued: Rev 10-28-66
Date Req'd: 10-28-66
Packaging: Display Pack

Contents: 635-25 "Union Pacific" Diesel Switcher; 6473-25 Rodeo Car; 6465-150 Tank Car; 6176-50 Hopper Car; 6059-50 Caboose; 1013-8 Curved Track (Bundle of 8 - 1013); 1018-30 Straight Track (Bundle of 3 - 1018); 6149-25 Remote Control Track; 1025-25 45-Watt Transformer; 1103-40 Envelope Packed; 11530-10 Instruction Sheet; 1-166 Warranty Card; 926-66 Service Station List; Form 3063 Parts Order Form

Boxes & Packing: 65-270 Box Top; 64-115 Box Bottom; 64-128 Corr. Insert; 65-273 Corr. Insert; 64-116 Shipper for 4 (1-4); 64-117 Shipper Pad (2-4); MT Mylar Tape (6")

19504 (1966)	C6	C7	C8	Rarity
Complete Outfit	300	515	875	R8
Outfit Box no. 65-270	150	300	500	R8

Comments: In 1966, Lionel issued 15 General Release Promotional outfits as part of its market development line. In reality, there were eight different outfits, seven of which were packaged in both display and RSC versions, with no. 19504 being the only one without an RSC counterpart. Each outfit was created to fulfill a different price point. (See outfit no. 19500 for a summary of the market development outfits for 1966.)

The contents of the 19504 were identical to those of the no. 19440 from 1965, except that the latter included a no. 3364-25 Log Dump Car.

The 19504, a Type IIb outfit, was led by a no. 635-25 Union Pacific Diesel Switcher. Included in promotional outfits only, this locomotive featured a two-position reversing unit, a headlight, a weight and a rubber tire as a traction aid.

The rolling stock in this outfit consisted of carryover items that were commonly used in outfits from 1966. The most notable item was the no. 6473-25 Rodeo Car. It used a Type IIIa body (cadmium yellow plastic with red lettering), which no longer exhibited the filled slot caused by broken tooling. During the course of 1966, Lionel finished removing the new date, a built date and number data from the heat-stamping of the black no. 6176-50 Hopper Car. This minimal decoration became the norm for the 6176-50.

The rolling stock in the 19504 followed the normal truck and coupler progression for 1966, with each of the cars having AAR types. All of them, including the no. 6059-50 Caboose, were equipped with one operating and one non-operating truck and coupler.

The no. 11530-10 Instruction Sheet was dated 6/65.

The no. 65-270 White Lift-Off with Full-Color 2037 Steam Freight Graphics Type D display outfit box was manufactured by Mead Containers and measured 24½ x 15½ x 3⅛ inches.

An original quantity of 1,000 units of the 19504 was to have been manufactured. This was subsequently reduced to 600. The 19504 is difficult to find complete and in collectible condition.

Outfit no. 19506 was Lionel's high-end diesel-powered market development outfit for 1966. It featured the promotional-only no. 215P-25 Santa Fe Diesel Power Car. This Alco appeared in 14 different outfits during its three-year run. Note the truck and coupler configuration on the no. 6059-50 Caboose – Lionel replaced the plain truck with a non-operating one in 1966. The "Toy 31.97" price was stamped on the left side of the outfit box by an unknown retailer.

Description: "O27" Promotional Outfit
Specification: "O27" Diesel Freight Outfit
Customer/No.: J. C. Penney Co., Inc.; 9808
Original Amount: 2,500
Factory Order Date: 2/22/1966
Date Issued: Rev 8-8-66
Date Req'd: 8-8-66
Packaging: Display Pack

Contents: 215P-25 "Santa Fe" Diesel Power Car; 212T-25 "Santa Fe" "A" Unit; 6050-100 Swift Savings Bank Car; 6465-150 Tank Car; 6142-100 Gondola Car; 6112-88 Canister (2); 6176-50 Hopper Car; 6059-50 Caboose; 1013-70 Curved Track (bundle of 12 - 1013); 1018-40 Straight Track (Bundle of 4 - 1018); 1018-30 Straight Track (Bundle of 3 - 1018); 1020-25 90° Crossing; 6149-25 Remote Control Track; 1073-25 60-Watt Transformer; 1103-40 Envelope Packed; 211-151 Instruction Sheet; 19506-10 Instruction Sheet; 1-166 Warranty Card; 926-66 Service Station List; Form 3063 Parts Order Form

Boxes & Packing: 65-270 Box Top; 64-112 Box Bottom; 64-122 Corr. Insert; 64-118 Corr. Insert; 64-121 Corr. Insert; 64-113 Shipper for 4 (1-4); 64-114 Shipper Pad (2-4); MT Mylar Tape (6")

19506 (1966)	C6	C7	C8	Rarity
Complete Outfit	260	425	625	R5
Outfit Box no. 65-270	75	125	150	R5

Comments: In 1966, Lionel issued 15 General Release Promotional outfits as part of its market development line. In reality, there were eight different outfits, seven of which were packaged in both display and RSC versions. Each outfit was created to fulfill a different price point. (See outfit no. 19500 for a summary of the market development outfits for 1966.)

The no. 19506 was likely sold through different retailers, but it has been linked only to J. C. Penney via a Lionel Billing Deck document as Penney no. 9808. Many retailers commonly carried the display-packed outfits in their stores and assigned them a different retail number than the ones in their catalog. When the 19506 appeared in Penney's catalog as the no. 19507, it was assigned the no. X 924-8279 A.

The nos. 19506 and 19507, both Type IIb outfits, included identical motive power and rolling stock. Each was led by a no. 215P-25 Santa Fe Diesel Power Car. This promotional-only Alco featured a two-position reversing unit, two traction tires, a headlight, a weight and an open pilot with a large ledge. It was paired with a no. 212T-25 Santa Fe "A" Unit.

The rolling stock in this outfit consisted of carryover items that were commonly used in outfits from 1966. The most notable item was the no. 6050-100 Swift Savings Bank Car, which used a Type III body. During the course of 1966, Lionel finished removing the new date, a built date and number data from the heat-stamping of the black no. 6176-50 Hopper Car. This minimal decoration became the norm for the 6176-50.

The rolling stock in the 19506 and 19507 followed the normal truck and coupler progression for 1966, with each of the cars having AAR types. All of them, including the no. 6059-50 Caboose, were equipped with one operating and one non-operating truck and coupler.

The difficult-to-find no. 19506-10 Instruction Sheet was unique to the 19506 and 19507. It detailed the figure-eight track layout and was dated 5/66. The 19506-10 was the same as the common no. 19214-10 Instruction Sheet, except that the former removed any reference to the transformer's direction control.

The no. 65-270 White Lift-Off with Full-Color 2037 Steam Freight Graphics Type D display outfit box was manufactured by Mead Containers and measured 24½ x 15½ x 3⅛ inches.

As with most outfits led by a Santa Fe engine, the 19506 and 19507 were very popular. An original quantity of 1,000 units of the 19506 was to have been manufactured. This was subsequently increased to 2,500. Due to this larger-than-average quantity, many 19506s have survived and one can be found with some patience.

Description: "O27" Promotional Outfit
Specification: "O27" Diesel Freight Outfit
Customer/No./Price: Aldens; 34 Y 5616E; $27.97
Cust./No./Price: J. C. Penney Co., Inc.; X 924-8279 A; $28.88
Customer/No./Price: Spiegel; R36 J 5260; $27.97
Original Amount: 1,125
Factory Order Date: 5/5/1966
Date Issued: Rev 11-21-66
Date Req'd: 11-21-66
Packaging: Mail Order Pack

Contents: 215P-25 "Santa Fe" Diesel Power Car; 212T-25 "Santa Fe" "A" Unit; 6050-100 Swift Savings Bank Car; 6465-150 Tank Car; 6142-100 Gondola Car; 6112-88 Canister (2); 6176-50 Hopper Car; 6059-50 Caboose; 1013-70 Curved Track (Bundle of 12 - 1013); 1018-40 Straight Track (Bundle of 4 - 1018); 1018-30 Straight Track (Bundle of 3 - 1018); 1020-25 90° Crossing; 6149-25 Remote Control Track; 1073-25 60-Watt Transformer; 1103-40 Envelope Packed; 211-151 Instruction Sheet; 19506-10 Instruction Sheet; 1-166 Warranty Card; 926-66 Service Station List; Form 3063 Parts Order Form

Boxes & Packing: 65-435 Outfit Box; 61-181 Corrugated Insert; 61-182 Corrugated Insert; 62-224 Corrugated Insert; 62-225 Corrugated Insert; 62-245 Corrugated Insert (2); 62-248 Corrugated Insert; 64-106 Corrugated Insert; 65-436 Shipper for 4 (1-4); 64-106 Shipper Pad (2-4)

19507 (1966)	C6	C7	C8	Rarity
Complete Outfit	310	500	725	R7
Outfit Box no. 65-435	125	200	250	R7

Comments: In 1966, Lionel issued 15 General Release Promotional outfits as part of its market development line. In reality, there were eight different outfits, seven of which were packaged in both display and RSC versions. Each outfit was created to fulfill a different price point. (See outfit no. 19500 for a summary of the market development outfits for 1966.)

The no. 19507, a Type IIb outfit, has been linked to Aldens (1966 Christmas Catalog page 153 as no. 34 Y 5616E for $27.97), J. C. Penney (1966 Christmas Catalog page 404 as no. X 924-8279 A for $28.88) and Spiegel (1966 Christmas Catalog page 398 as no. R36 J 5260 for $27.97). It likely was sold through other retailers as well.

The 19507 came with the same motive power and rolling stock as the no. 19506. (See the 19506 for information about the contents of this outfit.) The only difference was that the 19507 came in an RSC box. In this case, the no. 65-435 Tan RSC with Black Graphics outfit box, which was manufactured by the Mead Corporation and measured 12¾ x 12 x 6⅞ inches. These boxes were made of a thicker corrugated material (rated at 90 pounds rather than the normal 65 pounds gross weight) that allowed each outfit to be shipped in its outfit box. It included four lines of data as part of its box manufacturer's certificate as well as a reference to the N.M.F.C.

As with most outfits led by a Santa Fe engine, the 19506 and 19507 were very popular. An original quantity of 1,000 units of the 19507 was to have been manufactured. This was subsequently

Outfit no. 19507 was Lionel's high-end diesel-powered market development outfit for 1966. It was the RSC version of display-packed no. 19506. Both featured the promotional-only no. 215P-25 Santa Fe Diesel Power Car. The RSC version was shipped in its outfit box. As such, it is difficult to find without signs of this initial shipment. The "96 1086" stamped on this example is likely an unknown retailer's stock number.

increased to 1,125. With less than half as many 19507s made than 19506s, the former is more difficult to find.

Since these outfits were shipped in their outfit box, most show signs of this initial shipment. Therefore, a 19507 is difficult to find in C8 condition.

CONVENTIONAL PACK
65-435 BOX

TOP LAYER

6050-100		
61-182	1073-25	
6059-50	61-181	
6176-50	62-225	
1018-30		
1018-40	1020-25	
1013-70	TOP	
6149-25		

BOTTOM LAYER

62-245

215P-25 | 62-248 | 212T-25 | 62-224 | 6465-150 / 6142-100

62-245

64-106

Description: "O27" Promotional Outfit
Specification: "O27" Steam Type Freight Outfit W/Smoke & Whistle
Customer/No.: J. C. Penney Co., Inc.; 9804
Original Amount: 500
Factory Order Date: 2/22/1966
Date Issued: Rev 6-2-66
Date Req'd: 5-9-66
Packaging: Display

Contents: 241-25 Steam Type Locomotive with Smoke; 234W-25 Whistle Tender; 6473-25 Rodeo Car; 3364-25 Log Dump Car; 3364-8 Logs (3); 6176-50 Hopper Car; 6142-100 Gondola Car; 6112-88 Canister (2); 6130-25 Work Caboose - "Santa Fe"; 260-1 Illuminated Bumper; 1022-75 L.H. Manual Switch; 1013-8 Curved Track (Bundle of 8 - 1013); 1013-85 Curved Track (Loose); 1018-30 Straight Track (Bundle of 3 - 1018) (2); 1018-5 Straight Track (Bundle of 5 - 1018); 6149-25 Remote Control Track; 1073-25 60-Watt Transformer; 147-25 Horn & Whistle Controller; 1103-50

Envelope Packed; 909-20 Smoke Fluid; Form 3063 Parts Order Form; 1-165 Warranty Card; 926-66 Service Station List; 11460-10 Instruction Sheet; 3364-10 Instruction Sheet; 19442-10 Instruction Sheet; 237-11 Instruction Sheet

Boxes & Packing: 65-270 Box Top; 64-112 Box Bottom; 64-119 Corr. Insert; 64-120 Corr. Insert; 64-118 Corr. Insert; 64-121X Corr. Insert; 64-113 Shipper for 4 (1-4); 64-114 Shipper Pad (2-4); MT Mylar Tape (6")

19510 (1966)	C6	C7	C8	Rarity
Complete Outfit	500	800	1,150	R8
Outfit Box no. 65-270	225	350	500	R8

Comments: In 1966, Lionel issued 15 General Release Promotional outfits as part of its market development line. In reality, there were eight different outfits, seven of which were packaged in both display and RSC versions. Each outfit was created to fulfill a

Outfit no. 19510 was Lionel's high-end steam-powered market development outfit for 1966. It was a follow-up to the no. 19442 from 1965 and included identical motive power and rolling stock. This is the only display-packed outfit to include a no. 1022-series switch in its outfit box. To make room for the switch, the filler insert that was underneath the white inserts was cut in half. On this example, the inserts on the upper half of the outfit have been sunken slightly lower to accommodate the switch and extra track.

helium tanks. During the course of 1966, Lionel finished removing the new date, a built date and number data from the heat-stamping of the black no. 6176-50 Hopper Car. This minimal decoration became the norm for the 6176-50.

The unboxed no. 6130-25 Santa Fe Work Caboose was introduced in 1965. Previously, it always came boxed as a no. 6130-1 Santa Fe Work Caboose. The 6130-25 had a red-painted cab and tray and a black-painted frame with no stampings. There were slats below the Santa Fe herald, but not a builder's plate.

The rolling stock in the 19510 and 19511 followed the normal truck and coupler progression for 1966, with each of the cars having late AAR types. Every model except for the 234W-25 was equipped one operating and one non-operating truck and coupler; it came with one non-operating and one plain type. The 6130-25 had one operating and one non-operating truck and coupler, reflecting the trend at Lionel to replace the plain one with a non-operating type on most cabooses in 1966.

The no. 19442-10 Instruction Sheet is very difficult to find. It was dated 4/65 and detailed an oval layout with an interior spur. All the other sheets were dated from 1965 as well.

What is unique about this outfit was the inclusion of a no. 1022-75 L.H. Manual Switch in a display-packed box. Lionel created the no. 64-121X Corr. Insert that provided extra room underneath the top insert for the 1022-75 and the additional track. (See the section on Outfit Boxes and Inserts for more information about this insert.)

The no. 1103-50 Envelope Packed has been observed in a Type III envelope. The no. 909-20 Smoke Fluid came with a white paper backing.

The no. 65-270 White Lift-Off with Full-Color 2037 Steam Freight Graphics Type D display outfit box was manufactured by Mead Containers and measured 24½ x 15½ x 3⅛ inches.

An original quantity of 1,000 units of the 19510 was to have been manufactured. This was subsequently reduced to 500. One would think that the relatively small number of outfits produced would lead to the 19510 being difficult to obtain in collectible condition. Yet examples of this outfit can, with some patience, be found in C8 condition, although seldom do they have the 1022-75.

different price point. (See outfit no. 19500 for a summary of the market development outfits for 1966.)

The no. 19510 was likely sold through different retailers, but it has been linked only to J. C. Penney via a Lionel Billing Deck document as Penney no. 9804. Many retailers commonly carried the display-packed outfits in their stores and assigned them a different retail number than the ones in their catalog. When the 19510 appeared in Penney's catalog as the no. 19511, it was assigned the no. X 924-8287 A.

The nos. 19510 and 19511, both Type IIb outfits, included identical motive power and rolling stock. They were a follow-up to outfit no. 19442 from 1965, which included the same motive power and rolling stock. In fact, an early 19510 Factory Order was simply a 19442 Factory Order with "19442" crossed out and "19510" written below. Lionel even used the same sales glossy photographs by whiting out "19442" and typing "19510" at the bottom.

The 19510 and 19511 were led by a no. 241-25 Steam Type Locomotive with Smoke that was paired with a no. 234W-25 Whistle Tender. This die-cast Scout steamer, which appeared only in promotional outfits, featured a two-position reversing unit, a headlight and a rubber tire as a traction aid. The early version with a thin, rubber-stamped stripe has been observed in at least one 19510. Otherwise, the later version with a wide, white-painted stripe version is most common. Except for its 241 number and stripe, it was the same engine as a no. 239.

All the rolling stock in this outfit, including the two operating cars, consisted of carryover items. The no. 6473-25 Rodeo Car used a Type IIIa body (cadmium yellow plastic with red lettering), which no longer exhibited the filled slot caused by broken tooling. The no. 3364-25 Log Dump Car was identical to the no. 3362-25 Helium Tank Unloading Car, except that it carried logs instead of

Description: "O27" Promotional Outfit
Specification: "O27" Steam Type Freight Outfit W/Smoke & Whistle
Customer/No./Price: Bennett Brothers; 6502T3250; $50.00
Cust./No./Price: J. C. Penney Co., Inc.; X 924-8287 A; $37.77
Original Amount: 500
Factory Order Date: 5/5/1966
Date Issued: Rev 10-28-66
Date Req'd: 10-28-66
Packaging: Mail Order Pack

Contents: 241-25 Steam Type Locomotive with Smoke; 234W-25 Whistle Tender; 6473-25 Rodeo Car; 3364-25 Log Dump Car; 3364-8 Logs (3); 6176-50 Hopper Car; 6142-100 Gondola Car; 6112-88 Canister (2); 6130-25 Work Caboose - "Santa Fe"; 260-1 Illuminated Bumper; 1022-75 L.H. Manual Switch; 1013-8 Curved Track (Bundle of 8 - 1013); 1013-85 Curved Track (Loose); 1018-30 Straight Track (Bundle of 3 - 1018) (2); 1018-5 Straight Track (Bundle of 5 - 1018); 6149-25 Remote Control Track; 1073-25 60-Watt Transformer; 147-25 Horn & Whistle Controller; 1103-50 Envelope Packed; 909-20 Smoke Fluid; Form 3063 Parts Order Form; 1-165 Warranty Card; 926-66 Service Station List; 11460-10 Instruction Sheet; 3364-10 Instruction Sheet; 19442-10 Instruction Sheet; 237-11 Instruction Sheet

Boxes & Packing: 66-138 Outfit Box; 61-181 Corrugated Insert; 61-182 Corrugated Insert; 62-248 Corrugated Insert (2); 64-143 Corrugated Insert (3); 62-225 Corrugated Insert (2); 64-167 Shipper 4 (1-4); 64-114 Shipper Pad (2-4)

19511 (1966)	C6	C7	C8	Rarity
Complete Outfit	525	825	1,200	R9
Outfit Box no. 66-138	250	375	550	R9

Comments: In 1966, Lionel issued 15 General Release Promotional outfits as part of its market development line. In reality, there were eight different outfits, seven of which were packaged in both display and RSC versions. Each outfit was created to fulfill a different price point. (See outfit no. 19500 for a summary of the market development outfits for 1966.)

The no. 19511, a Type IIb outfit, has been linked to Bennett Brothers (1967 Bennett Blue Book page 774 as no. 6502T3250 for $50) and J. C. Penney (1966 Christmas Catalog page 404 as no. X 924-8287 A for $37.77). It likely was sold through other retailers as well.

The 19511 came with the same motive power and rolling stock as the no. 19510. (See the 19510 for information about the contents of this outfit.) The only difference was that the 19511 came in an RSC box. In this case, the no. 66-138 Tan RSC with Black Graphics outfit box, which was manufactured by Eastern Corrugated Container Corp. and measured 15¼ x 10⅝ x 7 inches. These boxes were made of a thicker corrugated material (rated at 90 pounds rather than the normal 65 pounds gross weight) that allowed each outfit to be shipped in its outfit box. It included four lines of data as part of its box manufacturer's certificate. This box was used for only two outfits, 19511 and the no. 19590.

As with the 19510, an original quantity of 1,000 units of the 19511 was to have been manufactured. This was subsequently reduced to 500. Unlike the 19510, this outfit is very difficult to find, hence its R9 rarity rating.

CONVENTIONAL PACK
66-138 BOX

TOP LAYER

1018-5 6149-25	6142-100
62-248 6176-50	
62-248 6130-25	
3364-25 3364-8 (3)	62-225

BOTTOM LAYER

1022-75	
1013-8 1013-85	1018-30 61-181
61-182 6473-25 234W-25	1073-25
241-25	260-1
64-143	

Description: "O27" Promotional Outfit
Specification: "O27" Diesel Freight Outfit
Customer/Price: Enloe Drug; $12.88
Original Amount: 1,922
Factory Order Date: 2/22/1966
Date Issued: Rev 10-21-66
Date Req'd: 10-22-66
Packaging: Display Pack

Contents: 221P-25 Diesel Locomotive; 6045-150 Tank Car; 6409-25 Flat Car; 6511-15 Pipes (3); 6042-25 Gondola Car; 6112-5 Canister (2); 6167-100 Caboose; 4-5 Elastic Band; 1013-8 Curved Track (Bundle of 8 - 1013); 1018-10 Straight Track (Loose) (2); 1025-25 45-Watt Transformer; 1103-20 Envelope Packed; 19512-10 Instruction Sheet; 1-166 Warranty Card; 926-66 Service Station List; Form 3063 Parts Order Form

Boxes & Packing: 65-260 Box Top; 64-102 Box Bottom; 64-107 Corr. Insert; 64-105 Shipper for 4 (1-4); 64-106 Shipper Pad (2-4); 64-103 Shipper for 6 (1-6); 64-104 Shipper Pad (2-6); MT Mylar Tape (6")

Alternate For Outfit Contents:
Note: For 66 outfits use 64-105 shipper (1-4) & 64-106 Shipper Pad (2-4).

19512 (1966)	C6	C7	C8	Rarity
Complete Outfit	200	325	500	R6
Outfit Box no. 65-260	75	125	200	R6

Comments: In 1966, Lionel issued 15 General Release Promotional outfits as part of its market development line. In reality, there were eight different outfits, seven of which were packaged in both display and RSC versions. Each outfit was created to fulfill a different price point. (See outfit no. 19500 for a summary of the market development outfits for 1966.)

The no. 19512 has been linked to Enloe Drug via a price tag for $12.88. The 19512 was likely sold through other retailers as well.

The 19512 and no. 19513, both Type IIb outfits, included identical motive power and rolling stock. Each was led by a no. 221P-25 Rio Grande Diesel Locomotive. This low-end, unpainted yellow Alco featured a two-position reversing unit, a traction tire

19500 Series

Outfit no. 19512 was Lionel's entry-level diesel-powered market development outfit for 1966. The 19512 and its RSC counterpart, the no. 19513, marked the final appearance of the nos. 221P-25 Rio Grande Diesel Locomotive and 6045-150 Tank Car. Most outfits are found without the no. 6511-15 Pipes.

and a closed pilot and lacked a headlight. It was making its final appearance in this outfit and the 19513 and no. 19533.

The rolling stock in this outfit consisted of carryover items that were commonly used in outfits from 1966. The no. 6409-25 Flat Car W/3 Pipes was a red no. 6511-series flat car that

had "Lionel" stamped on each side and lacked a car number and a brake wheel. The no. 6045-150 Tank Car was making its final appearance in this outfit and the 19513 and 19533.

The rolling stock in the 19512 and 19513 followed the normal truck and coupler progression for 1966, with each of the cars having late AAR types. All but one were equipped with non-operating trucks and couplers. The no. 6167-100 Caboose had one operating and one non-operating type.

The no. 19512-10 Instruction Sheet was dated 6/66 and made its first appearance in this outfit.

The no. 65-260 White Lift-Off with Full-Color 2037 Steam Freight Graphics Type D display outfit box was manufactured by Mead Containers and measured 23½ x 11½ x 3 inches.

An original quantity of 3,500 units of the 19512 was to have been manufactured. This was subsequently decreased to 1,922. Many of these outfits have survived, but it still takes effort to find one in C8 condition.

Description: "O27" Promotional Outfit
Specification: "O27" Diesel Freight Outfit
Original Amount: 300
Factory Order Date: 9/1/1966
Date Issued: 9-1-66
Date Req'd: 9-1-66
Packaging: MO Pack

Contents: 221P-25 Diesel Locomotive; 6045-150 Tank Car; 6409-25 Flat Car; 6511-15 Pipes (3); 6042-25 Gondola Car; 6112-5 Canister (2); 6167-100 Caboose; 4-5 Elastic Band; 1013-8 Curved Track (Bundle of 8 - 1013); 1018-10 Straight Track (Loose) (2); 1025-25 45-Watt Transformer; 1103-20 Envelope Packed; 19512-10 Instruction Sheet; 1-166 Warranty Card; 926-66 Service Station List; Form 3063 Parts Order Form

Boxes & Packing: 65-410 Outfit Box; 62-254 Corr. Insert; 62-264 Corr. Insert; 64-319 Corr. Insert; 65-330 Shipper for 6 (1-6); 64-104 Shipper Pad (2-6)

19513 (1966)	C6	C7	C8	Rarity
Complete Outfit	320	550	800	R10
Outfit Box no. 65-410	200	350	500	R10

Comments: In 1966, Lionel issued 15 General Release Promotional outfits as part of its market development line. In reality, there were eight different outfits, seven of which were packaged in both display and RSC versions. Each outfit was created to fulfill a different price point. (See outfit no. 19500 for a summary of the market development outfits for 1966.)

The no. 19513, a Type IIb outfit, likely was sold through a few retailers, although it has yet to be linked to a specific one.

The 19513 came with the same motive power and rolling stock as the no. 19512. (See the 19512 for information about the contents of this outfit.) The only difference was that the 19513 came in an RSC box. In this case, the no. 65-410 Tan RSC with

Black Graphics outfit box, which was manufactured by Mann Kraft Container Corporation and measured 11½ x 10 x 6¼ inches. It included four lines of data as part of the box manufacturer's certificate as well as a reference to the N.M.F.C.

An original quantity of 96 units of the 19513 was to have been manufactured. This was subsequently increased to 300. The small number of units produced makes this a difficult outfit to find, and it is seldom seen, hence its R10 rarity rating.

CONVENTIONAL PACK
65-410 BOX

TOP LAYER		BOTTOM LAYER	
6045-150		221P-25	
6409-25		6167-100	1025-25
6042-25		1013-8 1018-10	

64-319

Outfit no. 19514 was Lionel's third steam-powered market development outfit for 1966. The later version is shown with light gray no. 6511-15 Pipes and a no. 6059-50 Caboose with one operating and one non-operating late AAR truck and coupler. Also note the no. 909-20 Smoke Fluid with a white paper backing.

Description: "O27" Promotional Outfit
Specification: "O27" Steam Type Freight Outfit W/Smoke
Customer/No./Price: Goodyear; M22 6 6745-10; $24.98
Customer/No.: J. C. Penney Co., Inc.; 9802
Original Amount: 6,200
Factory Order Date: 2/24/1966
Date Issued: Rev 8-8-66
Date Req'd: 8-8-66
Packaging: Display Pack

Contents: 237-25 Steam Type Locomotive with Smoke; 242T-25 Tender; 6465-150 Tank Car; 6401-25 Flat Car; 6511-15 Pipes (3); 6050-100 Swift Savings Bank Car; 6059-50 Caboose; 4-5 Rubber Band; 1013-70 Curved Track (Bundle of 12 - 1013); 1018-30 Straight Track (Bundle of 3 - 1018); 1020-25 90° Crossing; 6149-25 Remote Control Track; 1025-25 45-Watt Transformer; 1103-40 Envelope Packed; 909-20 Smoke Fluid; 19214-10 Instruction

Sheet; 237-11 Instruction Sheet; 1-166 Warranty Card; 926-66 Service Station List; Form 3063 Parts Order Form

Boxes & Packing: 65-270 Box Top; 64-115 Box Bottom; 64-119 Corr. Insert; 64-120 Corr. Insert; 64-128 Corr. Insert; 64-116 Shipper for 4 (1-4); 64-117 Shipper Pad (2-4); MT Mylar Tape (6")

19514 (1966)	C6	C7	C8	Rarity
Complete Outfit	155	255	385	R4
Outfit Box no. 65-270	35	65	100	R4

Comments: In 1966, Lionel issued 15 General Release Promotional outfits as part of its market development line. In reality, there were eight different outfits, seven of which were packaged in both display and RSC versions. Each outfit was created to fulfill a different price point. (See outfit no. 19500 for a summary of the market development outfits for 1966.)

The no. 19514, which likely was sold through various retailers, has been linked to J. C. Penney via a Lionel Billing Deck document as Penney no. 9802. Many retailers commonly carried the display-packed outfits in their stores and assigned them a different retail number than the ones in their catalog. When the 19514 appeared in Penney's catalog as the no. 19515, it was assigned the no. X 924-8261 A. In addition, the 19514 has been observed with a Goodyear Service Stores price tag as no. M22 6 6745-10 for $24.98.

The 19514 and no. 19515, both Type IIa outfits, included identical motive power and rolling stock. Each was led by a no. 237-25 Steam Type Locomotive with Smoke. This Scout steamer featured a two-position reversing unit and a headlight and used a rubber tire as a traction aid. The later version with narrow running boards came in this outfit.

Two versions of the 19514 have been observed. The early version exhibited late-1965 or early-1966 features, while the later version had 1966 features. The early version had a no. 6059-50 Caboose with one operating and one plain AAR truck and coupler and no. 6511-15 Pipes that were opaque silver. The later version included a 6059-50 with one operating and one non-operating AAR truck and coupler and 6511-15 Pipes that were light gray. Original versions of these light gray pipes are difficult to find.

These differences were likely caused by the increase in the number of outfits ordered from 2,000 to 6,200.

The rolling stock in this outfit consisted of carryover items that were commonly used in outfits from 1966. The most notable item was the no. 6050-100 Swift Savings Bank Car, which used a Type III body.

The rolling stock in the 19514 and 19515 followed the normal truck and coupler progression for 1966, with each of the cars having late AAR types. Most were equipped with one operating and one non-operating truck and coupler. However, the no. 242T-25 Tender had one non-operating and one plain type and the 6059-50 had one operating and one plain type in the early outfits. Many outfits included cars with a washer riveted as part of their leaf spring assembly.

The no. 19214-10 Instruction Sheet was dated 6/66 and outlined the figure-eight track layout.

The no. 65-270 White Lift-Off with Full-Color 2037 Steam Freight Graphics Type D display outfit box was manufactured by Mead Containers and measured 24½ x 15½ x 3⅛ inches.

With 6,200 units produced, the 19514 is fairly common. However, finding the later version with original light gray pipes is a challenge.

Outfit no. 19515 was Lionel's third steam-powered market development outfit for 1966. It was the RSC version of display-packed no. 19514. To date, every outfit found has come with a no. 6059-50 Caboose with one operating and one plain AAR truck and coupler and no. 6511-15 Pipes that were opaque silver. This C9 example even boasted an original Lionel no. 4-5 Elastic Band.

Description: "O27" Promotional Outfit
Specification: "O27" Steam Type Freight Outfit W/Smoke
Customer/No./Price: Aldens; 34 Y 5618; $19.88
Customer/No./Price: Bennett Brothers; 6500T1950; $30.00
Customer/No./Price: Coast to Coast; TU0112-5; $19.97
Cust./No./Price: J. C. Penney Co., Inc.; X 924-8261 A; $19.88
Original Amount: 1,800
Factory Order Date: 5/5/1966
Date Issued: Rev 8-8-66
Date Req'd: 8-8-66
Packaging: Mail Order Pack

Contents: 237-25 Steam Type Locomotive with Smoke; 242T-25 Tender; 6465-150 Tank Car; 6401-25 Flat Car; 6511-15 Pipes (3); 6050-100 Swift Savings Bank Car; 6059-50 Caboose; 4-5 Rubber Band; 1013-70 Curved Track (Bundle of 12 - 1013); 1018-30 Straight Track (Bundle of 3 - 1018); 1020-25 90° Crossing; 6149-25 Remote Control Track; 1025-25 45-Watt Transformer; 1103-40 Envelope Packed; 909-20 Smoke Fluid; 19214-10 Instruction Sheet; 237-11 Instruction Sheet; 1-166 Warranty Card; 926-66 Service Station List; Form 3063 Parts Order Form

Boxes & Packing: 61-170 Outfit Box; 62-254 Corrugated Insert; 61-172 Corrugated Insert; 62-249 Corrugated Insert; 62-248 Corrugated Insert; 61-175 Shipper for 4 (1-4); 65-413 Shipper Pad (2-4)

19515 (1966)	C6	C7	C8	Rarity
Complete Outfit	195	325	485	R6
Outfit Box no. 61-170	75	135	200	R6

Comments: In 1966, Lionel issued 15 General Release Promotional outfits as part of its market development line. In reality, there were eight different outfits, seven of which were packaged in both display and RSC versions. Each outfit was created to fulfill a different price point. (See outfit no. 19500 for a summary of the market development outfits for 1966.)

The no. 19515, a Type IIa outfit, has been linked to Aldens (1966 Christmas Catalog page 152 as no. 34 Y 5618 for $19.88), Bennett Brothers (1967 Bennett Blue Book page 774 as no. 6500T1950 for $30), Coast to Coast Stores (unknown catalog page 18 as no. TU0112-5 for $19.97) and J. C. Penney (1966 Christmas Catalog page 404 as no. X 924-8261 A for $19.88). It likely was sold through other retailers as well.

The 19515 and no. 19514 included identical motive power and rolling stock. Keep in mind, though, that the 19515 has been observed only with a no. 6059-50 Caboose with one operating and one plain AAR truck and coupler and no. 6511-15 Pipes that were opaque silver. (See the 19514 for information about the contents of this outfit.)

The only difference between the 19514 and 19515 was that the latter came in a RSC box. In this case, the no. 61-170 Tan RSC with Black Graphics outfit box, which was manufactured by United Container Co. and measured 11½ x 10¼ x 6¼ inches. It included four lines of data, a "64" and two stars as part of the box manufacturer's certificate. Printed on the bottom was a reference to the N.M.F.C.

Be aware that the stamping on some outfits was carelessly applied and appeared to be stamped "19315" instead of "19515" (the "5" resembles a "3"). However, the 19315 was a completely different item, a Sears outfit from 1964 that came in a much larger box.

An original quantity of 2,500 units of the 19515 was to have been manufactured. This was subsequently reduced to 1,800. With so many large retailers cataloging this outfit and with 1,800 examples produced, a 19515 should appear more often than one does.

CONVENTIONAL PACK
61-170 BOX

TOP LAYER | BOTTOM LAYER 1020-25 TOP

6465-150	6401-25 6511-25 6149-25 1018-30	237-25
6050-100		1025-25 / 6059-50
242T-25		1013-70

61-172 BETWEEN LAYERS

19516
1966

Outfit no. 19516 was Lionel's fourth steam-powered market development outfit for 1966. The no. 241-25 Steam Type Locomotive with Smoke in this example featured a wide, white-painted stripe.

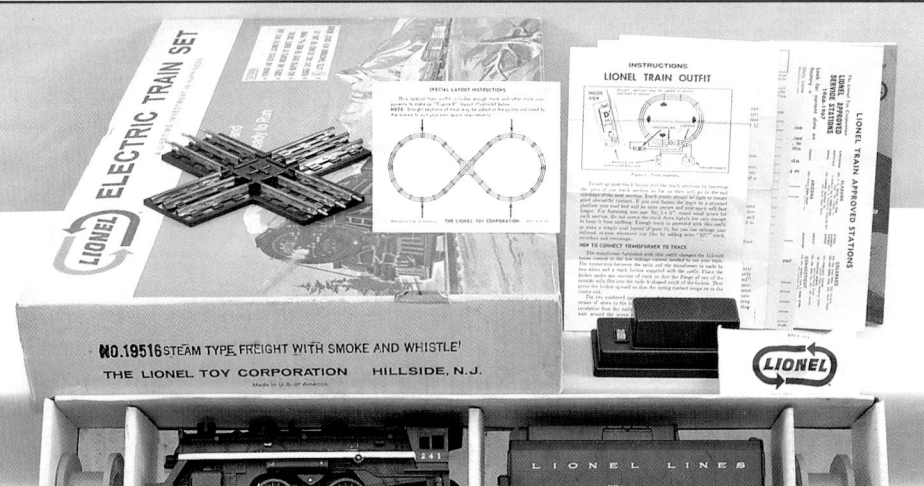

Description: "O27" Promotional Outfit
Specification: "O27" Steam Type Freight Outfit with Smoke & Whistle
Customer/No./Price: Children's Supermarket; 19516; $34.94
Original Amount: 2,400
Factory Order Date: 2/24/1966
Date Issued: Rev 10-28-66
Date Req'd: 10/28/66
Packaging: Display Pack

Contents: 241-25 Steam Type Locomotive with Smoke; 234W-25 Whistle Tender; 6050-100 Swift Savings Bank Car; 6465-150 Tank Car; 6142-150 Gondola Car; 40-11 Cable Reels (2); 6176-50 Hopper Car; 6059-50 Caboose; 1013-70 Curved Track (Bundle of 12 - 1013); 1018-30 Straight Track (Bundle of 3 - 1018); 1020-25 90° Crossing; 6149-25 Remote Control Track; 1018-40 Straight Track (Bundle of 4 - 1018); 1073-25 60-Watt Transformer; 147-25 Horn & Whistle Controller; 1103-50 Envelope Packed; 909-20 Smoke Fluid; 11460-10 Instruction Sheet; 1802-10 Instruction Sheet; 237-11 Instruction Sheet; 1-166 Warranty Card; 926-66 Service Station List; Form 3063 Parts Order Form

Boxes & Packing: 65-270 Box Top; 64-112 Box Bottom; 64-119 Corr. Insert; 64-120 Corr. Insert; 64-118 Corr. Insert; 64-121 Corr. Insert; 64-113 Shipper for 4 (1-4); 64-114 Shipper Pad (2-4); MT Mylar Tape (6")

19516 (1966)	C6	C7	C8	Rarity
Complete Outfit	260	440	650	R5
Outfit Box no. 65-270	50	75	125	R5

Comments: In 1966, Lionel issued 15 General Release Promotional outfits as part of its market development line. In reality, there were eight different outfits, seven of which were packaged in both display and RSC versions. Each outfit was created to fulfill a different price point. (See outfit no. 19500 for a summary of the market development outfits for 1966.)

The no. 19516 has been linked to Children's Supermarket via a price tag for $34.94. It likely was sold through other retailers as well.

The 19516 and no. 19517, both Type IIb outfits, included identical motive power and rolling stock. Each was led by a no. 241-25 Steam Type Locomotive with Smoke that was paired with a no. 234W-25 Whistle Tender. This die-cast Scout steamer, which appeared only in promotional outfits, featured a two-position reversing unit, a headlight and a rubber tire as a traction aid. The early version with a thin, rubber-stamped stripe as well as the later version with a wide, white-painted stripe have been observed in the 19516. Except for its 241 number and stripe, it was the same engine as a no. 239.

The rolling stock in this outfit consisted of carryover items that were commonly used in outfits from 1966. The most notable item was the no. 6050-100 Swift Savings Bank Car, which used a Type III body. During the course of 1966, Lionel finished removing the new date, a built date and number data from the heat-stamping of the black no. 6176-50 Hopper Car. This minimal decoration became the norm for the 6176-50.

The rolling stock in the 19516 and 19517 followed the normal truck and coupler progression for 1966, with each of the cars having late AAR types. All but two were equipped with one operating and one non-operating truck and coupler. The 234W-25 had one non-operating and one plain type, and the no. 6059-50 Caboose had one operating and one plain type in some outfits.

A no. 1802-10 Instruction Sheet detailed the figure-eight track layout.

The no. 65-270 White Lift-Off with Full-Color 2037 Steam Freight Graphics Type D display outfit box was manufactured by Mead Containers and measured 24½ x 15½ x 3⅛ inches.

An original quantity of 1,000 units of the 19516 was to have been manufactured. This was subsequently increased to 2,400. Many of these outfits have survived, and finding a 19516 is possible.

Description: "O27" Promotional Outfit
Specification: "O27" Steam Type Freight Outfit W/Smoke & Whistle
Customer/No./Price: Bennett Brothers; 6501T2600; $40.00
Customer/Price: Children's Supermarket; $34.94
Original Amount: 250
Factory Order Date: 5/5/1966
Date Issued: Rev 10-28-66
Date Req'd: 10-28-66
Packaging: Mail Order Pack

Contents: 241-25 Steam Type Locomotive with Smoke; 234W-25 Whistle Tender; 6050-100 Swift Savings Bank Car; 6465-150 Tank Car; 6142-150 Gondola Car; 40-11 Cable Reels (2); 6176-50 Hopper Car; 6059-50 Caboose; 1013-70 Curved Track (Bundle of 12 - 1013); 1018-7 Straight Track (Bundle of 7 - 1018); 1020-25 90° Crossing; 6149-25 Remote Control Track; 1073-25 60-Watt Transformer; 147-25 Horn & Whistle Controller; 1103-50 Envelope Packed; 909-20 Smoke Fluid; 11460-10 Instruction Sheet; 1802-10 Instruction Sheet; 237-11 Instruction Sheet; 1-166 Warranty Card; 926-66 Service Station List; Form 3063 Parts Order Form

Boxes & Packing: 65-435 Outfit Box; 62-225 Corrugated Insert; 62-251 Corrugated Insert; 62-264 Corrugated Insert; 64-106 Corrugated Insert; 64-169 Corrugated Insert; 64-323 Corrugated Insert; 65-436 Shipper for 4 (1-4); 64-106 Shipper Pad (2-4)

19517 (1966)	C6	C7	C8	Rarity
Complete Outfit	410	735	1,015	R9
Outfit Box no. 65-435	200	375	500	R9

Comments: In 1966, Lionel issued 15 General Release Promotional outfits as part of its market development line. In reality, there were eight different outfits, seven of which were packaged in both display and RSC versions. Each outfit was created to fulfill a different price point. (See outfit no. 19500 for a summary of the market

Outfit no. 19517 was Lionel's fourth steam-powered market development outfit for 1966. It was the RSC version of display-packed no. 19516. The no. 241-25 Steam Type Locomotive with Smoke in this example featured a thin, rubber-stamped stripe. For 1966, this was a higher-end starter outfit that any kid would have been excited to receive. In fact, this example came from the original owner with a photograph (not shown) of the owner's child playing with the outfit at Christmas of 1967.

Every marking on an outfit box likely meant something at one time. This no. 19517 included Bennett Brothers' stock number "6501T" written on the box.

development outfits for 1966.)

The no. 19517, a Type IIb outfit, has been linked to Bennett Brothers (1967 Bennett Blue Book page 774 as no. 6501T2600 for $40) and Children's Supermarket (a price tag for $34.94). It likely was sold through other retailers as well.

The 19517 and no. 19516 included identical motive power and rolling stock. Keep in mind, though, that the 19517 has been observed only with a no. 241-25 Steam Type Locomotive with Smoke and with a thin, rubber-stamped stripe. (See the 19516 for information about the contents of this outfit.)

The only difference between the 19516 and 19517 was that the latter came in a RSC box. In this case, the no. 65-435 Tan RSC with Black Graphics outfit box, which was manufactured by the Mead Corporation and measured 12¾ x 12 x 6⅞ inches. These boxes were made of a thicker corrugated material (rated at 90 pounds rather than the normal 65 pounds gross weight) that allowed each outfit to be shipped in its outfit box. It included four lines of data as part of its box manufacturer's certificate as well as a reference to the N.M.F.C.

An original quantity of 1,000 units of the 19517 was to have been manufactured. This was subsequently reduced to 250. Even with such a small number of outfits produced, the 19517 does appear from time to time.

19500 Series

CONVENTIONAL PACK
65-435 BOX

TOP LAYER				
6176-50	6465-150	6142-150	234W-25	
62-225	62-264		40-11 (2)	

BOTTOM LAYER			
6059-50	6050-100	241-25	1013-70
62-251	64-323	64-169	1018-7
			6149-25
			1020-25
1073-25			147-25

64-106

Description: "O27" Promotional Outfit
Specification: "O27" Steam Type Freight Outfit
Customer: Sperry & Hutchinson Co.
Original Amount: ~~7,500~~ Cancel
Factory Order Date: 2/24/1966
Date Issued: Rev 6-15-66
Date Req'd: 5-9-66
Packaging: Display Pack 4 / Master

Contents: 1062-75 Steam Type Loco. W/Light & Reversing Unit; 1062T-25 Tender; 6142-150 Gondola Car; 40-11 Cable Reels (2); 6176-75 Hopper Car; 6050-100 Swift Savings Bank Car; 6167-100 Caboose; 1013-8 Curved Track (Bundle of 8 - 1013); 1018-10 Straight Track (loose); 1008-50 Uncoupling Unit; 1025-25 45-Watt Transformer; 1103-40 Envelope Packed; 11580-15

Instruction Sheet; 1-166 Warranty Card; 926-66 Service Station List; Form 3063 Parts Order Form

Boxes & Packing: 65-260 Box Top; 64-102 Box Bottom; 65-261 Corr. Insert; 65-262 Corr. Insert; 64-105 Shipper for 4 (1-4); 64-106 Shipper Pad (2-4); MT Mylar Tape (6")

Alternate For Outfit Contents:
Note: Sub 6,500 - 1010-25 for 1025-25.

Comments: This was the last Factory Order to list Sperry & Hutchinson (S&H) as the customer. However, the original quantity was crossed out and the Factory Order marked "Cancel". A sales sample may have been made, but one has yet to be observed. This listing is provided for historical reference.

The no. 19530 was one of four outfits purchased by Western Auto in 1966. This low-end starter outfit was the only one to appear in a Western Auto catalog in that year. The later, light gray version of the no. 6511-15 Pipes was included; too bad that most outfits found now are missing these pipes.

Description: "O27" Promotional Outfit
Specification: "O27" Steam Type Freight Outfit
Customer/No./Price: Western Auto; E5002; $15.97
Original Amount: 6,500
Factory Order Date: 4/14/1966
Date Issued: Rev 10-28-66
Date Req'd: 10-28-66
Packaging: Display Pack (Units not Boxed), 4 per Master

Contents: 1062-75 Steam Type Loco. W/Light & Reversing Unit; 1062T-25 Tender; 6076-75 Hopper Car - Black; 6409-25 Flat Car; 6511-15 Pipes (3); 6167-100 Caboose; 1013-70 Curved Track (Bundle of 12 - 1013); 1018-40 Straight Track (Bundle of 4 - 1018); 1020-25 90° Crossing; 1025-25 45-Watt Transformer; 1103-20 Envelope Packed; Form 3063 Parts Order Form; 1-166 Warranty Card; 926-66 Service Station List; 19171-10 Instruction Sheet

Boxes & Packing: 65-260 Box Top; 64-102 Box Bottom; 65-264 Corr. Insert; 86925 Mylar Tape (4"); 64-105 Shipper for 4 (1-4); 64-106 Shipper Pad (2-4)

19530 (1966)	C6	C7	C8	Rarity
Complete Outfit	110	190	285	R4
Outfit Box no. 65-260	25	40	65	R4

Comments: Western Auto Stores purchased four outfits in 1966: nos. 11520, 19436, 19530 and 19910. The 19530, a Retailer Promotional Type Ib outfit, appeared in Western Auto's 1966 Christmas Gifts Catalog for $15.97 and its 1966-1967 Fall & Winter and Gift Catalog for $15.77.

The 19530 was led by a no. 1062-75 Steam Type Loco. W/ Light & Reversing Unit (new for 1966). This low-end Scout steamer featured a 2-4-2 wheel arrangement and a rubber tire as a traction aid. Except for its wheel arrangement, the 1062-75 was identical to the no. 1062-50 Steam Type Loco. W/Light & Reversing Unit.

The rolling stock in this outfit consisted of carryover items that were commonly used in outfits from 1966. During the course of that year, Lionel finished removing the new date, a built date and number data from the heat-stamping of the no. 6076-75 Hopper

Car – Black. This minimal decoration became the norm for the 6076-75. Even though this model lacked the new date, a built date and number data, it was designated a 6076-75 because it came with non-operating trucks and couplers.

The no. 6409-25 Flat Car W/3 Pipes was a red no. 6511-series flat car that had "Lionel" stamped on each side and lacked a car number and a brake wheel. It is most often found with the later, light gray version of the no. 6511-15 Pipes. Original light gray pipes are difficult to find.

The rolling stock in the 19530 followed the normal truck and coupler progression for 1966, with each of the cars having late AAR types. All but two were equipped with non-operating trucks and couplers. The no. 1062T-25 Tender had one non-operating and one plain type, and the no. 6167-100 Caboose had one operating and one non-operating type.

The no. 65-260 White Lift-Off with Full-Color 2037 Steam Freight Graphics Type D display outfit box was manufactured by Mead Containers and measured 23½ x 11½ x 3 inches.

An original quantity of 7,500 units of the 19530 was to have been manufactured. This was subsequently reduced to 6,500. With such a large number of outfits manufactured, this outfit can easily be found in collectible condition, although finding a complete example with original light gray pipes is a challenge.

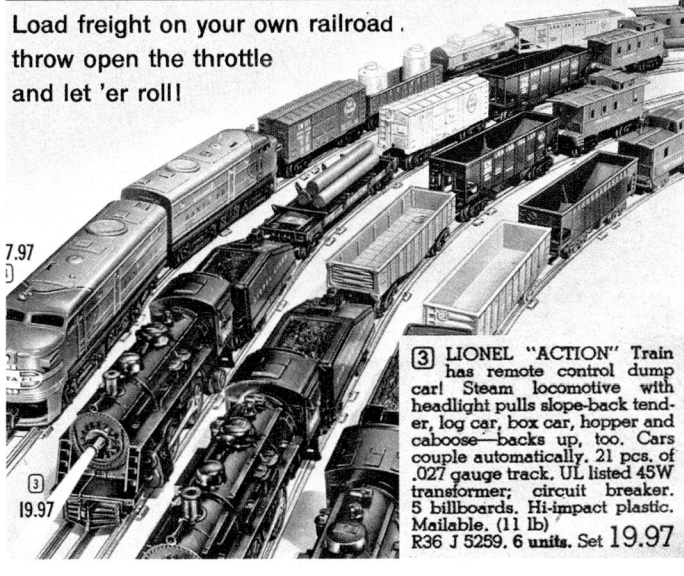

The no. 19541 appeared on page 398 of the 1966 Spiegel Christmas Catalog as no. R36 J 5259 for $19.97 (item no. 3). It was Spiegel's mid-level offering, pictured here between the nos. 19501 and 19507 (Spiegel nos. R36 J 5258 and R36 J 5260). Of note was a white no. 6050-100 Swift Savings Bank Car. Photographs used for retail catalogs often included prototype or non-production items. This difficult-to-find variation likely was used only for the photograph and not included in the final outfit.

Description: "O27" Promotional Outfit
Specification: "O27" Steam Type Freight Outfit
Customer/No./Price: Spiegel; R36 J 5259; $19.97
Original Amount: 1,105
Factory Order Date: 6/21/1966
Date Issued: 12-8-66
Date Req'd: 12-8-66
Packaging: MO Pack 4/Master (Units not Boxed)

Contents: 1062-75 Steam Type Loco. W/Light & Reversing Unit; 1062T-25 Tender; 3364-25 Log Dump Car; 3364-8 Logs; 6176-50 Hopper Car; 6050-100 Swift Savings Bank Car; 6167-100 Caboose; 1013-70 Curved Track (Bundle of 12 - 1013); 1018-7 Straight Track (Bundle of 7 - 1018); 6149-25 Remote Control Track; 1020-25 90° Crossing; 310-2 Set of (5) Billboards; 1025-25 45 Watt Transformer; 1103-40 Envelope Packed; Form 3063 Parts Order Form; 1-166 Warranty Card; 926-66 Service Station List; 19223-10 Instruction Sheet

Boxes & Packing: 65-415 Outfit Box; 62-223 Corr. Insert; 62-225 Corr. Insert; 62-254 Corr. Insert; 62-264 Corr. Insert; 62-244 Shipper for 4 (1-4); 64-106 Shipper Pad (2-4)

Alternate For Outfit Contents:
Note: Substitute 64-177 for 62-225 in last 50 sets.

19541 (1966)	C6	C7	C8	Rarity
Complete Outfit	270	425	625	R7
Outfit Box no. 65-415	150	225	300	R7

Comments: Due to Lionel's changing distribution policies, Spiegel was not permitted to purchase unique promotional outfits after 1964. Instead, Lionel limited it to General Release Promotional outfits and Spiegel had to compete head to head against other retailers with similar offerings. In 1966, Spiegel purchased three such outfits: nos. 19501, 19507 and 19541. All three appeared in the 1966 Spiegel Christmas Catalog and were likely sold through other retailers as well.

The 19541, a Type IIb outfit, was led by a no. 1062-75 Steam Type Loco. W/Light & Reversing Unit (new for 1966). This low-end Scout steamer featured a 2-4-2 wheel arrangement and a rubber tire as a traction aid. Except for its wheel arrangement, the 1062-75 was identical to the no. 1062-50 Steam Type Loco. W/Light & Reversing Unit.

The rolling stock in this outfit consisted of carryover items that were commonly used in outfits from 1966. The no. 3364-25 Log Dump Car was identical to the no. 3362-25 Helium Tank Unloading Car, except that it carried logs instead of helium tanks. The no. 6050-100 Swift Savings Bank Car in this outfit used a Type III body. During the course of 1966, Lionel finished removing the new date, a built date and number data from the heat-stamping of the black no. 6176-50 Hopper Car. This minimal decoration became the norm for the 6176-50.

The rolling stock in the 19541 followed the normal truck and coupler progression for 1966, with each of the cars having AAR types. All but one were equipped with one operating and one non-operating truck and coupler. The no. 1062T-25 Tender had one non-operating and one plain type.

This was one of only two outfits in 1966 to include a no. 310-2 Set of (5) Billboards. The other was the no. 19550, sold to Coast to Coast Stores.

The no. 19223-10 Instruction Sheet was dated 6/66 and outlined the figure-eight track layout.

The no. 65-415 Tan RSC with Black Graphics outfit box

was manufactured by Mann Kraft Container Corporation and measured 12 x 11½ x 6⅜ inches. These boxes were made of a thicker corrugated material (rated at 90 pounds rather than the normal 65 pounds gross weight) that allowed each outfit to be shipped in its outfit box. It included four lines of data as part of the box manufacturer's certificate, and printed on the bottom was a reference to the N.M.F.C.

An original quantity of 2,000 units of the 19541 was to have been manufactured. This was subsequently reduced to 1,105. Even with the larger-than-average number, this outfit is seldom seen.

CONVENTIONAL PACK
65-415 BOX

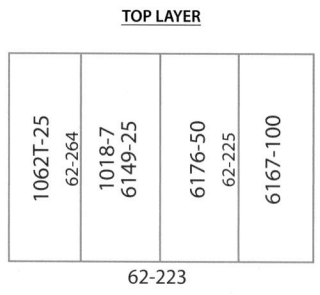

TOP LAYER

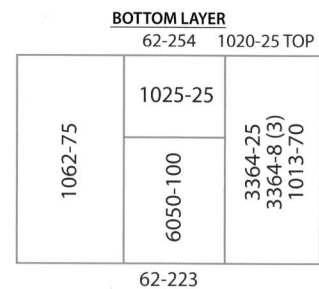

BOTTOM LAYER

Customer No. On Box: 48-21301
Description: "O27" Promotional Outfit
Specification: "O27" Steam Type Freight Outfit
Customer/No./Price: Montgomery Ward; 48 HT 21301; $16.99
Original Amount: 6,000
Factory Order Date: 6/10/1966
Date Issued: Rev 06-14-66
Date Req'd: 8-1-66
Packaging: WRSC 4/Master (Units Not Boxed)

Contents: 1062-75 Steam Type Loco. W/Light & Reversing Unit; 1062T-25 Tender; 6408-50 Flat Car W/3 Pipes; 6511-15 Pipes (3); 6465-150 Tank Car; 6167-100 Caboose; 110-75 Modified Trestle Set; 309-100 Yard Set; 1013-70 Curved Track (Bundle of 12 - 1013); 1018-5 Straight Track (Bundle of 5 - 1018); 1008-50 Uncoupling Unit; 1020-25 90° Crossing; 1025-25 45-Watt Transformer; 1103-20 Envelope Packed; Form 3063 Parts Order Form; 1-166 Warranty Card; 926-66 Service Station List; 19522-10 Instruction Sheet; 1008-11 Flyer; 239-18 Flyer

Boxes & Packing: 66-167 Outfit Box; 62-254 Corr. Insert; 64-177 Corr. Insert (3); 65-413 Corr. Insert; 66-168 Shipper for 4 (1-4); 64-106 Shipper Pad (2-4)

19542 (1966)	C6	C7	C8	Rarity
Complete Outfit	275	450	700	R6
Outfit Box no. 66-167	125	175	225	R5

Comments: In 1966, Montgomery Ward purchased four Retailer Promotional outfits, as shown on pages 352 and 353 of its Christmas Catalog. Three were available at the company's retail stores and came in specially decorated Ward RSCs: nos. 19542 (no.

48 HT 21301 for $16.99), 19544 (no. 48 HT 21302 for $24.99) and 19546 (no. 48 HT 21303 M for $39.50). The fourth outfit, as explained below, was available only through Ward's mail-order catalog and came in a plain tan RSC.

The 19542 and 19544 were also available via mail-order, but the 19546 was not because its weight made shipment in its special RSC problematic. As a consequence, Lionel created the no. 19547. Its contents were identical to those of the 19546, and it had the same Ward no. 48 HT 21303 M. However, the 19547 was packed in a plain tan RSC made of thicker corrugated material (rated at 90 pounds rather than the normal 65 pounds gross weight) to minimize damage during shipping.

The entry-level 19542, a Type Ib outfit, cost Ward $10.50 each. It was led by a no. 1062-75 Steam Type Loco. W/Light & Reversing Unit (new for 1966). This low-end Scout steamer featured a 2-4-2 wheel arrangement and a rubber tire as a traction aid. Except for its wheel arrangement, the 1062-75 was identical to the no. 1062-50 Steam Type Loco. W/Light & Reversing Unit.

The rolling stock in this outfit consisted of carryover items, with the exception of the no. 6408-50 Flat Car W/3 Pipes. Introduced in the 19542, this car was identical to the no. 6408-25 Flat Car W/5 Pipes, except that it had a smaller load. The 6408-50 was a red no. 6511-series model with "Lionel" stamped on each side and a brake wheel installed. It came with only three of the later light gray versions of the no. 6511-15 Pipes, which are difficult to find.

The rolling stock in the 19542 followed the normal truck and coupler progression for 1966, with each of the cars having late AAR types. All but one were equipped with one operating and one non-operating truck and coupler. The no. 1062T-25 Tender had one non-operating and one plain type. All the outfits observed included cars with a washer riveted as part of their leaf spring assembly.

Although the rolling stock is very common, the no. 110-75 Modified Trestle included in this outfit is not. The 110-75 included nine pairs of graduated trestle piers, or "bents," which were designed to elevate the figure-eight track layout to a height of

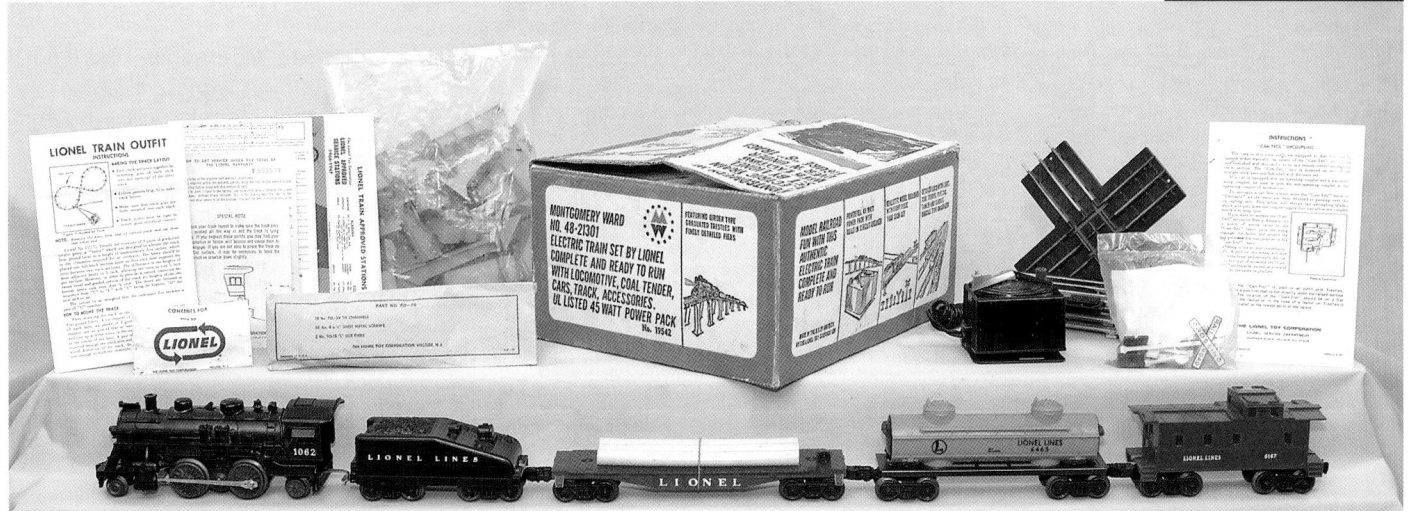

After a two-year hiatus, Lionel's relationship with Montgomery Ward was rekindled by Bruce Parmett, Lionel's Market Development Manager. The no. 19542 (Ward no. 48 HT 21301) was the first of four Retailer Promotional Type Ib outfits purchased by Ward in 1966. Three of the four outfits featured a uniquely decorated outfit box that listed all the outfit's contents and advertised other features. In 1966, peripherals such as the nos. 110-75 Modified Trestle Set and 309-100 Yard Set were packaged in plastic bags. The later and larger version of the no. 110-78 Envelop Packed is shown. Most outfits came with the earlier and smaller version that did not list the envelope's contents.

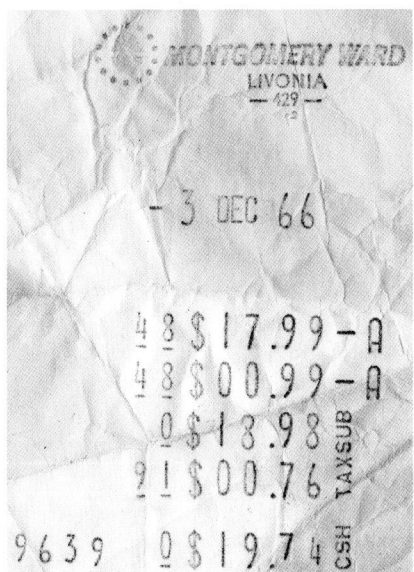

An original sales receipt for a no. 19542 (Montgomery Ward no. 48 HT 21301) was dated December 3, 1966, for $17.99. Price tags (not shown) also confirm the $17.99 over-the-counter-price, which was a $1.00 more than the catalog price of $16.99.

as a substitution because the bottom of each was melted to its base during assembly.

The elevated figure-eight layout and trestle assembly instructions were outlined on a no. 19522-10 Instruction Sheet dated 6/66. This difficult-to-find item was introduced in the 19542. The "19522" base number is curious because no records have surfaced regarding an outfit with that number. The outfit probably progressed far enough for an instruction sheet to have been created before the outfit was canceled.

The Factory Order for the 19542 represented the only instance when a no. 1008-11 Flyer for a "CAM-TROL" appeared. This difficult-to-find sheet was dated 5/66.

The no. 66-167 White RSC Montgomery Ward Design with Orange and Black Graphics outfit box was manufactured by United Container Co. and measured 13⅜ x 11⅜ x 6¾ inches. It included four lines of data, a "66" and five stars as part of the box manufacturer's certificate. Printed on the bottom was a reference to the N.M.F.C.

Even with 6,000 units manufactured and distributed through a major retailer, the 19542 is fairly difficult to obtain complete and in collectible condition. Most outfit boxes show signs of initial shipment or poor care. Complete examples of the 110-75 and 309-100 as well as light gray 6511-15s and correct paperwork are difficult to find. That's why the outfit box achieves an R5 rarity and a complete outfit with all peripherals is an R6.

approximately 5 inches. A no. 110-78 Envelope Packed included the Tie Channels and Screws to assemble the trestles. Most outfits are found with the later and smaller version of this envelope, which did not list its contents. All of these peripherals were sealed in a no. 1-41 Poly Bag. As with many promotional-only items, the packaging and packed envelope are very difficult to obtain, yet are necessary to complete the outfit (a point assumed in the outfit pricing). Be aware that the Ward catalog listing incorrectly states that the 19542 came with 16 graduated trestles.

Another uncommon and promotional-only peripheral contained in the 19542 was the no. 309-100 Yard Set. It was a cheapened version of the no. 309-1 Yard Set, which last appeared in 1959. The eight signs and bases in the "-100" came unassembled. They were combined with the difficult-to-find no. 309-35 Instruction Sheet and sealed in a small polyethylene bag. Even though a large quantity of 309-100s was made, they are very difficult to find sealed in the bag. A sealed 309-100 is required for a C8 outfit. Be aware that the signs from a 309-1 cannot be used

CONVENTIONAL PACK
66-167 BOX

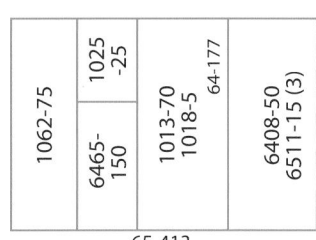

TOP LAYER				BOTTOM LAYER			
6167-100	64-177	110-75	64-177	1062T-25	1062-75	6465-150	1025-25 / 1013-70 1018-5 / 64-177 / 6408-50 6511-15 (3)

65-413

The no. 19544 (Montgomery Ward no. 48 HT 21302) was Ward's mid-level outfit purchase for 1966. It featured a uniquely decorated outfit box that listed all the outfit's contents and advertised other features. In 1966, Plasticville items returned to the Lionel product line. The nos. 1403 Signal Bridge and 1706 Suburban Station likely came packaged in plastic bags, yet an outfit configured this way has yet to be observed. Note that the outfit box included both the Lionel and Ward numbers.

Customer No. On Box: 48-21302
Description: "O27" Promotional Outfit
Specification: "O27" Steam Type Freight Outfit W/Smoke
Customer/No./Price: Montgomery Ward; 48 HT 21302; $24.99
Original Amount: 2,500
Factory Order Date: 6/10/1966
Date Issued: Rev 6-15-66
Date Req'd: 8-1-66
Packaging: WRSC 4/Master (Units Not Boxed)

Contents: 237-25 Steam Type Locomotive with Smoke; 242T-25 Tender; 6014-325 Frisco Box Car; 3364-25 Log Dump Car; 3364-8 Logs (3); 6176-50 Hopper Car; 6167-100 Caboose; 1706 Suburban Station; 1403 Signal Bridge; 309-100 Yard Set; 1013-70 Curved Track (Bundle of 12 - 1013); 1018-7 Straight Track (Bundle of 7 - 1018); 6149-25 Remote Control Track; 1020-25 90° Crossing; 1025-25 45-Watt Transformer; 909-20 Smoke Fluid; 1103-50 Envelope Packed; Form 3063 Parts Order Form; 1-166 Warranty Card; 926-66 Service Station List; 19544-10 Instruction Sheet; 237-11 Instruction Sheet; 3364-10 Instruction Sheet

Boxes & Packing: 66-169 Outfit Box; 62-225 Corr. Insert (2); 62-254 Corr. Insert; 62-264 Corr. Insert; 65-433 Corr. Insert; 66-171 Corr. Insert; 66-170 Shipper for 4 (1-4); 63-315 Shipper Pad (2-4)

19544 (1966)	C6	C7	C8	Rarity
Complete Outfit	310	450	650	R5
Outfit Box no. 66-169	100	135	175	R5

Comments: In 1966, Montgomery Ward purchased four Retailer Promotional outfits, as shown on pages 352 and 353 of its Christmas Catalog. Three were available at the company's retail stores and came in specially decorated Ward RSCs: nos. 19542 (no. 48 HT 21301 for $16.99), 19544 (no. 48 HT 21302 for $24.99) and 19546 (no. 48 HT 21303 M for $39.50). The fourth outfit, as explained below, was available only through Ward's mail-order catalog and came in a plain tan RSC.

The 19542 and 19544 were also available via mail-order, but the 19546 was not because its weight made shipment in its special RSC problematic. As a consequence, Lionel created the no. 19547. Its contents were identical to those of the 19546, and it had the same Ward no. 48 HT 21303 M. However, the 19547 was packed in a plain tan RSC made of thicker corrugated material (rated at 90 pounds rather than the normal 65 pounds gross weight) to minimize damage during shipping.

The mid-level 19544, a Type Ib outfit, cost Ward $15.78 each. It was led by a no. 237-25 Steam Type Locomotive with Smoke. This Scout steamer featured a two-position reversing unit and a headlight and used a rubber tire as a traction aid. The later version with narrow running boards came in this outfit.

The rolling stock in this outfit consisted of carryover items that were commonly used in outfits from 1966. The no. 3364-25 Log Dump Car was identical to the no. 3362-25 Helium Tank Unloading Car, except that it carried logs instead of helium tanks. The 6014-325 Frisco Box Car in this outfit used a Type III body. During the course of 1966, Lionel finished removing the new date, a built date and number data from the heat-stamping of the black no. 6176-50 Hopper Car. This minimal decoration became the norm for the 6176-50.

The rolling stock in the 19544 followed the normal truck and coupler progression for 1966, with each of the cars having late AAR types. All but one were equipped with one operating and one non-operating truck and coupler. The no. 242T-25 Tender had one non-operating and one plain type.

After a one-year absence, Plasticville items returned to Lionel outfits in 1966, although something was different. Instead of providing unique, individually boxed Lionel versions of Plasticville sets, as had been the rule in the past, Lionel now included the same Plasticville items that were available to any retailer. In fact, the Factory Order listed the Plasticville set numbers.

Also different was that now each Plasticville set presumably came packaged in a plastic bag. However, an example of the no. 1403 Signal Bridge or no. 1706 Suburban Station in its original plastic bag has yet to be observed, so we cannot state with certainty that this change in packaging did occur. We base this conclusion on the fact that the no. 1407 Watchman Shanty included in four other outfits has been observed in a plastic bag.

The outfit packing diagram also supports the contention that Plasticville sets came in plastic bags because it indicates that individually boxed items would not fit. A Signal Bridge instruction sheet from Bachmann Bros., the manufacturer of Plasticville, has been found loose in some 19544s, although it likely was originally included in that item's plastic bag.

The 19544 came with the uncommon no. 309-100 Yard Set. This promotional-only peripheral was a cheapened version of the no. 309-1 Yard Set, which last appeared in 1959. The eight signs and bases in the "-100" came unassembled. They were combined with the difficult-to-find no. 309-35 Instruction Sheet and sealed in a small polyethylene bag. Even though a large quantity of 309-100s was made, they are very difficult to find sealed in the bag. A sealed 309-100 is required for a C8 outfit. Be aware that the signs from a 309-1 cannot be used as a substitution because the bottom of each was melted to its base during assembly.

The figure-eight layout was outlined on the difficult-to-find no. 19544-10 Instruction Sheet dated 6/66. It was unique to this outfit.

The no. 66-169 White RSC Montgomery Ward Design with Orange and Black Graphics outfit box was manufactured by United Container Co. and measured 15⅝ x 11⅝ x 6¾ inches. It included four lines of data, a "66" and five stars as part of the box

manufacturer's certificate. Printed on the bottom was a reference to the N.M.F.C.

An original quantity of 3,000 units of the 19544 was to have been manufactured. This was subsequently reduced to 2,500. Even with 2,500 units produced and distributed through a major retailer, the 19544 is fairly difficult to obtain complete and in collectible condition. Most outfit boxes show signs of initial shipment or poor care. A complete version of the 309-100 is difficult to find, and original, plastic-bagged versions of the Plasticville items have yet to be observed.

CONVENTIONAL PACK
66-169 BOX

TOP LAYER

6176-50	62-264	1018-7	6167-100	1706 1403 309-100

BOTTOM LAYER

237-25	1025 -25	6014-325	1013-70	62-225	3364-25 3364-8 (3)	62-225	242T-25

65-433

The no. 19546 (Montgomery Ward no. 48 HT 21303 M) was Ward's high-end outfit purchase for 1966 and was offered through its retail stores. It featured a uniquely decorated outfit box listing all the outfit's contents and advertising other features.

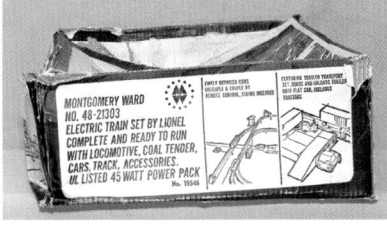

The side view of the no. 19546 (Montgomery Ward no. 48 HT 21303 M) shows both the Lionel and Ward numbers.

Customer No. On Box: 48-21303
Description: "O27" Promotional Outfit
Specification: "O27" Steam Type Freight Outfit W/Smoke
Cust./No./Price: Montgomery Ward; 48 HT 21303 M; $39.50
Original Amount: 750
Factory Order Date: 6/10/1966
Date Issued: Rev 8-29-66
Date Req'd: 8-29-66
Packaging: WRSC 4/Master (Units not Boxed)

Contents: 237-25 Steam Type Locomotive with Smoke; 242T-25 Tender; 6431-1 Trailer Flat Car W/2 Trailers; 6465-150 Tank Car; 6050-100 Swift Savings Bank Car; 6142-100 Gondola Car; 6112-88 Canister (2); 6167-100 Caboose; 309-100 Yard Set; 261-25 Non-Illuminated Bumper; 461-1 Unloading Platform; 1402 Switch Tower; 1403 Signal Girder; 1407 Watchman Shanty; 1013-82 Curved Track (Bundle of 6 - 1013); 1013-90 Curved Track (Bundle of 9 - 1013); 1018-7 Straight Track (Bundle of 7 - 1018); 1018-75 Straight Track (Bundle of 6 - 1018); 6149-25 Remote Control Track; 1022-1 Pr. Manual Switches; 1022-50 R.H. Manual Switch; CTC-1 Lockon (2); 1025-25 45-Watt Transformer; 909-20 Smoke Fluid; 1103-50 Envelope Packed; Form 3063 Parts Order Form; 1-166 Warranty Card; 926-66 Service Station List; 19546-5 Layout Sheet; 237-11 Instruction Sheet; 19214-10 Instruction Sheet; 461-13 Instruction Sheet

Boxes & Packing: 66-172 Outfit Box; 41110-23 Corr. Insert; 61-173 Corr. Insert; 61-182 Corr. Insert (2); 62-249 Corr. Insert; 62-254 Corr. Insert; 63-323 Corr. Insert; 65-256 Corr. Insert; 65-303 Corr. Insert; 66-173 Shipper for 4 (1-4); 41110-23 Shipper Pad (2-4)

Alternate For Outfit Contents:
Note: Do not use 62-249 & 65-256 inserts when Blistered B1022-50 is used.

19546 (1966)	C6	C7	C8	Rarity
Complete Outfit	825	1,225	1,825	R8
Complete Outfit With no. B1022-50	1,075	1,650	2,425	R8
Outfit Box no. 66-172	200	275	350	R8

Comments: In 1966, Montgomery Ward purchased four Retailer Promotional outfits, as shown on pages 352 and 353 of its Christmas Catalog. Three were available at the company's retail stores and came in specially decorated Ward RSCs: nos. 19542 (no. 48 HT 21301 for $16.99), 19544 (no. 48 HT 21302 for $24.99) and 19546 (no. 48 HT 21303 M for $39.50). The fourth outfit, as explained below, was available only through Ward's mail-order catalog and came in a plain tan RSC.

The 19542 and 19544 were also available via mail-order, but the 19546 was not because its weight made shipment in its special RSC problematic. As a consequence, Lionel created the no. 19547. Its contents were identical to those of the 19546, and it had the same Ward no. 48 HT 21303 M. However, the 19547 was packed in a plain tan RSC made of thicker corrugated material (rated at 90 pounds rather than the normal 65 pounds gross weight) to minimize damage during shipping.

The 19546 and 19547, both Type Ic outfits, were high-end offerings that cost Ward $26.41 each. They were led by a no. 237-25 Steam Type Locomotive with Smoke. This Scout steamer featured a two-position reversing unit and a headlight and used a rubber tire as a traction aid. The later version with narrow running boards came in this outfit.

The desirable 6431-1 Trailer Flat Car W/2 Trailers was the only new-for-1966 item in this outfit. As with many cars from the middle and late 1960s, "new" meant that it was derived from other cars. To be specific, the car was stamped "6430" and Lionel added a die-cast red no. 6431-150 Toy Tractor purchased from Midgetoy and two white no. 6430-150 Trailer Assemblies. Then it packaged everything in a Cellophane Window box.

The rolling stock in the 19546 followed the normal truck and coupler progression for 1966, with each of the cars having late AAR types. All but two were equipped with one operating and one non-operating truck and coupler. The no. 242T-25 Tender had one non-operating and one plain type, and the 6431-1 had operating types. Most of the cars had a washer riveted as part of their leaf spring assembly.

By far the most collectible item was the no. 461-1 Unloading Platform (new for 1966). This accessory was created exclusively for the 19546 and 19547. It included the nos. 461-200 Trailer Platform Complete, 6431-150 Toy Tractor and a white 6430-150 Trailer Assembly, all in a no. 461-10 Corr. Box. The trailer platform was unique to the 461-1 and did not include wheel depressions or a product number.

The 461-1's Production Control File indicated that the infrequently found no. 461-13 Instruction Sheet was to be included in its box; however, that entry was subsequently crossed out. This likely occurred because the sheet incorrectly stated that the 461-1 came with a flat car and a pair of truck trailers. By being placed loose with the outfit, which had a separately packed 6431-1, the sheet technically became correct.

After a one-year absence, Plasticville items returned to Lionel outfits in 1966, although something was different. Instead of providing unique, individually boxed Lionel versions of Plasticville sets, as had been the rule in the past, Lionel now included the same Plasticville items that were available to any retailer. In fact, the Factory Order listed the Plasticville set numbers.

Also different was that now each Plasticville set presumably came packaged in a plastic bag. However, an example of the no. 1402 Switch Tower or no. 1403 Signal Bridge in its original plastic bag has yet to be observed, so we cannot state with certainty that this change in packaging did occur. We base this conclusion on the fact that the no. 1407 Watchman Shanty has been observed in a plastic bag.

The outfit packing diagram also supports the contention that Plasticville sets came in plastic bags because it indicates that individually boxed items would not fit. A Signal Bridge instruction sheet from Bachmann Bros., the manufacturer of Plasticville, has been found loose in some outfits. Also, the 1407 came with a poorly copied piece of paper with "1407 Shanty" on it. These sheets likely were originally included in each item's plastic bag.

This outfit came with the uncommon no. 309-100 Yard Set. This promotional-only peripheral was a cheapened version of the no. 309-1 Yard Set, which last appeared in 1959. The eight signs and bases in the "-100" came unassembled. They were combined with the difficult-to-find no. 309-35 Instruction Sheet and sealed in a small polyethylene bag. Even though a large quantity of 309-100s was made, they are very difficult to find sealed in the bag. A sealed 309-100 is required for a C8 outfit. Be aware that the signs from a 309-1 cannot be used as a substitution because the bottom of each was melted to its base during assembly.

Further cheapening of the product line led to the no. 261-25 Non-Illuminated Bumper, which was molded in black plastic.

Some outfits came with a no. B1022-50 R.H. Manual Switch (Blister Packed). This item affects the outfit price, as listed in the pricing table.

The 19546/19547 included a unique track layout, as outlined on the no. 19546-5 Layout Sheet dated 6/66. This sheet commands a substantial premium.

The no. 66-172 White RSC Montgomery Ward Design with Black Graphics outfit box was manufactured by Bell Container Corp. and measured 20⅜ x 15⅞ x 7¼ inches. It included four lines of data as part of the box manufacturer's certificate. Printed on the bottom were "66-172" and a reference to the N.M.F.C.

An original quantity of 1,000 units of the 19546 was to have been manufactured. This was subsequently reduced to 750. This is the smallest quantity produced of any of the Ward outfits from 1966. As such, this outfit is the most difficult to find. In fact, complete outfits with all their peripherals and paperwork are very uncommon.

Of note, the reduction of 500 units total for both the 19546 and 19547 led to a large number of excess 461-1s. That is likely why this accessory can still be found sealed in its box.

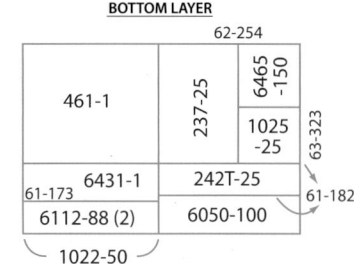

CONVENTIONAL PACK
66-172 BOX

The no. 19547 (Montgomery Ward no. 48 HT 21303 M) was Ward's high-end outfit purchase for 1966 and was offered only through its mail-order catalog. Except for the no. 6431-1 Trailer Flat Car W/2 Trailers, the trains in this outfit are inconsequential. What makes this outfit special are its difficult-to-obtain peripherals and paperwork. The no. 19546 and 19547 were the only outfits to include a no. 461-1 Unloading Platform. Also of note were the nos. 309-100 Yard Set and 1407 Watchman Shanty, shown in their original plastic bags.

Customer No. On Box: 48-21303
Description: "O27" Promotional Outfit
Specification: "O27" Steam Type Freight Outfit W/Smoke
Cust./No./Price: Montgomery Ward; 48 HT 21303 M; $39.50
Original Amount: 1,750
Factory Order Date: 6/10/1966
Date Issued: Rev 8-29-66
Date Req'd: 08/29/66
Packaging: RSC 4/Master (Units not Boxed)

Contents: 237-25 Steam Type Locomotive with Smoke; 242T-25 Tender; 6431-1 Trailer Flat Car W/2 Trailers; 6465-150 Tank Car; 6050-100 Swift Savings Bank Car; 6142-100 Gondola Car; 6112-88 Canister (2); 6167-100 Caboose; 309-100 Yard Set; 261-25 Non-Illuminated Bumper; 461-1 Unloading Platform; 1402 Switch Tower; 1403 Signal Bridge; 1407 Watchman Shanty; 1013-82 Curved Track (Bundle of 6 - 1013); 1013-90 Curved Track (Bundle of 9 - 1013); 1018-7 Straight Track (Bundle of 7 - 1018); 1018-75 Straight Track (Bundle of 6 - 1018); 6149-25 Remote Control Track; 1022-1 Pr. Manual Switches; 1022-50 R.H. Manual Switch; CTC-1 Lockon (2); 1025-25 45-Watt Transformer; 909-20 Smoke Fluid; 1103-50 Envelope Packed; Form 3063 Parts Order Form; 1-166 Warranty Card; 926-66 Service Station List; 19546-5 Layout Sheet; 237-11 Instruction Sheet; 19214-10 Instruction Sheet; 461-13 Instruction Sheet

Boxes & Packing: 66-174 Outfit Box; 41110-23 Corr. Insert; 61-173 Corr. Insert; 61-182 Corr. Insert (2); 62-249 Corr. Insert; 62-254 Corr. Insert; 63-323 Corr. Insert; 65-256 Corr. Insert; 65-303 Corr. Insert; 66-173 Shipper for 4 (1-4); 41110-23 Shipper Pad (2-4)

Alternate For Outfit Contents:
Note: Do not use 62-249 & 65-256 inserts when Blistered B1022-50 is used.

19547 (1966)	C6	C7	C8	Rarity
Complete Outfit	775	1,150	1,725	R7
Complete Outfit With no. B1022-50	1,025	1,575	2,325	R8
Outfit Box no. 66-174	150	200	250	R7

Comments: In 1966, Montgomery Ward purchased four Retailer Promotional outfits, as shown on pages 352 and 353 of its Christmas Catalog. Three were available at the company's retail stores and came in specially decorated Ward RSCs: nos. 19542 (no. 48 HT 21301 for $16.99), 19544 (no. 48 HT 21302 for $24.99) and 19546 (no. 48 HT 21303 M for $39.50). The fourth outfit, as explained below, was available only through Ward's mail-order catalog and came in a plain tan RSC.

The 19542 and 19544 were also available via mail-order, but the 19546 was not because its weight made shipment in its special RSC problematic. As a consequence, Lionel created the no. 19547. Its contents were identical to those of the 19546, and it had the same Ward no. 48 HT 21303 M. However, the 19547 was packed in a plain tan RSC made of thicker corrugated material (rated at 90 pounds rather than the normal 65 pounds gross weight) to minimize damage during shipping. (See the entry for the 19546 for complete information about the 19547's contents.)

The no. 66-174 Tan RSC Mailer with Black Graphics outfit box was manufactured by Bell Container Corp. and measured 20⅜ x 15⅞ x 7¼ inches. It included four lines of data as part of the box manufacturer's certificate and printed on the bottom was reference to the N.M.F.C.

An original quantity of 2,000 units of the 19547 was to have been manufactured. This was subsequently reduced to 1,750. Even with 1,750 units produced and distributed through a major retailer, the 19547 is difficult to obtain complete and in collectible condition. Most outfit boxes show signs of initial shipment or poor care.

Of note, the reduction of 500 units total for both the 19546 and 19547 led to a large number of excess no. 461-1 Unloading Platforms. That is likely why this accessory can still be found sealed in its box.

CONVENTIONAL PACK
66-174 BOX

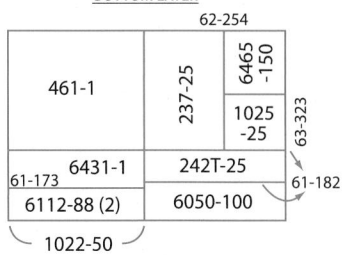

TOP LAYER

1022-1	1018-7 / 1018-75 / 1013-82 / 1013-90
1402	
62-249	65-303
6167-100	1403
6142-100	1407

BOTTOM LAYER

		62-254	
461-1	237-25	6465-150	63-323
		1025-25	
61-173 6431-1	242T-25		61-182
6112-88 (2)	6050-100		
1022-50			

19550
1966

Outfit no. 19550 was the entry-level offering in 1966 for Coast to Coast Stores (no. TU0106-3 for $14.97). It was similar to promotional outfit no. 19500, but the 19550 added two no. 40-11 Cable Reels, a no. 310-2 Set of (5) Billboards and a no. 309-100 Yard Set. Finding a sealed 309-100 is the most difficult part of completing this outfit.

Boxes & Packing: 65-260 Box Top; 64-102 Box Bottom; 64-107 Corr. Insert; MT Mylar Tape (6"); 64-105 Shipper for 4 (1-4); 64-106 Shipper Pad (2-4)

Description: "O27" Promotional Outfit
Specification: "O27" Steam Type Freight Outfit
Customer/No./Price: Coast to Coast; TU0106-3; $14.97
Original Amount: 2,675
Factory Order Date: 6/21/1966
Date Issued: Rev 11-11-66
Date Req'd: 11-11-66
Packaging: Display 4/Master (Units not Boxed)

19550 (1966)	C6	C7	C8	Rarity
Complete Outfit	115	205	315	R5
Outfit Box no. 65-260	20	45	75	R5

Comments: Coast to Coast Stores was a wholesaler that purchased two promotional outfits in 1966: nos. 19515 and 19550. The 19550, a Retailer Promotional Type Ib outfit, was Coast to Coast's low-end purchase.

The 19550 was led by a no. 1062-75 Steam Type Loco. W/ Light & Reversing Unit (new for 1966). This low-end Scout steamer featured a 2-4-2 wheel arrangement and a rubber tire as a traction aid. Except for its wheel arrangement, the 1062-75 was identical to the no. 1062-50 Steam Type Loco. W/Light & Reversing Unit.

The rolling stock in this outfit consisted of carryover items that were commonly used in outfits from 1966. One of those models, the no. 6042-75 Gondola Car (Less 2 Cable Reels), was making its final appearance in the 19550.

Contents: 1062-75 Steam Type Loco. W/Light & Reversing Unit; 1062T-25 Tender; 6042-75 Gondola Car (Less 2 Cable Reels); 40-11 Cable Reels (2); 6076-75 Hopper Car - Black; 6167-100 Caboose; 310-2 Set of (5) Billboards; 309-100 Yard Set; 1013-8 Curved Track (Bundle of 8 - 1013); 1018-10 Straight Track (Loose) (2); 1025-25 45-Watt Transformer; 1103-20 Envelope Packed; Form 3063 Parts Order Form; 1-166 Warranty Card; 926-66 Service Station List; 19500-10 Instruction Sheet

During the course of 1966, Lionel finished removing the new date, a built date and number data from the heat-stamping of the no. 6076-75 Hopper Car - Black. This minimal decoration became the norm for the 6076-75. Even though this model lacked the new date, a built date and number data, it was designated a 6076-75 because it came with non-operating trucks and couplers.

The rolling stock in the 19550 followed the normal truck and coupler progression for 1966, with each of the cars having late AAR types. All but two were equipped with non-operating trucks and couplers. The no. 1062T-25 Tender had one non-operating and one plain type, and the no. 6167-100 Caboose had one operating and one non-operating type.

The 19550 came with two peripheral items, and, as with many promotional outfits, these are what make it somewhat interesting. The no. 310-2 Set of (5) Billboards appeared in only one other outfit in 1966 (no. 19541). The no. 309-100 Yard Set was a cheapened version of the no. 309-1 Yard Set, which last appeared in 1959. The eight signs and bases in the "-100" came unassembled. They were combined with the difficult-to-find no. 309-35 Instruction Sheet and sealed in a small polyethylene bag. Even though a large quantity of 309-100s was made, they are very difficult to find sealed in the bag. A sealed 309-100 is required for a C8 outfit. Be aware that the signs from a 309-1 cannot be used as a substitution because the bottom of each was melted to its base during assembly.

DISPLAY PACK
65-260 BOX
3-14-66

1025-25	1062T-25	1062-75
6076-75		6042-75
309-100	6167-100	1018-10 (2) 1013-8

The no. 65-260 White Lift-Off with Full-Color 2037 Steam Freight Graphics Type D display outfit box was manufactured by Mead Containers and measured 23½ x 11½ x 3 inches.

An original quantity of 3,500 units of the 19550 was to have been manufactured. This was subsequently reduced to 2,675. Many of these outfits have survived and are easy to find complete with everything except the 309-100. Finding a 309-100 intact and sealed in its plastic bag can take time.

Description: "O27" Promotional Outfit
Specification: "O27" Diesel Freight Outfit
Original Amount: 200
Factory Order Date: 6/16/1966
Date Issued: Rev 6-20-66
Date Req'd: 6-16-66
Packaging: MO Pack (4/Master), (Units not Boxed)

Contents: 221P-25 Diesel Locomotive; 6045-150 Tank Car; 6409-25 Flat Car; 6511-15 Pipes (3); 6042-25 Gondola Car; 6112-5 Canister (2); 6828-1 Flat Car With Construction Crane; 6167-100 Caboose; 4-5 Elastic Band; 1013-8 Curved Track (Bundle of 8 - 1013); 1018-10 Straight Track (Loose) (2); 1025-25 45-Watt Transformer; 1103-20 Envelope Packed; Form 3063 Parts Order Form; 1-166 Warranty Card; 926-66 Service Station List; 19512-10 Instruction Sheet

Boxes & Packing: 65-415 Outfit Box; 62-254 Corr. Insert; 62-223 Corr. Insert; 62-251 Corr. Insert; 62-248 Corr. Insert; 64-177 Corr. Insert; 64-319 Corr. Insert (3); 62-244 Shipper for 4 (1-4); 65-413 Pad (2-4)

19553 (1966)	C6	C7	C8	Rarity
Complete Outfit	690	1,075	1,490	R10
Outfit Box no. 65-415	400	625	800	R10

Comments: The no. 19553 was a General Release Promotional Type IIb that has yet to be linked to a particular retailer. Its contents were identical to those of the nos. 19512/19513, except that it added a no. 6828-1 Flat Car With Construction Crane.

The 19553 was led by a no. 221P-25 Rio Grande Diesel Locomotive. This low-end, unpainted yellow Alco featured a two-position reversing unit, a traction tire and a closed pilot and lacked a headlight. It was making its final appearance in this outfit and the 19512 and 19513.

The 6828-1, which last appeared in Super O catalog outfit no. 13138 from 1963, returned to the Lionel product line in a Cellophane Window box in 1966. The 6828-1 included a boxed model of a Harnischfeger construction crane.

The remaining rolling stock in this outfit consisted of carryover items that were commonly used in outfits from 1966. The no. 6409-25 Flat Car W/3 Pipes was a red no. 6511-series flat car that had "Lionel" stamped on each side and lacked a car number and a brake wheel. The no. 6045-150 Tank Car was making its final appearance in this outfit and the 19512 and 19513.

The rolling stock in the 19553 followed the normal truck and coupler progression for 1966, with each of the cars having AAR types. All but two were equipped with non-operating trucks and couplers. The no. 6167-100 Caboose had one operating and one non-operating type, and the 6828-1 had operating types.

The no. 19512-10 Instruction Sheet was dated 6/66 and made its last appearance in this outfit.

The only other difference between this outfit and the 19512 and 19513 was the outfit packing. The 19553 came in a no. 65-415 Tan RSC with Black Graphics outfit box that measured 12 x 11½ x 6⅜ inches.

With only 200 units produced, the 19553 is extremely difficult to find in any condition, hence its R10 rarity rating.

CONVENTIONAL PACK
65-415 BOX

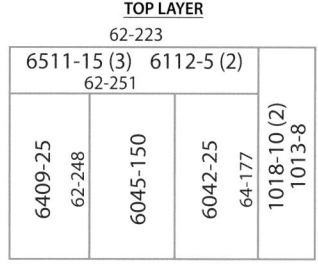

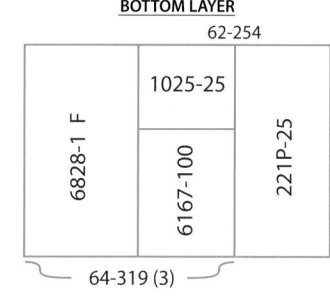

The no. 19555 was the last outfit to list incentive merchandiser Richie Premium on a Factory Order. As with most Richie outfits, it included the promotional-only no. X625-20 Cardboard Scenic Set. Surviving examples are extremely fragile and tend to fall apart over time. Note the 2-4-2 wheel arrangement on the no. 1061-75 Steam Type Locomotive (new for 1966). This locomotive appeared in only five outfits.

Description: "O27" Promotional Outfit
Specification: "O27" Steam Type Freight Outfit
Customer: Merbler Jewelry Co.
Customer: Richie Premium
Customer: Stix, Baer & Fuller
Original Amount: 5,000
Factory Order Date: 4/15/1966
Date Issued: Rev 10-28-66
Date Req'd: 10-28-66
Packaging: MO Pack

Contents: 1061-75 Steam Type Locomotive; 1062T-25 Tender; 6822-50 Searchlight Car; 6176-50 Hopper Car; 6142-100 Gondola Car; 6112-88 Canister (2); 6167-100 Caboose; 1013-70 Curved Track (Bundle of 12 - 1013); 1018-40 Straight Track (Bundle of 4 - 1018); 1020-25 90° Crossing; 1025-25 45-Watt Transformer; 1103-20 Envelope Packed; X625-20 Cardboard Scenic Set; Form 3063 Parts Order Form; 1-166 Warranty Card; 926-66 Service Station List; 19555-10 Instruction Sheet

Boxes & Packing: 65-415 Outfit Box; 62-254 Corr. Insert; 62-223 Corr. Insert; 61-173 Corr. Insert; 64-177 Corr. Insert; 62-244 Shipper for 4 (1-4); 65-413 Pad (2-4)

19555 (1966)	C6	C7	C8	Rarity
Complete Outfit	450	1,050	1,375	R9
Outfit Box no. 65-415	35	65	100	R4

Comments: This Retailer Promotional Type Ib outfit was the only outfit purchased by incentive merchandiser Richie Premium in 1966. Richie Premium outfits are highly collectible because all of them included at least one rare paper item.

Richie resold the 19555 to at least two end retailers: Stix Baer & Fuller (via a price tag) and Merbler Jewelry Co. (via a filled-in warranty card).

The 19555 was led by a no. 1061-75 Steam Type Locomotive (new for 1966). This low-end Scout steamer featured a 2-4-2

wheel arrangement and a rubber tire as a traction aid. It went forward only and lacked a headlight and lens. Except for its wheel arrangement, the 1061-75 was identical to the no. 1061-50 Steam Type Loco W/Tire.

All the rolling stock in this outfit, including the one operating car, consisted of carryover items. The no. 6822-50 Searchlight Car made its final outfit appearance in the 19555. During the course of 1966, Lionel finished removing the new date, a built date and number data from the heat-stamping of the black no. 6176-50 Hopper Car. This minimal decoration became the norm for the 6176-50.

The cars in the 19555 followed the normal truck and coupler progression for 1966, with each of them having AAR types. All but the no. 1062T-25 Tender came equipped with one operating and one non-operating truck and coupler. It had one non-operating and one plain type.

What makes this otherwise common and dull outfit highly collectible was the inclusion of a no. X625-20 Cardboard Scenic Set. This fragile item featured figures, railroad signs, automobiles and buildings that could be punched out, assembled and placed around a layout. The rarity of the X625-20 is linked to a lack of Lionel markings (it was identified with only "Printed in Japan"), which led to it frequently being separated from the trains and discarded before or after assembly.

The no. 19555-10 Instruction Sheet was unique to this outfit and remains very difficult to find. Dated 5/66, it described the figure-eight track layout.

The no. 65-415 Tan RSC with Black Graphics outfit box was manufactured by Mann Kraft Container Corporation and measured 12 x 11½ x 6⅜ inches. These boxes were made of a thicker corrugated material (rated at 90 pounds rather than the normal 65 pounds gross weight) that allowed each outfit to be shipped in its outfit box. It included four lines of data as part of the box manufacturer's certificate, and printed on the bottom was a reference to the N.M.F.C.

An original quantity of 6,500 units of the 19555 was to have been manufactured. This was subsequently reduced to 5,000. Even with so many outfits produced, a complete one with the Cardboard Scenic Set seldom surfaces. For that reason, the 19555 is one of those unusual outfits whose components, specifically the X625-20, make it an R9. The box by itself rates an R4.

CONVENTIONAL PACK
65-415 BOX

TOP LAYER			BOTTOM LAYER					
					1020-25 TOP			
1013-70 1018-40	1062T-25 61-173	6822-50	1061-75	62-254	1025-25	6176-50	64-177	6142-100 6112-88 (2)
					6167-100			
					62-223			

The early version of the no. 19557 (Sears no. 9808) came in a no. 66-139 White RSC Allstate By Lionel With Blue Steamer (With Smoke and Trees) and Orange and Blue Gift of Lifetime Graphics outfit box. This "Gift of Lifetime" decorating scheme was new for 1966 and was used for both the 19557 and 19561 (Sears no. 9810). Note the original, plastic-bagged version of the no. 1407 Watchman Shanty that came with this outfit. A photocopied handwritten sheet identified it as a 1407.

With the success of the 19557, Lionel ran out of uniquely decorated no. 66-139 outfit boxes. It substituted a no. 65-415 Tan RSC with Black Graphics outfit box and attached a no. 19557-15 Printed Label. Production Control Files show that 1,930 units were packaged this way. This version is more difficult to find.

No Factory Order exists for a no. 19557-100, but an empty hand-stamped no. 65-411 Outfit Box has been found. As with other hand-stamped boxes, its contents were likely assembled by a large retailer or distributor or even the Service Department at Lionel. The Production Control File for the 65-411 box stated that more than 400 units were supplied to the Service Department in 1966 and 1967. (See the section on Outfit Box Printing, Graphics and Labels for more information.)

Customer No. On Box: SR 9808
Description: "O27" Promotional Outfit
Specification: "O27" Steam Type Freight Outfit
Customer/No./Price: Sears, Roebuck and Co.; SR 9808; $19.99
Original Amount: 9,700
Factory Order Date: 6/7/1966
Date Issued: Rev 12-1-66
Date Req'd: 12-1-66
Packaging: WRSC 4/Master (Units not Boxed)

Contents: 1062-75 Steam Type Loco. W/Light & Reversing Unit; 1062T-25 Tender; 6176-50 Hopper Car; 6142-100 Gondola Car; 6112-88 Canister (2); 6167-100 Caboose; 1407 Watchman Shanty; 309-100 Yard Set; 1013-10 Curved Track (Bundle of 10 - 1013); 1018-7 Straight Track (Bundle of 7 - 1018); 1018-10 Straight Track (Loose); 1022-1 Pr. Manual Switches; 1008-50 Uncoupling Unit; 1025-25 45-Watt Transformer; 1103-20 Envelope Packed; Form 3063 Parts Order Form; 1-166 Warranty Card; 926-66 Service Station List; 19557-5 Layout Sheet; 11580-15 Instruction Sheet

Boxes & Packing: 66-139 Outfit Box; 62-254 Corr. Insert; 62-249 Corr. Insert; 64-177 Corr. Insert (3); 64-161 Corr. Insert (3); 65-436 Shipper for 4 (1-4); 64-106 Shipper Pad (2-4); 19557-15 Printed Label; 65-415 Outfit Box (When the 66-139 Outfit Box and Packing are depleted use this box and the following packing); 61-171 Corr. Insert; 61-192 Corr. Insert; 64-177 Corr. Insert; 62-248 Corr. Insert; 62-244 Shipper for 4 (1-4); 64-106 Shipper Pad (2-4); 19557-15 Printed Label (2); 62-247 Shipper for 3 (For 213 Sets use this shipper and the following) (1-3); 64-106 Shipper Pad (2-3)

Alternate For Outfit Contents:
Note: Use 62-244 for 500 sets; Use 62-247 (1-3) for 213 Sets W/64-106 (2-3).

19557 (1966)	C6	C7	C8	Rarity
Complete Outfit With no. 66-139 Box	185	285	430	R4
Outfit Box no. 66-139	35	55	90	R4
Complete Outfit With no. 65-415 Box	240	355	540	R6
Outfit Box no. 65-415	90	125	200	R6

Comments: In 1966, Sears purchased two Retailer Promotional Type Ib outfits: nos. 19557 and 19561. It also carried over the no. 19453 from 1965 by issuing a 1966 re-order of that outfit.

The 19557, for which Sears paid $12.00 each, appeared on page 464 of the 1966 Sears Christmas Catalog for $19.99. This outfit, Sears' low-end offering, included both the Lionel 19557 and the Sears no. SR 9808 on its outfit box.

The 19557 was led by a no. 1061-75 Steam Type Locomotive (new for 1966). This low-end Scout steamer featured a 2-4-2 wheel arrangement and a rubber tire as a traction aid. It went forward only and lacked a headlight and lens. Except for its wheel arrangement, the 1061-75 was identical to the no. 1061-50 Steam Type Loco W/Tire.

The rolling stock in this outfit consisted of carryover items that were commonly used in outfits from 1966. The black no. 6176-50 Hopper Car most often found in the 19557 lacked the new date,

a built date and number data from its heat-stamping. Exceptions have been observed stamped "BUILT 1-48" and "LIONEL 6076"; however, they still were considered a 6176 because they each came with one operating truck and coupler.

The rolling stock in the 19557 followed the normal truck and coupler progression for 1966, with each of the cars having late AAR types. All but one were equipped with one operating and one non-operating truck and coupler. The no. 1062T-25 Tender had one non-operating and one plain type. Most of the cars had a washer riveted as part of their leaf spring assembly.

After a one-year absence, Plasticville items returned to Lionel outfits in 1966, although something was different. Instead of providing unique, individually boxed Lionel versions of Plasticville sets, as had been the rule in the past, Lionel now included the same Plasticville items that were available to any retailer. In fact, the Factory Order listed the Plasticville set numbers.

Also different was that the no. 1407 Watchman Shanty included in this outfit came packaged in a plastic bag. It came with a poorly copied piece of paper with "1407 Shanty" on it.

This outfit also came with the uncommon no. 309-100 Yard Set. This promotional-only peripheral was a cheapened version of the no. 309-1 Yard Set, which last appeared in 1959. The eight signs and bases in the "-100" came unassembled. They were combined with the difficult-to-find no. 309-35 Instruction Sheet and sealed in a small polyethylene bag. Even though a large quantity of 309-100s was made, they are very difficult to find sealed in the bag. A sealed 309-100 is required for a C8 outfit. Be aware that the signs from a 309-1 cannot be used as a substitution because the bottom of each was melted to its base during assembly.

The difficult-to-find no. 19557-5 Layout Sheet was dated 6/66. This paper item was unique to the 19557.

Orders for this outfit exceeded original forecasts. The quantity was increased three times, going from 7,500 to 7,770 to 8,700 and finally to 9,700. These changes led to two different outfit boxes. The early version (first 7,770 units) used the no. 66-139 White RSC Allstate By Lionel With Blue Steamer (With Smoke and

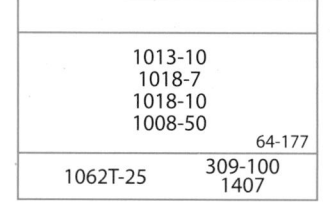

CONVENTIONAL PACK
66-139 BOX

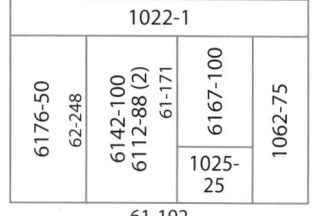

CONVENTIONAL PACK
65-415 BOX
SUB PACKING

Trees) and Orange and Blue Gift of Lifetime Graphics outfit box. It was manufactured by United Container Co. and measured 12¾ x 12 x 6⅝ inches. It included four lines of data, a "66" and five stars as part of the box manufacturer's certificate. Printed on the bottom was a reference to the N.M.F.C.

The remaining 1,930 outfits were packed in a no. 65-415 Tan RSC with Black Graphics outfit box that was manufactured by Mann Kraft Container Corporation and measured 12 x 11½ x 6⅜ inches. These boxes were made of a thicker corrugated material (rated at 90 pounds rather than the normal 65 pounds gross weight) that allowed each outfit to be shipped in its outfit box. It included

four lines of data as part of the box manufacturer's certificate, and printed on the bottom was a reference to the N.M.F.C.

Both outfit boxes featured a no. 19557-15 Printed Label that included a picture of the outfit and listed all its contents.

The large number of 66-139 outfit boxes produced means that it is fairly common. The 65-415 is more difficult to find. Still, finding either box in C6 or better condition takes time.

What is a real challenge is finding a complete outfit with all its peripherals and paperwork, especially the 309-100 and an original plastic-bagged version of the 1407.

The no. 19561 (Sears no. 9810) came in a unique box, the brand-new no. 66-165 White RSC Allstate By Lionel With Blue Steamer (With Smoke and Trees) and Orange and Blue Gift of Lifetime Graphics outfit box. The outfit's components are fairly common, but its peripherals are not. Lionel used promotional outfits to dump excess inventory, as was demonstrated here by the last appearance of the no. 346-1 Culvert Unloader and the only outfit appearance of the no. B1122-250 R.H. Remote Switch (Blister Packed). Note the original, plastic-bagged version of the no. 1407 Watchman Shanty.

Customer No. On Box: SR 9810
Description: "O27" Promotional Outfit
Specification: "O27" Diesel Freight Outfit
Customer/No.: Sears, Roebuck and Co.; SR 9810
Original Amount: 2,700
Factory Order Date: 6/7/1966
Date Issued: Rev 8-12-66
Date Req'd: 8-12-66
Packaging: WRSC 4/Master (Units not Boxed)

Contents: 635-25 "Union Pacific" Diesel Switcher; 6401-100 Flat Car W/3 Pipes; 6511-15 Pipes (3); 6014-325 Frisco Box Car; 6342-25 Culvert Pipe Car; 6465-150 Tank Car; 6176-50 Hopper Car; 6119-110 Work Caboose; 346-1 Culvert Unloader; 261-25 Non-Illuminated Bumper; 1706 Suburban Station; 1407

Watchman Shanty; 1013-10 Curved Track (Bundle of 10 - 1013); 1013-85 Curved Track (Loose); 1018-75 Straight Track (Bundle of 6 - 1018); 1018-7 Straight Track (Bundle of 7 - 1018) (2); 1018-30 Straight Track (Bundle of 3 - 1018); 6149-25 Remote Control Track; B1122-250 R.H. Remote Switch (Blister Packed); 1025-25 45-Watt Transformer; 1103-50 Envelope Packed; Form 3063 Parts Order Form; 1-166 Warranty Card; 926-66 Service Station List; 11341-10 Instruction Sheet; 19561-5 Layout Sheet; 346-21 Instruction Sheet

Boxes & Packing: 66-165 Outfit Box; 61-182 Corr. Insert; 62-254 Corr. Insert; 62-264 Corr. Insert; 64-106 Corr. Insert (4); 65-375 Corr. Insert; 65-376 Corr. Insert (2); 600-26 Corr. Insert (2); 66-166 Shipper for 2 (1-2); 41110-23 Shipper Pad (2-2); 19561-15 Printed Label; 41110-23 Corr. Insert

19500 Series

19561 (1966)	C6	C7	C8	Rarity
Complete Outfit	1,175	1,750	2,375	R6
Outfit Box no. 66-165	200	350	450	R6

Comments: In 1966, Sears purchased two Retailer Promotional Type Ib outfits: nos. 19557 and 19561. It also carried over the no. 19453 from 1965 by issuing a 1966 re-order of that outfit.

The 19561, for which Sears paid $24.00 each, was likely sold over the counter at Sears stores because it did not appear in the 1966 Sears Christmas Catalog. This outfit, Sears' high-end offering, included both the Lionel 19561 and the Sears no. SR 9810 on its outfit box.

The 19561 was led by a no. 635-25 Union Pacific Diesel Switcher. Included in promotional outfits only, this locomotive featured a two-position reversing unit, a headlight, a weight and a rubber tire as a traction aid.

The rolling stock in this outfit deserved attention, starting with the no. 6401-100 Flat Car W/3 Pipes, which appeared in only one other outfit (no. 19563). The suffix indicated that the flat car load was three no. 6511-15 Pipes; otherwise, the car was the same as a no. 6401-25 Flat Car.

The no. 6342-25 Culvert Car, last seen in the 1959 consumer catalog, had been re-introduced in outfit no. 19327 from 1964. The new version of this car found in the 19561 was equipped with one operating and one non-operating AAR truck and coupler riveted directly to the body.

During the course of 1966, Lionel finished removing the new date, a built date and number data from the heat-stamping of the black no. 6176-50 Hopper Car. This minimal decoration became the norm for the 6176-50. Finally, the "-110" suffix added to the no. 6119-110 Work Caboose in this outfit meant that it came unboxed.

The rolling stock in the 19561 followed the normal truck and coupler progression for 1966, with each of the cars having AAR types. The norm for all the cars was one operating and one non-operating truck and coupler. However, the 6119-110 could come with one operating and one plain in 1966.

As with many promotional outfits, the peripherals included in the 19561 make it a highly collectible outfit. Specifically, the no. 346-1 Culvert Unloader appeared only in five promotional outfits. The 346-1 was the manual version of the culvert unloader and was packed with seven culvert pipes in a no. 346-13 Corr. Box. The 6342-25 and no. 346-21 Instruction Sheet were included separately in the outfit.

After a one-year absence, Plasticville items returned to Lionel outfits in 1966, although something was different. Instead of providing unique, individually boxed Lionel versions of Plasticville sets, as had been the rule in the past, Lionel now included the same Plasticville items that were available to any retailer. In fact, the Factory Order listed the Plasticville set numbers.

Also different was that now each Plasticville set presumably came packaged in a plastic bag. However, an example of the no. 1706 Suburban Station in its original plastic bag has yet to be observed, so we cannot state with certainty that this change in packaging did occur. We base this conclusion on the fact that the no. 1407 Watchman Shanty included in this outfit has been observed in a plastic bag.

The outfit packing diagram also supports the contention that Plasticville sets came in plastic bags because it indicates that individually boxed items would not fit. The 1407 came with a poorly copied piece of paper with "1407 Shanty" on it.

Lionel had excess inventory of the no. B1122-250 R.H. Remote Switch (Blister Packed) so it used that instead of a no. 1122-250 R.H. Remote Switch. The 19561 represented the only instance when this blister-packed item came in an outfit. The B1122-250 is very difficult to find in collectible condition and adds a premium to the overall outfit price.

Further cheapening of the product line led to the no. 261-25 Non-Illuminated Bumper, which was molded in black plastic.

The 19561 included a unique track layout, as outlined on the no. 19561-5 Layout Sheet dated 8/66. This sheet commands a substantial premium. The no. 11341-10 Instruction Sheet was dated 6/66.

The no. 66-165 White RSC Allstate By Lionel With Blue Steamer (With Smoke and Trees) and Orange and Blue Gift of Lifetime Graphics outfit box was manufactured by United Container Co. and measured 24⅛ x 13⅛ x 10 inches. It included four lines of data, a "66" and five stars as part of the box manufacturer's certificate. Printed on the bottom was a reference to the N.M.F.C.

Orders for the 19561 exceeded original forecasts, and the quantity was increased from 600 to 1,500 units and then to 2,700. Even with the large number of outfits produced, few have survived intact. Sears outfits were destined for children and not collectors, which is why many boxes were damaged upon initial opening. Over time, the large space required to store the box has led to an extremely low quantity of boxes surviving in collectible condition. Even when a box is found, finding collectible versions of its peripherals and paperwork takes time and plenty of money.

CONVENTIONAL PACK
66-165 BOX

The no. 19563 was Mercury Model's high-end steam-powered offering for 1966. On the end of the outfit box was a no. 19563-15 Printed Label with a picture of the outfit and a listing of its contents. No longer were customers asked to purchase a plain white or tan box; now they could see what was included. This outfit came with an early version of the no. 110-78 Envelope Packed.

Description: "O27" Promotional Outfit
Specification: "O27" Steam Type Freight Outfit W/Smoke
Customer/No./Price: Gimbels; 740 S8 65; $29.99
Customer/No./Price: Hudson's Detroit; 664*11-7; $35.00
Customer: Mercury Model
Original Amount: 3,000
Factory Order Date: 6/1/1966
Date Issued: Rev 9-13-66
Date Req'd: 9-13-66
Packaging: WRSC 4/Master (Units not Boxed)

Contents: 241-25 Steam Type Locomotive with Smoke; 242T-25 Tender; 6401-100 Flat Car W/3 Pipes; 6511-15 Pipes (3); 6050-100 Swift Savings Bank Car; 6176-75 Hopper Car; 6142-125 Gondola Car; 6402-150 Flat Car W/Trailer; 6405-150 Van; 6167-100 Caboose; 1013-8 Curved Track (Bundle of 8 - 1013) (2); 1018-7 Straight Track (Bundle of 7 - 1018); 1018-40 Straight Track (Bundle of 4 - 1018); 6149-25 Remote Control Track; 1020-25 90° Crossing; 909-20 Smoke Fluid; 110-75 Modified Trestle Set; 1025-25 45-Watt Transformer; 1103-50 Envelope Packed; 1-166 Warranty Card; 926-66 Service Station List; Form 3063 Parts Order Form; 237-11 Instruction Sheet; 19563-10 Instruction Sheet; 19563-5 Track Layout; 239-18 Flyer

Boxes & Packing: 66-159 Outfit Box; 66-161 Corrugated Insert; 66-162 Corrugated Insert (6); 61-171 Corrugated Insert; 62-225 Corrugated Insert (2); 62-249 Corrugated Insert; 62-248 Corrugated Insert (2); 62-251 Corrugated Insert; 62-264 Corrugated Insert; 66-160 Shipper for 4 (1-4); 41110-23 Shipper Pad (2-4); 19563-15 Printed Label

19563 (1966)	C6	C7	C8	Rarity
Complete Outfit	325	575	820	R6
Outfit Box no. 66-159	75	125	150	R5

Comments: In 1966 Mercury Model, an important Lionel distributor purchased six Retailer Promotional outfits: steam-powered nos. 19563, 19567, 19567-500 and 19583 and diesel-powered nos. 19569 and 19571. Mercury paid Lionel $17.25 for each 19563 and then sold them to various retailers, including Gimbels (Gimbels Schuster's) and Hudson's Detroit.

The 19563, a Type Ic outfit, was Mercury's high-end steam-powered offering. It was led by a no. 241-25 Steam Type Locomotive with Smoke. This die-cast Scout steamer, which appeared only in promotional outfits, featured a two-position reversing unit, a headlight and a rubber tire as a traction aid. The later version with a wide, white-painted stripe was included in this outfit. Except for its 241 number and stripe, it was the same engine as a no. 239.

The rolling stock in this outfit deserves attention, starting with the no. 6401-100 Flat Car W/3 Pipes, which appeared in only one other outfit (no. 19561). The suffix indicated that the flat car load was three no. 6511-15 Pipes (the later, light gray version); otherwise, the car was the same as a no. 6401-25 Flat Car. Also, the yellow no. 6176-75 Hopper Car was stamped "BUILT 1-48" and "LIONEL 6176".

In 1966, Lionel added new suffixes to the no. 6402 Flat Car to indicate its load. The no. 6402-150 Flat Car W/Trailer, which appeared only in this outfit, carried a no. 6405-150 Van. All vans (trailers) have been observed with white bodies that do not have slots on the side. They were identical to the no. 6430-150 Trailer Assembly that came with the no. 6431-1 Trailer Flat Car W/2 Trailers. Even though the 6402 carried a "-150" suffix, it was identical to the common no. 6402-50 Flat Car W/2 Cable Reels.

The rolling stock in the 19563 followed the normal truck and coupler progression for 1966, with each of the cars having late AAR types. All but one were equipped with one operating and one non-operating truck and coupler. The no. 242T-25 Tender had one non-operating and one plain type. Most cars had a washer riveted as part of their leaf spring assembly.

Although the rolling stock is fairly common, the no. 110-75 Modified Trestle Set included in this outfit is not. The 110-75 included nine pairs of graduated trestle piers, or "bents," which were designed to elevate the figure-eight track layout to a height of approximately 5 inches. A no. 110-78 Envelope Packed included the Tie Channels and Screws to assemble the trestles. Both the earlier (larger) version as well as the later (smaller) version of this envelope has been observed in this outfit. All of these peripherals were sealed in a no. 1-41 Poly Bag. As with many promotional-only items, the packaging and packed envelope are very difficult to obtain. They are, nonetheless, necessary for completing this outfit (a point assumed in the outfit pricing).

The 19563 included a unique track layout, as outlined on the no. 19563-5 Track Layout dated 6/66. This sheet commands a substantial premium. Also unique to this outfit was the no. 19563-10 Instruction Sheet dated 6/66.

The no. 66-159 White RSC with Orange Graphics outfit box was manufactured by United Container Co. and measured 18¾ x 13½ x 7 inches. It included four lines of data, a "66" and two, six or seven stars as part of the box manufacturer's certificate. Printed on

the bottom was a reference to the N.M.F.C.

An original quantity of 5,000 units of the 19563 was to have been manufactured. This was subsequently reduced to 3,000. This large quantity makes the 19563 somewhat common, yet its larger-than-normal outfit box takes time to find in collectible condition. Even when a box is found, acquiring a complete 110-75 (with its 110-78 Envelope Packed), the three light gray pipes and the proper paperwork for this outfit remains a challenge. In fact, a complete 110-75 leads to an outfit rarity rating of R6.

CONVENTIONAL PACK
66-159 BOX

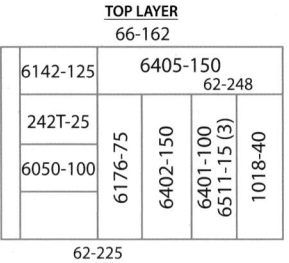
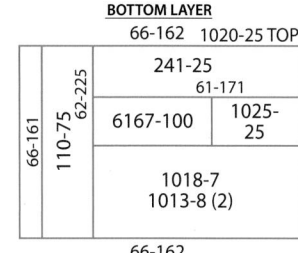

Description: "O27" Promotional Outfit
Specification: "O27" Steam Type Freight Outfit
Customer: Mercury Model
Original Amount: 1,600
Factory Order Date: 9/7/1966
Date Issued: Rev 11-15-66
Date Req'd: 11-15-66
Packaging: WRSC 4/Master (Units not Boxed)

Contents: 1062-125 Steam Type Loco. W/Light & Reversing Unit; 1061T-50 Tender; 6142-125 Gondola Car; 6401-25 Flat Car W/Auto; 6014-325 Frisco Box Car; 6176-25 Hopper Car; 6167-100 Caboose; 1013-70 Curved Track (Bundle of 12 - 1013); 1018-7 Straight Track (Bundle of 7 - 1018); 1018-30 Straight Track (Bundle of 3 - 1018); 110-75 Modified Trestle Set; 1025-25 45-Watt Transformer; 1103-20 Envelope Packed; 19567-21 Plastic Fuel Tank Car (1/2); 19567-22 Plastic Passenger Car (1/2); 1-166 Warranty Card; 926-66 Service Station List; Form 3063 Parts Order Form; 1-66 Flyer; 19522-10 Instruction Sheet; 19567-5 Track Layout; 239-18 Flyer; 19567-16 Flyer

Boxes & Packing: 66-159 Outfit Box; 1013-59 Corrugated Insert (6); 66-162 Corrugated Insert (3); 61-171 Corrugated Insert; 62-225 Corrugated Insert (2); 62-251 Corrugated Insert (3); 66-163 Corrugated Insert; 66-160 Shipper for 4 (1-4); 41110-23 Shipper Pad (2-4); 19567-20 Printed Label; 66-181 Corr. Insert (4)

Alternate For Outfit Contents:
Note: Mercury Model to supply auto to go with flat car; Sub. 6176-75 for 6176-25 as needed.

19567 (1966)	C6	C7	C8	Rarity
Complete Outfit	285	500	750	R6
Outfit Box no. 66-159	100	175	250	R5

Comments: In 1966 Mercury Model, an important Lionel distributor purchased six Retailer Promotional outfits: steam-powered nos. 19563, 19567, 19567-500 and 19583 and diesel-powered nos. 19569 and 19571. Mercury paid Lionel $10.37 for each 19567 and then likely sold them to various retailers, although this outfit has yet to be linked to a specific one.

The 19567 and 19567-500 were nearly identical because they originated as a 19567 and then evolved into either a 19567 or a 19567-500. In both cases, Mercury Model provided items to Lionel, which then included them in the outfit box. Specifically, the Factory Orders for the two outfits stated, "Mercury Model to supply auto to go with Flat Car".

In addition, the Factory Order for the 19567-500 noted, "Mercury to supply cutouts". These cutouts (actually, they were punch-outs), which Lionel designated no. 19567-511 Mercury Model Cutouts, and the no. 19567-510 Flyer were the only differences in the contents of the two outfits.

The 19567, a Type Ib outfit, was one of Mercury's low-end steam-powered offerings. Like the 19567-500, it was led by a no. 1062-125 Steam Type Loco. W/Light & Reversing Unit (new for 1966 and found in only these two outfits). This low-end Scout steamer featured a 2-4-0 wheel arrangement and a rubber tire as a traction aid. Except for its lack of rear wheels, the 1062-125 was identical to the no. 1062-75 Steam Type Loco. W/Light & Reversing Unit. Despite being somewhat difficult to find, the no. 1062-125 has not drawn much interest from collectors because until now its existence could not be substantiated.

The rolling stock in this outfit consisted of carryover items that were commonly used in outfits from 1966. Even though the hopper car was listed as a blank yellow no. 6176-25 Hopper Car, it is often found as a yellow no. 6176-75 Hopper Car lacking the new date, a built date and number data from its heat-stamping.

The rolling stock in the 19567 followed the normal truck and coupler progression for 1966, with each of the cars having late AAR types. All but one were equipped with one operating and one non-operating truck and coupler. The no. 1061T-50 Tender had one non-operating and one plain type. Some cars had a washer riveted

The no. 19567 was one of Mercury Model's low-end steam-powered offerings for 1966. Mercury supplied the Payton Products red plastic automobile included in this outfit. The no. 1062-125 Steam Type Loco. W/Light & Reversing Unit featured a 2-4-0 wheel arrangement and was unique to this outfit and no. 19567-500. Shown are the earlier (smaller) version of the no. 19567-5 Layout Sheet dated 5/66, the no. 19567-16 Flyer dated 9/66 and the yellow no. 6176-75 Hopper Car substitution.

as part of their leaf spring assembly.

Mercury Model provided Lionel with the automobile to be included in this outfit. Lionel listed this automobile as a no. 19567-21 Plastic Fuel Tank Car and a no. 19567-22 Plastic Passenger Car, each with a quantity of "1/2", which likely meant it split an equal number of each model between outfits. Observations of actual outfits have confirmed that the 19567-22 was a red automobile from Payton Products, but a 19567-21 has not yet been observed though we assume it also came from Payton (one of its models from that era matches the description). Even though these cars were almost always separated from the 19567, they were normal Payton production and so are easily obtained to complete an outfit.

A no. 19567-16 Flyer dated 9/66 was included in each outfit. It stated, "The toy auto in this set is not provided, manufactured nor warranted by the Lionel Toy Corporation." This is a difficult piece of paperwork to obtain.

Although the rolling stock is fairly common, the no. 110-75 Modified Trestle Set included in this outfit is not. The 110-75 included nine pairs of graduated trestle piers, or "bents," which were designed to elevate the figure-eight track layout to a height of approximately 5 inches. A no. 110-78 Envelope Packed included the Tie Channels and Screws to assemble the trestles. All of these peripherals were sealed in a no. 1-41 Poly Bag. As with many promotional-only items, the packaging and packed envelope are very difficult to obtain. They are, nonetheless, necessary for completing this outfit (a point assumed in the outfit pricing).

The 19567 and 19567-500 included a unique track layout, as outlined on the no. 19567-5 Track Layout. Two versions of this sheet exist. The earlier (smaller) one was dated 5/66, and the later (larger) one was dated 8/66. The difficult-to-find no. 19522-10 Instruction Sheet dated 6/66 included instructions for assembling the trestles.

The no. 66-159 White RSC with Orange Graphics outfit box was manufactured by United Container Co. and measured 18¾ x 13½ x 7 inches. It included four lines of data, a "66" and six or seven stars as part of the box manufacturer's certificate. Printed on the bottom was a reference to the N.M.F.C. A no. 15657-20 Printed Label was glued on the outfit box end. This detailed all the contents and provided a picture of the outfit.

After Lionel split the 19567 into a 19567 and 19567-500, an original quantity of 2,000 units of the 19567 was to have been manufactured. This was subsequently reduced to 1,600. Even with the larger-than-average number of units produced, the 19567 is difficult to find complete and in collectible condition. Especially difficult to find is the 110-75 (with its 110-78 Envelope Packed) and the outfit's paperwork. In fact, a complete 110-75 leads to an outfit rarity rating of R6.

CONVENTIONAL PACK
66-159 BOX

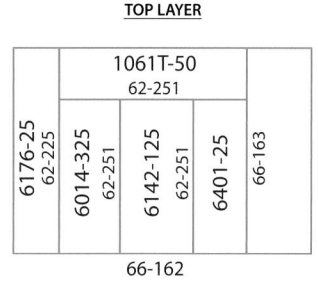

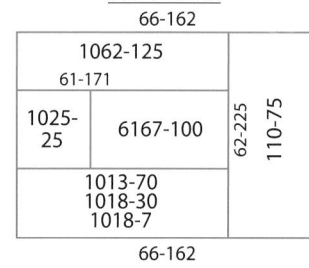

19567-500
1966

Mercury Model's no. 19567-500 was identical to outfit no. 19567, except that it added the no. 19567-511 Mercury Model Cutouts plus a no. 19567-510 Flyer saying that these peripheral items did not come from Lionel. Instead, Mercury Model supplied them, and a set is shown assembled. This outfit is the early version without any substitutions. It included a no. 19567-21 Plastic Fuel Tank Car or 19567-22 Plastic Passenger Car (shown) provided by Mercury to Lionel as well as the earlier (smaller) no. 19567-5 Track Layout dated 5/66.

The later version of Mercury Model's no. 19567-500 included the nos. 1062-75 Steam Type Loco. W/Light & Reversing Unit, 1062T-25 Tender and 6176-75 Hopper Car substitutions. Also note the later (larger) version of the no. 19567-5 Track Layout dated 8/66. Lionel apparently ran out of automobiles supplied by Mercury Model because later 19567-500s came with a no. 0068-3 Automobile Body (Maroon). When this occurred, Lionel correctly omitted the no. 19567-16 Flyer, which noted that the automobile had not been supplied by Lionel. The no. 19567-511 Mercury Model Cutouts is shown in its Kraft envelope (Mercury no. C 76591).

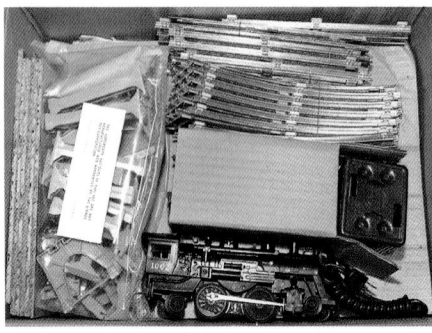

The ultimate in outfit research - a sealed later version of a no. 19567-500 was opened from the bottom to reveal its contents. This is a first look at the bottom layer of contents.

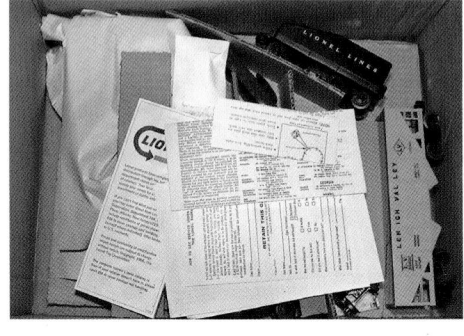

The top layer of a newly opened later version no. 19567-500 reveals the remainder of its contents, a no. 0068-3 Automobile Body (Maroon) and authentic Lionel Bogus Paper.

Description: "O27" Promotional Outfit
Specification: "O27" Steam Type Freight Outfit
Customer/No./Price: May - D&F; CL 12 B Dept. 63; $23.87
Customer: Mercury Model
Customer/No./Price: Titche's; 830 116; $13.88
Original Amount: 6,400
Factory Order Date: 11/4/1966
Date Issued: Rev 11-15-66
Date Req'd: 11-15-66
Packaging: WRSC 4/Master (Units not Boxed)

Contents: 1062-125 Steam Type Loco. W/Light & Reversing Unit; 1061T-50 Tender; 6142-125 Gondola Car; 6401-25 Flat Car W/Auto; 6014-325 Frisco Box Car; 6176-25 Hopper Car; 6167-100 Caboose; 1013-70 Curved Track (Bundle of 12 - 1013); 1018-7 Straight Track (Bundle of 7 - 1018); 1018-30 Straight Track (Bundle of 3 - 1018); 110-75 Modified Trestle Set; 1025-25 45-Watt Transformer; 1103-20 Envelope Packed; 1-166 Warranty Card; 926-66 Service Station List; Form 3063 Parts Order Form; 1-66 Flyer; 19522-10 Instruction Sheet; 19567-5 Track Layout; 239-18 Flyer; 19567-510 Flyer; 19567-16 Flyer; 19567-21 Plastic Fuel Tank Car (1/2); 19567-22 Plastic Passenger Car (1/2); 19567-511 Mercury Model Cutouts

Boxes & Packing: 66-159 Outfit Box; 1013-59 Corrugated Inserts (6); 66-162 Corrugated Insert (3); 61-171 Corrugated Insert; 62-225 Corrugated Insert (2); 62-251 Corrugated Insert (3); 66-163 Corrugated Insert; 66-160 Shipper for 4 (1-4); 41110-23 Shipper Pad (2-4); 19567-515 Printed Label; 66-181 Corr. Insert (3)

Alternate For Outfit Contents:
Note: Mercury to supply auto to go with flat car; Mercury to supply cutouts; Note: Sub 2,765 - 1062-75 for 1062-125; Sub. 16 - 1060T for 1061T-50; Sub. 36 - 1060T-50 for 1061T-50; Sub. 47 - 1050T-25 for 1061T-50; Sub. 31 - 244T-25 for 1061T-50; Sub. 2,390 - 1062T-25 for 1061T-50; Sub. 2,357 - 6176-75 for 6176-25; Sub. 0068-3 Automobile Body (Maroon) for Mercury auto as needed.

19567-500 (1966)	C6	C7	C8	Rarity
Complete Outfit	600	975	1,575	R7
Complete Outfit With no. 0068-5 Automobile Body (Maroon)	635	1,035	1,650	R7
Outfit Box no. 66-159	150	250	450	R4

Comments: In 1966 Mercury Model, an important Lionel distributor purchased six Retailer Promotional outfits: steam-powered nos. 19563, 19567, 19567-500 and 19583 and diesel-powered nos. 19569 and 19571. Mercury sold the 19567-500 to various retailers, including May - D&F and Titche's.

The 19567 and 19567-500 were nearly identical because they originated as a 19567 and then evolved into either a 19567 or a 19567-500. In both cases, Mercury Model provided items to Lionel, which then included them in the outfit box. Specifically, the Factory Orders for the two outfits stated, "Mercury Model to supply auto to go with Flat Car".

In addition, the Factory Order for the 19567-500 noted, "Mercury to supply cutouts". These cutouts (actually, they were punch-outs), which Lionel designated no. 19567-511 Mercury

Model Cutouts, and the no. 19567-510 Flyer were the only differences in the contents of the two outfits.

The 19567-500, a Type Ic outfit, was one of Mercury's low-end steam-powered offerings. Like the 19567, it was led by a no. 1062-125 Steam Type Loco. W/Light & Reversing Unit (new for 1966 and found in only these two outfits). This low-end Scout steamer featured a 2-4-0 wheel arrangement and a rubber tire as a traction aid. Except for its lack of rear wheels, the 1062-125 was identical to the no. 1062-75 Steam Type Loco. W/Light & Reversing Unit, which was used in the later production of this outfit. Despite being somewhat difficult to find, the no. 1062-125 has not drawn much interest from collectors because until now its existence could not be substantiated.

The rolling stock in the 19567-500 consisted of carryover items that were commonly used in outfits from 1966. The yellow no. 6176-75 Hopper Car substitution was stamped "BUILT 1-48" and "LIONEL 6176". The locomotive, tender and hopper car substitutions do not materially affect the outfit price.

Except for the tender substitutions, all the rolling stock in this outfit followed the normal truck and coupler progression for 1966, with each of the cars having late AAR types. All but one were equipped with one operating and one non-operating truck and coupler. The no. 1061T-50 Tender had one non-operating and one plain type. Most cars had a washer riveted as part of their leaf spring assembly.

Lionel used the 19567-500 to deplete the remaining inventory of four different tenders. All but one were equipped with one non-operating and one plain truck and coupler. The no. 244T-25 included one operating and one plain type.

Mercury Model provided Lionel with the automobile to be included in this outfit. Lionel listed this automobile as a no. 19567-21 Plastic Fuel Tank Car and a no. 19567-22 Plastic Passenger Car, each with a quantity of "1/2", which likely meant it split an equal number of each model between outfits. Observations of actual outfits have confirmed that the 19567-22 was a red automobile from Payton Products, but a 19567-21 has not yet been observed though we assume it also came from Payton (one of its models from that era matches the description). Even though these cars were almost always separated from the 19567-500, they were normal Payton production and so are easily obtained to complete an outfit.

A no. 19567-16 Flyer dated 9/66 was included in each outfit. It stated, "The toy auto in this set is not provided, manufactured nor warranted by the Lionel Toy Corporation." This is a difficult piece of paperwork to obtain.

Although the rolling stock is fairly common, the no. 110-75 Modified Trestle Set included in this outfit is not. The 110-75 included nine pairs of graduated trestle piers, or "bents," which were designed to elevate the figure-eight track layout to a height of approximately 5 inches. A no. 110-78 Envelope Packed included the Tie Channels and Screws to assemble the trestles. Both the earlier (larger) version as well as the later (smaller) version of this envelope has been observed in this outfit. All of these peripherals were sealed in a no. 1-41 Poly Bag. As with many promotional-only items, the packaging and packed envelope are very difficult to obtain. They are, nonetheless, necessary for completing this outfit (a point assumed in the outfit pricing).

Mercury Model provided Lionel with three sheets of cutouts packaged in a Kraft envelope. The envelope included a picture of the 19567-500 and had "44 Piece Railroad Accessory Set" and the part no. "C 76591" printed on the bottom right corner. As noted, Lionel designated these cutouts 19567-511 Mercury Model Cutouts, and they enabled Lionel to advertise the 19567-500 as an 87-piece electric train. The 19567-511 was intended to be assembled by the customer. It often became separated from the train outfit and ended up destroyed.

A no. 19567-510 Flyer dated 8/66 was included in each outfit. It stated, "The cardboard cut-outs in this set are not manufactured nor warranted by the Lionel Toy Corporation." This is a difficult flyer to obtain.

The 19567-500 and 19567 included a unique track layout, as outlined on the no. 19567-5 Track Layout. Two versions of this sheet exist. The earlier (smaller) one was dated 5/66, and the later (larger) one was dated 8/66. The difficult-to-find no. 19522-10 Instruction Sheet dated 6/66 provided instructions for assembling the trestles.

The no. 66-159 White RSC with Orange Graphics outfit box was manufactured by United Container Co. and measured 18¾ x 13½ x 7 inches. It included four lines of data, a "66" and two, six or seven stars as part of the box manufacturer's certificate. Printed on the bottom was a reference to the N.M.F.C. A no. 19567-515 Printed Label was glued on the outfit box end. This detailed all the contents and provided a picture of the outfit.

After Lionel split the 19567 into a 19567 and a 19567-500, an original quantity of 2,000 units of the 19567-500 was to have been manufactured. This was subsequently increased to 6,400. This change likely meant that Lionel ran out of automobiles because late-production 19567-500s have been observed with a no. 0068-3 Automobile Body (Maroon), also known as a "cheapie" automobile. This automobile substitution affects the price, as listed in the pricing table.

With such a large number of outfits produced, a 19567-500 outfit box is easy to obtain, although finding a complete outfit in collectible condition is a challenge. Acquiring the Mercury Model Cutouts, a complete 110-75 (with its 110-78 Envelope Packed) and the proper paperwork for this outfit are the greatest challenges when trying to complete this outfit. In fact, these peripherals give the complete outfit an R7 rarity rating.

CONVENTIONAL PACK
66-159 BOX

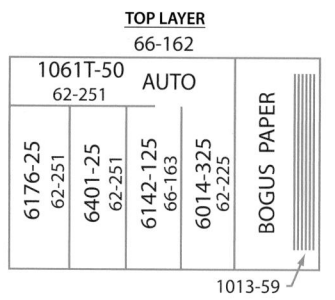

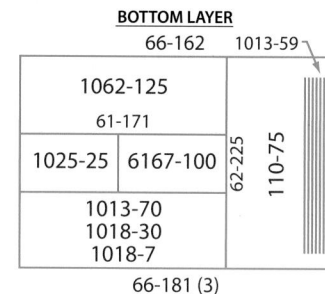

19569
1966

Description: "O27" Promotional Outfit
Specification: "O27" Diesel Type Freight Outfit
Customer/No./Price: Hudson's Detroit; 664*12-6; $29.99
Customer: Mercury Model
Customer/No./Price: Shillito's; 06; $29.99
Original Amount: 3,000
Factory Order Date: 6/2/1966
Date Issued: Rev 8-1-66
Date Req'd: 8-1-66
Packaging: WRSC 4/Master (Units not Boxed)

Contents: 215P-25 "Santa Fe" Diesel Power Car; 212T-25 "Santa Fe" "A" Unit; 6142-75 Gondola Car; 6112-88 Canister (2); 6050-100 Swift Savings Bank Car; 6176-50 Hopper Car; 6167-100 Caboose; 1013-70 Curved Track (Bundle of 12 - 1013); 1013-85 Curved Track (Loose) (3); 1018-30 Straight Track (Bundle of 3 - 1018); 1013-95 Half Section Curved (Loose) (2); 6149-25 Remote Control Track; 1023-25 45° Crossing; 1025-25 45-Watt Transformer; 1103-50 Envelope Packed; 1-166 Warranty Card; 926-66 Service Station List; Form 3063 Parts Order Form; 1802C Layout Instruction Sheet; 19214-10 Instruction Sheet; 211-151 Instruction Sheet

Boxes & Packing: 64-164 Outfit Box; 62-224 Corrugated Insert; 62-245 Corrugated Insert (2); 62-248 Corrugated Insert; 62-223 Corrugated Insert; 61-171 Corrugated Insert; 62-225 Corrugated Insert; 62-251 Corrugated Insert; 19569-15 Printed Label; 62-244 Shipper for 4 (1-4); 64-106 Shipper Pad (2-4)

19569 (1966)	C6	C7	C8	Rarity
Complete Outfit	265	400	600	R5
Outfit Box no. 64-164	65	95	125	R5

Comments: In 1966 Mercury Model, an important Lionel distributor purchased six Retailer Promotional outfits: steam-powered nos. 19563, 19567, 19567-500 and 19583 and diesel-powered nos. 19569 and 19571. Mercury paid Lionel $14.22 for each 19569 and then sold them to various retailers, including Hudson's Detroit and Shillito's.

The 19569, a Type Ib outfit, was Mercury's low-end diesel-powered offering. It was led by a no. 215P-25 Santa Fe Diesel Power Car. This promotional-only Alco featured a two-position reversing unit, two traction tires, a headlight, a weight and an open pilot with a large ledge. It was paired with a no. 212T-25 Santa Fe "A" Unit.

The rolling stock in this outfit consisted of carryover items that were commonly used in outfits from 1966. The no. 6050-100 Swift Savings Bank Car used a Type III body. During the course of 1966, Lionel finished removing the new date, a built date and number data from the heat-stamping of the black no. 6176-50 Hopper Car. This minimal decoration became the norm for the 6176-50.

The rolling stock in the 19569 followed the normal truck and coupler progression for 1966, with each of the cars having late AAR types. All were equipped with one operating and one non-operating truck and coupler. Some of the cars had a washer riveted as part of their leaf spring assembly.

The no. 1802C Track Layout sheet appeared only on the Factory Order for this outfit. It outlined the pretzel layout and was dated 6/66. Curiously, this track layout called for 14 pieces of

The no. 19569 was Mercury Model's low-end diesel-powered offering for 1966. It featured the no.1802C Track Layout, which was unique to this outfit. The outfit box included a no. 19569-15 Printed Label on the box end with a picture of the outfit and a list of its contents. The 19569 and no. 19563 were the only Mercury Model outfits from 1966 lacking an item supplied by Mercury.

curved track, four half-curves, three straights and one uncoupling section, but the Factory Order listed one additional curved track and only two half-curves. Outfits have been observed as listed on the Factory Order.

The no. 64-164 White RSC with Orange Graphics outfit box was manufactured by United Container Co. and measured 12⅛ x 11⅝ x 6½ inches. It included four lines of data, a "66" and four stars as part of the box manufacturer's certificate. Printed on the bottom was a reference to the N.M.F.C. A no. 19569-15 Printed Label was glued on the outfit box end. This detailed all the contents and provided a picture of the outfit.

An original quantity of 5,000 units of the 19569 was to have been manufactured. This was subsequently reduced to 3,000. This decrease likely explains why unused 19569-15 Printed Labels can be found. Even with this reduction, the 19569 is commonly

available. The only item that is somewhat difficult to find is the 1802C.

CONVENTIONAL PACK
64-164 BOX

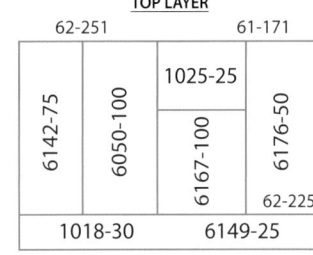

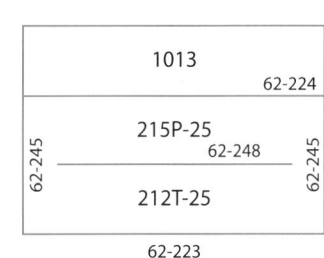

Description: "O27" Promotional Outfit
Specification: "O27" Diesel Type Freight Outfit with Horn
Customer/No./Price: Joseph Horne Co.; 661/2 19571; $23.95
Customer: Mercury Model
Original Amount: 500
Factory Order Date: 6/2/1966
Date Issued: Rev 9-9-66
Date Req'd: 9-9-66
Packaging: WRSC 4/Master (Units not Boxed)

Contents: 216P-25 "Minn. & St. Louis" Diesel Power Car With Horn; 213T-25 Motorless Unit; 6142-125 Gondola Car; 6050-100 Swift Savings Bank Car; 6401-25 Flat Car W/Auto; 6167-100 Caboose; 1013-8 Curved Track (Bundle of 8 - 1013); 1013-85 Curved Track (Loose) (4); 1018-10 Straight Track (Loose) (3); 6149-25 Remote Control Track; 1020-25 90° Crossing; 1025-25 45-Watt Transformer; 147-25 Horn & Whistle Controller; 1103-

50 Envelope Packed; 1-166 Warranty Card; 926-66 Service Station List; Form 3063 Parts Order Form; 212-64 Instruction Sheet; 19571-10 Instruction Sheet; 19567-16 Flyer

Boxes & Packing: 64-164 Outfit Box; 66-164 Corrugated Insert; 62-251 Corrugated Insert; 62-225 Corrugated Insert (2); 63-316 Corrugated Insert (2); 64-323 Corrugated Insert; 64-341 Corrugated Insert; 62-244 Shipper for 4 (1-4); 64-106 Shipper Pad (2-4); 64-169 Corr. Insert

Alternate For Outfit Contents:
Note: Mercury to supply auto to go with flat car.

19571 (1966)	C6	C7	C8	Rarity
Complete Outfit	525	800	1,085	R9
Outfit Box no. 64-164	250	375	500	R9

The no. 19571 was Mercury Model's high-end diesel-powered offering for 1966. Only 500 units were manufactured, making it difficult to find in any condition. The no. 216P-25 Minn. & St. Louis Diesel Power Car With Horn appeared in only this and outfit no. 19454-500 (Sears no. 9835). Since Mercury Model supplied the automobile, it took finding a complete and unaltered 19571 to confirm that it was a red automobile from Payton Products.

Comments: In 1966 Mercury Model, an important Lionel distributor purchased six Retailer Promotional outfits: steam-powered nos. 19563, 19567, 19567-500 and 19583 and diesel-powered nos. 19569 and 19571. Mercury paid Lionel $16.39 for each 19571 and then sold them to various retailers, including Joseph Horne Co. in Pittsburgh, Pennsylvania.

The 19571, a Type Ib outfit, was Mercury's high-end diesel-powered offering. It was led by a no. 216P-25 Minn. & St. Louis Diesel Power Car With Horn. This Alco featured a two-position reversing unit, a headlight and two rubber tires as traction aids. It appeared only in this outfit and promotional outfit no. 19454-500 (Sears no. 9835). In both it was paired with a no. 213T-25 Motorless Unit. Lionel produced only 2,000 of these difficult-to-find Alcos, which made their final appearance in this outfit.

The rolling stock in this outfit consisted of carryover items that were commonly used in outfits from 1966. The no. 6050-100 Swift Savings Bank Car used a Type III body.

The cars followed the normal truck and coupler progression for 1966, with each of them having late AAR types. All were equipped with one operating and one non-operating truck and coupler. The no. 6401-25 Flat Car W/Auto has been observed with a washer riveted as part of its leaf spring assembly.

As with outfit nos. 19567 and 19567-500, Mercury Model provided Lionel with the automobile to be included in this outfit. Unlike the 19567 and 19567-500, Lionel did not list the automobile separately on the Factory Order for this outfit. Observations of actual outfits have confirmed that Mercury supplied a red automobile from Payton Products. Even though these cars were almost always separated from the 19571, they were normal Payton production and so are easily obtained to complete an outfit.

A no. 19567-16 Flyer dated 9/66 was included in each outfit.

It stated, "The toy auto in this set is not provided, manufactured nor warranted by the Lionel Toy Corporation." The no. 19571-10 Instruction Sheet was unique to this outfit and dated 8/66. Both of these paper items are difficult to find.

The no. 64-164 White RSC with Orange Graphics outfit box was manufactured by United Container Co. and measured 12⅛ x 11⅝ x 6½ inches. It included four lines of data, a "66" and seven stars as part of the box manufacturer's certificate. Printed on the bottom was a reference to the N.M.F.C.

An original quantity of 1,500 units of the 19571 was to have been manufactured. This was subsequently reduced to 500. This small quantity, combined with the narrow availability of the 216P-25 and unique paperwork, makes this a difficult outfit to find complete and in collectible condition.

CONVENTIONAL PACK
64-164 BOX

TOP LAYER

1013-70 1018-10 (3)	62-225
6167-100	147-25 62-225
6401-25	

BOTTOM LAYER

	66-164	
63-316	216P-25	64-169 63-316
	213T-25	64-323
1025-25	6142-125	62-251
	6050-100	
	64-341	

Customer No. On Box: #5
Description: "O27" Promotional Outfit
Specification: "O27" Steam Type Freight Outfit
Customer/No.: Bronco Modelcraft; #5
Original Amount: 2,500
Factory Order Date: 6/2/1966
Date Issued: 6-7-66
Date Req'd: 7-11-66
Packaging: Display and Bulk (Units not Boxed)

Contents: 242-25 Steam Type Locomotive; 1062T-25 Tender; 3364-25 Log Dump Car; 3364-8 Logs (3); 6176-75 Hopper Car; 6142-100 Gondola Car; 6112-88 Canister (2); 6059-50 Caboose; 1013-8 Curved Track (Bundle of 8 - 1013); 1018-10 Straight Track (Loose); 6149-25 Remote Control Track; 1025-25 45-Watt Transformer; 1103-40 Envelope Packed; Form 3063 Parts Order Form; 1-166 Warranty Card; 926-66 Service Station List; 11450-10 Instruction Sheet; 3364-10 Instruction Sheet; (The following items are part of the 19578 Outfit but are to be Bulk Packed & not included in the 11500 Box.); 1020-25 90° Crossing; 1013-85 Curved Track (Loose) (12); 1018-10 Straight Track (Loose) (14); 1022-2 Right Hand Switch; 1022-3 Left Hand Switch; 1022-37 Envelope Packed; 6014-325 Frisco Box Car; 6142-125 Gondola Car

Boxes & Packing: 65-270 Box Top; 64-112 Box Bottom; 64-118 Corrugated Insert; 64-119 Corrugated Insert; 64-120 Corrugated Insert; 64-121 Corrugated Insert; 65-274 Shipper for 2 (1-2)

Alternate For Outfit Contents:
Note: This set to be packed in #11500 Box but omit number and do not seal lid. Master Carton (2 per) to be sealed on one side and stamp number 3 on Master Carton.

19578 (#5) (1966)	C6	C7	C8	Rarity
Complete Outfit Without Bulk Items	200	335	500	R6
Complete Outfit With Bulk Items	225	380	575	R6
Outfit Box no. 65-270	100	175	250	R6

Comments: In 1966, Bronco Modelcraft, a notable Lionel distributor, purchased four Retailer Promotional outfits: nos. 11520-500, 11540-500, 19578 and 19580.

The 19578, a Type Ia, was identical to Bronco's no. 11520-500, except that it listed additional items that were bulk-packed. All of

these items would not fit in the outfit box, so it is likely that only a few were included or Bronco packaged them separately. In any case, we have never seen a 19578 complete with all of these items. It is most often observed without any of the bulk-packed items. As such, pricing is provided with and without the bulk-packed items.

The Factory Order instructed Lionel not to stamp or seal the outfit boxes, only to stamp "No. 3" on the master carton. Even so, individual outfit boxes have been observed stamped "#5". It is believed that the 11520-500 from 1966 was stamped "#5" as well.

The generic numbering and additional bulk-packed items likely gave Bronco the flexibility to create unique outfits for its customers. To date, most #5s are found as listed on the Factory Order and some are found with additional pieces of track to make a figure-eight layout.

The 19578 was led by a no. 242-25 Steam Type Locomotive. This low-end Scout steamer featured a two-position reversing unit and a headlight, lacked smoke and used a rubber tire as a traction aid. The later version with narrow running boards was included in this outfit.

The rolling stock consisted of carryover items that were commonly used in outfits from 1966. The most notable item was the no. 3364-25 Log Dump Car, which was identical to the no. 3362-25 Helium Tank Unloading Car except that it carried logs instead of helium tanks. The yellow no. 6176-75 Hopper Car was stamped "BUILT 1-48" and "LIONEL". This variation did not include the "6176" number as part of its heat-stamping.

The rolling stock in the 19578 followed the normal truck and coupler progression for 1966, with each of the cars having AAR types. All but two were equipped with one late operating and one late non-operating truck and coupler. The no. 1062T-25 Tender had one late non-operating and one plain type, and the no. 6059-50 Caboose had one late operating and one plain type.

The no. 65-270 White Lift-Off with Full-Color 2037 Steam Freight Graphics Type D display outfit box was manufactured by Mead Containers and measured 24½ x 15½ x 3⅛ inches.

Interestingly, even though the Factory Order specified that the master carton for the 19578 was to be stamped with a "No. 3", the outfit boxes are observed stamped "#5". The opposite is true for Bronco's no. 19580: The Factory Order instructs that the master carton be stamped "No. 5", but the 19580's outfit box is observed stamped "#3".

It is our belief that the #5 was stamped on both Bronco's 11520-500 and 19578. As such, quantities are combined to determine rarity and pricing. (See the 11520-500 from 1966 for a photograph of this outfit.)

The no. 19580 (Bronco Modelcraft #3) was Bronco Modelcraft's high-end purchase for 1966. Bronco was likely responsible for stamping it with the "#3". This outfit was identical to Bronco's 11540-500, except that the Factory Order listed two additional cars and track that were to be bulk-packed as part of the outfit. This #3 is shown the way most outfits are found – without any of the bulk-packed items.

Customer No. On Box: #3
Description: "O27" Promotional Outfit
Specification: "O27" Steam Type Freight Outfit W/Smoke
Customer/No.: Bronco Modelcraft; #3
Original Amount: 2,500
Factory Order Date: 6/2/1966
Date Issued: 6-7-66
Date Req'd: 7-11-66
Packaging: Display & Bulk (Units not Boxed)

Contents: 239-25 Steam Locomotive With Smoke; 242T-25 Tender; 6473-25 Rodeo Car; 6465-150 Tank Car; 6176-50 Hopper Car; 6119-110 Work Caboose; 1013-8 Curved Track (Bundle of 8 - 1013); 1018-10 Straight Track (Loose); 6149-25 Remote Control Track; 1025-25 45-Watt Transformer; 1103-40 Envelope Packed; 909-20 Smoke Fluid; Form 3063 Parts Order Form; 1-166 Warranty Card; 926-66 Service Station List; 11450-10 Instruction Sheet; 237-11 Instruction Sheet; 239-18 Flyer; (The following items are part of the 19580 Outfit but are to be Bulk Packed & not included in the 11500 Box.); 1020-25 90° Crossing; 1013-85 Curved Track (Loose) (12); 1018-10 Straight Track (Loose) (14); 1022-2 Right Hand Switch; 1022-3 Left Hand Switch; 1022-37 Envelope Packed; 6014-325 Frisco Box Car; 6465-150 Tank Car

Boxes & Packing: 65-270 Box Top; 64-112 Box Bottom; 64-118 Corrugated Insert; 64-119 Corrugated Insert; 64-120 Corrugated Insert; 64-121 Corrugated Insert; 65-274 Shipper for 2 (1-2)

Alternate For Outfit Contents:
Note: This set to be packed in #11500 Box but omit number & do not seal lid. Master Carton (2 per) to be sealed on one side only & stamp No. 5 on Master Carton.

19580 (#3) (1966)	C6	C7	C8	Rarity
Complete Outfit Without Bulk Items	235	350	500	R6
Complete Outfit With Bulk Items	265	410	575	R6
Outfit Box no. 65-270	100	150	200	R6

Comments: In 1966, Bronco Modelcraft, a notable Lionel distributor, purchased four Retailer Promotional outfits: nos. 11520-500, 11540-500, 19578 and 19580.

The 19580, a Type Ia, was identical to Bronco's no. 11540-500, except that it listed additional items that were bulk-packed. All of these items would not fit in the outfit box, so it is likely that only a few were included or Bronco packaged them separately. In any case, we have never seen a 19580 complete with all of these items. It is most often observed without any of the bulk-packed items. As such, pricing is provided with and without the bulk-packed items.

The Factory Order instructed Lionel not to stamp or seal the outfit boxes, only to stamp "No. 5" on the master carton. Even so, individual outfit boxes have been observed stamped "#3". The generic numbering and additional bulk-packed items likely gave Bronco the flexibility to create unique outfits for its customers.

The 19580 was led by a no. 239-25 Steam Locomotive With Smoke. This die-cast Scout steamer featured a two-position reversing unit, a headlight and a rubber tire as a traction aid. Except for its 239 number and lack of stripe, it was the same engine as a no. 241.

The rolling stock in this outfit consisted of carryover items that were commonly used in outfits from 1966. The no. 6473-25 Rodeo Car used a Type IIIc body (cadmium yellow plastic with maroon lettering), which no longer exhibited the filled slot caused by broken tooling. During the course of 1966, Lionel finished removing the new date, a built date and number data from the heat-stamping of the black no. 6176-50 Hopper Car. This minimal decoration became the norm for the 6176-50. Finally, the "-110" suffix for the no. 6119-110 Work Caboose in this outfit meant that it came unboxed.

The rolling stock in the 19580 followed the normal truck and coupler progression for 1966, with each of the cars having AAR types. All but two were equipped with one late operating and one late non-operating truck and coupler. The no. 242T-25 Tender

had one late non-operating and one plain type, and the 6119-110 had one late operating and one plain type. Be aware that some 6176-50s featured a washer riveted above or below the leaf spring on their trucks and couplers.

The no. 65-270 White Lift-Off with Full-Color 2037 Steam Freight Graphics Type D display outfit box was manufactured by Mead Containers and measured 24½ x 15½ x 3⅛ inches.

Interestingly, even though the Factory Order specified that the master carton for the 19580 was to be stamped with a "No. 5", the outfit boxes are observed stamped "#3". The opposite is true for Bronco's nos. 11520-500 and 19578: The Factory Order instructs that the master carton be stamped "No. 3", but the outfit boxes are observed stamped "#5".

With 2,500 examples of the 19580 manufactured, this outfit does appear, although seldom complete and correct with bulk-packed items.

Description: "O27" Promotional Outfit
Specification: "O27" Steam Type Freight Outfit
Customer/No./Price: Arlan's Department Stores; 66 40; $16.88
Customer: Mercury Model
Original Amount: 3,680
Factory Order Date: 8/17/1966
Date Issued: Rev 11-3-66
Date Req'd: 11-3-66
Packaging: WRSC 4/Master (Units not Boxed)

Contents: 251-25 Steam Locomotive Without Smoke; 1062T-25 Tender; 6014-325 Frisco Box Car; 6142-125 Gondola Car; 6176-50 Hopper Car; 6167-100 Caboose; 1013-70 Curved Track (Bundle of 12 - 1013); 1018-30 Straight Track (Bundle of 3 - 1018); 1008-50 Uncoupling Unit; 1020-25 90° Crossing; 1025-25 45-Watt Transformer; 1103-20 Envelope Packed; 19333-10 Instruction Sheet; 1-166 Warranty Card; 926-66 Service Station List; Form 3063 Parts Order Form; 19583-16 Engineer Cap

Boxes & Packing: 64-164 Outfit Box; 19583-15 Printed Label; 62-254 Corr. Insert; 62-273 Corr. Insert; 64-319 Corr. Insert; 62-251 Corr. Insert; 64-177 Corr. Insert; 62-244 Shipper for 4 (1-4); 65-413 Shipper Pad (2-4)

Alternate For Outfit Contents:
Note: For first 3,440 outfits, Add Engineer Cap (Mercury Model to Supply); Note: For Additional 240 outfits, Add Engineer Cap (Use Lionel Cap instead of no. 19583-16) and Sub: 241-25 for 251-25.

19583 (1966)	C6	C7	C8	Rarity
Complete Outfit With no. 251-25	295	485	750	R8
Complete Outfit With no. 241-25 Substitution	230	405	590	R5
Outfit Box no. 64-164	75	125	200	R5

Comments: In 1966 Mercury Model, an important Lionel distributor purchased six Retailer Promotional outfits: steam-powered nos. 19563, 19567, 19567-500 and 19583 and diesel-powered nos. 19569 and 19571. Mercury sold the 19583 to various

retailers, including Arlan's Department Stores.

The 19583, a Type Ic outfit, was a higher-end steam-powered offering. It was led by a no. 251-25 Steam Locomotive Without Smoke (new for 1966). This rare die-cast Scout steamer was unique to this outfit and featured a two-position reversing unit and a headlight, lacked smoke and used a rubber tire as a traction aid. Except for its 251 number and lack of stripe, its body was the same as the no. 241 and its motor was the same as a no. 242-25 Steam Type Locomotive.

Orders for the 19583 exceeded original forecasts. When the quantity was increased from 3,400 to 3,680, Lionel issued a new Factory Order, referred to here as the *later version*, with a few changes. For this later version, Lionel ran out of 251-25s and substituted 240 units of the no. 241-25 Steam Type Locomotive with Smoke. The version with a wide, white-painted stripe was included in this outfit. Ironically, even though this was an upgraded engine with smoke, it is far more common than the 251-25. The price of this substitution is reflected in the pricing table.

The rolling stock consisted of carryover items that were commonly used in outfits from 1966. During the course of that year, Lionel finished removing the new date, a built date and number data from the heat-stamping of the black no. 6176-50 Hopper Car. This minimal decoration became the norm for the 6176-50.

The no. 6014-325 Frisco Box Car in this outfit used a Type III body, although at least one later 19583 was observed with a 6014-325 that had a Type IIa body with a coin slot and middle operating AAR trucks and couplers. Normally, a 6014-325 came with one operating and one non-operating type. Lionel likely found some old shells and frames and assembled them to create the additional units it needed.

Except for the Type IIa 6014-325, the rolling stock in the 19583 followed the normal truck and coupler progression for 1966, with each of the cars having late AAR types. All but one were equipped with one operating and one non-operating truck and coupler. The no. 1062T-25 Tender had one non-operating and one plain type. The no. 6167-100 Caboose has been observed with a washer riveted as part of its leaf spring assembly.

Mercury Model provided Lionel with the engineer cap to be

Mercury Model's no. 19583 was the only source of the rare no. 251-25 Steam Locomotive Without Smoke. Shown is the early version of the 19583 with the 251-25 and no. 19583-16 Engineer Cap (marked "Engineer") provided by Mercury to Lionel. Later versions (not shown) of the 19583 are most often observed with a cap marked "Lionel Engineer".

included in this outfit. Lionel listed this cap as a no. 19583-16 Engineer Cap on the early version of the 19583 Factory Order. Based on observations, we think that the caps supplied by Mercury were marked "Engineer" in yellow paint. The later version of the 19583 stated that Lionel was to supply the cap. Based on observations, these were marked "Lionel Engineer". In either case, there is no price or rarity difference for each cap.

The proper version of the no. 19333-10 Instruction Sheet was dated 9/66. It was slightly different and far more difficult to find than the one dated 6/64.

The no. 64-164 White RSC with Orange Graphics outfit box was manufactured by United Container Co. and measured 12⅛ x 11⅝ x 6½ inches. It included four lines of data, a "66" and seven stars as part of the box manufacturer's certificate. Printed on the bottom was a reference to the N.M.F.C. A no. 19583-15 Printed Label was glued on the outfit box end. This detailed all the contents and provided a picture of the outfit.

The early version of the 19583 is a highly desirable collectible because it is the only source of the rare 251-25 and the 1966 version of the 19333-10. Empty boxes are fairly easy to obtain and achieve an R5 rarity, but complete early versions of this outfit are an R8. Even though only 240 units of the later version were made, they did not contain a 251-25 and so earn only an R5 rating.

CONVENTIONAL PACK
64-164 BOX

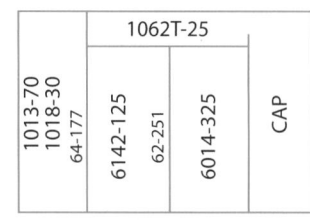

TOP LAYER

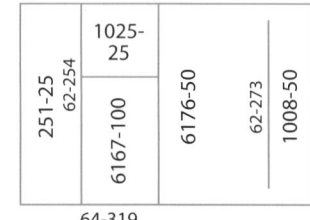

BOTTOM LAYER

64-319

Description: "O27" Promotional Outfit
Specification: "O27" Steam Type Freight Outfit
Customer/Price: G. C. Murphy; $19.99
Original Amount: 600
Factory Order Date: 8/15/1966
Date Issued: 8-15-66
Date Req'd: 8-29-66
Packaging: Display Pack (Units not Boxed)

Contents: 237-25 Steam Type Locomotive with Smoke; 242T-25 Tender; 6822-50 Searchlight Car; 6142-100 Gondola Car; 6112-88 Canister (2); 6176-50 Hopper Car; 6167-100 Caboose; 1013-70

Curved Track (Bundle of 12 - 1013); 1018-7 Straight Track (Bundle of 7 - 1018); 1020-25 90° Crossing; 6149-25 Remote Control Track; 1025-25 45-Watt Transformer; 1103-50 Envelope Packed; 909-20 Smoke Fluid; 19223-10 Instruction Sheet; 1-166 Warranty Card; 926-66 Service Station List; Form 3063 Parts Order Form

Boxes & Packing: 65-270 Box Top; 19586-15 Printed Label; 64-115 Box Bottom; 64-118 Corr. Insert; 64-119 Corr. Insert; 64-120 Corr. Insert; 64-116 Shipper for 4 (1-4); 64-117 Shipper Pad (2-4); MT Mylar Tape (6")

19586 (1966)	C6	C7	C8	Rarity
Complete Outfit	400	575	775	R8
Outfit Box no. 65-270	250	350	450	R8

The no. 19586 was retailer G. C. Murphy's only promotional outfit purchase after 1960. It featured the nos. 237-25 Steam Type Locomotive with Smoke and 6822-50 Searchlight Car plus a figure-eight layout. Note the lack of an outfit number on the box ends. The number was printed on the no. 19586-15 Printed Label.

No. 19586 FREIGHT
EXCITING G. C. MURPHY EXCLUSIVE BY LIONEL

STEAM TYPE LOCOMOTIVE PUFFS SMOKE,
HAS HEADLIGHT, INCLUDES TENDER, ILLUMINATED SEARCHLIGHT CAR, GONDOLA CAR WITH LOAD OF CANISTERS, HOPPER CAR AND CABOOSE.

EXTRA LARGE "027" FIGURE - "8" LAYOUT
REMOTE CONTROL TRACK AND CONTROLLER, 7 SECTIONS OF STRAIGHT AND 12 SECTIONS OF CURVED TRACK, 90° CROSSING TRACK.

45W HEAVY-DUTY SAFETY TRANSFORMER
Ⓤ LISTED, WITH BUILT-IN CIRCUIT BREAKER, 45 WATTS.

Set includes instructions, wire, lockon, warranty, and extra smoke fluid.
Made in the U. S. of America.
THE LEADER IN LIONEL MODEL RAILROADING

A no. 19586-15 Printed Label was affixed to every no. 19586. The practice of pictorially identifying an outfit's contents on the box was long overdue.

later version with narrow running boards came in this outfit.

All the rolling stock in this outfit, including the one operating car, consisted of carryover items. That model, a no. 6822-50 Searchlight Car, was the only item of note in this outfit. During the course of that year, Lionel finished removing the new date, a built date and number data from the heat-stamping of the black no. 6176-50 Hopper Car. This minimal decoration became the norm for the 6176-50.

The cars in the 19586 followed the normal truck and coupler progression for 1966, with each having late AAR types. All but one were equipped with one operating and one non-operating truck and coupler. The no. 242T-25 Tender had one non-operating and one plain type.

The proper version of the no. 19223-10 Instruction Sheet was dated 6/66.

The no. 65-270 White Lift-Off with Full-Color 2037 Steam Freight Graphics Type D display outfit box was manufactured by Mead Containers and measured 24½ x 15½ x 3⅛ inches. A no. 19586-15 Printed Label was glued on the outfit box top. This detailed all the contents and provided a picture of the outfit. It was the only indication of the outfit number because the number was not stamped anywhere else on the box.

Even though the 19586 was produced in above-average quantities, examples in any condition are seldom seen. Finding an outfit in C6 or better condition is quite difficult.

DISPLAY PACK
65-270 BOX

	237-25	242T-25	
6112-88	6176-50	6167-100	909-20 / 6112-88
6142-100		6149-25 / 1013-70	
6822-50	1025-25	1018-7	

Comments: The no. 19586 was the second and final instance of retailer G. C. Murphy appearing on a Factory Order. Its previous purchase was the no. X-524NA from 1960. G. C. Murphy paid Lionel $13.88 for each no. 19586, a Retailer Promotional Type Ia outfit.

The 19586 was led by a no. 237-25 Steam Type Locomotive with Smoke. This Scout steamer featured a two-position reversing unit and a headlight and used a rubber tire as a traction aid. The

The no. 19589 marked S. Klein's first Retailer Promotional outfit purchase since its no. 19273 in 1963. The contents of the 19589 duplicated those of outfit no. 11570, with the addition of a no. 6076-75 Hopper Car - Black. Note the S. Klein price tag still attached to the box; it listed a price of $11.88.

Comments: S. Klein was a discount retailer that purchased numerous promotional Lionel outfits in the 1960s. In 1966, it purchased Retailer Promotional Type Ib outfit no. 19589. This outfit was identical to the no. 11570, except that it came with one more item, a no. 6076-75 Hopper Car - Black.

The 19589 was led by a no. 1061-75 Steam Type Locomotive (new for 1966). This low-end Scout steamer featured a 2-4-2 wheel arrangement and a rubber tire as a traction aid. It went forward only and lacked a headlight and lens. Except for its wheel arrangement, the 1061-75 was identical to the no. 1061-50 Steam Type Loco W/Tire.

The rolling stock consisted of carryover items, with all but two of the cars being unmarked. The no. 1062T-25 Tender came stamped with "Lionel Lines". Also, during the course of that year, Lionel finished removing the new date, a built date and number data from the heat-stamping of the 6076-75 Hopper Car - Black. This minimal decoration became the norm for the 6076-75. Even though this model lacked the new date, a built date and number data, it was designated a 6076-75 because it came with non-operating trucks and couplers. Finally, the no. 6042-250 Gondola Car has been observed in light and dark shades of blue plastic.

The rolling stock in the 19589 followed the normal truck and coupler progression for 1966, with each of the cars having late AAR types. All but one were equipped with non-operating trucks and couplers. The 1062T-25 had one non-operating and one plain type. For many cabooses in 1966, including the no. 6167-25 Caboose in this outfit, Lionel replaced the plain truck with a non-operating one.

The no. 11570-10 Instruction Sheet was dated 2/66.

The no. 64-162 White RSC with Orange Graphics outfit box was manufactured by United Container Co. and measured 11⅜ x 9¾ x 6⅛ inches. It included four lines of data, a "66" and eight stars as part of the box manufacturer's certificate. Printed on the bottom were "64-162" and a reference to the N.M.F.C.

The 19589 is difficult to find, but it attracts little collector interest because it included low-end and common components. Even so, it is more desirable than its 11570 counterpart.

Description: "O27" Promotional Outfit
Specification: "O27" Steam Type Freight Outfit
Customer/No./Price: S. Klein; 12 T; $11.88
Original Amount: 1,200
Factory Order Date: 9/19/1966
Date Issued: 9-20-66
Date Req'd: 9-20-66
Packaging: WRSC

Contents: 1061-75 Steam Type Locomotive; 1062T-25 Tender; 6042-250 Gondola Car; 6112-88 Canister (2); 6402-25 Flat Car W/2 Cable Reels; 40-11 Cable Reels (2); 6076-75 Hopper Car - Black; 6167-25 Caboose; 1013-8 Curved Track (Bundle of 8 - 1013); 1018-10 Straight Track (Loose) (2); 1025-25 45-Watt Transformer; 1103-20 Envelope Packed; 11570-10 Instruction Sheet; 1-166 Warranty Card; 926-66 Service Station List; Form 3063 Parts Order Form

Boxes & Packing: 64-162 Outfit Box; 62-254 Corr. Insert; 61-173 Corr. Insert; 64-319 Corr. Insert; 63-384 Shipper for 4 (1-4); 64-106 Shipper Pad (2-4)

19589 (1966)	C6	C7	C8	Rarity
Complete Outfit	175	275	415	R7
Outfit Box no. 64-162	100	150	225	R7

Description: "O27" Promotional Outfit
Specification: "O27" Steam Type Freight Outfit
Customer: Polk
Original Amount: 500

Factory Order Date: 8/17/1966
Date Issued: Rev 8-22-66
Date Req'd: 8-22-66
Packaging: RSC (Units Boxed)

Contents: 239-1 Steam Locomotive With Smoke; 242T-1 Tender; 6464-650 "Denver & Rio Grande" Box Car; 6464-700

The no. 19590 was the sole Retailer Promotional outfit purchased by Polk Model Craft Hobbies in 1966. It represented the only instance in the 1960s when Lionel placed three no. 6464-series box cars in the same outfit. The rare boxes used for the nos. 239-1 Steam Locomotive With Smoke and 242T-1 Tender were unique to this outfit. The 242T-1 came in a no. 6429-10 Folding Box (shown) with a label marked "No 242T Tender" (not shown). These features make the 19590 a highly desirable outfit.

"Santa Fe" Box Car; 6464-250 "Western Pacific" Box Car; 6517-75 Bay Window Caboose - Illuminated; 1013-8 Curved Track (Bundle of 8 - 1013); 1018-5 Straight Track (Bundle of 5 - 1018); 6149-25 Remote Control Track; 1025-1 45-Watt Transformer; 1103-50 Envelope Packed; 11450-10 Instruction Sheet

Boxes & Packing: 66-138 Outfit Box; 1013-59 Corrugated Insert; 64-143 Corr. Insert (2); 64-167 Shipper 4 (1-4); 64-114 Shipper Pad (2-4); BP Bogus Paper

19590 (1966)	C6	C7	C8	Rarity
Complete Outfit	1,350	1,935	2,600	R10
Outfit Box no. 66-138	350	500	600	R9

Comments: In 1966, longtime Lionel customer Polk Model Craft Hobbies purchased Retailer Promotional Type Ic outfit no. 19590. This outfit stands out as a collector's treasure because it was one of the few promotional outfits from 1966 that boasted all boxed items. It was also the only outfit from the 1960s to include three no. 6464-series box cars.

The 19590 was led by a no. 239-1 Steam Locomotive With Smoke. This die-cast Scout steamer featured a two-position reversing unit, a headlight and a rubber tire as a traction aid. Except for its 239 number and lack of stripe, it was the same engine as a no. 241. What makes the 239-1 included in the 19590 interesting was that Lionel ran out of no. 239-12 Corr. Boxes, so it used an overstamped no. 2029-6 Corr. Box. Inside each box were the nos. TP-35 Tissue Paper, 1-165 Warranty Card, 237-11 Instruction Sheet and 909-20 Smoke Fluid.

The no. 242T-1 Tender was the only example of a 242T-25 appearing in a box. A memorandum attached to the Factory Order instructed the Outfit Packing Department to use a no. 6429-10 Folding Box (originally used for the no. 6429-1 Wrecking Car) and attach two labels with "No 242T Tender". The Hillside Orange Picture no. 6429-10 Folding Box is rare on its own, the overstickered version even more so.

The 19590 came with three 6464-series box cars that, according to their Production Control Files, were reinstated on 2/3/66. In reality, the orange no. 6464-250 Western Pacific Box Car was previously stamped "6464100" in 1954 and had its decoration updated for 1966. It was now stamped "6464250". In 1966, the cars generally used a Type IV body. All three box cars came packaged in Cellophane Window Boxes.

In 1966, Lionel originally reinstated the no. 6517-1 Bay Window Caboose - Illuminated. This was the caboose shown in the 1966 consumer catalog. Lionel subsequently changed direction and issued the no. 6517-75 Bay Window Caboose - Illuminated (new for 1966). This difficult-to-find car was stamped "Erie" and "C301" and equipped with no. 2400-series operating trucks and couplers. The 6517-75 came in a Cellophane Window box.

With the exception of the caboose, the rolling stock in the 19590 followed the normal truck and coupler progression for 1966, with each of the cars having late AAR types. All but one were equipped with operating trucks and couplers. The 242T-1 had one non-operating and one plain type.

The no. 1025-1 45-Watt Transformer came in a no. 12-142 Corrugated Box.

The no. 66-138 Tan RSC with Black Graphics outfit box was manufactured by Eastern Corrugated Container Corp. and measured 15¼ x 10⅝ x 7 inches. These boxes were made of a thicker corrugated material (rated at 90 pounds rather than the normal 65 pounds gross weight) that allowed each outfit to be shipped in its outfit box. It included four lines of data as part of its box manufacturer's certificate. This box was used for only two outfits, the 19590 and the no. 19511.

As with many outfits containing desirable individual items, the 19590 was most often split up and the contents sold.

The outfit box for the 19590 is difficult to find. Even more so is finding the proper boxes for the 239-1 and 242T-1. As such, the outfit box rates an R9; however, a complete outfit with correct boxes is an R10.

Now that the Factory Orders have validated the contents of this outfit, advanced collectors will seek to acquire one.

CONVENTIONAL PACK
66-138 BOX

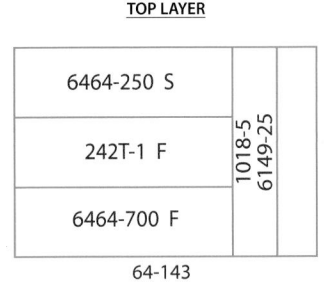

TOP LAYER

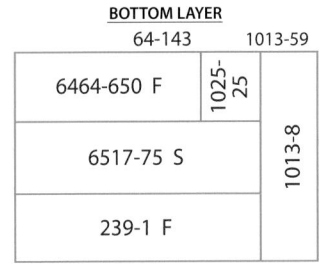

BOTTOM LAYER

The no. 19701 (Sears no. 49 N 9723) was Sears' low-end steam-powered offering for 1967. Even though it appeared for $18.44 in the Sears Christmas Catalog, this example included a price tag (not shown) with a $19.99 price. As with all 1967 outfits, this one was assembled from leftover inventory.

Through an error, the locomotive in the outfit, 49N9723, $18.44, was not equipped with a headlight as shown in the catalog illustration.

We are reducing the price $1.00 and trust you are satisfied with this merchandise.

This flyer accompanied the no. 19701 and explains the price reduction of the outfit caused by an error in the Sears catalog. Lionel had provided the incorrect description to Sears, which then published it. The text and illustration in the Sears catalog showed the no. 1061-75 Steam Type Locomotive as having a headlight.

Description: "O27" Promotional Outfit
Specification: 6 Unit "O27" Steam Freight
Customer/No./Price: Sears, Roebuck and Co.; 49 N 9723; $18.44
Original Amount: 11,793
Factory Order Date: 2/10/1967
Packaging: R.S.C. Outfit Packing

Contents: 1061-75 Steam Type Locomotive; 1062T-25 Tender; 6402-25 Flat Car W/3 Logs; 3364-8 Logs (3); 6042-250 Gondola Car; 40-11 Cable Reels (2); 6076-75 Hopper Car - Black; 6167-25 Caboose; 1013 Curved Track (8); 1018 Straight Track (2); 1025-25 45-Watt Transformer; 1103-20 Envelope Packed; 11570-10 Instruction Sheet; 1-165 Warranty Card; 926-66 Service Station List; Form 3063 Parts Order Form; 1-117 Accessory Catalog

Boxes & Packing: 64-162 Outfit Box; 61-172 Corr. Insert; 62-254 Corr. Insert; 64-319 Corr. Insert; 64-106 Corr. Pad (2-4); 63-384 Shipper For 4 (1-4)

19701 (1967)	C6	C7	C8	Rarity
Complete Outfit	85	155	235	R4
Outfit Box no. 64-162	10	20	35	R4

Comments: Although no new trains were cataloged in 1967 (Lionel reused the 1966 catalog), Lionel was still assembling catalog and promotional outfits from leftover inventory. Longtime Lionel customer Sears purchased four Retailer Promotional outfits in 1967: nos. 19701, 19703, 19705 and 19706.

The 19701, a Type Ib for which Sears paid $8.00 each, appeared on page 523 of the 1967 Sears Christmas Catalog as no. 49 N 9723 for $18.44.

This outfit was Sears' low-end steam-powered offering for 1967. Except for the flat car and gondola loads, it was identical to promotional outfit no. 19589 from 1966.

Both outfits were led by a no. 1061-75 Steam Type Locomotive. This low-end Scout steamer featured a 2-4-2 wheel arrangement and a rubber tire as a traction aid. It went forward only and lacked a headlight and lens. Other than its wheel arrangement, the 1061-75 was identical to the no. 1061-50 Steam Type Loco W/Tire.

Because there were no new trains in 1967, all the rolling stock in this outfit consisted of carryover models. They were, with two exceptions, completely unmarked. The no. 1062T-25 Tender was stamped with "Lionel Lines", and the no. 6076-75 Hopper Car - Black had Lehigh Valley markings though the new date, a built date and number data had been removed from its heat-stamping.

The rolling stock in the 19701 followed the normal truck and coupler progression for 1967, with each of the cars having late AAR types. All but one of them, including the no. 6167-25 Caboose, were equipped with non-operating trucks and couplers. The 1062T-25 had one non-operating and one plain type.

The no. 11570-10 Instruction Sheet was dated 2/66.

The no. 64-162 White RSC with Orange Graphics outfit box was manufactured by United Container Co. and measured 11⅜ x 9¾ x 6⅛ inches. It included four lines of data and has been observed with an "8-66" as part of the box manufacturer's certificate. Printed on the bottom were "64-162" and a reference to the N.M.F.C.

The 19701 was produced in large numbers, but examples do not often appear. Even with its Sears origin, this outfit attracts only minimal interest.

Description: "O27" Promotional Outfit
Original Amount: 1,964

Boxes & Packing: 61-170 Outfit Box; 65-415 Outfit Box; 65-428 Insert; 62-254 Corr. Insert; 62-264 Corr. Insert; 61-172 Corr. Insert; 62-223 Corrugated Insert; 61-175 Corr. Shipper for 4 (1-4)

Comments: In 1967, Lionel Production Control Files specified

that 1,964 boxes were used for outfit no. 19702. A no. 61-170 Tan RSC with Black Graphics outfit box was used for 1,320 units and a no. 65-415 Tan RSC with Black Graphics outfit box for 644 units. Neither box has thus far been observed, however, and documentation of the outfit's contents has not surfaced. Therefore, outfit pricing is unavailable. This listing is provided for historical reference because we believe this outfit was manufactured, but to date it has eluded the collecting community.

This no. 19703 (Sears no. 49 N 9724) was acquired from the original owner and is shown as it came from Sears. Note the no. 6825-25 Flat Car equipped with early operating AAR trucks and couplers that date it from 1959 or the early 1960s. Also note the Type III no. 6050-100 Swift Savings Bank Car with one non-operating Archbar and one operating AAR truck and coupler, circa 1963. These two cars were among the many being depleted in the outfits from 1967. The flyer that Sears provided explained the lack of remote-control uncoupling and the $2.50 price reduction.

Description: "O27" Promotional Outfit
Specification: 5 Unit "O27" Diesel Freight
Cust./No./Price: Sears, Roebuck and Co.; 49 N 9724; $22.50
Original Amount: 3,831
Factory Order Date: 2/10/1967
Packaging: R.S.C. Outfit Packing

Contents: 635-25 "Union Pacific" Diesel Switcher; 6050-100 Swift Savings Bank Car; 6176-50 Hopper Car; 6408-50 Flat Car W/Cable Reels; 40-11 Cable Reels (2); 6130-25 Work Caboose - "Santa Fe"; 1013-8 Curved Track (Bundle of 8 - 1013); 1018 Straight Track; 1008-50 Uncoupling Unit; 1025-25 45-Watt Transformer; 1103-20 Envelope Packed; 926-66 Service Station List; 11530-10 Instruction Sheet; 1-165 Warranty Card

Boxes & Packing: 65-411 Outfit Box; 65-413 Insert; 600-26 Insert (2); 65-428 Insert; 64-177 Insert; 62-254 Insert; 64-106 Corr. Pad (2-4); 65-412 Shipper for 4 (1-4)

19703 (1967)	C6	C7	C8	Rarity
Complete Outfit	170	300	500	R5
Outfit Box no. 65-411	25	75	125	R5

Comments: Although no new trains were cataloged in 1967 (Lionel reused the 1966 catalog), Lionel was still assembling catalog and promotional outfits from leftover inventory. Longtime Lionel customer Sears purchased four Retailer Promotional outfits in 1967: nos. 19701, 19703, 19705 and 19706.

The 19703, a Type Ib for which Sears paid $11.25 each, appeared on page 523 of the 1967 Sears Christmas Catalog as no. 49 N 9724 for $22.50.

This outfit was Sears' low-end diesel-powered offering for 1967. It was led by a no. 635-25 Union Pacific Diesel Switcher. Included in promotional outfits only, this locomotive featured a two-position reversing unit, a headlight, a weight and a rubber tire as a traction aid.

Because there were no new trains in 1967, all the rolling

stock in this outfit consisted of carryover models. Since leftover inventory was being used, Lionel was freely substituting different variations of most of the cars included in this outfit.

One example of Lionel's loose approach with the 19703 was the Lehigh Valley hopper car. Some outfits have been observed with a black no. 6176-50 Hopper Car that lacked the new date, a built date and number data from its heat-stamping. Other outfits have been observed with a gray no. 6176-75 that had "BUILT 1-48" and "LIONEL 6076" data. Even though this latter model was stamped "6076", it still was considered a 6176 because it had an operating truck and coupler. In fact, both hopper cars always came with one operating and one non-operating AAR truck and coupler.

A second example was the 6408-50 Flat Car W/Cable Reels in the 19703. This car, according to its Production Control File, was a red no. 6511-series model with "Lionel" stamped on each side, a brake wheel installed and one operating and one non-operating AAR truck and coupler. Some outfits have been observed with a 6408-50 that fit that description. Others have been seen with a 6408-50 equipped with one operating AAR type and one non-operating Archbar type.

But this mix is just the beginning. Other examples of the 19703 have been observed with cars stamped "6825" and equipped with early operating AAR trucks and couplers. Still others have unstamped flat cars whose frames featured holes for truck-mounting plates and came with one operating AAR truck and coupler and one non-operating Archbar type. Even a red flat car with two automobiles has been reported.

Finally, the no. 6130-25 Santa Fe Work Caboose also came with an odd mix of features. All of the models observed had slats below the Santa Fe herald and lacked a builder's plate. Some had a black frame without "Lionel", and others had "Lionel" stamped in sans-serif lettering. One interesting example included an unpainted gray tray that was heat-stamped with "6130". Each of these different cabooses was equipped with AAR trucks and couplers – either one operating and one plain type or one operating and one non-operating type.

The no. 6050-100 Swift Savings Bank Car used a Type III body. As for trucks and couplers, it always had at least one operating AAR type. On some models, the second one was a non-operating

Archbar type; on others, it was a second operating AAR type.

With all these variations, it appears that anything was possible, a circumstance that further supports the idea that Lionel was depleting existing inventory and probably assembling cars out of parts in its inventory. The different variations surely are interesting to collectors, but only the version of the 6130-25 with a gray tray (stamped "6130") really affects the price of this outfit.

As with the 19701, Lionel made a mistake when describing the 19703's contents to Sears. It stated that the 19703 had "Remote control uncoupling", but the outfit included a manual no. 1008-50 Uncoupling Unit. This error required Sears to include a flyer indicating that the description in its catalog was incorrect and offering a $2.50 price reduction.

The no. 11530-10 Instruction Sheet was dated 6/65. It also incorrectly stated that this outfit came with a remote-control uncoupling track section.

The no. 65-411 Tan RSC with Black Graphics outfit box was manufactured by Gem-Bilt Container Corp. and measured 13¼ x 11¼ x 6¼ inches. It included four lines of data as part of its box manufacturer's certificate as well as a reference to the N.M.F.C. Be aware that the stamping on some outfits was carelessly applied and appears to be stamped "19733" instead of "19703".

The 19703 was produced in smaller numbers than the 19701, but it seems to appear more often. Many combinations of rolling stock are possible. Therefore, to ensure that an outfit is just the way it was when it left the Lionel factory, anyone contemplating buying one should be sure of its provenance.

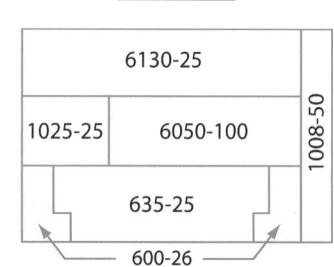

CONVENTIONAL PACK
65-411 BOX

| TOP LAYER | BOTTOM LAYER |

Description: "O27" Promotional Outfit
Specification: "O27" Steam Type Freight Outfit
Original Amount: 8,421
Packaging: W.R.S.C. Outfit Packing

Contents: 1062-75 Steam Type Loco. W/Light & Reversing Unit; 1062T-25 Tender; 6176-75 Hopper Car; 6401-25 Flat Car; 3364-8 Logs (3); 6167-100 Caboose; 1013-8 Curved Track (Bundle of 8 - 1013); 1018-10 Straight Track (Loose); 1008-50 Uncoupling Unit; 1025-25 45-Watt Transformer; 1103-20 Envelope Packed; 1-165 Warranty Card; 926-66 Service Station List; Form 3063 Parts Order Form; 1-117 Accessory Catalog; 11580-15 Instruction Sheet; 1-165 Warranty Card

Boxes & Packing: 64-162 Outfit Box; 62-254 Insert; 64-319 Insert; 61-173 Corr. Insert; 64-106 Corr. Pad (2-4); 63-384 Shipper For 4 (1-4)

19704 (1967)	C6	C7	C8	Rarity
Complete Outfit	100	175	270	R4
Outfit Box no. 64-162	25	50	75	R4

Comments: Although no new trains were cataloged in 1967 (Lionel reused the 1966 catalog), Lionel was still assembling catalog and promotional outfits from leftover inventory. The no. 19704 was a General Release Promotional Type IIb outfit that has yet to be linked to a retailer.

The 19704 was, with one exception, identical to promotional outfit no. 11580 from 1966 - the former had a yellow hopper instead of a black one. Each outfit was led by a no. 1062-75 Steam Type Loco. W/Light & Reversing Unit. This low-end Scout steamer featured a 2-4-2 wheel arrangement and a rubber tire as a traction

Outfit no. 19704 was one of the three General Release Promotional outfits issued by Lionel in 1967. It was nearly identical to promotional outfit no. 11580 from 1966, except the 19704 included a yellow hopper car instead of a black one. The 19704 was likely assembled from the excess inventory created when Lionel reduced the forecast of the 11580 from 50,000 units to 18,000 units.

aid. Except for its wheel arrangement, the 1062-75 was identical to the no. 1062-50 Steam Type Loco. W/Light & Reversing Unit.

Because there were no new trains in 1967, all the rolling stock in this outfit consisted of carryover models. The yellow no. 6176-75 Hopper Car observed in examples of the 19704 always omitted the "NEW 1-48" from its heat-stamping and might or might not have a built date and number data. As with the 11580 the no. 6401-25 Flat Car came with three no. 3364-8 Logs.

The rolling stock in the 19704 followed the normal truck and coupler progression for 1967, with all the cars having late AAR types. All but one of them, including the no. 6167-100 Caboose, were equipped with one operating and one non-operating truck

and coupler. The no. 1062T-25 Tender had one non-operating and one plain type.

The no. 11580-15 Instruction Sheet was dated 5/66.

The no. 64-162 White RSC with Orange Graphics outfit box was manufactured by United Container Co. and measured 11⅜ x 9¾ x 6⅛ inches. It included four lines of data and has been observed with a "66" and seven stars as part of the box manufacturer's certificate. Printed on the bottom were "64-162" and a reference to the N.M.F.C.

The 19704 frequently appears and attracts minimal interest from collectors. Its only feature of note is that it's one of the few outfits from 1967.

Description: "O27" Promotional Outfit
Specification: 7 Unit "O27" Steam Type Freight
Cust./No./Price: Sears, Roebuck and Co.; T49 C9733; $19.99
Original Amount: 9,541
Factory Order Date: 2/10/1967
Packaging: R.S.C. Outfit Packing

19705 (1967)	C6	C7	C8	Rarity
Complete Outfit	150	240	375	R4
Outfit Box no. 65-411	35	50	75	R4

Contents: 242-25 Steam Type Locomotive; 1062T-25 Tender; 6176-50 Hopper Car; 6142-150 Gondola Car; 6050-100 Swift Savings Bank Car; 3364-25 Log Dump Car; 3364-8 Logs (3); 6167-100 Caboose; 1013-8 Curved Track (Bundle of 8 - 1013); 1018-5 Straight Track (Bundle of 5 - 1018); 6149-25 Remote Control Track; 1025-25 45-Watt Transformer; 1103-40 Envelope Packed; 11450-10 Instruction Sheet; 1-165 Warranty Card; 3364-10 Instruction Sheet; 926-66 Service Station List; 1-117 Accessory Catalog; Form 3063 Parts Order Form

Boxes & Packing: 65-411 Outfit Box; 65-413 Insert; 62-254 Insert; 62-248 Insert (3); 64-177 Insert (2); 64-106 Corr. Pad (2-4); 65-412 Shipper for 4 (1-4)

Comments: Although no new trains were cataloged in 1967 (Lionel reused the 1966 catalog), Lionel was still assembling catalog and promotional outfits from leftover inventory. Longtime Lionel customer Sears purchased four Retailer Promotional outfits in 1967: nos. 19701, 19703, 19705 and 19706.

The 19705, a Type Ia for which Sears paid $11.85 each, appeared on page 40 of a 1967 Sears promotional mailer as no. T49 C9733 for $19.99.

The 19705 was Sears' high-end steam-powered offering for 1967. It was led by a no. 242-25 Steam Type Locomotive. This low-end Scout steamer featured a two-position reversing unit and a headlight, lacked smoke and used a rubber tire as a traction aid. The later version with narrow running boards was included in this outfit.

The no. 19705 (Sears no. T49 C9733) was Sears' high-end steam-powered offering for 1967. This example came from its original owner and included a sales receipt (not shown) for $19.99 that was dated October 30, 1967. It was shipped in its outfit box and still has the shipping label on its top.

Because there were no new trains in 1967, all the rolling stock in this outfit consisted of carryover models. The most notable item here was the no. 3364-25 Log Dump Car, which was identical to the no. 3362-25 Helium Tank Unloading Car except that it carried logs instead of helium tanks. The black no. 6176-50 Hopper Car omitted the new date, a built date and number data from its heat-stamping. The no. 6050-100 Swift Savings Bank Car used a Type III body.

The rolling stock in the 19705 followed the normal truck and coupler progression for 1967, with each of the cars having late AAR types. All but one of them, including the no. 6167-100 Caboose, were equipped with one operating and one non-operating truck and coupler. The no. 1062T-25 Tender had one non-operating and one plain type. Many cars had a washer riveted as part of their leaf spring assembly.

The no. 11450-10 Instruction Sheet was dated 6/65.

The no. 65-411 Tan RSC with Black Graphics outfit box was manufactured by Gem-Bilt Container Corp. and measured 13¼ x

11¼ x 6¼ inches. It included four lines of data as part of its box manufacturer's certificate as well as a reference to the N.M.F.C.

Even though 9,541 units of the 19705 were produced, one does not appear too often. This outfit attracts interest from collectors for two key reasons: It was a Sears outfit, and it came from 1967. Advanced collectors will be challenged to find the 1967 Sears promotional mailer that publicized the 19705.

CONVENTIONAL PACK
65-411 BOX

TOP LAYER						BOTTOM LAYER		
6176-50	1062T-25	6142-150	3364-25	6050-100	1018-5	1013-8 6149-25		
						1025-25	6167-100	
						242-25		

Description: "O27" Promotional Outfit
Specification: 6 Unit "O27" Diesel Freight
Customer/No./Price: Sears, Roebuck and Co.; 9732; $32.99
Original Amount: 2,343
Factory Order Date: 2/10/1967
Packaging: R.S.C. Outfit Packing

Contents: 215P-25 "Santa Fe" Diesel Power Car; 212T-25 "Santa Fe" "A" Unit; 6473-25 Rodeo Car; 6176-50 Hopper Car; 6465-150 Tank Car; 6059-50 Caboose; 1013-70 Curved Track (Bundle of

12 - 1013); 1018-30 Straight Track (Bundle of 3 - 1018); 6149-25 Remote Control Track; 1020-25 90° Crossing; 1025-25 45-Watt Transformer; 1103-40 Envelope Packed; 926-66 Service Station List; 19214-10 Instruction Sheet; 211-151 Instruction Sheet; Form 3063 Parts Order Form; 1-165 Warranty Card; 1-117 Accessory Catalog

Boxes & Packing: 65-411 Outfit Box; 65-413 Insert; 64-177 Insert (2); 62-224 Corrugated Insert; 62-245 Corr. Insert (2); 62-254 Corr. Insert; 62-248 Corr. Insert; 64-106 Corr. Pad (2-4); 65-412 Shipper for 4 (1-4)

The no. 19706 (Sears no. 9732) was Sears' high-end diesel-powered offering for 1967. It marked the last appearance of the nos. 215P-25 Santa Fe Diesel Power Car and 212T-25 Santa Fe "A" Unit. This example included remnants of a Sears price tag with no. 9732 for $32.99. The 19706 was the last Retailer Promotional outfit purchased by Sears in the postwar era.

19706 (1967)	C6	C7	C8	Rarity
Complete Outfit	265	410	625	R6
Outfit Box no. 65-411	75	125	175	R6

Comments: Although no new trains were cataloged in 1967 (Lionel reused the 1966 catalog), Lionel was still assembling catalog and promotional outfits from leftover inventory. Longtime Lionel customer Sears purchased four Retailer Promotional outfits in 1967: nos. 19701, 19703, 19705 and 19706.

The 19706, a Type Ib for which Sears paid $16.00 each, has yet to be observed in a Sears catalog. One has been observed with a Sears price tag as no. 9732 for $32.99.

The 19706 was Sears' high-end diesel-powered offering for 1967. It was led by a no. 215P-25 Santa Fe Diesel Power Car. This promotional-only Alco featured a two-position reversing unit, two traction tires, a headlight, a weight and an open pilot with a large ledge. It was paired with a no. 212T-25 Santa Fe "A" Unit. The 212T-25 had "BLT 8-57" stamped on its body, and the 215P-25 had "BLT" stamped on its body. This outfit marked the last appearance of the 212T-25 and 215P-25.

Because there were no new trains in 1967, all the rolling stock

in this outfit consisted of carryover models. The most notable item was the no. 6473-25 Rodeo Car. It used a Type IIIa body (cadmium yellow plastic with red lettering), which no longer exhibited the filled slot caused by broken tooling. The black no. 6176-50 Hopper Car omitted the new date, a built date and number data from its heat-stamping.

The rolling stock in the 19706 followed the normal truck and coupler progression for 1967, with each of the cars having late AAR types. All were equipped with one operating and one non-operating truck and coupler. Some cars had a washer riveted as part of their leaf spring assembly.

The no. 19214-10 Instruction Sheet was dated 6/66.

The no. 65-411 Tan RSC with Black Graphics outfit box was manufactured by Gem-Bilt Container Corp. and measured 13¼ x 11¼ x 6¼ inches. It included four lines of data as part of its box manufacturer's certificate as well as a reference to the N.M.F.C.

Of the four Sears outfits for 1967, the 19706 was produced in the smallest quantities and is the most difficult to find. It also featured the most desirable contents. Therefore, this is the most highly sought of the Sears outfits for 1967.

Description: "O27" Promotional Outfit
Specification: "O27" Steam Type Freight Outfit
Customer/No./Price: Arlan's Department Stores; -66; $19.99
Cust./No./Price: Children's Bargain Town USA; 19707; $27.97
Customer/No.: McKelvey's; E 350
Customer/No./Price: Titche's; 19707; $30.00
Original Amount: 3,548
Packaging: R.S.C. Outfit Packing

Contents: 241-25 Steam Type Locomotive with Smoke; 242T-25 Tender; 6176-75 Hopper Car; 6465-150 Tank Car; 6050-100 Swift Savings Bank Car; 6401-25 Flat Car; 3364-8 Logs (3); 6059-50 Caboose; 1013-70 Curved Track (Bundle of 12 - 1013); 1018-30 Straight Track (Bundle of 3 - 1018); 6149-25 Remote Control Track; 1020-25 90° Crossing; 1025-25 45-Watt Transformer; 1103-40 Envelope Packed; 909-

Outfit no. 19707 was one of the three General Release Promotional outfits issued by Lionel in 1967. This example featured a label mistakenly affixed upside down to the box side and detailing the outfit's contents and number. The 19707 was the last promotional outfit issued in 1967.

20 Smoke Fluid; 237-11 Instruction Sheet; 1-165 Warranty Card; 1802-10 Instruction Sheet; 926-66 Service Station List; 11450-10 Instruction Sheet; Form 3063 Parts Order Form

Boxes & Packing: 65-411 Box; 65-413 Insert; 62-254 Insert; 65-428 Insert; 64-177 Insert; 64-106 Corr. Pad (2-4); 65-412 Shipper for 4 (1-4)

19707 (1967)	C6	C7	C8	Rarity
Complete Outfit	210	375	525	R5
Outfit Box no. 65-411	40	75	125	R5

Comments: Although no new trains were cataloged in 1967 (Lionel reused the 1966 catalog), Lionel was still assembling catalog and promotional outfits from leftover inventory. The no. 19707 was a General Release Promotional Type IIb outfit that has been linked to Arlan's, Children's Bargain Town USA, McKelvey's and Titche's through price tags. It likely was sold through other retailers as well.

The 19707 was led by a no. 241-25 Steam Type Locomotive with Smoke. This die-cast Scout steamer, which appeared only in promotional outfits, featured a two-position reversing unit, a headlight and a rubber tire as a traction aid. The later version with a wide, white-painted stripe was included in this outfit. Except for its 241 number and stripe, it was the same engine as a no. 239.

Because there were no new trains in 1967, all the rolling stock in this outfit consisted of carryover models. The yellow no. 6176-75 Hopper Car omitted the new date, a built date and number data from its heat-stamping. The no. 6050-100 Swift Savings Bank Car used a Type III body. The no. 6401-25 Flat Car came with three no. 3364-8 Logs.

The rolling stock in the 19707 followed the normal truck and coupler progression for 1967, with all the cars having late AAR types. All but one of them, including the no. 6059-50 Caboose, were equipped with one operating and one non-operating truck

and coupler. The no. 242T-25 Tender had one non-operating and one plain type.

A no. 1802-10 Layout Instruction Sheet detailed the figure-eight track layout. The no. 11450-10 Instruction Sheet was dated 6/65.

The no. 65-411 Tan RSC with Black Graphics outfit box was manufactured by Gem-Bilt Container Corp. and measured 13¼ x 11¼ x 6¼ inches. It included four lines of data as part of its box manufacturer's certificate as well as a reference to the N.M.F.C. Most outfits included a label on the box side that featured a photograph of the outfit as well as a listing of its contents.

A large number of 19707s were produced and distributed to numerous retailers. Many outfits have survived, but finding one in C7 or better condition takes time and effort.

CONVENTIONAL PACK
65-411 BOX

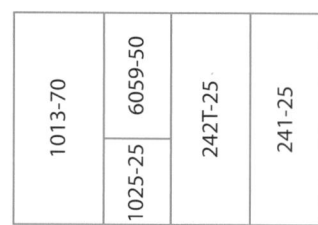

TOP LAYER

	1018-30 6149-25		
6050-100	6465-150	6176-75	6401-25 3364-8 (3)

BOTTOM LAYER

1013-70	6059-50	242T-25	241-25
	1025-25		

In late 1966, Lionel introduced the short-lived no. 19900 series of outfits by issuing the no. 19910. This low-end outfit was assembled with surplus inventory and packaging; consequently, two different outfit boxes (one small and one large) were used. Shown is the larger of the two, the no. 65-270 Box Top version.

Description: "O27" Promotional Outfit
Specification: "O27" Steam Type Freight Outfit
Customer/No./Price: Western Auto; E1002; $14.77
Original Amount: 12,400
Factory Order Date: 11/23/1966
Date Issued: 12-14-66
Date Req'd: 12-14-66
Packaging: Units not Boxed

Contents: 1062-75 Steam Type Loco. W/Light & Reversing Unit; 1062T-25 Tender; 6176-50 Hopper Car; 6142-100 Gondola Car; 6401-25 Flat Car; 6059-50 Caboose; 6112-88 Canister (2); 1013-8 Curved Track (Bundle of 8 - 1013); 1018-10 Straight Track (Loose) (2); 1025-25 45-Watt Transformer; 1103-20 Envelope Packed; Form 3063 Parts Order Form; 1-166 Warranty Card; 926-66 Service Station List; 19500-10 Instruction Sheet

Boxes & Packing: 65-270 Box Top; 64-115 Box Bottom; 64-119 Corr. Insert; 64-120 Corr. Insert; 64-128 Corr. Insert; 64-116 Shipper for 4 (1-4); 64-117 Shipper Pad (2-4); 65-260 Box Top (This Box And Following Packing to be used for 7,400 sets); 64-102 Box Bottom; 65-261 Corr. Insert; 65-262 Corr. Insert; 64-105 Shipper for 4 (1-4); 64-106 Shipper Pad (2-4)

Alternate For Outfit Contents:
Note: 1,000 Sets (only) are to be made less (2) 6112-88 Canisters.

19910 (1966)	C6	C7	C8	Rarity
Complete Outfit With Either Outfit Box	85	145	215	R2
Outfit Box nos. 65-260 Or 65-270	15	25	35	R2

Comments: Near the very end of 1966, Lionel issued two General Release Promotional Type IIb outfits: nos. 19910 and 19920. Along with the no. 19437 from 1966, these were the final outfits created in that year. By the time Lionel released these outfits, its executives realized that sales were substantially below projections. In response, the 19910 and 19920 were assembled to begin the long process of reducing the unsold inventory that had built up. It is unknown why Lionel initiated the no. 19900 series of numbers on these two outfits.

Longtime customer Western Auto was one retailer that purchased the 19910. The outfit appeared in its 1967 Christmas Gifts Catalog and 1967-1968 Fall & Winter and Gift Catalog as no. E1002 for $14.77. Earlier in 1966, Western Auto had purchased the nos. 11520, 19436 and 19530.

The 19910 was led by a no. 1062-75 Steam Type Loco. W/Light & Reversing Unit (new for 1966). This low-end Scout steamer featured a 2-4-2 wheel arrangement and a rubber tire as a traction aid. Except for its wheel arrangement, the 1062-75 was identical to the no. 1062-50 Steam Type Loco. W/Light & Reversing Unit.

The rolling stock in this outfit consisted of carryover items that were commonly used in outfits from 1966. The black no. 6176-50 Hopper Car observed in examples of the 19910 always omitted the "NEW 1-48" from its heat-stamping and might or might not have the "BUILT 1-48" and "LIONEL 6076" data. Despite being stamped "6076", this model still was considered a 6176 because it came with an operating truck and coupler. In 1966, the no. 6112-88 Canisters could be found molded in red plastic.

The rolling stock in this outfit followed the normal truck and coupler progression for 1966, with all the cars having late AAR types. Most were equipped with one operating and one non-operating truck and coupler. However, the no. 1062T-25 Tender had one non-operating and one plain type. In addition, a few outfits came with a no. 6059-50 Caboose that had one operating and one plain type. Many cars had a washer riveted as part of their leaf spring assembly.

The no. 1103-20 Envelope Packed has been observed in a Type III envelope.

Two different outfit boxes were used to pack the 19910. The first and larger of the two was the no. 65-270 White Lift-Off with Full-Color 2037 Steam Freight Graphics Type D display outfit box. It was manufactured by Mead Containers and measured 24½ x 15½ x 3⅛ inches. The second was a no. 65-260 White Lift-Off with Full-Color 2037 Steam Freight Graphics Type D display outfit box. It lacked manufacturer data and measured 23½ x 11½ x 3 inches. The outfit boxes are equally as common, and there is no premium for either one. Many collectors desire to own an example of each type.

The 19910 grew from 2,000 outfits to 12,400 over a series of several factory orders. Unfortunately for Lionel, a memorandum indicates that this increase was based more on the quantity of surplus trains and packaging available than heightened customer demand.

The 19910 is readily available in C8 condition.

In late 1966, Lionel introduced the short-lived no. 19900 series. The no. 19920 was the second and last of these outfits. It was led by a no. 635-25 Union Pacific Diesel Switcher, which appeared only in six promotional outfits. The 19920 was packed in a mail-order box, which meant it likely was sold to catalog retailers that shipped outfits direct in the outfit box. It has yet to be linked to a retailer.

Description: "O27" Promotional Outfit
Original Amount: 800
Factory Order Date: 12/1/1966
Date Issued: 12-14-66
Date Req'd: 12-14-66
Packaging: M.O. Pack (Units not Boxed)

Contents: 635-25 "Union Pacific" Diesel Switcher; 6176-50 Hopper Car; 6142-100 Gondola Car; 6112-88 Canister (2); 6050-100 Swift Savings Bank Car; 6401-25 Flat Car; 6059-50 Caboose; 1013-8 Curved Track (Bundle of 8 - 1013); 1018-10 Straight Track (Loose) (2); 1025-25 45-Watt Transformer; 1103-20 Envelope Packed; Form 3063 Parts Order Form; 1-166 Warranty Card; 926-66 Service Station List; 19152-10 Instruction Sheet

Boxes & Packing: 65-435 Outfit Box; 62-254 Insert; 62-245 Insert (2); 62-264 Insert; 64-177 Insert; 64-106 Insert (5); 65-436 Shipper for 4 (1-4); 64-106 Shipper Pad (2-4)

19920 (1966)	C6	C7	C8	Rarity
Complete Outfit	290	465	695	R8
Outfit Box no. 65-435	150	250	325	R8

Comments: Near the very end of 1966, Lionel issued two General Release Promotional Type IIb outfits: nos. 19910 and 19920. Along with the no. 19437 from 1966, these were the final outfits created in that year. By the time Lionel released these outfits, its executives realized that sales were substantially below projections. In response, the 19910 and 19920 were assembled to begin the long process of reducing the unsold inventory that had built up. It is unknown why Lionel initiated the no. 19900 series of numbers on these two outfits.

The 19920, which has yet to be linked to an end retailer, was led by a no. 635-25 Union Pacific Diesel Switcher. Included in promotional outfits only, this locomotive featured a two-position reversing unit, a headlight, a weight and a rubber tire as a traction aid.

The rolling stock in this outfit consisted of carryover items that were commonly used in outfits from 1966. The most notable item was the no. 6050-100 Swift Savings Bank Car, which used a Type III body. During the course of 1966, Lionel finished removing the new date, a built date and number data from the heat-stamping of the black no. 6176-50 Hopper Car. This minimal decoration became the norm for the 6176-50.

The rolling stock in this outfit followed the normal truck and coupler progression for 1966, with all the cars having late AAR types. All of them were equipped with one operating and one non-operating truck and coupler, and many had a washer riveted as part of their leaf spring assembly.

The no. 1103-20 Envelope Packed has been observed in a Type III envelope.

The no. 65-435 Tan RSC with Black Graphics outfit box was manufactured by Eastern Corrugated Container Corp. and measured 12¾ x 12 x 6⅞ inches. These boxes were made of a thicker corrugated material (rated at 90 pounds rather than the normal 65 pounds gross weight) that allowed each outfit to be shipped in its outfit box. The box listed Lionel's corporate name as "The Lionel Toy Corporation".

An original quantity of 500 units of the 19920 was to have been manufactured. This was subsequently increased to 800. Even with this increase, this outfit is seldom seen in any condition.

PART IV

The Appendices

APPENDIX A - OUTFITS ORGANIZED BY MOTIVE POWER

Appendix A lists the motive power featured in a promotional outfit. The list is sorted by motive power part number and includes the outfit number and year. Also included are diesel locomotive "B" and "C" units and steam locomotive tenders.

Part No.	Outfit Number (Year)
44-50	X-500NA (60)
45-1	X-676 (61); X-714 (61)
45-25	X-663 (61)
45-50	X-515NA (60); X-520NA (60); X-535NA (60)
50-1	X-576 (60); X-577 (60); 13255 (64); 19312 (63)
52-1	X-572NA (60); X-576 (60); X-577 (60)
54-1	19435 (65)
55-1	X-537NA (60); X-573NA (60)
58-1	X-578NA (60)
59-1	19311 (63); 19312 (63); 19324 (63)
65-1	19408 (64)
68-1	X-572NA (60)
211P-25	19115 (62); 19117 (62); 19133 (62); 19136 (62); 19141 (62); 19159 (62); 19181 (62); 19187 (62); 19219 (63); 19312 (63)
211P-150	11361-500 (63); 11361X (63); 11560-500 (65); 11560X (66); 19219 (63); 19225 (63); 19232 (63); 19238 (63); 19238-502 (63); 19249 (63); 19310 (63); 19396 (64)
211PX-1	19206 (62); 19396 (64)
211T-1	11361-500 (63); 19206 (62); 19310 (63); 19396 (64)
211T-25	11361-500 (63); 11560-500 (65); 11560X (66); 19115 (62); 19117 (62); 19133 (62); 19136 (62); 19141 (62); 19159 (62); 19187 (62); 19219 (63); 19225 (63); 19232 (63); 19238 (63); 19238-502 (63); 19249 (63); 19310 (63); 19396 (64)
212P-1	19410 (64)
212P-25	11385-500 (64); 19347 (64)
212T-1	19410 (64)
212T-25	11385-500 (64); 19335 (64); 19335 (65); 19347 (64); 19355 (64); 19372-500 (64); 19396 (64); 19399 (64); 19444 (65); 19444 (66); 19444-502 (65); 19506 (66); 19507 (66); 19569 (66); 19706 (67)
213LT	19406 (64)
213P-25	11482 (64); 19372 (64); 19392 (64); 19434 (65)
213T-25	11482 (64); 19372 (64); 19392 (64); 19454-500 (65); 19571 (66)
215P-25	19335 (64); 19335 (65); 19355 (64); 19372-500 (64); 19396 (64); 19399 (64); 19435 (65); 19444 (65); 19444 (66); 19444-502 (65); 19506 (66); 19507 (66); 19569 (66); 19706 (67)
216P-25	19454-500 (65); 19571 (66)
217C-1	9654 (60)
218C-1	X-636 (61); X-636 (62); X-688 (61); 9656 (62); 9673 (61)
218C-25	19271 (64)
218P-1	X-522NA (60); X-603 (61); X-636 (61); X-636 (62); X-643 (61); X-683 (61); X-802 (60); 9673 (61); 9693 (60); 19172 (62); 19231 (63); 19266 (63)
218P-25	9730 (63); 11361-500 (63); 19231 (63); 19231-500 (63); 19310 (63)
218T-1	X-522NA (60); X-603 (61); 9693 (60); 19231 (63)
218T-25	9730 (63); 11361-500 (63); 19231 (63); 19231-500 (63); 19310 (63)
220P-1	X-503NA (60); X-529NA (60); X-531NA (60); X-534NA (60); X-552NA (60); X-556NA (60); X-558NA (60); X-565NA (60); X-606 (61); X-688 (61); X-698 (61); X-801 (60)
220P-25	X-568NA (60)
220T-1	X-503NA (60); X-529NA (60); X-531NA (60); X-534NA (60); X-552NA (60); X-565NA (60)
220T-25	X-568NA (60)
221P-1	19301 (63)
221P-25	11341-500 (63); 19235 (63); 19237 (63); 19301 (63); 19314 (63); 19341 (64); 19370 (64); 19382 (64); 19433 (65); 19434 (65); 19512 (66); 19513 (66); 19553 (66)
221P-50	19334 (64); 19334-500 (64); 19334-500 (65); 19434 (65)
221P-75	19334 (64); 19343 (64); 19383 (64); 19434 (65)
222P-25	11011 (62); 11015 (62); 11341-500 (63); 19109 (62); 19312 (63); 19314 (63); 19314-500 (63)
223P-1	9656 (62); 19172 (62); 19317 (63); 19317A (63); 19322 (63)
223P-50	19271 (64)
224C-1	X-562NA (60); X-579NA (60); X-584NA (60); X-628 (61); 19201 (1) (62)
224C-25	X-646 (61); 9671 (61); 19145 (62); 19201 (2) (62)
224P-1	X-527NA (60); X-540NA (60); X-562NA (60); X-579NA (60); X-582 (60); X-584NA (60); X-628 (61); X-720 (61); 19201 (1) (62)
224P-25	X-646 (61); 9671 (61); 19145 (62); 19201 (2) (62)
225P-1	X-509NA (60); X-511NA (60); X-519NA (60); X-556NA (60); 9652 (60)
225P-25	X-240 (60)
226C-1	X-576 (60); X-577 (60); 1649NE (60); 9654 (60)
226P-1	X-576 (60); X-577 (60); 1649NE (60); 9654 (60)
227P-1	X-616 (61); X-670 (61); X-703 (61); 1113 (60); 1115 (60); 1125 (61); 19301 (63); 19301(A) (63); 19312 (63); 19394 (64)
228P-1	X-550NA (60); X-625 (61); 19203 (62)
228P-25	X-533NA (60)
229C-1	9730-500 (63); 19129 (62)
229P-1	9730-500 (63); 19129 (62)
230P-1	X-623 (61); X-632 (61); X-634 (61)
230P-25	19312 (63); 19319 (63)
231P-1	X-608 (61); X-641 (61); X-652 (61); X-658 (61); X-671 (61); X-679 (61); X-684 (61); X-698 (61); X-701 (61); X-708 (61); 19304 (63); 19395 (64); 19434 (65)
231P-25	X-614 (61); X-666 (61); 19112 (62); 19138 (62); 19164 (62); 19190 (62); 19202 (62); 19227 (63); 19238-501 (63); 19281 (63); 19304 (63); 19312 (63); 19313 (63); 19323 (63); 19349 (64); 19395 (64)
232P-25	19302 (63); 19395 (64)
233-1	X-607 (61); X-609 (61); X-633 (61); X-640 (61); X-653 (62); X-672 (61); 19186 (62)
233-25	X-639 (61); 9672 (61); 19103 (62); 19113 (62); 19161 (62); 19165 (62); 19229 (63); 19229-500 (63); 19229-501 (63); 19229-501X (63); 19233 (63)
233W-1	X-609 (61); X-633 (61); X-672 (61)
233W-25	9672 (61); 19332 (64); 19354 (64)
234T-25	11620 (68)
234W-1	9657 (62); 9733 (63); 11375-500 (63); 19177 (62); 19186 (62); 19204 (62); 19205 (62); 19230 (63); 19241-500 (63); 19250 (63); 19252 (63); 19400 (64)
234W-25	19103 (62); 19113 (62); 19161 (62); 19165 (62); 19230-500 (63); 19241 (63); 19254 (63); 19275 (63); 19337 (64); 19366 (64); 19390 (64); 19393 (64); 19397 (64); 19398 (64); 19411 (64); 19438 (65); 19438-502 (65); 19441 (65); 19442 (65); 19442 (66); 19510 (66); 19511 (66); 19516 (66); 19517 (66)
235-1	X-648 (61)
236-1	X-602 (61); X-607 (61); X-629 (61); X-640 (61); X-647 (61); X-653 (61); X-655 (61); X-691 (61); X-709 (61); X-717 (61)
236-25	X-639 (61); X-667 (61); X-702 (61); 19102 (62); 19108 (62); 19111 (62); 19124 (62); 19128 (62); 19132 (62); 19137 (62); 19143 (62); 19166 (62); 19176 (62); 19191 (62)
237-25	11351-500 (63); 11375-500 (63); 19218 (63); 19224 (63); 19226 (63); 19229 (63); 19229-502 (63); 19233 (63); 19242 (63); 19246 (63); 19262 (63); 19267 (63); 19273 (63); 19280 (63); 19327 (64); 19331 (64); 19344 (64); 19348 (64); 19351 (64); 19353 (64); 19366 (64); 19371 (64); 19380 (64); 19390 (64); 19416 (64); 19437 (65); 19437 (66); 19437-502 (65); 19441 (65); 19453 (65); 19453 (66); 19455 (65); 19514 (66); 19515 (66); 19544 (66); 19546 (66); 19547 (66); 19586 (66)
237X-1	19229-501 (63); 19229-501X (63); 19233-500 (63); 19241-500 (63)
238-25	19214 (63); 19214-500 (63); 19233 (63); 19241 (63); 19254 (63); 19275 (63); 19326 (65)
238LTS	19407 (64)
239-1	19590 (66)
239-25	11540-500 (65); 11540-500 (66); 11540X (66); 19337 (64); 19345 (64); 19346 (64); 19351-500 (64); 19371-500 (64); 19378 (64); 19391 (64); 19397 (64); 19419 (64); 19437 (66); 19580 (66)
240-25	19326 (64); 19350-500 (64); 19350-500 (65)
241-25	19438 (65); 19438-502 (65); 19442 (65); 19442 (66); 19510 (66); 19511 (66); 19516 (66); 19517 (66); 19563 (66); 19583 (66); 19707 (67)
242-25	X-604 (62); X-660 (62); X-705 (62); 9650 (62); 11520-500 (65); 11520-500 (66); 19106 (62); 19106-50 (62); 19106-100 (62); 19107 (62); 19110 (62); 19114 (62); 19116 (62); 19120 (62); 19121 (62); 19123 (62); 19127 (62); 19131 (62); 19134 (62); 19135 (62); 19140 (62); 19142 (62); 19142-50 (62); 19142-100 (62); 19142-500 (63); 19142-502 (63); 19148 (62); 19150 (62); 19153 (62); 19156 (62); 19160 (62); 19163 (62); 19168 (62); 19169 (62); 19171 (62); 19174 (62); 19175 (62); 19180 (62); 19183 (62); 19185 (62); 19188 (62); 19199 (62); 19210 (63); 19212 (63); 19229-500 (63); 19233-501 (63); 19234 (63); 19234-500 (63); 19255 (63); 19273-500 (63); 19336 (64); 19350 (64); 19350-500 (65); 19502 (66); 19503 (66); 19578 (66); 19705 (67)
242T-1	19590 (66)
242T-25	11540-500 (65); 11540-500 (66); 11540X (66); 19326 (64); 19326 (65); 19327 (64); 19329 (64); 19331 (64); 19333 (64); 19344 (64); 19345 (64); 19346 (64); 19350-500 (64); 19350-500 (65); 19350-501 (65); 19351 (64); 19351-500 (64); 19353 (64); 19371 (64); 19371-500 (64); 19380 (64); 19391 (64); 19437 (65); 19437 (66); 19437-502 (65); 19453 (65); 19453 (66); 19455 (65); 19502 (66); 19503 (66); 19514 (66); 19515 (66); 19544 (66); 19546 (66); 19547 (66); 19563 (66); 19580 (66); 19586 (66); 19707 (67)
243-1	X-514NA (60); X-555NA (60); X-573NA (60); X-585NA (60); 9653 (60); 9745 (60)
243-25	19105 (62); 19203X (62); 19204X (62)
243W	X-506NA (60); X-514NA (60); X-536NA (60); X-537NA (60); X-551NA (60); X-555NA (60); X-585NA (60); X-630 (61); X-642 (61); X-664 (61); X-692 (61); X-835 (60); 9653 (60); 9692 (60); 9692 (61)
244-1	X-505NA (60); X-518NA (60); X-528NA (60); X-542NA (60); X-547 (60); X-561NA (60)
244-25	X-532NA (60); X-546NA (60)
244-50	X-566NA (60)
244LT	X-501NA (60)
244T-1	X-505NA (60); X-518NA (60); X-528NA (60); X-542NA (60); X-547 (60); X-561NA (60); X-566NA (60); X-657 (61)
244T-25	X-532NA (60); X-546NA (60); X-605 (61); X-622 (61); X-627 (61); X-631 (61); X-669 (61); X-685 (61); X-689 (61); X-694 (61); 1123 (62); 9670 (61); 19567-500 (66)
245-1	X-604 (62)
245X-1	X-570NA (60); X-571NA (60)
246-1	X-502NA (60); X-510NA (60); X-516NA (60); X-517NA (60); X-521NA (60); X-523NA (60); X-526NA (60); X-530NA (60); X-539NA (60); X-544NA (60); X-545NA (60); X-548 (60); X-554NA (60); X-557 (60); X-559NA (60); X-560NA (60); X-563NA (60); X-569NA (60); X-574NA (60); X-583NA (60); X-604 (62); X-657 (61); X-678 (61); X-837 (60); X-875 (60); 9651 (60)
246-25	X-538NA (60); X-549NA (60); X-567NA (60); X-600 (61); X-601 (61); X-604 (61); X-604 (62); X-605 (61); X-612 (61); X-622 (61); X-627 (61); X-631 (61); X-638 (61); X-645 (61); X-650 (61); X-651 (61); X-659 (61); X-660 (61); X-669 (61); X-685 (61); X-689 (61); X-694 (61); X-704 (61); X-705 (61); X-710 (61); 1111 (60); 1117 (60); 1119 (60); 9670 (61); 19140 (62)
247-1	X-501NA (60); X-613 (61); X-680 (61); X-682 (61); X-697 (61)

Part No.	Outfit Number (Year)
247LT	X-874 (60)
247T-1	X-501NA (60); X-613 (61); X-680 (61); X-682 (61); X-697 (61)
249-1	X-874 (60)
251-25	19583 (66)
250T-1	X-874 (60)
614-1	X-513NA (60)
616X-1	9674 (61)
617X-1	19256 (63); 19318 (63)
633-25	19101 (62)
633-50	19149 (62); 19151 (62); 19152 (62); 19184 (62); 19198 (62); 19321 (63)
634-1	19248 (63)
634-25	19321 (63)
635-25	19440 (65); 19440-502 (65); 19504 (66); 19561 (66); 19703 (67); 19920 (66)
637X-1	13255 (64); 19196 (62); 19230-500 (63); 19308 (63)
736-1	X-564NA (60); 9694 (60); 12710X (66)
736LTS	12807 (64)
736X-1	9658 (62); 9675 (61); 19257 (63); 19309 (63)
736W-1	X-564NA (60); 9658 (62); 9675 (61); 9694 (60); 12710X (66); 12838 (64); 13255 (64); 13267 (64); 19196 (62); 19257 (63); 19308 (63); 19309 (63)
746-1	9694 (60)
746W-1	9694 (60)
773-1	12838 (64)
773LTS	12827 (64); 12847 (64); 12867 (64); 13277 (64)
773X-1	13267 (64)
1050-25	X-553NA (60); 1103 (60)
1050T-25	X-553NA (60); X-604 (61); X-612 (61); X-618 (61); X-620 (61); X-621 (61); X-624 (61); X-637 (61); X-638 (61); X-645 (61); X-650 (61); X-651 (61); X-659 (61); X-661 (61); X-665 (61); X-668 (61); X-673 (61); X-681 (61); X-686 (61); X-687 (61); X-690 (61); X-695 (61); X-696 (61); X-699 (61); X-700 (61); X-706 (61); X-707 (61); X-710 (61); X-715 (61); X-716 (61); 1103 (60); 1123 (61); 1123C (61); 1123C (62); 19567-500 (66)
1055-25	X-541NA (60); X-829 (60); 1107 (60); 1125 (61)
1060-25	X-508NA (60); X-543NA (60); X-575 (60); X-580NA (60); X-615 (61); X-618 (61); X-620 (61); X-621 (61); X-624 (61); X-635 (61); X-637 (61); X-661 (61); X-665 (61); X-668 (61); X-673 (61); X-681 (61); X-686 (61); X-687 (61); X-690 (61); X-695 (61); X-696 (61); X-699 (61); X-700 (61); X-706 (61); X-707 (61); X-707 (62); X-715 (61); X-716 (61); 1109 (60); 1123 (61); 1123 (62); 1123C (61); 1123C (62); 1123C (63); 1124 (61); 1124C (61); 1124P (61); 11001 (62); 11001 (63); 11005 (62); 19000 (62); 19100 (62); 19118 (62); 19119 (62); 19125 (62); 19126 (62); 19130 (62); 19139 (62); 19146 (62); 19147 (62); 19154 (62); 19155 (62); 19157 (62); 19158 (62); 19162 (62); 19167 (62); 19170 (62); 19173 (62); 19173-500 (63); 19179 (62); 19182 (62); 19189 (62); 19192 (62); 19193 (62); 19194 (62); 19195 (62); 19197 (62); 19200 (62); 19211 (62); 19215 (63); 19216 (63); 19357 (64); 19429 (65)
1060T-1	19428 (65)

Part No.	Outfit Number (Year)
1060T-25	X-508NA (60); X-543NA (60); X-549NA (60); X-575 (60); X-580NA (60); X-600 (61); X-604 (62); X-615 (61); X-635 (61); X-660 (61); X-660 (62); X-667 (61); X-704 (61); X-705 (61); X-705 (62); X-707 (62); 1109 (60); 1111 (60); 1117 (60); 1119 (60); 1124 (61); 1124C (61); 1124P (61); 9650 (62); 11001 (62); 11001 (63); 11005 (62); 11351-500 (63); 19000 (62); 19100 (62); 19102 (62); 19105 (62); 19106 (62); 19106-50 (62); 19106-100 (62); 19107 (62); 19108 (62); 19110 (62); 19111 (62); 19114 (62); 19116 (62); 19118 (62); 19119 (62); 19120 (62); 19121 (62); 19123 (62); 19124 (62); 19125 (62); 19126 (62); 19127 (62); 19128 (62); 19130 (62); 19131 (62); 19132 (62); 19134 (62); 19135 (62); 19137 (62); 19139 (62); 19140 (62); 19142 (62); 19142-50 (62); 19142-100 (62); 19143 (62); 19146 (62); 19147 (62); 19148 (62); 19150 (62); 19153 (62); 19154 (62); 19155 (62); 19156 (62); 19157 (62); 19158 (62); 19160 (62); 19162 (62); 19163 (62); 19166 (62); 19167 (62); 19168 (62); 19169 (62); 19170 (62); 19171 (62); 19173 (62); 19174 (62); 19175 (62); 19176 (62); 19179 (62); 19180 (62); 19182 (62); 19183 (62); 19185 (62); 19188 (62); 19189 (62); 19191 (62); 19192 (62); 19193 (62); 19194 (62); 19195 (62); 19197 (62); 19199 (62); 19200 (62); 19210 (63); 19211 (63); 19212 (63); 19214 (63); 19214-500 (63); 19216 (63); 19217 (63); 19218 (63); 19224 (63); 19226 (63); 19229 (63); 19229-500 (63); 19229-501 (63); 19229-501X (63); 19229-502 (63); 19233 (63); 19233-500 (63); 19233-501 (63); 19234 (63); 19242 (63); 19246 (63); 19255 (63); 19267 (63); 19273 (63); 19273-500 (63); 19280 (63); 19282 (64); 19328 (64); 19336 (64); 19350 (64); 19378 (64); 19419 (64); 19428 (65); 19567-500 (66)
1060T-50	19263 (63); 19328 (64); 19350 (64); 19428 (65); 19567-500 (66)
1061-25	11311X (63); 11415 (63); 19213 (63); 19216 (63); 19220 (63); 19221 (63); 19222 (63); 19223 (63); 19240 (63); 19240-500 (63); 19244 (63); 19244 (64); 19247 (63); 19258 (63); 19260 (63); 19272 (63); 19328 (64); 19338 (64); 19342 (64); 19368 (64); 19373 (64); 19386 (64); 19405 (64); 19409 (64); 19426 (65)
1061-50	19244-500 (64); 19325 (64); 19330 (64); 19339 (64); 19363 (64); 19363-500 (64); 19415 (64); 19426 (65); 19427 (65); 19428 (65); 19429 (65)
1061-75	10613SF (69); 11570 (66); 19555 (66); 19589 (66); 19701 (67)
1061T-25	1123C (63); 11311X (63); 11315 (63); 11415 (63); 19142-500 (63); 19142-502 (63); 19173-500 (63); 19213 (63); 19215 (63); 19220 (63); 19221 (63); 19222 (63); 19223 (63); 19228 (63); 19228-500 (63); 19236 (63); 19239 (63); 19240 (63); 19240-500 (63); 19243 (63); 19244 (63); 19244 (64); 19245 (63); 19245 (65); 19247 (63); 19253 (63); 19253 (64); 19258 (63); 19259 (63); 19260 (63); 19262 (63); 19269 (63); 19270 (63); 19272 (63); 19274 (63); 19274-500 (63); 19276 (63); 19348 (64); 19357 (64); 19358 (64); 19362 (64); 19373 (64); 19374 (64); 19376 (64); 19377 (64); 19377-500 (64); 19386 (64); 19405 (64); 19409 (64); 19412 (64); 19415 (64); 19426 (65); 19427 (65); 19428 (65); 19429 (65); 19430 (65); 19431 (65); 19432 (65)
1061T-50	19244-500 (64); 19325 (64); 19330 (64); 19338 (64); 19339 (64); 19340 (64); 19340 (65); 19342 (64); 19352 (64); 19363 (64); 19363-500 (64); 19364 (64); 19365 (64); 19367 (64); 19368 (64); 19369 (64); 19375 (64); 19379 (64); 19379 (65); 19385 (64); 19416 (64); 19418 (64); 19427 (65); 19428 (65); 19430 (65); 19431 (65); 19432 (65); 19567 (66); 19567-500 (66)
1062-25	11315 (63); 19217 (63); 19228 (63); 19228-500 (63); 19236 (63); 19239 (63); 19243 (63); 19245 (63); 19245 (65); 19253 (63); 19253 (64); 19259 (63); 19263 (63); 19269 (63); 19270 (63); 19274 (63); 19274-500 (63); 19276 (63); 19358 (64); 19374 (64); 19376 (64); 19377 (64); 19377-500 (64); 19379 (64); 19381 (64); 19389 (64); 19430 (65); 19431 (65)

Part No.	Outfit Number (Year)
1062-50	19282 (64); 19333 (64); 19340 (64); 19340 (65); 19352 (64); 19362 (64); 19364 (64); 19365 (64); 19367 (64); 19369 (64); 19375 (64); 19379 (65); 19385 (64); 19412 (64); 19418 (64); 19428 (65); 19432 (65); 19436 (65); 19439 (65); 19439 (66); 19439-502 (65); 19446 (65); 19450 (65); 19450 (66)
1062-50X	19350-501 (65)
1062-75	11580 (66); 19436 (66); 19439 (66); 19450 (66); 19500 (66); 19501 (66); 19520 (66); 19530 (66); 19541 (66); 19542 (66); 19550 (66); 19557 (66); 19567-500 (66); 19704 (67); 19910 (66)
1062-125	19567 (66); 19567-500 (66)
1062T-25	10613SF (69); 11520-500 (65); 11520-500 (66); 11570 (66); 11580 (66); 19333 (64); 19381 (64); 19389 (64); 19436 (65); 19436 (66); 19439 (65); 19439 (66); 19439-502 (65); 19446 (65); 19450 (65); 19450 (66); 19500 (66); 19501 (66); 19520 (66); 19530 (66); 19541 (66); 19542 (66); 19550 (66); 19555 (66); 19557 (66); 19567-500 (66); 19578 (66); 19583 (66); 19589 (66); 19701 (67); 19704 (67); 19705 (67); 19910 (66)
1065-25	X-626 (61); X-644 (61); X-654 (61); X-662 (61); X-703 (61); X-713 (61); 1125 (61); 1125C (61); 10653SF (69); X-704 (62); 19122 (62); 19144 (62); 19216 (63); 19303 (63); 19306 (63)
1066-25	19328 (64); 19389 (64)
1130T-1	X-502NA (60); X-510NA (60); X-512NA (60); X-516NA (60); X-517NA (60); X-521NA (60); X-523NA (60); X-524NA (60); X-526NA (60); X-530NA (60); X-539NA (60); X-544NA (60); X-545NA (60); X-548 (60); X-554NA (60); X-557 (60); X-559NA (60); X-560NA (60); X-563NA (60); X-569NA (60); X-570NA (60); X-571NA (60); X-573NA (60); X-574NA (60); X-583NA (60); X-602 (61); X-607 (61); X-629 (61); X-640 (61); X-647 (61); X-648 (61); X-653 (61); X-655 (61); X-678 (61); X-691 (61); X-709 (61); X-717 (61); X-718 (61); X-719 (61); X-800 (60); X-837 (60); X-875 (60); 9651 (60)
1130T-25	X-538NA (60); X-567NA (60); X-600 (61); X-601 (61); X-639 (61); X-653 (62); X-702 (61); 9745 (60); 19203X (62); 19204X (62); 19210 (63); 19211 (63); 19216 (63); 19217 (63); 19218 (63); 19229 (63); 19233 (63); 19234 (63); 19234-500 (63); 19273-500 (63)
1862-1	X-619 (61)
1862T-1	X-619 (61)
1872T-1	X-677 (61)
1872X-1	X-677 (61)
1882-25	X-507NA (60)
1882T-25	X-507NA (60)
2018	X-648 (61)
2018-1	X-504NA (60); X-512NA (60); X-524NA (60); X-536NA (60); X-551NA (60); X-630 (61); X-692 (61); X-718 (61); X-719 (61); X-800 (60)
2029-1	19400 (64)
2029-25	11620 (68); 19329 (64); 19332 (64); 19354 (64); 19393 (64); 19398 (64); 19411 (64)
2029LTS	19408 (64); 19417 (64)
2037-1	X-506NA (60); X-537NA (60); X-642 (61); X-664 (61); X-835 (60); 9657 (62); 9692 (60); 9692 (61); 9733 (63); 19177 (62); 19204 (62); 19205 (62); 19230 (62); 19230-500 (63); 19250 (63); 19252 (63)
2037LTS	19268 (63)
2322-1	12820-100 (65); 12850X (66)
2346-1	12800X (66)
2347-1	12885-500 (65)
2349X	X-586 (60)
2360-1	19251 (63)
2360X-1	X-693 (61); 19178 (62); 19320 (63)
2365-1	9655 (62); 19305 (63)
2383-1	12817 (64); 12857 (64)
2383P-1	X-572NA (60)
2383PX-1	19315 (63); 19316 (63)
2383T-1	X-572NA (60); 19315 (63); 19316 (63)
3927-1	X-572NA (60); X-576 (60); X-577 (60)
6026W-1	X-504NA (60); X-506NA (60)

APPENDIX B - OUTFITS ORGANIZED BY INDIVIDUAL ITEMS

Appendix B lists the individual items featured in a promotional outfit. Most major components are listed, with the exception of boxes and packing, flat car and gondola loads, paperwork, small peripherals, track, transformers and common trestles. Motive power is listed separately in Appendix A. The list is sorted by part number and includes the outfit number and year.

Part No.	Outfit Number (Year)
X625-20	X-624 (61); X-625 (61); 19142-502 (63); 19147 (62); 19216 (63); 19328 (64); 19450 (65); 19450 (66); 19555 (66)
0282	19365 (64)
76-1	12857 (64)
76-25	12885-500 (65); 19454-500 (65)
109-25	X-513NA (60)
110-75	19325 (64); 19542 (66); 19563 (66); 19567 (66); 19567-500 (66)
110-125	19454-500 (65)
111	X-576 (60); X-577 (60)
111-1	X-688 (61); 12817 (64); 12857 (64); 19276 (63); 19412 (64)
128	X-563NA (60); X-565NA (60)
128-1	X-573NA (60)
140-1	X-576 (60); 13277 (64); 19271 (64); 19392 (64)
145-1	13255 (64); 19268 (63); 19410 (64)
145-100	19454-500 (65)
151	X-577 (60)
151-1	13277 (64)
154-1	13277 (64)
161-1	19273-500 (63); 19304 (63); 19321 (63)
163-1	19309 (63)
175	X-564NA (60); X-569NA (60)
175-1	X-572NA (60); 9745 (60)
175-50	19105 (62)
195-1	19309 (63)
214-1	X-557 (60); 19305 (63)
214-3	19379 (64); 19379 (65); 19426 (65); 19427 (65); 19430 (65)
252	X-509NA (60)
252-1	X-576 (60); X-577 (60); X-636 (61); X-636 (62); 19398 (64)
262-1	9730-500 (63); 13255 (64); 13277 (64); 19268 (63); 19304 (63); 19312 (63); 19323 (63); 19410 (64)
264-1	X-530NA (60); X-537NA (60); X-555NA (60)
299-1	19309 (63); 19317 (63); 19317A (63); 19322 (63)
309-100	19542 (66); 19544 (66); 19546 (66); 19547 (66); 19550 (66); 19557 (66)
311-25	19332 (64)
321-1	X-572NA (60); 13255 (64); 19304 (63); 19327 (64)
321-100	12885-500 (65); 19454-500 (65)
332-1	X-572NA (60); 19407 (64)
334	X-563NA (60); X-565NA (60); X-570NA (60); X-571NA (60)
334-1	X-573NA (60)
346-1	12885-500 (65); 19327 (64); 19453 (65); 19453 (66); 19561 (66)
347-25	19326 (64); 19326 (65); 19434 (65)
350-1	X-564NA (60); X-572NA (60)
350-50	X-564NA (60); X-572NA (60)
353	X-577 (60)
353-1	X-576 (60)
375-1	12807 (64); 12827 (64); 12847 (64); 12867 (64); 19312 (63); 19406 (64)
419-1	19175 (62); 19434 (65)
443	X-520NA (60); X-522NA (60)
443-1	19323 (63); 19434 (65)
448-1	X-657 (61); 19311 (63)
452-1	19242 (63); 19308 (63)
461-1	19546 (66); 19547 (66)
462-1	19434 (65)
464	X-566NA (60); X-573NA (60)
464-1	X-680 (61)
470-1	X-501NA (60); X-515NA (60); X-531NA (60); X-579NA (60); X-583NA (60); X-647 (61); X-658 (61); X-676 (61); X-691 (61); 19196 (62); 19204X (62); 19311 (63)
494-1	12807 (64); 13255 (64); 19268 (63)
902	X-544NA (60); X-549NA (60); X-567NA (60); X-568NA (60); X-574NA (60); X-575 (60)
902-1	X-703 (61); X-704 (61)
903	X-549NA (60); X-567NA (60); X-574NA (60); X-829 (60); 9730-500 (63); 19142-502 (63); 19216 (63)
903-1	X-704 (61); 19322 (63)
903-25	19328 (64)
908-10	19224 (63); 19311 (63); 19318 (63); 19394 (64); 19395 (64)
910	X-515NA (60)
910-1	X-625 (61); X-676 (61); X-714 (61); 19201 (1) (62); 19201 (2) (62); 19203 (62); 19311 (63); 19394 (64)
920-8	X-829 (60)
943	X-505NA (60); X-514NA (60); X-515NA (60); X-518NA (60); X-519NA (60); X-550NA (60)
943-1	X-500NA (60); X-527NA (60); X-528NA (60); X-533NA (60); X-539NA (60); X-663 (61); X-676 (61); X-682 (61); X-714 (61); 19203X (62); 19217 (63); 19397 (64)
951	X-829 (60)
951-1	X-508NA (60)
953	X-557 (60)
953-1	X-542NA (60); X-543NA (60); X-544NA (60); X-637 (61); X-121 (61); 19146 (62); 19171 (62)
958-50	19331 (64); 19397 (64); 19405 (64); 19428 (65)
958-75	19326 (64); 19344 (64); 19434 (65)
958-100	19327 (64)
958-150	19326 (65); 19405 (64); 19434 (65)
958-175	19326 (65); 19405 (64); 19434 (65)
960	X-509NA (60); X-544NA (60); X-569NA (60)
960-1	X-510NA (60); X-563NA (60); X-637 (61)
961-1	X-564NA (60); X-569NA (60)
963-1	X-545NA (60)
963-100	X-507NA (60)
965-1	X-564NA (60); X-569NA (60)
972	X-509NA (60)
972-1	19267 (63); 19380 (64)
975-1	19326 (64); 19326 (65); 19334 (64); 19334-500 (64); 19334-500 (65); 19338 (64); 19343 (64); 19344 (64); 19405 (64); 19416 (64); 19434 (65)
980	X-567NA (60)
980-1	X-508NA (60); X-569NA (60)
981	X-557 (60); X-574NA (60); X-636 (61)
981-1	X-541NA (60)
984-1	X-636 (61); X-636 (62); 19146 (62); 19171 (62); 19175 (62)
987-1	19309 (63)
988-1	19309 (63)
1047-1	19255 (63); 19267 (63); 19366 (64); 19372-500 (64); 19398 (64); 19433 (65)
1402	19546 (66); 19547 (66)
1403	19544 (66); 19546 (66); 19547 (66)
1407	19546 (66); 19547 (66); 19557 (66); 19561 (66)
1706	19544 (66); 19561 (66)
1865-25	X-619 (61)
1866-25	X-507NA (60)
1875-1	X-576 (60); X-577 (60)
1875W-1	X-677 (61)
1876-1	X-576 (60); X-677 (61)
1877-1	X-554NA (60); X-719 (61)
1877-25	X-619 (61); 19132 (62)
1885-25	X-507NA (60)
1887-25	X-507NA (60)
2404-1	19400 (64); 19406 (64)
2405-1	19400 (64); 19406 (64)
2406-1	19400 (64); 19406 (64)
2432	X-801 (60)
2432-1	X-572NA (60); X-576 (60); X-577 (60)
2436	X-801 (60)
2436-1	X-572NA (60)
2521-1	12817 (64); 12857 (64); 19315 (63); 19406 (64)
2522-1	12817 (64); 12857 (64); 19315 (63); 19406 (64)
2523-1	12817 (64); 12857 (64); 19315 (63); 19406 (64)
3309-25	19100 (62); 19109 (62); 19125 (62); 19131 (62); 19135 (62); 19139 (62); 19142 (62); 19142-50 (62); 19142-100 (62); 19144 (62); 19146 (62); 19147 (62); 19148 (62); 19153 (62); 19155 (62); 19159 (62); 19160 (62); 19171 (62); 19173-500 (63); 19179 (62); 19183 (62); 19193 (62); 19194 (62); 19199 (62); 19235 (63); 19236 (63); 19273-500 (63); 19281 (63); 19325 (64); 19362 (64); 19432 (65)
3309-50	19334 (64); 19334-500 (64); 19334-500 (65); 19416 (64); 19432 (65)
3330-1	X-500NA (60); X-501NA (60); X-522NA (60); X-583NA (60); X-606 (61); X-608 (61); X-609 (61); X-625 (61); X-633 (61); X-643 (61); X-647 (61); X-653 (61); X-671 (61); X-698 (61); X-717 (61); 9694 (60); 19435 (65)
3330-25	X-614 (61); X-622 (61); X-627 (61); X-651 (61); X-662 (61); X-669 (61)
3349-1	9655 (62); 9656 (62); 11361-500 (63); 19129 (62); 19273-500 (63); 19274-500 (63); 19281 (63); 19309 (63); 19310 (63)
3349-25	19111 (62); 19115 (62); 19124 (62); 19128 (62); 19133 (62); 19137 (62); 19143 (62); 19151 (62); 19164 (62); 19168 (62); 19171 (62); 19185 (62); 19187 (62); 19190 (62); 19198 (62); 19273 (63)
3349-100	11385-500 (64); 19271 (64); 19341 (64); 19370 (64); 19382 (64); 19383 (64)
3356-1	12827 (64); 12838 (64); 12847 (64); 13267 (64); 19410 (64)
3357-1	19206 (62); 19430 (65); 19431 (65); 19433 (65)
3357-25	19110 (62); 19119 (62); 19121 (62); 19123 (62); 19127 (62); 19132 (62); 19139 (62); 19140 (62); 19150 (62); 19165 (62); 19167 (62); 19180 (62); 19184 (62); 19188 (62); 19189 (62); 19191 (62); 19195 (62); 19229 (63); 19229-500 (63); 19229-501 (63); 19229-501X (63); 19262 (63); 19380 (64); 19416 (64); 19430 (65)
3361-1	X-576 (60); X-577 (60); X-719 (61)
3361X	9675 (61)
3361X-1	X-566NA (60); X-680 (61); X-719 (61)
3362-1	9658 (62); 19177 (62); 19320 (63); 19435 (65)
3362-25	19102 (62); 19113 (62); 19140 (62); 19165 (62); 19201 (1) (62); 19201 (2) (62); 19203X (62); 19204X (62)
3364-25	11520-500 (65); 11520-500 (66); 19330 (64); 19335 (64); 19335 (65); 19336 (64); 19347 (64); 19353 (64); 19355 (64); 19372 (64); 19435 (65); 19436 (65); 19436 (66); 19440 (65); 19440-502 (65); 19442 (65); 19442 (66); 19446 (65); 19450 (65); 19450 (66); 19510 (66); 19511 (66); 19541 (66); 19544 (66); 19578 (66); 19705 (67)
3370-1	X-640 (61); X-677 (61); X-678 (61); X-684 (61); X-692 (61); X-708 (61); X-719 (61); 9657 (62); 19205 (62); 19229-501 (63); 19229-501X (63); 19233-500 (63); 19233-501 (63); 19256 (63); 19268 (63); 19433 (65)
3370-25	X-626 (61); X-645 (61); X-662 (61); X-666 (61); X-670 (61); X-685 (61); X-702 (61); X-710 (61); 19108 (62); 19191 (62); 19229-502 (63); 19240 (63); 19240-500 (63); 19280 (63)
3376-1	X-511NA (60); X-517NA (60); X-529NA (60); X-547 (60); X-551NA (60); X-554NA (60); X-560NA (60); X-570NA (60); X-571NA (60); X-573NA (60); X-576 (60); X-577 (60); X-584NA (60); X-652 (61); X-672 (61); X-692 (61); X-708 (61); X-719 (61); 9745 (60); 19433 (65)
3376-25	X-532NA (60); X-689 (61); X-696 (61); X-715 (61)
3376-150	19317A (63); 19321 (63); 19433 (65)
3376-160	9657 (62); 19229-500 (63); 19240-500 (63); 19273-500 (63); 19317 (63); 19433 (65)
3386-1	X-526NA (60); X-565NA (60); X-574NA (60)
3386-25	X-549NA (60); X-567NA (60); X-568NA (60); X-575 (60); 1109 (60); 1111 (60); 1117 (60)

Part No.	Outfit Number (Year)
3409-25	X-637 (61); X-638 (61); X-644 (61); X-650 (61); X-654 (61); X-661 (61); X-663 (61); X-665 (61); X-667 (61); X-668 (61); X-686 (61); X-690 (61); X-695 (61); X-700 (61); X-704 (61); X-705 (61); X-706 (61); 1124 (61); 1124C (61); 1124P (61)
3410-1	X-607 (61); X-608 (61); X-628 (61); X-633 (61); X-688 (61); X-701 (61); X-718 (61); 19248 (63)
3410-25	X-631 (61); X-646 (61); X-705 (62); 19115 (62); 19117 (62); 19128 (62); 19132 (62); 19137 (62); 19149 (62); 19156 (62); 19212 (63); 19227 (63); 19228 (63); 19228-500 (63); 19234 (63); 19237 (63); 19245 (63); 19258 (63); 19273 (63); 19276 (63); 19305 (63); 19350 (64)
3413-1	19129 (62); 19205 (62); 19305 (63); 19316 (63); 19317A (63); 19435 (65)
3413-25	19103 (62); 19112 (62); 19114 (62); 19117 (62); 19120 (62); 19124 (62); 19133 (62); 19136 (62); 19138 (62); 19141 (62); 19143 (62); 19149 (62); 19151 (62); 19161 (62); 19166 (62); 19168 (62); 19175 (62); 19176 (62); 19181 (62); 19183 (62); 19190 (62); 19192 (62); 19198 (62)
3413-150	11361X (63); 19232 (63)
3419-1	X-500NA (60); X-501NA (60); X-504NA (60); X-505NA (60); X-514NA (60); X-515NA (60); X-518NA (60); X-520NA (60); X-522NA (60); X-528NA (60); X-530NA (60); X-531NA (60); X-534NA (60); X-535NA (60); X-539NA (60); X-550NA (60); X-551NA (60); X-556NA (60); X-558NA (60); X-561NA (60); X-564NA (60); X-579NA (60); X-582 (60); X-584NA (60); X-585NA (60); X-586 (60); X-603 (61); X-609 (61); X-642 (61); X-671 (61); X-679 (61); X-720 (61); 9654 (60); 9656 (62); 9673 (61); 9693 (60); 9694 (60); 13277 (64); 19256 (63)
3419-25	X-524NA (60); X-533NA (60); X-546NA (60); 19331 (64)
3419-250	19241 (63); 19273 (63); 19337 (64); 19350-501 (65)
3434-1	12827 (64); 12838 (64); 13267 (64); 19407 (64)
3435	X-573NA (60)
3444-1	9693 (60)
3470-1	13277 (64); 19204 (62); 19205 (62); 19305 (63); 19309 (63); 19317 (63); 19323 (63)
3470-25	19115 (62); 19133 (62); 19139 (62); 19141 (62); 19153 (62); 19160 (62); 19164 (62); 19187 (62); 19194 (62)
3470-100	11385-500 (64); 19271 (64); 19435 (65)
3509-1	X-647 (61); X-648 (61); X-653 (61); X-653 (62); X-688 (61); X-697 (61); X-709 (61); X-717 (61); X-718 (61)
3509-25	X-627 (61); X-666 (61); X-669 (61); X-694 (61); 19105 (62)
3510-25	11011 (62); 11015 (62); 19101 (62); 19122 (62); 19148 (62); 19157 (62); 19162 (62); 19170 (62); 19181 (62); 19245 (65)
3512-1	X-522NA (60); X-537NA (60); X-564NA (60); X-566NA (60); X-573NA (60); 9693 (60)
3519-1	X-623 (61); X-629 (61); X-632 (61); X-634 (61); X-641 (61); X-658 (61); X-672 (61); X-676 (61); X-691 (61); X-714 (61); 11341-500 (63); 19129 (62); 19314 (63); 19314-500 (63); 19319 (63); 19408 (64); 19435 (65)
3519-25	19218 (63); 19229-501X (63); 19311 (63)
3535	X-573NA (60)
3535-1	X-514NA (60); X-583NA (60); X-586 (60); X-676 (61); X-714 (61); 9694 (60)
3540-1	9694 (60)
3545-1	X-671 (61); 19177 (62); 19196 (62); 19312 (63); 19319 (63); 19432 (65)
3619-1	19196 (62); 19204 (62); 19205 (62); 19228-500 (63); 19273-500 (63); 19305 (63); 19350-500 (65); 19408 (64)
3619-25	19103 (62); 19113 (62); 19120 (62); 19138 (62); 19141 (62); 19151 (62); 19160 (62); 19163 (62); 19168 (62); 19176 (62); 19190 (62); 19198 (62); 19350-500 (64); 19350-500 (65); 19350-501 (65)
3619-100	19271 (64)
3662-1	12807 (64); 12827 (64); 12838 (64); 12847 (64); 12850X (66); 12885-500 (65); 13267 (64); 19410 (64)

Part No.	Outfit Number (Year)
3665-1	X-628 (61); X-632 (61); X-643 (61); X-648 (61); X-658 (61); X-682 (61); X-701 (61); X-709 (61); X-717 (61); X-718 (61); 9656 (62); 9673 (61); 19204 (62); 19268 (63); 19350-501 (65); 19408 (64); 19434 (65)
3665-25	X-646 (61); X-694 (61); 19116 (62); 19195 (62)
3665-100	11361X (63); 19232 (63)
3666-25	19326 (64); 19326 (65); 19332 (64); 19434 (65)
3672-1	X-576 (60); X-577 (60)
3820-25	X-718 (61)
3830	X-576 (60)
3830-1	X-520NA (60); X-577 (60); X-579NA (60); X-602 (61); X-628 (61); X-653 (62); X-658 (61); X-676 (61); X-691 (61); X-709 (61); X-714 (61); 19142-500 (63); 19142-502 (63); 19196 (62); 19201 (1) (62); 19201 (2) (62); 19202 (62); 19203 (62); 19320 (63); 19432 (65); 19433 (65)
3830-75	11385-500 (64); 19271 (64)
6014-1	X-504NA (60); X-512NA (60); X-526NA (60); 9653 (60)
6014-75	10653SF (69)
6014-100	X-510NA (60); X-521NA (60); X-534NA (60); X-561NA (60); X-563NA (60); X-569NA (60); X-800 (60); X-835 (60); X-837 (60); X-875 (60)
6014-325	9730-500 (63); 11482 (64); 11540X (66); 11560X (66); 19142-500 (63); 19142-502 (63); 19212 (63); 19215 (63); 19237 (63); 19246 (63); 19273-500 (63); 19282 (64); 19301(A) (63); 19302 (63); 19303 (63); 19305 (63); 19306 (63); 19311 (63); 19313 (63); 19317 (63); 19322 (63); 19324 (63); 19328 (64); 19332 (64); 19345 (64); 19353 (64); 19354 (64); 19366 (64); 19370 (64); 19371 (64); 19371-500 (64); 19372 (64); 19372-500 (64); 19378 (64); 19391 (64); 19392 (64); 19393 (64); 19397 (64); 19398 (64); 19411 (64); 19437 (65); 19437-502 (65); 19438 (65); 19438-502 (65); 19441 (64); 19450 (65); 19450 (66); 19454-500 (65); 19502 (66); 19503 (66); 19544 (66); 19561 (66); 19567 (66); 19567-500 (66); 19578 (66); 19580 (66); 19583 (66)
6014-335	19248 (63)
6017-1	X-501NA (60); X-502NA (60); X-503NA (60); X-504NA (60); X-505NA (60); X-506NA (60); X-509NA (60); X-510NA (60); X-511NA (60); X-512NA (60); X-516NA (60); X-517NA (60); X-518NA (60); X-519NA (60); X-520NA (60); X-521NA (60); X-522NA (60); X-523NA (60); X-526NA (60); X-527NA (60); X-528NA (60); X-529NA (60); X-530NA (60); X-531NA (60); X-534NA (60); X-535NA (60); X-536NA (60); X-539NA (60); X-540NA (60); X-542NA (60); X-547 (60); X-550NA (60); X-551NA (60); X-552NA (60); X-554NA (60); X-559NA (60); X-561NA (60); X-562NA (60); X-563NA (60); X-565NA (60); X-569NA (60); X-570NA (60); X-571NA (60); X-573NA (60); X-579NA (60); X-582 (60); X-584NA (60); X-585NA (60); X-602 (61); X-603 (61); X-606 (61); X-607 (61); X-608 (61); X-609 (61); X-623 (61); X-625 (61); X-629 (61); X-632 (61); X-633 (61); X-634 (61); X-636 (61); X-636 (62); X-640 (61); X-641 (61); X-642 (61); X-643 (61); X-647 (61); X-648 (61); X-652 (61); X-653 (61); X-653 (62); X-655 (61); X-657 (61); X-658 (61); X-671 (61); X-672 (61); X-678 (61); X-679 (61); X-680 (61); X-682 (61); X-684 (61); X-688 (61); X-691 (61); X-697 (61); X-698 (61); X-701 (61); X-708 (61); X-709 (61); X-717 (61); X-718 (61); X-800 (60); X-835 (60); X-874 (60); X-875 (60); 1649NE (61); 9653 (60); 9654 (60); 9657 (62); 9673 (61); 9692 (60); 9692 (61); 9693 (60); 19129 (62); 19203 (62); 19205 (62); 19266 (62)
6017-25	X-524NA (60); X-532NA (60); X-533NA (60); X-538NA (60); X-546NA (60); X-600 (61); X-601 (61); X-605 (61); X-613 (61); X-614 (61); X-627 (61); X-639 (61); X-669 (61); X-685 (61); 9672 (61); 9730 (63); 9733 (63); 19103 (62); 19227 (63); 19230 (63); 19230-500 (63); 19231 (63); 19231-500 (63); 19238 (63); 19241-500 (63); 19250 (63); 19252 (63); 19281 (63); 19304 (63); 19351-500 (64)
6017-85	X-512NA (60)
6017-100	X-512NA (60)
6017-110	12800X (66)

Part No.	Outfit Number (Year)
6017-185	X-558NA (60)
6017-200	X-628 (61)
6017-210	X-628 (61); X-646 (61); 9671 (61); 19117 (62); 19201 (1) (62); 19201 (2) (62)
6017-225	19115 (62); 19133 (62)
6017-235	9656 (62)
6027-1	X-510NA (60); X-560NA (60); X-563NA (60)
6042-25	X-508NA (60); X-541NA (60); X-543NA (60); X-553NA (60); X-578NA (60); X-580NA (60); X-600 (61); X-612 (61); X-615 (61); X-616 (61); X-618 (61); X-620 (61); X-624 (61); X-635 (61); X-659 (61); X-662 (61); X-670 (61); X-673 (61); X-686 (61); X-687 (61); X-696 (61); X-700 (61); X-703 (61); X-706 (61); X-707 (61); X-707 (62); X-713 (61); X-715 (61); X-716 (61); X-829 (60); 1103 (61); 1107 (60); 1113 (60); 1115 (60); 1119 (60); 1123 (61); 1123 (62); 1123C (61); 1123C (62); 1123C (63); 11001 (62); 11001 (63); 11005 (62); 19118 (62); 19145 (62); 19146 (62); 19158 (62); 19169 (62); 19170 (62); 19189 (62); 19197 (62); 19217 (62); 19221 (62); 19224 (62); 19228-500 (63); 19235 (63); 19239 (63); 19240-500 (63); 19244 (63); 19244 (64); 19244-500 (64); 19247 (63); 19405 (64); 19409 (64); 19415 (64); 19512 (66); 19513 (66); 19553 (66)
6042-25X	19173 (62)
6042-50	1107 (60); 19386 (64); 19389 (64)
6042-75	19000 (62); 19107 (62); 19126 (62); 19127 (62); 19130 (62); 19147 (62); 19155 (62); 19159 (62); 19167 (62); 19171 (62); 19192 (62); 19200 (62); 19211 (63); 19219 (63); 19228 (63); 19239 (63); 19240 (63); 19240-500 (63); 19243 (63); 19245 (63); 19245 (65); 19249 (63); 19259 (63); 19272 (63); 19276 (63); 19381 (64); 19427 (65); 19500 (66); 19550 (66)
6042-100	19338 (64); 19426 (65)
6042-125	19325 (64); 19427 (65); 19500 (66); 19501 (66)
6042-250	11570 (66); 19173-500 (63); 19242 (63); 19339 (64); 19342 (64); 19357 (64); 19358 (64); 19362 (64); 19367 (64); 19368 (64); 19373 (64); 19374 (64); 19376 (64); 19377 (64); 19377-500 (64); 19428 (65); 19589 (66); 19701 (67)
6042-275	19260 (63)
6044-25	X-508NA (60); X-541NA (60); X-543NA (60); X-553NA (60); X-568NA (60); X-578NA (60); X-580NA (60); X-829 (60); 1103 (60); 1107 (60); 1113 (60); 1115 (60); 1117 (60)
6045-25	X-508NA (60); X-510NA (60); X-511NA (60); X-541NA (60); X-543NA (60); X-548 (60); X-549NA (60); X-553NA (60); X-563NA (60); X-567NA (60); X-568NA (60); X-578NA (60); X-829 (60); 1111 (60); 1115 (60); 1117 (60); 1119 (60)
6045-50	X-574NA (60); X-604 (61); X-604 (62); X-681 (61); X-704 (61); 19106 (62); 19106-50 (62); 19106-100 (62); 19210 (62)
6045-60	19210 (63); 19210 (63)
6045-150	11351-500 (63); 19210 (63); 19213 (63); 19216 (63); 19224 (63); 19233-500 (63); 19234-500 (63); 19238-501 (63); 19242 (63); 19312 (63); 19381 (64); 19512 (66); 19513 (66); 19553 (66)
6047-1	X-574NA (60)
6047-25	X-508NA (60); X-541NA (60); X-543NA (60); X-549NA (60); X-553NA (60); X-567NA (60); X-568NA (60); X-575 (60); X-578NA (60); X-580NA (60); X-829 (60); 1103 (60); 1107 (60); 1109 (60); 1111 (60); 1113 (60); 1115 (60); 1117 (60); 1119 (60); 1123 (61); 1123 (61); 19212 (63); 19229-500 (63); 19335 (65); 19349 (64); 19405 (64)
6050-1	X-606 (61); X-684 (61); X-698 (61)
6050-25	X-601 (61); X-613 (61); X-620 (61); X-626 (61); X-645 (61); X-651 (61); X-660 (61); X-664 (61); X-666 (61); X-670 (61); X-685 (61); X-702 (61); X-713 (61); X-716 (61); 9670 (61); 19108 (62); 19124 (62); 19364 (64)
6050-50	X-686 (61); X-713 (61); 19118 (62); 19134 (62); 19158 (62); 19159 (62); 19249 (63); 19250 (63); 19252 (63)

Part No.	Outfit Number (Year)
6050-100	19124 (62); 19229 (63); 19229-501 (63); 19229-501X (63); 19229-502 (63); 19230 (63); 19231 (63); 19231-500 (63); 19249 (63); 19250 (63); 19252 (63); 19255 (63); 19346 (64); 19348 (64); 19349 (64); 19390 (64); 19433 (65); 19502 (66); 19503 (66); 19506 (66); 19507 (66); 19514 (66); 19515 (66); 19516 (66); 19517 (66); 19520 (66); 19541 (66); 19546 (66); 19547 (66); 19563 (66); 19569 (66); 19571 (66); 19703 (67); 19705 (67); 19707 (67); 19920 (66)
6050-110	19206 (62)
6050-150	X-660 (62); 11351-500 (63); 11520-500 (65); 19000 (62); 19142 (62); 19142-50 (62); 19142-100 (62); 19158 (62); 19171 (62); 19197 (62); 19200 (62); 19211 (63); 19216 (63); 19217 (63); 19218 (63); 19219 (63); 19220 (63); 19224 (63); 19229-500 (63); 19230-500 (63); 19236 (63); 19239 (63); 19242 (63); 19259 (63); 19394 (64); 19419 (64)
6050-175	11520-500 (65); 19238-501 (63); 19263 (63); 19301 (63); 19304 (63); 19357 (64); 19362 (64); 19396 (64); 19399 (64); 19419 (64); 19429 (65); 19433 (65)
6057-1	X-544NA (60); X-545NA (60); X-548 (60); X-557 (60); X-837 (60); 9651 (60); 9655 (62)
6057-25	X-622 (61); X-631 (61); X-651 (61); X-664 (61); X-689 (61); X-694 (61); X-702 (61); 9650 (62); 9670 (61); 9745 (60); 19102 (62); 19105 (62); 19108 (62); 19110 (62); 19111 (62); 19112 (62); 19113 (62); 19114 (62); 19116 (62); 19120 (62); 19121 (62); 19123 (62); 19124 (62); 19128 (62); 19132 (62); 19136 (62); 19137 (62); 19138 (62); 19140 (62); 19141 (62); 19143 (62); 19149 (62); 19151 (62); 19155 (62); 19161 (62); 19163 (62); 19164 (62); 19165 (62); 19166 (62); 19168 (62); 19175 (62); 19176 (62); 19180 (62); 19181 (62); 19184 (62); 19185 (62); 19186 (62); 19187 (62); 19188 (62); 19190 (62); 19191 (62); 19198 (62); 19273 (63)
6057-50	19155 (62); 19202 (62); 19203X (62); 19204X (62)
6059-1	19248 (63)
6059-25	19212 (63); 19281 (63)
6059-50	9730 (63); 9730-500 (63); 11341-500 (63); 11361-500 (63); 11375-500 (63); 11520-500 (65); 11520-500 (66); 11560-500 (65); 11560X (66); 19237 (63); 19238-502 (63); 19245 (63); 19255 (63); 19281 (63); 19301(A) (63); 19302 (63); 19303 (63); 19305 (63); 19306 (63); 19308 (63); 19309 (63); 19310 (63); 19311 (63); 19312 (63); 19313 (63); 19314 (63); 19314-500 (63); 19316 (63); 19317A (63); 19318 (63); 19319 (63); 19321 (63); 19322 (63); 19323 (63); 19324 (63); 19327 (64); 19329 (64); 19332 (64); 19333 (64); 19335 (64); 19335 (65); 19336 (64); 19337 (64); 19348 (64); 19350 (64); 19350-500 (63); 19350-501 (65); 19351 (64); 19355 (64); 19364 (64); 19372 (64); 19372-500 (64); 19390 (64); 19396 (64); 19397 (64); 19398 (64); 19399 (64); 19434 (65); 19435 (65); 19436 (65); 19436 (66); 19437 (65); 19437-502 (65); 19438 (65); 19438-502 (65); 19439 (65); 19439 (66); 19439-502 (65); 19440 (65); 19440-502 (65); 19441 (65); 19446 (65); 19450 (65); 19450 (66); 19453 (65); 19453 (66); 19454-500 (65); 19455 (65); 19502 (66); 19504 (66); 19506 (66); 19507 (66); 19514 (66); 19515 (66); 19516 (66); 19517 (66); 19578 (66); 19706 (67); 19707 (67); 19910 (66); 19920 (66)
6062-1	X-502NA (60); X-504NA (60); X-506NA (60); X-509NA (60); X-516NA (60); X-517NA (60); X-521NA (60); X-526NA (60); X-529NA (60); X-530NA (60); X-534NA (60); X-536NA (60); X-542NA (60); X-547 (60); X-551NA (60); X-552NA (60); X-561NA (60); X-562NA (60); X-563NA (60); X-565NA (60); X-569NA (60); X-607 (61); X-623 (61); X-625 (61); X-642 (61); X-652 (61); X-655 (61); X-657 (61); 9651 (60); 9653 (60); 9692 (60); 9692 (61); 11341-500 (63); 19203 (62); 19314 (63); 19314-500 (63); 19318 (63); 19321 (63)

Part No.	Outfit Number (Year)
6062-25	X-532NA (60); X-546NA (60); X-601 (61); X-605 (61); X-613 (61); X-627 (61); X-631 (61); X-639 (61); X-646 (61); X-669 (61); X-702 (61); 11540X (66); 11620 (68); 19110 (62); 19163 (62); 19175 (62); 19186 (62); 19202 (62); 19203X (62); 19204X (62); 19216 (63); 19433 (65)
6067-25	X-600 (61); X-604 (61); X-604 (62); X-612 (61); X-616 (61); X-618 (61); X-620 (61); X-624 (61); X-626 (61); X-635 (61); X-637 (61); X-638 (61); X-644 (61); X-645 (61); X-650 (61); X-659 (61); X-660 (61); X-660 (61); X-661 (61); X-662 (61); X-663 (61); X-665 (61); X-666 (61); X-667 (61); X-668 (61); X-673 (61); X-681 (61); X-686 (61); X-687 (61); X-690 (61); X-695 (61); X-696 (61); X-699 (61); X-700 (61); X-703 (61); X-704 (61); X-705 (61); X-705 (61); X-706 (61); X-707 (61); X-707 (62); X-710 (61); X-713 (61); X-715 (61); X-716 (61); 1123 (61); 1123 (62); 1123C (61); 1123C (62); 1123C (63); 1124 (61); 1124C (61); 1124P (61); 11001 (62); 11001 (63); 11005 (62); 19000 (62); 19100 (62); 19101 (62); 19104 (62); 19106 (62); 19106-50 (62); 19106-100 (62); 19107 (62); 19109 (62); 19118 (62); 19119 (62); 19122 (62); 19125 (62); 19126 (62); 19127 (62); 19130 (62); 19131 (62); 19134 (62); 19135 (62); 19139 (62); 19142 (62); 19142-50 (62); 19142-100 (62); 19142-500 (62); 19144 (62); 19145 (62); 19146 (62); 19147 (62); 19148 (62); 19150 (62); 19152 (62); 19153 (62); 19154 (62); 19155 (62); 19156 (62); 19158 (62); 19159 (62); 19160 (62); 19162 (62); 19167 (62); 19169 (62); 19170 (62); 19171 (62); 19173 (62); 19174 (62); 19179 (62); 19182 (62); 19183 (62); 19189 (62); 19192 (62); 19193 (62); 19194 (62); 19195 (62); 19197 (62); 19199 (62); 19200 (62); 19210 (63); 19211 (63); 19216 (63); 19217 (63); 19218 (63); 19219 (63); 19223 (63); 19224 (63); 19225 (63); 19226 (63); 19228 (63); 19228-500 (63); 19229 (63); 19229-500 (63); 19229-501 (63); 19229-501X (63); 19229-502 (63); 19233 (63); 19234 (63); 19234-500 (63); 19236 (63); 19240 (63); 19240-500 (63); 19241 (63); 19242 (63); 19243 (63); 19244 (63); 19244 (64); 19244-500 (64); 19245 (63); 19245 (65); 19246 (63); 19247 (63); 19249 (63); 19258 (63); 19259 (63); 19260 (63); 19262 (63); 19267 (63); 19272 (63); 19273 (63); 19273-500 (63); 19274 (63); 19276 (63); 19358 (64); 19362 (64); 19380 (64); 19394 (64); 19395 (64); 19409 (64); 19428 (65)
6076-25	X-600 (61); X-624 (61); X-705 (62); X-716 (61); 11011 (62); 11015 (62); 19106 (62); 19106-50 (62); 19106-100 (62); 19118 (62); 19127 (62); 19130 (62); 19131 (62); 19134 (62); 19146 (62); 19150 (62); 19153 (62); 19154 (62); 19157 (62); 19158 (62); 19159 (62); 19162 (62); 19167 (62); 19169 (62); 19170 (62); 19182 (62); 19183 (62); 19189 (62); 19197 (62); 19200 (62); 19219 (63); 19249 (63)
6076-75	X-600 (61); X-612 (61); X-615 (61); X-618 (61); X-620 (61); X-624 (61); X-626 (61); X-635 (61); X-637 (61); X-638 (61); X-644 (61); X-645 (61); X-667 (61); X-668 (61); X-681 (61); X-687 (61); X-690 (61); X-695 (61); X-700 (61); X-705 (61); X-706 (61); X-707 (61); X-707 (62); X-710 (61); X-715 (61); X-716 (61); 1124 (61); 1124C (61); 1124P (61); 19213 (63); 19231-500 (63); 19235 (63); 19239 (63); 19242 (63); 19281 (63); 19282 (64); 19304 (63); 19363 (64); 19363-500 (64); 19367 (64); 19381 (64); 19382 (64); 19429 (65); 19500 (66); 19501 (66); 19530 (66); 19550 (66); 19589 (66); 19701 (67)
6076-100	9730-500 (63); 11311X (63); 11315 (63); 11351-500 (63); 11375-500 (63); 19215 (63); 19222 (63); 19230-500 (63); 19231-500 (63); 19234 (63); 19234-500 (63); 19245 (63); 19245 (65); 19249 (63); 19259 (63); 19262 (63); 19269 (63); 19270 (63); 19273-500 (63); 19281 (63); 19317 (63); 19394 (64); 19395 (64)
6076-125	19263 (63); 19301 (63); 19327 (64); 19333 (64)

Part No.	Outfit Number (Year)
6119-100	X-500NA (60); X-513NA (60); X-515NA (60); X-537NA (60); X-555NA (60); X-566NA (60); X-693 (61); 9652 (60); 11351-500 (63); 19233-500 (63); 19233-501 (63); 19239 (63); 19251 (63); 19280 (63); 19351-500 (64)
6119-110	11540-500 (65); 11540-500 (66); 11540X (66); 19331 (64); 19346 (64); 19347 (64); 19366 (64); 19371 (64); 19432 (65); 19561 (66); 19580 (66)
6119-125	19334 (64); 19334-500 (64); 19334-500 (65); 19344 (64); 19351-500 (64); 19391 (64); 19416 (64); 19432 (65)
6120-25	X-615 (61); X-619 (61); X-621 (61); X-654 (61); X-670 (61); 1125 (61); 1125C (61); 11011 (62); 11015 (62); 19142-500 (63); 19142-502 (63); 19157 (62); 19239 (63)
6130-1	X-630 (61); 9674 (61)
6130-25	11620 (68); 19442 (65); 19442 (66); 19444 (65); 19444 (66); 19444-502 (65); 19510 (66); 19511 (66); 19703 (67)
6142-25	9730-500 (63); 11361-500 (63); 19227 (63); 19229 (63); 19229-500 (63); 19229-501 (63); 19229-501X (63); 19229-502 (63); 19238-502 (63); 19252 (63); 19255 (63); 19258 (63); 19301(A) (63); 19302 (63); 19306 (63); 19308 (63); 19310 (63); 19311 (63); 19313 (63); 19316 (63); 19319 (63); 19335 (64); 19382 (64)
6142-50	10653SF (69); 19340 (64); 19340 (65); 19365 (64); 19369 (64); 19375 (64)
6142-75	19245 (65); 19331 (64); 19364 (64); 19393 (64); 19433 (65); 19434 (65); 19569 (66)
6142-100	11520-500 (65); 11520-500 (66); 11560-500 (65); 19345 (64); 19366 (64); 19371 (64); 19371-500 (64); 19378 (64); 19391 (64); 19436 (65); 19436 (66); 19437 (65); 19437 (66); 19437-502 (65); 19439 (65); 19439 (66); 19439-502 (65); 19442 (65); 19442 (66); 19444 (65); 19444 (66); 19444-502 (65); 19454-500 (65); 19506 (66); 19507 (66); 19510 (66); 19511 (66); 19546 (66); 19547 (66); 19555 (66); 19557 (66); 19578 (66); 19586 (66); 19910 (66); 19920 (66)
6142-125	19328 (64); 19329 (64); 19330 (64); 19335 (65); 19341 (64); 19346 (64); 19351 (64); 19352 (64); 19354 (64); 19363 (64); 19363-500 (64); 19370 (64); 19372-500 (64); 19383 (64); 19385 (64); 19396 (64); 19399 (64); 19411 (64); 19418 (64); 19435 (65); 19563 (66); 19567 (66); 19567-500 (66); 19571 (66); 19578 (66); 19583 (66)
6142-150	11482 (64); 19325 (64); 19335 (65); 19372 (64); 19392 (64); 19412 (64); 19516 (66); 19517 (66); 19520 (66); 19705 (67)
6142-175	19334 (64); 19334-500 (64); 19334-500 (65); 19343 (64); 19416 (64); 19427 (64); 19428 (65); 19431 (65); 19432 (65)
6162-1	X-504NA (60); X-544NA (60); X-545NA (60); X-557 (60); X-573NA (60); X-800 (60); X-835 (60); X-837 (60); X-874 (60); 9673 (61); 19206 (62)
6162-25	X-660 (61); X-660 (62); X-664 (61); X-689 (61); 9650 (62); 9670 (61); 9672 (61); 9733 (63); 9745 (60); 11351-500 (63); 11375-500 (63); 19102 (62); 19108 (62); 19112 (62); 19121 (62); 19123 (62); 19180 (62); 19184 (62); 19187 (62); 19188 (62); 19214 (63); 19214-500 (63); 19229-500 (63); 19229-501 (63); 19229-501X (63); 19234-500 (63); 19236 (63); 19238-501 (63); 19254 (63); 19275 (63); 19317A (63); 19324 (63); 19348 (64); 19349 (64); 19390 (64)
6162-100	19351-500 (64)
6162-110	12710X (66)
6167-25	11311X (63); 11315 (63); 11415 (63); 11570 (66); 19142-500 (63); 19173-500 (63); 19213 (63); 19215 (63); 19220 (63); 19221 (63); 19222 (63); 19228-500 (63); 19229-501 (63); 19229-501X (63); 19233-500 (63); 19233-501 (63); 19235 (63); 19253 (63); 19253 (64); 19274-500 (63); 19281 (63); 19317 (63); 19339 (64); 19342 (64); 19363 (64); 19363-500 (64); 19368 (64); 19373 (64); 19376 (64); 19377 (64); 19377-500 (64); 19379 (64); 19379 (65); 19381 (64); 19382 (64); 19386 (64); 19427 (65); 19429 (65); 19433 (65); 19589 (66); 19701 (67)

Part No.	Outfit Number (Year)
6167-50	19244-500 (64); 19269 (63); 19270 (63); 19281 (63); 19357 (64); 19374 (64); 19426 (65); 19427 (65)
6167-75	19238-501 (63); 19244-500 (64); 19263 (63); 19301 (63); 19367 (64); 19428 (65)
6167-100	10613SF (69); 10653SF (69); 11580 (66); 19282 (64); 19328 (64); 19330 (64); 19341 (64); 19345 (64); 19351-500 (64); 19352 (64); 19353 (64); 19370 (64); 19371-500 (64); 19378 (64); 19383 (64); 19385 (64); 19389 (64); 19411 (64); 19415 (64); 19500 (66); 19501 (66); 19512 (66); 19513 (66); 19520 (66); 19530 (66); 19541 (66); 19542 (66); 19544 (66); 19546 (66); 19547 (66); 19550 (66); 19553 (66); 19555 (66); 19557 (66); 19563 (66); 19567 (66); 19567-500 (66); 19569 (66); 19571 (66); 19583 (66); 19586 (66); 19704 (67); 19705 (67)
6167-125	19328 (64); 19340 (64); 19340 (65); 19345 (64); 19354 (64); 19365 (64); 19369 (64); 19375 (64); 19412 (64)
6167-150	19325 (64); 19428 (65)
6167-175	19338 (64); 19343 (64); 19418 (64); 19427 (65)
6175-1	X-664 (61); X-802 (60); X-835 (60); 19196 (62)
6175-25	X-524NA (60); 19105 (62)
6176-25	10613SF (69); 19340 (64); 19340 (65); 19342 (64); 19364 (64); 19365 (64); 19369 (64); 19375 (64); 19385 (64); 19567 (66); 19567-500 (66)
6176-50	11385-500 (64); 11482 (64); 11540-500 (65); 11540-500 (66); 11560-500 (65); 11560X (66); 11580 (66); 19330 (64); 19333 (64); 19336 (64); 19341 (64); 19370 (64); 19371 (64); 19372 (64); 19383 (64); 19392 (64); 19396 (64); 19399 (64); 19438 (65); 19438-502 (65); 19440 (65); 19440-502 (65); 19441 (65); 19442 (65); 19442 (66); 19450 (65); 19450 (66); 19454-500 (65); 19504 (66); 19506 (66); 19507 (66); 19510 (66); 19511 (66); 19516 (66); 19517 (66); 19541 (66); 19544 (66); 19555 (66); 19557 (66); 19561 (66); 19569 (66); 19580 (66); 19583 (66); 19586 (66); 19703 (67); 19705 (67); 19706 (67); 19910 (66); 19920 (66)
6176-75	11520-500 (65); 11520-500 (66); 19327 (64); 19332 (64); 19333 (64); 19350-500 (64); 19350-500 (65); 19350-501 (65); 19351 (64); 19352 (64); 19353 (64); 19354 (64); 19355 (64); 19366 (64); 19372 (64); 19393 (64); 19411 (64); 19430 (64); 19438-502 (65); 19444 (65); 19444 (66); 19444-502 (65); 19446 (65); 19450 (65); 19453 (65); 19453 (66); 19454-500 (65); 19455 (65); 19520 (66); 19563 (66); 19567-500 (66); 19578 (66); 19704 (67); 19707 (67)
6176-100	19334 (64); 19334-500 (64); 19334-500 (65); 19343 (64); 19344 (64); 19351-500 (64); 19372-500 (64); 19416 (64); 19418 (64); 19432 (65)
6219-1	X-556NA (60)
6219-25	X-240 (60)
6257-100	11361X (63); 11385-500 (64); 11482 (64); 19214 (63); 19214-500 (63); 19230-500 (63); 19231-500 (63); 19232 (63); 19240-500 (63); 19254 (63); 19271 (64); 19275 (63); 19392 (64); 19393 (64)
6315-60	9730 (63); 12820-100 (65); 13267 (64); 19251 (63); 19316 (63); 19417 (64)
6342-25	12885-500 (65); 19327 (64); 19453 (65); 19453 (66); 19561 (66)
6343-1	X-603 (61); X-636 (61); X-636 (62); X-672 (61); X-683 (61); 1649NE (61); 19172 (62); 19266 (63)
6343-25	X-605 (61); 11375-500 (63); 19201 (1) (62); 19201 (2) (62); 19202 (62); 19203X (62); 19204X (62); 19218 (63); 19267 (63); 19280 (63); 19301(A) (63); 19303 (63); 19306 (63); 19320 (63); 19324 (63); 19349 (64); 19351 (64); 19351-500 (64)
6357-1	X-683 (61); X-692 (61); 9675 (61)
6361	X-577 (60)
6361-1	X-513NA (60); X-537NA (60); X-540NA (60); X-566NA (60); X-603 (61); X-640 (61); 9652 (60); 9657 (62); 9692 (60); 9692 (61); 12820-100 (65); 12838 (64); 12850X (66); 13255 (64); 13267 (64); 19238-501 (63); 19317A (63); 19320 (63); 19324 (63); 19335 (65); 19372-500 (64); 19407 (64)

Part No.	Outfit Number (Year)
6401-25	11560X (66); 11580 (66); 19326 (64); 19326 (65); 19331 (64); 19344 (64); 19350-500 (65); 19350-501 (65); 19351-500 (64); 19397 (64); 19428 (65); 19514 (66); 19515 (66); 19567 (66); 19567-500 (66); 19571 (66); 19704 (67); 19707 (67); 19910 (66); 19920 (66)
6401-100	19561 (66); 19563 (66)
6402-25	11001 (62); 11001 (63); 11005 (62); 11341-500 (63); 11570 (66); 19152 (62); 19182 (62); 19269 (63); 19270 (63); 19281 (63); 19304 (63); 19314 (63); 19358 (64); 19374 (64); 19428 (65); 19432 (65); 19589 (66); 19701 (67)
6402-50	10613SF (69); 10653SF (69); 11620 (68); 13267 (64); 19329 (64); 19336 (64); 19350-500 (64); 19353 (64); 19375 (64); 19393 (64); 19398 (64); 19416 (64); 19437 (65); 19437 (66); 19437-502 (65); 19439 (65); 19439 (66); 19439-502 (65); 19446 (65); 19454-500 (65); 19455 (65); 19502 (66); 19503 (66)
6402-150	19563 (66)
6404-25	X-575 (60); X-580NA (60); 1109 (60); 1119 (60)
6405-1	X-607 (61); X-636 (61); X-636 (62); X-642 (61); 1649NE (61)
6405-25	X-664 (61); 19138 (62); 19173 (62); 19186 (62); 19228 (63)
6406-25	X-600 (61); X-604 (61); X-604 (62); X-616 (61); X-618 (61); X-620 (61); X-624 (61); X-637 (61); X-638 (61); X-659 (61); X-660 (61); X-660 (62); X-661 (61); X-666 (61); X-668 (61); X-673 (61); X-687 (61); X-690 (61); X-695 (61); X-696 (61); X-700 (61); X-703 (61); X-705 (61); X-705 (62); X-706 (61); X-707 (61); X-707 (62); 1123 (61); 1123 (62); 1123C (61); 1123C (62); 1123C (63); 19100 (62); 19118 (62); 19126 (62); 19134 (62); 19142 (62); 19142-50 (62); 19142-100 (62); 19142-500 (63); 19142-502 (63); 19154 (62); 19158 (62); 19173 (62); 19210 (63); 19212 (63); 19228 (63); 19228-500 (63); 19234 (63); 19234-500 (63); 19243 (63); 19244 (63); 19244 (64); 19262 (63); 19273-500 (63); 19276 (63); 19317 (63); 19428 (65)
6407-1	19309 (63); 19320 (63)
6407-25	9733 (63); 11385-500 (64); 19237 (63); 19241-500 (63); 19271 (64); 19348 (64); 19390 (64)
6408-25	9730-500 (63); 11361-500 (63); 19238-502 (63); 19302 (63); 19303 (63); 19306 (63); 19310 (63); 19349 (64); 19350 (64); 19354 (64); 19411 (64)
6408-50	19542 (66); 19703 (67)
6409-25	11311X (63); 11315 (63); 19215 (63); 19222 (63); 19223 (63); 19229 (63); 19229-500 (63); 19229-501 (63); 19229-501X (63); 19229-502 (63); 19247 (63); 19250 (63); 19259 (63); 19269 (63); 19270 (63); 19274 (63); 19274-500 (63); 19379 (64); 19385 (64); 19395 (64); 19405 (64); 19409 (64); 19428 (65); 19512 (66); 19513 (66); 19530 (66); 19553 (66)
6410-25	19223 (63); 19247 (63); 19250 (63); 19274 (63); 19428 (65)
6411-25	19260 (63); 19428 (65)
6413-1	9655 (62); 19431 (65)
6413-25	9733 (63); 11341-500 (63); 11361X (63); 19101 (62); 19109 (62); 19111 (62); 19114 (62); 19117 (62); 19144 (62); 19156 (62); 19161 (62); 19164 (62); 19174 (62); 19179 (62); 19199 (62); 19232 (63); 19241 (63); 19241-500 (63); 19273 (63); 19303 (63); 19314 (63); 19314-500 (63); 19416 (64); 19431 (65)
6414-1	X-540NA (60); X-555NA (60); 12710X (66); 12800X (66); 12885-500 (65); 19257 (63); 19268 (63)
6414-75	19380 (64); 19435 (65)
6414-85	12827 (64); 19417 (64); 19435 (65)
6414-150	19214 (63); 19214-500 (63); 19238 (63); 19254 (63); 19267 (63); 19275 (63)
6415-1	12807 (64); 12827 (64); 12838 (64); 12847 (64); 12867 (64); 12885-500 (65); 13267 (64); 19410 (64); 19417 (64)
6415-25	12800X (66)
6416-1	X-693 (61); 9674 (61); 11341-500 (63); 19172 (62); 19177 (62); 19206 (62); 19266 (63); 19274 (63); 19309 (63); 19314 (63)
6424-1	X-511NA (60); X-512NA (60); X-522NA (60)
6424-60	X-512NA (60)

Part No.	Outfit Number (Year)
6424-85	X-512NA (60)
6428	X-576 (60)
6428-1	X-572NA (60); X-678 (61); X-679 (61); X-680 (61); X-682 (61); X-801 (60); 9675 (61)
6428-25	12800X (66)
6429-1	19257 (63); 19320 (63); 19432 (65)
6431-1	12710X (66); 19546 (66); 19547 (66)
6436-100	12800X (66)
6436-110	12820-100 (65); 12838 (64); 12850X (66); 13255 (64); 13267 (64); 19251 (63); 19317A (63); 19321 (63); 19372-500 (64); 19417 (64)
6437-1	X-719 (61); X-720 (61); 9658 (62); 12710X (66); 12820-100 (65); 12838 (64); 12850X (66); 12885-500 (65); 13255 (64); 13267 (64); 19172 (62); 19177 (62); 19178 (62); 19196 (62); 19204 (62); 19206 (62); 19410 (64)
6440-1	X-693 (61); 9692 (61); 13255 (64); 19178 (62); 19230-500 (63); 19320 (63); 19435 (65)
6440-50	9730-500 (63); 19230 (63); 19231 (63); 19231-500 (63); 19238 (63); 19431 (65)
6445-1	X-636 (61); X-636 (62); X-640 (61); X-677 (61); X-692 (61); X-708 (61); 1649NE (61); 9657 (62); 11341-500 (63); 19313 (63); 19314 (63); 19395 (64)
6445-25	X-636 (61); X-710 (61); 19191 (62)
6446-1	19251 (63); 19256 (63); 19309 (63); 19435 (65)
6446-60	19435 (65)
6448-1	9655 (62); 9656 (62); 19268 (63); 19434 (65)
6448-25	9733 (63); 19111 (62); 19128 (62); 19137 (62); 19185 (62); 19225 (63); 19229-500 (63); 19241 (63); 19241-500 (63); 19272 (63); 19273 (63); 19322 (63); 19415 (64); 19434 (65)
6463-1	9655 (62); 19204 (62); 19248 (63); 19398 (64); 19431 (65)
6463-25	9733 (63); 11341-500 (63); 11361-500 (63); 19113 (62); 19116 (62); 19133 (62); 19135 (62); 19148 (62); 19149 (62); 19161 (62); 19164 (62); 19166 (62); 19175 (62); 19176 (62); 19181 (62); 19199 (62); 19237 (63); 19238-502 (63); 19241 (63); 19241-500 (63); 19308 (63); 19310 (63); 19314 (63); 19314-500 (63); 19431 (65)
6464	13267 (64)
6464-250	19590 (66)
6464-450	12850X (66)
6464-475	X-802 (60)
6464-485	12800X (66)
6464-525	19417 (64)
6464-650	19590 (66)
6464-700	19590 (66)
6464-735	12710X (66); 12820-100 (65); 12850X (66); 12885-500 (65); 13255 (64); 19308 (63); 19380 (64); 19407 (64); 19410 (64)
6464-750	9730 (63); 19308 (63); 19320 (63)
6464-900	X-572NA (60); X-576 (60); 11375-500 (63); 19251 (63); 19308 (63)
6464-925	9730 (63); 19229-501 (63); 19229-501X (63); 19231-500 (63)
6465	9651 (60)
6465-1	9651 (60); 9651 (60)
6465-60	9651 (60); 9651 (60)
6465-85	X-502NA (60); X-506NA (60); 9651 (60); 9651 (60)
6465-100	X-502NA (60); X-532NA (60); 9671 (61); 9672 (61)
6465-100X	X-559NA (60)
6465-110	X-506NA (60); X-517NA (60); X-560NA (60); X-569NA (60); X-655 (61); X-875 (60); 9651 (60); 9651 (60)

Part No.	Outfit Number (Year)
6465-150	9730 (63); 11540-500 (65); 11540-500 (66); 11540X (66); 11560-500 (65); 13267 (64); 19214 (63); 19214-500 (63); 19226 (63); 19229 (63); 19229-500 (63); 19229-501 (63); 19229-501X (63); 19229-502 (63); 19233 (63); 19233-500 (63); 19233-501 (63); 19238 (63); 19250 (63); 19254 (63); 19267 (63); 19275 (63); 19282 (64); 19303 (63); 19328 (64); 19329 (64); 19332 (64); 19337 (64); 19345 (64); 19346 (64); 19352 (64); 19353 (64); 19354 (64); 19355 (64); 19366 (64); 19371 (64); 19371-500 (64); 19378 (64); 19380 (64); 19389 (64); 19391 (64); 19393 (64); 19399 (64); 19411 (64); 19412 (64); 19418 (64); 19438 (65); 19438-502 (65); 19440 (65); 19440-502 (65); 19441 (65); 19444 (65); 19444 (66); 19444-502 (65); 19454-500 (65); 19455 (65); 19504 (66); 19506 (66); 19507 (66); 19514 (66); 19515 (66); 19516 (66); 19517 (66); 19542 (66); 19546 (66); 19547 (66); 19561 (66); 19580 (66); 19580 (66); 19706 (67); 19707 (67)
6465-160	19417 (64)
6469-1	19231-500 (63); 19251 (63); 19266 (63)
6469-50	9730 (63); 19227 (63); 19230 (63); 19230-500 (63); 19231 (63); 19231-500 (63); 19238 (63); 19316 (63); 19371-500 (64)
6470-1	X-505NA (60); X-519NA (60); X-520NA (60); X-522NA (60); X-523NA (60); X-527NA (60); X-528NA (60); X-536NA (60); X-550NA (60); X-556NA (60); X-558NA (60); X-570NA (60); X-571NA (60); X-582 (60); X-584NA (60); X-585NA (60); X-586 (60); X-602 (61); X-609 (61); X-629 (61); X-632 (61); X-634 (61); X-641 (61); X-643 (61); X-648 (61); X-688 (61); X-701 (61); X-709 (61); 9654 (60)
6470-25	X-240 (60); X-639 (61); X-694 (61); 9671 (61); 11361X (60); X-229-500 (63); 19229-501 (63); 19232 (63); 19272 (63); 19273 (63); 19326 (64); 19326 (65); 19337 (64); 19351 (64); 19351-500 (64); 19397 (64); 19434 (65)
6473-1	9657 (62); 19178 (62)
6473-25	9650 (62); 9730 (63); 11482 (64); 11540-500 (65); 11540-500 (66); 11540X (66); 11560-500 (65); 11560X (66); 19102 (62); 19119 (62); 19140 (62); 19150 (62); 19165 (62); 19184 (62); 19191 (62); 19227 (63); 19229 (63); 19229-500 (63); 19229-501 (63); 19229-501X (63); 19229-502 (63); 19233 (63); 19235 (63); 19239 (63); 19246 (63); 19255 (63); 19258 (63); 19281 (63); 19304 (63); 19331 (64); 19335 (64); 19335 (65); 19347 (64); 19353 (64); 19371 (64); 19379 (64); 19379 (65); 19380 (64); 19392 (64); 19393 (64); 19398 (64); 19412 (64); 19418 (64); 19440 (65); 19440-502 (65); 19442 (65); 19442 (66); 19455 (65); 19504 (66); 19510 (66); 19511 (66); 19580 (66); 19706 (67)
6475-1	X-577 (60); X-586 (60); X-636 (61); X-636 (62); 1649NE (61); 9658 (62); 19178 (62)
6475-25	19180 (62)
6475-50	19238-501 (63); 19263 (63); 19304 (63); 19373 (64); 19382 (64); 19389 (64); 19419 (64); 19435 (65)
6476-1	X-509NA (60); X-529NA (60); X-542NA (60); X-544NA (60); X-545NA (60); X-551NA (60); X-552NA (60); X-557 (60); X-562NA (60); X-574NA (60); X-606 (60); X-608 (61); X-698 (61); X-800 (60); X-874 (60); X-875 (60); 9651 (60); 9673 (61); 19266 (63)
6476-25	X-538NA (60); X-549NA (60); X-567NA (60); X-568NA (60); X-601 (61); X-622 (61); 1111 (60); 1117 (60); 9650 (62); 9670 (61); 9730 (63); 9745 (60); 19105 (62); 19108 (62); 19121 (62); 19123 (62); 19136 (62); 19163 (62); 19226 (63); 19230 (63); 19230-500 (63); 19231 (63); 19231-500 (63); 19233 (63); 19233-500 (63); 19233-501 (63); 19246 (63); 19250 (63); 19252 (63); 19255 (63); 19305 (63); 19309 (63); 19316 (63); 19319 (63); 19350 (64)
6476-75	19214 (63); 19245 (65); 19254 (63); 19275 (63)
6476-85	19248 (63); 19309 (63)
6476-125	11620 (68)

Part No.	Outfit Number (Year)
6476-135	12850X (66)
6480-25	X-621 (61); X-650 (61); X-654 (61); X-663 (61); X-665 (61); X-667 (61); X-699 (61); 1125 (61); 1125C (61); 9730-500 (63); 11361-500 (63); 19104 (62); 19107 (62); 19109 (62); 19122 (62); 19135 (62); 19144 (62); 19145 (62); 19147 (62); 19148 (62); 19152 (62); 19156 (62); 19174 (62); 19179 (62); 19193 (62); 19195 (62); 19238-502 (63); 19310 (63)
6484-25	19312 (63)
6500-1	19308 (63); 19309 (63); 19319 (63); 19323 (63); 19395 (64)
6500-25	19217 (63); 19218 (63); 19225 (63); 19246 (63); 19267 (63)
6501-1	19233-500 (63); 19233-501 (63); 19256 (63); 19317 (63); 19322 (63); 19396 (64); 19399 (64)
6501-25	19113 (62); 19115 (62); 19116 (62); 19125 (62); 19132 (62); 19137 (62); 19140 (62); 19165 (62); 19176 (62); 19184 (62); 19225 (63); 19227 (63); 19233 (63)
6502-25	11415 (63); 11415 (63); 19000 (62); 19159 (62); 19169 (62); 19219 (63); 19220 (63); 19249 (63); 19252 (63)
6502-50	11415 (63); 19211 (63); 19219 (63); 19220 (63); 19223 (63); 19240 (63); 19240-500 (63); 19242 (63); 19244-500 (64); 19245 (63); 19245 (65); 19249 (63); 19253 (63); 19253 (64); 19274 (63); 19301 (63); 19322 (63); 19367 (64); 19368 (64); 19376 (64); 19377 (64); 19377-500 (64); 19379 (64); 19379 (65); 19381 (64); 19382 (64); 19389 (64); 19394 (64); 19426 (65); 19427 (65)
6502-75	19333 (64); 19430 (65)
6512-1	19129 (62); 19204 (62); 19308 (63); 19313 (63); 19318 (63); 19435 (65)
6512-25	19103 (62); 19112 (62); 19114 (62); 19117 (62); 19124 (62); 19133 (62); 19136 (62); 19138 (62); 19141 (62); 19143 (62); 19149 (62); 19161 (62); 19166 (62); 19175 (62); 19181 (62); 19183 (62); 19190 (62); 19198 (62); 19435 (65)
6517-1	X-802 (60)
6517-75	19590 (66)
6519-1	X-630 (61); X-655 (61); X-678 (61); X-680 (61); X-684 (61); X-692 (61); X-802 (60); 9658 (62); 19309 (63)
6519-25	X-603 (61); X-623 (61); X-631 (61); X-640 (61); X-685 (61); 9674 (61); 19303 (63)
6530-1	X-633 (61); X-676 (61); X-679 (61); X-683 (61); X-693 (61); X-697 (61); X-714 (61); X-720 (61); 9675 (61)
6536-25	19233-501 (63); 19312 (63)
6544-1	X-518NA (60); X-528NA (60); X-539NA (60); X-550NA (60); X-571NA (60); X-572NA (60); X-579NA (60); X-582 (60); X-583NA (60); X-585NA (60); X-586 (60); X-694 (60); 19305 (63); 19435 (65)
6544-25	X-524NA (60); X-533NA (60); 11385-500 (64); 19272 (63)
6560-1	X-577 (60); 12827 (64); 19407 (64)
6560-25	X-572NA (60); X-693 (61); 19178 (62); 19251 (63); 19257 (63)
6560-50	19318 (63)
6630-25	X-621 (61); X-650 (61); X-654 (61); X-663 (61); X-665 (61); X-667 (61); X-699 (61); 1125 (61); 1125C (61); 9730-500 (63); 19104 (62); 19107 (62); 19122 (62); 19145 (62); 19152 (62); 19156 (62); 19202 (62); 19203X (62); 19217 (63); 19302 (63); 19313 (63); 19317 (63); 19317A (63); 19323 (63)
6640-25	9671 (61); 9671 (61)
6650-1	X-505NA (60); X-514NA (60); X-519NA (60); X-520NA (60); X-523NA (60); X-527NA (60); X-531NA (60); X-536NA (60); X-556NA (60); X-558NA (60); X-570NA (60); X-579NA (60); X-584NA (60); X-586 (60); X-602 (61); X-609 (61); X-629 (61); X-634 (61); X-641 (61); X-688 (61); X-720 (61); 9654 (60); 19316 (63); 19435 (65)
6650-25	X-240 (60); X-639 (61); 9671 (61); 9733 (63); 19141 (62); 19225 (63); 19241 (63); 19241-500 (63); 19273 (63); 19312 (63)

Part No.	Outfit Number (Year)
6651-25	19337 (64); 19343 (64); 19344 (64); 19397 (64); 19415 (64); 19419 (64); 19438 (65); 19438-502 (65)
6670-1	X-513NA (60); X-537NA (60); X-555NA (60); X-566NA (60); X-582 (60); X-583NA (60); X-585NA (60); 9652 (60)
6736-1	9675 (61); 19172 (62); 19178 (62)
6802-1	X-509NA (60); X-512NA (60)
6803-1	X-512NA (60); X-527NA (60)
6804-1	X-564NA (60)
6807-1	X-527NA (60); X-564NA (60); X-874 (60)
6809-1	X-561NA (60); X-564NA (60)
6812-1	X-511NA (60); X-513NA (60); X-528NA (60); X-537NA (60); X-540NA (60); X-552NA (60); X-555NA (60); X-556NA (60); X-558NA (60); X-562NA (60); X-564NA (60); X-565NA (60); X-573NA (60); X-630 (61); X-643 (61); X-682 (61); X-683 (61); X-692 (61); X-708 (61); X-717 (61); 9652 (60); 9674 (61); 19172 (62)
6812-25	X-704 (61); 9745 (60)
6816-1	9693 (60)
6817-1	X-513NA (60); X-540NA (60); X-566NA (60); X-630 (61); X-678 (61); X-679 (61); X-680 (61); X-683 (61); 9652 (60); 19172 (62)
6819-1	X-503NA (60); X-506NA (60)
6819-25	X-240 (60)
6820-1	X-509NA (60); X-519NA (60); X-632 (61); X-653 (61); X-720 (61); X-802 (60); 9658 (62); 19178 (62)
6820-25	X-653 (62); 9730-500 (63)
6821	X-526NA (60); X-569NA (60)
6821-1	X-521NA (60); X-875 (60); 9692 (60)
6822-1	9674 (61); 12820-100 (65); 12827 (64); 19177 (62); 19238-501 (63); 19238-502 (63); 19407 (64)
6822-25	19227 (63)
6822-50	11375-500 (63); 19214 (63); 19214-500 (63); 19227 (63); 19238 (63); 19275 (63); 19302 (63); 19327 (64); 19347 (64); 19453 (65); 19453 (66); 19555 (66); 19586 (66)
6823-1	X-503NA (60)
6824-50	19326 (64); 19326 (65); 19430 (65); 19431 (65); 19432 (65)
6825-1	X-502NA (60); X-504NA (60); X-510NA (60); X-516NA (60); X-521NA (60); X-529NA (60); X-530NA (60); X-536NA (60); X-542NA (60); X-547 (60); X-548 (60); X-552NA (60); X-554NA (60); X-560NA (60); X-562NA (60); X-563NA (60); X-569NA (60); X-625 (61); X-652 (61); X-657 (61); X-698 (61); X-701 (61); X-800 (60); 9651 (60); 9653 (60); 9692 (60); 9692 (61); 19203 (62); 19309 (63)
6825-25	X-538NA (60); X-546NA (60); X-605 (61); X-614 (61); 9650 (62); 9670 (61); 9672 (61); 19108 (62); 19110 (62); 19121 (62); 19312 (63)
6826-1	X-502NA (60)
6827-1	X-630 (61); X-693 (61); 9674 (61); 19238-501 (63); 19257 (63); 19320 (63)
6828-1	X-630 (61); X-693 (61); 19553 (66)
6830-1	X-503NA (60); X-514NA (60); X-515NA (60); X-519NA (60); X-531NA (60); X-535NA (60); 9654 (60)
6844-1	X-500NA (60); X-512NA (60); X-518NA (60); X-528NA (60); X-535NA (60); X-539NA (60); X-586 (60); X-800 (60); X-835 (60)
6844-25	X-533NA (60)
19567-511	19567-500 (66)

APPENDIX C - LEAST & MOST PRODUCED OUTFITS

Appendix C ranks the ten least and the ten most produced promotional and catalog outfits from the 1960s. Also featured is the motive power that appeared in the outfit.

Least Produced Outfits

Rank	Outfit Number	Year	Qty	Motive Power
1	X-559NA	60	6	246-1
	X-578NA	60		58-1
2	13267	64	12	773X-1
3	13255	64	20	637X-1, 50-1
4	X-682	61	24	247-1
	12857	64		2383-1
	12867	64		773LTS
5	12838	64	25	773-1
	19187	62		211P-25, 211T-25
6	X-677	61	30	1872X-1
	12807	64		736LTS
	12817	64		2383-1
7	9692	61	34	2037-1
8	X-534NA	60	36	220P-1, 220T-1
	X-547	60		244-1
9	19246	63	37	237-25
10	X-545NA	60	40	246-1
	X-586	60		2349X
	19275	63		238-25
	19409	64		1061-25

Most Produced Outfits

Rank	Outfit Number	Year	Qty	Motive Power
1	11415	63	85,000	1061-25
2	X-600	61	75,000	246-25
3	1123	61	69,000	1060-25
4	1107	60	65,000	1055-25
5	11520	65	62,700	242-25
6	1609	60	55,000	246-25
	11001	62		1060-25
7	1109	60	50,000	1060-25
	11570	66		1061-75
8	11540	65	38,850	239-25
9	1627S	60	32,500	244-25
10	19244	63	31,700	1061-25

APPENDIX D - PASSENGER CAR OUTFITS

Appendix D lists the promotional outfits that featured one or more passenger cars. Also included is the motive power that headed the outfit.

Outfit Number	Year	Motive Power	Passenger Cars in Outfit (Qty)
X-507NA	60	1882-25, 1882T-25	1866-25; 1885-25
X-572NA	60	2383P-1, 2383T-1	2432-1; 2436-1
X-576	60	226P-1, 226C-1	1875-1; 1876-1; 2432-1;
X-577	60	226P-1, 226C-1	1875-1; 2432-1
X-619	61	1862-1, 1862T-1	1865-25
X-677	61	1872X-1, 1872T-1	1875W-1; 1876-1
X-801	60	220P-1	2432; 2436
12817	64	2383-1	2521-1; 2522-1; 2523-1 (2)
12857	64	2383-1	2521-1; 2522-1 (3); 2523-1 (3)
19315	63	2383PX-1, 2383T-1	2521-1; 2522-1; 2523-1
19400	64	2029-1, 234W-1	2404-1; 2405-1 (2); 2406-1
19406	64	213LT	2404-1; 2405-1; 2406-1; 2521-1; 2522-1; 2523-1

APPENDIX E - O GAUGE AND SUPER O OUTFITS

Appendix E lists the O gauge and Super O promotional outfits that appear in this volume. Also shown are the quantity, motive power and customer (if available).

O Gauge Promotional Outfits

Outfit Number	Year	Qty	Motive Power	Customer
9658	62	600	736X-1	Sears, Roebuck and Co.
12710X	66	200	736-1	
12800X	66	300	2346-1	
12807	64	30	736LTS	Polk
12817	64	30	2383-1	
12820-100	65		2322-1	
12827	64	60	773LTS	Joe, The Motorists' Friend, Others
12838	64	25	773-1	Englewood Electric, Glen's Train Shop
12847	64	60	773LTS	Polk
12850X	66	150	2322-1	
12857	64	24	2383-1	Branch Brook Co.
12867	64	24	773LTS	
12885-500 (9836)	65	315	2347-1	Sears, Roebuck and Co.

Super O Promotional Outfits

Outfit Number	Year	Qty	Motive Power	Customer
X-522NA	60	240	218P-1, 218T-1	Gimbels
X-564NA	60	200	736-1	Madison Hardware
X-572NA	60	100	2383P-1, 2383T-1	
X-586	60	40	2349X	Beller Brothers
X-693	61	97	2360X-1	
9674	61	1,000	616X-1	Sears, Roebuck and Co.
9675	61	700	736X-1	
9692	60	1,300	2037-1	
	61	34	2037-1	
9693	60	1,600	218P-1, 218T-1	
9694	60	900	746-1 or 736-1	
13255	64	20	637X-1	National Association of Railroad Business Women
13267	64	12	773X-1	Jersey Model Distributors
13277	64	60	773LTS	Polk
19178	62	100	2360X-1	Joe, The Motorists' Friend
19196	62	60	637X-1	Broadway Stores
19251	63	72	2360-1	Joe, The Motorists' Friend
19257	63	200	736X-1	Beller Electric
19308	63	1,470	637X-1	Sears, Roebuck and Co.
19309	63	200	736X-1	
19315	63	75	2383PX-1, 2383T-1	
19316	63	200	2383PX-1, 2383T-1	
19320	63	200	2360X-1	

INDEX - OUTFITS SORTED BY YEAR

INDEX - OUTFITS SORTED BY NUMBER

INDEX - OUTFITS SORTED BY NUMBER

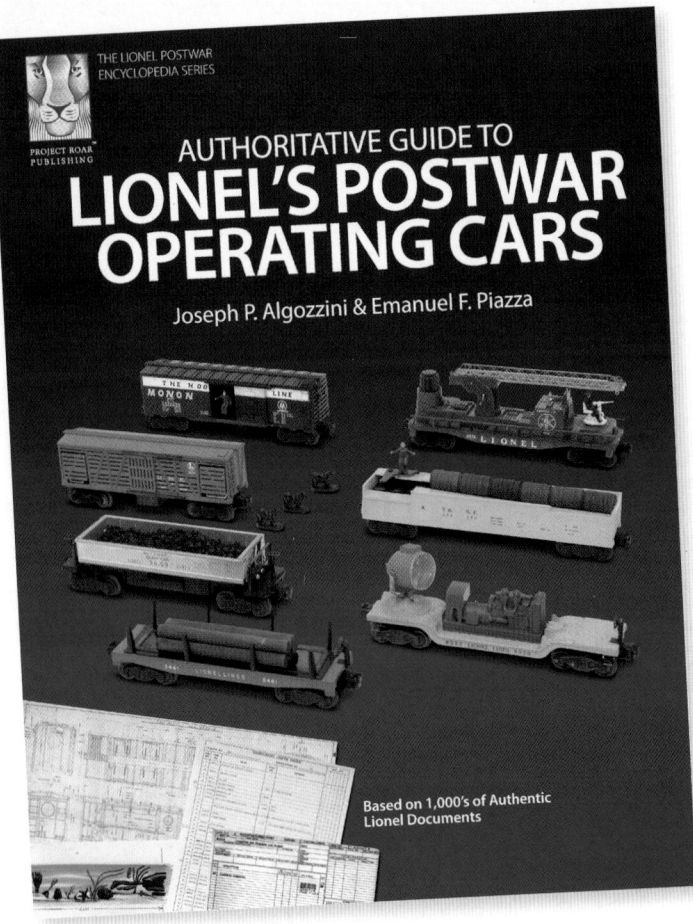